The Spor

POINT-TO-POINT

FORM & RESULTS

1996

Compiled by

Jonathan Neesom with Steven Payne

Published 1996 by The Sporting Life
One Canada Square, Canary Wharf, London E14 5AP

ISBN 0 901091 87 1

Irish Point-to-Point Results 1996 are reproduced by courtesy of *The Irish Field*

Editorial and Production by Martin Pickering Bloodstock Services
Cover designed by P.W. Reprosharp Ltd, London EC1
Cover printed by Graphic Techniques, Milton Keynes, Bucks
Preliminaries by LBJ Enterprises Ltd, Chilcompton and Aldermaston
Text printed by The Bath Press, Bath and London

Cover pictures

Main picture: Old Sport gives Stephen Gribble that crashing feeling in the Members at the Mid Surrey Farmers' meeting at Charing in February.

Insert picture: River Melody and Tim Moore clear the last to land the Confined Race at the Puckeridge Hunt's Horseheath meeting in April.

(Photographs: Reflex Sports Photography)

CONTENTS

REVIEW OF 1996

by Jonathan Neesom

(This article first appeared in *The Sporting Life* on June 11, 1996)

The usual glut of records were broken during the 1996 point-to-point season — 207 of the scheduled 213 fixtures survived, while there were 1,522 races, an increase of 27 on the previous season's record total.

Only four meetings had to be abandoned because of the horrendous early-season frosts and snows, in addition to the ever-absent Talybont and the little-lamented National Festival, which both bit the dust long before coming under starter's orders.

Fifty-five meetings took place on Sundays, an increase of 12 on last year's inaugural tally, although mutterings from several camps suggest this figure may not be reached next year, even though crowds tended to vary between large and massive.

Midweek fixtures have all but disappeared, which is a great pity given the crowds who flocked to Heythrop, Hockworthy, Andoversford and Brampton Bryan for the four which remained on the original list this year. A reversal of this trend would prove popular with many enthusiasts.

Two new courses were introduced with less than happy results. Cothelstone attracted 67 runners to its initial fixture on March 16, but a paltry 28 turned up the following week, and only 21 for the third meeting on April 13.

Most owners considered the ground too uneven to risk their horses and it is hoped that the promised overhaul for next season is successful.

Wolverhampton was added to the list of "proper" racecourses used for the sport, and while the lure of racecourse facilities can be pretty powerful on days when standing in a field getting thoroughly soaked seems a daft way of passing the time, the atmosphere at these courses smacks little of that associated with real point-to-pointing.

Sponsorship has proved difficult to attract in recent seasons and thanks are owed to Land Rover for its continued support — the series culminated in a high class final at Cheltenham in May, won by Ryming Cuplet, while the late acquisition of Vauxhall, in the shape of the Monterey Restricted series, shold prove a worthwhile addition to the cause if maintained next year.

The rule-change which prevented horses winning more than one Restricted, and which caused much controversy when announced at the end of last season, proved highly successful, and Intermediate races, until this year a rather forlorn spectacle, took on a far greater competitiveness — exactly the purpose of the change.

If congratulations are in order here, they would be more heartfelt if hunts were forced to give up their Members' races unless able to provide a proper race for the paying public — too many of them this season provided just the opposite. There is no worse way to start an afternoon than with a tiny field containing only one horse with a realistic chance of success.

The standard of bookmaking at point-to-points has improved out of all recognition in recent years and most areas offer punters a more-than-fair chance of losing their money at least in the knowledge that good value has been obtained.

The only exceptions to this commendation are the Yorkshire and South-East areas, the former because of the vastly over-round books on each race, and the latter because of its practice of offering each-way terms only on the first two horses in any race, irrespective of the number of runners.

Phar Too Touchy proved a worthy winner of the Grand Marnier trophy, especially as Becky Francis, who rode the nine-year-old to all but one of her ten victories, started the season with a career total of precisely nil.

An inauspicious beginning, when the partnership went their separate ways at the first fence at Barbury Castle in January, soon blossomed into a remarkable Spring, with only one further defeat, at the hands of Khattaf at Kilworthy in March, blemishing an otherwise unbeaten run.

Phar Too Touchy ("One win, ten places, 1994/95, ratio likely to continue.") — my astute comment in *The Sporting Life Point-to-Point Form & Results 1995* — bore ample testimony to the training skills of Victor Dartnall, who was also responsible for Chilipour and Butler John, among others, in a season where the stable secured a success rate of well over 50 per cent with their runners.

This level of success is old hat to Dick Baimbridge, of course, but even by his standards, 1996 was a vintage year.

Di Stefano and Down The Mine led the way but it was the maestro's ability to transform lost causes into fighting machines which once again served to remind us all of his genius.

Landsker Alfred had finished one of his six races the previous year but won four out of five in 1996, while the highly unpleasant Western Harmony emerged from the new yard just once to score an emphatic victory in a Maiden at Upper Sapey in March — a true triumph of mind over matter.

All of which leads neatly on to Alison Dare, who landed her sixth *Sporting Life* Ladies' Championship, with a personal record of 31 winners.

Fully-recovered from the broken leg which brought a premature end to her season in 1995, and which looked at the time likely to spell the end of a glittering career, Dare returned to the fray to display all the poise and tactical awareness that have been her trademarks. Her riding of Di Stefano at Whitwick in February will be an abiding delight for any who witnessed it.

At the beginning of the season, there was no betting on the Ladies' title, with bookmakers and enthusiasts alike assuming that Polly Curling had simply to turn up at the requisite number of meetings to claim her fourth consecutive championship.

In a rare moment of foresight, I suggested in *The Sporting Life* seasonal preview in January that such an outcome was by no means a foregone conclusion and no apologies are made for repeating what I wrote then:

"Curling can expect to steer a variety of horses, many of them inexperienced, over approximately 1,500 jumps during the course of the next five months."

The reigning champion suffered some heavy falls in mid-season, the one from Strong Tarquin at Didmarton in March being a prime example, and it was no surprise that stumps were virtually pulled in the closing weeks.

No loss of powers were in evidence at Umberleigh last Saturday, when she powered home on Fosbury, and we are privileged to be able to watch two outstanding women riders still in their prime.

Pip Jones was threatening to make life difficult for Dare and Curling until jinxed by injury in the last six weeks of the season and there are very few who would deny that her considerable talents should be rewarded with a title eventually — her partnership with Handsome Harvey provided clear testimony to her ability.

Jo Cumings secured 19 winners to achieve her best tally, while Emma James is perhaps the pick of those emerging from the younger ranks.

If Dare and Baimbridge maintained their formidable partnership, that Jamie Jukes and Bert Lavis was no less instrumental in helping the rider to a deserved first Men's title.

With Peter Bowen defecting to the ranks of the licensed trainers, and making a highly successful start to his professional career, Lavis resumed the mantle of the wizard of West Wales, and in Jukes had the ideal rider — strong, determined and highly skilled.

Virtually unconsidered in the pre-season betting, Jukes had ridden only 13 winners by mid-April but doubled that score in a three-week period to overtake defending champion Alastair Crow, and fairly sprinted away in the closing weeks, finally winning the title comfortably with 34 winners.

His performance on Northern Bluff at Bassaleg in May was an effort of real class — the horse hung left throughout the race on a course where going in a straight line is hard enough at the best of times — and he rounded off the season with a ride of tactical brilliance on Handsome Harvey to win the John Corbet Cup at Stratford.

Crow eventually ran out of opportunities when the ground dried up in May but at least made a bold bid to win his third title in four years and will no doubt be back thirsting for more next season.

Crow at least had the compensation of reaching the career landmark of 100 winners during the season — others to match this feat were Mandy Hand, George Cooper and Julian Pritchard, while Ron Treloggen took his total past the 150 mark.

Andrew Parker got off to a flier in the North in an attempt to lead all the way but was always going to be geographically disadvantaged in the closing weeks, while both Paul Hacking and Tim Mitchell enjoyed highly-successful seasons.

There was a real crop of talented young riders to emerge throughout the season. Joe Tizzard and Stuart Morris shared the Wilkinson Sword at the PPORA lunch, although Tizzard wins the novice title because of more placed rides. Add to these two the Yorkshire-based Richard Edwards, and the travel-anywhere Robert Thornton, and there is no shortage of potential challengers for the future.

At the other end of the scale, the dangers faced by riders were illustrated in double at the North Ledbury in March, when both Sue Sadler and Tommy Jackson suffered serious injuries. Jackson is happily well down the road to full recovery but the same process is taking much longer for Sadler, for whom a charity Ball has been arranged, which will take place at Evesham on August 16.

Sharinski won a competitive race for *The Sporting Life*-sponsored Lady Dudley Cup, and in the process secured *The Sporting Life* Classics Cup for owner Jo Yeomans, by virtue of winning at Upton-on-Severn 11 days earlier. Trained by Jonathan Rudge and qualified with the North Ledbury, Sharinski also earns a prize for his breeder, which may be hard to present as the horse is American-bred!

The other two legs of the Classics Cup saw Kettles steam home in the Heythrop four-miler while the Lord Grimthorpe Cup at the Middleton was won in more controversial circumstances by Highland Friend, who was adjudged to have pipped Cot Lane by the minimum margin.

The Taunton area again provided more than its share of promising horses during the season, and if Richard Barber could not match his all-conquering run of last year, he at least produced the usual number of potential stars — Bengers Moor, Calling Wild and Strong Chairman among them — while others in the region to impress include Arctic Chill, Tinotops and Emerald Knight.

Other horses who have given the impression during the season that greatness may await them include Bitofamixup (South-East), Teeton Mill (Midlands), Kaloore (Devon & Cornwall), Jigintime (North) and Launchselect (Yorkshire) — not an exhaustive list but enought to whet the appetite for next year.

Any recommendations for outstanding merit during the season must be based, perforce, on personal experience, but the vast majority of meetings I have attended around the country have been organised and run in exemplary fashion.

Certainly worthy of mention are the North Hereford (assuming its usual place with the most runners at any meeting — 133), the West Percy & Milvain, Tiverton, Lauderdale and Exmoor, but the honours go to the Lamerton, which provided all that any devotee of the sport could ask for.

The rider of the year has to be Alison Dare, while the riding performance goes to Adam Welsh for his effort on High Burnshot at Aldington on Easter Monday.

Finally, I would like to thank all those correspondents who braved the elements in order to return results and reports from all areas of the country — without their expertise and help, *The Sporting Life's* coverage would be impossible.

TOP HUNTER CHASERS/ POINT-TO-POINTERS 1996

by Jonathan Neesom

The horses selected here for extended commentary represent those who were, for a variety of reasons, outstanding during 1996 in Hunter chases or point-to-points. This list is not intended to be exhaustive, just a personal opinion of the merits of ten horses in each field; the reader is welcome to disagree with the comments made or to argue the case for any horse that has been omitted!

HUNTER CHASERS

PROUD SUN (39)

Dubbed, "The horse most likely to," at the start of the 1996 season, Proud Sun endured a frustrating time in February, when the weather continually foiled attempts to give him a race.

When he finally appeared at Kempton, at the end of that month, he started favourite against the likes of Cool Dawn and Teaplanter, but was bumped, and fell, a mile from home before the race had begun in earnest.

Mike Felton, who had ridden Proud Sun in all his races up to this point, lost the ride after this incident, and the fall of the ill-fated Synderborough Lad at Nottingham the following week — owners have the right to choose who they wish to partner their horses but this decision smacked of unwonted haste.

With no time for another outing prior to Cheltenham, Proud Sun was in the difficult position of making his attack on the Foxhunters there with only half a run under his belt, and a new rider, Sean Mulcaire, in the saddle. The result was no surprise; Proud Sun whipped round as the tapes rose, made numerous mistakes at the rear of the field and was never in the race with any hope — that he finished 4th, beaten only 13 lengths at the end, was some testimony to his ability.

Disaster struck again in his next outing, when he fell at Ascot, before a change of tack saw him appear at Cheltenham in April, where he won a valuable handicap off an attractive mark, prior to covering himself in glory by finishing fast in second place in the Whitbread at Sandown, at the end of that month, despite being well out of the handicap.

With the major prizes in National Hunt racing polished off for the season, attentions were turned back to Hunter chasing, with the services of the leading amateur Jim Culloty secured.

Horse and rider were beaten at Stratford in May, when Culloty gave the horse a great deal to do and then found Proud Sun making mistakes at the vital stage of the race, but it was a different scene when the partnership returned to the same course for the Horse and Hound Championship on the last day of the season.

Held up, as usual, Proud Sun was put into the race on the last circuit, sweeping to the front three from home in effortless style. What would probably have been a clear-cut success, however, became a real battle when he went lame between the last two fences and was pressed by Celtic Abbey on the run-in — the courage he displayed in holding off this challenge stamped his claims as a great hunter chaser.

Proud Sun will probably miss 1997 as a result of the injury sustained at Stratford and would be 10 years old, with a mere 16 races in his career, were he to return the following season — let us hope that he does.

ELEGANT LORD (38)

Elegant Lord started favourite for the 1995 running of the Cheltenham Foxhunters but finished a well beaten third to Fantus and Holland House, when he never appeared likely to justify the support, much of which emanated from his owner, who suffered mega-losses during the Festival that year.

Undaunted, connections once again aimed him at the race in 1996, and he started the season with a comfortable win at Leopardstown in February.

The money flowed strongly again at Cheltenham, but with a much more satisfactory outcome for his supporters, as Elegant Lord impressively brushed aside the challenge of the home contingent over the last three fences, cruising up the hill to win by six lengths from Cool Dawn, and reversing form with Holland House to the tune of nearly 25 lengths.

It is tempting fate to decry the form of any championship race but there are grounds for believing that this year's Cheltenham Foxhunters was below the normal standard of the race — neither Cool Dawn (qv) nor Proud Sun was seen to his best advantage, and the relative proximity of the likes of Goolds Gold and Clare Man, both beaten around 20 lengths, suggests this was not a vintage renewal.

Nothing should detract from Elegant Lord's performance on the day, however, and he could do no more than win as easily as he did — a feat he repeated in subsequent races at Fairyhouse and Punchestown.

Ridden in 1995 by the top Irish amateur Tony Martin, Elegant Lord was reunited in 1996 with Enda Bolger, who had appeared on the verge of retirement the previous season. His skill as a rider played no little part in Elegant Lord's development from "Great Irish Hope" to "Great Irish Champion."

Should Elegant Lord return to defend his crown next season, when he will be only nine years old, he may find the local challenge more of a test — nevertheless he would very much be the horse to beat.

COOL DAWN (38)

Cool Dawn's precocious talent was displayed to a wider audience in 1996 when his three outings culminated in an outstanding effort in the Irish National at Fairyhouse.

Reappearing at Kempton in February, Cool Dawn put up an impressive performance in the Corinthian Hunters Chase — making all the running and cruising away from the hard-ridden Teaplanter after the last fence, with the rest of the field unsighted. Kempton was the ideal place for horse and rider, being both flat and right-handed, and Dido Harding took the sensible option in making all the running.

Cheltenham poses different demands, particularly for a horse with a tendency to hang to the right, and in a field where dictating the pace was never going to be a straightforward exercise.

Cool Dawn managed to make most of the running in the Foxhunters but was passed by Elegant Lord before the home turn and lost valuable ground in the home straight by hanging across to the stands rail after the last fence; the cause was lost by that stage but Cool Dawn gave the clear impression that he had untapped reserves of energy at the end of the race.

The decision to allow him to be professionally-ridden in the Irish National prompted a flood of money in the ante-post market and Cool Dawn started the Irish National with expectations high that he could pull off a stunning victory.

He ran as well as his supporters could have hoped, making most of the running and having most of his rivals in trouble until giving way two from home, eventually finishing third.

There seems little point in returning to the hunter chase scene with Cool Dawn in 1997 — greater fame and fortune should await him in the professional sphere, and it is by no means stretching imaginations to ridiculous lengths to suggest that a tilt at the King George at Kempton would be worthwhile.

Only eight years old, Cool Dawn has shown his best form on all but heavy going, and is markedly suited by a right-handed course.

ROLLING BALL (36)

The winner of the 1991 Sun Alliance Chase at the Cheltenham Festival, Rolling Ball had suffered a series of setbacks in the following years which suggested that his future was all behind him when he reappeared in hunter chases at the age of 13, in 1996.

Warwick, at the start of March, was the chosen venue, and the mighty Double Silk provided as stern a test as any horse could want, even if he had to concede Rolling Ball 11lbs, including allowances.

Rolling Ball took Double Silk on at his own game, making virtually all the running, jumping quickly and fluently, and fighting off a last challenge five fences from home before drawing away to win by a distance.

Arguments that Double Silk was conceding weight, was eased when his chance had vanished, and was not the horse he once was all have varying degrees of validity but there is no doubt in this writer's view that Rolling Ball's performance at Warwick was not just the best hunter chase display of the season, but the best for many years.

Aintree beckoned, and 25 rivals rather than just Double Silk, but Rolling Ball again adopted front-running tactics. All went to plan until he took the scenic route at the Canal Turn and was sensibly given a breather when Sir Noddy overtook him two fences later.

Back in front by the last fence, Rolling Ball once again drifted away to the right after the elbow and looked sure to be beaten when Kerry Orchid loomed up on the far rail; it is a measure of his ability that he quickened again, under encouragement rather than force, to win a dramatic race by a length and a half.

Matters went sadly downhill after this. Sent to Uttoxeter in May, Rolling Ball was beaten by My Nominee and looked less than whole-hearted when overtaken by that horse four from home. Worse was to follow when he dropped out of the Horse and Hound Championship at Stratford after leading the field for two miles, and he presented a forlorn figure pulling up six fences from home.

We may well have seen the last of this enigmatic character — if that is the case, at least he had the chance to show his huge talent once more before slipping away. For this, much credit must go to Stephen Brookshaw's training, and particularly to the riding of Richard Ford, whose handling of the horse was both skilful and nerveless, especially at Aintree.

DOUBLE SILK (35)

No excuse needs to be made for including the legend of '90s hunter chasing, Double Silk, in this list once again.

He ran only three times in 1996, opening up with a win at Hereford, a track which does not suit him, on heavy ground and conceding lumps of weight to his rivals. If that win owed something to the fall of Howaryason two from home, when in a challenging position, it at least showed that Double Silk was still a potent force.

The defeat by Rolling Ball at Warwick appeared to convince many people that he had slid well off the top of the perch, although with the benefit of hindsight he faced an impossible task at the time.

Forced to miss the Cheltenham Foxhunters, Double Silk did not reappear until the hunter chase at the same track at the beinning of May.

A wet and miserable evening was illuminated by his performance there, when he once again adopted his role at the head of affairs and produced his customary round of impressive jumping. Pressed by the gallant Welsh mare Miss Millbrook at the top of the hill, Double Silk put paid to her chance, as he had done to so many others in the past, with his relentless galloping.

Well clear by the time they reached the home straight, he was assured of victory long before Miss Millbrook fell at the last through sheer exhaustion, and was allowed to canter up the run-in to resounding cheers from the stands, to record his fifth victory on the course.

There is no doubt that Double Silk has lost some of his powers but his career, which has encompassed two wins in the Cheltenham Foxhunters and one at Aintree, ensures his place amongst the immortals of hunter chasing.

COOME HILL (35)

Unbeaten in six races before the start of last season, Coome Hill had not beaten any significant rival, and had been made to work hard when winning a modest hunter chase at Wincanton the previous season.

He ran only twice in 1996 but both performances stamped him as a top-class hunter chaser and a real prospect for the major prizes next season.

Only four opponents faced him at Wincanton in early March, but they included the useful Still In Business and Dubit, as well as the consistent yardstick Sonofagipsy. With the ground on the fast side, and his rivals race-fit, the signs pointed to the end of the unbeaten record, and a price of 9–2 reflected this. In the race, Coome Hill left the rest for dead half a mile from home, beating Sonofagipsy by 30 lengths without coming under any pressure.

Wisely opting out of the Cheltenham Foxhunters only seven days later, Coome Hill's other outing came at Chepstow at the end of the month, when he was pitted against tough horses. The unbeaten record fell here, but not without the most tremendous effort on his part to maintain it, going under by a head to Holland House — another 20 yards and victory would have been his.

Put away for the rest of the season, Coome Hill will start 1997 with only eight races on the clock and the Cheltenham Foxhunters surely as his main objective — it is not hard to see him playing a major part of the outcome there if all goes to plan. He jumps well in the main, stays and can now be said to act on ground ranging from good to firm to heavy.

TEAPLANTER (32)

Teaplanter enjoyed a revival at the age of 13 in 1996 — it is an obvious temptation to ascribe this solely to the riding of Ben Pollock, but this would overlook the skills of his trainer, Caroline Saunders, and to the horse himself, who has been at or near the top of the tree for six years and deserves much credit for his toughness.

A win at Barbury Castle in January — his first point-to-point for six years, was the precurser for another successful campaign in hunter chases, when he won at Wetherby, his beloved Towcester (twice) and Bangor, each time stamping his authority on the field a long way from home.

The only defeats he suffered during this period were at the hands of Cool Dawn at Kempton, when he fought like a lion all the way up the home straight in the face of insurmountable odds, and at Towcester, when he was just outspeeded in a match with Call Home.

Sent to Towcester in May for the four miles race on that course's hunter chase evening, Teaplanter showed the effects of a long season and put up his only disappointing performance of the year in finishing fourth behind Young Brave — it was not the trip that undid him, as he would not have won the race at any stage.

Connections expressed their hope that Teaplanter will return at 14, when he should still be capable of adding to his tally of 25 victories, all but four of which have come in hunter chases.

KERRY ORCHID (32)

Favourite for the 1993 Cheltenham Foxhunters, when he was only five years old, Kerry Orchid discovered with a vengeance at what cost horses tackled Double Silk in his pomp; beaten off three times from the second last fence, Kerry Orchid was added to the list of hunter chasers who had been "bottomed" by Double Silk and never recovered their true form.

It says much for his talent that he returned in 1996 to produce two outstanding performances in the season's main events.

The winner of a point-to-point in January, Kerry Orchid was easily beaten by Elegant Lord at Leopardstown the following month, before winning comfortably enought at Fairyhouse.

From there it was on to Cheltenham and another crack at the race he had so nearly won three years earlier. He did not jump well enought in the Foxhunters there, but still battled on for third place, 13 lengths behind his compatriot.

His finest hour came at Aintree, where his chance appeared to have vanished at the first fence. Badly hampered by the usual melee which occurs there, Kerry orchid was all but tailed off for the first half of the race. Making relentless progress from the Canal Turn, he appeared on the scene in the home straight and looked the likely winner when Rolling Ball hung away to his right in the last 200 yards.

Unable to match the winner's speed near the line, Kerry Orchid did nothing but cement his reputation by his performance here, and of all the deserving causes, a win for this horse in a major event in 1997 would certainly be no more than he has earned.

RYMING CUPLET (32)

This really is a tough horse, and one of those whose form in point-to-points is little more than solid — it is hunter chasing that brings out his qualities of stamina and courage.

A well beaten last of four finishers behind West Quay at Cothelstone on his reappearance, and comprehensively outpointed by Young Brave at Larkhill, Ryming Cuplet showed that he was reaching his peak when just holding off Fosbury in the Land Rover qualifier at Badbury Rings in April.

There are not many objectives for a hunter chaser who is at his best in late season but does not appreciate Stratford — the Final of the highly-successful Land Rover Series at Cheltenham was the obvious target, and he duly took his place in a field worthy of the race.

West Quay and Fosbury lined up, but the clear favourite was the high-class Sheer Jest, who had won his qualifier on the first weekend of the season and was the form choice.

When Sheer Jest cruised through the field to join issue with Ryming Cuplet and West Quay as the field turned for home, it looked as if he would prevail, but a combination of the rain-softened ground and Ryming Cuplet's gameness saw the complexion of the race change on the run-in. Under strong driving, Ryming Cuplet refused to yield and it was Sheer Jest who cracked in the final hundred yards.

Two of Ryming Cuplet's previous hunter chase wins had been claimed at Uttoxeter's hunter chase meeting, but that fixture this year had a lop-sided look to it, with four of the races confined to novices, and there was no suitable event on the card. Probably against their better judgment, connections took him to Stratford for the Horse and Hound Championship, but ground, course and a breakneck pace were against him and he was pulled up with a circuit to go.

Ryming Cuplet will be 12 years old in 1997, but has had comparatively little racing for a horse of his age — he should be able to add to his tally of four hunter chase wins, and if it comes to a battle at the end of a race, he is certainly the horse you would want to be on.

JIGTIME (30)

There is always a feeling of satisfaction for those people who spot talent at the beginning of a horse's career, and Steven Payne, who has contributed much had work to this book over the last three years, can claim with justification that he was among those who saw Jigtime first!

Fifth of six finishers in a Maiden at Alnwick in February 1995, on her debut, and beaten nearly 40 lengths, Jigtime nevertheless caught the attention of our wandering race-reader, and justified the "improve" tag with a fluent win at Friars Haugh three weeks later.

Unraced for the rest of that year, Jigtime looked an obvious hope for a Restricted success in 1996, and duly won on her return, also at Friars Haugh, in March, under the promising Mark Bradburne.

No further conformation to the usual pattern followed, however, and for her next outing, only the fourth of her career, she was thrown in against some of the best Scottish hunter chasers at Kelso, on the same evening as the Cheltenham hunter chase fixure.

Whilst memories of Double Silk and Ryming Cuplet will live long in the memories of those of us present at Cheltenham, Jigtime's display at Kelso will also hold its place as forcefully.

Despite a mistake at the first fence, Jigtime was in the firing line throughout the race, and on the final circuit the question became not "If?" but "When?"

In the end, Jigtime beat the course specialist Royal Jester by six lengths, with Carousel Rocket and Green Times, by no means star material, not far behind. If the bare bones of the result are not that exciting, the performance certainly was, and Jigtime is a horse whose progress should be monitored closely at the start of 1997.

POINT-TO-POINTERS

PHAR TOO TOUCHY (29)

Phar Too Touchy may not have been the best horse to have run in point-to-points in 1996 but she certainly deserves pride of place at the top of the list.

In two previous season's racing, Phar Too Touchy had managed a solitary win, in a Welsh Maiden, from 13 attempts, and had looked extremely onepaced even in modest Restricted class races, but all that changed when she was acquired by Victor Dartnall on behalf of Becky Francis for the 1996 season.

The partnership came unstuck at the first fence at Barbury Castle in January — scarcely the most auspicious of beginnings — and Neil Harris was in the saddle when the mare next appeared, winning a Restricted at Wadebridge at the start of February.

That race looked nothing special at the time, although with African Bride as the runner-up, it was to prove to be one of the most hotly contested races in that class all season.

Miss Francis was back in the saddle the following week at Great Trethew; common opinion was that the partnership could be safely disregarded and odds of 7–1 were available about the horse's chance in the Intermediate.

Once again, what had looked to be no more than an average contest before the race turned out to be one of the most significant of he season, with Phar Too Touchy making most of the running — he placed horses, Kaloore, Vital Song and On Alert were all to prove hemselves highly useful performers by the end of the season.

In winning this race, Phar Too Touchy was also giving the rider her first success, and nine more followed over the next four months, he only blip occurring in a hot Ladies' Open at Kilworthy, when she could finish only third to Khattaf (". . . sixth race in seven weeks appears to have taken the edge off her for the moment," I wrote after he meeting — wrong again).

Far from taking the edge, that defeat seemed only to sharpen the blade and five further wins followed before the end of the season, and he Grand Marnier title was never in doubt.

Phar Too Touchy showed tremendous versatility during the eason, winning on ground ranging from firm to heavy, and also cantering home over four miles at Flete Park in May, while she raced from mid-January to late May.

Much of the credit for her success must be placed at the door of Dartnall, whose progression to join the ranks of the top point-to-point trainers has been lightning-quick, and whose record in 1996 bears the closest inspection — Chilipour, Slievenamon Mist, Wolf Winter, Butler John and Interpretation all winning good races.

The rider's role should not be overlooked either — it is hard to imagine that the Grand Marnier trophy will again be won by a horse whose rider started the season as a virtual beginner, and Francis showed plenty of tactical acumen despite the obvious pressures of riding in the full glare of public attention.

Phar Too Touchy has demonstrated that she is not just a decent pot-hunter but a top-class pointer — it will be no surprise to see her land some major prizes next season, when she is sure to prove hard to beat.

FAITHFUL STAR (32)

Unbeaten in five point-to-points in 1995, Faithful Star also won a hunters' chase at Uttoxeter in that season, and was unsurprisingly long odds-on when he made his reappearance at Barbury Castle in January, in a division of the Land Rover Open.

To say he ran badly is an understatement; he was never travelling easily, made several mistakes, and virtually walked across the line to finish a distant last of three behind Howaryason and Ru Valentino.

Matters were no less disturbing at Wadebridge two weeks later, when he looked thoroughly miserable at the back of the field before dislodging David Pipe after a circuit, and spectators appeared to be watching the rapid decline of one of the top pointers of the previous year.

A third behind Chilipour at Ottery two weeks later at least signalled something of a revival, a view confirmed when he gave Pipe his last winning ride at Milborne St Andrew in early March.

Shirley Vickery resumed her place in the saddle after this and five more victories were to follow before the end of the season, re-establishing Faithful Star's position at the top of his league.

Victor Dartnall's Interpretation gave him a severe test at Hockworthy in April in what was the best Confined race of the season, but that pretender was thrashed ten days later at Bratton Down — the lighter weights of Ladies' Opens seeming to suit Faithful Star particularly well.

Another crack at Stratford's Horse and Hound Championship (in which he started favourite the previous season but finished only fourth) was called for, but disappointment followed as he unseated Vickery four from home when holding every chance.

At 12 years old in 1997, Faithful Star, who acts on softish ground but is particularly well-suited to a fast surface, should have plenty more opportunities to add to his already impressive haul of victories.

Faithful Star is owned by Martin Pipe, which clearly gives him a marked advantage over horses hunted and trained in virtual isolation by their owners — nobody would assume that the horse is not given the same outstanding care that has led to the yard's success over the last 10 years. Similarly, horses trained by Dick Baimbridge, Richard Barber, Victor Dartnall and Caroline Saunders also benefit from the professional skills of their handlers, and the word "professional" is used as a tribute, not a criticism.

It may be galling for some people to witness the top stables mop up large numbers of races each season but their presence has raised the standard of point-to-pointing — the alternative is virtually to argue that pointers should not be allowed the facilities that have been developed over the years to maximise both their potential and well-being — and minimise the risk of injury caused by lack of fitness.

There will always be the opportunity for the small yard to produce a champion — one of the main reasons for Double Silk's popularity is that he is a true hunter, and yet became simply the best.

The suggestion that point-to-pointing should be thrown open to professional trainers to run any horses in their care, rather than just ones they own, opens up an entirely different can of worms, however.

Much of Irish point-to-pointing, in which many of the leading professional trainers participate, is little more than a shop window, displaying the goods for the benefit of English visitors with large hopes and larger wallets — this is not a situation which should be encouraged here, where the sport still retains the authentic taste of amateurs competing largely for glory, not gain.

The attraction of point-to-pointing is the fact that meetings are usually organised and run to high, professional standards in the 1990's, but still offer the spectator a genuinely amateur sport in content — long may it remain so.

DI STEFANO (29)

You can take your pick, really.

The evergreen, Stephens Pet, unbeaten in four outings, Rip Van Winkle, stirred from his slumbers to win four of his six races, Guiting

Gray, vastly improved and beautifully handled to win three times despite a tendency to swallow his tongue, Landsker Alfred, pulled up in five of his six races in 1995 for previous connections but the winner of four of his five starts in 1996, or Western Harmony, useless and dangerous in East Anglia but the winner of his only start in 1996 at Upper Sapey.

Whichever way you look at it, this was a vintage season, even by the standards set by Dick Baimbridge in the past, and exemplified by the performances of Di Stefano, unbeaten in seven starts and produced to run for his life each time.

He won two of his three races in 1995 but appeared to need an easy course to last the trip, and the close-up comments for this season bear testament to a plan of action to counteract any possible deficiency in this aspect — always taken steadily for half the race, moving through to lead three out or thereabouts, and quickening clear in seemingly effortless fashion.

On the first occasion, at the beautifully-run North Hereford meeting at Whitwick, the mutterings in the crowd were reaching vallium levels when Di Stefano was still lost in the pack of 21 runners as the field entered the final mile; in a matter of a few hundred yards he had swept through to lead two from home, drawing clear to win by six lengths.

This devastating burst of speed was unleashed on each of the other six occasions, and Di Stefano ended his season at Mollington by handing out a second thrashing to the very useful Sperrin View, confirming his status as a top pointer.

And what of the rider?

If we are honest with ourselves, most of us will admit that when Alison Dare broke her leg at Heythrop in March, 1995, on the same afternoon that she had become the first woman rider to reach the 200 mark in point-to-points, this seemed a sad but appropriate moment for her to slip into well-earned retirement.

Ten months later she was back, skipping home on Down The Mine (once considered the slowest Maiden winner in the North-West — but now a potent force in the speed stakes) at Barbury Castle, and confirming her return to full fitness.

In 1991, Dare achieved what seemed an unbeatable record when she won 26 races from only 38 rides — a ratio of more than two-thirds. Her score in 1996 was 31 from 43 rides, only a shade under three-quarters.

This is the stuff of legends and enabled the rider to secure her sixth Ladies' title with a total which is a personal record and has been beaten only by Polly Curling among women riders; who is to say that a seventh championship will not be secured in 1997?

FOSBURY (29)

The winner of three point-to-points in 1995, Fosbury was another horse who did not shine early in 1996 — persistently cold weather seemed to take its toll on many horses who thrive on the customary Spring warmth that was missing this year.

He failed to win any of his first six races, his best effort in this time coming when pipped by Ryming Cuplet at Badbury Rings in April, and he did not manage to win until finding a poor race at Holnicote on May 11.

However, he proved unstoppable from that point, until the end of the season, winning three more races with increasing authority.

He gave 7lbs to the useful pair of Vital Song and Tasmin Tyrant when beating them at Mounsey Hill Gate later that month before rounding off the season with two sparkling wins at Bratton Down and Umberleigh.

At the former, he powered home in the four miler, winning by a wide margin despite being heavily eased up the long run-in, and he is particularly well-suited to a stamina test of this nature.

Umberleigh does not normally pay host to the top horses at the season's end, but Fosbury's performance in winning the Ladies' Open there was one of the best displays of the season in any race. Faced by the ever-consistent Flame O'Frensi and the promising Not Mistaken, Fosbury took up the running with more than a circuit remaining and left the rest for dust climbing the hill for the final time, winning in a very fast time without being in any way extended.

This victory at least brought a happy conclusion to the season for Polly Curling, whose attempts to land a fourth consecutive Ladies championship were thwarted by a succession of bone-shaking (but fortunately not bone-breaking) falls during the first half of the season.

She is sure to return in 1997 with renewed determination, and without the pressure that unbridled success brings with it.

Should 1997 provide a warmer Spring, Fosbury, who needs good or fast ground to be seen at his best, is sure to win many more races, and he would be a tempting prospect in a four miles hunters' chase if conditions were suitable.

MASTER KIT (29)

Buying an Irish point-to-pointer is always fraught with potential problems — for every star in the making there are plenty of duds, non-stayers and horses who need a mudbath to enable them to show any ability — just like in England really!

Master Kit won a Maiden in Ulster, usually the weakest area of Irish pointing, at the fifth attempt in 1995, a record that would not automatically suggest potential greatness.

Bought by the comparative novice Jeremy Billinge to race in the Northern area in 1996, the partnership, rather like Phar Too Touchy and Becky Francis, made the less than ideal start of going their separate ways at the fourth fence in the Restricted at Friars Haugh in late February.

It was a different story just seven days later, when they romped home in a similar race at Corbridge, defying odds of 33–1 in the process and earning rave reviews from an appreciative audience.

Six more efforts in point-to-points produced four wins, a fall at the last fence when holding a clear lead, and a slip-up on a bend, and the last two victories saw the rise to Open class races taken in easy fashion.

With little to lose, Master Kit was despatched to Perth for a competitive hunters' chase against experienced opposition in mid-May. The result was not in doubt from a long way out, as he cruised behind the leaders before quickening to a clear-cut success approaching the last.

Billinge had to do little more than sit and steer here, as was the case in the pointing wins, and there is little doubt that he has unearthed a real treasure in Master Kit, who will only be eight years old in 1997.

With the ability to act on soft and firm ground, and effective from two and a half to four miles, Master Kit will provide a very interesting prospect for next season, if he remains in the amateur arena.

LUCKY CHRISTOPHER (28)

The strenuous effort made by Jimmy Tarry to land the Men's Title in 1995 appeared to have taken its toll on the stable's horses this season, and winners were at a premium for the first three months — the death of Fine Lace during the summer of 1995 robbing the yard of its flagship in Open races.

Lucky Christopher, who had won seven of his last eight races in 1995, was a case in point, and his performances for the first half of this season were disappointing. Pulled up at Kingston Blount, beaten at Ampton and thrashed in a hunters' chase at Towcester, he then scrambled home in a modest race at Horseheath before going under to Fiddlers Three at Eaton Hall.

Things only picked up from April onwards, and Lucky Christopher was to end the season with an unbeaten run of five victories, starting with wins in Opens at Kingston Blount and Clifton-on-Dunsmore, and moving on to a hunters' chase at Uttoxeter, where Tarry gave supporters several anxious moments by prematurely easing the horse on the run-in as the rallying Ledwyche Gate closed the gap.

Top form was not hit until the dying weeks of the season, when Lucky Christopher won the Open at the Melton Hunt Club before putting up a magnificent display at Dingley, romping home under Andrew Sansome in a very fast time.

The winner of 13 of his last 18 races, Lucky Christopher has now reached his prime at a comparitively elderly age — he was very lightly raced up until 1995 — and there should be more wins to come at the age of 12 next season. He has the precious ability to quicken, and acts on soft and fast conditions.

NETHERTARA (27)

The winner of four races in modest company in 1995, Nethertara developed into a very useful pointer this season, ascending the ranks by winning four of her five races, culminating in an Open win at Heathfield on Easter Monday.

Beaten at Cottenham on the first weekend of the season in an Intermediate, she made amends, if somewhat fortuitously, by taking advantage of the last-fence fall of the ill-fated Pakenham by winning a similar race at Horseheath in February.

A modest race at Charing followed, but it was a Confined win in March at Parham, a course which places real emphasis on stamina, that caught the eye. She bounded home from a fair field in by far the fastest time of the day, a feat repeated in the Open win two weeks later.

Off the course for more than a month after the last win, as the ground dried, Nethertara reappeared in a novice hunters' chase at Fakenham in mid-May — scarcely the ideal course for a horse whose forte is stamina, but the only one offering good, as opposed to firm ground, at that stage of the season.

Poised to challenge when blundering and unseating Paul Hacking two from home, Nethertara may find her mishap to her advantage at the start of next season, when she will be able to compete in hunter chases without a penalty. A powerful galloper who stays well and acts on good or soft going, Nethertara will be 10 years old in 1997, but this late developer looks the ideal sort to run up several wins in novice hunters' chases and is definitely one to watch for in these events.

CEDAR SQUARE (26)

This five year old is a real prospect, having won three of his four races in 1996 in West Wales, the last two in much the fastest time of the day.

Running green on his debut, Cedar Square finished third in a Maiden at Erw Lon in March, with the subsequent hunters' chase winner Northern Bluff in front of him. Two weeks later he cantered home in a similar race at Pantyderi before winning his Members' race at Lydstep on Easter Monday.

If this sounds like basement-league stuff, his final performance of the season, in beating the gallant veteran Lislary Lad, also at Lydstep, in the Men's Open, marked him out as a real hope for the future, and left connections contemplating a stab at hunters' chases.

It is perhaps wise that they declined the chance, as it leaves Cedar Square with plenty of options open to him in this area in 1997, when he looks sure to make his presence felt in much better company than he has so far encountered.

Cedar Square's rider on three of his four outings was Jamie Jukes, who became the first Welsh rider to win the Men's championship since the great John Llewellyn thirteen years earlier, and his performances during the season were worthy of the mantle he has inherited.

Strong, secure and very skilful, Jukes was seen to maximum advantage when riding Northern Bluff to win the Confined race at the first meeting at Bassaleg in May, when he had to contend with the unique character of the course and a horse whose natural inclination was to veer in the opposite direction. It was a tribute to Jukes' talent and determination that the partnership completed the course at all, let alone go on to win the race.

Jukes was assisted in his march to the title by the host of winners sent out by Bert Lavis, whose return to the peaks of point-to-point trainers was a feature of the season; with the same support in 1997, Jukes will have every chance of adding a second title, a feat even Llewellyn could not manage.

TINOTOPS (26)

Tinotops was sold in June 1995, after winning a very poor Maiden from four attempts as a five year old in East Anglia for Gurney Shephard — at five thousand guineas he looked expensive enough on what he had achieved thus far.

The money proved to have been wisely spent, however, judged on his displays in 1996, when he won three of his six starts.

A fall at Barbury Castle, followed by a fourth in a good Restricted at Ottery and a success in a modest event at Garnons signalled little more than satisfactory progress, but the last three efforts marked Tinotops as a force to be reckoned with among the crop of young hopefuls eager to make their names.

Tinotops finished second to Desert Waltz in an Intermediate at Larkhill, one of the hottest races in this class all season, with Apatura

Hati and Guiting Gray behind, before dishing out a comprehensive beating to the vastly more experienced Granville Grill at Heythrop in April.

On his final appearance, Tinotops beat the Barber-trained pair of Calling Wild and Bet With Baker in the PPORA race at Hockworthy; Calling Wild is himself no mean prospect and Tinotops was forced to show plenty of courage as well as ability to hold off a strong challenge.

Having shown form on firm and soft ground, Tinotops should have ample opportunity to climb the ladder further in 1997; what is impressive about his victories is that he has shown a tigerish attitude and responded gamely when the pressure has been applied — attributes that are sure to stand him in good stead in the future.

BITOFAMIXUP (20)

There does not appear to be a Hops and Pops or Davy Blake among this year's crop of first season horses — if there is, I haven't spotted it, but Bitofamixup is a worthy inclusion as a horse who should certainly make a name for himself in the future in much better company than he has met to date.

A potter round the back for a circuit at Tweseldown showed nothing other than the word "schooled" which appeared in the close-up comment was appropriate, but he really caught the eye a week later at Detling, under another highly-considerate ride from Paul Hacking in the Maiden there.

Loitering around the back of the field for much of the race, he finished fast and late in second place, without looking in any way as if he had been extended.

The Maiden win was forthcoming soon after at Barbury Castle, where poor rivals were beaten out of sight, and the Restricted success at Bexhill, again against weak opposition, only served to show that he could at least hand firm ground.

As is often the case with young horses, it is not just what they beat (in Bitofamixup's instance the answer is, "Not much,") but how they achieve it; he has shown that he is a possible star-in-the-making, and his progress will be closely monitored next season by all those who have seen him run.

INTRODUCTION

This introduction is little changed to that which appeared in previous years but is probably worth re-printing for anyone seeing the book for the first time.

The objective of this form book is to give the racegoer immediate access to all the information that is needed to assess the relative merits of each runner in any race.

To achieve this aim, the contents include:

a. results with 'close-ups' of all meetings in 1996;
b. Irish results of hunter' chases and point-to-points in full;
c. 'at a glance' form of all registered runners in point-to-points and hunter 'chases in 1996;
d. winning amateur riders under Rules and in point-to-points;
e. the weights of winning amateur riders licensed to ride under Rules;
f. course characteristics.

In order to see how a horse ran in all its races at different times of the season, at different courses, on different going and at different distances, the usual procedure is to look in the index for the horse, find the last race in which it ran and then thumb back through the results.

It seems, therefore, eminently sensible to present all this information in an 'at a glance' format, particularly for racegoers at point-to-points where there is little time between the runners being known and the betting market being formed.

This has been done in the Form section where a race rating is given each time a horse ran. From these figures an overall rating is given, not as a historical record of the past season, but as an indication as to how the horse might run in the future when it is one year older.

To ease the task of the racegoer further, the Irish runners are integrated into the main Index of runners rather than into a separate section.

In the Irish results section ratings are given for placed horses. The ratings are on the same scale as those in the main Index and are useful as a guide for horses that subsequently run in the U.K. Care should be taken, however, as there is often a marked difference with some of the younger horses improving significantly while others never run to the same mark again after leaving their professional yards.

The owners of some horses will be disappointed to read that their superb hunter and family pet has been dismissed as 'of no account'. The horse may have run his heart out and given the owner tremendous enjoyment. The comment simply implies that he is not a racehorse who should be treated seriously in the betting market.

Purposely excluded are unregistered hunters. These horses invariably have a rating of 0 and are ineligible to run in any race other than one specifically for hunt members of the host meeting. Their inclusion would clutter up the list to no purpose. Each horse is, of course, able to be found in the results section in the members' race in which it ran.

It is often of interest, particularly in low weighted hunter chases, to know whether or not the usual rider can make the weight and take full advantage of any allowance. It is also sometimes significant as to how much dead weight a horse carries in a point-to-point and the effects of a further penalty of 7 or 10lbs of lead. Consequently the weights are given of all riders who are licensed to ride under Rules who have had at least one success this season, either in a hunter 'chase or in a point-to-point. These weights are incorporated in the table of the record of winning riders.

The book is intended to be used as a working document rather than a library publication. From your local knowledge, if you believe that a race has been assessed wrongly and that horses have been rated either too high or too low then alter them and update as the season progresses. At the end of the book there are blank pages so that horses appearing for the first time next season can be added. These, of course, will be given a rating and, together with every other runner, have the rating updated each week in *Point-to-Point Entries Index.* This is published on Wednesdays to complement the detailed results, which appear on Mondays, in *The Sporting Life.*

Comments and criticisms of this publication will be welcomed. The compiler does not guarantee that each letter will be personally answered but does promise that its contents will be taken fully into consideration before the publication of next year's annual. Write to:

Point-to-Point Feedback, The Sporting Life,
One Canada Square, Canary Wharf, London E14 5AP

HOW TO USE THE RATINGS

Guide to Ratings

10–14	Moderate Form
15–17	Average Maiden Winner
18–19	Average Restricted Winner
20–21	Average Intermediate Winner
22–23	Average Confined Winner
24–26	Average Open Winner
27–29	Very good Pointer/Fair Hunter 'chaser
30–34	Very good Hunter 'chaser
35+	Top Class

Adjustment to Ratings for finding Winners

In Point-to-Points 1 point = 3lbs.
In Hunter 'chases 1 point = 2lbs.

Note: The 5lbs mares allowance and the 7lbs allowance for 5-yr-olds are already taken into account and no further adjustment is necessary.

Other Factors to be taken into account

Ratings, are valueless unless used sensibly, and therefore, must be used in conjunction with the summary given for each horse. This guides the reader, on the evidence available, on the suitability of particular going, distance and type of course. Suppose the comments and ratings of the four main contenders in a race are:

Horse A	25	Best in testing conditions over extreme distances; heavy
Horse B	24	Always needs a couple of runs to come to his best; any
Horse C	26	Useful hunter chaser at 2–2½m; best R/H; firm
Horse D	23	Resolute and consistent; runs less well on heavy

In an early season point-to-point on good ground on a left handed course, Horse D is the most sensible bet even though having the lowest rating.

The rating given after the horse comment in the Index section should be used for early races. Subsequently the rating will be amended weekly in *Point-to-Point Entries Index*.

BETTING

Withdrawn Horse

(a) A bet on a horse withdrawn before it comes under Starter's Orders, will be refunded.

(b) If a horse is withdrawn late, Tattersalls Committee has authorised the following deductions under Rule 4(c) from winnings, based on the price on the withdrawn horse to compensate bookmakers who are obliged to return stakes on the withdrawn horse, as they would have laid shorter odds about the other runners when compiling their book.

If the Current Odds are	Reduction by Bookmaker
3/10 or longer odds on	75p in the £
2/5 to 1/3	70p
8/15 to 4/9	65p
8/13 to 4/7	60p
4/5 to 4/6	55p
20/21 to 5/6	50p
Evens to 6/5	45p
5/4 to 6/4	40p
13/8 to 7/4	35p
15/8 to 9/4	30p
5/2 to 3/1	25p
10/3 to 4/1	20p
9/2 to 11/2	15p
6/1 to 9/1	10p
10/1 to 14/1	5p
over 14/1	No Reduction
2 or more horses being withdrawn	Maximum Reduction 75p in the £

Note: Remember that the full amount of your stake should be returned—it is only the winnings that are subject to a deduction:

Examples:

1. You have a winning bet of £5 at 3–1 but the favourite at even money was withdrawn

stake of £5 returned in full
Winnings of £15 subject to 45p in the £1 deduction
ie. winnings reduced to £8.25
Total Return £13.25

2. You have a winning bet of £6 at 4–6 made before a horse was withdrawn whose price was 4–1
   Stake of £6 returned in full
   Winnings of £4 subject to 20p in the £1 deduction
   ie. winnings reduced to £3.20
   Total Return £9.20

Dead Heat

You will be paid the full odds to half your stake. The other half of your stake is lost.

Example: The prices of two horses that dead heat are even money and 4–1. You have backed both with a stake of £10 on each.

On the even money chance
You have £5 on at evens and win £5
Your return will be £10

On the 4–1 chance
You have £5 on at 4–1 and win £20
Your return will be £25

Point-to-Point Races

MEMBERS', SUBSCRIBERS', FARMERS' or HUNT RACE For horses hunted with the promoting hunt or club.

MAIDEN For horses that have not won a race. They can have qualified from any hunt unless conditions specify certain hunts.

CONFINED For horses hunted with the promoting hunt or one of the confined hunts nominated for the particular meeting.

RESTRICTED For horses that have not won under Rules and have not won an open, intermediate or one restricted point-to-point.

INTERMEDIATE For horses that have not won under Rules, an open or two intermediate point-to-points.

OPEN For any qualified horse, to be ridden by men or women as specified unless mixed (open to both).

CLUB For members' horses.

INDEX TO HUNTS
Point-to-Point

INDEX TO MEETINGS
Point-to-Point

INDEX TO MEETINGS
Hunter Chase

Point-to-Point Results 1996

ARMY
Larkhill
Saturday January 13th
GOOD TO SOFT

1 - Saddle Club

DESERT WALTZ (IRE) .... **Maj O Ellwood** 1
(fav) mstks 2nd & 3rd,chsd ldrs,disp 15th-2 out,rallied to ld fin
Over The Edge .... **S Sporborg** 2
ld 4-5th, chsd ldr, disp 15th til ld 2 out, hdd post
Balisteros (Fr) .... **D Alers-Hankey** 3
hld up,prog & mskt 6th,rdn whn mstk 12th,outpcd,kpt on 3 out
Charden *ld to 4th & agn nxt, sn wll clr, wknd & hdd 15th, fin tired* 4
Shilgrove Place *reluc to race, t.o. whn f 1st* .... f
True Steel *hld up, lost tch 13th, bhnd whn p.u. 3 out* .. pu
Golden Mac *alwys bhnd, t.o. 8th, p.u. last* .... pu
7 ran. Nk, 20l, 10l. Time 6m 22.00s. SP 2-1.
H B Geddes (Beaufort).

2 - Open Maiden (5-8yo) Div I (12st)

AFRICAN BRIDE (IRE) 5a .... **Miss P Jones** 1
mid-div, prog to 2nd 12th, ld & mstk 3 out, ran on well
Upton Orbit .... **Miss S Sadler** 2
mid-div, prog to 3rd 13th, chsd wnr apr last, ran on
Tea Cee Kay .... **A Sansome** 3
ld 5th-3 out, no ext aft
Master Art *mstks, alwys chsng ldrs, outpcd frm 12th, no dang aft* 4
Sit Tight *chsd ldrs, outpcd frm 12th, no dang aft* 5
Scarlet Berry 5a *rear, effrt 11th, nvr nr ldrs* 6
Kingsthorpe *in tch to 10th, 9th & wll bhnd whn p.u. 13th* .... pu
Mac's Boy *mid-div, 7th & lost tch 13th, running on whn p.u. 15th* .... pu
Balance *ld to 3rd, prom whn f 5th* .... f
Two John's (Ire) *(fav) pllng, mskts, ld 3-5th, disp whn ran out & u.r. 12th* .... ro
Woodland Cutting *alwys rear, t.o. & p.u. 13th* .... pu
Heather Boy *prom to 10th, 8th & no ch 13th, wll bhnd whn p.u. 3 out* .... pu
Front Cover 5a *prom whn u.r. 3rd* .... ur
Muskerry Moya (Ire) 5a *rear whn f 6th* .... f
Rory'm (Ire) 2ow *rear whn f 2nd* .... f
Torsons Comet (Ire) *alwys bhnd, t.o. last whn p.u. 13th* .... pu
Peat Potheen *in tch whn blnd 6th, rear whn u.r. 9th* .. ur
17 ran. 3l, 10l, 30l, ½l, 20l. Time 6m 23.00s. SP 9-1.
David Brace (Llangeinor).

3 - Open Maiden (5-8yo) Div II Pt I (12st)

STRONG TARQUIN (IRE) .... **Miss P Curling** 1
(fav) hld up, rpd prog to 2nd 13th, ld aft 2 out, qcknd flat
Vulgan Prince .... **A Greig** 2
hld up, mstk 12th, prog to 3rd 14th, chal last,brshd aside
Gipsula 5a .... **S Slade** 3
chsd ldrs, ld 13th-aft 2 out, onepcd
Clobeever Boy *hld up bhnd, t.o. 13th, fin well, crashed thro rail aft fin* 4
Woodside Lady (Ire) 5a *ld to 13th, wknd rpdly & p.u. 15th* .... pu
Cherry Street 5a 4ow *n.j.w. chsd ldrs, 3rd whn f 11th* f
Barry Glen *chsd ldrs, blnd 5th, btn 13th, p.u. last* ..... pu
Filthy Reesh *prssd ldr til wknd 13th, p.u. 15th* ..... pu
Pharrago (Ire) *rear, bhnd 10th, t.o. whn ran out 14th* .. ro
Blucanoo 5a *20s-10s, jmpd lft, mid-div, no prog 14th, p.u. 2 out* .... pu
10 ran. 8l, 4l, nk. Time 6m 38.00s. SP 1-2.
Paul K Barber (Blackmore & Sparkford Vale).

4 - Open Maiden (5-8yo) Div II Pt II (12st)

TRUE FORTUNE .... **J Jukes** 1
(fav) in tch, blnd 6th, prog & ld 13-14th, ld apr last, styd on
Childsway .... **T Underwood** 2
pllng, ld til ran wd aft 12th, ld 14th-apr last, wknd
Gawcott Wood 5a .... **C Wadland** 3
hld up, prog to 3rd 14th, kpt on onepcd, hit last
Deep Moss (Ire) *mid-div, outpcd 12th, plodded on* 4
Sister Lark 5a *ld til aft 1st, t.o. last 7th, plodded on* ... 5
Blakes Beau *ld aft 1st, mstk 2nd, hdd 6th, wknd rpdly 4 out, p.u. 2 out* .... pu
Waipiro *last whn f 6th* .... f
Bridge House *rear, wll bhnd frm 12th, t.o. & p.u. 14th* pu
Gunner Boon *blnd 2nd, ran out nxt* .... ro
9 ran. 8l, ½l, 20l, 10l. Time 6m 36.00s. SP 7-4.
D J Miller (Pembrokeshire).
One fence omitted. 17 jumps.

5 - Ladies

FLAKED OATS .... **Miss P Curling** 1
(fav) w.w. chsd ldr 9th, ld 3 out, qcknd apr last, imprssv
Carrick Lanes .... **Miss P Jones** 2
mid-div, prog 11th, chsd wnr aft 3 out, outpcd apr last
Spacial (USA) .... **Miss M Hill** 3
ld to 3 out, sn btn
Upham Close 5a *last pair, lost tch 7th, nvr nr ldrs aft* 4
Daybrook's Gift *prom, mstk 6th, wknd rpdly 14th, t.o. & p.u. last* .... pu
Ski Nut *mid-div, lost tch 12th, poor 6th whn u.r. 3 out* ur
Give All *jmpd slwly 1st, t.o. whn nrly ref 6th & p.u.* .... pu
Tudor Henry *mstk 6th, in tch to 12th, wll bhnd whn p.u. 15th* .... pu
Slievenamon Mist *chsd ldrs til wknd rpdly 11th, t.o. & p.u. 13th* .... pu
I Is *chsd ldr 3-9th, wknd rpdly 12th, p.u. nxt* .... pu
10 ran. 15l, 6l, 30l. Time 6m 18.60s. SP 4-6.
E B Swaffield (Cattistock).

6 - Land Rover Open (12st)

WHAT A HAND 7ex .... **T Mitchell** 1
(fav) hld up,rpd prog 12th,2nd 14th,ld 3 out,slw last,ran on well
Wolf Winter 7ex .... **N Harris** 2
jmpd lft, prom, ld 9th-3 out, ev ch aft last, ran on onepcd
Buonarroti .... **M Batters** 3
prom, ld 6-9th, 3rd & outpcd frm 15th, fair effort
Nearly Splendid 7ex *mid-div, outpcd 13th, kpt on frm 3 out, bttr for race* 4
Mister Main Man (Ire) *sn prom, chsd ldr brfly 13th, outpcd 15th, fair effort* 5
Chibougama (USA) *alwys wll bhnd, t.o. frm 14th* 6
Phils Pride *nvr nr ldrs, t.o. & p.u. 15th* .... pu
Good Holidays 5a 3ow *ld to 6th, wknd 8th, t.o. & p.u. 15th* .... pu
Salcombe Harbour (NZ) *jmpd badly, t.o. 7th, p.u. 2 out* .... pu

Winter's Lane *mid-div, prog 12th, chsd ldrs 14th, wknd nxt, p.u. last* .... pu
Corrianne 5a (h) *prom to 10th, t.o. whn p.u. 3 out* .... pu
Sweatshirt *w.w. effrt 13th, 6th & btn whn blnd & u.r. 15th* .... ur
Holland House 7ex *trckd ldrs, blnd & u.r. 5th* .... ur
Daringly *mid-div, no ch frm 12th, t.o. & p.u. aft 3 out* .... pu
Light The Wick 2ow *alwys bhnd, t.o. & p.u. 13th* .... pu
Lighten The Load *well in rear whn f 11th* .... f
Master Kiwi (NZ) *mid-div, wknd 10th, t.o. & p.u. 15th* .... pu
Pro Bono (Ire) *prom to 10th, t.o. & p.u. 15th* .... pu

18 ran. 2l, 10l, 1l, 1l, 25l. Time 6m 23.40s. SP 4-5.
Mrs L J Roberts (Taunton Vale).

7 - Confined (12st)

GRANVILLE GUEST 1ow........D Pipe 1
in tch, prog 13th, disp nxt til ld 2 out, sn clr, rdn out
Earl Boon........Miss P Curling 2
(fav) trckd ldrs, prog to disp 14th-2 out, no ch wth wnr aft
Astound (Ire) 7a........Lt-Col R Webb-Bowen 3
hld up, lost tch 10th, t.o. 13th, fin strngly
Bang On Target *rear, prog to jn ldrs 13th, btn frm nxt* 4
Qualitair Memory (Ire) 7ex *in tch whn mstk 6th, bhnd whn hmpd 10th, no ch aft* 5
Zorro's Mark *in tch, effrt 12th, lost tch wth ldrs 14th, no dang aft* 6
Skinnhill (bl) *mstk 6th, prom to 14th, wknd rpdly* 7
Nathan Blake (bl) *ld til blnd 3rd, blnd nxt, sn last, t.o. & p.u. 3 out* .... pu
Iama Zulu 3ow *chsd ldr, lft in ld 10th, hdd 14th, 4th & btn whn f nxt* .... f
Not My Line (Ire) *ld 3rd til f 10th* .... f

10 ran. 12l, 20l, 5l, 15l, hd, 6l. Time 6m 30.00s. SP 7-2.
Mrs Bridget Nicholls (Blackmore & Sparkford Vale).
J.N.

CAMBRIDGESHIRE HARRIERS
Cottenham
Sunday January 14th
GOOD

8 - Confined (12st)

CARRIGEEN LAD........R Wakley 1
trckd ldrs going wl,jnd ldr & hit 2 out,ld last,rdn out
Copper Thistle (Ire) 6ex........P Taiano 2
(fav) in tch,ld apr 3 out,jnd & lft in ld 2 out, hdd & onepcd last
Gypsy King (Ire)........A Coe 3
in tch, 5th & rdn 16th, kpt on well apr last
Loughbrickland *ld/disp til ld 12th, jnd 14th, grad wknd frm 3 out* 4
Who's Next 7ex (bl) *in tch, prog to disp 14th, blnd 16th, rdn & btn nxt* 5
St Gregory *w.w. in tch, no prog frm 16th, fin with no irons* 6
Just Jack 7ex *w.w. in tch, outpcd apr 14th, no dang aft* 7
Mount Patrick *alwys last, t.o. frm 6th* 8
Jimstro *cls up, disp 6-11th, blnd nxt, no ch whn f 2 out* .... f
Abingdon Boy 3ex *in tch, outpcd 15th, p.u. apr last, bttr for race* .... pu

10 ran. 2l, 3l, 10l, 5l, 1l, 30l, dist. Time 6m 5.00s. SP 20-1.
Mrs Julie Read (Suffolk).

9 - Land Rover Open (12st)

SHEER JEST 7ex........A Hill 1
(fav) w.w. smooth prog to 2nd 13th, ld apr 2 out, clr last, easily
Peanuts Pet 7ex........R Walmsley 2
prom, disp ld 10-12th, ev ch til no ext apr last
Bright Burns 7ex (bl)........R Sweeting 3
mid-div, prog to 4th apr 2 out, kpt on steadily
Tammy's Friend 7ex (bl) *ld 2nd til jnd & hit 9th, outpcd 16th, styd on agn flat* 4
Green's Van Goyen (Ire) 4ex *ld 1st, sn hdd, jnd ldr 9th, ld 12th-3 out, eased whn btn* 5
Ten Of Spades *chsd ldrs, wknd 16th, p.u. last* .... pu
Shimshek (USA) *knckd over 2nd* .... f
Danribo *hmpd & u.r. 2nd* .... ur
Contact Kelvin *raced wd, lost tch 12th, p.u. 3 out* .... pu
Good Team *prom to 11th, losing tch whn u.r. 14th* .... ur
Wunderbar *b.d. 2nd* .... bd
Jerrigo *alwys rear, t.o. & p.u. 16th* .... pu
Bajan Affair 5a 7ex *mid-div, mstk 6th, bhnd frm 11th, p.u. 2 out* .... pu

13 ran. 6l, 2l, 4l, ¾l, 30l. Time 6m 1.00s. SP 4-6.
Mrs Judy Wilson (Pytchley).

10 - Intermediate (12st)

TIMBER'S BOY........R Gill 1
(fav) w.w. prog & cls up 11th, lft in ld 3 out, kpt on
Nethertara 5a........P Hacking 2
w.w. prog to 4th 3 out, lft 2nd nxt, kpt on und pres flat
Glitzy Lady (Ire) 5a 3ow........G Smith 3
7s-4s, w.w. in tch, prog to 3rd 2 out, nvr able to chal
The Right Kind *bhnd, prog & in tch 9th, lost tch 13th, ran on well frm 2out* 4
Couture Quality *ld to 7th, chsd ldrs til btn apr 3 out* 5
Fouracre *in tch to 14th, p.u. & dsmntd last* .... pu
Horace *prom, ld 8th, 6l clr whn f 3 out* .... f
Galzig *cls up, wkng whn blnd 15th, p.u. last* .... pu
Dynamite Dan (Ire) *blnd & u.r. 1st* .... ur
Good Old Chips *chsd ldrs to 4th, grad lost plc, last whn p.u. 11th* .... pu

10 ran. 2l, 20l, 7l, 10l. Time 6m 6.00s. SP 7-4.
B Clark (Puckeridge).

11 - Ladies

RICHARD HUNT........Miss L Rowe 1
(fav) chsd clr ldrs,clsd 9th,ld 15th,drew clr & blnd 2 out,easily
Douce Eclair 5a........Miss P Robson 2
ld/disp in clr ld to 9th,ld 14-15th,3rd & btn 3 out,styd on
Luck Money........Miss C Holliday 3
chsd clr ldrs, clsd 9th, 2nd apr 3 out, sn outpcd
Speculation *disp til wknd 13th, no ch whn f 16th, dead* .... f
Whistling Eddy *bhnd & pshd alng 5th, t.o. & p.u. 13th* pu
Mend *ref to race* 0
Ashboro (Ire) 7ow *alwys bhnd, t.o. & p.u. apr 2 out* .... pu

7 ran. 25l, 2l. Time 6m 6.00s. SP 2-5.
Mrs P Rowe (Puckeridge).

12 - Restricted

ZENISKA (USA)........R Wakley 1
chsd ldrs, went 2nd 3 out, ld nxt, clr & blnd last, rdn out
Busters Sister 5a........G Cooper 2
(fav) prom, chsd ldr 8th, rdn & btn 3 out, styd on agn flat
Sunset Run........Miss C Tuke 3
rear, prog 15th, went 2nd apr last, nvr nrr
Far View (Ire) *mstks, prog to 3rd 13th, btn apr 2 out, ran on agn flat* 4
Druid's Lodge *rear div, kpt on frm 16th, nvr nrr* 5
Parkers Hills (Ire) *ld 1st, sn hdd, prom til no prog frm 15th* 6
Cass *alwys mid-div, nvr able to chal* 7
Reviller's Glory *ld 2nd, went clr 13th, hdd 2 out, wknd rpdly* 8
Dream Packet *mid-div, in tch til outpcd apr 14th* 9
Russian Vision *mid-div whn f 6th* .... f
Familiar Friend (bl) *rear, effrt & blnd 11th, no ch aft, p.u. apr 14th* .... pu
Camogue-Valley (Ire) *rear, pshd alng 8th, blnd nxt, t.o. & p.u. 13th* .... pu

12 ran. 4l, nk, 2l, 3l, 15l, 3l, 10l, ½l. Time 6m 12.00s. SP 33-1.
Mrs P King (Suffolk).

13 - Open Maiden Div I (12st)

BLACK ERMINE (Ire) 7a 3ow..............R Ford 1
(fav) alwys going wl,ld 16th,clr whn swvrd & nrly ref last,rdn out
Auchendolly (Ire) ....S Sporborg 2
ld to 4th, cls up, mstk 13th, 3rd & btn 2 out
Montimezzo.............................C Ward 3
ld/disp 5-9th, 4th & btn 2 out, tk 2nd flat, eased cls hm
Charlie Kelly *in tch, wnet 3rd 14th, chsd wnr 3 out-flat, fin 4th, disq* 4D
Torali (Ire) *sn well bhnd, t.o. & f 9th* .... f
Salachy Run (Ire) *pllng, prom, ld 10-16th, p.u. rpdly apr nxt* .... pu
Dashboard Light *hld up, jmpd big 1st, in tch, slght mstk 14th,p.u.nxt,imprve* .... pu
Do You Know (Ire) 5a *bhnd whn jmpd slwly 8th & 9th, p.u. nxt* .... pu
Reformed Queen 5a *bhnd til p.u. 11th* .... pu
Springlark (Ire) 7a *rear & blnd 9th, t.o. & p.u. 13th* .... pu

10 ran. 4l, hd, 6l. Time 6m 18.00s. SP 2-1.
Mrs M Cooper (Middleton).
Charlie Kelly fin 4th, disq for taking wrong course.

14 - Open Maiden Div II (12st)

BARDAROS..........................P Hacking 1
prom, chsd ldr 13th, ld apr 3 out, lft well clr last
Derring Knight ....A Sansome 2
mid-div, lost tch 12th, lft 3rd 3 out, lft 2nd last
Sharp To Oblige *(fav) ld 5th, blnd 9th, hdd apr 3 out where f* .... f
Grain Merchant *in tch, went 3rd 14th, lft 2nd 3 out, 4l down whn f last* .... f
Run To Au Bon (Ire) *hld up, some prog 10th, 6th & no ch whn p.u. 16th, dsmntd* .... pu
Vernometum *ld to 4th, cls up, ran wd apr 10th, wknd 13th, p.u. 3 out* .... pu
Muddle Head (Ire) 3ow *pllng, went prom 4th til f 12th* .... f
Tiger Paws (Ire) 5a *cls up, f 7th* .... f
Boulevard Bay (Ire) 7a *jmpd stckly early, making prog whn b.d. 12th* .... bd
Daphni (Fr) 7a *w.w. blnd 11th, b.d. nxt* .... bd

10 ran. Dist. Time 6m 11.00s. SP 6-1.
Mrs D M Stevenson (East Sussex & Romney Marsh).

15 - Maiden (12st)

AL JAWWAL..........................R Wakley 1
chsd ldrs going well, ld apr last, pshd out
Just A Madam (Ire) 5a ....A Sansome 2
cls up, prog to ld 2 out, hdd apr last, no ext
Harry Lauder (Ire) 7a................S Sporborg 3
alwys prom, 5th 2 out, kpt on, improve
Shaab Turbo *(fav) prom, chsd ldr 4th, lft in ld 11th, hdd apr 2 out, wknd* 4
Ballysheil Star *in tch, blnd 10th, chsd ldr 14th, wknd apr 2 out* 5
Saffron Flame (Ire) *cls up to 9th, outpcd 13th, 6th whn blnd 2 out, improve* 6
Barmerville 5a *in tch in rear, outpcd 14th* 7
Aughnacloy Rose *alwys bhnd, t.o.* 8
Sign Performer *bhnd frm 10th, p.u. 16th* .... pu
Manor Cottage (Ire) *pllng, ld til f 11th* .... f
The Prior *rear, prog to mid-div whn blnd & u.r. 14th* .... ur
Fresh Ice (Ire) *w.w. prog & ev ch 14th, btn & eased apr 3 out, p.u. nxt* .... pu
Just Us (Ire) *in tch to 12th, bhnd & p.u. 16th* .... pu
Spartan's Conquest *n.j.w. sn bhnd, p.u. apr 13th* .... pu

14 ran. 2l, 6l, hd, 6l, 8l, 4l, dist. Time 6m 18.00s. SP 20-1.
Mrs P King (Suffolk).
S.P.

GARTH & SOUTH BERKS
Tweseldown
Sunday January 14th
GOOD TO SOFT

16 - Members (12st)

FRERE HOGAN (FR) 4ex...............P Scouller 1
made all, clr to 12th, kpt on gamely aft last
Olde Crescent.......................T Underwood 2
(fav) pllng, hld up, clsd 12th, rdn & ev ch last, not qckn flat

2 ran. 3l. Time 6m 47.00s. SP Evens.
P A D Scouller (Garth & South Berks).

17 - P P O A Maiden (12st)

ELITE GOVERNOR (IRE) ....L Baker 1
(fav) ld 4th, made rest, mstks 3 out & last, drvn out flat
Wholestone (Ire)..........................A Greig 2
alwys prom, chsd wnr 13th, rdn apr last, onepcd flat
Phil's Dream ....E James 3
w.w. clsd 12th,went 3rd & outpcd 4 out,styd on,improve
Local Manor *1st ride, prom til 5th & outpcd 15th, no prog aft* 4
Looking *rear, lost tch 11th, kpt on frm 15th, no dang* 5
Scratch Player (NZ) *mstk 2nd, in tch to 10th, sn outpcd, no dang frm 12th* 6
Rbf Arianne 5a *8s-5s, hld up, lost tch 11th, nvr on terms aft* 7
Final Option (Ire) *ld 3-4th, sn rear, t.o. 12th, p.u. 2 out, dsmntd* .... pu
Lazzaretto 1ow *alwys bhnd, t.o. 11th, p.u. 2 out* .... pu
Full Score (Ire) *ld to 3rd, chsd wnr & mstks 12,13 & nxt,drppd out & p.u.3out* .... pu
Stalbridge Gold 5a *prom, 3rd & outpcd 15th, wknd, hit 2 out & p.u.* .... pu

11 ran. 3l, 4l, 15l, 3l, 3l, 3l. Time 6m 37.00s. SP 2-1.
P Gardner (Berks & Bucks Drag).

18 - Mixed Open

ARDBRENNAN..........................C Bennett 1
chsd ldr 3rd, ld 11th, drew clr aft 2 out, hit last
Wild Illusion........................Miss P Curling 2
(fav) ld til hit 2nd, chsd wnr 11th, 2l down 3 out, rdn & btn nxt
Paco's Boy ....P York 3
alwys last, t.o. 8th, btn 2f
Qualified *nvr going well, t.o. 10th, poor 4th whn ran out & u.r. 12th* .... ro
Amber Ruler *ld 2nd-11th, wknd rpdly, fence bhnd 15th, stppd 2 out* .... pu
Bucksfern *3rd whn mstk & u.r. 4th* .... ur

6 ran. 25l, dist. Time 6m 34.00s. SP 33-1.
C C Bennett (Vine & Craven).

19 - Confined (12st)

DARTON RI..............................J Maxse 1
in tch,3rd & pshd alng 12th,chsd ldr 2 out,ld last,styd on
Copper Rose Hill 5a 3ex ....M Portman 2
prog 6th, chsd ldr 12th, ld 3 out, clr nxt,hdd & no ext last
Colonel O'Kelly (NZ) 9ex...............H Dunlop 3
rear, mstk 8th, lost tch 12th, ran on frm 2 out, nvr nrr
Mister Christian (NZ) (bl) *chsd ldr to 12th, 4th & btn frm 14th* 4
Yahoo *raced wd, hit 2nd, wll bhnd hlfwy, plodded on* 5
Afaltoun *(fav) ld to 3 out,wknd rpdly,no ch whn blnd last,p.u. flat,dsmntd* .... pu
Tomalley (bl) *1st ride, alwys last pair, t.o. whn f 11th* .... f
Cool It A Bit *mstk 2nd, mid-div, lost tch 11th, wll bhnd whn p.u. last* .... pu
Kites Hardwicke *u.r. 1st.* .... ur

9 ran. 3l, 10l, 5l, sht-hd, 20l. Time 6m 33.00s. SP 7-1.
Mrs S Maxse (Hampshire).

20 - Restricted (12st)

BARNEY BROOK.........................R Nuttall 1

5s-5/2,hld up,prog 10th,chsd ldr 14th,ld last,not extnd
Music In The Night.....................R White 2
ld, mstks 13 & 15th, hdd last, kpt on, no ch wth wnr
Turbulent Gale (Ire).....................R Bevis 3
(fav) nrly u.r. 1st,mstks,chsd ldng trio,outpcd frm 12th,t.o.
Royal Rupert *rear, mstk 9th, effrt 14th, sn wknd* 4
Pyro Pennant *rear, last whn u.r. 10th* .... ur
Reggie (v) *3rd til lft 2nd 10th, 3rd agn frm 14th, dist bhnd & f last* .... f
Endless Glee *chsd ldr til blnd & u.r. 10th* .... ur
Lewesdon Princess 5a *last & losing tch whn blnd & u.r. 7th* .... ur
Keep On Dreaming 5a *mstks, alwys rear, no ch whn f 3 out* .... f
9 ran. 1½l, dist, 4l. Time 6m 38.00s. SP 5-2.
R J Symonds (Blackmore & Sparkford Vale).
J.N.

P-TO-P OWNERS & RIDERS CLUB
Barbury Castle
Saturday January 20th
GOOD TO SOFT

21 - Members' Mares

FLAME O'FRENSI 5a 7ex........Miss J Cumings 1
made all, rdn whn lft clr 2 out, fin tired
Scally's Daughter 5a 7ex.............E Williams 2
(fav) mstks,prog & prom 10th,outpcd 15th,lft 2nd 2 out,styd on wl
Tapalong 5a *mid-div, 8th & lost tch 11th, p.u. 14th* .... pu
Loch Garanne 5a *reluc to race, t.o. til p.u. 4th* .... pu
Sisterly 5a *blnd 8th,prssd wnr to 10th,wknd 14th,lft 3rd 2 out,f last* .... f
Aintree Oats 5a *chsd ldrs to 8th, 6th & losing tch 11th, p.u. 15th* .... pu
Rainy Miss (Ire) 5a *alwys rear, t.o. & p.u. 12th* .... pu
Liddington Belle 5a *alwys bhnd, t.o. 7th, p.u. 9th* ...... pu
Little Martina (Ire) 5a *prom,chsd wnr 10-15th,3rd & btn whn hmpd & u.r. 2 out* .... ur
Woodmanton 5a *alwys bhnd, t.o. & p.u. 15th* .... pu
Arctic Madam 5a 1ow *w.w. prog 10th, chsd wnr 3 out, chal & f nxt* .... f
Copper Pan 5a *prom, f 3rd* .... f
Miss Millbrook 5a *mid-div, 7th & lost tch 11th, p.u. 15th* .... pu
High Lucy 5a *mstk 5th, alwys bhnd, t.o. & p.u. 13th* ... pu
Star Of Steane 5a *lost tch whn f 7th* .... f
Youbetya (Ire) 7a *mstk 5th, rear whn f 8th* .... f
16 ran. 7l. Time 6m 26.80s. SP 9-1.
P J Clarke (Devon & Somerset Staghounds).

22 - Novice Riders Div I (12st)

FAIR CROSSING 7ex...............M Emmanuel 1
chsd ldr,lft in ld 13th,in cmmnd whn lft clr last,ran on wll
19 **Kites Hardwicke ....Miss C Behrens** 2
rear til prog 10th, styd on frm 3 out, lft 2nd last
Dukes Son............................D Smith 3
rear, prog 13th, kpt on frm 2 out, nrst fin
Tenelord *hld up,prog to chs ldng trio 12th,no imp frm nxt* 4
Sevens Out 8ex *prom til lost plc 5th,sn bhnd,kpt on frm 14th,no dang* 5
Rubika (Fr) *unruly paddock, alwys wll bhnd, t.o.* 6
Prince Metternich *in tch to 5th, sn strggling, t.o.* 7
Robusti 5ex *alwys t.o.* 8
Espy 7ex (bl) *(fav) prom,lft 2nd 13th,ev ch apr 2 out,rdn & not run on,f last* .... f
9 Contact Kelvin 5ex *chsd ldrs til wknd 9th, p.u. 12th* ... pu
Secret Summit (USA) *bhnd til some prog 13th, nvr on terms, t.o. & p.u. 2 out* .... pu
Bright As A Button 11ex *nvr on terms, no ch frm 10th, p.u. 3 out* .... pu
All Weather *mid-div & out of tch,effrt 13th,nvr rchd ldrs,p.u. 2 out* .... pu
Tydelmore *mstk 5th, alwys bhnd, t.o. & p.u. 12th* ..... pu
Bellman *prom to 8th, steadily wknd, t.o. & p.u. 15th* ... pu
Dashing Brook *ld til jnd & f 13th* .... f
3 Pharrago (Ire) *alwys bhnd, t.o. 12th, p.u. last* .... pu
Gt Hayes Pommard *t.o. til u.r. 5th* .... ur
Posy Hill (Ire) 7a 1ow *t.o. in last trio til u.r. 10th* ...... ur
19 ran. 12l, 10l, ½l, 5l, dist, 6l, 1l. Time 6m 23.30s. SP 8-1.
Michael Emmanuel (Windsor Forest Drag).

23 - Novice Riders Div II Pt I (12st)

10 **GLITZY LADY (IRE) 5a..................G Smith** 1
4s-3s, prom, ld 12th, clr aft 3 out, mstk nxt, ran on well
Archie's Nephew 3ex (bl) ....Miss A Bush 2
prog 9th,outpcd 12th,styd on strngly frm 2 out,nrst fin
Gentleman's Jig (Can) ....P Hadden Wight 3
chsd ldrs, 3rd frm 14th, no imp frm 3 out
Brown Baby 5a *alwys bhnd, t.o. 10th* 4
Tattlejack (Ire) *(fav) prom,blnd 10th,wth wnr 12-14th,wknd 2 out,nrly ref last* 5
Tsagairt Paroiste *u.r. 2nd* .... ur
Run To Form *lft in ld 4th, hdd 12th, wknd nxt, t.o. & p.u. 2 out* .... pu
Windover Lodge *ld til ran out & u.r. 4th* .... ro
Electrolyte *mstk 7th, prom til wknd 10th, p.u. nxt* ..... pu
Mr Paddy Bell *blnd 6th & lost tch, t.o. & u.r. 11th* ..... ur
Phar Too Touchy 5a *u.r. 1st* .... ur
11 ran. 15l, 6l, 15l, 15l. Time 6m 34.40s. SP 3-1.
G Smith (Cranwell Bloodhounds).

24 - Novice Riders Div II Pt II (12st)

GETAWAY BLAKE...................R Thornton 1
chsd ldr, ld 14th, lft clr nxt, unchal
Tuffnut George.................Miss M Corbett 2
(fav) clr ldr til hdd 14th, blnd nxt, no ch wth wnr aft
The Jogger...........................J Tizzard 3
chsd ldrs, 4th & no prog 13th, lft 3rd nxt, no imp ldrs
Laundryman *alwys bhnd, t.o. 9th* 4
Barkin 3ex *rear whn f 1st* .... f
Punching Glory *chsd ldrs, 3rd frm 11th, no ch wth 1st pair whn u.r. 14th* .... ur
Flaxridge *rear whn u.r. 1st* .... ur
Rochester *last whn u.r. 1st* .... ur
Sprucefield *sn wll bhnd, t.o. & p.u. 9th* .... pu
Your Opinion *mstks, blnd 4th & lost plc, t.o. & p.u. 15th* .... pu
Drumceva 5ex *f 1st* .... f
Par-Bar (Ire) 5a *bhnd frm 8th, t.o. & p.u. 2 out* .... pu
12 ran. 30l, 12l, 30l. Time 6m 24.50s. SP 12-1.
Mrs C Mackness (Cotswold).

25 - Land Rover Open Div I (12st)

TEAPLANTER 7ex....................B Pollock 1
(Jt fav) ld to 2nd, ld agn 15th, clr aft nxt, all out flat
Good For Business 4ow..............T Mitchell 2
w.w. prog 10th, chsd wnr 15th, styd on strngly aft last
Welsh Legion 7ex......................J Jukes 3
hld up, prog frm 12th, disp 2nd aft 3 out, wknd last
6 Holland House 7ex *(Jt fav) mstk 3rd, rear, lost tch 12th, styd on frm 2 out, no dang* 4
Tangle Baron *w.w. prog 10th, chsd ldrs aft, 3rd 3 out, wknd nxt* 5
Roaming Shadow *alwys bhnd, kpt on frm 15th, nrst fin* 6
Woodhay Hill *trckd ldrs, pshd alng 11th, wknd frm 13th* 7
Duke Of Impney *alwys bhnd, blnd 8th, t.o. & p.u. 14th* pu
Old Road (USA) 5ow *ld 2-4th, wkng whn blnd 11th, p.u. 13th* .... pu
Quick Rapor 7ex *ld 4th til hdd & mstk 15th, wknd rpdly, p.u. 2 out* .... pu
Chip'N'run *prom to 10th, btn frm 12th, t.o. & p.u. 2 out* .... pu
Knowing 5a 3ow *rear, lost tch & p.u. 11th* .... pu
Prince Tino *prom to 9th, sn lost tch, t.o. & p.u. 2 out* .. pu

Ufano (Fr) 7ex *mid-div, prog 11th, wknd 14th, no ch whn u.r. 3 out* .... ur
14 ran. 2½l, 12l, 6l, 5l, 15l, 4l. Time 6m 24.60s. SP 7-4.
R G Russell (Pytchley).

26 - Land Rover Open Div II (12st)

HOWARYASUN (IRE) ....D S Jones 1
in tch,lft 2nd 13th,lkd hld til styd on und pres to ld post
Ru Valentino.........................G Hanmer 2
in tch, 3rd whn lft in ld 13th, clr aft til wknd & hdd post
Faithful Star 7ex ....D Pipe 3
(fav) blnd 6th,effrt 10th,outpcd 12th,lft 3rd nxt,wknd 3 out,tired
Pin's Pride *alwys last, t.o. & p.u. 13th* .... pu
Ryde Again *j.w. prom, trckd ldr 8th, going wll whn b.d. 13th* .... bd
Tekla (Fr) *33s-14s, cls up, 4th whn f 8th* .... f
Pont de Paix 4ex *trckd ldrs til wknd 11th, t.o. & p.u. 13th* .... pu
9 Wunderbar *prom to 8th, wknd rpdly & p.u. 10th* .... pu
6 Lighten The Load *mstk 3rd, rear, prog & cls up whn f 11th* .... f
5 I Is *bhnd frm 7th, t.o. & p.u. 12th* .... pu
John Roger *f 2nd* .... f
Fresh Prince *ld, 3l up whn f 13th* .... f
12 ran. Sht-hd, dist. Time 6m 34.10s. SP 20-1.
M R Watkins (Ross Harriers).

27 - Ladies

DOWN THE MINE ....Miss A Dare 1
(fav) j.w. made all, ran on strngly apr last
Workingforpeanuts (Ire) 5a ....Mrs D Smith 2
hld up bhnd, gd prog frm 12th, chsd wnr last, no imp flat
Pamela's Lad ....Miss J Priest 3
mstk 6th, rear, prog 10th, lft 2nd aft 2 out, onepcd
Fosbury *mid-div & outpcd, styd on frm 14th, nrst fin* 4
Thamesdown Tootsie 5a *prom til outpcd frm 13th, sn no ch* 5
Space Camp *w.w. prog to chs wnr 10-13th, wknd 3 out, fin tired* 6
Button Your Lip *chsd ldrs til f 10th* .... f
Garda Spirit 5a *alwys t.o. last, p.u. 14th* .... pu
Starember Lad *in tch, chsd wnr 13th, 2nd & hld whn p.u. aft 2 out, dead* .... pu
5 Ski Nut *wll bhnd frm 8th, t.o. & p.u. 2 out* .... pu
20 Pyro Pennant *t.o. 5th, p.u. 10th* .... pu
Little Thyne *t.o. 6th, mstk 8th, p.u. 14th* .... pu
Bold Man (NZ) *chsd ldrs to 9th, bhnd whn p.u. 15th* .... pu
Lavalight *chsd ldrs til wknd 12th, t.o. & p.u. 2 out* .... pu
Glenmavis *chsd ldrs to 9th, t.o. & p.u. 15th* .... pu
15 ran. 7l, 12l, 5l, 25l, 8l. Time 6m 24.10s. SP 9-4.
R T Baimbridge (Berkeley).
Last fence omitted, 17 jumps.

28 - Restricted Div I (12st)

BROAD STEANE.....................A Sansome 1
6s-3s, hld up in tch,prog to ld aft 3 out,mstk last,styd on
Glenrowan Lad ....T Marks 2
cls up, effrt to chs wnr 2 out, styd on, no imp nr fin
Sound Statement (Ire) ....T Hills 3
ld to 14th, lft in ld nxt, hdd aft 3 out, fdd
Hey Henry *in tch, prog 11th, cls up 3 out, wknd* 4
New Years Eve *mstk 7th, prom to 12th, wknd, p.u. 3 out* .... pu
17 Lazzaretto *last frm 4th, t.o. & p.u. 13th* .... pu
Cut The Corn *pllng, prom til f 8th* .... f
Parditino *rear til u.r. 8th* .... ur
Tinotops *chsd ldr, ld 14th, jnd & f nxt* .... f
Perish The Thought *mstk 7th, rear whn hmpd & u.r. 10th* .... ur
St Julien (Ire) *in tch in rear to 11th, nrly u.r. 13th, p.u. nxt* .... pu
Fathers Footprints *alwys rear, t.o. & p.u. 14th* .... pu
Highleeze (Ire) 2ow *(fav) hld up, in tch in rear whn f 10th* .... f
Monday Country *in tch to 11th, last & no ch 15th, p.u. 2 out* .... pu
14 ran. 2½l, 15l, 8l. Time 6m 37.60s. SP 3-1.
Sir Michael Connell (Grafton).

29 - Restricted Div II (12st)

TEX MEX (IRE)...........................J Maxse 1
ld, clr to 13th, rdn & hdd last, sn ld agn, ran on gamely
Lord Ellerton...........................B Pollock 2
chsd wnr, rdn 2 out, ld last, sn hdd & no ext flat
Calling Wild (Ire) 2ow ....T Mitchell 3
(fav) mstks, hld up, effrt 15th, styd on, not rch ldrs
2 Tea Cee Kay *hld up, prog frm 12th, styd on frm 3 out, nrst fin* 4
Dodgy Dealer (Ire) *prom til wknd 3 out, not disgraced* 5
17 Final Option (Ire) *rear, lost tch 10th, t.o. whn blnd & u.r. 12th* .... ur
Pavi's Brother *5s-7/2, trckd ldrs til wknd 13th, t.o. & p.u. 2 out* .... pu
My Boy Barney *f 3rd* .... f
Ice House Street (NZ) *prom to 11th, wknd 13th, t.o. & p.u. 2 out* .... pu
Roll-A-Dance *chsd ldrs to 8th, t.o. p.u. 12th* .... pu
Southern Flight *rear,prog 11th,chsd ldrs 14th,fair 5th but btn whn u.r. last* .... ur
Oh Lord (Ire) *alwys bhnd, t.o. & p.u. 13th* .... pu
12 ran. 1l, 5l, 1l, 30l. Time 6m 30.10s. SP 20-1.
Mrs S Maxse (Hampshire).
J.N.

WAVENEY
Higham
Saturday January 20th
GOOD TO FIRM

30 - Members (12st)

AS YOU WERE 7ex ....D Parravani 1
(fav) ld/disp til ld 11th, made rest, rddn out
Little Freddie ....Miss L Hollis 2
ld/disp til blnd 11th, ev ch last, onepaced
Muck Or Money 29ow *alwys 3rd, lst tch 12th, t.o. whn ref 3 out* .... ref
Here's Humphrey 8ow *last whn ref & u.r. 2nd* .... ref
4 ran. ¾l. Time 6m 52.00s. SP 1-3.
D Parravani (Waveney Harriers).

31 - Confined (12st)

CRAFTSMAN.......................Miss G Chown 1
cls up, ld 10th-11th & again 15th, clr nxt, ran on strngly
10 **Timber's Boy ....R Gill** 2
(fav) w.w. stdy prog 9th, hit 10th, chsd ldr 2 out, no ext last
Cardinal Red.............................S Cowell 3
prom, ld 5th-9th, rddn & no ex appr 2 out
Salmon River (USA) 7a *bhnd, kpt on stdly from 16th, nvr nrr, improve* 4
Way Of Life (Fr) 3ex *nvr put in race, sme prog 13th, no dang* 5
El Bae *nvr bttr than mid-div, t.o. & p.u. 2 out* .... pu
Frank Rich *prom, ld 12th-14th, sn wknd, p.u. 3 out* .... pu
15 The Prior *alwys bhnd, t.o. & p.u. appr 16th* .... pu
Minstrels Joy (Ire) *ld to 4th, wknd appr 13th, t.o. & p.u. appr last, dead* .... pu
9 ran. 3l, 3l, 20l, 20l. Time 6m 6.00s. SP 7-4.
G W Paul (Essex & Suffolk).

32 - Open

STRONG GOLD (bl)...................T McCarthy 1
(fav) ld/disp,rddn 12th,hd rdn to ld 3 out to flat,rlld to ld post
The Portsoy Loon ....A Hickman 2
prom, 3rd at 12th, jnd ldr 16th- nxt,ld flat til hdd post

Welsh Singer .... **R Lawther** 3
hit 2nd, alwys wll bhnd, kpt on from 16th, nvr nrr
Exclusive Edition (Ire) 5a *prom, disp ld 4th-15th, sn wknd*........ 4
9 Danribo *alwys bhnd t.o.*........ 5
Armagret *mid-div whn f 4th*........ 6
Pigeon Island *v.s.a. t.o. til p.u. 11th*........ pu
Nicknavar *chsd ldrs, hit 8th, 4th & lsing grnd whn f 14th*........ f
Rehab Venture *prom to 8th, sn bhnd p.u. appr 16th*... pu
Yeoman Farmer *in tch to 11th, p.u. 13th*........ pu
Mara Askari (v) *prom to 6th, sn lst plc, p.u. aft 11th*... pu
Laburnum *rr whn hmpd bnd appr 4th, t.o. & p.u. 12th* pu
Stede Quarter *chsd ldrs to 11th, wkng whn u.r. 13th*.. ur
Basher Bill *alwys bhnd, t.o. & p.u. aft 11th*........ pu
Tasmanite *bhnd til p.u. 11th*........ pu
15 ran. Hd, 20l, 10l, dist. Time 6m 8.00s. SP 4-7.
Peter Bonner (Old Surrey & Burstow).

33 - Ladies

11 **RICHARD HUNT** .... **Miss L Rowe** 1
(fav) alwys going wll, ld appr last, pushed out flat, clvrly
Counterbid 3ow .... **Miss Z Turner** 2
trkd ldrs, chall last, nt pace of wnnr flat
What A Gig .... **Miss P Ellison** 3
prom, ld 14th til appr last, onepcd
Crazy Otto *in tch, ev ch appr 3 out, onpcd*........ 4
Little Nod *in tch, ev ch appr 3 out, wknd 2 out*........ 5
11 Mend *hld up, in tch, ch 16th, btn appr 2 out*........ 6
Motor Cloak *u.r. 1st*........ ur
Ravens Hasey Moon *pllg, chsd ldr blnd 10th, wknd appr 12th, p.u. 3 out*........ pu
Swinging Song *pllg,jmpd rt, made most to 13th, sn wknd, p.u. 3 out*........ pu
9 ran. 1l, 3l, 1l, 4l, 6l. Time 6m 17.00s. SP 1-3.
Mrs P Rowe (Puckeridge).

34 - Maiden

SHAKE FIVE (IRE) 7a .... **S Sporborg** 1
chsd lding pr 12th, qknd to chall last, sn ld, clvrly
Ludoviciana 5a .... **Miss G Chown** 2
set fast pace to 15th,lft in ld last, sn hdd,rlld gmly flat
Kellys Nap .... **C Ward** 3
chsd ldr 11th, ld 16th,1l ld whn blnd & u.r. last, rmtd
Lunar Lunacy (Ire) 5a *disp ld whn u.r. 3rd*........ ur
Northern Reef (Fr) 7a *in tch til f 5th*........ 0
Coppinger's Cave *s.s. alwys bhnd, 5th & no ch whn p.u. 16th*........ pu
15 Manor Cottage (Ire) *(fav) alwys chsing lding grp, 4th & no ch whn p.u. 3 out*........ pu
Room To Manouver (Ire) *jmpd badly, sn t.o. p.u. 16th* pu
Kiwi Exile (NZ) *bhnd, blnd 8th, p.u. nxt, dead*........ pu
Ernie Fox *rr div, 5th & no ch whn ref & u.r. 13th*...... ref
Sheer Hope (bl) *chsd ldr to 10th, sn wknd, p.u. 12th*... pu
11 ran. ½l, dist. Time 6m 12.00s. SP 10-1.
Mrs C H Sporborg (Puckeridge & Thurlow).

35 - Restricted Div I (12st)

STORMHILL PILGRIM .... **P Hacking** 1
ld 3rd, clr 8th, ran on strngly whn chal 2 out
On The Beer (Ire) .... **S Sporborg** 2
(fav) prog to 4th at 11th, ev ch 3 out, rdn nxt, onepcd
Tough Minded .... **R Wakley** 3
mid-div, poor 4th at 16th, rpd prog to chal 2 out, no ext
Oflaherty's Babe (Ire) *alwys prom, ev ch 16th, wknd 2 out*........ 4
Holding The Aces *mid-div whn hmpd 13th, nvr trbld ldrs, improve*........ 5
Wistino *prom to 11th, grad lost plc frm nxt*........ 6
Alfredo Garcia (Ire) 7a *alwys bhnd, nvr nr ldrs*........ 7
Woodrow Call *bhnd frm 12th, t.o.*........ 8
Fort Diana *blnd & u.r. 4th*........ ur
Tel D'Or *bhnd frm 11th, t.o. & p.u. last*........ pu
Harpley Dual (Ire) *bhnd frm 11th, t.o. & p.u. last*...... pu
Doctor Dick (Ire) *cls up whn f 2nd*........ f
Swift Reward 5a *bhnd frm 10th, p.u. last*........ pu
Joyful Hero 5a *sn bhnd, p.u. 9th*........ pu
Prime Course (Ire) *prom to 10th, wkng whn f 13th*..... f
Borneo Days 5a *alwys rear, t.o. & p.u. 11th*........ pu
16 ran. 1½l, 3l, 10l, 15l, 3l, 6l, 30l. Time 6m 9.00s. SP 4-1.
Mike Roberts (East Sussex & Romney Marsh).

36 - Restricted Div II (12st)

MISS CONSTRUE 5a .... **N Bloom** 1
in tch, jnd ldr 16th, ld nxt, rdn out
Billion Dollarbill .... **M Gorman** 2
prom, ev ch apr 2 out, onepcd und pres flat
Major Neave .... **G Hopper** 3
w.w. prog 12th, went 3rd apr last, no ext flat
Cowage Brook *prom, chsd ldr 12-15th, wknd 2 out*... 4
Ryders Wells *mid-div, chsd ldrs apr 3 out, not pace to chal*........ 5
Corn Kingdom *in tch, rmndrs 11th, grad wknd frm 13th*........ 6
Cool Apollo (NZ) *wth ldr to 10th, wknd 12th*........ 7
8 Mount Patrick *sn t.o., p.u. 3 out*........ pu
12 Russian Vision *n.j.w. rear, brief effrt 12th, sn btn, p.u. 16th*........ pu
Ha-To-Siee (Ire) *(fav) 5/2-1/1,ld,hit 4th,clr 12th,hdd 3 out,immed btn,p.u. nxt*........ pu
Salmon Mead (Ire) *f 1st*........ f
Reaper *jmpd slwly 3rd, bhnd 8th, p.u. 12th*........ pu
12 ran. ¾l, 2l, ½l, 1l, 15l, 10l. Time 6m 17.00s. SP 20-1.
Mrs Kit Martin (North Norfolk).
S.P.

WETHERBY
Saturday February 3rd
GOOD TO SOFT

37 - 3m 110yds Hunt Chase

25 **TEAPLANTER 11.9 5a** .... **Mr B Pollock** 1
prom, ld 4 out, styd on well.
Wudimp 11.3 7a .... **Mr C Storey** 2
nvr far away, chsd wnr from 4 out, kept on, no impn.
Tipping Tim 11.5 5a .... **Mr M Rimell** 3
(fav) ld till hdd 4 out, no ext.
Southern Minstrel 11.3 7a *in tch, effort after 12th, ev ch 4 out, soon wknd.*........ 4
Off The Bru 11.3 7a (v) *chsd ldrs till wknd before 4 out, no ch when blnd 2 out, t.o.*........ 5
Carousel Rocket 11.3 7a *soon well bhnd, t.o.*........ 6
Quixall Crossett 11.3 7a *hmpd before 1st, lost tch from hfwy, t.o.*........ 7
Dark Dawn 12.4 *chsd ldrs till wknd before 4 out, losing tch when p.u. before 2 out.*........ pu
Astre Radieux (Fr) 11.3 7a *soon well bhnd, t.o. when p.u. after 8th*........ pu
Politico Pot 11.8 7a 5ow *bhnd from hfwy, lost tch and p.u. before 4 out.*........ pu
Carton 11.3 7a *lost tch from hfwy, t.o. when p.u. before 12th*........ pu
11 ran. 6l, 13l, 2½l, 30l, 20l, 8l. Time 6m 42.80s. SP 2-1.
R G Russell

NORTH CORNWALL
Wadebridge
Saturday February 3rd
GOOD TO FIRM

38 - Members (12st)

MYHAMET .... **A Farrant** 1
(fav) ld to 9th & frm 11th, pshd out flt, comf
Just My Bill .... **C Heard** 2
last til prog 6th, ld 9/11th, chsd wnr, no imp 2 out
Baron Rush .... **I Dowrick** 3
chsd wnr to 7th, disp 2nd 13th-3 out, wknd rpdly
Gymcrak Dawn *mstks, hld up, lost tch 11th, t.o. aft til fin fast*........ 4
4 ran. 4l, dist, 8l. Time 6m 16.00s. SP 4-7.

Paul C N Heywood (North Cornwall).

39 - Open (12st)

6 **WOLF WINTER 7ex ....N Harris 1**
ld to 8th, chsd ldr, hrd rdn last, ran on to ld flat
Stoke Hand 4ex.........................C Heard 2
trckd ldr, ld 8th, rdn last, hdd & no ext flat
Lady Llanfair 5a 7ex..................E Williams 3
prom til lost pl 12th, outpcd 15th, fin well
Anjubi *prom, chsd ldr 12th til rdn aft 14th, outpcd.....* 4
Moze Tidy *cls up, eff aft 14th, sn outpcd..........* 5
St Laycar *hld up, ev ch aft 14th, sn not qckn ....* 6
26 Faithful Star 7ex *(fav) msk 5th, last whn u.r. 8th......* ur
7 ran. 4l, 7l, 6l, 1l, 3l. Time 6m 20.00s. SP 5-4.
Victor Dartnall (Dulverton West).

40 - Ladies

BUTLER JOHN (IRE).............Miss J Cumings 1
j.w., ld 2nd, clr 14th, pshd out flat
5 **Carrick Lanes ....Miss P Jones 2**
(fav) in tch, chsd wnr 11th, hld whn blndrd 2 out, kpt on
Bootscraper ....Miss T Brown 3
hld up, pckd 8th, 3rd frm 12th, kpt on one pace
Pejawi 5a *chsd wnr 2nd-11th, outpcd 12th, kpt on....* 4
Heluva Season 5a *ld to 2nd, p.u. aft 4th, lame ......* pu
5 ran. 3½l, 2½l, 8l. Time 6m 6.00s. SP 7-2.
Nick Viney (Exmoor).

41 - Resticted (12st)

23 **PHAR TOO TOUCHY 5a ....N Harris 1**
made virt all, jnd 3 out, ran on gmly flat
2 **African Bride (Ire) 5a ....Miss P Jones 2**
(fav) mstk 1st, prog 8th, jnd wnr & mstk 3 out, not qckn
Caracol 2ow...........................T Mitchell 3
hld up, prog 11th, hmprd 15th, styd on agn flat
Ewhonosebest *10s-5s, wth wnr to 13th, outpcd 15th, kpt on..................................* 4
High Degree *prom to 11th, eff agn 15th, 3rd & btn whn blndrd last.................................* 5
Sherbrooks *in tch to 13th, rdn & outpcd aft nxt ....* 6
Moorland Abbot *in tchh to 13th, sn outpcd ....* 7
Saffron Moss *lost tch & msk 7th, sn t.o., btn 3 f.......* 8
Great Impostor (bl) *blndrd 2nd & 3rd, prom whn u.r. 5th..* ur
9 ran. 1l, 10l, 4l, 1l, 1l, 12l, dist. Time 6m 15.00s. SP 9-2.
Miss R A Francis (Dulverton West).

42 - Confined (12st)

WALKERS POINT......................A Farrant 1
ld to 8th, 11-13th & aft nxt, rdn clr 3 out, styd on
Oneovertheight.........................N Harris 2
ld 8-11th & 13th-aft nxt, kpt on frm 2 out
Early To Rise..........................J Creighton 3
tckd ldrs, eff & ev ch app 4 out, no ext
Sancreed *clse up til outpcd 12th, kpt on frm 2 out ....* 4
Ghofar *jmpd errctclly, bhnd frm 9th, kpt on frm 2 out..* 5
6 Phils Pride *last whn u.r. 8th ....* ur
Cardinal Bird (USA) *rlct to race, t.o. whn tried to ref 5th, p.u. nxt...................................* pu
Full Alirt 5a *(fav) u.r. 1st...........................* ur
8 ran. 6l, 1l, 3l, 4l. Time 6m 17.00s. SP 7-4.
T D H Hughes (Lamerton).

43 - Intermediate (12st)

JUST BERT (IRE).....................P Scholfield 1
w.w., mstk 3rd, prog 11th, ld 14th, rdn out
Lucky Ole Son.......................Miss P Jones 2
ld to 11th, outpcd, rlld 15th, ev ch last, kept on
1 **Balisteros (Fr)...................D Alers-Hankey 3**
in tch, prog 11th, ld 12-14th, one pace 3 out
Magnolia Man 5ex *(fav) prom, clse 3rd whn slppd & f 14th...* f
4 ran. 2l, 4l. Time 6m 8.00s. SP 7-4.
Mrs J Alford (Eggesford).

44 - Open Maiden Div I (12st)

17 **WHOLESTONE (IRE) ....A Greig 1**
(fav) ld 3rd-8th & 10th-aft 14th, ld 2 out, rdn out
Far Run ....A Farrant 2
hld up, prog 10th, ld aft 14th-2 out, no ext
Absent Minds 5a ....Miss S Young 3
trckd ldrs til outpcd 15th, fin tired
4 Sister Lark 5a *ld to 3rd, mid-div & rdn 12th, sn outpcd, fin well...* 4
Dharamshala (Ire) *trckd ldrs, rdn & outpcd aft 14th, no imp aft ....* 5
Great Precocity *mstk 2nd, alwyd bhnd, t.o. & p.u. 12th ....* pu
Happy Thought 5a *schoold rear, t.o. whn p.u. 2 out ..* pu
Charlie's Hideaway (Ire) *prom, ld 8-10th, wknd rpdly, t.o. & p.u. 15th..* pu
Hod Wood 7a *last whn ran out 3rd, rjnd, p.u. aft 4th ..* pu
9 ran. 4l, 15l, 1l, ½l. Time 6m 14.00s. SP 11-10.
D R Greig (Surrey Union).

45 - Open Maiden Div II (12st)

RUSHALONG..............................A Farrant 1
hld up rear, prog 11th, eff 3 out, ld flat, ran on well
17 **Stalbridge Gold 5a ....B Dixon 2**
tckd ldrs, ld 15th, clr 3 out, wknd & hdd flat
Baldhu Chance ....J Young 3
ld 4-15th, rlld & ev ch last, wknd flat
6 Master Kiwi (NZ) *prssdl ld to 12th, 4th whn hit 15th, rlld flat ....* 4
Mr Cherrypicker (Ire) *(fav) trckd ldrs gng wl, mstk 14th, sn wknd ....* 5
Namestaken *prom til wknd 12th, t.o. & p.u. 15th......* pu
2 Muskerry Moya (Ire) 5a *alwys rear, lost tch 11th, t.o. & p.u. 2 out ....* pu
2 Rory'm (Ire) *jmpd bdly in last til p.u. 6th ....* pu
Lets Go Polly 5a *prom till u.r. 10th ....* ur
Mrs Wumpkins (Ire) 7a *alwys rear, lost tch & p.u. 12th, dsmtd ....* pu
10 ran. 3l, 1½l, 1l, 25l. Time 6m 20.50s. SP 8-1.
George Ball (Spooners And W Dartmoor).
J.N.

WEST PERCY & MILVAIN
Alnwick
Sunday February 4th
GOOD

46 - Members (12st)

WASHAKIE 4ow 7ex.......................J Walton 1
trckd ldrs, ld 8th, rdn 2 out, hld on gmly
Hardihero................................A Robson 2
(fav) trckd ldrs app 3 out, rdn & not qckn nxt
The Healy 5a ....Mrs F Scales 3
chsd ldr, ld 7th-nxt, outpcd 3 out, ran on nxt
McNay *bhnd, prog & in tch 8th, no imp frm 12th......* 4
Loughlinstown Boy *ld to 7th, grad wknd frm 10th......* 5
Cynch *bhnd frm 5th, t.o. & p.u. 3 out...............* pu
Called To Account 5a *last whn u.r. 3rd...............* ur
7 ran. 2l, 5l, 30l, 8l. Time 6m 33.00s. SP 7-4.
Mrs F T Walton (West Percy).
One fence omitted all races; 16 jumps

47 - Resticted (12st)

FARRIERS FAVOURITE 5a ....A Parker 1
hld up, prog 11th, disp app 3 out til lft clr last drvn out
Prior Conviction (Ire)...................S Swiers 2
rear, prog 9th, chsd ldrs 3 out, lft 2nd last, no ext
Joli Exciting 5a ....C Storey 3
mid-div, prog & in tch 12th, one pacd 3 out, lft 3rd last
11 Douce Eclair 5a 1ow *(fav) ld to 3rd, ld 9th till app 3 out, sn wknd ....* 4
Sunnie Cruise 5a *hld up last pair, nvr nr, imprv.......* 5

Toaster Crumpet *mid-div, prog to trck ldr 12th, wknd 3 out* 6

Pennine View *ld 4-9th, grad wknd frm 13th* 7

12 Reviller's Glory *rear, blndrd 8th, eff 12th, wknd, p.u. 3 out* pu

Miss Eros 5a *rear, in tch 11th, eff 3 out, 4th whn hmprd & u.r. last* ur

Clone (Ire) *prom til blndrd & u.r. 3rd* ur

Deday *ld 3rd-4th, wknd 7th, t.o. & p.u. 3 out* pu

Kalajo *mid-div, prog 11th, disp app 3 out, just ld whn f last* f

Tall Fellow (Ire) *pllng, wth ld 4th-nxt, wknd rpdly, p.u. 10th* pu

Two Gun Tex *t.o. in last pair til p.u. 8th* pu

14 ran. 3l, 15l, 4l, hd, 8l, ½l. Time 6m 30.30s. SP 4-1.
Mrs J Leckenby (Braes Of Derwent).

48 - Ladies

THISTLE MONARCH ... Miss R Clark 1
sttld rear, prog 8th, ld 2 out, slow last, drvn out

Steele Justice ... Miss P Robson 2
tckd ldrs, eff 3 out, ev ch last, not qckn nr fin

Across The Lake ... Miss S Brotherton 3
(fav) rear, grad clsd frm 13th, eff & ev ch last, not qckn

Fish Quay *last til eff app 3 out, kpt on, nvr able to chal* 4

Another Dyer *ld to 6th & 12th-2 out, wknd* 5

Abitmorfun *mstk 5th, ld 6th-12th, btn aft nxt* 6

Iron Prince *clse up, eff & ev ch 13th, wknd nxt, fair effort* 7

Anzarna 5a *clse up to 8th, wknd & p.u. 11th* pu

Mandys Special 5a *in tch, mstk 8th & 9th, wknd, p.u. 13th* pu

9 ran. 1l, nk, 6l, 3l, 7l, 15l. Time 6m 30.40s. SP 7-1.
S B Clark (York & Ainsty South).

49 - Open

ROYAL STREAM ... A Parker 1
(fav) j.w., made all, wl clr 3 out, eased flat

9 **Peanuts Pet ... R Walmsley** 2
w.w., prog 11th, blndrd nxt, chsd wnr 2 out, no imp

Political Issue ... J Walton 3
in tch, chsd wnr 11th, no imp aft 13th, one pace

Tom Log *blndrd 9th, chsd wnr til blndrd 11th, one pace frm 13th* 4

Castle Gem 5a *chsd ldrs, outpcd 12th, kpt on agn frm 3 out* 5

Ready Steady *alwys outpcd in rear, nvr nr* 6

Fordstown (Ire) 2ow *alwys bhnd, t.o. hlfwy* 7

Trebonkers 16ow *alwys wl bhnd, t.o. & p.u. 3 out* pu

Who's In Charge *rear, t.o. & p.u. aft 8th* pu

General Brandy *chsd ldrs, 3rd frm 10th-3 out, 5th & btn, f last* f

Dundee Prince (NZ) *s.v.s., prog frm hlfwy, disp 4th whn f 13th* f

Kilminfoyle *blndrd 5th, prom to 11th, t.o. & p.u. 3 out* pu

Chickcharnie *t.o. last til f 5th* f

Judicious Captain *mstk 4th, rear, lost tch 12th, t.o. & p.u. 3 out* pu

14 ran. 8l, 1l, 4l, 6l, 15l, 20l. Time 6m 31.00s. SP 7-4.
Mrs D B Johnstone (Berwickshire).

50 - Confined (12st)

HEDLEY MILL 5a 7ex ... A Parker 1
(fav) hld up, prog 12th, mstk nxt, ld 2 out, v easily

Royella 5a ... A Robson 2
prom til lost pl 11th, ran on agn 2 out, fin well

Hallo Sensation ... Mrs V Jackson 3
ld to 4th & aft 12th til 3 out, one pace

Tod Law 5a *in tch, mstk 9th, ld 3 out-nxt, no ext* 4

Buckle It Up 3ex *prog 6th, clse up til 12th, no prog 3 out* 5

Bow Handy Man *prom til grad wknd frm 3 out* 6

Deplete 14ow *plld to ld 4th, hdd aft 12th, wknd, p.u. 2 out* pu

Sharp Opinion 6ex *in tch to 7th, t.o. & p.u. 11th* pu

Lion Of Vienna *hld up, prog 12th, disp 2nd & gng wl, f nxt* f

9 ran. 5l, 5l, 3l, 6l, 4l. Time 6m 31.40s. SP 5-4.
J W Hope (Braes Of Derwent).

51 - Open Maiden Div I (12st)

WEEJUMPAWUD 5a ... C Storey 1
tckd ldrs, ld 12th-2 out, lft in ld last, all out

Attle ... S Brisby 2
hmprd 1st, mid-div, prog 12th, lft 2nd last, kpt on

Roly Prior ... Miss P Robson 3
in tch, lost pl 11th, prog 4 out, mstk nxt, fin well

Canister Castle *tckd ldrs, clse up 13th, one pace frm 3 out* 4

Hungry Jack 12ex *alwys ldng grp, one pace app 3 out* 5

Steady Away (Ire) *rear, kpt on frm 3 out, nvr dang* 6

Trip Your Trigger (Ire) 7a *schoold rear, lost tch hlfwy, nvr nr* 7

Miss Cullane (Ire) 5a *in tch to 9th, no ch 13th, virt p.u. flat* 8

Jack's Croft *alwys bhnd, t.o. 9th, p.u. 11th* pu

Indian River (Ire) *7s-3s, ld to 4th, prom til wknd 13th, p.u. nxt* pu

Silver Shilling *alwys bhnd, t.o. & p.u. 3 out* pu

Need A Ladder *mid-div, wknd 11th, bhnd & p.u. 13th* pu

African Gold *prom, 5th whn f 10th* f

Cukeira 5a *f 1st* f

Eastlands Hi-Light *ld 4-12th, ld 2 out, 1l up whn blndrd & u.r. last* ur

14 Boulevard Bay (Ire) 7a 1ow *(fav) hld up, gd prog to jn ldrs 13th, wknd & p.u. nxt* pu

Alianne 5a *t.o. til p.u. 12th* pu

17 ran. 1½l, 1l, 3l, 6l, 12l, hd, 25l. Time 6m 37.20s. SP 3-1.
A J Carnegie (College Valley/ Northumberland).

52 - Open Maiden Div II (12st)

FROZEN STIFF (IRE) ... N Wilson 1
trckd ldr, ld 9th, clr whn blndrd 2 out, ran on well

Misskeira 5a ... C Paisley 2
tckd ldrs, eff 3 out, no imp wnr aft nxt

Weddicar Lady 5a ... Mrs J Williamson 3
made most til 9th, prom aft, one pace 3 out

Border Supreme (Ire) *rear, prog to chs ldrs 9th, one pce frm 3 out* 4

14 Sharp To Oblige *(fav) hld up wll bhnd, prog 10th, not rch ldrs, wknd 2 out* 5

Woolaw Lass (USA) 5a *prom, ld brfly 5th, wkng whn mst 9th, p.u. 3 out* pu

Jane's Feelings *rear, lost tch 8th, t.o. & p.u. 13th* pu

Terracotta Warrior *f 2nd* f

Doc Spot *prom, mstk 9th, blndrd 12th, not rcvr, p.u. nxt* pu

Malakie (Ire) *chsd ldrs, 6th & lsng tch whn blndrd & u.r. 12th* ur

Bucklands Cottage 5a *n.j.w., alws bhnd, t.o. & p.u. 13th* pu

11 ran. 4l, 4l, 1l, 25l. Time 6m 40.00s. SP 14-1.
Alan Brown (Buccleuch).

53 - Open Maiden Div III (12st)

ADMISSION (IRE) ... Miss C Metcalfe 1
prom, chsd ldr 3 out, styd on to ld nr fin

Castle Tyrant 5a ... P Atkinson 2
ld to 9th & frm 12th, clr 3 out, wknd & hd nr fin

Olive Branch 5a ... D Wood 3
rear, lost tch 8th, ran on frm 3 out, nrst fin

Buckwheat Lad (Ire) *wth ldr, ld 9-12th, no ext 3 out* 4

Are-Oh *(Jt fav) hld up, lost tch 9th, ran on frm 3 out, nvr nr* 5

Sparky's Decision (Ire) 7a *(Jt fav) hld up, prog 8th, ev ch aft 13th, wknd rpdly* 6

Wassl's Nanny (Ire) 5a *mid-div, 6th whn u.r. 11th* ur

Summer Dalliance *prom to 6th, sn wknd, t.o. & p.u. 13th* pu

Fair Grand *n.j.w., rear, t.o. & p.u. 10th* pu

Jamarsam (Ire) *mid-div, chsd ldrs 12th, sn btn, p.u. 3 out* pu

Mapalak 5a *t.d.e., plld into ld & ran out 3rd* .... ro
Starlin Sam *alwys bhnd, t.o. & p.u. 13th* .... pu
Scarlet Rising 5a *rear, wl bhnd hlfwy, t.o. & p.u. 11th* pu
13 ran. ¾l, 12l, 2l, 2½l, 20l. Time 6m 41.00s. SP 20-1.
N Chamberlain (South Durham).
J.N.

CAMBRIDGE UNIV DRAGHOUNDS
Cottenham
Saturday February 10th
GOOD TO SOFT

54 - Members

36 **SALMON MEAD (IRE) ....S Sporborg** 1
(fav) jmpd lft, wth ldr, ld 5th-aft 12th, jnd ldr & lft clr 3 out
Highland Laird ....M Barnard 2
ld to 5th, last & rdn 11th, sn lost tch
12 Sunset Run *pllng, hld up, ld aft 12th, jnd & ran out 3 out, lame* .... ro
3 ran. Dist. Time 6m 30.00s. SP 4-7.
Christopher Sporborg (Cambs Univ Draghounds).

55 - Confined (12st)

KELLY'S EYE (bl) ....L Lay 1
mstk 9th,disp,ld & mstk 14th,clr 16th,tried ref 2 out,allout
Sylvan Tempest..........................T Lane 2
(fav) jmpd slwly 4th, disp to 14th, btn 16th, slw 2 out, lame
2 ran. Dist. Time 6m 40.00s. SP 5-4.
Mrs M Kimber (Grafton).

56 - Open

32 **ARMAGRET.............................S Cowell** 1
trckd ldrs, 2nd 16th, ld 2 out, ran on well apr last
Quentin Durwood ....T McCarthy 2
hld up in tch, prog to ld 13th, hdd & no ext 2 out
32 **Stede Quarter ....A Hickman** 3
prom, ld 9th-13th, cls 3rd 3 out, no imp wnr nxt
32 Exclusive Edition (Ire) 5a *mstks, hld up in tch, prog & in tch 3 out, not qckn, kpt on* 4
Lights Out *hld up in tch, outpcd aft 16th, not pshd, promising* 5
Welshman's Creek *sttld mid-div, effrt & in tch 15th, wknd nxt* 6
Cromwell Point *(fav) n.j.w. ld to 2nd lft in ld 5th, hdd 7th, wknd 4 out* 7
32 Pigeon Island *33s-14s, ld 7-9th, wknd 13th, sn no ch* .. 8
The Forties *alwys last, t.o. 12th* 9
Blue Beat 5a *alwys rear, t.o. 14th, p.u. 16th* .... pu
Athnanurlainn 4ow *alwys bhnd, t.o. & p.u. 14th* .... pu
Jefferby *ld 2nd til ref 5th, cont t.o. til p.u. 13th* .... pu
12 ran. 10l, hd, hd, 8l, 15l, 12l, 2l, 1 fence. Time 6m 22.20s. SP 5-2.
B Kennedy (Essex Farmers & Union).

57 - Ladies

KAMBALDA RAMBLER ....Miss C Holliday 1
16s-7s, j.w. trckd ldr, ld 7th, wll clr frm 11th, unchal
Profligate.........................Miss P Ellison 2
hld up, effrt hlfwy, no imp wnr, lft poor 2nd 2 out
Quenby Girl (Ire) 5a.............Miss E Godfrey 3
chsd ldrs, lost tch 12th, nrly u.r. nxt, t.o.
22 Prince Metternich *hmpd & u.r. 1st* .... ur
Pardon Me Mum (bl) *(fav) hmpd & u.r. 1st* .... ur
33 Motor Cloak *mstks, ld to 7th, chsd wnr aft, dist 2nd whn u.r. 2 out* .... ur
11 Ashboro (Ire) *hmpd & u.r. 1st* .... ur
High Burnshot *hmpd & u.r. 1st* .... ur
33 Swinging Song *pllng, prom to 8th, strgglng 10th, t.o. & p.u. 3 out* .... pu
9 ran. Dist, 5l. Time 6m 10.00s. SP 7-1.
H Morton (Quorn).
1 fence omitted 2nd circuit. 18 jumps.

58 - Restricted Div I (12st)

36 **BILLION DOLLARBILL ....M Gorman** 1
wth ldrs, drvn to ld last, hld on well cls home
36 **Ryders Wells.......................Mrs M Morris** 2
made most to 2 out, ev ch last, just hld nr fin
Alansford...................................P Bull 3
sttld in tch, effrt aft 2 out, ran on onepcd flat
12 Familiar Friend (bl) *trckd ldrs, mstk 16th, ld 2 out, hdd & wknd last* 4
Half A Sov *prom til wknd aft 3 out, p.u. last* .... pu
Prince's Gift *(fav) blnd & u.r. 2nd* .... ur
Reign Dance 7a *schoold & t.o. til p.u. 12th* .... pu
7 ran. Hd, 4l, 6l. Time 6m 27.00s. SP 2-1.
Brian Tetley (Surrey Union).

59 - Restricted Div II (12st)

SAMSWORD.......................John Pritchard 1
(fav) mstks,prom,lost plc 12th,styd on 2 out,ld apr last,all out
Big Jack (Ire)..............................I Marsh 2
mstk 1st,ld 7th,clr 14th,reluc aft,not run on & hdd apr last
Iridophanes.......................Miss S Knight 3
prom til outpcd 14th, no ch 3 out, styd on agn flat
23 Brown Baby 5a *cls up, chs ldr 14th-aft 2 out, wknd* ... 4
Majestic Ride *withdrawn start - deemed to have come und orders* 0
Dangerosa 5a *prom til wknd sddnly & p.u. 13th* .... pu
35 Doctor Dick (Ire) *blnd & u.r. 2nd* .... ur
Broadcaster *ld to 6th, mstk & wknd 11th, p.u. 15th* .... pu
Late Start 5a *last & n.j.w. t.o. & p.u. 11th* .... pu
9 ran. 7l, 7l, 12l. Time 6m 32.60s. SP Evens.
B C Gurney (Warwickshire).

60 - Open Maiden (5-7yo) Div I (12st)

15 **SAFFRON FLAME (IRE) ....P Taiano** 1
w.w. mstk 14th, lft 2nd apr 3 out, ld aft 2 out, ran on well
Grassington (Ire) ....S Quirk 2
1st ride,pllng,hld up last,kpt on to go 2nd flat,no ch wnr
14 **Derring Knight ....A Sansome** 3
ld to 12th, lft in ld apr 3 out, mstk 2 out, hdd & wknd
Red Rory *mstk 4th,cls up,ld 12th,2l up whn hmpd & u.r. apr 3 out* .... ur
2 Upton Orbit *(fav) ld & f 1st* .... f
15 Fresh Ice (Ire) *prom, wth ldr whn f 11th* .... f
14 Daphni (Fr) 7a *in tch to 11th, last & no ch whn f 14th* .. f
7 ran. 8l, 5l. Time 6m 35.00s. SP 3-1.
Mrs M G Sheppard (Cambridgeshire).

61 - Open Maiden (5-7yo) Div II (12st)

PENLY...........................John Pritchard 1
out of tch, lft 2nd aft 15th, lft clr 2 out, all out
35 **Holding The Aces ....S R Andrews** 2
(fav) mstks,poor 3rd frm 6th,lft in ld & blnd 15th,hdd & tired aft
Reedfinch..............................R Barrett 3
out of tch,poor 4th 13th,lft in ld aft 15th,u.r 2 out,rmntd
Mister Spectator (Ire) *ld, drew away 13th, fence up & f 15th* .... f
13 Salachy Run (Ire) *alwys bhnd, t.o. & p.u. 14th* .... pu
14 Muddle Head (Ire) *wth ldr & clr of rest,blnd 11th, wknd rpdly & p.u. 14th* .... pu
Clonattin Lady (Ire) 5a *raced wd, alwys bhnd, t.o. last whn p.u. 13th* .... pu
Irish Genius (Ire) *alwys bhnd, t.o. & p.u. 14th* .... pu
8 ran. 10l. Time 6m 47.00s. SP 7-1.
R G Weaving (Warwickshire).

62 - Open Maiden (5-7yo) Div III (12st)

TANGLEWOOD BOY 7a ....R Thornton 1
hld up,prog 12th,mstk 15th,qcknd to ld 3 out,drvn out flat

Cantango (Ire) ....A Sansome 2
(fav) in tch, trckd ldr 10th-3 out, effrt apr last, no ext flat
Hullabaloo 5a 5ow ....T Lacey 3
ld to 3 out, wknd apr last
34 Room To Manouver (Ire) *in tch to 12th, no ch 15th, blnd 2 out* 4
Still Hopeful 5a *chsd ldr to 10th, last whn f 13th* ...... f
St Amour 7a *blnd & u.r. 2nd* .... ur
6 ran. ¾l, 15l, 20l. Time 6m 31.00s. SP 9-4.
S Aspinall (Warwickshire).
1 fence omitted 2nd circuit. 18 jumps. J.N.

EAST CORNWALL
Great Trethew
Saturday February 10th
SOFT

63 - Members (12st)

42 **FULL ALIRT 5a ....Miss S Young** 1
(fav) ld 4th,made rest, rdn out
Brother Bill.........................Mrs M Hand 2
off pace 7th, steady prog nxt, fin well
42 **Ghofar ....C Crosthwaite** 3
twrds rear til prog 14th, kpt on onepcd
Rathmichael (bl) *ld til apr 4th, in tch whn mstk 13th, sn btn*........ 4
Holly Fare *trckd ldrs til ref 7th* .... ref
41 Moorland Abbot *bhnd til hmpd & u.r. 7th, rmntd, t.o. & p.u. 2 out* .... pu
6 ran. 10l, 2l, 25l. Time 6m 41.00s. SP Evens.
B R J Young (East Cornwall).

64 - Confined (12st)

THE GENERAL'S DRUM ....K Heard 1
bhnd, godd prog to ld 14th, made rest, readily
Oriental Plume ....Mrs M Hand 2
ld 6th-14th, prssd wnr til outpcd last
42 **Sancreed..........................Miss L Long** 3
mid-div, prog past btn horses frm 15th
Senegalais (Fr) 4ow *ld 4th-nxt, wknd 9th, fin tired*..... 4
Casting Time (NZ) *(fav) prom til wknd 14th* 5
Confused Express 5a *ld til u.r. 4th* .... ur
Chandigarh *prom til lost tch 13th, p.u. 15th* .... pu
7 ran. 5l, dist, 5l, 10l. Time 6m 29.00s. SP 2-1.
Mrs R Fell (Dartmoor).

65 - Intermediate (12st)

41 **PHAR TOO TOUCHY 5a..........Miss R Francis** 1
ld 2nd, ld agn 8th, made rest, all out
Kaloore ....P Scholfield 2
mid-div til prog frm 13th, kpt on wll flat
Vital Song 2ow ....G Matthews 3
ld/disp 2nd-8th, no ext frm 3 out
On Alert (NZ) *nvr thrtnd ldrs, kpt on onepcd frm 3 out* 4
Pharynx 1ow *nvr a fctr, p.u. 10th* .... pu
24 Tuffnut George *mostly abt 5th-6th, wknd 13th, p.u. 16th*........ pu
Scorpio Sam *nvr nr ldrs, p.u. aft 13th* .... pu
27 Space Camp *nvr nr to chal, p.u. bef 2 out* .... pu
25 Good For Business *(fav) mid-div, prog 7th, mstk nxt, no imp whn p.u. 2 out* .... pu
25 Tangle Baron *mid-div, no imp whn p.u. aft 13th*........ pu
Lady Lir 5a *ld to 2nd, disp to 8th, wknd, p.u. aft 12th* .. pu
Henry Vajra *alwys bhnd, p.u. 2 out*........ pu
Saucy's Wolf *wll bhnd whn p.u. 13th* .... pu
13 ran. 3l, 15l, ½l. Time 6m 19.00s. SP 7-1.
Miss R A Francis (Dulverton West).

66 - Open (12st)

LEWESDON HILL ....T Mitchell 1
alwys going wll, ld last, ran on well
Chilipour 7ex..........................N Harris 2
ld til last, no ext flat
The Bird O'Donnell 7ex ....T Barry 3
chsd ldr til onepcd frm 3 out
Fearsome *alwys rear, no ch frm 3 out* 4
Far Too Loud 7ex *nvr bttr than 4th/5th, no ch frm 3 out*........ 5
Mr Lion *grad lost tch frm 10th, p.u. 2 out* .... pu
6 Nearly Splendid 7ex *disp brfly 3rd, fdng whn blnd 11th, p.u. 13th* .... pu
Kilmacthomas *twrds rear, p.u. 13th*........ pu
8 ran. 1l, 10l, 15l, ½l. Time 6m 26.00s. SP 7-1.
T C Frost (Seavington).

67 - Ladies

RURAL OUTFIT....................Miss P Curling 1
(Jt fav) alwys prom, ld 14th, made rest, comf
18 **Qualified.......................Mrs L Boscawen** 2
alwys cls up, kpt on onepcd frm 2 out, no imp wnr
Searcy..........................Miss L Blackford 3
chsd wnr 14th til last, wknd und pres
Kings Rank *clsd up 13th, no ext frm nxt* 4
Great Pokey *nvr bttr than mid-div, no ch frm 3 out*.... 5
Grey Guestino *ld to 4th, grad wknd*........ 6
Treleven 5a *alwys bhnd* 7
Unityfarm Oltowner *alwys bhnd, fin own time*........ 8
Galaxy High *nvr on terms*........ 9
Duchess Of Tubber (Ire) 5a *nvr a fctr, p.u. aft 14th* .... pu
40 Butler John (Ire) *(Jt fav) ld 4th-14th, sn fdd, p.u. 2 out* pu
11 ran. 3l, 4l, ½l, 8l, 10l, dist, 2l, 2l. Time 6m 35.00s. SP 7-4.
Mrs S Humphreys (Cattistock).

68 - Restricted (12st)

3 **STRONG TARQUIN (IRE) ....Miss P Curling** 1
(fav) mid-div til prog 5 out, ld 3 out, ran on well
Clandon Lad 3ow ....T Mitchell 2
steady prog frm 14th, onepcd frm 2 out
Strong Breeze ....Mrs R Pocock 3
alwys prom, unable to chal frm 2 out
Lonesome Traveller (NZ) *ld to 3rd, drppd back, styd on agn frm 3 out*........ 4
Pillow Spin *u.r. 3rd*........ ur
41 High Degree *nvr dang, p.u. aft 14th*........ pu
63 Holly Fare *2nd outing, bhnd whn p.u. aft 12th* .... pu
The Kimbler *nvr bttr than mid-div, p.u. 14th*........ pu
Roving Rebel *nvr trbld ldrs, p.u. aft 14th* .... pu
Monkton (Ire) *prom early, grad fdd, p.u. 5 out*........ pu
Millaroo *ld to 3rd, sn bhnd, p.u. aft 12th* .... pu
41 Sherbrooks *nvr seen wth ch, p.u. 14th*........ pu
17 Elite Governor (Ire) *trckd ldrs, p.u. bef 4 out, bandages loose* .... pu
21 Youbetya (Ire) 7a *nvr a fctr, p.u. aft 14th* .... pu
14 ran. 3l, 4l, 8l. Time 6m 37.00s. SP Evens.
Paul K Barber (Blackmore & Sparkford Vale).

69 - Open Maiden Div I (12st)

EARTHMOVER (IRE) 7a ....Miss P Curling 1
mid-div, prog 14th, chal nxt, sn ld, readily
4 **Waipiro ....I Dowrick** 2
alwys cls up, ev ch 2 out, no ext, promising
Moorland Highflyer 7a...........Miss D Mitchell 3
prom, ld 14th-nxt, kpt on und pres
Miss Pernickity 5a *alwys bhnd, t.o.*........ 4
Stormy Sunset 5a *1st ride, ld 7th til jnd & u.r. 14th* ..... ur
Eserie de Cores (USA) *(fav) alwys prom, blnd 14th, p.u. nxt*........ pu
Balmaha 7a *prom whn u.r. 13th*........ ur
Run With Joy (Ire) 7a *nvr dang, p.u. 14th* .... pu
Jay Em Ess (NZ) *u.r. 1st*........ ur
Itscountryman *ld to 7th, grad wknd, p.u. 3 out*........ pu
Karlimay 5a *prom, losing tch whn p.u. 14th* .... pu
Saint Joseph *twrds rear, p.u. 14th*........ pu
12 ran. 4l, 3l, dist. Time 6m 44.00s. SP 5-2.
R M Penny (Cattistock).

70 - Open Maiden Div II (12st)

2 **MAC'S BOY..............................J Jukes** 1
(fav) 6s-6/4, mid-div, prog to ld 15th, drew clr aft
Clonroche Lucky (Ire)..................I Dowrick 2
prom, ld 13th-15th, outpcd frm nxt
Chukamill ....R Mills 3

ld to 13th, sn btn
Sharrow Bay (NZ) *nvr bttr than mid-div, p.u. aft 14th* .. pu
Newstarsky *nvr a serious threat, p.u. aft 14th* .... pu
Say Charlie *bhnd whn p.u. aft 14th* .... pu
Mr Wideawake *chsd ldrs til lost ground & p.u. 13th* ... pu
Corporal Charlie *nvr on terms, p.u. bef 13th* .... pu
3 Gipsula 5a *mid-div whn f 11th* .... f
Pen-Alisa 5a *wll bhnd whn p.u. aft 7th* .... pu
Gigi Beach (Ire) 7a *s.s. mstk 1st, bhnd whn u.r. 13th* .. ur
Kanjo Olda 5a *bhnd whn p.u. 8th* .... pu
Spartans Dina 7a 2ow *f 4th* .... f
Bells Wood *chsd ldrs, 4th & btn whn f 2 out* .... f
14 ran. 10l, dist. Time 6m 42.00s. SP 6-4.
Julian P Allen (Llangeinor).

71 - Open Maiden Div III (12st)

TASMIN TYRANT (NZ) ....**L Jefford** 1
alwys prom, ld 3 out, drvn clr
Parson Flynn ....**R White** 2
prog frm mid-div 13th, rdn nxt, no imp wnr
Biddlestone Boy (NZ) ....**A Farrant** 3
mid-div, ran on onepcd frm 3 out, nrst fin
45 Baldhu Chance *ld 4th-3 out, grad fdd* 4
Sixth In Line (Ire) *bhnd frm 4th, p.u. 7th* .... pu
Zany Girl 5a (bl) *nvr a fctr, p.u. 13th* .... pu
Gay Muse 5a *alwys bhnd, p.u. 3 out* .... pu
Friendly Viking *nvr bttr than mid-div, p.u. 13th* .... pu
Mendip Son *(fav) chsng grp til mstk 10th, p.u. bef nxt* pu
Ashcombe Valley *bhnd whn p.u. 3 out* .... pu
Rosa's Revenge 5a *prom early, losing tch whn p.u. aft 13th* .... pu
Upton Gale (Ire) *disp to 3rd, grad wknd, p.u. 3 out* .... pu
Sgeir Bantighearna 5a *wll bhnd, p.u. 3 out* .... pu
Swing To The Left (Ire) 5a *ld 3rd-4th, cls up til wknd 14th, p.u. 3 out* .... pu
Crownhill Cross 7a *in rear whn p.u. aft 4th* .... pu
15 ran. 5l, 10l, 10l. Time 6m 34.00s. SP 5-1.
Mrs C Egalton (Axe Vale Harriers).
P.Ho.

BADSWORTH
Wetherby Point-To-Point Course
Sunday February 11th
GOOD TO SOFT

72 - Confined (12st)

48 **THISTLE MONARCH 5ex** ....**Miss R Clark** 1
(fav) cls up, ld 14th, hld off chal, styd on well
Mahana ....**D Coates** 2
mid-div, prog 12th, tk 2nd 14th, chsd wnr
49 **Tom Log** ....**W Burnell** 3
ld to 5th, disp 6-8th, in tch to 4 out, outpcd aft
Kellys Diamond *mid-div, prog 13th, 4th 4 out, no ext* .. 4
Convincing *alwys prom, disp 6-8th, styd on onepcd frm 4 out* 5
Earl Gray *alwys mid-div, nvr dang* 6
Fowling Piece *rear, nvr a fctr* 7
Arctic Paddy *cls up, 2nd at 10th, fdd rpdly 12th* 8
Major Rouge *cls up til p.u. 7th* .... pu
Celtic King *alwys rear, p.u. 4 out* .... pu
Valassy (v) *alwys rear, f 12th* .... f
Mr Snail *mid-div, rear whn u.r. 12th* .... ur
Shotivor 1ow *alwys rear, p.u. 3 out* .... pu
Simply A Star (Ire) *bhnd early, prog 14th, 3rd 4 out, chal whn u.r. 2 out* .... ur
Dear Jean 5a 1ow *cls up, ld 9th-12th, fdd rpdly, p.u. 3 out* .... pu
Charlcot Storm 7a *bhnd til p.u. 4th* .... pu
Primitive Penny 7a 2ow *s.s. t.o. & p.u. 10th* .... pu
Lakeland Venture 5a *rear whn ran out 6th* .... ro
18 ran. 8l, 6l, 5l, 8l, 6l, 1l, 5l. Time 7m 8.00s. SP Evens.
S B Clark (York & Ainsty South).

73 - Open Maiden (5-7yo) Div I (12st)

LATHERON (IRE) ....**S Swiers** 1
(fav) rear, prog 12th, disp last, styd on well flat
Anythingyoulike ....**T Stephenson** 2
disp 9th, ld 3 out, disp last, just outpcd flat
Rye Head 7a ....**N Tutty** 3
alwys prom, 2nd at 12th, 3rd 2 out, styd on onepcd
Priceless Sam 7a *rear, late prog, nvr nrr* 4
Greet The Greek *cls up, disp 9th, ld nxt-4 out, sn no ext* 5
Skyval 5a *mid-div, 3rd at 13th, onepcd aft* 6
Timber Topper *lost tch early, rear whn p.u. 4 out* ...... pu
Stride To Glory (Ire) 7a *rear, mstk 6th, outpcd, p.u. 4 out* .... pu
Whispers Hill 7a *f 4th* .... f
Flying Pan 5a *in tch, 5th at 10th, u.r. 12th* .... ur
Barneys Gold (Ire) *ld to 8th, 2nd at 13th, ran out nxt* ... ro
Red Star Queen 5a *alwys rear, p.u. 13th* .... pu
Mal's Castle (Ire) 5a *bhnd, outpcd, p.u. 13th* .... pu
Arras-Tina 5a *rear, prog whn hit wing & f 14th* .... f
Muscoates 7a *rear, p.u. 6th* .... pu
15 ran. 1l, 4l, 15l, 1l, 15l. Time 7m 11.00s. SP 5-2.
Mrs A M Easterby (Middleton).

74 - Open Maiden (5-7yo) Div II (12st)

THIRD TIME (IRE) 5a ....**A Phillips** 1
mid-div, prog 12th, ld 3 out, drew clr, comf
Morcat 5a ....**C Mulhall** 2
ld 8th-4 out, outpcd by wnr aft
Reefside (Ire) ....**N Tutty** 3
rear, prog 11th, lft dist 3rd at 14th, no ext
Pure Madness (USA) (bl) *ld to 7th, wknd, p.u. 12th* .... pu
Lingcool 5a *bhnd early, nvr a fctr, p.u. 4 out* .... pu
Another Hooligan *(fav) alwys rear, u.r. 9th* .... ur
Mount Faber *in tch, 3rd at 12th, fdd, p.u. 4 out* .... pu
City Buzz (Ire) *alwys prom, 2nd at 13th, f nxt* .... f
Sergent Kay *mid-div, fdd, f 12th* .... f
Tyndrum Gold *alwys rear, nvr dang, p.u. 14th* .... pu
Winters Melody 5a *f whn hit wing 4th* .... f
11 ran. 15l, dist. Time 7m 28.00s. SP 9-4.
Miss J Green (Ludlow).

75 - Open Maiden (5-7yo) Div III (12st)

POLITICAL SAM ....**A Rebori** 1
cls up, ld 4 out, prssd 2 out, drew clr flat, comf
Launchselect 7a ....**C Mulhall** 2
in tch, 3rd at 14th, tk 2nd flat, outpcd by wnr
Mr Busker (Ire) ....**C Barlow** 3
(fav) prom, ld 14th, hdd & no ext last
Goongor (Ire) *ran out 1st* .... ro
Living On The Edge (Ire) *prom, disp 12th-nxt, wknd, p.u. 4 out* .... pu
53 Fair Grand *in tch to 10th, outpcd whn u.r. 13th* .... ur
Ingleby Lodger *alwys rear, p.u. 10th* .... pu
Tinker's Hill 7a *ld to 11th, disp to 13th, fdd rpdly, p.u. 4 out* .... pu
8 ran. 10l, 10l. Time 7m 11.00s. SP 7-2.
J W Barker (Hurworth).

76 - Ladies

37 **SOUTHERN MINSTREL** ....**Miss C Metcalfe** 1
(fav) cls up, 3rd 4 out, drvn to ld flat, styd on well
Ridwan ....**Miss S Bonser** 2
cls up, 2nd at last, just hld flat
Final Hope (Ire) ....**Mrs F Needham** 3
rear early, prog 11th, ld 14th-last, no ext flat
Katies Argument 5a *alwys rear, nvr dang* 4
Carole's Delight 5a *mid-div, effrt 13th, onepcd aft* 5
Side Brace (NZ) *alwys wll in rear, p.u. 4 out* .... pu
Barry Owen *ld to 10th, fdd rpdly, p.u. 4 out* .... pu
27 Workingforpeanuts (Ire) 5a *in tch, ld 11th-13th, 2nd whn u.r. 3 out* .... ur
8 ran. 1l, 4l, 15l, 3l. Time 7m 4.00s. SP 5-4.
N Chamberlain (South Durham).

77 - Restricted (12st)

47 **PRIOR CONVICTION (IRE)** ....**S Swiers** 1
(fav) mid-div, prog 14th, ld 2 out, drvn out
Polynth ....**H Brown** 2
ld 9th-13th, 2nd 2 out, hrd rdn, just btn
Implicitly Suzie 5a ....**C Mulhall** 3

mid-div, late prog, 5th 2 out, styd on well
Miley Pike *alwys prom, 3rd at 12th, rnwd chal 2 out, nvr nrr* 4
Stag Fight *cls up, 3rd 2 out, no ext aft*....... 5
Ocean Rose 5a *prom, ld 14th-3 out, outpcd aft*....... 6
Current Attraction 5a *mid-div, onepcd, nvr nrr*....... 7
Missile Man *in tch, 3rd at 13th, no ext 4 out*....... 8
One For The Chief *alwys wll in rear, p.u. 4 out*....... pu
Hillview Lad *alwys rear, p.u. 10th*....... pu
Cairndhu Misty 5a *cls up, fdd 11th, p.u. 4 out*....... pu
Young Moss *alwys rear, nvr a fctr, p.u. 4 out*....... pu
Andretti's Heir *ld to 8th, u.r. 11th*....... ur
Cardinal Court (Ire) *ran out 2nd*....... ro
Kings Mischief (Ire) *rear, u.r. 11th*....... ur
Era's Imp *cls up, u.r. 11th*....... ur
Stilltodo 5a *bhnd early, p.u. 4 out*....... pu
Chummy's Last 5a *rear early, t.o. & p.u. 7th*....... pu
18 ran. Nk, 3l, 1l, 2l, 3l, 1l, 2l, 10l. Time 7m 10.00s. SP 6-4.
A Orkney (West Of Yore).

78 - Open

37 **POLITICO POT**.......**S Whitaker** 1
(Jt fav) ld to 3 out, disp last, drvn out to ld flat
Syrus P Turntable.......**P Murray** 2
mid-div, prog 4 out, ld 2 out, disp last, just btn
Quayside Cottage (Ire).......**C Mulhall** 3
alwys prom, 2nd at 13th, 3rd 4 out, onepcd
Nishkina *cls up, 4th frm 4 out, onepcd aft*....... 4
Cheeky Fox *mid-div, fdd, p.u. 11th*....... pu
The Right Guy *rear, t.o. 7th, p.u. 11th*....... pu
Mediator *(Jt fav) rmndrs 2nd, cls up at 10th, fdd rpdly, p.u. nxt*....... pu
Caman 5a *cls up, 2nd at 5th, wknd, p.u. 13th*....... pu
Dry Hill Lad 7a *alwys rear, p.u. 4 out*....... pu
Primitive Star 7a *rear, p.u. 13th*....... pu
10 ran. 1½l, 10l, 5l. Time 7m 15.00s. SP 6-4.
Charlie Peckitt (Sinnington).

79 - Open Maiden (8yo+) Div I

KAMADORA.......**S J Robinson** 1
cls up, ld 4 out, hld off chal flat
Rabble Rouser.......**R Edwards** 2
alwys prom, 2nd 2 out, chsd wnr, alwys hld
Meadow Gray.......**J Davies** 3
ld to 14th, 3rd frm 2 out, no ext
Lartington Lad *wll in rear, t.o. 11th, some late prog*....... 4
Hoofer Syd *mid-div, 5th at 14th, nvr dang*....... 5
Barichste *ran out 4th*....... ro
Prophet's Choice *f 1st*....... f
Scampton *bhnd early, t.o. 11th, p.u. nxt*....... pu
Cloud Cover *prom early, b.d. 10th*....... bd
Sweet Rose 5a *alwys rear, t.o. 11th, p.u. 4 out*....... pu
Bungy Bourke *cls up, 2nd at 8th, f 10th*....... f
Henceyem (Ire) *(fav) mid-div, 5th at 12th, fdd, p.u. 4 out*....... pu
12 ran. 2l, dist, 20l, 10l. Time 7m 25.00s. SP 5-1.
Milson Robinson (Burton).

80 - Open Maiden (8yo+) Div II

53 **BUCKWHEAT LAD (IRE)**.......**C Wilson** 1
cls up, disp 3 out, ld last, drvn out
Scottish Laird.......**T Garton** 2
(fav) prom, ld 14th-nxt, disp 3 out, hit last, just btn
Tribute To Dad.......**P Murray** 3
mid-div, prog 12th, went 3rd 2 out, nvr nrr
No Takers 5a *ld 6th-13th, 4th 2 out, no ext*....... 4
Here Comes Charter *ld to 5th, in tch to 4 out, outpcd.*....... 5
Cleric On Broadway (Ire) 5a *cls up whn f 11th*....... f
Ingleby Flyer 5a *bhnd early, onepcd, p.u. 4 out*....... pu
Quite A Character 5a *mid-div, fdd 12th, p.u. 4 out*....... pu
Keep Them Keen (Ire) *rear, nvr dang, p.u. 4 out*....... pu
Royal Recruit (Ire) *cls up, wknd 4th, p.u. 10th*....... pu
Malvern Cantina *prom, 4th at 8th, fdd, p.u. 10th*....... pu
Fethardonseafriend *alwys wll in rear, p.u. 4 out*....... pu
12 ran. ½l, 6l, 8l, 10l. Time 7m 19.00s. SP 4-1.
P Cheesbrough (South Durham).

81 - Members

MY TRUE CLOWN.......**Miss L Hampshire** 1
ld to 6th, agn 14th, disp 3 out, drew clr apr last
Breckenbrough Lad.......**I Bennett** 2
in tch, disp 3 out-nxt, no ext aft
Acertainhit.......**D Pritchard** 3
(fav) last frm 8th, outpcd, lft 3rd 4 out
Auntie Fay (Ire) 7a *ld 7th-13th, fdng whn f 4 out*....... f
4 ran. 10l, dist. Time 8m 1.00s. SP 5-1.
Mrs Peter Seels (Badsworth).
A.C.

COLLEGE VALLEY & N N'LAND
Alnwick
Sunday February 11th
GOOD TO SOFT

82 - Members (12st)

50 **DEPLETE 9ow**.......**T Smalley** 1
(fav) ld 2nd, drew clr frm 3 out, comf, cllpsd & died aft race
Harden Glen 7a.......**C Storey** 2
ld to 2nd, chsd wnr aft, ev ch apr 3 out, sn btn, fair debut
Ensign Ewart (Ire) 7a.......**Mrs J Storey** 3
jmpd slwly early, alwys 3rd, lost tch 13th, t.o.
Lounging 5a *last, effrt 12th, outpcd frm nxt, t.o.*....... 4
4 ran. 10l, 25l, 2½l. Time 6m 57.00s. SP 4-5.
T W B Smalley (College Valley/Northumberland).

83 - Confined (12st)

HOWAYMAN.......**A Parker** 1
(fav) trckd ldrs, ld apr 3 out, sn clr, rdn out flat
Across The Card.......**W Ramsay** 2
mid-div, outpcd 13th, ran on 3 out, tk 2nd flat, nrst fin
Astrac Trio (USA).......**Miss A Bowie** 3
prssd ldr, ld 14th-apr 3 out, onepcd aft
46 The Healy 5a *ld to 14th, sn outpcd, kpt on frm 2 out*....... 4
Royalist (Can) *mstk 2nd,trckd ldrs,cls up 15th,wknd nxt,fin tired*....... 5
46 Loughlinstown Boy *prom til grad wknd frm 13th*....... 6
Master Mischief 10ow *ran in snatches, in tch 15th, sn wknd*....... 7
49 Trebonkers 7ow *alwys last, t.o. & p.u. 2 out*....... pu
Equinoctial *trckd ldrs til mstk & u.r. 8th*....... ur
Yenoora (Ire) *prom til p.u. 7th, dsmntd*....... pu
10 ran. 5l, 1l, 12l, 15l, 10l, 3l. Time 6m 48.40s. SP 5-4.
Dennis Waggott (Dumfriesshire).

84 - Restricted (12st)

52 **FROZEN STIFF (IRE)**.......**N Wilson** 1
(fav) hld up,prog & mstk 9th,sn 2nd,rdn to ld 2 out,styd on well
Kinlea 4ow.......**P Diggle** 2
ld 4th-2 out, ran on onepcd aft
47 **Sunnie Cruise 5a**.......**P Johnson** 3
hld up, prog to trck ldng pair 14th, btn nxt, wknd 2 out
Royal Surprise *prom til 3rd & strggling 13th, sn lost plc, kpt on apr last*....... 4
47 Miss Eros 5a *rear, prog 8th, outpcd 10th, no imp aft, fin tired*....... 5
Merry Jerry *rear, effrt 9th, outpcd nxt, sn wll bhnd*....... 6
Jads Lad *mstk 1st, alwys bhnd, t.o. hlfwy*....... 7
Bonnie Scallywag 5a *ld to 4th, wknd 7th, mstk 10th, t.o. & p.u. 12th*....... pu
Polar Hat *prom whn f 2nd*....... f
47 Deday *alwys rear, wll bhnd hlfwy, t.o. & p.u. 13th*....... pu
Houselope Beck *mstk 4th,chsd ldrs,4th & outpcd 10th,no ch & p.u.15th,dsmntd*....... pu
11 ran. 6l, 30l, 8l, 1l, 20l, 20l. Time 6m 41.80s. SP 2-1.
Alan Brown (Buccleuch).

85 - Ladies

48 **STEELE JUSTICE.................Miss P Robson** 1
(fav) prom, ld 14th, clr 3 out, all out aft last
50 **Hallo Sensation.................Mrs V Jackson** 2
prom, 4th & outpcd 3 out, styd on strngly apr last, nrst fin
Marshalstoneswood...............Miss A Bowie 3
alwys prom, chsd wnr 15th, onepcd frm 2 out
48 Fish Quay *in tch,ld 10th,jmpd rght nxt,hdd 12th,disp 2nd 3 out,no ext* 4
48 Across The Lake *mid-div & outpcd, effrt 14th, kpt on, nvr able to chal* 5
Wall Game (USA) *mstk 8th, prom til wknd rpdly aft 3 out*.......... 6
48 Another Dyer *ld to 10th & 12th-14th, wknd rpdly nxt*... 7
Rarely At Odds *mstks 3rd & 8th, rear, lost tch 10th, t.o.*.......... 8
Upwell *last pair & alwys t.o.*.......... 9
Rushing Burn 5a *alwys rear, t.o. & p.u. 15th*.......... pu
Tappietourie 5a *last pair & t.o. til p.u. 12th*.......... pu

11 ran. 3l, 2l, 2l, ½l, 25l, 6l, 1 fence, 8l. Time 6m 42.50s. SP 7-4.
W Manners (Morpeth).

86 - Open

46 **WASHAKIE 3ow........................J Walton** 1
cls up,outpcd whn blnd 15th,rallied strngly 2 out,ld nr fin
Royal Jester............................C Storey 2
(fav) ld, rdn 3 out, slw nxt, styd on, hdd nr fin
37 **Off The Bru........................M Bradburne** 3
prssd ldr, chal 2 out, ev ch aft last, not qckn
Green Times *prom, mstk 12th, ev ch 14th, wknd rpdly, t.o.*.......... 4
49 Ready Steady *prog to jn ldrs 7th, 5th & in tch whn f 12th*.......... f
Paddy Hayton *bhnd frm 6th, t.o. & p.u. 12th*.......... pu
Tartan Tornado *reluc to race, t.o. til p.u. 10th*.......... pu
Its The Bidder (Ire) *wll bhnd frm 6th, t.o. & p.u. 10th*... pu

8 ran. ¾l, 2l, 1 fence. Time 6m 40.80s. SP 8-1.
Mrs F T Walton (Border).

87 - Open Maiden Div I (12st)

THE BUACHAILL (IRE)..................A Parker 1
(fav) hld up, trckd ldr 11th, ld apr 3 out, blnd nxt, easily
53 **Are-Oh ....Miss P Robson** 2
prom, rdn frm 9th, ld 11th-apr 3 out, no ch wnr aft
Niad *last & t.o. til p.u. 10th*.......... pu
Peat Stack *chsd ldrs, mstk 9th, wknd, t.o. & p.u. 3 out* pu
Lindon Run *ld 2nd-5th, bhnd frm 7th, t.o. & p.u. 11th*. pu
52 Border Supreme (Ire) *ld to 2nd & 5th-11th, wknd, tired & p.u. 3 out*.......... pu
Olympic Class *cls up til wknd 11th, no ch whn f hvly 4 out*.......... f

7 ran. 12l. Time 6m 57.00s. SP 6-4.
Mrs Alix Stevenson (Dumfriesshire).
Open ditch omitted last 3 races - 16 jumps.

88 - Open Maiden Div II (12st)

51 **STEADY AWAY (IRE)...............Miss S Nichol** 1
prom, ld 11th-nxt, rallied 3 out, ld last, styd on well
Arm Ah Man (Ire).......................N Wilson 2
(fav) hld up, prog to ld 12th, mstk 2 out, hdd & no ext last
51 **Canister Castle..........................R Shiels** 3
prom, ld 9-11th, 2nd whn mstk 13th, wknd
Willy Waffles (Ire) *ld to 7th, prom til wknd 4 out, t.o.*... 4
Fiscal Policy *sn wll bhnd, t.o. 6th, p.u. last*.......... pu
Wolf's Den *prom, ld 7-9th, wknd 11th, p.u. 2 out*.......... pu
Monynut 5a *cls up, 6th & in tch whn blnd 9th, wknd, p.u. 11th*.......... pu
Coolreny (Ire) 10ow *immed t.o. & schoold, f 2 out*.......... f
Murder Moss (Ire) *sn wll bhnd, t.o. 6th, p.u. 2 out*.......... pu
53 Mapalak 5a *immed t.o., p.u. aft 10th*.......... pu
51 Alianne 5a *out of tch in mid-div, t.o. 6th, p.u. 2 out*.... pu

11 ran. 3l, 30l, 15l. Time 6m 50.50s. SP 5-1.
Mrs J D Bulman (Cumberland Farmers).

89 - Open Maiden Div III (12st)

PARLEBIZ 5a ....A Wight 1
mstks, prom frm 5th, chsd ldr 3 out, ev ch whn lft clr nxt
Eostre ....A Parker 2
(fav) hld up, prog to chs ldr 12th, wknd 3 out, lft 2nd nxt
51 **Jack's Croft ....S Bainbridge** 3
prom til outpcd aft 9th, lft poor 3rd 2 out
52 Terracotta Warrior 4ow *alwys last, t.o. hlfwy*.......... 4
52 Woolaw Lass (USA) 5a *prom til f 6th*.......... f
Sovereigns Match *ld, prssd whn p.u. 2 out, dsmntd*... pu
Cool View 5a *trckd ldrs til f 5th*.......... f
46 Called To Account 5a *mstk 2nd,schoold & bhnd,some prog 11th,sn lost tch,p.u. 13th*.......... pu
53 Scarlet Rising 5a 1ow *mid-div, lost tch whn blnd 10th, p.u. nxt*.......... pu

9 ran. 15l, 25l, 30l. Time 6m 55.60s. SP 8-1.
A J Wight (Berwickshire).
J.N.

DUNSTON HARRIERS
Ampton
Sunday February 11th
GOOD TO FIRM

90 - Confined (12st)

8 **COPPER THISTLE (IRE) 6ex.............P Taiano** 1
(fav) made all, drew clr 3 out, not extndd
8 **St Gregory....................C Ward-Thomas** 2
mstk 2nd,rdn & chsd wnr 13th-15th,outpcd 3 out,2nd agn last
Melton Park 5ex..........................N Bloom 3
in tch, chsd wnr 16th, outpcd apr 3 out, lost 2nd last
Easy Over (USA) *pllng, chsd wnr to 12th, outpcd 15th, no ch 3 out*.......... 4
Old Dundalk 3ex (bl) *alwys last, lost tch 14th, no ch 3 out*.......... 5

5 ran. 6l, 4l, 15l, 4l. Time 6m 36.00s. SP 1-3.
M G Sheppard (Cambridgeshire).

91 - Open Maiden Div I

GOLDEN FELLOW (IRE) ....A Coe 1
(fav) ld 4th, made rest, clr whn blnd bdly 2 out, rdn out flat
Rebel Tom ....Miss L Hollis 2
rear, steady prog 7th, went 2nd 2 out, not rch wnr
15 **Ballysheil Star ....J Townson** 3
mid-div, prog 12th, went 3rd 3 out, no ext frm nxt
Canadian Boy (Ire) *alwys prom, ev ch 16th, wknd apr 2 out*.......... 4
Samuel Plimsol *prom, chsd wnr 5th, ev ch 16th, wknd nxt*.......... 5
35 Fort Diana *n.j.w. ld to 3rd, grad lost plc, t.o. & p.u. 16th*.......... pu
Nun On The Run 5a *mid-div, mod 6th & rdn 14th, no prog, p.u. 3 out*.......... pu
Ronlees *jmpd bdly, t.o. whn ref & u.r. 11th*.......... ref
15 Aughnacloy Rose *n.j.w. prom to 6th, t.o. 10th, p.u. last*.......... pu
15 Just Us (Ire) *mstk 2nd, mid-div, lost tch 10th, p.u. 13th* pu

10 ran. 3l, 5l, 10l, 12l. Time 6m 45.00s. SP 7-4.
Keith Coe (Essex Farmers & Union).

92 - Open Maiden Div II

GIVE IT A BASH (IRE) 5a ....T Moore 1
trckd ldrs going wl, disp 14th, ld 2 out, jmpd lft last,easy
Odysseus............................E Andrewes 2
ld/disp to 13th, ev ch til onepcd apr 2 out
Sharp Tactics ....N King 3
jmpd lft, ld/disp, mstks 12th & 15th, wknd 2 out
Learned Master *(fav) hmpd & u.r. 2nd*.......... ur
Loch Irish (Ire) 5a *f 2nd*.......... f

Rainbow Fantasia (Ire) *n.j.w. wll bhnd frm 3rd, ref 7th* ref
Als Diner *hmpd & u.r. 2nd* ur
7 ran. 8l, ¾l. Time 6m 53.00s. SP 11-2.
Miss S Wilson (Essex & Suffolk).

93 - Ladies

31 **CRAFTSMAN .... Miss G Chown** 1
(fav) made all, hit 8th, drew clr 3 out, easily
Mr Gossip .... Miss L Rowe 2
jmpd slwly 3rd, prog to 3rd at 15th, outpcd 17th, 2nd last
33 **Mend .... Miss A Embiricos** 3
trckd ldrs going wll, ev ch 17th, sn outpcd
Queen's Chaplain 7ex *prom, chsd wnr 12-13th, rdn 15th, sn lost tch* 4
57 Ashboro (Ire) *in tch til pshd alng & outpcd 15th, no ch aft* 5
32 Mara Askari (v) *blnd & u.r. 2nd* ur
Notary-Nowell 4ow *chsd wnr to 11th, last frm 15th, p.u. 2 out* pu
7 ran. 20l, 3l, 10l, 5l. Time 6m 39.00s. SP 1-4.
G W Paul (Essex & Suffolk).

94 - Open (12st)

1 **OVER THE EDGE .... S Sporborg** 1
(Jt fav) j.w. made virt all, shkn up & drew clr 2 out, comf
10 **Good Old Chips .... M Gingell** 2
wth wnr, ld brfly 14th, disp 3 out, unable qckn nxt
30 **As You Were .... D Parravani** 3
mid-div, ev ch 3 out, not qckn frm nxt
Saint Bene't (Ire) *hld up, prog 13th, chsd ldrs & ev ch 3 out, no prog nxt* 4
Linred *svrl pstns, ev ch 3 out, wknd nxt* 5
Glen Oak 7ex *alwys prom, drvn alng 15th, onepcd frm 3 out* 6
Catchapenny 7ex *(Jt fav) rear, in tch til outpcd 15th, no ch whn tried ref & u.r.17th* ur
31 El Bae *rear, lost tch 12th,, t.o. & p.u. last* pu
8 ran. 6l, 1½l, 1l, 1½l, 6l. Time 6m 43.00s. SP 2-1.
Christopher Sporborg (Puckeridge).

95 - Restricted (12st)

12 **DREAM PACKET .... C Ward-Thomas** 1
trckd ldrs going wll 9th, ld 3 out, clr nxt, imprssv
35 **Tough Minded .... R Wakley** 2
(fav) mid-div, jnd ldrs 13th, ev ch & rdn 3 out, btn nxt, lame
Unlucky For Some (Ire) .... B Pollock 3
ld/disp to 7th, prom, rdn to ld 17th-nxt, sn wknd
Talk Sence (Ire) (bl) *alwys wll bhnd, nvr nrr* 4
12 Camogue-Valley (Ire) *blnd 8th, rmndrs nxt, jnd ldrs 11th, wknd 13th, t.o.* 5
Alsemero *prom to 7th, grad lost plc, t.o. & p.u. 3 out* pu
36 Mount Patrick *wll bhnd 4th, t.o. & p.u. 2 out* pu
Young Gun *mid-div, outpcd 12th, p.u. 3 out* pu
35 Tel D'Or *disp to 7th, wknd 11th, p.u. 15th* pu
24 Par-Bar (Ire) 5a *not fluent, last frm 6th, t.o. & p.u. 15th* pu
54 Salmon Mead (Ire) *prom, ld 8th-16th, wknd nxt, p.u. 2 out* pu
11 ran. 20l, 6l, 30l, dist. Time 6m 38.00s. SP 10-1.
A Howland Jackson (Essex & Suffolk).

96 - BFSS Novice Riders

12 **DRUID'S LODGE .... T Bulgin** 1
w.w. prog 8th, rdn to ld 17th, hrd rdn 2 out, hld on flat
10 **Galzig .... W Tellwright** 2
prom,ld 10-11th,chsd ldr 3 out,kpt on wll und pres,jst faild
9 **Jerrigo .... J Knowles** 3
ld to 2nd, bhnd 8th, mod 6th 17th, ran on strngly,just faild
Hackett's Farm *cls up, ld 7-9th & 13-16th, wknd apr 2 out* 4
54 Highland Laird *in tch til outpcd 15th, no ch 17th* 5
8 Jimstro *disp til blnd 13th, losing tch whn blnd 15th, no ch aft* 6
8 Loughbrickland *(fav) chsd ldrs, strggling 12th, no ch frm 15th, dsmntd aft fin* 7
32 Danribo *prom, blnd 6th, bhnd frm 9th, p.u. 14th* pu
Merlyns Choice *alwys wll bhnd, t.o. & p.u. 15th* pu
9 Bajan Affair 5a *rear, lost tch 14th, t.o. & p.u. 3 out* pu
Arkay *rear, wll bhnd whn u.r. 11th* ur
11 ran. Hd, ¾l, 6l, 25l, 10l, 10l. Time 6m 42.00s. SP 7-2.
D J Lay (Essex & Suffolk).

97 - Members

CHATTERLEY .... N Bloom 1
(fav) ld til jnd 4th, ld agn 9th, lft solo nxt
George The Greek (Ire) *disp 5-8th, cls up whn stmbld & u.r. 10th* ur
2 ran. Time 7m 20.00s. SP 1-3.
Mrs J Bloom (Dunston Harriers).
S.P.

HEREFORD
Monday February 12th
HEAVY

98 - 3m 1f 110yds Hun Chase

DOUBLE SILK 12.7 3a .... Mr R Treloggen 1
(fav) ld after 2nd, left clr 2 out, unchal.
Drumard (Ire) 11.0 7a .... Mr A Sansome 2
ld till after 1st, remained prom till wknd 4 out, left poor 2nd 2 out.
Rusty Bridge 12.3 7a .... Mr R Thornton 3
mstk 5th, nvr on terms, t.o..
25 Welsh Legion 12.0 7a *held up, hdwy 10th, wknd 15th, t.o. when p.u. before 3 out* pu
Sword-Ash 11.7 7a *alwys bhnd, t.o. when p.u. before 4 out.* pu
Cape Cottage 11.7 7a *prom, weakening when left in 2nd pl and ref 2 out* ref
Horn Player (USA) 11.0 7a *alwys bhnd, t.o. when p.u. before 14th* pu
Merino Waltz (USA) 11.0 7a *not fluent, alwys bhnd, t.o. when p.u. before 15th.* pu
La Mezeray 10.10 7a 1ow *alwys bhnd, blnd and u.r. 7th* ur
23 Tattlejack (Ire) 11.1 7a 1ow *f 5th.* f
Jog-Along 11.2 5a *ld after 1st till after next, chsd wnr till apr 9th, weakening when hit 10th, t.o. when p.u. before 14th* pu
26 Howaryasun (Ire) 11.0 7a (v) *in tch, chsd wnr apr 9th, rdn when f 2 out.* f
12 ran. Dist, 15l. Time 7m 26.60s. SP 11-10.
R C Wilkins

LINGFIELD
Wednesday February 14th
HEAVY

99 - 3m Hun Chase

25 **HOLLAND HOUSE 11.7 7a .... Mr C Vigors** 1
(Jt fav) held up, hdwy after 6th, left in ld apr 10th, clr approaching 3 out, eased run-in.
6 **Buonarroti 11.7 7a .... Mr M Batters** 2
held up, left in 2nd apr 10th till 14th, left in second again 3 out, no impn on wnr.
Cool And Easy 12.2 5a .... Mr M Felton 3
in tch, wknd 7th, left mod 3rd 3 out.
Tryumphant Lad 11.7 7a *nvr on terms.* 4
37 Tipping Tim 12.2 5a *held up, hdwy 7th, left in 4th apr 10th, wknd quickly four out.* 5
Blue Danube (USA) 11.7 7a *alwys bhnd, t.o. when p.u. before 13th.* pu
Out For Fun 11.7 7a *in tch, chsd wnr from 14th, 2nd and held when f 3 out.* f
Mr Golightly 11.7 7a *(Jt fav) ld till rider tk wrong course apr 10th, p.u..* pu

Clare Man (Ire) 11.7 7a *chsd ldr till rider tk wrong course apr 10th, p.u.* .... pu
9 ran. 20l, 15l, 30l, nk. Time 6m 56.30s. SP 2-1.
E Knight

FAKENHAM
Friday February 16th
GOOD

100 - 2m 5f 110yds Hun Chase

9 **SHEER JEST 12.3 3a .... Mr A Hill** 1
(fav) held up, hdwy 10th, ld after 12th, clr last.
8 **Gypsy King (Ire) 11.3 7a .... Mr A Coe** 2
lding gp, mstk 3rd, rdn and not qckn from 2 out.
Duncan 11.5 5a .... Mr B Pollock 3
well pld, chsd wnr 12th, ran on one pace from 3 out.
8 Just Jack 11.12 3a 5ow *held up in tch, effort 10th, outpcd from 12th* 4
Professor Longhair 11.5 7a 2ow *mid div, hit 4th, bhnd from 6th* 5
Erins Bar (Ire) 11.3 7a *chsd ldr, mstk 8th, ld 10th till after 12th, soon wknd* 6
94 Saint Bene't (Ire) 11.3 7a *bhnd from 6th* 7
Doc Lodge 10.12 7a (bl) *ld, hit 5th, hdd after 10th, soon wknd, p.u. before 3 out* .... pu
Faringo 11.3 7a *in tch till outpcd 10th, t.o. when p.u. before 12th* .... pu
9 ran. 5l, 4l, 20l, 1½l, 14l, 2l. Time 5m 32.30s. SP 4-6.
Mrs Judy Wilson

ESSEX FARMERS & UNION
Marks Tey
Saturday February 17th
GOOD

101 - Members

10 **DYNAMITE DAN (IRE) .... S Cowell** 1
made all, blnd & jnd brfly 17th, in cmmnd whn lft solo last
56 **Exclusive Edition (Ire) 5a .... A Coe** 2
(fav) pllng, alwys 2nd, rddn 2 out, hld whn f last
Mister Rainman *hld up, in tch til f 14th* .... f
3 ran. Dist. Time 6m 55.00s. SP 6-4.
B Kennedy (Essex Farmers & Union).

102 - Confined (12st)

THE ARTFUL RASCAL .... N Bloom 1
prom, ld 6th 10l clr 15th, unchall
6 **Mister Main Man (Ire) .... S Sporborg** 2
(Jt fav) in tch, chsd ldr vainly frm 15th, no imp
94 **Glen Oak .... W Wales** 3
mid div, 9th hlfwy, styd on wll frm 16th, nvr nrr
8 Carrigeen Lad 3ex *(Jt fav) w.w.11th & in tch hlfwy, outpcd 13th, no dang after* 4
90 St Gregory *mid div, 10th & rddn hlfwy, 4th & no ch 16th* 5
90 Easy Over (USA) *ld to 5th, chsd ldr to 14th, grad wknd* 6
Loyal Note 3ex *in tch, 8th hlfwy,5th & wll btn 16th* 7
94 As You Were *rr, sme late prog nvr dang* 8
Major Inquiry (USA) *rr, prog & in tch 13th,sn outpcd* 9
95 Mount Patrick *prom to 12th, grad wknd* 10
94 El Bae *alwys rr div, nvr dang* 11
90 Old Dundalk 3ex (bl) *alwys rr, nvr dang* 12
The Grey Boreen *cls up to 9th, bhnd whn p.u. 2 out* .... pu
Santano *cls up til 7th, bhnd whn p.u. appr 11th* .... pu
31 Cardinal Red *prom to 12th, grad wknd, p.u. 2 out* .... pu
31 Frank Rich *in tch, rddn 11th, no ch whn u.r. 16th* .... ur
Plowshare Tortoise *schoold, last frm 11th, p. u. 3 out* .... pu
17 ran. 15l, 5l, 4l, ½l, 1l, 8l, 12l, 1l, 5l, 2l. Time 6m 42.00s. SP 14-1.
M A Kemp (Suffolk).

103 - Ladies

TOPPING-THE-BILL .... Mrs E Coveney 1
alwys going wll, ld 16th, qknd appr last, comf
33 **Counterbid .... Miss Z Turner** 2
(fav) trkd ldrs going wll, 2nd & rddn appr last, not qckn
33 **Crazy Otto .... Miss L Allen** 3
in tch, chsd ldr & ev ch 17th, onepcd 2 out
Kaim Park *disp til ld 11th- 15th, rddn & outpcd nxt* 4
11 Whistling Eddy *prom, disp ld 9th til appr 11th, wknd 16th* 5
Sacrosanct *disp ld til 10th, sn strggling, p.u. & dismntd 17th* .... pu
Fragment (Ire) *rr, lst tch appr 11th, t.o. & p.u. 17th* .... pu
7 ran. 3l, 4l, 12l, 30l. Time 6m 48.00s. SP 7-4.
Mrs Emma Coveney (Old Surrey & Burstow).

104 - Open

CELTIC SPARK .... P Hacking 1
made all, clr 16th, rddn aft 2 out, blnd last,styd on wll
Brown Windsor (bl) .... B Pollock 2
(fav) trkd ldrs, 3rd & rddn 17th, ch last, onepcd
32 **The Portsoy Loon .... A Hickman** 3
w.w. prog 10th, chsd ldr 16th, onepcd und press frm 2 out
90 Melton Park *j.s. 1st, mid div, styd on frm 15th, nvr nrr, lkd to fin 3rd* 4
56 Armagret *in tch, prog to 2nd 14th, wknd appr 16th* 5
9 Shimshek (USA) *prom to 11th, bhnd & p.u. appr 15th, lame* .... pu
J J Jimmy *pllng, wth ldr to 10th, wknd 12th, p.u. 17th* .... pu
Namoos *w.w. prog 8th, outpcd 12th, p.u. 17th* .... pu
Meritmoore *alwys bhnd, p.u. 13th* .... pu
56 Athnanurlainn 1ow *last & rddn 10th, t.o. &p.u. 13th* .... pu
31 Way Of Life (Fr) *chsd ldrs til blnd & u.r. 13th* .... ur
Jimmy Mac Jimmy *bhnd 10th, t.o. & p.u. 13th* .... pu
32 Laburnum *mid div, prog & cls up 11th, wknd appr 16th, p.u. 3 out* .... pu
Kates Castle 5a *rr, prog & in tch 12th, btn appr 15th, p.u. 3 out* .... pu
14 ran. 2l, 1l, ½l, dist. Time 6m 40.00s. SP 7-1.
M D Reed (Chid.Lec. & Cowdray).

105 - Restricted Div I (12st)

36 **MAJOR NEAVE .... G Hopper** 1
prog 12th, chall & rmdrs 3 out, ld last, rddn clr
Lantern Pike .... A Michael 2
ld 4th, 12l clr 15th, hdded last, onepcd
59 **Doctor Dick (Ire) .... S Cowell** 3
alwys bhnd, 5th & no ch 16th, went poor 3rd last
Hill Fort (Ire) *(fav) mid div, rddn 13th, 4th & hd rddn 16th,no prog* 4
36 Corn Kingdom (bl) *cls up til f 14th* .... f
36 Russian Vision *ld to 3rd, hit 6th, wknd 15th, p.u. appr last* .... pu
33 Ravens Hasey Moon *chsd ldrs til lst pl appr 11th, p.u. 12th* .... pu
Whats Another 5a *chsd ldrs, wkng whn u.r. 15th* .... ur
30 Here's Humphrey *ref 1st* .... ref
Miners Medic (Ire) 7a *rr, lsing tch whn p.u. appr 15th* .... pu
15 Spartan's Conquest *schoold in rr til p.u. 15th* .... pu
11 ran. 2½l, 20l, 10l. Time 6m 42.00s. SP 5-1.
J Jamieson (East Kent).

106 - Restricted Div II (12st)

PENDIL'S PLEASURE 5a .... W Wales 1
chsd ldrs, ld 11th clr & hit 2 out, sn rcvd, easy
35 **Alfredo Garcia (Ire) 7a .... T Moore** 2
prom, chsd ldr 14th, ev ch til rddn & no ex appr 2 out
35 **Harpley Dual (Ire) 7ow .... A Case** 3
in tch to 14th, 3rd & btn 16th, kpt on
Colonel Kenson *mid div, prog & ev ch 12th, wknd appr 17th* 4
36 Cool Apollo (NZ) *alwys bhnd, nvr dang* 5
36 Cowage Brook *in tch, 5th & rddn 11th, no ch whn ref 17th* .... ref
Joe Quality *alwys rr, t.o. & p.u. 17th* .... pu
22 Tenelord *(fav) in tch, 4th & blnd 12th, wknd appr 16th, p.u. & dism 17th* .... pu

57 High Burnshot *plng, ld, sn clr, blnd 10th, sn hdded & wknd, p.u. 12th* .... pu
12 Parkers Hills (Ire) *rr div, last & rmdrs 11th, no resp, p.u. 17th* .... pu
32 Tasmanite *rr whn p.u. 5th* .... pu
Peptic Lady (Ire) 5a *alwys rr, t.o. & p.u. 17th* .... pu
12 ran. 15l, 6l, 15l, 1l. Time 6m 42.00s. SP 9-2.
J R Heatley (West Norfolk).

107 - Maiden Div I (12st)

HIGHLAND RALLY (USA) ....N Bloom 1
(fav) made all, drw wll clr frm 14th, drvn along frm 2 out
13 **Charlie Kelly ....P Taiano** 2
mid div, outpcd 14th, 3rd & no ch 17th, went 2nd last
13 **Springlark (Ire) 7a ....A Coe** 3
alwys bhnd, nvr nr ldrs
13 Montimezzo *trkd ldrs, going wll 10th, 2nd & outpcd 15th, lst 2nd flat* 4
Alapa *r.o. & u.r. 4th* .... ro
34 Northern Reef (Fr) 7a *alwys rr div, p.u. 13th* .... pu
Funny Worry *cls up til f 14th* .... f
Andalucian Sun (Ire) *mstks, prog to 8th 11th, wkng whn p.u. 13th* .... pu
Steel Ice *chsd ldrs to 10th, wknd 12th, t.o. & p.u. 3 out* .... pu
Scout *chsd ldrs til wknd 11th, t.o. & p.u. 16th* .... pu
31 The Prior *wl bhnd frm 6th, t.o. & p.u. 3 out* .... pu
91 Rebel Tom *mstks, prog 9th, poor 3rd whn f 16th* .... f
96 Arkay *bhnd frm 7th, u.r. 11th* .... ur
Magic Fountain (Ire) 5a *alwys bhnd last whn p.u. 12th* .... pu
Charlie Andrews *mid div til f 11th* .... f
15 ran. Dist, 2l, 15l. Time 6m 42.00s. SP 2-1.
M W Ingle (Cambridgeshire).

108 - Maiden Div I (12st)

NIBBLE ....G Cooper 1
cls up,ld & blnd 2 out,blnd & hdd last,rallied to ld nr fin
15 **Harry Lauder (Ire) 7a................S Sporborg** 2
(fav) trkd ldrs, ld brfly 3 out, lft in ld last, hdd cls hme
34 **Coppinger's Cave ....N Bloom** 3
in tch 11th, kpt on wll frm 3 out, nt rch ldrs
91 Ballysheil Star *prog 10th, ev ch 16th, wknd 3 out* 4
Bruff Castle *ld/disp til 15th, wknd appr 3 out* 5
91 Aughnacloy Rose *jmpd rt, alwys bhnd* 6
Rhyming Moppet 5a *prog 10th, blnd 13th, 5th & ch whn blnd 17th, wlkd in* 7
Superforce *t.o. whn p.u. 7th* .... pu
Kerry My Home *rr & rmdrs 9th, bhnd whn p.u. 13th* .... pu
15 Shaab Turbo *plng, jnd ldrs 10th,ld 16th til appr 3 out,sn wkd,p.u. last* .... pu
62 Room To Manouver (Ire) *in tch to 10th, t.o. whn p.u. appr last* .... pu
34 Ernie Fox *rr, in tch, wkng whn r.o. & u.r. 14th* .... ro
Insulate 5a *f 2nd* .... f
Le Vienna (Ire) *cls up, blnd 7th, wknd 13th, p.u. 3 out* .... pu
Regal Bay *blnd 1st, bhnd til p.u. 16th* .... pu
Sustaining *mstks, made most 14th, sn wknd, t.o. whn p.u. 3 out* .... pu
Thereyougo 7a *alwys rr, last whn p.u. 15th* .... pu
17 ran. Hd, 3l, 6l, 4l, 20l, 4l. Time 6m 55.00s. SP 33-1.
G I Cooper (Essex & Suffolk).
S.P.

LANARKS & RENFREW
Lanark
Saturday February 17th
GOOD TO SOFT

109 - Members

DUNCANS DREAM................Miss C Wilson 1
mod 2nd frm 9th, no imp whn lft clr last
Crooked Streak...................W Shorthouse 2
clr frm 6th, blnd 2 out, rider lost irons, r.o. last, rjnd
Gold Profit 5a *(fav) f 2nd* .... f
Chaperall Lady 5a 13ow *disp to 5th, t.o. 10th, p.u. 4 out* .... pu
Midas Man 7a 9ow *u.r. 1st* .... ur
5 ran. Dist. Time 7m 28.00s. SP 10-1.
Ms C Wilson (Lanark & Renfrew).

110 - Confined (12st)

49 **FORDSTOWN (IRE) 7ex.............J Alexander** 1
steady prog frm 10th, just ld whn lft clr 2 out
50 **Sharp Opinion 6ex ....Miss P Robson** 2
(Jt fav) early rmndrs, cls up, no imp on wnr frm 2 out
Pantara Prince (Ire)......................T Scott 3
alwys prom, no ext frm 3 out
The Shade Matcher *mid-div, clsd up 4 out, no ext frm nxt* 4
Andrew *bhnd til rpd prog to ld 12th, wknd qckly frm nxt* 5
Toddlin Hame *ld to 12th, sn wknd* 6
Scottish Gold *alwys rear, t.o.* 7
Canny Chronicle *alwys wll bhnd, p.u. 4 out* .... pu
Hamilton Lady (Ire) 5a *prom early, losing tch whn p.u. 11th* .... pu
83 Astrac Trio (USA) *(Jt fav) alwys handy, ld 13th til just hdd & u.r. 2 out* .... ur
10 ran. 5l, 5l, 2l, dist. Time 6m 44.00s. SP 8-1.
Jamie Alexander (Fife).

111 - Restricted (12st)

84 **KINLEA ....P Diggle** 1
(fav) cls up, chal 3 out, ld last, all out
47 **Toaster Crumpet................Miss P Robson** 2
alwys handy, ld apr 3 out, hdd last, no ext flat
Sloothak...............................A Wight 3
ld til wknd rpdly apr 3 out
84 Jads Lad *handy til lost tch 4 out* 4
Corby Knowe *wll bhnd whn u.r. 4th* .... ur
85 Tappietourie 5a *lost tch by 11th, p.u. 4 out* .... pu
6 ran. 1l, 25l, nk. Time 6m 43.00s. SP 4-5.
Peter Diggle (Dumfriesshire).

112 - Ladies

PARLIAMENT HALL...............Miss S Forster 1
made all, drew wll clr apr last
47 **Farriers Favourite 5a............Miss P Robson** 2
(fav) 5th at 10th, some prog 4 out, no imp on wnr
85 **Marshalstoneswood...............Miss A Bowie** 3
3rd at 10th, kpt on well, no ch wth wnr
Hydropic *chsd wnr frm 7th til wknd rpdly 4 out* 4
Galadine *blnd 6th, alwys wll bhnd aft* 5
Granny's Bay *2nd til 7th, sn wknd, p.u. 13th* .... pu
Colonel James *u.r. 5th* .... ur
Royal Fife 5a *4th at 10th, disp 2nd whn f 3 out* .... f
8 ran. 25l, hd, dist, dist. Time 6m 42.00s. SP 3-1.
S H Shirley-Beavan (Jedforest).

113 - Land Rover Open (12st)

50 **HEDLEY MILL 5a 7ex...................A Parker** 1
(fav) alwys handy, 2nd 4 out, ld apr 2 out, sn clr
86 **Off The Bru.......................M Bradburne** 2
2nd til ld 8th, hdd apr 2 out, sn outpcd
Bowlands Way 7ex (bl)....................R Ford 3
ld to 8th, wklnd rpdly 4 out
86 Ready Steady 7ow *bhnd frm 10th, nvr dang* 4
Jimmy River 7ex *t.o. 10th, p.u. 3 out* .... pu
Dawn Coyote (USA) *not fluent, t.o. 10th, p.u. 3 out* .... pu
6 ran. 12l, dist, 8l. Time 6m 37.00s. SP 10-11.
J W Hope (Braes Of Derwent).

114 - Open Maiden (5-7yo) Div I (12st)

51 **EASTLANDS HI-LIGHT ....T Morrison** 1
(fav) made most frm 9th, drew clr frm 3 out
Pablowmore...............................R Green 2
wll bhnd 8th, gd prog 4 out, went 2nd flat
Solwaysands ....Mrs J Williamson 3
alwys handy, ld brfly 11th, outpcd frm 3 out

Villanella 5a *in tch til wknd rpdly 4 out* 4
Ballyargan (Ire) *wll bhnd by 8th, t.o.* 5
About Midnight 5a *nvr dang, p.u. 2 out* .... pu
87 Lindon Run *ld 4th til 9th, losing tch whn f 2 out* .... f
53 Summer Dalliance *nvr dang, p.u. 2 out* .... pu
Madame Beck 5a *cls up frm 11th, losing tch whn f 2 out* .... f
Little Flo 5a *ld til 4th, losing tch whn f 2 out* .... f
Aumale (Ire) 7a *nvr dang, p.u. 4 out* .... pu
Davy's Lad 7a *in tch to 10th, bhnd whn p.u. 4 out* .... pu
12 ran. 12l, 4l, dist, dist. Time 6m 59.00s. SP 6-4.
J G Staveley

115 - Open Maiden (5-7yo) Div II (12st)

DRAKEWRATH (IRE)........A Parker 1
(Jt fav) in tch, 2nd frm 10th, ld apr 3 out, comf
51 **Cukeira 5a........T Morrison** 2
(Jt fav) hld up, 4th at 10th, went 2nd 3 out, alwys hld
Eilid Anoir........R Shiels 3
ld til apr 3 out, sn wknd
Rough House 7a *nvr dang* 4
Normans Profit *2nd to 10th, sn wknd* 5
By Crikey (Ire) *ref 2nd* .... ref
Major Peril *f 3rd* .... f
Connie Leathart 7a *t.o. 4th, p.u. 10th* .... pu
8 ran. 1l, 25l, dist, 3l. Time 7m 11.00s. SP 5-2.
R A Bartlett (Fife).

116 - Open Maiden (8yo+)

51 **MISS CULLANE (IRE) 5a........R Neill** 1
alwys handy, ld last, hld on well
88 **Fiscal Policy........H Trotter** 2
sn bhnd, rpd prog frm 14th, chal last, just hld
53 **Olive Branch 5a........D Wood** 3
(fav) alwys handy, ld 11th til last, no ext flat
Moscow Mule *in tch til wknd rpdly 3 out* 4
48 Iron Prince *handy til wknd 4 out, p.u. 2 out* .... pu
89 Jack's Croft *sn wll bhnd, p.u. 4 out* .... pu
Bowlands Himself (Ire) *ld til f 11th* .... f
Connor The Second *prom early, bhnd whn p.u. 11th* .... pu
Prince Rossini (Ire) *sn bhnd, f 8th* .... f
88 Willy Waffles (Ire) *prom early, bhnd whn p.u. 12th* .... pu
10 ran. ½l, 1l, dist. Time 6m 58.00s. SP 10-1.
Robert Neill (Berwickshire).
R.J.

OLD RABY HUNT CLUB
Witton Castle
Saturday February 17th
SOFT

117 - Members

76 **FINAL HOPE (IRE)........Mrs F Needham** 1
(fav) rear, prog 7th, 2nd at 9th, ld 12th, clr 2 out, kpt on well
Computer Pickings 5a........C Wilson 2
rear of ldrs, smooth prog to 2nd 2 out, no ext apr last
85 **Wall Game (USA)........Miss H Delahooke** 3
ld to 6th, outpcd 8th, 4th 2 out, styd on apr last, 3rd flat
Pinewood Lad *handy, ld 6th-11th, 2nd aft til outpcd 2 out* 4
74 City Buzz (Ire) *in tch to 12th, wknd nxt, poor 5th 2 out* 5
79 Meadow Gray *cls up to 7th, wknd 12th, t.o. 2 out* 6
Into The Trees *mid-div whn f 6th* .... f
75 Goongor (Ire) *rear whn b.d. 6th* .... bd
80 Malvern Cantina *mid-div to 6th, rear whn p.u. 12th* .... pu
9 ran. 5l, 4l, 2l, 20l, 3l. Time 6m 21.00s. SP 1-2.
R Tate (Hurworth).
One fence omitted all races. 16 jumps.

118 - Intermediate

78 **QUAYSIDE COTTAGE (IRE)........N Wilson** 1
rear early, prog 10th, ld 12th, ran on well
77 **Stag Fight........S Walker** 2
(fav) rear, prog to 3rd at 12th, chsd wnr nxt, no imp aft
Jack Dwyer........D Coates 3
disp to 12th, outpcd nxt, onepcd aft
49 Castle Gem 5a *prom to 10th, wknd 12th, kpt on onepcd aft* 4
Beau Gem 5a *cls up to 6th, mid-div aft, no dang* 5
79 Lartington Lad *dwelt, t.o. 7th, fin own time* 6
Vienna Woods *rear, prog 10th, 7th & in tch whn b.d. 12th* .... bd
Some Flash *prom, cls up whn f 12th* .... f
51 Need A Ladder *mid-div til wknd 8th, hrd rdn nxt, rear & p.u. 12th* .... pu
9 ran. 2½l, 15l, 2l, 6l, dist. Time 6m 16.00s. SP 4-1.
R Marley (Braes Of Derwent).

119 - Ladies

72 **THISTLE MONARCH........Miss R Clark** 1
(fav) mstk 1st, cls 4th at 7th, lft 2nd 11th, rallied to ld flat
Grey Realm 5a........Miss J Wood 2
disp to 8th, lft in ld 11th, 2l clr last, wknd & hdd flat
76 **Barry Owen........Miss A Deniel** 3
disp to 8th, wknd 11th, nvr a dang aft
Indie Rock *hld up, smooth prog to ld 8th, going wll whn ran out 11th* .... ro
4 ran. 2l, 15l. Time 6m 17.00s. SP 2-5.
S B Clark (York & Ainsty South).

120 - Open

ELLERTON HILL........S Swiers 1
(Jt fav) j.w. made all, qcknd clr apr last, imprssv
56 **Jefferby........J Apiafi** 2
handy, 2nd 3 out, outpcd by wnr apr last
Fast Study........S Pittendrigh 3
cls up til outpcd 3 out, styd on onepcd aft
Speakers Corner *cls up til outpcd 13th, onepcd aft* 4
78 Syrus P Turntable *rear, styd on well frm 2 out, nvr dang* 5
72 Arctic Paddy *alwys rear, t.o. 10th* 6
Tobin Bronze *(Jt fav) mid-div, wknd 13th, p.u. 2 out* .... pu
7 ran. 7l, 8l, 5l, 2l, dist. Time 6m 8.00s. SP 7-4.
T W Thompson (Hurworth).

121 - Restricted (12st)

72 **KELLYS DIAMOND........S Walker** 1
(fav) rear, prog 11th, disp ld 13th til ld apr last, wknd nr fin
Flip The Lid (Ire) 5a........N Tutty 2
mid-div, prog to disp 10th-2 out, rallied flat, just faild
47 **Clone (Ire)........S Brisby** 3
rear, prog 10th, strng chal 2 out, onepcd apr last
Chapel Island *mid-div, effrt 2 out, no ext apr last* 4
77 Young Moss *ld/disp to 10th, wknd nxt, kpt on in mid-div aft* 5
80 Ingleby Flyer 5a *mid-div to 10th, rear aft, slght prog agn frm 2 out* 6
Hoistthestandard 5a *alwys mid to rear, nvr a dang* 7
72 Earl Gray *mid-div to 12th, rear aft* 8
79 Sweet Rose 5a *mid-div to 11th, rear whn mstk & u.r. nxt* .... ur
53 Jamarsam (Ire) *prom til wknd 10th, rear whn p.u. 2 out* .... pu
Country Chalice *2nd whn ran out 3rd* .... ro
11 ran. Hd, 7l, 4l, 5l, 6l, 4l, 2l. Time 6m 21.00s. SP 5-4.
Mrs P A Russell (Middleton).

122 - Open Maiden (5-7yo) Div I

53 **CASTLE TYRANT 5a........P Atkinson** 1
(fav) ld to 4th, cls 2nd aft, disp last, styd on best flat
Scotchie (Ire)........N Wilson 2
mid-div, prog 14th, ld 2 out, jnd last, outpcd flat
Yornoangel........G Markham 3
cls up, ld 4th, clr 6th-13th, wknd & hdd 3 out, onepcd aft
74 Sergent Kay *rear of ldrs, outpcd aft 3 out* 4

Aitch-A 7a *t.o. 6th, came home own time* 5
74 Pure Madness (USA) *rear whn ref 6th* .... ref
Armastoke (Ire) *mid-div whn f 3rd* .... f
Blank Cheque *mstk 2nd, not rcvr & ran out apr nxt* ... ro
8 ran. 1l, 10l, 15l, dist. Time 6m 20.00s. SP 5-4.
S Clark (Bedale).

123 - Open Maiden (5-7yo) Div II

FERN LEADER (IRE)..................C Wilson 1
ld/disp til ld 12th, jnd 2 out, ran on well apr last
Raise A Dollar 5a ....S Swiers 2
rear, smooth prog to trck ldrs 12th, ev ch 2 out, no ext aft
73 **Stride To Glory (Ire) 7a ....R Edwards** 3
mid-div, prog 12th, styd on strngly apr last, improve
74 Another Hooligan *(fav) numerous mstks, prom/disp 10th-2 out, outpcd apr last* 4
Private Jet (Ire) *prom to 10th, wknd nxt, kpt on in rear aft* 5
Lord Jester *in tch to 8th, wknd 10th, t.o. 13th* 6
53 Wassl's Nanny (Ire) 5a *rear whn mstk & u.r. 9th* .... ur
75 Fair Grand *rear whn p.u. 10th* .... pu
75 Ingleby Lodger *prom to 8th, wknd 10th, rear whn p.u. 13th* .... pu
73 Mal's Castle (Ire) 5a *rear whn f 9th* .... f
The Golly Ollybird 14ow *jmpd slwly 1st, last whn p.u. aft 11th* .... pu
11 ran. 10l, 2l, 2l, dist, dist. Time 6m 25.00s. SP 3-1.
W R Ward (South Durham).
R.W.

OXFORD UNIVERSITY HUNT CLUB
Kingston Blount
Saturday February 17th
GOOD TO SOFT

124 - Confined (12st)

PENLET ....John Pritchard 1
chsd ldrs, clsd 14th, ld nxt, clr 2 out, ran on well
Cawkwell Dean ....R Sweeting 2
prom in chsng grp, effrt 14th, chsd wnr 3 out, sn outpcd
6 **Daringly ....A Kilpatrick** 3
1st ride, rear, gd prog 14th, ran on onepcd frm 2 out
32 Welsh Singer 5ex *mstks, hld up bhnd, gd prog 14th, onepcd & no imp frm nxt* 4
Severn Invader *mid-div, lost tch wth ldrs 14th, kpt on frm 2 out* 5
Bit Of A Clown 3ex *mid-div, lost tch apr 14th, kpt on onepcd aft* 6
Saybright *ld to 2nd, prssd ldr, ld 9-11th, ev ch 15th, wknd, fin tired* 7
24 Sprucefield *chsd ldrs, effrt apr 14th, wknd nxt* 8
25 Old Road (USA) 4ow (bl) *ld 2nd-9th & 11-15th, wknd rpdly* 9
55 Kelly's Eye 3ex (bl) *chsng grp, effrt apr 14th, sn wknd* 10
Ramlosa (NZ) *1st ride, alwys bhnd, last frm 6th, t.o. 14th* 11
Celtic Flame 5ex *mid-div, lost tch aft 13th, t.o. & p.u. 2 out* .... pu
19 Cool It A Bit *mid-div, lost tch 13th, t.o. & p.u. 3 out* .... pu
21 Tapalong 5a *alwys bhnd, t.o. & p.u. 3 out* .... pu
22 Kites Hardwicke *s.v.s. last til u.r. aft 4th* .... ur
Bervie House (Ire) 2ow *(fav) 3s-6/4,w.w. prog to chs 1st 2 11th,wknd rpdly 15th,p.u.nxt* .... pu
Mr Rigsby (Ire) *mid-div,rdn & prog 10th,ev ch apr 14th,wknd rpdly,p.u.2 out* .... pu
17 ran. 10l, nk, 6l, 8l, 1l, 20l, ½l, 6l, 2l, 6l. Time 6m 25.00s. SP 25-1.
R G Weaving (Warwickshire).

125 - Open

18 **WILD ILLUSION ....R White** 1
(fav) j.w. trckd ldrs, lft in ld 12th, clr 2 out, easily
Mountshannon ....A Hill 2
hld up, prog 10th, ev ch 14th, no imp wnr frm 3 out
18 **Paco's Boy ....P York** 3
wth ldr to 5th, sn lost plc, t.o. 13th, btn a fence
Castlebay Lad *prom, chsd wnr 12-14th, wknd, poor 3rd whn ref last* .... ref
Grey Tudor *s.s. pllng, in tch to 11th, t.o. 13th, p.u. 15th* .... pu
Retail Runner *made most til mstk & u.r. 12th* .... ur
Lucky Christopher *hld up,outpcd 13th,effrt nxt,not rch ldrs,3rd 2 out,p.u.last* .... pu
Fighting Mariner *in tch til pshd alng & wknd 10th, p.u. nxt* .... pu
What About That (Ire) (bl) *prom til wknd 13th, t.o. & p.u. 15th* .... pu
26 John Roger *alwys rear, mstk 11th, lost tch whn p.u. 13th* .... pu
10 ran. 8l, dist. Time 6m 22.00s. SP 4-5.
G Pidgeon (Grafton).

126 - Ladies

SPERRIN VIEW 5a ....Mrs K Sunderland 1
trckd ldrs, prog 10th, mstk 14th, ld on innr 2 out, drvn out
27 **Thamesdown Tootsie 5a ....Miss V Lyon** 2
(fav) raced wd,ld/disp til ld 10th,hdd 2 out,rallied flat,hld off
27 **Button Your Lip ....Miss K Holmes** 3
chsd ldrs, 4th & lost tch aft 13th, styd on well apr last
Knight's Spur (USA) *prom, ev ch apr 14th, 3rd & btn nxt, wknd* 4
23 Run To Form *s.v.s. jmpd slwly, bhnd til prog aft 13th, no imp nxt, wknd* 5
Codger *mstk 6th, cls up to 9th, wll t.o. 13th* 6
Military Two Step *ld/disp til lost plc 10th, no ch 13th, 6th whn p.u. 2 out* .... pu
Sutton Lass 5a *in tch to 10th, t.o. 13th, p.u. aft 15th* ... pu
Icky's Five *alwys rear, last & wll t.o. 13th, p.u. 15th* ... pu
27 Little Thyne *last & strggling 8th, t.o. & p.u. 12th* .... pu
Arble March 5a *in tch to 10th, t.o. 13th, p.u. 2 out* .... pu
11 ran. ¾l, 15l, 6l, 25l, 6l. Time 6m 24.00s. SP 7-1.
Mrs Katie Sunderland (Bicester With Whaddon Chase).

127 - Members

GLEN CHERRY ....P Scouller 1
made all, clr aft 3 out, styd on well
19 **Mister Christian (NZ) (bl)................M Walters** 2
chsd wnr to 14th & agn apr 2 out, no imp
22 **Espy ....A James** 3
(fav) w.w. chsd wnr 14th, no imp whn blnd 3 out, wknd
22 Bright As A Button *prom til lost tch 13th,4th & styng on whn crawld nxt & p.u.* .... pu
Hill Island *5s-9/4, nvr going well, bhnd frm 5th, t.o. & p.u. 15th* .... pu
Bedwyn Bridge 7a 4ow *alwys last, t.o. 8th, p.u. aft 13th* .... pu
6 ran. 12l, 6l. Time 6m 27.00s. SP 7-1.
P A D Scouller (Garth & South Berks).

128 - Restricted (12st)

WARRIOR BARD (IRE) ....T Lacey 1
hld up, prog 10th, ld 13th, clr 15th, styd on well
28 **Sound Statement (Ire) ....T Hills** 2
prom,lft in ld 5th,sn hdd,chsd wnr 14th,styd on one-pcd 2 out
Wayward Sailor.................Miss C Spearing 3
sn prom, 4th & outpcd aft 13th, kpt on
Ravensdale Lad *ld aft 5th-13th, stdly wknd frm nxt* 4
1 Golden Mac 4ow *alwys rear, lost tch 10th, t.o. 13th* ... 5
65 Scorpio Sam *alwys rear, t.o. hlfwy* 6
Rain Down 2ow *(fav) hld up bhnd, prog 10th, no imp 13th, 5th & btn whn p.u. 14th* .... pu
Musical Mail *25s-8s, chsd ldrs, lost tch 11th, f 13th* ... f
Miss Solitaire 5a *rear & pshd alng, t.o. 13th, p.u. 15th* pu
Lily The Lark 5a *mid-div, mstk 8th, 6th & out of tch whn f 13th* .... f
Kingofnobles (Ire) *trckd ldrs, hit rail aft 8th, not rcvr, t.o. & p.u. 14th* .... pu
22 Gt Hayes Pommard *alwys bhnd, t.o. 11th, p.u. 15th* ... pu
Lord Macduff *last frm 6th, t.o. & p.u. 11th* .... pu

Autumn Light 5a *ld til u.r. 5th* .... ur
14 ran. 6l, 10l, 10l, 20l, 1 fence. Time 6m 28.00s. SP 25-1.
Miss S Stuart-Hunt (Beaufort).

129 - Maiden

SINGING CLOWN 5a ....**L Lay** 1
mid-div,outpcd 13th,styd on und pres 2 out,lft in ld last
Just Ballytoo ....**B Hodkin** 2
prom to 8th, sn outpcd, lft 4th 3 out, kpt on
17 **Looking** ....**R White** 3+
prog 12th,2nd 15th,lft in ld 3 out,wknd,nrly ref & hdd last
29 **Dodgy Dealer (Ire)**..........**E James** 3+
(Jt fav) ld 3rd-14th, lft 2nd 3 out, wknd, fin tired
Miners Rest 5a *cls up to 6th, t.o. 13th, no ch aft* 5
Miss Precocious 5a *rear, lost tch & mstk 11th, p.u. nxt*.......... pu
27 Bold Man (NZ) *20s-12s, prog to chs ldr 9th, ld 14th, 4l clr whn f 3 out*.......... f
Fortytimes More *alwys rear, t.o. 13th, p.u. 2 out*.......... pu
Tommy O'Dwyer (Ire) *raced wd, mid-div till f 5th*.......... f
21 Copper Pan 5a *rear, lost tch whn u.r. 13th* .... ur
Opus Winwood (Ire) *sn rear, wll bhnd 13th, no real prog aft, p.u. 2 out*.......... pu
Daring Daisy 5a *alwys well in rear, lost tch whn p.u. 13th*.......... pu
Apple Anthem 5a *ptom to 9th, sn wknd, t.o. & p.u. 14th*.......... pu
28 Hey Henry *(Jt fav) rear, mstk 5th, lost tch 13th, t.o. & p.u. 2 out*.......... pu
Bit Of An Idiot *12s-7s,keen hold,mstk 8th,prom to 13th,5th & no ch, p.u.last*.......... pu
15 ran. 12l, 5l, dd-ht, 10l. Time 6m 41.00s. SP 20-1.
R Jeffrey (Grafton).
J.N.

SOUTH POOL HARRIERS
Ottery St Mary
Saturday February 17th
GOOD TO SOFT

130 - Members

39 **MOZE TIDY** ....**I Dowrick** 1
cls up, lft in ld aft 7th, made rest, comf
First Design..........**W G Turner** 2
chsd wnr frm 8th, no imp frm 2 out
42 **Early To Rise**..........**J Creighton** 3
prom, virt c.o. aft 7th, outpcd frm 4 out
Bluechipenterprise 5a *(fav) alwys last, nvr going well* 4
40 Bootscraper *cls up whn blnd & u.r. 5th*.......... ur
69 Jay Em Ess (NZ) *prom whn blnd & u.r. 6th*.......... ur
6 ran. 20l, 8l, 10l. Time 6m 28.40s. SP 25-1.
Denis Williams (South Pool Harriers).

131 - Maiden Div I (12st)

70 **CHUKAMILL**..........**R Mills** 1
alwys prom, lft in ld 3 out, easily
Capstown Bay 7a..........**P Scholfield** 2
rear, some prog 14th, lft bttr by dfctns, nvr nrr
Kalokagathos..........**S Slade** 3
alwys mid-div, nvr on terms
Reptile Princess 5a *alwys wll bhnd, t.o. 13th*.......... 4
Good Appeal 5a *cls 4th whn f 12th* .... f
44 Far Run *(fav) cls up, slppd bnd 9th, rcvrd, slppd agn 16th, ev ch & f 3out* .... f
71 Biddlestone Boy (NZ) *ld/disp til blnd & u.r. 3 out* .... ur
70 Spartans Dina 7a *n.j.w. mid-div whn c.o. 10th*.......... co
The Ugly Duckling *in tch whn ran out & u.r. 10th* .... ro
Big Reward *sn bhnd, t.o. & p.u. 14th* .... pu
10 ran. Dist, 3l, dist. Time 6m 32.00s. SP 10-1.
Robin Mills (Dartmoor).

132 - Maiden Div II (12st)

69 **STORMY SUNSET 5a** ....**David Dennis** 1
(fav) j.w. alwys prom, ld 4 out, sn clr, imprssv
Far East (NZ)..........**I Dowrick** 2
rear early, prog 12th, 2nd at 16th, no ch wnr aft
Cardan..........**S Hornby** 3
alwys prom, ld 7th-15th, lost tch 4 out, onepcd aft
Here's Mary 5a *alwys bhnd, lost tch 10th* 4
44 Dharamshala (Ire) *in tch to 13th, wknd & p.u. 2 out*.......... pu
Cottage Light (bl) *cls up early, lost tch 12th, p.u. 4 out* .... pu
Father Malone (Ire) *mid-div til p.u. 11th, missed marker*.......... pu
Well Timed *sn rear, t.o. & p.u. 3 out* .... pu
69 Karlimay 5a *alwys rear, t.o. whn f 3 out* .... f
9 ran. 15l, 6l, dist. Time 6m 21.00s. SP 3-1.
Mrs Jill Dennis (Tetcott).

133 - Open

66 **CHILIPOUR**..........**N Harris** 1
(fav) hld up, prog 15th, ld 3 out, qcknd clr last
7 **Qualitair Memory (Ire)** ....**J Tizzard** 2
mid-div, prog 12th, went 2nd 2 out, alwys hld
39 **Faithful Star** ....**D Pipe** 3
hld up, prog 15th, went 3rd 2 out, no ext flat
39 Anjubi *mid-div, prog 14th, ev ch 3 out, wknd frm nxt* .. 4
6 Sweatshirt *hld up, prog 14th, ev ch 3 out, no ext aft*.. 5
Bargain And Sale *nvr on terms, onepcd*.......... 6
Pay-U-Cash *prom to 13th, lost tch 4 out*.......... 7
Ragtime Solo (bl) *alwys mid-div, bhnd whn p.u. 3 out* pu
66 Mr Lion *rear whn blnd & u.r. 7th*.......... ur
Fred Splendid *alwys mid-div, no ch whn p.u. 3 out* .. pu
Centenary Star *ld til 5 out, wknd nxt, p.u. 3 out*.......... pu
Departure 5a *sn bhnd, t.o. & p.u. 14th*.......... pu
64 Chandigarh *sn rear, t.o. & p.u. 3 out*.......... pu
Our Jackie *bolted to start, in tch til wknd 14th, p.u. 4 out*.......... pu
Serious Time *rear whn f 6th* .... f
Buckingham Gate *mid-div, bhnd whn p.u. 4 out* .... pu
39 Stoke Hand *cls up to 12th, lost tch 15th, p.u. 3 out*.......... pu
Be My Habitat *mid-div to 12th, lost tch & p.u. 4 out* .... pu
18 ran. 3l, 1l, 6l, 3l, 10l, 10l. Time 6m 24.00s. SP Evens.
Nick Viney (Dulverton (West)).

134 - Confined

43 **MAGNOLIA MAN**..........**N Harris** 1
hld up, prog 13th, disp 4 out, ev ch last, just got up
In The Navy ....**D Pipe** 2
n.j.w. mid-div, prog 14th, ld nxt, blnd last, hdd nr fin
66 **Fearsome** ....**G Penfold** 3
alwys mid-div, prog 15th, no ext frm 3 out
Double The Stakes (USA) *alwys prom, ld 8-14th, wknd nxt* 4
42 Cardinal Bird (USA) *alwys mid-div, nvr on terms* 5
Expressment *alwys mid-div, nvr in tch, bttr for race* .. 6
64 Casting Time (NZ) *alwys mid-div, nvr on terms* 7
42 Oneovertheight *n.j.w. lost tch frm 14th* 8
42 Phils Pride *prom, ld 2nd-7th, disp til blnd 13th, p.u. aft* .... pu
38 Just My Bill *ref to race*.......... 0
38 Myhamet *(fav) in tch, 3rd whn f 13th*.......... f
68 Millaroo *sn bhnd, t.o. & p.u. 4 out* .... pu
12 ran. Sht-hd, 10l, 25l, 20l, 10l, 6l, 20l. Time 6m 30.00s. SP 2-1.
Mrs D B Lunt (Tiverton Foxhounds).

135 - Ladies Div I

SOME-TOY ....**Mrs M Hand** 1
hld up, prog 13th, 2nd & hld whn lft clr 2 out
21 **Flame O'Frensi 5a** ....**Miss J Cumings** 2
ld/disp to 4 out, wknd nxt, lft 2nd 2 out
False Economy ....**Miss K Scorgie** 3
in tch, 3rd at 14th, outpcd frm 4 out, lft 3rd 2 out
67 Great Pokey *alwys mid-div, nvr on terms* 4
6 Winter's Lane *alwys mid-div, nvr on terms* 5
Unique New York (bl) *alwys bhnd, t.o. 14th* 6
Rapid Rascal *prom early, lost tch 7th, t.o. 14th*.......... 7
On His Own *rear til p.u. 3 out*.......... pu
Bianconi *alwys mid-div, lost tch 13th, bhnd whn p.u. 4 out*.......... pu
5 Flaked Oats *(fav) j.w. hld up, prog 7th, ld 4 out, 10l clr whn u.r. 2 out* .... ur

Celtic Goblin 5a *mid-div whn blnd & u.r. 10th* .... ur
11 ran. 4l, 5l, 25l, 25l, 15l, 12l. Time 6m 20.40s. SP 3-1.
John Squire (Stevenstone).

136 - Ladies Div II

KHATTAF ....Miss J Cumings 1
(fav) handy, prog 10th, ld 4 out, easily
5 **Daybrook's Gift....................Miss N Allen** 2
rear, prog 14th, styd on frm 4 out, nvr nrr
Quiet Confidence (Ire) 5a........Miss D Stafford 3
ld to 4 out, onepcd frm nxt
Sohail (USA) *w.w. prog 14th, onepcd frm 4 out* 4
67 Treleven 5a *prom early, lost tch frm 13th* 5
Go West (bl) *n.j.w. alwys rear, no ch frm 12th* 6
Eagle Trace *alwys rear, last whn p.u. 12th* .... pu
Friendly Lady 5a *in tch til f 12th* .... f
Blue-Bird Express 5a *in tch early, bhnd whn p.u. 14th* .... pu
9 ran. 5l, 6l, 5l, 12l, 25l. Time 6m 27.00s. SP Evens.
Mrs H C Johnson (Devon & Somerset Staghounds).

137 - Restricted Div I (12st)

CAUTIOUS REBEL ....J Creighton 1
mid-div, prog 12th, ld 14th, sn clr
Kings Reward ....C Heard 2
in tch, ld 8-11th, outpcd by wnr 3 out
Finnigan Free ....M Frith 3
handy, ld 13th-nxt, wknd frm 4 out
Tom Boy *alwys mid-div, nvr nrr* 4
Mountain Master *prom early, lost tch 14th, no dang aft* 5
The Copper Key *alwys rear, nvr on terms* 6
Roving Vagabond *alwys bhnd, t.o. & p.u. 2 out* .... pu
For Michael *mid-div, lost tch 12th, p.u. 14th* .... pu
Amadeo *sn bhnd, t.o. & p.u. 14th* .... pu
70 Newstarsky *alwys rear, t.o. & p.u. 2 out* .... pu
Northern Bride 5a *rear whn p.u. 13th* .... pu
Majestic Spirit *(fav) ld to 7th, wknd 14th, bhnd whn p.u. 2 out* .... pu
44 Happy Thought 5a *rear whn u.r. 7th* .... ur
Our Teddis *alwys bhnd, last whn f 3 out* .... f
7 Astound (Ire) 7a *mid-div til p.u. 12th* .... pu
15 ran. 4l, 5l, 6l, 8l, 10l. Time 6m 30.00s. SP 12-1.
Mrs L Roberts (Exmoor).

138 - Restricted Div II (12st)

ARCTIC CHILL (IRE) ....D Pipe 1
w.w. 4th at 13th, ld last, sn clr
Avril Showers 5a....................R Atkinson 2
ld til hdd apr last, outpcd
24 **The Jogger............................J Tizzard** 3
chsd ldr, ev ch 2 out, onepcd aft
28 Tinotops *mid-div, prog 12th, ev ch 3 out, wknd nxt*.... 4
Lawd Of Blisland *alwys mid-div, onepcd frm 3 out*..... 5
Call Avondale *alwys mid-div, outpcd frm 4 out* 6
No More Nice Guy (Ire) *rear, onepcd frm 13th*......... 7
69 Miss Pernickity 5a *alwys bhnd, t.o. frm 14th* 8
Darktown Strutter *cls up, f 7th* .... f
Just Silver *alwys bhnd, t.o. & p.u. 15th* .... pu
41 Great Impostor *alwys rear, t.o. & u.r. 14th* .... ur
68 Roving Rebel *mid-div, p.u. 12th* .... pu
Just Ben *prom early, lost tch 4 out, p.u. 2 out* .... pu
Langton Parmill *u.r. 2nd* .... ur
Hensue *mid-div, no ch whn p.u. 3 out* .... pu
Churchtown Chance (Ire) 5a *mid-div, wknd 14th, p.u. 3 out* .... pu
28 Highleeze (Ire) *(fav) mid-div, hmprd & u.r. 7th* .... ur
Copper And Chrome (Ire) 5a *alwys rear, t.o. & p.u. 3 out* .... pu
18 ran. 3l, 3l, 4l, 6l, 10l, 12l, dist. Time 6m 29.00s. SP 16-1.
M F Thorne (Blackmore & Sparkford Vale).
D.P.

UNITED SERVICES
Larkhill
Saturday February 17th
GOOD

139 - Confined Div I (12st)

7 **EARL BOON.......................Miss P Curling** 1
(fav) w.w. ld 15th, sn clr, not extndd
Country Style 5a.......................P Henley 2
ld to 5th, alwys prom, ran on frm 2 out
Cape Henry ....Dr P Pritchard 3
sttld rear, prog to ld 13th-15th, wknd nxt
26 Tekla (Fr) *prom, ld 8th-12th, sn wknd, onepcd* 4
Sirisat 5ex *prom, ld 5th-7th, wknd frm 15th, onepcd*... 5
American Black *tckd away in mid-div, not plcd to chal* 6
Gunner Stream *u.r. in mid-div 2nd* .... ur
Rambling Echo *sn rear & jmpd slwly, p.u. 7th*........ pu
Busteele 4ow *alwys last & y.o., p.u. 13th* .... pu
Paper Days 3ex *mid-div, wknd frm 13th, p.u. last*..... pu
Jabberwocky *alwys chsng ldrs, wknd & p.u. last* ..... pu
11 ran. 6l, 6l, 2l, 1l, 1l. Time 6m 11.00s. SP 1-2.
J A Keighley (Blackmore & Sparkford Vale).

140 - Confined Div II (12st)

65 **HENRY VAJRA.........................M Miller** 1
prom, ld & tk cmmnd 2 out, ran on well
19 **Darton Ri 3ex ....J Maxse** 2
(fav) prom, ld 13th-2 out, not able to qckn
25 **Roaming Shadow.....................J Hankinson** 3
sttld mid-div, ran on frm 3 out, nrst fin
7 Skinnhill (bl) *bhnd til prog 4 out, nrst fin* 4
Brack N Brandy *alwys mid-div, 4th at 13th, onepcd aft* 5
Smooth Escort 3ex *made most to 7th, wknd frm 13th, t.o.* 6
Cheeky Cheval 5ex *prom early, wknd frm 13th, t.o.*... 7
23 Windover Lodge 2ow *prom, ld 7th-12th, wknd nxt, t.o.* 8
Mary Borough 5a 2ow *sn rear, t.o. 13th* 9
Free Bear 2ow *ld to 2nd, qckly wknd, t.o. 12th*........ 10
Captain Jim *sn t.o., p.u. last* .... pu
Jimmy Cone *in rear whn u.r. 5th* .... ur
Four Star Line 1ow *alwys bhnd, p.u. 15th* .... pu
Dancing Doris 5a *alwys bhnd ldng grp, p.u. 15th* ..... pu
La Princesse 5a 1ow *prom, 3rd at 10th, wknd, p.u. 14th* .... pu
Palaman *sn bhnd, p.u. 13th* .... pu
Dormston Lad 8ow *alwys mid-div, wknd 12th, p.u. nxt* .... pu
17 ran. 6l, 20l, 5l, 2l, 4l, 4l, 1l, 20l, 5l. Time 6m 16.00s. SP 14-1.
Mrs H M Bridges (Portman).

141 - Members (12st)

1 **DESERT WALTZ (IRE) 5ex........D Alers-Hankey** 1
(fav) bhnd ldrs, smooth prog to ld 4 out, mstk last, ran on
Myliege 5ex ....Maj O Ellwood 2
ld to 6th, prom aft, onepcd frm 3 out
16 **Olde Crescent......................T Underwood** 3
plld hrd, ld 7th til mstk & hdd 15th, wknd
In The Choir 5a *alwys mid-div, nvr nrr* 4
Champagne Run *alwys bhnd, t.o. whn p.u. 4 out* ..... pu
Bryn's Story *sn rear, p.u. 9th* .... pu
6 ran. 6l, 3l, 20l. Time 6m 26.00s. SP 2-7.
H B Geddes (Beaufort).

142 - Mixed Open

6 **WHAT A HAND ....Miss P Curling** 1
(fav) tckd away, prog to ld 15th, ran on well frm last
Still In Business ....T Mitchell 2
ld 3rd til 4 out, chal agn last, ran on well
27 **Fosbury..........................D Alers-Hankey** 3
alwys cls up, not pace of ldng pair to chal
The Tartan Spartan *prom early, wknd frm 13th, onepcd* 4
Snowfire Chap *alwys bhnd, t.o. & p.u. 14th* .... pu
Virginia's Bay *chsd ldrs, wknd 12th, p.u. 14th*......... pu
J B Lad *prom til wknd rpdly 11th, p.u. 4 out*.......... pu
The Holy Golfer *sn rear, p.u. 5th* .... pu

18 Ardbrennan *mid-div whn f 5th* .... f
9 ran. 2½l, dist, 10l. Time 6m 12.00s. SP 2-5.
Mrs L J Roberts (Taunton Vale).

143 - Open Maiden (5-7yo) Div I (12st)

2 **TWO JOHN'S (IRE)** .... **Miss P Curling** 1
(fav) j.w. made all, not extndd
2 **Sit Tight** .... **M Portman** 2
alwys prom, ran on wll frm last, tk 2nd nr fin
Toms Choice (Ire) .... **G Barfoot-Saunt** 3
alwys prom, ch 3 out, unable to qckn, lost 2nd nr fin
Mostyn 7a *sn t.o., nvr nrr* 4
Ragtime *mid-div whn f 2nd* .... f
28 New Years Eve *mid-div whn f 5th* .... f
Ower Farm 5a *mid-div whn b.d. 5th* .... bd
Dragons Lady 5a *prom whn u.r. 4th* .... ur
Revels Hill (Ire) *schoold in rear, t.o. whn f last* .... f
Wolfie Smith *rear whn p.u. 4th* .... pu
Bet With Baker (Ire) 2ow *nvr bttr than mid-div, rear whn p.u. 14th* .... pu
Brooklyn Express 5a *prom whn f 8th* .... f
Sulason *prom til wknd frm 13th, p.u. 3 out* .... pu
Givus A Hand *sn rear, p.u. 6th* .... pu
14 ran. 20l, nk, dist. Time 6m 18.00s. SP 4-5.
Paul K Barber (Blackmore & Sparkford Vale).

144 - Open Maiden (5-7yo) Div II (12st)

MARKET GOSSIP .... **P Henley** 1
alwys prom, gd prog to ld last, ran on well
Wicked Thoughts .... **Mrs N Ledger** 2
tckd away, rpd prog 3 out, ev ch last, not qckn
Samule .... **G Barfoot-Saunt** 3
prom, ld 11th til apr last, no ext flat
29 Tea Cee Kay *sttld bhnd, some prog 14th, sn onepcd* 4
Is She Quick 5a *prom, ld 8th-10th, wknd 4 out, onepcd* 5
Good Looking Guy *alwys mid-div, nvr nr to chal* 6
Wesshaun 5a *in rear whn b.d. 6th* .... bd
3 Filthy Reesh *sttld bhnd ldrs, some prog 13th, wkng whn u.r. 3 out* .... ur
3 Blucanoo 5a *ld to 7th, losing plc whn u.r. 10th* .... ur
Definite Maybe (Ire) *(fav) rear, not fluent, t.o. & p.u. 12th* .... pu
Royal Pittance *sn t.o., p.u. 12th* .... pu
Inhurst 5a *mid-div whn f 6th* .... ur
The Blind Judge *rear whn u.r. 1st* .... ur
2 Master Art *alwys mid-div, wknd 3 out, p.u. last* .... pu
Derri Bride 7a 3ow *mid-div, u.r. 2nd* .... ur
15 ran. 1½l, 1½l, 1l, 10l, 4l. Time 6m 22.00s. SP 4-1.
R J Tory (Portman).

145 - Open Maiden (5-7yo) Div III (12st)

SKIP'N'TIME .... **M Miller** 1
ld 6th, hrd rdn apr last, styd on well
Erme Rose (Ire) 5a .... **P Henley** 2
alwys prom, chal 2 out, not qckn flat, improve
60 **Upton Orbit** .... **O McPhail** 3
prom, ev ch 2 out, ran on onepcd
Three And A Half *nvr bttr than mid-div* 4
Steel Street (Ire) *alwys rear, nvr nrr* 5
Roadrunner *prom, losing tch whn ref 14th* .... ref
Celtic Token *ld to 5th, sn wknd, p.u. 8th* .... pu
Seachest 5a *chsd ldrs, wknd 12th, p.u. 16th* .... pu
Aller Moor (Ire) 7a *sn rear, t.o. & p.u. 15th* .... pu
45 Muskerry Moya (Ire) 5a *rear whn u.r. 6th* .... ur
Count Balios (Ire) *mid-div, 3rd at 12th, wknd & p.u. 3 out* .... pu
Country Blue 7a *(fav) sttld rear, rpd prog 12th, sn wknd, p.u. 15th* .... pu
Rocky Rose 5a 12ow *rear whn u.r. 3rd* .... ur
13 ran. 1l, 15l, 10l, 15l. Time 6m 16.00s. SP 4-1.
M S Rose (Portman).
T.S.

VALE OF CLETTWR
Erw Lon
Saturday February 17th

GOOD

146 - Members

JUDGEROGER .... **G Lewis** 1
(fav) made all, 1l up 2 out, drew clr last
Origami .... **J P Keen** 2
rear, prog to chal 2 out, no ext aft
Robin Of Sherwood .... **Miss L Pearce** 3
last til prog to 3rd 14th, ch 2 out, onepcd
Live Rust (Ire) *1st ride, 2nd til lost plc hlfwy, t.o. 14th* 4
Carlowitz (USA) *rear, prog to 3rd 10th, wknd, p.u. 15th* .... pu
Katy Country Mouse 5a *3rd early, grad lost plc, p.u. 13th* .... pu
Deal Me One *cls 4th, prog to disp whn u.r. 6th* .... ur
7 ran. 8l, 8l, dist. Time 6m 20.00s. SP 4-6.
Grant Lewis (Vale Of Clettwr).

147 - Maiden Div I Pt I (12st)

JUST MARMALADE .... **J Tudor** 1
(Jt fav) cls up, rdn to ld 14th, jnd 2 out, ran on flat
Final Cruise 5a .... **R Thornton** 2
(Jt fav) alwys prom, ld 13th-nxt, chal 2 out, outpcd
The Mill Height (Ire) .... **D S Jones** 3
alwys cls up, ev ch 3 out, wknd nxt, improve
Mackabee (Ire) *t.o. 6th, fin own time* 4
Sea Search *mid-div, wknd 10th, p.u. 13th* .... pu
Parks Pride 7a *ld to 13th, wknd, f 15th* .... f
Steel Bee 5a *rear, lost tch 10th, p.u. 13th* .... pu
Ceffyl Gwyn *8s-3s, alwys last, u.r. 6th* .... ur
8 ran. 3l, 8l, dist. Time 6m 12.00s. SP 2-1.
J Tudor (Llangeinor).

148 - Maiden Div I Pt II (12st)

CRANAGH MOSS (IRE) .... **G Lewis** 1
ld 6th, prssd 15th, rdn & ran on well
Purple Melody (Ire) .... **V Hughes** 2
mid-div, prog to chal 15th, ev ch 2 out, styd on onepcd
Never So High .... **Miss A Meakins** 3
ld to 5th, cls 2nd til 3 out, no ext apr last
Amazing Air (USA) *rear, prog to 4th at 15th, 2l down 2 out, no ext* 4
Telephone *(fav) 4s-6/4, rear, some late prog 3 out, nvr nrr* 5
Icecapade (Bel) *alwys rear, nvr dang* 6
Spikeie Rose 5a *alwys rear, t.o. & p.u. 3 out* .... pu
Mister Jay Day *cls up to 14th, wknd & p.u. 2 out* .... pu
45 Lets Go Polly 5a *prom, blnd 12th, p.u. 14th* .... pu
9 ran. 3l, 5l, 5l, 15l. Time 6m 19.00s. SP 2-1.
Iwan Thomas (Carmarthenshire).

149 - Maiden Div II (12st)

45 **MRS WUMPKINS (IRE) 7a** .... **Miss P Jones** 1
hld up, 4th at 12th, 2nd 3 out, ran on to ld flat
Kinlogh Gale (Ire) .... **E Williams** 2
(fav) ld, 5l clr 13th, wknd aft 2 out, hdd & no ext flat
Le Gerard .... **M Daly** 3
rear, styd on to 3rd 2 out, no ch wth 1st 2
2 Peat Potheen *mid-div, prog to 2nd brfly 14th, mstk nxt & wknd* 4
Just For A Lark 5a *rear, lost tch frm 12th* 5
Cairneymount *rear whn f 4th* .... f
Pushlyn 5a *prom til wknd rpdly hlfwy, p.u. 14th* .... pu
Khandys Slave (Ire) 5a *rear, 7th at 11th, p.u. nxt* .... pu
Bold Alfie *prom in 3rd til f 14th* .... f
I'm A Bute 5a *t.o. hlfwy, p.u. 15th* .... pu
10 ran. 2½l, 10l, 10l, 15l. Time 6m 17.00s. SP 5-1.
David Brace (Llangeinor).

150 - Maiden Div III Pt I (12st)

STORMY WITNESS (IRE) 5a .... **J Jukes** 1
(fav) ld 2nd, made rrest, drvn clr flat
Oaklands Word .... **J P Keen** 2
alwys cls up, 2nd 2 out, chal last, outpcd flat

Buckley's Court ....**E Williams** 3
cls up, went 2nd 14th, poor jmps nxt 2, onepcd
Toucher (Ire) *ld 1st, disp whn u.r. 4th* .... ur
45 Rory'm (Ire) *rear, t.o. & p.u. 5th* .... pu
Forever In Debt 5a *5th whn ref 6th* .... ref
Miss Montgomery (Ire) 7a *cls up whn f 8th* .... f
Kerstin's Choice 7a *t.o. whn p.u. 5th* .... pu
8 ran. 1½l, dist. Time 6m 15.00s. SP 6-4.
D J Miller (Pembrokeshire).

151 - Maiden Div III Pt II (12st)

THE APPRENTICE ....**E Roberts** 1
made all, 20l clr 5th, 5l up 2 out, styd on
Magnetic Reel 7a ....**D S Jones** 2
alwys chsng wnr, clsd 2 out, alwys hld
Royal Oats 5a ....**J Tudor** 3
alwys 3rd/4th, styd on frm 13th, no ch 1st 2
Charles Quaker *(fav) rear, prog 3 out, 3rd nxt, wknd aft* 4
Trust Merci 5a *prom early, lost plc frm 12th* 5
Preseli View 7a *alwys rear, no ch frm hlfwy* 6
Jolly Swagman 7a *t.o. 6th, p.u 12th* .... pu
Mister McGaskill *mid-div, wknd 11th, p.u. 13th* .... pu
8 ran. 2½l, 10l, 4l, dist, 3l. Time 6m 18.00s. SP 8-1.
Robert Williams (Llangeinor).

152 - Maiden Div IV (12st)

CELTIC DAUGHTER 5a ....**J Jukes** 1
alwys cls up, disp 2nd frm 14th, alwys hld, fin 2nd, prmtd
Lady Romance (Ire) 5a ....**P Davis** 2
alwys prom, disp 2nd frm 14th, hld last, fin 3rd, plcd 2nd
44 **Great Precocity** ....**R Jones** 3
mid-div, 4th at 14th, onepcd aft, fin 4th, plcd 3rd
Moonlight Cruise 5a *(fav) rear, some prog frm 13th, no ch 2 out, fin 5th, plcd 4th* 4
Bay Leader 5a *alwys rear, fin 6th, plcd 5th* 5
4 Gunner Boon *2nd til lft in ld 13th, clr nxt, ran on, fin 1st, disq* 6D
21 Liddington Belle 5a *alwys rear, p.u. 11th* .... pu
44 Sister Lark 5a *ld, 5l clr 9th, p.u. qckly 13th* .... pu
Gatten's Brake *rear whn f 6th* .... f
Redoran 7a *alwys last, t.o. & p.u. 11th* .... pu
Tims Kick (Ire) 7a *alwys last pair, p.u. 15th* .... pu
11 ran. 4l, 2l, 4l, 10l, 1l. Time 6m 21.00s. SP 5-1.
Mrs E A Webber (Pembrokeshire).
Gunner Boon Disqualified for missing marker. Original distances.

153 - Open (12st)

GOOLDS GOLD 5a ....**J Jukes** 1
alwys prom, 3rd 14th, ran on 2 out, ld last
39 **Wolf Winter 7ex** ....**T Jones** 2
(fav) prom, ld 10th, hdd last, kpt on
21 **Scally's Daughter 5a 7ex** ....**E Williams** 3
ld to 8th, cls up aft, blnd 15th, no ext
22 Robusti 4ex *cls up, disp 8th-10th, outpcd frm 3 out* ... 4
Mummy's Song *mid-div, 10l 5th at 13th, no ch aft* 5
Noisy Welcome *rear, prog frm 3 out, nvr nrr* 6
Doubting Donna 5a *alwys mid-div, no ch frm 14th* 7
Lislary Lad *mid-div no prog frm 3 out* 8
The Batchlor *rear, t.o. & p.u. 15th* .... pu
Ittihaad *alwys rear, t.o. & p.u. 15th* .... pu
Forest Ranger *m.n.s, p.u.* .... pu
St Helens Boy *last trio, no prog, p.u. 14th* .... pu
Spirited Holme (Fr) *alwys rear, p.u. 13th* .... pu
Sandbrook *prom til wknd rpdly 13th, p.u. 3 out* .... pu
23 Electrolyte *u.r. 2nd* .... ur
15 ran. 3l, dist, 1l, 10l, 10l. Time 6m 6.00s. SP 12-1.
David Brace (Llangeinor).

154 - Ladies

HANDSOME HARVEY ....**Miss P Jones** 1
(fav) ld 10th, made rest, clr last, easily
76 **Workingforpeanuts (Ire) 5a** ....**Mrs D Smith** 2
hld up, steady prog frm 10th, 2nd 2 out, no ch wnr
Busman (Ire) ....**Miss L Pearce** 3
chsd wnr 10th, wknd apr last
Fast Freeze *rear, late prog, nrst fin* 4
Moving Force *prom, ld 5th-9th, wknd aft* 5
Dare Say *alwys 4th/5th, wknd frm 13th* 6
6 Good Holidays 5a *alwys mid-div, no ch frm hlfwy* 7
Mount Falcon *alwys rear* 8
Harwall Queen 5a *alwys last trio* 9
Geo Potheen *rear & no ch frm hlfwy* 10
6 Light The Wick *alwys last pair* 11
Black Russian *t.o. 3rd, btn 2 fences* 12
Travistown *alwys rear, p.u. 14th* .... pu
39 Lady Llanfair 5a *mid-div, no show frm hlfwy, p.u. 14th* .... pu
14 ran. 10l, 5l, 12l, 10l, 20l. Time 6m 1.00s. SP 1-2.
E L Harries (Pembrokeshire).

155 - Restricted Div I (12st)

41 **AFRICAN BRIDE (IRE) 5a** ....**Miss P Jones** 1
(fav) cls up til ld 10th, clr nxt, easily
Robbie's Boy ....**J P Keen** 2
rear til prog to 2nd at 15th, no ch wnr
Valiant Friend ....**Miss B Barton** 3
hld up, prog frm 3 out, nrst fin
Pick'n Hill (Ire) *mid-div, styd on frm hlfwy, nvr nrr* 4
98 Horn Player (USA) *prom, chsd wnr 9th-14th, wknd rpdly* 5
25 Knowing 5a *ld to 8th, wknd rpdly, p.u. 13th* .... pu
Equatime 5a *hld up, 5th at 10th, wknd rpdly, p.u. 13th* pu
My Harvinski *rear, gd prog to 3rd at 11th, wknd & p.u. 13th* .... pu
Willow Belle (Ire) 5a *alwys last, p.u. 12th* .... pu
9 ran. Dist, 4l, 20l, 10l. Time 6m 20.00s. SP 1-2.
David Brace (Llangeinor).

156 - Restricted Div II (12st)

MISTER HORATIO ....**M Lewis** 1
made all, wll clr 13th, easily
Celtic Bizarre 5a ....**Miss B Barton** 2
hld up, prog to 3rd 2 out, tk 2nd last, no ch wth wnr
Wolver's Pet (Ire) ....**V Hughes** 3
twrds rear, prog hlfwy, 6th at 15th, fin well
Push Along *alwys 3rd/4th, wknd frm 14th* 4
Notanotherone (Ire) *mid-div, lost tch 12th* 5
24 Flaxridge *prom, 2nd 10th, 15l down whn f 15th* .... f
Louis Farrell *alwys rear, p.u. 13th* .... pu
Cathgal *prom to hlfwy, wknd rpdly, p.u. 14th* .... pu
Box Of Delights *(fav) 4th til went 2nd at 15th, mstk nxt, p.u. 2 out* .... pu
Normski *alwys rear, p.u. 14th* .... pu
22 Pharrago (Ire) *p.u. 2nd* .... pu
Welsh Royal (Ire) 7a *schoold rear, f 14th* .... f
Royal Bula *alwys last pair, p.u. 12th* .... pu
13 ran. Dist, 1½l, 3l. Time 6m 12.00s. SP 3-1.
W D Lewis (Tivyside).

157 - Confined

21 **MISS MILLBROOK 5a** ....**V Hughes** 1
mid-div, rpd prog 3 out, styd on to ld flat
Metrostyle ....**J Jukes** 2
alwys prom, ld 12th, hdd & no ext flat
Proud Drifter ....**J Tudor** 3
mid-div, prog to 2nd 2 out, onepcd
43 Lucky Ole Son *(fav) rear, prog frm 13th, fin well, nvr nrr* 4
Butt And Ben *alwys 3rd/4th, wknd 3 out* 5
Heluva Battle *mid-div, 6th at 13th, onepcd aft* 6
Construction King *rear, some late prog, no dang* 7
27 Pyro Pennant *alwys rear, no dang* 8
6 Chibougama (USA) *8th at 9th, no prog aft* 9
City Entertainer *ld early, 3rd at 9th, lost plc aft* 10
My Pilot *alwys rear* 11
21 Loch Garanne 5a *ld 3rd-12th, wknd rpdly* 12
Bronze Effigy *alwys last pair, p.u. 13th* .... pu
No Panic *mid-div, t.o. hlfwy, p.u. 3 out* .... pu
McMahon's River 5a *last trio, p.u. 14th* .... pu
15 ran. 2l, 6l, 5l, 8l, 3l. Time 6m 21.00s. SP 10-1.
D T Goldsworthy (Llangeinor).
P.H.

WEST SHROPSHIRE DRAGHOUNDS
Weston Park
Saturday February 17th
GOOD

158 - Members

20 **TURBULENT GALE (IRE)................R Bevis** 1
6s-3s, ld/disp, clr 3 out, ran on well
Real Class..............................J Evans 2
(fav) cls up, chsd wnr frm 5 out, not qckn cls home
Principle Music (USA) (bl).............A Phillips 3
mid-div, clsd up 12th, onepcd frm 2 out
Saymore *hld up, nrst fin* 4
Palm Reader *chsng grp, no ext frm 3 out* 5
Woolstonwood 5a *mid-div, some late prog, nvr dang* 6
My Son John *t.o. hlfwy, p.u. 12th* .... pu
Autumn Green (Ire) *cls up til outpcd 12th, p.u. 3 out* ... pu
Winters Cottage (Ire) *ld/disp to 10th, wknd, p.u. 3 out* pu
Ballybeggan Parson (Ire) *mid-div, lost tch hlfwy, 6th & no ch whn f hvly last* .... f
Real Gent *f 1st* .... f

11 ran. ½l, 3l. Time 6m 45.00s. SP 3-1.
E E Williams (West Shropshire Drag).

159 - Confined

FIDDLERS THREE (bl)....................I Wynne 1
chsng grp, str chal 3 out, sn ld, ran on well
Korbell (Ire) 5a ....A Crow 2
(fav) ld to aft 3 out, sn btn whn hdd, bttr for race
Shoon Wind.............................A Dalton 3
hld up in tch, ran on clsng stgs, nrst fin
Formal *nvr bynd mid-div, no dang* 4
26 Ru Valentino *chsd ldr to 3 out, not run on* 5
Ultrason IV (Fr) *prom early, lost tch, not qckn frm 4 out* 6
Ambrose *prog hlfwy, prom 12th, lost tch & sn btn* 7
25 Duke Of Impney *alwys mid-div, no dang* 8
Christian *prom til outpcd 13th, sn btn* 9
Brompton Road *mid-div, nvr dang* 10
Rufo's Coup *mid to rear, nvr a fctr* 11
Queens Tour *prom early, fdd, p.u. 14th* .... pu
Quite So 5a (bl) *ref to start* 0
Dark Record *mid to hlfwy, sn btn, p.u. 4 out* .... pu
37 Astre Radieux (Fr) *prom whn f 6th* .... f
Nearctic Bay (USA) *mid to rear, no ch whn p.u. 14th* .. pu
Firehalms *prom in chsng grp, fdd, p.u. 2 out* .... pu
Charlie Chalk *mid to rear, outpcd, p.u. 2 out* .... pu
Ebony Gale *mid to rear, p.u. 3 out* .... pu
Spartan Pete *mid to rear, no ch whn p.u. 14th* .... pu
Twelth Man *chsd ldrs, fdd & p.u. 14th* .... pu
Ballyhannon (Ire) *n.j.w. alwys rear, f 14th* .... f

22 ran. 6l, 12l. Time 6m 38.00s. SP 6-1.
Ian Wynne (Cheshire).

160 - Open Div I (12st)

LOCHINGALL.....................T Stephenson 1
10s-9/2, hld up in tch, gd prog to ld apr last, ran on wll
Scally Muire 5a..........................A Crow 2
dwelt, steady prog frm rear to ld 3 out, wknd & hdd apr last
18 **Bucksfern 7ex ....R Bevis** 3
chsd ldrs, outpcd 3 out, onepcd
27 Pamela's Lad *mid-div, prog to chal 4 out, no ext frm nxt* 4
Barn Pool *mid to rear, some late prog, nvr dang* 5
Ross Venture 7ex *ld to 11th, stppd qckly, p.u. nxt* ..... pu
Parsons Son *mid to rear, p.u. 14th* .... pu
Top The Bid *rear, t.o. & p.u. 13th* .... pu
Scriven Boy *mid-div, nvr dang, p.u. 14th* .... pu
My Nominee 7ex (bl) *(fav) chsd ldrs, 2nd 13th, ld nxt, hdd 3 out, fdd, p.u. nxt* .... pu
22 Tydelmore *chsd ldrs to 9th, fdd, p.u. 12th* .... pu
37 Carton *cls up, ld 12th-nxt, sn btn, p.u. 3 out* .... pu
28 Cut The Corn *chsng grp, outpcd frm 14th, p.u. 2 out* .. pu
Mansun *mid-div, lost tch & p.u. 4 out* .... pu
Gal-A-Dor *t.o. hlfwy, p.u. 14th* .... pu
Better Future (Ire) *alwys rear, p.u. 14th* .... pu

16 ran. 8l, 6l. Time 6m 41.00s. SP 9-2.
Miss P Morris (Croome & West Warwickshire).

161 - Ladies Div I

27 **DOWN THE MINE ....Miss A Dare** 1
(fav) made all, ran on well whn prssd frm 4 out
Eastshaw ....Miss C Thomas 2
alwys chsng wnr, ev ch 4 out, no ext frm 2 out
Sooner Still (bl)..................Miss K Rimmer 3
cls up til outpcd 4 out, onepcd aft
Brockish Bay *mid-div, prog 10th, no ext frm 4 out* 4
Guild Street 5a *mid-div, no ch wth ldrs frm 11th, onepcd* 5
Saahi (USA) *prom, outpcd frm 11th* 6
22 Secret Summit (USA) *mid to rear, nvr rchd ldrs* 7
Kameo Style *f 1st* .... f
Love On The Rocks 5a *mid-div, fdd, p.u. 4 out* .... pu
Bidders Clown *chsng grp, mstks, fdd & p.u. 3 out* .... pu
96 Hackett's Farm *f 4th* .... f

11 ran. 6l, dist. Time 6m 36.00s. SP 2-5.
R T Baimbridge (Berkeley).
2 fences omitted. 14 jumps.

162 - Open Div II (12st)

ASK FRANK 7ex.......................H Wheeler 1
(fav) hld up rear, prog 11th, ld aft nxt, sn in cmmnd, eased flat
Garrylucas 7ex ....G Hanmer 2
chsng grp, chsd wnr 13th, nvr able to chal
Carly's Castle 5a 4ex.................S Jackson 3
prom, outpcd by ldng pair frm 4 out
Auction Law (NZ) 7ex *w.w. rear, prog 5 out, ran on, nvr nrr* 4
Tara Boy *chsd ldrs, outpcd frm 3 out* 5
Hagler *mid-div, nvr dang, p.u. 2 out* .... pu
Tipp Down *chsng grp, in tch to 13th, wknd rpdly, p.u. 3 out* .... pu
Ryton Guard 7ex *alwys rear, p.u. 4 out* .... pu
Bay Owl *f 2nd* .... f
Glenshane Lad *prom to hlfwy, outpcd 13th, p.u. 3 out* pu
25 Chip'N'run 7ex *chsd ldrs, ev ch 13th, sn wknd, p.u. 3 out* .... pu
Mr Tittle Tattle 7ex (bl) *ld to 5th, ld 8-11th, fdd rpdly 3 out, p.u. nxt* .... pu
Brook Cottage (Ire) (bl) *prom early, t.o. & p.u. 4 out* ... pu
Dannigale 7ex *mid to rear, p.u. aft 12th* .... pu
Treaty Bridge *prom, ld 6-7th, in tch to 5 out, fdd, p.u. 2 out* .... pu
Scotch II (Fr) *mid-div, t.o. & p.u. aft 12th* .... pu

16 ran. 8l, 8l. Time 6m 42.00s. SP 5-4.
Mrs R A Price (North Cotswold).

163 - Ladies Div II

MAJOR MATCH (NZ).............Miss C Thomas 1
(fav) prom, ld 6th, sn clr, unchal
Hornblower ....Miss C Burgess 2
ld to 3rd, in tch wth wnr 6th, onepcd aft
Soldiers Duty (USA) ....Mrs M Bryan 3
mid-div, styd on frm 4 out, nrst fin
Nodforms Dilemma (USA) *hld up, late prog, fin well, nrst fin* 4
Renard Quay *chsd ldrs, no ext frm 4 out* 5
Couture Tights *mid-div, nvr dang* 6
Roving Report *chsd ldrs to 5 out, wknd & p.u. 3 out* ... pu
Dice Off 5a 2ow *mid to rear, lost tch frm 12th, p.u. 4 out* .... pu
Sweet Petel 5a *mid-div, nvr nr ldrs, p.u. 4 out* .... pu
Andyworth *ld 4th-5th, mid-div whn f 9th* .... f

10 ran. 6l, 6l. Time 6m 44.00s. SP 6-4.
Mrs M Wiggin (Ludlow).

164 - Restricted Div I (12st)

WHATAFELLOW (IRE)......................A Crow 1
(fav) hld up, rpd prog to ld aft 3 out, sn clr
Worleston Farrier.....................G Hanmer 2

ld to aft 3 out, sn outpcd by wnr
Tropical Gabriel (Ire)...............Miss J Penny 3
mid-div, some late prog, nvr nrr
Rinky Dinky Doo *chsd ldrs, cls up 4 out, sn no ext....* 4
The Yokel *chsng grp to hlfwy, lost tch frm 3 out ......* 5
Flinters *mid to rear, losing tch whn u.r. 11th ....* ur
Foolish Fantasy *chsng grp, 4th at 15th, wknd rpdly, p.u. 2 out ....* pu
Merry Scorpion *chsd ldr to 11th, in tch in 3rd whn u.r. 5 out...* ur
Mastiff Lane *nvr bttr than mid-div, p.u. 12th ....* pu
Aunt Margaret 5a *prom early, mid-div whn ran out 10th...* ro
Juste Jo 5a *bhnd & strgglng, p.u. 11th.................* pu
11 ran. Dist, dist. Time 6m 48.00s. SP 5-4.
Gareth Samuel (North Shropshire).

165 - Restricted Div II (12st)

INCH FOUNTAIN (IRE) 7a.................A Crow 1
(fav) prom, prog to ld 3 out, comf
Miss Shaw 5a ....A Griffith 2
ld/disp to 3 out, no ext aft
The Barren Arctic.....................Mrs M Bryan 3
rear, mstks, ran on frm 4 out, nrst fin
Nothing Ventured *mid-div, no ch whn p.u. 4 out.......* pu
Spurious *mid-div, prog 13th, 3rd & in tch whn f 3 out..* f
Extraspecial Brew *chsd ldrs, fdd & p.u. 3 out ....* pu
Tina's Missile *ld/disp to 9th, sn btn, p.u. 4 out........* pu
Mr Bobbit (Ire) *cls up, losing tch whn f 12th...........* f
29 Roll-A-Dance *mid-div whn f 10th ....* f
9 ran. 7l, 10l. Time 6m 52.00s. SP 4-5.
M J Parr (North Shropshire).

166 - Maiden (5-7yo) Div I

ANTICA ROMA (IRE) 5a ....G Crank 1
(fav) ld 4th-nxt, ld agn 5 out, clr 3 out, ran on
King Keith ....Charles Barlow 2
mid-div, prog 4 out, styd on, nrst fin
Costermonger.........................A Griffith 3
rear, prog frm 4 out, nrst fin
The Last Joshua *hld up, prog 12th, unable to chal frm 4 out ....* 4
Agile King 7a *cls up, ld 7th-13th, fdd 3 out ....* 5
Bay Tiger *rear, t.o. 4th, p.u. 7th ....* pu
Sandy King (Ire) *chsd ldrs, in tch whn f 7th ....* f
Mickley Justtheone 5a *cls up, ld 5th-nxt, wknd rpdly, p.u. 13th...* pu
Scally Hicks 7a *f 1st...* f
Piptony *chsng grp, in tch 13th, wknd rpdly, p.u. 4 out* pu
10 ran. 10l, 6l. Time 7m 13.00s. SP Evens.
J Davenport (Cheshire).

167 - Maiden (5-7yo) Div II

WESTCOTE LAD ....W Bryan 1
(fav) prom, prog to ld 4 out, lft clr nxt, easily
Rejects Reply.............................R Owen 2
mid-div, btn whn lft poor 2nd 2 out
Niord *trckd ldrs, 3rd at 11th, fdd rpdly, p.u. 4 out .....* pu
Sargeants Choice *cls up, 2nd at 8th, 3rd at 13th, tired & p.u. 3 out.......................................* pu
Captiva Bay 5a *f 1st...* f
Antigua's Treasure (Ire) *ld to 4 out, 2nd & hld whn f nxt ....* f
Frank The Swank 7a *f 1st ....* f
Michelles Crystal 7a *mstks, t.o. 8th, p.u. 12th ....* pu
Stepasideboy *5th whn ran out 4th ....* ro
Mister Tinker *t.o. 3rd, p.u. 10th...........................* pu
10 ran. Dist. Time 7m 6.00s. SP 4-6.
David A Smith (South Shropshire).
V.S.

LINCS UNITED HUNTS CLUB
Market Rasen Point-To-Point
Sunday February 18th
GOOD TO FIRM

168 - Members

LAYEDBACK JACK ....Mrs J Dawson 1
(fav) cls up, hit 6th, wth ldr 9th, ld 4 out, sn clr
Carly Brrin...............................N Kent 2
mstks, made most to 15th, blnd nxt, sn rdn & btn
Ways And Means 5a ....K Green 3
trckd ldrs 7th, 4th & outpcd 11th, no ch aft
Somerby *in tch, outpcd 10th, t.o. 13th...................* 4
Pokey Grange *wth ldr to 6th, wknd apr 11th, t.o. 13th* 5
Mister Chippendale *chsd ldrs, 3rd & strgglng whn hit 12th, last whn p.u. 2 out ....* pu
Beckford *alwys last, t.o. 10th, u.r. 12th..............* ur
7 ran. Dist, 3l, 20l, 1l. Time 6m 30.00s. SP 2-5.
C D Dawson (Brocklesby).

169 - Confined (12st)

ZAM BEE ....N Bell 1
j.w. jnd ldr 10th, ld 15th, bttr jmps last 2, hld on
23 **Glitzy Lady (Ire) 5a.....................G Smith** 2
wll bhnd, prog 11th, chal 3 out, kpt on
Drawn'N'quartered 7ex..........Mrs J Dawson 3
hld up, prog 3 out, chsd ldng pair apr last, onepcd flat
72 Simply A Star (Ire) *(fav) w.w. prog 10th, hit 12th, 3rd & rdn apr 2 out, no ext ....* 4
78 Mediator 7ex *rear, prog to 5th apr 14th, no prog frm 3 out...* 5
Antrim County *prom, disp 6th-14th, wknd* 6
Trusty Friend *alwys mid-div, nvr dang ....* 7
59 Broadcaster *mid-div, hmpd 8th, 5th & rdn 11th, blnd 14th, wknd ....* 8
Rain Mark *nvr bttr than mid-div ....* 9
San Remo *alwys mid-div, nvr dang........................* 10
32 Rehab Venture *chsd ldrs to 10th, sn wknd ....* 11
Happy Breed *ld to 5th, disp to 8th, wknd 10th, p.u. 14th..* pu
Golden Moss 5ex *wth ldr to 4th, 6th whn f 8th..........* f
Lad Lane *rear 10th, t.o. & p.u. 15th ....* pu
Tresillian Bay (bl) *ld brfly 3rd, prom to 10th, t.o. & p.u. 2 out ....* pu
15 ran. ½l, 5l, 1l, 10l, 3l, hd, 10l, 3l, 10l, 6l. Time 6m 31.00s. SP 8-1.
Mrs A Bell (Belvoir).

170 - PPORA (12st)

ELDER PRINCE ....P Gee 1
(fav) pllng, trckd ldrs going wll, chal & ld last, comf
21 **Sisterly 5a..........................M Jackson** 2
ld 1st, sn hdd, prom, ld 2 out, hdd & onepcd last
Golden Savannah 4ex ....S Charlton 3
cls up, chsd ldr 7th, ld 9th-3 out, onepcd
Causeway Cruiser *hld up pllng, hit 14th, 5th & rdn 3 out, kpt on ....* 4
Park Drift 7ex *w.w. prog to 3rd going wl 10th,hit 12th,btn & eased apr last ....* 5
Arden *w.w. lost tch apr 14th, nvr nr ldrs...............* 6
Clare Lad 7ex *ld 2nd-8th, last frm 11th, no ch 14th....* 7
Osgathorpe 7ex *chsd ldr 4th-6th, prom til wknd 14th, p.u. last ....* pu
8 ran. ¾l, 2½l, hd, 12l, 8l, 15l. Time 6m 36.00s. SP 5-4.
Brian Gee (Grove & Rufford).

171 - Restricted Div I

21 **AINTREE OATS 5a ....J Docker** 1
(fav) cls up, chsd ldr 7th, ld 2 out, slwly drew clr apr last
Ginger Pink (bl) ....N Kent 2
ld 2nd, jnd 4 out, hdd 2 out, btn apr last
Politicians Prayer 5a.................S Charlton 3
w.w. hit 8th, ev ch 14th, sn rdn & btn
Mysterious Run (Ire) *cls up til blnd & u.r. 4th...........* ur
Kilmakee 5a *ld 1st, sn hdd, disp 3rd whn f 13th.......* f
5 ran. 4l, dist. Time 6m 47.00s. SP 2-5.
J R Holt (Atherstone).

172 - Restricted Div II

MISS PENNAL 5a .... M Jackson 1
in tch, jnd ldr going wl 9th, ld 11th, hit 14th,clr apr last
78 **Dry Hill Lad 7a .... N Kent** 2
chsd ldrs, rdn to chal 2 out, wknd rpdly apr last, fin tired
84 **Bonnie Scallywag 5a .... N Tutty** 3
chsd ldrs, 3rd & hit 2 out, no ext
14 Vernometum *raced wd, ld/disp to 15th, grad wknd* ... 4
Granby Gap *w.w. prog & in tch 11th, mstk nxt, outpcd 14th* ... 5
79 Kamadora *(fav) in tch, 3rd at 12th, rdn 4 out, btn nxt* .. 6
Midge 5a *w.w. prog & in tch 11th, wknd apr 14th, p.u. aft 2 out* ... pu
Strong Trace (Ire) *t.d.e. ld/disp to 8th, rmndrs apr 14th, sn wknd, p.u. nxt* ... pu
Buzzards Grange *alwys last, jmpd slwly, t.o. & p.u. 12th* ... pu

9 ran. 9l, 1l, 1l, 2l, 1l. Time 6m 42.00s. SP 4-1.
V Y Gethin (South Hereford).

173 - Restricted Div III

77 **OCEAN ROSE 5a .... W Burnell** 1
prom, jnd ldrs 14th, 2nd & hrd rdn 2 out, ld cls hm
Fragrant Fellow .... R Thornton 2
ld to 3rd, ld agn 14th, rdn apr 2 out, blnd last, hdd nr fin
58 **Ryders Wells .... Mrs M Morris** 3
(fav) in tch, blnd 5th & 10th, 4th & btn 15th
Kali Sana (Ire) *disp 4th til ld 7th, hit 9th, hdd 14th, wknd 3 out* ... 4
Final Nod *w.w. in tch, outpcd apr 14th, wll btn nxt* ... 5
Boscoe *alwys last, rmndrs 11th, no ch 14th, p.u. 2 out* ... pu

6 ran. Nk, 5l, 15l, 12l. Time 6m 43.00s. SP 6-4.
W M Burnell (Bramham Moor).

174 - 2m 5f Open Maiden (5-8yo) Div I

SPALEASE 5a .... A Hill 1
(fav) not alwys fluent, prog to ld 12th, hit 2 out, clr last, comf
Mr Dick .... S Swiers 2
prom, disp 6th-14th, rdn apr last, no ext
74 **Mount Faber .... S Charlton** 3
w.w. ev ch 11th, kpt on onepcd frm 2 out
Nobbutjust (Ire) 5a *prom, 3rd & rdn 3 out, no ext* ... 4
Rise Above It (Ire) *raced wd, pllng, ld 3rd, jnd 6th, blnd 11th, wknd,p.u.3out* ... pu
Boo's Delight 5a *ld to 2nd, in tch, wknd apr 11th, p.u. 2 out* ... pu
Dante's Pride (Ire) *rear 8th, sn outpcd, p.u. 11th* ... pu

7 ran. 3l, 3l, 2l. Time 5m 45.00s. SP 4-7.
Mrs Judy Wilson (Pytchley).

175 - 2m 5f Open Maiden (5-8yo) Div II

CARLY CLEVER CLOGS (IRE) 5a .... N Tutty 1
pllng, hld up, squeezed thro' & ld apr last, drvn out
Benbeath .... P Gee 2
(fav) pllng, chal going wll apr last, ran wd, ran on flat
Its Murphy Man .... A Martin 3
prom, disp 9th til ld apr 11th, jnd 3 out, unable qckn flat
72 Dear Jean 5a *cls up, disp ld 3 out til apr last, no ext flat* ... 4
62 Still Hopeful 5a *ld til jnd 9th, wknd apr 2 out* ... 5
Fortytwo Dee (Ire) 5a *pllng, prom to 11th, no dang aft* 6
Tiger *prog to 6th & in tch 11th, wknd 3 out* ... 7
Abbey Moss 7a *alwys rear, hit 6th, t.o. & p.u. last* ... pu

8 ran. ¾l, ½l, 1l, 20l, ½l, 1l. Time 5m 48.00s. SP 3-1.
Mrs P A Gaskin (Cleveland).

176 - 2m 5f Open Maiden (5-8yo) Div III

PETRIANA 5a .... E Andrews 1
1st ride, j.w. ld to 10th, ld on innr apr last, kpt on
Cadrillon (Fr) .... Miss A Deniel 2
mid-div, 3rd at 11th, mstk nxt, rdn & ch last, kpt on flat
Fair Ally .... S Charlton 3
(fav) jmpd rght,pllng,ld 11th,wd & hdd aft 2 out,rallied flat
Desert Hero *w.w. 4th & rdn 11th, ev ch 3 out, onepcd* 4
73 Skyval 5a *prog 9th, 4th & ch whn blnd 3 out, wknd* ... 5
74 Lingcool 5a *prog 8th, 5th whn hmpd & u.r. nxt* ... ur
Spanish Arch (Ire) *pllng, mstks, prom to 9th, t.o. & p.u. 12th* ... pu
Lindalighter 5a *chsd ldrs, 3rd whn f 9th* ... f
Flaxton King (Ire) 7a *alwys rear, last whn p.u. 10th* ... pu
Albert's Adventure (Ire) *mstk 2nd, ran out 4th* ... ro

10 ran. ¾l, 1l, 5l, 10l. Time 5m 40.00s. SP 20-1.
E Andrews (York & Ainsty South).
S.P.

THURLOW
Horseheath
Sunday February 18th
GOOD

177 - Confined (12st)

RIVER MELODY 5a 9ex .... T Moore 1
(fav) prom, ld 12th-15th & agn 3 out, ran on well flat
Millbay (Ire) .... N Bloom 2
prom,ld 7th-11th,effrt & ev ch 3 out,mstk nxt,onepcd aft
Cunninghams Ford (Ire) .... A Harvey 3
prom, ld 11-12th & 15th-nxt, onepcd aft, lame
31 Salmon River (USA) 7a *ld 2nd-7th, outpcd 15th, wknd 2 out* ... 4
95 Talk Sence (Ire) (bl) *alwys last, rdn 9th, sn t.o.* ... 5
96 Jimstro *prom, rdn & strgglng 10th, sn lost tch, p.u. 2 out* ... pu
Madagans Grey *rear, effrt to chs ldrs 13th, p.u. aft nxt, lame* ... pu
Divine Chance (Ire) *ld til mstk 2nd, 5th & in tch whn u.r. 11th* ... ur

8 ran. 4l, hd, 30l, 1 fence. Time 6m 40.00s. SP 4-5.
T W Moore (Essex).

178 - Intermediate (12st)

10 **NETHERTARA 5a 5ex .... P Hacking** 1
4s-2s,mstks,prog 11th,disp & hit 2 out,lft clr last,rdn out
10 **The Right Kind .... T Moore** 2
wth ldrs,lost plc 11th,rallied 3 out,lft 2nd last, styd on
31 **Timber's Boy 5ex .... N Bloom** 3
(fav) w.w. prog 12th, rdn & outpcd 3 out, styd on apr last
94 Good Old Chips *ld 4-11th & 13-15th, wknd rpdly nxt* .. 4
Santietown *blnd 2nd, alwys rear, t.o. & p.u. 14th* ... pu
12 Zeniska (USA) *in tch to 7th, last by 9th, t.o. & p.u. 2 out* ... pu
91 Fort Diana *bhnd, 10th whn f 9th* ... f
25 Woodhay Hill *prom til outpcd frm 15th, wll btn whn u.r. 2 out* ... ur
Pakenham 5ex *cls up,ld 11-13th & 15th, 1l up whn blnd & u.r. last* ... ur
Stanwick Farlap 5a *prom til wknd 15th, bhnd whn p.u. last* ... pu
New Day (Ire) 5a *20s-10s, mstk 10th, prom to 12th, bhnd 14th, p.u. last* ... pu

11 ran. 8l, 5l, dist. Time 6m 37.70s. SP 2-1.
Alan Cowing (East Sussex & Romney Marsh).
Last fence omitted. 17 jumps.

179 - Open (12st)

COLONIAL KELLY .... P Hacking 1
(fav) ld,blnd 9th,mstk & hdd nxt,ld agn 12th,ran on gamely flat
90 **Copper Thistle (Ire) .... P Taiano** 2

chsd wnr, disp 11th-nxt, 3l down 2 out, kpt on well aft
Shipmate ....R Hunnisett 3
t.o. 7th, btn over 2 fences
Alpha One 7ex *sn rdn,lost tch & slw jmp 12th,p.u. aft nxt,cont,p.u. last* .... pu
9 Green's Van Goyen (Ire) 4ex *trckd ldrs, ld 10th til jnd & f nxt* .... f
5 ran. 3l, dist. Time 6m 31.00s. SP 1-2.
Cockerell Cowing Racing (East Sussex & Romney Marsh).

180 - Ladies

33 **RICHARD HUNT ....Miss L Rowe** 1
(fav) not fluent, ld to 2nd & frm 6th, clr 3 out, easily
Emsee-H ....Miss Z Turner 2
ld 2nd-6th, wth wnr 10-14th, sn outpcd
General Picton *restrained, t.o. 5th, u.r. 9th* .... ur
3 ran. 6l. Time 6m 49.00s. SP 1-7.
Mrs P Rowe (Puckeridge).

181 - Restricted (12st)

12 **BUSTERS SISTER 5a ....G Cooper** 1
(fav) made all, mstk 9th, clr whn mstks 3 out & nxt, comf
Trimage (Ire) ....T Newton 2
chsd wnr to 9th, lost tch 14th, styd on to go 2nd agn flat
Radiant Monarch ....T Moore 3
cls up, chsd wnr 9th, mstk 12th, btn whn mstk 2 out, wknd
Picture This *alwys 4th, lost tch 10th, p.u. aft 12th* ..... pu
59 Late Start 5a *jmpd lft, sn wll bhnd, p.u. 8th* .... pu
5 ran. 15l, 5l. Time 6m 49.00s. SP 1-3.
G I Cooper (Essex & Suffolk).

182 - Open Maiden (5-7yo) (12st)

35 **PRIME COURSE (IRE) ....P Bull** 1+
cls up, prssd ldr 12th, styd on wll flat, got up fin
60 **FRESH ICE (IRE) ....S R Andrews** 1+
(fav) prom, ld 10th, blnd nxt, drvn & kpt on flat, jnd fin
97 **George The Greek (Ire).................A Coe** 3
ld to 10th, blnd 12th, onepcd frm 15th
Teeton Thomas *jmpd badly, in tch to 13th, kpt on* 4
14 Run To Au Bon (Ire) *20s-5s, in tch to 13th, losing tch whn p.u. 15th* .... pu
Kushdalay (Ire) *6s-7/2, trckd ldrs to 15th, no ch whn p.u. 2 out* .... pu
Cormeen Lord (Ire) *schoold in last, t.o. 14th, p.u. 2 out* .... pu
Morston Again *in tch til p.u. 11th, lame* .... pu
60 Derring Knight *in tch, blnd 12th,ev ch whn mstk 3 out,wknd rpdly, p.u.last* .... pu
61 Clonattin Lady (Ire) 5a *blnd 8th, in tch to 12th, t.o. 14th, p.u. 3 out* .... pu
92 Als Diner *f 1st* .... f
11 ran. Dd-ht, 20l, 4l. Time 6m 54.00s.
G Vergette/ E Farrant (Fitzwilliam/ E Sussex & Rm).
Fresh Ice, 6/4. Prime Course, 20/1. J.N.

MUSSELBURGH
Monday February 19th
GOOD TO FIRM

183 - 3m Hun Chase

ON THE OTHER HAND 12.0 7a ....Capt A Ogden 1
(fav) held up, steady hdwy to ld 14th, styd on well.
Carrickmines 12.0 7a..................Mr M Daly 2
held up, rdn and hdwy before 14th, soon chasing wnr, ridden and no impn from 2 out.
85 **Fish Quay 11.7 7a....................Miss S Lamb** 3
in tch, lost pl after 14th, kept on from 3 out.
Speech 11.7 7a *ld 3rd, hit 9th, mstk and hdd 14th, lost tch from 2 out, t.o.* 4
52 Weddicar Lady 11.4 5a *ld to 3rd, dropped rear after 10th, gradually lost tch, t.o.* 5
5 ran. 4l, ¾l, dist, 1l. Time 6m 23.30s. SP 4-6.
Robert Ogden

HAYDOCK
Friday February 23rd
GOOD TO SOFT

184 - 3m Hun Chase

99 **CLARE MAN (IRE) 12.2 5a...........Mr M Rimell** 1
(Jt fav) cl up, left in ld 5th, made rest, driven clr after last.
Simply Perfect 12.0 7a.........Miss K Swindells 2
in tch, chsd wnr from 15th, ev ch 2 out, no ext.
100 **Professor Longhair 11.11 7a ....Mr R Hicks** 3
chsd wnr 5th to 15th, fd.
The Major General 11.7 7a *in tch, effort after 15th, no hdwy* 4
120 Syrus P Turntable 11.7 7a *bhnd most of way, blnd 13th* 5
78 Cheeky Fox 12.0 7a (bl) *bhnd, tailing off when ref 9th.* .... ref
Hickelton Lad 11.11 7a *mstk 1st, in tch, wknd and p.u. before 15th* .... pu
Thornhill 11.2 7a *slowly into stride, soon in tch, tracking ldrs when blnd and u.r. 4th* .... ur
Country Tarrogen 12.2 5a *(Jt fav) ld till blnd and u.r. 5th* .... ur
9 ran. 9l, 20l, 12l, 2l. Time 6m 42.70s. SP 7-4.
M P Wareing

KEMPTON
Friday February 23rd
GOOD TO SOFT

185 - 3m Hun Chase

COOL DAWN (IRE) 12.0 7a ....Miss D Harding 1
made all, hit 5 out, ran on strly from last.
37 **Teaplanter 12.2 5a.................Mr B Pollock** 2
chsd wnr from 6th, hrd rdn apr 3 out, ev ch next, no ext approaching last.
Sonofagipsy 12.2 5a................Mr P Henley 3
trckd ldrs till wknd apr 13th, t.o..
The Real Unyoke 11.7 7a *held up in tch, chsd lding pair from 13th, outpcd from 5 out, t.o.* 4
Golden Freeze 11.11 7a *alwys bhnd, lost tch from 13th, t.o..* 5
Blakes Orphan 11.11 7a *mid div, dropped rear, 10th, t.o..* 6
1 Charden 11.11 7a *blnd 4th, bhnd, hdwy into 5th when blunded and u.r. 14th* .... ur
Goodshot Rich 11.7 7a *jmpd left, chsd ldrs to 12th, t.o. when p.u. before 3 out.* .... pu
Proud Sun 12.5 5a *(fav) held up, hmpd and f 12th.* .... f
9 ran. 6l, 25l, 15l, 7l, 11l. Time 6m 15.30s. SP 7-2.
The Hon Miss D Harding

BERWICKSHIRE
Friars Haugh
Saturday February 24th
SOFT

186 - Members

83 **ACROSS THE CARD ....W Ramsay** 1
(fav) hld up in tch, jnd ldr apr last, ld cls home
116 **Fiscal Policy ....H Trotter** 2
made most frm 8th, jnd apr last, hdd cls home
89 **Parlebiz 5a ....Miss J Wight** 3
wll in tch til outpcd frm 2 out
84 Merry Jerry *wll in tch til outpcd frm 2 out* 4
Staneshiel *ld brfly 14th, styd in tch til outpcd frm 2 out* 5
86 Paddy Hayton *ld til 8th, grad lost tch* 6
85 Rarely At Odds *nvr dang* 7
7 ran. Sht-hd, 10l, nk, 2l, 15l, 5l. Time 6m 51.00s. SP Evens.
Capt W B Ramsay (Berwickshire).

187 - Confined (12st)

86 **GREEN TIMES 7ex** .... **W Ramsay** 1
alwys handy, ld apr 2 out, just hdd whn lft clr last
110 **Fordstown (Ire) 10ex** .... **J Alexander** 2
mid-div, styd on frm 4 out, not rch wnr
Reed .... **R Robinson** 3
bhnd, kpt on frm 3 out, nvr dang
True Fair 6ex *5th hlfwy, nvr nr ldrs* 4
Little Glen *alwys twrds rear* 5
110 Toddlin Hame *prom til hlfwy* 6
110 Hamilton Lady (Ire) 5a 6ow *mid-div whn u.r. 8th* .... ur
Dancing Legend (Ire) (bl) *ld to 7th, sn wknd, p.u. 10th* pu
Worthy Spark 3ex *ld 7th til apr 2 out, just ld agn whn f last* .... f
Juniors Choice *wll bhnd p.u. 12th* .... pu
50 Tod Law 5a *nvr dang, p.u. 4 out* .... pu
Bit Of A Blether (Ire) *(fav) abt 5l 2nd & going well whn f 13th* .... f

12 ran. 10l, 12l, 20l, 8l, 2l. Time 6m 47.00s. SP 14-1.
Major General C A Ramsay (Berwickshire).

188 - Restricted Div I (12st)

KILLESHANDRA LASS (IRE) 5a .... **A Parker** 1
alwys handy, chal whn lft clr 3 out, fin lame
53 **Admission (Ire)** .... **Miss C Metcalfe** 2
5th hlfwy, styd on frm 3 out, not rch wnr
84 **Royal Surprise** .... **Miss P Robson** 3
bhnd til styd on frm 4 out, nvr dang
47 Pennine View *bhnd til styd on frm 4 out, nvr dang* 4
84 Deday *ld to 10th, grad wknd* 5
109 Crooked Streak *bhnd whn p.u. 14th* .... pu
Seteralite 5a *nvr dang, p.u. 15th* .... pu
Bullaford Fair 3ow *sn bhnd, p.u. 12th* .... pu
Blakes Folly (Ire) *ld 10th til f 3 out* .... f
Emu Park *prom early, bhnd whn p.u. 14th* .... pu
51 Weejumpawud 5a *(fav) 2nd whn mstk 14th, lost plc & p.u. aft nxt* .... pu
Master Kit (Ire) *2nd whn u.r. 4th* .... ur

12 ran. 5l, 2l, 2l, 25l. Time 6m 47.00s. SP 5-2.
Mrs B Eggo (Berwickshire).

189 - Restricted Div II (12st)

THE BLACK BISHOP (IRE) .... **P Williams** 1
5th hlfwy, ld 4 out, styd on well
51 **Roly Prior** .... **Miss P Robson** 2
4th hlfwy, went 2nd flat, not rch wnr
87 **The Buachaill (Ire)** .... **A Parker** 3
(fav) not fluent, 3rd hlfwy, no ext apr last
47 Joli Exciting 5a *hld up, kpt on frm 3 out, not rch ldrs* .. 4
47 Kalajo *2nd hlfwy, styd cls up til wknd 3 out* 5
88 Steady Away (Ire) *alwys twrds rear* 6
87 Peat Stack *made most til wknd rpdly 4 out* 7
Panto Lady 5a *sn bhnd, p.u. 4 out* .... pu
116 Moscow Mule *bhnd whn p.u. 4 out* .... pu

9 ran. 5l, ½l, 4l, 8l, 15l, 25l. Time 6m 53.00s. SP 14-1.
Martin F Edgar (Buccleuch).

190 - Ladies

85 **RUSHING BURN 5a** .... **Miss N Snowden** 1
alwys handy, ld 11th til 15th, ld agn 2 out, drew clr last
Amber Payne .... **Miss D Laidlaw** 2
3rd hlfwy, ld 15th til outpcd frm 2 out
85 **Hallo Sensation** .... **Mrs V Jackson** 3
(fav) hld up, some prog frm 4 out, nvr dang
Flypie *alwys abt same plc, no ext frm 4 out* 4
Beau Rose *nvr nr ldrs* 5
112 Hydropic *ld 7th til wknd rpdly 15th* 6
Handsome Gent *ld til 7th, wknd rpdly & p.u. 9th* ...... pu

7 ran. 10l, ½l, 15l, dist. Time 6m 51.00s. SP 6-1.
F D A Snowden (Berwickshire).

191 - Land Rover Open (12st)

49 **ROYAL STREAM 7ex** .... **A Parker** 1
(fav) j.w. sn clr, unchal
83 **Royalist (Can)** .... **C Storey** 2
chsd wnr to 4th & frm 2 out, no ch wth wnr
49 **Kilminfoyle 7ex** .... **R Hale** 3
chsd wnr frm 4th, mstks 13th & nxt, no ext frm 2 out
86 Tartan Tornado 7ex *wll bhnd til kpt on frm 3 out* 4
83 Trebonkers 8ow *alwys bhnd* 5

5 ran. 15l, 1l, 1l, dist. Time 6m 59.00s. SP 1-3.
Mrs D B Johnstone (Berwickshire).

192 - Maiden Div I

NOVA NITA 5a .... **A Parker** 1
alwys handy, mstk 2 out, kpt on well to ld cls home
88 **Wolf's Den** .... **Mrs V Jackson** 2
ld til hdd nr fin
88 **Canister Castle** .... **R Shiels** 3
alwys handy, no imp frm 3 out
116 Olive Branch 5a *alwys prom, no imp frm 3 out* 4
Sky Missile 5a *nvr nr ldrs* 5
51 Indian River (Ire) *in tch til grad wknd frm hlfwy* 6
89 Called To Account 5a *nvr nr ldrs* 7
Beltino 7a *alwys wll bhnd* 8
General Jack *prom early, lost tch frm hlfwy, p.u. 4 out* .... pu
Sweet Sergeant *sn wll bhnd, p.u. 4 out* .... pu
Megans Mystery (Ire) *(fav) some prog 15th, mstk nxt, wll hld whn p.u. 2 out* .... pu
114 Aumale (Ire) 7a (bl) *nvr nr ldrs, p.u. 4 out* .... pu

12 ran. Sht-hd, 6l, nk, 20l, 1l, 1l, dist. Time 7m 17.00s. SP 4-1.
Robert Black (Dumfriesshire).

193 - Maiden Div II

TODCRAG .... **T Scott** 1
(fav) 3rd hlfwy, ld 3 out, drew clr apr last
My Meadowsweet .... **C Storey** 2
poor 5th hlfwy, went cls 2nd 3 out, outpcd frm nxt
New Problem 5a *10l 2nd whn s.u. aft 10th* .... su
114 About Midnight 5a *remote 6th whn p.u. 10th* .... pu
88 Murder Moss (Ire) *sn bhnd, p.u. 10th* .... pu
Witness Of Truth 5a *sn bhnd, p.u. 10th* .... pu
Good Profit *4th hlfwy, bhnd whn p.u. 4 out* .... pu
115 Eilid Anoir *ld til 3 out, wknd rpdly, p.u. nxt* .... pu
47 Two Gun Tex *sn bhnd, p.u. 10th* .... pu
Joanna May 7a *bhnd whn p.u. 10th* .... pu

10 ran. 15l. Time 7m 7.00s. SP 2-1.
Mrs D Scott (Border).

194 - Maiden Div III

ELECTRIC ARC (FR) .... **R Green** 1
ld 5th, sn clr, unchal
Thief's Road .... **R Shiels** 2
bhnd early, went 2nd 11th, nvr nr wnr
Wang How .... **K Hargreave** 3
6th hlfwy, no imp on ldrs
Funny Feelings *ld til 5th, grad lost tch frm 11th* 4
89 Woolaw Lass (USA) 5a *bhnd whn p.u. 7th* .... pu
88 Mapalak 5a *15l 3rd whn f 11th* .... f
Peelinick *(fav) mod 5th whn s.u. aft 13th* .... su
115 Normans Profit *sn t.o., p.u. 12th* .... pu
Cogitate 5a *sn t.o., p.u. 12th* .... pu
Kings Token *sn t.o., p.u. 12th* .... pu
114 Ballyargan (Ire) *mod 4th whn f 13th* .... f

11 ran. Dist, 12l, 15l. Time 7m 15.00s. SP 5-1.
R W Green (Milvain).
R.J.

BOLVENTOR HARRIERS
Lemalla
Saturday February 24th
HEAVY

195 - Intermediate (12st)

65 **PHAR TOO TOUCHY 5a** .... **Miss R Francis** 1
(fav) ld til carried wd aft 6th, ld agn 3 out, sn clr, easily
134 **Expressment** .... **I Widdicombe** 2
chsd ldrs, lft 2nd 3 out, outpcd by wnr

63 Brother Bill *sn bhnd, p.u. 4 out* .... pu
71 Friendly Viking *mid-div whn ref 10th* .... ref
Karicleigh Boy *chsd ldrs, ld 4 out, jnd & f nxt* .... f
130 Jay Em Ess (NZ) *lft in ld 6th til u.r. 4 out* .... ur
Hanukkah 5a *plld hrd, cls up whn u.r. 4th* .... ur
7 ran. 6l. Time 6m 54.00s. SP 4-7.
Miss R A Francis (Dulverton West).

196 - Confined (12st)

64 **THE GENERAL'S DRUM 3ex** .... **K Heard** 1
(fav) alwys going wll, ld 2 out, styd on well
134 **Just My Bill 3ex** .... **C Heard** 2
alwys prom, ld 3 out, hdd & outpcd nxt
64 **Senegalais (Fr)** .... **M Venner** 3
mid-div, prog frm 14th, kpt on onepcd
42 Walkers Point 3ex *ld/disp frm 4th til hdd 3 out, onepcd aft* 4
68 The Kimbler *mid-div til some late prog, no dang, bttr for race* 5
64 Sancreed *alwys abt same pl* 6
63 Ghofar *unruly start, nvr trbld ldrs* 7
133 Buckingham Gate *alwys rear* 8
63 Moorland Abbot *prom early, grad wknd* 9
64 Confused Express 5a *ld to 3rd, grad wknd, sn bhnd* .. 10
Little Coombe 5a *nvr bttr than mid-div, lost tch 5 out* 11
134 Cardinal Bird (USA) (bl) *t.o. 3rd, p.u. 13th* .... pu
Laneast Lore *alwys bhnd, p.u. 13th* .... pu
134 Double The Stakes (USA) *t.d.e. rear til prog to chal 3 out, sn wknd, p.u. last* .... pu
14 ran. 1l, 1l, 1l, 2l, 2l, 8l, 5l, ½l, 2l, 1l. Time 6m 59.00s. SP 7-4.
Mrs R Fell (Dartmoor).

197 - Ladies

64 **ORIENTAL PLUME** .... **Mrs M Hand** 1
alwys prom, ld 9th, made rest, kpt on well
Tamar Lass 5a .... **Miss S Kirkpatrick** 2
disp to 3rd & frm 6th-9th, chal 3 out, no ext apr last
137 **Majestic Spirit** .... **Miss J Cumings** 3
alwys prom, unable to chal frm 2 out
67 Duchess Of Tubber (Ire) 5a *wll in rear till ran past tired horses* 4
67 Unityfarm Oltowner *nvr a fctr* 5
65 Lady Lir 5a *rear, t.o. 3 out* 6
Jokers Patch *alwys rear, p.u. 14th* .... pu
68 High Degree *nvr on terms, p.u. 2 out* .... pu
67 Searcy *(fav) mid-div, prog to chal 3 out whn ran out* .. ro
67 Grey Guestino *disp to 3rd, sn btn, p.u. 2 out* .... pu
Maboy Lady *ran wd aft 2nd, bhnd whn p.u. 4 out* ..... pu
137 Happy Thought 5a *rear, rdn & no prog whn p.u. aft 12th* .... pu
Marksway Boy *ld aft 4th, ran wd aft 6th, f nxt* ..... f
13 ran. 2l, 10l, ½l, 15l, 15l. Time 6m 50.00s. SP 7-4.
J F Weldhen (Fourburrow).
Open ditch omitted from 3rd race onwards. 16 jumps races 3-9.

198 - Land Rover Open (12st)

130 **BOOTSCRAPER 7ex** .... **A Farrant** 1
alwys prom, ld 2 out, ran on wll und pres
153 **Wolf Winter 7ex** .... **N Harris** 2
(fav) alwys prom, chal 3 out, ev ch nxt, no ext flat
Celtic Sport 7ex (bl) .... **R White** 3
ld to 3 out, no ext aft
Greenwine (USA) *chsd ldrs til no ext frm 4 out* 4
133 Departure 5a *bhnd frm 6th, ran on agn frm 2 out* 5
Charmers Wish 5a 3ow *alwys bhnd* 6
Badihar (USA) *sn bhnd, p.u. 3 out* .... pu
38 Gymcrak Dawn *nvr seen wth a ch, p.u. 2 out* .... pu
Batsi *nvr trbld ldrs, p.u. 2 out* .... pu
133 Chandigarh *alwys bhnd, p.u. 2 out* .... pu
133 Serious Time *bhnd whn p.u. aft 11th* .... pu
70 Pen-Alisa 5a *t.o. 2nd, p.u. 6th* .... pu
12 ran. 1½l, 3l, 1l, 20l, 20l. Time 6m 58.00s. SP 7-4.
Mrs Sarah Adams (South Cornwall).

199 - Restricted (12st)

29 **SOUTHERN FLIGHT** .... **Miss J Cumings** 1
alwys prom, ld 3 out, styd on well
68 **Lonesome Traveller (NZ)** .... **Mrs M Hand** 2
alwys cls up, chal 2 out, no ext
68 **Monkton (Ire)** .... **R White** 3
ld 9th-3 out, fdd aft
Green Hill *mid-div, styd on onepcd frm 2 out, nvr nrr* 4
Aristocratic Gold *alwys bhnd, t.o. & p.u. 13th* .... pu
41 Ewhonosebest *sn bhnd, p.u. 12th* .... pu
68 Holly Fare *prom to 4th, sn bhnd, p.u. 2 out* .... pu
Laneast Prince *sn wll bhnd, p.u. 12th* .... pu
137 Kings Reward *prom til wknd & p.u. 2 out* .... pu
134 Oneovertheight *wll bhnd whn p.u. 12th* .... pu
131 Chukamill *ld/disp to 9th, wknd rpdly, p.u. 2 out* ..... pu
38 Baron Rush *sn bhnd, t.o. & p.u. 2 out* .... pu
Neil's Way *mid-div til prog 4 out, sn wknd, p.u. 2 out* .. pu
71 Tasmin Tyrant (NZ) *(fav) nvr going wll, strggling whn p.u. 2 out* .... pu
132 Far East (NZ) *mid-div, 5th & no ch whn p.u. last* ..... pu
Ticket To The Moon 5a *mid-div, prog to chal 3 out, sn wknd, p.u. last* .... pu
138 Copper And Chrome (Ire) 5a *nvr a fctr, p.u. 8th* ..... pu
17 ran. 1l, 3l, 8l. Time 7m 1.00s. SP 8-1.
Mrs K J Cumings (Devon & Somerset Staghounds).

200 - Open Maiden Div I (12st)

69 **WAIPIRO** .... **I Dowrick** 1
(fav) alwys going wll, ld 4 out, in cmmnd aft, easily
Simply Joyful 5a .... **P King** 2
chsd ldrs, 2nd frm 4 out, no ch wth wnr
Quick Opinion .... **J Young** 3
ld to 6th, prom aft, no imp ldrs frm 4 out
70 Sharrow Bay (NZ) *nvr bttr than 4th, no dang frm 3 out* 4
Cool Work *alwys prom, ld 9th-4 out, wknd, fin tired* ... 5
137 Northern Bride 5a *cls up to hlfwy, wknd & p.u. 11th* ... pu
132 Cardan *ld 6th-9th, wknd, p.u. 3 out* .... pu
69 Eserie de Cores (USA) *prssd ldrs til blnd & u.r. 12th* .. ur
My Prides Way 5a *rear, t.o. & f 3 out* .... f
Moonbay Lady 5a *wll bhnd whn p.u. aft 12th* .... pu
71 Ashcombe Valley *alwys bhnd, p.u. 9th* .... pu
131 Spartans Dina 7a *strgglng frm 9th, p.u. 11th* .... pu
12 ran. 6l, 2l, 12l, 4l. Time 7m 14.00s. SP 7-4.
Mrs C A Furse (Tetcott).

201 - Open Maiden Div II (12st)

GOLDEN DROPS (NZ) .... **I Dowrick** 1
mid-div, prog to ld 3 out, ran on strngly
71 **Parson Flynn** .... **R White** 2
(fav) ld 9th til 3 out, no ext und pres
Mosside .... **N Harris** 3
mid-div til styd on onepcd clsng stgs
Robenko (USA) *prom til no ext frm 2 out* 4
Treassowe Oats *nvr nrr* 5
Dovedon Princess 5a *alwys rear, p.u. 2 out* .... pu
71 Baldhu Chance *s.u. bend aft 4th* .... su
Ianovitch *u.r. 4th* .... ur
71 Sixth In Line (Ire) *prom early, losing tch whn p.u. aft 11th* .... pu
71 Zany Girl 5a (bl) *alwys bhnd, p.u. aft 13th* .... pu
Springcombe 5a *rear, no ch whn p.u. aft 11th* .... pu
Chocolate Buttons 5a *mid-div, s.u. bend apr 4th* ..... su
Breeze-Bloc 5a *ld/disp to 9th, grad wknd, p.u. 2 out* .. pu
13 ran. 1l, 3l, 10l, 10l. Time 7m 15.00s. SP 7-1.
D H Barons (Dart Vale And South Pool Hrrs).

202 - Open Maiden Div III (12st)

71 **SWING TO THE LEFT (IRE) 5a** ... **Miss J Cumings** 1
alwys handy, ld 2 out, rdn out
70 **Bells Wood** .... **R White** 2
alwys chsng grp, slight ld 4 out-2 out, kpt on onepcd
Golden Eye (NZ) .... **I Dowrick** 3
prog to tck ldrs 4 out, onepcd frm nxt, improve
45 Master Kiwi (NZ) *alwys prom, not pace to chal frm 3 out* 4
69 Moorland Highflyer 7a *ld/disp 6th til 4 out, sn onepcd* 5
71 Rosa's Revenge 5a *prom til rdn 12th, no response* ... 6
138 Darktown Strutter *ld to 3rd, sn wll bhnd, p.u. 10th* ... pu
Skip Tracer *not alwys fluent, p.u. aft 9th* .... pu
Artistic Peace 5a 8ow *wll bhnd frm 3rd, p.u. 2 out* .... pu
Diana Moss (Ire) 5a *ld 3rd-6th, wknd & p.u. 9th* ...... pu

Coed Canlas *sn bhnd, p.u. aft 4th* .... pu
Tinstreamer Johnny 7a *bhnd frm 3rd, t.o. & p.u. 9th* .. pu
12 ran. ½l, 2l, 2l, 10l, 1l. Time 7m 18.00s. SP 7-1.
J Pryce (Devon & Somerset Staghounds).
P.Ho.

MENDIP FARMERS
Castle Of Comfort
Saturday February 24th
HEAVY

203 - Members (12st)

SAYYURE (USA)........................A Harris 1
(fav) chsd ldr, rdn 4 out, blnd nxt, ld last, styd on
Kings Gunner ....Miss S Vickery 2
j.w. ld to last, tired & hdd
Frozen Minstrel ....R Billing 3
sn t.o., btn 3 fences
Noble Minister *cls up early, lost tch 11th, t.o. & p.u. 4 out*........ pu
4 ran. 3l, dist. Time 7m 12.00s. SP 4-7.
A G Harris (Mendip Farmers).

204 - Open Maiden Div I (12st)

141 **BRYN'S STORY...................Maj G Wheeler** 1
wll bhnd til prog 15th, styd on to ld flat
28 **Fathers Footprints ....R Hicks** 2
rear til prog 14th, ev ch last, outpcd
152 **Lady Romance (Ire) 5a...................P Davis** 3
cls up to 12th, sn bhnd, styd on agn 3 out, no ext flat
Abit More Business (Ire) 7a *(fav) hld up,prog to disp 4 out,lft clr nxt wknd rpdly last,tired*........ 4
Romano Hati 5a *cls up early, sn lost tch, p.u. 11th*.... pu
Juniper Lodge *made most til 4 out, ev ch whn f nxt*.... f
Its A Mugs Game 5a *f 1st*........ f
Orchard Lady 5a *in tch, 4th at 12th, wknd nxt, p.u. 3 out*........ pu
Penny's Prince *f 1st*........ f
Trevella 5a *mid-div to 14th, wknd nxt, p.u. 3 out* .... pu
Hillview Star (Ire) 5a *alwys rear, t.o. & p.u. 3 out*.... pu
11 ran. 5l, 3l, dist. Time 7m 25.00s. SP 33-1.
G D Blagbrough (Avon Vale).
Two fences omitted this race, 16 jumps.

205 - Open Maiden Div II (12st)

MAMMY'S CHOICE (IRE) 5a.............M Miller 1
(fav) alwys prom, ld 12th, prssd 3 out, ran on well frm nxt
143 **Bet With Baker (Ire) ....Miss P Curling** 2
cls up, chsd ldr 13th, ev ch 3 out, outpcd aft nxt
152 Great Precocity *rear til f 7th*........ f
143 New Years Eve *sn bhnd, t.o. & p.u. 2 out*........ pu
Son Of Anun *handy to 8th, lost tch & p.u. 13th*........ pu
3 Woodside Lady (Ire) 5a *nvr on terms, t.o. 13th, p.u. last*........ pu
135 Celtic Goblin 5a *prom, ld 4-11th, wknd, t.o. & p.u. 4 out*........ pu
Between You And Me *mid-div til lost tch 12th, t.o. & p.u. 14th*........ pu
Itsstormingnorma 5a *sn rear, t.o. & p.u. 2 out*........ pu
9 ran. 8l. Time 7m 30.00s. SP 7-4.
David Young (Portman).

206 - Open Maiden Div III (12st)

143 **OWER FARM 5a ....D Dennis** 1
cls up, ld 4 out, ran on frm 2 out
Lake Mariner 5a..................Maj O Ellwood 2
mid-div to 12th, ev ch 3 out, no ext aft
Royal Swinger 5a *alwys bhnd, no ch whn p.u. 4 out* .. pu
Yet To Dance 5a *ld to 9th, wknd & p.u. 13th*........ pu
Prince Itsu *bhnd, t.o. & p.u. 10th*........ pu
Rymer's Express *sn rear, t.o. & p.u. 13th*........ pu
Electrofane (Ire) *prom to 3 out, wknd & p.u. last*........ pu
Masters Nephew *(fav) in tch, disp 11th-4 out, wknd nxt, p.u. last*........ pu
Annmount Lady (Ire) 5a *sn rear, t.o. til prog 12th, ev ch 4 out, wknd nxt, p.u.2out*........ pu
Sue's Quest 5a *sn t.o., last whn p.u. 4 out*........ pu
10 ran. 10l. Time 7m 42.00s. SP 5-1.
Mrs J E Purdie (South Dorset).

207 - Open Maiden Div IV (12st)

MISTY (NZ) ....M Felton 1
cls up, ld 13th, styd on well frm 2 out
70 **Clonroche Lucky (Ire) ....P Henley** 2
(fav) handy, ev ch 2 out, no ext last
He Is ....T Mitchell 3
rear, prog 12th, ev ch 2 out, no ext, promising
138 Langton Parmill *mid-div, prog 14th, ev ch 3 out, outpcd aft*........ 4
29 Oh Lord (Ire) *mid-div, ev ch 4 out, onepcd frm nxt* .. 5
26 I Is *ld/disp to 10th, wknd & p.u. nxt*........ pu
Stormy Fashion *rear til p.u. 13th*........ pu
Ive Called Time *alwys mid-div, no ch whn p.u. last* ... pu
152 Sister Lark 5a *alwys mid-div, t.o. & p.u. 14th*........ pu
Tullykyne Bells *in tch to 7th, ld 11th-nxt, wknd, t.o. & p.u. 15th*........ pu
Legal Vision 5a (bl) *rear til p.u. 14th*........ pu
Flights Lane 5a *rear til p.u. 12th*........ pu
Dirty Dancer *bhnd, t.o. & p.u. 12th*........ pu
71 Sgeir Bantighearna 5a *rear til p.u. 13th*........ pu
Sarah Dream (Ire) 5a *rear, prog 7th, cls up 11th, wknd & p.u. 13th*........ pu
15 ran. 3l, 4l, 1l, 6l. Time 7m 29.00s. SP 16-1.
Mrs J E Milne (Cotswold).

208 - Ladies

MY MELLOW MAN (bl)............Miss S Vickery 1
in tch, disp 4 out til ld 2 out, ran on
135 **On His Own ....Miss W Southcombe** 2
alwys prom, disp 4 out-2 out, no ext aft
67 **Galaxy High ....Miss L Horsey** 3
alwys mid-div, 4th at 14th, no ch frm nxt
Alpine Song 5a *rear til prog 14th, nrst fin*........ 4
Mendip Music *1st ride, alwys mid-div, nvr on terms* .. 5
Bridge Express *prom to 6th, outpcd frm 10th*........ 6
135 Unique New York *disp to 5th, cls up to 12th, outpcd frm nxt*........ 7
126 Little Thyne *alwys rear, nvr on terms*........ 8
136 Daybrook's Gift *alwys rear, nvr on terms*........ 9
140 Jimmy Cone *rear whn f 13th*........ f
Prince Nepal *rear til u.r. last*........ ur
Beyond Our Reach *2s-1/1, in tch, ld 13th, going clr whn f nxt*........ f
154 Light The Wick *sn t.o., wll bhnd whn p.u. 4 out*........ pu
Cock Finch *sn t.o., m bhnd whn p.u. 4 out*........ pu
14 ran. 5l, 15l, 20l, 4l, 6l, 3l, 10l, 30l. Time 7m 18.00s. SP 5-1.
W G Gooden (Mendip Farmers).

209 - Open (12st)

66 **THE BIRD O'DONNELL 7ex ....T Barry** 1
hld up, prog 13th, disp 4 out til ld 2 out, sn clr
Orujo (Ire)...............................M Felton 2
cls up, ld 14th-nxt, disp nxt, ev ch 2 out, wknd
142 **Ardbrennan ....C Bennett** 3
ld 6th-13th, no ext frm 3 out
Columbique 1ow *ld to 5th, cls up aft, wknd & lost tch frm 14th*........ 4
Southerly Buster *sn rear, t.o. whn blnd & u.r. 2 out* .... ur
133 Bargain And Sale *mid-div to 8th, wknd & p.u. 12th*.... pu
25 Prince Tino *rear til p.u. 13th*........ pu
66 Lewesdon Hill *(fav) handy, prog 13th, disp whn blnd & u.r. 4 out*........ ur
8 ran. 25l, 10l, dist. Time 7m 28.00s. SP 3-1.
Lady Sarah Barry (Taunton Vale Foxhounds).

210 - Intermediate Div I (12st)

SPACE CAPPA ....Miss V Stephens 1
made most, ran on well frm 2 out
Balmoral Boy (NZ) ....M Miller 2
handy, prog 12th, ev ch 2 out, onepcd
Binney Boy ....M Felton 3

(fav) mid-div, prog 13th, ev ch 3 out, wknd nxt
7 Zorro's Mark *cls up to 14th, no ext aft* 4
136 Eagle Trace *alwys rear, t.o. & p.u. last* .... pu
Cossack Strike (Ire) *rear til s.u. bend aft 13th* .... su
Therewego (Ire) *mid-div, lost tch 14th, t.o. & p.u. 2 out* pu
A Windy Citizen (Ire) 5a *cls up, ld 13th-nxt, wknd aft, p.u. 3 out* .... pu
156 Pharrago (Ire) *in rear til p.u. 12th* .... pu
Plan-A (Ire) *in tch, wknd 13th, t.o. & p.u. last* .... pu
10 ran. 4l, 2l, 20l. Time 7m 27.00s. SP 6-1.
D G Stephens (West Somerset Vale).

211 - Intermediate Div II (12st)

APATURA HATI 5a........P Henley 1
alwya prom, ld 10-13th, disp 4 out til ld 2 out, ran on
138 **The Jogger........J Tizzard** 2
handy, prog 12th, ld 14th til disp nxt, wknd 2 out
68 **Strong Breeze........Mrs R Pocock** 3
in tch, outpcd frm 4 out
157 Pyro Pennant *sn wll bhnd, t.o. & p.u. 14th* .... pu
65 Good For Business *(fav) cls up, 2nd whn blnd & u.r. 13th* .... ur
5 ran. 5l, 25l. Time 7m 31.00s. SP 5-2.
Mrs R O Hutchings (Portman).

212 - Confined (12st)

160 **BETTER FUTURE (IRE)........B Potts** 1
handy, disp frm 14th, ld 2 out, styd on
43 **Balisteros (Fr)........D Alers-Hankey** 2
hld up, prog 10th, ld/disp frm 13th til outpcd 2 out
Direct........T Edwards 3
(fav) rear, went 3rd at 14th, no ch frm nxt
133 Ragtime Solo *handy, lost tch 14th, t.o. & p.u. last* .... pu
136 Blue-Bird Express 5a *alwys rear, bhnd whn p.u. 13th* pu
Jupiter Moon *cls up, ld 3rd til blnd & u.r. 13th* .... ur
Bishops Truth *cls up til 10th, wknd, p.u. 13th* .... pu
7 ran. 3l, dist. Time 7m 26.00s. SP 7-1.
J A C Edwards (Berkeley).
D.P.

NORTH HEREFORDSHIRE
Newtown
Saturday February 24th
GOOD TO SOFT

213 - Members (12st)

CHARACTERISTIC........Miss E James 1
(fav) chsd ldr frm 8th, ld 2 out, lft clr last, styd on
156 **Cathgal (bl)........J Rees** 2
ld til hrd rdn & hdd 2 out, ev ch whn blnd last, not rcvr
Spanish Rouge........S Blackwell 3
mstks 3rd & 10th, in tch to 12th, sn t.o., btn 2 fences
Space Mariner 14ow 7ex *sn bhnd, t.o. frm 5th* 4
163 Sweet Petel 5a *chsd ldr til blnd 8th & rider lost irons, p.u. nxt* .... pu
Hennerwood Oak 5a *mstk 7th, prom til wknd 11th, sn t.o., p.u. 2 out* .... pu
So Easy 5a *sn wll bhnd, t.o. & p.u. 7th* .... pu
7 ran. 4l, dist, 12l. Time 6m 55.00s. SP 6-4.
D H Godfrey (North Hereford).

214 - Confined (12st)

DI STEFANO........Miss A Dare 1
(fav) hld up, rpd prog aft 13th, ld 2 out, pshd clr last
162 **Hagler........S Griffiths** 2
prom, chsd ldr 14th, ev ch 2 out, onepcd
170 **Sisterly 5a........M Jackson** 3
ld 6th, clr 13th, hdd & wknd 2 out
Sound Golly 3ow *wll bhnd til ran on frm 15th, nrst fin* 4
Homme D'Affaire *prom, chsd ldr 13th-nxt, btn frm nxt* 5
22 All Weather *mid-div, no ch frm 13th, kpt on* 6
Master Donnington *prom, ld 4-6th, outpcd aft 13th, no dang aft* 7
Gozone *ld to 2nd, chsd ldrs aft, outpcd frm 13th* 8
Ragtime Cowboy Joe *hld up bhnd, nvr nr to chal* 9
160 Barn Pool *alwys rear, nvr dang* 10
Troy Boy *wll bhnd, brf effrt 13th, no dang* 11
Caviss 5a *alwys bhnd, t.o. last whn f 10th* .... f
Paddy In Paris *rear, lost tch & p.u. 13th* .... pu
24 Punching Glory *alwys rear, t.o. & p.u. 3 out* .... pu
125 Grey Tudor *last whn p.u. 6th* .... pu
Arctic Quest 5a *chsd ldrs to hlfwy, wknd, t.o. & p.u. 2 out* .... pu
Agarb (USA) *alwys rear, lost tch & p.u. 12th* .... pu
Churchill Star *ld 2-4th, p.u. 10th, dead* .... pu
The Rum Mariner *chsd ldrs to 13th, sn wknd, p.u. 2 out* .... pu
153 Noisy Welcome *f 2nd* .... f
Flimsy Flame *prom, chsd ldr 6th-13th, wknd, p.u. 2 out* .... pu
21 ran. 6l, 3l, 15l, 2l, 4l, 5l, 12l, 3l, 1l, ½l. Time 6m 49.00s. SP 7-4.
Mike Gifford (Cotswold Vale).

215 - Open (12st)

162 **GARRYLUCAS 7ex........G Hanmer** 1
prom, prog to ld 14th, clr 2 out, rdn out
162 **Ask Frank 7ex........H Wheeler** 2
(fav) hld up bhnd, gd prog to disp 14th, chsd wnr nxt, no imp 2out
157 **Miss Millbrook 5a........V Hughes** 3
bhnd, prog to poor 5th aft 13th, kpt on, no dang
140 Roaming Shadow *rear, styd on frm 11th, no dang, nrst fin* 4
Nether Gobions *ld to 14th, wknd, fin tired* 5
Frampton House *mid-div, rdn 11th, sn btn, t.o. & p.u. 2 out* .... pu
Willie McGarr (USA) *s.s. wll bhnd, some prog 13th, no ch whn p.u. 2 out* .... pu
High Ham Blues *mid-div, no ch frm 13th, p.u. nxt* .... pu
Gee Double You *hld up wll bhnd, no prog 12th, t.o. & p.u. 3 out* .... pu
Athassel Abbey *chsd ldrs to 8th, wknd rpdly & p.u. 12th* .... pu
Sams Heritage 7ex *blnd 2nd, alwys bhnd, no prog 12th, p.u. 3 out* .... pu
162 Glenshane Lad 7ex *5th whn u.r. 8th* .... ur
Coombesbury Lane 5a *prom, 4th whn f 13th* .... f
157 Loch Garanne 5a *left, t.n.p.* 0
162 Chip'N'run *prom til 4th & btn apr 14th, 5th whn p.u. 2 out* .... pu
Proud Slave 5a *1st ride, alwys rear, last whn u.r. 12th* .... ur
153 Electrolyte *alwys rear, t.o. 13th, p.u. 2 out* .... pu
Nawrik (Ire) 7ex *ptom to 12th, sn wknd, t.o. & p.u. 2 out* .... pu
Macaabee Special (Ire) *t.o. & p.u. 7th* .... pu
Baptist John (Ire) *n.j.w. in tch to 12th, t.o. & p.u. 14th* .... pu
20 ran. 3l, dist, 3l, 10l. Time 6m 45.00s. SP 10-1.
J D Lomas (United).

216 - Ladies

BANKHEAD (IRE) 7ex........Miss C Spearing 1
7/2-9/4, 3rd frm 6th til chsd ldr 13th, ld 2 out, rdn out
126 **Thamesdown Tootsie 5a 7ex........Miss V Lyon** 2
ld, clr 12th, hdd 2 out, not qckn apr last
Derring Bud 4ex........Miss A Downes 3
s.s. hld up wll bhnd, prog 13th, ran on 2 out, fin strngly
161 Eastshaw 7ex *(fav) w.w. rmndrs 9th, chsd ldng pair 13th, no imp nxt, fin tired* 4
Pithy 4ex *alwys wll bhnd, t.o. & p.u. 11th* .... pu
Afaristoun (Fr) *prom, chsd ldr 5th-13th, wknd rpdly, t.o. & p.u. 15th* .... pu
Rectory Boy 7ow *t.o. last, 3 fences bhnd whn u.r. last* .... ur
They All Forgot Me 4ex *alwys rear, t.o. & p.u. 13th* .... pu
27 Ski Nut *rear, lost tch 10th, no prog 14th, p.u. 2 out* .... pu
Gan Awry 5a 4ex *chsd ldrs til wknd 12th, p.u. nxt* .... pu
Cantantivy 5a 1ow *rear, mstk 8th, p.u. nxt* .... pu
24 Drumceva 4ex *chsd ldrs, 6th & outpcd whn blnd & u.r. 12th* .... ur
163 Andyworth *in tch to 9th, sn wknd, t.o. & p.u. aft 13th* .... pu
13 ran. 2l, 20l, 6l. Time 6m 43.00s. SP 9-4.
A J Brazier (Croome & West Warwickshire).

217 - Restricted Div I (12st)

GUITING GRAY .... **Miss A Dare** 1
(fav) trckd ldrs, ld 12th, drew clr 2 out, easily
Ollardale (Ire) .... **W Bryan** 2
in tch, prog 12th, chsd wnr 2 out, kpt on, no imp
Kettles 5a .... **A Phillips** 3
chsd ldrs, 5th hlfwy, outpcd 14th, ran on agn 2 out
Saffron Glory *alwys prom, cls up 14th, no imp frm nxt* 4
Linantic *made most to 12th, wth wnr 14th, sn wknd* ... 5
Squeeze Play *alwys well bhnd, t.o. & p.u. 11th* .... pu
Kerry Hill *alwys rear, lost tch 13th, t.o. & p.u. 2 out* .. pu
Teega Suku *nvr nr ldrs, t.o. & p.u. 15th* .... pu
Welsh Clover 5a *chsd ldrs, lost tch aft 13th, p.u. 15th* pu
Plundering Star (Ire) *prom to 7th, lost plc, prog 11th, no imp 15th, p.u. last* .... pu
Barrafona (Ire) *prom to 8th, wknd 10th, wll bhnd whn u.r. 13th* .... ur
79 Cloud Cover *rear, prog 9th, lost tch aft 13th, mstk 15th, p.u., dsmntd* .... pu
146 Deal Me One *mstk 3rd, alwys bhnd, t.o. & p.u. 14th* ... pu
Sugi *f 5th* .... f
Bride Run (Ire) *chsd ldrs to hlfwy, no ch 13th, p.u. 15th* .... pu
Imike *t.o. last til p.u. 8th* .... pu
Forever Freddy *rear, lost tch 8th, t.o. & p.u. 12th* .... pu

17 ran. 8l, 5l, 8l, 6l. Time 6m 53.00s. SP 4-6.
A M Mason (V.W.H.).

218 - Maiden Div I (12st)

2 **SCARLET BERRY 5a** .... **Julian Pritchard** 1
hld up, prog 10th, ld 15th, clr last, styd on well
I Blame Theparents 5a .... **R Bevis** 2
in tch, ld 12-15th, ev ch 2 out, no ext apr last
Derring Ruler .... **S Jackson** 3
trckd ldrs, ev ch 14th, sn wknd, fin tired
Promethean Singer *prom, ev ch 14th, sn wknd* 4
Plucky Punter *ld 3-8th & 10-12th, wknd aft nxt, p.u. 15th* .... pu
23 Mr Paddy Bell *alwys bhnd, t.o. & p.u. 11th* .... pu
69 Balmaha 7a *rear, prog 11th, ev ch whn f 14th* .... f
Rosenthal 5a *mstks, alwys bhnd, t.o. 10th, p.u. 15th* pu
21 Woodmanton 5a *in tch to 10th, wknd & p.u. 13th* ..... pu
Mandys Lad *ld to 3rd & 8th til hdd & mstk 10th, wknd rpdly, p.u. 14th* .... pu
Cruise A Hoop *alwys rear, t.o. & p.u. 12th* .... pu
Tennessee Cruiser *last & t.o. til p.u. 3 out* .... pu
Bolshie Baron *(fav) in tch, mstk 8th, lost plc & p.u. 11th* .... pu
Lady Rosebury 5a *rear whn f 5th* .... f

14 ran. 6l, 30l, 8l. Time 6m 55.00s. SP 10-1.
Mrs C A Dance (North Ledbury).

219 - Restricted Div II (12st)

26 **LIGHTEN THE LOAD** .... **A Wintle** 1
rear, gd prog frm 12th, ld apr last, ran on well
41 **Caracol** .... **Julian Pritchard** 2
4s-9/4, alwys prom, ld apr 2 out, hdd & wknd apr last
70 **Mac's Boy** .... **J Jukes** 3
trckd ldrs going wll, lft in ld 12th, hdd & wknd apr 2 out
Judy Line 5a *last trio til prog 11th, poor 10th aft 13th, fin strngly* 4
156 Push Along *prom, cls 4th at 14th, sn btn* 5
Board Game *chsd ldrs, 6th aft 13th, wknd nxt* 6
Tenella's Last 5a *mid-div, lost tch 13th, no ch aft* 7
Banton Loch *mid-div, 7th aft 13th, wkng whn hit 3 out, p.u. nxt* .... pu
Dane Rose 5a *prom to 6th, wknd rpdly, p.u. 12th* ..... pu
Old Steine *mstk 3rd, prom to 8th, t.o. 12th, p.u. 15th* .. pu
155 Knowing 5a 1ow *blnd 7th, alwys bhnd, p.u. 13th* ..... pu
Rip Van Winkle *(fav) ld til f 12th* .... f
Callerose *mid-div, effrt 11th, lost tch 13th, p.u. 3 out* .. pu
Steel Faucon (Ire) *f 1st, dead* .... f
77 Kings Mischief (Ire) *cls up, mstk 10th & rmndrs, wknd 13th, p.u. 15th* .... pu
41 Saffron Moss *sn wll bhnd, t.o. & p.u. aft 13th* .... pu
150 Forever In Debt 5a *in tch to 8th, rdn & wknd 11th, t.o. & p.u. 15th* .... pu

17 ran. 6l, 5l, 25l, 3l, 4l, 15l. Time 6m 53.00s. SP 10-1.
J S Payne (Gelligaer).

220 - Maiden Div II (12st)

RIGHT ROSY 5a .... **R Jenkins** 1
rear, poor last 14th, ran on aft, ld last, sn clr
Most Rich (Ire) .... **R Evans** 2
jmpd rght, ld, clr frm 10th, wknd 2 out, hdd last
Big Buckley 5a .... **M Jackson** 3
(Jt fav) wth ldr, blnd 6th, chsng aft, tired frm 15th
Western Pearl (Ire) *(Jt fav) mstks, chsd ldng pair, wknd & p.u. 13th* .... pu
Joyney 5a 1ow *in tch til s.u. aft 8th* .... su
Perryline 5a *mstk 4th, prog frm rear 12th, lost tch & p.u. 15th* .... pu
Bel Lane 5a *alwys rear, t.o. & p.u. 14th* .... pu
Rusty Fellow *mstks, prog frm rear 12th, in tch whn blnd & u.r. nxt* .... ur
Must Be Murphy (Ire) 7a *t.o. in last pair til p.u. 11th* .. pu
Daisy's Pal 7a *in tch til eased & p.u. aft 11th* .... pu
70 Kanjo Olda 5a *mstks, chsd ldrs, wknd 13th, poor 4th whn p.u. 2 out* .... pu
Arms Park 5ow *t.o. in last pair til p.u. 11th* .... pu

12 ran. 5l, 30l. Time 7m 10.00s. SP 20-1.
Rhys Jenkins (Ledbury).

221 - Maiden Div III (12st)

73 **ANYTHINGYOULIKE** .... **T Stephenson** 1
(fav) trckd ldrs, ld 12th, lft clr 14th, easily
Mr Wendyl .... **J Rees** 2
mstk 2nd, prom til outpcd aft 13th, lft poor 2nd nxt, no imp
Demamo (Ire) .... **S Jackson** 3
chsd ldrs, outpcd whn lft poor 3rd 14th, no imp aft
143 Dragons Lady 5a *ld to 10th, wknd 12th, t.o.* 4
Silver Concord *10s-4s, hld up, prog aft 12th, sn lost tch, p.u. 2 out* .... pu
Romany Gold 5a (bl) *mstk 6th, alwys rear, t.o. & p.u. 13th* .... pu
Grey Watch 5a *rear, 8th whn mstk & u.r. 8th* .... ur
Cruise Ann 5a *cls up to 8th, losing tch whn mstk 12th, p.u. 15th* .... pu
The Hollow (Ire) 5a *prom, ld 10-12th, 2l bhnd wnr whn f 14th* .... f
Mis-E-Fishant 5a *mstk 5th, last whn p.u. 7th* .... pu
Saxon Smile *f 1st* .... f
Tanner *trckd ldrs going wll, mstk 11th, lost tch 13th, p.u. nxt* .... pu

12 ran. 15l, 15l, 1 fence. Time 7m 4.00s. SP 4-5.
Mrs D A Smith (North Ledbury).
J.N.

SINNINGTON
Duncombe Park
Saturday February 24th
GOOD TO SOFT

222 - Members

MIAMI BEAR .... **M Haigh** 1
ld/disp til ld 7th, made rest, clr & hit 3 out, comf
123 **Private Jet (Ire)** .... **I Brown** 2
prom, hit 7th, chsd wnr 12th, btn 3 out, fin tired
76 **Katies Argument 5a** .... **Mrs J Milburn** 3
disp to 4th, sn lost plc, no ch 15th, ran on flat
121 Earl Gray (bl) *w.w. jmpd lft 11th, sn strggling, t.o.* 4
79 Rabble Rouser *(fav) cls up, ev ch whn blnd 14th, not rcvr, no ch & u.r. 2 out* .... ur
73 Muscoates 7a *last whn u.r. 5th* .... ur

6 ran. 20l, 3l, 25l. Time 6m 23.00s. SP 3-1.
Mrs L M Fahey (Sinnington).

223 - Confined (12st)

169 **SIMPLY A STAR (IRE)** .... **S Swiers** 1

(fav) w.w. prog 9th, chal apr last, drew clr und pres flat
72 **Tom Log** .... **W Burnell** 2
chsd ldrs, hit 9th, ld 15th, hdd und pres flat, wknd nr fin
Just Charlie 6ow .... **D Easterby** 3
prog 9th, 6th & outpcd 3 out, styd on well aft
Advent Lady 5a *prom, ld 12th-14th, wknd apr last* 4
Sharpridge *ld to 11th, 5th & wkng 14th, no ch aft* 5
Hazel Crest *cls up to 13th, no ch frm 3 out* 6
81 Breckenbrough Lad 2ow *sn well bhnd, t.o. frm 5th* ... 7
121 Country Chalice *bhnd 5th, t.o. 8th* 8
81 Acertainhit 5ow (bl) *mid-div, strgglng & blnd 10th, p.u. 12th* .... pu
72 Fowling Piece *prom to 9th, no ch whn u.r. 3 out* ...... ur
Pri Neukin *sn bhnd, t.o. 5th, p.u. 12th* .... pu
Mr Elk *mid-div, lost tch 11th, t.o. & p.u. 14th* .... pu
73 Timber Topper *hmpd & u.r. 4th* .... ur
Constant Amusement 5a *jmpd slwly 1st, t.o. 5th, p.u. 12th* .... pu
Greenmount Lad (Ire) *f 4th* .... f
72 Charlcot Storm 7a *ran out 1st* .... ro
16 ran. 5l, 5l, hd, 20l, 10l, 20l, ½l. Time 6m 29.00s. SP 5-4.
Mrs A M Easterby (Middleton).

224 - Restricted Div I

77 **POLYNTH** .... **H Brown** 1
wth ldr, ld apr 10th, made rest, hit 3 out, styd on strngly
118 **Stag Fight** .... **S Walker** 2
chsd wnr 12th, rdn to chal 2 out, unable qckn flat
80 **Here Comes Charter** .... **A Pennock** 3
rear of main grp, steady prog to 3rd 15th, kpt on
Honest Expression 5a *chsd ldrs til 4th & wkng 3 out* .. 4
Glenbricken *ld to 9th, grad wknd, 5th & no ch 13th* 5
78 Caman 5a *sn wll bhnd, t.o. frm 7th* 6
79 Prophet's Choice *s.s. t.o. til f 13th* .... f
Broad Chare *ref to race* 0
73 Latheron (Ire) *(fav) mid-div whn blnd & u.r. 7th* .... ur
84 Polar Hat *rear 8th, prog nxt, in tch whn f 13th* .... f
79 Scampton *in tch, rdn 10th, t.o. & p.u. 15th* .... pu
121 Jamarsam (Ire) *f 2nd* .... f
12 ran. 1½l, 20l, 20l, 20l, 1 fence. Time 6m 26.00s. SP 2-1.
Mrs V Cunningham (Cleveland).
One fence omitted this race, 17 jumps.

225 - Restricted Div II

77 **ERA'S IMP** .... **Miss S Baskerville** 1
(fav) ld 4th, made rest, blnd 6th & 2 out, styd on strngly flat
77 **Miley Pike** .... **N Tutty** 2
ld to 3rd, chsd wnr, rdn to chal last, no ext flat
121 **Ingleby Flyer 5a** .... **P Frank** 3
in tch, chsd ldng pair 14th, blnd 3 out, fin tired
72 Primitive Penny 7a *prom to 10th, 4th & outpcd 14th, kpt on, improve* 4
Spartan Juliet 5a *in rear 9th, some late prog, nvr dang* 5
118 Lartington Lad *alwys rear, t.o. frm 14th. walked in* ... 6
Goodwill Hill *in tch, blnd 10th, no ch frm 14th* 7
77 Hillview Lad *prom to 10th, sn wknd, p.u. 13th* .... pu
Brother Minstrel *cls up til wknd 10th, p.u. 13th* .... pu
Roseberry Star 5a *in tch til f 6th* .... f
121 Sweet Rose 5a *rear but in tch whn u.r. 5th* .... ur
171 Politicians Prayer 5a *rear, brf effrt 10th, wkng whn blnd 14th, p.u. nxt* .... pu
12 ran. 5l, 25l, 12l, 2l, 12l, 10l. Time 6m 32.00s. SP Evens.
R E Baskerville (Vale Of Aylesbury).
One fence omitted from race 4 onwards, 16 jumps per race.

226 - Land Rover Open (12st)

78 **POLITICO POT** .... **S Whitaker** 1
(Jt fav) prom to 5th,prog 12th,lft 2nd nxt,styd on to ld flat,all out
37 **Quixall Crossett** .... **K Green** 2
prom, outpcd 12th, lft 3rd nxt, styd on und pres flat
Hyperion Son .... **M Haigh** 3
prom, ld 6th, lft clr 4 out, lkd wnr til tired & hdd flat
Furry Knowe 7ex *in tch, pshd alng 10th, lft mod 4th 4 out, kpt on* 4
78 The Right Guy *alwys rear, no ch frm 12th* 5
83 Equinoctial 7ex *ld to 5th, prom til wknd apr 4 out* 6
Ringmore *in tch, wknd 11th, t.o. & p.u. 4 out* .... pu
78 Nishkina *prog to jn ldrs 10th, 2nd & ev ch whn f 4 out* f
170 Golden Savannah *prom to 8th, wknd nxt, p.u. 12th* .... pu
Clontoura (Ire) 6ow *(Jt fav) in tch til blnd & u.r. 5th* ... ur
10 ran. 4l, 5l, 10l, 20l, 12l. Time 6m 29.00s. SP 6-4.
Charlie Peckitt (Sinnington).

227 - Ladies

85 **ACROSS THE LAKE** .... **Miss S Brotherton** 1
(fav) chsd ldr, disp 9th, ld 11th, made rest, styd on
76 **Carole's Delight 5a** .... **Mrs L Ward** 2
ld to 10th, chsd wnr aft, rallied gamely flat
117 **Wall Game (USA)** .... **Miss H Delahooke** 3
in tch, 3rd & rdn 3 out, kpt on flat
93 Queen's Chaplain *in tch to 12th, last & jmpd slwly 3 out & nxt* 4
Valiant Vicar 5ow *prom 6th-9th, last whn u.r. 12th* ..... ur
Dizzy Dealer 5a *in tch, rdn 11th, blnd nxt, t.o. & p.u. 13th* .... pu
6 ran. 1½l, 2l, 25l. Time 6m 31.00s. SP 4-5.
Mrs D R Brotherton (Middleton).

228 - Open Maiden (5-7yo) Div I

117 **CITY BUZZ (IRE)** .... **P Atkinson** 1
ld, drew clr 12th, lft 30l clr nxt, tired flat, all out
122 **Aitch-A 7a** .... **Mrs S Grant** 2
prom, outpcd 11th, lft poor 3rd 4 out, ran on well flat
75 **Living On The Edge (Ire)** .... **N Tutty** 3
w.w. lost tch 12th, lft 2nd nxt, ran on well flat
73 Greet The Greek *(fav) chsd ldr, outpcd 12th, 13l 3rd whn f nxt* .... f
Basil Grey *pllng, chsd ldrs, 3rd whn f 12th* .... f
122 Sergent Kay *pllng, mid-div whn f 5th* .... f
Lepton (Ire) 7a *w.w. steady prog to 12l 2nd going wll whn f 4 out* .... f
Lisband Lady (Ire) 5a *rear, t.o. & hmpd 5th, p.u. 9th* ... pu
Woody Dare *prom 8th til wknd apr 10th, p.u. nxt* ..... pu
9 ran. 2l, ½l. Time 6m 44.00s. SP 5-2.
Victor Ogden (Bedale).

229 - Open Maiden (5-7yo) Div II

75 **LAUNCHSELECT 7a** .... **R Edwards** 1
chsd ldrs, lft 3rd 4 out, chal last, sn ld, styd on strngly
51 **Attle** .... **S Brisby** 2
(Jt fav) in tch,lft 2nd 4 out,rdn & ch apr last,wknd,fin tired
Edinburgh Reel Ale 7a .... **P Atkinson** 3
alwys rear, tk mod 3rd flat, ran on
Oaklands Fred *blnd 1st, alwys bhnd, t.o. 12th* 4
73 Flying Pan 5a *chsd ldrs til f 5th* .... f
74 Reefside (Ire) *s.v.s. rear whn b.d. 5th* .... bd
74 Morcat 5a *pllng, jnd ldr 5th, wknd apr 10th, p.u. 12th* pu
123 Fair Grand *chsd ldr to 4th, lost plc & rear 8th, p.u. 12th* .... pu
122 Blank Cheque *ld til hdd flat, stppd to walk & p.u.* ..... pu
Ship The Builder *f 4th* .... f
River Ramble 5a *mid-div whn f 5th* .... f
Gypsy Race (Ire) 5a *w.w. steady prog to 10l 2nd whn f 4 out* .... f
74 Winters Melody 5a *jmpd lft, chsd ldng trio 5th, wd apr 9th, t.o. & p.u. 12th* .... pu
13 ran. Dist, 2l, dist. Time 6m 40.00s. SP 7-2.
M J Brown (Sinnington).
S.P.

SOUTH MIDLAND AREA HUNT CLUB
Heythrop
Saturday February 24th
GOOD TO SOFT

230 - Members

170 **CAUSEWAY CRUISER................R Lawther 1**
hld up, chsd ldrs hlfwy, 2nd 12th, ld 16th, drew clr
1 **True Steel......................J Trice-Rolph 2**
hld up, prog frm 11th, styd on frm 3 out, went 2nd nxt
124 **Cawkwell Dean ....R Sweeting 3**
rear to hlfwy, styd on onepcd aft, tk 3rd flat
24 Rochester *ld til 16th, grad wknd, lost 3rd flat* 4
Viascorit *chsd ldrs, wknd aft 7th, bhnd whn p.u. 10th*.. pu
Tell You What *cls up to hlfwy, bhnd whn p.u. 14th*..... pu
24 Getaway Blake *(fav) mid-div to hlfwy, ev ch 13th, wkng 3rd whn f 16th*.......... f
Tumbril *mostly mid-div til prog hlfwy, wkng whn p.u. 13th*.......... pu
Branwell Bronte *sn rear, t.o. & p.u. 11th*.......... pu
Bear's Flight *mid-div til u.r. 7th*.......... ur
Creeves Nephew *alwys well bhnd, t.o. & p.u. 12th*.... pu
Shortcastle *cls up to hlfwy, wknd, t.o. & p.u. last*..... pu
12 ran. 12l, 12l, 2l. SP 6-1.
J Tredwell (Grafton).

231 - Resttricted Div I

MY BEST MAN ....A Hill 1
hld up, prog 13th, blnd nxt, chsd ldr 16th, ld nxt, ran on
Moorside Lad.........................C Stockton 2
ld/disp til ld 13th, jnd 15th, ld nxt, hdd 2 out, ran on
124 **Ramlosa (NZ)..........................R Cope 3**
in tch, chsd ldrs 12th, tk 3rd cls home
95 Unlucky For Some (Ire) *alwys cls up, jnd ldr 12th, sn wknd, fdd flat*.......... 4
Sideliner *rear, prog to 3rd at 12th, grad wknd*.......... 5
Bilbo Baggins (Ire) *chsd ldrs to 10th, wknd rpdly* 6
Golden Companion *ld/disp to 9th, wknd rpdly, last at 11th & p.u.*.......... pu
Juranstan *nvr nr ldrs, mid-div whn blnd 10th, p.u. 15th*.......... pu
20 Endless Glee *in tch early, wkng whn p.u. 12th* .... pu
58 Prince's Gift *(fav) alwys rear, p.u. 6th*.......... pu
10 ran. 10l, 1l, 4l, 10l, 15l. SP 4-1.
Alan Hill (Vale Of Aylesbury).

232 - Open (12st)

9 **BRIGHT BURNS (bl)...................R Sweeting 1**
(fav) ld/disp til ld 5th, made rest, styd on well
Space Man ....F Crew 2
in tch, went 4th at 14th, chsd wnr 2 out, nvr nrr
Sandy Beau ....R Thornton 3
disp to 5th, chsd wnr aft to 2 out, styd on onepcd
Tango Tom *wll bhnd to hlfwy, steady prog 11th, ran past btn hrss*.......... 4
162 Tara Boy *chsd ldrs to hlfwy, 5th & wll btn whn f last*... f
Shadow Walker *alwys wll bhnd, t.o. & p.u. 13th* .... pu
6 Corrianne 5a *in tch, wknd hlfwy, t.o. & p.u. 12th*..... pu
Joburn 5a *hld up mid-div,3rd 13th,ev ch nxt,wknd,poor 5th & p.u.last*.......... pu
Halham Tarn (Ire) *disp til hlfwy, wknd rpdly, p.u. 12th* pu
Making Time 5a *mid-div, no ch whn p.u. 13th*.......... pu
10 ran. 8l, 12l, 6l. SP Evens.
Colin Gee (Heythrop).

233 - Maiden Div I

125 **JOHN ROGER...................A Charles-Jones 1+**
rear til prog to 4th at 14th, chal last, jnd ldr on line
ARCHIES OATS.....................J Trice-Rolph 1+
in tch, chsd ldr hlfwy, disp 13th, ld 3 out, styd on, jnd fn
129 **Copper Pan 5a ....Miss S Duckett 3**
mid-div til prog 11th, 3rd & ev ch 15th, onepcd
Crestafair 5a *alwys prom, disp frm hlfwy, ld 14th-16th, wknd*.......... 4
Specific Impulse *chsd ldr, cls up til wknd & p.u. 3 out* pu
Dilkush *nvr rchd ldrs, p.u. aft 11th*.......... pu
91 Canadian Boy (Ire) *(Jt fav) cls up to hlfwy, fdd & p.u. 2 out*.......... pu
Arctic Line *ld til jnd 4th, wknd 8th, p.u. aft 11th*....... pu
2 Balance *(Jt fav) rear, prog 11th, 3rd & wkng 14th, p.u. 2 out*.......... pu
21 Star Of Steane 5a *alwys rear, p.u. 12th* .... pu
Country Brew 5a *alwys bhnd, p.u. 12th*.......... pu
Dip The Lights 5a 1ow *mid-div til f 4th*.......... f
Tranquil Lord (Ire) *cls up, disp 5th, in tch whn u.r. 10th*.......... ur
Secret Truth 5a *mostly mid-div til wknd & p.u. 12th*... pu
14 ran. Dd-ht, 12l, 5l.
H J Manners/ J Trice-Rolph (V.W.H./ Heythrop).
Archies Oats, 7/1. John Roger, 9/2.

234 - Ladies

PHELIOFF ....Miss S Dawson 1+
(fav) hld up, chsd ldrs 12th, ld 2 out, jnd nr fin
124 **KITES HARDWICKE ....Miss C Behrens 1+**
ld to 8th, chsd ldr, 3rd at 15th, chal last, got up nr fin
126 **Codger ....Miss J Thame 3**
chsd ldr til ld 8th, jnd 3 out, hdd nxt, onepcd
Vital Shot 5a 1ow *mostly rear, nvr rchd ldrs*.......... 4
Mitchells Best *mostly rear, went 4th at 15th, p.u. last* pu
Rip The Calico (Ire) 5a *mostly rear, some prog 11th, wknd frm 15th, p.u. nxt*.......... pu
6 ran. Dd-ht, 10l, 25l. Time 7m 31.00s.
Miss S Dawson/ Miss C Behrens (Windsor Forest/ Berks & Bucks).
Kites Hardwicke, 5/2. Phelioff, 9/4.

235 - Restricted Div II

128 **GOLDEN MAC...............Capt R Fanshawe 1**
rear,poor 5th at 14th,styd on,still 5th last,ld 50 yrds out
Diamond Valley (Ire) ....Miss S Wallin 2
rear, gd prog hlfwy, ld 2 out, hdd last, no ext flat
126 **Arble March 5a 4ow ....A Hill 3**
alwys prom, ld hlfwy, hdd 14th, mstk nxt, styd on flat
156 Notanotherone (Ire) *wll bhnd, prog 11th, 3rd 2 out, slight ld last, outpcd flat*.......... 4
26 Fresh Prince *(fav) ld to 2nd, cls up til ld 14th, hdd 2 out, wknd last*.......... 5
Waterhay *prom til lost plc hlfwy, bhnd whn p.u. 14th*.. pu
Mr Patrick (bl) *ld 2nd-8th, wknd prdly, p.u. 11th*.......... pu
140 Mary Borough 5a *mid-div whn u.r. 3rd*.......... ur
Jellyband *alwys bhnd, p.u. 12th*.......... pu
Cool Ginger *nvr a fctr, p.u. 12th*.......... pu
10 ran. 2l, 4l, 8l, 20l. Time 7m 41.00s. SP 16-1.
R Fanshawe (V.W.H.).

236 - Maiden Div II

129 **TOMMY O'DWYER (IRE)........................A Hill 1**
hld up rear, prog to 3rd at 12th, ld 14th, made rest,rdn out
Sabre King ....L Lay 2
alwys prom, 6th hlfwy, jnd ldrs 11th, ld nxt-14th, rallied f
144 **Good Looking Guy ....A Charles-Jones 3**
rear to hlfwy, prog 12th, 3rd at 14th, styd on onepcd
17 Phil's Dream *(fav) sn bhnd, prog to 3rd hlfwy, wknd 14th*.......... 4
Hawaiian Reef *in tch early, bhnd & p.u. 11th*.......... pu
Di Moda *cls 2nd to 7th, lost plc, 5th whn f 13th*.......... f
Le Loubec 5a *s.s. sn t.o., p.u. 9th*.......... pu
Saxon Lass 5a *ld to 10th, wknd rpdly, p.u. 16th* ..... pu
Alias Silver *cls up, 2nd hlfwy, lost tch & p.u. aft 3 out*.. pu
129 Miners Rest 5a *chsd ldrs to 11th, rear whn p.u. 2 out* pu
Bettiville *mostly mid-div, wknd & p.u. 16th*.......... pu
Space Molly 5a *rear whn f 5th*.......... f
Dolly Bloom 5a *rear whn f 5th*.......... f
13 ran. 2½l, 6l, 15l. Time 7m 43.00s. SP 5-1.
A K Pritchard (Vale Of Aylesbury).
H.F.

CRANWELL BLOODHOUNDS
Southwell P-To-P Course
Sunday February 25th
HOLDING

237 - Members

SOLITARY REAPER.........................D Esden 1

3rd til went 2nd apr 3 out, not qckn flat, fin 2nd, promoted
175 **Still Hopeful 5a ....Miss E Osbourne** 2
last, t.o. 4 out, tk poor 3rd nr fin, promoted
Billhead ....Miss K O'Neill 3
ld to 14th, wknd apr 3 out, fin 4th, plcd 3rd
T.C. *(fav) wth ldr til ld 14th, ran on well flat, fin 1st, disq.* 0
4 ran. 2½l, 30l, nk. Time 7m 22.00s. SP 6-1.
R King (Cranwell Bloodhounds).
T.C. disqualified, failed to draw correct weight. Original distances.

238 - Open Maiden Div I Pt I

175 **DEAR JEAN 5a ....M Sowersby** 1
hld up,mstk 8th,prog 11th,hmpd 13th,hrd rdn & ld last,allout
Henry Darling.......................E Andrewes 2
ld, lft clr 13th, hmpd by loose horse & hdd last, no ext
73 **Barneys Gold (Ire).....................A Bealby** 3
trckd ldrs, mstk 10th & lost tch, t.o. 4 out, fin strngly
59 Iridophanes *in tch to 10th, steadily wknd, t.o. 4 out* ... 4
158 Winters Cottage (Ire) *trckd ldrs til wknd 11th, poor 3rd whn p.u. 4 out* .... pu
Mr Branigan (Ire) *prssd ldr, ev ch whn blnd & u.r. 13th* .... ur
73 Rye Head 7a *(fav) blnd 4th, mstk nxt, blnd & u.r. 6th* .. ur
181 Late Start 5a *prom whn mstk 6th, lost tch whn mstk 8th, t.o. & p.u. nxt* .... pu
Shakey Thyne (Ire) 5a *s.s. t.o. til p.u. aft 11th* .... pu
9 ran. 3l, 20l, 30l. Time 7m 2.00s. SP 8-1.
M E Sowersby (Holderness).

239 - Open Maiden Div I Pt II

GIVE IT A WHIRL.......................S Walker 1
made most to 4 out, 2l 2nd whn lft in ld 2 out, ran on well
Keep On Trying 5a...................M Portman 2
prom,disp 4 out,outpcd nxt,lft 2nd 2 out,btn whn blnd last
Charlotte's Oliver.........................P Gee 3
cls up, ev ch 4 out, wknd apr nxt
Glen Taylor *prom til wknd 12th, hmpd nxt, t.o.* 4
160 Gal-A-Dor *prom til f 5th* .... f
Split The Wind 5a *alwys last, t.o. & p.u. 9th* .... pu
92 Rainbow Fantasia (Ire) *hld up in tch, 5th whn f 13th* ... f
Greenhills Ruby 7a *f 2nd* .... f
Mrs Blobby (Ire) 5a *(fav) hld up in tch, qcknd to ld 4 out, 2l up whn f 2 out* .... f
9 ran. 10l, 25l, 1 fence. Time 7m 9.00s. SP 10-1.
Ross Haddow (Blankney).
One fence omitted second circuit, 17 jumps.

240 - Open Maiden Div II

WHATWILLBEWILLBE (IRE) ....G Hanmer 1
trckd ldrs, ld 13th, drew clr 2 out, ran on well
13 **Dashboard Light....................S R Andrews** 2
trckd ldrs, prog 12th, chsd wnr & ev ch 3 out, no ext nxt
176 **Fair Ally...........................M Sowersby** 3
hld up in poor last,gd prog frm 9th,ev ch 4 out,outpcd nxt
Relishing 5a *(fav) trckd ldrs, prog to disp 4 out, btn apr nxt* 4
Rallye Stripe *set mad gallop to 5th, wknd 9th, t.o. & p.u. 12th* .... pu
52 Sharp To Oblige *hld up, prog & in tch 11th, 5th & btn 4 out, p.u. nxt* .... pu
Eighty Eight *4th whn f 3rd* .... f
Master Enborne *mid-div, in tch 11th, wkng whn f 13th* ... f
Beat The Rap *wth ldr 5th-13th, wknd rpdly, p.u. 4 out* pu
The Tondy (Ire) *hld up bhnd, prog & in tch 11th, eased & p.u. 14th* .... pu
St Enton *alwys bhnd, t.o. 8th, p.u. aft 11th* .... pu
Im Ok (Ire) 5a *started 5 fences bhnd, cont til p.u. 12th* pu
Potato Fountain (Ire) 5a *rear, t.o. 8th, p.u. aft 11th* .... pu
Derring Floss 5a *5th whn f 7th* .... f
Ronson Royale *hld up, plld to disp 6th-9th, sn wknd, t.o. & p.u. 3 out* .... pu
15 ran. 8l, 15l, 10l. Time 6m 56.00s. SP 25-1.
P S Burke (Wheatland).

241 - Open Maiden Div III

BLUE IS THE COLOUR (IRE) ....S Walker 1
hld up, prog 9th, wth ldr frm 4 out, rdn to ld last 100 yrds
Chacer's Imp..........................B Pollock 2
prom, ld 12th, jnd 4 out, hdd & no ext last 100 yrds
182 **Cormeen Lord (Ire).....................J Sharp** 3
jmpd slwly, in tch, chsd 1st pair apr 3 out, no imp
173 Final Nod *prom, 3rd & ev ch 4 out, wknd apr nxt* 4
Hasty Cruise *prom til wknd 14th, t.o.* 5
167 Sargeants Choice *wth ldr 3rd-12th, sn wknd, t.o. 3 out* 6
Coolsythe 5a *in tch til rdn & strggling 11th, t.o. & p.u. 4 out* .... pu
166 Bay Tiger *pllng, in tch til p.u. 5th* .... pu
Huntsbydale 5a *hld up, prog to trck ldrs whn f 14th* ... f
128 Musical Mail *prom, wkng whn blnd & u.r. 14th* .... ur
172 Vernometum *ld to 3rd, mid-div whn f 5th* .... f
Bucklelone 5a *sn rear, t.o. & p.u. 12th* .... pu
Riverside Love 5a *made most 3rd-12th, sn wknd, t.o. & p.u. 3 out* .... pu
74 Tyndrum Gold *n.j.w. alwys bhnd, t.o. & p.u. 3 out* ..... pu
62 Cantango (Ire) *(fav) mid-div, effrt to 6th whn f 4 out* ... f
15 ran. 1½l, 20l, 8l, dist, 3l. Time 6m 59.00s. SP 12-1.
Miss E M Hewitt (Middleton).

242 - Restricted Div I (12st)

ROYAL SURVIVOR ....R Walker 1
j.w. lft in ld 3rd, hdd 4 out, lft in ld nxt, ran on well
I Did It My Way (bl)...................T Jackson 2
rdn & prog to jn ldrs 11th,4th & btn whn lft 3rd 3 out,kpton
Whinstone Mill ....R Thornton 3
trckd ldrs 6th, 3rd whn blnd 12th, rdn & onepcd frm 4 out
77 Stilltodo 5a *prom til outpcd 4 out, no ch aft nxt* 4
Cornamona 5a *ld to f 3rd* .... f
95 Tel D'Or *bhnd frm 6th, t.o. & p.u. aft 11th* .... pu
128 Miss Solitaire 5a *f 1st* .... f
Coolvawn Lady (Ire) 5a *trckd ldrs, mstk 10th, wknd frm 13th, t.o. & p.u. 3 out* .... pu
Rayman (Ire) *mstks, trckd ldrs til wknd rpdly 12th, p.u. 14th* .... pu
Teeton Mill *(fav) trckd ldrs, ld 4 out, clr whn f nxt* ..... f
166 The Last Joshua *rear, lost tch 8th, t.o. & p.u. 13th* .... pu
72 Lakeland Venture 5a *in tch til wknd 10th, t.o. & p.u. 12th* .... pu
12 ran. 15l, 12l, 10l. Time 6m 56.00s. SP 12-1.
A Godrich (Cottesmore).

243 - Restricted Div II (12st)

SISTER EMU 5a 4ow.....................A Crow 1
lost plc 4th,prog frm rear 4 out,ld 2 out,sn clr, drvn out
106 **Tenelord ....S Morris** 2
prom to 12th, rnwd effrt 4 out, kpt on onepcd frm 2 out
77 **Cairndhu Misty 5a ....P Gee** 3
mid-div, prog 13th, ld 3 out-nxt, sn no ext
47 Reviller's Glory *made most to 3 out, sn outpcd* 4
13 Black Ermine (Ire) 7a *(Jt fav) hld up,prog 9th,mstk 11th,no imp ldrs 3 out,fin tired* 5
Ocean Sovereign *prom to 13th, sn outpcd & no dang* 6
164 Foolish Fantasy *in tch, rdn 13th, sn btn, t.o. 2 out* 7
Ballyvoyle Bay 5a (bl) *trckd ldr 5th-12th, wknd rpdly, p.u. 3 out* .... pu
12 Cass *mstk 6th, alwys bhnd, t.o. & p.u. 2 out* .... pu
28 Glenrowan Lad *(Jt fav) trckd ldrs, chal 4 out, btn nxt, 4th whn f 2 out* .... f
159 Ballyhannon (Ire) *rear, prog whn mstk 12th & lost plc, t.o. & p.u. 3 out* .... pu
11 ran. 10l, 8l, 8l, 6l, 3l, 20l. Time 6m 56.00s. SP 14-1.
M D Gichero (North Shropshire).

244 - Confined (12st)

THE POINT IS.................................M Hewitt 1
mstks, made all, sn clr, styd on well frm 3 out
178 **Pakenham...............................H Nicholson** 2
(fav) hld up,prog 8th,chsd wnr 4 out,kpt on,nvr able to chal
Beau Dandy 3ex...........................B Pollock 3
trckd ldrs, 2nd frm 11th-15th, wknd 3 out
169 Lad Lane *lost tch 6th, t.o. aft*........................ 4
96 Merlyns Choice *sn t.o. in last, p.u. 4 out*............. pu
169 Antrim County *chsd wnr to 10th, wknd, p.u. 12th*....... pu
McCartney *mstk 3rd, alwys rear, t.o. 11th, p.u. 15th*... pu
96 Galzig *prom, mstk 11th, sn wknd, poor 5th 4 out, p.u. 3 out*.. pu
The Difference *alwys rear, t.o. 11th, styd on aft, poor 5th whn p.u. 3 out*................................ pu
Bowery Boy 3ex *mstks, trckd ldrs, rdn 11th, lost tch nxt, p.u. 4 out*................................ pu
Rambling Lord (Ire) *rear, 12th whn u.r. 5th*............ ur
Harmony Walk (Ire) *chsng grp til wknd 11th, p.u. nxt*.. pu
169 Glitzy Lady (Ire) 5a *mstks, chsd ldrs, 3rd at 12th, btn frm 14th, p.u. 3 out*................................ pu
13 ran. 3l, 30l, 2 fences. Time 6m 52.00s. SP 7-1.
P S Hewitt (Quorn).

245 - Ladies

PEAJADE.............................Miss J Wormall 1
(fav) ld to 3rd,wth ldr on innr aft, ld aft 4 out, jnd last,hld on
76 **Ridwan...............................Miss S Bonser** 2
ld 3-6th, wth ldrs aft, chal frm 3 out, lvl last, just hld
Shouldofdone......................Miss H Vickers 3
raced wd, made most frm 6th til aft 4 out, sn wknd
Grand Value *in tch to 9th, t.o. 12th*........................ 4
Directly *mstk 2nd, mstk & u.r. nxt*........................ ur
Affair Of Honour (Ire) *bhnd til p.u. 10th*.............. pu
118 Vienna Woods *s.s. trckd ldrs 7th, 8l 4th whn mstk & u.r. 12th*.. ur
Out The Door (Ire) *keen hld, hld up last, hmpd & u.r. 3rd*.. ur
8 ran. Nk, 30l, dist. Time 6m 58.00s. SP 6-4.
Mrs Janine Hall (Atherstone).

246 - Open

26 **RYDE AGAIN...............................S Morris** 1
(fav) w.w. prog 9th, ld 14th, all out
127 **Bright As A Button.........................G Tarry** 2
mstk 7th, trckd ldrs, chsd wnr 14th, no imp whn hit 2 out
Raise An Argument........................J Docker 3
mid-div, lost tch 9th, t.o. 12th
Leading Guest *4th whn f 5th*................................ f
Teacake *last & bhnd frm 6th, p.u. 9th*.................. pu
57 Kambalda Rambler *prom, ld 10th, blnd 13th, hdd & blnd nxt, p.u. 4 out*................................. pu
56 Blue Beat 5a *alwys bhnd, lost tch & p.u. 11th*......... pu
Anchor Express 5a (bl) *made most to 10th, rdn 12th, wknd & p.u. 15th*.................................... pu
Syd Green (Ire) *plling, prom to 9th, wknd & p.u. aft 11th*.. pu
9 ran. 4l, 1 fence. Time 7m 7.00s. SP 4-5.
Miss J E Hayward (Pytchley).
J.N.

MID SURREY FARMERS DRAG
Charing
Sunday February 25th
GOOD TO SOFT

247 - Members

GINGER TRISTAN 7ex....................D Robinson 1
(fav) ld to 4th, agn 10th, drew well clr aft 15th, easily
Bye Bye Baby (Fr) 5a.......................C Young 2
sn wll bhnd,ran on strngly frm 4 out,2nd apr last,no ch wnr
Dovehill...............................J Van Praagh 3
mstks, lost tch 15th, lft 3rd by dfctns
Time Star (NZ) 2ow *in tch to 13th, wll bhnd whn p.u. aft 15th*.. pu
Charleston Lad *chsd ldrs, 3rd final cct, wll btn whn p.u. last*.. pu
The Lager Lout *ld 4th-10th, chsd wnr aft, 3rd & wll btn whn ran out last*................................... ro
Old Sport *ref 1st,clmbrd over 3rd try,f 2nd,rmntd & jmpd 3rd,p.u.*.. f
7 ran. 12l, 25l. Time 6m 39.00s. SP 11-8.
D C Robinson (Mid Surrey Farmers Drag).

248 - Monterey Restricted

HIGHGATE MILD..............................E James 1
cls up, ld 15th, rdn 3 out, hld on gamely
58 **Alansford.....................................P Bull** 2
mid-div,jnd ldrs 13th,chsd wnr 4 out,chal 2 out,no ext flat
14 **Bardaros................................P Hacking** 3
(fav) trckd ldrs frm 8th, 3rd 4 out, rdn & no ext apr last
Sybillabee 5a *alwys prom, 3rd & blnd 4 out, no ch aft* 4
Bright Crusader *alwys twrds rear*.......................... 5
20 Royal Rupert *prom to 15th, fdd*.......................... 6
Harry-H *alwys in rear*.. 7
Golden Pele *alwys rear, t.o. & p.u. aft 14th*............ pu
Smart Work 5a *wll bhnd, steady prog frm 15th, 5th & no ch whn f last*..................................... f
Souldan (Ire) *ld til jmpd rght 15th, grad wknd, 6th whn f last*.. f
20 Lewesdon Princess 5a *in tch to 10th, bhnd whn p.u. 13th*.. pu
128 Autumn Light 5a *rear, prog to 2nd whn mstk 6th, lost plc, rear & p.u. 11th*.................................. pu
12 ran. 1l, 5l, 15l, 6l, 8l, 20l. Time 6m 42.00s. SP 6-4.
A R Hunt (Vine & Craven).

249 - SEH Members Moderate

56 **Stede Quarter...........................P Hickman** 1D
ld 6th-4 out, chal & ld 2 out, kpt on well
BURROMARINER............................S Cowell 1
alwys prom, mostly 3rd final cct, chal 2 out, kpt on
Barn Elms..............................J Van Praagh 2
rear,steady prog final cct,ld 4 out,hdd & mstk 2 out,no ext
56 **Quentin Durwood** *(fav) hld up, jnd issue 4 out, rdn & btn in 4th nxt*.................................... 3
99 Tryumphant Lad *wll in tch to 15th, no dang aft*......... 4
Cantorial *rear til p.u. 11th*................................ pu
9 Ten Of Spades *ld to 6th, wth ldr til wknd 15th, bhnd whn u.r. 2 out*.. ur
Sir Wager (bl) *t.o. 6th, p.u. 8th*.......................... pu
Highland Bounty *prom til jmpd slwly 10th, bhnd whn p.u. 14th*.. pu
104 Athnanurlainn 2ow *cls up til f 10th*.................... f
Mogwai (Ire) *in tch til f 10th*................................ f
11 ran. 3l, 6l, 6l, nk. Time 6m 45.00s. SP 11-4.
Stede Quarter disq, lost weight cloth.

250 - Ladies

DURBO...............................Mrs E Coveney 1
trckd ldrs, chal 2 out, ld last, rdn out
11 **Luck Money.........................Miss C Holliday** 2
handy, ld aft 3 out til last, not qckn
Sky Venture..........................Mrs S Hickman 3
wll in rear, gd prog 12th, 4th 4 out, kpt on
Magical Morris *wll in rear, steady prog frm 12th, styd on well frm 2 out*.................................... 4
27 Lavalight *ld to 3rd & frm 8th til aft 3 out, fdd, fin tired* 5
Take Issue *ld 3rd-8th, 2nd & wkng whn f 10th*............ f
Wellington Bay *prom to 15th, wkng whn p.u. 4 out*..... pu
57 Motor Cloak *sn rear, t.o. 14th, p.u. nxt*................ pu
33 What A Gig *(fav) mid-div, prog to cls 2nd 4 out, wknd nxt, p.u. 2 out*..................................... pu
33 Little Nod *prom, 5th & ev ch whn u.r. 14th*.............. ur
93 Ashboro (Ire) 2ow *twrds rear whn f 5th*.................. f

Target Time 5a 7ow *mid-div, f 2nd* .... f
12 ran. 3l, 1½l, 2l, 12l. Time 6m 39.00s. SP 5-1.
Mrs E J Champion (Old Surrey & Burstow).
One fence omitted 2nd circuit, 18 jumps.

251 - Open

124 **COOL IT A BIT** .... **P Scouller** 1
ld 9th, made rest, styd on well
177 **Divine Chance (Ire)** .... **S Cowell** 2
(fav) chsd wnr frm 12th, rdn to chal apr 2 out, wknd flat
32 **Yeoman Farmer** .... **P Hacking** 3
wll in rear early, steady prog 13th, 4th & ev ch 4 out, wknd
Bright Hour *alwys mid-div, lost tch 4 out* 4
Highly Decorated *mid-div, chsd wnr frm 12th, fdd 3 out, p.u. nxt* .... pu
Vultoro *s.s. alwys t.o., p.u. 2 out* .... pu
Tom Tucker 3ow *rear, t.o. & p.u. 14th* .... pu
Eddie Walshe *ld to 9th, rear & btn whn p.u. 14th* ...... pu
Sakil (Ire) *rear, prog to trck ldrs 6th, p.u. 9th* .... pu
Take The Town 1ow *in tch, pshd alng 12th, btn 15th, p.u. last* .... pu
10 ran. 4l, 12l, 1 fence. Time 6m 47.00s. SP 25-1.
P A D Scouller (Garth & South Berks).

252 - Intermediate (12st)

29 **TEX MEX (IRE)** .... **J Maxse** 1
made all, clr frm 4th, mstk 4 out, nvr chal
Country Vet 5a .... **P Bull** 2
chsd wnr, niggld alng hlfwy, kpt on, nvr able to chal
Pallingham Star (Ire) .... **P Hickman** 3
out of tch hlfwy, 4th frm 14th, kpt on, tk 3rd apr last
Bective Boy 5ex *chsd wnr frm 8th, jmpd slwly & btn 3 out* 4
Oberons Butterfly *last & strggling frm 7th, p.u. 10th* ... pu
Comers Gate *chsd wnr, wkng whn p.u. 11th* .... pu
20 Barney Brook *(fav) jmpd slwly early,chsd wnr 8th,3rd & no imp whn p.u.13th,lame* .... pu
7 ran. 8l, 1 fence, 3l. Time 6m 44.00s. SP 4-1.
Mrs S Maxse (Hampshire).

253 - Open Maiden Div I (12st)

BRAMBLEDOWN (IRE) 7a .... **Mrs B Sillars** 1
1st ride, lft in ld 12th, made rest, ran on strngly 2 out
Bric Lane (USA) .... **P Hickman** 2
alwys prom, cls 2nd 4 out, wknd nxt
178 **Fort Diana** .... **A Welsh** 3
in tch, 3rd frm 15th, btn 3 out
182 Clonattin Lady (Ire) 5a *t.o. 7th* 4
Shared Fortune (Ire) *(fav) ld to 3rd, prom aft, wkng in 4th whn p.u. 4 out* .... pu
Zallot *prom to 8th, bhnd whn p.u. 12th* .... pu
4 Childsway *plld into ld 3rd til u.r. 8th* .... ur
Shelley Street 5a *sn cls up, lft in clr ld 8th, still in ld whn p.u. 12th* .... pu
35 Borneo Days 5a *alwys rear, t.o. & p.u. 12th* .... pu
58 Reign Dance 7a *alwys rear, lost tch 10th, p.u. 14th* .... pu
10 ran. 1 fence, 10l, 2 fences. Time 6m 56.00s. SP 14-1.
Mrs B Sillars (West Street/Tickham).

254 - Open Maiden Div II (12st)

61 **SALACHY RUN (IRE)** .... **A Welsh** 1
pshd alng 12th, just ld 14th, forged clr 2 out, all out
60 **Red Rory** .... **T McCarthy** 2
(fav) trckd ldrs, wth wnr on bridle frm 14th, rdn & found nil 2out
Orphan Olly .... **P York** 3
alwys wll dtchd, jmpd bdly, strggld round
106 Joe Quality *ld, hdd 8th, lft in ld 10th, jnd & f 14th* ..... f
Vital Legacy *f 2nd* .... f
Sovereign Spray (Ire) *alwys rear, losing tch whn p.u. 14th* .... pu
35 Joyful Hero 5a *f 2nd* .... f
Polar Ana (Ire) 5a *f 2nd* .... f
Bomb The Bees 5a *wth ldr, ld 8th, blnd & u.r. 10th* ... ur
9 ran. 10l, 2 fences. Time 7m 1.00s. SP 12-1.
Mrs J P Gordon (Southdown & Eridge).
G.Ta.

TAUNTON
Wednesday February 28th
GOOD TO SOFT

255 - 4¼m 110yds Hun Chase

141 **MYLIEGE 11.12 7a** .... **Mr N Harris** 1
pressed ldrs from 9th, ld 21st to 4 out, led again 3 out, ran on gamely.
133 **Sweatshirt 11.12 7a** .... **Mr J Jukes** 2
steady hdwy from 17th, chsd wnr from 3 out, edged left and no ext run-in.
Afterkelly 11.12 7a .... **Mr Richard White** 3
(fav) ld to 10th, chal from 14th to after 19th, led 4 out, hdd 3 out, soon one pace.
185 Charden 11.12 7a *tk str hold, chsd ldrs 13th, ld after 19th, hdd 21st, styd on from 3 out but not pace to chal.* 4
99 Buonarroti 11.12 7a *prom till lost position 12th, t.o. when p.u. before 21st* .... pu
149 Le Gerard 11.5 7a *chsd ldrs 11th, wknd 18th, t.o. when p.u. before 21st* .... pu
157 Construction King 11.5 7a *soon well bhnd, t.o. when p.u. before 21st* .... pu
213 Space Mariner 11.5 7a *bhnd from 15th, t.o. when p.u. before 3 out* .... pu
99 Cool And Easy 12.7 5a *chsd ldrs, ld 10th to after 19th, styd pressing lders till wknd 3 out, p.u. before last.* ... pu
98 Rusty Bridge 12.8 7a *in tch when b.d. 6th* .... bd
22 Bellman 11.5 7a *mid div till hit 11th and wknd, t.o. when p.u. before 19th* .... pu
29 Final Option (Ire) 11.6 7a 1ow *effort 13th, soon wknd, t.o. when p.u. before 21st* .... pu
Bathwick Bobbie 11.5 7a *bhnd most of way, t.o. when p.u. before 3 out* .... pu
162 Carly's Castle 11.0 7a *chasing ldrs when f 6th, dead.* f
129 Just Ballytoo 11.5 7a *wknd 13th, t.o. when p.u. before 21st* .... pu
15 ran. 5l, 2½l, 2l. Time 9m 56.00s. SP 11-2.
Mrs C C Scott

LUDLOW
Thursday February 29th
GOOD

256 - 3m Hun Chase

125 **WILD ILLUSION 12.0 7a** .... **Mr Richard White** 1
(fav) prom, hit 9th, ld before 12th, hit 14th, drew clr from 4 out.
98 **Cape Cottage 11.7 7a** .... **Mr A Phillips** 2
in tch 6th, styd on from 4 out, tk 2nd run-in, no ch with wnr.
Another Coral 11.7 7a .... **Mr R Lawther** 3
in tch, pressed wnr from 12th till outpcd 4 out, lost 2nd run-in.
133 Anjubi 11.7 7a *mstk 2nd, well bhnd 6th, hdwy 14th, kept on from 4 out* 4
183 Carrickmines 11.7 7a *prom, one pace from 15th* 5
Romany King 12.0 *prom, lost pl 11th, kept on from 4 out* 6
Knockumshin 12.2 5a *hdwy 12th, chsd ldrs 15th, wknd 4 out* 7
155 Robbie's Boy 11.9 5a *chsd ldrs to 14th* 8
160 My Nominee 12.0 7a (bl) *mstk 4th, hdwy 12th, mistake next, wknd* 9
98 Welsh Legion 12.0 7a *well bhnd 10th, some prog 13th, f next* .... f
Kingfisher Bay 11.7 7a *ld till apr 12th, soon wknd, t.o. when p.u. before 4 out* .... pu
Shareef Star 11.7 7a *t.o. 6th, p.u. before 15th* .... pu
Double-U-Gee (Ire) 11.7 7a *n.j.w., t.o. 10th, p.u. after 12th* .... pu

Watchit Lad 11.7 7a *t.o. 10th, no ch when f last.* .... f
14 ran. 8l, 5l, 2l, 2½l, ½l, 6l, 14l, 2½l. Time 6m 6.90s. SP 5-4.
G Pidgeon

NOTTINGHAM
Thursday February 29th
GOOD

257 - 2½m Hun Chase

76 **SOUTHERN MINSTREL 11.7 7a Miss C Metcalfe** 1
patiently rdn, steady hdwy from 5 out, drew level last, soon ld, styd on strly to go clr run-in.
6 **Pro Bono (Ire) 11.7 7a ....Mr A Sansome** 2
soon handy, jmpd ahd 5 out, hrd pressed last 3, hdd and one pace run-in.
25 **Quick Rapor 11.7 7a ....Mr D Alers-Hankey** 3
bhnd and struggling to go pace after one cct, styd on from 3 out, nearest fin.
Hamper 11.7 7a (bl) *soon handily pld, joined ldrs final cct, ev ch till rdn and no ext from 2 out.* 4
Pastoral Pride (USA) 11.9 5a *alwys handy, ld 3rd, clr hfwy, hdd 5 out, fd und pres last 2.* 5
Al Hashimi 11.7 7a *in tch 1st cct, feeling pace and struggling 6 out, no impn last 4.* 6
Social Climber 11.7 7a *chsd ldrs for over a cct, struggling before 6 out, t.o..* 7
Lumberjack (USA) 11.9 5a (bl) *settld in tch, effort after one cct, struggling before 6 out, no ch when blnd and u.r. 3 out.* .... ur
Book Of Runes 11.7 7a *nvr going well, t.o. from hfwy, p.u. after 5 out.* .... pu
Synderborough Lad 12.5 5a *(fav) held up in rear when f 1st.* .... f
Percy Thrower 11.9 5a *ld to 3rd, 2nd when jmpd right and u.r. 5th.* .... ur
11 ran. 8l, 7l, ¾l, 8l, 15l, 20l. Time 5m 11.30s. SP 5-1.
N Chamberlain

258 - 3m 110yds Nov Hun Chase

LAND OF WONDER (USA) 11.12 7a ...Mr R Hicks 1
soon well bhnd, relentless prog final cct, effort and blnd last, ran on to ld last stride.
Royal Irish 12.0 5a.................Mr P Henley 2
alwys handy, ld 8th, clr after next, rdn along from 4 out, ct last stride.
97 **Chatterley 11.12 7a.................Mr N Bloom** 3
settld in tch, bustled along when pace qcknd final cct, no impn from 4 out.
96 Danribo 11.12 7a *well t.o. from 9th, cont 2 fences bhnd till p.u. before two out.* .... pu
R N Commander 11.12 7a *alwys handy, ld 5th to 8th, chsd wnr after, 2nd and staying on when blnd and u.r. 4 out.* .... ur
Bear Necessities 11.12 7a *chsd ldrs, driven along when pace lifted final cct, blnd and u.r. 7 out.* .... ur
169 San Remo 11.12 7a *ld to 5th, lost tch quickly final cct, t.o. when p.u. before 5 out.* .... pu
Squirrellsdaughter 11.7 7a *settld to track ldrs, blnd and u.r. 7th.* .... ur
No Joker (Ire) 11.12 7a *blnd and u.r. 3rd.* .... ur
Not Quite White 12.0 5a *(fav) pricker off side, settld in tch, p.u. lame before 7th.* .... pu
10 ran. Nk, dist. Time 6m 34.10s. SP 8-1.
Artisan Partnership

KELSO
Friday March 1st
GOOD TO SOFT

259 - 3m 1f Hun Chase

113 **OFF THE BRU 12.5 7a ....Mr M Bradburne** 1
j.w, made all, hrd pressed final 100 yards, held on well.
86 **Royal Jester 12.5 7a ....Mr C Storey** 2
(fav) chsd ldrs, kept on well from last, no ext und pres near fin.
37 **Carousel Rocket 12.5 7a............Mr J Davies** 3
soon chasing ldrs, pushed along after 15th, kept on und pres from last.
Ruber 12.1 7a (bl) *mstk 7th, soon bhnd, lost tch 13th, t.o.* 4
187 Toddlin Hame 11.12 7a *chsd ldrs, outpcd 12th, well bhnd when blnd and u.r. 16th.* .... ur
83 Loughlinstown Boy 12.1 7a *soon lost tch, t.o. when p.u. before 13th.* .... pu
Lisnavaragh 11.5 7a *prom till wknd after 14th, t.o. when ref 2 out.* .... ref
Whosthat 11.7 5a *bhnd when blnd and u.r. 9th.* .... ur
8 ran. Hd, 2l, dist. Time 6m 39.90s. SP 5-1.
J G Bradburne

NEWBURY
Friday March 1st
GOOD TO SOFT

260 - 3m Hun Chase

179 **COLONIAL KELLY 11.6 3a ....Mr P Hacking** 1
(Jt fav) chsd ldr, hit 10th, ld 14th, hit 2 out, driven and kept on well.
142 **Still In Business 11.10 5a ....Miss P Curling** 2
(Jt fav) hit 1st, hdwy 5th, hit 10th, chal 14th, blnd 4 out, rallied from 2 out, rdn and not qckn run-in.
Dubit 11.12 7a ....Miss S Vickery 3
ld to 14th, rallied and kept on from 2 out.
125 Paco's Boy 11.2 7a *hit 2nd, in tch, chasing ldrs 12th, mstk 13th and soon wknd, t.o..* 4
Wayside Boy 11.2 7a *hit 4th, t.o. 8th, p.u. after 13th...* pu
7 Bang On Target 11.4 5a (bl) *held up, steady hdwy to track ldrs when f 12th.* .... f
6 ran. 2½l, 3½l, dist. Time 6m 30.00s. SP 11-8.
Alan Cowing

WARWICK
Saturday March 2nd
GOOD

261 - 3¼m Hun Chase

ROLLING BALL (FR) 11.10 7a..........Mr R Ford 1
ld 2nd, made rest, drew clr from 3 out, easily.
98 **Double Silk 12.7 3a..............Mr R Treloggen** 2
(fav) ld to 2nd, chsd wnr after, chal from 16th, outpcd from 3 out, eased run-in, t.o..
185 **Goodshot Rich 11.10 7a (bl).........Mr E James** 3
held up, hdwy apr 4th, blnd 10th, soon wknd, t.o..
214 Barn Pool 11.10 7a *chsd ldng pair til apr 4th, not fluent 6th, soon t.o..* 4
New Mill House 11.10 7a *soon well bhnd, t.o. when blnd and u.r. 3 out.* .... ur
5 ran. Dist, dist, 20l. Time 6m 48.90s. SP 7-2.
Mrs H J Clarke

BEAUFORT
Didmarton
Saturday March 2nd
GOOD

262 - Members

141 **DESERT WALTZ (IRE)............D Alers-Hankey** 1
(fav) w.w. mstk 10th, ld 12th, sn clr, slw last, pshd out
Granville Grill ....J Deutsch 2
ld 3rd-12th, sn outpcd, rallied last, no ext flat
139 **Paper Days..............................S Bush** 3
mstk 1st, trckd ldrs, effrt 13th, clsd apr last, onepcd flat
Perseverance *prom til outpcd 12th, no ch frm 15th....* 4
212 Jupiter Moon 7ex *wll in rear, no ch 11th, styd on aft, nrst fin* 5
139 Sirisat 7ex *trckd ldrs, outpcd whn blnd 12th, wknd....* 6
140 Free Bear *alwys last pair, t.o. hlfwy.* 7
217 Teega Suku *alwys wll bhnd, t.o. 12th.* 8

140 Dancing Doris 5a *chsd ldrs, mstk 7th, lost tch 11th, 5th & no ch whn u.r.last* .... ur
235 Mary Borough 5a *s.s. last pair & wll bhnd,mod prog but still t.o. whn f last* .... f
125 What About That (Ire) (bl) *ld to 3rd, chsd ldr to 11th, 4th & hld whn u.r. 3 out* .... ur
11 ran. 1½l, 3l, 25l, 15l, 5l, 20l, 15l. Time 6m 9.00s. SP 2-5.
H B Geddes (Beaufort).

263 - Intermediate Div I (12st)

150 **OAKLANDS WORD** .... **J P Keen** 1
chsng grp, prog 12th, chal apr last, ran on to ld nr fin
156 **Mister Horatio** .... **M Lewis** 2
(fav) made most, hrd prssd frm 2 out, kpt on, hdd nr fin
28 **Broad Steane** .... **A Sansome** 3
in tch, chsd ldr 11th, ev ch whn mstk last, ran on, just hld
Dusky Day *wll in rear til prog frm 14th, nvr nrr, improve* 4
Offensive Weapon *chsng grp, 3rd apr 12th, lost tch aft nxt* 5
Plax *mid-div, lost tch 13th, t.o.* 6
98 Tattlejack (Ire) *mstk 2nd, chsd ldrs, wknd 13th, t.o.* 7
Short Shot *s.v.s. t.o. til p.u. 13th* .... pu
157 Metrostyle *mid-div, lost tch 12th, no ch aft, p.u. last* .... pu
Sylvan Sirocco *prssd ldr to 11th, wknd 14th, 5th & no ch whn u.r. last* .... ur
Country Life (USA) 7ow *t.o. frm 4th, p.u. 13th* .... pu
133 Our Jackie *f 1st* .... f
Howley Lad *s.s. t.o. til u.r. 2nd* .... ur
Lonesome Step 5a *rear, t.o. 12th, p.u. 2 out* .... pu
206 Royal Swinger 5a *chsng grp, lost tch 11th, 10th & no ch whn u.r. 13th* .... ur
Royal Fireworks *mid-div, wknd 13th, t.o. & p.u. last* .... pu
Titchwell Milly 5a *s.v.s. t.o. til p.u. 13th* .... pu
Beauty Pet 5a 3ow *s.v.s. mstk 1st, t.o. til u.r. 8th* .... ur
18 ran. Hd, nk, 25l, 20l, 3l, 12l. Time 6m 3.00s. SP 20-1.
F P Luff (Vale Of Clettwr).
One fence omitted 2nd circuit. 17 jumps.

264 - Intermediate Div II (12st)

FRENCH PLEASURE 5a .... **P Howse** 1
cls up, ev ch frm 3 out, pshd into ld flat, comf
161 **Hackett's Farm 5ex** .... **Julian Pritchard** 2
in tch, made most 11th-last,sn ld agn,hdd & no ext flat
Printemps (USA) .... **J Barnes** 3
in tch in rear, prog 15th, ev ch apr last, onepcd
Tumble Time *made most to 5th, wth ldrs aft, ld last, sn hdd & no ext* 4
Master Swillbrook *prom, ld 5th-11th, wknd 3 out* 5
Annson *wll in tch til wknd 14th, t.o.* 6
Kamtara *last pair, wll bhnd whn f 9th* .... f
My Last Buck (Ire) *last pair, wknd 11th, p.u. 13th* .... pu
Miss Corinthian 5a *u.r. 2nd* .... ur
Duques 5a *cls up til p.u. 9th* .... pu
Reply 5a *in tch in rear, wknd 12th, p.u. 14th* .... pu
68 Strong Tarquin (Ire) *(fav) trckd ldrs, cls 3rd whn f 9th* .... f
12 ran. 6l, 3l, 1l, 25l, 25l. Time 6m 18.00s. SP 6-1.
A J Mason (V.W.H.).
One fence omitted 2nd circuit. 17 jumps.

265 - Open (12st)

209 **LEWESDON HILL** .... **T Mitchell** 1
(fav) prom,wth ldr 11th til blnd 13th,rallied to ld aft last,ranon
7 **Granville Guest 7ex** .... **D Pipe** 2
prom, ld 8th, hrd rdn 2 out, hdd flat, ran on
232 **Shadow Walker 7ex** .... **T Stephenson** 3
ld to 8th, outpcd aft 11th, sn no ch
Spring Fun 7ex *cls up to 11th, sn btn, t.o. 3 out* 4
Flying Ziad (Can) *in tch to 11th, sn bhnd, t.o. 14th* 5
142 The Holy Golfer *n.j.w. alwys last, t.o. 5th* 6
6 ran. 3l, 30l, 15l, 3l, 1 fence. Time 6m 3.00s. SP 8-11.
T C Frost (Seavington).

266 - Ladies

135 **FLAKED OATS 4ex** .... **Miss P Gundry** 1
(fav) trckd ldrs, mstk 9th, chal 3 out, ld last, ran on well
163 **Roving Report** .... **Mrs A Rucker** 2
alwys prom, 3rd & not qckn whn mstk 3 out, ran on wll last
154 **Fast Freeze 4ex** .... **Mrs J Hawkins** 3
ld to last, ran on onepcd flat
News Review 7ex *in tch til outpcd 13th, kpt on onepcd frm 2 out* 4
Finally Fantazia 5a *wll bhnd til prog frm 11th, kpt on, nvr dang* 5
234 Rip The Calico (Ire) 5a *in tch, jnd ldrs 12th, wknd frm 15th* 6
Little Island 5a *mid-div, prog to jn ldrs 10th, 5th & outpcd 13th, no ch aft* 7
136 Friendly Lady 5a *hld up rear, t.o. 11th, ran on 3 out, nvr in race* 8
Gold Diver *prom to 10th, wknd rpdly aft nxt, t.o. 3 out* 9
Ocean Lad *u.r. 1st* .... ur
Woodway *sn last, t.o. whn u.r. 11th* .... ur
27 Garda Spirit 5a *mid-div til f 8th* .... f
Cool Rascal 5a *in tch in rear to 13th, wll bhnd whn p.u. 2 out* .... pu
13 ran. 3l, ¾l, 25l, ½l, ½l, 1l, 1l, 25l. Time 6m 8.00s. SP 2-5.
E B Swaffield (Cattistock).

267 - Maiden (5-7yo) Div I (12st)

145 **COUNT BALIOS (IRE)** .... **F Crew** 1
lft in ld 4th-8th, lft in ld 13th-15th, ld last, ran on
144 **Tea Cee Kay** .... **A Sansome** 2
(fav) mstks, chsd ldrs, clsd frm 3 uot, ev ch last, not qckn
233 **Dip The Lights 5a** .... **F Brennan** 3
jmpd all over the pl, sn wll bhnd, lft 3rd by dfctns
205 Son Of Anun *chsd ldrs til wknd 10th, wll bhnd whn u.r. 13th* .... ur
145 Celtic Token *ld til blnd & u.r. 4th* .... ur
Seahawk Retriever *prom,ld 8th til blnd 13th,ld 15th,hdd & lkd btn whn u.r.last* .... ur
29 My Boy Barney *t.o. whn crawld 1st & 2nd, cont til p.u. last* .... pu
236 Good Looking Guy *u.r. 3rd* .... ur
129 Apple Anthem 5a *mstk 6th, chsd ldrs til 4th & lost tch 12th, p.u. 15th* .... pu
Twilight Tom *rear til b.d. 4th* .... bd
Magical Cruise 5a *mstks, wll bhnd frm 6th, t.o. & p.u. 13th* .... pu
11 ran. 2l, 2 fences. Time 6m 12.00s. SP 4-1.
M H Wood (V.W.H.).

268 - Maiden (5-7yo) Div II (12st)

BEWDLEY BOY .... **Miss P Gundry** 1
j.w. ld 4th til apr last, sn ld agn, ran on well
144 **Definite Maybe (Ire)** .... **T Mitchell** 2
(fav) s.s. prog 6th,prssd wnr 12th,ld apr last,sn hdd,ran on flat
Stray Harmony 5a .... **J Trice-Rolph** 3
prom, ev ch 14th, outpcd by 1st pair frm 3 out
138 Churchtown Chance (Ire) 5a *mstks, prom, blnd 9th, ev ch 14th, sn outpcd.* 4
144 The Blind Judge *ld to 4th, wkng whn mstk 9th, t.o.* 5
205 New Years Eve *mid-div til f 8th* .... f
Haydon Hill 7a *rear, prog & in tch 9th, outpcd 12th, poor 5th & p.u. 14th* .... pu
143 Sit Tight *prom til blnd & u.r. 6th* .... ur
143 Givus A Hand *mid-div, lost plc 7th, t.o. & p.u. 9th* .... pu
Motor Trader *alwys rear, t.o. & p.u. 12th* .... pu
10 ran. 2l, 15l, 2l, 1 fence. Time 6m 18.00s. SP 9-1.
J E Grey (Berkeley).

269 - Restricted

29 **CALLING WILD (IRE)** .... **T Mitchell** 1
(Jt fav) mstks,hld up,prog 11th,chal & outjmpd last,qcknd to ld flat

145 **Skip'N'time................................M Miller** 2
(Jt fav) trckd ldrs, ld 15th, jnd & bttr jmp last, hdd & outpcd flat
129 **Bit Of An Idiot............................C Morlock** 3
ld 2-3rd & 10th-15th, no ext aft, promising
147 Just Marmalade *trckd ldrs, 4th & outpcd whn mstk 15th, no dang aft.* 4
155 Pick'n Hill (Ire) *ld to 2nd, lft in ld 8th, hdd 10th, wknd 14th, t.o.* 5
233 Arctic Line *cls up to 10th, sn lost tch, t.o.* 6
235 Jellyband *b.d. 1st* bd
Cutsdean Cross (Ire) *trckd ldrs til lost tch frm 13th, t.o. & p.u. 2 out* pu
Glenard (Ire) *b.d. 1st* bd
29 Pavi's Brother *8s-5s, ld 3rd til ran off course apr 8th* ro
Chalvey Grove *crawld 2nd, t.o. whn u.r. nxt* ur
206 Annmount Lady (Ire) 5a *f 1st* f
12 ran. 3l, 12l, 1l, 20l, 25l. Time 6m 13.00s. SP 2-1.
J A Keighley (Blackmore & Sparkford Vale).
J.N.

CHIDDINGFOLD,L'FIELD & COWDRAY
Parham
Saturday March 2nd
GOOD TO FIRM

270 - Members

26 **PIN'S PRIDE................................T Hills** 1
prom, disp 9th-nxt, made most aft, ran on well 2 out
Pat Alaska..........................Miss C Wates 2
(Jt fav) ld 3rd, disp 9th-nxt, 2nd aft, chal & blnd 3 out, no ext nxt
249 **Cantorial................................W Church** 3
in tch, effrt 13th, ld brfly nxt, kpt on onepcd
103 Kaim Park *(Jt fav) ld to 3rd, in tch aft, 4th & no dang frm 15th* 4
Vanity Fair 36ow *alwys last, lost tch 3rd, compltd own time* 5
5 ran. 5l, 2l, 10l, Bad. Time 6m 58.00s. SP 8-1.
Mrs E C Pinto (Chiddinfold, L'field & Cowdray).

271 - Confined (12st)

21 **LITTLE MARTINA (IRE) 5a 3ex...........A Welsh** 1
alwys wth ldrs, jst ld 12th, rdn 2 out, hld on, all out
58 **Billion Dollarbill........................M Gorman** 2
mid-div, prog 4 out, 4th 3 out, chal last, kpt on wll
104 **The Portsoy Loon......................A Hickman** 3
(fav) twrds rear, clsd up aft hlfwy, 3rd 14th, und pres & btn 2out
104 Kates Castle 5a 3ex *ld to 5th, cls up aft, prssd wnr 14th, wknd last* 4
Myverygoodfriend *mid-div, no dang frm 14th* 5
Pete's Sake *nvr trbld ldrs* 6
140 Skinnhill 1ow (bl) *nvr bttr than mid-div, wknd 4 out* 7
142 Snowfire Chap (bl) *prog to trck ldrs hlfwy, fdd 14th* 8
104 Namoos *nvr nr ldrs, wll bhnd whn p.u. 2 out* pu
249 Highland Bounty *rear, some prog 8th, wknd 13th, bhnd whn p.u. 2 out* pu
Supreme Dealer *ld 5th-12th, fdd, wll bhnd whn p.u. 2 out* pu
250 Wellington Bay *alwys rear, wll bhnd whn p.u. 2 out* pu
19 Colonel O'Kelly (NZ) 9ex *prom til u.r. 14th* ur
93 Mara Askari (v) *mid-div, rdn & wknd 12th, wll bhnd whn p.u. 4 out* pu
252 Country Vet 5a 3ex *prom,blnd & lost plc 4th, nvr going wll aft, bhnd & p.u.2out* pu
15 ran. ¾l, 2l, 6l, 8l, 10l, nk, 1l. Time 6m 44.00s. SP 11-4.
Christopher Newport (East Sussex & Romney Marsh).

272 - Restricted (12st)

MURBERRY (IRE) 5a..........................T Hills 1
5s-3s,handy,smooth prog to jn ldr 4 out,ld & clr 2 out
248 **Alansford..................................P Bull** 2
(fav) prog to 2nd 12th, ld 14th, hdd aft 3 out, 2nd best aft
20 **Reggie (v)...........................R Wilkinson** 3
alwys cls up, ld 3rd-4th, 3rd frm 3 out, onepcd
44 Wholestone (Ire) *ld 4th-14th, styd cls up til wknd 2 out* 4
140 Palaman *alwys rear* 5
140 Dormston Lad 5ow *prom til wknd 14th* 6
Firewater Station *alwys rear, p.u. 13th* pu
250 Motor Cloak *alwys strggIng in rear, last whn blnd & u.r. 8th* ur
Tau *alwys rear, wll bhnd whn p.u. 3 out* pu
Manaolana 5a *pllng, prom to hlfwy, bhnd whn p.u. 14th* pu
Philipintown (v) *ld to 3rd, bhnd frm 7th, u.r. 12th* ur
Prince Rua *alwys wll in rear, p.u. 15th* pu
Prince Ronan (Ire) *alwys mid-div, btn whn p.u. aft 14th* pu
13 ran. 10l, 3l, 10l, 15l, 10l. Time 6m 48.00s. SP 3-1.
Maurice E Pinto (Chiddingfold).

273 - Ladies

CLOVER COIN 5a.........................Miss J Grant 1
alwys prom, chal 2 out, und pres & drft lft, just ld flat
103 **Topping-The-Bill..................Mrs E Coveney** 2
(fav) alwys prom, ld 14th, rdn 2 out, hdd flat
Bossburg 5a 3ow.................Miss S French 3
ld 6th-14th, 3rd aft, wknd rpdly 2 out
Wendy Jane 5a *1st ride, rear, poor 5th frm 14th, lft 4th last* 4
Wrekin Hill *alwys well in rear, t.o. final cct.* 5
104 Meritmoore *immed dtchd, t.o. hlfwy, p.u. 3 out* pu
Our Survivor *ld, mstk 2nd, c.o. by loose horse 4th* co
Maltby Boy *lft in ld 4th, hdd 6th, wknd frm 12th, wll bhnd & p.u.3 out* pu
Coral Eddy *twrds rear, 6th & no ch whn u.r. 13th* ur
136 Quiet Confidence (Ire) 5a *3rd whn u.r. 3rd* ur
40 Pejawi 5a *mid-div, prog to chs ldng trio 11th, 3rd & no ch, r.o. last* ro
11 ran. ½l, 25l, 8l, 1 fence. Time 6m 41.00s. SP 9-2.
M E T Davies (Southdown & Eridge).

274 - Open (12st)

104 **CELTIC SPARK 4ex........................P Hacking** 1
(fav) wll plcd, ld apr 3 out, styd on well
125 **Retail Runner................................T Hills** 2
ld to 6th, agn 10th til aft 4 out,qcknd wth wnr, no ext last
32 **Strong Gold 7ex (bl)..................T McCarthy** 3
cls up, ld 6th-10th, outpcd in 3rd frm 3 out
Redelva 5a *twrds rear, prog 14th, 4th frm 3 out, nvr dang* 4
Folk Dance 8ow *alwys bhnd, t.o. frm 12th* 5
56 The Forties 3ow *alwys rear, t.o. 7th* 6
Toushtari (USA) *prom to 12th, 6th & wkng whn f 15th* f
Sunday Punch *prom to 7th, bhnd whn p.u. 3 out* pu
25 Ufano (Fr) 7ex *lost tch 8th, t.o. & p.u. 3 out.* pu
Centre Stage *last & nvr going wll, t.o. 7th, p.u. 12th.* pu
251 Take The Town 7ex *6th whn f 6th* f
Berrings Dasher *cls up, pshd alng 12th, wknd 15th, p.u. nxt* pu
12 ran. 3l, 20l, 3l, 1 fence, 25l. Time 6m 39.00s. SP 5-4.
M D Reed (Chiddingfold,l'field & Cowdray).

275 - Maiden (12st)

17 **LOCAL MANOR 3ow.......................H Dunlop** 1
(fav) 9/2-5/2, prog 8th, jnd ldrs 13th, ld aft 3 out, ran on well
252 **Pallingham Star (Ire)...............Mrs S Hickman** 2
rear, steady prog fnl cct, 2nd aft 3 out, not pace to chal
Dad's Pipe................................T Smith 3
handy, cls 3rd 3 out, just outpcd aft, styd on
253 Zallot *alwys well in rear, lost tch 13th* 4
247 Time Star (NZ) *ld & u.r. 1st* ur
252 Oberons Butterfly *nvr nr ldrs, blnd 11th, p.u. nxt* pu
St Robert *ld 1st, clr hlfwy, hdd 13th, wknd rpdly, p.u. aft nxt* pu
253 Fort Diana *nvr on terms, wll bhnd whn p.u. 4 out* pu
Moran Brig *wll in tch, wknd & p.u. 12th* pu

Times Are Changing 5a 8ow *in tch til mstk 7th, wll bhnd whn p.u. 12th* .... pu
253 Childsway *pllng,chsd ldr,ld 13th,mstk & hdd 3 out,wknd rpdly,p.u.last* .... pu
106 High Burnshot *mid-div whn ran out 5th* .... ro
144 Royal Pittance *rear, mstks, wll bhnd whn f 11th* .... f
Welshmans Canyon (Ire) *rear, losing tch whn p.u. 9th* pu
Bubbles Galore (Ire) 7a (bl) *rear, losing tch whn p.u. 9th* .... pu
15 ran. 5l, 1l, 1 fence. Time 6m 56.00s. SP 5-2.
J L Dunlop (Crawley & Horsham).
One fence omitted, 17 jumps. G.Ta.

EAST DEVON
Clyst St Mary
Saturday March 2nd
SOFT

276 - Members

66 **NEARLY SPLENDID .... T Greed** 1
(fav) made all, clr 15th, easily
Stainless Steel .... M Sweetland 2
last til prog 15th, went 2nd nxt, no ch wth wnr
Plain Sailing (Fr) .... Miss A Barnett 3
chsd wnr to 15th, wknd nxt, t.o. 3 out
137 The Copper Key *2nd whn blnd & u.r. 3rd* .... ur
4 ran. 20l, 25l. Time 7m 32.60s. SP 1-4.
S R Stevens (East Devon).

277 - Open (12st)

133 **CHILIPOUR 7ex .... N Harris** 1
(fav) hld up, blnd 14th, prog 17th, ld 3 out, sn clr, easily
130 **Early To Rise .... J Creighton** 2
ld to 3 out, outpcd aft
133 **Mr Lion .... P King** 3
chsd ldr to 16th, wknd nxt, outpcd
Querrin Lodge *sn bhnd, t.o. & p.u. 16th* .... pu
4 ran. 8l, 25l. Time 7m 29.60s. SP 2-9.
Nick Viney (Dulverton (West)).

278 - Confined

133 **QUALITAIR MEMORY (IRE) .... J Tizzard** 1
(fav) hld up, prog 12th, ld 16th, ran on well frm 3 out
Larky McIlroy 5a .... Miss S Vickery 2
cls up, ld 13th-16th, outpcd frm 3 out
198 **Badihar (USA) .... E Clarkson** 3
ld to 3rd, mid-div frm 5th, styd on frm 16th, no ch 2 out
66 Far Too Loud *alwys mid-div, nvr any ch, outpcd* 4
Deviosity (USA) *bhnd, no ch frm 14th, outpcd* 5
134 Phils Pride *ld 4th-15th, wknd & outpcd aft* 6
133 Fred Splendid *prom early, lost tch 12th, t.o. & p.u. 17th* .... pu
133 Be My Habitat *bhnd til f 15th* .... f
Dollybat 5a *alwys rear, t.o. & p.u. 15th* .... pu
9 ran. 4l, 2l, 8l, 25l, 20l. Time 7m 28.20s. SP Evens.
C Tizzard (Blackmore & Sparkford Vale).

279 - Ladies

195 **PHAR TOO TOUCHY 5a .... Miss R Francis** 1
(fav) prom, ld 14th, sn clr, easily
135 **Great Pokey .... Miss N Courtenay** 2
ld 5th-13th, hdd, easily hld frm 3 out
Seventh Lock .... Miss L Blackford 3
rear, 4th at 11th, no ch frm 3 out, outpcd
198 Departure 5a *alwys rear, no ch frm 13th* 4
135 Rapid Rascal *prom to 14th, lost tch frm 3 out* 5
136 Go West (bl) *alwys rear, t.o. & p.u. 2 out* .... pu
Tom Snout (Ire) *disp til blnd & u.r. 8th* .... ur
7 ran. 15l, 2½l, 2l, 10l. Time 7m 13.00s. SP 4-7.
Miss R A Francis (Dulverton West).
Open ditch omitted from this race onwards. 19 jumps per race.

280 - Restricted Div I (12st)

138 **JUST BEN .... Miss J Cumings** 1
(Co fav) alwys prom, ld 14th, styd on well frm 3 out
199 **Green Hill .... S Mulcaire** 2
hld up, prog 12th, ev ch 3 out, onepcd nxt
211 **Strong Breeze .... Mrs R Pocock** 3
(Co fav) ld/disp to 13th, chsd wnr frm nxt, ev ch 3 out, outpcd aft
276 The Copper Key *2nd outing, mid-div, lost tch 14th, t.o. nxt* 4
Ballysheil *sn rear, t.o. 12th* 5
Blake's Finesse 5a *disp early, lost tch 12th, wknd & p.u. 15th* .... pu
Palace King (Ire) *sn bhnd, t.o. & p.u. 12th* .... pu
69 Run With Joy (Ire) 7a *mid-div, lost tch 12th, t.o. & p.u. 14th* .... pu
138 Hensue *(Co fav) rear, prog 12th, wknd 15th, t.o. & p.u. 3 out* .... pu
Dula Model 5a *alwys mid-div, lost tch 13th, p.u. nxt* ... pu
131 The Ugly Duckling *rear, t.o. & p.u. 14th* .... pu
11 ran. 3l, 2l, dist, dist. Time 7m 21.00s. SP 4-1.
Roger Persey (Devon & Somerset Staghounds).

281 - Restricted Div II (12st)

THE PEDLAR 5a .... T Greed 1
handy, 3rd at 8th, ld 3 out, styd on well
137 **Mountain Master .... Miss L Blackford** 2
(fav) 7/2-5/4, in tch, ld 8th-3 out, outpcd frm nxt
28 **Parditino .... Miss V Nicholas** 3
unruly paddock, alwys mid-div, ran on frm 3 out, nrst fin
138 Great Impostor *alwys mid-div, no ch frm 14th* 4
68 Sherbrooks *alwys mid-div, nvr on terms* 5
204 Its A Mugs Game 5a *sn last, t.o. frm 12th* 6
Blakeington *cls up to 14th, wknd frm nxt* 7
Hedera Helix *ld til f 2nd* .... f
The Butler *sn rear, no ch whn p.u. 12th* .... pu
3 Cherry Street 5a *ld to 7th, lost tch 14th, t.o. & p.u. 3 out* .... pu
Tractorias (Ire) *sn rear, t.o. & p.u. 16th* .... pu
11 ran. 8l, 13l, 5l, 6l, 2l, hd. Time 7m 22.00s. SP 12-1.
Mrs Sally Hurst (Devon & Somerset Staghounds).

282 - Maiden Div I Pt I (12st)

BELMOUNT BEAUTY (IRE) 5a .... N Mitchell 1
mid-div, prog 12th, 2nd at 14th, ld 3 out, easily
Melling 7a .... Miss A Goschen 2
cls up early, lost plc 12th, ran on 4 out, no ch wnr
131 **Good Appeal 5a .... Miss L Blackford** 3
handy, ld 12th-4 out, wknd frm nxt
132 Here's Mary 5a *ld to 11th, in tch til wknd 13th, p.u. 3 out* .... pu
207 Langton Parmill *6s-5/2, cls up til f 3rd* .... f
137 Tom Boy *(fav) 3rd whn ran out 3rd* .... ro
Sam's Successor 7a *rear, lost tch 10th, t.o. & p.u. 12th* .... pu
Devonshire Lad 7a *cls up, ev ch 14th, wknd & f heavily 2 out* .... f
8 ran. 25l, dist. Time 7m 38.00s. SP 16-1.
G B Foot (Seavington).

283 - Maiden Div I Pt II (12st)

45 **STALBRIDGE GOLD 5a .... B Dixon** 1
cls up, ld 3 out, styd on well, easily
2 **Heather Boy .... Miss J Cumings** 2
(fav) ld 8th-3 out, onepcd frm nxt
Working Man (Ire) 7a .... M Hoskins 3
hld up, prog 14th, ev ch 3 out, outpcd aft
River Stream 5a *in tch to 14th, wknd nxt, p.u. 2 out* ... pu
201 Ianovitch (bl) *sn 25l clr, wkng whn f heavily 8th* .... f
Musbury Castle 5a *rear til p.u. 6th* .... pu
Elle Flavador 5a *hld up in rear, t.o. & p.u. 14th, improve* .... pu
7 ran. 25l, hd. Time 7m 35.00s. SP 6-4.
C J Barnes (Blackmore & Sparkford Vale).

284 - Maiden Div II (12st)

VENN BOY .... J Tizzard 1

w.w. prog 10th, in tch 14th, ld 3 out, sn clr, improve
70 **Say Charlie .... Miss J Cumings** **2**
prom, ld 12th-3 out, outpcd aft
Jolly Flier .... S Ellis **3**
(fav) ld to 12th, prom aft, wknd 3 out
138 Miss Pernickity 5a *handy, outpcd & no ch frm 14th* ... 4
Rogerson *mid-div, prog 12th, ev ch 15th, wknd 3 out, p.u. nxt* .... pu
132 Father Malone (Ire) *alwys mid-div, no ch whn p.u. 15th* .... pu
Suba Lin 5a *sn rear, t.o. & p.u. 14th* .... pu
Carumu 5a *mid-div til lost tch 14th, p.u. nxt* .... pu
Lochnaver 5a *mid-div, lost tch 10th, p.u. 12th* .... pu
Brook A Light 7a *alwys bhnd, t.o. & p.u. 12th* .... pu
Grey Jerry 7a *alwys rear, t.o. & p.u. 15th* .... pu
11 ran. 25l, 6l, 4l. Time 7m 24.00s. SP 6-1.
L G Tizzard (Blackmore & Sparkford Vale).
D.P.

SIR W W WYNN'S
Eaton Hall
Saturday March 2nd
GOOD

285 - Members

159 **AMBROSE .... W Ritson** **1**
(fav) cls up, lft in ld 4th, made rest, prssd 2 out, lft solo
75 **Mr Busker (Ire) .... C Barlow** **2**
w.w. prog 4 out, chal whn u.r. 2 out, rmntd
Wally Wrekin *ld til u.r. 4th* .... ur
Sale Ring *in tch to 8th, p.u. 11th* .... pu
Emma Clew (Ire) 5a *prom, cls up & ev ch whn u.r. 13th* .... ur
5 ran. Dist. Time 6m 52.00s. SP 4-5.
W A Ritson (Sir W W Wynn's).

286 - Open Maiden Div I

145 **UPTON ORBIT .... Miss S Sadler** **1**
mid-div, prog 12th, strng run to ld 2 out, ran on well
Pebble Rock .... R Ford **2**
handy, ld 7th-2 out, ran on onepcd
Micksdilemma .... A Phillips **3**
mid-div, prog 4 out, fin well
158 Autumn Green (Ire) *mid-div at 13th, steady prog aft, nrst fin* 4
166 Sandy King (Ire) *chsng grp, ev ch 4 out, not qckn nxt* .. 5
Blaze Of Majesty (USA) *chsd ldrs, no ext frm 4 out* ... 6
Nights Image (Ire) *s.s. prog last m, nrst fin* 7
164 The Yokel (bl) *ld to 6th, in tch whn f 13th* .... f
166 Costermonger *(fav) sttld mid-div, mstks, losing tch whn p.u. 11th* .... pu
Beeworthy 5a *mid to rear, hmpd & u.r. 13th* .... ur
164 Juste Jo 5a *u.r. 3rd* .... ur
167 Mister Tinker *mid-div hlfwy, fdd, p.u. 4 out* .... pu
Heriot Water (Ire) 5a *mid to rear, p.u. 11th* .... pu
Inglebrook 7a *mid-div, no ch whn p.u. 3 out* .... pu
14 ran. 2l, 5l. Time 6m 51.00s. SP 9-4.
J C Collett (North Cotswold).

287 - Open Maiden Div II

KINGQUILLO (IRE) .... G Hanmer **1**
j.w. made all, ran on well frm 2 out
Brabiner Lad .... J Townson **2**
w.w. prog frm 14th, chsd wnr frm 3 out, no ext
Little By Little .... R Bevis **3**
(fav) hld up, prog 12th, ev ch til wknd 4 out
J B Saucy Doris 5a *mid-div, no ch whn p.u. 4 out* .... pu
Kingfisher Blues (Ire) *mid to rear, no ch whn p.u. 4 out* .... pu
173 Kali Sana (Ire) *chsd ldrs to hlfwy, wknd, p.u. 4 out* .... pu
167 Frank The Swank 7a *mid to rear, nvr in race, p.u. 13th* .... pu
Jacky's Jaunt 5a *in tch, saddle slppd & p.u. 6th* .... pu
164 Aunt Margaret 5a *chsd ldrs to 7th, sn wknd, p.u. 11th* pu
Maesgwyn Bach 5a *prom to 13th, losing tch whn p.u. 3 out* .... pu
Colonian King *s.s. last whn f 3rd* .... f
11 ran. 10l, 10l. Time 6m 36.00s. SP 8-1.
Mrs B Shaw (West Shropshire).

288 - Open Maiden Div III

165 **MR BOBBIT (IRE) .... R Burton** **1**
prog frm mid-div to 2nd 13th, ld 5 out, ran on well 2 out
164 **Flinters (bl) .... D Barlow** **2**
chsng grp, prog to ld/disp 11-13th, not qckn frm nxt
Dee Light 5a .... C Barlow **3**
mid-div, prog 5 out, ev ch 3 out, no ext
Salmon Spring *chsng grp, ld/disp 11-13th, fdd* 4
North Hollow *prog last m, nrst fin* 5
Public Appeal *alwys rear, p.u. 5 out* .... pu
Moya's Tip Top 5a *prom to 10th, grad lost tch, p.u. 5 out* .... pu
164 Merry Scorpion *ld, set str pace, carried by loose horses 10th* .... co
80 Scottish Laird *(fav) hld up rear, nvr going wll, no ch whn p.u. 2 out* .... pu
167 Captiva Bay 5a *u.r. 5th* .... ur
Cloud Dancing *disp whn ran out aft 7th* .... ro
158 Ballybeggan Parson (Ire) *mid to rear, no ch whn p.u. 5 out* .... pu
221 The Hollow (Ire) 5a *rear, prog to 4th at 12th, fdd, p.u. 3 out* .... pu
166 King Keith *nvr going wl, p.u. 5 out* .... pu
Nial (Ire) *mid to rear, nvr dang, p.u. 4 out* .... pu
Leo The Lodger *mid to rear, no ch whn p.u. 4 out* .... pu
Lady Pokey 5a *mid-div, wknd & p.u. 4 out* .... pu
17 ran. 2l, 5l, 15l, 20l. Time 6m 34.00s. SP 5-1.
S J P Furniss (West Shropshire Drag).

289 - Confined

159 **KORBELL (IRE) 5a .... A Crow** **1**
(fav) n.j.w. mid-div,ld 8-11th,hit nxt 3,ld 2 out,jnd last,ran on
159 **Shoon Wind .... A Dalton** **2**
prog 6th, ld 12th-2 out, ev ch last, no ext nr line
159 **Ebony Gale .... Miss J Penney** **3**
mid-div, no ch wth 1st pair frm 5 out
Lattin General *1st ride, mid-div, outpcd hlfwy* 4
120 Arctic Paddy *prom to 10th, sn strggling* 5
On Your Way *mid to rear, no ch whn p.u. 5 out* .... pu
162 Tipp Down *ld to 7th, grad wknd, p.u. 4 out* .... pu
159 Astre Radieux (Fr) *chsng grp to 12th, sn btn, p.u. 4 out* .... pu
Sandstone Arch *mid to rear, nvr dang, p.u. 4 out* ..... pu
Wot Pet *chsd ldrs to 6th, outpcd frm 12th, p.u. 4 out* .. pu
10 ran. Nk, dist, 30l, 2l. Time 6m 26.00s. SP 1-4.
K J Mitchell (North Shropshire).

290 - Land Rover Open (12st)

160 **SCALLY MUIRE 5a .... A Crow** **1**
(fav) cls up, ld 12th, duelld wth 2dn frm 4 out, hdd last,ld line
162 **Mr Tittle Tattle 7ex .... D Barlow** **2**
ld to 12th, chal frm 4 out, ld last, hdd post
94 **Catchapenny 7ex (bl) .... W Tellwright** **3**
wll in tch til outpcd 4 out, no ext nxt
125 Castlebay Lad 7ex *prom, ev ch 4 out, onepcd* 4
24 Barkin *chsng grp to 4 out, sn outpcd* 5
Castle Cross 7ex *cls up to 12th, lost tch nxt, p.u. 3 out* .... pu
6 ran. ½l, 15l, 2l, 1l. Time 6m 30.00s. SP 2-5.
G L Edwards (North Shropshire).

291 - Ladies

STEPHENS PET .... Miss A Dare **1**
(fav) hld up, prog 12th, ld 2 out, ran on well flat, just hld on
163 **Hornblower .... Miss C Burgess** **2**
ld to 2 out, rallied flat, just hld
163 **Nodforms Dilemma (USA) ..... Miss H Brookshaw** **3**
w.w. prog frm 4 out, nrst fin
76 Side Brace (NZ) *mid-div, prog 6th, onepcd frm 4 out* .. 4

163 Renard Quay *mid-div, nrst fin.* 5
161 Brockish Bay *disp to 11th, lost tch wth 1st pair 14th, sn btn* 6
159 Queens Tour *mid-div, lost tch 10th, p.u. 14th* pu
161 Sooner Still (bl) *wll in tch til f 14th* f
Allow Gold *mstk 4th, f nxt* f
Pepperbox 5a *u.r. 2nd* ur
10 ran. Sht-hd, 15l, 10l, 4l, 2l. Time 6m 21.00s. SP 4-6.
Dr P P Brown (Berkeley).

292 - Restricted (12st)

219 **RIP VAN WINKLE ....Miss A Dare** 1
(fav) w.w. smooth prog to ld 14th, sn clr, easily
165 **The Barren Arctic..................Mrs M Bryan** 2
hld up rear, prog 4 out, ran in 2 out, fin well
165 **Miss Shaw 5a ....A Griffith** 3
ld to 4th, ld 12th-nxt, ev ch 4 out, outpcd aft
Grange Prize *w.w. prog 5 out, styd on, nrst fin* 4
77 One For The Chief *mid to rear, nvr dang* 5
Lindsey Doyle 5a *mid-div, prog frm 13th, not qckn aft* 6
165 Spurious *mid-div, prog 13th, 3rd 4 out, fdd nxt* 7
Gen-Tech *mid-div, outpcd frm hlfwy* 8
164 Rinky Dinky Doo *prom, chsng grp til outpcd 5 out, sn btn, p.u. 2 out* pu
Lakenheather (NZ) *mid-div whn u.r. 14th* ur
Rhine River (USA) *prom, outpcd hlfwy, p.u. 3 out* pu
Mighty Haggis *mid to rear, sn btn, p.u. 3 out* pu
Monarrow (Ire) *chsd ldrs to 9th, wknd rpdly, p.u. 4 out* pu
Mister Goodguy (Ire) *hld up, ld 5th-11th, wth ldrs whn f 5 out* f
165 Roll-A-Dance *mid-div, nvr dang, p.u. 3 out* pu
15 ran. 15l, nk, 8l, 6l, 30l. Time 6m 30.00s. SP 4-6.
Dr P P Brown (Berkeley).

293 - Intermediate (12st)

LANDSKER ALFRED ....Miss A Dare 1
(Jt fav) hld up, prog 13th, ld 5 out, ran on well 2 out
Three Potato Four ....D Barlow 2
(Jt fav) w.w. jnd chsng grp 13th, 2nd 2 out, no imp wnr
164 **Worleston Farrier.....................G Hanmer** 3
ld to 9th, cls up & ev ch, no ext last
Ledwyche Gate *prog 11th, ev ch 3 out, ran on onepcd* 4
Grey Gorden (Ire) *rear, nrly t.o. til styd on frm 14th, nvr rchd ldrs* 5
159 Formal *chsng grp, strggling 4 out* 6
159 Charlie Chalk *nvr bttr than mid-div, ran on onepcd* 7
160 Scriven Boy *prom, ld 10th til u.r. 14th* ur
Bally Muire 5a *mid to rear, p.u. 4 out* pu
160 Carton *chsd ldrs to 6th, lost tch 14th, p.u. 2 out* pu
Downtown *t.o. 8th, p.u. 14th* pu
11 ran. 3l, 1l, 4l, 12l. Time 6m 31.00s. SP 3-1.
Dr P P Brown (Berkeley).
V.S.

SOUTH CORNWALL
Great Trethew
Saturday March 2nd
GOOD

294 - Confined (12st)

196 **THE KIMBLER......................Miss S Young** 1
hld up, prog 16th, styd on wll to ld last
198 **Gymcrak Dawn ....I Hambly** 2
alwys prom, disp 2 out-last, no ext
Catch The Cross (bl)...................Mrs M Hand 3
made most aft 6th til wknd & hdd aft 2 out
196 Buckingham Gate *handy til lost plc 16th, styd on one-pcd* 4
196 Sancreed *4th hlfwy, steadily wknd* 5
Happy Valley 5a *alwys bhnd* 6
196 Laneast Lore *bhnd frm hlfwy* 7
198 Pen-Alisa 5a *jmpd lft, ld til wd aft 6th, bhnd nxt, p.u. 13th* pu
43 Just Bert (Ire) *(fav) w.w. prog 14th, cls 3rd whn u.r. 16th* ur
Noddy's Story 5a *rear til p.u. apr 13th* pu
10 ran. 3l, 6l, 10l, dist, dist, 1½l. Time 6m 22.60s. SP 7-1.
B R J Young (East Cornwall).

295 - Ladies

197 **ORIENTAL PLUME ....Mrs M Hand** 1
(fav) in tch, ld 14th, sn clr, easily
Playpen ....Miss S Crook 2
1st ride, prom, 2nd whn mstk 14th, kpt on onepcd
Mo's Chorister ....Miss S Young 3
ld/disp, hit 12th, 3rd & onepcd frm 14th
197 Jokers Patch *in tch to 15th, sn wknd, walked in* 4
136 Treleven 5a *sn rear, t.o. frm hlfwy* 5
Morgans Man *n.j.w. bhnd til p.u. 13th* pu
6 ran. 15l, 3l, 20l, hd. Time 6m 20.40s. SP 2-5.
J F Weldhen (Fourburrow).

296 - Open (12st)

198 **CELTIC SPORT 7ex (bl)..................R White** 1
made all, dictated pace, clr 3 out, styd on well
196 **The General's Drum ....K Heard** 2
(fav) hld up, chsd wnr 16th, not qckn clsng stgs
134 **Fearsome ....G Penfold** 3
handy, 2nd at 14th, 3rd & onepcd frm 16th
Glenform *in tch til wknd 14th* 4
Pillmere Lad *last til p.u. 3 out* pu
5 ran. 2l, 6l, dist. Time 6m 21.00s. SP 9-4.
Mrs A C Martin (Tiverton Foxhounds).

297 - Intermediate (12st)

65 **KALOORE.............................I Dowrick** 1
(fav) in tch, prog 14th, drvn to chal 2 out, ld last, sn clr
65 **Vital Song ....G Matthews** 2
ld to 16th, 3rd frm 3 out, styd on gamely flat
65 **On Alert (NZ)..........................R White** 3
trckd ldr til ld 16th, hdd & blnd badly last
195 Brother Bill *t.o. hlfwy* 4
198 Batsi *rear, strggling 7th, t.o. & p.u. 2 out* pu
130 First Design *cls 4th whn f 9th* f
Light The Bay 5a *7th hlfwy, bhnd whn p.u. 13th* pu
195 Friendly Viking *bhnd frm 7th til f 11th* f
211 Apatura Hati 5a *mid-div, poor 4th whn p.u. last* pu
195 Hanukkah 5a *rear, p.u. 13th* pu
10 ran. 6l, 2½l, 2 fences. Time 6m 14.00s. SP 4-5.
Mrs J Alford (Eggesford).

298 - Restricted (12st)

199 **MONKTON (IRE) ....R White** 1
hld up,prog to jn ldrs 12th,cls up whn lft in ld 2 out,hldon
201 **Golden Drops (NZ).....................I Dowrick** 2
handy, cls 4th at 15th, ev ch whn lft 2nd 2 out,no ext,imprv
199 **Copper And Chrome (Ire) 5a ....D Stephens** 3
raced wd, cls up, 5th aft 17th, kpt on
196 Moorland Abbot *rear, 10th hlfwy, ran on steadily, nrst fin* 4
199 Lonesome Traveller (NZ) *(Jt fav) ld 1st, ld agn 9-15th, sn outpcd* 5
199 Holly Fare *bhnd frm hlfwy* 6
137 Roving Vagabond *rear whn f 11th* f
Miss Moony 5a *bhnd til p.u. 17th* pu
188 Deday *ld 2nd til 9th, lost plc 11th, 8th whn f 17th* f
Play Poker (Ire) *twrds rear whn f 4th* f
Pines Express (Ire) *(Jt fav) w.w. gd prog 14th, ld 17th, cls 2nd whn b.d. 2 out* bd
Romany Anne 5a *bhnd til p.u. 14th* pu
210 Plan-A (Ire) *prom, ld 14th, ran wd apr 3 out, came agn, ld & f 2 out* f
13 ran. 1½l, 6l, 4l, 10l, 2 fences. Time 6m 27.50s. SP 4-1.
A J Scrimgeour (Devon & Somerset Staghounds).

299 - Open Maiden Div I (12st)

145 **ERME ROSE (IRE) 5a ....R Nuttall 1**
(fav) in tch, ld 15th, qcknd clr 2 out, comf
70 **Gipsula 5a ....S Slade 2**
ld til 15th, ev ch til outpcd apr 2 out
201 **Treassowe Oats ....Mrs M Hand 3**
8th hlfwy, went 3rd 16th, kpt on
201 Springcombe 5a *alwys rear* 4
131 Reptile Princess 5a *t.o. hlfwy* 5
Blade Of Fortune *prog to 5th hlfwy, not rch ldrs, p.u. 16th* .... pu
65 Pharynx *6th hlfwy, no prog, p.u. 3 out* .... pu
202 Artistic Peace 5a *mstk 7th, t.o. whn p.u. 15th* .... pu
Minstrals Boyo *prom, 4th whn f 14th* .... f
201 Sixth In Line (Ire) *twrds rear til p.u. 16th* .... pu
195 Jay Em Ess (NZ) *hld up, gd prog to jnd ldrs 12th, wknd 15th, p.u. nxt* .... pu
202 Coed Canlas *bhnd til p.u. 16th* .... pu
69 Saint Joseph *cls 5th at 12th, p.u. 14th, quiet run* .... pu
13 ran. 10l, 6l, 2 fences, 2l. Time 6m 28.60s. SP 4-5.
Mrs B C Willcocks (Portman).

300 - Open Maiden Div II (12st)

202 **ROSA'S REVENGE 5a (bl) ....D Jones 1**
made most til hdd 14th, renewed effrt 2 out,ld last,drvn out
131 **Biddlestone Boy (NZ) ....I Dowrick 2**
(Jt fav) prom, cls 2nd 15th, drvn to slight ld 2 out, hdd last
201 **Dovedon Princess 5a................D Stephens 3**
in tch, went 3rd apr 2 out, not qckn
200 Eserie de Cores (USA) *hld up rear, 5th & clsng 3 out, not chal ldrs* 4
132 Karlimay 5a *prog 10th, ld 14th til wknd rpdly apr 2 out* 5
131 Far Run *(Jt fav) cls 2nd at 10th, wknd 12th, 8th whn p.u. 15th* .... pu
201 Zany Girl 5a (bl) *mid-div, 6th whn mstk 14th, p.u. 16th* .... pu
Kahlo 5a 3ow *mid-div, 7th whn p.u. 16th* .... pu
145 Seachest 5a *s.s. rear til p.u. 2 out* .... pu
202 Tinstreamer Johnny 7a *lost plc rpdly aft 5th, last whn p.u. 9th* .... pu
10 ran. 1l, 3l, 4l, 6l. Time 6m 33.00s. SP 14-1.
G W Johnson (Dartmoor).

301 - Open Maiden Div III (12st)

201 **BALDHU CHANCE ....J Young 1**
made most, lkd wnr whn lft clr 2 out, mstk last
206 **Electrofane (Ire) ....L Jefford 2**
alwys prom, disp 14th-nxt, 3rd & onepcd 17th, lft 2nd 2 out
131 **Kalokagathos ....S Slade 3**
handy, 4th at 16th, lft 3rd & hld whn hmpd 2 out
Lucky Call (NZ) 7a *bhnd til ran on steadily clsng stgs, do better* 4
202 Diana Moss (Ire) 5a *prom whn hit 11th (broke fence), no ch 14th* 5
200 My Prides Way 5a *mstk 5th, 6th hlfwy, nvr dang* 6
Scallykenning *nvr dang, bhnd whn p.u. 15th* .... pu
Crucis (Ire) 7a *blnd badly 7th, t.o. & p.u. 16th* .... pu
200 Moonbay Lady 5a 7ow *6th at 12th, p.u. 14th* .... pu
Its A Doddle 5a *nvr dang, t.o. & p.u. 13th* .... pu
201 Breeze-Bloc 5a *5th hlfwy, went 2nd & styng on 17th, 3l 2nd whn f 2 out* .... f
Happy Henry (Ire) *(fav) no show, bhnd til p.u. 2 out* .... pu
Better By Half (Ire) *mstk 4th, t.o. & p.u. 13th* .... pu
13 ran. 10l, 5l, 8l, 6l, 15l. Time 6m 39.80s. SP 4-1.
Terry Long (Fourburrow).
G.T.

SOUTH DURHAM
Great Stainton
Saturday March 2nd
GOOD TO SOFT

302 - Members

51 **TRIP YOUR TRIGGER (IRE) 7a ....Mrs S Grant 1**
j.w. mid-div, prog to ld 13th, jnd last, forged clr nr fin
80 **Buckwheat Lad (Ire) 7ex ....C Wilson 2D**
(fav) handy, ld 12th-nxt, disp last, hdd nr fin, fin 2nd, disq
Flying Lion 10ex ....W Askew 2
1st ride, cls up, ev ch 2 out, onepcd, fin 3rd, promoted
224 **Jamarsam (Ire)........................S Charlton 3**
cls up, wknd 11th, styd on onepcd aft, fin 4th, promoted
224 Caman 5a *cls up to 12th, wknd aft, poor 5th 2 out, fin 5th, promoted* 4
Slieve Na Bar (Ire) *rear, effrt 11th, no imp, poor 6th 2 out, fin 6th, promoted* 5
May Be Tomorrow *1st ride, rear, t.o. 10th, p.u. nxt* .... pu
7 ran. Sht-hd, 8l, ½l, 10l, 2l. Time 6m 45.00s. SP 4-1.
Chris Grant (South Durham).
Buckwheat Lad finished 2nd, Disq, not weigh-in. Original distances.

303 - Confined (12st)

122 **CASTLE TYRANT 5a ....P Atkinson 1**
ld til 16th, rallied apr last, styd on wll to ld flat
118 **Quayside Cottage (Ire) ....N Wilson 2**
(fav) hld up, prog 11th, ld 16th til jnd last, outpcd flat
72 **Celtic King 4ow.......................K Needham 3**
mid-div, prog 11th, ev ch 2 out, onepcd apr last
223 Fowling Piece *disp til wknd 15th, styd on onepcd aft* 4
117 Computer Pickings 5a *cls up, outpcd frm 2 out* 5
Tammy My Girl 5a *1st ride, handy to 11th, outpcd nxt, styd on onepcd* 6
170 Arden *alwys rear, t.o. 3 out* 7
Languedoc 3ow *alwys rear, p.u. 11th* .... pu
Cleasby Hill *mid-div whn u.r. 6th* .... ur
223 Constant Amusement 5a *handy, wknd 12th, p.u. 3 out* .... pu
223 Charlcot Storm 7a *ref 1st* .... ref
11 ran. ¾l, 9l, 4l, 3l, 3l, 20l. Time 6m 35.00s. SP 5-1.
S Clark (Bedale).

304 - Open

72 **MAHANA ....D Coates 1**
rear, prog 15th, styd on wll 2 out, 2l 2nd last, ld cls hm
226 **Hyperion Son...........................M Haigh 2**
made most, 4l clr 4 out, 2l clr last, wknd flat, hdd cls hm
226 **Clontoura (Ire).........................D Easterby 3**
alwys abt 3rd, styd on onepcd frm 2 out
120 Speakers Corner *cls up til outpcd 3 out, styd on onepcd* 4
226 Equinoctial *rear, chsd alng 11th, no imp, wknd 15th* 5
Band Sargeant (Ire) *mid-div til wknd 15th* 6
120 Jefferby *(fav) mid-div whn u.r. 6th, dead* .... ur
224 Broad Chare (v) *ref to start* .... ref
Skipping Gale *cls up to 5th, lost tch 10th, p.u. 15th* .... pu
Celtic Lane 5a *mid-div, wknd 2 out, p.u. last* .... pu
10 ran. Nk, 6l, 8l, 5l, 10l. Time 6m 39.00s. SP 3-1.
D J Coates (Pendle Forest & Craven).

305 - Ladies

117 **FINAL HOPE (IRE) ....Mrs F Needham 1**
(fav) hld up, prog 15th, disp 2 out, sn ld & clr, easily
117 **Pinewood Lad ....Mrs S Grant 2**
j.w. cls up, ld 7th til jnd 2 out, outpcd by wnr apr last
119 **Grey Realm 5a.................Miss J Eastwood 3**
mid-div, prog 15th, styd on wll aft 2 out, nrst fin
Choctaw *cls up, disp ld til outpcd 3 out, styd on onepcd* 4
Colonel Popski *alwys mid-div, nvr a fctr, p.u. last* .... pu
Linebacker *1st ride, prom to 10th, wknd aft, rear whn p.u. 16th* .... pu
Rare Fire *1st ride, t.o. 8th, p.u. 13th* .... pu
119 Barry Owen *prom, 3l 3rd whn blnd & u.r. 14th* .... ur
245 Vienna Woods *rear whn u.r. 14th* .... ur
225 Spartan Juliet 5a *alwys rear, t.o. 7th, p.u. 13th* .... pu
225 Sweet Rose 5a *slw jmp 1st, t.o. 8th, p.u. 12th* .... pu
11 ran. 8l, 3l, 3l. Time 6m 34.00s. SP Evens.
R Tate (Hurworth).

306 - Intermediate

123 **FERN LEADER (IRE)....................C Wilson** 1
mid-div, prog 12th, cls 3rd 15th, disp nxt, ld last, ran on
224 **Honest Expression 5a................P Atkinson** 2
mid-div, prog 10th, disp 15th, outpcd apr last
Durham Hornet...................Miss S Horner 3
ld 1st til jnd 15th, disp aft til wknd apr last
173 Ocean Rose 5a *mid-div, styd on well frm 2 out, one-pcd last* 4
77 Prior Conviction (Ire) *(fav) hld up, prog 10th, effrt 2 out, wknd apr last* 5
118 Jack Dwyer *in tch til outpcd 3 out, styd on onepcd*.... 6
Go Miletrian *cls up til wknd 10th, t.o. 3 out*........ 7
What A Miss 5a *cls up til wknd 10th, rear whn p.u. 14th*........ pu
223 Hazel Crest *mid-div to 12th, rear whn p.u. 16th*........ pu
304 Broad Chare (v) *ref to race (again)*........ ref
118 Some Flash *alwys rear, p.u. 16th*........ pu
75 Political Sam *alwys last, t.o. 11th, blnd & u.r. 15th*.... ur
12 ran. 2l, 4l, 2l, 3l, 3l, 10l. Time 6m 43.00s. SP 6-1.
W R Ward (South Durham).

307 - Open Maiden Div I

228 **SERGENT KAY........................W Burnell** 1
mid-div, prog 15th, smooth run to ld apr last, styd on well
73 **Priceless Sam 7a....................S Charlton** 2
rear, prog 10th, gd hdwy 2 out, ev ch last, no ext flat
228 **Woody Dare..........................N Wilson** 3
mid-div, prog 11th, ld 15th til wknd apr last, onepcd flat
174 Mr Dick *(fav) rear of ldrs, prog 10th, 2nd 15th, onepcd frm 2 out*........ 4
Triple Value 5a *prom, ev ch 2 out, no ext apr last, improve*........ 5
225 Goodwill Hill *cls up, outpcd 16th, onepcd frm 2 out*.... 6
229 Oaklands Fred *alwys mid-div*........ 7
87 Olympic Class *alwys mid-div*........ 8
Byland Princess 5a *1st ride, prom, wknd 15th, t.o. 2 out*........ 9
Hutcel Bell 7a *plld hrd, cls up til wknd 10th, t.o. 2 out* 10
80 Fethardonseafriend *mid-div, wknd 12th, t.o. 2 out*.... 11
121 Hoisthestandard 5a *rear whn f 11th*........ f
79 Barichste *alwys mid-div, wkng whn p.u. 2 out*........ pu
Political Skirmish 5a *rear, effrt 10th, mid-div whn blnd & u.r. 12th*........ ur
73 Red Star Queen 5a *rear whn saddle slppd & u.r. flat apr 2nd*........ ur
222 Muscoates 7a *jmpd stickily, t.o. 3rd, p.u. 6th*........ pu
Scarth Nick *mid-div to 10th, rear whn p.u. 16th*........ pu
17 ran. 1½l, 1l, 5l, 2l, 2l, 3l, 6l, 15l, 10l, 2l. Time 6m 46.00s. SP 10-1.
Mrs C A Coward (York & Ainsty South).

308 - Open Maiden Div II

225 **PRIMITIVE PENNY 7a................R Edwards** 1
mid-div,prog 10th,cruised to ld apr last,ran on well,imprssv
80 **Quite A Character 5a..................R Barker** 2
handy, ld 2 out til ran wd apr last, outpcd by wnr flat
229 **Flying Pan 5a..........................N Wilson** 3
mid-div, prog 15th, ld nxt, 5l clr 4 out, wknd 2 out, onepcd
Highland Friend *prom, outpcd 2 out, styd on onepcd aft*........ 4
52 Doc Spot *1st ride, mid-div, wknd 15th, t.o. 3 out*........ 5
73 Whispers Hill 7a *alwys rear, t.o. 15th*........ 6
223 Timber Topper *alwys rear, t.o. 15th*........ 7
Tudor Lord *plld hrd, ld 4th til wknd 14th, rear whn p.u. 3 out*........ pu
51 Hungry Jack *(fav) mid-div, wkng whn blnd 14th, p.u. 3 out*........ pu
123 Lord Jester *rear, gd prog 11th, wknd rpdly 14th, p.u. 16th*........ pu
52 Malakie (Ire) *rear, slw jmp 4th, p.u. nxt*........ pu
77 Chummy's Last 5a *rear whn bkd & u.r. 4th*........ ur
12 ran. 3l, 1½l, ½l, 25l, 4l, 10l. Time 6m 47.00s. SP 4-1.
M J Brown (Sinnington).
R.W.

SUFFOLK
Ampton
Saturday March 2nd
GOOD

309 - Members

102 **OLD DUNDALK (bl)......................N King** 1
ld til jmpd slw 4th,lft disp 13th,ld 17th,sn clr,pshd out
102 **Major Inquiry (USA)....................W Pewter** 2
w.w. lft 3rd 13th, chsd wnr appr last, kpt on wll
106 **Cool Apollo (NZ)..................G Plenderleith** 3
ld 5th-8th, lft disp ld 13th til 16th, wknd next
180 Emsee-H *(fav) w.w. 4th & rddn appr 17th, no rspnse*.. 4
Strontino *cls up til 8th, last whn f 12th, dead*........ f
10 Couture Quality *cls up, ld 11th, rddn clr 12th, blnd & u.r. nxt*........ ur
6 ran. 3l, 15l, 5l. Time 6m 40.00s. SP 2-1.
R Oliver Smith (Suffolk).
one fence omitted. 19 jumps

310 - Confined (12st)

DUNBOY CASTLE (IRE)...........Miss G Chown 1
ld 4th, made rest, blnd 17th, styd on strngly frm 2 out
93 **Mr Gossip............................W Wales** 2
w.w. prog 7th, chsd wnr 2 out, kpt on onpcd
102 **Mister Main Man (Ire)..............S Sporborg** 3
(fav) cls up going wll,chsd ldr 14th,outpcd 3 out,ran on agn flat
95 Dream Packet *wth ldrs, ev ch 17th, no ex und press frm 3 out*........ 4
102 El Bae *w.w. prog 12th, chal 3 out, wknd appr last*.... 5
102 As You Were *rr, in tch, kpt on frm 3 out, nvr trbld ldrs* 6
96 Druid's Lodge *in tch, rddn 15th, blnd nxt, kpt on onpcd aft*........ 7
178 Stanwick Farlap 5a *prom, disp ld 9th-11th, ev ch til wknd 3 out*........ 8
Galloway Raider *ld til f 3rd*........ f
96 Highland Laird *b.d. 3rd*........ bd
177 Jimstro *mid div, blnd 12th, lst tch 14th, t.o. whn s.u. appr 2 out*........ su
104 Melton Park 7ex *nvr going, last & j.s. 5th, t.o. & p.u. 16th*........ pu
102 The Grey Boreen *hmpd & u.r. 3rd*........ ur
13 ran. 3l, 1l, ½l, 4l, nk, nk, nk. Time 6m 42.00s. SP 8-1.
Mrs F Chown (Essex & Suffolk).

311 - Ladies

102 **ST GREGORY (bl)....................Mrs L Gibbon** 1
mstks, made virt all, rddn & qknd clr appr 3 out, drvn out
Larry The Lamb..................Miss G Chown 2
(fav) trkd ldrs, sltly outpcd appr 3 out, rlld & ch last, no ex
93 **Notary-Nowell....................Miss L Hollis** 3
wth wnr til rddn & outpcd appr 3 out, kpt on onepcd aft
Sarazar (USA) *alwys last, lst tch 16th, t.o.*........ 4
4 ran. 3l, 6l, dist. Time 6m 42.00s. SP 7-4.
A Howland Jackson (Essex & Suffolk).

312 - Land Rover Open (12st)

179 **COPPER THISTLE (IRE)................P Taiano** 1
(fav) made all, drw clr appr 2 out,rddn & styd on wll appr last
125 **Lucky Christopher......................G Tarry** 2
in tch,rdn to chal 3 out,unable to qkn,hld whn slw jmp last
Cockstown Lad 4ex..............D Featherstone 3
blnd 2 nd, cls up til 3rd & outpcd appr 17th, no dang aft
100 Saint Bene't (Ire) *cls up, rmdrs 13th, no ch frm 16th*... 4

104 Jimmy Mac Jimmy *chsd ldr til 12th, 4th & rddn 15th, no ch frm nxt* 5
124 Celtic Flame 7ex *bhnd & pshd alng 8th, lst tch 10th, no ch 15th* 6
6 ran. 5l, 12l, 3l, 15l, 15l. Time 6m 33.00s. SP 1-2.
M G Sheppard (Cambridgeshire).

313 - Restricted (12st)

60 **SAFFRON FLAME (IRE) . . . . P Taiano** 1
(fav) w.w. jnd ldrs 13th, 3rd & hit 17th, ld appr last, rddn out
242 **Miss Solitaire 5a . . . . G Tarry** 2
mstks, prog 12th, chsd wnr appr last, no impr flat
180 **General Picton . . . . P Harding-Jones** 3
chsd ldr 7th, rddn to ld appr 3 out, hdd appr last, wknd
105 Doctor Dick (Ire) *pllng, ld 7th til appr 3 out, wknd appr 2 out* 4
92 Give It A Bash (Ire) 5a *pllng, in tch blnd 14th, rddn & wknd appr 3 out* 5
106 Parkers Hills (Ire) *1st ride, disp ld to 4th, grad lst pl, t.o. frm 16th* 6
105 Whats Another 5a *chsd ldrs to 15th, wknd appr 3 out, p.u. last* . . . . pu
181 Trimage (Ire) *disp til ld 4th to 6th, wknd 14th, blnd & u.r. 16th* . . . . ur
177 Talk Sence (Ire) (bl) *alwys bhnd, j.s. 10th, t.o. & p.u. appr 3 out* . . . . pu
9 ran. 5l, 3l, 10l, 12l, dist. Time 6m 49.00s. SP 7-4.
Mrs M G Sheppard (Cambridgeshire).

314 - Open Maiden Div I (12st)

NO QUITTING (IRE) . . . . N Bloom 1
ld to 2nd & agn 5th, made rest, drw clr appr 2 out, easy
107 **Rebel Tom . . . . Miss L Hollis** 2
(fav) ld 3-4th, disp ld 16th til rddn & btn appr 2 out
108 **Kerry My Home . . . . P Harding-Jones** 3
mstks,rmndrs 2nd, jnd ldrs 12th, ev ch til wknd appr 3 out
108 Aughnacloy Rose *nt fluent, alwys bhnd, t.o.* 4
108 Superforce *disp ld 8th, blnd 10th, wknd qkly 13th, p.u. 16th* . . . . pu
Countessa 5a *prom to 5th, bhnd 9th, t.o. & p.u. 16th* . . pu
Clonoghill (Ire) *cls up, 4th & wkng whn u.r. 16th* . . . . ur
108 Le Vienna (Ire) *mid div, hit 6th, lst tch 10th, p.u. 14th* . . pu
Go Magic *alwys bhnd, t.o. & p.u. 14th* . . . . pu
Ticklebay 7a *alwys bhnd,t.o. & p.u. 15th* . . . . pu
10 ran. 15l, 6l, dist. Time 6m 48.00s. SP 5-1.
M Kemp (Suffolk).

315 - Open Maiden Div II (12st)

129 **OPUS WINWOOD (IRE) . . . . A Martin** 1
in tch, j.s. 8th, ld 12th, clr frm 17th, easy
107 **The Prior . . . . P Rowe** 2
disp ld 5th-7th, chsd wnr aft, btn appr 3 out
13 **Auchendolly (Ire) . . . . S Sporborg** 3
(fav) made most til blnd 11th, 4th & btn appr 17th, plodded on
107 Arkay *alwys bhnd,t.o. frm 10th* 4
107 Alapa *rushed into ld & r.o. 3rd* . . . . ro
Lavins Thatch 5a *f 3rd* . . . . f
108 Bruff Castle *prom, rmdrs 6th, disp 11th-nxt, blnd 14th,bhnd & p.u. last* . . . . pu
Gayton Wilds *mstks,rmdrs 2nd,prom 7th ev ch til wknd 17th,3rd & p.u.last* . . . . pu
92 Learned Master *n.j.w. bhnd til p.u. 14th* . . . . pu
108 Thereyougo 7a *alws bhnd, p.u. appr 3 out* . . . . pu
10 ran. 25l, 8l, dist. Time 6m 53.00s. SP 14-1.
Bryan Allen (Vale Of Aylesbury).
s.p.

TYNEDALE
Corbridge
Saturday March 2nd
GOOD TO SOFT

316 - Members

GENERAL DELIGHT . . . . D Wood 1
mid-div, prog 10th, 2nd 12th, ld nxt, lft clr 15th, styd on
85 **Upwell . . . . Miss J Morton** 2
alwys prom, lft 2nd 15th, styd on, not pace to chal
183 **Weddicar Lady 5a . . . . Mrs J Williamson** 3
disp 3rd, prom whn mstk 11th, styd on frm 2 out
Sally Smith 5a *bhnd til ran on frm 2 out, nvr nrr* 4
87 Niad *alwys bhnd* 5
Deise Crusader *prom early, bhnd frm 6th, nvr dang aft* 6
Crocket Lass 5a *bhnd frm 3rd, blnd & u.r. 8th* . . . . ur
Merry Nutkin *last til prog 5th, ld brfly nxt, btn 3rd whn u.r. last* . . . . ur
Piper O'Drummond *(fav) alwys prom, ld 9th, going well whn f 15th* . . . . f
Welton Ceilidh *mid-div whn blnd & u.r. 4th* . . . . ur
10 ran. 15l, 3l, 15l, 6l. Time 6m 26.00s. SP 11-2.
Mrs A R Wood (Tynedale).

317 - Confined

83 **HOWAYMAN . . . . A Parker** 1
(fav) prom, disp 9th, ld 14th, clr 2 out, wkng nr fin
83 **Master Mischief . . . . J Walton** 2
mid-div early, prog 9th, cls up 15th, styd on onepcd
110 **Astrac Trio (USA) . . . . Miss A Bowie** 3
disp 2nd, styd prom, ev ch 3 out, no ext apr last
187 Little Glen *4th frm 6th, chsd ldrs 15th, styd on* 4
The Mosses *hld up, prog 12th, outpcd frm 14th* 5
183 Fish Quay *sn last, some prog 13th, nvr nrr* 6
186 Paddy Hayton *alwys bhnd, schoolmaster* 7
Killula King *ld 1st til mstk 6th, prom whn blnd 3 out, sn btn* 8
Old Comrades *bhnd frm 8th, p.u. 12th* . . . . pu
187 Dancing Legend (Ire) *mid-div, clsd up hlfwy, chsng ldrs und pres whn f 2 out* . . . . f
Lyford Cay (Ire) *mstks, last at 3rd, lost tch 8th, wll bhnd whn f 14th* . . . . f
11 ran. 1½l, 1l, 4l, 1l. Time 6m 27.00s. SP 4-7.
Dennis Waggott (Dumfriesshire).

318 - 3m 5f Ladies

113 **READY STEADY . . . . Mrs K Hargreave** 1
j.w. made all, wkng nr fin
227 **Across The Lake . . . . Miss S Brotherton** 2
bhnd,prog 13th,3rd at 15th,ran on to 2nd flat,too mch to do
112 **Marshalstoneswood . . . . Miss A Bowie** 3
mid-div, prog 11th, prom frm 17th, no ext apr last
84 Sunnie Cruise 5a *cls 3rd frm 4th, styd prom, onepcd frm 3 out* 4
85 Steele Justice *(fav) alwys abt same plc, nvr nrr* 5
222 Katies Argument 5a *prom to 9th, lost plc 14th, nvr dang aft* 6
83 The Healy 5a 2ow *nvr a fctr* 7
113 Dawn Coyote (USA) (v) *prom early, lost plc & bhnd frm 14th* 8
Carousel Calypso *2nd early, lost plc, wll bhnd whn p.u. 2 out* . . . . pu
Furry Venture 5a *last early, nvr rchd ldrs, blnd & u.r. 16th* . . . . ur
10 ran. 3l, 2l, 4l, 4l, 3l. Time 7m 45.00s. SP 8-1.
Lady Temple (Percy-West).

319 - Restricted (12st)

188 **MASTER KIT (IRE) . . . . J Billinge** 1
alwys prom, cls 2nd 11th, ld 3 out, ran on well, improve
110 **Pantara Prince (Ire) . . . . T Scott** 2
trckd ldrs, prog 15th, rdn 2 out, 2nd at last, no ext flat
Little Wenlock . . . . P Craggs 3
bhnd, prog 10th, prom & ev ch 3 out, outpcd
114 Eastlands Hi-Light *mid-div, prog hlfwy, chsd ldrs 15th, onepcd* 4

Ensign Ewart (Ire) *alwys abt same plc* 5
188 Royal Surprise *nvr nr ldrs* 6
189 Kalajo *alwys mid-div* 7
Acropol 5a 2ow *bhnd, last at 9th, p.u. 12th* .... pu
194 Electric Arc (Fr) *ld 1st til f 14th* .... f
193 New Problem 5a 2ow *prom, cls up 15th, wknd & u.r. nxt* .... ur
Sarona Smith 5a 11ow *last at 5th, t.o. & p.u. 2 out* .... pu
116 Connor The Second *bhnd whn p.u. 6th* .... pu
77 Andretti's Heir 2ow *2nd at 3rd, sn lost plc, p.u. 9th* .... pu
Neville *nvr nr ldrs, no ch whn u.r. 2nd cct* .... ur
84 Houselope Beck *mid-div, no ch whn p.u. 2 out* .... pu
115 Drakewrath (Ire) *(fav) mid-div whn f 14th* .... f

16 ran. 9l, 4l, 6l, 10l. Time 6m 21.00s. SP 33-1.
J Billinge (Fife).

320 - 3m 5f Open (12st)

50 **BOW HANDY MAN** .... **T Scott** 1
disp frm 2nd, ld 13th, clr 15th, mstks 3 out & last, unchal
191 **Tartan Tornado** .... **P Johnson** 2
mid-div, lft 2nd at 18th, onepcd
190 **Beau Rose** .... **S Brisby** 3
mid-div, lft 3rd 18th, nvr nrr
110 Scottish Gold 7ex *cls up early, mstks 4th & 7th, u.r. 16th* .... ur
113 Jimmy River 7ex *cls up early, nvr going wll, p.u. 11th* pu
49 Political Issue 6ow *(fav) disp 2nd til outpcd frm 15th, wknd & p.u. 3 out* .... pu
89 Terracotta Warrior *sn last, t.o. & u.r. 12th* .... ur
191 Kilminfoyle *mstk 3rd, prom, disp ld whn f 18th (4 out)* f

8 ran. Dist, dist. Time 7m 53.00s. SP 10-1.
J L Gledson (Border).

321 - Maiden Div I

JAYANDOUBLEU (IRE) .... **T Scott** 1
ld 1st, styd prom, disp til ld apr last, qcknd clr
192 **Canister Castle** .... **R Shiels** 2
mstk 1st, rear til prog 15th, styd on und pres frm last
82 **Harden Glen 7a** .... **C Storey** 3
rear early, styd on onepcd, nvr nr ldrs
186 Staneshiel *mid-div, prog 10th, not rch ldrs* 4
Warkswoodman *ld 4th, disp & ev ch til wknd 2 out* ... 5
194 Woolaw Lass (USA) 5a *mid-div whn f 14th* .... f
189 Roly Prior *(fav) trckng ldrs whn f 7th* .... f
116 Prince Rossini (Ire) *cls up early, lost plc 6th, t.o. frm 10th, f 14th* .... f
192 General Jack *alwys mid-div, u.r. 15th* .... ur
115 Cukeira 5a *cls up whn f 6th* .... f
Barney Cross *nvr going wll, p.u. 5th* .... pu
Sharpe Exit *mstk 2nd, t.o. & p.u. 11th* .... pu

12 ran. 6l, 3l, 3l, 10l. Time 6m 38.00s. SP 4-1.
W A Crozier (Haydon).

322 - Maiden Div II

OVERSTEP .... **T Scott** 1
alwys prom, ld 7th, ran on wll frm 3 out
82 **Lounging 5a** .... **P Johnson** 2
prom, disp 8th, ev ch 2 out, outpcd apr last
123 **Wassl's Nanny (Ire) 5a** .... **A Parker** 3
cls 4th frm 8th, prom, strng chal 2 out, wknd last
Trumpet Hill *cls up frm 10th, chsd ldrs 3 out, no ext nxt* 4
194 Peelinick *(fav) mstks, nvr going wll* 5
88 Alianne 5a 5ow *mid-div, last at 10th, nvr a fctr aft* ... 6
192 Sweet Sergeant *ld 1st, styd prom til wknd 14th* 7
193 Witness Of Truth 5a *trckng ldrs whn f 4th* .... f
K Walk 5a *sn bhnd, t.o. & p.u. 8th* .... pu
Phoza Moya (Ire) 7a *last at 6th, t.o. & p.u.* .... pu

10 ran. 4l, 3l, 6l, dist, 2l, dist. Time 6m 40.00s. SP 5-2.
R Douglas (Lauderdale).

323 - Maiden Div III

186 **FISCAL POLICY** .... **H Trotter** 1
(fav) mid-div 6th, prog 4 out, strng run to ld flat, ran on
89 **Cool View 5a** .... **C Storey** 2
cls 4th early, 2nd frm 13th, und pres 2 out, ld last, hdd flat
Man Of Moreef .... **D Wood** 3
prom frm 6th, went 3rd at 8th, ld 10th til hdd & no ext last
87 Are-Oh *alwys prom, cls up & ev ch 2 out, onepcd* ... 4
114 Solwaysands *mstks, last frm 7th, bhnd aft* 5
The Raskins 5a *alwys bhnd* 6
88 Monynut 5a *last at 6th, p.u. 12th* .... pu
114 Lindon Run *ld 2nd til 13th, lost plc, f 3 out* .... f
Lauras Teeara (Ire) 5a *ref 1st* .... ref
Whatoupa *prom whn f 4th* .... f
53 Starlin Sam *prom early, jmpd lft thro'out, p.u. 12th* ... pu
Keirose 5a *ref 1st* .... ref

12 ran. 4l, 3l, 1l. Time 6m 36.00s. SP 7-4.
A R Trotter (Berwickshire).
D.G.

BURTON
Market Rasen Point-To-Point
Sunday March 3rd
GOOD

324 - Members

168 **WAYS AND MEANS 5a** .... **K Green** 1
(fav) trckd ldrs, hit 14th, ld 2 out, clr last, easily
The Big Wheel .... **S J Robinson** 2
trckd ldr, ld 3 out, tried to ref & hdd nxt, onepcd
Emerald Queen 5a .... **Miss J Wormall** 3
set seady pace to 15th, no ext
Seabright Saga *pllng, in tch, reluc & lost plc aft 13th, p.u. nxt* .... pu

4 ran. 5l, 2l. Time 6m 54.00s. SP 1-4.
Mrs S Mollett (Burton).

325 - Ladies

168 **LAYEDBACK JACK 7ex** .... **Mrs J Dawson** 1
(fav) chsd ldrs, went 2nd 14th, ld 2 out, sn clr
245 **Out The Door (Ire) 7ex** .... **Miss S Baxter** 2
disp ld 4th til ld 11th, clr nxt, hdd & hit 2 out, no ext
Fettle Up 7ex .... **Miss S Brotherton** 3
prog 12th, chsd ldr brfly apr 14th, onepcd aft
Duntime 7ex *jmpd rght, ld to 10th, prom til outpcd apr 14th* 4
Strong Views *chsd ldrs 6th-10th, wknd apr 14th* 5
Proverb Prince *chsd ldr to 3rd, last frm 7th, t.o.* 6

6 ran. 10l, 15l, sht-hd, 12l, 10l. Time 6m 31.00s. SP 2-5.
C D Dawson (Brocklesby).

326 - Open (12st)

170 **ELDER PRINCE** .... **P Gee** 1
(fav) alwys going well, prog 10th, ld apr 2 out, eased flat
168 **Carly Brrin** .... **N Kent** 2+
ld 4th til apr 14th, rdn & onepcd frm nxt
Iveagh Lad 7ex .... **N Tutty** 2+
alwys prom, ev ch & rdn 3 out, unable qckn
125 Mountshannon 7ex *prom, ld 14th-3 out, blnd nxt, no ext und pres* 4
169 Rain Mark *nvr nr ldrs, 6th & no ch apr 14th, t.o.* ... 5
Okeetee 5ex *prom to 9th, sn wknd, p.u. 14th* .... pu
169 Happy Breed *prom til wknd 10th, t.o. & p.u. 2 out* ... pu
72 Convincing *mid-div, mod 5th & rdn 13th, no prog, p.u. last* .... pu
Minstrel Paddy *wll bhnd 10th, p.u. 2 out* .... pu
117 Into The Trees *nvr on terms, p.u. 13th* .... pu
Croft Mill 7ex *n.j.w. sn wll bhnd, t.o. & p.u. 15th* ... pu
Bennan March *t.o. 6th, p.u. last* .... pu
Grey Hussar (NZ) *nvr trbld ldrs, bhnd whn blnd 12th, p.u. nxt* .... pu
Saxon Fair *rshd into ld til ran wd apr 4th, p.u. 5th, bridle broke* .... pu

14 ran. 5l, dd-ht, sht-hd, 1 fence. Time 6m 31.00s. SP 2-1.
Brian Gee (Grove & Rufford).

327 - Confined (12st)

244 **GALZIG** ....W Tellwright 1
chsd ldrs, 3rd & outpcd 14th, tk 2nd last, promoted
121 **Kellys Diamond**........................S Walker 2
prom 7th,disp 13th til outpcd nxt,wknd 3 out,fin 3rd,prmtd
Easby Roc (Ire)........................A Rebori 3
alwys mid-div, no ch frm 14th, fin 4th, pld 3rd
Phrose 7ex *prom, hit 4th, wknd 8th, bhnd frm 11th, fin 5th, pld 4th* 4
244 McCartney *alwys wll bhnd, t.o. whn blnd badly 14th, fin 6th* 5
237 Solitary Reaper *alwys rear, p.u. 14th* .... pu
Golden Clogs *disp til p.u. aft 5th, dead* .... pu
223 Breckenbrough Lad *u.r. 2nd* .... ur
Rexy Boy *alwys chsng grp, no ch whn ran out 4 out* .. ro
169 Zam Bee 3ex *(fav) j.w. disp 4th, ld 11th, drew clr frm 14th, fin 1st, disq* 0
169 Mediator 7ex *w.w. hit 4th, effrt 11th, no prog 13th, p.u. 4 out* .... pu
168 Mister Chippendale *nvr bttr than mid-div, no ch 13th, p.u. 2 out* .... pu
Hobnobber *ld to 10th, wknd apr 14th, p.u. last* .... pu
169 Drawn'N'quartered *f 2nd* .... f
Rise In Politics 5a *alwys bhnd, t.o. 7th, p.u. 13th* .... pu
15 ran. 15l, 8l, 15l, 30l, 15l. Time 6m 34.00s. SP 12-1.
Mrs D E H Turner (Belvoir).
Zam Bee finished 1st, disq for missing 3 out. 1 fence omitted,17 jumps

328 - Restricted Div I (12st)

121 **FLIP THE LID (IRE) 5a**...................N Tutty 1
(fav) in tch, rdn to chal 3 out, ld last, hld on well
121 **Clone (Ire)**.............................S Brisby 2
prom, ld 13th, rdn 2 out, hdd last, kpt on
169 **Tresillian Bay (v)** ....N Kent 3+
in tch til 3rd & outpcd apr 14th, no ch aft
172 **Granby Gap** ....M Chatterton 3+
disp to 2nd, grad lost plc, no ch apr 14th
Tweed Valley *rear & hit 8th, t.o. & p.u. 13th* .... pu
222 Earl Gray (bl) *disp 3rd, ld 7th, hdd 12th, wknd, no ch whn u.r. 3 out* .... ur
Shore Lane *lost tch 13th, t.o. & p.u. last* .... pu
176 Flaxton King (Ire) 7a *mstks, prog to mod 3rd & blnd 14th, p.u. 3 out* .... pu
171 Kilmakee 5a *disp to 6th, wknd 11th, t.o. & p.u. 2 out* ... pu
9 ran. Sht-hd, dist, dd-ht. Time 6m 35.00s. SP 4-5.
Peter Sawney (Cleveland).

329 - Restricted Div II (12st)

244 **RAMBLING LORD (IRE)** ....T Betteridge 1
in tch, jnd ldrs 4 out, ld apr last, styd on
Ruff Song................................N Jelly 2
chsd ldr 4th, ld 7th-3 out, rallied apr last, kpt on
Jasilu 5a (bl)............................S Swiers 3
w.w. steady prog to ld 2 out, rdn & hdd apr last, wknd
171 Ginger Pink (bl) *rear, some prog 11th, nvr nr ldrs* 4
175 Carly Clever Clogs (Ire) 5a *(Jt fav) w.w. prog & ev ch apr 14th, wknd nxt* 5
121 Young Moss *alwys rear, nvr nr ldrs, some late prog* .. 6
The Chap *alwys rear, no ch frm 12th* 7
242 Cornamona 5a *set mad gallop, hdd & blnd 7th, sn wknd, p.u. 11th* .... pu
172 Midge 5a *alwys bhnd, t.o. 11th, p.u. last* .... pu
Bare Fisted *alwys rear, t.o. 11th, p.u.last* .... pu
243 Ocean Sovereign *prom to 12th, t.o. & p.u. 2 out* ...... pu
176 Petriana 5a *alwys prom, 4th & ev ch whn f 2 out* ...... f
12 ran. 1l, 6l, 15l, 10l, 7l, 15l. Time 6m 43.00s. SP 8-1.
J Betteridge (Meynell & South Staffs).

330 - Open Maiden Div I

176 **SKYVAL 5a**...............................K Green 1
chsd ldrs, hit 10th, chal 3 out, ld apr last, rdn clr
228 **Basil Grey** ....P Jenkins 2
ld/disp til ld 3 out, hdd apr last, no ext
175 **Fortytwo Dee (Ire) 5a**...............Mrs K Bevan 3
prog to 4th whn blnd 12th, outpcd nxt, lft 3rd 3 out
242 The Last Joshua *sn wll bhnd, some late prog* 4
239 Charlotte's Oliver *chsd ldrs til 5th & wkng 13th, t.o.* 5
80 No Takers 5a *(fav) blnd 5th, ld/disp to 15th, 3rd & lkd btn whn f nxt* .... f
Raike It In 5a *in tch, blnd 8th, 6th & outpcd 13th, p.u. nxt* .... pu
7 ran. 10l, 20l, dist, 25l. Time 6m 48.00s. SP 5-2.
T Peace (Farndale).

331 - Open Maiden Div II Pt I

168 **BECKFORD** ....A Pickering 1
chsd ldr, ld 11th, hrd prssd whn lft wll clr 3 out, tired
174 **Mount Faber** ....M Sowersby 2
hld up in tch, outpcd apr 14th, lft 2nd 3 out, fin tired
228 **Greet The Greek** ....A Rebori 3
n.j.w. lost tch 13th, lft poor 3rd 3 out, kpt on
Tristiorum *ld to 10th, wknd apr 14th, p.u. 2 out* .... pu
Blue Rosette *(fav) prom 8th, 6th whn hit 12th, rdn & btn 14th, p.u. nxt* .... pu
117 Malvern Cantina *prom, jnd ldr 14th, f 3 out* .... f
The Bold Abbot *lost tch 12th, p.u. 15th* .... pu
238 Shakey Thyne (Ire) 5a *bhnd frm 8th, p.u. 14th* .... pu
172 Buzzards Grange *prom to 7th, wknd 10th, last & p.u. 12th* .... pu
9 ran. 7l, 12l. Time 6m 51.00s. SP 14-1.
P D F Strawson (Brocklesby).

332 - Open Maiden Div II Pt II

165 **TINA'S MISSILE** ....Miss C Burgess 1
chsd ldr, ld 8th, jnd & lft clr 3 out
225 **Roseberry Star 5a**...............Miss T Jackson 2
prog to 4th at 11th, sn outpcd, lft poor 2nd 3 out, tired
241 **Bucklelone 5a** ....J Docker 3
rear & rmndrs 6th, no ch 13th, t.o.
Sunnyfield Boy *cls up, 3rd & wkng whn blnd & u.r. 14th* .... ur
Man Of Fashion *t.d.e. ld to 7th, sn wknd, last whn blnd 12th, p.u. 14th* .... pu
175 Benbeath *(fav) trckd ldrs going wll, jnd wnr & f 3 out* f
Joint Account *mstks, sn t.o., p.u. 11th* .... pu
240 Derring Floss 5a *rear, blnd & u.r. 5th* .... ur
8 ran. Dist, 25l. Time 6m 54.00s. SP 10-1.
M M Allen (West Shropshire Drag).

333 - Open Maiden Div III

228 **LEPTON (IRE) 7a** ....S Swiers 1
(fav) conf rdn, steady prog to ld apr last, easily
Engaging ....Miss T Jackson 2
ld, clr apr 14th, hdd apr last, no ext
169 **Broadcaster** ....P Picton-Warlow 3
bhnd 6th, prog 11th, styd on, nvr nrr
Mrs Tweed 5a *8s-4s, cls up, ev ch apr 14th, wknd 3 out* 4
240 Rallye Stripe *chsd ldrs 7th-12th, grad wknd* 5
240 St Enton *alwys rear, t.o. 13th, jmpd slwly last* 6
240 Im Ok (Ire) 5a *chsd ldrs til wknd apr 14th, no ch whn u.r. 3 out* .... ur
241 Riverside Love 5a *alwys mid-div, lost tch 12th, p.u. 14th* .... pu
176 Albert's Adventure (Ire) (bl) *chsd ldr 4th til f 6th* .... f
174 Dante's Pride (Ire) *hmpd 6th, 4th & rdn 11th, sn wknd, p.u. 15th* .... pu
Father's Gift 5a *bhnd, blnd 5th & 10th, p.u. 13th* ...... pu
11 ran. 8l, 15l, 10l, dist, dist. Time 6m 49.00s. SP Evens.
M W Easterby (Middleton).
S.P.

FARMERS BLOODHOUNDS
Heythrop
Sunday March 3rd
GOOD

334 - Members

AUTONOMOUS..................A Charles-Jones 1
(fav) made all, drew clr aft last
239 **Gal-A-Dor ....L Brown** 2
prssd wnr, ev ch 2 out, wknd last
Tokanda *chsd ldrs til wknd 12th, t.o. & p.u. 2 out* ..... pu
Great Legend *last & sn bhnd, t.o. 9th, u.r. 14th* .... ur
Elegant Bertie *n.j.w. blnd 9th & lost tch, t.o. & p.u. 13th* .... pu
Devil's Sting (Ire) *chsd ldrs, 3rd & outpcd 12th, p.u. 2 out* .... pu
6 ran. 12l. Time 7m 19.00s. SP 8-11.
Mrs Kate Whitehead (Farmers Bloodhounds).

335 - Intermediate (12st)

155 **AFRICAN BRIDE (IRE) 5a..........Miss P Jones** 1
(fav) prom, ld 11th, prssd frm 14th, ran on well flat
138 **Arctic Chill (Ire) ....Miss S Vickery** 2
prom, chsd wnr 12th, chal 14th til no ext frm last
Chita's Cone 5a.....................R Treloggen 3
prom, trckd ldng pair 12th, btn 2 out, hit last, eased
Anurag *outpcd & sn wll bhnd, nvr nrr* 4
96 Jerrigo *chsd ldrs, 4th & outpcd 12th, wknd 3 out* 5
127 Hill Island *outpcd & alwys wll bhnd* 6
Star Actor 5ex *set fast pace til hdd 11th, wknd nxt, p.u. 14th* .... pu
128 Lord Macduff *in tch to 7th, sn wknd, p.u. 11th* .... pu
Fiddlers Knap *alwys last, t.o. & p.u. 14th* .... pu
9 ran. 7l, dist, 10l, 4l, 20l. Time 7m 0.00s. SP 2-1.
David Brace (Llangeinor).

336 - Ladies

126 **SPERRIN VIEW 5a ....Mrs K Sunderland** 1
(fav) w.w. in tch, jnd ldr 3 out, ld last, rdn out
124 **Daringly ....Miss J Johnson** 2
hld up in tch, ld 14th, sn prssd, hdd last, not qckn
245 **Grand Value ....Mrs S Coupe** 3
ld 5th-14th, outpcd 3 out
126 Icky's Five *ld to 5th, strgglng frm 14th, t.o.* 4
230 Branwell Bronte *bhnd frm 6th, t.o. & p.u. 13th* ..... pu
5 ran. 3l, dist, 25l. Time 7m 9.00s. SP 8-15.
Mrs Katie Sunderland (Bicester With Whaddon Chase).

337 - Open

142 **THE TARTAN SPARTAN ....K Hollowell** 1
in tch, prog 11th, ld 14th, hdd & lft clr last
124 **Welsh Singer..........................R Lawther** 2
not fluent, hld up bhnd, prog 14th, lft 2nd last, no ch wnr
232 **Bright Burns (bl).....................R Sweeting** 3
(fav) ld to 14th, 3rd & btn frm nxt
Strong Beau *prom til outpcd aft 12th, no imp ldrs aft* .. 4
January Don *in tch, rdn & strgglng hlfwy, t.o. 15th* 5
230 Shortcastle *cls up to 12th, sn outpcd, wll btn whn slw jmp 2 out* 6
124 Old Road (USA) (bl) *prom to 11th, t.o. 15th* 7
King's Treasure (USA) *tubed,w.w. prog 12th, jnd wnr 14th, ld going wll & u.r. last* .... ur
Father Fortune *bolted bef start, last frm 6th, t.o. & p.u. 10th* .... pu
22 Dukes Son *prom til lost plc 10th, wknd 14th, t.o. & p.u. last* .... pu
10 ran. 12l, 12l, 10l, 12l, 1l, 12l. Time 7m 7.00s. SP 16-1.
Mrs Delyth Batchelor (Bicester With Whaddon Chase).

338 - Monterey Restricted Div I (12st)

128 **LILY THE LARK 5a ....Miss H Irving** 1
(Co fav) prom, prssd ldr 3 out, drvn to ld flat
219 **Tenella's Last 5a ....R Morgan** 2
cls up, ld 14th til hdd & no ext flat
124 **Tapalong 5a..................................L Lay** 3
bhnd 9th, sn t.o., styd on to poor 3rd flat
232 Making Time 5a *(Co fav) prom, ld 9th-13th, wknd aft nxt, lost 3rd flat* 4
235 Waterhay *wll bhnd 9th, sn t.o.* 5
235 Mr Patrick (bl) *(Co fav) bhnd frm 9th, t.o. & p.u. 13th* .. pu
231 Juranstan (bl) *prom, mstk 10th, blnd 12th & wknd, ref 14th* .... ref
231 Endless Glee *mstk 4th, sn last & bhnd, t.o. & p.u. 12th* .... pu
Tarry Awhile *(Co fav) ld to 9th, ld 13th til hdd & f nxt* ... f
9 ran. 3l, dist, 6l, 20l. Time 7m 16.20s. SP 4-1.
Miss H M Irving (Grafton).

339 - Monterey Restricted Div II (12st)

GRECIAN LARK ....G Tarry 1
rear,prog 14th,mod 3rd 3 out,styd on wll to ld last,rdn out
29 **Ice House Street (NZ) ....A Balding** 2
cls up, chsd ldr 12th, ld aft 2 out, hdd & not qckn last
128 **Kingofnobles (Ire) ....R Lawther** 3
ld to 9th & 11th til aft 2 out, btn whn mstk last
233 Archies Oats *(Jt fav) hld up, effrt & prog 13th, no imp on ldrs 3 out* 4
105 Hill Fort (Ire) *chsd ldrs, rdn 11th, outpcd frm 15th, no ch aft* 5
King Of The Clouds *prom, ld 9-11th, wknd rpdly 13th* 6
Transplant Blue *alwys last, t.o. 13th* 7
The Hon Company *prom, mstk 9th, wkng whn mstk 13th, p.u. nxt* .... pu
149 Mrs Wumpkins (Ire) 7a *(Jt fav) w.w. mstk 6th, effrt 13th, btn whn blnd nxt & p.u.* .... pu
Happy Enough 5a *in tch til lost plc & p.u. 12th* .... pu
10 ran. 3l, 15l, 12l, 1l, 30l, 12l. Time 7m 16.50s. SP 9-2.
G B Tarry (Grafton).

340 - Maiden Div I (12st)

ROYAL EXHIBITION.......................M Frith 1
rear, rdn hlfwy, styd on frm 15th, ld flat, kpt on well
233 **Tranquil Lord (Ire).......................D Smith** 2
(fav) in tch,lost plc 10th,ran on 3 out,mstk last,ev ch flat,no ex
Miss Cresta 5a..........................S Morris 3
mstk 6th, trckd ldrs, prog to ld 2 out, hdd & wknd flat
240 Eighty Eight *prom, ld 11th-2 out, wknd last* 4
Gusher 1ow *mstks, in tch to 14th, 4th & btn nxt* 5
Matchlessly 1ow *ld to 6th & 10-11th, ev ch 2 out, wknd, walked in* 6
Yabbadabbadoo *prom, ld 6-10th, wknd aft nxt, p.u. 13th* .... pu
Never So Lost *in tch to hlfwy, p.u. 12th* .... pu
St Martin *blnd & lost plc 4th, rear & mstk 9th, p.u. 12th* .... pu
233 Country Brew 5a *trckd ldrs, blnd 13th, sn lost tch, p.u. last* .... pu
True Sparkle 5a *s.s. sn trckd ldrs, wknd 12th, p.u. 14th* .... pu
Rickham Bay 5a *t.o. til p.u. 4th* .... pu
12 ran. 1l, 3l, 8l, 15l, 8l. Time 7m 33.50s. SP 7-1.
Mrs Jayne Barton (Bicester With Whaddon Chase).

341 - Maiden Div II (12st)

WHAT CHANCE (IRE) 5a.......Mrs K Sunderland 1
alwys in tch, chsd ldr 3 out, mstk last, rdn to ld flat
233 **Canadian Boy (Ire).......................A Tutton** 2
prom, ld 9th, clr 3 out, hdd & no ext flat
Fountain Of Fire (Ire) 5a...............C Vigors 3
(fav) 8s-5/2, mid-div, effrt & prog 13th, chsd ldrs 3 out, no imp
233 Copper Pan 5a *prom til wknd 3 out* 4
Horcum *wll in tch til 4th & wkng whn f 3 out* .... f
Sonny's Song *nvr dang, t.o. & p.u. 14th* .... pu
236 Saxon Lass 5a *prom, chsd ldr 9th til wknd 15th, p.u. 2 out* .... pu
Ballycanal Boy *rear, lost tch hlfwy, t.o. & p.u. 14th* .... pu
Lochinvar Lord (bl) *prom to 7th, lost plc hlfwy, t.o. & p.u. 14th* .... pu
The Man From Clare (Ire) *ld to 9th, wkng whn blnd 12th, p.u. 14th* .... pu
2 Woodland Cutting *in tch to hlfwy, no ch aft 13th, t.o. & p.u. 2 out* .... pu
Glenisla 5a *t.o. last til p.u.9th* .... pu
236 Dolly Bloom 5a *mid-div, no ch 13th, p.u. 2 out* .... pu
13 ran. 3l, 15l, 12l. Time 7m 24.00s. SP 7-2.
Mrs Helen Mobley (Bicester With Whaddon Chase).

J.N.

NORTH NORFOLK
Higham
Sunday March 3rd
GOOD

342 - Members (12st)

PENDIL'S JOY ....**C Carman** 1
(fav) ld 4th, made rest, ran on flat
Behokie VI ....**Mrs P Hurn** 2
ld to 3rd, cls 2nd aft, ran on frm 2 out
On Target 7ex........................**Miss L Hollis** 3
cls 2nd til onepcd 15th, mstk last
Rings Of Jasmine 12ow *ref 1st* .... ref
4 ran. 3l, 10l. Time 7m 5.00s. SP 4-7.
C Carman (North Norfolk).

343 - Open Maiden Div I

240 **BEAT THE RAP** ....**G Morrison** 1
mid-div til prog 11th, ld 14th, made rest, kpt on
Just Maisy 5a ....**C Ward** 2
handy in mid-div, chal 2 out, no ext cls home
Alien Corn (Ire) ....**Miss S French** 3
alwys prom, no ext last
129 Bold Man (NZ) *(fav) ld 8th-14th, wknd & btn 3 out*..... 4
34 Sheer Hope (bl) *in rear, jnd main grp 11-13th, wknd 4 out*.......... 5
315 Alapa *mid-div, wknd 14th, p.u. 16th* .... pu
107 Northern Reef (Fr) 7a *in rear til f 13th* .... f
101 Mister Rainman *rear, mstks, p.u. 13th* .... pu
108 Ernie Fox *ld to 7th, ev ch whn ref 14th* .... f
Stanwick Belfry 5a *rear, sn t.o., p.u. 3 out* .... pu
View Point (Ire) *t.o. 4th, p.u. 15th* .... pu
11 ran. ¾l, 3l, 8l, 1l. Time 6m 27.00s. SP 33-1.
Mrs R J Morrison (Fernie).
Stewards' Enquiry, result stands.

344 - Open Maiden Div II

108 **SHAAB TURBO** ....**A Coe** 1
ld to 3rd,cls 2nd aft til ld agn 13th,made rest,just hld on
15 **Just A Madam (Ire) 5a** ....**Miss E Tomlinson** 2
cls 2nd til ld 3rd-13th, prssd wnr aft, ran on, just faild
Kelburne Lad (Ire)........................**P Bull** 3
mid-div, prog to 3rd at 11th, not qckn 15th, mstk 3 out
Lockhill (Ire) *sn bhnd, t.o. 15th* 4
Tharif *cls up til u.r. 6th* .... ur
103 Fragment (Ire) *prom, mstk 4th, sn bhnd, p.u. 11th, stewards* .... pu
Worthy Memories 5a *handy, cls up 7th, p.u. nxt, saddle slppd* .... pu
Bozo Bailey *in rear, no ch whn p.u. 11th* .... pu
30 Little Freddie *sn bhnd, t.o. 11th, p.u. 14th* .... pu
107 Andalucian Sun (Ire) *mid-div, prog 11th, chsng ldrs whn f 13th* .... f
61 Holding The Aces *(fav) handy, ev ch in 4th whn f 13th* f
Stanwick Lass 5a *sn bhnd, t.o. & p.u. 11th*.......... pu
12 ran. Hd, 15l, 1 fence. Time 6m 21.00s. SP 5-1.
D Heath (Essex Farmers & Union).

345 - Open

100 **FARINGO**........................**C Ward** 1
(fav) cls 2nd til ld 8-11th, ld agn 14th, pshd clr, ran on well
102 **Frank Rich** ....**T Bulgin** 2
alwys cls up, effrt 2 out, slw jmp last, sn btn
John O'Dee ....**I Marsh** 3
ld to 8th, ld agn 12-14th, wknd 2 out
3 ran. 5l, 5l. Time 6m 34.00s. SP 1-3.
Fred Farrow (West Norfolk).

346 - Intermediate (12st)

35 **ON THE BEER (IRE)** ....**S Sporborg** 1
cls up, ran on 3 ut, chal last, ld nr fin
178 **Timber's Boy 5ex**..............**P Harding-Jones** 2
trckd ldrs, ld 12th, prssd last, hrd rdn, hdd nr fin
94 **Linred 7ex**........................**P Hacking** 3
(fav) ld to 12th, rmnd prom til no ext 16th
36 Miss Construe 5a *cls up on outer, prog 14th, styd on onepcd 2 out* 4
93 Mend *cls up til wknd 15th, no ch nxt* 5
Smart Pal 5ex *handy to 11th, wknd 14th, t.o. 16th, p.u. 2 out* .... pu
6 ran. Hd, 10l, 6l, 2l. Time 6m 19.00s. SP 4-1.
H D Hill (Puckeridge).

347 - Ladies

57 **PARDON ME MUM** ....**Mrs E Coveney** 1
ld to 2nd, trckd ldrs, chal 2 out, ld last, ran on well
Kelly's Original..................**Miss K Tolhurst** 2
trckd ldrs, prog 3 out, chal last, no ext flat
Dromin Leader ....**Mrs L Gibbon** 3
prom to 7th, lost plc & bhnd nxt, kpt on frm 2 out
Just Precious 5a *ld 3rd til hdd & wknd rpdly 3 out* 4
250 Ashboro (Ire) *cls up in mid-div til not qckn 15th, kpt on onepcd*.......... 5
57 Profligate *mid-div, outpcd 11th, bhnd 15th* 6
Legal Beagle *f 2nd* .... f
180 Richard Hunt *(fav) hld up, u.r. 3rd* .... ur
103 Crazy Otto *mid-div, wkng 11th, p.u. 13th* .... pu
250 Little Nod *t.o. 4th, p.u. 3 out* .... pu
10 ran. 3l, 6l, ½l, ¾l, 20l. Time 6m 16.00s. SP 7-1.
Dr D B A Silk (Old Surrey & Burstow).
One fence omitted last two races. 17 jumps.

348 - Restricted (12st)

105 **LANTERN PIKE** ....**A Michael** 1
ld 3rd, made rest, ran on well last
Bitter Aloe ....**R Wakley** 2
prom, chsd wnr 14th, effrt 2 out, no ext last
35 **Wistino** ....**Miss L Rowe** 3
alwys prom, onepcd apr last
95 Salmon Mead (Ire) *mid-div, prog to 4th 14th, btn whn mstk 3 out* 4
34 Shake Five (Ire) 7a *(fav) sweating, rear, nvr going wll, nvr dang* 5
Inch Gale 5a *t.o. frm 6th* 6
True Measure 5a *pckd & u.r. 2nd* .... ur
105 Russian Vision *prom til b.d. 2nd* .... bd
35 Woodrow Call *sn rear, t.o. 12th, p.u. 15th* .... pu
Rolleston Blade *prom, hit 1st, f 2nd* .... f
Nursery Story *sn rear, bhnd whn p.u. 12th* .... pu
91 Golden Fellow (Ire) *cls up in 3rd/4th til f 13th* .... f
12 ran. 4l, 3l, 25l, 2l, dist. Time 6m 15.00s. SP 8-1.
A H L Michael (Quantock Staghounds).
S.B.

ROSS HARRIERS
Garnons
Sunday March 3rd
GOOD TO SOFT

349 - Members

LAYSTON D'OR ....**A Dalton** 1
(fav) 3rd til chsd ldr 13th, ld last, pshd out flat
215 **High Ham Blues** ....**D S Jones** 2
2nd til ld 11th, jnd 2 out, kpt on und pres whn hdd flat
214 Caviss 5a *ld to 10th, wknd, t.o. & u.r. 13th* .... ur
Catbrook Chance *cls up whn hit 12 & 13th, lost tch nxt, t.o. whn u.r. 2 out* .... ur
4 ran. 2½l. Time 6m 37.00s. SP 4-7.
J W Russell (Ross Harriers).

350 - Confined (12st)

214 **DI STEFANO 3ex**..................**Miss A Dare** 1
(fav) conf rdn, hld up til prog 9th, ld 3 out, drew clr last

214 **Homme D'Affaire ....T Stephenson** 2
trckd ldrs, effrt 14th, outpcd nxt, styd on frm last
212 **Better Future (Ire) 8ex.................T Edwards** 3
10l 4th at 9th, not qckn 13th, styd on onepcd frm 3 out
154 Geo Potheen *chsd ldrs, hit 7th & 15th, no ch frm 3 out, kpt on* 4
Stanford Boy *hld up til effrt to ld 14th, jnd 3 out, wknd frm nxt* 5
215 Gee Double You *ld/disp til ld 12th-nxt, sn outpcd* 6
Roscoe's Gemma 5a *alwys rear, lost tch 8th, t.o. & p.u. 2 out* .... pu
213 Spanish Rouge *trckd ldng pair to 11th, wknd 13th, t.o. & p.u. 2 out* .... pu
27 Glenmavis *ld/disp to 11th, wknd, t.o. & p.u. 2 out* .... pu
Generator Boy *mid-div til lost tch 11th, t.o. & p.u. 14th* .... pu
221 Saxon Smile *rear frm 4th, p.u. 12th* .... pu
11 ran. 8l, 4l, 20l, 2l, 10l. Time 6m 34.00s. SP 2-5.
Mike Gifford (Cotswold Vale Farmers).

351 - Open (12st)

160 **LOCHINGALL 4ex ....T Stephenson** 1
trckd ldrs, chal 14th, ld 3 out, sn drew clr
232 **Sandy Beau 4ex ....T Jones** 2
prom til lost plc apr 14th, styd on frm 3 out
153 **Doubting Donna 5a...................V Hughes** 3
prom til ld 14th-nxt, outpcd frm 3 out, lost 2nd flat
215 Nawrik (Ire) 7ex *ld to 3rd, ev ch til not qckn 14th, kpt on onepcd 3 out* 4
Sharinski *trckd ldrs, effrt to 3l 4th at 14th, no ext nxt* . . 5
216 Drumceva *ld 7th-12th, outpcd aft nxt* 6
153 Mummy's Song *10l 7th at 12th, lost tch frm 14th* 7
153 The Batchlor *f 1st* .... f
215 Loch Garanne 5a *ref to race* 0
215 Ask Frank 7ex *(fav) mid-div whn u.r. 3rd* .... ur
153 Sandbrook *lost tch 7th, t.o. & p.u. 14th* .... pu
162 Treaty Bridge *mid-div whn u.r. 9th* .... ur
215 Macaabee Special (Ire) *t.o. 7th, p.u. 10th* .... pu
Jack Sun *t.o. 3rd, m bhnd whn p.u. 15th* .... pu
14 ran. 10l, 1½l, 4l, 1l, dist, 10l. Time 6m 39.00s. SP 3-1.
Miss P Morris (Croome & West Warwickshire).

352 - 2½m Maiden (5-7yo) Div I Pt I (12st)

204 **HILLVIEW STAR (IRE) 5a ....G Barfoot-Saunt** 1
lost tch 7th, lft alone by many fallers
Capture The Magic (Ire) 5a *ref to race* 0
Countrywide Lad *ld 4th-7th, cls 3rd whn f 10th* .... f
Surrendell *ld to 3rd & frm 8th, 8l up whn f 3 out, dead* f
Shadowgraff 5a *6l 3rd at 11th, lft 2l 2nd 3 out, ld & f nxt* .... f
Always Dreaming 5a *chsng ldrs whn b.d. 2nd* .... bd
Winter Gem 5a *cls up whn f 2nd* .... f
May Runner 5a *12l 4th & wkng whn f 11th* .... f
Swift Monday *(fav) chsd ldr 11th,lft in ld nxt,hdd & lft clr 2 out,f last* .... f
9 ran. Time 5m 50.00s. SP 12-1.
M F Harding (Berkeley).

353 - 2½m Maiden (5-7yo) Div I Pt II (12st)

CELTIC BERRY 5a ....T Jackson 1
ld/disp til drew clr frm 3 out
218 **Derring Ruler ....S Jackson** 2
chsd ldng pair frm 7th, no ch wth wnr, tk 2nd cls home
Susies Melody (Ire) 7a..................J Tudor 3
taken steadily in rear, prog 9th, nrst fin
Irish Marie 5a *ld/disp til outpcd frm 3 out, wknd flat* . . . 4
Native Missile 5a 1ow *6l 4th at 5th, lost tch 9th, t.o. & p.u. last* .... pu
Wattasupriseforus *alwys rear, lost tch 9th, p.u. 3 out*. . pu
Brown Bala 5a *rear, t.o. whn f 7th* .... f
7 ran. 20l, 1½l, 4l. Time 5m 44.00s. SP 4-1.
J T Jackson (North Ledbury).
Open ditch omitted from this race onwards. 13 jumps this race.

354 - 2½m Maiden (5-7yo) Div II (12st)

220 **PERRYLINE 5a ....A Wintle** 1
w.w. prog 9th, chsd ldrs 3 out, rdn to ld cls home
143 **Toms Choice (Ire).................G Barfoot-Saunt** 2
(fav) ld to 3rd, jmpd to ld 3 out, hdd flat
143 **Wolfie Smith....................Julian Pritchard** 3
alwys prom, ev ch 3 out, kpt on frm nxt
220 Bel Lane 5a *hld up til prog frm 9th, ran on 3 out, nrst fin* 4
Tigeritsi 5a *mid-div whn mstk 8th, lost tch nxt, t.o.* . 5
Murcot Melody 5a *nvr rchd ldrs, lost tch 9th, t.o. nxt* . . 6
Tuscania 5a *cls 4th at 7th, ev ch 10th, wkng whn u.r. 3 out* .... ur
Oats For Notes 5a *5s-3s, cls 5th & ev ch whn b.d. 10th* .... bd
Playing The Fool 5a *went cls 3rd 8th, ld & blnd 3 out, sn hdd, p.u. last* .... pu
176 Lindalighter 5a *ld 4th til f 10th* .... f
213 So Easy 5a *rear frm 6th, p.u. aft 9th* .... pu
Scottishhighlander *cls 6th at 5th, lost tch frm 9th, p.u. 2 out* .... pu
Layston Pinzal 7a *rear whn s.u. bend aft 3rd* .... su
13 ran. 1l, 1l, 1l, dist, dist. Time 5m 38.00s. SP 6-1.
R Fellows (Ledbury).

355 - Intermediate (12st)

230 **GETAWAY BLAKE ....D Duggan** 1
ld/disp to 12th, 2l down last, rallied to ld nr fin
172 **Miss Pennal 5a ....M Jackson** 2
ld/disp, hit 4th, ld 15th, hdd nr fin
157 **My Pilot ....J Price** 3
chsd ldrs, cls 5th at 11th, ran on frm 3 out
157 Proud Drifter *alwys cls up, outpcd frm 3 out* 4
Boddington Hill 5a *lost tch 8th, t.o. 11th* 5
215 Proud Slave 5a *lost tch 5th, t.o. & p.u. 3 out*........ pu
215 Nether Gobions *(fav) n.j.w. trckd ldrs, ev ch whn hit 3 out, p.u. nxt* .... pu
Vatacan Bank *alwys rear, t.o. & p.u. 3 out* .... pu
Open Agenda (Ire) *prom whn f 8th* .... f
147 Sea Search *cls up til blnd 12th, wknd nxt, p.u. 2 out* . . pu
10 ran. 1l, 7l, 15l, dist. Time 6m 34.00s. SP 5-2.
Mrs C Mackness (Cotswold).
One extra fence omitted this race. 15 jumps.

356 - Ladies

216 **BANKHEAD (IRE) ....Miss C Spearing** 1
(fav) cls up, ld frm 13th, jnd 3 out, drew clr aft nxt
136 **Khattaf.........................Miss J Cumings** 2
went 5th at 7th, chsd ldrs 12th, chal 3 out, hld frm nxt
216 **Derring Bud ....Miss A Downes** 3
s.v.s. prog frm 13th, nrst fin
98 La Mezeray 5a *ld to 12th, not qckn frm nxt, wknd 2 out* 4
126 Run To Form *prom to 9th, outpcd frm 11th* 5
154 Mount Falcon *cls up to 11th, wknd frm 13th* 6
146 Robin Of Sherwood *rear frm 6th, t.o. 13th* 7
Magnus Pym *prom to 3rd, outpcd frm 6th, t.o. & p.u. aft 12th* .... pu
154 Travistown *rear & lost tch frm 4th, t.o. & p.u. aft 6th* . . . pu
216 Rectory Boy *in tch til wknd 8th, t.o. & p.u. 13th* .... pu
221 Grey Watch 5a *15l 7th at 10th, wknd 12th, p.u. nxt* .... pu
Forest Fountain (Ire) 7a *chsd ldrs to 8th, wknd frm 10th, p.u. aft 13th* .... pu
12 ran. 5l, 20l, 8l, 8l, 25l, 6l. Time 6m 28.00s. SP 4-6.
A J Brazier (Croome & West Warwickshire).

357 - Restricted Div I (12st)

138 **TINOTOPS ....Miss S Vickery** 1
(fav) cls 5th at 9th, ld 13th, drew clr frm 2 out
Frozen Pipe 5a ....L Squire 2
trckd ldrs, effrt 13th, ev ch nxt, wknd apr last
217 **Plundering Star (Ire).....................A Crow** 3
chsd ldrs, ld brfly 11th, not qckn frm nxt, kpt on one-pcd
218 Scarlet Berry 5a *ld aft 12th-nxt, ev ch til not qckn apr 3 out* 4
Gillie's Fountain 7a 1ow *in tch in rear til no prog frm 12th, kpt on steadily* 5

152 Bay Leader 5a *wll bhnd frm 6th, nvr nr ldrs* 6
Tudor Oaks 5a *prom to 8th, wknd 11th, t.o. 3 out* 7
The Fun Of It *nvr rchd ldrs, no ch 13th, p.u. 2 out* ..... pu
220 Joyney 5a *cls 2nd at 7th, wknd 12th, p.u. 3 out* .... pu
155 My Harvinski *mstks, prom at 9th, not qckn frm 12th, p.u. 2 out* .... pu
217 Welsh Clover 5a *made most to 12th, outpcd frm nxt, tired whn ref 2 out* .... ref
217 Barrafona (Ire) *mid-div til wknd 11th, t.o. & p.u. 3 out* .. pu
Hazel Park *prom to 9th, wkng whn f 13th* .... f
241 Musical Mail *prom to 10th, lost tch 12th, p.u. 3 out* .... pu
14 ran. 8l, 8l, 6l, 8l, 20l, 6l. Time 6m 38.00s. SP 7-4.
R H H Targett (Blackmore & Sparkford Vale).

358 - Restricted Div II (12st)

219 **JUDY LINE 5a..................S Shinton** 1
trckd ldrs, went cls 3rd 11th, lft 2nd 3 out, ld last,kpt on
128 **Wayward Sailor.................Miss C Spearing** 2
ld 7th til jnd 13th, lft in ld nxt, hdd 2 out, kpt on well
Major Bert (Ire).......................H Wheeler 3
alwys mid-div, lost tch wth ldrs frm 12th
236 Le Loubec 5a *prom to 7th, outpcd, kpt on onepcd frm 13th* 4
First Command (NZ) *in ldng grp, chal & ev ch 13th, wknd apr nxt* 5
155 Horn Player (USA) (bl) *chsd ldrs til not qckn aft 12th, no ch frm nxt* 6
R Lad *s.s. p.u. bef 3rd, lame* .... pu
204 Romano Hati 5a *t.o. whn f 7th* .... f
Bold Imp *jnd ldrs 11th, chal 13th, 2l up whn u.r. nxt* ... ur
Striking Chimes *rear frm 4th, t.o. & p.u. 10th* .... pu
Plas-Hendy *clsd on ldrs 7th, sn wknd, p.u. aft 12th* ... pu
156 Wolver's Pet (Ire) *(fav) trckg ldrs whn f 2nd* .... f
155 Willow Belle (Ire) 5a *ld to 6th, sn wknd, p.u. aft 12th* ... pu
Bix 7a *s.s. ld 3rd, ran off course 6th* .... ro
213 Sweet Petel 5a *chsd ldrs til no prog frm 12th, p.u. 2 out* .... pu
Furious Oats (Ire) 5a *mid-div, just in tch whn f 12th* ... f
Greenhill Lady 5a *mid-div til prog twrds ldrs whn f 12th* .... f
Deryn Y Cwm (Ire) *bhnd frm 3rd, t.o. & p.u. 12th* ...... pu
18 ran. ½l, dist, 1l, 10l, 5l. Time 6m 43.00s. SP 9-2.
K C Lewis (Gelligaer).
P.R.

DONCASTER
Monday March 4th
GOOD

359 - 2m 3f 110yds Hun

99 **TIPPING TIM 11.9 5a.................Mr M Rimell** 1
made most, hdd briefly when left with advantage again 2 out, styd on well.
Space Fair 11.9 5a.................Mr T McCarthy 2
trckd ldr, feeling pace and rdn after 4 out, left 2nd 2 out, kept on one pace.
257 **Al Hashimi 12.1 7a.....................Mr N Ridout** 3
trckd ldrs, lost ground quickly when pace qcknd after 5 out, no impn after.
226 Furry Knowe 12.1 7a *in tch, mstk and reminders 5th, struggling from hfwy, t.o.* 4
102 Easy Over (USA) 11.7 7a *chsd ldrs, mstk and lost pl quickly 7th, t.o. from hfwy* 5
48 Abitmorfun 11.7 7a *struggling to stay in tch hfwy, t.o. when blnd 3 out* 6
100 Sheer Jest 12.5 3a *(fav) patiently rdn, smooth hdwy on bit 4 out, nosing ahd when f 2 out* .... f
Falconbridge Bay 12.1 7a *struggling to stay in tch hfwy, t.o. when p.u. before 6 out* .... pu
113 Hedley Mill 11.10 7a *waited with, imp to go handy before 4 out, effort next, 3rd and one pace when badly hmpd by faller and u.r. 2 out* .... ur
81 Auntie Fay (Ire) 10.7 7a *t.o. when ref 6th* .... ref
10 ran. 2½l, dist, 5l, 14l, ¾l. Time 4m 57.00s. SP 6-1.
Mrs J Mould

WINDSOR
Monday March 4th
GOOD TO SOFT

360 - 3m Hun

142 **WHAT A HAND 12.2 5a..............Mr T Mitchell** 1
(fav) patiently rdn, hdwy 12th, ld 2 out, ran on well.
104 **Brown Windsor 12.2 5a (bl).........Mr B Pollock** 2
chsd ldr from 5th, ld 3 out, mstk and hdd next, no ext.
258 **No Joker (Ire) 11.7 7a..................Mr R Hall** 3
soon ld, blnd 5th, hdd, mstk and rider lost irons 3 out, one pace.
100 Gypsy King (Ire) 11.7 7a *held up bhnd ldrs, rdn 4 out, soon btn* 4
198 Bootscraper 11.9 5a *held up, hdwy 11th, wknd apr 4 out* 5
219 Old Steine 11.8 7a 1ow *held up, hdwy 9th, wknd next, t.o.* 6
Ullswater 12.0 7a *chsd ldrs 2nd to 5th, wknd 9th, t.o.* . 7
208 My Mellow Man 12.0 7a (bl) *blnd and u.r. 1st* .... ur
8 ran. 8l, 3l, 2½l, 9l, dist, 2½l. Time 6m 29.70s. SP 4-6.
Mrs L J Roberts

LEICESTER
Tuesday March 5th
GOOD TO SOFT

361 - 2½m 110yds Mdn Hun

210 **A WINDY CITIZEN (IRE) 11.9 7a ......Mr R Hicks** 1
waited with, prog 9th, blnd badly 4 out, chal and switched apr last, ld cl home, cleverly.
160 **Pamela's Lad 12.0 7a..............Mr G Hanmer** 2
held up, smooth prog to ld 3 out, rdn last, ct cl home.
Freddie Fox 12.0 7a.................Mr T Garton 3
mid div, prog to dispute ld 3 out, wknd next, blnd last.
207 Misty (NZ) 12.2 5a *bhnd, prog 11th, chsd ldrs and rdn 3 out, no further progress* 4
309 Couture Quality 12.0 7a (bl) *chsd ldr, ld 5th, soon clr, hdd apr 3 out, btn and blnd 2 out* 5
58 Familiar Friend 12.0 7a (bl) *rear, prog 6th, blnd 10th, disp ld 3 out, wknd quickly* 6
Great Uncle 12.0 7a *soon well bhnd, t.o. from 7th* 7
210 Pharrago (Ire) 12.0 7a *soon well bhnd, t.o. 5th* 8
235 Notanotherone (Ire) 12.0 7a *chsd ldr 7th, ev ch 4 out, wknd apr next, t.o. when p.u. last* .... pu
59 Brown Baby 11.11 5a *chsd ldrs till wknd 9th, t.o. when p.u. 2 out* .... pu
Candle Glow 11.9 7a *ld to 4th, weakening when blnd 9th, t.o. when p.u. 3 out* .... pu
137 Newstarsky 12.0 7a *f 1st* .... f
Haye Buster 12.0 7a *prom to 9th, rdn and wknd 11th, t.o. when p.u. last* .... pu
68 Elite Governor (Ire) 12.0 7a *(fav) chsd ldrs till u.r. 3rd* .... ur
241 Chacer's Imp 12.2 5a *prom till f 5th* .... f
15 ran. ¾l, 20l, hd, 15l, dist, dist, dist. Time 5m 32.20s. SP 9-2.
Mrs J A Thomson

362 - 2½m 110yds Hun

135 **FLAME O'FRENSI 10.12 7a......Miss J Cumings** 1
(Jt fav) chsd ldr, ld 4th to 7th and 10th to 11th, led again 3 out, kept on gamely und pres.
246 **Kambalda Rambler 11.3 7a.........Mr R Crosby** 2
prom, chsd ldr 6th, disp ld 8th to next, ld 4 out till apr next, no ext.
Hermes Harvest 11.12 7a..........Mr A Balding 3
(Jt fav) reminders 3rd, bhnd and pushed along 7th, blnd 11th, styd on from 3 out, not reach ldrs.
244 Antrim County 11.3 7a *in tch to 6th, t.o. from 4 out* 4
Fergal's Delight 11.3 7a (bl) *ld to 3rd, wknd 11th, t.o.* . 5

Some Obligation 11.5 5a *in tch, blnd 4th, 3rd and btn four out, t.o. when p.u. last.* .... pu
230 Rochester 11.3 7a *held up, chasing ldrs when blnd and u.r. 7th.* .... ur
208 Light The Wick 11.3 7a *reminders 3rd, soon bhnd, blnd 5th, t.o. when p.u. 8th.* .... pu
8 ran. 5l, 5l, dist, 25l. Time 5m 32.30s. SP 6-4.
P J Clarke

363 - 3m Hun

246 **RYDE AGAIN 11.2 5a........Mr B Pollock** 1
disp ld to 5th, ld 9th, made rest, clr 3 out, rdn and kept on apr last.
245 **Peajade 11.0 7a........Miss J Wormall** 2
disp ld till ld 6th to 8th, outpcd apr 3 out, regained 2nd and blnd last, one pace.
256 **Wild Illusion 11.8 7a........Mr Richard White** 3
(fav) hit 1st, trckd ldrs, went 2nd 4 out, rdn and btn apr 2 out.
3 ran. 8l, 15l. Time 6m 20.10s. SP 9-4.
Miss J E Hayward

364 - 2m 1f Hun

232 **HALHAM TARN (IRE) 11.3 7a ......Mr A Charles-Jones** 1
chsd clr ldr 2nd, ld apr 2 out, clear last, styd on well.
154 **Busman (Ire) 11.3 7a........Mr D S Jones** 2
chasing gp, prog 7th, chsd ldr 2 out, no impn run-in.
Micherado (Fr) 11.6 7a 3ow........Mr R Ford 3
(fav) taken down early, ld, soon well clr, blnd 2nd, hdd apr 2 out, wknd.
158 Saymore 11.3 7a *prom in chasing gp, rdn and effort apr 3 out, btn 2 out.* 4
Monaughty Man 11.7 7a *alwys rear, some prog 4 out, nvr nrr.* 5
Trust The Gypsy 12.3 5a *rear and pushed along 5th, n.d..* 6
219 Knowing 11.5 7a 7ow *alwys rear, nvr on terms.* 7
Radical Views 12.5 3a *chsd ldr to 2nd, prom in chasing gp till rdn 6th, no ch 4 out, t.o..* 8
209 Orujo (Ire) 11.5 5a *chasing gp, rdn and blnd 4 out, n.d..* 9
Royal Gleason 11.3 7a *prom in chasing gp till wknd 11th, t.o..* 10
207 I Is 11.3 7a *prom in chasing gp till rdn and wknd apr 4 out, t.o..* 11
100 Doc Lodge 10.12 7a (bl) *alwys rear, t.o. when p.u. 4 out.* .... pu
12 ran. 15l, 7l, 4l, 20l, 5l, 12l, 14l, 1l, 12l, 25l. Time 4m 30.80s. SP 33-1.
H J Manners

365 - 3m Mdn Hun

98 **HOWARYASUN (IRE) 11.12 7a (v) ...Mr D S Jones** 1
(fav) alwys going well, chsd ldr 9th, ld 2 out, clr and wandered last, rdn out.
178 **Woodhay Hill 11.12 7a........Mr R Wakley** 2
bhnd 10th, styd on well from 4 out, nvr nrr.
65 **Tangle Baron 12.0 5a........Mr M Felton** 3
held up, prog 12th, chsd ldr and rdn 2 out, btn last.
First Harvest 11.12 7a *mstks, ld 5th, clr 9th, hdd apr 2 out, wknd.* 4
197 Searcy 11.12 7a *in tch till reminders and lost pl apr 9th, rdn and btn approaching 4 out.* 5
231 Bilbo Baggins (Ire) 11.12 7a *disp ld to 4th, chsd ldr to 8th, wknd 12th.* 6
231 My Best Man 12.2 3a *mstks, bhnd and rdn along apr 9th, n.d..* 7
157 McMahon's River 11.7 7a *disp ld till mstk 4th, weakening and blnd 12th, t.o. when p.u. 2 out.* .... pu
242 Whinstone Mill 11.12 7a *in tch to 12th, well bhnd when p.u. 2 out.* .... pu
98 Drumard (Ire) 11.12 7a *waited with, in tch, outpcd 14th, btn and blnd 4 out, p.u. next.* .... pu
10 ran. 5l, 4l, 13l, 20l, 8l, 20l. Time 6m 27.90s. SP 6-5.
M R Watkins

BANGOR
Wednesday March 6th
GOOD TO SOFT

366 - 3m 110yds Hun

258 **SQUIRRELLSDAUGHTER 11.2 7a....Miss S Beddoes** 1
(fav) patiently rdn, hdwy going well when hit 6 out, ld between last 2, readily.
292 **Spurious 11.7 7a........Mr A Griffith** 2
disp ld, ld 9th, joined and hit 2 out, soon hdd, mstk last, one pace.
292 **Rinky Dinky Doo 11.7 7a........Mr C J B Barlow** 3
slight ld to 9th, struggling to hold pl 4 out, t.o. next.
256 Watchit Lad 11.7 7a *in tch, disp 3rd and staying on when f 7 out.* .... f
4 ran. 1¾l, dist. Time 6m 33.00s. SP 8-15.
J W Beddoes

CATTERICK
Wednesday March 6th
GOOD

367 - 3m 1f 110yds Hun

37 **WUDIMP 11.7 7a........Mr C Storey** 1
(fav) nvr far away, ld 16th, clr after 3 out, eased run-in.
102 **Carrigeen Lad 11.7 7a........Mr R Wakley** 2
mid div, effort after 16th, styd on to go 2nd at last, no impn on wnr.
188 **Admission (Ire) 11.7 7a ....Miss C Metcalfe** 3
mstk 2nd, soon in tch, driven along before 3 out, kept on.
226 Politico Pot 11.10 7a 3ow *in tch, hdwy after 12th, chsd ldrs from 16th, wknd after 2 out.* 4
259 Lisnavaragh 11.7 7a *bhnd, hdwy into midfield hfwy, wknd after 16th.* 5
226 Quixall Crossett 11.7 7a (bl) *in tch till outpcd after 11th, bhnd after.* 6
56 Cromwell Point 11.9 5a *bhnd, t.o. when p.u. before 3 out.* .... pu
113 Bowlands Way 11.7 7a (bl) *cl up, ld 8th, hdd 12th, left in ld 15th, hded next, 2nd and no impn when p.u. lame after 3 out.* .... pu
305 Barry Owen 11.7 7a *mstks, in tch, hdwy hfwy, slight ld 12th till f 15th.* .... f
329 Cornamona 11.2 7a *keen, soon ld, blnd 5th, p.u. before 8th.* .... pu
333 Im Ok (Ire) 11.2 7a *well bhnd when mstk and u.r. 10th.* .... ur
147 Final Cruise 11.4 5a *in tch, slightly hmpd 15th, bhnd when f 2 out.* .... f
12 ran. 2l, 1½l, 9l, 25l, nk. Time 6m 45.70s. SP 1-2.
C Storey

LINGFIELD
Wednesday March 6th
SOFT

368 - 3m Hun

212 **DIRECT 11.12 7a........Mr B Potts** 1
held up, mstk 11th, hdwy 4 out, ld apr last, driven out run-in.
Amazon Lily 11.7 7a ....Mr M Gorman 2
jmpd right, left in ld 2nd, ran wd bend after 9th, pkd 3 out, hdd apr last, not qckn.
261 **Goodshot Rich 11.12 7a (bl)........Mr E James** 3
chsd ldrs, ev ch 5 out, rdn and one pace after 2 out.
248 Highgate Mild 12.0 5a *trckd ldrs, went 3rd after 6 out, wknd after 5 out, t.o..* 4
Deep Isle 12.7 5a *held up, lost tch after 10th, t.o. 5 out.* 5
210 Binney Boy 12.0 5a *held up, lost tch after 11th, t.o. when p.u. before 2 out.* .... pu

Ballyandrew 11.12 7a *(fav) ld til blnd badly and u.r. 2nd*.......... ur
7 ran. 8l, 14l, dist, 15l. Time 6m 52.10s. SP 13-2.
J A C Edwards

TOWCESTER
Thursday March 7th
GOOD

369 - 3m 1f Hun

185 **TEAPLANTER 12.1 5a..........Mr B Pollock** 1
(fav) ld 5th, clr 13th, easily.
347 **Richard Hunt 11.13 7a..........Miss L Rowe** 2
mstk 1st, hdwy 12th, went poor 2nd apr last, ran on.
312 **Lucky Christopher 11.7 5a..........Mr G Tarry** 3
chsd wnr from 14th till wknd apr last.
234 Kites Hardwicke 11.5 7a *well bhnd from 12th, t.o.*..... 4
256 Shareef Star 11.5 7a (v) *started slowly, t.o. till f 2 out.* f
185 Blakes Orphan 11.9 7a (bl) *ld to 5th, wknd 13th, 4th when blnd 3 out, ref next*.......... ref
6 ran. 30l, 3l, dist. Time 6m 48.40s. SP 4-9.
R G Russell

WINCANTON
Thursday March 7th
GOOD TO FIRM

370 - 3m 1f 110yds Hun

COOME HILL (IRE) 12.0 7a..........Mr T Dennis 1
alwys prom, ld 16th, clr 4 out, unchal.
185 **Sonofagipsy 12.2 5a..........Mr P Henley** 2
prom, rdn 13th, lost pl 16th, went remote 2nd 2 out.
260 **Still In Business 12.2 5a..........Mr T Mitchell** 3
(fav) held up, mstk 2nd, hdwy 13th, ld next to 16th, wknd 4 out.
260 Dubit 12.0 7a *ld to 14th, 3rd when p.u. before 17th*.... pu
Ragtime Boy 11.9 5a *held up, lost pl 13th, rallied 16th, f next*.......... f
5 ran. 30l, 6l. Time 6m 45.50s. SP 9-2.
W W Dennis

AYR
Friday March 8th
GOOD TO FIRM

371 - 2m 5f 110yds Nov Hun

186 **PARLEBIZ 10.12 7a..........Mr A Robson** 1
bhnd, lost tch after 12th, hdwy after 2 out, styd on well und pres to ld final 30 yards.
243 **Reviller's Glory 11.10..........Mr S Swiers** 2
chsd ldrs, hdwy before 4 out, ld after 2 out, hdd final 30 yards, no ext.
193 **Eilid Anoir 11.8 5a 3ow..........Mr R Shiels** 3
chsd ldr, ld after 14th, hdd after 2 out, soon wknd.
Sound Profit 10.12 7a *mstks, lost tch from 11th, t.o.*... 4
110 Canny Chronicle 11.3 7a *ld, clr till hfwy, hdd after 14th, 2nd and weakening when f 4 out*.......... f
Henrymyson 11.3 7a *blnd and u.r. 3rd*.......... ur
Risky Dee 11.7 3a *(fav) blnd and u.r. 6th*.......... ur
193 Good Profit 11.3 7a *f 7th*.......... f
8 ran. 1½l, 11l, dist. Time 5m 43.70s. SP 4-1.
A J Wight

MARKET RASEN
Friday March 8th
GOOD

372 - 3m 1f Hun

257 **PERCY THROWER 12.7 5a..........Mr M Rimell** 1
(fav) ld, mstk 5 out, hdd 3 out, rallied to ld next, pushed clr apr last.
256 **Another Coral 11.12 7a..........Mr R Lawther** 2
going well, hdwy to ld 3 out, hdd and mstk next, soon btn.
290 **Catchapenny 12.5 7a (bl)..........Mr W Tellwright** 3
chsd ldrs, blnd 10th, driven and outpcd 3 out, soon no dngr.
345 Faringo 12.5 7a *in tch, reminders apr 12th, t.o. approaching 4 out*.......... 4
258 R N Commander 11.12 7a *trckd ldrs, jmpd slowly 7th, lost tch 13th, soon t.o.*.......... 5
289 Astre Radieux (Fr) 11.12 7a *bhnd, jmpd slowly 7th, t.o. from 10th, p.u. after 13th*.......... pu
6 ran. 16l, 1¼l, dist, 1½l. Time 6m 35.90s. SP 13-8.
Mrs Marilyn Scudamore

SANDOWN
Friday March 8th
GOOD

373 - 3m 110yds Hun

94 **OVER THE EDGE 11.11 7a..........Mr S Sporborg** 1
pressed ldr, ld 15th, narrow ld when left clr 18th, driven and held on well run-in.
183 **On The Other Hand 12.4 7a..........Capt A Ogden** 2
(fav) held up in 4th, hit 12th, hdwy four out, str chal apr last, ran on, just faild.
235 **Golden Mac 11.13 7a 2ow..........Mr R L Fanshawe** 3
in 3rd pl msot of way, hit 12th, effort apr 3 out, soon oiutp aced.
360 No Joker (Ire) 11.11 7a *made most till hdd and mstk 15th, challenging wnr when f 18th*.......... f
4 ran. ½l, 20l. Time 6m 43.40s. SP 11-4.
Christopher Sporborg

SANDOWN
Saturday March 9th
GOOD TO SOFT

374 - 2½m 110yds Hun

184 **THE MAJOR GENERAL 11.7 7a..........Capt A Ogden** 1
(fav) hdwy 9th, ld 11th, mstk next, clr 2 out, rdn out.
230 **True Steel 11.9 5a..........Mr J Trice-Rolph** 2
lost pl 8th, shaken up 14th, styd on well apr last.
346 **On The Beer (Ire) 11.7 7a..........Mr S Sporborg** 3
cl up, ld 10th till next, one pace from 3 out.
184 Hickelton Lad 11.7 7a *chsd ldr, ld 7th till next, wknd apr 2 out*.......... 4
362 Some Obligation 11.7 7a *ld, mstk 3rd, hdd 7th, led 8th till 10th, weakening when mistake 13th, p.u. before 3 out*.......... pu
5 ran. 1¼l, 2½l, 6l. Time 5m 35.70s. SP 15-8.
Robert Ogden

AVON VALE
Barbury Castle
Saturday March 9th
GOOD TO SOFT

375 - Maiden (5-7yo) (12st)

STALBRIDGE BILL..........Miss A Goschen 1
alwys prom, ld 4 out, pshd out flat
Pontabula..........E James 2
sttld mid-div, prog & ev ch last, not qckn
267 **Good Looking Guy..........A Charles-Jones** 3
alwys mid-div, onepcd frm 3 out
144 Is She Quick 5a *mid-div whn f 7th*.......... f
268 New Years Eve *nvr trbld ldrs, t.o. & p.u. 15th*.......... pu
Wired For Sound *ld to 13th, wknd rpdly, p.u. 4 out*.... pu
144 Wesshaun 5a *sn well bhnd, f 8th*.......... f
Favlient 5a *alwys prom, ld 13-15th, f nxt*.......... f
267 Seahawk Retriever *(fav) sttld rear, smooth prog whn f 12th*.......... f
Gamay *mid-div whn u.r. 3rd*.......... ur
Members Cruise *sn rear, f 9th*.......... f
Horton Country 5a *schoold, p.u. 14th*.......... pu
Jestastar 7a *rear whn u.r. 6th*.......... ur

Shelley's Dream 5a *rear whn f 1st* .... f
14 ran. 4l, 20l. Time 6m 42.00s. SP 20-1.
Mrs J Frankland (Blackmore & Sparkford Vale).

376 - Members

215 **ROAMING SHADOW** ....J Hankinson 1
(fav) ld 7th, pshd clr 3 out, ran on flat
Sandford Orcas ....P Bevins 2
sttld rear, prog to 2nd at 11th, hrd rdn flat, alwys hld
Merchant Mile *ld til 7th, wknd rpdly 11th, p.u. nxt* ..... pu
128 Gt Hayes Pommard *2nd whn u.r. 5th* .... ur
4 ran. 1½l. Time 6m 55.00s. SP 4-6.
J D Hankinson (Avon Vale).

377 - Open (12st)

198 **WOLF WINTER 7ex**.....................T Lacey 1
(fav) made all, alwys in command, easily
262 **Paper Days**...........................S Bush 2
j.w. alwys prssng wnr, no ext apr last
Hizal...........................A Charles-Jones 3
sn bhnd, nvr a fctr
19 Yahoo 7ex *sn rear, t.o. frm 11th* 4
Game Fair *prom early, sn wknd, p.u. 15th* .... pu
5 ran. 6l, dist, 15l. Time 6m 38.00s. SP 1-3.
Victor Dartnall (Dulverton West).

378 - Ladies

5 **SPACIAL (USA)**.......................Miss M Hill 1
lft in ld 5th, sn wll clr, unchal, canter
266 **Roving Report**....................Mrs A Rucker 2
nvr able to chal wnr, onepcd
208 **Unique New York**...................Miss S Offord 3
sn rear, t.o. 11th
Deep In Greek *sn wll bhnd, t.o. frm 11th*.............. 4
237 Billhead *in rear whn p.u. 8th*.................... pu
67 Butler John (Ire) *(fav) ld til blnd & u.r. 5th*........... ur
6 ran. Dist, 12l, 10l. Time 6m 33.00s. SP 11-4.
Richard J Hill (Wilton).

379 - Novice Riders Div I

214 **ALL WEATHER** ....M Wilesmith 1
sttld rear, rpd prog to ld 14th, jnd & lft clr last
137 **Amadeo (bl)**.........................Miss J Lewis 2
alwys prom, wknd frm 3 out, lft 2nd last
139 **Tekla (Fr)** ....Miss D Olding 3
made most to 11th, wknd nxt, t.o.
248 Royal Rupert *prom early, wknd & t.o. frm 14th* 4
264 Miss Corinthian 5a *sn rear, t.o. 11th, btn 2 fences* 5
Todds Hall (Ire) *sn wll bhnd, btn 2 fences* 6
271 Myverygoodfriend *prom, wkng whn u.r. 3 out* .... ur
Interpretation (NZ) *rear, prog frm 14th, chal & ev ch whn f last*.......................... f
Rare Flutter 5a *(fav) sttld rear, limited prog 10th, wknd & p.u. 15th*.......................... pu
9 ran. Dist, 15l, 5l, 1 fence, 10l. Time 6m 40.00s. SP 7-1.
M S Wilesmith (Ledbury).

380 - Confined (12st)

BANTEL BUCCANEER ....C Vigors 1
lft in ld 7th, ran on whn chal flat
Arnold's Choice ....Miss G Young 2
alwys prom, chal last, not qckn flat
264 **French Pleasure 5a** ....P Howse 3
(fav) prom, ch 14th, unable to qckn aft, onepcd
265 The Holy Golfer *prom til wknd frm 13th, onepcd*...... 4
263 Country Life (USA) *t.o. 2nd, btn 2 fences* 5
19 Afaltoun (bl) *ld til u.r. 7th*.......................... ur
See You There *mid-div til wknd rpdly 14th, p.u. 2 out*.. pu
Major Wayne *sn wll bhnd, p.u. 12th* .... pu
Trimbush *sn rear, p.u. 12th* .... pu
212 Bishops Truth *mid-div whn u.r. 2nd*.................. ur
Buckland Filleigh (Ire) 5a 7ex *mid-div whn f 2nd*...... f
11 ran. 1l, 25l, 2l, 2 fences. Time 6m 47.00s. SP 8-1.
R W Fidler (Vine & Craven).

381 - Novice Riders Div II

279 **PHAR TOO TOUCHY 5a**...........Miss R Francis 1
(fav) prom, lft in ld 13th, in cmmnd aft, easily
136 **Sohail (USA)** ....T Cox 2
sttld mid-div, prog 4 out, unable to chal
23 **Archie's Nephew (bl)**................Miss A Bush 3
alwys prom, ch 4 out, ran on onepcd aft
214 Master Donnington *prom, 3rd at 8th, sn wknd, t.o.*...... 4
141 Champagne Run *sn bhnd, nvr a fctr, t.o.* 5
Swing Free *mstk 2nd, sn rear, t.o. & p.u. last* .... pu
Mr Mayfair *nvr nr ldrs, t.o. & p.u. 12th*.............. pu
264 Kamtara *sn t.o., f last*........................... f
230 Bear's Flight *ld, going wll whn ran out 13th*........... ro
9 ran. 15l, 8l, dist, 1l. Time 6m 43.00s. SP 4-5.
Miss R A Francis (Dulverton West).
T.S.

BRECON
Llanfrynach
Saturday March 9th
GOOD TO SOFT

382 - Members (12st)

147 **MACKABEE (IRE)** ....T Weale 1
trckd ldrs, mstks 2nd & 15th, rdn to ld last, jnd fin
Spring Bavard 5a 3ex....................J Tudor 2
prom, ld 12th, rdn & hdd last, rallied, lkd to d/h
365 **McMahon's River 5a 3ex** ....P Hamer 3
(fav) in tch, chsd ldr 12th-2 out, hrd rdn & onepcd
219 Dane Rose 5a 3ex *ld to 12th, outpcd 4 out, btn whn mstk 2 out* 4
351 Loch Garanne 5a *reluc to race, sn in tch, cls up & going wll 14th, btn nxt*.......................... 5
Astley Jack *s.v.s. rcvrd to 2nd at 3rd, last by 8th, t.o. & p.u. 13th*.......................... pu
Jobingo *hld up rear, lost tch & not pshd 12th, t.o. & p.u. 2 out* .... pu
7 ran. Nk, 5l, 15l, 4l. Time 6m 41.00s. SP 4-1.
P B Williams (Brecon).

383 - Confined (12st)

153 **Lislary Lad 6ex** ....M Daly 1D
cls up,prog to ld & lft clr 13th,hld on wll apr last,disq
214 **THE RUM MARINER**....................J Jukes 1
(fav) prom,lft 2nd 13th,hrd rdn 3 out,kpt on,unable qckn last,prmoted
217 **Linantic**..........................Miss P Jones 2
prom,3rd & outpcd 14th,no imp ldng pair 3 out,fin 3rd,prmtd
Banker's Gossip ....S Shinton 3
mid-div,outpcd 13th,kpt on onepcd frm 3 out,no dang,fin 4th,prmtd
350 Geo Potheen *rear, prog to mid-div hlfwy, outpcd 13th, no prog aft*.......................... 5
214 Noisy Welcome *wll bhnd frm 9th, t.o. 15th, mod late prog* 6
263 Lonesome Step 5a *mid-div, pshd algn 11th, sn wknd, t.o. 15th* 7
Silks Domino *mstks, rear, lost tch 13th, sn t.o.* 8
356 Magnus Pym *prom til lost plc & u.r. 7th* .... ur
356 Rectory Boy *sn bhnd, t.o. & p.u. 10th* .... pu
98 Sword-Ash *in tch til p.u. aft 4th* .... pu
266 Fast Freeze 5ex *ld til hdd, stumbld & u.r. 13th* .... ur
157 No Panic *lft, t.o. & u.r. 1st* .... ur
13 ran. 1½l, 15l, 2½l, 10l, 10l, 15l, 4l. Time 6m 40.00s. SP 7-1.
T A Rogers (Radnor & West Hereford).
Lislary Lad subsequently disq, carried wrong weight.Original distances

384 - Open (12st)

40 **CARRICK LANES** ....T Jones 1
(fav) alwys prom, ld 15th, slw jmp last, drvn out flat
215 **Willie McGarr (USA)** ....P Hamer 2
hld up rear,gd prog 14th,chsd wnr nxt,unable to qckn last

146 **Judgeroger..............................G Lewis** 3
alwys prom, 3rd & rdn 15th, sn outpcd, no imp ldrs aft
Sun Of Chance *ld/disp 2nd-14th, sn outpcd, ran on agn flat, lkd 3rd* 4
98 Merino Waltz (USA) *prom, cls up 15th, sn outpcd, kpt on apr last*.......... 5
153 St Helens Boy *lft, sn rcvrd, cls up til aft 14th, sn btn* .. 6
215 Electrolyte *rear, lost tch 14th, mod late prog, nvr dang*.......... 7
Cornish Cossack (NZ) *wll in tch til outpcd aft 15th, no ch aft* 8
256 Kingfisher Bay *ld/disp 2nd-15th, sn wknd*.......... 9
351 Doubting Donna 5a *ld to 2nd, sn mid-div, wknd aft 14th*.......... 10
The Wooden Hut *chsd ldrs to 14th, wknd nxt*.......... 11
Enchanted Man *prom til f 7th*.......... f
The Last Mistress 5a *alwys last pair, t.o. 14th, p.u. 2 out*.......... pu
Martiya 5a *alwys rear, t.o. & p.u. last* .... pu
214 Troy Boy 7ex *hld up, alwys rear, lost tch 15th, p.u. 2 out*.......... pu
Swahili Run *alwys last pair, t.o. whn blnd 14th, p.u. 2 out*.......... pu
16 ran. 3l, 8l, hd, sht-hd, 15l, 7l, 8l, 1l, 3l, 15l. Time 6m 41.00s. SP 6-4.
David Brace (Llangeinor).

385 - Ladies

154 **HANDSOME HARVEY ....Miss P Jones** 1
(fav) made all at fast pace, shkn up & ran on wll 2 out, clvrly
154 **Workingforpeanuts (Ire) 5a ....Mrs D Smith** 2
sttld in tch,effrt 3 out,chsd wnr apr last,fin wll,alwys hld
356 **La Mezeray 5a ....Mrs J Hawkins** 3
alwys prom, chsd wnr 13th til apr last, onepcd
154 Lady Llanfair 5a *alwys prom, outpcd aft 13th, effrt 2 out, kpt on* 4
208 Prince Nepal *alwys prom, onepcd frm 3 out, fair effrt* 5
154 Dare Say *prom, wkng whn mstk 3 out, sn btn* 6
143 Mostyn 7a *prssd wnr to 10th, wknd rpdly nxt, t.o.*.......... 7
157 Lucky Ole Son *s.s. alwys t.o. & mls bhnd* 8
154 Black Russian *t.o. frm 5th, sn mls bhnd* 9
Dewliner *t.o. 4th, 2 fences bhnd whn p.u. 11th*.......... pu
154 Good Holidays 5a *p.u. 3rd, tack problems*.......... pu
Golden Fare *t.o. 4th, mls bhnd aft, p.u. last* .... pu
Touch 'N' Pass *rear whn u.r. 2nd* .... ur
356 Grey Watch 5a *mid-div whn u.r. 2nd*.......... ur
14 ran. ½l, 8l, 5l, 3l, 20l, 1 fence, 2 fences, 1 fence. Time 6m 28.00s. SP 2-5.
E L Harries (Pembrokeshire).
1 fence omitted this race last two circuits. 16 jumps.

386 - Monterey Restricted Div I Pt I (12st)

152 **CELTIC DAUGHTER 5a ....J Jukes** 1
mstks, outpcd in mid-div, ran on 14th, rdn to ld last,sn clr
Carlsan ....M P Jones 2
prom, chsd ldr 10th, lft clr nxt, hdd & no ext last
148 Telephone *chsd ldrs,lft 2nd 11th,no imp,btn 3rd whn eased & p.u. 2 out* .... pu
149 Pushlyn 5a *bhnd frm 6th, t.o. & p.u. 10th* .... pu
219 Caracol *(fav) not fluent, ld, 1l up whn ran off course aft 11th*.......... ro
Rio Cisto 5a *s.s. schoold & jmpd badly til p.u. 5th* .... pu
Abbey Venture (Ire) 5a *prssd ldr to 10th, wknd rpdly, p.u. aft 11th*.......... pu
351 Macaabee Special (Ire) *bhnd frm 5th, poor 6th whn f 10th*.......... f
Delightfilly 7a *sn wll bhnd, t.o. & p.u. 9th* .... pu
217 Imike *in tch to 6th, t.o. 8th, p.u. 15th* .... pu
10 ran. 5l. Time 6m 42.30s. SP 3-1.
Mrs E A Webber (Pembrokeshire).

387 - Monterey Restricted Div I Pt II (12st)

151 **ROYAL OATS 5a ....D S Jones** 1
prom, ld 10-13th, ld 15th, drvn & styd on wll frm 2 out
Polly Pringle 5a ....A Price 2
rear, prog 10th, effrt to chs wnr 2 out, no imp, fair effrt
269 **Just Marmalade..........................J Tudor** 3
(fav) trckd ldrs, mstk 11th, ld 13-15th, hrd rdn & no ext 2 out
156 Celtic Bizarre 5a *chsd ldrs, not qckn apr 15th, onepcd aft* 4
217 Squeeze Play (bl) *prom til rdn & wknd 13th, t.o. & p.u. 2 out*.......... pu
205 Great Precocity *alwys rear, t.o. 14th, p.u. 3 out*.......... pu
155 Equatime 5a *ld to 10th, wknd rpdly, t.o. & p.u. 2 out*... pu
357 Welsh Clover 5a *cls up to 11th, sn wknd, t.o. & p.u. 2 out*.......... pu
150 Toucher (Ire) *in tch to 7th, last at 11th, t.o. & p.u. 15th* pu
264 Reply 5a *sn rear, last whn p.u. 7th* .... pu
Creme Zahilla 5a *schoold, last to 11th, t.o. 14th, p.u. 2 out*.......... pu
11 ran. 2½l, 5l, 10l. Time 6m 39.00s. SP 14-1.
E Tudor Harries (Pembrokeshire).

388 - Monterey Restricted Div II (12st)

219 **PUSH ALONG ....D Stephens** 1
prom, ld 13th, kicked clr nxt, in no dang frm 2 out, unchal
220 **Right Rosy 5a.........................R Jenkins** 2
mid-div, effrt 14th, styd on well frm 2 out, no ch wth wnr
150 **Stormy Witness (Ire) 5a ....J Jukes** 3
in tch, chsd wnr 14th, 4l down 3 out, sn btn
Benuad *alwys prom, 3rd & outpcd aft 14th, no prog frm nxt* 4
219 Mac's Boy *(fav) w.w. out of tch, kpt on frm 14th, nvr any dang*.......... 5
156 Flaxridge *mid-div, pshd alng & no prog 12th, nvr on terms*.......... 6
Antarctic Call *hld up rear, wll bhnd hlfwy, nvr nrr* 7
210 Cossack Strike (Ire) *prom to 10th, mid-div by 13th, steadily wknd* 8
Mystery Belle 5a *sn mid-div, lost tch 13th, no ch aft, t.o.*.......... 9
358 Horn Player (USA) (bl) *mid-div, no ch frm 14th, t.o. & p.u. 2 out* .... pu
151 The Apprentice *ld to 13th, sn wknd, p.u. 3 out*.......... pu
155 Valiant Friend *alwys bhnd, t.o. & p.u. 14th* .... pu
357 Tudor Oaks 5a *nvr bynd mid-div, no ch 14th, p.u. 2 out*.......... pu
Shannon King (Ire) *prom, rdn & wknd 10th, p.u. 12th* .. pu
385 Grey Watch 5a *2nd outing, alwys rear grp, t.o. & p.u. 2 out*.......... pu
358 Wolver's Pet (Ire) *rear whn p.u. aft 4th* .... pu
A Farm Bar *in tch to 11th, bhnd whn p.u. 14th*.......... pu
152 Gatten's Brake *wll in rear til p.u. 7th*.......... pu
150 Kerstin's Choice 7a *alwys wll bhnd, t.o. & p.u. 12th* ... pu
Queen's Equa 5a *bhnd, blnd 6th, t.o. & p.u. 8th* .... pu
20 ran. 20l, 8l, 5l, 6l, 12l, 6l, 20l, 6l. Time 6m 42.50s. SP 14-1.
G T Goldsworthy (Tredegar).

389 - Maiden Div I

MYLORDMAYOR ....A W Price 1
1st ride, j.w. raced wd,prom 7th,ld 3 out,sn wll clr
355 **Boddington Hill 5a ....I Johnson** 2
in tch in rear, prog 15th, chsd wnr 2 out, no imp
205 **Itsstormingnorma 5a ....K Cousins** 3
mstks, alwys prom, effrt 15th, sn wknd, fin tired
Aldington Kid *ld 8-10th & 13th-3 out, wknd, fin tired*... 4
149 I'm A Bute 5a *u.r. bef start,lft in ld 6-8th,ld 10-13th,wknd 3 out,tired* 5
Maytown *not fluent, rear, lost tch 12th, t.o. & p.u. 2 out*.......... pu
Bowland Girl (Ire) 5a *(fav) ld 2nd, mstk nxt, jnd, bmpd & f 6th*.......... f
352 Capture The Magic (Ire) 5a *t.d.e. ld to 2nd, jnd ldr whn bmpd & f 6th*.......... f
Tiger Lord 7a *mstks 1st & 2nd, in tch to 14th, t.o. & p.u. last* .... pu

353 Brown Bala 5a *rmndrs 2nd, t.o. 8th, crawld 12th & p.u.* .... pu
Forest Rose 5a *last whn ref & u.r. 1st* .... ref
11 ran. 15l, 25l, 1l, 6l. Time 6m 59.00s. SP 12-1.
T G Price (Llandeilo Farmers).

390 - Maiden Div II

SHAWN CUDDY 7a .... S Shinton 1
w.w. in tch,hmpd 12th,prog 14th,ld 2 out,rdn & all out flat
207 **Sister Lark 5a (bl) .... V Hughes** 2
clr ldr til hdd 2 out, rallied & ev ch last, just hld
221 **Cruise Ann 5a .... Miss C Thomas** 3
chsd ldr to 15th, 3rd & wll btn aft
Ludermain 5a *in tch to 10th, wknd, p.u. 13th* .... pu
148 Never So High *rear main grp, lost tch 13th, t.o. & p.u. 3 out* .... pu
357 The Fun Of It *ref 1st* .... ref
Gold Tip 5a *last trio, t.o. 8th, p.u. 12th* .... pu
204 Lady Romance (Ire) 5a *trckd ldrs, 4th & in tch whn f 12th* .... f
148 Mister Jay Day *prom, disp 2nd aft 14th, btn 3 out, eased & p.u. nxt* .... pu
Ask For Plenty (Ire) *ref 1st, cont, ref 2nd, cont, ref 6th (twice), gave up* .... ref
Buckwyn *n.j.w. in tch in rear to 10th, wknd & p.u. 12th* .... pu
354 Scottishhighlander *last trio, t.o. 8th, p.u. 12th* .... pu
Lennie The Lion 7a *green, last trio, t.o. 8th, p.u. 12th* .... pu
13 ran. ½l, 20l. Time 6m 52.00s. SP 14-1.
R T Jones (Tredegar Farmers).
Charles Quaker (favourite) withdrawn not under orders,.

391 - Maiden Div III

WARREN BOY .... Miss P Jones 1
(fav) mstks, ld aft 1st, drew clr frm 15th, promising
255 **Final Option (Ire) .... I Johnson** 2
bhnd til prog 7th,went poor 3rd 13th,no imp,.lft 2nd flat
218 **Rosenthal 5a .... M P Jones** 3
chsd ldng quartet, no imp & no ch 14th, kpt on
150 Miss Montgomery (Ire) 7a *chsd ldng pair to 13th, wll btn frm 15th* 4
358 Bix 7a *t.d.e. plld hrd, 2nd whn f 5th* .... f
148 Icecapade (Bel) *ld to 2nd,chsd wnr,ev ch 14th,sn btn,tired 2nd whn p.u. flat* .... pu
Caerffili's Bay 5a *sn wll bhnd, t.o. 7th, last whn p.u. 12th* .... pu
156 Royal Bula *jmpd badly, alwys rear, 6th & no ch 11th, p.u. 15th* .... pu
Lady Medusa (Ire) 7a *schoold in last pair, going easily whn p.u. aft 11th* .... pu
Forest Poppy 7a *sn wll bhnd, t.o. 7th, last whn crawld 13th & u.r.* .... ur
Miss Clare 5a *nrly u.r. 6th, alwys bhnd, 7th & t.o. 11th, p.u. nxt* .... pu
11 ran. 1 fence, 5l, 2½l. Time 6m 47.00s. SP Evens.
F J Ayres (Tredegar).
J.N.

COTTESMORE
Garthorpe
Saturday March 9th
GOOD

392 - Members (12st)

92 **ODYSSEUS .... E Andrewes** 1
(fav) made all at steady pace, drew away 2 out, comf
239 **Rainbow Fantasia (Ire) .... P Millington** 2
2nd frm 7th, chal 3 out, outpcd nxt
244 **Lad Lane .... J Borradaile** 3
mostly 3rd, outpcd by 1st pair 4 out
179 Shipmate 15ex *last pair frm 7th, t.o. 12th* 4
246 Teacake (bl) *2nd til p.u. aft 5th, b.b.v.* .... pu
171 Mysterious Run (Ire) *alwys rear hlf, last & t.o. 12th, p.u. 4 out* .... pu
6 ran. 6l, 20l, 20l. Time 6m 44.00s. SP 11-4.
Miss E Inman (Cottesmore).

393 - Confined (12st)

VALTORUS (IRE) .... J Turcan 1
ld frm 6th, lft clr 2 out
171 **Aintree Oats 5a .... J Docker** 2
ld to 6th, 3rd & outpcd 4 out, lft 2nd 2 out
Traders Choice (v) .... C Millington 3
cls up 3rd til wknd 9th, last & outpcd frm 12th
246 Blue Beat 5a *alwys last, t.o. 7th, p.u. 12th* .... pu
244 The Difference *5th & outpcd frm 7th, 4th & running on whn f 2 out* .... f
244 Pakenham *(fav) rear hlf whn s.u. apr 5th, dead* .... su
242 Coolvawn Lady (Ire) 5a *3rd frm 9th, 2nd 4 out, ev ch whn f 2 out* .... f
7 ran. 9l, dist. Time 6m 34.00s. SP 8-1.
W J Turcan (Fernie).

394 - Ladies

GENERAL HIGHWAY .... Mrs J Dawson 1
(fav) w.w. on outer, 2nd 6 out, chal 3 out, ld nxt, comf
Cruising On 5a .... Miss E Guest 2
ld frm 3rd til 3 out, chsd wnr gamely, no imp
57 **Prince Metternich .... Miss S Phizacklea** 3
mid-div on innr til 4th & outpcd 6 out, lft remote 3rd 4 out
Singing Seal *last frm 7th, t.o. 9th* 4
Nowhiski *ld to 2nd, cls 2nd til wknd rpdly 12th, p.u. nxt* .... pu
57 Quenby Girl (Ire) 5a *mostly 3rd/4th, 3rd & outpcd whn f 4 out* .... f
6 ran. 8l, dist, 1 fence. Time 6m 25.00s. SP 1-4.
C D Dawson (Brocklesby).

395 - Land Rover Open (12st)

246 **RAISE AN ARGUMENT .... J Docker** 1
(fav) made all, drrew away frm 4 out, comf
Padrigal 5a .... A Sansome 2
mid-div, 4th & outpcd at 11th, ran on well last m
169 **Rehab Venture .... D Esden** 3
3rd frm 7th, 2nd frm 11th, outpcd 4 out
169 Trusty Friend *last trio frm 3rd, 5th & t.o. 10th* 4
244 Merlyns Choice 7ex *alwys last pair, t.o. frm 10th* 5
Dubalea *cls 2nd til mstk 10th, wknd rpdly, p.u. 6 out* .... pu
178 Zeniska (USA) 2ow *alwys last pair, t.o. last frm 7th, p.u. 4 out* .... pu
7 ran. 20l, 5l, 12l, 1l. Time 6m 39.00s. SP 7-4.
Mrs J H Docker (Atherstone).

396 - Restricted

243 **TENELORD .... S Morris** 1
(fav) 2nd to 5 out, renewed chal 2 out, best spd flat, wll rdn
292 **Monarrow (Ire) .... W Tellwright** 2
mostly 3rd for 2m, chsd ldr 4 out, chal 2 out, outpcd flat
243 **Ballyvoyle Bay 5a (bl) .... J Docker** 3
tried to make all, ran on gamely whn chal 2 out, just outpcd
329 Bare Fisted *nvr dang, 5th & outpcd frm 6 out* 4
242 Tel D'Or *alwys last, blnd 6th, t.o. 8th, p.u. 11th* .... pu
243 Cass *mostly 4th, mstk 11th, in tch whn f 5 out* .... f
Royal Quarry *6th 1st m, fddd, t.o. 10th, p.u. 12th* .... pu
Dilly's Last 5a *twrds rear whn u.r. 3rd (ditch)* .... ur
172 Kamadora *alwys rear hlf, outpcd in 6th whn f 5 out* .... f
9 ran. 2l, nk, 25l. Time 6m 37.00s. SP 9-4.
C R Saunders (Pytchley).

397 - Maiden (12st)

SMART RHYTHM 5a .... J Docker 1
alwys prom, ld 5 out-nxt, hld til rvl blnd last, ld nr fin

Needwood Neptune ....A Sansome 2
prog 10th, ld 4 out, clr whn blnd last, just ct
238 **Henry Darling.......................E Andrewes** 3
(fav) ld to 6 out, chsd ldr, in tch whn blnd 2 out, eased
Loose Wheels *cls up 2nd/3rd til fdd frm 10th*.......... 4
331 The Bold Abbot *cls up, disp 10th-6 out, wknd rpdly nxt*.. 5
241 Final Nod *alwys rear hlf, outpcd 6 out, p.u. 3 out* ...... pu
238 Barneys Gold (Ire) *cls up til f 5th* .... f
333 Dante's Pride (Ire) *cls up til fdd 10th, bhnd whn p.u. 4 out*.. pu
217 Forever Freddy *last & jmpd slwly til p.u. 12th* .... pu
9 ran. Nk, 20l, 20l, 5l. Time 6m 33.00s. SP 11-4.
R H Woodward (Atherstone).
K.B.

CUMBERLAND FARMERS
Dalston
Saturday March 9th
GOOD

398 - Members (12st)

188 **PENNINE VIEW ....Mrs J Williamson** 1
(fav) alwys prom, ld 6th & agn 3 out, wnt clr 2 out, unchal
Sir Harry Rinus ....S Sullivan 2
cls up frm 8th, styd prom, chsd ldr frm 3 out, styd on sm pc
322 **Trumpet Hill ....T Morrison** 3
alwys hndy, cls up 7th, ld 11th-16th, no ex frm 2 out
85 Another Dyer *ld 1st, styd prom frm 6th, mstks, outpcd frm 16th*.. 4
Oughterby Jack *al in rr*.. 5
189 Steady Away (Ire) *prom whn mstk 7th, rmndrs 9th, nvr sn wth chnc*.. 6
All Or Nothing 5a *bhnd frm 9th*............................. 7
116 Jack's Croft *cls up 7th, not go pc frm 12th* 8
112 Galadine *2nd early, stdd, chsd ldrs frm hlfwy, one-pcd*.. 9
Budweiser *nvr sn wth chnce*................................. 10
Barton Royal (Ire) *prom whn f 9th*.......................... f
188 Bullaford Fair *u.r. 1st* .... ur
Shabaahn *bhnd frm 8th, wl btn whn f 2 out* .... f
13 ran. 15l, 3l, 2l, 1l, 3l. Time 6m 25.00s. SP 5-2.
J J Dixon (Cumberland Farmers).

399 - Confined

187 **WORTHY SPARK.........................P Craggs** 1
(fav) ld 2nd, clr at 8th tl jnd at last, qcknd away on flat
191 **Royalist (Can) ....C Storey** 2
2nd frm 4th, strng chal to jn wnr last, no ex flat
112 **Farriers Favourite 5a...................A Parker** 3
hld up, imprv 10th, chsd wnr frm 3 out, ev ch 2 out,not qckn
110 Sharp Opinion *prom early, lost plc hlfwy, ran on agn 3 out, no dang*.. 4
194 Wang How *cls 3rd at 4th, prom tl outpcd frm 15th* 5
Boreen Owen *sn last, al t.o., f at last*..................... 6
Teatime Girl 5a *u.r. 4th*...................................... ur
If I Fancy 5a *bhnd frm 3rd, t.o. 11th, p.u. nxt* .... pu
319 Neville *cls 2nd early, lst plc 11th, wl btn whn p.u. 2 out*.. pu
9 ran. 8l, hd, 25l, 10l. Time 6m 18.00s. SP 7-4.
A J Balmer (Morpeth).

400 - Ladies

MINIBRIG 5a..........................Miss P Robson 1
bhnd 7th,hdwy 9th,clsd up app 2 out,strng brst flt,ld nr ln
112 **Parliament Hall ....Miss S Forster** 2
(fav) prom, ld 3rd & 8th, md rst tl cght cls hm
190 **Amber Payne 1ow ....Miss D Laidlaw** 3
prom, lft 2nd at 14th, ev ch 2 out, no ex frm last
May Run *bhnd hlfwy, improve 14th, nvr nrr*.............. 4
318 Ready Steady *w.w., hdwy 8th, wnd 2nd 13th, u.r. nxt*.. ur
Heavenly Hoofer *2nd early, mstk 5th, lost pl, t.o. 10th, p.u. 3 out*.. pu
189 Panto Lady 5a *last frm 2nd, blndrd & u.r. 15th* .... ur
48 Mandys Special 5a *ld 1st, prom tl mstk 4 out, nt rcvr, p.u. 16th*.. pu
Authenticity (Ire) 5a *p.u. 6th*................................ pu
Tannock Brook *bhnd 8th, t.o. 9th, p.u. 3 out*............ pu
10 ran. 1½l, 3l, 20l. Time 6m 19.00s. SP 8-1.
Mrs Jane Clark (Berwickshire).

401 - Open (John Peel)

MAN'S BEST FRIEND.........................R Ford 1
jmpd wl, ld 1st, prom frm 4th, lft ld 11th, md rst, easily
120 **Fast Study.........................S Pittendrigh** 2
mid-div early, last at 8th, cls 2nd frm 15th, outpcd
Music Minstrel (bl) ....L Morgan 3
last & undr pres 11th, t.o.
Generals Boy *(fav) hld up, trckng ldrs whn bdly hmprd & u.r. 11th*.. ur
72 Mr Snail *3rd frm 4th, wth ldrs whn u.r. 13th*............ ur
Hurricane Ryan (Ire) *ld 4th til f 11th*...................... f
6 ran. 6l, dist. Time 6m 24.00s. SP 2-1.
Mrs M Dickinson (Middleton).

402 - PPORA (12st)

110 **THE SHADE MATCHER.....................A Parker** 1
ld 1st, prom frm 8th,strng chal appr last,ran on to ld flat
158 **Real Class..................................J Evans** 2
(fav) j.w. alwys prom, ld 14th til hdd & no ext flat
189 **The Black Bishop (Ire)...........Miss P Williams** 3
mid-div early, imprv 11th, chsd ldrs frm 3 out, one pace
317 Fish Quay *bhnd tl hdwy 14th, styd on, nvr nrr*.......... 4
187 Reed *mid-div through't, n.d.*................................. 5
46 Hardihero *nvr btr thn mid-div* 6
110 Andrew *mid-div early, bhnd frm hlfwy* 7
49 Judicious Captain *alwys abt sm plc* 8
191 Trebonkers 9ow *cu. 6th, sn lst plc, t.o. frm 12th* 9
289 Arctic Paddy *trckd ldrs 6th, ld 8th-14th, still prom whn u.r. 3 out*.. ur
South Stack *sn bhnd, mstk 13th, p.u. nxt*................ pu
Duntree *prom early, t.o. frm 11th, p.u. nxt* .... pu
Beccy Brown 5a 7ow *n.j.w. alwys strggling, p.u. 14th* pu
13 ran. 3l, 8l, 1l, 10l, 12l. Time 6m 22.00s. SP 4-1.
Mrs Alix Stevenson (Dumfriesshire).

403 - Restricted Div I (12st)

ABERCROMBY COMET...........Miss S Forster 1
mstk 2nd, tk ld 6th, wnt clr 15th, unchal
302 **Buckwheat Lad (Ire).......................A Parker** 2
prom, trckd ldrs frm 12th, wnt 2nd at 17th, no ch wth wnr
188 **Blakes Folly (Ire) ....N Hargreave** 3
ld 2nd, styd prom tl mstk 10th, r.o. frm 2 out
319 Houselope Beck *4th frm 8th, outpcd frm 3 out* 4
111 Toaster Crumpet *(fav) mid-div early, impr 12th, one-pcd frm 14th* 5
Givower 3ow *al mid-div*.. 6
316 Weddicar Lady 5a *prom at 6th, nt go pc frm 14th* 7
Reskue Line 2ow *bhnd 11th, nvr sn wth ch* 8
321 Prince Rossini (Ire) 8ow *last at 6th, p.u. 11th* .... pu
188 Emu Park *disp 3rd, prom 8th-12th, lost plc & p.u. aft 3 out*.. pu
I'll Skin Them (Ire) 5a *bhnd at 6th, nvr fctr* .... pu
11 ran. 15l, nk, 20l. Time 6m 20.00s. SP 10-1.
Mrs S Forster (Jedforest).

404 - Restricted Div II (12st)

SAYIN NOWT 5a...........................A Parker 1
w.w. prog hlfwy,cls up 3 out,qcknd & ran on to ld nr fin
193 **Todcrag ....T Scott** 2
(fav) ld 4th, nt fuent, disp aft, ran on frm last, jst outpcd
319 **Eastlands Hi-Light......................T Morrison** 3

ld 2nd, dispute frm 4th & ev chnc last, outpcd nr fin
116 Bowlands Himself (Ire) *al bhnd* 4
Fruids Park 5a *4th at 6th, t.o. frm 11th* 5
323 The Raskins 5a *3rd at 4th, bd mstk 14th, p.u. nxt* .... pu
116 Miss Cullane (Ire) 5a *f 3rd* .... f
7 ran. 3l, 3l, 25l, dist. Time 6m 20.00s. SP 5-2.
Dennis Waggott (Dumfriesshire).

405 - 2½m Open Maiden (5-7yo) Div I (12st)

52 **BUCKLANDS COTTAGE 5a ....T Morrison** 1
disp 2nd, prom til ld 3 out, ran on und pres frm last
In Demand 7a ....P Craggs 2
cls up frm 11th, lkd dang apr last, no ext nr fin
192 **Called To Account 5a..........R Hale** 3
prom, chsd ldrs frm 15th, nt quckn frm 2 out
323 Cool View 5a *(fav) prom til outpcd frm 3 out* 4
Disrespect 5a *mid-div, hdwy frm 14th, nvr nrr, improve* 5
302 Slieve Na Bar (Ire) *nvr sn wth chnc* 6
Fiddlers Brae *last at 4th, styd on frm 2 out* 7
322 K Walk 5a *al bhnd* 8
Border Glory 7a *prom early, grad lost plc frm 12th, n.d.* 9
Mr Sharp *al in rr* 10
189 Peat Stack 3ow *ld 2nd, mstks, prom tl wknd rpdly appr 13th, p.u. & dismnt* .... pu
Bridgnorth Lass 5a *f 8th* .... f
194 Mapalak 5a *wl bhnd whn p.u. 10th* .... pu
194 Cogitate 5a *prom early, lost plce frm 10th, t.o. & p.u. 13th* .... pu
228 Lisband Lady (Ire) 5a *blndrd & u.r. 3rd* .... ur
Gold Code 7a 4ow *mid-div early, wl btn whn u.r. 13th* .... ur
16 ran. 1l, 12l, 3l. Time 5m 23.00s. SP 10-1.
J C Hogg (Buccleuch).

406 - 2½m Open Maiden (5-7yo) Div II (12st)

194 **FUNNY FEELINGS ....Miss D Laidlaw** 1
ld 3rd, und pres apr last, hld on gmly nr fin
Denim Blue ....A Parker 2
(fav) mid-div,hdwy hlfwy,chal frm 2 out,hrd rdn run-in, jst faild
307 **Olympic Class..........S Pittendrigh** 3
hdwy 8th, ev ch frm 3 out, nt pc of frst 2
Rustic Bridge *cls up 9th, styd prom tl wknd frm 2 out, improve* 4
194 Kings Token 5ow *bhnd early, sm hdwy 7th, nvr nrr* 5
192 Sky Missile 5a *bhnd, hdwy frm 12th, sm pc frm 13th* 6
193 Murder Moss (Ire) *prom early, sn mid-div, n.d.* 7
308 Lord Jester *sm hdwy frm rr at 12th, n.d.* 8
307 Political Skirmish 5a *cls 2nd at 3rd, mstk 7th, lost plc, t.o. & p.u. 2 out* .... pu
321 Barney Cross *last whn ref 3rd* .... ref
166 Piptony *cls up frm 5th til f 10th* .... f
Whatashot *rlctnt to line up, al bhnd, p.u. last* .... pu
12 ran. Nk, 4l, 8l. Time 5m 26.00s. SP 6-1.
Mrs J Scott (College Valley).

407 - 2½m Open Maiden (5-7yo) Div III (12st)

321 **CUKEIRA 5a..........T Morrison** 1
prom, wnt 2nd at 12th, tk ld 14th, ran on wl
114 **Pablowmore..........R Green** 2
mid-div, gd hdwy 10th, lft 2nd at 14th, no ex appr last
192 **Megans Mystery (Ire) 5ow..........J Walton** 3
(Jt fav) hdwy frm hlfwy, cls up 13th, no ext apr last
321 Roly Prior *(Jt fav) alwys prom, with ldrs tl outpcd frm 14th* 4
323 Lindon Run *clse 2nd early, grad wknd, no ch frm 13th* 5
322 Lounging 5a *t.o. 6th, sm hdwy 11th, nvr nr* 6
Allerbank 7a *mstk 4th, bhnd 6th, wnt 4th 12th, outpcd frm nxt* 7
308 Doc Spot *bhnd 6th, mid-div whn f 8th* .... f
192 Wolf's Den *ld 1st, rdn & disp 3 out, still there when f 2 out* .... f
Stanwick Fort 5a *f 3rd* .... f
Canny Curate (Ire) *mid-div whn b.d. 8th* .... bd
Gemma Law 5a 4ow *nvr sn wth ch, p.u. 11th* .... pu
322 Phoza Moya (Ire) 7a *mid-div early, lost plc, bhnd whn ref 9th* .... ref
13 ran. 8l, 3l, 6l. Time 5m 22.00s. SP 5-2.
R Paisley (Cumberland Farmers).
D.G.

DERWENT
Charm Park
Saturday March 9th
GOOD

408 - Members

176 **CADRILLON (FR)..........N Tutty** 1
(fav) in tch, ld frm 4 out, hld off chal run-in
305 **Vienna Woods ....S Swiers** 2
cls up, lft 2nd 4 out, chsd wnr, jst btn
G Derek..........P Holder 3
md-div, lft 3rd 3 out, n.d.
176 Lingcool 5a *prom, ld 12-15, in tch whn f 3 out* .... f
225 Politicians Prayer 5a *cls up whn u.r. 7th* .... ur
307 Hutcel Bell 7a *ld to 11th, hdd, fdng whn f 14th* .... f
Another Chant *alwys wl in rr, p.u. 3 out* .... pu
7 ran. ½l, dist. Time 6m 44.00s. SP 11-10.
Chester Bosomworth & A Lockwood (Derwent).

409 - Confined

223 **JUST CHARLIE ....D Easterby** 1
alwys prom, ld frm 3 out, styd on wl
326 **Saxon Fair..........M Sowersby** 2
(fav) ld 12th to 4 out, ht nxt, hld by wnr
306 **Durham Hornet..........Miss S Horner** 3
ld to 11th, in tch 3rd 3 out, no extr nxt
303 Castle Tyrant 5a *alwys prom, 4th 4 out, outpcd by ldr after* 4
Wolvercastle 5a *rr early, tk 5th 3 out, nvr fctr* 5
292 One For The Chief *alwys mid-div, styd on sm pc* 6
224 Polynth *mid-div, nvr dang, styd on one pc* 7
War Head *mid-div early, fdd, p.u. 11th* .... pu
306 What A Miss 5a *alwys wl in rr, p.u. 4 out* .... pu
Vale Of York *ht 3rd, cls up 4th-8th, fdd 12th, p.u. 4 out* .... pu
Chuckleberry *prom early, wknd hlfwy, p.u. 3 out* .... pu
11 ran. 5l, 10l, 2l, 2l, 1l, 4l. Time 6m 29.00s. SP 5-1.
Mrs Susan E Mason (Middleton).

410 - Open

226 **GOLDEN SAVANNAH..........M Sowersby** 1
ld 5-14th, disp 4 out to last, drvn out flat
326 **Convincing ....S Whitaker** 2
ld to 4th, trckd ldr, disp 4 out to last, jst btn
223 **Simply A Star (Ire)..........S Swiers** 3
(fav) rr early, prog 12th, 20l 3rd 2 out, too much to do
304 Mahana *mid-div, 3rd 4 out, styd on one-pcd* 4
304 Clontoura (Ire) *mid-div to 14th, prog nxt, styd on 2 out, nvr nrr* 5
226 Nishkina *rr early, prog 12th, n.d.* 6
367 Cromwell Point *mid-div, 9th at 8th, styd on sm pc* 7
326 Grey Hussar (NZ) *c.u. 4th-13th, no ext, one-pcd aftr* 8
Amy's Mystery *rr early, effrt 10th-13th, wknd aftr* 9
49 Peanuts Pet *mid-div, nvr fctr* 10
326 Into The Trees *alwys prom, 3rd at 13th, fdd rpdly* 11
326 Minstrel Paddy *cls up early, wknd hlfwy, onepcd aft* 12
226 Ringmore *in tch to 4 out, fdd rpdly, cmpltd own tm* 13
Elegant Guest *prom early, wknd 9th, p.u. 12th* .... pu
170 Clare Lad *f 2nd* .... f
326 Carly Brrin *cls up, 4th at 6th, rr whn p.u. 9th* .... pu
120 Tobin Bronze *alwys wl in rr, p.u. 14th* .... pu
17 ran. ½l, 3l, 10l, 3l, 1l, 2l, 2l, 1l, 2l, 2l. Time 6m 33.00s. SP 16-1.
A W Reynard (York & Ainstey).

411 - Restricted (12st)

229 **LAUNCHSELECT 7a....................R Edwards** 1
(fav) alwys prom, ld last, drvn out, styd on wl
224 **Latheron (Ire).........................S Swiers** 2
cls up, 2nd at 14th, chsd wnr to post, jst btn
77 **Missile Man ....Miss J Eastwood** 3
rr early, prog 10th, 5th 4 out, tk 3rd run-in
Ellerton Park *ld to 2 out, hdd appr last, no ex flat* 4
121 Chapel Island *bhnd early, 8th 11th, rn on lt, nvr nrr* 5
329 The Chap *prom early, outpcd 11th, p.u. 3 out* .... pu
223 Mr Elk *u.r. 2nd* .... ur
302 Caman 5a *rr early, p.u. 10th* .... pu
329 Midge 5a *mid-div, nvr fctr, p.u. 3 out* .... pu
Ingleby Wot *cls up 7th, fdd, p.u. 10th* .... pu
305 Spartan Juliet 5a *alwys wl in rr, t.o. & p.u. 10th* ...... pu
224 Glenbricken *mid-div, n.d., p.u. 4 out* .... pu
Cumberland Blues (Ire) *alwys prom, 2nd 13th, wknd rpdly, p.u. 4 out* .... pu
Vaigly Grey 5a *alwys rr, sme pace thro'out, p.u. 4 out* pu
328 Shore Lane *in tch to hlfwy, wknd 13th, p.u. 4 out* ..... pu
223 Greenmount Lad (Ire) *bhnd early, p.u. 8th* .... pu
228 City Buzz (Ire) *b.d. 2nd* .... bd
307 Sergent Kay *mid-div, prog 12th, 3rd 4 out, u.r. nxt* .... ur
238 Dear Jean 5a *alwys wl in rr, p.u. 4 out* .... pu
306 Honest Expression 5a *cls up, 4th at 8th, no ext 14th, p.u. nxt* .... pu
20 ran. ½l, 8l, 5l, 4l. Time 6m 30.00s. SP 9-4.
M J & C Brown (Sinnington).

412 - Ladies

227 **CAROLE'S DELIGHT 5a..............Mrs L Ward** 1
(fav) ld 13th, wknd, rnwd chal, disp last, drvn out
John Corbet....................Miss S Brotherton 2
alwys prom, disp last, styd on, jst btn
119 **Indie Rock.......................Mrs F Needham** 3
rr early, prog 12th, ld 14th-2 out, hdd, no ext
305 Pinewood Lad *in tch 14th, wknd, effrt 2 out, nvr nrr* ... 4
190 Rushing Burn 5a *in tch 13th, fdd, styd on onepcd* 5
227 Valiant Vicar *alwys rr, last whn u.r. 9th* .... ur
305 Grey Realm 5a *u.r. 1st* .... ur
7 ran. 1l, 3l, 4l, 15l. Time 6m 31.00s. SP 6-4.
C Holden (Cleveland).

413 - Open Maiden (5-6yo) Div I (12st)

307 **MR DICK...............................S Swiers** 1
prom, ld frm 13th, styd on wl, imprv
240 **Fair Ally...........................M Sowersby** 2
(fav) jmpd rght,cls up,25l clr wth ldr 4 out,hit 2 out,no ch aft
Sergeant Pepper ....S Whitaker 3
mid-div early, tk 3rd rn-in, nvr nrr
Tom The Tank *prom 12th, lost tch 14th, no extr aftr* ... 4
242 Lakeland Venture 5a *mid-div, 4th at 11th, styd on one-pcd* 5
Not The Nadger 7a *bhnd early, 7th at 14th, no ext, p.u. 4 out* .... pu
229 Blank Cheque *ld to 5th, rr & outpcd aftr, ref last*...... ref
307 Red Star Queen 5a *mid-div, 6th at 11th, outpcd aftr, p.u. 3 out* .... pu
175 Abbey Moss 7a *mid-div, 5th at 10th, wknd 14th, p.u. 3 out*................................... pu
Just Takethe Micky *rr early, ht 1st, prog 9th, fdd 13th, p.u. 4 out* .... pu
229 Winters Melody 5a *ld 6th-13th, hdd, u.r. 15th*........... ur
327 Rise In Politics 5a *in tch to 10th, fdd rpdly 12th, p.u. 3 out*................................... pu
12 ran. Dist, 2l, 4l, 5l. Time 6m 38.00s. SP 2-1.
Mrs J Cooper (Middleton).

414 - Open Maiden (5-6yo) Div II (12st)

123 **STRIDE TO GLORY (IRE) 7a...........R Edwards** 1
(fav) mid-div, 3rd frm 14th-last, styd on wl to line
51 **Boulevard Bay (Ire) 7a.................N Wilson** 2
ld 12th-last, hdd & outpcd run-in
Blackwoodscountry ....K Green 3
ld 6th-11th, hdd, trckd ldr, no ext, lost 2nd on flat
229 River Ramble 5a *mid-div, lft 4th 4 out, nvr nrr*......... 4
308 Malakie (Ire) *in tch to 12th, wknd 4 out, cmpltd own tm* 5
Rich Asset (Ire) *ld to 3rd, lst tch 12th p.u. 4 out* .... pu
308 Whispers Hill 7a *cls up, 4th at 14th, ht wing 3 out*..... f
332 Joint Account *slw strt, prog, 6th at 10th, u.r. nxt*........ ur
King Fly *alwys wl in rr, p.u. 4 out* .... pu
307 Muscoates 7a *2nd whn r.o. 5th* .... ro
Profiler (Ire) 7a *ld 4-5th, 2nd at 8th, wknd 14th, p.u. 4 out*.. pu
11 ran. 2l, 3l, 10l, dist. Time 6m 49.00s. SP 4-7.
M J & C Brown (Sinnington).

415 - Open Maiden (7yo+) Div I (12st)

123 **ANOTHER HOOLIGAN...........Mrs F Needham** 1
rr early, prog 12th, disp last, styd on wl
Neladar 5a ....J Sinnott 2
al prom, ld 13th to 2 out, disp last, jst btn
330 **Basil Grey ....P Jenkins** 3
ld to 4th, hdd, 3rd 2 out, outpcd aftr
79 Henceyem (Ire) *mid-div, prog 11th, 4th 2 out, no extr*.. 4
308 Quite A Character 5a *in tch, mstks 8th & 11th, styd on same pace aft*................................. 5
333 Engaging *prom to hlfwy, wknd 12th, one pcd 4 out*.... 6
302 Jamarsam (Ire) *mid-div, wknd 10th, nvr fctr* 7
Sweet Wyn 5a *alws wl in rr, p.u. 11th* .... pu
330 No Takers 5a *bhnd early, errors, n.d., p.u. 4 out*....... pu
225 Ingleby Flyer 5a *cls up, early, fdng whn b.d. 4 out* ..... bd
Master Crozina *(fav) ld 5-12, hdd, f 4 out, lkd btn* ..... f
122 Yornoangel *cls up, 2nd 3 out, r.o. nxt* .... ro
Prickly Trout 5a *alws wl bhnd, mstk 12th, p.u. 4 out*.... pu
13 ran. 3l, 20l, 4l, 2l, 5l, 12l. Time 6m 37.00s. SP 6-1.
R Tate (Hurworth).

416 - Open Maiden (7yo+) Div II (12st)

307 **GOODWILL HILL..........................D Coates** 1
in tch, ld frm 3 out, hld off chal flat
307 **Hoistthestandard 5a...................Mrs S Grant** 2
al prom, tk 2nd bfr last, styd on, jst btn
229 **Morcat 5a.............................C Mulhall** 3
cls up, 2nd at 14th, 3rd appr last, outpcd aftr
Jack Little *rr early, prog 10th, mstk 4 out, styd on 2 out*...................................... 4
224 Prophet's Choice *al mid-div, 6th at 14th, nvr fctr* 5
Shildon (Ire) *ld 3rd-3 out, hdd, fdd rpdly aftr*........... 6
223 Country Chalice *prom early, wkn 13th, outpcd frm 4 out*....................................... 7
307 Triple Value 5a *alwys rr, n.d., p.u. 3 out* .... pu
118 Need A Ladder *mid-div, one pcd, p.u. 4 out*............ pu
Ninefiveo 5a *al wl bhnd, p.u. 11th* .... pu
228 Living On The Edge (Ire) *f 2nd* .... f
Pearl Bridge *cls up, 4th at 8th, mid-div whn u.r. 12th*.. ur
229 Attle *(fav) mid-div, prog 10th, u.r. nxt* .... ur
13 ran. 1l, 10l, 5l, 5l, 10l, 4l. Time 6m 51.00s. SP 10-1.
Mrs S J Gospel (Farndale).
A.C.

ESSEX
High Easter
Saturday March 9th
SOFT

417 - Members

312 **JIMMY MAC JIMMY................S R Andrews** 1
disp ld til lft clr 9th, lft solo 12th
344 Fragment (Ire) (bl) *disp til blnd bdly & u.r. 9th* .... ur
91 Ronlees (bl) *alwys last, j.s. 1st & 6th, t.o. whn ref 10th* ref
106 Alfredo Garcia (Ire) 7a *(fav) chsd lding pr,prog 8th, lft 2nd nxt, 3l down whn f 12th* .... f
4 ran. Time 7m 20.00s. SP 6-4.
D R Barnard (Essex).

418 - Confined

102 **CARDINAL RED......................Miss L Hollis** 1
keen hold,disp ld til 7th,chsd ldr til ld 2 out,clr last
Malachite Green.............................A Coe 2
w.w. prog to ld 14th, sn clr, hdded & blnd 2 out, no ex
8 **Abingdon Boy......................S R Andrews** 3

(fav) trkd ldrs,gng wll,outpcd 14th,no dang aft,kpt on frm 2 out
104 Way Of Life (Fr) *prom, ld 8th-13th, grad wknd frm 16th* 4
345 Frank Rich (bl) *mid div, prog 10th, 3rd appr 2 out, wknd* 5
346 Mend *in tch til outpcd appr 14th, no dang aft* 6
309 Major Inquiry (USA) *in tch, pshd along 11th, no ch 14th* 7
Vintage Lad *disp ld to 7th, wknd 11th, mstk 14th, t.o. & p.u. 15th* .... pu
310 El Bae *w.w. blnd & lst pl 9th, lst tch 13th, p.u. 15th* .... pu
Regal Shadow *rr, hit 10th, lst tch 13th, p.u. 16th* .... pu
10 ran. 8l, 4l, 10l, 2l, 15l, 4l. Time 6m 58.00s. SP 4-1.
J M Turner (Suffolk).

419 - Restricted (12st)

UNIQUE TRIBUTE .... Miss L Hollis 1
(Jt fav) prom, ld 14th, drw clr appr 2 out, styd on
313 **General Picton .... P Harding-Jones** 2
(Jt fav) ld to 4th, rddn to ld 11th, hdded 13th,hrd rddn & wknd 2 out
106 **Colonel Kenson .... M Gingell** 3
disp ld to 4th, blnd 13th, sn stgglng, no ch frm 16th
105 Ravens Hasey Moon *ld 5th-6th, prom til 13th, 3rd & no ch appr 2 out* 4
105 Corn Kingdom (bl) *cls up til outpcd 13th, t.o.* 5
15 Sign Performer *lst pl qkly aft 5th, p.u. nxt* .... pu
348 Russian Vision *w.w. lst tch 13th, no ch 15th, p.u. 2 out* pu
309 Cool Apollo (NZ) *rr, lst tch 9th, p.u. 11th* .... pu
Boy Basil *rr, prog to ld 7th, hdded 10th, f nxt* .... f
313 Doctor Dick (Ire) *pllng, in tch til outpcd 13th, t.o. & p.u. 2 out* .... pu
10 ran. 10l, dist, 3l, 1l. Time 6m 56.00s. SP 7-2.
Miss L Hollis & Mr J Parker (Waveney Harriers).

420 - Open (12st)

104 **ARMAGRET 7ex .... S Cowell** 1
(fav) trkd ldrs, ld 15th, hld on gamely und press flat
310 **Melton Park 7ex (bl) .... N Bloom** 2
nt alwys fluent,prom,chall 2 out,wnt lft flat, no ex cls hme
101 **Exclusive Edition (Ire) 5a 7ex .... A Coe** 3
w.w. prog gng wll 12th, ev ch 3 out, wknd appr nxt
309 Old Dundalk (bl) *rr, styd on wll frm 3 out, nvr nrr* 4
312 Cockstown Lad 4ex *disp til ld 4th-12th, blnd nxt, no ch frm 16th* 5
251 Divine Chance (Ire) 7ex *in tch, ld 13th to nxt, ev ch til wknd qkly 3 out* 6
102 Glen Oak 7ex *in tch, rddn alng 11th, sn strgglng, no ch frm 15th* 7
Pikeman *rr, last whn ref 13th* .... ref
102 Mount Patrick *disp ld to 3rd, prom til wknd 13th, t.o. & p.u. 2 out* .... pu
9 ran. ¾l, 8l, 4l, 12l, 5l, 7l. Time 6m 53.00s. SP 2-1.
B Kennedy (Essex Farmers & Union).
After a stewards enquiry. Result stands

421 - Ladies

311 **ST GREGORY (bl) .... Mrs L Gibbon** 1
rr,hit 2nd & 8th, pshd up to ld 11th,made rest,styd on wll
347 **Kelly's Original .... Miss K Tolhurst** 2
in tch, blnd 9th, outpcd 15th, mstk 3 out, kpt on frm nxt
250 **Durbo .... Mrs E Coveney** 3
ld to 10th, disp ld 15th to 3 out, wknd
103 Counterbid *cls up, rddn 12th, lst tch appr 14th, p.u. last* .... pu
310 Dunboy Castle (Ire) *(fav) cls up, pshd along & hit 15th, ev ch 2 out,hld whn u.r. last* .... ur
5 ran. 15l, 3l. Time 6m 55.00s. SP 4-1.
A Howland Jackson (Essex & Suffolk).

422 - Intermediate

177 **MILLBAY (IRE) .... N Bloom** 1
(fav) disp ld, hit 13th, ld nxt drw clr appr last, easy
310 **Druid's Lodge .... T Bulgin** 2
trkd ldrs, went 2nd 16th, rddn 2 out, sn btn
310 **The Grey Boreen .... S Cowell** 3
disp ld to 13th, last frm 16th, t.o.
3 ran. 8l, dist. Time 7m 9.00s. SP 1-4.
Mrs C Bailey (Dunston Harriers).

423 - Maiden Div I (12st)

TOP OF THE RANGE (IRE) .... A Harvey 1
chsng grp,prog 9th,hit16th,ld 2 out,in comm whn lft clr last
344 **Tharif .... Miss H Pewter** 2
clr wth ldr to 9th, wknd appr 14th, t.o. 3 out
344 Worthy Memories 5a *made most til blnd 14th,wknd 3 out,3rd & no ch whn p.u. last* .... pu
But Not Quite (Ire) *(fav) keen hold, chsd ldrs, cls 3rd whn blnd & u.r. 10th* .... ur
343 Ernie Fox (bl) *chsd ldrs,blnd 12th,ld 15th,j.s.3 out,hdded nxt,hld&ref last* .... ref
92 Loch Irish (Ire) 5a *n.j.w. blnd 2nd, bhnd sme prog whn hmpd 11th, p.u. nxt* .... pu
Potentilla (Ire) 7a *rr of mn grp, lst tch 12th, p.u. appr 14th* .... pu
108 Sustaining *chsng grp, lst tch 12th, p.u. appr 14th* .... pu
8 ran. Dist. Time 7m 19.00s. SP 7-2.
P C Cornwell (Suffolk).

424 - Maiden Div II (12st)

RAISE A LOAN .... N Bloom 1
(fav) j.w. ld 7th, made rest drw clr appr last, v. easy
344 **Andalucian Sun (Ire) .... C Ward** 2
w.w. prog 11th, chall gng wll 16th, wknd 2 out, fin tired
108 **Regal Bay .... W Wales** 3
w.w. in tch, outpcd appr 14th, no dang aft, kpt on
314 Superforce *rr, blnd 9th, outpcd & blnd 14th, 4th & no ch whn p.u. last* .... pu
Amaam Amaam *ld to 6th, cls up til wknd 14th, t.o. & p.u. 2 out* .... pu
108 Room To Manouver (Ire) *prom til u.r. 3rd* .... ur
107 Charlie Andrews *prom, hit 11th, wknd appr 14th, t.o. & p.u. 16th* .... pu
107 Springlark (Ire) 7a *prom, chsd ldr 14th, ev ch whn u.r. 3 out* .... ur
Another Comedy *alwys bhnd, lst tch 11th, t.o. & p.u. 16th* .... pu
Portman Road *prom 5th-7th, last & lsng tch whn f 10th* .... f
10 ran. 15l, 20l. Time 7m 10.00s. SP 3-1.
Lady Aldous (Essex & Suffolk).
S.P.

NORTH LEDBURY
Upton-On-Severn
Saturday March 9th
GOOD TO SOFT

425 - Members

264 **HACKETT'S FARM 5ex .... Julian Pritchard** 1
smooth run to ld 14th, clr nxt, easily
217 **Kerry Hill .... T Stephenson** 2
disp 14th, chal agn 2 out, outpcd
214 **Paddy In Paris 5ex .... Miss D Carrington** 3
wth ldrs til wknd 15th
Running Frau *ldng grp til wknd 11th* 4
Melburn March Playboy 2ow *t.o. hlfwy, hunted round* 5
353 Celtic Berry 5a *(fav) ld whn tried to ref & f 3rd* .... f
330 Fortytwo Dee (Ire) 5a *b.d. 3rd* .... bd
7 ran. 4l, 30l, 30l, 2 fences. Time 6m 15.00s. SP 6-4.
Miss Barbara Wilce (North Ledbury).
1 fence omitted, 17 jumps.

426 - Confined (12st)

214 **SISTERLY 5a .... M Jackson** 1
effrt frm 11th, disp 2 out, sn ld & clr
Docter Mac 5a .... J Bates 2

ld frm 10th til hdd & wknd 2 out
Leigh Boy (USA) 3ex (v)................D Duggan 3
(fav) effrt to 3rd 2 out, styd on well
234 Mitchells Best *effrt frm 10th, 4th 3 out, no ext* 4
362 Fergal's Delight *ld to 10th, 2nd til wknd rpdly 3 out*.... 5
214 Arctic Quest 5a *10th hlfwy, mod late prog* 6
Game Set *prom til wknd aft hlfwy* 7
161 Kameo Style *disp 6th/7th til onepcd frm 14th* 8
214 Ragtime Cowboy Joe *alwys strggling in rear* 9
328 Kilmakee 5a *lost tch ldrs hlfwy*........ 10
215 Frampton House *last frm hlfwy* 11
23 Tsagairt Paroiste *t.o. whn blnd 9th, p.u. 10th* .... pu
Emerald Gem *t.o. & p.u. 9th* .... pu
214 Grey Tudor *mid-div, f 11th*........ f
Shaker Maker *chsng ldrs whn b.d. 7th* .... bd
Stormhill Recruit *mid-div whn f 7th* .... f
16 ran. 8l, 8l, 5l, 10l, 3l, ½l, 3l, 20l, 6l, 10l. Time 6m 31.00s. SP 3-1.
Peter Nash (Clifton-On-Teme).
i fence omitted, 17 jumps.

427 - Open (12st)

LOST FORTUNE 4ex....................H Wheeler 1
(fav) 3rd at 14th, sustained run to ld apr last, ran on well
159 **Ru Valentino..........................D Duggan** 2
disp frm 11th, 5l clr 3 out, wknd nxt, hdd apr last
232 **Corrianne 5a (h)...............G Barfoot-Saunt** 3
j.w. disp til onepcd frm 3 out
265 Shadow Walker 7ex *disp to 8th, onepcd aft*........ 4
Dragon's Blood (USA) *lost tch ldrs 12th, p.u. 14th*........ pu
214 Agarb (USA) *dist last whn p.u. 15th*........ pu
6 ran. 2½l, 12l. Time 6m 37.00s. SP 4-9.
H W Wheeler (North Cotswold).

428 - Restricted (12st)

217 **KETTLES 5a.............................A Phillips** 1
disp ld 3 out, qcknd to ld apr last, ran on strngly
235 **Diamond Valley (Ire)................Miss S Wallin** 2
smooth prog 14th, ev ch 2 out, outpcd by wnr
Danbury Lad (Ire)....................Miss A Dare 3
(fav) prog 14th, 5th & ch 2 out, unable to sustain effrt
269 Cutsdean Cross (Ire) *alwys prom, cls 2nd & ch 3 out, onepcd*........ 4
263 Dusky Day *last hlfwy, steady run 14th, nvr nrr*........ 5
231 Sideliner *svrl pstns 1st cct, 4th at 15th, onepcd*........ 6
156 Louis Farrell *clr ldr frm 10th til wknd apr 2 out*........ 7
Members Rights 5a *disp ld til wknd frm 8th*........ 8
215 Athassel Abbey *alwys strggling, p.u. 14th*........ pu
Dixons Homefinder *wll bhnd whn p.u. 15th*........ pu
263 Plax *u.r. apr 1st*........ ur
263 Howley Lad *s.s. t.o. & p.u. 6th*........ pu
Red Furlong *wll bhnd whn p.u. 13th*........ pu
Sudanor (Ire) *ld/disp til wknd frm 13th, p.u. 3 out*........ pu
Really An Angel 5a *t.o. whn p.u. 14th*........ pu
215 Baptist John (Ire) *last whn p.u. 15th*........ pu
62 Tanglewood Boy 7a *losing tch whn p.u. 14th*........ pu
17 ran. 3l, 6l, 6l, 8l, 15l, 6l, 12l. Time 6m 37.00s. SP 20-1.
Mrs Joanna Daniell (Ledbury).

429 - Ladies

291 **STEPHENS PET.........................Miss A Dare** 1
(fav) 2nd til qcknd to ld 15th, sn clr, easily
216 **They All Forgot Me.................Miss C Dyson** 2
cls 3rd til wknd 13th, eased flat, almost lost 2nd
Legal Picnic.........................Miss C Bryan 3
20l 3rd 3 out, fin well, nrly snatched 2nd
Paris Of Troy *ld to 15th, 20l 2nd whn p.u. 2 out, sore*........ pu
4 ran. Dist, ½l. Time 6m 32.00s. SP 1-3.
Dr P P Brown (Berkeley).

430 - Open Maiden Div I (12st)

ALDINGTON CHARLIE.................H Wheeler 1
(fav) alwys prom, strng run to disp last, ran on wll flat
160 **Cut The Corn ....P Hanly** 2
ld, lft clr 15th, hdd & unable qckn last
236 **Bettiville..............................N Bradley** 3
5th 3 out, ran on frm 2 out, nrst fin
341 Fountain Of Fire (Ire) 5a *effrt to go 4th 3 out, no further prog, disq*........ 4D
234 Vital Shot 5a *alwys ldng grp, no ext frm 3 out*........ 5
218 Bolshie Baron *prog frm 14th, tk 6th apr 2 out, not rch ldrs*........ 6
233 Specific Impulse *wll btn 6th whn virt p.u. flat*........ 7
Social Vision (Ire) *mid-div to 11th, wknd, p.u. 3 out*........ pu
Close Control (Ire) *mstks, rear whn p.u. 14th*........ pu
Dustys Trail (Ire) *conf rdn, just ld whn f 15th*........ f
204 Fathers Footprints *chsd ldrs til 13th, bhnd & p.u. 2 out*........ pu
174 Boo's Delight 5a *t.o. & p.u. 14th*........ pu
Live Wire (Ire) 7a *alwys last, p.u. 14th*........ pu
220 Daisy's Pal 7a *mid-div til wknd 12th, p.u. 14th*........ pu
239 Greenhills Ruby 7a *losing tch whn p.u. 14th*........ pu
15 ran. 4l, 8l, 5l, 3l, 12l, 15l. Time 6m 44.00s. SP 7-2.
H W Wheeler (North Cotswold).
Fountain Of Fire disqualified, not W/I. Original distances.

431 - Open Maiden Div II (12st)

NATIONAL CASE 5a..................S Blackwell 1
effrt frm 14th to disp 2 out, ld last, ran on well
Nutcase 5a..............................A Phillips 2
(fav) prog frm 12th, disp ld 2out-last, outpcd flat
218 **Cruise A Hoop ....T Stephenson** 3
effrt frm 13th, went 3rd 2 out, styd on onepcd
221 Demamo (Ire) *6th at 12th, not pace to chal frm 4 out*........ 4
218 Promethean Singer *clr ldr to 10th, renewed effrt 3 out, wknd*........ 5
350 Roscoe's Gemma 5a *t.o. 1st cct, mod late prog*........ 6
Coddington Star 5a *10th hlfwy, styd on frm 15th, no dang*........ 7
341 Sonny's Song *disp 3rd til wknd frm 9th*........ 8
238 Winters Cottage (Ire) *12th hlfwy, mod late prog, nrst fin*........ 9
269 Annmount Lady (Ire) 5a *s.s. alwys wll bhnd*........ 10
Samuel Perry *mstks, mid-div, p.u. 14th*........ pu
Breeches Buoy *rear whn u.r. 6th*........ ur
2 Kingsthorpe *8th 7 wll btn whn b.d. 3 out*........ bd
Emmabella 5a *disp ld 12th til f 15th*........ f
Master Frith *t.o. & p.u. 14th*........ pu
220 Big Buckley 5a *7th & wkng whn f 3 out*........ f
Warm Relation (Ire) 7a *n.j.w. rear & p.u. 13th*........ pu
17 ran. 2½l, 8l, 5l, 20l, 5l, 10l, 4l, 3l, 8l. Time 6m 42.00s. SP 14-1.
Nigel Lilley (Clifton On Teme).

432 - Open Maiden Div III (12st)

FINAL ABBY 5a.......................R Thornton 1
(fav) conf rdn, ld 13th, mstks last 2, easily
128 **Ravensdale Lad.....................R Wakeham** 2
effrt from 15th, went 2nd 3 out, not trbl wnr
213 **Cathgal.....................................J Rees** 3
alwys prom, lost tch & 4th 3 out, lft poor 3rd last
334 Gal-A-Dor *ld brfly 7-8th, 2l 2nd at 15th, sn btn*........ 4
Orty *disp 4th-5th, wknd 8th, p.u. 12th*........ pu
221 Romany Gold 5a *wll bhnd til p.u. 2 out*........ pu
129 Looking *mid-div whn f 9th*........ f
160 Mansun *5th hlfwy, grad lost tch, p.u. 3 out*........ pu
358 Sweet Petel 5a *ld brfly 3rd, rear hlfwy, p.u. 15th*........ pu
Yarron King *disp 3rd-9th, wknd & p.u. 3 out*........ pu
221 Mis-E-Fishant 5a *last whn f 3 out*........ f
220 Rusty Fellow *mstks, wll bhnd whn b.d. 14th*........ bd
Brother Prim *wkng 3rd whn mstk 2 out, no ch whn u.r. last*........ ur
214 Flimsy Flame *ld frm 11th til f 13th*........ f
Master Trooper (Ire) *mid-div whn mstk 9th, p.u. dead*........ pu
335 Fiddlers Knap *prom early, wkng whn f 14th*........ f
Daisy Lane 5a *f 3rd*........ f
17 ran. 6l, 20l, 20l. Time 6m 43.00s. SP 9-4.
Mrs E A Thomas (Pembrokeshire).
P.M.

OAKLEY
Newton Bromswold
Saturday March 9th
GOOD TO SOFT

433 - Members

HENFIELD .... **M Turner** 1
ld/disp til mstk 11th, 12l 2nd nxt, lft clr 3 out
Just Donald .... **R Barrett** 2
ld 1st-2nd, cls up til wknd 11th, lft 2nd 3 out
Parting Hour *(fav) ld/disp til ld aft 12th, sn clr, 3l up whn u.r. 3 out* .... ur
3 ran. 10l. Time 7m 33.00s. SP 6-4.
G G Tawell (Oakley).

434 - Confined (12st)

230 **CAUSEWAY CRUISER** .... **R Lawther** 1
hld up rear, prog 12th, ld 3 out, made rest, comf
124 **Penlet 3ex** .... **John Pritchard** 2
(fav) hld up last, prog hlfwy, chsd ldrs 14th, ev ch 2 out, onepcd
124 **Saybright** .... **G Tarry** 3
chsd ldrs, ev ch 15th, lost plc, ran on agn 2 out
244 Beau Dandy *ld to 1st & frm nxt, hdd 3 out, wknd rpdly* 4
124 Sprucefield *alwys prom, wknd frm 3 out* 5
124 Mr Rigsby (Ire) *twrds rear til some prog frm 13th, nvr rchd ldrs* 6
124 Kelly's Eye 3ex (bl) *alwys rear, last & lost tch whn crawld 13th & p.u.* .... pu
Hostetler *chsd ldrs to hlfwy, fdd, p.u. 2 out* .... pu
124 Bervie House (Ire) *hld up rear,prog to jn ldrs 14th,ev ch 3 out,wknd, p.u. last* .... pu
Rare Knight *mid-div to hlfwy, wknd & wll bhnd whn p.u. 2 out* .... pu
Aylesford 7a *ld aft 1st-2nd, chsd ldrs to 9th, wknd & p.u. 11th* .... pu
11 ran. Dist, 10l, 10l, 25l, 25l. Time 6m 57.00s. SP 3-1.
J Tredwell (Grafton).

435 - Open

232 **JOBURN 5a** .... **John Pritchard** 1
sttld mid-div, 5th at 14th, prog 3 out, ld last, rdn clr
337 **Welsh Singer** .... **R Lawther** 2
last til apr hlfwy,prog & cls 3rd 15th,ld aft 3 out,hdd last
Vital Witness (Can) .... **M Ashton** 3
cls 2nd til lost plc 14th,ran on 3 out,fin well
Tompet *nvr rchd ldrs, styd on onepcd* 4
364 Radical Views *chsd ldrs til ld 14th, hdd 3 out, wknd* ... 5
334 Tokanda *chsd ldrs to 8th, fdd, t.o. 13th, p.u. 3 out* ..... pu
244 The Point Is *(fav) ld to 14th, cls 2nd & going wll whn u.r. nxt* .... ur
7 ran. 8l, ¾l, 20l, 4l. Time 7m 6.00s. SP 12-1.
Mrs G V Mackay (Warwickshire).

436 - Ladies

GREEN ARCHER .... **Miss S Duckett** 1
(fav) alwys prom, chsd ldr frm 4th, ld 9th, clr 3 out, idld flat
126 **Knight's Spur (USA)** .... **Mrs J Parris** 2
chsd ldrs, effrt apr last, ran on, just faild
310 **Stanwick Farlap 5a** .... **Mrs M Bellamy** 3
wll bhnd til prog 14th, gd run frm 2 out, styd on
126 Military Two Step *ld to 4th, chsd ldrs til lost plc 9th, styd on well frm 2out* 4
Chiasso Forte (Ity) *alwys prom, 2nd til outpcd frm 4 out, styd on* 5
245 Directly *wll bhnd til prog 9th, 3rd nxt & mstk, wknd 4 out* 6
336 Icky's Five *alwys twrds rear* 7
266 Finally Fantazia 5a *hld up rear, some prog to 4th 3 out, fdd, walked in* 8
264 Tumble Time *alwys wll bhnd* 9
Winged Whisper (USA) *bolted bef start, rear til plld to ld 4th-9th,wknd,p.u. 14th* .... pu
10 ran. ½l, 10l, 2l, 4l, 25l, dist, 10l, 1l. Time 7m 0.00s. SP 4-5.
Mrs S D Walter (Vale Of Aylesbury).

437 - Restricted (12st)

242 **TEETON MILL** .... **B Pollock** 1
(fav) hld up mid-div, prog 14th, ld 2 out, qcknd clr
129 **Singing Clown 5a** .... **L Lay** 2
chsd ldr til ld/disp 9th-2 out, styd on onepcd
243 **Glenrowan Lad** .... **T Marks** 3
hld up mid-div, cls up 4 out, styd on onepcd
Saffron Gale (Ire) *alwys in tch, ld apr 14th, disp aft til not qckn 2 out, wknd* 4
338 Tarry Awhile *alwys prom, ev ch 16th, wknd, walked in* 5
174 Spalease 5a 4ow *hld up rear, prog to chal 4 out, btn whn blnd 2 out* 6
61 Penly *sn prom, ld aft 10th, jnd 12th, outpcd frm 2 out* .. 7
338 Waterhay *ld to 9th, 3rd hlfwy, btn whn f 15th* ..... f
269 Glenard (Ire) *alwys rear, t.o. & p.u. 2 out* ..... pu
9 ran. 12l, ½l, 20l, 2l, 2l, 1l. Time 7m 7.00s. SP 5-4.
C R Saunders (Pytchley).

438 - Maiden Div I

TEETON NISHABALL 5a .... **R Barrett** 1
hld up, prog to 3rd at 11th, ld 3 out, drew clr
Dunloughan .... **Miss S Duckett** 2
mid-div, prog 13th, 2nd apr 2 out, styd on
236 **Alias Silver** .... **Miss H Irving** 3
alwys prom, ev ch 15th, styd on agn cls home
241 Cormeen Lord (Ire) *hld up mid-div, prssd ldrs & mstk 14th, not rcvr* 4
240 Relishing 5a *(fav) ld, 20l clr 5th, wknd & hdd 3 out, walked in* 5
129 Fortytimes More *chsd ldr to 8th, fdd, rear 11th, p.u. 14th* .... pu
Copper Bank *sn prom, going wll in 5th whn u.r. 15th* ur
4 Gawcott Wood 5a *chsd ldr til ran wd apr 9th & ran out* .... ro
233 Crestafair 5a *chsd ldrs til f 9th* .... f
Petoski Bay *last early, rpd prog to 3rd hlfwy, wknd & p.u. 13th* .... pu
10 ran. 20l, 2½l, 1l, 20l. Time 7m 10.00s. SP 20-1.
Mrs Joan Tice (Atherstone).

439 - Maiden Div II

238 **MR BRANIGAN (IRE)** .... **T Marks** 1
(fav) hld up rear,prog 14th,mod 4th 3 out,qcknd to ld last,sn clr
314 **Kerry My Home** .... **P Taiano** 2
chsd ldrs, cls 2nd at 14th, lost plc, ran on agn 2 out
Butlers Match (Ire) .... **L Lay** 3
alwys prom, ld 12th-nxt, ld 14th-last, outpcd
Apple Nicking *ld to 1st, chsd ldr, ld/disp 13th-3 out, wknd, f last* .... f
Lloyds Loser *ld aft 1st til 13th, dropped out, p.u. aft 16th* .... pu
Hehas *alwys rear, bhnd whn p.u. 16th* .... pu
Spring Sabre *jmpd slwly 1st & 2nd, bhnd whn p.u. 2 out* .... pu
7 ran. 3l, 12l. Time 7m 23.00s. SP 6-4.
G T H Bailey (Pytchley).

440 - Maiden Div III

236 **SABRE KING (bl)** .... **L Lay** 1
(fav) alwys prom, ld 12th, clr 2 out, ran on well
80 **Cleric On Broadway (Ire) 5a** .... **M Barnard** 2
hld up rear, prog to cls 4th 3 out, not rch wnr
341 **Horcum** .... **John Pritchard** 3
alwys cls up, 2nd 3 out, not qckn
Supreme Dream (Ire) 5a *ld to 12th, lost plc, 5th 2 out, fin fast* 4
Cruise Free *mid-div, nvr rchd ldrs* 5
Archie's Sister 5a *alwys bhnd, p.u. 15th* .... pu
Orelse *m.n.s. rear whn ref 7th* .... ref
Lucky Crest 5a *cls up, fdd & p.u. 14th* .... pu
Sparnova 5a *mostly mid-div, wkng whn p.u. 3 out* ..... pu
175 Tiger *sn prom, cls up whn blnd 15th, fdd, p.u. nxt* ..... pu
10 ran. 20l, 6l, 4l, hd. Time 7m 20.00s. SP 3-1.
J Tredwell (Grafton).
H.F.

SILVERTON

Haldon
Saturday March 9th
SOFT

441 - Members

296 **FEARSOME ....G Penfold** 1
(Jt fav) hld up in tch, rmndrs aft 13th, lft 2nd 3 out, ld cls home
279 **Seventh Lock ....Miss L Blackford** 2
handy,2nd 13th,lft in ld 3 out,lkd wnr til hng lft flat,hdd
280 **The Copper Key ....T Greed** 3
cls up,trckd ldr 6-13th,cls 3rd frm 3 out,blnd last,nt rcvr
195 Karicleigh Boy *(Jt fav) slght ld at slow pace til drew clr 14th, 20l clr whn f 3 out* .... f
200 Ashcombe Valley *lost tch frm 7th, bhnd whn f 12th*.... f
Philippastone *alwys last, t.o. 4th, p.u. 11th* .... pu
6 ran. 3l, 12l. Time 6m 53.00s. SP 11-8.
G W Penfold (Silverton).

442 - Confined

199 **SOUTHERN FLIGHT ....Miss J Cumings** 1
(fav) alwys wll plcd, ld 16th, drew clr nxt, comf, eased
196 **Senegalais (Fr) ....M Venner** 2
went 4th at 13th, prog frm off pace to take 2nd flat, ran on
294 **Catch The Cross (bl) ....Mrs M Hand** 3
prom, cls 3rd hlfwy, wknd grad frm 3 out
135 Bianconi *made most, mstk 11th, hdd aft 15th, fdd frm 2 out*.......... 4
The Doormaker *in tch, blnd 3rd, lost ground frm 11th, wll bhnd clsng stgs* 5
Nelson River (USA) *sn rear, bhnd frm 4th til p.u. 11th* pu
6 ran. 1l, 10l, 3l, 25l. Time 6m 40.00s. SP Evens.
Mrs K J Cumings (Devon & Somerset Staghounds).

443 - Ladies

356 **KHATTAF ....Miss J Cumings** 1
(fav) patiently rdn, prog to 2nd 3 out, ld nxt, drew clr, easily
199 **Aristocratic Gold ....Mrs M Hand** 2
mid-div, rpd prog to 2nd 14th, ld nxt, hdd & outpcd 2 out
295 **Playpen ....Miss S Crook** 3
ld/disp to 15th, mstk nxt, 3rd & onepcd frm 2 out
208 On His Own *in tch, went 2nd brfly at 15th, 4th & one-pcd frm 3 out*.......... 4
208 Little Thyne *mid-div, lost tch 13th, poor 5th frm 3 out*. 5
Kiltonga *tubed, sn bhnd, t.o. frm 10th* 6
197 Unityfarm Oltowner *5th hlfwy, lost ground frm 11th, t.o.*.......... 7
Qajar *rear til p.u. 3 out*.......... pu
197 Tamar Lass 5a *in tch, cls 4th at 13th, wknd rpdly & p.u. nxt, dead* .... pu
197 Majestic Spirit *ld/disp frm 7th til wknd aft 13th, p.u. 15th*.......... pu
10 ran. 6l, 3l, 2l, 25l, 5l, 3l. Time 6m 35.00s. SP 4-6.
Mrs H C Johnson (Devon & Somerset Staghounds).

444 - Land Rover Open (12st)

134 **MAGNOLIA MAN..........................N Harris** 1
(fav) j.w. disp frm 11th, ld aft 13th, drew clr 3 out, imprssv
130 **Bluechipenterprise 5a 7ex..............R Darke** 2
ld in to start, disp til outpcd aft 13th, tired 2 out
Prince Soloman ....W G Turner 3
disp,mstk 11th,3rd frm 13th,btn whn slw 2 out,hng lft flat
277 Querrin Lodge *alwys last, t.o. frm 7th til p.u. 3 out* .... pu
Hurricane Tommy 7ex *sn prom, cls up til 12th, wknd nxt, p.u. 14th* .... pu
5 ran. Dist, 20l. Time 6m 39.00s. SP 4-5.
Mrs D B Lunt (Tiverton Foxhounds).

445 - Restricted (12st)

45 **RUSHALONG ....A Farrant** 1
(fav) hld up, prog 11th, disp nxt, ld 14th & sn clr, easily
Big Seamus (Ire) ....J Creighton 2
mid-div, went 3rd & styng on 15th, tk 2nd flat
199 **Neil's Way.........................I Widdicombe** 3
prom, disp frm 8th til outpcd aft 13th, 2nd agn 3 out,no imp
197 Grey Guestino *ld to 8th, disp til lost plc 13th, bhnd & jmpd slw aft*.......... 4
281 Hedera Helix *mid-div, rmndrs 10th, mstk 12th, no ch nxt, p.u. 2 out* .... pu
Generous Scot *keen hold,cls 5th hlfwy,cls 2nd 13th, wknd 15th,p.u. 2 out*.......... pu
298 Roving Vagabond *rear & rmndr 10th, bhnd whn p.u. 14th*.......... pu
199 Chukamill *prom, disp 10-13th, sn outpcd, wll btn in 4th whn p.u. 2 out*.......... pu
280 Palace King (Ire) *rear til p.u. 14th*.......... 0
9 ran. 20l, ½l, dist. Time 6m 41.00s. SP Evens.
George Ball (Spooners & West Dartmoor).

446 - Open Maiden Div I (12st)

202 **DARKTOWN STRUTTER (bl) ....M Burrows** 1
ld/disp to 12th,cls 2nd nxt,lkd btn til rallied to ld cls hm
201 **Mosside...................................N Harris** 2
handy, ld 13th, pshd alng & lkd wnr 2 out, hdd cls hm
202 **Golden Eye (NZ) ....I Dowrick** 3
(fav) alwys wll plcd, effrt & 2nd aft 2 out, fdd flat
Drumbanes Pet *alwys in tch, ev ch til onepcd frm 3 out*.......... 4
200 Quick Opinion *in tch, ev ch whn cls 3rd 3 out, sn wknd*.......... 5
Dusty Furlong *mid-div, 8th at 13th, bhnd aft*.......... 6
Bright Road 5a *mid-div, poor 7th at 13th, t.o. & p.u. 2 out*.......... pu
132 Dharamshala (Ire) *sn rear, bhnd frm 9th, t.o. & p.u. 13th*.......... pu
Tacoment 5a *rear & rmndrs 11th, t.o. & p.u. 2 out* .... pu
Avin Fun Bar 5a *ld/disp to 12th, lost plc nxt, t.o. & p.u. 2 out*.......... pu
283 Musbury Castle 5a *bhnd til p.u. 10th*.......... pu
Prides Delight 5a *prom, 3rd at 9th, sn wknd, mstk 11th, p.u. nxt*.......... pu
301 Better By Half (Ire) *rear, some prog 9th, bhnd whn p.u. 13th*.......... pu
13 ran. ½l, 2½l, 6l, 20l, 2l. Time 6m 55.00s. SP 33-1.
R W Pincombe (Dulverton (East)).

447 - Open Maiden Div II (12st)

132 **WELL TIMED ....M Frith** 1
ld/disp frm 5th, hdd 3 out, renewed effrt last, sn clr
207 **Ive Called Time.........................T Greed** 2
prom, disp 13th-nxt, ld 3 out, jnd & blnd last, not rcvr
2 **Front Cover 5a.......................S Mulcaire** 3
(fav) hld up, prog 9th, 3rd & ev ch 15th, unable to chal aft
202 Skip Tracer *prog to 3rd whn crashed thro wing 7th* ... ro
200 Northern Bride 5a *rear & rmndrs 2nd, t.o. til p.u. 11th* pu
201 Parson Flynn *cls 5th hlfwy, just in tch whn slw jmp 14th, btn & p.u. 2out*.......... pu
300 Dovedon Princess 5a *twrds rear, 10th hlfwy, p.u. 12th* .... pu
Noble Auk (NZ) *mid-div, mstk 11th, 7th whn p.u. 14th* pu
One For The Cross (Ire) *ld to 5th, prom whn mstk 10th, wknd 13th, p.u. 15th*.......... pu
201 Chocolate Buttons 5a *gd prog to 3rd at 13th, wknd 15th, p.u. 2 out* .... pu
Anvil Corner 5a *mid-div, 6th at 14th, btn whn p.u. 2 out*.......... pu
296 Pillmere Lad *mid-div whn mstk 6th, sn rear, blnd 12th, p.u. nxt*.......... pu

284 Carumu 5a *prog 6th, disp 8th-10th, wknd 13th, p.u. 3 out* .... pu
13 ran. 3l, ½l. Time 6m 42.00s. SP 12-1.
Mrs G A Robarts (Dartmoor).

448 - Open Maiden Div III (12st)

206 **LAKE MARINER 5a** .... **L Jefford** 1
handy, disp 11th, cls up going wll 13th, ld 15th, sn clr
280 **The Ugly Duckling** .... **R Treloggen** 2
wll in tch, disp 10-11th, cls 3rd 14th, 2nd 2 out, no ch wnr
Spy Dessa .... **Miss S Rowe** 3
j.w. ld 3rd, disp 10-14th, wknd nxt, tired nr fin
Gloriki 5a *bhnd til p.u. apr 6th* .... pu
299 Artistic Peace 5a *prog to 6th at 13th, btn 4th whn f 3 out* .... f
200 Sharrow Bay (NZ) *(fav) prom til lost plc 6th, bhnd whn p.u. 10th, dsmntd* .... pu
Steamburd 5a *strng hld, prom, 3rd hlfwy, 4th & wkng 14th, p.u. 3 out* .... pu
301 Scallykenning *in tch, disp 3rd at 14th, wkng whn blnd nxt, mstk nxt & p.u.* .... pu
134 Millaroo *ld til apr 3rd, lost plc frm 7th, bhnd & p.u. 13th* .... pu
282 Sam's Successor 7a *sn bhnd & jmpd lft, t.o. & p.u. 10th* .... pu
10 ran. 20l, dist. Time 6m 59.00s. SP 3-1.
Mrs Lyn Brafield (Weston & Banwell).
G.T.

SOUTH EAST HUNTS CLUB
Charing
Saturday March 9th
GOOD

449 - Restricted (12st)

253 **BRAMBLEDOWN (IRE) 7a** .... **Mrs B Sillars** 1
(fav) cls up, outpcd & mstk 15th, strng run 4 out, ld on line
254 **Salachy Run (Ire)** .... **A Welsh** 2
alwys prom, 3rd at 15th, chal 2 out, ld flat, hdd on line
272 **Manaolana 5a** .... **G Hopper** 3
rear, gd prog 12th, ld 15th, drvn clr, jnd last, wknd flat
248 Bright Crusader *mid-div, nggld alng frm 4th, poor 5th 4 out, kpt on* 4
32 Basher Bill *prom to 7th, wll bhnd frm 15th* 5
247 Charleston Lad *ld to 7th, agn 10-15th, 3rd & btn 2 out, tired, walked in* 6
Killarney Man *rear, nvr going well, t.o. 15th* 7
Edged Weapon (Fr) *prom to 5th, last by 7th, p.u. nxt* .... pu
248 Golden Pele *twrds rear whn f 2nd* .... f
Cuckoo Pen *alwys rear, p.u. 13th* .... pu
King's Maverick (Ire) *rear, dived thro 8th, f 10th* .... f
Greenhill Fly Away *prom, ld aft 7th til u.r. 10th* .... ur
248 Lewesdon Princess 5a *rear, lost tch 10th, t.o. & p.u. 3 out* .... pu
13 ran. ½l, 2l, 20l, 20l, 8l, 10l. Time 6m 32.00s. SP 7-4.
Mrs B Sillars (West Street/Tickham).

450 - Club (12st)

178 **NETHERTARA 5a 3ex** .... **P Hacking** 1
(fav) wll plcd, ld aft 8th, made rest, ran on strngly, clr 4 out
271 **Country Vet 5a 3ex** .... **P Bull** 2
chsd wnr frm 8th, outpcd frm 4 out
American Eyre .... **Miss S Gladders** 3
rear but in tch, 4th at 13th, outpcd aft, kpt on same pace
Pacific Sound *cls up, 3rd at 12th, wknd 15th, p.u. 2 out* .... pu
271 Highland Bounty *f 5th in rear* .... f
Country Festival 5a 3ow *in tch,3rd whn blnd 11th,sn rdn,poor 4th whn p.u. last,lame* .... pu
249 Mogwai (Ire) *cls up, mstk 10th, wknd rpdly aft nxt, p.u. 14th, dsmntd* .... pu
Rough Aura *ld til blnd 7th, mstks & fdd aft, p.u. aft 12th* .... pu
8 ran. 12l, 5l. Time 6m 30.00s. SP 1-2.
Alan Cowing (East Sussex & Romney Marsh).

451 - Open (12st)

274 **FOLK DANCE 3ow 7ex** .... **F Jackson** 1
handy, ld apr last, rdn out
271 **Snowfire Chap (bl)** .... **T Underwood** 2
cls up, chal 2 out, lvl last, no ext flat
251 **Yeoman Farmer** .... **P Hacking** 3
w.w. dtchd 12th,rpd prog 4 out,wth wnr whn blnd last,nt rcvr
247 Ginger Tristan 7ex *(fav) 2s-4/6, ld to 7th, agn 9th, hdd apr last, onepcd* 4
251 Bright Hour *mid-div, clsd up to 4th & ev ch 4 out, onepcd* 5
274 Take The Town 7ex *wth ldr, ld 8-9th, 4th aft, drvn to 2nd 4 out, sn btn* 6
Darkbrook 7ex *in tch, nggld alng 12th, wknd und pres 4 out* 7
251 Highly Decorated *in tch til wknd 4 out, p.u. 2 out* .... pu
251 Cool It A Bit *mid-div whn b.d. 9th* .... bd
251 Sakil (Ire) *mid-div whn f 9th* .... f
Quarter Marker (Ire) 1ow *rear, blnd 8th, p.u. nxt* .... pu
11 ran. 1l, 5l, 4l, 6l, 6l, 8l. Time 6m 37.00s. SP 25-1.
F R Jackson (Old Surrey & Burstow).

452 - Ladies

273 **OUR SURVIVOR** .... **Miss C Savell** 1
mid-div, prog to ld 15th-3 out, rallied & ld flat
Forest Sun .... **Miss J Grant** 2
(fav) handy, ld 9th-15th, agn 3 out, rdn & hdd flat
250 **Magical Morris 4ex** .... **Miss C Grissell** 3
rear, prog final cct, 4th 3 out, kpt on
250 Luck Money *mstk 2nd, chsd ldrs frm 12th, 3rd whn pckd 3 out, no ch aft* 4
Jim Bowie *alwys prom, ld 3-5th, ev ch 4 out, wknd nxt* 5
Saxon Swinger *last frm 8th, t.o. 13th* 6
347 Profligate 4ex *alwys rear, nvr thrtnd, 6th & wll btn whn p.u. last* .... pu
No Say *ld 5th-9th, wth ldr whn p.u. qckly 11th* .... pu
Strong Suspicion *ld to 3rd, cls up aft, wknd & p.u. 14th* .... pu
9 ran. 1l, 5l, 3l, ½l, 2 fences. Time 6m 30.00s. SP 20-1.
Harry White (East Sussex & Romney Marsh).

453 - Moderate

249 **BURROMARINER** .... **A Welsh** 1
cls up, jmpd slwly 3 out, sn chal, ld apr last, drvn out
249 **Stede Quarter** .... **A Hickman** 2
(fav) ld 4th, blnd 11th & 15th, hdd apr last, no ext
249 Sir Wager (bl) *ld to 4th, lost tch 7th, wll bhnd whn p.u. aft 11th* .... pu
249 Barn Elms *trckd ldrs, 3rd & ev ch whn f 2 out* .... f
4 ran. 1½l. Time 6m 49.00s. SP 2-1.
Mrs A Blaker (Mid Surrey Farmers Draghounds).

454 - Maiden Div I (12st)

254 **SOVEREIGN SPRAY (IRE)** .... **P Hacking** 1
rear, clsd up 10th, ld 13th, prssd whn lft clr 3 out
Huckleberry Friend 5a .... **P Blagg** 2
lft in ld 8th, hdd 10th, strggling aft, t.o. 4 out
182 Run To Au Bon (Ire) *rear, jmpd slwly 8th, 9th & 10th, p.u. aft* .... pu
Linger Balinda 5a *mid-div to 10th, sn strggling, t.o. & p.u. 4 out* .... pu
250 Target Time 5a *mstk 2nd, twrds rear whn p.u. 10th* .... pu
61 Mister Spectator (Ire) *2nd, clr wth ldr whn ran out 8th* .... ro
Clean Sweep *mid-div whn f 7th* .... f
Galaroi (Ire) *(fav) ld 10th, just hdd whn f 13th* .... f
Pett Lad *ld, ran wd bend bef 8th, styd wide & ran out 8th* .... ro

254 Bomb The Bees 5a *14s-6s, prog 13th, wth wnr 4 out, f nxt* .... f
10 ran. 1 fence. Time 6m 43.00s. SP 14-1.
S P Tindall (Southdown & Eridge).

455 - Maiden Div II (12st)

275 **ST ROBERT** .... **T Hills** 1
made all, drew clr 3 out
275 **Time Star (NZ)** .... **R Crosby** 2
chsd wnr, nvr fluent, lost plc 15th, kpt on, tk 2nd 2 out
253 **Bric Lane (USA)** .... **J Van Praagh** 3
alwys prom, chsd wnr 15th, wknd rpdly 3 out, blnd last
60 Grassington (Ire) *(fav) s.s. t.o. 11th, ran on frm 4 out* .. 4
273 Coral Eddy *nvr nr ldrs, 5th frm 15th* 5
Larquill 5a *prom til wknd 14th* 6
254 Polar Ana (Ire) 5a *s.s. t.o. 11th* 7
Robcourt Hill *chsd ldrs, disp 3rd & btn whn f 2 out* .... f
Manor Ranger *ref to race* 0
Over The Clover (Ire) 5a *twrds rear, lost ground 7th, t.o. & p.u. 10th* .... pu
10 ran. 15l, 5l, 8l, 4l, 1 fence, 1l. Time 6m 40.00s. SP 7-2.
D A Cundle (Ashford Valley).
G.Ta.

TANATSIDE
Eyton-On-Severn
Saturday March 9th
GOOD

456 - Members

291 Allow Gold *(fav) jmpd stckly, trckd ldr tl gng on 12th, f 13th* .... f
Godor Spirit *ld tl hdd 12th, lft solo 13th, f 14th* .... f
2 ran.
Race void.

457 - Intermediate Div I (12st)

ORCHESTRAL SUITE (IRE) .... **R White** 1
(fav) tkd ldrs gng esly,ld 13th,in cmd whn lft clr last
293 **Scriven Boy** .... **W Bryan** 2
hld up mid-div, ran on one pc frm 4 out, lft poor 2nd last
Montykosky .... **Miss L Wallace** 3
prom, ev ch 5 out, sn btn
293 Ledwyche Gate *alwys bhnd, nvr nrr* 4
159 Firehalms *ld to 12th, wknd qkly, no ch whn p.u. 2 out* pu
159 Christian 5ex *2nd to 8th, sn btn, p.u. 4 out* .... pu
226 The Right Guy 5ex *rr 5th, t.o. 12th, p.u. 5 out* .... pu
Steel Plate 5ow *mid to rear, no ch whn p.u. 4 out* .... pu
293 Bally Muire 5a *chsd ldrs, lost tch aftr 8th, p.u. 2 out* ... pu
Haven Light *chsd ldrs,prog 4 out,chal 3 out,ev ch nxt,btn whn u.r. last* .... ur
288 Lady Pokey 5a *cls up in 4th at 13th, wknd rpdly 4 out, p.u. 2 out* .... pu
11 ran. Dist, 12l, 10l. Time 6m 35.00s. SP 4-5.
G Pidgeon (Grafton).

458 - Intermediate Div II (12st)

159 **ULTRASON IV (FR)** .... **Mrs M Bryan** 1
chsd ldrs, ld 10th-4 out, 1l down whn lft in ld 2 out
292 **Lakenheather (NZ)** .... **Miss L Wallace** 2
mid-div, clsr ordr to go 2nd at 12th, ran on one pce
Orton House .... **R Burton** 3
alwys prom, ev ch 4 out, no ext frm 2 out
162 Bay Owl *mid to rear, some late prog, no ch 1st 3* ... 4
330 The Last Joshua 3ow *alwys rear, passed btn horses from 3 out* 5
239 Glen Taylor *t.o. frm hlfwy, jmpd rnd in own tm, btn 2 fncs* 6
158 My Son John *mid-div, s-lvd effort to rch ldrs 13th, fdd, p.u. 2 out* .... pu
241 Bay Tiger *r.o. 2nd* .... ro
293 Downtown *ld/disp 5th, ld 6th-9th, 2nd & bd mstk 12th, p.u. 2 out* .... pu
286 Juste Jo 5a *ld/disp to 5th, cls up whn u.r. 7th* .... ur
164 Whatafellow (Ire) *(fav) w.w., 3rd 13th, tk ld 3 out, 2l clr gng wl, u.r. 2 out* .... ur
11 ran. 8l, 10l, 6l, 20l, dist. Time 6m 45.00s. SP 4-1.
David A Smith (North Shropshire).

459 - Open (12st)

215 **CHIP'N'RUN** .... **J Cornes** 1
cls up, ld 13th, ran on und pres frm 4 out
215 **Garrylucas 7ex** .... **G Hanmer** 2
(fav) chsng grp, ran on und pres frm 2 out, not rch wnr
160 **Bucksfern 7ex** .... **R Bevis** 3
prom, 2nd 13th, in tch & ev ch 3 out, no ex
232 Tara Boy *prom, 5th 4 out, styd on frm 2 out, nvr nrr* . 4
256 My Nominee 7ex (bl) *mid-div, clsr ordr 4 out, ev ch 3 out, nt qckn* 5
159 Duke Of Impney *ld to 12th, grd wknd frm 4 out* 6
159 Quite So 5a *alwys bhnd, t.o. whn p.u. 12th* .... pu
162 Ryton Guard 7ex *cls up til outpcd 13th, sn btn, p.u. 3 out* .... pu
King Of Shadows *mid-div early, lst tch, p.u. bfr 13th* .. pu
My Senor *mid-div, nvr trbld ldrs, p.u. 3 out* .... pu
Moss Castle 7ex *hld up, clsr ordr 11th, in tch whn p.u. lame 13th* .... pu
11 ran. 5l, 1l, 3l, 1l, dist. Time 6m 37.00s. SP 20-1.
F D Cornes (South Shropshire).

460 - Ladies

325 **OUT THE DOOR (IRE)** .... **Miss S Baxter** 1
hld up rr,prog frm 12th to ld 3 out,ran on wll frm nxt
184 **Simply Perfect** .... **Miss S Swindells** 2
(fav) mid-div, 3rd at 12th, lft 2nd 3 out,ran on one-pcd clsng stgs
291 **Nodforms Dilemma (USA)** ..... **Miss H Brookshaw** 3
chsng grp, outpcd frm hlfwy til ran on frm 3 out, nrst fin
163 Couture Tights *hld up in rr, some late prog, no dang* 4
291 Sooner Still (bl) *cls up to 8th, outpcd frm 4 out* 5
364 Saymore *in tch, ld 12th-4 out, 3l 2nd whn f 3 out* .... f
184 Cheeky Fox 3ow *rr 6th, t.o. hlfwy, p.u. 13th* .... pu
288 Moya's Tip Top 5a *nvr btr thn mid-div, sn btn, p.u. 4 out* .... pu
Kingfisher Lad 3ow *prom, sn btn aftr 12th, p.u. 3 out* .. pu
Glamdring 5a *ld to 11th, wkng whn u.r. 4 out* .... ur
10 ran. 3l, 8l, 15l, 10l. Time 6m 33.00s. SP 5-2.
M Mann (Wheatland).

461 - Restricted Div I

219 **BOARD GAME** .... **A Beedles** 1
mid-div, stdy prog frm 5 out, rn on wl frm 2 out to ld flat
Remembertom .... **A Crow** 2
hld up, ld 14th tl cght flat, fin lame
217 **Ollardale (Ire)** .... **W Bryan** 3
(fav) chsng grp, ev ch 3 out, nt qckn clsng stgs
Moydrum Prince *ld to 3rd, chsng grp tl wknd 4 out, p.u. 2 out* .... pu
225 Hillview Lad *mid to rear, p.u. 5 out* .... pu
Luke's The Bizz (Ire) *cls up, ld 7th-13th, sn btn, p.u. 2 out* .... pu
159 Spartan Pete *mid to rear, p.u. 4 out* .... pu
164 Mastiff Lane *cls up 13th, lsng tch wth 1st 4 whn f 4 out* .... f
216 Andyworth *ld 4th-10th, in tch to 5 out, fdd, p.u. 2 out* .. pu
291 Pepperbox 5a *alwys rear, p.u. 13th* .... pu
292 Roll-A-Dance *mid-div, sn btn, p.u. 4 out* .... pu
Ita's Fellow (Ire) *mid-div whn u.r. 7th* .... ur
Grecianlid *chsd ldrs, ev ch 13th, lost tch frm 4 out, p.u. bfr last* .... pu
Cut A Niche *mstks, lost tch frm 12th, p.u. 4 out* .... pu
288 Leo The Lodger *rr, n.d., p.u. 3 out* .... pu
15 ran. ½l, 5l. Time 6m 44.00s. SP 20-1.
A Beedles (South Shropshire).

462 - Restricted Div II

167 **WESTCOTE LAD** .... **W Bryan** 1

(fav) *w.w., clsr ordr 5 out, ld 3 out, ran out wll aft*
288 **Cloud Dancing..................M Worthington** 2
trckd ldrs, ld brfly 4 out, ran on onepcd frm 2 out
Foxy Blue........................Miss C Burgess 3
chsd ldrs, ld 4th-8th & agn 5 out-3 out, onepcd aft
166 Antica Roma (Ire) 5a *cls up, rdn & found nil frm 4 out* 4
217 Saffron Glory *t.o. hlfwy, sm lt prog, nrst fin* 5
Royal Entertainer *prom, ld 9th-10th, lost plc nxt, no chnc frm 4 out*........ 6
Embu-Meru *mstks, rr early, r.o. one pc frm 4 out*..... 7
243 Ballyhannon (Ire) *mid-div, ev ch 5 out, not quckn* 8
Ahalin *mid to rear, no ch whn p.u. last*........... pu
Fennorhill *ld to 3rd, cls up til outpcd 12th, p.u. 3 out* .. pu
286 Blaze Of Majesty (USA) *mid-to-rr, p.u. 3 out*......... 0
Howlin' Wolf *prom, bd mstk 8th, u.r. 10th*............ ur
12 ran. 5l, 12l, 2l, 2l, 10l. Time 6m 42.00s. SP Evens.
David A Smith (South Shropshire).

463 - 2½m Maiden (5-7yo) Div I (12st)

TAURA'S RASCAL........................R Bevis 1
(Jt fav) w.w. in tch, tk ld 3 out, ran on well
221 **Tanner.............................M Hammond** 2
t.o. hlfwy, schooling, btn fnce
167 Niord *ld to 8th, wknd quckly aftr 11th, p.u. 4 out*...... pu
Four Hearts (Ire) *(Jt fav) nvr shwd, p.u. 8th*........... pu
286 Costermonger *nvr btr thn mid-div, p.u. 3 out*.......... pu
Lydebrook *chsng grp, ld 9th-3 out, 2l 2nd whn slppd & u.r. last*........ ur
217 Sugi *f 1st*........ f
287 Frank The Swank 7a *prom early, fdd & sn btn 5 out, p.u. 3 out*........ pu
166 Mickley Justtheone 5a *c.u. to hlfwy, fdd 5 out, p.u. 3 out*........ pu
286 Nights Image (Ire) *chsng grp, 10l 3rd whn u.r. 4 out*... ur
Builder Boy *rr 5th, prog to chs ldrs 5 out, sn wknd, p.u. 2 out*........ pu
Po Cap Eel 5a *mid to rear, no dang, p.u. 3 out*......... pu
Sharsman (Ire) *w.w., rng on 3rd bt lkd hld whn f 3 out* f
174 Nobbutjust (Ire) 5a *rr, p.u. 3 out*........ pu
14 ran. Dist. Time 5m 17.00s. SP 5-2.
P A Jones (Tanatside).

464 - 2½m Maiden (5-7yo) Div II (12st)

GRAY ROSETTE 5a...............M Worthington 1
mid-div,prog 4 out, styd on to disp & lft in ld flat,readily
Shanballymore (Ire)......................J Tilley 2
mid-div,ran on frm 5 out, disp 2 out, not qckn, lft 2nd flat
288 **Merry Scorpion.........................T Marlow** 3
mid-div, nvr rchd ldrs, lft 3rd aftr last
165 Nothing Ventured *mid-div, sm prog frm 3 out, nrst fin* 4
241 Sargeants Choice *chsng grp, 2nd & ev ch whn c.o. by lse hrse 9th*........ co
167 Rejects Reply *md no shw, p.u. 4 out*........ pu
167 Antigua's Treasure (Ire) *(fav) prom, 2nd 4 out, disp 3rd & btn whn f last*........ f
Seymore Money *ld 4th, jnd 2 out, hdd & p.u. flat, dead*........ pu
286 Beeworthy 5a *s.s. sn in tch, outpcd 5 out, p.u. 3 out* .. pu
Bombadier Jack *u.r. 4th*........ ur
167 Michelles Crystal 7a *nvr btr thn mid-div, btn 8th, p.u. 3 out*........ pu
287 Little By Little *ldng grp whn r.o. 3rd*........ ro
166 Agile King 7a *ld tl f 3rd*........ f
13 ran. 3l, 3l, 5l. Time 5m 22.00s. SP 5-1.
Dr G M Thelwall Jones (Cheshire Forest).
V.S.

SOUTH DORSET
Milborne St Andrew
Sunday March 10th
GOOD

465 - Restricted Div I (12st)

EMERALD KNIGHT (IRE)...............P Henley 1
in tch, rdn 3 out, lft clr nxt, drvn out
211 **The Jogger...............................J Tizzard** 2
cls up, 3rd at 12th, ran on well frm 2 out, just hld
138 **Avril Showers 5a.....................R Atkinson** 3
chsd ldrs, 4th at 12th, outpcd frm 2 out
206 Sue's Quest 5a *rear, wll bhnd 12th, kpt on same pace*........ 4
Glamorous Guy *sn bhnd, t.o. 8th*........ 5
Lisahane Lad *sn rear, t.o. & p.u. 4 out*........ pu
Brendan's Way (Fr) *alwys mid-div, no ch whn p.u. 4 out*........ pu
Bill Of Rights *alwys mid-div, bhnd whn p.u. 13th*..... pu
205 Mammy's Choice (Ire) 5a *ld til blnd & u.r. 2 out*....... ur
68 Clandon Lad *(fav) cls up whn u.r. 3rd*........ ur
65 Saucy's Wolf *mid-div til lost tch 13th, blnd 15th & p.u.* pu
11 ran. Nk, 8l, dist, dist. Time 6m 14.00s. SP 9-2.
Peter Henley (Portman).

466 - Restricted Div II (12st)

69 **EARTHMOVER (IRE) 7a...........Miss P Curling** 1
in tch, ld 9th, ran on well frm 3 out
298 **Play Poker (Ire)..........................S Slade** 2
hld up, prog 12th, chal 2 out, alwys hld
144 **Market Gossip..........................P Henley** 3
(fav) ld to 8th, cls up aft, outpcd 15th
Thegoose *alwys mid-div, late prog frm 3 out, nvr nrr* 4
210 Balmoral Boy (NZ) *in tch to 4 out, wknd & onepcd frm nxt*........ 5
443 Majestic Spirit *alwys mid-div, outpcd frm 4 out*....... 6
Emily's Niece 5a *alwys bhnd, t.o. 15th*........ 7
Time Module *n.j.w. lost tch 12th, t.o. & p.u. 14th*...... pu
204 Bryn's Story *alwys mid-div, p.u. 11th*........ pu
200 Waipiro *mid-div til blnd & u.r. 7th*........ ur
Nearly A Mermaid 5a *prom til u.r. 7th*........ ur
205 Between You And Me *cls up early, mid-div whn f 13th*........ f
282 Belmount Beauty (Ire) 5a *cls up, ev ch 12th, lost tch 4 out, p.u. last*........ pu
13 ran. 3l, 4l, 2l, ½l, 1l, 25l. Time 6m 22.00s. SP 3-1.
R M Penny (Cattistock).

467 - Members

THE HUMBLE TILLER...........Miss L Knights 1
1st ride, 33s-11s, made all, clr 12th, ran on well 4 out
Mighty Falcon.......................Miss E Tory 2
1st ride, chsd ldrs, 4th at 15th, styd on frm 2 out, nrst fn
139 **Jabberwocky........................P MacEwan** 3
cls up, 3rd at 12th, outpcd frm 2 out
139 Country Style 5a *(fav) handy, chsd ldr 12th, wknd 3 out*........ 4
Beamish Boy *sn t.o.*........ 5
135 False Economy *cls up whn u.r. 7th*........ ur
210 Zorro's Mark *p.u. before 3rd, lame*........ pu
Inner Snu 5a *handy whn f 5th*........ f
8 ran. 15l, ½l, 10l, dist. Time 6m 20.00s. SP 11-1.
Miss L Knights (South Dorset).

468 - Open (12st)

133 **FAITHFUL STAR 7ex........................D Pipe** 1
(fav) hld up, prog 12th, ld 4 out, sn clr
209 **Bargain And Sale......................I Dowrick** 2
ld/disp to 4 out, outpcd by wnr aft
139 **Busteele...............................R White** 3
ld/disp to 14th, wknd nxt
142 Fosbury 7ex *hld up, ev ch 14th, not qckn frm 4 out* ... 4
Joe Penny *f 2nd*........ f
5 ran. 20l, 6l, 25l. Time 6m 19.00s. SP 4-6.
M C Pipe (Taunton Vale).

469 - Ladies

208 **DAYBROOK'S GIFT.................Miss N Allan** 1
bhnd, prog 14th, ld 2 out, sn clr
203 **Kings Gunner.....................Miss S Vickery** 2
handy, ld 13th-2 out, not qckn aft
273 **Wrekin Hill.....................Mrs J Wilkinson** 3
chsd ldrs, no ch & outpcd frm 3 out

208 Galaxy High *bhnd, late prog frm 4 out, not rch ldrs* . . . 4
139 Earl Boon *(fav) ld/disp to 12th, lost tch 4 out, b.b.v.* . . . 5
140 Brack N Brandy *ld/disp to 13th, wknd nxt, t.o.* . . . 6
279 Go West (bl) *sn rear, t.o. whn p.u. 15th* . . . pu
Temple Knight *mid-div, lost tch 12th, t.o. & p.u. 14th, lame* . . . pu
8 ran. 2l, 2l, 15l, 6l, 20l. Time 6m 17.00s. SP 9-1.
Miss N K Allan (Royal Artillery).

470 - Open Maiden Div I (12st)

BIRCHALL BOY............Miss W Southcombe 1
ld to 10th, ld agn last, ran on well
145 **Aller Moor (Ire) 7a......................P Henley** 2
(fav) hld up, prog 15th, ld 2 out, slppd final bnd,hdd & nt rcvr
Passing Fair 7a ....Miss S Vickery 3
mid-div, prog 12th, ld 4 out-2 out, outpcd aft
Final Express 5a *handy, ev ch 3 out, not qckn frm nxt* 4
Highway Lad *in tch, ev ch 15th, outpcd frm nxt* . . . 5
70 Gigi Beach (Ire) 7a *bhnd, some late prog, nrst fin* . . . 6
254 Vital Legacy *alwys mid-div, no ch frm 2 out* . . . 7
281 Blakeington *in tch, ld 11th-15th, wknd nxt* . . . 8
299 Reptile Princess 5a *sn bhnd, t.o. frm 14th* . . . 9
284 Say Charlie *alwys mid-div, no ch whn f last* . . . f
253 Shared Fortune (Ire) *cls up early, lost tch 14th, t.o. & p.u. last* . . . pu
280 Dula Model 5a *plld hrd, ld 4th til u.r. nxt* . . . ur
204 Orchard Lady 5a *rear whn u.r. 5th* . . . ur
143 Revels Hill (Ire) *alwys mid-div, no ch whn p.u. last* . . . pu
Byron Choice (Ire) *sn rear, some prog whn u.r. 14th* . . . ur
Miss Dotty 5a *mid-div til p.u. 15th* . . . pu
45 Mr Cherrypicker (Ire) *alwys mid-div, outpcd frm 4 out, p.u. last* . . . pu
Tempest Mead (Ire) *mid-div, no ch whn f 4 out* . . . f
18 ran. 1l, sht-hd, 4l, 2l, 1l, 1l, 10l, 25l. Time 6m 28.00s. SP 7-1.
P L Southcombe (Cattistock).

471 - Open Maiden Div II (12st)

BENGERS MOOR 7a.............Miss P Curling 1
handy, lft in ld 15th, sn clr, easily, imprssv
Master Mario ....P Henley 2
(fav) mid-div, prog 12th, chsd wnr vainly frm 15th
Coachroadstarboy ....B Dixon 3
mid-div, hmpd 5th, chsd ldr 15th, no imp 2 out
Laura's Flutter 5a *mid-div, ev ch 15th, outpcd frm nxt* 4
Nearly A Brook 5a *rear, prog 12th, outpcd frm 4 out, improve* . . . 5
200 Simply Joyful 5a *mid-div, lost tch 15th, onepcd aft* . . . 6
Orchestrated Chaos (Ire) 5a *in tch to 14th, wknd nxt, outpcd aft* . . . 7
Freemount Minstrel (Ire) *alwys rear, no ch frm 14th* . . . 8
207 Stormy Fashion *rear whn u.r. 8th* . . . ur
Green's Game *u.r. 2nd* . . . ur
Father Flattery *ld 5th til u.r. 15th* . . . ur
267 Celtic Token *ld to 4th, cls up whn u.r. 7th* . . . ur
272 Dormston Lad *alwys mid-div, no ch whn p.u. last* . . . pu
207 Tullykyne Bells *rear whn u.r. 5th* . . . ur
44 Hod Wood 7a *sn rear, t.o. & p.u. 2 out* . . . pu
Touch Of Wind 7a *mid-div, losing tch whn f 13th* . . . f
16 ran. 4l, 20l, 10l, 2l, 3l, 2l, 25l. Time 6m 27.00s. SP 7-2.
J R Townshend (Cattistock).

472 - Intermediate (12st)

297 **VITAL SONG ....G Matthews** 1
made all, ran on well frm 2 out
211 **Good For Business ....T Mitchell** 2
(fav) hld up, prog 14th, went 2nd nxt, rdn & not qckn last
212 **Balisteros (Fr)..................D Alers-Hankey** 3
mid-div, prog 14th, outpcd frm 3 out
137 Cautious Rebel *in tch to 12th, outpcd nxt* . . . 4
252 Bective Boy 5ex *sn rear, wll bhnd frm 15th* . . . 5
Captain Dimitris *sn rear, t.o. & p.u. 3 out* . . . pu
263 Our Jackie *chsd wnr to 11th, lost tch 13th, p.u. 15th* . . . pu
Suil Eile *mid-div til p.u. 9th, lame* . . . pu
8 ran. 6l, 20l, 15l, dist. Time 6m 15.00s. SP 5-2.
G Matthews (Blackmore & Sparkford Vale).
D.P.

STAFF COLLEGE & RMA DRAG
Tweseldown
Sunday March 10th
GOOD

473 - Members

275 **DAD'S PIPE...............................T Smith** 1
(fav) cls up, effrt 4 out, ld aft nxt, all out
Johnny Rose ....O Macphail 2
cls up til ld 12th, hdd aft 3 out, rallied last
Membering ....D Line 3
pllng, ld til apr 12th, wknd & btn 4 out
D-Day *1st ride, sn bhnd, t.o. 10th* . . . 4
248 Autumn Light 5a *dwelt, reluc to race, n.j.w. t.o. 5th, f 3 out* . . . f
5 ran. 1l, dist, dist. Time 6m 52.00s. SP 11-10.
T Smith (Staff College & Rmas Drag).

474 - Ladies

QANNAAS (bl) ....Miss P Jones 1
(fav) made all, qcknd clr frm 2 out, easily
216 **Ski Nut.........................Miss S Davison** 2
chsd wnr, clr 2nd frm 13th, ch whn blnd 3 out
5 **Tudor Henry ....Mrs C Mitchell** 3
chsd wnr to 13th, mstk 15th, sn btn
234 Phelioff *outpcd, t.o. 13th, nvr plcd to chal, stewards* . . . 4
250 Sky Venture *outpcd in rear, rdn frm hlfwy, t.o. 13th* . . . 5
336 Grand Value *outpcd, dtchd 4th whn u.r. 4th* . . . ur
270 Pat Alaska *u.r. 1st* . . . ur
7 ran. 8l, 8l, 20l, 7l. Time 6m 27.00s. SP 4-7.
Mrs Ann Leat (Hursley Hambledon).

475 - Confined (12st)

140 **DARTON RI 3ex..........................J Maxse** 1
(fav) disp til ld 3rd, made rest, mstk last, drvn out
232 **Space Man ....F Crew** 2
mid-div, prog 14th, styd on frm 2 out, nrst fin
140 **Smooth Escort 3ex..................T McCarthy** 3
hld up,prog 10th,rdn 3 out,styd on onepcd frm nxt
337 Strong Beau *trckd ldrs, 3rd & rmndrs 13th, ch 3 out, sn wknd* . . . 4
271 Skinnhill (bl) *2nd til mstk 10th, wknd rpdly, ran on agn cls home* . . . 5
Popeswood *mid-div, u.r. 2nd* . . . ur
What A To Do *mid-div, prog to 3rd hlfwy, sn wknd, bhnd whn u.r. 3 out* . . . ur
Charlton Yeoman *pllng, prom to 9th, t.o. whn p.u. 3 out* . . . pu
141 Olde Crescent *hld up rear, nvr in chal postn, p.u. 4 out* . . . pu
9 ran. 1l, hd, 12l, hd. Time 6m 33.50s. SP 6-4.
Mrs S Maxse (Hampshire).

476 - Open (12st)

209 **ARDBRENNAN.........................C Bennett** 1
2nd frm 9th, ld apr 2 out, pshd out, easily
346 **Linred...............................P Hacking** 2
handy, blnd badly 10th, styng on whn lft 2nd apr last, no ch
251 **Vultoro 4ex.......................T Underwood** 3
2nd to 9th, grad wknd, t.o. 2 out
271 Namoos 4ex *hld up, rear whn p.u. aft 9th, rein broke* pu
Freddy Owen 7ex *rear, jmpd lft 3rd, p.u. nxt, dsmntd* pu
Gormless (Ire) *handy, mstks frm 13th & wknd, p.u. 4 out* . . . pu
Swordella 5a *(fav) ld,blnd 12th,tired frm 4 out,hdd 2 out,p.u. aft,dsmntd* . . . pu
7 ran. 5l, dist. Time 6m 35.50s. SP 7-2.
C C Bennett (Vine & Craven).

477 - Open Maiden Div I (12st)

233 **BALANCE...................................T Cox** 1
3rd frm 9th til prog on bit 14th, ld 4 out, pshd out flat
255 **Just Ballytoo ....B Hodkin** 2

disp to 5th, 2nd aft til outpcd 15th, styd on 2 out,not qckn
3 **Vulgan Prince ....A Greig** 3
(fav) bhnd, mstk 14th, styd on frm 4 out, nrst fin
254 Joe Quality *mid-div, jnd ldrs 12th, ev ch til onepcd frm 4 out* 4
Trecometti 5a *ld, clr hlfwy, hdd 4 out, wknd rpdly*..... 5
252 Comers Gate *sn bhnd, t.o. & p.u. 4 out*........ pu
No Reply *disp to 5th, sn lost plc, p.u. 4 out*........ pu
341 Saxon Lass 5a *rear of ldng grp, in tch to 4 out, p.u. 2 out*........ pu
Queens Day 5a *rear of ldng grp to hlfwy, p.u. 4 out*... pu
264 Duques 5a *n.j.w. sn rear, t.o. 10th, p.u. 14th*........ pu
334 Devil's Sting (Ire) *prom to 10th, wknd nxt, p.u. 2 out*... pu
282 Tom Boy *trckd ldrs, ev ch 14th, lost plc frm nxt, p.u. 2 out*........ pu
253 Shelley Street 5a *schoold in rear, t.o. 11th, p.u. 4 out* pu
Wergild *u.r. 1st*........ ur
62 Hullabaloo 5a 3ow *bhnd whn u.r. 9th*........ ur
15 ran. 2½l, 12l, 8l, 25l. Time 6m 37.00s. SP 8-1.
Richard J Smith (Beaufort).

478 - Restricted (12st)

339 **TRANSPLANT BLUE ....S Goodings** 1
trckd ldrs, prog 3 out, ld apr last, rdn out
140 **Windover Lodge ....Miss M Hill** 2
j.w. ld, rdn 2 out, hdd apr last, no ext
269 **Pavi's Brother ....R Sweeting** 3
(fav) trckd ldrs,blnd 8th,2nd 13th,ev ch til onepcd frm 3 out
231 Ramlosa (NZ) *u.r. 3rd*........ ur
248 Souldan (Ire) *prom early, in pack whn p.u. aft 11th*.... pu
Celtic Demon *rear, prog & ch in 4th whn f 15th*...... f
272 Palaman *mostly 2nd to 12th, 4th & lkd btn whn u.r. 3 out*........ ur
Apple John *whppd round start, jmpd badly, wll btn whn f 2 out*........ f
341 Glenisla 5a *slw jmp 1st, tried to ref & rdr lost irons 2nd, p.u.*........ pu
9 ran. 3½l, 12l. Time 6m 39.00s. SP 25-1.
S J Goodings (Windsor Forest Drag).

479 - Open Maiden Div II (12st)

221 **SILVER CONCORD ....S Blackwell** 1
dist 5th hlfwy, prog 11th, lft clr 3 out, fin tired
Image Boy (Ire)................A Charles-Jones 2
schoold rear, t.o. 4th, lft remote 4th 3 out, tk 2nd flat
267 **Dip The Lights 5a ....F Brennan** 3
sn bhnd, lft remote 2nd 3 out, tired & lost plc flat
Roneo (USA) *4th & pshd alng whn f 10th*........ f
204 Juniper Lodge *6s-3s, disp to 6th, rdn & lkd hld whn f 3 out*........ f
341 The Man From Clare (Ire) *bhnd, some mod late prog whn f 3 out*........ f
221 Mr Wendyl *cls up, ld 13th, 2l up whn u.r. 3 out*........ ur
144 Wicked Thoughts *(fav) disp til ld 6th, hdd 13th, btn 4th whn f 4 out, winded*........ f
254 Orphan Olly *rear, t.o. 13th, lft remote 3rd 3 out, disp 2nd whn f last*........ f
Bitofamixup (Ire) 7a *schoold in rear, t.o. 4th, p.u. 10th* pu
10 ran. Dist, 2l. Time 6m 45.00s. SP 8-1.
Mrs D E Cheshire (Ross Harriers).
M.J.

PLUMPTON
Monday March 11th
GOOD TO SOFT

480 - 3m 1f 110yds Hun

102 **LOYAL NOTE 11.11 3a ....Mr Simon Andrews** 1
j.w, ld 2nd till 10th, led 14th, clr apr last.
258 **Royal Irish 11.9 5a..................Mr P Henley** 2
(fav) ld till 2nd, led 10th till 14th, ev ch 2 out, one pace.
260 **Paco's Boy 11.7 7a....................Mr P York** 3
hdwy 11th, ev ch after, one pace from 3 out.
274 Centre Stage 11.7 7a *blnd 2nd, alwys bhnd, t.o. from 11th*........ 4
360 Ullswater 11.7 7a *prom till wknd 9th, t.o. from 13th*... 5
265 Spring Fun 11.7 7a *prom till 9th, t.o. from 14th, p.u. before last*........ pu
6 ran. 6l, nk, dist, 24l. Time 7m 3.50s. SP 15-8.
R Andrews

TAUNTON
Monday March 11th
GOOD

481 - 3m Hun Chase

210 **SPACE CAPPA 11.12 7a ....Miss V Stephens** 1
prom, ld 4th to 10th, regained ld four out, in command when mstk 2 out, readily.
196 **Just My Bill 11.12 7a ....Mr C Heard** 2
waited with, hdwy 6th, chsd wnr from 4 out, no impn from next.
360 **My Mellow Man 12.7 5a (bl) ....Mr T Mitchell** 3
jmpd left, held up, hdwy apr 5th, blnd badly next, outpcd 4 out, kept on again from 2 out.
265 Granville Guest 12.5 7a *(fav) in tch, ld 10th, hdd 4 out, wknd next*........ 4
Father Dowling 12.5 7a *held up, hdwy 11th, wknd 15th*........ 5
135 Winter's Lane 12.5 7a *held up in tch, wknd from 15th.* 6
210 Eagle Trace 11.12 7a *alwys bhnd, t.o. from 9th*........ 7
294 Buckingham Gate 12.5 7a *bhnd 5th, t.o. from 9th*..... 8
Abba Lad 12.5 7a *ld, pkd 1st, hdd 4th, lost tch 8th, t.o. next*........ 9
Pactolus (USA) 11.12 7a *blnd 3rd, alwys bhnd, t.o. when tried to refuse 5th, soon p.u.*........ pu
198 Greenwine (USA) 12.5 7a *bhnd from 14th, t.o. when p.u. before 3 out*........ pu
11 ran. 5l, 3l, 16l, 6l, 11l, 7l, 21l, dist. Time 6m 19.20s. SP 3-1.
D G Stephens

NEWTON ABBOT
Wednesday March 13th
SOFT

482 - 2m 5f 110yds Nov Hun

296 **THE GENERAL'S DRUM 11.10 7a ....Mr K Heard** 1
held up in rear, steady hdwy from 10th, ld last, rdn out.
134 **Myhamet 11.12 5a ....Mr A Farrant** 2
alwys in tch, ld 6th out, hdd next, led and mstk 3 out, hrd rdn and hded last, no ext.
297 **On Alert (NZ) 11.10 7a.........Mr Richard White** 3
in tch, ld 6th, hdd 8th, led 10th to next, led 5 out to 3 out, wknd apr next.
432 Cathgal 11.10 7a *ld to 3rd, wknd 10th, t.o.*........ 4
360 Bootscraper 11.10 7a (bl) *(fav) f 2nd*........ f
Northern Optimist 11.7 5a *in tch till wknd 9th, p.u. before next*........ pu
281 Mountain Master 11.10 7a *bhnd till hdwy 6th, in tch when blnd and u.r. 10th*........ ur
Paid Elation 11.5 7a *alwys bhnd, t.o. when p.u. before 10th*........ pu
Sausalito Boy 11.10 7a *mid div till wknd 6th, p.u. before 9th*........ pu
132 Stormy Sunset 11.5 7a *ld 3rd to 6th, led 8th to 10th, weakening when blnd and u.r. 3 out*........ ur
277 Early To Rise 11.10 7a *chsd ldrs till f 4 out*........ f
300 Biddlestone Boy (NZ) 11.10 7a (v) *mstk 4th, prom till f 9th*........ f
202 Master Kiwi (NZ) 11.10 7a *alwys bhnd, t.o. when p.u. before 4 out*........ pu
445 Chukamill 11.10 7a *in tch to 6th, t.o. when p.u. before 4 out*........ pu
14 ran. 4l, 24l, dist. Time 6m 13.80s. SP 4-1.
Mrs R Fell

CHELTENHAM
Thursday March 14th

GOOD

483 - 3¼m 110yds Chase

ELEGANT LORD (IRE) 12.0 ....Mr E Bolger 1
(fav) alwys going well, hdwy on bit final cct, ld 3 out, qcknd clr 2 out, comf.
185 **Cool Dawn (Ire) 12.0 ....Miss D Harding** 2
soon ld, hdd 8th, led again 12th, hded 3 out, outpcd 2 out, kept on from last.
Kerry Orchid 12.0 (v) ....Mr P Fenton 3
midfield, n.j.w., gd hdwy to chase ldrs 5 out, hit next, one pace apr 2 out.
185 Proud Sun 12.0 *whipped round start, hmpd 3rd, n.j.w. after, blnd 9th and 13th, styd on from 2 out, n.d..* 4
99 Holland House 12.0 *held up, pushed along from 6 out, styd on steadily from 3 out, nvr nrr.* 5
153 Goolds Gold 12.0 *held up, pushed along towards rear 6 out, nvr able to chal.* 6
184 Clare Man (Ire) 12.0 *cl up, ld 8th, jmpd right 10th, hdd 12th, driven along and mstk 3 out, fd from next.* 7
209 The Bird O'Donnell 12.0 *mid div when hit 5th, hdwy to chase ldrs from 10th, disp 3rd when mstk 3 out, wknd apr next.* 8
265 Lewesdon Hill 12.0 *blnd in rear 6th, struggling final cct, t.o..* 9
Earlydue 12.0 *held up, struggling when blnd 6 out, t.o..* 10
184 Country Tarrogen 12.0 *went handy 8th, mstk and driven along 14th, lost tch 6 out, t.o..* 11
256 Cape Cottage 12.0 *bhnd, hmpd 3rd, struggling from hfwy, well t.o. when p.u. between last 2.* pu
191 Royal Stream 12.0 *midfield, hmpd 12th, bhnd when blnd 15th, p.u. before 3 out.* pu
362 Hermes Harvest 12.0 (v) *cl up when f 12th.* f
99 Mr Golightly 12.0 *chsd ldrs, mstk 10th, 6th and driven along when u.r. 4 out.* ur
260 Colonial Kelly 12.0 *hit 1st, cl up when f 3rd.* f
360 What A Hand 12.0 *f 1st.* f
17 ran. 6l, 7l, sht-hd, 3½l, 2½l, 4l, 2l, 15l, 15l, dist. Time 6m 50.80s. SP 3-1.
J P McManus

FAKENHAM
Friday March 15th
GOOD TO FIRM

484 - 2m 5f 110yds Nov Hun Chase

257 **PRO BONO (IRE) 11.2 7a.........Mr A Sansome** 1
chsd ldr, ld 12th, rdn and styd on well from last.
361 **A Windy Citizen (Ire) 11.3 7a ....Mr R Hicks** 2
(fav) well in tch, hit 5th, blnd and lost pl 9th, ran on again after 12th, fin well.
100 **Erins Bar (Ire) 11.12 3a 6ow ....Mr A Hill** 3
held up, imp 7th, cld on ldrs from 11th, ev ch 3 out, one pace apr last.
327 Galzig 11.3 7a 1ow *soon tracking ldrs, hit 3rd, rdn and no ext from 3 out.* 4
361 Familiar Friend 11.2 7a (bl) *mid div, gd hdwy from 12th, wknd from 2 out.* 5
419 Cool Apollo (NZ) 11.2 7a *nvr nrr.* 6
361 Couture Quality 11.2 7a (bl) *ld, hit 7th, hdd 12th, wknd 3 out.* 7
328 Tresillian Bay 11.2 7a *well pld till hit 3 out, soon btn..* 8
361 Candle Glow 10.13 7a 2ow *chsd ldrs till wknd 11th.* 9
346 Miss Construe 11.3 7a 6ow *alwys towards rear, lost tch from 10th, mstk 2 out.* 10
348 Wistino 11.2 7a *chsd ldrs till blnd and u.r. 4th.* ur
100 Just Jack 11.12 3a *u.r. 1st.* ur
104 Laburnum 11.2 7a *in 7th pl to hfwy, bhnd when p.u. before 11th.* pu
13 ran. 3l, ½l, ¾l, 6l, 8l, 6l, 15l, 10l, 18l. Time 5m 30.30s. SP 3-1.
P C Caudwell

HEREFORD
Saturday March 16th
SOFT

485 - 3m 1f 110yds Hun Chase

365 **HOWARYASUN (IRE) 11.11 7a (v) ...Mr D S Jones** 1
(fav) held up, hdwy 14th, ld last, ran on well.
379 **All Weather 11.7 7a............Mr J M Pritchard** 2
prom in chasing gp, cld from 14th, disp ld when jmpd left 3 out and next, hdd last, hung badly left, no ext flat.
Sir Noddy 11.11 7a..............Mr C Stockton 3
ld, clr to 11th, clear again 14th, joined 3 out, hdd last, soon btn.
185 Golden Freeze 11.11 7a *chsd ldr from 5th to 4 out, soon wknd, t.o..* 4
255 Rusty Bridge 12.0 7a *n.j.w., bhnd from 7th, soon pushed along, lost tch 11th, t.o..* 5
383 Lislary Lad 11.11 7a *midfield, mstk 5th, hit 9th, some hdwy 12th, wknd before 14th, t.o..* 6
360 Old Steine 11.7 7a *bhnd, t.o. from 7th.* 7
360 Brown Windsor 12.2 5a (bl) *prom till jmpd slowly 3rd, soon bhnd, t.o. when p.u. before 4 out.* pu
258 Land Of Wonder (USA) 11.11 7a *bhnd, t.o. when p.u. before 6th.* pu
372 Faringo 11.11 7a *cl up when blnd and u.r. 1st.* ur
458 Orton House 11.7 7a *jmpd slowly thrght, soon t.o., p.u. before 12th.* pu
Fine Timing 11.9 5a *chsd ldrs, wknd 11th, t.o. when p.u. before 15th.* pu
99 Out For Fun 11.7 7a *in tch, mstk 2nd, blnd 10th, soon lost pl, hdwy 12th, 3rd when f next (water).* f
13 ran. 8l, 8l, dist, 25l, 2l, dist. Time 7m 4.80s. SP 9-4.
M R Watkins

NEWCASTLE
Saturday March 16th
GOOD TO SOFT

486 - 3m Hun Chase

367 **WUDIMP 11.10 5a ....Mr C Storey** 1
(fav) held up in rear, blnd 12th, hdwy after 4 out, chal last, soon ld, kept on well.
298 **Deday 11.0 7a..................Mr M Bradburne** 2
prom, ld 7th, blnd 12th, hdd after last, not qckn.
367 **Quixall Crossett 11.0 7a...........Mr P Murray** 3
held up, hit 8th, rallied 11th, ev ch 3 out, one pace last.
291 Side Brace (NZ) 11.3 7a *in tch, lost pl before 9th, rallied 11th, struggling last 3.* 4
368 Ballyandrew 11.0 7a *pulld hrd and soon led, hdd 7th, prom, fd apr 3 out.* 5
259 Ruber 11.12 5a *chsd ldrs, lost pl 10th, no dngr after.* 6
223 Advent Lady 10.9 7a *prom, reminders 13th, blnd 5 out, soon struggling.* 7
320 Tartan Tornado 11.10 5a *not fluent in rear, nvr on terms.* 8
400 Panto Lady 10.9 7a *held up in tch, hdwy 8th, struggling 13th, t.o..* 9
9 ran. 1½l, 2l, 20l, 7l, 2l, 12l, 9l, dist. Time 6m 23.50s. SP 4-7.
C Storey

487 - 3m Hun Chase

37 **DARK DAWN 11.13 ....Mr S Swiers** 1
held up, hdwy hfwy, ld apr 3 out, soon clr, kept on.
86 **Washakie 11.5 5a.................Mr P Johnson** 2
(Co fav) held up, gd hdwy 8th, outpcd after 3 out, hung left, styd on well from last.
187 **Green Times 11.6 7a............Capt W Ramsay** 3
alwys prom, ld briefly after 4 out, styd on one pace.
259 Carousel Rocket 11.3 7a *(Co fav) settld towards rear, rdn along from 10th, soon outpcd, no dngr after.* 4
402 Fish Quay 11.3 7a *bhnd, mstk 14th, soon struggling, t.o..* 5
460 Simply Perfect 11.3 7a *(Co fav) settld in tch, chsd ldrs 7th, outpcd final 3.* 6
412 Pinewood Lad 11.3 7a *in tch, lost pl 9th, soon struggling, t.o..* 7
Mr Diplomatic 11.3 7a (bl) *cl up, ld 4th, stumbled and hdd after four out, p.u. next.* pu

Little General 11.5 5a *blnd 3rd, towards rear, imp after 8th, struggling after 6 out, p.u. 3 out* .... pu
259 Loughlinstown Boy 11.5 5a *ld to 4th, prom, blnd 8th, struggling when p.u. before 13th* .... pu
10 ran. 5l, 7l, 25l, 14l, 6l, 20l. Time 6m 19.10s. SP 11-2.
Mrs J M Newitt

488 - 2½m Nov Hun Chase

304 **HYPERION SON 12.0 7a ....Mr M Haigh** 1
(fav) alwys well pld, chal 9th, mstk 11th, driven after 4 out, rallied to ld between last 2, left clr last.
371 **Reviller's Glory 12.7 ....Mr S Swiers** 2
disp ld, went on 8th, hdd 5 out, left remote 2nd last.
190 **Flypie 12.2 5a ....Mr C Storey** 3
soon well bhnd till styd on last 2, n.d..
371 Eilid Anoir 12.2 5a *disp ld to 8th, soon pushed along, struggling last 5* 4
371 Henrymyson 12.0 7a *in tch, struggling before 6 out, soon btn* 5
303 Constant Amusement 11.11 5a *soon well bhnd, p.u. 7th* .... pu
308 Flying Pan 11.11 5a *settld in tch, challenging when u.r. 3 out* .... ur
88 Coolreny (Ire) 12.4 3a *nvr far away, hit 5th, ld 5 out, hit next, hdd after 2 out, five l 2nd when f last* .... f
405 Called To Account 11.11 5a *alwys bhnd, t.o. when p.u. before 12th* .... pu
9 ran. 30l, nk, 30l, 1½l. Time 5m 31.20s. SP 6-4.
John Mackley

CAMBRIDGESHIRE
Horseheath
Saturday March 16th
GOOD TO FIRM

489 - Members

418 **WAY OF LIFE (FR) 5ex ....J Ferguson** 1
sttld bhnd ldr, ld 7th-10th, ld 4 out, blnd 2 out, all out
315 **Bruff Castle ....Mrs L Gibbon** 2
lft in ld 4th-7th,ld 10th-4 out, mstk nxt, ev ch last,no ext
107 Highland Rally (USA) *(fav) rear, blnd & nrly u.r. 1st, mstk & u.r. 4th* .... ur
108 Ballysheil Star *rear frm 2nd, mstk & u.r. nxt* .... ur
4 ran. 2l. Time 6m 34.00s. SP 6-4.
John Ferguson (Thurlow).

490 - P P O R A (12st)

369 **LUCKY CHRISTOPHER 5ex ....G Tarry** 1
(fav) trckd ldrs, 2nd 4 out, chal nxt, ld aft 2 out, rdn out
335 **Jerrigo ....J Knowles** 2
j.w. ld aft 1st, hdd aft 2 out, kpt on well
420 **Glen Oak ....W Wales** 3
hld up, 6th & rdn aft 11th, prog 4 out, ev ch nxt, wknd 2out
Decent Gold *mid-div, prog to 4th at 10th, lost tch ldrs 13th, t.o. 4 out* 4
Parkbhride *rear of main grp, mstk 9th, und pres whn f heavily 12th* .... f
Mount Eaton Fox *alwys last, jmpd delib, lost tch 4th, t.o. & p.u. 10th* .... pu
Kelly's Twilight 5a *ld & mstk 1st, prom til wknd rpdly 12th, t.o. & p.u. 3 out* .... pu
7 ran. 1l, 3l, dist. Time 6m 28.00s. SP 2-7.
G B Tarry (Grafton).

491 - Confined (12st)

417 **JIMMY MAC JIMMY ....C Ward-Thomas** 1
j.w. made all, going wll 4 out, ran on strngly
310 **As You Were ....D Parravani** 2
rear, prog 13th, ev ch 3 out, onepcd
420 **Melton Park 5ex (bl) ....N Bloom** 3
(fav) mid-div, last at 5th, mstks 8 & 9th, ev ch 4 out, onepcd
311 Notary-Nowell *alwys in tch, 2nd & ev ch 3 out, wknd nxt* 4
310 Mr Gossip *w.w. rmndrs 5th, prog to jn ldrs 10th, ev ch 4 out, wknd* 5
5 ran. 3l, 4l, 10l, 15l. Time 6m 28.00s. SP 25-1.
D R Barnard (Essex).

492 - Open

312 **COPPER THISTLE (IRE) ....P Taiano** 1
(fav) j.w. made all at steady pace, qcknd clr last, easily
312 **Saint Bene't (Ire) ....A Coe** 2
alwys 2nd, jnd wnr 13th, ev ch 3 out, mstk nxt, btn last
433 **Parting Hour ....R Adderson** 3
alwys last, lost tch 12th, t.o. 4 out
3 ran. 4l, dist. Time 6m 36.00s. SP 1-6.
M G Sheppard (Cambridgeshire).

493 - Ladies

369 **RICHARD HUNT ....Miss L Rowe** 1+
(fav) ld at gd pace, hdd last, ran on well flat
311 **LARRY THE LAMB ....Miss G Chown** 1+
sttld in 2nd, hrd rdn to ld last, ld flat, lkd to hld on
421 **St Gregory ....Mrs L Gibbon** 3
s.v.s mstks 1st & 2nd, nvr on terms, wknd 12th,lft 3rd 4 out
311 Sarazar (USA) *prom, 2nd at 8th, mstk 12th, lost tch 13th, u.r. 4 out* .... ur
4 ran. Dd-ht, dist. Time 6m 26.00s.
Mrs P Rowe/ Mrs F Chown (Puckeridge/ Grafton).
Richard Hunt, 4/7. Larry The Lamb, 4/1.

494 - Restricted (12st)

313 **PARKERS HILLS (IRE) ....S Sporborg** 1
prom, rdn 4 out, btn 2nd whn lft clr 2 out, all out
106 **Harpley Dual (Ire) 7ow ....A Case** 2
hld up rear, ran on past btn horses frm 3 out, nvr nrr
313 **Miss Solitaire 5a ....G Tarry** 3
mid-div, prog 13th, lft remote 2nd 2 out, tired & dmtd flat
181 Radiant Monarch *alwys rear, prog 4 out, wknd rpdly nxt, t.o.* 4
Frenchlands Way *prom til f 4th* .... f
433 Just Donald *alwys mid-div, lost tch ldrs 12th, t.o. & p.u. 3 out* .... pu
Linlake Lightning 5a *alwys bhnd, lst tch 6th, t.o. & p.u. 10th* .... pu
236 Tommy O'Dwyer (Ire) *(fav) sttld rear,prog to trck ldrs 12th,blnd 4 out,wknd,p.u.2 out* .... pu
315 Opus Winwood (Ire) *cls up, 3rd whn f 11th* .... f
314 No Quitting (Ire) *sn ld, 4l clr 4 out, in cmmnd whn f 2 out* .... f
10 ran. 10l, 8l, 20l. Time 6m 31.00s. SP 25-1.
Christopher Sporborg (Puckeridge).

495 - Open Maiden Div I (12st)

341 **CANADIAN BOY (IRE) ....A Tutton** 1
alwys prom, ld 9th, prssd 4 out, ran on well, fin tired
182 **George The Greek (Ire) ....A Coe** 2
prom, chal wnr 4 out, no ext frm 2 out
439 **Apple Nicking ....A Hill** 3
(fav) sttld mid-div,prog 10th,mstks 12 & nxt,hrd rdn 4 out,onepcd
340 Yabbadabbadoo *hld up bhnd, rmndrs 10th, t.o. frm 12th* 4
314 Aughnacloy Rose *alwys rear, mstk 11th, t.o. 13th* 5
423 Loch Irish (Ire) 5a *alwys rear, effrt 14th, sn wknd, virt p.u. flat* 6
424 Superforce *prom early, lost tch 11th, bhnd whn mstk & u.r. 13th* .... ur
418 Regal Shadow *pllng, hld up, lost tch 10th, t.o. & p.u. 4 out* .... pu
61 Muddle Head (Ire) *pllng, disp 6th, lost plc 10th, wknd 13th, p.u. 4 out* .... pu

423 But Not Quite (Ire) *ld to 7th, wknd rpdly 10th, t.o. & p.u. 4 out* .... pu
438 Petoski Bay *mid-div, prog to jn ldrs 5th, wknd 9th, t.o. & p.u. 3 out* .... pu
341 Dolly Bloom 5a *mstk 3rd, in tch to 10th, t.o. & p.u. 4 out* .... pu
12 ran. 4l, 20l, 3l, 4l, 8l. Time 6m 33.00s. SP 7-2.
Mrs J Shirley (Farmers Bloodhounds).

496 - Open Maiden Div II (12st)

438 **ALIAS SILVER..........................Miss H Irving** 1
mid-div, prog 6th, ld 3 out, qckned clr 2 out, eased flat
315 **Lavins Thatch 5a.....................R Lawther** 2
prom, jnd ldrs 10th, und pres 13th, ev ch 3 out, sn btn
315 **Auchendolly (Ire)...................S Sporborg** 3
(fav) alwys wll plcd, 2nd at 7th, ld aft 10th, hdd & outpcd 3 out
424 Room To Manouver (Ire) *bhnd til ran on onepcd frm 2 out, nvr nrr* 4
454 Run To Au Bon (Ire) (bl) *restrnd, prog 11th, sn bhnd, ran on well flat* 5
343 Stanwick Belfry 5a 3ow *hld up rear, nvr on trms, t.o. 10th* 6
344 Bozo Bailey *prom to 10th, wknd, sn t.o.* 7
439 Lloyds Loser *sn ld, clr 6th, mstk & f 8th* .... f
105 Here's Humphrey *last whn ref 1st, cont, ref 2nd* .... ref
106 Tasmanite *alwys rear, blnd & nrly u.r. 9th, t.o. 3 out, p.u. nxt* .... pu
10 ran. 3l, 5l, dist, 1l, 15l, 8l. Time 6m 36.00s. SP 9-4.
J H Busby (Grafton).
J.W.

EGLINTON
Lanark
Saturday March 16th
GOOD

497 - Members

187 **HAMILTON LADY (IRE) 5a...............M Smith** 1
(fav) ld 10th, sn wll clr, fin alone
Bitofanatter *ld til 10th, sn lost tch, t.o. & u.r. last* .... ur
2 ran. Time 6m 59.00s. SP 4-5.
Alex Fergusson (Eglinton).

498 - Confined (12st)

319 **MASTER KIT (IRE)......................J Billinge** 1
(fav) alwys handy, ld 9th, drew clr frm 3 out
317 **Little Glen.............................T Scott** 2
ld 6th-9th, 3rd frm nxt, went 2nd 2 out, no ch wth wnr
187 **Fordstown (Ire) 10ex...............J Alexander** 3
ld to 5th, 20l 5th at 11th, styd on frm 4 out
316 Piper O'Drummond *chsd wnr frm 9th, wknd 3 out* 4
109 Duncans Dream *sn bhnd, some late prog, nvr dang* .. 5
317 Paddy Hayton *alwys wll bhnd* 6
190 Hydropic *alwys wll bhnd* 7
402 Andrew *ld brfly 5th, lost tch by 11th, p.u. 2 out* .... pu
371 Canny Chronicle *cls 4th at 11th, wknd 4 out, p.u. 2 out* .... pu
Leyden Lady 5a *alwys wll bhnd, p.u. 2 out* .... pu
10 ran. 20l, 2l, 6l, 5l, 15l, 12l. Time 6m 37.00s. SP 2-1.
J Billinge (Fife).

499 - Ladies

400 **READY STEADY...............Mrs K Hargreave** 1
cls up til ld 7th, made rest, lft wll clr 2 out
400 **Minibrig 5a.........................Miss P Robson** 2
(fav) hld up, went 2nd brfly 4 out, no imp whn lft 2nd agn 2 out
398 **Barton Royal (Ire)..................Miss F Barnes** 3
ld 4th-7th, lost tch 3 out
186 Rarely At Odds *nvr a dang* 4
398 Galadine *sn wll bhnd* 5
305 Rare Fire *sn well bhnd, p.u. 10th* .... pu
112 Colonel James *ld to 4th, wll bhnd whn p.u. 4 out* .... pu
318 Carousel Calypso *2nd at 11th, lost tch 3 out, poor 4th whn p.u. last* .... pu
190 Handsome Gent *sn bhnd, p.u. 4 out* .... pu
400 Tannock Brook *3rd at 11th, chsd wnr frm 3 out, 4l down whn u.r. 2 out* .... ur
10 ran. Dist, 12l, dist. Time 6m 32.00s. SP 6-4.
Lady Temple (Percy-West).

500 - Open

285 **WALLY WREKIN (bl).......................R Ford** 1
made all, kpt on wll
402 **Duntree..............................C Macmillan** 2
chsd wnr frm 12th, no real imp
399 **Boreen Owen..........................T Morrison** 3
3rd at 11th, nvr a serious dang
King Spring *(fav) alwys rear, lost tch by 4 out* 4
259 Toddlin Hame *2nd at 11th, wknd frm 13th* 5
49 Dundee Prince (NZ) *reluc to race, abt 2 fences bhnd by 4th, p.u. 13th* .... pu
6 ran. 5l, 5l, 15l, 6l. Time 6m 46.00s. SP 6-1.
Mrs C R Dutton (Sir W W Wynn's).

501 - Restricted (12st)

319 **DRAKEWRATH (IRE).....................A Parker** 1
(fav) alwys handy, slght ld apr 3 out, hld on well
407 **Cukeira 5a..........................T Morrison** 2
alwys handy, prssd wnr frm 3 out, just hld
398 **Pennine View...............................R Ford** 3
clsd up 4 out, no real imp on ldng pair aft
112 Royal Fife 5a *sn bhnd, t.o.* 4
111 Jads Lad *sn bhnd, t.o.* 5
111 Corby Knowe *nvr dang, bhnd whn u.r. 3 out* .... ur
193 About Midnight 5a *ld/disp til wknd frm 11th, bhnd whn p.u. 2 out* .... pu
400 Mandys Special 5a *prom early, losing tch whn f 11th* .... f
322 Overstep *sn bhnd, p.u. 13th* .... pu
332 Tina's Missile *disp til ld 11th, hdd aft 4 out, btn 4th whn f 2 out* .... f
Rallying Cry (Ire) *nvr dang, p.u. 2 out* .... pu
404 Miss Cullane (Ire) 5a *sn bhnd, p.u. 12th* .... pu
12 ran. ½l, 6l, dist, 8l. Time 6m 38.00s. SP 7-4.
R A Bartlett (Fife).

502 - Open Maiden Div I

404 **BOWLANDS HIMSELF (IRE)..............R Ford** 1
made all, clr 4 out, hld on well
406 **Denim Blue......................Miss P Robson** 2
(fav) wnet 2nd 12th, clsd on wnr frm 3 out, not quite get up
115 **Rough House 7a ....R Robinson** 3
4th at 11th, nvr dang
398 Bullaford Fair *in tch whn u.r. 9th* .... ur
158 Woolstonwood 5a *lost tch by 12th, p.u. 2 out* .... pu
114 Davy's Lad 7a *cls 2nd at 11th, wknd & p.u. apr nxt* .... pu
193 Two Gun Tex *in tch whn u.r. 6th* .... ur
7 ran. 1½l, dist. Time 6m 50.00s. SP 5-2.
Mrs Lynn Campion (Vale Of Lune Harriers).

503 - Open Maiden Div II

323 **SOLWAYSANDS..............................R Ford** 1
alwys handy, disp 4 out, drew clr apr nxt
194 **Ballyargan (Ire)....................R Westwood** 2
bhnd til prog frm 4 out, tk 2nd flat
406 **Rustic Bridge................................S Love** 3+
(fav) alwys handy, disp 4 out, outpcd frm nxt, blnd last
Saigon Lady (Ire) 5a....................A Parker 3+
cls up til outpcd frm 3 out
Claywalls 7a *alwys bhnd* 5
399 Wang How *mid-div whn u..r 9th* .... ur
Zoflo 5a *ld til 4 out, wknd rpdly, t.o. & p.u. aft last* .... pu
114 Madame Beck 5a *sn bhnd, p.u. 11th* .... pu
Copper Dial *sn bhnd, t.o. & p.u. 11th* .... pu
407 Gemma Law 5a *sn bhnd, t.o. & p.u. 11th* .... pu
10 ran. Dist, 6l, dd-ht, dist. Time 6m 50.00s. SP 3-1.
K Little (Dumfriesshire).
R.J.

GELLIGAER
Magor
Saturday March 16th
GOOD TO SOFT

504 - Members

357 **BAY LEADER 5a.................Miss E Tamplin** 1
made all, clr hlfwy, prssd 15th, qcknd clr
Auvillar (USA).........................P Doorhof 2
(fav) hld up, prog to mod 2nd 3 out, no imp
384 **Martiya 5a............................S Shinton** 3
chsd wnr, rdn to chal 15th, wknd rpdly aft
Colonel Frazer (Ire) *3rd til lost tch 12th, p.u. last* ...... pu
Trydan *cls 4th whn ran out 4th* .... ro
5 ran. 20l, 20l. Time 7m 19.00s. SP 3-1.
G I Isaac (Gelligaer Farmers).

505 - P P O R A (12st)

335 **AFRICAN BRIDE (IRE) 5a...........Miss P Jones** 1
(fav) 2nd til ld 7th, made rest, easily
267 **My Boy Barney.............................J Jukes** 2
hld up, prog to clr 2nd frm 15th, wknd flat
157 **Chibougama (USA)...................S Shinton** 3
cls up in 2nd frm 7-15th, 3rd & onepcd aft
379 Tekla (Fr) *rear, blnd 12th, lost tch aft* 4
157 Bronze Effigy *mod 4th til onepcd frm 12th, t.o. & ref last* .... ref
364 I Is *ld to 7th, wkng whn f nxt* .... f
219 Forever In Debt 5a *last pair whn p.u. 7th* .... pu
7 ran. 15l, 6l, dist. Time 6m 42.00s. SP 1-3.
David Brace (Llangeinor).

506 - Confined (12st)

385 **LA MEZERAY 5a 3ex.............Mrs J Hawkins** 1
(fav) hld up, prog to 2nd 14th, ld 2 out, easily
295 **Mo's Chorister ....Miss S Young** 2
chsng grp, 3rd 3 out, ran on to tk 2nd last
384 **St Helens Boy...........................J Tudor** 3
2nd til ld 10th, 5l clr 15th, hdd & onepcd 2 out
350 Gee Double You *rear, styd on frm 3 out, hrd rdn & nvr nrr* 4
385 Dewliner *last at hlfwy, t.o. & p.u. 2 out* .... pu
383 Silks Domino *cls up in 2nd/3rd to 13th, wknd rpdly, p.u. last* .... pu
351 Mummy's Song *ld to 10th, wknd, t.o. & p.u. last* ...... pu
28 Lazzaretto *t.o. 3rd, p.u. 6th* .... pu
8 ran. 15l, 15l, 10l. Time 6m 48.00s. SP 4-6.
C C Morgan (Tredegar Farmers).

507 - Mixed Open

219 **LIGHTEN THE LOAD....................A Wintle** 1
2s-6/4, hld up, rpd prog 12th, 2nd til ld 2 out, sn clr
385 **Touch 'N' Pass........................E Roberts** 2
rear, hrd rdn & prog to ld 15th, hdd 2 out, fin tired
351 **Sandy Beau...............................T Jones** 3
(fav) 2nd til ld 13th, hdd nxt, onepcd aft
362 Light The Wick *t.o. 6th, fin own time* 4
385 Prince Nepal *ld to 12th, wknd rpdly, p.u. 2 out* .... pu
5 ran. 30l, 15l, 10l. Time 6m 45.00s. SP 6-4.
J S Payne (Gelligaer Farmers).

508 - Intermediate (12st)

385 **LUCKY OLE SON ....Miss P Jones** 1
(Jt fav) cls 3rd til went 2nd 12th, ld 15th, qcknd away
255 **Construction King ....Mrs J Hawkins** 2
(Jt fav) n.j.w. last & lost tch 10th, ran on own pace, no dang
358 Plas-Hendy *2nd at 6th, lft in ld 9th, hdd 15th, wknd, p.u. last* .... pu
335 Star Actor *cls up in 5l 2nd whn p.u. 11th, lame* .... pu
432 Brother Prim *20s-6s, ld til u.r. 9th* .... ur
5 ran. Dist. Time 6m 48.00s. SP 9-4.
David Brace (Llangeinor).

509 - Maiden Div I

391 **ICECAPADE (BEL)...................S Blackwell** 1
(fav) made all, wll clr frm 8th, easily
358 **Willow Belle (Ire) 5a..................S Shinton** 2
rear, steady prog to 3rd at 11th, tk 2nd 2 out, no dang
Steel Valley (Ire) 5a ....R Rowsell 3
dist 2nd frm 9th, mstks 15th & nxt, lost 2nd 2 out
211 Pyro Pennant *prom early, wknd frm 11th* 4
149 Cairneymount *5l 2nd whn ran out 4th* .... ro
391 Caerffili's Bay 5a *mid-div til lost tch hlfwy, p.u. 13th* ... pu
Tarrtingo 5a *rear, losing tch whn p.u. 12th* .... pu
301 Its A Doddle 5a *rear, poor 5th frm 11th, t.o. & p.u. last* .... pu
Willows Wonderman *alwys last, t.o. & p.u. 6th* .... pu
9 ran. Dist, 5l, 5l. Time 7m 9.00s. SP 9-4.
P Riddick (Pentyrch).

510 - Maiden Div II

390 **THE FUN OF IT........................E Williams** 1
hld up, gd prog 13th, disp 15th, ld 2 out, ran on
217 **Bride Run (Ire)...........................A Price** 2
2nd til ld 13th, jnd 15th, hdd 2 out, no ext
Jimmy O'Goblin ....J Price 3
(fav) prom, cls 3rd at 10th, outpcd 15th, improve
Bonus Number (Ire) *mid-div, 6th at 9th, styd on own pace* 4
148 Lets Go Polly 5a *mid-div, poor 4th 2 out, fin own time* 5
386 Macaabee Special (Ire) *mid-div, lost tch frm 15th* 6
358 Romano Hati 5a *t.o. whn p.u. 13th* .... pu
386 Rio Cisto 5a *t.o. whn p.u. 12th* .... pu
152 Tims Kick (Ire) 7a *ld to 13th, wknd rpdly, p.u. 2 out*.... pu
9 ran. 2l, dist, 12l, 3l, 20l. Time 7m 14.00s. SP 3-1.
A Hazell (Llangibby).
P.H./J.C.

HOLDERNESS
Dalton Park
Saturday March 16th
GOOD

511 - Members

410 **GREY HUSSAR (NZ) 5ex...............S Walker** 1
(fav) not fluent or keen, in tch, rdn to ld & lft clr 16th, unchal
316 **Crocket Lass 5a ....Miss F Hunter** 2
plIng, ld 5-8th, last by 12th, sn t.o., lft poor 2nd 16th
Laganbrae *ld to 5th, ld 8th til hdd & u.r. 16th* .... ur
3 ran. Dist. Time 7m 23.00s. SP 8-15.
Mrs S Gray (Holderness).

512 - Confined

410 **TOBIN BRONZE 5ex..................R Edwards** 1
(fav) hld up rear, prog frm 14th, chal last, pshd out to ld flat
320 **Beau Rose ....S Brisby** 2
trckd ldrs, rdn 16th, ld 2 out, hdd & no ext flat
410 **Nishkina..............................C Cundall** 3
prom, ld 14th-4 out, ld agn apr 2 out, sn hdd & one-pcd
303 Cleasby Hill *prom til outpcd frm 14th, 6th 4 out, kpt on* 4
327 McCartney *keen hold, ld to 6th, 9-14th & 4 out-apr 2 out, wknd* 5
9 Good Team *prom, ld 6th-9th, grad wknd frm 16th*..... 6
223 Acertainhit *alwys bhnd, t.o. 15th* 7
409 War Head *rear frm 7th, t.o. & p.u. 13th* .... pu
412 Valiant Vicar *alwys rear, nrly u.r. 14th, t.o. & p.u. last* pu
327 Breckenbrough Lad *not fluent, alwys bhnd, t.o. 12th, p.u. aft 16th* .... pu
10 ran. 2l, 12l, 4l, 3l, 12l, 1 fence. Time 7m 10.20s. SP 2-1.
I Bray (York & Ainsty North).

513 - Open

327 **ZAM BEE ....N Bell** 1
(fav) prssd ldr frm 3rd til ld 15th, clr 3 out, easily
170 **Park Drift ....R Tate** 2
w.w. went 3rd & outpcd 14th, ran on to chs wnr 2 out,no imp
324 **Ways And Means 5a ....K Green** 3
made most frm 3-15th, outpcd by wnr 4 out, kpt on
410 Clontoura (Ire) *rear, nvr put in race, lft poor 4th 4 out, no ch* 4
359 Furry Knowe *pshd alng in tch, blnd 12th, sn bhnd & no ch* 5
410 Cromwell Point *chsd ldrs, rdn frm 8th, no ch frm 14th, t.o.* 6
324 The Big Wheel *ld to 2nd, chsd ldrs, 4th & btn whn f 4 out* .... f
303 Arden *jmpd slwly 1st, last & t.o. 3rd til p.u. 16th* ...... pu
367 Barry Owen *ld 2-3rd, prom til wknd 14th, t.o. & p.u. 16th* .... pu
9 ran. 10l, 2l, 25l, ½l, 15l. Time 6m 58.20s. SP 8-11.
Mrs A Bell (Belvoir).

514 - Ladies

363 **PEAJADE ....Miss J Wormall** 1
(fav) prom, ld apr 15th, hdd 3 out, ld & lft clr 2 out, pshd out
119 **Thistle Monarch ....Miss R Clark** 2
rear, prog 11th, 3rd 4 out, hmpd & lft 2nd 2 out,unable chal
412 **Grey Realm 5a.................Miss J Eastwood** 3
chsd ldrs, 5th & outpcd 4 out, hmpd 2 out, styd on
412 Carole's Delight 5a *ld til apr 15th, 4th & btn 3 out* 4
305 Linebacker *in tch to 10th, wll bhnd frm 13th*......... 5
170 Osgathorpe *hld up, prog & wth ldrs whn f 13th*....... f
325 Fettle Up (bl) *alwys prom, ld 3 out, just hdd whn f heavily nxt*.......... f
328 Earl Gray *last whn mstk 9th, t.o. 12th, p.u. 2 out* ...... pu
8 ran. 2l, 5l, 10l, 25l. Time 6m 58.40s. SP 5-4.
Mrs Janine Hall (Atherstone).

515 - B F S S (12st)

329 **RAMBLING LORD (IRE) 4ex ....T Betteridge** 1
in tch, 6th whn mstk 16th, ran on nxt, ld last, drvn out
303 **Celtic King..........................K Needham** 2
mstk 7th, in tch, prog to ld 4 out, hdd last, kpt on
410 **Golden Savannah 4ex ....M Sowersby** 3
(fav) ld to 5th & 12th-4 out, ev ch 2 out, onepcd
244 Glitzy Lady (Ire) 5a 4ex *w.w. prog 12th, rdn 16th, ev ch 2 out, onepcd*.......... 4
329 Jasilu 5a (bl) *alwys prom, rdn & ev ch 2 out, wknd apr last* 5
416 Pearl Bridge *rear, lost tch 15th, kpt on frm 3 out, nrst fin* 6
318 Katies Argument 5a *alwys rear, t.o. 16th, kpt on*...... 7
Bold Croft 5a *jmpd badly, rear til blnd & u.r. 5th* .... ur
329 Ginger Pink *ld 5th-12th, prom aft, 6th & btn whn u.r. 3 out*.......... ur
411 Midge 5a *blnd 7th, alwys rear, t.o. & p.u. aft 3 out* .... pu
224 Polar Hat *alwys rear, last & no ch 14th, t.o. & p.u. 2 out*.......... pu
308 Primitive Penny 7a *mstk & u.r. 2nd* .... ur
12 ran. 1l, 5l, 1l, 4l, 4l, 15l. Time 7m 1.70s. SP 7-2.
J Betteridge (Meynell & South Staffs).

516 - Open Maiden Div I Pt I

307 **BARICHSTE...........................A Ogden** 1
in tch, chsd ldr 15th, ld 2 out, comf
413 **Fair Ally ....M Sowersby** 2
(fav) hld up bhnd, prog 8th, ld 14th-2 out, hrd rdn & not qckn
332 **Roseberry Star 5a...............Miss T Jackson** 3
prom, disp 2nd 16th, wknd 3 out
Grange Gracie 5a *prom, lft in ld aft 10th, hdd 14th, sn wknd*.......... 4
Political Field 5a *rear, effrt 15th, sn wknd, t.o.*.......... 5
Justforgastrix (Ire) *hld up last, schoold & alwys t.o.*.... 6
308 Tudor Lord *plld hrd, sn ld, p.u. aft 10th, lame* .... pu
222 Rabble Rouser *n.j.w. mid-div & drvn alng, no ch whn ran out 3 out* .... ro
Lyningo *prom, 3rd whn f 9th* .... f
333 Albert's Adventure (Ire) (bl) *n.j.w. last frm 10th, t.o. aft til p.u. 15th*.......... pu
Stays Fresh *rear, effrt aft 14th, sn wknd, p.u. 16th* .... pu
11 ran. 2l, 30l, 15l, 6l, 25l. Time 7m 16.20s. SP 7-1.
Major M Watson (Middleton).

517 - Open Maiden Div I Pt II

416 **ATTLE..............................S Brisby** 1
trckd ldrs, went 2nd 16th, drvn to ld last, styd on flat
224 **Here Comes Charter ....A Pennock** 2
ld, qcknd 16th, hdd last, no ext flat
414 **Blackwoodscountry ....C Mulhall** 3
(fav) trckd ldr til not qckn & rdn 16th, styd on frm 2 out
415 Neladar 5a *hld up, prog 9th, rdn & effrt 4 out, no imp frm 2 out* 4
307 Scarth Nick *pllng, cls up til wknd frm 16th*.......... 5
415 Sweet Wyn 5a *bhnd, t.o. 8th, p.u. 11th, dsmntd*......... pu
416 Prophet's Choice *mstk 2nd, in tch whn no room & ran out 4th* .... ro
414 Rich Asset (Ire) *mstks, rear, 8th whn blnd & u.r. 7th*... ur
408 Lingcool 5a *w.w. in tch, prog to 4th & in tch whn p.u. 15th*.......... pu
333 Father's Gift 5a *prom to 6th, wknd rpdly, t.o. & p.u. aft 10th*.......... pu
10 ran. 1l, 3l, 4l, 30l. Time 7m 21.20s. SP 3-1.
J W Furness (Bedale).

518 - Open Maiden Div II

413 **TOM THE TANK ....C Mulhall** 1
in tch, 3rd frm 10th til effrt to ld apr 2 out, lft clr,comf
168 **Pokey Grange.................Capt S Robinson** 2
(fav) chsd ldr, ld 5 out til apr 2 out, onepcd
408 **Politicians Prayer 5a ....S Charlton** 3
hld up wll bhnd,prog hlfwy,cls up 5 out,outpcd aft 3 out
332 Derring Floss 5a *wll in tch til wknd frm 16th, t.o.*...... 4
333 St Enton *6th whn blnd & u.r. 7th*.......... ur
416 Shildon (Ire) *ld to 15th, 4th & in tch whn blnd & u.r. nxt* .... ur
305 Sweet Rose 5a *alwys rear, t.o. 14th, p.u. 2 out* .... pu
415 Prickly Trout 5a *wll in tch to 4 out, 4th & no ch whn p.u. last* .... pu
241 Tyndrum Gold *mid-div to 8th, sn wll bhnd, t.o. & p.u. 3 out*.......... pu
328 Flaxton King (Ire) 7a *alwys wll bhnd, t.o. hlfwy, p.u. 3 out*.......... pu
73 Arras-Tina 5a *prog frm mid-div hlfwy,jnd ldrs 4 out, 2nd & rdn whn f 2 out* .... f
High Mill *t.o. last whn p.u. 4th*.......... pu
413 Winters Melody 5a *plld hrd, mid-div til ran out 8th*.... ro
Just Johnie *schoold in last & t.o., poor 8th & running on whn p.u. 16th*.......... pu
414 Profiler (Ire) 7a *alwys rear, t.o. 14th, p.u. 2 out*......... pu
15 ran. 10l, 3l, 1 fence. Time 7m 20.30s. SP 7-1.
D Gill (Bramham Moor).
One fence omitted final circuit, 19 jumps. J.N.

NEW FOREST BUCKHOUNDS
Larkhill
Saturday March 16th
GOOD

519 - Confined

264 **STRONG TARQUIN (IRE) ....Miss P Curling** 1
(fav) restrnd, mstk 8th, prog to ld 13th, pshd out flat
467 **Mighty Falcon.........................Miss E Tory** 2
alwys prom, rallied frm 2 out, no ext flat
381 **Bear's Flight.....................J Hadden-Wight** 3
sttld bhnd, prog whn lost irons 4 out, onepcd aft
377 Game Fair *nvr trbld ldrs* 4
375 Wesshaun 5a *ld til wknd rpdly aft 12th, p.u. nxt* ...... pu
5 ran. 2l, 8l, dist. Time 6m 22.00s. SP 1-4.
Paul K Barber (Blackmore & Sparkford Vale).

520 - Open Maiden (5-8yo) Div I (12st)

471 **MASTER MARIO** ....P Henley 1
(fav) sttld mid-div, prog 13th, ld apr last, ran on well
269 **Bit Of An Idiot** ....C Morlock 2
ld, 10l clr 13th, wknd & hdd apr last
Constant Sula 5a ....Miss P Gundry 3
rear, prog 14th, ran on well frm 2 out, nrst fin
Pinber 5a *mid-div whn u.r. 1st* .... ur
263 Titchwell Milly 5a *mid-div whn u.r. 6th* .... ur
275 Royal Pittance *jmpd bdly, sn t.o., p.u. 9th* .... pu
143 Sulason *prom til wknd rpdly frm 14th, p.u. 2 out* ...... pu
Whod Of Thought It (Ire) 7a *nvr bttr than mid-div, no ch whn p.u. 14th* .... pu
267 Magical Cruise 5a *mid-div whn f 8th* .... f
Olive Basket 7a *dwelt & lost 30l start, p.u. 8th* .... pu
Stillmore Business 7a 6ow *sn wll bhnd, jmpd slwly, p.u. 6th* .... pu
11 ran. 6l, 20l. Time 6m 26.00s. SP Evens.
Mrs M A T Potter (Portman).

521 - Open Maiden (5-8yo) Div II (12st)

268 **DEFINITE MAYBE (IRE)** ....T Mitchell 1
(fav) n.j.w. no ch whn lft in ld last, lucky
236 **Phil's Dream** ....C Morlock 2
prom, ld 13th, 8l clr but tiring whn f last, rmntd
206 Yet To Dance 5a *ld, 20l clr 12th, p.u. nxt, lame* .... pu
Ted's Knight (Ire) 7a *sn t.o., f 11th* .... f
I'minonit *sttld wth chsng grp, bhnd whn f 4 out* .... f
Funny Farm 2ow *schoold in rear, t.o. & p.u. 3 out* .... pu
6 ran. Dist. Time 6m 41.00s. SP 4-5.
B C Kilby (Blackmore & Sparkford Vale).

522 - Open Maiden (5-8yo) Div III (12st)

APATURA KING ....T Mitchell 1
(fav) alwys prom, ld 2 out, ran on well whn prssd flat, promising
Plumbridge ....C Vigors 2
prom, ev ch apr last, ran on well flat
344 **Just A Madam (Ire) 5a** ....Miss E Tomlinson 3
ld to 2 out, ran on onepcd
477 Vulgan Prince *prom, mstk 8th, unable qckn frm 3 out* 4
Alex Thuscombe *prom early, no ch frm 14th, onepcd* 5
129 Miss Precocious 5a *nvr bttr than mid-div, p.u. 13th* ... pu
275 Moran Brig *sn t.o., nvr nrr, p.u. 2 out* .... pu
340 Never So Lost *alwys mid-div, wknd 13th, p.u. 15th*.... pu
269 Chalvey Grove *bhnd, prog 10th, 3rd 12th, wknd & p.u. nxt* .... pu
144 Derri Bride 7a *rear whn f 7th* .... f
Strong Chairman (Ire) 7a *w.w. prog 14th, cruising & lvl whn f last* .... f
Greenacre Girl 5a *bhnd & jmpd bdly, ref 3rd* .... ref
12 ran. Hd, 2l, 2l, 15l. Time 6m 28.00s. SP 2-1.
C Gibbs (Portman).

523 - Mixed Open (12st)

336 **DARINGLY 7ex** ....Maj O Ellwood 1
alwys cls up, ld aft 2 out, ran on well flat
Indian Knight ....C Vigors 2
alwys prom, ld 13th til apr last, ran on, bttr for race
443 **On His Own** ....Miss W Southcombe 3
ld to 13th, styd on frm 3 out
350 Stanford Boy *bhnd til ran on frm 4 out, nrst fin* 4
Touch Of Winter 7ex *(fav) alwys bhnd, nvr trbld ldng grp* 5
364 Orujo (Ire) 7ex *nvr bttr than mid-div*................ 6
Its All Over Now *alwys chsng ldrs, wknd 12th, t.o.* 7
Favoured Victor (USA) 9ow *plld hrd, prom, wknd 12th, p.u. nxt* .... pu
8 ran. 4l, 4l, 6l, hd, 20l, 1 fence. Time 6m 24.00s. SP 4-1.
M Appleby (Berks & Bucks Drag).

524 - Intermediate (12st)

262 **DESERT WALTZ (IRE) 5ex**.........Miss P Curling 1
mid-div, smooth prog to ld 14th, pshd clr apr last
357 **Tinotops** ....T Mitchell 2
rear til sustained prog frm 14th, fin well
297 **Apatura Hati 5a 5ex** ....P Henley 3
alwys prom, wknd frm 14th, onepcd
217 Guiting Gray *(fav) prom, brfly ld 13th, unable to qckn frm 2 out* 4
Beinn Mohr 5a 2ow *alwys mid-div, nvr nrr* 5
365 First Harvest *ld til 13th, wknd rpdly, onepcd* 6
348 Inch Gale 5a 1ow (bl) *prom, 3rd at 6th, wknd 12th, t.o.* 7
264 Master Swillbrook *t.o. 6th* 8
381 Champagne Run *sn rear, t.o. & p.u. 14th*............ pu
Steel Dance *prom to 10th, t.o. whn u.r. 14th* .... ur
Clobracken Lad *mid-div whn p.u. 8th* .... pu
11 ran. 4l, 8l, 4l, dist, 5l, 1 fence, 10l. Time 6m 14.00s. SP 7-4.
H B Geddes (Beaufort).

525 - Restricted Div I (12st)

428 **DUSKY DAY** ....Mrs N Sheppard 1
ld/disp, slght ld whn lft clr last
242 **Rayman (Ire)** ....J Trice-Rolph 2
nvr able to rch ldrs, lft poor 2nd last
266 **Cool Rascal 5a** ....L Lay 3
nvr trbld ldrs, t.o.
381 Kamtara *sn t.o., p.u. 15th* .... pu
231 Prince's Gift *prom til wknd 12th, p.u. nxt* .... pu
298 Plan-A (Ire) *(fav) alwys wth wnr, upsides but tired whn f last* .... f
340 Rickham Bay 5a *sn rear, f 10th* .... f
7 ran. 1 fence, 10l. Time 6m 26.00s. SP 5-2.
C J Hitchings (Ledbury).

526 - Restricted Div II (12st)

ALWAYS GREAT ....Dr P Pritchard 1
alwys prom, ld 3 out, hrd rdn flat
137 **Astound (Ire) 7a** ....Lt-Col R Webb-Bowen 2
sn rear, rpd prog frm 14th, ran on last, just faild
262 **Perseverance** ....Miss P Gundry 3
j.w. ld to 3 out, onepcd aft
365 Bilbo Baggins (Ire) *mid-div, mstk 6th, lost ground 10th, ran on frm 4 out* 4
361 Misty (NZ) *sn t.o., nvr nrr.* 5
242 I Did It My Way (bl) *alwys prom, onepcd frm 2 out, no ch whn ref last* .... ref
Master Bertie *mid-div, mstk 8th, wknd & p.u. 13th* ... pu
432 Looking *prom, 2nd at 9th, sn wknd, p.u. 15th*......... pu
298 Pines Express (Ire) *(fav) alwys mid-div, wknd rpdly 13th, p.u. last* .... pu
9 ran. 1l, 15l, 4l, 10l. Time 6m 30.00s. SP 20-1.
Miss Sarah George (Berkeley).

527 - Members

273 **QUIET CONFIDENCE (IRE) 5a** ....Miss D Stafford 1
(fav) made all, 10l clr 14th, unchal
Stirrup Cup..........................C Goulding 2
alwys chsng wnr, unable qckn 3 out
380 **Trimbush**........................Maj O Ellwood 3
sn wll bhnd, t.o.
Betty's Pearl *alwys rear, t.o. 8th, btn 2 fences*.......... 4
4 ran. 12l, 1 fence, 1 fence. Time 6m 26.00s. SP 4-5.
Mrs S Kerley (New Forest Buckhounds).
T.S.

QUANTOCK STAGHOUNDS
Cothelstone
Saturday March 16th
GOOD

528 - Members

FLY THE WIND 5a ....Miss L Blackford 1
(fav) chsd ldrs, disp ld 12th til ld 15th, clr 3 out, easy
Jaffa's Boy ....Miss H Pavey 2
chsd ldr to 11th, lst plc, 5th 4 out, styd on wll frm 3 out
348 **Lantern Pike**......................A Michael 3
ld to 14th, 3rd & blnd 3 out, no ex

280 Green Hill *w.w. prog to 2nd 15th, rddn appr 3 out, wknd* 4
277 Mr Lion *rr & blnd 10th, no ch 14th, p.u. 2 out* .... pu
Grey Sonata 5a *rr & hit 11th, rddn & lst tch 12th, p.u. appr 13th* .... pu
Dubata *w.w. prog 11th, 4th & blnd 14th, sn btn, p.u. 2 out* .... pu
284 Lochnaver 5a *rr, in tch whn f 6th* .... f
8 ran. 15l, 10l, 12l. Time 6m 25.00s. SP Evens.
Miss Helen L Pengelly (Quantock Staghounds).

529 - Ladies

296 **CELTIC SPORT (bl) .... Miss S Kirkpatrick** 1
trkd ldr, ld appr 4 out, drw clr appr last, styd on wll
362 **Flame O'Frensi 5a .... Miss J Cumings** 2
(fav) ld til 15th, rlld & disp 3 out, wknd appr last
Killelan Lad .... Miss K Dimarte 3
chsd ldrs, hit 5th, lst tch 11th, t.o.
212 Blue-Bird Express 5a (bl) *j.s 2nd, last whn blnd & u.r. 8th* .... ur
Jameswick *chsd ldrs, lst tch 11th, 3rd & no ch whn ref & u.r. 3 out* .... ref
5 ran. 3l, 1 fence. Time 6m 26.00s. SP 2-1.
Mrs A C Martin (Tiverton Foxhounds).
1 Fence Omitted. 18 Jumps

530 - Land Rover Open (12st)

WEST QUAY .... J Creighton 1
made all, in comm 3 out, eased flat, impress
378 **Butler John (Ire) .... N Harris** 2
hld up, prog to trk ldr 12th, rddn & btn appr 3 out
365 **Tangle Baron .... M Felton** 3
chsd ldr 5th-11th, 3rd & outpcd 15th, no dang aft
Ryming Cuplet 7ex *(fav) backward,prom,rmdr 8th,4th & strugg whn blnd 15th,no ch aft* 4
Billilla *in tch til 12th, p.u appr 14th, dead* .... pu
Feile Na Hinse *mstks, in tch to 12th, no ch whn p.u. & dism 4 out* .... pu
198 Charmers Wish 5a *in tch, last & rddn 11th, t.o. & p.u. 2 out* .... pu
7 ran. 4l, 25l, 1l. Time 6m 27.00s. SP 6-1.
C T Moate (West Somerset Vale).

531 - Confined

278 **QUALITAIR MEMORY (IRE) .... J Tizzard** 1
alwys prom, ld appr 3 out, clr nxt, easy
281 **The Pedlar 5a .... T Greed** 2
w.w.prog & in tch 13th,rddn 4 out, wnt 2nd flat,nt trbl wnr
278 **Larky McIlroy 5a .... L Jefford** 3
mid div, prog to disp 2nd 10th, ev ch & rddn 4 out, no ex
278 Deviosity (USA) *alwys rr div, 5th & no ch 15th* 4
255 Myliege *(fav) hit 6th, prog 11th, ld 13th til appr 4 out, sn btn* 5
278 Badihar (USA) *rr & blnd bdly 8th, p.u. appr nxt* .... pu
279 Rapid Rascal *chsd ldr 5th, disp bfly 6th, wknd 11th, u.r. 13th* .... ur
472 Our Jackie *ld, sn clr, hdded & wknd qkly 13th, wll bhnd whn u.r. 15th* .... ur
278 Be My Habitat *rr 7th, t.o. & p.u appr 13th* .... pu
298 Monkton (Ire) *mid div whn blnd bdly 6th, nt rcvr, bhnd & p.u. 11th* .... pu
280 Just Ben *bhnd frm 7th, t.o. & p.u. 15th* .... pu
Bay Blossom 5a *in tch til wknd 12th, t.o.& p.u. 4 out* .... pu
12 ran. 10l, 2½l, 15l, 10l. Time 6m 28.00s. SP 7-4.
C Tizzard (Blackmore & Sparkford Vale).

532 - Restricted (12st)

465 **THE JOGGER .... J Tizzard** 1
lft 2nd 7th, ld 4 out, kpt on und press frm 2 out
466 **Play Poker (Ire) .... S Slade** 2
(fav) keen hold, trkd ldrs, chall gng wll 2 out, sn rddn & fnd nil
Highway Jim .... Miss M Peck 3
prom,hit 13th, 4th & blnd bdly 15th, kpt on onpcd aft
281 Sherbrooks 2ow *in tch, blnd 10th, rddn & onpcd frm 14th* 4
281 Great Impostor *rr & hit 4th, t.o. frm 11th* 5
Liberty James *dashed into ld 2nd, wll clr whn f 7th* .... f
Link Copper *lft in ld 7th, hdded appr 4 out, wknd nxt,3rd whn p.u. 2 out* .... pu
357 Hazel Park *rr div, lst tch 11th, t.o. & p.u. 15th* .... pu
Hopefull Drummer *hld up, prog 11th, in tch & gng wll whn f 14th* .... f
299 Springcombe 5a *bhnd 8th, t.o. & p.u. last* .... pu
Northern Sensation 5a *prom til p.u. qkly appr 13th* .... pu
352 Always Dreaming 5a 5ow *bhnd, t.o 8th til p.u. 13th* .... pu
12 ran. 7l, 5l, 1l, dist. Time 6m 37.00s. SP 9-4.
Mrs P T Tizzard (Blackmore & Sparkford Vale).

533 - Maiden Div I (12st)

471 **FATHER FLATTERY .... I Dowrick** 1
5/2-1/1,ld to 11th,lft in ld 15th til 3 out,lft in ld last
Rushhome 5a .... A Farrant 2
prog 12th, ld 3 out til walked thro' last & hdded, fin tired
301 **Electrofane (Ire) .... R Payne** 3
prom to 10th, sn strugg, 3rd & no ch 4 out
207 Legal Vision 5a (v) *in tch til rddn & outpcd 13th, no ch 4 out* 4
299 Blade Of Fortune *keen hold, cls up, lft in ld 13th, gng stngly whn f 15th* .... f
Furry Loch *f 1st* .... f
283 River Stream 5a *alwys rr, t.o. & p.u. 13th* .... pu
447 Parson Flynn *prom, ld 12th til f nxt* .... f
280 Run With Joy (Ire) 7a *in tch til wknd 12th, t.o. & p.u. appr last* .... pu
Nearly All Right *f 2nd* .... f
Risky Bid 5a *rr, lst tch 11th, t.o. & p.u. 13th* .... pu
283 Working Man (Ire) 7a 2ow *b.d. 2nd* .... bd
Renshaw Ings *f 1st* .... f
13 ran. 6l, dist, 15l. Time 6m 42.00s. SP Evens.
Miss A V Handel & P Musgrave (Taunton Vale).

534 - Maiden Div II (12st)

SWANSEA GOLD (IRE) 7a .... D Alers-Hankey 1
cls up, disp 5th-10th, ld 3 out, clr last, just hld on
And What Else (Ire) .... B Dixon 2
in tch going wll,disp brfly apr 4 out,rallied flat,jst faild
283 **Heather Boy .... Miss J Cumings** 3
prom, ev ch 15th, wknd nxt
Supreme Warrior *w.w. in tch, ch 15th, onepcd frm nxt* 4
284 Jolly Flier *made most to 15th, rdn & wknd apr nxt* 5
278 Dollybat 5a *in tch to 12th, outpcd nxt, no dang aft* 6
Melody Mine 5a *rear, prog 10th, wkng whn blnd 13th, t.o. & p.u. 4 out* .... pu
284 Father Malone (Ire) *prom, chsd ldr 9-12th, sn wknd, p.u. 14th* .... pu
282 Melling 7a *keen hold, disp to 4th, wknd 11th, t.o. & p.u. 2 out* .... pu
207 Clonroche Lucky (Ire) *(fav) in tch, jnd ldrs 12th, p.u. 14th, dsmntd* .... pu
10 ran. Hd, 8l, 8l, 6l, 4l. Time 6m 44.00s. SP 20-1.
Mrs H E North (West Somerset).
S.P.

BLANKNEY
Southwell P-To-P Course
Sunday March 17th
GOOD TO SOFT

535 - Confined (12st)

393 **THE DIFFERENCE .... M Chatterton** 1
hld up mid-div, clsd 5 out, ran on frm 2 out, ld nr fin
327 **Hobnobber .... J Docker** 2
(fav) alwys cls up, ld 11th til hdd nr fin
327 **Phrose 7ex .... A Pickering** 3
chsd ldrs, no ext frm 3 out
244 Harmony Walk (Ire) *mid-div, prog 11th, outpcd frm 3 out* 4
Spanish Whisper *rear, mid-div by 12th, nvr rchd ldrs* 5

327 Solitary Reaper (bl) *in tch whn u.r. 6th* .... ur
Subsonic (Ire) *sn t.o., poor 6th whn p.u. last* .... pu
329 Ruff Song *ld 7-10th, in tch 4 out, fdd, p.u. 2 out* .... pu
258 San Remo *mid-div, fdd, no ch whn p.u. 3 out* .... pu
242 Royal Survivor *wth ldr 2nd til f 6th* .... f
10 ran. Hd, 8l, 20l, 20l. Time 6m 50.00s. SP 7-1.
M G Chatterton (Belvoir).

536 - Ladies

460 **OUT THE DOOR (IRE)**..............**Miss S Baxter** 1
hld up, prog 8th, trckd ldr aft, qcknd to ld flat
325 **Layedback Jack 7ex**.............**Mrs J Dawson** 2
(fav) w.w. 2nd at 9th, ld 5 out, 4l clr 2 out, hdd & no ext flat
47 **Douce Eclair 5a**.....................**Miss S Hogg** 3
mstks in rear, ran on onepcd frm 4 out, nrst fin
245 Ridwan *mid-div, no ch wth 1st 2 from 3 out* 4
394 Nowhiski *ld to 5 out, wknd frm 3 out* 5
347 Crazy Otto *mid to rear, alwys strgglng to keep in tch* 6
161 Guild Street 5a *prom early, no ch frm 12th* 7
Hawaiian Goddess (USA) 5a *prom to 10th, wknd rpdly, t.o.* 8
227 Queen's Chaplain *alwys rear, nvr going, p.u. 5 out* ... pu
9 ran. 2½l, dist, 10l, 5l, 2l. Time 6m 46.00s. SP 5-1.
M Mann (Wheatland).

537 - Open (12st)

434 **PENLET** ....**John Pritchard** 1
(fav) hld up, prog to ld 5 out, sn wll clr, unchal
290 **Castlebay Lad 7ex**......................**C Coyne** 2
chsd ldrs, ev ch 4 out, not qckn
246 **Bright As A Button** ....**J Connell** 3
cls up, ld 8th, nrly ref 13th, lost plc, ran on frm 3 out
337 Shortcastle *chsng grp, nvr dang* 4
395 Merlyns Choice (bl) *mid-div, lost tch, t.o.* 5
395 Dubalea *ld to 9th, wknd rpdly, p.u. 12th* .... pu
Blue Aeroplane *rear, t.o. 10th, p.u. 12th* .... pu
7 ran. 8l, sht-hd, dist, dist. Time 6m 50.00s. SP 10-11.
R G Weaving (Warwickshire).

538 - PPORA

263 **BROAD STEANE**......................**A Sansome** 1
(fav) hld up, prog 13th, rdn 3 out, lkd hld whn lft clr nxt
230 **Cawkwell Dean** ....**R Sweeting** 2
chsd ldr to 13th, onepcd frm 4 out, lft poor 2nd 2 out
327 **Kellys Diamond**......................**S Walker** 3
nvr bttr than mid-div, found little und pres
392 Shipmate *rear, prog to 4th & in tch 12th, sn wknd, t.o. & p.u. 3 out* .... pu
435 The Point Is *ld, clr & lkd wnr whn u.r. 2 out* .... ur
Back The Road (Ire) *cls up to 8th, wknd rpdly, p.u. 11th* .... pu
6 ran. Dist, 3l. Time 6m 50.00s. SP 5-4.
Sir Michael Connell (Grafton).

539 - Restricted

241 **BLUE IS THE COLOUR (IRE)** ....**S Walker** 1
cls up, ld 11th, sn clr, ran on well, easily
393 **Coolvawn Lady (Ire) 5a**..................**T Lane** 2
chsng grp, no ext whn wnr went clr
224 **Stag Fight**..............................**B Pollock** 3
(Jt fav) prom, unable to qckn 14th, onepcd
Easy Life (Ire) *mid-div, late prog, nvr dang* 4
Eastern Statesman *mid-div, mostly 4th/5th, onepcd frm 12th* 5
328 Tweed Valley (bl) *mid-div, prog 12th, 4th & btn whn p.u. 3 out* .... pu
411 Ellerton Park *(Jt fav) set str pace, hdd 13th, u.r. nxt* ... ur
365 Whinstone Mill *cls up to 12th, sn btn, p.u. 3 out* .... pu
396 Dilly's Last 5a *mid-div, in tch to 12th, wknd rpdly, p.u. 6 out* .... pu
Reel Rascal 5a *t.o. whn f 2nd* .... f
Pendle Witch 5a *lft a fence, t.o. til p.u. 8th* .... pu
11 ran. Dist, 12l, dist, nk. Time 6m 44.00s. SP 7-2.
Miss E M Hewitt (Middleton).

540 - Open Maiden Div I Pt I

397 **HENRY DARLING** ....**E Andrewes** 1
(fav) hld up mid-div, smooth prog to ld 13th, ran on well 3 out
Paradise Row (Ire).................**M Chatterton** 2
ld to 7th, in tch, 2nd 2 out, ran on onepcd
331 **Shakey Thyne (Ire) 5a**...............**D Sherlock** 3
mid-div, prog frm 4 out, nrst fin
Eazy Peazy (Ire) *chsng grp, ld 10-12th, onepcd whn hdd* 4
237 Still Hopeful 5a *alwys rear, p.u. 4 out* .... pu
239 Split The Wind 5a *schoold rear, p.u. 9th* .... pu
Remalone 5a (bl) *u.r. 1st* .... ur
392 Rainbow Fantasia (Ire) *mid-div, lost tch aft 12th, p.u. 3 out* .... pu
397 Forever Freddy *prom, ld 8-9th, sn btn aft mstks 12 & 13th, p.u. 3 out* .... pu
9 ran. 4l, dist, 15l. Time 7m 2.00s. SP 6-4.
Mrs B F Abraham (Quorn).

541 - Open Maiden Div I Pt II

240 **DASHBOARD LIGHT**..................**S R Andrews** 1
(fav) w.w. 3rd 4 out, disp 2 out, ld last, ran on well
414 **Boulevard Bay (Ire) 7a**.................**N Wilson** 2
hrd hld in rear, prog frm 3 out, ran on, nrst fin
332 **Bucklelone 5a** ....**J Docker** 3
ld to 2 out, ev ch last, not qckn flat
Littledale (USA) *chsng grp, cls 2nd 10th, no ext frm 2 out* 4
367 Im Ok (Ire) 5a *rear, prog 10th, ev ch 2 out, onepcd* 5
Griffin Lark 5a *rear, mstks, prog frm 8th to trck ldrs, wknd & p.u. 3 out* .... pu
397 The Bold Abbot *prom, chal & ev ch whn f last* .... f
Springfield Pet 5a *mid-div, fdng whn p.u. 3 out* ...... pu
Simply Stanley *prom, chsng grp to 3 out, btn whn p.u. last* .... pu
9 ran. 5l, ½l, 4l, 4l. Time 7m 16.00s. SP Evens.
A D Cooke (Cottesmore).

542 - Open Maiden Div II

218 **MANDYS LAD**.......................**M Hammond** 1
prom, ld 7th, ran on well, easily
Tempered Point (USA)...................**T Lane** 2
cls up, unable to cls on wnr frm 4 out
241 **Cantango (Ire)**..........................**J Turcan** 3
(fav) hld up, nvr rchd ldrs
392 Mysterious Run (Ire) *mid-div, nrst fin* 4
240 Master Enborne *mid-div, wll bhnd whn p.u. 3 out* ...... pu
367 Cornamona 5a *mid-div, lost tch whn p.u. 3 out* .... pu
160 Top The Bid *chsng grp to hlfwy, fdd, p.u. 3 out* ...... pu
220 Most Rich (Ire) *prom, ld 4-6th, strgglng frm 12th, p.u. 3 out* .... pu
287 Jacky's Jaunt 5a *cls up, 2nd at 10th, sn btn, p.u. 13th* pu
Gonalston Percy *rear whn p.u. 13th* .... pu
315 Gayton Wilds *f 2nd* .... f
174 Rise Above It (Ire) *wth ldrs to 5th, cls up til fdd 4 out, p.u. 2 out* .... pu
431 Warm Relation (Ire) 7a *ld to 3rd, in tch to 13th, p.u. 4 out* .... pu
61 Irish Genius (Ire) *mid to rear, p.u. 3 out* .... pu
397 Dante's Pride (Ire) *schoold rear, p.u. 6 out* .... pu
15 ran. Dist, dist, 1l. Time 7m 4.00s. SP 16-1.
Tony Walpole (Croome & West Warks).
One fence omitted this race, 17 jumps.

543 - Members

327 **MISTER CHIPPENDALE** ....**S Walker** 1
(fav) alternated ld til lft alone 13th
The Real McCoy 0
2 ran. SP 1-4.
Mrs D S R Watson (Blankney).
V.S.

CARMARTHENSHIRE
Erw Lon

Sunday March 17th
GOOD TO SOFT

544 - Members

MR MAD .... **P Hamer** 1
(fav) sttld rear, prog 11th, ld 13th, easily
Gus McCrae .... **Miss P Jones** 2
ld to 11th, wth wnr last, onepcd flat
157 **Butt And Ben** .... **D S Jones** 3
alwys 2nd/3rd, btn 2 out, lame
Never Be Great *ld 11-13th, wkng whn u.r. 15th* .... ur
388 Gatten's Brake *alwys rear, p.u. 15th* .... pu
5 ran. 1l, dist. Time 5m 59.00s. SP 4-7.
Gwynne Phillips (Carmarthenshire).

545 - Confined

263 **MISTER HORATIO** .... **M Lewis** 1
(fav) sttld in 2nd, ld 13th, nvr trbld aft
263 **Metrostyle** .... **J Jukes** 2
mid-div, prog frm 4 out, no ch wth wnr
Baron's Heir .... **S Lloyd** 3
mid-div, prog 13th, onepcd frm 3 out
266 Gold Diver *ld to 13th, fdd, fin tired* 4
508 Construction King *tongue-strap, 3rd/4th to 12th, no dang aft* 5
351 The Batchlor *nvr bttr than mid-div* 6
Miss Montana 5a *twrds rear til p.u. 14th* .... pu
383 No Panic *in rear, p.u. 13th* .... pu
146 Carlowitz (USA) *s.s. p.u. 3rd* .... pu
355 Proud Drifter *trckd ldrs, tiring whn p.u. aft 2 out, lame* .... pu
10 ran. 8l, 1l, ½l, 15l. Time 6m 3.00s. SP 1-2.
W D Lewis (Tivyside).

546 - Ladies

483 **GOOLDS GOLD 5a** .... **Miss P Jones** 1
(fav) 2nd/3rd til ld 2 out, unchal
266 **News Review** .... **Miss J Mathias** 2
mid-div, prog frm 15th, no ch wth wnr
364 **Busman (Ire)** .... **Miss L Pearce** 3
twrds rear to 8th, prog frm 13th, ran on gamely
216 Afaristoun (Fr) *mid-div & in tch til 3 out, onepcd* 4
383 Fast Freeze *nvr clsr than mid-div* 5
Medieval Queen 5a *t.o. 4 out, rpd late prog, nrst fin* .. 6
385 Good Holidays 5a *prom til wknd 3 out* 7
356 Mount Falcon *nvr nr ldrs* 8
385 Black Russian *twrds rear, wknd rpdly aft 11th, t.o.* 9
154 Moving Force *clr ldr to 3 out, tired 2nd whn u.r. last* .. ur
10 ran. 8l, 2l, 8l, 3l, ½l, 1l, 1l, 2 fences. Time 5m 56.00s. SP 1-4.
David Brace (Llangeinor).

547 - Open (12st)

214 **HAGLER** .... **S Griffiths** 1
prom til lft in ld 2 out, unchal aft
384 **Cornish Cossack (NZ)** .... **W Pugh** 2
chsd ldrs, lft 2nd 2 out, onepcd
146 **Origami (bl)** .... **A W Price** 3
mid-div, rpd prog 4 out, fdd 2 out
153 Ittihaad (bl) *nvr nrr than mid-div, u.r. 15th* .... ur
157 Heluva Battle *ld til u.r. 9th* .... ur
Bell Glass (Fr) *(fav) mid-div, p.u. 8th* .... pu
382 Loch Garanne 5a *ref to race* 0
545 Carlowitz (USA) *2nd outing, mstks, ld 10th, lkd wnr whn f 2 out* .... f
384 Electrolyte *u.r. 2nd* .... ur
Cefn Woodsman 7a *alwys rear, p.u. 12th* .... pu
10 ran. 10l, 6l. Time 6m 15.00s. SP 2-1.
R D Griffiths (Ludlow).

548 - Restricted Div I (12st)

391 **WARREN BOY** .... **Miss P Jones** 1
(fav) made all, easily
388 **Stormy Witness (Ire) 5a** .... **J Jukes** 2
chsd wnr, chal 13th, sn outpcd
387 **Celtic Bizarre 5a** .... **Miss B Barton** 3
alwys mid-div, onepcd
389 Mylordmayor *u.r. 3rd* .... ur
269 Pick'n Hill (Ire) *4th whn u.r. 11th* .... ur
Sheer Power (Ire) *p.u. 5th* .... pu
382 Mackabee (Ire) *nvr nrr than mid-div, f 11th* .... f
Final Rose 5a *mid-div, p.u. 10th* .... pu
8 ran. 15l, 4l. Time 5m 55.00s. SP Evens.
F J Ayres (Tredegar Farmers).

549 - Restricted Div II (12st)

386 **CARACOL** .... **T Jones** 1
(fav) 2nd til ld 13th, sn in cmmnd
Bancyfelin Boy .... **J P Keen** 2
twrds rear, prog frm 3 out, unable to chal
432 **Final Abby 5a** .... **R Thornton** 3
cls up til wknd 2 out
Penny Lark *ld to 13th, tired aft* 4
357 My Harvinski *alwys rear, nvr dang* 5
263 Short Shot *ref to race* 0
387 Equatime 5a *u.r. 1st* .... ur
357 Joyney 5a *twrds rear til p.u. 14th* .... pu
388 Mac's Boy *mid-div, p.u. 14th* .... pu
339 Mrs Wumpkins (Ire) 7a *in 3rd/4th til mstk 10th, p.u. nxt* .... pu
152 Redoran 7a *mid-div, f 6th* .... f
11 ran. 20l, 2l. Time 6m 9.00s. SP 6-4.
C G Bolton (Gelligaer Farmers).

550 - Maiden Div I

148 **PURPLE MELODY (IRE)** .... **V Hughes** 1
(fav) mid-div, prog to ld 4 out, ran on gamely
Northern Bluff .... **D S Jones** 2
mid-div, prog 3 out, nrst fin, improve
Cedar Square (Ire) 7a .... **J Jukes** 3
mid-div, prog to hld ev ch 3 out, ran green
355 Sea Search *chsd ldrs, prog 3 out, onepcd* 4
430 Dustys Trail (Ire) *4th/5th, onepcd frm 3 out* 5
149 Kinlogh Gale (Ire) *disp 8th-4 out, fdd aft* 6
387 Great Precocity *twrds rear, p.u. 11th* .... pu
152 Moonlight Cruise 5a *nvr dang, p.u. 11th* .... pu
Nanook *f 2nd, dead* .... f
Willows Engagement 5a *nvr dang, p.u. 14th* .... pu
Another Quince 5a *ld to 8th, fdd, p.u. 11th* .... pu
147 Parks Pride 7a *alwys rear, p.u. 9th* .... pu
206 Rymer's Express *alwys mid-div, p.u. 15th* .... pu
13 ran. 6l, 12l. Time 6m 9.00s. SP 5-4.
V Hughes (Llangeinor).

551 - Maiden Div II

150 **BUCKLEY'S COURT** .... **E Williams** 1
sttld mid-div, prog 4 out, ld last, styd on well
147 **The Mill Height (Ire)** .... **D S Jones** 2
2nd til ld 13th, hdd apr last, onepcd
390 **Never So High** .... **Miss A Meakins** 3
twrds rear, no ch 2 out, fin fast
390 Sister Lark 5a *(fav) ld to 4 out, wknd* 4
151 Preseli View 7a *alwys in rear* 5
Barnaby Boy *alwys prom, chal whn p.u. last, lame* ... pu
505 Forever In Debt 5a *ran out 3rd* .... ro
Ayyarose 5a *twrds rear, p.u. 11th* .... pu
8 ran. 6l, 2l. Time 6m 25.00s. SP 12-1.
R Weston (Pembrokeshire).

552 - Maiden Div III

CHERRY ISLAND (IRE) .... **J Jukes** 1
(fav) alwys prom, ld 3 out, easily
152 **Gunner Boon** .... **E Williams** 2
ld to 3 out, onepcd
Pendil's Delight 5a .... **D S Jones** 3
alwys prom, onepcd frm 3 out, improve
Chancy Oats *mid-div, prog whn blnd 4 out, not rcvr* .. 4
387 Toucher (Ire) *mid-div, wknd & p.u. 14th* .... pu
151 Jolly Swagman 7a *nvr nr ldrs, p.u. 9th* .... pu
386 Telephone *nvr bynd mid-div, p.u. 15th* .... pu
Harry From Barry *prom til blnd 3 out, p.u. bef nxt* .... pu
358 Deryn Y Cwm (Ire) *alwys bhnd, t.o. & p.u. 11th* .... pu

Appeal 5a *alwys bhnd, t.o. & p.u. 11th* .... pu
10 ran. 6l, 1l. Time 6m 23.00s. SP 6-4.
Mrs H Gibbon (Pembrokeshire).

553 - Maiden Div IV

DOWNHILL RACER 5a................**E Williams** 1
(fav) made all, unchal
Shuil's Star (Ire) 7a....................**P Hamer** 2
rear, nvr thrtnd wnr, ran on frm last
On The Book 5a *2nd whn u.r. 14th* .... ur
3 ran. 6l. Time 7m 0.00s. SP Evens.
Mrs J Barber (Pembrokeshire).
P.D.

DART VALE & HALDON
Ottery St Mary
Sunday March 17th
GOOD

554 - Members

279 **DEPARTURE 5a**........................**J Creighton** 1
ld 6-8th, ld agn 11th, clr aft 14th, comf
130 **Moze Tidy**..............................**I Dowrick** 2
(fav) in tch, chsd wnr 13th, outpcd 4 out, btn whn mstk last
Good King Henry....................**I Widdicombe** 3
hld up, ld brfly 8-9th, lost tch frm 14th
Glencoe Boy *1st ride, ld to 2nd, ld agn 4th, blnd & u.r. 5th*.......... ur
Miles More Fun 5a *plld hrd, ld aft 2nd til p.u. aft nxt, stewards*.......... pu
5 ran. 5l, dist. Time 6m 42.00s. SP 7-2.
W H Whitley (Dart Vale And South Pool Hrrs).

555 - Open Maiden Div I (12st)

207 **HE IS**..................................**T Mitchell** 1
hld up,prog 14th,cls 3rd & blnd 3 out,hld whn lft in ld last
Iades Boy (NZ) 7a ....**I Dowrick** 2
mid-div, out of tch 14th, slght prog 4 out,nvr plcd to chal
Temporary................................**S Slade** 3
prom, ld 6-10th, cls up to 4 out, outpcd aft
300 Eserie de Cores (USA) *sn bhnd, t.o. 14th* 4
131 Big Reward *ld to 3rd, sn lost plc, t.o. 15th* 5
431 Annmount Lady (Ire) 5a *alwys rear, nvr plcd to chal* .. 6
Get Stepping *cls up til blnd & u.r. 14th*.......... ur
Regent Son *sn rear, t.o. & p.u. 10th* .... pu
Southerly Gale *(fav) handy, ld 10th to 3 out, disp whn hit marker & u.r apr nxt* .... ur
300 Kahlo 5a (bl) *ld 4th til blnd & u.r. 7th*.......... ur
138 Lawd Of Blisland *alwys mid-div, lost tch 14th, t.o. & p.u. 3 out*.......... pu
294 Pen-Alisa 5a *mid-div til u.r. 7th* .... ur
Mountain-Linnet *mid-div, prog 13th, 4th whn f 15th* ... f
Petchburi Road (Ire) 7a *hld up, prog 15th, chal 3 out, lft clr nxt, f last*.......... f
520 Stillmore Business 7a *rear whn u.r. 4th*.......... ur
15 ran. 5l, 10l, 20l, dist, 2l. Time 6m 31.00s. SP 5-2.
T Hamlin (Devon & Somerset Staghounds).

556 - Open Maiden Div II (12st)

201 **ROBENKO (USA)**........................**A Farrant** 1
hld up,prog 10th, ld 13th-4 out, disp nxt, drew clr apr last
204 **Abit More Business (Ire) 7a**.......**Miss P Curling** 2
(fav) mid-div, prog 13th, disp 4 out-2 out, wknd apr last
137 **Our Teddis**............................**G Penfold** 3
mid-div, prog 10th, 2nd at 13th, ld nxt-4 out, wknd
Herhorse 5a *handy to 13th, lost plc nxt, ran on agn frm 2 out* 4
282 Langton Parmill *alwys mid-div, outpcd frm 13th* 5
Morchard Milly 5a *alwys rear, t.o. frm 13th* 6
284 Miss Pernickity 5a *alwys mid-div, t.o. frm 15th* 7
294 Happy Valley 5a *sn rear, t.o. frm 10th* 8
283 Ianovitch (bl) *cls up to 13th, wknd, mid-div whn f 4 out* .... f
Bright Work *ld 3rd til ran out 11th* .... ro
Cousin Amos *ld to 3rd, cls up to 12th, wknd & p.u. 15th*.......... pu
284 Suba Lin 5a *alwys rear, t.o. & p.u. 13th* .... pu
44 Charlie's Hideaway (Ire) *rear whn u.r. 7th*.......... ur
301 Lucky Call (NZ) 7a *cls up til f 10th* .... f
Harmony's Choice 7a *mid-div til p.u. 12th* .... pu
15 ran. 5l, 4l, nk, 15l, 1½l, dist, 20l. Time 6m 30.00s. SP 5-1.
Paul C N Heywood (East Cornwall).

557 - Maiden Div III Pt I (12st)

205 **BET WITH BAKER (IRE)**...........**Miss P Curling** 1
(fav) hld up, prog 13th, chal 3 out, ld nxt, sn clr
132 **Cottage Light (bl)**......................**M Miller** 2
2nd til lost plc 14th, ran on agn frm 3 out
430 **Fathers Footprints**......................**R Hicks** 3
mid-div, 4th at 14th, outpcd frm 4 out
299 Jay Em Ess (NZ) *ld to 3 out, wknd nxt, fin tired* 4
300 Zany Girl 5a (bl) *alwys rear, no ch frm 15th* 5
282 Good Appeal 5a *cls up to 13th, wknd, p.u. 3 out*.......... pu
301 Kalokagathos *alwys mid-div, t.o. & p.u. 2 out* .... pu
Nottarex *mid-div whn u.r. 7th* .... ur
301 Moonbay Lady 5a *sn t.o., u.r. 14th* .... ur
298 Romany Anne 5a *sn rear, t.o. & p.u. 11th*.......... pu
10 ran. 6l, 4l, 1l, 25l. Time 6m 33.00s. SP Evens.
George W Baker (Cattistock).

558 - Open Maiden Div III Pt II (12st)

M-REG ....**L Jefford** 1
handy, prog 13th, chal 4 out, disp nxt, qcknd clr flat
Time For Oats..........................**T Barry** 2
(fav) cls up, ld 10th-4out, disp til wknd apr last
446 **Drumbanes Pet**........................**G Penfold** 3
bhnd, plggd on frm 4 out, not trbl 1st pair
207 Flights Lane 5a *bhnd, lost tch 12th, outpcd* 4
138 Just Silver (bl) *ld til ran out 9th, rtrcd, cont t.o.* 5
282 Here's Mary 5a *mid-div, out of tch 12th, t.o. & p.u. last* .... pu
200 Cardan *prom, 2nd whn u.r. 7th*.......... ur
284 Rogerson *bhnd & mstks, t.o. & p.u. 3 out* .... pu
Medias Maid 5a *mid-div, out of tch whn f 13th* .... f
9 ran. 4l, dist, 3l, dist. Time 6m 29.00s. SP 3-1.
Mrs C Egalton (Axe Vale Harriers).

559 - Open

277 **CHILIPOUR**..............................**N Harris** 1
(fav) w.w. prog 13th, ld 3 out, easily
255 **Afterkelly**................................**R White** 2
ld/disp to 3 out, no ext aft
Colcombe Castle........................**M Miller** 3
handy, ev ch 5 out, outpcd frm nxt
Brabazon (USA) *bhnd early, prog 10th, styd on frm 4 out, nvr dang*.......... 4
278 Far Too Loud *in tch, 5th hlfwy, outpcd frm 4 out* 5
278 Fred Splendid *prom, disp 9-10th, wknd 13th, t.o. & p.u. 3 out* .... pu
Twice Knightly 7a *last til some prog frm 4 out, btn whn f 2 out*.......... f
7 ran. 4l, 3l, 2l, dist. Time 6m 31.60s. SP 1-3.
Nick Viney (Dulverton (West)).

560 - Confined

294 **GYMCRAK DAWN (bl)** ....**I Hambly** 1
cls up, ld 8th-3 out, btn 2nd whn handed race nxt
134 **In The Navy** ....**D Pipe** 2
(fav) hld up, prog to ld 7-8th, ld 3 out, blnd bdly nxt,nt rcvr
297 **Light The Bay 5a**........................**G Penfold** 3
handy, mstks, 3rd at 14th, nvr able to chal
294 Laneast Lore *ld to 7th, outpcd frm 13th*.......... 4
294 Noddy's Story 5a *cls up early, lost plc 7th, t.o. 10th*... 5
442 Senegalais (Fr) *2nd til f 6th* .... f
196 Cardinal Bird (USA) (bl) *ref 1st* .... ref
7 ran. 3l, 2l, 20l, dist. Time 6m 39.00s. SP 6-1.
A W Perkins (North Cornwall).

561 - Ladies

279 **GREAT POKEY................Miss N Courtenay** 1
made all, ran on well whn chal 3 out
279 **Tom Snout (Ire) ....Miss J Cumings** 2
hld up, went 3rd 11th, chal 3 out, no ext und pres aft
467 **False Economy ....Miss K Scorgie** 3
in tch til lost plc 12th, ran on frm 4 out, went 3rd nxt
443 Playpen *handy, 2nd at 12th, wknd frm 4 out*.......... 4
Reef Lark *alwys mid-div, nvr on terms*.......... 5
266 Friendly Lady 5a *alwys rear, nvr nrr*.......... 6
474 Ski Nut *alwys last, t.o. 13th*.......... 7
196 Little Coombe 5a *mid-div, outpcd frm 13th*.......... 8
212 Ragtime Solo (bl) *prom early, lost tch 13th, bhnd whn p.u. 3 out*.......... pu
67 Kings Rank *mid-div whn slowed 7th, p.u. bef nxt*.......... pu
208 Beyond Our Reach *(fav) hld up, mid-div whn hmpd & u.r. 7th*.......... ur
197 Happy Thought 5a *mid-div whn u.r. 6th*.......... ur
12 ran. 4l, 10l, 3l, 8l, 3l, 1l, 1l. Time 6m 24.00s. SP 12-1.
Miss Nell Courtenay (Taunton Vale Foxhounds).

562 - Monterey Retricted (12st)

199 **TICKET TO THE MOON 5a ....P Scholfield** 1
hld up, prog 12th, ld 4 out, ran on well
482 **Biddlestone Boy (NZ)...................A Farrant** 2
w.w. prog 14th, chsd wnr 3 out, no ext frm nxt
202 **Swing To The Left (Ire) 5a ....Miss J Cumings** 3
mid-div, prog 11th, 3rd nxt, lost plc nxt, ran on agn 3 out
284 Venn Boy *(fav) 3s-1/1, not fluent, prog 12th, ld 5 out-nxt, outpcd aft*.......... 4
199 Oneovertheight *ld to 14th, no ext & onepcd frm 3 out* 5
197 Lady Lir 5a *alwys rear, t.o. 14th*.......... 6
482 Mountain Master *mid-div, nvr on terms, p.u. 3 out*.......... pu
Remember Mac *sn rear, t.o. & p.u. 11th*.......... pu
Dark Reflection *sn rear, t.o. & p.u. 13th*.......... pu
283 Stalbridge Gold 5a *in tch to 13th, wknd & p.u. 4 out*.......... pu
206 Ower Farm 5a *cls 2nd til u.r. 10th*.......... ur
298 Copper And Chrome (Ire) 5a *cls up to 8th, wknd, t.o. & p.u. 4 out*.......... pu
12 ran. 5l, 5l, 5l, 3l, 6l, 20l. Time 6m 35.00s. SP 9-2.
Mrs Janita Scott (South Devon).
D.P.

NORTH WEST HUNT CLUB
Wolverhampton P-To-P Course
Sunday March 17th
GOOD TO SOFT

563 - Progressive

292 **RHINE RIVER (USA)...................C Stockton** 1
set slow pace til clr aft 13th, easily
288 **Nial (Ire).............................R Thomas** 2
disp to 13th, wknd
243 Sister Emu 5a *(fav) rear, mstk & u.r. 2nd*.......... ur
462 Howlin' Wolf *disp whn ref 4th*.......... ref
4 ran. 30l. Time 8m 11.00s. SP 7-2.
Brian Eardley (North Staffordshire).

564 - Restricted

461 **ITA'S FELLOW (IRE) ....Miss C Burgess** 1
hld up, ld 15th, ran on strngly frm 3 out
288 **Mr Bobbit (Ire) ....R Burton** 2
(fav) alwys prom, 2nd at 15th, ev ch 2 out, outpcd
Furry Fox (Ire) ....A Crow 3
chsd ldrs, ld 13th-15th, onepcd
366 Rinky Dinky Doo *ld to 5th, still cls up to 15th, no ext*.. 4
243 Foolish Fantasy *alwys rear, nvr dang*.......... 5
285 Emma Clew (Ire) 5a *s.s. ld 5th-13th, wknd, p.u. 3 out*.. pu
Jo-Su-Ki *nvr bynd mid-div, p.u. 16th*.......... pu
461 Mastiff Lane *alwys rear, p.u. 3 out*.......... pu
8 ran. 10l, 15l, 25l, 20l. Time 6m 36.00s. SP 6-1.
R Prince (Meynell & South Staffs).

565 - Open (12st)

290 **SCALLY MUIRE 5a 1ow ....A Crow** 1
(fav) hld up, drvn to ld 3 out, sn clr
459 **My Nominee 7ex (bl)...................A Griffith** 2
ld 14th-3 out, no ext
290 **Mr Tittle Tattle 7ex ....D Barlow** 3
chsd ldrs, 7l 3rd at 14th, wknd aft
289 Tipp Down *alwys rear, no dang*.......... 4
289 Sandstone Arch *alwys rear, p.u. 14th*.......... pu
Noble Angel (Ire) *ld to 14th, wknd & p.u. 3 out, fair effort*.......... pu
6 ran. 3l, 30l, 20l. Time 6m 36.00s. SP Evens.
G L Edwards (North Shropshire).

566 - Ladies

291 **HORNBLOWER...................Miss C Burgess** 1
(fav) made all, alwys in cmmnd
394 **Quenby Girl (Ire) 5a..............Miss E Godfrey** 2
chsd wnr, ev ch 3 out, styd on onepcd
River Trout ....Mrs S Coupe 3
s.s. nvr in race
458 Glen Taylor *cls up 1st cct, wknd aft*.......... 4
325 Strong Views *alwys rear, wknd rpdly 15th, p.u. 3 out*.. pu
5 ran. 3l, 30l, 1½l. Time 6m 44.00s. SP 1-4.
N J Barrowclough (North Shropshire).

567 - Members (12st)

246 **ANCHOR EXPRESS 5a 7ex...............A Crow** 1
ld, clr 3 out, easily
458 **Lakenheather (NZ)......................G Hanmer** 2
(fav) hld up, 2nd at 15th, ev ch til onepcd aft
459 **Duke Of Impney ....D Barlow** 3
2nd frm 8-15th, wknd rpdly
290 Castle Cross *cls up in 3rd whn f 11th*.......... f
4 ran. 25l, 8l. Time 6m 43.00s. SP 5-4.
D Malam (North Shropshire).

568 - Maiden Div I

167 **STEPASIDEBOY ....A Crow** 1
hld up, ld 3 out, styd on well
288 **Flinters...............................D Barlow** 2
(fav) ld to 3 out, mstk nxt, outpcd
464 **Bombadier Jack ....C Barlow** 3
cls up in 3rd to 3 out, no ext
458 My Son John *mid-div, 8l 3rd whn f 3 out*.......... f
458 Bay Tiger *rear, t.o. 14th, p.u. 2 out*.......... pu
463 Niord *s.s. bhnd whn f 8th*.......... f
285 Sale Ring *2nd to 13th, wknd rpdly, p.u. 3 out*.......... pu
464 Sargeants Choice *mid-div, 12l 4th whn hmpd & ran out 3 out*.......... ro
Son Of Ishka *cls up in 3rd whn u.r. 8th*.......... ur
9 ran. 8l, 5l. Time 6m 47.00s. SP 9-2.
E H Crow (North Shropshire).

569 - Maiden Div II

SIR GALEFORCE (IRE) ....A Crow 1
ld 9th, clr 3 out, styd on well
458 **The Last Joshua ....E Haddock** 2
prog to 2nd 4 out, styd on onepcd
286 The Yokel *ld to 9th, wknd rpdly, p.u. 16th*.......... pu
Shayna Maidel 5a *prog to 5l 2nd at 15th, wknd rpdly, p.u. 2 out*.......... pu
Parkinson's Law *alwys rear, p.u. 14th*.......... pu
285 Mr Busker (Ire) *(fav) 3rd whn f 9th*.......... f
288 Captiva Bay 5a *prom to 14th, wknd, btn 4th whn p.u. 3 out*.......... pu
463 Sugi *n.j.w. bhnd whn ran out 10th*.......... ro
Baronburn 5a *chsd ldrs, 3rd whn f 11th*.......... f
Sister Seat 5a *mid-div, no ch whn p.u. 14th*.......... pu
Gold Talisman 5a *jmpd bdly in rear, p.u. 9th*.......... pu
11 ran. 5l. Time 6m 52.00s. SP 5-1.
E H Crow (North Shropshire).
R.A.

WEST STREET-TICKHAM
Detling
Sunday March 17th
GOOD TO FIRM

570 - Members

BEACH TIGER .... **T Hills** 1
(fav) prog to trck ldr 12th, chal whn lft in ld 3 out, pshd clr
449 **Basher Bill** .... **K Giles** 2
chsd ldr to hlfwy, in tch aft, ran on frm 3 out, mstk nxt
451 **Bright Hour** .... **G Hopper** 3
alwys prom, cls 3rd 3 out, rdn & no ext nxt
Discain Boy *chsd ldr til mstk 11th, outpcd 4 out, kpt on frm 2 out* 4
249 Ten Of Spades *ld, prssd whn u.r. 3 out* .... ur
449 Bright Crusader 4ex *alwys last, pshd alng 9th, sn lost tch, p.u. 3 out* .... pu
6 ran. 5l, ½l, 2l. Time 6m 31.00s. SP 7-4.
T J Hills (Tickham).

571 - Confined (12st)

453 **BURROMARINER** .... **S Cowell** 1
(Jt fav) cls up, ld 3 out, drvn out
450 **American Eyre** .... **Miss S Gladders** 2
ld to 12th, outpcd aft, 5th 3 out, styd on wll, tk 2nd flat
347 **Little Nod** .... **P O'Keeffe** 3
alwys prom, ld 12th, hdd 3 out, 2nd & ev ch whn blnd last
Boycott *(Jt fav) handy, wth ldr 12-14th, cls 3rd aft, wknd 2 out* 4
270 Pin's Pride *mid-div, prog 12th, 4th 3 out, onepcd* 5
274 Toushtari (USA) *prom til wknd 4 out* 6
210 Therewego (Ire) (bl) *rear, mstk 16th, prog 4 out, 3rd 2 out, wknd & eased* 7
Mel's Rose *nvr trbld ldrs* 8
Kilsheelan Lad 5ex *alwys rear, t.o. 14th* 9
Glenavey *alwys rear, t.o. 14th* 10
274 The Forties *alwys rear, t.o. 14th* 11
249 Quentin Durwood *rear til p.u. 10th, lame* .... pu
449 Greenhill Fly Away *cls up whn u.r. 11th* .... ur
13 ran. 4l, 4l, 2l, ½l, 12l, 8l, 4l, 25l, 8l, 3l. Time 6m 17.00s. SP 5-2.
Mrs A Blaker (Mid Surrey Farmers Draghounds).

572 - Ladies

347 **PARDON ME MUM 4ex** .... **Mrs N Ledger** 1
(fav) hld up,smth prog to 2nd 13th,ld 15th,drew clr apr last,easy
273 **Clover Coin 5a 4ex** .... **Miss J Grant** 2
alwys prom, chsd wnr frm 15th, not pace to chal
250 **What A Gig** .... **Miss P Ellison** 3
rear, prog 14th, 3rd 4 out, wknd nxt
421 Durbo 4ex *alwys prom, mstk 7th, 3rd 2 out, wknd last* 4
452 Jim Bowie *ld to 3rd, prom aft, outpcd 15th, styd on frm 2 out* 5
273 Wendy Jane 5a *ld 3rd, jmpd rght, hdd 15th, fdd* 6
455 Larquill 5a *alwys rear, t.o. 10th* 7
273 Meritmoore *mid-div to hlfwy, wll bhnd 4 out* 8
271 Wellington Bay *rear, prog 10th, 5th & no ch whn u.r. 3 out.* .... ur
Silly Sovereign 5a *rear, t.o. & p.u. 12th* .... pu
10 ran. 8l, 15l, 6l, 6l, 10l, 20l, 12l. Time 6m 13.00s. SP 6-4.
Dr D B A Silk (Old Surrey & Burstow).

573 - 4m Open

474 **SKY VENTURE** .... **P Bull** 1
alwys prom, rdn to ld apr 2 out, hdd last, rallied & ld fin
271 **Billion Dollarbill** .... **S Cowell** 2
wll plcd, rdn to ld 3 out,hdd nxt,ld last,hdd line
274 **Strong Gold 7ex (bl)** .... **T McCarthy** 3
(fav) ld to 3 out, rallied apr last, lame
453 Stede Quarter *alwys prom, 4th whn jmpd slwly 4 out, no ch aft* 4
270 Kaim Park *rear, lost tch 10th, t.o. & p.u. 2 out* .... pu
249 Tryumphant Lad *f 4th* .... f
140 Cheeky Cheval *in tch til wknd 14th, wll bhnd whn p.u. 22nd* .... pu
248 Smart Work 5a 1ow *t.o. 8th, p.u. 21st* .... pu
451 Ginger Tristan 7ex *2nd til u.r. 10th* .... ur
9 ran. Nk, 1l, 15l. Time 8m 24.00s. SP 8-1.
Barry Briggs (Surrey Union).

574 - Restricted (12st)

128 **SOUND STATEMENT (IRE)** .... **T Hills** 1
(fav) made all, clr 13th, unchal
449 **Salachy Run (Ire)** .... **A Welsh** 2
chsd wnr, outpcd in 2nd frm 3 out
272 **Motor Cloak** .... **Miss C Savell** 3
prom, 5th at 17th, kpt on
348 Rolleston Blade *chsd wnr, 3rd & btn 3 out* 4
452 Saxon Swinger *2nd to 11th, fdd, t.o. 3 out* 5
272 Firewater Station *mid-div, some prog to 4th 3 out, no ch whn p.u. nxt* .... pu
449 Golden Pele *mid-div early, wll whn p.u. 13th* .... pu
272 Prince Rua *whppd round start, sn t.o., p.u. 10th* .... pu
449 Killarney Man *rear, prog to 5th at 10th, rmndrs nxt, 7th & btn whn f 15th* .... f
Mr Sunnyside *wth ldrs whn f 1st* .... f
275 Times Are Changing 5a *t.o. 6th, f 2 out* .... f
449 King's Maverick (Ire) *rear, wll bhnd whn p.u. 17th* .... pu
272 Prince Ronan (Ire) *b.d. 1st* .... bd
Fixed Liability *badly hmpd 1st, rear aft, nvr able to get into race,p.u.12th* .... pu
14 ran. 15l, 7l, 6l, 1 fence. Time 6m 13.00s. SP 6-4.
Maurice E Pinto (Chiddingfold,l'field & Cowdray).
1 fence omitted last 2 circuits, 19 jumps.

575 - Open Maiden (12st)

CHERRYGAYLE (IRE) 5a .... **Miss S French** 1
rear, poor 4th apr 3 out, styd on strngly to ld last
Velka 5a .... **Mrs S Hickman** 2
chsng grp,dist 3rd 4 out,lft 2nd nxt,ld 2 out,sn hdd & outpd
477 **Joe Quality** .... **M Loughnane** 3
chsd clr ldr,clr of rest 4 out,lft in ld nxt,fdd & hdd nxt
253 Clonattin Lady (Ire) 5a *sn wll in rear, t.o. 3 out* 4
275 Oberons Butterfly *in chsng grp, blnd 12th, wkng whn p.u. 4 out* .... pu
454 Target Time 5a *t.o. 9th, jmpd slwly & u.r. 13th* .... ur
275 High Burnshot *lft in ld 3rd, dist clr 10th, 20l up whn f 3 out.* .... f
Malingerer 7a *pllng, ld til ran out 3rd* .... ro
275 Welshmans Canyon (Ire) *bhnd whn f 13th* .... f
Croft Court 7a *rear, t.o. 9th, p.u. 12th* .... pu
10 ran. 8l, 20l, dist. Time 6m 26.00s. SP 12-1.
P Mercer (West Street).

576 - Maiden (12st)

454 **GALAROI (IRE) 5ow** .... **D Robinson** 1
alwys prom, chsd ldr 14th, chal whn lft clr last
479 **Bitofamixup (Ire) 7a** .... **P Hacking** 2
rear,wll bhnd til steady prog 14th,styd on wll,lft 2nd last
275 **Pallingham Star (Ire)** .... **P Hickman** 3
(fav) mid-div, nvr trbld ldrs, styd on
Captain Beal *prom, 3rd at 14th, wknd 3 out* 4
455 Grassington (Ire) *wll bhnd hlfwy, some late prog* 5
Eastern Evening *nvr bttr than mid-div, wll bhnd whn p.u. aft 4 out* .... pu
Iorwerth *in tch til wknd 14th, wll bhnd whn p.u. 3 out.* . pu
Custardorcream 5a 2ow *prom to 11th, bhnd whn p.u. 17th* .... pu
275 Fort Diana *alwys wll in rear, p.u. 14th* .... pu
455 Manor Ranger *ld 3rd-9th, lft in ld 13th, clr apr 3 out, prssd & u.r. last* .... ur
455 Coral Eddy *ld to 3rd, prom whn u.r. 6th* .... ur
275 Zallot *mid-div to 10th, bhnd whn p.u. 14th* .... pu
454 Huckleberry Friend 5a 3ow *rear, p.u. 13th* .... pu
344 Kelburne Lad (Ire) *prom, ld 9th til f 13th* .... f

Highland Romance 5a *rear til p.u. 15th* ..... pu
455 Over The Clover (Ire) 5a *rear, p.u. 10th* ..... pu
455 Polar Ana (Ire) 5a *wll in rear, some prog in 10th whn u.r. 15th* ..... ur
477 Wergild *rear, p.u. 9th* ..... pu
18 ran. 10l, 15l, 12l, 8l. Time 6m 19.00s. SP 7-1.
D C Robinson (Mid Surrey Farmers Drag).
G.Ta.

FONTWELL
Tuesday March 19th
GOOD TO FIRM

577 - 2m 3f Hun Chase

257 **HAMPER 11.7 7a (bl) ..... Mr N R Mitchell** 1
(fav) alwys in tch, challenging when hit 10th, ld next, left clr 12th, wknd run-in, fin tired.
369 **Blakes Orphan 11.13 7a (bl) ..... Mr P Scott** 2
ld till after 2nd, blnd next, styd on to go second 2 out, ran on strly run-in.
250 **Lavalight 11.9 5a ..... Mr P Henley** 3
pulld hrd, in rear, left poor 2nd 12th, wknd 2 out.
Welshman's Gully 11.7 7a *alwys bhnd, t.o. when p.u. after 4 out* ..... pu
251 Eddie Walshe 11.7 7a *pulld hrd, led apr 3rd, hdd 11th, f next* ..... f
5 ran. 1½l, 16l. Time 5m 3.80s. SP 5-4.
N J Hoare

LUDLOW
Wednesday March 20th
GOOD

578 - 3m Hun Chase

363 **WILD ILLUSION 11.7 7a ..... Mr Richard White** 1
(fav) alwys prom, left 2nd bend after 11th, ld apr 4 out, soon clr.
160 **Ross Venture 12.0 7a ..... Mr C Stockton** 2
ld, blnd 7th, hdd apr 4 out, no ch with wnr.
215 **Sams Heritage 11.7 7a ..... Mr M Daly** 3
slowly into stride, hdwy 6th, left 3rd bend after 11th, wknd next.
261 Barn Pool 11.7 7a *prom, hit 3rd, soon lost pl and well bhnd, t.o. when blnd and u.r. last* ..... ur
Fox Pointer 11.7 7a *in rear when hmpd and u.r. bend after 11th* ..... ur
461 Roll-A-Dance 11.7 7a *started slowly, soon prom, rdn when blnd and u.r. 10th* ..... ur
372 Percy Thrower 11.13 5a *chsd ldr, f bend after 11th* ..... f
7 ran. 15l, dist. Time 6m 17.40s. SP 5-6.
G Pidgeon

579 - 2½m Hun Chase

374 **HICKELTON LAD 11.7 7a ..... Miss S Higgins** 1
prom, mstk and lost pl 5 out, rallied 2 out, styd on to ld final 50 yards.
65 **Tuffnut George 11.7 7a ..... Mr A Phillips** 2
held up, hdwy 5 out, left in ld flat, hdd final 50 yards.
362 **Kambalda Rambler 12.0 7a ..... Mr R Crosby** 3
mid div, hdwy 5 out, btn when left 4th last, kept on.
359 Al Hashimi 12.0 7a *alwys prom, 2nd and btn when left in ld and hmpd last, soon hdd and wknd* 4
365 Searcy 11.7 7a *prom, rdn 5 out, gradually wknd* 5
359 Falconbridge Bay 11.11 7a *prom to 6th, t.o. from from 12th* 6
257 Pastoral Pride (USA) 11.9 5a *(fav) ld, clr 4 out, f last* ..... f
Tytherington 11.7 7a *ref to race* ..... f
385 Golden Fare 11.7 7a *mid div, lost tch hfwy, t.o. and p.u. before 2 out* ..... pu
374 Some Obligation 11.7 7a (bl) *mid div when blnd and u.r. 5th* ..... ur
361 Pamela's Lad 11.7 7a *held up, hdwy 10th, 3rd when f 4 out* ..... f
459 King Of Shadows 11.7 7a *bhnd from hfwy, t.o. when p.u. before 2 out* ..... pu
Hook Line'N'sinker 11.7 7a *mstk 3rd, alwys in rear, t.o. when p.u. before 2 out* ..... pu
Warner Forpleasure 11.7 7a (bl) *prom to hfwy, soon bhnd, p.u. before 5 out* ..... pu
461 Luke's The Bizz (Ire) 11.7 7a *prom to 10th, bhnd when p.u. before 5 out* ..... pu
287 Kali Sana (Ire) 11.7 7a *blnd and u.r. 1st* ..... ur
Derring Run 11.2 7a *started slowly, mstk and hmpd 1st, t.o. when p.u. before 10th* ..... pu
17 ran. ¾l, ½l, 6l, 15l, dist. Time 5m 11.60s. SP 20-1.
Miss B W Palmer

TOWCESTER
Wednesday March 20th
GOOD

580 - 2¾m Hun Chase

CALL HOME (IRE) 11.7 7a ..... Mr T Hills 1
chsd ldr, ld 12th, joined 2 out, driven out run-in.
369 **Teaplanter 12.3 5a ..... Mr B Pollock** 2
(fav) ld, mstk 11th, hdd next, str chal from 2 out, no ext run-in.
Vulcan Star 11.9 5a ..... Mr T Byrne 3
soon t.o..
362 Antrim County 11.7 7a *t.o. from 6th* 4
481 Abba Lad 11.7 7a *soon t.o.* 5
5 ran. ½l, dist, 8l, dist. Time 5m 58.90s. SP 11-4.
Maurice E Pinto

WINCANTON
Thursday March 21st
SOFT

581 - 2m 5f Nov Hun Chase

263 **OAKLANDS WORD 11.7 7a ..... Mr J Jukes** 1
alwys prom, ld 4 out, ran on well.
337 **King's Treasure (USA) 11.7 7a ..... Mr A Balding** 2
alwys prom, ev ch apr 3 out, not qckn.
337 **Bright Burns 11.7 7a (bl) ..... Mr Rupert Sweeting** 3
ld to 4 out, ran on one pace.
358 Bold Imp 12.0 *hdwy 10th, ev ch 4 out, one pace* 4
370 Still In Business 12.1 5a *(fav) hdwy 10th, wknd apr 3 out* 5
Four Rivers 11.7 7a *chsd ldr, weakening when mstk 9th, p.u. before 5 out* ..... pu
208 Alpine Song 11.2 7a *t.o. when p.u. before 5 out* ..... pu
361 Notanotherone (Ire) 11.7 7a *t.o. when p.u. before 4 out* ..... pu
361 Great Uncle 11.7 7a *mstks 5th and 11th, t.o. when p.u. before 4 out* ..... pu
367 Carrigeen Lad 11.7 7a *chsd ldrs to 5 out, weakening when f 4 out* ..... f
361 Haye Buster 11.7 7a *t.o. when p.u. before 12th* ..... pu
Precis 11.2 7a *t.o. when p.u. before 5 out* ..... pu
260 Bang On Target 11.9 5a (bl) *bhnd from 10th, t.o. when ref last* ..... ref
13 ran. 4l, 13l, 2l, 20l. Time 5m 46.70s. SP 6-1.
F P Luff

KELSO
Friday March 22nd
GOOD

582 - 3½m Hun Chase

259 **ROYAL JESTER 11.11 5a ..... Mr C Storey** 1
(fav) trckd ldrs, hdwy 11th, ld 16th, blnd badly and hdd 3 out, rallied to chal last, led flat and ran on.
320 **Political Issue 11.5 5a ..... Mr P Johnson** 2
alwys prom, blnd 10th, effort and ld 3 out, soon rdn, hdd and no ext flat.
371 **Parlebiz 11.4 7a ..... Mr A Robson** 3
held up, blnd 2nd, hit 7th, blunded 11th, hdwy 14th, rdn 3 out and one pace.
487 Mr Diplomatic 11.3 7a (bl) *rdn and hdd 16th, gradually wknd from 3 out* 4

500 Toddlin Hame 11.6 7a 3ow *u.r. 2nd.* .... ur
320 Bow Handy Man 11.3 7a *prom till blnd badly and u.r. 14th.* .... ur
Birtley Girl 11.0 5a *n.j.w., soon bhnd, t.o. 10th, p.u. before 3 out.* .... pu
305 Final Hope (Ire) 11.9 7a *held up in rear, steady hdwy 12th, trckd ldrs when f next.* .... f
8 ran. 7l, 25l, 13l. Time 7m 36.80s. SP 4-5.
Mrs A D Wauchope

BRAMHAM MOOR
Wetherby Point-To-Point Course
Saturday March 23rd
SOFT

583 - Members

COT LANE .... R Walmsley 1
cls up, ld 13th, ran on well 2 out
306 **Ocean Rose 5a .... W Burnell** 2
(fav) prom, outpcd 14th, styd on onepcd aft
512 **Good Team .... D Crossland** 3
cls up, 2nd & ev ch 3 out, wknd nxt
Certain Rhythm *prom, wknd 12th, t.o. 14th, p.u. 3 out* pu
409 One For The Chief *rear whn ran out 8th* .... ro
Winston (Mem) *1st ride, t.o. 5th, f 7th* .... f
6 ran. 12l, 15l. Time 7m 26.00s. SP 6-4.
J W Walmsley (Bramham Moor).

584 - Restricted Div I

539 **STAG FIGHT .... S Walker** 1
(fav) 2nd til ld 12th, styd on well frm 2 out
415 **Another Hooligan .... R Tate** 2
hld up, prog 14th, ev ch 2 out, outpcd by wnr
515 **Primitive Penny 7a .... C Mulhall** 3
alwys prom, onepcd frm 2 out
T'int (Ire) 5a *mid-div, kpt on onepcd frm 2 out, nvr nrr* 4
411 Missile Man *cls up, outpcd4 out, styd on wll 2 out, no ext flat* 5
Kenilworth (Ire) *mid-div, prog 11th, cls up til wknd 4 out.* 6
81 My True Clown *t.o. 3rd, p.u. 10th* .... pu
403 Buckwheat Lad (Ire) *alwys mid-div, btn whn f 3 out* ... f
515 Polar Hat (bl) *cls up til wknd 10th, rear whn p.u. 14th* pu
411 Cumberland Blues (Ire) *ld to 12th, in tch whn f 14th* ... f
416 Goodwill Hill *mid-div, wknd 3 out, p.u. last.* .... pu
Spanish Fly (Ire) 5a *mid-div, f 6th.* .... f
303 Charlcot Storm 7a *ref 1st* .... ref
13 ran. 1½l, 4l, ½l, 10l, ½l. Time 7m 25.00s. SP 2-1.
Mrs P A Russell (Middleton).

585 - Restricted Div II

411 **LATHERON (IRE) .... S Swiers** 1
(fav) rear, prog 10th, 4th 4 out, ran on on outer to ld flat
306 **Political Sam .... A Rebori** 2
rear, prog 12th, 3rd 4 out, no imp til rallied wll flat
515 **Jasilu 5a .... N Wilson** 3
prom, ld 10th-aft 12th, lft in ld 4 out, hdd & no ext flat
329 Young Moss *alwys mid-div, kpt on onepcd frm 3 out, no dang* 4
411 Caman 5a *t.o. 6th, fin own time* 5
411 The Chap *alwys mid-div, no ch whn p.u. last* .... pu
408 G Derek *t.o. 6th, p.u. 2 out.* .... pu
411 Mr Elk *mid-div till f 14th* .... f
221 Anythingyoulike *prom, ld aft 12th til f 4 out* .... f
303 Computer Pickings 5a *alwys twrds rear, no ch whn p.u. 3 out* .... pu
414 Stride To Glory (Ire) 7a *mid-div whn blnd & u.r. 4th* ... ur
718 Shildon (Ire) *ld til nrly c.o. 10th, wknd nxt, p.u. 14th* ... pu
Pin Up Boy *mid-div to 10th, rear whn p.u. 13th.* .... pu
13 ran. 2l, ½l, 25l, dist. Time 7m 23.00s. SP 5-4.
Mrs A M Easterby (Middleton).

586 - Ladies

385 **WORKINGFORPEANUTS (IRE) 5a ... Miss S Jackson** 1
(fav) mid-div, gd prog to ld last, ran on well
515 **Katies Argument 5a .... Mrs J Milburn** 2
handy, outpcd 3 out, styd on well, tk 2nd nr fin
318 **Across The Lake .... Miss S Brotherton** 3
mid-div, prog 12th, ld 3 out-last, eased & lost 2nd flat
514 Linebacker *33s-20s, made most to 4 o ut, wknd nxt* ... 4
306 Prior Conviction (Ire) *alwys mid-div, no dang* 5
536 Douce Eclair 5a *cls up til wknd 10th, no dang aft* 6
227 Wall Game (USA) *alwys rear, t.o. & p.u. 10th* .... pu
225 Era's Imp *prom whn p.u. 11th, dead* .... pu
8 ran. 5l, ¾l, 10l, 5l, 10l. Time 7m 25.00s. SP Evens.
Mrs D A Smith (North Ledbury).

587 - Open

401 **MAN'S BEST FRIEND .... R Ford** 1
(fav) cls up, disp 14th til ld last, hdd flat, rallied to ld fin
410 **Peanuts Pet .... R Walmsley** 2
mid-div, prog 12th, disp 14th-last, ld flat, hdd nr fin
512 **Tobin Bronze .... R Edwards** 3
hld up, prog 14th, styd on well 3 out, no ext apr last
367 Politico Pot *cls up, ld 11-14th, outpcd nxt, onepcd* ... 4
513 Furry Knowe *prom to 10th, sn outpcd* 5
304 Equinoctial *handy til wknd 14th* 6
512 Nishkina *mid-div, blnd 12th, t.o. 3 out* 7
303 Tammy My Girl 5a *alwys rear, t.o. 3 out* 8
410 Amy's Mystery *alwys twrds rear, p.u. last* .... pu
410 Minstrel Paddy *rear frm 10th, bhnd whn p.u. 14th* .... pu
513 Barry Owen *mid-div, f 7th, dead.* .... f
326 Croft Mill *mstks, rear, t.o. & p.u. 11th* .... pu
Oaksey *rear frm 10th, bhnd whn p.u. 13th* .... pu
304 Skipping Gale *ld to 10th, wknd 12th, p.u. 14th* .... pu
Gaelic Warrior *mid-div, no ch whn p.u. 3 out* .... pu
15 ran. Sht-hd, 10l, 15l, 5l, 3l, 20l, 10l. Time 7m 22.00s. SP 4-6.
Mrs M Dickinson (Middleton).

588 - Intermediate (12st)

303 **QUAYSIDE COTTAGE (IRE) .... N Wilson** 1
hld up, prog 14th, ran on well 2 out, disp last, ld flat
293 **Three Potato Four .... D Barlow** 2
rear, gd prog 14th, ld 3 out, hdd & no ext flat
328 **Flip The Lid (Ire) 5a .... N Tutty** 3
cls up, outpcd 4 out, styd on onepcd frm nxt
409 Castle Tyrant 5a *made msot to 4 out, onepcd aft* 4
306 Jack Dwyer *handy wil wknd 4 out* 5
409 Just Charlie *alwys mid-div, nvr a fctr* 6
223 Tom Log *alwys mid-div, nvr dang* 7
303 Fowling Piece *rear by 10th, t.o. 12th, fin own time* 8
416 Country Chalice *t.o. 10th, fin own time* 9
512 War Head *rear by 10th, t.o. & p.u. 13th* .... pu
512 Breckenbrough Lad *rear, t.o. 12th, p.u. nxt* .... pu
306 Go Miletrian *rear frm 10th, p.u. 14th* .... pu
413 Mr Dick *mid-div whn f 4 out* .... f
408 Vienna Woods *mid-div, blnd 12th, p.u. nxt* .... pu
411 Launchselect 7a *(fav) prom, rdn whn mstk 13th, not rcvr, p.u. last* .... pu
409 Polynth *alwys mid-div, no ch whn p.u. last* .... pu
539 Pendle Witch 5a *mstks, t.o. 4th, p.u. 8th* .... pu
17 ran. 2l, 10l, 3l, 8l, 4l, dist, 15l, 2l. Time 7m 25.00s. SP 10-1.
B Marley (Braes Of Derwent).

589 - Open Maiden Div I

308 **HIGHLAND FRIEND .... A Rebori** 1
(Jt fav) handy, ld 13th-4 out, styd on apr last, ld flat
517 **Lingcool 5a .... N Wilson** 2
mid-div, prog 12th, lft 2nd 14th, ld last, hdd & no ext flat
238 **Rye Head 7a .... P Atkinson** 3
(Jt fav) mstks, mid-div, styd on well 3 out, nrst fin
718 Tyndrum Gold *rear, prog 14th, styd on frm 3 out, nvr nrr.* 4
307 Oaklands Fred *alwys mid-div, nvr dang* 5
331 Greet The Greek *alwys mid-div, nvr dang* 6
359 Auntie Fay (Ire) 7a *rear whn p.u. 4th* .... pu
117 Goongor (Ire) *cls up to 10th, rear whn p.u. 12th.* ...... pu

516 Grange Gracie 5a *ld to 12th, cls up whn f 14th* .... f
516 Roseberry Star 5a *hmpd 1st, alwys rear, t.o. 10th, p.u. 14th* .... pu
Fleeced *prom, mstk 4th, wknd 10th, rear & p.u. 14th* .. pu
287 Colonian King *f 1st* .... f
286 Micksdilemma *mid-div, prog 12th, disp whn f 2 out* .. f
413 Just Takethe Micky *mid-div, btn whn mstk & u.r. 3 out* .... ur
517 Father's Gift 5a *mid-div to 10th, sn rear, p.u. 14th* .... pu
Lively Lil (Ire) 5a *t.o. 6th, p.u. 10th* .... pu
16 ran. 3l, 2l, 15l, 5l, 3l. Time 7m 40.00s. SP 5-2.
Henry Bell (Bilsdale).

590 - Open Maiden Div II

409 **WOLVERCASTLE 5a**..................**S Charlton** 1
mid-div, prog 11th, disp nxt, lft dist clr 4 out, easily
416 **Triple Value 5a**....................**Miss R Clark** 2
mid-div, prog to 3rd 14th, lft poor 2nd nxt, no ch wnr
397 **Barneys Gold (Ire)**....................**A Bealby** 3
cls up til wknd 14th, poor 3rd frm nxt
288 Salmon Spring *alwys mid-div, no ch whn p.u. 4 out* ... pu
415 Ingleby Flyer 5a *mid-div to 10th, t.o. whn f 12th*.......... f
413 Not The Nadger 7a *f 1st*........ f
71 Mendip Son *rear til p.u. 9th* .... pu
331 Malvern Cantina *prom, disp 12th til f 4 out*........ f
Tortula 5a *ld to 11th, wknd, p.u. 4 out* .... pu
414 River Ramble 5a *alwys mid-div, no ch whn p.u. 4 out* pu
541 Boulevard Bay (Ire) 7a *(fav) prom, wknd 12th, p.u. 15th*........ pu
414 Muscoates 7a *rear whn p.u. 12th* .... pu
Just Jessica 5a *f 2nd* .... f
416 Jack Little *mid-div whn f 12th* .... f
Magic Song 5a *mid-div, ran out 9th* .... ro
Bucksum (Ire) 7a *mid-div, f 4th*........ f
16 ran. 15l, dist. Time 7m 40.00s. SP 5-2.
Ian Wormald (Bilsdale).

591 - Open Maiden Div III

431 **NUTCASE 5a** ....**T Stephenson** 1
(fav) mid-div, prog 12th, ld 4 out, ran on well
516 **Rabble Rouser**.........................**R Edwards** 2
cls up, ld 11th-4 out, onepcd aft
415 **Basil Grey** ....**P Jenkins** 3
prom til grad wknd frm 3 out
218 Balmaha 7a *alwys mid-div, kpt on onepcd frm 4 out* .. 4
Tricycling (Ire) *alwys rear, p.u. 14th*........ pu
Zin Zan (Ire) *plld hrd, ld to 3rd, lft in ld nxt, wknd 10th, p.u. 14th*........ pu
308 Timber Topper *rear, p.u. 3rd, saddle slppd* .... pu
Sarvo (Ire) *ld 3rd, 20l clr whn f nxt, dead* .... f
416 Ninefiveo 5a *t.o. 7th, p.u. nxt*........ pu
515 Pearl Bridge *mid-div, wkng whn ref 3 out*........ ref
413 Lakeland Venture 5a (bl) *cls up to 12th, wknd nxt, p.u. 4 out* .... pu
516 Stays Fresh *rear whn blnd & u.r. 10th*........ ur
413 Sergeant Pepper *mstks, mid-div, wknd 10th, p.u. 14th* pu
516 Justforgastrix (Ire) *alwys rear, p.u. 14th* .... pu
14 ran. 7l, 15l, 3l. Time 7m 37.00s. SP 2-1.
N Shutts (Albrighton Woodland).
R.W.

CRAWLEY & HORSHAM
Parham
Saturday March 23rd
GOOD TO SOFT

592 - Members

DREWITTS DANCER..................**M Gorman** 1
plIng,cls up,ld aft 8th,lft dist clr 13th,hacked round
271 Colonel O'Kelly (NZ) *(fav) trckd ldrs, 2nd 9th, mstk 11th, chsng wnr whn u.r. 13th* .... ur
Sir Hugo 26ow *ld to aft 8th,t.o. 12th,lft bad 2nd nxt,u.r. 3 out,evntl fin*........ 0
576 Wergild *immed dtchd, t.o. whn ref 4th*........ ref
4 ran. Time 7m 2.00s. SP 5-2.
Mrs A A Hawkins (Crawley & Horsham).

593 - Restricted (12st)

248 **BARDAROS**...........................**P Hacking** 1
rear, prog 9th, ld 14th, made rest, comf
574 **Fixed Liability 1ow**.....................**P Hickman** 2
handy, mstk 13th, prog to chs wnr 4 out, ev ch 2 out, wknd
275 **Local Manor**.............................**H Dunlop** 3
sn prom, 3rd frm 3 out, not pace to chal
108 Nibble *cls up, jmpd slwly 14th whn 3rd, 4th & no dang frm 4 out*........ 4
378 Billhead *mid-div, wknd & p.u. 12th*........ pu
272 Tau *prom til wknd 13th, wll bhnd whn p.u. 2 out* ..... pu
Tufter's Garth *plld into ld 2nd,prssd frm 8th,hdd 14th,wll bhnd & p.u.2 out*........ pu
478 Palaman 2ow *rear, mstk 3rd, lost tch whn p.u. aft 13th*........ pu
449 Lewesdon Princess 5a *alwys wll in rear, t.o. & p.u. 3 out*........ pu
428 Diamond Valley (Ire) *(fav) ld to 2nd, mid-div aft, 7th whn u.r. 10th*........ ur
Indiway *alwys rear, p.u. 11th* .... pu
11 ran. 6l, 6l, 15l. Time 6m 55.00s. SP 3-1.
Mrs D M Stevenson (East Sussex & Romney Marsh).

594 - Confined (12st)

450 **NETHERTARA 5a 3ex**..................**P Hacking** 1
mid-div, smooth prog to ld 12th, ran on strngly 3 out,sn clr
271 **The Portsoy Loon**....................**A Hickman** 2
alwys prom, chsd wnr 4 out, outpcd 2 out
271 **Kates Castle 5a** ....**Mrs S Hickman** 3
ld, blnd 10th, hdd 12th, 3rd frm 14th, btn 3 out
272 Murberry (Ire) 5a *(fav) cls up til mstk 11th, 4th frm 14th, no ch frm 3 out* 4
573 Kaim Park *rear, lost tch 12th, p.u. 2 out* .... pu
450 Highland Bounty *alwys rear, rmndrs hlfwy, wll bhnd whn p.u. 13th*........ pu
474 Pat Alaska *mid-div to hlfwy, wll bhnd whn p.u. 3 out* .. pu
451 Cool It A Bit 5ex *nvr bttr than mid-div, losing tch whn p.u. 14th*........ pu
475 Olde Crescent *rear whn u.r. 2nd* .... ur
249 Athnanurlainn 2ow *alwys wll in rear, blnd 8th, t.o. aft, p.u. last* .... pu
Sure Pride (USA) *mid-div, 5th & wkng 14th, wll bhnd whn p.u. 3 out*........ pu
450 Country Vet 5a 3ex *alwys twrds rear, lost tch 11th, p.u. last* .... pu
274 Berrings Dasher *cls up til wknd rpdly 13th, p.u. nxt* ... pu
13 ran. 20l, 8l, 6l. Time 6m 48.00s. SP 2-1.
Alan Cowing (East Sussex & Romney Marsh).

595 - Open (12st)

271 **LITTLE MARTINA (IRE) 5a**...............**A Welsh** 1
sn wth ldr, ld 11th, clr 4 out, unchal
274 **Retail Runner** ....**T Hills** 2
ld/disp to 11th, 2nd aft, outpcd 4 out, wknd last
480 **Paco's Boy 4ex**...........................**P York** 3
in tch, nvr on terms, styd on well apr last
573 Ginger Tristan 7ex *sn chsng ldng pair, nvr on terms, rdn out flat*........ 4
274 Celtic Spark 7ex *(fav) mid-div,mstk 5th,nvr thrntd,some prog to 3rd 4 out,eased flt* 5
451 Folk Dance 4ow 4ex *in tch to 14th, bhnd whn p.u. 3 out*........ pu
476 Vultoro 7ex *alwys rear & strgglng to stay in tch, p.u. 13th*........ pu
379 Myverygoodfriend *rear, sn strgglng to stay in tch, bhnd whn p.u. 12th*........ pu
274 Sunday Punch *ref to race* 0
451 Darkbrook *mstks, mid-div, rmndrs hlfwy, 7th & no ch whn f 12th* .... f
480 Centre Stage *alwys rear, nvr going wll, p.u. 13th*.... pu
451 Quarter Marker (Ire) 1ow *prom, mstk 2nd, wknd rpdly 8th, bhnd whn p.u. 10th* .... pu
12 ran. 15l, 5l, 1l, 10l. Time 6m 54.00s. SP 5-2.
Christopher Newport (East Sussex & Romney Marsh).

596 - Ladies

572 **WELLINGTON BAY**..............**Miss C Grissell** 1
rear,out of tch 13th,rdn & styd on 4 out,2nd 2 out, ld flat
452 **Forest Sun**..........................**Miss J Grant** 2
prom, ld aft 4 out, clr 2 out, wknd aft, hdd flat
452 **Our Survivor 4ex**...................**Miss C Savell** 3
ld to 3rd, prom aft, outpcd 12th, 4th 2 out, styd on strngly
273 Topping-The-Bill 4ex *(fav) rear, jnd ldrs 9th, mstks aft, chsd ldr 4 out, btn 2 out* 4
473 Johnny Rose *ld 6th til aft 4 out, kpt on same pace* 5
Mountaico *ld apr 3rd-6th, wknd 8th, rear & p.u. 11th* .. pu
273 Maltby Boy *in tch to 13th, wll bhnd p.u. 2 out* .... pu
Scotch Law *plIng, prom to 10th, rear & strggIng 12th, u.r. 14th* .... ur

8 ran. ½l, ½l, 10l, 6l. Time 7m 3.00s. SP 20-1.
L R Vine (East Sussex & Romney Marsh).

597 - Open Maiden (12st)

575 **CROFT COURT 7a**...................**P Hacking** 1
rear, 50l 6th at 12th,prog aft,3rd 4 out,styd on to ld last
576 **Pallingham Star (Ire)**...............**P O'Keeffe** 2
2nd, clsd on clr ldr 9th, ld & lft clr 14th, hdd last,tired
Saun (Cze).........................**Miss C Elliott** 3
1st ride, alwys rear & outpcd, dist 2nd frm 14th, 3rd 3 out
477 No Reply *alwys rear & outpcd, dist 4th 4 out, plodded round* 4
455 Time Star (NZ) *alwys strggIng, wll bhnd whn p.u. 14th* .... pu
454 Mister Spectator (Ire) *(fav) ld, clr to 10th, just hdd whn f 14th* .... f
576 Kelburne Lad (Ire) *chsd ldr, clsd in 3rd whn f 10th* .... f
314 Clonoghill (Ire) *trckng ldrs whn u.r. 2nd* .... ur
314 Le Vienna (Ire) *rear, wll bhnd whn p.u. 9th* .... pu

9 ran. 8l, 1 fence, 4l. Time 7m 9.00s. SP 9-1.
Barry J Cockerell (East Sussex & Romney Marsh).
G.Ta.

CURRE
Howick
Saturday March 23rd
SOFT

598 - Members (12st)

506 **GEE DOUBLE YOU**...................**B Tulloch** 1
(fav) cls 2nd, ld 10th, clr aft, easily
267 **Twilight Tom**...........................**A Price** 2
hld up, ran on onepcd frm 14th, tk 2nd 3 out
Bee Moy Do (Ire).........................**J Price** 3
ld to 10th, wknd 14th, lost 2nd 3 out
379 Miss Corinthian 5a *alwys 3rd/4th, onepcd frm hlfwy* .. 4
388 Cossack Strike (Ire) *cls 4th whn u.r. 9th* .... ur
Miss Rems Girl Vii *10l last whn f 6th* .... f

6 ran. Dist, dist, 8l. Time 7m 14.00s. SP 11-8.
J D Watkins (Curre).

599 - Restricted Div I (12st)

MISS ISLE 5a....................**Miss C Thomas** 1
cls 2nd til ld 11th, ran on well whn chal 3 out
357 **Scarlet Berry 5a**................**Julian Pritchard** 2
hld up, prog frm 12th, 2l down 3 out, alwys hld
428 **Louis Farrell**.......................**S Blackwell** 3
mostly 3rd, cls 2nd 11th, wknd 14th, poor 3rd aft
508 Plas-Hendy 2ow *alwys last, p.u. 13th* .... pu
387 Welsh Clover 5a *mid-div, wknd hlfwy, p.u. 14th* ..... pu
Inch Empress (Ire) *ld 4-10th, wknd rpdly, p.u. 3 out* .... pu
235 Fresh Prince *(fav) ld to 4th, lost plc, lost tch 11th, p.u. 3 out* .... pu

7 ran. 6l, dist. Time 7m 6.00s. SP 6-1.
M F Clifford (Warwickshire).

600 - Restricted Div II (12st)

OSCEOLA.............................**P Williams** 1
alwys prom, clr 2nd 12th, drvn to ld 3 out, hld on
256 **Robbie's Boy**..........................**J P Keen** 2
3rd/4th til ld 12th, hdd 3 out, ran on last, alwys hld
388 **Right Rosy 5a**.........................**R Jenkins** 3
mid-div, mstk 9th, ran on 15th, 3l down 2 out, just hld
379 Amadeo (bl) *hld up, prog 13th, no ext frm nxt* 4
387 Polly Pringle 5a *mid-div, styd on to 4th at 15th, wknd aft* 5
219 Saffron Moss *last at 2nd, fin own time* 6
350 Spanish Rouge *4th/5th to 12th, wknd, fin own time* 7
Parson's Corner *alwys rear, p.u. 3 out* .... pu
388 Tudor Oaks 5a *alwys rear, p.u. 14th* .... pu
383 Linantic *(fav) ld 6-11th, hdd & fdd, p.u. 3 out* .... pu
Cottage Raider (Ire) *ld til f 6th* .... f
Majic Belle 5a *prom to 6th, wknd grad, p.u. 15th* ..... pu
Dromin Chat (Ire) 1ow *3rd to 6th, wknd & p.u. 12th* .... pu
386 Delightfilly 7a *rear, p.u. 6th* .... pu

14 ran. Hd, 1l, 5l, 8l, 20l, 5l. Time 7m 9.00s. SP 4-1.
J Bryant (Glamorgan).
Objection by 2nd to winner, over-ruled.

601 - Confined (12st)

384 **SUN OF CHANCE**......................**P Williams** 1
mstk 4th, prom aft, rdn to 2nd 3 out, ld nxt, sn clr
505 **Chibougama (USA)**....................**S Shinton** 2
mid-div, ld 11th-14th & 3 out-nxt, onepcd aft
388 **Push Along**.........................**D Stephens** 3
(fav) hld up, went 3rd 3 out, not rch ldng pair
384 Troy Boy *4th frm 11th, styd on onepcd aft* 4
507 Prince Nepal *cls up, ld 14th-nxt, wknd rpdly aft* 5
383 Noisy Welcome *rear, lost irons 12th, fin well* 6
255 Space Mariner *t.o. 6th, fin own time* 7
Harken Premier *t.o. 10th, p.u. nxt* .... pu
232 Tango Tom *rear of ldng grp, f 7th* .... f
Smoulder (USA) *mid-div, lost plc 10th, p.u. 12th* ..... pu

10 ran. 8l, 6l, 7l, 3l, 5l, dist. Time 7m 12.00s. SP 7-2.
Miss M Ree (Glamorgan).

602 - Land Rover Open (12st)

256 **WELSH LEGION 7ex**.....................**J Jukes** 1
(fav) hld up, prog to ld 11th, made rest, alwys in cmmnd
Hugli 7ex............................**E Roberts** 2
rear, prog to 3rd at 13th, chsd wnr 3 out, no imp
507 **Sandy Beau 4ex**........................**T Jones** 3
ld 8-10th, chsd wnr, onepcd frm 15th
504 Auvillar (USA) *alwys rear, no ch frm 14th* 4
545 The Batchlor *mid-div, t.o. & p.u. 3 out* .... pu
506 Mummy's Song *ld to 7th, wknd rpdly, p.u. 13th* .... pu
384 Kingfisher Bay 7ex *cls up to 8th, wknd, p.u. 12th* ..... pu
Provence 7ex *alwys rear, some prog to 5th at 11th, wknd & p.u. 3 out* .... pu
547 Loch Garanne 5a *ref to race* 0
426 Stormhill Recruit *cls up whn u.r. 6th* .... ur
Barton Bulldozer (Ire) *t.o. whn u.r. 6th* .... ur

11 ran. 5l, 3l, 12l. Time 7m 14.00s. SP 2-5.
G W Lewis (Carmarthenshire).

603 - Ladies

385 **HANDSOME HARVEY 7ex**..........**Miss P Jones** 1
(fav) made all, chal 2 out, qcknd away
506 **La Mezeray 5a**...................**Mrs J Hawkins** 2
mstk 8th, 2nd frm 13th, chal 2 out, alwys hld
385 **Dare Say**.......................**Miss R Williams** 3
prom til 4th at 15th, wknd, lft poor 3rd 3 out
508 Lucky Ole Son *last, lft remote 4th by dfctns 3 out* 4
339 King Of The Clouds *mid-div, wknd & p.u. 3 out* .... pu
385 Lady Llanfair 5a 3ex *rear, gd prog 13th, 8l 3rd nxt, p.u. 3 out, lame* .... pu
216 Cantantivy 5a *chsd wnr to 12th, wknd & p.u. 3 out* .... pu
507 Light The Wick *alwys rear, t.o. 9th, p.u. 11th* .... pu

8 ran. 3l, dist, 10l. Time 7m 9.00s. SP 2-5.
E L Harries (Pembrokeshire).

604 - Intermediate (12st)

215 **MISS MILLBROOK 5a 5ex ....V Hughes** 1
6s-4s, cls up, went 2nd 10th, ld 14th, drew clr
358 **Judy Line 5a ....S Shinton** 2
rear, prog to 4th at 12th, styd on 3 out, nrst fin
262 **Dancing Doris 5a ....T Cox** 3
hld up, prog to 2nd at 9th, wknd frm 12th, lft 3rd 3 out
383 Lonesome Step 5a *cls up to hlfwy, wknd rpdly, p.u. 3 out* .... pu
549 Equatime 5a *2nd early, wknd frm 6th, t.o. & p.u. 12th* pu
386 Celtic Daughter 5a *rear, prog to 3rd at 13th, tired & p.u. 3 out* .... pu
505 African Bride (Ire) 5a 5ex *(fav) ld & clr to 13th, hdd nxt, wkng whn p.u. 3 out, distressed* .... pu
7 ran. Dist, 5l. Time 7m 14.00s. SP 4-1.
D T Goldsworthy (Llangeinor).

605 - Maiden Div I (12st)

391 **ROSENTHAL 5a ....M P Jones** 1
mid-div, prog to 3rd 12th, disp 14th-3 out, ld flat, all out
Brownscroft 5a......................S Jackson 2
2nd til disp 14th, ld 3 out, hdd flat, no ext und pres
432 **Yarron King (bl) ....S Blackwell** 3
(fav) ld to 13th, disp to 15th, wknd, fin tired
149 Khandys Slave (Ire) 5a *cls up early, lost plc frm 13th, tk 4th last* 4
485 Old Steine *cls up, lost tch wth 1st 3 frm 12th, fin tired* 5
389 Aldington Kid *prom to hlfwy, poor 6th whn p.u. 3 out.* pu
510 Romano Hati 5a *t.o. 5th, p.u. nxt* .... pu
Flying Roofer 5a *t.o. 8th, p.u. 11th* .... pu
Puttingonthestyle *mid-div, wknd 9th, p.u. 11th* .... pu
504 Colonel Frazer (Ire) *rear, wknd 7th, p.u. 11th* .... pu
504 Trydan *u.r. 2nd* .... ur
510 Rio Cisto 5a *mid-div, dtchd at 10th, p.u. nxt* .... pu
390 Lennie The Lion 7a *cls up whn f 6th* .... f
13 ran. ½l, dist, dist, 5l. Time 7m 32.00s. SP 5-1.
M P Jones (South Herefordshire).

606 - Maiden Div II (12st)

391 **BIX 7a...............................P Doorhof** 1
hld up, rpd prog to ld 12th, sn clr, impressive
431 **Roscoe's Gemma 5a.............Miss J Houldey** 2
rear, prog steadily frm 13th, 3rd 3 out, tk 2nd flat
510 **Bride Run (Ire)...........................A Price** 3
prom til went 2nd 13th, chsd wnr, alwys hld
509 Pyro Pennant *ld/disp to 11th, 2nd til wknd 13th, fin tired* 4
380 Country Life (USA) *t.o. 8th, fin own time* 5
263 Royal Swinger 5a *prom to hlfwy, wknd & p.u. 3 out* .... pu
510 Jimmy O'Goblin *just ld whn f 6th* .... f
389 Boddington Hill 5a *mid-div whn f 6th* .... f
509 Willow Belle (Ire) 5a *alwys rear, p.u. 3 out* .... pu
Buckskin Clover (Ire) *cls 5th whn f 8th* .... f
432 Mansun *f 2nd* .... f
389 I'm A Bute 5a *prom to 6th, wknd rpdly, p.u. 11th* .... pu
354 Wolfie Smith *(fav) ld/disp to 11th, wknd grad, p.u. 3 out* .... pu
13 ran. 10l, 2l, dist, dist. Time 7m 21.00s. SP 33-1.
J Parfitt (Gelligaer).

607 - Maiden Div III (12st)

DAUPHIN BLEU (FR)......................J Jukes 1
ld & clr by 4th, drew wll away 10th, easily
361 **Pharrago (Ire) ....Miss P Cooper** 2
chsd wnr frm 9th, styd on, no imp
391 **Miss Montgomery (Ire) 7a ....E Roberts** 3
9th at 11th, ran on own pace, lft 3rd by dfctns
391 Final Option (Ire) *cls 4th at 11th, wknd, fin own time* 4
390 Ludermain 5a *mod 5th whn f 13th* .... f
It's So Sweet 5a *rear, p.u. 10th* .... pu
506 Lazzaretto *mid-div, t.o. & p.u. 14th* .... pu
431 Demamo (Ire) *(fav) cls 2nd whn f 9th* .... f
Nutsil 5a *rear, p.u. 9th* .... pu
509 Steel Valley (Ire) 5a *alwys 3rd/4th, wknd frm 13th, clr 3rd whn f 3 out* .... f
389 Tiger Lord 7a *t.o. hlfwy, p.u. 15th* .... pu
Just Danny *rear, t.o. & p.u. 10th* .... pu
12 ran. Dist, dist, 5l. Time 7m 26.00s. SP 6-1.
Miss Victoria Roberts (Berkeley).
P.H./J.C.

DUKE OF BUCCLEUCH'S
Friars Haugh
Saturday March 23rd
GOOD

608 - Restricted (12st)

JIGTIME 5a.........................M Bradburne 1
disp ld frm 11th, ld 4 out, styd on wll
404 **Eastlands Hi-Light...................T Morrison** 2
4th hlfwy, wnt 2nd 2 out, no impr on wnnr
319 **Kalajo 2ow ....R Shiels** 3
5th hlfwy, styd on frm 3 out, nrst fin
403 Blakes Folly (Ire) *ld 7th untl jnd 11th, wknd 3 out* 4
189 Joli Exciting 5a *nvr bttr thn mdfld* 5
316 General Delight *nvr bttr thn mdfld* 6
323 Fiscal Policy 3ow *(fav) alwys rr* 7
318 Sunnie Cruise 5a *alwys rr* 8
404 Fruids Park 5a *bhnd 4th, u.r. 14th* .... pu
48 Anzarna 5a *t.o. 7th, p.u. 13th.* .... pu
406 Funny Feelings *made most til f 7th* .... f
498 Leyden Lady 5a *not fluent, 3rd hlfway, sn wknd, p.u. 4 out* .... pu
321 Jayandoubleu (Ire) *mid-div whn f 8th* .... f
13 ran. 6l, nk, 20l, 8l, 4l, 2l, 20l. Time 6m 33.00s. SP 10-1.
J W Hughes (Buccleuch).

609 - P P O R A (12st)

399 **WORTHY SPARK.......................P Craggs** 1
(fav) made all, blnd 13th, hrd prssd apr last, styd on gamely
399 **Royalist (Can)..........................C Storey** 2
2nd frm 11th, strng chal frm 2 out, no ext flat
186 **Across The Card ....W Ramsay** 3
not fluent in rear, some hdwy frm 4 out, nvr dang
402 Hardihero *not fluent, nvr dngrs* 4
499 Rarely At Odds *2nd hlfwy, sn wknd* 5
318 The Healy 5a *10l 4th whn u.r. 4 out* .... ur
Gay Vixen VI 5a *3rd hlfwy, lost tch 15th, p.u. next* .... pu
7 ran. 3l, 20l, 2l, 20l. Time 6m 36.00s. SP 4-6.
A J Balmer (Tynedale).

610 - Confined (12st)

404 **SAYIN NOWT 5a..........................A Parker** 1
(fav) 4th hlfwy, ld apr 2 out, sn clr, comf
498 **Little Glen...............................T Scott** 2
3rd hlfwy, styd on to take 2nd cl home
187 **True Fair 6ex..........................A Robson** 3
ld til apr 2 out, no ext apr last
498 Fordstown (Ire) 10ex *5th hlfwy, styd on frm 3 out, nrst fin* 4
402 Reed *2nd hlfwy, clse up untl wknd 2 out* 5
50 Buckle It Up 3ex *alwys twrds rr* 6
498 Paddy Hayton *sn bhnd* 7
Redediver (bl) *t.o. hlfwy* 8
318 Dawn Coyote (USA) *6th hlfwy, sn lost tch, p.u. bfr last* 0
Jade Shoon *missed start, virt t.n.p., p.u. 8th* .... pu
Davimport *nvr dngrs, bhnd whn p.u. 4 out* .... pu
11 ran. 8l, sht-hd, hd, 6l, dist, 2l, dist. Time 6m 41.00s. SP Evens.
Dennis Waggott (Dumfriesshire).

611 - Ladies

412 **RUSHING BURN 5a............Miss N Snowden** 1
hld up, hdwy to ld 3 out, styd on wll
319 **Royal Surprise...................Miss P Robson** 2
4th hlfwy, chal apr last, no ext flat
359 **Abitmorfun ....Miss K McLintock** 3
made most til grad wknd frm 4 out

400 Amber Payne *ld brfly 4 out, wknd frm nxt* 4
318 Furry Venture 5a *sn bhnd, some late hdwy, nrst fin* ... 5
Wigtown Bay *2nd frm 4th, remained clse up until wknd 4 out* 6
403 Emu Park *3rd hlfwy, sn wknd* 7
499 Carousel Calypso *alwys rr* 8
318 Marshalstoneswood *(fav) mdfld, some hdwy frm 13th, 5l 4th whn u.r. 3 out* 9
501 Royal Fife 5a *5th hlfwy, u.r. 11th* .... ur
10 ran. 3l, 4l, 4l, nk, 20l, 1l, 5l. Time 6m 44.00s. SP 9-2.
F D A Snowden (Berwickshire).

612 - Open

317 **HOWAYMAN** .... **A Parker** **1**
2nd hlfwy, ld 15th, pshd out flat
486 **Ruber** .... **R Hale** **2**
ld til mstk & lost plc 6th, wnt 2nd 4 out, no ex apr last
500 **Boreen Owen** .... **T Morrison** **3**
ld 6th until 8th, wknd frm 15th
402 Judicious Captain *3rd hlfwy, sn wknd* 4
401 Generals Boy *(fav) ld 8th-15th, 3rd & wkng whn f 3 out, dead* .... f
83 Yenoora (Ire) *sn bhnd, t.o. whn p.u. 11th* .... pu
Fortinas Flyer 5a (bl) *4th hlfwy, u.r. 11th* .... ur
500 Dundee Prince (NZ) *s.s. 8l bhnd ldr whn f 13th* .... f
8 ran. 4l, 20l, dist. Time 6m 45.00s. SP 5-2.
Dennis Waggott (Dumfriesshire).

613 - Maiden Div I

405 **IN DEMAND 7a** .... **P Craggs** **1**
5th hlfwy, ld 4 out, sn clr, comf
407 **Roly Prior** .... **Miss P Robson** **2**
(fav) mid-div, prog 4 out, went 2nd apr last, no imp on wnr
398 **All Or Nothing 5a** .... **J Ewart** **3**
ld until 15th, kpt on one pace
488 Called To Account 5a *2nd hlfwy, ld brfly 15th, no ext frm nxt* 4
407 Lounging 5a *alwys same pl* 5
193 My Meadowsweet *4th hlfwy, no ex. frm 15th* 6
323 Monynut 5a *alwys mdfld* 7
Red Hot Boogie (Ire) *prom til wknd frm hlfwy* 8
406 Sky Missile 5a *nvr dang* 9
398 Trumpet Hill *alwys bhnd* 10
321 Woolaw Lass (USA) 5a *bhnd whn p.u. 4th* .... pu
402 Beccy Brown 5a *sn bhnd, p.u. 4 out* .... pu
322 Sweet Sergeant *sn bhnd, p.u. 4 out* .... pu
Moore View 5a *t.o. hlfwy, p.u. 4 out* .... pu
Senora D'Or 5a *3rd hlfwy, sn wknd, p.u. 4 out* .... pu
15 ran. 4l, 4l, 5l, 3l, 10l, 3l, ½l, 2l, 5l. Time 6m 44.00s. SP 3-1.
A J Balmer (Tynedale).

614 - Maiden Div II

321 **STANESHIEL** .... **Miss D Calder** **1**
3rd hlfwy, ld 4 out, styd on wll
503 **Ballyargan (Ire)** .... **R Westwood** **2**
2nd hlfwy, cl up, kpt on wll.
405 **Mapalak 5a** .... **Miss P Robson** **3**
5th hlfwy, hdwy 4 out, no ext apr last
407 Megans Mystery (Ire) *(fav) 7th hlfwy, hdwy to have ch 3 out, no ext frm 2 out* 4
405 Mr Sharp *alwys wll bhnd, t.o.* 5
403 Prince Rossini (Ire) *alwys wll bhnd, t.o.* 6
405 Cool View 5a *6th hlfwy, strgglng whn ref 13th* .... ref
503 Saigon Lady (Ire) 5a *4th hlfwy, blnd 12th, p.u. nxt* 0
502 Davy's Lad 7a *ld until wknd quckly 4 out, p.u. aftr 2 out* .... pu
Craig Burn 5a *u.r. 7th* .... ur
10 ran. 4l, 6l, 2l, dist, 1l. Time 6m 58.00s. SP 8-1.
Miss D M M Calder (Berwickshire).

615 - Members

BEAU-SUN .... **Mrs P Marjoribanks** **1**
made virt all, jnd apr last, found ext flat
Battle Hero .... **Miss M Bremner** **2**
bhnd til stdy prog frm hlfwy, jnd wnr apr last, no ext
Majestic Ring (Can) .... **Miss M Bowie** **3**
(fav) 2nd hlfwy, cl up until wknd 4 out.
Seymour Fiddles 7a *4th hlfwy, went 2nd 13th, wknd quckly 4 out* 4
French Pink *wll bhnd by 7th* 5
Tim Bobbin 14ex *3rd hlfwy, wknd frm 11th* 6
Roscoe 10ow 14ex *alwys bhnd* 7
502 Two Gun Tex 2ow *wll bhnd by 7th* 8
Sox 2ow 14ex *disp until 6th, t.o. whn p.u. 4 out* .... pu
9 ran. 1½l, dist, 15l, 20l. Time 7m 9.00s. SP 6-1.
Mrs P M Marjoribanks (Duke Of Buccleuch's).
R.J.

EASTON HARRIERS
Higham
Saturday March 23rd
GOOD TO FIRM

616 - Members

GILSON'S COVE .... **Miss L Rowe** **1**
(fav) ld 3rd-10th, chal 3 out, ld last, ran on well
419 **Colonel Kenson** .... **R Barr** **2**
ld & mstk 1st, mstk 5th, disp 9th til hdd last, ran on
315 **Arkay** .... **R Kerry** **3**
prom til last frm 4th, blnd & wknd 10th, t.o.
3 ran. Hd, dist. Time 6m 30.00s. SP 1-3.
A Merriam (Easton Harriers).

617 - Open Maiden Div I (12st)

340 **MISS CRESTA 5a** .... **S Morris** **1**
alwys prom, mstk 6th, ld nxt, clr 9th, lft clr 3 out
254 **Red Rory** .... **T McCarthy** **2**
(fav) pllng in rear,last at 4th,prog 11th,rdn 13th,lft 2nd last
440 **Cruise Free** .... **B Pollock** **3**
mid-div, wknd 11th, lft poor 3rd last
343 Alapa *w.w. 5th at 13th, gd prog 4 out, chal & going wll,r.o.nxt* .... ro
423 Tharif *rear, prog 3 out, 2nd & btn whn ran out last* .... ro
424 Amaam Amaam *ld to 1st, prom, p.u. 12th, dsmntd* .... pu
343 Just Maisy 5a *sttld rear,prog 11th,styd on one-pcd,u.r.4 out,saddle slppd* .... ur
My Last Penny (Ire) 5a *alwys rear, rdn aft 3rd, lost tch 7th, t.o. & p.u. 11th* .... pu
Zap (Ire) 5a *prom, wknd rpdly 7th, t.o. & u.r. 10th* .... ur
314 Go Magic *mid-div, wknd 7th, bhnd & p.u. 10th* .... pu
423 Sustaining *in rear whn mstk 2nd, prog 6th, ch 11th, wknd nxt, p.u. 3out* .... pu
11 ran. 20l, 12l. Time 6m 24.00s. SP 4-1.
R Wale (Pytchley).

618 - Open Maiden Div II (12st)

TOMORROW'S TIMES .... **B Pollock** **1**
hld up, prog to 3rd at 10th, chal 4 out til lft clr last
57 **Swinging Song** .... **Miss K Gilman** **2**
alwys prom, lost plc 11th, styd on frm 3 out, lft 2nd last
344 **Little Freddie** .... **Miss L Hollis** **3**
mid-div, lost tch 11th, slight prog 13th, sn btn, t.o.
423 Worthy Memories 5a *ld 4th, still prom but und pres whn mstk & u.r. 13th* .... ur
314 Countessa 5a *in rear, mstk 1st, dtchd 4th, t.o. & p.u. 12th* .... pu
348 Nursery Story *alwys wll plcd, disp 7th til tired & f last* .... f
424 Andalucian Sun (Ire) *wth ldrs whn u.r. 5th* .... ur
489 Ballyshell Star *(Jt fav) prom early, mid-div whn mstk & u.r. 8th* .... ur
Royal Bav (Ire) *alwys bhnd, lost tch 5th, t.o. til p.u. 2 out* .... pu
Flight Of Love 5a 12ow *plld to ld 2nd, p.u. aft 3rd* .... pu
423 Ernie Fox *rear of main grp whn ref 8th* .... ref
542 Gayton Wilds *(Jt fav) 5s-3s, mid-div whn f 2nd* .... f
343 View Point (Ire) *rear whn u.r. 2nd* .... ur
105 Spartan's Conquest *alwys bhnd, lost tch 4th, t.o. & p.u. 12th* .... pu
14 ran. 15l, dist. Time 6m 35.00s. SP 8-1.
Miss F Robinson (Pytchley).

619 - Open

484 **LABURNUM....................P Harding-Jones** 1
sttld mid-div, mstk 8th, prog to disp 4 out, ld 2 out,hld on
420 **Exclusive Edition (Ire) 5a..................A Coe** 2
hld up rear,prog to cls on ldrs 11th,chal 3 out,one-pcd flat
420 **Armagret ....S Cowell** 3
(fav) chsd ldrs, prog to 3rd at 9th, ev ch 2 out, no ext last
451 Sakil (Ire) *pllng, prog to mid-div 12th, ev ch 3 out, wknd rpdly*.......... 4
420 Cockstown Lad *rear of main grp, mstks 2nd & 8th, rdn 12th, styd on 3 out*.......... 5
418 El Bae *wth ldrs early, rmndrs 10th, grad lost tch 13th* 6
418 Mend *ld to 3rd, mstk & rdn 10th, btn aft 13th*.......... 7
258 Danribo *prom early, lost plc aft 4th, blnd 10th, t.o. & p.u. 3 out*.......... pu
490 Parkbhride *mid-div,prog to 2nd 9th, und pres 12th, wknd 14th, p.u.2 out*.......... pu
Fast Recovery *ld 3rd-4 out, wknd rpdly, cllpsd flat, dead*.......... pu
10 ran. 4l, 4l, 3l, 8l, 4l, ½l. Time 6m 29.00s. SP 33-1.
R Barr (Easton Harriers).

620 - Ladies

484 **WISTINO............................Miss L Rowe** 1
alwys prom, clr 2nd at 14th, ld 3 out, clr last, easily
421 **Kelly's Original..................Miss K Tolhurst** 2
mid-div, prog 12th, 3rd 15th, mstk 4 out, ran on to 2nd flat
572 **What A Gig ....Miss P Ellison** 3
hld up bhnd, gd prog to 3rd 12th, ev ch 3 out, no ext
421 Counterbid (bl) *(fav) ld at fast pace, hdd 3 out, wknd rpdly*.......... 4
Cherry Chap *sttld off pace, prog to 5th at 12th, ev ch 14th, no ext nxt*.......... 5
106 Cowage Brook *lost tch ldrs 7th, t.o. 11th, p.u. 14th*.... pu
347 Just Precious 5a *pllng, jnd ldrs 3rd, prom to 11th, wknd, p.u. 14th*.......... pu
102 Santano *prom, wknd rpdly 7th, t.o. & p.u. 11th*...... pu
Lord Richard *alwys bhnd, t.o. 8th, p.u. 14th*.......... pu
9 ran. 10l, 3l, 7l, 6l. Time 6m 16.00s. SP 6-1.
A W K Merriam (Easton Harriers).

621 - Intermediate (12st)

528 **LANTERN PIKE ....A Michael** 1
bhnd, prog to ld 4th, clr 9th, chal 3 out, sn qcknd away
419 **General Picton................P Harding-Jones** 2
mid-div, prog to 2nd at 14th, chal 3 out, sn outpcd
346 **Timber's Boy 5ex..........................R Gill** 3
(fav) hld up rear, blnd 5th, prog to 4th at 15th, no ext 2 out
Cleddau King 7ow *ld to 5th, lost tch 12th, sn t.o.* 4
395 Zeniska (USA) *alwys rear, lost tch 8th, t.o. & p.u. last* pu
419 Corn Kingdom *alwys rear, mstk 4th, t.o. & p.u. 2 out*.. pu
484 Couture Quality (bl) *chsd ldrs to 11th, wknd nxt, t.o. & p.u. last*.......... pu
58 Half A Sov *alwys bhnd, slight prog 15th, sn btn, p.u. last*.......... pu
313 Whats Another 5a *mid-div, rdn to cls 11th, wknd 14th, t.o. & p.u. 2 out*.......... pu
348 Salmon Mead (Ire) *disp to 4th, und pres 10th, wknd 12th, t.o. & p.u. 2 out*.......... pu
618 Ballysheil Star *2nd outing, prom, wknd 10th, t.o. & p.u. 2 out*.......... pu
231 Unlucky For Some (Ire) *alwys prom, cls up whn f 10th* f
12 ran. 6l, 5l, 30l. Time 6m 17.00s. SP 4-1.
A H L Michael (Quantock Staghounds).

622 - Confined (12st)

374 **ON THE BEER (IRE)...................S Sporborg** 1
(fav) j.w. alwys prom, ld 15th, qcknd clr last, comf
420 **Old Dundalk 3ex ....N King** 2
sttld rear of grp, prog 14th, chal 3 out, mstk last, no ext
177 **Salmon River (USA) 7a.................R Wakley** 3
alwys rear, nvr rchd ldrs, lft poor 3rd 3 out
359 Easy Over (USA) *alwys rear, blnd 8th, no ch wth ldrs 4 out*.......... 4
418 Major Inquiry (USA) *alwys rear, wknd 11th, t.o. 13th* .. 5
418 Cardinal Red *unruly start, mstks, rdn to ld 11th, hdd 15th, sn btn*.......... 6
Owd Henry *alwys prom, disp 4th, mstk & f 7th* ...... f
420 Mount Patrick *mid-div whn mstk & u.r. 7th* .... ur
77 Current Attraction 5a *chsd ldrs,prog to ld 9th,mstk nxt,hdd 11th,3rd whn f 3 out*.......... f
618 Flight Of Love 5a 7ow *2nd outing, wth ldrs til wknd 8th, t.o. 11th, p.u. aft nxt*.......... pu
10 ran. 4l, 25l, 2l, 10l, 30l. Time 6m 22.00s. SP 7-4.
H D Hill (Puckeridge).
J.W.

LAMERTON
Kilworthy
Saturday March 23rd
GOOD TO SOFT

623 - Members

196 **WALKERS POINT.......................A Farrant** 1
(fav) made all, slw jmps 3 & 11th (ditch), shkn up & drw clr 2 out
447 **Anvil Corner 5a.........................D Dennis** 2
alwys 2nd, cls enough 15th, rdn & btn aft nxt
560 Cardinal Bird (USA) (bl) *1st ride, s.s. last til ref 5th*.... ref
448 The Ugly Duckling *raced 3rd, losing tch whn blnd 12th, p.u. aft nxt*.......... pu
4 ran. 15l. Time 6m 52.50s. SP 1-4.
T D H Hughes (Lamerton).

624 - Ladies

443 **KHATTAF ....Miss J Cumings** 1
race wd, j.w. prom, ld 15th, clr nxt, ran on well
381 **Phar Too Touchy 5a ....Miss R Francis** 2
(fav) ld to 4th & 9-11th,blnd nxt,rallied to chs wnr 3 out,no imp
135 **Some-Toy.......................Miss L Blackford** 3
prom, ld 11-15th, 3rd & wkng whn blnd 2 out
298 Moorland Abbot *last to 10th, t.o. frm 12th, plodded on*.......... 4
443 Aristocratic Gold *chsd ldng quartet, strgglng 11th, no dang aft, fin tired*.......... 5
295 Jokers Patch *mstk 9th, alwys last pair, t.o. 12th*...... 6
295 Treleven 5a *ld 4-9th, 4th & btn frm 11th til p.u. last, dsmntd*.......... pu
7 ran. 8l, 15l, 25l, 4l, 30l. Time 6m 30.00s. SP 3-1.
Mrs H C Johnson (Devon & Somerset Staghounds).

625 - Confined (12st)

482 **STORMY SUNSET 5a ....D Dennis** 1
prom, ld 8th, made rest, clr last, drvn out flat
294 **Just Bert (Ire)......................P Scholfield** 2
(fav) not fluent,lost plc 7th,prog to 2nd 14th,ev ch 2 out,nt qckn
199 **Ewhonosebest ....Miss S Young** 3
prom til outpcd 14th, ran on frm 2 out, fin well
444 Prince Soloman *wll in tch til outpcd 14th, styd on one-pcd frm 3 out*.......... 4
294 Sancreed *prom til outpcd 13th, sn rear, styd on frm 3 out*.......... 5
560 Gymcrak Dawn 3ex (bl) *trckd ldrs going wll, effrt 14th, sn outpcd, no imp aft*.......... 6
442 Catch The Cross *ld to 8th, chsd wnr to 14th, fdd frm nxt*.......... 7
198 Chandigarh *alwys bhnd, t.o. 13th*.......... 8
560 Noddy's Story 5a *alwys bhnd, t.o. 13th*.......... 9
278 Phils Pride *nrly u.r. 3rd & ran off course, p.u. nxt*.. pu
Whats Your Game (bl) *rear, wknd rpdly 11th, t.o. & p.u. 14th*.......... pu
11 ran. 2l, nk, 10l, 8l, ½l, 6l, dist, 15l. Time 6m 37.00s. SP 7-2.
Mrs Jill Dennis (Tetcott).

626 - Open

276 **NEARLY SPLENDID .... L Jefford** 1
prom, ld 11th, hrd rdn flat, hld on gamely nr fin
482 **The General's Drum .... K Heard** 2
wll in rear to gd prog to chs wnr 15th,chal flat,just hld
482 **Bootscraper....................... W G Turner** 3
prom, chsd wnr 12th-15th, onepcd und pres 2 out
559 Afterkelly *ld to 7th, rdn frm 10th, sn outpcd, no ch aft* 4
296 Glenform *rear, poor 9th whn nrly u.r. 11th, t.o. aft, fin well*........ 5
Parson's Way *rear, 8th & rdn aft 10th, sn t.o., rdn rght out*........ 6
468 Bargain And Sale *prom, ld 7-11th, wknd 14th, t.o.*..... 7
559 Chilipour *(fav) w.w. trckd ldrs 12th, 4th & btn whn blnd 3 out, p.u. last* pu
559 Far Too Loud *ref & u.r. 1st* .... ref
Whats The Crack (bl) *rel to race, t.o. whn ref 1st* ..... ref
561 Little Coombe 5a *alwys bhnd, t.o. 12th, p.u. last*...... pu
Indian Rabi *in tch, ran wd apr 7th, wkng whn mstk 12th,t.o. & p.u.15th* .... pu
12 ran. Nk, 15l, 25l, 12l, 8l, 6l. Time 6m 30.00s. SP 8-1.
S R Stevens (East Devon).

627 - Restricted (12st)

199 **TASMIN TYRANT (NZ) .... L Jefford** 1
alwys prom, chal whn lft in ld 2 out, styd on well, rdn out
447 **Well Timed .... M Frith** 2
mstk 3rd,cls up,outpcd 15th,styd on to chs wnr last,ran on
299 **Erme Rose (Ire) 5a................... A Farrant** 3
(fav) blnd 3rd & lost plc,prog und pres 13th,kpt on 3 out,nrst fin
528 Green Hill *in tch,prog 11th,ld 13th,sn clr,blnd & hdd 2 out,wknd* 4
298 Lonesome Traveller (NZ) *mid-div, mstk 5th & rmndr, effrt 13th, nvr rchd ldrs* 5
300 Rosa's Revenge 5a *prom to 12th, sn lost plc, kpt on onepcd frm 2 out* 6
280 Strong Breeze *ld to 13th, outpcd frm nxt, sn no ch* 7
301 Baldhu Chance *prom to 10th, wknd rpdly & p.u. 13th* pu
445 Neil's Way *trckd ldrs, mstk 11th, sn wknd, no ch whn p.u. 15th* .... pu
466 Waipiro *nvr nrr ldrs, lost tch 12th, p.u. 15th* .... pu
532 Springcombe 5a *alwys bhnd, t.o. & p.u. 15th* .... pu
562 Lady Lir 5a *alwys rear, t.o. & p.u. 14th* .... pu
Tangle Kelly *w.w. in rear til lost tch 12th, t.o. & p.u. 15th* .... pu
13 ran. 6l, 6l, 10l, 6l, 1l, 10l. Time 6m 32.00s. SP 6-1.
Mrs C Egalton (Axe Vale Harriers).

628 - Intermediate

297 **KALOORE .... P Scholfield** 1
(fav) w.w. prog to ld 12th, clr 15th, shkn up flat, unchal
441 **Karicleigh Boy .... S Slade** 2
hld up,hmpd 4th,prog 11th,chsd wnr aft 15th,no real imp
531 **Monkton (Ire) (bl)........................ R White** 3
ran in sntchs,mstk 4th,outpcd aft 14th,kpt on 2 out,no dang
531 Just Ben *prom, mstk 8th, ld 11-12th, wknd rpdly apr 3 out*........ 4
Straight Brandy *wth ldr to 8th, wknd rpdly 11th, p.u. nxt*........ pu
298 Miss Moony 5a *f 4th*........ f
524 Beinn Mohr 5a *made most til blnd & hdd 11th, not rcvr, p.u. 13th* .... pu
7 ran. 10l, 2l, 20l. Time 6m 39.00s. SP 4-6.
Mrs J Alford (Eggesford).

629 - Maiden Div I (12st)

556 **OUR TEDDIS......................... G Penfold** 1
(fav) ld 3rd, drew wll clr 15th, unchal, eased flat
70 **Mr Wideawake .... W G Turner** 2
ld to 3rd, chsd wnr frm 12th, rdn & btn 15th
200 **Cool Work .... T Dennis** 3
sttld rear, prog 10th, sn outpcd, ran on 15th, no imp aft
470 Reptile Princess 5a *last whn jmpd slwly 3rd, sn t.o., nvr nrr* 4
299 Coed Canlas *in tch to 10th, t.o. frm 14th*........ 5
557 Romany Anne 5a *chsd ldrs to 10th, sn wknd, t.o.*..... 6
Plenary *alwys bhnd, t.o. 9th* 7
446 Quick Opinion *c.o. by loose horse 2nd*........ co
Collard Tor *in tch to 10th, sn wknd, p.u. 13th* .... pu
301 Diana Moss (Ire) 5a *prom, chsd wnr 10-12th, wknd, poor 4th whn u.r. 3 out* .... ur
Flying Maria 7a *10s-3s, ran out 1st* .... ro
11 ran. 12l, 1l, 30l, 30l, 6l, 10l, 1 fence. Time 6m 54.50s. SP 5-2.
E Sussex (Stevenstone).

630 - Maiden Div II (12st)

131 **CAPSTOWN BAY 7a................ P Scholfield** 1
(fav) 2s-1/1, lost plc 7th, prog to ld 14th, mstk 3 out, drvn out
202 **Moorland Highflyer 7a........... Miss D Mitchell** 2
prssd ldr, lft in ld 12th, hdd 14th, ev ch 2 out, not qckn
300 **Karlimay 5a .... K Heard** 3
hld up wll bhnd,rpd prog 15th,clsd & blnd last,too mch to do
299 Sixth In Line (Ire) *prom, mstk 8th, 3rd & outpcd 15th, no imp ldrs aft* 4
448 Artistic Peace 5a *t.d.e. mid-div, outpcd aft 14th, no prog frm 3 out*........ 5
297 Hanukkah 5a *mid-div, outpcd aft 14th, no dang aft*.... 6
Bally Sky *prom, mstk 8th, lost tch 15th, fin tired* 7
448 Steamburd 5a *ld, narrow ld whn u.r. 12th* .... ur
301 My Prides Way 5a *alwys last pair, wkng whn f 11th*... f
300 Tinstreamer Johnny 7a *mid-div, wknd 9th, last whn f 11th*........ f
10 ran. 6l, 6l, 10l, 6l, 3l, 25l. Time 6m 50.50s. SP Evens.
Mrs J Alford (Mid Devon).
J.N.

SOUTH WOLD
Market Rasen Point-To-Point
Saturday March 23rd
GOOD TO FIRM

631 - Members (12st)

536 **HAWAIIAN GODDESS (USA) 5a ..... Miss H Fines** 1
cls up on outer, effrt 2 out, ld last, ran on
484 **Tresillian Bay 4ex (v) .... N Kent** 2
(fav) tried to make all, hdd apr last, no ext
541 **Springfield Pet 5a.................... K Needham** 3
cls up, outpcd 2 out
3 ran. 3l, 12l. Time 6m 48.00s. SP 7-1.
Mrs C W Pinney (South Wold).

632 - Confined (12st)

410 **CARLY BRRIN.............................. N Kent** 1
ld, 12l clr 11th, ct 4 out, hdd flat, came again
513 **Ways And Means 5a .... K Green** 2
alwys prom, 2nd frm 11th, chal 4 out, ld flat, just outpcd
411 **Greenmount Lad (Ire) .... P Cornforth** 3
rear, prog 10th, 3rd 5 out, outpcd nxt
327 Drawn'N'quartered *(fav) s.s. 7th 6 out, ran on past btn horses* 4
434 Rare Knight *mid-div, 8th & outpcd 6 out* 5
326 Happy Breed *cls up 2nd to 9th, 3rd & fdng whn f 12th (ditch)*........ f
Write The Music (bl) *rider hit by clod in eye & p.u. 4th* .... pu
327 Rexy Boy *mid-div, 6th whn b.d. 12th*........ bd
Father Liam *4th for 2m, cls enough whn ran out 5 out* ro
Nearly There (Ire) 5a *t.o. last til p.u. 8th*........ pu
10 ran. 1l, 15l, 4l, 1 fence. Time 6m 27.00s. SP 7-2.
J R Buckley (Brocklesby).

633 - Ladies

394 **CRUISING ON 5a** .... **Miss E Guest** **1**
(Jt fav) j.w. ld frm 3rd, ran on well last m, well rdn
326 **Okeetee** .... **Mrs J Dawson** **2**
alwys prom, prssd wnr 5 out, outpcd bef last
325 **Duntime** .... **Mrs M Morris** **3**
(Jt fav) trckd ldrs, mstk 6 out, 3rd nxt, ran on one-pcd
536 Nowhiski *ld to 3rd, cls up til outpcd frm 10th* 4
397 Loose Wheels *nvr dang, 7th & outpcd frm 7th, ran on onepcd* 5
333 Rallye Stripe 3ow *nvr dang, last pair frm 6th, outpcd nxt* 6
436 Winged Whisper (USA) *s.s. alwys last trio, outpcd frm 10th* 7
511 Crocket Lass 5a 5ow *rear, last & outpcd frm 7th* 8
Monk's Mistake *6th & in tch for 2m, fdd 6 out, p.u. 3 out* .... pu
Adamare *ldng quartet, 2nd 10th-6 out, fdd nxt, p.u. 2 out* .... pu
10 ran. 6l, 3l, 1 fence, 10l, 5l, 10l, 5l. Time 6m 29.00s. SP 5-2.
Mrs J E Goodall (Meynell & South Staffs).

634 - Land Rover Open (12st)

169 **GOLDEN MOSS** .... **Capt S Robinson** **1**
ld to 5 out & frm 3 out, ran on gamely
632 **Write The Music 4ex (bl)** .... **T Lane** **2**
2nd outing, rear in tch, 4th 2 out, ran on well, just hld
326 **Elder Prince** .... **P Gee** **3**
(fav) w.w. cls up, chal 4 out, 2nd nxt, no ext frm 2 out
326 Bennan March 7ex *cls up, mostly 3rd to 2 out, wknd rpdly* 4
512 McCartney *cls up, 2nd frm 11th, chal 4 out, f nxt* .... f
537 Blue Aeroplane *2nd to 6th, last frm 8th, t.o. 11th, p.u. 4 out* .... pu
6 ran. 2l, 3l, 15l. Time 6m 36.00s. SP 7-2.
C Cottingham (Brocklesby).

635 - Restricted (12st)

396 **Cass** .... **P Picton-Warlow** **1D**
12s-6s, w.w. prog 6 out, ran on well to ld last
396 **BARE FISTED** .... **Miss H Phizacklea** **1**
2nd til lft in ld 12th, ct last, no ext
396 **Kamadora** .... **S J Robinson** **2**
prog 10th, 2nd 6 out, wknd nxt
424 **Another Comedy** *nvr dang, last pair frm 3rd, outpcd frm 11th* 3
331 Beckford *w.w. prog 6 out, 2nd nxt, ev ch whn squeezed aft 2 out,s.u.* .... su
239 Give It A Whirl *(Jt fav) ld, 50l clr frm 6th, still wll clr whn f 12th (ditch)* .... f
172 Dry Hill Lad 7a *(Jt fav) overjmpd & f 1st* .... f
Step-Aside *alwys last pair, outpcd 11th, p.u. 4 out* .... pu
8 ran. 2l, 25l, 8l. Time 6m 45.00s. SP 6-1.
Cass was disq, traces of banned substance.

636 - Maiden

535 **RUFF SONG** .... **N Jelley** **1**
(fav) ld 2nd-6 out, ran on agn frm 4th 4 out, chal last, ran on
397 **Final Nod** .... **J Apiafi** **2**
alwys prom, lft in ld 3 out, jnd last, just outpcd
539 **Reel Rascal 5a** .... **T Lane** **3**
mid-div, prog 10th, 2nd 3 out, fdd frm nxt
Gay Boots 5a *t.o. in 8th at 6th, f 8th, rmntd* 4
517 Sweet Wyn 5a *prom til wknd 10th, t.o. 6 out, p.u. nxt* .... pu
330 Charlotte's Oliver *mostly 6th til f 12th (ditch)* .... f
Nash Brakes *t.o. 1st, p.u. 6 out* .... pu
Shireoak's Flyer *broke leather 1st, p.u. 4th* .... pu
241 Huntsbydale 5a *cls up, ld 6 out, in cmmnd whn blnd & u.r. 3 out* .... ur
540 Split The Wind 5a *t.o. in 9th at 6th, hmpd & u.r. 8th* .... ur
78 Primitive Star 7a *rear, t.o. 10th, p.u. 12th* .... pu
11 ran. 1l, 15l, dist. Time 6m 42.00s. SP 5-4.
N Jelley (Fernie).
K.B.

VALE OF THE WHITE HORSE
Siddington
Saturday March 23rd
SOFT

637 - Members

505 **TEKLA (FR)** .... **Miss D Olding** **1**
ld/disp thro'out,rddn 2 out, lft in ld last, kpt on flat
477 **Saxon Lass 5a** .... **A Martin** **2**
jmpd lft, ld/disp thro'out, slt ld & blnd last, no ex flat
475 **Space Man** .... **F Crew** **3**
in tch, chall & rddn 3 out, not much room flat,one-pcd
260 Wayside Boy *trkd ldrs, 4th & rddn 3 out, onepcd* 4
477 Just Ballytoo *disp ld to 6th, prom til wknd appr 15th* 5
373 Golden Mac *(fav) mid div, 8th & rddn 13th, no dang aft* 6
524 Master Swillbrook *prom til appr 10th, no ch frm 14th* 7
230 Creeves Nephew *rr, sme prog 10th, nvr trbld ldrs* 8
28 St Julien (Ire) *prog 10th, chsd ldrs & ch appr 15th, wknd qkly 3 out* 9
Sentimentality (Ire) *sn bhnd, t.o. frm 12th* 10
479 Image Boy (Ire) *rr, lst tch 8th, t.o. & p.u. 13th* .... pu
Ben *mstk 2nd, u.r. 3rd* .... ur
Nesselnite 5a *s.s. hit 1st, u.r. 3rd* .... ur
Tu Piece *j.s. 1st, in tch to 13th, p.u. appr 15th* .... pu
14 ran. 1l, sht-hd, 4l, 10l, sht-hd, sht-hd, 3l, 6l, 20l. Time 6m 21.00s. SP 8-1.
E H Lodge (Vale Of The White Horse).

638 - Confined (12st)

262 **GRANVILLE GRILL 9ex** .... **J Deutsch** **1**
(fav) ld, clr 3rd, hdded 3 out, ld appr last, in comm whn lft clr
263 **Tattlejack (Ire) (v)** .... **E Walker** **2**
chsd lding pr & rddn 13th, kpt on frm 2 out, lft 2nd last
337 **Dukes Son** .... **D Smith** **3**
hld up, bhnd, ran on wll frm 15th, nvr nrr
434 Saybright *chsd lding pr to 12th, 4th & onepcd aft, lft 3rd last* 4
426 Ragtime Cowboy Joe *mid div, rddn appr 10th, kpt on frm 14th, nvr trbld ldrs* 5
380 The Holy Golfer *nvr bttr than mid div, nvr dang* 6
434 Kelly's Eye (bl) *chsd ldrs til appr 10th, no ch frm 14th* 7
380 Major Wayne *rr & blnd 7th, t.o. frm 12th* 8
266 Ocean Lad *mstk 2nd, bhnd til p.u. 12th* .... pu
368 Highgate Mild *chsd ldr, rddn to ld 3 out- nxt,2l dwn & hld whn f last,dead* .... f
369 Kites Hardwicke 5ex *last whn u.r. 7th* .... ur
262 What About That (Ire) *mid div, rddn 10th, no ch whn blnd & u.r. 14th* .... ur
335 Hill Island *in tch til u.r. 6th* .... ur
Salmon Poutcher 5a *schoold, in tch til appr 10th, p.u. 15th* .... pu
351 Jack Sun *nt fluent, rr, whn f 8th* .... f
268 Motor Trader *mstk 5th, bhnd til p.u. 12th* .... pu
16 ran. 8l, 6l, hd, nk, 10l, 2l, dist. Time 6m 15.00s. SP 4-5.
E W Smith (Beaufort).

639 - Open (12st)

365 **MY BEST MAN** .... **A Hill** **1**
jnd ldr 7th, kicked clr 11th, 15l ld 14th, blnd last, kpt on
434 **Causeway Cruiser** .... **R Lawther** **2**
(fav) w.w. prog 10th, mod 3rd & rddn 3 out, ran on, nt rch wnnr
475 **Strong Beau** .... **L Lay** **3**
in tch, rmdrs 9th, chsd ldr appr 15th,styd on, nt rch wnnr
537 Bright As A Button *chsd ldrs, outpcd 11th, 4th & one-pcd appr 15th* 4
22 Sevens Out *rr div, 8th & rddn appr 10th, kpt on frm 15th, nvr dang* 5

Gallic Belle 5a *in tch til appr 10th, no dang aft* 6
265 Flying Ziad (Can) *wll bhnd frm 9th* 7
Royle Speedmaster *f 2nd* .... f
475 What A To Do *p.u appr 3rd* .... pu
Sunshine Manor *ld to 3rd,2nd whn hit 10 & 12th,wknd 14th,5th whn p.u.2 out* .... pu
230 Tumbril *ld 4th, blnd 6th, hdded 10th, wknd 13th, p.u. appr 3 out* .... pu
Mountfosse *j.s. 1st, sn wll bhnd, hit 5th, t.o. & p.u. 11th* .... pu

12 ran. 3l, 3l, 4l, 2l, 15l, 30l. Time 6m 8.00s. SP 8-1.
Alan Hill (Vale Of Aylesbury).
One fence omitted. 16 Jumps

640 - Ladies

336 **SPERRIN VIEW 5a ....Mrs K Sunderland** 1
trkd ldrs going wll 11th, ld 3 out, sn clr, easy
266 **Little Island 5a ....Miss V Hardman** 2
prom, lft in ld 9th, hdded 3 out, no ex
Solar Rocket 5a ....Miss H Irving 3
plIng, cls up, ev ch 3 out, onepcd
236 Miners Rest 5a *rr, prog & in tch 13th, wknd appr 15th* 4
443 Little Thyne *jmpd slwly, wll bhnd frm 13th, t.o.* 5
266 Woodway *ld 2nd til 5th, last frm 10th, t.o.* 6
436 Green Archer *(fav) 4th & pshd alng 11th, ch appr 15th, no prog,wll btn & f last* .... f
239 Keep On Trying 5a *w.w. lst tch & p.u. 10th* .... pu
Cardschool 5a *ld & hit 6th, blnd bdly 8th, pulld out nxt* .... pu

9 ran. 15l, 2l, 20l, 30l, 5l. Time 6m 15.00s. SP 9-4.
Mrs Katie Sunderland (Bicester With Whaddon Chase).

641 - Restricted Div I (12st)

438 **COPPER BANK ....F Hutsby** 1
in tch,disp ld appr 15th,ld 3 out,clr nxt,rddn out,impress
437 **Tarry Awhile...............................G Tarry** 2
chsd ldrs, 3rd & rddn 3 out, kpt on onepcd
This I'll Do Us (Ire) ....A Morley 3
bhnd, ran on wll frm 15th, nvr pld to chall, improve
264 Printemps (USA) *mid div, stdy prog 14th, 3rd & hit 2 out, nt rch ldrs* 4
263 Sylvan Sirocco *mid div, in tch, kpt on onepcd frm 15th* 5
267 Count Balios (Ire) *(Jt fav) jnd ldrs 11th, disp ld appr 15th, wknd qkly appr 3 out* 6
375 Good Looking Guy *alwys mid div, kpt on frm 15th, nvr dang* 7
339 Kingofnobles (Ire) *(Jt fav) disp ld to 4th, rmdrs & lst pl appr 10th, no dang aft* 8
428 Plax *ld 7th-13th, wknd appr 15th* 9
Goldtopper 5a *ld/disp to 6th, prom til grad wknd frm 14th* 10
338 Endless Glee *mid div til rddn 10th, sn bhnd* 11
236 Di Moda *alwys wll bhnd, t.o. frm 10th* 12
Home To Tara *bhnd frm 11th, p.u appr 15th* .... pu
Golden Sound *prom til wknd 11th, p.u. 14th* .... pu
437 Singing Clown 5a *chsd ldrs, strugg 13th, no ch whn p.u. 2 out* .... pu
357 Frozen Pipe 5a *w.w. mstks 3rd & 7th, prog 11th, 7th & in tch whn f 14th* .... f
339 Archies Oats *prom til rddn 14th, wknd appr nxt, p.u. last* .... pu
Totally Optimistic *bhnd whn blnd 8th, p.u. appr 10th* .. pu
Barney Boy *n.j.w. sn bhnd, p.u. appr 5th* .... pu
Mr Drake (Ire) *schoold in rr til p.u. appr 15th* .... pu

20 ran. 3l, 3l, 2l, 12l, 2l, 1½l, ½l, 10l, 5l, sht-hd. Time 6m 20.00s. SP 12-1.
Mrs H Hutsby (Warwickshire).

642 - Restricted Div II (12st)

440 **SABRE KING ....L Lay** 1
disp ld 7th,ld 10th- 3 out, gd jmp to ld nxt,hld on und pres
341 **What Chance (Ire) 5a ....Mrs K Sunderland** 2
w.w. hit 8th, prog nxt, ld 3 out, outjmpd & hdded nxt,no ex
428 **Cutsdean Cross (Ire) ....J Trice-Rolph** 3
cls up, outpcd appr 15th, 3rd & btn whn blnd 2 out
235 Arble March 5a *disp ld to 9th, 3rd & rddn 11th, wknd appr 15th* 4
437 Glenard (Ire) *rr, prog & in tch 8th, outpcd 13th, no dang aft* 5
478 Ramlosa (NZ) *wll bhnd frm 13th, t.o.* 6
358 R Lad *prom til wknd appr 10th, bhnd & p.u 14th* ...... pu
Happy Paddy (bl) *chsd ldrs to 10th, wkng & blnd 12th, p.u. nxt* .... pu
Spartan's Saint *n.j.w. bhnd frm 6th, p.u.10th* .... pu
Coolmoreen (Ire) *w.w. mstks 7th & 8th, lsing tch whn p.u. 13th* .... pu
Silver Hollow *tubed, wll bhnd frm 5th, t.o. whn ref 10th* .... ref
438 Dunloughan *disp ld 3rd-6th, wknd 14th, p.u. 2 out* .... pu
361 Elite Governor (Ire) *(fav) prog to 2nd 11th, blnd badly 14th, nt rcvr, p.u nxt* .... pu
437 Penly *chsd ldrs til appr 10th, sn wknd, p.u. 13th* ...... pu
Suny Mill *nt fluent, rr til p.u. 14th* .... pu

15 ran. ¾l, 20l, 8l, 1½l, 20l. Time 6m 20.00s. SP 5-1.
J Tredwell (Grafton).

643 - Maiden

505 **MY BOY BARNEY.........................A Wintle** 1
(fav) mid div, chall & rddn 3 out, lft in ld nxt, kpt on und press
375 **Pontabula ....A Charles-Jones** 2
trkd ldrs, ev ch 3 out, lft 2nd nxt, no ex und press flat
340 **Tranquil Lord (Ire).......................D Smith** 3
prom, blnd 6th, wknd 13th, lft poor 3rd 2 out
267 Apple Anthem 5a *prom, jmpd slwly 3rd, wknd frm 13th* 4
Colonel Fairfax *made most to 15th, wknd rpdly nxt* ... 5
Roark's Chukka *in tch til wknd rpdly 10th, p.u. nxt* .... pu
264 Annson 3ow *bhnd til u.r. 4th* .... ur
375 Wired For Sound *chsd ldr 6th, wkng whn blnd 12th, p.u. 14th* .... pu
267 Son Of Anun *blnd 2nd, t.o. & p.u. 14th* .... pu
479 Dip The Lights 5a *rear, rdn 7th, crashed thro' wing 9th* .... ro
375 Gamay *w.w. prog 10th, cls 4th & running on whn blnd & u.r. 2 out* .... ur
268 Sit Tight *disp whn blnd 11th, ld 3 out, blnd & u.r. nxt* .. ur
268 The Blind Judge *mid-div til f 6th* .... f
Harry Tartar 7a *rear & mstk 4th, bhnd whn p.u. 13th* .. pu
375 Jestastar 7a *schoold in rear, blnd 5th, p.u. 11th* ..... pu
Bay Hobnob 7a *schoold in rear til p.u. 13th* .... pu

16 ran. 1l, 20l, 10l, 4l. Time 6m 27.00s. SP 6-4.
Mrs A T Lodge (Vale Of The White Horse).
One fence omitted 2nd circuit, 17 jumps. S.P.

WESTON & BANWELL
Cothelstone
Saturday March 23rd
SOFT

644 - Members

335 **CHITA'S CONE 5a...................R Treloggen** 1
(fav) hndy, ld 6th, clr 12th, easily
Colonel Crumpet 4ow.....................T Lee 2
chsd ldr tll left clr 2nd 5 out
Cootamundra.......................Miss S Rant 3
bhnd frm 4th, blndrd 7th, t.o. next.
465 Bill Of Rights *rluctnt to stt, 3rd 4 out, tired nxt, p.u. 2 out* .... pu
466 Between You And Me *cl 3rd till 7th, t.o. from 13th, p.u. bfr 4 out* .... pu
531 Bay Blossom 5a *ld to 5th, chsd ldr aftr p.u. lame bfr 15th* .... pu

6 ran. Dist, dist. Time 6m 56.00s. SP 2-9.
I M Ham (Weston And Banwell).

645 - Open Maiden Div I (12st)

268 **CHURCHTOWN CHANCE (IRE) 5a ...R Treloggen** 1
(fav) hrd hld, ld or disp till wnt clr appr last, easily
465 **Glamorous Guy...................D Fitch-Peyton** 2

ld or disp tll outpcd appr last
203 Noble Minister *alwys 3rd, lst tch 14th, t.o. whn p.u. 2 out*........ pu
3 ran. 4l. Time 7m 25.00s. SP 4-7.
Miss Kim Tripp (Weston & Banwell Harriers).

646 - Open Maiden Div II (12st)

447 **IVE CALLED TIME** .... **T Greed** 1
(Jt fav) chsd ldrs, wnt 2nd 12th, styd on frm 3 out to ld cls home
533 **Blade Of Fortune** .... **R Treloggen** 2
(Jt fav) plld hrd, ld 7th till wknd 2 out, hdd clse home.
Nothing To Fear .... **G Barfoot-Saunt** 3
last at 6th, styd on for 3rd from 2 out, not trble 1st 2.
533 River Stream 5a *ld to 6th, in tch to 12th, wknd 3 out, fin tired* 4
Noble Comic 7a *schoold in rr till p.u. 4 out* .... pu
5 ran. ½l, dist, 6l. Time 6m 53.00s. SP 5-4.
Mrs M de Burgh (Devon & Somerset Staghounds).

647 - Confined (12st)

531 **THE PEDLAR 5a** .... **T Greed** 1
hld up, prog 12th, ld 15th, ran on wll whn chllg
472 **Balisteros (Fr)** .... **D Alers-Hankey** 2
(fav) waited with, prog 9th, ld 12th-14th, rnwd eff 2 out, no extr
209 **Columbique** .... **D Moffett** 3
alwys rear
531 Be My Habitat 7ex (bl) *cl up till 12th, mstk 13th, lost tch aftr* 4
443 Unityfarm Oltowner *clse up tll blun 7th, t.o. 13th, walked in* 5
208 Bridge Express 3ex *ld to 11th, wknd 15th, t.o. whn p.u. 3 out* .... pu
6 ran. 4l, dist, 25l, 5l. Time 6m 48.00s. SP 6-4.
Mrs Sally Hurst (Devon And Somerset Staghounds).

648 - Open (12st)

203 **SAYYURE (USA)** .... **R Treloggen** 1
walked over
A G Harris (Mendip Farmers).

649 - Ladies

529 **KILLELAN LAD** .... **Miss K Di Marte** 1
(Jt fav) made all, clr 12th, ran on wll whn chall 2 out
472 **Captain Dimitris** .... **Miss M Coombe** 2
(Jt fav) chsd ldr, 5l bhnd 3 out, rdn, no impn from last
Best Left 5a *ref 1st* .... ref
3 ran. 3l. Time 7m 9.00s. SP 6-4.
Miss K Di Marte (Tiverton Staghounds).

650 - Restricted (12st)

280 **HENSUE** .... **R Treloggen** 1
trckd ldr, ld aftr 3 out, rddn clr 2 out
268 **Bewdley Boy** .... **Miss P Gundry** 2
(fav) blnd 6th, ld to 2 out, hdd and one pace aftr.
526 **Astound (Ire) 7a** .... **Lt-Col R Webb-Bowen** 3
sn last, prog 7th, styd on frm 3 out, not trbl 1st 2
465 Brendan's Way (Fr) *sn rr, t.o. whn p.u. 10th* .... pu
562 Venn Boy *4s-2s, mostly 3rd, blnd 5 out, t.o. whn p.u. 2 out* .... pu
5 ran. 5l, 30l. Time 6m 45.00s. SP 12-1.
Miss P J Boundy (Devon & Somerset Staghounds).
D.P.

WILTON
Badbury Rings
Saturday March 23rd
GOOD

651 - Members

SPITFIRE JUBILEE .... **M Felton** 1
(fav) made all, clr 15th, unchall, canter
Elegant Sun .... **Miss S King** 2
prom early, wknd 10th, tk 2nd 15th, hld on
471 **Dormston Lad** .... **C Jowett** 3
rr, bhnd 10th, ran on frm 15th, kpt on flat
469 Brack N Brandy *settld, prog 10th-15th, wknd nxt, p.u. last* .... pu
4 ran. Dist, ½l. Time 6m 17.00s. SP 4-6.
Mrs Z S Clark (Wilton).

652 - Open Maiden Div I (12st)

470 **VITAL LEGACY** .... **Miss A Goschen** 1
alwys prom, left in ld 3 out, held on flat
470 **Say Charlie** .... **T Mitchell** 2
bhnd, prog 13th, strngly rdn run-in, just faild
471 **Tullykyne Bells** .... **Miss D Stafford** 3
frnt rnk untl lost plc 13th, lost plc from 3 out
466 Time Module *mid-div, wknd frm 14th, one pace aftr* 4
205 Woodside Lady (Ire) 5a *alwys prom, ld 10th-14th, wknd next, t.o.* 5
471 Freemount Minstrel (Ire) *mid-div untl wknd, t.o. 15th* 6
471 Stormy Fashion *sn wll bhnd, t.o. whn p.u. 12th* .... pu
Kilmington (Ire) *ld 4th-9th & 14-15th, upsides whn f 3 out* .... f
470 Revels Hill (Ire) *nvr trbld ldrs, wknd 11th, p.u. 14th* .... pu
447 Front Cover 5a *(fav) mid-div, ld 4 out, going well whn f. next* .... f
144 Master Art *ld to 3rd, prom whn f 14th* .... f
284 Grey Jerry 7a *midfld untl wknd 12th, p.u. 14th* .... pu
Tamaimo (Ire) 7a *settld and schooled in rear, p.u. 12th* .... pu
13 ran. 1l, dist, dist, 10l, 10l. Time 6m 27.00s. SP 20-1.
J Bugg (Portman).

653 - Open Maiden Div II (12st)

470 **FINAL EXPRESS 5a** .... **M Hoskins** 1
settld mid-div, left 2nd 12th, ld appr last, ran on.
471 **Coachroadstarboy** .... **M Felton** 2
ld 6th-9th and 12th to appr last, ran on run-in
425 **Fortytwo Dee (Ire) 5a** .... **Mrs K Bevan** 3
ld to 5th, alwys prom until one pace from 15th
470 Gigi Beach (Ire) 7a *(fav) patiently rdn, nvr plcd to chall* 4
Janejolawrieclaire *alwys chsng ldng grp, t.o. from 13th, one pace* 5
Crock D'Or *prom, ld 10th, going well whn ran out 12th* .... ro
Heatherton Park 7a *jmpd poorly, crawld over 6th, u.r.* .... ur
Rosanda 5a *sn bhnd, nvr nvr, p.u. 10th* .... pu
520 Olive Basket 7a *mid-div til lost plc 11th, t.o. & f last* .... f
9 ran. 1½l, 12l, 5l, dist. Time 6m 32.00s. SP 5-1.
J A G Meaden (Blackmore & Sparkford).

654 - Open (12st)

472 **VITAL SONG** .... **G Matthews** 1
(fav) made all, clr frm 14th, not extnd, easily
530 **Butler John (Ire) 7ex** .... **T Mitchell** 2
rr, prog 8th, no ch wth wnnr
475 **Popeswood 4ex** .... **D Dennis** 3
cl up untl outpcd from 13th
480 Spring Fun 7ex *prom till wknd 14th, one pace final m* 4
559 Fred Splendid *cl up untl wknd and t.o. frm 15th* 5
5 ran. 6l, dist, ½l, 4l. Time 6m 15.00s. SP 4-5.
M H Dare (Blackmore & Sparkford Vale).

655 - Ladies

378 **SPACIAL (USA)** .... **Miss M Hill** 1
made all, jmpd well, ran on flat
266 **Flaked Oats** .... **Miss P Curling** 2
(fav) bhnd, prog 13th, 2nd when mstk 3 out, no chnc wth wnnr
561 **False Economy** .... **Miss K Scorgie** 3
prom early, wknd 10th, ran on frm 4 out
469 Daybrook's Gift *rr untl ran on one pace from 16th* 4
561 Friendly Lady 5a *nvr bttr than mid-div* 5

469 Kings Gunner *front rank untl wknd 15th, mstk 16th, t.o.* 6
561 Kings Rank (bl) *front rank, 2nd 10th, hmpd 12th, t.o.* ... 7
481 Winter's Lane *prom and 2nd whn u.r. 6th,* .... ur
8 ran. 4l, 10l, 10l, dist, 20l, 20l. Time 6m 11.00s. SP 7-2.
Richard J Hill (Wilton).

656 - Restricted

466 **THEGOOSE** .... **P King** 1
tucked away, prog to ld 4 out, left clr 2 out, ran on
Ely Island .... **J Thatcher** 2
in rear untl rpd prog 14th, left 2nd 2 out, ran on well
Caundle Steps .... **M Felton** 3
front rank, ld 13th-16th, not qckn 2 out
379 Royal Rupert *alwys prom, not qckn frm 4 out* 4
466 Balmoral Boy (NZ) *wth ldrs untl wknd 13th, ran on from 2 out* 5
526 Pines Express (Ire) *ld 6th-12th, fdd next, one pace from 4 out* 6
465 Lisahane Lad *prom early, wknd frm 10th, t.o.* 7
426 Kilmakee 5a *ld to 5th, prom untl wknd 11th, t.o.* 8
562 Ower Farm 5a *sn in rr, t.o. 11th* 9
445 Palace King (Ire) *sn bhnd, t.o. 11th, p.u. 14th* .... pu
465 Clandon Lad *(fav) settld mid-div, prog 15th, ev ch when f 2 out* .... f
11 ran. 1½l, dist, 5l, 4l, 5l, dist, 1l, 5l. Time 6m 25.00s. SP 5-1.
A Palmer (Cotley).

657 - Intermediate (12st)

PANDA SHANDY 5a 5ex .... **Miss A Goschen** 1
rstrnd in last, prog to ld 4 out, qckn clr
466 **Earthmover (Ire) 7a** .... **Miss P Curling** 2
(fav) ld/disp til 16th, not qckn whn hdd, kpt on
Pabrey .... **N Mitchell** 3
ld/disp untl 16th, wknd next, no ch with 1st 2
3 ran. 15l, 5l. Time 6m 27.00s. SP 5-4.
Mrs R H Woodhouse (Portman).

658 - Open Maiden Div III (12st)

556 **LANGTON PARMILL** .... **P Shaw** 1
ld to 5th, again from 4 out, pushed out flat
207 **Sgeir Bantighearna 5a** .... **Miss M Tory** 2
ld 6th untl 3 out, not able to qckn wth wnnr
467 **Inner Snu 5a** .... **G Baines** 3
sn wll bhnd, ran through btn horses frm 4 out
Sandy Etna (Ire) 5a *prom untl 14th, wknd 15th, t.o. from 3 out* 4
471 Green's Game *(fav) patiently rdn, 2nd at 11th, wknd, t.o. frm 15th* 5
471 Simply Joyful 5a *whipped round and u.r. start* .... ur
470 Orchard Lady 5a *wth ldng grp until wknd whn u.r. 14th* .... ur
520 Sulason *hmpd start, rpd prog whn f. 5th* .... f
8 ran. 8l, dist, 6l, dist. Time 6m 36.00s. SP 9-2.
Miss J Hodgkinson (Cattistock).
T.S.

FLINT & DENBIGH
Eaton Hall
Sunday March 24th
SOFT

659 - Members

464 **MERRY SCORPION 4ow** .... **R Owen** 1
cls up, disp frm 11th, ld 13th, prssd last, ran on well
462 **Embu-Meru** .... **I Lowe** 2
ld/disp to 12th, lost plc nxt, rallied 3 out, just faild
464 **Shanballymore (Ire)** .... **J Tilley** 3
(fav) chsd ldrs, ev ch 2 out, not qckn
In Hand *alwys rear, t.o.* 4
289 Lattin General *in tch whn u.r. 7th* .... ur
Coddington Village *cls up til lost tch 12th, sn btn, p.u. 14th* .... pu
6 ran. Hd, 5l, dist. Time 6m 49.00s. SP 5-2.
T D Marlow (Flint & Denbigh).

660 - Maiden Div I

569 **MR BUSKER (IRE)** .... **C Barlow** 1
(fav) prom, blnd 5th, lft in ld 13th, prssd 2 out, ran on well
463 **Nights Image (Ire)** .... **O Macphail** 2
chsng grp, ld 7-10th, in tch aft, chal 2 out, onepcd
Call Coup (Ire) 5a .... **M Smith** 3
lost tch 7th, ran on steadily frm 4 out, no dang
463 Mickley Justtheone 5a *chsng grp, in tch wth ldrs whn f heavily 10th* .... f
463 Builder Boy *mid-div, prog to 3rd 13th, f nxt* .... f
463 Po Cap Eel 5a *mid to rear, lost tch whn p.u. 3 out* .... pu
286 Inglebrook 7a *ld to 6th, ld 11th, clr nxt, blnd & u.r. 13th* .... ur
7 ran. 10l, dist. Time 6m 58.00s. SP 4-5.
C J B Barlow (Sir W W Wynn's).

661 - Maiden Div II

288 **BALLYBEGGAN PARSON (IRE)** .... **G Hanmer** 1
jmpd slwly, ld/disp to 3rd, prog to ld 13th, styd on well 2 out
288 **King Keith** .... **Charles Barlow** 2
mid-div, prog to disp 8-10th, chal 2 out, not qckn
464 **Little By Little** .... **R Bevis** 3
mstks, mid-div, some prog 14th, ran on onepcd
407 Canny Curate (Ire) *mid-div, 4th & ev ch 3 out, onepcd* 4
Mophead Kelly *mid-div, blnd 11th & lost tch, p.u. 4 out* .... pu
464 Beeworthy 5a *mid to rear, nvr dang, p.u. 3 out* .... pu
Maes Gwyn Dreamer *prom to 6th, wknd rpdly, p.u. 8th* .... pu
Rough Echo *mstks in rear, p.u. 8th, lame* .... pu
464 Agile King 7a *plld hrd, ld to 13th, still going wll whn u.r. nxt* .... ur
9 ran. 5l, 7l, 10l. Time 6m 59.00s. SP 10-1.
P E Mills (West Shropshire Draghounds).

662 - Open (12st)

159 **FIDDLERS THREE 7ex (bl)** .... **I Wynne** 1
trckd ldrs, 2nd 7th til ld apr last, ran on well, comf
490 **Lucky Christopher** .... **G Tarry** 2
(fav) w.w. mid-div, clsd 13th, ran on und pres 4 out, tk 2nd flat
153 **Scally's Daughter 5a 7ex** .... **E Williams** 3
ld til apr last, fdd flat
459 Tara Boy *mid-div in tch, not qckn frm 3 out, sn btn* 4
162 Auction Law (NZ) 7ex *hld up rear, nvr in race, p.u. 2 out* .... pu
215 Glenshane Lad 7ex *chsd ldrs to 8th, fdd, p.u. 5 out* ... pu
401 Mr Snail *mstks in rear, t.o. & p.u. 5 out* .... pu
459 Chip'N'run 4ex *prom, disp 2nd whn u.r. 5 out* .... ur
304 Band Sargeant (Ire) *mid-div, 5th & in tch 4 out, sn wknd, p.u. nxt* .... pu
162 Dannigale *nvr bynd mid-div, t.o. 12th, p.u. 4 out* .... pu
10 ran. 15l, 5l, 8l. Time 6m 37.00s. SP 2-1.
Ian Wynne (Cheshire).

663 - Ladies

429 **STEPHENS PET** .... **Miss A Dare** 1
(fav) hld up in tch, prog to ld 10th, comf
Fell Mist .... **Miss A Sykes** 2
cls up, tried to chal last, alwys hld
291 **Renard Quay** .... **Miss C Wilberforce** 3
rear, out of tch wth ldrs, late prog, nrst fin
569 Captiva Bay 5a *prom to 4 out, sn btn* 4
457 Montykosky *sn t.o., p.u. 11th* .... pu
Inch Maid 5a *mid-div, cls up whn u.r. 6th* .... ur
460 Moya's Tip Top 5a *mid to rear, nvr bttr than 5th, p.u. 4 out* .... pu
460 Glamdring 5a *ld to 9th, mstks aft, no ch whn f 3 out* ... f
8 ran. 2l, 20l, 4l. Time 6m 48.00s. SP 1-5.
Dr P P Brown (Berkeley).

664 - Confined

285 **AMBROSE** .... **W Ritson** 1

chsng grp, ran on well frm 3 out to ld last
289 **Korbell (Ire) 5a ....A Crow** 2
(fav) handy, ld 3 out, sn clr, hdd last, no ext
289 **Shoon Wind.........................A Dalton** 3
mid-div, styd on frm 3 out, no ch 1st pair
290 Barkin *ld/disp 5th-4 out, ev ch nxt, onepcd* 4
563 Howlin' Wolf *mid-div, nvr rchd ldrs* 5
402 Real Class *mid to rear, onepcd, nvr dang* 6
289 Wot Pet *mid-div whn u.r. 9th* .... ur
458 Bay Owl *nvr going well, p.u. 8th* .... pu
369 Shareef Star *mid to rear, no ch whn p.u. 5 out* .... pu
Logical Fun *ld/disp to 14th, sn lost tch & btn, p.u. 3 out*......... pu
568 Bay Tiger *rear, p.u. 11th* .... pu
461 Hillview Lad *rear whn u.r. 7th*......................... ur
289 Ebony Gale *mid to rear, no ch whn p.u. 4 out* .... pu
Strathbogie Mist (Ire) 7ex *rear, p.u. 6th* .... pu
538 Back The Road (Ire) *prom to hlfwy, sn btn, p.u. 4 out*... pu
15 ran. 2l, dist, 10l. Time 6m 42.00s. SP 33-1.
W A Ritson (Sir W. W. Wynn's).

665 - Restricted Div I (12st)

292 **GEN-TECH ....A Gribbin** 1
cls up, ld 5th, made rest, comf
Made Of Talent 5a ....A Crow 2
(fav) w.w. in rear, prog to prss wnr 4 out, onepcd & hld last
219 **Kings Mischief (Ire)......................A Price** 3
mid-div, prog last m, nvr dang
Friary Lad (Ire) *rear, some late prog, nrst fin* 4
462 Foxy Blue *prom to hlfwy, sn btn, p.u. 4 out* .... pu
231 Moorside Lad *prom, chsd wnr 5-13th, grad fdd, p.u. 3 out*......... pu
Annyban 5a *p.u. 2nd, dsmntd* .... pu
Crimson Mary 5a *mid to rear, no ch frm hlfwy, p.u. 5 out*......... pu
464 Gray Rosette 5a *mid-div to 10th, prog 12th, ev ch whn u.r. 2 out* .... ur
Kiltrose Lad *f 1st* .... f
462 Ballyhannon (Ire) *t.o. & p.u. 8th*......... pu
461 Grecianlid *t.o. & p.u. 11th* .... pu
Cader Idris *ld to 2nd, chsng grp to 4 out, no ch whn p.u. nxt*......... pu
458 Juste Jo 5a *prom, ld 3rd-4th, fdd rpdly, p.u. 9th* ...... pu
14 ran. 10l, 10l, 15l. Time 6m 51.00s. SP 20-1.
A D Gribbin (Cheshire Forest).

666 - Restricted Div II (12st)

ORAGAS ....R Thornton 1
chsng grp, 20l 3rd 5 out, ran on to ld apr last
292 **Miss Shaw 5a ....A Griffith** 2
prom, ld 8th til hdd apr last, onepcd
292 **Lindsey Doyle 5a...............Miss C Burgess** 3
alwys rear, t.o.
569 The Yokel *cls up, 2nd at 12th, btn whn blnd 2 out, p.u. last*......... pu
461 Moydrum Prince *trckd ldrs to 6 out, wknd, p.u. 3 out*.. pu
565 Noble Angel (Ire) *ld/disp to 8th, hmpd by loose horse, p.u. 11th*......... pu
159 Twelth Man *alwys rear, p.u. 5 out* .... pu
462 Royal Entertainer *f 1st* .... f
462 Saffron Glory *mid-div, 3rd at 10th, grad wknd, p.u. 4 out*......... pu
461 Pepperbox 5a *mid to rear, nvr in race, p.u. 4 out*..... pu
240 Whatwillbewillbe (Ire) *(fav) hld up in tch, going easily in 3rd whn f 13th*......... f
287 Maesgwyn Bach 5a *mid to rear, no ch whn p.u. 5 out* pu
Reckless Lord (Ire) *ld to 4th, cls up whn u.r. 7th* ..... ur
13 ran. Dist, 3l, dist. Time 6m 54.00s. SP 50-1.
G J L Orchard (Ludlow).

667 - Intermediate (12st)

339 **GRECIAN LARK ....G Tarry** 1
hld up, prog 2 out, lvl last, sn ld, ran on well
293 **Landsker Alfred 5ex ....Miss A Dare** 2
(fav) w.w. prog 7th, ld 3 out, clr nxt, hdd & onepcd flat
458 **Whatafellow (Ire) ....A Crow** 3
hld up rear, ran on frm 3 out, outpcd by ldng pair
293 Worleston Farrier *ld to 3 out, outpcd aft* 4
457 The Right Guy *sn bhnd, t.o.* 5
Alex-Path *rear to 12th, sn lost tch, p.u. 4 out*......... pu
Brazen Gold *chsd ldr to 8th, lost tch 12th, p.u. 3 out* .. pu
457 Bally Muire 5a *rear whn p.u. 11th* .... pu
563 Rhine River (USA) *prom early, lost tch, p.u. 4 out*..... pu
383 The Rum Mariner *mid-div, prog to 2nd 11th, fdd. p.u. 2 out*......... pu
Ring Bank 7a *rear, p.u. 10th*......... pu
11 ran. 3l, 10l, dist, dist. Time 6m 54.00s. SP 10-1.
G B Tarry (Grafton).
V.S.

SANDOWN
Tuesday March 26th
GOOD TO SOFT

668 - 2½m 110yds Hun

COOL RELATION 11.9 7a...........Mr A Phillips 1
(fav) trckd ldrs, ld 8th, left clr 5 out, blnd 2 out, shaken up and ran on well from last.
Beau Bo's Return 10.4 5a...........Mr J Culloty 2
mstk 5th, bhnd, lost tch 8th, hdwy to chase wnr from 3 out, no ext run-in.
257 **Social Climber 11.5 7a ....Mr L Lay** 3
cl up, ld briefly 7th, outpcd 9th, t.o..
481 Father Dowling 11.5 7a *alwys bhnd, lost tch from 8th, t.o.*......... 4
345 John O'Dee 11.10 7a 5ow *ld till hdd 4th, bhnd from 6th, t.o. from 8th.* 5
104 J J Jimmy 11.5 7a *mstk 7th, soon bhnd, t.o. when mistake 9th, p.u. before 11th.*......... pu
363 Ryde Again 11.13 7a *nvr far away, trckd wnr from 8th, 2 l 2nd when f 5 out.*......... f
Crossofspancilhill 11.5 7a *keen hold, ld 4th to 7th, soon outpcd, t.o. when p.u. before 6 out.*......... pu
8 ran. 2½l, 27l, 7l, dist. Time 5m 36.00s. SP 4-5.
D J Caro

CHEPSTOW
Wednesday March 27th
SOFT

669 - 3m Hun

483 **HOLLAND HOUSE 11.13 5a..........Mr C Vigors** 1
held up, hdwy to go 2nd 7th, ld 13th, rdn run-in, just held on.
370 **Coome Hill (Ire) 11.11 7a...........Mr T Dennis** 2
(fav) in tch till jmpd slowly and lost pl 11th, rallied to go 2nd 5 out, rdn and ran on run-in, just faild.
546 **Goolds Gold 11.7 5a..............Miss P Jones** 3
prom till lost pl apr 8th, effort approaching 5 out, n.d..
485 Howaryasun (Ire) 11.11 7a (v) *prom, jmpd badly right 13th, soon rcvred, rdn and wknd 4 out.* 4
485 Rusty Bridge 11.11 7a *alwys bhnd, t.o..* 5
Skerry Meadow 11.6 7a 1ow *ld to 2nd, bhnd from 6th, t.o. when p.u. before 12th.*......... pu
481 My Mellow Man 11.8 7a *t.o. 7th, p.u. before 11th.* .... pu
606 Pyro Pennant 11.7 5a *prom till blnd 7th, soon t.o., p.u. before 9th.*......... pu
507 Lighten The Load 11.5 7a *soon well bhnd, t.o. when p.u. before 2 out.*......... pu
578 Percy Thrower 11.12 3a *ld 2nd, hit 7th, hdd 13th, wknd quickly, t.o. when p.u. before last.*......... pu
10 ran. Hd, 29l, 11l, dist. Time 6m 42.30s. SP 11-4.
E Knight

AINTREE
Thursday March 28th
GOOD

670 - 3m 1f Nov Hun

486 **WUDIMP 12.0.........................Mr C Storey** 1

(fav) midfield, ld 12th, mstk next, driven clr apr last, kept on well und pres.
483 **Colonial Kelly 12.0 ....Mr P Hacking** 2
cl up, mstk 4th, ld 11th, mistake and hdd next, kept on from 2 out.
Bally Riot (Ire) 12.0 ....Mr P Fenton 3
cl up, ld 6th to 11th, driven along to chase wnr from 5 out, no ext 2 out.
Johnny The Fox (Ire) 12.0 *pressed ldrs, chal 13th, driven along from 3 out, held when jmpd slowly last...* 4
366 Squirrellsdaughter 11.9 *jmpd poorly, alwys rear, well bhnd from 4 out, t.o. when p.u. after 2 out............* pu
484 A Windy Citizen (Ire) 11.9 *f 1st......................* f
484 Erins Bar (Ire) 12.0 *held up rear, mstk 5th, effort to chase ldrs hfwy, struggling when hit 5 out, t.o. when p.u. before 3 out..............................* pu
481 Space Cappa 12.0 *soon ld, hdd 6th, dropped rear apr 9th, bhnd when blnd and u.r. 5 out..............* ur
476 Ardbrennan 12.0 *pressed ldrs, disp 2nd when f 11th.* f
9 ran. 4l, 1l, 3½l. Time 6m 36.30s. SP 15-8.
C Storey

TAUNTON
Thursday March 28th
SOFT

671 - 3m Hun Chase

482 **ON ALERT (NZ) 11.7 7a........Mr Richard White** 1
ld 3rd, jmpd slowly and hdd 5th, left in clr ld 15th, unchal.
485 **Golden Freeze 12.0 7a..............Mr E James** 2
prom, jmpd slowly 5th and 14th, chsd wnr from next, one pace.
195 **Expressment 11.7 7a ....Mr I Widdicombe** 3
bhnd, mstk 13th, hdwy 15th, one pace 3 out.
481 Just My Bill 11.7 7a *bhnd, hdwy 14th, wknd before 3 out.....................................* 4
480 Loyal Note 11.11 3a *(fav) ld to 3rd, regained ld 5th, hdd 7th, wknd 13th..............................* 5
255 Sweatshirt 11.7 7a *bhnd, gd hdwy 11th, blnd next, wknd 15th...................................* 6
554 Moze Tidy 11.7 7a *blnd 11th, nvr on terms...........* 7
601 Chibougama (USA) 11.7 7a *prom early, bhnd when mstks 7th and next, soon t.o...........................* 8
534 And What Else (Ire) 11.7 7a *bhnd, mstk 4th, t.o. from 13th...................................* 9
482 Myhamet 11.9 5a *mid div, mstk 6th, effort 13th, wknd after next, t.o.................................* 10
261 New Mill House 12.0 7a *bhnd from 13th, t.o. when p.u. before 3 out...............................* pu
560 Light The Bay 11.2 7a *not fluent, held up, hdwy from 12th, wknd 15th, t.o. when p.u. before 2 out...........* pu
63 Full Alirt 11.2 7a *trckd ldrs, ld 7th, mstks 9th and 14th, f next......................................* f
13 ran. 14l, 1¾l, 3½l, 15l, 14l, 2l, 9l, 10l, 19l. Time 6m 19.60s. SP 9-1.
V G Greenway

AINTREE
Friday March 29th
GOOD

672 - 2¾m Hun

261 **ROLLING BALL (FR) 12.0.............Mr R Ford** 1
(fav) raced freely, soon ld, clr when ran wd 12th (Canal Turn), hdd 4 out, rallied to ld last, edged right run-in, held on well.
483 **Kerry Orchid 12.0 (v) ....Mr P Fenton** 2
hmpd 1st, soon well bhnd, bumped 12th (Canal Turn), hdwy 4 out, jmpd right 2 out, ran on strly from last, held cl home.
485 **Sir Noddy 12.0 ....Mr C Stockton** 3
pressed ldr, ld 4 out to last, kept on well till no ext cl home.
257 Synderborough Lad 12.0 *patiently rdn, imp hfwy, hdwy to chal 2 out, ridden and one pace run-in.......* 4
483 The Bird O'Donnell 12.0 *held up, pushed along and outpcd hfwy, some hdwy apr 2 out, n.d..............* 5
370 Sonofagipsy 12.0 *chsd ldrs, outpcd hfwy, driven along from 5 out, no impn 3 out..................* 6
577 Hamper 12.0 (bl) *held up, struggling hfwy, nvr a factor.......................................* 7
257 Southern Minstrel 12.0 *hmpd 1st, alwys well bhnd, t.o. hfwy...................................* 8
523 Daringly 12.0 *held up, struggling 9th, well bhnd after. ....* 9
Jumbeau 12.0 *held up, outpcd 9th, struggling when blnd 14th, t.o.................................* 10
373 Over The Edge 12.0 *jmpd slowly rear, struggling hfwy, t.o. 6 out................................* 11
373 On The Other Hand 12.0 *held up, losing tch when pkd 10th (Becher's), well bhnd after...............* 12
184 Professor Longhair 12.0 *n.j.w., alwys rear, t.o. hfwy.* 13
257 Quick Rapor 12.0 (bl) *jmpd slowly rear, well bhnd when blnd 13th (Valentine's), t.o..................* 14
480 Ullswater 12.0 *jmpd slowly, alwys well bhnd, t.o. hfwy.....................................* 15
368 Direct 12.0 *f 1st..................................* f
485 Brown Windsor 12.0 (bl) *held up, midfield when b.d. 9th.....................................* bd
491 As You Were 12.0 *rear when u.r. 1st.................* ur
487 Dark Dawn 12.0 *chsd ldrs till bumped and u.r. 5th....* ur
587 Furry Knowe 12.0 *hmpd and useated rider 1st.........* ur
259 Off The Bru 12.0 *hmpd 1st, rear when f 3rd (Chair)...* f
579 Kambalda Rambler 12.0 *alwys rear, t.o. hfwy, blnd and u.r. 13th (Valentine's) ....* ur
565 My Nominee 12.0 (bl) *chsd ldrs, 3rd when blnd 7th, losing pl when f 9th..............................* f
The Country Trader 12.0 (bl) *f 1st....................* f
483 Clare Man (Ire) 12.0 *f 1st...............................* f
483 Earlydue 12.0 *f 1st......................................* f
26 ran. 1½l, 6l, 4l, 6l, 15l, 12l, 2l, 2½l, 1¼l, 10l. Time 5m 38.80s. SP 7-2.
Mrs H J Clarke

SEDGEFIELD
Friday March 29th
GOOD TO FIRM

673 - 3m 3f Hun Chase

371 **RISKY DEE 11.4 5a................Mr N Wilson** 1
alwys handy, ld 5 out, pushed clr after next.
582 **Final Hope (Ire) 11.2 7a ....Mrs F Needham** 2
(fav) settld in tch, chsd wnr 4 out, driven 2 out, no impn.
612 **Boreen Owen 11.2 7a.............Mr T Morrison** 3
nvr far away, ld 13th, hdd 5 out, outpcd last 3.
487 Fish Quay 11.2 7a *alwys prom, left in ld 12th, hdd next, struggling 5 out, btn when ref last.............* ref
536 Queen's Chaplain 11.2 7a *hit 2nd, in tch, f heavily 12th...................................* f
587 Politico Pot 11.9 7a 7ow *not fluent, bhnd, t.o. when p.u. before 3 out................................* pu
259 Whosthat 11.4 5a *jmpd right, ld and soon clr, mstk 3rd, blnd and u.r. 12th.........................* ur
7 ran. 4l, 6l. Time 7m 7.90s. SP 6-1.
James Hepburn

HEREFORD
Saturday March 30th
SOFT

674 - 2m Nov Hun Chase

484 **FAMILIAR FRIEND 11.7 7a (bl) ....Mr L Lay** 1
held up, hdwy 4 out, ld 2 out, clr when hit last, rdn out.
480 **Royal Irish 11.7 7a (bl) ....Mr E James** 2
(fav) prom, ld 5th, hdd 7th, rdn after 4 out, chal 2 out, kept on one pace run-in.
482 **Cathgal 11.7 7a ....Miss C Thomas** 3
held up, hdwy 6th, ld next, mstk and hdd 2 out, kept on one pace.
364 Doc Lodge 11.10 7a 8ow (bl) *started slowly, f 1st....* f

666 Noble Angel (Ire) 11.7 7a *left in ld 2nd, mstk and hdd 5th, 4th when f 7th* .... f
Ideal 11.7 7a *ld, blnd and u.r. 2nd.* .... ur
Peppermill Lane 11.7 7a *blnd 4th, alwys bhnd, t.o. from 7th, p.u. before last* .... pu
184 Thornhill 11.2 7a *bhnd when blnd 1st, f 3rd* .... f
8 ran. 2½l, 1½l. Time 4m 20.80s. SP 4-1.
M H G Lang

CAMBRIDGE UNIV UNITED HUNTS
Cottenham
Saturday March 30th
GOOD TO FIRM

675 - Members

581 **BRIGHT BURNS** .... **R Sweeting** 1
(fav) made all, clr 4 out, eased flat
310 **Highland Laird** .... **Miss J Holmes** 2
chsd wnr to til mstk 14th, went 2nd agn last, no ch
571 **Glenavey** .... **C Hall** 3
last pair, clsd 3 out, styd on well flat, nrst fin
344 Stanwick Lass 5a *in tch, chsd wnr 14th-last, kpt on onepcd* 4
618 View Point (Ire) *jmpd slwly, last pair, nrly u.r. 13th, effrt 3 out,wknd nxt* 5
490 Mount Eaton Fox *raced wd, 3rd til slw jmps 6 & 7th, p.u. nxt* .... pu
6 ran. 1½l, ¾l, ¾l, 25l. Time 6m 17.20s. SP 1-3.
Colin Gee (Heythrop).

676 - Intermediate (12st)

434 **BEAU DANDY 5ex** .... **T Marks** 1
pllng, prom, ld 12th, lft clr aft 2 out, drvn & hld on well
422 **Druid's Lodge** .... **T Bulgin** 2
mid-div, effrt 3 out, styd on well apr last, just hld
313 **Saffron Flame (Ire)** .... **P Taiano** 3
(Jt fav) hld up, prog 13th, outpcd 16th, ran on 2 out, fin well
621 Timber's Boy 5ex *(Jt fav) hld up rear, outpcd 14th, ran on 3 out, too mch to do* 4
235 Cool Ginger *prom til wknd frm 3 out* 5
535 Royal Survivor *ld til mstk & hdd 7th, mstk 9th, sn lost plc, no dang aft* 6
419 Ravens Hasey Moon *wll in tch til wknd 3 out* 7
576 Coral Eddy *alwys last pair, t.o. 9th* 8
Alzamina 5a *trckd ldrs to 15th, no ch whn p.u. 2 out* .... pu
Nee-Argee 5a *alwys last pair, t.o. 9th, p.u. 2 out* .... pu
Ovac Star 5ex *chsd ldrs, effrt 13th, wknd 16th, no ch whn p.u. 2 out* .... pu
Aldington Baron *prom, ld 8-12th, wknd rpdly, p.u. 15th* .... pu
105 Major Neave *mstks 3 & 5th,prog 11th,jnd wnr 3 out,ran wd aft nxt,p.u.* .... pu
13 ran. 1l, ¾l, 8l, 20l, hd, 12l, 1 fence. Time 6m 3.10s. SP 4-1.
C C Shand Kydd (Pytchley).

677 - Open

619 **COCKSTOWN LAD** .... **D Featherstone** 1
in tch,prog 16th,ld 2 out-last,rallied flat,lkd to fin 2nd
177 **River Melody 5a** .... **T Moore** 2
(fav) w.w. prog 3 out,ld last,rdn & found lttl flat,lkd to fin 1st
581 **Carrigeen Lad** .... **R Wakley** 3
mstk 9th, chsd ldr 14th-3 out, chal last, onepcd flat
492 Saint Bene't (Ire) *alwys prom, cls 5th 2 out, onepcd aft* 4
One More Run *ld to 2 out, wknd apr last* 5
435 Tompet *prom to 11th, wknd frm 4 out* 6
622 Owd Henry *prog & prom 10th, wknd 16th, no ch whn p.u. 2 out* .... pu
619 El Bae *alwys last, t.o. & p.u. 10th* .... pu
491 Jimmy Mac Jimmy *mstk 7th, prom, mstk 14th, rdr lost irons & p.u. 3 out* .... pu
538 The Point Is *f 1st* .... f
393 Traders Choice *in tch to 14th, sn wknd, t.o. & p.u. 2 out* .... pu
11 ran. Hd, 2½l, 7l, 6l, 20l. Time 6m 3.10s. SP 14-1.
Mrs E R Featherstone (Puckeridge).

678 - Ladies

493 **RICHARD HUNT** .... **Miss L Rowe** 1
(fav) w.w. prog 11th,ld 3 out,outjmpd & hdd nxt,sn ld agn,rdn out
347 **Dromin Leader** .... **Miss G Chown** 2
j.w. chsd ldr, ld 12th-3 out, ld agn brfly nxt, kpt on flat
620 **Cherry Chap** .... **Miss L Hollis** 3
hld up, lost tch 13th, went 3rd 15th, no imp aft
493 Sarazar (USA) 2ow *wll in tch til outpcd 14th, sn no ch* 4
572 Wendy Jane 5a *jmpd rght, clr ldr til aft 12th, sn lost plc & btn* 5
535 Spanish Whisper *chsd ldrs, lost plc whn pckd 10th, bhnd frm 13th* 6
6 ran. 2l, 15l, 15l, 4l, 12l. Time 6m 3.50s. SP 2-7.
Mrs P Rowe (Puckeridge).

679 - Restricted

419 **RUSSIAN VISION (bl)** .... **C Ward-Thomas** 1
wth ldr, blnd 10th, ld 13th, clr 2 out, pshd out
348 **Shake Five (Ire) 7a** .... **S Sporborg** 2
w.w. prog to 3rd 16th, mstk 2 out, styd on to 2nd flat
541 **Dashboard Light** .... **S R Andrews** 3
blnd 1st, rear, prog 10th, chsd wnr 16th, no imp apr last
494 Radiant Monarch *in tch in rear, outpcd 15th, no imp on ldrs 3 out* 4
484 Cool Apollo (NZ) *chsd ldrs til wknd frm 16th* 5
494 Just Donald *chsd ldrs, mstk 13th, sn wknd, t.o.* 6
620 Cowage Brook *mid-div, b.d. 5th* .... bd
490 Kelly's Twilight 5a *bhnd frm 7th, t.o. 10th, p.u. aft 12th* pu
449 Charleston Lad *in tch, outpcd 16th, 4th & btn whn mstk 2 out, p.u. last* .... pu
348 Woodrow Call *in tch whn b.d. 5th* .... bd
524 Inch Gale 5a (bl) *lft in ld 2nd, hdd 13th, sn wknd, poor 7th whn u.r. 2 out* .... ur
173 Ryders Wells *ld til blnd & u.r. 2nd* .... ur
15 Al Jawwal *3rd whn f 5th* .... f
437 Glenrowan Lad *(fav) hld up, in tch whn b.d. 5th* .... bd
59 Big Jack (Ire) *hld up, lost tch rpdly 13th, p.u. nxt* .... pu
15 ran. 4l, 2l, 20l, 10l, dist. Time 6m 1.40s. SP 20-1.
Mrs Alexander Scott (Thurlow).
One fence omitted 2nd circuit, 18 jumps.

680 - Open Maiden Div I (12st)

522 **JUST A MADAM (IRE) 5a** .... **Miss E Tomlinson** 1
made all, clr 13th, mstk last, unchal
479 **Mr Wendyl** .... **M Emmanuel** 2
prom, chsd wnr 10-16th, went 2nd agn last, no imp
424 **Springlark (Ire) 7a** .... **A Coe** 3
mid-div, mstk 11th, prog 14th, chsd wnr 16th-last, no imp
314 Rebel Tom *rear, kpt on to poor 4th at 14th, nvr dang* 4
Anita's Son *schoold in last, t.o. 10th* 5
618 Nursery Story *wth wrn to 8th, wknd 10th, t.o. & p.u. 16th* .... pu
Tarry No More 5a *mstk 5th, trckd ldrs, blnd 13th, sn btn, p.u. 15th* .... pu
495 Muddle Head (Ire) (bl) *pllng, prom to 10th, sn wknd, t.o. & p.u. 15th* .... pu
Kings Romance 5a *mid-div, wknd 8th, t.o. & p.u. 15th* pu
239 Mrs Blobby (Ire) 5a *(fav) hld up bhnd, mstk 12th, no prog 14th, p.u. 3 out* .... pu
Suny Bertie *mid-div, ran wd aft 12th & lost tch, t.o. & p.u. 15th* .... pu
11 ran. 15l, 5l, 20l, 25l. Time 6m 7.20s. SP 3-1.
Miss E Tomlinson (Cambridge Univ Drag).

681 - Open Maiden Div II (12st)

439 **KERRY MY HOME** .... **T Marks** 1
in tch, rmndr 11th, prog to ld 15th, rdn out frm last
617 **Alapa** .... **J Townson** 2

in tch, prog 14th, chsd wnr & ev ch last, no qckn flat
495 **George The Greek (Ire)....................A Coe** 3
trckd ldrs, chsd wnr 3 out, ev ch nxt, wknd apr last
576 Grassington (Ire) *rear, mod 5th & no ch 3 out, kpt on, nrst fin* 4
718 Derring Floss 5a *prom, ld 8-15th, 4th & wkng whn mstk 2 out* 5
56 Lights Out *(fav) mstk 3rd, rear, lost tch 14th, no dang aft* 6
240 Ronson Royale *mstk 4th, alwys rear, no ch 15th, t.o.* .. 7
Shelter *blnd 1st, last pair til hmpd & u.r. 9th* .... ur
455 Bric Lane (USA) *mid-div, outpcd 15th, 7th & btn whn f nxt* .... f
618 Little Freddie *wth ldr to 14th, cls 5th whn f 3 out* ...... f
344 Holding The Aces *ld to 8th, cls 3rd whn f 12th* .... f
Joyful Joan (Ire) 7a *in tch in rear til f 9th* .... f
12 ran. 2l, 12l, ¾l, 8l, 20l, 15l. Time 6m 12.20s. SP 3-1.
M J Norman (Fitzwilliam).

682 - Open Maiden Div III (12st)

HURRICANE GILBERT ....C Ward-Thomas 1
(fav) prom, 2nd whn blnd 3 out, lft in ld apr last, all out
495 **Dolly Bloom 5a ....A Sansome** 2
w.w.prog to ld aft 3 out,hmpd loose hrs apr last,rallied flt
618 **Royal Bav (Ire)...........................R Gill** 3
mid-div, last & outpcd 16th, kpt on
617 Tharif *ld to 4th, ld 12th, sn clr, wknd & hdd aft 3 out* ... 4
496 Bozo Bailey *n.j.w. alwys bhnd, last whn p.u. 12th*..... pu
107 Funny Worry *plld to ld 4th,sn clr,nrly u.r.10th,hdd 12th,wknd,p.u.16th* .... pu
617 Zap (Ire) 5a *mid-div, blnd 13th, not rcvr, p.u. nxt*...... pu
Lend Us A Buck 5a *bhnd frm 6th, no ch whn hit 12th, p.u. nxt* .... pu
Broadway Swinger 7a *last whn u.r. 4th* .... ur
9 ran. ½l, 15l, 1l. Time 6m 10.00s. SP 3-1.
Mrs A Villar (Suffolk).
J.N.

HARKAWAY CLUB
Chaddesley Corbett
Saturday March 30th
GOOD

683 - Members

JOLLY BOAT..............................A Crow 1
(Jt fav) chsd ldr 5th, ld 2 out, sn hdd, lft in ld last, drvn out
538 **Cawkwell Dean.............................L Lay** 2
chsd ldrs, ev ch & rdn 15th, lft 2nd last, onepcd
355 **Nether Gobions ....E Williams** 3
ld to 3 out, onepcd und pres aft
427 Shadow Walker *mid-div, 10th & pshd alng hlfwy, nvr trbld ldrs* 4
381 Master Donnington *hld up, 11th hlfwy, nvr on terms* .. 5
569 The Last Joshua *alwys wll bhnd, t.o. frm 4th*......... 6
Durzi *chsd ldrs to 7th, wknd 10th, p.u. 13th* .... pu
Wildnite *mid-div, no ch whn blnd 12th, p.u. 14th*...... pu
214 Punching Glory *bhnd frm 7th, t.o. & p.u. last*......... pu
Raido *blnd 1st, in tch, 6th & outpcd 12th, p.u. 3 out* ... pu
458 Ultrason IV (Fr) 7ex *chsd ldrs to 11th, sn wknd, p.u. 3 out* .... pu
426 Shaker Maker *alwys bhnd, t.o. & p.u. 13th*.......... pu
535 Hobnobber *(Jt fav) prog 11th, ld aft 2 out, in cmmnd whn ran out last* .... ro
579 Kali Sana (Ire) *chsd ldrs to 6th, sn wknd, t.o. & p.u. 12th* .... pu
French Stick *chsd ldr, blnd 3rd, wknd 7th, t.o. & p.u. 14th* .... pu
139 American Black *hld up rear, nvr dang, p.u. 3 out*..... pu
Westwood March *rear, p.u. 9th* .... pu
17 ran. 1l, 2l, 15l, nk, 2 fences. Time 6m 5.00s. SP 4-1.
Gareth Samuel (North Shropshire).

684 - Restricted

526 **PERSEVERANCE.................Miss P Gundry** 1
t.d.e. prom, lft 2nd 12th, ld 4 out, rdn 2 out, hld on flat
286 **Upton Orbit ....O Macphail** 2
chsd ldr 11th, lft in ld nxt, hdd 4 out, kpt on wll flat
461 **Ollardale (Ire) ....W Bryan** 3
w.w. prog 11th, rdn apr 3 out, kpt on well flat
349 Layston D'Or *mstks, hld up, prog 9th, 4th & ch whn blnd 2 out, no ext* 4
428 Sideliner *mid-div, pshd alng 11th, 5th & ch 3 out, onepcd* 5
425 Kerry Hill *tubed, chsd ldrs, wknd apr 15th* 6
459 Quite So 5a *s.v.s. t.o. til f 9th* .... f
231 Golden Companion *chsd ldrs til wknd 11th, bhnd whn p.u. 13th* .... pu
462 Fennorhill *bhnd frm 4th, t.o. & p.u. 12th* .... pu
269 Jellyband *chsd ldr 5-9th, wkng whn blnd 11th, t.o. & p.u. 3 out* .... pu
542 Mandys Lad *ld, 5l clr whn f 12th* .... f
Quick Quick Sloe 5a *(fav) bmpd & u.r. 1st*.......... ur
569 Sir Galeforce (Ire) *plld hrd, chsd ldr 4th til u.r. 6th* .... ur
Thank The Lord 7a *schoold, bhnd, some prog whn f 12th* .... f
14 ran. ½l, hd, 5l, 1l, 12l. Time 6m 16.80s. SP 8-1.
D H Bennett (Beaufort).

685 - Ladies

RUSSKI...........................Miss A Dare 1
chsd ldng pair 10th,rdn 3 out,rnunning on whn lft in ld last
436 **Knight's Spur (USA).................Mrs J Parris** 2
w.w. prog 11th, 4th & hit 3 out, lft 2nd last, no imp
Mister Gebo ....Miss C Dyson 3
blnd 8th,ld/disp to 11th, ev ch 4 out, blnd 2 out, no ext
Redben *s.s. alwys wll bhnd, t.o. frm 11th*........... 4
566 River Trout *ld 3-4th, sn wknd, t.o. frm 12th* 5
Blue Cheek *disp 5th til ld 12th, clr 3 out, 2l up whn u.r. last* .... ur
292 The Barren Arctic *prom, cls 4th whn ran out 11th*..... ro
662 Dannigale *raced wd, prom til u.r. 9th* .... ur
356 Bankhead (Ire) *(fav) in tch til u.r. 5th* .... ur
9 ran. 3l, 5l, dist, ½l. Time 6m 12.00s. SP 8-1.
D V A Willis (Berkeley).
One fence omitted, 17 jumps.

686 - Open

351 **LOCHINGALL ....T Stephenson** 1
(fav) hld up, smooth prog to chal 2 out, ld last, ran on, clvrly
459 **Garrylucas ....G Hanmer** 2
w.w. prog to ld 12th, hdd last, onepcd
537 **Penlet...........................John Pritchard** 3
chsd ldr, disp 8-11th, ev ch til onepcd frm 3 out
427 Ru Valentino *prom, ev ch 12th, wknd 3 out*........... 4
Bumptious Boy *cls up til outpcd apr 12th, p.u. 14th* ... pu
Greek Chime (Ire) *blnd 1st, jmpd dtckly in rear, t.o. & ref 13th* .... ref
6 ran. 1½l, 10l, 1½l. Time 6m 12.00s. SP Evens.
Miss P Morris (Croome & West Warwickshire).

687 - Confined (12st)

664 **KORBELL (IRE) 5a 6ex...................A Crow** 1
(fav) chsd ldr 8-14th, hrd rdn 3 out, ld last, gamely
426 **Docter Mac 5a ....J Bates** 2
blnd 1st, ld nxt, clr 6th, hdd apr last, no ext flat
Carbery Arctic ....Miss P Gundry 3
in tch, outpcd 13th, 5th 2 out, ran on well flat
426 Mitchells Best *rear, prog 12th, chsd ldr & ev ch 15th, wknd 2 out* 4
425 Hackett's Farm 3ex *ld 1st, sn hdd, outpcd 13th, kpt on agn frm 2 out* 5
163 Soldiers Duty (USA) *w.w. prog & in tch 10th, wknd 13th, p.u. 2 out* .... pu
Master Dancer 3ex *blnd & rmndrs 4th, lost tch 12th, p.u. 3 out* .... pu
427 Corrianne 5a (h) *wth ldr 4th til lost plc 8th, last frm 10th, p.u. 3 out* .... pu

638 Ragtime Cowboy Joe *cls up, rdn 10th, outpcd nxt, p.u. 14th* .... pu
664 Back The Road (Ire) *w.w. prog to 4th & blnd 12th, not rcvr, p.u. aft nxt* .... pu
10 ran. 1½l, 8l, ½l, 3l. Time 6m 12.00s. SP 6-4.
K J Mitchell (North Shropshire).

688 - Maiden Div I (12st)

356 **FOREST FOUNTAIN (IRE) 7a ....A Dalton** 1
chsd ldrs going wll, prog to ld 2 out, sn clr, comf
542 **Most Rich (Ire) ....M Jackson** 2
prom, 4th & rdn 4 out, kpt on, no ch wth wnr
Bucks Flea 5a ....R Burton 3
ld 2nd-11th, ev ch & rdn 3 out, onepcd
438 Gawcott Wood 5a *cls up, ld 12th-3 out, wknd* 4
218 I Blame Theparents 5a *chsd ldrs, ev ch 12th, outpcd apr 15th* 5
431 Sonny's Song *alwys rear, some late prog, nvr dang* 6
Lord Rattle (Ire) *mid-div, 6th & outpcd apr 12th, no ch aft* 7
Meadow Cottage *f 1st* .... f
Nordross 5a 1ex *mstks, bhnd 11th, t.o. & p.u. 3 out* .... pu
430 Close Control (Ire) *alwys rear, last at 12th, p.u. 4 out* .... pu
218 Mr Paddy Bell *mid-div, blnd 4th, strggling whn u.r. 11th* .... ur
Silver Fig 5a *(fav) mounted on course, w.w. mid-div, lsot tch 11th, p.u. 13th* .... pu
Miss Madge 5a *s.v.s. jmpd badly, t.o. til p.u. 9th* .... pu
540 Remalone 5a (bl) *t.o. 8th, last whn p.u. 11th* .... pu
Smart Song 7a *mstk 3rd, in tch to 11th, p.u. apr 4 out* .... pu
Another Chancer 7a *s.v.s. bhnd, some prog 9th, t.o. & p.u. 3 out* .... pu
End Of The Run 7a *twrds rear, f 9th* .... f
17 ran. 5l, 6l, ½l, 12l, 6l, 1l. Time 6m 15.00s. SP 6-1.
J D Callow (Albrighton Woodland).
One fence omitted, 17 jumps.

689 - Maiden Div II (12st)

MAGGIES FELLOW (IRE) ....G Barfoot-Saunt 1
in tch, disp 12th, ld 3 out, clr nxt, rdn out
439 **Hehas ....C Wadland** 2
rear of main grp, prog to 5th 4 out, styd on, nvr nrr
665 **Kiltrose Lad ....Julian Pritchard** 3
ld 2nd-nxt, blnd 10th, outpcd 14th, kpt on frm 2 out
269 Arctic Line *disp 4th, lft in ld 11th, hdd & wknd rpdly apr 3 out* 4
432 Mis-E-Fishant 5a *prom to 10th, sn wknd, t.o.* 5
Plateman *u.r. 2nd* .... ur
144 Blucanoo 5a *prom, disp 3rd whn blnd 12th, sn wknd, ref & u.r. 15th* .... ref
352 Shadowgraff 5a *(fav) mid-div til f 5th* .... f
Heather Wood 5a *sn bhnd, t.o. 8th, p.u. 14th* .... pu
569 Baronburn 5a *chsd ldrs, ev ch 3 out, blnd nxt, 2nd & btn whn f last* .... f
428 Baptist John (Ire) *disp 3rd, blnd nxt, f 11th* .... f
Philelwyn (Ire) 7a *in tch, blnd 9th & 10th, last frm nxt, p.u. 15th* .... pu
590 Bucksum (Ire) 7a *schoold in rear til p.u. 11th* .... pu
Caprice de Cotte (Fr) *schoold rear, p.u. 11th* .... pu
Sutton Lighter *plld hrd, chsd ldr to 3rd, wknd 6th, t.o. & p.u. 12th* .... pu
15 ran. 4l, 5l, 15l, 1 fence. Time 6m 21.00s. SP 12-1.
John Eaton (Ledbury).
S.P.

MONMOUTHSHIRE
Llanvapley
Saturday March 30th
GOOD TO SOFT

690 - Members (12st)

HATTERILL RIDGE ....C Richards 1
cls up in last til disp 3 out, ld nxt, clr last
358 **Major Bert (Ire) ....H Wheeler** 2
(fav) alwys cls up, ld 11th, jnd 3 out, outpcd frm nxt
Paper Fair 5a 5ex *ld to 11th, cls up til wknd rpdly 15th, p.u. nxt* .... pu
218 Tennessee Cruiser 4ex *cls up, wknd 10th, t.o. 13th, p.u. 3 out* .... pu
4 ran. 10l. Time 7m 35.00s. SP 7-1.
A C James (Monmouthshire).

691 - Confined (12st)

MINERS FORTUNE (IRE) ....B Potts 1
prom, 2nd at 8th, ld 13th, made rest, hit 2 out, ran on flat
601 **Push Along ....D Stephens** 2
cls up, 3rd at 13th, chsd wnr 15th, 5l dwn 3 out, just hld
Pat Cullen 3ex ....S Blackwell 3
3rd/4th til wknd frm 14th
578 Barn Pool *alwys rear, lft 4th by dfctns* 4
601 Noisy Welcome (bl) *alwys last, fin own time* 5
505 Bronze Effigy (bl) *mid-div, no prog frm 13th, btn 4th whn ref last* .... ref
384 Enchanted Man *rear whn p.u. 9th* .... pu
506 Silks Domino *5th/6th to hlfwy, lost plc & p.u. 15th* .... pu
Co-Tack *rear, lost tch 8th, p.u. 10th* .... pu
382 Astley Jack 6ex *u.r. 1st* .... ur
The Dark Watch *last pair, t.o. & p.u. 15th* .... pu
506 Mo's Chorister *mid-div, wknd 12th, p.u. 15th* .... pu
605 Old Steine *rear, went 6th at 13th, wknd rpdly, p.u. 3 out* .... pu
355 Vatacan Bank *rear, no ch frm 10th, p.u. 15th* .... pu
548 Warren Boy *(fav) ld to 13th, chsd wnr til wknd rpdly 15th, p.u. nxt* .... pu
15 ran. 1l, dist, 15l, dist. Time 7m 5.00s. SP 5-1.
J A C Edwards (South Hereford).

692 - Open (12st)

350 **BETTER FUTURE (IRE) ....B Potts** 1
(fav) rear, prog to 2nd at 14th, 2l down last, qcknd to ld flat
485 **Lislary Lad ....M Daly** 2
rear, prog to ld 11th, 2l up last, hdd & no ext nr fin
384 The Wooden Hut *ld 3-9th, wknd rpdly, t.o. 13th, ref last* .... ref
142 Virginia's Bay *alwys rear, lost tch 10th, p.u. 15th* .... pu
602 Provence 7ex (bl) *3rd/4th til clr 3rd frm 14th, 15l down whn u.r. nxt* .... ur
547 Bell Glass (Fr) 7ex *cls up, ld 9-11th, wknd rpdly, p.u. 13th* .... pu
6 ran. 1l. Time 7m 8.00s. SP 6-4.
J A C Edwards (Berkeley).

693 - Ladies

603 **HANDSOME HARVEY 7ex ....Miss P Jones** 1
(fav) made all, qcknd flat
208 **Mendip Music ....Miss E Crawford** 2
alwys 2nd, strng chal 15th, just hld
536 **Out The Door (Ire) 5ex ....Miss S Baxter** 3
mostly 3rd, clsd 3 out, unable qckn frm nxt
545 Construction King *rear, t.o. 13th, p.u. 3 out* .... pu
603 Light The Wick *alwys last, t.o. 12th, p.u. 15th* .... pu
388 Grey Watch 5a *mostly 4th/5th, lost plc hlfwy, p.u. 3 out* .... pu
6 ran. ¾l, 10l. Time 7m 9.00s. SP 4-7.
E L Harries (Pembrokeshire).

694 - Restricted Div I (12st)

600 **POLLY PRINGLE 5a ....A Price** 1
(fav) 7/2-7/4, cls up 2nd at 11th, lft in ld 13th, sn clr, easily
606 **Boddington Hill 5a ....I Johnson** 2
mid-div, prog to 3rd at 12th, lft 2nd aft nxt, not rch wnr
504 **Bay Leader 5a ....Miss E Tamplin** 3
alwys last, styd on own pace
598 Cossack Strike (Ire) *lost tch 6th, p.u. 10th* .... pu
549 Penny Lark *4th at 7th, wknd rpdly & p.u. 11th* .... pu
600 Linantic *1/1-5/2, ld to 5th, 2nd til p.u. aft 13th, lame* .... pu
552 Toucher (Ire) *mid-div, 5th at 11th, wknd aft, p.u. 3 out* .... pu
358 Greenhill Lady 5a *ld 6th til f 13th* .... f

391 Miss Clare 5a *rear, blnd 7th, lost tch 11th, p.u. 3 out* .. pu
9 ran. 8l, dist. Time 7m 7.00s. SP 7-4.
Mrs C E Goldsworthy (Tredegar Farmers).

695 - Restricted Div II (12st)

387 **JUST MARMALADE** ....**J Tudor** 1
(fav) hld up,prog 11th,ld & lft clr 14th,hdd 3 out,lft clr 2 out
388 **Horn Player (USA)** ....**M P Jones** 2
cls up, 3rd & outpcd 15th, styd on
509 **Icecapade (Bel)** ....**S Blackwell** 3
ld 9-12th, grad lost tch
607 Final Option (Ire) *alwys rear, fin own time* 4
Cistolena 5a *rear, no ch whn p.u. 10th* .... pu
Bob-Cam *t.o. 5th, p.u. 3 out* .... pu
548 Mylordmayor *mid-div, prog to 2nd 11th, ld nxt til f 13th* .... f
Moonlight Shift *alwys rear, p.u. 3 out* .... pu
388 Flaxridge *ld 7-8th, cls 4th whn b.d. 13th* .... bd
Strong Secret *alwys rear, p.u. 11th* .... pu
607 Lazzaretto *alwys last pair, p.u. 10th* .... pu
600 Cottage Raider (Ire) *rear, prog to chal 14th, sn ld, wknd & jnd whn f 2 out* .... f
600 Dromin Chat (Ire) *ld to 6th, wknd rpdly, p.u. 9th* .... pu
13 ran. 4l, 25l, dist. Time 7m 11.00s. SP 5-2.
J Tudor (Llangeinor).

696 - Maiden (5-7yo) Div I (12st)

552 **TELEPHONE** ....**P Hamer** 1
hld up, mod 6th at 15th, prog nxt, qcknd to ld flat
148 **Spikeie Rose 5a** ....**J Jukes** 2
ld, 3l clr 2 out, wknd last, hdd flat
390 **Mister Jay Day** ....**A Price** 3
alwys cls up, 3rd 13th, chsd ldr 3 out, ev ch last, not qckn
551 Sister Lark 5a (v) *(Jt fav) alwys prom, 2nd 13th-3 out, ev ch last, wknd, tired* 4
389 Capture The Magic (Ire) 5a *alwys rear, dist 5th whn p.u. flat* .... pu
390 Cruise Ann 5a *(Jt fav) 3rd at 11th, 5th 13th, wknd & p.u. 3 out* .... pu
509 Its A Doddle 5a *mid-div, no prog frm hlfwy, p.u. 15th* pu
353 Native Missile 5a *2nd to 13th, wknd rpdly, p.u. 3 out* .. pu
Sweet Blue 5a *rear, wkng whn ref 12th* .... ref
388 Queen's Equa 5a *alwys rear, p.u. 11th* .... pu
510 Bonus Number (Ire) *mid-div whn u.r. 6th* .... ur
Irish Thinker 7a *mid-div, losing tch whn p.u. 12th* ..... pu
Balinger Boy *rear, ref 12th* .... ref
13 ran. 2l, 8l, 4l. Time 7m 21.00s. SP 7-2.
R J Hamer (Llangeinor).

697 - Maiden (5-7yo) Div II (12st)

598 **TWILIGHT TOM** ....**A Price** 1
2nd/3rd til disp 15th, ld 2 out, ran on well
354 **Bel Lane 5a** ....**D S Jones** 2
(fav) alwys prom, clsd 15th, disp to 2 out, just outpcd
213 **Hennerwood Oak 5a** ....**M P Jones** 3
ld & clr to 14th, wknd & hdd nxt, scrambld over last
548 Sheer Power (Ire) *4th at 7th, wkng whn p.u. 14th* ...... pu
607 Pharrago (Ire) *mid-div whn u.r. 6th* .... ur
607 Nutsil 5a *last trio, t.o. & p.u. 10th* .... pu
510 Lets Go Polly 5a *prom to 14th, wknd & p.u. nxt* ...... pu
390 Scottishhighlander *2nd at 9th, wknd, 5th whn u.r. 13th* .... ur
389 Brown Bala 5a *last trio, t.o. & p.u. 10th* .... pu
391 Lady Medusa (Ire) 7a *hld up, 4th at 14th, p.u. 3 out* ... pu
Nadanny (Ire) *last trio, t.o. & p.u. 10th* .... pu
11 ran. 2½l, dist. Time 7m 10.00s. SP 9-4.
L J Williams (Curre).
P.H/J.C.

MORPETH
Tranwell
Saturday March 30th
GOOD TO SOFT

698 - Members

400 **MAY RUN** ....**Mrs V Jackson** 1
(fav) trckd ldrs, prog 15th, ld 2 out, ran on strngly
Park Slave ....**P Craggs** 2
ld, jnd 15th, hdd & onpcd und pres 2 out
Newbrano 5a (bl) ....**I Carmichael** 3
4th at 10th, nvr nrr
The Marching Grey *last at 8th, t.o. 10th* 4
399 Teatime Girl 5a *prom, disp 15th, cls up 2 out, btn whn f last* .... f
5 ran. 15l, 20l. Time 6m 35.00s. SP 11-10.
W R Middleton (Morpeth).

699 - Confined (12st)

306 **FERN LEADER (IRE)** ....**N Wilson** 1
(fav) alwys prom, ld 10th, hrd rdn last, hld on flat
Free Transfer (Ire) ....**A Robson** 2
mid-div, prog 14th, chal 2 out, came again nr fin
317 **Master Mischief 2ow** ....**J Walton** 3
mid-div, prog 9th, cls up 15th, rdn & wknd 2 out
399 Neville *last early, prog hlfwy, cls up 4 out, wknd aft nxt* 4
86 Its The Bidder (Ire) (bl) *bhnd 8th, prog to chs ldrs 14th, no ext frm 3 out* 5
610 Dawn Coyote (USA) (bl) *not fluent, 4th at 12th, sn outpcd* 6
317 Old Comrades *sn rear, t.o. & p.u. 14th* .... pu
303 Languedoc 4ow *not fluent, ld 2nd til f 10th* .... ur
8 ran. 1l, 15l, 15l. Time 6m 26.00s. SP 4-5.
W R Ward (South Durham).

700 - Ladies

499 **READY STEADY 7ex** ....**Miss P Robson** 1
(fav) ld 2nd, lft clr 15th, unchal
501 **Mandys Special 5a** ....**Mrs M Robinson** 2
not fluent, t.o. frm 14th, lft poor 2nd nxt
611 Royal Fife 5a *ptchd & u.r. 1st* .... ur
403 Houselope Beck *chsd wnr 3rd, outpcd whn f 15th* .... f
4 ran. Dist. Time 6m 28.00s. SP 2-9.
Lady Temple (West Percy).

701 - Open

587 **EQUINOCTIAL** ....**N Wilson** 1
prom,ld 4-9th,chsd ldr 15th,hrd rdn to ld apr last,drvn out
401 **Fast Study** ....**S Robinson** 2
(fav) prog to disp 10th, ld 14th til hdd apr last, no ext flat
317 **The Mosses** ....**D Wood** 3
prog 12th, cls up 3 out, ev ch last, no ext flat
486 Tartan Tornado *wll bhnd, prog 13th, outpcd frm nxt, ran on agn 2 out,no ext* 4
401 Music Minstrel (bl) *prom early, bhnd frm 11th* 5
410 Elegant Guest *alwys rear, last at 9th, p.u. 13th* ...... pu
183 Speech *mstks 6th, ld 2nd-10th, disp til wknd 14th, p.u. 2 out* .... pu
612 Yenoora (Ire) *prom to 8th, bhnd whn f 10th* .... f
8 ran. 6l, 1½l, 1l. Time 6m 30.00s. SP 7-2.
John Sisterson (Braes Of Derwent).

702 - P P O R A (12st)

611 **WIGTOWN BAY** ....**Miss N Stirling** 1+
disp to 13th, chal und pres last, jnd ldr fin
242 **STILLTODO 5a** ....**N Wilson** 1+
(fav) disp til ld 13th, hrd rdn last, jnd fin
609 **Gay Vixen VI 5a** ....**T Scott** 3
alwys last, outpcd frm 12th
3 ran. Dd-ht, dist. Time 6m 31.00s.
W R Wilson/ Mrs P Stirling (Zetland/ Fife).
S.P's. Wigtown Bay, 5/2. Stilltodo, 11/10.

703 - Restricted

404 **TODCRAG** ....**T Scott** 1
(fav) not alwys fluent, ld 2nd, made rest, comf

611 **Royal Surprise....................Miss P Robson** 2
chsd wnr 4th, ev ch 3 out, wnd apr last
501 **Miss Cullane (Ire) 5a....................C Storey** 3
mid-div, rmndrs 9th, ran in sntchs, outpcd 3 out
319 Sarona Smith 5a *prom til mstk 12th, no dang aft* 4
172 Bonnie Scallywag 5a *alwys bhnd, p.u. 3 out* .... pu
Heathfield (USA) 1ow *s.s. last frm 9th, f 14th*......... f
Say Milady 5a *mid-div, prog 13th, wknd rpdly 3 out, p.u. nxt*.......... pu
7 ran. 10l, 10l, 1l. Time 6m 26.00s. SP 4-5.
Mrs D Scott (Border).

704 - Open Maiden Div I (12st)

613 **ROLY PRIOR...........................A Parker** 1
(fav) trckd ldrs, 2nd frm 13th, lft in ld 15th, ran on well
414 **King Fly.........................Miss S Horner** 2
bhnd to hlfwy, gd prog 14th, kpt on, no ext apr last
321 **Warkswoodman..................Mrs H Dickson** 3
bhnd, prog 10th, styd on frm 3 out, not rch ldrs
330 Raike It In 5a *mid-div whn mstk 13th, no dang aft*. . 4
404 The Raskins 5a *prom, 4th at 13th, outpcd frm nxt*.... 5
Amanda Bay *prom early, btn whn blnd 14th, p.u. nxt*.. pu
Strong Chance *nvr rchd ldrs, bhnd frm 10th, p.u. 3 out*........ pu
407 Doc Spot *disp 5th, styd prom til wknd 15th, p.u. 2 out* pu
Corsage 7a 7ow *mstk 6th, wll bhnd whn p.u. 3 out* ... pu
323 Lauras Teeara (Ire) 5a *mid-div til mstk 7th, f 10th*.... f
114 Little Flo 5a *nvr nr ldrs, wll bhnd whn p.u. 2 out*...... pu
The Camair Flyer (Ire) *ld 2-4th, disp nxt, ld 11th til f 15th*........ f
322 Alianne 5a *last whn mstks 1st & 2nd, p.u. nxt* .... pu
123 The Golly Ollybird 21ow *last frm 3rd, t.o. til p.u. aft 13th*........ pu
321 Sharpe Exit 1ow *t.o. & p.u. 14th*........ pu
405 Slieve Na Bar (Ire) *prom, ld 4th til jnd & f 10th*........ f
16 ran. 3l, 6l, 3l. Time 6m 32.00s. SP 4-5.
Ian Hamilton (Tynedale).

705 - Open Maiden Div II (12st)

319 **ENSIGN EWART (IRE)...................C Storey** 1
mid-div, prog 14th, disp nxt, ld 2 out, ran on well
Snapper 7a............................S Love 2
mstk 4th, trckd ldrs frm 13th, ev ch 2 out, not pace of wnr
406 **Kings Token 2ow.......................J Walton** 3
(fav) prom, disp 12th, hrd rdn 3 out, hdd nxt, no ext apr last
322 Wassl's Nanny (Ire) 5a *bhnd, prog 14th, disp nxt til bmpd 3 out, not rcvr* 4
415 Jamarsam (Ire) *ld 2-5th, prom til mstk 12th, no dang aft* 5
Tolmin *sn mid-div, wll bhnd frm 13th*........ 6
323 Starlin Sam *mstks, last frm 3rd, nvr dang* 7
Ruecastle *cls up, ld 8-12th, lost plc 14th, p.u. 2 out* ... pu
414 Malakie (Ire) *cls up frm 5th, disp 12th til f 14th*........ f
9 ran. 5l, 2½l, 6l. Time 6m 36.00s. SP 7-2.
Major M Sample (Collge Valley).
D.G.

TEDWORTH
Barbury Castle
Saturday March 30th
GOOD

706 - Members

523 **TOUCH OF WINTER.....................T Lacey** 1
(fav) n.j.w. hld up, prog 10th, ld 3 out, sn clr, easily
380 **Arnold's Choice (bl) ....Miss G Young** 2
handy, ld 10th-3 out, outpcd aft
Madiyan (USA) ....J Hankinson 3
in tch to 14th, onepcd frm nxt
380 See You There *cls up to 10th, lost tch & outpcd frm 13th*........ 4
Unscrupulous Gent *ld to 9th, grad wknd frm nxt, t.o. 3 out*........ 5
379 Todds Hall (Ire) *sn bhnd, t.o. 10th*........ 6
381 Swing Free *mid-div til blnd & u.r. 13th* .... ur
7 ran. 15l, 3l, dist, 5l, dist. Time 6m 37.00s. SP 4-6.
M W Kwiatkowski (Tedworth).

707 - Monterey Restricted (12st)

557 **BET WITH BAKER (IRE)...........Miss P Curling** 1
(fav) 3s-9/4, hld up, prog 10th, ld 4 out, ran on frm 2 out
525 **Plan-A (Ire) ....R Nuttall** 2
w.w. prog 13th, ev ch 2 out, wknd, rallied wll flat
377 **Hizal ....A Harvey** 3
mid-div, went 3rd 2 out, not trble 1st pair
526 Misty (NZ) *n.j.w. mid-div, cls 4th 4 out, wknd nxt* 4
496 Alias Silver *alwys mid-div, nvr on terms with ldrs*..... 5
375 Stalbridge Bill *bhnd, some prog frm 12th, sn outpcd* .. 6
652 Time Module *rear whn u.r. 7th*........ ur
428 Howley Lad *mid-div whn u.r. 2nd*........ ur
600 Amadeo (bl) *cls up whn u.r. 3rd*........ ur
Everso Irish *sn bhnd, t.o. & p.u. 4 out*........ pu
262 Mary Borough 5a *alwys mid-div, t.o. & p.u. 3 out*..... pu
519 Game Fair *alwys rear, t.o. & p.u. 4 out*........ pu
Sula Pride *sn rear, t.o. 5th, p.u. 3 out*........ pu
477 Balance *ld/disp til blnd 4 out, wkng whn u.r. nxt*...... ur
338 Making Time 5a *ld/disp to 12th, wknd nxt, t.o. & p.u. 2 out*........ pu
627 Waipiro *rear, outpcd frm 10th, t.o. & p.u. 3 out* .... pu
448 Lake Mariner 5a *alwys mid-div, no ch whn p.u. 2 out* pu
525 Rayman (Ire) *prom to 4 out, wkng whn f nxt*........ f
18 ran. ½l, 8l, 6l, 5l, 6l. Time 6m 35.80s. SP 9-4.
George W Baker (Cattistock).

708 - Ladies

379 **INTERPRETATION (NZ) ....Miss R Francis** 1
in tch, 2nd frm 9th, strng chal apr last, ld nr fin
529 **Flame O'Frensi 5a ....Miss J Cumings** 2
j.w. ld til hdd final 50 yrds
381 **Sohail (USA).........................Miss M Hill** 3
in tch, effrt 13th, ev ch 3 out, onepcd aft
266 Rip The Calico (Ire) 5a *sn bhnd, some prog frm 13th, not trbl 1st 3*........ 4
Track Angel 5a *cls up to 8th, wknd nxt, t.o. & p.u. 11th, lame*........ pu
481 Pactolus (USA) *bhnd, t.o. 11th, p.u. 3 out*........ pu
593 Billhead *cls up til blnd & u.r. 11th*........ ur
443 Kiltonga *sn rear, t.o. & p.u. 9th*........ pu
561 Beyond Our Reach *(fav) cls 3rd whn f 9th*........ f
273 Pejawi 5a *alwys rear, t.o. & p.u. last*........ pu
10 ran. 2l, 6l, 25l. Time 6m 31.00s. SP 14-1.
Nick Viney (Dulverton (West)).

709 - Open (12st)

639 **ROYLE SPEEDMASTER ....A Harvey** 1
hld up, prog 10th, ld 12th, ran on well frm 3 out
Trifast Lad.............................P Hacking 2
(fav) 7/2-6/4, in tch, chsd wnr 13th, chal 2 out, alwys hld aft
523 **Indian Knight ....C Vigors** 3
hld up, prog 12th, ev ch 3 out, outpcd nxt
355 Getaway Blake *sttld mid-div, prog 12th, ev ch 3 out, not qckn aft*........ 4
524 Clobracken Lad *alwys mid-div, no ch frm 3 out* 5
559 Colcombe Castle (bl) *rear, nvr on terms frm 12th, outpcd*........ 6
654 Fred Splendid *ld 4-6th, wknd nxt, t.o. 13th*........ 7
644 Bill Of Rights *ld to 4th, ld agn 7-11th, grad wknd aft*... 8
654 Popeswood 4ex *mid-div, no ch frm 13th, t.o. & p.u. last*........ pu
Bloxham *sn bhnd, t.o. & p.u. 11th*........ pu
528 Grey Sonata 5a *alwys bhnd, t.o. & p.u. 2 out*........ pu
524 Steel Dance *alwys mid-div, nvr on terms, t.o. & p.u. 2 out*........ pu
Walkonthemoon 5a *sn rear, t.o. & p.u. 11th*........ pu
Russell Rover *sn rear, t.o. & p.u. 11th*........ pu
537 Shortcastle *cls up to 9th, lost tch 11th, t.o. & u.r. 13th* ur
15 ran. 8l, 3l, 2l, 1l, 6l, 20l, 25l. Time 6m 33.00s. SP 33-1.
Miss S J Cutcliffe (V W H).

710 - Confined (12st)

UP AND COMING ....**Miss M Bentham** 1
j.w. ld 6th, went clr frm 2 out
524 **Desert Waltz (Ire) 3ex** ....**Miss P Curling** 2
(fav) hld up, prog 12th, chsd ldr aft, outpcd frm 2 out
638 **Kites Hardwicke** ....**Mrs C Behrens** 3
ld to 2nd, lost tch 12th, outpcd aft
380 Bantel Buccaneer *ld 3-6th, wknd, lost tch 13th, t.o. & p.u. 4 out* .... pu
601 Tango Tom *cls up to 12th, lost tch 4 out, p.u. last* ..... pu
376 Roaming Shadow *alwys bhnd, t.o. & p.u. 4 out* .... pu
6 ran. 8l, dist. Time 6m 34.00s. SP 25-1.
Miss M C Bentham (Vine & Craven).

711 - Open Maiden Div I (12st)

576 **BITOFAMIXUP (IRE) 7a**...............**P Hacking** 1
(fav) j.w. trckd ldrs, ld 4 out, sn clr, easily
375 **Favlient 5a**..............................**A Martin** 2
ld to 4 out, outpcd frm nxt
375 **Is She Quick 5a**..........................**J Price** 3
in tch to 12th, outpcd aft
558 Just Silver (bl) *cls up til blnd 10th, p.u. bef nxt*........ pu
Nearly Five Too 5a *f 2nd* .... f
Uncle Bruce *f 1st*.......... f
Crosswell Star (Ire) 7a *n.j.w. rear til f 7th* .... f
Mine's A Gin (Ire) 7a *schoold in rear til p.u. 12th*...... pu
8 ran. Dist, dist. Time 6m 39.00s. SP 4-6.
Mike Roberts (East Sussex & Romney Marsh).

712 - Open Maiden Div II (12st)

432 **RAVENSDALE LAD** ....**R Wakeham** 1
in tch, ld 8th, clr 4 out, easily
522 **Vulgan Prince** ....**A Greig** 2
(fav) handy, chsd wnr 11th, outpcd frm 4 out
341 **Lochinvar Lord (bl)** ....**D Renney** 3
ld to 5th, wknd, lost tch 12th, outpcd aft
520 Pinber 5a *alwys mid-div, no ch whn p.u. 14th* .... pu
534 Heather Boy *cls 3rd whn f 2nd*.......... f
534 Melling 7a *handy, ld 6-8th, cls up whn f 10th*.......... f
175 Its Murphy Man *alwys mid-div, no ch whn p.u. 13th*.... pu
Baron Bigfoot *alwys rear, t.o. & p.u. 14th*.......... pu
638 Salmon Poutcher 5a *in tch to 11th, rdn nxt, outpcd & p.u. 14th*.......... pu
439 Spring Sabre *33s-14s, rear, prog 10th, 3rd nxt, wkng whn ran out 4 out*.......... ro
10 ran. Dist, 15l. Time 6m 40.00s. SP 4-1.
Miss S Hogbin (Meynell & South Staffs).

713 - Open Maiden Div III (12st)

522 **PLUMBRIDGE** ....**C Vigors** 1
(fav) hld up, prog 11th, ld 14th, sn clr, easily
341 **Woodland Cutting** ....**J Trice-Rolph** 2
handy, 3rd at 11th, ev ch 4 out, no ext frm 2 out
479 **Juniper Lodge**............................**S Bush** 3
ld/disp to 13th, outpcd frm 4 out
248 Sybillabee 5a *in tch, ev ch 13th, wknd whn f 2 out* .... f
430 Vital Shot 5a *alwys rear, t.o. & p.u. 4 out*.......... pu
69 Itscountryman *alwys mid-div, no ch whn p.u. 4 out* ... pu
376 Gt Hayes Pommard *ld/disp to 12th, lost tch 3 out, tired whn f last*.......... f
Colourful Boy *alwys rear, t.o. 10th, p.u. 4 out* .... pu
202 Bells Wood *8s-5s, sttld mid-div, effrt 12th, no rspns, t.o. & p.u. 2out*.......... pu
375 Horton Country 5a *mid-div, lost tch 12th, p.u. 4 out* ... pu
10 ran. 10l, 20l. Time 6m 36.00s. SP 4-5.
D R Chamings (Vine & Craven).
D.P.

WESTERN
Wadebridge
Saturday March 30th
GOOD TO FIRM

714 - Members (12st)

562 **DARK REFLECTION**...................**D Curnow** 1
(fav) made all, drew clr frm 14th, unchal
557 **Zany Girl 5a (bl)** ....**I Hambly** 2
chsd wnr, lkd reluc, some prog 13th, sn rdn & wknd
555 **Pen-Alisa 5a (bl)** ....**J Young** 3
strgglng in 3rd & reluc thro'out
3 ran. 20l, 25l. Time 6m 21.00s. SP 1-2.
J D Curnow (Western).

715 - Confined (12st)

625 **PRINCE SOLOMAN** ....**W G Turner** 1
handy,lft in ld 12th,tried to p.u. aft 14th,ld nxt,all out
625 **Catch The Cross (bl)** ....**Mrs M Hand** 2
prog 11th,lft 2nd nxt,ld brfly aft 14th,hmpd bnd aft nxt,kpt
Roses In May 5a..................**Miss S Young** 3
mid-div, hmpd & lft 3rd 12th, sn rdn & wknd
626 Whats The Crack *lost tch aft 7th, t.o. whn hmpd 10 & 12th*.......... 4
625 Whats Your Game (bl) *in tch til p.u. 10th, lame* .... pu
281 The Butler *ld til f heavily 12th (ditch)*.......... f
625 Sancreed *raced wd, mid-div, virt c.o. apr 10th & p.u.* pu
623 Walkers Point 3ex *(fav) prom, cls 2nd whn f 10th* ..... f
8 ran. 2l, 25l, 2 fences. Time 6m 16.50s. SP 6-4.
W G Turner (Spooners & West Dartmoor).
Objection to winner by 2nd for bumping - over-ruled.

716 - Ladies

197 **DUCHESS OF TUBBER (IRE) 5a** ...**Miss S Young** 1
prog 12th, cls 3rd 14th, ld 3 out, pshd out, ran on gamely
441 **Seventh Lock**..................**Miss L Blackford** 2
(Co fav) ld 5th til hdd 3 out, rnwd effrt cls home
481 **Greenwine (USA)**.....................**Miss A Lamb** 3
(Co fav) hld up rear, nvr dang, went 3rd 2 out, nrst fin
624 Aristocratic Gold *(Co fav) ld to 5th, prom til lost plc aft 15th, eased flat*.......... 4
624 Jokers Patch *in tch til lost plc steadily frm 13th, t.o. & p.u. 3 out*.......... pu
197 High Degree *last but in tch whn u.r. 5th (ditch)*....... ur
6 ran. 5l, 1l, 5l. Time 6m 7.00s. SP 4-1.
R J S Linne (East Cornwall).

717 - Open (12st)

554 **DEPARTURE 5a** ....**J Creighton** 1
j.w. made all, drew clr aft 15th, easily
444 **Magnolia Man** ....**N Harris** 2
(fav) hld up in tch, effrt & hmpd 15th, unable qckn clsng stgs
626 **Bootscraper 7ex (bl)**.................**W G Turner** 3
trckd ldr, rdn aft 14th, wkng whn mstk nxt, t.o. & blnd last
3 ran. 5l, dist. Time 6m 9.00s. SP 3-1.
W H Whitley (Dart Vale And South Pool Hrrs).

718 - Open Maiden Div I (12st)

446 **MOSSIDE** ....**N Harris** 1
handy,disp 8th-aft 14th,drvn to ld last 50 yrds,just hld on
447 **Dovedon Princess 5a**...............**D Stephens** 2
in tch,cls 4th hlfwy,mstk 14th,4th nxt til strng burst flat
555 **Temporary** ....**S Slade** 3
(fav) lft in ld 5th,ld/disp to aft 14th,styd on onepcd aft
448 Scallykenning *hld up in tch, prog aft 14th, ld 15th-aft last, wknd rpdly* 4
630 Hanukkah 5a *twrds rear, mstk 10th, poor 5th frm 14th* 5
Fire Of Troy 5a *in tch to 8th, lost plc rpdly aft 11th, p.u. nxt*.......... pu
Gamblers Refrain *rear & strgglng frm 7th, t.o. & p.u. 3 out*.......... pu
My Boy Buster *mstk 3rd, bolted clr aft nxt, u.r. 5th (ditch)*.......... ur

446 Tacoment 5a *ld 2nd-4th, disp 7-8th, 5tha t 11th, wknd, p.u. 3 out* .... pu
556 Charlie's Hideaway (Ire) *sn rear, 6th at 16th, p.u. apr last, schooling* .... pu
630 Tinstreamer Johnny 7a *twrds rear whn u.r. 4th* .... ur
11 ran. Nk, ½l, 2½l, 20l. Time 6m 12.00s. SP 5-2.
B W Gillbard (Dulverton (East)).
One fence omitted, 17 jumps.

719 - Open Maiden Div II (12st)

445 **BIG SEAMUS (IRE) .... J Creighton** 1
(fav) hld up in tch, went 2nd 9th, ld 15th, pshd out
555 **Big Reward .... K Crook** 2
slght ld 8th til hdd 15th, 3l 2nd whn mstk 2 out, ran on wll
478 **Glenisla 5a .... S Hornby** 3
keen hold, cls 3rd 12th, mstk 14th, blnd 3 out, mstk last
629 Flying Maria 7a *not fluent, some prog aft 14th, no imp whn pckd 2 out* 4
446 Musbury Castle 5a *mid-div, 5th & no ch 14th* 5
Maverick's Creek (NZ) *raced keenly, jmpd boldy, ld 2nd-apr 8th, p.u. 12th, dsmntd* .... pu
282 Devonshire Lad 7a *hld up rear, not fluent 12th, sn lost tch, p.u. 15th, school* .... pu
7 ran. ½l, 8l, ½l, 12l. Time 6m 32.00s. SP 4-5.
Mrs J M Whitley (Dartmoor).

720 - Restricted (12st)

627 **BALDHU CHANCE .... J Young** 1
jmpd rght,made virt all,drew clr 3 out,hung rght flat,hld on
562 **Mountain Master .... Miss L Blackford** 2
handy, chsd wnr 11th, outpcd 3 out, rallied flat, styd on
Sunwind .... D Heath 3
in tch, cls 4th hlfwy, wknd, lft poor 3rd at 15th
Cornish Ways *sn rear, last frm 7th, t.o.* 4
532 Highway Jim *mid-div whn u.r. 6th* .... ur
556 Robenko (USA) *(fav) rear, steady prog 11th, 3rd 13th, 5l 3rd whn f 15th* .... f
562 Oneovertheight *prom til lost ground 12th, 5th & wkng 14th, p.u. nxt* .... pu
554 Miles More Fun 5a *2nd whn blnd & u.r. 5th (ditch)* .... ur
562 Copper And Chrome (Ire) 5a *sn rear, bhnd til p.u. 15th* .... pu
9 ran. 1l, dist, 8l. Time 6m 4.00s. SP 10-1.
Terry Long (Fourburrow).

721 - Intermediate

63 **RATHMICHAEL (bl) .... A Farrant** 1
ld,sn drvn,hdd brfly 12th,6l clr 3 out,drvn out
472 **Cautious Rebel .... J Creighton** 2
(fav) chsd wnr,not alwys fluent,ld brfly 12th,drvn & no imp,eased
297 **Brother Bill .... Mrs M Hand** 3
alwys outpcd, blnd 6th, t.o.
3 ran. 15l, dist. Time 6m 9.00s. SP 13-8.
P C N Heywood (East Cornwall).
G.T.

BELVOIR
Garthorpe
Sunday March 31st
GOOD

722 - Members

396 **MONARROW (IRE) .... W Tellwright** 1
(fav) ld arp 5th-9th, ld 12th, pshd out flat
326 **Rain Mark .... M Chatterton** 2
ld to apr 5th, ld 11th-12th, rdn & kpt on frm 2 out
Arpal Breeze .... J Henderson 3
alwys last, no ch frm 13th
394 Singing Seal *prom, ld 9-11th, 3rd & btn whn u.r. 14th.* .... ur
4 ran. 2l, 20l. Time 6m 35.00s. SP 4-7.
William Tellwright (Belvoir).

723 - Confined (12st)

436 **STANWICK FARLAP 5a 2ow .... T Marks** 1
in tch, clsd frm 11th, chsd ldr aft 15th, ld last, rdn out
580 **Antrim County .... J Cornwall** 2
prom, ld 7th, hdd last, no ext flat
396 **Tenelord .... S Morris** 3
ld 4-5th, chsd ldr 13th-aft 15th, not qckn 3 out, styd on
490 Glen Oak *rear, 9th hlfwy, styd on frm 15th, no dang, nrst fin* 4
633 Okeetee *chsd ldrs, 7th hlfwy, prog 15th, 6th & btn whn nrly u.r.2out* 5
513 The Big Wheel *mid-div, 8th hlfwy, prog to 4th aft 15th, btn 3 out* 6
436 Chiasso Forte (Ity) *alwys rear, 11th hlfwy, nvr nrr* 7
535 The Difference 3ex *alwys rear, 12th & wll bhnd hlfwy, nvr dang* 8
540 Henry Darling *alwys rear, 10th hlfwy, no prog* 9
515 Ginger Pink *ld 3-4th & 5-7th, 6th whn blnd 9th, sn strg-glng* 10
537 Merlyns Choice *s.s. alwys last grp, t.o. 7th* 11
392 Lad Lane *sn bhnd, 14th & wll bhnd hlfwy, t.o.* 12
634 Write The Music (bl) *alwys bhnd, t.o. 7th, last whn u.r. 15th* .... ur
Arbitrageur *blnd & u.r. 3rd* .... ur
Valatch 3ow *blnd 3rd, sn wll bhnd, t.o. last whn p.u. 9th* .... pu
434 Hostetler *sn bhnd, 15th & t.o. hlfwy, p.u. 3 out* .... pu
393 Aintree Oats 5a *ld to 3rd, wth ldrs aft, 3rd & ev ch whn f 15th* .... f
440 Cleric On Broadway (Ire) 5a *20s-8s, f 2nd* .... f
393 Valtorus (Ire) 3ex *(fav) wth ldrs til mstk 11th, sn drppd out, t.o. & p.u. 3 out* .... pu
19 ran. 2½l, 2l, 15l, ½l, 12l, ½l, 15l, 10l, 3l, 15l. Time 6m 22.00s. SP 10-1.
T F G Marks (Fitzwilliam).

724 - Ladies

394 **GENERAL HIGHWAY .... Mrs J Dawson** 1
ld to 3rd, trckd ldr aft, ld 2 out, rdn out nr fin
513 **Zam Bee .... Miss S Bell** 2
(fav) s.s. rcvrd to ld 3rd, hdd 2 out, mstk last, rallied flat
536 **Ridwan .... Miss S Bonser** 3
jmpd slwly, lost tch ldng pair 8th, t.o.
Sea Clipper (Ire) *s.s. alwys last, t.o. 11th, p.u. 3 out* .... pu
434 Mr Rigsby (Ire) *f 2nd, dead* .... f
5 ran. 2l, dist. Time 6m 21.00s. SP 5-4.
C D Dawson (Brocklesby).
One fence (10/18) omitted, 16 jumps.

725 - Open (12st)

515 **CELTIC KING .... K Needham** 1
trckd ldrs, prog 14th, ld last, rdn out flat
634 **Golden Moss 4ex .... Capt S Robinson** 2
mstk 3rd, prssd ldr, ld 11th, hdd last, unable qckn flat
395 **Raise An Argument .... J Docker** 3
(fav) wth ldr, ld 5-11th, outpcd 15th, rallied 2 out, no ext last
515 Glitzy Lady (Ire) 5a *cls up, prssd ldr 13th til aft 3 out, onepcd* 4
The Dancing Parson 5a *bhnd, lost tch hlfwy, ran on 14th, 5th 3 out, no more prog* 5
395 Trusty Friend *in tch in rear, nrly u.r. 7th, outpcd 14th, onepcd aft* 6
395 Rehab Venture *in tch in mid-div to 13th, sn strgglng, t.o.* 7
395 Padrigal 5a *ld to 5th, wknd rpdly 12th, t.o.* 8
490 Decent Gold *nvr going wll, alwys last, t.o. & p.u. 9th* .... pu
9 ran. 1½l, 4l, 3l, 5l, 6l, 25l, 30l. Time 6m 22.80s. SP 4-1.
John E Needham (Bilsdale).

726 - Restricted (12st)

439 **MR BRANIGAN (IRE) .... T Marks** 1

w.w. prog 8th, ld 15th, qcknd clr apr last, imprssv
182 **Fresh Ice (Ire) .... S R Andrews** 2
prom, ld 11-15th, outpcd 3 out, kpt on flat
396 **Ballyvoyle Bay 5a (bl) .... J Docker** 3
alwys prom, chal & ev ch 2 out, brshd aside apr last
540 Forever Freddy *wll bhnd, 11th hlfwy, styd on frm 15th, nrst fin* 4
539 Dilly's Last 5a *rear, prog to 7th hlfwy, rchd 4th 3 out, sn btn* 5
339 Hill Fort (Ire) *bhnd, 12th & rdn hlfwy, kpt on frm 15th, no dang* 6
635 Beckford *mid-div, 8th hlfwy, effrt 14th, 5th 3 out, no prog aft* 7
539 Easy Life (Ire) *handy to 12th, sn outpcd & btn* 8
Damers Treasure *prom to 6th,bhnd & rdn 10th,effrt to mid-div 13th,sn btn* 9
Full Song 5a *hld up last trio, nvr put in race* 10
328 Clone (Ire) *(fav) 4s-5/2,n.j.w. nvr gong well, effrt 11th, sn btn, no ch 15th* 11
Crawn Hawk *prom til f 12th* .... f
633 Rallye Stripe *sn ld, hdd 11th, stppd to nil, p.u. 3 out* ... pu
Merlins Girl 5a *f 1st* .... f
636 Shireoak's Flyer *s.s. last til u.r. 3rd* .... ur
329 Ocean Sovereign *alwys bhnd, t.o. & p.u. 15th* .... pu
16 ran. 15l, ½l, 8l, 6l, 1l, 1l, 8l, 8l, 8l, 4l. Time 6m 28.30s. SP 3-1.
G T H Bailey (Pytchley).

727 - Open Maiden (5-7yo) (12st)

397 **NEEDWOOD NEPTUNE .... A Sansome** 1
(fav) w.w. in rear,prog 11th,ld 2 out,clr last,rdn & all out fin
540 **Paradise Row (Ire) .... M Chatterton** 2
chsd ldr til apr 3 out, styd on to tk 2nd agn flat
635 **Dry Hill Lad 7a .... N Kent** 3
sttld last,prog frm 12th, ran on frm 2 out, nrst fin,improve
361 Chacer's Imp *jmpd lft, ld til hng lft & hdd 2 out, rdn & wknd last* 4
424 Regal Bay *sttld rear, prog to 5th aft 15th, kpt on one-pcd, improve* 5
61 Reedfinch *lost plc 7th, wll bhnd frm 13th, t.o. & p.u. 3 out* .... pu
541 Bucklelone 5a *in tch in rear to 11th, wll bhnd 13th, t.o. & p.u. 3 out* .... pu
440 Supreme Dream (Ire) 5a *chsd ldrs til u.r. aft 8th* ...... ur
182 Derring Knight *chsd ldrs, rdn 10th, sn lost tch, ref 14th* .... ref
Dark Rhytham *prom to 13th, sn lost plc, t.o. & p.u. 3 out* .... pu
542 Irish Genius (Ire) *in tch til wknd rpdly 11th, p.u. 14th* ... pu
542 Dante's Pride (Ire) *prom til wknd rpdly 12th, p.u. nxt* .. pu
12 ran. 5l, 2l, 1½l, 8l. Time 6m 29.10s. SP 5-4.
P A Bennett (Atherstone).
J.N.

CATTISTOCK
Little Windsor
Sunday March 31st
GOOD TO SOFT

728 - Members (12st)

465 **AVRIL SHOWERS 5a 7ex .... R Atkinson** 1
(fav) in tch, hdwy to 2nd 14th, efft to disp last, sn clr
523 **On His Own .... Miss W Southcombe** 2
tried to make all, j.w., 5l clr 2 out, cght last, wknd rpdly
649 **Captain Dimitris .... Miss M Coombe** 3
prom to 11th, sn outpcd, kpt on onepcd frm 3 out
658 Langton Parmill 7ex *mid-div, efft 3 out, no ch ldrs* 4
381 Archie's Nephew 7ex (bl) *rmndr 11th, lost plc steadd frm 12th* 5
656 Lisahane Lad 7ex *lost tch frm 14th, t.o.* 6
Handy Spider 5a 2ow *rear, no ch whn blndrd 3 out, t.o. p.u. 2 out* .... pu
7 ran. 6l, 10l, 1l, 12l, 10l. Time 6m 46.00s. SP 6-4.
Mrs R Atkinson (Cattistock).

729 - Restricted (12st)

478 **APPLE JOHN .... P Henley** 1
ld & sn clr,wll clr til hdd3 out,ld agn aft 2 out,ran on wll
471 **Bengers Moor 7a .... Miss P Curling** 2
(fav) hld up,hdwy 11th,ld 3 out,hdd & wknd qckly 2 out,eased runin
646 **Ive Called Time .... T Greed** 3
5th 12th, not rchd ldrs whn 3rd apr last
520 Master Mario *hdwy to 3rd 12th, onepcd frm 3 out, blndrd last* 4
656 Balmoral Boy (NZ) *midfld, 6th 15th, no prog* 5
653 Final Express 5a 3ow *mid-div, 6th & pshd alng 12th, nvr dang* 6
532 Great Impostor (bl) *mstk 4th, 8th 12th, nvr near* 7
532 Hazel Park *prom til lost plc 8th, bhnd whn hit 14th, fin tired* 8
Sullivans Choice *prom til rddn aft 12th, blndrd 13th, p.u. & destroyed* .... pu
558 Here's Mary 5a *bhnd til p.u. apr 11th* .... pu
644 Between You And Me *rear til p.u. apr 2 out* .... pu
Race Against Time 5a *sn bhnd, t.o. p.u. apr 11th* ..... pu
12 ran. 8l, 3l, 8l, 2½l, 2l, dist, 12l. Time 6m 38.00s. SP 5-2.
J D Roberts (Berkeley).

730 - Ladies

483 **LEWESDON HILL .... Miss P Curling** 1
(fav) hld up in tch, ld 14th, clr 3 out, eased run in
467 **The Humble Tiller .... Miss L Knights** 2
ld til hdd 14th, kpt on wll, not qckn clsng stgs
378 **Unique New York (v) .... Miss S Offord** 3
prom til lost plc stdly frm 15th
519 Mighty Falcon 8ow *in tch til aft 14th, no ch clsng stgs* 4
469 Go West *just in tch til outpcd aft 14th, t.o. p.u. aft 3 out* .... pu
469 Galaxy High (v) *rmmndrs aft 6th, in tch, 8l 3rd whn blndrd & u.r. 3 out* .... ur
6 ran. 4l, 15l, 2l. Time 6m 42.00s. SP 1-2.
T C Frost (Seavington).

731 - Open (12st)

YOUNG BRAVE 7ex .... M Miller 1
(Jt fav) j.w., disp ld thruout til qcknd clr 2 out, imp
530 **Ryming Cuplet 7ex .... R White** 2
disp ld til aft 14th, rddn apr 3 out, styd on clsng stgs
531 **Qualitair Memory (Ire) 7ex .... J Tizzard** 3
(Jt fav) cls up thruout, disp aft 14th til blndrd 3 out, not rcvr
626 Far Too Loud *ref 3rd* .... ref
444 Hurricane Tommy 7ex *in tch til outpcd aft 14th, bhnd whn ref 15th* .... ref
5 ran. 5l, 8l. Time 6m 43.00s. SP 6-4.
David Young (Portman).

732 - Intermediate (12st)

524 **APATURA HATI 5a 5ex .... T Mitchell** 1
j.w.,ld til 14th,disp nxt,ld agn apr 3 out,styd on strngly
465 **Emerald Knight (Ire) .... P Henley** 2
hld up in tch, wnt 2nd 3 out, no ext frm 2 out
644 **Chita's Cone 5a .... R Treloggen** 3
(fav) trckd ldr til ld brfly 14th,disp nxt til outpcd 3 out,eased
379 Rare Flutter 5a *towrds rear, lost tch aft 14th* 4
470 Birchall Boy *alwys towrds rear, no ch frm 14th* 5
War Baron *bhnd til p.u. apr 10th* .... pu
6 ran. 4l, dist, 10l, 1l. Time 6m 35.00s. SP 4-1.
Mrs R O Hutchings (Portman).

733 - Open Maiden Div I (12st)

470 **ALLER MOOR (IRE) 7a .... P Henley** 1
(fav) cls 2nd frm 14th, efft & ld aft last, pushd clr
Ruth's Boy (Ire) .... R White 2
2nd til ld 12th,slght ld last,not qckn run in,gd efft
558 **Drumbanes Pet .... G Penfold** 3

hdwy frm rear aft 14th, tk 3rd aft 3 out, fin tired
448 Spy Dessa *prom til outpcd 15th, tired clsng stgs* 4
482 Paid Elation 5a *rear til p.u. apr 2 out*.......... pu
4 Blakes Beau *ld & sn 20l clr, hdd 12th, wknd & p.u. apr 15th*.......... pu
Think It Out 7a *rear whn f hvly 12th*.......... f
468 Joe Penny *6th 11th, wknd, t.o. p.u. apr 3 out*.......... pu
520 Constant Sula 5a *midfld til hdwy 15th, tk 3rd whn blndrd & u.r. 3 out*.......... ur
555 Mountain-Linnet *not alwys fluent,gd hdwy to 3rd 15th,wknd 3 out,p.u. apr nxt*.......... pu
Girls In Business 5a *bhnd & jmp nvcy til p.u. apr 16th, schoold*.......... pu
533 Working Man (Ire) 7a *not fluent, rear til p.u. apr 10th*.. pu
528 Lochnaver 5a *hdwy to 5th whn mstk 13th, p.u. nxt*.... pu
13 ran. 4l, dist, 25l. Time 6m 45.00s. SP Evens.
G Keirle (Portman).
Fence 19 omitted

734 - Open Maiden Div II (12st)

521 **I'MINONIT ....P Henley** 1
(fav) hdwy to 2nd 10th, ld apr 2 out, drvn out
Four Leaf Clover 5a..........L Jefford 2
prom,slght ld whn carrd wd by lose horse apr 2 out,not rcvr
Ridemore Balladeer 7a ....Miss S Cobden 3
hdwy frm rear 12th, 4th 3 out, bad mstk 2 out, should imprv
204 Penny's Prince *4th whn mstk 12th, hdwy 16th, not rch ldrs, do bttr*.......... 4
470 Blakeington (bl) *prom, 2nd whn mstk 10th, cls up til rddn 15th, fdd*.......... 5
Timells Brook *prom, mstk 8th, lost plc 11th, p.u. aft 13th*.......... pu
532 Always Dreaming 5a 1ow *sn bhnd & strggling, t.o. p.u. apr 13th*.......... pu
Young Tiger *mstk 1st, ld & jmp slwly 3rd, 6th whn ref 6th*.......... ref
465 Saucy's Wolf *hdwy to 3rd 15th, outpcd 17th, 6th whn f 2 out*.......... f
533 Renshaw Ings *3rd whn f 9th*.......... f
555 Stillmore Business 7a *slght mstk 7th, towrds rear whn badly hmpd & u.r. 9th*.......... ur
11 ran. 2l, 8l, 3l, 4l. Time 6m 57.00s. SP 7-4.
P S Macrae (Portman).
G.T.

CHESHIRE FOREST
Sudlow Farm
Sunday March 31st
GOOD

735 - Members

361 **FREDDIE FOX..........T Garton** 1
(fav) in tch, gng wll, chsd ldr 13th, ld last, rddn clr
163 **Dice Off 5a..........G Crank** 2
chsd ldr til ld 6th, hdd apr last, no ext
293 **Charlie Chalk..........A Griffith** 3
not fluent, chsd ldr 6-12th, ev ch & blndrd 2 out, wknd
Melsonby *cls up, ev ch 15th, wknd 2 out*.......... 4
458 Downtown *ld to 5th, grdly wknd, t.o. frm 13th*.......... 5
159 Nearctic Bay (USA) 26ow *tubed, sn wll bhnd, t.o. frm 5th*.......... 6
Gitche Gumme *rmndrs 4th, rddn & lost tch 7th, p.u. 13th*.......... pu
7 ran. 5l, 15l, 1½l, 1 fence, 10l. Time 6m 48.00s. SP 4-5.
Mrs A B Garton (Cheshire Forest).

736 - Confined (12st)

293 **GREY GORDEN (IRE)..........A Crow** 1
(fav) made virtly all, 4l clr 2 out, styd on und pres
486 **Side Brace (NZ)..........Miss K Swindells** 2
chsd wnnr to 12th & agn 2 out, onepcd und pres
664 **Bay Owl 3ex ....M Worthington** 3
prog to chs ldr 13th, ev ch til wknd 2 out, fin lame
659 Lattin General 1ow *prom to 11th, 5th & no ch 3 out* ... 4
664 Wot Pet *sn wll bhnd, t.o. frm 6th*.......... 5
565 Sandstone Arch *rear, blndrd 9th & 10th, t.o. & p.u. 12th*.......... pu
662 Mr Snail *prog & cls up 11th, outpcd 14th, 4th & wll btn whn u.r. last*.......... ur
664 Strathbogie Mist (Ire) *s.s, bhnd til p.u. 4th*.......... pu
667 Ring Bank 7a *ref to race*.......... ref
9 ran. 3l, 12l, 15l, 2 fences. Time 6m 40.00s. SP Evens.
R H W Major (North Shropshire).

737 - Land Rover Open (12st)

565 **MR TITTLE TATTLE 7ex (bl) ....D Barlow** 1
ld to 7th & agn 11th, 2l ld 2 out, kpt on wll
565 **Scally Muire 5a 4ex..........A Crow** 2
(fav) ld 8-10th, disp ld 14-15th, rddn & onepcd aft
179 Alpha One 7ex *last & rddn 4th, ref 7th*.......... ref
579 Warner Forpleasure (bl) *chsd ldr to 7th & 11-12th, sn lost tch, p.u. 3 out*.......... pu
4 ran. 4l. Time 6m 34.00s. SP 3-1.
H A Shone (Cheshire Forest).

738 - Ladies Open

566 **HORNBLOWER..........Miss C Burgess** 1
(fav) made all, alwys in commd, pushd out flat
664 **Ebony Gale ....Miss J Penney** 2
chas ldrs, whn 2nd 13th, kpt on, not trbl wnnr
426 **Kameo Style (bl) ....Miss J Priest** 3
chsd 4-12th, sn outpcd
Mrs Cadogan 5a *alwys last, losng tch & jmpd slwly 6th, p.u. nxt*.......... pu
Sheppie's Reality *chsd ldr to 3rd, blndrd nxt, bhnd frm 7th, p.u. 12th*.......... pu
5 ran. 5l, 30l. Time 6m 47.00s. SP 1-4.
N J Barrowclough (West Shropshire).

739 - Restricted (12st)

667 **WORLESTON FARRIER..........G Hanmer** 1
ld to 8th, chsd ldr, ld apr last, sn clr, rddn out
502 **Bowlands Himself (Ire) ....R Ford** 2
trckd ldrs, ld 9th, 6l clr 2 out, hdd apr last, fin lame
461 **Andyworth..........Miss K Chilton** 3
prom, chsd ldng pair frm 10th, kpt on onepcd
286 Autumn Green (Ire) *mid-div, outpcd 11th, no dang aft* 4
165 Extraspecial Brew *rear & blndrd 8th, some late prog, nvr dang* 5
564 Jo-Su-Ki *mid-div, outpcd 10th, no ch frm 13th*.......... 6
665 Foxy Blue *rear div, no ch 13th, u.r. 2 out*.......... ur
564 Rinky Dinky Doo *mid-div, blndrd 5th, f 7th*.......... f
665 Moorside Lad (bl) *mstks,chsd ldr to 7th, outpcd 12th, blndrd 2 out, p.u. last*.......... pu
578 Roll-A-Dance *alwys rear, lost tch 11th, p.u. last*.......... pu
666 Reckless Lord (Ire) *(fav) lost 30l at start, prog to 5th 15th, no ext, p.u. apr last*.......... pu
11 ran. 6l, 4l, 12l, 2l, 12l. Time 6m 38.00s. SP 3-1.
Mrs A J Flanders (Cheshire).

740 - Maiden

659 **EMBU-MERU..........I Lowe** 1
mid-div, mod 6th 14th, styd on wll aft, ld flat
568 **Flinters (bl) ....D Barlow** 2
ld 3rd-12th, lft 8l 2nd 2 out, ld last, sn hdd
Bubble N Squeek..........R Ford 3
trckd ldrs, 5th & strggling 13th, lft 4th last, wnt 3rd flat
661 King Keith *mstks, in tch, 4th & ch whn blndrd 14th, wknd*.......... 4
287 Kingfisher Blues (Ire) *mstks, nvr bttr thn mid-div*.......... 5
New Cruiser 5a *schoold, last trio, nvr dang*.......... 6
568 Son Of Ishka *cls up, wknd 7th, t.o. 13th*.......... 7
288 North Hollow (bl) *alwys rear, last frm 11th, t.o. & p.u. last*.......... pu
Cloud Dancing *(fav) prog 9th, disp ld 3 out, lft clr nxt, wknd, hdd & f last*.......... f
485 Orton House *ld to 2nd, chsd ldr til ld 13th, jnd 3 out, f nxt*.......... f
Analystic (Ire) *chsd ldrs til u.r. 5th*.......... ur

22 Posy Hill (Ire) 7a *mid-div, rddn 11th, no ch 13th, p.u. apr last* .... pu
Eller's Reflection 5a *schoold, rear of main grp til p.u. 12th* .... pu
589 Lively Lil (Ire) 5a *ran out 5th* .... ro
Dream Flight 7a *bhnd til p.u. 10th* .... pu
Gold Top 7a *schoold in last trio til p.u. 10th* .... pu
16 ran. 1l, 30l, ¾l, 30l, 8l, 1 fence. Time 6m 47.00s. SP 6-1.
R G Owen (Flint & Denbigh).
S.P.

CLIFTON-ON-TEME
Upper Sapey
Sunday March 31st
GOOD TO SOFT

741 - Members

457 **HAVEN LIGHT** .... **A Dalton** 1
(fav) made all, 10l clr hlfwy, unchal frm 15th
Invite D'Honneur (NZ) .... **N Oliver** 2
disp 2nd/3rd til outpcd frm 15th
Aldington Bell (bl) *disp 2nd/3rd til u.r. 13th* .... ur
Detinu 7a *2nd whn f 2nd* .... f
4 ran. 15l. Time 6m 20.00s. SP 4-9.
Mrs J P Spencer (Clifton On Teme).

742 - Restricted (12st)

641 **FROZEN PIPE 5a** .... **L Squire** 1
effrt to disp 15th, qcknd clr apr last
656 **Kilmakee 5a** .... **M Jackson** 2
mostly 2nd, disp ld frm 16th til outpcd flat
430 **Aldington Charlie** .... **H Wheeler** 3
(fav) cls 4th, ev ch til outpcd frm 4 out
431 Breeches Buoy *6th whn f 4th* .... f
Back-Bencher *u.r. 2nd* .... ur
339 The Hon Company *strgglng frm 13th, last whn p.u. 2 out* .... pu
388 Shannon King (Ire) *clr ldr til wknd 14th, p.u. 2 out* .... pu
354 Perryline 5a *hld up, effrt frm 3 out, ev ch whn f last* .... f
Slight Panic 5a *6th whn f 10th* .... f
9 ran. 4l, 10l. Time 6m 17.00s. SP 4-1.
Alan P Brewer (North Ledbury).

743 - Ladies

663 **STEPHENS PET** .... **Miss A Dare** 1
(fav) mstks, prog to disp 3 out-nxt, rnwd effrt to ld last, sn clr
378 **Roving Report** .... **Mrs A Rucker** 2
3rd at 15th, effrt to disp nxt, ld 2 out, hdd & outpcd flat
356 **Run To Form** .... **Miss E Wilesmith** 3
ld 8th, disp 3 out til mstk nxt, outpcd
429 They All Forgot Me *cls up in 4th til outpcd frm 15th* 4
429 Legal Picnic *last at 14th, fin strngly frm 2 out* 5
426 Fergal's Delight (bl) *clr ldr to 7th, 4th aft til wknd 14th* 6
492 Parting Hour 2ow *wkng in 5th whn u.r. 2 out* .... ur
7 ran. 1l, 5l, 12l, 6l, 20l. Time 6m 7.00s. SP 1-3.
Dr P P Brown (Berkeley).

744 - Open (12st)

427 **LOST FORTUNE 7ex** .... **H Wheeler** 1
(fav) effrt to disp 3 out, sn clr, pshd out flat
337 **January Don (bl)** .... **A Dalton** 2
ld, jnd 15th, outpcd frm 2 out
215 **Coombesbury Lane 5a** .... **G Barfoot-Saunt** 3
mstk 12th, disp frm 15th, outpcd frm 3 out
426 Grey Tudor *2nd/3rd til outpcd 11th, 50l 4th whn p.u. last* .... pu
351 Drumceva *ran out & u.r. apr 2nd* .... ro
5 ran. 2½l, 30l. Time 6m 15.00s. SP 2-7.
H W Wheeler (North Cotswold).

745 - Intermediate (12st)

292 **RIP VAN WINKLE** .... **Miss A Dare** 1
(fav) hld up, smooth prog to disp 3 out, just ld whn lft clr nxt
674 **Ideal** .... **J Rees** 2
ld, 20l clr hlfwy, still disp & ev ch til outpcd 2 out
545 **Baron's Heir** .... **S Lloyd** 3
cls up til outpcd 12th, lft 3rd 2 out
426 Game Set *alwys strgglng frm 10th* 4
355 Miss Pennal 5a *effrt to disp 15th, 2nd & ch whn f 2 out* .... f
Minstrels Jazz 5a *mid-div whn f 4th* .... f
6 ran. 4l, 12l, dist. Time 6m 12.00s. SP 4-5.
Dr P P Brown (Berkeley).

746 - Confined

350 **DI STEFANO** .... **Miss A Dare** 1
(fav) smooth prog to disp 3 out, sn qcknd clr, easily
351 **Ask Frank** .... **H Wheeler** 2
ld to 6th, agn 8-15th, outpcd frm 2 out
426 **Frampton House** .... **F Hutsby** 3
ld 6-8th, outpcd frm 12th
3 ran. 6l, dist. Time 6m 17.00s. SP 4-6.
Mike Gifford (Cotswold Vale).

747 - Open Maiden Div I Pt I (12st)

WESTERN HARMONY .... **E Williams** 1
disp frm 12th, qcknd clr apr last
464 **Nothing Ventured** .... **A Beedles** 2
disp 3 out, cls 2nd til outpcd frm 2 out
389 **Bowland Girl (Ire) 5a** .... **Miss C Thomas** 3
(fav) disp 3rd frm hlfwy, no ext frm 2 out
431 Kingsthorpe *mid-div, effrt to go 3rd brfly 15th, sn no ext* 4
340 Matchlessly *ld til wknd 9th* 5
Sweet Joanna 5a *prom to hlfwy, wknd, p.u. 12th* .... pu
Dorn Retreat *25l last whn u.r. last* .... ur
688 Miss Madge 5a *t.o. whn ref 15th* .... ref
350 Saxon Smile *bhnd whn u.r. 11th* .... ur
220 Must Be Murphy (Ire) 7a *losing tch whn p.u. aft 11th* .... pu
389 Forest Rose 5a *t.o. whn p.u. 11th* .... pu
11 ran. 1½l, 1½l, 4l, dist. Time 6m 19.00s. SP 4-1.
R T Baimbridge (Berkeley).

748 - Open Maiden Div I Pt II (12st)

430 **LIVE WIRE (IRE) 7a** .... **T Cox** 1
ld frm 14th, drew clr frm 2 out
641 **Home To Tara** .... **Mrs C McCarthy** 2
4th at 14th, strng run frm 2 out, tk 2nd flat
352 **Countrywide Lad** .... **B Potts** 3
prog 11th, 2nd at 15th, ev ch til outpcd 2 out
Think Twice *effrt frm hlfwy to 3rd at 15th, wknd apr last* 4
602 Stormhill Recruit *chsd ldrs, nvr on terms, nrst fin* 5
Pridewood Target *alwys last, mod prog frm hlfwy* 6
Amerous Lad *t.o. frm 12th* 7
Sioux Perfick 5a *rmndrs 2nd, t.o. whn p.u. 16th* .... pu
432 Sweet Petel 5a *effrt to ld brfly 13th, wkng in 5th whn f 2 out* .... f
590 Mendip Son (bl) *clr ldr to 10th, wknd rpdly, last whn p.u. 15th* .... pu
431 Cruise A Hoop *(fav) 5th whn f 10th* .... f
11 ran. 10l, 5l, 1l, 12l, ½l, 5l. Time 6m 24.00s. SP 7-1.
C C Trietline (Clifton On Teme).

749 - Open Maiden Div II (12st)

GROMIT (NZ) .... **Julian Pritchard** 1
w.w. strng run frm 3 out, disp last, ran on wll flat
340 **Eighty Eight** .... **E Walker** 2
alwys prom, disp 14th til outpcd flat
549 **Joyney 5a** .... **L Squire** 3
prog frm 2 out, ev ch last, just outpcd flat
354 Oats For Notes 5a *(Jt fav) prog frm 15th, ev ch 2 out, wknd apr last* 4
Rap Up Fast (USA) *(Jt fav) ld/disp til wknd frm 2 out* 5
689 Shadowgraff 5a *4th at hlfwy, still 4th til wknd 2 out* 6
387 Creme Zahilla 5a *mstks, cls up til outpcd frm 3 out* 7
358 First Command (NZ) *prom til grad outpcd frm 15th* 8
Welsh Lightning *disp to 11th, wknd rpdly frm 15th* 9

358 Le Loubec 5a *rear whn p.u. 8th, dsmntd* .... pu
Mariner's Walk *disp to 8th, wknd & p.u. 14th* .... pu
219 Callerose *u.r. 2nd* .... ur
741 Detinu 7a *2nd outing, t.o. til p.u. 11th* .... pu
354 So Easy 5a *prom to hlfwy, wknd, p.u. 14th* .... pu
432 Rusty Fellow *ref 3rd* .... ref
431 Big Buckley 5a *alwys strgglng, last whn p.u. last* .... pu
220 Arms Park *t.o. hlfwy, p.u. 13th* .... pu
17 ran. Nk, 2l, 2l, 2l, 1l, 2l, 3l. Time 6m 26.00s. SP 12-1.
Miss Sarah Eaton (Croome & West Warwickshire).
P.M.

DUMFRIESSHIRE
Lockerbie
Sunday March 31st
GOOD

750 - Members

503 **SOLWAYSANDS 2ow 7ex.................K Little** 1
(fav) abt 4l clr thruout, eased cls home
608 **Fruids Park 5a ....L Morgan** 2
not alwys fluent, nvr lkd like wnng
2 ran. 1l. Time 7m 40.00s. SP 1-4.
K Little (Dumfriesshire).

751 - Confined (12st)

610 **FORDSTOWN (IRE) 10ex ....J Alexander** 1
ld 10th, made rest, 2l ld whn lft clr last
402 **The Shade Matcher ....A Parker** 2
ld til 5th, lost plc, styd on agn frm 4 out, no imp
317 **Astrac Trio (USA) ....Miss A Bowie** 3
alwys prom, no ext frm 3 out
399 Sharp Opinion 6ex *nvr nr ldrs* 4
320 Scottish Gold *alwys wll bhnd* 5
498 Hydropic *bhnd by 9th, t.o.* 6
405 Bridgnorth Lass 5a *bhnd by 13th, t.o.* 7
Sunset Reins Free *u.r. 3rd* .... ur
497 Hamilton Lady (Ire) 5a *3rd hlfwy, sn lost plc, p.u. 2 out* .... pu
665 Crimson Mary 5a *ran out 2nd* .... ro
610 Little Glen *ld 5th til 8th, rmnd cls up, 2l 2nd whn u.r. last* .... ur
498 Master Kit (Ire) 3ex *(fav) ld 8th til 10th, cls 2nd whn s.u. apr 12th* .... su
12 ran. 6l, 4l, 20l, dist. Time 7m 22.00s. SP 14-1.
J F Alexander (Fife).

752 - Ladies

320 **KILMINFOYLE....................Miss S Forster** 1
blndrd 2nd, 3rd hlfwy, jnd ldr 2 out, ld last stride
609 **The Healy 5a ....Mrs F Scales** 2
ld frm 10th, jnd 2 out, hdd last stride
514 **Fettle Up (bl) ....Miss S Brotherton** 3
(Jt fav) alwys hndy, 4th hlfwy, no ext frm 2 out
Agathist (USA) *(Jt fav) 6th hlfwy, no hdwy frm 3 out* 4
611 Marshalstoneswood *7th hlfwy, nvr rchd ldrs* 5
398 Another Dyer *ld til 10th, grdly wknd* 6
608 Sunnie Cruise 5a *8th hlfwy, nvr a dang* 7
611 Carousel Calypso *cls 2nd whn u.r. 6th* .... ur
611 Furry Venture 5a *sn strgglng in rear, p.u. 3 out* .... pu
499 Tannock Brook *5th hlfwy, lost tch by 13th, p.u. 3 out* .... pu
10 ran. Sht-hd, 8l, 3l, 5l, 25l, 5l. Time 7m 9.00s. SP 7-1.
Mrs S Shirley-Beavan (Jedforest).

753 - Open

673 **BOREEN OWEN.......................T Morrison** 1
(fav) ld by abt 3l til drew wll clr frm 13th
614 **Craig Burn 5a ....J Ewart** 2
chsd wnnr til wknd rpdly frm 13th
2 ran. Dist. Time 7m 55.00s. SP 2-7.
David Alan Harrison (Cumberland Farmers).

754 - Restricted

403 **TOASTER CRUMPET ....Miss P Robson** 1
alwys hndy, ld 15th, styd on strngly
192 **Nova Nita 5a ....A Parker** 2
(fav) chsd wnnr frm 16th, no imp frm 2 out
403 **Givower.....................................P Diggle** 3
ld frm 9th til wknd 15th
498 Duncans Dream *sn strgglng in rear, p.u. 3 out* .... pu
319 Little Wenlock *in tch whn u.r. 9th* .... ur
614 Staneshiel *cls up whn p.u. lame aft 10th* .... pu
Luvly Bubbly *2nd whn f 3rd* .... f
398 Steady Away (Ire) (bl) *ld til ran out 9th* .... ro
8 ran. 6l, 25l. Time 7m 24.00s. SP 9-2.
Miss P Robson (Tynedale).

755 - Maiden Div I (12st)

502 **DENIM BLUE.....................Miss P Robson** 1
(fav) alwys hndy, 4th hlfwy, ld 4 out, kpt on wll
407 **Lindon Run ....R Morgan** 2
ld til 7th, ld agn 14th-4 out, styd on wll
407 **Pablowmore.............................R Green** 3
towrds rear til hdwy frm 14th, no ext run in
398 Sir Harry Rinus *alwys hndy, 3rd hlfwy, wknd 3 out* 4
Highland River 5a *nvr bttr then midfld* 5
613 All Or Nothing 5a *alwys abt same plc* 6
503 Rustic Bridge *bhnd early, 6th hlfwy, wknd 4 out* 7
614 Mr Sharp *alwys bhnd* 8
Kincardine Bridge (USA) *ld 7th til u.r. 14th* .... ur
502 Bullaford Fair *5th hlfwy, sn wknd, b.d. 2 out* .... bd
Mattella (Ire) 5a *nvr dang, p.u. 3 out* .... pu
371 Good Profit *bhnd whn f 2 out* .... f
89 Eostre *midfld whn f 13th* .... f
Mordington Lass 5a *sn bhnd, p.u. 10th* .... pu
Gypsey Royle 5a *sn bhnd, p.u. 13th* .... pu
The Early Bird 7a *sn bhnd, p.u. 13th* .... pu
613 Senora D'Or 5a *sn bhnd, p.u. 3 out* .... pu
17 ran. 1½l, 1l, dist, 2l, 6l, 4l, 20l. Time 7m 27.00s. SP 2-1.
Mrs L Walby (Tynedale).

756 - Maiden Div II (12st)

KIRCHWYN LAD ....R Shiels 1
jmp wll, made all, styd on wll
406 **Murder Moss (Ire)......................M Ruddy** 2
wnt 4th 4 out, kpt on wll, no imp on wnnr
Fort Alicia 5a ....M Bradburne 3
3rd hlfwy, kpt on wll but no ch wth wnnr
403 I'll Skin Them (Ire) 5a *4th hlfwy, wnt 2nd 15th, no ext apr last* 4
613 Sweet Sergeant *2nd hlfwy, rmnd cls up til no ext frm 3 out* 5
614 Mapalak 5a *(fav) last hlfwy, nvr got into contention* 6
503 Zoflo 5a *5th hlfwy, no ext frm 4 out* 7
614 Prince Rossini (Ire) *alwys towrds rear* 8
398 Jack's Croft *nvr dang, p.u. 3 out* .... pu
Red Scot *sn bhnd, p.u. 12th* .... pu
611 Emu Park *nvr dang, p.u. 3 out* .... pu
614 Saigon Lady (Ire) 5a *not fluent, some hdwy hlfwy, bhnd whn p.u. 3 out* .... pu
405 Cogitate 5a *prom early, t.o. whn p.u. 11th* .... pu
503 Gemma Law 5a *sn bhnd, p.u. 3 out* .... pu
14 ran. 10l, ½l, 1½l, 8l, 2l, 4l, dist. Time 7m 32.00s. SP 8-1.
Dr Bernard Lawley (Tynedale).
R.J.

HURWORTH
Great Stainton
Sunday March 31st
GOOD TO SOFT

757 - Members

411 **CHAPEL ISLAND 10ex.....................G Tuer** 1
sttld in tch,went 2nd 8th,ld 3 out,clr last,idld flat
516 **Lyningo ....A Wood** 2
ld til 3 out, sn rdn, kpt on well cls home
590 **Ingleby Flyer 5a..........................P Frank** 3
chsd ldrs, wknd 14th, t.o.
Slim King 7ow *prom, jmpd rght 4th, mstk 11th, wknd nxt, t.o. & p.u. 2 out* .... pu

415 Henceyem (Ire) *(fav) last & outpcd frm 8th, rdn hlfwy, sn t.o., p.u. 14th* .... pu
5 ran. Nk, 30l. Time 6m 41.00s. SP 11-8.
E W & M Tuer (Hurworth).

758 - Restricted

JR-KAY (IRE)..........................**N Bannister** 1
made all, drvn out flat
718 **Tom The Tank**..........................**C Mulhall** 2
chsd ldrs, ev ch 3 out, went 2nd nxt, styd on well flat
302 **Flying Lion**..........................**M Haigh** 3
alwys prom, prog to 2nd 4 out, onepcd frm nxt
411 Honest Expression 5a *mid-div, prog to trck ldrs hlfwy, rdn 3 out, onepcd* 4
584 Missile Man *prom, mstk 6th, chsd ldr hlfwy, ev ch 3 out, onepcd* 5
411 Glenbricken *mid-div, mstk 11th, outpcd frm 3 out* 6
411 Sergent Kay *mstk 1st, mid-div, rdn 15th, sn no ext*.... 7
584 Buckwheat Lad (Ire) *alwys rear, rdn 11th, onepcd frm 4 out* 8
408 Cadrillon (Fr) *mid-div, fdd frm 5 out* 9
585 Computer Pickings 5a *mid-div, went prom hlfwy, no prog aft, wknd 5 out, t.o.* 10
319 Acropol 5a *rear, last frm 4th, t.o. 7th* 11
584 Goodwill Hill *mid-div, outpcd frm 14th, t.o.* 12
516 Barichste *chsd ldrs til p.u. bef 4th* .... pu
584 Polar Hat *mid-div, u.r. 15th* .... ur
584 Another Hooligan *(fav) n.j.w. alwys bhnd, t.o. & p.u. 15th* .... pu
584 Charlcot Storm 7a (bl) *ref 1st* .... ref
Lord Lander 7a *rdn & lost tch 7th, p.u. aft 11th* .... pu
17 ran. Nk, 5l, 3l, 6l, 4l, 7l, 3l, 6l, 2l, 12l. Time 6m 31.00s. SP 33-1.
N W A Bannister (Pendle Forest & Craven).

759 - Ladies

412 **INDIE ROCK**..........................**Mrs F Needham** 1
hld up going wll,went 2nd 6th, qcknd to ld last, kpt on flat
Integrity Boy..........................**Miss A Armitage** 2
sttld wth ldrs, disp 3 out, hdd last, rallied flat
305 **Colonel Popski**..........................**Mrs J Barr** 3
mid-div, went prom 6th, styd on frm 15th, disp 3 out,onepcd
Cheeky Pot *prom, 3rd hlfwy, kpt on onepcd frm 4 out* 4
514 Grey Realm 5a 2ow *(fav) mid-div, rdn 8th, mstk 11th, mod prog frm 3 out, no dang* 5
412 John Corbet *ld til hdd & wknd 3 out* 6
316 Upwell *prom til fdd 4 out* 7
586 Linebacker *mid-div, drppd rear 9th, bhnd whn u.r. 14th* .... ur
514 Earl Gray (bl) *rear, dtchd 9th, rdn 11th, t.o. & p.u. 14th* pu
413 Red Star Queen 5a *keen hld, prom til wknd rpdly 9th, t.o. & p.u. 3 out* .... pu
10 ran. ½l, 4l, 3l, 8l, 8l, 10l. Time 6m 30.00s. SP 3-1.
R Tate (Hurworth).

760 - Land Rover Open (12st)

FIERY SUN..........................**N Wilson** 1
ld to 5 out, rallied to ld 2 out, sn clr
587 **Gaelic Warrior 4ex**..........................**S Swiers** 2
prom, 2nd hlfwy, chal 5 out, ld 3 out-nxt, onepcd
488 **Hyperion Son 7ex**..........................**M Haigh** 3
(fav) chsd ldrs, 2nd 13th, disp 5 out, fdd 3 out, onepcd
306 Some Flash *alwys mid-div, onepcd frm 3 out* 4
587 Skipping Gale 7ex *blnd 1st, chsd ldrs til rdn & fdd frm 13th* 5
583 Cot Lane 7ex (bl) *nvr going wll, rear & rdn 11th, nvr dang* 6
587 Tammy My Girl 5a *mid-div, u.r. 7th* .... ur
634 Bennan March 7ex *mid-div, rmndr 4th, wknd frm 7th, t.o. & p.u. 11th* .... pu
8 ran. 10l, 2l, 3l, 5l, 7l. Time 6m 32.00s. SP 5-1.
P Cartmell (Cleveland).

761 - Intermediate

588 **FLIP THE LID (IRE) 5a**..........................**N Wilson** 1
(fav) j.w. disp til ld 4th, qcknd clr apr last
588 **Castle Tyrant 5a**..........................**P Atkinson** 2
disp to 4th, chsd wnr aft, ev ch 2 out, no ext last
588 **Jack Dwyer**..........................**D Coates** 3
chsd ldrs til mstk 3 out, onepcd
486 Advent Lady 5a *rear, jmpd rght 4th, chsd ldrs til wknd 13th, t.o.* 4
223 Sharpridge *alwys rear, t.o. & p.u. 8th* .... pu
588 Fowling Piece *rear, outpcd 4th, bhnd 6th, t.o. & p.u. aft 11th* .... pu
409 What A Miss 5a *rear & lost tch 6th, p.u. aft 11th* ...... pu
7 ran. 2½l, 30l, 30l. Time 6m 27.00s. SP 4-6.
Peter Sawney (Cleveland).

762 - Maiden Div I Pt I (12st)

414 **WHISPERS HILL 7a**..........................**C Mulhall** 1
mid-div, prog to chs ldrs hlfwy, ld 2 out, sn clr, easily
590 **River Ramble 5a**..........................**Miss T Jackson** 2
prom, mstk 11th, prog to ld 15th, hdd & no ext 2 out
591 **Zin Zan (Ire)**..........................**M Mawhinney** 3
rear, prog 12th, styd on frm 3 out
718 Sweet Rose 5a *alwys chsng ldrs, onepcd frm 3 out*... 4
416 Hoistthestandard 5a *(fav) mid-div, fdd hlfwy, t.o. & p.u. 11th* .... pu
223 Pri Neukin *rear, prog und pres 11th, no frthr hdwy, wknd 14th, p.u.last* .... pu
308 Hungry Jack *prom, ld 3rd, disp 8th, ld agn 13th,hdd 15th,wknd,p.u. flat* .... pu
409 Vale Of York *chsd ldr, disp 8th, hdd 13th, wknd rpdly, p.u. 3 out* .... pu
409 Chuckleberry *mid-div, mstk 6th, prom hlfwy, wknd 3 out, t.o. & p.u. last* .... pu
308 Chummy's Last 5a *rear, prog 12th, ev ch whn f 14th*.. f
Another Class 6ow *last & t.o. 7th, p.u. 9th* .... pu
11 ran. 6l, 2l, 8l. Time 6m 46.00s. SP 4-1.
Roy Robinson (Derwent).

763 - Maiden Div I Pt II (12st)

RUFF ACCOUNT..........................**Miss J Eastwood** 1
prom, ld 10th, sn wll clr, unchal
Think Pink..........................**A Bonson** 2
mid-div, prog 6th, ld 8th-10th, wknd 2 out
590 **Magic Song 5a 4ow**..........................**C Denny** 3
mid-div, mstk 4th, prom hlfwy, no prog aft, tk 3rd nr fin
517 Rich Asset (Ire) *mid-div whn blnd 6th, sn prom, wknd frm 2 out* 4
589 Goongor (Ire) *chsd ldrs, went 3rd hlfwy, no prog aft, wknd* 5
Multi Purpose *ld to 8th, wknd rpdly 10th, p.u. 3 out* .... pu
488 Flying Pan 5a *(fav) rear, prog hlfwy, ev ch whn f 14th* f
Patey Court 7a *mid-div, lost tch 10th, p.u. nxt* .... pu
Redwood Boy *rear, wknd 6th, t.o. & p.u. 10th* .... pu
Jonah's Jest (Ire) *prom, mstk 11th, sn wknd, p.u. aft 14th* .... pu
588 Pendle Witch 5a *rear & mstk 5th, t.o. 9th, p.u. 14th* ... pu
11 ran. Dist, 7l, sht-hd, 2l. Time 6m 46.00s. SP 20-1.
R G Brader (Middleton).

764 - Maiden Div II (12st)

591 **RABBLE ROUSER**..........................**R Edwards** 1
chsd ldrs, prog 4 out, chal whn mstk last, sn ld, ran on wll
307 **Priceless Sam 7a**..........................**S Charlton** 2
(fav) mid-div, prog hlfwy, 2nd 12th, ld aft 2 out, hdd flat,no ext
415 **Yornoangel**..........................**G Markham** 3
rear, prog frm 7th, ev ch aft 2 out, not qckn
316 Niad *alwys prom, ld 12th til hdd & wknd 2 out*...... 4
222 Private Jet (Ire) *prom, mstk 8th, chsd ldrs til wknd 4 out, t.o.* 5
517 Here Comes Charter *chsd ldng grp, rdn 13th, sn wknd, t.o.* 6
415 Quite A Character 5a *prom, ld 7th-hlfwy, wknd rpdly, p.u. 3 out* .... pu
117 Meadow Gray *ld to 7th, sn wknd, p.u. 3 out* .... pu

Canny's Fort 5a *chsd ldrs til wknd hlfwy, t.o. & p.u. 14th* .... pu
406 Lord Jester *tubed, rear, lost tch 5th, t.o. & p.u. 3 out* .. pu
416 Living On The Edge (Ire) *strng hld, hld up, ev ch whn blnd & u.r. 12th* .... ur
Fountain View (Ire) *prom til fdd hlfwy, p.u. 3 out* .... pu
408 Hutcel Bell 7a *last & sn t.o., p.u. 3 out* .... pu
Flashlight 7a *mid-div whn mstk 8th, sn lost tch, p.u. 14th* .... pu
Mighty Wizard *mid-div, wknd 12th, p.u. 3 out* .... pu
591 Justforgastrix (Ire) *mid-div, wknd 14th, t.o. & p.u. 3 out* .... pu

16 ran. 4l, 2l, 10l, 20l, 20l. Time 6m 37.00s. SP 7-1.
M J Brown (Sinnington).
N.E.

TIVYSIDE
Pantyderi
Sunday March 31st
GOOD

765 - Members

548 **CELTIC BIZARRE 5a** .... **Miss B Barton** 1
(fav) ld 3rd, sn clr, unchal
551 **Preseli View 7a** .... **M Lewis** 2
chsd wnr, ran green t.o.
Zamanayn (Ire) *bolted into ld, f 2nd* .... f

3 ran. Dist. Time 6m 13.00s. SP 1-3.
R R Smedley (Tivyside).

766 - Confined (12st)

549 **BANCYFELIN BOY** .... **J P Keen** 1
mid-div, mstk 13th, rpd prog 15th, hrd rdn to ld last
603 **Lucky Ole Son** .... **Miss P Jones** 2
alwys prom, ran on frm last, just hld
604 **Celtic Daughter 5a** .... **J Jukes** 3
ld 11th, hdd & onepcd last
387 Royal Oats 5a *(fav) ld to 11th, fdd, no ext frm 15th* ... 4
507 Touch 'N' Pass *alwys in rear* 5
547 Carlowitz (USA) *s.s. ref 2nd* .... ref

6 ran. Nk, 1l, 10l, ½l. Time 6m 1.00s. SP 6-1.
Miss A L Williams (South Pembrokeshire).

767 - Intermediate (12st)

545 **MISTER HORATIO 5ex** .... **M Lewis** 1
(fav) alwys prom, ld 4 out, easily
545 **Metrostyle** .... **J Jukes** 2
alwys prom, chsd wnr 4 out, no imp
Kumada .... **V Hughes** 3
ld to 3rd, agn 9th-4 out, no ext aft
Tricky Dex (USA) *nvr bttr than mid-div* 4
547 Heluva Battle *ld 4-9th, outpcd aft 4 out* 5
545 Miss Montana 5a *nvr trbld ldrs* 6
Magic Ripple 5a *in rear, mstk 13th, p.u. nxt* .... pu

7 ran. 6l, 4l, 2l, 20l, 20l. Time 5m 52.00s. SP 1-2.
W D Lewis (Tivyside).

768 - Open (12st)

766 **CARLOWITZ (USA)** .... **J Price** 1
2nd outing, ld 13th-4 out, agn nxt, comf, lame
384 **Willie McGarr (USA)** .... **P Hamer** 2
(fav) s.s. ld brfly 11th, hrd rdn 2 out, no ext
552 **Cherry Island (Ire)** .... **J Jukes** 3
alwys prom, ev ch last, no ext flat
546 Medieval Queen 5a *ld to 13th, fdd* 4
547 Origami (bl) *mid-div, prog to ld 4 out, hdd nxt, onepcd aft* 5
384 Doubting Donna 5a *nvr nrr enough to chal* 6
547 Cornish Cossack (NZ) 2ow *alwys mid-div, no dang* ... 7
383 Banker's Gossip *alwys rear* 8
547 Electrolyte *alwys wll in rear* 9
602 Mummy's Song *prom to 8th, fdd, p.u. 11th* .... pu

10 ran. 4l, 2l, 2l, 5l, 5l, 1l, 10l, 2l. Time 5m 54.00s. SP 20-1.
Mrs J Sidebottom (Vale Of Clettwr).

769 - Ladies

669 **GOOLDS GOLD** .... **Miss P Jones** 1
(fav) ld chsng grp, ct ldr 4 out, sn clr, easily
546 **Busman (Ire)** .... **Miss L Pearce** 2
mid-div, mstk 10th, rallied frm 2 out, nrst fin
546 **Moving Force** .... **Miss C Williams** 3
clr ldr til 4 out, sn btn, kpt on frm 2 out
546 Fast Freeze *nvr rchd ldrs* 4
603 Dare Say *u.r. 1st* .... ur
546 Mount Falcon *in rear whn u.r. 13th* .... ur

6 ran. 5l, nk, dist. Time 5m 38.00s. SP 1-2.
David Brace (Llangeinor).

770 - Restricted (12st)

600 **ROBBIE'S BOY** .... **J P Keen** 1
(fav) ld chsng grp, ld 2 out, easily
388 **The Apprentice** .... **E Roberts** 2
dist ldr til hdd 2 out, kpt on
148 **Cranagh Moss (Ire)** .... **G Lewis** 3
chsng grp, ev ch 3 out, onepcd aft
Highland Minstrel *nvr bttr than mid-div* 4
549 My Harvinski *mstk 3rd, plodded round* 5
600 Saffron Moss *nvr nr to chal* 6
695 Mylordmayor *twrds rear, p.u. aft 15th* .... pu
553 Downhill Racer 5a *tried to ref 4th, u.r. 6th* .... ur
547 Cefn Woodsman 7a *in rear whn p.u. 14th* .... pu

9 ran. 6l, 3l, 4l, 3l, 10l. Time 6m 0.00s. SP Evens.
J L Brown (Llandeilo Farmers).

771 - Maiden Div I (12st)

550 **DUSTYS TRAIL (IRE)** .... **R Thornton** 1
(fav) mid-div, und pres 15th, hrd rdn to ld nr fin
552 **Gunner Boon** .... **Miss P Jones** 2
ld to 9th, agn 15th, jnd last, hrd rdn, just ct
551 **Barnaby Boy** .... **J P Keen** 3
trckd ldrs, ev ch 2 out-last, kpt on flat
509 Cairneymount *alwys mid-div* 4
600 Parson's Corner *alwys twrds rear* 5
550 Northern Bluff *twrds rear whn u.r. 5th* .... ur
606 Jimmy O'Goblin *ld 9-15th, fdd, p.u. 2 out* .... pu
553 On The Book 5a *u.r. 3rd* .... ur
Fumi D'Oro 5a *nvr nr to chal, p.u. 15th* .... pu
509 Tarrtingo 5a *in rear whn p.u. 13th* .... pu
552 Chancy Oats *trckd ldrs, f 13th, dead* .... f
391 Royal Bula *rear whn p.u. 2 out* .... pu
552 Deryn Y Cwm (Ire) *mstks 2nd & 4th, p.u. aft 8th* .... pu
Hil Lady 7a *t.o. 7th, p.u. 9th* .... pu

14 ran. Hd, 2l, 4l, dist. Time 5m 55.00s. SP 2-1.
G Morris (Pembrokeshire).
Objection to judge's result (!), result stands.

772 - Maiden Div II Pt I (12st)

550 **CEDAR SQUARE (IRE) 7a** .... **D S Jones** 1
made all, unchal
550 **Moonlight Cruise 5a** .... **P Williams** 2
chsd ldrs, nvr thrtnd wnr
Hansom Marshal *prom til f 5th* .... f
552 Jolly Swagman 7a *in rear whn p.u. 9th* .... pu
146 Katy Country Mouse 5a *1st ride, trckd ldr to 8th, fdd rpdly, p.u. 11th* .... pu
544 Gatten's Brake *mid-div whn f 14th* .... f
367 Final Cruise 5a *(fav) prom whn u.r. 13th* .... ur
Classic Edition 7a *twrds rear, ran green, p.u. 11th* ... pu

8 ran. 6l. Time 5m 59.00s. SP 2-1.
A J Rhead (South Pembrokeshire).

773 - Maiden Div II Pt II (12st)

553 **SHUIL'S STAR (IRE) 7a** .... **P Hamer** 1
s.s. rear, prog 4 out, hrd rdn to ld flat
390 **Lady Romance (Ire) 5a** .... **A Price** 2
ld 12th, hdd flat, kpt on well
550 **Kinlogh Gale (Ire)** .... **J Price** 3
(fav) ld to 11th, onepcd frm 2 out
Kirby's Charm *alwys mid-div, ran green, improve* 4
Mr Ffitch *trckd ldrs, wkng whn f 14th* .... ur

550 Rymer's Express *trckd ldrs til ran out 6th* ro
Stephleys Girl 5a *mid-div, p.u. 11th, lame* pu
549 Redoran 7a *nvr nr ldrs, u.r. 13th* ur
8 ran. 1l, 2l, 3l. Time 6m 11.00s. SP 5-2.
Bob Mason (Carmarthenshire).
P.D.

WEST KENT
Penshurst
Sunday March 31st
GOOD TO SOFT

774 - Members

574 **PRINCE RONAN (IRE)** ....**A Welsh** 1
cls up, ld 12th, made rest, rddn out flat
272 **Reggie (v)**...........................**R Wilkinson** 2
(fav) ld to 6th, agn 9-12th, chal 4 out, no ext last
574 **Prince Rua**.............................**P Blagg** 3
ld 6-9th, 3rd aft, ev ch 3 out, rddn & btn nxt
3 ran. 2½l, 10l. Time 7m 14.00s. SP 5-2.
J A C Ayton (West Kent).

775 - Confined (12st)

571 **BURROMARINER 3ex** ....**S Cowell** 1
(fav) cls up, prssd ldr 14th, ld apr 2 out, rddn out
570 **Ten Of Spades**..................**Miss A Sansom** 2
ld to apr 2 out, no ext last
571 **American Eyre** ....**Miss S Gladders** 3
alwys prom, wth ldr 6-8th, chal 4 out, ev ch whn blndrd last
247 Bye Bye Baby (Fr) 5a *trckd ldrs til mstk 7th, no dang aft, ran on frm 3 out* 4
571 Mel's Rose *alwys rear, lost tch 14th* 5
476 Namoos *alwys rear, in tch to 14th, p.u. 2 out* pu
577 Welshman's Gully *trckd ldrs, wknd 14th, bhnd whn p.u. aft 3 out* pu
573 Stede Quarter *in tch, hdwy 12th, cls up in 3rd whn f nxt* f
8 ran. 4l, hd, 5l, 25l. Time 6m 57.00s. SP 6-4.
Mrs A Blaker (Mid Surrey Farmers Drag).

776 - Open (12st)

595 **CENTRE STAGE**..........................**A Warr** 1
hndy, 2nd aft 3 out, chal last, ld cls home
573 **Strong Gold 7ex (bl)** ....**T McCarthy** 2
(fav) ld, prssd frm 10th, styd on, hdd line
451 **Yeoman Farmer** ....**P Hacking** 3
in tch in rear, drvn up to 3rd 2 out, no ext flat
527 Stirrup Cup 5ow *in tch in rear, nvr dang, mstk 2 out, kpt on* 4
451 Take The Town 7ex *2nd, prssd ldr frm 10th til rddn & wknd apr 2 out* 5
Colne Valley Kid *trckd ldrs, wknng whn p.u 13th* pu
6 ran. Hd, 5l, 8l, ½l. Time 6m 55.00s. SP 25-1.
L J Bowman (Kent & Surrey Bloodhounds).

777 - Ladies

421 **DUNBOY CASTLE (IRE)** ....**Miss G Chown** 1
trckd ldrs, 4th final ctt, ran on wll frm 3 out to ld flat
596 **Forest Sun**..........................**Miss J Grant** 2
hndy, ld apr 2 out, und press & hdd flat
572 **Pardon Me Mum 7ex**............**Mrs E Coveney** 3
(fav) sn cls up, chal 3 out, 3rd & btn nxt
452 Magical Morris *alwys rear, styd on, nvr nrr* 4
Zilfi (USA) *prom early, wll bhnd whn p.u. 11th* pu
596 Scotch Law *5th whn f 7th* f
Monksfort *ld, hdd aft 3 out, wknd & p.u. nxt* pu
7 ran. 1½l, 12l, 2l. Time 6m 51.00s. SP 3-1.
Miss G Chown (Essex & Suffolk).

778 - Intermediate (12st)

310 **DREAM PACKET** ....**M Gorman** 1
(fav) hld up, imprvd to ld 12th, hdd brfly 3 out, drew clr last
594 **Berrings Dasher 5ex**.....................**A Welsh** 2
cls up, ld 10-12th & brfly 3 out, wknd nxt
335 **Anurag (bl)** ....**R Lawther** 3
prom, 3rd frm 11th, blndrd nxt, strgglng aft, t.o. 2 out
570 Beach Tiger *alwys last & detached,jmp slwly thruout,t.o. whn p.u. aft9th* pu
Netherby Cheese *immed detached, t.o. whn p.u. 10th* pu
595 Quarter Marker (Ire) 2ow *ld to 10th, bhnd whn p.u. aft 11th* pu
6 ran. 10l, 1 fence. Time 6m 57.00s. SP 5-4.
A Howland Jackson (Essex & Suffolk).

779 - Restricted (12st)

272 **ALANSFORD**..............................**P Bull** 1
(fav) towrds rear, clsd up 12th, chal 3 out, ld nxt, ran on wll
574 **King's Maverick (Ire)**..................**P Hacking** 2
rear, gd prog to 3rd 10th, ld 4-2 out, rddn & no ext
574 **Motor Cloak**.........................**Miss C Savell** 3
alwys prom, 4th & mstk 3 out, no ch aft
593 Tau *in tch in mid-div, kpt on same pce* 4
455 St Robert *ld to 14th, fdd, tired & walked in* 5
574 Firewater Station *prom to 11th, bhnd whn p.u. aft 13th* pu
449 Manaolana 5a *in tch to 10th, p.u. 12th* pu
570 Basher Bill *f 1st* f
Brief Sleep 5a *in tch to 10th, p.u. 12th* pu
571 Greenhill Fly Away *rear, prog 11th, 3rd 3 out, wknd & p.u. last* pu
576 Huckleberry Friend 5a *cls up, 3rd whn f 8th* f
Miss Beal 5a *b.d. 1st* bd
Cumberland Gap 7a *f 1st* f
13 ran. 6l, 7l, 10l, dist. Time 6m 59.00s. SP Evens.
E J Farrant (East Sussex & Romney Marsh).

780 - Maiden Div I (12st)

ELMORE ....**P Hacking** 1
(fav) (5s-5/2),hndy, ld 4 out, rddn out whn chal last
454 **Bomb The Bees 5a**...................**Miss P Ellison** 2
alwys prom, chal 2 out, kpt on onepce flat
495 **Loch Irish (Ire) 5a** ....**S Cowell** 3
mid-div, mstk 7th, prog to ld 10th-4 out, wknd
Tommy Springer *mid-div, jnd ldrs 8th, wknd 3 out* 4
576 Manor Ranger *u.r. 1st* ur
572 Silly Sovereign 5a (bl) *ld to 2nd, styd in tch, wknng in 6th whn p.u. 13th* pu
597 Saun (Cze) *mid-div whn u.r. 4th* ur
Tamborito (Ire) *alwys rear, wll bhnd whn p.u. 13th* pu
454 Pett Lad *plld to ld 2nd, sn clr, ran out bnd aft 7th, rddr baild out* ro
576 Polar Ana (Ire) 5a *alwys wll in rear, p.u. 13th* pu
Tartan Glory 5a *prog frm rear 9th, 4th 12th, wknng & jmp slwly 14th & p.u.* pu
479 Orphan Olly *prom til f 11th* f
12 ran. 4l, 6l, 20l. Time 7m 17.00s. SP 5-2.
Mrs R R Day (East Sussex & Romney Marsh).

781 - Maiden Div II (12st)

576 **IORWERTH**.........................**Miss C Savell** 1
in tch, lft 2nd 14th, ld aft 3 out, kpt on
576 **Over The Clover (Ire) 5a**..................**A Welsh** 2
(10s-9/2),prom,rddn final ctt,lft 3rd 14th,kpt on,2nd 2 out
Mandenka ....**G Cooper** 3
(fav) (6s-5/2),ld 6-12th, lft in ld 14th, hdd 3 out, fdd
575 Oberons Butterfly *alwys detached, t.o. whn p.u. aft 12th* pu
Cherry Anne 5a *alwys towrds rear, wll bhnd whn p.u. 13th* pu
574 Times Are Changing 5a *in tch, hmpd 9th, rddn & wknd 12th, p.u. 14th* pu
575 Target Time 5a (bl) *cls up til f 9th* f
Sunley Line (bl) *sn rear, p.u. 12th* pu
575 Welshmans Canyon (Ire) *mstks in rear, wll bhnd whn p.u. 13th* pu
253 Reign Dance 7a *ld to 6th, wth ldr aft, ld agn 12th til p.u. 14th* pu

Phantom Slipper *prom til p.u. 8th* .... pu
1 ran. 6l, dist. Time 7m 21.00s. SP 4-1.
arry White (East Sussex & Romney Marsh).
.Ta.

WINDSOR FOREST BLOODHOUNDS
Tweseldown
Sunday March 31st
GOOD

782 - City Of London

377 **YAHOO ....S Astaire** 1+
16s-12s,cls up,ld 9th,qcknd clr 4 out,idld flat,jnd fin
126 **BUTTON YOUR LIP ....Mrs J Enderby** 1+
ld 3-9th, chsd ldr til not qckn 4 out, styd on wll flat
274 **Redelva 5a ....Mrs D Rowell** 3
mstks, plld, ld to 3rd, outpcd frm 13th, styd on wll 2 out
622 Mount Patrick *outpcd in rear, btn frm 4 out* 4
381 Mr Mayfair *sn rear, btn frm 4 out* 5
640 Little Island 5a *(fav) trckd ldrs,pshd alng hlfwy,bhnd whn mstk 13th,p.u.nxt,dsmntd* .... pu
ran. Dd-ht, 1l, 15l, 2½l. Time 6m 36.00s.
Astaire/Mrs J Enderby (Bicester With Whaddon Chase).
utton Your Lip, 3/1. Yahoo, 12/1.

783 - Members

469 **WREKIN HILL ....Mrs J Wilkinson** 1
(fav) w.w. prog to ld 10th, jnd 12th, hdd 3out, ld nxt, pshd out
478 **Transplant Blue ....S Goodings** 2
hld up, went 2nd & ev ch aft 2 out, no ext flat
575 **Joe Quality.............................C Coyne** 3
w.w. prog to disp 12th,ld 3 out,rdn & hdd nxt,immed btn
452 Strong Suspicion *made most til p.u. aft 9th, dsmntd* .. pu
592 Sir Hugo 21ow *cls 2nd til lft in ld aft 9th, hdd & wknd nxt, u.r. 4 out* .... ur
ran. ½l, 12l. Time 6m 43.00s. SP 5-4.
rs J V Wilkinson (Windsor Forest Bloodhounds).

784 - Confined (12st)

252 **TEX MEX (IRE)..........................J Maxse** 1
(fav) made all, clr 4 out, eased flat, cllpsd & died
99 **Blue Danube (USA).......................A Martin** 2
pshd alng hlfwy, styd on onepcd frm 4 out, no ch wth wnr
475 **Skinnhill (bl) ....C Mason** 3
chsd wnr to 11th, sn wknd, lft 3rd apr last
472 Bective Boy 3ex *chsd wnr 11th til blnd 4 out, not rcvr* 4
594 Olde Crescent *hld up, prog 7th, 2nd 4 out, wknd 2 out, p.u. last* .... pu
ran. 15l, 8l. Time 6m 22.00s. SP 4-7.
rs S Maxse (Hampshire).

785 - Open

380 **AFALTOUN...............................T Lacey** 1
ld to 6th, hrd rdn & no ext 4 out, lft clr last
337 **Old Road (USA) (bl) ....C Coyne** 2
trckd ldrs to 12th, outpcd 4 out, t.o. 2 out, lft 2nd last
595 Vultoro *cls up, ld 6th, clr 4 out, 15l clr whn blnd & u.r. last* .... ur
475 Darton Ri *(fav) trckd ldr, 2l 2nd whn u.r. 14th* .... ur
262 Jupiter Moon *f 1st*.................. f
ran. Dist. Time 6m 36.00s. SP 11-4.
iss J Winch (Vine & Craven).

786 - Ladies

474 **QANNAAS (bl) ....Miss L Parrott** 1
(fav) cls up, lft in ld 10th, clr 12th, pshd out flat
Sunley Street 5a (v) ....Miss S Vickery 2
hld up rear, prog 7th, not qckn 12th, styd on frm last,no ch
474 **Tudor Henry ....Mrs C Mitchell** 3
cls up, chsd wnr 10th, outpcd 12th, no ext 2 out
475 Charlton Yeoman *outpcd in rear, nvr able to chal* 4
Sam Shorrock *1st ride, sn rear, t.o. 11th* 5
474 Phelioff *chsd ldrs til pshd alng hlfwy, sn bhnd, t.o. 13th*.................. 6
Astroar *rear, u.r. 1st*.................. ur
478 Windover Lodge *ld, dstrctd by loose horse & ran out 10th*.................. ro
8 ran. 12l, 5l, 20l, 3l, 3l. Time 6m 18.00s. SP Evens.
Mrs Ann Leat (Hursley Hambledon).
One fence omitted last two circuits, 17 jumps.

787 - Restricted (12st)

479 **SILVER CONCORD ....S Blackwell** 1
8s-4s,w.w. prog 12th,styd on wll to ld apr last,all out
473 **Dad's Pipe ....T Smith** 2
prom, mstly 2nd frm 12th, ev ch last, no ext flat
640 **Keep On Trying 5a....................M Portman** 3
alwys prom, ld 11th, qcknd 13th, hdd apr last, no ext
219 Banton Loch *rear, not qckn 13th, late prog frm 2 out*. . 4
526 Bilbo Baggins (Ire) *made most to 11th, wknd frm nxt, sn btn*.................. 5
574 Mr Sunnyside *trckd ldrs, outpcd frm 12th, t.o. 2 out* ... 6
Daring Trouble 5a *mid-div, prog 8th, wknd 12th, bhnd whn p.u. 3 out*.................. pu
520 Titchwell Milly 5a *rear, gd prog 3 out, 3rd & ev ch whn no room & u.r. last* .... ur
272 Wholestone (Ire) *(fav) n.j.w. blnd 3rd, wknd 12th, blnd 4 out & p.u.*.................. pu
9 ran. 2½l, 2½l, 2½l, 10l, 25l. Time 6m 40.00s. SP 4-1.
Mrs D E Cheshire (Ross Harriers).

788 - Open Maiden

557 **FATHERS FOOTPRINTS..................R Hicks** 1
cls up, ld 11th, qcknd 13th, styd on well 2 out, pshd out
525 **Cool Rascal 5a ....L Lay** 2
mid-div, prog hlfwy, pshd alng 14th, ev ch last, one-pcd
267 **Tea Cee Kay.......................R Sweeting** 3
trckd ldrs, not qckn & rdn 13th, styd on onepcd frm 2 out
Mariners Maid 5a *prom, rmndrs 2nd, 2nd & ev ch 3 out, wknd nxt*.................. 4
597 No Reply *sn rear, t.o. 4 out*.................. 5
521 Phil's Dream *(fav) cls 4th whn u.r. 9th*.................. ur
Dicks Delight (Ire) *ld to 11th, sn rdn, t.o. & p.u. last* ... pu
Barrow Street *dwelt, last, mstk & lost iron 5th, blnd nxt & p.u.*.................. pu
8 ran. 2l, 5l, 25l, 5l. Time 6m 42.00s. SP 8-1.
Mrs M Thomson (Cotswold).
M.J.

KELSO
Monday April 1st
GOOD TO FIRM

789 - 3m 1f Mdn Hun

403 **ABERCROMBY COMET 11.7 7a...Miss S Forster** 1
settld midfield, imp hfwy, led 6 out to 3 out, rallied und pres to ld run-in, soon clr.
609 **Worthy Spark 12.0 ....Mr P Craggs** 2
(fav) j.w, ld to 6 out, led 3 out, hdd run-in, no ext.
Damnification 11.7 7a ....Mr A Parker 3
in tch, left to chase lding pair after 8 out, kept on same pace from 3 out.
501 Rallying Cry (Ire) 11.7 7a *struggling to keep up after one cct, t.o.*.................. 4
486 Panto Lady 11.2 7a *soon struggling, t.o.*.................. 5
609 Royalist (Can) 11.9 5a *struggling to stay in tch after one cct, t.o. when ref last.* .... ref
403 Weddicar Lady 11.2 7a *settld with chasing gp, blnd and u.r. 11th*.................. ur
499 Minibrig 11.2 7a *settld with chasing gp, 5th and one pace when f 6 out*.................. f
486 Deday 11.7 7a *pressed ldr, blnd and u.r. 8 out*....... ur
321 Canister Castle 11.10 5a 1ow *blnd 2nd, chsd ldrs till lost tch quickly and p.u. before 7 out*.................. pu

613 Monynut 11.2 7a *soon bhnd, p.u. before 7 out* .... pu
11 ran. 7l, 15l, dist, 1¼l. Time 6m 32.00s. SP 7-1.
Mrs S Forster

790 - 3m 1f Hun

582 **ROYAL JESTER 11.9 5a ....Mr C Storey** 1
settld with chasing gp, imp before 5 out, outpcd after next, styd on strly to ld run-in.
672 **Off The Bru 12.0 7a ....Mr M Bradburne** 2
pressed lea der, ld 2 out, hdd briefly last, rallied, hded and one pace run-in.
359 **Hedley Mill 11.6 7a ....Mr A Parker** 3
(fav) patiently rdn, hdwy 5 out, ld briefly last, ridden and not qckn run-in, broke down.
487 Washakie 12.0 *in tch one cct, soon outpcd and driven along, kept on from 3 out, no impn.* 4
The Green Fool 12.1 3a *chsd ldrs, effort hfwy, struggling when pace qcknd 5 out, no impn after.* 5
120 Ellerton Hill 12.0 *ld till hdd and hit 2 out, wknd quickly before last.* 6
487 Green Times 12.0 7a *struggling to keep up after one cct, t.o.* 7
612 Ruber 11.7 7a *soon struggling, t.o.* 8
487 Loughlinstown Boy 11.13 5a *chsd ldrs till p.u. before 12th.* .... pu
Secret Sceptre 11.9 5a *driven along and outpcd after one cct, t.o. when p.u. before 2 out.* .... pu
582 Parlebiz 11.2 7a *settld off the pace, f 5th* .... f
11 ran. 4l, 3½l, 20l, 2½l, 1½l, 10l, dist. Time 6m 24.10s. SP 5-2.
Mrs A D Wauchope

HEYTHROP
Heythrop
Tuesday April 2nd
FIRM

791 - Members

SAILOR'S DELIGHT ....T Lacey 1
(fav) made all, hrd rdn flat, kpt on
643 **Tranquil Lord (Ire)........................D Smith** 2
trckd wnr, 4l down last, ran on flat, too much to do
643 **Colonel Fairfax..................Miss K Matthews** 3
hld up, nvr on terms, no dang
Sad Old Red *chsd 1st pair, mstk 14th, 8l 3rd whn f nxt* .... f
The Last Straw *t.o. 6th, rest fin whn walked out & u.r. 3 out* .... ro
5 ran. 2l, 20l. Time 7m 3.00s. SP 8-15.
Alan Bosley (Heythrop).

792 - 3¾m Sporting Life Ladies

262 **SIRISAT..............................Miss T Blazey** 1
prssd ldr to 13th, 3rd aft til ran on last, ld nr fin
436 **Military Two Step ....Miss A Plunkett** 2
ld to 15th & frm 17th, 5l clr 2 out, hdd nr fin
525 **Dusky Day.......................Mrs N Sheppard** 3
(fav) n.j.w. rear,prog to ld 15-17th,ran on agn flat,just faild
436 Icky's Five (bl) *chsd ldrs to hlfwy, outpcd frm 15th, wknd 2 out* 4
234 Codger *mid-div, no imp on ldrs 4 out, wknd 2 out* 5
684 Jellyband *alwys last pair, t.o. frm 15th* 6
474 Grand Value *3rd whn f 5th* .... f
7 ran. Nk, nk, 20l, 12l, 20l. Time 8m 6.00s. SP 4-1.
Miss Tessa Blazey (Beaufort).
One fence omitted, 21 jumps.

793 - 4m Sporting Life Open

428 **KETTLES 5a ....A Phillips** 1
mstks,rear,prog 10th,prssd ldrs 4 out,rdn to ld last 100yrds
639 **Strong Beau.......................................L Lay** 2
prom, ld 16th, hrd prssd frm 3 out, hdd last 100 yrds
744 **January Don (bl) ....A Dalton** 3+
prssd ldr,ld 14-16th,sn rdn,ev ch last,not qckn flat
124 **Bit Of A Clown..........................A Mobley** 3
hld up,prog 18th,cls up 3 out,onepcd whn hit last,fin 4th
639 Sevens Out *prom,ld/disp 12-16th,ev ch whn blnd 2 out,not rcvr* ....
538 Shipmate *lost tch 10th, t.o. 14th* ....
337 The Tartan Spartan *trckd ldrs,rdn & lost tch aft 17th,t.o. & p.u. 2 out, dsmntd* .... p
579 Tytherington *ld to 12th, prom til wknd 17th, t.o. & p.u. 2 out* .... p
657 Panda Shandy 5a *(fav) hld up,prog to disp whn blnd 18th,nt rcvr,no ch whn p.u.flat* .... p
637 Golden Mac *mstk 9th, lost tch 14th, p.u. 17th.* .... p
10 ran. 1½l, 5l, ½l, 8l, 1 fence. Time 8m 30.00s. SP 10-1.
Mrs Joanna Daniell (Ledbury).

794 - Confined (12st)

524 **GUITING GRAY ....Miss A Dare**
(fav) j.w. ld 10th, clr 2 out, easy
334 **Autonomous ....A Charles-Jones**
ld to 10th, chsd wnr til pckd 3 out, kpt on, tk 2nd agn fin
380 **French Pleasure 5a ....P Howse**
not fluent, in tch, prog to chs wnr aft 3 out, no imp
712 Its Murphy Man *chsd ldrs til outpcd 14th, sn no ch* ....
338 Lily The Lark 5a *w.w. strgglng whn mstk 14th, no dang aft* ....
637 Nesselnite 5a 7ow *s.s. t.o. last til mstk & u.r. 6th* .... u
6 ran. 15l, nk, 15l, sht-hd. Time 6m 41.00s. SP 4-5.
A M Mason (V.W.H.).

795 - B F S S

524 **TINOTOPS ....Miss S Vickery**
trckd ldr, ld 14th, clr 3 out, drvn out frm last
638 **Granville Grill ....J Deutsch**
(fav) jmpd lft, ld to 14th, btn frm 2 out
451 **Snowfire Chap (bl)..................T Underwood**
cls up to 12th, btn whn blnd nxt, kpt on
358 Striking Chimes *t.o. 3rd, 2 fences bhnd whn p.u. 3 out* .... p
4 ran. 8l, 15l. Time 6m 45.00s. SP 11-8.
R H H Targett (Blackmore & Sparkford Vale).

796 - Maiden Div I

607 **DEMAMO (IRE) ....S Jackson**
prom, ld 9th, clr last, all out nr fin
641 **Good Looking Guy ....A Charles-Jones**
ran in sntchs,outpcd frm 15th,mod 4th 2 out,fin strngly
430 **Specific Impulse ....L Lay**
mstk 1st, prom, prssd wnr 14th, rdn & no ext apr last
221 Dragons Lady 5a *ld to 9th, prom aft, ev ch 3 out, no ext frm nxt* ....
643 Dip The Lights 5a *chsd ldrs til grad wknd frm 15th* ....
639 Mountfosse *in tch to 12th, wll bhnd frm 3 out* ....
440 Archie's Sister 5a *pllng, in tch to 15th, wknd rpdly, t.o. whn blnd last* ....
525 Rickham Bay 5a *jmpd slwly, alwys last, t.o. 12th* ....
430 Fountain Of Fire (Ire) 5a *(fav) cls up to 13th, wknd nxt, t.o. & p.u. 3 out* .... p
641 Totally Optimistic *mstks, in tch to hlfwy, t.o. whn blnd 13th, p.u. 15th* .... p
643 Bay Hobnob 7a *mstk 5th, in tch to 12th, t.o. & p.u. 2 out* .... p
11 ran. ¾l, 4l, 3l, 20l, dist, 12l, 20l. Time 6m 56.00s. SP 6-1.
H Bricknell (Cotswold Vale Farmers).

797 - Maiden Div II

440 **SPARNOVA 5a ....R Barrett**
cls up, chsd ldr 2 out, chal last, ld nr fin
432 **Fiddlers Knap ....J Hobbs**
ld to 6th,lost plc & poor last 9th,rpd prog 2 out,just faild
Autumn Ride (Ire) 5a (bl) ....F Brennan
(fav) cls up,mstk 11th,ld 13th & sn clr,not run on 3 out,hdd fin
340 Country Brew 5a *prom til outpcd aft 2 out* ....

477 Devil's Sting (Ire) *prom, ld 12-13th, outpcd frm 2 out...* 5
479 The Man From Clare (Ire) *hld up, nvr plcd to chal.....* 6
Furious Avenger *ld 6-12th, wknd 3 out* 7
643 Roark's Chukka *cls up, wknd whn mstk 11th, p.u. nxt* pu
606 Mansun *14s-8s, blnd 9th, cls up to 12th, t.o. whn blnd 3 out & p.u.* ..... pu
Princess Letitia 5a *mstk 1st, t.o. whn ref 2nd.........* ref
Mr Robstee 7a *ref 1st, cont, ref 2nd* ..... ref
11 ran. Nk, nk, 10l, 1l, 15l, 2l. Time 7m 6.00s. SP 5-1.
V T Bradshaw (Bicester With Whaddon Chase).
J.N.

ASCOT
Wednesday April 3rd
GOOD TO FIRM

798 - 2m 3f 110yds Hun

483 **MR GOLIGHTLY 12.1 7a ....Mrs J Reed** 1
trckd ldrs, ld 8th, made rest, mstk last, styd on well.
670 **A Windy Citizen (Ire) 11.6 7a ....Mr R Hicks** 2
held up, mstk 9th, hdwy to chal 11th, ev ch last, no ext.
Amari King 12.1 7a ....Mr C Ward Thomas 3
chsd ldrs, ev ch 2 out, one pace apr last.
364 Trust The Gypsy 11.13 5a *trckd ldrs till wknd after 10th, soon driven along, styd on one pace.* 4
668 Social Climber 11.7 7a *keen hold early, trckd ldr to 7th, cl up till rdn and wknd apr 3 out.* 5
595 Paco's Boy 11.7 7a *bhnd, mstk 7th, cld 11th, soon lost tch, t.o..* 6
359 Tipping Tim 12.1 3a *ld to 8th, rallied 10th, wknd next, t.o..* 7
Rah Wan (USA) 11.13 5a *held up, f 8th.* ..... f
581 Four Rivers 11.7 7a *alwys bhnd, t.o. when p.u. before 4 out.* ..... pu
483 Proud Sun 12.1 7a *(fav) keen hold, held up, f 8th.* ..... f
10 ran. 2½l, 6l, 13l, 8l, nk, 15l. Time 4m 56.20s. SP 5-2.
Mrs B I Cobden

LUDLOW
Wednesday April 3rd
GOOD TO FIRM

799 - 3m Hun

581 **OAKLANDS WORD 11.12 7a ....Mr J Jukes** 1
in tch, ld 11th, drew clr between last 2, pushed out.
530 **West Quay 11.7 7a...............Mr J Creighton** 2
(fav) ld till after 2nd, blnd next, led 8th till mstk and hdd 11th, only horse to jump 15th, blunded 2 out, no ext.
256 **Carrickmines 11.12 7a ....Miss D J Jones** 3
chsd ldrs, in tch when blnd 3 out, soon one pace.
256 Knockumshin 12.0 5a *held up, pushed along and outpcd apr 2 out.* 4
669 Rusty Bridge 11.12 7a *ld 4th, blnd next, hdd 8th, one pace from 3 out.* 5
683 Kali Sana (Ire) 11.7 7a (bl) *bhnd, t.o. when p.u. before 9th.* ..... pu
674 Thornhill 11.2 7a *ld after 2nd to 4th, midfield when f 7th.* ..... f
366 Watchit Lad 11.7 7a *bhnd when blnd and u.r. 6th.....* ur
8 ran. 5l, ½l, 1¾l, 4l. Time 6m 2.90s. SP 2-1.
F P Luff

MID DEVON
Clyst St Mary
Thursday April 4th
GOOD TO SOFT

800 - Members

630 **ARTISTIC PEACE 5a ....D Stephens** 1
trckd ldr, b.d. 15th, rmntd, fin alone
560 Senegalais (Fr) *(fav) ld at slow pace, f heavily 15th (ditch)* ..... f
Nattadon-Hill 5a *jmpd lft 1st, ref & u.r. 2nd* ..... ref
3 ran. Time 8m 48.00s. SP 5-1.
Mrs Diane Jackson (Mid Devon).
One fence omitted this race, 19 jumps instead of 22.

801 - Confined (12st)

531 **DEVIOSITY (USA) (bl)...........Miss L Blackford** 1
disp til slght ld aft 14th, pshd 3l clr apr 2 out
531 **Larky McIlroy 5a ....Miss S Vickery** 2
(fav) disp to 14th, ev ch til outpcd apr nxt, eased whn btn
2 ran. 10l. Time 6m 42.00s. SP 11-4.
Merv Rowe (Devon & Somerset Staghounds).
Open ditch omitted from this race onwards, 16 jumps per race.

802 - Open

626 **CHILIPOUR.............................N Harris** 1
(fav) lft solo 2nd, jmpd slwly 3rd & 4th, grad warmed up
442 Nelson River (USA) *tried to ref, blnd & u.r. 2nd.......* ur
2 ran. Time 7m 47.00s. SP 1-10.
Nick Viney (Dulverton (West)).

803 - Ladies

624 **PHAR TOO TOUCHY 5a...........Miss R Francis** 1
(fav) hld up in tch, disp 9th til drew clr frm 12th, easily
730 **Unique New York (bl) ....Miss S Offord** 2
prom, hit 8th, disp 11th-nxt, sn outpcd
716 **Aristocratic Gold ....Mrs M Hand** 3
rear, slight prog 4 out, nvr nr, reluc clsng stgs
531 Rapid Rascal *slght ld til aft 8th, disp 11th-nxt, sn wknd.* 4
4 ran. 5l, 30l, hd. Time 6m 39.00s. SP 2-7.
Miss R A Francis (Dulverton West).

804 - Intermediate (12st)

647 **THE PEDLAR 5a 5ex ....T Greed** 1
(fav) made all, mstk 6th, drew wll clr aft 3 out, easily
446 **Darktown Strutter (bl).................M Burrows** 2
chsd wnr, outpcd 3 out
444 **Querrin Lodge ....I Widdicombe** 3
alwys last, strgglng final ctt
3 ran. 15l, 6l. Time 6m 54.00s. SP 2-5.
D Hurst (Deven & Somerset Staghounds).

805 - Restricted (12st)

627 **LONESOME TRAVELLER (NZ) ....Mrs M Hand** 1
ld to 4th, sttld 3rd, prog 3 out, ld nxt, styd on
720 **Oneovertheight...........................N Harris** 2
disp frm 5th, mstk 8th, ld 11th til hdd aft 2 out, no ext
720 **Mountain Master ....Miss L Blackford** 3
(fav) disp 5th til ld 8th, hdd & blnd 11th, sn wknd & mstks
352 Hillview Star (Ire) 5a *n.j.w. t.o. frm 9th* 4
441 The Copper Key *mstk 1st, rear til p.u. aft 6th* ..... pu
554 Good King Henry *nvr dang, poor 4th at 8th, t.o. & p.u. 13th.* ..... pu
Kingdom Lad 7a *rear, not fluent, p.u. 8th.* ..... pu
7 ran. 4l, 12l, 2 fences. Time 6m 37.00s. SP 5-2.
Reg Hand (Dartmoor).

806 - Open Maiden Div I (12st)

CHASING CHARLIE ....Miss A Goschen 1
tubed, chsd ldrs, prog 3 out, ld nxt, pshd clr
557 **Good Appeal 5a...............Miss L Blackford** 2
handy, ld & hmpd apr 12th, ld agn aft 3 out-nxt, no ext
446 **Avin Fun Bar 5a..........................T Greed** 3
ld to 11th, agn 12th, hdd aft 3 out, onepcd
718 Scallykenning *(Jt fav) prom, cls 3rd whn blnd & u.r. 11th.* ..... ur
301 Breeze-Bloc 5a *(Jt fav) n.j.w. blnd 5th, poor 4th frm 11th til p.u. 2 out* ..... pu
Poppy Cleo 5a *bhnd & strgglng til p.u. 12th, schoold* pu

Legal Affair 7a *not fluent, bhnd til p.u. 13th, schoold* .. pu
7 ran. 10l, 12l. Time 6m 49.50s. SP 8-1.
Mrs S Hooper (Portman).

807 - Open Maiden Div II (12st)

734 **BLAKEINGTON (bl) ....N Mitchell** 1
cls 2nd til lft in ld 10th, hdd 12th, drvn & lft clr 2 out
446 **Dusty Furlong ....Miss K Baily** 2
poor 5th at 14th, ran on clsng stgs, nrst fin
534 **Jolly Flier ....S Ellis** 3
in tch, 3rd & rdn 14th, wknd, lft 3rd last
627 Springcombe 5a *bhnd frm 8th, t.o.* 4
733 Working Man (Ire) 7a *not fluent, alwys rear* 5
355 Open Agenda (Ire) *sn bhnd, t.o. & p.u. 10th* .... pu
734 Four Leaf Clover 5a *(fav) in tch, ld 12th, assured wnr whn f 2 out* .... f
446 Prides Delight 5a *mid-div, 5th whn blnd & u.r. 13th* ... ur
471 Touch Of Wind 7a *slght ld til f 10th* .... f
556 Harmony's Choice 7a *rear, prog 13th, ran on to 3rd whn f last* .... f
10 ran. 8l, 25l, 10l, 20l. Time 6m 50.00s. SP 6-1.
Mrs Jackie Bugg (South Dorset).
G.T.

TOWCESTER
Saturday April 6th
FIRM

808 - 3m 1f Hun

483 **HERMES HARVEST 12.5 5a ....Mr J Culloty** 1
alwys in tch, ld 3 out, pushed clr.
580 **Call Home (Ire) 11.11 7a ....Mr T Hills** 2
(fav) blnd 2nd, ld 3rd, soon clr, hdd 3 out, soon outpcd.
671 **New Mill House 11.7 7a ....Mr P Scott** 3
lost tch 9th, t.o. when hit 12th.
Windy Ways 11.9 5a *ld to 3rd, styd chasing ldr till p.u. before 14th, lame.* .... pu
4 ran. 9l, dist. Time 6m 20.60s. SP 7-4.
Miss B W Palmer

ASHFORD VALLEY
Charing
Saturday April 6th
FIRM

809 - Members (12st)

676 **ALZAMINA 5a ....A Welsh** 1
(fav) hld up, chal apr 4 out, qcknd to ld nxt, ran on well
452 **Profligate....................Miss P Ellison** 2
ld to 2nd, ld 11th-14th, agn apr 4 out-nxt, no ext 2 out
780 **Polar Ana (Ire) 5a ....Miss S Gladders** 3
prom, ld 14th til hdd & outpcd apr 4 out
Scarning Gizmo 5a *ld 2nd, clr 8th til u.r. 11th* .... ur
4 ran. 4l, 4l. Time 6m 38.00s. SP 4-5.
J C Window (Ashford Valley).

810 - Restricted (12st)

454 **SOVEREIGN SPRAY (IRE)..............P Hacking** 1
(fav) wll plcd, ld apr 3 out, rdn out whn chal last
576 **Galaroi (Ire) 2ow ....D Robinson** 2
disp 6th til ld 13th, hdd apr 3 out, rallied, no ext flat
574 **Salachy Run (Ire) ....A Welsh** 3
trckd ldrs, 3rd frm 14th, rddn 4 out, no imp, wknd 2 out
Second Time Round *in tch, no dang final cct* 4
779 Basher Bill *ld/disp to 13th, grad wknd aft* 5
574 Golden Pele *in tch, und pres 13th, last nxt, wll bhnd whn p.u. aft 2 out* .... pu
6 ran. 2l, 7l, 15l, ¾l. Time 6m 26.00s. SP 7-4.
S P Tindall (Southdown & Eridge).

811 - Land Rover Open (12st)

776 **STRONG GOLD 7ex (bl)..............T McCarthy** 1
sn prom, ld 9th, disp 13-15th, made rest, ran on wll 2 out
595 **Ginger Tristan 7ex ....D Robinson** 2
alwys wth ldrs, prssd wnr 4 out-2 out, onepcd
677 **Cockstown Lad 7ex ....D Featherstone** 3
(fav) sn rear, hdwy 15th, 3rd 2 out, nvr nrr
573 Sky Venture *alwys mid-div, 8l 3rd 4 out, onepcd*...... 4
570 Bright Hour *mid-div to 12th, rear & no ch frm 4 out* ... 5
776 Yeoman Farmer *alwys rear, mstk 12th, nvr thrtnd* 6
571 Kilsheelan Lad 2ow *t.o. hlfwy* 7
595 Sunday Punch *ld to 9th, disp 13-15th, wknd & p.u. 4 out*.......... pu
595 Darkbrook 7ex *mid-div, strggling 12th, rear whn p.u. 14th*.......... pu
9 ran. 5l, 4l, 5l, 2l, 1l, 2 fences. Time 6m 11.00s. SP 9-4.
Peter Bonner (Old Surrey & Burstow).

812 - Ladies

633 **ADAMARE ....Miss C Holliday** 1
made all, prssd 13th-2 out, styd on well
620 **What A Gig ....Miss P Ellison** 2
rear, clsd 13th, outpcd 15th, rdn & ran on 4 out,tk 2nd last
572 **Durbo 4ex ....Mrs E Coveney** 3
alwys prom, jmpd rght, effrt apr 4 out, 4th & btn 2 out
596 Our Survivor 4ex *(fav) alwys rear, nvr going wll, wll bhnd whn p.u. 2 out*.......... pu
783 Strong Suspicion *alwys rear, blnd 4th, last & no ch whn u.r. 4 out* .... ur
337 Father Fortune *cls up, prssd wnr 13th til wknd 2 out, 3rd whn ran out last*.......... ro
6 ran. 4l, 10l. Time 6m 2.00s. SP 11-4.
H Morton (Quorn).

813 - Club

775 **STEDE QUARTER ....P Hickman** 1
(fav) clsd up 12th, disp 14-15th, 2nd aft, chal 2 out, ld last
775 **American Eyre ....Miss S Gladders** 2
ld/disp frm 2nd, def adv 4 out, jnd last, hdd & onepcd flat
450 **Pacific Sound ....J Van Praagh** 3
ld to 2nd, disp 3-10th, 3rd frm 12th, rmndrs nxt,wknd 2 out
779 Huckleberry Friend 5a *in tch to 3 out, wknd*.......... 4
453 Sir Wager (bl) *sn last, jmpd slwly & nvr going, p.u. aft 6th*.......... pu
5 ran. 1½l, 25l, 10l. Time 6m 24.00s. SP 11-10.
Mrs S Dench (Ashford Valley).

814 - 2½m Open Maiden (5-7yo) (12st)

597 **KELBURNE LAD (IRE) ....P Bull** 1
alwys prom, ld apr 9th, blnd & hdd 2 out, rallied to ld flat
575 **Velka 5a....................Mrs S Hickman** 2
(fav) ld to 4th, cls aft, chal 3 out, ld nxt, hdd flat
Prom's Mohock ....G Hopper 3
nvr fluent & jmpd rght, ld 4th-apr 9th, chal 3 out, wknd nxt
Little Petherick 5a *schoold in rear, out of tch hlfwy* ... 4
781 Target Time 5a 3ow (bl) *prom, 4th & btn whn f 2 out*... f
Hit The Bid (Ire) 7a *rear, schoold, out of tch hlfwy, p.u. 4 out* .... pu
781 Phantom Slipper *alwys rear, lost tch 6th, p.u. aft 11th* pu
Rugans Hope *rear, out of tch whn p.u. 8th*.......... pu
8 ran. ½l, 6l, dist. Time 5m 13.00s. SP 7-2.
Mrs D B A Silk (Kent & Surrey Bloodhounds).
G.Ta.

BLACKMORE & SPARKFORD VALE
Charlton Horethorne
Saturday April 6th

GOOD TO FIRM

815 - Members

532 **THE JOGGER**..........................**J Tizzard** 1
in tch, ld 12th, sn clr, easily
Arctic Baron.....................**Miss S Vickery** 2
ld/disp to 12th, kpt on frm 4 out
519 **Strong Tarquin (Ire)**...............**Miss P Curling** 3
(fav) held up,mstk 11th & rmmndrs,prog nxt,3rd & outpcd frm 3 out
707 Sula Pride *midfld, styd on onepce frm 3 out* 4
709 Fred Splendid *hndy to 12th, lost tch frm 4 out* 5
655 Kings Rank *alwys rear, t.o. 14th, p.u. & dismntd 4 out* pu
Spar Copse *sn rear, t.o. whn p.u. 12th* .... pu
Devonia (NZ) 5a *ld/disp to 12th, lost tch 4 out, p.u. apr last* .... pu
8 ran. 10l, 15l, 1l, 10l. Time 6m 20.70s. SP 5-2.
Mrs P T Tizzard (Blackmore & Sparkford Vale).

816 - Intermediate (12st)

335 **ARCTIC CHILL (IRE)**.............**Miss S Vickery** 1
(fav) prom, ld 3rd, ran on wll frm 3 out, easily
656 **Thegoose**...............................**P King** 2
held up, prog 12th, ev ch 3 out, onepcd aft
472 **Good For Business**...................**T Mitchell** 3
in tch to 15th, lost ch whn hit 2 out, onepcd aft
530 Tangle Baron *chsd ldrs, lost tch 13th, outpcd frm nxt* .. 4
476 Gormless (Ire) *midfld, cls 3rd 12th, wknd frm 5 out* 5
652 Vital Legacy *alwys rear, lost tch frm 14th* 6
657 Pabrey *in tch to 12th, rddn nxt, outpcd frm 4 out* 7
7 ran. 3l, 4l, 8l, 10l, 2l, 20l. Time 6m 19.90s. SP 2-1.
M F Thorne/ B G Hobbs (Blackmore & Sparkford Vale).

817 - Open (12st)

648 **SAYYURE (USA)**.....................**R Treloggen** 1
chsd ldr, ld aft 3 out, clr nxt, rddn out
654 **Vital Song**..........................**G Matthews** 2
(fav) ld til aft 3 out, rlld apr last, not qckn aft
651 **Spitfire Jubilee 7ex**..................**R Nuttall** 3
in tch to 12th, outpcd frm 14th
731 Qualitair Memory (Ire) 7ex *chsd ldr, btn 3rd whn f 14th* .... f
469 Earl Boon *last thruout, lost tch 12th, p.u. apr 5 out* .... pu
5 ran. 1½l, dist. Time 6m 15.00s. SP 12-1.
A G Harris (Mendip Farmers).

818 - Ladies

561 **TOM SNOUT (IRE)**..............**Miss S Vickery** 1
(Jt fav) made all, ran on wll frm 4 out
654 **Butler John (Ire)**.................**Miss R Francis** 2
chsd ldr, chal 13th, alwys held frm 3 out
581 **Great Uncle**.......................**Miss A Goschen** 3
in tch til 9th, t.o. frm 13th
708 Kiltonga *in tch til f 8th* .... f
708 Beyond Our Reach *(Jt fav) held up, in 4th whn u.r. 6th* .... ur
469 Temple Knight *in tch til 10th, t.o. & p.u. lame 3 out* .... pu
6 ran. 6l, dist. Time 6m 12.00s. SP 7-4.
J M Kinnear (Blackmore & Sparkford Vale).

819 - Maiden (5-7yo) Div I (12st)

283 **ELLE FLAVADOR 5a**..............**Miss S Vickery** 1
j.w., ld 4th, styd on wll frm 3 out, easily
653 **Crock D'Or**............................**M Felton** 2
(fav) held up, prog 10th, chsd wnnr vainly aft
465 **Sue's Quest 5a**..................**G Barfoot-Saunt** 3
rear til 10th, prog 12th, nvr on terms wth 1st 2
534 Dollybat 5a *alwys midfld, nvr on terms wth ldrs* 4
653 Olive Basket 7a *alwys midfld, outpcd frm 5 out* 5
557 Nottarex *rear, no ch frm 12th, u.r. 14th* .... ur
145 Country Blue 7a *held up, prog 12th, 3rd nxt, btn whn f last* .... f
653 Rosanda 5a *u.r. 1st* .... ur
448 Sam's Successor 7a *alwys rear, t.o. & p.u. 12th* .... pu
652 Tamaimo (Ire) 7a 7ow *alwys rear, p.u. & dismntd 14th* pu
10 ran. 12l, 20l, ½l, 20l. Time 6m 37.00s. SP 4-1.
Mrs A B Watts (Blackmore & Sparkford Vale).

820 - Maiden (5-7yo) Div II (12st)

522 **STRONG CHAIRMAN (IRE) 7a 3ow**.....**N Mitchell** 1
(Jt fav) held up, prog 12th, wnt 3rd 3 out, ld aft 2 out, ran on wll
734 **Ridemore Balladeer 7a**..........**Miss S Cobden** 2
alwys prom, ld 13-15th, outpcd nxt, rlld apr last
646 **Noble Comic 7a**.......................**J Tizzard** 3
in tch, 3rd 11th, ld 3 out til hdd aft nxt, not qckn aft
712 Melling 7a *j.w., hndy, ev ch 14th-3 out, no ext frm nxt* 4D
Old Harry's Wife 5a *midfld, 4th 11th, ev ch 14th, no ext frm 2 out, imprv* 4
712 Heather Boy *ld 3rd-12th, rddn 4 out, onepcd aft* 5
Model Countess (Ire) 5a *cls up til 7th, lost tch 9th, p.u. apr 12th* .... pu
658 Sandy Etna (Ire) 5a *ld to 3rd, lost tch 11th, t.o. & p.u. 2 out* .... pu
556 Suba Lin 5a *rear til blndrd & u.r. 7th* .... ur
653 Heatherton Park 7a *alwys rear, t.o. & p.u. 3 out* ...... pu
734 Stillmore Business 7a 7ow *n.j.w., alwys rear, t.o. whn p.u. 4 out* .... pu
470 Passing Fair 7a *(Jt fav) held up in midfld, gng wll whn f 11th* .... f
12 ran. 8l, 2l, ½l, dist. Time 6m 31.00s. SP 6-4.
J A Keighley (Blackmore & Sparkford Vale).

821 - Maiden (8y & Up) (12st)

653 **COACHROADSTARBOY**................**M Felton** 1
held up, prog 13th, efft 3 out, ld nxt, ran on wll
646 **Blade Of Fortune**....................**R Treloggen** 2
(fav) held up, ld 13th-2 out, outpcd aft, eased
527 **Trimbush**...............................**T Lacey** 3
mid-div thruout, nvr on terms wth ldrs
733 Mountain-Linnet *in tch til 12th, outpcd frm 4 out* 4
532 Liberty James *prom, ld 9-13th, grdly wknd frm 4 out* .. 5
733 Paid Elation 5a *cls up early, rear frm 9th, outpcd* 6
533 Rushhome 5a *held up in tch, wknng whn p.u. & dismntd 4 out* .... pu
Goblins Light 5a *ld til 8th, wknd 10th, p.u. apr 13th* ... pu
652 Say Charlie *alwys rear, t.o. whn p.u. 4 out* .... pu
138 Call Avondale *(7s-3s), alwys rear, t.o. whn p.u. bfr 12th* .... pu
10 ran. 10l, 20l, 10l, 15l, 15l. Time 6m 19.00s. SP 6-1.
F G Gingell (Blackmore & Sparkford Vale).

822 - Restricted (12st)

368 **BINNEY BOY**...........................**M Felton** 1
(Jt fav) ld 13th-3 out, mstks 11th & 14th, disp aft, ld line
645 **Churchtown Chance (Ire) 5a**........**R Treloggen** 2
held up, prog 13th, disp 3 out til hdd line
521 **Definite Maybe (Ire) (bl)**..............**T Mitchell** 3
in tch, ev ch 3 out, outpcd aft, rlld aft last
Prince Amanda *rear, outpcd & no ch frm 14th* 4
728 Lisahane Lad *mid-div, no ch frm 13th, outpcd* 5
280 Blake's Finesse 5a *ld til 13th, wknd 3 out, p.u. apr last* .... pu
138 Highleeze (Ire) *(Jt fav) mid-div,rmmndrs 7th,4th 12th,rddn nxt,f hvly 14th (dead)* .... f
7 ran. Sht-hd, ¾l, 25l, 20l. Time 6m 19.00s. SP 2-1.
A D Wardall (Blackmore & Sparkford Vale).
D.P.

CLEVELAND
Stainton
Saturday April 6th
GOOD TO FIRM

823 - Members

591 **BASIL GREY**...........................**P Jenkins** 1
prom,ld 14th-3 out, ran wd straight, rallied to ld last
704 **Raike It In 5a**...........................**N Tutty** 2

sttld rear, prog 4 out, ld nxt til hdd & hit last, not rcvr
517 **Neladar 5a ....J Sinnott** 3
(fav) alwys handy, prog 4 out, ev ch nxt, sn onepcd
762 Sweet Rose 5a *disp til ld 5th, hdd 14th, lost plc & wknd 3 out* 4
515 Bold Croft 5a *alwys strggling, wll bhnd whn ran out bef 12th* .... ro
415 Engaging *disp til wknd 5th, p.u. 7th* .... pu
6 ran. 8l, 6l, 15l. Time 6m 14.00s. SP 5-1.
S G Jones (Cleveland).

824 - Confined (12st)

761 **FLIP THE LID (IRE) 5a....................N Tutty** 1
(fav) chsd ldrs, ld 8th, drew clr 3 out, comf
513 **Cromwell Point 3ex ....N Wilson** 2+
prom, pshd alng 9th, 2nd 16th, styd on onepcd
758 **Flying Lion ....M Haigh** 2+
alwys prom, rdn 15th, styd on frm 2 out
487 Pinewood Lad *chsd ldrs, blnd 16th, no prog frm 4 out* 4
512 Beau Rose *rear, rdn & prog 9th, jmpd slwly 14th, sn wknd, t.o.* 5
512 Valiant Vicar *last & lost tch 9th, blnd 13th, t.o. & p.u. 4 out* .... pu
586 Wall Game (USA) 5ex (bl) *mid-div, rdn 9th, sn strggling, t.o. & p.u. last* .... pu
760 Tammy My Girl 5a *mid-div, rdn 6th, u.r. nxt* .... ur
760 Some Flash *twrds rear, rdn 6th, u.r. nxt* .... ur
Gold Choice *ld to 8th, fdng whn blnd 12th, p.u. 15th* .... pu
758 Charlcot Storm 7a *strng rmndrs to jmp 1st, ref nxt* .... ref
11 ran. 2l, dd-ht, 10l, dist. Time 6m 9.00s. SP Evens.
Peter Sawney (Cleveland).

825 - Restricted (12st)

588 **MR DICK..............................S Swiers** 1
(fav) prom & going wll, ld 2 out, sn qcknd clr
329 **Carly Clever Clogs (Ire) 5a.............N Wilson** 2
rear, prog 6th, ev ch 2 out, btn whn mstk last
757 **Chapel Island ....G Tuer** 3
hld up, mstk 11th, prog 15th, ev ch 2 out, no ext
589 Highland Friend *alwys abt same plc, not pace to chal* 4
584 Cumberland Blues (Ire) *ld, blnd 7th, hdd 2 out, wknd* .. 5
225 Miley Pike *chsd ldrs, grad wknd frm 6 out, t.o.* 6
411 Spartan Juliet 5a *prom, pshd alng 6th, fdd 10th, t.o. 4 out* 7
7 ran. 6l, ½l, 5l, 7l, 20l, dist. Time 6m 12.00s. SP 4-5.
Mrs J Cooper (Middleton).

826 - Open

760 **FIERY SUN.............................N Wilson** 1
(fav) prom, went 2nd apr 14th, chal last, qcknd to ld flat
760 **Skipping Gale.........................P Atkinson** 2
alwys prom, mstk 13th, kpt on well frm 2 out
Knowe Head ....S Brisby 3
ld til last, onepcd
410 Convincing (v) *alwys prom, ev ch 4 out, wknd und pres 2 out* 4
410 Ringmore *twrds rear, dtchd by 11th, t.o. 4 out* 5
512 Cleasby Hill *nvr going wll, lost tch 8th, p.u. aft nxt* .... pu
Gospel Rock (NZ) *s.s. bhnd whn p.u. 3rd* .... pu
Frome Boy *mid-div, mstk 2nd, p.u. nxt* .... pu
8 ran. ½l, 2l, 15l, dist. Time 6m 9.00s. SP Evens.
P Cartmel (Cleveland).

827 - Ladies

514 **CAROLE'S DELIGHT 5a..............Mrs L Ward** 1
(fav) trckd ldr, disp 2 out, ld last, ran on well
Hellcatmudwrestler....................Miss T Gray 2
jmpd lft, ld til jnd 2 out, hdd last, kpt on well
759 **Cheeky Pot..........................Mrs S Grant** 3
mid-div, prog 16th, onepcd frm 2 out
759 John Corbet *prom til outpcd bef 2 out* 4
759 Grey Realm 5a *mid-div, mstk 7th, wknd apr 2 out* 5
759 Colonel Popski *mid-div, gd prog to go prom 14th, wknd 3 out* 6
759 Earl Gray (bl) *rear, mstk 8th, outpcd 10th, lost tch 14th, t.o.* 7
7 ran. ½l, 8l, 1l, 5l, 12l, 25l. Time 6m 4.00s. SP Evens.
C Holden (Cleveland).

828 - Open Maiden Div I

415 **MASTER CROZINA....................P Cornforth** 1
(fav) ld to 3rd,ld 7th,hdd 6 out,lft in ld nxt,styd on well
762 **Vale Of York........................Miss R Clark** 2
prom, ld 3rd-7th, onepcd frm 4 out
758 **Acropol 5a ....A Gribben** 3
twrds rear, pshd along 6th, nvr a dang
589 Roseberry Star 5a *chsd ldrs, outpcd 10th, sn t.o.* 4
763 Flying Pan 5a *chsd ldrs, ld 6 out, going wll whn p.u. 5 out, dead* .... pu
762 Chummy's Last 5a *rear, mstk 4th, ran wd & ran out bef nxt* .... ro
Swiss Comfort (Ire) 7a *n.j.w. alwys bhnd, t.o. 13th, ref & u.r. nxt* .... ref
7 ran. 8l, 25l, 20l. Time 6m 17.00s. SP Evens.
J Cornforth (York & Ainsty North).

829 - Open Maiden Div II

590 **MALVERN CANTINA.....................S Swiers** 1
(fav) hld up rear,prog 12th,lft in ld 4 out,jnd 2 out,rdn to ld fn
764 **Meadow Gray ....J Davies** 2
prom, went 2nd 8th, chal 2 out, ev ch flat, kpt on well
704 **Doc Spot ....P Allan** 3
mid-div, prog 7th, wknd 4 out
757 Slim King *alwys rear, jmpd lft 3rd, wll bhnd frm 5 out* 4
636 Primitive Star 7a *mid-div, prog 9th, no hdwy aft, sn wknd* 5
415 No Takers 5a *prom, ld aft 6th til u.r. 4 out* .... ur
590 Not The Nadger 7a *prom whn blnd 5th, outpcd 9th, t.o. & p.u. 14th* .... pu
759 Red Star Queen 5a *plldn hrd, ld & ran wd apr 5th, blnd 7th, wknd, p.u. 15th* .... pu
517 Scarth Nick *alwys rear, t.o. & p.u. 2 out* .... pu
9 ran. Hd, 20l, 15l, hd. Time 6m 18.00s. SP 4-5.
M J Hill (Hurworth).
N.E.

EAST ESSEX
Marks Tey
Saturday April 6th
GOOD

830 - Maiden

618 **SPARTAN'S CONQUEST ....C Ward** 1
prom, ld 11th-13th, disp 15th til forged clr flat
107 **Scout ....T Bulgin** 2D
mid-div,prog to ld 14th,disp 15th,no ext last,fin 2nd,disq
423 **Potentilla (Ire) 7a.......................W Wales** 2
mid-div, prog to 3rd 12th, ev ch til wknd aft 2 out,promoted
496 **Auchendolly (Ire) ....S Sporborg** 3
(fav) mid-div, bhnd & no ch 16th, fin 4th, promoted
597 Le Vienna (Ire) *cls up, trckd ldrs, 3rd at 14th, wknd nxt, no ch 16th* 5
343 Alien Corn (Ire) *mid-div, not rch ldrs, rear & no ch 15th* 6
618 Ernie Fox *mid-div til ref 5th* .... ref
108 Insulate 5a *in rear whn blnd & u.r. 4th* .... ur
424 Charlie Andrews *prom, cls up 4th at 12th, wknd nxt, rear 16th, p.u. 2 out* .... pu
Hendora (Ire) 7a *in tch to 12th, wll in rear whn p.u. 16th* .... pu
Thurles Pickpocket (Ire) 7a *rear, t.o. 4th, schoold til p.u. 16th* .... pu
424 Portman Road *plld into ld 3rd, jnd & blnd 11th, not rcvr, p.u. 13th* .... pu
Secret Music 7a *rear, f 5th* .... f

92 Sharp Tactics *pllng, cls up til lost plc 10th, rear whn p.u. 13th* .... pu
14 ran. 3l, 2l, 8l, 10l, 15l. Time 7m 0.00s. SP 12-1.
O Vaughan-Jones (Essex & Suffolk).
Scout disqualified, rider not W/I. Original distances.

831 - Confined

422 **MILLBAY (IRE)** .... **N Bloom** 1
(fav) cls up, trckd ldr 16th, ld last, ran on, just hld on
676 **Druid's Lodge** .... **T Bulgin** 2
hld up in tch, prog 15th, chal 2 out, ran on last, just hld
622 **Salmon River (USA) 7a** .... **R Wakley** 3
cls up til 5th at 14th, rdn 16th, kpt on onepcd,lft 3rd last
494 Parkers Hills (Ire) *ld to 15th, wknd steadily, bhnd 3 out* 4
622 Major Inquiry (USA) *last pair, t.o. 15th, p.u. last* .... pu
677 Owd Henry *cls up, 2nd 12th, ld aft 15th-17th, btn 3rd whn f last* .... f
6 ran. Nk, 3l, 5l. Time 6m 51.00s. SP 1-3.
Mrs C Bailey (Dunston Harriers).

832 - Ladies

493 **ST GREGORY (bl)** .... **Miss A Plunkett** 1
ld to 3rd, prog agn 13th, ld aft 15th, ran on whn chal flat
678 **Richard Hunt** .... **Miss L Rowe** 2
(fav) hld up, chsd ldrs 11th, 2nd 15th, chal 2 out, no ext flat
93 **Craftsman** .... **Miss A Embiricos** 3
ld 3rd, made most to 16th, wknd & no ext nxt
622 Cardinal Red *prom/disp, wknd rpdly 15th, t.o. 17th* ... 4
616 Gilson's Cove *mid-div, dist 5th at 11th, no ch aft, t.o.* .. 5
594 Kaim Park *twrds rear whn f 5th* .... f
347 Legal Beagle *sn rear, t.o. last at 9th, p.u. 11th* .... pu
Ryme And Run 5a *rear, n.j.w. t.o. 12th, p.u. 17th* ..... pu
8 ran. 1l, 8l, 10l. Time 6m 43.00s. SP 5-1.
A Howland Jackson (Essex & Suffolk).

833 - Open

595 **Celtic Spark** .... **M Loughnane** 1D
chsd ldr, clsd 16th, ran on to disp last, ld flat, lame,disq
677 **SAINT BENE'T (IRE)** .... **A Coe** 1
ld 2nd,sn clr,10l clr 17th,jnd last,hdd flat,fin 2nd,promotd
677 **River Melody 5a** .... **T Moore** 2
(fav) mostly 3rd, no ext frm 17th, btn 2 out, fin 3rd, plcd 2nd
619 **Laburnum** .... **P Harding-Jones** 3
hld up in 4th, rdn & btn 17th, fin 4th, plcd 3rd
4 ran. Hd, 8l, 10l. Time 6m 52.00s. SP 12-1.
George Prodromou (Dunston Harriers).
Celtic Spark disqualified, rider failed to draw correct weight.

834 - Restricted

419 **BOY BASIL** .... **W Wales** 1
mid-div,prog to 2nd 15th,lkd hld whn lft disp 2 out,ld last
621 **Corn Kingdom (bl)** .... **A Coe** 2
ld til jnd aft 15th,hdd nxt,lft disp 2 out,hdd last,kpt on
621 **Salmon Mead (Ire)** .... **S Sporborg** 3
4th/5th,lost plc 10th,rear 14th,styd on onepcd frm 3 out
313 Give It A Bash (Ire) 5a *mid-div, not pace to rch ldrs, styd on onepcd frm 3 out* 4
681 Shelter *blnd 3rd & p.u.* .... pu
494 Harpley Dual (Ire) *rear, wll bhnd whn p.u. 18th* .... pu
618 Andalucian Sun (Ire) *last at 3rd, jmpd badly, t.o. 10th, p.u. 11th* .... pu
679 Al Jawwal *handy, wknd 15th, p.u. 17th, dsmntd* .... pu
423 Top Of The Range (Ire) *alwys rear, nvr going wll, p.u. 17th* .... pu
Tenderman (Ire) 7a *prom, wknd aft 14th, rear whn p.u. 2 out* .... pu
424 Raise A Loan *(fav) trckd ldr going wll, ld 16th, in cmmnd whn f 2 out* .... f
11 ran. 3l, 5l, 10l. Time 6m 54.00s. SP 5-1.
Exors Of The Late Capt W H Bulwer-Long (North Norfolk Harriers).

835 - Members

621 **HALF A SOV** .... **S March** 1
(fav) trckd ldr, ld apr last, ran on flat, just hld on
495 **Aughnacloy Rose** .... **R Page** 2
sttld rear, prog to 2nd 16th, rdn 2 out, styd on,just faild
Celtic Hawk .... **P Chinery** 3
rshd to ld 10th, hdd apr last, onepcd
675 Mount Eaton Fox *ld, sn clr, wknd & hdd 10th, t.o. & p.u. nxt* .... pu
4 ran. Sht-hd, 2l. Time 7m 10.00s. SP Evens.
Mrs Anne Butler (East Essex).
S.B.

LEDBURY
Maisemore Park
Saturday April 6th
GOOD TO FIRM

836 - Members (12st)

744 **DRUMCEVA** .... **M Wilesmith** 1
mstk 2nd, trckd ldrs til ld 8th, 12l clr 13th, unchall
683 **Master Donnington** .... **Miss E Wilesmith** 2
cls up, chsd ldr 10th, nvr able to chall
683 **Punching Glory** .... **Miss S Brewer** 3
cls up, 4th & outpcd 11th, no dang after, wnt 3rd appr last
747 Saxon Smile *cls up,jmpd right 6th,lft 3rd 10th,sn strugg,no ch frm 14th* 4
606 Roscoe's Gemma 5a *prom to 3rd, sn bhnd, last frm 7th, no ch frm 12th* 5
523 Stanford Boy *(fav) w.w. prog 9th, b.d. nxt* .... bd
How Friendly *ld, blnd 4th, hdded appr 8th, cls up whn f 10th* .... f
7 ran. 15l, 10l, 6l, 8l. Time 6m 38.50s. SP 11-2.
M S Wilesmith (Ledbury).
One fence omitted. 17 Jumps

837 - Confined (12st)

667 **LANDSKER ALFRED** .... **Miss A Dare** 1
(fav) disp ld til blnd 4th, ld 15th, drw clr appr 2 out, easy
686 **Bumptious Boy** .... **S Hanks** 2
j.w. disp til lft in ld 4th, hdded 15th, outpcd appr 2 out
579 **Hook Line'N'sinker** .... **L Brown** 3
cls up, 3rd & blnd 12th, outpcd appr 14th, no dang after
707 Howley Lad *hld up last, efft 13th, sn strugg, t.o. whn blnd last* 4
4 ran. 8l, 4l, 1 fence. Time 6m 39.00s. SP 1-4.
Dr P P Brown & Mrs S Birks (Berkeley).

838 - Open (12st)

669 **LIGHTEN THE LOAD** .... **A Wintle** 1
w.w. prog to 2nd 13th-nxt, sn rddn, rallied 2 out, ld flat
662 **Scally's Daughter 5a 7ex** .... **E Williams** 2
(fav) ld,jmpd rght 6th,qcknd 8l clr 15th,jmpd slwly last,hdd flat
426 **Leigh Boy (USA)** .... **Julian Pritchard** 3
chsd ldr to 12th, & agn 15th, kpt on wll frm 2 out
744 Grey Tudor *chsd ldrs, ev ch 12th, wkng & blnd nxt, t.o.* 4
4 ran. 2l, ½l, 1 fence. Time 6m 32.00s. SP 7-4.
J S Payne (Gelligaer Farmers).

839 - Ladies

SPLIT SECOND .... **Miss A Dare** 1
(fav) blnd 1st & 11th, disp til ld 15th, clr 2 out, easy

743 **They All Forgot Me** .... **Miss C Dyson** 2
disp ld til hit 14th, 4l down whn jmpd slwly 2 out,no ch aft
2 ran. 10l. Time 6m 47.60s. SP 1-4.
Mrs P J Willis (Berkeley).

840 - Restricted (12st)

581 **NOTANOTHERONE (IRE)** .... **S Lloyd** 1
chsd ldr to 3 out, gd jmp to ld last, ran on wll
544 **Mr Mad** .... **P Hamer** 2
(fav) mstks,last trio frm 4th,rpd hdwy appr 2out,hit last,nvr nr
551 **Buckley's Court** .... **E Williams** 3
slw jmp 5th,prog to ld apr 2 out,slw jmp & hdd last,no ext
641 Plax *jmpd slwly 4th, disp 2nd 8th-14th,kpt on onepcd frm 3 out* 4
641 Endless Glee *sn clr ld, 12l clr 14th, hdded appr 2 out, wknd rpdly* 5
387 Squeeze Play (bl) *alwys mid-div, nvr trbld ldrs* 6
642 Coolmoreen (Ire) *hld up in rr, 7th & rddn 14th, no prog* 7
428 Really An Angel 5a *alwys rr, last & blnd 12th, t.o. & p.u. 3 out* .... pu
350 Generator Boy *chsd ldrs, 5th whn f 11th* .... f
9 ran. 3l, 2l, 10l, 3l, 10l, 12l. Time 6m 43.90s. SP 11-2.
R Light (Brecon).

841 - Maiden Div I (12st)

430 **BETTIVILLE** .... **A Milner** 1
(fav) in tch, ld 14th, clr 3 out, jmpd slwly last, drvn out
Sterling Buck (USA) .... **Julian Pritchard** 2
sttld, in tch, prog to chs wnnr 2 out, hit last, nt qkn flat
773 **Mr Ffitch** .... **L Stephens** 3
rcd wd,chsd ldr 6th,disp ld bfly 12th,3rd & wkng appr 2 out
45 Namestaken *in tch, ld 12th-nxt, rddn & wknd appr 3 out* 4
Ginge *t.d.e. unruly start, ref to race* 0
218 Woodmanton 5a *prom til r.o. 5th* .... ro
Golden Nectar *ld to 11th, wknd appr 13th, last frm 15th, p.u. appr last* .... pu
771 Royal Bula *hld up, in tch,outpcd 14th, 3rd & wll btn whn u.r. 2 out* .... ur
Nearly Amaboobalee 5a *sn wll bhnd, t.o & p.u. appr 13th* .... pu
9 ran. 1½l, 15l, 1l. Time 6m 41.10s. SP 2-1.
R D Russell (Heythrop).

842 - Maiden Div II (12st)

688 **MEADOW COTTAGE** .... **T Stephenson** 1
w.w. prog to ld 14th, made rest, gd jmp last, hld on wll
354 **Layston Pinzal 7a** .... **Miss S Wallin** 2
prog to 4th 12th,prssd wnnr frm 15th,unable to qkn frm 2 out
773 **Lady Romance (Ire) 5a** .... **P Davis** 3
ld bfly 1st, prom, 3rd & ev ch 2 out, wknd appr last
637 Tu Piece *in tch,outpcd 14th, ran on agn frm 2 out, fin wll.* 4
Highland Chase *chsd ldr 7th, lft in ld 11th-nxt, wknd 15th* 5
697 Sheer Power (Ire) *rr of mn grp, 10th & outpcd 12th, no ch aft* 6
Pocket Pest 5a *rr, prog & in tch 8th, lst pl 10th, last frm 14th* 7
695 Moonlight Shift *ld 2nd,blnd 8th, clr whn p.u. & dism 11th* .... pu
742 Back-Bencher 3ow *prom, cls 3rd whn f 12th* .... f
606 Royal Swinger 5a *prom, blnd 11th, wknd appr 15th, no ch whn b.d. last* .... bd
334 Elegant Bertie *mstks, mid-div, prog to 4th 15th, wknd nxt, 6th whn f last* .... f
749 Rusty Fellow *jmpd slwly 1st, ref & u.r. 2nd* .... ref
352 Swift Monday *(fav) w.w. prog 11th, cls 6th whn f 14th* .... f
Thats Different *jmpd badly, t.o. 3rd til ref 7th* .... ref
607 Just Danny *alwys rr, last frm 9th til p.u. 13th* .... pu
Silk Oats 5a *sttld rr, blnd 4th, lst tch 9th, bhnd & p.u. appr 13th* .... pu
Alcofrolic 5a *jmpd badly, t.o. 3rd til ref 7th* .... ref
17 ran. 1l, 6l, 12l, 6l, 12l, 10l. Time 6m 50.50s. SP 4-1.
N F Williams & G Mucklow (N. Ledbury).
S.P.

LLANGIBBY
Howick
Saturday April 6th
GOOD TO FIRM

843 - Members (12st)

600 **TUDOR OAKS 5a** .... **S Shinton** 1
rear, prog 10th, 2nd 15th, ld nxt, drvn out
691 **Co-Tack** .... **S Lloyd** 2
3rd/4th, rpd prog 15th, 2nd 2 out, alwys hld
604 **Lonesome Step 5a** .... **A Price** 3
(fav) alwys 2nd/3rd, 2l down 2 out, wknd apr last, lame
204 Trevella 5a *mstks 2nd & 11th, alwys rear, btn frm 13th* 4
383 Magnus Pym *alwys rear, no ch hlfwy, poor 5th whn p.u. flat* .... pu
389 Maytown (bl) *2nd til ld 13th, hdd 3 out, 3rd & hld whn u.r. last* .... ur
598 Bee Moy Do (Ire) *ld to 12th, cls 2nd til f 3 out* .... f
7 ran. 2l, 5l, 20l. Time 6m 40.00s. SP 9-1.
S Gallagher (Llangibby).

844 - Restricted (12st)

695 **ICECAPADE (BEL)** .... **Miss E Jones** 1
ld to 7th & frm 11th, disp 14th, went clr 3 out
599 **Louis Farrell** .... **S Blackwell** 2
2nd til ld 8-10th, disp 14th, outpcd frm 3 out
388 **Benuad** .... **A Price** 3
rear, prog to 2nd at 9th, lost plc nxt, 3rd 14th, styd on
694 Cossack Strike (Ire) *rear, 25l down 14th, ran on late* 4
Cosa Nostra *prom to 8th, grad lost tch* 5
669 Pyro Pennant *alwys last pair, fin own time* 6
695 Cistolena 5a *rear, some prog 12th, no ch 14th, p.u. nxt* .... pu
549 Short Shot *ref 1st* .... ref
770 Saffron Moss *disp 3rd whn f 5th* .... f
549 Mrs Wumpkins (Ire) 7a *(fav) 5th hlfwy, no prog, p.u. 3 out* .... pu
10 ran. 15l, 3l, 2l, 15l, dist. Time 6m 33.00s. SP 6-1.
P Riddick (Gelligaer).
One fence omitted, 17 jumps.

845 - Confined (12st)

598 **GEE DOUBLE YOU** .... **B Tulloch** 1
12s-6s, rear, prog to ld 11th, chal frm 3 out, ran on well
604 **Miss Millbrook 5a 3ex** .... **V Hughes** 2
3rd/4th, went 2nd 11th, chal 3 out, just hld frm nxt
692 **Lislary Lad 6ex** .... **D S Jones** 3
(fav) cls up, 3rd 4 out, chal nxt, outpcd
691 Mo's Chorister *ld to 10th, wknd aft, no ch frm 14th* 4
691 Vatacan Bank *alwys rear, fin own time* 5
Brabiner King *4th/5th, 3rd brfly 9th, lost plc aft* 6
601 Harken Premier *alwys rear, p.u. 13th* .... pu
602 The Batchlor *last pair, f 4th* .... f
691 Silks Domino (bl) *alwys rear, t.o. hlfwy, p.u. 3 out* .... pu
601 Prince Nepal 3ow *rear til prog to 4th at 14th, wll btn whn p.u. 3 out* .... pu
693 Construction King *last pair, no ch whn p.u. 3 out* .... pu
693 Light The Wick 7ex *cls 3rd whn u.r. 6th* .... ur
12 ran. 2l, 10l, 20l, 15l, 10l. Time 6m 24.00s. SP 6-1.
J D Watkins (Curre).

846 - Open (12st)

602 **WELSH LEGION 7ex** .... **J Jukes** 1
(fav) hld up, steady prog to 2nd 15th, ld nxt, easily

384 **Merino Waltz (USA)** ....**J Price** 2
hld up, prog to ld 12th, hdd 3 out, styd on, no ch wnr
691 **Pat Cullen** ....**S Blackwell** 3
ld to 11th, grad wknd, 3rd frm 15th
602 Kingfisher Bay 7ex *mid-div, drvn to cls 4th at 11th, wknd & no ch 14th* 4
691 Bronze Effigy (bl) *4th to 10th, lost tch wth ldrs frm nxt* 5
601 Smoulder (USA) *10s-4s, alwys last, lost tch 9th, p.u. 14th*........ pu
768 Doubting Donna 5a *2nd to 10th, wknd rpdly, p.u. 14th* pu
7 ran. 8l, 10l, 8l, dist. Time 6m 29.00s. SP 2-5.
G W Lewis (Carmarthenshire).

847 - Ladies

766 **LUCKY OLE SON** ....**Miss P Jones** 1
hld up,prog to 3rd at 14th, 15l 2nd nxt, clsd to ld apr last
603 **La Mezeray 5a** ....**Mrs J Hawkins** 2
(fav) handy,2nd 12th,ld nxt,clr 15th,blnd nxt,not run on,hdd last
Algaihabane (USA) (bl)............**Miss P Gundry** 3
ld to 13th, wknd rpdly, t.o.
607 Miss Montgomery (Ire) 7a *rear, t.o. 12th*........ 4
356 Travistown *alwys rear, t.o. 12th* 5
Adanac *5th whn u.r. 6th*........ ur
693 Mendip Music *mid-div, hmpd & p.u. 9th, saddle slppd* .... pu
604 Judy Line 5a *1st ride, 15l 2nd whn u.r. 7th*........ ur
Wooly Town 5a *alwys last pair, t.o. & p.u. 15th*........ pu
9 ran. 3l, dist, dist, dist. Time 6m 39.00s. SP 5-1.
David Brace (Llangeinor).

848 - Maiden Div I (12st)

SWEET KILDARE 5a ....**J Jukes** 1
trckd ldrs, ld 13th, clr nxt, unchal
151 **Charles Quaker** ....**Miss P Jones** 2
(fav) s.s. rear til steady prog 11th,3rd 3 out,styd on,nt rch wnr
255 **Le Gerard** ....**J Price** 3
chsng grp, 30l bhnd hlfwy, styd on frm 14th
389 Itsstormingnorma 5a *ld to 9th, chsd nwr frm 13th, alwys hld*........ 4
605 Khandys Slave (Ire) 5a *chsd ldr to 9th, lost plc, rdn to 2nd agn 12th, wknd rpdly* 5
262 Free Bear *alwys rear, some late prog*........ 6
599 Plas-Hendy *prom in ldng grp til wknd frm 14th*........ 7
550 Great Precocity *last pair, no ch frm 11th* 8
695 Final Option (Ire) *ld chsng grp til wknd 10th, t.o. 13th*.. 9
606 Country Life (USA) *rear, fin own time, t.o.*........ 10
She Goes 5a *rear, clsd frm 14th, 15l down 3 out, p.u. nxt*........ pu
697 Pharrago (Ire) *alwys rear, no ch hlfwy, p.u. 3 out*........ pu
606 I'm A Bute 5a *alwys rear, p.u. 10th*........ pu
Lady Orr (Ire) 7a *rear, no ch whn p.u. 14th*........ pu
14 ran. 8l, 1l, 3l. Time 6m 37.00s. SP 16-1.
V J Thomas (Ystrad).

849 - Maiden Div II (12st)

CELESTIAL STREAM ....**A Price** 1
made all, drew clr 13th, easily
Pine Timber..........................**P Williams** 2
hld up, 6th at 13th, ran on, nrst fin
696 **Sister Lark 5a**..........................**V Hughes** 3
3rd/4th til chsd wnr 15th, no imp, lost 2nd flat
694 Boddington Hill 5a *rear, prog frm 13th, nrst fin*........ 4
Always Allied (Ire) *(fav) hld up, prog frm 10th, 15l 3rd 3 out, wknd, lame*........ 5
382 Jobingo *prom to 10th, grad lost tch*........ 6
Snippetoff *2nd/3rd to 13th, drppd out rpdly*........ 7
691 Astley Jack *2nd to 9th, wknd rpdly, p.u. 12th*........ pu
City Rhythm *last to 7th, p.u. 10th*........ pu
Itsgonnashine 5a *7th hlfwy, t.o. & p.u. last*........ pu
690 Tennessee Cruiser *t.o. whn ref 12th*........ ref
772 Classic Edition 7a *rear, f 3rd*........ f
696 Queen's Equa 5a *mid-div, f 4th*........ f
Saronica-R *u.r. 1st*........ ur
14 ran. 15l, 1l, 4l, 5l, 10l. Time 6m 30.00s. SP 7-1.
J Williams (Curre).

850 - Maiden Div III (12st)

268 **HAYDON HILL 7a**....................**M FitzGerald** 1
mid-div,prog to 4th at 14th, ld nxt, mstk 3 out, ran on well
598 **Miss Corinthian 5a**.......................**M Flynn** 2
hld up, prog to 4th at 11th, 3rd 3 out, chal nxt, alwys hld
691 **Old Steine** ....**I Johnson** 3
chsd ldr to 13th, ld brfly til hdd & onepcd frm nxt
606 Willow Belle (Ire) 5a *mid-div, prog to 5l down 14th, no imp aft*........ 4
605 Yarron King (bl) *(fav) ld to 13th, wknd rpdly*........ 5
Annaben 5a *alwys last pair*........ 6
773 Rymer's Express *alwys last trio, fin own time*........ 7
605 Puttingonthestyle *t.o. 10th, p.u. 12th*........ pu
605 Trydan *t.o. 8th, p.u. 10th*........ pu
697 Nutsil 5a *last pair, f 3rd*........ f
697 Lets Go Polly 5a *prom to 12th, wknd rpdly, p.u. 14th*.. pu
602 Barton Bulldozer (Ire) *t.o. 9th, p.u. 12th*........ pu
Myitsu *cls up whn f heavily 9th*........ f
607 Steel Valley (Ire) 5a *rear, p.u. 6th*........ pu
14 ran. 8l, 10l, 5l, 20l, dist. Time 6m 41.00s. SP 7-1.
Mrs E Kulbicki (Curre).
P.H./J.C.

NORTH STAFFORDSHIRE
Sandon
Saturday April 6th
GOOD TO FIRM

851 - Members

667 **RHINE RIVER (USA)**..................**C Stockton** 1
(Jt fav) held up, cls order 11th, ld 3 out, ran on srgly apr last
664 **Howlin' Wolf**..........................**M Pennell** 2
(Jt fav) ld to 5th,trckd ldr lft in ld 14th,chal by wnr 3 out,outpcd
Barney Rubble 14ow ....**M Slater** 3
outpcd, nvr nrr then 3rd
Sonnett *(25s-4s) alwys last 2, nvr in race*........ 4
663 Glamdring 5a *cls up, ld 6th til u.r. 14th*........ ur
The Thug 14ow *alwys rear, t.o. whn p.u. bfr last*........ pu
6 ran. 3l, dist, 4l. Time 6m 52.00s. SP 7-4.
Brian Eardley (North Staffordshire).

852 - Maiden (12st)

DENBY HOUSE LAD (CAN)................**S Prior** 1
cls order 10th, tk ld 14th, ran on wll frm 3 out
666 **The Yokel**..........................**T Garton** 2
(fav) held up,smth prog frm 12th to be up sides 3 out,no ext 2 out
460 **Kingfisher Lad**.......................**C Stockton** 3
prom, ld 3rd-8th, in tch to 4 out, outpcd
566 Glen Taylor *ld to 2nd, in tch, ld 9-13th, onepce frm 4 out*........ 4
736 Ring Bank 7a *chsng grp to 10th, lost tch wth ldrs 13th* 5
569 Sister Seat 5a *chsdng grp to hlf way, fdd qckly, wll btn*........ 6
664 Bay Tiger *mstks, rear, p.u. 13th*........ pu
740 Son Of Ishka *chsd ldrs to 11th, wknng & btn whn u.r. 14th*........ ur
740 Analystic (Ire) *f 2nd*........ f
9 ran. 12l, 20l, 3l, 10l, dist. Time 6m 35.00s. SP 7-1.
K J Shone (Saddleworth).

853 - Ladies

693 **OUT THE DOOR (IRE)**..............**Miss S Baxter** 1
(fav) hld up in rear,cls order 10th,rlld apr last,ld flat,all out
633 **Cruising On 5a** ....**Miss E Guest** 2
j.w., made all, 8l clr 2 out, idld apr last, cght run in
Fly For Us 5a.........................**Miss C Burgess** 3
w.w., cls order 14th, 2nd 2 out, no ext, will imprv

460 Nodforms Dilemma (USA) *chsng grp, not qckn whn pce increased 4 out* 4
427 Agarb (USA) 2ow (bl) *alwys rear, p.u. 4 out* pu
663 Moya's Tip Top 5a *msrly 2nd, in tch & ev ch whn u.r. 3 out* ur
738 Sheppie's Reality *sn t.o., no ch whn p.u. 12th* pu
7 ran. ¾l, 3l, 10l. Time 6m 30.00s. SP 4-5.
M Mann (Wheatland).

854 - Open

672 **MY NOMINEE (bl)** .... **A Griffith** 1
(fav) ld/disp to 7th whn lft clr,hld off chal frm 6 out,ran on wll
459 **Bucksfern** .... **R Bevis** 2
prom, lft 2nd 7th, cls up & ev ch 11th, not qckn frm 2 out
372 **Catchapenny** .... **W Tellwright** 3
sn outpcd, nvr dang
567 Anchor Express 5a (bl) *ld/disp til f hvly 7th* f
4 ran. 6l, dist. Time 6m 25.00s. SP Evens.
D E Nicholls (West Shropshire).

855 - Confined

739 **WORLESTON FARRIER** .... **N Gittins** 1
(Jt fav) j.w., made all, conf rddn
663 **Inch Maid 5a** .... **Miss H Brookshaw** 2
mid-div,cls order 12th,up sides btwn last 2,outpcd cls home
665 **Gen-Tech** .... **A Griffith** 3
(Jt fav) chsd wnnr, ev ch til outpcd 5 out
667 Bally Muire 5a *mid-div, nvr rchd chal position* 4
736 Wot Pet *sn rear, jmp round in own time, btn 2 fences* 5
685 Dannigale *mid-div, disp 4th whn u.r. last* ur
6 ran. 3l, 10l, dist, dist. Time 6m 25.00s. SP 6-4.
Mrs A J Flanders (Cheshire).

856 - Restricted (12st)

291 **BROCKISH BAY** .... **Miss S Baxter** 1
w.w. in rear, cls order 4 out, strng chal apr last, readly
665 **Gray Rosette 5a** .... **A Griffith** 2
rear early, prog 5 out to join chsng grp, ev ch last no ext
722 **Monarrow (Ire)** .... **W Tellwright** 3
ld grp thruout, unable to qckn whn pce increased
659 Shanballymore (Ire) *mid-div in tch, no ext frm 2 out* 4
501 Tina's Missile *ld 3rd to 2 out, outpcd* 5
564 Mastiff Lane *chsd ldrs, ev ch to 2 out, wknd* 6
Mr Gee *cls up,ld 2 out,hdd btwn last 2 fences,disp 3rd whn ro last* ro
564 Foolish Fantasy (bl) *alwys rear, p.u. 2 out* pu
665 Made Of Talent 5a *(fav) ld to 2nd,restrain in rear 4th,rpd hdwy to cls whn f2 out* f
9 ran. 3l, 8l, 4l, 4l, dist. Time 6m 34.00s. SP 10-1.
Roy Baxter (Meynell & South Staffs).
V.S.

PERCY
Alnwick
Saturday April 6th
GOOD TO FIRM

857 - Members (12st)

790 **LOUGHLINSTOWN BOY** .... **P Craggs** 1
ld/disp til 15th, styd on, unchall
752 **The Healy 5a** .... **Mrs F Scales** 2
(Jt fav) chsd ldr, disp ld 10th-14th, no ex frm 3 out
610 **True Fair** .... **A Robson** 3
(Jt fav) alwys 3rd,mstk 13th, onepcd & no dang aft
789 Panto Lady 5a *soon last, t.o. whn p.u. 3 out* pu
4 ran. 8l, 6l. Time 6m 15.00s. SP 9-2.
J A Riddell (Percy).

858 - Restricted

608 **FISCAL POLICY** .... **J Walton** 1
prom,ld 10th-12th,lkd btn 3 out, strng run flat, ld cls hme
608 **Eastlands Hi-Light** .... **J Cookson** 2
mid-div,prog to 3rd hlfwy, clsd appr last, just outpcd flat
608 **Kalajo** .... **R Shiels** 3
(fav) disp ld 6-9th,ld 13th,clr 3 out, wknd rpdly last, hdded flat
186 Merry Jerry (bl) *bhnd 6th, pshd alng 9th, ran on frm 2 out, no dang* 4
608 Anzarna 5a *alwys same pl, nvr dang* 5
501 Jads Lad *ld 3rd-5th, lst pl, mstk 14th, no dang aft* 6
754 Luvly Bubbly *not fluent, 4th hlfwy, wll bhnd whn p.u. 3 out* pu
7 ran. 1l, 1l, dist. Time 6m 16.00s. SP 4-1.
Major A Trotter (Berwickshire).

859 - 2½m Open Maiden (5-7yo)

488 **EILID ANOIR** .... **R Shiels** 1
disp ld til ld 4th, clr 8th, hdded & lft clr 2 out
192 **Beltino 7a** .... **T Scott** 2
chsd ldrs thro'out, t.o. frm 15th
323 Keirose 5a *sn bhnd, t.o. & p.u. 3 out* pu
321 Harden Glen 7a *(fav) disp ld to 3rd, trkd ldr, ld & f 2 out* ur
Pennyman (Ire) *nvr nr ldrs, p.u. 11th* pu
5 ran. Dist. Time 5m 21.00s. SP 2-1.
J Shearer (Lanark & Renfrewshire).

860 - 4m 1f Mixed Open (12st)

582 **BOW HANDY MAN** .... **T Scott** 1
chsd ldrs, prog 15th, chsng ldr whn lft in ld last
700 **Ready Steady** .... **Miss P Robson** 2
w.w. prog to ld 14th, mstk & hdd nxt, no ex frm 2 out
790 **Green Times** .... **W Ramsay** 3
chsd ldrs, ev ch 3 out, onepcd
609 Rarely At Odds *alwys abt same pl.* 4
610 Redediver (bl) *sn last, t.o. & p.u. appr 15th.* pu
750 Fruids Park 5a *bhnd 8th, blnd 14th, t.o. & p.u. 3 out* pu
751 Master Kit (Ire) *(fav) w.w. prog to ld 10th-13th,ld agn 21st, clr whn f last* f
7 ran. 5l, 4l, dist. Time 8m 48.00s. SP 4-1.
J L Gledson (Border).

861 - Confined (12st)

609 **ACROSS THE CARD** .... **W Ramsay** 1
mid-div, prog to 2nd 10th, ld 16th, in comm whn lft clr last
751 **Astrac Trio (USA)** .... **Miss A Bowie** 2
ld 3rd til 12th, outpcd frm 15th
673 **Fish Quay** .... **Miss S Lamb** 3
alwys bhnd, nvr dang
751 Bridgnorth Lass 5a *rr, prog to ld 12th-15th, wknd* 4
701 Music Minstrel (bl) *mid-div, pshd alng 9th, t.o. 13th* 5
699 Free Transfer (Ire) *(fav) w.w. prog to chs wnnr 16th, hd rddn & ev ch whn f last* ur
701 Yenoora (Ire) *ld 1st-2nd, lsng pl whn u.r. 10th* ur
7 ran. 20l, 6l, dist. Time 6m 15.00s. SP 6-1.
Capt W B Ramsay (Berwickshire).

862 - Maiden

DRUID'S BROOK .... **A Parker** 1
w.w., hdwy 10th, ld 3 out, sn drew clr, imprv further
789 **Weddicar Lady 5a** .... **R Hale** 2
prom, ld 7-15th, no ext
613 **My Meadowsweet** .... **C Storey** 3
mid-div early, prog 9th, outpcd frm 14th
52 Misskeira 5a *(fav) cls up til p.u. 11th, dismntd* pu
704 Lauras Teeara (Ire) 5a (bl) *m.n.s., p.u. 13th* pu
116 Willy Waffles (Ire) *chsd ldr, blndrd 8th-nxt, sn wknd, t.o. & p.u. 3 out* pu
Jay Ceevee *mid-div 4th, grdly lost plc, bhnd & p.u. 2 out* pu
755 Mordington Lass 5a *t.o. 7th, p.u. apr 12th* pu
8 ran. 10l, 30l. Time 6m 25.00s. SP 7-2.
Mrs D B Johnstone (Berwickshire).
D.G.

ROYAL ARTILLERY
Larkhill
Saturday April 6th
FIRM

863 - Members

655 **DAYBROOK'S GIFT 7ex............Miss N Allan** 1
(fav) hld up, cls 2nd frm 12th, ld 3 out, rddn out flat, unimprssv
707 **Game Fair..............................G Burton** 2
ld til mstk 3rd, ld agn 9th til pckd 3 out, rlld flat
524 **Champagne Run.......................C Farr** 3
cls up, lft ld 7th til hmp 11th, outpcd frm nxt & sn btn
Space Lab *ld 3rd til blndrd & u.r. 7th* .... ur
4 ran. ¾l, 25l. Time 6m 21.00s. SP 1-3.
Miss N K Allan (Royal Artillery).

864 - 2½m Maiden (5-7yo)

643 **PONTABULA...................A Charles-Jones** 1
(fav) trckd ldng pair, cls 2nd 10th, lft ld 4 out, pushd out
652 **Tullykyne Bells....................Miss D Stafford** 2
made most to 4 out, onepcd whn hdd, no ch with wnnr
658 **Sulason.................................M Miller** 3
w.w., clsd up 5 out, 2nd & ch whn hit 2 out, not rcvr
643 Wired For Sound *alwys rear, no ch frm 10th, u.r. 4 out*.......... ur
519 Wesshaun 5a *alwys towrds rear, t.o. 9th, p.u. nxt*..... pu
Doujas 5a *ld in, bhnd whn bldrd & u.r. 1st*.......... ur
Eatons 7a *pulld hrd, cls 2nd til wknd frm 5 out, u.r. 3 out*.......... ur
711 Uncle Bruce *trckd ldrs til wknd frm 9th, t.o. whn ref 4 out*.......... ref
301 Happy Henry (Ire) *plld, clsd up 5 out, narrow adv & gng wll whn f nxt*.......... f
9 ran. 5l, 4l. Time 5m 24.00s. SP 5-4.
P Greenwood /H J Manners (V.W.H.).
15 jumps.

865 - Confined (12st)

785 **JUPITER MOON 7ex....................C Casey** 1
not fluent & jmp lft, lft in ld 2nd, clr frm 5 out
207 **Dirty Dancer ....M Miller** 2
not fluent, trckd wnnr 2nd til outpcd frm 13th
709 Indian Knight *(fav) narrow ld whn u.r. 2nd*.......... ur
3 ran. Dist. Time 6m 33.00s. SP 3-1.
Mrs I N McCallum (Beaufort).

866 - Intermediate (12st)

526 **ALWAYS GREAT ....Dr P Pritchard** 1
(fav) made virt all, qcknd frm 12th, clr frm 3 out, pushd out
604 **Dancing Doris 5a ....T Cox** 2
trckd wnnr, outpcd frm apr 13th, wnt 2nd nxt, no ch wth wnnr
628 **Beinn Mohr 5a.........................P Henley** 3
trckd wnnr, outpcd 12th, wll btn frm 5 out
710 Roaming Shadow *trckd wnnr, rddn apr 13th, btn & wknd rpdly nxt, p.u. last*.......... pu
4 ran. 15l, 20l. Time 6m 5.00s. SP Evens.
Miss Sarah George (Berkley).

867 - 4m Mixed Open (12st)

639 **WHAT A TO DO.......................R Sweeting** 1
prom, disp 5-12th & 5 out til wnt on apr 2 out, cosily
783 **Wrekin Hill.......................Mrs J Wilkinson** 2
(fav) hndy,ld 13th,jnd 5 out,blndrd nxt,hd 2 out,ev ch last outpcd
561 **Ski Nut...............................J Hankinson** 3
ld til jnd 5th, hdd 13th, rddn 5 out, no ext, sn btn
728 Captain Dimitris *sn rear, outpcd 10th, t.o. 13th* 4
475 Smooth Escort *cls up, lost plc & rddn frm 11th, t.o. 17th, p.u. 3 out*.......... pu
643 Annson *hld up, 5th whn f 10th*.......... f
6 ran. 2l, dist, 12l. Time 8m 5.00s. SP 4-1.
C J R Sweeting (Heythrop).
22 Jumps.

868 - Restricted (12st)

527 **QUIET CONFIDENCE (IRE) 5a....Miss D Stafford** 1
j.w., made all, sn clr, slow 4 out, jnd last, ran on gamely
627 **Erme Rose (Ire) 5a.......................M Miller** 2
(fav) hld up, stdy prog frm 11th, disp & blndrd last, no ext
676 **Cool Ginger...........................R Sweeting** 3
down early, outpcd 11th, btn frm 13th
656 Pines Express (Ire) (bl) *chsd wnnr til wknd frm 12th, sn bhnd, p.u. 4 out*.......... pu
4 ran. Sht-hd, dist. Time 6m 3.00s. SP 6-4.
Mrs S E Kerley (New Forest Buck Hounds).

869 - Kings Troop Members (12st)

HAVANA ....Sgt W Goudie 1
Lightning..........................Capt A Wood 2
Henley ....Bdr M Watson 3
Legion 2ow *(fav)* 4
Loxley 5
Libel 6
Halfpenny 15ow .... pu
7 ran. 15l, ¾l, 6l, dist, dist. Time 6m 51.00s. SP 5-2.
Capt A W Wood (Royal Artillery).
M.J.

SPOONERS & WEST DARTMOOR
Higher Kilworthy
Saturday April 6th
GOOD TO FIRM

870 - Members

626 **LITTLE COOMBE 5a.......................R Cole** 1
in tch, went 2nd 15th, chal 2 out, ld last, sn clr
671 **Light The Bay 5a......................G Penfold** 2
(fav) hld up, ld 13th, ev ch whn blnd last, not rcvr
280 **Ballysheil.............................S Edwards** 3
ld/disp til aft 12th, wknd
Christmas Hols *ld/disp to 9th, 4th & rdn 15th, no ch aft*.......... 4
555 Kahlo 5a *16s-8s, rear, lost tch 13th* 5
5 ran. 6l, 5l, 30l, ½l. Time 6m 6.00s. SP 5-2.
M Wilkins (Spooners & West Dartmoor).

871 - Restricted (12st)

627 **GREEN HILL ....Miss L Blackford** 1
hld up in tch, prog to disp 3 out, just ld last, drvn out
720 **Copper And Chrome (Ire) 5a.........D Stephens** 2
tongue-strap, sn prom, ld 15th, jnd 3 out, hrd rdn, not qckn
629 **Our Teddis...........................G Penfold** 3
(fav) mid-div, outpcd 12th, ran on steadily frm 3 out, sore
624 Moorland Abbot *6th hlfwy, nvr dang, nrst fin* 4
556 Happy Valley 5a *sn rear, nvr dang, t.o. & p.u. 3 out*... pu
Druid Blue *slght ld to 12th, lost plc steadily, bhnd & p.u. 3 out*.......... pu
199 Baron Rush *7s-3s, in tch, ld 13th-15th, 3rd whn p.u. 2 out, lame*.......... pu
Polly's Corner 5a *twrds rear, not fluent, t.o. & p.u. 3 out*.......... pu
Trolly 7a *bhnd til p.u. apr 15th, schoold* .... pu
9 ran. Nk, 15l, 15l. Time 6m 1.50s. SP 7-4.
P C Pocock (Quantock Staghounds).

872 - Ladies

624 **SOME-TOY** ....**Miss L Blackford** 1
(fav) j.w. disp til drew clr aft 15th, canter
561 **Playpen** ....**Miss S Crook** 2
disp til outpcd 15th, no ext
276 Plain Sailing (Fr) *lost tch aft 5th, t.o. & p.u. 11th* .... pu
3 ran. 15l. Time 5m 55.00s. SP 4-11.
John Squire (Stevenstone).

873 - Confined

626 **THE GENERAL'S DRUM** ....**K Heard** 1
(fav) in tch, ld apr 15th, sn clr, comf
721 **Rathmichael (bl)**.........................**A Farrant** 2
ld, jmpd hstntly 5th & 12th (ditch), hdd apr 15th, no ext
623 **Cardinal Bird (USA) (bl)** ....**A Holdsworth** 3
prog to cls 3rd 9th, in tch til outpcd aft 14th
196 Ghofar *lost tch frm 8th, t.o.* 4
4 ran. 12l, 6l, 25l. Time 5m 59.00s. SP 1-2.
Mrs R Fell (Dartmoor).

874 - Open

TRY IT ALONE.............................**S Slade** 1
hld up in tch, prog 14th, went 2nd nxt, ld 2 out, drew clr
444 **Bluechipenterprise 5a** ....**R Darke** 2
ld/disp til hdd 2 out, no ext
717 **Departure 5a** ....**J Creighton** 3
(fav) sn prom, disp 4-12th, wknd 15th, sn btn, eased
Perfect Stranger *7s-3s, hld up in tch, outpcd aft 13th, no ch clsng stgs* 4
Shalchlo Boy *lost ground frm 10th, t.o. 13th* 5
625 Chandigarh *last whn ran out 7th* .... ro
6 ran. 5l, 20l. Time 5m 49.50s. SP 10-1.
M Biddick (North Cornwall).

875 - Maiden Div I (12st)

630 **KARLIMAY 5a** ....**K Heard** 1
(Jt fav) hld up in tch, qcknd to ld apr 2 out, comf
630 **Moorland Highflyer 7a**...........**Miss D Mitchell** 2
ld til hdd apr 2 out, kpt on onepcd
629 **Romany Anne 5a** ....**Miss S Young** 3
cls 3rd mostly, 5l 3rd 3 out, no ext, blnd last
557 Cottage Light (bl) *(Jt fav) trckd ldr til aft 14th, sn wknd* 4
Barrette 5a *just in tch til crashd thro wing 9th*........ ro
Lady Goldrush 5a *rear but in tch til blnd 11th, t.o. & p.u. 14th* .... pu
6 ran. 5l, 6l, 1 fence. Time 6m 24.00s. SP 6-4.
Mrs R Fell (Dartmoor).

876 - Maiden Div II (12st)

KINDLY LADY 5a.....................**P Scholfield** 1
(fav) keen hold, conf rdn, prog 15th, disp 3 out, pshd clr flat
441 **Ashcombe Valley**...............**Miss L Blackford** 2
hld up in tch,ld apr 15th,jnd & rdn 3 out,cls 3rd,hmpd last
629 **Mr Wideawake** ....**C Heard** 3
in tch, prog 15th, ev ch til wknd 2 out
625 Noddy's Story 5a *ld 8th til aft 14th, lost plc 3 out* 4
719 Big Reward *prom til lost plc aft 6th, no ch frm 13th* ... 5
555 Get Stepping *in tch, cls 3rd 13-15th, wknd nxt, t.o. & p.u. 2 out* .... pu
629 Collard Tor *ld to 8th, lost plc rpdly 11th, t.o. & p.u. 3 out*.. pu
556 Herhorse 5a *rear whn mstk 8th, p.u. nxt*............ pu
Baron Knayber *bhnd,last at 13th,prog 15th,disp 2 out,ev ch whn f last* .... f
623 The Ugly Duckling *prom, no prog frm 15th, 6th whn blnd & u.r. 2 out* .... ur
Rhyme And Chime 7a *sn bhnd, t.o. & p.u. 11th*....... pu
11 ran. 2½l, 2½l, 10l, 20l. Time 6m 11.00s. SP 6-4.
David Fisher (Mid Devon).
G.T.

UNITED

Brampton Bryan
Saturday April 6th
GOOD TO FIRM

877 - Members

COMEDIE FLEUR 5a.....................**A Dalton** 1
walked-over
Miss Caroline Nicholas (United).

878 - Open (12st)

524 **FIRST HARVEST**..........................**P Hanly** 1
ld 3rd, rmndrs 7th, 8l clr 13th, rdn & clr 3 out
579 **Pamela's Lad 7ex**.....................**G Hanmer** 2
(fav) hld up, prog 14th, chsd wnr nxt, nvr on terms
All Greek To Me (Ire) 7ex...............**W Bryan** 3
rear til some prog 15th, kpt on onepcd frm 3 out
506 St Helens Boy *ld to 2nd, chsd wnr til slw jmp 15th, no ch aft* 4
692 The Wooden Hut *6l 3rd at 12th, cls enough 15th, wknd apr nxt* 5
5 ran. 15l, 5l, 4l, 30l. Time 6m 43.00s. SP 3-1.
C J Bennett (Ledbury).

879 - Ladies

579 **TUFFNUT GEORGE** ....**Miss A Corbett** 1
(fav) chsd ldr til ld 9th, 4l up 13th, styd on strngly 3 out
Czermno 7ex ....**Miss J Priest** 2
ld to 9th, lost plc aft 16th, rallied frm 2 out
743 **Legal Picnic 7ex**...................**Miss C Bryan** 3
alwys 3rd, 5l down 10th, kpt on onepcd frm 16th
687 Soldiers Duty (USA) *4th/5th til effrt & ch apr 16th, no prog frm 3 out*.. 4
693 Grey Watch 5a *rear til prog 14th, cls up 16th, no ext aft 3 out* 5
579 Golden Fare *hld up, nvr rchd ldrs, no ch frm 16th* 6
In The Water *alwys rear, t.o. 9th* 7
684 Fennorhill *rear frm 6th, t.o. 9th* 8
603 Cantantivy 5a *mid-div, 21l 5th at 11th, wknd frm 14th, t.o.*.. 9
9 ran. 8l, 6l, 3l, 1l, 30l, 15l, 12l, 1l. Time 6m 40.00s. SP 4-5.
P T Cartridge (Worcestershire).

880 - P P O R A (12st)

664 **SHOON WIND** ....**A Dalton** 1
(fav) mid-div, prog 9th, trckd ldr 12th, ld 3 out, easily
386 **Carlsan** ....**M P Jones** 2
prom, ld 9th-15th, no ext whn hdd, kpt on onepcd
214 **Sound Golly**...............................**R Pike** 3
ld to 8th, lost plc 13th, styd on frm 3 out
738 Kameo Style *rear & lost tch 11th, t.o. 16th, tk 4th on line* 4
687 Corrianne 5a *prom to 4th, grad lost tch frm 12th*...... 5
426 Emerald Gem (bl) *alwys rear, lost tch 14th, t.o.*....... 6
Volcanic Dancer (USA) 4ex *strtd 3 fences bhnd, p.u. 13th*.. pu
567 Lakenheather (NZ) *cls 2nd whn u.r. 6th* .... ur
8 ran. 8l, 2l, 20l, nk, dist. Time 6m 51.00s. SP 1-2.
J N Dalton (Wheatland).

881 - Confined (12st)

383 **GEO POTHEEN** ....**Mrs N Sheppard** 1
mid-div, prog 16th, styd on to ld last, pshd out
457 **Scriven Boy** ....**W Bryan** 2
prog to 3rd at 13th, chal 3 out, ld nxt, hdd & not qckn last
667 **The Rum Mariner** ....**M Harris** 3
ld chsng grp, clsd on ldr 15th, disp 3 out, no ext frm nxt
691 Barn Pool *nvr nr ldrs, ran on strngly frm 16th*.......... 4
601 Space Mariner *35l 3rd at 12th, kpt on onepcd frm 16th* 5
662 Tara Boy *last frm 4th, fin well frm 3 out*.............. 6
745 Ideal *clr ldr til ct apr 16th, wknd rpdly nxt* 7

877 Comedie Fleur 5a *prog frm 14th, disp 3 out, wknd & p.u. last* .... pu
Oakers Hill *last at 12th, t.o. 15th, p.u. 2 out* .... pu
9 ran. 2l, 8l, 5l, 2l, hd, 15l. Time 6m 43.00s. SP 16-1.
T H Sheppard (Golden Valley).

882 - Restricted (12st)

695 **HORN PLAYER (USA) ....M P Jones** 1
ld to 4th, chsd ldrs, styd on frm 16th, ld flat
548 **Mackabee (Ire)..........T Weale** 2
trckd ldrs, effrt 16th, lft in ld 3 out, jnd last, no ext
382 **Dane Rose 5a..........A Dalton** 3
prog frm 13th, rdn 16th, chal whn mstk last, no ext flat
Katie Parson 5a *cls 2nd at 9th, ev ch 16th, wknd frm 3 out* 4
Young Parson *just in tch 12th, no ch frm 15th* 5
390 Buckwyn *alwys trailing, no ch frm 13th* 6
Lorenza Lad *t.o. 4th, u.r. 10th* .... ur
382 Spring Bavard 5a *(fav) prog to chs ldr 15th, lft in ld nxt, 3l up whn f 3 out* .... f
Lles Le Bucflow *chsd ldrs, just in tch 12th, wknd 14th, p.u. 3 out* .... pu
666 Saffron Glory (bl) *ld 5th, 6l up whn f 16th* .... f
425 Celtic Berry 5a *mid-div, effrt 14th, wknd 16th, p.u. nxt* .... pu
661 Ballybeggan Parson (Ire) *mid-div, mstk 6th, hmpd 10th, lost tch 13th, p.u. 3 out* .... pu
661 Maes Gwyn Dreamer *t.o. 3rd, p.u. 12th* .... pu
Pulltheplug 7a *mid-div whn f 10th* .... f
14 ran. Hd, 1l, 12l, 25l, 8l. Time 6m 45.00s. SP 12-1.
Stephen J Fletcher (Golden Valley).

883 - Maiden Div I (12st)

696 **CAPTURE THE MAGIC (IRE) 5a..........C Richards** 1
cls 4th at 13th, ld 16th, jmpd lft 2 out, rdn out flat
Rising Sap..........A Dalton 2
rear til ran on frm 16th, fin well, not rch wnr
689 **Baptist John (Ire)..........M Harris** 3
trckd ldrs going wll, ev ch 16th, no ext frm 3 out
748 Amerous Lad *ld to 3rd, styd prom, no ext frm 3 out* 4
Derring Ann 5a *chsd ldrs, nvr rchd chal pstn* 5
Woodzee *cls up, ev ch 16th, wknd frm 2 out* 6
661 Agile King 7a *(fav) ld 4-8th & 13th-15th, wknd apr 3 out* 7
431 Master Frith (bl) *cls up 9th, prom whn ran out 12th* .... ro
689 Mis-E-Fishant 5a *strtd fence bhnd, p.u. 5th* .... pu
Seven Cruise *prom til wknd 13th, p.u. 16th* .... pu
I've Copped It (Ire) *ld 9-12th, wknd frm 15th, p.u. flat* .... pu
Tot Of Rum 5a *rear, still in tch 11th, wknd 13th, p.u. 15th* .... pu
Day Girl 5a *trckng ldrs whn f 8th* .... f
13 ran. 6l, 3l, nk, 6l, 8l. Time 6m 59.00s. SP 5-1.
H Morris (Golden Valley).

884 - Maiden Div II (12st)

747 **SWEET JOANNA 5a..........Miss E James** 1
alwys prom, kpt on to ld 2 out, drew clr flat
689 **Kiltrose Lad..........A Dalton** 2
rdn to chs ldr 15th, kpt on onepcd
748 **Stormhill Recruit..........J Rees** 3
wth ldrs, ev ch til wknd aft 2 out
353 Susies Melody (Ire) 7a *trckd ldrs, went 2nd apr 3 out, wknd nxt* 4
749 Creme Zahilla 5a *ld 9th til jnd apr 2 out, wknd last* 5
748 Sioux Perfick 5a *prom at 8th, in tch til wknd aft 16th, p.u. last* .... pu
True Fred *rear frm 5th, lost tch 15th, p.u. 3 out* .... pu
696 Cruise Ann 5a *cls up at 8th, hit 13th, wknd 15th, p.u. 3 out* .... pu
463 Frank The Swank 7a *ld to 8th, wknd frm 13th, p.u. 16th* .... pu
745 Minstrels Jazz 5a *hit 6th, wknd 14th, p.u. 16th, lame* .... pu
Spartan Eric *hld up, nvr rchd ldrs, p.u. 3 out* .... pu
683 Westwood March *in tch to 12th, wknd 14th, p.u. 3 out* .... pu
12 ran. 5l, 3l, 5l, 6l. Time 6m 55.00s. SP 12-1.
Miss P Kerby (Clifton On Teme).
P.R.

VALE OF AYLESBURY
Kimble
Saturday April 6th
GOOD TO FIRM

885 - Members

312 **CELTIC FLAME 7ex..........Miss C Mee** 1
1st ride, ld to 2 out, ld last, ran on well
435 **Radical Views..........A Hill** 2
hld up, chsd wnr aft 12th, ld 2 out-last, no ext
Truely Royal 4ex..........Miss S Baskerville 3
w.w. chsd ldng pair 13th, onepcd frm 3 out
Polecroft *1st ride, chsd wnr to 12th, 4th & wkng whn u.r. nxt* .... ur
642 Ramlosa (NZ) 4ex *in tch in rear, 5th & btn whn u.r. 13th* .... ur
5 ran. 4l, 7l. Time 6m 35.00s. SP 4-1.
Bryan Allen (Vale Of Aylesbury).
Kingofnobles (favourite) withdrawn start, not undr orders.

886 - Confined (12st)

639 **MY BEST MAN 5ex..........A Hill** 1
(fav) chsd ldr,mstk 8th,rdn 14th,outpjmpd aft,ld last,all out
743 **Parting Hour..........Mrs S Adderson** 2
j.w. ld 2nd til mstk & hdd last, just hld nr fin
Admiral Rous 7a..........A Tutton 3
chsd ldrs, mstk 10th, cls 3rd whn blnd 12th, not rcvr, t.o.
434 Sprucefield *ld to 2nd, strgglng frm 5th, t.o. 12th* 4
709 Walkonthemoon 5a *alwys last, t.o. 12th* 5
5 ran. Nk, dist, 3l, 25l. Time 6m 32.50s. SP 1-2.
Alan Hill (Vale Of Aylesbury).

887 - Open

435 **WELSH SINGER..........R Lawther** 1
(fav) ld aft 1st, made rest, rdn out flat
638 **Saybright..........G Tarry** 2
not fluent, ld til mstk 1st, chal last, alwys hld flat
2 ran. 1l. Time 6m 39.00s. SP 4-6.
K B Rogers (Vine & Craven).

888 - Ladies

493 **LARRY THE LAMB..........Miss G Chown** 1
(fav) trckd ldrs, mstk 11th, ld aft 3 out, clr nxt, eased nr fin
640 **Green Archer..........Miss S Duckett** 2
trckd ldr, ld 13th-aft 3 out, outpcd frm nxt
786 **Astroar..........Mrs J Parris** 3
ld to 13th, 3rd & btn aft 3 out, onepcd
782 Button Your Lip *last frm 4th, t.o. 13th* 4
4 ran. 4l, 10l, 1 fence. Time 6m 23.00s. SP 4-5.
Mrs F E Chown (Grafton).

889 - Monterey Restricted (12st)

707 **MAKING TIME 5a..........A Martin** 1
made all, mstks 14th & 3 out, rdn & just hld on flat
641 **Goldtopper 5a..........A Tutton** 2
(fav) cls up, chsd wnr 10th, mstk 2 out, hrd rdn flat,just faild
593 **Fixed Liability 1ow..........A Hill** 3
chsd ldrs, mstk 14th, 3rd & btn frm 3 out
338 Tenella's Last 5a *cls up to 12th, 4th & btn frm 16th* 4
706 Arnold's Choice (bl) *cls up, mstk 5th, bhnd frm 8th, t.o. 13th* 5
Why Ever Not *chsd wnr 4-10th, 3rd whn blnd 15th, not rcvr, p.u. nxt* .... pu
641 Archies Oats *prom to 3rd, last frm nxt, t.o. 10th, p.u. 12th* .... pu
7 ran. Hd, 20l, 15l, 1 fence. Time 6m 31.00s. SP 12-1.
M F Loggin (Bicester With Whaddon Chase).

890 - Maiden

688 **GAWCOTT WOOD 5a..................C Wadland** 1
cls up, prog to ld 15th, clr last, ran on well
495 **Yabbadabbadoo......................R Lawther** 2
rear, gd prog 14th, chsd wnr 3 out, btn whn mstk last
680 **Mr Wendyl..........................M Emmanuel** 3
(Jt fav) prom til lost plc 12th,8th at 14th,ran on & 3rd 2 out,no imp
Miss Kenmac 5a *ld 5-8th, outpcd apr 3 out, no dang aft*.......... 4
Multi Line 5a *mid-div, prog 10th, outpcd apr 3 out, no dang aft*.......... 5
Tinsun 7a *hld up last trio, prog & in tch 15th, btn 3 out, improve*.......... 6
689 Arctic Line *alwys last trio, bhnd frm 12th, p.u. last, dsmntd*.......... pu
495 Apple Nicking *(Jt fav) ld aft 3rd-5th, blnd 11th, wknd 14th, p.u. 3 out*.......... pu
642 Dunloughan *mid-div, prog to ld 13-15th, wknd rpdly aft 3 out, p.u. last*.......... pu
640 Cardschool 5a *hld up, mstk 8th, rear 12th, wll bhnd whn p.u. 2 out*.......... pu
641 Mr Drake (Ire) *ld to aft 3rd & 8th til mstk & hdd 13th, wknd 15th, p.u.2out*.......... pu
11 ran. 12l, 10l, 2l, 4l, 4l. Time 6m 39.00s. SP 6-1.
Mrs E C Cockburn (Warwickshire).
J.N.

VALE OF LUNE
Whittington
Saturday April 6th
FIRM

891 - Members

NENNI (FR)...............................R Ford 1
(fav) ld 11th, clr 13th, rasily
664 **Hillview Lad.........................G Thomas** 2
ld til 6th, ran wd bnds, 2nd 13th, blndrd last
Felix...................................Miss P Smith 3
ld 6-11th, wknd grdly aft
Maximillian *alwys rear, nvr dang*.......... 4
667 The Right Guy *alwys rear, sn t.o., crawld over 14th, immed p.u.*.......... pu
751 Crimson Mary 5a *3l 2nd whn u.r. 11th*.......... ur
6 ran. Dist, 10l, 30l. Time 6m 54.00s. SP 4-9.
Mrs P Robertson (Vale Of Lune).

892 - Confined

664 **AMBROSE.............................D Barlow** 1
(fav) w.w., ld 3 out, clr nxt, canter
588 **Go Miletrian.........................T Bannister** 2
held up, cls 2nd 3 out, outpcd aft
289 **On Your Way..........................D Sherlock** 3
ld 8th to 3 out, wknd qckly
667 Alex-Path *ld, mssd marker aft 2nd, hdd apr 8th, p.u. 11th*.......... pu
4 ran. 6l, 15l. Time 6m 48.00s. SP 1-5.
W A Ritson (Sir W. W. Wynn's).

893 - Ladies

586 **ACROSS THE LAKE (bl).......Miss S Brotherton** 1
w.w., lft in ld apr 3 out, clr nxt, styd on wll
487 **Simply Perfect..................Miss K Swindells** 2
(fav) lft 1l 2nd 3 out, rddn & no ext
400 **Heavenly Hoofer..................Miss F Barnes** 3
chsd ldrs to 13th, wknd & t.o. nxt
Royle Burchlin *ld, mssd marker aft 13th, p.u. apr 3 out*.......... pu
4 ran. 15l, 1 fence. Time 6m 29.00s. SP 5-4.
Mrs D R Brotherton (Middleton).

894 - Open

761 **JACK DWYER...........................D Coates** 1
ld most, styd on wll whn chal 2 out
500 **Wally Wrekin (bl).....................R Ford** 2
(fav) held up, n.j.w., ev ch whn chal 2 out to last, no ext
892 **Alex-Path.............................T Whittaker** 3
2nd outing, alwys bhnd, styd on onepce to take 3rd 2 out
410 Clare Lad *(3s-2s), alwys rear, t.o. 6th*.......... 4
736 Strathbogie Mist (Ire) *2nd to 3 out, wknd rpdly, p.u. last*.......... pu
5 ran. 1½l, 12l, dist. Time 6m 35.00s. SP 5-1.
J J Coates (Pendle Forest & Craven).

895 - Restricted (12st)

501 **PENNINE VIEW..........................R Ford** 1
ld 4th, clr aft 3 out, easily
591 **Nutcase 5a...........................A Phillips** 2
(fav) held up,2nd 11th,ev ch whn chal 3 out,mstks last 3,eased flt
586 **Douce Eclair 5a....................Miss N Hogg** 3
chsd ldrs, lost plc 14th, styd on wll frm 2 out
The Ginger Tom *in tch to 13th, wknd qckly aft*.......... 4
754 Steady Away (Ire) (bl) *chsd ldrs to 11th, wknd & p.u. apr 14th*.......... pu
5 ran. 20l, hd, 12l. Time 6m 40.00s. SP 3-1.
J J Dixon (Cumberland Farmers).

896 - Open Maiden

463 **FOUR HEARTS (IRE)....................D Barlow** 1
2nd til ld apr 13th, kpt on wll whn chal flat
589 **Micksdilemma.........................A Phillips** 2
(fav) w.w., 2nd 14th, mstk last, drvn to chal flat, outpcd
589 **Greet The Greek........................R Ford** 3
(4s-2s), ld to 12th, grdly wknd aft
756 Jack's Croft *alwys bhnd, nvr dang*.......... 4
613 Moore View 5a *rear whn f 4th*.......... f
5 ran. 1½l, dist, 12l. Time 6m 48.00s. SP 3-1.
T D B Barlow (Cheshire).
R.A.

WOODLAND PYTCHLEY
Dingley
Saturday April 6th
GOOD TO SOFT

897 - Confined (12st)

676 **BEAU DANDY 3ex.......................T Marks** 1
(fav) cls up, hrd hld, ld 11th, drew clr 4 out, comf
490 **Jerrigo 3ex.........................J Knowles** 2
ld to 3rd, contd cls up, outpcd 4 out
Oh So Windy 5a.......................S Morris 3
prog 8th, 4th 4 out, ran on, not rch 1st 2
632 Rare Knight (bl) *last pair to 8th, stdy prog, nrst at fin*.......... 4
Obie's Train 3ow *cls up, rnng wd, outpcd by 1st trio 3 out*.......... 5
Hellbrunn *s.s., mid-div frm 11th, outpcd 6 out*.......... 6
535 Subsonic (Ire) *cls up, chsd wnnr 6 out, wknd 2 out*.......... 7
638 Kelly's Eye 3ex (bl) *prog 8th, 6th brfly 11th, sn fdd*.......... 8
622 Current Attraction 5a *cls up 5th/6th 2 m, wknd qckly 5 out*.......... 9
Kellys Pal *cls up til mstk 5th, no ch frm 10th*.......... 10
678 Spanish Whisper *prom to 3rd, sn wknd, last trio frm 10th*.......... 11
334 Great Legend *u.r. 1st*.......... ur
676 Aldington Baron *ld 4-10th, fdd, p.u. 2 out*.......... pu
535 San Remo *cls up 5-8th, fdd, bhnd whn f 3 out*.......... f
Menature (Ire) *mid-div to 8th, fdd, p.u. aft 4 out*.......... pu
15 ran. 20l, 2½l, 3l, nk, 10l, 5l, 8l, 8l, 8l, 30l. Time 6m 44.00s. SP 11-10.
C C Shand Kydd (Pytchley).

898 - 2m 5f Maiden (5-7yo) Div I (12st)

NAUGHTY NELLIE 7a.............Mrs J Dawson 1
(Co fav) ld (safest plc) frm 4th, mstk 5 out, ran on wll
727 **Bucklelone 5a.........................J Docker** 2
2nd frm 4th, chsd wnnr last m, no imp

636 **Reel Rascal 5a..........................T Lane** 3
(Co fav) mid-div, 4th 5 out, lft 3rd 3 out, ran on onepce
540 Still Hopeful 5a *imprvng 3rd whn u.r. 5th (ditch)*...... ur
324 Emerald Queen 5a *ld jmpng lft til ran out 4th*........ ro
541 The Bold Abbot *(Co fav) in tch last pair whn blkd loose horse 7th*.......... bd
Minstrel's Night (Ire) 7a *in tch last pair whn blkd by loose horse 7th*.......... bd
675 View Point (Ire) *3rd frm 7th, wknd 6 out, b.d. 3 out*.... bd
Rough Light (Ire) *mid-div, chsd 1st pair 6 out, u.r. 3 out*.......... ur
Malvern Lad *nvr dang, mstly 6th frm 10th, outpcd whn u.r. 3 out*.......... ur
10 ran. 15l, 4l. Time 5m 56.00s. SP 7-2.
C D Dawson (Brocklesby).

899 - Members

392 **TEACAKE (bl)..........................H Nicholson** 1
reluctant ldr slow pce, ran on gamely frm 2 out
393 **Blue Beat 5a..........................M Hewitt** 2
alwys prom, chal 2 out, jst outpcd
438 **Cormeen Lord (Ire)..........................J Sharp** 3
(fav) cls up, hrd hld, chal 2 out, sn outpcd
635 Cass *cls up, chal 2 out, ran on onepce*.......... 4
4 ran. 3l, 5l, nk. Time 8m 7.00s. SP 3-1.
J G Nicholson (Woodland Pytchley).

900 - 2m 5f Maiden (5-7yo) Div II Pt I (12st)

WESTON MOON (IRE) 5a..........................N Bell 1
made all, 20l clr 6 out, unchal
Rymerole..........................Mrs J Dawson 2
(fav) mid-div, ran on frm 6 out, no threat to wnnr
Pocket Watch..........................T Lane 3
2nd frm 1st til wknd 2 out
542 Cantango (Ire) *4th, lft 3rd 6 out, f nxt*.......... f
542 Warm Relation (Ire) 7a *3rd frm 1st, wknd qckly 10th, p.u. nxt*.......... pu
Oliver Himself 7a *last jmpng slwly til p.u. 9th*.......... pu
See The Lord (Ire) *6th til f 9th*.......... f
Brenda's Dream 7a *remote 7th whn ref 9th*.......... ref
8 ran. 20l, 15l. Time 5m 55.00s. SP 12-1.
Mr & Mrs N R J Bell (Fernie).

901 - 2m 5f Maiden (5-7yo) Div II Pt II (12st)

KENALAN LAD..........................N Kent 1
made all, clr ld, hmp by loose horses 10th, ran on wll
635 **Another Comedy..........................J Knowles** 2
remote 2nd frm 4th, ran on onepce
540 **Rainbow Fantasia (Ire)..........................P Millington** 3
nvr dang, kpt gng whn rest stopped
688 Remalone 5a *3rd til rddn & wknd 8th, t.o. 6 out*.......... 4
Batcho Missile *in rear whn u.r. 2nd*.......... ur
727 Dark Rhytham *(fav) 6l 2nd whn f 4th*.......... f
Storm Alive (Ire) 7a *last jmpng slwly til p.u. 9th*.......... pu
682 Lend Us A Buck 5a 3ow *3rd/4th to 6 out, fdd, p.u. 4 out*.......... pu
Master Pug (bl) *alwys last pair, p.u. 9th*.......... pu
9 ran. 20l, 12l, 2 fences. Time 5m 50.00s. SP 4-1.
Mrs Sally Thornton (Belvoir).

902 - Land Rover Open (12st)

725 **RAISE AN ARGUMENT..........................J Docker** 1
(fav) 2nd til ld 12th, battld back whn hdd 2 out, remarkable
639 **Bright As A Button..........................J Connell** 2
cls up, 2nd frm 12th, chal & ld 2 out, outpcd bfr last
723 **Write The Music 4ex (bl)..........................T Lane** 3D
cls up,jmp rght,3rd 6 out,lost wght clth 2 out,fin fast,disq
537 **Dubalea..........................P Millington** 3
ld to 11th, wknd qckly, t.o. 5 out, fin 4th, promoted
4 ran. 4l, nk, 1 fence. Time 6m 48.00s. SP Evens.
Mrs J H Docker (Atherstone).

903 - Ladies

633 **LOOSE WHEELS (bl)..........................Miss K Makinson** 1
made most, ran on gamely frm 2 out
640 **Miners Rest 5a..........................Mrs C McCarthy** 2
cls up, 3rd 6 out, chsd wnnr 3 out, alwys held
633 **Winged Whisper (USA)..........................Miss A Wells** 3
alwys prom, cont 7-11th, 3rd reluctant 3 out
724 Sea Clipper (Ire) *last pair frm 5th, no ch frm 6 out*.... 4
676 Ovac Star *cls up 3rd/4th til outpcd 6 out*.......... 5
436 Directly *(fav) jmp slwly in rear til ref 8th*.......... ref
536 Guild Street 5a *in tch 4th/5th til p.u. qckly 6 out*...... pu
7 ran. 4l, 12l, 1 fence, 5l. Time 6m 57.00s. SP 3-1.
Miss K Makinson (Fitzwilliam).

904 - Restricted (12st)

539 **COOLVAWN LADY (IRE) 5a..........................T Lane** 1
alwys prom, 3rd frm 5th, 2nd 6 out, ld 4 out, ran on wll
358 **Wayward Sailor (bl)..........................Miss C Spearing** 2
prom bhnd ldrs, 5th 6 out, ran on, not rch wnnr
484 **Candle Glow 5a..........................S Morris** 3
ld to 5 out, ran on onepce whn hdd
494 Linlake Lightning 5a *rear div, 12th 10th, ran on passed btn horses last m*.......... 4
539 Whinstone Mill *prom bhnd ldrs, 3rd 6-3 out, fdd*...... 5
343 Beat The Rap *prog 10th, 6th 6 out, no ext*.......... 6
428 Dixons Homefinder *mid-div whn f 7th*.......... f
897 Great Legend 10ow *2nd outing, rear div whn f 7th (ditch)*.......... f
241 Coolsythe 5a *alwys rear div, t.o. 8th, p.u. 6 out*.......... pu
726 Merlins Girl 5a *rear div til floundd p.u. 8th*.......... pu
392 Odysseus *cls up 1st m, sn fdd, p.u. 5 out*.......... pu
681 Kerry My Home *abt 10th 1st m, p.u. 10th*.......... pu
Grange Missile 5a *alwys rear hlf, outpcd 6 out, p.u. 3 out*.......... pu
397 Smart Rhythm 5a *last trio frm 5th, t.o. 8th, p.u. 12th*.. pu
432 Gal-A-Dor *prom for 2 m, 2nd 5-11th, wknd qckly, p.u. 4 out*.......... pu
621 Unlucky For Some (Ire) *nvr dang, remote 7th 2 out, p.u. last*.......... pu
679 Glenrowan Lad *(fav) abt 6th for 2 m, 4th 6 out, fdd, p.u. 2 out*.......... pu
726 Forever Freddy *mid-div, abt 7th whn u.r. 5 out*.......... ur
Cawkwell Win 7a *t.o. last til p.u. 8th*.......... pu
Just Like Madge 3ow *t.o. 19th frm 2nd, p.u. 8th*.......... pu
20 ran. 10l, 10l, 5l, 20l, 10l. Time 6m 49.00s. SP 6-1.
W R Halliday (Cranwell Bloodhounds).
K.B.

CARLISLE
Monday April 8th
FIRM

905 - 3¼m Mdn Hun Chase

667 **BRAZEN GOLD 12.0 7a..........................Mr D Barlow** 1
(fav) cl up, ld twelfth, shaken up apr last, ran on.
758 **Glenbricken 12.0 7a..........................Mr R Barker** 2
alwys prom, chal twelfth and ev ch till rdn and one pace apr last.
673 **Whosthat 12.0 7a..........................Mr J Davies** 3
ld till hdd twelfth, soon wknd.
503 Madame Beck 11.6 7a 4ow *held up in rear when f 6th, rmt and t.o. after*.......... 4
789 Royalist (Can) 12.0 7a *prom till lost pl quickly 6th, t.o. 10th, p.u. before 2 out*.......... pu
5 ran. 3½l, dist, 28l. Time 7m 7.10s. SP 6-4.
Sir John Barlow Bt

FAKENHAM
Monday April 8th
GOOD

906 - 2m 5f 110yds Nov Hun Chase

PRINZAL 12.0..........................Mr M Armytage 1
chsd ldrs, hdwy 4th, ld before 7th, hdd after 9th, mstk next, led again before 3 out, soon clr, impressive.

621 **Lantern Pike 11.7 7a ....Mr A Michael 2**
chsd ldrs, mstk 4th, ld after 9th, hdd before 3 out, no ext from next.
255 **Bathwick Bobbie 11.7 7a.........Miss S Higgins 3**
soon prom, styd on same pace from 3 out.
622 On The Beer (Ire) 11.7 7a *(fav) bhnd early, prog 5th, styd on one pace clsg stgs.* 4
484 Just Jack 11.13 7a *n.d.* 5
581 Bold Imp 11.7 7a *chsd ldrs to 8th, soon bhnd.* 6
491 Notary-Nowell 11.7 7a *chsd ldrs to 11th, soon well bhnd.* 7
420 Divine Chance (Ire) 11.9 5a *alwys bhnd, t.o.* 8
622 Easy Over (USA) 11.9 5a *made most to 6th, blnd 8th, soon bhnd, t.o. when p.u. 12th.* .... pu
633 Nowhiski 11.7 7a *u.r. 2nd.* .... ur
621 Couture Quality 11.7 7a (bl) *with ldrs, bad mstk 11th, t.o. when p.u. before next.* .... pu
11 ran. 25l, 4l, 2½l, 13l, 2½l, 1l, 24l. Time 5m 25.90s. SP 3-1.
Mrs Pam Froud

907 - 3m 110yds Hun Chase

676 **TIMBER'S BOY 11.1 7a..................Mr R Gill 1**
bhnd early, gd hdwy after 9th, chsd ldr from 15th, left well clr 2 out, unchal.
485 **Faringo 11.5 7a ....Mr C Ward 2**
(Jt fav) chsd ldr, no ext after 4 out.
620 **Wistino 11.1 7a ....Mr P Taiano 3**
(Jt fav) ld 3rd, bad mstk when hdd 4 out, no ext.
620 Counterbid 11.7 5a (bl) *chsd ldr, ev ch 5 out, wknd from next.* 4
309 Emsee-H 11.5 7a *alwys bhnd, n.d.* 5
621 General Picton 11.4 5a 1ow *chsd ldrs, ld 4 out, going well when f 2 out.* .... f
723 Antrim County 11.5 7a *ld to 3rd, slow jump 4th, soon struggling, t.o. when p.u. before four out.* .... pu
489 Way Of Life (Fr) 11.5 7a *soon bhnd, mstk 13th, t.o. when p.u. before 2 out.* .... pu
678 Dromin Leader 11.5 7a *cl up when u.r. 10th.* .... ur
677 Carrigeen Lad 11.5 7a (bl) *prog to go 2nd twelfth, p.u. before 5 out, fin lame.* .... pu
679 Cool Apollo (NZ) 11.1 7a *bhnd from 11th, p.u. before 4 out.* .... pu
11 ran. Dist, 10l, 1½l, 22l. Time 6m 20.50s. SP 7-1.
B G Clark

HEREFORD
Monday April 8th
GOOD TO FIRM

908 - 2m 3f Hun

674 **FAMILIAR FRIEND 12.0 7a (bl) ....Mr L Lay 1**
held up, hdwy 6th, ld 4 out, rdn out.
670 **Squirrellsdaughter 11.9 7a......Miss S Beddoes 2**
(fav) held up, hdwy 6th, chsd ldr and mstk 9th, ev ch from 3 out, kept on run-in.
691 **Enchanted Man 11.7 7a.............Mr M Harris 3**
prom, rdn 9th, styd on same pace from 4 out.
364 Knowing 11.2 7a *held up, hdwy 7th, joined ldrs 10th, wknd 2 out.* 4
637 Tekla (Fr) 11.7 7a *mid div, hit 5th, outpcd from 4 out.* 5
737 Warner Forpleasure 11.8 7a 1ow (bl) *prom, ld 6th, rdn and hdd 4 out, soon wknd.* 6
709 Bill Of Rights 11.3 7a *prom till rdn and wknd 10th.* 7
291 Queens Tour 11.3 7a *bhnd from 6th, t.o. when p.u. before 2 out.* .... pu
Ebony Star 11.7 7a *p.u. before 1st.* .... pu
579 Hickelton Lad 12.0 7a *held up, hit 1st, mstks 3rd, f next.* .... f
807 Open Agenda (Ire) 11.3 7a *ld to 6th, wknd 8th, t.o. when p.u. before 10th.* .... pu
674 Cathgal 11.7 7a *blnd and u.r. 3rd.* .... ur
12 ran. 2l, 15l, 5l, 4l, 3l, dist. Time 4m 47.80s. SP 9-2.
M H G Lang

TOWCESTER
Monday April 8th
FIRM

909 - 2¾m Hun

580 **TEAPLANTER 12.0 5a...............Mr B Pollock 1**
(fav) ld to 7th, led apr 9th, mstk 12th, clr approaching 3 out, unchal.
799 **Knockumshin 12.0 5a ....Mr T Byrne 2**
bhnd, mstk 10th, hdwy next, chsd wnr apr 2 out, no impn.
Treyford 11.7 7a.....................Mr D Verco 3
prom, wknd apr 3 out.
577 Blakes Orphan 11.12 7a *mstk 13th, nvr trbl ldrs.* 4
Woodlands Genhire 11.7 7a (v) *held up in tch, ld 7th, hdd apr 9th, wknd 11th.* 5
Biblical 11.2 7a *bhnd from 8th, t.o. when p.u. before 2 out.* .... pu
6 ran. 30l, 2½l, 1½l, 6l. Time 5m 31.40s. SP 4-11.
R G Russell

BRAES OF DERWENT
Tranwell
Monday April 8th
GOOD TO FIRM

910 - Members

764 **JUSTFORGASTRIX (IRE) ....S Bowden 1**
made all, j.w. 25l clr 14th, styd on strngly
320 **Terracotta Warrior 2ow.................A Kirtley 2**
(fav) chsd wnr, wknd to 3rd at 12th, tk remote 2nd last
704 **Corsage 7a........................B Stonehouse 3**
3rd til chsd wnr 12th, no imp 4 out, wknd last
763 Multi Purpose *1st ride, alwys last, blnd & u.r. 7th.* .... ur
4 ran. Dist, 4l. Time 6m 29.00s. SP 3-1.
Eddy Luke (Braes Of Derwent).

911 - Confined (12st)

703 **TODCRAG..............................T Scott 1**
trckd ldr til ld/disp 9th-2 out, just ld last, found ext
699 **Master Mischief 1ow..................J Walton 2**
ran in sntchs, 10l 6th at 14th, prog 2 out, ran on wll flat
701 **The Mosses..........................D Wood 3**
mid-div, prog to handy 3rd 2 out, styd on, not rch ldrs
699 Neville *alwys prom in chsng grp, 3rd frm 9-14th, no ext frm 2 out* 4
317 Dancing Legend (Ire) *prom to hlfwy, not rch ldrs frm 14th.* 5
702 Gay Vixen VI 5a *ld/disp til wknd rpdly aft 2 out* 6
Just Maskaraider *prom early, wknd into 7th hlfwy, lost tch 12th.* 7
608 Joli Exciting 5a *alwys rear, last at 9th, lost tch 12th* 8
Mill Knock *alwys rear, last whn mstk 12th, t.o.* 9
9 ran. 2l, 6l, 2½l, 20l, 10l, 5l, 1l, 20l. Time 6m 5.00s. SP 4-7.
Mrs D Scott (Border).

912 - Open

790 **WASHAKIE............................J Walton 1**
(fav) chsd ldng pair, cls up 4 out, ld & mstk nxt, clr 2 out
857 **True Fair...........................A Robson 2**
ld, outpcd & wknd into 3rd 3 out, lft 2nd apr nxt
701 **Tartan Tornado......................P Johnson 3**
rear, prog to 4th hlfwy, styd on wll 4 out, not trbl ldrs
701 Fast Study *6th hlfwy, nvr on terms wth ldrs* 4
753 Boreen Owen *alwys rear, 7th hlfwy, not rch ldrs* 5
701 Equinoctial *trckd ldr to 14th, going wll whn p.u. aft 3 out, dead* .... pu
500 Duntree *mid-div whn f 3rd, dead* .... f
699 Its The Bidder (Ire) *handy 5th hlfwy, outpcd & wknd rpdly 14th, p.u. last* .... pu
8 ran. 8l, 1l, 2l, 15l, dist. Time 6m 3.00s. SP 4-6.
Mrs F T Walton (Border).
One fence omitted, 17 jumps.

913 - Ladies

752 **FETTLE UP (bl)** .... **Miss S Brotherton** 1
(fav) ld to 4th, ld nxt, jnd 13th, clr nxt, imprssv
611 **Amber Payne** .... **Miss D Laidlaw** 2
chsd ldr, ld 4-5th, 3l down 14th, outpcd 2 out
700 **Houselope Beck** .... **Miss S Forster** 3
tongue-strap, 5l 4th hlfwy, 3rd frm 12th, outpcd 14th
488 Flypie *nvr on terms, disp 5th hlfwy, no imp aft* 4
752 Furry Venture 5a *outpcd, poor 6th at 13th, plodded on* 5
698 May Run *nvr going wll, last at 13th, p.u. nxt* .... pu
756 Zoflo 5a *chsd ldng pair to hlfwy, wknd 13th, p.u. 3 out* .... pu
7 ran. 20l, 1l, 6l, 20l. Time 6m 2.00s. SP 4-6.
Mrs D R Brotherton (Middleton).

914 - Restricted (12st)

613 **IN DEMAND 7a** .... **P Craggs** 1
(fav) hld up, prog 14th, disp nxt, qcknd to ld last, clvrly
754 **Little Wenlock** .... **Mrs V Jackson** 2
cls up, smooth prog to ld 3 out, hdd & outpcd last
703 **Royal Surprise** .... **Miss P Robson** 3
chsd ldr til ld 11th, hdd 4 out, sn btn
608 Blakes Folly (Ire) *ld to 3rd, cls up hlfwy, outpcd 4 out, wknd 2 out* 4
Wire Lass 5a *ld/disp 4-10th, wknd 12th, p.u. 2 out* .... pu
703 Say Milady 5a *whppd round start, tk no part* 0
6 ran. 4l, 10l, 15l. Time 6m 13.00s. SP 4-5.
A J Balmer (Morpeth).

915 - Open Maiden

705 **RUECASTLE** .... **A Robson** 1
made all, clr 9th, easily
763 **Goongor (Ire)** .... **P Jenkins** 2
lft clr 2nd at 4th, chsd wnr aft, no ch frm 15th, tired
705 **Wassl's Nanny (Ire) 5a** .... **A Parker** 3
(fav) nvr on terms wth ldrs, 20l 3rd hlfwy, und pres 5 out, no imp
704 The Raskins 5a *mid-div whn b.d. 4th* .... bd
698 Teatime Girl 5a *alwys last, nvr going wll, t.o. & p.u. aft 9th* .... pu
416 Need A Ladder (bl) *mid-div, b.d. 4th* .... bd
704 The Camair Flyer (Ire) *chsd ldr, disp 2nd whn f 4th* .... f
7 ran. 12l, dist. Time 6m 19.00s. SP 14-1.
Miss Simone Park (Braes Of Derwent).

916 - 2½m Open Maiden (5-7yo)

755 **LINDON RUN** .... **R Morgan** 1
made all, j.w. qcknd clr last, styd on well
613 **Called To Account 5a** .... **A Parker** 2
(fav) alwys prom, ev ch 4 out, lft 4l 2nd 2 out, outpcd
705 **Starlin Sam** .... **A Kirtley** 3
mid-div, handy 4th at 6th, wknd 11th, lost tch nxt
406 Political Skirmish 5a *u.r. 1st* .... ur
Cookie Boy 7a *alwys rear, remote 5th at 11th, t.o. & p.u. nxt* .... pu
704 Sharpe Exit *alwys strgglng, lost tch 10th, f nxt* .... f
704 Slieve Na Bar (Ire) *alwys prom, trckd wnr til wknd und pres 3 out, f nxt,dead* .... f
Little Hawk *nvr going wll, p.u. 7th* .... pu
8 ran. 20l, 20l. Time 5m 12.00s. SP 2-1.
T D Donaldson (Tynedale).
P.B.

EAST KENT
Aldington
Monday April 8th
FIRM

917 - Restricted (12st)

574 **ROLLESTON BLADE** .... **P Bull** 1
(fav) hld up, ld 13th, clr 2 out, pshd out flat
810 **Basher Bill** .... **K Giles** 2
mstk 4th, cls up, outpcd 12th, ran on 3 out, no imp flat
Political Man *ld 3-6th,chsd wnr 15th,no imp 2 out,p.u.last,dsmntd* .... pu
774 Prince Rua *ld to 3rd & 6-13th, wth wnr whn u.r. 15th* .... ur
4 ran. 3l. Time 6m 46.00s. SP 1-2.
H J Jarvis (Ashford Valley).

918 - Confined (12st)

775 **BURROMARINER 6ex** .... **A Welsh** 1
cls up, prog to ld 3 out, clr apr last, easily
574 **Sound Statement (Ire)** .... **T Hills** 2
(fav) jmpd rght, ld to 12th, wth wnr 3 out, btn whn mstk nxt
775 **Welshman's Gully** .... **P Bull** 3
prssd ldr, ld 12th til hdd & wknd 3 out
594 The Portsoy Loon *cls up in last, effrt apr 3 out, found nil* 4
4 ran. 8l, 12l, 3l. Time 6m 37.80s. SP 2-1.
Mrs A Blaker (Mid Surrey Farmers Draghounds).

919 - Ladies

596 **TOPPING-THE-BILL 7ex** .... **Mrs E Coveney** 1
(fav) steadied start,prog to jn ldr 11th,mstk 14th,ld last,pshdout
596 **Wellington Bay 4ex** .... **Miss C Grissell** 2
ld, jnd 12th, outjmpd wnr aft, hdd last, ran on und pres
Shamrock Star .... **Miss C Townsley** 3
cls up to 13th, t.o. 16th
572 Larquill 5a *chsd ldr to 6th, last frm nxt, blnd 11th,t.o.14th,p.u. 2 out* .... pu
4 ran. ½l, 1 fence. Time 6m 35.90s. SP 1-2.
Mrs Emma Coveney (Old Surrey & Burstow).

920 - Open (12st)

179 **GREEN'S VAN GOYEN (IRE) 4ex** ...... **T McCarthy** 1
ld to 15th,3rd & outpcd aft nxt,rallied to ld last,drvn out
Rose King 7ex .... **T Hills** 2
(fav) nt fluent early,prog 12th,ld 15th,hrd rdn & hdd last,nt qckn
571 **Little Nod** .... **M FitzGerald** 3
cls up, wth ldr 15th-3 out, 2nd & btn whn blnd nxt, nt rcvr
776 Colne Valley Kid *chsd ldr to 10th, wknd rpdly 15th, t.o. & p.u. 3 out* .... pu
594 Athnanurlainn 6ow *cls up to 10th, rdn & wknd nxt, t.o. & p.u. aft 15th* .... pu
813 Stede Quarter 1ow *sttld last, lost tch 14th, t.o. & p.u. aft 16th* .... pu
6 ran. 1½l, 30l. Time 6m 39.30s. SP 13-8.
Mrs D H McCarthy (Kent & Surrey Bloodhounds).

921 - Open Maiden (12st)

575 **HIGH BURNSHOT** .... **A Welsh** 1
(fav) plld to ld 2nd,stdd & hdd 11th,ld aft 2 out,sn clr,wll rdn
576 **Fort Diana** .... **G Hopper** 2
mstks, ld to 2nd, chsd ldr, ld 11th-aft 2 out, immed btn
778 **Netherby Cheese** .... **P Hickman** 3
mod 4th til went 3rd frm 11th, kpt on, nvr rchd 1st pair
254 Joyful Hero 5a *strtd 30l bhnd,schoold & t.o.,fin full of running,stewards* 4
780 Silly Sovereign 5a *raced in 5th/6th wth stablemate, t.o. 10th, p.u. 15th* .... pu
781 Sunley Line (bl) *raced in 5th/6th wth stablemate, t.o. 10th, p.u. 15th* .... pu
253 Borneo Days 5a *5th whn ran out 4th* .... ro
275 Bubbles Galore (Ire) 7a *chsd ldng pair to 11th,4th & no ch 14th,p.u. aft 16th,green* .... pu
8 ran. 15l, 8l, 1 fence. Time 6m 54.60s. SP Evens.
Mrs G M Gladders (Ashford Valley).

922 - Members

PRINCE ZEUS.......................T McCarthy 1
(fav) chsd ldr til lft m clr aft 10th, lft alone nxt
668 J J Jimmy *pllng, ld til p.u. aft 10th, lame* .... pu
496 Tasmanite *alwys last, t.o. 6th, 2 fences bhnd whn p.u. 11th* .... pu
Hatchit *1st ride, mod 3rd til ref & u.r. 6th* .... ref
4 ran. Time 7m 6.00s. SP 2-5.
D G Knowles (East Kent).
J.N.

EGGESFORD
Bishopsleigh
Monday April 8th
GOOD

923 - Members

625 PHILS PRIDE *ld 1st, ran out 2nd* .... ro
625 Just Bert (Ire) *(fav) lft in ld 2nd,u.r. 9th, rider unable to remnt, injured* .... ur
2 ran.
Race Void.

924 - Ladies

624 **KHATTAF ....Miss J Cumings** 1
ld/disp til clr ldr 3rd, nvr hdd, ran on strngly
528 **Fly The Wind 5a................Miss L Blackford** 2
(fav) disp ld 1st-2nd, chsd nwr aft, nvr able to chal aft last
716 **Greenwine (USA)..................Miss A Lamb** 3
mstk 9th, cls order frm 13th, no ext frm 3 out
640 Little Thyne *alwys rear, jmp big, fin race own pce*.... 4
669 Skerry Meadow *in front rank chal whn u.r. 14th* ..... ur
Gallery Lady (Ire) 5a *towrds rear frm 1st, f 4th*........ f
Typographer (Ire) 7a *u.r. 1st* .... ur
7 ran. 1l, 8l, dist. Time 6m 42.00s. SP 5-4.
Mr H C Johnson (Devon & Somerset Staghounds).

925 - Confined

708 **FLAME O'FRENSI 5a ....Miss J Cumings** 1
(fav) ld 2nd, front rank til clr 11th, clvrly
650 **Hensue ....N Harris** 2
wll bhnd til rppd hdwy 3 out, nvr nrr
804 Querrin Lodge *bhnd frm 10th, t.o. p.u. 3 out*.......... pu
Bert House *ld 4th, front rank til 11th, wknd qckly, p.u. 2 out* .... pu
Bincombe Top *alwys wll bhnd, t.o. whn p.u. bfr 11th* .. pu
628 Monkton (Ire) (bl) *ld 1st, lsng grnd frm 7th, f 9th* ...... f
6 ran. 2l. Time 6m 49.00s. SP 4-7.
P J Clarke (Devon & Somerset Staghounds).

926 - Restricted (12st)

558 **M-REG ....L Jefford** 1
(fav) alwys wll plcd, ld 3 out, won wll
532 **Link Copper ....Miss L Blackford** 2
ld 2nd & 5th til hdd 7th, fronk rank, no ext aft last
482 **Chukamill ....R Mills** 3
ld 3rd & 8th til no ext 4 out
718 Mosside *mid-div whn lsng grnd frm 16th, styd on onepcd*.................. 4
804 Darktown Strutter (bl) *midfld, bad mstk 12th, wknd rpdly, p.u. 17th whn wll bhnd*.................. pu
445 Roving Vagabond *lost grnd frm 5th, t.o. whn p.u. 4 out*.................. pu
562 Remember Mac (bl) *bhnd frm 1st, p.u. 5th whn t.o.* ... pu
276 Stainless Steel *wll bhnd frm 10th, p.u. 4 out* .... pu
447 One For The Cross (Ire) *t.o. whn p.u. 5 out*........... pu
9 ran. 3l, 5l, 10l. Time 6m 44.00s. SP Evens.
Mrs C Egalton (Axe Vale Harriers).

927 - Open

441 **FEARSOME...........................R White** 1
raced at rear til cls order frm 13th, ld 3 out, easy
717 **Magnolia Man ....N Harris** 2
(fav) alwys frnt rank til clr 11th, no ext frm 3 out
671 **Moze Tidy.............................I Dowrick** 3
mid-div til grdly wknd frm 16th
626 Bargain And Sale *mid-div til cls order 9th, bad mstk 16th, wknd qckly*.................. 4
731 Far Too Loud *ref 1st*.................. ref
718 Gamblers Refrain *ld 1st til hdd 11th, frnt rank whn u.r. 13th*.................. ur
Admirals Realm *p.u. aft 2nd* .... pu
7 ran. 10l, 15l, 25l. Time 6m 45.00s. SP 3-1.
G W Penfold (Silverton).

928 - Maiden

482 **MASTER KIWI (NZ)....................L Jefford** 1
ld 4th, nvr hdd, won readly
558 **Medias Maid 5a ....A Holdsworth** 2
towrds rear til hdwy 10th, lft 2nd 3 out, nvr trbld wnnr
Sgt Childcraft............................S Slade 3
towrds rear, some prog frm 12th, nvr nrr
556 Miss Pernickity 5a *alwys wll bhnd, t.o. frm 13th* 4
534 Melody Mine 5a *towrds rear early, p.u. aft 11th* .... pu
807 Dusty Furlong *ld 1st-4th, stil frnt rank whn f 13th* ..... f
719 Musbury Castle 5a *mid-div whn f 9th* .... f
627 Tangle Kelly *(fav) mntng chal & hrd rddn whn f 3 out*.. f
Fair Lark *f 1st*.................. f
9 ran. 15l, dist, dist. Time 6m 57.00s. SP 5-2.
F G Hollis (Dulverton (East)).
G.H.

ESSEX FARMERS & UNION
Marks Tey
Monday April 8th
GOOD

929 - Open Maiden Div I

BRACKENHEATH (IRE) 7a...............T Bulgin 1
sttld rear, prog to chal 2 out, ld apr last, hld on flat
830 **Insulate 5a 1ow ....S March** 2
chsd ldrs, disp 7th, last by 9th, outpcd 15th,styd on 2 out
780 **Loch Irish (Ire) 5a ....S R Andrews** 3
(fav) set steady pace, clr 15th, hdd apr last, no ext flat
495 Superforce *rear whn slw jmp & nrly ref 1st, ref 2nd*... ref
617 Go Magic *trckd ldrs, mstk 13th, ch whn mstk 4 out, wknd rpdly,p.u.nxt* .... pu
5 ran. 1½l, 2l. Time 7m 16.00s. SP 2-1.
G H Barber (Essex Farmers & Union).

930 - Open Maiden Div II

489 **BRUFF CASTLE (bl) ....A Coe** 1
(Jt fav) prom, ld 8-12th, lft in ld nxt-4out, ld 3 out, hld on flat
343 **Mister Rainman ....T Bulgin** 2
hld up,mstk 9th,prog 11th,ld 4 out-nxt,ev ch last, no ext
781 **Mandenka ....G Cooper** 3
(Jt fav) wth ldrs, lft 2nd 13th, outpcd frm 16th
419 Sign Performer *alwys bhnd, lost tch 12th, t.o. 16th*.... 4
681 Alapa *prom whn ran out 4th* .... ro
Nova Star 7a *mid-div, mstk 1st, prog 11th, ld nxt, going wll whn u.r. nxt* .... ur
6 ran. ¾l, 8l, dist. Time 7m 14.00s. SP 2-1.
D L Claydon (Puckeridge & Thurlow).

931 - Restricted (12st)

593 **NIBBLE ....G Cooper** 1
trckd ldrs, ld 6th-10th, rdn 15th, ld apr 2 out, blnd last
620 **Kelly's Original...................Miss K Tolhurst** 2
(fav) mid-div, prog to 2nd 14th, ld 16th-apr 2 out, onepcd aft
417 **Alfredo Garcia (Ire) 7a ....T Moore** 3
ld to 4th, ev ch 3 out, wknd frm nxt

782 Mount Patrick *alwys prom, ld aft 4th-6th, ld 10th-16th, outpcd* 4
682 Tharif *alwys rear, mstk & rdn 10th, t.o. whn u.r. 12th* .. ur
676 Ravens Hasey Moon *hld up rear, in tch whn p.u. qckly 11th* .... pu
621 Whats Another 5a *s.v.s. t.o. 3rd, p.u. 12th* .... pu
682 Zap (Ire) 5a *slw jmp 1st, alwys rear, lost tch 10th, p.u. 13th* .... pu
8 ran. 4l, 15l, 10l. Time 6m 44.00s. SP 2-1.
G I Cooper (Essex & Suffolk).

932 - Open

491 **MELTON PARK (bl)....................N Bloom** 1
trckd ldr, mstk 11th, disp 13th, lft clr nxt, fin alone
671 Loyal Note *(fav) ld, jnd 13th, f nxt* .... f
Morstons Express *keen hold, alwys last, lft dist 2nd 14th, p.u. 2 out, lame* .... pu
3 ran. Time 7m 8.00s. SP 6-4.
A J Papworth (Dunston).

933 - Ladies

832 **ST GREGORY (bl) ....Miss A Plunkett** 1
(fav) made all, drew clr 4 out, unchal
680 **Springlark (Ire) 7a ....Mrs L Wrighton** 2
s.i.s. prog to cls 2nd 14th, outpcd 16th, styd on
678 **Sarazar (USA) ....Miss H Pewter** 3
chsd wnr til last frm 14th, btn whn mstk 16th
3 ran. 8l, 6l. Time 6m 58.00s. SP 1-3.
A Howland Jackson (Essex & Suffolk).

934 - Confined (12st)

778 **DREAM PACKET ....S R Andrews** 1
(fav) hld up, prog 8th, mstks 12 & 13th, ld apr last, rdn out
418 **Malachite Green ....S Cowell** 2
hld up, mstk 6th, prog 10th, disp 16th-2 out, slw jmp last
484 **Miss Construe 5a ....M Spillane** 3
hld up,prog 6th,blnd 9th,4th & ev ch 15th,sn outpcd,virt p.u
620 Lord Richard *ld to 11th, prom to 16th, wknd rpdly aft..* 4
832 Legal Beagle *prom, ld 11th, p.u. 13th, dsmntd* .... pu
Lovely Clonmoyle (Ire) 5a (bl) *wth ldrs til lost plc 6th, bhnd whn p.u. aft 11th* .... pu
6 ran. 4l, 20l, 2l. Time 6m 50.00s. SP 5-4.
A Howland Jackson (Essex & Suffolk).

935 - Members

619 **EXCLUSIVE EDITION (IRE) 5a ....A Coe** 1
(fav) made all, clr 6th, jnd 10th, drew clr 16th, lft alone 3 out
679 Woodrow Call *alwys 2nd, rdn to disp brfly 10th, wknd 16th, p.u. 3 out* .... pu
Saffron Queen 7a *mstks 1st & 2nd, lost tch 6th, t.o. & p.u. aft 10th* .... pu
3 ran. Time 6m 57.00s. SP 2-5.
Robert J Foster (Essex Farmers & Union).
J.W.

FOUR BURROW
Wadebridge
Monday April 8th
FIRM

936 - Members

720 **BALDHU CHANCE ....J Young** 1
(fav) made all, j.w., easy
629 **Plenary...................................D Curnow** 2
chsd wnnr frm start, no imp, wknd clsng stgs
2 ran. 20l. Time 6m 18.00s. SP 4-6.
Terry Long (Fourburrow).

937 - Intermediate (12st)

720 **CORNISH WAYS ....Miss S Young** 1
alwys trckng ldr, strng run to ld last stride
714 **Dark Reflection.......................D Curnow** 2
(fav) ld 1st til cght cls home
557 **Moonbay Lady 5a 9ow ....G Andrews** 3
bhnd, pshd alng frm 10th, grdly lost tch, btn 2 fences
721 Brother Bill (bl) *u.r. 3rd* .... ur
4 ran. Hd, dist. Time 6m 10.00s. SP 9-4.
R J S Linne (East Cornwall).

938 - Open (12st)

870 **LITTLE COOMBE 5a..................J Creighton** 1
mstk 2nd, ld to 8th agn 11th, made rest, ran on wll
625 **Gymcrak Dawn (bl) ....I Hambly** 2
(fav) ld 8-11th, mstk 15th, no imp aft
800 **Artistic Peace 5a....................D Stephens** 3
prom til lost grnd aft 12th, pckd 15th, sn outpcd
3 ran. 10l, 10l. Time 6m 6.00s. SP 5-4.
M Wilkins (Spooners & West Dartmoor).

939 - Restricted (12st)

715 **ROSES IN MAY 5a ....Miss S Young** 1
ld to 8th, mstk 9th, ld agn 15th, made rest, comf
719 **Big Seamus (Ire) ....J Creighton** 2
(fav) ld 8-15th, rmndrs nxt, kpt on und pres
2 ran. 3l. Time 6m 19.00s. SP 11-8.
R J S Linne (East Cornwall).

940 - Ladies

803 **PHAR TOO TOUCHY 5a..........Miss R Francis** 1
(fav) made all, 10l clr 2nd, raced clr, ran on wll
716 **Duchess Of Tubber (Ire) 5a ....Miss S Young** 2
2nd best frm start, nvr engh to chal
716 **Jokers Patch ....Mrs D Gillies** 3
raced off the pce, til tk 3rd cls home
803 Aristocratic Gold *mstly 3rd til wknd qckly cls home...* 4
4 ran. 4l, dist, 2l. Time 6m 4.00s. SP 2-5.
Miss R A Francis (Dulverton West).

941 - Maiden (12st)

718 **DOVEDON PRINCESS 5a...............D Stephens** 1
(fav) ld/disp til ld 12th, made rest, ran on wll
629 **Diana Moss (Ire) 5a ....C Heard** 2
ld/disp to 8th, drppd back, came agn run in
St Morwenna 5a ....J Creighton 3
pssd ldr 12th-last, no ext run in
Diamond Flier (Ire) *ld/disp to 12th, grdly fdd, p.u. 3 out* .... pu
Rose's Lady Day 7a *bhnd whn u.r. 12th* .... ur
5 ran. 3l, 1l. Time 6m 21.00s. SP 4-6.
D Stephens (South Cornwall).
P.H.

NORTH COTSWOLD
Andoversford
Monday April 8th
GOOD TO FIRM

942 - Members

683 **WILDNITE...........................H Wheeler** 1
alwys in tch, ld 13th, made rest, styd on
Springfield Lad ....Miss E Walker 2
carried 14st, wll bhnd to 13th, prog aft, nrst fin
Straight Bat ....M Rollett 3
carried 14st, ld to aft 8th, lost plc, ran on agn 16th
Clonroche Gazette *carried 14st, alwys wll bhnd, fin own time* 4
791 The Last Straw *sn bhnd, t.o. 9th* 5
683 Durzi *chsd ldrs, cls 2nd at 16th, wknd rpdly, p.u. 2 out* .... pu
338 Juranstan *chsd ldrs, ld bef 12th, almost ref nxt, 4th whn ref 14th* .... ref
797 Fiddlers Knap *(fav) cls 2nd at 14th, wknd & p.u. last ..* pu
8 ran. 4l, 25l, 2 fences, Bad. Time 6m 24.00s. SP 2-1.
Miss L Robbins (North Cotswold).

943 - Confined (12st)

683 **NETHER GOBIONS ....E Williams** 1
ld/disp til ld aft 12th, made rest, drew clr frm 2 out
793 **January Don (bl) ....A Dalton** 2
alwys chsng ldng 4, effrt 15th, ran on to tk 2nd flat
795 **Granville Grill 12ex...........................J Deutsch** 3
(fav) ld/disp to 12th, outpcd frm 3 out, lost 2nd flat
687 Mitchells Best *alwys in chsg grp, onepcd frm 3 out* 4
230 Tell You What *in tch til wknd frm 13th, t.o. 2 out* 5
639 Flying Ziad (Can) *chsd ldrs to hlfwy, wknd, last whn p.u. aft 12th* .... pu
794 Nesselnite 5a *last whn u.r. 1st* .... ur
Smart Teacher (USA) *chsd ldrs til aft 12th, wknd & p.u. 14th* .... pu
Very Cavalier 7a *last whn f 4th* .... f
9 ran. 15l, 10l, 12l, dist. Time 6m 7.30s. SP 6-4.
P Clutterbuck (Berkeley).

944 - Ladies

746 **DI STEFANO.........................Miss A Dare** 1
(fav) hld up in tch,mstk 15 & 16th, ld aft 3 out, qcknd clr
743 **Roving Report......................Mrs A Rucker** 2
last early, 2nd at 9th, ld 14th til hdd 3 out, unable qckn
786 **Phelioff ....Miss S Dawson** 3
made most to 13th, cls 2nd to 3 out, outpcd
639 Gallic Belle 5a *chsd ldr to 8th, wknd 12th, last nxt, p.u. 2 out* .... pu
4 ran. 8l, 10l. Time 6m 7.80s. SP 1-4.
Mike Gifford (Cotswold Vale).

945 - Open (12st)

744 **COOMBESBURY LANE 5a ....T Stephenson** 1
hld up rear, prog to ld 13th, qcknd clr frm 2 out
746 **Ask Frank 7ex..........................H Wheeler** 2
(fav) reluc ldr, hdd 13th, mstk nxt, effrt 2 out, sn outpcd
683 **Shadow Walker 7ex ....G Barfoot-Saunt** 3
hld up bhnd ldrs, ran on frm 2 uot, unable to chal
3 ran. 10l, 2½l. Time 6m 22.30s. SP 6-1.
N F Williams (North Ledbury).

946 - Restricted (12st)

428 **DANBURY LAD (IRE) ....Miss A Dare** 1
(fav) hld up rear,prog whn slw jmp 15th, disp 3 out,sn ld,pshd out
Bakmalad...............................H Wheeler 2
hld up rear, styd on frm 15th, went 2nd flat
684 **Sideliner.........................G Barfoot-Saunt** 3
alwys prom, ld 14th til jnd 3 out, sn hdd, onepcd
599 Scarlet Berry 5a *alwys prom, not qckn frm 2 out* 4
707 Rayman (Ire) *mostly mid-div, nvr nrr* 5
707 Mary Borough 5a *in tch early, rear by hlfwy* 6
684 Golden Companion (bl) *cls up, ld 10th, sn clr, wknd & hdd 14th, p.u. last* .... pu
Moorechurch Glen *plld hrd, ld aft 2nd, sn clr, hdd 10th, wknd, p.u. 13th* .... pu
742 Perryline 5a *mid-div whn u.r. 5th* .... ur
797 Country Brew 5a *ld to 2nd, sn lost plc, rear hlfwy, p.u. last* .... pu
10 ran. 6l, 4l, 1l, 8l, 30l. Time 6m 15.70s. SP 4-6.
Dr P P Brown (Berkeley).

947 - Maiden (12st)

637 **SAXON LASS 5a........................A Martin** 1
ld to 3rd, steadied, ld 13th, drew clr
796 **Dragons Lady 5a ....A Dalton** 2
(fav) hld up mid-div, prog 10th, ev ch 15th, outpcd
787 **Daring Trouble 5a......................R Hicks** 3
rear, last at 13th, ran on, lft 3rd at last
749 Shadowgraff 5a *sn rear, ran on thro' btn horses* 4
747 Matchlessly *cls up, ld 6th, sn hdd, grad wknd frm 11th* 5
791 Colonel Fairfax *disp to 2nd, ld 4-6th, agn 8-13th, wknd, p.u. last* .... pu
797 Roark's Chukka *mid-div, btn whn p.u. 15th* .... pu
747 Dorn Retreat *hld up,prog to 10l 2nd at 15th, wll btn 3rd whn u.r. last* .... ur
477 Duques 5a *in tch early, wknd, rear whn p.u. 15th*..... pu
643 The Blind Judge *alwys last, t.o. & p.u. 15th* .... pu
Easter Prince *alwys bhnd, p.u. 13th*........ pu
11 ran. 10l, dist, 5l, 20l. Time 6m 18.50s. SP 3-1.
M N J Sparkes (V.W.H.).
H.F.

NORTH SHROPSHIRE
Eyton-On-Severn
Monday April 8th
GOOD TO FIRM

948 - Members (12st)

667 **WHATAFELLOW (IRE) ....A Crow** 1
(fav) cls up, gng easily, ld 2 out, ran on wll frm last
855 **Inch Maid 5a.................Miss H Brookshaw** 2
made all to 2 out, ran on und pres frm last
462 **Ahalin................................J Austin** 3
cls up to 12th, lost tch whn pce increased 4 out
881 Scriven Boy *w.w. in tch, ev ch whn f 12th*.......... f
4 ran. 2l, 25l. Time 6m 31.00s. SP 4-6.
Gareth Samuel (North Shropshire).

949 - Maiden (12st)

431 **WINTERS COTTAGE (IRE).............A Phillips** 1
held up, cls order 10th, ld 2 out, ran on
852 **The Yokel..............................T Garton** 2
made all til bad mstk 3 out, hdd 2 out, onepcd
661 **Beeworthy 5a ....A Beedles** 3
(fav) cls up til pce increased 3 out, not qckn frm 2 out
287 J B Saucy Doris 5a *wth ldrs to 10th, grdly wknd frm 3 out.* 4
660 Builder Boy *alwys in tch, ev ch whn f 5 out* .... f
5 ran. 2½l, 3l, 15l. Time 6m 32.00s. SP 2-1.
M A Lloyd (West Shropshire).

950 - Open (12st)

662 **CHIP'N'RUN 4ex ....J Cornes** 1
(fav) ld to 6th, steadd, ld 4 out, ran on strgly
686 **Ru Valentino ....A Phillips** 2
cls up,ld 7-12th,chsd wnr frm 4 out,ran on, cllpsd & died
662 **Glenshane Lad 7ex....................A Griffith** 3
prom, ld 13th til apr 4 out, onepcd
662 Auction Law (NZ) 7ex *in tch til pce increased 13th, onepcd frm 4 out* 4
4 ran. 10l, 15l, 15l. Time 6m 21.00s. SP 4-5.
F D Cornes (South Shropshire).

951 - Ladies

685 **THE BARREN ARCTIC..............Mrs M Bryan** 1
mid-div to 10th,smth prog to disp ld 3 out,clr 2 out,ran on
663 **Fell Mist..........................Miss A Sykes** 2
(fav) mstly 2nd to 12th, ld 13th-3 out, not qckn
Air Commander ....Miss T Spearing 3
held up in rear, cls order 13th, no ext cls home
739 Andyworth *ld to 12th, in tch til outpcd 3 out*....... 4
685 River Trout *prom to 8th, fdd 10th, no ch whn p.u. 3 out* .... pu
Running Frau 5a *rear, t.o. 6th, cont in own time, p.u. bfr last* .... pu
6 ran. 5l, 3l, 15l. Time 6m 25.00s. SP 3-1.
David A Smith (South Shropshire).

952 - Restricted (12st)

665 **FRIARY LAD (IRE)......................W Bryan** 1
held up, cls order 12th, hndy, ld 3 out, ran on strgly
564 **Mr Bobbit (Ire) ....R Burton** 2

(fav) ldng grp thruout, chsd wnr frm 3 out, outpcd
666 **Miss Shaw 5a ....A Griffith** 3
chsd ldrs, ld 13th-4 out, ran on onepce
739 Foxy Blue *ld to 5th, cls up til lost tch 13th, no ch whn p.u. 3 out* .... pu
739 Rinky Dinky Doo *prom, disp 5th, ld 6-10th, wknd 2 out, p.u. last* .... pu
599 Welsh Clover 5a *cls up,disp 10th,ld 11-12th,wknd qckly frm 4 out,p.u. last* .... pu
666 Pepperbox 5a *s.s., t.o., p.u. 13th* .... pu
7 ran. 5l, 15l. Time 6m 24.00s. SP 5-2.
D Rogers (North Shropshire).

953 - 2½m Open Maiden (5-7yo) Div I (12st)

661 **LITTLE BY LITTLE......................R Bevis** 1
(fav) chsng grp, cls order 9th, chal & wnt clr 2 out, readly
Scorpotina 5a ....R Thomas 2
ld 4th-4 out, ran on clsng stgs
Dalusaway (Ire) 5a....................A Griffith 3
chsd ldrs, disp 3 out, hdd by wnr 2 out, onepcd
456 Godor Spirit *mid-div, onepcd frm 3 out, nvr dang.....* 4
354 Playing The Fool 5a *mid-div, lkd btn in 4th whn f 4 out* .... f
542 Jacky's Jaunt 5a *ld til u.r. 4th* .... ur
352 Winter Gem 5a *in tch whn f 6th* .... f
Aralier Man (Ire) 7a *mid to rear, no ch in 5th whn u.r. 5 out* .... ur
Sweet Jesterday 5a *rear to 7th, t.o. & p.u. 10th.......* pu
Gunner Be A Lady 5a *rear, t.o. 8th, p.u. 3 out ....* pu
10 ran. 4l, 15l, dist. Time 5m 6.00s. SP 2-1.
D Pugh (North Shropshire).

954 - 2½m Open Maiden (5-7yo) Div II (12st)

747 **NOTHING VENTURED................A Beedles** 1
made virt all, ran on strgly frm 3 out, comf
331 **Blue Rosette 2ow ....A Hill** 2
(fav) disp to 4th, cls 2nd til outpcd frm 3 out
697 **Brown Bala 5a ....I Lowe** 3
alwys mid-div, in tch to 5 out, no ext frm 4 out
Muckle Jack *rear early, prog 5 out, ran on, nrst fin...* 4
569 Shayna Maidel 5a *cls up to 9th, sn wknd & t.o., p.u. 3 out* .... pu
Lady Barbarosa (Ire) 5a *prom to hlfwy, t.o. & no ch whn p.u. 3 out* .... pu
6 ran. 15l, 15l, 1½l. Time 5m 12.00s. SP 6-4.
Mrs Susie Farquhar (South Shropshire).
V.S.

OLD BERKSHIRE
Lockinge
Monday April 8th
GOOD TO FIRM

955 - Members

638 **THE HOLY GOLFER.....................C Smyth** 1
in tch, efft 3 out, ld apr last, ran on
22 **Rubika (Fr).....................Mrs S Shoemark** 2
(Jt fav) ld/disp til apr last, not qckn aft
Wild Fortune..........................R Delgety 3
(Jt fav) cls up, efft 4 out, ev ch nxt, wknd aft
Dark Sirona 5a *prom early, lost tch frm 14th ....* 4
580 Abba Lad *alwys rear, no ch & t.o. frm 14th ....* 5
5 ran. 3½l, 10l, 20l, 25l. Time 6m 32.70s. SP 9-4.
C Smyth (Old Berkshire).

956 - Maiden (5-7yo)

788 **TEA CEE KAY ....R Sweeting** 1
(fav) ld til 3rd, cls up til ld 13th, ran on wll, easily
461 **Cut A Niche ....R Lawther** 2
held up, 3rd 10th, chsd wnr frm 4 out, no imp frm 2 out
713 **Horton Country 5a ....P Howse** 3
alwys mid-div, wll bhnd frm 14th, not trbld 1st 2
713 Gt Hayes Pommard *plld hrd, ld 4-14th, wknd & onepcd aft* 4
643 Son Of Anun *n.j.w., hndy til lost tch 14th, t.o. & p.u. 3 out* .... pu
Ragtimer *cls up til 12th, wknd, t.o. & p.u. 5 out ....* pu
Nossi Be *alwys last, schoold til p.u. 11th ....* pu
7 ran. 10l, 25l, 6l. Time 6m 38.00s. SP 7-4.
C O King (Old Berkshire).

957 - Confined (12st)

783 **TRANSPLANT BLUE.................S Goodings** 1
(fav) prom, ld 4-11th, cls up til ld 2 out, ran on wll
638 **Major Wayne ....M Walters** 2
ld 2nd-3rd, agn 12th-2 out, outpcd aft
786 **Sam Shorrock...................Miss H Thorner** 3
last til prog 14th, ran on frm 4 out, nrst fin
Proplus *ld to 2nd, prom til wknd & onepcd frm 5 out ..* 4
434 Aylesford 7a *held up, prog 9th,cls up til wknd 14th,t.o. & p.u. bfr 3 out* 5
5 ran. 4l, 10l, dist. Time 6m 31.80s. SP 6-4.
S J Goodings (Windsor Forest Drag).

958 - Mixed Open

377 **WOLF WINTER ....N Mitchell** 1
(fav) cls up, ld 10th, mstks 3 & 2 out, kpt on whn chal
709 **Royle Speedmaster.....................A Harvey** 2
in tch, wnt 2nd 3 out, alwys held frm 2 out
792 **Sirisat ....Miss T Blazey** 3
mstly 4th, nvr on terms wth 1st 2
708 Sohail (USA) *sn bhnd, nvr on terms to chal ....* 4
785 Old Road (USA) (bl) *ld til 9th, wknd & outpcd frm 12th* 5
364 Halham Tarn (Ire) *in tch til 13th, wknd nxt, t.o. & p.u. 5 out* .... pu
6 ran. 1½l, 25l, 2l, dist. Time 6m 18.70s. SP 5-4.
Victor Dartnall (Dulverton West).

959 - Maiden (6yo+)

712 **LOCHINVAR LORD (bl)...............D Renney** 1
ld to 3rd, outpcd 12th, prog frm 5 out, ld apr last, ran on
637 **Image Boy (Ire)................A Charles-Jones** 2
held up, prog 13th, disp 3 out til wknd apr last
Joven Top.............................R Sweeting 3
ld 4-10th, prom aft, disp 3 out til wknd apr last
438 Crestafair 5a *(fav) held up, prog 9th, ld 11th-4 out, wknd qckly nxt, outpcd* 4
713 Colourful Boy *alwys rear, t.o. whn p.u. 5 out........* pu
Bidore *prom early, lost tch 12th, p.u. 4 out...........* pu
6 ran. 1l, nk, 10l. Time 6m 35.50s. SP 11-4.
D J Renney (North Cotswold).

960 - Restricted

642 **GLENARD (IRE) ....R Smith** 1
ld/disp til wnt clr 3 out, styd on wll
707 **Balance ....T Cox** 2
prom, disp 5-3 out, ran on und pres frm 2 out
706 **Madiyan (USA) ....J Hankinson** 3
hndy, 4th 10th, outpcd frm 4 out
707 Alias Silver *cls up to 14th, outpcd frm 4 out ....* 4
707 Everso Irish *mid-div, prog 14th, ev ch 5 out til wknd apr 3 out, onepcd* 5
478 Pavi's Brother *sn bhnd, shrt livd efft 14th, outpcd frm 4 out* 6
525 Kamtara *sn bhnd, t.o. frm 12th, p.u. 4 out...........* pu
707 Amadeo (bl) *ld til 9th, outpcd frm 11th, t.o. & p.u. 4 out* .... pu
707 Hizal *(fav) rear early, prog 10th, outpcd frm 13th, p.u. 4 out* .... pu
9 ran. 4l, 12l, 2l, 3l, 4l. Time 6m 26.20s. SP 5-1.
W Booth (Grafton).
D.P.

SOUTHDOWN & ERIDGE
Heathfield
Monday April 8th

GOOD

961 - Members

675 **GLENAVEY ....C Hall** 1
last & detached, stdy prog 13th, wnt 2nd 2 out,ld flat
Stately Lover ....Miss J Grant 2
(fav) lft 2nd 11th,ld 4 out,8l clr nxt, rdn 2 out, wknd & hdd flat
Present Times ....Miss Sheena West 3
ld 1st, sn hdd, chsd ldr, disp 14th-16th, wknd 4 out
596 Mountaico (bl) *lft in ld 11th, blnd 14th, sn hdd, rdn nxt,sn btn,p.u. 2 out* .... pu
593 Tufter's Garth *ld 2nd til u.r. 11th* .... ur
5 ran. 2l, dist. Time 6m 43.00s. SP 6-4.
C J Hall (Southdown & Eridge).

962 - B F S S Nov Riders

594 **KATES CASTLE 5a.................J Van Praagh** 1
(fav) made all, blnd 10th & 3 out, rdn & drw clr 2 out, comf
786 **Charlton Yeoman...................Mrs D Rowell** 2
chsd wnr 5th, 3l down 4 out, rdn & wknd 2 out
592 **Colonel O'Kelly (NZ) ....H Dunlop** 3
trkd ldrs, 10l 3rd & outpcd 13th, no dang aft, kpt on flat
571 The Forties *tubed, chsd wnr to 4th, lst tch 12th, t.o. frm 14th* 4
4 ran. 8l, 1l, 1 fence. Time 6m 39.00s. SP 4-5.
B Van Praagh (East Sussex & Romney Marsh).

963 - Mixed Open (12st)

594 **NETHERTARA 5a ....P Hacking** 1
(fav) prssd ldr til ld 4 out, qknd clr, impress
572 **Clover Coin 5a.....................Miss J Grant** 2
trkd ldrs, 3rd & ev ch 16th, outpcd nxt, tk 2nd flat
811 **Ginger Tristan 7ex ....D Robinson** 3
ld til appr 4 out, sn outpcd, lst 2nd flat
594 Sure Pride (USA) *hld up, effort to 4th 14th, wknd appr 4 out* 4
451 Highly Decorated 7ex *mstks, prom til lst pl & rmdrs 7th, bhnd frm 14th,p.u. 3 out* .... pu
594 Highland Bounty *ld into start, in tch, blnd 13th, sn rdn & btn, p.u. 2 out* .... pu
777 Zilfi (USA) *s.s. sn rcvd, lst tch 10th, t.o. & p.u. 4 out* ... pu
7 ran. 12l, 1l, 30l. Time 6m 26.00s. SP 1-3.
Alan Cowing (East Sussex & Romney Marsh).

964 - Restricted (12st)

810 **GALAROI (IRE) 2ow..................D Robinson** 1
chsd ldr til 7th, made rest, drw clr appr 3 out, impress
597 **Croft Court 7a 1ow ....P Hacking** 2
(fav) w.w. prog to 2nd 16th, 5l down 4 out,rdn & btn appr nxt
779 **Tau ....A Warr** 3
in tch, blnd 14th, rdn & onepcd frm 16th
779 Motor Cloak *w.w in tch, 4th & rdn appr 4 out, no prog* 4
779 St Robert *ld til jmpd lft & hdd 6th, in tch til wknd appr 4 out* 5
576 Captain Beal *in tch to 10th, wll bhnd whn p.u. appr 14th* .... pu
593 Local Manor *prom til squeezed & r.o. 8th, cont, pld 3rd, disq* .... ro
7 ran. 12l, 1l, ½l, 1½l, dist. Time 6m 41.00s. SP 6-4.
D C Robinson (Mid Surrey Farmers Drag).
ORIGINAL DISTANCES

965 - Intermediate (12st)

593 **BARDAROS...........................P Hacking** 1
(fav) mid-div, prog 12th, lft in ld 14th, drw clr 4 out, easy
573 **Billion Dollarbill........................M Gorman** 2
in tch, lft 2nd 14th, rdn 4 out, sn btn
453 **Barn Elms ....J Van Praagh** 3
w.w. prog to 4l 3rd 16th, btn nxt, jmpd slwly last, wlkd in
778 Quarter Marker (Ire) 2ow *hdstrng, chsd ldr 3rd til f 7th* .... f
59 Dangerosa 5a *ld, hd prssd whn u.r. 14th* .... ur
779 Miss Beal 5a 1ow *sn wll bhnd, blnd 5-6th, hmpd nxt, t.o. & p.u 9th* .... pu
6 ran. 20l, dist. Time 6m 36.00s. SP 4-7.
Mrs D M Stevenson (East Sussex & Romney Marsh).

966 - Open Maiden (12st)

780 **SAUN (CZE) ....Miss C Elliot** 1
in tch, lft 4th 16th, chall appr last, ran on wll, ld flat
780 **Manor Ranger..................P Picton-Warlow** 2
ld til appr last, rallied gamely flat
681 **Grassington (Ire) ....S Quirk** 3
chsd ldrs, wnt 2nd 13th, ld last, hdd & no ex flat
454 Clean Sweep *chsd ldrs, rdn to chall 2 out, wknd appr last* 4
809 Scarning Gizmo 5a *t.d.e. alwys rr, lst tch 11th, t.o. frm 14th* 5
780 Tamborito (Ire) *pllng, disp ld 7-11th, wknd 13th, slpd & u.r. appr 16th* .... ur
Prince Buck (Ire) *(fav) blnd 1st, rr hit 7th, prog 12th, jnd ldrs & r.o. 16th* .... ro
7 ran. 1l, 1l, 4l, 1 fence. Time 6m 56.00s. SP 7-1.
Miss C J Elliott (East Sussex & Romney Marsh).

SOUTH NOTTS
Thorpe Lodge
Monday April 8th
GOOD TO FIRM

967 - Members

539 **TWEED VALLEY (bl)..................E Andrewes** 1
prog 9th, 3rd nxt, 2nd 5 out, chal innr & ld 2 out, ran on
237 **T.C. ....G Smith** 2
(fav) s.s. prog 9th, 2nd nxt, ld 5 out, hdd & no ext 2 out
726 **Full Song 5a.............................S Morris** 3
nvr dang, last trio, prog 11th, 3rd & outpcd 4 out
Royal Mile *4th til fdd 6th, t.o. 10th* 4
Craggaunowen Chief (Ire) *prom, ld 9th-6 out, fdd, p.u. 3 out* .... pu
590 Barneys Gold (Ire) *disp til ran out 7th, cont, p.u. nxt*... pu
Jeffrey Perfect *disp to 7th, ld 8th, wknd rpdly, p.u. 13th* .... pu
7 ran. 4l, 6l, 2 fences. Time 6m 42.00s. SP 7-2.
Mrs Susan Crawford (South Notts).

968 - Confined (12st)

583 **GOOD TEAM ....D Crossland** 1
mostly 3rd til effrt & ld 3 out, ran on well
244 **Bowery Boy 3ex ....E Andrewes** 2
(fav) n.j.w. w.w. 20l 4th 6 out, clsd rpdly 3 out, nt rch wnr
723 **The Big Wheel.......................S J Robinson** 3
prog 7th, 2nd at 9th, ld 4 out, onepcd frm nxt
723 Arbitrageur *ld, 25l clr 5th-13th, hdd & wknd rpdly 4 out* 4
542 Gonalston Percy *alwys last, t.o. 9th, p.u. 4 out* .... pu
5 ran. 1l, 10l, 1 fence. Time 6m 37.00s. SP 5-2.
Miss J E McGivern (Bramham Moor).

969 - Open (12st)

677 **THE POINT IS.........................M Hewitt** 1
(fav) made all, waited in front, clvrly
632 **Rexy Boy ....P Gee** 2
3rd til chsd wnr frm 12th, 5l down 6 out-last, outpcd flat
723 **Valatch ....J Henderson** 3
last, t.o. 12th, stole 3rd on line
535 Solitary Reaper (bl) *chsd wnr to 12th, outpcd 4 out, mstk 2 out, lost 2nd nr fin* 4
4 ran. 12l, dist, 1l. Time 6m 27.00s. SP 4-7.

P S Hewitt (Quorn).

970 - Ladies

672 **KAMBALDA RAMBLER** .... **Miss C Holliday** 1
(fav) disp til ld 4th, drew away 10th, easily
Nishvamitra .... **Mrs J Dawson** 2
disp to 4th, chsd wnr, outpcd 10th, fair 1st effort
631 **Hawaiian Goddess (USA) 5a** .... **Miss H Fines** 3
t.o. 4th, ran on past wkng rivals last m
675 Highland Laird *4th, disp 3rd 11th-4 out, 4th agn & outpcd nxt* 4
633 Monk's Mistake *3rd to 11th, disp 3rd to 4 out, fdd, p.u. 2 out* .... pu
722 Singing Seal *nvr dang, t.o. 10th, p.u. flat* .... pu
6 ran. 1 fence, 4l, 8l. Time 6m 27.00s. SP 4-6.
H Morton (Quorn).

971 - Restricted (12st)

635 **BARE FISTED** .... **Miss H Phizacklea** 1
(fav) ld to 5 out, jmpd wll to ld agn 2 out, ran on
679 **Ryders Wells** .... **Mrs M Morris** 2
cls up, ld 4 out til blnd 2 out, not rcvr
584 **T'int (Ire) 5a** .... **J Burley** 3
mostly 3rd, chsd ldr & cls up 3 out, just outpcd frm nxt
726 Dilly's Last 5a *mostly last, cls up til outpcd 4 out, p.u. flat* .... pu
4 ran. 5l, ½l. Time 6m 34.00s. SP 11-8.
R W Phizacklea (Atherstone).

972 - Open Maiden Div I (12st)

542 **TEMPERED POINT (USA)** .... **T Lane** 1
cls up, 3rd 6 out, chal 3 out, ld nxt, ran on
Class Meo .... **J Henderson** 2
prog 11th, 2nd 6 out, ld 5 out-3 out, outpcd bef nxt
Boot-On 5a .... **G Brewer** 3
2nd til ld 11th-5 out, outpcd frm 3 out
542 Top The Bid *rear hlf, ran on onepcd into 4th, no ch wth 1st 3 5 out* 4
541 Griffin Lark 5a *alwys rear hlf, 5th & outpcd frm 6 out* .. 5
636 Charlotte's Oliver (bl) *3rd til 8th, fdd, t.o. 6 out, p.u. 2 out* .... pu
Anvadabo *ld, 12l clr 5th, hdd 11th, fdd 13th, f 5 out* ... f
Disneys Hill *alwys last trio, t.o. last frm 6 out, p.u. 3 out* .... pu
675 Stanwick Lass 5a *(fav) alwys rear hlf, outpcd in 6th 6 out, p.u. 3 out* .... pu
9 ran. 5l, 8l, 8l, 20l. Time 6m 33.00s. SP 7-2.
Mrs R Smith (Bicester With Whaddon Chase).

973 - Open Maiden Div II (12st)

542 **MYSTERIOUS RUN (IRE)** .... **Miss S Samworth** 1
w.w. cls up, well-timed chal 3 out, ld nxt, ran on gamely
541 **Littledale (USA)** .... **T Lane** 2
mostly 3rd til ld 5 out, hdd 2 out, ran on und pres
618 **Swinging Song** .... **Miss K Gilman** 3
(fav) ld to 6th, cls up til outpcd by 1st pair frm 3 out
Stone Broom 5a *rear hlf, prog to disp 9-13th, 5th & outpcd 6 out* 4
726 Rallye Stripe *alwys prom, ld 6th-5 out, cls up whn f 2 out* .... f
396 Royal Quarry *6th & strggling whn u.r. 11th* .... ur
967 Barneys Gold (Ire) *2nd outing, ran out bend aft 2nd, cont, p.u. 12th* .... pu
7 ran. 1½l, 10l, 1 fence. Time 6m 39.00s. SP 6-1.
Mrs D C Samworth (Cottesmore).
K.B.

SOUTH PEMBROKESHIRE
Lydstep
Monday April 8th
GOOD

974 - Members (12st)

772 **CEDAR SQUARE (IRE) 7a** .... **J Jukes** 1
(fav) ld 4th, unchal frm 16th
768 **Medieval Queen 5a** .... **Miss A Meakin** 2
mid-div til prog 15th, ran on, unable to chal
766 **Bancyfelin Boy** .... **J P Keen** 3
mstk 3rd, prom, onepcd frm 2 out
767 Miss Montana 5a *chsd ldrs to 13th, fdd aft* 4
766 Royal Oats 5a *ld to 3rd, sn mid-div, no prog* 5
Mellaston Tom *1st ride, alwys rear* 6
152 Liddington Belle 5a *1st ride, rear, p.u. 3 out* .... pu
Blair House (Ire) 5a *prom whn u.r. 6th* .... ur
767 Magic Ripple 5a *1st ride, mid-div, u.r. 4th* .... ur
Cistina Brown *1st ride, prom til u.r. 14th* .... ur
10 ran. 20l, 8l, 30l, 5l, dist. Time 6m 43.00s. SP 6-4.
A J Rhead (South Pembrokeshire).

975 - Open Maiden Div I

552 **PENDIL'S DELIGHT 5a** .... **D S Jones** 1
sttld mid-div, prog 8th, ld 2 out, easily
772 **Final Cruise 5a** .... **R Ford** 2
3rd/4th, mstk 10th, ev ch 2 out, onepcd
550 **Another Quince 5a** .... **Miss P Jones** 3
ld to 2 out, no ext
773 Kinlogh Gale (Ire) *alwys mid-div, no dang* 4
550 Sea Search *nvr nrr enough to chal* 5
770 Highland Minstrel *(fav) prom to 10th, fdd, p.u. 2 out* .... pu
772 Katy Country Mouse 5a *mid-div, p.u. aft 6th, b.b.v.* .... pu
510 Macaabee Special (Ire) *rear, p.u. 5th* .... pu
696 Irish Thinker 7a *rear, u.r. 6th* .... ur
9 ran. 10l, 8l, 12l, 12l. Time 6m 14.00s. SP 7-2.
A Simpson (Pembrokeshire).

976 - Open Maiden Div II

551 **THE MILL HEIGHT (IRE)** .... **D S Jones** 1
(fav) alwys ldng grp, in ld last, easily
771 **Parson's Corner** .... **V Hughes** 2
ld til tired & in 2nd last, no ext
771 **Cairneymount** .... **J Price** 3
wth ldrs, 3rd & btn last
694 Greenhill Lady 5a *mstk 3rd, alwys mid-div, unable to chal* 4
772 Jolly Swagman 7a *nvr nrr than 4th, p.u. 14th* .... pu
552 Harry From Barry *mid-div, p.u. 2 out* .... pu
771 Fumi D'Oro 5a *f 9th* .... f
151 Mister McGaskill *mid-div, p.u. 2 out* .... pu
509 Willows Wonderman *f 3rd* .... f
552 Appeal 5a *p.u. 9th* .... pu
771 Hil Lady 7a *in rear, u.r. 12th* .... ur
Rosieplant 5a *twrds rear, p.u. 10th* .... pu
12 ran. 15l, 6l, 10l. Time 6m 26.00s. SP 6-4.
Mrs J Mathias (South Pembrokeshire).
Visibility poor from this race onwards - restricted comments.

977 - Open Maiden Div III

551 **AYYAROSE 5a** .... **J Price** 1
trckd ldrs, ld aft last, all out
354 **Tuscania 5a** .... **V Hughes** 2
ld til hdd aft last, just hld
772 **Moonlight Cruise 5a** .... **P Williams** 3
(Jt fav) nvr nr enough to chal
773 Kirby's Charm *(Jt fav) alwys mid-div* 4
747 Bowland Girl (Ire) 5a *prom, rdn 12th, btn whn p.u. 16th* .... pu
772 Hansom Marshal *p.u. 8th* .... pu
Quaker Pep *twrds rear, p.u. 14th* .... pu
Royal Barge *twrds rear, p.u. 14th* .... pu
8 ran. Hd, 10l, 8l. Time 6m 22.00s. SP 10-1.
Mrs C Higgon (South Pembrokeshire).

978 - Open (12st)

766 **TOUCH 'N' PASS** .... **J Tudor** 1
made all, easily
767 **Mister Horatio** .... **M Lewis** 2
(fav) alwys chsng wnr, nvr able to chal
767 **Metrostyle** .... **J Jukes** 3
nvr nrr enough to chal
768 Origami (bl) *mid-div, p.u. 3 out* .... pu

602 Hugli *mid-div, p.u. 3 out* .... pu
768 Electrolyte *alwys mid-div, p.u. 3 out* .... pu
6 ran. 25l, 2l, 8l. Time 6m 20.00s. SP 12-1.
David Vaughan-Morgan (Llangeinor).

979 - Ladies

769 **BUSMAN (IRE) 3ex**........**Miss L Pearce** 1
wth ldrs, in ld last, easily
546 **News Review**........**Miss J Mathias** 2
prom, 2nd at last, unable to chal
769 **Dare Say**........**Miss A Meakin** 3
prom, hrd rdn in 3rd aft last
769 Moving Force *made most til 4th & wkng at last* 4
847 La Mezeray 5a *alwys twrds rear* 5
769 Mount Falcon *alwys in rear* 6
Atlaal *1st ride, p.u. 10th in mid-div* .... pu
545 Gold Diver *mid-div, p.u. 14th* .... pu
769 Goolds Gold 7ex *(fav) u.r. 2nd* .... ur
9 ran. 12l, ¾l, 1l, 5l, dist. Time 6m 2.00s. SP 5-1.
Keith R Pearce (Carmarthenshire).

980 - Restricted (12st)

544 **GUS MCCRAE**........**Miss P Jones** 1
disp, in ld apr last, easily
768 **Cherry Island (Ire)**........**J Jukes** 2
(fav) prom, 2nd & onepcd frm last
770 **My Harvinski (bl)**........**J Price** 3
nvr nr to chal
771 Dustys Trail (Ire) *alwys mid-div* 4
770 Mylordmayor *mid-div, rear whn u.r. last* .... ur
770 The Apprentice *disp to 14th, p.u. 16th* .... pu
Prince Theo *mid-div, p.u. 14th* .... pu
696 Telephone *trckd ldrs, btn whn p.u. last* .... pu
976 Fumi D'Oro 5a *2nd outing, twrds rear, p.u. 13th* .... pu
770 Downhill Racer 5a *f 6th* .... f
770 Cranagh Moss (Ire) *mid-div, u.r. 10th* .... ur
11 ran. 10l, 25l, 10l. Time 6m 16.00s. SP 8-1.
Miss P Philipps (Carmarthenshire).

981 - Intermediate (12st)

767 **KUMADA**........**V Hughes** 1
alwys disp, hrd rdn whn lft clr last
600 **Osceola**........**P Williams** 2
chsd ldng pair, lft 2nd & ev ch last, no ext flat
766 **Celtic Daughter 5a**........**J Jukes** 3
alwys 4th, tired whn lft 3rd last
691 Noisy Welcome *alwys rear, f 13th* .... f
604 African Bride (Ire) 5a *(fav) alwys disp, lkd wnr whn f last* .... f
5 ran. 1l, dist. Time 6m 16.00s. SP 5-1.
Miss Lisa Llewellyn (Llangeinor).
P.D.

STAINTONDALE
Charm Park
Monday April 8th
GOOD TO FIRM

982 - Members (12st)

764 **HERE COMES CHARTER**........**A Pennock** 1
(fav) ld & made all, eased apr line
585 **G Derek**........**P Holder** 2
trckd to 12th, no ext aft, nvr nrr
408 **Another Chant**........**H Brown** 3
alwys 3rd, outpcd 14th, lost tch 3 out
3 ran. 4l, dist. Time 6m 42.00s. SP 4-9.
E Pennock (Staintondale).

983 - Restricted (12st)

758 **TOM THE TANK**........**C Mulhall** 1
(Jt fav) cls up, disp 4 out, ld nxt, drew clr, comf
758 **Another Hooligan**........**Mrs F Needham** 2
rear early, prog 10th, tk 2nd apr last, styd on wll
758 **Missile Man**........**H Brown** 3
alwys prom, 6th 12th, 3rd 2 out, drvn out
539 Ellerton Park (bl) *ld to 15th, disp nxt, hdd, no ext aft* 4
758 Cadrillon (Fr) *in tch, 8th 9th, onepcd frm 4 out* 5
758 Goodwill Hill *cls up, 5th 10th, no ext 4 out* 6
761 Advent Lady 5a *prom, 2nd 10th, fdd rpdly frm 12th* 7
758 Polar Hat *alwys rear, 11th 9th, nvr dang* 8
411 City Buzz (Ire) *alwys rear, onepcd thruout* 9
585 Stride To Glory (Ire) 7a *(Jt fav) alwys wll in rear, nvr a factor* 10
Tooting Times *towrds rear, lost tch, p.u. 12th* .... pu
726 Clone (Ire) *prom early, 2nd 11th, wknd, rear whn p.u. 2 out* .... pu
511 Laganbrae *mid-div, fdd 11th, p.u. 13th* .... pu
13 ran. 5l, 2l, 4l, 7l, 2l, 8l, 4l, 10l, 5l. Time 6m 23.00s. SP 3-1.
D Gill (Bramham Moor).

984 - Mixed Open (12st)

826 **GOSPEL ROCK (NZ)**........**C Mulhall** 1
disp 4th-2 out, hdd apr last, drvn out to line
515 **Golden Savannah 7ex**........**M Sowersby** 2
(fav) disp to 2 out, ld to last, hdd & just btn flat
514 **Osgathorpe**........**Mrs F Needham** 3
rear early, prog 4 out, late chal, nvr nrr
583 Certain Rhythm *mid-div, 4th 4 out, styd on onepcd* 4
587 Nishkina *cls up, 3rd 2 out, no ext aft* 5
587 Amy's Mystery *rear early, 3rd 10th, outpcd 14th, 6th frm 3 out* 6
673 Politico Pot 4ex *disp to 3rd, fdd, last frm 10th, p.u. 2 out* .... pu
7 ran. Hd, 10l, ½l, 3l, 8l. Time 6m 19.00s. SP 33-1.
M A Humphreys (Sinnington).

985 - Intermediate

588 **JUST CHARLIE**........**D Easterby** 1
ld frm 7th, drew clr apr last, comf
306 **Hazel Crest**........**S Charlton** 2
rear early, prog 10th, 3rd frm 13th, tk 2nd run in
409 **Saxon Fair**........**M Sowersby** 3
(fav) ld to 6th, in tch, 2nd 3 out, hit nxt, lost 2nd on flat
517 Attle *in tch, 2nd 12th, 4th frm 4 out, no ext* 4
515 Midge 5a *mid-div, prog hlfwy, nvr dang* 5
588 Tom Log *rear early, outpcd 13th, nvr a factor* 6
761 Sharpridge *rear early, outpcd frm 11th, p.u. nxt* .... pu
761 What A Miss 5a *rear early, onepcd frm 12th, p.u. 3 out* .... pu
718 Prickly Trout 5a *mid-div, fdd 4 out, p.u. apr last* .... pu
9 ran. 9l, 3l, 2l, 2l, 20l. Time 6m 23.00s. SP 6-4.
Mrs Susan E Mason (Middleton).

986 - Maiden (7yo+)

757 **LYNINGO**........**M Sowersby** 1
ld 3rd-8th, disp 12th-3 out, ld nxt, drew clr comf
416 **Morcat 5a**........**C Mulhall** 2
ld 10th-nxt, disp 12th-3 out, hdd, no ext
764 **Yornoangel**........**G Markham** 3
(fav) mid-div, prog 9th, 3rd frm 3 out, outpcd aft
585 Shildon (Ire) *cls up, 3rd 13th, 4th frm 4 out, nvr nrr* 4
Greatfull Fred *prom early, 2nd 7th, onepcd frm 13th* 5
517 Prophet's Choice *in tch, 3rd 10th, fdd rpdly, p.u. 4 out* .... pu
591 Pearl Bridge *bhnd early, onepcd, nvr a factor, p.u. 4 out* .... pu
588 Country Chalice *ld to 2nd agn 9th, lost saddle & u.r. apr 10th* .... ur
763 Magic Song 5a *rear early, 7th 9th, p.u. 3 out* .... pu
762 Another Class *mid-div, fdd 10th, p.u. 12th* .... pu
10 ran. 11l, 4l, 9l, 8l. Time 6m 30.00s. SP 7-1.
Mrs M J Ward (Hurworth).

987 - Maiden (5 & 6yo)

517 **BLACKWOODSCOUNTRY**........**C Mulhall** 1
(fav) ld 10th agn frm 13th, styd on wll
516 **Political Field 5a**........**M Haigh** 2
cls up early, 3rd 4 out, lft 2nd last, no ch wth wnnr
122 **Pure Madness (USA) (bl)**........**R Edwards** 3
ld to 9th, hdd, cls up to 4 out, outpcd aft
589 Fleeced *alwys mid-div, 5th 15th, no ext* 4

763 Rich Asset (Ire) (bl) *alwys wll in rear, nvr dang, completed own time* 5
590 Muscoates 7a *mid-div, 5th 13th, onepcd aft* 6
516 Fair Ally *mid-div, prog 12th, hit 14th & p.u.* .... pu
414 Joint Account *f 1st* .... f
589 Tyndrum Gold *alwys wll in rear, nvr a factor, p.u. 3 out* .... pu
828 Chummy's Last 5a *alwys wll in rear, outpcd, p.u. 14th* .... pu
542 Rise Above It (Ire) *ld 11th-nxt, hdd, 2nd whn f last, lkd btn* .... f
763 Patey Court 7a *rear early, fdd & p.u. 10th* .... pu
718 High Mill *bhnd early, lost tch & p.u. 10th* .... pu

13 ran. 15l, 18l, 1l, 10l, ½l. Time 6m 34.00s. SP 7-4.
Mrs Winifred A Birkinshaw (Sinnington).
A.C.

TAUNTON VALE
Kingston St Mary
Monday April 8th
FIRM

988 - Members

468 **FAITHFUL STAR** .... **Miss S Vickery** 1
(fav) hld up in tch, ld 12th, pshd clr 14th
561 **Great Pokey** .... **E Clarkson** 2
ld to 12th, 6l 2nd 14-15th, fdd
733 **Blakes Beau** .... **T Barry** 3
s.s. prog to 10l 3rd at 12th, rdn 14th, fdd
647 Unityfarm Oltowner *in tch to 11th, 20l 4th at 13th, t.o. & p.u. aft 15th* .... pu
Fosabud *twrds rear, last whn f 12th* .... f
Flemings Fleur *last whn u.r. 11th* .... ur
733 Spy Dessa *keen hld, prog to cls 2nd 6th til u.r. 9th* .... ur

7 ran. 25l, 20l. Time 6m 1.00s. SP 1-3.
M C Pipe (Taunton Vale Harriers).

989 - Confined (12st)

732 **CHITA'S CONE 5a** .... **R Treloggen** 1
(fav) hld up in tch, 2nd at 10th, ld aft 14th, comf
647 **Bridge Express 3ex** .... **Miss H Pavey** 2
ld til aft 14th, onepcd
728 **Archie's Nephew 3ex (bl)** .... **Miss A Bush** 3
2nd whn mstk 8th, lost tch frm 12th
802 Nelson River (USA) *5th & just in tch 9th, wknd, t.o. & p.u. 12th* .... pu
732 Rare Flutter 5a *went 2nd & mstk 9th, u.r. 10th* .... ur
707 Lake Mariner 5a *handy til blnd 7th, bhnd frm 12th, p.u. 2 out* .... pu

6 ran. 4l, 25l. Time 5m 59.00s. SP 4-6.
I M Ham (Weston & Banwell).

990 - Open (12st)

581 **STILL IN BUSINESS 7ex** .... **T Mitchell** 1
(fav) prom til ld 11th, drew clr 3 out, comf
528 **Dubata** .... **J Tizzard** 2
j.w. prog to cls 2nd 12th, ev ch til outpcd aft 15th
528 **Mr Lion** .... **P King** 3
prog to cls 2nd 9th, cls 3rd frm 13th, wknd steadily
709 Grey Sonata 5a (bl) *in tch, cls 4th at 14th, wknd* 4
709 Russell Rover *ld 4th, slght ld to 11th, sn wknd* 5
807 Jolly Flier *ld to 4th, wknd 8th, t.o. & p.u. 2 out* .... pu

6 ran. 5l, 8l, 25l, 30l. Time 6m 4.50s. SP 2-5.
R G Williams (Taunton Vale Foxhounds).

991 - Ladies

730 **LEWESDON HILL** .... **Miss S Cobden** 1
(fav) not fluent,hld up,lot to do 15th,ran on wll 3 out,just got p
728 **On His Own** .... **Miss W Southcombe** 2
hld up in tch, cls 5th at 15th, ld 2 out, ct nr post
803 **Rapid Rascal** .... **Miss S West** 3
ld to 7th, ld 12-15th, 5th 2 out, ran on agn cls home
529 Jameswick *prog 15th, cls 2nd & rdn nxt, 3rd 2 out, no ext und pres* 4
655 False Economy *twrds rear, 25l 6th at 10th, nvr dang* 5
560 In The Navy *tongue-strap, ld 8-12th & 15th, 3l clr 3 out, hdd nxt,sn btn* 6
561 Ragtime Solo (bl) *7th at 10th, f 12th* .... f
730 The Humble Tiller *last & strgglng, nvr put into race, p.u. 12th* .... pu

8 ran. Sht-hd, 8l, hd, 10l, 5l. Time 6m 0.00s. SP 4-7.
T C Frost (Seavington).

992 - Restricted (12st)

627 **STRONG BREEZE** .... **Mrs R Pocock** 1
j.w. made all, ran on gamely frm 2 out
728 **Avril Showers 5a** .... **R Atkinson** 2
(fav) hld up, went 4l 3rd 15th, 2nd 2 out, ran on, just hld
720 **Highway Jim** .... **P King** 3
sn prom, 2nd mostly, ev ch til onepcd aft 3 out
729 Great Impostor *nvr dang, hit 8th, tk 4th 3 out, nvr nr ldrs* 4
656 Palace King (Ire) *in tch til lost plc 15th, t.o.* 5
445 Hedera Helix *some prog 12th, wkng whn hit 14th, t.o. & p.u. 2 out* .... pu

6 ran. Nk, 2½l, 20l, 25l. Time 6m 11.00s. SP 4-1.
I J Pocock (Taunton Vale Foxhounds).

993 - Open Maiden (12st)

375 **SEAHAWK RETRIEVER** .... **T Mitchell** 1
(fav) alwys prom, cls 3rd 13th, ld 16th, sn clr, comf
300 **Seachest 5a** .... **Miss V Stephens** 2
ld to 7th, handy til outpcd aft 15th, ran on agn 2 out
471 **Nearly A Brook 5a** .... **Miss S Cobden** 3
7th at 11th, prog to 15l 4th 4 out, kpt on to 3rd flat
788 Barrow Street *pllng, cls up til ld 7th, tiring whn blnd & hdd 3 out,wknd* 4
733 Girls In Business 5a *schoold round in mid-div, late prog, nrst fin, improve* 5
671 And What Else (Ire) *sn rear, m.n.s* 6
646 River Stream 5a *mid-div, 8th at 15th, nvr dang* 7
645 Glamorous Guy *sn rear, bhnd & alwys strgglng* 8
658 Orchard Lady 5a *in tch, wll plcd til lost ground frm 15th* 9
807 Springcombe 5a *sn rear, t.o. frm hlfwy* 10
470 Highway Lad *mid-div, swrd & u.r. 7th* .... ur
Joli High Note 5a *sn bhnd, t.o. til p.u. 15th* .... pu
733 Joe Penny (v) *mid-div, 6th at 11th, nvr dang, p.u. 3 out* .... pu
734 Young Tiger *prom, jmpd lft 4th, 3rd whn f 7th* .... f
446 Better By Half (Ire) *10th hlfwy, f heavily 15th* .... f
733 Lochnaver 5a *some prog to 8th at 11th, nvr dang, btn 7th whn p.u. 2 out* .... pu
734 Renshaw Ings *in tch, 5th at 11th, wknd nxt, rear & p.u. 15th* .... pu

17 ran. 8l, 25l, 6l, 2l, 8l, 12l, 5l, 8l, 2l. Time 6m 10.00s. SP 2-1.
H B Geddes (Beaufort).
G.T.

VINE & CRAVEN
Hackwood Park
Monday April 8th
GOOD TO FIRM

994 - Members

127 **ESPY** .... **A James** 1
(fav) trckd ldr frm 6th, ld last, qcknd easily
274 **Ufano (Fr)** .... **Miss J Waites** 2
ld to last, outpcd
712 **Vulgan Prince** .... **A Greig** 3
in rear, jmp rght, rddn 12th, fdd
Express Reale *cls up to 10th, wknd qckly, t.o.* 4

4 ran. 6l, dist, 15l. Time 6m 28.00s. SP 4-7.
C James (Vine & Craven).

995 - B F S S (Nov Riders) (12st)

782 **MR MAYFAIR** .... **R Irving** 1
alwys 1st trio, jnd ldr 14th, outpcd nxt, lft clr 2 out
708 **Pejawi 5a** .... **Miss J Waites** 2
rear to hlfwy, mstk 15th, ran on

637 **Master Swillbrook ....Miss E Wood** 3
remote 4th aft 3 out, no imp
792 Icky's Five *mstk 2nd, alwys trling*.................. 4
709 Popeswood *in rear whn u.r. 7th* .... ur
784 Skinnhill *(fav) ld frm 7th,ran in sntchs,qcknd up 15th,3l clr whn u.r.2 out*.................. ur
Prince's Court *rear early,cls up hlfwy,1l 3rd whn mstk leather brk u.r.16th* .... ur
706 Todds Hall (Ire) *ld to 6th, wknd qckly 9th, ref 12th* .... ref
8 ran. 6l, 10l, 3l. Time 6m 27.00s. SP 4-1.
R C Irving (Berks & Bucks).

996 - Mixed Open (12st)

795 **SNOWFIRE CHAP (bl)..............T Underwood** 1
sweating,3rd til cls up 2 out, hrd rdn, ld last, ran on wll
710 **Bantel Buccaneer..........................C Vigors** 2
2nd til ld 14th, hrd rdn 2 out, hdd last, ran on
594 **Cool It A Bit 7ex.........................P Scouller** 3
ld to 14th, hrd rdn, outpcd
706 Touch Of Winter 7ex *(fav) alwys trlld, wknd qckly 3 out*.................. 4
4 ran. 2l, 10l, 5l. Time 6m 24.00s. SP 3-1.
T D B Underwood (Garth & South Berks).

997 - Open Maiden (12st)

713 **VITAL SHOT 5a...................Mrs R Baldwin** 1
ld frm 6th, jnd 2 out, held on, all out
275 **Childsway..........................T Underwood** 2
held up, 2nd frm 11th, chal 2 out, wandered & no imp flat
651 **Dormston Lad ....C Jowett** 3
ld to 5th, outpcd hlfwy, ran on last 2
281 Tractorias (Ire) *alwys in 1st 4, onepcd* 4
788 No Reply *nvr bttr thn 4th, onepcd* 5
522 Moran Brig *alwys rear, mstk 16th, nvr a factor* 6
605 Flying Roofer 5a *2nd whn mstk 10th, f nxt* .... f
522 Chalvey Grove *rear til p.u. aft 9th* .... pu
643 Sit Tight *(fav) nvr in contention, p.u. aft 13th* .... pu
521 Ted's Knight (Ire) 7a *mstk 1st, rear whn mstk & p.u. aft 8th*.................. pu
520 Whod Of Thought It (Ire) 7a *mstly rear, 10l 4th hlfwy, wknd qckly 16th, p.u.*.................. pu
11 ran. 2l, 4l, 2l, 6l, 2l. Time 6m 29.00s. SP 5-1.
M C Hillier (Beaufort).

998 - Confined (12st)

784 **OLDE CRESCENT...................Maj G Wheeler** 1
rear early, ld 10th, strchd clr 12th, rddn out
271 **Pete's Sake ....C Vigors** 2
(fav) 2nd to 8th, outpcd, no imp
573 **Cheeky Cheval ....D Dennis** 3
mstks, nvr a factor
706 See You There *drppd away 4th, rddn 6th, cont slwly & rmtly*.................. 4
785 Afaltoun *set gd pce to 9th, chsd ldr to 14th, wknd & p.u. aft 16th* .... pu
5 ran. 20l, 30l, dist. Time 6m 18.00s. SP 6-1.
T Underwood/ C Shanklin (Garth & South Berks).

999 - Restricted (12st)

466 **EMILY'S NIECE 5a ....T Woolridge** 1
ld 7th, hdd 9-16th, ld agn 2 out, ran on strgly
712 **Ravensdale Lad.......................R Wakeham** 2
(fav) ld 9-16th, outpcd
787 **Mr Sunnyside ....S Claisse** 3
last to hlfwy, ran on, no imp
126 Sutton Lass 5a *ld early, 3rd hlfwy, wknd* 4
787 Keep On Trying 5a *alwys in rear, rddn hlfwy, t.o.*...... 5
637 Just Ballytoo *ld to 4th, 2nd to 8th, wknd, t.o.* 6
6 ran. 4l, 8l, 10l, 20l, dist. Time 6m 21.00s. SP 8-1.
T Woolridge (New Forest Buckhounds).
P.M.

WETHERBY
Tuesday April 9th
GOOD

1000 - 3m 110yds Nov Hun

374 **THE MAJOR GENERAL 11.5 7a....Capt A Ogden** 1
held up, hdwy to track ldrs hfwy, ld before 4 out, soon clr.
492 **Copper Thistle (Ire) 11.5 7a ....Mr P Taiano** 2
(fav) ld 2nd till before 4 out, soon outpcd, fin tired.
585 **Jasilu 11.7 (bl).....................Mr S Swiers** 3
mstks, in tch, hdwy hfwy, chsd clr ldrs from 11th, no impn.
760 Cot Lane 11.5 7a (bl) *chsd ldrs till wknd after 11th*.... 4
372 R N Commander 11.5 7a *ld to 2nd, bhnd hfwy*.......... 5
634 McCartney 11.5 7a *in tch till outpcd after 11th, t.o.*..... 6
740 Orton House 11.5 7a *bhnd hfwy, t.o. when p.u. before 12th*.................. pu
409 Durham Hornet 11.5 7a *chsd ldrs early, wknd before 10th, t.o. when p.u. before 4 out*.................. pu
488 Constant Amusement 11.0 7a (bl) *soon t.o., p.u. before 10th*.................. pu
789 Deday 11.5 7a *disp ld when blnd 8th, weakening when blunded 10th, p.u. before next*.................. pu
10 ran. Dist, 1l, 16l, 2½l, 21l. Time 6m 23.10s. SP 5-2.
Robert Ogden

CROOME & WEST WARWICKS
Upton-On-Severn
Tuesday April 9th
FIRM

1001 - Members

743 **FERGAL'S DELIGHT (bl).........Julian Pritchard** 1
ld to 8th, chsd ldr to 14th, rlld to ld app 2 out, all out
904 **Wayward Sailor (bl).............Miss C Spearing** 2
not fluent, chsd ld 14th, slpd app 3 out, ev ch, not qckn
726 **Damers Treasure 3ex................A Sansome** 3
chsd ldrs, rdn & lost tch frm 9th, mstk 12th, kpt on
Yeoman Cricketer *last, t.o. frm 8th, fin well* 4
684 Mandys Lad *(fav) jmpd lft, ld 8th til app 2 out, immed btn, virt p.u.*.................. 5
687 Ragtime Cowboy Joe *5th til p.u. 7th* .... pu
6 ran. 2l, 20l, 30l, 8l. Time 6m 18.00s. SP 16-1.
Mrs Caroline Chadney (Croome & West Warks).

1002 - Restricted (12st)

428 **SUDANOR (IRE)..................Julian Pritchard** 1
ld to 2nd, agn 6-9th & frm 11th, drw wl clr 3 out, esd flat
642 **Cutsdean Cross (Ire) ....J Trice-Rolph** 2
c.u., chsd wnr 12-13th, sn outpcd, kpt on mod 2nd last
549 **Final Abby 5a ....J Jukes** 3
(fav) w.w., prog 9th, chsd wnr 14th, sn outpcd, mstk 2 out
642 Happy Paddy (bl) *prog to ld 9-11th, sn btn, t.o. last 3 out*.................. 4
840 Plax *mstks, in tch, outpcd 13th, poor 4th whn p.u. last* pu
428 Members Rights 5a 1ow *ld 2nd-6th, wknd qckly 12th, p.u. nxt*.................. pu
840 Really An Angel 5a *mstk 7th, last & stgng 9th, t.o. whn p.u. 11th*.................. pu
650 Bewdley Boy *c.u., chsd wnr 13-14th, wknd qckly, p.u. 15th*.................. pu
8 ran. 25l, 10l, dist. Time 6m 18.00s. SP 11-4.
Miss Jane Fellows (Ledbury).

1003 - Ladies

586 **WORKINGFORPEANUTS (IRE) 5a 7ex.....Miss P Jones** 1
tckd ldr to 6th & frm 14th, ld app last, qckn clr flat
161 **Down The Mine 7ex.................Miss A Dare** 2
(fav) ld, shkn up & hdd app last, eased whn btn
River Galaxy.......................Miss S Duckett 3
chsd ldr 6-14th, wknd rpdly, t.o.

Tom Smith *j.s., t.o. 6th, 2 fences bhnd whn p.u. 2 out* pu
4 ran. 5l, dist. Time 6m 21.00s. SP 9-4.
Mrs D A Smith (North Ledbury).

1004 - Land Rover Open (12st)

351 **SHARINSKI ....M Jackson** 1
(fav) ld 3rd, mstks 11-12th, clr aft 15th, easily
578 **Sams Heritage 7ex....................M Daly** 2
chsd wnr 8th, jmpd lft nxt, not qckn 15th, wl btn 2 out
640 **Woodway....................Dr P Pritchard** 3
ld to 3rd, last frm 8th, t.o. 11th, dsmntd aft fin
3 ran. 15l, dist. Time 6m 41.00s. SP 4-6.
Mrs Jo Yeomans (North Ledbury).

1005 - Confined (12st)

881 **THE RUM MARINER....................J Jukes** 1
ld 2nd, made rest, wl clr 2 out, rdn out
603 **King Of The Clouds....................Mrs N Sheppard** 2
prog frm rear 13th, chsd wnr 15th, btn whn mstk 2 out
793 **Tytherington....................M Hammond** 3
ld to 2nd, rdn 11th, 4th & outpcd 15th, no dang aft
638 Ocean Lad *last pair, t.o. 13th, p.u. 15th* .... pu
Tap Dancing 3ex *tckd ldrs, mstk 10th, not qckn 12th, p.u. qckly 14th* .... pu
745 Miss Pennal 5a *(fav) tckd ldrs, not qckn 15th, no ch & p.u. last, lame* .... pu
6 ran. 10l, 20l. Time 6m 17.00s. SP 5-2.
T A Rogers (Radnor & West Hereford).

1006 - Maiden (12st)

747 **KINGSTHORPE....................A Phillips** 1
c.u., trckd ldr 14th, ld aft 2 out, hrd rdn, hld on wl
430 **Bolshie Baron....................M Harris** 2
(fav) ld 6th til hrd rdn & hdd aft 2 out, gd jmp last, jst hld
749 **Eighty Eight ....E Walker** 3
c.u., chsd ldr 10-14th, rdn & one pace frm 3 out
697 Scottishhighlander *rear, outpcd 12th, prog to 4th at 14th, not rch ldrs* 4
555 Annmount Lady (Ire) 5a *mstks, chsd ldrs, outpcd 13th, no imp aft* 5
Rocket Radar 7a *schoold & alws wl bhnd, nvr nrr* 6
842 Rusty Fellow 3ow *immediately t.o. & crawld fences, btn 3 fences* 7
749 Mariner's Walk *ld to 6th, wknd 13th, t.o. & p.u. 2 out* .... pu
688 Mr Paddy Bell *with ldr to 6th, wknd 11th, t.o. whn p.u. 14th* .... pu
Central Lass 5a 4ow *t.d.e., in tch to 11th, t.o. 14th, p.u. 3 out* .... pu
Carlingford Lad (Ire) *sn wl bhnd, 10th whn r.o. & u.r. 4th* .... ro
11 ran. Hd, 5l, 20l, 10l, 15l, Bad. Time 6m 24.00s. SP 7-2.
Mervyn Jones (Ledbury).
J.N.

HIGH PEAK HARRIERS
Flagg Moor
Tuesday April 9th
GOOD

1007 - Members (Stone Walls Div)

CARLI'S STAR....................Miss S Rodman 1
(fav)
Busy Going Nowhere 13ow....................R Godfrey 2
Francesca ....Miss K Tobin 3
Maesgwyn Star 4
Preview 2ow 5
Andante 6
565 Tipp Down 8ow .... ur
7 ran. 5l, 30l. Time 6m 45.00s. SP 4-5.

1008 - 2½m Open Maiden (5-7yo) (12st)

590 **TORTULA 5a....................R Ford** 1
made all, blndrd 10th, drew clr app 2 out, easily
Hot Advice (Ire)....................D Barlow 2
w.w., prog 5th, chsd wnr 3 out, sn rdn & btn
540 **Shakey Thyne (Ire) 5a....................D Sherlock** 3
chsd ldr to 6th, outpcd app 8th, no ch 11th, tk 3rd on post
901 Rainbow Fantasia (Ire) *(fav) chsd ldr 7-11th, rdn app 3 out, 3rd & btn whn blndrd last* 4
502 Woolstonwood 5a *t.d.e., jmpd bdly, sn wl bhnd, t.o. & p.u. 10th* .... pu
852 Ring Bank 7a *t.d.e., w.w., hmprd 6th, lost tch 8th, crwld 3 out & p.u.* .... pu
740 Gold Top 7a *in tch, 4th whn f 6th* .... f
7 ran. 30l, 6l, sht-hd. Time 5m 52.00s. SP 4-1.
N S Bostock (Pendle Forest & Craven).

1009 - Confined

735 **CHARLIE CHALK ....A Griffith** 1
ld to 5th & 14th, jnd app 2 out, kpt on gmly flat
735 **Freddie Fox....................T Garton** 2
(fav) in tch, ld 11-13th, disp 2 out, unable to qckn und pres
563 **Sister Emu 5a....................M Smith** 3
prog 10th, ev ch 15th, wknd qckly app 2 out
736 Lattin General *pllng, chsd ldr til ld 6-10th, wknd app 15th* 4
Portknockie 5a *last frm 8th, t.o. & ref 13th* .... ref
567 Castle Cross *chsd ldr to 11th, t.o. frm 15th, p.u. 2 out* pu
740 Embu-Meru *tbd, rear, 6th & pshd alng whn u.r. 12th* .. ur
7 ran. ¾l, 20l, 30l. Time 7m 17.00s. SP 5-1.
Mrs R A Schofield (Cheshire Forest).

1010 - Ladies

305 **CHOCTAW....................Mrs A Farrell** 1
j.w., made all, rdn 2 out, styd on strngly
514 **Peajade....................Miss J Wormall** 2
(fav) not alwys fluent, chsd ldr, ev ch 15th, one pace frm 2 out
738 **Mrs Cadogan 5a....................Miss L Dix** 3
chsd ldng trio, lost tch 10th, lft poor 3rd 12th
683 The Last Joshua *sn wl bhnd, t.o. frm 7th* 4
666 Lindsey Doyle 5a *alwys 3rd, outpcd 10th, p.u. 12th* .... pu
541 Im Ok (Ire) 5a *sn wl bhnd, p.u. 8th, stirrup broke* .... pu
6 ran. 3l, 2 fences, dist. Time 7m 7.00s. SP 3-1.
Mrs Anthea L Farrell (Middleton).

1011 - Land Rover Open (12st)

737 **SCALLY MUIRE 5a 4ex....................A Crow** 1
(fav) ld to 5th, chsd ldr, rdn to ld app last, drw clr flat
854 **My Nominee 7ex (bl) ....A Griffith** 2
ld 6th, rdn 2 out, sn hdd, no ex
855 **Dannigale ....E Haddock** 3
chsd ldr 3-5th, lost tch 11th, t.o. frm 14th
725 Trusty Friend *in tch, 3rd & outpcd 12th, btn whn swrvd & u.r. aft 15th* .... ur
4 ran. 8l, dist. Time 7m 1.00s. SP 4-5.
G L Edwards (North Shropshire).

1012 - PPORA

735 **DICE OFF 5a ....G Crank** 1
chsd ldr 3rd, lft dsptng ld 13th, hrd rdn flat, ld cls home
664 **Real Class....................J Evans** 2
in tch, prog 7th, lft dsptng ld 14th, no ex und pres flat
726 **Ballyvoyle Bay 5a (bl) ....J Docker** 3
chsd ldrs, ev ch 3 out, sn rdn & wknd
739 Autumn Green (Ire) *jmpd rght, prog 11th, 4th & ch 15th, wknd nxt* 4
586 Prior Conviction (Ire) *(fav) chsd ldr to 2nd, lost pl nxt, nvr gng wl aft, no ch 15th* 5
683 Ultrason IV (Fr) *mid-div til u.r. 6th* .... ur

Kingoftheswingers *hdstr, ld, hrd prsd whn f 13th* ..... f
7 ran. 1½l, 12l, 12l, 10l. Time 7m 11.00s. SP 4-1.
H A Shone (Cheshire Forest).
S.P.

ASCOT
Saturday April 13th
GOOD TO SOFT

1013 - 3m 110yds Nov Hun Chase

595 **LITTLE MARTINA (IRE) 11.6 3a......Mr J Culloty** 1
(fav) held up, steady hdwy 15th, ld after 3 out, soon clr.
581 **King's Treasure (USA) 11.7 7a......Mr A Balding** 2
pushed along 9th, hdwy 14th, chsd ldrs 3 out, kept on from next but no ch with wnr.
732 **Birchall Boy 11.7 7a........Miss W Southcombe** 3
ld 3rd then made most to 13th, led again 15th, hdd and left in ld 4 out, hded after next, soon lost tch.
674 Royal Irish 11.9 5a (bl) *in tch 10th, lost touch 15th, no ch when went badly left last, t.o.* 4
788 Fathers Footprints 11.7 7a *ld to 2nd, with ldrs 10th, wknd from 4 out, t.o.* 5
672 Daringly 11.7 7a *mstk 3rd, bhnd from 11th, t.o. when p.u. before last.* .... pu
872 Some-Toy 11.7 7a *chsd ldrs 7th, still with lders when mstk and u.r. 4 out.* .... ur
Fiddlers Glen (Ire) 11.7 7a *blundred 6th, soon well bhnd, t.o. when p.u. before 15th.* .... pu
35 Stormhill Pilgrim 12.0 *prom till ld and u.r. 5th.* .... ur
549 Caracol 11.7 7a *hdwy 11th, wknd 3 out, t.o. when p.u. before last, taild off..* .... pu
670 Ardbrennan 11.7 7a *ld 2nd to 3rd, with ldrs till led 13th, hdd 15th, led again and u.r.e 4 out..* .... ur
11 ran. 12l, dist, 13l, 3l. Time 6m 30.80s. SP 11-4.
Christopher Newport

BICESTER WITH WHADDON CHASE
Kingston Blount
Saturday April 13th
GOOD

1014 - Pegasus Members

891 **CRIMSON MARY 5a...............Miss M Maher** 1
pllng, mstks, in tch, pshd into ld last, styd on
Celtic Caber 5ow ....D Turner 2
last til prog 14th, ld 2 out-last, not qckn
677 **Tompet ....J Connell** 3
(fav) chsd ldr, ld 10-13th & 14th-2 out, not qckn
558 Cardan *ld, blnd 9th, hdd nxt, ld 13th-nxt, wknd, virt p.u. flat* 4
4 ran. 3½l, 1½l, dist. Time 6m 44.00s. SP 7-1.
Sir Sanderson Temple (Vale Of Lune).

1015 - Members

683 **CAWKWELL DEAN ....R Sweeting** 1
(fav) ld to 2nd & frm 4th, clr 15th, easily
792 **Codger ....Miss J Thame** 2
cls up, chsd wnr 13th, no imp 15th, kpt on
788 **Cool Rascal 5a ....L Lay** 3
cls up, chsd wnr 7-13th, 3rd & outpcd 15th, no prog aft
888 Button Your Lip *chsd wnr 6-7th, lost plc 10th, effrt 14th, onepcd* 4
782 Yahoo 4ex *last, prog hlfwy, outpcd 14th, no prog aft* .. 5
709 Shortcastle *cls up, rider lost irons svrl fences, outpcd 14th, no ch aft* 6
792 Military Two Step 4ow *chsd ldrs, outpcd 14th, no prog aft* 7
Stilts 14ow *ld 2-4th, t.o. 12th* 8
I'm-A-Gypsy *rear, mstk 11th, lost tch 13th, t.o. & f 2 out.* .... f
9 ran. 4l, 20l, 1l, 1l, hd, hd, 2 fences. Time 6m 39.00s. SP 6-4.
J N Hutchinson (Bicester With Whaddon Chase).

1016 - Confined (12st)

897 **KELLY'S EYE 3ex (bl) ....L Lay** 1
cls up,disp apr 14th,hrd rdn & hdd last,rallied to ld flat
887 **Saybright ....G Tarry** 2
(fav) ld to 2nd, disp apr 14th til ld last, hdd & no ext flat
Lady Kay-Lee 5a ....Mrs C Mitchell 3
s.s. prog & cls up 11th, wknd 13th, t.o. nxt, fin tired
523 Favoured Victor (USA) 5ow *pllng, mstks, bhnd frm 9th, sn t.o.* 4
246 Leading Guest *prom til wknd 11th, 5th & no ch whn f 13th* .... f
Valibus (Fr) 3ex *n.j.w. made most 2nd-apr 14th,wknd rpdly,poor 3rd & p.u.3out* .... pu
6 ran. Nk, 2 fences, dist. Time 6m 38.00s. SP 5-1.
Mrs M Kimber (Grafton).

1017 - Open

662 **LUCKY CHRISTOPHER ....G Tarry** 1
(fav) cls up, chsd ldr 13th, chal 2 out, ld last, rdn out
686 **Penlet ....John Pritchard** 2
trckd ldr, ld 11th, 3l clr whn blnd 3 out, hdd last, onepcd
791 **Sailor's Delight ....T Lacey** 3
jmpd rght, ld to 11th, last & outpcd 14th, nrly ref last
902 Bright As A Button *jmpd slwly, in tch til outpcd 14th, t.o. whn ref last.* .... ref
4 ran. 2l, 30l. Time 6m 33.00s. SP 11-10.
G B Tarry (Grafton).

1018 - Ladies

685 **BANKHEAD (IRE) ....Miss C Spearing** 1
(fav) 2nd til ld 11th,clr 14th,blnd 3 out,hdd last,rallied,ld post
640 **Sperrin View 5a..............Mrs K Sunderland** 2
w.w. chsd wnr 13th, qcknd to ld last, hdd post
786 **Tudor Henry ....Mrs C Mitchell** 3
ld to 11th, 3rd frm 13th, kpt on onepcd
957 Sam Shorrock *rear frm 9th, t.o. 5th at 13th, no prog* .. 4
708 Rip The Calico (Ire) 5a *in tch to 10th, 4th & btn 13th, t.o.* 5
710 Up And Coming *prom, j.w. til blnd 10th, not rcvr, t.o. & p.u. 15th* .... pu
903 Miners Rest 5a *bhnd frm 9th, t.o. & p.u. 3 out* .... pu
890 Cardschool 5a *alwys bhnd, t.o. last whn p.u. 11th* .... pu
8 ran. Sht-hd, 20l, 25l, 12l. Time 6m 27.00s. SP 6-4.
A J Brazier (Croome & West Warwickshire).

1019 - Intermediate (12st)

667 **GRECIAN LARK 7ex ....G Tarry** 1
(fav) chsd ldrs, went 2nd 14th, ld 3 out, rdn out flat
641 **Kingofnobles (Ire) (bl)...............R Lawther** 2
ld to 14th, 3rd & outpcd nxt, rallied 2 out, clsng flat
638 **Tattlejack (Ire) (v) ....E Walker** 3
prssd ldr 6th, ld 14th-3 out, wknd apr last
885 Ramlosa (NZ) *bhnd frm 6th, t.o. 13th, fin well* 4
708 Billhead *s.s. prom to 6th, wknd 8th, t.o. & p.u. 11th* ... pu
638 What About That (Ire) (bl) *mstks, chsd ldrs, rdn 9th, 4th & btn whn p.u. 12th, dsmntd* .... pu
6 ran. 1½l, 12l, 15l. Time 6m 40.00s. SP 8-11.
G B Tarry (Grafton).

1020 - Maiden

797 **THE MAN FROM CLARE (IRE) ....L Lay** 1
prom, ld/disp 7th til ld 14th, clr 2 out, styd on
440 **Horcum ....M Frith** 2
hld up, prog 10th, chsd wnr 3 out, rdn & no imp aft nxt
Witches Promise 5a ....R Lawther 3
prom, disp 10th-14th, lost 2nd 3 out, wknd, walked in
Truly Optimistic 5a *prom to 6th, last 9th, t.o. & p.u. 12th* .... pu

496 Lloyds Loser *made most to 7th, wknd rpdly 12th, t.o. & p.u. 14th* .... pu
643 Apple Anthem 5a *in tch to 10th, wknd & p.u. 12th, dsmntd* .... pu
796 Mountfosse *tubed, n.j.w. alwys bhnd, t.o. 13th, p.u. last* .... pu
791 Tranquil Lord (Ire) *(fav) w.w. prog to jn ldrs 11th til u.r. 13th* .... ur
Top Trump 7a 2ow *cls up, mstk 10th & pshd alng, wknd & t.o. 14th, p.u. nxt* .... pu
Not To Be Trusted *mstks 2nd & 3rd, f 5th* .... f
10 ran. 8l, dist. Time 6m 45.00s. SP 5-1.
Mrs R C Matheson (Old Berkshire).
J.N.

BROCKLESBY
Brocklesby Park
Saturday April 13th
GOOD TO FIRM

1021 - Members

718 **POKEY GRANGE** ....**Capt S Robinson** 1
(fav) made all, drew clr frm 8th
718 **St Enton** ....**K Green** 2
alwys 2nd, outpcd frm 8th
636 **Nash Brakes** ....**A Forman** 3
alwys last, t.o. frm 7th
3 ran. 1 fence, 3 fences. Time 6m 43.00s. SP 2-9.
S N Burt (Brocklesby).

1022 - Confined (12st)

632 **WAYS AND MEANS 5a** ....**K Green** 1
(fav) w.w., last pair for 2 m, prog 4 out, ld 2 out, comf
969 **Rexy Boy** ....**P Gee** 2
cls up, mstly 3rd til ld 5 out, hdd & no ext bfr 2 out
722 **Rain Mark** ....**M Chatterton** 3
ld for 2 m, ran on onepce, 3rd outpcd frm 3 out
543 Mister Chippendale *alwys abt 4th, cls up til outpcd 3 out* 4
793 Shipmate 2ow *alwys rear, last whn hit 8th & t.o.* 5
968 Bowery Boy 3ex *mstly 2nd til bad mstk gd rcvr 5 out (ditch), p.u. nxt* .... pu
6 ran. 15l, 10l, 4l, 1 fence. Time 6m 11.00s. SP Evens.
Mrs S Mollett (Burton).

1023 - Ladies

759 **INTEGRITY BOY** ....**Miss A Armitage** 1
(fav) dict pce, ran on wll whn chal 3 out, drew clr frm last
984 **Osgathorpe** ....**Mrs F Needham** 2
cls up, chal frm 3 out, outpcd flat
633 **Crocket Lass 5a 1ow** ....**Miss F Hunter** 3
alwys last, t.o. frm 7th
3 ran. 4l, 1 fence. Time 6m 18.00s. SP 4-5.
R P Watts (Staintondale).

1024 - Open

513 **PARK DRIFT** ....**R Tate** 1
w.w., prog 6 out, ld nxt, ran on strgly last m
725 **Golden Moss** ....**Capt S Robinson** 2
nvr dang, 25l 4th 4 out, ran on into rmte 2nd 2 out
760 **Bennan March** ....**N Bannister** 3
alwys last, t.o. frm 4th
902 Dubalea *3rd to 8th, fdd, t.o. 5th 6 out, p.u. 4 out* .... pu
632 Carly Brrin *(fav) cont to 6 out, chsd wnnr nxt, 3l down whn f 3 out* .... f
246 Syd Green (Ire) *cont to 6 out, wknd qckly nxt, rmte 3rd whn u.r. last* .... ur
6 ran. 1 fence, 1 fence. Time 6m 5.00s. SP 9-4.
G Thornton (York & Ainsty North).

1025 - Monterey Retricted

723 **GINGER PINK (bl)** ....**Capt S Robinson** 1
cls up 2nd-4 out,cls 4th nxt,ran on wll frm 2out,ld cls home
904 **Merlins Girl 5a** ....**R Armson** 2
last pair for 2 m,prog 4 out,slght ld 2 out,cght clse home
726 **Easy Life (Ire) (bl)** ....**Miss J Wormall** 3
made most, ran on whn jnd 3 out, just outpcd flat
904 Beat The Rap *mid-div, prog 5 out, 2nd 3 out, wknd nxt* 4
985 Midge 5a *cls up for 2 m,cont 3 out,on terms whn bldnrd & u.r.last* .... ur
726 Beckford *mid-div, cont 4th wth wnr 3 out, fdd, p.u. last* .... pu
635 Give It A Whirl *cls up 3rd til u.r. 6th (ditch)* .... ur
330 Skyval 5a *t.o. last frm 7th, p.u. 11th* .... pu
679 Dashboard Light *(fav) w.w, prog 8th, 2nd imprvng whn f 12th* .... f
9 ran. 2l, 1½l, 15l. Time 6m 14.00s. SP 10-1.
C Cottingham (Brocklesby).

1026 - Maiden Div I

240 **SHARP TO OBLIGE** ....**S Swiers** 1
w.w., rpd prog 6 out, 2nd 5 out, ld 3 out, sn clr
898 **The Bold Abbot** ....**P Millington** 2
(fav) cls up, ld 5 out, hdd bfr 3 out, ran on onepce
Quiet Arrogance (USA) 5a *ld to 12th, wknng whn broke leg bfr 4 out, (dead)* .... pu
636 Final Nod *mid-div, prog 9th, chal ld & f 6 out, (dead)* .. f
591 Ninefiveo 5a *2nd to 8th, fdd, t.o. 10th, f 5 out (ditch)* ... f
904 Cawkwell Win 7a *n.j.w., t.o. 4th, f 6th* .... f
6 ran. 10l. Time 6m 19.00s. SP 5-2.
Miss S J Rodgers (Bramham Moor).

1027 - Maiden Div II

676 **NEE-ARGEE 5a** ....**C Millington** 1
mstly 3rd, ran wll frm 3 out, chal last, ran on
240 **The Tondy (Ire)** ....**S Brisby** 2
w.w., prog 4 out, chal nxt, ld aft 2 out, just outpcd flat
727 **Paradise Row (Ire)** ....**M Chatterton** 3
(fav) ld to 3 out, wknd whn hdd frm nxt
898 Emerald Queen 5a *nvr dang, 5th frm 8th, outpcd 3 out* 4
718 Flaxton King (Ire) 7a *cls up, 2nd 12th-4 out, wknd bfr nxt* 5
542 Master Enborne *cls up, last pair whn f 7th* .... f
516 Albert's Adventure (Ire) (bl) *2nd jmpng lft til ran out 5th* .... ro
7 ran. 1½l, 6l, 25l, 5l. Time 6m 23.00s. SP 6-1.
Miss Carole Baylis (Fernie).
K.B.

CHESHIRE
Alpraham
Saturday April 13th
GOOD TO SOFT

1028 - Members

664 **BARKIN** ....**C Stockton** 1
(fav) cls up, lft in ld 10th, hrd rddn 4 out, just held on
736 **Side Brace (NZ)** ....**Miss S Swindells** 2
chsd ldrs, not alwys fluent, ev ch frm 3 out, just btn
567 Duke Of Impney 1ow *rider lost irons 1st, veered lft & ran out 2nd* .... ro
Sir George Chuffy (Ire) *ld most to 10th, qckly p.u. apr nxt* .... pu
286 Mister Tinker *alwys rear, t.o. 12th, crawld over nxt, cont & ref 2 out* .... ref
5 ran. Hd. Time 7m 42.00s. SP 4-5.
Peter Saville (Cheshire).

1029 - Open Maiden (12st)

740 **FLINTERS (bl)** ....**D Barlow** 1
(fav) ld to 13th & apr last, rddn & held on wll
663 **Captiva Bay 5a** ....**Miss D Hockenhull** 2

chsd ldr til ld 13th, hdd apr last, no ext
740 **Dream Flight 7a....................J R Barlow** 3
bhnd, prog 14th, 3rd 2 out, nrst fin
740 North Hollow (bl) *4th whn u.r. 4th.* ur
852 Glen Taylor *mid-div, 6th whn blndrd & u.r. 8th.* ur
852 Son Of Ishka *chsd ldrs to 9th, wknd nxt, t.o. 11th, p.u. 13th.* pu
852 Analystic (Ire) *mstks, rear & sn t.o., p.u. 11th.* pu
569 Gold Talisman 5a *held up, 3rd 10th-3 out, wknd & p.u. nxt.* pu
8 ran. 2½l, 2l. Time 7m 49.00s. SP 4-7.
John Halewood (Cheshire).

1030 - Monterey Restricted (12st)

585 **PIN UP BOY ....A Crow** 1
ld 2nd, clr 3 out, styd on wll, impress
856 **Gray Rosette 5a ....A Griffith** 2
(fav) last to 11th, steadd prog to 4l 3rd 15th, lft 2nd last
851 **Howlin' Wolf....................M Pennell** 3
cls up 13th, lost plc & wknd nxt, lft 3rd last
739 Moorside Lad (bl) *ld to 2nd, still cls up whn f 5th* f
739 Extraspecial Brew *chsd ldng pair, hmp & u.r. 5th.* ur
739 Jo-Su-Ki *chas ldrs to 12th, wknd qckly, t.o. & p.u. 3 out.* pu
Will De-Brooke *rear, p.u. bfr 5th, broke pelvis (dead)* pu
660 Mr Busker (Ire) *held up, impd & u.r. flat aft 5th* ur
665 Kings Mischief (Ire) *mid-div, 8l 4th & styng on wll whn u.r. 3 out* ur
665 Grecianlid *2nd 5th-2 out, onepcd & wll btn whn u.r. last* ur
10 ran. 20l, 10l. Time 7m 50.00s. SP 4-1.
Mrs P Tollit (Worcestershire).

1031 - Mixed Open (12st)

1011 **SCALLY MUIRE 5a 7ex....................A Crow** 1
(fav) held up, prog to 2nd 3 out, ld aft nxt, styd on wll
1012 **Real Class....................J Evans** 2
alwys prom, ld 14th-2 out, outpcd aft
578 **Ross Venture....................C Stockton** 3
ld til hdd 14th, rddn & no ext frm 3 out
894 Wally Wrekin 4ex (bl) *in tch to 12th, t.o. nxt* 4
662 Band Sargeant (Ire) *rear, bad mstk 8th, rider lost iron & p.u. bfr nxt* pu
5 ran. 5l, 25l. Time 7m 30.00s. SP 8-11.
G L Edwards (North Shropshire).

1032 - Confined (12st)

736 **GREY GORDEN (IRE) 3ex ....A Crow** 1
w.w., rddn 13th, ran on wll 4 out, ld bfr last
672 **Sir Noddy ....C Stockton** 2
(fav) ld til hdd apr last, no ext
663 **Renard Quay 5ex ....Miss C Wilberforce** 3
nvr bynd mid-div
735 Melsonby *rear, last & t.o. 6th, p.u. aft 11th.* pu
735 Gitche Gumme *alwys rear, sn t.o., p.u. 7th* pu
460 Cheeky Fox 7ex (bl) *mid-div, 5th whn f 4th.* f
893 Royle Burchlin *chsd ldr to 4 out, wknd nxt, p.u. last* pu
1009 Charlie Chalk 6ex *alwys bhhd, t.o. 6th, p.u. 2 out* pu
855 Bally Muire 5a *bhnd whn s.u. aft 4th* su
9 ran. 2l, dist. Time 7m 26.00s. SP 5-2.
R Major (North Shropshire).

1033 - 2½m Open Maiden (5-7yo) (12st)

856 **SHANBALLYMORE (IRE)....................J Tilley** 1
alwys prom, ld apr 3 out, drew clr aft nxt
568 **Sargeants Choice....................J R Barlow** 2
lft in ld 8th, hdd bfr 3 out, outpcd
665 **Annyban 5a....................S Prior** 3
3rd/4th thruout, ev ch 4 out, no ext
740 New Cruiser 5a *held up, stead prog 11th, rddn & no ext frm 3 out* 4
661 Canny Curate (Ire) *mid-div frm 6th, onepcd aft* 5
568 Niord *rear thruout, some late prog, nvr nrr* 6
463 Lydebrook *(fav) ld sn 10l clr, u.r. flat several strides aft 4th* ur
954 Lady Barbarosa (Ire) 5a *prog 8th, wknd 11th, 7th whn p.u. last* pu
286 Heriot Water (Ire) 5a *last pair in rear, t.o. 4th, p.u. 8th* pu
High Handed (Ire) 7a *ld 6th til ran out thru wing 8th* ro
406 Piptony *bhnd whn ref 8th* ref
Sky Runner 7a *last pair in rear, t.o. 4th, p.u. 8th* pu
Chip Pan 7a *nvr bynd mid-div, 6th whn p.u. last* pu
740 Eller's Reflection 5a *rear, t.o. 7th, p.u. 10th* pu
Scally Blue 7a *cls up 4th whn hmp & u.r. 8th* ur
15 ran. 8l, 2l, 8l, 12l, 8l. Time 5m 36.00s. SP 7-2.
Mrs C S Tilley (Flint & Denbigh).
R.A.

GLAMORGAN
St Hilary
Saturday April 13th
GOOD

1034 - Members

979 **NEWS REVIEW 3ex ....Miss J Mathias** 1
(fav) ld to 5th & frm 13th, drew clr
844 **Cosa Nostra....................K Cousins** 2
ld 6-12th, chsd wnr, alwys hld
976 **Hil Lady 7a..........Miss S McGillivary** 3
cls 3rd to 9th, grad lost tch
3 ran. 25l, dist. Time 6m 38.00s. SP 1-5.
Mrs S Mathias (Glamorgan).

1035 - Confined (12st)

846 **BRONZE EFFIGY (bl) ....R Jones** 1+
mid-div, gd prog to ld 15th, bttr jmp last, jnd line
847 **Lucky Ole Son 5ex..........Miss P Jones** 1+
hld up, prog to 5l 4th 3 out, ran on apr last, jnd ldr line
382 **McMahon's River 5a ....C Richards** 3
prom, ld brfly 15th, ev ch 2 out, no ext
767 Tricky Dex (USA) *prom til ld 12th, hdd 15th, cls enough 3 out, not run on* 4
845 Vatacan Bank *alwys rear, t.o. 13th* 5
845 The Batchlor *rear, 20l 5th at 14th, p.u. 2 out* pu
843 Magnus Pym (bl) *ld 6th-12th, wknd rpdly, p.u. 14th.* pu
545 No Panic *alwys rear, p.u. 14th* pu
845 Light The Wick 7ex *rear, t.o. & p.u. 14th* pu
691 Push Along *(fav) ld til f 6th* f
10 ran. Dd-ht, 6l, 2l, 20l. Time 6m 25.00s.
David Brace/ W Pugh (Llangeinor).
Bronze Effigy 40-1. Lucky Ole Son 3-1.

1036 - Ladies

979 **GOOLDS GOLD 7ex..........Miss P Jones** 1
(fav) cls 2nd til ld 11th, clr 14th, easily
546 **Afaristoun (Fr)..........Miss J Morse** 2
rear, 3rd at 14th, ran on 3 out, nrst fin, no ch wnr
975 **Kinlogh Gale (Ire) (bl)..........Miss H Williams** 3
ld to 10th, hdd & wknd aft
544 Never Be Great 3ex *cls up, 2nd frm 12th, wknd rpdly 16th, fin tired* 4
847 Adanac *t.o. 7th, p.u. 13th* pu
847 Mendip Music *mostly 5th, prog to 7l 4th whn u.r. 14th* ur
6 ran. 12l, 15l, 10l. Time 6m 21.00s. SP 4-9.
David Brace (Llangeinor).

1037 - Open (12st)

602 **SANDY BEAU 4ex ....T Jones** 1
ld to 12th, disp to 15th, 5l down 3 out, ran on to ld nxt
694 **Polly Pringle 5a ....A Price** 2
prom in 3rd, disp 15th, ld 3 out, wknd & hdd nxt
768 **Cornish Cossack (NZ) ....J Jukes** 3
alwys cls up, prog to disp 15th til wknd 3 out
846 Kingfisher Bay 7ex *disp til p.u. 12th, lame* pu
770 Robbie's Boy *(fav) last til prog 11th, ld/disp til f 16th* f
5 ran. 6l, 1½l. Time 6m 23.00s. SP 5-2.
Mrs Vanessa Ramm (Cotswold).

1038 - Restricted (12st)

773 **SHUIL'S STAR (IRE) 7a....................P Hamer** 1
(fav) rear, gd prog 14th, disp 2 out, ld last & lft clr
388 **Antarctic Call..........................N Richards** 2
mid-div, 3rd at 12th, no ext 3 out, lft 2nd last
690 **Paper Fair 5a.............................J Price** 3
rear, no ch 15th, lft 3rd by dfctns
844 Louis Farrell *cls 2nd til lft clr apr 12th, hdd 15th, wknd* 4
980 Mylordmayor *rear, t.o. whn f 14th* f
695 Flaxridge *ld til s.u. flat apr 12th* su
Silver Step *alwys rear, p.u. 3 out* pu
695 Cottage Raider (Ire) *3rd til lft 2nd apr 12th, ld 15th, 3l up nxt, hdd & u.r.last* ur
Rymin Thyne *prom, grad lost tch, p.u. 14th* pu
840 Buckley's Court *rear, prog to 4th at 14th, wkng whn ran out 3 out* ro
643 My Boy Barney *rear, prog to cls 3rd 15th, ev ch whn ran out 3 out* ro
844 Saffron Moss *rear, p.u. 3 out* pu
599 Fresh Prince *clr 3rd whn p.u. 9th* pu
844 Mrs Wumpkins (Ire) 7a *rear, no prog whn p.u. 14th* pu
690 Hatterill Ridge *alwys rear, p.u. 13th* pu
15 ran. 10l, dist, 8l. Time 6m 26.00s. SP 7-2.
Bob Mason (Carmarthenshire).

1039 - Maiden (5-7yo)

848 **PHARRAGO (IRE).................Miss P Cooper** 1
rear, prog to 4th at 14th, 2nd 2 out, ld flat
849 **Sister Lark 5a..........................V Hughes** 2
ld, clr 14th, tired 3 out, ct flat
847 **Miss Montgomery (Ire) 7a ....Miss A Meakins** 3
mid-div, went 4th at 14th, wknd, lft poor 3rd 16th
976 Rosieplant 5a *schoold, styd on late* 4
849 City Rhythm *rear, fin own time* 5
771 On The Book 5a *alwys last pair, p.u. 15th* pu
976 Jolly Swagman 7a *prom, 3rd whn f 11th* f
696 Spikeie Rose 5a *4th/5th, badly hmpd 9th, some prog 13th, p.u. 15th* pu
850 Lets Go Polly 5a *rear, went 5th at 14th, p.u. 2 out* pu
771 Gunner Boon *(fav) cls 3rd, went 2nd at 8th, f nxt* f
605 Lennie The Lion 7a *cls 2nd whn f 8th* f
607 Tiger Lord 7a *prom to 12th, wknd & p.u. 3 out* pu
773 Redoran 7a *alwys rear, p.u. 16th* pu
975 Irish Thinker 7a *mid-div, prog to 3rd whn u.r. 13th* ur
14 ran. 2½l, dist, 15l, 1l. Time 6m 37.00s. SP 14-1.
Miss E Saunders (Tredegar Farmers).

1040 - Maiden (8yo+)

771 **BARNABY BOY ....J P Keen** 1
(fav) rear, rpd prog to 2nd 13th, ld nxt, ran on whn chal 2 out
975 **Sea Search................................J Price** 2
hld up, went 3rd at 13th, ran on to chal 2 out, just hld
976 **Parson's Corner.........................V Hughes** 3
mid-div, cls 4th at 14th, no ext aft
844 Pyro Pennant *mid-div til wknd frm 13th* 4
849 Astley Jack *wll clr 6th, ct 14th, fdng whn f 16th* f
848 Great Precocity *rear, p.u. 9th* pu
390 Gold Tip 5a *2nd to 12th, wknd rpdly, p.u. 3 out* pu
848 Plas-Hendy *cls 4th/5th till f 12th* f
976 Cairneymount *rear trio whn u.r. 5th* ur
605 Colonel Frazer (Ire) *prom in 3rd whn f 13th* f
Frontrunner 5a *cls up, 6th whn p.u. 9th* pu
843 Trevella 5a *rear whn f 13th* f
12 ran. ¾l, dist, dist. Time 6m 32.00s. SP 6-4.
J L Brown (Llandeilo Farmer).
P.H./ J.C.

LUDLOW
Bitterley
Saturday April 13th
GOOD

1041 - Members

457 **LEDWYCHE GATE (bl) ....M Jackson** 1
made virt all, drew clr frm 3 out
666 **Oragas....................................R Bevis** 2
(fav) w.w. cls 3rd at 10th, effrt 14th, not qckn nxt, btn 2 out
749 **First Command (NZ)..................M Munrowd** 3
disp 5th, chal 13-14th, wknd apr 3 out
547 Hagler 7ex *hld up, p.u. 8th, lame* pu
748 Mendip Son (bl) *tk str hld, ran out 4th* ro
689 Bucksum (Ire) 7a *jmpd novicey, cls 4th at 10th, wknd 12th, p.u. nxt* pu
6 ran. 15l, 15l. Time 6m 27.00s. SP 9-4.
L Evans (Ludlow).

1042 - Confined (12st)

880 **SHOON WIND ....A Dalton** 1
cls 2nd til ld 8th, gd jmp & drew clr frm 15th
Gay Ruffian ....Miss C Dyson 2
cls up, chsd wnr 12th, no ext frm 15th
881 **Geo Potheen 3ex ....Mrs N Sheppard** 3
mid-div, prog 12th, chsd 2nd frm 3 out
943 Mitchells Best *cls up til outpcd frm 11th, styd on one-pcd frm 3 out* 4
691 The Dark Watch *trckd ldrs, 8l 3rd 13th, outpcd frm nxt* 5
881 Barn Pool *ld to 7th, outpcd aft 12th* 6
881 Space Mariner 5ex *tubed, prom to 4th, lost tch aft 12th, t.o. 14th* 7
878 All Greek To Me (Ire) *alwys last, no ch whn p.u. 12th* pu
691 Miners Fortune (Ire) 3ex *(fav) hit 4th, mid-div whn s.u. bend apr 8th* su
9 ran. 15l, 4l, 5l, 8l, 4l, dist. Time 6m 21.00s. SP 3-1.
J N Dalton (Wheatland).

1043 - Land Rover Open (12st)

854 **BUCKSFERN 7ex..........................R Bevis** 1
(fav) cls up til ld 12th, hrd prssd 2 out, drew clr last
836 **Drumceva..........................M Wilesmith** 2
disp 9-10th, rdn & lost plc 13th, chal 3 out-nxt, blnd last
683 **Raido....................................M Jackson** 3
ld 5-8th, 3l 2nd & ev ch 13th, onepcd frm 15th
687 Hackett's Farm *cls 5th at 11th, not qckn frm nxt, styd on into 4th at 15th* 4
671 Chibougama (USA) *alwys last, not keen to jn ldrs, no ch 13th, late prog* 5
881 Tara Boy (bl) *ld to 4th, slw jmp nxt, cls 4th at 11th, wknd 13th* 6
837 Bumptious Boy *blnd badly & u.r. 1st* ur
880 Volcanic Dancer (USA) 7ex (bl) *started 3 fences bhnd (again), p.u. 2nd* pu
741 Invite D'Honneur (NZ) *6l 6th at 11th, lost tch nxt, t.o. & p.u. 15th* pu
9 ran. 15l, 4l, 12l, 6l, 15l. Time 6m 21.00s. SP Evens.
E E Williams (West Shropshire Drag).

1044 - Open Maiden (5-7yo) Div I (12st)

688 **ANOTHER CHANCER 7a..............M Harris** 1
30l 3rd 7th, chsd ldr 12th, ld nxt, lft clr 15th, solo 2 out
697 **Bel Lane 5a ....D S Jones** 2
(fav) 40l 4th at 7th, 6l 3rd 12th, tired 2nd & ref 2 out, cont
Promitto 5a *whppd round start, tk no part* 0
748 Countrywide Lad *t.o. in 3rd whn ref 15th* ref
884 True Fred *dist 4th whn u.r. 12th* ur
748 Cruise A Hoop *chsng grp whn f 4th* f
697 Hennerwood Oak 5a *ld to 4th & frm 9th, jnd 13th, ev ch whn f 15th* f
884 Frank The Swank 7a *ld 5-8th, wknd rpdly 10th, p.u. nxt* pu
Wrenbury Farmer *nvr going pace, t.o. & ref 4th* ref
749 So Easy 5a *nvr nr ldrs, eased & p.u. 10th* pu
3 Clobeever Boy *chsg grp whn b.d. 4th* bd
Fancytalkintinker (Ire) *alwys rear, in tch whn f 9th* f
Bunchoffives 7a *hit marker & u.r. apr 5th* ur
354 Tigeritsi 5a *mid-div, remote 4th whn p.u. 15th, cont, f 2 out* f
689 Philelwyn (Ire) 7a *in tch til eased 10th, p.u. aft nxt* pu
15 ran. Dist. Time 6m 35.00s. SP 6-1.
K C G Edwards (Ludlow).

One fence omitted, 17 jumps.

1045 - Open Maiden (5-7yo) Div II (12st)

LITTLE NOTICE (IRE) 7a ....R Bevis 1
trckd ldrs, effrt 15th, ld nxt, rallied to chal last,ld post
977 **Bowland Girl (Ire) 5a ....Miss E James** 2
trckd ldrs, prog to ld 2 out, hdd nr fin
688 **Bucks Flea 5a ....R Burton** 3
(fav) alwys prom, ev ch til no ext frm 2 out
606 Wolfie Smith *ld 2-4th, cls up to 14th, kpt on onepcd frm 3 out* 4
696 Native Missile 5a *cls 5th at 7th, ldng grp til not qckn 14th, kpt on* 5
799 Watchit Lad *alwys rear, late prog frm 15th* 6
430 Greenhills Ruby 7a *prom to 10th, in tch til no ext frm 15th* 7
748 Think Twice *chsd ldrs, ev ch 13th, wknd frm 15th* 8
550 Parks Pride 7a *nvr rchd ldrs, wknd frm 13th* 9
841 Ginge *ld 9th til jnd 15th, wknd & p.u. last* .... pu
883 Seven Cruise *outpcd & lost tch 11th, t.o. & p.u. 3 out* .... pu
Corview (Ire) 7a *cls up at 10th, ev ch whn blnd 13th, p.u. 15th* .... pu
463 Tanner *ld 5-8th, lost plc 13th, p.u. 3 out* .... pu
Asante Sana 7a *alwys rear, p.u. 10th* .... pu
Crimson Bow 5a 7ow *trckng ldrs whn u.r. 5th* .... ur
689 Sutton Lighter *cls up til wknd 12th, t.o. & p.u. 3 out* .... pu

16 ran. Nk, 3l, 15l, 2l, 4l, 1l, ½l, 20l. Time 6m 33.00s. SP 4-1.
Capt T Forster (Berkeley).

1046 - Ladies

743 **RUN TO FORM.................Miss E Wilesmith** 1
chsd ldr frm 7th, ld 12th, kpt on well frm 2 out
Night Wind.......................Mrs A Rucker 2
ld to 11th, cls up, chal aft 2 out, not qckn flat
687 **Carbery Arctic..................Miss T Spearing** 3
(fav) prog 9th, trckd ldrs 12th, ev ch 14th, kpt on frm 3 out
836 Stanford Boy *hld up, prog 9th, effrt 12th, onepcd frm 15th* 4
879 Golden Fare *cls up til not qckn frm 13th, no ch frm 15th* 5
879 In The Water *prom til slppd bnd apr 8th, lost tch 13th, t.o. 15th* 6
945 Shadow Walker *cls up til outpcd frm 12th, lost tch & p.u. 15th* .... pu
687 Master Dancer *chsd ldrs til not qckn 13th, p.u. last* .... pu
The City Minstrel *cls up til lost plc 9th, wknd 13th, p.u. last* .... pu

9 ran. 1l, 3l, 8l, 15l, dist. Time 6m 22.00s. SP 8-1.
M S Wilesmith (Ledbury).

1047 - Open Maiden (8yo+) Div I (12st)

688 **SILVER FIG 5a ....N Bradley** 1
ld 3rd, lft clr 12th, kpt on frm 2 out
908 **Cathgal..J Rees** 2
prog 9th, went 10l 2nd 14th, not get on terms wnr
733 **Constant Sula 5a.................Miss P Gundry** 3
(fav) rear of mid-div, some prog 13th, styd on 3 out, nrst fin
883 Baptist John (Ire) *prog to cls 3rd at 7th, ev ch 11th, not qckn nxt, kpt on* 4
688 Close Control (Ire) *prom til wknd 13th, t.o. 3 out* 5
695 Bob-Cam *s.s. t.o. 4th, p.u. last* .... pu
688 I Blame Theparents 5a *trckd ldrs, prom 11th, chal whn f nxt* .... f
Itsallamatter (Ire) *rear frm 4th, lost tch & p.u. 10th* .... pu
883 Master Frith (bl) *cls up to 10th, outpcd 13th, p.u. 2 out* .... pu
Flying Wild *alwys rear, losing tch whn p.u. 11th* .... pu
357 Musical Mail *mid-div to 10th, wknd & p.u. aft 12th* .... pu
605 Brownscroft 5a *ld to 3rd, cls up til wknd 12th, p.u. 15th* .... pu
749 Welsh Lightning *in tch til no prog 11th, no ch 14th, p.u. 3 out* .... pu

13 ran. 3l, 10l, 3l, dist. Time 6m 26.00s. SP 5-1.
J Mahon (Croome & West Warwickshire).

1048 - Open Maiden (8yo+) Div II (12st)

880 **CARLSAN.......................Miss E James** 1
alwys chsng ldrs, styd on to ld 2 out, rdn out flat
896 **Micksdilemma ....A Phillips** 2
cls 3rd at 8th, ev ch 15th, not qckn 3 out, tk 2nd flat
749 **Joyney 5a...................................L Squire** 3
prog to lng grp 9th, ld 3 out, wknd frm nxt
688 Most Rich (Ire) *(fav) prom til ld 12th, mstk 15th, hdd & wknd nxt* 4
883 Mis-E-Fishant 5a *made most to 4th, wknd 11th, t.o. 15th* 5
568 My Son John *in tch in rear til wknd 11th, p.u. nxt* .... pu
742 Breeches Buoy *last at 4th, lost tch & p.u. 12th* .... pu
683 Shaker Maker *mid-div, outpcd apr 13th, p.u. 15th* .... pu
350 Glenmavis *chsd ldrs, grad wknd 12th, p.u. last* .... pu
748 Sweet Petel 5a *s.s. prog to disp whn u.r. 7th* .... ur
841 Woodmanton 5a *ld 4th til hdd & f 12th* .... f
600 Majic Belle 5a *last at 10th, reluc aft nxt & p.u.* .... pu

12 ran. 6l, 3l, 12l, dist. Time 6m 32.00s. SP 4-1.
Mrs A Price (Teme Valley (United)).
P.R.

OLD SURREY & BURSTOW
Penshurst
Saturday April 13th
GOOD

1049 - Nat Country Members

BANOGUE HILL...................Mrs A Blaker 1
(fav)
Siltack..............................Miss S Temple 2
O'Max ....Mrs C Scott 3
Prestor John 4
Collooney Blue 5
Forest Canyon 6
The Hook 11ow 7
Jaffa 8
Master Troy .... ur
Major Max .... pu
Joint Venture .... ur

11 ran. 3l, 3l. Time 7m 39.00s. SP 2-1.
Mrs A Blaker (Old Surrey & Burstow).

1050 - Confined

779 **ALANSFORD..................................P Bull** 1
sn prom, cls 3rd whn blnd 14th, styd on 3 out to ld frm last
594 **Murberry (Ire) 5a ....T Hills** 2
(fav) mid-div, clsd up 13th, wth ldr aft, ld 2 out-last,kpt on wll
778 **Berrings Dasher..........................A Welsh** 3
jnd ldrs 7th, ld 12th, hrd prssd 4 out, hdd & wknd 2 out
813 American Eyre *cls up to 8th, lost plc, in tch 10th, kpt on* 4
811 Yeoman Farmer *in tch, 4th & btn 4 out* 5
775 Mel's Rose *mid-div, nvr dang, wknd 3 out* 6
963 Highland Bounty (v) *s.s. sn prom, 5th whn f 12th* .... f
776 Take The Town 2ow *ld, just hdd whn u.r. 12th* .... ur

8 ran. ½l, 10l, 12l, 1l, 8l. Time 6m 50.00s. SP 3-1.
E J Farrant (East Sussex & Romney Marsh).

1051 - Members

777 **MONKSFORT....................Miss C Holliday** 1
(fav) made all, blnd & nrly u.r. 1st, styd on, drew clr 3 out
779 **Firewater Station ....Mrs E Coveney** 2
2nd at 7th, wth wnr 14th, wknd nxt, fin tired, walked in
496 **Run To Au Bon (Ire) (bl) ....T McCarthy** 3
strgglng to stay in tch 7th, 3rd & wknd 13th
Divine Problem *t.o. 5th, fin own time* 4

780 Tommy Springer *chsd ldr to 7th, steadily wknd, bhnd & p.u. 12th* .... pu
5 ran. 30l, 10l, 2 fences. Time 7m 10.00s. SP 1-2.
Miss C Holliday (Old Surrey & Burstow).

1052 - Open (12st)

595 **RETAIL RUNNER** .... **T Hills** 1
(fav) handy, ld frm 11th, made rest, clr 4 out, easily
776 **Centre Stage** .... **A Warr** 2
rear, prog 11th, 2nd 4 out, not pace to chal
537 **Castlebay Lad 7ex** .... **C Coyne** 3
alwys prom, chsd wnr 11th, nvr on terms, 3rd & wknd 4 out
813 Pacific Sound *in tch to 13th, fdd* 4
577 Eddie Walshe *ld to 11th, fdd, p.u. 13th* .... pu
619 Sakil (Ire) 7ex *rear, losing tch whn p.u. bef 12th* .... pu
965 Quarter Marker (Ire) *wll in tch to 11th, wknd aft, p.u. aft 13th* .... pu
7 ran. 7l, 15l, 1 fence. Time 6m 46.00s. SP 1-2.
Maurice E Pinto (Chiddingfold,I'field & Cowdray).

1053 - Ladies

572 **MERITMOORE** .... **Miss F Hatfield** 1
jnd ldrs 10th, lost plc 13th, ran on strngly 2 out, ld last
812 **Adamare 4ex** .... **Miss C Holliday** 2
(fav) ld, mstk 2nd, clr 2 out, wknd aft, jmpd slwly & hdd last
961 **Mountaico (bl)** .... **Miss J Grant** 3
ran in sntchs, 2nd & btn 2 out
782 Redelva 5a *sn cls up, 2nd 4 out, wknd* 4
Golden Huntress 5a (bl) *rear, lost tch 11th, p.u. 13th* .... pu
5 ran. 2l, 20l, 6l. Time 6m 58.00s. SP 25-1.
K Tork (Surrey Union).

1054 - Restricted (12st)

779 **KING'S MAVERICK (IRE)** .... **P Hacking** 1
(fav) hld up, gd prog 4 out, ld apr 2 out, drew wll clr
774 **Prince Ronan (Ire)** .... **Miss F Taylor** 2
ld to 2nd, prom in chsng grp aft, 4th 3 out, ran on onepcd
182 **Prime Course (Ire)** .... **P Bull** 3
prom in chsng grp, 3rd frm 3 out, onepcd
592 Drewitts Dancer *chsng grp,lft in ld 12th,clr 14th,wknd rpdly 3 out,hdd nxt* 4
781 Iorwerth *alwys rear, t.o. 7th, p.u. 12th* .... pu
779 Brief Sleep 5a *ld 4th, clr nxt, still wll clr whn f 12th* .... f
593 Lewesdon Princess 5a *ld 2-4th, styd in tch til wknd 12th, p.u. 3 out* .... pu
810 Salachy Run (Ire) *s.i.s. sn in tch, 3rd & rmndrs 13th, wknd nxt, p.u. aft 2out* .... pu
8 ran. Dist, ¾l, 12l. Time 6m 59.00s. SP 6-4.
C J Ells (Southdown & Eridge).

1055 - Open Maiden (12st)

809 **POLAR ANA (IRE) 5a** .... **Miss S Gladders** 1
alwys prom, qcknd to ld 4 out, sn clr, easily
830 **Le Vienna (Ire)** .... **P Hacking** 2
(Jt fav) handy, ev ch 4 out, wknd nxt, fin tired
783 **Joe Quality** .... **M Loughnane** 3
ld til mstk 2nd, prom aft, ld 12th & 14th, 3rd nxt & btn
597 Time Star (NZ) 6ow *ld 2nd, hdd 12th, hmpd aft nxt, wll bhnd whn p.u. 2 out* .... pu
681 Bric Lane (USA) *mid-div til u.r. 11th* .... ur
814 Prom's Mohock *prom, jmpd rght, jmpd rght 6th & f* .... f
965 Miss Beal 5a *alwys rear, p.u. 12th* .... pu
781 Over The Clover (Ire) 5a (bl) *alwys rear, p.u. 12th* .... pu
780 Bomb The Bees 5a *(Jt fav) mid-div, prog 10th, just ld whn u.r. 13th* .... ur
779 Cumberland Gap 7a *schoold in rear til p.u. 12th* .... pu
Don'tcallmegeorge 7a *schoold in rear, blnd 5th, some prog 10th, p.u. 12th* .... pu
11 ran. 15l, 15l. Time 7m 3.00s. SP 5-1.
Mrs P A McIntyre (Ashford Valley).
G.Ta.

PORTMAN
Badbury Rings
Saturday April 13th
GOOD TO FIRM

1056 - Restricted (12st)

522 **APATURA KING** .... **T Mitchell** 1
(Jt fav) hld up, prog 13th, 2nd nxt, ld 3 out, styd on
729 **Final Express 5a 3ow** .... **M Hoskins** 2
in tch to 13th, lost plc, renewed effrt 2 out, styd on
581 **Bang On Target** .... **T Barry** 3
prom, ld 7th-3 out, wknd & onepcd aft
707 Misty (NZ) *mid-div, prog 10th, prom to 4 out, wknd & blnd last* 4
656 Royal Rupert *in tch to 10th, outpcd frm 14th* 5
707 Time Module *n.j.w. alwys bhnd, t.o. 12th, p.u. 3 out* .... pu
562 Stalbridge Gold 5a *cls up to 7th, p.u. 9th, tack broke* .... pu
728 Langton Parmill *ld 3rd-7th, in tch aft, 4th whn b.d. 3 out* .... bd
466 Nearly A Mermaid 5a *mid-div to 9th, lost tch 11th, t.o. & p.u. 4 out* .... pu
465 Mammy's Choice (Ire) 5a *(Jt fav) ld to 3rd, prom, 3rd & ev ch whn f 3 out* .... f
10 ran. 3l, 20l, 8l, dist. Time 6m 12.00s. SP 5-4.
C E Gibbs (Portman).

1057 - Members (12st)

654 **SPRING FUN** .... **Miss Y Young** 1
j.w. chsd ldr, ld apr last, ran on well
707 **Plan-A (Ire)** .... **R Nuttall** 2
(fav) n.j.w. last til 13th, prom nxt, rdn 3 out, chal flat, hld
Kala Dawn 5a .... **Miss M Tory** 3
ld til hdd apr last, onepcd flat
816 Vital Legacy *3rd til 13th, lost tch nxt, ref 15th* .... ref
4 ran. ½l, 2l. Time 6m 12.00s. SP 14-1.
David Young (Portman).

1058 - Ladies

655 **SPACIAL (USA)** .... **Miss M Hill** 1
(fav) made all, mstk last, unchal
786 **Sunley Street 5a (bl)** .... **Miss S Vickery** 2
chsd wnr, blnd 15th, styd on onepcd frm 2 out
818 **Great Uncle** .... **Miss A Goschen** 3
handy til lost tch 12th, onepcd frm 4 out
730 Mighty Falcon *in tch to 4 out, 3rd & wkng whn mssd marker aft last, rtrcd* 4
651 Elegant Sun *alwys last, losing tch whn f 14th* .... f
5 ran. 8l, dist, 25l. Time 6m 4.60s. SP 1-2.
Richard J Hill (Wilton).

1059 - Land Rover Open (12st)

731 **RYMING CUPLET 7ex** .... **R White** 1
(fav) in tch, ld 3 out, slw jmp last, rdn & just hld on
468 **Fosbury 7ex** .... **T Mitchell** 2
ld 3rd-3 out, rallied aft last, just faild
669 **My Mellow Man 7ex** .... **N Mitchell** 3
ld to 2nd, cls up to 12th, lost tch frm 4 out
523 Orujo (Ire) *handy to 15th, lost tch frm 4 out, onepcd* 4
139 Gunner Stream *n.j.w. alwys rear, t.o. & p.u. 4 out* .... pu
5 ran. Sht-hd, 20l, 25l. Time 6m 7.70s. SP 4-7.
Gerald Tanner (Dulverton West).

1060 - Open Maiden (12st)

652 **FRONT COVER 5a** .... **S Mulcaire** 1
(fav) hld up, prog 14th, ld 4 out, sn clr, easily
522 **Alex Thuscombe** .... **P Shaw** 2
handy, 4th at 14th, chsd wnr apr last, not trbl wnr
713 **Sybillabee 5a** .... **D Dennis** 3
prom, ld 15th-4 out, outpcd frm 2 out
533 Legal Vision 5a *alwys mid-div, no ch frm 4 out* 4
815 Spar Copse *cls up, 3rd at 10th, wknd & outpcd frm 4 out* 5
728 Handy Spider 5a *alwys bhnd, nvr able to chal* 6

471 Celtic Token *ld to 14th, wknd & onepcd aft* 7
997 Moran Brig *mid-div til u.r. 9th* .... ur
711 Nearly Five Too 5a *mid-div whn u.r. 5th* .... ur
Springvilla (Ire) *hld up, prog 14th, 4th & ev ch whn f 3 out* .... f
712 Pinber 5a *mid-div, lost tch 10th, t.o. & p.u. 13th* ...... pu
145 Rocky Rose 5a 10ow *last whn bkd 3rd* .... ref
819 Rosanda 5a *rear whn ref & u.r. 3rd* .... ref
652 Grey Jerry 7a *alwys mid-div, t.o. & p.u. 15th* .... pu
14 ran. 8l, 15l, 10l, ½l, 6l, 2l. Time 6m 7.00s. SP 5-4.
Stewart Pike (East Devon).

1061 - Intermediate (12st)

709 **CLOBRACKEN LAD** .... **Miss M Coombe** 1
j.w. ld/disp til went clr 2 out, hld on und pres
467 **Country Style 5a** .... **R Nuttall** 2
(fav) ld/disp til blnd 2 out, rdn aft last, alwys hld
532 **Sherbrooks** .... **M Hoskins** 3
alwys 3rd, wll bhnd frm 15th
3 ran. Nk, dist. Time 6m 6.00s. SP 5-2.
T Swaffield (Devon & Somerset Staghounds).
D.P.

PUCKERIDGE
Horseheath
Saturday April 13th
FIRM

1062 - Members

679 **SHAKE FIVE (IRE) 7a** .... **S Sporborg** 1
(fav) chsd ldr, qknd to ld last, rdn out
668 **John O'Dee** .... **I Marsh** 2
ld til appr last, onepcd
Blumix *1st ride, disp ld 7th-9th, lst tch 12th, t.o. & ref 15th* .... ref
3 ran. 2l. Time 6m 40.00s. SP 1-3.
Mrs C H Sporborg (Puckeridge).

1063 - Open Maiden 5-6yo (12st)

830 **AUCHENDOLLY (IRE)** .... **S Sporborg** 1
prom, ld 3rd-5th, jmpd to ld 15th, rdn nxt, kpt on gamely
681 **George The Greek (Ire)** .... **A Coe** 2
(fav) cls up, ld 7th-14th, unable to qkn und press frm nxt
Remilan (Ire) 7a .... **P Taiano** 3
j.s. 1st & 3rd, in tch to 13th, lft poor 3rd 15th, t.o.
835 Celtic Hawk *ld 1st, drpd rr 3rd, prog & ev ch 13th, 3rd & btn whn f 15th* .... f
830 Hendora (Ire) 7a *ld 2nd-nxt, prom til wknd 13th, p.u. nxt* .... pu
5 ran. 2½l, dist. Time 6m 31.00s. SP 5-2.
Christopher Sporborg (Puckeridge).

1064 - Open Maiden 7yo & Up (12st)

622 **FLIGHT OF LOVE 5a 13ow** .... **J Buckle** 1
made all, ran on wll flat
972 **Stanwick Lass 5a** .... **T Marks** 2
(fav) alwys 2nd, ev ch 2 out, rdn & nt qkn flat
835 **Aughnacloy Rose** .... **R Page** 3
alwys last, nt fluent, outpcd 14th, ran on flat, fin wll
3 ran. 1½l, hd. Time 6m 49.00s. SP 6-1.
James Buckle (Essex & Suffolk).

1065 - Confined (12st)

833 **RIVER MELODY 5a 7ex** .... **T Moore** 1
(fav) alwys gng wll, ld 13th-15th, qknd to ld 2 out, pshd clr
834 **Salmon Mead (Ire)** .... **S Sporborg** 2
cls up, ld appr 3 out til 2 out, onepcd und press
672 **As You Were** .... **D Parravani** 3
ld/disp to 12th, ev ch 15th, sn outpcd
832 Cardinal Red 3ex *keen hold,ld/disp to 12th,ev ch 3 out,3rd & btn whn u.r. nxt* .... ur
4 ran. 5l, 10l. Time 6m 31.00s. SP 4-6.
T W Moore (Essex).

1066 - Ladies

347 **ASHBORO (IRE)** .... **Miss L Hollis** 1
chsd ldr, blnd 9th, efft to ld 15th, sn clr
325 **Proverb Prince** .... **Miss S Samworth** 2
(fav) ld, sn clr, hdd 15th, wknd appr nxt
2 ran. 20l. Time 6m 28.00s. SP 6-4.
J M Turner (Suffolk).

1067 - Open

672 **OVER THE EDGE** .... **S Sporborg** 1
(fav) ld/disp, hit 12th, ld 3 out, clr nxt rddn out
932 **Melton Park (bl)** .... **N Bloom** 2
last & pshd alng, clsd appr 15th, chsd wnr 2 out, kpt on
677 **Jimmy Mac Jimmy** .... **C Ward-Thomas** 3
ld /disp til ld 15th, hdd & wknd nxt
3 ran. 2l, 20l. Time 6m 25.00s. SP 4-7.
Christopher Sporborg (Puckeridge).

1068 - Intermediate (12st)

676 **SAFFRON FLAME (IRE)** .... **P Taiano** 1
(fav) w.w. prog to chal 3 out, ld last, rdn out
679 **Russian Vision (bl)** .... **C Ward-Thomas** 2
ld to 5th, & agn 9th, hdd last, no ex
723 **Stanwick Farlap 5a 5ex** .... **T Marks** 3
chsd ldr 10th-15th, rdn & onepcd frm 3 out
679 Kelly's Twilight 5a *prom, ld 6th-8th, wknd appr 14th, no ch whn j.s. last 2* 4
906 Couture Quality *blnd 4th, 5th & rdn 12th, no hdwy, wll btn whn u.r. 15th* .... ur
934 Lovely Clonmoyle (Ire) 5a *rear, lst tch 12th, t.o. & p.u. 14th* .... pu
831 Parkers Hills (Ire) *prom, hit 6th, lst pl & bhnd 8th,rdn & no resp 12th,p.u 14th* .... pu
7 ran. 2l, 15l, dist. Time 6m 19.00s. SP 6-4.
Mrs M G Sheppard (Cambridgeshire).
S.P.

TETCOTT
Lifton
Saturday April 13th
SOFT

1069 - Confined (12st)

628 **JUST BEN** .... **Miss J Cumings** 1
hndy, outpcd 15th, wnt 3rd 3 out, ld last, pshd out
715 **Walkers Point 3ex** .... **A Farrant** 2
(fav) prom, disp 6-14th, slght ld und pres 2 out,hdd & no ext last
715 **Prince Soloman 3ex** .... **L Jefford** 3
cls 3rd mstly, mstk 3 out, ev ch 2 out, ran on onepce
715 Catch The Cross (bl) *sn rear, poor 7th 14th, nvr nr to chal* 4
715 Sancreed *rear, ran on stdly 5th 16th, nrst at fin* 5
874 Chandigarh *disp 6th til slght ld 14th, hdd & wknd 3 out* 6
805 Oneovertheight *7th & just in tch 12th, bhnd frm 3 out* 7
923 Phils Pride *cls 6th whn mstk 13th,blndrd bdly nxt,last whn p.u. apr 15th* .... pu
938 Gymcrak Dawn 3ex (bl) *plld hrd, 4th 13th, 5th & pshd alng 3 out, t.o., p.u. last* .... pu
9 ran. 3l, nk, 1l, hd, 1½l, 30l. Time 6m 24.00s. SP 5-1.
Roger Persey (Devon & Somerset Staghounds).

1070 - Maiden Div I (12st)

627 **LADY LIR 5a** .... **Miss S Young** 1
cls 2nd 6th til ld 12th, wll clr 3 out, unchal
555 **Lawd Of Blisland** .... **A Farrant** 2
hld up, hdwy 16th, wnt 2nd 3 out, no imp
718 **Hanukkah 5a** .... **I Hambley** 3
chsd ldrs til wknd & onepcd frm 3 out
928 Dusty Furlong *several postns, 5th 10th, wnt poor 4th 16th, no ch* 4

623 Anvil Corner 5a *(Jt fav) midfld, 7th 12th, rddn nxt, poor 5th & no ch frm 3 out* 5
806 Scallykenning *(Jt fav) in tch, 2nd & mstk 13th, blndrd 15th, btn 6th p.u. apr 3 out* .... pu
718 Charlie's Hideaway (Ire) *keen hold & ld to 12th,wknd qckly & mstk 13th,rear,p.u.15th* .... pu
200 Spartans Dina 7a *hd strng,restrained in rear,last 12th,bhnd whn f hvly16th* .... f
718 Tinstreamer Johnny 7a *towrds rear, bad mstk 9th, bhnd, p.u. apr 13th* .... pu
9 ran. 12l, 3l, 20l, 15l. Time 6m 31.00s. SP 12-1.
B R J Young/ Mrs J Holden-White (East Cornwall).

1071 - Maiden Div II (12st)

875 **MOORLAND HIGHFLYER 7a......Miss D Mitchell** 1
prom, disp frm 12th, just ld cls home
629 **Quick Opinion ....J Young** 2
cls 2nd 7th, disp frm 12th, hrd rddn, no ext cls home
871 **Happy Valley 5a ....Miss P Baker** 3
midfld, pckd bdly 16th, wnt poor 3rd apr 2 out
630 Sixth In Line (Ire) *mid-div, 4th & no ch frm 3 out, walked in* 4
713 Itscountryman *(fav) (7/2-2s),cls 3rd til outpcd 15th, sn btn & eased* 5
714 Zany Girl 5a (bl) *n.j.w., lost tch 15th, reluctant & jmp slwly clsng stgs* 6
Uckerby Lad 7a *pllng & ld 3rd-6th,jmp slwly 7th,bhnd frm 8th til p.u. 11th* .... pu
876 Noddy's Story 5a *not fluent, 7th & outpcd 13th, t.o., p.u. aft 3 out* .... pu
876 Rhyme And Chime 7a *blndrd & u.r. 3rd* .... ur
941 Rose's Lady Day 7a 9ow *imdly t.o., p.u. apr 13th* .... pu
10 ran. Hd, 20l, 10l, 8l, 12l. Time 6m 29.00s. SP 11-4.
Miss P D Mitchell (East Cornwall).

1072 - Ladies

466 **MAJESTIC SPIRIT ....Miss T Cave** 1
j.w., ld apr 9th, ran on strgly whn chal frm 2 out
924 **Khattaf..........................Miss J Cumings** 2
(fav) wnt 2nd 9th, efft to chal 2 out, not qckn clsng stgs
445 **Grey Guestino ....Miss L Delve** 3
prom, cls 3rd 10th, lost grnd stdly frm 3 out
940 Jokers Patch *rear, wnt dist 4th 15th, hit last, virtly p.u. flat* 4
Bidston Mill *nov rddn, alwys towrds rear, t.o., p.u. apr 2 out* .... pu
Baman Powerhouse *ld & sn clr, swrvd lft 7th, hdd 9th, t.o., p.u. apr 13th* .... pu
561 Happy Thought 5a *wnt 4th 12th & just in tch, 5th whn blndrd & u.r. 13th* .... ur
7 ran. 1l, 25l, dist. Time 6m 23.00s. SP 7-1.
Alan Raymond (Blackmore & Sparkford Vale).

1073 - Open (12st)

802 **CHILIPOUR 7ex........................N Harris** 1
hld up in tch, hdwy 12th, ld 3 out, sn qcknd clr, imp
873 **The General's Drum 7ex ....K Heard** 2
(Jt fav) in tch, ld brfly aft 16th, outpcd nxt, styd on clsng stgs
Mystic Gale (Ire) 5a 7ex................L Jefford 3
j.w., slght ld mstly, hdd aft 16th, kpt on wll
671 Myhamet *alwys prom, cls up & ev ch 3 out, outpcd clsng stgs* 4
625 Stormy Sunset 5a *(Jt fav) hld up in tch, gd hdwy to disp 16-17th, sn outpcd* 5
800 Senegalais (Fr) 2ow *towrds rear, 6th frm hlfwy, not able to chal* 6
874 Shalchlo Boy 7ex *rear, jmp slwly 13th, hit 14th, p.u. apr nxt* .... pu
Snuggle 5a *ref 1st* .... ref
927 Far Too Loud 7ex *ref 1st* .... ref
715 Whats The Crack *ref to race* .... ref
10 ran. 5l, 4l, 2l, 6l, 15l. Time 6m 22.00s. SP 3-1.
Nick Viney (Dulverton (West)).

1074 - Intermediate (12st)

627 **TASMIN TYRANT (NZ)...................L Jefford** 1
(fav) j.w., 2nd til ld aft 14th, drew clr 3 out, easily
445 **Rushalong ....A Farrant** 2
hld up, gd hdwy to 3rd 15th,ran on wll und pres clsng stgs
562 **Ticket To The Moon 5a.................K Heard** 3
hld up, hdwy to cls 2nd 14th, ev ch til rddn & outpcd 3 out
936 Baldhu Chance *ld til hdd aft 14th, wknd, eased clsng stgs* 4
Philippastone 7a *s.s., sn t.o. & jmp slwly, fin in own time* 5
925 Querrin Lodge *disp 3rd 10th, poor 5th 13th, t.o., p.u. apr 2 out* .... pu
294 The Kimbler 5ex *in tch til lost plc 11th, 6th whn p.u. apr 13th* .... pu
Oldham Joker *bhnd, p.u. apr 13th* .... pu
937 Moonbay Lady 5a 8ow *bhnd whn p.u. apr 13th* .... pu
9 ran. 2½l, 2l, 25l, 3 fences. Time 6m 22.00s. SP 7-4.
Mrs C Egalton (Axe Vale Harriers).

1075 - Restricted (12st)

875 **KARLIMAY 5a ....K Heard** 1
conf rddn, wnt 3rd 16th, qcknd to ld 2 out, sn clr comf
684 **Quick Quick Sloe 5a................Miss T Cave** 2
(fav) hld up,wnt 2nd 16th,ld nxt,lkd wnr til hdd & no ext 2 out
532 **Northern Sensation 5a................L Jefford** 3
ld/disp frm 4th,ld apr 11th til hdd 3 out,btn whn blnd 2 out
301 Crucis (Ire) 7a *not fluent early, prog to 6th 3 out, nrst at fin,shld imprv* 4
871 Moorland Abbot *mid-div thruout, not pce to chal* 5
715 The Butler *ld til 3rd, 2nd 11-14th, sn wknd* 6
555 Regent Son *towrds rear, bhnd 11th til p.u. aft 3 out* .... pu
807 Four Leaf Clover 5a *disp 3rd-10th, outpcd 15th, disp 3rd whn u.r. last* .... ur
Dinkies Quest 5a *prom til lost plc hlfwy, rear whn f 16th* .... f
718 Tacoment 5a 3ow *wll plc til lost grng 13th, mstk 14th, p.u. bfr nxt* .... pu
Secret Siphoner *sn towrds rear, bhnd, blndrd bdly 14th, p.u. apr nxt* .... pu
711 Mine's A Gin (Ire) 7a *in tch til lost grnd stdly frm 12th,p.u. apr 2 out,schld,imp* .... pu
12 ran. 5l, 10l, 5l, 10l, 6l. Time 6m 38.00s. SP 2-1.
Mrs R Fell (Dartmoor).
G.T.

WEST SOMERSET VALE
Cothelstone
Saturday April 13th
GOOD TO FIRM

1076 - Members

528 **JAFFA'S BOY.......................Miss H Pavey** 1
(fav) ld 11th, wll clr 2 out, easily
Admirals Landing ....Miss S Robinson 2
ld, hit 5th, hdd 11th, wll btn whn u.r. last, rmntd
2 ran. Dist. Time 6m 40.00s. SP 1-3.
Dr Robert Sharpe (West Somerset Vale).

1077 - Restricted (12st)

992 **HIGHWAY JIM.....................Miss M Peck** 1
(fav) made all, mstk 9th, 4l clr 12th, easily
695 **Strong Secret ....S Lloyd** 2
chsd wnr, 4l down 12th, mstk 15th, no ext 2 out
2 ran. 10l. Time 7m 10.00s. SP 2-9.
David Staddon (Cotley).

1078 - Mixed Open (12st)

579 **SEARCY ....J Creighton** 1
4th til prog 15th, ld last, rdn out
626 **Afterkelly 7ex ....R Treloggen** 2
(fav) 3rd til prog to disp 8th, ld 15th, hdd last, no ext

845 **Prince Nepal** .... **G Barfoot-Saunt** 3
2nd early, 3rd at 15th, no ext und pres aft
730 Go West *rear, und pres whn p.u. aft 10th* .... pu
708 Pactolus (USA) *tried to ref & u.r. 1st* .... ur
991 Rapid Rascal *ld to 8th, b.d. bend aft 10th* .... bd
6 ran. 1½l, 20l. Time 6m 23.00s. SP 6-4.
K Haynes (Quantock Staghounds).
Two fences omitted fences, 17 jumps.

1079 - Intermediate (12st)

989 **BRIDGE EXPRESS** .... **Miss H Pavey** 1
made all, clr 10th, 3l clr 3 out, comf
850 **Miss Corinthian 5a** .... **M Flynn** 2
disp 2nd, effrt und pres 14th, no imp wnr
710 **Tango Tom 5ex** .... **M Walters** 3
4th til 2nd frm 8th, rdn 12th, no ext
721 Cautious Rebel *(fav) well in rear, n.j.w. p.u. 2 out* .... pu
993 Springcombe 5a *rear, no ch whn p.u. 2 out* .... pu
5 ran. 6l, 10l. Time 6m 30.00s. SP 7-4.
C T Moate (West Somerset Vale).

1080 - P P O R A (12st)

925 **HENSUE** .... **R Treloggen** 1
(fav) made all, 4l clr 15th, easily
990 **Grey Sonata 5a** .... **I Dowrick** 2
wth wnr to 13th, sn no imp
2 ran. 10l. Time 6m 36.00s. SP 1-6.
Miss P J Boundy (Dulverton East).

1081 - Maiden (12st)

646 **NOTHING TO FEAR** .... **G Barfoot-Saunt** 1
disp til ld 2 out, hld on wll und pres
645 **Noble Minister** .... **M Wells** 2
disp, ld brfly 13th, hdd 2 out, no ext last
732 War Baron *(fav) rear, mstk 15th, no ch whn p.u. last* .. pu
Miss Ricus 7a *alwys rear, p.u. last* .... pu
4 ran. 4l. Time 6m 49.00s. SP 2-1.
Miss A S White (West Somerset).
M.C.

JEDFOREST
Friars Haugh
Sunday April 14th
FIRM

1082 - Members

858 **KALAJO** .... **R Shiels** 1
(fav) chal ldr frm 4 out, upsides last, ld flat
756 **Sweet Sergeant** .... **Miss S Forster** 2
made most til jnd last, outpcd flat
De Grey *plld hrd, ld 8-10th, 3l 2nd whn f nxt* .... f
3 ran. 2l. Time 6m 27.00s. SP 1-3.
M J McGovern (Jedforest).

1083 - Confined (12st)

861 **FREE TRANSFER (IRE)** .... **C Storey** 1
4th hlfwy, ld 4 out, clr 2 out
790 **Secret Sceptre** .... **A Parker** 2
3rd hlfwy, went 2nd 4 out, outpcd frm 3 out
789 **Worthy Spark 6ex** .... **P Craggs** 3
(fav) ld til hdd & wknd 4 out
751 Fordstown (Ire) 15ex *bhnd til some late prog, nvr dang* 4
912 True Fair 6ex *2nd mostly til 10th, grad wknd* 5
610 Reed *nvr rchd ldrs* 6
911 Dancing Legend (Ire) *alwys bhnd* 7
751 Hydropic 4ow *alwys bhnd* 8
861 Music Minstrel (bl) *sn wll bhnd, t.o. whn u.r. last* .... ur
699 Old Comrades *bhnd whn u.r. 9th* .... ur
10 ran. 15l, 3l, 8l, 8l, ½l, 20l, 6l. Time 6m 18.00s. SP 4-1.
D J Fairbairn (Berwickshire).

1084 - Ladies

857 **THE HEALY 5a** .... **Mrs F Scales** 1
made all, drew clr frm 2 out
752 **Marshalstoneswood** .... **Miss A Bowie** 2
chsd wnr frm 11th, outpcd frm 2 out
913 **Furry Venture 5a** .... **Miss D Calder** 3
sn strggling in rear, lft 3rd at last
Golesa *chsd wnr to 10th, sn wknd* 4
702 Wigtown Bay *nvr dang, poor 3rd whn f last* .... f
615 Battle Hero *u.r. 8th* .... ur
913 Flypie *ran out apr 6th* .... ro
790 Ruber *(fav) c.o. apr 6th* .... co
8 ran. 8l, 25l, 20l. Time 6m 26.00s. SP 5-2.
Mrs M Sircus (Percy).

1085 - Open

857 **LOUGHLINSTOWN BOY** .... **P Craggs** 1
sn ld, drew wll clr frm 2 out
912 **Tartan Tornado** .... **P Johnson** 2
chsd wnr frm 9th, outpcd frm 2 out
Miss Enrico 5a .... **A Parker** 3
(fav) 3rd frm 10th, nvr rchd chal pstn
753 Craig Burn 5a *2nd til 9th, sn lost tch* 4
701 Speech *wll bhnd by 11th* 5
612 Dundee Prince (NZ) *reluc to race, ref 1st* .... ref
6 ran. 25l, 2l, dist, 2l. Time 6m 27.00s. SP 9-4.
J A Riddell (Percy).

1086 - Restricted (12st)

914 **LITTLE WENLOCK** .... **Mrs V Jackson** 1
patiently rdn, 4th hlfwy, ld apr last, comf
608 **Funny Feelings** .... **Miss D Laidlaw** 2
2nd mostly, ld brfly 2 out, sn hdd & outpcd
914 **Blakes Folly (Ire)** .... **N Hargreave** 3
5th hlfwy, styd on frm 3 out, not rch 1st pair
858 Anzarna 5a *made most til hdd & wknd 2 out* 4
858 Eastlands Hi-Light *(fav) alwys bhnd, plenty to do whn blnd 15th, no ch aft* 5
860 Fruids Park 5a *last hlfwy, t.o. whn p.u. 2 out* ...... pu
914 Say Milady 5a *cls 3rd whn p.u. aft 10th* .... pu
7 ran. 6l, 4l, 10l, 8l. Time 6m 31.00s. SP 9-4.
Mrs D S C Gibson (Tynedale).

1087 - Open Maiden Div I

789 **CANISTER CASTLE** .... **R Shiels** 1
(fav) alwys handy, ld apr last, kpt on well
755 **Rustic Bridge** .... **S Love** 2
ld frm 9th til hdd & no ext apr last
704 **Warkswoodman** .... **Mrs H Dickson** 3
3rd hlfwy, outpcd 3 out, styd on agn apr last
704 Amanda Bay *ran out 2nd* .... ro
789 Rallying Cry (Ire) *lost tch 12th, p.u. 4 out* .... pu
610 Davimport *made most til 9th, sn wknd, t.o. & p.u. 4 out* .... pu
755 Good Profit *lost tch by 12th, p.u. 4 out* .... pu
756 Red Scot *cls up whn f 14th* .... f
405 Border Glory 7a *u.r. 6th* .... ur
9 ran. 2l, nk. Time 6m 36.00s. SP 6-4.
Miss Z A Green (Jedforest).

1088 - Open Maiden Div II

755 **KINCARDINE BRIDGE (USA)** .... **M Bradburne** 1
(fav) made virt all, drew wll clr frm 2 out
858 **Luvly Bubbly** .... **A Robson** 2
5th hlfwy, styd on frm 4 out, no ch wth wnr
Bagots Park .... **R Shiels** 3
3rd hlfwy, chal wnr 4 out, wknd 2 out
705 Tolmin *6th hlfwy, nvr rchd ldrs* 4
755 Bullaford Fair *2nd hlfwy, cls up til wknd 15th, p.u. apr last* .... pu
Exile Run (Ire) *f 6th* .... f
613 Red Hot Boogie (Ire) *4th hlfwy, styd in tch til wknd 4 out, p.u. 2 out* .... pu
Bavington 7a *sn t.o., p.u. 4 out* .... pu
I'm Joking *nvr nr ldrs, p.u. 2 out* .... pu
Pandandy 7a *sn bhnd, p.u. aft 7th* .... pu
10 ran. 20l, 1½l, 20l. Time 6m 39.00s. SP 5-4.
J G Bradburne (Fife).

1089 - Mares Maiden

755 **SENORA D'OR 5a........................R Shiels** 1
alwys handy, kpt on wll frm 2 out to ld apr last
700 **Royal Fife 5a............................A Parker** 2
patiently rdn, ld 4 out til hdd & no ext apr last
698 **Newbrano 5a (bl)......................P Johnson** 3
ld 14th til 4 out, no ext apr last
913 Zoflo 5a *made most frm 3rd til 14th, no ext frm 3 out..* 4
755 All Or Nothing 5a *ld til u.r. 3rd* ur
704 Little Flo 5a *bhnd by hlfwy, p.u. 4 out* pu
756 Mapalak 5a *(fav) ld brfly 10th, losing plc whn f 12th...* f
756 Saigon Lady (Ire) 5a *f 6th* f
755 The Early Bird 7a *nvr dang, t.o. & p.u. 2 out* pu
615 Seymour Fiddles 7a *in tch whn u.r. 12th* ur
10 ran. 3l, 2l, 15l. Time 6m 41.00s. SP 16-1.
Mrs Ann Rutherford (Lauderdale).
R.J.

MIDDLETON
Whitwell-On-The-Hill
Sunday April 14th
GOOD

1090 - Restricted (12st)

584 **KENILWORTH (IRE)......................C Mulhall** 1
alwys prom, ld 4 out, sn clr, styd on strngly
985 **Attle ....S Brisby** 2
rear, prog to chs ldrs 5 out, styd on well frm 2 out
758 **Honest Expression 5a................P Atkinson** 3
alwys prom, ld brfly 10th, onepcd frm 3 out
823 Basil Grey *trckd ldrs, ld 11th til jnd 4 out, fdd nxt, onepcd* 4
983 Advent Lady 5a *ld 2nd-10th, steadily fdd frm 12th* 5
827 Earl Gray (bl) *trckd ldrs, onepcd frm 13th* 6
758 Barichste *mid-div, prog 13th, no hdwy aft, onepcd.* 7
895 Douce Eclair 5a *drppd out rear, imprvd 9th, no prog aft, wknd 14th* 8
1010 Im Ok (Ire) 5a *sttld mid-div, prog 8th, fdd frm 12th, sn wknd* 9
828 Acropol 5a *rear, dtchd frm 3rd, nvr a fctr* 10
983 Cadrillon (Fr) *alwys rear, nvr dang, t.o.* 11
952 Pepperbox 5a *chsd ldrs til wknd 12th, t.o.* 12
895 The Ginger Tom *f 1st* f
585 Mr Elk *mid-div, blnd 10th, p.u. nxt* pu
635 Kamadora *mid-div, drppd rear 7th, rallied 11th, sn wknd, p.u. 3 out* pu
590 Wolvercastle 5a *(fav) mid-div, prog 13th, chal 4 out, sn onepcd, 2nd & btn, f last* f
763 Pendle Witch 5a *mid-div, mstk 3rd, drppd rear 6th, t.o. & p.u. 3 out* pu
17 ran. 10l, 3l, 5l, 4l, 7l, 6l, 8l, 2l, 3l, ½l. Time 6m 29.00s. SP 4-1.
Mrs D D Osborne (Holderness).

1091 - P P O R A (12st)

585 **LATHERON (IRE) ....S Swiers** 1
(fav) hld up rear, prog to trck ldrs 4 out, rdn 2 out, ld nr fin
588 **Polynth ....H Brown** 2
mid-div, prog 11th, chal 5 out, ld nxt, mstk last, hdd flat
761 **Fowling Piece ....Miss L Horner** 3
disp,ld 3rd at slw pace,qcknd clr 13th,hdd aft 14th,kpt on
584 Stag Fight *sttld mid-div, ev ch 5 out, onepcd nxt* 4
824 Some Flash *trckd ldrs, disp 9th, mstk nxt, sn fdd, t.o. & p.u. last* pu
983 City Buzz (Ire) *disp ld til mstk 4th, lost plc 7th, wknd 10th, p.u. 4 out* pu
6 ran. 1l, 1½l, 12l. Time 6m 32.00s. SP 1-2.
Mrs A M Easterby (Middleton).

1092 - Confined

761 **CASTLE TYRANT 5a ....P Atkinson** 1
disp to 5 out, rallied to ld 3 out, rdn & ran on well
587 **Peanuts Pet..........................R Walmsley** 2
rear, prog 7th, effrt 4 out, rdn & styd on nxt
824 **Cromwell Point ....N Wilson** 3
mid-div, prog to jn ldrs 12th, onepcd frm 4 out
985 Just Charlie *(fav) alwys prom, ld 5 out-3 out, no ext...* 4
701 Elegant Guest *trckd ldrs til lost plc 10th, wkng whn u.r. 13th* ur
587 Minstrel Paddy *rear whn mstk 8th, wknd 13th, t.o. & p.u. 2 out* pu
585 Caman 5a 4ow *rear & dtchd 3rd, sn t.o., p.u. 2 out* pu
1000 Durham Hornet *disp to 5 out, wknd rpdly, t.o. & p.u. 2 out* pu
824 Gold Choice *prom til lost plc 7th, sn t.o., p.u. 4 out* pu
241 Hasty Cruise *rear & mstk 10th, mod prog 13th, sn wknd, t.o. & p.u. 2 out* pu
10 ran. 2l, 5l, 2l. Time 6m 27.00s. SP 8-1.
S Clark (Bedale (West Of Yore)).

1093 - 4m Mixed Open (12st)

825 **HIGHLAND FRIEND ....P Atkinson** 1
prom, disp 13th-16th, rallied to ld last, jnd fin,plcd 1st
1000 **Cot Lane (bl) ....R Walmsley** 2
(fav) prom,disp 7th-16th,ran on to ld 4 out,hdd last,rallied fin
760 **Hyperion Son...........................M Haigh** 3
wth ldrs, disp 7-13th, ld 16th-4 out, onepcd
826 Convincing (v) *alwys wll there, ev ch 4 out, wknd nxt* 4
585 The Chap *alwys trckng ldrs, lost plc frm 19th* 5
585 Political Sam *alwys bhnd, t.o. 17th* 6
894 Clare Lad *mid-div, wll bhnd frm 18th, t.o.* 7
759 Linebacker *trckd ldng grp til wknd 14th, f 4 out* f
982 G Derek *rear & lost tch 12th, sn t.o., p.u. 2 out* pu
824 Tammy My Girl 5a *mid-div whn b.d. 6th* bd
586 Katies Argument 5a *mid-div whn b.d. 6th* bd
826 Frome Boy *s.v.s. rear whn b.d. 6th* bd
723 The Difference *chsd ldrs til b.d. 6th* bd
Polishing *ref 1st* ref
587 Oaksey *mid-div, prog 14th, ev ch whn f nxt* f
1009 Castle Cross *alwys rear, blnd 15th, p.u. nxt* pu
224 Scampton (bl) *ld til f 6th* f
760 Gaelic Warrior *rear, prog 9th, no hdwy aft, fdng whn u.r. 15th* ur
589 Oaklands Fred *t.o. 7th, p.u. 17th* pu
19 ran. Sht-hd, 15l, 25l, 1½l, 7l, 15l. Time 8m 47.00s. SP 8-1.
Henry Bell (Bilsdale).
Stewards' Enquiry, result stands.

1094 - 2½m 88yds Open Maiden (5-7yo) Div I (12st)

589 **RYE HEAD 7a...............................N Tutty** 1
prom, ld 7th-10th, ld agn 4 out, drew wll clr, easily
987 **Rich Asset (Ire).......................G Markham** 2
mid-div, late prog frm 3 out, styd on to tk 2nd cls hm
762 **River Ramble 5a ....Miss T Jackson** 3
alwys prom, no prog frm 3 out, onepcd
331 Mount Faber *prom, ld 10th, hdd 4 out, onepcd aft* 4
762 Chuckleberry *prom til onepcd frm 4 out* 5
764 Hutcel Bell 7a *alwys twrds rear, bhnd frm 3 out* 6
591 Stays Fresh *twrds rear, nvr a threat* 7
413 Blank Cheque *bhnd & sn t.o.* 8
764 Private Jet (Ire) *mid-div whn f 7th* f
589 Lingcool 5a *chsd ldrs, mod prog 4 out, sn wknd, p.u. last* pu
589 Grange Gracie 5a *mid-div whn u.r. 7th* ur
411 Shore Lane *mid-div, prog 7th, ev ch 5 out, wknd nxt, p.u. last* pu
590 Boulevard Bay (Ire) 7a *(fav) rear, t.o. & p.u. 10th* pu
704 King Fly *prom, ld 5th, hdd nxt, prom aft, und pres & btn whn f 2 out* f
589 Just Takethe Micky *ld, mstk 4th, hdd nxt, sn lost plc, t.o. & p.u. 10th* pu
953 Gunner Be A Lady 5a *rear, t.o. & p.u. 4 out* pu
16 ran. 20l, ½l, 5l, 2l, 3l, 12l, 3l. Time 5m 21.00s. SP 5-1.
Mrs K Tutty (Hurworth).

1095 - 2½m 88yds Open Maiden (5-7yo) Div II (12st)

764 **LIVING ON THE EDGE (IRE) ....N Tutty** 1

rear, prog rpdly to ld 7th, sn drew wll clr, easily
987 **Rise Above It (Ire) ....S Brisby** 2
(fav) ld til wd & hdd apr 7th,sn drppd bck,prog 5 out,2nd 2 out
987 **Pure Madness (USA) (bl)..............R Edwards** 3
keen hold, chsd ldrs, outpcd 5 out, kpt on 2 out
705 Malakie (Ire) *nvr bttr than mid-div* 4
229 Ship The Builder *rear, gd prog to chs ldrs 10th, no imp aft* 5
986 Morcat 5a *alwys prom, remote 2nd 3 out, sn wknd* ... 6
987 Fleeced *mid-div til wknd 5 out* 7
589 Auntie Fay (Ire) 7a *jmpd slwly 1st, t.o. & p.u. 10th* ..... pu
764 Canny's Fort 5a *mid-div whn f 7th* .... f
Makin' Doo (Ire) *rear, t.o. 8th, p.u. 10th* .... pu
406 Olympic Class *rear whn f 7th* .... f
987 High Mill *alwys rear, t.o. & p.u. 10th* .... pu
590 Just Jessica 5a *alwys rear, t.o. & p.u. 8th* .... pu
718 Just Johnie *chsd ldrs til wknd 7th, t.o. & p.u. 3 out*.... pu
14 ran. Dist, 20l, 4l, 1l, 2l, 3l. Time 5m 20.00s. SP 4-1.
Mrs D Ibbotson (York & Ainsty South).

1096 - Members (12st)

763 **RUFF ACCOUNT ....C Brader** 1
made all, styd on strngly frm 2 out, gamely
1000 **Jasilu 5a (bl) ....S Swiers** 2
(Jt fav) plldn hrd in rear, prog 10th, ev ch 2 out, kpt on flat
538 **Kellys Diamond ....N Wilson** 3
mid-div, prog 7th, chal 2 out, onepcd
986 Prophet's Choice *alwys prom, ev ch til fdd 3 out* 4
Commander Swaine 19ow *chsd ldrs, wknd 8th, sn t.o.* 5
Playboy *alwys wll in rear, u.r. 9th* .... ur
Hurricane Linda 5a *(Jt fav) hld up rear, f 2nd* .... f
Jeune Garcon (Ire) 7a *mid-div, blnd 10th, p.u. nxt*..... pu
Ruben 5ow *rear, t.o. 4th, p.u. 7th*............ pu
9 ran. ½l, 4l, 12l, 2 fences. Time 6m 35.00s. SP 5-1.
R G Brader (Middleton).
N.E.

PYTCHLEY
Guilsborough
Sunday April 14th
GOOD

1097 - Members

723 **TENELORD.............................S Morris** 1
mstk 7th,ld to 13th & frm 15th,clr 3 out,rdn & lft clr last
438 **Teeton Nishaball 5a ....R Barrett** 2
(fav) prssd wnr 9th,ld 13th til mstk 15th,btn 3 out,lft 2nd last
723 **Hostetler ....J Stephenson** 3
bhnd frm 6th, t.o. 13th
897 Jerrigo *cls up til u.r. bnd apr 5th* .... ur
727 Supreme Dream (Ire) 5a *hld up,mod 3rd 12th,chsd wnr 2 out,clsng fast whn u.r. last*............ ur
900 See The Lord (Ire) *chsd wnr to 9th, wkng whn mstk 11th, p.u. nxt* .... pu
6 ran. 25l, dist. Time 6m 34.00s. SP 2-1.
C R Saunders (Pytchley).

1098 - Confined (12st)

638 **HILL ISLAND ....R Sweeting** 1
alwys prom, lft in ld 14th, hdd 4 out, drvn to ld flat
726 **Mr Branigan (Ire) ....T Marks** 2
(fav) trckd ldrs,prog to ld 16th,1l up whn mstk last,sn hdd,ralld
683 **Hobnobber ....J Docker** 3
prog & prom 9th,chsd ldng pair 16th,styd on onepcd frm 3 out
725 The Dancing Parson 5a 2ow *mstks, prom to 12th, sn strgglng, kpt on agn frm 2 out* 4
901 Kenalan Lad *14s-8s, lft in ld 1st, blnd & hdd 14th, not rcvr* 5
434 Bervie House (Ire) *prom, mstk 13th, rdn in 5th & btn apr 3 out, wknd* 6
793 Sevens Out 8ex *novie rdn, alwys wll bhnd, t.o. 9th, nvr nrr* 7
725 Decent Gold *bhnd & sn drvn alng, t.o. 9th, nvr on terms* 8
723 Lad Lane 1ow *alwys rear, t.o. 12th* 9
722 Arpal Breeze *rear til b.d. by loose horse 6th* .... bd
899 Teacake (bl) *alwys wll bhnd, t.o. 10th, p.u. 3 out* ...... pu
899 Blue Beat 5a *hmpd 6th, in tch til 7th & btn whn p.u. 3 out* .... pu
639 Tumbril *mid-div, ran wd bnd apr 9th, p.u. & dsmntd*... pu
636 Ruff Song *lft 30l start, rcvrd to jnd rear of grp, 10th whn u.r. 10th* .... ur
676 Royal Survivor *ld, blnd & u.r. 1st* .... ur
641 Copper Bank *hld up, mstks 6th & nxt, bhnd frm 9th, t.o. & p.u. 13th* .... pu
642 Sabre King (bl) *chsd ldrs, in tch 13th, btn whn p.u. 15th* .... pu
17 ran. Nk, 5l, 25l, 4l, 4l, 10l, 15l, ¾l. Time 6m 28.00s. SP 20-1.
Colin Gee (Heythrop).

1099 - Ladies

777 **DUNBOY CASTLE (IRE) ....Miss G Chown** 1
(fav) trckd ldrs, ld 16th, clr 2 out, comf
723 **Okeetee..............................Mrs J Dawson** 2
prom, ld 9-11th, outpcd 14th, rallied apr 3 out, onepcd nxt
East River ....Mrs K Sunderland 3
rear, pshd alng & prog 13th, chsd ldng pair 2 out, onepcd
903 Loose Wheels (bl) *mstks, mid-div, outpcd 14th, kpt on onepcd frm 3 out* 4
486 Ballyandrew *ld to 9th & 11-16th, wknd 3 out, tired*.... 5
903 Winged Whisper (USA) *prom to 15th, sn wknd* 6
Sanamar *rear frm 10th, last & wll btn whn f 3 out*...... f
725 Padrigal 5a *bhnd frm 8th, t.o. & p.u. 16th* .... pu
951 Air Commander *hld up, prog 9th, cls 5th whn blnd & u.r. 13th* .... ur
9 ran. 10l, 5l, 12l, 2l, 8l. Time 6m 31.00s. SP Evens.
Miss Gi Chown (Essex & Suffolk).

1100 - Open

904 **COOLVAWN LADY (IRE) 5a...............T Lane** 1
ld 6-7th & frm 15th, jnd 2 out, ld last, hld on gamely
709 **Trifast Lad............................P Hacking** 2
prom, ld 7-15th, jnd wnr 2 out, kpt on flat, just hld
672 **Brown Windsor (bl) ....B Pollock** 3
(fav) trckd ldrs, chal 13th, 3rd & rdn 3 out, kpt on flat
723 Glen Oak *mid-div, rdn 11th, outpcd 14th, kpt on* 4
897 Current Attraction 5a *chsd ldrs, outpcd frm 15th, no imp on ldrs aft* 5
903 Directly *jmpd badly, t.o. & p.u. 7th* .... pu
897 Kellys Pal *ld til hdd & blnd 6th, sn rdn, t.o. & p.u. 13th* pu
634 Blue Aeroplane *in tch til mstks 11 & 12th, t.o. 14th, p.u. 2 out* .... pu
579 Falconbridge Bay *mstk 1st, chsd ldrs, in tch whn blnd 15th, t.o. & p.u. 2 out* .... pu
9 ran. 1l, 1½l, 10l, 1l. Time 6m 34.00s. SP 9-2.
W R Halliday (Cranwell Bloodhounds).

1101 - Restricted Div I (12st)

960 **ALIAS SILVER.......................Miss H Irving** 1
rear, gd prog 13th, ld 3 out, styd on wll frm nxt, rdn out
682 **Hurricane Gilbert ....N Bloom** 2
wll in tch, chsd ldrs 16th, ran on onepcd frm 2 out
726 **Hill Fort (Ire)...........................B Pollock** 3
prom, lft in ld 13-15th & agn aft nxt-3 out,hrd rdn,onepcd
641 Tarry Awhile *mstks, bhnd & pshd alng hlfwy, styd on frm 3 out, nrst fin* 4
338 Tapalong 5a *bhnd, prog 12th, chsd ldrs 16th, kpt on, lame* 5
617 Miss Cresta 5a *mstk 3rd, rear, no imp on ldrs 16th, kpt on* 6
904 Kerry My Home *trckd ldrs, effrt & 4th apr 3 out, wknd nxt* 7
904 Grange Missile 5a *rear, prog & in tch 14th, sn wknd, t.o.* 8

726 Crawn Hawk *(fav) ld 5th, 2l up whn blnd & u.r. 13th* ... ur
641 Singing Clown 5a *mstk 3rd, alwys bhnd, t.o. & p.u. 13th* ... pu
Sinberto 5a *ld to 5th, prom til wknd rpdly & p.u. 13th* pu
641 This I'll Do Us (Ire) *mid-div, 7th & in tch whn blnd & u.r. 14th* ... ur
904 Smart Rhythm 5a *in tch to 13th, t.o. & p.u. 3 out* ... pu
437 Saffron Gale (Ire) *prom, ld 15th til p.u. aft nxt, broke down* ... pu
Rakish Queen 5a *6th whn u.r. 6th* ... ur
901 Another Comedy *mstks, alwys rear, lost tch hlfwy, t.o. & p.u. last* ... pu
16 ran. 2½l, 1l, 2½l, 4l, 6l, 8l, 1 fence. Time 6m 38.00s. SP 20-1.
J H Busby (Grafton).

1102 - Restricted Div II (12st)

564 **FURRY FOX (IRE) ... A Crow** 1
prom, ld 9-13th, ld agn aft 2 out, forged clr
128 **Rain Down ... A Hill** 2
prom, ld 13th til aft 2 out, no ch wth wnr aft
665 **Cader Idris ... G Tarry** 3
mstks, ld til blnd 9th, lost tch whn blnd 15th, styd on 2out
904 Linlake Lightning 5a *mstks, wll bhnd hlfwy, t.o. 16th, styd on wll frm 3 out* ... 4
495 Canadian Boy (Ire) *chsd ldrs, rdn 9th, mstk 14th, wll btn 3 out* ... 5
618 Tomorrow's Times *trckd ldrs going wll, mstks 13 & 15th, btn frm nxt* ... 6
684 Upton Orbit *(fav) mid-div, out of tch & rdn hlfwy, nvr rchd ldrs* ... 7
897 Menature (Ire) *rear hlfwy,lost tch 13th,kpt on,disp poor 4th whn blnd last* ... 8
Why Not Flopsy 5a *alwys wll bhnd, t.o. hlfwy, no real prog* ... 9
748 Home To Tara *alwys rear, t.o. last 3 out, p.u. last* ... pu
Polo Prince *in tch to 8th, sn wknd, t.o. & p.u. 12th* ... pu
904 Whinstone Mill *wth ldrs til reluc frm 15th, t.o. & p.u. 2 out* ... pu
Sporting Lark 5a *alwys bhnd, t.o. & p.u. 14th* ... pu
680 Kings Romance 5a *drppd out aft 6th, t.o. 9th, p.u. 11th* ... pu
Coptic Dancer 5a *alwys bhnd, t.o. & p.u. 13th* ... pu
15 ran. 10l, 6l, 20l, 2l, nk, 2l, 10l, 2l. Time 6m 35.00s. SP 8-1.
E H Crow (North Shropshire).

1103 - Maiden Div I

727 **CHACER'S IMP ... B Pollock** 1
(Jt fav) alwys prom, ld 3 out, clr nxt, hld on nr fin
899 **Cormeen Lord (Ire) ... J Sharp** 2
prom, chal & mstk 3 out, rallied aft nxt, just faild
967 **Full Song 5a ... S Morris** 3
hld up bhnd, steady prog frm 13th, kpt on to tk 3rd aft last
689 Plateman *clr ldr til wknd & hdd 3 out, lame* ... 4
904 Coolsythe 5a *alwys bhnd, t.o. & p.u. 10th* ... pu
890 Apple Nicking *race wd, ldng grp, wknd 15th, bhnd whn p.u. 3 out* ... pu
680 Tarry No More 5a *chsd ldrs, mstk 7th, wknd & p.u. 16th* ... pu
440 Lucky Crest 5a *blnd badly 6th, wll bhnd hlfwy, t.o. & p.u. 15th* ... pu
959 Crestafair 5a *rear, lost tch hlfwy, t.o. & p.u. 14th* ... pu
439 Butlers Match (Ire) *(Jt fav) mstk 3rd, chsd ldrs, wknd 15th, t.o. & p.u. last* ... pu
898 Reel Rascal 5a *s.s. mstks, alwys rear, t.o. & p.u. 15th* pu
727 Dante's Pride (Ire) *chsd ldr to 6th, wknd rpdly 9th, t.o. & p.u. 13th* ... pu
682 Broadway Swinger 7a *s.s. bhnd til prog 10th, 5th & in tch whn p.u. 15th, improve* ... pu
Orton Actress 5a *mstks, rear til prog & in tch 13th, wknd & p.u. 15th* ... pu
904 Just Like Madge (bl) *t.d.e. alwys bhnd, t.o. & p.u. 13th* ... pu
15 ran. Nk, 20l, 1½l. Time 6m 37.00s. SP 2-1.
Michael Farnan (Bicester With Whaddon Chase).

1104 - Maiden Div II

689 **HEHAS ... C Wadland** 1
(fav) alwys prom, ld apr 3 out, styd on well und pres
856 **Mr Gee ... L Hicks** 2
prom, chsd wnr 3 out, chal frm nxt, not qckn apr last
901 **Dark Rhytham ... S Morris** 3
ld 3rd-12th, chsng aft, no imp frm 3 out
Stab In The Dark *prom, ld 12th-3 out, wknd, fin tired* ... 4
712 Spring Sabre *mstks, hld up, some prog 11th, nvr rchd ldrs* ... 5
Sparkling Clown 5a *mid-div, jmpd slwly 5th, in tch to 14th, no dang aft,improve* ... 6
903 Sea Clipper (Ire) *alwys well in rear, t.o. whn mstk 11th* ... 7
Turkish Island 5a *alwys wll bhnd, t.o. & p.u. 14th* ... pu
Arley Gale 5a *mid-div, f 5th* ... f
723 Cleric On Broadway (Ire) 5a *mstks, alwys bhnd, t.o. 11th, p.u. 3 out* ... pu
898 Bucklelone 5a *rear frm 7th, t.o. & p.u. 15th* ... pu
495 Petoski Bay *trckd ldrs, cls 5th whn f 14th* ... f
681 Holding The Aces *bmpd & u.r. 1st* ... ur
901 Remalone 5a *ld to 3rd, wknd 8th, t.o. whn blnd 10th, p.u. 12th* ... pu
440 Tiger *prom to 11th, wknd rpdly, t.o. & p.u. 3 out* ... pu
540 Eazy Peazy (Ire) *rear,prog & in tch 11th, 5th & btn 4 out, t.o. & p.u. 2 out* ... pu
898 Malvern Lad *rear, prog & in tch 11th, 6th & btn 4 out, p.u. nxt* ... pu
Seaton Mill *mid-div, f 5th* ... f
18 ran. 1l, 15l, 5l, 15l, 1l, 20l. Time 6m 41.00s. SP 7-2.
Mrs E C Cockburn (Warwickshire).

1105 - Maiden Div III

897 **OH SO WINDY 5a ... S Morris** 1
(fav) prom, ld 9-15th & frm 3 out, sn clr, unchal
Bubbly Boy ... G Tarry 2
mid-div,outpcd & poor 4th 16th,styd on wll 2 out,tk 2nd last
Foolish Soprano 5a ... John Pritchard 3
w.w. prog to ld 15th, hdd & wknd 3 out
900 Oliver Himself 7a 1ow *prom, ld 7-9th, mstk 11th, ev ch apr 3 out, wknd, improve* ... 4
522 Never So Lost *prom til wknd 13th, t.o.* ... 5
904 Great Legend 1ow *trckd ldrs, cls 5th whn u.r. 13th* ... ur
901 Batcho Missile *plld hrd,hld up bhnd,prog 10th,last & wkng whn f 15th* ... f
Strong Account (Ire) *prom whn u.r. 2nd* ... ur
Witch Doctor *made most to 7th, wknd rpdly, t.o. & p.u. 12th* ... pu
Singh Song 5a *rear, effrt 9th, rdn 12th, sn wknd & p.u. nxt* ... pu
Beachborough *plIng, hld up, bhnd frm 10th, blnd badly 12th & p.u.* ... pu
632 Nearly There (Ire) 5a *t.o. 9th, p.u. 11th* ... pu
12 ran. 15l, 5l, 1l, 15l. Time 6m 46.00s. SP Evens.
Rupert Cottrell (Pytchley).
J.N.

HEXHAM
Monday April 15th
GOOD TO FIRM

1106 - 3m 1f Mdn Hun Chase

861 **ACROSS THE CARD 12.0 7a ... Capt W Ramsay** 1
held up in tch, effort after 3 out, left in ld between last 2, styd on strly.
Amadeus (Fr) 12.4 3a ... Mr C Bonner 2
in tch, effort before 2 out, chsd wnr between last two, no impn.
914 **Wire Lass 11.9 7a ... Mr R Morgan** 3
ld to 3rd, cl up, led 16th, soon hdd, wknd between last 2.
582 Birtley Girl 11.9 7a *ld 3rd, mstk 15th, hdd next, wknd quickly after 3 out, t.o. when blnd last* ... 4
764 Niad 12.2 5a *chasing ldrs when blnd 10th (water), soon lost tch, p.u. before 13th* ... pu
703 Sarona Smith 12.2 *soon well bhnd, t.o. when p.u. before 12th* ... pu

367 Admission (Ire) 12.0 7a *chsd ldrs till blnd and u.r. 7th.* .... ur
588 Quayside Cottage (Ire) 12.2 5a *(fav) well bhnd early, steady hdwy after hfwy, ev ch 3 out, wknd after next and p.u. lame* .... pu
702 Stilltodo 11.9 7a *chsd ldrs, ld after 16th, just ahd when tk wrong course between last 2* .... ro
9 ran. 7l, 19l, dist. Time 6m 39.60s. SP 9-2.
Capt W B Ramsay

SOUTHWELL
Monday April 15th
GOOD

1107 - 3m 110yds Nov Hun Chase

670 **COLONIAL KELLY 12.4 3a ....Mr P Hacking** 1
(fav) made all, hit 4th, hrd pressed final 3, gamely.
971 **Ryders Wells 11.9 5a..............Mr A Sansome** 2
pressed wnr, ev ch from 3 out, one pace after last.
798 **A Windy Citizen (Ire) 11.9 7a ....Mr R Hicks** 3
mstks, held up, smooth hdwy to chase ldrs 5 out, hung left 3 out, btn next.
897 Beau Dandy 11.7 7a *nvr far away, pushed along 14th, btn last 3* 4
788 Phil's Dream 11.7 7a *in tch, rdn along after 12th, outpcd last 4* 5
907 Timber's Boy 12.0 7a *held up, rdn and outpcd final cct, nvr able to chal* 6
1000 R N Commander 11.7 7a *chsd ldrs, lost pl before 10th, soon struggling, p.u. before 13th* .... pu
580 Vulcan Star 11.9 5a *in rear when blnd and u.r. 2nd* .... ur
564 Emma Clew (Ire) 11.2 7a *bhnd when blnd and u.r. 11th* .... ur
674 Peppermill Lane 11.7 7a *in tch, blnd 9th, soon struggling, t.o. when p.u. before 3 out* .... pu
10 ran. 3l, 6l, 7l, 1¾l, 3l. Time 6m 29.00s. SP 11-8.
Cockerell Cowing Racing

CHELTENHAM
Wednesday April 17th
GOOD TO SOFT

1108 - 4m 1f Hun Chase

669 **HOLLAND HOUSE 12.2 5a...........Mr C Vigors** 1
(fav) alwys prom, blnd 1st, ld after 3rd, mstk 12th, hdd 19th, challenging when hit 4 out, led apr last, ran on.
808 **Hermes Harvest 12.4 3a............Mr C Bonner** 2
not fluent, held up, hdwy 11th, mstk 4 out, ld apr 2 out, hdd before last, no ext.
854 **Catchapenny 11.10 7a (bl) ......Mr W Tellwright** 3
alwys prom, lost pl 4 out, styd on after 2 out.
626 Nearly Splendid 11.7 7a *alwys in tch, ld 19th, hdd after 3 out, mstk next, soon wknd* 4
909 Woodlands Genhire 11.7 7a (v) *mid div when mstks 11th and 13th, bhnd final cct, t.o.* 5
798 Paco's Boy 11.7 7a *well bhnd from 18th, t.o.* 6
672 Professor Longhair 11.7 7a *alwys bhnd, t.o.* 7
637 Space Man 11.10 7a 3ow *bhnd when mstk 8th, t.o.* 8
805 Lonesome Traveller (NZ) 11.7 7a *alwys bhnd, mstk 14th, t.o.* 9
907 Faringo 11.10 7a *alwys bhnd, t.o.* 10
784 Blue Danube (USA) 11.7 7a *ld till after 3rd, mstk 11th, bhnd when blnd 18th, p.u. before next* .... pu
808 New Mill House 11.7 7a *t.o. 9th, p.u. before 19th* .... pu
908 Tekla (Fr) 11.7 7a *prom, mstk 10th, wknd when mistake 17th, blnd 20th, p.u. before 22nd* .... pu
672 Clare Man (Ire) 11.7 7a *prom, weakening when mstks 21st and next, t.o. when p.u. before 2 out* .... pu
14 ran. 7l, 2½l, 7l, dist, 13l, hd, dist, 19l. Time 9m 0.80s. SP 6-4.
E Knight

TIVERTON
Hockworthy
Wednesday April 17th
GOOD TO SOFT

1109 - Members

801 **LARKY MCILROY 5a ....L Jefford** 1
ld 4th, made most aft, mstk 14th, lft wl clr 2 out
Gratuity ....R Payne 2
ld to 4th, wth wnr to 12th, btn 14th, lft 2nd 2 out
871 **Polly's Corner 5a ....R Emmett** 3
in tch to 12th, btn 14th, lft 3rd 2 out
927 Magnolia Man *(fav) w.w., tckd wnr 12th, mstk 14th, ev ch whn f 2 out* .... f
4 ran. 20l, 12l. Time 6m 45.20s. SP 5-1.
D Luxton (Tiverton Foxhounds).

1110 - Confined

988 **FAITHFUL STAR.................Miss S Vickery** 1
(fav) prog 5th, trckd ldr 10th, ld 15th, drvn out flat
708 **Interpretation (NZ)...................N Harris** 2
prog 6th, chsd wnr 2 out, hrd rdn & ran on, just held
655 **Friendly Lady 5a ....Miss A Bush** 3
sn mid-div, 4th & outpcd 12th, kpt on to mod 3rd post
925 Flame O'Frensi 5a *ld to 15th, 3rd & btn frm 2 out, wknd* 4
671 Expressment *rr, eff to 5th hlfwy, sn lost tch, walked in* 5
818 Kiltonga *rr, lost tch & p.u. aft 11th* .... pu
925 Bert House *chsd ldr to 10th, wknd, 6th whn f 13th* .... f
925 Bincombe Top *alwys rr, 8th & out of tch whn u.r. 11th* ur
647 Be My Habitat (bl) *n.j.w., alwys bhnd, t.o. & u.r. 15th* .... ur
9 ran. 1l, 25l, sht-hd, 25l. Time 6m 28.90s. SP Evens.
M C Pipe (Taunton Vale Harriers).

1111 - Mixed Open (12st)

655 **FLAKED OATS ....Miss P Curling** 1
(fav) early rmndrs, rr, prog to ld aft 13th, clr last, rdn out
581 **Alpine Song 5a.................Miss V Stephens** 2
33s-14s, cls up, ld brfly 13th, prsd wnr aft, no ex app last
1013 **Some-Toy.....................Miss L Blackford** 3
mstks, w.w., prog 13th, 3rd & in tch whn blndrd 2 out, no ex
671 Full Alirt 5a *w.w, prog 12th, outpcd 15th, kpt on one pace* 4
1059 My Mellow Man 7ex (bl) *whpd rnd strt, in tch, hrd rdn to ld 12th, hdd & btn nxt* 5
1037 Sandy Beau 7ex *ld to 9th, outpcd frm 12th, no dang aft* 6
1043 Chibougama (USA) *cls up, chsd ldr 10th, sn outpcd & no ch* 7
1078 Pactolus (USA) *reluct to race, bhnd & nrly ref 7th, t.o. & f 9th* .... f
815 Kings Rank 4ex (bl) *prom, ld 9-12th, wknd rpdly, t.o. & ref 15th* .... ref
Dibloom 7ex *in tch to 10th, lost pl, t.o. & p.u. 14th* .... pu
927 Bargain And Sale *prom to 10th, wkng whn mstk 13th, t.o. & p.u. last* .... pu
If You Say So 7ex *sn last & nvr gng wl, t.o. & u.r. 7th* ur
990 Russell Rover *prom to 7th, t.o. & p.u. 11th* .... pu
13 ran. 8l, 8l, 2l, 3l, 12l, hd. Time 6m 32.40s. SP Evens.
E B Swaffield (Cattistock).

1112 - P P O R A (12st)

795 **TINOTOPS ....Miss S Vickery** 1
(fav) cls up, ld 15th, clr last, drvn out
269 **Calling Wild (Ire)......................T Mitchell** 2
mstks, hld up, chsd wnr aft 2 out, hrd rdn & ran on
707 **Bet With Baker (Ire) ....Miss P Curling** 3
hld up, prog 8th, mstks 12th & nxt, 4th & btn 2 out, kpt on
804 The Pedlar 5a *ld 3rd-6th & 9-15th, chsd wnr til wknd aft 2 out* 4
709 Getaway Blake *ld to 3rd, outpcd 12th, ran on agn 14th, btn whn mstk 2 out* 5
866 Beinn Mohr 5a *ld 6th til hdd & mstk 9th, bhnd 13th, rdn out flat* 6

684 Perseverance *in tch til outpcd 12th, no ch aft, t.o. & p.u. last* .... pu
926 Remember Mac (bl) *mstk 1st, prom, rdn & wknd 10th, p.u. 12th* .... pu
Nice To No *s.s., t.o. & jmpd bdly til p.u. 11th* .... pu
9 ran. 1½l, 10l, 6l, 6l. Time 6m 33.80s. SP 9-4.
R H H Targett (Blackmore & Sparkford Vale).

1113 - Restricted Div I (12st)

607 **DAUPHIN BLEU (FR)........J Jukes** 1
made all, clr 12th, blndrd 2 out, impressive
822 **Definite Maybe (Ire) (bl) ....T Mitchell** 2
w.w., rmnds 4th, chsd wnr 13th, no imp 2 out, wknd, eased
562 **Swing To The Left (Ire) 5a ......Miss J Cumings** 3
prom, chsd wnr 11-13th, 3rd & btn frm nxt
805 The Copper Key *chsd ldrs, 4th & outpcd frm 13th, no prog aft* 4
992 Great Impostor *rr, t.o. 10th, kpt on late* 5
807 Blakeington (bl) *alwys bhnd, t.o. frm 10th* 6
822 Prince Amanda *mstk 1st, last whn u.r. 2nd* .... ur
650 Brendan's Way (Fr) (bl) *chsd wnr to 11th, wkng whn blndrd nxt & p.u.* .... pu
926 Link Copper *chsd ldrs to 8th, sn strgglng, t.o. & p.u. 14th* .... pu
627 Well Timed *(fav) rr, rdn 10th, 7th whn blndrd 11th, no ch & p.u. 14th* .... pu
993 Glamorous Guy *rr frm 8th, t.o. & p.u. 13th* .... pu
11 ran. 25l, 10l, 12l, hd, dist. Time 6m 32.60s. SP 5-2.
Miss Victoria Roberts (Berkeley).

1114 - Restricted Div II (12st)

868 **ERME ROSE (IRE) 5a........R Nuttall** 1
made all, rdn clr app last, ran on well
656 **Clandon Lad........T Mitchell** 2
(fav) hld up, chsd wnr 12th, clse up 2 out, sn btn, eased
805 **Mountain Master ....Miss L Blackford** 3
chsd wnr to 12th, btn 15th, t.o. & u.r. last, rmntd
992 Palace King (Ire) *mstks 4th & 6th, in tch to 10th, p.u. aft nxt* .... pu
4 ran. 10l, dist. Time 6m 40.80s. SP 5-4.
Mrs B C Willcocks (Portman).

1115 - Open Maiden Div I (12st)

643 **GAMAY........N Mitchell** 1
hld up bhnd, prog 12th, lft 2nd 2 out, sn ld, drvn out
447 **Chocolate Buttons 5a........H Thomas** 2
cls up, chsd ldr 15th, lft in ld 2 out, sn hdd & wknd
928 **Melody Mine 5a........J Creighton** 3
lft in ld 6th, hdd 14th, btn whn lft 3rd 2 out
734 Timells Brook *prom to 8th, wknd, bhnd whn p.u. 12th* pu
Riggledown Regent *jmpd bdly, ld til ran out 6th* .... ro
Nearly At Sea 5a *(fav) prom, ld 14th, 1l up whn f 2 out* .... f
448 Millaroo *in tch til wknd & p.u. 14th* .... pu
556 Cousin Amos *chsd ldrs, 3rd at 11th, p.u. bef nxt* .... pu
734 Penny's Prince *prom to u.r. 4th* .... ur
819 Sam's Successor 7a *jmpd slwly, t.o. last whn p.u. 7th* pu
10 ran. 8l, 20l. Time 6m 58.60s. SP 2-1.
Mrs L M Boulter (V.W.H.).

1116 - Open Maiden Div II Pt I (12st)

713 **BELLS WOOD........R Nuttall** 1
sn trckd ldr, ld 11th, clr aft 2 out, comf
630 **Bally Sky ....R Wakeham** 2
in tch, lft 3rd 13th, chsd wnr 3 out, rdn & btn nxt
630 **Steamburd 5a........Miss J Sleep** 3
ld to 11th, chsd wnr to 3 out, 3rd & btn aft
993 River Stream 5a *pllng, cls up til rdn 10th, t.o. & p.u. last* .... pu
875 Barrette 5a *t.o. & p.u. 3rd* .... pu
Ducky Pool (Ire) *(fav) mstk 4th, trckd ldrds, cls 4th whn bdly hmprd 13th & p.u.* .... pu
299 Saint Joseph *prom til f 4th* .... f
806 Legal Affair 7a *rr, prog & cls up whn b.d. 13th* .... bd
Clatter Brook 5a *trckd ldrs, cls 3rd whn f 13th, dead* .. f
9 ran. 8l, 20l. Time 6m 57.80s. SP 9-4.
A J K Dunn (Minehead Harriers).

1117 - Open Maiden Div II Pt II (12st)

YQUEM (IRE) ....T Mitchell 1
(fav) tckd ldrs, ld 13th, clr app 2 out, easily
556 **Morchard Milly 5a........J Auvray** 2
alwys prom, chsd wnr frm 13th, no imp app 2 out, wknd
385 **Mostyn 7a ....Miss P Gundry** 3
mstks, prom, 4th & btn whn bkd 15th, cont'd
924 Gallery Lady (Ire) 5a *n.j.w., sn last, t.o. & blndrd 10th & 11th, p.u. nxt* .... pu
927 Gamblers Refrain *mstk 4th, ld to 13th, 3rd & wkng whn ref 15th* .... ref
446 Bright Road 5a *wl bhnd, t.o. whn f hvly 12th* .... f
928 Fair Lark *out of tch in rr, 5th & rdn 10th, p.u. aft nxt* ... pu
876 The Ugly Duckling *chsd ldn quartet, wknd 9th, p.u. 11th* .... pu
8 ran. 20l, dist. Time 6m 51.80s. SP 11-10.
Mrs L M Boulter (V.W.H).

1118 - Open Maiden Div III (12st)

OTTER MILL........J Jukes 1
cls up, ld 12th, 2l up whn lft wl clr 2 out
928 **Miss Pernickity 5a........Miss J Cumings** 2
chsd ldrs, 4th & rdn 10th, sn wknd, lft dist 2nd 2 out
820 **Heatherton Park 7a........R Nuttall** 3
mstks,prog 9th,chsd wnr 14th,clsng whn ran out 2 out, rjnd
988 Fosabud *alwys bhnd, t.o. & p.u. 12th* .... pu
658 Green's Game *prssd ldr to 11th, wknd, mstks 13th & nxt, p.u. 3 out* .... pu
988 Flemings Fleur *mid-div, 8th & btn 11th, hmprd & u.r. nxt* .... ur
733 Ruth's Boy (Ire) *(fav) 4/7-4/9, cls up till f 4th* .... f
941 Diana Moss (Ire) 5a *mid-div, 6th & btn at 11th, b.d. nxt* .... bd
629 Coed Canlas *mstk 2nd, alwys bhnd, mstk 11th, t.o. & p.u. nxt* .... pu
806 Avin Fun Bar 5a *ld til hdd & f 12th* .... f
928 Medias Maid 5a *6th whn f 6th* .... f
143 Brooklyn Express 5a *last & t.o. til p.u. 4th* .... pu
875 Romany Anne 5a *alwys rr, lft poor 5th 12th, stppd aft 3 out* .... pu
268 Givus A Hand *mid-div, 7th & btn at 11th, b.d. nxt* ..... bd
14 ran. Dist, sht-hd. Time 6m 53.00s. SP 14-1.
O J Carter (Axevale).
J.N.

AYR
Thursday April 18th
GOOD TO SOFT

1119 - 3m 3f 110yds Hun

790 **ROYAL JESTER 11.9 5a........Mr C Storey** 1
(fav) trckd ldrs, ld 12th, styd on well from 3 out.
487 **Carousel Rocket 11.11 3a........Mr C Bonner** 2
ld or disp ld till outpcd after 14th, rallied after 17th, kept on well und pres from 3 out.
672 **Southern Minstrel 11.7 7a ......Miss C Metcalfe** 3
held up, tk clr order hfwy, outpcd before 17th, styd on from 3 out.
790 Off The Bru 11.7 7a *j.w, ld or disp ld till hdd 12th, remained cl up, weakening when hit 2 out.* 4
483 Country Tarrogen 11.9 5a *in tch, pushed along before 14th, outpcd after 16th, rallied after 4 out, wknd after next.* 5
672 Direct 11.7 7a *lost tch from 12th, t.o. when p.u. before 3 out.* .... pu
912 Boreen Owen 12.0 *soon lost tch, t.o. when p.u. before 13th.* .... pu
582 Political Issue 11.9 5a *lost tch and p.u. before 13th.* .. pu
483 Royal Stream 11.7 7a *prom, disp ld 14th, rdn and wknd before 17th, lost tch and p.u. before 3 out.* .... pu
9 ran. 2½l, 10l, 7l, 3½l. Time 7m 14.20s. SP 5-2.

Mrs A D Wauchope

BANGOR
Saturday April 20th
SOFT

1120 - 2½m 110yds Hun Chase

1011 **MY NOMINEE 12.0 7a (bl)..........Mr A Griffith** 1
prom, ld 8th, clr from 4 out till rdn 2 out, hdd last, rallied to regain ld flat, kept on.
892 **Ambrose 11.7 7a..................Mr W Ritson** 2
held up, hdwy from 7th, chsd wnr 4 out, ld last, hdd flat, no ext.
257 **Lumberjack (USA) 12.2 5a (bl) ....Mr A Sansome** 3
trckd ldrs, no ch with front 2 from 4 out.
893 Simply Perfect 11.7 7a *bhnd, mstk 4th, t.o. 7th, kept on steadily from four out, n.d.* 4
579 Al Hashimi 12.0 7a *in tch, niggld along 4 out, wknd quickly, t.o.* 5
911 The Mosses 11.7 7a *rear, pushed along and t.o. from 7th, fin lame* 6
668 Ryde Again 12.0 7a *(fav) in tch till b.d. 6th* .... bd
674 Doc Lodge 11.9 7a 7ow (bl) *prom till f 6th* .... f
400 Parliament Hall 11.7 7a *ld, hdd 8th, blnd next, wknd quickly 10th, t.o. when p.u. before 4 out* .... pu
664 Shareef Star 11.7 7a *bhnd, f 8th (water)* .... f
579 King Of Shadows 11.7 7a *bhnd, reminders after 6th, soon t.o., p.u. before 11th* .... pu
Elegant Friend 11.7 7a *in tch, rdn and wknd before 9th, t.o. when mstk next, p.u. before 11th* .... pu
908 Squirrellsdaughter 11.9 7a *rear, mstk 1st, hdwy to track ldrs 7th, outpcd from 4 out, fourth and btn when f heavily 2 out* .... f
13 ran. 2l, 29l, 5l, 18l, 4l. Time 5m 22.10s. SP 6-1.
D E Nicholls

1121 - 3m 110yds Hun Chase

909 **TEAPLANTER 12.2 5a.............Mr B Pollock** 1
(fav) made all, clr from 3 out, easily.
1010 **Peajade 11.7 7a................Miss J Wormall** 2
prom, lost pl 12th, soon und pres and outpcd, kept on to take 2nd apr last, no ch with wnr.
669 **Howaryasun (Ire) 12.0 7a (v) ....Mr D S Jones** 3
held up, hdwy 11th, went 2nd 14th, outpcd by wnr from 3 out, lost second apr last.
860 Green Times 12.0 7a *handily pld, not fluent 4 out, fd.* 4
752 Kilminfoyle 12.0 7a *in tch till no dngr from 12th* 5
662 Fiddlers Three 12.0 7a (bl) *held up in tch, lost pl 11th, no dngr after, t.o.* 6
673 Queen's Chaplain 11.13 5a *rear, jmpd slowly 3rd, rdn after next, ref 6th* .... ref
482 Sausalito Boy 11.9 5a *in tch early, bhnd from 10th, t.o. when p.u. before 13th* .... pu
8 ran. 23l, 3½l, 5l, 1l, 24l. Time 6m 30.30s. SP 4-6.
R G Russell

STRATFORD
Saturday April 20th
GOOD TO FIRM

1122 - 2m 5f 110yds Hun

798 **MR GOLIGHTLY 12.0 7a ....Mrs J Reed** 1
alwys prom, ld 12th, hdd 3 out, mstk next, rallied to ld flat, styd on.
359 **Sheer Jest 12.7 3a.....................Mr A Hill** 2
(fav) held up, hdwy 9th, ld 3 out, hdd and no ext flat.
359 **Space Fair 11.9 5a...............Mr T McCarthy** 3
chsd ldrs, ld 9th to 12th, wknd apr 2 out, dead.
798 Amari King 11.7 7a *prom, rdn 12th, wknd apr 2 out.* .. 4
685 Blue Cheek 11.7 7a *prom, mstk 11th, soon rdn, wknd 4 out* 5
372 Another Coral 11.7 7a *held up, nvr troubld ldrs* 6
1054 Drewitts Dancer 11.7 7a *nvr near to chal* 7
675 Bright Burns 11.7 7a (bl) *ld to 2nd, wknd 12th* 8
943 Flying Ziad (Can) 11.7 7a *alwys in rear* 9
641 Sylvan Sirocco 11.7 7a *alwys bhnd* 10
383 Rectory Boy 11.9 5a *ld 2nd to 5th, gradually lost pl, t.o. when p.u. before 9th* .... pu
798 Social Climber 11.7 7a *prom to 8th, bhnd when p.u. before 12th* .... pu
838 Grey Tudor 11.9 5a *mid div, hit 4th, gradually lost pl, bhnd when p.u. before 12th* .... pu
907 Antrim County 11.7 7a *alwys in rear, t.o. when p.u. before 11th* .... pu
216 Gan Awry 11.2 7a *hdwy 5th, wknd 12th, bhnd when p.u. before 3 out* .... pu
669 Percy Thrower 11.7 7a *prom, ld 5th to 9th, ev ch when blnd and u.r. 4 out* .... ur
16 ran. 1¼l, 8l, 8l, 10l, 15l, 1¼l, 1l, dist, 10l. Time 5m 18.20s. SP 9-2
Mrs B I Cobden

AXE VALE HARRIERS
Stafford Cross
Saturday April 20th
SOFT

1123 - Members

1074 **TASMIN TYRANT (NZ)...................L Jefford** 1
(fav) ld 5th, wnt clr 3 out, easily
926 **Stainless Steel ....M Sweetland** 2
disp to 4th, chsd ldr aft, no imp frm 3 out
924 **Skerry Meadow..............Miss A Bodenham** 3
disp to 4th, cls up til lost tch 4 out
3 ran. 8l, dist. Time 6m 21.00s. SP 2-9.
Mrs C Egalton (Axe Vale Harriers).

1124 - Confined (12st)

992 **STRONG BREEZE.................Mrs R Pocock** 1
ld til 8th agn 11th-3 out, hdd, rlld to ld 2 out, rdn out
815 **Arctic Baron ....Miss S Vickery** 2
chsd ldrs, lost tch 4 out, rlld nxt, chal strgly flat
927 **Fearsome 5ex ....G Penfold** 3
(fav) bhnd, prog frm 3 out, nrst at fin
716 Seventh Lock *sn bhnd, out of tch 12th, mod late prog* 4
991 False Economy *cls up til ld 9-10th, prom til wknd 4 out* 5
655 Winter's Lane *hndy, 2nd 12th, ld 3 out til wknd qckly frm 2 out* 6
1072 Bidston Mill *rear whn f 4th* .... f
7 ran. ¾l, 5l, 10l, 2l, 1l. Time 6m 28.00s. SP 9-2.
Mrs R Pocock (Taunton Vale Fox Hounds).

1125 - Open (12st)

817 **QUALITAIR MEMORY (IRE) 7ex ....J Tizzard** 1
prom, ld 5th til wnt clr 3 out, easily
874 **Perfect Stranger.......................G Penfold** 2
held up, prog 12th, styd on frm 3 out, not trbld wnr
Pintail Bay (bl) ....Maj G Wheeler 3
in tch, 2nd 12th, wknd & no ch frm 2 out
709 Colcombe Castle *rear til some late prog frm 3 out* ... 4
559 Brabazon (USA) 7ex *cls up til 14th, rdn & onepce frm 3 out* 5
647 Columbique *ld to 4th, prom til mstk 11th, lost tch frm 4 out* 6
990 Still In Business 7ex *(fav) hndy whn f 2nd* .... f
7 ran. 8l, 3l, 10l, 4l, dist. Time 6m 32.80s. SP 5-2.
C Tizzard (Blackmore & Sparkford Vale).

1126 - Ladies

818 **BUTLER JOHN (IRE)............Miss J Cumings** 1
made all, lft wll clr frm 3 out
1072 **Majestic Spirit......................Miss T Cave** 2
chsd ldr til lost tch 12th, lft 2nd 3 out
991 **On His Own ....Miss W Southcombe** 3
sn rear, wll bhnd & no ch frm 4 out
655 Kings Gunner *2nd early, lost tch 12th, t.o. frm 3 out* ... 4
1059 Fosbury *held up, 3rd & in tch whn f 12th* .... f
581 Precis 5a *in tch til 10th, wknng whn f 14th* .... f
816 Arctic Chill (Ire) *(fav) held up, prog 11th, 2nd & gng wll whn slppd & f 3 out* .... f
7 ran. 20l, 6l, 25l. Time 6m 18.00s. SP 8-1.
Nick Viney (Dulverton (West)).

1127 - Intermediate (12st)

871 **GREEN HILL ....Miss L Blackford** 1
w.w., prog 12th, ld 3 out, sn clr, easily
815 **The Jogger ....J Tizzard** 2
(fav) hndy, ld 11th-3 out, onepcd whn hdd
870 **Light The Bay 5a ....G Penfold** 3
alwys 3rd/4th, nvr on terms wth ldrs
989 Rare Flutter 5a *ld til 10th, bndrd nxt, rmmdrs, t.o. & p.u. 4 out* .... pu
4 ran. 25l, dist. Time 6m 28.00s. SP 6-1.
P C Pocock (Quantock Staghounds).

1128 - Restricted (12st)

729 **BENGERS MOOR 7a ....Miss P Curling** 1
(fav) held up, prog 10th, 2nd 3 out, strgly rdn to ld cls home
Kinesiology (Ire) ....R Treloggen 2
ld til 10th & agn 12th til hdd cls home
992 **Avril Showers 5a ....R Atkinson** 3
alwys prom, 2nd 12th, no further prog frm 3 out
988 Spy Dessa *midfld, wnt 4th 12th, nvr nrr* 4
822 Lisahane Lad *alwys midfld, nvr any ch* 5
711 Just Silver *midfld til lost tch 10th, p.u. 12th* .... pu
1075 The Butler *midfld til lost tch 10th, p.u. 12th* .... pu
1060 Nearly Five Too 5a *sn bhnd, t.o. whn p.u. 12th* .... pu
Anstey Gadabout *in tch early, wknd 9th, t.o. & p.u. 12th* .... pu
558 Rogerson *sn bhnd, t.o. & p.u. 11th* .... pu
1118 Otter Mill *in tch til 11th, btn whn blndrd & u.r. 14th* .... ur
Drumcolliher *sn last, t.o. & p.u. 12th* .... pu
197 Maboy Lady *rear whn f 4th* .... f
656 Ower Farm 5a *prom early, lsng tch whn ref 13th* .... ref
1060 Handy Spider 5a *u.r. 2nd* .... ur
993 And What Else (Ire) *rear, t.o. whn p.u. 10th* .... pu
729 Race Against Time 5a *rear whn f 4th* .... f
17 ran. ½l, 20l, dist, 6l. Time 6m 25.00s. SP 6-4.
J R Townshend (Cattistock).

1129 - Open Maiden (5-7yo) (12st)

653 **GIGI BEACH (IRE) 7a ....Miss P Curling** 1
(8s-3s),w.w.,prog 11th,2nd 14th,disp nxt til wnt clr aprlast
1118 **Ruth's Boy (Ire) ....T Mitchell** 2
(fav) ld til 4 out, disp nxt, outpcd apr last
819 **Dollybat 5a ....M Frith** 3
mid-div til 10th, wnt 3rd 3 out, not trbl 1st 2
637 St Julien (Ire) *in tch, prog 11th, ev ch 14th, wknd frm 3 out* 4
819 Nottarex *alwys midfld, nvr on terms wth ldrs* 5
658 Inner Snu 5a *rear til blndrd & u.r. 11th* .... ur
928 Musbury Castle 5a *sn rear, t.o. & p.u. 9th* .... pu
820 Noble Comic 7a *prom to 14th, lost tch nxt, p.u. apr 2 out* .... pu
820 Old Harry's Wife 5a *2nd til 9th, lost tch & p.u. 13th* .... pu
807 Prides Delight 5a *mid-div whn u.r. 11th* .... ur
807 Touch Of Wind 7a *sn rear, t.o. & p.u. 7th* .... pu
11 ran. 8l, 15l, 20l, 25l. Time 6m 38.00s. SP 3-1.
Mrs Susan Humphreys (Cattistock).
D.P.

BEDALE & WEST OF YORE
Hornby Castle
Saturday April 20th
GOOD

1130 - Confined (12st)

827 **GREY REALM 5a ....S Swiers** 1
mid-div, prog to ld 13th, lft clr 3 out, easily
1091 **Fowling Piece ....Miss C Horner** 2
disp to 4th, jmpd slwly 8th, onepcd whn lft 2nd 3 out
632 **Greenmount Lad (Ire) ....P Cornforth** 3
rear, prog frm 3 out, kpt on well frm nxt
699 Fern Leader (Ire) 3ex *(fav) disp to 4th, prom, ev ch whn mstk 12th, onepcd frm 3 out* 4
910 Justforgastrix (Ire) *prom til steadily fdd frm 4 out* 5
824 Flying Lion *chsd ldrs til u.r. 11th* .... ur
985 Sharpridge *prom, ld 4th-11th, wknd rpdly, t.o. & u.r. 3 out* .... ur
1093 Katies Argument 5a *mid-div whn u.r. 4th* .... ur
985 What A Miss 5a *mid-div, wknd frm 13th, t.o. & p.u. last* .... pu
1091 Some Flash *handy, ld brfly 11th, wknd frm 4 out, t.o. & p.u. last* .... pu
764 Rabble Rouser *not fluent, alwys strgglng, t.o. & p.u. 3 out* .... pu
1096 Hurricane Linda 5a *rear, prog hlfwy, 2nd & going wll whn f 3 out* .... f
1091 Polynth *mid-div, wknd 14th, t.o. & p.u. 3 out* .... pu
13 ran. 20l, nk, 4l, 8l. Time 6m 29.00s. SP 10-1.
R E Barr (Cleveland).

1131 - Restricted (12st)

983 **ANOTHER HOOLIGAN ....Mrs F Needham** 1
(Jt fav) sttld rear, prog 13th, chal 15th, ld nxt, sn drew clr
825 **Chapel Island ....G Tuer** 2
mid-div, prog 12th, ev ch 4 out, kpt on frm 2 out
825 **Spartan Juliet 5a ....P Jenkins** 3
mid-div, prog 14th, styd on wll frm 3 out
825 Carly Clever Clogs (Ire) 5a *chsd ldrs, mstk 4th, outpcd 13th, kpt on frm 3 out* 4
828 Master Crozina *prom, ld 8th, jnd 15th, wknd rpdly* 5
704 Roly Prior *mostly mid-div, no prog frm 4 out* 6
1096 Ruff Account *mid-div, prog 11th, blnd 15th, no ext* 7
983 Stride To Glory (Ire) 7a *twrds rear, mstk 5th, t.o. 5 out* 8
1092 Caman 5a *prom early, lost plc hlfwy, t.o. 11th* 9
1093 The Chap *alwys rear, t.o. & p.u. 2 out* .... pu
982 Here Comes Charter *keen hld, nvr bttr than mid-div, wknd 14th, t.o. & p.u. 3out* .... pu
1090 Barichste *disp early, prom til wknd 12th, t.o. & p.u. 14th* .... pu
1090 Earl Gray *chsd ldrs, lost plc 11th, t.o. 13th, p.u. 2 out* .... pu
983 Laganbrae *disp early, ld 3rd-8th, wknd 11th, t.o. & p.u. aft 13th* .... pu
1090 Wolvercastle 5a *mid-div whn u.r. 2nd* .... ur
323 Whatoupa *last frm 3rd, sn trailing, t.o. 10th, p.u. aft 13th* .... pu
987 Blackwoodscountry *mid-div most of way, wknd 13th, p.u. 2 out* .... pu
17 ran. 5l, 8l, 1½l, ½l, 4l, 5l, 10l, 12l. Time 6m 24.00s. SP 2-1.
R Tate (Hurworth).

1132 - Ladies

827 **HELLCATMUDWRESTLER ....Miss T Gray** 1
raced solo for 10 fences, unchal
1023 **Crocket Lass 5a ....Miss F Hunter** 2
p.u. bef 1st, restrted 10 fences bhnd wnr, compltd own time
Portavogie ....Miss L Foxton 3
p.u. bef 1st, restrtd 11 fences bhnd wnr, cmpltd own time
633 Duntime *p.u. bef 1st, rstrtd 10 fences bhnd wnr, p.u. agn 3rd* .... pu
827 Cheeky Pot *p.u. bef 1st, rider thought false start* .... pu
827 Carole's Delight 5a *p.u. bef 1st, rider thought false start* .... pu
1092 Durham Hornet *p.u. bef 1st, rider thought false start* .... pu
759 Indie Rock *(fav) p.u. bef 1st, rider thought false start* .... pu
825 Cumberland Blues (Ire) *whppd round start, ref to race* 0
9 ran. Dist, dist. Time 6m 36.00s. SP 3-1.
Henry Bell (Bilsdale).

1133 - Land Rover Open (12st)

1092 **PEANUTS PET 7ex ....R Walmsley** 1
alwys cls up, went 2nd apr 3 out, ld nxt, ran on strngly
724 **Zam Bee 7ex ....N Bell** 2
(fav) alwys handy, prog to ld 4 out, hdd & onepcd 2 out
1024 **Park Drift 7ex ....R Tate** 3
prom, prog to jn ldr 11th, hdd 13th, onepcd frm 3 out

725 Celtic King *mstk 1st, mid-div, no prog frm 14th, sn wknd*. 4
632 Father Liam *ld to 5th, rmnd prom til wknd 4 out* 5
1092 Cromwell Point *nvr bttr than mid-div, t.o. 3 out* 6
1093 Tammy My Girl 5a *rear & pshd alng 2nd, sn strggling, t.o.* 7
513 Arden *rear, t.o. 8th* 8
1093 Clare Lad *twrds rear, mstk 4th, outpcd 7th, t.o. 3 out, u.r. last* ur
790 Ellerton Hill 4ex *alwys wth ldrs, ld 13th, hdd 4 out, ev ch whn f 2 out* f
672 Furry Knowe *alwys rear, bhnd whn u.r. 11th* ur
984 Gospel Rock (NZ) *ld 5th, jnd 11th, hdd 13th, sn lost plc, t.o. & p.u. 2 out* pu
912 Fast Study 7ex *mid-div, rdn 8th, lost tch 13th, blnd 2 out & p.u.* pu
861 Yenoora (Ire) 7ex *rear, sn strggling, t.o. & p.u. aft 12th* pu
14 ran. 4l, 6l, 20l, ½l, 12l, sht-hd, 8l. Time 6m 24.00s. SP 6-1.
J W Walmsley (Bramham Moor).

1134 - Members

905 **GLENBRICKEN 5ex** .... **R Barker** 1
w.w. prog 7th, ld nxt, kpt on strngly
824 **Beau Rose** .... **A Ogden** 2
alwys prom, ev ch 3 out, not qckn flat
826 **Skipping Gale** .... **P Atkinson** 3
(fav) rear, prog 8th, hit nxt, 2nd 15th, no hdwy aft, onepcd
1092 Gold Choice *ld to 5th, sn lost plc, t.o.* 4
1012 Prior Conviction (Ire) 5ex *prom,jmpd slwly 7th,lost tch 9th,t.o. & u.r.last,rmntd* 5
307 Byland Princess 5a *wth ldrs whn u.r. 3rd* ur
6 ran. 1l, 3l, 15l, dist. Time 6m 43.00s. SP 2-1.
H R Barker (Bedale (West Of Yore)).

1135 - Maiden Div I Pt I

823 **NELADAR 5a** .... **S Charlton** 1
reluc to race,clsd 3rd,prog 11th,ld 14th,qcknd wll clr
986 **Greatfull Fred** .... **Miss K Pickersgill** 2
plld hrd, prom, ld 4th til mstk & hdd 7th, ld 9-14th,onepcd
829 **Meadow Gray** .... **J Davies** 3
(fav) alwys handy, ev ch 4 out, onepcd
503 Claywalls 7a *ld to 5th, prom, mstk 11th, no ext frm 3 out* 4
823 Sweet Rose 5a *alwys rear, lost tch 9th, t.o.* 5
764 Quite A Character 5a *rear, mstk 3rd, sn strggling, p.u. 2 out* pu
1094 Lingcool 5a *alwys rear, t.o. & p.u. 12th* pu
1094 Grange Gracie 5a *mid-div, lost plc 9th, t.o. & p.u. 2 out* pu
1092 Hasty Cruise *n.j.w. prom til wknd rpdly & p.u. 9th* pu
1094 Just Takethe Micky *prom, ld 7th-9th, hld in 3rd whn f 3 out* f
10 ran. 30l, ½l, 7l, dist. Time 6m 37.00s. SP 3-1.
T D Smith (Cleveland).

1136 - Maiden Div I Pt II

1094 **MOUNT FABER (bl)** .... **M Sowersby** 1
wth ldrs, ld 12th, qcknd 3 out, blnd nxt, styd on strngly
762 **Hungry Jack** .... **P Atkinson** 2
hld up, prog 12th, ev ch whn blnd 2 out, not rcvr
823 **Engaging** .... **Miss T Jackson** 3
ld to 5th, wth ldrs til not qckn frm 3 out
828 Vale Of York *chsd ldrs, ld 5th, hdd 12th, outpcd frm 2 out* 4
332 Benbeath *(fav) alwys prom, ev ch whn mstk 15th, no imp aft* 5
910 Terracotta Warrior *wth ldrs, outpcd 13th, sn t.o.* 6
1090 Acropol 5a *bhnd 3rd, t.o. 12th, p.u. last* pu
Master Frisk *s.s. jmpd poorly, alwys t.o., p.u. 8th* pu
915 The Raskins 5a *mid-div whn u.r. 10th* ur
Shine A Light *prom til lost plc 9th, t.o. & p.u. 12th* pu
987 Joint Account *keen hold, mid-div whn u.r. 10th* ur
11 ran. 5l, 3l, 12l, 3l, 10l. Time 6m 39.00s. SP 2-1.
R G Watson (Bramham Moor).

1137 - Maiden Div II

987 **POLITICAL FIELD 5a** .... **M Sowersby** 1
rear, prog 10th, rmndrs 12th, ran on to ld 3 out, kpt on
762 **Zin Zan (Ire)** .... **M Mawhinney** 2
disp mostly, ev ch flat, kpt on well
1095 **Pure Madness (USA)** .... **R Edwards** 3
keen hold, alwys prom, ev ch 3 out, onepcd
762 Hoistthestandard 5a *disp to 14th, lost plc, onepcd aft* 4
1095 Canny's Fort 5a *alwys wth ldrs, no prog frm 3 out, onepcd* 5
828 Roseberry Star 5a *mid-div, rmndrs 9th, sn wknd, t.o.* 6
Noble Norman 7a *mid-div, drppd rear 7th, sn t.o.* 7
823 Bold Croft 5a *mstk 1st, chsd ldrs to 9th, not keen, t.o. & p.u. 14th* pu
Wild Expression *mid-div, wknd 13th, t.o. & p.u. 15th* pu
987 Chummy's Last 5a *in rear whn u.r. 3rd* ur
764 Priceless Sam 7a *(fav) mid-div,prog to jn ldrs 11th,ld 15th,hdd & p.u. 3 out,dsmntd* pu
1095 High Mill *rear, prog 13th, ev ch nxt, sn wknd, p.u. 2 out* pu
1095 Just Jessica 5a *rear, not fluent, bhnd whn p.u. aft 5th* pu
13 ran. Sht-hd, 3l, 20l, 8l, 10l, dist. Time 6m 40.00s. SP 4-1.
R G Watson (Bramham Moor).
N.E.

DARTMOOR
Flete Park
Saturday April 20th
SOFT

1138 - Members

1069 **CATCH THE CROSS (bl)** .... **Mrs M Hand** 1
trckd ldr 6th til ld 14th, clr 3 out, kpt on
1075 **Karlimay 5a** .... **K Heard** 2
(fav) hld up rear, went 2nd 16th, effrt apr last, not qckn
926 **Roving Vagabond** .... **A Holdsworth** 3
ld til 14th, wll bhnd frm 17th
627 Neil's Way *6s-3s, 2l 2nd whn blnd & u.r. 6th* ur
4 ran. 6l, dist. Time 7m 6.00s. SP 7-4.
Reg Hand (Dartmoor).

1139 - Restricted (12st)

729 **IVE CALLED TIME** .... **T Greed** 1
(fav) in tch, prog 14th, went 2nd 17th, strng run to ld 2 out,comf
1071 **Moorland Highflyer 7a** .... **Miss D Mitchell** 2
ld/disp to 17th, in tch til outpcd aft 3 out, ran on steadly
805 **Good King Henry** .... **I Widdicombe** 3
cls up in 3rd to 14th, rdn & no ext frm 17th
960 Madiyan (USA) *5th hlfwy, in tch to 14th, no ch clsng stgs* 4
Brown Rebel *ld/disp, ld 17th til wknd rpdly 2 out, eased* 5
992 Hedera Helix *sn rear, wll bhnd til p.u. last* pu
1073 Snuggle 5a *ref 1st, cont, t.o. & ref 2nd* ref
557 Kalokagathos *twrds rear, 8th hlfwy, bhnd whn p.u. 17th* pu
871 Druid Blue *mstk 2nd, nvr dang, bhnd whn p.u. 14th* pu
941 Dovedon Princess 5a *mid-div, 6th at 10th, bhnd whn p.u. 17th* pu
926 Mosside *cls 6th whn blnd & u.r. 9th* ur
Baashful Blaze 5a *rear whn f 5th* f
875 Lady Goldrush 5a *twrds rear whn blnd & u.r. 4th* ur
Sydney Boon 7a *in tch til mstk 11th, eased & p.u. 13th, quiet run* pu
14 ran. 12l, 8l, ¾l, 5l. Time 7m 1.00s. SP 2-1.
C M Shadbolt (Devon & Somerset Staghounds).

1140 - 4m Open (12st)

1073 **THE GENERAL'S DRUM 7ex** .... **K Heard** 1
(fav) hld up, prog 14th, trckd ldr 4 out til ld apr last, easily

1078 **Afterkelly 7ex ....I Dowrick** 2
ld/disp, ld 4 out til hdd apr last, onepcd
1109 **Magnolia Man ....N Harris** 3
hld up, prog to 3rd 3 out, ev ch til wknd nxt
1069 Gymcrak Dawn (bl) *rear, losing tch whn p.u. 20th* .... pu
658 Simply Joyful 5a *cls 3rd til lost plc 14th, bhnd whn p.u. 4 out* .... pu
626 Parson's Way 7ex (bl) *ld/disp til wknd 20th, bhnd whn p.u. last* .... pu
6 ran. 5l, 15l. Time 8m 31.00s. SP 4-7.
Mrs R Fell (Dartmoor).

1141 - Ladies

940 **PHAR TOO TOUCHY 5a..........Miss R Francis** 1
(fav) ld 4th, sn clr, unchal
924 **Greenwine (USA)....................Miss A Lamb** 2
4th hlfwy, disp 2nd frm 15th, no ch wnr
872 **Playpen ....Miss S Crook** 3
mid-div, ran on steadily, tk remote 3rd apr last
1077 Highway Jim *disp 2nd frm 15th, wkng in 4th whn blnd last* 4
1072 Grey Guestino *ld to 4th, chsd ldr til wknd 12th, bhnd & strggling 16th* 5
939 Roses In May 5a *sn rear, t.o. & p.u. 12th* .... pu
940 Aristocratic Gold *rear, 7th at 10th, nvr going wll, t.o. & p.u. last* .... pu
Mistress Rosie 5a *prog to 3rd brfly 10th, wkng whn hit 13th, p.u. aft 3 out* .... pu
8 ran. 25l, 8l, 6l, 1 fence. Time 6m 54.50s. SP 1-2.
Miss R A Francis (Dulverton West).

1142 - Confined (12st)

1073 **SENEGALAIS (FR) 1ow ....M Venner** 1
handy, cls 5th frm hlfwy, 2nd aft 3 out, ld nxt, sn clr
1069 **Walkers Point 3ex ....A Farrant** 2
in tch, cls 3rd 14th, wknd grad frm 3 out
1075 **Moorland Abbot.................Miss D Mitchell** 3
sn rear, t.o. frm hlfwy, lft remote 3rd apr last
1073 Shalchlo Boy *bhnd & strggling frm 10th, t.o.* 4
870 Christmas Hols *t.o. & p.u. 13th* .... pu
873 Cardinal Bird (USA) *prog 9th,rpd prog to ld aft 4 out,wknd & hdd apr 2 out,p.u.* .... pu
927 Moze Tidy *in tch, ld 14th-nxt, sn wknd, poor 5th whn p.u. last* .... pu
937 Brother Bill (v) *ld til apr 3rd, blnd badly 5th, rear whn ref 7th (ditch)* .... ref
Poacher's Delight *(fav) ld 3rd til 14th, wknd rpdly, p.u. 16th* .... pu
1069 Prince Soloman 3ex *handy,blnd 4th,drvn 13th,ld brfly 4 out,tired 4th & p.u.last* .... pu
937 Cornish Ways *rear whn f 9th* .... f
11 ran. 20l, dist, 4l. Time 7m 1.00s. SP 14-1.
M S Venner (Mid Devon).
One fence omitted, 19 jumps.

1143 - Maiden (12st)

MUTUAL AGREEMENT 5a...............R Darke 1
(Co fav) hld up bhnd, mstk 5th, prog 3 out, strng run to ld last,comf
1071 **Happy Valley 5a ....Miss P Baker** 2
in tch, 6th at 10th, prog to 2nd 3 out, ev ch nxt, no ext
448 **Sharrow Bay (NZ).........................I Dowrick** 3
went 3rd 10th, ld 15th, clr 3 out, hdd & wknd apr last
718 Fire Of Troy 5a *prog to 5th at 12th, 4th whn slw jmp 3 out, no ch nxt* 4
718 Temporary *(Co fav) handy,cls 3rd frm 13th, wknd aft 3 out, btn 5th whn p.u.last* .... pu
1075 Regent Son *some prog to 7th at 12th, sn wknd, t.o. & p.u. last* .... pu
1072 Baman Powerhouse *keen hold, tore into ld 7th, wknd rpdly & hdd 12th,p.u. 14th* .... pu
729 Here's Mary 5a *6th at 12th, wknd 15th, t.o. & p.u. last* .... pu
876 Mr Wideawake *(Co fav) mid-div, til p.u. aft 10th, lame* .... pu
1075 Tacoment 5a 3ow *rear, some prog to 7th at 14th, not rch ldrs, p.u. last* .... pu
1115 Millaroo *alwys bhnd, t.o. & p.u. last* .... pu
876 Herhorse 5a *prog to 6th at 14th,hit 17th,6l 2nd whn ran wd & p.u.2out* .... pu
1074 Oldham Joker *mstk 2nd, 12th hlfwy, mstks 15th & nxt, p.u. 17th* .... pu
Rusty Light (Ire) *hmpd & u.r. 1st* .... ur
1070 Spartans Dina 7a 1ow *plld hrd, ld 2-7th & 12-15th, wknd rpdly, p.u. 16th* .... pu
800 Nattadon-Hill 5a 10ow *f 1st* .... f
876 Big Reward *alwys bhnd, p.u. last* .... pu
17 ran. 3l, 6l, 30l. Time 7m 20.50s. SP 3-1.
Edward Darke (Dart Vale & South Pool).
G.T.

ESSEX & SUFFOLK
Higham
Saturday April 20th
FIRM

1144 - Members

832 **CRAFTSMAN......................Miss G Chown** 1
(fav) not fluent, ld 8th, lft wll clr 12th, idld 2 out, pshd out
1064 **Flight Of Love 5a..............Miss N Robertson** 2
1st ride, last, t.o. 10th, lft 2nd 12th, ran on frm 2 out
621 Cleddau King *ld to 8th, cls 2nd whn blnd & u.r. 12th* .. ur
934 Lord Richard *blnd & u.r. 2nd* .... ur
4 ran. 3l. Time 6m 13.00s. SP 1-5.
G W Paul (Essex & Suffolk).
One fence omitted last two circuits, 17 jumps.

1145 - Restricted (12st)

904 **CANDLE GLOW 5a...........................S Morris** 1
made all, sn wll clr, 25l up final cct, unchal
907 **General Picton.................P Harding-Jones** 2
chsg grp, pshd alng hlfwy, chsd wnr 12th, no imp
1065 **Salmon Mead (Ire) ....S Sporborg** 3
bhnd til prog 5th,chsng grp aft,styd on onepcd frm 16th
1101 Hurricane Gilbert *(fav) chsd wnr 8-12th, no imp, onepcd frm 16th* 4
834 Top Of The Range (Ire) *prom in chsng grp, onepcd frm 16th* 5
907 Cool Apollo (NZ) *alwys rear of main grp, t.o. 16th* 6
1068 Kelly's Twilight 5a *chsng grp, wknd 12th, t.o.* 7
834 Give It A Bash (Ire) 5a *20s-8s,chsng grp,strggling whn mstk 13th,wknd,p.u.2 out* .... pu
931 Kelly's Original *alwys rear, last at 12th, p.u. nxt* .... pu
814 Kelburne Lad (Ire) *u.r. 1st* .... ur
1102 Cader Idris *prom in chsng grp to 11th, los ttch nxt, t.o. & p.u. 2 out* .... pu
834 Tenderman (Ire) 7a *rear of chsng grp, lost tch 12th, t.o. & p.u. 16th* .... pu
12 ran. 25l, nk, ½l, ½l, 25l, ½l. Time 6m 4.40s. SP 25-1.
Mrs P J Hutchinson (Fernie).

1146 - Open (12st)

906 **LANTERN PIKE ....A Michael** 1
(Jt fav) ld 4th, made rest, drvn & hld on well flat
933 **St Gregory (bl) ....S R Andrews** 2
(Jt fav) chsd ldng pair,mstk 14th,chal 2 out,ran on flat,just hld
639 **Sunshine Manor..........................G Tarry** 3
ld to 4th, prssd wnr to 2 out, rdn & onepcd
918 Welshman's Gully *rear, lost tch 13th, wll bhnd whn p.u. 16th* .... pu
811 Cockstown Lad 7ex *outpcd, wll bhnd frm 4th, t.o. & u.r. 9th* .... ur
1052 Sakil (Ire) 7ex *w.w. rdn 12th, no prog, p.u. 15th* .... pu
935 Exclusive Edition (Ire) 5a 7ex *hld up, no prog in 5th whn p.u. 13th* .... pu
7 ran. Nk, 10l. Time 6m 4.20s. SP 2-1.
A H L Michael (Quantock Staghounds).

1147 - Ladies

907 **DROMIN LEADER ....Miss G Chown** 1
ld 3-4th & frm 10th, mstk 2 out, clr last, rdn out flat

678 **Cherry Chap ....Miss L Hollis** 2
mid-div, effrt 12th, chsd wnr 2 out, no imp flat
907 **Wistino ....Miss L Rowe** 3
ld to 3rd & 4-10th, chsd wnr to 2 out, onepcd, lame
777 Pardon Me Mum *(fav) w.w. prog to 3rd at 11th, mstk 15th, no prog frm nxt* 4
812 Strong Suspicion *ran wd bnd apr 4th, strgglng aft, t.o.* 5
620 Just Precious 5a *u.r. 1st* .... ur
812 What A Gig *hld up, prog 5th, 6th whn s.u. bnd apr 9th* su
906 Nowhiski *mstk 3rd, chsd ldrs til wknd 11th, p.u. 13th* .. pu
933 Sarazar (USA) *in tch to 8th, t.o. 11th, p.u. nxt* .... pu
9 ran. 2½l, 4l, 1l, 1 fence. Time 6m 5.80s. SP 2-1.
J M Turner (Suffolk).
One fence omitted last two circuits, 17 jumps.

1148 - Confined (12st)

907 **EMSEE-H ....Miss L Hollis** 1
wth ldr, ld 10th, qcknd clr aft 16th, rdn & hld on flat
906 **On The Beer (Ire) 3ex ....S Sporborg** 2
(fav) trckd wnr 12th, outpcd 16th, ran on 2 out, not qckn flat
931 **Mount Patrick ....C Lawson** 3
ld to 10th, last frm 15th, t.o.
831 Owd Henry *trckd ldrs, 3rd & outpcd 16th, btn whn p.u. 2 out, lame* .... pu
831 Druid's Lodge *mstks, in tch, 4th whn u.r. bnd apr 16th* .... ur
5 ran. 6l, dist. Time 6m 9.70s. SP 14-1.
J M Turner (Suffolk).

1149 - Open Maiden (12st)

973 **SWINGING SONG.................Miss K Gilman** 1
rdn into fences,prom,ld 8th,made most aft,clr 3 out,rdn out
617 **Just Maisy 5a.............................A Coe** 2
(fav) rear, outpcd 12th, styd on to chs wnr 3 out, no imp
1063 **Celtic Hawk 3ow.....................P Chinery** 3
sn in tch, 4th & outpcd whn mstk 16th, kpt on
830 Scout *mid-div, prog to prss wnr 13-16th, wknd nxt*.... 4
973 Royal Quarry 1ow *1st ride, alwys bhnd, t.o. 10th* 5
834 Shelter *alwys rear, bhnd frm 12th, t.o. & p.u. 3 out*.... pu
681 Little Freddie *rear, lsot tch 12th, t.o. & p.u. 16th* ...... pu
680 Nursery Story *prom to 12th, wknd 15th, wll bhnd whn p.u. 2 out* .... pu
Warner For Sport *bhnd frm 8th, t.o. & p.u. 11th* .... pu
901 Lend Us A Buck 5a *ld to 8th, prom aft, 3rd whn s.u. bnd apr 3 out* .... su
10 ran. 15l, 8l, 8l. Time 6m 18.20s. SP 3-1.
Mrs F E Gilman (Cottesmore).
J.N.

HOLCOMBE HARRIERS
Whittington
Saturday April 20th
GOOD

1150 - Members

463 **NOBBUTJUST (IRE) 5a ....J R Barlow** 1D
2nd 8th, mssd marker apr 14th, ld 3 out, held on wll,disq
894 **Strathbogie Mist (Ire) ....C Way** 1
(fav) w.w., cls 2nd & ev ch 3 out, no ext
Tarka ....Miss B Steele 2
sn wll clr, mssd marker apr 14th, hdd 3 out, wknd
892 **On Your Way.............................A Gilby** 3
rear, sn t.o., tk 4th aft 3 out
Captain Kelly *2nd 4-8th, wknd qckly, wnt round in own time* 4
Couture Color *cls 2nd whn u.r. 4th* .... ur
6 ran. 1l, dist, 2 fences, 6l. Time 7m 21.00s. SP Evens.
C Way (Holcombe Harriers).
Nobbutjust disqualified, missed marker. Original distances.

1151 - Intermediate (12st)

758 **JR-KAY (IRE).........................N Bannister** 1
chsd ldr, lft in ld 14th, chal flat, just held on
895 **Pennine View ....R Ford** 2
(fav) bhnd, prog 14th, 2nd aft 2 out, ran on strgly
754 **Toaster Crumpet................Miss P Robson** 3
held up, hdwy 13th, lft 2nd nxt, ev ch frm 3 out, no ext
855 Gen-Tech *alwys ldng grp & cls up, onepcd frm 3 out*.. 4
1083 Hydropic 4ow *chsd ldrs to 14th, wknd nxt* 5
952 Foxy Blue *nvr bynd mid-div* 6
895 Steady Away (Ire) (bl) *nvr bynd mid-div* 7
1030 Kings Mischief (Ire) (bl) *alwys rear, nvr dang*........ 8
736 Bay Owl 5ex *alwys rear, p.u. 3 out* .... pu
896 Four Hearts (Ire) *mid-div, fdd final ctt, p.u. 2 out* .... pu
1030 Pin Up Boy *ld thruout, gng wll & 2l up whn f 14th*..... f
Steel Guest (Ire) *mid-div, wknd 7th, rear & t.o. whn p.u. 11th* .... pu
12 ran. ½l, 4l, ½l, 25l, 20l, 1l, 5l. Time 6m 41.00s. SP 7-2.
N W A Bannister (Pendle Forest & Craven).

1152 - Confined

1031 **REAL CLASS.............................J Evans** 1
prom, ld aft 3 out, eased flat
1014 **Crimson Mary 5a..........................R Ford** 2
held up, 3rd 14th, ran on wll frm 2 out
1028 **Barkin...............................C J B Barlow** 3
ld mstly til aft 3 out, hdd & no ext
892 Go Miletrian *nvr bynd mid-div* 4
Harley *ld/disp to 6th,still cls up 11th,wknd, t.o. 14th,p.u. 3 out* .... pu
402 South Stack *6l 4th 14th, wknd nxt, wll btn 4th whn p.u. & dismntd flat* .... pu
Potiphar *bhnd, some prog 9th, fdd 14th, p.u. 3 out* ..... pu
1032 Grey Gorden (Ire) *(fav) f 1st* .... f
1009 Embu-Meru *rear, t.o. 6th, p.u. 8th* .... pu
9 ran. Nk, 15l, dist. Time 6m 45.00s. SP 5-2.
J W Evans (West Shropshire Drag Hounds).

1153 - Ladies

498 **PIPER O'DRUMMOND............Miss P Robson** 1
not alwys fluent, 3rd 11th, hrd rdn 2 out, ld flat
853 **Fly For Us 5a...................Miss C Burgess** 2
held up, ld 3 out til outpcd flat
460 **Sooner Still (bl)..................Miss K Rimmer** 3
ld 12th-3 out, outpcd aft
499 Barton Royal (Ire) (bl) *ld 6-12th, wknd 14th* 4
860 Ready Steady *(Jt fav) 4th whn f 8th* .... f
893 Across The Lake (bl) *(Jt fav) last plc thruout, alwys strgglng, p.u. 14th* .... pu
752 Another Dyer (bl) *ld to 6th, cls up 3rd whn collided & u.r. flat apr 10th* .... ur
1032 Royle Burchlin *2nd whn u.r. 2nd* .... ur
738 Ebony Gale *alwys rear, wll btn 5th whn p.u. 2 out* .... pu
Stormhead *2nd whn u.r. 1st* .... ur
10 ran. 1½l, 30l, dist. Time 6m 35.00s. SP 7-2.
Mrs L Walby (Tyndale).
Three fences omitted.

1154 - Land Rover Open (12st)

737 **MR TITTLE TATTLE 7ex (bl) ....D Barlow** 1
ld thruout, wnt clr 15th, easily
587 **Man's Best Friend 7ex.....................R Ford** 2
(fav) cls 3rd 15th, outpcd by wnr aft
1028 **Duke Of Impney ....C J B Barlow** 3
bhnd, 4th 3 out, styd on wll frm nxt
894 Alex-Path *alwys rear, t.o. 14th, lft 4th 2 out* 4
894 Jack Dwyer *nvr dang, btn 5th whn blkd & u.r. apr 2 out*........ ur
1031 Band Sargeant (Ire) 7ex (bl) *chsd ldr to 15th, wknd, tired & btn 4th whn ref 4 out*........ ref
1024 Bennan March 7ex *3rd whn f 13th* .... f
7 ran. 8l, 3l, dist. Time 6m 44.00s. SP 9-4.
H A Shone (Cheshire Forest).

1155 - Maiden

HEKNOWYOU (IRE)..........................R Ford 1
ld thruout, ran on whn chal 2 out
400 **Authenticity (Ire) 5a ....Miss C Burgess** 2

ldng grp, lft 2nd 14th, chal 2 out, no ext aft
1095 **Makin' Doo (Ire) ....K Green** 3
mid-div, 3rd 3 out, fin wll
763 Think Pink *4th/5th frm 11th, nvr nrr* 4
590 Salmon Spring (bl) *cls up 3rd to 15th, wknd aft* 5
Bessie Love 5a (bl) *last pair in rear, sn t.o. & p.u. 11th* .... pu
896 Jack's Croft *2nd whn f 4th* .... f
861 Bridgnorth Lass 5a *last pair in rear, sn t.o., p.u. 9th dismntd* .... pu
1029 Analystic (Ire) *chsng ldr, 4l 2nd whn f 14th* .... f
1087 Border Glory 7a *nvr bynd mid-div, p.u. 17th* .... pu
916 Cookie Boy 7a *4th whn f 4th* .... f
1045 Crimson Bow 5a *bhnd, nvr dang, p.u. 12th* .... pu
Scally Lass 5a *alwys bhnd, p.u. 11th* .... pu
1090 Pendle Witch 5a *alwys rear, t.o. 7th, p.u. last* .... pu
14 ran. 10l, 15l, 30l, 3l. Time 6m 50.00s. SP 5-1.
Mrs Lynn Campion (Vale Of Lune Harriers).
Gold Talisman (fav) withdrawn not under orders. R.A.

PENTYRCH
Llantwit Major
Saturday April 20th
GOOD TO SOFT

1156 - Members

1036 **ADANAC..........................S Blackwell** 1
prssd ldr to ld 12th, qcknd clr apr 2 out, easy
850 **Steel Valley (Ire) 5a..........................K Cousins** 2
w.w., prog to jn wnr 16th-nxt, sn outpcd
980 **My Harvinski (bl)..........................J Price** 3
mstks, prog to 3rd 11th, hrd rdn 3 out, no prog
844 Cistolena 5a *in tch, blndrd 10th, 4th & outpcd frm 16th* 4
Captain Equaty *ld to 11th, sn wknd, p.u. 14th* .... pu
849 Pine Timber *(fav) held up, f 2nd* .... f
696 Its A Doddle 5a *chsd ldrs, strgglng & rmmdrs 9th, t.o. & f 14th* .... f
7 ran. 12l, 8l, 25l. Time 6m 39.00s. SP 8-1.
Barton L Williams (Pentyrch).

1157 - Confined (12st)

1037 **POLLY PRINGLE 5a..........................A Price** 1
in tch, lft 2nd 14th, rdn to ld 2 out, held on wll flat
1035 **Bronze Effigy 3ex (bl)..........................R Jones** 2
mid-div, lft 4th 14th, ran on 3 out, ev ch last, kpt on
Golden Arctic..........................J Tudor 3
prom, lft in ld 14th, hdd & blndrd 2 out, wknd,bttr for race
1035 The Batchlor *prog 9th, lft 3rd 14th, wknd 3 out* 4
845 Harken Premier *mid-div, prog to 3rd 10th, wknng whn f 14th* .... f
845 Silks Domino *rear til blndrd & u.r. 11th* .... ur
981 Kumada *(fav) disp ld to 3rd, ld 8th til f 14th* .... f
979 Gold Diver 3ex *disp ld til ld 4-7th, wknd qckly & p.u. apr 11th* .... pu
384 The Last Mistress 5a *rear div til p.u. apr 12th* .... pu
1035 Light The Wick *alwys rear, t.o. 12th, p.u. 3 out* .... pu
844 Icecapade (Bel) *chsd ldrs, mstks 4th & 6th, lost plc 8th, bhnd & f 14th* .... f
11 ran. 1l, 20l, 10l. Time 6m 38.00s. SP 4-1.
Mrs C E Goldsworthy (Tredegar Farmers).

1158 - 4m Open (12st)

1035 **MCMAHON'S RIVER 5a..........................C Richards** 1
w.w., prog to jn ldr 22nd, rdn to ld apr last, held on wll
880 **Sound Golly 2ow..........................R Pike** 2
disp 2nd til chsd ldr 11th, ld 21st-2 out, just onepcd
881 **Ideal..........................J Rees** 3
ld 2nd til blndrd 20th, sn hdd, rlld 3 out, onepcd
878 St Helens Boy *in tch, 3rd & rdn 3 out, no hdwy aft* 4
1042 Barn Pool *alwys rear, lost tch 20th, 5th & no ch frm 3 out* 5
1111 Chibougama (USA) *in tch til outpcd 17th, no ch frm 20th* 6
943 January Don (bl) *disp 2nd,rmdrs 11th,sn drvn alng,drpd to rear 16th,p.u. 18th* .... pu
1035 Lucky Ole Son *(fav) held up bhnd, rdn & no resp 20th, t.o. & p.u. 2 out* .... pu
694 Bay Leader 5a *rear, lost tch 18th, t.o. & p.u. 2 out* .... pu
9 ran. 1l, 2l, 10l, 2l, 5l. Time 8m 34.00s. SP 7-1.
J V C Davenport (Brechin).
25 jumps.

1159 - Ladies

1036 **NEVER BE GREAT 3ex..........................Miss L Pearce** 1
disp til ld 4-6th, ld aft 3 out, lft wll clr nxt
1037 **Kingfisher Bay 3ex..........................Miss E Jones** 2
chsd ldng pair, lost tch 15th, lft poor 2nd 2 out
880 **Emerald Gem 6ow (bl)..........................Miss J Short** 3
s.s., sn wll bhnd, t.o.
979 Moving Force *(fav) disp ld to 3rd, ld 7th-3 out,3l down whn blndrd & u.r. 2 out* .... ur
850 Rymer's Express *mstks, alwys 4th, t.o. whn ref 12th* .... ref
5 ran. 1 fence, 1 fence. Time 6m 33.00s. SP 5-2.
Keith R Pearce (Carmarthenshire).

1160 - Restricted (12st)

848 **SWEET KILDARE 5a..........................J Jukes** 1
chsd ldrs, prog to ld apr 2 out, sn clr, rddn out
1038 **Antarctic Call..........................Miss N Richards** 2
mid-div, prog 11th, chsd wnr 2 out, kpt on, unable to chal
843 **Tudor Oaks 5a..........................S Shinton** 3
alwys rear, lost tch 12th, no ch frm 16th
604 Equatime 5a *chsd ldrs til wknd 15th, 4th whn f last, remntd* 4
844 Benuad *ld to 5th, bhnd & rdn 10th, t.o. & p.u. 2 out* .... pu
844 Cossack Strike (Ire) *s.s., last whn f 12th* .... f
765 Celtic Bizarre 5a *alwys rear, nvr trbld ldrs, p.u. 2 out* .... pu
1038 Paper Fair 5a *mid-div til outpcd 12th, t.o. & p.u. last* .... pu
849 Celestial Stream *(fav) hngng on bnds, ld 6th-3 out, immed btn, p.u. last* .... pu
1038 Cottage Raider (Ire) *mid-div whn f 6th* .... f
980 Downhill Racer 5a *alwys rear, no ch 11th, p.u. 14th* .... pu
1038 Hatterill Ridge *wll bhnd, prog 8th, outpcd 12th, f 14th* .... f
12 ran. 4l, 25l, 1 fence. Time 6m 38.00s. SP 5-1.
V J Thomas (Ystrad).

1161 - Open Maiden Div I (12st)

947 **DRAGONS LADY 5a..........................M FitzGerald** 1
cls up, ld 8th, 6l clr 2 out, hit last, pushd out, comf
1040 **Cairneymount..........................J Tudor** 2
cls up, chsd ldr 15th, rdn apr 2 out, no ext
849 **Snippetoff..........................Miss F Wilson** 3
bhnd, steady prog to 4th 14th, no prog frm 3 out
849 Boddington Hill 5a *bhnd frm 4th, no ch frm 14th, tk 4th on line* 4
771 Jimmy O'Goblin *ld to 7th, wth ldrs til wknd 16th* 5
976 Mister McGaskill *in tch til 5th & outpcd 14th, t.o.* 6
842 Lady Romance (Ire) 5a *held up, some prog 9th, nvr rchd ldrs, p.u. 16th* .... pu
1047 Cathgal *(fav) cls 4th whn hit by loose horse & u.r. 11th* .... ur
505 I Is *prom to 11th, sn wknd, p.u. 3 out* .... pu
694 Toucher (Ire) *in tch til u.r. 6th* .... ur
848 Khandys Slave (Ire) 5a *prom, hrd rdn 9th, wknd 12th, p.u. 3 out* .... pu
848 I'm A Bute 5a *alwys rear, no ch whn f 14th* .... f
883 Derring Ann 5a *mid-div til 11th, no ch & f 14th* .... f
694 Miss Clare 5a *mstks, wll bhnd til f 14th* .... f
Top Tor 5a *bhnd & hit 5th, t.o. 12th, p.u. 2 out* .... pu
15 ran. 12l, 15l, 15l, hd, 20l. Time 6m 41.00s. SP 5-1.
J S Warner (Cotswold Vale Farmers).

1162 - Open Maiden Div II (12st)

510 **TIMS KICK (IRE) 7a..........................J Tudor** 1
chsd ldrs, ld 3 out, blndrd nxt & last, drvn out
1040 **Colonel Frazer (Ire)..........................G Lewis** 2
ld/disp to 5th, til ld 14-16th, kpt on und pres flat
841 **Royal Bula..........................J Jukes** 3
in tch, last & strgglng 14th, lft poor 3rd 3 out

1040 Gold Tip 5a *wll bhnd, prog & in tch 11th, wknd 15th, p.u. 3 out* .... pu
842 Sheer Power (Ire) *disp ld til ld 6-13th, wknd 15th, p.u. 2 out* .... pu
976 Greenhill Lady 5a *hmp & f 2nd* .... f
696 Mister Jay Day *(fav) trckd ldrs, 4th whn hmp 3 out, not rcvr, p.u. nxt* .... pu
850 Nutsil 5a *hmp & f 2nd (dead)* .... f
850 Barton Bulldozer (Ire) *blndrd bdly & u.r. 2nd* .... ur
696 Sweet Blue 5a *hmp & ref 2nd* .... ref
1039 Miss Montgomery (Ire) 7a *w.w., prog 11th, cls 3rd whn f 3 out* .... f
977 Royal Barge *t.d.e., mid-div whn ref 2nd* .... ref
12 ran. 4l, 25l. Time 6m 48.00s. SP 7-1.
Mrs L Richardson (Llangeinor).
One fence omitted (18 jumps). S P.

SOUTH & WEST WILTS
Larkhill
Saturday April 20th
GOOD TO FIRM

1163 - Members

906 **BOLD IMP** .... **J Maxse** 1
(fav) made all at sedate pce, clr frm 3 out, canter
652 **Kilmington (Ire)** .... **M Felton** 2
n.j.w. early, ev ch 14th, wknd qckly nxt
1060 **Pinber 5a** .... **Maj O Ellwood** 3
alwys chsng ldng 2, t.o. frm 13th
3 ran. Dist, 1 fence. Time 6m 23.00s. SP 4-5.
J T Heritage (South & West Wilts).

1164 - Maiden (12st)

796 **GOOD LOOKING GUY** .... **A Charles-Jones** 1
(Jt fav) tckd awy, smooth prog to ld 3 out, ran on wll
1060 **Spar Copse** .... **Miss A Goschen** 2
ld to 6th & 13-15th, not able to qckn wth wnr
787 **Titchwell Milly 5a** .... **L Lay** 3
mid-div, prog 13th, onepce frm 3 out
997 Childsway *tckd awy, prog 12th, ch 14th, wknd nxt* 4
956 Nossi Be *sn rear, nvr a factor, t.o.* 5
864 Wired For Sound *mid-div til wknd frm 12th, t.o. frm 14th* 6
821 Paid Elation 5a *prom, ld 7th til c.o. by loose horse 9th* .... co
997 Dormston Lad 5ow *prom, ld 9-12th, wknd nxt, p.u. 3 out* .... pu
993 Joli High Note 5a *rear whn u.r. 2nd* .... ur
864 Happy Henry (Ire) *(Jt fav) mid-div whn f 3rd* .... f
780 Orphan Olly *sn in rear, t.o., p.u. 13th* .... pu
1003 Tom Smith *prom early, wknd frm 8th, t.o., p.u. 13th* .... pu
12 ran. 12l, 6l, 1l, 20l, 6l. Time 6m 21.00s. SP 9-4.
Mrs Judy Young (Beaufort).

1165 - Ladies

863 **DAYBROOK'S GIFT** .... **Miss N Allan** 1
(fav) rear, prog, ld 10-12th, qcknd into clr ld frm 3 out
958 **Sirisat 5ow** .... **Miss T Blazey** 2
ld til 10th, styd prom, ev ch 3 out, not qckn
812 **Father Fortune** .... **Miss C Townsley** 3
unruley lost 30l stt, prog & ld 13-14th, wknd nxt
958 Sohail (USA) *prom thruout til ran on onepce frm 4 out* 4
803 Unique New York (v) *alwys ldng grp, prom whn ran out 12th* .... ro
955 Rubika (Fr) *prom, mstk 6th, wknd frm 13th, p.u. 3 out* .... pu
842 Pocket Pest 5a *mid-div whn u.r. 2nd* .... ur
7 ran. 5l, 8l, 2l. Time 6m 12.00s. SP 7-4.
Miss N K Allan (Royal Artillery).
One fence omitted.

1166 - Open

731 **YOUNG BRAVE** .... **M Miller** 1
(fav) tckd awy in rear, prog frm 13th, ld apr last, easily
817 **Spitfire Jubilee** .... **M Felton** 2
front rank, ld 10th til no match for wnr whn chal last
815 **Devonia (NZ) 5a** .... **Maj O Ellwood** 3
ldng grp throut til wknd frm 14th, t.o.
1059 Gunner Stream *sn wll bhnd, t.o. frm 12th, btn one fence* 4
Sandmoor Prince *1st ride, ld pllng hrd til 9th, wknd 12th, p.u. 3 out* .... pu
863 Game Fair *prom til wknd qckly frm 13th, p.u. 3 out* .... pu
6 ran. 4l, 1 fence, 10l. Time 6m 11.00s. SP 1-4.
David Young (Portman).

1167 - B F S S Members

1046 **RUN TO FORM** .... **Miss E Wilesmith** 1
(fav) ld to 6th, styd frnt rank, ld agn 14th, ran on wll
1058 **Mighty Falcon** .... **Miss E Tory** 2
frnt rank, ld 6-14th, ran on to chs wnr frm 2 out
1057 **Spring Fun** .... **Miss Y Young** 3
prom thruout, ch 4 out, no able to qckn
865 Jupiter Moon *nvr bttr thn mid-div, not pce to chal* 4
960 Amadeo (bl) *prom early til wknd frm 12th, t.o. nxt* 5
957 Major Wayne *alwys bhnd ldng grp, t.o. frm 13th* 6
863 Space Lab *sn in rear, t.o. frm 13th* 7
863 Champagne Run *jmp poorly in rear whn p.u. 4th* .... pu
815 Sula Pride *mid-div whn mstk & u.r. 5th* .... ur
9 ran. 15l, 6l, 3l, 25l, 4l, 20l. Time 6m 13.00s. SP Evens.
M S Wilesmith (Ledbury).

1168 - Restricted

821 **COACHROADSTARBOY** .... **M Felton** 1
mid-div,chsd ldr 14th,hrd rdn to ld apr last,pshd out flat
729 **Master Mario** .... **S Bush** 2
frnt rank,lft in ld 14th,tired,hdd & wandered apr last
959 **Lochinvar Lord (bl)** .... **D Renney** 3
nvr bttr thn mid-div, t.o. frm 14th, onepcd
1056 Bang On Target (bl) *prom early, wknd frm 12th, t.o. frm 14th* 4
1056 Langton Parmill *mid-div whn u.r. 11th* .... ur
864 Pontabula *alwys frnt rank, ld 13th, gng wll whn f nxt* .... f
269 Skip'N'time *(fav) ld & gng wll til lost action & p.u. lame aft 12th* .... pu
1060 Rocky Rose 5a 10ow *prom early, wknd frm 7th, t.o. & p.u. 10th* .... pu
8 ran. 2l, dist, 3l. Time 6m 15.00s. SP 3-1.
F G Gingell (Blackmore & Sparkford Vale).
T.S.

WORCESTERSHIRE
Chaddesley Corbett
Saturday April 20th
GOOD

1169 - Members

1042 **MITCHELLS BEST** .... **T Stephenson** 1
cls up til lost plc 12th, styd on 16th, rdn to ld flat
944 **Roving Report** .... **Mrs A Rucker** 2
(fav) trckd ldrs, ld 16th, jnd & not qckn flat
1002 **Members Rights 5a 1ow** .... **M Keel** 3
ld to 10th, outpcd frm 16th, won race for 3rd
1005 Tytherington *disp frm 10th til ld 12th, hdd 16th, one-pcd frm nxt* 4
354 Lindalighter 5a *patiently rdn, prog frm 9th, ev ch 16th, no ext frm nxt* 5
909 Treyford *alwys last, t.o. 8th, completed own time* 6
African Minstrel *chsd ldrs til lost tch 13th, t.o. & p.u. 3 out* .... pu
581 Haye Buster *cls up til wknd 14th, no ch nxt, t.o. & p.u. 17th* .... pu
Contradict *strgglng frm 6th, lost tch 12th, p.u. 14th* .... pu
9 ran. ¾l, 15l, 1l, 2l, dist. Time 6m 50.00s. SP 6-1.
A Hollingsworth (Worcestershire).

1170 - Confined (12st)

942 **SPRINGFIELD LAD 2ow** .... **Miss E Walker** 1
prog 10th, chsd ldr 12th, ld 2 out, drew clr last

1046 **Stanford Boy ....Julian Pritchard** 2
prog 10th,hit 13th & lost plc,styd on 3 out,rdn to 2nd flat
837 **Hook Line'N'sinker ....L Brown** 3
trckd ldr til ld 5th, hdd & wknd 2 out
1042 Gay Ruffian *(fav) mid-div, effrt 12th, 3l 3rd 14th, ev ch 16th, wknd nxt* 4
1043 Bumptious Boy *chsd ldr 6-12th, wknd 14th, t.o. & p.u. 3 out* .... pu
1042 The Dark Watch *chsd ldrs, 5th & in tch 13th, outpcd nxt, p.u. 3 out* .... pu
853 Agarb (USA) (bl) *ld to 4th, wknd 6th, t.o. whn ref 14th* .. ref
689 Caprice de Cotte (Fr) *rear, short-lived effrt 8th, wknd 12th, p.u. nxt* .... pu
951 Running Frau 5a *s.s. prog twrds ldrs whn u.r. 4th* .... ur
9 ran. 6l, 1l, 2l. Time 6m 38.00s. SP 5-1.
J L Robbins (North Cotswold).

1171 - Open (Lady Dudley)

1004 **SHARINSKI ....M Jackson** 1
trckd ldrs, prog to ld 17th, styd on wll frm nxt
1042 **Shoon Wind..........................A Dalton** 2
ld 2nd, cls 2nd til ld 14th, hdd & no ext 17th, kpt on
692 **Better Future (Ire) ....B Potts** 3
w.w. prog 12th, chsd ldr 14th, ev ch til no ext frm 3 out
840 Notanotherone (Ire) *ld 1st, chsd ldrs aft, not qckn 14th, styd on frm 17th* 4
838 Leigh Boy (USA) *mid-div, rdn 14th, 4th 3 out, unable to chal* 5
838 Lighten The Load *hld up til gd prog 15th, ev ch nxt, wknd 3 out* 6
793 Kettles 5a *(fav) alwys rear, last at 10th, ran on one-pcd frm 15th* 7
1004 Sams Heritage *cls up til not qckn aft 14th, no ch frm 17th* 8
1046 Shadow Walker *nvr rchd ldrs, bhnd frm 13th* 9
1005 Tap Dancing *s.s. prom at 8th, wknd 12th, p.u. 14th* .... pu
945 Coombesbury Lane 5a *mid-div, lost tch frm 12th, p.u. 14th* .... pu
950 Chip'N'run *trckng ldrs whn u.r. 5th* .... ur
519 Bear's Flight *s.s. nvr rchd ldrs, t.o. & p.u. last* .... pu
1005 The Rum Mariner *ld 3-13th, ev ch 15th, wknd nxt, p.u. 3 out* .... pu
1042 Miners Fortune (Ire) *alwys cls up, ev ch 16th, 5th & btn 2 out, p.u. last* .... pu
15 ran. 3l, 2l, 7l, 3l, 2l, 2l, 5l, 20l. Time 6m 40.00s. SP 9-1.
Mrs Jo Yeomans (North Ledbury).

1172 - Ladies

1018 **BANKHEAD (IRE) ....Miss C Spearing** 1
chsd ldr & alwys outjmpd, chal 2 out, ld last, pshd clr
1003 **Down The Mine......................Miss A Dare** 2
(fav) j.w. ld, 5l up aft 17th, jnd & no ext frm 2 out
685 **Mister Gebo ....Miss C Dyson** 3
cls up til outpcd frm 6th
3 ran. 5l, dist. Time 6m 36.00s. SP 5-4.
A J Brazier (Croome & West Warwickshire).

1173 - Monterey Restricted (12st)

688 **FOREST FOUNTAIN (IRE) 7a ....A Dalton** 1
(fav) 2s-1/1, hld up, gd prog 15th, ld 2 out, sn clr
Glitterbird 5a...................Julian Pritchard 2
ld frm 3rd til hit 10th, ld 13th, hdd 2 out, rgnd 2nd flat
1005 **King Of The Clouds............Mrs N Sheppard** 3
ld chsng grp, clsd 16th, ev ch til no ext aft 3 out
949 Winters Cottage (Ire) *prom in chsng grp, prog frm 15th, ev ch 3 out, wknd nxt* 4
684 Kerry Hill *rear of main grp, styd on frm 15th, not rch ldrs* 5
1001 Damers Treasure 4ow *nvr bynd mid-div, 8th at 14th, kpt on frm 16th* 6
Disco Dan *s.s. rear til mod prog frm 14th* 7
946 Sideliner *mid-div, 25l 6th aft 14th, wknd frm 3 out* 8
1002 Really An Angel 5a *rear frm 10th, nvr nr ldrs* 9
59 Majestic Ride *rear frm 10th, t.o. & p.u. 16th* .... pu
882 Lorenza Lad *blnd & u.r. 3rd* .... ur
879 Fennorhill 1ow *mid-div, lost tch 10th, p.u. 17th* .... pu
1077 Strong Secret *mid-div, fair 8th at 9th, outpcd 14th, p.u. 3 out* .... pu
1001 Mandys Lad *ld to 2nd & 11th-nxt, cls 2nd til wknd 17th, p.u. 3 out* .... pu
840 Generator Boy *7th at 9th, mstk nxt, lost tch 15th, p.u. 3 out* .... pu
890 Gawcott Wood 5a *prom, cls 3rd whn u.r. 6th* .... ur
525 Prince's Gift *nvr bynd mid-div, no ch 15th, p.u. 3 out* .. pu
742 Kilmakee 5a *chsd ldrs to 12th, wknd 15th, p.u. 3 out* .. pu
18 ran. 6l, ¾l, 3l, 10l, 6l, 8l, 20l, 15l. Time 6m 50.00s. SP Evens.
J D Callow (Albrighton Woodland).

1174 - Maiden Div I (12st)

883 **RISING SAP ....A Dalton** 1
(fav) hld up, rpd prog 16th, chal & pckd 2 out, pshd into ld flat
997 **Ted's Knight (Ire) 7a ....A Phillips** 2
mid-div til prog 15th, ld 3 out, hdd & outpcd flat
Ora Pronobis ....T Stephenson 3
went prom 6th, ev ch 17th, wknd 3 out
842 Just Danny (bl) *alwys rear, in tch til not qckn 14th, no ch frm 17th* 4
Boys Rocks *ld to 12th, cls 3rd whn mstk 14th, grad wknd frm 17th* 5
1008 Rainbow Fantasia (Ire) *prom, ld 12th til hdd 17th, wknd frm nxt* 6
841 Namestaken *cls up, cls 2nd whn u.r. 13th* .... ur
1006 Mr Paddy Bell (v) *chsd ldrs,cls 5th at 13th,rdn & ev ch 16th, wknd & p.u.3out* .... pu
240 Potato Fountain (Ire) 5a (bl) *prom whn u.r. 6th* .... ur
883 Amerous Lad *prom to 6th, lost plc nxt, t.o. 13th, p.u. 17th* .... pu
10 ran. 1½l, 8l, 25l, nk, 12l. Time 7m 8.00s. SP 4-5.
J Downes (Wheatland).

1175 - Maiden Div II (12st)

1047 **I BLAME THEPARENTS 5a.........Miss E James** 1
trckd dlrs, cls 2nd 14th, ld 16th, drew clr 2 out
884 **Kiltrose Lad..............................A Dalton** 2
ld til ran wd bnd apr 13th,ld 15th-nxt,no ext frm 2 out
797 **Autumn Ride (Ire) 5a....................F Brennan** 3
alwys cls up, ev ch 15th, not qckn 3 out
841 Sterling Buck (USA) *(fav) w.w. gd prog frm rear 16th, no ext frm 3 out* 4
841 Mr Ffitch *prom, chsd ldrs, 6l 3rd whn f 16th* .... f
Fiddler's Lane *s.s. alwys last, lost tch & p.u. aft 16th* .. pu
1006 Rusty Fellow *prom,lost plc 5th,cls 2nd 10th,ld 13th,tried ref & u.r.nxt* .... ur
688 Lord Rattle (Ire) *cls 6th at 12th, ev ch 14th, wknd 17th, p.u. 2 out* .... pu
653 Janejolawrieclaire *cls last at 6th, losing tch whn f 8th* f
9 ran. 6l, 12l, 1l. Time 7m 1.00s. SP 4-1.
P J Corbett (Ludlow).
P.R.

GRAFTON
Mollington
Sunday April 21st
FIRM

1176 - Members

960 **GLENARD (IRE) ....R Smith** 1
(fav) ld 3rd, made most aft, jnd 12th-last, styd on well flat
1101 **Tarry Awhile...............................G Tarry** 2
cls up, wth wnr 12th til wknd aft last
1015 **Cawkwell Dean...................J Hutchinson** 3
prom til ran wd bnd apr 11th, sn wll bhnd, kpt on 2 out
1101 Alias Silver *ld to 2nd, cls up til outpcd 11th, sn no ch* .. 4
361 Brown Baby 5a *ld 2-3rd, wth wnr 9-10th, wknd nxt, t.o.* 5
1101 Singing Clown 5a *1st ride, t.o. 4th, nrly ref 7th & p.u.* pu
6 ran. 6l, 15l, 2l, 4l. Time 6m 21.80s. SP 7-4.

C W Booth (Grafton).

1177 - Intermediate (12st)

1098 **HILL ISLAND 5ex .... R Sweeting** 1
(Jt fav) ld to 2nd, made most frm 5th, drew clr last, comf
889 **Making Time 5a .... A Martin** 2
prom, wth wnr frm 5th, mstk 15th, ev ch 2 out, one-pcd
599 **Miss Isle 5a .... Miss S Duckett** 3
(Jt fav) in tch, outpcd 11th, styd on to 3rd 14th, no imp apr 2 out
745 Baron's Heir *rmnrds 3rd,sn wll bhnd,9th hlfwy,styd on to poor 4th 3 out* 4
886 Sprucefield 5ex *mid-div, 6th & effrt hlfwy, no prog frm 13th* 5
436 Tumble Time *wll bhnd, ran past btn horses to 6th 3 out, no dang* 6
897 San Remo *ldng grp til wknd aft 12th, no ch frm nxt* ... 7
971 Bare Fisted *in tch til 8th & rear hlfwy, no prog aft* 8
Berkana Run *last pair & sn t.o.* 9
955 Wild Fortune 10ex *ld 2-5th, wkng whn mstk 11th, t.o.* .. 10
1019 Ramlosa (NZ) (bl) *alwys wll in rear, 10th hlfwy, t.o. & p.u. 2 out* .... pu
Bet A Lot 5a *mid-div & out of tch by 5th, no ch whn p.u. 12th* .... pu
1105 Batcho Missile *n.j.w. last pair & t.o. til p.u. 11th* ...... pu
794 Its Murphy Man *prom, 3rd whn hit 13th, 4th & wkng whn p.u. nxt* .... pu

14 ran. 10l, 8l, 6l, 10l, 3l, 10l, dist, 2l. Time 6m 20.00s. SP 9-4.
Colin Gee (Heythrop).

1178 - Restricted Div I

1002 **CUTSDEAN CROSS (IRE) .... J Trice-Rolph** 1
(Jt fav) made virt all, clr 13th, rdn apr last, all ot fin, lame
1001 **Wayward Sailor (bl) .... Miss C Spearing** 2
(Jt fav) cls up, prssd wnr 9-11th, slw jmps aft & not qckn
742 **Slight Panic 5a .... T Stephenson** 3
hld up, prog to 3rd at 11th, no imp 1st pair frm 3 out
642 Spartan's Saint *in tch, rdn 11th, sn wll bhnd, mod prog agn 2 out* 4
1012 Ballyvoyle Bay 5a (bl) *cls up, hrd rdn 10th, sn strg-glng in rear* 5
642 Arble March 5a *wth wnr, mstk 7th, rdn 10th, sn btn, t.o. & p.u. 2 out* .... pu
Weston Gale 5a *alwys last, t.o. 8th, p.u. 11th* .... pu

7 ran. 2l, 12l, 4l, 20l. Time 6m 26.00s. SP 7-4.
Mrs H Clarke (North Cotswold).

1179 - Sporting Life Ladies

888 **LARRY THE LAMB .... Miss G Chown** 1
(fav) w.w. prog 11th, effrt 3 out, rdn to ld last, ran on strngly
642 **What Chance (Ire) 5a .... Mrs K Sunderland** 2
w.w. going wll,trckd ldr 11th,ld 3 out,hdd & mstk last,eased
124 **Severn Invader .... Miss H Gosling** 3
prom, ld & qcknd aft 10th, hdd 3 out, styd on onepcd
888 Green Archer *prom, ld 4-6th, outpcd 11th, kpt on one-pcd frm 3 out* 4
723 Chiasso Forte (Ity) *chsd ldrs, in tch to 11th, outpcd aft, no ch frm 13th* 5
888 Astroar *ld to 4th & 6th-aft 10th, sn outpcd & no ch* ... 6
792 Jellyband *mstk 5th, alwys wll bhnd, t.o. 10th* 7
Wild Moon 5a *alwys bhnd, t.o. 10th* 8
1022 Shipmate *1st ride, prom to 3rd, rear whn u.r. 8th* ..... ur
1015 Codger *rear frm 5th, t.o. & p.u. 12th* .... pu

10 ran. 7l, 4l, 7l, 20l, ½l, 25l, 20l. Time 6m 13.10s. SP 4-6.
Mrs F E Chown (Grafton).

1180 - Land Rover Open (12st)

1000 **COPPER THISTLE (IRE) 4ex .... P Taiano** 1
(fav) j.w. made all, wll clr 13th, easily
793 **Strong Beau .... L Lay** 2
cls up, outpcd 13th, mstk 15th, kpt on to mod 2nd flat
887 **Welsh Singer 4ex .... R Lawther** 3
hld up,chsd wnr 12th,sn outpcd,mstk 3 out,wknd badly flat
943 Tell You What *chsd wnr to 12th, last & btn frm nxt* 4
1015 Shortcastle *s.s. last til p.u. aft 8th* .... pu

5 ran. 25l, 10l, 5l. Time 6m 16.20s. SP 2-5.
M G Sheppard (Cambridgeshire).

1181 - Restricted Div II

834 **RAISE A LOAN .... N Bloom** 1
(fav) ld 3rd, wll clr frm 15th, unchal
889 **Goldtopper 5a .... A Tutton** 2
outpcd,last & mstk 4th,wll bhnd 8th,ran on 15th,nvr nrr
797 **Sparnova 5a .... R Barrett** 3
mid-div, 4th & wll outpcd 13th, ran on 3 out, nrst fin
1101 Crawn Hawk *ld to 3rd, prom til 3rd & outpcd 12th, kpt on onepcd 3 out* 4
904 Odysseus *rear, 8th & wll bhnd 8th, t.o. aft til p.u. last* pu
1025 Give It A Whirl *cls up, trckd wnr 11th, blnd 14th, wknd 3 out, p.u. last* .... pu
904 Glenrowan Lad *prom til p.u. aft 10th, lame* .... pu
1101 Rakish Queen 5a *alwys rear, blnd 11th, p.u. 13th* ..... pu
642 Penly *alwys rear, no ch frm 10th, t.o. & p.u. 15th* ..... pu
901 Storm Alive (Ire) 7a *alwys last, t.o. & p.u. 11th* .... pu

10 ran. 6l, hd, 4l. Time 6m 28.10s. SP 5-4.
Mrs C Bailey (Essex & Suffolk).

1182 - Maiden Div I

LOYAL GAIT (NZ) .... P Atkins 1
tubed, ld 2nd, made rest, wll clr 3 out, unchal
1020 **Not To Be Trusted .... R Barrett** 2
in tch, 3rd & outpcd 14th, rdn & kpt on frm 3 out
909 **Biblical 5a .... R Mumford** 3
ld to 2nd, rear 8th, no ch 13th, ran on 3 out, tk 3rd last
Deep Song *wll in rear, prog 12th, chsd wnr aft 3 out, wknd apr last* 4
1104 Turkish Island 5a *prssd wnr 4th til mstk 7th, wknd 11th, t.o.* 5
890 Yabbadabbadoo *(fav) w.w. prog to jn wnr 14th, btn aft nxt, p.u. 2 out, lame* .... pu
947 Roark's Chukka *prom, mstk 13th, sn wknd, t.o. & p.u. 2 out* .... pu
236 Space Molly 5a *rear, pshd alng 10th, sn btn, t.o. & p.u. 13th* .... pu
Sally's Song 7a *slw jmp 5th, last frm 8th, t.o. & p.u. 11th* .... pu
797 Princess Letitia 5a *jmpd slwly, t.o. til ref 5th* .... ref

10 ran. 20l, 10l, 5l, 30l. Time 6m 28.50s. SP 16-1.
P Atkins (Windsor Forest).

1183 - Maiden Div II

1020 **TRANQUIL LORD (IRE) .... D Smith** 1
prom, ld 14th, drew clr apr last, ran on well
1015 **Cool Rascal 5a .... L Lay** 2
trckd ldr, ld apr 13th-14th, onepcd frm 2 out
890 **Multi Line 5a .... R Barrett** 3
trckd ldrs, chal 15th, ev ch 2 out, wknd apr last, tired
1104 Arley Gale 5a *pllng, hld up, prog 13th, cls 4th whn hit 2 out, wknd* 4
1097 Supreme Dream (Ire) 5a *(fav) prom to 9th, lost plc, wll bhnd 3 out, fin fast* 5
1020 Horcum *in tch in rear, 7th & btn whn p.u. 15th* ...... pu
1020 Lloyds Loser *14s-8s, ld to apr 13th, sn wknd, t.o. & p.u. 3 out* .... pu
1105 Witch Doctor *mstk 3rd, in tch til wknd 9th, last whn p.u. 11th* .... pu
1104 Spring Sabre *jmpd sketchily, last pair in tch til ran out 9th* .... ro
901 Master Pug 7a *last pair, in tch to 12th, no ch nxt, p.u. 3 out* .... pu

10 ran. 10l, 6l, 4l, ½l. Time 6m 28.10s. SP 4-1.
D P Smith (Heythrop).
J.N.

ISLE OF WIGHT
Tweseldown
Sunday April 21st
GOOD TO FIRM

1184 - Members (12st)

995 **SKINNHILL (bl) ....C Mason** 1
(fav) ran in sntchs, disp til rdn 6th, ld 14th, pshd out
995 **Popeswood 7ex ....D Dennis** 2
disp til made most frm 6th, hdd & onepcd frm 14th
Benson 10ow ....L Brown 3
1st ride,plld hrd,mstks,ld 8-9th,t.o. 14th,u.r.3out,rmntd
Tudor Fathom *prom til outpcd frm 14th, wll btn 3rd whn f 3 out* .... f
4 ran. 20l, dist. Time 6m 27.00s. SP 4-6.
P Mason (Hursley Hambledon).

1185 - Confined (12st)

998 **PETE'S SAKE ....C Vigors** 1
trckd ldrs, ld 10-14th, rdn 2 out, ld flat, all out
732 **Apatura Hati 5a 6ow ....T Mitchell** 2
(fav) cls 2nd,ld 7-10th,rdn 13th,ld 15th,not fluent last,hdd,no ex
867 **Smooth Escort 3ex (bl) ....Miss P Curling** 3
made most to 7th, sn lost tch whn hdd, t.o. 15th
706 Swing Free *s.s. sn rdn, alwys rear, t.o. 14th* 4
4 ran. 1l, dist, 12l. Time 6m 12.00s. SP 5-2.
Mrs Michael Ennever (Hampshire).

1186 - Ladies

786 **QANNAAS (bl) ....Miss P Curling** 1
(fav) j.w. rdn to disp 1st, made rest, imprssv
867 **Ski Nut ....Miss S Davison** 2
immed outpcd, t.o. 8th, lft remote 2nd last
919 **Shamrock Star ....Miss C Townsley** 3
immed outpcd, t.o. 8th, lft remote 3rd last
885 Celtic Flame *outpcd,styng on whn lft clr 2nd 3 out,btn whn u.r. last,lame* .... ur
944 Phelioff *disp 1st, chsd wnr til u.r. 7th* .... ur
818 Tom Snout (Ire) *n.j.w. chsd wnr, blnd 6th, btn & wknd whn ref & u.r. 3 out* .... ref
6 ran. Dist, 30l. Time 6m 9.00s. SP 8-11.
Mrs Ann Leat (Hursley Hambledon).

1187 - Maiden

959 **IMAGE BOY (IRE) ....A Charles-Jones** 1
(fav) j.w. w.w. prog 8th, ld 14th, slw 2 out, pshd out
999 **Keep On Trying 5a ....M Portman** 2
rear, outpcd hlfwy, styd on well frm 3 out, nrst fin
997 **No Reply ....Mrs C Mitchell** 3
trckd ldrs, 4th & rdn 15th, sn btn
1060 Legal Vision 5a *mid-div, prog 9th, hit 12th, sn pshd alng & btn* 4
Academicallybright *not fluent in rear, p.u. aft 9th, dsmntd* .... pu
966 Manor Ranger *ld 1st, hdd & mstk 2nd, sn strgglng, p.u. 9th* .... pu
Shining Gem 5a *prom, hit 2nd, wknd 9th, f heavily 12th, winded* .... f
470 Shared Fortune (Ire) *ld 2nd til f 8th* .... f
820 Model Countess (Ire) 5a *trckd ldrs, 3rd at 11th, wknd nxt, p.u. 15th* .... pu
993 Barrow Street *prom, lft in ld 8th, hdd 14th, btn 3 out, p.u. last* .... pu
814 Phantom Slipper *schoold rear, hng lft & ran out bnd aft 9th, u.r.* .... ro
11 ran. 2l, 10l, nk. Time 6m 27.00s. SP 5-2.
Mrs R D Greenwood (V.W.H.).

1188 - Open (12st)

793 **PANDA SHANDY 5a ....R Nuttall** 1
(fav) ld to 3rd & 13th-aft 2 out, all out to ld agn nr fin
787 **Silver Concord ....S Shinton** 2
cls up frm 12th, rdn 4 out, ld aft 2 out, hdd nr fin
957 **Transplant Blue ....S Goodings** 3
rear, outpcd 12th, styd on onepcd frm 3 out
785 Vultoro 4ex *plld, ld 3rd, jmpd lft frm 10th, hdd 13th, wknd frm 4 out* 4
965 Billion Dollarbill *n.j.w. cls up til outpcd frm 13th, sn btn* 5
885 Truely Royal 7ex *hit 3rd & rmndrs, pshd alng hlfwy, outpcd 12th, sn bhnd* 6
6 ran. 4l, 15l, 6l, 8l, 8l. Time 6m 20.00s. SP 11-10.
Mrs R H Woodhouse (Portman).

1189 - Monterey Restricted

787 **BANTON LOCH ....J Hankinson** 1
w.w. went dist 2nd 13th, ld aft 3 out, untidy last, easily
889 **Arnold's Choice (bl) ....Miss G Young** 2
chsd ldrs, styd on onepcd frm 2 out, nrst fin
946 **Moorechurch Glen ....J Owen** 3
ld in start, plld, ld 2nd, sn clr, tired & hdd aft 3 out
1060 Moran Brig *outpcd rear, nvr able to chal, some mod late prog* 4
999 Mr Sunnyside *w.w. prog to dist 2nd hlfwy, onepcd frm 14th* 5
810 Second Time Round *outpcd rear, p.u. 10th* .... pu
787 Bilbo Baggins (Ire) *hit 1st, nvr going wll, prom til wknd 8th, last & p.u. 2 out* .... pu
593 Palaman *ld to 2nd, chsd ldr til mstk 12th, wknd rpdly, p.u. 2 out* .... pu
997 Vital Shot 5a *4s-5/2, twrds rear whn p.u. aft 4th* .... pu
868 Pines Express (Ire) (bl) *(fav) n.j.w. in mid-div, strgglng 10th, bhn 5th whn p.u. 2 out* .... pu
10 ran. 10l, 10l, 3l, 10l. Time 6m 25.00s. SP 8-1.
J D Hankinson (Avon Vale).

1190 - Tweseldown Members (12st)

998 **OLDE CRESCENT ....T Underwood** 1
(fav) plld hrd in 2nd, rdn to disp last, drvn out flat
1015 **Yahoo ....S Astaire** 2
j.w. ld, jnd last, no ext flat, dead
867 Wrekin Hill *hld up in 3rd, blnd & u.r. 3rd, rmntd, ref 4th* .... ref
3 ran. 2l. Time 6m 25.00s. SP 4-5.
T D B Underwood (Garth & South Berks).
M.J.

MEYNELL & SOUTH STAFFS
Sandon
Sunday April 21st
GOOD

1191 - Members

564 **ITA'S FELLOW (IRE) ....Miss S Baxter** 1
(fav) hld up, prog 8th, ld nxt, sn clr, easily
1011 **Dannigale ....E Haddock** 2
ld 2-8th, chsd wnr, no imp
665 **Ballyhannon (Ire) ....Miss J Froggatt** 3
alwys rear, 3rd at 9th, nvr dang
949 The Yokel *ld & u.r. 1st* .... ur
Just Jody *cls up to 8th, sn wknd, t.o. & p.u. 13th* .... pu
5 ran. 20l, dist. Time 6m 32.00s. SP 1-3.
R Prince (Meynell & South Staffs).

1192 - Confined (12st)

948 **WHATAFELLOW (IRE) ....A Crow** 1
(fav) hld up rear, smooth prog 11th, ld 3 out, ran on well
999 **Ravensdale Lad.....................R Wakeham** 2
prom, 3rd at 11th, ld 14th, sn clr, hdd 3 out, onepcd
1032 **Renard Quay ....Miss C Wilberforce** 3
outpcd, ran on frm 3 out, nrst fin
950 Glenshane Lad *ld 6-10th, wknd rpdly* 4
1024 Dubalea *cls 3rd at 7th, lost tch 12th, no ch aft* 5
1032 Melsonby *rear 7th, lost tch 10th, p.u. 13th* .... pu
856 Brockish Bay *mid-div whn f 11th* .... f
851 Rhine River (USA) *mid to rear, outpcd, p.u. 4 out* .... pu

1107 Emma Clew (Ire) 5a *mid-div, u.r. 11th* .... ur
687 Back The Road (Ire) *ld to 5th, trckd ldr, ld 11-13th, sn btn, p.u. 3 out* .... pu
952 Mr Bobbit (Ire) *mid-div in tch, u.r. 13th* .... ur
11 ran. 3l, 25l, 25l. Time 6m 25.00s. SP Evens.
Gareth Samuel (North Shropshire).

1193 - Open

683 **JOLLY BOAT..........A Crow** 1
(fav) w.w. ld 3 out, sn clr, comf
664 **Logical Fun..........A Griffith** 2
cls up, ld 11th-3 out, ran on onepcd, improve
Le Piccolage..........C Barlow 3
rear, some late prog frm 5 out, onepcd
366 Spurious *ld to 10th, not qckn frm 5 out* 4
1043 Tara Boy (bl) *rear of chsng grp, onepcd frm 5 out*..... 5
Pressure Game *cls up to 8th, wknd rpdly, p.u. 10th* ... pu
1032 Cheeky Fox (bl) *alwys rear, losing tch whn p.u. 8th* ... pu
737 Alpha One (bl) *sn rear, no ch whn ref 8th* .... ref
8 ran. 10l, 15l, 3l, 25l. Time 6m 29.00s. SP 1-3.
Gareth Samuel (North Shropshire).

1194 - Ladies

948 **INCH MAID 5a..........Miss H Brookshaw** 1
steadied bhnd ldr, drvn to ld apr last, ran on well
853 **Out The Door (Ire)..........Miss S Baxter** 2
(fav) trckd ldr, ld aft 2 out, slw jmp last, hdd flat
853 **Cruising On 5a..........Miss E Guest** 3
ld til hdd aft 2 out, ran on onepcd, no ext flat
839 They All Forgot Me *chsng grp til outpcd 4 out*.......... 4
908 Queens Tour *alwys rear, t.o. & p.u. 8th*................ pu
Penllyne's Pride *cls up, p.u. qckly apr 6th* .... pu
Taurian Princess 5a *mid-div, 5th & in tch 4 out, wknd rpdly, p.u. nxt* .... pu
7 ran. 2l, 4l, 12l. Time 6m 25.00s. SP 4-1.
S A Brookshaw (North Shropshire).

1195 - PPORA

687 **KORBELL (IRE) 5a..........A Crow** 1
(fav) hld up, prog 11th, ld 3 out, sn clr, easily
1012 **Dice Off 5a..........S Crank** 2
ld to 4 out, no ch wth wnr frm nxt
1000 **Orton House..........R Burton** 3
w.w. prog 4 out, outpcd frm nxt
880 Kameo Style *rear, styd on onepcd frm 3 out* 4
396 Tel D'Or *rear, t.o. 12th, p.u. 3 out* .... pu
897 Aldington Baron *prom, 2nd to 11th, fdd 14th, p.u. 3 out*................ pu
856 Mastiff Lane *mid to rear, p.u. 3 out* .... pu
463 Costermonger *mid to rear, p.u. 4 out* .... pu
1090 Pepperbox 5a *mid-div, u.r. 5th*................ ur
9 ran. 20l, 3l, dist. Time 6m 30.00s. SP 1-3.
K J Mitchell (North Shropshire).

1196 - Maiden (12st)

749 **CALLEROSE..........R Burton** 1
cls up, ld 5 out, sn clr, eased nr fin
688 **Nordross 5a..........G Hanmer** 2
mid-div & out of tch, prog 3 out, ran on, nrst fin
1094 **Gunner Be A Lady 5a..........S Prior** 3
outpcd early, ran on frm 2 out, nrst fin
1033 Lydebrook *(fav) ld til wknd & hdd 5 out, onepcd*...... 4
1029 Glen Taylor *mid to rear & outpcd, no ch ldrs*.......... 5
852 Bay Tiger *mid to rear, t.o. & p.u. 4 out* .... pu
1033 Niord *mid-div, btn whn f 5 out*................ f
1033 Sargeants Choice *disp 3rd & no ch 1st pair whn u.r. apr last, (tack broke)* .... ur
1047 Musical Mail *ldng trio clr of rest whn s.u. flat apr 13th* .... su
1012 Kingoftheswingers *chsng grp whn f 5th* .... f
1010 The Last Joshua *mid to rear, p.u. 4 out* .... pu
853 Sheppie's Reality *rear frm 3rd, t.o. & p.u. 13th* .... pu
1033 Heriot Water (Ire) 5a *p.u. aft 2nd*................ pu
1033 High Handed (Ire) 7a *mid-div, prog to 4th going wll whn ran out bnd apr 5 out* .... ref
Bettys Rose (Ire) 7a *mid-div, u.r. 11th*................ ur
681 Ronson Royale *mid to rear, p.u. 5 out* .... pu

1008 Ring Bank 7a *nvr bttr than mid-div, p.u. 3 out*........ pu
17 ran. 8l, 25l, 10l, dist. Time 6m 45.00s. SP 3-1.
R J Bevis (West Shropshire Drag).
V.S.

PEMBROKESHIRE
Lydstep
Sunday April 21st
SOFT

1197 - Members

980 **CHERRY ISLAND (IRE)..........J Jukes** 1
(fav) made all, easily
1038 **Buckley's Court..........E Williams** 2
chsd wnr, cls enough 2 out, no dang aft
388 **Kerstin's Choice 7a..........D Llewellyn** 3
alwys rear, do better
3 ran. 15l, dist. Time 6m 54.00s. SP 1-3.
Mrs Heather Gibbon (Pembrokeshire).

1198 - Intermediate (12st)

978 **ORIGAMI..........J P Keen** 1
twrds rear,steady prog frm 12th,hrd rdn 2 out,ld flat,hld on
974 **Royal Oats 5a..........D S Jones** 2
ld to 6th, agn 11th til flat, just hld
695 **Just Marmalade..........J Tudor** 3
(fav) in tch, ev ch 5 out, onepcd frm 2 out
974 Miss Montana 5a *alwys rear, p.u. 11th* .... pu
1157 The Last Mistress 5a *ld 6th-11th, fdd, p.u. 2 out* ...... pu
5 ran. Hd, 10l. Time 6m 41.00s. SP 6-1.
Alex Rhodes (Vale Of Clettwr).

1199 - Open (12st)

974 **CEDAR SQUARE (IRE) 7a..........J Jukes** 1
(fav) made all, unchal, imprssv
845 **Lislary Lad..........D S Jones** 2
alwys 2nd/3rd, chsd wnr frm 15th, no imp
978 **Electrolyte (bl)..........J P Keen** 3
prog 12th, blnd 14th, fdd aft
Abbreviation *2nd whn u.r. 12th*................ ur
846 Doubting Donna 5a *rear whn b.d. 12th*................ bd
5 ran. 15l, dist. Time 6m 35.00s. SP 4-6.
A J Rhead (South Pembrokeshire).

1200 - Maiden Div I (12st)

975 **HIGHLAND MINSTREL..........J Jukes** 1
prom, ld 3 out, rdn out
975 **Another Quince 5a..........J Price** 2
(fav) ld to 16th, wknd, fin tired
548 **Final Rose 5a..........D Llewellyn** 3
rear to 6th, prog 10th, nvr able to chal
976 Appeal 5a *mid-div, prog frm 14th, rpd hdwy 2 out, blnd last,lost 2nd* 4
1040 Sea Search *mid-div whn f 6th*................ f
607 It's So Sweet 5a *9th whn u.r. 5th* .... ur
974 Liddington Belle 5a *alwys rear, p.u. 10th* .... pu
975 Katy Country Mouse 5a *prom to 11th, p.u. 14th* ...... pu
1045 Parks Pride 7a *5th whn f 10th*................ f
974 Magic Ripple 5a *nvr nrr than 8th, p.u. 14th* .... pu
10 ran. 2l, ¾l, 5l. Time 6m 45.00s. SP 5-2.
J Lewis (Pembrokeshire).

1201 - Maiden Div II (12st)

771 **NORTHERN BLUFF..........J Jukes** 1
(fav) ld/disp til ld 2 out, hrd rdn flat
Wayward Edward..........J Price 2
ld/disp to 2 out, rallied flat, just hld
977 **Moonlight Cruise 5a..........P Williams** 3
sttld in 6th, prog frm 4 out, 3rd 2 out, tired
980 Prince Theo *prog 9th, mstk 14th, wknd, p.u. 3 out*..... pu
1040 Frontrunner 5a *nvr nrr than 5th, p.u. 9th*................ pu
975 Final Cruise 5a *prom to 14th, fdd, p.u. 2 out*.......... pu
Good Boy Charlie 7a *alwys rear, p.u. 14th* .... pu
770 Cefn Woodsman 7a *nvr nrr than 7th, p.u. 12th*........ pu

Euromill Star 5a *twrds rear whn f 6th* .... f
9 ran. 1½l, 6l. Time 6m 47.00s. SP 5-4.
H Gibbon (Pembrokeshire).

1202 - Ladies

979 **BUSMAN (IRE) 3ex................Miss L Pearce** 1
(fav) sttld bhnd ldr, ld 12th, unchal aft
769 **Fast Freeze.....................Mrs J Hawkins** 2
prom, nvr able to chal wnr
979 **Mount Falcon....................Miss C Morgan** 3
ld to 12th, onepcd aft
1158 Lucky Ole Son 3ex *nvr nrr than 4th*.......... 4
4 ran. Dist, 1½l, 6l. Time 6m 47.00s. SP 1-2.
Keith R Pearce (Carmarthenshire).
Objection to winner by runner-up, over-ruled.

1203 - Restricted (12st)

975 **PENDIL'S DELIGHT 5a...............D S Jones** 1
(fav) trckd ldr til ld 4 out, in cmmnd aft, unchal
694 **Penny Lark...................Miss G McGillvray** 2
rear, prog 3 out, hrd rdn last to tk 2nd flat
1038 **Saffron Moss............................A Price** 3
alwys prom, tired & lost 2nd aft last
977 Ayyarose 5a *ld to 4 out, fdd, fin tired*........ 4
1038 Silver Step *rear, p.u. 4th*.................... pu
5 ran. 3l, 1½l, 20l. Time 6m 49.00s. SP 1-2.
A Simpson (Pembrokeshire).

1204 - Confined (12st)

546 **GOOD HOLIDAYS 5a....................D S Jones** 1
ld/disp til ld 2 out, blnd last, all out
974 **Medieval Queen 5a.......................J Jukes** 2
(fav) ld/disp til blnd badly 3 out, mstk 2 out, rallied flat
1111 Dibloom *alwys rear, p.u. 12th*.................. pu
3 ran. 2l. Time 7m 2.00s. SP 2-1.
Caleb Davies (Llangeinor).
P.D.

SOUTHDOWN & ERIDGE
Heathfield
Sunday April 21st
FIRM

1205 - Members

961 **TUFTER'S GARTH......................S Garrott** 1
(fav) ld/disp to 6th, ld 9-10th, agn 16th, kpt on wll 2 out
Capulet 7ow.........................Miss L Jones 2
last & in tch, prog to ld 10-16th, 2nd aft, onepcd, lame
1049 **Joint Venture.....................Miss J Moffatt** 3
disp 2-6th, ld nxt-9th, fdd, t.o. 16th
593 Indiway *in tch to 13th, bhnd whn blnd & u.r. 15th* .... ur
4 ran. 3l, 2 fences. Time 6m 45.00s. SP Evens.
Mrs M Rigg (Southdown & Eridge).

1206 - Restricted (12st)

964 **LOCAL MANOR........................H Dunlop** 1
trckd ldrs, chsd ldr 16th, styd on to ld line
964 **Motor Cloak...........................G Hopper** 2
ld, blnd 7th, rdn clr frm 16th, hdd line
1145 **Kelburne Lad (Ire)........................P Bull** 3
rear, prog 12th, 3rd frm 15th, rdn 4 out, kpt on
917 Prince Rua *prom to hlfwy, t.o. 4 out*............. 4
Hyluna 5a *t.o. whn p.u. aft 10th* .... pu
348 True Measure 5a *sn rear, wll bhnd whn p.u. 16th* ..... pu
780 Elmore *(fav) mid-div, rmndrs 14th, btn 16th, p.u. nxt lame*........ pu
1054 Lewesdon Princess 5a (bl) *wth ldr to 14th, fdd & p.u. 4 out*........ pu
8 ran. Nk, 4l, 20l. Time 6m 29.00s. SP 3-1.
J L Dunlop (Crawley & Horsham).

1207 - Confined (12st)

964 **GALAROI (IRE) 3ow..................D Robinson** 1
(fav) disp 6-8th, ld nxt, made rest, pshd clr 2 out, blnd last
1053 **Redelva 5a.........................Mrs D Rowell** 2
alwys prom, 4th 4 out, styd on to tk 2nd flat
811 **Bright Hour...........................Miss J Grant** 3
ld/disp to 9th, cls aft til blnd 16th, ran on frm 2 out
920 Stede Quarter *in tch, 6th & no ch 4 out, kpt on frm 2 out*........ 4
809 Alzamina 5a *mid-div, mstk 8th, prog to chs wnr 16th, wknd last*........ 5
965 Barn Elms *rear, prog 16th, 3rd 4 out, wknd apr last*.. 6
832 Kaim Park *sn rear, lost tch 14th*.................. 7
917 Political Man *rear, in tch to 14th, p.u. 2 out* .... pu
962 Colonel O'Kelly (NZ) 9ex *in rear whn u.r. 6th* .... ur
9 ran. 3l, 4l, 3l, 4l, 6l, 20l. Time 6m 29.00s. SP 7-4.
D C Robinson (Mid Surrey Farmers Drag).

1208 - Ladies

777 **MAGICAL MORRIS..............Miss C Grissell** 1
alwys prom, 5th 4 out, chal 2 out, styd on wll to ld flat
922 **Prince Zeus.....................Miss S Gladders** 2
in tch, prog to ld 4 out, hrd prssd aft, hdd flat
832 **Gilson's Cove.......................Miss L Rowe** 3
ld 6-9th,disp til ld 14th,blnd 16th & hdd,chal nxt,no ex las
811 Sky Venture *(fav) rear, clsd up 10th, 2nd 14th-4 out, onepcd*........ 4
965 Dangerosa 5a *wll in tch, cls 3rd 4 out, rdn & wknd nxt*........ 5
963 Zilfi (USA) *ld to 6th & agn 9th, disp 10-13th, cls up whn ran out nxt* .... ro
6 ran. ½l, 2l, 5l, 12l. Time 6m 28.00s. SP 11-2.
Mrs D M Grissell (East Sussex & Romney Marsh).

1209 - Land Rover Open (12st)

963 **GINGER TRISTAN 7ex..............D Robinson** 1
(fav) made virt all, chal 4 out, rdn clr nxt
963 **Highly Decorated 7ex (bl)..........J Van Praagh** 2
wth wnr to 10th, chal 16th, wknd apr 3 out
595 **Folk Dance 3ow 4ex..................F Jackson** 3
prom, outpcd & no dang frm 16th
619 Parkbhride *wll in tch, blnd 9th, last & btn 13th, p.u. 4 out*........ pu
1052 Quarter Marker (Ire) *wll in tch, 4th whn f 14th*........ f
5 ran. 12l, 10l. Time 6m 52.00s. SP 10-11.
D C Robinson (Mid Surrey Farmers Drag).

1210 - Open Maiden (12st)

966 **GRASSINGTON (IRE)......................S Quirk** 1
(fav) rear, steady prog 9th, 3rd 16th, ld 3 out, ran on wll last
1051 **Run To Au Bon (Ire) (bl)..............T McCarthy** 2
made most to 16th,rdn to ld nxt,hdd & mstk 3 out,wknd
921 **Joyful Hero 5a..........................A Welsh** 3
trckd ldrs, 3rd 13th, ld 16th, hdd nxt, wknd
921 Netherby Cheese *prom, ld brfly 9th, cls 5th at 16th, 3rd 2 out, wknd flat*........ 4
1055 Time Star (NZ) 6ow *cls up, 4th at 16th, steadily wknd* 5
966 Scarning Gizmo 5a *alwys rear, lost tch 13th*........ 6
449 Edged Weapon (Fr) *sn prom, wknd 8th, t.o. & p.u. 13th*........ pu
575 Malingerer 7a *rear, hmpd & f 2nd* .... f
781 Welshmans Canyon (Ire) *in tch, blnd 10th, wll bhnd whn p.u. 14th*........ pu
921 Borneo Days 5a *prom, 6th & btn 14th, t.o. & p.u. 2 out*........ pu
780 Tartan Glory 5a *rear, n.j.w. p.u. aft 9th*........ pu
814 Little Petherick 5a *schoold in rear, lost tch & p.u. 13th*........ pu
922 Hatchit *last, lost tch 5th, jmpd slwly nxt, ref 7th* ...... ref
13 ran. 12l, 10l, 1l, 10l, 1 fence. Time 6m 37.00s. SP 7-2.
Scott Patrick Quirk (West Kent).

G.Ta.

CHEPSTOW
Tuesday April 23rd
SOFT

1211 - 3m Hun

845 **MISS MILLBROOK 11.5 7a ....Mr E Williams** 1
ld 9th, ran on well.
846 **Welsh Legion 12.1 7a................Mr J Jukes** 2
ld to 4th, mstk and lost pl 11th, hdwy to chase wnr 14th, wknd 3 out.
981 **Osceola 11.10 7a ....Mr P Williams** 3
ld 4th to 8th, ev ch 13th, one pace from four out.
1036 Goolds Gold 12.3 5a *(fav) joined ldrs 6th, mstk and lost pl 12th, no ch after.........* 4
846 Pat Cullen 11.10 7a *prom till wknd 4 out.........* 5
845 Gee Double You 11.10 7a *hdwy to ld 8th, hdd and wknd 9th, t.o. when p.u. after 13th..........* pu
Writer's Quay 11.10 7a *hdwy 9th, ev ch 13th, wknd next, p.u. before 4 out..........* pu
978 Metrostyle 11.10 7a *bhnd from 7th, t.o. when p.u. before 4 out..........* pu
978 Touch 'N' Pass 11.13 7a *prom till wknd 8th, t.o. when p.u. before 14th..........* pu
974 Bancyfelin Boy 11.10 7a *bhnd from 9th, t.o. when p.u. before 12th..........* pu
690 Major Bert (Ire) 11.5 7a *mstk 11th, t.o. when p.u. before 4 out..........* pu
981 Celtic Daughter 11.5 7a *t.o. from 7th, p.u. before 11th..........* pu
1013 Caracol 11.10 7a *mstk 2nd, hdwy 10th, wknd 13th, bhnd when p.u. before 4 out..........* pu
13 ran. 25l, 2½l, 10l, 14l. Time 6m 46.50s. SP 9-1.
D T Goldsworthy

COTSWOLD
Andoversford
Wednesday April 24th
GOOD

1212 - Members

1038 **FRESH PRINCE ....T Jones** 1
(fav) made all at stdy pace, pshd clr app last, comf
1170 **Bumptious Boy ....S Hanks** 2
chsd wnr, chal 2 out, one pcd
1006 **Annmount Lady (Ire) 5a....................R Hicks** 3
cl up, hit 5th, 3rd & outpcd 12th, no dang aft
Nelloes Pet (Ire) 5a *v rlctnt to race, ref 1st..........* ref
Shuil Poipin (Ire) 5a 3ow *last & jmpd slwly 2nd & 3rd, blndrd 4th, ref & u.r. 5th..........* ref
5 ran. 3½l, 1 fence. Time 6m 47.00s. SP 11-10.
Mrs Vanessa Ramm (Cotswold).

1213 - Confined (12st)

946 **DANBURY LAD (IRE) ....Miss A Dare** 1
(fav) trckd ldng pair 6th, ld 16th, drw clr 2 out, easily
866 **Always Great......................Dr P Pritchard** 2
cl up, ld 4-12th, ev ch 3 out, sn outpcd
668 **Crossofspancilhill ....N Bradley** 3
ld to 3rd & 13-15th, rdn & wknd app 2 out
745 Game Set *in tch, 4th & outpcd 6th, t.o. frm 13th ......* 4
943 Nesselnite 5a *n.j.w., t.o. 6th til p.u. 11th..........* pu
5 ran. 15l, 15l, dist. Time 6m 30.00s. SP 2-5.
Dr P P Brown (Berkeley).

1214 - Ladies

944 **DI STEFANO..........................Miss A Dare** 1
(fav) w.w., chsd ld 13th, ld 3 out, sn clr, easily
1018 **Sperrin View 5a..............Mrs K Sunderland** 2
ld, jmpd lft 7th, hd 3 out, sn rdn & btn
942 **Straight Bat ....Miss S Duckett** 3
hld up, prog to ch ldr 8-12th, outpcd nxt, t.o.
1005 Ocean Lad *chsd ldr to 6th, sn bhnd, t.o..........* 4
4 ran. 12l, 1 fence, 1 fence. Time 6m 22.00s. SP 1-2.
Mike Gifford (Cotswold Vale).

1215 - Land Rover Open (12st)

943 **GRANVILLE GRILL.......................J Deutsch** 1
made all, jmpd lft, styd on wl frm 2 out
26 **Pont de Paix 4ex..........................R White** 2
(fav) w.w., chsd ldr 9th, rdn 2 out, ev ch last, no ex
1111 **Sandy Beau 7ex ....T Jones** 3
in tch til 4th & outpcd 13th, kpt on frm 2 out
1013 Daringly 7ex *chsd ldr 2-9; wknd 3 out; poor 4th when ref last..........* ref
671 Golden Freeze 7ex *jmpd slwly & drpd last 5th, rlctnt 12th, t.o. & ref 14th..........* ref
5 ran. 1½l, 8l. Time 6m 22.00s. SP 3-1.
E W Smith (Beaufort).

1216 - Intermediate (12st)

1112 **GETAWAY BLAKE 5ex....................T Jones** 1
disp to 3rd, 2nd 13th-3 out, rlld undr pres to ld flat
794 **Guiting Gray 5ex....................Miss A Dare** 2
(fav) pllng, hit 7th, ld nxt, sn clr, wknd 2 out, hd flat
866 **Roaming Shadow....................J Hankinson** 3
w.w., prog 4th, 2nd app 2 out, one pcd
793 Golden Mac *disp til ld 4-7th, 4th & one pcd frm 3 out* 4
338 Mr Patrick (bl) *cl up, hit 3rd, lost pl 10th, last & p.u. 13th..........* pu
749 Gromit (NZ) *in tch, blndrd 12th, sn strglng, t.o. & p.u. app 2 out..........* pu
375 Members Cruise *rr, prog 8th, 4th whn f 15th ....* f
7 ran. ½l, 5l, 15l. Time 6m 27.00s. SP 7-2.
Mrs C Mackness (Cotswold).

1217 - Open Maiden (12st)

1006 **EIGHTY EIGHT..........................E Walker** 1
prom, lft in ld 14th, made rest, hrd prssd & lft clr last
947 **Daring Trouble 5a........................R Hicks** 2
w.w., mid-div, prog to ch wnr 3 out-nxt, one pcd
713 **Juniper Lodge............................S Bush** 3
wth ldr, ld 12th, blndrd & hd 15th, not rcvr, kpt on 2 out
Inky 5a *in tch, prog to 5th 12th, ev ch til wknd app 2 out..........* 4
641 Di Moda *bhnd til kpt on frm 3 out, nvr dang..........* 5
1026 The Bold Abbot *in tch, chsd ldr 15-16th, wknd nxt ....* 6
947 Duques 5a *rr, prog & rmndrs 12th, no hdwy frm 15th* 7
947 Matchlessly *rcd wd, prom to 13th, t.o. & p.u. last .....* pu
1048 Shaker Maker *(fav) w.w., prog to 3rd 12th, wknd app 3 out, p.u. last..........* pu
867 Annson *bhnd, sm prog 9th, sn stglng, p.u. aft 12th....* pu
711 Favlient 5a *prom, mstks 3rd & 6th, lost pl 12th, b.d. 14th..........* bd
1060 Sybillabee 5a *hld up, prog 14th, 2nd 2 out, chal & lkd wnr whn f last..........* f
993 Seachest 5a *made most to 12th, grad lost pl, t.o. & p.u. 2 out..........* pu
848 Free Bear *rr div, prog 12th, blndrd & u.r. nxt..........* ur
959 Colourful Boy *cl up to 4th, grad lost plc, mid-div & f 14th..........* f
796 Bay Hobnob 7a *alwys last trio, blndrd 6th, last & blndrd 16th, p.u. nxt..........* pu
16 ran. 6l, 15l, 3l, 10l, 12l, 2l. Time 6m 31.00s. SP 4-1.
Mrs H B Dowson (North Cotswold).
S.P.

TEME VALLEY
Brampton Bryan
Wednesday April 24th
GOOD

1218 - Members

1045 **TANNER ....M Hammond** 1
(fav) chal 5th, lft in ld 6th, lft virt solo 12th
1045 **Seven Cruise..............................R Jones** 2
lft 2nd at 6th, chal 9th til lost irons 11th, p.u. nxt, cont

1046 In The Water *3l 3rd whn u.r. 6th* .... ur
Cwm Bye 7a *ld/disp til u.r. 6th* .... ur
4 ran. 1 fence. Time 7m 49.00s. SP 5-4.
Mrs S E Vaughan (Teme Valley).

1219 - Confined (12st)

1171 **SHOON WIND 3ex .... A Dalton** 1
(fav) ld 1st & frm 11th, drw clr aft nxt, unchal
952 **Friary Lad (Ire) .... A Crow** 2
w.w., prog 13th, nvr rch ldr, lft clr 2nd at last
882 **Horn Player (USA) .... M P Jones** 3
chsd ldrs til lost pl 12th, no ch frm 15th, kpt on
461 Spartan Pete *cl up til outpcd 14th, kpt on one pace frm nxt* 4
1194 Penllyne's Pride *ld 2nd-10th, wknd 12th, p.u. aft 15th* .. pu
1042 Geo Potheen 3ex *rpd prog to ch ldr 14th, disp btn 2nd whn f 3 out, dead* .... f
214 Gozone *rr frm 6th, lost tch 14th, p.u. aft nxt* .... pu
602 Loch Garanne 5a *ref to race (again), stewards* 0
1041 Oragas *mid-div, rdn 14th, kpt on, disp 2nd whn f last* f
9 ran. 12l, 8l, 1½l. Time 6m 50.00s. SP 1-2.
J N Dalton (Wheatland).

1220 - Open (12st)

659 **MERRY SCORPION .... T Marlow** 1
wnt 2nd 10th, clsd on ldr til ld 16th, just hld on
1177 **Baron's Heir .... S Lloyd** 2
20l 3rd at 12th, styd on frm 15th, clsng flat
908 Enchanted Man *25l 5th at 12th, rdn 14th, no ch whn p.u. 2 out* .... pu
Scottish Dream *rr frm 4th, t.o. 6th, p.u. 8th* .... pu
854 Anchor Express 5a 7ex (bl) *chsng ldr whn msd mrkr bef 8th, p.u.* .... pu
Alamir (USA) *chsd ldrs to 4th, lost pl & ref 8th* .... ref
1171 Chip'N'run 7ex *(fav) 3rd whn msd mrkr bef 8th, p.u.* .. pu
Speedy Sioux 5a 7ex *alws rr, ref 4th* .... ref
Killy's Filly 5a *23l 4th at 12th, t.o. frm 14th, p.u. 16th* .. pu
384 Swahili Run *ld, msd mrkr app 8th, hd 16th, fin 3rd, disq.* 0
10 ran. Nk, dist. Time 7m 4.00s. SP 14-1.
T D Marlow (Flint & Denbigh).

1221 - Ladies

951 **FELL MIST .... Miss A Sykes** 1
(fav) made all, prsd whn lft wl clr 16th
879 **Grey Watch 5a .... Miss E James** 2
cl 4th whn hit 12th, wnt 2nd 3 out, no ch wth wnr
1046 **Golden Fare (v) .... Miss L Wallace** 3
cl up til outpcd 13th, lft 2nd, no ch frm 16th
Harpley *alws last, grad lost tch, t.o. whn p.u. aft 2 out* pu
908 Warner Forpleasure (bl) *cl up til wknd 13th, p.u. 15th* .. pu
1043 Drumceva *chsd ldr, hit 12th, 2l 2nd nxt, chal whn f 16th* .... f
6 ran. 20l, 15l. Time 6m 56.00s. SP Evens.
Mrs W D Sykes (South Shropshire).

1222 - Monterey Restricted Div I (12st)

882 **SPRING BAVARD 5a .... J Tudor** 1
(fav) ld 2nd-4th, 4l 3rd 15th, rdn to ld 3 out, kpt on wl
683 **French Stick .... E Williams** 2
ld frm 5th til aft 16th, rlld frm 2 out
1047 **Silver Fig 5a .... B Pollock** 3
2nd/3rd til chsd ldr 3 out, no ex nxt, lost 2nd flat
882 Mackabee (Ire) *prog frm rr 8th, ev ch 12th, not qckn frm 15th* 4
796 Demamo (Ire) *cl up to 11th, lost tch frm 14th* 5
953 Little By Little *chsd ldrs to 11th, wknd frm 13th, t.o.* 6
605 Rosenthal 5a *outpcd frm 10th, t.o. frm 14th* 7
Carriglawn *mid-div til wknd 13th, p.u. 16th* .... pu
883 Capture The Magic (Ire) 5a *s.a., alwys rr, p.u. 14th* .... pu
882 Pulltheplug 7a *wth ldrs til wknd 12th, p.u. 15th* .... pu
1044 Another Chancer 7a *mid-div 11th, wknd 15th, p.u. 3 out* .... pu
11 ran. 4l, nk, 8l, 10l, dist, 30l. Time 6m 58.00s. SP 6-4.
K Jones (Brecon).

1223 - Monterey Restricted Div II (12st)

882 **DANE ROSE 5a .... A Dalton** 1
prog to 3rd at 14th, lft in ld nxt, clr last
1048 **Carlsan .... Miss E James** 2
trckd ldrs, prog 14th, lft 2nd 16th, died aft race
952 **Miss Shaw 5a .... A Griffith** 3
ld to 6th, chsd ldr, ev ch whn hmprd 16th, not rcvr
600 Right Rosy 5a *lost tch 12th, ran on strngly frm 3 out* .. 4
742 Shannon King (Ire) *chsd ldrs rdn 14th, hmprds 16th, t.o. 2 out* 5
1038 Flaxridge *prom, ld 6th til f 16th* .... f
1173 Kerry Hill *outpcd frm 13th, t.o. & p.u. 16th* .... pu
882 Lles Le Bucflow *chsd ldrs to 13th, wknd nxt, p.u. 16th* pu
952 Welsh Clover 5a *prom to 12th, wknd nxt, p.u. 16th* .... pu
882 Ballybeggan Parson (Ire) *prom to 4th, cls 6th at 8th, wknd 13th, p.u. 3 out* .... pu
684 Sir Galeforce (Ire) *(fav) rr til prog 14th, not rch ldrs, p.u. 3 out* .... pu
11 ran. 12l, 2l, 10l, dist. Time 7m 1.00s. SP 7-1.
P J Sheppard (Brecon).

1224 - Open Maiden Div I (12st)

1175 **KILTROSE LAD .... A Dalton** 1
(fav) ld 4-7th & frm 13th, kpt on und pres frm 3 out
464 **Antigua's Treasure (Ire) .... G Hanmer** 2
cls 2nd at 13th, ev ch 16th, no ex frm 3 out
1012 **Autumn Green (Ire) .... R Burton** 3
prom, ev ch til rdn & no ex frm 3 out
1045 Ginge *cls up frm 8th, chsd ldrs til wknd 2 out* 4
1044 Wrenbury Farmer *v slw jmp 5th, t.o. frm 8th* 5
432 Orty *ld 8-12th, wknd frm 15th, t.o. 3 out* 6
884 Sioux Perfick 5a *rr frm 6th, lost tch & p.u. 12th* .... pu
Lucky Domino *rr frm 6th, lost tch 13th, p.u. 3 out* .... pu
1047 Master Frith (bl) *rr frm 6th, p.u. 9th* .... pu
Vital Wonder *jmpd nvcy in rr, nvr rch ldrs, p.u. 13th* .. pu
1047 Flying Wild *ld to 3rd, lost pl 8th, t.o. & p.u. 3 out* .... pu
1044 True Fred *wth ldrs, 5th whn p.u. lame app 14th* .... pu
1045 Native Missile 5a *prom to 6th, rdn 12th, no resp, p.u. 14th* .... pu
882 Maes Gwyn Dreamer *prom, fair 6th whn f 14th* .... f
1045 Asante Sana 7a *nvr rch frnt rnk, in rr whn u.r. 10th* ... ur
883 Day Girl 5a *in tch in mid-div til wknd 14th, p.u. 3 out* .. pu
953 Sweet Jesterday 5a *rr frm 6th, lost tch 13th, p.u. nxt* .. pu
17 ran. 5l, 1l, 8l, dist, 7l. Time 6m 59.00s. SP 6-4.
Mrs Elizabeth Gutteridge (Clifton-On-Teme).

1225 - Open Maiden Div II (12st)

1175 **FIDDLER'S LANE .... K Hibbert** 1
mid-div til prog 16th, strng run frm last to ld flat
1045 **Bowland Girl (Ire) 5a .... Miss E James** 2
(fav) prog 8th, chal 2 out to last, not qckn flat
1048 **Majic Belle 5a (bl) .... G Barfoot-Saunt** 3
cls up 11th, chal 3 out, ld nxt, hd flat
842 Alcofrolic 5a *mid-div 12th, prog 14th, 3rd 3 out, chal nxt, no ex flat* 4
849 Jobingo *mid-div til prog frm 15th, fin wl frm 2 out* 5
1044 Cruise A Hoop *trckd ldrs, eff 14th, ld nxt, wknd 2 out* .. 6
Diamond Light *prom to 4th, cls up 9th, grad wknd frm 14th* 7
1040 Astley Jack *ref to race* 0
799 Thornhill 5a (bl) *last frm 9th, lost tch 14th, f nxt* .... f
1048 Sweet Petel 5a *ld 4th, 4l up 9th, jnd app 15th, wknd & p.u. 3 out* .... pu
1044 Frank The Swank 7a 1ow *alwys mid-div, wknd 13th, p.u. 16th* .... pu
1033 Lady Barbarosa (Ire) 5a *eff frm mid-div 9th, prom 12th, wknd 14th, p.u. 3 out* .... pu
666 Maesgwyn Bach 5a *nvr rch ldrs, lost tch 14th, p.u. 16th* .... pu
1045 Watchit Lad *rr & mstk 8th, mod prog 13th, no ch whn f 16th* .... f
149 Peat Potheen *ld to 3rd, wth ldrs to 11th, wkng whn hit 14th, p.u. nxt* .... pu
1044 Fancytalkintinker (Ire) *rr 9th, sm prog frm 14th, not rch ldrs, p.u. 3 out* .... pu
747 Forest Rose 5a *t.o. frm 4th, ran out 6th* .... ro

748 Pridewood Target *cls 3rd at 11th, ev ch 14th, wknd & p.u. 3 out* .... pu
18 ran. 3l, hd, nk, hd, 10l, 30l. Time 7m 8.00s. SP 14-1.
Miss P Kerby (Clifton-On-Teme).
P.R.

PERTH
Thursday April 25th
SOFT

1226 - 3m Hun

1086 **LITTLE WENLOCK 11.7 7a ....Mrs V Jackson** 1
well bhnd early, hdwy after 14th, challenging when bumped run-in, styd on strly.
256 **Romany King 11.11 3a ....Mr C Bonner** 2
trckd ldrs, ld 15th, clr 2 out, wknd, edged left und pres and hdd run-in, no ext.
1119 **Southern Minstrel 12.5 ....Mr S Swiers** 3
trckd ldrs, mstk and ld 11th (water), hdd 15th, kept on same pace.
1083 Secret Sceptre 11.9 5a *prom, driven along after 13th, lost tch from 3 out, jmpd badly left and blnd next.....* 4
861 Fish Quay 11.7 7a *n.j.w., soon lost tch, t.o. when p.u. after 11th.* .... pu
582 Mr Diplomatic 11.7 7a (bl) *ld, mstk 10th, hdd next, soon wknd, t.o. when p.u. before 15th.........* pu
612 Howayman 11.7 7a *(fav) in tch, ev ch 15th, weakening when f 3 out* .... f
7 ran. 3l, 9l, 29l. Time 6m 44.70s. SP 25-1.
Mrs D S C Gibson

LUDLOW
Friday April 26th
GOOD

1227 - 2½m Hun

1122 **AMARI KING 12.0 7a.........Mr C Ward Thomas** 1
chsd ldrs, ld 11th, styd on well.
1107 **A Windy Citizen (Ire) 11.9 7a ....Mr R Hicks** 2
(fav) held up, hdwy 10th, rdn apr last, ran on one pace.
879 **Tuffnut George 11.7 7a.............Mr A Phillips** 3
prom, driven along apr 2 out, styd on same pace.
908 Familiar Friend 12.0 7a (bl) *held up, hdwy 10th, wknd apr last.* 4
1120 King Of Shadows 11.7 7a *mid div, effort apr 6 out, not reach ldrs.* 5
685 Knight's Spur (USA) 11.7 7a *chsd ldrs, rdn 3 out, wknd next.* 6
577 Lavalight 11.7 7a *n.d.* 7
998 Afaltoun 12.0 7a *prom to 10th, wknd.* 8
1007 Tipp Down 11.7 7a *bhnd hfwy.* 9
1122 Flying Ziad (Can) 11.7 7a *bhnd 9th.* 10
No More The Fool 11.7 7a *mstk 3rd, alwys rear.* 11
1169 Haye Buster 11.7 7a (bl) *bhnd hfwy.* 12
578 Fox Pointer 12.0 7a *bhnd, staying on when blnd and u.r. 4 out.* .... ur
579 Luke's The Bizz (Ire) 11.7 7a *n.j.w., ld to 11th, wknd 5 out, bhnd when f 2 out, dead.* .... f
373 No Joker (Ire) 11.7 7a *alwys bhnd, t.o. when blnd and u.r. 4 out.* .... ur
569 Parkinson's Law 11.7 7a *mid div, lost pl hfwy, t.o. when p.u. before 3 out.* .... pu
16 ran. 5l, 8l, 13l, ½l, 7l, 1¼l, 11l, ¾l, 1¾l, 24l. Time 5m 0.80s. SP 11-2.
M Ward-Thomas

WORCESTER
Saturday April 27th
GOOD

1228 - 2m 7f Nov Hun

IDIOTIC 11.9 5a...................Mr C Vigors 1
hdwy 12th, blnd 2 out, ld apr last, driven out.
1112 **The Pedlar 11.2 7a ....Mr T Greed** 2
gd hdwy 4 out, mstk 2 out, ran on, not reach wnr.
906 **Prinzal 12.7 ....Mr M Armytage** 3
(fav) alwys prom, ld 10th to 12th, led 4 out, hit next 2, hdd apr last, not qckn.
924 Fly The Wind 11.2 7a *with ldr, ld 12th to 4 out, hrd rdn and one pace from next.* 4
878 First Harvest 11.7 7a *left in ld 4th, hdd 10th, wknd four out.* 5
956 Tea Cee Kay 11.9 5a *hdwy 10th, wknd 14th.* 6
1033 Shanballymore (Ire) 11.7 7a *alwys bhnd.* 7
1108 Tekla (Fr) 11.7 7a *prom to 9th.* 8
874 Try It Alone 11.11 3a *hdwy 10th, rdn and wknd 12th...* 9
597 Pallingham Star (Ire) 11.7 7a *alwys bhnd, t.o.* 10
794 Autonomous 11.7 7a *jmpd badly, t.o. till ref 5th.* ...... ref
1122 Gan Awry 11.2 7a *mid div when f 8th.* .... f
National Choice 11.9 5a *mstks, hdwy 6th, blnd and wknd 10th, t.o. when p.u. before 4 out.* .... pu
963 Sure Pride (USA) 11.7 7a *mid div when blnd and u.r. 10th.* .... ur
833 Laburnum 11.9 5a *mstks, t.o. when p.u. before 4 out.* pu
1107 Vulcan Star 11.9 5a *t.o. when p.u. before 4 out.* .... pu
1079 Bridge Express 11.7 7a *ld till f 4th.* .... f
17 ran. 3l, 4l, 2½l, 10l, 15l, 10l, 1½l, 6l, dist. Time 5m 54.80s. SP 6-1.
E Knight

ALBRIGHTON
Weston Park
Saturday April 27th
GOOD

1229 - Members

1196 **GLEN TAYLOR ....Mrs M Wall** 1
made all, steadd pce, jmp rght, lft solo 3 out
Achieved Ambition (Ire) *(fav) hrd held, cls up, ev ch whn f 3 out* .... f
2 ran. Time 7m 42.00s. SP 5-4.
Mrs G A Spencer / Mrs P Derbyshire (Albrighton).
Finished alone.

1230 - Confined (12st)

1102 **FURRY FOX (IRE) ....A Crow** 1
(fav) ld/disp 3rd-3 out, qcknd 2 out, ran on wll
1192 **Back The Road (Ire)......................G Hamner** 2
cls up frm 3rd, disp 8th-3 out, no ext frm 2 out
1154 **Duke Of Impney ....C Barlow** 3
rear early, cls order 13th, unable to qckn frm 3 out
1192 Brockish Bay *mid-div, ran on onepcd frm 4 out* 4
879 Soldiers Duty (USA) *held up, 3rd 10th, mstk 13th, not qckn frm 3 out.* 5
1153 Ebony Gale *ld to 2nd, chsng grp to 12th, onepcd frm 5 out.* 6
1151 Bay Owl 3ex *mid-div to hlfwy, mstks, sn btn* 7
7 ran. 3l, 1l, 1l, 1l, 4l, 15l. Time 6m 43.00s. SP 4-7.
E H Crow (North Shropshire).

1231 - Open

1193 **JOLLY BOAT..............................A Crow** 1
(fav) ld/disp to 4th,steadd,ld 10th,strng chal frm 3 out,ran onwll
1193 **Le Piccolage ....C Barlow** 2
rear early,prog 11th,cls up 13th,strng chal 3 out, fdd last
1052 **Castlebay Lad..............................C Coyne** 3
mstly 2nd/3rd, ev ch 3 out, not qckn
1193 Tara Boy (bl) *chsng grp, outpcd frm 13th, nvr dang* ... 4
459 Ryton Guard *prom, ld 5-9th, onepcd frm 4 out* 5
948 Ahalin *in tch to 12th, outpcd aft, no ch in rear, p.u. 2 out.* .... pu
6 ran. 2½l, 10l, 1l, 10l. Time 6m 45.00s. SP 2-5.
Gareth Samuel (North Shropshire).

1232 - Ladies

1194 **INCH MAID 5a...................Miss H Brookshaw** 1
cls 3rd/4th til wnt on 12th, sn clr, easy
879 **Czermno ....Miss J Priest** 2
ld/disp to 11th, hdd 12th, ran on onepce

1153 **Sooner Still 1ow (bl) ....Miss K Rimmer** 3
held up, prog 2nd 13th, no ext frm 4 out
1219 Penllyne's Pride *cls up, ld/disp til bad mstk & u.r. 12th* ..... ur
738 Hornblower *(fav) chsd ldrs, nvr gng wll, cls 3rd whn f 11th* ..... f
951 The Barren Arctic *w.w.,rear hlfwy,bad mstk 13th,one-pcd,4th last,p.u.runin lame* ..... pu
6 ran. 20l, 5l. Time 6m 39.00s. SP 2-1.
S A Brookshaw (North Shropshire).

1233 - Restricted (12st)

880 **LAKENHEATHER (NZ) ....G Hanmer** 1
mid-div, cls order 12th, ran on frm 3 out,lkd held bfr last
1193 **Spurious ....A Griffith** 2
disp frm 8th,lft ld 4 out,clr whn carred wd by loose horse
1153 **Royle Burchlin ....S Prior** 3
chsng grp, outpcd frm 12th, styd on, nrst fin
1030 Jo-Su-Ki *prom, ldng grp thruout, not qckn frm 3 out* .. 4
882 Saffron Glory (bl) *chsd ldrs to 10th, in tch to 3 out, onepcd* 5
952 Rinky Dinky Doo (bl) *ld/disp to 4th, cls up 12th, out-pcd* 6
1030 Grecianlid *mid-div, nvr dang* 7
1195 Mastiff Lane *mid to rear* 8
1120 Shareef Star *s.s., alwys rear, grdly lost tch, btn 1 fence* 9
1151 Foxy Blue *ld/disp to 4th, mid-div to 12th, lost tch, p.u. bfr last* ..... pu
1006 Kingsthorpe *chsd ldrs, hndy whn f hvly 4th* ..... f
1029 Flinters (bl) *chsng grp, in tch whn p.u. qckly bfr 10th* .. pu
Yukon Gale (Ire) *(fav) cls up, ld/disp 5th, clr 12th, gng wll f 4 out* ..... f
1028 Mister Tinker *mid-div, p.u. qckly & dismntd bfr 10th* ... pu
14 ran. 2l, dist, 2l, 1l, 1l. Time 6m 42.00s. SP 8-1.
Mrs Pat Mullen (West Shropshire Drag).

1234 - Open Maiden (12st)

1195 **ORTON HOUSE ....R Burton** 1
(fav) w.w., cls order 10th, ld 5 out, ran on strgly, comf
462 **Cloud Dancing....................M Worthington** 2
mid-div, chsd ldr frm 5 out, ran on onepce
1195 **Costermonger.........................A Griffith** 3
cls up, ld 10-12th, ev ch til wknd 3 out
464 Rejects Reply *held up mid-div, some late prog, ran on, nrst fin* 4
1155 Salmon Spring 2ow *mid-div, not qckn, nvr trbld ldrs* .. 5
1196 Sheppie's Reality *alwys rear, t.o. frm 8th* 6
288 Public Appeal *plld hrd, mid to rear, diff ride, p.u. 5 out* ..... pu
740 Kingfisher Blues (Ire) *mid-div whn u.r. 4th* ..... ur
Country Loch 5a *mstks, mid to rear, t.o. whn p.u. 5 out* ..... pu
1029 Son Of Ishka *ld 7-9th, cls up, ld 13th, wknd 4 out, p.u. 2 out* ..... pu
842 Highland Chase *ld to 6th, lost tch 12th, fdd, p.u. 2 out* pu
Bee-A-Scally 7a *rear, jmp novcy, no ch whn p.u. 6 out* ..... pu
Whats Money 7a *mid to rear, lost cth, p.u. 4 out* .... pu
13 ran. 6l, 15l, 4l, nk, dist. Time 6m 52.00s. SP 5-4.
Mrs A P Kelly (Flint & Denbigh).
V.S.

ATHERSTONE
Clifton On Dunsmore
Saturday April 27th
GOOD TO FIRM

1235 - Members

723 **AINTREE OATS 5a ....J Holt** 1
(fav) ld 2nd, made rest, clr last, eased flat
1100 **Falconbridge Bay ....R Armson** 2
jmpd slwly 4th, jnd wnr 7th, hrd rdn & ev ch 2 out, sn btn
1011 **Trusty Friend ....J Oldring** 3
ld to 2nd, 3rd & outpcd 12th, no ch whn nrly ref 15th
1101 Smart Rhythm 5a *cls up to 8th, last & no ch frm 12th* 4
4 ran. 6l, 30l, 12l. Time 6m 14.10s. SP 8-15.
J R Holt (Atherstone).

1236 - Confined (12st)

1105 **OH SO WINDY 5a.....................B Pollock** 1
(fav) trckd ldrs, 2nd 13th, rdn to ld 2 out, clr last, all out
1098 **Bervie House (Ire) ....A Hill** 2
trckd ldrs, ld 13th, rdn & hdd 2 out, btn whn mstk last
1180 **Tell You What ....N Ridout** 3
ld/disp to 12th, 3rd & outpcd frm nxt, kpt on
1191 Dannigale *ld/disp to 12th, 4th & outpcd nxt, no prog aft* 4
1097 Hostetler *rear frm 5th, bhnd frm 12th, t.o.* 5
1099 Sanamar *alwys rear, wll bhnd frm 12th, t.o.* 6
1122 Grey Tudor *rdr lost irons 4th, bhnd frm 11th, 6th & t.o. whn u.r. 16th* ..... ur
1016 Kelly's Eye 6ex *nvr going wll, alwys rear, poor 5th whn p.u. 2 out* ..... pu
8 ran. 5l, 12l, 20l, 30l, 4l. Time 6m 2.00s. SP 11-8.
Rupert Cottrell (Pytchley).

1237 - Open

1017 **LUCKY CHRISTOPHER ....G Tarry** 1
(fav) mstk 1st, cls up, ld 12th, drvn clr 2 out, ran on well
1100 **Brown Windsor (bl) ....B Pollock** 2
cls up, prssd wnr 13th til not qckn 2 out
902 **Write The Music (bl).....................T Lane** 3
sn pshd alng, in tch, chsd 1st pair 4 out, sn outpcd
1098 Decent Gold *jmpd rght, ld 3-5th, last & outpcd 13th, no ch aft* 4
1100 Blue Aeroplane *ld to 3rd & 5th-12th, disp 3rd & in tch whn f 4 out* ..... f
5 ran. 7l, 25l, 15l. Time 6m 5.70s. SP 4-7.
G B Tarry (Grafton).

1238 - Ladies

724 **GENERAL HIGHWAY..............Mrs J Dawson** 1
(fav) ld to 2nd, ld 14th, sn wll clr, hvly eased flat
394 **Prince Metternich ....Miss C Arthers** 2
pllng,ld 2-10th,4th & outpcd 13th,kpt on 2 out,tk 2nd flat
1099 **Okeetee.............................Miss C Tarratt** 3
chsd ldrs, 3rd & outpcd 13th, chsd wnr 2 out, no imp
1003 River Galaxy *prom, ld 10-14th, outpcd by wnr aft, wknd 2 out* 4
995 Prince's Court *alwys bhnd, kpt on frm 2 out, nvr nrr* .. 5
999 Sutton Lass 5a *rear, mstk 12th & sn strggling, t.o.* 6
6 ran. 12l, 2l, 8l, 1l, 25l. Time 6m 2.90s. SP 1-4.
C D Dawson (Brocklesby).

1239 - Restricted (12st)

1102 **WHINSTONE MILL....................R Thornton** 1
prom, ld/disp frm 8th, drvn clr 2 out, hng left flat
1173 **Majestic Ride........................R Armson** 2
mstk 6th,in tch,outpcd & mstk 14th,ran on 3 out,tk 2nd flat
727 **Needwood Neptune ....A Sansome** 3
(fav) cls up, jnd wnr 14th, blnd 16th, hrd rdn & one-pcd frm 2 out
1101 Miss Cresta 5a *plIng, prom, wth wnr 4 out, wknd aft nxt* 4
1104 Hehas *w.w., going wll 12th, outpcd nxt, no imp on ldrs 4 out* 5
433 Henfield *mstks, raced wd, rear, outpcd 13th, kpt on* ... 6
1195 Tel D'Or *mstk 4th, alwys rear, t.o. 14th* 7
1102 Sporting Lark 5a *prom to 8th, sn rear, wll bhnd whn p.u. 15th* ..... pu
904 Unlucky For Some (Ire) *ld to 8th, prom til lost tch 15th, wll bhnd whn p.u. last* ..... pu
9 ran. 10l, 1l, 5l, 3l, 6l, dist. Time 6m 9.20s. SP 25-1.
Mrs Bambi Hornbuckle (Belvoir).

1240 - Open Maiden Div I (12st)

1104 **MR GEE ....L Hicks** 1
(fav) cls up, chal 16th, not qckn nxt, styd on frm last to ld post
1103 **Apple Nicking ....A Hill** 2
prom, ld 14th, clr whn mstk last, wknd & hdd post
1018 **Miners Rest 5a...............................L Lay** 3
w.w. cls up 12th, ev ch 15th, outpcd frm 3 out
1103 Full Song 5a *alwys prom, ev ch 15th, wknd apr 3 out* 4
972 Top The Bid *prom, ld 12th til mstk 14th, wknd apr 3 out.* 5
1105 Great Legend *12s-8s, made most to 12th, ev ch 15th, wknd, 6th whn f 2 out.* f
173 Boscoe *alwys bhnd, t.o. & p.u. 14th* pu
1104 Remalone 5a *alwys bhnd, t.o. last whn ran out apr 9th.* ro
900 Brenda's Dream 7a *rear, 7th & in tch whn f 11th* f
1104 Seaton Mill *pllng, prom, mstk 7th, mid-div whn u.r. bnd apr 9th* ur
10 ran. Sht-hd, 15l, 6l, 4l. Time 6m 6.00s. SP 7-4.
M W Conway (Quorn).

1241 - Open Maiden Div II (12st)

1183 **SUPREME DREAM (IRE) 5a ....Mrs P Adams** 1
cls up, ld 13th, jnd 2 out-last, found ext flat
890 **Mr Wendyl.........................M Emmanuel** 2
prom, chsd wnr 13th, chal & lvl 2 out-last, not qckn flat
1105 **Foolish Soprano 5a ....John Pritchard** 3
(fav) hld up last, prog 13th, 3rd 4 out, found nil frm 2 out
1177 Bet A Lot 5a *cls up til mstk & wknd 16th, t.o.* 4
Lord Kilton *ld/disp to 12th, 6th & wkng whn crashed thro wing 14th* ro
1182 Space Molly 5a *last frm 11th, t.o. & p.u. 16th* pu
1105 Strong Account (Ire) *pllng, prom/disp to 10th, wknd 15th, t.o. & p.u. 2 out* pu
Dancing Supreme *prom, ld 10-12th, 7th & wkng whn f nxt.* f
8 ran. 1l, 10l, 25l. Time 6m 8.00s. SP 3-1.
Mrs Pauline Adams (Pytchley).
J.N.

BERKELEY
Woodford
Saturday April 27th
GOOD

1242 - Restricted (12st)

466 **MARKET GOSSIP ....M Miller** 1
in tch, chsd ldr 10th, ld 16th, styd on strgly frm 2 out
947 **Saxon Lass 5a ....A Martin** 2
alwys prom, wth wnr 2 out, no ext und pres last
820 **Strong Chairman (Ire) 7a ....Miss P Curling** 3
(fav) held up, prog to 3rd 16th, not qckn nxt, kpt on flat
946 Bakmalad *mid-div, 8th & in tch hlfwy, onepcd frm 3 out.* 4
822 Churchtown Chance (Ire) 5a *chsd ldrs, 3rd hlfwy, ld 15-16th, grdly wknd* 5
1101 This I'll Do Us (Ire) *alwys rear, 13th hlfwy, nvr trbld ldrs* 6
1225 Astley Jack *unruly stt, blndrd 4th, chsd ldr to 8th, wll bhnd, p.u. 13th* pu
960 Kamtara *chsd ldrs to 7th, soon lost plc, p.u. apr 11th* pu
1101 Sinberto 5a *ld to 14th, wknd rpdly & p.u. nxt* pu
Red Russe *p.u. 5th, (lame)* pu
466 Bryn's Story *bhnd, blndrd 3rd, last frm 7th, t.o. & p.u. 3 out* pu
956 Son Of Anun *nvr trbld ldrs, 10th hlfwy, t.o. & p.u. 16th* pu
840 Coolmoreen (Ire) *w.w, prog to 7th & in tch hlfwy, wknd 16th, p.u. 3 out* pu
742 Aldington Charlie *blndrd & u.r. 1st.* ur
1223 Right Rosy 5a *mstks, alwys rear div, 12th hlfwy, t.o. & p.u. 3 out* pu
997 Sit Tight *chsd ldrs, 4th hlfwy, wknd apr 3 out, 6th whn p.u. 2 out* pu
712 Baron Bigfoot *s.s., some prog to 9th hlfwy, nvr on terms, p.u. 16th.* pu
734 I'minonit 1ow *alwys rear, jmp lft 5th, no ch frm 11th, p.u. 3 out* pu
18 ran. 2l, 1l, 8l, 10l, 12l. Time 6m 33.00s. SP 7-1.
R J Tory (Portman).

1243 - Members

837 **LANDSKER ALFRED ....Miss A Dare** 1
(fav) blndrd 3rd, chsd ldr 6th, ld apr 16th, clr 3 out, easy
Ardell Boy.........................Miss P Gundry 2
ld, blndrd 10th, hdd apr 16th, blndrd nxt, soon outpcd
1078 **Prince Nepal ....G Barfoot-Saunt** 3
chsd ldrs, 3rd & outpcd 15th, no ch whn blndrd last
848 Country Life (USA) *chsd ldrs to 3rd, soon bhnd, t.o. 7th, fin lame, (disq)* 4D
1213 Always Great *held up, 4th & blndrd 13th, soon lost tch, t.o. & p.u. 3 out* pu
Budget *chsd ldr to 6th, soon wll bhnd, u.r. 8th* ur
6 ran. 12l, 10l, 2 fences. Time 6m 33.00s. SP 1-3.
Dr P Brown / Mrs S Birks (Berkeley).
Country Life disq failed to weigh-in.

1244 - Intermediate (12st)

1112 **CALLING WILD (IRE) ....T Mitchell** 1
(fav) chsd ldr til lft in ld 14th,slght mstk 3out,clr nxt,pshd out
657 **Earthmover (Ire) 7a..............Miss P Curling** 2
held up, prog to chs wnr 16th, ev ch nxt, no ext
1046 **Carbery Arctic ....G Barfoot-Saunt** 3
prom in chsng grp, 4th & rddn 16th, onepcd
1112 Perseverance *tkn down early,8th hlfwy,lost tch 14th,styd on 3 out,nvrdang* 4
847 Judy Line 5a *prom in chsng grp til outpcd apr 16th* 5
1019 Tattlejack (Ire) *chsd ldrs, 4th & blndrd 13th, sn rddn, outpcd apr 16th.* 6
1171 Bear's Flight 5ex *mid-div, lost tch apr 16th, last whn nrly ref last, t.o.* 7
784 Bective Boy 5ex *prog 8th, 3rd & ev ch 16th, sn btn, p.u. & dismntd last* pu
995 Master Swillbrook *blnd 1st, lost tch 11th, t.o. & p.u. 3 out.* pu
943 Nether Gobions 5ex *ld, blnd 8th, f 14th.* f
1047 Itsallamatter (Ire) *s.s., blnd 8th, 11th & no ch hlfwy, p.u. 14th* pu
Nicolinsky 5a *alwys bhnd, last hlfwy, t.o. & p.u. 3 out* pu
12 ran. 3l, 12l, 2l, 12l, 15l, 30l. Time 6m 29.00s. SP 6-4.
J A Keighley (Blackmore & Sparkford Vale).

1245 - Ladies

839 **SPLIT SECOND ....Miss A Dare** 1
(fav) trckd ldrs, lft 2nd 9th, ld 3 out, easy
1018 **Tudor Henry ....Mrs C Mitchell** 2
ld to 16th, onepcd aft
1035 **Vatacan Bank...................Miss B Williams** 3
alwys rear, wnt poor 3rd 13th, nvr dang
1170 Running Frau 5a *alwys rear, last frm 9th, t.o.* 4
924 Little Thyne *chsd ldr to 3rd, lost tch 7th, lost iron 12th, p.u. 15th* pu
815 Strong Tarquin (Ire) *chsd ldr 4th, disp 2nd whn f 9th* f
6 ran. 5l, 25l, dist. Time 6m 31.00s. SP 4-5.
Mrs P J Willis (Berkeley).

1246 - Open (12st)

1211 **GEE DOUBLE YOU.......................B Tulloch** 1
in tch, ld 9th, drew clr 2 out, comf
998 **Cheeky Cheval ....D Dennis** 2
prog 10th, lft 3rd 15th, rdn & btn 3 out, tk 2nd cls home
817 **Sayyure (USA) 4ex ....A Harris** 3
(fav) raced wd, prom, ev ch 3 out, sn btn, eased cls home
955 Dark Sirona 5a *chsd ldr to 7th, wll bhnd frm 13th, t.o.* 4

230 Viascorit *keen hold, ld to 8th, sn bhnd, last & p.u. 13th* .... pu
1220 Killy's Filly 5a *trckd ldrs, jnd ldr 11th til ran out & u.r. 15th* .... ro
6 ran. 15l, 1½l, 1 fence. Time 6m 29.00s. SP 7-4.
J D Watkins (Curre).

1247 - Confined (12st)

745 **RIP VAN WINKLE .... Miss A Dare 1**
lft 2nd 11th, ld 15th, clr nxt, hung rght frm 3 out,kpt on
710 **Desert Waltz (Ire) 3ex .... Miss P Curling 2**
(fav) prog 8th, lft in ld 11-14th, chsd wnr, rdn 2 out, onepcd
523 **Its All Over Now .... D Renney 3**
mid-div, 4th & outpcd 14th, wnt mod 3rd cls home
Epileny *lft in ld 9th til ran wd apr 11th, 3rd & outpcd frm 14th* 4
1167 Major Wayne *last frm 7th, t.o.* 5
Devils Elbow *sn clr ld, 30l clr whn f 9th* .... f
845 Brabiner King *chsd ldrs, outpcd & blnd 14th, 5th & no ch whn f 3 out* .... f
7 ran. 5l, 30l, 1l, dist. Time 6m 27.00s. SP Evens.
Dr P Brown / Mrs S Birks (Berkeley).

1248 - Maiden (12st)

849 **ALWAYS ALLIED (IRE) .... Miss V Roberts 1**
prom, ld 15th, kckd clr, lft wll clr 3 out, unchal
712 **Salmon Poutcher 5a .... J Trice-Rolph 2**
in tch, 4th 13th, outpcd 15th, lft 2nd 3 out, kpt on
1164 **Wired For Sound .... P Howse 3**
blnd 3rd, bhnd, 9th hlfwy, kpt on frm 3 out, nvr nrr
842 Royal Swinger 5a *chsd ldr 6-10th, outpcd apr 16th, no dang aft* 4
1006 Bolshie Baron *prom, chsd ldr 11-16th, wknd* 5
1128 Nearly Five Too 5a *blnd 4th, 12th & no ch hlfwy, f 14th* .... f
1107 Peppermill Lane *mid-div, 8th hlfwy, rdn & lost tch 13th, p.u. 2 out* .... pu
1161 Snippetoff *rear div, some prog whn f 8th* .... f
1081 Noble Minister *alwys rear, 11th hlfwy, t.o. & p.u. 3 out (lame)* .... pu
1039 City Rhythm *ld til hdd & f 15th* .... f
956 Gt Hayes Pommard *s.s., jmp bdly, fence bhnd whn p.u. aft 5th* .... pu
1175 Rusty Fellow *held up,10th hlfwy,prog to 2nd 16th,clsng whn blnd & u.r.nxt* .... ur
1047 Constant Sula 5a *(fav) chsd ldr til blnd 5th, rdn & strglng 13th, no ch & p.u. last* .... pu
956 Ragtimer *mid-div, mstk & rmmdr 9th, 6th whn hmp & u.r. 15th* .... ur
Flashmans Mistress 5a *alwys rear, last hlfwy, p.u. 13th* .... pu
15 ran. 10l, 6l, 2l, 20l. Time 6m 41.00s. SP 5-2.
Miss Victoria Roberts (Berkeley).
S.P.

FIFE
Balcormo Mains
Saturday April 27th
GOOD TO SOFT

1249 - Restricted

82 **ENSIGN EWART (IRE) 7a .... C Storey 1**
(fav) 5th hlfwy, hdwy to ld aft 3 out, sn clr
914 **Royal Surprise .... Miss P Robson 2**
rmmndrs aft 4th, 2nd hlfwy, ld 13th til outpcd aft 3 out
1106 **Wire Lass 5a .... R Morgan 3**
6th hlfwy, tk 3rd cls home, nvr dang
189 The Buachaill (Ire) *ld til 13th, grdly wknd* 4
1106 Sarona Smith 5a *bhnd by 6th, nvr dang* 5
501 Corby Knowe *bhnd by hlfwy, t.o.* 6
1131 Roly Prior *3rd hlfwy, lost tch by 3 out, p.u. bfr last* .... pu
1000 Deday *t.o. by 5th, p.u. aft 12th* .... pu
1082 Kalajo *bhnd whn p.u. bfr 12th* .... pu
750 Solwaysands *4th hlfwy, sn lost tch, p.u. 4 out* .... pu
10 ran. 8l, 15l, 1½l, 25l, dist. Time 7m 32.00s. SP 7-2.
Maj M Sample (College Valley).

1250 - Ladies

913 **HOUSELOPE BECK .... Miss S Forster 1**
made all, drew clr 2 out
911 **Joli Exciting 5a .... Miss D Laidlaw 2**
not alwys fluent, chsd wnr frm 11th, no ext frm 2 out
789 **Minibrig 5a .... Miss P Robson 3**
(fav) bhnd, some hdwy frm 3 out, nvr nrr
860 Rarely At Odds *alwys bhnd* 4
1084 Golesa *chsd wnr til wknd frm 11th, t.o. whn p.u. apr 3 out* .... pu
5 ran. 8l, 8l, dist. Time 7m 33.00s. SP 3-1.
F V White (Percy).

1251 - Open (12st)

860 **MASTER KIT (IRE) .... J Billinge 1**
(fav) disp ld frm 6th til wnt clr frm 2 out
610 **Buckle It Up .... R Hale 2**
ld til 5th, disp frm 13th until outpcd frm 2 out
1106 **Across The Card 7ex .... W Ramsay 3**
held up, some hdwy frm 4 out, nvr dang
1226 Mr Diplomatic *ld/disp frm 5th til wknd frm 13th* 4
1083 Reed *3rd hlfwy, sn lost tch* 5
751 Sharp Opinion *sn last, lost tch by 12th, p.u. apr 3 out* .... pu
6 ran. 12l, 10l, dist. Time 7m 23.00s. SP 4-5.
J Billinge (Fife).

1252 - Intermediate (12st)

647 **BALISTEROS (FR) .... A Parker 1**
alwys in tch, ld 3 out, sn clr
858 **Fiscal Policy .... H Trotter 2**
ld til 6th, last & plenty to do 13th,styd on wll frm 4 out
1151 **Toaster Crumpet .... Miss P Robson 3**
ld 6th til outpcd frm 3 out
914 In Demand 7a *(fav) held up in tch til wknd qckly 4 out* 4
1088 Kincardine Bridge (USA) *cls up til wknd qckly apr 13th, p.u. bfr nxt* .... pu
5 ran. 8l, ½l, dist. Time 7m 34.00s. SP 11-2.
Mrs B K Thomson (Berwickshire).

1253 - Open Maiden Div I

705 **SNAPPER 7a .... R Hale 1**
(fav) ld aft 12th, made rest, held on wll
1089 **All Or Nothing 5a .... J Ewart 2+**
gd hdwy frm 4 out, fin strgly, not rch wnr
Nothingtotellme (Ire) 7a .... A Parker 2+
ev ch frm 4 out, no ext run in
905 Madame Beck 5a *alwys hndy, ev ch til no ext frm 2 out* 4
1087 Good Profit *nvr rch ldrs* 5
614 Megans Mystery (Ire) *bhnd early, wnt hndy 4 out, wknd qckly frm nxt* 6
Mossiman (Ire) *not fluent, hndy til wknd qckly 4 out* 7
1088 Exile Run (Ire) *prom to hlfwy, sn wknd* 8
1136 Terracotta Warrior *prom early, lost tch frm hlfwy* 9
704 Strong Chance *p.u. aft 4th, (broke leg)* .... pu
1089 Zoflo 5a *prom to hlfwy, bhnd whn p.u. 4 out* .... pu
405 K Walk 5a *ld til wknd frm 12th, p.u. 4 out* .... pu
Buckaroo 7a *bhnd by hlfwy, p.u. aft 12th* .... pu
Fragrant Lord *bhnd whn p.u. aft 12th* .... pu
407 Phoza Moya (Ire) 7a *bhnd whn p.u. aft 12th* .... pu
916 Little Hawk *bhnd by hlfwy, p.u. aft 12th* .... pu
16 ran. 3l, dd-ht, 4l, 20l, 6l, 6l, 20l, ½l. Time 7m 43.00s. SP 5-4.
R H Black (Fife).

1254 - Open Maiden Div II

1089 **ROYAL FIFE 5a .... R Hale 1**
last early, steadd prog to ld last, drvn out
755 **Eostre .... A Parker 2**
alwys hndy, 4th hlfwy, ld apr 2 out, no ext flat
614 **Ballyargan (Ire) .... R Westwood 3**
alwys hndy, 3rd hlfwy, styd on onepcd frm 3 out

Price War *ld/disp frm 8th til no ext frm 2 out* 4
613 Trumpet Hill *ld til 4th, grdly lost tch* 5
1087 Amanda Bay *bhnd whn p.u. aft 12th* .... pu
1087 Rustic Bridge *5th hlfwy, bhnd whn p.u. 2 out* .... pu
1089 Newbrano 5a (bl) *prom early, bhnd whn p.u. 4 out* .... pu
756 Murder Moss (Ire) *nvr dang, p.u. 3 out* .... pu
405 Disrespect 5a *bhnd whn p.u. aft 12th* .... pu
1089 Mapalak 5a *f 5th* .... f
1088 I'm Joking *prom to hlfwy, bhnd whn p.u. 2 out* .... pu
705 Kings Token *(fav) ld/disp frm 4th til wknd qckly 15th, p.u. 2 out* .... pu
1088 Pandandy 7a *bhnd whn p.u. aft 12th* .... pu
14 ran. 3l, nk, 8l, 20l. Time 7m 43.00s. SP 8-1.
Mrs C G Braithwaite (Fife).

1255 - Members

1083 **FORDSTOWN (IRE)** .... **J Alexander** 1
(fav) made all, unchal
Bruce's Castle .... **Miss K Durie** 2
nvr a threat, wll bhnd frm 3 out
2 ran. Dist. Time 7m 59.00s. SP 2-9.
Jamie Alexander (Fife).
R.J.

FITZWILLIAM
Cottenham
Saturday April 27th
FIRM

1256 - Members

1100 **CURRENT ATTRACTION 5a** .... **Miss L Allan** 1
ld 2nd, hdd brfly 4th, hdd 10th, ld 4 out, rdn clr flat
1101 **Kerry My Home** .... **T Marks** 2
(fav) prom, mstk 1st, ld brfly 4th, ld 10th-4 out, no ext 2 out
969 **Valatch** .... **J Henderson** 3
ld to 2nd, chsd ldng pair 8th, outpcd 4 out
Sultan *s.s. alwys bhnd, lost tch 10th, t.o. 12th* 4
1064 Stanwick Lass 5a *hld up rear, mstk 10th, lost tch nxt, sn t.o.* 5
970 Highland Laird *alwys rear, mstks 2nd & 4th, strgglng 7th, t.o. 12th,f 4 out* .... f
6 ran. 15l, 20l, 5l, 20l. Time 6m 7.00s. SP Evens.
R H Fox (Fitzwilliam).

1257 - Confined (12st)

1068 **STANWICK FARLAP 5a 3ex** .... **T Marks** 1
(fav) alwys prom, ld aft 12th, prssd 3 out, rdn out flat, comf
906 **Notary-Nowell** .... **Miss L Hollis** 2
mid-div, prog to cls 3rd 13th, chal 3 out, ev ch last, hld
310 **Jimstro** .... **R Wakley** 3
alwys prom, disp to 8th & 9-12th, chal 3 out, blnd nxt,no ex
Pike's Glory *prom to 3rd, last by nxt, mstk 5th, sn lost tch, t.o.* 4
Daisy Pond (Ire) 5a *rear,mstks 10 & 11th, lost tch 13th, crawld 2 out, ref last* .... ref
5 ran. 1½l, 6l, 1 fence. Time 6m 13.00s. SP 1-2.
T F G Marks (Fitzwilliam).

1258 - Open (12st)

1065 **RIVER MELODY 5a** .... **T Moore** 1
hld up, ld 5th-8th, chal last, bttr pace flat
634 **Elder Prince** .... **P Gee** 2
(fav) ld 3-5th, ld 8th, qcknd 4 out, hdd & outpcd flat
835 **Mount Eaton Fox** .... **R Page** 3
ld to 2nd, lost tch 8th, t.o.
3 ran. 3l, 1 fence. Time 6m 29.00s. SP Evens.
T W Moore (Essex).

1259 - Ladies

1147 **CHERRY CHAP** .... **Miss L Hollis** 1
(fav) chsd ldrs,prog to 2nd 13th,disp 15th til ld apr last,rdn out
903 **Ovac Star** .... **Miss S Gritton** 2
mid-div, prog 12th, outpcd 14th, styd on 2 out, tk 2nd flat
1066 **Ashboro (Ire)** .... **Miss G Chown** 3
rear, outpcd 12th, styd on wll frm 3 out, nrst fin
1208 Gilson's Cove *alwys prom, ld 4th, jnd 4 out, hdd apr last, wknd flat* 4
1186 Phelioff *wth ldrs til wknd frm 15th, btn whn mstk nxt, t.o.* 5
5 ran. 2½l, ½l, 1l, 20l. Time 5m 59.00s. SP 6-4.
J Bowles (Waveney Harriers).

1260 - Restricted (12st)

868 **COOL GINGER** .... **R Sweeting** 1
(fav) ld,wd bnd aft 3rd,hdd 4 out,ld agn 2 out,hdd flat,ld nr fn
1145 **Tenderman (Ire) 7a** .... **S Cowell** 2
chsd ldr to 9th,ld 15th,hdd 2 out,ld flat,hdd cls hm
679 **Radiant Monarch** .... **R Gill** 3
sttld rear,2nd at 9th,rdn 13th,outpcd frm 4 out
3 ran. ½l, dist. Time 6m 6.00s. SP 4-5.
C J R Sweeting (Heythrop).

1261 - Open Maiden (12st)

1064 **AUGHNACLOY ROSE** .... **R Page** 1
outpcd, mstk 9th, styd on 3 out, 6l down last, fin wll,ld fn
681 **Lights Out** .... **R Wakley** 2
(fav) chsd ldr, mstk 11th, ld 15th-4 out, ld last, hdd nr fin
1149 **Shelter** .... **N King** 3
ld at gd pace to 15th, ld 4 out-last, no ext flat
1149 Royal Quarry *wth ldrs til outpcd frm 14th, wknd 4 out* 4
496 Lavins Thatch 5a *alwys rear, blnd 4th, last nxt, rdn 10th, onepcd aft* 5
1149 Little Freddie *mid-div, lost tch ldrs 12th, wknd rpdly nxt, fin tired* 6
930 Sign Performer *mid-div whn u.r. 1st* .... ur
814 Hit The Bid (Ire) 7a *trckd ldrs, prog to 4th at 12th, mstk nxt,wknd, p.u. 4 out* .... pu
1104 Malvern Lad *mid-div, mstks 6 & 8th, bhnd whn p.u. 12th, dsmntd* .... pu
935 Saffron Queen 7a *withdrawn und orders start* 0
10 ran. ¾l, 1½l, 20l, 5l. Time 6m 11.00s. SP 16-1.
D Etheridge (East Essex).
J.W.

LLANGEINOR
Pyle
Saturday April 27th
GOOD

1262 - Members

1035 **TRICKY DEX (USA)** .... **J Tudor** 1
(fav) w.w. prog 11th, ld 13th, hit 2 out, clr last
1199 **Doubting Donna 5a** .... **D Hughes** 2
8s-7/2, 10l 4th at 10th, rdn 14th, styd on to 2nd flat
1157 **Bronze Effigy (bl)** .... **R Jones** 3
last til prog 13th, no ext frm nxt, tk 3rd flat
1199 Abbreviation *prom, chsd ldr 14th, still 2nd last, reluc flat* 4
1202 Lucky Ole Son *ld to 5th, cls up til wknd 13th, t.o. & u.r. 2 out* .... ur
Sharing Thoughts 5a *ld 6-12th, p.u. lame aft nxt* .... pu
6 ran. 10l, 10l, 3l. Time 6m 23.00s. SP 7-4.
D Gibbs (Llangeinor).

1263 - Confined (12st)

1197 **CHERRY ISLAND (IRE)** .... **J Jukes** 1
(fav) cls up til ld 8th, kicked clr 14th, unchal
1204 **Good Holidays 5a** .... **D S Jones** 2
ld 5-7th, wth wnr til outpcd frm 14th
1157 **The Batchlor** .... **J P Keen** 3
rear, cls 7th at 7th, went remote 3rd 14th, styd on

980 Gus McCrae *nvr rchd front rank, 10l 5th at 13th, no ch frm nxt* 4
1157 Golden Arctic *5l 3rd at 10th, not qckn 13th, wknd 15th, p.u. 2 out* 5
1157 Harken Premier *cls up whn f 2nd* .... f
154 Harwall Queen 5a *rear 5th, lost tch 11th, t.o. & p.u. 14th* .... pu
1157 Light The Wick 7ex *cls up til outpcd 11th, t.o. & p.u. 15th* .... pu
1157 Icecapade (Bel) *ld to 4th, lost plc 11th, t.o. & p.u. 14th* pu
9 ran. Dist, 12l, 2l. Time 6m 16.00s. SP 7-4.
Mrs Heather Gibbon (Pembrokeshire).

1264 - Ladies

1036 **MENDIP MUSIC** .... **Miss E Crawford** 1
w.w. prog 13th, rdn to ld last, kpt on
1159 **Never Be Great 5ex** .... **Miss L Pearce** 2
cls 4th at 11th, ev ch til not qckn frm 2 out,fin 3rd,promtd
1199 **Lislary Lad** .... **Miss H Evans** 3
15l 3rd at 10th,prog to ld 15th,hdd aft 2 out,fin 4th,prmtd
1159 Moving Force *ld 2-12th, ev ch 14th, outpcd frm nxt* ... 5
1046 Night Wind *(fav) chsd ldr, ld 13th, hdd & wknd 3 out* .. 6
1036 Afaristoun (Fr) *in tch til outpcd 11th, no ch frm 13th* ... 7
1202 Mount Falcon *s.v.s. fence bhnd frm 8th* 8
1034 News Review 7ex *ld 1st,rstrnd,prog to 3rd 14th,styd on apr last,fin 2nd,disq* 0
1159 Emerald Gem (bl) *rear 2nd, dist 9th whn u.r. flat apr 7th* .... ur
1078 Rapid Rascal *8l 3rd at 6th, wknd 14th, no ch whn f 2 out* .... f
10 ran. 2½l, 1½l, 1l, 5l, 6l, 25l, 25l. Time 6m 17.00s. SP 7-1.
Miss E Crawford (Curre).
New Review finished 2nd, disqualified, missed marker. Original dists.

1265 - Open (12st)

693 **HANDSOME HARVEY** .... **J Jukes** 1
(fav) ld frm 4th, prssd frm 14th, rdn & hld on flat
1211 **Touch 'N' Pass** .... **J Tudor** 2
trckd ldrs, chal und pres 14th, disp 2 out, just hld
1156 **Adanac** .... **A Price** 3
ld to 3rd, chal 14th, wknd frm nxt
1037 Robbie's Boy *chsd ldrs til outpcd 14th* 4
1037 Cornish Cossack (NZ) *cls up til outpcd frm 13th, no ch frm 15th* 5
996 Cool It A Bit *alwys rear, cls 7th at 6th, outpcd 8th, p.u. 13th* .... pu
1043 Volcanic Dancer (USA) *wppd round & u.r. start, rmntd, p.u. 13th* .... pu
1204 Dibloom 7ex *cls up til lost plc 8th, wknd & p.u. 12th* .. pu
8 ran. Hd, dist, nk, dist. Time 6m 16.00s. SP 2-5.
E L Harries (Pembrokeshire).

1266 - Restricted Div I (12st)

1040 **BARNABY BOY** .... **J P Keen** 1
hld up,prog 7th,cls up 14th,strng run 2 out,ld flat
1160 **Cottage Raider (Ire)** .... **T Jones** 2
ld 3rd-3 out, rallied nxt, ld last, hdd flat
1200 **Highland Minstrel** .... **J Jukes** 3
(fav) went 3l 3rd 13th, ld on inner 3 out, wknd aft nxt
980 Cranagh Moss (Ire) *cls up, 10l 5th at 14th, wknd frm 3 out* 4
1156 Cistolena 5a *cls up til lost plc & rdn 10th, t.o. 15th* 5
510 The Fun Of It *rear frm 4th, in tch 10th, wknd & p.u. 13th* .... pu
1034 Cosa Nostra *ld to 2nd, cls 2nd at 14th, wknd nxt, p.u. last* .... pu
1160 Benuad *mid-div, lost plc 13th, no ch nxt, p.u. 2 out* .. pu
1203 Silver Step *chsd ldr to 8th, wknd 12th, p.u. 14th* .... pu
1222 Rosenthal 5a *rear frm 5th, t.o. & p.u. 9th* .... pu
10 ran. 1l, 15l, 10l, dist. Time 6m 18.00s. SP 4-1.
J L Brown (Llandeilo Farmers).

1267 - Restricted Div II (12st)

980 **THE APPRENTICE** .... **J Tudor** 1
made all, clr 5th, tired apr last, hld on well
1160 **Antarctic Call** .... **Miss N Richards** 2
alwys 2nd, styd on frm 15th, clsng flat
980 **Telephone** .... **P Hamer** 3
(fav) w.w. effrt & prog 13th, rdn & kpt on onepcd frm 15th
1203 Penny Lark *hld up, prog 9th, rdn & clsng frm 15th, hit last, wknd flat* 4
1160 Tudor Oaks 5a *12l 3rd at 8th, outpcd frm 12th, no ch 14th* 5
1160 Downhill Racer 5a *prom in chsng grp til 9th, wknd 11th, p.u. 14th* .... pu
1160 Hatterill Ridge *20l 6th at 10th, no prog nxt, t.o. & p.u. 14th* .... pu
7 ran. ½l, 1l, 30l, 10l. Time 6m 20.00s. SP 7-2.
Robert Williams (Llangeinor).

1268 - Intermediate (12st)

981 **AFRICAN BRIDE (IRE) 5a 7ex** .... **T Jones** 1
(fav) ld 6th, drew clr 15th, easily
1157 **Polly Pringle 5a 7ex** .... **A Price** 2
10l 6th at 10th, effrt 13th, rdn into 2nd last, no ch wnr
1198 **Just Marmalade** .... **J Tudor** 3
ld to 5th, chsd wnr, 4l down 14th, rdn & no ext frm nxt
1198 Royal Oats 5a *8l 4th at 8th, just outpcd frm 12th, no ch frm 14th* 4
1198 The Last Mistress 5a *rmndrs 10th, lost tch 12th, styd on und pres 3 out* 5
1198 Origami *drppd rear 5th, lost tch 13th, t.o. & p.u. 2 out* pu
881 Oakers Hill *prom, cls 3rd whn hit 11th, wknd 13th, p.u. 15th* .... pu
1039 Pharrago (Ire) *rear frm 3rd, no ch frm 12th, t.o. & p.u. 3 out* .... pu
8 ran. 8l, 7l, 15l, 6l. Time 6m 17.00s. SP 4-5.
David Brace (Llangeinor).

1269 - Open Maiden Div I Pt I (12st)

1201 **MOONLIGHT CRUISE 5a** .... **P Williams** 1
ld 6-9th & 11-14th, rallied 3 out, ld last, ran on
1161 **Top Tor 5a** .... **T Vaughan** 2
prom, ld 10th, agn 15th, jnd 2 out, hdd & no ext last
1161 **Lady Romance (Ire) 5a** .... **J Jukes** 3
prog 10th, 3rd frm 13th, rdn & not rch ldrs frm 15th
1161 Boddington Hill 5a *lft in ld 5th, cls 5th apr 14th, onepcd frm nxt* 4
848 Le Gerard *cls up, cls 4th & ev ch 14th, wknd frm nxt* .. 5
1161 Cairneymount *(fav) ld til ran out & u.r. 5th* .... ro
Solars Sister 5a *rear 7th, no ch 11th, t.o. & p.u. 13th* .. pu
977 Quaker Pep *n.j.w. dtchd last til some prog 7th, no ch 10th, p.u. 2 out* .... pu
771 Deryn Y Cwm (Ire) *last frm 6th, ran off course apr 9th, p.u. 11th* .... pu
9 ran. 2l, 8l, 3l, 15l. Time 6m 29.00s. SP 6-1.
W J G Hughes (South Pembrokeshire).

1270 - Open Maiden Div I Pt II (12st)

1200 **SEA SEARCH** .... **J P Keen** 1
(fav) trckd ldrs going wll, ld 3 out, sn in cmmnd
1200 **It's So Sweet 5a** .... **A Price** 2
chsd ldrs,chal 13th,ld apr 15th, sn jnd, no ext und pres
1161 **Toucher (Ire)** .... **M Munrowd** 3
cls up til lft in ld 10th, hdd apr 15th, rdn & wknd
1040 Pyro Pennant *alwys prom, ev ch 14th, rdn & onepcd frm nxt* 4
605 Aldington Kid *ld til f 10th* .... f
1162 Greenhill Lady 5a *cls up, ev ch whn u.r. 11th* .... ur
976 Willows Wonderman *last frm 5th, ran out wing nxt* ... ro
1162 Royal Barge *rear whn ran out & u.r. 3rd* .... ro
Channel Island 5a *trailing frm 4th,short-lived effrt apr 14th, t.o. & p.u.3out* .... pu
9 ran. 5l, 10l, 3l. Time 6m 39.00s. SP 5-4.
C R Johnson (Llandeilo Farmers).

1271 - Open Maiden Div II (12st)

1039 **ROSIEPLANT 5a** .... **M Lewis** 1

alwys prom, ld 13th, rdn clr 3 out
976 **Harry From Barry....................J Tudor** 2
ld to 4th, cls up til chal 3 out, wknd frm nxt
849 **Classic Edition 7a....................S Shinton** 3
w.w. prog to 5l 3rd 14th, no ext frm nxt
1161 I'm A Bute 5a *mid-div, prog 8th, not qckn frm 13th, no ch frm 3 out* 4
842 Moonlight Shift *prog to ld 11th, wknd & p.u. aft 13th* .. pu
1201 Prince Theo *14s-8s, ld 5-10th, wknd aft 13th, no ch whn p.u. 2 out* .... pu
1039 Jolly Swagman 7a *prom, ev ch 13th, wknd nxt, p.u. 3 out.* .... pu
974 Blair House (Ire) 5a *in tch in mid-div whn f 11th, dead* f
847 Wooly Town 5a *alwys rear, t.o. 10th, p.u. nxt* .... pu
1201 Frontrunner 5a *cls up to 7th, no ch 10th, p.u. 12th* ...... pu
1162 Sweet Blue 5a *prom, cls up whn f 11th* .... f
1162 Royal Bula *(fav) trckd ldrs, cls up 11th, p.u. nxt* .... pu
Sea Tarth 7a *rear 6th, f 11th* .... f
849 Queen's Equa 5a *rear, losing tch 8th, t.o. 10th, p.u. 12th* .... pu
Mountain Slave 5a *alwys rear, t.o. 4th, p.u. 7th* .... pu
15 ran. Dist, 15l, 10l. Time 6m 35.00s. SP 3-1.
A Plant (Curre).

1272 - Open Maiden Div III Pt I (12st)

1162 **COLONEL FRAZER (IRE)..................G Lewis** 1
(fav) ld/disp til rdn clr frm 14th, kpt on und pres flat
1162 **Gold Tip 5a..........................J P Keen** 2
mostly 3rd/4th, lft chsng wnr 14th, kpt on onepcd frm 3 out
843 **Maytown (bl)..........................R Nolan** 3
last at 5th, t.o. 12th, styd on frm 14th
1201 Cefn Woodsman 7a *cls up til outpcd frm 13th* 4
850 Old Steine *p.u. lame apr 4th* .... pu
850 Puttingonthestyle *ld/disp til wknd aft 13th, dist 3rd whn ref 2 out* .... ref
883 Woodzee *trckd ldrs til p.u. lame aft 6th* .... pu
349 Catbrook Chance *cls 4th at 10th, 1l 2nd whn ran out 14th* .... ref
696 Bonus Number (Ire) *chsd ldrs, outpcd 11th, t.o. & p.u. 15th* .... pu
9 ran. 8l, 30l, 1l. Time 6m 39.00s. SP 9-4.
Ray Perkins (Gelligaer).

1273 - Open Maiden Div III Pt II (12st)

1161 **MISTER MCGASKILL....................P Williams** 1
cls up til chal 14th, ld nxt, lft solo 3 out
1047 Bob-Cam *prom, 15l 4th whn b.d 13th* .... bd
1161 I Is *chsd ldrs, 10l 3rd whn f 13th, dead* .... f
1200 Katy Country Mouse 5a *ld to 7th,wknd 11th,p.u. aft nxt,cont, fin aft evone lft* .... pu
1039 Spikeie Rose 5a *(fav) mid-div,lft dist 3rd whn ref 13th,cont,fin aft evone left* .... ref
550 Willows Engagement 5a *ld 8-14th, 2l down & lkd hld whn f 3 out* .... f
1156 Steel Valley (Ire) 5a *last at 5th, t.o. nxt, p.u. 11th* .... pu
1039 Irish Thinker 7a *mstks, cls up, ev ch whn u.r. 12th* .... ur
1201 Euromill Star 5a *mostly last, t.o. whn blnd 10th & p.u.* pu
9 ran. Time 6m 35.00s. SP 16-1.
P L Thomas (Glamorgan).
P.R.

TIVERTON STAGHOUNDS
Bratton Down
Saturday April 27th
GOOD TO FIRM

1274 - Members

1114 **MOUNTAIN MASTER...........Miss L Blackford** 1
(fav) made all, lft clr last
Just Rose 5a..........................R White 2
in tch early, 6th at 12th, prog 14th, btn whn lft 2nd last
926 **Darktown Strutter (bl)...............M Burrows** 3
prom to 14th, wknd & outpcd frm nxt
Play Risky (Ire) *rear, mstk 7th, wll bhnd 15th* 4
Glencommon *in tch to 11th, wknd & p.u. 14th* .... pu
Just As Hopeful (NZ) *alwys last, t.o. whn ref 4th* ...... ref
1117 Morchard Milly 5a *handy, 3rd at 12th, 2nd 14th, ev ch whn blnd & u.r. last* .... ur
7 ran. Dist, 3l, dist. Time 6m 21.50s. SP 10-11.
Mrs Sue Rowe (Tiverton Staghounds).

1275 - Open

817 **VITAL SONG..........................G Matthews** 1
ld til apr last,hdd,rallied & ran on wll,fin 1st,disq
1073 **Chilipour.............................N Harris** 2
(fav) hld up,2nd 12th,chal last,hld whn switchd flat,fin 2nd,prmtd
1108 **Nearly Splendid.......................T Greed** 3
hld up, prog 13th, ev ch 4 out, not qckn frm 2 out
1139 Good King Henry *in tch to 12th, outpcd frm 14th, walked in* 4
1125 Brabazon (USA) *sn bhnd, rdn 12th, nvr on terms* 5
1073 Whats The Crack *prom early, lost plc 9th, t.o. 13th* ... 6
1142 Cardinal Bird (USA) (bl) *bhnd, out of tch 13th, t.o. & p.u. last* .... pu
1109 Gratuity *handy to 13th, lost tch, p.u. 3 out, dsmntd* .... pu
8 ran. 3l, 15l, 30l, 1l, dist. Time 6m 3.70s. SP 4-5.
Vital Song finished 1st, placed 2nd after objection by runner-up. But reinstated on appeal.

1276 - Ladies

1110 **FAITHFUL STAR..................Miss S Vickery** 1
(fav) mstks, ld 6th, sn clr, easily
1110 **Interpretation (NZ)..............Miss R Francis** 2
hld up, went 2nd 3 out, no further prog aft
1069 **Chandigarh.........................Miss K Baily** 3
in tch, 2nd frm 6th til wknd frm 3 out
1074 The Kimbler *sn bhnd, t.o. 12th* 4
1072 Jokers Patch *sn wll bhnd, t.o. 11th* 5
Newski Express 5a *ld/disp til u.r. 5th* .... ur
1072 Happy Thought 5a *ld/disp early, in tch aft, cls 4th whn u.r. 11th* .... ur
7 ran. 12l, dist, dist, 10l. Time 5m 58.00s. SP 1-2.
M C Pipe (Taunton Vale).

1277 - Confined (12st)

5 **SLIEVENAMON MIST....................N Harris** 1
hld up, prog 10th, 2nd 12th, disp 15th til clr 2 out, easily
370 **Ragtime Boy..........................A Farrant** 2
mid-div, prog 15th, 2nd apr last, no ch wth wnr
1110 **Expressment 3ex....................I Widdicombe** 3
in tch, chsd ldrs 4 out, not qckn frm last
1111 Alpine Song 5a *in tch, ld 8th-14th, disp til outpcd frm 2 out* 4
1069 Just Ben *(fav) ld to 7th, cls up til wknd & outpcd frm 2 out.* 5
718 My Boy Buster *bhnd, t.o. 12th, outpcd* 6
1124 Bidston Mill *mid-div, outpcd 12th, no ch whn p.u. 2 out.* .... pu
1110 Friendly Lady 5a *prom, 4th at 12th, btn 4th whn u.r. last* .... ur
1117 Bright Road 5a (bl) *alwys rear, t.o. & p.u. 3 out* .... pu
1143 Here's Mary 5a *cls up, 7th at 12th, outpcd 14th, t.o. & p.u. 3 out* .... pu
1112 Remember Mac *mid-div, lost tch 9th, t.o. & p.u. 13th* .. pu
925 Monkton (Ire) *mid-div, p.u. 13th, dsmntd* .... pu
1128 Maboy Lady *rear whn blnd & u.r. 5th* .... ur
1112 Nice To No *mid-div, lost tch 11th, t.o. & p.u. 14th* .... pu
1081 Nothing To Fear *handy, 5th at 12th, wknd whn crashd thro wing 4 out* .... ro
15 ran. 10l, ½l, 4l, 10l, 2 fences. Time 6m 5.00s. SP 6-1.
Nick Viney (Dulverton (West)).

1278 - Intermediate (12st)

1123 **TASMIN TYRANT (NZ) 5ex..............L Jefford** 1
(fav) prom, disp 9th til ld 14th, styd on wll frm 3 out
816 **Thegoose..............................P King** 2
w.w. prog 4 out, ev ch 2 out, ran on wll frm last
1114 **Erme Rose (Ire) 5a..................R Nuttall** 3
ld/disp to 8th, cls up til not qckn frm last

1108 Lonesome Traveller (NZ) *ld/disp to 13th, outpcd frm 3 out* 4
Fellow Sioux *alwys mid-div, ev ch 4 out, outpcd frm nxt* 5
1139 Madiyan (USA) *rear, some prog 14th, outpcd frm 3 out* 6
1079 Cautious Rebel *in tch, 5th at 12th, btn whn f 16th* ..... f
529 Blue-Bird Express 5a *sn rear, t.o. 7th, p.u. 11th* ...... pu
1142 Brother Bill *alwys rear, nvr any ch, t.o. & p.u. last* .... pu
1074 Baldhu Chance *alwys prom, cls 2nd whn f 15th* ...... f
Alfree *mid-div whn f 5th* .... f
I Like The Deal 7a *alwys rear, no ch whn p.u. 3 out* ... pu
12 ran. 1l, 3l, 6l, 20l, 4l. Time 6m 4.00s. SP 5-4.
Mrs C Egalton (Axe Vale Harriers).

1279 - Open Maiden (5-7yo) Div I (12st)

1115 **NEARLY AT SEA 5a..............I Widdicombe** 1
(fav) w.w. 6th at 12th, prog 3 out, strng run to ld last 100 yrds
556 **Lucky Call (NZ) 7a....................A Farrant** 2
handy, 3rd at 12th, disp 3 out til hdd last 100 yrds
928 **Tangle Kelly ....Miss J Cumings** 3
ld/disp til hdd & outpcd aft last
284 Brook A Light 7a *handy, 2nd at 12th, ev ch 2 out, wknd last* 4
533 Risky Bid 5a *mid-div, 4th at 12th, outpcd frm 3 out* 5
1118 Medias Maid 5a *in tch, 5th at 12th, lost plc & wknd 4 out* 6
1118 Flemings Fleur *prom whn u.r. 4th* .... ur
1075 Crucis (Ire) 7a *5s-5/2, plld hrd, cls up whn f 11th* ...... f
820 Melling 7a *prom whn c.o. by loose horse 5th* .... co
1116 Saint Joseph *mid-div, lost tch 14th, p.u. last* .... pu
1070 Tinstreamer Johnny 7a *rear, no ch whn p.u. 4 out, dsmntd* .... pu
719 Devonshire Lad 7a *prom, disp whn c.o. by loose horse 8th* .... co
871 Trolly 7a *mid-div, lost tch 13th, t.o. & p.u. 3 out* ..... pu
Lucky Thursday *rear, blnd & u.r. 2nd* .... ur
14 ran. 2l, 2l, 12l, 10l, 2l. Time 6m 27.00s. SP 7-4.
C J Down (East Devon).

1280 - Open Maiden (5-7yo) Div II (12st)

1115 **PENNY'S PRINCE...............Miss A Goschen** 1
w.w. prog 14th, chal aft last, ran on wll to ld flat
1116 **Steamburd 5a......................Miss J Sleep** 2
ld/disp to 13th, chsd ldr aft, onepcd 2 out, fin 3rd, prmtd
1109 **Polly's Corner 5a ....R Emmett** 3
mid-div, prog 14th, nrst fin, fin 4th, promoted
819 Olive Basket 7a *j.w. alwys prom, 3rd at 12th, wknd frm 3 out, improve* 5
870 Kahlo 5a *alwys rear, no ch frm 4 out* 6
145 Three And A Half *handy, 2nd at 12th, ld 14th til hdd cls hm, fin 2nd, disq.* 0
1071 Itscountryman *prom to 13th, wknd nxt, p.u. 15th, dsmntd* .... pu
1117 Fair Lark *alwys mid-div, no ch whn p.u. last* ...... pu
734 Saucy's Wolf *rear, no show, t.o. & p.u. 13th* .... pu
1075 Secret Siphoner *sn rear, t.o. & p.u. 11th* .... pu
1116 Ducky Pool (Ire) *w.w. prog 14th, 3rd & chal whn u.r. flat, dead* .... ur
1118 Heatherton Park 7a *(fav) w.w. prog 12th, ev ch 3 out, wknd nxt, btn 4th whn f last* .... f
521 Funny Farm *16s-10s, plld hrd, ran wd bnd aft 2nd, ran out nxt* .... ro
1116 Legal Affair 7a *sn rear, t.o. & ref 14th* .... ref
14 ran. ½l, 10l, 5l, 2l, 15l. Time 6m 18.00s. SP 6-1.
J Sprake (Blackmore & Sparkford Vale).
Three And A Half fin 2nd, disq, rider not W/I. Original dists. D.P.

YORK & AINSTY
Easingwold
Saturday April 27th
GOOD

1281 - Confined (12st)

824 **FLIP THE LID (IRE) 5a 3ex...............N Tutty** 1
(fav) hld up, prog to chs ldrs 5th, ld 10th, jnd flat, ran on wll
1092 **Just Charlie 3ex ....S Swiers** 2
ld to 3rd, prom, chsd wnr 3 out, chal flat, not qckn cls hm
984 **Golden Savannah 5ex ....M Sowersby** 3
alwys prom, 2nd at 15th, no prog aft, onepcd
1154 Band Sargeant (Ire) *alwys prom, disp ld 7-9th, onepcd frm 4 out* 4
1130 Flying Lion *rear, pshd alng 7th, nvr on terms* 5
824 Pinewood Lad *mid-div, lost plc 11th, nvr dang aft* 6
968 Good Team 3ex *rear, mstk 5th, wknd 11th, sn lost tch* 7
Jolly Fellow *rear, sn bhnd, t.o.* 8
1130 Sharpridge *nvr bttr than mid-div, wknd 10th, t.o. & p.u. 15th* .... pu
1023 Osgathorpe 5ex *alwys rear, lost tch 11th, p.u. 14th* ... pu
824 Valiant Vicar *sn rear, rdn 11th, lost tch, t.o. & p.u. 14th* .... pu
826 Cleasby Hill *prom, rdn 9th, sn lost plc, t.o. & p.u. 13th* pu
1130 Fowling Piece *prom, ld 3rd til disp 7th, grad fdd, wll btn whn f 2 out* .... f
1131 Caman 5a *rear, mid-div whn u.r. 9th* .... ur
983 Tom The Tank *sn rear, mstk 11th, wll bhnd whn p.u. 14th* .... pu
15 ran. 1l, 6l, 3l, 7l, 7l, 1l, dist. Time 5m 52.00s. SP 7-4.
Peter Sawney (Cleveland).

1282 - Open

1133 **PARK DRIFT................................R Tate** 1
keen hold,alwys prom,ld 10th-12th,ld 14th,clr 2 out,easily
1093 **Hyperion Son..............................M Haigh** 2
alwys chsng ldrs, pshd alng 15th, kpt on frm 2 out
1091 **Latheron (Ire) (bl).......................S Swiers** 3
sttld mid-div, prog 13th, lft 2nd 3 out, ev ch & wd nxt
826 Fiery Sun *(fav) ld to 10th, sn lost plc, onepcd frm 4 out* 4
984 Amy's Mystery *mstk 1st, mid-div, rdn 11th, t.o. frm 15th* 5
1092 Minstrel Paddy (v) *rear, mstk 5th, lost tch 7th, t.o. & p.u. 14th* .... pu
1093 Frome Boy *n.j.w. sn dtchd, ran out & u.r. 10th* .... ro
985 Saxon Fair *keen hld,trckd ldrs,ld 12th-14th, ev ch whn p.u. 3 out,lame* .... pu
8 ran. 5l, 1½l, 15l, dist. Time 5m 54.00s. SP 5-2.
G Thornton (York & Ainsty North).

1283 - Ladies

1132 **DUNTIME.......................Miss J Eastwood** 1
trckd ldr, disp 7th, ld nxt, qcknd 2 out, ran on strngly
1023 **Integrity Boy ....Miss A Armitage** 2
rear, prog 12th, ev ch 4 out, sn outpcd, ran on well flat
1132 **Carole's Delight 5a ....Mrs L Ward** 3
sttld 3rd, ev ch frm 3 out, not qckn nxt
1132 Hellcatmudwrestler *ld til jnd 7th, disp 10th til wknd bef 2 out* 4
1132 Durham Hornet *chsd ldrs, mstk 2nd, outpcd 10th, sn no dang* 5
1132 Cheeky Pot *rear, jmpd slwly 6th, wknd 10th, t.o. 13th* 6
827 Colonel Popski *mid-div, drppd rear 7th, t.o. 13th* 7
588 Vienna Woods *sn rear, mstk 5th, wll bhnd whn u.r. 13th* .... ur
1132 Indie Rock *plld hrd in rear, prog 10th, going wll whn ran out 12th* .... ro
1132 Cumberland Blues (Ire) *rear, prog 5th, no hdwy 13th, wknd, t.o. & p.u. 2 out* .... pu
10 ran. 3l, 1½l, 5l, 3l, 15l, 10l. Time 5m 50.00s. SP 33-1.
Mrs S Gray (Holderness).

1284 - Restricted (12st)

1096 **JASILU 5a (bl)..........................W Burnell** 1
alwys prom, 2nd 4 out, chal nxt, ld 2 out, ran on wll flat
1131 **Spartan Juliet 5a ....P Jenkins** 2+
alwys prom, ev ch 3 out, styd on wll flat
1090 **Honest Expression 5a..................P Atkinson** 2+
prom, ld 6th, jnd 3 out, hdd nxt, unable qckn

1131 Chapel Island *sttld mid-div, prog 10th, trckd ldrs 14th, onepcd frm 3 out* 4
1131 Earl Gray (bl) *alwys bhnd, mod prog frm 4 out* 5
986 Lyningo *mid-div, nvr a dang* 6
1131 Wolvercastle 5a *prom, rdn 4 out, sn wknd* 7
1090 Douce Eclair 5a *ld to 4th, sn lost plc, t.o.* 8
1026 Sharp To Oblige *alwys rear, wll bhnd whn p.u. 14th* pu
1025 Midge 5a *alwys mid-div, rdn 10th, hmpd & c.o. 4 out* co
1095 Auntie Fay (Ire) 7a *s.s. n.j.w. alwys t.o., p.u. 14th* pu
1131 Master Crozina *prom, ld 4th-6th, mstk & wknd 15th, t.o. & p.u. last* pu
1095 Living On The Edge (Ire) *(fav) hld up, gd prog 10th, poised to chal whn u.r. nxt* ur
1136 Mount Faber (bl) *alwys bhnd, blnd 5th, p.u. nxt* pu

14 ran. 4l, dd-ht, 5l, 7l, 8l, 12l, 8l. Time 5m 54.00s. SP 6-1.
Mrs Susan E Mason (Middleton).

1285 - Open Maiden Div I

591 **SERGEANT PEPPER** .... **S Swiers** 1
(fav) mid-div,mstk 12th,went poor 2nd 4 out, btn whn lft clr 2 out
1096 **Prophet's Choice** .... **M Haigh** 2
alwys prom, steadily wknd frm 13th, lft remote 2nd 2 out
1137 Hoistthestandard 5a *prom, jmpd slwly 3rd, lost plc 8th, blnd 13th, s.u. 2 out* su
319 Andretti's Heir *ld, drew clr 14th, 12l ld whn f 2 out, unlucky* f
1137 Chummy's Last 5a *alwys rear, t.o. 8th, p.u. aft 10th* pu
987 Patey Court 7a 5ow *not fluent, rear, t.o. & p.u. aft 10th* pu
1027 Flaxton King (Ire) 7a *prom, chsd ldr 10th, losing tch whn f 14th* f
987 Muscoates 7a *rear, jmpd slwly 2nd, lost tch 5th, t.o. & p.u. 7th* pu
Highland Miss 5a *rear, t.o. 8th, p.u. aft 10th* pu

9 ran. 30l. Time 6m 6.00s. SP 5-4.
Mrs D N B Pearson (Hurworth).

1286 - Open Maiden Div II

14 **GRAIN MERCHANT** .... **R Walmsley** 1
(Jt fav) in tch, prog 4 out, ld 2 out, hrd prssd flat, hld on wll
1137 **Pure Madness (USA)** .... **R Edwards** 2
mid-div, prog 10th, ev ch 2 out, drvn & kpt on wll flat
1094 **Private Jet (Ire)** .... **G Markham** 3
handy, wth ldrs 4 out, not qckn 2 out, kpt on wll flat
1136 Hungry Jack *ld to 3rd, sn lost plc, outpcd 9th, kpt on frm 4 out* 4
307 Fethardonseafriend *wth ldrs, steadily fdd frm 4 out* 5
1095 Morcat 5a *mstk 1st, prom, ld 8th til hdd 2 out, wknd rpdly* 6
1090 Im Ok (Ire) 5a *alwys rear, rdn 10th, sn t.o.* 7
705 Jamarsam (Ire) *mid-div, blnd 8th, sn t.o.* 8
910 Multi Purpose *rear, rmndr 3rd, t.o. 6th, p.u. 11th* pu
986 Shildon (Ire) *mid-div, u.r. 2nd* ur
1135 Sweet Rose 5a *prom, ld 3rd- 8th, wknd 11th, t.o. & u.r. 2 out* ur
987 Fair Ally (bl) *nvr going wll, bhnd whn p.u. 12th* pu
1095 Ship The Builder *(Jt fav) mid-div, mstk 5th, s.u. apr 9th* su

13 ran. ½l, ½l, 12l, 3l, 3l, 15l, 12l. Time 6m 2.00s. SP 4-1.
J W Walmsley (Bramham Moor).

1287 - Members (12st)

1130 **GREENMOUNT LAD (IRE)** .... **P Cornforth** 1
prom, chsd ldr 10th, chal last, ran on gamely to ld nr fin
1093 **Gaelic Warrior** .... **S Swiers** 2
(fav) ld til jnd last, hdd & no ext nr fin
758 **Sergent Kay** .... **W Burnell** 3
last & outpcd 7th, hmpd & lost ground 9th, sn t.o.
1094 Chuckleberry *prom til lost ground 10th, sn rdn & wknd, t.o.* 4
985 Hazel Crest 24ow *plld hrd, prom, cls 2nd whn u.r. 9th* ur

5 ran. Hd, dist, 12l. Time 5m 58.00s. SP 7-2.
J Cornforth (York & Ainsty North).

N.E.

BERKS & BUCKS DRAGHOUNDS
Barbury Castle
Sunday April 28th
FIRM

1288 - Members

642 **ELITE GOVERNOR (IRE)** .... **B Hodkin** 1
(fav) n.j.w. ld 4-6th & frm 10th, sn wll clr, blnd last
1187 **Keep On Trying 5a** .... **M Portman** 2
hld up, went mod 2nd 12th, no imp on wnr
706 **Unscrupulous Gent** .... **Mrs E Huttinger** 3
carried 14st, ld to 4th, wll bhnd frm 9th, t.o.
Castle Jester *ld 6-10th, sn outpcd, t.o. whn ref 2 out* ref
Hassle *carried 14st, sn wll bhnd, t.o. & p.u. 7th* pu

5 ran. 15l, dist. Time 6m 40.00s. SP 4-5.
Paul Gardner (Berks & Bucks Draghounds).

1289 - Confined (12st)

1018 **UP AND COMING 3ex** .... **Miss M Bentham** 1
(fav) cls up, ld 14th, alwys in cmmnd aft, clvrly
1184 **Skinnhill (bl)** .... **C Mason** 2
ld, rdn 11th, hdd 14th, prssd wnr aft, alwys hld
1018 **Sam Shorrock** .... **Miss H Thorner** 3
chsd ldrs, 4th & outpcd 14th, kpt on to tk 3rd last
996 Bantel Buccaneer 3ex *chsd ldrs, 3rd & outpcd frm 14th, lost 3rd last* 4
1079 Tango Tom *mstk 7th, chsd ldrs, rdn frm 11th, no prog frm 3 out* 5
1165 Rubika (Fr) *prom to 10th, bhnd frm 12th, no ch aft* 6
955 The Holy Golfer *in tch in rear, blnd 10th, last & no ch frm 12th* 7
1216 Roaming Shadow *last til 10th, outpcd 13th, 6th & btn whn u.r. 3 out* ur

8 ran. ½l, 15l, 1½l, 6l, 10l, 10l. Time 6m 26.00s. SP Evens.
Miss M C Bentham (Vine & Craven).
Objection by 2nd to winner overruled.

1290 - Open

996 **TOUCH OF WINTER** .... **T Lacey** 1
made all, kicked clr 3 out, rdn out, unchal
1166 **Game Fair** .... **G Burton** 2
alwys chsng wnr, outpcd 3 out, no imp aft
958 **Royle Speedmaster** .... **A Harvey** 3
(fav) hld up, prog 10th, not qckn 15th, no ch whn mstk 2 out
865 Indian Knight *mstks, cls up til not qckn 15th, no ch aft 3 out* 4
816 Gormless (Ire) *n.j.w. in tch to 12th, bhnd frm 14th, t.o. & p.u. last* pu

5 ran. 10l, 5l, 1l. Time 6m 24.00s. SP 11-2.
M W Kwiatkowski (Tedworth).

1291 - Ladies

1072 **KHATTAF** .... **Miss J Cumings** 1
(fav) trckd ldrs, ld 13th, comf
1165 **Sirisat 4ow** .... **Miss T Blazey** 2
prog & cls up 11th, ld 12th-nxt, chsd wnr, no imp 2 out
864 **Doujas 5a** .... **Mrs B Bloomfield** 3
mstks, ld 2-12th, wknd 14th, t.o.
1179 Wild Moon 5a *ld to 2nd, last frm 8th, sn t.o.* 0
1046 The City Minstrel *cls up to 11th, sn wll bhnd, t.o. & p.u. last, lame* ref

5 ran. 8l, 25l. Time 6m 27.00s. SP 2-7.
Mrs H C Johnson (Devon & Somerset Staghounds).

1292 - Restricted (12st)

1168 **PONTABULA** .... **A Charles-Jones** 1
(fav) cls up,ld 14th,rdn & hdd aft 2 out,lft in ld last,all out
960 **Hizal** .... **A Harvey** 2
wll in rear til gd prog 14th, styd on frm 2 out,tk 2nd fin

960 **Balance** .... **A Farrant** 3
mstks,rear,prog 11th,rdn to ld aft 2 out,blnd last,nt rcvr
960 Everso Irish *mstks, bhnd, gd prog 13th, ev ch 15th, wknd apr last* 4
1056 Misty (NZ) *ld to 2nd & 7-14th, slw jumps aft, virt p.u. flat* 5
946 Golden Companion (bl) *drppd last & lost tch 10th, t.o. & p.u. 14th* .... pu
1189 Arnold's Choice (bl) *cls up to 10th, wknd rpdly & mstk 12th, t.o. & p.u. aft 2out* .... pu
946 Mary Borough 5a *last whn u.r. 1st* .... ur
1102 Canadian Boy (Ire) *made most to 6th, wth ldrs whn f 9th, dead* .... f
841 Bettiville *prom, ld 6-7th, wknd 15th, wll bhnd whn p.u. last* .... pu
1173 Gawcott Wood 5a *mid-div, rdn & btn aft 11th, t.o. & p.u. 2 out* .... pu
11 ran. 1½l, hd, 10l, 20l. Time 6m 26.00s. SP 7-2.
H J Manners & P Greenwood (V.W.H.).
One fence omitted, 17 jumps.

1293 - Open Maiden (12st)

1217 **COLOURFUL BOY** .... **A Charles-Jones** 1
prom, mstk 9th, 2nd frm 11th, pshd into ld last, rdn out
1079 **Miss Corinthian 5a** .... **M Flynn** 2
(fav) mstks, trckd ldrs, rdn to chal last, ev ch, just hld
1165 **Pocket Pest 5a** .... **G Baines** 3
prom, disp 5th til ld 10th, mstk 3 out, hdd last, kpt on wll
1103 Lucky Crest 5a *n.j.w. in tch to 9th, t.o. frm 11th* 4
Discipline 5a *chsd ldrs, 5th & in tch whn blnd & u.r. 9th* .... ur
Man Of Ice 1ow *cls up to 9th, eased & p.u. nxt* .... pu
375 New Years Eve *s.s. rear til hmpd & u.r. 2nd* .... ur
1175 Autumn Ride (Ire) 5a (bl) *ld/disp til mstk 10th, 4th whn mstk & u.r. nxt* .... ur
1128 Handy Spider 5a *cls up, f 2nd* .... f
1075 Mine's A Gin (Ire) 7a *jmpd slwly, wll bhnd frm 8th, t.o. & p.u. 10th* .... pu
Spirit Of Success *jmpd badly, t.o. til p.u. 6th* .... pu
11 ran. Hd, nk, 1 fence. Time 6m 32.00s. SP 20-1.
H J Manners (Berks & Bucks Drag).
One fence (1, 9 & 15) omitted, 15 jumps. J.N.

EAST SUSSEX & ROMNEY MARSH
Bexhill
Sunday April 28th
FIRM

1294 - Members

RUSTIC RAMBLE .... **P Hacking** 1
hld up, ld 15th, clr 2 out, easily
918 **The Portsoy Loon** .... **A Hickman** 2
(fav) ld to 15th, rdn & chsd wnr aft, wknd 2 out
1054 **Iorwerth** .... **Miss C Savell** 3
blnd 1st, 3rd & in tch frm 7th, btn whn r.o. 4 out, cont
No Parole *chsd ldr til f 5th* .... f
4 ran. 20l, Bad. Time 7m 0.00s. SP 5-2.
Peter Tipples (East Sussex & Romney Marsh).

1295 - Restricted (12st)

711 **BITOFAMIXUP (IRE) 7a** .... **P Hacking** 1
(fav) lft in ld 9th, in cmmnd aft, eased clr apr last
779 **Manaolana 5a** .... **G Hopper** 2
lft 2nd 9th, pshd alng to sty wth wnr 14th, wknd 2 out
1205 **Tufter's Garth** .... **S Garrott** 3
lost tch 4th, fin own time
High Revs *mstks, alwys rear, t.o. & p.u. aft 11th* .... pu
1054 Brief Sleep 5a *lft in ld 2nd, clr whn f 9th* .... f
921 High Burnshot *ld til f 2nd* .... f
889 Fixed Liability (bl) *2nd whn u.r. 6th* .... ur
7 ran. 10l, 1 fence. Time 6m 56.00s. SP 1-2.
Mike Roberts (East Sussex & Romney Marsh).

1296 - Open (12st)

1209 **GINGER TRISTAN 7ex** .... **D Robinson** 1
(fav) ld to apr 7th, agn aft 11th, made rest, drew clr 2 out
1188 **Vultoro 4ex** .... **T Underwood** 2D
restrnd, ld apr 7th-aft 11th, wknd 2 out, fin 2nd, disq
1209 Parkbhride *trckd ldrs, 4th & btn 14th, p.u. 4 out* .... pu
1209 Quarter Marker (Ire) *trckd ldrs, rmndrs aft 4th, 3rd & ev ch whn u.r. 4 out* .... ur
4 ran. 12l. Time 6m 49.00s. SP 1-2.
D C Robinson (Mid Surrey Farmers Drag).

1297 - Ladies

1053 **MOUNTAICO (bl)** .... **Miss J Grant** 1
cls up, ld 15th, hrd prssd 3 out, hld on gamely flat
1055 **Polar Ana (Ire) 5a** .... **Miss S Gladders** 2
mstks in rear, clsd up 4 out, chal 2 out, ran on,jst faild
812 **Durbo 4ex** .... **Mrs E Coveney** 3
ld 4th, hdd 15th, chal 2 out, no ext flat
812 Our Survivor 4ex *(fav) cls up, ev ch 3 out, mstk & btn nxt* 4
962 Charlton Yeoman *wth ldr to 15th, steadily wknd 3 out* 5
1053 Golden Huntress 5a (bl) *blnd 1st, plld into ld 2nd, slppd & u.r. bnd aft 3rd* .... ur
1208 Zilfi (USA) *ld to 2nd, cls up whn ran out bnd apr 4th* ro
7 ran. Hd, 1½l, 8l, 10l. Time 6m 54.00s. SP 14-1.
L J Bowman (Southdown & Eridge).

1298 - Confined (12st)

962 **KATES CASTLE 5a** .... **J Van Praagh** 1
(fav) ld til disp 13-16th, advtg 3 out, ran on well
1016 **Valibus (Fr) 3ex** .... **P Scouller** 2
cls 2nd, disp 13-16th, 2nd aft, wknd 2 out
1207 **Kaim Park** .... **Miss C Wates** 3
alwys 3rd, lost tch 12th
1207 Redelva 5a *in tch to 11th, wll bhnd whn u.r. 15th* ..... ur
4 ran. 25l, 10l. Time 6m 42.00s. SP 4-7.
B Van Praagh (East Sussex & Romney Marsh).

1299 - Open Maiden (5-7yo) (12st)

814 **VELKA 5a** .... **Mrs S Hickman** 1
rear, prog to ld apr 8th, clr 4 out, kpt on well
966 **Prince Buck (Ire)** .... **P Hacking** 2
(fav) trckd ldrs, 2nd frm 14th, ev ch 3 out, ran on same pace
966 Tamborito (Ire) *ld aft 3rd-7th, wknd rpdly 12th, t.o. & p.u. 14th* .... pu
1210 Malingerer 7a *last, t.o. & p.u. 9th* .... pu
922 Tasmanite *wll plcd, cls 4th whn f 14th* .... f
1164 Orphan Olly *strng hld, cls up til f 14th whn 3rd* .... f
681 Joyful Joan (Ire) 7a *ld to 3rd, cls aft, 3rd frm 14th, wknd 4 out, p.u. 2 out* .... pu
7 ran. 4l. Time 6m 59.00s. SP 5-2.
R Mair (East Sussex & Romney Marsh).

1300 - Open Maiden (12st)

966 **CLEAN SWEEP** .... **M Jones** 1
patiently rdn, prog to ld 14th, hrd prssd 3 out, hld on wll
1210 **Netherby Cheese** .... **P Hickman** 2
ld 7th,ran wd & hdd bnd bef nxt,chal 3 out,not qckn flat
1055 **Le Vienna (Ire)** .... **P Hacking** 3
(fav) ld to 5th, agn 8-14th, rdn to chal 3 out, ran on gamely
1210 Scarning Gizmo 5a *rear & in tch til wknd 2 out* 4
921 Fort Diana *wth ldr whn f 4th* .... f
921 Sunley Line (bl) *prom, ld brfly 5-6th, steadily wknd, bhnd whn p.u. aft 11th* .... pu
1187 Phantom Slipper (bl) *cls up, mstk 6th, und pres & wkng 13th, p.u. 3 out* .... pu
7 ran. 1l, 1l, 12l. Time 7m 5.00s. SP 5-2.
Miss Janet Menzies (West Kent).
G.Ta.

GROVE & RUFFORD
Southwell P-To-P Course
Sunday April 28th
GOOD TO FIRM

1301 - Open Maiden (12st)

1096 **JEUNE GARCON (IRE) 7a..............N Wilson** 1
hld up, prog 10th, chal 2 out, clr last, imprssv
1095 **Rise Above It (Ire) ....S Brisby** 2
(Jt fav) cls up, ld/disp 5th til blnd 2 out, ran on und pres
972 **Boot-On 5a.............................G Brewer** 3
ld to 4th, wll in tch, disp 11th-3 out, no ext cls hm
1217 The Bold Abbot *chsd ldrs, ev ch 3 out, not qckn..........* 4
1094 Stays Fresh *prom early, mid-div hlfwy, onepcd ......* 5
973 Littledale (USA) *(Jt fav) chsng grp til wknd 6 out, poor 6th whn p.u. 2 out......................................* pu
973 Rallye Stripe *ld & f 1st ....* f
680 Anita's Son *chsng grp, 4th whn u.r. 6 out ....* ur
1183 Witch Doctor (v) *mid to rear, t.o. & p.u. 13th ....* pu
Midnight Runner 5a *ref 1st ....* ref
10 ran. 4l, 12l, ½l, 1l. Time 6m 22.00s. SP 4-1.
M Hogg (Middleton).
Fences 8 & 15 omitted, 16 jumps.

1302 - Intermediate

1024 **SYD GREEN (IRE) ....S Walker** 1
(Jt fav) mid-div, prog 11th, ld 13th, sn in cmmnd, ran on well
1000 **McCartney ....K Green** 2
hld up, prog to 2nd 5 out, ran on, not rch wnr
972 **Tempered Point (USA).......................T Lane** 3
alwys 1st 3, outpcd frm 4 out
1195 Aldington Baron *chsg grp, onepcd, nvr on terms .....* 4
1009 Sister Emu 5a *(Jt fav) hld up, hrd rdn 6 out, no imp ...* 5
1025 Ginger Pink (bl) *cls up, ld 9-12th, drppd away tamely nxt..* 6
1093 The Difference *hld up rear, prog to ldrs whn u.r. 12th* ur
1025 Merlins Girl 5a *sn rear, t.o. & p.u. 5 out ....* pu
1131 Laganbrae (bl) *chsd ldrs, going wll to 9th, wknd rpdly, p.u. 12th..* pu
1098 Royal Survivor *ld til f 8th, dead..................................* f
10 ran. 5l, 5l, 25l, 10l, dist. Time 6m 24.00s. SP 3-1.
P Hodges (Middleton).

1303 - Confined

1177 **SAN REMO.......................Miss S Samworth** 1
cls up, ld 4th, jnd & lft clr 11th, ran on gamely 3 out
1022 **Bowery Boy.................................E Andrewes** 2
(fav) hld up, no ext whn asked to qckn 3 out
969 **Solitary Reaper (bl) ....T Lane** 3
prom, chsg grp, not qckn frm 4 out
1192 Dubalea *mid-div, p.u. apr 12th, dead ....* pu
1022 Mister Chippendale *mid-div, going wll whn f 11th .....* f
1181 Odysseus *disp whn u.r. 11th...................................* ur
1090 Kamadora *mid to rear, lost tch 8th, ran out 11th.......* ro
7 ran. 2l, 20l. Time 6m 31.00s. SP 7-1.
Mrs D C Samworth (Quorn).

1304 - Open

1133 **FATHER LIAM ....M Appleyard** 1
lft 2nd at 3rd, clsd 13th, ld 5 out, ran on well
826 **Knowe Head ....N Wilson** 2
(fav) ld 4th, sn clr, breather 13th, ct 5 out, not qckn
950 **Auction Law (NZ) ....A Crow** 3
2nd til blnd 8th & lost 40l, not rch ldrs aft
1133 Clare Lad (bl) *chsg grp to 7th, sn t.o., fin own time, tk 4th on line ....* 4
967 Royal Mile *chsd ldr to 5 out, wknd rpdly..................* 5
5 ran. 8l, 12l, dist, nk. Time 6m 21.00s. SP 12-1.
M G Appleyard (York & Ainsty).

1305 - Ladies

1147 **NOWHISKI.................................Miss C Tarratt** 1
made all, set strng pace, breather 5 out, ran on wll 3 out
1025 **Easy Life (Ire) (bl) ....Miss J Wormall** 2
3rd & cls up, went 2nd 3 out, onepcd
970 **Hawaiian Goddess (USA) 5a........Miss H Fines** 3
t.o. 4th
1053 Adamare *(fav) 2nd to 4 out, wknd rpdly, p.u. 3 out, lame ....* pu
4 ran. 20l, dist. Time 6m 20.00s. SP 14-1.
Tim Tarratt (Cottesmore).

1306 - Members

1022 **REXY BOY...P Gee** 1
(fav) 2nd til ld 7th, duelld frm 8th, ran on well
726 **Ocean Sovereign ....S Walker** 2
3rd til prssd wnr 7th, duelld wth wnr, onepcd apr last
Harvey ....A Hook 3
ran round own pace, alwys bhnd
636 Gay Boots 5a 5ow *ld to 6th, 3rd frm nxt, sn lost tch, t.o. & f 5 out...* f
4 ran. 1l, dist. Time 6m 42.00s. SP 4-9.
P Swift (Grove & Rufford).
V.S.

SEAVINGTON
Little Windsor
Sunday April 28th
GOOD

1307 - Members

1125 **COLUMBIQUE.............................D Moffett** 1
walked over
S D Moffett (Seavington).

1308 - Open Maiden (12st)

820 **RIDEMORE BALLADEER 7a ......Miss P Curling** 1
(fav) hld up in tch, ld 3 out, ran on well
1075 **Four Leaf Clover 5a....................R Woollacott** 2
prog 15th, 4th 3 out, styd on onepcd
1279 **Melling 7a..............................Miss A Goschen** 3
made most, hdd 3 out, no ext und pres
1129 Inner Snu 5a *rear, prog 14th, wknd frm 3 out ....* 4
Bramble Pink 5a *mstk 1st, in tch til lost plc 15th, btn whn p.u. 2 out...* pu
1164 Happy Henry (Ire) *rear, prog to 3rd aft 16th, ev ch nxt, 3rd & und pres,f 2out..* f
6 ran. 4l, 3l, 20l. Time 6m 35.50s. SP 11-8.
D Barron (Cattistock).

1309 - Open (12st)

1125 **STILL IN BUSINESS 7ex..............T Mitchell** 1
(fav) j.w. hld up, cls 3rd 14th, ld nxt, drew clr aft 3 out,easily
1124 **Fearsome ....G Penfold** 2
hld up, 4th & off pace 15th, styd on to 2nd 2 out, no ch wnr
531 **Myliege 7ex ....N Harris** 3
in tch, cls 4th at 12th, 4l 2nd whn hit 3 out, sn outpcd
672 Hamper 7ex (bl) *ld 10th til aft 14th, 3rd at 17th, fdd......* 4
730 Galaxy High (bl) *in tch til outpcd aft 13th, sn btn.........* 5
468 Busteele (bl) *slight ld to 8th, grad wknd, rear & p.u. 14th...* pu
1110 Bincombe Top *5th whn mstk 10th, rear whn p.u. 14th* pu
Nanda Moon *prom, ld brfly 9th, sn pshd alng, lost tch 14th, p.u. nxt ....* pu
8 ran. 10l, 10l, 4l, 7l. Time 6m 24.00s. SP 4-6.
R G Williams (Taunton Vale).

1310 - Ladies

991 **LEWESDON HILL.....................Miss P Curling** 1
(fav) ld 7th, made rest, easily, collapsed & died aft race
1124 **False Economy ....Miss K Scorgie** 2
ld to 7th, chsd wnr, no imp

1190 **Wrekin Hill......................Mrs J Wilkinson** 3
rear, prog 15th, tk 3rd clsng stgs
1126 On His Own *3rd whn blnd 10th, 6l 3rd 3 out, fdd*...... 4
4 ran. 4l, 3l, 2½l. Time 6m 20.50s. SP 1-4.
T C Frost (Seavington).

1311 - Intermediate (12st)

729 **APPLE JOHN ....M Miller** 1
(fav) j.w. made all, 10l clr hlfwy, unchal, imprssv
1139 **Ive Called Time ....T Greed** 2
chsd wnr, mstk 13th, unable to get on terms
1056 **Apatura King ....T Mitchell** 3
hld up rear, went 3rd 12th, lot to do 15th, mstk 2 out
1112 Beinn Mohr 5a *rear, pshd alng 12th, out of tch 15th, styd on to 4th last*.......... 4
1127 Light The Bay 5a *4th whn hit 13th, nvr dang* 5
867 Captain Dimitris *last but in tch whn u.r. 4th*.......... ur
6 ran. 12l, 15l, 3l, 8l. Time 6m 20.00s. SP 4-5.
J D Roberts (Berkeley).

1312 - PPORA (Novice Riders) (12st)

991 **THE HUMBLE TILLER ....Miss L Knights** 1
(fav) blnd 6th, prog 12th, ld apr 15th, mstk 2 out, kpt on
1165 **Unique New York (bl) ....Miss S Offord** 2
prom, ld brfly 14th, chsd wnr, ev ch 2 out, onepcd
1061 **Sherbrooks 3ow.......................M Hoskins** 3
rear, prog 16th, cls 3rd & ev ch 3 out, no ext
989 Archie's Nephew (bl) *3rd at 10th, outpcd 14th, sn trailing*.......... 4
1113 Great Impostor *nvr going wll, t.o. 12th* 5
651 Brack N Brandy *ld to 14th, lost ground steadily, bhnd & p.u. 2 out, dsmntd*.......... pu
6 ran. 3l, 2l, 20l. Time 6m 26.50s. SP 6-4.
Miss L Knights (South Dorset).

1313 - Restricted (12st)

NOT MISTAKEN ....Miss S Vickery 1
hld up mid-div, prog 9th, ld 13th, ran on strngly whn prssd
1117 **Yquem (Ire) ....T Mitchell** 2
(fav) hld up rear, prog to 5th at 14th, went 2nd 16th, not qckn
1057 **Plan-A (Ire)...........................I Dowrick** 3
9th hlfwy, steady prog, cls 4th 15th, kpt on well
870 Ballysheil *rear but in tch, 7th at 14th, prog to 5th 3 out, kpt on*.......... 4
1061 Country Style 5a *keen hold, ld 9-10th, lost plc 15th, ran on agn clsg stgs*.......... 5
729 Balmoral Boy (NZ) *mid-div, some prog to 6th at 15th, outpcd frm nxt*.......... 6
806 Chasing Charlie *handy, cls 6th at 9th, rdn & lost plc 13th, no ch 15th*.......... 7
733 Aller Moor (Ire) 7a *last whn blnd 5th, nvr got into race* 8
1113 Blakeington (bl) *ld/disp to 8th, cls 3rd at 15th, lost plc rpdly*.......... 9
1113 The Copper Key *ld 1st, styd prom til lost plc 12th, bhnd frm 15th*.......... 10
656 Caundle Steps *mid-div, cls 6th at 13th, outpcd nxt, bhnd & p.u. last*.......... pu
650 Venn Boy *in tch, cls 7th at 11th, lost plc aft 14th, bhnd & p.u. last*.......... pu
1114 Clandon Lad *rear whn f 2nd*.......... f
1116 Bells Wood *cls 7th at 9th,ev ch 4 out,wknd rpdly, p.u.2 out,lost shoe*.......... pu
14 ran. 6l, 12l, 4l, 3l, 1l, 4l, 8l, 4l, 8l. Time 6m 21.00s. SP 6-1.
Mrs S A Turner (Gelligaer).
G.T.

WEST MIDS & WELSH BORDER CLUB
Bitterley
Sunday April 28th
GOOD

1314 - Members (12st)

1171 **THE RUM MARINER.......................J Jukes** 1
(fav) made all, gd jmp & in cmmnd 13th, pshd out flat
1041 **Ledwyche Gate (bl) ....M Jackson** 2
cls up, not fluent 1st cct, chsd wnr 12th, hld frm 15th
1171 **Tap Dancing ....N Bradley** 3
rdn & prog 10th, lost tch 1st pair frm 13th, tk 3rd flat
350 Homme D'Affaire *alwys mid-div, styd on onepcd frm 14th*.......... 4
1043 Hackett's Farm *chsd ldrs, went 3rd 14th, no ch 1st pair, wknd flat*.......... 5
1221 Golden Fare (v) *cls 5th whn mstk 5th, in tch 11th, outpcd frm nxt*.......... 6
836 Punching Glory *rear frm 6th, losing tch 11th, no ch nxt*.......... 7
1220 Alamir (USA) *prssd wnr to 8th, wknd 11th, p.u. 15th* ... pu
Carn Count *rdn & no prog 11th, p.u. 13th*.......... pu
1223 Welsh Clover 5a *mid-div, cls 5th at 10th, rdn 12th, wknd & p.u. 15th*.......... pu
Onemoreanwego 5a *sttld mid-div, cls 8th at 10th, wknd 12th, p.u. 15th*.......... pu
1173 Kilmakee 5a *nvr rchd ldrs, in tch til wknd 11th, p.u. 3 out*.......... pu
1222 Pulltheplug 7a *chsd ldrs, cls up whn f 12th* .... f
13 ran. 8l, 10l, nk, 2l, 15l, 10l. Time 6m 8.00s. SP 5-4.
T A Rogers (Radnor & West Hereford).

1315 - Open Mares Maiden (12st)

1044 **HENNERWOOD OAK 5a 2ow..........M P Jones** 1
made all & sn clr, j.w. kpt on frm 3 out
1048 **Joyney 5a...............................A Dalton** 2
(fav) hld up, last at 11th, prog 14th, 2nd 3 out, no ext last
1044 **Promitto 5a ....A Phillips** 3
mid-div, 20l 5th at 12th, kpt on steadily frm 14th
796 Fountain Of Fire (Ire) 5a *7th & just in tch 10th, kpt on frm 13th, no ch ldrs*.......... 4
842 Silk Oats 5a *chsd clr ldr, effrt 12th, 15l down 14th, wknd nxt*.......... 5
1033 Annyban 5a *15l 3rd at 10th, wknd frm 13th, p.u. 15th* .. pu
388 Mystery Belle 5a *prom in chsg grp, 20l 4th whn f 12th* f
233 Secret Truth 5a *plld hrd, 2nd at 4th, saddle slppd & p.u. nxt*.......... pu
954 Brown Bala 5a *mid-div at 10th, rdn 12th, no imp, poor 5th & p.u. last*.......... pu
1224 Asante Sana 7a *mid-div, drppd rear 8th, p.u. nxt*...... pu
10 ran. 7l, 10l, 15l, 15l. Time 6m 20.00s. SP 5-1.
Cyril Thomas (North Hereford).

1316 - Open (12st)

1220 **CHIP'N'RUN 7ex ....J Cornes** 1
trckd ldrs, went 4l 2nd 12th, chal last, drew clr flat
1113 **Dauphin Bleu (Fr) ....J Jukes** 2
(fav) cls 2nd til ld 6th, 2-3l up aft til wknd apr last, hdd flat
1001 **Fergal's Delight (bl) ....Julian Pritchard** 3
set fast pace til hdd 6th, wknd frm 12th
1043 Raido *feeling pace frm 3rd, 10l 5th 11th, remote 4th 13th*.......... 4
Mirpur *chsd ldrs til outpcd 12th, wknd & p.u. 15th* .... pu
5 ran. 2l, dist, dist. Time 6m 4.00s. SP 7-4.
F D Cornes (South Shropshire).

1317 - Ladies

1194 **OUT THE DOOR (IRE)..............Miss S Baxter** 1
(Jt fav) trckd ldr, pace qckng whn lft solo 13th
685 Russki *(Jt fav) ld by 2-3l, going wll whn f 13th*....... f
2 ran. Time 6m 30.00s. SP 10-11.
M Mann (Wheatland).

1318 - Novice Riders (12st)

485 **ALL WEATHER ....M Wilesmith** 1
(fav) w.w. cls 5th at 10th, chal 14th, ld nxt, just hld on
1098 **Sevens Out 7ex ....Miss S Brewer** 2
alwys prom, chal 14th, chsd wnr, rallied apr last
748 **Live Wire (Ire) 7a.............................T Cox** 3
trckd ldrs, outpcd 12th, prog 15th, not rch 1st pair

942 Durzi *trckd ldrs, cls 2nd at 13th, ev ch nxt, wknd 15th* 4
1195 Kameo Style *cls up til outpcd 12th, styng on in 3rd whn f 3 out* f
1170 Agarb (USA) (bl) *last frm 3rd, t.o. 6th, p.u. nxt* pu
1158 McMahon's River 5a 7ex *ld,jmpd rght 3 & 11th,mstk & hdd 14th,wknd,p.u. 3 out* pu
1218 In The Water *blnd & u.r. 1st* ur
8 ran. Hd, 15l, 15l. Time 6m 18.00s. SP 5-4.
M S Wilesmith (Ledbury).

1319 - Maiden (12st)

1161 **CATHGAL** ..... **J Rees** 1
w.w. prog 14th, lft in clr ld 3 out, hng lft flat
1048 **Micksdilemma** ..... **A Phillips** 2
ld 1st, alwys prom, hit 14th, lft 2nd 3 out
1041 **First Command (NZ)** ..... **M Munrowd** 3
hld up, effrt & prog 14th, wknd frm 3 out
1006 Mariner's Walk *ld to 11th, chsd ldrs til outpcd frm 15th* 4
688 Sonny's Song *cls up to 8th, lost tch ldrs 14th* 5
749 Rap Up Fast (USA) *(fav) w.w. prog 13th, ld 15th, 2l up whn f nxt* f
1174 Namestaken *prom, ev ch 14th, wknd bef nxt, t.o. & p.u. last* pu
1224 Master Frith (bl) *hit 3rd, last at 10th, t.o. & p.u. 13th* pu
1047 Close Control (Ire) *ld 12th, hdd aft 14th, 3rd whn b.d. 3 out, dead* bd
841 Golden Nectar *prom to 10th, outpcd 12th, t.o. & p.u. 15th* pu
1044 Bunchoffives 7a *alwys prom, 2nd & ev ch whn b.d. 3 out* bd
1033 Sky Runner 7a 2ow *mid-div, in tch 11th, lost tch 13th, t.o.& p.u. 3 out* pu
1045 Sutton Lighter *jmpd novicey in rear, lost tch 10th, p.u. aft nxt* pu
13 ran. 10l, 5l, 6l, 6l. Time 6m 18.00s. SP 4-1.
Richard Mathias (North Hereford).
P.R.

WEST NORFOLK
Fakenham P-To-P Course
Sunday April 28th
GOOD

1320 - Members

834 **HARPLEY DUAL (IRE)** ..... **A Case** 1
(fav) made most til apr 2 out, rallied und pres to ld flat
1145 **Kelly's Twilight 5a** ..... **Miss S French** 2
chsd wnr, disp & blnd 13th, ld 2 out, hdd & no ext flat
1101 **Another Comedy** ..... **J Knowles** 3
mostly 3rd, disp ld brfly aft 12th, blnd 2 out, onepcd
3 ran. ¾l, 2l. Time 6m 41.00s. SP 4-7.
R J Case (West Norfolk).

1321 - Confined

MANOR MIEO ..... **A Coe** 1
(fav) made all, blnd 7th, drew clr 3 out, easily
906 **Just Jack** ..... **S R Andrews** 2
hld up going wll, 2nd whn blnd 13th & 15th, outpcd nxt
831 **Salmon River (USA) 7a** ..... **R Wakley** 3
chsd ldr 4th-12th, 4th & outpcd 15th, onepcd und pres
931 Whats Another 5a *in tch, blnd 4th, 3rd & outpcd 15th, no dang aft* 4
1068 Lovely Clonmoyle (Ire) 5a *chsd ldr to 3rd, last frm 11th, t.o.* 5
5 ran. 6l, 8l, 7l, dist. Time 6m 22.00s. SP 4-5.
George Prodromou (Essex Farmers & Union).

1322 - Restricted (12st)

348 **BITTER ALOE** ..... **R Wakley** 1
(fav) jmpd slwly 3rd & nxt, ld 10th, made rest, rdn & kpt on last
1145 **Hurricane Gilbert** ..... **N Bloom** 2
ld to 9th, rdn apr 15th, onepcd und pres
1063 **Auchendolly (Ire)** ..... **S Sporborg** 3
nvr going wll, 4th whn blnd 7th & 9th, no ch 14th
342 Pendil's Joy *alwys last, lost tch 5th, t.o.* 4
835 Half A Sov *chsd ldrs, 3rd & btn whn u.r. 3 out* ur
5 ran. 2l, 1 fence, 1l. Time 6m 21.00s. SP Evens.
Mrs Julie Read (Suffolk).

1323 - Open (12st)

1108 **FARINGO 7ex** ..... **C Ward** 1
prom going wll, ld 15th, rdn apr last, styd on
1067 **Jimmy Mac Jimmy** ..... **C Ward-Thomas** 2
chsd ldrs, went 2nd 15th, blnd 3 out, not qckn last
833 **Saint Bene't (Ire) (bl)** ..... **A Coe** 3
disp 5th-12th, 3rd & rdn 3 out, kpt on flat
1065 As You Were *bhnd, prog 15th, 4th & ch 2 out, no ext, lame* 4
1148 Druid's Lodge *alwys abt same plc, onepcd und pres frm 3 out* 5
1067 Over The Edge 7ex *(fav) ld to 4th, prom til 5th & rdn 13th, no dang aft* 6
831 Major Inquiry (USA) *blnd 3rd, in tch, pshd alng 10th, last & no frm 14th* 7
834 Boy Basil *hld up, mid-div whn f 12th* f
8 ran. 3l, hd, 3l, 5l, 10l, 2l. Time 6m 20.00s. SP 8-1.
Fred Farrow (West Norfolk).

1324 - Ladies

1065 **CARDINAL RED** ..... **Miss L Hollis** 1
disp til lft in ld 11th-12th, rdn 3 out, ld last, all out
1144 **Craftsman** ..... **Miss A Embiricos** 2
chsd ldrs, lft 2nd 11th, ld 13th, rdn 3 out, hdd last,onepcd
1147 **Sarazar (USA)** ..... **Miss H Pewter** 3
sn bhnd, t.o. frm 5th
1146 St Gregory (bl) *5th whn blnd & u.r. 7th* ur
1099 Dunboy Castle (Ire) *(fav) disp ld til blnd & u.r. 11th* ur
898 Naughty Nellie 7a *keen hold, disp to 8th, cls 3rd whn f nxt* f
6 ran. ½l, dist. Time 6m 20.00s. SP 10-1.
J M Turner (Suffolk).
One fence omitted, 17 jumps.

1325 - Open Maiden (5-7yo) (12st)

1063 **GEORGE THE GREEK (IRE)** ..... **A Coe** 1
(fav) prom, lft 2nd 5th, ld apr 4 out, lft wll clr 2 out
830 **Secret Music 7a** ..... **Miss L Hollis** 2
in tch, last & outpcd 12th, lft poor 2nd 2 out
Lara's Princess 5a 1ow *jmpd lft & u.r. 1st* ur
930 Mister Rainman *w.w. prog 10th, 5l 3rd whn f 4 out* f
1104 Holding The Aces *ld, mstk 11th, hdd apr 4 out, blnd nxt,5l dwn whn u.r. 2 out* ur
1103 Broadway Swinger 7a *chsd ldr til jmpd lft & u.r. 5th* ur
6 ran. Dist. Time 6m 46.00s. SP Evens.
George Prodromou (Dunston Harriers).
One fence omitted, 16 jumps.

1326 - Open Maiden (8yo+)

446 **GOLDEN EYE (NZ)** ..... **N King** 1
(fav) chsd ldr 9th, ld 14th, in cmmnd whn lft solo 2 out
931 Tharif *chsd ldrs to 7th, no ch 13th, p.u. 15th* pu
1149 Just Maisy 5a *in tch, rdn 14th, 8l 3rd whn b.d. 2 out* bd
621 Ballysheil Star *ld to 3rd, blnd 10th, 3rd & rdn 14th, 5l 2nd whn f 2 out* f
495 But Not Quite (Ire) *hld up, mstk 5th, sn lost tch, p.u. apr 7th* pu
238 Late Start 5a *blnd 3rd & 5th, last frm 10th, p.u. 13th* pu
972 Class Meo *ld 4th-13th, 4th & btn whn hmpd & u.r. 2 out* ur
7 ran. Time 6m 33.00s. SP 2-1.
Mrs Jill McVay (Dart Vale & South Pool).
S.P.

HUNTINGDON

Tuesday April 30th
GOOD TO FIRM

1327 - 3m Hun

578 **WILD ILLUSION 12.0 7a ....Mr Richard White** 1
(fav) trckd ldrs, left 2nd 16th, ld apr 2 out, pushed out.
672 **Sonofagipsy 11.11 3a...............Mr J Culloty** 2
chsd ldr, driven to ld 15th, hdd apr 2 out, kept on und pres run-in.
909 **Knockumshin 11.9 5a ....Mr T Byrne** 3
in tch, left 3rd 16th, rdn and btn apr 2 out.
1108 Woodlands Genhire 11.7 7a (v) *in tch, pushed along 5th, lost touch 14th, t.o.* 4
1213 Crossofspancilhill 11.7 7a *u.r. before start, prom, lost iron 2nd, weakening and blnd 13th, t.o..* 5
920 Green's Van Goyen (Ire) 11.9 5a *ld to 15th, blnd and u.r. next.* .... ur
6 ran. 1½l, 27l, 11l, dist. Time 6m 6.30s. SP 8-11.
G Pidgeon

1328 - 3m Nov Hun

1165 **FATHER FORTUNE 11.7 7a .....Miss C Townsley** 1
ld till joined 13th, hdd 16th, rallied to ld run-in, drew clr.
673 **Final Hope (Ire) 12.0 7a ....Mrs F Needham** 2
(fav) in tch, joined ldr 13th, ld 16th, pushed clr apr 2 out, rdn approaching last, hdd run-in, soon btn.
1213 **Game Set 11.9 5a ....Mr A Sansome** 3
in tch till rdn and lost touch 14th, t.o..
931 Ravens Hasey Moon 11.7 7a *chsd ldr to 10th, f 13th.* f
4 ran. 4l, dist. Time 6m 7.30s. SP 10-1.
Mrs Pru Townsley

1329 - 3m Hun

1145 **CANDLE GLOW 11.2 7a ....Mr P Hutchinson** 1
made all, soon well clr, rdn run-in, all out.
1176 **Tarry Awhile 11.9 5a ....Mr G Tarry** 2
prom in chasing gp, went 2nd 3 out, rdn apr last, kept on.
1177 **Making Time 11.2 7a ....Mr Andrew Martin** 3
outpcd in mid div, styd on from 16th, went 3rd last, nvr nrr.
1146 Lantern Pike 11.11 7a *outpcd in mid div, prog 11th, chsd wnr 15th to next, wknd 2 out.* 4
616 Colonel Kenson 11.11 3a *bhnd and rdn 10th, kept on from 2 out, n.d..* 5
1100 Coolvawn Lady (Ire) 11.6 7a *(fav) chsd ldr to 14th, wknd 16th, t.o..* 6
917 Basher Bill 11.7 7a *well bhnd from 11th, t.o..* 7
1206 Motor Cloak 11.7 7a *mstks, alwys well bhnd, t.o.*..... 8
676 Major Neave 11.7 7a *mstks, nvr on terms, t.o. when p.u. before 2 out.* .... pu
1107 Ryders Wells 11.9 5a *n.j.w., outpcd and rdn 6th, nvr on terms, t.o. when p.u. before last.* .... pu
917 Rolleston Blade 11.7 7a *mid div, blnd 5th and 12th, fifth when f next.* .... f
1019 Kingofnobles (Ire) 11.7 7a (bl) *soon well bhnd, last and t.o. when p.u. before 9th.* .... pu
679 Big Jack (Ire) 11.7 7a *disp 2nd from 6th till f 12th.* ..... f
904 Forever Freddy 11.7 7a *bhnd and rdn 11th, t.o. when p.u. before 14th.* .... pu
14 ran. 5l, 2l, 17l, 29l, 1½l, 2½l, 2l. Time 6m 6.40s. SP 12-1.
Mrs P J Hutchinson

1330 - 2½m 110yds Hun

1186 **QANNAAS 12.2 3a (bl) ....Mr J Culloty** 1
(fav) made virtually all, rdn clr 2 out, easily.
1120 **Simply Perfect 11.7 7a.........Miss K Swindells** 2
prog 9th, blnd next, rdn apr 2 out, went 2nd run-in, not trbl wnr.
579 **Some Obligation 11.9 5a (bl) ....Mr B Pollock** 3
prom, disp ld 5th to 9th and 11th to 3 out, wknd next.
907 Counterbid 12.0 5a (bl) *trckd ldrs, disp ld 8th to 9th, 3rd and rdn 3 out, well btn next.* 4
920 Rose King 11.7 7a *waited with, mstks 8th and 9th, well btn 3 out, walked in.* 5
1066 Proverb Prince 11.7 7a *mstks, t.o. from 8th, p.u. before 12th.* .... pu
1024 Carly Brrin 11.7 7a *disp ld to 4th, mstks 6th and 7th, rdn 10th, no ch when p.u. before last.* .... pu
920 Little Nod 11.7 7a *cl up to 4th, bhnd and blnd 8th, t.o. when p.u. before 12th.* .... pu
8 ran. 9l, 2l, 7l, dist. Time 5m 4.40s. SP Evens.
Mrs Ann Leat

CHELTENHAM
Wednesday May 1st
GOOD

1331 2m 5f Keyline Builders Merchants Hunters' Chase Class H

1120[1] **MY NOMINEE 12.0 7a (bl)..........Mr A Griffith** 1
chsd ldrs, ld 6th, made rest, hrd rdn run-in, just held on.
1122[1] **Mr Golightly 12.0 7a.................Mrs J Reed** 2
(fav) prog to chase ldr 8th, mstk 11th, rdn apr last, drifted right run-in, just faild.
672[4] **Synderborough Lad 12.0 7a.......Mr S Mulcaire** 3
soon pushed along, prog 10th, lost tch 14th, went poor 3rd apr last.
672 Jumbeau 11.9 5a *waited with, prog 8th, outpcd 11th, no ch after*............Mr C Vigors 4
1110[4] Flame O'Frensi 11.2 7a *ld to 5th, chsd ldrs till wknd 11th, t.o.*............Miss J Cumings 5
1159[2] Kingfisher Bay 11.7 7a *cl up to 3rd, well bhnd when blnd 10th, t.o..*............Mr D S Jones 6
1122[6] Another Coral 11.7 7a *in tch, 3rd and outpcd 13th, t.o. and p.u. before 2 out.*............Mr R Lawther pu
1108 Blue Danube (USA) 11.7 7a *cl up, rdn apr 8th, lost tch 10th, t.o. and p.u. before 2 out.* .....Mr Andrew Martin pu
1080[2] Grey Sonata 11.2 7a (bl) *mstk 5th, t.o. from 8th till u.r. 2 out.*............Mr B Dixon ur
9 ran. Hd, dist, 12l, 27l, dist. Time 5m 30.70s. SP 9-1.
D E Nicholls

1332 3m 1f 110yds Colin Nash Memorial United Hunts' Challenge Cup Hunters' Chase Class H

261[2] **DOUBLE SILK 12.0 3a ....Mr R Treloggen** 1
(fav) j.w, made all, drew clr from 3 out, easily.
799[5] **Rusty Bridge 11.10 7a............Mr R Thornton** 2
soon driven along, chsd ldrs, lost tch 12th, left 2nd last.
1111[5] **My Mellow Man 11.10 7a (bl) .....Miss S Vickery** 3
mid div, prog to 3rd 11th, soon lost tch, blnd 2 out, left third last.
377[2] Paper Days 11.12 5a *bhnd and blnd 6th, nvr on terms after, t.o.*............Mr S Bush 4
1170[2] Stanford Boy 11.10 7a *bhnd, rdn and lost tch apr 12th, t.o.*............Mr J M Pritchard 5
1158 January Don 11.10 7a (bl) *chsd ldrs, driven along 11th, no ch 13th, t.o. and p.u. before 3 out.* ....Mr A Dalton pu
1122 Sylvan Sirocco 11.10 7a *bhnd and rdn 10th, t.o. and p.u. before 12th.*............Mr D Drinkwater pu
1170[3] Hook Line'N'sinker 11.10 7a *chsd ldrs, reminder 8th, blnd 9th, lost tch 11th, t.o. and p.u. before 3 out.* ....Mr L Brown pu
1108[7] Professor Longhair 11.10 7a *mid div, lost tch 11th, t.o. and p.u. before 18th.*............Mr R Hicks pu
1170[1] Springfield Lad 11.12 7a 2ow *veered right at start, jmpd badly right, t.o. from 3rd, p.u. before 2 out.* ....Miss E Walker pu
1211[1] Miss Millbrook 11.7 5a *chsd ldr 10th, mstks 12th and 14th, ev ch and hit 17th, btn 2nd when f last.* ....Mr M Rimell f
11 ran. 16l, 9l, 23l, 3½l. Time 7m 0.20s. SP 10-11.
R C Wilkins

1333 3m 1f 110yds Land Rover Gentleman's Championship Hunters' Chase Class H

1059[1] **RYMING CUPLET 12.4**.........**Mr Richard White** 1
mid div, prog to chase ldr 16th, disp ld apr 2 out, hrd rdn run-in, ld cl home, all out.
1122[2] **Sheer Jest 12.7**.........................**Mr A Hill** 2
(fav) held up, steady prog to 4th 13th, joined ldrs 3 out, hrd rdn run-in, wknd cl home.
799[2] **West Quay 11.9**..................**Mr J Creighton** 3
prog to 2nd 10th, ld 15th, hit 4 out, joined and hit next, btn apr last, eased run-in.
1211[2] Welsh Legion 12.7 *mid div, prog 12th, 4th and rdn apr 3 out, no progress*...................Mr J Jukes 4
1126 Fosbury 12.4 *bhnd and hit 4th, t.o. 12th, ran on from 3 out, fin well*.....................Mr T Mitchell 5
1043[1] Bucksfern 12.4 *chsd ldr to 9th, prom till wknd apr 18th*.................................Mr R Bevis 6
1209[3] Folk Dance 12.4 *bhnd from 7th, t.o.*.....Mr F Jackson 7
811[1] Strong Gold 12.4 (bl) *cl up, reminders 11th, well bhnd from 14th, t.o. when p.u. before 18th.* ..Mr T McCarthy pu
725[7] Rehab Venture 12.4 *mstk 1st, jmpd slowly 3rd, t.o. when p.u. before 12th*.......................Mr T Lane pu
1180[2] Strong Beau 12.4 *chsd ldrs, rdn 11th, soon lost tch, t.o. and p.u. before last*.....................Mr L Lay pu
1142 Prince Soloman 11.9 *mstks, bhnd and rdn 7th, t.o. and p.u. before 12th*...................Mr L Jefford pu
1236[4] Dannigale 11.10 1ow *f 1st*...........Mr E Haddock f
1180[1] Copper Thistle (Ire) 11.9 *ld, blnd 11th, hdd and blunded 15th, wknd quickly, t.o. and p.u. before 2 out.* ....Mr P Taiano pu

13 ran. 2½l, 16l, 7l, ¾l, 21l, dist. Time 6m 57.60s. SP 7-1.
Gerald Tanner

1334 3¼m 110yds Range Rover Champion Hunters' Chase Class H

1166[1] **YOUNG BRAVE 12.0**...............**Mr M G Miller** 1
(fav) with ldr, blnd 5th, left in ld 10th, clr 3 out, idld run-in, driven out.
255[4] **Charden 12.0**.............**Lt-Col R Webb-Bowen** 2
steadied in 3rd, left 2nd 10th to 11th, blnd 15th and 19th, chsd wnr 2 out, driven and ran on well flat.
1120 **Ryde Again 12.6**.....................**Mr T Marks** 3
ld till slpd on lndg 10th, with wnr and blnd 12th, rdn apr 19th, wknd 3 out, virtually p.u. run-in.

3 ran. 1½l, dist. Time 7m 37.40s. SP 8-11.
David Young

1335 2m 5f Land Rover Defender Maiden Hunters' Chase Class H

1111[3] **SOME-TOY 11.7 7a**...........**Miss L Blackford** 1
(fav) mid div, prog to dispute ld 14th, ld apr 2 out, clr last, rdn out.
1061[1] **Clobracken Lad 11.7 7a**............**Mr G Baines** 2
mstk 5th, 4th and outpcd 12th, styd on from 3 out, went 2nd run-in, not trbl wnr.
1073[5] **Stormy Sunset 11.2 7a**.............**Mr D Dennis** 3
ld 2nd to 10th, led 14th till apr 2 out, wknd.
1122[8] Bright Burns 11.7 7a (bl) *chsd ldrs, went 2nd 8th, ld 11th to 13th, wknd apr 3 out*.......Mr Rupert Sweeting 4
555 Southerly Gale 11.9 5a *held up rear, prog 8th, wknd 13th, t.o.*...............................Mr A Farrant 5
978[2] Mister Horatio 11.7 7a *blnd badly 3rd, bhnd and blunded 7th, n.d., t.o.*..........................Mr M Lewis 6
1039[2] Sister Lark 11.4 5a *chsd ldrs 7th, rdn and lost pl 8th, blnd 11th, t.o.*...........................Mr A Sansome 7
1013[5] Fathers Footprints 11.7 7a *raced wd, cl up to 4th, bhnd from 8th, t.o.*.........................Mr R Hicks 8
822 Blake's Finesse 11.2 7a *keen hold, ld 1st, soon hdd, chsd ldr to 7th, wknd 9th, p.u. before 14th.* ....Miss S Vickery pu
1013[4] Royal Irish 11.9 5a (bl) *bhnd and rdn along 5th, t.o. and p.u. before 3 out*.................Mr P Henley pu

10 ran. 12l, 7l, ½l, 21l, 2l, dist, hd. Time 5m 38.90s. SP 11-4.
John Squire

1336 2m 110yds Land Rover Discovery Hunters' Chase Class H

1013[2] **KING'S TREASURE (USA) 11.13 7a Mr A Balding** 1
prog 6th, cld up 10th, ld after 4 out, drew clr 2 out, blnd last, pushed out.
958 **Halham Tarn (Ire) 12.3 7a ...Mr A Charles-Jones** 2
chsd ldr 4th, ld 10th till 11th, rdn and blnd 2 out, fin tired.
579 **Pastoral Pride (USA) 12.1 5a......Miss P Curling** 3
(fav) raced wd, chsd ldrs, pkd 10th, ev ch 11th, wknd apr 2 out.
908[4] Knowing 11.8 7a *mstk 1st, prog to 5th 10th, styd on one pace*..............................Miss E James 4
364[3] Micherado (Fr) 11.13 7a *taken steadily to start, ld 2nd, soon clr, hit 3rd, hdd 10th, wknd apr 3 out.* ....Mr R Ford 5
798[4] Trust The Gypsy 12.5 5a *blnd 1st, alwys bhnd, t.o. from 8th*...............................Mr P Henley 6
1122 Rectory Boy 12.1 5a *bhnd and blnd 5th, t.o. and p.u. before last*..........................Mr J L Llewellyn pu
1221 Warner Forpleasure 11.13 7a (bl) *ld 1st, chsd ldr to 3rd, well bhnd 8th, t.o. and p.u. before 3 out.* ....Mr G Hanmer pu
256 Double-U-Gee (Ire) 11.13 7a *well bhnd from 6th, t.o. and f 11th*..............................Mr I Johnson f

9 ran. 23l, 1¾l, 2½l, 14l, dist. Time 4m 27.80s. SP 2-1.
Tunnel Vision

KELSO
Wednesday May 1st
SOFT

1337 3m 1f Bell Lawrie White United Border Hunters' Chase Class H

608[1] **JIGTIME 11.0 7a**...............**Mr M Bradburne** 1
mstk 1st, disp ld 4th till ld 3 out, hdd next, led last, styd on well.
1119[1] **Royal Jester 11.13 5a**...............**Mr C Storey** 2
(fav) cl up, disp ld from 12th, slight lead 2 out, hdd last, no ext.
1119[2] **Carousel Rocket 11.9 3a**...........**Mr C Bonner** 3
prom, rdn after 11th, soon lost pl, styd on from 2 out.
1121[4] Green Times 11.11 7a *made most to 3 out, ev ch till wknd apr last*..........................Capt W Ramsay 4
1084 Ruber 11.13 5a *mstks, alwys bhnd, t.o.*.....Mr R Hale 5
912[1] Washakie 11.12 *mstks, in tch when blnd 13th, soon wknd, t.o.*..................................Mr J Walton 6
1119 Boreen Owen 11.5 7a *bhnd when blnd 11th, t.o. when p.u. before 3 out*.............................Mr A Parker pu
1092[1] Castle Tyrant 11.0 7a *held up, joined ldrs 12th, wknd before 14th, lost tch and p.u. after 2 out.* ....Mr P Atkinson pu
Mountain Fox (Ire) 11.9 3a *in tch when blundd and u.r. 9th*..............................Mr M Thompson ur

9 ran. 6l, 2½l, 3l, dist, 6l. Time 6m 55.40s. SP 5-1.
J W Hughes

BANGOR
Friday May 3rd
SOFT

1338 3m 110yds Eastern Destiny Novices' Hunters' Chase Class H for the James Griffith Memorial Trophy

1202[1] **BUSMAN (IRE) 11.10 7a**...........**Mr D S Jones** 1
pulld hrd, chsd ldrs, went 2nd 7th, led after 9th, ran on, pushed clr run-in.
1196[1] **Callerose 11.10 7a**...................**Mr R Bevis** 2
rear, hdwy to go prom 13th, challenging when not fluent 2 out, soon one pace.
1233[2] **Spurious 11.10 7a**.....................**Mr A Griffith** 3
keen hold, mstk 2nd, in tch, effort 13th, btn 3 out.
1185[2] Apatura Hati 11.7 5a *midfield, mstk 7th, rdn to track ldrs 13th, mistake next, blnd 4 out, soon btn.* ....Mr P Henley 4
1151[4] Gen-Tech 11.10 7a *alwys bhnd, struggling final cct.* ....Mr A Gribbin 5
1336 Warner Forpleasure 11.10 7a (bl) *ld, reminders after 3rd, clr to 8th, hdd after next, wknd quickly 12th, t.o. when mstk next, p.u. before 3 out.* ..Mr M Worthington pu

1013[1] Little Martina (Ire) 11.12 7a *(fav) handy, 2nd when blnd and u.r. 4 out.* .... Mr A Welsh ur
1013 Stormhill Pilgrim 12.0 3a *alwys rear, struggling 10th, t.o. when p.u. before 4 out.* .... Mr P Hacking pu
8 ran. 6l, 22l, 1¼l, 4l. Time 6m 29.40s. SP 7-1.
Keith R Pearce

HEREFORD
Saturday May 4th
FIRM

1339 2m 3f Jail-break Hunters' Chase Class H

1227[3] **TUFFNUT GEORGE 11.7 7a......... Mr A Phillips** 1
alwys prom, ld 7th till after 11th, regained ld apr 3 out, mstk next, hdd last, rallied to lead again cl home.
1227[1] **Amari King 12.0 7a .... Mr C Ward Thomas** 2
(fav) held up, smooth hdwy apr 3 out, chsd wnr from next, ld last, hdd cl home.
1270[1] **Sea Search 11.7 7a .... Mr R Thornton** 3
held up, gd hdwy 8th, mstk next, rdn apr 3 out, wknd before next.
1227[4] Familiar Friend 12.0 7a (bl) *held up in tch, mstk 10th, ld after next, hdd apr 3 out, soon wknd.* .... Mr L Lay 4
1120[5] Al Hashimi 12.0 7a *chsd ldrs, ld 4th till 7th, bhnd from 9th.* .... Mr N Ridout 5
1309[4] Hamper 11.11 7a (bl) *held up, bhnd from 10th.* .... Mr N R Mitchell 6
1176[5] Brown Baby 11.4 5a *ld to 4th, lost pl next, rallied 9th, wknd four out, bhnd when f last.* ..... Mr T Byrne f
7 ran. Sht-hd, 14l, 3l, 2l, 1¼l. Time 4m 42.30s. SP 7-2.
P T Cartridge

HEXHAM
Saturday May 4th
SOFT

1340 3m 1f Gilesgate Volvo Heart Of All England Maiden Hunters' Chase Class H

1090[1] **KENILWORTH (IRE) 11.7 7a......... Mr C Mulhall** 1
in tch, ld 12th, styd on strly apr last.
1249[2] **Royal Surprise 11.7 7a........... Miss P Robson** 2
in tch, effort before 3 out, driven along between last 2, kept on, no impn on wnr.
1106 **Admission (Ire) 12.0 .... Mr S Swiers** 3
(fav) held up, hdwy after 13th, driven along after 2 out, styd on same pace.
1106 Stilltodo 11.2 7a *cl up, ld 9th, hdd 12th, chsd wnr after till wknd apr last.* .... Mr A Parker 4
1106[4] Birtley Girl 11.4 5a *chsd ldrs, driven along after 2 out, soon btn.* .... Mr R Hale 5
486[3] Quixall Crossett 11.7 7a *bhnd most of way.* .... Mr P Murray 6
1093[1] Highland Friend 11.7 7a *in tch, effort before 3 out, soon btn.* .... Mr P Atkinson 7
611[3] Abitmorfun 11.7 7a *prom till wknd before 3 out, t.o..* .... Mrs K McLintock 8
751 Little Glen 11.7 7a *losing tch when blnd badly 12th, well t.o..* .... Mr T Scott 9
1249[3] Wire Lass 11.2 7a *in tch when blnd and u.r. 8th.* .... Mr R Morgan ur
1249 Deday 11.7 7a *in tch when blnd and u.r. 8th.* .... Mr M Bradburne ur
Spanish Money 11.9 5a *ld till hdd 9th, soon wknd, t.o. when p.u. before 14th.* .... Mr N Wilson pu
1286[8] Jamarsam (Ire) 11.7 7a (bl) *mstks, soon well bhnd, t.o. when p.u. after 12th.* .... Mr J Davies pu
13 ran. 6l, 3½l, 3l, 5l, 22l, 2l, dist, dist. Time 6m 43.50s. SP 7-2.
Mrs D D Osborne

WARWICK
Saturday May 4th
GOOD TO FIRM

1341 2½m 110yds Willoughby de Broke Challenge Trophy Novices' Hunters' Chase Class H

1121[3] **HOWARYASUN (IRE) 12.0 7a (v) .... Mr D S Jones** 1
alwys prom, mstk 4 out, ld run-in, styd on strly.
1122[5] **Blue Cheek 11.12 7a .... Mr N Bradley** 2
alwys prom, joined ldr 7th, ld 5 out, hdd and no ext run-in.
1227[2] **A Windy Citizen (Ire) 11.9 7a .... Mr R Hicks** 3
(fav) chsd ldrs, ev ch when blnd 2 out, ran on one pace.
946[5] Rayman (Ire) 11.9 5a *prom to 10th, gradually lost pl, kept on from 2 out.* .... Mr J Trice-Rolph 4
1215[2] Pont de Paix 11.7 7a *ld, hit 7th, hdd 5 out, wknd apr 2 out.* .... Mr R Lawther 5
1319[1] Cathgal 11.7 7a *started slowly, effort 8th, wknd 11th.* .... Mr J Rees 6
1228[7] Shanballymore (Ire) 11.7 7a *prom to 10th, soon wknd.* .... Mr W J N Tilley 7
1025[4] Beat The Rap 11.7 7a *alwys in rear, bhnd and rdn 8th, t.o..* .... Mr G Morrison 8
947 Colonel Fairfax 11.7 7a *mstk 1st, bhnd and hit 6th, t.o. when p.u. before 2 out.* .... Mr A Wintle pu
842 Back-Bencher 11.7 7a *alwys in rear, t.o. when p.u. before 12th.* .... Mr F Hutsby pu
1187 Manor Ranger 11.7 7a *alwys in rear, bhnd when mstk 4th, t.o. and p.u. before 12th.* .... Mr E Babington pu
485 Fine Timing 11.9 5a *mid div, hdwy to chase ldrs 7th, wknd 12th, t.o. when p.u. before 2 out.* ...... Mr M Rimell pu
12 ran. 5l, sht-hd, 10l, 6l, 1¼l, 19l, dist. Time 5m 12.60s. SP 7-2.
M R Watkins

DEVON & SOMERSET STAGHOUNDS
Holnicote
Saturday May 4th
GOOD TO SOFT

1342 Members

1278[5] **FELLOW SIOUX .... I Dowrick** 1
alwys going wll, trckd ldrs, ld 2 out, ran on well
1277 **Friendly Lady 5a .... Miss A Bush** 2
(fav) ld/disp to 15th, ld 16th-2 out, ev ch til just outpcd nr fin
1075 **Dinkies Quest 5a...................... S Kidston** 3
alwys prom, unable to chal frm 3 out
820[5] Heather Boy *ld/disp to 15th, sn wknd* Miss J Cumings 4
442[5] The Doormaker *ld to 3rd, grad lost tch* ...... B Trickey 5
1280 Three And A Half 2ow *alwys bhnd* .... J M Scott 6
Tuffnut Tom *alwys last, p.u. 3 out* .... J Scott pu
7 ran. Nk, 5l, ½l, 15l, dist. Time 6m 57.00s. SP 9-4.
T B Stevens (Devon & Somerset Staghounds).

1343 Open

1125[1] **QUALITAIR MEMORY (IRE) .... J Tizzard** 1
(fav) made all, not extnd
1243[3] **Prince Nepal .... G Barfoot-Saunt** 2
mostly 2nd, effrt 3 out, kpt on onepcd
530 **Charmers Wish 5a .... H Thomas** 3
nvr nrr
874[3] Departure 5a *mostly 3rd/4th, prog 15th, efft short-lived, sn fdd* .... J Creighton 4
1124[6] Winter's Lane *s.s. nvr a serious threat* .... R White 5
1111 Russell Rover *cls up early, fdd frm 15th, sn bhnd* .... Maj O Ellwood 6
6 ran. 10l, 10l, 1l, 2l, dist. Time 6m 55.00s. SP 2-5.
C Tizzard (Blackmore & Sparkford Vale).

1344 Confined

1277[3] **EXPRESSMENT .... G Penfold** 1
trckd ldr, ld 8th, made rest, kpt on well
Flood Mark .... S Mulcaire 2
chsd wnr 8th, no real imp
Senor Tomas .... R Woolacott 3
chsd 1st pair, wknd frm 3 out

1109[1] Larky McIlroy 5a *(fav) ld til u.r. 8th* ....Miss S Vickery ur
4 ran. 5l, dist. Time 7m 6.00s. SP 13-8.
Miss A S Ross (Eggesford).

1345 Restricted (12st)

1313[6] **BALMORAL BOY (NZ) ....M Miller** 1
mid-div, gd prog 15th, ld last, ran on well
1313 **Caundle Steps ....J Tizzard** 2
ld 14th-last, kpt on und pres
819[1] **Elle Flavador 5a...............Miss S Vickery** 3
(fav) ld 7-14th, grad fdd
1056 Nearly A Mermaid 5a *rear til some prog 9-10th, ev ch 3 out, wknd clsng stgs*..................R White 4
1277 Remember Mac *nvr seen wth ch* ......Miss C Hayes 5
939[2] Big Seamus (Ire) *nvr bttr than mid-div* ....J Creighton 6
679[6] Just Donald *u.r. 2nd*...................A Honeyball ur
532 Hopefull Drummer *ld to 7th, grad lost tch, p.u. 4 out* ....N Harris pu
864 Eatons 7a *plld hrd, rear whn p.u. 14th* ......P Shaw pu
1313 Clandon Lad *rear whn b.d. 6th*..............T Mitchell bd
Windwhistle Joker *rear whn f 6th* ....B Dixon f
11 ran. 2l, 20l, 3l, 15l, ½l. Time 6m 45.00s. SP 10-1.
M G Miller (Portman).
Open Ditch omitted from this race onwards. 18 jumps per race.

1346 Ladies

1276[1] **FAITHFUL STAR ....Miss S Vickery** 1
(fav) ld 14th, made rest, not extnd
988[2] **Great Pokey ....Miss N Courtenay** 2
ld 8-14th, no imp wnr aft
1126[2] **Majestic Spirit ....Miss T Cave** 3
ld to 8th, kpt on onepcd aft
1165[1] Daybrook's Gift *nvr trbld ldrs*...........Miss N Allan 4
1110 Be My Habitat (bl) *sn bhnd, p.u. 14th* Miss L Hawkins pu
5 ran. 10l, 2½l, 10l. Time 6m 42.00s. SP 1-3.
M C Pipe (Taunton Vale).

1347 Open Maiden Div I (12st)

FOR CHRISTIE (IRE) ....J Tizzard 1
ld 14th, made rest, ran on wll whn chal
821[5] **Liberty James ....N Harris** 2
rear til gd prog 14th, fin well, just hld
820 **Stillmore Business 7a ....Maj O Ellwood** 3
mid-div, prog 3 out, no ext frm nxt
Jolly Sensible 5a *prom, 3rd & ev ch til outpcd frm 2 out*..................J Creighton 4
1274 Morchard Milly 5a *prom early, 2nd at 9th, grad lost tch*..................J Auvray 5
1076[2] Admirals Landing *ld/disp to 7th, grad fdd* ....Miss S Robinson 6
Inner Temple *(fav) ld/disp til f 6th*............R White pu
1128 Rogerson *2nd & ev ch whn u.r. 3 out*......S Mulcaire ur
1248 Noble Minister *nvr on terms, p.u. 2 out*.......M Wells pu
1128[4] Spy Dessa *cls up, disp 4-6th, chsd ldrs aft til fdd 14th, p.u. aft nxt*..................Miss S Rowe pu
1115[2] Chocolate Buttons 5a *chsd ldrs til u.r. 10th* ....H Thomas ur
Blue Night 5a *ld 7th til jnd & u.r. 14th*..........J Scott ur
1129[3] Dollybat 5a *prom early, fdng whn p.u. 3 out*...M Frith pu
206 Masters Nephew *cls 3rd whn ran out 6th* B O'Doherty ro
1280 Fair Lark *ld/disp 4th til wknd & u.r. 15th*.....I Dowrick ur
1081 Miss Ricus 7a *prom early, sn bhnd, p.u. 2 out* ....R Treloggen pu
16 ran. Hd, 4l, 10l, 2l, 20l. Time 6m 53.70s. SP 10-1.
Miss A V Handel (Taunton Vale).

1348 Open Maiden Div II Pt I (12st)

1129[2] **RUTH'S BOY (IRE) ....R White** 1
(fav) set gd pace, made all, clr 3 out, styd on well
1057[3] **Kala Dawn 5a.......................Miss M Tory** 2
2nd at 8th, chsd wnr at onepcd aft
1279 **Flemings Fleur ....P King** 3
bhnd til some prog 14th, went 3rd nxt, no imp aft
1277 Here's Mary 5a *alwys well bhnd* ....G Penfold 4
1187 Model Countess (Ire) 5a *bhnd whn u.r. 14th* ....T Atkinson ur
1279[6] Medias Maid 5a *mstks, 3rd at 8th, grad wknd, p.u. 3 out*..................J Auvray pu
876[2] Ashcombe Valley *f 1st* ....Miss L Blackford f
1129 Touch Of Wind 7a *p.u. 2nd*..........Miss S Vickery pu
1279 Devonshire Lad 7a *nvr a fctr, p.u. 14th*.......N Harris pu
9 ran. 10l, 25l, 25l. Time 6m 50.00s. SP 4-6.
Capt T A Forster (Devon & Somerset Staghounds).

1349 Open Maiden Div II Pt II (12st)

1060[7] **CELTIC TOKEN ....J Barnes** 1
ld to 7th, ld 10th, made rest, ran on well
1279[5] **Risky Bid 5a.............................H Thomas** 2
mid-div, effrt 14th, kpt on onepcd frm nxt
1118[2] **Miss Pernickity 5a..................R Woolacott** 3
alwys prom, no ext frm 2 out
993 Lochnaver 5a *alwys abt same pl*......Miss P Gundry 4
941[3] St Morwenna 5a *(fav) nvr going wll, bhnd til p.u. 14th* ....J Creighton pu
1118 Fosabud *in 5th & no ch whn ref last* ....M Sweetland ref
470 Dula Model 5a *ld 8-9th, sn fdd, p.u. 13th*.....J Tizzard pu
1164 Joli High Note 5a *wll bhnd, t.o. & p.u. 9th* ....Miss T Honeyball pu
8 ran. 15l, 25l, 10l. Time 6m 55.80s. SP 3-1.
Mrs Kin Lundberg-Young (South & West Wilts).
P.Ho.

LAUDERDALE
Mosshouses
Saturday May 4th
GOOD TO SOFT

1350 Members

608 **LEYDEN LADY 5a...............Miss H Dudgeon** 1
mstks, sn 30l bhnd, 15l down & clsng whn lft alone 11th
187 Juniors Choice *(fav) sn wll clr, 15l up & wkng whn f 11th* ....Miss J Hollands f
2 ran. Time 7m 28.70s. SP 11-8.
Miss J Fisher (Lauderdale).

1351 Confined (12st)

911[1] **TODCRAG 3ex...............................T Scott** 1
mstk 2nd, alwys going wll, ld 2 out, sn clr, comf
1252[2] **Fiscal Policy ....H Trotter** 2
prog 9th, ld 13th-2 out, kpt on onepcd
1083[1] **Free Transfer (Ire) 3ex..................A Parker** 3
(fav) hld up, prog 9th, ev ch apr 2 out, wknd
861[2] Astrac Trio (USA) *ld 3-5th & 9-12th, 4th & outpcd aft nxt, no prog 3 out*..................Miss A Bowie 4
905 Royalist (Can) *in tch til 5th & outpcd aft 13th, kpt on und pres frm 3 out* ....C Storey 5
699[6] Dawn Coyote (USA) (bl) *in tch to 12th, sn outpcd, no imp frm 3 out*..................M Bradburne 6
1151[5] Hydropic *mstk 2nd, ld 5-9th, wknd 12th, sn bhnd* ....Miss K Miller 7
860 Redediver *rear, wll bhnd frm 7th, t.o.*........P Forster 8
1251[2] Buckle It Up 3ex *ld to 3rd, lost plc & rdn 8th, btn 13th, p.u. 2 out*..................R Hale pu
1083[7] Dancing Legend (Ire) *in tch to 12th, wknd rpdly, t.o. & p.u. 15th*..................T Oates pu
Ink Flicker (Ire) *alwys last, t.o. whn u.r. 10th* ....J Cookson ur
11 ran. 10l, 15l, 12l, ½l, 15l, 6l, 1 fence. Time 6m 52.20s. SP 3-1.
Mrs D Scott (Border).

1352 Ladies

1084[2] **MARSHALSTONESWOOD ....Miss A Bowie** 1
cls up, ld aft 12th, made rest, clr 2 out, idld flat
1084 **Wigtown Bay ....Miss S Foster** 2
trckd ldrs, mstk 10th, chsd wnr 3 out, not qckn nxt, kpt on
1250[3] **Minibrig 5a ....Mrs V Jackson** 3
drppd last 6th, mstk 11th, ran on 15th, kpt on und pres flat
1153[1] Piper O'Drummond *(fav) prom, 2nd whn blnd 15th & lost plc, not qckn und pres,kpt on* .....Miss P Robson 4

1250[2] Joli Exciting 5a *jmpd slwly 6th, outpcd 13th, no prog frm 3 out* ....Miss D Laidlaw 5
1226 Fish Quay *mstks, rear, lost tch 13th, effrt 3 out, sn wknd* ....Miss S Lamb 6
1250[4] Rarely At Odds *alwys rear, last by 13th, t.o.* ....Miss R Ramsay 7
1084 Battle Hero *prom, ld 9th-aft 12th, wknd 15th, p.u. 2 out* ....Miss M Bremner pu
501 About Midnight 5a *t.d.e. pllng,wd bnds,ld to 9th,hit hedge bef 12th* ....Miss M Robinson ro
1254 Disrespect 5a *u.r. 3rd* ....Miss M Macmillan ur
10 ran. 1l, 2l, hd, 15l, 12l, 1 fence. Time 7m 2.00s. SP 7-1.
Miss A C Bowie (Duke Of Buccleuch).

1353 Monterey Restricted (12st)

862[1] **DRUID'S BROOK** ....**A Parker** 1
(fav) hld up, prog 9th, ld 14th-nxt, ld apr 2 out, sn clr, imprssv
1086[5] **Eastlands Hi-Light** ....**T Morrison** 2
chsd ldr 9th, ld 15th-apr 2 out, no ch wnr aft
911[6] **Gay Vixen VI 5a** ....**T Scott** 3
made most to 14th, 3rd & outpcd nxt, fin tired
1254[1] Royal Fife 5a *last trio, poor 9th hlfwy, prog to 6th at 14th, styd on* ....R Hale 4
1086[2] Funny Feelings *chsd ldr to 9th, grad outpcd frm 14th, no ch 2 out* ....Miss D Laidlaw 5
1089[1] Senora D'Or 5a 5ow *wth ldrs til wknd 14th, t.o.* ....R Shiels 6
Fisherman's Quay *in tch til 7th & outpcd hlfwy, no ch whn mstk 13th & p.u.* ....Miss A Bowie pu
1249[6] Corby Knowe *alwys last trio, no ch 11th, t.o. & p.u. 3 out* ....Miss M Fotheringham pu
1254 Murder Moss (Ire) *mstk 2nd, rear, 8th & lost tch hlfwy, t.o. & p.u. 2 out* ....M Ruddy pu
915[1] Ruecastle *chsd ldrs, 6th & strgglng 12th, sn btn, p.u. 3 out* ....A Robson pu
703[3] Miss Cullane (Ire) 5a *sn last, t.o. 9th, p.u. 2 out* R Neill pu
11 ran. 15l, 12l, ½l, 2l, 30l. Time 6m 56.20s. SP 11-10.
Mrs D B Johnstone (Berwickshire).

1354 Open

1251[1] **MASTER KIT (IRE)** ....**J Billinge** 1
(fav) cls up, ld 14th, clr 2 out, easily
612[4] **Judicious Captain** ....**C Storey** 2
66s-10s, mstks, ld 9-12th, ev ch 3 out, sn rdn & btn
1085[1] **Loughlinstown Boy** ....**P Craggs** 3
made most to 9th, 3rd & outpcd 15th, eased whn no ch 2 out
1085[3] Miss Enrico 5a *cls up, ld 12-14th, btn whn blnd 3 out, t.o. & u.r. last* ....A Parker ur
4 ran. 20l, 20l. Time 6m 56.00s. SP 4-7.
J Billinge (Fife).

1355 Open Maiden Div I

1254[2] **EOSTRE** ....**A Parker** 1
(fav) trckd ldng pair, ld apr 2 out, rdn out flat
1253[4] **Madame Beck 5a** ....**M Smith** 2
cls up, mstk 12th, chsd wnr 2 out, unable qckn last
407[7] **Allerbank 7a** ....**C Storey** 3
keen hld,hld up,lost tch 13th,styd on 2 out,fin wll,improve
194[2] Thief's Road *wth ldr til mstk 3 out, wknd aft nxt* ....R Shiels 4
1088 Red Hot Boogie (Ire) *made most to apr 2 out, wknd, crawld last, improve* ....T Scott 5
1085[4] Craig Burn 5a *rear, lost tch 13th, sn no ch, kpt on frm 2 out* ....J Ewart 6
April Cracker 5a *ld & blnd 2nd, p.u. bef nxt* ....Mrs W Nichol pu
789 Monynut 5a *rear, lost tch 13th, p.u. 15th* ....A Robson pu
1254 Pandandy 7a *mstks 7 & 8th & lost tch, t.o. & p.u. aft 11th* ....R Robinson pu
1253 Little Hawk *mstk 5th & last, t.o. & p.u. 13th* ..R Morgan pu
10 ran. 1½l, 20l, 3l, 2l, 1l. Time 7m 7.20s. SP Evens.
Mrs J M Lancaster (Dumfriesshire).

1356 Open Maiden Div II

1253[2] **ALL OR NOTHING 5a** ....**J Ewart** 1
(fav) lost plc 8th,hmpd 12th,ran on 15th,ld aft last,sn clr
1155 **Jack's Croft** ....**R Hale** 2
prom,lost plc 7th,ran on 3 out,lft disp nxt,hdd & no ext flt
1088[3] **Bagots Park** ....**R Shiels** 3
prom,ld 12th,hdd & mstk 3 out,lft disp nxt,hdd & no ext flat
1136 Shine A Light *mstk 8th, rear, no ch 14th, styd on frm 2 out* ....A Robson 4
1082[2] Sweet Sergeant *ld to 12th, wknd 3 out* Miss S Forster 5
1253 Phoza Moya (Ire) 7a *alwys rear, no ch 14th, kpt on* ....M Bradburne 6
1253[8] Exile Run (Ire) *mstk 6th, rear, wll bhnd 13th, p.u. 3 out* ....Mrs W Nichol pu
1253[5] Good Profit *trckd ldrs, 5th & wll in tch whn u.r. 12th* ....P Craggs ur
859[2] Beltino 7a *12s-6s, trckd ldrs, 6th & strgglng whn f 14th* ....C Storey f
1253 Buckaroo 7a *schoold, mstk 2nd, in tch whn f 11th* ....A Parker f
502[3] Rough House 7a *in tch til blnd 10th, sn bhnd, t.o. & p.u. 3 out* ....R Robinson pu
405[7] Fiddlers Brae *cls up,2nd 14th,ld 3 out,going wll whn ran out nxt* ....Miss D Calder ro
12 ran. 4l, 1½l, 20l, ¾l, 3l. Time 7m 15.00s. SP 11-4.
N M L Ewart (Cumberland Farmers).
J.N.

MODBURY HARRIERS
Flete Park
Saturday May 4th
GOOD

1357 Members

1139 **SYDNEY BOON 7a** ....**R Darke** 1
(fav) made all at slow pace, forged clr 15th, easily
Over The Lake (Ire) 5a ....**S Hornby** 2
chsd wnr, lost tch 15th, onepcd
1139 **Baashful Blaze 5a** ....**A Holdsworth** 3
sn bhnd, jmpd slwly & t.o. 12th, iron broke
3 ran. 6l, dist. Time 7m 36.00s. SP 4-6.
Mrs M E Doidge (Modbury Harriers).

1358 Restricted (12st)

928[1] **MASTER KIWI (NZ)** ....**L Jefford** 1
(fav) handy, raced keenly, ld aft 10th, ran on strngly
1143[1] **Mutual Agreement 5a** ....**R Darke** 2
w.w. prog 12th, ev ch til not qckn frm 2 out
1138 **Neil's Way** ....**I Widdicombe** 3
prom, cls 2nd frm 12th, wknd 3 out, onepcd
1139 Dovedon Princess 5a *6th hlfwy, not pace to chal* ....D Stephens 4
1277 Maboy Lady *keen hld, ld early & agn brfly 10th, rear nxt, blnd last* ....Miss K Baily 5
1139 Snuggle 5a *ref 1st (twice), cont, ref 2nd, cont, t.o. & p.u. 11th* ....T Cole pu
1138[3] Roving Vagabond (bl) *prom, 3rd at 12th, sn lost plc, last whn f 15th (ditch)* ....A Holdsworth f
1139[5] Brown Rebel *not alwys fluent, prog 14th, lost plc aft 16th, p.u. last* ....S Slade pu
8 ran. 2½l, 8l, 8l, 5l. Time 6m 54.00s. SP 6-4.
F G Hollis (Dulverton (East)).

1359 4m Ladies

1141[1] **PHAR TOO TOUCHY 5a** ....**Miss R Francis** 1
(fav) made all, wll clr final cct, unchal
1141[3] **Playpen** ....**Miss S Crook** 2
went 2nd apr 4 out, no ch wnr
1278[4] **Lonesome Traveller (NZ)** ....**Mrs M Hand** 3
chsd wnr, no imp, wknd & lost 2nd 4 out
1142[3] Moorland Abbot *last & out of tch, sntchd remote 4th nr fin* ....Miss D Mitchell 4

1069^5 Sancreed 1ow *3rd/4th & nvr in cont, lost 4th nr fin* ....Miss L Long 5
5 ran. Dist, 10l, 1 fence, ¾l. Time 8m 3.50s. SP 2-5.
Miss R A Francis (Dulverton West).

1360 Open (12st)

1140^1 **THE GENERAL'S DRUM 7ex............K Heard 1**
(fav) ld/disp til ld 15th, ran on gamely whn chal 2 out
874^2 **Bluechipenterprise 5a 7ex..............R Darke 2**
s.v.s. went 3rd aft 10th, effrt & ld brfly 2 out, no ext
1278 **Baldhu Chance ....J Young 3**
ld/disp til aft 14th, sn outpcd
1275^6 Whats The Crack (bl) *lost tch & reluc 11th, t.o.* ....N Rossiter 4
938^1 Little Coombe 5a *in tch, 4th & tail swishing 12th, bhnd whn p.u. 17th*....................S Slade pu
5 ran. 1l, dist, 2 fences. Time 6m 45.00s. SP 8-11.
Mrs R Fell (Dartmoor).

1361 Confined (12st)

1142 **MOZE TIDY ....A Farrant 1**
hld up, steady prog to disp apr 2 out, ld last, pshd out
1138^2 **Karlimay 5a ....K Heard 2**
(fav) hld up, prog 3 out, short-lived effrt whn blnd last, sn btn
1138^1 **Catch The Cross (bl) ....Mrs M Hand 3**
ld til 4th, ld 15th, disp & ev ch 2 out, wknd
626^5 Glenform *twrds rear, 7th at 14th, poor 5th 3 out, nvr nr*...T Cole 4
Christmas Bash 5a *lft in ld 7th, hit 11th, hdd 15th, wknd rpdly 17th* ....L Jefford 5
628 Miss Moony 5a *alwys rear, last hlfwy, t.o. frm 3 out* ....I Widdicombe 6
1142 Christmas Hols *twrds rear, 6th at 14th, bhnd frm 15th, p.u. last*...............................D Stephens pu
1111 If You Say So *plld hrd, ld apr 4th til ref & u.r. 7th (ditch)* ....S Ellis ref
Cornish Harp *went 3rd 9th, in tch til lost ground 15th, bhnd & p.u. last* ....R Darke pu
9 ran. 6l, 6l, 10l, 30l, 2l. Time 6m 54.50s. SP 6-1.
Denis Williams (Dart Vale & Haldon Harriers).

1362 Open Maiden (12st)

1276 **NEWSKI EXPRESS 5a..................L Jefford 1**
(fav) w.w. in rear, prog 3 out, slght ld nxt, drew clr apr last
446 **Dharamshala (Ire) ....Mrs M Hand 2**
went 2nd 15th, ld apr 3 out, ran wd & jnd apr nxt,sn wknd
875^4 **Cottage Light (bl) ....I Widdicombe 3**
ld 6th til apr 3 out, onepcd
1143 Rusty Light (Ire) *1st ride, mid-div, 6th at 16th, nvr dang*...A Moir 4
807 Harmony's Choice 7a *in tch til lost ground frm 17th, tired whn mstk last* ....A Farrant 5
1071^6 Zany Girl 5a *twrds rear, 6th at 14th, bhnd frm 17th* ....I Hambly 6
719 Maverick's Creek (NZ) *ld to 6th, wll in tch til wknd 16th, t.o. & p.u. last*....................D Stephens pu
1143 Herhorse 5a (bl) *cls 4th at 10th, ran wd & plld herself up apr 11th* ....R Darke pu
1139 Lady Goldrush 5a *alwys rear, no ch frm 15th, t.o. & p.u. last* ....S Slade pu
9 ran. 12l, 4l, 10l, 6l, 12l. Time 7m 13.00s. SP 2-1.
John Lister (Dart Vale & South Pool).
G.T.

PENDLE FOREST & CRAVEN
Gisburn
Saturday May 4th
GOOD

1363 Members

983^8 **POLAR HAT ....Miss J Foster 1**
hld up, ld 14th, clr 2 out
1152 **South Stack ....D Coates 2**
chsd ldrs, cls up to 15th, onepcd aft
1154 **Bennan March (bl) ....N Bannister 3**
(fav) s.s. lft 30l, ld 5th, rdn & hdd 14th, no ext
1154^4 Alex-Path *mid-div whn p.u. 5th* ....T Whittaker pu
1134^4 Gold Choice *chsng ldr whn u.r. 13th*........V Ogden ur
5 ran. 8l, ½l. Time 7m 41.00s. SP 8-1.
Miss J E Foster (Pendle Forest & Craven).

1364 Open Maiden Div I

1029^3 **DREAM FLIGHT 7a.....................J Barlow 1**
(fav) 5/2-6/4, ld 7th, clr 3 out, ran on strngly
April Suprise 5a ....G Hanmer 2
hld up, 2nd 3 out, nvr nrr
569 **Sugi ....A Griffith 3**
bhnd, late prog to 3rd apr last, nvr nrr
1093 Oaklands Fred *mid-div, blnd 11th, 3rd frm 13th-last, onepcd* ....T Glass 4
1234^5 Salmon Spring (bl) *ld to 6th, 2nd to 15th, wknd rpdly aft*..R Williams 5
1155^2 Authenticity (Ire) 5a *prom, wknd 10th, p.u. 2 out* ....Miss C Burgess pu
740^4 King Keith *alwys prom, 5th whn u.r. 14th* ....C J M Barlow ur
987 Tyndrum Gold *ldng grp, 4th whn p.u. 13th*......N Tutty pu
1095^7 Fleeced *alwys rear, t.o. 9th, p.u. 3 out*......W Burnell pu
1196 High Handed (Ire) 7a *rear whn hmpd & f 6th* ....C J B Barlow f
1196 Ring Bank 7a *rear whn hmpd & u.r. 6th* ....M Worthington ur
11 ran. 15l, 3l, 12l, 25l. Time 7m 23.00s. SP 6-4.
Mrs Lorraine Lomax (Staff College & R.M.A.S. Drag).

1365 Open Maiden Div II

1224^3 **AUTUMN GREEN (IRE) ....G Hanmer 1**
(fav) w.w. 2nd 3 out, ld flat, well rdn
1094 **King Fly ....Miss S Horner 2**
cls up, ld 12th til hdd & outpcd flat
229^3 **Edinburgh Reel Ale 7a.................S Brisby 3**
bhnd, prog to 3l 3rd 16th, onepcd aft
1286^6 Morcat 5a *prog to 5th 3 out, lft 3rd last, no ext* ....C Mulhall 4
740^3 Bubble N Squeek *mid-div, nvr dang* ....C J B Barlow 5
1286^7 Im Ok (Ire) 5a *ldng grp, rdn 3 out, fin tired* ....Miss V Haigh 6
Colonial King *alwys rear, t.o. 10th* ....M Smith 7
Sambrian (bl) *rear, ref 1st (twice)* ....I Baker ref
762 Pri Neukin *chsd ldrs to 12th, wknd & p.u. 3 out* ....D Coates pu
590^2 Triple Value 5a *alwys bhnd, p.u. 2 out* ...Miss R Clark pu
1136^3 Engaging *ld/disp to 12th, wknd rpdly, p.u. 15th* ....Miss T Jackson pu
1234^3 Costermonger *hrd rdn to jn ldr 15th, wknd & p.u. 2 out*..A Griffith pu
1095^4 Malakie (Ire) *f 1st* ....Mrs S Grant f
1155 Analystic (Ire) *prog 15th, 3rd nxt, 15l down whn f last* ....M Worthington f
764 Flashlight 7a *cls up, mstks 6th & 8th, sn wknd, t.o. & u.r. 10th* ....S Whitaker ur
1029 Gold Talisman 5a *alwys rear, p.u. 9th*.......D Barlow pu
1008 Gold Top 7a *mstks, rear, u.r. 6th* ....R Bevis ur
17 ran. 2l, 20l, ½l, dist, 2l, 12l. Time 7m 31.00s. SP 9-4.
S J P Furniss (West Shropshire).

1366 Ladies

1121^2 **PEAJADE ....Miss J Wormall 1**
(fav) chsd ldrs, ld 14th, ran on well, eased flat
1153 **Across The Lake (bl).........Miss S Brotherton 2**
alwys prom, ev ch 3 out, styd on onepcd
1328^2 **Final Hope (Ire) ....Mrs F Needham 3**
bhnd, 3rd frm 2 out, nvr nrr
1232^3 Sooner Still (bl) *made most to 14th, onepcd aft* ....Miss K Rimmer 4
1192^3 Renard Quay *alwys 4th/5th, nvr dang* ....Miss C Wilberforce 5
1133^7 Tammy My Girl 5a *mid-div, nvr trbld ldrs* ....Miss A Armitage 6

1221 Harpley *mstks, t.o. 9th*..................Miss J Priest 7
1132² Crocket Lass 5a *alwys rear, t.o. 10th*...Miss F Hunter 8
1093 Linebacker *bhnd whn u.r. 7th*..........Miss S Leach ur
1153² Fly For Us 5a *chal 14th, wknd rpdly nxt, btn 5th whn f last*..............................Miss C Burgess f
1130 Katies Argument 5a *rear, t.o. 7th, p.u. 13th*..................................Mrs J Milburn pu
514² Thistle Monarch *nvr bynd mid-div, t.o. 13th, p.u. nxt*..................................Miss R Clark pu
12 ran. 2l, 10l, 4l, 6l, 12l, 1 fence, 1 fence. Time 7m 18.00s. SP 5-4.
Mrs Pauline Vernon (Atherstone).

1367 Open (12st)

1031¹ **SCALLY MUIRE 5a 7ex.....................A Crow** 1
(fav) chsd ldrs til ld 15th, clr 2 out, easily
1154¹ **Mr Tittle Tattle 7ex (bl)..................D Barlow** 2
ld to 14th, sn btn
1231⁵ **Ryton Guard 7ex ....A Gribbin** 3
alwys 3rd, 5l down 14th, onepcd aft
1304⁴ Clare Lad 7ex (v) *alwys rear, t.o. 14th*......Dr M Tate 4
4 ran. 10l, 12l, 1 fence. Time 7m 27.00s. SP 4-7.
G L Edwards (North Shropshire).

1368 Restricted

583 **ONE FOR THE CHIEF (v).................D Curren** 1
chsd ldrs, lft in ld 13th, clr 2 out
856 **Made Of Talent 5a..........................A Crow** 2
bhnd, prog 14th, 3rd nxt, rdn & styd on onepcd
1131⁷ **Ruff Account ....Miss J Eastwood** 3
cls up, 2l 2nd 14th-2 out, no ext aft
983⁶ Goodwill Hill *alwys rear, nvr dang*..........D Coates 4
1233⁷ Grecianlid *alwys prom, lft 2nd 13th, wknd rpdly nxt*..................................Miss S Hopkins 5
1131 The Chap *bhnd, t.o. 10th, p.u. 2 out*......Miss R Clark pu
1284 Midge 5a *6th whn f 8th*..............Mrs F Needham f
158¹ Turbulent Gale (Ire) *(fav) ld 4th, going wll whn c.o. by loose horse apr 13th*..........................R Bevis co
740 Posy Hill (Ire) 7a *8l 3rd at 10th, wknd 14th, p.u. 2 out*..................................G Hanmer pu
9 ran. 6l, 2l, 1 fence, 1 fence. Time 7m 33.00s. SP 16-1.
D Curren (Bramham Moor).

1369 Confined (12st)

1152³ **BARKIN 3ex ....C J B Barlow** 1
lft in ld 15th, styd on well
1032 **Charlie Chalk 6ex ....A Griffith** 2
lft 3l 2nd 15th, ev ch aft, no ext
1093⁶ **Political Sam ....A Rebori** 3
alwys bhnd, lft poor 3rd 15th
1150³ On Your Way *mstks, rear 9th, t.o. nxt*.....D Sherlock 4
1134² Beau Rose *alwys bhnd, p.u. 15th*............A Ogden pu
1281 Fowling Piece *bhnd, rear whn p.u. 15th*..................................Miss L Horner pu
1230⁶ Ebony Gale *mid-div, 5th whn f 15th*....Miss J Penney f
1152² Crimson Mary 5a *cls up in 3rd whn f 15th*..................................Miss C Burgess f
1091⁴ Stag Fight *4l 5th whn f 14th*.................S Walker f
1151¹ Jr-Kay (Ire) *(fav) ld til f 15th whn going wll*..................................N Bannister f
10 ran. 2l, dist, 2 fences. Time 7m 32.00s. SP 10-1.
Peter Saville (Cheshire).
R.A.

SURREY UNION
Peper Harow
Saturday May 4th
FIRM

1370 Members

MILBIRD ....M Gorman 1
tubed, cls up, ld 13th, clr 3 out, eased flat,
1108⁶ **Paco's Boy ....P York** 2
(fav) made most to 13th, rdn appr 3 out, no resp
1210 **Little Petherick 5a.......................P Bull** 3
cls up, disp ld 10-12th, onepcd frm 15th
3 ran. 4l, 10l. Time 6m 55.00s. SP 2-1.
Lady Huntley & Mrs P Tetley (Surrey Union).

1371 Restricted (12st)

1295 **FIXED LIABILITY (bl)................T Underwood** 1
(fav) mstks, chsd ldr 15th, chal on inner 2 out, ld last, rdn out
679 **Charleston Lad ....P Bull** 2
prom,ld 13th, hmpd 2 out, sn hdded, no ex
1189 **Second Time Round ....Capt D Parker** 3
bhnd, lst tch appr 13th, styd on frm 3 out, nvr dang
1206 Lewesdon Princess 5a (bl) *ld,clr 3-7th,hdded appr 13th,wknd 3 out,wl btn & blnd last*..............T Hills 4
1189⁵ Mr Sunnyside *chsd ldr 7-10th,strng chall whn bmpd & u.r. appr 2 out*............................S Claisse ur
5 ran. 4l, 12l, 20l. Time 6m 50.00s. SP Evens.
T D B Underwood (Warwickshire).

1372 Open (12st)

1296¹ **GINGER TRISTAN 7ex ....D Robinson** 1
ld 8-12th, jmpd to ld nxt, made rest, clr 3 out, comf, lame
1208⁴ **Sky Venture ....P Bull** 2
prom, ld bfly appr 13th, outpcd nxt, kpt on und press 2 out
1246² **Cheeky Cheval ....D Dennis** 3
hld up, prog 12th, ev ch nxt, sn strugg, no ch frm 3 out
1209² Highly Decorated 7ex (bl) *made most to 6th, lst pl & rmdrs 10th, no ch whn p.u. 15th*..........J Van Praagh pu
918¹ Burromariner *(fav) in tch, 4th whn reluctant & j.s. 14th, lsng tch whn ref nxt*...................S Cowell ref
1296 Quarter Marker (Ire) *keen hold, hld up, lst tch appr 13th, p.u. 15th*.........................M Loughnane pu
6 ran. 8l, 20l. Time 6m 41.00s. SP 2-1.
D C Robinson (Mid Surrey Farmers Drag).

1373 Ladies

1208¹ **MAGICAL MORRIS 4ex...........Miss C Grissell** 1
(fav) chsd ldr, clsd appr 13th, ld appr 3 out, clr nxt, easy
596⁵ **Johnny Rose ....Mrs C Mitchell** 2
ld, 12l clr 11th, hdded appr 3 out, rdn & btn apppr 2 out
995² Pejawi 5a *blnd & u.r. 1st*...........Miss M Bentham ur
3 ran. 15l. Time 6m 54.00s. SP 1-2.
Mrs D M Grissell (East Sussex & Romney Marsh).

1374 Open Maiden (12st)

1164⁴ **CHILDSWAY ....T Underwood** 1
restrained in rr, prog to 2nd 3 out, ld nxt, drvn out flat
1228 **Pallingham Star (Ire) ....P O'Keeffe** 2
(fav) chsd ldrs, disp ld 13th, ld 15th-2 out, onepcd und press
1210² **Run To Au Bon (Ire) (bl)...............T McCarthy** 3
ld to 14th, 3rd & rdn appr 2 out, wknd appr last
1187³ No Reply *keen hold, chsd ldr 4-12th, rdn & wknd appr 2 out*..............................Mrs C Mitchell 4
1055 Bric Lane (USA) *nt fluent, last frm 7th, t.o 15th*..................................Miss D French 5
1187 Shared Fortune (Ire) *f 1st*..................D Dennis f
994³ Vulgan Prince *in tch til u.r. 6th*...............A Greig ur
1300 Phantom Slipper (bl) *n.j.w. mid-div, lst tch appr 13th, p.u. 14th*......................................P York pu
8 ran. 1l, 5l, 3l, dist. Time 6m 57.00s. SP 6-1.
Charles Kay (Garth & South Berks).

1375 Confined (12st)

1298² **VALIBUS (FR) 3ex.....................P Scouller** 1
prog 9th, chsd ldr 13th, ld appr last, std on strngly
1207¹ **Galaroi (Ire) 3ex....................D Robinson** 2
(fav) 3/1-1/1,prom, ld 13th til appr last, no ex
1289² **Skinnhill (bl) ....C Mason** 3
prom to 8th, last & pshd alng 11th, styd on frm 3 out, n.d.

1298 Redelva 5a *chsd ldr, ld 11th til appr 13th, wknd 3 out* ....M Gorman 4
961[1] Glenavey *bhnd 3rd, p.u. 5th* ....P Hall pu
920 Colne Valley Kid *mid-div til lst pl appr 7th, t.o. whn p.u. 10th* ....A Welsh pu
Lucas Court *bhnd til p.u. aft 6th* ....S Garrott pu
1190[1] Olde Crescent 3ex *hld up, effrt 13th, 5th & btn whn p.u. aft 3 out* ....T Underwood pu
1298[1] Kates Castle 5a 6ex *(fav) ld to 10th, 4th whn p.u. qkly aft 12th* ....J Van Praagh pu
9 ran. 4l, 10l, 20l. Time 6m 35.00s. SP 16-1.
P A D Scouller (Garth & South Berks).
S.P.

FERNIE
Dingley
Sunday May 5th
GOOD TO FIRM

1376 Members

1237[3] **WRITE THE MUSIC (bl) ....D Esden** 1
(fav) in tch, mstk 3 out, sn trckd ldr, ld aft last, sn clr,easily
1174 **Potato Fountain (Ire) 5a (bl) ....P Millington** 2
ld 5-9th & 12th-aft last, immed outpcd by wnr
897[6] **Hellbrunn ....N Bell** 3
ld 2-5th, cls up til outpcd 3 out, kpt on agn apr last
1103 Coolsythe 5a *ld to 2nd & 9-12th, 3rd & outpcd 2 out, onepcd* ....C Millington 4
1027[1] Nee-Argee 5a *alwys bhnd, no ch whn nrly u.r. 3 out, walked in* ....P Ikin 5
1100 Kellys Pal *cls up til blnd 11th, not rcvr, t.o. & p.u. 2 out* ....C Weaver pu
1177 Batcho Missile *last til prog 3rd,prom whn mstk & u.r. 5th* ....J Dillon ur
7 ran. 4l, nk, 2l, 20l. Time 6m 46.70s. SP 4-5.
Miss E M Davison (Fernie).

1377 Confined (12st)

538[1] **BROAD STEANE ....A Sansome** 1
(Co fav) j.w. trckd ldrs, ld 14th, bttr jump last, ran on well
1239[1] **Whinstone Mill ....R Thornton** 2
mid-div,prog 10th,chsd wnr 3 out,ch whn slw jmp last,onepcd
794[5] **Lily The Lark 5a ....Miss H Irving** 3
mstks, cls up til hit 13th, strggling 3 out, kpt on
1068[1] Saffron Flame (Ire) *(Co fav) w.w. effrt 13th, nvr rchd ldrs, btn apr 2 out* ....P Taiano 4
1236[1] Oh So Windy 5a 3ex *(Co fav) mid-div, prog 9th, cls up 13th, rdn 15th, sn btn* ....S Morris 5
1179[5] Chiasso Forte (Ity) (bl) *ld 3rd, sn clr, hdd 14th, grad fdd* ....Mrs P Adams 6
1099[4] Loose Wheels (v) *ld to 3rd, prom aft til wknd 15th* ....Miss K Makinson 7
897 Spanish Whisper *alwys rear, t.o. 13th* ....T Lane 8
1236[5] Hostetler *alwys last pair, t.o. frm 8th* ...J Stephenson 9
970 Monk's Mistake *alwys last pair, t.o. frm 8th* ....Miss S Bonser 10
1236[6] Sanamar *alwys rear grp, t.o. 12th, p.u. 2 out*...D Ingle pu
1022[3] Rain Mark *prom til wknd 10th, poor 8th whn u.r. 15th* ....M Chatterton ur
12 ran. 6l, 20l, 4l, ½l, 3l, 15l, 30l, 10l, 10l. Time 6m 24.20s. SP 9-4.
Sir Michael Connell (Grafton).

1378 2½m Open Maiden

1104[3] **DARK RHYTHAM ....S Morris** 1
(fav) made all, 1l up & lkd wnr whn lft clr last
1104 **Tiger ....P Cowley** 2
prom, chsd wnr 6th-4 out, 4th & btn aft nxt, lft 2nd last
898 **View Point (Ire) ....M Gingell** 3
in tch, chsd wnr 4 out-aft nxt, wknd, lft 3rd last
1174[6] Rainbow Fantasia (Ire) *mid-div, 8th & btn whn nrly f 11th, no ch aft* ....P Millington 4
1105[5] Never So Lost *wth ldrs, prog to chal 2 out, 1l down & lkd btn whn u.r.last* ....J Trice-Rolph ur
1103 Tarry No More 5a *chsd ldrs, in tch whn p.u. 10th* ....A Sansome pu
1376 Batcho Missile *2nd outing, s.s. last til f 5th*....J Dillon f
Broadnote 5a *mstk 2nd, mid-div, 8th whn f 6th* ....S R Andrews f
1319 Golden Nectar *ldng grp, 6th & still in tch whn f heavily 4 out* ....E Walker f
1224[5] Wrenbury Farmer *rear, prog & in tch hlfwy, sn btn, t.o. & p.u. last* ....M Jackson pu
1240 Remalone 5a *alwys bhnd, t.o. & p.u. 10th* ....D Ingle pu
727 Derring Knight (v) *last & t.o. 8th, p.u. 11th* E Andrewes pu
1105 Beachborough *ldng grp til p.u. 10th* ....T Marks pu
1026 Cawkwell Win 7a *alwys rear, 12th & no ch whn f 9th* ....K Needham f
Holmby Copse *schoold,clsd hlfwy,prog to 3rd apr last,lost action & p.u.* ....B Pollock pu
Tomcappagh (Ire) 7a *schoold in last trio, t.o. & p.u. 4 out* ....Miss S French pu
16 ran. 15l, ¾l, 20l. Time 5m 34.00s. SP 3-1.
G Coombe (Quorn).
One fence omitted 2nd circuit. 15 jumps.

1379 Mixed Open

902[1] **RAISE AN ARGUMENT ....J Docker** 1
trckd ldrs, chal 14th, ld nxt, clr 2 out, ran on strngly
1235[2] **Falconbridge Bay ....R Armson** 2
prom, chal & lft in ld 14th, hdd nxt, wknd 2 out, fin tired
1235[3] **Trusty Friend ....J Oldring** 3
last pair, t.o. 12th, styd on apr last
1179 Shipmate *last pair, t.o. 12th, styd on apr last* ....R Hunnisett 4
906 Easy Over (USA) *ld 2-6th, mstk 12th, wknd, poor 4th whn hmpd apr 2 out* ....M Gingell 5
1237 Blue Aeroplane *prom, blnd 12th, 3rd & no ch whn badly hmpd apr 2 out* ....A Sansome 6
1329[6] Coolvawn Lady (Ire) 5a *(fav) 5/4-4/6, ld 6th, just in ld whn f 14th* ....T Lane f
7 ran. 30l, 6l, 1l, 12l, 20l. Time 6m 35.80s. SP 7-4.
Mrs J H Docker (Atherstone).

1380 Restricted (12st)

GRIMLEY GALE (IRE) 5a........M Jackson 1
(fav) mstk 5th, trckd ldrs, ld aft 12th, drew clr apr last, comf
1145 **Cader Idris ....G Tarry** 2
ld to 2nd,prom,ev ch 15th,not qckn,styd on to chs wnr last
1241[1] **Supreme Dream (Ire) 5a ....Mrs P Adams** 3
chsd ldrs, mstk 12th, strggling 3 out, styd on apr last
1178[5] Ballyvoyle Bay 5a (bl) *chsd ldrs, cls up 3 out, sn outpcde & btn* ....J Docker 4
680[1] Just A Madam (Ire) 5a *mstks, ld 2-3rd & 9-10th, btn frm 3 out* ....Miss E Tomlinson 5
1239[2] Majestic Ride *in tch, gd prog to chal wnr 2 out, wknd rpdly apr last* ....R Armson 6
1168[3] Lochinvar Lord (bl) *rear, lost tch 10th, bhnd aft, kpt on apr last* ....D Renney 7
679 Inch Gale 5a (bl) *wll in tch til wknd frm 14th* M Gingell 8
1306[2] Ocean Sovereign *ld 3-9th & 10th-aft 12th, wknd rpdly, walked in* ....A Sansome 9
1025 Dashboard Light *j.w. in tch, chal 15th, wknd rpdly 2 out, p.u. last* ....S R Andrews pu
973[1] Mysterious Run (Ire) *mstk 8th, sn lost tch, t.o. & p.u. 11th* ....Miss S Samworth pu
11 ran. 8l, 7l, 12l, 8l, 1l, ½l, nk, 1 fence. Time 6m 24.50s. SP 5-2.
R M Phillips (Clifton-On-Teme).

1381 Open Maiden

1248[5] **BOLSHIE BARON ....M Harris** 1
j.w. made all, pckd 12th, clr 15th, eased flat
1242 **Sit Tight ....M Portman** 2
in tch, went 3rd & outpcd 14th, kpt on to chs wnr apr last
682[2] **Dolly Bloom 5a ....G Tarry** 3
(Jt fav) prom,chsd wnr 10th,outpcd 15th,no imp,fin 4th,promoted

1103² Cormeen Lord (Ire) *(Jt fav) prom, 5th & wll outpcd 14th, kpt on 2 out, no dang* .... J Sharp 5
1103 Dante's Pride (Ire) *in tch to 11th, sn wknd, t.o.* .... C Weaver 6
1217 Matchlessly *chsd wnr to 10th, wknd frm 12th, t.o.* .... Miss E Walker 7
1301⁴ The Bold Abbot *alwys rear, t.o. 14th* .... P Millington 8
1301 Littledale (USA) *prom to 12th, sn wknd, t.o. & p.u. last* .... R Armson pu
1240 Boscoe *alwys rear, last & lost tch 10th, t.o. & p.u. 13th* .... G Brewer pu
1240⁴ Full Song 5a *hld up,prog 11th,sn outpcd,kpt on frm 3 out,fin 3rd,disq* .... S Morris 0
898 Minstrel's Night (Ire) 7a *in tch to 10th, t.o. & f 13th, dead* .... C Ward f
1063³ Remilan (Ire) 7a *alwys rear, t.o. last whn p.u. 10th* .... P Taiano pu
1097 See The Lord (Ire) *in tch til blnd 11th, not rcvr, p.u. nxt* .... B Pollock pu
930 Nova Star 7a *n.j.w. alwys rear, t.o. & p.u. 9th* .... S R Andrews pu
1240 Seaton Mill *mid-div til f 6th* .... M Hewitt f
Plat Du Jour 5a *mid-div til f 8th* .... R Barrett f

16 ran. 15l, 1½l, 4l, 3l, dist, 2½l, 2½l. Time 6m 35.80s. SP 8-1.
M H Weston (Croome & West Warwickshire).
Full Song disqualified, rider not W/I. Original distances. J.N.

EXETER
Monday May 6th
GOOD TO FIRM

1382 2m 7f 110yds West Of England Open Hunters' Chase Class H

1275¹ **CHILIPOUR 11.2 7a 3ow** .... **Mr Richard White** 1
(fav) alwys prom, ld 10th, ran on well.
1226² **Romany King 11.6** .... **Mr M Armytage** 2
held up, steady hdwy 11th, ev ch 2 out, rdn and not qckn after last.
940² **Duchess Of Tubber (Ire) 10.9 7a 1ow** .... **Miss S Young** 3
joined wnr 10th, ev ch 4 out, one pace from next.
1327² Sonofagipsy 11.1 5a *ld to 10th, wknd apr 4 out.* .... Mr P Henley 4
1123³ Skerry Meadow 11.3 3a *alwys well bhnd.* .... Mr J Culloty 5
672 Ullswater 10.13 7a *t.o. from 6th, blnd 9th, p.u. before next.* .... Miss G Russell pu
1228⁸ Tekla (Fr) 10.13 7a *with ldr till wknd 9th, t.o. when p.u. before 5 out.* .... Miss D Olding pu
1122 Percy Thrower 11.6 5a *f 3rd.* .... Mr M Rimell f

8 ran. 1l, 6l, 13l, 11l. Time 5m 51.60s. SP 5-2.
Nick Viney

TOWCESTER
Monday May 6th
GOOD TO FIRM

1383 2¾m New 96.6 Northants FM & FM 103 Horizon Novices' Hunters' Chase Class H

1107⁴ **BEAU DANDY 11.7 7a** .... **Mr T Marks** 1
(fav) ld to 4th, regained ld 6th, made rest, rdn out.
906³ **Bathwick Bobbie 11.11 3a** .... **Mr C Bonner** 2
held up in tch, mstk 5th, ev ch 2 out, no ext last.
1228⁶ **Tea Cee Kay 11.9 5a** .... **Mr A Sansome** 3
in tch, mstk 5th, jmpd slowly and lost pl 10th, no dngr after.
909⁴ Blakes Orphan 12.0 7a (bl) *pressed wnr, ld 4th to 6th, jmpd slowly 11th, 3rd and held when mstk 2 out.* .... Mr P Scott 4
1107⁶ Timber's Boy 12.0 7a *alwys bhnd, t.o.* .... Mr R Gill 5
746³ Frampton House 11.7 7a *mstk 8th, alwys bhnd, t.o. when p.u. before 4 out.* .... Mr F Hutsby pu
263 Royal Fireworks 11.7 7a *blnd 6th, bhnd from 8th, t.o. when f 12th.* .... Miss S Higgins f

7 ran. 2½l, 10l, 12l, dist. Time 5m 41.90s. SP 11-8.
C C Shand Kydd

BANWEN MINERS
Pantyderi
Monday May 6th
GOOD TO FIRM

1384 Members

LITTLE SQUAW 7a .... **P Hamer** 1
(fav) sttld cls up, hrd rdn to ld aft last, ran green
Woodlight Dawn 5a .... **J Tudor** 2
mstks, ld til aft last, no ext

2 ran. ¾l. Time 7m 12.00s. SP 1-2.
W Hancock (Banwen Miners).

1385 Confined (12st)

1211 **CELTIC DAUGHTER 5a** .... **J Jukes** 1
hld up, prog 12th, ld aft 15th, comf
1264⁵ **Moving Force** .... **J P Keen** 2
ld til aft 15th, breather, drvn & unable chal frm 2 out
1262 **Lucky Ole Son** .... **Miss P Jones** 3
sttld 5th, prog 15th, hrd rdn 2 out, onepcd aft
846² Merino Waltz (USA) *(fav) trckd ldrs to 13th, mstk nxt, wknd, tired* .... D S Jones 4
1263 Harken Premier *alwys rear, p.u. 11th* .... A Price pu
1268³ Just Marmalade *prom to hlfwy, rmndr 10th, mstk nxt, p.u. 12th* .... J Tudor pu

6 ran. 8l, 3l, 30l. Time 5m 40.00s. SP 2-1.
Mrs E A Webber (Pembrokeshire).

1386 Open (12st)

1265² **TOUCH 'N' PASS** .... **J Tudor** 1
(fav) sttld rear, prog 10th, ld aft 15th, ran om gamely flat
1262² **Doubting Donna 5a** .... **J Jukes** 2
ld 2nd til aft 15th, prssd wnr aft, no ext flat
1264³ **Lislary Lad** .... **D S Jones** 3
nvr bttr than 3rd, onepcd
Tinas Lad *trckd ldrs, mstk 12th, wknd, p.u. nxt, dead* .... A W Price pu
601¹ Sun Of Chance *strng hld, trckd ldrs, mstk 10th, wknd aft, p.u. 12th* .... P Williams pu

5 ran. 3l, 2l. Time 5m 44.00s. SP 4-5.
David Vaughan-Morgan (Llangeinor).

1387 Ladies

1157 **GOLD DIVER** .... **Miss E Jones** 1
alwys prom, mstk 10th, ld 15th, comf
1264² **Never Be Great 3ex** .... **Miss L Pearce** 2
sttld off pace, prog frm 15th, hrd rdn 3 out, no ch wnr
1264⁷ **Afaristoun (Fr)** .... **Miss J Morse** 3
ld to 13th, fin tired
1264⁸ Mount Falcon *alwys rear* .... Miss C Morgan 4
979 Atlaal *ref 1st* .... Miss D Bowen ref
1211⁴ Goolds Gold 7ex *(fav) mid-div, s.u. flat aft 7th* .... Miss P Jones su

6 ran. 10l, ½l, 10l. Time 5m 47.00s. SP 6-1.
Linden Rogers (Llangeinor).

1388 Restricted (12st)

1201¹ **NORTHERN BLUFF** .... **J Jukes** 1
(fav) made all, wll clr last, eased flat
980⁴ **Dustys Trail (Ire)** .... **R Thornton** 2
sttld cls up, rmndr aft 10th, prog to 2nd 13th, no ch wnr
1160 **Celtic Bizarre 5a** .... **Miss B Barton** 3
trckd ldr to hlfwy, wknd 11th, lame
1203³ Saffron Moss *sttld 4th/5th, prog 8th, fdd 11th, onepcd* .... A Price 4
1203⁴ Ayyarose 5a *nvr nrr than 5th, btn whn f 14th* .... J Price f
1162¹ Tims Kick (Ire) 7a *mid-div, no ch whn p.u. 2 out* .... J Tudor pu
1273 Euromill Star 5a *s.s. t.o. whn ref 3rd* .... M Lewis ref

7 ran. 12l, dist, 30l. Time 5m 46.00s. SP 4-5.
H Gibbon (Pembrokeshire).

1389 Intermediate (12st)

1203[1] **PENDIL'S DELIGHT 5a ....D S Jones** 1
(fav) prom, ld aft 15th, hrd rdn 2 out, all out
1160[1] **Sweet Kildare 5a ....J Jukes** 2
strng hld, chsd ldr 9th, chsd wnr 3 out, kpt on flat
1268 **Origami 4ex ....J P Keen** 3
rear, effrt 3 out, onepcd nxt, ref last, cont
1267[1] The Apprentice *ld til aft 15th, wknd rpdly, p.u. 3 out* ....J Tudor pu
1263[4] Gus McCrae *alwys rear, onepcd, p.u. 11th* . .P Hamer pu
5 ran. 4l, dist. Time 5m 44.00s. SP Evens.
A Simpson (Pembrokeshire).

1390 Open Maiden Div I (12st)

151[2] **MAGNETIC REEL 7a ....J Jukes** 1
(fav) ld/disp, hdd brfly aft 2 out, drvn out flat
1200 **Parks Pride 7a ....R Thornton** 2
sttld rear,prog 9th,mstk nxt,ld aft 2 out,sn hdd & no ext
1175 **Mr Ffitch ....L Stephens** 3
prom til wknd frm 15th, kpt on apr last
1271 Jolly Swagman 7a *rear, prog 8th, ld 10-15th, fdd, fin tired* ....G Perkins 4
765[2] Preseli View 7a *3rd/4th til wknd 15th* ....M Lewis 5
1040 Great Precocity (v) *chsd ldrs to hlfwy, wknd frm 15th* ....R Jones 6
1272[4] Cefn Woodsman 7a *nvr nrr, nvr dang* . . . .D S Jones 7
1201[2] Wayward Edward *alwys mid-div, p.u. 14th* . . . .J Price pu
1270[2] It's So Sweet 5a *nvr dang, bhnd whn p.u. aft 14th* ....P Williams pu
1271[2] Harry From Barry *ld til f 4th* ....J Tudor f
Relatively High 7a *alwys wll bhnd, t.o. & p.u. 3 out* ....S Lloyd pu
980 Fumi D'Oro 5a *rear, p.u. 8th*.............D Llewellyn pu
1271[4] I'm A Bute 5a *ran out 7th* ....T Vaughan ro
1201 Good Boy Charlie 7a *alwys bhnd, p.u. 3 out*. . .A Price pu
977[4] Kirby's Charm *3rd/4th til wknd 15th, p.u. last* ....J P Keen pu
15 ran. 3l, 3l, 7l, 20l, 2l, dist. Time 5m 54.00s. SP Evens.
Mrs E A Webber (Pembrokeshire).

1391 Open Maiden Div II (12st)

1269 **CAIRNEYMOUNT ....J Tudor** 1
trckd ldrs til ld 15th, sn clr, comf
1200[2] **Another Quince 5a........................J Price** 2
(fav) ld to 7th, mstk 14th, chsd wnr aft, no imp
1272[2] **Gold Tip 5a ....J P Keen** 3
ld 7th-15th, wknd 2 out
1040 Trevella 5a (bl) *nvr nrr than 4th, strgglng frm 14th* ....D Stephens 4
Agapanthus 5a *3rd/4th til fdd frm 2 out*.......S Lloyd 5
1271 Prince Theo *c.o. 3rd* ....M Lewis co
1269 Solars Sister 5a *u.r. 1st*......................R Jones ur
1271 Frontrunner 5a *u.r. 1st* ....A W Price ur
1162 Miss Montgomery (Ire) 7a *blnd 2nd, p.u. 8th* ....D S Jones pu
1269 Deryn Y Cwm (Ire) *b.d. 1st*...........Miss C Morgan bd
1271 Sea Tarth 7a *alwys rear, ref 14th* ....J Jukes ref
1197[3] Kerstin's Choice 7a *in rear whn p.u. 10th* D Llewellyn pu
697 Lady Medusa (Ire) 7a *ran out 3rd*.........R Thornton ro
13 ran. 10l, 5l, 10l, ½l. Time 5m 56.00s. SP 4-1.
Robert Williams (Llangeinor).
P.D.

COTLEY
Cotley Farm
Monday May 6th
GOOD TO FIRM

1392 Members

1278[2] **THEGOOSE ....P King** 1
(fav) j.w., hld up, disp 3 out, ld app last, rdn out
1114 **Palace King (Ire) ....G Baines** 2
chsd ldr, prog 10th, disp nxt til outpcd app last, rlld flat
Beltane The Smith ....Maj G Wheeler 3
ld to 11th, disp to 3 out, outpcd aft
1079 Springcombe 5a *prom early, 4th frm 5th, clsng whn blndrd & u.r. 13th* ....Miss S Eames ur
993 Better By Half (Ire) *alws last, t.o. whn p.u. 13th* ....J Tizzard pu
5 ran. 1½l, 20l. Time 6m 32.80s. SP 2-7.
A Palmer (Cotley).

1393 B F S S (Nov Riders)

1127 **RARE FLUTTER 5a...................B O'Doherty** 1
rr early, prog 8th, ld nxt, ran on wl frm 2 out
1167[3] **Spring Fun ....Miss Y Young** 2
in tch, 4th at 9th, ev ch 4 out, one pace aft
1141[4] **Highway Jim ....Miss M Peck** 3
alwys prom, 2nd at 10th, ev ch 3 out, outpcd aft
1312[4] Archie's Nephew (bl) *rr early, 6th at 10th, outpcd frm nxt*..................................P Griffiths 4
1312[1] The Humble Tiller *rr, no ch 10th, btn 5th whn u.r. 2 out* ....Miss L Knights ur
1167 Champagne Run *mid-div, lost tch 10th, t.o. & p.u. 3 out* ....G Chanter pu
1124[1] Strong Breeze *(fav) ld til blndrd 9th, rdr lost irns, p.u. bef nxt*...........................Mrs R Pocock pu
1310[2] False Economy *mid-div, 5th at 10th, lost tch 4 out, p.u. app last* ....Miss K Scorgie pu
1168 Langton Parmill *mid-div early, 3rd at 10th, 2nd 12th, ev ch & f last* ....P Shaw f
1113 Glamorous Guy *sn bhnd, t.o. 14th, p.u. 2 out*. .D Fitch-Peyton pu
10 ran. 6l, ½l, 25l. Time 6m 26.60s. SP 14-1.
H J Panes (Taunton Vale Foxhounds).

1394 Mixed Open (12st)

1310[4] **ON HIS OWN ....Miss W Southcombe** 1
j.r., ld 5th, clr 10th, easily
1291[2] **Sirisat ....Miss T Blazey** 2
(fav) w.w., 4th at 10th, 2nd 12th, outpcd frm 3 out
1309[5] **Galaxy High ....I Dowrick** 3
alwys bhnd, no ch frm 14th
1166[4] Gunner Stream *alwys rr, no ch frm 11th* . . .G Chanter 4
1309 Nanda Moon *ld to 5th, prom to 11th, wknd & p.u. 14th* ....G Baines pu
5 ran. 20l, 20l, 10l. Time 6m 25.30s. SP 3-1.
P L Southcombe (Cattistock).

1395 Restricted (12st)

1128[3] **AVRIL SHOWERS 5a ....R Atkinson** 1
rr, stdy prog frm 4 out, ld last, ran on
1060[1] **Front Cover 5a.......................S Mulcaire** 2
(fav) w.w., prog frm 11th, ld app last, not qckn whn hdd
1113[2] **Definite Maybe (Ire) ....N Mitchell** 3
alwys prom, ld 11th-2 out, outpcd aft
1335 Blake's Finesse 5a *ld to 10th, cl up til ld agn 2 out, no ex whn hdd* ....Miss S Vickery 4
1345 Just Donald *sn bhnd, t.o. frm 13th* ....A Honeyball 5
993[1] Seahawk Retriever *hld up, prog frm 10th, ev ch 3 out, wknd nxt & p.u.*................................T Mitchell pu
Stalbridge Return 5a *sn rr, t.o. whn p.u. 8th* ....S Parfimowicz pu
1189 Pines Express (Ire) (bl) *cl up to 10th, wknd nxt, p.u. 14th* ....I Dowrick pu
8 ran. 2l, 3l, 10l, dist. Time 6m 21.50s. SP 4-1.
Mr And Mrs R Atkinson (Cattistock).

1396 Open Maiden (12st)

1060[2] **ALEX THUSCOMBE (v)...................P Shaw** 1
prom, ld to 4th, disp frm 10th til ld 4 out, ran on well
820 **Passing Fair 7a ....Miss S Vickery** 2
(fav) hld up, prog to disp 10th, hdd 4 out, no ex aft
1140 **Simply Joyful 5a ....P King** 3
alwys mid-div, 3rd 4 out, not trble 1st 2
1129[4] St Julien (Ire) *alwys mid-div, no ch frm 4 out, onepcd* ....T Mitchell 4
Royal Turn *alwys rr, t.o. frm 14th, outpcd* A Honeyball 5

1308[4] Inner Snu 5a *alwys mid-div, no ch whn p.u. app last* ....N Mitchell pu
1349 Dula Model 5a *mid-div whn blndrd & u.r. aft 3rd* ....J Tizzard ur
1279 Crucis (Ire) 7a *mid-div, prog 10th, ev ch 3 out, btn 4th whn f last* ....I Dowrick f
1187 Barrow Street *prom, ld 5th til ran out aft 9th* ....Maj G Wheeler ro
993[5] Girls In Business 5a *mstk 1st, sn rr, t.o. whn p.u. 13th* ....P Griffiths pu
Jim Crow *mid-div, wknd 10th, t.o. whn p.u. 13th* ....M Miller pu
11 ran. 10l, 20l, 3l, dist. Time 6m 33.50s. SP 6-1.
Mrs F Shaw (Tavistock).

1397 Confined (12st)

1311[4] **BEINN MOHR 5a....N Mitchell 1**
cl up, ld 9th, styd on wl frm 2 out
1124[2] **Arctic Baron ....Miss S Vickery 2**
ld to 9th, prom aft, rlld frm last, just fld
1125[3] **Pintail Bay ....Maj G Wheeler 3**
hld up, ev ch 10th, outpcd frm 12th
1307[1] Columbique *alwys last, no ch frm 13th* ....D Moffett 4
4 ran. Nk, 30l, 10l. Time 6m 29.00s. SP 5-1.
Mrs B C Willcocks (Portman).
D.P.

ENFIELD CHACE
Northaw
Monday May 6th
FIRM

1398 Members (12st)

1148[3] **MOUNT PATRICK ....C Lawson 1**
j.w. ld 3rd, made rest, clr 2 out, easy
1300[3] **Le Vienna (Ire) ....S R Andrews 2**
(fav) n.j.w. rmdrs 2nd, chsd wnr 5th,ev ch & rdn 3 out, sn btn
Target Moon ....Mrs K Pilkington 3
1st ride, ld to 2nd, lst tch appr 8th, no ch frm 10th
Ash-Leigh 7ow *alwys last, lst tch 7th, disp poor 3rd whn f 13th* ....Miss S Harrington f
4 ran. 8l, 2 fences. Time 6m 20.00s. SP 7-4.
C J Lawson (Enfield Chace).

1399 Confined (12st)

1257[3] **JIMSTRO ....T Moore 1**
chsd ldr 4th-12th,3rd & rdn 3 out, strng run flat,ld cls hme
1321[3] **Salmon River (USA) 7a 3ow....N King 2**
(fav) in tch,wnt 2nd 13th,ld appr last,nt qkn und pres,hdd cls hme
1144 **Lord Richard ....S R Andrews 3**
ld 3rd til appr last, onepcd und press
1256[3] Valatch *chsd ldrs, 4th & outpcd 13th, kpt on onepcd frm 3 out* ....J Henderson 4
1188[6] Truely Royal *nt fluent early, prog to 6th 12th, no imp on ldrs frm 15th* ....Miss S Gritton 5
677 El Bae *w.w. in tch, outpcd 13th, no dang frm 15th* ....P Taiano 6
1068 Parkers Hills (Ire) *ld to 2nd, lst pl appr 8th, t.o frm 15th* ....S Sporborg 7
1062 Blumix *prog to disp ld bfly 7th, bhnd frm 11th, t.o.* ....N Strain 8
8 ran. ½l, 2l, 12l, 5l, 8l, dist, 1l. Time 5m 47.00s. SP 10-1.
K F Clutterbuck (Puckeridge).

1400 Open (12st)

1323[6] **OVER THE EDGE 7ex ....S Sporborg 1**
ld to 11th, ld agn 14th, hld on gamely und press flat
1258[1] **River Melody 5a ....T Moore 2**
(fav) trkd ldrs, chal 3 out, rdn nxt, unable to qkn flat
1372 **Quarter Marker (Ire) ....M Loughnane 3**
in tch, hit 9th, ld 13th, hdd & blnd nxt, sn wknd
1376 Kellys Pal (bl) *wth ldr, ld 12th, sn hdd, wknd 14th, t.o.* ....P Millington 4
1257[4] Pike's Glory *last frm 3rd, t.o. whn p.u 8th* ....J Henderson pu
1228 Laburnum 7ex *blnd & rmdr 1st,prom 5th,lst pl & rdn 11th,last & p.u. 13th* ....P Harding-Jones pu
6 ran. Hd, 1 fence, 2l. Time 5m 54.00s. SP 5-4.
Christopher Sporborg (Puckeridge).

1401 Ladies

1324 **ST GREGORY 7ex (bl) ....Miss L Hollis 1**
chsd ldr 4th,lft disp 8th,ld 12th-15th,sn ld agn & drw clr
1321[4] **Whats Another 5a 5ow....Miss K Bridge 2**
lft disp ld 8th, blnd nxt,hdd 12th,ld bfly 15th,sn outpcd
1324[3] **Sarazar (USA) ....Miss H Pewter 3**
j.s. 3rd, lst tch appr 11th, t.o. frm 13th
1324 Dunboy Castle (Ire) 7ex *(fav) ld til u.r. 8th* ....Miss G Chown ur
4 ran. 15l, dist. Time 6m 2.00s. SP 5-4.
A Howland Jackson (Essex & Suffolk).

1402 Restricted (12st)

1145[2] **GENERAL PICTON ....P Harding-Jones 1**
(fav) trkd ldrs,2nd & blnd 9th,ld 14th,rdn 2 out,forged clr flat
River Spirit (USA) ....G Smith 2
ld to 5th, ld 10-11th,ev ch frm 3 out, no ex flat
1181[3] **Sparnova 5a....R Barrett 3**
in tch,lst pl appr 8th,pshd alng 10th,n.d. aft,wnt 3rd 3 out
1322[3] Auchendolly (Ire) *ld 6-9th, ld 12th, blnd nxt, sn hdd, wknd qkly 15th, t.o.* ....S Sporborg 4
1239[6] Henfield *alwys bhnd, mstk 7th, lst tch 14th, t.o.* ....G Tawell 5
5 ran. 3l, 15l, 30l, ½l. Time 6m 2.00s. SP 11-10.
Mrs C S Knowles (East Essex).

1403 Open Maiden (12st)

1325 **LARA'S PRINCESS 5a....S March 1**
prom, disp ld 10th, ld 13th, made rest,styd on wll frm 2 out
1326 **Just Maisy 5a....A Coe 2**
chsd ldr to 4th, in tch, ev ch 3 out, nt qkn flat
1261[4] **Royal Quarry ....Miss A Eaton 3**
in tch,lst pl 11th, prog to 2nd 15th, onepcd frm 2 out
1149[4] Scout *ld to 12th, wknd appr 2 out* ....Miss J Templeton 4
1182[2] Not To Be Trusted *(fav) in tch, blnd 13-14th, 5th & strugg nxt, no dang aft* ....R Barrett 5
834 Andalucian Sun (Ire) *keen hold, hld up, prog & cls up 12th, wknd 15th* ....C Ward 6
1326 But Not Quite (Ire) *keen hold, prom til wknd qkly 15th, bhnd & p.u. appr nxt* ....P Harding-Jones pu
1256[5] Stanwick Lass 5a (bl) *rr, in tch til f 8th* Miss N McKim f
8 ran. 1l, 1½l, 15l, 8l, 10l. Time 6m 6.00s. SP 6-1.
R W Gardiner (East Essex).
ONE FENCE OMITTED (17 JUMPS) S.P.

HAMPSHIRE
Hackwood Park
Monday May 6th
FIRM

1404 Members (12st)

1189 **PALAMAN ....H Rowsell 1**
(fav) disp ld til lft alone 10th
788 Dicks Delight (Ire) *u.r. paddock, plld hrd disp ld til f 10th.* ....S Baker f
2 ran. Time 6m 50.00s. SP 4-9.
C D Aikenhead (Hampshire).

1405 Confined (12st)

1185[1] **PETE'S SAKE 5ex ....C Vigors 1**
(fav) hld up, chall 2 out, ld last, ran on wll
1312 **Brack N Brandy ....Miss R David 2**
ld frm 3rd, j.w. hdd last. ran on

1290[2] **Game Fair** ....**G Burton** 3
alwys cls up, 3l 3rd 2 out, wknd
1375[3] Skinnhill (bl) *reluctant, hd rdn thro'out, nvr dang* ....C Mason 4
958[5] Old Road (USA) (bl) *ld 1st, cls up to 2 out, wknd qkly* ....C Coyne 5
1375 Olde Crescent 5ex *reluctant, alwys bhnd, p.u before last*..........T Underwood pu
6 ran. 1½l, 10l, 6l, 4l. Time 6m 17.00s. SP 5-4.
Mrs K Ennever (Hampshire).

1406 Mixed Open (12st)

1166[2] **SPITFIRE JUBILEE 7ex**.................**R Nuttall** 1
(fav) made most, j.w. qknd 4l clr aft 3 out, jnd last, ran on wll
1290[1] **Touch Of Winter 7ex** ....**T Lacey** 2
hld up, 20l off pace aft 12th, prog 2 out, chall last, no ex
998[4] **See You There** ....**M Portman** 3
mostly 2nd/3rd, ld bfly 13th, fdd 2 out
1264 Rapid Rascal *2nd til wknd frm hlfwy*.....Miss S West 4
1184[2] Popeswood 4ex *alwys bhnd, p.u. 15th*......D Dennis pu
5 ran. ¾l, 20l, 7l. Time 6m 15.00s. SP 11-8.
Mrs Z S Clark (Wilton).

1407 B F S S (12st)

1165[4] **SOHAIL (USA) 7ex** ....**Miss M Hill** 1
(fav) lft in ld 7th, made rest, all out
1373 **Pejawi 5a**..............................**T Lacey** 2
ld to 2nd, cls up, ran on wll
1242 **Kamtara** ....**R Hicks** 3
last to hlfwy, prog 12th, sn outpcd
1185[3] Smooth Escort 7ex *rdn along, cls up to 11th, fdd* ....J Maxse 4
1438[5] Tompet 7ex *ld 3rd til r.o. 7th* ....B McKim ro
5 ran. 4l, 15l, 20l. Time 6m 19.00s. SP 6-4.
Mrs Carrie Janaway (Beaufort).

1408 Intermediate (12st)

1290 **GORMLESS (IRE)** ....**Miss M Hill** 1
(fav) 2nd to 12th, ld aft, 10l clr last, canter
1166[3] **Devonia (NZ) 5a** ....**Maj O Ellwood** 2
ld to 12th, cls up to 2 out, no ch wth wnr, eased flat
2 ran. Dist. Time 6m 33.00s. SP 1-3.
Sir Richard Cooper (Cattistock).

1409 Open Maiden (12st)

1293 **NEW YEARS EVE** ....**C Vigors** 1
hld up, wnt 2nd 12th, qknd clr 3 out, easy
343[4] **Bold Man (NZ)** ....**Miss T Honeyball** 2
rr til styd on frm 2 out, nvr pld to chall
997[4] **Tractorias (Ire)** ....**T Woolridge** 3
ld 11th, hdd 3 out, ran on onepcd
864[2] Tullykyne Bells *(fav) ld to 10th, outpcd aft* ....Miss D Stafford 4
1299 Orphan Olly *cls up til u.r 15th* ....P York ur
956[3] Horton Country 5a *last at 12th, p.u. 2 out*....P Howse pu
6 ran. 6l, 3l, 4l. Time 6m 32.00s. SP 8-1.
Miss V C Sturgis (Beaufort).
P.M.

RADNOR & WEST HEREFORD
Cursneh Hill
Monday May 6th
GOOD TO FIRM

1410 Members (12st)

1158[5] **BARN POOL** ....**E Collins** 1
made all, 8l up 9th, prssd whn lft clr last
1314 **Welsh Clover 5a** ....**Miss E James** 2
chsd ldr, hit 4th & 11th, wknd 15th, lft 2nd last
884 **Cruise Ann 5a** ....**Miss L Skelton** 3
alwys last, t.o. frm 6th, btn 1 1/2 fences
1225[2] Bowland Girl (Ire) 5a *(fav) w.w., chsd ldr 15th, chllng whn blnd & u.r. last* ....Miss C Thomas ur
4 ran. 10l, dist. Time 6m 15.00s. SP 7-2.
E S Collins (Radnor & West Hereford).

1411 Confined (12st)

1169[2] **ROVING REPORT** ....**Mrs A Rucker** 1
(fav) 3rd til clsd up 11th, ld 15th, in commd frm 3 out
1314[4] **Homme D'Affaire** ....**T Stephenson** 2
w.w., efft 14th, chsd wnr frm nxt, alwys held
1316[3] **Fergal's Delight** ....**Julian Pritchard** 3
ld 1st & 6-9th, ld 13th til hdd & onepcd aft nxt
1219 Oragas *outpcd thruout, no ch frm 15th* ....A Dalton 4
1315[1] Hennerwood Oak 5a 1ow *ld 2nd-5th & 10-12th, wknd frm nxt, p.u. last* ....M P Jones pu
5 ran. 1½l, 15l, 30l. Time 6m 10.00s. SP 4-5.
Mrs A Rucker (Worcestershire).

1412 Open (12st)

1244 **NETHER GOBIONS** ....**Julian Pritchard** 1
(fav) made all, clr frm 6th, fence ahd frm 13th
1042[7] **Space Mariner** ....**O McPhail** 2
alwys 3rd, chal for 2nd frm 15th, styd on
1332 **January Don** ....**A Dalton** 3
rddn 1st, last til chal for 2nd 3 out, no ext flat
1043 Invite D'Honneur (NZ) *remote 2nd til wknd frm 3 out* ....M Munrowd 4
4 ran. Dist, 1½l, 12l. Time 6m 9.00s. SP 4-9.
P Clutterbuck (Berkeley).

1413 Intermediate (12st)

1213[1] **DANBURY LAD (IRE) 5ex** ....**Miss A Dare** 1
(fav) 3l 3rd 12th, prog to ld 3 out, clr last
1314[5] **Hackett's Farm 5ex**.............**Julian Pritchard** 2
made most til hdd & mstk 3 out, kpt on onepce
1219[3] **Horn Player (USA)** ....**M P Jones** 3
prom, ld brfly 8th, rddn & outpcd frm 15th
845 Construction King *drppd rear 6th, in tch til outpcd frm 13th* ....Mrs J Hawkins 4
742[1] Frozen Pipe 5a *held up til prog 14th, slw jmp & no ch frm 2 out*....................M Jackson 5
942[1] Wildnite *cls up, ld 6th, wknd frm 14th, t.o. 3 out* ....J Jackson 6
6 ran. 3l, 10l, 15l, 1½l, 20l. Time 6m 18.00s. SP 2-5.
Dr P P Brown (Berkeley).

1414 Ladies

1214[1] **DI STEFANO 7ex**....................**Miss A Dare** 1
(fav) held up, prog to ld aft 15th, lft clr last
1157 **Kumada** ....**Miss S Wallin** 2
ld til hdd aft 15th, btn frm 2 out, lft 2nd last
979[5] **La Mezeray 5a** ....**Mrs J Hawkins** 3
chsd ldr, ev ch til outpcd frm 15th
1245[3] Vatacan Bank *rear frm 6th, lost tch 11th, styd on frm 14th*....................Miss B Williams 4
1263 Light The Wick 7ex *chsd ldrs, cls 5th 9th, outpcd frm 13th, t.o.*....................Miss P Cooper 5
1214[4] Ocean Lad *t.o. frm 7th, f 10th*..........Miss H Bevan f
847[5] Travistown *t.o. frm 7th, p.u. 13th*.....Miss N Richards pu
1264[1] Mendip Music 7ex *chsd ldrs, styd on frm 15th, 2nd & lkd held whn u.r. last*..............Miss E Crawford ur
1221[2] Grey Watch 5a *cls up to 13th, wknd frm nxt, p.u. aft 15th*....................Miss E James pu
9 ran. 10l, 3l, 30l, dist. Time 6m 13.00s. SP 1-3.
Mike Gifford (Cotswold Vale Farmers).

1415 Restricted (12st)

1216 **GROMIT (NZ)** ....**T Stephenson** 1
cls 4th 11th,wnt 2nd 2 out,lft in ld bfr last,drew clr flat
836 **How Friendly** ....**Julian Pritchard** 2
(fav) ld 1st, alwys prom, not qckn frm 15th, styd on onepce
879[9] **Cantantivy 5a** ....**Miss D Carrington** 3
ld frm 2nd til hdd aft 15th, wknd frm nxt

1169[3] Members Rights 5a 1ow *cls up til outpcd frm 15th, no ch frm nxt* .... M Keel 4
1158 Bay Leader 5a 4ow *7th & in tch 9th, no qckn frm 12th* .... S Shinton 5
1223 Lles Le Bucflow *rear whn mstk 5th, no ch frm 13th* .... A Dalton 6
Guarena (USA) *alwys rear, short lived efft 9th, t.o. & p.u. aft 13th* .... C Richards pu
600[7] Spanish Rouge *prom, ld 3 out, lkd wnnr whn reins broke & ran out bfr last* .... M Jackson ro
1242 Coolmoreen (Ire) 1ow *midfld whn mstk 6th, lost tch frm 13th, p.u. nxt* .... C Campbell pu
1268 Pharrago (Ire) *chsd ldrs, rddn & lost tch frm 14th, p.u. nxt* .... Miss P Cooper pu
1314 Kilmakee 5a *last 12th, t.o. & p.u. 14th*. . . .Mrs K Bevan pu
11 ran. 6l, 2l, 25l, 10l, 10l. Time 6m 15.00s. SP 9-2.
Miss Sarah Eaton (North Cotswold).

1416 Open Maiden Div I (12st)

1319[3] **FIRST COMMAND (NZ) .... M Munrowd 1**
(fav) chsd ldr, ld aft 2 out, pushd clr apr last
1225 **Sweet Petel 5a .... M FitzGerald 2**
ld frm 3rd, hit 10th, hdd & wknd aft 2 out
900 **Warm Relation (Ire) 7a.......... T Cox 3**
chsd ldrs, ev ch til not qckn frm 14th, kpt on
1044 Tigeritsi 5a *pllng, held up, efft & clsng 14th, no ext frm 3 out* .... T Stephenson 4
1248 City Rhythm *alwys rear, lost tch frm 11th, styd on frm 2 out* .... C Packer 5
1224[6] Orty *chsng ldrs whn slppd & f aft 3rd* . . . .Miss J Short f
Just Eve 5a *midfld, in tch til wknd 3 out, p.u. aft nxt* .... M Jackson pu
749 Big Buckley 5a *held up, trckng ldrs whn mstk & u.r. 6th* .... Julian Pritchard ur
1161 Derring Ann 5a *slwly away, t.o. til p.u. 6th*. .G Shenkin pu
9 ran. 5l, 8l, nk, 7l. Time 6m 22.00s. SP 3-1.
P Newey (Ludlow).
One fence omitted, 2nd & 3rd circuits (16 jumps).

1417 Open Maiden Div II (12st)

1314 **ONEMOREANWEGO 5a .... Miss E James 1**
cls 3rd 8th, prog to ld 15th, kpt on wll frm nxt
1248 **Rusty Fellow .... D Mansell 2**
rear whn mstk 9th, gd prog frm 14th, fin wll, not rch wnr
1315[2] **Joyney 5a .... Julian Pritchard 3**
(fav) cls up frm 11th, ev ch 15th, rddn & no ext frm nxt
1196 Musical Mail *nvr rchd ldrs, styd on onepcd frm 14th* .... M Munrowd 4
1225[6] Cruise A Hoop *held up, prog 13th, ev ch 15th, wknd frm 2 out* .... T Stephenson 5
1269[4] Boddington Hill 5a *mstk 9th, rear frm nxt, no ch frm 13th* .... S Shinton 6
1319 Namestaken *rear frm 9th, t.o. frm 13th, p.u. 15th* .... Mrs K Bevan pu
1044 Countrywide Lad *ld 7-14th, wknd frm nxt, p.u. last* .... A Dalton pu
1270 Greenhill Lady 5a *rear frm 4th, t.o. 13th, p.u. 15th* .... M P Jones pu
1047 Brownscroft 5a *ld to 6th, styd cls up til wknd 14th, p.u. nxt* .... Miss T Spearing pu
1169[5] Lindalighter 5a *midfld whn mstk 8th, no prog frm 12th, p.u. 15th* .... M Jackson pu
Miss Jcb (Ire) 6ow *started 3 fences bhnd, p.u. aft 5th* .... C Campbell pu
1224 Sweet Jesterday 5a *cls 4th 8th, in tch whn p.u. aft 12th* .... O McPhail pu
Kerry Soldier Blue *midfld til prog 9th, wknd 14th, p.u. nxt* .... M FitzGerald pu
14 ran. 7l, 8l, hd, 1l, 10l. Time 6m 16.00s. SP 4-1.
P J Corbett (Ludlow).
P.R.

SOUTH SHROPSHIRE
Eyton-On-Severn
Monday May 6th
GOOD TO FIRM

1418 Members (12st)

954[1] **NOTHING VENTURED 5ex.......... A Beedles 1**
hld up in 9th, ld 5 out, ran on strngly frm 3 out, easily
1231[4] **Tara Boy (bl) .... R Cambray 2**
hld up in rr, 2nd 9th, ran on one pace
666 **Moydrum Prince .... Miss L Wallace 3**
disp to 2nd, chsng grp to 4 out, wknd frm 3 out
462[1] Westcote Lad 7ex *(fav) ld to 2nd, cl up, ld 8-9th, trckd ldr, u.r. 12th, rmntd* .... W Bryan 4
1225 Frank The Swank 7a 1ow *rr early, 2nd 8th, ld 10-11th, wknd qckly* .... N Gittens 5
1232 Penllyne's Pride 2ow *prom, ld 3-7th, cl up & ev ch whn u.r. 12th* .... J Chilton ur
1224 Maes Gwyn Dreamer *prom early, lost tch 6th, t.o. 5 out, p.u. 2 out* .... J Cornes pu
7 ran. 25l, dist, 2l, 20l. Time 6m 30.00s. SP 2-1.
Mrs Susie Farquhar (South Shropshire).

1419 Open (12st)

1316[1] **CHIP'N'RUN 7ex .... J Cornes 1**
made all sttng strng pace, ran on whn rnnr-up clsd 3 out
1231[1] **Jolly Boat 4ex .... A Crow 2**
(fav) 3rd in rr, clsr ordr 9th, 2nd 13th, chsd wnr, alwys hld
1192[4] **Glenshane Lad .... A Griffith 3**
cls up, 2nd to 13th, ran on one pce frm 5 out
1093 Castle Cross *rr early, lost tch 8th, t.o. 13th* . . . .S Prior 4
4 ran. 15l, 15l. Time 6m 17.00s. SP 10-11.
F D Cornes (South Shropshire).

1420 Ladies

460[4] **COUTURE TIGHTS .... Miss J Priest 1**
2nd 3-12th, clr 2nd 13th, chal whn lft in ld 4 out
1314[6] **Golden Fare .... Miss L Wallace 2**
2nd 3-12th, lost tch 13th, lft 2nd 4 out
1232[1] Inch Maid 5a 7ex *(fav) ld stng stdy pce, qcknd frm 13th, chal whn ran out 4 out* . . . . . . .Miss H Brookshaw ro
3 ran. 15l. Time 6m 31.00s. SP 2-1.
M A Lloyd (Albrighton Woodland).

1421 Restricted (12st)

292 **MISTER GOODGUY (IRE) .... A Crow 1**
(Jt fav) ld frm 2nd, set gd pce, clr whn mstk last, rcvrd wl
1173[4] **Winters Cottage (Ire) .... G Hanmer 2**
(Jt fav) hld up mid-div, prog 5 out, strng chal 2 out, ran on
1151 **Four Hearts (Ire) .... David Barlow 3**
chsng grp, 2nd frm 8th-3 out, not qckn nr fin
1233 Foxy Blue *ld 1st, ldng 4 thro'out, ev ch whn outpcd fr 3 out* .... Miss C Burgess 4
1030 Mr Busker (Ire) *cl up, dsp 5th, ev ch 4 out, not qckn* .... C Barlow 5
1222[6] Little By Little *chsd ldrs to 4 out, no ex frm 3 out* .... R Bevis 6
1231 Ahalin *alwys mid-to-rr, t.o. hlfwy* . . . . J Austin 7
1195 Pepperbox 5a *mid-to-rr, one pce, t.o.* . . . . .S Prior 8
1314 Alamir (USA) *mid-to-rr, bd mstk 13th, not rcvr, lost tch, p.u. 3 out* .... M Hammond pu
1233[8] Mastiff Lane *mid-to-rr, t.o. & trd whn u.r. last* .... D Sherlock ur
Dara's Course (Ire) 5a 5ow *u.r. in rr 2nd, rmntd & cont 3 fncs bhnd, p.u. 5 out* .... Miss J Oakey pu
11 ran. ½l, 1l, 1l, 3l, 25l, 1l, 25l. Time 6m 30.00s. SP 5-2.
E H Crow (North Shropshire).

1422 Confined (12st)

1231[2] **LE PICCOLAGE .... C J B Barlow 1**
cl up, ld 7-9th, in tch, ld 4 out, sn clr, comf
1230[1] **Furry Fox (Ire) 3ex .... A Crow 2**
(fav) ld to 4th, cl up, ld 10th-5 out, not qckn frm 4 out
1230[3] **Duke Of Impney .... David Barlow 3**

in tch, ld 5-6th, outpcd frm 13th, ran on frm 2 out
3 ran. 25l, 10l. Time 6m 21.00s. SP 5-4.
P H Morris (West Shropshire).

1423 Open Maiden (12st)

BUCKINTIME 5a .... **G Hanmer** 1
ld 7th, made rest, ran on strngly frm 3 out, comf
1234[2] **Cloud Dancing** .... **M Worthington** 2
(Jt fav) chsng grp, drvn to chal 3 out, not qckn
1196 **Niord** .... **S Prior** 3
cl up, ev ch 4 out, ran on one pce, cght for 2nd flat
Contradict *rr, t.o. 9th, btn over 1 fence* ...... M Harris 4
674 Noble Angel (Ire) *ld to 6th whr sdle slpd, in tch, lkd hld whn u.r. 2 out* .... John Barlow ur
953[4] Godor Spirit *mid-div whn f 6th* .... N Gittens f
1033 Scally Blue 7a *(Jt fav) hld up, tk clsr ordr 10th, 2nd 13th, rng on whn f 2 out* .... A Crow f
7 ran. Dist, nk, dist. Time 6m 27.00s. SP 4-1.
Mrs B Shaw (West Shropshire Hunt).
V.S.

STEVENSTONE
High Bickington
Monday May 6th
GOOD

1424 Members (12st)

HIDDEN DOLLAR .... **G Penfold** 1
jmp wll, ld/disp til ld 14th, drew clr apr last
1118 **Romany Anne 5a** .... **Miss S Young** 2
(fav) w.w. in tch, efft 3 out, not qckn
1128 **Drumcolliher** .... **Miss K Baily** 3
ld/disp til wknd 15th, sn btn
Westcountry Lad *lost tch aft 11th, t.o. p.u. aft 13th* .... Miss J Sleep pu
4 ran. 10l, 20l. Time 6m 48.00s. SP 6-4.
G Heal (Stevenstone).

1425 Open

1140 **PARSON'S WAY (bl)** .... **A Farrant** 1
made all, ran on wll und pres whn chal
1140[3] **Magnolia Man** .... **N Harris** 2
held up, jmp lft, ev ch 14th, wknd, no ch whn lft 2nd last
1074 **Querrin Lodge** .... **T Greed** 3
lost tch 14th, t.o.
1228[9] Try It Alone *(fav) trckd ldr,3rd 14th,2nd apr 3 out,chal und pres whn f last* .... S Slade f
4 ran. 10l, dist. Time 6m 39.00s. SP 7-2.
Paul C N Heywood (North Cornwall).

1426 Ladies

1141[2] **GREENWINE (USA)** .... **Miss A Lamb** 1
(fav) cls up, ld 16th, clr 2 out, comf
1141 **Mistress Rosie 5a** .... **Miss G Linley** 2
raced outer, made most til hdd 16th, onepce
1277 **Bidston Mill** .... **Miss P Platt** 3
sn rear, lost tch 12th
3 ran. 8l, dist. Time 6m 39.00s. SP 4-9.
T Winzer (Modbury).

1427 Confined (12st)

1309[2] **FEARSOME 5ex** .... **G Penfold** 1
(fav) held up, prog 14th, 2nd 3 out, drvn to ld last 75 yards
1277[5] **Just Ben 3ex** .... **Miss J Cumings** 2
chsd ldr, ld 3 out, cght in last 75 yards
1309 **Bincombe Top** .... **L Jefford** 3
mid-div, some late hdwy
873[2] Rathmichael 3ex (bl) *prom in chsng grp til wknd 14th* .... A Farrant 4
Horwood Ghost 3ex *ld, wll clr til hdd & wknd 3 out, lost 3rd nr line* .... R Treloggen 5
Clear Call (Fr) *towrds rear, bhnd whn p.u. apr 15th* .... Miss L Blackford pu
1275 Cardinal Bird (USA) (bl) *t.o. whn ref 6th* .. Miss K Baily ref
1140 Gymcrak Dawn 3ex *towrds rear, bhnd whn p.u. apr 15th* .... I Hambley pu
1110 Bert House *mid-div, btn 6th whn p.u. aft 16th* S Slade pu
1277[6] My Boy Buster *rear whn f 7th* .... D Jones f
10 ran. 1l, 10l, sht-hd, 1l. Time 6m 34.00s. SP 9-4.
G W Penfold (Silverton).

1428 Restricted (12st)

1313 **THE COPPER KEY** .... **T Greed** 1
ld til hdd aft 2 out, drvn to ld agn last 50 yards
1313[4] **Ballysheil** .... **S Edwards** 2
prog 15th, ld aft 2 out til not ran on & hdd cls home
1358[4] **Dovedon Princess 5a** .... **D Stephens** 3
prog & ev ch 15th, ran on onepce
1141 Aristocratic Gold *hdwy 12th, ev ch til wknd 3 out* .... Mrs M Hand 4
720[3] Sunwind *alwys mid-div, no ch frm 16th* ...... D Heath 5
1277 Bright Road 5a 3ow (bl) *towrds rear til p.u. 15th* .... H Thomas pu
1128 Anstey Gadabout *last whn f 14th* .... A Holdsworth f
Gypsy Luck 5a *prom til f 4th* .... Miss J Cumings f
1075[3] Northern Sensation 5a *(fav) held up, 2nd & rddn 13th, sn wknd, p.u. apr 17th* .... L Jefford pu
1139 Mosside *not fluent, rear 14th til p.u. apr 16th* N Harris pu
10 ran. 1l, 8l, 1l, 2½l. Time 6m 37.00s. SP 14-1.
Mrs S M Trump (Silverton).

1429 Open Maiden Div I Pt I (12st)

1279[3] **TANGLE KELLY** .... **Miss J Cumings** 1
(Jt fav) j.w. cls up, outpcd 16th, styd on to ld last
1118 **Diana Moss (Ire) 5a** .... **C Heard** 2
hndy, qcknd to ld 16th, cght last
1117 **The Ugly Duckling** .... **R Treloggen** 3
made most frm 5th, not alwys fluent, hdd 16th, sn wknd
1348 Ashcombe Valley *(Jt fav) in tch, rddn 14th, onepce, walked in* .... Miss L Blackford 4
1116 River Stream 5a *ld til blnd 5th, sn strllng, t.o. p.u. aft 13th* .... M Burrows pu
1129 Musbury Castle 5a *rear til p.u. apr 16th* .... S Kidston pu
1362 Lady Goldrush 5a *rear til p.u. apr 16th* .... S Slade pu
1071 Rose's Lady Day 7a *bhnd til p.u. apr 17th* G Andrews pu
8 ran. 1l, 20l, dist. Time 6m 46.00s. SP 7-4.
Michael Lanz (Devon & Somerset Staghounds).

1430 Open Maiden Div I Pt II (12st)

626 **INDIAN RABI** .... **G Penfold** 1
(fav) in tch, outpcd 16th, lkd btn 2 out, lft in ld last
1280 **Funny Farm** .... **L Jefford** 2
held up bhnd, late hdwy to take 2nd cls home
1143 **Big Reward** .... **K Crook** 3
prom til 14th, sn lost plc
1071[4] Sixth In Line (Ire) *ld/disp, lft in ld whn blnd badly last, not rcvrd* .... T Cole 4
1070 Scallykenning *wnt 2nd 6th, ld 2 out, lkd wnnr whn ran out last* .... J Young ro
1071 Rhyme And Chime 7a *rear whn hmpd by loose horse & rddr k/o on bnd* .... T Dennis ur
1279 Lucky Thursday *bhnd & jmp novcy til p.u. apr 15th* .... S Hornby pu
Pixie In Purple (Ire) 7a *rear til crashed thru wing 4th* .... D Stephens ro
8 ran. 1l, 3l, 8l. Time 6m 53.00s. SP 6-4.
Mrs E M Roberts (Silverton).

1431 Open Maiden Div II Pt I (12st)

533 **PARSON FLYNN** .... **R White** 1
(fav) hdwy 12th, ld 15th, slight ld 2 out, drvn clr
719[4] **Flying Maria 7a** .... **C Heard** 2
rear, hdwy 15th, ev ch 2 out, no ext apr last
Location .... **L Jefford** 3
prom til lost plc 14th, onepcd
1070[2] Lawd Of Blisland *hdwy 14th, ev ch til wknd 17th* .... A Farrant 4
1115[3] Melody Mine 5a *in tch til wknd 15th* ...... J Creighton 5

1293 Mine's A Gin (Ire) 7a *prom til lost plc 9th, bhnd frm 15th* ....Miss J Cumings 6
806^{2} Good Appeal 5a *towrds rear, lost tch 15th, p.u. apr 17th*..........Miss L Blackford pu
1118 Avin Fun Bar 5a *ld til 15th, sn wknd, btn 6th whn p.u. apr 18th*..........T Greed pu
Eskimo Star 5a *rear whn blnd bdly & u.r. 8th*...S Ellis ur
9 ran. 5l, 8l, 6l, 25l, 8l. Time 6m 43.00s. SP 7-4.
Mrs M J Trickey (Devon & Somerset Staghounds).

1432 Open Maiden Div II Pt II (12st)

RISEUPWILLIEREILLY ....A Holdsworth 1
ld 4th til hdd brfly run in, rlld to ld cls home
1308^{2} **Four Leaf Clover 5a ....R Woollacott** 2
(fav) in tch, wnt 2nd 16th, ld brfly run in, no ext cls home
1143 **Baman Powerhouse ....Miss K Baily** 3
hdwy to 2nd 12th,wknd 15th,blnd bdly & p.u. 17th,rmntd t.o.
1071^{2} Quick Opinion *ld to 4th, cls 3rd whn p.u. & dismntd apr 8th*..........J Young pu
1117 Gamblers Refrain *prom til lost plc & rmmndrs 11th, ref 13th*..........D Jones ref
1115 Cousin Amos *n.j.w., bhnd til p.u. apr 17th*..........Miss J Sleep pu
1070^{5} Anvil Corner 5a *mid-div, 5th whn u.r. 9th*....D Dennis ur
1074 Moonbay Lady 5a (bl) *rear, blnd bdly 6th, strgglng til p.u. aft 13th*..........G Andrew pu
447 Carumu 5a 7ow *bhnd til p.u. apr 17th*......S Hornby pu
9 ran. 1l, 3 fences. Time 6m 46.00s. SP 12-1.
D F Bassett (Eggesford).
G.T.

WARWICKSHIRE
Ashorne
Monday May 6th
GOOD

1433 Open Maiden Div I

1182^{3} **BIBLICAL 5a..........R Mumford** 1
ld 3-5th & frm 8th, clr 3 out, styd on und pres flat
1242 **Baron Bigfoot ....A Charles-Jones** 2
alwys 1st trio, chsd wnr 14th, kpt on, unable chal
1315^{4} **Fountain Of Fire (Ire) 5a.......Miss S Duckett** 3
cls up til outpcd 13th, styd on wll frm 2 out, tk 3rd nr fin
1183^{2} Cool Rascal 5a *in tch til outpcd 13th, ran on 15th, not rch ldrs, wknd flat*..........L Lay 4
796 Totally Optimistic *prom to 14th, wll btn frm nxt* ....C Wadland 5
1105^{4} Oliver Himself 7a 1ow *(fav) w.w. rear, prog 11th, cls 3rd 15th, wknd nxt*..........A Hill 6
1174 Mr Paddy Bell (v) *ld 5-6th, prom aft til wknd 13th, t.o.* ....B Potts 7
1173 Lorenza Lad *sn wll bhnd, t.o. & p.u. aft 12th*...N Cook pu
1182^{5} Turkish Island 5a *alwys rear, lost tch & p.u. 9th* ....M Cowley pu
1183^{4} Arley Gale 5a *w.w. lost tch 10th, t.o. & p.u. 12th* ....John Pritchard pu
904 Gal-A-Dor *ld to 3rd & 6-8th, wknd 12th, t.o. & p.u. 15th* ....L Brown pu
1224^{4} Ginge *5s-7/2, unruly start, s.s. alwys bhnd, t.o. & p.u. 9th*..........J Bates pu
1241 Strong Account (Ire) *mid-div, 10th whn u.r. 7th* ....A Mobley ur
1182 Sally's Song 7a *bhnd frm 6th, t.o. & p.u. 9th*...J Trice-Rolph pu
688 Smart Song 7a *schoold, lost tch 13th, no ch whn hit 2 out & p.u.*..........A Phillips pu
1183 Spring Sabre (bl) *chsd ldrs til ran out bnd apr 11th* ....R Lawther ro
16 ran. 2½l, 20l, ½l, 10l, 20l, 10l. Time 6m 34.50s. SP 14-1.
D Jeffries (Bicester With Whaddon Chase).

1434 Open Maiden Div II

1183 **HORCUM ....M Frith** 1
in tch, clsd 13th, ld aft 2 out, styd on well
954^{2} **Blue Rosette ....A Hill** 2
w.w. in tch, ld aft 12th til aft 2 out, sn no ext
1217^{3} **Juniper Lodge ....S Bush** 3
(fav) alwys prom, ld 11-12th, ev ch 14th, fdd frm 3 out
1341 Colonel Fairfax *hld up bhnd, prog frm 12th, ev ch 3 out, wknd rpdly nxt*..........R Lawther 4
1225^{3} Majic Belle 5a (v) *prom, ld brfly 12th, sn wknd, t.o.* ....G Barfoot-Saunt 5
1319^{5} Sonny's Song *alwys bhnd, t.o. 14th*..........L Brown 6
1182 Roark's Chukka *alwys rear, lost tch 11th, t.o.& p.u. 13th*..........D Smith pu
1241 Space Molly 5a *mid-div, 10th whn u.r. 7th*...N Ridout ur
1020 Truly Optimistic 5a *chsd ldr, ld 8-11th, wknd rpdly, t.o. & p.u. 13th*..........C Wadland pu
1183 Lloyds Loser *ld to 8th, wknd 12th, t.o. & p.u. 2 out* ....G Tarry pu
890^{4} Miss Kenmac 5a *in tch to 12th, lost plc whn p.u. 14th* ....J Trice-Rolph pu
1175 Lord Rattle (Ire) *alwys rear, bhnd frm 10th, t.o. & p.u. 13th*..........E Walker pu
1301 Midnight Runner 5a *rear, 13th whn u.r. 8th* R Armson ur
1381 Plat Du Jour 5a *alwys bhnd, t.o. & p.u. 11th* B Pollock pu
Royal Credit 5a *bhnd, prog to 7th & in tch 10th, lost tch 13th, p.u. 2 out*..........John Pritchard pu
15 ran. 10l, 4l, 8l, 30l, 8l. Time 6m 29.90s. SP 10-1.
Mrs Jayne Barton (Bicester With Whaddon Chase).

1435 Confined (12st)

639^{2} **CAUSEWAY CRUISER 3ex ....R Lawther** 1
(fav) hld up, prog 5th, ld 10th, clr 13th, easily
1244^{3} **Carbery Arctic ....G Barfoot-Saunt** 2
mid-div,7th & out of tch 11th,ran on wll frm 14th,tk 2nd fin
1169^{1} **Mitchells Best ....J Trice-Rolph** 3
prom, chsd wnr 11th, no imp 3 out, wknd flat, lost 2nd nr fn
867^{1} What A To Do 5ex *ld to 2nd, prom aft til 3rd & outpcd 13th, no dang aft*..........R Sweeting 4
1244^{6} Tattlejack (Ire) *chsd ldrs, outpcd frm 12th, no ch nxt* ....E Walker 5
Nick The Brief 6ow *1st ride, alwys bhnd, t.o. 13th* ....P Sheppard 6
1289^{3} Sam Shorrock *alwys wll in rear, t.o. 13th* ....Miss H Thorner 7
1214^{3} Straight Bat 5ex *ld 2-6th, wknd rpdly 8th, t.o. & p.u. 13th*..........Miss S Duckett pu
Keeler Rider (USA) *mid-div, out of tch, effrt nxt, wknd 13th, p.u. 3 out*..........B Potts pu
1122 Social Climber *prom, ld 6-10th, wknd 13th, wll bhnd whn p.u. last*..........L Lay pu
1302^{4} Aldington Baron *wll in rear, effrt 10th, sn wknd, t.o. & p.u. 13th*..........M Hewitt pu
947 Easter Prince *last whn mstk 7th, t.o. & p.u. 11th* ....C Wadland pu
12 ran. 20l, 3l, 8l, 12l, 5l, 6l. Time 6m 18.60s. SP 4-6.
J Tredwell (Grafton).

1436 Members

1177^{3} **MISS ISLE 5a..........Miss S Duckett** 1
(fav) mstk 3rd & rmndr,prog to ld 11th,sn wll clr,wknd 2 out,unchl
1239^{5} **Hehas ....C Wadland** 2
rear, t.o. & rdn 12th,ran on 15th,chsd wnr 2 out,nrst fin
1236^{3} **Tell You What ....N Ridout** 3
prom, outpcd 12th, lft 2nd 15th, no imp, fin tired
A Lad Insane *1st ride, mid-div & out of tch, t.o. 12th, mod late prog*..........Miss T Cowper 4
904 Dixons Homefinder *mstks, in tch, chsd wnr 13th, wll btn in 2nd whn f 15th*..........A Barnett f
1241^{3} Foolish Soprano 5a *ld 4-11th, wknd 13th, t.o. & p.u. last*..........John Pritchard pu
890 Arctic Line *last frm 8th, t.o. & p.u. 12th*.......S Green pu
7 ran. 6l, 8l, 20l. Time 6m 30.00s. SP 4-6.
M F Clifford (Warwickshire).

1437 Mixed Open (12st)

1215[1] **GRANVILLE GRILL 4ow ....J Deutsch 1**
jmpd lft,ld apr 5th,narrow ld aft,pshd out flat
1017[2] **Penlet ....John Pritchard 2**
(fav) rear, prog 10th, cls 3rd 15th, rdn to chal apr last, styd on
1146[3] **Sunshine Manor ....G Tarry 3**
plling,ld to 4th,mstk 8th,chal & mstk 3 out,ev ch last,no ext
1228 Autonomous *mstk 4th, prom, blnd 11th, cls 4th 2 out-last, no ext flat* ....A Charles-Jones 4
1171[9] Shadow Walker 7ex *rear til prog 11th, 5th & in tch 15th, chal apr last, wknd*...............J Trice-Rolph 5
1289 Roaming Shadow 1ow *last pair, wll bhnd 10th, kpt on frm 13th, nrst fin*...........................J Hankinson 6
1246 Killy's Filly 5a *in tch in mid-div til fdd frm 14th* ....G Barfoot-Saunt 7
995[4] Icky's Five *mid-div, prog to 5th at 11th, lost tch frm 13th*..Miss T Habgood 8
1001 Ragtime Cowboy Joe *last at 4th, alwys bhnd aft* ....N Bradley 9
1316 Mirpur *cls up to 10th, sn wknd, t.o. & p.u. 13th* ....H Wheeler pu
1017[3] Sailor's Delight *mstks, prom to 12th, wknd & p.u. 15th* ....L Lay pu
1046 Master Dancer *alwys rear, lost tch 9th, t.o. & p.u. 15th* ....Miss C Dyson pu
880[5] Corrianne 5a (h) *ld brfly 4th, wknd rpdly 8th, t.o. & p.u. 13th*..R Ford pu
13 ran. 1½l, 2½l, 4l, 4l, 20l, 6l, 12l, 5l. Time 6m 24.50s. SP 2-1.
E W Smith (Beaufort).

1438 Novice Riders (12st)

1318[2] **SEVENS OUT 8ex ....Miss A Plunkett 1**
prom, ld 7th, clr wth chsr 13th, rdn & all out flat,wll rdn
1177[5] **Sprucefield ....A Barlow 2**
chsng grp,went mod 3rd 13th,ran on strngly 2 out,jst faild
1179[3] **Severn Invader ....Miss H Gosling 3+**
(fav) chsng grp,5th hlfwy,poor 5th 3 out,ran on strngly,just faild
1176[3] **Cawkwell Dean ....Mrs C McCarthy 3+**
ld to 2nd,mstk 4th,chsd wnr 12th,mstk nxt,kpt on onepcd flat
1014[3] Tompet 5ex *2nd meeting (!),rear of chsng grp,no ch frm 15th,kpt on*...........................B McKim 5
1108[8] Space Man 5ow *mstk 4th, chsg grp out of tch, poor 4th 3 out, wknd*...........................F Crew 6
1238[5] Prince's Court *mid-div out of tch, 9th hlfwy, effrt 12th, nvr on terms*...........................Mrs J Kimber 7
1098[4] The Dancing Parson 5a *chsd ldrs, clsd 10th, wknd 13th, t.o.*...........................M Brown 8
437 Waterhay *alwys bhnd, t.o. 7th*...........R Mumford 9
1291 Wild Moon 5a *alwys bhnd, t.o. 7th* .....Miss R Tutton 10
1217[5] Di Moda *alwys bhnd, t.o. 8th* ....Miss S Firmin 11
1177[9] Berkana Run *9th & wll out of tch whn u.r. 6th* R Bailey ur
1180 Shortcastle *alwys bhnd, t.o. 7th, ref 13th, lame* ....T Sunderland ref
1103[4] Plateman *ld 2-7th, chsd wnr, mstk 11th, wknd nxt, p.u. 15th*...........................F Hutsby pu
14 ran. 1½l, sht-hd, dd-ht, 15l, 10l, hd, 25l, 30l, 3l, 4l. Time 6m 27.00s. SP 5-1.
Gerard Nock (Heythrop).

1439 Restricted (12st)

1212[1] **FRESH PRINCE 2ow ....A Hill 1**
made virt all, qcknd clr 12th, blnd 2 out, all out, well rdn
1222[3] **Silver Fig 5a ....F Hutsby 2**
t.d.e. prom til lost plc & outpcd 12th,ran on 2 out,nrst fin
1242[4] **Bakmalad ....H Wheeler 3**
(fav) prog 5th,lost plc 11th,effrt 15th,chsd wnr 2 out,kpt on flat
967[1] Tweed Valley (bl) *in tch, outpcd 12th, effrt to 4th 3 out, kpt on*...........................E Andrewes 4
1102[4] Linlake Lightning 5a *in tch til outpcd 12th, onepcd aft* ....Miss H Irving 5
1239[4] Miss Cresta 5a *t.d.e. prom,mstk 11th,outpcd nxt,chsd wnr 15th-2 out, wknd* ....S Morris 6
1178[2] Wayward Sailor (bl) *mstks, prom to 7th, outpcd 12th, no prog aft*...........................Miss C Spearing 7
1238[4] River Galaxy *rear of main grp, outpcd 12th, effrt 14th, sn no prog*...........................R Lawther 8
1169 African Minstrel *rear, rpd prog to chs wnr 13th, wknd 15th, t.o.*...........................L Brown 9
1239 Sporting Lark 5a *in tch, outpcd 12th, wknd 14th, t.o. & p.u. 2 out*...........................G Tarry pu
1164[3] Titchwell Milly 5a *in tch, outpcd 12th, wknd & p.u. 14th*...........................L Lay pu
11 ran. 2l, 1l, 4l, 8l, 3l, ½l, hd, 15l. Time 6m 28.00s. SP 8-1.
Mrs Vanessa Ramm (Cotswold).
J.N.

WEST STREET-TICKHAM
Aldington
Monday May 6th
HARD

1440 Intermediate (12st)

1294[1] **RUSTIC RAMBLE ....P Hacking 1**
(fav) reluctant ldr crawl 1st,ld 11-15th,chal 3 out,ld nxt,all out
1207[4] **Stede Quarter ....P Hickman 2**
cls up, ld 15th-2 out, kpt on gamely
1206[1] **Local Manor ....H Dunlop 3**
ld 3rd-11th, 3rd frm 12th, kpt on same pce 2 out
1207[6] Barn Elms *trckd ldrs, rddn & outpcd 2 out* ....J Van Praagh 4
1207[5] Alzamina 5a *last slpd & nrr u.r. bnd aft 10th,in tch aft,wkng & p.u.3out*...........................A Welsh pu
5 ran. ½l, 6l, 1l. Time 7m 6.00s. SP 6-4.
Peter Tipples (East Sussex & Romney Marsh).

1441 Members

1329[7] **BASHER BILL ....K Giles 1**
(fav) wth ldr, ld 11th, kpt on wll whn chal 2 out
570[4] **Discain Boy ....G Hopper 2**
ld hdd 11th, rddn & cls aft, chal 2 out, no ext last
1207 **Political Man ....T Hills 3**
alwys 3rd,8l down 15th,clsd 3 out,ev ch nxt,no ext flat,lame
1206 Hyluna 5a *alwys last, t.o. 8th*...............D Maitland 4
4 ran. 1½l, hd, 3 fences. Time 6m 36.00s. SP 6-4.
K D Giles (West Street-Tickham).

1442 Restricted (12st)

964[3] **TAU ....A Warr 1**
(12s-5s),hndy,ld 11th,hdd whn lft in ld 2 out,drvn out flat
1297[2] **Polar Ana (Ire) 5a ....Miss S Gladders 2**
(fav) rear,hdwy to cls 3rd 15th,chal 2 out,level last,not qckn flt
1294[3] **Iorwerth ....Miss C Savell 3**
alwys rear, t.o. 4 out
1210 Edged Weapon (Fr) *chsd ldr, 3rd whn u.r. 10th* ....Mrs L Stock ur
810 Golden Pele *alwys rear, wll bhnd whn p.u. bfr 15th* ....P Hall pu
778 Beach Tiger *ld to 2nd, prom aft, wknd 15th, poor 3rd whn p.u. 2 out*...........................T Hills pu
1295 High Burnshot *pulld into ld 2nd, sn clr, stead & hdd 11th, ld & f 2 out*...........................A Welsh f
7 ran. 1½l, 1 fence. Time 6m 38.00s. SP 5-1.
Miss Felicity McLachlan (Ashford Valley).

1443 Ladies

1305 **ADAMARE 4ex ....Miss C Holliday 1**
(4s-9/4),made all, ran on wll whn chal 2 out
919[1] **Topping-The-Bill 7ex.............Mrs E Coveney 2**
(fav) chsd wnnr frm 5th, chal 2 out, kpt on onepce
1373[1] **Magical Morris 7ex ....Miss C Grissell 3**
last & detached, ran on frm 12th, nvr dang, eased flat, lame

1207[3] Bright Hour *3rd frm 5th, nvr nrr 1st 2, last frm 4 out* ....Miss J Grant 4
4 ran. 3l, 30l, 10l. Time 6m 33.00s. SP 9-4.
H Moreton (Quorn).

1444 Open (12st)

1372 **BURROMARINER ....S Cowell 1**
(fav) trckd ldr, lft in ld 11th, made rest, pushd clr flat
1050[3] **Berrings Dasher ....A Welsh 2**
held up, clsd 15th, chal frm 3 out, wknd last
1050[5] **Yeoman Farmer ....P Hacking 3**
sttld off pce, efft 15th, 3rd aft 2 out, not pce to chal
1050 Highland Bounty (bl) *prom, rmmndrs 11th, feeling pce 3 out, wknd last* ....M Jones 4
1330 Little Nod *mstks, alwys wll in tch, nvr dang, wknd 2 out* ....P O'Keeffe 5
247 The Lager Lout *pulld into ld aft 1st til p.u. qckly apr 11th, dismntd* ....N Benstead pu
6 ran. 4l, 5l, 3l, 3l. Time 6m 35.00s. SP 5-4.
Mrs A Blaker (Mid Surrey Farmers Draghounds).

1445 Open Maiden (12st)

1300 **FORT DIANA ....G Hopper 1**
alwys prom, prssd ldr 4 out, ld 2 out, drvn out flat
1300[4] **Scarning Gizmo 5a....D Maitland 2**
mid-div, imprvd to 2nd 13th, wknd 15th, fin 3rd prom 2nd
1300[2] Netherby Cheese *(Jt fav) cls up til ran wd bnd bfr 11th, 3rd aft, btn whn p.u.2 out*....P Hickman pu
676[8] Coral Eddy *alwys towrds rear, in tch in 5th & btn whn u.r. 4 out*....Mrs L Stock ur
814 Target Time 5a (bl) *cls up, ran wd bnd bfr 2nd, ld 6th til f 12th* ....P Blagg f
1149 Warner For Sport *ld to 6th, last final cct, t.o. 4 out, u.r. last*....Miss F Worley ur
1210[3] Joyful Hero 5a *(Jt fav) rr,jnd ldrs 10th,lft in ld 12th,hdd 2 out,rlld undpres,disq* ....A Welsh 0
Isabella Morn 5a *wll detached whn ref 2nd*....P Hall ref
8 ran. 1l, dist. Time 6m 48.00s. SP 4-1.
J H Berwick (East Sussex & Romney Marsh).
Joyful Hero disqualified, rider not W/I. Original ditances. G.Ta.

ZETLAND
Witton Castle
Monday May 6th
GOOD

1446 Confined (12st)

1282[3] **LATHERON (IRE) ....S Swiers 1**
(fav) rear, prog 13th, hrd rdn nxt,hdwy 4 out,ld 2 out,ran on wll
1281 **Tom The Tank ....C Mulhall 2**
prom, ld 3-2 out, no ext whn hdd
1130[1] **Grey Realm 5a 5ex....Miss P Robson 3**
prom, ld 6th til wknd 3 out, onepcd aft
1369 Fowling Piece *cls up, wknd 3 out, kpt on onepce* ....Miss L Horner 4
1281 Caman 5a *rear, t.o. 14th, came home own time* ....Miss S Duell 5
1133 Gospel Rock (NZ) 5ex *ld til ran wd apr 6th, cls up til wknd 13th, p.u. 3 out*....S Brisby pu
1155 Bridgnorth Lass 5a *cls up til ran wd apr 13th, wknd nxt,rear whn p.u. bfr 3 out*....Miss J Percy pu
7 ran. 4l, 3½l, 6l, dist. Time 6m 5.00s. SP 4-5.
Mrs A M Easterby (Middleton).

1447 Restricted

1281[5] **FLYING LION ....S Swiers 1**
midfld, prog 14th, 2l 2nd 3 out, ld nxt, ran on wll
1281[8] **Jolly Fellow (bl) ....N Wilson 2**
hndy, ld 14th-2 out, outpcd by wnnr
755[1] **Denim Blue ....Miss P Robson 3**
(fav) midfld, slght hdwy 3 out, no ext apr last
1284[4] Chapel Island *midfld, efft 3 out, no imp*....G Tuer 4
1284[6] Lyningo *cls up, outpcd 14th, made slght hdwy frm 2 out* ....A Wood 5
1287[1] Greenmount Lad (Ire) *in tch in midfld whn bad mstk 7th, nvr a dang aft*....P Cornforth 6
1284[5] Earl Gray (bl) *alwys rear, t.o. 14th, p.u. last* ....Miss T Jackson pu
983[4] Ellerton Park (bl) *pulld hrd,ld, 20l clr 7th, wknd 12th, rear whn p.u. 3 out*....D Raw pu
1284 Mount Faber (bl) *hndy, wknd 14th, p.u. 3 out* ....M Sowersby pu
1090 Cadrillon (Fr) *alwys rear, p.u. 3 out*....S Charlton pu
1284[2] Honest Expression 5a *cls up, outpcd 14th, midfld whn p.u. 3 out, (lame)*....P Atkinson pu
11 ran. 2l, 5l, 3l, 2l, 10l. Time 6m 6.00s. SP 4-1.
John Mackley (South Durham).

1448 Open

1282[1] **PARK DRIFT ....R Tate 1**
cls up in 3rd,outpcd 14th,styd on wll 3 out,ld nxt,ran on wl
1133 **Ellerton Hill ....S Swiers 2**
(fav) (4/6-6/4)cls 2nd,ld 14th-apr 4 out, outpcd by wnnr
1304[2] **Knowe Head ....N Wilson 3**
ld til hdd 14th, wknd nxt, poor 3rd 3 out
1281 Sharpridge *rear by 5th, t.o. 14th, p.u. nxt* ....M Mawhinney pu
1351[2] Fiscal Policy *rear by 5th, t.o. 14th, p.u. 3 out* H Trotter pu
5 ran. 5l, dist. Time 6m 0.00s. SP 7-4.
G Thornton (York & Ainsty North).

1449 Ladies

1283 **INDIE ROCK ....Mrs F Needham 1**
held up in rear, prog 8th, ld 5 out, 2l clr last, ran on wll
827[4] **John Corbet ....Miss S Brotherton 2**
midfld, styd on wll apr 2 out, tk 2nd cls home
1283[3] **Carole's Delight 5a ....Mrs L Ward 3**
hndy,disp 4th-5 out,rlld apr 2 out,no ext last,lost 2nd flat
1281[4] Band Sargeant (Ire) *cls up, 2l 2nd 3 out, wknd aft* ....Miss J Foster 4
1283[6] Cheeky Pot *outpcd in midfld, made slight late hdwy* ....Mrs S Grant 5
1283[5] Durham Hornet *outpcd in midfld, nvr a dang* ....Miss S Horner 6
1282[4] Fiery Sun *outpcd in midfld, nvr a dang* ....Miss P Robson 7
1283[4] Hellcatmudwrestler *cls up, disp ld 4th til wknd 13th, rear whn p.u. 3 out*....Miss T Gray pu
1283[1] Duntime *(fav) ld til jmp rght 4th, wknd 5th, p.u. nxt (broke down)* ....Miss J Eastwood pu
1120 Parliament Hall *sn in rear, t.o. 7th, p.u. 10th* ....Miss S Foster pu
10 ran. 3l, nk, 5l, 8l, 10l, 8l. Time 6m 2.00s. SP 4-1.
R Tate (Hurworth).

1450 Open Maiden Div I (12st)

1286[2] **PURE MADNESS (USA) ....R Edwards 1**
midfld,prog 14th,2l 2nd 2 out,hrd rdn & rld flat,ld nr line
1137[2] **Zin Zan (Ire) ....M Mawhinney 2**
(fav) made most, 2l clr 2 out, ran on flat, just hdd nr line
1106 **Niad ....Miss J Morton 3**
midfld, prog 4 out, gng wll whn bad mstk 2 out, not rcvrd
756 Emu Park *alwys midfld, kpt on onepce* ....P Craggs 4
1301[5] Stays Fresh *rear, gd hdwy 12th, cls 2nd 14th til wknd 3 out*....N Wilson 5
1087 Rallying Cry (Ire) *midfld thruout, nvr a dang* ...T Scott 6
1136 Acropol 5a *alwys rear, nvr a dang*....S Gibbon 7
1286 Sweet Rose 5a *alwys rear, t.o. 4 out* ....Mrs L Ward 8
1137 Bold Croft 5a *in tch in midfld til bad mstk 14th, not rcvrd, p.u. 4 out*....M Haigh pu
1136 Joint Account *pulld hrd, cls up to 10th, wknd nxt, p.u. 12th* ....Mrs F Needham pu
1285 Patey Court 7a *alwys rear, p.u. 13th* ....C Mulhall pu
1155 Cookie Boy 7a *alwys rear, p.u. 12th* ....Miss H Delahooke pu

763 Redwood Boy *jmpng errors, sn in rear, t.o. whn p.u. 10th*..........D Raw pu
1285 Highland Miss 5a *pulld hrd, cls up til wknd 10th, ran out nxt*..........S Charlton ro
14 ran. ¾l, 15l, 15l, 10l, 3l, 10l, dist. Time 6m 17.00s. SP 9-4.
M J Brown (Sinnington).

1451 Open Maiden Div II (12st)

829 **NO TAKERS 5a..........S Swiers** 1
cls up in 2nd, disp ld 3 out, ld nxt, ran on wll
1286 **Ship The Builder..........S Brisby** 2
rear, prog 8th, cls up 4 out, 2nd aft 2 out, outpcd by wnnr
1286⁴ **Hungry Jack..........P Atkinson** 3
ran in sntche,ld to 4th,rear by 11th,styd on 4 out,wknd last
1094² Rich Asset (Ire) *alwys abt same plc, styd on onepce*..........G Markham 4
1134 Byland Princess 5a *midfld to rear, made slght late hdwy*..........N Tutty 5
1285 Hoistthestandard 5a (v) *ld 4-14th, grdly wknd aft*..........Mrs S Grant 6
915 Need A Ladder (bl) *jmpng errors, sn in rear, t.o. 13th, p.u. nxt*..........S Charlton pu
1135 Lingcool 5a *alwys rear, p.u. 14th*..........C Mulhall pu
The Way North *midfld whn ran out 3rd*...R Wakeham ro
1285 Chummy's Last 5a *rear whn f 2nd*...Mrs F Needham f
Crocket Prince *rear whn p.u. 11th*..........P Craggs pu
1094 Boulevard Bay (Ire) 7a *(fav) rear,prog 8th,ld 14th til jnd & mstk 3 out,wknd nxt,p.u.last*..........N Wilson pu
12 ran. 4l, 4l, 4l, 2l, 2l. Time 6m 15.00s. SP 3-1.
Miss C A Blakeborough (Bedale).

1452 Members

758 **COMPUTER PICKINGS 5a..........C Gibbon** 1
hndy, ld 4 out, lft wll clr 2 out, cruised home
Joe's Blackjack..........N Wilson 2
ld til wknd 4 out, lft 10l 2nd 2 out, kpt on onepce
Didgeridoo..........C Graham 3
t.o. 6th, came home in own time
824 Wall Game (USA) *cls up, wknd 4 out, rear whn ran out 2 out*..........Miss H Delahooke ro
1135³ Meadow Gray *(fav) cls up whn f 11th*..........J Davies f
1137⁵ Canny's Fort 5a *pulld hrd, cls up whn f 10th* S Gibbon f
1095 Olympic Class *hndy, cls 2nd 4 out, 5l 2nd & held whn f nxt*..........S Robinson f
7 ran. 12l, dist. Time 6m 11.00s. SP 4-1.
John E Wright (Zetland).
R.W.

WINCANTON
Tuesday May 7th
FIRM

1453 2m 5f R. K. Harrison Insurance Brokers Novices' Hunters' Chase Class H

1127² **THE JOGGER 11.7 7a..........Mr J Tizzard** 1
j.w, alwys prom, ld 12th, ran on well.
1227 **No Joker (Ire) 11.9 5a..........Mr M Rimell** 2
with ldr, ld 11th to 12th, rdn 5 out, ev ch 3 out, hit 2 out, no impn.
1309¹ **Still In Business 11.13 5a..........Mr T Mitchell** 3
(fav) hdwy 6th, hrd rdn 12th, one pace from 3 out.
1290⁴ Indian Knight 11.9 5a *hdwy 10th, rdn 5 out, styd on one pace*..........Mr C Vigors 4
1126⁴ Kings Gunner 11.7 7a *well bhnd, some hdwy from 4 out*..........Miss L Blackford 5
816⁴ Tangle Baron 11.9 5a *alwys bhnd, t.o.*...Mr M Felton 6
1164 Paid Elation 11.2 7a *mstks, t.o. from 12th.*..........Mr J Wingfield Digby 7
1055³ Joe Quality 11.7 7a *t.o. when p.u. before 4 out.*..........Mr J Van Praagh pu
Tom Furze 11.7 7a *ld to 11th, blnd and wknd 12th, t.o. when p.u. before 3 out.*..........Mr R Nuttall pu
9 ran. 4l, ½l, ¾l, 20l, 30l, dist. Time 5m 9.00s. SP 3-1.
Mrs P Tizzard

NEWTON ABBOT
Tuesday May 7th
GOOD TO SOFT

1454 2m 5f 110yds Totnes And Bridgetown Novices' Hunters' Chase Class H

1127¹ **GREEN HILL 11.7 7a..........Miss L Blackford** 1
held up in rear, hdwy 8th, ld 6 out, shaken up apr last, ran on.
1335⁵ **Southerly Gale 11.9 5a..........Mr A Farrant** 2
nvr far away, went 2nd 4 out, rdn and no impn from 2 out.
1113 **Well Timed 11.7 7a..........Mr M Frith** 3
held up in rear, hdwy when mstk 5 out, no impn from 3 out.
1275⁴ Good King Henry 11.7 7a *chsd ldrs, wknd 5 out.*..........Mr I Widdicombe 4
1276³ Chandigarh 11.7 7a *in rear from 10th.*..........Mr A Holdsworth 5
1227⁷ Lavalight 11.7 7a *ld to 5th, led apr 8th, hdd 6 out, wknd quickly, p.u. before last.*..........Mr R Nuttall pu
1335³ Stormy Sunset 11.2 7a *(fav) trckd ldr, ld 5th, hdd apr 8th, f next.*..........Mr D Dennis f
1311² Ive Called Time 11.7 7a *in tch early, wknd 9th, t.o. when p.u. before 2 out.*..........Mr T Greed pu
8 ran. 2½l, 4l, 23l, 1½l. Time 5m 29.20s. SP 3-1.
P C Pocock

UTTOXETER
Wednesday May 8th
GOOD

1455 2m 5f Bradshaw Bros. Novices' Hunters' Chase Class H

1227⁵ **KING OF SHADOWS 11.7 7a..........Mr S Prior** 1
ld till after 12th, led after 3 out, clr last, rdn out.
1191 **The Yokel 11.9 5a..........Mr P Henley** 2
chsd ldr to 2nd and from 9th to 12th, rdn apr next, one pace 2 out.
1329² **Tarry Awhile 11.9 5a..........Mr G Tarry** 3
in tch, rdn 11th, 4th and outpcd apr four out, no dngr after.
1337 Mountain Fox (Ire) 11.11 3a *chsd ldr 7th to 9th, wknd apr 12th.*..........Mr M Thompson 4
1227⁹ Tipp Down 11.8 7a 1ow *chsd ldr 3rd till u.r. 6th.*..........Mr R Thomas ur
1338 Warner Forpleasure 11.9 5a *in tch, rdn 9th, wknd apr 12th, t.o. when p.u. before 4 out.*..........Mr B Pollock pu
1228 Gan Awry 11.2 7a *in tch, wknd 11th, t.o. when p.u. before 4 out.*..........Miss S Duckett pu
1126 Precis 11.2 7a *waited with, prog 10th, blnd 12th, soon wknd, t.o. when p.u. 2 out.*..........Mr J Jukes pu
1341³ A Windy Citizen (Ire) 11.9 7a *(fav) held up, mstk 3rd, prog and mistake 9th, ld apr 4 out till after next, cl third when blnd and u.r. 2 out.*..........Mr R Hicks ur
9 ran. 7l, 17l, 19l. Time 5m 25.50s. SP 25-1.
Ceri James

1456 2m 5f Lucia Farmer Maiden Hunters' Chase Class H for the Pat Wint Cup

1009² **FREDDIE FOX 11.12 7a..........Mr T Garton** 1
prog 9th, with ldr apr 4 out, ld last, driven out.
1098³ **Hobnobber 11.12 7a..........Mr J Docker** 2
(fav) cl up, ld apr 4 out, jmpd left next, blnd and hdd last, went left and no ext.
878² **Pamela's Lad 11.12 7a..........Miss J Priest** 3
bhnd, prog 9th, 3rd and rdn apr last, one pace.
1230² Back The Road (Ire) 11.12 7a *cl up, ev ch 4 out, 3rd when slpd on lndg 2 out, no chance after.*..........Mr G Hanmer 4
1128 Otter Mill 11.12 7a *prom, blnd 7th, lost pl 10th, rdn and rallied 12th, btn next.*..........Mr J Jukes 5

1338[3] Spurious 11.12 7a *cl up, ld apr 9th to next, wknd quickly 12th, bhnd when p.u. before 4 out.* ....Mr A Griffith pu
1223[3] Miss Shaw 11.7 7a *in tch, strugling when f 12th.* ....Mr C J B Barlow f
1236[2] Bervie House (Ire) 12.2 3a *waited with, in tch till f 8th.* ....Mr A Hill f
488 Coolreny (Ire) 12.2 3a *bhnd 4th, jmpd left 6th, p.u. before 12th.*....Mr M Thompson pu
1103[1] Chacer's Imp 12.0 5a *ld till after 8th, led 10th till after 12th, soon wknd, bhnd when p.u. before 3 out.* ....Mr B Pollock pu
Very Daring 11.12 7a *alwys bhnd, t.o. when p.u. before 4 out.*....Miss S Sharratt pu
11 ran. 2½l, 2l, 7l, ½l. Time 5m 24.60s. SP 11-1.
Mrs A B Garton

1457 3¼m Strebel Boilers & Radiators Novices' Hunters' Chase Class H

1237[1] **LUCKY CHRISTOPHER 11.9 5a ....Mr G Tarry** 1
(fav) prom, blnd 16th, ld 3 out, clr last, eased cl home.
1314[2] **Ledwyche Gate 11.7 7a (bl) ....Mr M Jackson** 2
chaed ldr 12th, ld 14th to 3 out, rallied und pres run-in.
1168[2] **Master Mario 11.9 5a....Mr P Henley** 3
mid div, rdn 15th, went poor 3rd 2 out, not trbl ldrs.
1323[3] Saint Bene't (Ire) 11.7 7a (v) *ld to 14th, wknd.* ....Mr A Coe 4
1028[2] Side Brace (NZ) 11.7 7a *mstk 3rd, in tch till outpcd 15th.*....Miss K Swindells 5
1234[1] Orton House 11.7 7a *prom, ev ch 16th, soon rdn, wknd quickly after 4 out.*....Mr R Thornton 6
1335 Royal Irish 11.7 7a (bl) *mid div, rdn 14th, some prog next, no hdwy 4 out.*....Mr E James 7
1133[6] Cromwell Point 11.9 5a *alwys bhnd, t.o. when p.u. before 4 out.*....Mr N Wilson pu
1221[1] Fell Mist 11.7 7a *prom, wknd 14th, t.o. when p.u. before 4 out.* ....Miss A Sykes pu
1015[7] Military Two Step 11.7 7a *rdn and lost pl after 12th, t.o. when p.u. before 4 out.*....Miss A Plunkett pu
Babil 11.7 7a *bhnd when p.u. before 13th.* Mr R Hicks pu
1314[3] Tap Dancing 11.7 7a *mstk 8th, prog and in tch 12th, soon rdn and btn, t.o. when p.u. before 16th.* ....Mr N Bradley pu
1133[4] Celtic King 11.7 7a *in tch, bhnd when blnd 11th, t.o. when p.u. before 2 out.* ....Mr K Needham pu
1229 Achieved Ambition (Ire) 11.7 7a *jmpd right, soon bhnd, t.o. when p.u. before 10th.*....Mr G Hanmer pu
1134[1] Glenbricken 11.9 7a 2ow *bhnd 5th, t.o. when p.u. before 4 out.*....Mr R Barker pu
1365 Costermonger 11.7 7a *prom, blnd and lost pl 10th, wknd 14th, bhnd when p.u. before 16th.*...Mr A Griffith pu
16 ran. ½l, 20l, 5l, 11l, 5l, 15l. Time 6m 53.30s. SP 7-4.
G B Tarry

1458 3¼m Vauxhall Monterey Championship Final A Hunters' Chase Class H For The Ingestre Trophy

1284[1] **JASILU 11.9 (bl) ....Mr S Swiers** 1
in tch, chsd ldr 16th, ev ch when blnd 3 out, held when left clr last.
1292[5] **Misty (NZ) 11.11 3a....Mr J Culloty** 2
ld to 14th, rdn and wknd 16th, tk poor 2nd run-in.
548[2] **Stormy Witness (Ire) 11.2 7a ....Mr J Jukes** 3
trckd ldrs, ev ch 4 out, soon rdn and btn, left remote 2nd at last, fin tired.
1177[8] Bare Fisted 11.7 7a *wd, chsd ldr, pkd 10th, wknd 15th, t.o. 4 out.*....Miss H Phizacklea 4
1329[3] Making Time 11.2 7a *chsd ldrs, rdn and outpcd 15th, 4th and no ch from four out, fin tired.* ....Mr Andrew Martin 5
1189[1] Banton Loch 11.7 7a *mstks, bhnd, lost tch 15th, t.o. when p.u. before 3 out.*....Mr R Hicks pu
1030[2] Gray Rosette 11.2 7a *mstks, bhnd 8th, last when p.u. and dismntd before 13th.* ....Mr A Griffith pu
1019[1] Grecian Lark 11.9 5a *(fav) cl up, ld 14th, drew clr apr 2 out, f last.*....Mr G Tarry f
8 ran. Dist, 3l, 3l, 7l. SP 4-1.
Mrs Susan E Mason

1459 4¼m Vauxhall Monterey Open Hunters' Chase Class H for the Uttoxeter Premier Trophy

1334[1] **YOUNG BRAVE 11.12 7a....Mr M G Miller** 1
held up, prog into 3rd 18th, ld 3 out, clr when mstk next, hit last, comf.
1332[2] **Rusty Bridge 11.12 7a....Mr R Thornton** 2
ld till after 5th, soon rdn along, chsd ldr 11th to 14th, outpcd 20th, styd on from 2 out.
1366[1] **Peajade 11.7 7a ....Miss J Wormall** 3
with ldr, ld after 5th to 15th, led 20th, clr apr next, hdd 3 out, no ext.
1121[1] Teaplanter 12.2 5a *(fav) chsd ldr 7th to 11th and 14th till ld 16th, hdd 20th, wknd apr next.* ....Mr B Pollock 4
1309[3] Myliege 11.10 7a *waited with in tch, mstk 10th, reminders 15th, lost touch 18th, t.o. and p.u. before 2 out.*....Mr N Harris pu
1179[4] Green Archer 11.10 7a *rear, in tch till u.r. 13th.* ....Miss S Duckett ur
1382[5] Skerry Meadow 11.7 7a *in tch, mstk 9th, lost touch 18th, t.o. and p.u. before 4 out.* ....Mr J Jukes pu
860[1] Bow Handy Man 11.7 7a *bhnd 10th, jmpd slowly next, t.o. and p.u. before 17th.* ....Mr T Scott pu
8 ran. 7l, 6l, 14l. Time 8m 58.70s. SP 9-4.
David Young

1460 2m 7f Sir Geoffrey Congreve Cup Open Hunters' Chase Class H

1331[1] **MY NOMINEE 12.0 7a (bl)....Mr A Griffith** 1
chsd ldr,mstk 11th, ld 4 out, clr last, comf.
672[1] **Rolling Ball (Fr) 12.0 7a ....Mr R Ford** 2
(fav) ld to 4 out, switched right next, 2 l bhnd when blnd two out, no ch after.
1318 **Kameo Style 11.7 7a....Miss J Priest** 3
bhnd, lost tch 10th, tk poor 3rd run-in, t.o..
1227 No More The Fool 11.7 7a *prog into 3rd 6th, lost tch apr 11th, t.o.*....Mr L Brennan 4
1122 Antrim County 11.7 7a *jmpd right, chsd lding pair to 6th, t.o. 12th.*....Mr J R Cornwall 5
5 ran. 7l, dist, 1¼l, dist. Time 5m 54.10s. SP 9-4.
D E Nicholls

SEDGEFIELD
Thursday May 9th
FIRM

1461 2m 5f Guy Cunard Hunters' Chase Class H

1226[1] **LITTLE WENLOCK 12.3 7a ....Mrs V Jackson** 1
(fav) held up, tk clr order hfwy, ld last, rdn and styd on.
1286[3] **Private Jet (Ire) 12.0 7a ....Mr G Markham** 2
nvr far away, ld before 3 out, mstk and hdd last, no ext.
1287 **Hazel Crest 12.0 7a ....Mr M Sowersby** 3
held up, hdwy to track ldrs 8th, ld 13th, soon hdd, wknd before 2 out.
1093[4] Convincing 12.0 7a (v) *ld to 3rd, led 9th till hdd 13th, gradually wknd.*....Mr P Cornforth 4
1353 Fisherman's Quay 12.0 7a *ld 3rd till hdd 9th, chsd ldrs till gradually wknd from 3 out.*....Mr A Parker 5
862[2] Weddicar Lady 11.9 7a *soon bhnd, reminders after 7th, some late hdwy, n.d.*....Mr R Morgan 6
857 Panto Lady 11.9 7a *bhnd from 10th, n.d..* ....Miss S Lamb 7
1130 Some Flash 12.0 7a *mstks, in tch, blnd 5th, hdwy to join ldrs hfwy, hit 11th, soon wknd.* ....Mr Simon Robinson 8
1088[4] Tolmin 12.0 7a *soon well bhnd.*....Mr P Forster 9
1084 Flypie 12.2 5a *in tch, 6th and no ch when blnd and u.r. 2 out.*....Mr C Storey ur
10 ran. 1l, 15l, 2l, ½l, 7l, 9l, 2½l, 13l. Time 5m 22.40s. SP 11-8.
Mrs D S C Gibson

MARKET RASEN
Friday May 10th
GOOD

1462 2¾m 110yds Geostar Novices' Hunters' Chase Class H

1336[1] **KING'S TREASURE (USA) 11.11 7a Mr A Balding** 1
(fav) held up in rear, hmpd by faller 4th, steady hdwy from 9th, ld soon after four out, clr 2 out, comf.
1281[3] **Golden Savannah 11.7 7a ....Mr M Sowersby** 2
alwys prom, mstks, ld 8th, hdd soon after 4 out, no impn from next.
1302[2] **McCartney 11.7 7a ....Mr K Green** 3
held up, hdwy 11th, went 3rd apr 3 out, one pace.
1281 Osgathorpe 11.7 7a *in tch, outpcd 4 out, wknd next.* ....Mrs F Needham 4
913[1] Fettle Up 11.7 7a (bl) *ld early, prom till wknd 4 out.* ....Miss S Brotherton 5
1330 Carly Brrin 11.7 7a *ld 2nd, hit 7th, hdd next, in tch till wknd apr 3 out*...........................Mr J Docker 6
1024[2] Golden Moss 11.7 7a *in rear when f 4th.* ....Capt S J Robinson f
1321[2] Just Jack 12.4 3a *in tch to 10th, soon wknd, t.o. when p.u. before 3 out*..................Mr Simon Andrews pu
1107 R N Commander 11.7 7a (bl) *slowly away, some hdwy 8th, bhnd when p.u. before 12th.* ....Mr J R Cornwall pu
1284 Master Crozina 11.7 7a *chsd ldrs till wknd quickly apr 3 out, p.u. before last*.............Mr P Cornforth pu
1286 Shildon (Ire) 11.7 7a *ld apr 1st, hit and hdd next, rdn approaching 9th, soon wknd, t.o. when p.u. after 12th.* ....Mr W Burnell pu
11 ran. 9l, 2l, 11l, 1¼l, 4l. Time 5m 46.00s. SP 8-11.
Tunnel Vision

STRATFORD
Friday May 10th
GOOD TO FIRM

1463 3m John And Nigel Thorne Memorial Cup Class H Hunters' Chase

1435[4] **WHAT A TO DO 11.7 7a .....Mr Rupert Sweeting** 1
ld to 3rd, led 6th, ran on well.
1133[2] **Zam Bee 11.7 7a...................Mr N M Bell** 2
(fav) ld 3rd to 6th, chsd wnr after, hmpd apr 5 out, no impn.
1330[2] **Simply Perfect 11.7 7a.........Miss S Swindells** 3
cld 12th, rdn 4 out, one pace.
1310[3] Wrekin Hill 11.7 7a *in tch to 10th, soon bhnd.* ....Mrs J Wilkinson 4
1370[2] Paco's Boy 11.7 7a (bl) *in tch till wknd apr 5 out.* ....Mr P York 5
1170[4] Gay Ruffian 11.7 7a *lost tch 11th, t.o.*...Miss C Dyson 6
6 ran. 6l, 12l, 5l, 10l, 10l. Time 6m 0.80s. SP 9-2.
C J R Sweeting

WARWICK
Saturday May 11th
FIRM

1464 3¼m Season's End Novices' Hunters' Chase Class H

1332 **PROFESSOR LONGHAIR 11.12 7a....Mr R Hicks** 1
trckd ldr, left in ld 13th, styd on from 2 out.
1344[1] **Expressment 11.7 7a ....Mr G Penfold** 2
held up, hdwy when hit 14th, went 2nd 5 out, kept on one pace from 2 out.
1173[6] **Damers Treasure 11.9 5a.........Mr A Sansome** 3
ld till blnd and hdd 13th, wknd 5 out.
1329 Ryders Wells 11.7 7a *alwys bhnd, t.o. hfwy, p.u. before 4 out*..............................Mr S Walker pu
1182[1] Loyal Gait (NZ) 11.7 7a *(fav) trckd ldrs, f 9th.* ....Mr P Atkins f
1164[1] Good Looking Guy 11.7 7a *in tch till blnd badly and u.r. 12th*..........................Mr A Charles-Jones ur
6 ran. ½l, 28l. Time 6m 42.70s. SP 5-1.
Huw Davies

BILSDALE
Easingwold
Saturday May 11th
GOOD

1465 Members

1449 **HELLCATMUDWRESTLER 5ex.......Miss T Gray** 1
(fav) j.w. ld to 6th & frm 9th, lft clr 14th, unchal
1448 **Sharpridge ....M Mawhinney** 2
nvr going wl,jmpd slwly 3rd,sn t.o.,lft 3rd 14th,tk 2nd 2out
1135[2] **Greatfull Fred ....Miss K Pickersgill** 3
sttld 2nd, mstk 11th, outpcd nxt, lft 2nd 14th, sn wknd
1450 Joint Account *pllng,prom,ld 6th,wd & hdd 9th,blnd 11th,ev ch & f 14th*..................Mrs F Needham f
4 ran. 20l, 6l. Time 6m 13.00s. SP 1-2.
Henry Bell (Bilsdale).

1466 Confined (12st)

1450[1] **PURE MADNESS (USA) ....R Edwards** 1
(Jt fav) hld up going wl,prog 8th,chal 2 out,rdn & qcknd clr apr last
1447[4] **Chapel Island ....G Tuer** 2
mid-div, mstk 5th, prog 11th, ev ch 2 out, not qckn
1134[3] **Skipping Gale ....P Atkinson** 3
disp til hdd & onepcd 2 out
1368[1] One For The Chief (v) *alwsy abt same plc, onepcd frm 4 out*..................................S Whitaker 4
1446[4] Fowling Piece *chsd ldrs, lost plc 10th, kpt on onepcd 4 out*..................................Miss L Horner 5
1447 Earl Gray (bl) *keen hld, alwys mid-div, onepcd frm 4 out*..................................Miss T Jackson 6
1446[5] Caman 5a *rear, dtchd 7th, t.o. 10th*.....Miss S Duell 7
1447 Cadrillon (Fr) *rear, rdn 10th, nvr on terms, p.u. 2 out, saddle slppd*..............................Miss A Deniel pu
1131 Blackwoodscountry *(Jt fav) keen, disp til ld aft 3 out, sn jnd, ev ch whn f nxt*......................C Mulhall f
Political Trout 5a *n.j.w. last & sn t.o., p.u. 13th* ....M Sowersby pu
10 ran. 4l, 5l, 3l, 1l, 12l, 20l. Time 6m 4.00s. SP 3-1.
M J Brown (Sinnington).

1467 Open

1448[1] **PARK DRIFT ....R Tate** 1
(fav) prom, lft 2nd apr 7th, disp 14th, ld nxt, sn clr, eased flat
1287[2] **Gaelic Warrior ....S Swiers** 2
chsd ldrs, mstk 5th, lft in ld apr 7th, hdd 15th, onepcd
1306[1] **Rexy Boy ....P Gee** 3
pllng,rear,prog 8th,trckd 1st 2,outpcd 12th,blnd 15th,onepcd
1281[7] Good Team *rear, dtchd 7th, nvr dang*....D Crossland 4
1448[3] Knowe Head *j.w. ld til s.u. apr 7th*..........S Brisby su
1282 Frome Boy *prom to 7th, lost plc, wknd 10th, t.o. & f last*..................................P Johnson f
6 ran. 4l, 8l, 8l. Time 6m 1.00s. SP 1-2.
G Thornton (York & Ainsty North).

1468 Restricted

1283 **CUMBERLAND BLUES (IRE) ....Miss A Deniel** 1
walked over
B Rickaby (Sinnington).

1469 Ladies

1449[5] **CHEEKY POT (bl) ....Mrs S Grant** 1
ld to 15th, ld nxt-apr last, switched rght flat, ld nr fin
1449[1] **Indie Rock ....Mrs F Needham** 2

(fav) prog 4th, ld 15th-nxt, ld apr last, hrd rdn & hdd cls hm
1366 **Linebacker ....Miss S Leach** 3
mstk 4th, mid-div, blnd 13th, sn strgglng, t.o.
970[2] Nishvamitra *handy, outpcd 14th, sn btn, t.o.* ....Mrs J Dawson 4
1283 Vienna Woods *prog 7th, fdd 11th, mstk nxt, strgglng whn f 14th*.............................Miss F Mudd f
1450[8] Sweet Rose 5a *mstks, alwys bhnd, t.o. & p.u. 10th* ....Mrs L Ward pu
6 ran. ½l, dist, 1½l. Time 5m 58.00s. SP 7-1.
Mrs E I L Tate (Cleveland).

1470 Open Maiden

1451[3] **HUNGRY JACK (bl)...................P Atkinson** 1
(fav) prom, ld 8th, disp 11th, hdd 3 out, ld last, ran on strngly
1287[4] **Chuckleberry ....N Tutty** 2
alwys prom, cls 3rd 14th, mstk nxt, ld 3 out-last, not qckn
1285[2] **Prophet's Choice ....M Haigh** 3
mstk 1st, alwys handy, disp 11th-3 out, onepcd
1451 Chummy's Last 5a *rear,prog 5th,mstk 9th,outpcd 13th,kpt on wll 3 out,improve* ....Mrs F Needham 4
1094 Shore Lane *bhnd frm 8th, strgglng 14th, t.o.* C Mulhall 5
1365 Engaging *ld to 8th, fdd, t.o. & p.u. 3 out* ....Miss T Jackson pu
1284 Auntie Fay (Ire) 7a *n.j.w. alwys wll bhnd, t.o. & p.u. 15th* ....I Baker pu
Wally's Girl 5a *dtchd 8th, t.o. & p.u. 14th* ....W Burnell pu
1135 Hasty Cruise *prom whn s.u. flat apr 7th* ......A Rebori su
1285 Flaxton King (Ire) 7a *mid-div, mstk 5th, clsd 7th, no prog aft, wknd 13th,p.u. nxt* ....M Sowersby pu
10 ran. 6l, 1½l, 8l, 15l. Time 6m 10.00s. SP 6-4.
D G Atkinson (Bedale (West Of Yore)).
N.E.

CUMBERLAND
Aspatria
Saturday May 11th
GOOD TO FIRM

1471 Members

754[3] **GIVOWER 1ow ....P Diggle** 1
(fav) ld aft 7th, hit 10th, hdd 11th, ld 14th, clr 16th, v easy
1337 **Boreen Owen 7ow................Miss F Barnes** 2
last frm 4th, mstk 11th, styd on frm 2 out, not trbl wnnr
Big Mac 14ow *in tch, ld apr 12-14th, 2nd & btn whn blndrd & u.r. last*...........................I McMath ur
700[2] Mandys Special 5a *rcd wd,ld to 7th,ld 11th,sn hdd,wknd 16th,last whn u.r.2 out* .....Miss A Creedon ur
4 ran. 7l. Time 6m 23.30s. SP Evens.
A J Smith (Cumberland).

1472 Restricted (12st)

1353[5] **Funny Feelings ....Miss D Laidlaw** 1D
ld 9th, blndrd & hdd 2 out, btn whn lft clr last, disq
1353[6] **SENORA D'OR 5a........................R Shiels** 1
ld 4-9th,prom,wknd apr 3 out,lft 2nd last,fin 2nd plcd 1st
501[2] **Cukeira 5a...............................C Paisley** 2
(fav) prog 11th,5th & outpcd nxt,kpt on frm 2 out,fin 3rd plcd 2nd
1086[3] **Blakes Folly (Ire) ....N Hargreave** 3
hld up, prog 12th, 4th & outpcd nxt, fin 4th plcd 3rd
1353[3] Gay Vixen Vl 5a *ld to 4th, bhnd frm 12th, t.o.* . .T Scott 4
1447[3] Denim Blue *prog 8th, prssd ldr 12th, ld 2 out, clr whn blnd & u.r. last*......................Miss P Robson ur
1252 Kincardine Bridge (USA) *trckd ldrs, lost plc qckly 10th, t.o. & p.u. bfr 12th* ....M Bradburne pu
188 Weejumpawud 5a *pullng, mstks, prom to 11th, t.o. whn p.u. 2 out* ....C Storey pu
8 ran. 10l, 2l, 1l, 30l. Time 6m 7.20s. SP 10-1.
Mrs Ann Rutherford (Lauderdale).
Funny Feelings fin 1st disq not weigh-in. Original distances.

1473 Ladies

1317[1] **OUT THE DOOR (IRE) ....Miss S Baxter** 1
(fav) conf rddn, ld 15th, shaken up apr last, rddn out flat
1250[1] **Houselope Beck ....Miss S Foster** 2
chsd ldr apr 12th, rddn to chal apr last, unable to qckn
1366[2] **Across The Lake (bl) ....Miss S Brotherton** 3
in tch, 4th & outpcd 15th, kpt on onepce aft
Matrace 5a *ld to 15th, 3rd & wknng nxt, fin tired* ....Miss D Laidlaw 4
Czaryne 5a *chsd ldr 3rd til aft 11th, sn wknd* ....Miss J Percy 5
1352[1] Marshalstoneswood *in tch til p.u. & dismntd bfr 10th* ....Miss A Bowie pu
1250 Golesa *in tch til wknd 12th, t.o. & p.u. bfr 16th* ....Miss L Bradburne pu
7 ran. 1l, 10l, 20l, 2 fences. Time 6m 2.20s. SP 4-5.
M Mann (Wheatland).

1474 Open

1226[4] **SECRET SCEPTRE ....A Parker** 1
(fav) w.w., ld 10th, clr 12th, canter
1133 Yenoora (Ire) (bl) *pulld hrd, ld aft 1st-8th, sn t.o., p.u. bfr 16th* ....J Carmichael pu
317[8] Killula King *ld til aft 1st,ld 8-10th,wknd 12th,v tired & stppd bfr last* ....R Morgan pu
3 ran. Time 6m 17.20s. SP 1-4.
R A Bartlett (Fife).

1475 Confined (12st)

1354[3] **LOUGHLINSTOWN BOY 5ex............P Craggs** 1
(fav) j.w., ld 6th til apr last, gd jmp to ld agn, ran on
1340[9] **Little Glen ....T Scott** 2
mstks, in tch, chal & ld apr last, mstk & hdd, not rcvrd
1252[3] **Toaster Crumpet ....Miss P Robson** 3
ld 4-6th, chsd ldr 15-16th, wknd nxt
1351[7] Hydropic *chsd ldrs, mstk 11th, 4th whn blndrd 15th, no ch aft* ....Miss K Miller 4
751 Sunset Reins Free *mstk 3rd, prog to 2nd 12th, wknd qckly 14th, p.u. nxt*......................S O'Sullivan pu
49 Who's In Charge *ld to 4th, bhnd & reluctant frm 7th, t.o. & p.u. bfr 12th*...........................R Morgan pu
6 ran. 2l, 15l, 7l. Time 6m 10.30s. SP 5-4.
J A Riddell (Percy).

1476 Open Maiden

613 **BECCY BROWN 5a.....................J Walton** 1
mid-div, prog 9th, ld 15th, clr whn blnd last, comf
1356[2] **Jack's Croft (bl) ....R Hale** 2
ld to 3rd, ld 12-15th, sn rddn, onepcd
1356 **Good Profit ....T Scott** 3
bhnd 11th, styd on frm 16th, wnt poor 3rd last, nvr dang
1451 The Way North *tubed, prog 11th, cls 3rd 15th, wknd nxt, fin tired*............................R Wakeham 4
1254 Rustic Bridge *tubed, chsd ldr 6-12th, sn strgglng, t.o.* ....S Love 5
1356 Beltino 7a *prom, blnd & lost plc 10th, no ch aft, t.o. frm 15th* ....C Storey 6
1136 The Raskins 5a *bhnd frm 6th, t.o. frm 13th* . .R Morgan 7
1155 Bessie Love 5a (bl) *u.r. 1st*...........Miss F Barnes ur
1365[6] Im Ok (Ire) 5a (bl) *prom til b.d. 11th* ....Miss V Haigh bd
1355[2] Madame Beck 5a *tubed, chsd ldrs til blnd & u.r. 7th* ....N Smith ur
1087 Red Scot *prog 8th, wll in tch whn f 11th* . .S O'Sullivan f
1356[3] Bagots Park *(fav) ld 3rd-12th, blnd nxt, wll btn 15th, p.u. last* ....R Shiels pu
859 Keirose 5a *n.j.w., bhnd til p.u. bfr 10th* ....C Paisley pu
1033 Chip Pan 7a *prom, mstk 8th, 5th & wknng 14th, p.u. 3 out* ....D Barlow pu
1089 The Early Bird 7a *mstks, alwys last, t.o. & p.u. bfr 12th* ....A Parker pu

Lethem Laird 7a *alwys rear, t.o. & p.u. bfr 13th* ....M Bradburne pu
16 ran. 12l, 20l, 10l, 20l, 10l, 5l. Time 6m 13.80s. SP 20-1.
Mrs F T Walton (Border).
Last fence omitted 18 jumps. S.P.

GOLDEN VALLEY
Bredwardine
Saturday May 11th
GOOD

1477 Members

1042 **ALL GREEK TO ME (IRE) 7ex..........W Bryan** 1
hld up, clsr order 14th, ld 3 out, clr nxt, pshd out
1225[7] **Diamond Light ....S Lloyd** 2
w.w. in 2nd, effrt to ld 15th, no ext frm nxt
1413[3] **Horn Player (USA) ....M P Jones** 3
(fav) ld to 14th, rdn & not qckn frm nxt
3 ran. 6l, 6l. Time 6m 51.00s. SP 5-4.
J Ashmole (Golden Valley).

1478 Confined (12st)

CELTIC ABBEY ....D S Jones 1
(fav) mid-div, prog to cls 2nd 10th, hmpd 12th, ld 3 out, kpt on
1435[2] **Carbery Arctic ....A Phillips** 2
w.w. prog 11th, chsd wnr 3 out, clsng flat
1435[3] **Mitchells Best ....M Jackson** 3
ld 1st, styd prom, rdn 12th, kpt on onepcd frm 15th
1223[1] Dane Rose 5a *hld up, prog 11th, no ext frm 15th* ....Miss A Sheppard 4
1245[4] Running Frau 5a *cls 10th at 9th, kpt on steadily frm 14th* ....D Milton 5
1410[1] Barn Pool (bl) *lost tch 5th, t.o. & p.u. last* ....E Collins pu
1411[2] Homme D'Affaire *mid-div whn u.r. flat bef 3rd* ....T Stephenson ur
1437 Corrianne 5a (bl) *ld 2nd-nxt, cls up til wknd 12th, p.u. 15th* ....G Hanmer pu
1268 Oakers Hill *prom to 10th, wknd & p.u. 14th* ....M Munrowd pu
1158[3] Ideal *ld 4th-15th, wknd rpdly, p.u. nxt* ....J Rees pu
1413[5] Frozen Pipe 5a *hld up rear, prog 13th, no ext frm 15th, p.u. last* ....A Wintle pu
1151 Pin Up Boy *trckd ldrs, effrt apr 14th, no ext frm nxt, p.u. 2 out* ....A Crow pu
12 ran. 1l, 12l, 10l, 3l. Time 6m 27.00s. SP 4-6.
G J Powell (Ross Harriers).

1479 Open (12st)

1386[3] **LISLARY LAD ....D S Jones** 1
prog to trck ldr 11th, ld 2 out, pshd clr flat
1304[3] **Auction Law (NZ) 7ex..........A Crow** 2
pshd alng frm 4th, rdn 14th, went 2nd flat
1228[5] **First Harvest ....P Hanly** 3
(fav) ld frm 5th, rdn 15th, ran wd & hdd 2 out, wknd flat
1265[3] Adanac *chsd ldrs, not qckn frm 14th, kpt on onepcd* ....A Price 4
1437[5] Shadow Walker 4ex *cls up til not qckn frm 14th* ....M Jackson 5
1331[6] Kingfisher Bay *prom, rdn 12th, wknd frm 14th* ....A Wintle 6
692 Virginia's Bay *chsd ldrs 4th-8th, wknd 10th, p.u. 12th* ....K Hibbert pu
1220 Swahili Run *ld to 5th, ran out & u.r. nxt* ....A Dalton ro
8 ran. 4l, 1½l, 12l, 7l, 25l. Time 6m 32.00s. SP 4-1.
Lee Bowles (Talybont).

1480 Ladies

1172[1] **BANKHEAD (IRE) 7ex..........Miss C Spearing** 1
trckd ldr frm 8th, chal 2 out, drew clr last
1247[1] **Rip Van Winkle ....Miss A Dare** 2
(fav) ld frm 4th, clr wth wnr 14th, hdd & no ext frm 2 out
1420[1] **Couture Tights 7ex ....Miss J Priest** 3
chsd ldrs to 12th, went dist 3rd 2 out
1230[5] Soldiers Duty (USA) *chsd ldrs til outpcd frm 13th, styd on frm 3 out* ....Mrs M Bryan 4
1264 News Review 7ex *cls up to 11th, outpcd frm 14th* ....Miss J Mathias 5
1172[3] Mister Gebo 7ex *disp 5th, chsd ldr 11th, wknd frm 14th* ....Miss C Dyson 6
741 Aldington Bell (bl) *prog to cls 3rd at 7th, lost tch 1st 2 15th, wknd nxt* ....Miss J Butler 7
1316[4] Raido *ld to 3rd, cls up whn r.o. & u.r. 6th* ....Miss L Wallace ro
1245 Little Thyne *rear frm 6th, lost tch & p.u. 12th* ....Miss S Trotman pu
1219 Loch Garanne 5a *trotted twards 1st & stppd* ....Miss E James ref
1414[4] Vatacan Bank *rear frm 4th, rmndrs nxt, lost tch 7th, t.o. & u.r. 15th* ....Miss B Williams ur
1318 In The Water *s.s. t.o. 2nd, p.u. aft 11th* Miss A Murphy pu
12 ran. 6l, 30l, 2½l, 3l, hd, 15l. Time 6m 24.00s. SP 11-8.
A J Brazier (Croome & West Warwickshire).

1481 Restricted Div I (12st)

568[1] **STEPASIDEBOY ....A Crow** 1
s.s. clsd by 11th, strng run to ld 2 out, kpt on well
1224[1] **Kiltrose Lad ....A Dalton** 2
prom, went 2nd 13th, ld 15th, hdd & kpt on onepcd 2 out
1439[3] **Bakmalad ....H Wheeler** 3
5s-7/2, rear & rmndrs 5th, last at 10th, fin wll frm 3 out
1173[8] Sideliner *cls up til not qckn frm 14th* ....M Jackson 4
1411 Hennerwood Oak 5a *ld 2nd til hdd & wknd aft 15th* ....M P Jones 5
1178[3] Slight Panic 5a *cls 5th at 7th, chsd ldrs til not qckn frm 13th* ....C Richards 6
1439[9] African Minstrel *mid-div, cls enough 12th, outpcd frm 14th* ....L Brown 7
1223 Kerry Hill *mid-div 8th, rdn 11th, no prog frm 13th, t.o. 2 out* ....T Stephenson 8
1223 Flaxridge *(fav) ld 1st, trckd ldr til mstk 13th, rallied 3 out, wknd flat* ....T Jones 9
1173[3] King Of The Clouds *mid-div at 8th, lost tch aft 15th, p.u. last* ....Mrs N Sheppard pu
1233 Kingsthorpe *mid-div & going wll 11th, effrt 13th, wknd 15th, p.u. 2 out* ....A Phillips pu
1211 Major Bert (Ire) *nvr rchd ldrs, in tch 11th, wknd 14th, p.u. 2 out* ....G Hanmer pu
882 Celtic Berry 5a *rear, mstk 5th, no ch 14th, t.o. & p.u. 2 out* ....W Bryan pu
843 Bee Moy Do (Ire) *prom to 5th, lost plc 8th, t.o. 14th, p.u. nxt* ....A Price pu
14 ran. 2½l, 4l, 12l, 1l, 7l, 10l, 8l, hd. Time 6m 38.00s. SP 5-1.
E H Crow (North Shropshire).

1482 Restricted Div II (12st)

1421 **DARA'S COURSE (IRE) 5a..........A Phillips** 1
alwys prom, rdn 14th, ld 3 out, drew wll clr
842[1] **Meadow Cottage ....T Stephenson** 2
alwys prom, ev ch 15th, outpcd nxt, tk 2nd flat
1381[1] **Bolshie Baron ....M Harris** 3
ld til hdd aft 15th, wknd frm 2 out
1175[1] I Blame Theparents 5a *trckd ldrs, cls 4tha t 15th, kpt on onepcd frm nxt* ....Miss E James 4
1242 Aldington Charlie *alwys rear, lost tch frm 15th* ....H Wheeler 5
1421 Alamir (USA) *prom, cls 5th whn mstk 12th, wknd & p.u. 15th* ....M Munrowd pu
287[1] Kingquillo (Ire) *2nd whn f 3rd* ....G Hanmer f
390[1] Shawn Cuddy 7a *rdn 11th, lost tch frm 15th, p.u. 2 out* ....S Shinton pu
1266 Rosenthal 5a *rdn alng in rear 4th, t.o. & ref 6th* ....M P Jones ref
1222[4] Mackabee (Ire) *mid-div whn s.u. bnd bef 6th* ..T Weale su
1075[2] Quick Quick Sloe 5a *(fav) s.s. u.r. 2nd* ..Miss T Cave ur
1267 Hatterill Ridge *chsd ldrs til p.u. aft 8th* ....C Richards pu
Scally Hill 7a *s.s. t.o. frm 5th, p.u. 10th* ....A Dalton pu
13 ran. 15l, 1l, 2l, 20l. Time 6m 39.00s. SP 20-1.
Miss Julia Oakey (Teme Valley).

1483 Open Maiden Div I (12st)

1319[4] **MARINER'S WALK** ....**H Wheeler** 1
ld to 3rd, cls up til chal 3 out, rdn to ld flat
1417[5] **Cruise A Hoop** ....**T Stephenson** 2
prog 8th, ld frm 11th til jnd last, no ext flat
1410 **Bowland Girl (Ire) 5a** ....**Miss E James** 3
(fav) w..w in mid-div, prog 13th, ev ch 3 out, no ext apr last
1196[2] Nordross 5a *prog frm rear 6th, kpt on steadily frm 15th, nrst fin* ....G Hanmer 4
1273 Bob-Cam *ld frm 5th, ran wd nxt, hdd 11th, ev ch 15th, wknd nxt* ....P Doorhof 5
1048[4] Most Rich (Ire) *cls up til wknd 14th, p.u. 3 out* ....M Jackson pu
1270[3] Toucher (Ire) *nvr rchd ldrs, wknd 10th, p.u. 12th* ....M Munrowd pu
953 Playing The Fool 5a *prom to 11th, wknd 13th, p.u. 15th* ....P Hanly pu
1218[2] Seven Cruise *lost tch 8th, t.o. & p.u. 15th* ..M P Jones pu
1271 Sweet Blue 5a *rear frm 4th, lost tch 14th, t.o. & p.u. last* ....C Richards pu
1315 Mystery Belle 5a *ld 4th, prom til wknd 15th, p.u. 2 out* ....D S Jones pu
849 Tennessee Cruiser *in tch til outpcd frm 12th, t.o. & p.u. 2 out* ....D Harrison pu
1045[8] Think Twice *trckd ldrs, cls up til wknd rdply 14th, p.u. nxt* ....A Dalton pu
1417 Miss Jcb (Ire) *ref to race* ....M FitzGerald 0
1039 Tiger Lord 7a *mstk 5th, rdn frm 7th, lost tch & p.u. 12th* ....A Price pu

15 ran. 1½l, 3½l, 10l, 10l. Time 6m 43.00s. SP 10-1.
Mrs V Miles (North Cotswold).

1484 Open Maiden Div II (12st)

1319[2] **MICKSDILEMMA** ....**A Phillips** 1
cls 3rd at 10th, ld 14th, jnd 3 out, rdn nxt, just hld on
1175[4] **Sterling Buck (USA)** ....**T Jones** 2
prom til not qckn frm 15th, styd on 2 out, clsng flat
1006[6] **Rocket Radar 7a**.........................**M Jackson** 3
prom frm 6th, ev ch 15th, 2nd at last, no ext flat
357[5] Gillie's Fountain 7a *(fav) w.w. 8th at 11th, chal 15th, disp nxt, wknd apr last*..........A Dalton 4
1225[5] Jobingo *6th & pshd alng 11th, no prog frm 14th* ....D Stephens 5
1234 Kingfisher Blues (Ire) *rear til effrt 12th, no prog frm 14th* ....G Hanmer 6
1269[5] Le Gerard (bl) *nvr rchd ldrs, no ch frm 3 out* ....D S Jones 7
1391[3] Gold Tip 5a *ld to 3rd, ev ch 15th, wknd & p.u. 2 out* ....A Price pu
1224 Vital Wonder *s.s. mstk & u.r. 3rd* ....P Doorhof ur
1224 Flying Wild *chsng ldrs whn blnd & u.r. 6th* ....Miss S Walker ur
1416[2] Sweet Petel 5a *ld 3rd-13th, wknd & p.u. nxt* ....M FitzGerald pu
1416[5] City Rhythm *mid-div, lost plc 11th, wknd & p.u. 14th* ....C Packer pu
949 Builder Boy *rear frm 11th, no ch 15th, t.o. & p.u. 2 out* ....S Prior pu
1271[3] Classic Edition 7a *rdn alng in rear 12th, lost tch 14th, p.u. 3 out* ....S Shinton pu
1368 Posy Hill (Ire) 7a *mid-div til p.u. 9th, dsmntd* ....Miss J Priest pu
1315 Asante Sana 7a *outpcd & lost tch 4th, tried to ref 6th & p.u.* ....K Hibbert pu
1319 Sutton Lighter *alwys rear, t.o. 8th, p.u. 10th* ..M Harris pu

17 ran. ½l, 3l, 15l, 6l, 10l, 5l. Time 6m 40.00s. SP 5-1.
N Shutts (North Shropshire).

1485 Open Maiden Div III (12st)

1416 **DERRING ANN 5a**.....................**D S Jones** 1
rear of main grp 9th, prog 11th, styd on to ld flat
1218 **Cwm Bye 7a** ....**M Jackson** 2
trckd ldrs frm 11th, ld 14th, rdn, hdd & no ext flat
1416 **Big Buckley 5a**.....................**T Stephenson** 3
alwys prom, 6l 4th 3 out, hit nxt, no ext apr last
1417[4] Musical Mail *cls up frm 8th, hmpd 13th, cls 2nd 3 out, kpt on onepcd nxt* ....M Munrowd 4
1242 Astley Jack *ld 2nd til p.u. aft 6th* ....C Pennycate pu
1434[6] Sonny's Song *prog to ld 7th, hdd 14th, wknd & p.u. 3 out* ....L Brown pu
1288[2] Keep On Trying 5a *(fav) 2nd whn blnd 2nd, t.o. 4th, p.u. nxt* ....M Portman pu
1315[3] Promitto 5a *trckd ldrs, effrt 13th, no prog & p.u. nxt* ....A Phillips pu
1434[5] Majic Belle 5a (v) *cls up 9th, ev ch til wknd 14th, p.u. 2 out* ....Miss S Jackson pu
1417 Greenhill Lady 5a *mstk 7th, last frm nxt, t.o. & u.r. 14th* ....M P Jones ur
953 Jacky's Jaunt 5a *in rear whn ref 8th* ....S Prior ref
1234 Highland Chase *ld 1st, cls up til wknd 13th, p.u. 15th* ....A Wintle pu
1161 Miss Clare 5a *cls up 9th, lost tch ldrs 11th, t.o. & p.u. 2 out* ....S Lloyd pu
Eventsinternashnal *ran out 1st* ....A Dalton ro
Sun Setting 7a *l.w. rear whn f 3rd*..........R Sweeting f

15 ran. 3l, 10l, 7l. Time 6m 44.00s. SP 5-1.
R B Davies (Radnor & West Hereford).
P.R.

LLANDEILO
Erw Lon
Saturday May 11th
FIRM

1486 Members

1266[1] **BARNABY BOY** ....**J P Keen** 1
(fav) settld rear to 6th, prog frm 9th, hrd rdn to ld aft last
1339[3] **Sea Search** ....**Miss A Meakins** 2
prom, ld 14th-aft last, rallied und pres
1160[4] **Equatime 5a** ....**P Williams** 3
ld to 13th, wknd
1391 Frontrunner 5a *in tch to 8th, fdd, fin t.o.*.......M Lewis 4

4 ran. 3l, dist, dist. Time 6m 0.00s. SP 1-2.
J L Brown (Llandeilo).

1487 Confined (12st)

1388[1] **NORTHERN BLUFF** ....**J Jukes** 1
(fav) made all, in no dang frm 13th
1413[4] **Construction King** ....**Mrs J Hawkins** 2
trckd ldr til bad mstk 13th, renewd aft 2 out, not trbl wnr
1385[3] **Lucky Ole Son 8ex**.......................**J Price** 3
nvr nrr then dist 3rd
1262[3] Bronze Effigy 3ex (bl) *alwys in rear*..........W Pugh 4

4 ran. 6l, dist, 10l. Time 6m 10.00s. SP 1-3.
H Gibbon (Pembrokeshire).

1488 Open (12st)

1385[2] **MOVING FORCE** ....**J Jukes** 1
(fav) made all, clr 8th, unchal
1265[5] **Cornish Cossack (NZ)** ....**J P Keen** 2
2nd/3rd thruout, nvr nrr to chal
768[1] Carlowitz (USA) *2nd/3rd thruout, 3rd whn ref last, (sore)* ....J Price ref
1268[4] Royal Oats 5a *in rear whn p.u. 9th*..........J Tudor pu

4 ran. Dist. Time 5m 40.00s. SP 4-5.
Mrs Louise Meyrick (South Pembrokeshire).

1489 Ladies

1414[2] **KUMADA 7ex**......................**Miss S Wallin** 1
ld to 7th & agn 14th, no threat aft, easy
1265[1] **Handsome Harvey 7ex**...........**Miss C Thomas** 2
(fav) svrl mstks, ld 7-13th, strgglng aft, eased flat
1414[3] **La Mezeray 5a** ....**Mrs J Hawkins** 3
in rear til ran on 2 out, nvr able to chal
1387[1] Gold Diver 3ex *settld 2nd/3rd, outpcd aft 13th, no dang aft* ....Miss E Jones 4

4 ran. 10l, 2l, 10l. Time 5m 47.00s. SP 7-2.
Miss Lisa Llewellyn (Llangeinor).

1490 Restricted (12st)

1388² **DUSTYS TRAIL (IRE) ....R Thornton** 1
(fav) ld frm 12th, drew clr frm 2 out
1266² **Cottage Raider (Ire) ....P Williams** 2
ld to 12th, cont to chal til btn 2 out
1266⁴ **Cranagh Moss (Ire) ....J Lewis** 3
nvr nrr to chal
1197² Buckley's Court *cls up 3rd, ev ch whn f 14th* ..J Jukes f
1267 Downhill Racer 5a *in rear whn p.u. 11th*.....J P Keen pu
1038 Mrs Wumpkins (Ire) 7a *prom to 9th, wknd, p.u. 13th* ....Miss C Thomas pu
6 ran. 12l, dist. Time 5m 45.00s. SP 7-4.
G Morris (Pembrokeshire).

1491 P P O R A (12st)

691 **WARREN BOY ....J Jukes** 1
(fav) ld to 10th & agn aft 13th whn lft alone
1262¹ Tricky Dex (USA) *ld 11th til aft 13th, p.u. lame* J Tudor pu
2 ran. Time 6m 8.00s. SP 4-6.
F J Ayres (Tredegar).

1492 Open Maiden (12st)

1335⁷ **SISTER LARK 5a ....P Williams** 1
(fav) ld/disp til ld 14th, easily
1391 **Miss Montgomery (Ire) 7a ....Miss A Meakins** 2
settld mi-div to 8th, rpd prog frm 3 out, no dang to wnr
1390 **Relatively High 7a ....M Lewis** 3
settld towrds rear, impvd frm 13th, mstk 3 out, no ch aft
1390 I'm A Bute 5a *nvr nrr to chal* ....J Price 4
1272 Puttingonthestyle *ld/disp til ran out 13th* ..L Stephens ro
1273 Katy Country Mouse 5a *in tch to 9th, wknd & p.u. 11th* ....D Davies pu
1390 Fumi D'Oro 5a *wth ldrs til 13th, fdd, p.u. 2 out* ....R Thornton pu
1390 Kirby's Charm *alwys towrds rear, p.u. 2 out* J P Keen pu
1271 Mountain Slave 5a *in rear til 4th, imprvd 7-13th, wknd & p.u. 15th* ....T Vaughan pu
1384² Woodlight Dawn 5a *alwys towrds rear, p.u. 11th* ....J Tudor pu
10 ran. 10l, 2l, 10l. Time 6m 0.00s. SP 6-4.
N B Jones (Ystrad).
P.D.

MINEHEAD & WEST SOMERSET
Holnicote
Saturday May 11th
GOOD

1493 Members

1342 **TUFFNUT TOM ....R Payne** 1
(Jt fav) in tch, prog 16th, ld apr last, comf
1277 **Nothing To Fear ....G Barfoot-Saunt** 2
(Jt fav) cls up, ev ch til outpcd 16th, ran on stdly, tk 2nd run in
1139 **Hedera Helix ....S Ellis** 3
not fluent, ld 12th, slght ld til hdd & wknd qckly apr last
1277 Nice To No *in tch, ev ch whn pckd 16th, wknd* S Slade 4
1129⁵ Nottarex *ld til 12th, wknd, lost tch 14th* ......B Wright 5
5 ran. 3½l, 3½l, 8l, 30l. Time 6m 54.00s. SP 2-1.
Mrs R Lamacraft (Minehead Harriers).

1494 Open Maiden Div I

1392 **SPRINGCOMBE 5a................Miss S Eames** 1
made most til hdd aft 2 out, rlld to ld agn last, ran on
1347 **Rogerson ....S Mulcaire** 2
hld up, gd hdwy 15th, ld 2 out til last, no ext
1430 **Lucky Thursday ....S Hornby** 3
not fluent, hndy til outpcd 16th, no ch clsng stgs
1187⁴ Legal Vision 5a *(fav) prom til rddn & wknd aft 16th, sn btn* ....B Dixon 4
1349³ Miss Pernickity 5a *prom til wknd 14th, no ch frm 16th* ....R Woolacott 5
1429 Musbury Castle 5a *wll in tch til lost plc 16th, mstk nxt, t.o.* ....S Kidston 6
652 Stormy Fashion *tubed, hld up rear, mkng gd hdwy 4th whn f 3 out* ....Maj G Wheeler f
French Invasion 5a *towrds rear, nvr dang, p.u. 15th* ....S Parfimowicz pu
8 ran. 3l, 20l, 8l, 10l, 8l. Time 6m 48.00s. SP 7-1.
Mrs E Eames (Cotley).

1495 Open Maiden Div II

1243² **ARDELL BOY ....Miss P Gundry** 1
made all, mstk 16th, ran on wll whn chal frm 4 out
1347² **Liberty James ....N Harris** 2
(fav) hld up,hdwy 11th,trckd wnr & ev ch til not qckn clsng stgs
1347 **Miss Ricus 7a ....R Treloggen** 3
midfld, ran on steadd clsng stgs, tk 3rd run in
1347 Masters Nephew *in tch, 3rd mstly, mstk 17th, onepcd frm 3 out* ....B O'Doherty 4
821⁴ Mountain-Linnet *prom til mstk 12th, disp poor 3rd 4 out, fdd* ....Miss A Goschen 5
1348³ Flemings Fleur (v) *towrds rear, hit 9th, no ch frm hlfwy* ....P King 6
1432 Gamblers Refrain *in tch til wknd 12th, t.o.* ....D Jones 7
1274⁴ Play Risky (Ire) *bhnd, blndrd bdly 16th, t.o.* R Emmett 8
1395 Stalbridge Return 5a *bhnd til p.u. 11th* S Parfimowicz pu
150 Rory'm (Ire) *sn bhnd, last whn ref 6th*........R Payne ref
1347 Dollybat 5a *rear til p.u. 15th*..................M Frith pu
11 ran. 2½l, 15l, 3l, 5l, dist, 2l, 3l. Time 6m 31.50s. SP 5-2.
J E Grey (Berkeley).

1496 Ladies

1333⁵ **FOSBURY ....Miss P Curling** 1
(fav) hld up, prog 11th, ld 16th, comf
1359² **Playpen ....Miss S Crook** 2
slght ld frm 9th til hdd aft 15th, blndrd 16th,kpt on onepce
991⁴ **Jameswick ....Miss A Goschen** 3
hld up in tch, rddn & no response frm 17th
1332³ My Mellow Man (bl) *ld til 9th,in tch til rmdrs & no imp 16th,no ch clsng stgs*..................Miss S Vickery 4
4 ran. 8l, 5l, 5l. Time 6m 31.00s. SP 1-2.
Mrs Susan Humphreys (Cattistock).

1497 Restricted (12st)

1342¹ **FELLOW SIOUX ....I Dowrick** 1
hdwy 9th, cls up til ld 3 out, ran on strgly
1345 **Clandon Lad ....T Mitchell** 2
(fav) prog 11th, cls 3rd & ev ch 4 out, wnt 2nd apr last, no ext
1056 **Stalbridge Gold 5a..............Miss A Goschen** 3
wll in tch 14th, wknd 18th, lft 3rd last
1345⁴ Nearly A Mermaid 5a *ld/disp to 7th, lost plc 15th, no ch frm 3 out* ....R Nuttall 4
1312³ Sherbrooks 3ow *midfld, no ch & jmp lft clsng stgs* ....M Hoskins 5
1392² Palace King (Ire) *just in tch 13th, outpcd frm 15th* ....G Baines 6
1395⁵ Just Donald *keen hold, ld apr 8th til ran out 14th* ....A Honeyball ro
1113 Link Copper *ld/disp til f 8th (ditch)* ..Miss L Blackford f
1345² Caundle Steps *prom, cls 2nd 4 out til aft 2 out,wknng in 3rd whn f last* ....J Tizzard f
1128 And What Else (Ire) *jmp slwly in rear, t.o. p.u. apr 8th* ....B Dixon pu
10 ran. 3l, 15l, 8l, 2l, 3l. Time 6m 35.00s. SP 5-1.
T B Stevens (Devon & Somerset Staghounds).

1498 Open (12st)

1397³ **PINTAIL BAY (v) ....Maj G Wheeler** 1
w.w. in tch, hdwy to 2nd 2 out, ld aft last, pushd clr
1343⁶ **Russell Rover ....L Jefford** 2
lft in ld 7th,disp 9-11th,ld agn 15th til hdd & no ext flat
1343³ **Charmers Wish 5a........................H Thomas** 3

hdwy to disp 9th, ld 12-15th, wknd qckly 2 out
1331 Grey Sonata 5a (bl) *chsd ldr, not fluent, rddn & lost grnd 16th* ....B Dixon 4
1427[5] Horwood Ghost *(fav) ld, hit 2nd, sn clr, slppd up bnd apr 7th* ....R Treloggen su
5 ran. 2l, 4l, 5l. Time 6m 44.00s. SP 3-1.
J C Sweetland (Cotley).

1499 Confined (12st)

1453[6] **TANGLE BARON ....M Felton** 1
ld 13th,drvn clr 2 out,clr whn trd to stop & hit rlls 50yout
1344 **Larky McIlroy 5a ....Miss S Vickery** 2
hndy, chsd wnnr und strng pres 3 out, no real imp
1080[1] **Hensue ....R Treloggen** 3
wnt 3rd 14th, rddn & disp 2nd apr 2 out, onepcd
1393 Strong Breeze 3ex *(Jt fav) ld til 7th, mstk 8th, lost plc, no ch frm hlfwy* ....Mrs R Pocock 4
1406[4] Rapid Rascal 5ex *pullng & sn prom, ld brfly 9th, lost plc 15th* ....Miss S West 5
1228 Bridge Express *(Jt fav) sn bhnd, t.o. frm 12th* ....Miss H Pavey 6
1278 Blue-Bird Express 5a (bl) *prom, ld 11-13th, wknd & reluctant frm 15th, t.o.* ....L Jefford 7
1344[2] Flood Mark *last, outpcd thruout, mstk 13th, p.u. nxt* ....S Mulcaire pu
8 ran. 3l, 10l, 4l, 1l, 6l, 12l. Time 6m 33.00s. SP 7-1.
P J Clarke (Devon & Somerset Staghounds).
G.T.

VALE OF AYLESBURY
Kingston Blount
Saturday May 11th
GOOD

1500 Confined (12st)

1438[3] **CAWKWELL DEAN ....R Sweeting** 1
(fav) made all, drew clr apr last, comf
1436[3] **Tell You What ....N Ridout** 2
prssd wnr to 13th, chal agn 3 out, no ext apr last
1333 **Strong Beau ....L Lay** 3
chsd ldng pair, pshd alng hlfwy, chal 14th, 3rd & btn 2 out
1177[6] Tumble Time *chsd ldng trio, easily outpcd frm 13th, no ch aft* ....Miss H Gosling 4
1289[7] The Holy Golfer *last & well bhnd, t.o. 14th, fin strngly* ....C Smyth 5
886[5] Walkonthemoon 5a *chsg grp, rdn 10th, no ch aft 13th* ....A Martin 6
1177 Wild Fortune *sn pshd alng, chsg grp to 12th, t.o. 14th* ....R Dalgety 7
7 ran. 6l, 1l, 20l, 4l, 8l, dist. Time 6m 27.00s. SP 4-5.
J N Hutchinson (Grafton).

1501 Restricted (12st)

1288[1] **ELITE GOVERNOR (IRE) ....B Hodkin** 1
(fav) made virt all, in cmmnd frm 2 out, easily
1439 **Sporting Lark 5a ....G Tarry** 2
prom, chsd wnr 10th, 3l down last, no imp
1402[3] **Sparnova 5a........R Barrett** 3
mstk 3rd,in tch,effrt 11th,ch whn mstk 15th,wknd aft 2 out
1434[1] Horcum *chsd ldrs, 4th & in tch 13th, same & btn nxt* ....L Lay 4
1238[6] Sutton Lass 5a *chsd wnr to 10th, sn wknd & bhnd* ....R Lawther 5
1371[3] Second Time Round *mstks, bhnd, t.o. & p.u. 9th* ....Capt D Parker pu
1402[5] Henfield *in tch til lost plc & mstk 6th, sn bhnd, t.o. & p.u. last* ....M Turner pu
1217[2] Daring Trouble 5a *raced wd, cls up to 7th, bhnd frm 11th, t.o. & p.u. last* ....R Hicks pu
1374[1] Childsway *hld up bhnd, prog 10th, rdn 12th, sn wknd, p.u. 15th*........T Underwood pu
Fearless Bertie 7a *schoold in last pair, t.o. & p.u. 11th* ....J Trice-Rolph pu
10 ran. 4l, 10l, 12l, 15l. Time 6m 26.00s. SP 7-4.
Paul Gardner (Berks & Bucks Draghounds).

1502 Ladies

1214[2] **SPERRIN VIEW 5a ....Mrs K Sunderland** 1
prom, ld 8th, clr 14th, ran on well, comf
1179[1] **Larry The Lamb ....Miss G Chown** 2
(fav) in tch, chsd wnr 11th, nvr able to chal
1438[3] **Severn Invader ....Miss H Gosling** 3
ld to 2nd, lost plc 5th, 3rd frm 13th, kpt on
1215 Daringly *ld 2-8th, outpcd frm 10th, t.o. 15th* ....Miss D Olding 4
1437[8] Icky's Five (bl) *chsd ldrs, lost tch frm 11th, t.o. 14th* ....Miss T Habgood 5
1288[3] Unscrupulous Gent *sn wll bhnd, t.o. 5th, p.u. 15th* ....Mrs E Huttinger pu
1291[3] Doujas 5a *prom til f 5th*........Mrs B Bloomfield f
7 ran. 8l, 1½l, 1 fence, 15l. Time 6m 19.00s. SP 7-4.
Mrs Katie Sunderland (Bicester With Whaddon Chase).

1503 Open

1375[1] **VALIBUS (FR) ....P Scouller** 1
(fav) made all, drew wll clr 2 out, ran on strngly
1375 **Lucas Court ....S Garrott** 2
chsd wnr 5th, 4l down 15th, btn nxt
1236 **Kelly's Eye (bl)........L Lay** 3
chsd wnr to 5th, rmndrs 11th, no ch frm 13th
3 ran. 15l, 15l. Time 6m 39.00s. SP 8-13.
P A D Scouller (Garth & South Berks).

1504 Open Maiden

1217 **SYBILLABEE 5a ....Daniel Dennis** 1
(fav) rcd wd,cls up,rdn to chs ldr 13th,kpt on to ld last,all out
1164[5] **Nossi Be ....Capt D Parker** 2
s.s. bhnd,prog 9th,poor 3rd aft 13th,styd on,tk 2nd nr fin
1103 **Crestafair 5a ....R Lawther** 3
in tch, prog to ld 8th, clr 13th, wknd 2 out, hdd last,tired
1434 Miss Kenmac 5a *ld 5-8th, prom aft to 13th, sn lost tch & no dang* ....J Trice-Rolph 4
1240[3] Miners Rest 5a *in tch to 12th, wll btn aft nxt, no real prog* ....L Lay 5
1293 Man Of Ice *mstk 6th, bhnd frm 10th, t.o. & p.u. 13th* ....C Coyne pu
1433 Turkish Island 5a *sn mid-div, 9th whn u.r. 9th* ....P Cowley ur
1187 Shining Gem 5a *sn last, t.o. & p.u. 10th* .....B Hodkin pu
1241 Lord Kilton (bl) *cls up to 11th, wknd & p.u. 13th* ....M Cowley pu
1241[2] Mr Wendyl *prom til ran out 4th* ....M Emmanuel ro
1434 Space Molly 5a *made most to 5th, wknd 11th, t.o. 13th, p.u. 15th* ....N Ridout pu
1434 Truly Optimistic 5a *20s-7s, chsng grp, rdn & lost tch 11th, no ch whn f 13th* ....C Wadland f
1055 Cumberland Gap 7a *s.s. schoold rear, blnd 7th, t.o. & p.u. aft 13th*........T McCarthy pu
13 ran. 3½l, 1l, 15l, 2l. Time 6m 32.50s. SP 2-1.
R A Horne (Hursley Hambledon).

1505 Members

885[2] **RADICAL VIEWS ....A Hill** 1
w.w. trckd ldr 9th, ld on innr apr 2 out, sn clr
1329 **Kingofnobles (Ire) ....R Lawther** 2
(fav) ld to 6th,lft in ld apr 9th,wd & hdd apr 2 out,not qckn
1177 **Ramlosa (NZ) ....R Cope** 3
chsd ldrs, pshd alng 7th, outpcd 13th, onepcd aft
885 Polecroft *alwys last, t.o. & u.r. 13th, rmntd, ref last, cont* ....Miss P Hance 4
798 Four Rivers *pllng, ld 6th til u.r. bend apr 9th* ....Miss T Honeyball ur
5 ran. 8l, 15l, Bad. Time 6m 35.00s. SP 7-4.
M A Walter (Vale Of Aylesbury).
J.N.

COTSWOLD VALE FARMERS
Maisemore Park
Sunday May 12th
FIRM

1506 Members

1412[3] **JANUARY DON (bl) ....M FitzGerald** 1
drvn into fences, ld to 5th & aft 9th, clr 5 out, rdn out
1244 **Itsallamatter (Ire) ....P Newth** 2
ld 5th-aft 9th, chsd wnr 14th, btn 3 out
1248 **Flashmans Mistress 5a ....M Davis** 3
jmpd v slwly, t.o. 7th, fence bhnd 14th, fin fast
797 Mansun *n.j.w. prssd wnr aft 9th til blnd 11th, wknd 15th, walked in* ....G Barfoot-Saunt 4
1415 Coolmoreen (Ire) *plng, trckd wnr til f 3rd* .....A Wintle f
5 ran. 25l, 1 fence, 1l. Time 6m 51.50s. SP 4-7.
J S Warner (Cotswold Vale Farmers).

1507 Confined (12st)

1243[1] **LANDSKER ALFRED 3ex ....Miss A Dare** 1
(fav) in tch, prog 9th, ld 12th, clr 3 out, comf
1332 **Hook Line'N'sinker ....L Brown** 2
w.w. prog to jn wnr 12-14th, rdn & no imp aft 3 out
1212[2] **Bumptious Boy ....S Hanks** 3
chsd ldrs, outpcd & lft 3rd aft 13th, mstk 3 out, t.o.
1247[3] Its All Over Now *chsd ldrs, outpcd aft 12th, no ch aft, t.o.* ....D Renney 4
1264 Emerald Gem (bl) *chsd ldr 2-9th, outpcd frm 12th, t.o.* ....H Wheeler 5
1314[7] Punching Glory *bhnd whn nrly u.r. 3rd, t.o. 9th* ....Miss S Brewer 6
1412[2] Space Mariner 5ex *bhnd frm 5th, t.o. 9th*...G Barfoot-Saunt 7
1332 Springfield Lad 3ex *alwys last & bhnd, t.o. 8th* ....Miss E Walker 8
1247 Devils Elbow *sn clr, blnd 4th, hdd 12th, 3rd & wkng whn s.u. bnd aft 13th*..........................T Cox su
1436 Dixons Homefinder 2ow *chsd ldr to 2nd,mstk 4th,strgglng frm 7th,t.o. 9th,p.u.3 out*........A Barnett pu
10 ran. 6l, dist, 15l, 3l, 15l, ½l, 25l. Time 6m 33.70s. SP 2-5.
Dr P P Brown & Mrs S Birks (Berkeley).

1508 Ladies

1415[3] **CANTANTIVY 5a 2ow ....Miss S Jackson** 1
2nd brfly 9th,poor 3rd frm 12th,styd on 3 out,lft in ld last
1316[2] **Dauphin Bleu (Fr) ....Miss V Roberts** 2
(fav) mstks,ld 3rd,sn clr,dist up whn f last,rmntd,just faild
1439[8] **River Galaxy ....Miss S Duckett** 3
chsd ldr aft 9th,no imp, lft ev ch last, wknd, dead
1245[2] Tudor Henry *ld to 3rd, mstk nxt, wknd 9th, sn t.o.* ....Mrs C Mitchell 4
1387[3] Afaristoun (Fr) *chsng grp, wknd 10th, poor 4th whn f 13th*..................................Miss J Morse f
1455 Gan Awry 5a *blnd 4th, last aft, t.o. & p.u. 13th* ....Miss S Wallin pu
6 ran. 1l, 4l, 25l. Time 6m 33.80s. SP 14-1.
T N Bailey (North Hereford).

1509 Open (12st)

1220[2] **BARON'S HEIR ....S Lloyd** 1
3rd/4th til chsd clr ldr 15th, styd on to ld flat, sn clr
1220 **Enchanted Man ....A Dalton** 2
chsd ldr, ld aft 9th, clr 15th, wknd & hdd aft last
1246 Viascorit *ld to aft 9th, last frm 12th, t.o. & p.u. 15th* ....R Hawker pu
1171[1] Sharinski 4ex *(fav) cls up, wth ldr 11-13th, wknd frm nxt, t.o. & p.u. last*..........................M Jackson pu
4 ran. 2l. Time 6m 40.50s. SP 6-1.
Mrs J L Livermore (Llangibby).

1510 P P O R A (12st)

1216[2] **GUITING GRAY ....Miss A Dare** 1
(fav) made all, blnd 12th, wll clr nxt, mstk 14th, imprssv
1314[1] **The Rum Mariner ....J Jukes** 2
4s-9/4, sn chsng wnr, 10l down 12th, lost tch frm nxt
1169[4] **Tytherington ....M Hammond** 3
chsd ldng pair 3rd, no ch aft 13th, plggd on
994[1] Espy *rear, rmndr 5th, rdn 10th, last & no ch whn p.u. aft 15th* ....A James pu
1437 Mirpur 4ex *mstk 6th, t.o. last whn ref 9th* ....Miss C Spearing ref
1313[1] Not Mistaken *mstk 4th, 4th whn u.r. 8th* ....Miss S Vickery ur
1173[9] Really An Angel 5a *t.o. til u.r. 7th* ....Mrs K Bevan ur
1347 Noble Minister *in tch, 4th whn s.u. bend apr 7th* ....M Wells su
8 ran. Dist, 5l. Time 6m 22.30s. SP 11-8.
A M Mason (V.W.H.).

1511 Open Maiden (12st)

1293[3] **POCKET PEST 5a......................G Baines** 1
alwys 1st trio, chsd ldr 3 out, ld & lft clr last, rdn out
1217[7] **Duques 5a ....C Wadland** 2
mstk 3rd, mid-div, prog 12th, 3rd 2 out,lft 2nd last, kpt on
Mondino ....L Lay 3
mstk 7th & rdr lost iron, rear til kpt on frm 14th, fin well
1270 Aldington Kid *mstks, ld to aft 15th, grad wknd* ....L Stephens 4
1381[7] Matchlessly *chsd ldrs to 11th, sn strgglng* ....Miss E Walker 5
1248[4] Royal Swinger 5a *alwys last trio, t.o. & p.u. 14th* ....Dr P Pritchard pu
1391[5] Agapanthus 5a *chsd ldrs to 10th, sn lost tch, t.o. & p.u. last*..................................S Lloyd pu
711[3] Is She Quick 5a *10s-6s, alwys rear, no ch frm 14th, t.o. & p.u. last* ....G Barfoot-Saunt pu
1293[2] Miss Corinthian 5a *prom,mstk 12th,ld aft 15th,clr apr 2 out,hdd & ref last,lame* ....M Flynn ref
848[2] Charles Quaker *(fav) mid-div, prog to 4th at 11th til p.u. in tch at 15th, dsmntd*.......................J Jukes pu
60 Daphni (Fr) 7a *alwys well in rear, t.o. & p.u. 15th* ....E James pu
1272 Bonus Number (Ire) *sn last, t.o. & p.u.11th* ....A Price pu
1244 Nicolinsky 5a *trckd ldrs til nrly ran off course & p.u. bef 6th* ....Julian Pritchard pu
Chism (Ire) 7a *schoold & bhnd, some prog 8th, nvr rchd ldrs, p.u. 15th*..........................M Miller pu
14 ran. 4l, 12l, 1l, 6l. Time 6m 42.00s. SP 5-1.
Ms S West (Berks & Bucks Draghounds).
J.N.

HAYDON
Hexham Point-To-Point Course
Sunday May 12th
HEAVY

1512 Members (12st)

911[9] **MILL KNOCK ....J Thompson** 1
(fav) trckd ldr 6th, ld apr 10th, grad drew clr, canter
Raffles ....Miss S Walton 2
jmpd rght, ld to 5th, 3rd frm nxt, t.o. 9th, 2nd agn 3 out
1254 **Amanda Bay ....Miss T Hammond** 3
ld 5th til apr 10th, grad lost tch wth wnr, demoted 3 out
862 Mordington Lass 5a *last frm 3rd, t.o. frm 5th* ....Miss V Burn 4
862 Willy Waffles (Ire) *last whn blnd & u.r. 3rd* ....Miss M Blakey ur
Larkin Girl 5a *jmpd badly rght, bhnd til u.r. 6th* ....Miss J Martin ur
6 ran. 2 fences, 4l, 2 fences. Time 8m 10.60s. SP 6-4.
J D Thompson (North Tyne).

1513 Confined (12st)

1351[1] **TODCRAG 6ex............................T Scott** 1

(fav) ld/disp til ld 3 out, clr whn jmpd rght last 2, rdn & ran on
1351 **Buckle It Up 3ex ....R Hale** **2**
ld/disp til apr 3 out, blnd badly nxt, rallied last, one-pcd
1251 **Sharp Opinion 6ex ....Miss P Robson** **3**
trckd ldrs going wll, 3rd & outpcd 3 out, no ch frm nxt
911² Master Mischief *nvr going wll, wll bhnd frm 7th, nvr dang* ....J Walton 4
911⁷ Just Maskaraider *last frm 4th, t.o. & p.u. 6th* ....Mrs H Dickson pu
1351 Dancing Legend (Ire) *trckd ldrs til lost tch 14th, last & reluc 16th, p.u. 2 out* ....T Oates pu
6 ran. 6l, 25l, 1l. Time 7m 46.20s. SP 4-5.
Mrs D Scott (Border).

1514 Restricted (12st)

1340 **WIRE LASS 5a ....R Morgan** **1**
10s-5s, ld/disp til ld 3 out, jmpd lft last, rdn out
1249⁵ **Sarona Smith 5a 4ow ....J Walton** **2**
ld til aft 1st, disp 7-9th, mstk 16th, ev ch 3 out, one-pcd
1461⁹ **Tolmin ....P Forster** **3**
jmpd slwly 1st, disp 11th-3 out, onepcd und pres aft
Hunting Country *blnd 3rd, lost tch apr 9th, p.u. nxt* ....T Scott pu
1340² Royal Surprise *(fav) disp aft 2nd, blnd nxt, blnd & u.r. 5th* ....Miss P Robson ur
5 ran. 2½l, 2½l. Time 8m 13.00s. SP 5-1.
Mrs M Armstrong (Tynedale).

1515 Open

1340 **DEDAY ....M Bradburne** **1**
j.w. made all, drew clr apr 3 out, easily
1304¹ **Father Liam ....M Appleyard** **2**
(fav) chsd wnr 5-8th & 13-16th & apr 2 out, no imp
1363² **South Stack ....R Ford** **3**
bhnd,rdn 14th,no prog,p.u. 2 out, cont, blnd last, walked in
1351⁶ Dawn Coyote (USA) (bl) *in tch, rdn apr 3 out, 2nd whn blnd 3 out, wknd rpdly, p.u.* ....R Hale pu
487 Little General *33s-10s, in tch, 2nd apr 3 out, sn wknd, no ch & p.u. last* ....A Robson pu
1133 Fast Study *chsd wnr to 5th & frm 8th til blnd 11th, p.u. nxt* ....S Robinson pu
6 ran. 30l, 2 fences. Time 8m 0.00s. SP 5-1.
Mrs H O Graham (Jedforest).

1516 Ladies

1010¹ **CHOCTAW ....Mrs A Farrell** **1**
(fav) reluc to line up, disp til ld 13th, grad drew clr
Hawaiian Prince ....Miss T Hammond **2**
disp, blnd 7th, hit 12th, outpcd frm nxt
2 ran. 1 fence. Time 8m 17.00s. SP 1-10.
Mrs Anthea L Farrell (Middleton).

1517 Maiden (12st)

1353 **MURDER MOSS (IRE) ....M Ruddy** **1**
in tch, ld 2 out, styd on
1253⁹ **Terracotta Warrior ....N Wilson** **2**
in tch, lost plc & rdn 13th, rallied & ev ch 3 out, one-pcd
1253² **Nothingtotellme (Ire) 7a ....A Parker** **3**
(fav) trckd ldrs going wll, ld 3 out, rdn & hdd nxt, wknd
1254 Kings Token *wll bhnd, steady prog to 2nd 3 out, no ext frm nxt* ....J Walton 4
1355 April Cracker 5a *chsd ldrs to 8th, wll bhnd 10th, p.u. 12th* ....Mrs W Nichol pu
1364 Authenticity (Ire) 5a *w.w. prog to 2nd aft 14th, blnd 16th, sn wknd, p.u. nxt* ....Miss C Burgess pu
1254 Mapalak 5a *t.d.e. in tch, wknd apr 3 out, p.u. 2 out* ....T Scott pu
316⁴ Sally Smith 5a *wll bhnd frm 6th, blnd 13th, t.o. & p.u. 2 out* ....Miss J Percy pu
915 The Camair Flyer (Ire) *disp ld til ld 11th, hdd 3 out, 5th & wll btn whn f nxt* ....P Forster f
1450 Cookie Boy 7a *ld/disp to 10th, ev ch til wknd apr 3 out, p.u. 2 out* ....Miss H Delahooke pu
10 ran. 5l, ½l, ½l. Time 8m 3.60s. SP 10-1.
S Coltherd (Buccleuch).
S.P.

QUORN
Garthorpe
Sunday May 12th
GOOD TO FIRM

1518 Members (12st)

1378¹ **DARK RHYTHAM 3ex ....S Morris** **1**
(Jt fav) made all, set str pace, ran on wll und pres 2 out
1302 **Merlins Girl 5a 3ex.......................T Lane** **2**
chsd ldrs, alwys 2nd/3rd, lft 2nd 3 out, ran on
1377 **Monk's Mistake 3ex ....Miss S Bonser** **3**
rear frm 3rd, outpcd, nvr dang
1333 Rehab Venture *wll in tch to 9th, wknd & p.u. 12th* ....D Esden pu
1239⁷ Tel D'Or (bl) *rear, t.o. 9th, p.u. 13th* ....P Millington pu
723⁹ Henry Darling 3ex *(Jt fav) chsd ldr, mostly 2nd, cls up but lkd hld whn f 2 out* ....E Andrewes f
6 ran. 4l, dist. Time 6m 27.00s. SP 7-4.
G Coombe (Quorn).

1519 Open

1379 **COOLVAWN LADY (IRE) 5a...............T Lane** **1**
(fav) cls up, ld 7th & frm 10th, sn in cmnd, ran on
1238³ **Okeetee ....S R Andrews** **2**
ld to 6th, cls up, tk 2nd 10th, not qckn cls home
1379¹ **Raise An Argument ....J Docker** **3**
prom, ld 8-9th, n.j.w. frm hlfwy, onepcd frm 3 out
1400⁴ Kellys Pal (bl) *mid-div, f heavily 3rd* .....P Millington f
1400 Pike's Glory (bl) *rear to 5th, t.o. & p.u. 8th* . .M Barnard pu
1098 Blue Beat 5a *cls up to 6th, lost tch 13th, p.u. 4 out* ....M Hewitt pu
1379² Falconbridge Bay *rear, clsd on ldrs 11th, 4th & hld whn p.u. 2 out, lame* ....R Armson pu
7 ran. 15l, 10l. Time 6m 19.00s. SP Evens.
W R Halliday (Cranwell Bloodhounds).
Fence 11 omitted, 17 jumps.

1520 Ladies

1305¹ **NOWHISKI ....Miss C Tarratt** **1**
cls 3rd to 12th, 2nd nxt, ld apr last, ran on well
1443¹ **Adamare ....Miss C Holliday** **2**
2nd til ld 5th, in cmmnd til ct apr last, not qckn
1377 **Sanamar ....Mrs C McCarthy** **3**
alwys 4th & just in tch, lft 3rd 3 out
1377⁷ Loose Wheels (v) *rear 5th, nvr nr to chal* ....Miss K Makinson 4
1379⁴ Shipmate *t.o. 12th, ran on own pace* ....Miss H Walsgrove 5
1377⁶ Chiasso Forte (Ity) (bl) *mid to rear, u.r. 6th* ....Mrs P Adams ur
1238¹ General Highway *(fav) ld to 4th, disp 2n/3rd til hit 15th, p.u. lame nxt* ....Mrs J Dawson pu
1259⁴ Gilson's Cove *mid-div whn u.r. 6th* .....Miss L Rowe ur
8 ran. 1l, dist, dist, 10l. Time 6m 17.00s. SP 8-1.
Tim Tarratt (Cottesmore).

1521 Intermediate

1302 **THE DIFFERENCE ....M Chatterton** **1**
ld to 2nd, hld up, prog 3 out, disp nxt, ld last, ran on wll
1257¹ **Stanwick Farlap 5a ....T Marks** **2**
(fav) cls up, ld 4th til ct last, ran on onepcd
1176⁴ **Alias Silver ....Miss H Irving** **3**
prom, ld 3rd-4th, disp 5-6th, outpcd frm 3 out
346 Smart Pal *mid to rear, nvr on terms wth ldrs, not qckn.* ....K Needham 4

1237^{4} Decent Gold *mid to rear, no ext whn asked to qckn 4 out* ....J Stephenson 5
1328^{3} Game Set *chsng grp, 4th at 9th, lost tch apr 12th, onepcd* ....A Sansome 6
1068^{2} Russian Vision (bl) *mid-div, mstk 3rd, chal whn mstk 11th, sn btn, p.u. 3 out* ....C Ward-Thomas pu
7 ran. 4l, 8l, 6l. Time 6m 28.00s. SP 8-1.
M G Chatterton (Belvoir).

1522 Restricted (12st)

1380^{6} **MAJESTIC RIDE ....R Armson** 1
w.w. rear, grad prog to 3rd 3 out, 20l 3rd whn lft clr last
1178^{4} **Spartan's Saint ....G Tarry** 2
mid-div, running on onepcd & no ch whn lft 2nd last
1302^{3} **Tempered Point (USA) ....T Lane** 3
chsd ldrs, ev ch til wknd 4 out, lft 3rd last, not qckn
1256^{2} Kerry My Home (bl) *mid to rear, nrst fin, nvr dang* ....T Marks 4
1303 Odysseus *ld/disp to 4th, cls up til outpcd 4 out, sn btn* ....E Andrewes 5
1240^{1} Mr Gee *ld/disp til ld 4th,hdd 7th, disp 3 out, going wll whn f last* ....L Hicks f
1284 Sharp To Oblige *chsd ldrs, prog 3 out, upsides whn f last* ....S Swiers f
1217^{1} Eighty Eight *mid-div going wll whn u.r. 12th* E Walker ur
1462 R N Commander *mid-div, outpcd frm 13th, t.o. & p.u. 4 out* ....J Cornwall pu
1101^{3} Hill Fort (Ire) (bl) *(fav) cls up, ld 8-12th, wknd rpdly, p.u. 3 out*..B Pollock pu
1102^{8} Menature (Ire) *prom, ld 14th, disp whn f nxt* . . J Seth-Smith f
618 Gayton Wilds *s.s. ref 1st* ....C Ward-Thomas ref
12 ran. 10l, 6l, dist, 12l. Time 6m 26.00s. SP 14-1.
Rob Woods (Cranwell Bloodhounds).

1523 Open Maiden (12st)

1196 **SARGEANTS CHOICE ....J Barlow** 1
ld/disp til lft clr 11th, ran on well, drew clr apr 3 out
1381 **Full Song 5a...............................S Morris** 2
chsd ldrs, alwys cls up, ev ch 4 out, not qckn
617^{3} **Cruise Free ....B Pollock** 3
rear, prog & cls up 4 out, not rch wnr
1378 Broadnote 5a *alwys cls up, mstks, ran on onepcd frm 3 out* ....S R Andrews 4
1403 Stanwick Lass 5a (bl) *(fav) prom, 4th at 8th, 3rd frm 10th til wknd 4 out* ....T Marks 5
1301 Rallye Stripe *s.s. prog & cls up 12th, sn btn, p.u. 4 out* ....S Allen pu
1326 Late Start 5a *s.s. rear, t.o. & p.u. 14th* . . . .P Andrew pu
1315 Secret Truth 5a *ld/disp at gd pace til u.r. 11th (ditch)* ....A Martin ur
1329 Forever Freddy *cls up, 2nd at 12th, 3l 2nd & lkd hld whn f 2 out* ....G Brewer f
1434 Midnight Runner 5a *mid to rear, no ch whn p.u. 13th* ....R Armson pu
The Birdie Song 5a *mid to rear, no prog whn f 11th* ....A Sansome f
11 ran. 8l, 6l, 6l. Time 6m 31.00s. SP 5-1.
John Sargeant (Albrighton).
V.S.

SOUTH DEVON
Ottery St Mary
Sunday May 12th
GOOD TO FIRM

1524 Members

1426^{2} **MISTRESS ROSIE 5a ....I Widdicombe** 1
(fav) cls up, slght ld 14th, disp nxt til forged clr apr last
1349 **St Morwenna 5a ....J Creighton** 2
plld hrd,made most to 14th, disp & ev ch til no ext apr last
1143 **Tacoment 5a ....S Hornby** 3
keen hld, prom til outpcd 15th, bhnd whn blnd 2 out
3 ran. 2l, 4l. Time 6m 34.50s. SP 2-5.
Martin Hill (South Devon).

1525 Confined (12st)

1342^{2} **FRIENDLY LADY 5a..................Miss A Bush** 1
in tch, cls 3rd 3 out, ld apr last, drew clr
1343^{4} **Departure 5a ....J Creighton** 2
handy, ld 16th, hdd aft 2 out, no ext
1427^{1} **Fearsome 8ex ....G Penfold** 3
alwys prom, cls 3rd & ev ch 2 out, just outpcd
1343^{5} Winter's Lane *hld up, some prog to 4th 3 out, nvr dang* ....Miss P Curling 4
1361^{3} Catch The Cross (bl) *rear, some late prog, nvr nr to chal* ....Mrs M Hand 5
1361 Christmas Hols *twrds rear frm hlfwy* Miss L Blackford 6
1142^{4} Shalchlo Boy *ld til hdd & wknd rpdly 12th, t.o. 16th* ....D Stephens 7
1142 Poacher's Delight *(fav) 4s-2s, chsd ldr til ld 13th, blnd & lost plc 16th, f nxt* ....L Jefford f
1357^{1} Sydney Boon 7a *in tch, mstk 12th, lost plc, t.o. & p.u. 2 out*..R Darke pu
9 ran. 5l, 2l, 10l, 3l, 4l, 25l. Time 6m 2.00s. SP 4-1.
J Grant Cann (Devon & Somerset Staghounds).

1526 Ladies

1331^{5} **FLAME O'FRENSI 5a............Miss J Cumings** 1
made all, j.w. ran on gamely
1247^{2} **Desert Waltz (Ire) ....Miss P Curling** 2
(fav) hld up, prog & rdn 15th, cls 2nd & ev ch 2 out, no ext
1454^{5} **Chandigarh ....Miss K Baily** 3
prom, disp 2nd mostly, ev ch til no ext aft 3 out
1361^{5} Christmas Bash 5a *in tch til outpcd 15th* Miss A Lamb 4
1346 Be My Habitat (bl) *not fluent, sn bhnd, t.o.* ....Miss L Hawkings 5
5 ran. 2l, 10l, 8l, dist. Time 5m 54.00s. SP 6-4.
P J Clarke (Devon & Somerset Staghounds).

1527 Restricted Div I (12st)

1395 **SEAHAWK RETRIEVER ....T Mitchell** 1
(fav) prom, went 2nd 15th, ld nxt, drew clr 2 out, easily
1342^{3} **Dinkies Quest 5a ....Miss L Blackford** 2
cls 5th hlfwy, went 3rd 3 out, ran on to tk 2nd nr fin
1456^{5} **Otter Mill....................................J Jukes** 3
ld 1st & agn 9-16th, sn rdn & no ext
1428^{5} Sunwind *plld hrd, ld 2nd til mstk 9th, lost ground frm 15th* ....C Heard 4
1349 Fosabud *twrds rear, bhnd frm 14th* . . . . .M Sweetland 5
313 Talk Sence (Ire) *alwys rear* ....G Penfold 6
1396^{5} Royal Turn *alwys last, t.o. hlfwy* . . . . .A Honeyball 7
1128 Ower Farm 5a *n.j.w. in tch til 14th, bhnd whn ref 16th* ....D Dennis ref
8 ran. 15l, 1l, 6l, dist, 5l, dist. Time 6m 5.50s. SP 6-4.
H B Geddes (Berkeley).

1528 Restricted Div II (12st)

1345^{6} **BIG SEAMUS (IRE) (bl)................J Creighton** 1
handy, cls 3rd frm 9th, effrt 2 out, ld last, drvn clr
1274^{1} **Mountain Master ....Miss L Blackford** 2
in tch, 4th whn hit 16th, prog & ev ch 2 out, onepcd
1128 **Just Silver (bl) ....R Wakeham** 3
alwys prom, lft in ld 3 out, hdd last, collapsed & died aft
1069^{7} Oneovertheight *mid-div, plenty to do 15th, styd on wll clsng stgs* ....N Harris 4
1428 Gypsy Luck 5a *mid-div, 5th at 13th, not able to chal* ....Miss J Cumings 5
1358^{2} Mutual Agreement 5a *rear frm hlfwy, blnd 14th, t.o.* ....R Darke 6
1428^{3} Dovedon Princess 5a *bhnd frm 13th, t.o.* . .D Stephens 7
1358 Snuggle 5a *bhnd til p.u. apr 12th, dead* . . . . . . .T Cole pu
549 Mac's Boy *(fav) not alwys fluent, tried to make all, clr whn blnd & u.r.3out* ....J Jukes ur
1056^{2} Final Express 5a *alwys rear, t.o. & p.u. 4 out* ....M Hoskins pu
10 ran. 5l, ½l, 1½l, 10l, 2l, dist. Time 6m 4.00s. SP 12-1.
Mrs J M Whitley (Dartmoor).

1529 Open (12st)

1111 **BARGAIN AND SALE ... T Greed** 1
ld aft 2nd til 3 out, rallied to disp nxt, ld last,drvn clr
1427 **Gymcrak Dawn ... S Slade** 2
trckd ldr til ld 3 out, disp nxt, ev ch til no ext last
1333 **Prince Soloman ... L Jefford** 3
3rd & rdn 15th, outpcd
1361[4] Glenform *mid-div, 5th at 13th, nvr dang* ... T Cole 4
1199[3] Electrolyte (bl) *ld til jmpd slwly 2nd, ran in sntchs, no ch frm 15th* ... G Austin 5
1360[2] Bluechipenterprise 5a 7ex *(fav) just in tch til jmpd slwly 13th, reluc, bhnd & p.u. 15th* ... R Darke pu
1425[2] Magnolia Man *alwys last & nvr going wll, p.u. 13th* ... N Harris pu
7 ran. 2l, 20l, 3l, 10l. Time 6m 5.00s. SP 16-1.
D J Minty (Dulverton).

1530 Open Maiden Div I (12st)

1431 **GOOD APPEAL 5a ... Miss L Blackford** 1
prom til ld 15th, lft clr last
1276 **Happy Thought 5a ... N Harris** 2
in tch, 3rd & rdn 15th, wll btn whn lft 2nd last
1348[4] **Here's Mary 5a ... G Penfold** 3
mstk 6th, rear & rmndrs 11th, wll btn frm 15th
1143 Spartans Dina 7a *plld hrd, ld & sn clr, hdd 15th, sn wknd* ... T Cole 4
1347[4] Jolly Sensible 5a *(fav) not fluent, prog 6th, 3rd whn hit 12th, p.u. nxt* ... J Creighton pu
1280[3] Polly's Corner 5a *mid-div, 4th whn f 13th* ... R Emmett f
Check On Tessa 5a *s.s. schoold & well bhnd, blnd & u.r. 7th* ... D Stephens ur
1279 Trolly 7a *rear,hit 11th,bhnd 15th,ran on to 2nd 2 out,2l 2nd f last* ... S Kidston f
8 ran. 25l, 20l, 20l. Time 6m 8.50s. SP 100-30.
Roy Bolitho (Silverton).

1531 Open Maiden Div II (12st)

1431 **AVIN FUN BAR 5a ... T Greed** 1
made all, styd on wll clsng stgs
1430[3] **Big Reward ... K Crook** 2
prom, mstk 7th, 4th & rdn 15th, went 2nd 3 out, one-pcd
1278 **I Like The Deal 7a ... S Slade** 3
bhnd til prog 14th, ran on to 3rd 2 out, promising
Kenstown (Ire) *mid-div, 5th at 14th, prog aft 3 out, should improve* ... G Penfold 4
1129 Old Harry's Wife 5a *(fav) mstks, 2nd whn blnd 15th, no ch frm nxt* ... D Dennis 5
1429[4] Ashcombe Valley *cls up, rmndrs 13th, went 2nd 16th, sn wknd* ... Miss L Blackford 6
1357[3] Baashful Blaze 5a *n.j.w. alwys rear* ... A Holdsworth 7
993 Young Tiger *6th hlfwy, wkng whn mstk 14th, wll btn 4 out* ... S Parfimowicz 8
Haven *last whn ref 1st* ... R Wakeham ref
9 ran. 4l, 8l, 2½l, 2l, 5l, 8l, 15l. Time 6m 19.50s. SP 9-2.
Mrs S M Trump (East Devon).
G.T.

TOWCESTER
Monday May 13th
GOOD TO FIRM

1532 2m 110yds Larry Connell Memorial Hunters' Chase Class H

1383[1] **BEAU DANDY 11.9 7a ... Mr T Marks** 1
(fav) ld 4th to four out, rallied to ld 100 yards out, edged right, ran on.
1346[2] **Great Pokey 11.6 7a ... Miss N Courtenay** 2
alwys prom, ld 3rd to 4th, led apr 2 out till final 100 yards.
1455[1] **King Of Shadows 11.9 7a ... Mr S Prior** 3
alwys prom, ev ch apr 2 out, ran on one pace.
1435 Social Climber 11.6 7a *alwys prom, rdn 3 out, one pace from 2 out* ... Mr L Lay 4
1339[5] Al Hashimi 11.6 7a *hdwy 3 out, nvr near to chal.* ... Mr N Ridout 5
1327[3] Knockumshin 11.8 5a *hdwy apr 2 out, nvr on terms.* ... Mr T Byrne 6
1336[3] Pastoral Pride (USA) 11.8 5a *ld 2nd to 3rd, led 4 out till wknd apr 2 out.* ... Miss P Curling 7
1014[4] Cardan 11.6 7a *nvr better than mid div.* .. Mr R Darke 8
1226[3] Southern Minstrel 12.2 *prom early, not trbl ldrs from 6th.* ... Mr S Swiers 9
1339 Brown Baby 11.1 7a *well bhnd from 6th, t.o..* ... Mr P Scott 10
1379[6] Blue Aeroplane 11.8 5a *ld to 2nd, wknd 5th, t.o..* ... Mr A Sansome 11
1227[8] Afaltoun 11.6 7a *outpcd, t.o. when p.u. before 2 out.* ... Mr T Lacey pu
768 Mummy's Song 11.6 7a *mid div when f 2 out.* ... Mr M Lewis f
798 Rah Wan (USA) 11.8 5a *hdwy 6th, 7th when mstk and wknd 4 out, p.u. before 2 out* ... Mr C Vigors pu
1336[4] Knowing 11.1 7a *soon well bhnd, t.o. when p.u. before 2 out* ... Miss E James pu
1333 Dannigale 12.1 7a 9ow *soon t.o., p.u. before 2 out.* ... Mr E Haddock pu
16 ran. 1½l, 2l, 5l, 1¾l, 2½l, 9l, 1l, sht-hd, 20l, 30l. Time 4m 7.30s. SP 11-4.
C C Shand Kydd

CHEPSTOW
Tuesday May 14th
FIRM

1533 3m Jorrocks Novices' Hunters' Chase Class H

1453[1] **THE JOGGER 11.12 7a ... Mr J Tizzard** 1
(fav) trckd ldr, rdn and held when left clr 3 out, ridden when mstk last, all out.
1335[2] **Clobracken Lad 11.7 7a ... Mr G Baines** 2
in rear, hdwy 5 out, styd on to go 2nd apr last, kept on run-in.
1332[4] **Paper Days 11.9 5a ... Mr S Bush** 3
trckd ldrs, disp ld apr 8th, lost pl 11th, rallied 3 out, kept on.
1246[1] Gee Double You 11.7 7a *prom, mstk 3rd, ld after 7th, mistakes 12th and 13th, blnd and u.r. 3 out.* ... Mr B Tulloch ur
1393[3] Highway Jim 11.7 7a *pulld hrd, prom when hit 9th, wknd next, blnd and u.r. 4 out..* ... Mr P King ur
1267[2] Antarctic Call 11.8 7a 1ow *ld till hdd after 7th, wknd 10th, bhnd when blnd and u.r. 4 out..* .. Mr C Richards ur
6 ran. 1l, 2½l. Time 6m 2.90s. SP 13-8.
Mrs P Tizzard

HEREFORD
Wednesday May 15th
FIRM

1534 3m 1f 110yds Brockhampton Hunters' Chase Class H

1333[4] **WELSH LEGION 12.2 5a ... Mr M Rimell** 1
alwys prom, ld 12th, rdn out.
1327[1] **Wild Illusion 12.0 7a ... Mr Richard White** 2
(fav) alwys prom, rdn apr 4 out, styd on run-in.
1459[2] **Rusty Bridge 12.0 7a ... Mr R Thornton** 3
ld to 12th, outpcd 14th, styd on again from 3 out.
1292[2] Hizal 11.7 7a *whipped round start, alwys well bhnd, t.o. when p.u. before 12th.* ... Mr A Charles-Jones pu
4 ran. 2½l, 5l. Time 6m 26.70s. SP 3-1.
G W Lewis

AINTREE
Thursday May 16th
GOOD TO FIRM

1535 3m 1f Aintree Novices' Hunters' Chase Class H

1302[1] **SYD GREEN (IRE) 11.7 7a............Mr S Walker** 1
keen hold, midfield, hdwy 7th, ld 10th, mstk and hdd 14th, left in ld next, soon clr, easily.
1377[2] **Whinstone Mill 11.7 7a...........Mr R Thornton** 2
rear, mstk 7th, hdwy 12th, und pres and chasing ldrs 4 out, went 2nd 2 out, no impn on wnr.
1340[4] **Stilltodo 11.2 7a....................Mr A Parker** 3
prom, ld apr 8th to 10th, hit next, struggling to go pace 15th.
1338[5] Gen-Tech 11.7 7a *midfield, lost pl 5th, struggling final cct.* ....Mr A Gribbin 4
1456[1] Freddie Fox 11.12 7a *held up, hmpd 4th, reminders 8th, pushed along and hdwy 11th, wknd 13th, t.o..* ....Mr T Garton 5
1422[3] Duke Of Impney 11.7 7a *held up, hdwy into midfield when f 12th.* ....Mr A Dalton f
1233[6] Rinky Dinky Doo 11.8 7a 1ow (bl) *ld till apr 8th, reminders 10th, mstk next, soon wknd, t.o. when mistake 13th, p.u. before next.* ....Mr C J B Barlow pu
1457[6] Orton House 11.7 7a *trckd ldrs, wknd 12th, t.o. when blnd and u.r. 2 out.* ....Mr R Burton ur
1458 Gray Rosette 11.6 3a *soon bhnd, lost tch final cct, t.o. when p.u. before 3 out.* ....Mr J Culloty pu
1340[1] Kenilworth (Ire) 11.12 7a *(fav) midfield, cld 8th, ld 14th, f next.* ....Mr C Mulhall f
1457 Costermonger 11.7 7a (bl) *trckd ldr, mstk 3rd, f next.* ....Mr A Griffith f

11 ran. 21l, 21l, 9l, 30l. Time 6m 39.80s. SP 5-1.
P M Hodges

FOLKESTONE
Thursday May 16th
GOOD TO FIRM

1536 2m 5f Pett Farm Equestrian Services Challenge Cup Maiden Hunters' Chase Class H

1453 **TOM FURZE 12.0 7a...............Mr R Nuttall** 1
ld to 10th, mstk next, led last, driven clr.
1444[2] **Berrings Dasher 12.0 7a............Mr A Welsh** 2
(fav) mid div, went 2nd 8th, ld 10th, hdd last, wknd run-in.
921 **Bubbles Galore (Ire) 11.9 5a......Mr T McCarthy** 3
mstks, held up, prog into 3rd 11th, kept on from 2 out.
1440 Alzamina 11.9 7a *bhnd, some prog 8th, no ch from 10th.* ....Mr P O'Keeffe 4
1441[1] Basher Bill 12.0 7a *cl up, reminders 7th, lost pl next, t.o..* ....Mrs E Coveney 5
1442 Beach Tiger 12.0 7a *mid div, prog to chase ldrs 9th, lost tch 11th, t.o. when p.u. before last.* ......Mr T Hills pu
1504 Man Of Ice 12.0 7a *cl up, jmpd left 6th, wknd 9th, bhnd when p.u. before 3 out.* ....Mr C Coyne pu
1440[1] Rustic Ramble 12.4 3a *waited with, rdn and no response 9th, no ch when p.u. before 2 out.* ....Mr P Hacking pu
1174[2] Ted's Knight (Ire) 11.7 7a *in tch to 8th, bhnd when p.u. before 13th, saddle slpd.* ....Mr A Phillips pu

9 ran. 7l, 4l, 18l, 24l. Time 5m 27.80s. SP 12-1.
R A Horne

1537 3¼m Eurocharing Novices' Hunters' Chase Class H for the Guy Peate Memorial Challenge Trophy

1440[2] **STEDE QUARTER 12.0 7a.........Mr P Hickman** 1
ld after 5th to 2 out, rallied gamely to ld run-in.
1329 **Rolleston Blade 12.0 7a ....Mr P Bull** 2
ld 1st till after 3rd, chsd ldr 10th to 12th and again 16th, led 2 out, hdd and one pace run-in.
1399[2] **Salmon River (USA) 11.7 7a.........Mr R Wakley** 3
held up, mstk 2nd, prog to chase ldr 13th, one pace next.
1442[1] Tau 12.0 7a *in tch till pushed along and outpcd 16th.* ....Mr A Warr 4
1443[4] Bright Hour 12.0 7a *bhnd 7th, prog 11th, outpcd apr 3 out.* ....Mr M Gorman 5
1188[3] Transplant Blue 12.0 7a *(fav) ld after 3rd till after 5th, lost pl quickly 12th, p.u. before next, broke blood vessel.* ....Mr S Goodings pu
1295[2] Manaolana 11.9 7a *mstks, ld to 1st, in tch till wknd 15th, no ch when ref 3 out.* ....Mr G Hopper ref
1206 True Measure 11.9 7a *in tch, last and struggling when f 13th.* ....Mr A Welsh f

8 ran. 1¼l, 12l, 18l, 5l. Time 6m 56.10s. SP 4-1.
Mrs S Dench

1538 3¼m IBS Appeal Open Hunters' Chase Class H for the Royal Judgement Challenge Trophy

1324[1] **CARDINAL RED 11.7 7a............Miss L Hollis** 1
ld into start, in tch, chsd ldr apr 2 out, rdn approaching last, led run-in, just held on.
1333 **Strong Gold 12.2 5a (bl)..........Mr T McCarthy** 2
(fav) ld 2nd, rdn and hdd run-in, rallied cl home, just failed.
1336[6] **Trust The Gypsy 12.0 7a ....Mr R Nuttall** 3
ld to 2nd, chsd ldr 7th to 13th and from 15th till after 3 out, no ext next.
1050[4] American Eyre 12.0 7a *in tch, prog to chase ldr 14th to next, outpcd 3 out.* ....Miss S Gladders 4
1333[7] Folk Dance 12.6 7a 6ow (v) *prog and cl up 11th, wknd apr 13th, t.o. next.* ....Mr F Jackson 5
1062[2] John O'Dee 12.4 7a 4ow *chsd ldr 4th to 7th, soon bhnd, t.o. when u.r. 15th.* ....Mr I Marsh ur

6 ran. Sht-hd, 6l, 15l. Time 6m 51.30s. SP 3-1.
J M Turner

1539 3m 7f Shepherd Neame United Hunts Open Champion Hunters' Chase Class H

1400[1] **OVER THE EDGE 11.10 7a........Mr S Sporborg** 1
ld till after 1st, chsd ldr, led 11th to 15th, led 2 out, rdn, styd on well.
1327[4] **Woodlands Genhire 11.7 7a (v) ..Mr J I Pritchard** 2
prom, chsd ldr 13th, ld after 15th to 2 out, one pace und pres.
1375 **Kates Castle 11.2 7a ....Mr J Van Praagh** 3
mid div, prog 13th, blnd 18th, ev ch 2 out, unable to qckn und pres.
594 Pat Alaska 11.7 7a *mid div, prog when mstk 15th, outpcd next, styd on from 2 out.* ....Miss C Wates 4
1382[4] Sonofagipsy 11.10 7a *(fav) prom, blnd 10th, 4th and rdn when mstk 16th, btn 3 out.* ....Mr R Nuttall 5
1148[1] Emsee-H 11.7 7a *held up bhnd, n.d..* .....Miss L Hollis 6
1329[5] Colonel Kenson 11.7 7a *mstk 2nd, well bhnd 4th, t.o..* ....Mr M Gingell 7
1329[8] Motor Cloak 11.7 7a (bl) *ld after 1st to 11th, blnd and u.r. 13th.* ....Miss C Savell ur
1534 Hizal 11.7 7a *in tch, 5th and rdn when blnd 16th, no ch after, p.u. before last.* ....Mr A Charles-Jones pu

9 ran. 1¼l, hd, 5l, 14l, 14l, dist. Time 8m 22.10s. SP 15-8.
Christopher Sporborg

1540 2m 5f Grant's Cherry Brandy South East Champion Novices' Hunters' Chase Final Class H

1292[1] **PONTABULA 12.0 7a........Mr A Charles-Jones** 1
(fav) chsd ldr apr 9th, ld 3 out, jmpd left next, clr last, driven out.
1335[8] **Fathers Footprints 12.0 7a...........Mr R Hicks** 2
chsd ldrs, ld apr 9th to 3 out, wknd approaching last.
1164[2] **Spar Copse 12.0 7a............Miss A Goschen** 3
chsd ldrs, rdn 11th, hdwy 3 out, ev ch next, soon wknd.
1206[3] Kelburne Lad (Ire) 12.0 7a *held up, mstk 2nd, prog 7th, joined ldrs next, wknd 2 out.* ....Mr P Bull 4
1299[1] Velka 11.9 7a *chsd ldr 3rd, left in ld 8th, soon hdd, no hdwy from 3 out.* ....Mrs S Hickman 5
1341[8] Beat The Rap 12.0 7a *ld to 3rd, prom till wknd apr 2 out.* ....Mr G Morrison 6
1374[2] Pallingham Star (Ire) 12.0 7a *bhnd and rdn 8th, t.o. from 3 out.* ....Mr P O'Keeffe 7

1440[3] Local Manor 12.0 7a *started slowly, soon in tch, cl 5th when u.r. 11th.* .... Mr H Dunlop ur
1442 High Burnshot 12.0 7a *whipped round start, pulld hrd, led 3rd, mstk next, f 8th.* .... Mr A Welsh f
1326[1] Golden Eye (NZ) 12.0 7a *mstk 5th, bhnd from next, t.o. and p.u. before 3 out.* .... Mr N King pu
10 ran. 7l, 7l, 2½l, 10l, 26l, 1¼l. Time 5m 41.80s. SP 9-4.
H J Manners

1541 2m 5f Kent & Surrey Bloodhounds United Hunts Open Challenge Cup Hunters' Chase Class H

1382[1] **CHILIPOUR 12.4 7a .... Mr N Harris** 1
(fav) waited with, prog to chase ldr after 10th, mstk next, rdn to ld after 2 out, driven clr run-in.
1052[1] **Retail Runner 12.0 7a .... Mr T Hills** 2
ld, went clr 11th, hdd after 2 out, no ext run-in.
1330[4] **Counterbid 12.6 5a (bl) .... Mr A Sansome** 3
chsd ldrs, went 2nd 9th to next, 3rd and outpcd from next.
1257[2] Notary-Nowell 12.4 3a (bl) *pressed ldr to 9th, 4th and well btn from 11th.* .... Mr Simon Andrews 4
1208[2] Prince Zeus 12.2 5a *b.d. 3rd.* .... Mr T McCarthy bd
1339[2] Amari King 12.4 7a *third when f 3rd.* .... Mr C Ward Thomas f
1532 Rah Wan (USA) 12.2 5a *started slowly, prog and in tch when f 8th.* .... Mr C Vigors f
1400[3] Quarter Marker (Ire) 12.0 7a *held up, rdn and lost tch apr 9th, t.o. when p.u. before 3 out.* .... Mr D M Loughnane pu
8 ran. 5l, 30l, dist. Time 5m 36.70s. SP 4-5.
Nick Viney

PERTH
Thursday May 16th
FIRM

1542 2½m 110yds Linlithgow & Stirlingshire Hunt Novices' Hunters' Chase Class H

1354[1] **MASTER KIT (IRE) 11.7 7a .... Mr J Billinge** 1
trckd ldrs going well, ev ch 4 out, ld apr last, qcknd run-in, comf.
1351[3] **Free Transfer (Ire) 11.11 3a .... Mr C Bonner** 2
prom, ld 8th to next, cl up and ev ch 3 out, not qckn run-in.
789[1] **Abercromby Comet 11.12 7a ..... Miss S Forster** 3
ld to 8th, led again next till hdd apr last, soon wknd.
1461[1] Little Wenlock 12.3 5a *held up and bhnd, outpcd till hdwy after 4 out, kept on one pace.* ..... Mrs V Jackson 4
673[1] Risky Dee 12.2 3a *alwys chasing ldrs, hit 7th, ev ch when mstk 4 out, soon btn.* .... Mr M Thompson 5
670[1] Wudimp 12.3 5a *(fav) held up, hit 9th, driven along after 6 out, no impn apr 2 out.* .... Mr C Storey 6
1340[6] Quixall Crossett 11.7 7a (bl) *pressed ldrs, mstk 7th, wknd after 6 out, bhnd when p.u. before 3 out.* .... Mr M H Naughton pu
1476 Madame Beck 11.2 7a *tubed, not fluent, lost tch after 8th, last when blnd and u.r. 10th.* .... Mr R M Smith ur
8 ran. 7l, 9l, ½l, 11l, hd. Time 5m 4.70s. SP 4-1.
J N R Billinge

NEWTON ABBOT
Friday May 17th
GOOD

1543 3¼m 110yds Mike Howard & Dick Spencer Memorial Hunters' Chase Class H

1454[2] **SOUTHERLY GALE 11.2 5a .... Mr A Farrant** 1
made all, not fluent 3 out, all out.
1454[4] **Good King Henry 11.7 7a 7ow .. Mr I Widdicombe** 2
alwys in tch, chal from 2 out, ev ch when not fluent last, ran on.
1382[2] **Romany King 11.7 .... Mr M Armytage** 3
(fav) held up bhnd ldrs, rdn when mstk 3 out, soon btn.
1393[2] Spring Fun 11.10 7a *in tch till wknd apr 16th, t.o..* .... Mr M G Miller 4
1387[2] Never Be Great 11.0 7a *chsd wnr till wknd 15th, t.o..* .... Mr D S Jones 5
1499 Flood Mark 11.0 7a *held up, lost tch apr 14th, t.o. when p.u. before 16th.* .... Mr S Mulcaire pu
297 Batsi 11.0 7a *lways bhnd, t.o. 7th, p.u. before 12th.* .... Mr L Jefford pu
1494 Stormy Fashion 11.1 7a 1ow *alwys bhnd, t.o. when p.u. after 6th..* .... Major G Wheeler pu
8 ran. Hd, 14l, dist, 5l. Time 6m 44.90s. SP 5-2.
M C Pipe

STRATFORD
Friday May 17th
GOOD TO FIRM

1544 3m U.K. Petroleum Hunters' Chase Class H For the Gay and Eve Sheppard Memorial Challenge Trophy

1462[1] **KING'S TREASURE (USA) 12.0 7a... Mr A Balding** 1
held up, hdwy 12th, went 3rd after 4 out, chal last, qcknd and soon ld, held on well.
1331[4] **Jumbeau 11.11 3a .... Mr C Bonner** 2
chsd ldr, rdn to ld last, soon hdd, not qckn.
798 **Proud Sun 12.7 3a .... Mr J Culloty** 3
(fav) held up, hdwy after 6 out, mstk 4 out, soon rdn, mistake 2 out, styd on well run-in.
1227 Fox Pointer 11.7 7a *ld to last, soon wknd.* .... Mr R Thornton 4
1334[2] Charden 11.7 7a *held up bhnd, blnd 13th, styd on well from 4 out, nvr nrr.* .... Lt-Col R Webb-Bowen 5
1457 Babil 11.7 7a *chsd lding pair till rdn and wknd quickly 3 out.* .... Mr R Hicks 6
1453[4] Indian Knight 11.9 5a *held up, mid div when blnd 4 out, wknd quickly.* .... Mr C Vigors 7
362 Rochester 11.7 7a *chsd lding gp, wknd 13th, soon bhnd, t.o..* .... Mr E James 8
1479[6] Kingfisher Bay 11.7 7a *chsd ldrs, wknd quickly after 11th, soon t.o..* .... Mr G Shenkin 9
1233[9] Shareef Star 11.7 7a *alwys last, t.o. after 5th.* .... Mr D Sherlock 10
10 ran. 1½l, ¾l, 1¼l, 13l, 1½l, 9l, 30l, 30l, dist. Time 6m 3.50s. SP 2-1.
I A Balding

BANGOR
Saturday May 18th
GOOD

1545 3m 110yds North Western Area Point-to-point Championship Final Hunters' Chase Class H for the Wynnstay Hunt Challenge Cup

1367[1] **SCALLY MUIRE 11.5 7a .... Mr A H Crow** 1
held up, hdwy apr 13th, ld 4 out, left clr 2 out, easily.
1420 **Inch Maid 11.5 7a .... Mr R Ford** 2
in tch, outpcd after 13th, hdwy after 3 out, left 2nd next, no impn on wnr.
1460[1] **My Nominee 12.3 7a (bl) .... Mr A Griffith** 3
(fav) ld, raced wd and hdd briefly after 9th, hded 4 out, soon und pres, btn apr 2 out.
1457 Fell Mist 11.10 7a *handily pld, rdn after 13th, fd.* .... Miss A Sykes 4
1422[1] Le Piccolage 11.10 7a *cl up, mstk 11th (water), weakening when mistake 4 out, soon bhnd.* .... Mr C J B Barlow 5
1120[2] Ambrose 11.10 7a *held up, prom 5th, cl 2nd and und pres when f 2 out.* .... Mr W Ritson f
1419[1] Chip'N'run 11.10 7a *in tch, ld briefly after 9th, wknd 14th, t.o. when p.u. before 2 out.* .... Mr J Cornes pu

1195² Dice Off 11.8 7a 3ow *alwys bhnd, blnd 12th, struggling when mstk next, no ch when f 3 out, dead.* ....Mr G Crank f
8 ran. 10l, 21l, 15l, 14l. Time 6m 22.30s. SP 4-1.
G L Edwards

FAKENHAM
Saturday May 18th
GOOD

1546 3m 110yds Hood, Vores And Allwood Hunters' Chase Class H For The Essandem Trophy

1333² **SHEER JEST 12.5 3a ....Mr A Hill** 1
(fav) held up rear, prog 12th, ld 3 out, driven and held on cl home.
1463² **Zam Bee 11.5 7a ....Mr N M Bell** 2
ld till hdd 3 out, rallied last, just failed.
1331 **Blue Danube (USA) 11.7 5a.....Mr J Trice-Rolph** 3
mid div, chsd ldr 9th to 13th, lost pl next, styd on again one pace from 2 out.
1147¹ Dromin Leader 11.7 5a *lding gp, chsd ldr 13th to 3 out, outpcd from next*..........Mr A Sansome 4
1258² Elder Prince 11.5 7a *chsd ldrs till blnd 9th, no impn after*..........Mr P Gee 5
1540 Golden Eye (NZ) 11.1 7a *rear till imp from 14th, nvr nrr*..........Mr N King 6
1228 Sure Pride (USA) 11.5 7a *trckd lding gp to 12th, lost tch from 14th*..........Mr C Ward 7
1457⁴ Saint Bene't (Ire) 11.5 7a (v) *well pld till lost position 8th, t.o. from 14th*..........Mr A Coe 8
1379⁵ Easy Over (USA) 11.5 7a (bl) *jmpd slowly in rear most of way, t.o. 14th*..........Mr R Wakley 9
1399⁶ El Bae 11.5 7a *alwys rear gp, lost tch 12th.* ....Mr P Taiano 10
1352⁶ Fish Quay 11.5 7a *struggling in rear most of way, t.o. 13th*..........Miss S Lamb 11
1259¹ Cherry Chap 11.5 7a *mid div to 12th, p.u. in rear before last*..........Mr S Cowell pu
1323² Jimmy Mac Jimmy 11.5 7a *chsd ldrs till wknd apr 14th, p.u. before 2 out*..........Mr C Ward Thomas pu
13 ran. Hd, 16l, 8l, 9l, ½l, 7l, 2l, 10l, 18l, 18l. Time 6m 19.50s. SP 8-11.
Mrs Judy Wilson

1547 2m 5f 110yds Barclays Bank Maiden Hunters' Chase Class H

1321¹ **MANOR MIEO 12.0 7a ....Mr A Coe** 1
j.w, ld 3rd, left well clr 2 out, unchal, tried to pull up after last.
1453² **No Joker (Ire) 12.2 5a ....Mr M Rimell** 2
ld to 3rd, with ldrs, hit 9th, blnd 11th, soon outpcd, left poor 2nd 2 out.
1341⁴ **Rayman (Ire) 12.2 5a ....Mr J Trice-Rolph** 3
mstk 1st, chsd ldrs till outpcd 12th, left poor 3rd 2 out.
1292⁴ Everso Irish 12.0 7a *towards rear and rdn 6th, nvr on terms after*..........Mr F Brennan 4
378⁴ Deep In Greek 12.0 7a *towards rear to hfwy, lost tch from 12th, t.o.*..........Mr A Balding 5
1322 Half A Sov 12.0 7a *soon bhnd, lost tch from 4th, p.u. before 13th*..........Mr P Taiano pu
1328 Ravens Hasey Moon 12.0 7a *lding gp, rdn and wknd 8th, t.o. when p.u. before 13th*..........Mr N Bloom pu
963¹ Nethertara 11.13 3a *(fav) in tch till ran on to chase wnr 10th, cl 2nd when blnd and u.r. 2 out.* ....Mr P Hacking ur
1399³ Lord Richard 12.4 3a *pressed ldrs to 5th, lost pl 8th, f 10th*..........Mr Simon Andrews f
1533³ Paper Days 12.2 5a *held up in mid div when blnd and u.r. 9th*..........Mr S Bush ur
1456 Bervie House (Ire) 12.4 3a *alwys rear, t.o. when p.u. before 3 out*..........Mr A Hill pu
11 ran. 3½l, 8l, 9l, 15l. Time 5m 33.40s. SP 11-4.
George Prodromou

SOUTHWELL
Saturday May 18th
GOOD TO FIRM

1548 3m 110yds Thorp Novices' Hunters' Chase Class H

960⁶ **PAVI'S BROTHER 11.7 7a ...Mr Rupert Sweeting** 1
hdwy 6th, ld 15th to last, rallied to ld final 25 yards.
1456² **Hobnobber 11.7 7a ....Mr J Docker** 2
hdwy 13th, slight ld last, hdd final 25 yards.
1461² **Private Jet (Ire) 11.7 7a ....Mr G Markham** 3
held up, styd on from 4 out, nearest fin.
1329¹ Candle Glow 11.9 7a *ld till apr 3rd, led 7th till approaching 10th, ran on from 2 out.* Mr P Hutchinson 4
1457 Cromwell Point 11.7 7a *slight mstks, kept on one pace from 3 out*..........Mr C Mulhall 5
1522 Eighty Eight 11.7 7a *mid div, no ch from 4 out.* ....Mr A Charles-Jones 6
1455 A Windy Citizen (Ire) 11.9 7a *alwys prom, ev ch 3 out, wknd 2 out*..........Mr R Hicks 7
1468¹ Cumberland Blues (Ire) 11.7 7a *ld apr 3rd to 5th, led approaching 10th to 15th, wknd quickly 3 out, t.o..* ....Miss A Deniel 8
1467¹ Park Drift 11.11 3a *(fav) nvr going well, alwys rear, p.u. 4 out*..........Mr C Bonner pu
1458¹ Jasilu 12.2 (bl) *rear till p.u. 4 out*..........Mr S Swiers pu
1458⁴ Bare Fisted 11.7 7a *ld 5th to 7th, soon wknd, t.o. when p.u. 4 out*..........Miss H Phizacklea pu
11 ran. Nk, 9l, 3l, nk, 18l, 6l, hd. Time 6m 26.60s. SP 25-1.
C J R Sweeting

DULVERTON WEST
Bratton Down
Saturday May 18th
FIRM

1549 Members

1359¹ **PHAR TOO TOUCHY 5a..........Miss R Francis** 1
(fav) made all, clr 3 out, easily
1495² **Liberty James ....N Harris** 2
hld up, went 2nd 2 out, no imp flat
1345⁵ **Remember Mac (bl) ....Miss C Hayes** 3
chsd wnr, cls up til wknd aft 3 out
1428 Anstey Gadabout *sttld 3rd, cls up til wknd 3 out* ....R Pipe 4
4 ran. 5l, 5l, 7l. Time 6m 14.00s. SP 1-7.
Miss R A Francis (Dulverton West).

1550 Confined

1453³ **STILL IN BUSINESS ....T Mitchell** 1
(fav) hld up, prog 14th, ld 3 out, ran on well whn chal flat
1499¹ **Tangle Baron ....M Felton** 2
hld up, went 2nd 2 out, chal und pres last, no ext flat
1529¹ **Bargain And Sale ....I Dowrick** 3
handy, ld aft 14th til 3 out, kpt on onepcd
1393¹ Rare Flutter 5a *in tch, cls 5th at 16th, outpcd aft 3 out* ....B O'Doherty 4
1499⁵ Rapid Rascal *ld to 3rd & frm 5th-14th, cls up til outpcd frm 3 out*..........Miss S West 5
1498³ Charmers Wish 5a *sn rear, hit 13th, bhnd whn p.u. apr nxt*..........H Thomas pu
1427 Bert House (bl) *ld 3rd-5th, cls up til wknd 14th, last whn u.r. 16th (ditch)*..........S Ellis ur
1497 Link Copper *went 3rd at 10th, lost ground 14th, bhnd & p.u. 3 out*..........Miss L Blackford pu
8 ran. 1½l, 8l, 6l, 6l. Time 5m 57.00s. SP 4-7.
R G Williams (Taunton Vale).

1551 Open (12st)

1459 **MYLIEGE 7ex..........N Harris** 1
ld 6th, clr 16th, styd on wll whn chal flat
1525³ **Fearsome ....G Penfold** 2
w.w. in tch, 3rd frm 16th, kpt on to tk 2nd cls home
1360¹ **The General's Drum 7ex ....K Heard** 3

(fav) in tch, went 2nd 15th, ev ch und pres apr last, not qckn
1290[3] Royle Speedmaster 7ex *prom, disp brfly 10th, lost plc 15th, onepcd* ....A Harvey 4
1396[1] Alex Thuscombe (v) *ld/disp to 6th, lost plc 15th, bhnd frm nxt* ....P Shaw 5
1528 Final Express 5a *ld/disp to 6th, cls up til lost plc 14th, no ch frm 16th* ....J Tizzard 6
1113 Prince Amanda *wll in tch, 4th at 16th, fdd* ...I Dowrick 7
1428 Bright Road 5a (bl) *mstk 2nd, sn rear, pshd alng 12th, t.o. frm 16th* ....H Thomas 8
8 ran. 2l, 1½l, 2l, 8l, 1l, 10l, 25l. Time 6m 10.50s. SP 8-1.
J Scott (Devon & Somerset Staghounds).

1552 Ladies

1346[1] **FAITHFUL STAR ....Miss S Vickery 1**
(fav) handy, mstk 4th, ld 14th, sn clr, unchal, eased flat
1346[4] **Daybrook's Gift ....Miss N Allan 2**
went 3rd 10th, tk 2nd 3 out, no imp wnr
1524[1] **Mistress Rosie 5a....Miss L Blackford 3**
ld apr 6th til 14th, lost 2nd 3 out, grad fdd
1393 False Economy *made most til aft 5th, lost plc 10th, poor 4th frm nxt* ....Miss K Scorgie 4
1058[3] Great Uncle *sn twrds rear, bhnd frm 12th* ....Miss A Goschen 5
1426[3] Bidston Mill *rear, t.o. frm 9th, p.u. 12th* ...Miss P Platt pu
1280[5] Olive Basket 7a *blnd & u.r. 3rd*..Miss W Southcombe ur
7 ran. 12l, 20l, 8l, 4l. Time 5m 54.00s. SP 2-9.
M C Pipe (Taunton Vale).

1553 P P O R A (12st)

1397[1] **BEINN MOHR 5a....N Mitchell 1**
j.w. ld apr 6th, made rest, lft clr 3 out, comf
1397[2] **Arctic Baron ....Miss S Vickery 2**
mstk & lost plc 5th, prog to 3rd 16th, styd on clsng stgs
1499[3] **Hensue ....R Treloggen 3**
prog 7th, 4th at 16th, disp 2nd aft 3 out til wknd apr last
1395[1] Avril Showers 5a *prom til stmbld & lost plc apr 6th,sn wll bhnd,poor 4th 3out* ....R Atkinson 4
1361[6] Miss Moony 5a *mid-div, rmndrs 12th, 6th at 14th, no dang* ....I Widdicombe 5
1527[6] Talk Sence (Ire) *sn rear, t.o. frm 10th*....G Penfold 6
1393[4] Archie's Nephew (bl) *ld/disp 2nd-5th, lost plc, t.o. frm 10th, lame* ....Miss A Bush 7
1445[1] Fort Diana *in tch, cls 4th at 12th til f 15th* ...G Hopper f
1361 If You Say So *rear til prog 11th, 2l 2nd whn f 15th* ....S Ellis f
1168[1] Coachroadstarboy *(fav) prog 12th, 2nd frm 15th, cls up whn f 3 out, dead* ....M Felton f
10 ran. 6l, 8l, 10l, 15l, 20l, 2l. Time 6m 0.50s. SP 8-1.
Mrs B C Willcocks (Portman).

1554 Open Maiden Div I (12st)

1511 **CHISM (IRE) 7a....M Miller 1**
(Jt fav) handy,5th at 13th,lft 2nd 15th,ld aft last,ran on strngly
1396 **Inner Snu 5a ....N Mitchell 2**
hld up bhnd,prog to 5th 3 out,strng run to disp last,jst hld
1347[5] **Morchard Milly 5a....J Auvray 3**
cls 2nd mostly,lft in ld 15th,jnd aft 3 out,ev ch,wknd last
1527[7] Royal Turn *mid-div,prog to 4th 3 out,kpt on onepcd* ....A Honeyball 4
1493[4] Nice To No *sn rear, not alwys fluent, t.o. 13th* S Slade 5
1430[4] Sixth In Line (Ire) *mid-div, 7th & wd bnd aft 13th, no dang clsg stgs*....T Cole 6
1530[3] Here's Mary 5a *mid-div, 8th whn mstk 14th, no ch clsng stgs* ....G Penfold 7
1430 Pixie In Purple (Ire) 7a *alwys strgglng in rear* ....D Stephens 8
1430 Scallykenning *mid-div, prog 15th, cls 3rd whn blnd & u.r. nxt (ditch)*....J Young ur
1432[2] Four Leaf Clover 5a *(Jt fav) prom, ld brfly aft 13th, cls up whn c.o. 15th* ....R Woolacott co
1396 Dula Model 5a *rear whn mstk 7th, 10th hlfwy, bhnd whn u.r. last* ....S Ellis ur
1495 Dollybat 5a *made most til s.u. apr 15th* ....M Frith su
1432 Carumu 5a *s.u. bnd apr 6th* ....S Hornby su
Master Buckley *schoold in rear til p.u. 14th* ..N Harris pu
1308 Happy Henry (Ire) *s.s. rear til gd prog 16th,3rd & ev ch whn blnd & u.r.2out* ....I Dowrick ur
Willsan *s.s. gd prog 9th, cls 4th at 11th, fdd & p.u. aft 13th*....Miss S Vickery pu
16 ran. 1½l, 6l, 3l, 30l, 10l, 8l, 30l. Time 6m 8.00s. SP 3-1.
N R Freak (Portman).

1555 Open Maiden Div II (12st)

1348 **MEDIAS MAID 5a....A Holdsworth 1**
4th hlfwy,ld apr 14th til cls 3rd 2 out,ld flat,drvn out
1349 **Joli High Note 5a ....Miss T Honeyball 2**
9th hlfwy, wll off pace til prog 2 out, fin wll
876 **Get Stepping ....J Creighton 3**
in tch, went 3rd 15th, 4th frm 3 out, tk 3rd cls home
1510 Noble Minister *ld 9th til wd bnd apr 14th,ran on to ld 2 out,hdd & fdd flat* ....M Wells 4
556 Bright Work *rear, 10th hlfwy, nrst fin*.......D Curnow 5
1432[3] Baman Powerhouse *twrds rear, 8th hlfwy, nvr dang* ....Miss K Baily 6
1279[4] Brook A Light 7a *(fav) mid-div, nvr a fctr* ....S Slade 7
1453[7] Paid Elation 5a *ld to 9th, lost ground steadily frm 14th, no ch* ....J Wingfield-Digby 8
1431[5] Melody Mine 5a *prog 12th,disp 15th,jst ld nxt-2 out,cls 3rd,blnd & u.r.last* ....T Greed ur
1424[3] Drumcolliher *mid-div whn u.r.4th*....C Farr ur
1493[5] Nottarex *alwys bhnd, u.r. last*....B Wright ur
1143 Oldham Joker *nvr dang, t.o. & p.u. last* .....I Hambly pu
1431 Eskimo Star 5a *crashed through wing 2nd*.....S Ellis ro
13 ran. 3l, 6l, 4l, 8l, 3l, 10l, 2l. Time 6m 13.00s. SP 7-1.
R T Grant (Tiverton Staghounds).
G.T.

YSTRAD
Bassaleg
Saturday May 18th
FIRM

1556 Members

1389[2] **SWEET KILDARE 5a ....V Thomas 1**
(fav) made all, clr 3-14th, kpt on whn prssd apr last
1388[4] **Saffron Moss ....Mrs S Farr 2**
mod 3rd til clsd 14th,chsd wnr nxt,ev ch last,not qckn
1492 **Puttingonthestyle ....K Cousins 3**
16s-6s, chsd wnr, clsd 14th, lost 2nd nxt, wknd 3 out
1385 Harken Premier *jmpd slwly, t.o. whn nrly ref 8th, sntchd 4th on line*....C Richards 4
Rebel Yell *alwys bhnd, t.o. 8th* ....N Jones 5
1039 Lennie The Lion 7a *f 1st*....L Stevens f
6 ran. 1l, 30l, 1 fence, ½l. Time 6m 37.40s. SP 4-6.
V J Thomas (Ystrad).

1557 Restricted (12st)

1391[1] **CAIRNEYMOUNT ....J Tudor 1**
ldng grp, ld 12th-2 out, rallied to ld last, drvn out
1486[2] **Sea Search ....Miss A Meakin 2**
cls up, prog 14th, sn chsd wnr, ld 2 out-last, not qckn
1390[1] **Magnetic Reel 7a ....J Jukes 3**
(fav) prom, ld 4th-12th, chsd wnr aft, rdn & btn 3 out
The Foolish One 5a *prom til wknd frm 3 out* ....M Jackson 4
1267[5] Tudor Oaks 5a *mstk 3rd, sn wll in rear, t.o. 10th* ....S Shinton 5
1266[5] Cistolena 5a *cls up til wkd 12th, t.o. & p.u. 15th* ....D S Jones pu
1156 Captain Equaty *in tch whn b.d. 7th*....M Lewis bd
1481[9] Flaxridge *prom, prssd ldr 10th-12th, sn wknd, p.u. 3 out* ....A Price pu
1272[1] Colonel Frazer (Ire) *ld to 4th, prom whn f nxt*..G Lewis f
1415[2] How Friendly *prom, chsd ldr & blnd 8th, lost plc rpdly 12th, p.u. 14th* ....T Jones pu

850[1] Haydon Hill 7a *hld up, prog 6th, cls up til wknd 12th, p.u. 15th* ....M FitzGerald pu
1490 Mrs Wumpkins (Ire) 7a *last whn u.r. 7th* Miss S Wallin ur
1391 Sea Tarth 7a *in tch whn u.r. 7th* ....D Davies ur
1271 Queen's Equa 5a *alwys bhnd, t.o. & p.u. 12th* . J Price pu
14 ran. 2l, 25l, 4l, 2 fences. Time 6m 19.80s. SP 10-1.
Robert Williams (Llangeinor).

1558 Confined (12st)

1487[1] **NORTHERN BLUFF 3ex.................J Jukes 1**
(fav) hanging lft,ld to 8th & 15-3 out,wd nxt,lft in ld last,kpton
1490[1] **Dustys Trail (Ire) ....M Jackson 2**
rdn to prss wnr,ld 8-15th & 3 out til nrly ref last,not rcvr
1263 **Icecapade (Bel) ....J P Keen 3**
chsd ldng pair abt 15l down,unable to cls,wknd apr last
1487[4] Bronze Effigy 3ex (bl) *sn poor 4th, t.o. 12th, kpt on* ....W Pugh 4
1487[3] Lucky Ole Son 5ex *sn t.o. in last, mstk 3rd, p.u. 15th* ....Miss S Wallin pu
1487[2] Construction King *sn t.o. in 5th, nrly ref 8th, p.u. 15th* ....Mrs J Hawkins pu
6 ran. 3l, 25l, 15l. Time 6m 23.80s. SP 4-6.
H Gibbon (Pembrokeshire).

1559 Ladies

1414 **MENDIP MUSIC 3ex...........Miss E Crawford 1**
pllng, cls up, ld 8th, qcknd 11th, jnd 14th-last, ran on wll
1489[1] **Kumada 3ex.......................Miss S Wallin 2**
(fav) ld til nrly ref 8th,sn outpcd,ran on to jn wnr 15th,just hld
978 **Hugli ....Miss L Pearce 3**
in tch, ev ch 13th, outpcd by 1st pair frm 3 out
1414 Travistown *last frm 4th, t.o. 12th* .....Miss N Richards 4
4 ran. 1l, 15l, 2 fences. Time 6m 34.90s. SP 5-4.
Miss E Crawford (Curre).

1560 Open (12st)

1489[2] **HANDSOME HARVEY ....J Jukes 1**
(fav) ld 3rd, hrd prssd frm 15th, drvn & ran on well flat
1438[6] **Space Man ....F Crew 2**
ld to 3rd, prssd wnr aft, ev ch 2 out, not qckn apr last
1506[1] **January Don (bl) ....A Dalton 3**
in tch, rdn 10th, bhnd frm 12th, wll t.o.
1479[1] Lislary Lad *w.w. in tch, hmpd & u.r. apr 9th* D S Jones ur
1479[4] Adanac *chsd ldrs til s.u. flat apr 9th*..........A Price su
1343[2] Prince Nepal *lost tch 8th, wll t.o. whn ref 15th* ....T Hopkins ref
1386[1] Touch 'N' Pass 4ex *chsd ldrs, prog & cls 3rd whn blnd & u.r. 12th* ....J Tudor ur
7 ran. 2l, Bad. Time 6m 16.00s. SP 5-4.
E L Harries (Pembrokeshire).

1561 Open Maiden

1484[2] **STERLING BUCK (USA) ....T Jones 1**
(fav) ld to 7th, trckd ldr aft, ld 3 out, clr last, easily
1484 **Gold Tip 5a ....J P Keen 2**
hld up, prog 5th, ld 7th-3 out, not run on und pres
1272[3] **Maytown ....R Nolan 3**
rear frm 6th, t.o. 10th, sntchd dist 3rd nr fin
1492[4] I'm A Bute 5a *prom, mstk & wknd 12th, sn t.o.* J Price 4
1486[4] Frontrunner 5a *lost tch 7th, t.o. 10th, p.u. aft 3 out as rest fin*..................................M Lewis pu
1390[2] Parks Pride 7a *not fluent, cls up, mstk 12th, 4th & btn whn f nxt*..............................D S Jones f
1273 Steel Valley (Ire) 5a *mstks 3 & 4th,prog 11th, 3rd & ev ch whn s.u. apr 2 out* ....A Price su
Bruna Alpina 5a *ref & u.r. 1st*...................J Cook ref
8 ran. 6l, 2 fences, ½l. Time 6m 37.20s. SP Evens.
D J Clapham (Ledbury).
J.N.

BICESTER WITH WHADDON CHASE
Mollington
Sunday May 19th
GOOD TO SOFT

1562 Members

1502[3] **SEVERN INVADER ....Miss H Gosling 1**
(fav) cls up, jnd ldr 13th, ld 3 out, clr nxt, comf
793[3] **Bit Of A Clown ....J Owen 2**
wth ldr, ld 9th, jnd 15th, hdd 3 out, fin tired, retired
1433[4] **Cool Rascal 5a ....L Lay 3**
4th til chsd ldng pair 11th, no imp, fin tired
Funchen View *1st ride, last, t.o. 6th, tk poor 4th apr 2 out*..Miss S Loggin 4
1015[4] Button Your Lip *sn bhnd, t.o. 6th, p.u. 11th* ....Mrs J Enderby pu
1433[1] Biblical 5a *ld to 9th, wknd 11th, sn t.o., p.u. last* ....R Mumford pu
6 ran. 25l, 25l, 20l. Time 6m 38.00s. SP 4-5.
Captain Miles Gosling (Bicester With Whaddon Chase).

1563 Confined (12st)

1177[1] **HILL ISLAND 3ex ....R Sweeting 1**
(fav) ld 3rd til aft 3 out, rallied to ld last, all out
1016[2] **Saybright ....G Tarry 2**
prom, chsd wnr 14th, ld aft 3 out-last, kpt on flat
1407 **Tompet 5ex ....J Connell 3**
prom, chsd wnr 11-14th, outpcd 3 out, styd on
1500[2] Tell You What *prom to 12th, sn strgglng, t.o.* N Ridout 4
1500[7] Wild Fortune *ld to 3rd, wknd 7th, t.o. & p.u. 13th* ....R Dalgety pu
1438 Berkana Run *alwys bhnd, t.o. last at 8th, p.u. 12th* ....R Bailey pu
1341[5] Pont de Paix 5ex *cls up til wknd 12th, poor 4th whn p.u. 3 out* ....R White pu
1500[5] The Holy Golfer *sn last & wll bhnd, prog 10th, no imp aft, t.o. & p.u. 3 out*........................C Smyth pu
8 ran. 1l, 15l, 1 fence. Time 6m 33.00s. SP 4-5.
Colin Gee (Heythrop).

1564 P P O R A (12st)

1395[2] **FRONT COVER 5a...............Miss S Vickery 1**
(fav) alwys prom, ld 13th, drew clr 2 out, ran on strngly
1380[2] **Cader Idris ....G Tarry 2**
prom, ld 11-13th, ev ch apr 2 out, sn btn, fin tired
1365[1] **Autumn Green (Ire) ....R Burton 3**
trckd ldrs, outpcd frm 14th, kpt on frm 2 out
1293[1] Colourful Boy *cls up til outpcd 14th, disp 3rd aft 3 out, onepcd*..........................A Charles-Jones 4
1437[6] Roaming Shadow 7ex *hld up, prog 13th, nvr rchd ldrs, onepcd frm 3 out*..................J Hankinson 5
1522 Menature (Ire) 2ow *mid-div, outpcd frm 13th, kpt on onepcd frm 2 out*......................J Seth-Smith 6
1407[2] Pejawi 5a *rear, lost tch 12th, kpt on agn frm 14th, no dang*..R Lawther 7
1371[1] Fixed Liability (bl) *in tch to 13th, 7th & no ch 3 out* ....T Underwood 8
1407[3] Kamtara *n.j.w. wll bhnd frm 4th, t.o. aft, kpt on frm 3 out*..R Hicks 9
1438[9] Waterhay *cls up to 12th, t.o. 3 out* ....R Mumford 10
1292 Golden Companion (bl) *ld to 11th, stppd bef nxt* L Lay pu
1173[2] Glitterbird 5a *hld up, prog & cls up whn blnd 13th, sn wknd, p.u. 3 out* ....Julian Pritchard pu
1439[5] Linlake Lightning 5a *in tch in rear til rdn & wknd 10th, t.o. & p.u. 14th* ....Miss H Irving pu
494 Tommy O'Dwyer (Ire) 3ow *hld up, prog 11th, cls up nxt, sn wknd, t.o. & p.u. 2 out* ....A Hill pu
14 ran. 15l, 12l, 3l, 3l, 6l, 8l, 15l, 8l, 3l. Time 6m 38.00s. SP 2-1.
Stewart Pike (East Devon).

1565 Open (12st)

1335[4] **BRIGHT BURNS 7ex (bl)..............R Sweeting 1**
chsd ldr,15l down whn lft wll clr 15th,stpping rpdly flat

1437[7] **Killy's Filly 5a ....G Barfoot-Saunt** **2**
chsd ldrs, outpcd 12th, lft disp dist 2nd 3 out, kpt on
1383[4] **Blakes Orphan 7ex ....B Pollock** **3**
sn pshd alng & nvr going wll, lft disp dist 2nd 3 out,no imp
1411[3] Fergal's Delight (bl) *outpcd frm 5th, t.o. 7th* ....Julian Pritchard 4
1146 Cockstown Lad 7ex *n.j.w. last & t.o. til p.u. 12th* ....D Featherstone pu
1017 Bright As A Button *chsd ldrs, no ch whn lft poor 2nd 15th, ref nxt*..........................J Connell ref
1437[3] Sunshine Manor *ld, clr 11th, 15l up & in cmmnd whn f 15th* ....G Tarry f
1435[1] Causeway Cruiser *(fav) hld up, 5th whn mstk & u.r. 5th*..........................R Lawther ur
8 ran. 12l, 10l, 1 fence. Time 6m 46.00s. SP 5-1.
Colin Gee (Heythrop).

1566 Ladies

1414[1] **DI STEFANO ....Miss A Dare** **1**
(fav) not fluent early, w.w., chsd ldr 13th,ld 15th,sn clr,easily
1502[1] **Sperrin View 5a...............Mrs K Sunderland** **2**
w.w. rdn & qcknd to ld 12th, hdd 15th, wknd apr 2 out
1459 **Green Archer ....Miss S Duckett** **3**
in tch til outpcd 12th, no ch nxt, kpt on slwly
1502[5] Icky's Five (bl) *prom to 12th, strgglng frm nxt* ....Miss T Habgood 4
1480[7] Aldington Bell (bl) *in tch to 11th, t.o. whn f 13th* ....Miss J Butler f
1259[5] Phelioff *last frm 5th, t.o. & p.u. 11th* . . .Miss S Dawson pu
1051[1] Monksfort *ld to 12th, sn wknd, t.o. & p.u. last* ....Miss C Holliday pu
7 ran. 30l, 1½l, 12l. Time 6m 32.00s. SP 2-5.
Mike Gifford (Cotswold Vale Farmers).

1567 Intermediate (12st)

1510 **NOT MISTAKEN ....Miss S Vickery** **1**
prom, ld 9-14th, mstk 3 out, ld nxt, drvn clr
1377[1] **Broad Steane 5ex ....A Sansome** **2**
(fav) cls up, ld 14th-2 out, rdn & no ext apr last
1380[1] **Grimley Gale (Ire) 5a ....M Jackson** **3**
mstk 3rd, in tch, chal & ev ch 15th, rdn & no ext aft 3 out
1413[2] Hackett's Farm 5ex *chsd ldrs, 5th & outpcd 14th, no imp ldrs aft* ....Julian Pritchard 4
1377[3] Lily The Lark 5a *prom til 5th & outpcd 13th, no ch whn blnd 2 out* ....Miss H Irving 5
1505[3] Ramlosa (NZ) *alwys bhnd, t.o. 11th, styd on* . . .R Cope 6
1481 King Of The Clouds *pllng, hld up, gd prog 9th, wth ldrs whn u.r. 13th* ....Mrs N Sheppard ur
1500[4] Tumble Time *alwys last pair, t.o. 11th, poor 6th whn f last*..........................Miss H Gosling f
1374[4] No Reply *prom to 8th, wknd, 7th & no ch whn blnd 12th, p.u. 3 out* ....Mrs C Mitchell pu
1405[3] Game Fair 3ow *ld to 2nd, rear whn mstk 5th, t.o. 11th, p.u. 2 out* ....G Burton pu
637[8] Creeves Nephew *alwys bhnd, t.o. 10th, p.u. last* ....Capt D Parker pu
1505[2] Kingofnobles (Ire) (bl) *ld 2nd-9th, rdn & not run on, t.o. & p.u. 13th* ....L Lay pu
12 ran. 10l, 8l, 15l, 6l, 25l. Time 6m 34.00s. SP 11-4.
Mrs S A Turner (Gelligaer).

1568 Open Maiden Div I

1438 **PLATEMAN ....F Hutsby** **1**
hld up, prog 8th, ld 14th, lft wll clr nxt, solo 3 out
Banjo Paterson ....A Charles-Jones **2**
ld to 3rd & 5th-14th, wknd, crawld 3 out & u.r., rmntd
Glenmere Prince *rear, lost tch 10th, t.o. & p.u. 13th* ....R Armson pu
1511[3] Mondino *n.j.w. rear 7th, rdn 10th, t.o. & p.u. 15th* ....L Lay pu
1504 Mr Wendyl *(fav) prom, chsd wnr 14th, 2l down whn u.r. nxt*..........................M Emmanuel ur
1378 Derring Knight *in tch til rdn & wknd 10th, ref nxt* ....A Sansome ref
1523 Secret Truth 5a *ld 3-5th, wknd 8th, t.o. last whn p.u. 11th*..........................A Martin pu
1378 Beachborough *33s-4s, prom, wth ldr whn f 11th* ....T Marks f
Fighting For Good (Ire) *trckd ldrs, pshd alng & wknd 10th, p.u. nxt* ....B Pollock pu
9 ran. 2 fences. Time 7m 3.00s. SP 7-1.
K Hutsby (Warwickshire).

1569 Open Maiden Div II

1434[4] **COLONEL FAIRFAX ....J Trice-Rolph** **1**
20s-6s,prom,ld 9-13th,ld agn 2 out,clr last,all out flat
1403[5] **Not To Be Trusted ....R Barrett** **2**
alwys prom,ev ch whn mstk 3 out,kpt on und pres,not rch wnr
890 **Mr Drake (Ire) ....R Thornton** **3**
prom, ld 13th-2 out, wknd last
1523[2] Full Song 5a *(fav) 4s-9/4, w.w. rear, effrt whn outpcd 12th, no imp ldrs 3 out*..........................S Morris 4
749 Detinu 7a *ld to 9th, outpcd 13th, effrt agn 3 out, wknd nxt*..........................M Jackson 5
1523 Rallye Stripe *s.s. last & wll bhnd, t.o. 11th* ....Capt J Holmes 6
1396 Barrow Street *prom, chal & mstk 13th, wknd aft 15th, walked in*..........................R Treloggen 7
1504 Space Molly 5a *prom til rdn & wknd 10th, t.o. & p.u. 13th*..........................N Ridout pu
643 Harry Tartar 7a *rear, rdr lost irons 4th, p.u. nxt* ....Capt D Parker pu
680 Mrs Blobby (Ire) 5a 1ow *cls up, mstk 7th, rdn & wknd 11th, p.u. 13th* ....A Hill pu
10 ran. 2l, 3l, 12l, 4l, dist, 5l. Time 6m 56.00s. SP 6-1.
Mrs N R Matthews (Heythrop).
J.N.

BORDER
Corbridge
Sunday May 19th
GOOD

1570 Confined (12st)

1475[1] **LOUGHLINSTOWN BOY 3ex............P Craggs** **1**
(Jt fav) made most, styd on wll flat
1513[4] **Master Mischief ....J Walton** **2**
mid-div, prog 3 out, gd hdwy apr last, not qckn flat
1351[5] **Royalist (Can) ....C Storey** **3**
alwys prom, cls 2nd at 13th, chsd wnr til wknd 2 out
1475[2] Little Glen *(Jt fav) mstks, prog 13th, went 3rd nxt, fdd 3 out*..........................T Scott 4
1514[1] Wire Lass 5a *alwys mid-div, no dang* ......R Morgan 5
1513 Just Maskaraider *alwys bhnd, styd on onepcd frm 2 out* ....Mrs H Dickson 6
50 Lion Of Vienna *last at 4th, nvr seen wth ch* . . .D Wood 7
1352[7] Rarely At Odds *cls up, disp 4th, sn lost plc, t.o. 16th* ....Miss R Ramsay 8
8 ran. 2½l, 4l, 5l. Time 6m 17.00s. SP 5-2.
J A Riddell (Percy).

1571 Restricted (12st)

1517[1] **MURDER MOSS (IRE) ....M Ruddy** **1**
mstk 3rd, prog hlfwy, ld aft 2 out, ran on wll, improve
1450[4] **Emu Park ....P Craggs** **2**
last early, prog 9th, gd hdwy 15th, rdn & ev ch 2 out,outpcd
1457 **Glenbricken 2ow..........................R Barker** **3**
mid-div, prog 4 out, styd on apr last, no ext flat
1447[6] Greenmount Lad (Ire) *mstk 9th, prog & prom 16th, onepcd frm nxt*..........................P Cornforth 4
1447[5] Lyningo *alwys mid-div, nvr able to chal* .....S Brisby 5
1447[2] Jolly Fellow (bl) *(fav) hld up rear, prog 8th, nvr rchd ldrs*..........................S Swiers 6
1353[4] Royal Fife 5a *cls up at 11th, outpcd frm 14th* A Parker 7
1466[7] Caman 5a *alwys bhnd*..................Miss S Duell 8
1353 Ruecastle *ld/disp til mstk 3 out, not rcvr* . . .A Robson 9
1461[5] Fisherman's Quay *prom early, mstk 11th, no dang aft* ....Miss A Bowie 10

1363[1] Polar Hat *not fluent, alwys bhnd, p.u. 2 out* ....Miss J Foster pu
1470[1] Hungry Jack *mstks, mid-div, wknd & p.u. 2 out* ....P Atkinson pu
1350[1] Leyden Lady 5a *sn prom, disp 7th til outpcd 15th, p.u. nxt* ....T Scott pu
13 ran. 4l, ½l. Time 6m 19.00s. SP 10-1.
S Coltherd (Buccleuch).

1572 Ladies

1351[4] **ASTRAC TRIO (USA) ....Miss A Bowie** 1
ld/disp til ld 7th, made rest, ran on und pres flat
1366[3] **Final Hope (Ire) ....Mrs F Needham** 2
disp 4th, prom til outpcd 14th, lft 2nd nxt, no ext apr last
1352[3] **Minibrig 5a ....Mrs V Jackson** 3
mid-div, prog to chs ldrs hlfwy, nvr nrr
1461 Flypie *trckd ldrs, disp brfly 9th, outpcd frm 13th* ....Mrs J Storey 4
1352 Battle Hero *sn last, u.r. 3rd* ....Miss M Bremner ur
1251[3] Across The Card *u.r. 2nd*....Miss R Ramsay ur
1472 Funny Feelings *cls up 7th, disp 9th, 2nd nxt til blnd & u.r. 15th*....Miss D Laidlaw ur
1473[2] Houselope Beck *(fav) mid-div, prog to 3rd at 13th, cls up whn u.r. 15th* ....Miss S Forster ur
8 ran. 5l, 15l, 6l. Time 6m 18.00s. SP 5-1.
Mrs M A Bowie (Buccleuch).

1573 Open

1337[6] **WASHAKIE ....J Walton** 1
(fav) mid-div, prog 4 out, disp last, drvn to ld nr fin gamely
1515[1] **Deday ....M Bradburne** 2
prom, made most frm 8th, jnd last, no ext und pres nr fin
1340[7] **Highland Friend (bl) ....P Atkinson** 3
bhnd, prog 14th, styd on wll frm 2 out, not rch ldrs flat
1447[1] Flying Lion *bhnd at 9th, some prog 14th, nvr nrr* ....S Swiers 4
1515 Fast Study *alwys mid-div*....S Robinson 5
1474[1] Secret Sceptre *prom to 7th, disp 11th, outpcd frm 15th*....A Parker 6
1093[2] Cot Lane *prom, disp 8th, styd prom til fdd 4 out* ....R Walmsley 7
1471[2] Boreen Owen *ld 2nd, lost plc hlfwy, outpcd frm 13th* ....T Morrison 8
1352[2] Wigtown Bay *alwys mid-div, no ch & p.u. 4 out* ....A Robson pu
1515 Dawn Coyote (USA) *mid-div early, bhnd whn p.u. aft 10th*....J Billinge pu
1474 Yenoora (Ire) *bhnd whn f 3rd* ....J Nicholl f
1085[2] Tartan Tornado *wll bhnd 9th, t.o. & p.u. 12th* ....P Johnson pu
12 ran. Nk, ¾l. Time 6m 12.00s. SP Evens.
Mrs F T Walton (Border).

1574 Open Maiden Div I

1476[2] **JACK'S CROFT ....R Hale** 1
(fav) made virt all, shakn up 2 out, hld on und pres flat
1517 **Mapalak 5a....T Scott** 2
prom, chsd wnr 12th, outpcd 16th, rallied apr last, ran on
1514[3] **Tolmin ....P Forster** 3
trckd ldrs,rmndrs 9th,prog 14th,ev ch 2 out,styd on und pres
1476 Red Scot *not fluent, alwys abt same plc*....J Walton 4
1476[7] The Raskins 5a *not fluent, lost plc 12th, f nxt* J Nicholl f
1517 Sally Smith 5a *f 2nd*....Miss J Percy f
6 ran. 1½l, ½l. Time 6m 28.00s. SP Evens.
R R Bainbridge (Cumberland Farmers).

1575 Open Maiden Div II

1517[4] **KINGS TOKEN ....J Walton** 1
(fav) mid-div, prog 9th, ld 3 out, comf, improve
1473[5] **Czaryne 5a ....Miss J Percy** 2
prom, cls 3rd at 12th, ld 14th-3 out, no ch wnr aft
1450[5] **Stays Fresh ....S Swiers** 3
mid-div, prog hlfwy, chsd ldrs 14th, nvr dang
1476[5] Rustic Bridge *cls up, rmndrs 11th, hmpd 14th, no dang aft*....S Love 4
1452 Olympic Class *mid-div whn hmpd 15th, not rcvr* ....S Robinson 5
1476 Bagots Park *sn bhnd, nvr nrr*....R Sheils 6
1461[6] Weddicar Lady 5a *prom til rdn & wknd 10th, bhnd whn p.u. 2 out*....R Morgan pu
1512 Willy Waffles (Ire) *3rd at 6th, cls up whn f 15th* T Scott f
916 Sharpe Exit *last at 4th, t.o. & p.u. 9th*....P Forster pu
1351 Ink Flicker (Ire) *ld 3rd-14th, f nxt* ....J Cookson f
10 ran. 10l, 20l, 10l. Time 6m 28.00s. SP 2-1.
J B Walton (Border).

1576 Members (12st)

1513[1] **TODCRAG ....T Scott** 1
(fav) made all, clr 6th, eased flat
1512[1] **Mill Knock ....J Thompson** 2
blnd 1st, sn rcvrd, chsd wnr 9th, no ch
1514[2] **Sarona Smith 5a ....Miss J Hutchinson** 3
outpcd frm 9th, t.o. 15th
1512[2] Raffles *f 3rd* ....Miss S Walton f
4 ran. 6l, dist. Time 6m 23.00s. SP 1-10.
Mrs D Scott (Border).
D.G.

WHEATLAND
Wolverhampton P-To-P Course
Sunday May 19th
GOOD

1577 Confined

1195[1] **KORBELL (IRE) 5a ....A Crow** 1
(fav) ld to 5th & 8-10th, ld apr 3 out, sn drew clr
158[5] **Palm Reader 7ex ....C Barlow** 2
hld up, prog to mod 3rd 14th, no real hdwy nxt, tk 2nd last
1418 **Penllyne's Pride 7ex ....J Chilton** 3
race wd, ld 6-8th, & 10th-apr 3 out, sn btn
1191[3] Ballyhannon (Ire) *chsd ldr to 3rd, lost plc & rmndrs 7th, no ch frm 14th*....R Ford 4
1412[4] Invite D'Honneur (NZ) 7ex *chsd ldrs 3-5th, lost tch 10th, t.o. & p.u. 3 out* ....M Munrowd pu
1230[4] Brockish Bay *hld up, alwys bhnd, blnd 9th, t.o. & p.u. 3 out*....Miss S Baxter pu
6 ran. 15l, ½l, 10l. Time 6m 47.00s. SP 1-3.
K J Mitchell (North Shropshire).

1578 Open (12st)

1456[4] **BACK THE ROAD (IRE) ....G Hanmer** 1
tubed,ld to 4th,chsd ldr 10th,ld apr 3 out,clr nxt,all out
1510[2] **The Rum Mariner ....J Jukes** 2
ld 4th til apr 3 out, rallied und pres flat, just faild
1152 **Grey Gorden (Ire) ....A Crow** 3
(fav) prog to chs ldr 9-10th, 4th & outpcd 14th, no dang aft
1367[3] Ryton Guard 7ex *w.w. in tch to 13th, sn strgglng, t.o. & p.u. 3 out*....A Gribbin pu
1545[5] Le Piccolage *w.w. effrt to 3rd 14th, btn nxt, t.o. & p.u. 2 out*....C Barlow pu
1544 Shareef Star (v) *s.s. sn prom, rmndrs 7th, bhnd 11th, t.o. & p.u. 2 out* ....D Sherlock pu
1532 Dannigale 7ow *chsd ldr 6th-8th, lost tch 14th, t.o. & p.u. 3 out* ....E Haddock pu
7 ran. Nk, 20l. Time 6m 38.00s. SP 6-1.
M Mann (Wheatland).

1579 Ladies

1473[1] **OUT THE DOOR (IRE) 7ex ....Miss S Baxter** 1
(fav) hld up, smooth prog to ld 16th, rdn out flat, comf
1264[6] **Night Wind ....Miss S Wallin** 2
chsd ldr to 5th, ld 15th-nxt, onepcd und pres 2 out

1194 **Taurian Princess 5a................Miss E James** 3
in tch, pckd 12th, ev ch 16th, lft 3rd nxt, onepcd
1193[2] Logical Fun *w.w. nvr nr ldrs, no dang frm 16th*
..................................Miss L Wallace 4
1232[2] Czermno *ld to 14th, wknd frm 16th*..........Miss J Priest 5
1520[3] Sanamar *prom to 4th, bhnd 7th, t.o. 15th*
..................................Mrs C McCarthy 6
1438[7] Prince's Court *in tch, chsd ldr 10-15th, cls 3rd & btn whn u.r. 3 out*..........................Mrs J Kimber ur
1480 Raido *chsd ldr 5-10th, wknd apr 14th, t.o. & p.u. 3 out*
..................................Miss C Thomas pu
1229[1] Glen Taylor *prom, losing plc whn mstk 9th, t.o. & p.u. 14th*..................................Mrs M Wall pu
9 ran. 1½l, 5l, 20l, 10l, 6l. Time 6m 37.00s. SP 1-2.
M Mann (Wheatland).

1580 Open Maiden Div I (12st)

1196 **THE LAST JOSHUA 4ow..............E Haddock** 1
(fav) mid-div, lft 2nd 12th, ld apr 14th, drew wll clr nxt
1482 **Scally Hill 7a..........................A Dalton** 2
blnd 1st, bhnd & pshd alng 7th, lft poor 2nd 16th
1301 **Witch Doctor.................Miss S Phizacklea** 3
chsd ldrs to 9th, t.o. frm 14th
1483 Seven Cruise *mid-div, disp poor 3rd 14th, exhausted frm 3 out, walked in*......................D Mansell 4
1485 Astley Jack *sn clr, reluc & hdd apr 8th, sn ld agn, clr whn u.r. 12th*..........................B Tulloch ur
1336 Double-U-Gee (Ire) *jmpd bdly, sn wll bhnd, t.o. & p.u. aft 10th, dsmntd*...........................C Yates pu
1483 Miss Jcb (Ire) *lft in ld apr 8th,sn hdd,lft in ld 12th-nxt,btn & u.r. 16th*......................M FitzGerald ur
1365 Gold Top 7a *n.j.w. t.o. & jmpd slwly 14th, p.u. nxt*
..................................R Bevis pu
8 ran. 2 fences, 20l, dist. Time 7m 5.00s. SP 5-2.
E Haddock (Meynell & South Staffs).

1581 Open Maiden Div II (12st)

1150 **NOBBUTJUST (IRE) 5a............John Barlow** 1
w.w. steady prog to 2nd 14th, ld 16th, clr 2 out, rdn out
463 **Sharsman (Ire)..........................A Crow** 2
mid-div, prog 13th, prssd wnr 16th, rdn & hit nxt, no ext
1364[2] **April Suprise 5a......................G Hanmer** 3
(fav) s.s. alwys rear, 5th & rdn 14th, nvr nrr
1483 Playing The Fool 5a *chsd ldr 5th, ld 13th, clr nxt, hdd 16th, sn wknd, tired*......................P Hanly 4
Rare Gift (USA) 7a 17ow *jmpd slwly 1st, sn wll bhnd, t.o. 5th*..................................B Smith 5
1517 Authenticity (Ire) 5a *ld to aft 4th, ev ch 14th, sn wknd, t.o. & p.u. 3 out*...................Miss C Burgess pu
661 Mophead Kelly *chsd ldrs, mstk 5th, lost plc 9th, t.o. & p.u. 14th*..............................D Barlow pu
1485 Jacky's Jaunt 5a *mstks, in tch to 10th, t.o. & p.u. 14th*
..................................S Prior pu
1364 Ring Bank 7a *ld apr 5th-13th, 6th & wknd whn f nxt*
..................................D Sherlock f
1417 Sweet Jesterday 5a *sn bhnd, jmpd slwly 9th, t.o. whn blnd & u.r. 11th*..........................O McPhail ur
10 ran. 8l, 25l, dist, Bad. Time 6m 50.00s. SP 5-1.
C H Birch (Holcombe Harriers).

1582 Restricted (12st)

1233[4] **JO-SU-KI..........................C Barlow** 1
w.w. in tch, jnd ldrs 14th, ld apr last, drvn clr flat
1233[3] **Royle Burchlin........................D Barlow** 2
prom, went 2nd 14th, ld 16th-3 out, onepcd und pres
1456 **Miss Shaw 5a..........................A Griffith** 3
chsd ldr apr 8-13th, ld 3 out-apr last, wknd und pres
1482 Hatterill Ridge *bhnd, prog to 5th & blnd 14th, wll btn nxt, t.o.*..................................C Richards 4
1368[5] Grecianlid *chsd ldr 5th til apr 8th, lost tch apr 14th, t.o.*..................................Miss S Hopkins 5
1421[4] Foxy Blue *in tch, went 3rd 10th, rdn & wknd apr 14th, t.o. & p.u. 3out*......................Miss C Burgess pu
1421 Mastiff Lane *bhnd, lost tch 9th, t.o. & p.u. 12th* S Prior pu

1222[5] Demamo (Ire) *12s-4s, whppd round & u.r. start*
..................................N Bradley ur
1233 Yukon Gale (Ire) *(fav) ld, slppd lndg 12th, hdd 16th, 4th & btn, p.u. nxt*..............................A Crow pu
1218[1] Tanner *in tch, mstk 9th, sn wknd, t.o. & p.u. 11th*
..................................M Hammond pu
10 ran. 6l, 3l, 1 fence, 3l. Time 6m 55.00s. SP 16-1.
Peter Saville (Cheshire).

1583 Members

1578[1] **BACK THE ROAD (IRE) 5ex..........G Hanmer** 1
walked over
M Mann (Wheatland).
S.P.

TOWCESTER
Friday May 24th
GOOD TO SOFT

1584 3m 1f Wayside Hunters' Chase Class H

1108[2] **HERMES HARVEST 12.4 3a........Mr C Bonner** 1
(fav) held up, hdwy 11th, pushed along after 5 out, ld 2 out, driven clr run-in.
1544[4] **Fox Pointer 12.0 7a..............Mr R Thornton** 2
ld 5th til hdd 2 out, rdn and styd on one pace between last two.
1108 **Clare Man (Ire) 12.2 5a..............Mr M Rimell** 3
chsd ldr from 7th, went 2nd 6 out, ev ch 3 out, soon rdn and one pace.
370 Dubit 12.0 7a *held up, hdwy 12th, soon pushed along, styd on one pace but no ch after 4 out.*
..................................Mr J Tizzard 4
1553[2] Arctic Baron 12.0 7a (bl) *mstks, reminders after 3rd, pushed along and chsd ldrs til wknd after 5 out, t.o..*
..................................Miss S Vickery 5
1539[4] Pat Alaska 12.0 7a *bhnd, lost tch after 12th, t.o. when p.u. before 2 out*..........................Miss C Wates pu
1133 Furry Knowe 12.0 7a *soon struggling in rear, t.o. after 9th, p.u. after 6 out*..................Mr D Pritchard pu
1247[4] Epileny 11.10 7a *blnd and u.r. 1st*......Mr G Barfoot-Saunt ur
1566[4] Icky's Five 11.10 7a (bl) *ld to 5th, wknd 9th, t.o. when p.u. before 12th*..........................Mr R Lawther pu
1406[2] Touch Of Winter 12.0 7a *u.r. after 3rd*....Mr T Lacey ur
1532[1] Beau Dandy 12.0 7a *chsd ldr from 6th, prom till wknd after six out, bhnd when p.u. before 2 out.* Mr T Marks pu
11 ran. 7l, 3½l, 13l, dist. Time 6m 40.90s. SP 5-4.
Miss B W Palmer

CARTMEL
Saturday May 25th
GOOD TO FIRM

1585 3¼m Caffrey's Maiden Hunters' Chase Class H for the Fraser Cup

1369 **JR-KAY (IRE) 11.7 7a...........Mr N Bannister** 1
(fav) trckd ldrs, hdwy to ld 4 out, driven out flat.
1353[2] **Eastlands Hi-Light 11.7 7a.........Mr T Morrison** 2
mstks, chsd ldrs, effort and blnd 13th and next, styd on flat, no ext near fin.
1535[3] **Stilltodo 11.2 7a......................Mr A Parker** 3
prom, effort 4 out, rdn flat and ev ch till no ext near fin.
1572 Houselope Beck 11.7 7a *in tch, effort 12th, rdn and wknd 3 out.*..............................Mr A Robson 4
1285 Andretti's Heir 12.2 7a 9ow *ld 2nd to 4 out, wknd flat.*
..................................Mr A Bonson 5
1548[5] Cromwell Point 11.7 7a *soon well bhnd.* Mr C Mulhall 6
1535[4] Gen-Tech 11.7 7a *blnd 7th, soon bhnd, t.o. hfwy.*
..................................Mr A Gribbin 7
1571[2] Emu Park 12.0 *prom to 6th, soon lost pl and bhnd from 12th, t.o..*..............................Mr P Craggs 8
1545[4] Fell Mist 11.7 7a *not fluent, chsd ldrs till wknd 12th, t.o. when p.u. before 3 out.*..............Miss A Sykes pu
1570[5] Wire Lass 11.2 7a *f 2nd*....................Mr R Morgan f

1340^{5} Birtley Girl 11.4 5a *alwys rear, bhnd when p.u. before 14th.* ....Mr R Hale pu
1466^{1} Pure Madness (USA) 11.7 7a *n.j.w., soon bhnd, t.o. when p.u. before last.* ....Mr R Edwards pu
1151^{2} Pennine View 11.9 5a *blnd 1st, alwys bhnd, t.o. 5th, p.u. before 13th.* ....Mrs J Williamson pu
1155^{1} Heknowyou (Ire) 11.7 7a *ld to 2nd, cl up till blnd 4 out and next, weakening when f last.* ....Mr R Ford f
14 ran. 3l, 1l, 12l, 6l, 25l, 14l, dist. Time 6m 32.90s. SP 7-2.
N W A Bannister

HEXHAM
Saturday May 25th
GOOD TO FIRM

1586 2½m 110yds Flying Ace Hunters' Chase Class H

1467 **KNOWE HEAD 11.7 7a ....Mr S Brisby** 1
(Jt fav) j.w, made all, clr thrght, unchal.
1548^{8} **Cumberland Blues (Ire) 11.7 7a....Miss A Deniel** 2
chsd wnr most of way, not fluent 4 out and next, kept on, no impn.
1466^{2} **Chapel Island 11.7 7a ....Mr P Atkinson** 3
settld with chasing gp, challenging for 2nd when not fluent 3 out, one pace after.
1489^{3} La Mezeray 11.2 7a *settld bhnd, styd on from 3 out, nearest fin.* ....Mrs J Hawkins 4
1449^{2} John Corbet 11.7 7a *settld with chasing gp, kept on from 3 out, not pace to chal.* ....Miss S Brotherton 5
1570^{3} Royalist (Can) 11.7 7a *settld bhnd, imp final cct, staying on fin.* ....Mrs C Amos 6
1455^{2} The Yokel 11.7 7a *chsd lding pair 1st cct, rdn along before 3 out, one pace.* ....Mr J Davies 7
1573 Tartan Tornado 12.2 5a *chsd along to go pace, nvr reach challenging position.* ....Mr P Johnson 8
1572^{4} Flypie 11.9 5a *with chasing gp, struggling to go pace hfwy, n.d.* ....Mr C Storey 9
1472^{4} Gay Vixen VI 11.2 7a *well bhnd hfwy, t.o..*..Mr T Scott 10
1571^{6} Jolly Fellow 11.9 5a (bl) *waited with, steady hdwy when nearly u.r. 6 out, not rcvr, t.o..*..Mr N Wilson 11
1571 Fisherman's Quay 11.7 7a *driven along to go pace, t.o. when p.u. before 4 out.* ....Miss A Bowie pu
1542^{4} Little Wenlock 12.2 5a *(Jt fav) patiently rdn, steady hdwy to go 4th when f 6 out.* ....Mrs V Jackson f
1461^{8} Some Flash 11.7 7a *alwys well bhnd, t.o. when pulld before 6 out.* ....Mr Simon Robinson pu
14 ran. 25l, 10l, 1l, 1¼l, 9l, nk, 8l, 30l, 1¼l, dist. Time 5m 9.60s. SP 11-4.
J Hodgson

DULVERTON EAST
Mounsey Hill Gate
Saturday May 25th
GOOD

1587 Members (12st)

1554^{3} **MORCHARD MILLY 5a....J Auvray** 1
cls up, disp 7th, lft in ld 16th, clr 2 out, styd on
1553^{3} **Hensue ....R Treloggen** 2
(fav) cls up, blnd 3rd, disp 7th til blnd 16th, onepcd aft
1549^{3} **Remember Mac (bl) ....Miss C Hayes** 3
in tch, went 3rd 10th, lost tch 15th, ref 2 out, cont
1274^{3} Darktown Strutter (bl) *ld to 7th, 4th & in tch whn p.u. 11th, dsmntd* ....R White pu
1274 Glencommon *alwys bhnd, t.o. & p.u. 9th, dsmntd* ....D Jones pu
447 Northern Bride 5a *alwys bhnd, t.o. & p.u. 13th* ....S Kidston pu
1530^{2} Happy Thought 5a *chsd ldr to 4th, 4th & rdn 13th, sn wknd, p.u. 16th* ....N Harris pu
7 ran. 8l, dist. Time 7m 3.00s. SP 8-1.
R T Grant (Dulverton East).

1588 Ladies

1480^{2} **RIP VAN WINKLE ....Miss A Dare** 1
(fav) ld 6th-13th, ld 16th-nxt, rallied flat, ld post
1526^{2} **Desert Waltz (Ire) ....Miss P Curling** 2
chsd wnr 7th, ld 13-16th,ld 3 out, hrd rdn flat, hdd post
1426^{1} **Greenwine (USA) ....Miss A Lamb** 3
prog to jn ldrs 6th, 3rd & strggllng 12th, t.o. 14th
Frosty Reception (bl) *keen hold, in tch to 11th, t.o. frm 14th.* ....Miss L Pope 4
1276^{4} The Kimbler *jmpd lft, bhnd frm 7th, t.o. & p.u. 14th* ....Miss S Young pu
1552 Olive Basket 7a *ld to 6th, lost tch 11th, t.o. & p.u. 15th* ....Miss W Southcombe pu
6 ran. Hd, 1 fence, 25l. Time 6m 47.00s. SP 4-7.
Dr P P Brown/ Mrs S Birks (Berkeley).

1589 Open (12st)

1496^{1} **FOSBURY 7ex ....T Mitchell** 1
steady prog 7th, went 3rd 13th, chal last, sn ld, drew clr
1275^{2} **Vital Song ....G Matthews** 2
(fav) ld til hdd & pckd 17th, styd on onepcd frm 2 out
1278^{1} **Tasmin Tyrant (NZ) ....L Jefford** 3
chsd ldr, ld 17th til aft last, wknd
1529^{4} Glenform *chsd ldrs, 4th & outpcd 11th, no ch frm 14th* ....T Cole 4
1125^{2} Perfect Stranger *alwys bhnd, t.o. frm 14th* ..G Penfold 5
1552 Bidston Mill *alwys bhnd, t.o. 7th, p.u. 14th* ..S Kidston pu
1407^{1} Sohail (USA) 7ex *wll bhnd 12th, t.o. & p.u. 14th* ....G Maundrell pu
1342^{5} The Doormaker *alwys rear, t.o. & p.u. 15th* ....R Woolacott pu
1525^{2} Departure 5a *f 3rd* ....J Creighton f
1078^{1} Searcy *mstk 2nd, mid-div, rdn 9th, no ch 14th, p.u. last* ....R White pu
1228^{2} The Pedlar 5a *chsd ldrs to 7th, lost plc 10th, p.u. 15th* ....R Wakeham pu
1529 Magnolia Man *mid-div, blnd 8th, no ch 13th, p.u. 17th* ....N Harris pu
12 ran. 4l, 5l, dist, dist. Time 6m 47.00s. SP 3-1.
Mrs Susan Humphreys (Cattistock).

1590 Intermediate (12st)

926^{1} **M-REG ....L Jefford** 1
in tch, went 2nd 15th, ld 2 out, clr last, comf
1454 **Ive Called Time ....T Greed** 2
w.w. prog 14th, ev ch 3 out, no ext apr last
1428 **Northern Sensation 5a....N Harris** 3
prom, mstk 14th, rdn nxt, btn 3 out, lft 3rd last
1345^{1} Balmoral Boy (NZ) *hld up bhnd, nvr nr ldrs, t.o. 14th* ....M Miller 4
1499^{7} Blue-Bird Express 5a (bl) *ld til aft 3 out, wknd rpdly, p.u. nxt* ....R Treloggen pu
1427^{3} Bincombe Top *in tch til wknd 15th, p.u. 2 out* ....I Widdicombe pu
1550^{4} Rare Flutter 5a *cls up, rdn 15th, 3rd & btn whn u.r. last* ....B O'Doherty ur
1497^{1} Fellow Sioux *(fav) hld up in tch til f 11th* ....I Dowrick f
8 ran. 10l, dist, dist. Time 6m 56.50s. SP 4-1.
Mrs C Egalton (Axe Vale Harriers).

1591 Restricted (12st)

1277^{2} **Ragtime Boy ....A Farrant** 1D
(fav) chsd ldrs,ld apr 2 out,lft wll clr nxt,fin 1st, disq
1528^{4} **ONEOVERTHEIGHT ....N Harris** 1
prssd ldr,ld 15th-17th,sn wknd,lft poor 2nd 2 out,promoted
1345^{3} **Elle Flavador 5a....Miss S Vickery** 2
chsd ldrs,5th & wkng 16th,lft 3rd 2 out,fin 3rd,plcd 2nd
1428^{2} **Ballysheil ....S Edwards** 3
mid-div, 8th at 14th, sn lost tch, p.u. last,cont,pld 3rd
1493^{3} Hedera Helix *jmpd rght, alwys rear, t.o. & p.u. 15th* ....S Ellis pu
1553^{5} Miss Moony 5a *bhnd frm 6th, t.o. & p.u. 14th* ....I Widdicombe pu
1553 Fort Diana *prog 6th, chsd ldrs 8-12th, bhnd whn p.u. 14th* ....G Hopper pu

1427 My Boy Buster *t.d.e. blnd 1st, alwys bhnd, t.o. & p.u. 14th* ....D Jones pu
1551[7] Prince Amanda *in tch to 9th, bhnd & p.u. 14th* ....I Dowrick pu
1550 Link Copper *ld to 15th, sn wknd, p.u. apr 2 out* ....Miss L Blackford pu
1348[1] Ruth's Boy (Ire) *w.w. in tch whn f 12th*....R White f
1482 Quick Quick Sloe 5a *chsd ldr to 6th, lost plc nxt, bhnd & p.u. 2 out* ....Miss T Cave pu
532[2] Play Poker (Ire) *w.w. prog to ld 17th,hdd aft 3 out,ev ch whn f nxt*....S Slade f
1494[1] Springcombe 5a *wll bhnd frm 6th, t.o. & p.u. 14th* ....Miss S Eames pu
1429[1] Tangle Kelly *chsd ldrs to 14th, btn whn blnd bdly 17th, p.u. aft*....Miss J Cumings pu
15 ran. Dist, 3l, 1 fence. Time 6m 52.00s. SP 14-1.
Miss K Cook (Tetcott).
Ragtime Boy disq, took wrong course. Original distances. 19 jumps.

1592 Open Maiden Div I (12st)

1495[3] **MISS RICUS 7a ....R Treloggen** 1
cls up, hit 8th, rdn 2 out, ld last, ran on well
820 **Sandy Etna (Ire) 5a ....M Miller** 2
ld to 6th, chsd ldr, ld agn apr 2 out, hdd last, no ext
1555[2] **Joli High Note 5a ....Miss T Honeyball** 3
bhnd 8th, went poor 4th 3 out, nvr nrr
1494[4] Legal Vision 5a (bl) *in tch, cls 3rd 14th, sn rdn, btn 3 out* ....B Dixon 4
Tom's Apache *jmpd lft, ld 6th, clr 10th, hdd aft 3 out, wknd, p.u. last*....I Widdicombe pu
1347 Inner Temple *(fav) u.r. 1st*....I Dowrick ur
1347 Chocolate Buttons 5a *w.w. blnd 12th, 5th & in tch whn f 17th*....H Thomas f
1554 Dula Model 5a *hld up rear, ran off course apr 5th* ....S Ellis ro
1531[3] I Like The Deal 7a *w.w. jmpd slwly 7th, rdn & btn 16th, p.u. 2 out*....S Slade pu
9 ran. 1l, 15l, 20l. Time 7m 13.00s. SP 9-2.
Miss P J Boundy (Eggesford).

1593 Open Maiden Div II (12st)

1347 **BLUE NIGHT 5a....J Scott** 1
hld up, prog to ld 13th, clr 16th, rdn 2 out, all out
1555 **Drumcolliher ....Miss K Baily** 2
disp to 8th, chsd ldr apr 2 out, kpt on flat
1495[5] **Mountain-Linnet ....Miss A Goschen** 3
(Jt fav) disp 5th til ld 8th, hdd 13th, 4th & btn 3 out
1494[5] Miss Pernickity 5a *disp to 4th, bhnd 12th, t.o. 3 out* ....R Woolacott 4
1554 Carumu 5a *mstk 1st, chsd ldrs to 10th, bhnd frm 13th, t.o.*....S Hornby 5
1524[2] St Morwenna 5a *in tch, prog to 3rd at 16th, wll btn 3 out, p.u. nxt*....J Creighton pu
Tom's Gemini Star *w.w. prog to 5th at 14th, btn 16th, p.u. 2 out*....I Widdicombe pu
1349[2] Risky Bid 5a *(Jt fav) bhnd, some prog 12th, nvr on terms, p.u. 16th*....H Thomas pu
1554 Master Buckley *in tch, 6th & outpcd 14th, p.u. 17th, improve*....N Harris pu
1279 Saint Joseph *mid-div, 7th whn ran wd apr 15th, t.o. & p.u. 2 out*....Miss S Young pu
1396 Jim Crow *in tch til bhnd & rdn 13th, t.o. & u.r. 2 out* ....M Miller ur
11 ran. 2l, 9l, dist, 5l. Time 7m 3.00s. SP 5-1.
Mrs E Scott (Minehead Harriers).
S.P.

MELTON HUNT CLUB
Garthorpe
Saturday May 25th
GOOD

1594 Members (12st)

1563[1] **HILL ISLAND ....R Sweeting** 1
(fav) 2nd til ld 8th, drew away frm 2 out, comf
1457 **Celtic King 4ex ....K Needham** 2
3rd frm 10th, chsd wnr 3 out, no imp
1521[2] **Stanwick Farlap 5a ....T Marks** 3
prog 6th, 2nd 10th-4 out, 3rd aft, just hld for 2nd
1192[1] Whatafellow (Ire) *w.w. 15l 5th 6 out, ran on 3 out, not rch 1st trio* ....A Crow 4
1377[8] Spanish Whisper *alwys last trio, 7th & outpcd 6 out* ....T Lane 5
1519 Blue Beat 5a *mid-div, 4th frm 10th, in tch to 3 out, wknd nxt & p.u.*....M Hewitt pu
1281[6] Pinewood Lad *alwys last, t.o. 10th, p.u. 2 out* ....Miss K Ford pu
1449[4] Band Sargeant (Ire) *ld to 8th, cls 2nd whn u.r. 9th* ....Miss J Foster ur
1097[1] Tenelord *cls up 1st m, wknd 7th, 7th at 10th, p.u. 12th* ....S Morris pu
1321[5] Lovely Clonmoyle (Ire) 5a *4th/5th for 2m, 6th & outpcd 5 out, p.u. 2 out*....N Bloom pu
10 ran. 6l, 1½l, 4l, 1 fence. Time 6m 23.50s. SP 5-4.
Colin Gee (Heythrop).

1595 Conditional

1535[2] **WHINSTONE MILL ....R Thornton** 1
(fav) 3rd frm 11th, ld 6 out, ran on gamely whn hdd 2 out,ld last
1505[1] **Radical Views ....A Hill** 2
3rd 6 out, chsd wnr 4 out, ld brfly 2 out, no ext last
1479[2] **Auction Law (NZ) ....A Crow** 3
rear for 2m, ran on past btn horses, too mch to do
1521[4] Smart Pal *2nd til ld 10th-6 out, 3rd & outpcd 3 out* ....K Needham 4
1522 R N Commander *alwys abt 5th, outpcd by 1st pair frm 4 out*....J Cornwall 5
1067[2] Melton Park (bl) *alwys rear hlf, prog past btn horses last m*....N Bloom 6
1462 Golden Moss *ld to 9th, cls up til wknd rpdly frm 6 out* ....Capt S Robinson 7
1455[3] Tarry Awhile *alwys mid-div, outpcd frm 6 out* ....J Connell 8
1522[1] Majestic Ride *alwys last trio, no ch frm 6 out* ....R Armson 9
1521[5] Decent Gold *last til p.u. 11th*....J Stephenson pu
1564 Waterhay *abt 6th 1st m, fdd 7th, mstk 12th, p.u. nxt* ....R Mumford pu
1465[2] Sharpridge *cls up in 3rd til chsd ldr 12th, wknd nxt, f 4 out*....M Mawhinney f
1259[2] Ovac Star *alwys rear hlf, outpcd 6 out, p.u. 3 out* ....S R Andrews pu
1546 El Bae *5th 1st m, fdd, bhnd whn p.u. 4 out* ...P Taiano pu
1518[2] Merlins Girl 5a *abt 7th 1st m, fdd, bhnd whn p.u. 2 out* ....T Lane pu
15 ran. 5l, 8l, 5l, ½l, 8l, 2l, 2l, 2l. Time 6m 22.00s. SP 2-1.
Mrs Bambi Hornbuckle (Belvoir).

1596 Ladies

1520[1] **NOWHISKI ....Miss C Tarratt** 1
alwys ld/disp, qcknd gamely flat to ld cls home
1563[2] **Saybright ....Miss H Irving** 2
alwys 1st 4, chal 3 out, ld last, just outpcd flat
1541[4] **Notary-Nowell (bl) ....Miss S Gritton** 3
3rd to 9th, 5th & outpcd frm 11th, lft remote 3rd 2 out
1579[6] Sanamar *alwys last pair, t.o. last frm 7th, p.u. 3 out* ....Mrs C McCarthy pu
1238[2] Prince Metternich *t.o. frm 7th, f 10th*...Miss C Arthers f
1520[2] Adamare *disp til f 6th*....Miss C Holliday f
1502[2] Larry The Lamb *(fav) prog 7th, 3rd frm 9th, rdn & disp 3rd whn f 2 out*....Miss G Chown f
1411[1] Roving Report *ref to race*....Mrs A Rucker 0
1469[2] Indie Rock *prog 7th, disp 10th-4 out, disp 3rd & ev ch whn f 2 out*....Mrs F Needham f
9 ran. 1l, dist. Time 6m 17.00s. SP 4-1.
Tim Tarratt (Cottesmore).

1597 Novice Championship (12st)

1415[1] **GROMIT (NZ) ....Julian Pritchard** 1
prog 11th, chsd ldr 4 out, ld aft 2 out, comf
1522[4] **Kerry My Home ....T Marks** 2
mostly 5th for 2m, ran on well frm 4 out, not rch wnr
1564 **Tommy O'Dwyer (Ire) 2ow....A Hill** 3
cls up, ld 12th, 10l clr 3 out, wknd rpdly & hdd nxt

1522 Sharp To Oblige *(fav) rpd prog 9th, disp 10-11th, 3rd 6 out, outpcd 4 out*............................S Swiers 4
1522 Mr Gee *cls up in 2nd/3rd to 9th, fdd, 8th & outpcd 6 out*............................L Hicks 5
1522³ Tempered Point (USA) *ld to 9th, fdd, 6th & outpcd 4 out*............................T Lane 6
1286¹ Grain Merchant *alwys rear hlf, last & outpcd 6 out*............................R Walmsley 7
1523¹ Sargeants Choice *cls up, 2nd frm 7th-5 out, went backwards nxt*............................J Barlow 8
1380³ Supreme Dream (Ire) 5a *alwys rear hlf, 7th whn f 5 out*............................Mrs P Adams f
9 ran. 5l, 6l, 15l, 5l, 2l, 30l, 3l. Time 6m 27.00s. SP 7-2.
Miss Sarah Eaton (North Cotswold).

1598 Open

1457¹ **LUCKY CHRISTOPHER** ....**A Sansome** 1
(fav) w.w. 2nd 6 out, ld 3 out, drew away und pres apr last
1133¹ **Peanuts Pet** ....**R Walmsley** 2
cls up, 3rd 12th-3 out, chsd wnr nxt, no imp
1519¹ **Coolvawn Lady (Ire) 5a**..................**T Lane** 3
2nd til ld 5th, hdd 3 out, outpcd frm nxt
1231³ Castlebay Lad *cls up in 3rd to 11th, 4th & outpcd frm nxt*............................C Coyne 4
1379³ Trusty Friend *alwys last, t.o. frm 5th* ....J Oldring 5
1519³ Raise An Argument *ld to 5th, 2nd til squeezed out apr 11th*............................J Docker ro
6 ran. 10l, 4l, 1 fence, 1l. Time 6m 20.00s. SP 5-6.
G B Tarry (Grafton).

1599 Open Maiden (12st)

1240² **APPLE NICKING** ....**A Hill** 1
w.w. prog 8th, ld 5 out, clr frm nxt, easily
1381³ **Dolly Bloom 5a** ....**A Sansome** 2
(fav) w.w. prog 8th, chsd wnr 5 out, blnd nxt, no ch aft
1434 **Plat Du Jour 5a** ....**B Pollock** 3
2nd/disp to 11th, outpcd nxt, completed own time
1399⁸ Blumix *alwys rear hlf, t.o. frm 7th, p.u. 12th* ..N Strain pu
1376⁴ Coolsythe 5a (bl) *ld/disp to 11th, 4th & fdng whn f aft 4 out*............................C Millington f
1523 Forever Freddy *cls up,ld 10th-6 out,3rd & outpcd 4 out, tired whn ref 3 out*......................G Brewer ref
1581⁵ Rare Gift (USA) 7a 16ow *3rd 1st m, 5th whn f 9th*............................B Smith f
7 ran. 20l, dist. Time 6m 33.00s. SP 7-4.
Mrs M Upstone (Bicester With Whaddon Chase).
K.B.

TREDEGAR FARMERS
Bassaleg
Saturday May 25th
GOOD TO SOFT

1600 Members

1268² **POLLY PRINGLE 5a**......................**A Price** 1
(fav) ld, mstk 2nd, clr 10th, easily
1414⁵ **Light The Wick** ....**C Pennycate** 2
chsd wnr to 10th, lft 2nd nxt, btn 2 fences
1270⁴ **Pyro Pennant** ....**Miss P Cooper** 3
3rd til dist 2nd frm 10th, u.r. nxt, rmntd
3 ran. Dist, dist. Time 7m 1.00s. SP 1-6.
Mrs C E Goldsworthy (Tredegar Farmers).
One fence omitted all races, 16 jumps.

1601 Restricted (12st)

1561¹ **STERLING BUCK (USA)** ....**T Jones** 1
(Jt fav) ld to 4th, 2nd til prog to ld 3 out, ran on
1482² **Meadow Cottage** ....**T Stephenson** 2
(Jt fav) rear, steady prog 10th, 8l down 3 out, nrst fin
1557 **Haydon Hill 7a** ....**M FitzGerald** 3
ld 4th, 15l clr 10th, hdd 3 out, onepcd aft
1415⁵ Bay Leader 5a *alwys last, lft 4th by dfctns* ..S Shinton 4
1557 Captain Equaty *mid-div, lost tch hlfwy, p.u. 10th*............................J P Keen pu
1557⁴ The Foolish One 5a *mid-div, lost tch 9th, p.u. last*............................M Jackson pu
1557 Colonel Frazer (Ire) *prom, 4th hlfwy, wknd, poor 5th whn p.u. last*............................G Lewis pu
1410² Welsh Clover 5a *3rd at 7th, wknd rpdly, p.u. 10th*............................G Barfoot-Saunt pu
1582 Demamo (Ire) *rear, some prog to 5th apr 10th where p.u. rpdly*............................A Phillips pu
217 Deal Me One *cls up, gd 3rd at 9th, wknd rpdly & p.u. 11th*............................J Jukes pu
1485¹ Derring Ann 5a *ref to race* ....D S Jones 0
1557 Sea Tarth 7a *mid-div, no ch whn u.r. 11th* ...D Davies ur
12 ran. 4l, 3l, 25l. Time 6m 33.00s. SP 7-2.
D J Clapham (Ledbury).

1602 Confined (12st)

1557¹ **CAIRNEYMOUNT** ....**J Tudor** 1
(fav) 2nd til ld 10th, clr 13th, easily
1415 **Pharrago (Ire)** ....**Miss P Cooper** 2
mid-div, poor 3rd 3 out, lft dist 2nd nxt
1558⁴ Bronze Effigy 3ex (bl) *mid-div, poor 4th whn ref 3 out*............................W Pugh ref
1262⁴ Abbreviation *cls up til wknd 10th, disp poor 4th whn hmpd & ref 3 out* ....J Williams ref
1560 Adanac *alwys rear, mstks 10th & nxt & p.u.* ...A Price pu
1560 Prince Nepal *ld to 9th, 15l 2nd whn s.u. apr 3 out*............................G Barfoot-Saunt su
1492¹ Sister Lark 5a *prom to 5th, wknd 9th, p.u. nxt*............................P Williams pu
1558³ Icecapade (Bel) *rear, steady prog to 4th at 10th, f nxt*............................J P Keen f
8 ran. Dist. Time 6m 43.00s. SP 8-11.
Robert Williams (Llangeinor).

1603 Ladies

1559¹ **MENDIP MUSIC 5ex**............**Miss E Crawford** 1
(fav) cls up, ld apr 10th, made rest, alwys in cmmnd
1543⁵ **Never Be Great** ....**Miss L Pearce** 2
cls up, 2nd frm 10th, clsd 3 out, alwys hld
1557 **How Friendly** ....**Miss E James** 3
ld to 8th, 3rd frm 10th, no ch 3 out
1387⁴ Mount Falcon *s.s. cls 4th at 8th, grad lost tch*............................Miss C Morgan 4
4 ran. 5l, 8l, dist. Time 6m 29.00s. SP 4-9.
Miss E Crawford (Curre).

1604 Open (12st)

1560 **TOUCH 'N' PASS 4ex**......................**J Tudor** 1
(fav) hld up, prog to ld 10th, qcknd away nxt, easily
1411⁴ **Oragas** ....**J Jukes** 2
cls up in 3rd/4th, chsd wnr 11th, styd on, no imp
1488² **Cornish Cossack (NZ)** ....**W Pugh** 3
prom to 9th, lost plc, remote 4th 3 out
1508 Afaristoun (Fr) *last at 4th, dtchd 9th, p.u. nxt* ...J Lilley 4
1171 Coombesbury Lane 5a *cls up to 9th, wknd rpdly, almost ref & f nxt*......................T Stephenson f
1439¹ Fresh Prince *ld to 9th, 2nd aft, grad wknd 13th, p.u. 2 out*............................T Jones pu
6 ran. 15l, dist. Time 6m 33.00s. SP Evens.
David Vaughan-Morgan (Llangeinor).

1605 Open Maiden Div I (12st)

1390 **HARRY FROM BARRY** ....**J Tudor** 1
4th til ld apr 10th, clr nxt, prssd 2 out, lft clr last
1417⁶ **Boddington Hill 5a** ....**S Shinton** 2
2nd at 10th, 3rd nxt, ran on 3 out, hld whn lft 2nd last
1561 **Steel Valley (Ire) 5a**.....................**A Dalton** 3
(fav) 4/5-7/4, rear, prog to 3rd 10th, lost plc 12th,ran on late
1483 Toucher (Ire) *alwys rear, fin own time* ....J Cook 4
1511 Agapanthus 5a *25s-12s, cls 3rd whn u.r. 7th* ..S Lloyd ur
1390 Good Boy Charlie 7a *hld up,prog to chs wnr 10th,chal 2 out,lkd hld whn u.r. last*......................J Jukes ur

1557 Queen's Equa 5a *cls up til lost plc 8th, p.u. 13th* ....M Lewis pu
1506[3] Flashmans Mistress 5a *33s-5s, cls up to 9th, lost tch nxt, p.u. 12th*....................D Stephens pu
8 ran. 1l, 4l, 25l. Time 6m 51.00s. SP 6-1.
Gwyn R Davies (Llangeinor).

1606 Open Maiden Div II (12st)

1483[3] **BOWLAND GIRL (IRE) 5a ....Miss E James** 1
(fav) prom, ld 13th, disp nxt til qckND apr last, all out
1492[3] **Relatively High 7a ....D S Jones** 2
hld up, gd prog to 3rd at 10th, disp 3 out,no ext apr last
1483 **Tennessee Cruiser ....D Harrison** 3
rear, lost tch 7th, poor 4th 3 out, tk 3rd flat
1561[2] Gold Tip 5a *ld til aft 9th, wknd rpdly, t.o. 3 out* ....J P Keen 4
1561[3] Maytown 5ow (v) *disp whn u.r. 4th* ....R Nolan ur
1200[4] Appeal 5a *mstk 3rd, 2nd til just ld 10th, f nxt* ..D Evatt f
1485 Miss Clare 5a *hld up, lost plc 8th, drvn to cls 5th whn f 11th*....................M FitzGerald f
7 ran. 3l, dist, 1½l. Time 6m 56.00s. SP 7-4.
G H Davies (Ludlow).
P.H./J.C.

THAMES VALLEY HUNTS CLUB
Tweseldown
Sunday May 26th
GOOD

1607 Members (12st)

1501 **CHILDSWAY ....T Underwood** 1
(fav) hld up, ld 9th, qcknd 3 out, rdn out flat
1405[5] **Old Road (USA) ....C Coyne** 2
hld up, ld 8-9th,not qckn 3 out, rdn & effrt apr last,kpt on
1567 **No Reply ....Mrs C Mitchell** 3
jmpd slwly, ld to 4th & 7-8th, outpcd frm 3 out
3 ran. 1½l, 15l. Time 7m 2.00s. SP 8-11.
Charles Kay (Garth & South Berks).

1608 Confined (12st)

1562[1] **SEVERN INVADER ....Miss H Gosling** 1
mstk 2nd,chsd ldr to 3rd,effrt & ld 13th,clr 3 out,ran on wl
1501[1] **Elite Governor (Ire) ....B Hodkin** 2
(fav) mstks,jmpd lft,ld aft 10-13th,outpcd 3 out,btn whn blnd last
1246[4] **Dark Sirona 5a ....D Lines** 3
immed outpcd in 4th, t.o. 8th, lft dist 3rd 3 out
1502 Unscrupulous Gent *immed outpcd in 5th, t.o. frm 8th* ....Mrs E Huttinger 4
1505[4] Polecroft *alwys last, t.o. 6th*..........Miss P Hance 5
1374 Shared Fortune (Ire) *st fast pace til hdd aft 10th,3rd frm 13th,btn whn f 3out*....................D Dennis f
6 ran. 12l, dist, 6l, 1 fence. Time 6m 19.00s. SP Evens.
Captain Miles Gosling (Bicester With Whaddon Chase).
Winner not favourite.

1609 Mixed Open (12st)

1566 **MONKSFORT 7ex ....Miss C Holliday** 1
ju.w. made all, jmpd lft 11th, ran on gamely apr last
1565 **Sunshine Manor ....A Sansome** 2
(fav) prom, prssd wnr 10th, outjmpd aft, no ext apr last
785 **Darton Ri ....J Maxse** 3
bckwrd,chsd ldrs,outpcd 11th,kpt on to mod 3rd at last
1260[1] Cool Ginger *mstk 4th & last,effrt 12th,lost plc 15th,kpt on agn 2 out*....................R Sweeting 4
1505 Four Rivers *prom til outpcd 11th,chsd ldng pair 14th,no imp,wknd last*....................R Lawther 5
1536[4] Alzamina 5a 3ow *in tch in rear,mstk 6th,outpcd 11th,no prog,p.u.2 out*....................T Hills pu
1532 Afaltoun 7ex *chsd wnr to 10th, outpcd nxt, wknd 14th, p.u. 3 out*....................T Lacey pu
1372[3] Cheeky Cheval *mstk 7th, in tch in rear til last frm 10th, bhnd & p.u.2 out*..........D Dennis pu
1536 Rustic Ramble *in tch in rear, mstk & lost plc 10th, wll btn & p.u. 2 out*....................P Hacking pu
9 ran. 5l, 20l, 4l, ¾l. Time 6m 19.00s. SP 16-1.
Miss C Holliday (Old Surrey & Burstow).

1610 Open Maiden

1540[7] **PALLINGHAM STAR (IRE) ....P O'Keeffe** 1
ld to 3rd,rdn & outpcd 12th,ran on to ld & mstk last,drvnout
1540[3] **Spar Copse ....Miss A Goschen** 2
ld 3rd, lft clr 15th, tired 2 out, hdd last no ext
1501 Daring Trouble 5a *hld up, in tch til last & n.j.w. frm 11th, t.o. & p.u.2 out*....................R Hicks pu
1485 Keep On Trying 5a *(fav) prom til f 10th* .....M Portman f
1434 Lloyds Loser *hld up,chsd ldr 12th,ev ch & f 15th,even rmntd & fin* ....A Sansome f
5 ran. 2l. Time 6m 38.00s. SP 7-2.
Mrs Carrie Zetter-Wells (Chiddingfold).

1611 Novice Riders

1563 **THE HOLY GOLFER ....C Smyth** 1
rear & in tch,prog to 3rd 12th,ld apr last where blnd,rdnout
1405[2] **Brack N Brandy ....Miss R David** 2
(fav) t.d.e. ld, lft clr 11th, hdd apr last, no ext
1507[6] **Punching Glory ....Miss S Brewer** 3
raced wd, chsd ldrs, 4th frm 12th, lft poor 3rd last
1562[4] Funchen View *last pair, t.o. 9th, retired* ....Miss S Loggin 4
1510 Espy 7ex *prom, cls 2nd whn f 11th*..........A James f
1562 Button Your Lip *chsd ldrs, disp 3rd whn u.r. 10th* ....Mrs J Enderby ur
1563 Berkana Run *chsd ldrs,lft 2nd 11th-aft 3 out,3rd & btn,blnd & u.r. last*....................R Bailey ur
1550[5] Rapid Rascal 7ex *prom to 9th, sn outpcd, t.o. & p.u. 15th*....................Miss S West pu
1551[6] Final Express 5a *n.j.w. last pair til nrly u.r. 5th, p.u. nxt*....................M Hoskins pu
9 ran. 10l, dist, 20l. Time 6m 22.00s. SP 16-1.
C Smyth (Old Berkshire).

1612 Restricted (12st)

1551[5] **ALEX THUSCOMBE ....P Shaw** 1
ld 3-6th & 9-13th,lft in ld 16th,clr 2 out, ran on well
1501[2] **Sporting Lark 5a....................Miss H Irving** 2
chsd ldrs, lft 2nd & hmpd 16th, outjmpd 2 out, btn aft
1481[3] **Bakmalad ....H Wheeler** 3
(fav) chsd ldrs, mstk 10th & rmndr, outpcd 14th, ran on 2 out
1564[4] Colourful Boy *lost plc 8th, effrt 12th, ev ch 15th, grad wknd 3 out*....................A Charles-Jones 4
1501[5] Sutton Lass 5a *chsd ldrs, mstk 11th, outpcd frm 13th, wknd 3 out*....................R Lawther 5
1564[9] Kamtara *mstks, wll bhnd, t.o. 11th, ran on 15th, nrst fin*....................R Hicks 6
1441[3] Political Man *ld to 3rd, sn lost plc, t.o. & p.u. 12th* ....T Hills pu
1395[4] Blake's Finesse 5a *j.w. ld 6-9th & frm 13th, 1l up wn f 16th, dead*....................Miss S Vickery f
1295 Brief Sleep 5a *t.d.e. hld up bhnd, nvr in race, t.o. & u.r. 12th*....................Miss J Wickens ur
1371 Mr Sunnyside *in tch to 13th, no ch whn blnd 16th, t.o. & p.u. 2 out*....................D Dennis pu
1371[4] Lewesdon Princess 5a (bl) *mid-div, jmpd slwly 8th, wknd 12th, t.o. & p.u. last*..........Miss S Gladders pu
11 ran. 15l, 6l, ¾l, 20l, 6l. Time 6m 21.00s. SP 3-1.
Mrs Peter Shaw (Cattistock).
J.N.

FONTWELL
Monday May 27th
GOOD

1613 3¼m 110yds South Coast Radio Hunters' Chase Class H

1541[1] **CHILIPOUR 12.0 7a ....Mr N Harris 1**
(fav) in tch, chsd ldr 11th, ld 2 out, styd on well.
1584[2] **Fox Pointer 11.7 7a ....Mr R Thornton 2**
ld, hdd and jmpd right 2 out, rdn and kept on gamely.
1463[4] **Wrekin Hill 11.0 7a.............Mrs J Wilkinson 3**
well bhnd till hdwy 13th, chsd ldrs 18th, one pace from next.
1560 Lislary Lad 11.0 7a *hdwy 13th, chsd lding pair 18th, wknd 3 out.*..........................Mr D S Jones 4
1464[1] Professor Longhair 12.0 7a *prom, outpcd 13th, no hdwy from 18th.*........................Mr R Hicks 5
1546[3] Blue Danube (USA) 11.7 7a *chsd ldrs till wknd 18th.* ....Mr T Hills 6
1538[3] Trust The Gypsy 11.7 7a *prom till wknd 18th, t.o. when virtually p.u. run-in.*..................Mr R Nuttall 7
1297[4] Our Survivor 11.0 7a *bhnd, mstk 10th, t.o. when p.u. after 19th.*...........................Miss C Savell pu
1323[7] Major Inquiry (USA) 11.7 7a *bhnd from 12th, t.o. 16th, p.u. before 18th.*..................Miss H C Pewter pu
1539 Motor Cloak 11.0 7a (bl) *mid div, wknd 15th, bhnd when p.u. after 17th.*.......................Mr P Bull pu
1546[7] Sure Pride (USA) 11.0 7a *mid div, mstk 2nd, wknd 13th, bhnd when p.u. before 18th.*......Mr P O'Keeffe pu
1294[2] The Portsoy Loon 11.7 7a (bl) *bhnd, hdwy 10th, wknd 17th, t.o. when p.u. before 2 out.*......Mrs S Hickman pu
12 ran. 2½l, 20l, 2½l, 3½l, 5l, dist. Time 7m 6.50s. SP Evens.
Nick Viney

HEREFORD
Monday May 27th
GOOD

1614 3m 1f 110yds Clive Maiden Hunters' Chase Class H

1464[2] **EXPRESSMENT 11.10 7a ....Mr G Penfold 1**
held up, hdwy 12th, went 2nd 4 out, ld after next, soon drew clr, easily.
1509[1] **Baron's Heir 11.10 7a ....Mr S Lloyd 2**
midfield, outpcd hfwy, styd on 2 out, tk 2nd run-in, not trbl wnr.
1557[2] **Sea Search 11.12 5a ....Mr J Llewellyn 3**
held up, hdwy 5th, ld 15th till after 3 out, rdn when blnd next, one pace.
470 Miss Dotty 11.5 7a *bhnd, struggling 11th, styd on from 3 out, nvr nrr.*................Miss A Plunkett 4
1508[1] Cantantivy 11.7 5a *handily pld, rdn 15th, outpcd 3 out.*..Mr M Rimell 5
1547[3] Rayman (Ire) 11.12 5a *midfield, hdwy to chase ldrs 4 out, wknd 2 out.* ....Mr J Trice-Rolph 6
1464[3] Damers Treasure 11.12 5a *held up, struggling 11th, t.o.*...Mr A Sansome 7
1478 Corrianne 11.5 7a (h) *ld till after 7th, lost ground quickly, soon bhnd, t.o. when p.u. before 4 out.* ....Mr O McPhail pu
1458[2] Misty (NZ) 12.0 3a *prom till lost pl quickly before 7th, bhnd when p.u. before next.*............Mr J Culloty pu
1211 Bancyfelin Boy 11.10 7a *in tch, not fleunt 13th (water), weakening when mstk 4 out, t.o. when p.u. before next.*..................................Mr A Price pu
1547[2] No Joker (Ire) 11.10 7a *bhnd, blnd 10th, hdwy 4 out, staying on in fourth when mstk and u.r. 2 out.* ....Mr R Hall ur
1582[1] Jo-Su-Ki 11.10 7a *alwys bhnd, lost tch 14th, t.o. when p.u. before 3 out.*............Mr C J B Barlow pu
1533[2] Clobracken Lad 11.10 7a *(fav) n.j.w., in tch, reminders 10th, wknd 14th, t.o. when p.u. before 3 out.* ....Mr G Baines pu
1458[5] Making Time 11.5 7a *cl up, ld after 7th till 15th, wknd quickly next, bhnd when p.u. before 3 out.* ....Mr Andrew Martin pu
1481[5] Hennerwood Oak 11.5 7a *nvr far away, cl 3rd when blnd and u.r. 14th.*.........................Mr M Jackson ur
1385[1] Celtic Daughter 11.5 7a *held up in rear when blnd and u.r. 5th.*..Mr J Rees ur
16 ran. 9l, 1¾l, ¾l, 4l, 4l, 29l. Time 6m 34.70s. SP 4-1.
Miss A S Ross

WETHERBY
Monday May 27th
GOOD

1615 2½m 110yds Guy Cunard Hunters' Chase Class H

1277[1] **SLIEVENAMON MIST 11.7 7a ..Mr Richard White 1**
ld till after 1st, chsd ldrs, led after 9th, drew well clr from 4 out.
1463[3] **Simply Perfect 11.7 7a........Miss S Swindells 2**
in tch, went 2nd between last 2, no ch with wnr.
1545[3] **My Nominee 12.0 7a (bl) ....Mr D Sherlock 3**
ld after 1st till hdd after 9th, wknd from 4 out.
1544[2] Jumbeau 11.11 3a *(fav) in tch till outpcd after 8th, no dngr after.*..............................Mr C Bonner 4
1532[9] Southern Minstrel 11.11 7a *soon well bhnd, t.o..* ....Miss C Metcalfe 5
1283[7] Colonel Popski 11.2 7a *soon well bhnd, t.o. when p.u. before 4 out.*.........................Mr C Mulhall pu
672 On The Other Hand 12.0 7a (v) *soon well bhnd, p.u. before 7th.*...................................Capt A Ogden pu
1586 Little Wenlock 12.2 5a *mstks, soon bhnd, t.o. when p.u. before last.* ....Mrs V Jackson pu
1337[4] Green Times 11.13 7a 2ow *soon well bhnd, t.o. when p.u. before 9th.* ....Capt W Ramsay pu
1462[2] Golden Savannah 11.3 7a 1ow *chsd ldrs, mstk 7th, lost tch and p.u. before 9th.*..........Mr M Sowersby pu
1467[2] Gaelic Warrior 11.4 5a *cl up till wknd after 8th, poor 4th when f four out.*............................Mr N Tutty f
11 ran. Dist, 6l, 1l, dist. Time 5m 11.30s. SP 11-2.
Nick Viney

ALBRIGHTON WOODLAND
Chaddesley Corbett
Monday May 27th
GOOD TO FIRM

1616 Members

1460[3] **KAMEO STYLE ....Miss J Priest 1**
walked over
S Rammell (Albrighton Woodland).

1617 Ladies

1480[1] **BANKHEAD (IRE) ....Miss C Spearing 1**
(fav) n.j.w. cls up, lft in ld 14th, jnd last, qcknd flat
1480[6] **Mister Gebo ....Miss C Dyson 2**
prom,not qckn 12th,lft 2nd 15th,ev ch last,no ext flat
1545[2] **Inch Maid 5a.................Miss H Brookshaw 3**
mstks,nrly u.r. 1st,pshd alng hlfwy,nvr able to chal,nvr nrr
1533 Antarctic Call *in tch til last & strgglng hlfwy, t.o. 3 out* ....Miss N Richards 4
1488[1] Moving Force *ld to 12th, cls 2nd whn hmpd & u.r. 14th* ....Miss C Williams ur
1420[2] Golden Fare *mstk 3rd, t.o. 6th, p.u. 10th* ....Miss L Wallace pu
1341[2] Blue Cheek *cls up, ld 12th, going wll whn u.r. 14th* ....Miss T Spearing ur
1579[2] Night Wind *cls up, lft 2nd 14th, ev ch whn f nxt* ....Mrs A Rucker f
8 ran. 4l, 3l, dist. Time 6m 0.60s. SP 8-13.
A J Brazier (Croome & West Warwickshire).

1618 Confined (12st)

1219[1] **SHOON WIND ....A Dalton 1**
(fav) chsd ldr til ld 5th, clr 15th, unchal
1596 **Roving Report ....Julian Pritchard 2**
in tch,mstk 6th,outpcd 13th,ran on to 2nd 2 out,no ch wnr
1422[2] **Furry Fox (Ire) ....A Crow 3**
ld to 5th, chsd wnr aft, btn 15th, lost 2nd 2 out
1478 Homme D'Affaire *rear, effrt & prog 12th, no imp ldrs frm 15th*................................T Stephenson 4

1507[2] Hook Line'N'sinker *rear, rdn 10th, no ch frm 14th* ....L Brown 5
1478[5] Running Frau 5a 3ow *alwys well in rear, nvr nrr* ....D Minton 6
1481 Kingsthorpe *rear, mstk 12th, sn no ch, t.o.* ..A Phillips 7
1510 Really An Angel 5a *alwys last, sn t.o.* ...Mrs K Bevan 8
1318[4] Durzi *s.s. sn mid-div, wknd rpdly & p.u. 14th* E Walker pu
1577[3] Penllyne's Pride 4ow *cls up whn u.r. 4th* ....J Chilton ur
1435 Keeler Rider (USA) 1ow *w.w. prog going wll 12th, wknd rpdly 14th, p.u. 3 out* ....B Potts pu
1437 Master Dancer *chsd ldrs, 3rd & wkng 15th, no ch whn p.u. last, dsmntd* ....Miss C Dyson pu
1577 Invite D'Honneur (NZ) *alwys rear, wll bhnd whn p.u. 3 out* ....A Wallett pu
1006 Central Lass 5a *alwys last trio, t.o. & p.u. 11th* ....D Mansell pu

14 ran. 8l, 3l, 8l, 30l, 4l, 15l. Time 6m 1.00s. SP 4-5.
J N Dalton (Wheatland).

1619 Open (12st)

1412[1] **NETHER GOBIONS ....Julian Pritchard** 1
(fav) made all, clr 15th, blnd 3 out, unchal
1480[3] **Couture Tights ....G Hanmer** 2
in tch, chsd wnr 10th, no imp frm 15th
1595[3] **Auction Law (NZ) 7ex ....A Crow** 3
rmndr 2nd, chsd ldrs, 3rd & outpcd 14th, wknd 3 out
1506 Coolmoreen (Ire) *alwys last, pair, blnd 9th, t.o. 12th* ....T Stephenson 4
1565[2] Killy's Filly 5a *last frm 6th, t.o. 12th* ...G Barfoot-Saunt 5
1532 Mummy's Song *chsd wnr til p.u. 10th, lame* ..M Lewis pu
1386 Sun Of Chance *chsd ldrs til wknd 9th, t.o. & p.u. 13th* ....P Williams pu

7 ran. 8l, 15l, 8l, nk. Time 6m 2.00s. SP 8-15.
P Clutterbuck (Berkeley).

1620 PPORA

1567[4] **HACKETT'S FARM ....Julian Pritchard** 1
ld 3-12th, lft in ld 14th, gd jmp last, drvn out
1413[1] **Danbury Lad (Ire) ....Miss A Dare** 2
(fav) not fluent, cls up, jnd wnr 3 out, outjmpd last, not qckn
1456[3] **Pamela's Lad ....G Hanmer** 3
w.w. prog 12th, jnd wnr 15th, not qckn 3 out
1507[8] Springfield Lad *trckd ldrs til easily outpcd frm 13th* ....Miss E Walker 4
1418[3] Moydrum Prince *ld to 3rd, cls up til wknd 14th* ....Miss L Wallace 5
1415 Guarena (USA) *n.j.w. rear, t.o. 13th, p.u. 3 out* ....C Richards pu
1292 Gawcott Wood 5a *mstk 4th, cls up, ld 12th til ran out & u.r. 14th* ....C Wadland ro
1325[2] Secret Music 7a *mstk 8th, in tch to 11th, t.o. & p.u. 3 out* ....Capt D Parker pu

8 ran. 3l, 6l, 20l, 10l. Time 6m 15.50s. SP 10-1.
Miss Barbara Wilce (North Ledbury).

1621 Open Maiden (12st)

1483[2] **CRUISE A HOOP ....Julian Pritchard** 1
hld up,gd prog frm 12th,clsng whn lft in ld 2 out,all out
1581 **Mophead Kelly ....J Barlow** 2
alwys prom, chsd ldr 11th-apr 3 out, lft 2nd nxt, no imp
1511[5] **Matchlessly 1ow ....Miss E Walker** 3
mid-div, outpcd frm 11th, kpt on frm 15th, nrst fin
1569 Harry Tartar 7a *last frm 3rd, lft 4th by dfctns* ....Capt D Parker 4
1580 Astley Jack *s.v.s. ld aft 2nd,made most to apr 12th, wknd & p.u. 15th* ....M FitzGerald pu
Karamazov *s.v.s. last til ran out 3rd* ....P Finnegan ro
1485 Sonny's Song (bl) *mid-div, in tch til wknd 14th, wll bhnd & p.u. 2 out* ....L Brown pu
1504 Turkish Island 5a *alwys wll in rear, t.o. & p.u. 12th* ....P Cowley pu
1511 Royal Swinger 5a *in tch, prog 12th, 4th & btn whn p.u. 3 out, dsmntd* ....Dr P Pritchard pu
842 Elegant Bertie *rear, wll bhnd whn p.u. 10th* ..E Walker pu
1504 Lord Kilton (bl) *prom, mstk 12th, sn btn, wll bhnd whn p.u. 3 out* ....M Cowley pu
1555[4] Noble Minister *prom til wknd 12th, wll btn whn p.u. 3 out* ....M Wells pu
1504[3] Crestafair 5a *hld up, bhnd, blnd & u.r. 3rd* ..R Lawther ur
1217[4] Inky 5a *prom, ld apr 12th, 2l up whn f 2 out* ..A Phillips f
1485[3] Big Buckley 5a *nvr nr ldrs, wll bhnd whn p.u. 14th* ....T Stephenson pu
1319 Bunchoffives 7a *(fav) trckd ldrs til p.u. aft 10th, lame* ....M Hammond pu
1319 Sky Runner 7a *bolted bef start, alwys rear, t.o. & p.u. 11th* ....D Barlow pu

17 ran. 8l, 8l, 20l. Time 6m 15.00s. SP 5-1.
W M A Davies (North Ledbury).
J.N.

SOUTH TETCOTT
Lifton
Monday May 27th
GOOD TO SOFT

1622 Confined (12st)

1142[2] **WALKERS POINT 3ex ....J Jukes** 1
(fav) in tch, 4th 3 out, chal und pres & just ld last, drvn out
1428[1] **The Copper Key ....T Greed** 2
6th at 13th, went 3rd 3 out, effrt und pres nxt, just faild
1589[4] **Glenform (bl) ....T Cole** 3
ld 6th-8th & agn 13th-2 out, no ext apr last
1529[3] Prince Soloman 3ex *7th hlfwy, went 5th 3 out, not pace to chal ldrs* ....L Jefford 4
1360[3] Baldhu Chance *5th hlfwy, cls up & ev ch 14th til wknd aft 3 out* ....J Young 5
1358[5] Maboy Lady *11th hlfwy, nrst fin* ....Miss K Baily 6
1527[4] Sunwind *alwys rear grp* ....D Heath 7
1530[1] Good Appeal 5a *prom, losing ground whn mstk 6th, p.u. nxt* ....Miss L Blackford pu
1427 Clear Call (Fr) *pllng, ld 1st, prom til lost plc 10th, bhnd & p.u. 2 out* ....S Kidston pu
1553 If You Say So *hld up, prog to 4th at 13th, 3rd whn f 16th* ....S Ellis f
1549[4] Anstey Gadabout *ld 2nd-6th & agn 9-13th, lost plc aft nxt, bhnd & p.u. 2 out* ....A Holdsworth pu
1588 The Kimbler 3ex *mid-div, 8th at 12th, rear whn p.u. 2 out* ....Miss S Young pu
1359[4] Moorland Abbot *sn rear, bhnd til p.u. 2 out, lame* ....Miss D Mitchell pu
1361 Cornish Harp *not fluent, t.o. & p.u. aft 11th* ...R Darke pu

14 ran. Nk, 3l, 6l, 1½l, 5l, 25l. Time 6m 21.00s. SP 5-4.
T D H Hughes (Lamerton).

1623 Open

1425[1] **PARSON'S WAY (bl) ....J Jukes** 1
ld til 13th & agn 3 out, hrd rdn & ran on gamely nxt
1551[3] **The General's Drum ....K Heard** 2
(fav) in tch, prog to 2nd & rdn aft 3 out, ev ch til not qckn nxt
1339[6] **Hamper (bl) ....N Mitchell** 3
cls up, ld 14th-3 out, sn outpcd
1529[2] Gymcrak Dawn *lost tch frm 14th, p.u. apr 2 out, lame* ....S Slade pu
1550 Bert House *lost ground & rmndrs apr 14th, bhnd & p.u. 2 out, lame* ....S Ellis pu

5 ran. 4l, 4l. Time 6m 21.00s. SP 3-1.
Paul C N Heywood (Avon Vale).

1624 Ladies

1526[1] **FLAME O'FRENSI 5a ....Miss J Cumings** 1
(fav) j.w. made all, ran on gamely
1525[5] **Catch The Cross (bl) ....Mrs M Hand** 2
hld up, prog 14th, ev ch aft 3 out, not qckn und pres
1425 **Try It Alone ....Miss L Blackford** 3
prog to 2nd 12th, chsd wnr til wknd 16th, onepcd aft
1139[2] Moorland Highflyer 7a *prom, 4th at 12th, in tch til onepcd frm 3 out* ....Miss D Mitchell 4

1526[4] Christmas Bash 5a *twrds rear, some prog 15th, not nr to chal* ...Miss A Lamb 5
1141[5] Grey Guestino *chsd ldr til hlfwy, lost ground frm 15th* ...Miss L Delve 6
1525[7] Shalchlo Boy *twrds rear whn u.r. 4th* ...Miss G Linley ur
1525[4] Winter's Lane *rear, no ch whn blnd & u.r. last* ...Miss P Curling ur
1276[5] Jokers Patch *t.o. & p.u. 3 out* ...Mrs D Gillies pu
9 ran. 3l, 7l, 4l, 6l, 3l. Time 6m 16.00s. SP 4-7.
P J Clarke (Devon & Somerset Staghounds).

1625 Intermediate

1427[2] **JUST BEN** ...**Miss J Cumings** 1
(Jt fav) trckd ldr frm 8th, ld 4 out, styd on strngly und pres
1553[4] **Avril Showers 5a** ...**R Atkinson** 2
(Jt fav) w.w. prog 16th, went 2nd aft 3 out, ev ch til no ext nr fin
1359[3] **Lonesome Traveller (NZ)** ...**Mrs M Hand** 3
ld til 4 out, onepcd clsng stgs
1425[3] Querrin Lodge *4th at 10th, lost ground steadily frm 14th* ...T Greed 4
1591 Fort Diana *chsd ldr to 6th, grad wknd, rear & mstk 13th, p.u. nxt* ...G Hopper pu
1497 Just Donald *5th at 15th, unable to chal, bhnd whn u.r. last* ...A Honeyball ur
1142 Cornish Ways *t.o. & p.u. 13th, lame* ...Miss S Young pu
1527[2] Dinkies Quest 5a *handy, cls 3rd 15th, effrt & cls 2nd 3 out, fdd, p.u. last* ...Miss L Blackford pu
8 ran. 2½l, 8l, 30l. Time 6m 26.00s. SP 7-4.
Roger Persey (Devon & Somerset Staghounds).

1626 Open Maiden Div I (12st)

1554[8] **PIXIE IN PURPLE (IRE) 7a** ...**D Stephens** 1
ld 10th-nxt, agn 14th, mstk 16th, styd on well
1396[2] **Passing Fair 7a** ...**Miss S Vickery** 2
(fav) handy, prog to 2nd 4 out, ev ch til rdn & no ext 2 out
1554[4] **Royal Turn** ...**A Honeyball** 3
prog 15th, styd on steadily clsng stgs, tk 3rd nr fin
1429[2] Diana Moss (Ire) 5a *mid-div, 7th at 13th, went 3rd 3 out, lost 3rd cls home* ...C Heard 4
1429[3] The Ugly Duckling *mid-div, rdn 13th, no prog* ...R Treloggen 5
1554 Scallykenning *mid-div, 7th at 11th, nvr able to chal ldrs* ...J Young 6
1555[6] Baman Powerhouse *plld hrd, jmpd lft, ld to 10th & 11-14th, wknd, p.u. 3 out* ...Miss K Baily pu
1531[7] Baashful Blaze 5a *jmpd slwly in rear, wll bhnd til p.u. 16th* ...A Holdsworth pu
1143 Nattadon-Hill 5a 10ow *last whn ref 2nd* ...M Shields ref
1429 Lady Goldrush 5a *not fluent, bhnd til p.u. 16th* ...S Slade pu
1074[5] Philippastone 7a *u.r. going to start, t.o. whn p.u. 7th* ...Miss L Delve pu
1429 Rose's Lady Day 7a *t.o. til p.u. 13th* ...Mrs M Hand pu
1494 French Invasion 5a *twrds rear whn blnd & u.r. 7th (ditch)* ...S Parfimowicz ur
13 ran. 2½l, 4l, nk, 30l, 3l. Time 6m 28.00s. SP 25-1.
D Stephens (South Cornwall).

1627 Open Maiden Div II (12st)

1431[6] **MINE'S A GIN (IRE) 7a** ...**Miss J Cumings** 1
blnd 7th,prog to 2nd at 13th,lft in ld 3 out, pshd clr flat
1362[2] **Dharamshala (Ire)** ...**Mrs M Hand** 2
5th at 10th, prog to 3rd 15th, jnd wnr 2 out-last,no ex flat
1431[4] **Lawd Of Blisland** ...**J Jukes** 3
(fav) ld til 5th, cls up til wknd 12th, no ch aft
1531[2] Big Reward *not alwys fluent, 6th at 10th, lost tch 13th* ...K Crook 4
1495[8] Play Risky (Ire) *7th at 10th, rear whn u.r. 14th (ditch)* ...R Emmett ur
1554[6] Sixth In Line (Ire) *sn prom, slght ld 12th til f 3 out* ...T Cole f
1555[5] Bright Work *ld/disp 6-10th, 2nd til 13th, 4th whn f 4 out* ...D Curnow f
1432 Moonbay Lady 5a 12ow *rear & rmndrs 12th, jmpd slwly nxt, p.u. 14th* ...G Andrew pu
1593 Saint Joseph *rear til p.u. aft 10th* ...Miss S Young pu
9 ran. 2½l, 20l, 25l. Time 6m 32.50s. SP 3-1.
Mrs H C Johnson (Devon & Somerset Staghounds).

1628 Members

1526[3] **CHANDIGARH** ...**Miss K Baily** 1
(fav) f 4th,rmntd,2f bhnd,clsd,ld apr 2 out
Dittisscombe Amber 4ow ...**D Rowe** 2
ld aft 5th,clr til mssd mrkr 15th,rjnd,ld 3 out,outpcd nxt
1278 **Alfree** ...**A Holdsworth** 3
lft in ld apr 15th,slwd & hdd 3 out, fin tired
1555 Oldham Joker (bl) *tubed, lost tch 10th, t.o. & p.u. 13th* ...I Hambly pu
1530 Check On Tessa 5a *3rd whn blnd & u.r. 2nd* ...D Stephens ur
5 ran. 8l, 20l. Time 6m 58.00s. SP 1-2.
F R Bown (South Tetcott).
G.T.

UTTOXETER
Thursday May 30th
GOOD TO SOFT

1629 2m 5f Douglas Macmillan Hospice Novices' Hunters' Chase Class H for the Feilden Challenge Cup

1558[1] **NORTHERN BLUFF 11.7 7a** ...**Mr J Jukes** 1
ld till after 1st, left in ld 4th, made rest, just held on.
1567[2] **Broad Steane 11.9 5a** ...**Mr A Sansome** 2
(fav) held up bhnd ldrs, rdn apr 4 out, left in 2nd 2 out, ran on well from last, just faild.
1572 **Across The Card 11.13 7a** ...**Capt W Ramsay** 3
chsd ldrs, gradually wknd from 10th.
1482[1] Dara's Course (Ire) 11.2 7a *held up in tch, wknd apr 4 out.* ...Mr G Barfoot-Saunt 4
1548[7] A Windy Citizen (Ire) 11.12 7a *alwys bhnd.* ...Mr R Hicks 5
1423 Noble Angel (Ire) 11.7 7a *chsd ldrs, weakening when blnd 10th, t.o. when p.u. before 12th.* ...Mr A Dalton pu
1583[1] Back The Road (Ire) 11.7 7a *held up bhnd ldrs, effort 4 out, 2nd and rdn when blnd and u.r. 2 out.* ...Mr G Hanmer ur
1528 Mac's Boy 11.7 7a *mid div when f 5th.* ..Mr D S Jones f
1591 Ragtime Boy 11.9 5a *held up, rdn along 11th, 5th and no ch when f 4 out.* ...Mr Richard White f
1476 Im Ok (Ire) 11.2 7a (bl) *bhnd till f 5th* ...Mr D Sherlock f
1421[3] Four Hearts (Ire) 11.7 7a (bl) *ld after 1st till blnd and hdd 4th, wknd 9th, t.o. when p.u. before 11th.* ...Mr D Barlow pu
1417 Lindalighter 11.2 7a *alwys bhnd, t.o. when p.u. before 9th.* ...Mr M Jackson pu
1536 Ted's Knight (Ire) 11.0 7a *alwys bhnd, t.o. when p.u. before 12th.* ...Mr A Phillips pu
13 ran. ½l, 28l, 9l, 9l. Time 5m 25.40s. SP 7-2.
Mrs Heather Gibbon

STRATFORD
Friday May 31st
GOOD TO FIRM

1630 3½m Horse And Hound Champion Novices' Hunters' Chase Class H for the John Corbet Cup

1560[1] **HANDSOME HARVEY 11.7 7a** ...**Mr J Jukes** 1
jmpd right, made all, mstk 2 out, styd on gamely run-in.
1535[1] **Syd Green (Ire) 11.7 7a** ...**Mr S Walker** 2
alwys handy, effort 3 out, unable to qckn from last.
1545[1] **Scally Muire 11.2 7a** ...**Mr A H Crow** 3
(fav) chsd ldrs, lost pl after 10th, rallied 16th, one pace 2 out.
1171[7] Kettles 11.2 7a *towards rear, styd on 4 out, nvr able to chal.* ...Mr A Phillips 4

1623[2] The General's Drum 11.7 7a *nvr near to chal.* ....Mr K Heard 5
1543[1] Southerly Gale 11.9 5a *held up in tch, rdn 17th, one pace after next.* ....Mr A Farrant 6
1614[3] Sea Search 11.7 7a *nvr near to chal.* Miss A Meakins 7
1535 Kenilworth (Ire) 11.7 7a *held up in tch, effort 3 out, wknd quickly last.* ....Mr C Mulhall 8
1565 Causeway Cruiser 11.7 7a *started slowly, hdwy 6th, lost pl after 14th, taied off when p.u. before 17th.* ....Mr R Lawther pu
1537[1] Stede Quarter 11.11 3a *nvr on terms, t.o. when p.u. before 17th.* ....Mr P Hacking pu
1333[3] West Quay 11.7 7a *prom till f 16th.* ....Mr J Creighton f
1457[2] Ledwyche Gate 11.7 7a (bl) *chsd ldrs, wknd 11th, taild of when p.u. before 17th.* ....Mr M Jackson pu
1573[3] Highland Friend 11.7 7a (bl) *in tch, mstk 15th, soon wknd, t.o. when p.u. before 3 out.* ....Mr P Atkinson pu
1543[2] Good King Henry 11.8 7a 1ow *in tch to 16th, t.o. when p.u. before 2 out.* ....Mr I Widdicombe pu
1228[1] Idiotic 11.9 5a *mid div, smooth hdwy from 13th, tracking ldrs when b.d. 16th.* ....Mr C Vigors bd
1542[6] Wudimp 11.9 5a *mid div when blnd 15th, soon wknd, t.o. when p.u. before 2 out.* ....Mr C Storey pu
16 ran. 3l, 4l, ½l, nk, nk, 7l, 15l. Time 7m 8.00s. SP 6-1.
E L Harries

STRATFORD
Saturday June 1st
GOOD TO FIRM

1631 3½m 37th Year Of The Horse And Hound Cup Final Champion Hunters' Chase Class B

1544[3] **PROUD SUN 12.0 ....Mr J Culloty 1**
(fav) towards rear, hdwy 14th, ld 3 out, all out run-in, fin lame.
1478[1] **Celtic Abbey 12.0 ....Mr D S Jones 2**
in tch, ld 17th to 3 out, ran on cl home.
1546[1] **Sheer Jest 12.1 1ow ....Mr A Hill 3**
held up, hdwy 12th, rdn apr 2 out, kept on same pace.
1584[1] Hermes Harvest 12.0 (v) *held up bhnd ldrs, blnd 15th, rdn 17th, soon btn.* ....Mr C Bonner 4
1546[2] Zam Bee 12.0 *prom till wknd 10th* ....Mr N M Bell 5
1534[1] Welsh Legion 12.0 *not fluent, mid div when blnd 7th, bhnd when mstk 13th.* ....Mr M Rimell 6
1570[1] Loughlinstown Boy 12.0 *mid div, lost pl 11th, no dngr after.* ....Mr P Craggs 7
1534[3] Rusty Bridge 12.0 (bl) *blnd 10th, alwys bhnd.* ....Mr R Thornton 8
1460[2] Rolling Ball (Fr) 12.0 *ld to 12th, wknd quickly 14th, t.o. when p.u. before 16th.* ....Mr R Ford pu
1552[1] Faithful Star 12.0 *prom, mstks 2nd and 9th, ld 12th to 17th, second when blnd and u.r. 4 out.* Miss S Vickery ur
1333[1] Ryming Cuplet 12.0 *alwys bhnd, t.o. when blnd 14th, p.u. before next.* ....Mr Richard White pu
1584[4] Dubit 12.0 (v) *chsd ldrs, wknd rpdly and p.u. before 4 out.* ....Mr J Tizzard pu
1331[2] Mr Golightly 12.0 *chsd ldrs to 16th, soon wknd, t.o. when p.u. before 2 out.* ....Mrs J Reed pu
483 What A Hand 12.0 *alwys bhnd, t.o. when p.u. before 16th.* ....Mr N R Mitchell pu
14 ran. 1¼l, 4l, 22l, 5l, 5l, 2½l, 25l. Time 6m 57.60s. SP 7-4.
Stewart Pike

EXMOOR
Bratton Down
Saturday June 1st
GOOD

1632 Members

1278 **CAUTIOUS REBEL (v) ....T Greed 1**
made all, clr 12th, mstks 16th & nxt, unchal
1591 **Tangle Kelly ....Miss J Cumings 2**
(fav) chsd wnr 4th til rdn & slwd 14th,2nd agn 3 out,no ch
1550 **Charmers Wish 5a ....H Thomas 3**
chsd wnr to 4th & 14th-3 out, no imp
3 ran. Dist, 3l. Time 6m 26.00s. SP 2-1.
Mrs L Roberts (Exmoor).

1633 B F S S (12st)

1550[1] **STILL IN BUSINESS 7ex ....T Mitchell 1**
(fav) j.w. ld 8th, clr 16th, eased flat
1567[1] **Not Mistaken ....Miss P Curling 2**
hld up, prog 9th, chsd wnr 14th, blnd nxt, no imp aft
1587[1] **Morchard Milly 5a ....S Holdsworth 3**
prom til rdn & outpcd 12th, ran on agn frm 16th, kpt on well
1589 The Pedlar 5a *w.w. last at 12th, effrt 15th, no imp frm 3 out* ....T Greed 4
1553[1] Beinn Mohr 5a *6s-3s, ld & slw jmp 2nd, hdd 8th, rdn & wknd 14th* ....I Dowrick 5
1587[3] Remember Mac (bl) *cls up to 14th, sn wknd.* .L Jefford 6
1498[4] Grey Sonata 5a (bl) *prom to 10th, rdn & strggling 12th, p.u. 16th* ....M Frith pu
1604[1] Touch 'N' Pass 7ex *ld to 2nd, f nxt* ....J Tudor f
8 ran. 8l, 4l, 12l, 12l, 10l. Time 6m 19.50s. SP 2-1.
R G Williams (Taunton Vale Foxhounds).
One fence omitted final two circuits. 17 jumps.

1634 Intermediate (12st)

1550[2] **Tangle Baron 5ex ....Miss J Cumings 1D**
made most to 15th,ld agn 3 out,rdn clr aft last,fin 1st,disq
1590[2] **IVE CALLED TIME ....T Greed 1**
mid-div,prog frm 14th,went 2nd flat,no imp,fin 2nd,promoted
1362[1] **Newski Express 5a ....A Farrant 2**
well in rear,prog 11th,ran on 3 out,nvr nrr,fin 3rd,promoted
1591 **Link Copper ....Miss L Blackford 3**
alwys prom,ld 15th-3 out,ev ch apr last,wknd,fin 4th,prmtd
1590 Fellow Sioux *mid-div,prog 11th,3rd 3 out,hung lft & wknd flat* ....I Dowrick 5
1590 Blue-Bird Express 5a *prom, jnd wnr 14th, wknd frm 3 out* ....R Treloggen 6
1622[2] The Copper Key *n.j.w. mid-div, lost tch frm 14th* ....G Penfold 7
1497[6] Palace King (Ire) *mstk 1st, prssd wnr til wknd & mstk 14th, no ch aft* ....G Baines 8
1528[7] Dovedon Princess 5a *in tch to hlfwy, bhnd frm 12th, t.o.* ....D Stephens 9
1567 King Of The Clouds *alwys rear, t.o. 11th, blnd 14th, p.u. nxt* ....Mrs N Sheppard pu
1591[1] Oneovertheight *bhnd, 12th whn p.u. 8th, dsmntd* ....N Harris pu
1527[1] Seahawk Retriever *pllng, prog 8th,trckd ldrs til lost plc & 6th whn u.r. 15th* ....Miss P Curling ur
1590[1] M-Reg 5ex *(fav) in tch til p.u. 6th, saddle slpd* ....L Jefford pu
1553[6] Talk Sence (Ire) *alwys rear, t.o. & p.u. 2 out* ..C Heard pu
820 Suba Lin 5a *9/4-33s (!), s.s. alwys last, t.o. & p.u. 11th* ....M Frith pu
15 ran. 5l, 5l, 6l, 10l, 15l, 10l, 6l, 20l. Time 6m 23.20s. SP 10-1.
Mrs M de Burgh (Devon & Somerset Staghounds).
Tangle Baron disqualified, rider not W/I. Original distances.

1635 Ladies

1245[1] **SPLIT SECOND ....Miss A Dare 1**
(fav) w.w. gd prog to ld 2 out, sn hdd, ld flat, ran on well
1588[2] **Desert Waltz (Ire) ....Miss P Curling 2**
w.w. rpd prog to ld aft 2 out, hdd & no ext flat
1228[4] **Fly The Wind 5a ....Miss L Blackford 3**
trckd ldrs, rdn 15th, cls up 3 out, immed outpcd aft nxt
1628[1] Chandigarh *prom, wll there 3 out, immed outpcd frm nxt* ....Miss K Baily 4
1589[5] Perfect Stranger *ld 4-6th, prssd ldr, ld brfly apr 2 out, sn hdd & btn* ....Miss J Cumings 5
1552[4] False Economy *mid-div, lost tch 12th, kpt on onepcd frm 2 out, no dang* ....Miss K Scorgie 6

1552^{2} Daybrook's Gift *wll bhnd in last pair til ran on 14th, nvr on terms* .... Miss N Allan 7

1586^{4} La Mezeray 5a 5ow *alwys rear, 11th & rdn at 13th, no ch aft* .... Mrs J Hawkins 8

1559^{2} Kumada *ran in snctchs, ld to 4th, in tch 15th, sn wknd, walked in* .... Miss S Wallin 9

1624^{2} Catch The Cross *sn rdn & reluc, still in tch 15th, no ch aft nxt, walked in* .... Mrs M Hand 10

1614^{5} Cantantivy 5a *ld 6th til aft 3 out, wknd nxt, walked in* .... Miss T Spearing 11

1588^{4} Frosty Reception *not fluent, alwys rear, no ch frm 14th, t.o.* .... Miss L Pope 12

1589 Bidston Mill *mstk 3rd, sn last, t.o. frm 9th* .... Miss D Green 13

13 ran. 4l, 15l, 8l, 6l, 8l, 25l, 8l, 6l, 3l, 1l. Time 6m 15.50s. SP 4-6.
Mrs P J Willis (Berkeley).
Extended distances, 8l, 20l.

1636 4m Open

1589^{1} **FOSBURY** .... **T Mitchell** 1
(fav) w.w. gd prog to ld 20th, clr 4 out, heavily eased flat

1611 **Final Express 5a** .... **M Hoskins** 2
last & rdn 10th, ran on 20th, went 3rd 4 out, tk 2nd nr fin

1551^{1} **Myliege** .... **N Harris** 3
prom/disp,chsd wnr 20th,mstk nxt,sn outpcd,lost 2nd nr fin

1602^{1} Cairneymount *in tch til outpcd 20th, no dang aft* .... W Stephens 4

1550^{3} Bargain And Sale *ld/disp to 19th, 3rd & outpcd nxt, demoted frm 4 out* .... I Dowrick 5

1551^{2} Fearsome *cls up til outpcd 20th, sn rdn & no imp* .... G Penfold 6

1427 Cardinal Bird (USA) (bl) *wll in tch til outpcd 20th, wknd 2 out, last whn p.u. flat* .... A Holdsworth pu

1507^{7} Space Mariner *rear & rdn 12th, wknd rpdly 19th, t.o. & p.u. 21st* .... O McPhail pu

1529^{5} Electrolyte (bl) *prom, disp 15th-17th, cls up whn u.r. 19th* .... G Austin ur

1591 Springcombe 5a *blnd & u.r. 1st* .... A Farrant ur

1493^{2} Nothing To Fear *prom, disp 7th, f nxt* G Barfoot-Saunt f

11 ran. 15l, ¾l, 10l, 4l, 2l. Time 8m 29.40s. SP 4-6.
Mrs Susan Humphreys (Cattistock).
One fence omitted 2nd circuit only, 24 jumps.

1637 Open Maiden Div I (12st)

1626^{4} **DIANA MOSS (IRE) 5a** .... **C Heard** 1
pllng, prom, chsd ldr 15th, ld last, rdn clr

1626^{6} **Scallykenning** .... **J Young** 2
alwys in tch, effrt & prog 2 out, ran on, no imp wnr flat

1549^{2} **Liberty James** .... **N Harris** 3
hld up bhnd,rpd prog to ld 14th,mstk nxt,hdd & wknd last

1319 Rap Up Fast (USA) *(fav) w.w. mstk 9th,5th 3 out,prog nxt,in tch apr last,wknd flat* .... Julian Pritchard 4

1554^{5} Nice To No *cls up, ld 10-14th, chsd ldrs til wknd 2 out* .... S Slade 5

1621^{4} Harry Tartar 7a *bhnd, last frm 10th, t.o. 15th* .... Capt D Parker 6

1593^{5} Carumu 5a *ld 2-6th, wknd 13th, t.o. 16th* ... S Hornsby 7

1342^{6} Three And A Half *n.j.w. mid-div, lost tch 13th, t.o. 16th* .... Maj O Ellwood 8

1555 Nottarex *ld to 2nd & 6th-10th, 7th & btn whn u.r. 15th* .... B Wright ur

1592 Dula Model 5a *trckd ldrs til f 11th* .... S Ellis f

1531^{4} Kenstown (Ire) *blnd 1st, rear aft, lost tch & p.u. 14th* .... G Penfold pu

11 ran. 7l, 4l, nk, 10l, 25l, nk, 10l. Time 6m 34.00s. SP 7-1.
J S Papworth (Four Burrow).

1638 Open Maiden Div II (12st)

1511 **DAPHNI (FR) 7a** .... **E James** 1
rear & just in tch, 6th 3 out, gd prog nxt, drvn to ld nr fn

1532^{8} **Cardan** .... **R Darke** 2
ld 6th, clr 15th, 6l up last, wknd & hdd nr fin

1348^{2} **Kala Dawn 5a** .... **Miss M Tory** 3
mid-div, effrt to chs ldrs 14th, onepcd frm 2 out

1554 Four Leaf Clover 5a *trckd ldrs, not qckn frm 15th, btn 2 out* .... R Woolacott 4

1591 My Boy Buster *last pair & wll bhnd, t.o. 14th, fin strngly* .... J Young 5

1495^{4} Masters Nephew *pllng, chsd ldr 7th, no imp apr 2 out, wnd apr last* .... B O'Doherty 6

1592 Chocolate Buttons 5a *(fav) 6s-2s, wll bhnd 7th,effrt 13th, nvr able to rch ldrs* .... N Harris 7

1592^{3} Joli High Note 5a *hld up bhnd, rpd prog to jn ldrs 12th, wknd frm 15th* .... Miss T Honeyball 8

1511 Is She Quick 5a *mid-div til f 8th* .... Dr P Pritchard f

1608 Shared Fortune (Ire) *ld to 4th, wknd 13th, t.o. & p.u. 2 out* .... D Dennis pu

1621 Noble Minister *ld 4-6th,mstk & wknd 12th,exhausted aft,f heavily 16th* .... M Wells f

1554 Dollybat 5a *rear whn hmpd 8th, p.u. nxt, dsmntd* .... M Frith pu

1555^{7} Brook A Light 7a *in tch in rear til b.d. 8th* ..... S Slade bd

13 ran. ½l, 10l, 4l, 12l, 12l, 12l, 8l. Time 6m 26.70s. SP 33-1.
Mrs L M Boulter (V.W.H.).
J.N.

HARBOROUGH HUNT CLUB
Dingley
Sunday June 2nd
GOOD TO FIRM

1639 Members

1564^{6} **MENATURE (IRE)** .... **J Seth-Smith** 1
in tch, chsd ldr 10th, ld 14th, clr 2 out, unchal

1595 **Decent Gold** .... **J Stephenson** 2
prog & cl up 13th, chsd wnr aft nxt, no imp, mstk last

1520 **Chiasso Forte (Ity) (bl)** .... **Mrs P Adams** 3
ld 3rd, sn clr, mstks 4th & 12th, hdd 14th, one pace

494^{3} Miss Solitaire 5a *(fav) not flnt, outpcd frm 6th, nvr nr ldrs* .... S Morris 4

1540^{6} Beat The Rap *ld to 3rd, wknd 12th, t.o. 2 out, walked in* .... G Morrison 5

1594^{5} Spanish Whisper 12ow *alwys rr, t.o. 12th* .... M Lane 6

1599 Coolsythe 5a (bl) *last til p.u. 6th, dsmntd* C Millington pu

7 ran. 15l, hd, 3l, 20l, 20l. Time 6m 33.00s. SP 3-1.
J Seth-Smith (Fernie).

1640 Restricted Div I (12st)

1482^{3} **BOLSHIE BARON** .... **M Harris** 1
(fav) j.w., made all, hrd prssd & mstk 2 out, drvn out

1612^{2} **Sporting Lark 5a** .... **Miss H Irving** 2
prom, chsd wnr 13th, chal 2 out, not qckn app last

1595^{8} **Tarry Awhile** .... **J Connell** 3
prom, chsd wnr 9-13th, styd on undr pres frm 2 out

1597^{6} Tempered Point (USA) *prom gng wl, not qckn 15th, no imp 2 out* .... T Lane 4

1564^{7} Pejawi 5a *1st ride, rr, no ch whn mstk 14th, kpt on* .... Mrs S Faber 5

1002^{4} Happy Paddy *rr, eff 11th, sn wknd, t.o. whn p.u. 3 out* .... A Sansome pu

1595 Waterhay *rr til u.r. 7th* .... R Mumford ur

1568^{1} Plateman *hld up, prog 10th, 3rd whn mstk 15th, wknd, p.u. last* .... F Hutsby pu

1324 Naughty Nellie 7a *pllng, mstks, lost pl rpdly 10th, last & p.u. 14th* .... Mrs J Dawson pu

9 ran. 2½l, ½l, 6l, 6l. Time 6m 31.00s. SP 2-1.
M H Weston (Croome & West Warwickshire).

1641 Restricted Div II (12st)

1599^{1} **APPLE NICKING** .... **A Hill** 1
w.w., prog 13th, ld 2 out, sn clr, rdn out

1586 **Jolly Fellow (bl)** .... **N Wilson** 2
mid-div, prog to ch ldr 13th, not qckn 3 out,kpt on und pres

1564^{2} **Cader Idris** .... **A Sansome** 3
(fav) trckd ldrs, rdn & not qckn 15th, styd on, nvr nr

1507 Dixons Homefinder *raced wd, in tch, outpcd 2 out, kpt on* .... A Barnett 4

597[5] Mr Gee *last whn jmpd slwly 2nd, mstk 8th, nvr on trms*..........................L Hicks 5
601 The Foolish One 5a 2ow *ld 5th, clr 13th, hdd 2 out, wknd rpdly*..............................A Dalton 6
562 Biblical 5a *prom to 8th, rr & rdn 10th, p.u. 13th*..............................R Mumford pu
439[7] Wayward Sailor (bl) *rr, mstk 8th, blndrd 11th, p.u. nxt*..............................Miss T Spearing pu
501[2] Meadow Cottage *in tch in rr til s.u. bnd app 9th*..............................T Stephenson su
564 Linlake Lightning 5a *slw jmp 2nd & rdn, in tch to 11th, t.o. whn p.u. last*..............................Miss H Irving pu
597 Supreme Dream (Ire) 5a *prom to 14th, 7th & btn whn f 2 out*..............................Mrs P Adams f
540[2] Fathers Footprints *ld to 5th, chsd ldr til mstk 11th, wknd, p.u. 2 out*..............................R Hicks pu
Quite A Miss 5a *jmpd badly, last frm 3rd, t.o. & p.u. 9th*..............................A Martin pu

ran. 6l, 1½l, nk, 15l, 10l. Time 6m 29.00s. SP 5-1.
s M Upstone (Bicester With Whaddon Chase).

1642 Ladies

567[5] **LILY THE LARK 5a ....Miss H Irving** 1
chsd ldr 10th, ld 15th, styd on well app last
596 **Larry The Lamb ....Miss G Chown** 2
(fav) w.w., in tch whn blndrd 14th, chsd wnr 2 out, not qckn last
520[4] **Loose Wheels ....Miss K Makinson** 3
ld to 15th, outpcd aft 3 out
494[4] They All Forgot Me *chsd ldr 4-10th, outpcd frm 3 out*..............................Miss C Dyson 4
584 Icky's Five *chsd ldr to 4th, sn rr, wknd 3 out, t.o.*..............................Miss T Habgood 5
579 Prince's Court *in tch til slpd & u.r. bnd app 9th*..............................Mrs C McCarthy ur

an. 1l, 20l, ½l, 12l. Time 6m 29.00s. SP 5-1.
ss H M Irving (Grafton).

1643 Open

598[1] **LUCKY CHRISTOPHER ....A Sansome** 1
(fav) w.w., prog 11th, left 2nd 14th, ld 2 out, sn clr, impressv
598[3] **Coolvawn Lady (Ire) 5a ....T Lane** 2
lft 2nd app 9th, ld 13th, lft clr nxt, hdd aft 2 out, no ex
585[6] **Cromwell Point ....C Mulhall** 3
rr & rdn 4th, 8th & no ch hlfwy, lft 3rd by dfctns
595[1] Whinstone Mill *7th & pshd alng hlfwy, nvr a dang, t.o.*..............................R Thornton 4
598[5] Trusty Friend *alwys bhnd, t.o. 7th* ....J Oldring 5
1618 Penllyne's Pride *s.s., alwys bhnd, t.o. 9th*....J Chilton 6
1584 Touch Of Winter *mid-div, mstk 5th, 6th & btn hlfwy, wlkd in*..............................T Lacey 7
618[1] Shoon Wind *fast away, ld to 13th, with ldr whn f nxt*..............................A Dalton f
613[6] Blue Danube (USA) *outpcd in rr, 10th whn p.u. 9th*..............................J Trice-Rolph pu
1565 Bright As A Button *chsd ldrs, 3rd hlfwy, sn outpcd, bhnd & p.u. 15th*..............................T Marks pu
1604 Coombesbury Lane 5a *chsd ldr 4th til s.u. bnd app 9th*..............................T Stephenson su
563[3] Tompet *chsd ldrs, rdn hlfwy, poor 3rd whn s.u. bnd app 2 out*..............................J Connell su
377[9] Hostetler *t.o. 8th, last whn f 11th*.......J Stephenson f

ran. 8l, 1 fence, 8l, 25l, 2l, 6l. Time 6m 19.00s. SP Evens.
B Tarry (Grafton).

1644 Open Maiden

504[2] **NOSSI BE ....Capt D Parker** 1
mid-div, prog 14th, 3rd at last, ran on well, ld nr fin
599[2] **Dolly Bloom 5a ....A Sansome** 2
(fav) lost pl 6th, prog 10th, chsd ldr 2 out, hrd rdn, not qckn
1621 **Crestafair 5a ....R Lawther** 3
hld up, prog 7th, ld 3 out, lkd wnr til wknd & hdd nr fin
1610 Keep On Trying 5a *chsd ldrs, eff 14th, unble to chal frm 2 out* ....M Portman 4
1610 Lloyds Loser *prom, ld 14th-3 out, wknd nxt*. . .A Martin 5
1568[2] Banjo Paterson *alwys rr, kpt on frm 3 out, no dang*..............................A Charles-Jones 6
1523[3] Cruise Free *nvr gng well, alwys bhnd* ....B Pollock 7
1020 Mountfosse *n.j.w., alwys wl bhnd, t.o. off* . . .A Barnett 8
1568 Glenmere Prince *pllng, hmprd 3rd, in tch, 7th whn f 13th*..............................R Armson f
1416 Just Eve 5a *made most to 14th, wknd rpdly, well btn & p.u. last*..............................M Jackson pu
1569[4] Full Song 5a *rr, mstk 5th, in tch whn hmprd 12th, sn btn, p.u. 2 out*..............................S Morris pu
1378 Remalone 5a *s.s., alwys bhnd, t.o. whn p.u. 11th*..............................D Ingle pu
1580[3] Witch Doctor *prom, ld & f 3rd* .....Miss S Phizacklea f
1433[6] Oliver Himself 7a *prom, ld gng well whn f 12th* . .A Hill f
1568 Beachborough *hld up, prog & mstk 11th, sn btn, t.o. whn p.u. 3 out*..............................T Marks pu
1599 Forever Freddy *prom til rdn & reluc 9th, stpd aft nxt*..............................R Thornton pu

16 ran. 1l, hd, 15l, 5l, 20l, 8l, dist. Time 6m 36.50s. SP 4-1.
Mrs T Arthur (Old Berks).

1645 Intermediate

1567[3] **GRIMLEY GALE (IRE) 5a..............M Jackson** 1
(fav) prom, ld 9th til blnd 12th, ld 2 out, sn clr, comf
1594[3] **Stanwick Farlap 5a ....T Marks** 2
ld 5-9th, lft in ld 12th-2 out, kpt on one pace
1595[9] **Majestic Ride ....R Armson** 3
pllng, in tch, outpcd 10th, stynd on 2 out, nrst fin
1595 Sharpridge *alwys rr, lost tch 12th, t.o., sntchd 4th nr fin*..............................M Mawhinney 4
1604[2] Oragas *ld to 5th, rdn 10th, no ch whn nrly ref 2 out, t.o.*..............................R Thornton 5

5 ran. 6l, 1½l, 1 fence, 2½l. Time 6m 34.00s. SP 8-13.
R M Phillips (Clifton-On-Teme).
J.N.

TORRINGTON FARMERS
Umberleigh
Saturday June 8th
GOOD TO FIRM

1646 Members (12st)

1494[3] **LUCKY THURSDAY ....R Treloggen** 1
(fav) ld 7-11th & frm 15th, clr 2 out, rdn out
1627 **Play Risky (Ire) ....R Emmett** 2
prom, ld 11-14th, chsd wnr nxt, not qckn 2 out
628 Straight Brandy *ld to 7th, ld 14th-15th, wknd nxt, p.u. last, dsmntd* ....Mrs M Hand pu
1280 Secret Siphoner *in tch, mstk 9th, ev ch 13th, wknd & p.u. 15th, dsmntd*..............................Miss A Barnett pu

4 ran. 2l. Time 6m 42.70s. SP 1-2.
A W Congdon (Torrington Farmers).

1647 Open

1406[1] **SPITFIRE JUBILEE ....M Miller** 1
(fav) mstk 8th,prom to 10th,renewd effrt whn lft clr 3 out,unchal
1607[2] **Old Road (USA) ....C Coyne** 2
prom til mstk 13th, btn whn lft 2nd 3 out, no imp
1584 Furry Knowe *prom, slw jmp 5th, nrly u.r. 10th, p.u. nxt, sddle slppd* ....D Pritchard pu
1595[2] Radical Views *hld up, prog 13th, went 2nd & b.d. 3 out*..............................A Hill bd
1624 Winter's Lane *made most, 2l up whn f 3 out* . .R White f
1636 Electrolyte (bl) *jmpd slwly, rear frm 6th, last whn f 12th*..............................G Austin f
720 Miles More Fun 5a *hld up, prog 7th, cls 3rd whn hmpd & u.r. 3 out*..............................L Jefford ur

7 ran. 10l. Time 6m 26.90s. SP 4-5.
Mrs Z S Clark (Wilton).
Last fence omitted - 17 jumps.

1648 Ladies

1636[1] **FOSBURY ....Miss P Curling** 1
(fav) w.w. prog 6th, ld 11th, drew clr 3 out, easily

1633[2] **Not Mistaken** .... **Miss S Vickery** **2**
ld to 2nd, mstks 10 & 12th, ev ch 15th, sn btn, fin tired
1635 **Catch The Cross (bl)** .... **Mrs M Hand** **3**
wll bhnd, t.o. 11th, ran on frm 15th, tk 3rd 2 out
1624[3] Try It Alone *lost plc 5th, nvr on trms aft, 4th & no ch 13th, no prog*.......................Miss L Blackford 4
1624[1] Flame O'Frensi 5a *ld 2-4th, chal 13th til mstk nxt, wknd aft 3 out*......................Miss J Cumings 5
1635[4] Chandigarh *s.s. ran in sntchs, in tch to 13th, sn wll bhnd*..................................Miss K Baily 6
1624[6] Grey Guestino *mid-div, outpcd frm 7th, t.o. 13th* ....Miss L Delve 7
1635 Bidston Mill *sn last & wll bhnd, t.o. 7th* . . .Miss P Platt 8
1558 Construction King *alwys wll bhnd, t.o. frm 13th* ....Mrs J Hawkins 9
1611[2] Brack N Brandy *ld 4-7th, mstk 9th, wknd 12th, t.o. & p.u. 2 out*..........................Miss R David pu
1624[5] Christmas Bash 5a *rear til u.r. aft 4th* . . .Miss A Lamb ur
11 ran. 20l, 6l, 6l, 12l, 2l, 20l, 2l, 8l. Time 6m 5.90s. SP 4-5.
Mrs Susan Humphreys (Cattistock).

1649 Restricted (12st)

1637[1] **DIANA MOSS (IRE) 5a** .... **C Heard** **1**
w.w. prog 11th, chal & mstk 14th,chal 2 out,ld last,rdn out
1591 **Ruth's Boy (Ire)** .... **Miss P Curling** **2**
(fav) ld 2nd-7th, ld agn apr 2 out-last where mstk, no ext
1634[3] **Link Copper** .... **Miss L Blackford** **3**
prom, ld 7th-apr 2 out, not qckn aft, styd on
1636 Springcombe 5a *rear & pshd along, wll bhnd 12th, styd on wll apr 2 out*..................Miss S Eames 4
1603[3] How Friendly *hld up, outpcd & wll bhnd 12th, kpt on frm 2 out, nvr dang* ....Julian Pritchard 5
1612[5] Sutton Lass 5a *ld to 2nd, prom to 10th, sn lost tch* ....R Lawther 6
1501 Second Time Round *alwys bhnd, t.o. & p.u. 2 out* ....Capt D Parker pu
1622[7] Sunwind *s.s. rear til b.d. 10th* ....D Heath bd
1633[6] Remember Mac (bl) *chsd ldrs til outpcd 13th, wknd 3 out, p.u. last* ....L Jefford pu
1622 Anstey Gadabout *chsd ldrs til f 10th* ....G Penfold f
1634[9] Dovedon Princess 5a *rear, mstk 7th, wll bhnd 12th, p.u. 14th* ....D Stephens pu
1619[4] Coolmoreen (Ire) *mid-div, hmpd 10th, no ch aft nxt, p.u. 2 out*...........................T Stephenson pu
1632[2] Tangle Kelly *prom, disp brfly 8th, wknd 12th, t.o. & p.u. last*.........................Miss J Cumings pu
1428 Mosside *last & n.j.w. til p.u. 6th*.............N Harris pu
14 ran. 1l, 3l, 5l, 1l, 20l. Time 6m 18.40s. SP 9-2.
J S Papworth (Four Burrow).
3rd last fence omitted - 17 jumps.

1650 Confined

1635 **FROSTY RECEPTION (bl)**............ **Miss L Pope** **1**
in tch, prog to chs ldr 15th, styd on to ld post
1634 **Tangle Baron** .... **Miss J Cumings** **2**
(fav) prom, ld 12th, 3l clr & rdn 2 out, hdd post
1634 **Oneovertheight** .... **N Harris** **3**
in tch, pshd alng 11th, ld 13th-15th, wknd nxt
1611 Rapid Rascal *ld to 12th, wknd nxt* ....Miss S West 4
1636 Cardinal Bird (USA) (bl) *reluc to race, ref 2nd* ....A Holdsworth ref
1636[5] Bargain And Sale *chsd ldrs, mstks 8 & 9th, wknd & p.u. aft nxt*..............................I Dowrick pu
1626 Baman Powerhouse *rear but in tch til outpcd & mstk 13th, t.o. & p.u. 2 out* ....Miss K Baily pu
7 ran. Nk, 25l, 15l. Time 6m 17.00s. SP 33-1.
R J Baker (Tiverton Foxhounds).

1651 Open Maiden Div I (12st)

1627[2] **DHARAMSHALA (IRE)** .... **Mrs M Hand** **1**
w.w. in tch, effrt to chs ldr aft 3 out, ld last, drvn out
1495[7] **Gamblers Refrain** .... **A Holdsworth** **2**
ld to 6th, lft in ld 10th, hdd & no ext last
1593[2] **Drumcolliher** .... **Miss K Baily** **3**
mstks, rear, gd prog 13th, rdn & outpcd 3 out, kpt on
1342[4] Heather Boy *prom, chsd ldr 11th til aft 3 out, wknd nxt, lame*..........................Miss J Cumings 4
1638[3] Kala Dawn 5a *alwys in tch, not qckn frm 3 out* ....Miss M Tory 5
1362 Maverick's Creek (NZ) *bhnd frm 6th, t.o. & p.u. 11th* ....D Stephens pu
1606[4] Gold Tip 5a *in tch, cls enough 14th, wknd 3 out, p.u. flat, dsmntd*................................J P Keen pu
1593 St Morwenna 5a *prom til wnd frm 14th, stppd aft 2 out* ....Miss L Blackford pu
1605 Agapanthus 5a *sn rear, t.o. 11th, p.u. 15th* . . . .S Lloyd pu
1638[2] Cardan *(fav) prom, ld 6th til ran out & u.r. 10th* ....R Darke ro
1637 Nottarex *alwys bhnd, t.o. & p.u. 13th*........B Wright pu
11 ran. 1½l, 8l, ½l, 2l. Time 6m 25.00s. SP 6-1.
P D Jones (Dart Vale & South Pool).

1652 Open Maiden Div II (12st)

1638[5] **MY BOY BUSTER** .... **J Young** **1**
t.d.e. prog 6th, ld & mstk 15th, clr 2 out, ran on well
1610[2] **Spar Copse** .... **N Mitchell** **2**
(fav) prom, disp 14th, chsd wnr aft, no imp 2 out, tired
1637[7] **Carumu 5a** .... **S Hornby** **3**
prog 8th, ld 11th-13th, btn frm nxt
1536 Man Of Ice *ld to 11th & 13th til aft nxt, stppd bef 3 out, lame*....................................C Coyne pu
1593[4] Miss Pernickity 5a *strgglng frm 8th, t.o. & p.u. 12th* ....R Woolacott pu
1115 Riggledown Regent *in tch to 11th, t.o. & p.u. 2 out* ....A Holdsworth pu
1587 Happy Thought 5a *rear, lost tch whn p.u. 7th* N Harris pu
1555 Eskimo Star 5a *rear, lost tch whn p.u. 7th*......S Ellis pu
1626 Philippastone 7a *t.d.e. crawld fnces, 2f bhnd whn u.r. 10th* ....Miss L Delve ur
1128 Race Against Time 5a *in tch, prog 11th, rdn nxt, wknd 14th, f heavily 3 out* ....Miss L Blackford f
10 ran. 12l, 20l. Time 6m 32.00s. SP 7-2.
Miss L J Smale (Torrington Farmers).
Here endeth the season. J.N.

Irish Point-to-Point Results 1996

(Reproduced by Courtesy of *The Irish Field*)

SOUTH UNION FOXHOUNDS
Rochestown
Monday January 1st
HEAVY

1 - Adjacent Maiden

Run Rose Run ....**J Motherway** 1
Prophets Thumb 2
Also: Persian Packer (f), Change The Pace (pu), Sparky Joe (pu)
5 ran. Hd.

2 - Geldings Maiden 5yo

Get Real ....**P Fenton** 1
Hazy Supreme 2
Thunder Road 3
Also: Ebbzeado Willfurr (4), Donickmore (5), John's Right (pu), Meldante VI (pu), Dukes Castle (pu), Leemount Lad (pu), Dancing Dessie (pu), You Know Best (pu), Full Of Bounce (pu), Hannigan's Bridge (pu), The Magic Slabber (f)
14 ran. 6l, nk, 10l.

3 - Open Lightweight

Earlydue VI...............................**M Scanlon** 1
Loftus Lad 2
Knocknacarra Lad 3
Also: Very Evident (4), River Water (pu), Araqueepa (pu), Trimmer Wonder (pu), Another Rustle (f)
8 ran. 1l, 10l, 20l.

4 - Geldings Maiden 6yo+ I

Dixon Varner ....**E Bolger** 1
Only Time 2
Tearaway King 3
Also: Ace Ventura (4), Another Point (5), Finnow Thyne (pu), Pat The Hat (pu), Minehill (pu), Western Fort (ur), Coolteen Hero (f), Amazing Hill (pu)
11 ran. 15l, 3l, 4l.

5 - Geldings Maiden 6yo+ II

Wellane Boy...............................**E Bolger** 1
Celtic Park 2
Owning 3
Also: Elwill Glory (4), Another Pickle (pu), Ardavillan Prince (pu), Supremcan (pu), Whitebarn Grit (pu), Just The Duke (pu), Stay In Touch (f), Ivegotyounow (pu)
11 ran. ½l, 8l, 10l.

6 - Winners Of Two

Just A Breeze ....**T Cloke** 1
Art Prince 2
Also: Princess Lena (pu), Derry's Diamond (pu), Holly Moss (pu), Carrolls Rock (pu), Scarteen Lower (pu), Tobarella (pu), Dromgurrihy Lad (pu), Kilcully-Pride (pu), Henleydown (pu), Mr Pipeman (pu)
12 ran. 4l.

7 - Mares Maiden 7yo+

Misgivings.................................**P Kelly** 1
Faulty Rap 2
Ruby Belle 3
Also: Sezu (4), Evie's Party (5), Rascal Street Lad (6), Bucks Reward (pu), Coolbawn Bramble (pu), Curraheen Bride (pu), Punteille (f), Artistic Quay (pu), Convamore Queen (pu), Candy Is Dandy (pu), Bright Moonbeam (pu), Selm Mary (pu), Kiama Bay (pu), Beet Spray (pu)
17 ran. 7l, 20l, 10l.

UNITED FOXHOUNDS
Lisgoold
Sunday January 7th
SOFT

8 - Confined Maiden

Carbery Minstrel [17] ....**T Lombard** 1
prom, ev ch last, rallied to ld nr fin
Dublin Hill [17]*prom, ld last, hdd nr fin* 2
Silent Sneeze [16]*prom, onepcd frm 2 out* 3
Also: Buladante (4), Rio Star (f), Glorious Gale (pu), Phardante's Way (pu), Glenselier (pu), Mountainous Valley (f), Luciano The Yuppi (pu), Lady Of Means (ur), Kilcully Night (pu), Witchiewah (pu), Dante Lad (pu), Royal Chapeau (f), Have A Drop (pu), Mags Super Toi (pu)
17 ran. ½l, 4l, dist. SP 10-1.

9 - Adjacent Maiden 5yo

2[2] **Hazy Supreme [15]** ....**A O'Shea** 1
trckd ldrs, ld apr last, sn clr
Terrano Star [11]*ld to apr last, sn btn* 2
Also: Frangapini (pu), Love Actinium (pu), 2 Hannigan's Bridge (su), Sweet Merenda (f), Monadante (f), Colmans Hope (pu), Rockview Supreme (f), Jack's Well (pu), Valley Erne (pu), O So Breezy (pu), Fools Courage (pu), Parish Ranger (ur), Dromod Magic (pu)
15 ran. 10l. SP 5-2.

10 - Open Lightweight

Kerry Orchid [27] ....**P Fenton** 1
prog to 2nd 5 out, ld 2 out, styd on well
Johnny The Fox [25]*prog to ld 5 out, hdd & no ext 2 out* 2
3 **Very Evident [25]***prog to 4th 5 out, ev ch apr 2 out, onepcd* 3
Also: 3 Another Rustle [20] (4), Lovely Citizen [16] (5), Colligan River (pu), Rossi Novae (f), Beaudel (pu), Bocock's Pride (pu), Seeandbeseen (pu), Castlelack (f)
11 ran. 4l, sht-hd, 15l, 12l. SP 2-1.

11 - Mares Maiden 6yo+ I

Supreme Arctic [18] ....**D Costello** 1
hld up, prog 4 out, ld apr last, sn clr
Bula Vogue [15]*prom, ld 3 out, hdd & outpcd apr last* 2
Lantern Spark [12]*nvr nrr* 3
Also: Ballinvuskig Lady [12] (4), Tourig Dante (pu), Laura's Leap (pu), Anniversary Annie (f), 7 Rascal Street Lad (f), Tacky Lady (pu), Victim Of Slander (pu), Something Sheer (f), Pass The Basket (pu)
12 ran. 10l, 10l, 1½l. SP 6-4.

12 - Mares Maiden 6yo+ II

Ore Engineeress [16]...................**D Murphy** 1
prom, ld 2 out, styd on well
Cappagh Glen [13]*chsd wnr 2 out, no imp* 2
Pharditu [13]*prom, onepcd frm 2 out* 3
Also: Shamron (pu), Ann Black (ur), Over Decent (f), 7 Punteille (pu),

She Wont Stop (pu), Solar Castle (pu), Holiday Time (pu), Lantern Lotto (pu), Meldap (pu)
12 ran. 7l, 1½l. SP 8-1.

13 - Maiden 6yo+ I

Baby Jake [19] .... **B Hassett** 1
prom, ld 3 out, clr last, easily
Saradante [15] *prom, ev ch 2 out, sn btn* 2
Maypole Fountain [10] *nvr dang* 3
Also: 4 Minehill (4), Kings Cave (ur), Warning Call (pu), Shining Minstrel (pu), 4 Pat The Hat (pu), Park Duke (pu), Safety Factor (pu), Percy Hannon (pu), Dawn Lad (pu), 5 Another Pickle (f)
13 ran. 6l, 15l, 2l. SP 4-1.

14 - Maiden 6yo+ II

5 **Stay In Touch [21]** .... **D Costello** 1
prom, ld 5 out, clr 3 out, unchal
Radical River [16] *chsd wnr 3 out, no imp* 2
Silver Buckle *t.o* 3
Also: Earl Of Mirth (4), Blue Mosse (pu), Geata Bawn (f), Brian Og (f), Rusnetto (pu), Buckhill (pu), Have Another (pu), Caribo Express (pu), Stroll Home (f), Greywood (pu)
13 ran. 10l, dist, dist. SP Evens.

15 - Winners Of Two

Blackwater Lady [17] .... **E Fehily** 1
prom, ld last, rdn out
Corymandel [17] *ld to last, no ext* 2
6 **Kilcully-Pride [12]** *nvr dang* 3
Also: Badalka (pu), Crazy Dreams (pu), Bayview Prince (pu), Cool Bandit (ref), Myalup (pu)
8 ran. 1l, 15l. SP 8-1.

WESTMEATH HARRIERS
Slanemore
Sunday January 7th
HEAVY

16 - Maiden 5yo

Irish Stout [14] .... **A Martin** 1
4th 4 out, ld & lft clr 2 out, crawld last
Also: Riberetto's Girl (f), Irish Reef (pu), Jensalee (pu), Garethson (f), Twentyfivequid (pu), Wonder Dawn (pu), Remainder Star (f), Rare House (f), Butler Brennan (ref), Bradleys Corner (pu), Big Bad John (ur), Blackie Connors (pu), Coolree Lord (pu)
14 ran. SP 5-2.

17 - Winners Of Three

Dennistownthriller [20] .... **J Codd** 1
hld up, 3rd 4 out, ld last, all out
Private Yashkan [19] *4th 4 out, lft in ld nxt, hdd & no ext und pres last* 2
Find Out More [18] *ld 4 out-nxt, onepcd frm last* 3
Also: Greenfield Tiger [17] (4), Ballinaveen Bridge (pu), Palmura (pu), Westwiththenight (pu), October (pu), Friday Thirteenth (su), Chene Rose (pu), Slaney Wind (pu), Jaybe's Friend (pu), Over The Maine (f), Timeless River (pu), Hilton Mill (pu)
15 ran. 1½l, 3l, 1½l. SP 3-1.

18 - Open Lightweight

Elegant Lord [31] .... **E Bolger** 1
made all, sn clr, easily
Laura's Beau [22] *prog to chs wnr 2 out, no imp* 2
Colin's Hatch [20] *chsd wnr, no imp, dmtd 2 out* 3
Also: Slaney Standard [14] (4), Teal Bridge (pu), Schweppes Tonic (pu), Temporale (pu), Voldi (pu), Lamh Eile (pu), Loch Garman Hotel (f), Farney Glen (pu), Jims Choice (pu)
12 ran. 25l, 7l, 15l. SP 1-4.

19 - Mares Maiden I

Over The Wall [15] .... **G Elliott** 1
ld 9th, clr 3 out, unchal
The Vendor *chsd wnr 2 out, no imp* 2
Arctic Leader *nvr dang* 3
Also: What A Choice (4), Pleasing Melody (5), The Frairy Sister (pu), Pinehill (pu), Sideways Sally (f), Rathcarrick Lass (pu), Codology (pu), Ballet Knees (f), In The Future (pu), Very Tense (pu), Black Beth (pu), Gold Leader (f), Memory Harbour (pu), Duirse Dairse (f), Sapphire 'N' Silver (f)
18 ran. Dist, 8l, 3l, dist. SP 4-1.

20 - Mares Maiden II

Call Me Connie [15] .... **P Graffin** 1
prom, disp whn lft clr 3 out, unchal
Le Hachette *chsd ldrs, lft 2nd 3 out, no dang* 2
Also: Lady Elise (pu), Pitmar (f), Satin Talker (pu), Warrenstown Lass (f), Moneycarragh (pu), Brook Hill Lady (ur), Blennerville (pu), Push Gently (pu), Kilmainhwood (pu), La Maja (f), Ballybriken Castle (pu), Another Idea (f), Gerry's Delight (pu), Miss Trout (pu), Teralisa (f)
17 ran. Dist. SP 3-1.

21 - Maiden 6yo+ I

Stanley Steamer [18] .... **C McCarren** 1
made most, clr 3 out, unchal
Midnight Service [13] *rear, styd on frm 2 out, tk 2nd flat* 2
Cahills Hill [13] *chsd wnr, no imp 3 out, lost 2nd flat* ... 3
Also: Benny The Bishop (pu), Sam's Man (f), Fearless Hunter (pu), Noble Knight (pu), Sinergia (pu), Flairline Bay (f), Loughdoo (pu), Annie's Arthur (pu), Rushing Waters (f), Who's Your Man (pu), Both Sides (f), Saucy Poll (pu), Cottoneyejoe (ur)
16 ran. 15l, ½l. SP 5-2.

22 - Maiden 6yo+ II

Manhattan Prince [16] .... **L Gracey** 1
w.w. prog to ld last, styd on
Credo Is King [15] *prog to ld 4 out, hdd last, no ext* ... 2
Shuil Daingean [14] *ld 5 out-4 out, onepcd frm 2 out* .. 3
Also: Radical Dual (4), Only One (ur), Oldson (pu), Rath An Uisce (pu), Clanmany (pu), Bayline Lad (ur), The Punters Pal (pu), Tricyclic (f), Irenes Treasure (pu), Cebu Gale (pu), Talk Of Excitement (pu), Fill Your Boots (pu), Gawn Inn (f)
16 ran. 2½l, 4l, dist. SP 12-1.

23 - Maiden 6yo+ III

Viscount Thurls [18] .... **A Martin** 1
prom, ld 5 out-2 out, rallied to ld nr fin
No Mistake VI [18] *prog to chs wnr 3 out, ld nxt, hdd nr fin* 2
Cool Rocket *t.o* 3
Also: O'Fiaich's Hope (4), Four Zeros (pu), Tip The Skip (ur), South East Sun (pu), Bashindora (pu), Coshla Expresso (pu), Up And Under (f), Kilmacrew (f), Glendine (pu), Palma D'Or (pu), Corries Hill (pu), Harry's Secret (pu)
15 ran. Hd, dist, 3l. SP 5-2.

24 - Mares Lightweight

Duchess Of Padua [16] .... **D Keane** 1
blnd 2nd, prog 4 out, ld nxt, drvn out
No One Knows [15] *rear, styd on frm 2 out, nrst fin* ... 2
Missing Lady [14] *ld to 3 out, no ext* 3
Also: 3 Trimmer Wonder (4), Beet Statement (pu), Gale Griffin (pu), Fidsprit (pu), Amme Enaek (su), Blu Blizzard (pu)
9 ran. 2l, 1½l, 25l. SP 10-1.

SHILLELAGH & DISTRICT
Tinahely
Sunday January 14th
SOFT

25 - Winners Of One

One Eyed Ger VI [16] .... **A Coyle** 1
prom, ld 3 out, hld on

Dromhana [16]*prog to chal 3 out, ev ch last, no ext* ... 2
24[2] **No One Knows [13]***nvr nrr* ... 3
Also: 15 Badalka [13] (4), Trimmer Princess [10] (5), Ta Se Ag Teacht (6), 17 Greenfield Tiger (7)
7 ran. 1l, 8l, 1l, 10l, 4l, 1l. SP 2-1.

26 - Maiden 7yo+ I

Slaney Goddess [14]........**Lillian Doyle** 1
chsd ldr, ld last, pshd out, clvrly ...
Ardbei [13]*chsd ldr, chal last, hrd rdn & kpt on* ... 2
22 **Oldson [13]***ld to last, no ext* ... 3
Also: 21 Loughdoo [12] (4), 14[3] Silver Buckle [10] (5), Drumcairn (6), Final Statement (7), Harvemac (pu), Red Mollie (pu), Dun Belle (pu), 23 Corries Hill (f), Arctic Lake (pu), Tara River (pu)
13 ran. 1l, 1l, ½l, 10l, 12l, 3l, 12l. SP 4-1.

27 - Maiden 7yo+ II

Salemhady [16]........**H Cleary** 1
chsd ldrs, ld 4 out-last, rallied to ld nr fin ...
23[2] **No Mistake VI [16]***3rd 4 out, jnd wnr 2 out, ld last, hdd nr fin* ... 2
Strong Performance*4th 4 out, wknd apr 2 out* ... 3
Also: Beau Cinq (4), Baileys Dream (pu), Mullinello (pu), Shimano (pu), Fric Facile (f), Clarkes Cross (pu), 23 Kilmacrew (pu), Galloping Giggs (pu), Trina's Cottage (pu), Divine Saint (pu)
13 ran. Nk, dist, dist. SP 4-1.

28 - Winners Of Two

Ozier Hill [19]........**J Berry** 1
trckd ldrs, ld 3 out, clr nxt, unchal ...
Cool Yule [14]*disp to 4 out, kpt on agn frm last* ... 2
24 **Amme Enaek [14]***prog to chs wnr 3 out, no imp* ... 2
Also: 17 Palmura (4), 17 Timeless River (5), Christy's Girl (ur), Mister Ross (f)
7 ran. 15l, dd-ht, dist, 10l. SP 4-5.

29 - Open Lightweight

Credit Transfer [24]........**H Cleary** 1
ld 8th til aft last, rallied to ld nr fin ...
18 **Slaney Standard [24]***4th 4 out, sn chsd wnr, ld flat, hdd nr fin* ... 2
18 **Teal Bridge [20]***chsd wnr & mstk 4 out, 3rd & btn nxt* .. 3
Also: 24 Beet Statement [12] (4), 18[2] Laura's Beau [10] (5), After The Number (pu), Clonrosh Slave (pu), Tasse Du The (pu), 18 Loch Garman Hotel (pu)
9 ran. ½l, 12l, 25l, 5l. SP 4-5.

30 - Maiden 5 & 6yo I

Garrynisk [17]........**J Berry** 1
trckd ldrs, ld apr last, rdn out ...
Speckled Glen [16]*disp, ld 7th, hdd & no ext apr last* 2
Andy's Birthday [12]*disp to 7th, chsd ldr to 3 out, no ext* ... 3
Also: Donal's Choice [12] (4), Difficult Decision (5), Rising Paddy (pu), Tullibards Rainbow (f), Greedy Johno (f), More Rain (pu), Lucky Hope (pu), 21 Sam's Man (f), Carrarea (pu), Captain Guinness (pu), Peggys Leg (pu)
14 ran. 2l, 12l, ½l, 30l. SP 3-1.

31 - Maiden 5 & 6yo II

16 **Irish Reef [15]**........**D O'Brien** 1
made all, jnd & lft clr 2 out ...
Highland Ark [10]*chsd ldrs, btn whn lft 2nd 2 out, blnd last* ... 2
13 **Kings Cave***nvr dang* ... 3
Also: Clonee Lane (pu), Dusty Track (pu), Quattro (f), Sweetmount Lad (f), Shillelagh Oak (pu), Rat Race (pu), 4 Western Fort (pu), Mite Have Bean (pu), Lord Amethyst (pu), Royal Basis [14] (f)
13 ran. 15l, 12l. SP 4-1.

32 - Mares Maiden I

Sandy Pearl [15]........**J Quigley** 1
made all, clr 2 out, styd on ...
Nurney Minstrel [12]*chsd ldrs, kpt on to tk 2nd last* .. 2
Alamillo [12]*chsd wnr, no imp 2 out, wknd last* ... 3
Also: Lollia Paulina (pu), Aloha (ro), Faras Flight (pu), Trembles Choice (pu), Hazel Ring (pu), 20 Teralisa (pu), 19[3] Arctic Leader (pu), Baby Whale (pu), 7 Bright Moonbeam (f), 19 Black Beth (bd), Phantoms Girl (pu), Tullbeg Bloom (f), Hollybuck (pu)
16 ran. 10l, 2l. SP 6-1.

33 - Mares Maiden II

Slemish Mist [15]........**D O'Brien** 1
hld up, prog 3 out, disp last, ld nr fin ...
Ballinaclash Pride [15]*prom, ld 3 out, jnd last, hdd nr fin* ... 2
Little Minute [12]*prom til onepcd frm 2 out* ... 3
Also: 20 Brook Hill Lady [11] (4), Orlas Fancy (pu), 19 Duirse Dairse (f), Trimmer Lady (pu), Lady Sally (pu), Sally Willows (pu), Knights Pleasure (pu), Flaherty's Best VI (pu), Trembling Rose (pu), Carriglegan Gem (pu), Moll's Choice (pu), 20 Miss Trout (pu), Miss Lurgan (pu)
16 ran. Nk, 8l, 2l. SP 5-2.

LIMERICK FOXHOUNDS
Patrickswell
Sunday January 14th
HEAVY

34 - Winners Of One

13[1] **Baby Jake [17]**........**B Hassett** 1
prog 3 out, chal & lft clr last ...
I Haven't A Buck [13]*chsd ldrs, btn whn lft 2nd last* .. 2
Royal Ziero [10]*chsd ldrs, btn whn lft 3rd last* ... 3
Also: 17 Ballinaveen Bridge (4), Grants Carouse (pu), 17 Friday Thirteenth (pu), Duke Of Hades (f), 6 Carrolls Rock (pu), Legitman (pu)
9 ran. 12l, 10l, 4l. SP 9-4.

35 - Maiden 5yo I

2 **You Know Best [16]**........**D Costello** 1
prom, ld 4 out, lft clr 2 out, comf ...
Strong Vision [13]*chsd ldrs, lft 2nd 2 out, no imp* ... 2
2 **Ebbzeado Willfurr [12]***chsd ldrs, onepcd frm 3 out* ... 3
Also: Thirtysomething (pu), Mr Tom Tom (pu), Clarkes Gorse (pu), Fools With Horses (pu), Action Lad (ref), 2[3] Thunder Road (f), Cruisin On Credit (f), Dorgan (pu), Dysart O'Dea (f)
12 ran. 6l, 4l. SP Evens.

36 - Maiden 5yo II

16 **Coolree Lord [17]**........**E Bolger** 1
cls up, ld & lft clr last, ran on ...
Lakefield Leader [15]*cls up, chal & hmpd last, kpt on*
Jeepers [15]*chsd ldrs, styd on wl frm last* ... 3
Also: Irregular Planting (4), Killerk Lady (pu), Silver Blend (pu), 2 Full Of Bounce [15] (f), The Alamo (pu), Johnny's Echo (pu), Jaffa Man (f), Camla Lad (f), The Red Devil (pu)
12 ran. 2l, 1l, dist. SP Evens.

37 - Open Lightweight

4[1] **Dixon Varner [25]**........**E Bolger** 1
cls up, ld 3 out, easily ...
Divali [20]*lft in ld 4th, hdd 3 out, no ch wnr aft* ... 2
10 **Another Rustle [18]***chsd ldrs, onepcd frm 3 out* ... 3
Also: Howarya Harry [18] (4), La Cienaga (f), Mooncaper (ur), Tenpence Princess (pu), Stevie Be (pu), Common Coin (f), Guirns Shop (f)
10 ran. 6l, 7l, 1l. SP 1-2.

38 - Maiden 6yo+ I

Welcome Call [16]........**A Costello** 1
prom, ld 3 out, styd on ...
Shareza River [14]*prom, chsd wnr 3 out, onepcd* ... 2

Dooneal Hero*t.o.* 3
Also: Supreme Flyer (4), Skulldugery (5), Mr Beak (pu), 21 Cottoneye-joe (pu), An Fear Dubh (pu), Glenbrowne (pu), I Have You Now (f), Lets Twist Again (f), O'Sullivan's Choise (pu), Not Convinced (pu), Boots Madden (f), Carramore Hill (pu)
15 ran. 4l, dist, 1l. SP 5-4.

39 - Maiden 6yo+ II

Five Circles [15] ....**L Temple** 1
prom, ld apr last, rdn out ....
Level Vibes [14]*in tch, chsd wnr last, kpt on* 2
Ballhopping [12]*chsd ldrs, onepcd frm 2 out*........ 3
Also: Sultan Of Swing [12] (4), Pearl Dante (5), Festival Light (pu), Polished Diamond (pu), Deep Wave (f), Nollaig (pu), Rhetoric House (pu), Irish Society (pu), Mount Buda (pu), 17 Jaybe's Friend (pu), 4 Finnow Thyne (f)
14 ran. 2l, 6l, nk. SP 3-1.

40 - Maiden 6yo+ III

4 **Another Point [15]**.......................**E Bolger** 1
prom, ld 2 out, styd on..................................
4[3] **Tearaway King [14]***prom, ev ch 2 out, onepcd* 2
For Josh*t.o.*.. 3
Also: 23 Coshla Expresso (4), Flood Relief (pu), Leaders View (pu), Debonair Duke (f), September Stephen (f), The Breaser Fawl (pu), 22 Bayline Lad (f), Fifth Generation (f), Dunkel (pu), Winter Breeze (pu)
13 ran. 4l, dist, 4l. SP 4-1.

41 - Mares Maiden I

Marillo [15] ....**E Bolger** 1
prom, disp whn bmpd 2 out, ld flat, all out............
Late Call [15]*prom, disp whn bmpd 2 out, sn ld, hdd nr fin*.. 2
Lishillaun*t.o.*.. 3
Also: Answer That (su), 12 Over Decent (pu), Snipe Lodge (pu), Ivy Glen (pu), 20 Ballybriken Castle (pu), Flo Again (pu), Watt A Buzz (pu), Aine Hencey (pu), Thyne Please (pu), Blame Barney (pu), Manley Girl (pu), Killeen Countess (pu)
15 ran. 1l, dist. SP 3-1.

42 - Mares Maiden II

Glenview Rose [15].......................**D Keane** 1
in tch, ld 4 out, styd on well ....
Holly Lake [12]*chsd wnr 3 out, no imp nxt* 2
12 **Solar Castle***t.o.*.. 3
Also: Gala Vote (4), Queen Of The Suir (f), 9 Love Actinium (f), Naida (pu), Native Success (f), Burren Valley (pu), Dannys Girl (pu), Tiger Dolly (pu), Spinning Melody (pu), Camden Lamp (pu), 11 Victim Of Slander (pu), Just Placed (pu)
15 ran. 10l, dist, dist. SP 6-1.

43 - Mares Maiden III

Fernhill [16]..............................**W Ewing** 1
prom, ld 3 out, clr apr last, unchal ....
16 **Jensalee***chsd wnr 2 out, sn btn* 2
Ring Mam*nvr dang*...................................... 3
Also: Henbits Dream (4), Granny Bid (5), 9 Frangapini (pu), Barmur (f), Taylors Twist (pu), Nagle Rice (pu), Sheshia (pu), Bay Lough (pu), Ballycar Princess (pu), 11[3] Lantern Spark (pu), 12 Lantern Lotto (pu), Galatasori Jane (pu)
15 ran. Dist, 12l, 8l. SP 9-4.

44 - Mares Race

6[1] **Just A Breeze [20]** ....**T Cloke** 1
ld 5 out, hld on aft last...................................
20[1] **Call Me Connie [19]***rear, prog 3 out, styd on, not rch wnr* 2
24[1] **Duchess Of Padua***nvr dang* 3
Also: Hi-Way's Gale (4), Tara Lodge (pu), Killoskehan Queen (f), Carling Lass (pu), Dromin Pride (pu), 6 Derry's Diamond (pu), The Vicarette (pu), Kizzy Rose (pu), Mrs Giggs (pu), Dont Waste It (pu)
13 ran. 3l, dist, 3l. SP 2-1.

TRAMORE
Thursday January 18th
SOFT

45 - 2¾m Hun Chase

Corymandel (Ire) 12.0..................**Mr P Fenton** 1
(Jt fav) ....
Johnny The Fox (Ire) 11.11 3a......**Mr T Lombard** 2
(Jt fav) in tch, chsd wnr 4 out, no ext aft 2 out..........
No Mistake VI (Ire) 11.7 7a..........**Mr A Fleming** 3
prom til outpcd 4 out, kpt on frm 2 out ....
Fays Folly (Ire) 11.2 7a 4
Princess Lena (Ire) 11.2 7a 5
Dromin Chat (Ire) 12.0 .... pu
Gracemarie Kate (Ire) 11.2 7a .... f
7 ran. 8l, hd, dist, 3l. Time 6m 5.5s. SP 7-4.

MUSKERRY FOXHOUNDS
Aghabullogue
Saturday January 20th
HEAVY

46 - Maiden 5yo

9 **Valley Erne [17]** ....**T Lombard** 1
hld up, ld last, sn well clr ....
Duke's Castle [11]*chsd ldr, ld 2 out-last, no ch wnr*... 2
2 **John's Right***t.o.*.. 3
Also: 2 Leemount Lad (pu), 2 Meldante VI (pu)
5 ran. 15l, dist. SP 4-6.

47 - Maiden 6yo+

5 **Elwill Glory [16]**........................**D Murphy** 1
made all, hld on wll flat...................................
14[2] **Radical River [15]***chsd wnr, chal last, kpt on* 2
Fundy [15]*chsd ldrs, chal apr last, kpt on* 3
Also: 14 Geata Bawn (pu), 8 Glenselier (pu), Frightening Child (pu), Classis King (pu), Bally Riot (pu), Supreme Odds (pu), 13 Safety Factor (pu), 11 Pass The Basket (pu), Riverdale Express (ro), 14 Brian Og (pu), Tavern Tale (pu), 39[3] Ballhopping (pu), Quirina Majano (pu)
16 ran. 2l, ½l. SP 8-1.

48 - Open Lightweight

10[1] **Kerry Orchid [25]** ....**P Fenton** 1
in tch, rdn to chal 2 out, ld aft last, all out ....
3[1] **Earlydue VI [25]***ld, jnd last, hdd flat, just hld*......... 2
Faha Gig [22]*nvr nrr*.................................... 3
Also: 10[3] Very Evident (pu), Ashton Court (pu)
5 ran. ½l, 5l. SP 4-6.

49 - Adjacent Maiden

7[2] **Faulty Rap [15]**.........................**T Lombard** 1
prom, chal 2 out, lft wll clr last.........................
1[2] **Prophets Thumb***nvr dang, lft 2nd last*................ 2
Tom The Boy VI*t.o.*....................................... 3
Also: 7 Kiama Bay (4), Nearhaan (pu), Forest Musk (pu), 5 Ivegotyounow (pu), Ruby Invite (pu), 7 Evie's Party (pu), Ormond Beach (pu), Desertmore [15] (f)
11 ran. 25l, dist, dist. SP 9-4.

50 - Mares Maiden

7 **Artistic Quay [17]** ....**J Collins** 1
made all, styd on well.....................................
7 **Sezu [15]***chsd ldrs, kpt on onepcd frm 2 out*........... 2
8[3] **Silent Sneeze [14]***chsd ldrs, onepcd frm 2 out* 3
Also: Minstrel Madame [12] (4), Stuarts Point (f), Ann Toni (pu), 7 Curraheen Bride (pu), Scarlet River (pu), 8 Rio Star (f), 9 Sweet Merenda (pu), Hurricane Iris (ur), Shannon Rugby Club (f), Hopper-dante (pu), 11 Rascal Street Lad (pu), Harvest Delight (pu), Teamtalk (pu)
16 ran. 5l, 4l, 5l. SP 3-1.

51 - Winners Of One

5[1] **Wellane Boy [21]** .... **E Bolger** 1
hld up, ld 3 out, comf ....
Ballinlovane Eile [18]*chsd wnr aft 3 out, rdn & no imp* 2
The Criosra*t.o.* 3
Also: Inch Emperor (pu), 1[1] Run Rose Run (pu), 6 Scarteen Lower (f), 15 Cool Bandit (pu)
7 ran. 5l, 25l. SP 4-7.

KILLEAGH HARRIERS
Killeagh
Sunday January 21st
HEAVY

52 - Maiden 5yo I

36 **Full Of Bounce [18]** .... **A Costello** 1
prom, ld 5 out, lft clr 3 out ....
Mickey's Dream [10]*no ch whn lft 2nd 3 out, no imp* .. 2
Droum Ross*t.o.* 3
Also: Geragh Road (pu), 9 Colmans Hope (f), Determined Man (pu), Courier's Way (f), Lightoak Lad (bd), Conor Mac (f), 36 Silver Blend (pu), 36 Jaffa Man (f), 9 Parish Ranger (pu)
12 ran. Dist, dist. SP 5-4.

53 - Maiden 5yo II

35 **Fools With Horses [15]** .... **J McNamara** 1
prog hlfwy, ld 3 out, lft clr nxt, hdd flat, ld post ....
35 **Mr Tom Tom [15]***chsd ldrs, lft 2nd 3 out, ld flat, hdd post* 2
Never Heard [15]*rear, ran on well 2 out, just faild* 3
Also: 2 Dancing Dessie (4), For Cathal (pu), Duky River (f), Black Abbey (f), 2 Donickmore (ro), 2 The Magic Slabber (pu), Clastinium (pu), Neelisagin (pu), 9[2] Terrano Star (co)
12 ran. Hd, ½l, 25l. SP 2-1.

54 - Winners Of Two

14[1] **Stay In Touch [24]** .... **D Costello** 1
prom, ld 4 out, sn wll clr ....
Chalwood [15]*chsd ldrs, no ch wth wnr frm 3 out* 2
The Miner's Fate*t.o.* 3
Also: Make A Line (pu), 6[2] Art Prince (pu), 15[3] Kilcully-Pride (pu), Cooladerra Lady (pu), 17[1] Dennistownthriller (pu), 42[1] Glenview Rose (pu), 37[2] Divali (pu), Roman Gale (pu)
11 ran. Dist, dist. SP 4-6.

55 - Confined Maiden

12[3] **Pharditu [15]** .... **J Motherway** 1
prom, ld 3 out, hld on nr fin ....
5 **Whitebarn Grit [14]***rear, ran on frm 2 out, not rch wnr* 2
Run For Brownie [13]*chsd ldrs, onepcd apr last* 3
Also: 11 Laura's Leap [12] (4), Finnuala Supreme (5), Gluais Linn (pu), Cahermone Lady (pu), Black Fountain (pu), 9 Monadante (pu), 11 Tourig Dante (pu)
10 ran. 1l, 2l, 2l. SP 4-1.

56 - Maiden 6yo I

30 **Lucky Hope [17]** .... **D O'Brien** 1
cls up, ld 4 out, clr whn jmpd rght last, styd on ....
8[2] **Dublin Hill [15]***chsd wnr 3 out, no imp last* 2
Gerry And Tom [14]*chsd ldrs, onepcd frm 3 out* 3
Also: Emerald Statement [12] (4), 4 Coolteen Hero (5), Just-N-James (ro), 14 Rusnetto (pu), Supreme Hooker (pu), 13 Park Duke (f), 4 Amazing Hill (pu), Sir Frederick (pu)
11 ran. 4l, 3l, 5l. SP 4-1.

57 - Maiden 6yo II

13 **Warning Call [15]** .... **J Motherway** 1
prom, ld 3 out, drvn out ....
5[3] **Owning [15]***prog to chal 2 out, just hld flat* 2
Minella Miller [15]*prog to chal 2 out, no ext nr fin* 3
Also: 14 Caribo Express [10] (4), 14 Stroll Home (5), Dante's Reward (pu), Bushmiller (pu), 13 Percy Hannon (f), 40 Flood Relief (pu), 39 Irish Society (pu)
10 ran. ½l, ½l, 20l. SP 6-1.

58 - Open Lightweight

37[3] **Another Rustle [21]** .... **M Cahill** 1
prom, ld 5 out, sn clr, unchal ....
24 **Trimmer Wonder [13]***chsd wnr 4 out, no imp* 2
6 **Holly Moss***nvr dang* 3
Also: 44 The Vicarette (4), 6 Mr Pipeman (5), 10 Seeandbeseen (pu), 37 Mooncaper (pu), 10 Beaudel (pu), 10 Lovely Citizen [29] (pu)
9 ran. 20l, 20l, ½l. SP 2-1.

59 - Mares Maiden 5yo I

Rosie's Pride [15] .... **A Hickey** 1
prom, rdn 3 out, styd on agn to ld last ....
Bit Of A Citizen [13]*prom, ld 3 out-last, no ext* 2
9 **Rockview Supreme***chsd ldrs, onepcd frm 2 out* 3
Also: Ellenmae Rose (f), Determined Okie (ro), Leamlara Rose (ref), 41 Watt A Buzz (ref), I'm Happy Now (f), Ballinacubby Pride (ur), Broad Valley (pu)
10 ran. 4l, 15l. SP 8-1.

60 - Mares Maiden 5yo II

20 **Lady Elise [15]** .... **J Codd** 1
prom, ld 4 out, sn clr
Parson River*chsd wnr 3 out, no imp* 2
Also: Round Tower Lady (pu), 42 Love Actinium (ur), Lee Valley Lady (pu), Pharleng (pu), Ballyhest Fountain (f), Noneofyourbusiness (pu), Ask Me In (pu), 9 Fools Courage (f)
10 ran. 25l. SP 6-1.

DUNGARVAN HARRIERS
Dungarvan
Sunday January 28th
HEAVY

61 - Maiden 5yo I

Gerone [16] .... **P Fenton** 1
w.w. 4th 5 out, hmpd & lft in ld 2 out, ran on well ....
53 **Donickmore [14]***5th 5 out, lft 2nd 2 out, onepcd* 2
Davy Lamp [13]*3rd 5 out, onepcd frm 2 out* 3
Also: 9 Hannigan's Bridge (f), Tomasins Choice (pu), Smiling Minstrel (pu), 35 Thirtysomething (pu), Where's Noel (pu), 35[3] Ebbzeado Willfurr (ur), 36 The Red Devil (f), 49 Forest Musk (pu), 53[3] Never Heard (pu), Poachers Lamp (ur)
13 ran. 3l, 4l. SP 5-1.

62 - Maiden 5yo II

30[3] **Andy's Birthday [15]** .... **J Codd** 1
prom, ld 5 out, clr 2 out, hld on und pres ....
35 **Clarkes Gorse [15]***chsd wnr & mstk 2 out, fin well* 2
35 **Thunder Road [15]***prom, outpcd 3 out, styd on agn last* 3
Also: 35 Dysart O'Dea [13] (4), 35 Action Lad [11] (5), Ballybeggan Boy (6), Gasmark (pu), Colmans Hatch (f), 30 Tullibards Rainbow (pu), Red Bronze (pu), 52 Courier's Way (pu), Executive Class (pu), Spirit Of A King (pu)
13 ran. ½l, 1l, 6l. SP 4-1.

63 - Mares Maiden 5 & 6yo I

Lake Tour [17] .... **K Whelan** 1
chsd ldr & lft in ld 5 out, drvn clr last ....
50[3] **Silent Sneeze [14]***chsd ldrs, kpt on to tk 2nd flat* 2
Supersonia [14]*chal 4 out til wknd apr last* 3
Also: 8 Royal Chapeau (4), Sweet Castlehyde (5), 1 Change The Pace (6), Mr K's Winterblues (7), Foherish Mist (f), 50 Hopperdante (pu), Appendix Lady (pu), 8 Lady Of Means (pu), Lunar Approach (pu), Bright Prospect (f), Shirdante (f), 55 Finnuala Supreme (f), 55 Gluais Linn (pu), 41 Blame Barney (pu)
17 ran. 10l, 4l, dist. SP 5-1.

64 - Mares Maiden 5 & 6yo II

50 **Sweet Merenda [16]....................E Gallagher** 1
prog 4 out, ld 2 out, sn clr
43 **Henbits Dream [12]***chsd wnr 2 out, onepcd* 2
47 **Frightening Child [11]***chsd ldrs, onepcd 2 out* 3
Also: The Pulpit (4), 8 Have A Drop (5), 60 Love Actinium (6), 42³ Solar Castle (7), 11² Bula Vogue (8), 50 Ann Toni (9), 11 Ballinvuskig Lady (10), Dante's Skip (11), Warlockfoe (pu), Farran Garrett (ref), 60² Parson River (pu), 8 Kilcully Night (pu), Dunmoon Lady (pu), 60 Ballyhest Fountain (pu)
17 ran. 8l, 2l, 15l. SP 12-1.

65 - Winners Of Two

38¹ **Welcome Call [21]....................A Costello** 1
w.w. hmpd 4 out, prog nxt, ld last, rdn out
9¹ **Hazy Supreme [20]***cls up, chal last, no ext flat* 2
54² **Chalwood [19]***ld to last, onepcd* 3
Also: 43¹ Fernhill [17] (4), Gracemarie Kate [14] (5), The Miners Fate [12] (6), 6 Princess Lena (7), 34 Ballinaveen Bridge (8), 15 Bayview Prince (9), Escheat (10), 3² Loftus Lad (11), 58 Seeandbeseen (pu)
12 ran. 1½l, 3l, 5l, 8l. SP 7-4.

66 - Confined Maiden

Sidcup Hill [16]....................T Lombard 1
chsd ldr, ld 2 out, sn clr
Mahon River [12]*ld to 2 out, no ext* 2
Dumont Lady*t.o.* 3
Also: Clodagh River (4), 60 Round Tower Lady (f), Brown Berry (f), 56 Supreme Hooker (pu), Stratton Park (pu), 12 Shamron (bd), 59 I'm Happy Now (pu)
10 ran. 8l, dist, 15l. SP 9-4.

67 - Open Lightweight

37¹ **Dixon Varner [26]....................E Bolger** 1
prom, ld 5 out, easily
48³ **Faha Gig [22]***chsd wnr 4 out, kpt on, no imp* 2
48² **Earlydue Vl [19]***chsd ldrs, kpt on onepcd 3 out* 3
Also: 10 Rossi Novae [15] (4), Awbeg Rover [13] (5), 15 Myalup (6), 10 Colligan River (7)
7 ran. 3l, 8l, 10l. SP 4-7.

68 - Maiden 7yo+ I

47 **Bally Riot [16]....................J Collins** 1
rear, prog to chal last, styd on to ld nr fin
Big Bo [15]*prom, ld 3 out, wknd & hdd flat* 2
Mighty Trust [14]*chsd ldrs, no ext apr last* 3
Also: Prayon Parson [11] (4), Dohney Boy (5), 8 Mountainous Valley (6), Milenkeh (ur), 14 Buckhill (pu), 14 Have Another (pu), Sandyrock (ro), Bush Telegraph (pu), 8 Luciano The Yuppi (pu), 47 Safety Factor (pu)
13 ran. 1l, 3l, 7l. SP 3-1.

69 - Maiden 7yo+ II

40³ **For Josh [16]....................M Phillips** 1
prom, ld last, styd on
West Lyn [15]*prom, ld 3 out-last, no ext* 2
13 **Minehill [12]***chsd ldrs, onepcd 3 out* 3
Also: 13 Dawn Lad [11] (4), 49² Prophets Thumb (5), 40 Coshla Expresso (6), Bartlemy King (7), Digacre (8), Bone Idol (pu), Bramble Run (ur), Aislings Toi (f), Fruit Town (f), 8 Buladante (pu)
13 ran. 3l, 10l, 3l. SP 10-1.

UNITED FOXHOUNDS
Carrigtwohill
Sunday February 4th
HEAVY

70 - Confined Maiden I

4² **Only Time [15]....................D Murphy** 1
prom, ld 4 out, in cmmnd whn lft clr last
47 **Supreme Odds***nvr dang, lft 2nd last* 2
64 **Have A Drop***nvr dang, lft 3rd last* 3
Also: 63 Lady Of Means (4), 8 Glorious Gale (5), Alice Sheer Thorn (6), Super Fred (pu), Castle Shelley (pu), 50 Hurricane Iris (pu), Black Perrin (pu), 68 Luciano The Yuppi (pu), 68 Mountainous Valley [13] (ur), Could Be A'ntin (pu), Get Cracking (pu), 63 Mr K's Winterblues (pu)
15 ran. 20l, 2l, 2l. SP 2-1.

71 - Confined Maiden II

56² **Dublin Hill [16]....................S O'Callaghan** 1
made all, mstk last, drvn out
68 **Bush Telegraph [15]***prom, chal aft last, alwys hld* 2
8 **Dante Lad [14]***chsd ldrs, kpt on onepcd frm 2 out* 3
Also: 46³ John's Right [13] (4), 8 Mags Super Toi [11] (5), 47 Glenselier (6), Fennells Bay (pu), 64³ Frightening Child (pu), Fountain House (f), Shady Prince (pu), Queen Of Clubs (pu), 68 Safety Factor (pu), 64 Kilcully Night (pu), 50 Rio Star (pu), Skipping Chick (pu)
15 ran. ¾l, 4l, 1l. SP 3-1.

72 - Winners Of One

Swans Wish [20]....................N Fahily 1
w.w. ld aft 4 out, hld on wll
35¹ **You Know Best [20]***prom, wth wnr aft 4 out, just hld* 2
66¹ **Sidcup Hill [18]***cls up, kpt on onepcd frm 3 out* 3
Also: 34² I Haven't A Buck [17] (4), 57¹ Warning Call [16] (5), 47¹ Elwill Glory [13] (6), 51³ The Criosra [11] (7), 51² Ballinlovane Eile (8), 51 Scarteen Lower (9), 10 Bocock's Pride (pu), Coole Cherry (pu), 34 Grants Carouse (pu), 65 Gracemarie Kate (f), 44 Dromin Pride (f), 55¹ Pharditu (pu), 65 Princess Lena (pu), Lakeview Lad (pu), 65 Bayview Prince (pu)
18 ran. ¾l, 4l, 2l. SP 10-1.

73 - Maiden 5yo I

53 **For Cathal [15]....................P Cloke** 1
trckd ldrs, 5th 2 out, strng run to ld flat
Another Lafontaine [14]*prom, ld 3 out til hdd flat* 2
Kippins [12]*prom, onepcd frm 2 out* 3
Also: 61 Tomasins Choice [12] (4), Camogue Bridge [10] (5), 52 Parish Ranger (6), 61 Thirtysomething (pu), 53 Dancing Dessie (pu), 36 Johnny's Echo (ur), Lord Pat (ro), Robin Of Loxley (pu), As Things Go (f)
12 ran. ½l, 4l, 1l. SP Evens.

74 - Maiden 5yo II

2 **Dukes Castle [15]....................K O'Sullivan** 1
prom, disp 3 out til lft clr last, styd on well
53² **Mr Tom Tom [13]***prom, disp 3 out til hit last, no ext* 2
62 **Ballybeggan Boy***nvr dang* 3
Also: Glenaboy (4), 61 Poachers Lamp (pu), 55 Black Fountain (f), 52² Mickey's Dream (pu), 52 Geragh Road (pu), Sirrah Aris (f), Silver Bow (pu), 9 Jack's Well (pu)
11 ran. 10l, 20l, dist. SP 9-4.

75 - Open Lightweight

67³ **Earlydue Vl [20]....................D Costello** 1
prom, disp 4 out, lft clr last, styd on
48 **Ashton Court [19]***prom, disp 4 out til blnd last, not rcvr* 2
58³ **Holly Moss [16]***chsd ldrs, no imp frm 3 out* 3
Also: 49¹ Faulty Rap [14] (4), 58 The Vicarette [11] (5), 58¹ Another Rustle [10] (6), Next Right (pu), What Thing (pu), Hotchpot (pu)
9 ran. 4l, 10l, 4l. SP 5-4.

76 - Mares Maiden I

59² **Bit Of A Citizen [15]....................W O'Sullivan** 1
chsd ldr 4 out, hrd rdn & styd on to ld flat
60 **Ask Me In [14]***ld, clr 2 out, wknd & hdd flat* 2
55 **Cahermone Lady [13]***nvr nrr* 3
Also: 63 Sweet Castlehyde [12] (4), 55 Monadante (pu), Hot Scent (f), Carlingford Gale (f), Dusty's Delight (f), Funny Habits (pu), Blackwater Fox (f)
10 ran. 4l, 1l, 1l. SP 7-2.

77 - Mares Maiden II

Tack Room Lady [17] .... **D Costello** 1
prog to ld 3 out, styd on strngly ....
66 I'm Happy Now [14]*prog & ev ch 3 out, no imp wnr nxt* 2
Daytime Dancer*nvr dang* 3
so: 63 Foherish Mist (4), High Park Lady (pu), 60 Noneofyourbusiss (pu), 64 Warlockfoe (pu), 66 Round Tower Lady (pu), 59[3] ckview Supreme (f), Dante's Whistle (pu), Janice Price (pu)
11 ran. 6l, 20l, 4l. SP 9-4.

78 - Maiden 6yo I

5[2] Celtic Park [20] .... **D Costello** 1
w.w. prog to ld 5 out, sn clr, easily ....
4 Ace Ventura [10]*chsd wnr 4 out, no ch* 2
57 Bushmiller*nvr dang* 3
so: Irish Display (pu), 49 Nearhaan (pu), Know Something VI (f), 57 ribo Express (f), Strong Stuff (pu), 57 Dante's Reward (f), 57[3] nella Miller (pu), Barnadown (pu), 56[3] Gerry And Tom (pu), An Oon An Owl (pu), 38 Supreme Flyer (pu), 40[2] Tearaway King (f), 57 oll Home (pu), 13[3] Maypole Fountain (pu), No Such Parson (pu), Desertmore (f)
19 ran. Dist, 10l. SP 5-4.

79 - Maiden 6yo II

Brighter Shade [15] .... **D Costello** 1
prom, disp 2 out, just hld on flat ....
3[2] Saradante [15]*prom, disp 2 out, just hld flat* 2
39 Finnow Thyne*nvr dang* 3
so: 56 Sir Frederick (4), Ross Quay (pu), Aesops Fables (pu), Round und (pu), Rain Spirit (pu), Driminamore (pu), 56 Park Duke (pu), nella Midget (pu), 47 Classis King (pu), See Just There (pu), Tor), Blackwood (pu), 56 Just-N-James (pu), 13 Pat The Hat (pu), stery Aristocrat (pu)
18 ran. Nk, dist, 4l. SP 4-1.

CARLOW FARMERS
Ballon
Sunday February 4th
SOFT

80 - Winners Of One

1[3] Kings Cave [15] .... **P Kelly** 1
hld up, prog 3 out, ld last, styd on ....
17 Slaney Wind [13]*trckd ldrs, outpcd 3 out, rallied last, no ext* 2
The Wee Fellow [12]*cls up, ld 3 out-apr last, no ext* .. 3
so: 25 Badalka [10] (4), Derby O'Gill (5), 25 Trimmer Princess (6), 33 arriglegan Gem (pu), Andy Joe (pu), Mount Nugent Jack (pu)
9 ran. 4l, 3l, 6l, 6l, ¾l. SP 7-1.

81 - Maiden 5yo

16 Remainder Star [16] .... **A Martin** 1
cls up, ld apr last where lft clr, comf ....
33 Moll's Choice [14]*rear, styd on wll apr last, nvr nrr* ... 2
Timeforgoing [10]*nrst fin* 3
so: Mr Lovely [10] (4), 16 Riberetto's Girl (5), Into The Web (ur), nely Castle (pu), 62 Tullibards Rainbow (pu), 62 Gasmark (ur), Wyn an Soon (pu), 31 Dusty Track (pu), 30 Peggys Leg (pu), Dearstershatter (pu), 16 Butler Brennan (pu)
14 ran. 4l, 12l, nk. SP 1-2.

82 - Open Lightweight

29[3] Teal Bridge [22] .... **G Elliott** 1
3rd 5 out, ld apr 2 out, rdn out ....
29 Loch Garman Hotel [21]*prog 3 out, chsd wnr apr last, no ext flat* 2
18 Farney Glen [16]*prog 3 out, chsd wnr nxt, sn btn* 3
so: 29 Clonrosh Slave [10] (4), 29 Tasse Du The (pu), Cool It (ro), 27[3] rong Performance (pu), 28 Palmura (pu), Ballinaboola Grove (pu), [3] Duchess Of Padua (ur), 19[1] Over The Wall (pu)
11 ran. 1½l, 15l, 20l. SP 5-1.

83 - Mares Maiden I

Sandfair [15] .... **R O'Keeffe** 1
w.w. chsd ldr 3 out, ld nxt, styd on ....
31 Clonee Lane [14]*prom, ld 4 out-2 out, onepcd* 2
19 Pleasing Melody [14]*4th 3 out, styd on onepcd frm nxt* 3
Also: 33 Flaherty's Best VI (4), Mauradonna (5), 59 Determined Okie (6), Loughlins Pride (f), Instrumental (f), 19 Pinehill (pu), 32 Baby Whale (pu), 49 Kiama Bay (ur), 19 The Frairy Sister (pu), 32 Faras Flight (pu), Royal Star (f), Cosie Cartel (f)
15 ran. 3l, 1l, 25l, dist, dist. SP 5-1.

84 - Mares Maiden II

Kilbricken Maid [16] .... **R O'Keeffe** 1
w.w. prog 3 out, 3rd last, rdn to ld flat ....
33[3] Little Minute [15]*prom, ev ch last, onepcd flat* 2
Sunczech [15]*prom, ld 3 out til hdd aft last, no ext* 3
Also: Cappajune [14] (4), Still Optimistic (5), 20 Gerry's Delight (6), 33 Duirse Dairse (7), Goldwren (pu), I'm Not Shes Girl (pu), 20 Push Gently (pu), Nectar Bloom (pu), 32 Phantoms Girl (pu), Brave Commitment (ur), 33 Miss Trout (pu), 32 Black Beth (pu)
15 ran. 3l, 1l, 2l, dist, 3l, 1½l. SP 6-4.

85 - Mares Maiden III

42[2] Holly Lake [17] .... **W Ewing** 1
prog 4 out, ld apr last, sn clr ....
33 Brook Hill Lady [13]*ld to apr last, no ch wnr aft* 2
32 Tullbeg Bloom*t.o.* 3
Also: 20 Pitmar (pu), 43[2] Jensalee (pu), 42 Dannys Girl (pu), 33 Orlas Fancy (ur), Short Of A Buck (f), 41 Over Decent (pu), Lusmagh River (f), 33 Trimmer Lady (pu), Sixty-One (pu), 43 Bay Lough (pu), Hazels Dream (pu), Cool Cailin (pu)
15 ran. 6l, dist. SP 2-1.

86 - Maiden 6yo I

Millfrone [18] .... **T Cloke** 1
made all, clr 2 out, unchal ....
38 Boots Madden [11]*chsd ldrs, lft 2nd 2 out, no ch wnr* 2
King Torus*t.o.* 3
Also: 23 Glendine (4), 21 Who's Your Man (5), 30 Greedy Johno (pu), 30 Sam's Man (f), 31 Lord Amethyst (pu), 31 Quattro (ur), Deerpark King (pu), Newtown Rambler (pu), 14 Greywood (pu), 22 Rath An Uisce (pu)
13 ran. 20l, dist, 4l, 8l. SP 10-1.

87 - Maiden 6yo II

23 Harry's Secret [15] .... **D Breen** 1
prog 4 out, ld apr 2 out, hld on ....
30[2] Speckled Glen [15]*prom, ld 4 out, blnd nxt, hdd apr 2 out, just hld* 2
22[2] Credo Is King [14]*rear, styd on frm 2 out, nvr nrr* 3
Also: Oul Larry Andy [11] (4), Rosevalley (pu), Tullebard Beetman (f), 30 Captain Guinness (pu), 37 Common Coin (pu), 31 Rat Race (pu), 22 Only One (pu), Diorraing (pu), Buffalo House (f), 22 Irenes Treasure (pu)
13 ran. ½l, 4l, 8l. SP 12-1.

88 - Maiden 7yo+ I

Remrar [14] .... **A Martin** 1
4th hlfwy, prog to ld 2 out, drvn out flat ....
22 The Punters Pal [13]*5th hlfwy, prog & lft in ld 4 out-2 out, rallied last,no ext* 2
Duncaha Hero [12]*prog 3 out, disp nxt, no ext apr last* 3
Also: 68 Prayon Parson [11] (4), 27[2] No Mistake VI (5), The Defender (pu), 26 Tara River (pu), 23 Four Zeros (pu), 23 Up And Under (f), Another Believer (ur), 26 Arctic Lake (pu), 26 Final Statement (pu), 40 Dunkel (pu), Queen Of Eagles (pu)
14 ran. 3l, 4l, 3l, 15l. SP 3-1.

89 - Maiden 7yo+ II

26 **Dun Belle [14] ....D Coakley** 1
3rd 5 out, chal last, rdn to ld flat ....
Will Travel [13]*prog 3 out, ev ch last, kpt on* 2
26 **Loughdoo [13]***prog 3 out, ld nxt, hdd & no ext flat* 3
Also: 22 Radical Dual (4), 27 Shimano (5), 39² Level Vibes (pu), 39 Festival Light (pu), Desmarfran (pu), 38 O'Sullivan's Choise (ro), 21 Both Sides (pu), 23 Tip The Skip (pu), Siamsa Brae (pu), Well Recovered (0)
13 ran. ½l, ¾l, 20l, 15l. SP 10-1.

90 - Maiden 7yo+ III

21² **Midnight Service [14] ....G Harford** 1
prom, ld 5 out, lft clr 2 out, just hld on ....
26² **Ardbei [14]***ld to 5 out, lft 2nd 2 out, rallied, just faild*... 2
39 **Jaybe's Friend***nvr dang* 3
Also: 27 Divine Saint (pu), Big Murt (pu), 69 Bramble Run (ur), 22 Fill Your Boots (pu), Trackman (pu), 39 Sultan Of Swing (pu), 38 Carramore Hill (pu), Glenmore Star (pu), Venetian Star (pu)
12 ran. ½l, 15l. SP 3-1.

CLONMEL
Thursday February 8th
HEAVY

91 - 3m Hun Chase

Stay In Touch (Ire) 11.11 3a.......Mr D P Costello 1
(fav) ld 7th-12th, ld 3 out, clr last, comf..............
45² **Johnny The Fox (Ire) 11.11 3a ......Mr T Lombard** 2
Dublin Hill (Ire) 11.7 7a ....Mr S O'Callaghan 3
66² Mahon River 12.0 4
90³ Jaybe's Friend 12.0 5
Ardubh 12.0 .... pu
The Vicarette (Ire) 11.2 7a (bl) .... f
Bally Riot (Ire) 11.7 7a .... f
45 Princess Lena (Ire) 11.5 7a 3ow .... bd
Thresa-Anita (Ire) 11.2 7a .... bd
Five Circles (Ire) 11.7 7a .... f
For Josh (Ire) 12.0 .... f
Ballhopping (Ire) 11.7 7a .... pu
Just A Breeze (Ire) 11.2 7a .... ur
14 ran. 11l, 13l, 2l, 14l. Time 7m 0.7s. SP 8-11.

EAST DOWN FOXHOUNDS
Tyrella
Saturday February 10th
GOOD

92 - Winners Of Two

16¹ **Irish Stout [19].........................A Martin** 1
chsd ldrs, prog 2 out, ld flat, sn clr ....
Mister Black [17]*clr ldr, mstk 2 out, hdd & no ext flat* 2
24 **Gale Griffin [12]***chsd clr ldr to 2 out, sn btn*......... 3
Also: 17 Over The Maine (4), Quay Fly (pu), 24 Fidsprit (pu), 28² Cool Yule (ur), Moylena (f), Half Scotch (pu), Chariot Del (pu), More Than Most (pu), Halens Match (pu)
12 ran. 3l, 20l, 15l. SP 2-1.

93 - Maiden 5 & 6yo

22 **Gawn Inn [15]...........................R Patton** 1
chsd ldrs, 2nd 4 out, styd on to ld flat.................
16 **Twentyfivequid [14]***ld til aft last, no ext*............. 2
Ballyarnott [12]*chsd ldrs, 3rd whn blnd 2 out, no imp aft* 3
Also: Rolier (4), Foyleside (5), Oriel Flight (pu), Hows Your Luck (ur), Kaspair Arrow (pu), Malt Man (pu), Kenellen (pu), Farmlea Dancer (pu)
11 ran. ¾l, 7l, dist, 5l. SP 3-1.

94 - Open Lightweight

82³ **Farney Glen [23]..........................P Kelly** 1
cls up, ld last, readily ....
Lacken Beau [21]*prom, ld 4 out, hdd & mstk last, no ext*...
82¹ **Teal Bridge [16]***prog 3 out, no imp on ldrs nxt* ....
Also: 28² Amme Enaek [14] (4), 18 Jims Choice [10] (5), Handyfellc (6), Young Entry (pu), Calliealla (pu), 18 Schweppes Tonic (pu), Wo Louse (pu), Cutter's Wharf (pu), Bald Joker (pu)
12 ran. 3l, 20l, 6l, 12l, 12l. SP 10-1.

95 - Mares Maiden 5 & 6yo I

Hiltonstown Lass [14] ....G Coulter
trckd ldr, ld last, pshd out.............................
Bonnington Lass [13]*ld to last, no ext*...............
Wolverbank*nvr dang*...................................
Also: 32 Teralisa (4), Ellies Pride (5), Greenfield Lass (6), Glen Thy (ur), Hillview Lizzie (pu), Sally Gee (su), 32 Hazel Ring (pu), Ma O'Tully (f)
11 ran. 2½l, 25l, 2l, 25l, 3l. SP 8-1.

96 - Mares Maiden 5 & 6yo II

Miss Elizabeth [15]......................A Martin
trckd ldr, ld aft last, pshd clr..........................
20 **Blennerville [14]***ld 3rd til mstk last, sn hdd & no ext* ..
Maccarrons Run*nvr dang* ....
Also: 33 Knights Pleasure (4D), Creighton (pu), 19 Sideways Sa (pu), Glenbrin (f), Kitzberg (pu), Ngala (pu), Tyrella Clear View (f Salaran (pu)
11 ran. 2l, 20l, ¾l. SP 5-4.

97 - Maiden 6yo

Genial Gent [15].........................A Martin
made virt all, drvn out ....
Tobermore [14]*prog 3 out, chsd wnr nxt, nrst fin* .....
87 **Irenes Treasure [10]***nvr nrr* ....
Also: 23 O'Fiaich's Hope (4), Longmore Boy (5), Florida Or Bust (f Cheri's Rival (pu), O'Moss (pu), Myown Treasure (pu), The Convinc (pu), Hanleys Call (pu)
11 ran. 2½l, 12l, 7l, 6l, 10l. SP 1-2.

98 - Maiden 7yo+ I

Rontom [14] ....P Graffin
made all, clr apr last, styd on..........................
Lingering Hope [12]*chsd wnr 5 out, mstk nxt, no imp apr last*...
Stag Hunt*chsd wnr to 5 out, sn btn* ....
Also: 26 Harvemac (4), Hollow Suspicion (5), Knocans Pride (f C-Mac (pu), Mongie (pu), Miners Valley (pu), 20 Moneycarragh (f Lord Sammy (pu), 89 Well Recovered (pu), 90 Fill Your Boots (f)
13 ran. 6l, 20l, ½l, ¾l. SP 4-5.

99 - Maiden 7yo+ II

Lord Loving [14] ....L Gracey
ld til aft 2 out, btn whn lft clr last ....
Takeithandy*nvr dang, lft 2nd last* ....
Errigal Bay*prom to 4 out, t.o.*..........................
Also: Dick's Cabin (pu), Ahogill [15] (f), Fidoon (pu), Iveagh Lady (p Cherryflame (pu), Farlough Lady (ur), 23³ Cool Rocket (f), Fair Avo (f), Sea Ovac (f)
12 ran. 20l, dist. SP 8-1.

LEOPARDSTOWN
Sunday February 11th
SOFT

100 - 3m Hun Chase

Elegant Lord (Ire) 12.2...............Mr E Bolger
(fav) ....
Credit Transfer (Ire) 11.8 ....Mr H F Cleary
48¹ **Kerry Orchid 11.4...................Mr P Fenton**
Baby Jake (Ire) 10.11 7a ....
18³ Colin's Hatch 11.9 ....
45¹ Corymandel (Ire) 11.2 7a ....

Call Me Connie (Ire) 10.6 7a .... f
7 ran. 3½l, 7l, ½l, 14l. Time 6m 26.6s. SP 8-11.

KILDARE FOXHOUNDS
Punchestown P-To-P Course
Sunday February 11th
HOLDING

101 - Farmers

25[3] **No One Knows [18]** ....**J Dempsey** 1
prog to 2nd 3 out, ld flat, styd on
30 **Difficult Decision [18]***prog to ld 4 out, mstk 2 out, hdd & no ext flat* 2
Fays Folly [17]*styd on frm 2 out, nvr nrr* 3
Also: 80[3] The Wee Fellow [16] (4), Carrig Conn [16] (5), Lineker [16] (6), Mornay Des Garnes [10] (7), Jester Jack (bd), M T Pockets (f), Sue Wood Bay (pu), Tamer's Run (bd), Thought Reader (f), Flower Of Grange (f), Maries Call (pu), Miss Annagaul (ur)
15 ran. ¾l, 1½l, 2l, 1l, 12l, 1l. SP 8-1.

102 - Winners Of One

Newtown Rosie [19]......................**S Mahon** 1
prog to disp whn lft in ld 5 out, sn clr, easily
Buaile Bos*t.o. whn lft 2nd 2 out* 2
Chesham Lord*t.o. whn lft 3rd 2 out* 3
Also: 88 Four Zeros (4), Charlesfield (f), 82 Cool It (ur), Thethreetoms (pu), 27[1] Salemhady (f), 33[1] Slemish Mist (pu), Spring Beau (f), The Toor Trail (pu)
11 ran. Dist, 3l, 5l. SP 5-1.

103 - Open Lightweight I

29 **Laura's Beau [21]**........................**T Farrell** 1
trckd ldrs, effrt 2 out, ld last, ran on well
17[2] **Private Yashkan [20]***prog 3 out, ld nxt, hdd last, alwys hld flat* 2
Carrigans Lad [14]*prom, ev ch 3 out, wknd nxt* 3
Also: 28 Timeless River (4D), Cloughan Boy (4), Satin Emma (5), 54 Art Prince (ur), Best Interest (ur), Fingerhill (pu), Norrismount (pu), Sexton Gleam (pu), Walshestown (pu)
12 ran. ½l, 25l, dist, 25l, 3l. SP 7-2.

104 - Open Lightweight II

82 **Clonrosh Slave [20]**........................**P Kelly** 1
prog 4 out, ld aft nxt, drvn out
Red Express VI [20]*trckd ldrs, chal 2 out, just hld* 2
17[3] **Find Out More [19]***trckd ldrs, chal 2 out, no ext flat* 3
Also: 24[3] Missing Lady [19] (4), Ounavarra Creek [19] (5), Astounded [14] (6), Captains View (pu), Forever Gold (pu), Selkoline (pu), Snuggledown (pu), Tul Na Gcarn (pu)
11 ran. ½l, ½l, nk, 1l, 12l. SP 8-1.

105 - Mares Maiden I

32[3] **Alamillo [16]** ....**A Martin** 1
trckd ldrs, prog 3 out, ld last, sn clr
19 **Rathcarrick Lass [12]***wth ldr 5 out-last, sn btn* 2
32 **Arctic Leader [11]***ld 5 out til hdd & wknd last* 3
Also: 42 Tiger Dolly (4), Barnish Rose (pu), Dusky Run (pu), 83 Faras Flight (f), 19 In The Future (pu), Larkin's Cross (pu), 12 Meldap (f), Mordella Lass (pu), 85 Orlas Fancy (ur), Poor Reception (f), Starling Lake (pu), 85[3] Tullbeg Bloom (f)
15 ran. 12l, 3l, dist. SP 5-4.

106 - Mares Maiden II

20 **Another Idea [17]** ....**D McAteer** 1
prom, ld 2 out, sn clr, styd on wll
84 **Cappajune [12]***ld til mstk 4 out, lft 2nd last, kpt on* 2
20 **La Maja***prog 4 out, ld 3 out-nxt, wknd rpdly* 3
Also: Aylesbury Beau (f), Early News (f), Gerry's Rose (f), Lismoy (pu), 19 Memory Harbour (f), 32[2] Nurney Minstrel [13] (f), 83 Pinehill (pu), Proud Princess (pu), 33 Sally Willows (pu), Theblondebarrister (pu), 81[3] Timeforgoing (pu), Windmill Star (pu)
15 ran. 10l, dist. SP 4-1.

107 - Mares Maiden III

83 **Instrumental [15]**..........................**A Martin** 1
trckd ldrs, 2nd 3 out, hit last, sn ld & clr
84 **Push Gently [13]***ld 4 out, hit last, sn hdd & no ext* 2
Another Tangle [12]*ran on frm 2 out, nrst fin* 3
Also: 19[2] The Vendor [11] (4), Ballylime Again [10] (5), 83 Mauradonna (6), 19 Codology (pu), Executive Bill (pu), Lantina (ur), Midi Minstrel (ur), New Legislation (pu), 85 Pitmar (f), 19 Sapphire 'N' Silver (pu), 32 Trembles Choice (f)
14 ran. 4l, 2l, 3l, 3l, 12l. SP 3-1.

108 - Maiden 5 & 6yo I

87[3] **Credo Is King [16]** ....**J Dempsey** 1
prom, chal last, ld flat, rdn out
55[2] **Whitebarn Grit [15]***prssd ldr 3 out, lft in ld nxt, hdd & no ext flat* 2
87 **Diorraing [14]***prssd ldr 3 out, eased whn btn flat* 3
Also: 86 Sam's Man (4), Boycetrus (5), Prince Sabi (6), Lord Knox (7), Almost An Angel (f), Fortynine Plus (pu), Golden Walk (pu), Jacksorbetter (pu), Normus (ur), 39 Pearl Dante (pu), Sporting Vision (pu), Talboy Maye (pu)
15 ran. 1½l, 4l, 25l, dist, 6l, dist. SP 5-1.

109 - Maiden 5 & 6yo II

86 **Quattro [16]**................................**A Coyle** 1
prog 5 out, ld nxt, lft clr last
30 **Donal's Choice [15]***nvr dang, lft 2nd last, kpt on* 2
Also: Ballymacrevan (ro), Connaught Boy (pu), 40 Debonair Duke (pu), 16 Garethson [14] (f), Graiguesallagh (pu), Lancastrian Pride (f), Louis Fourteen (f), 87 Only One (pu), Pearl Of Orient (pu), 31 Shillelagh Oak (pu), 21 Sinergia (pu), Uncle Art (pu)
14 ran. 3l. SP 3-1.

110 - Maiden 5 & 6yo III

Parahandy [15]...........................**D O'Brien** 1
prog 3 out, ld apr last where lft wll clr
87 **Rat Race***ld 5 out-3 out, 4th & btn whn lft 2nd last* 2
16 **Blackie Connors***3rd 5 out, 3rd & btn whn f last, rmntd* 3
Also: Coq Hardi Dancer (pu), Digin For Gold (f), Easy Catch (f), Glenbride Boy (pu), 36 Irregular Planting (f), Lislooney (f), Mile Mill (pu), Pilbara (pu), Some Man (pu), Staffy's Boy (f), Whatforsurprise (pu)
14 ran. 25l, dist. SP 4-1.

111 - Maiden 7yo+ I

26 **Silver Buckle [16]**..........................**J Roche** 1
trckd ldrs, prog 2 out, ld aft last, ran on well
Pats Cross [14]*prom, ld 4 out, mstk last, sn hdd & no ext* 2
38[3] **Dooneal Hero***wth ldr 4 out-nxt, wknd* 3
Also: 89[3] Loughdoo (4), Murcheen Durken (5), Miller King (6), 80 Andy Joe (pu), Ballybrit (pu), Big Spender (pu), Bredinthepurple (pu), 22 Clanmany (pu), 21 Fearless Hunter (pu), Harsh Decision (pu), Lisnagree Boy (f), 26[3] Oldson (pu), 88 The Defender (pu), 22 Tricyclic (pu)
17 ran. 4l, 20l, 12l, 1l, 8l. SP 8-1.

112 - Maiden 7yo+ II

88 **Another Believer [15]** ....**G Elliott** 1
prom, ld 4 out, styd on well
88 **No Mistake VI [11]***chsd wnr 3 out, no imp* 2
Sheer Mystery*nvr dang* 3
Also: 89 Desmarfran (4), Mahankhali (5), 90 Big Murt (f), 89 Both Sides (pu), Celtic Kinship (pu), Erinsborough (pu), 89 Festival Light (pu), Highland Buck (pu), Locklan (pu), 27 Mullinello (pu), Ordain (pu), Thorn Cottage (f)
15 ran. 12l, 25l, 8l, 4l. SP 3-1.

WEST WATERFORD
Tallow
Sunday February 11th
HEAVY

113 - Confined Maiden

Our Blossom [16] .... **J Flynn** 1
made all, drew clr 4 out, comf
47² **Radical River [11]** *not fluent, ev ch 5 out, sn btn* 2
78 **Stroll Home [10]** *chsd ldrs, ev ch 5 out, sn btn* 3
Also: 78 Gerry And Tom (4), Lady Steel (5), Major Bill (f), Golden Cygneture (pu), Tina Ore (pu), Glengarra Maid (pu), Amandawill (pu), 68 Buckhill (pu), 74 Glenaboy (pu), 50 Teamtalk (pu), Matchmaker Seamus (pu), Keep Flowing (pu)
15 ran. 15l, 3l, 6l. SP 6-1.

114 - Maiden 5yo

62² **Clarkes Gorse [17]** 1
ld hlfwy, wandrered 2 out, drew clr last
62 **Red Bronze [14]** *3rd 4 out, chsd wnr 2 out, no ext* 2
36² **Lakefield Leader** *chsd wnr 4 out, btn aft nxt* 3
Also: 61 Never Heard (4), 30 More Rain (5), 53 Black Abbey (pu), 53 Duky River (pu), Brother Nicholas (pu), 61 Where's Noel (pu), 70 Super Fred (pu), 62 Executive Class (pu), Mr Boomaleen (pu), 73 Dancing Dessie (f), 52 Conor Mac (pu), 73 Johnny's Echo (pu), 61² Donickmore (f), Castle Bailey (pu), 74 Sirrah Aris (pu), Dual Or Bust (pu)
19 ran. 10l, 20l, 6l. SP 7-4.

115 - Open Lightweight

67² **Faha Gig [22]** .... **K O'Sullivan** 1
hld up, ld 3 out, sn clr, easily
67 **Rossi Novae [16]** *ld to 3 out, sn btn* 2
65 **The Miners Fate [12]** *nvr dang* 3
Also: 67 Myalup [10] (4), Amoristic Top (5), 67 Awbeg Rover (f), 75 What Thing (pu)
7 ran. 10l, 10l, 5l. SP 4-7.

116 - Winners Of One

63¹ **Lake Tour [21]** .... **K Whelan** 1
prom, ld 4 out, styd on well
52¹ **Full Of Bounce [17]** *in tch, chsd wnr 3 out, no imp* 2
60¹ **Lady Elise [12]** *nvr dang* 3
Also: 72 Elwill Glory [11] (4), 65 Escheat (5), 62¹ Andy's Birthday (pu), Burkean Melody (f), Some Tourist (pu), 72 Coole Cherry (pu), 11¹ Supreme Arctic (pu), 64¹ Sweet Merenda (pu), Kilcannon House (pu)
12 ran. 10l, 15l, 4l. SP 3-1.

117 - Maiden 6 & 7yo I

56 **Emerald Statement [16]** .... **M Phillips** 1
prog 3 out, ld aft nxt, styd on well
57 **Irish Society [12]** *prom, ev ch whn blnd 4 out, not rcvr*
Mythical Approach [12] *ld 5 out til aft 2 out, wknd* 3
Also: 68³ Mighty Trust (4), What Is The Plan (5), 79 Tor (pu), Des The Architect (pu), 69 Bone Idol (pu), 69 Prophets Thumb (pu), 66 Supreme Hooker (pu), Barrys Avenue (pu), 69 Buladante (pu), 78 Barnadown (pu), 79 Park Duke (pu), 68 Dohney Boy (pu), 79 See Just There (pu), 5 Just The Duke (pu)
17 ran. 15l, hd, 12l. SP 4-1.

118 - Maiden 6 & 7yo II

39 **Mount Buda [17]** .... **K O'Sullivan** 1
made all, clr 3 out, hld on flat
47³ **Fundy [17]** *chsd ldrs, ran on well apr last, just hld* 2
70 **Castle Shelley [10]** *chsd ldrs, btn frm 3 out* 3
Also: I'm A Chippy (4), Cashel Moss (pu), Carbery Boy (pu), Theairyman (pu), Raggety Man (pu), 71 Mags Super Toi (pu), Ajar (pu), 79 Ross Quay (f), Blazing Crack (pu), Sarcoid (pu), 66 Stratton Park (pu), 79 Pat The Hat (pu), 79 Mystery Aristocrat (pu), 47 Quirina Majano (pu)
17 ran. ½l, 25l, dist. SP 7-2.

119 - Mares Maiden 5 & 6yo I

63² **Silent Sneeze [18]** .... **K Beecher** 1
prom, ld 4 out, styd on well
76 **Carlingford Gale [11]** *cls up, chal 3 out, sn btn* 2
50 **Scarlet River** *nvr dang* 3
Also: Highways Sister (4), Aston Braes (pu), Suite Cottage Lady (pu), 77 Round Tower Lady (pu), Kochnie (pu), 64 Ann Toni (pu), 42 Victim Of Slander (pu), 70 Lady Of Means (pu), 64 Dante's Skip (f), Nans Pet (pu), 60 Pharleng (f), 77 Rockview Supreme (pu), 76 Dusty's Delight (pu), 77 Warlockfoe (pu), 76 Blackwater Fox (pu), 77 Dante's Whistle (f)
19 ran. 25l, 10l, dist. SP 4-1.

120 - Mares Maiden 5 & 6yo II

Arctic Pearl [15] .... **D Keane** 1
prom, ld 5 out, styd on
55 **Tourig Dante [14]** *chsd wnr 4 out, kpt on* 2
Dominant Lady *t.o.* 3
Also: 66 Shamron (pu), 60 Fools Courage (pu), 64 Love Actinium (pu), Idiot's Surprise (pu), 77³ Daytime Dancer (f), 85 Lusmagh River (f), Scarra Darragh (pu), Princess Diga (f), 63 Finnuala Supreme (su), Liskilnewabbey (f), 60 Lee Valley Lady (pu), Ballintee Belle (f), Clogheen Lass (f), 77 Janice Price (pu), Rose's Luck (pu), Montohouse (pu)
19 ran. 3l, dist. SP 12-1.

STONEHALL HARRIERS
Askeaton
Sunday February 11th
HEAVY

121 - Confined Maiden

In The Blood [14] .... **J McNamara** 1
cls up, prog to ld 2 out, styd on
38² **Shareza River [13]** *disp to 2 out, no ext last* 2
57 **Flood Relief [11]** *prog to disp 3 out, onepcd* 3
Also: 39 Deep Wave [10] (4), 53 Neelisagin (5), Sammy Sunshine (6), Jodesi (co), Tom Deely (ur), 39 Rhetoric House (pu)
9 ran. 2l, 6l, 3l. SP 8-1.

122 - Maiden 5yo

61 **The Red Devil [17]** .... **J McNamara** 1
ld 5 out, in cmmnd whn lft clr last
74² **Mr Tom Tom** *nvr dang, lft 2nd last* 2
Serenade Star *t.o.* 3
Also: Fort Deely [14] (4), Drumline Castle (f), 61 Forest Musk (f), Tom The Saint (f), Banner Year (pu), General Ari (pu), Educate Me (pu), 81 Riberetto's Girl (pu), La Mon Dere (pu), 73 As Things Go (f)
13 ran. Dist, 20l, dist. SP 7-4.

123 - Open Lightweight

Itsalltheonetodev [20] .... **W Ewing** 1
made all, drvn clr apr last
44 **Killoskehan Queen [16]** *chsd wnr, ev ch 2 out, no ext* 2
58 **Lovely Citizen** *t.o.* 3
Also: Jigg's Forge VI (pu), Bit Of A Touch (f)
5 ran. 12l, dist. SP 6-4.

124 - Maiden 6yo+ I

21 **Flairline Bay [16]** .... **N Kelleher** 1
prog 3 out, sn ld & clr, unchal
88 **Dunkel** *chsd ldrs, no ch wnr frm 2 out* 2
Master Kemal *ld to aft 3 out, wknd* 3
Also: 68 Have Another (4), 69 Digacre (f), 40 Leaders View (f), Tinerana Boy (f), 68 Milenkeh (f), 38 Skulldugery (f), 21 Rushing Waters (pu), 90 Carramore Hill (pu), 87 Common Coin (pu), 37 Guirns Shop (pu), 26 Corries Hill (pu)
14 ran. Dist, dist, 10l. SP 5-4.

125 - Maiden 6yo+ II

69² **West Lyn [17]** .... **B Moran** 1
made all, styd on well frm last
78 **Tearaway King [15]** *chsd wnr 4 out, chal apr last, no ext* ... 2
Over In McGanns *nvr dang* 3
Also: 69 Fruit Town (4), 86 Glendine (5), Wylfa Boy (6), 40 The Breaser Fawl (7), Daffydown Breeze VI (pu), 40 Winter Breeze (pu), 78 Irish

Display (pu), St Aidan (pu), 90 Sultan Of Swing (f), 47 Riverdale Express (f), 89 O'Sullivan's Choise (f)
14 ran. 5l, 25l, 20l. SP 3-1.

126 - Winners Of One

72 **I Haven't A Buck [16]** .... **R Hurley** 1
ld/disp, all out frm last.
Young Mrs Kelly [16] *in tch, lft 2nd 3 out, chal apr last, just hld* 2
54 **Make A Line** *t.o.* 3
Also: 72 Lakeview Lad (pu), 34 Carrolls Rock (pu)
5 ran. 1l, dist. SP Evens.

127 - Mares Maiden I

44 **Hi-Way's Gale [15]** .... **D Daly** 1
made all, ran on well....
7 **Selm Mary** *chsd wnr, no imp 3 out* 2
41 **Ballybriken Castle** *t.o.* 3
Also: Brook Queen (4), 83 Flaherty's Best VI (5), Lancastrian Lass (pu), No Swap (pu), 41 Aine Hencey (pu), 11 Something Sheer (f), 42 Gala Vote (pu), Fort Rouge (pu), Six Of Spades (pu), Killbally Castle (pu), 41 Snipe Lodge (f)
14 ran. 20l, dist, 15l. SP 4-1.

128 - Mares Maiden II

85² **Brook Hill Lady [14]** .... **D Duggan** 1
made all, clr whn blnd last, styd on
41³ **Lishillaun [12]** *chsd wnr, no imp aft last* 2
49 **Evie's Party** *t.o.* 3
Also: 41 Ivy Glen (4), 83 Baby Whale (f), Lisnagar Lady (pu), 47 Pass The Basket (pu), 41 Manley Girl (pu), 42 Camden Lamp (pu), 64 Ballyhest Fountain (f), Trembling Lady (f), 42 Just Placed (pu)
12 ran. 4l, dist, 15l. SP 5-2.

BRAY HARRIERS
Ashford
Sunday February 11th
GOOD TO SOFT

129 - Open Farmers

54 **Dennistownthriller [22]** .... **P Fenton** 1
made all, hld on wll flat....
94¹ **Farney Glen [22]** *hld up, prog to chal 2 out, ev ch, no ext nr fin* 2
88 **Tara River [17]** *chsd wnr 4 out-nxt, sn btn* 3
Also: Cedarbelle (4), 25 Greenfield Tiger (f)
5 ran. Nk, 15l, dist. SP 6-4.

130 - Winners Of Two

25² **Dromhana [18]** .... **J Berry** 1
cls up, 2nd 3 out, ld nxt, drvn out....
Coolafinka [17] *made most to 2 out, kpt on well* 2
82 **Ballinaboola Grove [15]** 3D
87¹ **Harry's Secret [14]** *nvr dang, fin 4th, promoted* 3
Also: Delgany Deer [14] (4), Msadi Mhulu (pu)
6 ran. 1l, 6l, 2½l, nk. SP 1-2.

131 - Maiden 5 & 6yo

86 **Rath An Uisce [14]** .... **V Devereux** 1
prom, chsd ldr 2 out, btn whn lft clr last....
Muskin More [11] *styd on frm 2 out, lft 2nd last* 2
Knights Crest *prom til onepcd frm 3 out* 3
Also: 86 Greedy Johno (4), Sarshill Lap (5), Golden Performance (pu), Stillorgan Park (pu), Louis de Palmer (pu), Bracing Breeze [16] (f), Gypsy Gerry (pu), Keepitsafe (f), 81 Dusty Track (f), I Cant Wait (pu), 81 Wyn Wan Soon (ro)
14 ran. 10l, 10l, 1l, 15l. SP 6-4.

132 - Mares Maiden

Asteal [15] .... **D Coakley** 1
prog 5 out, ld aft 2 out, styd on well....
Wishing Velvet [13] *alwys prom, chsd wnr apr last, no imp flat* 2
83 **Kiama Bay [13]** *chsd ldrs, kpt on onepcd frm 2 out* 3
Also: 59 Broad Valley [13] (4), 41 Thyne Please (5), Warkey Lady (pu), Miss Tornado (pu), Callys Run (bd), Pampered Society (f), 33 Miss Lurgan (pu), Spritly Lady (bd), 7 Beet Spray (pu), 85 Hazels Dream (f), Miner's Sunset (pu), Pils Invader (f), Choretine Lady (pu), 84 Nectar Bloom (pu)
17 ran. 4l, ½l, ½l, 12l. SP 8-1.

133 - Maiden 7yo+

Seemingly So [14] .... **D McCartney** 1
chsd ldrs, styd on to ld last, drvn out....
88³ **Duncaha Hero [13]** *prssd ldr to 2 out, kpt on onepcd* .. 2
21 **Noble Knight [12]** *ld to 2 out, onepcd.* 3
Also: 89 Shimano [12] (4), Eastern Fox (pu), 27 Galloping Giggs (pu), Orange Dream (pu), Scar Statement (pu)
8 ran. 2l, 2l, ½l. SP 8-1.

134 - Nomination

26 **Drumcairn [13]** .... **P Cloke** 1
ld 4th, made rest, styd on....
Ash Plant [12] *chsd wnr 4 out, no imp last* 2
84 **Black Beth** *nvr dang, lft 3rd 2 out* 3
Also: 27 Beau Cinq (f), Sorry Sarah (pu), Solitary Spirit (ur), Windgates Zone (pu), 32 Aloha (f)
8 ran. 4l, 15l. SP 4-1.

THURLES
Thursday February 15th
YIELDING TO SOFT

135 - 3m Hun Chase

91¹ **Stay In Touch (Ire) 11.9 3a 3ow** ... **Mr D P Costello** 1
(fav)
91² **Johnny The Fox (Ire) 11.1 3a** .... **Mr T Lombard** 2
82 **Tasse Du The 11.6 7a** .... **Mr G Elliot** 3
Fairy Mist (Ire) 10.11 7a 4
91 Thresa-Anita (Ire) 10.11 7a 5ow 5
91 Jaybe's Friend 11.4 6
91 Mahon River 11.4 .... pu
Dixon Varner (Ire) 11.8 4ow .... f
8 ran. 13l, 7l, 20l, 5½l. Time 6m 34.6s. SP 9-10.

AVONDHU FOXHOUNDS
Knockenard
Sunday February 18th
HEAVY

136 - Winners Of Two

68¹ **Bally Riot [22]** .... **J Collins** 1
prom, ld 3 out, styd on strngly....
The Parish Pump [20] *prom, ev ch 2 out, not qckn* 2
129 **Greenfield Tiger [17]** *prom til no ext frm 2 out* 3
Also: 22¹ Manhattan Prince [15] (4), 72 Bocock's Pride (f), 116 Burkean Melody (pu), 103 Art Prince (pu)
7 ran. 3l, 10l, 4l. SP 3-1.

137 - Maiden 5 & 6yo I

61³ **Davy Lamp [16]** .... **R Hurley** 1
prog to disp 4 out, hrd rdn to ld flat....
86² **Boots Madden [15]** *prom, ld 4 out, hdd & no ext flat* ... 2
Weak Moment [15] *styd on frm 2 out, nrst fin* 3
Also: 79 Rain Spirit [13] (4), Alone Home (f), Militation (pu), Sandy Valley (pu), Call Me Paris (pu), High Charges (pu), 79 Blackwood (pu), 131 I Cant Wait (pu), Upton Steamer (pu), Spectre Brown [10] (pu), 40 Fifth Generation (ro)
14 ran. 1½l, 1l, 6l. SP 2-1.

138 - Maiden 5 & 6yo II

78 **Maypole Fountain [17]** .... **W O'Sullivan** 1
prom, ld apr 2 out, in cmmnd whn lft clr last..........
8 **Phardante's Way***nvr dang, btn 4th whn lft 2nd last*.... 2
113³ **Stroll Home***t.o.* 3
Also: 8 Witchiewah (f), 79 Just-N-James (pu), 79² Saradante (f), The Road To Moscow (pu), 78 Know Something VI (f), Lordinthesky (pu), Mr Weiser (pu), 78³ Bushmiller (pu), 73 Camogue Bridge (pu), Carnmore House (pu), Timmy Tuff (pu)
14 ran. 20l, dist. SP 3-1.

139 - Maiden 5 & 6yo III

121 **Jodesi [17]** .... **D Costello** 1
ld 5 out, wll clr last, easily ....
Galebreaker*nvr dang, no ch wnr* 2
Saol Sona*t.o.* 3
Also: 118 Ross Quay (pu), Cash For Bash (pu), 71 Shady Prince (pu), Roskeen Bridge (f), 113 Major Bill (pu), Long Drive (pu), 39 Nollaig (pu), 131 Wyn Wan Soon (pu), Nutty Solera (pu), 118 Stratton Park (pu)
13 ran. 20l, dist. SP Evens.

140 - Open Lightweight

115¹ **Faha Gig [23]** .... **Rose Ring** 1
hld up, prog to ld aft 2 out, easily ....
15 **Crazy Dreams [18]***prom, disp 2 out, sn outpcd*....... 2
44¹ **Just A Breeze [17]***prom, disp 2 out, sn outpcd*....... 3
Also: 115³ The Miners Fate (4), 75 Next Right (f), 37 La Cienaga (pu), 58 Mr Pipeman (pu), 104 Snuggledown (ur), 123³ Lovely Citizen (0)
9 ran. 7l, 2l, dist. SP 6-4.

141 - Mares Winners Of Two

72 **Gracemarie Kate [20]** .... **R Hurley** 1
chsd ldrs, lft 2nd last, hrd rdn to ld flat...............
72³ **Sidcup Hill [19]***disp 4 out, lft clr last, wknd & hdd flat* 2
72 **Pharditu***t.o.* 3
Also: 116 Escheat (4), 12¹ Ore Engineeress (pu), 54 Glenview Rose (pu), 83¹ Sandfair (pu), Summerhill Express (pu), 116¹ Lake Tour [19] (f), 82 Duchess Of Padua (pu), 76¹ Bit Of A Citizen (pu), 82 Over The Wall (pu), 80 Trimmer Princess (pu), Looking Ahead (pu), 75 Faulty Rap (pu), 75³ Holly Moss (pu), 116 Supreme Arctic (pu)
17 ran. 3l, dist, dist. SP 10-1.

142 - Adjacent Maiden

7³ **Ruby Belle [16]** .... **W O'Sullivan** 1
prog to ld 3 out, sn drew clr ....
88 **Prayon Parson [10]***ev ch 3 out, sn btn* 2
Kerry Glen*ev ch 3 out, sn btn* 3
Also: 78² Ace Ventura (4), Ellesmere (pu), Anyone Whoknows Me (pu), 50 Shannon Rugby Club (pu), 77 High Park Lady (f), 114 Dancing Dessie (pu), 76 Sweet Castlehyde (pu), Brigade Leader (pu), Reen-O-Foil (pu), 117 Barrys Avenue (pu), 117 Des The Architect (pu), 83 Loughlins Pride (pu), 118 Raggety Man (pu)
16 ran. 20l, 3l, 10l. SP 3-1.

143 - Mares Maiden 6yo+ I

70 **Get Cracking [16]** .... **R Hurley** 1
prom, outpcd 4 out, rallied ot ld aft 2 out, kpt on ....
Sharoujack [14]*chsd ldrs, ev ch 2 out, onepcd* 2
64 **The Pulpit [13]***chsd ldrs, ev ch 2 out, onepcd* 3
Also: 119 Nans Pet (4), 119 Suite Cottage Lady (pu), 12 Ann Black (pu), 88 Queen Of Eagles (pu), 71 Kilcully Night (pu), 120 Scarra Darragh (pu), Ore Galore (pu), 64 Dunmoon Lady (pu), 85 Trimmer Lady (pu), 64 Solar Castle (pu), 113 Amandawill (pu), 127 Brook Queen (pu), 70 Could Be A'ntin (pu), 70 Hurricane Iris (pu), 127 Snipe Lodge (pu), 132 Thyne Please (pu)
19 ran. 6l, 3l, 20l. SP 8-1.

144 - Mares Maiden 6yo+ II

64 **Bula Vogue [17]** .... **J Lombard** 1
hld up, prog to ld last, styd on well ....
63 **Blame Barney [15]***prom, ev ch apr last, wknd* 2
120 **Ballintee Belle [14]***wll bhnd til styd on 2 out, nvr nrr*.. 3
Also: Eagles Witch (pu), 70² Supreme Odds (pu), Celia's Pride (ur), Metal Miss (pu), 50 Rascal Street Lad (f), Tipperaryenteprise (pu), 50² Sezu (pu), 7 Convamore Queen (pu), Flashy Leader (f), 120 Finnuala Supreme (pu), Lady Fountain (pu), 71 Rio Star (pu), 128 Baby Whale (pu), 113 Glengarra Maid (pu), Hootenany (pu)
18 ran. 6l, 2l. SP 5-2.

FAIRYHOUSE
Sunday February 25th
GOOD TO YIELDING

145 - 3m 1f Hun Chase

100³ **Kerry Orchid 11.4 (bl)** .... **Mr P Fenton** 1
(fav)
91 **Bally Riot (Ire) 10.11 7a** .... **Mr J A Collins** 2
Lakeview Lad (Ire) 10.11 7a .... **Mr B M Cash** 3
101 Lineker 12.0 4
Tullbeg Bloom (Ire) 10.4 5
45 Fays Folly (Ire) 10.6 7a .... pu
6 ran. Dist, dist, 11l, 1l. Time 6m 50.3s. SP 1-3.

DUHALLOW FOXHOUNDS
Kildorrery
Sunday February 25th
HEAVY

146 - Adjacent Maiden

Greenfield George [15] .... **P Coleman** 1
disp to 2 out, chal & lft clr last ....
79³ **Finnow Thyne [13]***chsd ldrs, btn whn lft 2nd last*..... 2
Ballybeggan Lady [10]*nvr dang* 3
Also: 114 Never Heard (4), 118 Theairyman (pu), 137 Rain Spirit [14] (f), 143 Brook Queen (pu)
7 ran. 4l, 10l, 10l. SP 4-1.

147 - Maiden 5yo I

122 **Fort Deely [16]** .... **J McNamara** 1
prom, ld 4 out, styd on well ....
62 **Action Lad [15]***prog 2 out, styd on apr last, nrst fin* ... 2
122 **Forest Musk [14]***prog 2 out, styd on apr last, nrst fin* 3
Also: 62 Dysart O'Dea [13] (4), 53 Terrano Star [11] (5), Wintry Willow (6), 122 Tom The Saint (7), 114 Brother Nicholas (8), 138 Mr Weiser (pu), Gentle Leader (pu), Ask Me Another (pu), 81 Into The Web (pu), 122 La Mon Dere (pu), 1 Persian Packer (pu), Coolflugh Hero (pu), 74 Jack's Well (pu), 74 Poachers Lamp (pu)
17 ran. 2l, 2l, 1l. SP 2-1.

148 - Maiden 5yo II

35² **Strong Vision [18]** .... **J McNamara** 1
prom, ld 4 out, clr nxt, styd on well ....
Short Circuit [16]*prog to chs wnr 3 out, no imp apr last* 2
53 **The Magic Slabber [14]***nvr nrr* 3
Also: 71 John's Right [13] (4), 139² Galebreaker [10] (5), 122³ Serenade Star (6), 74 Black Fountain (f), 139 Long Drive (pu), 122 Drumline Castle (pu), 74³ Ballybeggan Boy (pu), 138 Witchiewah (pu), Willbrook (pu), 114 Executive Class (pu), 114 Sirrah Aris (pu), Ten Bob Down (pu), 122 As Things Go (f)
16 ran. 4l, 5l, 3l. SP Evens.

149 - Mares Maiden 5 & 6yo I

70 **Mr K's Winterblues [17]** .... **T Lombard** 1
prom, ld 2 out, styd on well ....
120 **Lusmagh River [16]***prom, wth wnr 2 out, no ext last*.. 2
Lady Clarina [14]*chsd ldrs, onepcd 2 out*............ 3
Also: 143 Hurricane Iris [10] (4), 119 Kochnie (5), Deciding Dance (pu), Divine Rapture (pu), 63 Appendix Lady (pu), Bright Choice (pu), 119 Dante's Skip (pu), The Wild Wave (pu), 64 Farran Garrett (f), Midnight Society (pu), 71 Skipping Chick (pu), 59 Ballinacubby Pride (f), 120 Rose's Luck (pu)
16 ran. 2l, 5l, 10l. SP 3-1.

150 - Mares Maiden 5 & 6yo II

41 Answer That [16]......................W Ewing 1
prom, ld 3 out, styd on well
128² Lishillaun [13] 2
119 Highways Sister [10]*nvr dang* **3**
Also: 128 Just Placed (4), Merry Castle (5), Northern Katie (pu), 106 Early News (pu), 71 Queen Of Clubs (pu), 122 Riberetto's Girl (f), 120² Tourig Dante (pu), Some Day (pu), 120 Princess Diga (pu), 85 Over Decent (f), 43 Barmur (pu), Everlaughing (pu)
15 ran. 10l, 10l, 15l. SP 10-1.

151 - Mares Maiden 5 & 6yo III

127 Something Sheer [15] ....B Moran 1
ld hlfwy, drvn out flat
63 Change The Pace [15]*chsd wnr 3 out, chal last, just hld* **2**
63 Hopperdante [12]*nvr nrr* **3**
Also: 63³ Supersonia (pu), 113 Tina Ore (pu), 50 Minstrel Madame (ur), Crabeg Hazel (pu), 119 Warlockfoe (pu), Brogeen Dubh (pu), 120 Daytime Dancer (pu), Riot Lady (pu), 120 Love Actinium (pu), 128 Ballyhest Fountain (pu), 77 Noneofyourbusiness (pu), Dereenavurrig (pu)
15 ran. ¾l, 10l, 15l. SP 4-1.

152 - Open Lightweight

72¹ Swans Wish [22]......................N Fehily 1
prom, disp 4 out til ld 2 out, styd on well
67 Colligan River [19]*prom, disp 4 out-2 out, no ext* **2**
140¹ Faha Gig [19]*prom, ev ch 4 out, onepcd frm 2 out* **3**
Also: 65 Loftus Lad [13] (4), 123 Bit Of A Touch (5), 115 What Thing (pu), 115 Amoristic Top (pu), 140 Snuggledown (pu), 144 Celia's Pride (pu)
9 ran. 4l, nk, 20l. SP 6-4.

153 - Winners Of Two

Okdo [18]..........................D Murphy 1
chsd ldr, btn whn lft clr last
72 Scarteen Lower [16]*chsd ldrs, btn whn lft 2nd last* **2**
125¹ West Lyn [16]*chsd ldrs, btn whn lft 3rd last* **3**
Also: 141 Ore Engineeress (pu), 8¹ Carbery Minstrel [19] (ur), 124¹ Flairline Bay (pu), 122¹ The Red Devil (pu), 72 Dromin Pride (pu)
8 ran. 5l, 1l. SP 14-1.

154 - Maiden 6yo+ I

118 I'm A Chippy [14]......................D Budds 1
prom, ld 3 out, drvn out
69³ Minehill [13]*ld to 3 out, hrd rdn & no ext flat* **2**
137 Blackwood*nvr dang* **3**
Also: 124 Tinerana Boy (4), 71 Glenselier (5), 124 Milenkeh (6), Dunbeacon (pu), 125 Riverdale Express (pu), 118 Cashel Moss (pu), Flash Of White (pu), 125 Winter Breeze (pu), Noble Protector (pu), Andy Gawe (pu), 38 Glenbrowne (pu)
14 ran. 1½l, 15l, 2l. SP 6-1.

155 - Maiden 6yo+ II

71² Bush Telegraph [15] ....J Nash 1
w.w. chsd ldr 3 out, ld apr last, sn clr
124 Skulldugery [12]*prom, ld 5 out-apr last, sn outpcd* **2**
118 Carbery Boy [10]*nvr nrr* **3**
Also: 124² Dunkel (4), 118² Fundy (5), 121 Sammy Sunshine (6), 118 Pat The Hat (pu), Forold (pu), 70 Mountainous Valley (pu), 121² Shareza River (pu), Emyvale Boy (pu), 117 Just The Duke (pu), 70 Luciano The Yuppi (pu)
13 ran. 7l, 7l, 12l. SP 5-2.

156 - Maiden 6yo+ III

117 See Just There [15] ....J Lombard 1
trckd ldr 5 out, ld 2 out, styd on well
118 Sarcoid [13]*prom, ld 5 out-2 out, no ext* **2**
Emerald Gale [11]*chsd ldrs, onepcd frm 3 out* **3**
Also: 138 Know Something VI (4), 121 Deep Wave (5), 79 Drimnamore (pu), 117 Tor (pu), 117 Park Duke (pu), 78 Caribo Express (ur), Lazy Acres (pu), 118 Mystery Aristocrat (f), First Bash (pu), 125³ Over In McGanns (pu)
13 ran. 6l, 6l, 10l. SP 6-4.

NORTH KILKENNY
Ballyragget
Sunday February 25th
GOOD TO SOFT

157 - Adjacent Maiden

117 Mighty Trust [14]......................T Cloke 1
chsd ldr 3 out, lft in ld last, kpt on
112 Locklan [14]*ld 3 out, clr whn blnd & hdd last, not rcvr* **2**
81 Gasmark [11]*chsd ldrs, onepcd 3 out* **3**
Also: 125 Glendine [11] (4), 30 Rising Paddy (5), Horgans Quay VI (pu), Sataldo (pu), 80 Mount Nugent Jack (pu), 117 Barnadown (f)
9 ran. 3½l, 4l, 1l. SP Evens.

158 - Open Lightweight

82² Loch Garman Hotel [21] ....J P Berry 1
prog 3 out, ld nxt, hld on flat
Aiguille [20]*prog to chal 2 out, ev ch til no ext flat* **2**
130² Coolafinka [18]*chsd ldrs, onepcd frm 2 out* **3**
Also: Talk To You Later [17] (4), 103¹ Laura's Beau [16] (5), 103 Fingerhill [12] (6), 115² Rossi Novae [11] (7), 58² Trimmer Wonder (8), 104¹ Clonrosh Slave (9), 104² Red Express VI (10), 109 Graiguesallagh (pu), Treens Folly (f), 104 Tul Na Gcarn (pu), 104 Selkoline (pu), Slaney Food (pu), Have A Brandy (pu)
16 ran. 1l, 6l, 3l. SP 2-1.

159 - Winners Of One I

85¹ Holly Lake [17] ....B Hamilton 1
chsd ldr 2 out, styd on to ld post
112¹ Another Believer [17]*s.s. ld 2nd til hdd post* **2**
90¹ Midnight Service [10]*nvr dang* **3**
Also: 124 Common Coin [10] (4), Sandy Pearl Two (5), 130 Ballinaboola Grove (6), 106¹ Another Idea (7), 129 Cedarbelle (8), 103 Sexton Gleam (pu), Brownroselad (pu), 80 Derby O'Gill (pu)
11 ran. Hd, 20l, 1l. SP 9-4.

160 - Winners Of One II

89¹ Dun Belle [19] ....D Coakley 1
prom, ld 4 out, jnd last, styd on well
80² Slaney Wind [18]*chsd wnr 2 out, chal last, no ext flat* **2**
116 Andy's Birthday [13]*chsd ldrs, onepcd frm 3 out* **3**
Also: 128¹ Brook Hill Lady (4), 141 Escheat (5), 102² Buaile Bos (6), 101 M T Pockets (pu), Happy Hangover (pu), 27 Clarkes Cross (pu), 111¹ Silver Buckle (pu), 102 Salemhady (pu)
11 ran. 2l, 15l, 12l. SP 5-1.

161 - Maiden 5 & 6yo I

109 Lancastrian Pride [14]..................W Ross 1
chsd ldr, btn whn lft disp 2 out, drvn out
131 Greedy Johno [12]*chsd ldr, btn whn lft disp 2 out, no ext* **2**
81 Dearmistershatter*t.o.* **3**
Also: 102 The Toor Trail (4), 108 Golden Walk (5), Treasuresox (6), 131 Stillorgan Park (7), 108 Lord Knox (8), 131 Dusty Track (pu), 101 Thought Reader (pu), 108 Sporting Vision (f), 131 Gypsy Gerry (f), Away In A Hack (pu), 108 Fortynine Plus (pu), Poulgillie (pu), 87 Buffalo House (pu), 87 Captain Guinness (ur), Buck River (pu)
18 ran. 6l, dist, sht-hd. SP 7-1.

162 - Maiden 5 & 6yo II

108³ Diorraing [17]..........................A Martin 1
prog 4 out, ld nxt, mstk last, rdn out
28 Mister Ross [16]*prog to chs wnr 2 out, hmpd apr last, kpt on flat* **2**
86³ King Torus [10]*ld 5 out-3 out, wknd* **3**
Also: 110² Rat Race (4), 137 Militation (pu), 131 Louis de Palmer (pu), 102³ Chesham Lord (pu), Tinamona (pu), Money Low (pu), Fort Zeddaan (f), Mineral Al (f), 87² Speckled Glen (pu), 103 Cloughan Boy (pu), 139 Nutty Solera (pu), 110 Glenbride Boy (pu), Sir Larry (f),

86 Lord Amethyst (pu)
17 ran. 2½l, dist, dist. SP 5-2.

163 - Mares Maiden I

105 **Poor Reception [15] ....B Hamilton** 1
prog to ld 2 out, rdn out flat ....
84[3] **Sunczech [14]***chsd wnr 2 out, no ext flat* 2
83 **Royal Star***t.o.* 3
Also: 106 Timeforgoing (4), 85 Dannys Girl (pu), 28 Christy's Girl (pu), 32 Hollybuck (f), Curraduff Moll (pu), 105 Meldap (f), 33 Trembling Rose (pu), Edermine Sunset (pu), 105 Dusky Run (pu), Oneofthеclan (pu), Eadie (f), Tearaway Sarah (pu)
15 ran. 1l, dist, dist. SP 2-1.

164 - Mares Maiden II

106[2] **Cappajune [15] ....F Kiernan** 1
prom, ld 5 out, kpt on..
83 **The Frairy Sister [13]***chsd wnr 3 out, no imp nxt*..... 2
Also: 105 Mordella Lass (f), 107 New Legislation (pu), Thank You (pu), 106 Aylesbury Beau (pu), Divine Thyme (f), 105 Larkin's Cross (pu), 130 Msadi Mhulu (pu), 132 Pampered Society (pu), 106 Proud Princess (pu), 105 Orlas Fancy (pu), 107 Codology (pu), Handy Sally (pu), 132 Hazels Dream (pu)
15 ran. 5l. SP 4-1.

165 - Mares Maiden III

81[2] **Moll's Choice [15] ....J Codd** 1
prog 4 out, ld 2 out, styd on ....
120[3] **Dominant Lady [14]***prog 4 out, chsd wnr aft 2 out, kpt on* 2
132 **Pils Invader [10]***disp & lft in ld 4 out, hdd & wknd 2 out*.. 3
Also: Kinross (4), 132 Callys Run (5), 84 Still Optimistic (6), 85 Short Of A Buck (pu), 106 Gerry's Rose (pu), 107[2] Push Gently (pu), 106 Theblondebarrister (pu), 107 Lantina (pu), 132 Broad Valley (pu), Lipstick Lady (pu)
13 ran. 2½l, 12l, 10l. SP 8-1.

166 - Maiden 7yo+ I

Rosel Walk [14] ....D O'Brien 1
prog to ld 3 out, kpt on.....................................
111 **Murcheen Durken [13]***chsd wnr 2 out, kpt on flat* 2
112 **Celtic Kinship [10]***nvr nrr* 3
Also: 112 Festival Light (4), The Territorian (5), 112 Mahankhali (6), Taste Of Freedom (pu), The Dance (f), 112 Highland Buck (pu), 80 Carriglegan Gem (pu), 133[2] Duncaha Hero (pu), Big Jimmy (pu), 90 Venetian Star (f), 134[2] Ash Plant (pu), Brewery Light (pu), Brmable Run (pu), 133[3] Noble Knight (pu)
17 ran. 2l, 8l, 10l. SP 5-1.

167 - Maiden 7yo+ II

111 **Miller King [14] ....A Fleming** 1
prom, ld 2 out, jnd post ....
71[3] **Dante Lad [14] ....A Martin** 1
prog 2 out, styd on to jn ldr post ....
89[2] **Will Travel [12]***chsd ldrs, onepcd apr last* 3
Also: 133 Scar Statement (4), Reel Him In (5), 124 Guirns Shop (6), 124 Digacre (f), 111 Lisnagree Boy (pu), Monksland (f), 111 Bredinthepurple (pu), 27 Baileys Dream (pu), 111 Ballybrit (bd), 112[3] Sheer Mystery (pu), 90 Divine Saint (pu), 90 Trackman (pu), 112 Desmarfran (pu)
16 ran. Dd-ht, 6l, 10l.
Miller King, 10-1. Dante Lad, 3-1.

DOWNPATRICK
Wednesday February 28th
SOFT

168 - 3m Hun Chase

100 **Corymandel (Ire) 12.0.................Mr P Fenton** 1
....
135[3] **Tasse Du The 12.0..................Mr A J Martin** 2
(fav) ....
94[3] **Teal Bridge 11.2 7a...................Mr G Elliot**
....
Amme Enaek (Ire) 11.4 ....
Mister Black (Ire) 11.9 ....
Find Out More (Ire) 11.2 7a ....
100 Colin's Hatch 11.7 7a ....
Glensport VI 11.4 7a 7ow ....
Seemingly So (Ire) 11.2 7a ....
Captain's View (Ire) 11.2 7a 1
92 Moylena 10.11 7a .... p
Lingering Hope (Ire) 11.9 .... p
Chene Rose (Ire) 11.1 7a 4ow .... p
94 Young Entry 11.3 7a 1ow .... p
Rontom (Ire) 11.3 7a 1ow ....
15 ran. 6l, 14l, 14l, 6l. SP 4-1.

FERMANAGH HARRIERS
Enniskillen
Saturday March 2nd
SOFT

169 - Adjacent Lightweight

158[2] **Aiguille [20] ....G Elliott**
w.w. prog 5 out, ld 3 out, drvn out..........................
104 **Missing Lady [19]***ld hlfwy-3 out, rallied last, no ext flat*..
44 **Mrs Giggs [14]***prom, effrt 3 out, sn btn* ....
Also: 21 Annie's Arthur [10] (4), 99[1] Lord Loving (5), 112 Ordain (6 109 Sinergia (7), Kylnhill (pu), Welsh Sitara (f), Willowmere (pu Portawaud (f), Dernamay (pu), Gilloway Princess (pu), Listrakelt (pu 96 Kitzberg (f), Seymour Lad (pu)
16 ran. 3l, 15l, 15l, 12l, 8l, 1l. SP 1-2.

170 - Winners Of Two I

103[2] **Private Yashkan [21] ....A Martin**
prom, ld hlfwy, in cmmnd whn lft clr last...................
92[3] **Gale Griffin [16]***chsd ldrs, btn whn lft 2nd last* ....
Duprey [15]*prom til fdd 3 out*..................................
Also: 136 Manhattan Prince [14] (4), Hall's Mill [12] (5), Quayfield [1((6), 17 October (7), 94 Callieаlla (8), 93[1] Gawn Inn [18] (ur), Clyd Emperor (pu), Salvation (pu), 95[1] Hiltonstown Lass (pu)
12 ran. 10l, 3l, 2l, 5l, 6l, 2l, 3l. SP 4-6.

171 - Winners Of Two II

96[1] **Miss Elizabeth [20].......................A Martin**
disp to 3 out, rallied und pres last, ld flat, sn clr........
92[2] **Mister Black [18]***disp til ld 3 out, hdd & no ext flat*.....
92 **Over The Maine [17]***chsd ldng pair, onepcd frm 2 out*
Also: Links Way [15] (4), Moyavo Lady [10] (5), Serious Note (6 Leave It Be (f), 17 Chene Rose (f), River Magnet (pu), 17 Hilton M (pu), Castledell (bd), Ballywoodock VI (pu)
12 ran. 6l, 2l, 4l, 20l, 1½l. SP 5-2.

172 - Maiden 5 & 6yo I

22[3] **Shuil Daingean [15] ....K Whelan**
made all, hrd rdn last, all out..............................
Drop The Act [14]*prog to chs wnr 4 out, ev ch last, no ext*...
Olumo [14]*prom, onepcd frm 2 out*..........................
Also: Fair Island [13] (4), Bell Hunter (pu), Just Horseplay (f), 93 Ballyarnott (pu), Thats My Luck (pu), Cabra Boy (pu), Springfarr Rath (pu), Wanclasstrain (pu), The Conawarey (f), 97[3] Irenes Treasur (pu), Willie Be Brave (pu), 110 Coq Hardi Dancer (pu)
15 ran. 3l, 1l, 2l. SP 6-4.

173 - Maiden 5 & 6yo II

Over The Way [16]......................I Buchanan
prog 4 out, ld nxt, sn clr......................................
Give Us A Lead*nvr dang, t.o. whn lft 2nd last*...........
97 **Longmore Boy***t.o. whn lft 3rd last*..........................
Also: Just Spellbound (4), Sharimage (su), 97 Myown Treasure (pu 97 Hanleys Call (pu), 109 Uncle Art (pu), 108 Jacksorbetter (pu), 10 Ballymacrevan (ur), Secret Prince (f), 97 Florida Or Bust (f), Shuil Mc (pu), Wayside Spin (pu)

14 ran. Dist, 25l, dist. SP 5-1.

174 - Maiden 5 & 6yo III

110 **Staffy's Boy [15]** ....K Ross 1
hld up, prog to ld 2 out, styd on flat....................
Sand de Vince [15]*prog to chs wnr apr last, alwys hld*
110 **Pilbara [13]***chsd ldrs, 3rd & btn last, eased flat*....... 3
Also: 93 Kenellen (4), Trimfold (5), Grove Victor (6), 108 Normus (ro), Pharbrook Lad (f), Malahide Michael (pu), 137 Spectre Brown (pu), 108 Sam's Man (pu), Shimna River (ur), 93 Farmlea Dancer (pu), 93 Foyleside (pu), 109 Garethson (pu)
15 ran. ½l, 8l, 10l, 20l, nk. SP 6-1.

175 - Open Lightweight

94 **Jims Choice [19]** ....R Patton 1
trckd ldr, ld aft 2 out, styd on well....................
94 **Cutter's Wharf [16]***lds til aft 2 out, no ext*........... 2
Fay Lin [11]*nvr dang*.................................... 3
Also: 18 Voldi (4), Dunluce Castle (pu), 103 Norrismount (pu), Moyavo Lad (f)
7 ran. 5l, 20l, dist. SP Evens.

176 - Mares Maiden I

106³ **La Maja [15]** ....W Ewing 1
ld 5 out, sn clr, comf....................
Golden Start [10]*chsd wnr 3 out, no imp*............... 2
107 **Midi Minstrel***chsd ldrs, no prog frm 3 out*.............. 3
Also: Miss Top (4), Follow Your Dream (5), Musical Patch (f), 96 Creighton (ur), Cardinals Lady (bd), Lake Majestic (pu), Tierfergus (pu), 106 Windmill Star (pu), 96 Glenbrin (pu), Let Her Run Wild (f), Bolesa's Joy (ref), 20 Kilmainhwood (f)
15 ran. 15l, 3l, 7l, 10l. SP 5-2.

177 - Mares Maiden II

Cabbery Rose [15] ....P Graffin 1
ld 4 out, clr 2 out, comf....................
107 **The Vendor [10]***chsd wnr 3 out, no imp nxt*.......... 2
107³ **Another Tangle [10]***chsd ldrs, onepcd frm 3 out*..... 3
Also: 96 Sideways Sally (4), 105³ Arctic Leader (5), 96² Blennerville (f), 95 Greenfield Lass (pu), Hidden Play (pu), Coloured Thyme (f), 107 Sapphire 'N' Silver (ur), Bobby Blazer (f), Friendly Bid (f), 19 Gold Leader (pu), Sarah's Cherrie (pu)
14 ran. 12l, 1l, 3l, 25l. SP 5-2.

178 - Mares Maiden III

You Name It [14] ....K Ross 1
prog 3 out, chal last, rdn to ld flat....................
96 **Knights Pleasure [14]***prom, ld 3 out, rdn & hdd flat*.. 2
96 **Ngala***no dang, lft 3rd last*.............................. 3
Also: Denel de (pu), Roselynhill (pu), 98 Moneycarragh (pu), Cheerio Fidel VI (pu), Damolly Rose (f), Mourne Miner (f), Blue Bay (ur), Incense Doll (f), Floruceva (pu), 84 Goldwren (ro), Melodic Lady (pu)
14 ran. Nk, 20l. SP 3-1.

179 - Maiden 7yo+ I

High Star [14] ....I Buchanan 1
cls up, 2nd 3 out, ld & lft clr last, all out..............
21³ **Cahills Hill [14]***chsd ldrs, lft 2nd last, styd on*.......... 2
99 **Cool Rocket [13]***chsd ldrs, kpt on onepcd frm 3 out*.. 3
Also: 98³ Stag Hunt (4), 166 Highland Buck (pu), 99 Iveagh Lady (pu), 27 Kilmacrew (f), Kimbry (pu), 98 Hollow Suspicion (pu), 99 Fidoon (pu), 104 Forever Gold (su), Bold Boreen (pu), 99 Ahogill (ro), Northern Granite (pu)
14 ran. ½l, 3l, dist. SP 2-1.

180 - Maiden 7yo+ II

111² **Pats Cross [13]** ....B Hamilton 1
prom, ld 3 out, just hld on....................
99² **Takeithandy [13]***chsd wnr 2 out, styd on, just faild*.... 2
111 **Loughdoo [11]***chsd ldrs, onepcd frm 2 out*.......... 3
Also: Sheer Indulgence (4), Neely (5), 99 Cherryflame (6), Andrea's Prince (7), 99 Fair Avoca (pu), Craigelle (pu), 99 Dick's Cabin (pu), 98 Miners Valley (pu), 111 Clanmany (pu), Laergy Cripperty (f), Ballinahowna Lad (f), Giorgione (pu)
15 ran. Nk, 4l, 20l, 5l, dist, 1l. SP 4-5.

KILWORTH & ARAGLEN
Kilworth
Saturday March 2nd
GOOD

181 - Maiden 4yo

Super Dealer [14] ....T Nagle 1
chsd ldr, gd jmp to ld last, hld on....................
Artistic Plan [14]*ld til hdd last, just hld*.............. 2
Shanagore Warrior*chsd ldrs, 3rd & onepcd frm 3 out* 3
Also: Acey Deucey (4), Proud Lady (5), Springford (6), La Riviera (pu)
7 ran. Nk, 15l, 1l. SP 5-1.

182 - Mares Maiden 6yo+ I

151 **Minstrel Madame [15]** ....D Keane 1
prom, ld 2 out, lft clr apr last, unchal..............
144³ **Ballintee Belle [12]***chsd ldrs, btn whn lft 2nd apr last* 2
Killatty Player*nvr dang*.................................... 3
Also: 143³ The Pulpit (4), 143 Nans Pet (f), Waterloo Princess (pu), 143 Ann Black (pu), Handball (pu), 70 Alice Sheer Thorn (pu), 144 Rascal Street Lad [13] (su)
10 ran. 10l, 12l, 1l. SP 8-1.

183 - Mares Maiden 6yo+ II

55 **Laura's Leap [15]** ....S O'Callaghan 1
cls up, ld 3 out, styd on well....................
119³ **Scarlet River [14]***chsd wnr 2 out, no ext flat*......... 2
143 **Solar Castle [12]***cvhsd ldrs, onepcd frm 3 out*....... 3
Also: 143² Sharoujack (4), 144 Rio Star (ur), 144 Lady Fountain (ur), 143 Kilcully Night (pu), 127 Killbally Castle (pu), 151 Dereenavurrig (pu), 70³ Have A Drop (pu)
10 ran. 1½l, 6l, 8l. SP 3-1.

184 - Open Lightweight

Try God [22] ....N Fehily 1
prom, disp 2 out til just ld nr fin....................
152³ **Faha Gig [22]***prom, disp 2 out til just hdd nr fin*....... 2
Sir-Eile [18]*rear, styd on 2 out, nvr nrr*................ 3
Also: Riszard [18] (4), 141³ Pharditu (pu), 152 What Thing (pu), 69¹ For Josh (pu), 141 Holly Moss (pu), 140 Lovely Citizen (pu), 75 The Vicarette (pu), 140 The Miners Fate (pu)
11 ran. Hd, 12l, ½l. SP 4-1.

185 - Adjacent Maiden

142 **Reen-O-Foil [15]** ....D Costello 1
prog 4 out, ld 2 out, sn clr....................
69 **Dawn Lad [12]***prog 5 out, ld nxt-2 out, sn outpcd*..... 2
Ilengar [11]*nvr nrr*.. 3
Also: The Gaffer (4), 142 Ace Ventura (pu), 142 Anyone Whoknows Me (pu), 142 Des The Architect (pu), 142 Barrys Avenue (ur), Slumber Hill (pu), 142 Brigade Leader (pu), Fileo (pu), Gallant Gale (pu)
12 ran. 7l, 4l, 20l. SP 2-1.

186 - Winners Of Two

153³ **West Lyn [17]** ....A O'Shea 1
alwys prom, ld 2 out, clr last, easily....................
140² **Crazy Dreams [13]***chsd wnr frm 2 out, no imp*....... 2
72 **Warning Call [12]***chsd ldrs, onepcd frm 3 out*........ 3
Also: 72 The Criosra (4), 141 Supreme Arctic (pu), 136 Burkean Melody (pu), 51 Inch Emperor (pu)
7 ran. 7l, 4l, 8l. SP 2-1.

187 - Maiden 5yo+ I

154² **Minehill [14]** ....D Murphy 1
disp til ld 4 out, jnd last, styd on well....................
Ecologic [13]*trckd ldrs, chal & ev ch last, no ext*...... 2

Castle Tiger Bay*t.o.* ... 3
Also: 70 Black Perrin (4), Icantsay (pu), 135 Mahon River (pu), Foxwoods Valley (pu), 47 Brian Og (f), Sandy's Choice (pu), 79 Round Pound (pu), Faha Moss (pu)
11 ran. 2l, dist, 12l. SP 5-1.

188 - Maiden 5yo+ II

117[3] **Mythical Approach [18]**...............**D Costello** 1
ld hlfwy, clr 2 out, easily ...
124[3] **Master Kemal [14]***chsd wnr 3 out, no imp* ... 2
137[3] **Weak Moment [13]***chsd ldrs, onepcd 3 out* ... 3
Also: 154 Glenselier [10] (4), 57 Percy Hannon (pu), 147 Persian Packer (pu), 138[3] Stroll Home (f), 155 Pat The Hat (pu), 79 Sir Frederick (pu), 78 Dante's Reward (pu)
10 ran. 5l, 5l, 8l. SP 5-4.

KILKENNY & KILMOGANNY
Gowran Point-To-Point Course
Sunday March 3rd
HOLDING

190 - Adjacent Maiden I

47 **Geata Bawn [15]** ....**M Scanlon** 1
hld up, prog 2 out, ld last, ran on ...
157 **Glendine [14]***ld 6 out, mstk & hdd last, no ext* ... 2
166 **Brewery Light [10]***nvr nrr* ... 3
Also: King Tyrant [10] (4), Drimeen (pu), Bourbon County (pu), Flying Fellow (pu), Pauper Boice (f), 166 Festival Light (pu), 89 Level Vibes (pu)
10 ran. 2l, 12l, 3l. SP 10-1.

191 - Adjacent Maiden II

162[3] **King Torus [16]**...............**A Martin** 1
w.w. prog aft 3 out, ld last, styd on well ...
Wejem [15]*chsd ldr, ld aft 3 out, hdd & no ext last* ... 2
Bramble Dale [13]*prog to chs ldr 2 out-apr last, no ext* ... 3
Also: 105 Tiger Dolly (f), Torus Spa (ur), 109[2] Donal's Choice (pu), 157 Rising Paddy (ur), Black Santa (pu), Windy Bee (pu), Mr Dennehy (pu)
10 ran. 1½l, 5l. SP 3-1.

192 - Maiden 4 & 5yo I

131[2] **Muskin More [16]** ....**P Fenton** 1
ld 3rd, clr 3 out, comf ...
101[2] **Difficult Decision [11]***prog to chs wnr 2 out, no imp* .. 2
102 **Spring Beau***nvr dang* ... 3
Also: 106 Nurney Minstrel (pu), 81 Lonely Castle (f), Mak's Dream (pu), Command (pu), Keelson (pu), Haven't An Ocean (pu), Dusty Maid (f), 157 Horgans Quay VI (pu)
11 ran. 15l, 10l. SP Evens.

193 - Maiden 4 & 5yo II

Killasheelan [16]...............**J Cash** 1
ld 6th, clr aft 3 out, unchal ...
114 **More Rain***chsd wnr 2 out, no imp* ... 2
110 **Mile Mill***t.o.* ... 3
Also: 31 Sweetmount Lad (f), 110[3] Blackie Connors (pu), 137 I Cant Wait (pu), Lovable Outlaw (pu), 139 Wyn Wan Soon (ur), 165 Lantina (f), Pejays Duca (f), 157 Mount Nugent Jack (ro)
11 ran. 20l, dist. SP 10-1.

194 - Winners Of Two

109[1] **Quattro [19]**...............**A Coyle** 1
prom, ld 4 out, clr 2 out, styd on well ...
110[1] **Parahandy [16]***prom, hmpd 6th, ld nxt-4 out, onepcd* .. 2
Kilburry [16]*prog 4 out, onepcd frm 2 out* ... 3
Also: 135 Jaybe's Friend [10] (4), 102 Four Zeros (5), 131 Golden Performance (pu), Venture On (pu), All For Max (f), 130[1] Dromhana (pu), 158 Tul Na Gcarn (pu), Footsy Murray (pu), 112 Both Sides (pu)
12 ran. 8l, ¾l, 15l. SP 6-1.

195 - Mares Maiden I

164 **Aylesbury Beau [14]**...............**E Sheehy** 1
prom, ld 4 out, mstk 2 out, hrd rdn & drew clr last ...
66 **Clodagh River [11]***prog 4 out, ev ch nxt, onepcd und pres aft nxt* ... 2
Geneva Steele*prom to 3 out, wknd* ... 3
Also: 163 Tearaway Sarah (4), 165 Push Gently (pu), 107 Ballylime Again (f), Dribs And Drabs (pu), Raheen River (pu), Handsome Maid (pu), 85 Sixty-One (pu), Sup A Whiskey (ur), 164 Hazels Dream (pu), Swaping Luck (pu), 157 Sataldo (f), 164 Orlas Fancy (pu), Slade Valley Lady (f)
16 ran. 8l, dist, 1½l. SP 10-1.

196 - Mares Maiden II

Milwaukee [16]...............**J Finn** 1
prom, ld aft last, pshd out ...
Rural Run [15]*mstks, ld til aft last, no ext* ... 2
Time To Smile [10]*nvr nrr* ... 3
Also: Potential Threat (pu), Natural Lady (pu), Randy Rose (pu), Slip Along Sally (pu), 163 Meldap (pu), 163 Hollybuck (pu), 165 Lipstick Lady (pu), 107 Trembles Choice (pu), Key Door (pu), Belle Of Kilbride (f), 165 Kinross (pu), 164 Proud Princess (pu)
15 ran. 3l, 15l. SP 5-2.

197 - Open Lightweight

159 **Ballinaboola Grove [19]** ....**L Winters** 1
made most, drew clr frm 2 out ...
Derali [15]*chsd wnr, ev ch 5 out, no ext 2 out* ... 2
Also: 158 Selkoline (ur), 123[2] Killoskehan Queen (f), Up In The Air (pu), 162 Louis de Palmer (f), 132 Miss Tornado (pu), Patty's Pride (pu), 162 Tinamona (pu), Baybuck (ur), 154 Cashel Moss (pu)
11 ran. 12l. SP 8-1.

198 - Farmers

Frazer Island [20]...............**T Hyde** 1
hld up, prog 3 out, ld last, easily ...
160 **Escheat [17]***chsd ldr 4 out, ld nxt, hdd & no ext last* ... 2
158 **Clonrosh Slave [16]***ld to 3 out, onepcd* ... 3
Also: It's A Deal [16] (4), 140[3] Just A Breeze [14] (5), 129[3] Tara River (pu), 80[1] Kings Cave (pu), 83 Determined Okie (pu), 52 Determined Man (pu), 90 Glenmore Star (f), 117 Bone Idol (pu), Spinans Hill (pu), 159 Sandy Pearl Two (pu)
13 ran. 3l, 3l, ½l, 6l. SP 8-1.

CO CLARE HARRIERS
Quin
Sunday March 3rd
SOFT

199 - Maiden 4 & 5yo I

Ballyline [17]...............**B Hassett** 1
made all, sn clr, styd on strngly ...
138 **Camogue Bridge***chsd wnr 5 out, no imp 2 out, wknd* .. 2
147 **Brother Nicholas***nvr dang, styd on frm 2 out* ... 3
Also: 139 Roskeen Bridge (4), Michael Ugene (f), 52[3] Droum Ross (pu), Oneofourown (pu), Ballymuckamore (pu), 35 Cruisin On Credit (pu)
9 ran. Dist, hd, dist. SP 5-2.

200 - Maiden 4 & 5yo II

61 **Ebbzeado Willfurr [16]**...............**B Moran** 1
chsd ldrs, rdn 3 out, ld last, all out ...
62[3] **Thunder Road [16]***made most to last, rallied flat* ... 2
Mr Freeman [11]*ran on frm 2 out, nvr nrr* ... 3
Also: 114 Where's Noel (4), Nobodywantsme (5), 122 Educate Me (6), 122 Banner Year (pu), Mr Campus (pu)
8 ran. ¾l, 15l, 8l, 20l, 20l. SP 3-1.

201 - Maiden 6yo

154 **Tinerana Boy [16]** ....**R Hurley** 1
chsd ldr, ld 2 out, clr last, styd on ...

108[2] **Whitebarn Grit [12]***hld up, prog 2 out, chsd wnr flat, no imp* 2
78 **An Oon Iss An Owl [11]***in tch, chsd wnr aft 2 out, no imp* 3
Also: 47 Ballhopping (4), 40 Bayline Lad (5), Head Bottle Washer (6), Lostyndyke (7), 87 Rosevalley (8), 125 Wylfa Boy (9), 124 Rushing Waters (10), Cangort King (11), 139 Nollaig (f), 162 Rat Race (f), 138 Carnmore House (pu), Rare Spread (f)
15 ran. 10l, 2½l, 10l, 7l, ½l, 15l, 5l, 15l, dist, 5l. SP 4-1.

202 - Open Lightweight

34[3] **Royal Ziero [21]........................W Ewing** 1
prom, ld 3 out, hrd rdn & hld on flat
Up For Ransome [21]*cls up, chal apr last, ev ch, just hld* 2
54 **Divali [18]***disp to 3 out, sn btn* 3
Also: 44 Kizzy Rose [14] (4), 72 Bayview Prince [13] (5), Starlight Fountain (pu), 140 La Cienaga (pu), 123 Jigg's Forge VI (ref), 127[3] Ballybriken Castle (pu), 141 Duchess Of Padua (ur)
10 ran. Hd, 10l, 10l, 3l. SP 4-1.

203 - Mares Maiden I

127 **Six Of Spades [14] ....J McNamara** 1
w.w. prog & 2nd 4 out, chal & lft clr last, drvn out
127[2] **Selm Mary [13]***4th 4 out, outpcd frm 2 out, lft 2nd last, styd on* 2
143 **Snipe Lodge [11]***3rd 4 out, outpcd frm 2 out, lft 3rd last* 3
Also: 128 Ivy Glen (4), 149 Midnight Society (5), 143 Scarra Darragh (ro), Knocktoran Lady (pu), 151 Love Actinium [14] (ur), Yasgourra (pu), 119 Victim Of Slander (ur), 85 Jensalee (pu), 119 Rockview Supreme (f)
12 ran. 2½l, 5l, 6l, 25l. SP 5-4.

204 - Mares Maiden II

Princess Henry [16] ....J McNamara 1
ld 4th, clr 3 out, unchal
43 **Galatasori Jane***chsd ldrs, no imp wnr frm 3 out* 2
Thorny Bridge*nvr dang* 3
Also: 43 Lantern Spark (4), 150 Barmur (5), 43 Taylors Twist (f), My New Merc (pu), 149 Kochnie (f), 120 Idiot's Surprise (f), Mona Lita (pu), 42 Queen Of The Suir (ur), Bunny Lightening (pu)
12 ran. 25l, 10l, 20l, 2l. SP Evens.

205 - Confined Maiden

147 **Dysart O'Dea [15] ....B Hassett** 1
trckd ldrs, ld 2 out, drvn out
148 **Drumline Castle [13]***disp to 2 out, kpt on* 2
162 **Fort Zeddaan***disp to 2 out, wknd* 3
Also: 147 La Mon Dere (4), Rathwiladoon (5)
5 ran. 5l, 20l, ½l, dist. SP 1-3.

206 - Maiden 7yo+

Murphys Lady [15].....................J Moloney 1
prom, ld 5 out, clr last, styd on
125 **Fruit Town [12]***prog to chs wnr aft 3 out, no imp apr last* 2
69 **Coshla Expresso [10]***styd on frm 2 out, nvr nrr* 3
Also: 167 Guirns Shop (4), 156 Deep Wave (5), 128 Camden Lamp (6), Mr Connie Vee (pu), 111[3] Dooneal Hero (pu), 117 What Is The Plan (pu), 111 The Defender (pu), 125 St Aidan (ur), 154 Winter Breeze (f)
12 ran. 8l, 5l, 8l, 5l, dist. SP 8-1.

WEST WATERFORD
Lismore
Sunday March 3rd
GOOD

207 - Confined Maiden

73 **Parish Ranger [17] ....T Lombard** 1
prom, disp last, sn ld & drvn clr
139[3] **Saol Sona [15]***cls up, disp last, outpcd by wnr* 2
151 **Supersonia [14]***prom, disp last, sn outpcd* 3
Also: 183 Sharoujack [12] (4), 154 Andy Gawe (5), 113 Lady Steel (6), Always Drumming (pu), Dons Pride (f), 144 Glengarra Maid (pu), Take It Away (pu), 149 Appendix Lady (pu), 151 Tina Ore (f), 119 Ann Toni (pu), 143 Amandawill (pu)
14 ran. 6l, 4l, 6l. SP 5-2.

208 - Maiden 4yo

Florida Pearl [15].......................A Costello 1
chsd ldr 3 out, ld flat, styd on
Perky Lad [14]*ld, clr 3 out, hdd & no ext flat* 2
Lord Harry [13]*rear, ran on 2 out, nrst fin* 3
Also: Claudia Electric (4), Executive Fox (5), Vasiliki (pu), Clonageera (f), Kilcully Carrig (f), Kilcully Talbot (f)
9 ran. 3l, 2l, dist. SP 4-5.

209 - Open Lightweight

119[1] **Silent Sneeze [21]......................K Beecher** 1
chsd ldr 5 out, ld aft last, ran on well
152[2] **Colligan River [20]***ld 5 out til aft last, no ext* 2
142[1] **Ruby Belle [17]***nvr nrr* 3
Also: 115 Myalup [14] (4), 115 Awbeg Rover [11] (5), 141 Looking Ahead (6), 6 Dromgurrihy Lad (pu), 113[1] Our Blossom (pu), 54 Cooladerra Lady (pu)
9 ran. 3l, 10l, 10l. SP 3-1.

210 - Mares Maiden I

77[2] **I'm Happy Now [15] ....K Whelan** 1
prom, rdn & disp whn lft clr last
76 **Hot Scent***nvr dang, lft poor 2nd last* 2
147 **Gentle Leader***t.o. whn lft poor 3rd last* 3
Also: 120 Fools Courage (4), 150 Queen Of Clubs (pu), 149 Farran Garrett (pu), 120 Liskilnewabbey (pu), 120 Janice Price [15] (f), 150 Northern Katie (pu), Classie Claire (pu), 63 Gluais Linn (pu), Another Brandy (pu), 119 Dusty's Delight (pu), Lady Brigida (pu)
14 ran. Dist, dist, 6l. SP 3-1.

211 - Mares Maiden II

149[2] **Lusmagh River [15]....................D Costello** 1
ld 5 out, clr 2 out, unchal
150 **Early News [10]***chsd wnr 3 out, no imp* 2
119 **Round Tower Lady***nvr dang* 3
Also: 76[3] Cahermone Lady (4), 149 Deciding Dance (5), 119 Blackwater Fox (pu), 49 Ruby Invite (f), 149 Bright Choice (pu), Macklette (pu), 149 Divine Rapture (f), 150 Princess Diga (bd), Harvey's Cream (pu), 81 Peggys Leg (pu), 149 Ballinacubby Pride (f)
14 ran. 15l, 20l, 10l. SP 6-4.

212 - Winners Of One

121[1] **In The Blood [17].......................K Whelan** 1
cls up, ld 2 out, rdn clr
Sleepy Rock [15]*chsd wnr frm 2 out, no imp last* 2
156[1] **See Just There [14]***chsd wnr 2 out, no imp last* 3
Also: 116 Elwill Glory [14] (4), 153[2] Scarteen Lower [12] (5), 153 Carbery Minstrel (6), 126 Carrolls Rock (7), 141 Trimmer Princess (8), 143[1] Get Cracking (pu), 116 Sweet Merenda (pu), Fine Affair (pu), 116 Kilcannon House (f), 3 River Water (pu), 167[1] Dante Lad (pu), 120[1] Arctic Pearl (pu)
15 ran. 2½l, 2l, 1l. SP 3-1.

213 - Maiden 5yo

148 **John's Right [15] ....K Beecher** 1
made most, drvn out frm last
114 **Dual Or Bust [14]***prog to chal apr last, no ext flat* 2
61 **Hannigan's Bridge** 3D
Hardy Breeze*nvr nrr, fin 4th, pld 3rd* 3
Also: 146 Never Heard (4), 114 Johnny's Echo (pu), 73 Robin Of Loxley (pu), The Stag (f), Spanish Castle (pu), Milford Road (pu), Bosco's Touch (pu), 148 Witchiewah (pu), 137 Upton Steamer (f), 137 High Charges (pu), Up And Over (pu), 35 Dorgan (ur), 121 Neelisagin (pu), Fernhill House (pu)
18 ran. 1l, 20l, 10l. SP 3-1.

EAST DOWN
Tyrella
Saturday March 9th
SOFT

214 - Confined Lightweight

170[3] **Duprey [16]**..............................G Martin 1
ld 5 out, clr 3 out, easily
177 **Sideways Sally***ld to 5 out, sn btn* 2
95 **Ellies Pride***nvr dang* 3
Also: 96 Tyrella Clear View (4), 92 Fidsprit (pu)
5 ran. 20l, 6l, dist. SP 1-4.

215 - Mares Maiden

177 **Blennerville [17]**..........................A Martin 1
trckd ldr, ld apr last, sn clr
Blossom World [13]*ld, clr 5 out, wknd & hdd apr last* 2
92 **Half Scotch***nvr dang* 3
Also: 179 Iveagh Lady (4), 178 Melodic Lady (5), 95 Glen Thyne (pu), 176 Lake Majestic (pu), 180 Fair Avoca (pu), 178 Blue Bay (pu), 178 Cheerio Fidel VI (pu), 178 Moneycarragh (f), 95 Teralisa (pu), 169 Dernamay (pu), 177 Sapphire 'N' Silver (pu)
14 ran. 8l, 15l, dist. SP 4-7.

216 - Open Lightweight

94[2] **Lacken Beau [22]**..........................R Arthur 1
disp to 5 out, ran on to ld last, sn clr.
94 **Bald Joker [19]***ld 5 out til apr last, onepcd* 2
98[1] **Rontom [15]***prom, ev ch 2 out, onepcd apr last* 3
Also: 94 Schweppes Tonic [15] (4), J J's Hope (pu), 180 Cherryflame (f)
6 ran. 8l, 4l, 8l. SP 4-6.

217 - Maiden 4 & 5yo

French Lady [14]..........................A Martin 1
trckd ldr, ld last, styd on well
174 **Pharbrook Lad [13]***ld to last, no ext* 2
81 **Butler Brennan [11]***nvr dang* 3
Also: Chase The Sun (ur)
4 ran. 2l, 6l. SP 4-5.

218 - Winners Of Two

171[3] **Over The Maine [19]**......................R Arthur 1
ld 5 out-nxt, ld 2 out, sn clr
170 **Hiltonstown Lass [15]***prom, ld 4 out-2 out, onepcd* 2
Folly Road*nvr dang* 3
Also: 134[1] Drumcairn (ur), 169 Lord Loving (pu)
5 ran. 8l, 20l. SP 6-4.

219 - Maiden 6yo+

169 **Kylnhill [14]**..........................I Buchanan 1
trckd ldrs, disp 4 out til ld 2 out, hrd rdn, ct post
98[2] **Lingering Hope [14]**......................A Martin 1
trckd ldrs, disp 4 out-2 out, hrd rdn, jnd ldr post.
172 **Irenes Treasure [11]***prog 4 out, no imp ldrs 2 out* 3
Also: 98 Harvemac (4), 179 Stag Hunt (5), Leannes Man (ur), 174 Trimfold (pu), 180 Sheer Indulgence (ur), Proceedwithcaution (pu), 179 Hollow Suspicion (pu), 93 Rolier (f), 98 Fill Your Boots (pu)
12 ran. Dd-ht, 10l, 4l, 15l.
Kylnhill, 8/1. Lingering Hope, 1/1.

KILLINICK HARRIERS
Killinick
Sunday March 10th
GOOD TO SOFT

220 - Winners Of One

155[1] **Bush Telegraph [18]**......................J Nash 1
trckd ldrs, ld 2 out, clr whn mstk last, rdn out
160[2] **Slaney Wind [16]***ld to 2 out, styd on wll agn flat* 2
194[2] **Parahandy [14]***nvr nrr* 3
Also: Foreign Cover [12] (4), 116[3] Lady Elise [11] (5), 157[1] Mighty Trust (6), 141 Sandfair (7), 130 Delgany Deer (8), Rathfardon (f), 159 Cedarbelle (pu), Do Drop In (pu), Annesley Lady (pu), 163[1] Poor Reception (pu), Proud Toby (f)
14 ran. 1½l, 5l. SP Evens.

221 - Open Lightweight

194 **Dromhana [21]**..........................J Berry 1
prom, ld 2 out, hrd rdn & styd on
158[1] **Loch Garman Hotel [20]***ld to 2 out, no ext flat* 2
158 **Slaney Food [18]***kpt on frm 2 out, nrst fin* 3
Also: 198[3] Clonrosh Slave [15] (4), 129[1] Dennistownthriller [13] (5), 197 Selkoline (6), 152 Amoristic Top (7), Give It A Lash (pu)
8 ran. 1l, 6l. SP 2-1.

222 - Maiden 4 & 5yo I

Sean's Quarter [16]......................J Codd 1
prom, ld apr 2 out, in cmmnd whn lft wll clr last
191 **Torus Spa***nvr dang, lft poor 2nd last* 2
Mardon [13]*chsd wnr 4 out, btn whn f last, rmntd* 3
Also: Polar Ridge (4), 132 Spritly Lady (pu), Sister Seven (f), 138 The Road To Moscow (f), Cracker Alley (pu), Side Stepper (pu), Riverrunsthroughit (pu), Gentle Mossy (pu), 193 Pejays Duca (pu), Ringaheen (pu), Punters Fortune (pu), 196 Natural Lady (pu)
15 ran. Dist, dist. SP 4-1.

223 - Maiden 4 & 5yo II

192 **Keelson [17]**..........................H Cleary 1
trckd ldrs, ld last, ran on well
193 **Wyn Wan Soon [15]***ld to last, sn no ext* 2
161 **Dusty Track***t.o.* 3
Also: 193 Mount Nugent Jack (4), 162 Mineral Al (5), 157[3] Gasmark (ur), Sinead's Joy (pu), 162 Sir Larry (pu), 132 Choretine Lady (f), Bart Eile (pu), Margarets Tocracy (pu), Luthier Girl (f), 192 Mak's Dream (pu), Apollodorus (pu), Woodbinesandroses (pu)
15 ran. 3l, dist. SP 7-4.

224 - Maiden 4 & 5yo III

Well Armed [15]..........................J Flynn 1
made most, all out flat
161 **Buck River [15]***prog to chs wnr aft 2 out, just hld* 2
198 **Determined Okie [12]***chsd wnr, mstk 2 out, sn btn* 3
Also: 192 Dusty Maid (4), 193 Lovable Outlaw (pu), Mary's Delight (pu), Back Withavengeance (pu), Cool Chic (pu), Leatansceil (pu), 196 Lipstick Lady (f), 195 Dribs And Drabs (pu), Namoilltear (pu), 193 Sweetmount Lad (ro), Whitestown Boy (pu)
14 ran. Nk, 10l, dist. SP 6-4.

225 - Mares Maiden 6yo+ I

Call Queen [15]..........................J Quigley 1
in tch, ld 2 out, rdn out
132 **Warkey Lady [14]***cls up, chal 2 out, onepcd flat* 2
132 **Miss Lurgan [12]***chsd ldrs, onepcd frm 2 out* 3
Also: 83[2] Clonee Lane [10] (4), 149 Hurricane Iris (5), 143 Trimmer Lady (6), Larry's Penny (f), 165[2] Dominant Lady (pu), 196 Key Door (pu), 163 Eadie (pu)
10 ran. 2l, 4l. SP 8-1.

226 - Mares Maiden 6yo+ II

195 **Swaping Luck [14]**......................D O'Brien 1
prog to chal 2 out, hld whn lft clr last
Talbot's Hollow [10]*nvr dang, lft 2nd last* 2
Also: Seaview Star (pu), 182 Handball [15] (f), Playful Princess (pu), 195 Sixty-One (pu), 196 Belle Of Kilbride (f), Betty Balfour (pu), Josalady (f), Buzz About (pu)
10 ran. 10l. SP 10-1.

227 - Maiden 6yo+ I

201[2] **Whitebarn Grit [17]**......................D O'Brien 1
prom, ld 3 out, drw clr last

162 Nutty Solera [14]*chsd ldrs, rdn 2 out, kpt on onepcd* . . 2
Little-K [12]*prom, wth wnr 2 out, wknd last* 3
Also: 162 Money Low (4), 31 Mite Have Bean (pu), Bens Unyoke (pu), 154³ Blackwood (pu), Even Call (pu), 167³ Will Travel (pu), Up The Rock (pu), 86 Newtown Rambler (pu), 198 Bone Idol (pu), 109 Shillelagh Oak (pu), The Caffler (pu), 156 Caribo Express (pu)
15 ran. 8l, 6l. SP 3-1.

228 - Maiden 6yo+ II

167 Bredinthepurple [14] . . . . J P Berry 1
prog to ld 2 out, hld on well . . . .
161² Greedy Johno [13]*prog & ev ch apr last, kpt on* 2
161 Gypsy Gerry [13]*chsd ldrs, hrd rdn apr last, kpt on* . . . 3
Also: 167 Scar Statement [10] (4), Glenfontaine (5), 133 Eastern Fox (pu), 161 Stillorgan Park (f), 133 Shimano (pu), 155³ Carbery Boy (pu), 161 Away In A Hack (pu), Shrule Hill (pu), 191 Mr Dennehy (pu), 111 Harsh Decision (pu), Over The Barrow (pu), River Bargy (pu)
15 ran. 1l, ½l. SP 10-1.

229 - Nomination

Ragged River . . . . K Roche 1
made all, styd on wll . . . .
160 Silver Buckle*chal 2 out, no ext last* 2
194 Tul Na Gcarn*nvr dang* 3
Also: Go Meekly (4), Dunamase Dandy (pu)
5 ran. 4l, 8l. SP Evens.

SOUTH WESTMEATH
The Pigeons
Sunday March 10th
GOOD

230 - Confined

164¹ Cappajune [17] . . . . F Kiernan 1
made all, comf . . . .
162 Cloughan Boy [10]*chsd wnr, no imp 2 out* 2
164 Mordella Lass*nvr dang* 3
Also: 103 Satin Emma (4), Castlepook (f)
5 ran. 6l, 20l, 6l. SP 1-3.

231 - Maiden 4 & 5yo

131 Keepitsafe [15] . . . . D McCartan 1
mstks, ld 6 out, kpt on well . . . .
Castleconner [13]*chsd wnr 2 out, no imp last* 2
161 Sporting Vision*nvr dang* 3
Also: 173 Jacksorbetter (4), 161 Fortynine Plus (5), 177 Coloured Thyme (f), Falas Lad (ro), Mr Peoples (pu), 101 Jester Jack (pu), Huntsman's Lodge (pu)
10 ran. 5l, 25l, 25l, 2½l. SP 4-1.

232 - Mares Maiden I

144 Baby Whale [15] . . . . G Elliott 1
sn trckd ldr, ld apr last, styd on well . . . .
195³ Geneva Steele [12]*ld to apr last, no ext* 2
105² Rathcarrick Lass*nvr dang* 3
Also: 107 Executive Bill (4), 127 Gala Vote (5), 165 Short Of A Buck (f), 106 Memory Harbour (f), Little Doe (bd), 165 Gerry's Rose (pu), 195 Slade Valley Lady (bd), 204 Taylors Twist (pu), Tobar Bhride (f), 204 Mona Lita (pu), Brooklawn (bd)
14 ran. 7l, 20l, 5l, dist. SP 12-1.

233 - Mares Maiden II

Slavica [18] . . . . J Shaw 1
hld up, prog 4 out, ld 2 out, sn wll clr . . . .
202 Ballybriken Castle [11]*prom, ld 4 out-2 out, sn btn* 2
195 Handsome Maid*nvr nrr* 3
Also: 203 Ivy Glen (4), 128 Trembling Lady (5), 164 New Legislation (6), 163 Dannys Girl (7), Howesshecutting (ur), 84 Gerry's Delight (pu), Palmrock Queen (pu), 164 Handy Sally (pu), Aunt Emeralds (pu), 177 Friendly Bid (pu), Wewillsee (ur)
14 ran. 20l, 8l, 6l, 2½l, 2½l, dist. SP 8-1.

234 - Winners Of One

161¹ Lancastrian Pride [19] . . . . W Ross 1
w.w. prog aft 3 out, ld last, hld on well . . . .
72² You Know Best [19]*prom, ld 4 out-last, just hld flat* . . . 2
Toby's Friend [16]*nvr nrr* 3
Also: River Of Dreams [15] (4), 160 Brook Hill Lady [13] (5), 159 Another Idea [13] (6), 160 Happy Hangover [11] (7), 92 Cool Yule (8), 133¹ Seemingly So (9), 160 Buaile Bos (10), 132¹ Asteal (11), Flo Jo's Boy (pu)
12 ran. Hd, 8l, 2l, 5l, 1l, 6l, 30l, ½l, 1l, 2l. SP 7-1.

235 - Open Lightweight

198¹ Frazer Island [22] . . . . T Hyde 1
prog 5 out, chsd ldr 2 out, ld last, hld on . . . .
175 Voldi [22]*ld 6 out til mstk & hdd last, rallied* 2
158 Talk To You Later [21]*prssd ldr 6 out-2 out, no ext.* 3
Also: 158 Red Express VI [18] (4), 18 Temporale (5), Final Issue (6), 171¹ Miss Elizabeth (pu), Rathventure (pu), 104³ Find Out More (f), 103³ Carrigans Lad (pu)
10 ran. Nk, 2l, 10l, 30l, 3l. SP 2-1.

236 - Maiden 6yo+ I

Spire Hill [15] . . . . K Ross 1
prom, ld 5 out,. lft clr 3 out, unchal aft . . . .
56 Coolteen Hero [12]*prog to jn wnr whn blnd 3 out, not rcvr* 2
169 Annie's Arthur*no dang frm 3 out* 3
Also: 21 Benny The Bishop (4), 108 Almost An Angel (5), Inactualfact (pu), 124 Leaders View (pu), 206 St Aidan (pu), 88² The Punters Pal (pu), Knock Ranger (pu), 180 Andrea's Prince (pu), 109 Connaught Boy (pu), 156 First Bash (f), Magic Caller (pu), 190² Glendine (pu)
15 ran. 12l, 8l, 3l, dist. SP 6-1.

237 - Maiden 6yo+ II

166² Murcheen Durken [15] . . . . G Elliott 1
prom, ld 2 out, clr last, comf . . . .
206³ Coshla Expresso [12]*ld 6 out-2 out, sn outpcd* 2
Rovet*nvr dang* 3
Also: Tassagh Boy (4), Prince Of Thyne (5), 180 Clanmany (pu), Thinkaboutthat (pu), 167 Lisnagree Boy (f), 133 Galloping Giggs (ur), 167 Reel Him In (pu), 166 Mahankhali (pu), 201 Carnmore House (pu), Almaurita (pu), 167 Trackman (pu), Open Champion (pu)
15 ran. 5l, 25l, 10l, dist. SP Evens.

WEST CARBERY
Skibbereen
Sunday March 10th
SOFT

238 - Maiden 4yo

New Line Girl [15] . . . . K O'Sullivan 1
trckd ldr, lft in ld 7 out, styd on well . . . .
Ardfert Minstrel [12]*chsd wnr 4 out, no imp last* 2
Clashbridane [11]*nvr nrr* 3
Also: Madam Aside (pu), Arthur (pu), Faha Point (f), Nissan Star (f)
7 ran. 6l, 2l, dist. SP 3-1.

239 - Mares Maiden 5yo+ I

151³ Hopperdante [16] . . . . K Taylor 1
made virt all, styd on wll frm 3 out, rdn out . . . .
144² Blame Barney [15]*prog to chal 3 out, no ext last* 2
185 Brigade Leader [14]*kpt on frm 2 out, nrst fin* 3
Also: 150³ Highways Sister [11] (4), Whitebarn Cailin (5), 203 Victim Of Slander (6), 149 Rose's Luck (7), Electric Can (pu), 127 Lancastrian Lass (pu), McFepend (f), 203 Scarra Darragh (f), Carrigfern (pu), 182 Rascal Street Lad (bd), 210 Dusty's Delight (f)
14 ran. 2l, 1l, 10l. SP 10-1.

240 - Mares Maiden 5yo+ II

Janice Pride [15] . . . . M Walsh 1
chsd ldrs, lft disp 2 out, ld nr fin . . . .

63 **Lunar Approach [15]***chsd ldrs, lft disp 2 out, hdd nr fin* 2
146[3] **Ballybeggan Lady [10]***nvr dang* 3
Also: 203 Rockview Supreme (4), 151 Brogeen Dubh (5), 183 Rio Star (6), Statoil (7), Real Rascal (pu), 149 The Wild Wave (pu), Irene's Call [16] (f), Inch Valley (f), 50 Harvest Delight (pu), 150 Merry Castle (f), 151 Ballyhest Fountain (pu)
14 ran. Nk, 15l, 1l. SP 6-4.

241 - Winners Of Two

184[1] **Try God [21]** ....**N Fehily** 1
prom, ld 4 out, styd on well flat ....
77[1] **Tack Room Lady [20]***prog to chal 3 out, no ext flat* ... 2
165[1] **Moll's Choice [18]***chsd ldrs, onepcd frm 2 out* 3
Also: Coolgreen [18] (4), 140 Mr Pipeman [14] (5), 3 Araqueepa (pu), 50[1] Artistic Quay (pu), 186 Inch Emperor (pu), 186[1] West Lyn (f)
9 ran. 1½l, 4l, hd. SP 7-4.

242 - Mares Lightweight

141 **Faulty Rap [19]**.........................**T Lombard** 1
hld up, prog to ld 2 out, styd on strngly ....
212 **Scarteen Lower [18]***chsd ldrs, kpt on well frm 2 out*.. 2
141 **Summerhill Express [17]***ld to 2 out, onepcd* 3
Also: 153 Ore Engineeress [12] (4), 158 Trimmer Wonder (5), 144[1] Bula Vogue (6), Fixed Assets (7), 209[1] Silent Sneeze (8), 184 Pharditu (pu), 212 Get Cracking (pu)
10 ran. 2l, 1l, 15l. SP 4-1.

243 - Adjacent Maiden

155 **Fundy [16]** ....**E Gallagher** 1
rear, prog 3 out, ld last, styd on well ....
117 **Dohney Boy [15]***chsd ldr, ld 6 out-last, onepcd*....... 2
138 **Just-N-James [10]***chsd ldrs, no dang frm 3 out*...... 3
Also: 64 Ballinvuskig Lady (4), Beans (pu), 117 Prophets Thumb (f), 77 Foherish Mist (f), 49 Ormond Beach (pu), 49[3] Tom The Boy VI (pu), Radical-Times (ro), 144 Metal Miss (pu), Queen Of The Gales (pu), 148[2] Short Circuit (pu)
13 ran. 3l, 14l, 3l. SP 3-1.

244 - Maiden 5yo+ I

185[3] **Ilengar [16]** ....**E Gallagher** 1
made all, styd on well 2 out ....
142 **Raggety Man [14]***chsd ldrs, onepcd frm 2 out*........ 2
147[3] **Forest Musk [14]***chsd ldrs, onepcd frm 2 out* 3
Also: 185 Des The Architect (4), 147 Coolflugh Hero (5), 155 Luciano The Yuppi (pu), 118[3] Castle Shelley (pu), 148 Black Fountain (pu), Clover Nook (pu), 138 Lordinthesky (pu), 156 Lazy Acres (pu), Jacky Flynn (f)
12 ran. 3l, 1l, dist. SP 2-1.

245 - Maiden 5yo+ II

188[2] **Master Kemal [17]** ....**T Lombard** 1
w.w. prog to ld 2 out, comf ....
187 **Brian Og [14]***prom, ev ch 2 out, sn outpcd* 2
185 **The Gaffer [12]***prom, ev ch 2 out, onepcd* 3
Also: 148 Galebreaker (4), Buckle Up (pu), Jorodec (f), 71 Fountain House (pu), The Snuffman (pu), 185[2] Dawn Lad (f), 55[3] Run For Brownie (f), 69 Bartlemy King (pu), 147 Terrano Star (pu)
12 ran. 4l, 5l, dist. SP 5-2.

LIMERICK FOXHOUNDS
Bruff
Sunday March 10th
SOFT

246 - Winners Of Three

141[1] **Gracemarie Kate [18]** ....**R Hurley** 1
prom, ld aft 2 out, rdn out flat..........................
206[1] **Murphys Lady [16]***prom, chsd wnr aft 2 out, onepcd*.. 2
202 **Duchess Of Padua [14]***prom, ev ch 2 out, wknd apr last* 3
Also: 127[1] Hi-Way's Gale [13] (4), 209 Looking Ahead [11] (5), 151[1] Something Sheer (pu), 44[2] Call Me Connie (pu), 153 Dromin Pride (ro)
8 ran. 4l, 4l, 2l, 6l. SP 4-1.

247 - Maiden 4 & 5yo I

Mike Stan [16] ....**B Hassett** 1
trckd ldrs, ld 2 out, styd on ....
148 **Long Drive [14]***ld to 2 out, unable qckn* 2
Cromogue Minstrel [12]*chsd ldrs, onepcd frm 2 out* 3
Also: 137 Alone Home [12] (4), 200 Where's Noel (f), Linda's Paradise (f), 199 Cruisin On Credit (f), Sam Quale (pu), Antics (pu), Ellies Nelson (pu)
10 ran. 4l, 6l, ½l. SP 7-2.

248 - Maiden 4 & 5yo II

199[2] **Camogue Bridge [16]**....................**W Ewing** 1
prom, ld & lft clr 2 out, lft clr last ....
148 **Executive Class***no dang, lft 2nd by dfctns* 2
Lucky Ross*t.o.* 3
Also: 200 Banner Year (4), Runabout (f), 148 Willbrook (f), 213 Dorgan (f), Bosco's Thatch [15] (f), Rathkerry [15] (f), 200 Mr Campus (pu)
10 ran. Dist, dist. SP 3-1.

249 - Winners Of Two

202[1] **Royal Ziero [18]** ....**W Ewing** 1
chsd ldr, btn whn lft clr last ....
204[1] **Princess Henry***t.o. whn lft 2nd last*.................. 2
Also: 126[1] I Haven't A Buck [20] (ur)
3 ran. Dist. SP 5-4.

250 - Maiden 6yo+

125[2] **Tearaway King [21]**......................**E Bolger** 1
ld/disp til ld 2 out, sn wll clr ....
137 **Fifth Generation [15]***ld/disp to 2 out, no ch wth wnr aft* 2
Minor Key [10]*prom til wknd 2 out* 3
Also: 206 Guirns Shop (4), 78 Supreme Flyer (5), 167 Digacre (6), 155 Sammy Sunshine (f), 79 Aesops Fables (bd), 154 Milenkeh (ur), 155 Forold (pu), 201[3] An Oon Iss An Owl (f), 206[2] Fruit Town (pu), 201 Nollaig (pu), 201 Wylfa Boy (pu), 206 Mr Connie Vee (pu), 205[3] Fort Zeddaan (f), 201 Head Bottle Washer (f), Take The Pledge (f), Mount Druid (pu)
19 ran. Dist, dist, 1l, dist. SP 5-2.

251 - Open Lightweight

123[1] **Itsalltheonetodev [17]**..................**B Hassett** 1
made all, clr 3 out, unchal ....
152 **Bit Of A Touch [10]***chsd wnr, no imp frm 3 out*....... 2
37 **Howarya Harry***t.o.* 3
Also: Hopefully True (f)
4 ran. 25l, dist. SP Evens.

252 - Mares Maiden I

203[2] **Selm Mary [15]**...........................**W Ewing** 1
prom, ld 5 out, styd on wll flat ....
151 **Crabeg Hazel [13]***prom, 3rd 5 out, chal last, no ext*... 2
204 **Idiot's Surprise [12]***prom, outpcd 3 out, kpt on*....... 3
Also: 204 Bunny Lightening [12] (4), 107 Mauradonna (5), 151 Daytime Dancer (f), Mounthenry Lady (pu), Strong Stern (f), Forgoodnessjake VI (f), Knock Derk (pu), Scottish Socks (pu), 204 Lantern Spark (f), Lothian Magic (pu), 43 Ballycar Princess (pu)
14 ran. 5l, 3l, 1l, dist. SP 2-1.

253 - Mares Maiden II

183[2] **Scarlet River [15]**.........................**B Moran** 1
prom, ld 5 out, mstk last, styd on well ....
203 **Love Actinium [13]***chal 3 out, ev ch last, no ext*...... 2
Oriental Blaze [10]*chsd wnr 5 out-3 out, onepcd* 3
Also: 206 Camden Lamp (4), 204 My New Merc (5), 43 Frangapini (pu), 203 Yasgourra (f), 12 She Wont Stop (pu), 204 Queen Of The Suir (pu), 149[3] Lady Clarina (f), Katies Kisses VI (pu), Miss Lynch (pu), Seatyrn (pu), 203 Knocktoran Lady (f)
14 ran. 4l, 10l, 2l, dist. SP 5-4.

IVEAGH HARRIERS
Maralin
Saturday March 16th
HEAVY

254 - Open Lightweight

175[1] **Jims Choice [21]** ....**R Patton** 1
ld to 5 out, ld apr last, ran on well
216[1] **Lacken Beau [19]***ld 5 out til rdn & hdd apr last, one-pcd* 2
170[2] **Gale Griffin***t.o.* 3
Also: 216 J J's Hope (pu), 175[3] Fay Lin (ur), 170 Quayfield (ur)
6 ran. 4l, dist. SP 6-4.

255 - Maiden 5 & 6yo I

172 **Coq Hardi Dancer [18]** ....**W Ewing** 1
prom, ld 3 out, clr apr last, comf
Donard Son [13]*ld 5 out-3 out, no ch wnr aft* 2
174[2] **Sand de Vince [10]***prom, ev ch 3 out, sn btn* 3
Also: 172 Thats My Luck (4), Bridge End (pu), 172 Bell Hunter (pu), 172 Just Horseplay (pu), 172 Cabra Boy (pu), Denfield (pu), 217 Chase The Sun (ur)
10 ran. 15l, 10l, 3l. SP 3-1.

256 - Maiden 5 & 6yo II

97 **The Convincer [15]** ....**A Martin** 1
ld 3rd, clr 3 out, styd on
219 **Rolier [12]***chsd wnr to 4 out, lft 2nd nxt, no imp* 2
173[3] **Longmore Boy [11]***chsd ldrs, onepcd frm 3 out* 3
Also: Just Harvey (pu), 173 Secret Prince (f), Che Amigo (pu), 173 Just Spellbound (f), 231 Falas Lad (pu), Ballinavary VI (pu), Raleagh Muggins (ur), MC Clatchey (pu)
11 ran. 6l, 2l. SP 3-1.

257 - Winners Of One

Claire Me [17] ....**A Tate** 1
prog 3 out, ld apr last, styd on well
170 **Gawn Inn [16]***prom, ev ch last, no ext* 2
177[1] **Cabbery Rose [14]***ld to apr last, no ext* 3
Also: 174[1] Staffy's Boy [12] (4), 170 Hall's Mill (pu), Longmore (pu), 92 More Than Most (pu), 217[1] French Lady (pu), 176[1] La Maja (pu), 170 Manhattan Prince (pu), Hillview Susie (pu), 234 Cool Yule (pu), 180[1] Pats Cross (f), 171 Chene Rose (pu)
14 ran. 1l, 10l, 4l. SP 12-1.

258 - Mares Maiden I

176 **Kilmainhwood [15]** ....**P Graffin** 1
ld 5 out, clr whn blnd 2 out, fin tired
215[3] **Half Scotch [12]***chsd wnr 4 out, no imp* 2
176 **Musical Patch [10]***ld to 5 out, 3rd & btn nxt* 3
Also: 215 Iveagh Lady (4), 215 Dernamay (pu), 99 Farlough Lady (pu), 169 Willowmere (ur), 95 Maid O'Tully (pu), 178 Mourne Miner (pu), 176 Miss Top (pu), 176 Bolesa's Joy (pu), 169 Gilloway Princess (pu), Lillooet (pu), 178 Damolly Rose (pu), 178 Floruceva (ur), 215 Lake Majestic (pu), Little Bopper (pu), 176 Let Her Run Wild (pu), Royal Aristocrat (pu)
19 ran. 8l, 8l, 4l. SP 3-1.

259 - Mares Maiden II

178[2] **Knights Pleasure [14]** ....**A Fleming** 1
hld up, prog 3 out, ld apr last, drvn out
214 **Fidsprit [13]***ld 5 out til jmpd rght & hdd 2 out, no ext* .. 2
178 **Goldwren [12]***prog to disp 3 out, hdd & btn aft nxt* 3
Also: 96[3] Maccarrons Run [11] (4), 177 Sarah's Cherrie (f), 216 Cherryflame (pu), 176 Glenbrin (pu), 176 Cardinals Lady (pu), 176[2] Golden Start (pu), Ollar Lady (pu), 177 Greenfield Lass (pu), 177 Arctic Leader (pu), Chanauley (pu), 215 Melodic Lady (f), Island Harriet (ur), 178 Denel de (pu), 177 Bobby Blazer (pu), 176[3] Midi Minstrel (pu), 215 Sapphire 'N' Silver (f)
19 ran. 2l, 2l, 2l. SP 2-1.

260 - Maiden 5yo+ I

180[3] **Loughdoo [15]** ....**L Gracey** 1
hld up, ld 4 out, sn clr
173 **Sharimage [10]***chsd ldrs, 2nd frm 3 out, no imp* 2
219 **Stag Hunt***clr ldr til wknd & hdd 4 out* 3
Also: Castle Royal (pu), 173 Florida Or Bust (pu), 180 Dick's Cabin (pu), Bonquist (pu), Panda Nova (pu), 180 Miners Valley (pu), Christimatt (ur), 180 Laergy Cripperty (pu), Steady Johnny (pu)
12 ran. 15l, 15l. SP 4-5.

261 - Maiden 5yo+ II

179 **Ahogill [15]** ....**P Graffin** 1
prom, ld 3 out, clr apr last, kpt on
180[2] **Takeithandy [12]***cls up, chsd wnr 2 out, btn whn mstk last* 2
180 **Craigelle***nvr dang, t.o.* 3
Also: 179 Fidoon (4), A Bit Of A Monkey (pu), Leslieshill (pu), 179[2] Cahills Hill (ur), 179 Kilmacrew (f), Rashee Lady (pu), 214 Tyrella Clear View (pu), 219 Fill Your Boots (ro), Swaning Around (pu)
12 ran. 10l, dist, dist. SP 4-1.

262 - Winners Of Two

235 **Miss Elizabeth [18]** ....**A Martin** 1
prom, ld apr 3 out, sn clr
197[1] **Ballinaboola Grove [13]***chsd ldrs, no imp wnr frm 3 out* 2
171 **River Magnet [11]***nvr dang* 3
Also: 170 Salvation (pu), 216[3] Rontom (pu)
5 ran. 15l, 6l. SP Evens.

LIMERICK
Sunday March 17th

263 - 2¾m Hun Chase

145[2] **Bally Riot (Ire) 12.0** ....**Mr P Fenton** 1
194[1] **Quattro 11.7 7a** ....**Mr A C Coyle** 2
Divali (Ire) 11.7 7a ....**Mr J P Moloney** 3
Lake Tour (Ire) 11.6 3a 4
Loftus Lad (Ire) 11.9 5a 5
Duchess Of Padua (Ire) 11.4 7a 2ow 6
153[1] Okdo 11.7 7a 7
Elwill Glory (Ire) 11.7 7a 8
198[2] Escheat 11.2 7a 9
Bit Of A Citizen (Ire) 10.8 7a 10
The Parish Pump (Ire) 12.0 *(fav)* .... f
145[3] Lakeview Lad (Ire) 11.7 7a .... ur
Prayon Parson (Ire) 12.0 .... pu
Carrolls Rock (Ire) 10.13 7a .... ur
14 ran. Hd, ¾l, 1½l, 11l. Time 5m 57.7s. SP 7-2.

SOUTH CO DUBLIN
Naas Point-To-Point Course
Sunday March 17th
SOFT

264 - Winners Of Two

220[3] **Parahandy [20]** ....**D O'Brien** 1
prom, chal 2 out, ld flat, ran on well
102[1] **Newtown Rosie [18]***prom, ld 3 out til hdd & no ext flat* 2
191[1] **King Torus [15]***chsd ldrs, onepcd aft 3 out* 3
Also: 169[3] Mrs Giggs (4), 102 Slemish Mist (pu), Princess Breda (pu)
6 ran. 2l, 10l, dist. SP 9-4.

265 - Open Lightweight

168[2] **Tasse Du The [22]** ....**A Martin** 1
made all, rdn 3 out, styd on well
158 **Laura's Beau [21]***prog hlfwy, chal 3 out, no ext aft nxt* 2

169² **Missing Lady [10]***nvr dang* 3
Also: 104 Astounded (4), Upshepops (pu), 161 Poulgillie (pu)
6 ran. 3l, dist, 6l. SP Evens.

266 - Maiden I

Not A Razu [16]. . . . . .D Costello 1
prom, chal 3 out, rdn to ld nr fin, tired . . . .
192² **Difficult Decision [16]***prom, ld 3 out, hdd nr fin, tired* 2
109 **Pearl Of Orient [14]***chsd ldrs, kpt on onepcd frm 3 out*. 3
Also: Venerdi Santo [13] (4), Father Prescott [10] (5), Noble Street (6), 237 Almaurita (pu), 227 Bens Unyoke (pu), Boreen Boy (f), Curragh Ranger (pu), 161 Golden Walk (ur), 158 Graiguesallagh (f), 227 Shillelagh Oak (pu), 56 Rusnetto (pu), 161 Thought Reader (pu), Blackmountaingiant (pu), 227 Up The Rock (pu)
17 ran. Hd, 6l, 2l, 10l, dist. SP 7-2.

267 - Maiden II

201 **Rat Race [15] . . . . .S Mahon** 1
prom, ld 5 out-3 out, lf tin ld nxt, kpt on . . . .
Grafy Hill [14]*chsd ldrs, lft 2nd 2 out, styd on, nrst fin* 2
110 **Digin For Gold [13]***mstks, chsd ldrs, kpt on frm 2 out, nvr nrr* 3
Also: 223 Sir Larry [12] (4), 156 Park Duke (5), Awalkintheclouds (pu), 193 Blackie Connors (pu), 139 Cash For Bash (f), 161³ Dearmistershatter (pu), Executive Chief (f), 194 Footsy Murray (pu), Jasper Jack (pu), 174 Normus (pu), Perryman (f), 161 The Toor Trail (pu), Turos (f), Kelly's Perk (pu)
17 ran. 2l, 4l, 3l, dist. SP 3-1.

268 - Maiden 7yo+ I

Into The Swing [19] . . . . .A Martin 1
ld hlfwy, qcknd clr frm last . . . .
Stonewall Curtin [17]*prog hlfwy, chsd wnr apr 2 out, no imp last*. 2
101 **Tamer's Run [14]***chsd wnr hlfwy til apr 2 out, onepcd* 3
Also: Youcat [12] (4), 111 Big Spender (pu), 197 Cashel Moss (pu), 166 Duncaha Hero (pu), 112 Erinsborough (ref), M Macg (f), 160 M T Pockets (f), 68 Sandyrock (pu), 134 Solitary Spirit (pu), 194 Venture On (pu), 98 Well Recovered (pu), 190³ Brewery Light (f), 237 Reel Him In (pu)
16 ran. 4l, 10l, 5l. SP Evens.

269 - Maiden 7yo+ II

191² **Wejem [18]. . . . . .Lucy Townsley** 1
prom frm hlfwy, ld 4 out, styd on well . . . .
194 **Jaybe's Friend [17]***prom frm hlfwy, prssd wnr 4 out, no ext last* 2
101 **Mornay Des Garnes***ld to 4 out, sn btn*. 3
Also: 190 Pauper Boice (4), 228 Shrule Hill (5), Givemeyourhand (6), Double Opportunity (pu), 228 Eastern Fox (pu), 250 Milenkeh (f), 89 Siamsa Brae (pu), Station Man (pu), 166 Taste Of Freedom (pu), Woodhaven Lad (pu), Castle Union (pu)
14 ran. 3l, dist, 10l, 10l, 15l. SP 5-2.

270 - Mares Maiden I

101 **Carrig Conn [15] . . . . .H Cleary** 1
w.w. prog to ld 4 out, rdn out flat. . . . .
225 **Key Door [14]***prom, chal apr last, kpt on well* 2
163³ **Royal Star [13]***rear, styd on frm 3 out, nrst fin*. 3
Also: 195 Push Gently [13] (4), Stradbally Jane (5), Moydanganrye (6), 215 Teralisa (7), Awaytoday (pu), Cynical Wit (ro), Killaligam Kim (pu), Kings Alibi (pu), 107 Pitmar (pu), 195 Tearaway Sarah (pu), The Buck Pony (pu)
14 ran. 1l, 4l, 1l, 15l, dist, 3l. SP 6-4.

271 - Mares Maiden II

233³ **Handsome Maid [15] . . . . .D Valentine** 1
prom, ld 4 out, mstks 3 out & nxt, styd on . . . .
36 **Killerk Lady [14]***prog to chs wnr 3 out, no ext last* 2
Brian's Delight [13]*prog 3 out, no ext apr last* 3
Also: 196³ Time To Smile (4), 196 Trembles Choice (5), Currasilla (f), 106 Lismoy (f), 233 New Legislation (pu), 196 Proud Princess (pu), 26 Red Mollie (pu), Satcotino (f), Calico Drum (pu), 195 Sataldo (pu)
13 ran. 2l, 2l, dist, dist. SP 5-2.

272 - Adjacent Maiden

Seventh Symphony [14] . . . . .J O'Connell 1
prom, ld 5 out, blnd 3 out, all out. . . . .
236 **Almost An Angel [14]***prssd wnr 4 out, ev ch flat, not qckn* 2
104 **Captains View [10]***nvr dang*. 3
Also: An Tuiodoir (4), Castle Hero (f), 102 Cool It (pu), 237 Galloping Giggs (f), 219 Harvemac (pu), 200 Nobodywantsme (bd), On The Way Home (pu), 198 Spinans Hill (pu), 166 The Dance (pu), 232 Tobar Bhride (pu), 233 Wewillsee (pu)
14 ran. ¾l, 10l. SP 3-1.

DOWN ROYAL
Monday March 18th
YIELDING

273 - 3m 1f Hun Chase

Over The Maine (Ire) 11.11 3a. . . .Mr B R Hamilton 1
See Just There (Ire) 11.7 7a. . . . . .Miss L Townsley 2
(fav)
168 **Amme Enaek (Ire) 11.2 7a (bl) . . . . . . .Mr B M Cash** 3

168 Mister Black (Ire) 12.0 4
Cool Rocket (Ire) 11.7 7a 5
168 Moylena 11.2 7a . . . . f
No One Knows (Ire) 11.9 . . . . pu
Blennerville (Ire) 11.2 7a . . . . f
Spire Hill (Ire) 11.7 7a . . . . ur
Pilbara (Ire) 11.7 7a . . . . f
10 ran. 3l, 11l, 9l, 15l. SP 7-1.

CLOYNE HARRIERS
Cloyne
Saturday March 23rd
HEAVY

274 - Maiden 4yo

College Land [16] . . . . .D Costello 1
prom, ld 3 out, styd on well . . . .
Wayward King [14]*chsd wnr aft 3 out, kpt on onepcd* 2
Fountain Page [13]*chsd ldrs, styd on onepcd frm 3 out*. 3
Also: Wishing William [11] (4), 208 Claudia Electric (5), 208 Clonageera (6), Water Font (f), Clash Of The Gales (pu), Boss Doyle (pu)
9 ran. 3l, 1l, 6l. SP 4-5.

275 - Maiden 5yo

Buck Related [16] . . . . .D Costello 1
made all, clr 2 out, styd on well. . . . .
244 **Coolflugh Hero [13]***chsd ldrs, 2nd frm 3 out, no imp wnr* 2
No Problem*nvr nrr*. 3
Also: 147 Poachers Lamp (4), Martha's Boy (5), 213 Robin Of Loxley (6), 74 Geragh Road (pu), Castle Avenue (pu), Silent Pond (pu), 213 Bosco's Touch (pu), 114 Super Fred (pu), Master Jake (pu), Another Berry (f), Flashing Rock (pu), 245 Jorodec (f), 138 Timmy Tuff (pu)
16 ran. 10l, 15l, 2l. SP 5-2.

276 - Winners Of One

186³ **Warning Call [19] . . . . .J Motherway** 1
prom, chal 3 out, ld last, styd on well . . . .
212 **Fine Affair [17]***prom, ld 5 out-last, wknd flat* 2
245¹ **Master Kemal***chsd ldrs 3 out, sn btn* 3
Also: 154¹ I'm A Chippy (pu), Minstrel Sam (pu), 186 Burkean Melody (pu), 209 Our Blossom (pu), 242 Bula Vogue (pu), 212 Trimmer Princess (pu), 36¹ Coolree Lord (pu)
10 ran. 5l, dist. SP 5-2.

277 - Confined Maiden

144 **Finnuala Supreme [14] ....D Budds** 1
trckd ldrs, ld 3 out, hld on
244 **Black Fountain [14]***chal 3 out, just hld flat* 2
Also: 245 Run For Brownie (pu), Monagurra (pu), 150 Tourig Dante (pu), 76 Monadante (pu), Miss Josephine (pu), Ardvillan Prince (pu), 211 Cahermone Lady (pu), 150 Everlaughing (ur)
10 ran. 1l. SP 3-1.

278 - Open Lightweight

184² **Faha Gig [20] ....K O'Sullivan** 1
hld up, prog to ld 2 out, styd on well
242 **Trimmer Wonder [18]***prog 3 out, chsd wnr apr last, no imp* 2
242 **Pharditu [17]***nvr nrr* 3
Also: 152 Loftus Lad (4), 209 Cooladerra Lady (pu), 224¹ Well Armed (pu)
6 ran. 3l, 3l, dist. SP 4-5.

279 - Mares Maiden 5yo+ I

182 **The Pulpit [15] ....D Budds** 1
prom, ld hlfwy, styd on well 2 out
211 **Ballinacubby Pride [12]***chsd wnr 5 out, no imp 2 out* 2
119 **Lady Of Means [10]***nvr nrr* 3
Also: Lios Na Maol (f), 211 Princess Diga (pu), 142 High Park Lady (pu), 210 Liskilnewabbey (pu), 182³ Killatty Player (pu), 43 Nagle Rice (pu), 120 Clogheen Lass (f), 113 Teamtalk (f)
11 ran. 10l, 5l. SP 7-4.

280 - Mares Maiden 5yo+ II

182 **Alice Sheer Thorn [15] ....M Phillips** 1
in tch, lft in ld 3 out, styd on well frm last
207³ **Supersonia***prog to chal 2 out, wknd rpdly apr last* 2
Also: 239 Scarra Darragh (pu), 210³ Gentle Leader (pu), 144 Tipperaryenteprise (pu), 252 Forgoodnessjake VI (pu), 243 Foherish Mist (pu), 211 Harvey's Cream (pu), Miss Metal (ur), Haven Lady (pu), Frosty Morn (pu)
11 ran. Dist. SP 4-1.

TYNAN & ARMAGH
Farmacaffley
Saturday March 23rd
SOFT

281 - Confined Lightweight

97 **O'Fiaich's Hope [20] ....P Graffin** 1
made all, styd on well frm 2 out
219¹ **Kylnhill [17]***prog 5 out, chal nxt, sn outpcd* 2
258 **Dernamay [11]***nvr dang, no ch whn hmpd & lft 3rd last* 3
Also: 237 Tassagh Boy (4), 179 Highland Buck (f), 178¹ You Name It (f), Drumorgan (su)
7 ran. 6l, 20l, dist. SP 7-1.

282 - Maiden 4-6yo I

173 **Ballymacrevan [15] ....K Ross** 1
ld 5th, made rest, rdn & styd on apr last
108 **Boycetrus [14]***chsd ldrs, mstk 4 out, kpt on wll apr last* 2
256² **Rolier***nvr dang* 3
Also: 255 Bell Hunter (4), Inspector Stalker (pu), 255 Cabra Boy (pu), 260 Bonquist (pu), 172³ Olumo (pu), 217² Pharbrook Lad (pu), 173 Shuil Mor (pu), 172 Springfarm Rath (pu), 174 Grove Victor (pu), 174 Kenellen (pu)
13 ran. 2l, 20l, 20l. SP 5-1.

283 - Maiden 4-6yo II

173 **Uncle Art [16] ....B Hamilton** 1
cls up, chal 3 out, ld apr last, styd on well
256 **MC Clatchey [11]***disp til ld 4 out, hdd & wknd apr last* 2
169 **Sinergia [10]***prom, mstk 4 out, sn btn* 3
Also: 261 Leslieshill (4), Oldtown Glen (5), Lord Basil (pu), Lynx Marine (ref), 173 Wayside Spin (su), Half Brandy (pu), Ballydesmond (pu), The Client (f), Opening Quote (pu)
12 ran. 15l, 2l, 3l, dist. SP 6-4.

284 - Open Lightweight

254¹ **Jims Choice [21] ....R Patton** 1
trckd ldr, ld 4 out, drvn out frm last
173¹ **Over The Way [20]***prog 4 out, sn chsd wnr, chal last, hng lft flat* 2
235 **Temporale [10]***ld to 4 out, sn btn* 3
Also: Copper Friend (pu), 171 Moyavo Lady (pu), Karens Leader (pu), 254 J J's Hope (pu), 171 Ballywoodock VI (pu)
8 ran. 2l, dist. SP 6-4.

285 - Mares Maiden I

171 **Castledell [13] ....Julia Murdoch** 1
disp 5th til hdd & mstk 3 out, btn whn lft clr last
214² **Sideways Sally [10]***disp 5th til rdn & wknd 3 out, lft 2nd last* 2
176 **Follow Your Dream***no dang, lft 3rd last* 3
Also: 258 Iveagh Lady (4), 96 Salaran (ro), 258 Willowmere (pu), Darshaba (f), It'snotsimple (pu), 259 Glenbrin [15] (f), 178 Incense Doll (pu)
10 ran. 12l, 6l, 8l. SP 12-1.

286 - Mares Maiden II

258 **Royal Aristocrat [15] ....R Arthur** 1
prog 4 out, ld apr last, styd on well
258 **Floruceva [12]***pllng, ld 4 out til apr last, wknd* 2
259 **Arctic Leader [10]***chsd ldrs, no imp frm 2 out* 3
Also: 258 Gilloway Princess (4), 215 Cheerio Fidel VI (5), 259 Ollar Lady (6), 261 Rashee Lady (pu), Quickly (pu), 178³ Ngala (pu)
9 ran. 7l, 7l, 6l, 6l, 20l. SP 3-1.

287 - Winners Of Two

Layitontheline [20].....................P Graffin 1
trckd ldr, ld apr last, all out
172¹ **Shuil Daingean [20]***trckd ldr 5 out, chal last, just hld* 2
254 **Quayfield [17]***ld to apr last, onepcd* 3
Also: 170¹ Private Yashkan [15] (4), 257 Manhattan Prince [13] (5), 170 Callieálla (ur), 180 Giorgione (pu), 179¹ High Star (f), 255¹ Coq Hardi Dancer (f), 218² Hiltonstown Lass (ur), 255 Chase The Sun (pu), 173 Hanleys Call (pu)
12 ran. ½l, 6l, 6l, 5l. SP 10-1.

288 - Maiden 7yo+

260 **Castle Royal [17].......................W Ewing** 1
cls up, ld 5 out, styd on well apr last
261³ **Craigelle [10]***cls up, chsd wnr 5 out, btn apr last* 2
219 **Sheer Indulgence***chsd ldng pair 4 out, mstk nxt, btn aft* 3
Also: 261 Fidoon (4), 169 Ordain (5), Zieg (6), Political Star (pu), 219 Proceedwithcaution (pu), Flodart (pu), 175 Moyavo Lad (pu), Rath Mear (pu), 260 Laergy Cripperty (pu), Pauls Point (ro), 261 Kilmacrew (pu), Sir Gallop (pu), 260 Steady Johnny (pu), 180 Neely (pu)
17 ran. 20l, 5l, 6l, 3l, dist. SP 4-5.

SCARTEEN FOXHOUNDS
Tipperary P-To-P Course
Sunday March 24th
HEAVY

289 - Confined Maiden

250 **Digacre [16]............................R Hurley** 1
trckd ldr hlfwy, ld 4 out, clr last, styd on well
125 **Sultan Of Swing [13]***ld hlfwy-4 out, onepcd* 2
128 **Manley Girl [11]***4th hlfwy, styd on onepcd frm 3 out* 3
Also: 247 Antics (4), 40 September Stephen (pu), Cozy Cottage (f), 248³ Lucky Ross (pu), Loslomos (pu), 204 Kochnie (f), Dinan (pu), Another Check (pu)
11 ran. 8l, 4l, 15l. SP 8-1.

290 - Mares Maiden I

253² Love Actinium [16] ....G Mulcaire 1
ld 4 out, kpt on wll frm 2 out ....
252³ Idiot's Surprise [14]*prog to chal 2 out, no ext last* 2
142 Sweet Castlehyde [11]*prog to chal 2 out, sn btn* 3
Also: 253 Yasgourra (4), 150 Just Placed (5), 83³ Pleasing Melody (pu), 252 Mauradonna (pu), Moneyfromaustralia (pu), Nine Out Of Ten (su), 270 Kings Alibi (pu), 239 Dusty's Delight (pu), 64² Henbits Dream (pu), 142 Loughlins Pride (pu), 252 Ballycar Princess (pu), 207 Appendix Lady (pu), 252 Bunny Lightening (f)
16 ran. 5l, 10l, 15l. SP 3-1.

291 - Mares Maiden II

Cloncannon Bell [15]..............Lulu Olivefalk 1
prog 3 out, ld nxt, sn clr ....
226 Handball*mstks, ld to 2 out, sn btn* 2
127 No Swap*nvr dang* 3
Also: 233² Ballybriken Castle (4), Swiss Thyne (pu), 253 Camden Lamp (pu), 163² Sunczech (pu), 252 Daytime Dancer (pu), 226 Betty Balfour (f), 253 My New Merc (pu), 253 She Wont Stop (pu), Fairy Thorn (f), 232 Mona Lita (pu), Solo Minstrel (pu), 253 Miss Lynch (pu), 239 Lancastrian Lass (pu), Thady's Remedy (pu), 253 Frangapini (pu)
18 ran. 20l, 20l, hd. SP 10-1.

292 - Maiden 4 & 5yo I

Granstown Lake [15] ....D Harney 1
prom, ld 3 out, styd on well ....
247 Sam Quale [13]*chsd wnr 3 out, no ext apr last* 2
248 Willbrook [12]*bhnd til ran on 2 out, nvr nrr* 3
Also: 150 Riberetto's Girl (4), 248 Banner Year (5), Hunters Chorus (f), The Fuzz Buzz Wuzz (pu), Legal Whisper (pu), 46 Meldante VI (ur), Up The Banner VI (pu), Hazy Mist (pu)
11 ran. 5l, 3l, 20l. SP 4-1.

293 - Maiden 4 & 5yo II

114 Black Abbey [16] ....M Cahill 1
prog 4 out, ld nxt, sn clr ....
248² Executive Class*prom, chsd wnr 3 out, sn btn* 2
187³ Castle Tiger Bay*ld to 3 out, wknd* 3
Also: 52 Lightoak Lad (f), 147² Action Lad (ref), 213 Milford Road (f), 190 Flying Fellow (bd), 247 Linda's Paradise (f), Well Doctor (pu), Odds On (pu), 121 Tom Deely (f)
11 ran. Dist, dist. SP 6-1.

294 - Winners Of One

250¹ Tearaway King [24]....................E Bolger 1
hld up, ld 3 out, sn clr, easily ....
202² Up For Ransome [18]*disp to 3 out, no ch wth wnr aft* 2
Also: 202 Bayview Prince (f), 125 The Breaser Fawl (pu), 157² Locklan (pu), 233¹ Slavica (f), 265 Upshepops (pu), 202 Jigg's Forge VI (pu)
8 ran. 20l. SP 4-6.

295 - Mares

198 Just A Breeze [20] ....T Cloke 1
hld up, prog 3 out, ld nxt, styd on well ....
202 Kizzy Rose [16]*prom, ld 5 out-2 out, sn btn* 2
184 The Vicarette [13]*prom til wknd 3 out* 3
Also: 246 Looking Ahead [10] (4), 242 Ore Engineeress (5), 234³ Toby's Friend (6), 246 Hi-Way's Gale (7), 246³ Duchess Of Padua (pu), 246² Murphys Lady (pu), 242³ Summerhill Express (pu), 230 Satin Emma (pu), 184 What Thing (co), 252¹ Selm Mary (pu)
13 ran. 12l, 8l, 10l. SP 4-1.

296 - Maiden 6yo+ I

250³ Minor Key [17] ....R Hurley 1
made all, clr 2 out, unchal ....
Minella Star [14]*prog to chs wnr 2 out, no imp* 2
190 Festival Light*nvr dang* 3
Also: 201 Rosevalley (4), 86 Greywood (pu), 269 Milenkeh (pu), 244 Clover Nook (pu), 197 Baybuck (pu), Reinskea (pu), 250 Guirns Shop (ur), 155 Dunkel (pu)
11 ran. 8l, 20l, 10l. SP Evens.

297 - Maiden 6yo+ II

Decor [17] ....C Murphy 1
prog 5 out, ld apr 2 out, sn clr ....
237 Trackman [14]*ld to apr 2 out, onepcd* 2
250 Sammy Sunshine [14]*chsd ldrs, onepcd frm 3 out* 3
Also: 250 Forold (f), Cooling Chimes (pu), Junior Moss (pu), 124 Corries Hill (pu), Cahergowan (f), 142² Prayon Parson (f)
9 ran. 10l, ½l. SP 5-1.

ORIEL HARRIERS
Dundalk Point-To-Point Course
Sunday March 24th
HEAVY

298 - Adjacent Lightweight

235³ Talk To You Later [23] ....R Barnwell 1
lft in ld 5th, clr last, unchal ....
235 Find Out More [18]*chsd wnr 4 out, no imp* 2
272³ Captains View*t.o.* 3
Also: 216 Schweppes Tonic (f), 232 Executive Bill (f), 214¹ Duprey (bd), 171 Leave It Be (bd), 219¹ Lingering Hope (f), 257 French Lady (pu), 259¹ Knights Pleasure (bd), 82 Strong Performance (pu), 268 Well Recovered (pu)
12 ran. 15l, dist. SP 6-1.

299 - Maiden 4-6yo I

109 Only One [16] ....J O'Connell 1
prom, ld 5 out, hld on well flat ....
230² Cloughan Boy [15] 2D
174 Sam's Man [14]*prog to chal apr 2 out, onepcd, fin 3rd, promoted* 2
Killaligan Kim [11]*prssd wnr 3 out, bnt nxt, fin 4th, promoted* 3
Also: 256 Secret Prince (4), 256 Raleagh Muggins (5), 266 Curragh Ranger (6), 260² Sharimage (f), Burrell Wharf (f), Glendarragh (pu), 231³ Sporting Vision (pu), Clifford (pu), Awalkinthewoods (pu), 256 Ballinavary VI (pu)
14 ran. 1l, 4l, 10l, 4l, 7l, 6l. SP 12-1.

300 - Maiden 4-6yo II

174 Garethson [14]........................A Martin 1
prog to disp aft 3 out, ld flat, jnd post ....
255 Denfield [14] ....I Buchanan 1
prog to disp aft 3 out, hdd flat, rallied post ....
231² Castleconner [11]*chsd ldrs, lft in ld 3 out, sn hdd & no ext* 3
Also: 267 Dearmistershatter (4), 267 Normus (ur), Cairncross (f), 260 Florida Or Bust (f), 272 Nobodywantsme (pu), Herb Superb (f), 172² Drop The Act (f), 219³ Irenes Treasure (pu), 272 On The Way Home (pu), Robotic (ur), 174 Spectre Brown [10] (ur)
14 ran. Dd-ht, 8l, 8l.
Garethson, 2/1. Denfield, 3/1.

301 - Mares Maiden I

270³ Royal Star [15] ....J O'Connell 1
trckd ldrs, ld apr last, sn clr ....
233 Friendly Bid*ld/disp til apr last, wknd* 2
Also: 214³ Ellies Pride (f), Tremollina (f), 259 Cardinals Lady (f), 258 Let Her Run Wild (f), 215 Moneycarragh (f), 233 Gerry's Delight (pu), Red Shoon (f), 232 Little Doe (f), 259 Golden Start (f), 233 Aunt Emeralds (f)
12 ran. Dist. SP 5-2.

302 - Mares Maiden II

230³ Mordella Lass [15]....................L Lennon 1
made all, clr apr last, kpt on ....
106 Sally Willows [12]*chsd ldrs, styd on to tk 2nd nr fin* ... 2
259 Sapphire 'N' Silver [12]*prom, ev ch 3 out, no ext apr last* 3
Also: 259 Melodic Lady (4), Skin Graft (bd), 259 Bobby Blazer (pu), 259 Denel de (ur), 165³ Pils Invader (ur), Manhattan Jewel (ur), Young

Bebe (pu), 233 Howesshecutting (f)
11 ran. 8l, nk, dist. SP 14-1.

303 - Open Lightweight

168[3] **Teal Bridge [22]..........................G Elliott** 1
trckd ldr hlfwy, ld 2 out, sn clr
235 **Red Express VI [18]***disp til ld 6th, hdd & no ext 2 out* 2
262[1] **Miss Elizabeth***chsd ldrs, rdn & btn 5 out* 3
Also: 235[2] Voldi (4), 234 Buaile Bos (5), Torenaga Hill (pu)
6 ran. 10l, dist, 4l, dist. SP 6-4.

304 - Winners Of Two

264[2] **Newtown Rosie [22]....................S Mahon** 1
made all, in cmmnd whn lft clr last
162[1] **Diorraing [11]***prog 5 out, disp 2nd 3 out, sn btn, lft 2nd agn last* 2
257 **Pats Cross [11]***alwys bhnd* 3
Also: 257 La Maja (f), 287 Private Yashkan [19] (f), 262 Salvation (pu), 130[3] Harry's Secret (pu)
7 ran. Dist, 1½l. SP 7-2.

305 - Maiden 7yo+

269[2] **Jaybe's Friend [16] ....P Graffin** 1
cls up, lft in ld 5 out, drvn out
236[3] **Annie's Arthur [16]***chsd wnr 5 out, chal apr last, kpt on* 2
Toss Up*t.o.* 3
Also: 269 Siamsa Brae (4), 260 Dick's Cabin (5), 268 Solitary Spirit (6), Darker Still (pu), Dara Knight (pu), 219 Leannes Man (f), 260[3] Stag Hunt (f), With Credit (f), 261 Cahills Hill (f), 167 Ballybrit (ur), 111 Oldson (f)
14 ran. 1l, dist, 25l, 8l, 8l. SP 5-4.

DUHALLOW FOXHOUNDS
Dromahane
Sunday March 24th
HEAVY

306 - Confined Maiden

138 **Saradante [15]........................E Gallagher** 1
prom, ld 3 out, kpt on well
146[2] **Finnow Thyne [14]***chsd wnr 3 out, styd on* 2
244[3] **Forest Musk [11]***chsd ldrs, onepcd 3 out* 3
Also: 183[3] Solar Castle (4), Old Trafford (5), 114 Mr Boomaleen (6), 182 Ann Black (pu), 245[2] Brian Og (ur), Nicenames (pu), Glitter Girl (pu), 187 Round Pound (pu), 245 Bartlemy King (pu), 240 Statoil (pu), 154 Riverdale Express (f), 200[3] Mr Freeman (ro)
15 ran. 2l, 10l, 5l. SP 5-2.

307 - Maiden 4yo

One For Navigation [18] ....D Costello 1
cls up, ld 4 out, mstk 2 out, sn clr
274 **Water Font [12]***chsd wnr 3 out, no imp* 2
Brickanmore*nvr dang.* 3
Also: 238 Nissan Star (4), Tonmarie Chance (pu), 208[3] Lord Harry (f), Hydro Brook (pu), 208 Kilcully Talbot (pu)
8 ran. 15l, 10l, 2l. SP 6-4.

308 - Mares Maiden 5yo+ I

182[2] **Ballintee Belle [15] ....J Flynn** 1
prom, ld 4 out-apr last, lft in ld last, drvn out
151 **Riot Lady [15]***chsd ldrs, btn whn lft wth ev ch last, no ext* 2
239[2] **Blame Barney [11]***chsd ldrs, onepcd 3 out* 3
Also: 240[3] Ballybeggan Lady (f), 83 Cosie Cartel (f), Keep Strong (pu), Castlemore Leader (f), Miss Thornton (pu), 211 Deciding Dance (pu), 149 Dante's Skip [16] (f), Cherry Glen (pu), 239[3] Brigade Leader (pu), 252 Strong Stern (pu), Leaping Three (pu), 185 Fileo (f), 225 Trimmer Lady (pu), 252 Mounthenry Lady (pu), Moss's Beauty (pu)
18 ran. 1l, 12l. SP 3-1.

309 - Mares Maiden 5yo+ II

207 **Sharoujack [15] ....K Beecher** 1
prom, ld 5 out, hdd last, drvn to ld flat
239 **Rascal Street Lad [14]***prog 4 out, ld last, hdd & not qckn flat* 2
253 **Queen Of The Suir [14]***styd on frm 2 out, nrst fin* 3
Also: 128 Lisnagar Lady [11] (4), 144 Sezu (5), Slowly But Surely (pu), 127 Fort Rouge (pu), 43[3] Ring Mam (pu), Emerald Lake (pu), 183 Lady Fountain (pu), Dromroe Lady (pu), 210 Northern Katie (pu), 239 Electric Can (pu), 183 Kilcully Night (ur), 210 Farran Garrett (pu), Keep The Change (pu), 151 Noneofyourbusiness (ur), 277 Everlaughing (pu), 146 Brook Queen (pu)
19 ran. 1l, 1½l, 6l. SP 5-1.

310 - Open Lightweight

116 **Coole Cherry [22]...........................J Flynn** 1
prom, ld apr 3 out, styd on wll nr fin
235[1] **Frazer Island [22]***prog 3 out, chal apr last, no ext nr fin* 2
241[1] **Try God [21]***prog 3 out, chal apr last, no ext flat* 3
Also: 184 Holly Moss [18] (4), 241[2] Tack Room Lady [14] (5), Battle Hard (pu), 184 Riszard (f)
7 ran. ½l, 1l, 5l. SP 10-1.

311 - Maiden 5yo+ I

156[3] **Emerald Gale [19]......................T Lombard** 1
prog 4 out, ld nxt, easily
It's A Gamble [13]*styd on frm 2 out, no ch wth wnr* 2
156 **Know Something VI [13]***disp 5 out-3 out, onepcd aft* 3
Also: 228 Mr Dennehy (4), 243 Prophets Thumb (5), 148[3] The Magic Slabber (pu), 243 Tom The Boy VI (pu), 187 Foxwoods Valley (pu), 243 Radical-Times (pu), Castle Ventry (pu), Jimmy The Tailor (pu), 244 Castle Shelley (pu), Glentoralda (pu), 244 Jacky Flynn (pu), 237 Prince Of Thyne (pu), 139 Shady Prince (pu), 14 Earl Of Mirth (pu), Komori (pu)
18 ran. 12l, 1l, 15l. SP 5-4.

312 - Maiden 5yo+ II

227 **The Caffler [16] ....D Murphy** 1
prom, ld 3 out, slw last, rdn out
188[3] **Weak Moment [14]***chsd wnr 3 out, no imp apr last* 2
188 **Dante's Reward [12]***chsd ldrs, onepcd frm 3 out* 3
Also: 113 Gerry And Tom (4), 244[2] Raggety Man (pu), 207 Always Drumming (pu), 155 Mountainous Valley (pu), 243[3] Just-N-James (pu), Comic Act (pu), Remmy Cruz (pu), 148 Ballybeggan Boy (pu), Mountain Hall (pu), 47 Tavern Tale (pu), 69 Aislings Toi (f), 244 Luciano The Yuppi (pu), Island Echo (pu)
16 ran. 2l, 6l, 10l. SP 3-1.

313 - Winners Of One

65[3] **Chalwood [22] ....P Coleman** 1
ld 5 out, clr 3 out, comf
242[2] **Scarteen Lower [15]***chsd wnr 4 out, no imp aft* 2
186[2] **Crazy Dreams [13]***chsd ldrs, onepcd frm 4 out* 3
Also: 241[3] Moll's Choice [12] (4), 190[1] Geata Bawn [10] (5), 148[1] Strong Vision (pu), 244[1] Ilengar (pu), 116 Some Tourist (pu), 74[1] Dukes Castle (pu), 234 Flo Jo's Boy (pu), 141 Bit Of A Citizen (ur)
11 ran. 15l, 5l, 2l. SP 7-4.

DOWNPATRICK
Wednesday March 27th
YIELDING

314 - 3m Hun Chase

Aiguille (Ire) 11.2 7a ....Mr G Elliot 1
273 **Cool Rocket (Ire) 11.7 7a (bl) ....Mr W Ewing** 2
Hiltonstown Lass (Ire) 11.6 3a....Mr B R Hamilton 3
273[2] See Just There (Ire) 12.0 *(fav)* 4
Time To Smile (Ire) 11.2 7a 5

273 Moylena 11.9 6
6 ran. 4½l, 15l, 7l, 9l. SP 11-8.

CO DOWN
Loughbrickland
Saturday March 30th
HEAVY

315 - Winners Of Two

254³ **Gale Griffin [17]** ....L Lennon 1
disp 5th til ld 2 out, sn clr
281² **Kylnhill [14]***hld up, last of 3 frm 5th, ev ch 3 out, one-pcd* 2
262 **Rontom***disp 5th til wknd 2 out* 3
Also: 301 Cardinals Lady (f), Handsome Anthony (bd), 284 J J's Hope (bd), 171 Hilton Mill (bd), 298 Lingering Hope (bd), 286¹ Royal Aristocrat (bd), 257¹ Claire Me (f)
10 ran. 10l, 20l. SP 10-1.

316 - Winners Of One

287 **High Star [16]** ....I Buchanan 1
2nd til ld 5 out, sn clr, comf
Kildowney Lady [13]*prog 4 out, styd on, nvr nrr* 2
Also: 257 Chene Rose (f), 256¹ The Convincer (f), 284 Moyavo Lady (pu), 304 Salvation (pu), 257² Gawn Inn (ur)
7 ran. 6l. SP 7-4.

317 - Open Lightweight

254² **Lacken Beau [22]** ....R Arthur 1
hld up, ld 2 out, sn clr, easily
298² **Find Out More [19]***chsd ldrs, kpt on to tk 2nd last* 2
284¹ **Jims Choice [17]***ld to 2 out, sn btn* 3
Also: 298 Schweppes Tonic (4)
4 ran. 8l, 6l, dist. SP 5-4.

318 - Maiden 5 & 6yo

Lough Tully [17] ....G Martin 1
pllng, hld up, ld 3 out, sn clr, comf
299 **Burrell Wharf [12]***chsd ldrs, kpt on onepcd 2 out* 2
Anns Display [10]*prom, onepcd frm 3 out* 3
Also: 282 Grove Victor (4), 282 Bonquist (pu), 261 A Bit Of A Monkey (ur), 256 Che Amigo (pu), Parman (pu), Cascum Lad (pu), 283 Ballydesmond (pu), 283 Opening Quote (pu), 260 Panda Nova (pu)
12 ran. 12l, 4l, 2l. SP 2-1.

319 - Mares Maiden I

20 **Satin Talker [15]** ....A Martin 1
ld 5th, made rest, unchal
286³ **Arctic Leader [13]***chsd ldrs, no imp wnr frm 2 out* 2
285 **Glenbrin***chsd ldrs, onepcd frm 3 out* 3
Also: 286 Gilloway Princess (4), 301 Ellies Pride (pu), Glen Deal (pu), 257 Hillview Susie (pu), Grey Rock (pu), Scotts Cross (pu), 259 Chanauley (pu), Winsome Blends (pu), 258 Lake Majestic (f), Nancy Hill (pu), 259 Island Harriet (ref), 259 Cherryflame (pu)
15 ran. 5l, 15l, 10l. SP 7-2.

320 - Mares Maiden II

259³ **Goldwren [15]** ....A Martin 1
chsd ldrs, lft in ld 3 out, styd on
258 **Lillooet [13]***prog 4 out, lft 3rd nxt, kpt on* 2
281³ **Dernamay [11]***prog 4 out, lft 2nd nxt, onepcd* 3
Also: 285 Iveagh Lady (4), 288 Fidoon (5), 259² Fidsprit (ur), 215 Glen Thyne (pu), Loch Saland (ur), Buckie Thistle (pu), 259 Midi Minstrel (ur), 288 Rath Mear (pu), Kanann (pu), 301 Let Her Run Wild (ur), 231 Coloured Thyme (f)
14 ran. 2l, 4l, 6l, dist. SP 2-1.

321 - Maiden 6yo+

288 **Steady Johnny [15]** ....W Ewing 1
prom, ld 4 out, jnd & lft clr last
Triple Bush [10]*nvr dang, lft 2nd last* 2
281 **Highland Buck***t.o.* 3
Also: 288 Ordain (4), Travarians Gold (pu), Oneman's Choice (pu), 288 Neely (ur), 288 Pauls Point (ur), 215 Fair Avoca (pu), Fernhill Way (ur), 288² Craigelle [15] (f), 261 Fill Your Boots (ur), 287 Hanleys Call (pu), 288 Zieg (pu), 172 Wanclasstrain (pu), 288 Flodart (f), 287 Giorgione (pu), Penylan Jack (pu)
18 ran. 15l, dist, dist. SP 6-1.

TIPPERARY FOXHOUNDS
Clonmel Point-To-Point Course
Sunday March 31st
GOOD TO SOFT

322 - Maiden 4yo

274 **Boss Doyle [15]** ....T Cloke 1
prom, disp 4 out til lft clr 3 out, unchal
Dry Highline [10]*chd ldrs, lft 2nd 3 out, onepcd* 2
238 **Arthur***t.o.* 3
Also: 274 Clash Of The Gales (pu), Ryder Cup (f), 270 The Buck Pony (pu), 231 Mr Peoples (pu), 222 Pejays Duca (f), Cirvin (pu), 307 Tonmarie Chance (pu)
10 ran. 15l, dist. SP 6-1.

323 - Maiden 5yo

Lucky Town [17] ....E Bolger 1
w.w. prog 2 out, ld last, sn clr
292 **Hunters Chorus [13]***chsd ldrs, kpt on onepcd frm 2 out* 2
223 **Gasmark [13]***chsd ldrs, kpt on onepcd frm 2 out* 3
Also: 292 Meldante VI [10] (4), 293 Lightoak Lad (5), 293 Milford Road (f), 192 Horgans Quay VI (pu), 293 Linda's Paradise (f), The Thin Fellow (pu), Cockpit (pu), 223 Mount Nugent Jack (pu), Appollo Vision (pu), Beyond Belief (pu), Vice Captain (pu), Prospect Star (pu)
15 ran. 10l, 1l, 10l, 2l. SP Evens.

324 - Mares Maiden 5yo+ I

271² **Killerk Lady [16]** ....S Durack 1
ld hlfwy, in cmmnd whn lft clr 2 out
222³ **Mardon [10]***disp hlfwy-4 out, lft 2nd 2 out* 2
291 **Lancastrian Lass***bhnd, nvr nrr* 3
Also: 291 Thady's Remedy (4), Off You Sail (pu), Pat Barry (f), 226 Belle Of Kilbride (pu), 306 Nicenames (pu), 142 Ellesmere (pu), 271 Sataldo [13] (f), 253 Knocktoran Lady (f), Yashgans Vision (pu), Right Pocket (pu), 290 Dusty's Delight (pu), The Lazy Cat (pu), 196 Randy Rose (f)
16 ran. 20l, 15l, 10l. SP 6-4.

325 - Mares Maiden 5yo+ II

291 **Betty Balfour [15]** ....E Norris 1
prog hlfwy, ld 2 out, styd on
290³ **Sweet Castlehyde [13]***in tch, ev ch 2 out, no ext* 2
195² **Clodagh River [11]***in tch, ev ch 2 out, onepcd* 3
Also: 271 Trembles Choice (4), 85 Bay Lough (5), 240 Rockview Supreme (6), 210² Hot Scent (pu), 290 Pleasing Melody (pu), 280 Harvey's Cream (pu), Mrs Maginn (pu), 289 Cozy Cottage (pu), 290 Just Placed (pu), 290 Appendix Lady (pu), Kilbally Castle (pu), Lady Bremur (pu), Pharding (pu)
16 ran. 5l, 4l, 5l, 4l, 10l. SP 7-2.

326 - Winners Of One

313 **Geata Bawn [16]** ....D Lanigan 1
made all, drvn out from last
153 **The Red Devil [14]***chsd wnr, ev ch 2 out, no ext* 2
Also: 291¹ Cloncannon Bell [14] (f)
3 ran. 4l. SP 6-4.

327 - Maiden 6yo+ I

131³ **Knights Crest [17]** ....T Hyde 1
trckd ldr, ld 2 out, comf
110 **Easy Catch [15]***hld up, prog to chs wnr apr last, no imp* 2
228 **Carbery Boy [13]***trckd ldrs, styd on onepcd 2 out* 3
Also: 187 Mahon River [12] (4), Supreme Athlete [11] (5), Wintry Dawn

[10] (6), Mac-Duagh (7), Decent Scotch (pu), 297 Forold (pu), 190 Level Vibes (pu), 268 Brewery Light (f), 296³ Festival Light (pu)

12 ran. ½l, 6l, 1½l, 3l, 2l, dist. SP 2-1.

328 - Maiden 6yo+ II

112 Big Murt [15] ....D Harney 1
prom, ld & lft clr 2 out, unchal aft
78 Minella Miller*prom, btn 3 out, lft 2nd nxt* 2
250² Fifth Generation 3D
124 Have Another*alwys bhnd, t.o.* 3
Also: 197 Tinamona (pu), 78 Nearhaan (pu), 118 Blazing Crack (pu), 206 Dooneal Hero (pu), 137² Boots Madden (ro), Lord Vince (pu), 297 Prayon Parson [12] (f), Tidy Village (pu)

12 ran. 20l, dist. SP 8-1.

329 - Open Lightweight

136² The Parish Pump [23] ....E Bolger 1
made all, styd on well frm 2 out
310² Frazer Island [20]*chsd wnr, no imp frm 2 out* 2
Miley Sweeney [18]*chsd ldrs, onepcd frm 3 out* 3
Also: 242 Fixed Assets [12] (4), 221 Amoristic Top [12] (5), Hurricane Eden (6), 158 Rossi Novae (7), 209² Colligan River (pu)

8 ran. 5l, 5l, 15l, 1l, 6l, 4l. SP 2-1.

DERRYGALLON
Liscarroll
Sunday March 31st
GOOD

330 - Maiden 4yo

Toni's Tip [16] ....K Whelan 1
prom, ld apr last, rdn out
248 Runabout [14]*prog 3 out, chsd wnr last, no ext* 2
Glen Empress [13]*ld 3rd til apr last, no ext* 3
Also: 274² Wayward King [12] (4), Ahead Of My Time (5), 208² Perky Lad (6), Nick Dundee (7), Kings Success (8), Club Caribbean (9), 208 Vasiliki (pu), Carol Style (pu), Anodfromalord (pu), Four From Home (f)

13 ran. 4l, 3l, 3l. SP 2-1.

331 - Open Lightweight

295 What Thing [21] ....D Costello 1
trckd ldr, ld last, sn clr, comf
242 Silent Sneeze [17]*rdn & prog 3 out, styd on to tk 2nd flat* 2
295 Summerhill Express [17]*prom, ld 5 out-last, no ext* 3
Also: 313² Scarteen Lower [16] (4), 309¹ Sharoujack [13] (5), 278 Cooladerra Lady (6), 241 Coolgreen (pu), 241 Mr Pipeman (pu)

8 ran. 5l, ½l, 2l. SP Evens.

332 - Maiden 5yo

247 Alone Home [16] ....P Fenton 1
prog 3 out, ld nxt, hld on well
114² Red Bronze [16]*hld up, prog to chal 2 out, just hld* 2
Mac's Legend [13]*ld to 2 out, onepcd* 3
Also: 247 Ellies Nelson [12] (4), 275 Castle Avenue (5), 247² Long Drive (6), 185 Slumber Hill (7), Stags Rock (8), 147 Ask Me Another (9), The Village Way (10), Phar Desert (11), 306 Mr Boomaleen (12), Ashburton Lord (pu), Boreens Secret (pu), Sheer Mischief (f), 312 Remmy Cruz (pu), 293 Tom Deely (ur), Matchmaker (pu)

18 ran. Nk, 8l, 3l. SP 5-1.

333 - Winners Of One

243¹ Fundy [17] ....N Fehily 1
made all, hld on well flat
117¹ Emerald Statement [17]*prog to chs wnr 2 out, ev ch whn outjmpd last, rallied* 2
220 Lady Elise [13]*chsd wnr to 2 out, onepcd* 3
Also: 310 Holly Moss [12] (4), 212 Elwill Glory (5), 276 Minstrel Sam (pu), 246 Dromin Pride (pu), 54 Kilcully-Pride (pu), 276 Bula Vogue (pu), July Schoon (pu), 313 Bit Of A Citizen (pu)

11 ran. ½l, 12l, 3l. SP 5-1.

334 - Maiden 6yo+

268 Youcat [15] ....P Fenton 1
prog 5 out, chal 2 out, lft clr last
206 Deep Wave [12]*chsd ldrs, btn whn lft 2nd last, no imp* 2
243² Dohney Boy [11]*chsd ldrs, btn whn lft 3rd last, no imp* 3
Also: 312 Tavern Tale [10] (4), 306² Finnow Thyne (5), 117 Buladante (6), 311 Prince Of Thyne (7), 185 Ace Ventura (pu), Kendor Pass (pu), 185 Barrys Avenue (pu), Broe's Cross (pu), Caddy Man [15] (ur), An Fear Og (ur), 312 Always Drumming (pu), Drominargle (pu), 250 An Oon Iss An Owl (pu), 312 Aislings Toi (pu)

17 ran. 8l, 3l, 3l. SP 7-4.

335 - Mares Maiden 6yo

279 Clogheen Lass [15] ....M Phillips 1
prog 4 out, ld 2 out, sn clr
239 Highways Sister [12]*chsd ldrs, styd on onepcd frm 2 out* 2
279 Killatty Player [12]*disp to 2 out, onepcd* 3
Also: 240 Brogeen Dubh [11] (4), 150² Lishillaun (5), 239 Victim Of Slander (6), Shamrock Lube (pu), 143 Suite Cottage Lady (pu), 12 Holiday Time (f), 252 Lantern Spark (pu), 290 Nine Out Of Ten (pu), Gale Tan (pu), 280 Miss Metal (ro), 308³ Blame Barney (pu)

14 ran. 6l, 1l, 2l. SP 4-1.

LOUTH FOXHOUNDS
Tallanstown
Sunday March 31st
GOOD

336 - Adjacent 5yo+

267¹ Rat Race [16] ....G Elliott 1
prom, lft in ld 3 out, rdn out
272 Cool It [15]*prom, lft cls 2nd 3 out, ev ch last, no ext* 2
302 Skin Graft [10]*nvr dang* 3
Also: 269 Woodhaven Lad (pu), 270 Moydanganrye (f), We Will See (ur)

6 ran. 1l, 15l. SP 2-5.

337 - Maiden 4-6yo

227 Mite Have Bean [15] ....A Martin 1
w.w. ld 3 out, lft clr nxt, comf
218³ Folly Road [12]*chsd ldrs, lft 2nd 2 out, no imp* 2
131 Bracing Breeze*chsd ldrs, lft 3rd & hmpd 2 out, no ch aft* 3
Also: 300 Spectre Brown [10] (4), 299 Sporting Vision (pu), 299² Sam's Man (pu), 267 Perryman (pu), 266 Boreen Boy (f), 300 On The Way Home (pu), 267 Awalkintheclouds (pu), 282² Boycetrus (f), Kilclare King (pu), Collooney Squire (f), 299 Cloughan Boy (ur), 299 Clifford (pu)

15 ran. 8l, 12l, ¾l. SP 3-1.

338 - Open Lightweight

262² Ballinaboola Grove [22] ....L Winters 1
hld up, prog 3 out, ld & lft clr nxt, just hld on
298 Duprey [22]*prom, lft 2nd 2 out, chal flat, just faild* 2
216² Bald Joker [20]*prom, onepcd frm 2 out* 3
Also: 303² Red Express VI [20] (4), 235 Final Issue (5), 101¹ No One Knows (pu), 303 Voldi (f), 298 Knights Pleasure (pu)

8 ran. Sht-hd, 4l, ½l, dist. SP 6-4.

339 - Novice

218 Drumcairn [13] ....A Martin 1
wth ldr til lft alone 2 out
Also: 171 Serious Note (ur)

2 ran. SP Evens.

340 - Mares Maiden

302 Pils Invader [15] ....D Valentine 1
chsd ldr 3 out, ev ch whn lft wll clr 2 out
270 Awaytoday*chsd ldrs, lft 3rd 3 out, lft 2nd nxt, no imp* 2
Also: Collon Mission (ur), 301 Tremollina (pu), 258 Damolly Rose (f),

271 New Legislation (pu), Mum's The Word (f), 98 Knocans Pride (ur), 195 Ballylime Again (pu), 301 Little Doe (pu), 298 Executive Bill (ur), 232 Brooklawn (pu), 134 Windgates Zone (pu), 302 Young Bebe (ro), 177² The Vendor (f), 163 Trembling Rose (ur), Peacefull River (pu)
17 ran. 20l. SP 6-1.

341 - Maiden 7yo+

305² Annie's Arthur [16]........................J Vance 1
prom, ld 4 out, clr apr last, styd on well
261² Takeithandy [14]*ld to 4 out, sn outpcd, styd on apr last* 2
194 Four Zeros [12]*prog to chs wnr 2 out, sn no imp* 3
Also: 237 Mahankhali [11] (4), 305 Ballybrit (5), 268 Big Spender (ur), 288 Laergy Cripperty (pu), 321 Fill Your Boots (ur), 269 Eastern Fox (pu), 288 Sir Gallop (ur), The Financier (ur), Drumriga (pu)
12 ran. 5l, 5l, 2l, 12l. SP 2-1.

WEXFORD FOXHOUNDS
Lingstown
Sunday March 31st
GOOD TO SOFT

342 - Winners Of Two

194 All For Max [18]...........................J Berry 1
hld up, ld 2 out, sn clr, comf
158³ Coolafinka [15]*prom, ld 4 out-2 out, outpcd* 2
220 Cedarbelle [12]*nvr dang, btn whn lft 3rd 2 out* 3
Also: 220 Sandfair (4), Royal Arctic (pu), 220² Slaney Wind (su)
6 ran. 10l, 10l, 7l. SP 11-10.

343 - Maiden 4 & 5yo

Jimmy The Forge [16]...................K Kirwan 1
prom, ld 6th, hrd rdn & hld on gamely flat
222 Gentle Mossy [16]*prog 3 out, chal last, just hld* 2
224² Buck River [15]*prog 3 out, chal & mstk last, no ext* 3
Also: 193² More Rain [13] (4), 222 The Road To Moscow [11] (5), 224 Sweetmount Lad [10] (6), 223³ Dusty Track (7), 224 Lovable Outlaw (8), 223 Apollodorus (pu), 224 Back Withavengeance (pu), 222 Cracker Alley (pu), Give It A Laugh (f), Master Chuzzlewit (pu), 222 Punters Fortune (pu), Radio Days (pu), 222 Ringaheen (f), 222 Side Stepper (f), 224 Whitestown Boy (pu)
18 ran. ½l, 4l, 3l, 5l, 3l, 8l, 20l. SP 4-1.

344 - Open Lightweight

221¹ Dromhana [18] ....J Berry 1
w.w. ld 2 out, styd on well
Irish Peace [16]*chsd wnr 2 out, not qckn* 2
221³ Slaney Food [15]*chsd ldrs, onepcd 3 out* 3
Also: 84¹ Kilbricken Maid (4)
4 ran. 4l, 1l, 12l. SP 4-6.

345 - Maiden 6yo+ I

Hearns Hill [16] ....H Cleary 1
made all, lft clr 4 out, styd on well
228 Shimano [14]*rear ran on 2 out, tk 2nd flat* 2
161 Captain Guinness [13]*chsd ldrs, lft 2nd 4 out, onepcd aft* 3
Also: Get Into It [10] (4), Daddy Warbucks (5), Clon Caw (6), 228 Away In A Hack (pu), Captain Scurlough (pu), 228 Glenfontaine (f), Hey Chief (pu), Major Man (pu), Maxxum Plus (co), 162² Mister Ross (pu), 137 Sandy Valley (pu)
14 ran. 4l, 3l, 8l, 15l, 20l. SP 8-1.

346 - Maiden 6yo+ II

227² Nutty Solera [16] ....J Berry 1
prom, ld 2 out, easily
227³ Little-K [12]*ld to 2 out, sn outpcd* 2
227 Money Low [10]*mid-div, styd on 2 out, nrst fin* 3
Also: 166³ Celtic Kinship (4), 220 Proud Toby (5), 86 Who's Your Man (6), 197 Louis de Palmer (7), 266 Bens Unyoke (f), 190 Drimeen (pu), Little Len (pu), 197 Patty's Pride (pu), 268 Sandyrock (pu), 268 Venture On (pu)
13 ran. 10l, 6l, 3l, 2l, 4l, 20l. SP 4-6.

347 - Mares Maiden 5yo+ I

222 Sister Seven [15] ....J P Berry 1
ld/disp til ld 4 out, styd on well
271 Satcotino [14]*rear, ran on 2 out, nrst fin* 2
193 Lantina [12]*rear, ran on 2 out, nrst fin* 3
Also: 220 Annesley Lady [11] (4), 224³ Determined Okie [10] (5), 198 Tara River (6), Cool Native (f), Magnetic Image (pu), Magnum Bullum (pu), 226 Playful Princess (pu), 222 Riverrunsthroughit (pu), 223 Sinead's Joy (pu), Sweepin Bends (pu), Thieving Sands (bd), Tinnecarrig Hill (pu), Trasna Na Cungaim (pu), Widow Twanky (pu)
17 ran. 2l, 4l, 3l, 3l, 2l. SP 4-1.

348 - Mares Maiden 5yo+ II

195 Raheen River [15] ....J Berry 1
hld up, prog to ld 2 out, sn clr
84² Little Minute [10]*lft 2nd 8th, onepcd frm 2 out* 2
222 Spritly Lady*lft in ld 8th, hdd & wknd 2 out* 3
Also: 224 Mary's Delight (4), Na Moilltear (5), Castle Kate (pu), 223 Choretine Lady (f), 270 Cynical Wit (f), 224 Dribs And Drabs (pu), 163 Edermine Sunset (f), Keeragh (pu), 270² Key Door (pu), 196 Kinross (pu), 196 Meldap (pu), Nash Na Habhainn (pu), 222 Natural Lady (f), Orafeno (pu), Over The Tavern (pu)
18 ran. 20l, 20l, 10l, 10l. SP 6-4.

349 - Nomination

229 Dunamase Dandy [18]....................P Cloke 1
made all, sn clr, rdn whn lft clr 2 out, all out
229¹ Ragged River [18]*chsd ldrs, lft 2nd 2 out, kpt on, just faild* 2
229³ Tul Na Gcarn*t.o.* 3
Also: 198 Glenmore Star (4), 221 Dennistownthriller (f), Kingeochy (f), 229² Silver Buckle (pu)
7 ran. ½l, dist, dist. SP 10-1.

DOWN ROYAL
Wednesday April 3rd
GOOD

350 - 3m Hun Chase

303¹ Teal Bridge 11.2 7a....................Mr G Elliot 1
265¹ Tasse Du The 12.0..................Mr A J Martin 2
(fav)
273³ Amme Enaek (Ire) 10.13 5a (bl) ......Mr B M Cash 3
273¹ Over The Maine (Ire) 11.7 7a 4
Ballymacrevan (Ire) 11.2 7a 5
338³ Bald Joker 11.7 7a (bl) 6
Handsome Maid (Ire) 11.1 3a 7
314² Cool Rocket (Ire) 11.2 7a (bl) ur
8 ran. 5l, 1l, 9l, 2l. SP 6-1.

KILLEAGH HARRIERS
Inch
Wednesday April 3rd
GOOD

351 - Maiden 4 & 5yo I

148 Sirrah Aris [15].........................D Costello 1
trckd ldrs, ld 3 out, comf
309 Farran Garrett [13]*2nd hlfwy, styd on onepcd frm 2 out* 2
308 Fileo [12]*prog 2 out, chal apr last, no ext* 3
Also: Graignamanagh [11] (4), 275 Timmy Tuff (5), 275 Robin Of Loxley (6), 277 Monadante (7), Juverna River (8), Our Own Way (9), 309 Electric Can (pu), 309 Northern Katie (ro), Chamsy (pu), 308 Leaping Three (ur), 211 Blackwater Fox (ur), Mr Matchit (f), 243 Queen Of The Gales (ur)
16 ran. 2l, 3l, 3l. SP 5-2.

352 - Maiden 4 & 5yo II

Tarrs Bridge [18] .... **E Gallagher** 1
trckd ldr, ld 3 out, easily ....
245 **Galebreaker [13]***chsd ldrs, kpt on onepcd frm 3 out* .. 2
275 **Bosco's Touch [12]***ld to 3 out, sn btn* 3
Also: Gee-Gee (4), 311 Jacky Flynn (5), 137 Call Me Paris (6), 114 Conor Mac (pu), 275 Super Fred (pu), 275 Another Berry (pu), 73 Lord Pat (ur), 119 Pharleng (ur), White Wyandotte (pu), 308 Moss's Beauty (f), 275 Poachers Lamp (pu), 240 The Wild Wave (pu), 308 Keep Strong (0)
16 ran. 15l, 2l, 20l. SP 2-1.

353 - Mares Maiden 6yo+ I

280² **Supersonia [14]** .... **E Gallagher** 1
prom, ld 2 out, drvn out ....
309² **Rascal Street Lad [13]***prom, ev ch last, no ext* 2
277 **Miss Josephine [12]***prom, ev ch last, no ext* 3
Also: 243 Ballinvuskig Lady [12] (4), 308 Brigade Leader (5), 226 Josalady (6), Shuilnamon (7), 308 Dante's Skip (8), 309 Lady Fountain (9), 308 Miss Thornton (10), 66 Brown Berry (11), 240 Rio Star (ur), 252 Scottish Socks (f), 309 Sezu (ur), 309 Emerald Lake (pu), 71 Fennells Bay (pu), 280 Tipperaryenteprise (pu), Vital Approach (f), 280 Haven Lady (ref)
19 ran. 1½l, 2l, 1l. SP 7-1.

354 - Mares Maiden 6yo+ II

240 **Irene's Call [16]** .... **K O'Sullivan** 1
prog 4 out, ld nxt, comf ....
50 **Curraheen Bride [13]***ld to 3 out, no ch wth wnr aft* ... 2
Sleetmore Gale [12]*chsd ldrs, styd on onepcd frm 2 out* 3
Also: 151² Change The Pace [11] (4), 240² Lunar Approach (5), 207 Amandawill (6), 71 Frightening Child (7), 308 Ballybeggan Lady (8), Highland Call (f), 279 Nagle Rice (f), 243 Metal Miss (pu), 280 Scarra Darragh (pu), 128 Pass The Basket (pu), 207 Tina Ore (pu), 308 Trimmer Lady (pu), 335 Miss Metal (pu), 306 Statoil (pu), 240 Harvest Delight (pu)
18 ran. 3l, 2l, 2l. SP 9-4.

355 - Open Lightweight

158 **Have A Brandy [22]** .... **P Fenton** 1
made all, styd on well frm 2 out ....
310 **Riszard [20]***chsd wnr, effrt 4 out, nvr able to chal* 2
My Sunny Way [18]*chsd ldrs, styd on onepcd 2 out* ... 3
Also: 209 Myalup [15] (4), 136 Bocock's Pride [12] (5), 278² Trimmer Wonder (6), Fair Revival (7), Lisadante (f)
8 ran. 4l, 4l, 8l. SP 9-4.

356 - Adjacent Maiden

312 **Gerry And Tom [15]** .... **D Budds** 1
prom, ld 4 out, styd on well ....
312 **Mountainous Valley [13]***chsd wnr 4 out, no ext 2 out* 2
113 **Glenaboy [13]***chsd ldrs, styd on onepcd frm 2 out* ... 3
Also: 277 Tourig Dante (4), 277 Monagurra (5), 275 Jorodec (6), Woodville Princess (7), 187 Icantsay (pu), 277 Cahermone Lady (pu), 245 Fountain House (pu), Garryross (f), 291 Solo Minstrel (pu)
12 ran. 4l, 1l, 12l. SP 4-1.

357 - Winners Of Two

Slaney Goodness [18] .... **Lilian Doyle** 1
chsd ldrs, lkd btn whn lft ch last, ld nr fin ....
276³ **Master Kemal [18]***ld hlfwy, clr whn blnd last, hdd nr fin* 2
313 **Some Tourist [16]***chsd ldrs, styd on onepcd frm 2 out* 3
Also: 276 Our Blossom [14] (4), 276² Fine Affair [12] (5), Saddle Her Well (pu), 312¹ The Caffler (pu), 276 Burkean Melody (pu), Ad Extra (pu)
9 ran. ½l, 3l, 5l. SP 5-1.

358 - Maiden 6yo+

188 **Stroll Home [18]** .... **E Gallagher** 1
ld/disp til ld 4 out, easily ....
312 **Mountain Hall [13]***chsd wnr 3 out, no imp* 2
306 **Brian Og [11]***chsd ldrs, onepcd frm 3 out* 3
Also: 334 Ace Ventura [11] (4), 312 Comic Act (5), 79 Classis King (6), 311 Foxwoods Valley (pu), 296 Baybuck (pu), 312 Just-N-James (pu), 296 Clover Nook (pu), 207 Andy Gawe (f), Prince Owen (pu), 311³ Know Something VI (pu), 188 Pat The Hat (f), Young Cal (pu), 312 Luciano The Yuppi (pu), Matt Moss (f)
17 ran. 5l, 4l, 1l. SP 2-1.

TIPPERARY
Saturday April 6th
GOOD TO YIELDING

359 - 3m Hun Chase

314¹ **Aiguille (Ire) 11.0 7a** .... **Mr J T McNamara** 1
Silent Sneeze (Ire) 10.9 7a (bl) ..... **Mr E Gallagher** 2
263³ **Divali (Ire) 11.0 7a** .... **Mr J P Moloney** 3
Crazy Dreams (Ire) 11.7 4
Faha Gig (Ire) 11.5 7a *(fav)* 5
329³ Miley Sweeney 11.7 6
Maypole Fountain (Ire) 11.2 5a 7
263 Lakeview Lad (Ire) 11.0 7a .... pu
Trackman (Ire) 11.0 7a .... f
Pharditu (Ire) 10.9 7a (bl) .... pu
10 ran. 3l, 1½l, 2½l, 13l. Time 6m 12.1s. SP 7-2.

NORTH DOWN
Comber
Saturday April 6th
GOOD

360 - Confined Lightweight

Ballyalla [17] .... **A Murdoch** 1
made all, clr 2 out, comf ....
305 **Dick's Cabin [10]***chsd wnr, chal apr 2 out, sn btn* 2
258² **Half Scotch***t.o.* 3
Also: 285¹ Castledell (4), 315 J J's Hope (5), Three Town Rock (ur), Little Celia (ref)
7 ran. 20l, dist, 6l, 10l. SP 2-1.

361 - Maiden

300 **Cairncross [15]** .... **J Bright** 1
prom, ld 5 out, kpt on well flat ....
341² **Takeithandy [12]***s.s. prog 3 out, chal last, sn no ext* .. 2
318 **Ballydesmond***chsd wnr 3 out-nxt, wknd* 3
Also: 305 Stag Hunt (4), 287 Chase The Sun (f), 298 Strong Performance (pu), 321 Craigelle (pu), Pibara (pu), 283 Lord Basil (pu)
9 ran. 10l, dist, dist. SP 2-1.

362 - Winners Of Two

341¹ **Annie's Arthur [16]** .... **J Vance** 1
chsd ldrs, 3rd & btn whn lft clr last, kpt on ....
315 **Royal Aristocrat [15]***chsd ldrs, 4th & btn whn lft 2nd last, no ext* 2
316 **Chene Rose [12]***nvr dang, lft 3rd last* 3
Also: 257³ Cabbery Rose [18] (bd), 288¹ Castle Royal [19] (f), 321¹ Steady Johnny (pu), 316 Salvation (pu), 257 More Than Most (pu), 298 French Lady (pu)
9 ran. 3l, 8l. SP 3-1.

363 - Open Lightweight

317² **Find Out More [20]** .... **N Toal** 1
prog to 2nd 3 out, ld flat, styd on ....
303³ **Miss Elizabeth [20]***cls up, ld 5 out, mstks 3 out & nxt, hdd & no ext flat* 2
338 **Voldi [17]***cls up til onepcd frm 3 out* 3
Also: 168 Young Entry [16] (4), 284 Copper Friend (5), It's A Fiddle (pu)
6 ran. 1l, 8l, 3l, dist. SP 4-1.

364 - Mares Maiden

302[3] **Sapphire 'N' Silver [14]** .... **B Hamilton** 1
chsd ldrs, 2nd 3 out, lft in ld aft last, kpt on ....
Brookview VI [13]*chsd ldr, ld 3 out, wd bnd aft last, hdd & no ext* 2
320[3] **Dernamay [11]***chsd ldrs, 3rd 3 out, no imp aft* 3
Also: 105 In The Future (4), 320 Kanann (pu), 320 Let Her Run Wild (ur), 286 Rashee Lady (pu), 169 Welsh Sitara (f), 286 Ollar Lady (pu), Thyne Valley (pu), 285 Incense Doll (f)
11 ran. 4l, 6l, dist. SP 4-1.

365 - Unplaced Maiden

Noluckmate [14] .... **B Hamilton** 1
in tch, trckd ldr 2 out, hrd rdn to ld nr fin ....
321 **Flodart [14]***ld til hdd nr fin* 2
318 **Grove Victor [11]***trckd ldr to 2 out, onepcd* 3
Also: Extra Stout (4), 300 Florida Or Bust (5), 321 Oneman's Choice (6), 321 Fernhill Way (7), 283 Oldtown Glen (pu), Bit Of A Song (pu), Major Scandal (pu), 260 Christimatt (pu), 318 A Bit Of A Monkey (pu), 319 Grey Rock (pu), 282 Inspector Stalker (pu), 215 Blue Bay (pu), 337 Clifford (pu)
16 ran. Nk, 10l, 10l, 20l, nk, dist. SP 2-1.

CO CLARE
Dromoland
Sunday April 7th
GOOD TO FIRM

366 - Maiden 4 & 5yo

Wooloomooloo [16] .... **P Fenton** 1
in tch, ld 4 out, lft clr 2 out, comf ....
293[2] **Executive Class [13]***chsd ldrs, 3rd & btn whn lft 2nd 2 out, kpt on* 2
200 **Educate Me [12]***chsd ldrs, btn whn lft 2nd 2 out, no ext* 3
Also: 122[2] Mr Tom Tom [11] (4), 293[3] Castle Tiger Bay (5), 289 Dinan (6), 292 Legal Whisper (ro), Lord O'The Rye [16] (f), Alberts Gamble (pu), 323 The Thin Fellow (pu), 323 Lightoak Lad (pu), Tom's Tune (pu), 332 Tom Deely (pu), Satco Supreme (ur), Jakes Dilemma (pu)
15 ran. 5l, 2l, 2l. SP 9-4.

367 - Maiden 6yo+ I

327 **Wintry Dawn [16]** .... **P Fenton** 1
prog 3 out, ld last, rdn out ....
290[2] **Idiot's Surprise [15]***made msot til hdd & no ext last* .. 2
296 **Rosevalley***nvr dang* 3
Also: 297 Cahergowan (4), 38 Cottoneyejoe (f), 124 Carramore Hill (pu), 289 September Stephen (f), 325 Kilbally Castle (pu), 250 Head Bottle Washer (pu), 180 Ballinahowna Lad (pu), 156 Over In McGanns (f)
11 ran. ½l, dist. SP 2-1.

368 - Maiden 6yo+ II

201 **Rare Spread [17]** .... **B Hassett** 1
prog hlfwy, ld 2 out, rdn out ....
121[3] **Flood Relief [15]***chsd ldrs, 4th & rdn 2 out, sn chsd wnr, no ext flat* 2
206 **The Defender [14]***chsd ldrs, rdn & btn 2 out, kpt on* .. 3
Also: 206 Winter Breeze [12] (4), Autumn Call (5), Meneduke (ur), 328 Nearhaan (pu), 328 Tidy Village (pu), 334[2] Deep Wave (f), 289 Another Check (pu)
10 ran. 2l, 2l, 4l. SP 4-6.

369 - Mares Maiden I

252[2] **Crabeg Hazel [15]** .... **J McNamara** 1
prom, ld 3 out, rdn out ....
291 **Sunczech [14]***chsd ldrs, kpt on well frm 2 out* 2
335 **Lishillaun [12]***chsd ldrs, styd on onepcd frm 2 out* 3
Also: 324 Knocktoran Lady [11] (4), 43 Sheshia (5), 290 Ballycar Princess (6), 289 Kochnie (su), 308 Strong Stern (f), 335 Lantern Spark (pu), Coolshamrock (pu), Rosetown Girl (pu)
11 ran. 1½l, 4l, 2l. SP 5-1.

370 - Mares Maiden II

Vain Princess [15] .... **W Ewing** 1
prom, ld 3 out, styd on well ....
309 **Ring Mam [12]***chsd wnr 2 out, no imp* 2
335 **Victim Of Slander [10]***chsd ldrs, onepcd frm 3 out* 3
Also: 290 Yasgourra (4), 296 Reinskea (pu), Sell And Regret (pu), 280 Forgoodnessjake VI (pu), 290 Bunny Lightening (pu), 203[3] Snipe Lodge (pu), 325 Rockview Supreme (su)
10 ran. 10l, 5l, 10l. SP 6-4.

371 - Winners Of One

201[1] **Tinerana Boy [18]** .... **R Hurley** 1
ld 4 out, clr last, comf ....
295 **Hi-Way's Gale [16]***chsd wnr 3 out, kpt on, no ch* 2
276 **Coolree Lord***t.o.* 3
Also: 248[1] Camogue Bridge (pu), Dreaming Idle (pu), 294 The Breaser Fawl (pu), 294 Bayview Prince (pu)
7 ran. ¾l, dist. SP 2-1.

372 - Open Lightweight

294[2] **Up For Ransome [22]** .... **R Hurley** 1
lft in ld 5 out, drew clr frm 2 out ....
326[2] **The Red Devil [19]***prog 3 out, no imp on wnr nxt* 2
251[2] **Bit Of A Touch [15]***chsd ldrs, no prog frm 3 out* 3
Also: 295[2] Kizzy Rose (4), Gabrielle's Boy (pu), 251 Hopefully True (pu)
6 ran. 6l, 10l, 20l. SP 6-4.

373 - Nomination

292 **Up The Banner VI** .... **M Casey** 1
Kolman-K 2
Mr Barney 3
Also: 294 Jigg's Forge VI (4)
4 ran. 4l, 10l, dist. SP 2-1.

UNITED FOXHOUNDS
Ballynoe
Sunday April 7th
GOOD TO FIRM

374 - Confined Maiden 5yo+

311 **Castle Shelley [15]** .... **A O'Shea** 1
chsd ldrs, btn whn lft disp 2 out, kpt on wll flat ....
334 **Buladante [14]***chsd ldrs, btn whn lft disp 2 out, no ext und pres flat* 2
280 **Gentle Leader***nvr dang, lft 3rd 2 out* 3
Also: 356 Garryross (4), 275 Master Jake (5), 183 Have A Drop (6), 353 Fennells Bay (pu), 71 Safety Factor (f)
8 ran. 1l, 15l, 6l. SP 4-1.

375 - Maiden 4 & 5yo

323 **Milford Road [15]** .... **J Motherway** 1
ld/disp til ld 3 out, sn clr ....
142 **Dancing Dessie [11]***chsd ldrs, onepcd frm 3 out* 2
332 **Ellies Nelson [10]***ld/disp til btn frm 3 out* 3
Also: 311 The Magic Slabber (4), Prestigious Man (5), 199 Oneofourown (pu), 199 Roskeen Bridge (ur), 311 Jimmy The Tailor (pu), 322 Cirvin (pu), 213 Up And Over (pu), 312 Ballybeggan Boy (pu), 323 Appollo Vision (f)
12 ran. 10l, 2l, 3l. SP 5-4.

376 - Mares Final

149[1] **Mr K's Winterblues [19]** .... **E Gallagher** 1
4th til ld 3 out, styd on well ....
239[1] **Hopperdante [17]***disp to 3 out, styd on well aft* 2
294 **Slavica [17]***prog 3 out, styd on frm nxt, nrst fin* 3
Also: 278[3] Pharditu [13] (4), 324[1] Killerk Lady (5), 333 Bula Vogue (6), 295 Ore Engineeress (pu), 310 Tack Room Lady (pu), 253[1] Scarlet River (pu), 141 Glenview Rose (f), 242[1] Faulty Rap (pu), 241 Artistic Quay (pu)
12 ran. 3l, 1l, 10l. SP 7-4.

377 - Maiden 6yo+

45 **Dawn Lad [16]** ....**E Gallagher** 1
prog to ld 3 out, styd on well ....
11 **Castle Ventry [13]***prog to chs wnr aft 3 out, no imp last* 2
56 **Rusnetto [12]***nvr nrr* 3
o: 312 Raggety Man (4), 190 King Tyrant (5), 297³ Sammy Sunne (6), 358 Andy Gawe (ro)
7 ran. 6l, 3l, 10l. SP 7-2.

378 - Open Lightweight

1¹ **What Thing [26]** ....**D Costello** 1
disp 4 out, sn ld & clr, easily ....
29 **Colligan River [20]***rear, styd on 2 out, no ch wth wnr* 2
2² **Sleepy Rock [17]***chsd ldrs, onepcd 3 out* 3
o: 184³ Sir-Eile [17] (4), 355 Lisadante [14] (5), 6 Tobarella (pu), 209 beg Rover (pu), 212 Carbery Minstrel (pu), 251³ Howarya Harry (f 13¹ John's Right (pu), 313 Ilengar (pu), 184 Lovely Citizen [29] (pu)
12 ran. 12l, 10l, ½l. SP 5-4.

379 - Mares Maiden I

07 **Lady Steel [15]**......................**T Lombard** 1
made all, clr 4 out, unchal ....
06 **Solar Castle***nvr dang, lft 2nd 2 out* 2
51 **Northern Katie***nvr dang* 3
o: 291 She Wont Stop (4), 306 Ann Black (5), 290 Loughlins Pride), 353 Scottish Socks (pu), Little Simba (pu), 211² Early News (f), rrygra Fountain (pu), Derrygallon Fancy (pu), 309 Brook Queen (f),) Frosty Morn (pu)
13 ran. 20l, 20l, dist. SP 8-1.

380 - Mares Maiden II

9² **Carlingford Gale [16]** 1
3rd 4 out, ld 2 out, sn clr, easily ....
09 **Lisnagar Lady [12]***2nd 4 out, chsd wnr 2 out, no imp* 2
8² **Riot Lady [10]***nvr nrr* 3
so: Sumakano (4), 270 Stradbally Jane (5), 274 Claudia Electric (6), 4 Nagle Rice (7), 309 Slowly But Surely (8), Dromroe Dante (f), 4³ Lancastrian Lass (pu), 280 Foherish Mist (pu), Langretta (su), 76 nny Habits (f)
13 ran. 10l, 6l, 15l. SP 3-1.

ISLAND FOXHOUNDS
Camolin
Sunday April 7th
GOOD

381 - Confined Maiden

45 **Maxxum Plus [16]** ....**D Valentine** 1
trckd ldr, ld 3 out, drw clr last ....
6³ **Money Low [13]***ld to 3 out, btn last* 2
8² **Greedy Johno [10]***chsd ldrs, onepcd 3 out* 3
so: 270 Push Gently (4), 348 Kinross (5), The Podger (pu), 345 aptain Scurlough (pu), 348³ Spritly Lady (pu), Menedream (pu), 161 ffalo House (f)
10 ran. 7l, 8l, 25l, 5l. SP Evens.

382 - Open Lightweight

4³ **Slaney Food [22]** ....**J Quigley** 1
disp 5 out, mstk 3 out, ld nxt, styd on well ....
21² **Loch Garman Hotel [19]***disp 5 out-2 out, no ext* 2
49 **Dennistownthriller [16]***nvr nrr* 3
so: Glen Og Lane [12] (4), 29 Beet Statement (pu)
5 ran. 6l, 4l, 12l. SP 4-1.

383 - Winners Of Two

42 **Slaney Wind [19]** ....**H Cleary** 1
trckd ldrs, ld 2 out, styd on well ....
42² **Coolafinka [18]***prog 5 out, chsd wnr last, no ext* 2
Another Star [15]*clr ldr til hdd & wknd 2 out* 3
so: 345¹ Hearns Hill (4), 342³ Cedarbelle (5), Catch The Mouse (pu), 264 Princess Breda (pu), 225¹ Call Queen (pu), 313 Moll's Choice (pu)
9 ran. 2½l, 10l, 20l, 25l. SP 9-4.

384 - Mares Maiden I

347 **Magnum Bullum [16]** ....**H Cleary** 1
w.w. ld apr last, styd on well ....
324 **Randy Rose [14]***prog 3 out, chsd wnr apr last, no ext flat* 2
33² **Ballinaclash Pride [12]***made most to apr 2 out, onepcd* 3
Also: 348 Key Door (4), 348 Meldap (5), Tullibards Again (6), 347 Tara River (co), 348 Cynical Wit (pu), Heymoll (ur), 348 Orafeno (pu), 224 Lipstick Lady (pu), 226² Talbot's Hollow (pu), Harlin Lady (pu), Ballyedmond (pu), Hardtobegood (pu)
15 ran. 3l, 5l, 8l, 6l, dist. SP 2-1.

385 - Mares Maiden II

347³ **Lantina [15]** ....**C Donnelly** 1
chsd ldrs, prog 2 out, ld flat, rdn out ....
196 **Hollybuck [14]***ld, blnd 2 out, hdd flat, no ext* 2
348 **Castle Kate***nvr nrr* 3
Also: 223 Luthier Girl (4), 195 Hazels Dream (5), 299³ Killaligan Kim (6), 348 Choretine Lady (7), Bedahokey (pu), Key Of The Nile (pu), 347 Tinnecarrig Hill (pu), Carrigmore Lady (pu), 347 Thieving Sands (pu), 163 Curraduff Moll (pu), 347 Magnetic Image (f), Glenroe Gal (ro), 347 Sweepin Bends (f)
16 ran. 1½l, 20l, 6l, 4l, 3l, 15l. SP 4-1.

386 - Maiden 4 & 5yo

223 **Mak's Dream [16]** ....**P Kelly** 1
prog 4 out, chal & lft in ld 2 out, styd on ....
192 **Lonely Castle [14]***lost plc hlfwy, ran on 2 out, nrst fin* 2
293 **Flying Fellow [13]***chsd ldr to 3 out, lft 2nd nxt, no imp* 3
Also: All But (4), 343 Dusty Track (5), 343 Apollodorus (f), Steppy Boy (f), Prologue (pu), Montel Express (ro), Nobodys Boy (pu), 223² Wyn Wan Soon (ro), 343 Ringaheen (pu), 347 Cool Native (f), Torduff Express (pu), 164 Msadi Mhulu (pu)
15 ran. 4l, 3l, 25l, 8l. SP 2-1.

387 - Maiden 6yo+ I

267 **Cash For Bash [16]**......................**P Cloke** 1
trckd ldrs, ld 2 out, ran on well ....
265 **Poulgillie [14]***ld to 2 out, kpt on aft* 2
227 **Will Travel [14]***wth ldr to 2 out, onepcd* 3
Also: 346 Drimeen (4), 266 Thought Reader (5), 161 Lord Knox (6), 272 Spinans Hill (7), Royal Road (pu), Glenville Breeze (pu), 346 Who's Your Man (ur), Gallic Twister (pu)
11 ran. 5l, hd, 25l, 10l, 1l, 25l. SP 4-5.

388 - Maiden 6yo+ II

228 **Stillorgan Park [15]** ....**P Cloke** 1
trckd ldr 4 out, ld aft last, rdn out ....
266 **Shillelagh Oak [14]***ld to aft last, not qckn* 2
345 **Glenfontaine [13]***chsd ldrs, styd on frm 2 out, nrst fin* 3
Also: 297 Junior Moss (4), 162 Lord Amethyst (5), 345 Sandy Valley (6), 346 Louis de Palmer (7), 305 Siamsa Brae (pu), 228 Over The Barrow (f), 346 Little Len (ro), 272 Galloping Giggs (pu)
11 ran. 1l, 2l, 20l, 5l, 6l, 4l. SP 6-4.

WESTMEATH FOXHOUNDS
Castletown-Geoghegan
Sunday April 7th
GOOD

389 - Adjacent Lightweight

230¹ **Cappajune [20]** ....**F Kiernan** 1
ld 3rd, made rest, ran on well ....
230 **Castlepook [16]***rear, styd on wll frm 2 out, no ch wth wnr* 2
234 **Another Idea [15]***chsd wnr, onepcd 3 out* 3
Also: 302¹ Mordella Lass [13] (4), 303 Torenaga Hill [12] (5), Morabito (pu), 267 Park Duke (pu), 159 Sexton Gleam (pu), 23 South East Sun (pu)

9 ran. 6l, 1½l, 6l, 3l. SP 3-1.

390 - Maiden 4 & 5yo

300 **Dearmistershatter [16]**..............**J O'Connell** 1
mid-div, prog 3 out, ld aft nxt, easily..........
267 **Executive Chief [11]***chsd ldrs, styd on onepcd 2 out, tk 2nd flat*.......... 2
267 **Blackie Connors [11]***mstks, ld til aft 2 out, sn btn* 3
Also: Scarvey Bridge (4), No Other Hill (5), 292 Riberetto's Girl (6), Big Charlie (pu), Condonstown (pu), Three Heads (pu)
9 ran. 12l, nk, 30l, 10l, 2l. SP 3-1.

391 - Mares Maiden

232³ **Rathcarrick Lass [14]**....................**R Pugh** 1
ld til aft 2 out, rallied to ld last, all out ....
340 **Ballylime Again [13]***prom, ld aft 2 out-last, not qckn* .. 2
291 **Ballybriken Castle [13]***prom, wth ldr 2 out-last, no ext*.......... 3
Also: Mountview Sue (4), 336³ Skin Graft (5), 271 Currasilla (pu), Garwell (f), Rathcore Lady (pu), 340 Young Bebe (pu)
9 ran. 1l, nk, 20l, 5l. SP 7-4.

392 - Open Lightweight

82 **Palmura [18]**..........................**G Harford** 1
made most, lft clr by dfctns, comf ....
284³ **Temporale [13]***chsd ldrs, lft 2nd by dfctns* 2
Also: 235 Carrigans Lad (ur), Fethard Orchid (ur), 158 Fingerhill (co), The Illiad (pu), Youngandfair (ur)
7 ran. 7l. SP 6-1.

393 - Winners Of Two

Show Your Hand [16]...................**A Martin** 1
hld up, ld last, sn clr ....
301¹ **Royal Star [14]** 2D
Field Of Destiny*set slw pace to 5 out, sn outpcd, fin 3rd, promoted*.......... 2
Also: Mr Moss Trooper (pu)
4 ran. 2l, dist. SP 6-4.

394 - Maiden 6yo+ I

294 **Locklan [15]** ....**Lulu Olivefalk** 1
ld to 5th & frm 9th, styd on well 2 out ....
269 **Givemeyourhand [12]***prog to chal 3 out, outpcd frm nxt*.......... 2
337 **Spectre Brown [10]***prom to 4 out, wknd*.......... 3
Also: 272 An Tuiodoir (4), 341³ Four Zeros (5), Charlie Hawes (ur), 269 Double Opportunity (pu), Drumriza (f), 268 M Macg (ur), Regular Beat (ur), Stoneyacre (pu)
11 ran. 8l, dist, 1½l, 20l. SP 4-1.

395 - Maiden 6yo+ II

298³ **Captains View [16]**......................**T Angel** 1
ld 4th, drew clr apr last ....
341 **Mahankhali [13]***ld to 4th, prssd wnr til outpcd apr last*
300 **Robotic [12]***prog 4 out, ev ch 2 out, onepcd*.......... 3
Also: 103 Timeless River [10] (4), 269 Castle Union (5), 269 Taste Of Freedom (6), 337 Collooney Squire (pu), 300 Herb Superb (pu), 179 Northern Granite (pu), 283³ Sinergia (pu), 341 The Financier (pu), 266 Venerdi Santo (f)
12 ran. 6l, 3l, 5l, dist, 1l. SP 2-1.

FAIRYHOUSE
Tuesday April 9th
GOOD

396 - 3m 1f Hun Chase

100¹ **Elegant Lord (Ire) 12.10** ....**Mr E Bolger** 1
(fav) ....
168¹ **Corymandel (Ire) 12.4**...............**Mr P Fenton** 2
359 **Faha Gig (Ire) 11.6 7a**.............**Mr K O'Sullivan** 3
....
Fifth Generation (Ire) 10.13 7a ....
273 Spire Hill (Ire) 11.6 ....
5 ran. 9l, dist. Time 6m 25.6s. SP 1-5.

ROUTE HARRIERS
Limavady
Tuesday April 9th
FIRM

397 - Mares Maiden

319 **Gilloway Princess [12]** ....**G Martin**
prog 5 out, chal & lft in ld last ....
258 **Miss Top [10]***2nd to 4 out, btn whn lft 2nd last*..........
364³ **Dernamay***t.o.*..........
Also: 261 Tyrella Clear View (bd), 320 Midi Minstrel (pu), 320 Buck Thistle (f), Tilly Lamp [13] (f)
7 ran. 5l, dist. SP 5-1.

398 - Winners Of One

171² **Mister Black [18]** ....**P Graffin**
ld 4 out, comf..........
218 **Lord Loving [12]***ld to 4 out, sn btn*..........
2 ran. 10l. SP 1-3.

399 - 4m Open Lightweight

317¹ **Lacken Beau [20]** ....**R Arthur**
ld 4 out, easily..........
317 **Schweppes Tonic [13]***ld to 4 out, sn btn* ....
2 ran. 3l. SP 1-8.

400 - Maiden 4 & 5yo

283² **MC Clatchey [13]** ....**P Graffin**
ld 5 out, easily..........
285 **It'snotsimple***ld to 5 out, sn btn* ....
2 ran. 8l. SP 1-5.

401 - Confined Lightweight

287³ **Quayfield [18]**.....................**J Mawhinney**
ld 4 out, easily..........
286 **Cheerio Fidel VI [11]***chsd wnr 3 out, no dang*..........
98 **Lord Sammy***t.o.*..........
Also: 172 Willie Be Brave (4), 319 Glen Deal (ur)
5 ran. 12l, dist, 1½l. SP 1-3.

402 - Maiden 6yo+

288 **Kilmacrew [14]** ....**L Gracey**
made all, all out ....
318 **Bonquist [13]***prog 4 out, hrd rdn last, no ext*..........
365 **Oneman's Choice [13]***prog 3 out, hrd rdn & styd on*..
Also: 341 Sir Gallop (4), 172 The Conawarey (5), 361 Stag Hunt (288³ Sheer Indulgence (ro)
7 ran. 1l, 1l, 20l, 3l, 15l. SP 16-1.

EAST ANTRIM
Loughanmore
Friday April 12th
SOFT

403 - Maiden 7yo+ I

269 **Shrule Hill [16]** ....**A Martin**
chsd ldng pair, ld 3 out, clr nxt, styd on wll ....
321 **Giorgione [13]***4th til kpt on frm 2 out, tk 2nd last*......
215² **Blossom World***chsd ldr, ld hlfwy-3 out, wknd*..........
Also: 340 Knocans Pride (4), 401³ Lord Sammy (pu), 365² Flodart (My Guitar (f), 402 Sir Gallop (pu), 365 Fernhill Way (ro), 302 Meloc Lady (pu), 321 Neely (pu)
11 ran. 10l, dist, 2l. SP 3-1.

404 - Maiden 7yo+ II

360² Dick's Cabin [12] ....**B Hamilton** 1
ld, clr 2 out, hdd sn aft, 3rd & btn whn lft clr last........
321 Zieg [10]*chsd ldrs, 4th 3 out, btn whn lft 2nd last......* 2
305 Cahills Hill [15]*hld up, ld aft 2 out, clr whn f last, rmntd* 3
Also: 179 Kimbry (pu), 305 Dara Knight (ur), 321³ Highland Buck (ur), 360 Little Celia (ur), 321² Triple Bush (f), 305 Leannes Man [13] (f), Gotsomeofthat (pu)
10 ran. 6l, dist. SP 6-1.

405 - Winners Of Two

281¹ O'Fiaich's Hope [18] ....**P Graffin** 1
made all, hld on wll flat..........................
316¹ High Star [18]*chsd wnr, ev ch whn mstk 2 out, rallied flat*.............................. 2
228¹ Bredinthepurple [17]*mstly 3rd, fin wll, nrst fin........* 3
Also: 362 Castle Royal [14] (4), Shanecracken [13] (5), 315² Kylnhill (6), 304³ Pats Cross (ur), 398² Lord Loving (pu), 360 J J's Hope (pu)
9 ran. ½l, 1l, 10l, 2l, 30l. SP 14-1.

406 - Mares Lightweight

362 Cabbery Rose [21] ....**P Graffin** 1
made all, clr 2 out, easily ....
315¹ Gale Griffin [15]*chsd wnr hlfwy, no imp 2 out ....* 2
316² Kildowney Lady [14]*chsd wnr to hlfwy, no imp 3 out..* 3
Also: 258¹ Kilmainhwood [12] (4), 347¹ Sister Seven (5), 320 Fidsprit (pu), 302 Manhattan Jewel (f), 316 Moyavo Lady (pu)
8 ran. 12l, 4l, 6l, 10l. SP 5-1.

407 - Maiden 4 & 5yo

361³ Ballydesmond [15] ....**G McKeever** 1
w.w. 3rd 5 out, ld 3 out, styd on wll ....
299 Raleagh Muggins [13]*prog 4 out, chsd wnr 2 out, no imp* 2
318 Panda Nova [11]*chsd ldr 5 out, onepcd aft..........* 3
Also: 282 Pharbrook Lad (pu), Coq Au Vin (pu), Jackie's Boy (pu), 318³ Anns Display (pu), 174 Shimna River (pu), 299 Secret Prince (pu), Yankie Lord (pu), 299 Ballinavary VI (pu), Bluagale (pu), 255 Bridge End (f), Millerman (pu)
14 ran. 5l, 6l. SP 16-1.

408 - Mares Maiden 4-6yo

285² Sideways Sally [15] ....**E Magee** 1
made all, clr 2 out, mstk last ....
364 In The Future*prog to chs wnr 4 out, chal nxt, btn 2 out*
Also: 286 Ngala (pu), 320 Coloured Thyme (pu), 365 Bit Of A Song (pu), 302 Denel de (f), 319 Hillview Susie (f), 319 Nancy Hill (pu), 320² Lillooet (f)
9 ran. 20l. SP 7-1.

409 - Unplaced Maiden

283 Wayside Spin [13]....................**B Hamilton** 1
ld to 4th, lft in ld 6 out, drw clr apr last..............
365 Florida Or Bust [11]*4th 5 out, prog & ev ch 2 out, onepcd*.............................. 2
365 Christimatt*rear, prog 4 out, ev ch nxt, sn outpcd .....* 3
Also: 173 Myown Treasure (pu), Willy Wee (f), 231 Jacksorbetter (pu), Doc-Halliday (pu), 319 Scotts Cross (pu), 318 Opening Quote (pu), 256 Just Spellbound (ur), Chat Run (pu), Irish Oats (pu)
12 ran. 6l, 6l. SP 6-1.

EAST ANTRIM
Loughanmore
Saturday April 13th
SOFT

410 - Winners Of Two

219 Hollow Suspicion [14] ....**G Coulter** 1
prog 4 out, ld 2 out, kpt on ....
282³ Rolier [12]*ld 5 out-2 out, not qckn ....* 2
Also: 284 Ballywoodock VI (pu), 288 Political Star (pu), 259 Sarah's Cherrie (pu), 319³ Glenbrin (f), 409 Just Spellbound (f)
7 ran. 5l. SP 16-1.

411 - 5 & 6yo Final

300¹ Garethson [17]..........................**A Martin** 1
prog 4 out, ld aft 2 out, jnd post ....
316 Gawn Inn [17]..........................**R Patton** 1
prog 4 out, chal last, styd on to jn ldr post............
282¹ Ballymacrevan [16]*ld to 4 out, ev ch apr last, kpt on flat*.............................. 3
Also: 316 The Convincer [15] (4), 283¹ Uncle Art (5), 300¹ Denfield (pu), 287 Coq Hardi Dancer (f), 282 Bell Hunter (pu)
8 ran. Dd-ht, 1l, 4l, 30l.
Both winners 6/1.

412 - Open Lightweight

382¹ Slaney Food [23] ....**J Quigley** 1
hld up, prog 4 out, chal nxt, ld flat, ran on well.........
317³ Jims Choice [22]*ld hlfwy til aft last, no ext ....* 2
363¹ Find Out More [12]*bhnd, prog whn mstk 3 out, no ch aft* 3
Also: 363 It's A Fiddle [12] (4), 363 Young Entry (5), 392² Temporale (6), 218¹ Over The Maine (pu), 363 Copper Friend (pu)
8 ran. 1½l, dist, ½l, 10l, 25l. SP 5-4.

413 - Maiden

404 Leannes Man [15] ....**P Gault** 1
made all, lft clr 4 out, drvn out flat..................
Man Of Iron [15]*prog & lft 3rd 4 out, chal flat, just hld* 2
365³ Grove Victor [14]*prog to jn wnr whn blnd 4 out, kpt on agn flat* 3
Also: 256³ Longmore Boy [11] (4), 301 Golden Start (5), 282 Springfarm Rath (6), 395 Sinergia (pu), 174³ Pilbara (pu), 365 A Bit Of A Monkey (ur), 321 Ordain (pu), 97² Tobermore (f), 179 Forever Gold (f)
12 ran. ½l, 7l, 2l, 30l, dist. SP 3-1.

414 - Winners Of Two Mares

406¹ Cabbery Rose [22] ....**P Graffin** 1
cls up, ld 4 out, clr 2 out, easily ....
304 La Maja [15]*prog 5 out, chsd wnr 3 out, no imp.........* 2
319¹ Satin Talker [12]*ld to 4 out, 3rd & btn nxt............* 3
Also: 362² Royal Aristocrat (4), 389 Mordella Lass (ur), 339 Serious Note (pu)
6 ran. 20l, 10l, 10l. SP Evens.

415 - Unplaced Maiden

Who Is Ed [16] ....**A Martin** 1
made most to 6 out, lft in ld 3 out, clr whn blnd last.....
320 Fidoon [12]*prog to 3rd 2 out, kpt on onepcd..........* 2
258 Farlough Lady [10]*in tch, chsd wnr 2 out, no imp......* 3
Also: 391 Young Bebe (4), 409 Jacksorbetter (5), 285 Darshaba (pu), 261 Swaning Around (f), 288 Moyavo Lad (pu), 360 Three Town Rock (pu), 341 Fill Your Boots (pu), 321 Penylan Jack (pu), 321 Wanclasstrain (pu), 255 Just Horseplay (ur), 365 Grey Rock (pu)
14 ran. 6l, 8l, dist, 5l. SP 4-5.

WICKLOW FOXHOUNDS
Camolin
Sunday April 14th
HEAVY

416 - Maiden 7yo+

387³ Will Travel [15] ....**H Cleary** 1
wth ldr to 3 out, rallied to ld flat, styd on ....
166 Noble Knight [15]*ld, clr 2 out, hdd & no ext flat ......* 2
Tomeko [14]*styd on frm 2 out, nrst fin ....* 3
Also: 345² Shimano [14] (4), 341 Eastern Fox [12] (5), 228 Scar Statement [10] (6), 388 Junior Moss (7), 305 Solitary Spirit (8), 345 Get Into It (ur), 154 Dunbeacon (pu), 349 Kingeochy (pu), 387 Gallic Twister (pu)
12 ran. 1l, 2l, 1l, 6l, 4l, dist, dist. SP 7-4.

417 - Mares Maiden I

Fiddling The Facts [16]..................**P Graffin** 1
prom, ld 4 out, styd on wll 2 out.....................
384 **Key Door [15]***ld to 4 out, ev ch 2 out, no ext*.......... 2
225[2] **Warkey Lady [14]***cls up, onepcd frm 2 out*........... 3
Also: 348[2] Little Minute [13] (4), Rehey Lady [13] (5), Kilannadrum (6), 167 Baileys Dream (7), 347 Riverrunsthroughit (8), Deep Salmon (pu), Lady Sandalay (pu), 384 Harlin Lady (pu), 232 Short Of A Buck (f), Lady Windgates (pu), 384 Ballyedmond (pu), Regular Rose (pu), 384 Talbot's Hollow (pu), 385 Glenroe Gal (pu), 226 Buzz About (pu), 340 Brooklawn (f)
19 ran. 3l, 2l, 2l, ½l, 25l, dist, ½l. SP 4-1.

418 - Mares Maiden II

Mullabawn [15]...........................**J Finn** 1
prom, ld 5 out, rdn out............................
384 **Orafeno [14]***chsd wnr 4 out, ev ch apr last, no ext*.... 2
Ballyday Step [10]*chsd ldrs, onepcd 3 out*........... 3
Also: 324 Yashgans Vision (4), 163 Timeforgoing (5), 340[2] Awaytoday (6), 324 Sataldo (f), Noble Melody (pu), 226 Seaview Star (pu), 385 Killaligan Kim (pu), 322 The Buck Pony (pu), Tremble Valley (pu), Dowhatyouhavetodo (f), 384 Hardtobegood (pu), 325 Lady Bremur (pu), Wandering Choice (pu), 381 Menedream (pu), Accountancy Perk (pu)
18 ran. 1½l, 12l, 20l, 12l, 15l. SP 14-1.

419 - Winners Of One

333[3] **Lady Elise [17]**...........................**J Codd** 1
made all, clr whn mstk last, unchal....................
Priceless Buck [15]*chsd wnr 4 out, no real imp*...... 2
383 **Princess Breda [14]***chsd wnr to 4 out, onepcd*....... 3
Also: 198 It's A Deal [14] (4), 383 Cedarbelle (5)
5 ran. 2l, 3l, ½l, 20l. SP 5-2.

420 - Maiden 4-6yo I

192 **Haven't An Ocean [15]**....................**J Berry** 1
prog 4 out, disp & lft clr 2 out, styd on...............
345[3] **Captain Guinness [13]***prom, 4th & btn whn lft 2nd 2 out, onepcd*.................................. 2
345 **Major Man [10]***nvr nrr*.......................... 3
Also: 387 Lord Knox (4), 231 Fortynine Plus (5), 388 Over The Barrow (6), 381 The Podger (pu), 343 Side Stepper (pu), 343 Master Chuzzlewit (f), 386 Torduff Express (pu), 311 Glentoralda (pu), 386 Nobodys Boy (pu), 220 Do Drop In (pu), 343 More Rain (f), 342 Royal Arctic (f)
15 ran. 4l, 8l, 3l, 20l, dist. SP 7-4.

421 - Maiden 4-6yo II

343 **Lovable Outlaw [15]**.....................**D Whelan** 1
chsd ldrs, lft 2nd 2 out, styd on to ld flat...............
387 **Who's Your Man [14]***chsd ldng pair, lft in ld 2 out, wknd & hdd flat*.................................. 2
343 **Punters Fortune [12]***chsd ldrs, kpt on onepcd frm 2 out*.. 3
Also: 388 Louis de Palmer (4), Gaelic Glen (5), 343 Cracker Alley (pu), 381[3] Greedy Johno (pu), Newtown Road (f), 343 Sweetmount Lad (f), Chas Randall (f), 345 Hey Chief (pu), Kimber Sissons (ur), 386 Montel Express (pu)
13 ran. 2l, 5l, 12l, 10l. SP 4-1.

422 - Open Lightweight

382[2] **Loch Garman Hotel [22]**.................**A Martin** 1
ld 4th, drw clr 3 out, comf............................
383[2] **Coolafinka [20]***ld to 4th, chal 4 out, btn frm nxt*....... 2
344[1] **Dromhana [20]***chsd ldrs, unable qckn 3 out, styd on*.. 3
Also: 355 Trimmer Wonder [14] (4), 197 Miss Tornado (pu), 338[1] Ballinaboola Grove (pu), 382 Glen Og Lane (su)
7 ran. 2l, ½l, 15l. SP 7-4.

423 - Nomination

383[1] **Slaney Wind [19]**.........................**H Cleary** 1
prom, ld 3 out, ran on well............................
84 **Duirse Dairse [16]***ld to 3 out, onepcd*................ 2
276 **Trimmer Princess [15]***alwys prom, onepcd frm 4 out* 3
Also: 386 Dusty Track [10] (4), Deeyehfollyme (f), 384 Tara River (pu)
6 ran. 6l, 3l, 15l. SP 2-5.

CO GALWAY
Athenry
Sunday April 14th
GOOD

424 - Maiden 4 & 5yo

114[3] **Lakefield Leader [15]**...............**J O'Connell** 1
made most to 3 out, mstk nxt, styd on to ld flat.........
274[3] **Fountain Page [14]***prog to ld 3 out, wknd & hdd flat*.. 2
147 **Into The Web***nvr dang*............................ 3
Also: 147 Wintry Willow (4), 390 Riberetto's Girl (5), 366 Legal Whisper (f), 205[2] Drumline Castle (pu), 366 Satco Supreme (pu), Amewsing (pu), 247 Cruisin On Credit (pu)
10 ran. 2l, 20l, 2l, 20l. SP 4-1.

425 - Winners Of Two

393[2] **Field Of Destiny [17]**..................**G Harford** 1
ld to 2 out, btn whn lft clr last.........................
126 **Lakeview Lad [14]***chsd ldrs, 3rd & btn whn lft 2nd last*... 2
Also: 296[1] Minor Key (ur), 327[1] Knights Crest (f), 328[1] Big Murt [18] (f), 39[1] Five Circles (pu)
6 ran. 4l. SP 4-1.

426 - Open Lightweight

357[1] **Slaney Goodness [21]**..............**Lillian Doyle** 1
prom, chal & lft in ld last, hld on gamely.............
372[1] **Up For Ransome [21]***prom, hmpd last, chal flat, alwys hld*..................................... 2
338 **Red Express VI [19]***w.w. prog 2 out, nvr nrr*......... 3
Also: 326[1] Geata Bawn [14] (4), 265[3] Missing Lady [12] (5), 329[2] Frazer Island [21] (f)
6 ran. ½l, 4l, 15l, 6l. SP 5-2.

427 - Mares Maiden I

354[3] **Sleetmore Gale [16]**....................**B Hassett** 1
ld 5th, clr 5 out, unchal..............................
Bet With Rosie*effrt 5 out, sn btn*...................... 2
232 **Gala Vote***effrt 5 out, sn btn, t.o.*..................... 3
Also: 309[3] Queen Of The Suir (f), Expensive Pleasure (f), Castlelake Lady (f), 127 Aine Hencey (f), Hogan (ur), 291 Mona Lita (pu), 301[2] Friendly Bid (f), 369 Lantern Spark (pu)
11 ran. Dist, dist. SP 2-1.

428 - Mares Maiden II

291[3] **No Swap [17]**......................**Lulu Olivefalk** 1
3rd til chsd ldr 5 out, styd on to ld last, sn clr..........
Cool Della [15]*plld hrd, clr ldr til wknd & hdd last*.... 2
391[3] **Ballybriken Castle***chsd ldr to 5 out, wknd*........... 3
Also: 370 Reinskea (4), 324 The Lazy Cat (ur), 340 Mum's The Word (pu), Moyode Lady (pu), 232 Taylors Twist (ur), 204 Barmur (pu), 369 Rosetown Girl (pu)
10 ran. 5l, dist, dist. SP 3-1.

429 - Maiden 6yo+ I

394[2] **Givemeyourhand [16]**.............**Lulu Olivefalk** 1
trckd ldrs, ld 2 out, comf..............................
367 **Carramore Hill [14]***prom, lft in ld 3 out, hdd & outpcd nxt*.. 2
300 **Drop The Act [10]***styd on frm 2 out, nrst fin*.......... 3
Also: 297[2] Trackman (4), The Deane Delegate (5), 237[3] Rovet (pu), Once In A Lifetime (f), 311 Komori (f), 266 Almaurita (pu), 367 Ballinahowna Lad (ur), 395 Castle Union (f), 389[2] Castlepook (f), 158 Treens Folly (pu)
13 ran. 4l, 12l, 6l, dist. SP 2-1.

430 - Maiden 6yo+ II

Debonair Dude [16]..................**J O'Connell** 1
ld 5 out, lft clr 3 out, styd on.........................

368[2] **Flood Relief [11]***chal & mstk 3 out, btn aft* 2
311 Mr Dennehy [10]*chsd ldrs & onepcd frm 3 out* 3
Also: 236 St Aidan (4), 367 September Stephen (5), 300 Normus (pu), 236 Knock Ranger (f), Belville Pond (pu), 394 Charlie Hawes (ur), 108 Pearl Dante (pu), 125 Daffydown Breeze VI (pu)
11 ran. 15l, 4l, 5l, dist. SP 3-1.

431 - Adjacent Maiden

367 Cahergowan [15] ....**D Duggan** 1
prom, ld 3 out, clr nxt, styd on ....
368[3] **The Defender***prom, ld 5 out-3 out, wknd nxt*.......... 2
201 Rushing Waters*kpt on frm 2 out, no dang*.......... 3
Also: 233 Ivy Glen (4), 237 Carnmore House (pu), 368 Autumn Call (f), 334 Prince Of Thyne (pu), Pigeonstown (f)
8 ran. 25l, 1l, 20l. SP 5-1.

CARBERY FOXHOUNDS
Bandon
Sunday April 14th
GOOD

432 - Adjacent Maiden

245 Terrano Star [16] ....**N Fehily** 1
made all, clr 2 out, easily ....
358 Classis King*hrd rdn to chal 3 out, sn wknd*........... 2
311 Tom The Boy Vl*alwys bhnd* 3
Also: 353 Lady Fountain (pu), 274 Clonageera (pu), 309 Noneofyourbusiness (pu), 354 Harvest Delight (pu)
7 ran. Dist, 10l. SP 4-5.

433 - Mares Maiden I

353 Brigade Leader [15] ....**K O'Sullivan** 1
prom, ld 3 out, hld on wll flat ....
379[2] **Solar Castle [15]***cls up, chal apr last, no ext flat* 2
353[2] **Rascal Street Lad [15]***prom, ld 5 out-3 out, ev ch last, no ext flat* 3
Also: 353 Rio Star [10] (4), 185 Anyone Whoknows Me (5), 279 Lios Na Maol (pu), 279[3] Lady Of Means (pu), 353 Brown Berry (pu), 325 Pharding (pu), Miss Bertaine (pu), 307 Nissan Star (pu)
11 ran. ½l, nk, 15l. SP 6-1.

434 - Mares Maiden II

330[3] **Glen Empress [17]**....................**K O'Sullivan** 1
prom, ld hlfwy, easily ....
356 Tourig Dante [12]*chsd wnr 4 out, no imp* 2
380[3] **Riot Lady [12]***chsd wnr 4 out, no imp* 3
Also: 211[3] Round Tower Lady (4), 279 High Park Lady (pu), 152 Celia's Pride (pu), 335 Suite Cottage Lady (pu), Fountain Lady (pu), 324 Ellesmere (bd), 308 Castlemore Leader (pu), Araglen Lass (pu)
11 ran. 10l, ½l, dist. SP 4-7.

435 - Open Lightweight

378 Awbeg Rover [20]....................**K O'Sullivan** 1
prog to ld aft 3 out, styd on wll flat ....
355 Myalup [18]*prog 3 out, chal apr last, alwys hld* 2
378 Lisadante [15]*disp 4 out-aft nxt, onepcd aft*.......... 3
Also: 331 Mr Pipeman (4), 310[3] Try God (5), 357[3] Some Tourist (pu), 310 Battle Hard (pu)
7 ran. 2l, 10l, 20l. SP 3-1.

436 - Winners Of One

354[1] **Irene's Call [19]**......................**K O'Sullivan** 1
ld 4 out, sn clr, mstk last ....
59[1] **Rosie's Pride [13]***ld to 4 out, no ch wth wnr aft*........ 2
186 The Criosra [13]*kpt on frm 2 out, no dang* 3
Also: 355 Fair Revival (4), 140 Next Right (pu), 357 Saddle Her Well (pu), 279[1] The Pulpit (pu), 333 July Schoon (pu)
8 ran. 20l, nk, 20l. SP 6-4.

437 - Maiden 6yo+

78 Desertmore [17] ....**N Fehily** 1
prog to ld 4 out, easily..............................
312[2] **Weak Moment [13]***chsd wnr 2 out, no imp* 2
374 Safety Factor*disp to 4 out, sn outpcd* 3
Also: 328 Prayon Parson (4), 353 Vital Approach (5), 244 Des The Architect (6), 297 Cooling Chimes (7), 334 Kendor Pass (pu), 358[3] Brian Og (ur), 227 Caribo Express (pu), 244 Lazy Acres (pu)
11 ran. 10l, 15l, 6l. SP 5-2.

438 - Maiden 4 & 5yo

352[2] **Galebreaker [15]** ....**D Murphy** 1
made virt all, drew clr frm 3 out ....
330 Four From Home*chsd wnr 5 out, btn frm nxt* 2
351 Monadante*nvr dang* 3
Also: 243 Short Circuit (4), 351 Electric Can (pu), 275 Martha's Boy (pu), 52 Silver Blend (pu), 352 Jacky Flynn (pu), 275[3] No Problem (f)
9 ran. Dist, 6l, 2l. SP 3-1.

LIMERICK FOXHOUNDS
Kilmallock
Sunday April 14th
GOOD TO FIRM

439 - Maiden 4yo

330 Ahead Of My Time [16]..................**P Fenton** 1
chsd ldr, disp last, just hld on ....
330[2] **Runabout [16]***chsd ldr, disp last, just hld*............ 2
Stormyfairweather [13]*ld to last, wknd*.............. 3
Also: 307[3] Brickanmore [10] (4), Hill Of Grace (pu), Irish Frolic (pu), Dirra Minstrel (pu), 292[2] Sam Quale (f)
8 ran. Hd, 10l, 8l. SP 4-1.

440 - Maiden 5yo

205 La Mon Dere [15] ....**R Flavin** 1
prom, ld 2 out, hld on wll ....
323 Meldante Vl [15]*prom, chal 2 out, just hld*.......... 2
293 Action Lad [12]*chsd ldrs, onepcd frm 2 out*.......... 3
Also: 293 Odds On (4), 200[2] Thunder Road (5), 366 Lightoak Lad (6), Rodo (7), Buckshee (8), 352 Lord Pat (9), 275 Silent Pond (10), Cash Flow (11), 366 Tom Deely (pu), 292 Banner Year (pu), 277[2] Black Fountain (f), 332 Mr Boomaleen (pu), 248 Mr Campus (pu), 275[2] Coolflugh Hero (f), 148 Serenade Star (pu), 352[3] Bosco's Touch (pu)
19 ran. Hd, 8l, 8l. SP 10-1.

441 - Winners Of One

The Yellow Bog [17] ....**E Bolger** 1
mid-div, prog 4 out, ld apr last, styd on ....
153 Flairline Bay [16]*disp til ld 4 out, hdd & no ext apr last* 2
72 Grants Carouse [11]*disp to 4 out, wknd 2 out*........ 3
Also: 289[1] Digacre [10] (4), 294 Upshepops (5), 333 Dromin Pride (pu), 313 Strong Vision (f), 295 Selm Mary (pu), 392 Fethard Orchid (pu), 371 Camogue Bridge (pu)
10 ran. 2l, 15l, 2½l. SP 4-1.

442 - Open Lightweight

295[1] **Just A Breeze [20]** ....**T Cloke** 1
hld up, prog 2 out, hrd rdn to ld flat ....
372 Hopefully True [20]*ld to flat, just hld*.............. 2
378 Howarya Harry [17]*chsd ldrs, onepcd frm 2out* 3
Also: Master Julian (pu), 372[3] Bit Of A Touch (pu)
5 ran. Hd, 5l. SP 11-10.

443 - Mares Maiden I

369[3] **Lishillaun [16]** ....**J Collins** 1
hld up, ld 3 out, clr last ....
369 Strong Stern*chsd wnr 3 out, no imp*.............. 2
325 Bay Lough*chsd ldrs, no imp 3 out*.............. 3
Also: 369 Kochnie (4), 253 Lady Clarina (5), 291 My New Merc (6), 370 Rockview Supreme (pu), 289[3] Manley Girl (bd), 370[2] Ring Mam (f), Buxom Orlov (pu), Special Company (pu), 37 Tenpence Princess (pu)
12 ran. 20l, 2l, 1l. SP 7-2.

444 - Mares Maiden II

369 Knocktoran Lady [15] ....S Hennessy 1
made all, hld on wll flat...........................
325 Cozy Cottage [14]*prog to chal last, no ext flat* 2
335 Brogeen Dubh [13]*chsd ldrs, kpt on onepcd apr last* 3
Also: 253³ Oriental Blaze (4), 370 Forgoodnessjake VI (5), 354 Scarra Darragh (6), 120 Lee Valley Lady (pu), 309 Fort Rouge (pu), Grannys Cottage (f), 291 Daytime Dancer (pu), 379 Scottish Socks (pu), Tacmahack (pu)
12 ran. 1½l, 2l, 20l. SP 5-1.

445 - Maiden 6yo+ I

155 Shareza River [16] ....W Ewing 1
prog to ld 5 out, easily...........................
334 Tavern Tale [10]*chsd wnr 3 out, no imp* 2
311 Earl Of Mirth*nvr dang* 3
Also: 296² Minella Star (4), Sonny Sullivan (pu), Speedy Dan (pu), Abettortime (pu), 389 Park Duke (pu), Tullaghfin (pu), 250 Mr Connie Vee (pu), Invincible Lad (pu)
11 ran. 15l, 6l, 6l. SP 2-1.

446 - Maiden 6yo+ II

327² Easy Catch [17] ....E Bolger 1
trckd ldrs, ld 2 out, comf ....
334 An Oon Iss An Owl [14]*styd on frm 2 out, no ch wth wnr* 2
237² Coshla Expresso [12]*ld to 2 out, onepcd*............ 3
Also: 86 Deerpark King (4), 78 Strong Stuff (5), 328³ Have Another (6), 328 Blazing Crack (pu), 38 Lets Twist Again (pu), Mirromark (pu), 377 Sammy Sunshine (pu), Proven Schedule (pu)
11 ran. 5l, 4l, 8l. SP Evens.

GOWRAN PARK
Wednesday April 17th
HEAVY

447 - 3m Hun Chase

100² Credit Transfer (Ire) 11.10 ....Mr H F Cleary 1
378¹ What Thing 10.12 7a.............Mr J G Sheehan 2
359¹ Aiguille (Ire) 11.3 7a...........Mr J T McNamara 3
396 Fifth Generation (Ire) 11.3 7a 4
135¹ Stay In Touch (Ire) 11.12 3a *(fav)* 5
346 Patty's Pride 11.7 3a (bl) .... pu
426³ Red Express VI 11.13 .... pu
396² Corymandel (Ire) 12.1 .... pu
359 Crazy Dreams (Ire) 11.10 .... pu
91³ Dublin Hill (Ire) 11.3 7a .... pu
359² Silent Sneeze (Ire) 10.12 7a (bl) .... pu
Kilburry (Ire) 11.3 7a .... pu
Minstrel Madame (Ire) 11.0 7a 2ow .... pu
13 ran. Dist, 25l, 8l, dist. Time 6m 41.8s. SP 2-1.

NEWRY HARRIERS
Taylorstown
Saturday April 20th
SOFT

448 - Mares Maiden I

406 Manhattan Jewel [15]...............L McBratney 1
ld 6 out, clr 3 out, comf ....
406 Fidsprit [11]*disp to 6 out, kpt on agn to go 2nd last* ... 2
360³ Half Scotch [10]*disp to 6 out, chsd wnr aft til wknd apr last*............................ 3
Also: 319 Ellies Pride (4), 403 Knocans Pride (5), 408 Denel de (pu), 321 Fair Avoca (pu), 364 Welsh Sitara (f), 415² Fidoon (pu), 320 Iveagh Lady (ur), 409 Scotts Cross (pu), 415³ Farlough Lady (pu)
12 ran. 10l, 4l, 20l, 1½l. SP 6-4.

449 - Mares Maiden II

403³ Blossom World [15]...................I Buchanan 1
lft in ld 3 out, easily ....
319² Arctic Leader [10]*chsd wnr frm 3 out, no imp*........ 2
408 Coloured Thyme*t.o.* 3
Also: 397 Tyrella Clear View (4), 284 Karens Leader (pu), 340 Damolly Rose (ur), Principal Peace (pu), 319 Island Harriet (pu), 408 Nancy Hill (pu), 301 Gerry's Delight (ro), Princess Guillaume (pu), 391 Skin Graft (pu)
12 ran. 10l, dist, 6l. SP 5-4.

450 - Maiden I

361² Takeithandy [16] ....L Lennon 1
w.w. chsd ldr 3 out, ld apr last, styd on well ....
403 Neely [14]*ld hlfwy, clr 2 out, hdd & no ext apr last*..... 2
413 Ordain [12]*kpt on frm 2 out, nrst fin* 3
Also: 404 Kimbry [11] (4), 415 Moyavo Lad (5), 407 Bridge End (pu), 407 Jackie's Boy (pu), 318 Cascum Lad (pu), 407 Shimna River (pu), 409³ Christimatt (pu), 300 Irenes Treasure (pu)
11 ran. 4l, 6l, 3l, dist. SP 2-1.

451 - Maiden II

Amazing All [18].......................I Buchanan 1
made all, drew clr 3 out, easily ....
407³ Panda Nova [12]*chsd ldrs, 3rd 5 out, kpt on frm last, no ch wth wnr* 2
413³ Grove Victor [11]*chsd wnr, no imp 3 out, wknd last*... 3
Also: 402² Bonquist [10] (4), 404 Highland Buck (pu), 413 A Bit Of A Monkey (pu), 318 Parman (pu), 407 Bluagale (pu), 407 Anns Display (pu), 409 Irish Oats (pu), Excuse Me (f)
11 ran. 15l, 4l, 4l. SP 8-1.

452 - Winners Of Two

405² High Star [20] ....I Buchanan 1
made all, drew clr 4 out, easily ....
362¹ Annie's Arthur [11]*chsd wnr & cls up 5 out, no ch aft* 2
257 Cool Yule*nvr dang* 3
Also: 315 Claire Me (4), 400¹ MC Clatchey (pu)
5 ran. Dist, 6l, 3l. SP Evens.

453 - Open Lightweight

399¹ Lacken Beau [24] ....R Arthur 1
hld up, ld 4 out, sn wll clr ....
412³ Find Out More [15]*rear, kpt on to poor 2nd aft last* ... 2
406² Gale Griffin [14]*prom, ld 5 out-nxt, no ch wth wnr aft* 3
Also: 412 It's A Fiddle (pu), 399² Schweppes Tonic (pu), 412 Copper Friend (pu)
6 ran. Dist, 4l. SP 4-6.

454 - Winners Of One

236¹ Spire Hill [18].............................K Ross 1
prom, ld 4 out, clr 2 out, mstk last, rdn out ....
430¹ Debonair Dude [16]*cls up, chsd wnr 3 out, btn nxt, kpt on wll flat*........................... 2
362³ Chene Rose*nvr dang*........................... 3
Also: 406³ Kildowney Lady (4), 362 More Than Most (pu), 287 Manhattan Prince (pu), 411 The Convincer (pu), 413¹ Leannes Man (f), 397¹ Gilloway Princess (f), 364¹ Sapphire 'N' Silver (pu), 261¹ Ahogill (pu)
11 ran. 3l, dist, 6l. SP 4-1.

455 - Unplaced Maiden I

341 Ballybrit [14]...........................G Harford 1
in tch, chal whn lft clr aft 2 out, in no dang aft.........
321 Pauls Point*lft poor 2nd aft 2 out, no imp wnr* 2
404 Dara Knight*t.o.*........................... 3
Also: 176 Windmill Star (pu), 112 Thorn Cottage (pu), Four North (pu), Fair Tree (pu), 403 Fernhill Way (f), 415 Penylan Jack (pu), 408 Bit Of A Song (pu), 415 Young Bebe (f)
11 ran. Dist, dist. SP 5-4.

456 - Unplaced Maiden II

411 **Bell Hunter [12]** .... **N Toal** 1
ld 4 out, clr whn blnd last
415 **Grey Rock***blnd 6 out, chsd wnr 3 out, no imp* 2
Also: 110 Some Man (f), 415 Fill Your Boots (ref), One Eleven (f), Ballysadare Bay (pu), 409 Opening Quote (pu), 415 Wanclasstrain (pu), 321 Travarians Gold (f), Farm Lodge (pu), Macken Money (pu)
11 ran. 8l. SP 5-1.

DONERAILE HARRIERS
Dromahane
Sunday April 21st
HEAVY

457 - Adjacent Maiden

358 **Know Something Vl [15]**............... **D Murphy** 1
made all, hld on wll flat
334 **Finnow Thyne [15]***chsd wnr whn blnd 4 out, rallied last, just hld*.......... 2
375 **Roskeen Bridge [12]***nvr nrr*.......... 3
Also: 354 Ballybeggan Lady (4), 332 Ask Me Another (5), Cnoc-Breac (pu), 324 Nicenames (pu), Leadtheboys (pu), Fountain Moss (pu), Conors Bluebird (f), 439 Hill Of Grace (pu), The Airy Man (pu), 306 Bartlemy King (pu), 379 Derrygallon Fancy (pu)
14 ran. 1l, 8l, 8l. SP 5-1.

458 - Maiden 5yo

375³ **Ellies Nelson [15]** .... **J Collins** 1
made all, styd on wll frm 2 out..........
Struggles Glory [14]*prog to chal 2 out, no ext flat* 2
244 **Lordinthesky***nvr dang*.......... 3
Also: 440 Lightoak Lad (4), 332 Ashburton Lord (5), 438 Jacky Flynn (pu), 332 Boreens Secret (pu), Minstrel's Quay (ro), 245 The Snuffman (pu), 332 Sheer Mischief (pu), Romeo's Brother (pu), 147 Jack's Well (f), 312 Island Echo (pu), 332 Castle Avenue (pu), 213 Fernhill House (pu)
15 ran. 2l, dist, 2l. SP 6-4.

459 - Mares Maiden I

351³ **Fileo [14]** .... **B Walsh** 1
made all, drew clr 4 out, hld on gamely flat ....
182 **Nans Pet [14]***w.w. prog to chal apr last, just hld*....... 2
354 **Frightening Child [12]***chsd ldrs, onepcd frm 2 out* 3
Also: 374 Have A Drop (4), 335³ Killatty Player (5), Call Her Lib (pu), 211 Macklette (pu), 434 Castlemore Leader (f), Macks Moss (bd), 352 White Wyandotte (f), 309 Everlaughing (pu), 335² Highways Sister (pu), 356 Woodville Princess (pu)
13 ran. Nk, 4l, dist. SP 10-1.

460 - Mares Maiden II

239 **Rose's Luck [14]** .... **E Gallagher** 1
prom, ld last, kpt on well..........
444³ **Brogeen Dubh [14]***prom, ld 3 out-last, no ext flat*..... 2
308 **Cherry Glen***nvr dang*.......... 3
Also: Carhoo Surprise (f), 335 Gale Tan (pu), 379³ Northern Katie (pu), Will I Or Wont I (pu), 352 The Wild Wave (pu), No Planning (bd), 351 Leaping Three (pu), 354 Miss Metal (pu), 444 Scarra Darragh (pu)
12 ran. ½l, dist. SP 5-2.

461 - Open Lightweight

209³ **Ruby Belle [21]**...................... **W O'Sullivan** 1
alwys going wll, ld 3 out, comf..........
355² **Riszard [18]***chsd wnr 3 out, rdn & no imp*.......... 2
263 **Okdo [15]***nvr nrr*.......... 3
Also: 355 Bocock's Pride (pu), 333 Minstrel Sam (pu), 212 Sweet Merenda (pu), 185¹ Reen-O-Foil (pu)
7 ran. 5l, 10l. SP 9-4.

462 - Maiden 6yo+

113² **Radical River [16]**..................... **T Lombard** 1
lft in ld 7 out, made rest, pshd out..........
358² **Mountain Hall [14]***chsd wnr 5 out, no imp 2 out*..... 2
358 **Foxwoods Valley [13]***chsd ldrs, onepcd frm 2 out* 3
Also: 327 Supreme Athlete [11] (4), Toytown King (pu), 268² Stonewall Curtin (f), A Little Help (pu), 312³ Dante's Reward (pu), 358 Luciano The Yuppi (pu), 445³ Earl Of Mirth (pu), 306 Round Pound (f), 207² Saol Sona (pu)
12 ran. 4l, 3l, 5l. SP 4-1.

463 - Winners Of One

437¹ **Desertmore [19]**......................... **N Fehily** 1
prom, ld 4 out, easily..........
331 **Sharoujack [16]***prog to chs wnr 3 out, no imp nxt* 2
378 **Carbery Minstrel***nvr dang*.......... 3
Also: 333 Elwill Glory (pu), 376 Scarlet River (pu), 186 Supreme Arctic (pu), 371³ Coolree Lord (pu)
7 ran. 6l, 25l. SP 6-4.

GOLDEN VALE
Thurles Point-To-Point Course
Sunday April 21st
HEAVY

464 - Maiden 4yo

Silver Sirocco [16].................... **M Scanlon** 1
trckd ldrs, ld 2 out, sn clr, comf..........
Lady Sylvie [12]*disp to 2 out, onepcd* 2
366 **Dinan [12]***disp to 2 out, onepcd*.......... 3
Also: Via Del Quatro [10] (4), 418 The Buck Pony (5), Kinnahalla (6), 384 Heymoll (ur), Cherishthelady (pu)
8 ran. 8l, 1l, 6l, 12l, 2l. SP 5-1.

465 - Maiden 5 & 6yo I

328 **Boots Madden [15]**...................... **W Ewing** 1
bhnd & rdn 4 out, styd on nxt, ld flat, drvn out ....
Shaws Cross [14]*prom, ld 3 out-flat, no ext*.......... 2
431³ **Rushing Waters***no dang frm 3 out, t.o.*.......... 3
Also: King's Banker (4), Mister Salvo (pu), 327 Mac-Duagh (pu), 125 Irish Display (ur), 446 Lets Twist Again (pu), Old Cavalier (pu), 386 Ringaheen (pu), 113 Keep Flowing (pu), 386³ Flying Fellow (pu)
12 ran. 2½l, dist, 10l. SP Evens.

466 - Maiden 5 & 6yo II

381² **Money Low [15]** .... **M Kavanagh** 1
disp 5 out til ld 2 out, drvn out..........
Hum 'N' Haw [14]*prog aft 4 out, ev ch 2 out, no ext flat*.......... 2
Tea Box [14]*disp 5 out-2 out, onepcd und pres* 3
Also: 356³ Glenaboy (pu), 38 An Fear Dubh (pu), 424 Legal Whisper (ro), Inch Cross (f), 375 Oneofourown (ur), 366 The Thin Fellow (pu), Clodiaghranger (bd), 424 Amewsing (f), 267 Footsy Murray (pu)
12 ran. 2½l, ½l. SP 3-1.

467 - Winners Of One

381¹ **Maxxum Plus [20]** .... **D Valentine** 1
ld 5 out, clr whn mstk last, easily..........
326 **Cloncannon Bell [14]***chsd wnr 3 out, no imp* 2
441 **Fethard Orchid [11]***nvr dang*.......... 3
Also: 358¹ Stroll Home [10] (4), 376 Killerk Lady (pu)
5 ran. 12l, 8l, 3l. SP Evens.

468 - Open Lightweight

Celtic Buck [23]...................... **P O'Keeffe** 1
trckd ldr, ld hlfwy, jnd & lft clr 2 out, unchal aft..........
295 **Duchess Of Padua [17]***3rd 5 out, btn whn lft 2nd 2 out, no imp*.......... 2
295 **Looking Ahead [16]***2nd 5 out, btn frm 2 out*.......... 3
Also: 435² Myalup [15] (4), 329 Hurricane Eden [14] (5), 441 Upshepops (f), Best Vintage (pu)
7 ran. 15l, 4l, 3l, 4l. SP 3-1.

469 - Mares Maiden 5yo+

291² **Handball [15]** ....**T Cloke** 1
prom, ld 5 out-3 out, ld nxt, styd on..................
204² **Galatasori Jane [13]***ld hlfwy-5 out, outpcd 3 out, kpt on* 2
427 **Castlelake Lady [12]***prog 4 out, ld 3 out-nxt, wknd last* 3
Also: 233 Handy Sally (4), 390 Condonstown (5), 325 Pleasing Melody (pu), Dockmaid (f), 428 Reinskea (pu), 164 Thank You (pu), Bucks Image (pu)
10 ran. 6l, 3l, 20l, 2l. SP 2-1.

470 - Unplaced Maiden

416 **Get Into It [13]** ....**P Curran** 1
n.j.w. bhnd, rpd prog aft 2 out, ld nr fin ....
327 **Forold [12]***rpd prog 2 out, ld flat, hdd nr fin* 2
377 **King Tyrant [10]***chsd ldr til aft 2 out, onepcd*......... 3
Also: 430 Charlie Hawes [10] (4), 237 Thinkaboutthat (5), The Cass Man (pu), 296 Guirns Shop (f), Pabelo (ur), Derring River (pu)
9 ran. 2l, 5l, 2l, 10l. SP 3-1.

LIMERICK HARRIERS
Friarstown
Sunday April 21st
GOOD

471 - Confined Maiden

366² **Executive Class [15]** ....**J McNamara** 1
trckd ldrs, ld aft 2 out, styd on wll ....
428 **Rosetown Girl [13]***chsd ldrs, kpt on frm 2 out, nrst fin* 2
370 **Yasgourra [12]***ld/disp til aft 2 out, no ext* 3
Also: 368 Winter Breeze [11] (4), 443 Buxom Orlov (pu), Kingsland (pu), 444 Forgoodnessjake VI (su)
7 ran. 3l, 4l, 2½l. SP Evens.

472 - Maiden 4 & 5yo

439² **Runabout [16]**.......................**J McNamara** 1
rear, prog 4 out, ld last, styd on strngly ....
440² **Meldante VI [12]***prom, ev ch last, sn no ext*........... 2
122 **General Ari [12]***prom til onepcd apr last* 3
Also: 366 Mr Tom Tom (4), 440 Banner Year (5), 323 Linda's Paradise (6), 292³ Willbrook (f), 332 Long Drive (pu), 366 Alberts Gamble (pu), 213 Neelisagin (f), 440 Odds On (pu), 440 Tom Deely (pu)
12 ran. 12l, ¾l, 15l. SP 7-2.

473 - Open Lightweight

368¹ **Rare Spread [21]**.......................**B Hassett** 1
cls up, ld last, pshd out ....
442² **Hopefully True [20]***ld to last, no ext flat* 2
441 **Dromin Pride [13]***nvr dang*.................................. 3
Also: Lurriga Glitter (4), Youbetya (5), Money Saved (pu), 372 Kizzy Rose (pu)
7 ran. 1l, 20l, 20l. SP 5-4.

474 - Maiden 6yo+

437 **Prayon Parson [16]**.......................**D Daly** 1
prom, ld 3 out, clr last, comf..................................
445 **Tullaghfin [10]***ld hlfwy-3 out, outpcd apr last*.......... 2
327 **Festival Light***nvr dang* 3
Also: 430 September Stephen (4D), 430 Belville Pond (pu), 370 Bunny Lightening (pu), Sweeney Lee (pu), 430³ Mr Dennehy (f), 368 Deep Wave (f)
9 ran. 20l, 15l, dist. SP 4-1.

475 - Mares Maiden

427² **Bet With Rosie [14]**.......................**B Moran** 1
chsd ldr, chal 2 out, ld nr fin..................................
232² **Geneva Steele [14]***ld, jnd 2 out, hdd nr fin* 2
443 **Manley Girl***nvr dang* 3
Also: 379 Brook Queen (4), 369 Ballycar Princess (5), 428 Taylors Twist (6), 427 Aine Hencey (pu), Rainproof (pu), 325 Just Placed (pu), 443 Ring Mam (pu), 380 Foherish Mist (pu)
11 ran. 1l, 20l, 8l. SP 5-1.

476 - Nomination

Nan's Dream VI ....**B Clohessy** 1
....
Crokers Cottage VI 2
368 **Meneduke** 3
Also: Kilpeacon Lady VI (4), Mulcaire Boy VI (pu)
5 ran. 15l, dist, 1½l. SP 5-1.

MEATH & TARA
Summerhill
Sunday April 21st
SOFT

477 - Confined

94 **Amme Enaek [20]**.......................**B Cash** 1
prom, ld 2 ou t, sn wll clr..................................
159³ **Midnight Service***rear, kpt on to tk poor 2nd nr fin* 2
234 **Happy Hangover***ld to 2 out, wknd rpdly* 3
Also: 336² Cool It (4), 394 Four Zeros (5), 395¹ Captains View (6), 237¹ Murcheen Durken (pu), 390² Executive Chief (ro), Kate Gale (pu), 393 Mr Moss Trooper (pu), 336 Woodhaven Lad (pu), 395 The Financier (pu)
12 ran. Dist, 1l, 1l, 25l, 2l. SP 2-1.

478 - Maiden 4 & 5yo I

Breath Of Scandal [20] ....**G Harford** 1
made all, sn clr, unchal..................................
300³ **Castleconner [10]***chsd wnr 6 out, no imp* 2
418 **Dowhatyouhavetodo***nvr dang, t.o.* 3
Also: 337 Awalkintheclouds (pu), Buckskins Babe (pu), 267³ Digin For Gold (pu), Glenpine (pu), Mast (pu), 421 Newtown Road (pu), 266³ Pearl Of Orient (pu), Spring Tour (pu), 340 Tremollina (f)
12 ran. Dist, dist. SP Evens.

479 - Maiden 4 & 5yo II

271³ **Brian's Delight [16]** ....**G Elliott** 1
chsd ldrs, prog 2 out, ld last, styd on well..............
337 **Cloughan Boy [14]***prom, ld 2 out-last, no ext* 2
337 **Perryman [11]***chsd ldrs, prog 2 out, sn onepcd*....... 3
Also: 420 Fortynine Plus (4), 390³ Blackie Connors (pu), Can She Do It (pu), 417 Lady Sandalay (pu), Mystery Pet (ro), 266 Noble Street (pu), The Bleary Flyer (pu), 385 Carrigmore Lady (f), Golden Mist (pu)
12 ran. 6l, 8l, dist. SP 2-1.

480 - Open Lightweight

392 **The Illiad [19]** ....**R Geraghty** 1
lft in ld 8th, clr 2 out, all out nr fin ....
350¹ **Teal Bridge [19]***rdn to chs wnr whn mstk 2 out, rallied flat*.. 2
265 **Astounded [11]***nvr dang* 3
Also: 422 Ballinaboola Grove (f), Coqualla (pu), 392¹ Palmura (pu)
6 ran. ½l, 25l. SP 8-1.

481 - Maiden 6yo

337² **Folly Road [16]**.........................**G Harford** 1
trckd ldrs, effrt 2 out, ld last, sn clr ....
Dress Hire [13]*ld to 2 out, styd on agn flat* 2
Hollybank Buck [13]*alwys prom, onepcd frm 2 out* 3
Also: Shillelegh Oak [13] (4), 429 Almaurita (pu), 236 Benny The Bishop (pu), 337 Boreen Boy (pu), 272 Castle Hero (ur), Celticair (pu), 299 Curragh Ranger (pu), 395 Herb Superb (pu), Moores Cross (pu), 430 Normus (pu), 237 Open Champion (pu), 271 Proud Princess (pu), 164² The Frairy Sister (pu)
16 ran. 8l, 1l, ½l. SP 4-1.

482 - Winners Of Two

361¹ **Cairncross [17]** ....**J Bright** 1
made most, edged lft flat, drvn out ....
298 **Leave It Be [16]***hld up, prog 5 out, chal 3 out, just hld* 2
Also: 390¹ Dearmistershatter (pu), 304² Diorraing (pu), 272 Harvemac (pu), 383 Hearns Hill (pu), 425 Knights Crest (pu),

oundsgoodtome (pu), 389 South East Sun (pu), 269 Station Man u), 429 Treens Folly (pu)
11 ran. 1l. SP 6-4.

483 - Mares Lightweight

382 **Beet Statement [20]** ....B Valentine 1
rpd prog to ld aft 4 out, hld on nr fin
264 **Slemish Mist [20]** *disp 5 out-aft nxt, rallied flat, just faild* 2
393 **Royal Star [19]** *disp 5 out-aft nxt, onepcd frm 2 out* 3
so: 389[3] Another Idea [14] (4), 426 Missing Lady [11] (5), 295 Satin mma (pu), 340 Collon Mission (pu), 417 Glenroe Gal (ur), 302 owesshecutting (pu), Megs Moment (pu), 271 Red Mollie (f), 301 ed Shoon (pu), 389 Torenaga Hill (pu), Winning Sally (pu), 340 Little oe (pu)
15 ran. Nk, 4l, 15l, 10l. SP 7-1.

PUNCHESTOWN
Tuesday April 23rd
SOFT

484 - 2½m Hun Chase

445 **Fays Folly (Ire) 10.13 7a**............Mr T J Farrell 1
273 **No One Knows (Ire) 11.6** ....Mr J P Dempsey 2
Sally Willows (Ire) 10.13 7a ....Mr G Elliot 3
Spinans Hill (Ire) 11.5 7a 1ow 4
268[3] Tamer's Run 11.11 .... f
350[2] Tasse Du The 12.7 *(fav)* .... pu
Mornay Des Garnes (Fr) 11.6 5a .... f
Carrig Conn (Ire) 11.6 .... ur
8 ran. 11l, 9l, 1½l. Time 5m 29.9s. SP 7-1.

485 - 3m Hun Chase

453 **No Mistake Vl (Ire) 11.6 7a** ....Mr A Fleming 1
Dennistownthriller (Ire) 11.13.........Mr P Fenton 2
Digacre (Ire) 11.13 ....Mr R Hurley 3
401[1] Quayfield 11.5 3a 4
Man With A Plan Vl (Ire) 11.6 7a 5
91 Just A Breeze (Ire) 11.1 7a 6
Dunamase Dandy (Ire) 11.6 7a 7
268 Duncaha Hero 11.6 7a 8
371 Dreaming Idle 11.13 .... pu
373[3] Mr Barney 11.6 7a .... ur
Drumcairn (Ire) 11.13 .... pu
Howarya Harry (Ire) 11.6 7a .... f
Silver Buckle (Ire) 11.6 7a .... pu
Tearaway King (Ire) 11.13 *(fav)* .... ur
14 ran. 2l, 13l, 2½l, 5l. Time 6m 38.6s. SP 7-1.

PUNCHESTOWN
Wednesday April 24th
SOFT

486 - 3m 1f Hun Chase

361 **Elegant Lord (Ire) 12.0**................Mr E Bolger 1
(fav)
593 **Divali (Ire) 12.0** ....Mr P Fenton 2
471 **Credit Transfer (Ire) 11.9** ....Mr H F Cleary 3
359 Miley Sweeney 12.0 4
4 ran. 7l, 8l, 15l. Time 6m 58.6s. SP 2-5.

LISTOWEL
Saturday April 27th
SOFT

487 - 3m Hun Chase

Caddy Man (Ire) 11.7 7a ....Mr P Cashman 1
447 **Crazy Dreams (Ire) 12.0**..............Mr P J Healy 2
447[2] **What Thing 11.6 3a**..............Mr D P Costello 3
(fav)
484 Carrig Conn (Ire) 11.9 4
359 Maypole Fountain (Ire) 11.9 5a 5
447 Kilburry (Ire) 11.7 7a 6
Youcat (Ire) 12.0 .... f
359 Lakeview Lad (Ire) 11.7 7a .... f
447 Dublin Hill (Ire) 11.7 7a .... pu
447 Silent Sneeze (Ire) 11.2 7a (bl) .... pu
447 Minstrel Madame (Ire) 11.2 7a .... pu
11 ran. 6l, sht-hd, 4½l, dist. Time 6m 38.9s. SP 7-1.

KILLULTAGH, OLD ROCK & C'ESTER
Lennymore
Saturday April 27th
HEAVY

488 - Confined Lightweight

411[3] **Ballymacrevan [16]**.....................G Coulter 1
ld 5 out, easily
365 **Inspector Stalker** *chsd wnr 4 out, sn btn* 2
402 **Stag Hunt** *ld to 5 out, wknd* 3
Also: 455[3] Dara Knight (f)
4 ran. Dist, dist. SP 1-5.

489 - Winners Of Two

405 **Shanecracken [17]**.......................L Gracey 1
cls up, ld 3 out, all out
257 **Staffy's Boy [17]** *prog 4 out, chsd wnr last, kpt on wll* .. 2
482[2] **Leave It Be [16]** *prom, 2nd whn blnd 3 out, mstk nxt, no ext last* 3
Also: 362 Steady Johnny [11] (4), 407[1] Ballydesmond (5), 410 Ballywoodock Vl (6), 398[1] Mister Black (7), 454 Manhattan Prince (pu), 454 More Than Most (pu), 454 Gilloway Princess (pu), 451[1] Amazing All (f)
11 ran. ½l, 3l, 15l, 6l, 1l, 1l. SP 16-1.

490 - Mares Final

414[1] **Cabbery Rose [23]** ....P Graffin 1
ld hlfwy, shkn up 2 out, styd on well
287 **Hiltonstown Lass [18]** *prog hlfwy, chsd wnr 5 out, no imp last* 2
410 **Glenbrin [12]** *nvr nrr* 3
Also: 397 Midi Minstrel (4), 408[1] Sideways Sally (5), 320[1] Goldwren (pu), 449 Island Harriet (pu), 408 Hillview Susie (pu)
8 ran. 3l, 20l, 10l, 15l. SP 4-5.

491 - Open Lightweight

452[1] **High Star [25]** ....I Buchanan 1
made all, clr 4 out, unchal aft
412[2] **Jims Choice [18]** *mid-div, chsd wnr 2 out, no imp* 2
454[1] **Spire Hill [15]** *prom til outpcd 4 out, no ch aft* 3
Also: Hayes Corner (pu), 405 J J's Hope (pu), 453 Copper Friend (pu), 257 Hall's Mill (pu), 392 Carrigans Lad (pu)
8 ran. 20l, 10l. SP 2-1.

492 - Maiden 4 & 5yo I

407[2] **Raleagh Muggins [16]** ....I Buchanan 1
made all, drrew clr frm 3 out
93[2] **Twentyfivequid** *prom, no ch wth wnr frm 3 out* 2
Also: 256 Falas Lad (pu), 455 Four North (pu), Hi-Jamie (pu), 456[2] Grey Rock (pu), 451 Anns Display (pu), 449 Nancy Hill (pu), Can I Come Too (pu), 449 Principal Peace (pu), 283 The Client (pu), 407 Millerman (pu), 479 The Bleary Flyer (pu)
13 ran. Dist. SP 6-4.

493 - Maiden 4 & 5yo II

299 **Sharimage [14]**........................**L Lennon** 1
hld up, prog 5 out, chal & hmpd last, ran on, promoted
413 **Golden Start [14]***prom, ld 5 out, swrvd apr last, hld on, fin 1st, disq*.................................... 2
413 **Springfarm Rath [13]***prom, outpcd aft 2 out*......... 3
Also: 451² Panda Nova [12] (4), 456 One Eleven (pu), 257 Longmore (pu), 450 Shimna River (pu), Rock Cottage (pu), Riverdance Rosie (f), 407 Yankie Lord (pu), Bannagh Moor (pu), Moses Man (pu)
12 ran. 1l, 2l, 1l. SP 2-1.

494 - Maiden 6yo+ I

477 **The Financier [15]**......................**P Graffin** 1
blnd 2nd, rear til prog to ld 5 out, drew clr............
413 **Longmore Boy [10]***ld to 5 out, no ext*............... 2
415 **Three Town Rock***nvr dang*.......................... 3
Also: 410 Political Star (pu), 320 Rath Mear (pu), 448 Scotts Cross (pu), Truth To Tell (pu), 448³ Half Scotch (ref), 456 Travarians Gold (pu), 361 Craigelle (pu), Choice Company (pu), Amorous Sailor (pu), Silken Ash (f)
13 ran. 15l, 20l. SP 5-1.

495 - Maiden 6yo+ II

429³ **Drop The Act [15]**........................**R Pugh** 1
prom, ld 4 out, sn clr..
451 **Bonquist***nvr dang, lft poor 2nd 2 out*................ 2
404² **Zieg***nvr dang, lft poor 3rd 2 out*...................... 3
Also: 281 Tassagh Boy (pu), 394³ Spectre Brown [10] (pu), 364 Rashee Lady (pu), Tacova's Gift (pu), 450 Christimatt (f), 404 Gotsomeofthat [11] (pu), 455² Pauls Point (ur), 403 Sir Gallop (pu), 450 Moyavo Lad (pu), 397 Tilly Lamp (pu)
13 ran. Dist, 4l. SP Evens.

GOLDEN VALE
Thurles Point-To-Point Course
Sunday April 28th
GOOD

496 - Open Lightweight

483¹ **Beet Statement [20]**..................**B Valentine** 1
chsd ldr 3 out, ld last, styd on well...........................
480¹ **The Illiad [19]***ld to last, no ext*.......................... 2
419³ **Princess Breda [15]***chsd ldrs, onepcd 3 out*......... 3
Also: Watercourse [13] (4), 329 Rossi Novae (5), 480 Palmura (6), 468 Hurricane Eden (f), Passer-By (pu)
8 ran. 2l, 12l, 6l. SP 4-1.

497 - Maiden 4 & 5yo

479³ **Perryman [15]**............................**P Kelly** 1
prog 5 out, ld last, hld on well..............................
421 **Sweetmount Lad [14]***ld to last, rallied flat, alwys hld* 2
465 **Flying Fellow***nvr dang*.................................... 3
Also: 440 Buckshee (4), 466 Inch Cross (pu), 466 Amewsing (ur), 390 Scarvey Bridge (pu)
7 ran. 2l, dist, dist. SP 7-2.

498 - Winners Of Two

421¹ **Lovable Outlaw [19]**......................**J Berry** 1
hld up, prog 3 out, disp aft nxt til ld flat, all out.........
393¹ **Show Your Hand [18]***prog to disp aft 2 out til hdd & no ext flat*.. 2
357 **Ad Extra [10]***clr ldr til wknd & hdd aft 2 out*.......... 3
Also: 295 Toby's Friend (4), 425 Big Murt (5), 482 Dearmistershatter (f)
6 ran. 1½l, 25l, 4l. SP 5-2.

499 - Mares Maiden 6yo+

379 **Loughlins Pride [16]**...................**M Phillips** 1
prog 3 out, ld nxt, clr last, styd on well.................
384³ **Ballinaclash Pride [13]***prog to chs wnr apr last, no imp flat*... 2
469 **Handy Sally [10]***prom, ld 5 out-2 out, sn btn*.........
Also: 369² Sunczech (4), 418 Awaytoday (5), 469³ Castlelake Lac (6), Baunfaun Run (f), 417 Rehey Lady (pu), Miss Nivels (pu), 324 C You Sail (pu), 428² Cool Della (f)
11 ran. 8l, 8l, 20l. SP 5-2.

500 - Maiden 6yo+

470³ **King Tyrant [16]**........................**S Durack**
made all, styd on wll apr last...................................
470 **Pabelo [15]***chsd wnr 3 out, no ext apr last*............
446 **Have Another [12]***chsd ldrs, onepcd frm 2 out*.......
Also: 465 Lets Twist Again [11] (4), Dromlar (5), 429 Castlepook (6 Bennetts Hill (7), 416 Shimano (f), 470² Forold (f), Fernboy (f), 42 Lord Knox (pu), 328 Tinamona (pu), 420 Glentoralda (pu), 421 Gael Glen (pu), Cantelier (pu), 394 Double Opportunity (pu), Gerry O'Ma ley (f), 421 Hey Chief (f)
18 ran. 2½l, 10l, 2½l. SP 5-1.

501 - Mares Maiden 4 & 5yo

347 **Annesley Lady [16]**.......................**P Cloke**
prog 3 out, ld aft 2 out, kpt on well.........................
Bella Brownie [15]*prog 3 out, wth wnr aft 2 out til no ext last*..
84 **Brave Commitment [14]***lft in ld apr 5 out, hdd & no ext aft 2 out*..
Also: 385 Sweepin Bends [11] (4), 324 Pat Barry (su), 469 Condons town (f), 464² Lady Sylvie (pu), 223 Woodbinesandroses (pu), 34 Natural Lady (f), Mystery Pat (pu), 469 Dockmaid (pu)
11 ran. 3l, 3l, 10l. SP 5-4.

KILLEADY HARRIERS
Waterfall
Sunday April 28th
GOOD

502 - Maiden 4 & 5yo

330 **Kings Success [16]**....................**G Crowley**
trckd ldrs, ld 3 out, styd on wll flat.........................
457³ **Roskeen Bridge [14]***prog 3 out, chal nxt, rdr lost irons last, no ext*...
181³ **Shanagore Warrior [13]***chsd ldrs, onepcd frm 2 out*..
Also: 466.0 Glenaboy (4D), 375.0² Dancing Dessie [13] (4), 458.C Lordinthesky [11] (5), 351.0 Robin Of Loxley (6), 440.0 Rodo (7 438.0³ Monadante (8), Asthefellasays (pu), Lisselan Lass (f), 351 Our Own Way (pu), 457.0 Conors Bluebird (pu), Lomond Hill (f), Lor Egross (pu), 459.0 Castlemore Leader (pu), 352.0 Another Berry (p
17 ran. 6l, 2l, ½l. SP 8-1.

503 - Mares Maiden I

356 **Cahermone Lady [15]**...................**J Collins**
chsd ldrs, rdn 3 out, styd on to ld flat......................
Merry River [15]*prom, ld 4 out, hdd & no ext flat*.....
308 **Deciding Dance [14]***chsd ldrs, kpt on frm 3 out, nrst fin*..
Also: 433³ Rascal Street Lad [14] (4), 335 Blame Barney [11] (5), 459 Frightening Child (6), Miss Thimble (7), Mosslen (8), 352 Moss Beauty (9), 324 Dusty's Delight (pu), 459 Killatty Player (f), 43 Araglen Lass (pu), 434 Fountain Lady (pu), 279² Ballinacubby Prid (pu), 434³ Riot Lady (f)
15 ran. ½l, ½l, ½l. SP 14-1.

504 - Mares Maiden II

354² **Curraheen Bride [16]**..................**J Sheehan**
prom, ld 3 out, rdn clr last......................................
437 **Vital Approach [13]***prog 3 out, chsd wnr apr last, sn no ext*..
433² **Solar Castle [11]***chsd ldrs, onepcd frm 2 out*........
Also: Ivy Breeze (4), 433 Miss Bertaine (5), 353 Sezu (6), Kamat Eyre (7), 460 Scarra Darragh (8), 379 Derrygra Fountain (9), 46C Brogeen Dubh (f), 380 Langretta (f), 438 Electric Can (pu), 460 N Planning (f), 434 Ellesmere (f)
14 ran. 6l, 6l, 20l. SP 2-1.

505 - Open Lightweight

331 **Coolgreen [21]** .... **D Keane** 1
disp til lft in ld apr 2 out, hld on well
435[1] **Awbeg Rover [20]***trckd ldrs, lft 2nd apr 2 out, chal last, no ext* 2
Mulders Friend [10]*nvr dang* 3
Also: 461 Minstrel Sam (4), 436 Fair Revival (5), 436 Next Right (6), 461 Bocock's Pride (bd), 437 Brian Og (bd), 378 Sir-Eile (su), 351[1] Sirrah Aris (ur)
10 ran. 1l, dist, 2l. SP 6-1.

506 - Confined Maiden

446[2] **An Oon Iss An Owl [15]** .... **R Flavin** 1
trckd ldrs, ld aft 2 out, pshd out
Ar Aghaidh Abhaile [14]*cls up, ld 2 out, sn hdd, no ext flat* 2
188 **Persian Packer***nvr dang* 3
Also: 7 Bucks Reward (4), 351 Timmy Tuff (5), Happy Hula Girl (pu), The Last One (pu), 460 The Wild Wave (pu), 354 Metal Miss (ur), 9 O So Breezy (pu)
10 ran. 1l, dist, 3l. SP Evens.

507 - Unplaced Maiden

239 **McFepend [15]** .... **T Lombard** 1
ld 5 out, styd on well frm 2 out
459 **Macklette [12]***chsd wnr 3 out, no imp nxt* 2
Ever True [10]*chsd ldrs, onepcd frm 2 out* 3
Also: 458 Jack's Well [10] (4), 460 Leaping Three (5), 458 Lightoak Lad (6), 434 Celia's Pride (7), 377 Andy Gawe (8), 462 Toytown King (f), 146 Theairyman (bd), Miss Paleface (f), 149 Skipping Chick (f), 437 Kendor Pass (pu), 352 Call Me Paris (pu), 332 Stags Rock (f), 118 Quirina Majano (pu)
16 ran. 6l, 5l, ½l. SP Evens.

508 - Winners Of One

463 **Scarlet River [18]** .... **J Collins** 1
made all, wll clr 2 out, just hld on
331 **Scarteen Lower [17]***chsd ldrs, rdn 2 out, fin wll, just faild* 2
436[2] **Rosie's Pride [14]***chsd ldrs, onepcd frm 2 out* 3
Also: 433[1] Brigade Leader (4), 357 Our Blossom (pu), 378[3] Sleepy Rock (pu), 459[1] Fileo (f), Cush Maid (pu)
8 ran. 1l, 10l, dist. SP 7-1.

EAST CLARE
Killaloe
Sunday April 28th
GOOD TO SOFT

509 - Maiden 4 & 5yo

424[3] **Into The Web [15]** .... **D Quinn** 1
prom, ld 4 out, kpt on well
440 **Thunder Road [14]***chsd wnr 3 out, not qckn last* 2
289 **Loslomos [12]***prom, onepcd frm 2 out* 3
Also: 472 Neelisagin [10] (4), 466 Oneofourown (5), 472 Tom Deely (6), 472 Alberts Gamble (pu), Florida Light (ur), 466 Legal Whisper (ro), Missfitz (pu)
10 ran. 2l, 4l, 6l, 8l, 2l. SP 4-1.

510 - Mares Maiden

369 **Coolshamrock [15]** .... **B Hassett** 1
chsd ldrs, ld 2 out, drvn out
427 **Lantern Spark [15]***rear, styd on wll frm 2 out, just faild* 2
457 **Ballybeggan Lady [14]***cls up, styd on onepcd frm 2 out* 3
Also: 471[3] Yasgourra [12] (4), 428[3] Ballybriken Castle [11] (5), 469 Bucks Image (f), 464 Cherishthelady (pu), 444[2] Cozy Cottage (pu), Dream Gale (bd), Gallant Dream (pu), Megs Law (bd), 443 My New Merc (pu)
12 ran. Hd, 2l, 5l, 4l. SP 7-1.

511 - Maiden 6yo+

431[2] **The Defender [17]** .... **J McNamara** 1
trckd ldr hlfwy, ld apr last, styd on well
446[3] **Coshla Expresso [16]***prog 2 out, chsd wnr last, fin well* 2
328 **Fifth Generation [15]***ld to apr last, rdn & not qckn* ... 3
Also: 465[3] Rushing Waters [12] (4), 430 Pearl Dante [11] (5), 30 Carrarea (pu), 367 Cottoneyejoe (pu), Hope's Delight (pu), 465 Irish Display (pu), 469 Reinskea (pu), Rowlandsons Bridge (pu), 31 Western Fort (pu), 471 Winter Breeze (pu)
13 ran. 2l, 1½l, 8l, 4l. SP 3-1.

512 - Mares

370[1] **Vain Princess [18]** .... **J McNamara** 1
ld 4 out, rdn out flat
435[3] **Lisadante [17]***ld to 4 out, rallied last, alwys hld* 2
468[2] **Duchess Of Padua [16]***prog to chal 2 out, sn onepcd* 3
Also: 473 Kizzy Rose (pu)
4 ran. ¾l, 3l. SP 5-4.

513 - Open Lightweight

249[1] **Royal Ziero [20]** .... **B Hamilton** 1
ld 4 out, sn in cmmnd
470 **Guirns Shop***sn strgglng, t.o. whn lft 2nd last* 2
Also: 441[1] The Yellow Bog (pu)
3 ran. Dist. SP 5-4.

514 - Winners Of One

446[1] **Easy Catch [18]** .... **E Bolger** 1
ld 4 out, sn clr, comf.
441[2] **Flairline Bay [15]***ld 5th-4 out, no ch wth wnr aft* 2
441 **Selm Mary***t.o. frm 5 out* 3
Also: Doon River (pu)
4 ran. 6l, 30l. SP 4-6.

WATERFORD FOXHOUNDS
Kill
Sunday April 28th
GOOD TO SOFT

515 - Confined Maiden

225 **Dominant Lady [12]** .... **D O'Brien** 1
ld to 2 out, ld last, drvn out
196 **Slip Along Sally [10]***chsd wnr, ld & blnd 2 out, hdd & wknd last* 2
Also: 353 Josalady (ur), 358 Comic Act (0), Minella Lass (ur)
5 ran. 6l. SP 5-2.

516 - Maiden 5yo+ I

387 **Drimeen [15]** .... **M Budds** 1
hld up, prog to 2nd 5 out, ld aft last, drvn out
Magical Approach [15]*chsd ldrs, chal & mstk 2 out, rallied wll flat* 2
458[2] **Struggles Glory [14]***ld to aft last, no ext.* 3
Also: 109 Louis Fourteen (4), 327 Decent Scotch (pu), 458 Minstrel's Quay (ro), 375 Appollo Vision (pu), 327[3] Carbery Boy (f), 420 Over The Barrow (pu), Loch Bran Lad (ro), 138 Bushmiller (pu)
11 ran. 1l, 2l, 15l. SP 3-1.

517 - Maiden 5yo+ II

445[2] **Tavern Tale [15]** .... **J Lombard** 1
prom, ld aft 3 out, sn hdd, ld last, drvn out
420 **More Rain [13]***prom, ld apr 2 out, hdd & no ext last* ... 2
374 **Garryross [11]***chsd ldrs, onepcd frm 2 out* 3
Also: Moonvoor (4), 227 Bone Idol (5), 191 Rising Paddy (f), 139 Ross Quay (f), 386 Steppy Boy (f), 323 Mount Nugent Jack (pu), 228 River Bargy (pu)
10 ran. 6l, 6l, 15l, 20l. SP 4-1.

518 - Maiden 4yo

330 Nick Dundee [19] ....W O'Sullivan 1
trckd ldrs, ld last, qcknd clr
343² Gentle Mossy [14]*ld to last, sn btn* **2**
Roughshod [14]*chsd ldr, ev ch 2 out, onepcd* **3**
Also: 322 Ryder Cup (4), Finnure (5), Coole Abbey (pu), 208 Kilcully Carrig (pu), Dukes Town (pu), Battys Bearings (ro), 464 Kinnahalla (ur), Gleeming Lace (pu), T J Goodtyme (f), The Happy Client (ur), Pedlar's Cross (pu)
14 ran. 8l, hd, 15l, nk. SP 9-4.

519 - Winners Of One

334¹ Youcat [18]...........................D Costello 1
trckd ldrs, 2nd 4 out, ld aft 2 out, easily
419² Priceless Buck [15]*ld hlfwy-aft 2 out, sn outpcd*...... **2**
463² Sharoujack [13]*prom, onepcd frm 2 out* **3**
Also: 436 July Schoon [12] (4), 383 Moll's Choice (5), 333 Kilcully-Pride (6), 308¹ Ballintee Belle (7), 356¹ Gerry And Tom (8), 136 Art Prince (ur), 378 John's Right (ur)
10 ran. 6l, 6l, 3l, 20l, 2l, 6l, 15l. SP 2-1.

520 - Open Lightweight

376 Pharditu [18] ....J Motherway 1
mstks, prog 4 out, hrd rdn to ld flat, just hld on
355³ My Sunny Way [18]*prom, hrd rdn aft 2 out, rallied flat, just faild* **2**
461 Sweet Merenda [18]*made most til hdd flat, kpt on well*........ **3**
Also: 329 Amoristic Top [15] (4), 221 Selkoline [12] (5), 378² Colligan River (f)
6 ran. Nk, hd, 10l, 7l. SP 4-1.

521 - Mares Maiden 5yo+ I

433 Anyone Whoknows Me [15]..............L Murphy 1
prom, ld apr 2 out where lft clr, rdn out
347 Determined Okie [13]*rear, styd on frm 2 out, tk 2nd nr fin* **2**
144 Flashy Leader [13]*chsd ldrs, lft 2nd & hmpd 2 out, wknd flat*........ **3**
Also: 113 Golden Cygneture (pu), 434 Round Tower Lady (f), 380 Stradbally Jane (pu), Rose Of Stradbally (pu), Mrs Bean (pu), 384 Cynical Wit (pu), 354 Lunar Approach (f), Jellaride (pu), Glen Of Bargy (pu), 385 Luthier Girl (ur), 418 Yashgans Vision (pu)
14 ran. 4l, nk. SP 3-1.

522 - Mares Maiden 5yo+ II

417 Kilannadrum [13] ....B Doyle 1
prog 3 out, ld apr nxt, all out
380² Lisnagar Lady [13]*chsd ldr & blnd 3 out, rallied to chal last, just hld* **2**
351² Farran Garrett [10]*ld 5 out-apr 2 out, sn rdn & btn* ... **3**
Also: 417 Buzz About (4), 385 Choretine Lady (5), 349 Glenmore Star (6), 384 Tullibards Again (7), 143 Dunmoon Lady (8), 144 Convamore Queen (pu), 325 Trembles Choice (pu), Hopeful Deal (pu), 354 Trimmer Lady (pu), Davids Pride (pu)
13 ran. Nk, 8l, 8l, dist, 6l, 8l, 8l. SP 7-2.

TRAMORE
Thursday May 2nd
GOOD

523 - 2¾m Hun Chase

487³ What Thing 11.2 7a ....Mr J G Sheehan 1
484¹ Fays Folly (Ire) 11.9 7a..............Mr T J Farrell 2
331 Cooladerra Lady 11.6 3a ....Mr T Lombard 3
Faulty Rap (Ire) 11.2 7a 4
Mr K's Winterblues (Ire) 11.2 7a *(fav)* 5
327 Mahon River 11.11 3a 6
Looking Ahead (Ire) 11.9 7
227 Even Call 11.9 7a 2ow .... pu
8 ran. 9l, 1½l, 1l, 15l. Time 5m 32.4s. SP 7-2.

DUNDALK
Friday May 3rd
YIELDING

524 - 3m Hun Chase

350³ Amme Enaek (Ire) 11.4 5a (bl) ....Mr B M Cash 1
(fav)
484² No One Knows (Ire) 11.9 ....Mr J P Dempsey 2
480 Ballinaboola Grove 11.7 7a .... ur
Cool It (Ire) 11.7 7a .... ur
4 ran. 12l. Time 6m 42.6s. SP Evens.

BREE FOXHOUNDS
Wexford Point-To-Point Course
Friday May 3rd
GOOD

525 - Winners Of Two

519 Art Prince [19] ....D O'Brien 1
ld 2nd, clr 2 out, styd on well
422² Coolafinka [15]*prom, chsd wnr 4 out, no imp 2 out* ... **2**
353¹ Supersonia [12]*prog 4 out, onepcd frm nxt* **3**
Also: 419¹ Lady Elise [10] (4), 496³ Princess Breda (5), 498² Show Your Hand (pu), 466¹ Money Low (pu), 270¹ Carrig Conn (pu), Slaney Beef (pu), 419 Cedarbelle (pu), 386¹ Mak's Dream (pu)
11 ran. 10l, 8l, 6l. SP 4-1.

526 - Maiden 4 & 5yo

465² Shaws Cross [16] ....P Fenton 1
ld to apr 2 out, rallied to ld last, styd on well
Lucky Hero [14]*chsd ldrs, ld apr 2 out-last, no ext* **2**
421 Montel Express*nvr dang* **3**
Also: 420 Master Chuzzlewit (4), 421 Chas Randall (pu), 386 All But (pu), Show The Light (f), 420 The Podger (pu), Forward On (pu), 386 Apollodorus (ro), 421³ Punters Fortune (pu), 517² More Rain (pu), 465 Ringaheen (pu), Cooper's Clan (pu), 193 I Cant Wait (pu)
15 ran. 4l, dist, 3l. SP 7-4.

527 - Maiden 6yo I

346 Proud Toby [16] ....D Costello 1
chsd ldrs, rdn 2 out, ld flat, ran on well
421² Who's Your Man [15]*prom, ld 2 out, hdd & no ext flat* **2**
163 Oneofthelan [14]*prom, ev ch apr last, onepcd*...... **3**
Also: 421 Greedy Johno [11] (4), 417 Talbot's Hollow (5), 516 Over The Barrow (6), 421 Louis de Palmer (7), 517 River Bargy (pu), 418 Lady Bremur (pu), 481 Moores Cross (f), 516 Loch Bran Lad (pu), 421 Kimber Sissons (f), 418 Noble Melody (f), 500 Lord Knox (pu), 381 Buffalo House (pu), 521 Mrs Bean (pu)
16 ran. 3l, 2l, 8l. SP 4-1.

528 - Maiden 6yo II

346² Little-K [15]...........................B Hallahan 1
chsd ldrs, ld 2 out, styd on wll
388² Shillelagh Oak [14]*ld to 2 out, not qckn* **2**
420 Royal Arctic [12]*chsd ldrs, onepcd frm 2 out*........ **3**
Also: 388 Lord Amethyst [12] (4), 521 Glen Of Bargy (5), 522 Buzz About (f), Pharmacy Prophet (pu), 156 Tor (f), Cuckroo (f), 379 She Wont Stop (pu), 500 Lets Twist Again (pu), Chuck (pu), Evening Empire (pu), 388 Sandy Valley (pu), 521 Jellaride (f), 420² Captain Guinness (bd)
16 ran. 4l, 6l, ½l. SP 4-1.

529 - Open Lightweight

412¹ Slaney Food [20] ....J Quigley 1
prom, ld 4 out, rdn out frm 2 out
422 Trimmer Wonder [18]*prog 3 out, chsd wnr apr last, no ext flat*........ **2**
418¹ Mullabawn [17]*chsd ldrs, onepcd frm 2 out*........ **3**
Also: Kinky Lady (f), 381 Kinross (pu), 382³ Dennistownthriller (pu)
6 ran. 4l, 3l. SP 4-5.

530 - Maiden 7 & 8yo I

416[3] Tomeko [16] ....P Curran 1
cls up, ld 3 out, sn clr, comf
388[3] Glenfontaine [10]*prog to chs wnr 2 out, no imp* 2
500[3] Have Another*nvr nrr* 3
Also: 225[3] Miss Lurgan (4), 522 Glenmore Star (5), 418 Seaview Star (pu), 521 Cynical Wit (pu), 90 Bramble Run (pu), 474 Mr Dennehy (f), Boderan Bridge (pu), 515[2] Slip Along Sally (pu), Supreme Friend (pu), Sweetly Sensitive (pu)
13 ran. 15l, 3l, 8l. SP 3-1.

531 - Maiden 7 & 8yo II

507 Miss Paleface [14] ....K Beecher 1
ld/disp, ld 2 out, rdn out
416 Scar Statement [13]*prom, chsd wnr 2 out, no ext last*
118 Mags Super Toi [12]*chsd ldrs, onepcd frm 2 out* 3
Also: Ten Past Ten (4), 422 Miss Tornado (5), 470 Derring River (pu), 423 Tara River (pu), 416 Eastern Fox (pu), 269 Pauper Boice (pu), Greenfield Lodge (f), 387 Royal Road (pu), 515 Josalady (pu), 423[2] Duirse Dairse (pu)
13 ran. 1½l, 3l, dist. SP 8-1.

532 - Mares Maiden 5yo I

418 Tremble Valley [15]......................H Cleary 1
made most, styd on wll frm 2 out
418 Sataldo [14]*prom, chsd wnr 2 out, no imp last* 2
418 Hardtobegood [13]*ran in sntchs, styd on frm 2 out* 3
Also: 381 Spritly Lady [11] (4), 522 Tullibards Again (5), 348 Mary's Delight (6), 417 Riverrunsthroughit (pu), 521 Luthier Girl (pu), Thats My Wife (pu), 469 Thank You (pu), Cianiclo (pu)
11 ran. 3l, 4l, 5l. SP 3-1.

533 - Mares Maiden 5yo II

385 Curraduff Moll [16]....................D O'Brien 1
alwys prom, ld hlfwy, drew clr frm 3 out
84 Phantoms Girl*ld to hlfwy, no ch wth wnr frm 3 out* 2
418[2] Orafeno*nvr dang* 3
Also: 501 Pat Barry (f), 522 Davids Pride (pu), 417 Lady Windgates (pu), 501 Sweepin Bends (pu), Kyle Lamp (ref), Loveable Lady (pu), Priory Street (f), 418 Menedream (pu)
11 ran. Dist, 12l. SP 3-1.

MID-ANTRIM
Ballymena
Saturday May 4th
HEAVY

534 - Winners Of Two

92 Chariot Del [14] ....D Clugston 1
chsd ldrs, 3rd whn lft in ld 4 out, unchal aft
489 Ballydesmond*trckd ldrs, 2nd whn b.d. 4 out, rmntd* 2
454 Leannes Man*ld til f 4 out, rmntd* 3
Also: 282 Kenellen (pu), 451[3] Grove Victor (pu), 448 Knocans Pride (ur), 450 Kimbry (pu), 456 Farm Lodge (pu), 493 Riverdance Rosie (f)
9 ran. Dist, nk. SP 33-1.

535 - Mares Maiden

Collon Diamond [15] ....G Elliott 1
in tch, chal & blnd 3 out, rallied to ld flat
493[2] Golden Start [14]*ld 5 out, lft clr 3 out, hdd & no ext flat* 2
448[2] Fidsprit [10]*ld to 5 out, onepcd* 3
Also: 449[2] Arctic Leader (4), 490 Midi Minstrel (pu), 492 Grey Rock (pu), 401 Glen Deal (pu), 448 Denel de (f), 258 Maid O'Tully (ur), 408 Ngala (pu), 319 Cherryflame (pu)
11 ran. 1½l, 10l, 20l. SP 4-7.

536 - Open Lightweight

412 Young Entry [19] ....C Andrews 1
chsd ldrs, ld 2 out, styd on well
489 Ballywoodock Vl [17]*ld to 2 out, no ext* 2
489 Mister Black [14]*chsd ldr 4 out, chal nxt, onepcd frm 2 out* 3
Also: 453 Schweppes Tonic (4), 491 Hayes Corner (pu), 453[2] Find Out More (pu)
6 ran. 6l, 10l, dist. SP 20-1.

537 - Winners Of One

454[3] Chene Rose [18].....................I Buchanan 1
chsd ldr 5 out, ld flat, styd on well
454 The Convincer [16]*prog 3 out, chal last, sn outpcd* 2
414 Serious Note [15]*prog 3 out, ld nxt, hdd & wknd flat* 3
Also: 405 Castle Royal [13] (4), 411 Uncle Art [11] (5), 405 Kylnhill (6), 260[1] Loughdoo (7), 405 Pats Cross (8), 404[1] Dick's Cabin (pu), 409[1] Wayside Spin (pu), 489 More Than Most (pu), 287 Calliealla (pu), 456[1] Bell Hunter (pu), 452 MC Clatchey (f)
14 ran. 6l, 2l, 5l, 6l, 8l, 12l, ½l. SP 14-1.

538 - Maiden 4 & 5yo

492[2] Twentyfivequid [15]....................P Graffin 1
made all, clr 3 out, unchal
407 Secret Prince*chsd wnr, no ch frm 3 out* 2
493 Panda Nova*nvr dang, lft poor 3rd last* 3
Also: 493 Moses Man (pu), 451 Bluagale (pu), 493 Longmore (f), Oneedin Glory (ur)
7 ran. Dist, 5l. SP 5-4.

539 - Maiden 6yo+

413 Pilbara [15] ....P Graffin 1
mstks, made all, clr 3 out, unchal
404 Triple Bush*chsd ldrs, rdn whn blnd 4 out, no ch aft* 2
402 Sheer Indulgence*chsd ldrs, no ch wth wnr frm 3 out* 3
Also: 455 Fernhill Way (4), 495[2] Bonquist (pu), 494 Silken Ash (pu), 169 Listrakelt (pu), 456 Wanclasstrain (pu), Mandingo (f)
9 ran. Dist, 2l, dist. SP 6-1.

STONEHALL HARRIERS
Ballysteen
Saturday May 4th
GOOD TO FIRM

540 - Confined Maiden

121 Rhetoric House [15]..................J McNamara 1
hld up, prog 5 out, ld 3 out, blnd nxt, clr last
509 Oneofourown [13]*mstks, chsd ldrs, no imp on wnr frm 2 out* 2
430[2] Flood Relief [13]*1st ride, chsd ldrs, styd on onepcd frm 2 out* 3
Also: 509 Tom Deely [10] (4), 472 Linda's Paradise (5), 250 Aesops Fables (6), 474 Bunny Lightening (ro), Real To Real (pu), 474 Sweeney Lee (pu)
9 ran. 5l, 1l, 8l, 1l, 12l. SP 4-1.

541 - Maiden 4 & 5yo

Aghawada Gold [17].................J McNamara 1
prom, ld 5 out, clr nxt, easily
440 Bosco's Touch [13]*mid-div, styd on 3 out, no ch wnr* 2
323[3] Gasmark [11]*rear, kpt on 2 out, nrst fin* 3
Also: 472[2] Meldante Vl [10] (4), 472[3] General Ari (5), 366[3] Educate Me (6), 509 Legal Whisper (7), 366 Tom's Tune (pu), 472 Banner Year (pu), 502 Dancing Dessie (pu), Cauteen River (pu), Kincora (pu), 440[3] Action Lad (pu), 466 The Thin Fellow (pu), 440 Silent Pond (pu), Royal Leader (pu)
16 ran. 8l, 6l, 3l, 8l, nk, dist. SP 5-1.

542 - Open Lightweight

473[3] Dromin Pride [21].........................P Carey 1
ld to 3 out, rallied to ld & nrly u.r. last, styd on well
512[1] Vain Princess [19]*chsd wnr, ld 3 out-last, no ext* 2
473[2] Hopefully True [18]*chsd ldrs, onepcd frm 2 out* 3
Also: 442 Bit Of A Touch (4), 473 Lurriga Glitter (f), 426[2] Up For Ransome (pu)
6 ran. 4l, 2l, dist. SP 14-1.

543 - Maiden 6yo+

Thefirstone [15]......................J McNamara 1
prog 6 out, ld 3 out, styd on well
465 **Mac-Duagh [12]***prom, ld 5 out-3 o ut, no ext nxt* 2
474 **Deep Wave***cls up, 3rd whn blnd 3 out, not rcvr* 3
Also: Stand Alone (4), 416 Junior Moss (5), 511 Western Fort (6), Seattle Fountain (7), 474² Tullaghfin (8), 367 Head Bottle Washer (ro), 462 Dante's Reward (co), Parsons Fort (f), 429 Komori (pu), 500 Dromlar (pu)
13 ran. 7l, 15l, 8l, 2l, 8l, 30l, nk. SP 10-1.

544 - Winners Of One

441 **Strong Vision [16]......................J McNamara** 1
wll bhnd, t.o. 5 out, styd on 3 out, ld last, all out
474¹ **Prayon Parson [16]***chsd ldrs, disp 2 out-last, no ext* .. 2
441³ **Grants Carouse [15]***disp, lft in ld 3 out, wknd & hdd last* 3
Also: 438¹ Galebreaker [10] (4), 425 Minor Key (5), 445¹ Shareza River (f), 441 Camogue Bridge (ro), 498 Toby's Friend (co), 369¹ Crabeg Hazel (pu), Miss Playtoi (pu)
10 ran. ½l, 4l, 15l, 3l. SP 2-1.

545 - Mares Maiden

469² **Galatasori Jane [16]......................E Bolger** 1
made all, clr 4 out, unchal, fin tired
510 **Dream Gale [13]***chsd ldrs, no imp wnr frm 3 out* 2
510² **Lantern Spark [13]***chsd ldrs, no imp wnr frm 3 out* ... 3
Also: 510 Cozy Cottage [12] (4), 475 Aine Hencey (5), 428 Moyode Lady (6), 510 Megs Law (7), 471 Forgoodnessjake VI (f), Set For Free (pu), Mali (pu), 444 Fort Rouge (pu)
11 ran. 7l, ½l, 1½l, 10l, 15l, 10l. SP 6-4.

MUSKERRY FOXHOUNDS
Waterfall
Sunday May 5th
FIRM

546 - Maiden 5yo

502 **Glenaboy [13]......................J Sheehan** 1
chsd ldrs, rdn 2 out, ld aft last, hld on
352 **Gee-Gee [13]***chsd ldrs, prog to chal flat, just hld* 2
352 **Poachers Lamp [11]***prom, ld 3 out, jmpd slwly last, sn hdd & btn* 3
Also: 506³ Persian Packer [11] (4), Lisas Delight (f), 502 Another Berry (pu)
6 ran. 1l, 5l, 1l. SP 6-4.

547 - Winners Of Two

505 **Sirrah Aris [18]......................E Gallagher** 1
prog 3 out, ld last, sn clr
512² **Lisadante [15]***ld to last, no ext* 2
435 **Mr Pipeman [14]***chsd ldrs, onepcd frm 2 out* 3
Also: 505 Fair Revival [14] (4), 521¹ Anyone Whoknows Me [12] (5), 435 Some Tourist (6), 357 Burkean Melody (7)
7 ran. 5l, 2l, 1l. SP 2-1.

548 - 4yo Championship

307 **Lord Harry [15]......................N Fehily** 1
prom, ld 3 out, hld on well
464 **Via Del Quatro [14]***cls up, chal 2 out, no ext flat* 2
322 **Tonmarie Chance***ld to 3 out, wknd* 3
Also: 351 Mr Matchit (4), 518 Battys Bearings (5)
5 ran. 1l, dist, 10l. SP 5-2.

549 - Open Lightweight

467 **Stroll Home [20]......................E Gallagher** 1
prom, ld 2 out, comf
519 **July Schoon [17]***ld to 2 out, no ch wnr aft* 2
519 **John's Right***t.o.* 3
Also: 468 Best Vintage (4)
4 ran. 2l, dist, 1l. SP 4-7.

550 - Mares Maiden

521 **Round Tower Lady [14]......................N Fehily** 1
prom, ld apr last, styd on well
504 **Scarra Darragh [13]***prom, ld 5 out-apr last, no ext flat*
522 **Convamore Queen***nvr dang* 3
Also: Coming Soon (4), 504 Sezu (5), Marys Friend (6), 354 Amandawill (7), Catch Me Kiss (8), 433 Brown Berry (pu), 143 Could Be A'ntin (pu), 432 Lady Fountain (pu)
11 ran. 1½l, dist, 2l. SP 4-1.

551 - Maiden 6yo+

437³ **Safety Factor [14]......................E Gallagher** 1
cls up, ld 3 out, rdn out flat
507 **Kendor Pass [13]***prom, chsd wnr 2 out, no ext flat* 2
245³ **The Gaffer [10]***ld to 3 out, onepcd* 3
Also: 500 Fernboy (4), 462 Luciano The Yuppi (5), 517 Ross Quay (ro), Thorn Hill Valley (f)
7 ran. 1l, 10l, dist. SP 7-4.

EAST GALWAY
Eyrecourt
Sunday May 5th
GOOD TO FIRM

552 - Maiden 4 & 5yo

479² **Cloughan Boy [14]......................P Gilligan** 1
cls up, ld aft 4 out, clr 2 out, comf
Hollow Wood [10]*mid-div, styd on frm 2 out, no ch wth wnr* 2
366 **Castle Tiger Bay [10]***ld til aft 4 out, onepcd* 3
Also: 497 Amewsing (4), 415 Jacksorbetter (ur), 509 Alberts Gamble (pu)
6 ran. 12l, hd, 8l. SP Evens.

553 - Open Lightweight

486 **Miley Sweeney [19]......................Lulu Olivefalk** 1
trckd ldrs, ld apr last, styd on well, lame
Native Venture [17]*chsd ldr, ld 3 out-apr last, no ext* 2
412 **Temporale [11]***ld to 3 out, sn btn* 3
Also: 426¹ Slaney Goodness (4)
4 ran. 3l, 25l, 10l. SP 2-1.

554 - Maiden 6yo+

236 **Glendine [14]......................D Harney** 1
prom, ld 5 out, drew clr apr last
413 **Sinergia***nvr dang, lft poor 2nd last* 2
367 **Over In McGanns [12]***jnd wnr aft 5 out, btn 2 out, f last, rmntd* 3
Also: 429² Carramore Hill (4), 297 Corries Hill (pu), Partyonjason (pu)
6 ran. Dist, 2l, 25l. SP 2-1.

555 - Winners Of One

485 **Dreaming Idle [18]......................D Harney** 1
prog 4 out, ld nxt, sn clr, easily
419 **It's A Deal [14]***ld to 3 out, no ch wth wnr aft* 2
473 **Youbetya***nvr dang* 3
Also: 372² The Red Devil (4), 483 Torenaga Hill (5), 470¹ Get Into It (ur)
6 ran. 8l, 20l, 3l. SP 5-2.

556 - Mares Maiden

499 **Rehey Lady [14]......................C Murphy** 1
made all, lft clr 3 out, unchal
510 **Ballybriken Castle***chsd wnr, cls 2nd whn blnd 3 out, no ch aft* 2
469 **Pleasing Melody***nvr dang* 3
Also: 418 Wandering Choice (pu), 471² Rosetown Girl (pu), 443 Lady Clarina (f), Laurens Pride (pu), 501 Dockmaid (ref)
8 ran. 25l, 5l. SP 7-1.

557 - Unplaced Maiden

511 **Pearl Dante [14]**........................**E Bolger** 1
made all, unchal.......................................
Vagabond Collonges [11]*chsd wnr 3 out, no imp* 2
368 **Tidy Village [10]***chsd ldrs, onepcd frm 3 out* 3
Also: 429 Castle Union (4), 424 Riberetto's Girl (5), 466 An Fear Dubh (f), 511 Cottoneyejoe (f), 474 September Stephen (pu), 431 Pigeonstown (pu), 509 Neelisagin (pu), 500 Hey Chief (pu), 445 Speedy Dan (f), Just My Harry (f)
13 ran. 6l, 5l, dist. SP 5-2.

BALLYMACAD
Oldcastle
Sunday May 5th
GOOD

558 - Adjacent

483 **Missing Lady [18]**....................**C McCarren** 1
chsd ldrs, ld last, styd on well.........................
477³ **Happy Hangover [16]***ld to last, no ext* 2
452² **Annie's Arthur [14]***chsd ldrs, onepcd frm 2 out* 3
Also: 483 Another Idea [13] (4), 449 Skin Graft (5), 414 Mordella Lass (pu), Moynalvy Future VI (pu), 483 Satin Emma (ro), 336 We Will See (ur), Belgrove Star (pu)
10 ran. 4l, 5l, 3l, dist. SP 7-1.

559 - Maiden 4-6yo

Impeccable Buck [16]..................**G Harford** 1
prog 3 out, lft in ld aft last, styd on......................
Highest Call [16]*chsd ldr 5 out, sn ld, slppd lndg last, hdd & not rcvr*.. 2
481 **Boreen Boy [13]***chsd ldr 4 out, onepcd frm 2 out* 3
Also: Cotton Eyed Jimmy [12] (4), George Finglas (5), 481 Almaurita (pu), 479 Blackie Connors (pu), 478² Castleconner (ro), 481 Curragh Ranger (0), 481² Dress Hire (f), 500 Gaelic Glen (bd), 420³ Major Man (pu), 478 Mast (pu), 465 Mister Salvo (pu), 478 Newtown Road (pu), 481 Normus (pu), Red Conker (bd), 429 Rovet (ref), 495 Spectre Brown [10] (pu)
19 ran. 3l, 10l, 2l, dist. SP 3-1.

560 - Winners Of Two

482 **Diorraing [18]**...........................**P Graffin** 1
ld 5th, clr 5 out, easily...................................
455¹ **Ballybrit [12]***chsd wnr 5 out, no imp*.................. 2
477 **Kate Gale***prom to hlfwy*.................................. 3
Also: 525 Show Your Hand (4), 234 Seemingly So (5)
5 ran. 15l, 8l, 15l, 15l. SP 9-2.

561 - Open Lightweight

447 **Red Express VI [21]** ....**G Harford** 1
disp til ld nr fin...
422¹ **Loch Garman Hotel [21]***disp til hdd nr fin*........... 2
392 **Fingerhill [18]***chsd ldrs, mstk 3 out, no imp aft* 3
Also: 483³ Royal Star [16] (4), 496² The Illiad [10] (5), 495 Sir Gallop (ur), 392 Youngandfair (ro)
7 ran. Hd, 10l, 6l, 20l. SP 7-1.

562 - Mares Maiden

340 **The Vendor [16]**......................**M O'Connor** 1
ld til blnd & lost plc 5 out, rallied 3 out, ld flat, sn clr....
Persian Amore [14]*prog to ld 5 out, hdd & no ext last* 2
340 **New Legislation [11]***chsd ldrs, onepcd frm 3 out*..... 3
Also: 483 Collon Mission (4), 449 Damolly Rose (pu), 478 Glenpine (pu), 417 Harlin Lady (pu), 479 Lady Sandalay (pu), 397² Miss Top (f), 478³ Dowhatyouhavetodo (f), 479 Golden Mist (pu)
11 ran. 3l, 8l, dist. SP 5-4.

563 - Maiden 7yo+

482 **South East Sun [14]** ....**G Elliott** 1
chsd ldrs, prog to ld 2 out, kpt on..........................
394 **M Macg [13]***chsd ldrs, went 2nd apr last, no ext*...... 2
305 **Oldson [11]***prom, ld 4 out, mstk & hdd 2 out, onepcd* .. 3
Also: 395² Mahankhali (4), 482 Harvemac (5), Ardee Gale (f), Bought The Aces (pu), 477 Four Zeros (pu), 451 Highland Buck (pu), Iolara (pu), Local Race (pu), 477 Mr Moss Trooper (f), 395 Taste Of Freedom (pu), 482 Treens Folly (pu), 477 Woodhaven Lad (f)
15 ran. 2½l, 5l, 25l, 2½l. SP 8-1.

MUSKERRY FOXHOUNDS
Dawstown
Monday May 6th
GOOD

564 - Adjacent Maiden

380 **Sumakano [14]**...........................**D Murphy** 1
w.w. prog 2 out, drvn to ld last, styd on well..............
311 **Radical-Times [13]***chsd ldrs, styd on apr last, no imp wnr flat*... 2
462 **Earl Of Mirth [12]***chsd ldrs, styd on onepcd frm last* .. 3
Also: 353 Ballinvuskig Lady [12] (4), 354 Change The Pace [11] (5), 546 Persian Packer (6), Brush Me Up (7), 506 Bucks Reward (8), 507 Theairyman (9), 358 Matt Moss (pu), 502 Castlemore Leader (pu), Davids Sister (pu)
12 ran. 3l, 3l, nk. SP 4-1.

565 - Maiden 4 & 5yo

458 **Castle Avenue [15]**......................**J Collins** 1
made most, styd on wll apr last............................
Knock Leader [13]*rear, prog to jn wnr 2 out, no ext* .. 2
9 **Dromod Magic [10]***nvr nrr* 3
Also: 507 Call Me Paris (4), 458 Jacky Flynn (f), Act In Time (ur), Inch Champion (f), 438 No Problem (ur), Regal Absence (f), Just A Playboy (pu), 518 The Happy Client (pu), Tommy Tuff (f)
12 ran. 5l, 10l, 4l. SP 4-1.

566 - Open Lightweight

549¹ **Stroll Home [21]**......................**E Gallagher** 1
made all, easily ....
278 **Loftus Lad [17]***chsd ldrs, onepcd & no imp frm 2 out* 2
468³ **Looking Ahead [17]***chsd ldrs, onepcd & no imp frm 2 out*.. 3
Also: 505 Bocock's Pride [16] (4), 505² Awbeg Rover [14] (5), 505 Next Right (ur)
6 ran. 6l, 1l, ½l. SP 4-5.

567 - Maiden 6yo+

437 **Cooling Chimes [16]** ....**M Phillips** 1
trckd ldrs, ld 5 out, sn clr, unchal ....
462³ **Foxwoods Valley [12]***chsd ldrs, 2nd whn slppd apr 2 out, no ch wnr aft*.. 2
437 **Lazy Acres [11]***chsd ldrs, onepcd frm 4 out*.......... 3
Also: Muskerry Express [11] (4), 306 Riverdale Express (5), 462 A Little Help (pu), 207 Take It Away (pu), 377 Raggety Man (pu), 377² Castle Ventry (pu), 334 Broe's Cross (pu), 507 Toytown King (pu)
11 ran. 10l, 2l, 1l. SP 2-1.

568 - Winners Of Two

357² **Master Kemal [19]** ....**W O'Sullivan** 1
made all, drew clr apr last, styd on well ....
440¹ **La Mon Dere [16]***prog to chal 2 out, no ext apr last*... 2
519³ **Sharoujack [14]***prog to chal 2 out, sn onepcd*........ 3
Also: Glenbower Queen (ur)
4 ran. 4l, 5l. SP 4-6.

569 - Mares Maiden 4-6yo

443 **Special Company [15]**..................**J Lombard** 1
prom, ld 6 out, lft clr 4 out, styd on ....
504³ **Solar Castle [14]***chsd ldrs, lft 2nd 4 out, kpt on onepcd* 2
459 **Highways Sister [10]***nvr nrr*............................ 3
Also: 503 Killatty Player (4), 507 Skipping Chick (5), 460 Will I Or Wont I (pu), 504² Vital Approach (ur), Bayloughbess (pu), 504 Derrygra Fountain (ro), Ballyhooly Belle (pu), 459 Have A Drop (pu), 434² Tourig Dante (pu), 504 Ellesmere (pu), Supreme Caution (pu)
14 ran. 3l, 12l, dist. SP 5-2.

DOWNPATRICK
Friday May 10th
GOOD TO FIRM

570 - 3m Hun Chase

536[1] Young Entry 11.7 7a ....Mr C Andrews 1

524 Ballinaboola Grove 11.7 7a..........Mr L Winters 2

413[2] Man Of Iron 11.7 7a ....Mr G Elliott 3
(fav)
168 Chene Rose (Ire) 11.2 7a 4
Kildowney Lady (Ire) 11.9 5
524[2] No One Knows (Ire) 11.9 6
314[3] Hiltonstown Lass (Ire) 11.6 3a 7
168 Seemingly So (Ire) 11.7 7a 8
Half Scotch (Ire) 11.2 7a 9
9 ran. ¾l, 4½l, nk, 7l. SP 10-1.

DERRYGALLON
Listowel Point-To-Point Course
Saturday May 11th
GOOD TO FIRM

571 - Maiden 4 & 5yo

502 Lordinthesky [14]...................J Motherway 1
ld 5 out-3 out, ld agn nxt, styd on well
502[2] Roskeen Bridge [13]*prog 3 out, ev ch last, no ext flat* 2
458 Island Echo [12]*chsd ldrs, styd on onepcd frm 2 out* .. 3
Also: 518 Finnure (4), 564 Brush Me Up (5), 440 Coolflugh Hero (6), 565 Jacky Flynn (7), Not For Parrot (ur), 565 No Problem (f), 440 Lord Pat (ro), Solvang (ur), 541 Silent Pond (pu), Shocking Scouse (pu)
13 ran. 2½l, 3l, 8l, 8l, 25l, 3l. SP 14-1.

572 - Mares Maiden 4 & 5yo

504 Ivy Breeze [17]..........................D Keane 1
made all, sn wll clr, unchal
503[3] Deciding Dance*chsd ldrs, nvr nr wnr* 2
502 Lisselan Lass*nvr dang, lft poor 3rd last* 3
Also: 253 Katies Kisses VI (f), 457 Derrygallon Fancy (f), 569 Will I Or Wont I (f), 439 Dirra Minstrel (pu), Peachy Girl (pu), Park Serenade (pu)
9 ran. Dist, 25l. SP 5-1.

573 - Open Lightweight

505 Sir-Eile [16] ....G Crowley 1
ld 3rd, made rest, easily
520[2] My Sunny Way [11]*chsd wnr 3rd, no imp, lame* 2
2 ran. 12l. SP 5-4.

574 - Maiden 6yo+

446 Strong Stuff [15] ....J McNamara 1
disp 6 out til ld 2 out, clr last, rdn out
358 Pat The Hat [13]*mid-div, styd on wll 2 out, tk 2nd flat* 2
543 Dante's Reward [12]*disp 6 out-2 out, onepcd* 3
Also: 462 Saol Sona (4), 543[3] Deep Wave (5), 505 Brian Og (6), 432[3] Tom The Boy VI (ur), 432[2] Classis King (pu), 528 Tor (pu), 543 Western Fort (pu), 551[2] Kendor Pass (pu), 358 Prince Owen (pu)
12 ran. 6l, 3l, 15l, 4l, 10l. SP 6-4.

575 - Mares Maiden 6yo+

522[2] Lisnagar Lady [15] ....E Gallagher 1
chsd ldr 5 out, hrd rdn apr last where lft in ld, drvn out
522 Dunmoon Lady [15]*ld, clr whn blnd & hdd last, not rcvr* 2
Viviennes Joy [14]*3rd 5 out, styd on wll apr last, nrst fin* 3
Also: 545[2] Dream Gale [12] (4), 550[3] Convamore Queen (5), 380 Nagle Rice (6), 545 Set For Free (ur), 503 Rascal Street Lad (su), 504 Miss Bertaine (ur), 504 Brogeen Dubh (pu)
10 ran. ½l, hd, 5l, 25l, 15l. SP 5-2.

576 - Winners Of One

463 Elwill Glory [16] ....K O'Sullivan 1
prom, ld 5 out, blnd last, styd on
357 Fine Affair [15]*prssd wnr 4 out, no ext flat* 2
519 Gerry And Tom [12]*chsd ldrs, onepcd frm 4 out* 3
Also: 333 Bit Of A Citizen (4), 508[3] Rosie's Pride (pu), Up Trumps (pu)
6 ran. 3l, 8l, 8l. SP 5-1.

NORTH TIPPERARY
Nenagh
Sunday May 12th
FIRM

577 - Winners Of One

556[1] Rehey Lady [17]........................C Murphy 1
ld to 3 out, ld & lft clr nxt
388[1] Stillorgan Park [13]*chsd ldrs, lft 2nd 2 out, no imp* 2
Also: 198 Sandy Pearl Two (ur), 544 Toby's Friend (f), 467[2] Cloncannon Bell (ur)
5 ran. 8l. SP 4-1.

578 - Mares Maiden 4-6yo

521 Stradbally Jane [14]...................D O'Brien 1
prom,disp whn lft in ld apr 2 out,hdd last,ralld to ld flat
556 Lady Clarina [14]*trckd ldrs, ld last, hdd & no ext flat* 2
528 She Wont Stop*nvr dang, lft poor 3rd apr 2 out* 3
Also: 224 Dusty Maid (4), 476[3] Meneduke (5), 444 Grannys Cottage (su), Theatre Sister (pu), 501 Mystery Pat (ref), 533 Pat Barry (pu), Hi Marble (f), 475 Taylors Twist (f)
11 ran. ½l, dist, 4l. SP 5-1.

579 - Maiden 7yo+

511[2] Coshla Expresso [15] ....G Mulcaire 1
prog 6 out, ld nxt, kpt on well flat
563[2] M Macg [14]*jnd wnr 4 out, ev ch til no ext last* 2
543 Junior Moss*nvr dang* 3
Also: 499[3] Handy Sally (4), 543 Parsons Fort (5), Cappanagrane Hill (pu), 530 Sweetly Sensitive (pu), 499 Cool Della (pu), 563 Mahankhali (pu), 429 Trackman (f), 511 Winter Breeze (su)
11 ran. 4l, dist, 10l. SP 6-4.

580 - Open Lightweight

496 Passer-By [20] ....R Kehoe 1
ld 5th-apr 3 out, rallied & ld 2 out, drvn out
529 Kinky Lady [19]*prog 3 out, chal apr last, no ext* 2
513 The Yellow Bog [18]*prog to ld apr 3 out, hdd & no ext 2 out* 3
Also: 555[1] Dreaming Idle [18] (4), 542[3] Hopefully True (ro)
5 ran. 2l, 2l, 1l. SP 4-1.

581 - Unplaced Maiden

557 Cottoneyejoe [13].........................D O'Brien 1
prom, ld 4 out, lft clr 2 out, easily
527 Louis de Palmer*chsd ldrs, btn whn lft 2nd apr 2 out, no ch wnr* 2
528 Lets Twist Again [13]*prom, chal & s.u. apr 2 out, rmntd* 3
Also: 470 Charlie Hawes (4), 443 Kochnie (5), 417 Short Of A Buck (6), 531 Miss Tornado (pu), 545 Forgoodnessjake VI (pu), 556 Dockmaid (pu), 545 Aine Hencey (f), 557 Castle Union (pu), 543 Head Bottle Washer (ro)
12 ran. 6l, 2l, 2l. SP 7-1.

582 - Maiden 4-6yo

345 Mister Ross [16] ....P Cloke 1
prom, ld 3 out, styd on well
527 Greedy Johno [13]*chsd wnr 2 out, sn no imp* 2
516 Louis Fourteen [12]*chsd ldrs, onepcd frm 2 out* 3
Also: 554 Partyonjason [10] (4), 540 Sweeney Lee (5), 541 Educate Me (6), 541 Tom's Tune (ur), 541 Kincora (pu), 527 Loch Bran Lad (pu), 343 Whitestown Boy (ur), 466 Clodiaghranger (f), 541 Legal

Whisper (ro), Kilgobbin (pu)
13 ran. 8l, 2l, 6l. SP 3-1.

CO SLIGO & NORTH MAYO
Sligo Point-To-Point Course
Sunday May 12th
GOOD

583 - Maiden 4 & 5yo

492 Falas Lad [15] ....B Potts 1
made all, wll clr 2 out, unchal
323 Prospect Star*chsd ldrs, went 2nd flat, no dang* **2**
557 Riberetto's Girl*chsd wnr to last, no imp* **3**
Also: 493 One Eleven (4), 492 Millerman (f), 478 Pearl Of Orient (f), 558 Belgrove Star (f), 538 Oneedin Glory (ro), Kidstuff (ro)
9 ran. 20l, 1l, dist. SP 5-2.

584 - Open Lightweight

553² Native Venture [22]......................E Bolger 1
chsd ldr 3 out, clsd last, ld flat, sn clr
561³ Fingerhill [20]*ld, clr 3 out, hdd & no ext flat* **2**
558³ Annie's Arthur [15]*chsd ldrs, onepcd frm 3 out* **3**
Also: 491 Carrigans Lad [15] (4), 553³ Temporale [14] (5), 425¹ Field Of Destiny (6), 423¹ Slaney Wind (su)
7 ran. 3l, 15l, 1l, 3l, dist. SP Evens.

585 - Maiden 6yo+

563³ Oldson [15] ....M McNulty 1
made all, hld on well frm 2 out
416² Noble Knight [14]*prog to chal 2 out, no ext flat*....... **2**
539 Bonquist*chsd ldrs, btn frm 2 out* **3**
Also: 559 George Finglas (4), 483 Red Shoon (5), 431 Ivy Glen (6), 554² Sinergia (7), 539 Listrakelt (pu), 431 Carnmore House (pu), Mr Duncan (su)
10 ran. 3l, 15l, 1l, 6l, 1½l, dist. SP 4-1.

586 - Winners Of Two

495¹ Drop The Act [18]..........................R Pugh 1
prog to jn ldr 2 out, ld flat, just hld on
489 Manhattan Prince [18]*chsd ldrs, 3rd at last, fin well, just faild* **2**
537 Uncle Art [18]*ld to aft last, kpt on well* **3**
Also: 427 Hogan (pu), 514¹ Easy Catch (f)
5 ran. Hd, hd. SP 3-1.

587 - Mares Maiden

556² Ballybriken Castle [14]..................D Duggan 1
w.w. prog 5 out, ld 3 out, sn clr
101 Maries Call [10]*wll bhnd til styd on well 2 out, nrst fin*
418 Killaligan Kim*nvr dang*.............................. **3**
Also: 562 Miss Top (4), 391 Rathcore Lady (5), 528 Jellaride (6), Harvest Time (f), 364 Let Her Run Wild (ur), 495 Tilly Lamp (pu), 427 Friendly Bid (pu)
10 ran. 10l, 20l, 2l, 3l, 10l. SP 3-1.

588 - Unplaced Maiden 7yo+

511 Hope's Delight [12] ....R Pugh 1
prog to ld 3 out, kpt on.
395 Northern Granite [11]*ld to 3 out, ev ch whn mstk last, no ext* **2**
563 Treens Folly [10]*chsd ldrs, onepcd frm 3 out*......... **3**
Also: 403 My Guitar (f), 561 Sir Gallop (ro)
5 ran. 3l, 3l. SP 4-6.

UNITED FOXHOUNDS
Ballindenisk
Sunday May 12th
FIRM

589 - Confined Maiden

569 Have A Drop [13] ....A O'Shea 1
ld to hlfwy, ld 3 out, drvn out
518 Kilcully Carrig [11]*ld hlfwy til 3 out, no ext* **2**
356 Fountain House [10]*nvr nrr* **3**
Also: 551 Luciano The Yuppi (4), 569 Bayloughbess (5), Kerry Story (pu), 356² Mountainous Valley (f), 516 Minstrel's Quay (pu)
8 ran. 6l, 1½l, 10l. SP 5-1.

590 - Maiden 4 & 5yo

62 Courier's Way [13].....................J McGrath 1
cls up, ld 2 out, comf
432 Noneofyourbusiness [10]*set mod gallop to 2 out, outpcd.* **2**
506 Happy Hula Girl [10]*cls up til outpcd 2 out* **3**
3 ran. 4l, 1l. SP 4-5.

591 - Open Lightweight

566² Loftus Lad [20].....................W O'Sullivan 1
w.w. prog to jn ldr 2 out, ld last, styd on well
566¹ Stroll Home [19]*ld, jnd 2 out, hdd & mstk last, no ext* **2**
566³ Looking Ahead [15]*wth ldr, rdn 4 out, btn 2 out* **3**
Also: 505 Minstrel Sam (4), 520 Colligan River (pu)
5 ran. 2l, 12l, dist. SP 4-1.

592 - Mares Maiden

475 Brook Queen [12] ....W O'Sullivan 1
made all, pshd out
Miss Catherine [10]*chsd wnr, btn 2 out*............ **2**
2 ran. 3l. SP 1-2.

593 - Winners Of One

519 Kilcully-Pride [17] ....S Jackson 1
prom, ld 2 out, styd on well
547³ Mr Pipeman [14]*prom, ld 6 out-2 out, no ext*......... **2**
551¹ Safety Factor [13]*chsd ldrs, onepcd frm 3 out* **3**
Also: 547 Fair Revival [12] (4), 516¹ Drimeen (5), 550¹ Round Tower Lady (6), 568 Glenbower Queen (7), 508 Cush Maid (pu), 547 Burkean Melody (f), 498³ Ad Extra (ur)
10 ran. 7l, 2l, 2l. SP 3-1.

594 - Maiden 6yo+

523 Even Call [16] ....D Costello 1
ld 6 out til apr last, rallied und pres to ld flat
567³ Lazy Acres [15]*prom, ld apr last, hdd & no ext flat*.... **2**
551³ The Gaffer [12]*nvr nrr* **3**
Also: 358 Ace Ventura (4), 564³ Earl Of Mirth (5), 49 Ivegotyouno w (6), 574 Classis King (ro)
7 ran. 1½l, 8l, 12l. SP 7-4.

KILLARNEY
Wednesday May 15th
GOOD TO FIRM

595 - 3m Hun Chase

263 Lake Tour (Ire) 10.8 5a ....Mr B M Cash 1
Meldante VI (Ire) 10.4 7a (bl) ..Mr John P Moloney 2
480² Teal Bridge 11.4 7a....................Mr G Elliott 3
Loch Garman Hotel (Ire) 10.11 7a 4
523² Fays Folly (Ire) 10.13 7a 5
523 Faulty Rap (Ire) 10.7 7a 1ow 6
Pat The Hat (Ire) 10.11 7a 7
Mullabawn (Ire) 10.6 7a 8
Glendine (Ire) 10.11 7a........ 9
485 Mr Barney 10.11 7a .... pu
461³ Okdo 10.11 7a .... bd
523¹ What Thing 10.13 7a .... ur
Rhetoric House (Ire) 10.11 7a .... f
486² Divali (Ire) 11.4 *(fav)* l
Sleepy Rock (Ire) 10.6 7a (bl) .... pu
15 ran. 11l, hd, sht-hd, 20l. Time 6m 18.1s. SP 9-1.

NORTH DOWN
Comber
Saturday May 18th
GOOD TO FIRM

596 - Confined Lightweight

537 **Castle Royal [20]** .... **L Lennon** 1
prog to 2nd 3 out, ld last, ran on well ....
583[1] **Falas Lad [17]***prog to ld 3 out, hdd & onepcd last*..... 2
360[1] **Ballyalla [10]***nvr dang*............................... 3
Also: 537 More Than Most [10] (4), 537 Dick's Cabin (5), 492[1] Raleagh Muggins (6), 539 Fernhill Way (7)
7 ran. 8l, 20l, ¾l, 20l, dist, dist. SP 2-1.

597 - Open Lightweight

491[2] **Jims Choice [22]**.......................... **R Patton** 1
trckd ldrs, jnd ldr last, hrd rdn to ld nr fin ....
350 **Bald Joker [22]***ld, jnd last, hdd nr fin* 2
537 **Kylnhill** 3D
Also: 534[1] Chariot Del (f), 536[2] Ballywoodock VI (pu), 584 Temporale (pu), 534[3] Leannes Man (pu), 537 Loughdoo (pu), 584[3] Annie's Arthur (pu)
9 ran. Hd. SP 9-4.

598 - Maiden 4 & 5yo

538 **Longmore [15]**.......................... **I Buchanan** 1
disp til ld 4 out, drew clr 2 out ....
Rainbow Riot [13]*trckd ldrs, jnd wnr apr 2 out, sn onepcd*... 2
534 **Grove Victor***disp to 4 out, wknd* 3
Also: 538[2] Secret Prince (4), 493 Shimna River (f), Ballywee Penny (f), 456 Ballysadare Bay (pu)
7 ran. 6l, 20l, 25l. SP 5-4.

599 - Maiden 6yo+

403[2] **Giorgione [14]**.......................... **I Buchanan** 1
made most, drew clr 2 out, mstk last, hld on...........
585[3] **Bonquist [13]***prog 4 out, outpcd 2 out, styd on wll flat* 2
495 **Christimatt***prom til outpcd frm 3 out* 3
Also: 494 Rath Mear (4), 563 Harvemac (5), 450[3] Ordain (6), 403 Lord Sammy (pu), 455 Penylan Jack (pu), 494 Amorous Sailor (pu), 488[3] Stag Hunt (pu), 404 Little Celia (pu), 588 My Guitar (pu), 585 Sinergia (pu), 588 Sir Gallop (pu), 585 Mr Duncan (pu)
15 ran. 1½l, 20l, 6l, 8l, 3½l. SP Evens.

600 - Winners Of Two

454 **Kildowney Lady [17]** .... **P Graffin** 1
made all, easily ....
490 **Goldwren***chsd wnr, nvr dang*.......................... 2
483 **Red Mollie***chsd wnr, nvr dang*........................ 3
3 ran. Dist, 1½l. SP 2-5.

601 - Mares Maiden

534 **Knocans Pride [15]** .... **P Graffin** 1
made most, drew clr frm 2 out......................
535[2] **Golden Start [12]***chsd ldrs, no imp on wnr frm 2 out*.. 2
535[3] **Fidsprit***prom til onepcd frm 4 out* 3
Also: 535 Arctic Leader (4), 494 Half Scotch (5), 535 Glen Deal (6), 562 Dowhatyouhavetodo (7), 535 Ngala (pu), 535 Cherryflame (pu), Runtarra (pu), 449 Tyrella Clear View (pu), Betsy Gray (f)
12 ran. 8l, 12l, dist, 1l, nk, dist. SP 12-1.

TIPPERARY FOXHOUNDS
Cashel
Saturday May 18th
GOOD

602 - Maiden 4yo

518 **Ryder Cup [15]**...................... **W O'Sullivan** 1
cls up, ld 2 out, hld on wll flat.......................
548[2] **Via Del Quatro [14]***prog 3 out, chal last, no ext flat* ... 2
548[3] **Tonmarie Chance [11]***ld to 2 out, sn btn* 3
Also: 572 Dirra Minstrel (pu), Jolly Gypsy (pu), Running On Thyne (pu)
6 ran. ½l, 10l. SP 5-4.

603 - Maiden 5yo

465 **King's Banker [16]**...................... **D Costello** 1
prom, ld aft 3 out, clr last, styd on well..............
541[3] **Gasmark [14]***trckd ldrs, outpcd 3 out, styd on well flat* 2
571 **No Problem [11]***trckd ldrs, ld 5 out-aft 3 out, onepcd* .. 3
Also: 582 Kilgobbin [11] (4), 557 Just My Harry [10] (5), Welsh Lane (ro), 517 Rising Paddy (pu), Empty Wagon (f), No Matter (pu)
9 ran. 4l, 8l, 1l, 2l. SP 5-2.

604 - Mares Maiden 5yo+

578[2] **Lady Clarina [14]** .... **P Costello** 1
made all, clr 2 out, wknd flat, just hld on ....
578 **Hi Marble [14]***chsd ldrs, ran on well apr last, just faild*
581 **Aine Hencey [13]***chsd ldrs, styd on wll apr last, nrst* 2
fin 3
Also: 550[2] Scarra Darragh [13] (4), 572 Peachy Girl [10] (5), 195 Sup A Whiskey (6), 481 Proud Princess (7), 556[3] Pleasing Melody (8), 532 Thank You (ur), 504 No Planning (pu), 530 Slip Along Sally (ur), 550 Coming Soon (f), 579 Cool Della (pu), 578[3] She Wont Stop (pu), 578 Grannys Cottage (pu), 528 Pharmacy Prophet (pu)
16 ran. ½l, 1l, 1l, 8l, 2l, 6l, 4l. SP 4-1.

605 - Open Lightweight

542[1] **Dromin Pride [24]**........................ **P Carey** 1
made all, clr 2 out, easily ....
580[2] **Kinky Lady [16]***chsd wnr, btn frm 2 out*............. 2
544[3] **Grants Carouse [14]***nvr dang* 3
Also: 579 Cappanagrane Hill [14] (4)
4 ran. 20l, 6l, ½l. SP 4-5.

606 - Winners Of Two

482 **Hearns Hill [19]**........................ **D Costello** 1
ld 5 out, made rest, comf ....
577 **Toby's Friend [17]***chsd ldrs, styd on frm 2 out, nrst fin*
547[2] **Lisadante [11]***ld to 5 out, sn outpcd*.................. 3
Also: 542 Lurriga Glitter (4), 564[1] Sumakano (5), 543[1] Thefirstone (ro), 580 Hopefully True (ro), 525 Slaney Beef (pu)
8 ran. 3l, 20l, 15l, 2l. SP 3-1.

607 - Maiden 6yo+

Suir Side [15] .... **E Gallagher** 1
prom, ld 5 out, styd on well flat ....
582[3] **Louis Fourteen [13]***prog 4 out, chsd wnr aft nxt, no ext last* 2
530[3] **Have Another [12]***chsd ldrs, styd on onepcd frm 2 out* 3
Also: 581[3] Lets Twist Again (4), 579 Trackman (5), 516 Decent Scotch (ur), 564[2] Radical-Times (pu), 531 Derring River (ref), 543[2] Mac-Duagh (f), 582 Clodiaghranger (pu), 540[3] Flood Relief (pu), 528 Evening Empire (pu)
12 ran. 4l, 3l, 8l, 1l. SP 3-1.

UNITED FOXHOUNDS
Bartlemy
Sunday May 19th
GOOD TO FIRM

608 - Confined Maiden

589 **Mountainous Valley [14]**........... **F Cunningham** 1
cls up, ld 3 out, sn clr.................................
458 **Sheer Mischief [11]***rear, prog 4 out, chsd wnr aft nxt, no imp* 2
503[2] **Merry River [10]***ld to 3 out, onepcd*.................. 3
Also: 567 Toytown King (4), 374 Master Jake (5), 550 Could Be A'ntin (6), 565 Call Me Paris (7), 517[3] Garryross (8), 589 Minstrel's Quay (9), 589 Luciano The Yuppi (10), 213[3] Hardy Breeze (f), 567 Broe's Cross (f), 433 Lady Of Means (ur), Dark Friend (pu), Ben Ore (pu), Fair Mane

(pu), 550 Marys Friend (f)
17 ran. 9l, 4l, 1l. SP 9-2.

609 - Mares Maiden 4 & 5yo I

Cailin Chuinne [14] ....**E Gallagher** 1
chsd ldr aft 2 out, kpt on to ld nr fin
504 Langretta [14]*prom, ld 2 out, slw last, hdd nr fin* 2
460[3] Cherry Glen [12]*prom, onepcd frm 2 out* 3
Also: 569 Skipping Chick (4), 240 Merry Castle (5), Dont Tell Nell (ro), Bawnavinogue Lady (pu), 502 Monadante (pu), Alpine Castle (pu), Rosey Ellen (pu)
10 ran. Hd, 4l, 15l. SP 3-1.

610 - Mares Maiden 4 & 5yo II

76[2] Ask Me In [17]..........................**D Costello** 1
made all, clr apr last, easily
434 High Park Lady [14]*chsd ldrs, effrt 2 out, no imp wnr aft* 2
572[2] Deciding Dance*chsd ldrs til wknd rpdly aft 2 out* 3
Also: 324[2] Mardon (4), 590[2] Noneofyourbusiness (pu), 475 Ring Mam (pu), Fahoora (pu), 457 Cnoc-Breac (pu), 578 Theatre Sister (f), 459 Everlaughing (pu)
10 ran. 5l, dist, 1l. SP 5-4.

611 - Open Lightweight

15[1] Blackwater Lady [21] ....**N Fehily** 1
prog 3 out, ld nxt, rdn out
591[1] Loftus Lad [20]*prog 3 out, wth wnr nxt til outpcd flat* .. 2
549[2] July Schoon [17]*styd on frm 2 out, onepcd* 3
Also: 547[1] Sirrah Aris (4), 566 Awbeg Rover (5), 573[1] Sir-Eile (f), 606 Hopefully True (ur)
7 ran. 2l, 9l, dist. SP 7-4.

612 - Maiden 4 & 5yo

571 Jacky Flynn [14] ....**D Murphy** 1
prog 3 out, sn disp, hrd rdn to ld nr fin
518 T J Goodtyme [14]*prom, disp 3 out til hdd nr fin* 2
518 Pedlar's Cross [12]*styd on frm 2 out, nrst fin* 3
Also: 332 Phar Desert [10] (4), Monteba (5), Chevin Lad (6), 139 Major Bill (pu), 238[3] Clashbridane (pu), Cool Cormack (pu), 571 Solvang (ro), 438[2] Four From Home (f), 507 Lightoak Lad (pu), 458 Romeo's Brother (pu)
13 ran. Nk, 4l, 6l. SP 5-2.

613 - Winners Of One

525[3] Supersonia [18] ....**N Fehily** 1
hld up, prog 4 out, ld 2 out, ran on well
574[1] Strong Stuff [17]*prog 4 out, ld brfly apr 2 out, sn outpcd* 2
576[2] Fine Affair [12]*prom, ld 3 out-apr nxt, sn btn* 3
Also: 566 Bocock's Pride [12] (4), 593[2] Mr Pipeman (5), 593[3] Safety Factor (6), 500[1] King Tyrant (7), 593 Fair Revival (pu), 593 Cush Maid (pu), 589[1] Have A Drop (pu), 504[1] Curraheen Bride (pu), 594[1] Even Call (pu)
12 ran. 3l, 15l, 1l. SP 3-1.

614 - Maiden 6yo+ I

531[3] Mags Super Toi [14] ....**K Beecher** 1
chsd clr ldr, styd on to disp 2 out, ld nr fin
516 Carbery Boy [14]*chsd clr ldr, styd on to disp 2 out, hdd nr fin* 2
567[2] Foxwoods Valley [14]*chsd clr ldr, styd on to disp 2 out, hdd nr fin* 3
Also: 594 Ace Ventura [12] (4), 564 Ballinvuskig Lady (5), 569 Ballyhooly Belle (pu), 185 Gallant Gale (pu), Teeline Terrapin (pu), 353 Miss Thornton (pu), Torloc (pu), 567 Riverdale Express (pu)
11 ran. Nk, nk, 5l. SP 5-1.

615 - Maiden 6yo+ II

377[3] Rusnetto [14]...........................**S Durack** 1
prog 3 out, chal last, ld flat, styd on
575 Rascal Street Lad [13]*chsd ldr 3 out, ld last, sn hdd & no ext* 2
569[2] Solar Castle [12]*ld 3 out-apr last, onepcd* 3
Also: Cloneenverb (pu), 445 Park Duke (pu), Sean O'Coinin (pu), 551 Fernboy (pu), Dante Alainn (pu), 550 Brown Berry (pu), Tearfull (pu)
10 ran. 1l, 5l. SP 4-1.

ISLAND FOXHOUNDS
Camolin
Sunday May 19th
GOOD TO FIRM

616 - Maiden 4 & 5yo

526[3] Montel Express [14].......................**B Doyle** 1
prog 3 out, ld last, styd on well
351 Graignamanagh [12]*ld 4 out-last, no ext* 2
526 The Podger*lft in ld 2nd til hdd 4 out, onepcd* 3
Also: 526 Forward On (4), 526 Ringaheen (5), 526 Chas Randall (pu), 420 Nobodys Boy (pu), 343 The Road To Moscow (bd), 526 Apollodorus (pu), 559 Blackie Connors (su), Lough Cullen (pu), 522 Choretine Lady (pu), 582 Whitestown Boy (pu)
13 ran. 4l, 10l, 10l. SP 6-1.

617 - Winners Of One

528[1] Little-K [20]..........................**B Hallahan** 1
trckd ldr, ld 4 out, sn drw clr
416[1] Will Travel [10]*ld to 4 out, sn rdn & btn* 2
525 Princess Breda*nvr dang, t.o.* 3
Also: 493[1] Sharimage (4), 555 Get Into It (f)
5 ran. Dist, 12l, 2l. SP Evens.

618 - Maiden 6yo+

531 Pauper Boice [14] ....**H Cleary** 1
cls up, 3rd 5 out, ld 3 out, rdn out
559 Major Man [12]*prog 3 out, chsd wnr last, no ext flat* .. 2
585[2] Noble Knight*ld/disp to 3 out, sn wknd* 3
Also: 381 Captain Scurlough (pu), 515 Comic Act (f), 416 Kingeochy (ro), 531 Eastern Fox (pu), 528 Cuckroo (pu), 500 Shimano (pu), 388 Little Len (pu)
10 ran. 6l, dist. SP 4-1.

619 - Mares Lightweight

525[2] Coolafinka [20].........................**D Whelan** 1
trckd ldr, ld 4 out, drew clr last
529[2] Trimmer Wonder [14]*chsd ldrs, styd on to tk 2nd flat, no dang* 2
577 Sandy Pearl Two [14]*ld to 4 out, btn aft 2 out* 3
Also: 454 Sapphire 'N' Silver (pu)
4 ran. 15l, ½l. SP 9-10.

620 - Open Lightweight

344[2] Irish Peace [19] ....**H Cleary** 1
prom, ld & lft clr 3 out, unchal
422 Glen Og Lane [11]*nvr dang, lft 2nd 3 out* 2
Also: 553 Slaney Goodness (su), 584 Slaney Wind (f)
4 ran. 15l. SP 9-10.

621 - Mares Maiden I

499[2] Ballinaclash Pride [14] ....**P Cloke** 1
trckd ldr, ld 5 out, clr last, drvn out
581 Miss Tornado [13]*prog 2 out, chal flat, no ext* 2
532[3] Hardtobegood [11]*nvr dang, kpt on frm 2 out, nrst fin* 3
Also: 385 Hazels Dream [11] (4), 531 Ten Past Ten (5), 530 Supreme Friend (6), 530 Glenmore Star (7), Rachels Plan (su), 533[2] Phantoms Girl (pu), 385[2] Hollybuck (pu), 483 Glenroe Gal (su), 527 Talbot's Hollow (pu)
12 ran. 2l, 4l, ½l. SP 4-1.

622 - Mares Maiden II

Sandy Jay [14] ....**C Murphy** 1
alwys prom, ld 3 out, clr last, styd on

532 Spritly Lady [12]*ld to 2 out, no ext last* 2
530 Miss Lurgan*chsd ldrs, onepcd frm 2 out* 3
Also: 384 Meldap (4), 562 Lady Sandalay (5), 417 Regular Rose (pu), 533 Lady Windgates (pu), 418 Accountancy Perk (f), 533 Loveable Lady (f), 533 Davids Pride (pu), 587 Jellaride (pu), 535 Denel de (pu)
12 ran. 4l, 12l, 6l. SP 6-1.

WESTMEATH & LONGFORD
Castletown-Geoghegan
Sunday May 19th
GOOD TO FIRM

623 - Mares Lightweight

558 Another Idea [20] ....**G Harford** 1
4th whn blnd 3 out, rdn to ld nxt, styd on well..........
558[1] Missing Lady [17]*ld to 2 out, sn outpcd* 2
584 Field Of Destiny [13]*prom, outpcd frm 2 out*.......... 3
Also: 338 No One Knows [10] (4), 544 Crabeg Hazel (5), 558 Satin Emma (pu)
6 ran. 8l, 10l, 8l, 20l. SP 5-1.

624 - Maiden 4 & 5yo

559 Mast [10] ....**W Hayes** 1
n.j.w. made virt all, just ld whn lft alone last...........
Also: 559 Newtown Road (f)
2 ran. SP 5-4.

625 - Mares Maiden

545 Cozy Cottage [16]....................**G Mulcaire** 1
prog to chal 3 out, rdn to ld flat ....
587 Harvest Time [16]*prog to ld 3 out, mstk nxt, hdd & no ext flat*.......... 2
483 Megs Moment [13]*mid-div, styd on frm 2 out, nrst fin* 3
Also: 558 We Will See [11] (4), 558 Skin Graft (5), 585 Red Shoon (6), 562 Collon Mission (pu), 586 Hogan (pu), 562[3] New Legislation (f), Super Secretary (f), 578 Taylors Twist (pu), 587 Rathcore Lady (pu)
12 ran. ½l, 10l, 5l, 15l, 10l. SP 2-1.

626 - Open Lightweight

584[2] Fingerhill [19] ....**G Elliott** 1
trckd ldrs, ld last, styd on well..........
584 Carrigans Lad [18]*disp til ld 3 out, hdd & no ext last*.. 2
552[1] Cloughan Boy [15]*chsd ldrs, onepcd frm 3 out*....... 3
Also: 496 Palmura (4), 500 Castlepook (ur), 579[1] Coshla Expresso (0), Winkelweg (f)
7 ran. 3l, 10l, dist. SP Evens.

627 - Winners Of Two

560[1] Diorraing [16] ....**G Elliott** 1
ld 4th, made rest, styd on well..........
561 Royal Star [14]*hld up, chal 2 out, no ext last* 2
477 Captains View*chsd wnr, btn 2 out* 3
3 ran. 3l, 15l. SP 4-9.

628 - Maiden 6yo+

481 Benny The Bishop [16]...................**A Ross** 1
hld up, prog 3 out, ld nxt, sn clr..........
559[3] Boreen Boy*trckd ldr, chal & lft in ld 3 out, hdd & wknd nxt*.......... 2
563 Mr Moss Trooper*bhnd, kpt on 2 out, no dang* 3
Also: 298 Well Recovered (4), 588[3] Treens Folly (5), 585 George Finglas (f), 599 Harvemac (pu), 563 Local Race (ro), 582 Partyonjason (pu), Red Hugh (pu), 563 Taste Of Freedom (pu), 563 Woodhaven Lad (pu)
12 ran. 25l, 15l, ½l, 20l. SP 6-1.

ORMOND FOXHOUNDS
Ballingarry
Sunday May 26th
SOFT

629 - Winners Of Two

544 Minor Key [17] ....**J Collins** 1
chsd ldr, lft in ld 2 out, drvn out flat..........
628[1] Benny The Bishop [16]*prog 3 out, chal nxt, no ext flat*.......... 2
606[2] Toby's Friend [14]*chsd ldrs, onepcd 2 out, lft 3rd last* 3
Also: 597 Loughdoo [14] (4), 65 Ballinaveen Bridge [13] (5), 619 Sapphire 'N' Silver (pu), 593 Drimeen [16] (ur), 444[1] Knocktoran Lady (pu), 619[3] Sandy Pearl Two (pu), 626 Coshla Expresso (pu), 623 Crabeg Hazel (pu), 313 Flo Jo's Boy (ur)
12 ran. 2l, 5l, 1l, 2l. SP 8-1.

630 - Maiden 4 & 5yo

518[2] Gentle Mossy [15].......................**B Doyle** 1
prog 3 out, chal nxt, ld flat, drvn out..........
540[2] Oneofourown [15]*prog 3 out, sn ld, hdd & no ext flat* 2
541[2] Bosco's Touch*chsd ldrs 3 out, blnd nxt, wknd* 3
Also: 497[2] Sweetmount Lad (4), 409 Doc-Halliday (5), 598[2] Rainbow Riot (f), 616 Forward On (pu), 616 Ringaheen (pu), 110 Irregular Planting (pu), 552[3] Castle Tiger Bay (pu), 540 Linda's Paradise (pu), 603 Just My Harry (f)
12 ran. ¾l, dist, 2l, 2l. SP 3-1.

631 - Mares Maiden I

575 Dream Gale [15].....................**J McNamara** 1
chsd ldrs, lft 2nd 3 out, ld last, styd on..........
609[3] Cherry Glen [14]*chsd ldrs, lft in ld 3 out, hdd & no ext last*.......... 2
587[3] Killaligan Kim*nvr dang*.......... 3
Also: 621[3] Hardtobegood (4), 625[3] Megs Moment (pu), 510 Yasgourra (pu), 622 Lady Sandalay (pu), 604 Sup A Whiskey (pu), 622 Davids Pride (pu), 622 Loveable Lady (pu), Ringhill Beauty (pu), 164 Codology (ro), 562[2] Persian Amore (pu), Marians Own (pu), 604 Thank You (pu)
15 ran. 3l, 25l, 5l. SP 4-1.

632 - Mares Maiden II

604[2] Hi Marble [17].......................**J McNamara** 1
prom, ld 2 out, comf..........
475[3] Manley Girl [13]*rear, styd on frm 2 out, tk 2nd last*.... 2
604 Proud Princess*prom, ld 3 out, hdd & wknd nxt* 3
Also: 621 Glenroe Gal (4), 621 Talbot's Hollow (5), 272 Wewillsee (6), Accountancy Park (pu), 622[3] Miss Lurgan (pu), 527[3] Oneofthec lan (pu), 506 The Wild Wave (pu), 585 Ivy Glen (pu), 625 Super Secretary (pu), 610 Theatre Sister (pu), 601 Betsy Gray (f), 545 Moyode Lady (pu)
15 ran. 6l, 15l, 20l, 15l, 10l. SP Evens.

633 - Open Lightweight

619[1] Coolafinka [21].........................**D Whelan** 1
disp 5 out, sn rdn & hdd, rallied to ld last, jnd post .....
561[2] Loch Garman Hotel [21] ....**T Cloke** 1
disp 5 out, ld 2 out, hdd last, rallied to jn ldr post ......
591[2] Stroll Home [20]*disp 5 out-2 out, no ext apr last*...... 3
Also: 613 King Tyrant (pu), 626[3] Cloughan Boy (pu), 496[1] Beet Statement (pu), 623[2] Missing Lady (pu)
7 ran. Dd-ht, 1½l.
Coolafinka, 4/1. Loch Garman Hotel, 6/4.

634 - Maiden 6yo+ I

579[2] M Macg [15] ....**A Fleming** 1
chsd ldrs, lft in ld 2 out, styd on..........
206 What Is The Plan [12]*chsd ldrs, lft 2nd 2 out, onepcd* 2
345 Daddy Warbucks*chsd ldrs, onepcd 3 out* 3
Also: Spanish Pal (4), 628 Well Recovered (pu), 527 Kimber Sissons (pu), 500 Gerry O'Malley (f), 618 Cuckroo (pu), 599[2] Bonquist (pu), 574 Western Fort (pu), 236 First Bash (f)
11 ran. 8l, 6l, dist. SP 7-2.

635 - Maiden 6yo+ II

618 Kingeochy [14]...........................**T Cloke** 1
made all, clr 2 out, styd on well..........

607 **Mac-Duagh***prog to chs wnr 2 out, sn no imp* 2
607 **Lets Twist Again***chsd ldrs, onepcd frm 3 out* 3
Also: 582² Greedy Johno (4), 628² Boreen Boy (pu), 607 Evening Empire (pu), 387 Glenville Breeze (pu), 530² Glenfontaine (pu), 511 Carrarea (pu), 236 Magic Caller (pu)
10 ran. 15l, 1½l, 6l. SP 3-1.

636 - Unplaced Maiden

Do Pop In [14]..........................**D Whelan** 1
chsd ldr 2 out, styd on to ld nr fin ....
616 **The Road To Moscow [14]***ld til hdd nr fin* 2
526 **Master Chuzzlewit [13]***chsd ldrs, styd on 2 out, nrst fin* 3
Also: 612 Phar Desert (4), 528 Glen Of Bargy (f), 582 Tom's Tune (pu), 429 Once In A Lifetime (pu), 607 Decent Scotch (pu), 581 Charlie Hawes (ur), 628 Partyonjason (pu), 605 Cappanagrane Hill (pu), 557 Speedy Dan (pu), 603 Kilgobbin (bd), 345 Clon Caw (pu)
14 ran. ¾l, 1½l, dist. SP 4-1.

DUHALLOW FOXHOUNDS
Dromahane
Sunday May 26th
GOOD TO SOFT

637 - Confined Maiden

574² **Pat The Hat [14]**..........................**B Walsh** 1
w.w. ld 2 out, pshd out ....
571 **Lord Pat [13]***prog to chal last, alwys hld*. 2
594 **Earl Of Mirth [11]***prom, onepcd frm 2 out* 3
Also: 614 Riverdale Express (4), 379 Ann Black (5), 564 Davids Sister (6), 614 Torloc (7), 457 Fountain Moss (8)
8 ran. 1l, 6l, 10l. SP 4-5.

638 - Maiden 4yo

565 **Act In Time [15]** ....**D Costello** 1
ld 2nd, made rest, easily..........................
571 **Brush Me Up [12]***chsd wnr 3 out, no imp* 2
502 **Asthefellasays***nvr dang* 3
Also: 439 Irish Frolic (f), Miracle Me (pu)
5 ran. 3l, 8l. SP 1-2.

639 - Open Lightweight

611¹ **Blackwater Lady [20]** ....**E Fehily** 1
hld up, ld 2 out, comf..........................
595 **Okdo [15]***ld to 2 out, sn outpcd* 2
593¹ **Kilcully-Pride [15]***chsd ldrs, styd on onepcd frm 2 out* 3
Also: 576 Bit Of A Citizen [13] (4), 549 Best Vintage (5), 611 Awbeg Rover (pu), 611³ July Schoon (su)
7 ran. 5l, ½l, 6l. SP 5-4.

640 - Mares Maiden 6yo+

569 **Killatty Player [14]** ....**A Hickey** 1
prom, ld 2 out, styd on flat ....
615² **Rascal Street Lad [13]***prog to chal 2 out, not qckn last* 2
569 **Vital Approach [12]***chsd ldrs, styd on onepcd frm 2 out*.. 3
Also: 459² Nans Pet [11] (4), 615 Tearfull (5), 615³ Solar Castle (6), 604 Pharmacy Prophet (7), 569³ Highways Sister (8), 592² Miss Catherine (9), Hamshire Gale (10), 354 Highland Call (11), 615 Brown Berry (12), 604 No Planning (13), 531 Josalady (su), 604 Scarra Darragh (f), 564 Bucks Reward (bd), 575 Miss Bertaine (bd), Irish Pride (pu), 144 Supreme Odds (f)
19 ran. 2l, 3l, 3l. SP 12-1.

641 - Winners Of One

569¹ **Special Company [18]**..........................**J Lombard** 1
disp 3 out til ld last, hld on well..........................
507¹ **McFepend [18]***disp 3 out til mstk last, just hld flat* 2
568³ **Sharoujack [16]***ev ch 3 out, sn onepcd*................ 3
Also: 593 Glenbower Queen [14] (4), 506¹ An Oon Iss An Owl (ro), Chestnut Shoon (ur)
6 ran. ½l, 4l, 4l. SP Evens.

642 - Maiden 5yo+

213 **Spanish Castle [15]** ....**D Keane** 1
prom, ld 2 out, rdn out..........................
614² **Carbery Boy [14]***chsd wnr 2 out, no ext last* 2
607 **Radical-Times [12]***chsd ldrs, onepcd frm 2 out* 3
Also: 608 Toytown King [11] (4), 541 Meldante VI (5), 574 Tom The Boy VI (pu), Trakswayboy (pu), 608 Hardy Breeze (bd), 615 Sean O'Coinin (pu), 328 Lord Vince (pu), 608 Ben Ore (pu), 275 Geragh Road (pu), Jolly Tear (su), Ise The Driver (pu), 615 Fernboy (pu), 507 Jack's Well (pu), 567 Muskerry Express (pu)
17 ran. 3l, 6l, 3l. SP 12-1.

KILBEGGAN
Monday May 27th
GOOD

643 - 3m 1f Hun Chase

595 **What Thing 10.13 7a**..........................**Mr E Gallagher** 1
595³ **Teal Bridge 11.4 7a**..........................**Mr G Elliott** 2
595 **Fays Folly (Ire) 10.13 7a**..........................**Mr T J Farrell** 3
561¹ Red Express VI 11.11 4
Leave It Be (Ire) 10.13 7a 5
447 Fifth Generation (Ire) 10.13 7a 6
570¹ Young Entry 11.4 7a 7
523 Looking Ahead (Ire) 11.0 5a 4ow 8
Up For Ransome (Ire) 10.13 7a 9
Fingerhill (Ire) 11.1 5a 10
570 Kildowney Lady (Ire) 11.3 2ow 11
447 Corymandel (Ire) 12.2 *(fav)* .... pu
Pauper Boice (Ire) 11.6 .... pu
Happy Hangover (Ire) 11.2 7a 3ow .... f
Educate Me (Ire) 10.6 7a .... pu
Locklan (Ire) 10.13 7a .... pu
16 ran. 3l, 25l, 2½l, 5l. Time 6m 22.9s. SP 4-1.

SOUTH UNION
Kinsale
Saturday June 1st
GOOD TO SOFT

644 - Maiden 4 & 5yo I

465 **Old Cavalier [16]**..........................**P Fenton** 1
trckd ldr, ld flat, pshd out..........................
517 **Moonvoor [15]***ld to flat, no ext* 2
603² **Gasmark [14]***chsd ldrs, onepcd frm 2 out*............ 3
Also: 636 Kilgobbin [10] (4), 630 Forward On (5), 466² Hum 'N' Haw (6), 582 Kincora (7), Glic Go Leor (pu), 608 Master Jake (pu), 616³ The Podger (pu), 616 Whitestown Boy (pu)
11 ran. ½l, 2½l, 12l. SP 7-2.

645 - Maiden 4 & 5yo II

616² **Graignamanagh [14]**..........................**B Cash** 1
made all, rdn whn lft clr 2 out ....
Cullaun*no dang, lft 2nd 2 out* 2
608 **Minstrel's Quay***no dang, lft 3rd 2 out*............ 3
Also: 571 Silent Pond (4), 612 Major Bill (pu), 502 Conors Bluebird (pu), 637² Lord Pat (f), 608 Call Me Paris (pu), 440 Cash Flow (bd), 642 Hardy Breeze (f), 630 Linda's Paradise (f)
11 ran. 20l, 1l, 2l. SP 6-4.

646 - Winners Of One

613 **Mr Pipeman [20]**..........................**D Costello** 1
hld up, prog 3 out, ld nxt, sn clr..........................
640¹ **Killatty Player [10]***prom, outpcd frm 2 out*........... 2
564 **Change The Pace***nvr dang, btn whn f 2 out, rmntd*.... 3
Also: 564 Persian Packer (pu), 432¹ Terrano Star (ro)
5 ran. Dist, dist. SP 2-1.

647 - Winners Of Two

641³ **Sharoujack [18]**....................Mary Horgan 1
cls up, ld last, just hld on
333¹ **Fundy [18]***cls up, chal last, just faild* 2
591³ **Looking Ahead [17]***chsd ldrs, ran on apr last, nrst fin*
Also: 560² Ballybrit [15] (4), 544 Miss Playtoi [13] (5), 636 Cappanagrane Hill [12] (6), 608 Luciano The Yuppi (7), 606 Slaney Beef (ur), 614 Ballinvuskig Lady (ur), 641 Chestnut Shoon (pu)
10 ran. Sht-hd, 2l, 5l. SP 5-1.

648 - Open Lightweight

633 **Beet Statement [20]**..................B Valentine 1
prom, ld 2 out, styd on well
611² **Loftus Lad [19]***prom, chal 2 out, no ext flat* 2
620 **Slaney Goodness [18]***chsd ldrs, onepcd apr last.* 3
Also: 639³ Kilcully-Pride [17] (4), 639 July Schoon [15] (5), 631¹ Dream Gale [14] (6), 606 Lurriga Glitter [12] (7), 629 Loughdoo (8), January Don (9), 503¹ Cahermone Lady (10), 593 Burkean Melody (f), 611 Sir-Eile (f)
12 ran. 2l, 3l, 2l. SP 3-1.

649 - Mares Maiden 4 & 5yo I

604 **Grannys Cottage [15]**....................M Cahill 1
cls up, ld apr last, styd on well
503 **Ballinacubby Pride [14]***prom, chal apr last, no ext flat* 2
602² **Via Del Quatro [14]***prom, no ext last.* 3
Also: Kilcannon Sophie [13] (4), 622² Spritly Lady [11] (5), 572³ Lisselan Lass (pu), 631 Marians Own (pu), 569 Derrygra Fountain (pu), Clonea (pu), 632 The Wild Wave (pu), 610 Fahoora (pu), 443³ Bay Lough (pu), 609 Bawnavinogue Lady (f)
13 ran. 2l, ½l, 2l. SP 3-1.

650 - Mares Maiden 4 & 5yo II

609 **Rosey Ellen [16]**.....................E Gallagher 1
ld 5 out, sn clr, easily.
631 **Ringhill Beauty***chsd wnr 3 out, nvr dang* 2
572 **Derrygallon Fancy***chsd ldrs, no ch frm 4 out* 3
Also: Flowery Fern (f), Bold Louise (f), Donna (f), 609 Skipping Chick (f), 610 Everlaughing (bd), Dunkitt Lady (pu), 279 Princess Diga (ur), 631 Sup A Whiskey (f), 609 Alpine Castle (pu)
12 ran. Dist, 1l. SP 5-2.

651 - Unplaced Maiden I

621 **Hazels Dream [13]**.......................J Cullen 1
prog 3 out, chal last, ld nr fin
634 **First Bash [13]***prom, ld 2 out, hdd nr fin* 2
631 **Codology [12]***prom, onepcd apr last* 3
Also: 636 Speedy Dan [10] (4), 604 Coming Soon (5), 608 Could Be A'ntin (6), 618 Comic Act (0), 569 Supreme Caution (pu), 640 No Planning (pu), 640 Hamshire Gale (f), Caherlag (f), 637 Davids Sister (f)
12 ran. Nk, 2l, 5l. SP 5-2.

652 - Unplaced Maiden II

Supremo [15]..........................C Murphy 1
prog 5 out, ld 2 out, comf
70 **Glorious Gale [12]***ld 3 out-nxt, no ch wnr aft* 2
642 **Toytown King [10]***chsd ldrs, onepcd frm 2 out* 3
Also: 636 Charlie Hawes (4), 640 Tearfull (5), 589 Bayloughbess (6), 368 Nearhaan (pu), 642 Ben Ore (ro), 445 Mr Connie Vee (pu), 550 Amandawill (pu), 356 Solo Minstrel (pu), 635 Magic Caller (pu)
12 ran. 4l, 4l, 10l. SP 5-1.

SOUTH UNION
Kinsale
Sunday June 2nd
GOOD

653 - Maiden 4yo

638 **Miracle Me [15]**........................D Costello 1
prog 2 out, rdn to ld flat.
638 **Irish Frolic [14]***prog to ld 3 out, hdd & no ext flat* 2
565² **Knock Leader [13]***ld to 3 out, onepcd apr last* 3
Also: 638³ Asthefellasays (4), 501 Lady Sylvie (5), 609 Dont Tell Nell (pu), 565 The Happy Client (pu), 590³ Happy Hula Girl (pu)
8 ran. 1l, 3l, 15l. SP 7-4.

654 - Maiden 6yo+ I

634² **What Is The Plan [15]**..................D Costello 1
trckd ldrs, ld 2 out, styd on well
640² **Rascal Street Lad [13]***prom, ev ch 2 out, not qckn* 2
640³ **Vital Approach [13]***prom, ld 5 out-2 out, onepcd* 3
Also: 604³ Aine Hencey [11] (4), Irish Court (pu), 632³ Proud Princess (pu), 594² Lazy Acres (pu), Hopeful Gamble (ro), 608 Broe's Cross (pu), 640 Supreme Odds (pu), 614 Ace Ventura (pu), 575 Convamore Queen (pu), 374 Fennells Bay (pu), 635 Glenville Breeze (pu)
14 ran. 3l, ½l, 6l. SP 3-1.

655 - Maiden 6yo+ II

628 **Red Hugh [16]**........................G Mulcaire 1
made all, drew clr 2 out
607³ **Have Another [11]***chsd wnr 3 out, no imp nxt* 2
635³ **Lets Twist Again [11]***chsd ldrs, styd on onepcd 2 out* 3
Also: 634³ Daddy Warbucks (4), 618³ Noble Knight (5), 608 Lady Of Means (6), 615 Dante Alainn (7), 634 Kimber Sissons (pu), 642 Trakswayboy (pu), 640 Brown Berry (pu), 594³ The Gaffer (pu), 528 Chuck (f), 637³ Earl Of Mirth (pu)
13 ran. 10l, ½l, 20l. SP 10-1.

656 - 4m Open Lightweight

643¹ **What Thing [23]**.......................D Costello 1
mid-div, prog to ld aft 2 out, sn clr.
648 **July Schoon [18]***ld 6 out-aft 2 out, no ch wth wnr* 2
620 **Slaney Wind***no dang, t.o.* 3
Also: 639 Bit Of A Citizen (4), 621 Glenmore Star (5), 468 Upshepops (pu), Man With A Plan VI (f), 593 Ad Extra (pu), 648 January Don (f)
9 ran. 5l, dist, 3l. SP 1-3.

657 - Open Lightweight

639¹ **Blackwater Lady [22]**...................N Fehily 1
prom, chal 2 out, ld last, styd on well
648¹ **Beet Statement [21]***prom, ld 2 out, hdd & no ext last* 2
633³ **Stroll Home [20]***prom, ev ch 2 out, no ext last* 3
Also: The Rum Mariner [20] (4), 520¹ Pharditu (pu), 580¹ Passer-By (pu), 648³ Slaney Goodness (pu), 547 Some Tourist (pu), 576 Up Trumps (pu)
9 ran. 1l, 3l, 1l. SP 7-4.

658 - Winners Of One I

614¹ **Mags Super Toi [16]**..................E Gallagher 1
prog 3 out, ld apr last, styd on well.
568² **La Mon Dere [15]***prog 3 out, ev ch apr last, onepcd* 2
648 **Loughdoo [15]***ld to apr last, no ext* 3
Also: 635¹ Kingeochy [13] (4), 613 Fair Revival (pu), 608¹ Mountainous Valley (pu), 596 More Than Most (pu), Slaney Supreme (pu), 641 Glenbower Queen (pu), 641² McFepend (pu)
10 ran. 3l, ½l, 4l. SP 5-1.

659 - Winners Of One II

604¹ **Lady Clarina [16]**......................P Costello 1
prom, ld last, drvn out
648 **Lurriga Glitter [16]***prom, ld 3 out-last, no ext* 2
606 **Thefirstone [10]***chsd ldrs, onepcd 3 out.* 3
Also: Derring Ann [13] (4), 547 Anyone Whoknows Me (5), 605³ Grants Carouse (6), 613 Safety Factor (pu), 647 Miss Playtoi (pu), 613 Curraheen Bride (pu), 629 Flo Jo's Boy (pu)
10 ran. 1l, 15l, 3l. SP 4-1.

660 - Maiden I

618² **Major Man [14]**..........................J Cullen 1
prog 3 out, ld nxt, styd on

615 Cloneenverb [13]*prom, ev ch 2 out, onepcd* 2
589³ Fountain House [11]*chsd ldrs, onepcd aft 2 out* 3
Also: 569 Ellesmere (4), 165 Theblondebarrister (pu), Healing Thought (pu), 649 The Wild Wave (pu), 610 Noneofyourbusiness (pu), 646 Persian Packer (pu), 546³ Poachers Lamp (pu)
10 ran. 2l, 6l, 6l. SP 3-1.

661 - Maiden II

636² The Road To Moscow [14].............B Hallahan 1
made all, clr 4 out, easily ....
614 Ballyhooly Belle [10]*chsd ldrs, no imp wnr 3 out* 2
621² Miss Tornado [10]*chsd ldrs, no imp wnr 3 out* 3
Also: 640 Miss Catherine (4), Rossi Beg (pu), 642 Tom The Boy VI (pu), Blarneys Trick (0), 652 Nearhaan (pu), 497 Buckshee (pu), 640 Scarra Darragh (pu), 645 Linda's Paradise (pu)
11 ran. 10l, 1l, 20l. SP 2-1.

Index to Point-to-Point Runners 1996

KEY TO INDEX

HORSE'S NAME Colour Sex Age Breeding Owner
Last year's record and Merit Rating for each race
Position (Rating) **Bold** indicates Hunter Chase **NH** other NH races
Race Number Date Course Left or Right Handed
(cross refers to Results Section)
Type of Race (refer to Results Section)
Distance to nearest furlong
No. of Runners Going Close-up Finishing Position Merit Rating for the race
Horse Comment .... **Merit Rating**
(This rating should be used until updated in Point-to-Point Entries Index)

ABBA LAD ch.g. 14 Le Bavard (FR) - Rosina Royal by Skyros — Mrs Annita Taylor

481	11/3	Taunton	(R)	HC	3m	11	G	*ld, pkd 1st, hdd 4th, lost tch 8th, t.o. next.*	9	0
580	20/3	Towcester	(R)	HC	2 3/4m	5	G	*soon t.o..*	5	0
955	8/4	Lockinge	(L)	MEM	3m	5	GF	*alwys rear, no ch & t.o. frm 14th*	5	0

Winning chaser; well past it now. **0**

ABBEY MOSS ch.g. 5 Executive Man - Mickley Vulstar by Sea Moss — Charlie Peckitt

175	18/2	Market Rase'	(L)	MDO	2m 5f	8	GF	*alwys rear, hit 6th, t.o. & p.u. last*	P	0
413	9/3	Charm Park	(L)	MDO	3m	12	G	*mid-div, 5th at 10th, wknd 14th, p.u. 3 out*	P	0

Just learning so far; probably capable of better. **0**

ABBEY VENTURE(IRE) b.m. 7 Ovac (ITY) - Dawn Of Spring Vii — Miss N A Showers

1995 P(0)

386	9/3	Llanfrynach	(R)	RES	3m	10	GS	*prssd ldr to 10th, wknd rpdly, p.u. aft 11th*	P	0

Yet to go further than 2 miles on on her annual appearances **0**

ABBREVIATION b.g. 13 Torus - Worldling by Linacre — John Williams

1995 P(0),R(-),R(-)

1199	21/4	Lydstep	(L)	OPE	3m	5	S	*2nd whn u.r. 12th*	U	-
1262	27/4	Pyle	(R)	MEM	3m	6	G	*prom, chsd ldr 14th, still 2nd last, reluc flat*	4	0
1602	25/5	Bassaleg	(R)	CON	3m	8	GS	*cls up til wknd 10th, disp poor 4th whn hmpd & ref 3 out*	R	-

Ungenuine and best avoided now. **0**

ABERCROMBY COMET br.g. 11 Strong Gale - Star-Pit by Queen's Hussar — Mrs S Forster

403	9/3	Dalston	(R)	RES	3m	11	G	*mstk 2nd, tk ld 6th, wnt clr 15th, unchal*	1	19
789	1/4	Kelso	(L)	HC	3m 1f	11	GF	*settld midfield, imp hfwy, led 6 out to 3 out, rallied und pres to ld run-in, soon clr.*	1	23
1542	16/5	Perth	(R)	HC	2 1/2m 110yds	8	F	*ld to 8th, led again next till hdd apr last, soon wknd.*	3	20

Missed 95; vastly improved; won modest H/Chase; prospects at 12 limited **22**

ABETTORTIME (Irish) — I 445P

ABINGDON BOY ch.g. 11 Balinger - Sharpie by Roan Rocket — Michael A Johnson

1995 F(-),2(17),2(20),1(21)

8	14/1	Cottenham	(R)	CON	3m	10	G	*in tch, outpcd 15th, p.u. apr last, bttr for race*	P	0
418	9/3	High Easter	(L)	CON	3m	10	S	*(fav) trkd ldrs,gng wll,outpcd 14th,no dang aft,kpt on frm 2 out*	3	16

Cottenham specialist(4 wins); lightly raced now; may find another win; G/F-G/S **20**

ABIT MORE BUSINESS(IRE) b.g. 5 Henbit (USA) - Driven Snow by Deep Run — R G Williams

204	24/2	Castle Of C'	(R)	MDO	3m	11	HY	*(fav) hld up,prog to disp 4 out,lft clr nxt wknd rpdly last,tired*	4	0
556	17/3	Ottery St M'	(L)	MDO	3m	15	G	*(fav) mid-div, prog 13th, disp 4 out-2 out, wknd apr last*	2	14

Promising; stamina problems at present; should win in 97; **15**

ABITMORFUN ch.g. 10 Baron Blakeney - Mary Mile by Athenius — James Bennett

1995 P(0),4(0),**P(0)**,P(0),4(0)

48 4/2 Alnwick (L) LAD 3m 9 G *mstk 5th, ld 6th-12th, btn aft nxt* 6 13
359 4/3 Doncaster (L) HC 2m 3f 110yds 10 G *struggling to stay in tch hfwy, t.o. when blnd 3 out.* 6 0
611 23/3 Friars Haugh (L) LAD 3m 10 G *made most til grad wknd frm 4 out* 3 14
1340 4/5 Hexham (L) HC 3m 1f 13 S *prom till wknd before 3 out, t.o..* 8 0

Beaten last 23 races; not really threatening to break the sequence. 14

A BIT OF A MONKEY (Irish) — I 261^{P}, I 318^{U}, I 365^{P}, I 413^{U}, I 451^{P}

ABOUT MIDNIGHT b.m. 7 Jester - Princess Andromeda by Corvaro (USA) Mrs L Moore

114 17/2 Lanark (R) MDO 3m 12 GS *nvr dang, p.u. 2 out* P 0
193 24/2 Friars Haugh (L) MDN 3m 10 S *remote 6th whn p.u. 10th* P 0
501 16/3 Lanark (R) RES 3m 12 G *ld/disp til wknd frm 11th, bhnd whn p.u. 2 out* P 0
1352 4/5 Mosshouses (L) LAD 3m 10 GS *t.d.e. pllng,wd bnds,ld to 9th,hit hedge bef 12th* r -

Defective brakes and steering so far; unpromising 0

ABSENT MINDS br.m. 10 Lir - Forgotten by Forlorn River B R J Young

44 3/2 Wadebridge (L) MDO 3m 9 GF *trckd ldrs til outpcd 15th, fin tired* 3 10

Very lightly-raced - missed 94/5 - & time running out 10

ACADEMICALLYBRIGHT b.g. 10 Pitpan - Own Acre by Linacre D R Greig

1187 21/4 Tweseldown (R) MDN 3m 11 GF *not fluent in rear, p.u. aft 9th, dsmntd* P 0

Very lightly-raced & may be finished now 0

ACCOUNTANCY PARK (Irish) — I 632^{P}

ACCOUNTANCY PERK (Irish) — I 418^{P}, I 622^{F}

ACERTAINHIT b.g. 12 Ascendant - Hit The Button by Red Alert David Pritchard

1995 1(0),**P(0)**,**P(0)**,P(0),**F(-)**,**P(0)**,**P(0)**

81 11/2 Wetherby Po' (L) MEM 3m 4 GS *(fav) last frm 8th, outpcd, lft 3rd 4 out* 3 0
223 24/2 Duncombe Pa' (R) CON 3m 16 GS *(bl) mid-div, strgglng & blnd 10th, p.u. 12th* P 0
512 16/3 Dalton Park (R) CON 3m 10 G *alwys bhnd, t.o. 15th* 7 0

Only effective in his members; well in it in 96; need luck to win again. 0

ACE VENTURA (Irish) — I 4^{4}, I 78^{2}, I 142^{4}, I 185^{P}, I 334^{P}, I 358^{4}, I 594^{4}, I 614^{4}, I 654^{P}

ACEY DEUCEY (Irish) — I 181^{4}

ACHIEVED AMBITION(IRE) gr.g. 8 Derring Rose - In Paris by Last Fandango Paul Morris

1995 **8(NH)**

1229 27/4 Weston Park (L) MEM 3m 2 G *(fav) hrd held, cls up, ev ch whn f 3 out* F -
1457 8/5 Uttoxeter (L) HC 3 1/4m 16 G *jmpd right, soon bhnd, t.o. when p.u. before 10th.* P 0

Poor novice hurdler; probably unlucky in joke members; more needed. 0

ACROPOL b.m. 14 Politico (USA) - Acroma by Tobrouk (FR) P F Gibbon

319 2/3 Corbridge (R) RES 3m 16 GS *bhnd, last at 9th, p.u. 12th* P 0
758 31/3 Great Stain' (L) RES 3m 17 GS *rear, last frm 4th, t.o. 7th* 11 0
828 6/4 Stainton (R) MDO 3m 7 GF *twrds rear, pshd along 6th, nvr a dang* 3 0
1090 14/4 Whitwell-On' (R) RES 3m 17 G *rear, dtchd frm 3rd, nvr a fctr* 10 0
1136 20/4 Hornby Cast' (L) MDN 3m 11 G *bhnd 3rd, t.o. 12th, p.u. last* P 0
1450 6/5 Witton Cast' (R) MDO 3m 14 G *alwys rear, nvr a dang* 7 0

Missed 95; an elderly maiden and will remain one. 0

ACROSS THE CARD b.g. 8 Lir - Cornish Susie by Fair Season Capt W B Ramsay

1995 3(13),4(0),1(14),4(13),1(16),4(13),1(16),4(13)

83 11/2 Alnwick (L) CON 3m 10 GS *mid-div, outpcd 13th, ran on 3 out, tk 2nd flat, nrst fin* 2 17
186 24/2 Friars Haugh (L) MEM 3m 7 S *(fav) hld up in tch, jnd ldr apr last, ld cls home* 1 15
609 23/3 Friars Haugh (L) PPO 3m 7 G *not fluent in rear, some hdwy frm 4 out, nvr dang* 3 12
861 6/4 Alnwick (L) CON 3m 7 GF *mid-div, prog to 2nd 10th, ld 16th, in comm whn lft clr last* 1 21
1106 15/4 Hexham (L) HC 3m 1f 9 GF *held up in tch, effort after 3 out, left in ld between last 2, styd on strly.* 1 21
1251 27/4 Balcormo Ma' (R) OPE 3m 6 GS *held up, some hdwy frm 4 out, nvr dang* 3 17
1572 19/5 Corbridge (R) LAD 3m 8 G *u.r. 2nd* U -
1629 30/5 Uttoxeter (L) HC 2m 5f 13 GS *chsd ldrs, gradually wknd from 10th.* 3 16

Changed hands 96; solid, consistent; weak H/Chase success makes life difficult in 97; Any 21

ACROSS THE LAKE b.g. 12 Over The River (FR) - Golden Highway by Royal Highway Mrs D R Brotherton

1995 2(21),F(-),2(20),2(21),5(19),1(22)

48 4/2 Alnwick (L) LAD 3m 9 G *(fav) rear, grad clsd frm 13th, eff & ev ch last, not qckn* 3 20
85 11/2 Alnwick (L) LAD 3m 11 GS *mid-div & outpcd, effrt 14th, kpt on, nvr able to chal* 5 18
227 24/2 Duncombe Pa' (R) LAD 3m 6 GS *(fav) chsd ldr, disp 9th, ld 11th, made rest, styd on* 1 19

318 2/3 Corbridge (R) LAD 3m 5f 10 GS *bhnd,prog 13th,3rd at 15th,ran on to 2nd flat,too mch to do* 2 19
586 23/3 Wetherby Po' (L) LAD 3m 8 S *mid-div, prog 12th, ld 3 out-last, eased & lost 2nd flat* 3 19
893 6/4 Whittington (L) LAD 3m 4 F *(bl) w.w., lft in ld apr 3 out, clr nxt, styd on wll* 1 23
1153 20/4 Whittington (L) LAD 3m 10 G *(Jt fav) (bl) last plc thruout, alwys strggling, p.u. 14th* P 0
1366 4/5 Gisburn (R) LAD 3m 12 G *(bl) alwys prom, ev ch 3 out, styd on onepcd* 2 22
1473 11/5 Aspatria (L) LAD 3m 7 GF *(bl) in tch, 4th & outpcd 15th, kpt on onepce aft* 3 17

Consistent ladies horse; stays well but rather indolent; can win again; G/F-SuG/F-S 21

ACT IN TIME (Irish) — **I** 565^{U}, **I** 638^{1}

ACTION LAD (Irish) — **I** 35^{R}, **I** 62^{5}, **I** 147^{2}, **I** 293^{R}, **I** 440^{3}, **I** 541^{P}

ADAMARE br.g. 12 Chukaroo - Coxmoore Sweaters by Wynkell R Crosby
1995 **F(-),F(NH)**

633 23/3 Market Rase' (L) LAD 3m 10 GF *ldng quartet, 2nd 10th-6 out, fdd nxt, p.u. 2 out* P 0
812 6/4 Charing (L) LAD 3m 6 F *made all, prssd 13th-2 out, styd on well* 1 23
1053 13/4 Penshurst (L) LAD 3m 5 G *(fav) ld, mstk 2nd, clr 2 out, wknd aft, jmpd slwly & hdd last* 2 16
1305 28/4 Southwell P' (L) LAD 3m 4 GF *(fav) 2nd to 4 out, wknd rpdly, p.u. 3 out, lame* P 0
1443 6/5 Aldington (L) LAD 3m 4 HD *(4s-9/4),made all, ran on wll whn chal 2 out* 1 19
1520 12/5 Garthorpe (R) LAD 3m 8 GF *2nd til ld 5th, in cmmnd til ct apr last, not qckn* 2 19
1596 25/5 Garthorpe (R) LAD 3m 9 G *disp til f 6th* F -

Front runner; won modest ladies; best L/H & fast ground; can win again. 19

ADANAC b.g. 13 Buckskin (FR) - Rosslea by Klairon Barton L Williams
1995 P(0),F(-),6(0),6(0),P(0),1(10)

847 6/4 Howick (L) LAD 3m 9 GF *5th whn u.r. 6th* U -
1036 13/4 St Hilary (R) LAD 3m 6 G *t.o. 7th, p.u. 13th* P 0
1156 20/4 Llanwit Maj' (R) MEM 3m 7 GS *prssd ldr to ld 12th, qcknd clr apr 2 out, easy* 1 14
1265 27/4 Pyle (R) OPE 3m 8 G *ld to 3rd, chal 14th, wknd frm nxt* 3 13
1479 11/5 Bredwardine (R) OPE 3m 8 G *chsd ldrs, not qckn frm 14th, kpt on onepcd* 4 14
1560 18/5 Bassaleg (R) OPE 3m 7 F *chsd ldrs til s.u. flat apr 9th* S -
1602 25/5 Bassaleg (R) CON 3m 8 GS *alwys rear, mstks 10th & nxt & p.u.* P 0

Dual Members winner 95/96; outclassed in Opens;G/S-F.oor race - offers only chance at 13; G-F 15

AD EXTRA (Irish) — **I** 357^{P}, **I** 498^{3}, **I** 593^{U}, **I** 656^{P}

ADMIRAL ROUS b.g. 5 Rousillon (USA) - Bireme by Grundy Miss E Keir

886 6/4 Kimble (L) CON 3m 5 GF *chsd ldrs, mstk 10th, cls 3rd whn blnd 12th, not rcvr, t.o.* 3 0

Flat winner 94; not disgraced on debut; vanished after; capable of better. 12

ADMIRALS LANDING b.g. 11 Dubassoff (USA) - Elysium Dream Vii C T Moate
1995 2(10),P(0)

1076 13/4 Cothelstone (L) MEM 3m 2 GF *ld, hit 5th, hdd 11th, wll btn whn u.r. last, rmntd* 2 0
1347 4/5 Holnicote (L) MDO 3m 16 GS *ld/disp to 7th, grad fdd* 6 0

Only 6 runs in 3 seasons; barely hanging on to a rating; time against him now. 11

ADMIRALS REALM gr.g. 7 Another Realm - Bedeni by Parthia D F Gillard
1995 **P(NH)**

927 8/4 Bishopsleigh (R) OPE 3m 7 G *p.u. aft 2nd* P 0

Sprinter on the Flat who unsurprisingly failed to take to pointing 0

ADMISSION(IRE) br.g. 6 Glow (USA) - Admit by Welsh Pageant N Chamberlain
1995 **7(NH),10(NH),11(NH)**

53 4/2 Alnwick (L) MDO 3m 13 G *prom, chsd ldr 3 out, styd on to ld nr fin* 1 14
188 24/2 Friars Haugh (L) RES 3m 12 S *5th hlfwy, styd on frm 3 out, not rch wnr* 2 16
367 6/3 Catterick (L) HC 3m 1f 110yds 12 G *mstk 2nd, soon in tch, driven along before 3 out, kept on.* 3 22
1106 15/4 Hexham (L) HC 3m 1f 9 GF *chsd ldrs till blnd and u.r. 7th.* U -
1340 4/5 Hexham (L) HC 3m 1f 13 S *(fav) held up, hdwy after 13th, driven along after 2 out, styd on same pace.* 3 20

Poor hurdler; steady improvement; placed weak H/chase; stays; sure to win again. 20

ADVENT LADY ch.m. 9 Kemal (FR) - Armantine by Brave Invader (USA) Mrs A J Haigh
1995 8(0),3(10),**9(0)**,3(11),2(12),1(13),**R(-)**,4(14),R(-)

223 24/2 Duncombe Pa' (R) CON 3m 16 GS *prom, ld 12th-14th, wknd apr last* 4 17
486 16/3 Newcastle (L) HC 3m 9 GS *prom, reminders 13th, blnd 5 out, soon struggling.* 7 0
761 31/3 Great Stain' (L) INT 3m 7 GS *rear, jmpd rght 4th, chsd ldrs til wknd 13th, t.o.* 4 0
983 8/4 Charm Park (L) RES 3m 13 GF *prom, 2nd 10th, fdd rpdly frm 12th* 7 0
1090 14/4 Whitwell-On' (R) RES 3m 17 G *ld 2nd-10th, steadily fdd frm 12th* 5 11

Maiden winner 95; safe but outclassed in 96 & Restricted win looks most unlikely now 12

AESOPS FABLES (Irish) — **I** 79^{P}, **I** 250^{B}, **I** 540^{6}

AFALTOUN b.g. 11 High Line - Afeefa by Lyphard (USA) Richard Lee

1995 F(-)
19 14/1 Tweseldown (R) CON 3m 9 GS *(fav) ld to 3 out,wknd rpdly,no ch whn blnd last,p.u. flat,dsmntd* P 0
380 9/3 Barbury Cas' (L) CON 3m 11 GS *(bl) ld til u.r. 7th* U -
785 31/3 Tweseldown (R) OPE 3m 5 G *ld to 6th, hrd rdn & no ext 4 out, lft clr last* 1 12
998 8/4 Hackwood Pa' (L) CON 3m 5 GF *set gd pce to 9th, chsd ldr to 14th, wknd & p.u. aft 16th* P 0
1227 26/4 Ludlow (R) HC 2 1/2m 16 G *prom to 10th, wknd.* 8 0
1532 13/5 Towcester (R) HC 2m 110yds 16 GF *outpcd, t.o. when p.u. before 2 out.* P 0
1609 26/5 Tweseldown (R) MXO 3m 9 G *chsd wnr to 10th, outpcd nxt, wknd 14th, p.u. 3 out* P 0

Problems 95; not regain form and a lucky winner; can only be watched now. 10

AFARISTOUN(FR) b.g. 12 Top Ville - Afrique (FR) by Exbury — Miss Joanne Morse
1995 U(-),4(13),U(-),S(-)
216 24/2 Newtown (L) LAD 3m 13 GS *prom, chsd ldr 5th-13th, wknd rpdly, t.o. & p.u. 15th* P 0
546 17/3 Erw Lon (L) LAD 3m 10 GS *mid-div & in tch til 3 out, onepcd* 4 17
1036 13/4 St Hilary (R) LAD 3m 6 G *rear, 3rd at 14th, ran on 3 out, nrst fin, no ch wnr* 2 17
1264 27/4 Pyle (R) LAD 3m 10 G *in tch til outpcd 11th, no ch frm 13th* 7 0
1387 6/5 Pantyderi (R) LAD 3m 6 GF *ld to 13th, fin tired* 3 14
1508 12/5 Maisemore P' (L) LAD 3m 6 F *chsng grp, wknd 10th, poor 4th whn f 13th* F -
1604 25/5 Bassaleg (R) OPE 3m 6 GS *last at 4th, dtchd 9th, p.u. nxt* 4 0

Ran better in 96; does not really stay and will need fortune to score. 14

A FARM BAR b.g. 9 Arkan - Evening Bar by Pardigras — P Dando
1995 P(0),1(15),**F(-)**,**P(0)**
388 9/3 Llanfrynach (R) RES 3m 20 GS *in tch to 11th, bhnd whn p.u. 14th* P 0

Won poor maiden 95; hardly seen in 96 and more needed for restricted. 14

AFFAIR OF HONOUR(IRE) ch.g. 8 Ahonoora - Good Relations by Be My Guest (USA) — Roger Milward
1995 4(14),1(17),U(-),3(13)
245 25/2 Southwell P' (L) LAD 3m 8 HO *bhnd til p.u. 10th* P 0

Won weak ladies 95; problems in 96; still young enough and may revive. 18

AFRICAN BRIDE(IRE) b.m. 6 Lancastrian - African Nelly by Pitpan — David Brace
2 13/1 Larkhill (R) MDO 3m 17 GS *mid-div, prog to 2nd 12th, ld & mstk 3 out, ran on well* 1 20
41 3/2 Wadebridge (L) XX 3m 9 GF *(fav) mstk 1st, prog 8th, jnd wnr & mstk 3 out, not qckn* 2 18
155 17/2 Erw Lon (L) RES 3m 9 G *(fav) cls up til ld 10th, clr nxt, easily* 1 19
335 3/3 Heythrop (R) INT 3m 9 G *(fav) prom, ld 11th, prssd frm 14th, ran on well flat* 1 24
505 16/3 Magor (R) PPO 3m 7 GS *(fav) 2nd til ld 7th, made rest, easily* 1 23
604 23/3 Howick (L) INT 3m 7 S *(fav) ld & clr to 13th, hdd nxt, wkng whn p.u. 3 out, distressed* P 0
981 8/4 Lydstep (L) INT 3m 5 G *(fav) alwys disp, lkd wnr whn f last* F 21
1268 27/4 Pyle (R) INT 3m 8 G *(fav) ld 6th, drew clr 15th, easily* 1 24

Ex-Irish; speedy & useful; plenty of options open in 97; H/Chase possible; Good 26

AFRICAN GOLD b.g. 8 Sonnen Gold - Lennoxlove by Lear Jet — Elliot Graham
51 4/2 Alnwick (L) MDO 3m 17 G *prom, 5th whn f 10th* F -

.... 0

AFRICAN MINSTREL b.g. 11 Longleat (USA) - Bewitched by African Sky — Mrs K E Steel
1169 20/4 Chaddesley ' (L) MEM 3m 9 G *chsd ldrs til lost tch 13th, t.o. & p.u. 3 out* P 0
1439 6/5 Ashorne (R) RES 3m 11 G *rear, rpd prog to chs wnr 13th, wknd 15th, t.o.* 9 0
1481 11/5 Bredwardine (R) RES 3m 14 G *mid-div, cls enough 12th, outpcd frm 14th* 7 0

All out to win a poor maiden, a hard ride and needs to improve for res 10

AFTERKELLY b.g. 11 Le Moss - Vamble by Vulgan — Mrs T White
1995 2(15),**1(24)**,**P(0)**,**P(0)**,2(23),1(18)
255 28/2 Taunton (R) HC 4 1/4m 110yds 15 GS *(fav) ld to 10th, chal from 14th to after 19th, led 4 out, hdd 3 out, soon one pace.* 3 21
559 17/3 Ottery St M' (L) OPE 3m 7 G *ld/disp to 3 out, no ext aft* 2 22
626 23/3 Kilworthy (L) OPE 3m 12 GS *ld to 7th, rdn frm 10th, sn outpcd, no ch aft* 4 15
1078 13/4 Cothelstone (L) MXO 3m 6 GF *(fav) 3rd til prog to disp 8th, ld 15th, hdd last, no ext* 2 20
1140 20/4 Flete Park (R) OPE 4m 6 S *ld/disp, ld 4 out til hdd apr last, onepcd* 2 24

Thorough stayer; very safe; outclassed in competitive company over 3m; Any 22

AFTER THE NUMBER (Irish) — I 29P

AGAPANTHUS ch.m. 9 True Song - Town Flirt by Charlottown — R J Myram
1995 R(-),**P(0)**,3(0),P(0),P(0),F(-),R(-)
1391 6/5 Pantyderi (R) MDO 3m 13 GF *3rd/4th til fdd frm 2 out* 5 0
1511 12/5 Maisemore P' (L) MDO 3m 14 F *chsd ldrs to 10th, sn lost tch, t.o. & p.u. last* P 0
1605 25/5 Bassaleg (R) MDO 3m 8 GS *25s-12s, cls 3rd whn u.r. 7th* U -
1651 8/6 Umberleigh (L) MDO 3m 11 GF *sn rear, t.o. 11th, p.u. 15th* P 0

INDEX TO POINT-TO-POINT RUNNERS 1996

Changed hands; ungenuine and most unlikely to consent to win. 0

AGARB(USA) b.g. 11 Key To The Mint (USA) - Knight's Promise (USA) by Sir Ivor — Mrs R Corn

214 24/2 Newtown (L) CON 3m 21 GS *alwys rear, lost tch & p.u. 12th* P 0
427 9/3 Upton-On-Se' (R) OPE 3m 6 GS *dist last whn p.u. 15th* P 0
853 6/4 Sandon (L) LAD 3m 7 GF *(bl) alwys rear, p.u. 4 out* P 0
1170 20/4 Chaddesley ' (L) CON 3m 9 G *(bl) ld to 4th, wknd 6th, t.o. whn ref 14th* R -
1318 28/4 Bitterley (L) XX 3m 8 G *(bl) last frm 3rd, t.o. 6th, p.u. nxt* P 0

Of no account 0

AGATHIST(USA) ch.g. 13 Bon Mot III - We Try Harder by Blue Prince II — Mrs C McClymont

752 31/3 Lockerbie (R) LAD 3m 10 G *(Jt fav) 6th hlfwy, no hdwy frm 3 out* 4 16

Very useful 92-94; only 1 run since; could still win if fit in 97; S-F. 20

AGHAWADA GOLD (Irish) — I 541[1]

AGILE KING b.g. 5 Rakaposhi King - My Aisling by John de Coombe — J E Potter

166 17/2 Weston Park (L) MDN 3m 10 G *cls up, ld 7th-13th, fdd 3 out* 5 0
464 9/3 Eyton-On-Se' (L) MDN 2 1/2m 13 G *ld tl f 3rd* F -
661 24/3 Eaton Hall (R) MDN 3m 9 S *plld hrd, ld to 13th, still going wll whn u.r. nxt* U -
883 6/4 Brampton Br' (R) MDN 3m 13 GF *(fav) ld 4-8th & 13th-15th, wknd apr 3 out* 7 0

Shows ability but burns himself out; go close if settling in 97. 13

AHALIN ch.g. 14 Laurence O - Reaper's Own by Master Owen — A C Austin

1995 S(-),6(0)

462 9/3 Eyton-On-Se' (L) RES 3m 12 G *mid to rear, no ch whn p.u. last* P 0
948 8/4 Eyton-On-Se' (L) MEM 3m 4 GF *cls up to 12th, lost tch whn pce increased 4 out* 3 0
1231 27/4 Weston Park (L) OPE 3m 6 G *in tch to 12th, outpcd aft, no ch in rear, p.u. 2 out* P 0
1421 6/5 Eyton-On-Se' (L) RES 3m 11 GF *alwys mid-to-rr, t.o. hlfwy* 7 0

Only beaten 1 horse 95/96; of no account now. 0

AHEAD OF MY TIME (Irish) — I 330[5], I 439[1]

AHOGILL (Irish) — I 99[F], I 179, , I 261[1], I 454[P]

AIGUILLE (Irish) — I 158[2], I 169[1]

AINE HENCEY (Irish) — I 41[P], I 127[P], I 427[F], I 475[P], I 545[5], I 581[F], I 604[3], I 654[4]

AINTREE OATS b.m. 9 Oats - Lucy Parker by Milan — J R Holt

1995 5(0),F(-),2+(12),1(14),4(0),1(18),2(18)

21 20/1 Barbury Cas' (L) MEM 3m 16 GS *chsd ldrs to 8th, 6th & losing tch 11th, p.u. 15th* P 0
171 18/2 Market Rase' (L) RES 3m 5 GF *(fav) cls up, chsd ldr 7th, ld 2 out, slwly drew clr apr last* 1 16
393 9/3 Garthorpe (R) CON 3m 7 G *ld to 6th, 3rd & outpcd 4 out, lft 2nd 2 out* 2 16
723 31/3 Garthorpe (R) CON 3m 19 G *ld to 3rd, wth ldrs aft, 3rd & ev ch whn f 15th* F -
1235 27/4 Clifton On ' (L) MEM 3m 4 GF *(fav) ld 2nd, made rest, clr last, eased flat* 1 15

Won weak races; honest & stays well; may find a weak confined; G-F. 19

AIR COMMANDER br.g. 11 Strong Gale - Southern Slave by Arctic Slave — Miss C Spearing

1995 **4(21),P(0)**,U(-),**P(0)**,1(20),**3(16),9(NH)**

951 8/4 Eyton-On-Se' (L) LAD 3m 6 GF *held up in rear, cls order 13th, no ext cls home* 3 17
1099 14/4 Guilsborough (L) LAD 3m 9 G *hld up, prog 9th, cls 5th whn blnd & u.r. 13th* U -

Ladies winner 95; season lasted 6 days in 96 & best watched at 12; G-F 16

AISLINGS TOI (Irish) — I 69[F], I 312[F], I 334[P]

AITCH-A gr.g. 5 Malaspina - Double Stretch by Double-U-Jay — Harry Atkinson

122 17/2 Witton Cast' (R) MDO 3m 8 S *t.o. 6th, came home own time* 5 0
228 24/2 Duncombe Pa' (R) MDO 3m 9 GS *prom, outpcd 11th, lft poor 3rd 4 out, ran on well flat* 2 11

Beaten 2 lengths in bad race; only young and can do better. 13

AJAR (Irish) — I 118[P]

A LAD INSANE br.g. 15 Al Sirat (USA) - Endora by Royal Palm — Miss Sarah Wills

1995 P(0)

1436 6/5 Ashorne (R) MEM 3m 7 G *1st ride, mid-div & out of tch, t.o. 12th, mod late prog* 4 0

Winning chaser; past it now. 0

ALAMILLO (Irish) — I 32[3], I 105[1]

ALAMIR(USA) b.g. 8 Shadeed (USA) - Glamour Girl (FR) by Riverman (USA) — M Darby

1995 P(0),7(0)

1220 24/4 Brampton Br' (R) OPE 3m 10 G *chsd ldrs to 4th, lost pl & ref 8th* R -
1314 28/4 Bitterley (L) MEM 3m 13 G *prssd wnr to 8th, wknd 11th, p.u. 15th* P 0

1421	6/5	Eyton-On-Se'	(L)	RES	3m	11	GF	*mid-to-rr, bd mstk 13th, not rcvr, lost tch, p.u. 3 out*	P	0
1482	11/5	Bredwardine	(R)	RES	3m	13	G	*prom, cls 5th whn mstk 12th, wknd & p.u. 15th*	P	0

Won short Maiden 94; does not stay and no further prospects. 10

ALANSFORD ch.g. 9 Carlingford Castle - Inneen Alainn by Prince Hansel — E J Farrant

1995 **7(NH),3(NH),7(NH),9(NH),3(NH),3(NH),3(NH),5(NH),4(NH)**

58	10/2	Cottenham	(R)	RES	3m	7	GS	*sttld in tch, effrt aft 2 out, ran on onepcd flat*	3	15
248	25/2	Charing	(L)	RES	3m	12	GS	*mid-div,jnd ldrs 13th,chsd wnr 4 out,chal 2 out,no ext flat*	2	17
272	2/3	Parham	(R)	RES	3m	13	GF	*(fav) prog to 2nd 12th, ld 14th, hdd aft 3 out, 2nd best aft*	2	16
779	31/3	Penshurst	(L)	RES	3m	13	GS	*(fav) towrds rear, clsd up 12th, chal 3 out, ld nxt, ran on wll*	1	20
1050	13/4	Penshurst	(L)	CON	3m	8	G	*sn prom, cls 3rd whn blnd 14th, styd on 3 out to ld frm last*	1	21

Ex-Irish; improved each start; quite useful now; stays well; Opens likely in 97; G-S 22

ALAPA b.h. 9 Alzao (USA) - Gay Folly by Wolver Hollow — A B Coogan

107	17/2	Marks Tey	(L)	MDN	3m	15	G	*r.o. & u.r. 4th*	r	-
315	2/3	Ampton	(R)	MDO	3m	10	G	*rushed into ld & r.o. 3rd*	r	-
343	3/3	Higham	(L)	MDO	3m	11	G	*mid-div, wknd 14th, p.u. 16th*	P	0
617	23/3	Higham	(L)	MDO	3m	11	GF	*w.w. 5th at 13th, gd prog 4 out, chal & going wll,r.o.nxt*	r	-
681	30/3	Cottenham	(R)	MDO	3m	12	GF	*in tch, prog 14th, chsd wnr & ev ch last, no qckn flat*	2	13
930	8/4	Marks Tey	(L)	MDO	3m	6	G	*prom whn ran out 4th*	r	-

Subsequent winners behind when placed; a real nutcase though,could win if more amenable in 97. 13

ALBERT'S ADVENTURE(IRE) ch.g. 6 Le Moss - Berry Street by Class Distinction — C Cottingham

176	18/2	Market Rase'	(L)	MDO	2m 5f	10	GF	*mstk 2nd, ran out 4th*	r	-
333	3/3	Market Rase'	(L)	MDO	3m	11	G	*(bl) chsd ldr 4th til f 6th*	F	-
516	16/3	Dalton Park	(R)	MDO	3m	11	G	*(bl) n.j.w. last frm 10th, t.o. aft til p.u. 15th*	P	0
1027	13/4	Brocklesby '	(L)	MDN	3m	7	GF	*(bl) 2nd jmpng lft til ran out 5th*	r	-

Very wayward at present; can only be watched. 0

ALBERTS GAMBLE (Irish) — **I** 366P, **I** 472P, **I** 509P, **I** 552P

ALCOFROLIC b.m. 7 Brando - Champagne Peri by The Malster — P J Houldey

842	6/4	Maisemore P'	(L)	MDN	3m	17	GF	*jmpd badly, t.o. 3rd til ref 7th*	R	-
1225	24/4	Brampton Br'	(R)	MDO	3m	18	G	*mid-div 12th, prog 14th, 3rd 3 out, chal nxt, no ex flat*	4	13

Incredible improvement 2nd start; beaten less than 4 lengths; should score in 97. 14

ALDINGTON BARON b.g. 9 Baron Blakeney - Aldington Princess by Cavo Doro — A Rogers

676	30/3	Cottenham	(R)	INT	3m	13	GF	*prom, ld 8-12th, wknd rpdly, p.u. 15th*	P	0
897	6/4	Dingley	(R)	CON	3m	15	GS	*ld 4-10th, fdd, p.u. 2 out*	P	0
1195	21/4	Sandon	(L)	XX	3m	9	G	*prom, 2nd to 11th, fdd 14th, p.u. 3 out*	P	0
1302	28/4	Southwell P'	(L)	INT	3m	10	GF	*chsg grp, onepcd, nvr on terms*	4	0
1435	6/5	Ashorne	(R)	CON	3m	12	G	*wll in rear, effrt 10th, sn wknd, t.o. & p.u. 13th*	P	0

Promising 92; problems and shown little since; can only be watched now. 12

ALDINGTON BELL b.g. 13 Legal Eagle - Dear Catalpa by Dear Gazelle — C C Trietline

1995 **4(NH),3(NH),3(NH),4(NH),6(NH),5(NH)**

741	31/3	Upper Sapey	(R)	MEM	3m	4	GS	*(bl) disp 2nd/3rd til u.r. 13th*	U	-
1480	11/5	Bredwardine	(R)	LAD	3m	12	G	*(bl) prog to cls 3rd at 7th, lost tch 1st 2 15th, wknd nxt*	7	0
1566	19/5	Mollington	(R)	LAD	3m	7	GS	*(bl) in tch to 11th, t.o. whn f 13th*	F	-

Dead 0

ALDINGTON CHARLIE gr.g. 7 Baron Blakeney - Aldington Princess by Cavo Doro — H W Wheeler

1995 2(13),5(0)

430	9/3	Upton-On-Se'	(R)	MDO	3m	15	GS	*(fav) alwys prom, strng run to disp last, ran on wll flat*	1	16
742	31/3	Upper Sapey	(R)	RES	3m	9	GS	*(fav) cls 4th, ev ch til outpcd frm 4 out*	3	11
1242	27/4	Woodford	(L)	RES	3m	18	G	*blndrd & u.r. 1st*	U	-
1482	11/5	Bredwardine	(R)	RES	3m	13	G	*alwys rear, lost tch frm 15th*	5	0

Confirmed 95 promise when winning; ran badly after (last both completions) & best watched start 97 .. 14

ALDINGTON KID ch.g. 12 Creetown - Mae Mae by Communication — Mrs Caroline Dix

1995 P(0),U(-),P(0)

389	9/3	Llanfrynach	(R)	MDN	3m	11	GS	*ld 8-10th & 13th-3 out, wknd, fin tired*	4	0
605	23/3	Howick	(L)	MDN	3m	13	S	*prom to hlfwy, poor 6th whn p.u. 3 out*	P	0
1270	27/4	Pyle	(R)	MDO	3m	9	G	*ld til f 10th*	F	-
1511	12/5	Maisemore P'	(L)	MDO	3m	14	F	*mstks, ld to aft 15th, grad wknd*	4	10

Very moderate; most unlikely to win now. 11

ALEX-PATH b.g. 13 Warpath - Alexandra by Song — Mrs S G Currie

1995 P(0),7(0),7(0),2(11),1(0),4(0),9(0)

667	24/3	Eaton Hall	(R)	INT	3m	11	S	*rear to 12th, sn lost tch, p.u. 4 out*	P	0
892	6/4	Whittington	(L)	CON	3m	4	F	*ld, mssd marker aft 2nd, hdd apr 8th, p.u. 11th*	P	0

894 6/4 Whittington (L) OPE 3m 5 F *2nd outing, alwys bhnd, styd on onepce to take 3rd 2 out* 3 12
1154 20/4 Whittington (L) OPE 3m 7 G *alwys rear, t.o. 14th, lft 4th 2 out* 4 0
1363 4/5 Gisburn (R) MEM 3m 5 G *mid-div whn p.u. 5th* P 0

Lucky winner 95; no real prospects of another win. 0

ALEX THUSCOMBE ch.g. 8 Takachiho - Portate by Articulate — Mrs Peter Shaw
1995 3(0),C(-),8(0),U(-),S(-),3(10),2(10)

522 16/3 Larkhill (R) MDO 3m 12 G *prom early, no ch frm 14th, onepcd* 5 10
1060 13/4 Badbury Rin' (L) MDO 3m 14 GF *handy, 4th at 14th, chsd wnr apr last, not trbl wnr* 2 13
1396 6/5 Cotley Farm (L) MDO 3m 11 GF *(vis) prom, ld to 4th, disp frm 10th til ld 4 out, ran on well* 1 15
1551 18/5 Bratton Down (L) OPE 3m 8 F *(vis) ld/disp to 6th, lost plc 15th, bhnd frm nxt* 5 14
1612 26/5 Tweseldown (R) RES 3m 11 G *ld 3-6th & 9-13th,lft in ld 16th,clr 2 out, ran on well* 1 19

Improved 96; safe & stays; novice-ridden; weak Confined may be best chance 97; G-F 19

ALFREDO GARCIA(IRE) b.g. 5 Lancastrian - The Tame Fairy by Bluerullah — S H Marriage

35 20/1 Higham (L) RES 3m 16 GF *alwys bhnd, nvr nr ldrs* 7 0
106 17/2 Marks Tey (L) RES 3m 12 G *prom, chsd ldr 14th, ev ch til rddn & no ex appr 2 out* 2 13
417 9/3 High Easter (L) MEM 3m 4 S *(fav) chsd lding pr,prog 8th, lft 2nd nxt, 3l down whn f 12th* F -
931 8/4 Marks Tey (L) RES 3m 8 G *ld to 4th, ev ch 3 out, wknd frm nxt* 3 10

Irish Maiden winner; ran passably and can find a weak restricted; may prefer an easy course. 15

ALFREE b.g. 8 Son Of Shaka - Super Brown by Gold Rod — F R Bown

1278 27/4 Bratton Down (L) INT 3m 12 GF *mid-div whn f 5th* F -
1628 27/5 Lifton (R) MEM 3m 5 GS *lft in ld apr 15th,slwd & hdd 3 out, fin tired* 3 0

Beaten by his remounted stablemate in Members; no prospects. 0

ALGAIHABANE(USA) b.g. 10 Roberto (USA) - Sassabunda by Sassafras (FR) — John Tuck
1995 P(0),F(-)

847 6/4 Howick (L) LAD 3m 9 GF *(bl) ld to 13th, wknd rpdly, t.o.* 3 0

Maiden winner 93; only 3 runs since and of no account now. 11

AL HASHIMI b.g. 12 Ile de Bourbon (USA) - Parmesh by Home Guard (USA) — Bruce Sarson
1995 **7(13),10(0),2(15),2(20)**

257 29/2 Nottingham (L) HC 2 1/2m 11 G *in tch 1st cct, feeling pace and struggling 6 out, no impn last 4.* 6 12
359 4/3 Doncaster (L) HC 2m 3f 110yds 10 G *trckd ldrs, lost ground quickly when pace qcknd after 5 out, no impn after.* 3 12
579 20/3 Ludlow (R) HC 2 1/2m 17 G *alwys prom, 2nd and btn when left in ld and hmpd last, soon hdd and wknd.* 4 21
1120 20/4 Bangor (L) HC 2 1/2m 110yds 13 S *in tch, nigglд along 4 out, wknd quickly, t.o..* 5 0
1339 4/5 Hereford (R) HC 2m 3f 7 F *chsd ldrs, ld 4th till 7th, bhnd from 9th.* 5 17
1532 13/5 Towcester (R) HC 2m 110yds 16 GF *hdwy 3 out, nvr near to chal.* 5 19

Winning chaser; sticks to short H/chases; declining now and unlikely to win one at 13. G-F. 16

ALIANNE ch.m. 6 Alias Smith (USA) - Anne de Bretagne by Ardross — Miss C M Martin

51 4/2 Alnwick (L) MDO 3m 17 G *t.o. til p.u. 12th* P 0
88 11/2 Alnwick (L) MDO 3m 11 GS *out of tch in mid-div, t.o. 6th, p.u. 2 out* P 0
322 2/3 Corbridge (R) MDN 3m 10 GS *mid-div, last at 10th, nvr a fctr aft* 6 0
704 30/3 Tranwell (L) MDO 3m 16 GS *last whn mstks 1st & 2nd, p.u. nxt* P 0

Well beaten when completing; much more needed. 0

ALIAS SILVER gr.g. 9 Alias Smith (USA) - Duresme by Starry Halo — J H Busby

236 24/2 Heythrop (R) MDN 3m 13 GS *cls up, 2nd hlfwy, lost tch & p.u. aft 3 out* P 0
438 9/3 Newton Brom' (R) MDN 3m 10 GS *alwys prom, ev ch 15th, styd on agn cls home* 3 0
496 16/3 Horseheath (R) MDO 3m 10 GF *mid-div, prog 6th, ld 3 out, qcknd clr 2 out, eased flat* 1 14
707 30/3 Barbury Cas' (L) RES 3m 18 G *alwys mid-div, nvr on terms with ldrs* 5 12
960 8/4 Lockinge (L) RES 3m 9 GF *cls up to 14th, outpcd frm 4 out* 4 11
1101 14/4 Guilsborough (L) RES 3m 16 G *rear, gd prog 13th, ld 3 out, styd on wll frm nxt, rdn out* 1 17
1176 21/4 Mollington (R) MEM 3m 6 F *ld to 2nd, cls up til outpcd 11th, sn no ch* 4 11
1521 12/5 Garthorpe (R) INT 3m 7 GF *prom, ld 3rd-4th, disp 5-6th, outpcd frm 3 out* 3 13

Won two modest races & inconsistent; may struggle in better company in 97; G-F 17

ALICE SHEER THORN (Irish) — **I** 70^{6}, **I** 182^{P}, **I** 280^{1}

ALIEN CORN(IRE) b.g. 6 Celestial Storm (USA) - Coup de Veine (FR) by Gift Card (FR) — Mrs M J Thorogood

343 3/3 Higham (L) MDO 3m 11 G *alwys prom, no ext last* 3 11
830 6/4 Marks Tey (L) MDN 3m 14 G *mid-div, not rch ldrs, rear & no ch 15th* 6 0

Barely rateable as yet; still young and may improve. 11

A LITTLE HELP (Irish) — **I** 462^{P}, **I** 567^{P}

INDEX TO POINT-TO-POINT RUNNERS 1996

AL JAWWAL ch.g. 6 Lead On Time (USA) - Littlefield by Bay Express — Mrs P King

1995 P(0),P(0)

15	14/1	Cottenham	(R)	MDN	3m	14 G	*chsd ldrs going well, ld apr last, pshd out*	1	15
679	30/3	Cottenham	(R)	RES	3m	15 GF	*3rd whn f 5th*	F	-
834	6/4	Marks Tey	(L)	RES	3m	11 G	*handy, wknd 15th, p.u. 17th, dsmntd*	P	0

Fit early and won fair Maiden; problems last start; could win modest restricted if fit in 97; Good. 16

ALL BUT (Irish) — I 386^{4}, I 526^{P}

ALLERBANK b.g. 5 Meadowbrook - Allerdale by Chebs Lad — C Storey

407	9/3	Dalston	(R)	MDO	2 1/2m	13 G	*mstk 4th, bhnd 6th, wnt 4th 12th, outpcd frm nxt*	7	0
1355	4/5	Mosshouses	(L)	MDO	3m	10 GS	*keen hld,hld up,lost tch 13th,styd on 2 out,fin wll,improve*	3	0

Only on educational outings in 96 & sure to do much better in 97 - Maiden win likely 13

ALLER MOOR(IRE) b.g. 5 Dry Dock - Boggy Peak by Shirley Heights — G Keirle

1995 **8(NH)**

145	17/2	Larkhill	(R)	MDO	3m	13 G	*sn rear, t.o. & p.u. 15th*	P	0
470	10/3	Milborne St'	(L)	MDO	3m	18 G	*(fav) hld up, prog 15th, ld 2 out, slppd final bnd,hdd & nt rcvr*	2	15
733	31/3	Little Wind'	(R)	MDO	3m	13 GS	*(fav) cls 2nd frm 14th, efft & ld aft last, pushd clr*	1	18
1313	28/4	Little Wind'	(R)	RES	3m	14 G	*last whn blnd 5th, nvr got into race*	8	0

Promising; beat subsequent scorer when winning & Restricted more than likely early 97; G-S 19

ALL FOR MAX (Irish) — I 194^{F}, I 342^{1}

ALL GREEK TO ME(IRE) b.g. 8 Trojan Fen - Do We Know by Derrylin — W J Bryan

1995 P(0),r(-),4(17)

878	6/4	Brampton Br'	(R)	OPE	3m	5 GF	*rear til some prog 15th, kpt on onepcd frm 3 out*	3	14
1042	13/4	Bitterley	(L)	CON	3m	9 G	*alwys last, no ch whn p.u. 12th*	P	0
1477	11/5	Bredwardine	(R)	MEM	3m	3 G	*hld up, clsr order 14th, ld 3 out, clr nxt, pshd out*	1	11

Winning hurdler 94; struggling in points 95/6 & won very weak contest; Members best hope 97 14

ALL OR NOTHING ch.m. 8 Scorpio (FR) - Kelton Lass by Lord Nelson (FR) — N M L Ewart

1995 2(12),2(12),P(0),3(12)

398	9/3	Dalston	(R)	MEM	3m	13 G	*bhnd frm 9th*	7	0
613	23/3	Friars Haugh	(L)	MDN	3m	15 G	*ld untl 15th, kpt on one pace*	3	13
755	31/3	Lockerbie	(R)	MDN	3m	17 G	*alwys abt same plc*	6	0
1089	14/4	Friars Haugh	(L)	MDN	3m	10 F	*ld til u.r. 3rd*	U	-
1253	27/4	Balcormo Ma'	(R)	MDO	3m	16 GS	*gd hdwy frm 4 out, fin strgly, not rch wnr*	2	14
1356	4/5	Mosshouses	(L)	MDO	3m	12 GS	*(fav) lost plc 8th,hmpd 12th,ran on 15th,ld aft last,sn clr*	1	14

Placed 5 times before winning at 16th attempt; novice-ridden; Restricted not on cards at present 15

ALLOW GOLD ch.g. 9 Golden Love - Knockduff Surprise by Monseigneur (USA) — Mrs N M E Jones

1995 P(0),P(0),P(0),8(0),P(0),F(-),6(0),4(0)

291	2/3	Eaton Hall	(R)	LAD	3m	10 G	*mstk 4th, f nxt*	F	-
456	9/3	Eyton-On-Se'	(L)	MEM	3m	2 G	*(fav) jmpd stckly, trckd ldr tl gng on 12th, f 13th*	F	-

Irish Maiden winner 93; rarely compleats; Members only hope of success.othing 10

ALL WEATHER b.g. 10 Air Trooper - Modom by Compensation — M S Wilesmith

1995 1(20),P(0),P(0),5(16)

22	20/1	Barbury Cas'	(L)	XX	3m	19 GS	*mid-div & out of tch,effrt 13th,nvr rchd ldrs,p.u. 2 out*	P	0
214	24/2	Newtown	(L)	CON	3m	21 GS	*mid-div, no ch frm 13th, kpt on*	6	12
379	9/3	Barbury Cas'	(L)	XX	3m	9 GS	*sttld rear, rpd prog to ld 14th, jnd & lft clr last*	1	19
485	16/3	Hereford	(R)	HC	3m 1f 110yds	13 S	*prom in chasing gp, cld from 14th, disp ld when jmpd left 3 out and next, hdd last, hung badly left, no ext flat.*	2	23
1318	28/4	Bitterley	(L)	XX	3m	8 G	*(fav) w.w. cls 5th at 10th, chal 14th, ld nxt, just hld on*	1	19

Quite able at best & stable in form 96; likes Barbury; can go well fresh; should win again; G-S 22

ALMAURITA (Irish) — I 237^{P}, I 266^{P}, I 429^{P}, I 481^{P}, I 559^{P}

ALMOST AN ANGEL (Irish) — I 108^{F}, I 236^{5}, I 272^{2}

ALOHA (Irish) — I 32, , I 134^{F}

ALONE HOME (Irish) — I 137^{F}, I 247^{4}, I 332^{1}

ALPHA ONE ch.g. 11 Belfalas - Clonaslee Foam by Quayside — C W C Tregoning

1995 5(16),4(0),3(21),4(17),2(19),4(19),1(20),**P(0)**

179	18/2	Horseheath	(R)	OPE	3m	5 G	*sn rdn,lost tch & slw jmp 12th,p.u. aft nxt,cont,p.u. last*	P	0
737	31/3	Sudlow Farm	(R)	OPE	3m	4 G	*last & rddn 4th, ref 7th*	R	-
1193	21/4	Sandon	(L)	OPE	3m	8 G	*(bl) sn rear, no ch whn ref 8th*	R	-

Won 5 94/95; changed hands after, and again mid-season; gone to pieces now.. 0

ALPINE CASTLE (Irish) — I 609^{P}, I 650^{P}

ALPINE SONG b.m. 11 True Song - Alpine Orchid by Mon Capitaine — D G Stephens

1995 3(0),F(-),2(22),5(12)

208 24/2 Castle Of C' (R) LAD 3m 14 HY *rear til prog 14th, nrst fin* 4 10
581 21/3 Wincanton (R) HC 2m 5f 13 S *t.o. when p.u. before 5 out.* P 0
1111 17/4 Hockworthy (L) MXO 3m 13 GS *33s-14s, cls up, ld brfly 13th, prsd wnr aft, no ex app last* 2 23
1277 27/4 Bratton Down (L) CON 3m 15 GF *in tch, ld 8th-14th, disp til outpcd frm 2 out* 4 18

Has ability but inconsistent & outclassed in good races; may find a chance at 12; G-S 20

ALS DINER ch.g. 6 Scallywag - Saucy Eater by Saucy Kit Mike Roberts

92 11/2 Ampton (R) MDO 3m 7 GF *hmpd & u.r. 2nd* U -
182 18/2 Horseheath (R) MDO 3m 11 G *f 1st* F -

Good stable but only negotiated one fence so far. 0

ALSEMERO gr.g. 10 Another Realm - Sky Miss by Skymaster J B Dale

1995 2(14),2(14),1(15),P(0)

95 11/2 Ampton (R) RES 3m 11 GF *prom to 7th, grad lost plc, t.o. & p.u. 3 out* P 0

Lightly raced; changed hands and vanished quickly in 96; best watched now. 14

ALWAYS ALLIED(IRE) b.g. 8 Dalsaan - Novesia by Sir Gaylord Miss Victoria Roberts

1995 P(0),3(16),2(14),2(17)

849 6/4 Howick (L) MDN 3m 14 GF *(fav) hld up, prog frm 10th, 15l 3rd 3 out, wknd, lame* 5 0
1248 27/4 Woodford (L) MDN 3m 15 G *prom, ld 15th, kckd clr, lft wll clr 3 out, unchal* 1 16

Deserved winner; onepaced and needs to get clear; can win modest Restricted; promising jockey. 17

ALWAYS DREAMING ch.m. 6 Farajullah - Lady Almscliffe by Plenty Spirit R J Butterworth

1995 P(0)

352 3/3 Garnons (L) MDN 2 1/2m 9 GS *chsng ldrs whn b.d. 2nd* B -
532 16/3 Cothelstone (L) RES 3m 12 G *bhnd, t.o 8th til p.u. 13th* P 0
734 31/3 Little Wind' (R) MDO 3m 11 GS *sn bhnd & strgglng, t.o. p.u. apr 13th* P 0

Yet to wake up 0

ALWAYS DRUMMING (Irish) — **I** 207P, **I** 312P, **I** 334P

ALWAYS GREAT b.g. 10 Vaigly Great - Jinja by St Paddy Miss Sarah George

1995 10(0),4D(12)

526 16/3 Larkhill (R) RES 3m 9 G *alwys prom, ld 3 out, hrd rdn flat* 1 17
866 6/4 Larkhill (R) INT 3m 4 F *(fav) made virt all, qcknd frm 12th, clr frm 3 out, pushd out* 1 20
1213 24/4 Andoversford (R) CON 3m 5 G *cl up, ld 4-12th, ev ch 3 out, sn outpcd* 2 15
1243 27/4 Woodford (L) MEM 3m 6 G *held up, 4th & blndrd 13th, soon lost tch, t.o. & p.u. 3 out* P 0

Lightly-raced; improved 96; best front-running; can win Confined if fit 97; Firm 19

ALZAMINA b.m. 10 Alzao (USA) - Timinala by Mansingh (USA) J C Window

676 30/3 Cottenham (R) INT 3m 13 GF *trckd ldrs to 15th, no ch whn p.u. 2 out* P 0
809 6/4 Charing (L) MEM 3m 4 F *(fav) hld up, chal apr 4 out, qcknd to ld nxt, ran on well* 1 14
1207 21/4 Heathfield (R) CON 3m 9 F *mid-div, mstk 8th, prog to chs wnr 16th, wknd last* 5 13
1440 6/5 Aldington (L) INT 3m 5 HD *last slpd & nrr u.r. bnd aft 10th,in tch aft,wkng & p.u.3out* P 0
1536 16/5 Folkestone (R) HC 2m 5f 9 GF *bhnd, some prog 8th, no ch from 10th.* 4 0
1609 26/5 Tweseldown (R) MXO 3m 9 G *in tch in rear,mstk 6th,outpcd 11th,no prog,p.u.2 out* P 0

Dual winner 94; missed 95; won weak race & outclassed after; may struggle again 97; G/S-F 14

AMAAM AMAAM b.g. 6 Last Tycoon - What A Pity by Blakeney M B Clarke

1995 **P(NH),5(NH),9(NH),11(NH)**

424 9/3 High Easter (L) MDN 3m 10 S *ld to 6th, cls up til wknd 14th, t.o. & p.u. 2 out* P 0
617 23/3 Higham (L) MDO 3m 11 GF *ld to 1st, prom, p.u. 12th, dsmntd* P 0

Ex novice hurdler; problems last start; looks a non-stayer. 0

AMADEO ch.g. 10 Le Moss - Pops Girl by Deep Run Mrs Carrie Janaway

1995 P(0),P(0),F(-)

137 17/2 Ottery St M' (L) RES 3m 15 GS *sn bhnd, t.o. & p.u. 14th* P 0
379 9/3 Barbury Cas' (L) XX 3m 9 GS *(bl) alwys prom, wknd frm 3 out, lft 2nd last* 2 10
600 23/3 Howick (L) RES 3m 14 S *(bl) hld up, prog 13th, no ext frm nxt* 4 16
707 30/3 Barbury Cas' (L) RES 3m 18 G *(bl) cls up whn u.r. 3rd* U -
960 8/4 Lockinge (L) RES 3m 9 GF *(bl) ld til 9th, outpcd frm 11th, t.o. & p.u. 4 out* P 0
1167 20/4 Larkhill (R) MEM 3m 9 GF *(bl) prom early til wknd frm 12th, t.o. nxt* 5 0

Ran well at Howick; not 100% genuine and unlikely to be bothered to win. 14

AMADEUS(FR) b.g. 8 Pamponi (FR) - Katy Collonge (FR) by Trenel Trevor Hemmings

1106 15/4 Hexham (L) HC 3m 1f 9 GF *in tch, effort before 2 out, chsd wnr between last two, no impn.* 2 18

Modest novice chaser; beaten in weak H/Chase; likely to remain under Rules in future 19

AMANDA BAY b.g. 11 Paddy's Stream - Vultang Lady by Le Bavard (FR) — Miss Tina Hammond

1995 F(-),10(0),6(0),U(-),P(0)

704	30/3	Tranwell	(L)	MDO	3m	16	GS	*prom early, btn whn blnd 14th, p.u. nxt*	P	0
1087	14/4	Friars Haugh	(L)	MDO	3m	9	F	*ran out 2nd*	r	-
1254	27/4	Balcormo Ma'	(R)	MDO	3m	14	GS	*bhnd whn p.u. aft 12th*	P	0
1512	12/5	Hexham Poin'	(L)	MEM	3m	6	HY	*ld 5th til apr 10th, grad lost tch wth wnr, demoted 3 out*	3	0

Beaten by a hunter at Hexham and has no prospects. 0

AMANDAWILL (Irish) — **I** 113[P], **I** 143[P], **I** 207[P], **I** 354[6], **I** 550, , **I** 652[P]

AMARI KING b.g. 12 Sit In The Corner (USA) - Maywell by Harwell — M Ward-Thomas

1995 **3(26),11(18),B(-),P(0)**

798	3/4	Ascot	(R)	HC	2m 3f 110yds	10	GF	*chsd ldrs, ev ch 2 out, one pace apr last.*	3	24
1122	20/4	Stratford	(L)	HC	2m 5f 110yds	16	GF	*prom, rdn 12th, wknd apr 2 out.*	4	23
1227	26/4	Ludlow	(R)	HC	2 1/2m	16	G	*chsd ldrs, ld 11th, styd on well.*	1	25
1339	4/5	Hereford	(R)	HC	2m 3f	7	F	*(fav) held up, smooth hdwy apr 3 out, chsd wnr from next, ld last, hdd cl home.*	2	25
1541	16/5	Folkestone	(R)	HC	2m 5f	8	G	*third when f 3rd.*	F	-

Much revived in 96; always has short campaigns; best at 2 1/2m; could win H/Chase at 13; F-G/S 24

AMAZING AIR(USA) ch.g. 6 Air Forbes Won (USA) - Amoriah (USA) by Norcliffe (CAN) — Paul C Blackwell

1995 **7(NH)**

148	17/2	Erw Lon	(L)	MDN	3m	9	G	*rear, prog to 4th at 15th, 2l down 2 out, no ext*	4	0

Fair debut (beat two subsequent winners) but disappeared; could go close if fit 97 13

AMAZING ALL (Irish) — **I** 451[1], **I** 489[F]

AMAZING HILL (Irish) — **I** 4[P], **I** 56[P]

AMAZON LILY ch.m. 9 Man Of France - Lady Amazon by Spartan General — Mrs J E Eales

1995 1(19)

368	6/3	Lingfield	(L)	HC	3m	7	S	*jmpd right, left in ld 2nd, ran v wd bend after 9th, pkd 3 out, hdd apr last, not qckn.*	2	19

Only 4 runs 94-6; quite decent and could win Opens; R/H looks essential. 23

AMBER PAYNE ch.g. 12 Amoristic (USA) - Payne's Lady by Lock Diamond — Mrs Linda C Balmer

1995 P(0),U(-),7(0),1(19),3(17),3(13),4(14)

190	24/2	Friars Haugh	(L)	LAD	3m	7	S	*3rd hlfwy, ld 15th til outpcd frm 2 out*	2	14
400	9/3	Dalston	(R)	LAD	3m	10	G	*prom, lft 2nd at 14th, ev ch 2 out, no ex frm last*	3	20
611	23/3	Friars Haugh	(L)	LAD	3m	10	G	*ld brfly 4 out, wknd frm nxt*	4	13
913	8/4	Tranwell	(L)	LAD	3m	7	GF	*chsd ldr, ld 4-5th, 3l down 14th, outpcd 2 out*	2	15

One win from 27 points; needs sharp track & firm; hard to win at 13. 17

AMBER RULER ch.g. 10 Tumble Wind (USA) - Matjup by Simbir — D J Line

18	14/1	Tweseldown	(R)	MXO	3m	6	GS	*ld 2nd-11th, wknd rpdly, fence bhnd 15th, stppd 2 out*	P	0

Finished 1st weekend & no prospects now 0

AMBROSE b.g. 9 Ile de Bourbon (USA) - Famous Band (USA) by Banderilla (USA) — W A Ritson

1995 P(0),1(16),2(18),**P(0)**

159	17/2	Weston Park	(L)	CON	3m	22	G	*prog hlfwy, prom 12th, lost tch & sn btn*	7	0
285	2/3	Eaton Hall	(R)	MEM	3m	5	G	*(fav) cls up, lft in ld 4th, made rest, prssd 2 out, lft solo*	1	16
664	24/3	Eaton Hall	(R)	CON	3m	15	S	*chsng grp, ran on well frm 3 out to ld last*	1	25
892	6/4	Whittington	(L)	CON	3m	4	F	*(fav) w.w., ld 3 out, clr nxt, canter*	1	22
1120	20/4	Bangor	(L)	HC	2 1/2m 110yds	13	S	*held up, hdwy from 7th, chsd wnr 4 out, ld last, hdd flat, no ext.*	2	24
1545	18/5	Bangor	(L)	HC	3m 110yds	8	G	*held up, prom 5th, cl 2nd and und pres when f 2 out.*	F	-

Much improved 96; likes Eaton Hall; can win more Confineds, possibly Open in 97; Any 23

AMERICAN BLACK b.g. 8 Lepanto (GER) - Cherry Morello by Bargello — Mrs D Fox-Ledger

1995 1(12),4(12),5(11),1(17)

139	17/2	Larkhill	(R)	CON	3m	11	G	*tckd away in mid-div, not plcd to chal*	6	16
683	30/3	Chaddesley '	(L)	MEM	3m	17	G	*hld up rear, nvr dang, p.u. 3 out*	P	0

Dual winner and promising 95; finished early and not progress 96; still young enough to revive; G-F. 19

AMERICAN EYRE gr.g. 11 Step Together (USA) - Jane Eyre by Master Buck — Mrs G M Gladders

1995 **13(NH),5(NH),5(NH),P(NH),7(NH),4(NH)**

450	9/3	Charing	(L)	XX	3m	8	G	*rear but in tch, 4th at 13th, outpcd aft, kpt on same pace*	3	16
571	17/3	Detling	(L)	CON	3m	13	GF	*ld to 12th, outpcd aft, 5th 3 out, styd on wll, tk 2nd flat*	2	17
775	31/3	Penshurst	(L)	CON	3m	8	GS	*alwys prom, wth ldr 6-8th, chal 4 out, ev ch whn blndrd last*	3	18

813 6/4 Charing (L) XX 3m 5 F *ld/disp frm 2nd, def adv 4 out, jnd last, hdd & onepcd flat* 2 16
1050 13/4 Penshurst (L) CON 3m 8 G *cls up to 8th, lost plc, in tch 10th, kpt on* 4 14
1538 16/5 Folkestone (R) HC 3 1/4m 6 G *in tch, prog to chase ldr 14th to next, outpcd 3 out.* 4 12

Ex Irish chaser; consistent but woefully onepaced; should try his Members; G/F-G/S 17

AMEROUS LAD b.g. 11 Amboise - Falla Dalla by Blandford Lad B R W Phillips

748 31/3 Upper Sapey (R) MDO 3m 11 GS *t.o. frm 12th* 7 0
883 6/4 Brampton Br' (R) MDN 3m 13 GF *ld to 3rd, styd prom, no ext frm 3 out* 4 12
1174 20/4 Chaddesley ' (L) MDN 3m 10 G *prom to 6th, lost plc nxt, t.o. 13th, p.u. 17th* P 0

Ran passably when 11l 4th but too old for a win now 10

AMEWSING (Irish) — I 424^{P}, I 466^{F}, I 497^{U}, I 552^{4}

AMME ENAEK (Irish) — I 24^{S}, I 28^{2}, I 94^{4}, I 477^{1}

AMORISTIC TOP (Irish) — I 115^{5}, I 152^{P}, I 221, , I 329^{5}, I 520^{4}

AMOROUS SAILOR (Irish) — I 494^{P}, I 599^{P}

AMY'S MYSTERY b or br.g. 15 Bivouac - Mystery Trip by Kadir Cup Clifford Thompson

1995 P(0),P(0),5(0),2(0),2(15),4(16)

410 9/3 Charm Park (L) OPE 3m 17 G *rr early, effrt 10th-13th, wknd aftr* 9 13
587 23/3 Wetherby Po' (L) OPE 3m 15 S *alwys twrds rear, p.u. last* P 0
984 8/4 Charm Park (L) MXO 3m 7 GF *rear early, 3rd 10th, outpcd 14th, 6th frm 3 out* 6 13
1282 27/4 Easingwold (L) OPE 3m 8 G *mstk 1st, mid-div, rdn 11th, t.o. frm 15th* 5 0

Confined winner 94; too old now. 13

ANALYSTIC(IRE) br.g. 6 Kambalda - Burlington Miss by Burlington II Ken Liscombe

740 31/3 Sudlow Farm (R) MDN 3m 16 G *chsd ldrs til u.r. 5th* U -
852 6/4 Sandon (L) MDN 3m 9 GF *f 2nd* F -
1029 13/4 Alpraham (R) MDO 3m 8 GS *mstks, rear & sn t.o., p.u. 11th* P 0
1155 20/4 Whittington (L) MDN 3m 14 G *chsng ldr, 4l 2nd whn f 14th* F -
1365 4/5 Gisburn (R) MDO 3m 17 G *prog 15th, 3rd nxt, 15l down whn f last* F -

Has ability but very clumsy at present; go close when jumping is sorted out. 12

ANCHOR EXPRESS ch.m. 10 Carlingford Castle - Bruff Gypsy by Even Money E H Crow

1995 **U(NH)**

246 25/2 Southwell P' (L) OPE 3m 9 HO *(bl) made most to 10th, rdn 12th, wknd & p.u. 15th* P 0
567 17/3 Wolverhampt' (L) MEM 3m 4 GS *ld, clr 3 out, easily* 1 16
854 6/4 Sandon (L) OPE 3m 4 GF *(bl) ld/disp til f hvly 7th* F -
1220 24/4 Brampton Br' (R) OPE 3m 10 G *(bl) chsng ldr whn msd mrkr bef 8th, p.u.* P 0

Won weak race easily but problems other starts; best watched 15

ANDALUCIAN SUN(IRE) ch.g. 8 Le Bavard (FR) - Sun Spray by Nice Guy R Barr

1995 5(0),P(0),**4(NH)**,**F(NH)**

107 17/2 Marks Tey (L) MDN 3m 15 G *mstks, prog to 8th 11th, wkng whn p.u. 13th* P 0
344 3/3 Higham (L) MDO 3m 12 G *mid-div, prog 11th, chsng ldrs whn f 13th* F -
424 9/3 High Easter (L) MDN 3m 10 S *w.w. prog 11th, chall gng wll 16th, wknd 2 out, fin tired* 2 10
618 23/3 Higham (L) MDO 3m 14 GF *wth ldrs whn u.r. 5th* U -
834 6/4 Marks Tey (L) RES 3m 11 G *last at 3rd, jmpd badly, t.o. 10th, p.u. 11th* P 0
1403 6/5 Northaw (L) MDO 3m 8 F *keen hold, hld up, prog & cls up 12th, wknd 15th* 6 0

Beaten by good horse when 2nd; pulls hard and does not stay; hard to see him winning. 12

ANDANTE 6

1007 9/4 Flagg Moor (L) MEM 3m 7 G 6 0

.. 0

ANDREA'S PRINCE (Irish) — I 180, , I 236^{P}

ANDRETTI'S HEIR ch.g. 10 Andretti - Mounemara by Ballymore T S Sharpe

1995 1(10)

77 11/2 Wetherby Po' (L) RES 3m 18 GS *ld to 8th, u.r. 11th* U -
319 2/3 Corbridge (R) RES 3m 16 GS *2nd at 3rd, sn lost plc, p.u. 9th* P 0
1285 27/4 Easingwold (L) MDO 3m 9 G *ld, drew clr 14th, 12l ld whn f 2 out, unlucky* F 13
1585 25/5 Cartmel (L) HC 3 1/4m 14 GF *ld 2nd to 4 out, wknd flat.* 5 12

Won Members 95 (subsequently disqualified); easily good enough for Maidens; likes sharp course. 15

ANDREW b.g. 13 Le Coq D'Or - Turkish Suspicion by Above Suspicion R D Pullar

110 17/2 Lanark (R) CON 3m 10 GS *bhnd til rpd prog to ld 12th, wknd qckly frm nxt* 5 0
402 9/3 Dalston (R) XX 3m 13 G *mid-div early, bhnd frm hlfwy* 7 0
498 16/3 Lanark (R) CON 3m 10 G *ld brfly 5th, lost tch by 11th, p.u. 2 out* P 0

Open winner 93, past it now. 0

AND WHAT ELSE(IRE) ch.g. 7 Parliament - San Patrice by Random Shot — Mrs D A Wetheral
1995 **P(NH)**
534 16/3 Cothelstone (L) MDN 3m 10 G *in tch going wll,disp brfly apr 4 out,rallied flat,jst faild* 2 15
671 28/3 Taunton (R) HC 3m 13 S *bhnd, mstk 4th, t.o. from 13th.* 9
993 8/4 Kingston St' (R) MDO 3m 17 F *sn rear, m.n.s* 6
1128 20/4 Stafford Cr' (R) RES 3m 17 S *rear, t.o. whn p.u. 10th* P
1497 11/5 Holnicote (L) RES 3m 10 G *jmp slwly in rear, t.o. p.u. apr 8th* P
Just failed on debut; poorly campaigned after; still young enough to regain the plot. 14

ANDY GAWE (Irish) — I 154^{P}, I 207^{5}, I 358^{F}, I 377, , I 507,
ANDY JOE (Irish) — I 80^{P}, I 111^{P}
ANDY'S BIRTHDAY (Irish) — I 30^{3}, I 62^{1}, I 116^{P}, I 160^{3}
ANDYWORTH b.g. 8 Andy Rew - Worth While by Sexton Blake — J D W Chilton
163 17/2 Weston Park (L) LAD 3m 10 G *ld 4th-5th, mid-div whn f 9th* F
216 24/2 Newtown (L) LAD 3m 13 GS *in tch to 9th, sn wknd, t.o. & p.u. aft 13th* P
461 9/3 Eyton-On-Se' (L) RES 3m 15 G *ld 4th-10th, in tch to 5 out, fdd, p.u. 2 out* P
739 31/3 Sudlow Farm (R) RES 3m 11 G *prom, chsd ldng pair frm 10th, kpt on onepcd* 3 15
951 8/4 Eyton-On-Se' (L) LAD 3m 6 GF *ld to 12th, in tch til outpcd 3 out* 4 11
Dual winner 94; missed 95; disappointing & beat only 3 other finishers 96; can only be watched 13

AN FEAR DUBH (Irish) — I 38^{P}, I 466^{P}, I 557^{F}
AN FEAR OG (Irish) — I 334^{U}
ANITA'S SON b.g. 9 Anita's Prince - Jubilaire by Gala Performance (USA) — Mrs B F Abraham
680 30/3 Cottenham (R) MDO 3m 11 GF *schoold in last, t.o. 10th* 5
1301 28/4 Southwell P' (L) MDO 3m 10 GF *chsng grp, 4th whn u.r. 6 out* U
No real signs of ability & time already passing him by 0

ANJUBI b.g. 11 Sunyboy - Dyna Bell by Double Jump — W H Whitley
1995 P(0),3(16),1(20),U(-),B(-),1(14),2(18),**3(18)**,U(-)
39 3/2 Wadebridge (L) OPE 3m 7 GF *prom, chsd ldr 12th til rdn aft 14th, outpcd* 4 16
133 17/2 Ottery St M' (L) OPE 3m 18 GS *mid-div, prog 14th, ev ch 3 out, wknd frm nxt* 4 20
256 29/2 Ludlow (R) HC 3m 14 G *mstk 2nd, well bhnd 6th, hdwy 14th, kept on from 4 out.* 4 22
Dual winner 95; outclassed in competitive races; bare stayer; finished early 96; best watched 19

ANNABEN ch.m. 13 Hotfoot - Northern Empress by Northfields (USA) — D T Goldsworthy
1995 2(0),U(-),P(0)
850 6/4 Howick (L) MDN 3m 14 GF *alwys last pair* 6
Of no account now. 2nd & has little chance of a win now 0

ANN BLACK (Irish) — I 12^{U}, I 143^{P}, I 182^{P}, I 306^{P}, I 379^{5}, I 637^{5}
ANNESLEY LADY (Irish) — I 220^{P}, I 347^{4}, I 501^{1}
ANNIE'S ARTHUR (Irish) — I 21^{P}, I 169^{4}, I 236^{3}, I 305^{2}, I 341^{1}, I 362^{1}, I 452^{2}, I 558^{3}, I 584^{3}, I 597^{P}
ANNIVERSARY ANNIE (Irish) — I 11^{F}
ANNMOUNT LADY(IRE) b.m. 8 Arapaho - Croziers Jewel by Crozier — Mrs A Eas
1995 4(0),2(12),3(0)
206 24/2 Castle Of C' (R) MDO 3m 10 HY *sn rear, t.o. til prog 12th, ev ch 4 out, wknd nxt, p.u.2out* P
269 2/3 Didmarton (L) RES 3m 12 G *f 1st* F
431 9/3 Upton-On-Se' (R) MDO 3m 17 GS *s.s. alwys wll bhnd* 10
555 17/3 Ottery St M' (L) MDO 3m 15 G *alwys rear, nvr plcd to chal* 6
1006 9/4 Upton-On-Se' (R) MDN 3m 11 F *mstks, chsd ldrs, outpcd 13th, no imp aft* 5
1212 24/4 Andoversford (R) MEM 3m 5 G *cl up, hit 5th, 3rd & outpcd 12th, no dang aft* 3
Ex Irish; very moderate and does not stay; need luck to win. 12

ANNS DISPLAY (Irish) — I 318^{3}, I 407^{P}, I 451^{P}, I 492^{P}
ANNSON bl.g. 10 Impecunious - Anns Valley by Hanover — Mrs S Stratford
264 2/3 Didmarton (L) INT 3m 12 G *wll in tch til wknd 14th, t.o.* 6
643 23/3 Siddington (L) MDN 3m 16 S *bhnd til u.r. 4th* U
867 6/4 Larkhill (R) MXO 4m 6 F *hld up, 5th whn f 10th* F
1217 24/4 Andoversford (R) MDO 3m 16 G *bhnd, sm prog 9th, sn stglng, p.u. aft 12th* P
Of no account now. 0

ANN TONI (Irish) — I 50^{P}, I 64, , I 119^{P}, I 207^{P}
ANNYBAN b.m. 6 Bairn (USA) - Mandrian by Mandamus — James Baniste
665 24/3 Eaton Hall (R) RES 3m 14 S *p.u. 2nd, dsmntd* P
1033 13/4 Alpraham (R) MDO 2 1/2m 15 GS *3rd/4th thruout, ev ch 4 out, no ext* 3 1
1315 28/4 Bitterley (L) MDO 3m 10 G *15l 3rd at 10th, wknd frm 13th, p.u. 15th* P

A hint of ability but more stamina needed. **10**

ANODFROMALORD (Irish) — I 330P

AN OON ISS AN OWL (Irish) — I 78P, I 2013, I 250F, I 334P, I 4462, I 5061, I 641,

ANOTHER BELIEVER (Irish) — I 88U, I 1121, I 1592

ANOTHER BERRY (Irish) — I 275F, I 352P, I 502P, I 546P

ANOTHER BRANDY (Irish) — I 210P

ANOTHER CHANCER ch.g. 5 Scallywag - Acuity by Sharp Edge — K C G Edwards

688	30/3	Chaddesley '	(L)	MDN	3m	17	G	*s.v.s. bhnd, some prog 9th, t.o. & p.u. 3 out*	P 0
1044	13/4	Bitterley	(L)	MDO	3m	15	G	*30l 3rd 7th, chsd ldr 12th, ld nxt, lft clr 15th, solo 2 out*	1 15
1222	24/4	Brampton Br'	(R)	RES	3m	11	G	*mid-div 11th, wknd 15th, p.u. 3 out*	P 0

Only one to go clear when winning; very young but much more needed. **15**

ANOTHER CHANT b.g. 6 Chas Sawyer - Golden Chorus by Golden Mallard — D A D Brydon

408	9/3	Charm Park	(L)	MEM	3m	7	G	*alwys wl in rr, p.u. 3 out*	P 0
982	8/4	Charm Park	(L)	MEM	3m	3	GF	*alwys 3rd, outpcd 14th, lost tch 3 out*	3 0

Well beaten last when 3rd; needes much more. **0**

ANOTHER CHECK (Irish) — I 289P, I 368P

ANOTHER CLASS ch.g. 8 Tower Joy - Diamond Deed by Casino Boy — Miss Elizabeth Richmond

762	31/3	Great Stain'	(L)	MDN	3m	11	GS	*last & t.o. 7th, p.u. 9th*	P 0
986	8/4	Charm Park	(L)	MDN	3m	10	GF	*mid-div, fdd 10th, p.u. 12th*	P 0

No signs of ability yet. **0**

ANOTHER COMEDY b.g. 6 El Conquistador - Miss Comedy by Comedy Star (USA) — Marten Julian (Turf Club) Ltd

424	9/3	High Easter	(L)	MDN	3m	10	S	*alwys bhnd, lst tch 11th, t.o. & p.u. 16th*	P 0
635	23/3	Market Rase'	(L)	RES	3m	8	GF	*nvr dang, last pair frm 3rd, outpcd frm 11th*	4 0
901	6/4	Dingley	(R)	MDN	2m 5f	9	GS	*remote 2nd frm 4th, ran on onepce*	2 0
1101	14/4	Guilsborough	(L)	RES	3m	16	G	*mstks, alwys rear, lost tch hlfwy, t.o. & p.u. last*	P 0
1320	28/4	Fakenham P-'	(L)	MEM	3m	3	G	*mostly 3rd, disp ld brfly aft 12th, blnd 2 out, onepcd*	3 0

Placings are virtually meaningless (last twice); barely worth a rating yet. **10**

ANOTHER CORAL br.g. 13 Green Shoon - Myralette by Deep Run — M R Deeley

1995 **5(NH),5(NH)**

256	29/2	Ludlow	(R)	HC	3m	14	G	*in tch, pressed wnr from 12th till outpcd 4 out, lost 2nd run-in.*	3 23
372	8/3	Market Rasen	(R)	HC	3m 1f	6	G	*going well, hdwy to ld 3 out, hdd and mstk next, soon btn.*	2 19
1122	20/4	Stratford	(L)	HC	2m 5f 110yds	16	GF	*held up, nvr troubld ldrs.*	6 14
1331	1/5	Cheltenham	(L)	HC	2m 5f	9	G	*in tch, 3rd and outpcd 13th, t.o. and p.u. before 2 out.*	P 0

Formerly useful chaser; retired now. **20**

ANOTHER DYER ch.g. 12 Deep Run - Saint Society by Saint Denys — Mrs M A Kendall

1995 **5(NH),1(NH),P(NH),3(NH)**

48	4/2	Alnwick	(L)	LAD	3m	9	G	*ld to 6th & 12th-2 out, wknd*	5 16
85	11/2	Alnwick	(L)	LAD	3m	11	GS	*ld to 10th & 12th-14th, wknd rpdly nxt*	7 0
398	9/3	Dalston	(R)	MEM	3m	13	G	*ld 1st, styd prom frm 6th, mstks, outpcd frm 16th*	4 0
752	31/3	Lockerbie	(R)	LAD	3m	10	G	*ld til 10th, grdly wknd*	6 0
1153	20/4	Whittington	(L)	LAD	3m	10	G	*(bl) ld to 6th, cls up 3rd whn collided & u.r. flat apr 10th*	U -

Winning chaser; front runner; does not stay and will need fortune to win. **15**

ANOTHER HOOLIGAN gr.g. 7 Scallywag - Chumolaori by Indian Ruler — R Tate

1995 F(-),P(0),2(10),2(11),P(0)

74	11/2	Wetherby Po'	(L)	MDO	3m	11	GS	*(fav) alwys rear, u.r. 9th*	U -
123	17/2	Witton Cast'	(R)	MDO	3m	11	S	*(fav) numerous mstks, prom/disp 10th-2 out, outpcd apr last*	4 0
415	9/3	Charm Park	(L)	MDO	3m	13	G	*rr early, prog 12th, disp last, styd on wl*	1 16
584	23/3	Wetherby Po'	(L)	RES	3m	13	S	*hld up, prog 14th, ev ch 2 out, outpcd by wnr*	2 18
758	31/3	Great Stain'	(L)	RES	3m	17	GS	*(fav) n.j.w. alwys bhnd, t.o. & p.u. 15th*	P 0
983	8/4	Charm Park	(L)	RES	3m	13	GF	*rear early, prog 10th, tk 2nd apr last, styd on wll*	2 16
1131	20/4	Hornby Cast'	(L)	RES	3m	17	G	*(Jt fav) sttld rear, prog 13th, chal 15th, ld nxt, sn drew clr*	1 20

Improved; stays well; mistakes but won competitive races; should win Confined in 97; G/F-S **20**

ANOTHER IDEA (Irish) — I 20F, I 1061, I 159,, I 2346, I 3893, I 4834, I 5584, I 6231

ANOTHER LAFONTAINE (Irish) — I 732

ANOTHER PICKLE (Irish) — I 5P, I 13F

ANOTHER POINT (Irish) — I 45, I 401

ANOTHER QUINCE b.m. 8 Ayyabaan - Dewy's Quince by Quorum — Mrs C Higgin

1995 U(-),P(0)

550	17/3	Erw Lon	(L)	MDN	3m	13	GS	*ld to 8th, fdd, p.u. 11th*	P	0
975	8/4	Lydstep	(L)	MDO	3m	9	G	*ld to 2 out, no ext*	3	0
1200	21/4	Lydstep	(L)	MDN	3m	10	S	*(fav) ld to 16th, wknd, fin tired*	2	12
1391	6/5	Pantyderi	(R)	MDO	3m	13	GF	*(fav) ld to 7th, mstk 14th, chsd wnr aft, no imp*	2	11

Placed 6 times 94/6; front runs and should find a win in 97. 14

ANOTHER RUSTLE (Irish) — **I** 3^{F}, **I** 10^{4}, **I** 37^{3}, **I** 58^{1}, **I** 75^{6}

ANOTHER STAR (Irish) — **I** 383^{3}

ANOTHER TANGLE (Irish) — **I** 107^{3}, **I** 177^{3}

ANSTEY GADABOUT ch.g. 10 Sixpenny Moon - Tikiland — D F Bassett

1995 **P(NH),F(NH),U(NH),P(NH),P(NH),F(NH)**

1128	20/4	Stafford Cr'	(R)	RES	3m	17	S	*in tch early, wknd 9th, t.o. & p.u. 12th*	P	0
1428	6/5	High Bickin'	(R)	RES	3m	10	G	*last whn f 14th*	F	-
1549	18/5	Bratton Down	(L)	MEM	3m	4	F	*sttld 3rd, cls up til wknd 3 out*	4	0
1622	27/5	Lifton	(R)	CON	3m	14	GS	*ld 2nd-6th & agn 9-13th, lost plc aft nxt, bhnd & p.u. 2 out*	P	0
1649	8/6	Umberleigh	(L)	RES	3m	14	GF	*chsd ldrs til f 10th*	F	-

Maiden winner 93; unsuccessful under Rules since; looks beyond redemption now 0

ANSWER THAT (Irish) — **I** 41^{S}, **I** 150^{1}

ANTARCTIC CALL b.g. 9 Callernish - Polarogan by Tarqogan — M Lewis

1995 3(0),1(14),P(0),4(10)

388	9/3	Llanfrynach	(R)	RES	3m	20	GS	*hld up rear, wll bhnd hlfwy, nvr nrr*	7	0
1038	13/4	St Hilary	(R)	RES	3m	15	G	*mid-div, 3rd at 12th, no ext 3 out, lft 2nd last*	2	14
1160	20/4	Llanwit Maj'	(R)	RES	3m	12	GS	*mid-div, prog 11th, chsd wnr 2 out, kpt on, unable to chal*	2	15
1267	27/4	Pyle	(R)	RES	3m	7	G	*alwys 2nd, styd on frm 15th, clsng flat*	2	16
1533	14/5	Chepstow	(L)	HC	3m	6	F	*ld till hdd after 7th, wknd 10th, bhnd when blnd and u.r. 4 out.*	U	-
1617	27/5	Chaddesley '	(L)	LAD	3m	8	GF	*in tch til last & strgglng hlfwy, t.o. 3 out*	4	10

Won weak Maiden 95; consistent but onepaced; can win modest restricted on long course. 17

ANTICA ROMA(IRE) ch.m. 7 Denel (FR) - Struell Course by Green Shoon — J Davenport

1995 F(-),2(12),F(-)

166	17/2	Weston Park	(L)	MDN	3m	10	G	*(fav) ld 4th-nxt, ld agn 5 out, clr 3 out, ran on*	1	15
462	9/3	Eyton-On-Se'	(L)	RES	3m	12	G	*cls up, rdn & found nil frm 4 out*	4	10

Won slowly run 3 finisher race; stamina doubts and well below restricted class. 14

ANTICS (Irish) — **I** 247^{P}, **I** 289^{4}

ANTIGUA'S TREASURE(IRE) ch.g. 7 Treasure Hunter - Sansculotte (FR) by Roi Dagrobert — Alan Harrington

1995 P(0),F(-),F(-),P(0)

167	17/2	Weston Park	(L)	MDN	3m	10	G	*ld to 4 out, 2nd & hld whn f nxt*	F	-
464	9/3	Eyton-On-Se'	(L)	MDN	2 1/2m	13	G	*(fav) prom, 2nd 4 out, disp 3rd & btn whn f last*	F	-
1224	24/4	Brampton Br'	(R)	MDO	3m	17	G	*cls 2nd at 13th, ev ch 16th, no ex frm 3 out*	2	14

Beat subsequent winner; non-finisher in other points; can win maiden if repeating the trick. 14

ANTRIM COUNTY ch.g. 11 Deep Run - Gothic Arch by Gail Star — J R Cornwall

1995 P(0),U(-),P(0),3(0),3(10),5(11),4(0),4(12),6(0)

169	18/2	Market Rase'	(L)	CON	3m	15	GF	*prom, disp 6th-14th, wknd*	6	13
244	25/2	Southwell P'	(L)	CON	3m	13	HO	*chsd wnr to 10th, wknd, p.u. 12th*	P	0
362	5/3	Leicester	(R)	HC	2 1/2m 110yds	8	GS	*in tch to 6th, t.o. from 4 out.*	4	0
580	20/3	Towcester	(R)	HC	2 3/4m	5	G	*t.o. from 6th.*	4	0
723	31/3	Garthorpe	(R)	CON	3m	19	G	*prom, ld 7th, hdd last, no ext flat*	2	17
907	8/4	Fakenham	(L)	HC	3m 110yds	11	G	*ld to 3rd, slow jump 4th, soon struggling, t.o. when p.u. before four out.*	P	0
1122	20/4	Stratford	(L)	HC	2m 5f 110yds	16	GF	*alwys in rear, t.o. when p.u. before 11th.*	P	0
1460	8/5	Uttoxeter	(L)	HC	2m 7f	5	G	*jmpd right, chsd lding pair to 6th, t.o. 12th.*	5	0

Safe but slow; not threatening to win now. 14

AN TUIODOIR (Irish) — **I** 272^{4}, **I** 394^{4}

ANURAG br.g. 10 Indian King (USA) - Merta (USA) by Jaipur — G Pidgeon

1995 P(0)

335	3/3	Heythrop	(R)	INT	3m	9	G	*outpcd & sn wll bhnd, nvr nrr*	4	0
778	31/3	Penshurst	(L)	INT	3m	6	GS	*(bl) prom, 3rd frm 11th, blndrd nxt, strgglng aft, t.o. 2 out*	3	0

Dual winner 93; only 5 runs since; blinkered to no effect last start; can only be watched. 15

ANVADABO br.g. 11 Kafu - Tassie by Lochnager — Mrs Sara Pepper

972	8/4	Thorpe Lodge	(L)	MDO	3m	9	GF	*ld, 12l clr 5th, hdd 11th, fdd 13th, f 5 out*	F	-

Hard-puller; has no prospects. 0

ANVIL CORNER ch.m. 7 Smackover - Douraine by Doubtless II — Miss Jane Wakeham

447	9/3	Haldon	(R)	MDO	3m	13	S	*mid-div, 6th at 14th, btn whn p.u. 2 out*	P	0
623	23/3	Kilworthy	(L)	MEM	3m	4	GS	*alwys 2nd, cls enough 15th, rdn & btn aft nxt*	2	11
1070	13/4	Lifton	(R)	MDN	3m	9	S	*(Jt fav) midfld, 7th 12th, rddn nxt, poor 5th & no ch frm 3 out*	5	0
1432	6/5	High Bickin'	(R)	MDO	3m	9	G	*mid-div, 5th whn u.r. 9th*	U	-

Ran well in Members but struggling in Maidens still; lightly raced; more needed for a win 12

ANYONE WHOKNOWS ME (Irish) — I 142^{P}, I 185^{P}, I 433^{5}, I 521^{1}, I 547^{5}, I 659^{5}

ANYTHINGYOULIKE b.g. 7 Lighter - Mill Miss by Typhoon — Mrs D A Smith

73	11/2	Wetherby Po'	(L)	MDO	3m	15	GS	*disp 9th, ld 3 out, disp last, just outpcd flat*	2	15
221	24/2	Newtown	(L)	MDN	3m	12	GS	*(fav) trckd ldrs, ld 12th, lft clr 14th, easily*	1	15
585	23/3	Wetherby Po'	(L)	RES	3m	13	S	*prom, ld aft 12th til f 4 out*	F	-

Quite promising; cantered home in modest Maiden; finished after fall but Restricted certain if fit 97 ... 17

ANZARNA b.m. 11 Zambrano - Angerton Annie by Waterfall — Mrs Susan Corbett

48	4/2	Alnwick	(L)	LAD	3m	9	G	*clse up to 8th, wknd & p.u. 11th*	P	0
608	23/3	Friars Haugh	(L)	RES	3m	13	G	*t.o. 7th, p.u. 13th*	P	0
858	6/4	Alnwick	(L)	RES	3m	7	GF	*alwys same pl, nvr dang*	5	0
1086	14/4	Friars Haugh	(L)	RES	3m	7	F	*made most til hdd & wknd 2 out*	4	10

Maiden winner 94; missed 95; not regain form and a win looks beyond her now. 10

APATURA HATI br.m. 7 Senang Hati - Apatura Iris by Space King — Mrs R O Hutchings

1995 F(-),2(14),1(16),5(13)

211	24/2	Castle Of C'	(R)	INT	3m	5	HY	*alwya prom, ld 10-13th, disp 4 out til ld 2 out, ran on*	1	19
297	2/3	Great Treth'	(R)	INT	3m	10	G	*mid-div, poor 4th whn p.u. last*	P	0
524	16/3	Larkhill	(R)	INT	3m	11	G	*alwys prom, wknd frm 14th, onepcd*	3	20
732	31/3	Little Wind'	(R)	INT	3m	6	GS	*j.w.,ld til 14th,disp nxt,ld agn apr 3 out,styd on strngly*	1	24
1185	21/4	Tweseldown	(R)	CON	3m	4	GF	*(fav) cls 2nd,ld 7-10th,rdn 13th,ld 15th,not fluent last,hdd,no ex*	2	21
1338	3/5	Bangor	(L)	HC	3m 110yds	8	S	*midfield, mstk 7th, rdn to track ldrs 13th, mistake next, blnd 4 out, soon btn.*	4	14

Maintained promise; ran in hot races; Opens likely in 97 - worth trying in H/Chase again; G-S 24

APATURA KING ch.g. 6 Button Bright (USA) - Apatura Iris by Space King — Baron E de Wykerslooth

522	16/3	Larkhill	(R)	MDO	3m	12	G	*(fav) alwys prom, ld 2 out, ran on well whn prssd flat, promising*	1	17
1056	13/4	Badbury Rin'	(L)	RES	3m	10	GF	*(Jt fav) hld up, prog 13th, 2nd nxt, ld 3 out, styd on*	1	19
1311	28/4	Little Wind'	(R)	INT	3m	6	G	*hld up rear, went 3rd 12th, lot to do 15th, mstk 2 out*	3	11

Decent start; put in his place last start but Intermediate awaits 97; stays; Good 20

APOLLODORUS (Irish) — I 223^{P}, I 343^{P}, I 386^{F}, I 526, , I 616^{P}

APPEAL ch.m. 6 Sunley Builds - Pastures Green by Monksfield — Chris Wall

552	17/3	Erw Lon	(L)	MDN	3m	10	GS	*alwys bhnd, t.o. & p.u. 11th*	P	0
976	8/4	Lydstep	(L)	MDO	3m	12	G	*p.u. 9th*	P	0
1200	21/4	Lydstep	(L)	MDN	3m	10	S	*mid-div, prog frm 14th, rpd hdwy 2 out, blnd last,lost 2nd*	4	10
1606	25/5	Bassaleg	(R)	MDO	3m	7	GS	*mstk 3rd, 2nd til just ld 10th, f nxt*	F	-

Shows some ability but last on only completion & makes limited appeal at present 11

APPENDIX LADY (Irish) — I 63^{P}, I 149^{P}, I 207^{P}, I 290^{P}, I 325^{P}

APPLE ANTHEM ch.m. 7 True Song - Windfall VI by Master Owen — M Wilson

1995 P(0),3D(0)

129	17/2	Kingston Bl'	(L)	MDN	3m	15	GS	*ptom to 9th, sn wknd, t.o. & p.u. 14th*	P	0
267	2/3	Didmarton	(L)	MDN	3m	11	G	*mstk 6th, chsd ldrs til 4th & lost tch 12th, p.u. 15th*	P	0
643	23/3	Siddington	(L)	MDN	3m	16	S	*prom, jmpd slwly 3rd, wknd frm 13th*	4	0
1020	13/4	Kingston Bl'	(L)	MDN	3m	10	G	*in tch to 10th, wknd & p.u. 12th, dsmntd*	P	0

Only beaten one horse so far; problems last start and nothing to sing about yet. 10

APPLE JOHN b.g. 7 Sula Bula - Hazelwain by Hard Fact — Derward Roberts

478	10/3	Tweseldown	(R)	RES	3m	9	G	*whppd round start, jmpd badly, wll btn whn f 2 out*	F	-
729	31/3	Little Wind'	(R)	RES	3m	12	GS	*ld & sn clr,wll clr til hdd3 out,ld agn aft 2 out,ran on wll*	1	23
1311	28/4	Little Wind'	(R)	INT	3m	6	G	*(fav) j.w. made all, 10l clr hlfwy, unchal, imprssv*	1	21

Maiden winner 94; missed 95; progressive front runner; can reach Open class in 97. 24

APPLE NICKING b.g. 9 Nickel King - Apple Crumble by Pony Express — Mrs M Upstone

1995 P(0),F(-),2(12),2(15),2(13)

439	9/3	Newton Brom'	(R)	MDN	3m	7	GS	*ld to 1st, chsd ldr, ld/disp 13th-3 out, wknd, f last*	F	-
495	16/3	Horseheath	(R)	MDO	3m	12	GF	*(fav) sttld mid-div,prog 10th,mstks 12 & nxt,hrd rdn 4 out,onepcd*	3	0
890	6/4	Kimble	(L)	MDN	3m	11	GF	*(Jt fav) ld aft 3rd-5th, blnd 11th, wknd 14th, p.u. 3 out*	P	0
1103	14/4	Guilsborough	(L)	MDN	3m	15	G	*race wd, ldng grp, wknd 15th, bhnd whn p.u. 3 out*	P	0

1240 27/4 Clifton On ' (L) MDO 3m 10 GF *prom, ld 14th, clr whn mstk last, wknd & hdd post* 2 15
1599 25/5 Garthorpe (R) MDO 3m 7 G *w.w. prog 8th, ld 5 out, clr frm nxt, easily* 1 16
1641 2/6 Dingley (R) RES 3m 13 GF *w.w., prog 13th, ld 2 out, sn clr, rdn out* 1 20

Improved late season; easily won competitive restricted; needs more for confineds. 19

APPOLLO VISION (Irish) — **I** 323^{P}, **I** 375^{F}, **I** 516^{P}

APRIL CRACKER b.m. 9 Cragador - Chanita by Averof — Mrs W Nichol

1355 4/5 Mosshouses (L) MDO 3m 10 GS *ld & blnd 2nd, p.u. bef nxt* P 0
1517 12/5 Hexham Poin' (L) MDN 3m 10 HY *chsd ldrs to 8th, wll bhnd 10th, p.u. 12th* P 0

no signs of ability. 0

APRIL SUPRISE b.m. 10 Saunter - Kefhalik by Precipice Wood — Dr A J Cooper

1995 4(0),3(14)

1364 4/5 Gisburn (R) MDO 3m 11 G *hld up, 2nd 3 out, nvr nrr* 2 11
1581 19/5 Wolverhampt' (L) MDO 3m 10 G *(fav) s.s. alwys rear, 5th & rdn 14th, nvr nrr* 3 0

Lightly raced; good enough to win but disappointed last start and becoming frusrating. 13

AR AGHAIDH ABHAILE (Irish) — **I** 506^{2}

ARAGLEN LASS (Irish) — **I** 434^{P}, **I** 503^{P}

ARALIER MAN(IRE) ch.g. 5 Roselier (FR) - Ara Go On by Sandalay — E H Crow

953 8/4 Eyton-On-Se' (L) MDO 2 1/2m 10 GF *mid to rear, no ch in 5th whn u.r. 5 out* U -

A quite start; successful stable and should improve. 0

ARAQUEEPA (Irish) — **I** 3^{P}, **I** 241^{P}

ARBITRAGEUR b.g. 9 Ile de Bourbon (USA) - Jenny Diver (USA) by Hatchet Man (USA) — Mrs Joanne Woods

723 31/3 Garthorpe (R) CON 3m 19 G *blnd & u.r. 3rd* U -
968 8/4 Thorpe Lodge (L) CON 3m 5 GF *ld, 25l clr 5th-13th, hdd & wknd rpdly 4 out* 4 0

Tailed off when completing & does not stay 0

ARBLE MARCH gr.m. 7 Baron Blakeney - Eventime by Hot Brandy — R Mann

1995 2(15),P(0),1(14),2(14)

126 17/2 Kingston Bl' (L) LAD 3m 11 GS *in tch to 10th, t.o. 13th, p.u. 2 out* P 0
235 24/2 Heythrop (R) RES 3m 10 GS *alwys prom, ld hlfwy, hdd 14th, mstk nxt, styd on flat* 3 16
642 23/3 Siddington (L) RES 3m 15 S *disp ld to 9th, 3rd & rddn 11th, wknd appr 15th* 4 10
1178 21/4 Mollington (R) RES 3m 7 F *wth wnr, mstk 7th, rdn 10th, sn btn, t.o. & p.u. 2 out* P 0

Maiden winner 95; moderate & struggling in better company; Members best hope; G/F-S. 14

ARCHIE'S NEPHEW b.g. 15 Royben - Lady London by London Gazette — Richard Barber

1995 4(18),3(0),4(15),1(18),F(-),1(18)

23 20/1 Barbury Cas' (L) XX 3m 11 GS *(bl) prog 9th,outpcd 12th,styd on strngly frm 2 out,nrst fin* 2 17
381 9/3 Barbury Cas' (L) XX 3m 9 GS *(bl) alwys prom, ch 4 out, ran on onepcd aft* 3 12
728 31/3 Little Wind' (R) MEM 3m 7 GS *(bl) rmndr 11th, lost plc steadd frm 12th* 5 0
989 8/4 Kingston St' (R) CON 3m 6 F *(bl) 2nd whn mstk 8th, lost tch frm 12th* 3 11
1312 28/4 Little Wind' (R) XX 3m 6 G *(bl) 3rd at 10th, outpcd 14th, sn trailing* 4 10
1393 6/5 Cotley Farm (L) XX 3m 10 GF *(bl) rr early, 6th at 10th, outpcd frm nxt* 4 0
1553 18/5 Bratton Down (L) XX 3m 10 F *(bl) ld/disp 2nd-5th, lost plc, t.o. frm 10th, lame* 7 0

Good servant; declined in 96; problems last start and may have reached the end of the road. 15

ARCHIES OATS ch.g. 7 Oats - Archetype by Over The River (FR) — Jon Trice-Rolph

1995 B(-),P(0),P(0)

233 24/2 Heythrop (R) MDN 3m 14 GS *in tch, chsd ldr hlfwy, disp 13th, ld 3 out, styd on, jnd fn* 1 14
339 3/3 Heythrop (R) RES 3m 10 G *(Jt fav) hld up, effrt & prog 13th, no imp on ldrs 3 out* 4 0
641 23/3 Siddington (L) RES 3m 20 S *prom til rddn 14th, wknd appr nxt, p.u. last* P 0
889 6/4 Kimble (L) RES 3m 7 GF *prom to 3rd, last frm nxt, t.o. 10th, p.u. 12th* P 0

Dead-heated in Maiden (no winners behind); disappointing after; more needed. 15

ARCHIE'S SISTER gr.m. 7 Pitpan - Lo-Incost by Impecunious — Mrs R Hurley

440 9/3 Newton Brom' (R) MDN 3m 10 GS *alwys bhnd, p.u. 15th* P 0
796 2/4 Heythrop (R) MDN 3m 11 F *pllng, in tch to 15th, wknd rpdly, t.o. whn blnd last* 7 0

Not without hope; needs to settle; can improve. 0

ARCTIC BARON b.g. 11 Baron Blakeney - Learctic by Lepanto (GER) — A C Raymond

1995 5(13),3(15),U(-)

815 6/4 Charlton Ho' (L) MEM 3m 8 GF *ld/disp to 12th, kpt on frm 4 out* 2 18
1124 20/4 Stafford Cr' (R) CON 3m 7 S *chsd ldrs, lost tch 4 out, rlld nxt, chal strgly flat* 2 20
1397 6/5 Cotley Farm (L) CON 3m 4 GF *ld to 9th, prom aft, rlld frm last, just fld* 2 20
1553 18/5 Bratton Down (L) XX 3m 10 F *mstk & lost plc 5th, prog to 3rd 16th, styd on clsng stgs* 2 18

1584 24/5 Towcester (R) HC 3m 1f 11 GS *(bl) mstks, reminders after 3rd, pushed along and chsd ldrs til wknd after 5 out, t.o..* 5 0

Finished 14 of 15 starts 94-6 & fair form in 96 but win may continue to prove elusive; F-S 19

ARCTIC CHILL(IRE) b.g. 6 Tremblant - Lady Zalona by Arctic Slave — M F Thorne

138 17/2 Ottery St M' (L) RES 3m 18 GS *w.w. 4th at 13th, ld last, sn clr* 1 20
335 3/3 Heythrop (R) INT 3m 9 G *prom, chsd wnr 12th, chal 14th til no ext frm last* 2 21
816 6/4 Charlton Ho' (L) INT 3m 7 GF *(fav) prom, ld 3rd, ran on wll frm 3 out, easily* 1 24
1126 20/4 Stafford Cr' (R) LAD 3m 7 S *(fav) held up, prog 11th, 2nd & gng wll whn slppd & f 3 out* F -

Promising; beaten by decent prospect when 2nd & should prosper if all's well in 97; G/F-S 25

ARCTIC LAKE (Irish) — **I** 26^{P}, **I** 88^{P}

ARCTIC LEADER (Irish) — **I** 19^{3}, **I** 32^{P}, **I** 105^{3}, **I** 177^{5}, **I** 259^{P}, **I** 286^{3}, **I** 319^{2}, **I** 449^{2}, **I** 535^{4}, **I** 601^{4}

ARCTIC LINE b.g. 8 Green Ruby (USA) - Sally Ann III by Port Corsair — S R Green

1995 **P(0)**,3(0),r(-),6(0),P(0),6(0),4(0),5(0),**12(0)**,2(12)

233 24/2 Heythrop (R) MDN 3m 14 GS *ld til jnd 4th, wknd 8th, p.u. aft 11th* P 0
269 2/3 Didmarton (L) RES 3m 12 G *cls up to 10th, sn lost tch, t.o.* 6 0
689 30/3 Chaddesley ' (L) MDN 3m 15 G *disp 4th, lft in ld 11th, hdd & wknd rpdly apr 3 out* 4 0
890 6/4 Kimble (L) MDN 3m 11 GF *alwys last trio, bhnd frm 12th, p.u. last, dsmntd* P 0
1436 6/5 Ashorne (R) MEM 3m 7 G *last frm 8th, t.o. & p.u. 12th* P 0

Lost all 27 points and will need a miracle to break the sequence. 0

ARCTIC MADAM b.m. 7 Town And Country - Arctic Servant by Goldhill — C L Barber

1995 1(13),1(17)

21 20/1 Barbury Cas' (L) MEM 3m 16 GS *w.w. prog 10th, chsd wnr 3 out, chal & f nxt* F 24

Won both starts 95; able but injured only outing 96 & may not return 25

ARCTIC PADDY ch.g. 13 Paddy's Stream - Chorabelle by Choral Society — K Rosier

1995 4(0),U(-),4(0),4(0)

72 11/2 Wetherby Po' (L) CON 3m 18 GS *cls up, 2nd at 10th, fdd rpdly 12th* 8 11
120 17/2 Witton Cast' (R) OPE 3m 7 S *alwys rear, t.o. 10th* 6 0
289 2/3 Eaton Hall (R) CON 3m 10 G *prom to 10th, sn strggling* 5 0
402 9/3 Dalston (R) XX 3m 13 G *trckd ldrs 6th, ld 8th-14th, still prom whn u.r. 3 out* U -

Safe but not threatening to win now. 12

ARCTIC PEARL (Irish) — **I** 120^{1}, **I** 212^{P}

ARCTIC QUEST ch.m. 11 Abednego - Frozen Ground by Arctic Slave — Mrs B Bebb

1995 P(0),B(-),5(0),U(-)

214 24/2 Newtown (L) CON 3m 21 GS *chsd ldrs to hlfwy, wknd, t.o. & p.u. 2 out* P 0
426 9/3 Upton-On-Se' (R) CON 3m 16 GS *10th hlfwy, mod late prog* 6 0

Maiden winner 94; shown nothing since and best avoided now. 12

ARDAVILLAN PRINCE (Irish) — **I** 5^{P}

ARDBEI (Irish) — **I** 26^{2}, **I** 90^{2}

ARDBRENNAN b.g. 9 Deep Run - Callan River — C C Bennett

1995 **10(NH)**

18 14/1 Tweseldown (R) MXO 3m 6 GS *chsd ldr 3rd, ld 11th, drew clr aft 2 out, hit last* 1 27
142 17/2 Larkhill (R) MXO 3m 9 G *mid-div whn f 5th* F -
209 24/2 Castle Of C' (R) OPE 3m 8 HY *ld 6th-13th, no ext frm 3 out* 3 14
476 10/3 Tweseldown (R) OPE 3m 7 G *2nd frm 9th, ld apr 2 out, pshd out, easily* 1 22
670 28/3 Aintree (L) HC 3m 1f 9 G *pressed ldrs, disp 2nd when f 11th.* F -
1013 13/4 Ascot (R) HC 3m 110yds 11 GS *ld 2nd to 3rd, with ldrs till led 13th, hdd 15th, led again and u.r.e 4 out.* U -

Ex-Irish; useful at best; veteran-ridden; Opens in 97 & H/Chase possible with right rider; G-S 24

ARDEE GALE (Irish) — **I** 563^{F}

ARDELL BOY b.g. 8 Cisto (FR) - Muses Doom by Fate — J E Grey

1243 27/4 Woodford (L) MEM 3m 6 G *ld, blndrd 10th, hdd apr 16th, blndrd nxt, soon outpcd* 2 15
1495 11/5 Holnicote (L) MDO 3m 11 G *made all, mstk 16th, ran on wll whn chal frm 4 out* 1 16

Missed 95; deserved winner (winner behind); tries hard and can win a modest restricted. 16

ARDEN b.g. 12 Ardross - Kereolle by Riverman (USA) — Michael D Abrahams

1995 r(-),5(18),U(-),5(13),5(10),2(16),F(-)

170 18/2 Market Rase' (L) XX 3m 8 GF *w.w. lost tch apr 14th, nvr nr ldrs* 6 12
303 2/3 Great Stain' (L) CON 3m 11 GS *alwys rear, t.o. 3 out* 7 0
513 16/3 Dalton Park (R) OPE 3m 9 G *jmpd slwly 1st, last & t.o. 3rd til p.u. 16th* P 0
1133 20/4 Hornby Cast' (L) OPE 3m 14 G *rear, t.o. 8th* 8 0

Showed no interest in 96; no prospects now. 0

ARDFERT MINSTREL (Irish) — **I** 238²

ARDVILLAN PRINCE (Irish) — **I** 277ᴾ

ARE-OH ch.g. 7 Noalto - Miss Racine by Dom Racine (FR) — W Manners

1995 6(0),6(0),5(0),4(13)

53	4/2	Alnwick	(L)	MDO 3m	13	G	*(Jt fav) hld up, lost tch 9th, ran on frm 3 out, nvr nr*	5	0
87	11/2	Alnwick	(L)	MDO 3m	7	GS	*prom, rdn frm 9th, ld 11th-apr 3 out, no ch wnr aft*	2	10
323	2/3	Corbridge	(R)	MDN 3m	12	GS	*alwys prom, cls up & ev ch 2 out, onepcd*	4	13

Not realised early promise and becoming frusrating; finished early and best watched initially in 97. 13

ARISTOCRATIC GOLD gr.g. 10 Nishapour (FR) - Lady Broke by Busted — J F Weldhen

1995 5(0),2(12),U(-),2(13),2(0),2(11),F(-),1(14),5(11)

199	24/2	Lemalla	(R)	RES 3m	17	HY	*alwys bhnd, t.o. & p.u. 13th*	P	0
443	9/3	Haldon	(R)	LAD 3m	10	S	*mid-div, rpd prog to 2nd 14th, ld nxt, hdd & outpcd 2 out*	2	19
624	23/3	Kilworthy	(L)	LAD 3m	7	GS	*chsd ldng quartet, strgglng 11th, no dang aft, fin tired*	5	0
716	30/3	Wadebridge	(L)	LAD 3m	6	GF	*(Co fav) ld to 5th, prom til lost plc aft 15th, eased flat*	4	16
803	4/4	Clyst St Ma'	(L)	LAD 3m	4	GS	*rear, slight prog 4 out, nvr nr, reluc clsng stgs*	3	0
940	8/4	Wadebridge	(L)	LAD 3m	4	F	*mstly 3rd til wknd qckly cls home*	4	0
1141	20/4	Flete Park	(R)	LAD 3m	8	S	*rear, 7th at 10th, nvr going wll, t.o. & p.u. last*	P	0
1428	6/5	High Bickin'	(R)	RES 3m	10	G	*hdwy 12th, ev ch til wknd 3 out*	4	15

1 win 14 places in points; ungenuine and unlikely to a ladies. 15

ARKAY ch.g. 6 Good Times (ITY) - Evening Crystal by Evening All — Russell C Kerry

1995 F(-),P(0),U(-)

96	11/2	Ampton	(R)	XX 3m	11	GF	*rear, wll bhnd whn u.r. 11th*	U	-
107	17/2	Marks Tey	(L)	MDN 3m	15	G	*bhnd frm 7th, u.r. 11th*	U	-
315	2/3	Ampton	(R)	MDO 3m	10	G	*alwys bhnd,t.o. frm 10th*	4	0
616	23/3	Higham	(L)	MEM 3m	3	GF	*prom til last frm 4th, blnd & wknd 10th, t.o.*	3	0

Last when completing and looks useless. 0

ARLEY GALE ch.m. 8 Scallywag - Lady Letitia by Le Bavard (FR) — Mrs A D Pritchard

1995 F(-)

1104	14/4	Guilsborough	(L)	MDN 3m	18	G	*mid-div, f 5th*	F	-
1183	21/4	Mollington	(R)	MDN 3m	10	F	*pllng, hld up, prog 13th, cls 4th whn hit 2 out, wknd*	4	10
1433	6/5	Ashorne	(R)	MDO 3m	16	G	*w.w. lost tch 10th, t.o. & p.u. 12th*	P	0

Ran well when completing but more stamina needed before going closer. 12

ARMAGRET b.g. 11 Mandrake Major - Friendly Glen by Furry Glen — B Kennedy

1995 **3(NH),9(NH),2(NH),4(NH),3(NH),4(NH)**

32	20/1	Higham	(L)	OPE 3m	15	GF	*mid-div whn f 4th*	6	0
56	10/2	Cottenham	(R)	OPE 3m	12	GS	*trckd ldrs, 2nd 16th, ld 2 out, ran on well apr last*	1	24
104	17/2	Marks Tey	(L)	OPE 3m	14	G	*in tch, prog to 2nd 14th, wknd appr 16th*	5	13
420	9/3	High Easter	(L)	OPE 3m	9	S	*(fav) trkd ldrs, ld 15th, hld on gamely und press flat*	1	22
619	23/3	Higham	(L)	OPE 3m	10	GF	*(fav) chsd ldrs, prog to 3rd at 9th, ev ch 2 out, no ext last*	3	16

Formerly useful chaser; won modest Opens; neededs easy 3 miles; can win again;G-S. 23

ARM AH MAN(IRE) br.g. 6 Mandalus - Peacocks Call by Peacock (FR) — Miss Elizabeth Robinson

1995 3(0)

88	11/2	Alnwick	(L)	MDO 3m	11	GS	*(fav) hld up, prog to ld 12th, mstk 2 out, hdd & no ext last*	2	15

Only appears annually; promising and must win if fit in 97. 16

ARMASTOKE(IRE) b.g. 6 Strong Statement (USA) - Cassagh Lady by Paddy's Stream — R G Makin

1995 U(-),P(0)

122	17/2	Witton Cast'	(R)	MDO 3m	8	S	*mid-div whn f 3rd*	F	-

Yet to complete and vanished in 96; 0

ARMS PARK br.g. 11 Park Row - Sable Cortes by Sable Skinflint — W M Kathrens

220	24/2	Newtown	(L)	MDN 3m	12	GS	*t.o. in last pair til p.u. 11th*	P	0
749	31/3	Upper Sapey	(R)	MDO 3m	17	GS	*t.o. hlfwy, p.u. 13th*	P	0

No prospects 0

ARNOLD'S CHOICE ch.g. 12 Vitiges (FR) - Never A Lady by Pontifex (USA) — Mrs J Young

1995 7(0),3(10),6(0),3(11),2(10)

380	9/3	Barbury Cas'	(L)	CON 3m	11	GS	*alwys prom, chal last, not qckn flat*	2	16
706	30/3	Barbury Cas'	(L)	MEM 3m	7	G	*(bl) handy, ld 10th-3 out, outpcd aft*	2	13
889	6/4	Kimble	(L)	RES 3m	7	GF	*(bl) cls up, mstk 5th, bhnd frm 8th, t.o. 13th*	5	0
1189	21/4	Tweseldown	(R)	RES 3m	10	GF	*(bl) chsd ldrs, styd on onepcd frm 2 out, nrst fin*	2	12
1292	28/4	Barbury Cas'	(L)	RES 3m	11	F	*(bl) cls up to 10th, wknd rpdly & mstk 12th, t.o. & p.u. aft 2out*	P	0

Maiden winner 92; safe but ungenuine; will be lucky to find a race now. 12

ARPAL BREEZE ch.g. 11 Deep Run - Arpal Magic by Master Owen — J H Henderson

1995 6(0),P(0),4(0),P(0),5(0)

722	31/3	Garthorpe	(R)	MEM 3m	4	G	*alwys last, no ch frm 13th*	3	0
098	14/4	Guilsborough	(L)	CON 3m	17	G	*rear til b.d. by loose horse 6th*	B	-

No longer of any account 0

ARRAS-TINA b.m. 6 State Diplomacy (USA) - Arras Style by Nicholas Bill — G E Mason

73	11/2	Wetherby Po'	(L)	MDO 3m	15	GS	*rear, prog whn hit wing & f 14th*	F	-
518	16/3	Dalton Park	(R)	MDO 3m	15	G	*prog frm mid-div hlfwy,jnd ldrs 4 out, 2nd & rdn whn f 2 out*	F	13

Promising but unfortunate so far; should go close in 97; 14

ARTHUR (Irish) — I 238^{P}, I 322^{3}

ARTISTIC PEACE b.m. 9 Prince Of Peace - Rising Artist by Mandamus — Mrs Diane Jackson

1995 F(-),r(-),2(0),U(-)

202	24/2	Lemalla	(R)	MDO 3m	12	HY	*wll bhnd frm 3rd, p.u. 2 out*	P	0
299	2/3	Great Treth'	(R)	MDO 3m	13	G	*mstk 7th, t.o. whn p.u. 15th*	P	0
448	9/3	Haldon	(R)	MDO 3m	10	S	*prog to 6th at 13th, btn 4th whn f 3 out*	F	-
630	23/3	Kilworthy	(L)	MDN 3m	10	GS	*t.d.e. mid-div, outpcd aft 14th, no prog frm 3 out*	5	0
800	4/4	Clyst St Ma'	(L)	MEM 3m	3	GS	*trckd ldr, b.d. 15th, rmntd, fin alone*	1	0
938	8/4	Wadebridge	(L)	OPE 3m	3	F	*prom til lost grnd aft 12th, pckd 15th, sn outpcd*	3	10

Won a joke contest; no hope in proper races. 10

ARTISTIC PLAN (Irish) — I 181^{2}

ARTISTIC QUAY (Irish) — I 7^{P}, I 50^{1}, I 241^{P}, I 376^{P}

ART PRINCE (Irish) — I 6^{2}, I 54^{P}, I 103^{U}, I 136^{P}, I 519^{U}, I 525^{1}

ASANTE SANA gr.m. 5 Scallywag - Paddy Will by Dublin Taxi — Mrs E Weaver

045	13/4	Bitterley	(L)	MDO 3m	16	G	*alwys rear, p.u. 10th*	P	0
224	24/4	Brampton Br'	(R)	MDO 3m	17	G	*nvr rch frnt rnk, in rr whn u.r. 10th*	U	-
315	28/4	Bitterley	(L)	MDO 3m	10	G	*mid-div, drppd rear 8th, p.u. nxt*	P	0
484	11/5	Bredwardine	(R)	MDO 3m	17	G	*outpcd & lost tch 4th, tried to ref 6th & p.u.*	P	0

Unpromising start. 0

ASHBORO(IRE) b.g. 7 Drumalis - Crecora by Royal Captive — J M Turner

1995 4(13),U(-),3(10),4(12),2(11)

11	14/1	Cottenham	(R)	LAD 3m	7	G	*alwys bhnd, t.o. & p.u. apr 2 out*	P	0
57	10/2	Cottenham	(R)	LAD 3m	9	GS	*hmpd & u.r. 1st*	U	-
93	11/2	Ampton	(R)	LAD 3m	7	GF	*in tch til pshd alng & outpcd 15th, no ch aft*	5	0
250	25/2	Charing	(L)	LAD 3m	12	GS	*twrds rear whn f 5th*	F	-
347	3/3	Higham	(L)	LAD 3m	10	G	*cls up in mid-div til not qckn 15th, kpt on onepcd*	5	16
066	13/4	Horseheath	(R)	LAD 3m	2	F	*chsd ldr, blnd 9th, efft to ld 15th, sn clr*	1	17
259	27/4	Cottenham	(R)	LAD 3m	5	F	*rear, outpcd 12th, styd on wll frm 3 out, nrst fin*	3	19

Won a pathetic ladies; only effective in poor on the firm; barely stays. 15

ASHBURTON LORD (Irish) — I 332^{P}, I 458^{5}

ASHCOMBE VALLEY gr.g. 8 Almutanabbi - Lady Of Egremont by Hill Farmer — Major Ranulf Rayner

1995 P(0),5(0),6(0)

71	10/2	Great Treth'	(R)	MDO 3m	15	S	*bhnd whn p.u. 3 out*	P	0
200	24/2	Lemalla	(R)	MDO 3m	12	HY	*alwys bhnd, p.u. 9th*	P	0
441	9/3	Haldon	(R)	MEM 3m	6	S	*lost tch frm 7th, bhnd whn f 12th*	F	-
876	6/4	Higher Kilw'	(L)	MDN 3m	11	GF	*hld up in tch,ld apr 15th,jnd & rdn 3 out,cls 3rd,hmpd last*	2	14
348	4/5	Holnicote	(L)	MDO 3m	9	GS	*f 1st*	F	-
429	6/5	High Bickin'	(R)	MDO 3m	8	G	*(Jt fav) in tch, rddn 14th, onepce, walked in*	4	0
531	12/5	Ottery St M'	(L)	MDO 3m	9	GF	*cls up, rmndrs 13th, went 2nd 16th, sn wknd*	6	0

A little ability but stamina a big problem, may find a win elusive. 12

ASH PLANT (Irish) — I 134^{2}, I 166^{P}

ASHTON COURT (Irish) — I 48^{P}, I 75^{2}

ASK FOR PLENTY(IRE) b.g. 7 Royal Fountain - Not So Dear by Dhaudevi (FR) — Mrs A Price

1995 U(-),R(-)

390	9/3	Llanfrynach	(R)	MDN 3m	13	GS	*ref 1st, cont, ref 2nd, cont, ref 6th (twice), gave up*	R	-

Not worth a carrot. 0

ASK FRANK b.g. 10 Seymour Hicks (FR) - West Bank by Martinmas — Mrs R A Price

1995 1(24),2(23),1(24),4(24)

162	17/2	Weston Park	(L)	OPE 3m	16	G	*(fav) hld up rear, prog 11th, ld aft nxt, sn in cmmnd, eased flat*	1	26
215	24/2	Newtown	(L)	OPE 3m	20	GS	*(fav) hld up bhnd, gd prog to disp 14th, chsd wnr nxt, no imp 2out*	2	25
351	3/3	Garnons	(L)	OPE 3m	14	GS	*(fav) mid-div whn u.r. 3rd*	U	-
746	31/3	Upper Sapey	(R)	CON 3m	3	GS	*ld to 6th, agn 8-15th, outpcd frm 2 out*	2	22

945 8/4 Andoversford (R) OPE 3m 3 GF *(fav) reluc ldr, hdd 13th, mstk nxt, effrt 2 out, sn outpcd* 2 1

Good pointer; consistent, stays; goes well fresh; can win again; G-Hy. 24

ASK ME ANOTHER (Irish) — **I** 147^{P}, **I** 332, , **I** 457^{5}
ASK ME IN (Irish) — **I** 60^{P}, **I** 76^{2}, **I** 610^{1}
ASTEAL (Irish) — **I** 132^{1}, **I** 234,
ASTHEFELLASAYS (Irish) — **I** 502^{P}, **I** 638^{3}, **I** 653^{4}
AS THINGS GO (Irish) — **I** 73^{F}, **I** 122^{F}, **I** 148^{F}

ASTLEY JACK gr.g. 10 Belfort (FR) - Brigado by Brigadier Gerard R J Cotto
1995 5(0),P(0)

382 9/3 Llanfrynach (R) MEM 3m 7 GS *s.v.s. rcvrd to 2nd at 3rd, last by 8th, t.o. & p.u. 13th* P
691 30/3 Llanvapley (L) CON 3m 15 GS *u.r. 1st* U
849 6/4 Howick (L) MDN 3m 14 GF *2nd to 9th, wknd rpdly, p.u. 12th* P
1040 13/4 St Hilary (R) MDN 3m 12 G *wll clr 6th, ct 14th, fdng whn f 16th* F
1225 24/4 Brampton Br' (R) MDO 3m 18 G *ref to race* 0
1242 27/4 Woodford (L) RES 3m 18 G *unruly stt, blndrd 4th, chsd ldr to 8th, wll bhnd, p.u. 13th* P
1485 11/5 Bredwardine (R) MDO 3m 15 G *ld 2nd til p.u. aft 6th* P
1580 19/5 Wolverhampt' (L) MDO 3m 8 G *sn clr, reluc & hdd apr 8th, sn ld agn, clr whn u.r. 12th* U
1621 27/5 Chaddesley ' (L) MDO 3m 17 GF *s.v.s. ld aft 2nd,made most to apr 12th, wknd & p.u. 15th* P

Completly overwhelmed by his temperament. 0

ASTON BRAES (Irish) — **I** 119^{P}

ASTOUND(IRE) ch.g. 5 Avocat - Clement Queen by Lucifer (USA) Miss Suzannah Cotter

7 13/1 Larkhill (R) CON 3m 10 GS *hld up, lost tch 10th, t.o. 13th, fin strngly* 3 1
137 17/2 Ottery St M' (L) RES 3m 15 GS *mid-div til p.u. 12th* P
526 16/3 Larkhill (R) RES 3m 9 G *sn rear, rpd prog frm 14th, ran on last, just faild* 2 1
650 23/3 Cothelstone (L) RES 3m 5 S *sn last, prog 7th, styd on frm 3 out, not trbl 1st 2* 3

Irish Maiden winner; unfortunate; surely win restricted when ridden with better judgement. 15

ASTOUNDED (Irish) — **I** 104^{6}, **I** 265^{4}, **I** 480^{3}

ASTRAC TRIO(USA) ro.g. 6 Timeless Moment (USA) - Fairway Flag (USA) by Fairway Phantom (USA) Mrs M Bowi
1995 **4(NH),7(NH),6(NH),U(NH),U(NH),11(NH),4(NH),P(NH)**

83 11/2 Alnwick (L) CON 3m 10 GS *prssd ldr, ld 14th-apr 3 out, onepcd aft* 3 1
110 17/2 Lanark (R) CON 3m 10 GS *(Jt fav) alwys handy, ld 13th til just hdd & u.r. 2 out* U
317 2/3 Corbridge (R) CON 3m 11 GS *disp 2nd, styd prom, ev ch 3 out, no ext apr last* 3 1
751 31/3 Lockerbie (R) CON 3m 12 G *alwys prom, no ext frm 3 out* 3 1
861 6/4 Alnwick (L) CON 3m 7 GF *ld 3rd til 12th, outpcd frm 15th* 2 1
1351 4/5 Mosshouses (L) CON 3m 11 GS *ld 3-5th & 9-12th, 4th & outpcd aft nxt, no prog 3 out* 4 1
1572 19/5 Corbridge (R) LAD 3m 8 G *ld/disp til ld 7th, made rest, ran on und pres flat* 1 2

Struggles to stay & switch to Ladies ideal; can win in that class again in 97; G/F-G/S 20

ASTRE RADIEUX(FR) b.g. 11 Gay Mecene (USA) - Divine Etoile (USA) by Nijinsky (CAN) Philip McKi

37 3/2 Wetherby (L) HC 3m 110yds 11 GS *soon well bhnd, t.o. when p.u. after 8th.* P
159 17/2 Weston Park (L) CON 3m 22 G *prom whn f 6th* F
289 2/3 Eaton Hall (R) CON 3m 10 G *chsng grp to 12th, sn btn, p.u. 4 out* P
372 8/3 Market Rasen (R) HC 3m 1f 6 G *bhnd, jmpd slowly 7th, t.o. from 10th, p.u. after 13th.* P

Ex-chaser,outclassed in 96; should try his Members. 0

ASTROAR b.g. 15 Indiaro - Astrador by Golden Catch J Perr

786 31/3 Tweseldown (R) LAD 3m 8 G *rear, u.r. 1st* U
888 6/4 Kimble (L) LAD 3m 4 GF *ld to 13th, 3rd & btn aft 3 out, onepcd* 3 1
1179 21/4 Mollington (R) LAD 3m 10 F *ld to 4th & 6th-aft 10th, sn outpcd & no ch* 6 1

Missed 95; gallant old stager but surely too old to win now. 13

AS YOU WERE b.g. 14 Beau Charmeur (FR) - Leaney Escort by Escart III D Parravar
1995 5(13),2(19),P(0),1(15),5(16),4(22),**4(18)**,3(18),**4(19)**,**3(22)**

30 20/1 Higham (L) MEM 3m 4 GF *(fav) ld/disp til ld 11th, made rest, rddn out* 1 1
94 11/2 Ampton (R) OPE 3m 8 GF *mid-div, ev ch 3 out, not qckn frm nxt* 3 1
102 17/2 Marks Tey (L) CON 3m 17 G *rr, sme late prog nvr dang* 8 1
310 2/3 Ampton (R) CON 3m 13 G *rr, in tch, kpt on frm 3 out, nvr trbld ldrs* 6 1
491 16/3 Horseheath (R) CON 3m 5 GF *rear, prog 13th, ev ch 3 out, onepcd* 2 1
672 29/3 Aintree (L) HC 2 3/4m 26 G *rear when u.r. 1st.* U
1065 13/4 Horseheath (R) CON 3m 4 F *ld/disp to 12th, ev ch 15th, sn outpcd* 3 1
1323 28/4 Fakenham P-' (L) OPE 3m 8 G *bhnd, prog 15th, 4th & ch 2 out, no ext, lame* 4 1

Members winner 95/96; declined in 96 and unlikely to win competitive races now. 15

ATHASSEL ABBEY b.g. 10 Tender King - Pearl Creek by Gulf Pearl Mrs K Munrow

215 24/2 Newtown (L) OPE 3m 20 GS *chsd ldrs to 8th, wknd rpdly & p.u. 12th* P 0
428 9/3 Upton-On-Se' (R) RES 3m 17 GS *alwys strgglng, p.u. 14th* P 0

poor hurdler; of no account now. 0

ATHNANURLAINN b.g. 11 Belfalas - Lights Off — Mrs John Seyfried
1995 P(0),7(0),U(-),P(0),4(0)
56 10/2 Cottenham (R) OPE 3m 12 GS *alwys bhnd, t.o. & p.u. 14th* P 0
104 17/2 Marks Tey (L) OPE 3m 14 G *last & rddn 10th, t.o. &p.u. 13th* P 0
249 25/2 Charing (L) XX 3m 11 GS *cls up til f 10th* F -
594 23/3 Parham (R) CON 3m 13 GS *alwys wll in rear, blnd 8th, t.o. aft, p.u. last* P 0
920 8/4 Aldington (L) OPE 3m 6 F *cls up to 10th, rdn & wknd nxt, t.o. & p.u. aft 15th* P 0

Schoolmaster now; safe but pedestrian. no prospects. 0

ATLAAL b.g. 11 Shareef Dancer (USA) - Anna Paola (GER) by Prince Ippi (GER) — O J Donnelly
1995 **5(NH),2(NH),5(NH),5(NH)**
979 8/4 Lydstep (L) LAD 3m 9 G *1st ride, p.u. 10th in mid-div* P 0
1387 6/5 Pantyderi (R) LAD 3m 6 GF *ref 1st* R -

Former winning hurdler/chaser; disinterested now. 15

ATTLE b.g. 7 Oats - Knockananna by Torus — J W Furness
51 4/2 Alnwick (L) MDO 3m 17 G *hmprd 1st, mid-div, prog 12th, lft 2nd last, kpt on* 2 14
229 24/2 Duncombe Pa' (R) MDO 3m 13 GS *(Jt fav) in tch,lft 2nd 4 out,rdn & ch apr last,wknd,fin tired* 2 0
416 9/3 Charm Park (L) MDO 3m 13 G *(fav) mid-div, prog 10th, u.r. nxt* U -
517 16/3 Dalton Park (R) MDO 3m 10 G *trckd ldrs, went 2nd 16th, drvn to ld last, styd on flat* 1 14
985 8/4 Charm Park (L) INT 3m 9 GF *in tch, 2nd 12th, 4th frm 4 out, no ext* 4 15
1090 14/4 Whitwell-On' (R) RES 3m 17 G *rear, prog to chs ldrs 5 out, styd on well frm 2 out* 2 15

Ex Irish; solid season; consistent, stays; should progress to restricteds; Good. 18

AUCHENDOLLY(IRE) b.g. 6 Mandalus - Advance Notice by Le Bavard (FR) — Christopher Sporborg
1995 2(0),U(-)
13 14/1 Cottenham (R) MDO 3m 10 G *ld to 4th, cls up, mstk 13th, 3rd & btn 2 out* 2 10
315 2/3 Ampton (R) MDO 3m 10 G *(fav) made most til blnd 11th, 4th & btn appr 17th, plodded on* 3 0
496 16/3 Horseheath (R) MDO 3m 10 GF *(fav) alwys wll plcd, 2nd at 7th, ld aft 10th, hdd & outpcd 3 out* 3 10
830 6/4 Marks Tey (L) MDN 3m 14 G *(fav) mid-div, bhnd & no ch 16th, fin 4th, promoted* 3 0
1063 13/4 Horseheath (R) MDO 3m 5 F *prom, ld 3rd-5th, jmpd to ld 15th, rdn nxt, kpt on gamely* 1 14
1322 28/4 Fakenham P-' (L) RES 3m 5 G *nvr going wll, 4th whn blnd 7th & 9th, no ch 14th* 3 0
1402 6/5 Northaw (L) RES 3m 5 F *ld 6-9th, ld 12th, blnd nxt, sn hdd, wknd qkly 15th, t.o.* 4 0

Beat subsequent winner; ran badly after; sold Ascot June; much more needed. 13

AUCTION LAW(NZ) ch.g. 12 Pevero - High Plateau (NZ) by Oncidium — Mrs Brenda Gittins
1995 3(17),2(21),1(23),1(22),3(23),2(22)
162 17/2 Weston Park (L) OPE 3m 16 G *w.w. rear, prog 5 out, ran on, nvr nrr* 4 17
662 24/3 Eaton Hall (R) OPE 3m 10 S *hld up rear, nvr in race, p.u. 2 out* P 0
950 8/4 Eyton-On-Se' (L) OPE 3m 4 GF *in tch til pce increased 13th, onepcd frm 4 out* 4 0
1304 28/4 Southwell P' (L) OPE 3m 5 GF *2nd til blnd 8th & lost 40l, not rch ldrs aft* 3 13
1479 11/5 Bredwardine (R) OPE 3m 8 G *pshd alng frm 4th, rdn 14th, went 2nd flat* 2 21
1595 25/5 Garthorpe (R) CON 3m 15 G *rear for 2m, ran on past btn horses, too mch to do* 3 15
1619 27/5 Chaddesley ' (L) OPE 3m 7 GF *rmndr 2nd, chsd ldrs, 3rd & outpcd 14th, wknd 3 out* 3 17

Winning chaser; declined in 96; may prefer a return to ladies; Good. 18

AUGHNACLOY ROSE gr.g. 8 Derring Rose - Tower Road by Polaroid — D Etheridge
15 14/1 Cottenham (R) MDN 3m 14 G *alwys bhnd, t.o.* 8 0
91 11/2 Ampton (R) MDO 3m 10 GF *n.j.w. prom to 6th, t.o. 10th, p.u. last* P 0
108 17/2 Marks Tey (L) MDN 3m 17 G *jmpd rt, alwys bhnd* 6 0
314 2/3 Ampton (R) MDO 3m 10 G *nt fluent, alwys bhnd, t.o.* 4 0
495 16/3 Horseheath (R) MDO 3m 12 GF *alwys rear, mstk 11th, t.o. 13th* 5 0
835 6/4 Marks Tey (L) MEM 3m 4 G *stlld rear, prog to 2nd 16th, rdn 2 out, styd on,just faild* 2 10
1064 13/4 Horseheath (R) MDO 3m 3 F *alwys last, nt fluent, outpcd 14th, ran on flat, fin wll* 3 0
1261 27/4 Cottenham (R) MDO 3m 10 F *outpcd, mstk 9th, styd on 3 out, 6l down last, fin wll,ld fn* 1 13

Ex Irish; gadually improved; not fluent; well below restricteds; Members best hope 97. 14

AUMALE(IRE) ch.g. 5 Be My Guest (USA) - Marie de Chantilly (USA) by Alleged (USA) — D Sundin
1995 **4(NH),7(NH)**
114 17/2 Lanark (R) MDO 3m 12 GS *nvr dang, p.u. 4 out* P 0
192 24/2 Friars Haugh (L) MDN 3m 12 S *(bl) nvr nr ldrs, p.u. 4 out* P 0

Ex-Irish; showed nothing & season lasted a week 0

AUNT EMERALDS (Irish) — **I** 233[P], **I** 301[F]

AUNTIE FAY(IRE) ch.m. 5 Fayruz - Auntie Ponny by Last Fandango — S P Hudson
81 11/2 Wetherby Po' (L) MEM 3m 4 GS *ld 7th-13th, fdng whn f 4 out* F -

359 4/3 Doncaster (L) HC 2m 3f 110yds 10 G *t.o. when ref 6th.* R
589 23/3 Wetherby Po' (L) MDO 3m 16 S *rear whn p.u. 4th* P
1095 14/4 Whitwell-On' (R) MDO 2 1/2m 88yds 14 G *jmpd slwly 1st, t.o. & p.u. 10th* P
1284 27/4 Easingwold (L) RES 3m 14 G *s.s. n.j.w. alwys t.o., p.u. 14th* P
1470 11/5 Easingwold (L) MDO 3m 10 G *n.j.w. alwys wll bhnd, t.o. & p.u. 15th* P

Ex novice hurdler; very unpromising. **0**

AUNT MARGARET ch.m. 11 Balinger - Commander Alice by Spartan General R Cambra

1995 U(-),P(0),6(0)

164 17/2 Weston Park (L) RES 3m 11 G *prom early, mid-div whn ran out 10th* r
287 2/3 Eaton Hall (R) MDO 3m 11 G *chsd ldrs to 7th, sn wknd, p.u. 11th* P

of no account. **0**

AUTHENTICITY(IRE) b.m. 8 Sheer Grit - Immunity by Brave Shot Miss C Billingto

400 9/3 Dalston (R) LAD 3m 10 G *p.u. 6th* P
1155 20/4 Whittington (L) MDN 3m 14 G *ldng grp, lft 2nd 14th, chal 2 out, no ext aft* 2 1
1364 4/5 Gisburn (R) MDO 3m 11 G *prom, wknd 10th, p.u. 2 out* P
1517 12/5 Hexham Poin' (L) MDN 3m 10 HY *w.w. prog to 2nd aft 14th, blnd 16th, sn wknd, p.u. nxt* P
1581 19/5 Wolverhampt' (L) MDO 3m 10 G *ld to aft 4th, ev ch 14th, sn wknd, t.o. & p.u. 3 out* P

Ex Irish, beaten 10 lengths when completing; more needed for a win. **13**

AUTONOMOUS b.g. 11 Milford - Mandrian by Mandamus Mrs Kate Whitehea

1995 4(0),U(-),F(-),4(15)

334 3/3 Heythrop (R) MEM 3m 6 G *(fav) made all, drew clr aft last* 1 1
794 2/4 Heythrop (R) CON 3m 6 F *ld to 10th, chsd wnr til pckd 3 out, kpt on, tk 2nd agn fin* 2 1
1228 27/4 Worcester (L) HC 2m 7f 17 G *jmpd badly, t.o. till ref 5th.* R
1437 6/5 Ashorne (R) MXO 3m 13 G *mstk 4th, prom, blnd 11th, cls 4th 2 out-last, no ext flat* 4 1

Won weak Members; ran better after; win Members again if retaining form. **18**

AUTUMN CALL (Irish) — **I** 368[5], **I** 431[F]

AUTUMN GREEN(IRE) ch.g. 8 Le Moss - Judy Green by Green God S J P Furnis

158 17/2 Weston Park (L) MEM 3m 11 G *cls up til outpcd 12th, p.u. 3 out* P
286 2/3 Eaton Hall (R) MDO 3m 14 G *mid-div at 13th, steady prog aft, nrst fin* 4
739 31/3 Sudlow Farm (R) RES 3m 11 G *mid-div, outpcd 11th, no dang aft* 4 1
1012 9/4 Flagg Moor (L) XX 3m 7 G *jmpd rght, prog 11th, 4th & ch 15th, wknd nxt* 4
1224 24/4 Brampton Br' (R) MDO 3m 17 G *prom, ev ch til rdn & no ex frm 3 out* 3 1
1365 4/5 Gisburn (R) MDO 3m 17 G *(fav) w.w. 2nd 3 out, ld flat, well rdn* 1 1
1564 19/5 Mollington (R) XX 3m 14 GS *trckd ldrs, outpcd frm 14th, kpt on frm 2 out* 3 1

Ex Irish; moderate but stays well; more needed for restricteds; probably best R/H. **17**

AUTUMN LIGHT b.m. 6 Pitpan - Fidelight by Fidel R H York

128 17/2 Kingston Bl' (L) RES 3m 14 GS *ld til u.r. 5th* U
248 25/2 Charing (L) RES 3m 12 GS *rear, prog to 2nd whn mstk 6th, lost plc, rear & p.u. 11th* P
473 10/3 Tweseldown (R) MEM 3m 5 G *dwelt, reluc to race, n.j.w. t.o. 5th, f 3 out* F

Going the wrong way. **0**

AUTUMN RIDE(IRE) b.m. 8 King's Ride - Natflat by Barrons Court H French

1995 P(0),3(11)

797 2/4 Heythrop (R) MDN 3m 11 F *(fav) (bl) cls up,mstk 11th,ld 13th & sn clr,not run on 3 out,hdd fin* 3 14
1175 20/4 Chaddesley ' (L) MDN 3m 9 G *alwys cls up, ev ch 15th, not qckn 3 out* 3 10
1293 28/4 Barbury Cas' (L) MDO 3m 11 F *(bl) ld/disp til mstk 10th, 4th whn mstk & u.r. nxt* U

Good enough to win but not one ti trust. **12**

AUVILLAR(USA) br.g. 8 Temperence Hill (USA) - Exquisita (USA) by Cougar (CHI) J Parfit

1995 **4(NH),3(NH),13(NH),1(NH),6(NH),2(NH)**

504 16/3 Magor (R) MEM 3m 5 GS *(fav) hld up, prog to mod 2nd 3 out, no imp* 2 0
602 23/3 Howick (L) OPE 3m 11 S *alwys rear, no ch frm 14th* 4 14

Winning hurdler/chaser; (often blinkered); lacks scope and disappointed in 96; best watched. **17**

AVIN FUN BAR b.m. 8 Sergeant Drummer (USA) - Cinbar by Cintrist Mrs S M Trump

1995 P(0),P(0),P(0),5(0),5(0)

446 9/3 Haldon (R) MDO 3m 13 S *ld/disp to 12th, lost plc nxt, t.o. & p.u. 2 out* P 0
806 4/4 Clyst St Ma' (L) MDO 3m 7 GS *ld to 11th, agn 12th, hdd aft 3 out, onepcd* 3 0
1118 17/4 Hockworthy (L) MDO 3m 14 GS *ld til hdd & f 12th* F
1431 6/5 High Bickin' (R) MDO 3m 9 G *ld til 15th, sn wknd, btn 6th whn p.u. apr 18th* P 0
1531 12/5 Ottery St M' (L) MDO 3m 9 GF *made all, styd on wll clsng stgs* 1 14

Front runner; won slow Maiden; stamina doubts and needs to improve. **16**

VRIL SHOWERS b.m. 7 Vital Season - April's Crook by Crozier — Mrs R Atkinson

1995 U(-),1(18),5(14),F(-)

138 17/2 Ottery St M' (L) RES 3m 18 GS *ld til hdd apr last, outpcd* 2 18
465 10/3 Milborne St' (L) RES 3m 11 G *chsd ldrs, 4th at 12th, outpcd frm 2 out* 3 17
728 31/3 Little Wind' (R) MEM 3m 7 GS *(fav) in tch, hdwy to 2nd 14th, efft to disp last, sn clr* 1 20
992 8/4 Kingston St' (R) RES 3m 6 F *(fav) hld up, went 4l 3rd 15th, 2nd 2 out, ran on, just hld* 2 18
128 20/4 Stafford Cr' (R) RES 3m 17 S *alwys prom, 2nd 12th, no further prog frm 3 out* 3 13
395 6/5 Cotley Farm (L) RES 3m 8 GF *rr, stdy prog frm 4 out, ld last, ran on* 1 21
553 18/5 Bratton Down (L) XX 3m 10 F *prom til stmbld & lost plc apr 6th,sn wll bhnd,poor 4th 3out* 4 12
525 27/5 Lifton (R) INT 3m 8 GS *(Jt fav) w.w. prog 16th, went 2nd aft 3 out, ev ch til no ext nr fin* 2 18

Solid, consistent & safe; veteran-ridden; Intermediate likely 97; stays well; F-G/S G-S 21

WALKINTHECLOUDS (Irish) — I 267P, I 337P, I 478P

WALKINTHEWOODS (Irish) — I 299P

WAY IN A HACK (Irish) — I 161P, I 228P, I 345P

WAYTODAY (Irish) — I 270P, I 3402, I 4186, I 4995

WBEG ROVER (Irish) — I 675, I 115F, I 2095, I 378P, I 4351, I 5052, I 5665, I 6115, I 639P

WINDY CITIZEN(IRE) ch.m. 7 Phardante (FR) - Candolcis by Candy Cane — Mrs J A Thomson

1995 P(0),P(0),5(14),F(-),P(0),F(-),4(16),1(21),1(19),**U(-)**,2(0)

210 24/2 Castle Of C' (R) INT 3m 10 HY *cls up, ld 13th-nxt, wknd aft, p.u. 3 out* P 0
361 5/3 Leicester (R) HC 2 1/2m 110yds 15 GS *waited with, prog 9th, blnd badly 4 out, chal and switched apr last, ld cl home, cleverly.* 1 22
484 15/3 Fakenham (L) HC 2m 5f 110yds 13 GF *(fav) well in tch, hit 5th, blnd and lost pl 9th, ran on again after 12th, fin well.* 2 22
570 28/3 Aintree (L) HC 3m 1f 9 G *f 1st.* F -
798 3/4 Ascot (R) HC 2m 3f 110yds 10 GF *held up, mstk 9th, hdwy to chal 11th, ev ch last, no ext.* 2 27
107 15/4 Southwell (L) HC 3m 110yds 10 G *mstks, held up, smooth hdwy to chase ldrs 5 out, hung left 3 out, btn next.* 3 21
227 26/4 Ludlow (R) HC 2 1/2m 16 G *(fav) held up, hdwy 10th, rdn apr last, ran on one pace.* 2 23
341 4/5 Warwick (L) HC 2 1/2m 110yds 12 GF *(fav) chsd ldrs, ev ch when blnd 2 out, ran on one pace.* 3 24
455 8/5 Uttoxeter (L) HC 2m 5f 9 G *(fav) held up, mstk 3rd, prog and mistake 9th, ld apr 4 out till after next, cl third when blnd and u.r. 2 out.* U -
548 18/5 Southwell (L) HC 3m 110yds 11 GF *alwys prom, ev ch 3 out, wknd 2 out.* 7 0
629 30/5 Uttoxeter (L) HC 2m 5f 13 GS *alwys bhnd.* 5 12

Won weak H/chase; struggling under penalty after; best below 3 miles; another win looks tough. 22

YLESBURY BEAU (Irish) — I 106F, I 164P, I 1951

YLESFORD b.g. 5 Efisio - My Myra by Auction Ring (USA) — Miss S Willis

434 9/3 Newton Brom' (R) CON 3m 11 GS *ld aft 1st-2nd, chsd ldrs to 9th, wknd & p.u. 11th* P 0
957 8/4 Lockinge (L) CON 3m 5 GF *held up, prog 9th,cls up til wknd 14th,t.o. & p.u. bfr 3 out* 5 0

.. 0

YYAROSE b.m. 8 Ayyabaan - Pinzarose by Pinzan — Mrs C Higgon

1995 P(0),2(10)

551 17/3 Erw Lon (L) MDN 3m 8 GS *twrds rear, p.u. 11th* P 0
977 8/4 Lydstep (L) MDO 3m 8 G *trckd ldrs, ld aft last, all out* 1 13
203 21/4 Lydstep (L) RES 3m 5 S *ld to 4 out, fdd, fin tired* 4 0
388 6/5 Pantyderi (R) RES 3m 7 GF *nvr nr than 5th, btn whn f 14th* F -

Scraped home in modest race & well beaten after; may eventually find weak Restricted 14

AASHFUL BLAZE ch.m. 10 Shaab - Barney's Blaze by Spitsbergen — Mrs Mary Trueman

139 20/4 Flete Park (R) RES 3m 14 S *rear whn f 5th* F -
357 4/5 Flete Park (R) MEM 3m 3 G *sn bhnd, jmpd slwly & t.o. 12th, iron broke* 3 0
531 12/5 Ottery St M' (L) MDO 3m 9 GF *n.j.w. alwys rear* 7 0
626 27/5 Lifton (R) MDO 3m 13 GS *jmpd slwly in rear, wll bhnd til p.u. 16th* P 0

No signs of ability. 0

ABIL b.g. 11 Welsh Pageant - Princess Eboli by Brigadier Gerard — Mrs C Hicks

457 8/5 Uttoxeter (L) HC 3 1/4m 16 G *bhnd when p.u. before 13th.* P 0
544 17/5 Stratford (L) HC 3m 10 GF *chsd lding pair till rdn and wknd quickly 3 out.* 6 18

Former good hurdler; hardly seen since 90; still has ability. 18

ABY JAKE (Irish) — I 131, I 341

ABY WHALE (Irish) — I 32P, I 83P, I 128F, I 144P, I 2321

ACK-BENCHER b.g. 9 Mummy's Treasure - Night Dreamer — A D Peachey

742 31/3 Upper Sapey (R) RES 3m 9 GS *u.r. 2nd* U -

842 6/4 Maisemore P' (L) MDN 3m 17 GF *prom, cls 3rd whn f 12th* F
1341 4/5 Warwick (L) HC 2 1/2m 110yds 12 GF *alwys in rear, t.o. when p.u. before 12th.* P

Ex-Irish; of no account **0**

BACK THE ROAD(IRE) ch.g. 8 Mister Lord (USA) - Salvation Sue by Mon Capitaine M Ma
1995 **P(0)**

538 17/3 Southwell P' (L) XX 3m 6 GS *cls up to 8th, wknd rpdly, p.u. 11th* P
664 24/3 Eaton Hall (R) CON 3m 15 S *prom to hlfwy, sn btn, p.u. 4 out* P
687 30/3 Chaddesley ' (L) CON 3m 10 G *w.w. prog to 4th & blnd 12th, not rcvr, p.u. aft nxt* P
1192 21/4 Sandon (L) CON 3m 11 G *ld to 5th, trckd ldr, ld 11-13th, sn btn, p.u. 3 out* P
1230 27/4 Weston Park (L) CON 3m 7 G *cls up frm 3rd, disp 8th-3 out, no ext frm 2 out* 2
1456 8/5 Uttoxeter (L) HC 2m 5f 11 G *cl up, ev ch 4 out, 3rd when slpd on lndg 2 out, no chance after.* 4
1578 19/5 Wolverhampt' (L) OPE 3m 7 G *tubed,ld to 4th,chsd ldr 10th,ld apr 3 out,clr nxt,all out* 1
1583 19/5 Wolverhampt' (L) MEM 3m 1 G *walked over* 1
1629 30/5 Uttoxeter (L) HC 2m 5f 13 GS *held up bhnd ldrs, effort 4 out, 2nd and rdn when blnd and u.r. 2 out.* U

Returned to form late season; ran well H/chases but unlikely to win one; tubed. **18**

BACK WITHAVENGEANCE (Irish) — **I** 224[P], **I** 343[P]
BADALKA (Irish) — **I** 15[P], **I** 25[4], **I** 80[4]
BADIHAR(USA) ch.g. 12 Nijinsky (CAN) - Mofida by Right Tack E R H Clarks
1995 3(15),2(15),P(0)

198 24/2 Lemalla (R) OPE 3m 12 HY *sn bhnd, p.u. 3 out* P
278 2/3 Clyst St Ma' (L) CON 3m 9 S *ld to 3rd, mid-div frm 5th, styd on frm 16th, no ch 2 out* 3
531 16/3 Cothelstone (L) CON 3m 12 G *rr & blnd bdly 8th, p.u. appr nxt* P

Moderate; problems last start and unlikely to win now. **15**

BAGOTS PARK ro.g. 7 Alias Smith (USA) - Newfield Green by Deep Run S J Leadbet
1995 **3(NH)**

1088 14/4 Friars Haugh (L) MDO 3m 10 F *3rd hlfwy, chal wnr 4 out, wknd 2 out* 3
1356 4/5 Mosshouses (L) MDO 3m 12 GS *prom,ld 12th,hdd & mstk 3 out,lft disp nxt,hdd & no ext flat* 3
1476 11/5 Aspatria (L) MDO 3m 16 GF *(fav) ld 3rd-12th, blnd nxt, wll btn 15th, p.u. last* P
1575 19/5 Corbridge (R) MDO 3m 10 G *sn bhnd, nvr nrr* 6

Ability under Rules & in points but stamina & courage in question; could continue to frustrate **13**

BAILEYS DREAM (Irish) — **I** 27[P], **I** 167[P], **I** 417,
BAJAN AFFAIR b.m. 6 Bold Owl - Silvery Moon by Lorenzaccio Keith Loa
1995 **P(NH),9(NH),3(NH),13(NH),8(NH),5(NH),4(NH)**

9 14/1 Cottenham (R) OPE 3m 13 G *mid-div, mstk 6th, bhnd frm 11th, p.u. 2 out* P
96 11/2 Ampton (R) XX 3m 11 GF *rear, lost tch 14th, t.o. & p.u. 3 out* P

Winning hurdler; small and has no prospects in points. **0**

BAKMALAD ch.g. 10 Kambalda - Joyspir by Master Buck N L Steve
1995 2(13),2(14),P(0)

946 8/4 Andoversford (R) RES 3m 10 GF *hld up rear, styd on frm 15th, went 2nd flat* 2
1242 27/4 Woodford (L) RES 3m 18 G *mid-div, 8th & in tch hlfwy, onepcd frm 3 out* 4
1439 6/5 Ashorne (R) RES 3m 11 G *(fav) prog 5th,lost plc 11th,effrt 15th,chsd wnr 2 out,kpt on flat* 3
1481 11/5 Bredwardine (R) RES 3m 14 G *5s-7/2, rear & rmndrs 5th, last at 10th, fin wll frm 3 out* 3
1612 26/5 Tweseldown (R) RES 3m 11 G *(fav) chsd ldrs, mstk 10th & rmndr, outpcd 14th, ran on 2 out* 3

Maiden winner 94; placed in 7 of 8 races 95/6 but runs in snatches now & Restricted win unlikely **16**

BALANCE b.g. 8 Balinger - Dance Partner by Manicou Richard J Smi
1995 F(-),P(0),3(0)

2 13/1 Larkhill (R) MDO 3m 17 GS *ld to 3rd, prom whn f 5th* F
233 24/2 Heythrop (R) MDN 3m 14 GS *(Jt fav) rear, prog 11th, 3rd & wkng 14th, p.u. 2 out* P
477 10/3 Tweseldown (R) MDO 3m 15 G *3rd frm 9th til prog on bit 14th, ld 4 out, pshd out flat* 1
707 30/3 Barbury Cas' (L) RES 3m 18 G *ld/disp til blnd 4 out, wkng whn u.r. nxt* U
960 8/4 Lockinge (L) RES 3m 9 GF *prom, disp 5-3 out, ran on und pres frm 2 out* 2
1292 28/4 Barbury Cas' (L) RES 3m 11 F *mstks,rear,prog 11th,rdn to ld aft 2 out,blnd last,nt rcvr* 3

Finally confirmed promise in modest race; unlucky last start & could win Restricted 97; G-F **18**

BALDHU CHANCE ch.g. 8 Chaparly (FR) - Galla Currency by Galeopsis Terry Lor
1995 **7(NH),15(NH)**

45 3/2 Wadebridge (L) MDO 3m 10 GF *ld 4-15th, rlld & ev ch last, wknd flat* 3
71 10/2 Great Treth' (R) MDO 3m 15 S *ld 4th-3 out, grad fdd* 4
201 24/2 Lemalla (R) MDO 3m 13 HY *s.u. bend aft 4th* S
301 2/3 Great Treth' (R) MDO 3m 13 G *made most, lkd wnr whn lft clr 2 out, mstk last* 1
627 23/3 Kilworthy (L) RES 3m 13 GS *prom to 10th, wknd rpdly & p.u. 13th* P
720 30/3 Wadebridge (L) RES 3m 9 GF *jmpd rght,made virt all,drew clr 3 out,hung rght flat,hld on* 1
936 8/4 Wadebridge (L) MEM 3m 2 F *(fav) made all, j.w., v easy* 1

1074	13/4	Lifton	(R)	INT	3m	9	S	*ld til hdd aft 14th, wknd, eased clsng stgs*	4 10
1278	27/4	Bratton Down	(L)	INT	3m	12	GF	*alwys prom, cls 2nd whn f 15th*	F -
1360	4/5	Flete Park	(R)	OPE	3m	5	G	*ld/disp til aft 14th, sn outpcd*	3 12
1622	27/5	Lifton	(R)	CON	3m	14	GS	*5th hlfwy, cls up & ev ch 14th til wknd aft 3 out*	5 15

Found right openings for successful season; struggling in better company & more wins hard; Any 17

BALD JOKER (Irish) — **I** 94^{P}, **I** 216^{2}, **I** 338^{3}, **I** 350^{6}, **I** 597^{2}

BALINGER BOY b.g. 6 Balinger - Young Gipsy by The Brianstan — L J Williams

696	30/3	Llanvapley	(L)	MDN	3m	13	GS	*rear, ref 12th*	R -

No signs on debut. 0

BALISTEROS(FR) b.g. 7 Bad Conduct (USA) - Oldburry (FR) by Fin Bon — Mrs B K Thomson

1995 U(-),2(15),1(17),1(20),4(14),2(17)

1	13/1	Larkhill	(R)	XX	3m	7	GS	*hld up,prog & mskt 6th,rdn whn mstk 12th,outpcd,kpt on 3 out*	3 17
43	3/2	Wadebridge	(L)	INT	3m	5	GF	*in tch, prog 11th, ld 12-14th, one pace 3 out*	3 18
212	24/2	Castle Of C'	(R)	CON	3m	7	HY	*hld up, prog 10th, ld/disp frm 13th til outpcd 2 out*	2 19
472	10/3	Milborne St'	(L)	INT	3m	8	G	*mid-div, prog 14th, outpcd frm 3 out*	3 13
647	23/3	Cothelstone	(L)	CON	3m	6	S	*(fav) waited with, prog 9th, ld 12th-14th, rnwd eff 2 out, no extr*	2 16
1252	27/4	Balcormo Ma'	(R)	INT	3m	5	GS	*alwys in tch, ld 3 out, sn clr*	1 19

Changed hands before final race; stays but onepaced; should win confined. 21

BALLET KNEES (Irish) — **I** 19^{F}

BALLHOPPING (Irish) — **I** 39^{3}, **I** 47^{P}, **I** 201^{4}

BALLINABOOLA GROVE (Irish) — **I** 82^{P}, **I** 130, , **I** 159^{6}, **I** 197^{1}, **I** 262^{2}, **I** 338^{1}, **I** 422^{P}, **I** 480^{F}, **I** 524^{U}, **I** 570^{2}

BALLINACLASH PRIDE (Irish) — **I** 33^{2}, **I** 384^{3}, **I** 499^{2}, **I** 621^{1}

BALLINACUBBY PRIDE (Irish) — **I** 59^{U}, **I** 149^{F}, **I** 211^{F}, **I** 279^{2}, **I** 503^{P}, **I** 649^{2}

BALLINAHOWNA LAD (Irish) — **I** 180^{F}, **I** 367^{P}, **I** 429^{U}

BALLINAVARY VI (Irish) — **I** 256^{P}, **I** 299^{P}, **I** 407^{P}

BALLINAVEEN BRIDGE (Irish) — **I** 17^{P}, **I** 34^{4}, **I** 65, , **I** 629^{5}

BALLINLOVANE EILE (Irish) — **I** 51^{2}, **I** 72,

BALLINTEE BELLE (Irish) — **I** 120^{F}, **I** 144^{3}, **I** 182^{2}, **I** 308^{1}, **I** 519,

BALLINVUSKIG LADY (Irish) — **I** 11^{4}, **I** 64, , **I** 243^{4}, **I** 353^{4}, **I** 564^{4}, **I** 614^{5}, **I** 647^{U}

BALLYALLA (Irish) — **I** 360^{1}, **I** 596^{3}

BALLYANDREW b.g. 11 Leading Man - Dunoon Court by Dunoon Star — A H B Hodge

1995 2(19),3(12),4(19),1(19),1(23),1(21)

368	6/3	Lingfield	(L)	HC	3m	7	S	*(fav) ld til blnd badly and u.r. 2nd.*	U -
486	16/3	Newcastle	(L)	HC	3m	9	GS	*pulld hrd and soon led, hdd 7th, prom, fd apr 3 out.*	5 10
1099	14/4	Guilsborough	(L)	LAD	3m	9	G	*ld to 9th & 11-16th, wknd 3 out, tired*	5 10

Won 3 ladies 95; below best in 96; still win ladies if fit 97; jumps well; needs easy surface. 20

BALLYARGAN(IRE) ch.g. 7 Long Pond - Glencorrin by Wishing Star — R V Westwood

114	17/2	Lanark	(R)	MDO	3m	12	GS	*wll bhnd by 8th, t.o.*	5 0
194	24/2	Friars Haugh	(L)	MDN	3m	11	S	*mod 4th whn f 13th*	F -
503	16/3	Lanark	(R)	MDO	3m	10	G	*bhnd til prog frm 4 out, tk 2nd flat*	2 0
614	23/3	Friars Haugh	(L)	MDN	3m	10	G	*2nd hlfwy, cl up, kpt on wll.*	2 12
1254	27/4	Balcormo Ma'	(R)	MDO	3m	14	GS	*alwys hndy, 3rd hlfwy, styd on onepcd frm 3 out*	3 14

Consistent, stays but novice-ridden & may need fortune to win 14

BALLYARNOTT (Irish) — **I** 93^{3}, **I** 172^{P}

BALLYBEGGAN BOY (Irish) — **I** 62^{6}, **I** 74^{3}, **I** 148^{P}, **I** 312^{P}, **I** 375^{P}

BALLYBEGGAN LADY (Irish) — **I** 146^{3}, **I** 240^{3}, **I** 308^{F}, **I** 354, , **I** 457^{4}, **I** 510^{3}

BALLYBEGGAN PARSON(IRE) b.g. 7 The Parson - Papadrim — P E Mills

1995 **14(NH)**,**11(NH)**

158	17/2	Weston Park	(L)	MEM	3m	11	G	*mid-div, lost tch hlfwy, 6th & no ch whn f hvly last*	F -
288	2/3	Eaton Hall	(R)	MDO	3m	17	G	*mid to rear, no ch whn p.u. 5 out*	P 0
661	24/3	Eaton Hall	(R)	MDN	3m	9	S	*jmpd slwly, ld/disp to 3rd, prog to ld 13th, styd on well 2 out*	1 15
882	6/4	Brampton Br'	(R)	RES	3m	14	GF	*mid-div, mstk 6th, hmpd 10th, lost tch 13th, p.u. 3 out*	P 0
1223	24/4	Brampton Br'	(R)	RES	3m	11	G	*prom to 4th, cls 6th at 8th, wknd 13th, p.u. 3 out*	P 0

Won modest race (nearly 7 mins) on only outing in Soft & may have prospects in similar Restricted 15

BALLYBRIKEN CASTLE (Irish) — **I** 20^{P}, **I** 41^{P}, **I** 127^{3}, **I** 202^{P}, **I** 233^{2}, **I** 291^{4}, **I** 391^{3}, **I** 428^{3}, **I** 510^{5}, **I** 556^{2}, **I** 587^{1}

BALLYBRIT (Irish) — **I** 111^{P}, **I** 167^{B}, **I** 305^{U}, **I** 341^{5}, **I** 455^{1}, **I** 560^{2}, **I** 647^{4}

BALLYCANAL BOY ch.g. 9 Deep Run - Super Straight by Our Mirage — D E Fletcher

1995 F(-),P(0),P(0),7(0)

341	3/3	Heythrop	(R)	MDN	3m	13 G	*rear, lost tch hlfwy, t.o. & p.u. 14th*	P	(

No real signs of ability yet. 0

BALLYCAR PRINCESS (Irish) — I 43P, I 252P, I 290P, I 369[6], I 475[5]

BALLYDAY STEP (Irish) — I 418[3]

BALLYDESMOND (Irish) — I 283P, I 318P, I 361[3], I 407[1], I 489[5], I 534[2]

BALLYEDMOND (Irish) — I 384P, I 417P

BALLYHANNON(IRE) b.g. 7 Strong Gale - Chestnut Fire by Deep Run — Miss J Froggat

159	17/2	Weston Park	(L)	CON	3m	22 G	*n.j.w. alwys rear, f 14th*	F	
243	25/2	Southwell P'	(L)	RES	3m	11 HO	*rear, prog whn mstk 12th & lost plc, t.o. & p.u. 3 out*	P	(
462	9/3	Eyton-On-Se'	(L)	RES	3m	12 G	*mid-div, ev ch 5 out, not quckn*	8	(
665	24/3	Eaton Hall	(R)	RES	3m	14 S	*t.o. & p.u. 8th*	P	(
1191	21/4	Sandon	(L)	MEM	3m	5 G	*alwys rear, 3rd at 9th, nvr dang*	3	(
1577	19/5	Wolverhampt'	(L)	CON	3m	6 G	*chsd ldr to 3rd, lost plc & rmndrs 7th, no ch frm 14th*	4	1(

Irish Maiden winner 94; showed nothing in 96 and can only be watched. 0

BALLYHEST FOUNTAIN (Irish) — I 60F, I 64P, I 128F, I 151P, I 240P

BALLYHOOLY BELLE (Irish) — I 569P, I 614P, I 661[2]

BALLYLIME AGAIN (Irish) — I 107[5], I 195F, I 340P, I 391[2]

BALLYLINE (Irish) — I 199[1]

BALLYMACREVAN (Irish) — I 109, , I 173U, I 282[1], I 411[3], I 488[1]

BALLYMUCKAMORE (Irish) — I 199P

BALLY MUIRE ch.m. 11 Bali Dancer - Coroin Muire by Perspex — B W Timmis

1995 P(0),5(11),P(0),4(0),P(0),1(15)

293	2/3	Eaton Hall	(R)	INT	3m	11 G	*mid to rear, p.u. 4 out*	P	(
457	9/3	Eyton-On-Se'	(L)	INT	3m	11 G	*chsd ldrs, lost tch aftr 8th, p.u. 2 out*	P	(
667	24/3	Eaton Hall	(R)	INT	3m	11 S	*rear whn p.u. 11th*	P	(
855	6/4	Sandon	(L)	CON	3m	6 GF	*mid-div, nvr rchd chal position*	4	(
1032	13/4	Alpraham	(R)	CON	3m	9 GS	*bhnd whn s.u. aft 4th*	S	(

Surprise winner 95 (20/1); best late season but finished early 96; struggle to win again. 15

BALLY RIOT (Irish) — I 47P, I 68[1], I 136[1]

BALLYSADARE BAY (Irish) — I 456P, I 598P

BALLYSHEIL b.g. 10 Roi Guillaume (FR) - Paldamask by Native Prince — P M Hun

1995 P(0),2(12),4(13),5(11),2(16)

280	2/3	Clyst St Ma'	(L)	RES	3m	11 S	*sn rear, t.o. 12th*	5	(
870	6/4	Higher Kilw'	(L)	MEM	3m	5 GF	*ld/disp til aft 12th, wknd*	3	1
1313	28/4	Little Wind'	(R)	RES	3m	14 G	*rear but in tch, 7th at 14th, prog to 5th 3 out, kpt on*	4	12
1428	6/5	High Bickin'	(R)	RES	3m	10 G	*prog 15th, ld aft 2 out til not ran on & hdd cls home*	2	1
1591	25/5	Mounsey Hil'	(R)	RES	3m	15 G	*mid-div, 8th at 14th, sn lost tch, p.u. last,cont,pld 3rd*	3	(

Capable of fair efforts but inconsistent; could win restricted on best form. 16

BALLYSHEIL STAR b.g. 10 Monksfield - Dynamic Girl by Martinmas — P Jonasor

1995 P(0),3(0),P(0),4(0),2(13),2(12)

15	14/1	Cottenham	(R)	MDN	3m	14 G	*in tch, blnd 10th, chsd ldr 14th, wknd apr 2 out*	5	1(
91	11/2	Ampton	(R)	MDO	3m	10 GF	*mid-div, prog 12th, went 3rd 3 out, no ext frm nxt*	3	12
108	17/2	Marks Tey	(L)	MDN	3m	17 G	*prog 10th, ev ch 16th, wknd 3 out*	4	12
489	16/3	Horseheath	(R)	MEM	3m	4 GF	*rear frm 2nd, mstk & u.r. nxt*	U	
618	23/3	Higham	(L)	MDO	3m	14 GF	*(Jt fav) prom early, mid-div whn mstk & u.r. 8th*	U	
621	23/3	Higham	(L)	INT	3m	12 GF	*2nd outing, prom, wknd 10th, t.o. & p.u. 2 out*	P	(
1326	28/4	Fakenham P-'	(L)	MDO	3m	7 G	*ld to 3rd, blnd 10th, 3rd & rdn 14th, 5l 2nd whn f 2 out*	F	

Improved in 95; jumping gone to pieces again now; may have missed his chances. 12

BALLY SKY b.g. 7 Karlinsky (USA) - Bally River by River Beau — Mrs L Bloomfielc

630	23/3	Kilworthy	(L)	MDN	3m	10 GS	*prom, mstk 8th, lost tch 15th, fin tired*	7	(
1116	17/4	Hockworthy	(L)	MDO	3m	9 GS	*in tch, lft 3rd 13th, chsd wnr 3 out, rdn & btn nxt*	2	1

A satisfactory start; placed in 3 finisher race; can do better. 14

BALLYVOYLE BAY b.m. 11 Paddy's Stream - Dancing Daisy by Arctic Slave — J R Holt

1995 2(0),7(0),4(0),9(0),2(15),3(13),3(13)

243	25/2	Southwell P'	(L)	RES	3m	11 HO	*(bl) trckd ldr 5th-12th, wknd rpdly, p.u. 3 out*	P	(
396	9/3	Garthorpe	(R)	RES	3m	9 G	*(bl) tried to make all, ran on gamely whn chal 2 out, just outpcd*	3	14
726	31/3	Garthorpe	(R)	RES	3m	16 G	*(bl) alwys prom, chal & ev ch 2 out, brshd aside apr last*	3	17
1012	9/4	Flagg Moor	(L)	XX	3m	7 G	*(bl) chsd ldrs, ev ch 3 out, sn rdn & wknd*	3	13
1178	21/4	Mollington	(R)	RES	3m	7 F	*(bl) cls up, hrd rdn 10th, sn strgglng in rear*	5	(
1380	5/5	Dingley	(R)	RES	3m	11 GF	*(bl) chsd ldrs, cls up 3 out, sn outpcde & btn*	4	12

Maiden winner 92; become disappointing; very onepaced and usually easily beaten. 15

BALLYWEE PENNY (Irish) — **I** 598[F]

BALLYWOODOCK VI (Irish) — **I** 171[P], **I** 284[P], **I** 410[P], **I** 489[6], **I** 536[2], **I** 597[P]

BALMAHA b.m. 5 Absalom - Mo Ceri by Kampala — Nick Shutts

69 10/2 Great Treth' (R) MDO 3m 12 S *prom whn u.r. 13th* U -
218 24/2 Newtown (L) MDN 3m 14 GS *rear, prog 11th, ev ch whn f 14th* F -
591 23/3 Wetherby Po' (L) MDO 3m 14 S *alwys mid-div, kpt on onepcd frm 4 out* 4 0

Last but not disgraced when completing; can go much closer in 97. 14

BALMORAL BOY(NZ) b.g. 8 Prince Simbir (NZ) - Barbee's Dream (NZ) by Silver Dream — M G Miller
1995 4(0),5(10),2(13),1(15)

210 24/2 Castle Of C' (R) INT 3m 10 HY *handy, prog 12th, ev ch 2 out, onepcd* 2 18
466 10/3 Milborne St' (L) RES 3m 13 G *in tch to 4 out, wknd & onepcd frm nxt* 5 15
656 23/3 Badbury Rin' (L) RES 3m 11 G *wth ldrs untl wknd 13th, ran on from 2 out* 5 0
729 31/3 Little Wind' (R) RES 3m 12 GS *midfld, 6th 15th, no prog* 5 15
313 28/4 Little Wind' (R) RES 3m 14 G *mid-div, some prog to 6th at 15th, outpcd frm nxt* 6 11
345 4/5 Holnicote (L) RES 3m 11 GS *mid-div, gd prog 15th, ld last, ran on well* 1 19
590 25/5 Mounsey Hil' (R) INT 3m 8 G *hld up bhnd, nvr nr ldrs, t.o. 14th* 4 0

Consistent & finished last 14 races; found modest Restricted; virtues may see Intermediate win; G-Hy 18

BAMAN POWERHOUSE b.g. 8 Bold Owl - Bella Abzug by Karabas — Graham Kivell
1995 4(0),S(-)

072 13/4 Lifton (R) LAD 3m 7 S *ld & sn clr, swrvd lft 7th, hdd 9th, t.o., p.u. apr 13th* P 0
143 20/4 Flete Park (R) MDN 3m 17 S *keen hold, tore into ld 7th, wknd rpdly & hdd 12th,p.u. 14th* P 0
432 6/5 High Bickin' (R) MDO 3m 9 G *hdwy to 2nd 12th,wknd 15th,blnd bdly & p.u. 17th,rmntd t.o.* 3 0
555 18/5 Bratton Down (L) MDO 3m 13 F *twrds rear, 8th hlfwy, nvr dang* 6 0
626 27/5 Lifton (R) MDO 3m 13 GS *plld hrd, jmpd lft, ld to 10th & 11-14th, wknd, p.u. 3 out* P 0
650 8/6 Umberleigh (L) CON 3m 7 GF *rear but in tch til outpcd & mstk 13th, t.o. & p.u. 2 out* P 0

Far too headstrong and has no prospects unless learning to settle. 11

BANCYFELIN BOY ch.g. 9 Old Lucky - Eve Darlin by Arcticeelagh — Miss A L Williams
1995 P(0),5(11),1(15),P(0)

549 17/3 Erw Lon (L) RES 3m 11 GS *twrds rear, prog frm 3 out, unable to chal* 2 11
766 31/3 Pantyderi (R) CON 3m 6 G *mid-div, mstk 13th, rpd prog 15th, hrd rdn to ld last* 1 18
974 8/4 Lydstep (L) MEM 3m 10 G *mstk 3rd, prom, onepcd frm 2 out* 3 13
211 23/4 Chepstow (L) HC 3m 13 S *bhnd from 9th, t.o. when p.u. before 12th.* P 0
614 27/5 Hereford (R) HC 3m 1f 110yds 16 G *in tch, not fleunt 13th (water), weakening when mstk 4 out, t.o. when p.u. before next.* P 0

Inconsistent but popped up with annnual win; no chance in H/Chases; may find another chance; Good 17

BAND SARGEANT(IRE) b.g. 7 Nashamaa - Indian Honey by Indian King (USA) — Miss J E Foster

304 2/3 Great Stain' (L) OPE 3m 10 GS *mid-div til wknd 15th* 6 10
662 24/3 Eaton Hall (R) OPE 3m 10 S *mid-div, 5th & in tch 4 out, sn wknd, p.u. nxt* P 0
031 13/4 Alpraham (R) MXO 3m 5 GS *rear, bad mstk 8th, rider lost iron & p.u. bfr nxt* P 0
154 20/4 Whittington (L) OPE 3m 7 G *(bl) chsd ldr to 15th, wknd, tired & btn 4th whn ref 4 out* R -
281 27/4 Easingwold (L) CON 3m 15 G *alwys prom, disp ld 7-9th, onepcd frm 4 out* 4 19
449 6/5 Witton Cast' (R) LAD 3m 10 G *cls up, 2l 2nd 3 out, wknd aft* 4 16
594 25/5 Garthorpe (R) MEM 3m 10 G *ld to 8th, cls 2nd whn u.r. 9th* U -

.. 16

BANG ON TARGET ch.g. 8 Cruise Missile - Airy Fairy by Space King — John Bowen
1995 **3(NH),U(NH),4(NH),6(NH)**

7 13/1 Larkhill (R) CON 3m 10 GS *rear, prog to jn ldrs 13th, btn frm nxt* 4 13
260 1/3 Newbury (L) HC 3m 6 GS *(bl) held up, steady hdwy to track ldrs when f 12th.* F -
581 21/3 Wincanton (R) HC 2m 5f 13 S *(bl) bhnd from 10th, t.o. when ref last.* R -
056 13/4 Badbury Rin' (L) RES 3m 10 GF *prom, ld 7th-3 out, wknd & onepcd aft* 3 12
168 20/4 Larkhill (R) RES 3m 8 GF *(bl) prom early, wknd frm 12th, t.o. frm 14th* 4 0

Does not stay and outclassed in H/chases; weak race on firm only hope. 14

BANJO PATERSON b.g. 9 Rymer - Roman Rock by Rockavon — C Goulding
1995 F(-)

568 19/5 Mollington (R) MDO 3m 9 GS *ld to 3rd & 5th-14th, wknd, crawld 3 out & u.r., rmntd* 2 0
644 2/6 Dingley (R) MDO 3m 16 GF *alwys rr, kpt on frm 3 out, no dang* 6 0

Very lightly raced; ran best ever last start ; but win still unlikely. 10

BANKER'S GOSSIP b.g. 12 Le Bavard (FR) - Gracious View by Sir Herbert — R T Jones
1995 4(16),4(0),5(11),4(0)

383 9/3 Llanfrynach (R) CON 3m 13 GS *mid-div,outpcd 13th,kpt on onepcd frm 3 out,no dang,fin 4th,prmtd* 3 14

768 31/3 Pantyderi (R) OPE 3m 10 G *alwys rear* 8 0

Ungenuine and will not win again. 13

BANKHEAD(IRE) gr.g. 7 Roselier (FR) - Coolcanute by Hardicanute A J Brazier

1995 **3(NH),1(NH),2(NH)**

216 24/2 Newtown (L) LAD 3m 13 GS *7/2-9/4, 3rd frm 6th til chsd ldr 13th, ld 2 out, rdn out* 1 25

356 3/3 Garnons (L) LAD 3m 12 GS *(fav) cls up, ld frm 13th, jnd 3 out, drew clr aft nxt* 1 26

685 30/3 Chaddesley ' (L) LAD 3m 9 G *(fav) in tch til u.r. 5th* U

1018 13/4 Kingston Bl' (L) LAD 3m 8 G *(fav) 2nd til ld 11th,clr 14th,blnd 3 out,hdd last,rallied,ld post* 1 26

1172 20/4 Chaddesley ' (L) LAD 3m 3 G *chsd ldr & alwys outjmpd, chal 2 out, ld last, pshd clr* 1 27

1480 11/5 Bredwardine (R) LAD 3m 12 G *trckd ldr frm 8th, chal 2 out, drew clr last* 1 28

1617 27/5 Chaddesley ' (L) LAD 3m 8 GF *(fav) n.j.w. cls up, lft in ld 14th, jnd last, qcknd flat* 1 23

Winning hurdler; very useful; not fluent, game & quickens; win H/chase if jumping holds up. 28

BANNAGH MOOR (Irish) — **I** 493[P]

BANNER YEAR (Irish) — **I** 122[P], **I** 200[P], **I** 248[4], **I** 292[5], **I** 440[P], **I** 472[5], **I** 541[P]

BANTEL BUCCANEER b.g. 14 Jellaby - Highview Jill by Proud Chieftain R W Fidler

1995 4(14),3(16),4(17),2(16)

380 9/3 Barbury Cas' (L) CON 3m 11 GS *lft in ld 7th, ran on whn chal flat* 1 17

710 30/3 Barbury Cas' (L) CON 3m 6 G *ld 3-6th, wknd, lost tch 13th, t.o. & p.u. 4 out* P 0

996 8/4 Hackwood Pa' (L) MXO 3m 4 GF *2nd til ld 14th, hrd rdn 2 out, hdd last, ran on* 2 16

1289 28/4 Barbury Cas' (L) CON 3m 8 F *chsd ldrs, 3rd & outpcd frm 14th, lost 3rd last* 4 14

Moderate but consistent; needs easy 3 miles; tough to find a race at 15. 16

BANTON LOCH br.g. 9 Lochnager - Balgownie by Prince Tenderfoot (USA) J D Hankinson

1995 1(14),P(0)

219 24/2 Newtown (L) RES 3m 17 GS *mid-div, 7th aft 13th, wkng whn hit 3 out, p.u. nxt* P 0

787 31/3 Tweseldown (R) RES 3m 9 G *rear, not qckn 13th, late prog frm 2 out* 4 13

1189 21/4 Tweseldown (R) RES 3m 10 GF *w.w. went dist 2nd 13th, ld aft 3 out, untidy last, easily* 1 17

1458 8/5 Uttoxeter (L) HC 3 1/4m 8 G *mstks, bhnd, lost tch 15th, t.o. when p.u. before 3 out.* P 0

Has won 2 weak races; barely stays and will need to find same to win again. 17

BAPTIST JOHN(IRE) b.g. 8 The Parson - Corrielek by Menelek P R M Philips

215 24/2 Newtown (L) OPE 3m 20 GS *n.j.w. in tch to 12th, t.o. & p.u. 14th* P 0

428 9/3 Upton-On-Se' (R) RES 3m 17 GS *last whn p.u. 15th* P 0

689 30/3 Chaddesley ' (L) MDN 3m 15 G *disp 3rd, blnd nxt, f 11th* F

883 6/4 Brampton Br' (R) MDN 3m 13 GF *trckd ldrs going wll, ev ch 16th, no ext frm 3 out* 3 12

1047 13/4 Bitterley (L) MDO 3m 13 G *prog to cls 3rd at 7th, ev ch 11th, not qckn nxt, kpt on* 4 11

Gradually finding form & not disgraced last two starts; may win if truly staying in 97 13

BARDAROS b.g. 7 Lighter - Suttons Hill by Le Bavard (FR) Mrs D M Stevenson

14 14/1 Cottenham (R) MDO 3m 10 G *prom, chsd ldr 13th, ld apr 3 out, lft well clr last* 1 17

248 25/2 Charing (L) RES 3m 12 GS *(fav) trckd ldrs frm 8th, 3rd 4 out, rdn & no ext apr last* 3 15

593 23/3 Parham (R) RES 3m 11 GS *rear, prog 9th, ld 14th, made rest, comf* 1 18

965 8/4 Heathfield (R) INT 3m 6 G *(fav) mid-div, prog 12th, lft in ld 14th, drw clr 4 out, easy* 1 20

Useful novice pointer; sold Ascot June to Lucinda Russell; best R/H. 21

BARE FISTED ch.g. 8 Nearly A Hand - Ba Ba Belle by Petit Instant R W Phizacklea

1995 P(0),P(0),5(0),3(0),7(0),P(0),5(0),1(13)

329 3/3 Market Rase' (L) RES 3m 12 G *alwys rear, t.o. 11th, p.u.last* P 0

396 9/3 Garthorpe (R) RES 3m 9 G *nvr dang, 5th & outpcd frm 6 out* 4 0

635 23/3 Market Rase' (L) RES 3m 8 GF *2nd til lft in ld 12th, ct last, no ext* 2 11

971 8/4 Thorpe Lodge (L) RES 3m 4 GF *(fav) ld to 5 out, jmpd wll to ld agn 2 out, ran on* 1 15

1177 21/4 Mollington (R) INT 3m 14 F *in tch til 8th & rear hlfwy, no prog aft* 8 0

1458 8/5 Uttoxeter (L) HC 3 1/4m 8 G *wd, chsd ldr, pkd 10th, wknd 15th, t.o. 4 out.* 4 0

1548 18/5 Southwell (L) HC 3m 110yds 11 GF *ld 5th to 7th, soon wknd, t.o. when p.u. 4 out.* P 0

Won 2 modest races; novice-ridden; jumps well but well below confined class. nil 14

BARGAIN AND SALE br.g. 11 Torenaga - Miss Woodville by Master Buck D J Minty

1995 **P(NH),9(NH),3(NH),3(NH),P(NH),U(NH),3(NH),8(NH),12(NH),P(NH)**

133 17/2 Ottery St M' (L) OPE 3m 18 GS *nvr on terms, onepcd* 6 16

209 24/2 Castle Of C' (R) OPE 3m 8 HY *mid-div to 8th, wknd & p.u. 12th* P 0

468 10/3 Milborne St' (L) OPE 3m 5 G *ld/disp to 4 out, outpcd by wnr aft* 2 17

626 23/3 Kilworthy (L) OPE 3m 12 GS *prom, ld 7-11th, wknd 14th, t.o.* 7 0

927 8/4 Bishopsleigh (R) OPE 3m 7 G *mid-div til cls order 9th, bad mstk 16th, wknd qckly* 4 0

1111 17/4 Hockworthy (L) MXO 3m 13 GS *prom to 10th, wkng whn mstk 13th, t.o. & p.u. last* P 0

1529 12/5 Ottery St M' (L) OPE 3m 7 GF *ld aft 2nd til 3 out, rallied to disp nxt, ld last,drvn clr* 1 19

1550 18/5 Bratton Down (L) CON 3m 8 F *handy, ld aft 14th til 3 out, kpt on onepcd* 3 18

1636 1/6 Bratton Down (L) OPE 4m 11 G *ld/disp to 19th, 3rd & outpcd nxt, demoted frm 4 out* 5 16

1650 8/6 Umberleigh (L) CON 3m 7 GF *chsd ldrs, mstks 8 & 9th, wknd & p.u. aft nxt* P 0

Tough & battle-hardened; found weak race & Confineds needed for win at 12; Any 18

BARICHSTE ch.g. 8 Electric - Be Sharp by Sharpen Up — Major M Watson
1995 **3(NH),U(NH)**
79 11/2 Wetherby Po' (L) MDO 3m 12 GS *ran out 4th* r -
307 2/3 Great Stain' (L) MDO 3m 17 GS *alwys mid-div, wkng whn p.u. 2 out* P 0
516 16/3 Dalton Park (R) MDO 3m 11 G *in tch, chsd ldr 15th, ld 2 out, comf* 1 14
758 31/3 Great Stain' (L) RES 3m 17 GS *chsd ldrs til p.u. bef 4th* P 0
1090 14/4 Whitwell-On' (R) RES 3m 17 G *mid-div, prog 13th, no hdwy aft, onepcd* 7 0
1131 20/4 Hornby Cast' (L) RES 3m 17 G *disp early, prom til wknd 12th, t.o. & p.u. 14th* P 0

Lightly-raced till 96; beat a poor lot & struggling in Restricteds since 13

BARKIN b.g. 13 Crash Course - Annie Augusta by Master Owen — Peter Saville
1995 P(0),P(0),1(16),1(16),**P(0)**,4(15),2(17),**P(0)**
24 20/1 Barbury Cas' (L) XX 3m 12 GS *rear whn f 1st* F -
290 2/3 Eaton Hall (R) OPE 3m 6 G *chsng grp to 4 out, sn outpcd* 5 13
664 24/3 Eaton Hall (R) CON 3m 15 S *ld/disp 5th-4 out, ev ch nxt, onepcd* 4 10
1028 13/4 Alpraham (R) MEM 3m 5 GS *(fav) cls up, lft in ld 10th, hrd rddn 4 out, just held on* 1 16
1152 20/4 Whittington (L) CON 3m 9 G *ld mstly til aft 3 out, hdd & no ext* 3 11
1369 4/5 Gisburn (R) CON 3m 10 G *lft in ld 15th, styd on well* 1 18

Dual winner 95; slow now & fortunate last start; Members best hope at 14; G-S 15

BARMERVILLE br.m. 7 Tudorville - Mateta by Whistling Top — Mrs C Mason
1995 P(0),F(-),2(12)
15 14/1 Cottenham (R) MDN 3m 14 G *in tch in rear, outpcd 14th* 7 0

A little promise 95; brief campaign 96; go close if fit in 97. 13

BARMUR (Irish) — **I** 43^{F}, **I** 150^{P}, **I** 204^{5}, **I** 428^{P}

BARNABY BOY b.g. 8 Ayyabaan - Owen's Hobby by Owen Anthony — J L Brown
1995 F(-),3(12),F(-)
551 17/3 Erw Lon (L) MDN 3m 8 GS *alwys prom, chal whn p.u. last, lame* P 0
771 31/3 Pantyderi (R) MDN 3m 14 G *trckd ldrs, ev ch 2 out-last, kpt on flat* 3 14
1040 13/4 St Hilary (R) MDN 3m 12 G *(fav) rear, rpd prog to 2nd 13th, ld nxt, ran on whn chal 2 out* 1 15
1266 27/4 Pyle (R) RES 3m 10 G *hld up,prog 7th,cls up 14th,strng run 2 out,ld flat* 1 17
1486 11/5 Erw Lon (L) MEM 3m 4 F *(fav) settld rear to 6th, prog frm 9th, hrd rdn to ld aft last* 1 17

Improved & showed right attitude; Confineds well within grasp 97; Opens need more; G-F 19

BARNADOWN (Irish) — **I** 78^{P}, **I** 117^{P}, **I** 157^{F}

BARN ELMS ch.g. 9 Deep Run - Leara by Leander — Mrs S J Hickman
1995 P(0),1(14),U(-),**4(14),4(NH),4(NH),4(NH),6(NH)**
249 25/2 Charing (L) XX 3m 11 GS *rear,steady prog final cct,ld 4 out,hdd & mstk 2 out,no ext* 3 15
453 9/3 Charing (L) XX 3m 4 G *trckd ldrs, 3rd & ev ch whn f 2 out* F -
965 8/4 Heathfield (R) INT 3m 6 G *w.w. prog to 4l 3rd 16th, btn nxt, jmpd slwly last, wlkd in* 3 0
1207 21/4 Heathfield (R) CON 3m 9 F *rear, prog 16th, 3rd 4 out, wknd apr last* 6 11
1440 6/5 Aldington (L) INT 3m 5 HD *trckd ldrs, rddn & outpcd 2 out* 4 13

Placed novice chases 95; changed hands; struggles to stay and will need poor race to win again. 13

BARNEY BOY b.g. 6 Lightning Dealer - True Poet by True Song — J H Caplin
641 23/3 Siddington (L) RES 3m 20 S *n.j.w. sn bhnd, p.u. appr 5th* P 0

Looked clueless on debut. 0

BARNEY BROOK ro.g. 9 Neltino - Binney Brook by Roman Warrior — R J Symonds
20 14/1 Tweseldown (R) RES 3m 9 GS *5s-5/2,hld up,prog 10th,chsd ldr 14th,ld last,not extnd* 1 21
252 25/2 Charing (L) INT 3m 7 GS *(fav) jmpd slwly early,chsd wnr 8th,3rd & no imp whn p.u.13th,lame* P 0

Maiden winner 93; missed 94/5; quite able but problems again last start; G/S 21

BARNEY CROSS gr.g. 6 Silly Prices - Queen Bell by King Sitric — K Waters
321 2/3 Corbridge (R) MDN 3m 12 GS *nvr going wll, p.u. 5th* P 0
406 9/3 Dalston (R) MDO 2 1/2m 12 G *last whn ref 3rd* R -

An unpromising start. 0

BARNEY RUBBLE b or br.g. 11 Politico (USA) - Peak Princess by Charlottown — M R Slater
1995 **4(NH),1(NH),4(NH),4(NH)**
851 6/4 Sandon (L) MEM 3m 6 GF *outpcd, nvr nrr then 3rd* 3 0

Fair winner under Rules & in points but looks finished now 0

BARNEYS GOLD(IRE) ch.g. 7 Orchestra - Fair Corina by Menelek — Mrs R White

1995 **4(NH),8(NH)**

73 11/2 Wetherby Po' (L) MDO 3m 15 GS *ld to 8th, 2nd at 13th, ran out nxt* r
238 25/2 Southwell P' (L) MDO 3m 9 HO *trckd ldrs, mstk 10th & lost tch, t.o. 4 out, fin strngly* 3 1
397 9/3 Garthorpe (R) MDN 3m 9 G *cls up til f 5th* F
590 23/3 Wetherby Po' (L) MDO 3m 16 S *cls up til wknd 14th, poor 3rd frm nxt* 3
967 8/4 Thorpe Lodge (L) MEM 3m 7 GF *disp til ran out 7th, cont, p.u. nxt* P
973 8/4 Thorpe Lodge (L) MDO 3m 7 GF *2nd outing, ran out bend aft 2nd, cont, p.u. 12th* P

Beat only one other finisher & taking the mickey; best avoided 10

BARNISH ROSE (Irish) — I 105[P]

BARN POOL b.g. 14 High Season - Mint Express by Pony Express E S Collins
1995 7(0),P(0),4(0),7(0),2(12),P(0),3(14),5(0)

160 17/2 Weston Park (L) OPE 3m 16 G *mid to rear, some late prog, nvr dang* 5 11
214 24/2 Newtown (L) CON 3m 21 GS *alwys rear, nvr dang* 10
261 2/3 Warwick (L) HC 3 1/4m 5 G *chsd lding pair til apr 4th, not fluent 6th, soon t.o..* 4 1
578 20/3 Ludlow (R) HC 3m 7 G *prom, hit 3rd, soon lost pl and well bhnd, t.o. when blnd and u.r. last.* U
691 30/3 Llanvapley (L) CON 3m 15 GS *alwys rear, lft 4th by dfctns* 4
881 6/4 Brampton Br' (R) CON 3m 9 GF *nvr nr ldrs, ran on strngly frm 16th* 4 13
1042 13/4 Bitterley (L) CON 3m 9 G *ld to 7th, outpcd aft 12th* 6 10
1158 20/4 Llanwit Maj' (R) OPE 4m 9 GS *alwys rear, lost tch 20th, 5th & no ch frm 3 out* 5 14
1410 6/5 Cursneh Hill (L) MEM 3m 4 GF *made all, 8l up 9th, prssd whn lft clr last* 1 12
1478 11/5 Bredwardine (R) CON 3m 12 G *(bl) lost tch 5th, t.o. & p.u. last* P

Ultra-safe but just a schoolmaster now but popped up to land bad Members 12

BARON BIGFOOT b.g. 7 Baron Blakeney - Elvira by Master Spiritus Mrs J H North Lewis
1995 3(10)

712 30/3 Barbury Cas' (L) MDO 3m 10 G *alwys rear, t.o. & p.u. 14th* P
1242 27/4 Woodford (L) RES 3m 18 G *s.s., some prog to 9th hlfwy, nvr on terms, p.u. 16th* P
1433 6/5 Ashorne (R) MDO 3m 16 G *alwys 1st trio, chsd wnr 14th, kpt on, unable chal* 2 13

Lightly-raced so far but ran well last start & should win in 97 if appearing regularly 14

BARONBURN b.m. 6 Baron Blakeney - Stella Romana by Roman Warrior Martin Kemp
1995 **11(NH),9(NH)**

569 17/3 Wolverhampt' (L) MDN 3m 11 GS *chsd ldrs, 3rd whn f 11th* F
689 30/3 Chaddesley ' (L) MDN 3m 15 G *chsd ldrs, ev ch 3 out, blnd nxt, 2nd & btn whn f last* F

Shows some ability but season lasted 2 weeks; may go close if fit in 97 13

BARON KNAYBER b.g. 7 Karlinsky (USA) - Moon Girl by Impersonator S G Edwards

876 6/4 Higher Kilw' (L) MDN 3m 11 GF *bhnd,last at 13th,prog 15th,disp 2 out,ev ch whn f last* F

Very lightly-raced but good enough to win if standing full season in 97 15

BARON RUSH b.g. 8 Baron Blakeney - Orvotus C Rush
1995 P(0),P(0),2(13),1(13),3(13),P(0),4(10),U(-)

38 3/2 Wadebridge (L) MEM 3m 4 GF *chsd wnr to 7th, disp 2nd 13th-3 out, wknd rpdly* 3
199 24/2 Lemalla (R) RES 3m 17 HY *sn bhnd, t.o. & p.u. 2 out* P
871 6/4 Higher Kilw' (L) RES 3m 9 GF *7s-3s, in tch, ld 13th-15th, 3rd whn p.u. 2 out, lame* P

Won a poor Maiden 95 & struggling since; problems last start & can only be watched 13

BARON'S HEIR b.g. 9 Town And Country - Lady London by London Gazette Mrs J L Livermore

545 17/3 Erw Lon (L) CON 3m 10 GS *mid-div, prog 13th, onepcd frm 3 out* 3 1
745 31/3 Upper Sapey (R) INT 3m 6 GS *cls up til outpcd 12th, lft 3rd 2 out* 3 15
1177 21/4 Mollington (R) INT 3m 14 F *rmnrds 3rd,sn wll bhnd,9th hlfwy,styd on to poor 4th 3 out* 4 13
1220 24/4 Brampton Br' (R) OPE 3m 10 G *20l 3rd at 12th, styd on frm 15th, clsng flat* 2 1
1509 12/5 Maisemore P' (L) OPE 3m 4 F *3rd/4th til chsd clr ldr 15th, styd on to ld flat, sn clr* 1 17
1614 27/5 Hereford (R) HC 3m 1f 110yds 16 G *midfield, outpcd hfwy, styd on 2 out, tk 2nd run-in, not trbl wnr.* 2 1

Missed 95; safe & stays but onepaced & found easy chance; may win again 97; G-F 19

BARRAFONA(IRE) ch.g. 8 Green Shoon - Bulabos by Proverb G A Fynn
1995 P(0),F(-),P(0),3(0)

217 24/2 Newtown (L) RES 3m 17 GS *prom to 8th, wknd 10th, wll bhnd whn u.r. 13th* U
357 3/3 Garnons (L) RES 3m 14 GS *mid-div til wknd 11th, t.o. & p.u. 3 out* P

Ex-Irish; shown nothing in England. 0

BARRETTE b.m. 6 Sergeant Drummer (USA) - Cinbar by Cintrist N E Lethbridge

875 6/4 Higher Kilw' (L) MDN 3m 6 GF *just in tch til crashd thro wing 9th* r
1116 17/4 Hockworthy (L) MDO 3m 9 GS *t.o. & p.u. 3rd* P

Uninspiring start; can only do better. 0

BARROW STREET b.g. 6 Sula Bula - Kerry Street by Dairialatan Mrs R A Vickery
1995 r(-),P(0)
788 31/3 Tweseldown (R) MDO 3m 8 G *dwelt, last, mstk & lost iron 5th, blnd nxt & p.u.* P 0
993 8/4 Kingston St' (R) MDO 3m 17 F *pllng, cls up til ld 7th, tiring whn blnd & hdd 3 out,wknd* 4 0
187 21/4 Tweseldown (R) MDN 3m 11 GF *prom, lft in ld 8th, hdd 14th, btn 3 out, p.u. last* P 0
396 6/5 Cotley Farm (L) MDO 3m 11 GF *prom, ld 5th til ran out aft 9th* r -
569 19/5 Mollington (R) MDO 3m 10 GS *prom, chal & mstk 13th, wknd aft 15th, walked in* 7 0
Shows speed but devoid of stamina; jumps poorly as well. 12

BARRY GLEN ch.g. 7 Vital Season - Polo Pam by Tiepolo II G F Wheeler
1995 F(-)
3 13/1 Larkhill (R) MDO 3m 10 GS *chsd ldrs, blnd 5th, btn 13th, p.u. last* P 0
Showed promise 94; only 2 runs since; best watched now. 12

BARRY OWEN b.g. 10 Owen Anthony - Tacita by Tacitus Mrs A Lockwood
1995 P(0),1(17),1(20),1(21),7(15),1(18),F(-),P(0),1(22),**F(-)**
76 11/2 Wetherby Po' (L) LAD 3m 8 GS *ld to 10th, fdd rpdly, p.u. 4 out* P 0
119 17/2 Witton Cast' (R) LAD 3m 4 S *disp to 8th, wknd 11th, nvr a dang aft* 3 13
305 2/3 Great Stain' (L) LAD 3m 11 GS *prom, 3l 3rd whn blnd & u.r. 14th* U -
367 6/3 Catterick (L) HC 3m 1f 110yds 12 G *mstks, in tch, hdwy hfwy, slight ld 12th till f 15th.* F -
513 16/3 Dalton Park (R) OPE 3m 9 G *ld 2-3rd, prom til wknd 14th, t.o. & p.u. 16th* P 0
587 23/3 Wetherby Po' (L) OPE 3m 15 S *mid-div, f 7th, dead* F -
Dead 18

BARRYS AVENUE (Irish) — **I** 117P, **I** 142P, **I** 185U, **I** 334P
BART EILE (Irish) — **I** 223P
BARTLEMY KING (Irish) — **I** 69, , **I** 245P, **I** 306P, **I** 457P
BARTON BULLDOZER(IRE) b.g. 6 Bulldozer - Black Pilot by Linacre Mrs G B Balding
1995 R(-)
602 23/3 Howick (L) OPE 3m 11 S *t.o. whn u.r. 6th* U -
850 6/4 Howick (L) MDN 3m 14 GF *t.o. 9th, p.u. 12th* P 0
162 20/4 Llanwit Maj' (R) MDO 3m 12 GS *blndrd bdly & u.r. 2nd* U -
Bulldozing the fences at present. 0

BARTON ROYAL(IRE) b.g. 6 Petorius - Royal Sensation by Prince Regent (FR) J Barnes
1995 **5(NH),U(NH)**
398 9/3 Dalston (R) MEM 3m 13 G *prom whn f 9th* F -
499 16/3 Lanark (R) LAD 3m 10 G *ld 4th-7th, lost tch 3 out* 3 0
153 20/4 Whittington (L) LAD 3m 10 G *(bl) ld 6-12th, wknd 14th* 4 0
Beaten miles both completions & does not stay 0

BASHER BILL b.g. 13 Maystreak - Rugby Princess by El Gallo K D Giles
1995 P(0),P(0),11(0),4(0),3(10),3(10),5(11),2(12),P(0),2(11),**9(0)**
32 20/1 Higham (L) OPE 3m 15 GF *alwys bhnd, t.o. & p.u. aft 11th* P 0
449 9/3 Charing (L) RES 3m 13 G *prom to 7th, wll bhnd frm 15th* 5 0
570 17/3 Detling (L) MEM 3m 6 GF *chsd ldr to hlfwy, in tch aft, ran on frm 3 out, mstk nxt* 2 10
779 31/3 Penshurst (L) RES 3m 13 GS *f 1st* F -
810 6/4 Charing (L) RES 3m 6 F *ld/disp to 13th, grad wknd aft* 5 0
917 8/4 Aldington (L) RES 3m 4 F *mstk 4th, cls up, outpcd 12th, ran on 3 out, no imp flat* 2 13
329 30/4 Huntingdon (R) HC 3m 14 GF *well bhnd from 11th, t.o..* 7 0
441 6/5 Aldington (L) MEM 3m 4 HD *(fav) wth ldr, ld 11th, kpt on wll whn chal 2 out* 1 12
536 16/5 Folkestone (R) HC 2m 5f 9 GF *cl up, reminders 7th, lost pl next, t.o..* 5 0
Very moderate; 2 wins last 35 starts; fortunate to have 2 Members; G-Hd. 12

BASHINDORA (Irish) — **I** 23P
BASIL GREY gr.g. 7 Grey Ghost - Lady Buttons by New Brig S G Jones
1995 r(-),U(-),P(0),U(-)
228 24/2 Duncombe Pa' (R) MDO 3m 9 GS *pllng, chsd ldrs, 3rd whn f 12th* F -
330 3/3 Market Rase' (L) MDO 3m 7 G *ld/disp til ld 3 out, hdd apr last, no ext* 2 10
415 9/3 Charm Park (L) MDO 3m 13 G *ld to 4th, hdd, 3rd 2 out, outpcd aftr* 3 10
591 23/3 Wetherby Po' (L) MDO 3m 14 S *prom til grad wknd frm 3 out* 3 0
823 6/4 Stainton (R) MEM 3m 6 GF *prom,ld 14th-3 out, ran wd straight, rallied to ld last* 1 15
090 14/4 Whitwell-On' (R) RES 3m 17 G *trckd ldrs, ld 11th til jnd 4 out, fdd nxt, onepcd* 4 12
Failed to finish first 5 races but improved; just stays; may have Restricted chances on easy 3m; G-F ... 15

BATCHO MISSILE ch.g. 7 Cruise Missile - Peticienne by Mummy's Pet Ian Gilbert
1995 P(0)
901 6/4 Dingley (R) MDN 2m 5f 9 GS *in rear whn u.r. 2nd* U -
105 14/4 Guilsborough (L) MDN 3m 12 G *plld hrd,hld up bhnd,prog 10th,last & wkng whn f 15th* F -

1177 21/4 Mollington (R) INT 3m 14 F *n.j.w. last pair & t.o. til p.u. 11th* P
1376 5/5 Dingley (R) MEM 3m 7 GF *last til prog 3rd, prom whn mstk & u.r. 5th* U
1378 5/5 Dingley (R) MDO 2 1/2m 16 GF *2nd outing, s.s. last til f 5th* F

Way off course at present; unpromising. **0**

BATHWICK BOBBIE b.g. 9 Netherkelly - Sunwise by Roi Soleil W Cliffor

255 28/2 Taunton (R) HC 4 1/4m 110yds 15 GS *bhnd most of way, t.o. when p.u. before 3 out.* P
906 8/4 Fakenham (L) HC 2m 5f 110yds 11 G *soon prom, styd on same pace from 3 out.* 3 2
1383 6/5 Towcester (R) HC 2 3/4m 7 GF *held up in tch, mstk 5th, ev ch 2 out, no ext last.* 2 2

Mixed novice chasing & H/Chases but struggling to win; Rules looks better option **20**

BATSI b.g. 12 Battlement - Bright Upham by Paridel Mrs E A Hex
1995 P(0),2(17),F(-),4(0),3(16),**P(0)**,1(18)

198 24/2 Lemalla (R) OPE 3m 12 HY *nvr trbld ldrs, p.u. 2 out* P
297 2/3 Great Treth' (R) INT 3m 10 G *rear, strgglng 7th, t.o. & p.u. 2 out* P
1543 17/5 Newton Abbot (L) HC 3 1/4m 110yds 8 G *lways bhnd, t.o. 7th, p.u. before 12th.* P

Restricted winner 95; interrupted season 96 & showed nothing; can only be watched at 13 .... **11**

BATTLE HARD (Irish) — I 310^{P}, I 435^{P}

BATTLE HERO gr.g. 13 Miami Springs - Smeralda by Grey Sovereign J W Hughe
1995 **P(0)**

615 23/3 Friars Haugh (L) MEM 3m 9 G *bhnd til stdy prog frm hlfwy, jnd wnr apr last, no ext* 2 1
1084 14/4 Friars Haugh (L) LAD 3m 8 F *u.r. 8th* U
1352 4/5 Mosshouses (L) LAD 3m 10 GS *prom, ld 9th-aft 12th, wknd 15th, p.u. 2 out* P
1572 19/5 Corbridge (R) LAD 3m 8 G *sn last, u.r. 3rd* U

2nd in dire Members; no chance in normal races. **0**

BATTYS BEARINGS (Irish) — I 518, , I 548^{5}

BAUNFAUN RUN (Irish) — I 499^{F}

BAVINGTON b.g. 5 Meadowbrook - Bargello's Lady by Bargello Ian Hamilto

1088 14/4 Friars Haugh (L) MDO 3m 10 F *sn t.o., p.u. 4 out* P

A gentle introduction; can do better. **0**

BAWNAVINOGUE LADY (Irish) — I 609^{P}, I 649^{F}

BAY BLOSSOM b.m. 6 El Conquistador - Apple Blossom by Orange Bay Miss Kim Trip

531 16/3 Cothelstone (L) CON 3m 12 G *in tch til wknd 12th, t.o.& p.u. 4 out* P
644 23/3 Cothelstone (L) MEM 3m 6 S *ld to 5th, chsd ldr aftr p.u. lame bfr 15th* P

A glimmer of hope but problems last start; more needed. **0**

BAYBUCK (Irish) — I 197^{U}, I 296^{P}, I 358^{P}

BAY HOBNOB b.g. 5 Buzzards Bay - Woody Isle by Precipice Wood A J Maso

643 23/3 Siddington (L) MDN 3m 16 S *schoold in rear til p.u. 13th* P
796 2/4 Heythrop (R) MDN 3m 11 F *mstk 5th, in tch to 12th, t.o. & p.u. 2 out* P
1217 24/4 Andoversford (R) MDO 3m 16 G *alwys last trio, blndrd 6th, last & blndrd 16th, p.u. nxt* P

Only schooling so far; looks capable of improving. **0**

BAY LEADER b.m. 8 Leander - Cascade Bay Vii G I Isaa
1995 **U(NH),P(NH),10(NH)**

152 17/2 Erw Lon (L) MDN 3m 11 G *alwys rear, fin 6th, plcd 5th* 5
357 3/3 Garnons (L) RES 3m 14 GS *wll bhnd frm 6th, nvr nr ldrs* 6
504 16/3 Magor (R) MEM 3m 5 GS *made all, clr hlfwy, prssd 15th, qcknd clr* 1
694 30/3 Llanvapley (L) RES 3m 9 GS *alwys last, styd on own pace* 3
1158 20/4 Llanwit Maj' (R) OPE 4m 9 GS *rear, lost tch 18th, t.o. & p.u. 2 out* P
1415 6/5 Cursneh Hill (L) RES 3m 11 GF *7th & in tch 9th, no qckn frm 12th* 5
1601 25/5 Bassaleg (R) RES 3m 12 GS *alwys last, lft 4th by dfctns* 4

Won a really bad contest & thrashed all other starts; future prospects unappealing **10**

BAYLINE LAD (Irish) — I 22^{U}, I 40^{F}, I 201^{5}

BAY LOUGH (Irish) — I 43^{P}, I 85^{P}, I 325^{5}, I 443^{3}, I 649^{P}

BAYLOUGHBESS (Irish) — I 569^{P}, I 589^{5}, I 652^{6}

BAY OWL b.g. 12 Paico - Dietrich by Sardis Mrs A P Glassfor
1995 P(0),P(0),F(-),U(-),U(-),1(20),1(17)

162 17/2 Weston Park (L) OPE 3m 16 G *f 2nd* F
458 9/3 Eyton-On-Se' (L) INT 3m 11 G *mid to rear, some late prog, no ch 1st 3* 4

664 24/3 Eaton Hall (R) CON 3m 15 S *nvr going well, p.u. 8th* P 0
736 31/3 Sudlow Farm (R) CON 3m 9 G *prog to chs ldr 13th, ev ch til wknd 2 out, fin lame* 3 14
1151 20/4 Whittington (L) INT 3m 12 G *alwys rear, p.u. 3 out* P 0
1230 27/4 Weston Park (L) CON 3m 7 G *mid-div to hlfwy, mstks, sn btn* 7 0

Dual winner 95; showed virtually nil in 96; tough to win at 13; G-F. 16

BAY TIGER b.g. 8 Bay Express - Perang's Niece by High Award Miss J Froggatt
1995 r(-),P(0),r(-),P(0)
166 17/2 Weston Park (L) MDN 3m 10 G *rear, t.o. 4th, p.u. 7th* P 0
241 25/2 Southwell P' (L) MDO 3m 15 HO *pllng, in tch til p.u. 5th* P 0
458 9/3 Eyton-On-Se' (L) INT 3m 11 G *r.o. 2nd* r -
568 17/3 Wolverhampt' (L) MDN 3m 9 GS *rear, t.o. 14th, p.u. 2 out* P 0
664 24/3 Eaton Hall (R) CON 3m 15 S *rear, p.u. 11th* P 0
852 6/4 Sandon (L) MDN 3m 9 GF *mstks, rear, p.u. 13th* P 0
1196 21/4 Sandon (L) MDN 3m 17 G *mid to rear, t.o. & p.u. 4 out* P 0

Yet to get round and looks hopeless. 0

BAYVIEW PRINCE (Irish) — I 15^{P}, I 65, , I 72^{P}, I 202^{5}, I 294^{F}, I 371^{P}
BEACHBOROUGH b.g. 6 Sizzling Melody - Appleby Park by Bay Express Exors Of The Late Mr G W Mills
1105 14/4 Guilsborough (L) MDN 3m 12 G *pllng, hld up, bhnd frm 10th, blnd badly 12th & p.u.* P 0
1378 5/5 Dingley (R) MDO 2 1/2m 16 GF *ldng grp til p.u. 10th* P 0
1568 19/5 Mollington (R) MDO 3m 9 GS *33s-4s, prom, wth ldr whn f 11th* F -
1644 2/6 Dingley (R) MDO 3m 16 GF *hld up, prog & mstk 11th, sn btn, t.o. whn p.u. 3 out* P 0

Looks the part but jumping needs attention; proabably worth keeping an eye on. 12

BEACH TIGER gr.g. 12 Java Tiger - Lido Light by Good Light T R Hills
1995 3(15),U(-),2(13),4(0),**2(10)**
570 17/3 Detling (L) MEM 3m 6 GF *(fav) prog to trck ldr 12th, chal whn lft in ld 3 out, pshd clr* 1 12
778 31/3 Penshurst (L) INT 3m 6 GS *alwys last & detached,jmp slwly thruout,t.o. whn p.u. aft9th* P 0
1442 6/5 Aldington (L) RES 3m 7 HD *ld to 2nd, prom aft, wknd 15th, poor 3rd whn p.u. 2 out* P 0
1536 16/5 Folkestone (R) HC 2m 5f 9 GF *mid div, prog to chase ldrs 9th, lost tch 11th, t.o. when p.u. before last.* P 0

Won awful Members; does not stay in proper races; Members only chance again. 12

BEANS (Irish) — I 243^{P}
BEAR NECESSITIES b.g. 11 Ya Zaman (USA) - Flower Parade by Mill Reef (USA) D E Fletcher
1995 P(0),**F(-)**,3(16),**U(-)**,2(13),**3(13)**
258 29/2 Nottingham (L) HC 3m 110yds 10 G *chsd ldrs, driven along when pace lifted final cct, blnd and u.r. 7 out.* U -

Good enough for Maiden win but badly placed; finished early 96; can win Maiden at 12. 15

BEAR'S FLIGHT ch.g. 9 Royal Vulcan - Semi-Colon by Colonist II Mrs J Hadden-Wight
1995 1(20)
230 24/2 Heythrop (R) MEM 3m 12 GS *mid-div til u.r. 7th* U -
381 9/3 Barbury Cas' (L) XX 3m 9 GS *ld, going wll whn ran out 13th* r -
519 16/3 Larkhill (R) CON 3m 5 G *sttld bhnd, prog whn lost irons 4 out, onepcd aft* 3 17
1171 20/4 Chaddesley ' (L) OPE 3m 15 G *s.s. nvr rchd ldrs, t.o. & p.u. last* P 0
1244 27/4 Woodford (L) INT 3m 12 G *mid-div, lost tch apr 16th, last whn nrly ref last, t.o.* 7 0

Lightly raced but good pointer to 95; changed hands; novice ridden & declined in 96; best watched. ... 15

BEAT THE RAP b.g. 10 Wolverlife - Juries Slip Mrs R J Morrison
240 25/2 Southwell P' (L) MDO 3m 15 HO *wth ldr 5th-13th, wknd rpdly, p.u. 4 out* P 0
343 3/3 Higham (L) MDO 3m 11 G *mid-div til prog 11th, ld 14th, made rest, kpt on* 1 12
904 6/4 Dingley (R) RES 3m 20 GS *prog 10th, 6th 6 out, no ext* 6 0
1025 13/4 Brocklesby ' (L) XX 3m 9 GF *mid-div, prog 5 out, 2nd 3 out, wknd nxt* 4 10
1341 4/5 Warwick (L) HC 2 1/2m 110yds 12 GF *alwys in rear, bhnd and rdn 8th, t.o..* 8 0
1540 16/5 Folkestone (R) HC 2m 5f 10 G *ld to 3rd, prom till wknd apr 2 out.* 6 0
1639 2/6 Dingley (R) MEM 3m 7 GF *ld to 3rd, wknd 12th, t.o. 2 out, walked in* 5 0

Won poor Maiden; well beaten after and stamina doubts; another win looks tough. 13

BEAU BO'S RETURN b.m. 5 Jupiter Island - Formidable Lady by Formidable (USA) Harold Winton
1995 **8(NH)**
668 26/3 Sandown (R) HC 2 1/2m 110yds 8 GS *mstk 5th, bhnd, lost tch 8th, hdwy to chase wnr from 3 out, no ext run-in.* 2 24

Sensational H/Chase debut & could prove highly useful in future 29

BEAU CINQ (Irish) — I 27^{4}, I 134^{F}
BEAU DANDY ch.g. 9 Le Bavard (FR) - Best Dressed by Pumps (USA) C C Shand Kydd
1995 1(21),1(20)

244	25/2	Southwell P'	(L)	CON	3m	13	HO	*trckd ldrs, 2nd frm 11th-15th, wknd 3 out*	3 14
434	9/3	Newton Brom'	(R)	CON	3m	11	GS	*ld to 1st & frm nxt, hdd 3 out, wknd rpdly*	4 10
676	30/3	Cottenham	(R)	INT	3m	13	GF	*pllng, prom, ld 12th, lft clr aft 2 out, drvn & hld on well*	1 22
897	6/4	Dingley	(R)	CON	3m	15	GS	*(fav) cls up, hrd hld, ld 11th, drew clr 4 out, comf*	1 23
1107	15/4	Southwell	(L)	HC	3m 110yds	10	G	*nvr far away, pushed along 14th, btn last 3.*	4 17
1383	6/5	Towcester	(R)	HC	2 3/4m	7	GF	*(fav) ld to 4th, regained ld 6th, made rest, rdn out.*	1 22
1532	13/5	Towcester	(R)	HC	2m 110yds	16	GF	*(fav) ld 4th to four out, rallied to ld 100 yards out, edged right, ran on.*	1 25
1584	24/5	Towcester	(R)	HC	3m 1f	11	GS	*chsd ldr from 6th, prom till wknd after six out, bhnd when p.u. before 2 out.*	P 0

Tough, solid, versatile; won 8 of last 14; best R/H; can win more H/Chases 97; Any 26

BEAUDEL (Irish) — **I** 10^P, **I** 58^P

BEAU GEM b.m. 8 Kalaglow - Tentraco Lady by Gay Fandango (USA) Ian Wormald

1995 P(0),4(0),2(13),5(0),1(15),4(15)

118	17/2	Witton Cast'	(R)	INT	3m	9	S	*cls up to 6th, mid-div aft, no dang*	5 0

Improved 95; finished early 96; may still win short course restricted if fit 97;G-F 16

BEAU ROSE b.g. 13 Beau Charmeur (FR) - Rosantus by Anthony Miss C A Blakeborough

1995 2(17),P(0),2(10)

190	24/2	Friars Haugh	(L)	LAD	3m	7	S	*nvr nr ldrs*	5 0
320	2/3	Corbridge	(R)	OPE	3m 5f	8	GS	*mid-div, lft 3rd 18th, nvr nrr*	3 0
512	16/3	Dalton Park	(R)	CON	3m	10	G	*trckd ldrs, rdn 16th, ld 2 out, hdd & no ext flat*	2 16
824	6/4	Stainton	(R)	CON	3m	11	GF	*rear, rdn & prog 9th, jmpd slwly 14th, sn wknd, t.o.*	5 0
1134	20/4	Hornby Cast'	(L)	MEM	3m	6	G	*alwys prom, ev ch 3 out, not qckn flat*	2 14
1369	4/5	Gisburn	(R)	CON	3m	10	G	*alwys bhnd, p.u. 15th*	P 0

Formerly useful; runs the odd good race now but unlikely to win at 14. 14

BEAUTY PET b.m. 7 Ayyabaan - Miss Beauty by Hollywood Star E H Williams

1995 F(-)

263	2/3	Didmarton	(L)	INT	3m	18	G	*s.v.s. mstk 1st, t.o. til u.r. 8th*	U -

Yet to reach halfway on 2 starts 95/6. 0

BECCY BROWN b.m. 8 Rabdan - Sarona by Lord Of Verona Mrs F T Walton

1995 U(-),2(11),9(0),**6(NH),F(NH)**

402	9/3	Dalston	(R)	XX	3m	13	G	*n.j.w. alwys strgglng, p.u. 14th*	P 0
613	23/3	Friars Haugh	(L)	MDN	3m	15	G	*sn bhnd, p.u. 4 out.*	P 0
1476	11/5	Aspatria	(L)	MDO	3m	16	GF	*mid-div, prog 9th, ld 15th, clr whn blnd last, comf*	1 15

Hacked up in competitive race (winner behind); inconsistent but can improve. 16

BECKFORD b.g. 7 Stanford - Combe Hill by Crozier P D F Strawson

168	18/2	Market Rase'	(L)	MEM	3m	7	GF	*alwys last, t.o. 10th, u.r. 12th*	U -
331	3/3	Market Rase'	(L)	MDO	3m	9	G	*chsd ldr, ld 11th, hrd prssd whn lft wll clr 3 out, tired*	1 13
635	23/3	Market Rase'	(L)	RES	3m	8	GF	*w.w. prog 6 out, 2nd nxt, ev ch whn squeezed aft 2 out,s.u.*	S -
726	31/3	Garthorpe	(R)	RES	3m	16	G	*mid-div, 8th hlfwy, effrt 14th, 5th 3 out, no prog aft*	7 12
1025	13/4	Brocklesby '	(L)	XX	3m	9	GF	*mid-div, cont 4th wth wnr 3 out, fdd, p.u. last*	P 0

Won a poor race & struggling after; Restricted prospects slight 13

BECTIVE BOY ch.g. 14 Wolverlife - Al Radegonde by St Alphage A S Jones

1995 P(0),1(21),3(19),**3(19),P(0)**

252	25/2	Charing	(L)	INT	3m	7	GS	*chsd wnr frm 8th, jmpd slwly & btn 3 out*	4 0
472	10/3	Milborne St'	(L)	INT	3m	8	G	*sn rear, wll bhnd frm 15th*	5 0
784	31/3	Tweseldown	(R)	CON	3m	5	G	*chsd wnr 11th til blnd 4 out, not rcvr*	4 0
1244	27/4	Woodford	(L)	INT	3m	12	G	*prog 8th, 3rd & ev ch 16th, sn btn, p.u. & dismntd last*	P 0

Won confined 95; problems later; below form in 96 and unlikely to win again;G-S. 16

BEDAHOKEY (Irish) — **I** 385^P

BEDWYN BRIDGE ch.m. 5 Over The River (FR) - Grotto Princess by Pollerton Gavin Hudson

127	17/2	Kingston Bl'	(L)	MEM	3m	6	GS	*alwys last, t.o. 8th, p.u. aft 13th*	P 0

No show on debut 0

BEE-A-SCALLY ch.m. 5 Scallywag - Beringa Bee by Sunley Builds Mrs C E Whiteway

1234	27/4	Weston Park	(L)	MDO	3m	13	G	*rear, jmp novcy, no ch whn p.u. 6 out*	P 0

Only learning on debut. 0

BEE MOY DO(IRE) b.g. 8 Kambalda - Gentle Goose by Push On A Leigh

1995 **8(NH),3(NH),3(NH),11(NH),P(NH)**

598	23/3	Howick	(L)	MEM	3m	6	S	*ld to 10th, wknd 14th, lost 2nd 3 out*	3 0

843 6/4 Howick (L) MEM 3m 7 GF *ld to 12th, cls 2nd til f 3 out* F -
1481 11/5 Bredwardine (R) RES 3m 14 G *prom to 5th, lost plc 8th, t.o. 14th, p.u. nxt* P 0

Beaten miles when 3rd & has no prospects in points 0

BEET SPRAY (Irish) — **I** 7^P, **I** 132^P

BEET STATEMENT (Irish) — **I** 24^P, **I** 29^4, **I** 382^P, **I** 483^1, **I** 496^1, **I** 633^P, **I** 648^1, **I** 657^2

BEEWORTHY b.m. 6 Gunner B - Miss Starworthy by Twilight Alley — J Swinnerton

1995 P(0),U(-)

286 2/3 Eaton Hall (R) MDO 3m 14 G *mid to rear, hmpd & u.r. 13th* U -
464 9/3 Eyton-On-Se' (L) MDN 2 1/2m 13 G *s.s. sn in tch, outpcd 5 out, p.u. 3 out* P 0
661 24/3 Eaton Hall (R) MDN 3m 9 S *mid to rear, nvr dang, p.u. 3 out* P 0
949 8/4 Eyton-On-Se' (L) MDN 3m 5 GF *(fav) cls up til pce increased 3 out, not qckn frm 2 out* 3 13

Beaten under 6 lengths on only completion (favourite?); more needed 12

BEINN MOHR b.m. 9 Rymer - Misty Sky by Hot Brandy — Mrs B C Willcocks

1995 2(18),**3(0)**,7(0),3(15)

524 16/3 Larkhill (R) INT 3m 11 G *alwys mid-div, nvr nrr* 5 0
628 23/3 Kilworthy (L) INT 3m 7 GS *made most til blnd & hdd 11th, not rcvr, p.u. 13th* P 0
866 6/4 Larkhill (R) INT 3m 4 F *trckd wnnr, outpcd 12th, wll btn frm 5 out* 3 0
1112 17/4 Hockworthy (L) PPO 3m 9 GS *ld 6th til hdd & mstk 9th, bhnd 13th, rdn out flat* 6 0
1311 28/4 Little Wind' (R) INT 3m 6 G *rear, pshd alng 12th, out of tch 15th, styd on to 4th last* 4 10
1397 6/5 Cotley Farm (L) CON 3m 4 GF *cl up, ld 9th, styd on wl frm 2 out* 1 20
1553 18/5 Bratton Down (L) XX 3m 10 F *j.w. ld apr 6th, made rest, lft clr 3 out, comf* 1 20
1633 1/6 Bratton Down (L) XX 3m 8 G *6s-3s, ld & slw jmp 2nd, hdd 8th, rdn & wknd 14th* 5 11

Fair at best but needs to dominate & makes mistakes; hard ride; may win again; G-F 20

BELGROVE STAR (Irish) — **I** 558^P, **I** 583^F

BELLA BROWNIE (Irish) — **I** 501^2

BEL LANE b.m. 7 Brotherly (USA) - Bow Lane by Idiot's Delight — M R Watkins

1995 P(0),P(0),U(-),P(0)

220 24/2 Newtown (L) MDN 3m 12 GS *alwys rear, t.o. & p.u. 14th* P 0
354 3/3 Garnons (L) MDN 2 1/2m 13 GS *hld up til prog frm 9th, ran on 3 out, nrst fin* 4 14
697 30/3 Llanvapley (L) MDN 3m 11 GS *(fav) alwys prom, clsd 15th, disp to 2 out, just outpcd* 2 14
1044 13/4 Bitterley (L) MDO 3m 15 G *(fav) 40l 4th at 7th, 6l 3rd 12th, tired 2nd & ref 2 out, cont* 2 0

Improved & good enough for a win but may need easy three miles & fortune 14

BELLE OF KILBRIDE (Irish) — **I** 196^F, **I** 226^F, **I** 324^P

BELL GLASS(FR) gr.g. 10 Bellypha - Greener Pastures (FR) by Rheingold — G Walters

1995 **7(NH)**,**4(NH)**,**1(NH)**

547 17/3 Erw Lon (L) OPE 3m 10 GS *(fav) mid-div, p.u. 8th* P 0
692 30/3 Llanvapley (L) OPE 3m 6 GS *cls up, ld 9-11th, wknd rpdly, p.u. 13th* P 0

Useful at best but short season 96 & all not well; best watched 16

BELL HUNTER (Irish) — **I** 172^P, **I** 255^P, **I** 282^4, **I** 411^P, **I** 456^1, **I** 537^P

BELLMAN b.g. 11 Barley Hill - Bellote by Seven Bells — R H T Cox

22 20/1 Barbury Cas' (L) XX 3m 19 GS *prom to 8th, steadily wknd, t.o. & p.u. 15th* P 0
255 28/2 Taunton (R) HC 4 1/4m 110yds 15 GS *mid div till hit 11th and wknd, t.o. when p.u. before 19th.* P 0

Shock open winner 93; of no account now. 10

BELLS WOOD br.g. 7 Sousa - Virtuosity by Reliance II — A J K Dunn

70 10/2 Great Treth' (R) MDO 3m 14 S *chsd ldrs, 4th & btn whn f 2 out* F -
202 24/2 Lemalla (R) MDO 3m 12 HY *alwys chsng grp, slight ld 4 out-2 out, kpt on onepcd* 2 14
713 30/3 Barbury Cas' (L) MDO 3m 10 G *8s-5s, sttld mid-div, effrt 12th, no rspns, t.o. & p.u. 2out* P 0
1116 17/4 Hockworthy (L) MDO 3m 9 GS *sn trckd ldr, ld 11th, clr aft 2 out, comf* 1 14
1313 28/4 Little Wind' (R) RES 3m 14 G *cls 7th at 9th,ev ch 4 out,wknd rpdly, p.u.2 out,lost shoe* P 0

Found a weak race but ran well last start (good contest) & may have Restricted chances 97 16

BELMOUNT BEAUTY(IRE) b or br.m. 7 Sheer Grit - Kakala by Bargello — G B Foot

282 2/3 Clyst St Ma' (L) MDN 3m 8 S *mid-div, prog 12th, 2nd at 14th, ld 3 out, easily* 1 13
466 10/3 Milborne St' (L) RES 3m 13 G *cls up, ev ch 12th, lost tch 4 out, p.u. last* P 0

Ex-Irish; trotted up at Clyst & ran in hot race after; short season; win Restricted if fit 97; Soft 16

BELTANE THE SMITH ch.g. 16 Owen Anthony - North Bovey by Flush Royal — J C Sweetland

1392 6/5 Cotley Farm (L) MEM 3m 5 GF *ld to 11th, disp to 3 out, outpcd aft* 3 0

Winning pointer/hurdler; only 2 runs 94-6; too old now. 14

BELTINO gr.g. 5 Neltino - Thorganby Bella by Porto Bello — Mrs S A Sutton

192	24/2	Friars Haugh	(L) MDN 3m	12	S	*alwys wll bhnd*	8	0
859	6/4	Alnwick	(L) MDO 2 1/2m	5	GF	*chsd ldrs thro'out, t.o. frm 15th*	2	0
1356	4/5	Mosshouses	(L) MDO 3m	12	GS	*12s-6s, trckd ldrs, 6th & strggling whn f 14th*	F	-
1476	11/5	Aspatria	(L) MDO 3m	16	GF	*prom, blnd & lost plc 10th, no ch aft, t.o. frm 15th*	6	0

Only beaten one horse so far; makes mistakes; more needed. 10

BELVILLE POND (Irish) — **I** 430P, **I** 474P

BE MY HABITAT ch.g. 7 Be My Guest (USA) - Fur Hat by Habitat — L J Hawkings

1995 **P(NH),P(NH),5(NH),P(NH),4(NH),P(NH),P(NH)**

133	17/2	Ottery St M'	(L) OPE 3m	18	GS	*mid-div to 12th, lost tch & p.u. 4 out*	P	0
278	2/3	Clyst St Ma'	(L) CON 3m	9	S	*bhnd til f 15th*	F	-
531	16/3	Cothelstone	(L) CON 3m	12	G	*rr 7th, t.o. & p.u appr 13th*	P	0
647	23/3	Cothelstone	(L) CON 3m	6	S	*(bl) cl up till 12th, mstk 13th, lost tch aftr.*	4	0
1110	17/4	Hockworthy	(L) CON 3m	9	GS	*(bl) n.j.w., alwys bhnd, t.o. & u.r. 15th*	U	-
1346	4/5	Holnicote	(L) LAD 3m	5	GS	*(bl) sn bhnd, p.u. 14th*	P	0
1526	12/5	Ottery St M'	(L) LAD 3m	5	GF	*(bl) not fluent, sn bhnd, t.o.*	5	0

Winning hurdler; shows no apptitude for pointing. 0

BENBEATH b.g. 6 Dunbeath (USA) - Steelock by Lochnager — C Batty

1995 **5(NH)**

175	18/2	Market Rase'	(L) MDO 2m 5f	8	GF	*(fav) pllng, chal going wll apr last, ran wd, ran on flat*	2	14
332	3/3	Market Rase'	(L) MDO 3m	8	G	*(fav) trckd ldrs going wll, jnd wnr & f 3 out*	F	-
1136	20/4	Hornby Cast'	(L) MDN 3m	11	G	*(fav) alwys prom, ev ch whn mstk 15th, no imp aft*	5	0

Ran well novice hurdle 94/5; unlucky not to win yet; should recoup losses in 97. 14

BENGERS MOOR b.g. 5 Town And Country - Quilpee Mai by Pee Mai — J R Townshend

471	10/3	Milborne St'	(L) MDO 3m	16	G	*handy, lft in ld 15th, sn clr, easily, imprssv*	1	16
729	31/3	Little Wind'	(R) RES 3m	12	GS	*(fav) hld up,hdwy 11th,ld 3 out,hdd & wknd qckly 2 out,eased runin*	2	20
1128	20/4	Stafford Cr'	(R) RES 3m	17	S	*(fav) held up, prog 10th, 2nd 3 out, strgly rdn to ld cls home*	1	20

Useful youngster; beaten by good horses; one to watch; G-S. 24

BENNAN MARCH br.g. 9 Daring March - Sweet And Shiny by Siliconn — N W A Bannister

1995 **P(NH),7(NH)**

326	3/3	Market Rase'	(L) OPE 3m	14	G	*t.o. 6th, p.u. last*	P	0
634	23/3	Market Rase'	(L) OPE 3m	6	GF	*cls up, mostly 3rd to 2 out, wknd rpdly*	4	13
760	31/3	Great Stain'	(L) OPE 3m	8	GS	*mid-div, rmndr 4th, wknd frm 7th, t.o. & p.u. 11th*	P	0
1024	13/4	Brocklesby '	(L) OPE 3m	6	GF	*alwys last, t.o. frm 4th*	3	0
1154	20/4	Whittington	(L) OPE 3m	7	G	*3rd whn f 13th*	F	-
1363	4/5	Gisburn	(R) MEM 3m	5	G	*(fav) (bl) s.s. lft 30l, ld 5th, rdn & hdd 14th, no ext*	3	0

Winning chaser; did not beat another horse; looks jaded & best avoided. 12

BENNETTS HILL (Irish) — **I** 500,

BENNY THE BISHOP (Irish) — **I** 21P, **I** 236[4], **I** 481P, **I** 628[1], **I** 629[2]

BEN ORE (Irish) — **I** 608P, **I** 642P, **I** 652,

BENS UNYOKE (Irish) — **I** 227P, **I** 266P, **I** 346F

BENUAD ch.g. 10 Le Moss - Hogan's Cherry by General Ironside — J R W Hole

1995 3(0),2(12),2(15),1(15)

388	9/3	Llanfrynach	(R) RES 3m	20	GS	*alwys prom, 3rd & outpcd aft 14th, no prog frm nxt*	4	0
844	6/4	Howick	(L) RES 3m	10	GF	*rear, prog to 2nd at 9th, lost plc nxt, 3rd 14th, styd on*	3	0
1160	20/4	Llanwit Maj'	(R) RES 3m	12	GS	*ld to 5th, bhnd & rdn 10th, t.o. & p.u. 2 out*	P	0
1266	27/4	Pyle	(R) RES 3m	10	G	*mid-div, lost plc 13th, no ch nxt, p.u. 2 out*	P	0

Lucky " winner" 95; struggling now upgraded; late season restricted best hope. G-F.; G-F 15

BERKANA RUN ch.g. 11 Deep Run - Geraldine's Pet by Laurence O — R J Bailey

1995 4(11),4(0),**5(0)**,U(-)

1177	21/4	Mollington	(R) INT 3m	14	F	*last pair & sn t.o.*	9	0
1438	6/5	Ashorne	(R) XX 3m	14	G	*9th & wll out of tch whn u.r. 6th*	U	-
1563	19/5	Mollington	(R) CON 3m	8	GS	*alwys bhnd, t.o. last at 8th, p.u. 12th*	P	0
1611	26/5	Tweseldown	(R) XX 3m	9	G	*chsd ldrs,lft 2nd 11th-aft 3 out,3rd & btn,blnd & u.r. last*	U	-

Dual winner 93; lost last 15 races; of no real account now. 10

BERRINGS DASHER ch.g. 9 Slippered - Lady Actress by Arctic Slave — J A C Ayton

1995 1(20),**3(21)**

274	2/3	Parham	(R) OPE 3m	12	GF	*cls up, pshd alng 12th, wknd 15th, p.u. nxt*	P	0
594	23/3	Parham	(R) CON 3m	13	GS	*cls up til wknd rpdly 13th, p.u. nxt*	P	0
778	31/3	Penshurst	(L) INT 3m	6	GS	*cls up, ld 10-12th & brfly 3 out, wknd nxt*	2	16
1050	13/4	Penshurst	(L) CON 3m	8	G	*jnd ldrs 7th, ld 12th, hrd prssd 4 out, hdd & wknd 2 out*	3	18

1444 6/5 Aldington (L) OPE 3m 6 HD *held up, clsd 15th, chal frm 3 out, wknd last* 2 18
1536 16/5 Folkestone (R) HC 2m 5f 9 GF *(fav) mid div, went 2nd 8th, ld 10th, hdd last, wknd run-in.* 2 17

Irish Maiden winner 94; placed in weak H/chases; deserves win but stamina problems deny him. 19

BERT HOUSE b.g. 10 Brianston Zipper - Salmon Spirit by Big Deal A J Cottle

925 8/4 Bishopsleigh (R) CON 3m 6 G *ld 4th, front rank til 11th, wknd qckly, p.u. 2 out* P 0
1110 17/4 Hockworthy (L) CON 3m 9 GS *chsd ldr to 10th, wknd, 6th whn f 13th* F -
1427 6/5 High Bickin' (R) CON 3m 10 G *mid-div, btn 6th whn p.u. aft 16th* P 0
1550 18/5 Bratton Down (L) CON 3m 8 F *(bl) ld 3rd-5th, cls up til wknd 14th, last whn u.r. 16th (ditch)* U -
1623 27/5 Lifton (R) OPE 3m 5 GS *lost ground & rmndrs apr 14th, bhnd & p.u. 2 out, lame* P 0

Does not stay & problems last start 0

BERVIE HOUSE(IRE) br.g. 8 Strong Gale - Bramble Hill by Goldhill Mrs Judy Wilson

1995 **F(-)**,1(18),1(20)

124 17/2 Kingston Bl' (L) CON 3m 17 GS *(fav) 3s-6/4,w.w. prog to chs 1st 2 11th,wknd rpdly 15th,p.u.nxt* P 0
434 9/3 Newton Brom' (R) CON 3m 11 GS *hld up rear,prog to jn ldrs 14th,ev ch 3 out,wknd, p.u. last* P 0
1098 14/4 Guilsborough (L) CON 3m 17 G *prom, mstk 13th, rdn in 5th & btn apr 3 out, wknd* 6 12
1236 27/4 Clifton On ' (L) CON 3m 8 GF *trckd ldrs, ld 13th, rdn & hdd 2 out, btn whn mstk last* 2 18
1456 8/5 Uttoxeter (L) HC 2m 5f 11 G *waited with, in tch till f 8th.* F -
1547 18/5 Fakenham (L) HC 2m 5f 110yds 11 G *alwys rear, t.o. when p.u. before 3 out.* P 0

Changed hands; good stable but disappointing 96; best watched. 16

BESSIE LOVE b.m. 14 Trusmadoor - Evening Surprize by Willipeg R Dixon

1155 20/4 Whittington (L) MDN 3m 14 G *(bl) last pair in rear, sn t.o. & p.u. 11th* P 0
1476 11/5 Aspatria (L) MDO 3m 16 GF *(bl) u.r. 1st* U -

Of no account. 0

BEST INTEREST (Irish) — **I** 103U

BEST LEFT br.m. 6 Gennaro (FR) - Right Lady by Right Flare P L Southcombe

649 23/3 Cothelstone (L) LAD 3m 3 S *ref 1st* R -

Well named so far. 0

BEST VINTAGE (Irish) — **I** 468P, **I** 5494, **I** 6395

BET A LOT ch.m. 7 Balinger - Crimson Flag by Kinglet R Hutchison

1995 P(0)

1177 21/4 Mollington (R) INT 3m 14 F *mid-div & out of tch by 5th, no ch whn p.u. 12th* P 0
1241 27/4 Clifton On ' (L) MDO 3m 8 GF *cls up til mstk & wknd 16th, t.o.* 4 0

Season lasted 6 days in 96 & yet to achieve much; may still do better 12

BETSY GRAY (Irish) — **I** 601F, **I** 632F

BETTER BY HALF(IRE) br.g. 8 Strong Gale - Belle Bavard by Le Bavard (FR) J F Symes

301 2/3 Great Treth' (R) MDO 3m 13 G *mstk 4th, t.o. & p.u. 13th* P 0
446 9/3 Haldon (R) MDO 3m 13 S *rear, some prog 9th, bhnd whn p.u. 13th* P 0
993 8/4 Kingston St' (R) MDO 3m 17 F *10th hlfwy, f heavily 15th* F -
1392 6/5 Cotley Farm (L) MEM 3m 5 GF *alws last, t.o. whn p.u. 13th* P 0

No signs of ability. 0

BETTER FUTURE(IRE) br.g. 7 Good Thyne (USA) - Little Else C J Hitchings

160 17/2 Weston Park (L) OPE 3m 16 G *alwys rear, p.u. 14th* P 0
212 24/2 Castle Of C' (R) CON 3m 7 HY *handy, disp frm 14th, ld 2 out, styd on* 1 20
350 3/3 Garnons (L) CON 3m 11 GS *10l 4th at 9th, not qckn 13th, styd on onepcd frm 3 out* 3 18
692 30/3 Llanvapley (L) OPE 3m 6 GS *(fav) rear, prog to 2nd at 14th, 2l down last, qcknd to ld flat* 1 20
1171 20/4 Chaddesley ' (L) OPE 3m 15 G *w.w. prog 12th, chsd ldr 14th, ev ch til no ext frm 3 out* 3 23

Ex-Irish; stays & consistent; ran well last start; more Opens likely in 97; G-Hy 23

BETTIVILLE b.g. 9 Sandalay - Kylenora by Dusky Boy R D Russell

1995 P(0),4(0),F(-),4(10),3(12),3(16)

236 24/2 Heythrop (R) MDN 3m 13 GS *mostly mid-div, wknd & p.u. 16th* P 0
430 9/3 Upton-On-Se' (R) MDO 3m 15 GS *5th 3 out, ran on frm 2 out, nrst fin* 3 11
841 6/4 Maisemore P' (L) MDN 3m 9 GF *(fav) in tch, ld 14th, clr 3 out, jmpd slwly last, drvn out* 1 15
1292 28/4 Barbury Cas' (L) RES 3m 11 F *prom, ld 6-7th, wknd 15th, wll bhnd whn p.u. last* P 0

Beat subsequent winner when scoring but modest at best & more needed for Restricted chances 97; G-S 15

BETTY BALFOUR (Irish) — **I** 226P, **I** 291F, **I** 3251

BETTY'S PEARL ch.g. 15 Gulf Pearl - Paiukiri by Ballyciptic Miss Gillian A Russell

527 16/3 Larkhill (R) MEM 3m 4 G *alwys rear, t.o. 8th, btn 2 fences* 4 0

Crept round in his Members(as usual). 0

BETTYS ROSE(IRE) ch.m. 5 Roselier (FR) - Bail Out by Quayside E H Crow

1196 21/4 Sandon (L) MDN 3m 17 G *mid-div, u.r. 11th* U -

Only learning on debut. 0

BETWEEN YOU AND ME gr.g. 6 Baron Blakeney - Win Shoon Please by Sheshoon Philip Simmonds

205 24/2 Castle Of C' (R) MDO 3m 9 HY *mid-div til lost tch 12th, t.o. & p.u. 14th* P 0
466 10/3 Milborne St' (L) RES 3m 13 G *cls up early, mid-div whn f 13th* F -
644 23/3 Cothelstone (L) MEM 3m 6 S *cl 3rd till 7th, t.o. from 13th, p.u. bfr 4 out* P 0
729 31/3 Little Wind' (R) RES 3m 12 GS *rear til p.u. apr 2 out* P 0

Shows speed but no stamina so far. 0

BET WITH BAKER(IRE) br.g. 6 Ovac (ITY) - Moate Gypsy by Fine Blade (USA) George W Baker

143 17/2 Larkhill (R) MDO 3m 14 G *nvr bttr than mid-div, rear whn p.u. 14th* P 0
205 24/2 Castle Of C' (R) MDO 3m 9 HY *cls up, chsd ldr 13th, ev ch 3 out, outpcd aft nxt* 2 11
557 17/3 Ottery St M' (L) MDN 3m 10 G *(fav) hld up, prog 13th, chal 3 out, ld nxt, sn clr* 1 15
707 30/3 Barbury Cas' (L) RES 3m 18 G *(fav) 3s-9/4, hld up, prog 10th, ld 4 out, ran on frm 2 out* 1 20
1112 17/4 Hockworthy (L) PPO 3m 9 GS *hld up, prog 8th, mstks 12th & nxt, 4th & btn 2 out, kpt on* 3 21

Top stable, promising & ran well in hot race last start; could do well in 97; Good 23

BET WITH ROSIE (Irish) — I 427[2], I 475[1]

BEWDLEY BOY ch.g. 7 Brando - Quiet Queen by Richboy J E Grey

1995 3(0),6(0)

268 2/3 Didmarton (L) MDN 3m 10 G *j.w. ld 4th til apr last, sn ld agn, ran on well* 1 15
650 23/3 Cothelstone (L) RES 3m 5 S *(fav) blnd 6th, ld to 2 out, hdd and one pace aftr.* 2 17
1002 9/4 Upton-On-Se' (R) RES 3m 8 F *c.u., chsd wnr 13-14th, wknd qckly, p.u. 15th* P 0

Won well but problems last start; jumps well; can win Restricted if fit 97; G-S 18

BEYOND BELIEF (Irish) — I 323[P]

BEYOND OUR REACH br.g. 8 Reach - Over Beyond by Bold Lad (IRE) Hunt & Co (Bournemouth) Ltd

1995 **1(NH),3(NH),2(NH),P(NH),6(NH)**

208 24/2 Castle Of C' (R) LAD 3m 14 HY *2s-1/1, in tch, ld 13th, going clr whn f nxt* F -
561 17/3 Ottery St M' (L) LAD 3m 12 G *(fav) hld up, mid-div whn hmpd & u.r. 7th* U -
708 30/3 Barbury Cas' (L) LAD 3m 10 G *(fav) cls 3rd whn f 9th* F -
818 6/4 Charlton Ho' (L) LAD 3m 6 GF *(Jt fav) held up, in 4th whn u.r. 6th* U -

Winning hurdler and has returned to that field; too Miss Curling's relief no doubt. 22

BIANCONI b.g. 10 I'm A Star - Coach Road by Brave Invader (USA) D Luxton

1995 **5(NH),P(NH),4(NH),11(NH)**

135 17/2 Ottery St M' (L) LAD 3m 11 GS *alwys mid-div, lost tch 13th, bhnd whn p.u. 4 out* P 0
442 9/3 Haldon (R) CON 3m 6 S *made most, mstk 11th, hdd aft 15th, fdd frm 2 out* 4 13

Winning chaser; lightly raced now; weak Confined in Soft only hope. 17

BIBLICAL b.m. 9 Montekin - Bap's Miracle by Track Spare D Jeffries

909 8/4 Towcester (R) HC 2 3/4m 6 F *bhnd from 8th, t.o. when p.u. before 2 out.* P 0
1182 21/4 Mollington (R) MDN 3m 10 F *ld to 2nd, rear 8th, no ch 13th, ran on 3 out, tk 3rd last* 3 0
1433 6/5 Ashorne (R) MDO 3m 16 G *ld 3-5th & frm 8th, clr 3 out, styd on und pres flat* 1 14
1562 19/5 Mollington (R) MEM 3m 6 GS *ld to 9th, wknd 11th, sn t.o., p.u. last* P 0
1641 2/6 Dingley (R) RES 3m 13 GF *prom to 8th, rr & rdn 10th, p.u. 13th* P 0

Missed 95; lasted home in weak Maiden; stamina problems make a follow up tough. 16

BIDDERS CLOWN b.g. 11 Ring Bidder - Lucky Joker by Cawston's Clown Mrs M J Wall

161 17/2 Weston Park (L) LAD 3m 11 G *chsng grp, mstks, fdd & p.u. 3 out* P 0

No prospects now 0

BIDDLESTONE BOY(NZ) b.g. 9 Wolverton - In Liefde (NZ) by In The Purple (FR) D H Barons

71 10/2 Great Treth' (R) MDO 3m 15 S *mid-div, ran on onepcd frm 3 out, nrst fin* 3 11
131 17/2 Ottery St M' (L) MDN 3m 10 GS *ld/disp til blnd & u.r. 3 out* U -
300 2/3 Great Treth' (R) MDO 3m 10 G *(Jt fav) prom, cls 2nd 15th, drvn to slight ld 2 out, hdd last* 2 14
482 13/3 Newton Abbot (L) HC 2m 5f 110yds 14 S *(vis) mstk 4th, prom till f 9th.* F -
562 17/3 Ottery St M' (L) XX 3m 12 G *w.w. prog 14th, chsd wnr 3 out, no ext frm nxt* 2 15

Ran really well last start & a certainty for Maiden win on that form if fit in 97; G-S 16

BIDORE b.g. 8 Ore - Pleasure Bid by Mon Plaisir Mrs R Hurley

959 8/4 Lockinge (L) MDN 3m 6 GF *prom early, lost tch 12th, p.u. 4 out* P 0

Not yet of any account 0

BIDSTON MILL ch.g. 11 Main Reef - Allotria by Red God — S Kidston

1995 7(0),5(10),C(-),F(-),3(0),4(11),6(0),2(14),4(0),5(0)

1072	13/4	Lifton	(R)	LAD	3m	7	S	*nov rddn, alwys towrds rear, t.o., p.u. apr 2 out*	P	0
1124	20/4	Stafford Cr'	(R)	CON	3m	7	S	*rear whn f 4th*	F	-
1277	27/4	Bratton Down	(L)	CON	3m	15	GF	*mid-div, outpcd 12th, no ch whn p.u. 2 out*	P	0
1426	6/5	High Bickin'	(R)	LAD	3m	3	G	*sn rear, lost tch 12th*	3	0
1552	18/5	Bratton Down	(L)	LAD	3m	7	F	*rear, t.o. frm 9th, p.u. 12th*	P	0
1589	25/5	Mounsey Hil'	(R)	OPE	3m	12	G	*alwys bhnd, t.o. 7th, p.u. 14th*	P	0
1635	1/6	Bratton Down	(L)	LAD	3m	13	G	*mstk 3rd, sn last, t.o. frm 9th*	13	0
1648	8/6	Umberleigh	(L)	LAD	3m	11	GF	*sn last & wll bhnd, t.o. 7th*	8	0

Lost last 29 races and will not break the sequence. 10

BIG BAD JOHN (Irish) — **I** 16^{U}

BIG BO (Irish) — **I** 68^{2}

BIG BUCKLEY b.m. 6 Buckley - Cadenette by Brigadier Gerard — R M Phillips

1995 4(0),2(10)

220	24/2	Newtown	(L)	MDN	3m	12	GS	*(Jt fav) wth ldr, blnd 6th, chsng aft, tired frm 15th*	3	0
431	9/3	Upton-On-Se'	(R)	MDO	3m	17	GS	*7th & wkng whn f 3 out*	F	-
749	31/3	Upper Sapey	(R)	MDO	3m	17	GS	*alwys strggling, last whn p.u. last*	P	0
1416	6/5	Cursneh Hill	(L)	MDO	3m	9	GF	*held up, trckng ldrs whn mstk & u.r. 6th*	U	-
1485	11/5	Bredwardine	(R)	MDO	3m	15	G	*alwys prom, 6l 4th 3 out, hit nxt, no ext apr last*	3	11
1621	27/5	Chaddesley '	(L)	MDO	3m	17	GF	*nvr nr ldrs, wll bhnd whn p.u. 14th*	P	0

Placed 4 times 95/6 but beat only one other finisher 96 & most unlikely to win 10

BIG CHARLIE (Irish) — **I** 390^{P}

BIG JACK(IRE) b.g. 6 Phardante (FR) - Sketch Plan — M Murphy

59	10/2	Cottenham	(R)	RES	3m	9	GS	*mstk 1st,ld 7th,clr 14th,reluc aft,not run on & hdd apr last*	2	13
679	30/3	Cottenham	(R)	RES	3m	15	GF	*hld up, lost tch rpdly 13th, p.u. nxt*	P	0
1329	30/4	Huntingdon	(R)	HC	3m	14	GF	*disp 2nd from 6th till f 12th.*	F	-

Irish Maiden winner 95; very mulish on debut and one to avoid; changed hands after 2nd run. 12

BIG JIMMY (Irish) — **I** 166^{P}

BIG MAC gr.g. 9 Warpath - Susan McIntyre by Double Jump — I L Davies

1995 **6(NH),2(NH),F(NH),6(NH)**

1471	11/5	Aspatria	(L)	MEM	3m	4	GF	*in tch, ld apr 12-14th, 2nd & btn whn blndrd & u.r. last*	U	-

Just a hunter now 0

BIG MURT (Irish) — **I** 90^{P}, **I** 112^{F}, **I** 328^{1}, **I** 425^{F}, **I** 498^{5}

BIG REWARD b.g. 7 Big Connaught - Wardbrook by Damsire Unknown — P D Jones

131	17/2	Ottery St M'	(L)	MDN	3m	10	GS	*sn bhnd, t.o. & p.u. 14th*	P	0
555	17/3	Ottery St M'	(L)	MDO	3m	15	G	*ld to 3rd, sn lost plc, t.o. 15th*	5	0
719	30/3	Wadebridge	(L)	MDO	3m	7	GF	*slght ld 8th til hdd 15th, 3l 2nd whn mstk 2 out, ran on wll*	2	12
876	6/4	Higher Kilw'	(L)	MDN	3m	11	GF	*prom til lost plc aft 6th, no ch frm 13th*	5	0
1143	20/4	Flete Park	(R)	MDN	3m	17	S	*alwys bhnd, p.u. last*	P	0
1430	6/5	High Bickin'	(R)	MDO	3m	8	G	*prom til 14th, sn lost plc*	3	12
1531	12/5	Ottery St M'	(L)	MDO	3m	9	GF	*prom, mstk 7th, 4th & rdn 15th, went 2nd 3 out, onepcd*	2	13
1627	27/5	Lifton	(R)	MDO	3m	9	GS	*not alwys fluent, 6th at 10th, lost tch 13th*	4	0

Beaten 4l or less three times but not progressing; may strike lucky eventually; G-F 13

BIG SEAMUS(IRE) ch.g. 6 Carlingford Castle - Galla's Pride by Quayside — Mrs J M Whitley

445	9/3	Haldon	(R)	RES	3m	9	S	*mid-div, went 3rd & styng on 15th, tk 2nd flat*	2	14
719	30/3	Wadebridge	(L)	MDO	3m	7	GF	*(fav) hld up in tch, went 2nd 9th, ld 15th, pshd out*	1	12
939	8/4	Wadebridge	(L)	RES	3m	2	F	*(fav) ld 8-15th, rmndrs nxt, kpt on und pres*	2	12
1345	4/5	Holnicote	(L)	RES	3m	11	GS	*nvr bttr than mid-div*	6	0
1528	12/5	Ottery St M'	(L)	RES	3m	10	GF	*(bl) handy, cls 3rd frm 9th, effrt 2 out, ld last, drvn clr*	1	18

Safe but modest & hard ride; improved by blinkers; may struggle to win in better company; G-F 17

BIG SPENDER (Irish) — **I** 111^{P}, **I** 268^{P}, **I** 341^{U}

BILBO BAGGINS(IRE) ch.g. 8 Beau Charmeur (FR) - Hiking by Royal Highway — Mrs J Pitman

1995 F(-),3(0),6(0),U(-),4(10),4(0),2(14),1(17),P(0)

231	24/2	Heythrop	(R)	XX	3m	10	GS	*chsd ldrs to 10th, wknd rpdly*	6	0
365	5/3	Leicester	(R)	HC	3m	10	GS	*disp ld to 4th, chsd ldr to 8th, wknd 12th.*	6	0
526	16/3	Larkhill	(R)	RES	3m	9	G	*mid-div, mstk 6th, lost ground 10th, ran on frm 4 out*	4	11
787	31/3	Tweseldown	(R)	RES	3m	9	G	*made most to 11th, wknd frm nxt, sn btn*	5	0
1189	21/4	Tweseldown	(R)	RES	3m	10	GF	*hit 1st, nvr going wll, prom til wknd 8th, last & p.u. 2 out*	P	0

Barely stays and must have G/F.will be fortunate to find another win. 14

BILLHEAD b.g. 10 Nicholas Bill - Time-Table by Mansingh (USA) Miss Katie O'Neill
1995 F(-),4(0),**P(0)**,4(0),P(0),1(15),**8(0)**,**8(0)**,**6(0)**,P(0)
237 25/2 Southwell P' (L) MEM 3m 4 HO *ld to 14th, wknd apr 3 out, fin 4th, plcd 3rd* 3 0
378 9/3 Barbury Cas' (L) LAD 3m 6 GS *in rear whn p.u. 8th* P 0
593 23/3 Parham (R) RES 3m 11 GS *mid-div, wknd & p.u. 12th* P 0
708 30/3 Barbury Cas' (L) LAD 3m 10 G *cls up til blnd & u.r. 11th* U -
1019 13/4 Kingston Bl' (L) INT 3m 6 G *s.s. prom to 6th, wknd 8th, t.o. & p.u. 11th* P 0
Won Maiden 95; only form and outclassed in better company; unlikely to win again.ly 12

BILLILLA ch.g. 13 Nicholas Bill - Thorganby Bella by Porto Bello Mrs G Greenwood
1995 **P(0)**,P(0),4(18)
530 16/3 Cothelstone (L) OPE 3m 7 G *in tch til 12th, p.u appr 14th, dead* P 0
Dead. 16

BILLION DOLLARBILL ch.g. 8 Nicholas Bill - Rest Hill Dolly by Balinger Brian Tetley
1995 P(0),P(0),3(0),F(-),1(10),2(14),**5(10)**
36 20/1 Higham (L) RES 3m 12 GF *prom, ev ch apr 2 out, onepcd und pres flat* 2 16
58 10/2 Cottenham (R) RES 3m 7 GS *wth ldrs, drvn to ld last, hld on well cls home* 1 16
271 2/3 Parham (R) CON 3m 15 GF *mid-div, prog 4 out, 4th 3 out, chal last, kpt on wll* 2 20
573 17/3 Detling (L) OPE 4m 9 GF *wll plcd, rdn to ld 3 out,hdd nxt,ld last,hdd line* 2 21
965 8/4 Heathfield (R) INT 3m 6 G *in tch, lft 2nd 14th, rdn 4 out, sn btn* 2 13
1188 21/4 Tweseldown (R) OPE 3m 6 GF *n.j.w. cls up til outpcd frm 13th, sn btn* 5 0
Won modest Restricted; ran well after but not Open class; stays well; can win another race; G/S-F. 18

BILL OF RIGHTS b.g. 8 Nicholas Bill - Cold Line by Exdirectory Mrs E B Scott
465 10/3 Milborne St' (L) RES 3m 11 G *alwys mid-div, bhnd whn p.u. 13th* P 0
644 23/3 Cothelstone (L) MEM 3m 6 S *rluctnt to stt, 3rd 4 out, tired nxt, p.u. 2 out* P 0
709 30/3 Barbury Cas' (L) OPE 3m 15 G *ld to 4th, ld agn 7-11th, grad wknd aft* 8 0
908 8/4 Hereford (R) HC 2m 3f 12 GF *prom till rdn and wknd 10th.* 7 0
Last on both completions & shows no stamina 0

BINCOMBE TOP gr.g. 12 Revlow - Flying Streak by Blue Streak W J Hayes
1995 P(0),**P(0)**,P(0)
925 8/4 Bishopsleigh (R) CON 3m 6 G *alwys wll bhnd, t.o. whn p.u. bfr 11th* P 0
1110 17/4 Hockworthy (L) CON 3m 9 GS *alwys rr, 8th & out of tch whn u.r. 11th* U -
1309 28/4 Little Wind' (R) OPE 3m 8 G *5th whn mstk 10th, rear whn p.u. 14th* P 0
1427 6/5 High Bickin' (R) CON 3m 10 G *mid-div, some late hdwy* 3 17
1590 25/5 Mounsey Hil' (R) INT 3m 8 G *in tch til wknd 15th, p.u. 2 out* P 0
Dual winner 93; ran well when 3rd but not threatening to win now. 0

BINNEY BOY b.g. 7 Broadsword (USA) - Binney Brook by Roman Warrior A D Wardall
1995 1(12)
210 24/2 Castle Of C' (R) INT 3m 10 HY *(fav) mid-div, prog 13th, ev ch 3 out, wknd nxt* 3 17
368 6/3 Lingfield (L) HC 3m 7 S *held up, lost tch after 11th, t.o. when p.u. before 2 out.* P 0
822 6/4 Charlton Ho' (L) RES 3m 7 GF *(Jt fav) ld 13th-3 out, mstks 11th & 14th, disp aft, ld line* 1 18
Lightly raced; won 2 modest races 95/6; more needed for Confineds. 18

BIRCHALL BOY br.g. 8 Julio Mariner - Polarita by Arctic Kanda P L Southcombe
470 10/3 Milborne St' (L) MDO 3m 18 G *ld to 10th, ld agn last, ran on well* 1 15
732 31/3 Little Wind' (R) INT 3m 6 GS *alwys towrds rear, no ch frm 14th* 5 0
1013 13/4 Ascot (R) HC 3m 110yds 11 GS *ld 3rd then made most to 13th, led again 15th, hdd and left in ld 4 out, hded after next, soon lost tch.* 3 12
Ability under Rules & began well in points; outclassed after; Restricted possible; lightly-raced;G/S 17

BIRTLEY GIRL b.m. 12 Le Coq D'Or - Goldness Abbey by Blackness Dennis Hutchinson
582 22/3 Kelso (L) HC 3 1/2m 8 G *n.j.w., soon bhnd, t.o. 10th, p.u. before 3 out.* P 0
1106 15/4 Hexham (L) HC 3m 1f 9 GF *ld 3rd, mstk 15th, hdd next, wknd quickly after 3 out, t.o. when blnd last.* 4 0
1340 4/5 Hexham (L) HC 3m 1f 13 S *chsd ldrs, driven along after 2 out, soon btn.* 5 17
1585 25/5 Cartmel (L) HC 3 1/4m 14 GF *alwys rear, bhnd when p.u. before 14th.* P 0
Won Confined 94; missed 95 and totally outclassed in H/chases. best watched now. 14

BISHOPS TRUTH gr.g. 10 Scallywag - Coumenole by Beau Chapeau Capt T L S Livingstone-Learmonth
1995 **6(NH)**
212 24/2 Castle Of C' (R) CON 3m 7 HY *cls up til 10th, wknd, p.u. 13th* P 0
380 9/3 Barbury Cas' (L) CON 3m 11 GS *mid-div whn u.r. 2nd* U -
Rarely seen & no form in 96; unlikely to figure in future 0

BIT OF A BLETHER(IRE) b.g. 7 Strong Gale - Chatty Actress by Le Bavard (FR) Mrs Alix Stevenson

1995 3(13),1(15),1(19)

187 24/2 Friars Haugh (L) CON 3m 12 S *(fav) abt 5l 2nd & going well whn f 13th* F -

Dual winner 95 (unextended) vanished after falling in 96; one to watch if fit in 97. 23

BIT OF A CITIZEN (Irish) — I 59^{2}, I 76^{1}, I 141^{P}, I 313^{U}, I 333^{P}, I 576^{4}, I 639^{4}, I 656^{4}

BIT OF A CLOWN b.g. 13 Callernish - Gusserane Lark by Napoleon Bonaparte — Mrs Ian McKie

1995 1(22),**2(NH)**,**3(NH)**,**7(0)**

124 17/2 Kingston Bl' (L) CON 3m 17 GS *mid-div, lost tch apr 14th, kpt on onepcd aft* 6 16
793 2/4 Heythrop (R) OPE 4m 10 F *hld up,prog 18th,cls up 3 out,onepcd whn hit last,fin 4th* 3 19
1562 19/5 Mollington (R) MEM 3m 6 GS *wth ldr, ld 9th, jnd 15th, hdd 3 out, fin tired, retired* 2 15

Retired. 19

BITOFAMIXUP(IRE) br.g. 5 Strong Gale - Geeaway by Gala Performance (USA) — Mike Roberts

479 10/3 Tweseldown (R) MDO 3m 10 G *schoold in rear, t.o. 4th, p.u. 10th* P 0
576 17/3 Detling (L) MDN 3m 18 GF *rear,wll bhnd til steady prog 14th,styd on wll,lft 2nd last* 2 11
711 30/3 Barbury Cas' (L) MDO 3m 8 G *(fav) j.w. trckd ldrs, ld 4 out, sn clr, easily* 1 16
1295 28/4 Bexhill (R) RES 3m 7 F *(fav) lft in ld 9th, in cmmnd aft, eased clr apr last* 1 17

Unextended when winning; good stable; one to keep an eye on; G-F. 20

BITOFANATTER ch.g. 8 Palm Track - Little Ginger by Cawston's Clown — David Caldwell

1995 2(12),5(0)

497 16/3 Lanark (R) MEM 3m 2 G *ld til 10th, sn lost tch, t.o. & u.r. last* U -

Promising debut but disappointing since; finished early 96 ; needs to recapture the plot. 11

BIT OF AN IDIOT b.g. 8 Idiot's Delight - Deep Dora by Deep Run — Mrs D E S Surman

1995 U(-),12(0)

129 17/2 Kingston Bl' (L) MDN 3m 15 GS *12s-7s,keen hold,mstk 8th,prom to 13th,5th & no ch, p.u.last* P 0
269 2/3 Didmarton (L) RES 3m 12 G *ld 2-3rd & 10th-15th, no ext aft, promising* 3 16
520 16/3 Larkhill (R) MDO 3m 11 G *ld, 10l clr 13th, wknd & hdd apr last* 2 16

Lightly raced but Maiden looks a formality; needs easy course. 17

BIT OF A SONG (Irish) — I 365^{P}, I 408^{P}, I 455^{P}

BIT OF A TOUCH (Irish) — I 123^{F}, I 152^{5}, I 251^{2}, I 372^{3}, I 442^{P}, I 542^{4}

BITTER ALOE b.g. 7 Green Desert (USA) - Sometime Lucky by Levmoss — Don Cantillon

1995 1(15),P(0)

348 3/3 Higham (L) RES 3m 12 G *prom, chsd wnr 14th, effrt 2 out, no ext last* 2 17
1322 28/4 Fakenham P-' (L) RES 3m 5 G *(fav) jmpd slwly 3rd & nxt, ld 10th, made rest, rdn & kpt on last* 1 18

Lightly raced; won 2 weak races; more needed for confineds; Good 17

BIX b or br.g. 5 Adbass (USA) - Valiant Dancer by Northfields (USA) — J Parfitt

1995 **P(NH)**

358 3/3 Garnons (L) RES 3m 18 GS *s.s. ld 3rd, ran off course 6th* r -
391 9/3 Llanfrynach (R) MDN 3m 11 GS *t.d.e. plld hrd, 2nd whn f 5th* F -
606 23/3 Howick (L) MDN 3m 13 S *hld up, rpd prog to ld 12th, sn clr, impressive* 1 16

Very headstrong but faster time than Dauphin Bleu; could prove useful if keeping sane. 17

BLACK ABBEY (Irish) — I 53^{F}, I 114^{P}, I 293^{1}

BLACK BETH (Irish) — I 19^{P}, I 32^{B}, I 84^{P}, I 134^{3}

BLACK ERMINE(IRE) br.g. 5 Wylfa - Corston Velvet by Bruni — Mrs M Cooper

13 14/1 Cottenham (R) MDO 3m 10 G *(fav) alwys going wl,ld 16th,clr whn swvrd & nrly ref last,rdn out* 1 15
243 25/2 Southwell P' (L) RES 3m 11 HO *(Jt fav) hld up,prog 9th,mstk 11th,no imp ldrs 3 out,fin tired* 5 0

Impressive start; stable out of form 96 and can be excused next run; still potentially decent. 17

BLACK FOUNTAIN (Irish) — I 55^{P}, I 74^{F}, I 148^{F}, I 244^{P}, I 277^{2}, I 440^{F}

BLACKIE CONNORS (Irish) — I 16^{P}, I 110^{3}, I 193^{P}, I 267^{P}, I 390^{3}, I 479^{P}, I 559^{P}, I 616^{S}

BLACKMOUNTAINGIANT (Irish) — I 266^{P}

BLACK PERRIN (Irish) — I 70^{P}, I 187^{4}

BLACK RUSSIAN br.g. 13 Crozier - Adamstown Girl by Lucifer (USA) — Miss M Watson

154 17/2 Erw Lon (L) LAD 3m 14 G *t.o. 3rd, btn 2 fences* 12 0
385 9/3 Llanfrynach (R) LAD 3m 14 GS *t.o. frm 5th, sn mls bhnd* 9 0
546 17/3 Erw Lon (L) LAD 3m 10 GS *twrds rear, wknd rpdly aft 11th, t.o.* 9 0

Last on all three starts & beaten two fences minimum each time! 0

BLACK SANTA (Irish) — I 191^{P}

BLACKWATER FOX (Irish) — I 76^{F}, I 119^{P}, I 211^{P}, I 351^{U}

BLACKWATER LADY (Irish) — **I** 15^{1}, **I** 611^{1}, **I** 639^{1}, **I** 657^{1}

BLACKWOOD, (Irish) — **I** 79^{P}, **I** 137^{P}, **I** 154^{3}, **I** 227^{P}

BLACKWOODSCOUNTRY b.g. 6 Town And Country - Sweet Spice by Native Bazaar — Mrs Winifred A Birkinshaw

1995 P(0),5(0)

414	9/3	Charm Park	(L)	MDO	3m	11	G	*ld 6th-11th, hdd, trckd ldr, no ext, lost 2nd on flat*	3	12
517	16/3	Dalton Park	(R)	MDO	3m	10	G	*(fav) trckd ldr til not qckn & rdn 16th, styd on frm 2 out*	3	13
987	8/4	Charm Park	(L)	MDN	3m	13	GF	*(fav) ld 10th agn frm 13th, styd on wll*	1	16
1131	20/4	Hornby Cast'	(L)	RES	3m	17	G	*mid-div most of way, wknd 13th, p.u. 2 out*	P	0
1466	11/5	Easingwold	(L)	CON	3m	10	G	*(Jt fav) keen, disp til ld aft 3 out, sn jnd, ev ch whn f nxt*	F	-

Improving; ran well in modest Confined; looks good for Restricted in 97;G/F-G. 19

BLADE OF FORTUNE b.g. 8 Beldale Flutter (USA) - Foil 'em (USA) by Blade (USA) — V G Greenway

299	2/3	Great Treth'	(R)	MDO	3m	13	G	*prog to 5th hlfwy, not rch ldrs, p.u. 16th*	P	0
533	16/3	Cothelstone	(L)	MDN	3m	13	G	*keen hold, cls up, lft in ld 13th, gng stngly whn f 15th*	F	-
646	23/3	Cothelstone	(L)	MDO	3m	5	S	*(Jt fav) plld hrd, ld 7th till wknd 2 out, hdd clse home.*	2	16
821	6/4	Charlton Ho'	(L)	MDN	3m	10	GF	*(fav) held up, ld 13th-2 out, outpcd aft, eased*	2	14

Only 5 runs last 3 seasons; headstrong; unfortunate in 96; should gain compensation. 15

BLAIR HOUSE(IRE) b.m. 7 Heraldiste (USA) - Mrs Baggins by English Prince — R Goldsworthy

974	8/4	Lydstep	(L)	MEM	3m	10	G	*prom whn u.r. 6th*	U	-
1271	27/4	Pyle	(R)	MDO	3m	15	G	*in tch in mid-div whn f 11th, dead*	F	-

Dead 0

BLAKEINGTON b.g. 10 Baron Blakeney - Camina by Don Carlos — Mrs Jackie Bugg

281	2/3	Clyst St Ma'	(L)	RES	3m	11	S	*cls up to 14th, wknd frm nxt*	7	0
470	10/3	Milborne St'	(L)	MDO	3m	18	G	*in tch, ld 11th-15th, wknd nxt*	8	0
734	31/3	Little Wind'	(R)	MDO	3m	11	GS	*(bl) prom, 2nd whn mstk 10th, cls up til rddn 15th, fdd*	5	0
807	4/4	Clyst St Ma'	(L)	MDO	3m	10	GS	*(bl) cls 2nd til lft in ld 10th, hdd 12th, drvn & lft clr 2 out*	1	13
1113	17/4	Hockworthy	(L)	RES	3m	11	GS	*(bl) alwys bhnd, t.o. frm 10th*	6	0
1313	28/4	Little Wind'	(R)	RES	3m	14	G	*(bl) ld/disp to 8th, cls 3rd at 15th, lost plc rpdly*	9	0

Poor novice chaser; lucky winner; looks ungenuine and hard to find another win. 14

BLAKES BEAU br.g. 6 Blakeney - Beaufort Star by Great Nephew — Lady Sarah Barry

4	13/1	Larkhill	(R)	MDO	3m	9	GS	*ld aft 1st, mstk 2nd, hdd 6th, wknd rpdly 4 out, p.u. 2 out*	P	0
733	31/3	Little Wind'	(R)	MDO	3m	13	GS	*ld & sn 20l clr, hdd 12th, wknd & p.u. apr 15th*	P	0
988	8/4	Kingston St'	(R)	MEM	3m	7	F	*s.s. prog to 10l 3rd at 12th, rdn 14th, fdd*	3	11

Top stable; devoid of stamina at present; may improve. 12

BLAKE'S FINESSE gr.m. 9 Baron Blakeney - True Finesse by True Song — Miss C A James

1995 P(0),1(15)

280	2/3	Clyst St Ma'	(L)	RES	3m	11	S	*disp early, lost tch 12th, wknd & p.u. 15th*	P	0
822	6/4	Charlton Ho'	(L)	RES	3m	7	GF	*ld til 13th, wknd 3 out, p.u. apr last*	P	0
1335	1/5	Cheltenham	(L)	HC	2m 5f	10	G	*keen hold, ld 1st, soon hdd, chsd ldr to 7th, wknd 9th, p.u. before 14th.*	P	0
1395	6/5	Cotley Farm	(L)	RES	3m	8	GF	*ld to 10th, cl up til ld agn 2 out, no ex whn hdd*	4	16
1612	26/5	Tweseldown	(R)	RES	3m	11	G	*j.w. ld 6-9th & frm 13th, 1l up wn f 16th, dead*	F	-

Dead. 14

BLAKES FOLLY(IRE) gr.g. 8 Sexton Blake - Welsh Folly by Welsh Saint — R H M Hargreave

1995 3(10),6(0),4(0),1(14),5(0)

188	24/2	Friars Haugh	(L)	RES	3m	12	S	*ld 10th til f 3 out*	F	-
403	9/3	Dalston	(R)	RES	3m	11	G	*ld 2nd, styd prom tl mstk 10th, r.o. frm 2 out*	3	14
608	23/3	Friars Haugh	(L)	RES	3m	13	G	*ld 7th untl jnd 11th, wknd 3 out*	4	10
914	8/4	Tranwell	(L)	RES	3m	6	GF	*ld to 3rd, cls up hlfwy, outpcd 4 out, wknd 2 out*	4	10
1086	14/4	Friars Haugh	(L)	RES	3m	7	F	*5th hlfwy, styd on frm 3 out, not rch 1st pair*	3	14
1472	11/5	Aspatria	(L)	RES	3m	8	GF	*hld up, prog 12th, 4th & outpcd nxt, fin 4th plcd 3rd*	3	13

Maiden winner 95; safe but beaten 10l minimum all completions 96; Restricted unlikely now 14

BLAKES ORPHAN gr.g. 10 Baron Blakeney - Orphan Grey by Crash Course — B Finch

1995 3(23),**2(22)**,**1(24)**,**P(0)**

185	23/2	Kempton	(R)	HC	3m	9	GS	*mid div, dropped rear, 10th, t.o..*	6	0
369	7/3	Towcester	(R)	HC	3m 1f	6	G	*(bl) ld to 5th, wknd 13th, 4th when blnd 3 out, ref next.*	R	-
577	19/3	Fontwell	(R)	HC	2m 3f	5	GF	*(bl) ld till after 2nd, blnd next, styd on to go second 2 out, ran on strly run-in.*	2	19
909	8/4	Towcester	(R)	HC	2 3/4m	6	F	*mstk 13th, nvr trbl ldrs.*	4	18
1383	6/5	Towcester	(R)	HC	2 3/4m	7	GF	*(bl) pressed wnr, ld 4th to 6th, jmpd slowly 11th, 3rd and held when mstk 2 out.*	4	12
1565	19/5	Mollington	(R)	OPE	3m	8	GS	*sn pshd alng & nvr going wll, lft disp dist 2nd 3 out,no imp*	3	14

Formerly useful; inconsistent now; likes a stiff track; treat with caution now. 17

BLAME BARNEY (Irish) — **I** 41^{P}, **I** 63^{P}, **I** 144^{2}, **I** 239^{2}, **I** 308^{3}, **I** 335^{P}, **I** 503^{5}

BLANK CHEQUE b.g. 6 Idiot's Delight - Quickapenny by Espresso — D J Coates

1995 **5(NH),8(NH),3(NH),P(NH)**

122	17/2	Witton Cast'	(R)	MDO	3m	8	S	*mstk 2nd, not rcvr & ran out apr nxt*	r	-
229	24/2	Duncombe Pa'	(R)	MDO	3m	13	GS	*ld til hdd flat, stppd to walk & p.u.*	P	0
413	9/3	Charm Park	(L)	MDO	3m	12	G	*ld to 5th, rr & outpcd aftr, ref last*	R	-
1094	14/4	Whitwell-On'	(R)	MDO	2 1/2m 88yds	16	G	*bhnd & sn t.o.*	8	0

Ex novice-hurdler; has ability but going the wrong way at present; best watched initially in 97. 10

BLARNEYS TRICK (Irish) — **I** 661,

BLAZE OF MAJESTY(USA) b.g. 8 Majestic Light (USA) - Uncommitted (USA) by Buckpasser — T H Caldwell

1995 P(0),P(0),4(0),2(0),**3(11),4(NH)**

286	2/3	Eaton Hall	(R)	MDO	3m	14	G	*chsd ldrs, no ext frm 4 out*	6	0
462	9/3	Eyton-On-Se'	(L)	RES	3m	12	G	*mid-to-rr, p.u. 3 out*	0	0

Well beaten when completing & barely worth a rating yet. 10

BLAZING CRACK (Irish) — **I** 118^{P}, **I** 328^{P}, **I** 446^{P}

BLENNERVILLE (Irish) — **I** 20^{P}, **I** 96^{2}, **I** 177^{F}, **I** 215^{1}

BLOSSOM WORLD (Irish) — **I** 215^{2}, **I** 403^{3}, **I** 449^{1}

BLOXHAM b.g. 11 The Brianstan - Sur Les Roches by Sea Break — Miss R S Newell

709	30/3	Barbury Cas'	(L)	OPE	3m	15	G	*sn bhnd, t.o. & p.u. 11th*	P	0

Chasing winner 91; of no account now. 12

BLUAGALE (Irish) — **I** 407^{P}, **I** 451^{P}, **I** 538^{P}

BLU BLIZZARD (Irish) — **I** 24^{P}

BLUCANOO ch.m. 6 Lighter - Lunar Monarch by Lone Star — J C Collett

1995 **13(NH)**

3	13/1	Larkhill	(R)	MDO	3m	10	GS	*20s-10s, jmpd lft, mid-div, no prog 14th, p.u. 2 out*	P	0
144	17/2	Larkhill	(R)	MDO	3m	15	G	*ld to 7th, losing plc whn u.r. 10th*	U	-
689	30/3	Chaddesley '	(L)	MDN	3m	15	G	*prom, disp 3rd whn blnd 12th, sn wknd, ref & u.r. 15th*	R	-

Does not stay; transfered to D. Nicholson & has won over hurdles. 0

BLUE AEROPLANE ch.g. 8 Reach - Shelton Song by Song — R R Collier

537	17/3	Southwell P'	(L)	OPE	3m	7	GS	*rear, t.o. 10th, p.u. 12th*	P	0
634	23/3	Market Rase'	(L)	OPE	3m	6	GF	*2nd to 6th, last frm 8th, t.o. 11th, p.u. 4 out*	P	0
1100	14/4	Guilsborough	(L)	OPE	3m	9	G	*in tch til mstks 11 & 12th, t.o. 14th, p.u. 2 out*	P	0
1237	27/4	Clifton On '	(L)	OPE	3m	5	GF	*ld to 3rd & 5th-12th, disp 3rd & in tch whn f 4 out*	F	-
1379	5/5	Dingley	(R)	MXO	3m	7	GF	*prom, blnd 12th, 3rd & no ch whn badly hmpd apr 2 out*	6	0
1532	13/5	Towcester	(R)	HC	2m 110yds	16	GF	*ld to 2nd, wknd 5th, t.o..*	11	0

Flat winner (7 furlongs maximum); no prospects in points. 0

BLUE BAY (Irish) — **I** 178^{U}, **I** 215^{P}, **I** 365^{P}

BLUE BEAT b.m. 11 Rymer - Coolek by Menelek — N P Morgan

1995 1(0),7(10),2(16),6(0),P(0),8(0),P(0)

56	10/2	Cottenham	(R)	OPE	3m	12	GS	*alwys rear, t.o. 14th, p.u. 16th*	P	0
246	25/2	Southwell P'	(L)	OPE	3m	9	HO	*alwys bhnd, lost tch & p.u. 11th*	P	0
393	9/3	Garthorpe	(R)	CON	3m	7	G	*alwys last, t.o. 7th, p.u. 12th*	P	0
899	6/4	Dingley	(R)	MEM	3m	4	GS	*alwys prom, chal 2 out, jst outpcd*	2	0
1098	14/4	Guilsborough	(L)	CON	3m	17	G	*hmpd 6th, in tch til 7th & btn whn p.u. 3 out*	P	0
1519	12/5	Garthorpe	(R)	OPE	3m	7	GF	*cls up to 6th, lost tch 13th, p.u. 4 out*	P	0
1594	25/5	Garthorpe	(R)	MEM	3m	10	G	*mid-div, 4th frm 10th, in tch to 3 out, wknd nxt & p.u.*	P	0

Won bad race 95; changed hands & deteriorated in 96; members only hope.G-Hy. 10

BLUE-BIRD EXPRESS ch.m. 11 Pony Express - Sheridans Daughter by Majority Blue — W G Kittow

1995 P(0),1(16),5(0),3(18),4(10),3(16)

136	17/2	Ottery St M'	(L)	LAD	3m	9	GS	*in tch early, bhnd whn p.u. 14th*	P	0
212	24/2	Castle Of C'	(R)	CON	3m	7	HY	*alwys rear, bhnd whn p.u. 13th*	P	0
529	16/3	Cothelstone	(L)	LAD	3m	5	G	*(bl) j.s 2nd, last whn blnd & u.r. 8th*	U	-
1278	27/4	Bratton Down	(L)	INT	3m	12	GF	*sn rear, t.o. 7th, p.u. 11th*	P	0
1499	11/5	Holnicote	(L)	CON	3m	8	G	*(bl) prom, ld 11-13th, wknd & reluctant frm 15th, t.o.*	7	0
1590	25/5	Mounsey Hil'	(R)	INT	3m	8	G	*(bl) ld til aft 3 out, wknd rpdly, p.u. nxt*	P	0
1634	1/6	Bratton Down	(L)	INT	3m	15	G	*prom, jnd wnr 14th, wknd frm 3 out*	6	0

Modest but consistent in 95; out of sorts and showed nothing in 96; can only be watched now.G-F. 12

BLUE CHEEK b or br.g. 10 Strong Gale - Star Streaker by Star Moss — J Mahon

1995 1(23),**1(26),P(0)**

685	30/3	Chaddesley '	(L)	LAD	3m	9	G	*disp 5th til ld 12th, clr 3 out, 2l up whn u.r. last*	U	24
1122	20/4	Stratford	(L)	HC	2m 5f 110yds	16	GF	*prom, mstk 11th, soon rdn, wknd 4 out.*	5	19
1341	4/5	Warwick	(L)	HC	2 1/2m 110yds	12	GF	*alwys prom, joined ldr 7th, ld 5 out, hdd and no ext run-in.*	2	24
1617	27/5	Chaddesley '	(L)	LAD	3m	8	GF	*cls up, ld 12th, going wll whn u.r. 14th*	U	-

Useful pointer; unlucky in ladies 96; always lightly raced and best on easy courses; can win in 97. 26

BLUECHIPENTERPRISE br.m. 10 Blakeney - Hey Skip (USA) by Bold Skipper (USA) — Richard C Darke

1995 1(23),1(24),**1(27)**,1(25),1(27),**1(29)**,**R(-)**

130	17/2	Ottery St M'	(L)	MEM	3m	6	GS	*(fav) alwys last, nvr going well*	4	0
444	9/3	Haldon	(R)	OPE	3m	5	S	*ld in to start, disp til outpcd aft 13th, tired 2 out*	2	16
874	6/4	Higher Kilw'	(L)	OPE	3m	6	GF	*ld/disp til hdd 2 out, no ext*	2	21
1360	4/5	Flete Park	(R)	OPE	3m	5	G	*s.v.s. went 3rd aft 10th, effrt & ld brfly 2 out, no ext*	2	23
1529	12/5	Ottery St M'	(L)	OPE	3m	7	GF	*(fav) just in tch til jmpd slwly 13th, reluc, bhnd & p.u. 15th*	P	0

Very useful in 95; temperament has got the better of her; best watched now; any. 20

BLUE DANUBE(USA) ch.g. 12 Riverman (USA) - Wintergrace (USA) — S G Allen

1995 **P(0)**,4(10),**5(23)**

99	14/2	Lingfield	(L)	HC	3m	9	HY	*alwys bhnd, t.o. when p.u. before 13th.*	P	0
784	31/3	Tweseldown	(R)	CON	3m	5	G	*pshd alng hlfwy, styd on onepcd frm 4 out, no ch wth wnr*	2	17
1108	17/4	Cheltenham	(L)	HC	4m 1f	14	GS	*ld till after 3rd, mstk 11th, bhnd when blnd 18th, p.u. before next.*	P	0
1331	1/5	Cheltenham	(L)	HC	2m 5f	9	G	*cl up, rdn apr 8th, lost tch 10th, t.o. and p.u. before 2 out.*	P	0
1546	18/5	Fakenham	(L)	HC	3m 110yds	13	G	*mid div, chsd ldr 9th to 13th, lost pl next, styd on again one pace from 2 out.*	3	20
1613	27/5	Fontwell	(R)	HC	3 1/4m 110yds	12	G	*chsd ldrs till wknd 18th.*	6	12
1643	2/6	Dingley	(R)	OPE	3m	13	GF	*outpcd in rr, 10th whn p.u. 9th*	P	0

H/Chase winner 94; retains some ability but inconsistent; weak Confined possible; G-S. 19

BLUE IS THE COLOUR(IRE) ch.g. 7 The Parson - Avocan by Avocat — Miss E M Hewitt

1995 **9(NH)**,**8(NH)**,**9(NH)**,**6(NH)**,**3(NH)**

241	25/2	Southwell P'	(L)	MDO	3m	15	HO	*hld up, prog 9th, wth ldr frm 4 out, rdn to ld last 100 yrds*	1	14
539	17/3	Southwell P'	(L)	RES	3m	11	GS	*cls up, ld 11th, sn clr, ran on well, easily*	1	20

Poor under Rules but outstanding start in points; prove useful if ready in 97; Soft 23

BLUE MOSSE (Irish) — **I** 14ᴾ

BLUE NIGHT b.m. 7 Latest Model - Midinette by Midsummer Night II — Mrs E Scott

1995 **9(NH)**,**7(NH)**,**8(NH)**

1347	4/5	Holnicote	(L)	MDO	3m	16	GS	*ld 7th til jnd & u.r. 14th*	U	-
1593	25/5	Mounsey Hil'	(R)	MDO	3m	11	G	*hld up, prog to ld 13th, clr 16th, rdn 2 out, all out*	1	15

No form under rules; won modest Maiden; looks capable of better; may prefer shorter course. 16

BLUE ROSETTE b.g. 7 Lucky Wednesday - Cadenette by Brigadier Gerard — Mrs Judy Wilson

331	3/3	Market Rase'	(L)	MDO	3m	9	G	*(fav) prom 8th, 6th whn hit 12th, rdn & btn 14th, p.u. nxt*	P	0
954	8/4	Eyton-On-Se'	(L)	MDO	2 1/2m	6	GF	*(fav) disp to 4th, cls 2nd til outpcd frm 3 out*	2	0
1434	6/5	Ashorne	(R)	MDO	3m	15	G	*w.w. in tch, ld aft 12th til aft 2 out, sn no ext*	2	13

Good stable but lightly-raced & struggles to stay; may find weak race eventually 13

BLUMIX ch.g. 14 Bluffer - Dolly Mixture by Sweet Ration — R Foulds

1995 P(0)

1062	13/4	Horseheath	(R)	MEM	3m	3	F	*1st ride, disp ld 7th-9th, lst tch 12th, t.o. & ref 15th*	R	-
1399	6/5	Northaw	(L)	CON	3m	8	F	*prog to disp ld bfly 7th, bhnd frm 11th, t.o.*	8	0
1599	25/5	Garthorpe	(R)	MDO	3m	7	G	*alwys rear hlf, t.o. frm 7th, p.u. 12th*	P	0

Schoolmaster in 96; of no account. 0

BOARD GAME b.g. 11 Angel Aboard - Rusty Lowe by Rustam — A Beedles

1995 P(0),1(13),4(10)

219	24/2	Newtown	(L)	RES	3m	17	GS	*chsd ldrs, 6th aft 13th, wknd nxt*	6	0
461	9/3	Eyton-On-Se'	(L)	RES	3m	15	G	*mid-div, stdy prog frm 5 out, rn on wl frm 2 out to ld flat*	1	16

Lightly raced; won two weak races 95/96; short of Confined class; hard to place now. 16

BOBBY BLAZER (Irish) — **I** 177ᶠ, **I** 259ᴾ, **I** 302ᴾ

BOB-CAM ch.g. 12 Scallywag - Stolen Girl by Mountain Call — J Parfitt

695	30/3	Llanvapley	(L)	RES	3m	13	GS	*t.o. 5th, p.u. 3 out*	P	0
1047	13/4	Bitterley	(L)	MDO	3m	13	G	*s.s. t.o. 4th, p.u. last*	P	0
1273	27/4	Pyle	(R)	MDO	3m	9	G	*prom, 15l 4th whn b.d. 13th*	B	-
1483	11/5	Bredwardine	(R)	MDO	3m	15	G	*ld frm 5th, ran wd nxt, hdd 11th, ev ch 15th, wknd nxt*	5	0

Last when finishing & an elderly maiden with no prospects 0

BOCOCK'S PRIDE (Irish) — **I** 10^{P}, **I** 72^{P}, **I** 136^{F}, **I** 355^{5}, **I** 461^{P}, **I** 505^{B}, **I** 566^{4}, **I** 613^{4}

BODDINGTON HILL b.m. 8 St Columbus - Dane Hole by Past Petition — B A Hall

1995 U(-),P(0),4(0)

355	3/3	Garnons	(L)	INT	3m	10	GS	*lost tch 8th, t.o. 11th*	5	0
389	9/3	Llanfrynach	(R)	MDN	3m	11	GS	*in tch in rear, prog 15th, chsd wnr 2 out, no imp*	2	0
606	23/3	Howick	(L)	MDN	3m	13	S	*mid-div whn f 6th*	F	-
694	30/3	Llanvapley	(L)	RES	3m	9	GS	*mid-div, prog to 3rd at 12th, lft 2nd aft nxt, not rch wnr*	2	15
849	6/4	Howick	(L)	MDN	3m	14	GF	*rear, prog frm 13th, nrst fin*	4	0
1161	20/4	Llanwit Maj'	(R)	MDO	3m	15	GS	*bhnd frm 4th, no ch frm 14th, tk 4th on line*	4	0
1269	27/4	Pyle	(R)	MDO	3m	9	G	*lft in ld 5th, cls 5th apr 14th, onepcd frm nxt*	4	0
1417	6/5	Cursneh Hill	(L)	MDO	3m	14	GF	*mstk 9th, rear frm nxt, no ch frm 13th*	6	0
1605	25/5	Bassaleg	(R)	MDO	3m	8	GS	*2nd at 10th, 3rd nxt, ran on 3 out, hld whn lft 2nd last*	2	13

Slow but usually completes; beaten 1 length last start and reliability may see her home one day. 11

BODERAN BRIDGE (Irish) — **I** 530^{P}

BOLD ALFIE br.g. 6 Sulaafah (USA) - Miss Boldly by Flandre II — D R Thomas

1995 P(0),F(-),6(0),7(0)

149	17/2	Erw Lon	(L)	MDN	3m	10	G	*prom in 3rd til f 14th*	F	-

Last in both completions in 95; vanished quickly in 96. 0

BOLD BOREEN (Irish) — **I** 179^{P}

BOLD CROFT b.m. 9 Crofter (USA) - Blajina by Bold Lad (IRE) — R E Barr

515	16/3	Dalton Park	(R)	XX	3m	12	G	*jmpd badly, rear til blnd & u.r. 5th*	U	-
823	6/4	Stainton	(R)	MEM	3m	6	GF	*alwys strggling, wll bhnd whn ran out bef 12th*	r	-
1137	20/4	Hornby Cast'	(L)	MDN	3m	13	G	*mstk 1st, chsd ldrs to 9th, not keen, t.o. & p.u. 14th*	P	0
1450	6/5	Witton Cast'	(R)	MDO	3m	14	G	*in tch in midfld til bad mstk 14th, not rcvrd, p.u. 4 out*	P	0

A poor jumper and most unpromising. 0

BOLD IMP bl.g. 11 Dubassoff (USA) - Woodlands Girl by Weepers Boy — J T Heritage

1995 **3(10)**,**6(0)**

358	3/3	Garnons	(L)	RES	3m	18	GS	*jnd ldrs 11th, chal 13th, 2l up whn u.r. nxt*	U	-
581	21/3	Wincanton	(R)	HC	2m 5f	13	S	*hdwy 10th, ev ch 4 out, one pace.*	4	21
906	8/4	Fakenham	(L)	HC	2m 5f 110yds	11	G	*chsd ldrs to 8th, soon bhnd.*	6	13
1163	20/4	Larkhill	(R)	MEM	3m	3	GF	*(fav) made all at sedate pce, clr frm 3 out, canter*	1	11

Won joke Members; ran well at Wincanton & could go close in a Restricted. 17

BOLD LOUISE (Irish) — **I** 650^{F}

BOLD MAN(NZ) b.g. 9 So Bold (NZ) - If It Wishes (NZ) by Zamazaan — R E Baskerville

27	20/1	Barbury Cas'	(L)	LAD	3m	15	GS	*chsd ldrs to 9th, bhnd whn p.u. 15th*	P	0
129	17/2	Kingston Bl'	(L)	MDN	3m	15	GS	*20s-12s, prog to chs ldr 9th, ld 14th, 4l clr whn f 3 out*	F	-
343	3/3	Higham	(L)	MDO	3m	11	G	*(fav) ld 8th-14th, wknd & btn 3 out*	4	0
1409	6/5	Hackwood Pa'	(L)	MDO	3m	6	F	*rr til styd on frm 2 out, nvr pld to chall*	2	0

Possibly unlucky 2nd start but beaten in bad races after; win most unlikely 10

BOLESA'S JOY (Irish) — **I** 176^{R}, **I** 258^{P}

BOLSHIE BARON b.g. 7 Baron Blakeney - Contrary Lady by Conwyn — M H Weston

1995 3(16),P(0),F(-)

218	24/2	Newtown	(L)	MDN	3m	14	GS	*(fav) in tch, mstk 8th, lost plc & p.u. 11th*	P	0
430	9/3	Upton-On-Se'	(R)	MDO	3m	15	GS	*prog frm 14th, tk 6th apr 2 out, not rch ldrs*	6	0
1006	9/4	Upton-On-Se'	(R)	MDN	3m	11	F	*(fav) ld 6th til hrd rdn & hdd aft 2 out, gd jmp last, jst hld*	2	15
1248	27/4	Woodford	(L)	MDN	3m	15	G	*prom, chsd ldr 11-16th, wknd*	5	0
1381	5/5	Dingley	(R)	MDO	3m	16	GF	*j.w. made all, pckd 12th, clr 15th, eased flat*	1	17
1482	11/5	Bredwardine	(R)	RES	3m	13	G	*ld til hdd aft 15th, wknd frm 2 out*	3	14
1640	2/6	Dingley	(R)	RES	3m	9	GF	*(fav) j.w., made all, hrd prssd & mstk 2 out, drvn out*	1	19

Improved; front runs & R/H essential ; more needed for Confineds; G-F. 18

BOMBADIER JACK b.g. 6 Primitive Rising (USA) - Palmister by Palm Track — M M Allen

1995 3(11)

464	9/3	Eyton-On-Se'	(L)	MDN	2 1/2m	13	G	*u.r. 4th*	U	-
568	17/3	Wolverhampt'	(L)	MDN	3m	9	GS	*cls up in 3rd to 3 out, no ext*	3	10

Lightly raced; only beaten one horse but beaten 13 lengths maximum; go closer if fit in 97. 13

BOMB THE BEES ch.m. 9 Cruise Missile - Honey's Sweet by Songedor — Mrs A Furnival

254	25/2	Charing	(L)	MDO	3m	9	GS	*wth ldr, ld 8th, blnd & u.r. 10th*	U	-
454	9/3	Charing	(L)	MDN	3m	10	G	*14s-6s, prog 13th, wth wnr 4 out, f nxt*	F	11
780	31/3	Penshurst	(L)	MDN	3m	12	GS	*alwys prom, chal 2 out, kpt on onepce flat*	2	12
1055	13/4	Penshurst	(L)	MDO	3m	11	G	*(Jt fav) mid-div, prog 10th, just ld whn u.r. 13th*	U	-

Rather clumsy & probably unlucky not to have won yet; should gain compensation in 97. 13

BONE IDOL (Irish) — **I** 69^{P}, **I** 117^{P}, **I** 198^{P}, **I** 227^{P}, **I** 517^{5}

BONNIE SCALLYWAG br.m. 10 Scallywag - Bonnie Lorraine by Sea Wolf — B A Husband

1995 P(0),9(14)

84	11/2	Alnwick	(L)	RES	3m	11	GS	*ld to 4th, wknd 7th, mstk 10th, t.o. & p.u. 12th*	P 0
172	18/2	Market Rase'	(L)	RES	3m	9	GF	*chsd ldrs, 3rd & hit 2 out, no ext*	3 12
703	30/3	Tranwell	(L)	RES	3m	7	GS	*alwys bhnd, p.u. 3 out*	P 0

Lightly raced; placed in weak Restricted and not threatening to win one. 12

BONNINGTON LASS (Irish) — **I** 95^{2}

BONQUIST (Irish) — **I** 260^{P}, **I** 282^{P}, **I** 318^{P}, **I** 402^{2}, **I** 451^{4}, **I** 495^{2}, **I** 539^{P}, **I** 585^{3}, **I** 599^{2}, **I** 634^{P}

BONUS NUMBER(IRE) br.g. 7 Roselier (FR) - Nelly Gleason by Gleason (USA) — Mrs Caroline Dix

510	16/3	Magor	(R)	MDN	3m	9	GS	*mid-div, 6th at 9th, styd on own pace*	4 0
696	30/3	Llanvapley	(L)	MDN	3m	13	GS	*mid-div whn u.r. 6th*	U -
1272	27/4	Pyle	(R)	MDO	3m	9	G	*chsd ldrs, outpcd 11th, t.o. & p.u. 15th*	P 0
1511	12/5	Maisemore P'	(L)	MDO	3m	14	F	*sn last, t.o. & p.u.11th*	P 0

Well beaten when completing and not threatening to hit the jackpot yet. 0

BOOK OF RUNES b.g. 11 Deep Run - Wychelm by Allangrange — Miss Y T Coleman

1995 P(0),**3(17),P(0)**,4(15)

257	29/2	Nottingham	(L)	HC	2 1/2m	11	G	*nvr going well, t.o. from hfwy, p.u. after 5 out.*	P 0

Winning hurdler 93; finished early in 96; needs to stick to points. win looks tough. 16

BOO'S DELIGHT b.m. 6 Idiot's Delight - Lucys Willing by Will Hays (USA) — R M Phillips

1995 **15(NH)**

174	18/2	Market Rase'	(L)	MDO	2m 5f	7	GF	*ld to 2nd, in tch, wknd apr 11th, p.u. 2 out*	P 0
430	9/3	Upton-On-Se'	(R)	MDO	3m	15	GS	*t.o. & p.u. 14th*	P 0

Ex n/h flat; no signs yet but still young enough to do better. 0

BOOT-ON b.m. 9 Welsh Captain - Deise Girl by Stranger — A Witcomb

1995 U(-),4(0),F(-),P(0)

972	8/4	Thorpe Lodge	(L)	MDO	3m	9	GF	*2nd til ld 11th-5 out, outpcd frm 3 out*	3 0
1301	28/4	Southwell P'	(L)	MDO	3m	10	GF	*ld to 4th, wll in tch, disp 11th-3 out, no ext cls hm*	3 11

Dead 12

BOOTSCRAPER ch.g. 9 Doc Marten - Impish Ears by Import — Mrs Sarah Adams

1995 1(22),1(24),**U(-)**,1(22),1(23),1(21)

40	3/2	Wadebridge	(L)	LAD	3m	5	GF	*hld up, pckd 8th, 3rd frm 12th, kpt on one pace*	3 21
130	17/2	Ottery St M'	(L)	MEM	3m	6	GS	*cls up whn blnd & u.r. 5th*	U -
198	24/2	Lemalla	(R)	OPE	3m	12	HY	*alwys prom, ld 2 out, ran on wll und pres*	1 26
360	4/3	Windsor	(R)	HC	3m	8	GS	*held up, hdwy 11th, wknd apr 4 out.*	5 17
482	13/3	Newton Abbot	(L)	HC	2m 5f 110yds	14	S	*(fav) (bl) f 2nd.*	F -
626	23/3	Kilworthy	(L)	OPE	3m	12	GS	*prom, chsd wnr 12th-15th, onepcd und pres 2 out*	3 23
717	30/3	Wadebridge	(L)	OPE	3m	3	GF	*(bl) trckd ldr, rdn aft 14th, wkng whn mstk nxt, t.o. & blnd last*	3 0

Useful pointer at best; goes best for A Farrant; no form in H/Chases; win more Opens; G-Hy 24

BOOTS MADDEN (Irish) — **I** 38^{F}, **I** 86^{2}, **I** 137^{2}, **I** 328, , **I** 465^{1}

BORDER GLORY ch.g. 5 Derrylin - Boreen's Glory by Boreen (FR) — J W Hughes

405	9/3	Dalston	(R)	MDO	2 1/2m	16	G	*prom early, grad lost plc frm 12th, n.d.*	9 0
1087	14/4	Friars Haugh	(L)	MDO	3m	9	F	*u.r. 6th*	U -
1155	20/4	Whittington	(L)	MDN	3m	14	G	*nvr bynd mid-div, p.u. 17th*	P 0

Only learning so far. 0

BORDER SUPREME(IRE) b.g. 7 Supreme Leader - Burren Maid by Lucifer (USA) — J W Hughes

1995 P(0),P(0),3(0),P(0),**7(0)**,P(0)

52	4/2	Alnwick	(L)	MDO	3m	11	G	*rear, prog to chs ldrs 9th, one pce frm 3 out*	4 10
87	11/2	Alnwick	(L)	MDO	3m	7	GS	*ld to 2nd & 5th-11th, wknd, v tired & p.u. 3 out*	P 0

Not disgraced on 1st outing; problems after; more needed 10

BOREEN BOY (Irish) — **I** 266^{F}, **I** 337^{F}, **I** 481^{P}, **I** 559^{3}, **I** 628^{2}, **I** 635^{P}

BOREEN OWEN b.g. 12 Boreen (FR) - Marble Owen by Master Owen — David Alan Harrison

1995 **3(NH),P(NH),12(NH)**

399	9/3	Dalston	(R)	CON	3m	9	G	*sn last, al t.o., f at last*	6 0
500	16/3	Lanark	(R)	OPE	3m	6	G	*3rd at 11th, nvr a serious dang*	3 13
612	23/3	Friars Haugh	(L)	OPE	3m	8	G	*ld 6th untl 8th, wknd frm 15th*	3 14
673	29/3	Sedgefield	(L)	HC	3m 3f	7	GF	*nvr far away, ld 13th, hdd 5 out, outpcd last 3.*	3 16
753	31/3	Lockerbie	(R)	OPE	3m	2	G	*(fav) ld by abt 3l til drew wll clr frm 13th*	1 13
912	8/4	Tranwell	(L)	OPE	3m	8	GF	*alwys rear, 7th hlfwy, not rch ldrs*	5 12

1119 18/4 Ayr (L) HC 3m 3f 110yds 9 GS *soon lost tch, t.o. when p.u. before 13th.* P 0
1337 1/5 Kelso (L) HC 3m 1f 9 S *bhnd when blnd 11th, t.o. when p.u. before 3 out.* P 0
1471 11/5 Aspatria (L) MEM 3m 4 GF *last frm 4th, mstk 11th, styd on frm 2 out, not trbl wnnr* 2 10
1573 19/5 Corbridge (R) OPE 3m 12 G *ld 2nd, lost plc hlfwy, outpcd frm 13th* 8 10
Winning chaser; won a joke open; mega safe but need similar to win again. 13

BOREENS SECRET (Irish) — I 332P, I 458P
BORNEO DAYS b.m. 6 Royal Vulcan - Cissac by Indian Ruler Mrs B G Blake
35 20/1 Higham (L) RES 3m 16 GF *alwys rear, t.o. & p.u. 11th* P 0
253 25/2 Charing (L) MDO 3m 10 GS *alwys rear, t.o. & p.u. 12th* P 0
921 8/4 Aldington (L) MDO 3m 8 F *5th whn ran out 4th* r -
1210 21/4 Heathfield (R) MDO 3m 13 F *prom, 6th & btn 14th, t.o. & p.u. 2 out* P 0
No real signs; looks short on stamina. 0

BOSCOE br.g. 10 Cidrax (FR) - Crest Cappagh P Hudson
1995 P(0),P(0),U(-)
173 18/2 Market Rase' (L) RES 3m 6 GF *alwys last, rmndrs 11th, no ch 14th, p.u. 2 out* P 0
1240 27/4 Clifton On ' (L) MDO 3m 10 GF *alwys bhnd, t.o. & p.u. 14th* P 0
1381 5/5 Dingley (R) MDO 3m 16 GF *alwys rear, last & lost tch 10th, t.o. & p.u. 13th* P 0
Of no account.shows no ability 0

BOSCO'S THATCH (Irish) — I 248F
BOSCO'S TOUCH (Irish) — I 213P, I 275P, I 352[3], I 440P, I 541[2], I 630[3]
BOSSBURG b.m. 9 Celtic Cone - Born Bossy by Eborneezer Mrs K S Clark
1995 **4(NH),5(NH),P(NH),3(NH),5(NH)**
273 2/3 Parham (R) LAD 3m 11 GF *ld 6th-14th, 3rd aft, wknd rpdly 2 out* 3 14
Well beaten when 3rd & promptly disappeared 16

BOSS DOYLE (Irish) — I 274P, I 322[1]
BOTH SIDES (Irish) — I 21F, I 89P, I 112P, I 194P
BOUGHT THE ACES (Irish) — I 563P
BOULEVARD BAY(IRE) b.g. 5 Royal Fountain - Cairita by Pitcairn J R Burns
14 14/1 Cottenham (R) MDO 3m 10 G *jmpd stckly early, making prog whn b.d. 12th* B -
51 4/2 Alnwick (L) MDO 3m 17 G *(fav) hld up, gd prog to jn ldrs 13th, wknd & p.u. nxt* P 0
414 9/3 Charm Park (L) MDO 3m 11 G *ld 12th-last, hdd & outpcd run-in* 2 13
541 17/3 Southwell P' (L) MDO 3m 9 GS *hrd hld in rear, prog frm 3 out, ran on, nrst fin* 2 12
590 23/3 Wetherby Po' (L) MDO 3m 16 GS *(fav) prom, wknd 12th, p.u. 15th* P 0
1094 14/4 Whitwell-On' (R) MDO 2 1/2m 88yds 16 G *(fav) rear, t.o. & p.u. 10th* P 0
1451 6/5 Witton Cast' (R) MDO 3m 12 G *(fav) rear,prog 8th,ld 14th til jnd & mstk 3 out,wknd nxt,p.u.last* P 0
Expensive to follow; stable out of sorts in 96; may be worth another chance. 13

BOURBON COUNTY (Irish) — I 190P
BOWERY BOY b.g. 9 Broadsword (USA) - Bowery Babe by Tantivy J R Knight
1995 1(20),U(-),6(0)
244 25/2 Southwell P' (L) CON 3m 13 HO *mstks, trckd ldrs, rdn 11th, lost tch nxt, p.u. 4 out* P 0
968 8/4 Thorpe Lodge (L) CON 3m 5 GF *(fav) n.j.w. w.w. 20l 4th 6 out, clsd rpdly 3 out, nt rch wnr* 2 15
1022 13/4 Brocklesby ' (L) CON 3m 6 GF *mstly 2nd til bad mstk gd rcvr 5 out (ditch), p.u. nxt* P 0
1303 28/4 Southwell P' (L) CON 3m 7 GF *(fav) hld up, no ext whn asked to qckn 3 out* 2 13
Below best in 96; usually goes well fresh; could still win weak Confined; G/F-S. 16

BOW HANDY MAN ch.g. 14 Nearly A Hand - Bellemarie by Beau Chapeau J L Gledson
1995 U(-),2(19),r(-),3(17),r(-),2(17),r(-),3(20),4(0),6(0),1(17),**2(19),5(NH)**
50 4/2 Alnwick (L) CON 3m 9 G *prom til grad wknd frm 3 out* 6 13
320 2/3 Corbridge (R) OPE 3m 5f 8 GS *disp frm 2nd, ld 13th, clr 15th, mstks 3 out & last, unchal* 1 22
582 22/3 Kelso (L) HC 3 1/2m 8 G *prom till blnd badly and u.r. 14th.* U -
860 6/4 Alnwick (L) MXO 4m 1f 7 GF *chsd ldrs, prog 15th, chsng ldr whn lft in ld last* 1 23
1459 8/5 Uttoxeter (L) HC 4 1/4m 8 G *bhnd 10th, jmpd slowly next, t.o. and p.u. before 17th.* P 0
Dour stayer; T Scott essential; won weak Open & lucky at Alnwick; win still possible at 15; Any. 20

BOWLAND GIRL(IRE) b.m. 7 Supreme Leader - El Marica by Buckskin (FR) G H Davies
1995 2(13),U(-),4(10)
389 9/3 Llanfrynach (R) MDN 3m 11 GS *(fav) ld 2nd, mstk nxt, jnd, bmpd & f 6th* F -
747 31/3 Upper Sapey (R) MDO 3m 11 GS *(fav) disp 3rd frm hlfwy, no ext frm 2 out* 3 13
977 8/4 Lydstep (L) MDO 3m 8 G *prom, rdn 12th, btn whn p.u. 16th* P 0
1045 13/4 Bitterley (L) MDO 3m 16 G *trckd ldrs, prog to ld 2 out, hdd nr fin* 2 15
1225 24/4 Brampton Br' (R) MDO 3m 18 G *(fav) prog 8th, chal 2 out to last, not qckn flat* 2 13
1410 6/5 Cursneh Hill (L) MEM 3m 4 GF *(fav) w.w., chsd ldr 15th, chllng whn blnd & u.r. last* U -

1483 11/5 Bredwardine (R) MDO 3m 15 G *(fav) w..w in mid-div, prog 13th, ev ch 3 out, no ext apr last* 3 13
1606 25/5 Bassaleg (R) MDO 3m 7 GS *(fav) prom, ld 13th, disp nxt til qcknd apr last, all out* 1 13

Not winning out of turn; barely stays; Restricted looks very tough. 14

BOWLANDS HIMSELF(IRE) b.g. 8 The Parson - Yellow Canary by Miner's Lamp — Mrs Lynn Campion

116 17/2 Lanark (R) MDO 3m 10 GS *ld til f 11th* F -
404 9/3 Dalston (R) RES 3m 7 G *al bhnd* 4 0
502 16/3 Lanark (R) MDO 3m 7 G *made all, clr 4 out, hld on well* 1 13
739 31/3 Sudlow Farm (R) RES 3m 11 G *trckd ldrs, ld 9th, 6l clr 2 out, hdd apr last, fin lame* 2 16

Beat subsequent winner; unlucky & problems next start; strong galloper; win Restricted if fit in 97. 18

BOWLANDS WAY b.g. 12 Al Sirat (USA) - Kilbride Lady VI by Menelek — Mrs Lynn Campion

113 17/2 Lanark (R) OPE 3m 6 GS *(bl) ld to 8th, wklnd rpdly 4 out* 3 0
367 6/3 Catterick (L) HC 3m 1f 110yds 12 G *(bl) cl up, ld 8th, hdd 12th, left in ld 15th, hded next, 2nd and no impn when p.u. lame after 3 out.* P 0

Ran well 2nd start but looks to have reached the end of the line 15

BOX OF DELIGHTS br.g. 8 Idiot's Delight - Pretty Useful by Firestreak — Mrs Jeanne Thomas

1995 3(14),1(16)

156 17/2 Erw Lon (L) RES 3m 13 G *(fav) 4th til went 2nd at 15th, mstk nxt, p.u. 2 out* P 0

Maiden winner 95; brief campaign 96; top stable and can win Restricted if fit in 97. 19

BOY BASIL b.g. 8 Balinger - Miss Behave by Don't Look — Exors Of The Late Capt W H Bulwer-Long

419 9/3 High Easter (L) RES 3m 10 S *rr, prog to ld 7th, hdded 10th, f nxt* F -
834 6/4 Marks Tey (L) RES 3m 11 G *mid-div,prog to 2nd 15th,lkd hld whn lft disp 2 out,ld last* 1 17
1323 28/4 Fakenham P-' (L) OPE 3m 8 G *hld up, mid-div whn f 12th* F -

Maiden winner 93; missed 95; fortunate winner; 2 wins 4 falls and brought down last 7 starts. 17

BOYCETRUS (Irish) — I 108[5], I 282[2], I 337[F]

BOYCOTT b.g. 9 Buckskin (FR) - Natanya by Menelek — Mrs Jean R Bishop

571 17/3 Detling (L) CON 3m 13 GF *(Jt fav) handy, wth ldr 12-14th, cls 3rd aft, wknd 2 out* 4 16

Winning hurdler; last ran 92/93; easily good enough to win but very fragile. 20

BOYS ROCKS ch.g. 8 Lighter - Nelodor by Nelcius — A Sparey

1174 20/4 Chaddesley ' (L) MDN 3m 10 G *ld to 12th, cls 3rd whn mstk 14th, grad wknd frm 17th* 5 0

A satisfactory debut; should go closer in 97. 12

BOZO BAILEY gr.g. 6 Hadeer - Perceive (USA) by Nureyev (USA) — Mrs Lucy Gibbon

344 3/3 Higham (L) MDO 3m 12 G *in rear, no ch whn p.u. 11th* P 0
496 16/3 Horseheath (R) MDO 3m 10 GF *prom to 10th, wknd, sn t.o.* 7 0
682 30/3 Cottenham (R) MDO 3m 9 GF *n.j.w. alwys bhnd, last whn p.u. 12th* P 0

Placed in novice hurdles 93/94; showed no aptitude for pointing. 0

BRABAZON(USA) b.g. 11 Cresta Rider (USA) - Brilliant Touch (USA) by Gleaming (USA) — H F T Scott

559 17/3 Ottery St M' (L) OPE 3m 7 G *bhnd early, prog 10th, styd on frm 4 out, nvr dang* 4 19
1125 20/4 Stafford Cr' (R) OPE 3m 7 S *cls up til 14th, rdn & onepce frm 3 out* 5 15
1275 27/4 Bratton Down (L) OPE 3m 8 GF *sn bhnd, rdn 12th, nvr on terms* 5 12

Former useful hurdler; ran well debut; disappointing after and best watched now. 15

BRABINER KING ch.g. 11 Posse (USA) - High Finale by High Line — Mrs M J Tuck

845 6/4 Howick (L) CON 3m 12 GF *4th/5th, 3rd brfly 9th, lost plc aft* 6 0
1247 27/4 Woodford (L) CON 3m 7 G *chsd ldrs, outpcd & blnd 14th, 5th & no ch whn f 3 out* F -

Lightly-raced & 2nd in a poor race; win at 13 looks well beyond him 11

BRABINER LAD ch.g. 12 Celtic Cone - Bit Of A Madam by Richboy — T Laxton

1995 **F(NH),P(NH)**

287 2/3 Eaton Hall (R) MDO 3m 11 G *w.w. prog frm 14th, chsd wnr frm 3 out, no ext* 2 13

Unpromising 13

BRACING BREEZE (Irish) — I 131[F], I 337[3]

BRACKENHEATH(IRE) b.g. 5 Le Moss - Stable Lass by Golden Love — G H Barber

929 8/4 Marks Tey (L) MDO 3m 5 G *sttld rear, prog to chal 2 out, ld apr last, hld on flat* 1 11

Won a bad & slowly run Maiden; very young but much more needed for Restricted. 12

BRACK N BRANDY b.g. 11 Skyliner - Pretty Gift by Realm — Miss Rachel David

1995 P(0),P(0),1(19),**P(0)**,**3(10)**,1(17)

140 17/2 Larkhill (R) CON 3m 17 G *alwys mid-div, 4th at 13th, onepcd aft* 5 10
469 10/3 Milborne St' (L) LAD 3m 8 G *ld/disp to 13th, wknd nxt, t.o.* 6 0
651 23/3 Badbury Rin' (L) MEM 3m 4 G *settld, prog 10th-15th, wknd nxt, p.u. last* P 0
1312 28/4 Little Wind' (R) XX 3m 6 G *ld to 14th, lost ground steadily, bhnd & p.u. 2 out, dsmntd* P 0
1405 6/5 Hackwood Pa' (L) CON 3m 6 F *ld frm 3rd, j.w. hdd last. ran on* 2 19
1611 26/5 Tweseldown (R) XX 3m 9 G *(fav) t.d.e. ld, lft clr 11th, hdd apr last, no ext* 2 14
1648 8/6 Umberleigh (L) LAD 3m 11 GF *ld 4-7th, mstk 9th, wknd 12th, t.o. & p.u. 2 out* P 0

Won poor race 95; novice ridden; best late season; another win looks tough.Firm. 15

BRADLEYS CORNER (Irish) — I 16P
BRAMBLE DALE (Irish) — I 191³
BRAMBLEDOWN(IRE) b.m. 5 Sheer Grit - Kilbeg Jackie by Beau Chapeau Mrs B Sillars

253 25/2 Charing (L) MDO 3m 10 GS *1st ride, lft in ld 12th, made rest, ran on strngly 2 out* 1 15
449 9/3 Charing (L) RES 3m 13 G *(fav) cls up, outpcd & mstk 15th, strng run 4 out, ld on line* 1 17

Dream start for horse & rider; season lasted 2 weeks; should win again if fit in 97; G-S 18

BRAMBLE PINK b.m. 10 Brando - Celtic Pink by Dumbarnie J A C Sheppard

1308 28/4 Little Wind' (R) MDO 3m 6 G *mstk 1st, in tch til lost plc 15th, btn whn p.u. 2 out* P 0

No real signs. 0

BRAMBLE RUN (Irish) — I 69U, I 90U, I 530P
BRANWELL BRONTE b.g. 11 The Parson - Woodford Belle by Harwell M F Loggin

1995 P(0),P(0)

230 24/2 Heythrop (R) MEM 3m 12 GS *sn rear, t.o. & p.u. 11th* P 0
336 3/3 Heythrop (R) LAD 3m 5 G *bhnd frm 6th, t.o. & p.u. 13th* P 0

Of no account 0

BRAVE COMMITMENT (Irish) — I 84U, I 501³
BRAZEN GOLD b.g. 10 Boreen (FR) - Flashy Gold by Le Bavard (FR) Sir John Barlow Bt

1995 **5(13)**,**7(0)**,1(17),**2(16)**,1(18)

667 24/3 Eaton Hall (R) INT 3m 11 S *chsd ldr to 8th, lost tch 12th, p.u. 3 out* P 0
905 8/4 Carlisle (R) HC 3 1/4m 5 F *(fav) cl up, ld twelfth, shaken up apr last, ran on.* 1 17

Won a dire H/chase; well below Open class and very hard to place now; stays. 18

BREATH OF SCANDAL (Irish) — I 478¹
BRECKENBROUGH LAD b.g. 9 Uncle Pokey - Fabulous Beauty by Royal Avenue Mrs M R Bennett

1995 **17(NH)**,**6(NH)**,**13(NH)**,**P(NH)**,**P(NH)**

81 11/2 Wetherby Po' (L) MEM 3m 4 GS *in tch, disp 3 out-nxt, no ext aft* 2 0
223 24/2 Duncombe Pa' (R) CON 3m 16 GS *sn well bhnd, t.o. frm 5th* 7 0
327 3/3 Market Rase' (L) CON 3m 15 G *u.r. 2nd* U -
512 16/3 Dalton Park (R) CON 3m 10 G *not fluent, alwys bhnd, t.o. 12th, p.u. aft 16th* P 0
588 23/3 Wetherby Po' (L) INT 3m 17 S *rear, t.o. 12th, p.u. nxt* P 0

A/W hurdle winner; novice ridden & no meaningful form in 96. 0

BREDINTHEPURPLE (Irish) — I 111P, I 167P, I 228¹, I 405³
BREECHES BUOY ch.g. 10 Buckskin (FR) - Sea Fog by Menelek J Pearson

431 9/3 Upton-On-Se' (R) MDO 3m 17 GS *rear whn u.r. 6th* U -
742 31/3 Upper Sapey (R) RES 3m 9 GS *6th whn f 4th* F -
1048 13/4 Bitterley (L) MDO 3m 12 G *last at 4th, lost tch & p.u. 12th* P 0

No signs of ability. 0

BREEZE-BLOC ch.m. 6 Sunley Builds - Sunny Breeze by Roi Soleil J B Shears

1995 R(-)

201 24/2 Lemalla (R) MDO 3m 13 HY *ld/disp to 9th, grad wknd, p.u. 2 out* P 0
301 2/3 Great Treth' (R) MDO 3m 13 G *5th hlfwy, went 2nd & styng on 17th, 3l 2nd whn f 2 out* F -
806 4/4 Clyst St Ma' (L) MDO 3m 7 GS *(Jt fav) n.j.w. blnd 5th, poor 4th frm 11th til p.u. 2 out* P 0

Showed ability 2nd start but yet to get round; go close when jumping sorted. 13

BRENDAN'S WAY(FR) b or br.g. 9 Kilian - Rambling by Wrekin Rambler P G Bailey

1995 1(10),P(0)

465 10/3 Milborne St' (L) RES 3m 11 G *alwys mid-div, no ch whn p.u. 4 out* P 0
650 23/3 Cothelstone (L) RES 3m 5 S *sn rr, t.o. whn p.u. 10th* P 0
1113 17/4 Hockworthy (L) RES 3m 11 GS *(bl) chsd wnr to 11th, wkng whn blndrd nxt & p.u.* P 0

Won bad race 95; non-finisher otherwise; no real prospects. 10

BRENDA'S DREAM b.g. 5 Dreams To Reality (USA) - Jenny Regrets by Piaffer (USA) A Witcomb

900 6/4 Dingley (R) MDN 2m 5f 8 GS *remote 7th whn ref 9th* R -

1240	27/4	Clifton On '	(L)	MDO	3m	10	GF	*rear, 7th & in tch whn f 11th*	F	-

Dead **0**

BREWERY LIGHT (Irish) — I 166^{P}, I 190^{3}, I 268^{F}, I 327^{F}

BRIAN OG (Irish) — I 14^{F}, I 47^{P}, I 187^{F}, I 245^{2}, I 306^{U}, I 358^{3}, I 437^{U}, I 505^{B}, I 574^{6}

BRIAN'S DELIGHT (Irish) — I 271^{3}, I 479^{1}

BRICKANMORE (Irish) — I 307^{3}, I 439^{4}

BRIC LANE(USA) br.g. 9 Arctic Tern (USA) - Spring Is Sprung (USA) by Herbager — Jamie Poulton

1995 **P(NH),7(NH),P(NH),P(NH)**

253	25/2	Charing	(L)	MDO	3m	10	GS	*alwys prom, cls 2nd 4 out, wknd nxt*	2	0
455	9/3	Charing	(L)	MDN	3m	10	G	*alwys prom, chsd wnr 15th, wknd rpdly 3 out, blnd last*	3	0
681	30/3	Cottenham	(R)	MDO	3m	12	GF	*mid-div, outpcd 15th, 7th & btn whn f nxt*	F	-
1055	13/4	Penshurst	(L)	MDO	3m	11	G	*mid-div til u.r. 11th*	U	-
1374	4/5	Peper Harow	(L)	MDO	3m	8	F	*nt fluent, last frm 7th, t.o 15th*	5	0

Poor hurdler; well beaten & non stayer; need a miracle to win. **0**

BRIDE RUN(IRE) ch.g. 7 Le Moss - Mariner's Run by Deep Run — Mrs C M Marles

217	24/2	Newtown	(L)	RES	3m	17	GS	*chsd ldrs to hlfwy, no ch 13th, p.u. 15th*	P	0
510	16/3	Magor	(R)	MDN	3m	9	GS	*2nd til ld 13th, jnd 15th, hdd 2 out, no ext*	2	10
606	23/3	Howick	(L)	MDN	3m	13	S	*prom til went 2nd 13th, chsd wnr, alwys hld*	3	11

Placed in weak races but not disgraced & may find a chance if ready in 97 .... **13**

BRIDGE END (Irish) — I 255^{P}, I 407^{F}, I 450^{P}

BRIDGE EXPRESS b.g. 9 Pony Express - Elysium Dream Vii — C T Moate

1995 P(0),2(15),5(12),6(0),1(15)

208	24/2	Castle Of C'	(R)	LAD	3m	14	HY	*prom to 6th, outpcd frm 10th*	6	0
647	23/3	Cothelstone	(L)	CON	3m	6	S	*ld to 11th, wknd 15th, t.o. whn p.u. 3 out*	P	0
989	8/4	Kingston St'	(R)	CON	3m	6	F	*ld til aft 14th, onepcd*	2	19
1079	13/4	Cothelstone	(L)	INT	3m	5	GF	*made all, clr 10th, 3l clr 3 out, comf*	1	15
1228	27/4	Worcester	(L)	HC	2m 7f	17	G	*ld till f 4th.*	F	-
1499	11/5	Holnicote	(L)	CON	3m	8	G	*(Jt fav) sn bhnd, t.o. frm 12th*	6	12

Moderate but safe; onepaced and only effective in weak races; need same to win again. **15**

BRIDGE HOUSE b.g. 7 Headin' Up - My Aisling by John de Coombe — Lee Bowles

1995 P(0),P(0)

4	13/1	Larkhill	(R)	MDO	3m	9	GS	*rear, wll bhnd frm 12th, t.o. & p.u. 14th*	P	0

Lightly raced; looks hopeless. **0**

BRIDGNORTH LASS b.m. 7 Say Primula - Muskcat Rambler by Pollerton — S Wanless

1995 U(-),4(0)

405	9/3	Dalston	(R)	MDO	2 1/2m	16	G	*f 8th*	F	-
751	31/3	Lockerbie	(R)	CON	3m	12	G	*bhnd by 13th, t.o.*	7	0
861	6/4	Alnwick	(L)	CON	3m	7	GF	*rr, prog to ld 12th-15th, wknd*	4	0
1155	20/4	Whittington	(L)	MDN	3m	14	G	*last pair in rear, sn t.o., p.u. 9th dismntd*	P	0
1446	6/5	Witton Cast'	(R)	CON	3m	7	G	*cls up til ran wd apr 13th, wknd nxt,rear whn p.u. bfr 3 out*	P	0

Tailed off on all completions; well short of a win. **0**

BRIEF SLEEP b.m. 10 Shua Jo - Madame Demelza — Miss Kim Tripp

779	31/3	Penshurst	(L)	RES	3m	13	GS	*in tch to 10th, p.u. 12th*	P	0
1054	13/4	Penshurst	(L)	RES	3m	8	G	*ld 4th, clr nxt, still wll clr whn f 12th*	F	-
1295	28/4	Bexhill	(R)	RES	3m	7	F	*lft in ld 2nd, clr whn f 9th*	F	-
1612	26/5	Tweseldown	(R)	RES	3m	11	G	*t.d.e. hld up bhnd, nvr in race, t.o. & u.r. 12th*	U	-

Won bad Members 93; missed 94/95; headstrong and need luck to win again. **10**

BRIGADE LEADER (Irish) — I 142^{P}, I 185^{P}, I 239^{3}, I 308^{P}, I 353^{5}, I 433^{1}, I 508^{4}

BRIGHT AS A BUTTON ch.g. 12 True Song - Bright Exploit by Exploitation — Sir Michael Connell

1995 1(21),1(23),F(-),F(-),2(21),P(0),1(21),1(23),U(-)

22	20/1	Barbury Cas'	(L)	XX	3m	19	GS	*nvr on terms, no ch frm 10th, p.u. 3 out*	P	0
127	17/2	Kingston Bl'	(L)	MEM	3m	6	GS	*prom til lost tch 13th,4th & styng on whn crawld nxt & p.u.*	P	0
246	25/2	Southwell P'	(L)	OPE	3m	9	HO	*mstk 7th, trckd ldrs, chsd wnr 14th, no imp whn hit 2 out*	2	21
537	17/3	Southwell P'	(L)	OPE	3m	7	GS	*cls up, ld 8th, nrly ref 13th, lost plc, ran on frm 3 out*	3	20
639	23/3	Siddington	(L)	OPE	3m	12	S	*chsd ldrs, outpcd 11th, 4th & onepcd appr 15th*	4	19
902	6/4	Dingley	(R)	OPE	3m	4	GS	*cls up, 2nd frm 12th, chal & ld 2 out, outpcd bfr last*	2	18
1017	13/4	Kingston Bl'	(L)	OPE	3m	4	G	*jmpd slwly, in tch til outpcd 14th, t.o. whn ref last*	R	-
1565	19/5	Mollington	(R)	OPE	3m	8	GS	*chsd ldrs, no ch whn lft poor 2nd 15th, ref nxt*	R	-
1643	2/6	Dingley	(R)	OPE	3m	13	GF	*chsd ldrs, 3rd hlfwy, sn outpcd, bhnd & p.u. 15th*	P	0

Good pointer in 95; novice ridden 96 & declined; may revive with stronger handling;G-S. **17**

BRIGHT BURNS b.g. 11 Celtic Cone - Chanter Mark by River Chanter — Colin Gee

1995 2(25),4(26),1(24),2(22),**P(0)**,2(0)

9	14/1 Cottenham	(R) OPE	3m	13	G	*(bl) mid-div, prog to 4th apr 2 out, kpt on steadily*	3	24
232	24/2 Heythrop	(R) OPE	3m	10	GS	*(fav) (bl) ld/disp til ld 5th, made rest, styd on well*	1	23
337	3/3 Heythrop	(R) OPE	3m	10	G	*(fav) (bl) ld to 14th, 3rd & btn frm nxt*	3	14
581	21/3 Wincanton	(R) HC	2m 5f	13	S	*(bl) ld to 4 out, ran on one pace.*	3	22
675	30/3 Cottenham	(R) MEM	3m	6	GF	*(fav) made all, clr 4 out, eased flat*	1	18
1122	20/4 Stratford	(L) HC	2m 5f 110yds	16	GF	*(bl) ld to 2nd, wknd 12th.*	8	12
1335	1/5 Cheltenham	(L) HC	2m 5f	10	G	*(bl) chsd ldrs, went 2nd 8th, ld 11th to 13th, wknd apr 3 out.*	4	17
1565	19/5 Mollington	(R) OPE	3m	8	GS	*(bl) chsd ldr,15l down whn lft wll clr 15th,stpping rpdly flat*	1	19

Fair pointer; tubed; finds little under pressure; best easy 3 miles; win points in 97; blinkers. 22

BRIGHT CHOICE (Irish) — I 149P, I 211P

BRIGHT CRUSADER b.g. 10 Lepanto (GER) - Snowdra's Daughter by Down Cloud — Mrs N Simm

1995 3(15),6(13),1(14),4(10),P(0)

248	25/2 Charing	(L) RES	3m	12 GS	*alwys twrds rear*	5	0
449	9/3 Charing	(L) RES	3m	13 G	*mid-div, nggld alng frm 4th, poor 5th 4 out, kpt on*	4	10
570	17/3 Detling	(L) MEM	3m	6 GF	*alwys last, pshd alng 9th, sn lost tch, p.u. 3 out*	P	0

Members winner 95; finished early & swwed nothing in 96; Members(2 chances) best hope 97. 11

BRIGHTER SHADE (Irish) — I 791

BRIGHT HOUR ro.g. 11 Kabour - Amber Vale by Warpath — Mrs B Ansell

1995 U(-),P(0),P(0),P(0),2(10),8(0)

251	25/2 Charing	(L) OPE	3m	10 GS	*alwys mid-div, lost tch 4 out*	4	0
451	9/3 Charing	(L) OPE	3m	11 G	*mid-div, clsd up to 4th & ev ch 4 out, onepcd*	5	10
570	17/3 Detling	(L) MEM	3m	6 GF	*alwys prom, cls 3rd 3 out, rdn & no ext nxt*	3	10
811	6/4 Charing	(L) OPE	3m	9 F	*mid-div to 12th, rear & no ch frm 4 out*	5	14
1207	21/4 Heathfield	(R) CON	3m	9 F	*ld/disp to 9th, cls aft til blnd 16th, ran on frm 2 out*	3	15
1443	6/5 Aldington	(L) LAD	3m	4 HD	*3rd frm 5th, nvr nrr 1st 2, last frm 4 out*	4	0
1537	16/5 Folkestone	(R) HC	3 1/4m	8 GF	*bhnd 7th, prog 11th, outpcd apr 3 out.*	5	0

Very moderate; placed in bad races; last won in 92 and unlikely to change that. 14

BRIGHT MOONBEAM (Irish) — I 7P, I 32F

BRIGHT PROSPECT (Irish) — I 63F

BRIGHT ROAD ch.m. 10 Button Bright (USA) - Road Express by Pony Express — J R Thomas

446	9/3 Haldon	(R) MDO	3m	13 S	*mid-div, poor 7th at 13th, t.o. & p.u. 2 out*	P	0
1117	17/4 Hockworthy	(L) MDO	3m	8 GS	*wl bhnd, t.o. whn f hvly 12th*	F	-
1277	27/4 Bratton Down	(L) CON	3m	15 GF	*(bl) alwys rear, t.o. & p.u. 3 out*	P	0
1428	6/5 High Bickin'	(R) RES	3m	10 G	*(bl) towrds rear til p.u. 15th*	P	0
1551	18/5 Bratton Down	(L) OPE	3m	8 F	*(bl) mstk 2nd, sn rear, pshd alng 12th, t.o. frm 16th*	8	0

Of no account. 0

BRIGHT WORK br.g. 9 Teamwork - Bright Performance by Gala Performance (USA) — J D Curnow

556	17/3 Ottery St M'	(L) MDO	3m	15 G	*ld 3rd til ran out 11th*	r	-
1555	18/5 Bratton Down	(L) MDO	3m	13 F	*rear, 10th hlfwy, nrst fin*	5	0
1627	27/5 Lifton	(R) MDO	3m	9 GS	*ld/disp 6-10th, 2nd til 13th, 4th whn f 4 out*	F	-

6 runs in 4 seasons; a little ability but barely worth a rating. 10

BRMABLE RUN (Irish) — I 166P

BROADCASTER b.g. 8 Broadsword (USA) - Rosepic by Seaepic (USA) — Richard Chandler

1995 P(0),P(0),3(0),3(0)

59	10/2 Cottenham	(R) RES	3m	9 GS	*ld to 6th, mstk & wknd 11th, p.u. 15th*	P	0
169	18/2 Market Rase'	(L) CON	3m	15 GF	*mid-div, hmpd 8th, 5th & rdn 11th, blnd 14th, wknd*	8	10
333	3/3 Market Rase'	(L) MDO	3m	11 G	*bhnd 6th, prog 11th, styd on, nvr nrr*	3	0

5 placings 94/96; does not really stay and not threatening to win; finished early in 96. 10

BROAD CHARE b.g. 9 Bishop Of Orange - Faultys Call Vii — James Byrne

1995 P(0),R(-),P(0),P(0),R(-)

224	24/2 Duncombe Pa'	(R) RES	3m	12 GS	*ref to race*	0	0
304	2/3 Great Stain'	(L) OPE	3m	10 GS	*(vis) ref to start*	R	-
306	2/3 Great Stain'	(L) INT	3m	12 GS	*(vis) ref to race (again)*	R	-

Maiden winner 94; seems to retired himself. 0

BROADNOTE b.m. 7 Broadsword (USA) - Maynote by Maystreak — R Andrews

1378	5/5 Dingley	(R) MDO	2 1/2m	16 GF	*mstk 2nd, mid-div, 8th whn f 6th*	F	-
1523	12/5 Garthorpe	(R) MDO	3m	11 GF	*alwys cls up, mstks, ran on onepcd frm 3 out*	4	0

Satisfactory 2nd run; should progress when jumping better. 12

BROAD STEANE b.g. 7 Broadsword (USA) - Banbury Cake by Seaepic (USA) — Sir Michael Connell

1995 3(10),1(15)

28	20/1 Barbury Cas'	(L)	RES	3m	14	GS	*6s-3s, hld up in tch,prog to ld aft 3 out,mstk last,styd on*	1	19
263	2/3 Didmarton	(L)	INT	3m	18	G	*in tch, chsd ldr 11th, ev ch whn mstk last, ran on, just hld*	3	21
538	17/3 Southwell P'	(L)	XX	3m	6	GS	*(fav) hld up, prog 13th, rdn 3 out, lkd hld whn lft clr nxt*	1	20
1377	5/5 Dingley	(R)	CON	3m	12	GF	*(Co fav) j.w. trckd ldrs, ld 14th, bttr jump last, ran on well*	1	24
1567	19/5 Mollington	(R)	INT	3m	12	GS	*(fav) cls up, ld 14th-2 out, rdn & no ext apr last*	2	21
1629	30/5 Uttoxeter	(L)	HC	2m 5f	13	GS	*(fav) held up bhnd ldrs, rdn apr 4 out, left in 2nd 2 out, ran on well from last, just faild.*	2	25

Improving; just failed in novice H/chase; can win one in 97; G/F-G/S. 25

BROAD VALLEY (Irish) — I 59P, I 1324, I 165P

BROADWAY SWINGER b.g. 5 Sulaafah (USA) - River Culm by Royal Salmon — P E D Cooke

682	30/3 Cottenham	(R)	MDO	3m	9	GF	*last whn u.r. 4th*	U	-
1103	14/4 Guilsborough	(L)	MDN	3m	15	G	*s.s. bhnd til prog 10th, 5th & in tch whn p.u. 15th, improve*	P	0
1325	28/4 Fakenham P-'	(L)	MDO	3m	6	G	*chsd ldr til jmpd lft & u.r. 5th*	U	-

Shows promise; needs to jump better; go close in 97. 14

BROCKISH BAY ch.g. 9 Le Bavard (FR) - Almanac by London Gazette — Roy Baxter

161	17/2 Weston Park	(L)	LAD	3m	11	G	*mid-div, prog 10th, no ext frm 4 out*	4	11
291	2/3 Eaton Hall	(R)	LAD	3m	10	G	*disp to 11th, lost tch wth 1st pair 14th, sn btn*	6	12
856	6/4 Sandon	(L)	RES	3m	9	GF	*w.w. in rear, cls order 4 out, strng chal apr last, readly*	1	17
1192	21/4 Sandon	(L)	CON	3m	11	G	*mid-div whn f 11th*	F	-
1230	27/4 Weston Park	(L)	CON	3m	7	G	*mid-div, ran on onepcd frm 4 out*	4	15
1577	19/5 Wolverhampt'	(L)	CON	3m	6	G	*hld up, alwys bhnd, blnd 9th, t.o. & p.u. 3 out*	P	0

Missed 95; inconsistent and not 100% genuine;L/H only; may surprise again. 16

BROE'S CROSS (Irish) — I 334P, I 567P, I 608F, I 654P

BROGEEN DUBH (Irish) — I 151P, I 2405, I 3354, I 4443, I 4602, I 504F, I 575P

BROMPTON ROAD b.g. 13 Derring Rose - London Gem by London Gazette — Mrs S M Graves

159	17/2 Weston Park	(L)	CON	3m	22	G	*mid-div, nvr dang*	10	0

Winning chaser but looks finished now 0

BRONZE EFFIGY ch.g. 14 Vaigly Great - Sea Fern by Klondyke Bill — W H Pugh

1995 P(0),F(-),P(0),2(14),5(0),5(0),2(0),P(0),2(14),4(0),**P(0)**,5(0),8(0)

157	17/2 Erw Lon	(L)	CON	3m	15	G	*alwys last pair, p.u. 13th*	P	0
505	16/3 Magor	(R)	PPO	3m	7	GS	*mod 4th til onepcd frm 12th, t.o. & ref last*	R	-
691	30/3 Llanvapley	(L)	CON	3m	15	GS	*(bl) mid-div, no prog frm 13th, btn 4th whn ref last*	R	-
846	6/4 Howick	(L)	OPE	3m	7	GF	*(bl) 4th to 10th, lost tch wth ldrs frm nxt*	5	0
1035	13/4 St Hilary	(R)	CON	3m	10	G	*(bl) mid-div, gd prog to ld 15th, bttr jmp last, jnd line*	1	18
1157	20/4 Llanwit Maj'	(R)	CON	3m	11	GS	*(bl) mid-div, lft 4th 14th, ran on 3 out, ev ch last, kpt on*	2	18
1262	27/4 Pyle	(R)	MEM	3m	6	G	*(bl) last til prog 13th, no ext frm nxt, tk 3rd flat*	3	10
1487	11/5 Erw Lon	(L)	CON	3m	4	F	*(bl) alwys in rear*	4	0
1558	18/5 Bassaleg	(R)	CON	3m	6	F	*(bl) sn poor 4th, t.o. 12th, kpt on*	4	0
1602	25/5 Bassaleg	(R)	CON	3m	8	GS	*(bl) mid-div, poor 4th whn ref 3 out*	R	-

Shock winner (40/1); change of jockey(R. Jones) bucked his ideas up; win at 15 looks tough. 14

BROOK A LIGHT ch.g. 5 Lighter - Elmley Brook by Paddy's Stream — W Westacott

284	2/3 Clyst St Ma'	(L)	MDN	3m	11	S	*alwys bhnd, t.o. & p.u. 12th*	P	0
1279	27/4 Bratton Down	(L)	MDO	3m	14	GF	*handy, 2nd at 12th, ev ch 2 out, wknd last*	4	0
1555	18/5 Bratton Down	(L)	MDO	3m	13	F	*(fav) mid-div, nvr a fctr*	7	0
1638	1/6 Bratton Down	(L)	MDO	3m	13	G	*in tch in rear til b.d. 8th*	B	-

Beaten 16 lengths when 4th; more needed; young and should do better. 11

BROOK COTTAGE(IRE) b or br.g. 8 Petorius - Slaney Maid by Furry Glen — J S Swindells

1995 4(10),**U(-)**,F(-),9(0),P(0),1(14)

162	17/2 Weston Park	(L)	OPE	3m	16	G	*(bl) prom early, t.o. & p.u. 4 out*	P	0

Shock winner 95; vanished quickly in 96 and few prospects. 12

BROOK HILL LADY (Irish) — I 20U, I 334, I 852, I 1281, I 1604, I 2345

BROOKLAWN (Irish) — I 232B, I 340P, I 417F

BROOKLYN EXPRESS b.m. 7 Sula Bula - Lady Brooklyn by Streak — E J Legg

1995 r(-),3(0)

143	17/2 Larkhill	(R)	MDO	3m	14	G	*prom whn f 8th*	F	-
1118	17/4 Hockworthy	(L)	MDO	3m	14	GS	*last & t.o. til p.u. 4th*	P	0

Tailed off on only completion and unpromising. 0

BROOK QUEEN (Irish) — I 1274, I 143P, I 146P, I 309P, I 379F, I 4754, I 5921

BROOKVIEW VI (Irish) — I 3642

BROTHER BILL ch.g. 11 Sovereign Bill - Queen's Brook by Daybrook Lad — D Bloomfield

63	10/2	Great Treth'	(R)	MEM	3m	6	S	*off pace 7th, steady prog nxt, fin well*	2	17
195	24/2	Lemalla	(R)	INT	3m	7	HY	*sn bhnd, p.u. 4 out*	P	0
297	2/3	Great Treth'	(R)	INT	3m	10	G	*t.o. hlfwy*	4	0
721	30/3	Wadebridge	(L)	INT	3m	3	GF	*alwys outpcd, blnd 6th, t.o.*	3	0
937	8/4	Wadebridge	(L)	INT	3m	4	F	*(bl) u.r. 3rd*	U	-
1142	20/4	Flete Park	(R)	CON	3m	11	S	*(vis) ld til apr 3rd, blnd badly 5th, rear whn ref 7th (ditch)*	R	-
1278	27/4	Bratton Down	(L)	INT	3m	12	GF	*alwys rear, nvr any ch, t.o. & p.u. last*	P	0

Restricted winner 93; fair 1st start but fell to pieces; 97 debut may be last hope; Soft 14

BROTHER MINSTREL ch.g. 9 Brotherly (USA) - Lady Peggy by Young Nelson — J V Hodgson

1995 P(0),5(11),4(0),P(0),4(0)

225	24/2	Duncombe Pa'	(R)	RES	3m	12	GS	*cls up til wknd 10th, p.u. 13th*	P	0

Finished early in 96; short of winning standard yet. 10

BROTHER NICHOLAS (Irish) — I 114[P], I 147, , I 199[3]

BROTHER PRIM gr.g. 7 Brotherly (USA) - Tudor Primrose by Tudor Sam — A G L Taylor

1995 P(0)

432	9/3	Upton-On-Se'	(R)	MDO	3m	17	GS	*wkng 3rd whn mstk 2 out, no ch whn u.r. last*	U	-
508	16/3	Magor	(R)	INT	3m	5	GS	*20s-6s, ld til u.r. 9th*	U	-

Yet to complete; punted at Magor, so someone thinks he has ability. 12

BROWN BABY br.m. 10 Full Of Hope - Funny Baby by Fable Amusant — R I Bird

1995 P(0),2(15),4(10),4(0),7(10),P(0),6(10),r(-),8(0)

23	20/1	Barbury Cas'	(L)	XX	3m	11	GS	*alwys bhnd, t.o. 10th*	4	10
59	10/2	Cottenham	(R)	RES	3m	9	GS	*cls up, chs ldr 14th-aft 2 out, wknd*	4	0
361	5/3	Leicester	(R)	HC	2 1/2m 110yds	15	GS	*chsd ldrs till wknd 9th, t.o. when p.u. 2 out.*	P	0
1176	21/4	Mollington	(R)	MEM	3m	6	F	*ld 2-3rd, wth wnr 9-10th, wknd nxt, t.o.*	5	10
1339	4/5	Hereford	(R)	HC	2m 3f	7	F	*ld to 4th, lost pl next, rallied 9th, wknd four out, bhnd when f last.*	F	-
1532	13/5	Towcester	(R)	HC	2m 110yds	16	GF	*well bhnd from 6th, t.o..*	10	0

Non stayer; lost her last 30 starts and will not break the sequence. 10

BROWN BALA b or br.m. 7 Balinger - Brown Veil by Don't Look — Mrs J A Skelton

353	3/3	Garnons	(L)	MDN	2 1/2m	7	GS	*rear, t.o. whn f 7th*	F	-
389	9/3	Llanfrynach	(R)	MDN	3m	11	GS	*rmndrs 2nd, t.o. 8th, crawld 12th & p.u.*	P	0
697	30/3	Llanvapley	(L)	MDN	3m	11	GS	*last trio, t.o. & p.u. 10th*	P	0
954	8/4	Eyton-On-Se'	(L)	MDO	2 1/2m	6	GF	*alwys mid-div, in tch to 5 out, no ext frm 4 out*	3	0
1315	28/4	Bitterley	(L)	MDO	3m	10	G	*mid-div at 10th, rdn 12th, no imp, poor 5th & p.u. last*	P	0

Beaten 30 lengths in short Maiden; stamina problems and much more needed. 0

BROWN BERRY (Irish) — I 66[F], I 353, , I 433[P], I 550[P], I 615[P], I 640, , I 655[P]

BROWN REBEL b.g. 10 Royal Boxer - Brown Rose by Rose Knight — Mrs A G Lawe

1995 4(0),1(15),2(15),P(0)

1139	20/4	Flete Park	(R)	RES	3m	14	S	*ld/disp, ld 17th til wknd rpdly 2 out, eased*	5	10
1358	4/5	Flete Park	(R)	RES	3m	8	G	*not alwys fluent, prog 14th, lost plc aft 16th, p.u. last*	P	0

Maiden winner 95; stopped quickly in 96 and maybe problems; best watched now. 14

BROWNROSELAD (Irish) — I 159[P]

BROWNSCROFT b.m. 8 Dubassoff (USA) - Keino by Kautokeino (FR) — Mrs Wendy Smith

1995 P(0),P(0),3(0),P(0),3(10)

605	23/3	Howick	(L)	MDN	3m	13	S	*2nd til disp 14th, ld 3 out, hdd flat, no ext und pres*	2	12
1047	13/4	Bitterley	(L)	MDO	3m	13	G	*ld to 3rd, cls up til wknd 12th, p.u. 15th*	P	0
1417	6/5	Cursneh Hill	(L)	MDO	3m	14	GF	*ld to 6th, styd cls up til wknd 14th, p.u. nxt*	P	0

Staying better now and only beaten 1/2 length; may find a weak Maiden. 12

BROWN WINDSOR b.g. 14 Kinglet - Cauldron by Kabale — C C Shand Kydd

1995 1(26),1(26),1(23),**2(31)**,**F(-)**,1(22)

104	17/2	Marks Tey	(L)	OPE	3m	14	G	*(fav) (bl) trkd ldrs, 3rd & rddn 17th, ch last, onepcd*	2	25
360	4/3	Windsor	(R)	HC	3m	8	GS	*(bl) chsd ldr from 5th, ld 3 out, mstk and hdd next, no ext.*	2	25
485	16/3	Hereford	(R)	HC	3m 1f 110yds	13	S	*(bl) prom till jmpd slowly 3rd, soon bhnd, t.o. when p.u. before 4 out.*	P	0
672	29/3	Aintree	(L)	HC	2 3/4m	26	G	*(bl) held up, midfield when b.d. 9th.*	B	-
1100	14/4	Guilsborough	(L)	OPE	3m	9	G	*(fav) (bl) trckd ldrs, chal 13th, 3rd & rdn 3 out, kpt on flat*	3	22
1237	27/4	Clifton On '	(L)	OPE	3m	5	GF	*(bl) cls up, prssd wnr 13th til not qckn 2 out*	2	19

A grand servent but declined in 96; another win looks tough at 15; any. 21

BRUCE'S CASTLE b.g. 10 Beau Charmeur (FR) - Maid In The Mist by Pry — M Walsh

1255 27/4 Balcormo Ma' (R) MEM 3m 2 GS *nvr a threat, wll bhnd frm 3 out* 2 0

Promising dual winner 94; beaten in a match and prospects look bleak now. 0

BRUFF CASTLE ch.g. 9 Carlingford Castle - Bruff Gypsy by Even Money D L Claydon

1995 P(0),U(-),5(0),P(0),2(11),4(0),2(11),**P(0)**

108 17/2 Marks Tey (L) MDN 3m 17 G *ld/disp til 15th, wknd appr 3 out* 5 10
315 2/3 Ampton (R) MDO 3m 10 G *prom, rmdrs 6th, disp 11th-nxt, blnd 14th,bhnd & p.u. last* P 0
489 16/3 Horseheath (R) MEM 3m 4 GF *lft in ld 4th-7th,ld 10th-4 out, mstk nxt, ev ch last,no ext* 2 12
930 8/4 Marks Tey (L) MDO 3m 6 G *(Jt fav) (bl) prom, ld 8-12th, lft in ld nxt-4out, ld 3 out, hld on flat* 1 12

Ex Irish; won at 15th attempt (bad race); not 100% genuine and Restricted looks to hard. 13

BRUNA ALPINA b.m. 11 Magnolia Lad - Cwm Rhondda by Celtic Cone E M Vitalini

1561 18/5 Bassaleg (R) MDO 3m 8 F *ref & u.r. 1st* R -

A late and obviously reluctant starter. 0

BRUSH ME UP (Irish) — **I** 564, , **I** 571⁵, **I** 638²

BRYN'S STORY b.g. 9 Push On - Lido Legend by Good Light G D Blagbrough

1995 P(0)

141 17/2 Larkhill (R) MEM 3m 6 G *sn rear, p.u. 9th* P 0
204 24/2 Castle Of C' (R) MDO 3m 11 HY *wll bhnd til prog 15th, styd on to ld flat* 1 13
466 10/3 Milborne St' (L) RES 3m 13 G *alwys mid-div, p.u.11th* P 0
1242 27/4 Woodford (L) RES 3m 18 G *bhnd, blndrd 3rd, last frm 7th, t.o. & p.u. 3 out* P 0

Only 5 runs 95/96; slogged home in mud; no form otherwise. 14

BUAILE BOS (Irish) — **I** 102², **I** 160⁶, **I** 234, , **I** 303⁵

BUBBLE N SQUEEK ch.g. 7 Celtic Cone - Booterstown by Master Owen C J B Barlow

1995 F(-)

740 31/3 Sudlow Farm (R) MDN 3m 16 G *trckd ldrs, 5th & strgglng 13th, lft 4th last, wnt 3rd flat* 3 0
1365 4/5 Gisburn (R) MDO 3m 17 G *mid-div, nvr dang* 5 0

Well beaten so far but has scope to do better. 12

BUBBLES GALORE(IRE) ch.g. 5 Hubbly Bubbly (USA) - New Top by New Brig Mrs D H McCarthy

275 2/3 Parham (R) MDN 3m 15 GF *(bl) rear, losing tch whn p.u. 9th* P 0
921 8/4 Aldington (L) MDO 3m 8 F *chsd ldng pair to 11th,4th & no ch 14th,p.u. aft 16th,green* P 0
1536 16/5 Folkestone (R) HC 2m 5f 9 GF *mstks, held up, prog into 3rd 11th, kept on from 2 out.* 3 15

Very green but ran really well in weak H/chase; good stable and looks sure to win in 97. 16

BUBBLY BOY ch.g. 9 St Columbus - Spartan Lace by Spartan General G B Tarry

1995 P(0)

1105 14/4 Guilsborough (L) MDN 3m 12 G *mid-div,outpcd & poor 4th 16th,styd on wll 2 out,tk 2nd last* 2 10

Only run twice; beaten 20 lengths and no winners behind; can win if racing regularly in 97. 14

BUCKAROO b.m. 5 Escapism (USA) - Come On Clover by Oats K Anderson

1253 27/4 Balcormo Ma' (R) MDO 3m 16 GS *bhnd by hlfwy, p.u. aft 12th* P 0
1356 4/5 Mosshouses (L) MDO 3m 12 GS *schoold, mstk 2nd, in tch whn f 11th* F -

Only learning so far; good stable. 0

BUCKHILL (Irish) — **I** 14ᴾ, **I** 68ᴾ, **I** 113ᴾ

BUCKIE THISTLE (Irish) — **I** 320ᴾ, **I** 397ᶠ

BUCKINGHAM GATE b.g. 10 Tap On Wood - Place Dauphine by Sea Hawk II T J Whitley

1995 **13(NH),6(NH)**

133 17/2 Ottery St M' (L) OPE 3m 18 GS *mid-div, bhnd whn p.u. 4 out* P 0
196 24/2 Lemalla (R) CON 3m 14 HY *alwys rear* 8 11
294 2/3 Great Treth' (R) CON 3m 10 G *handy til lost plc 16th, styd on onepcd* 4 11
481 11/3 Taunton (R) HC 3m 11 G *bhnd 5th, t.o. from 9th.* 8 0

Well beaten when completing and a win in points looks well beyond him now 12

BUCKINTIME ch.m. 9 Buckskin (FR) - Summerville Lass by Deep Run Mrs B Shaw

1423 6/5 Eyton-On-Se' (L) MDO 3m 7 GF *ld 7th, made rest, ran on strngly frm 3 out, comf* 1 15

Lightly-raced; missed 95; handed modest race on plate; may have Restricted hopes if fit 97 15

BUCKLAND FILLEIGH(IRE) ch.m. 6 Buckskin (FR) - Free Choice by Paddy's Stream R J Francome

1995 **B(NH),9(NH),12(NH),1(NH),9(NH)**

380 9/3 Barbury Cas' (L) CON 3m 11 GS *mid-div whn f 2nd* F -

.. 0

BUCKLANDS COTTAGE gr.m. 7 Roaring Riva - Nothing Happened by General Ironside J C Hogg

52	4/2	Alnwick	(L)	MDO 3m	11	G	*n.j.w., alws bhnd, t.o. & p.u. 13th*	P	0
405	9/3	Dalston	(R)	MDO 2 1/2m	16	G	*disp 2nd, prom til ld 3 out, ran on und pres frm last*	1	13

Much improvement to win modest Maiden; more needed but looks a progressive sort. 15

BUCKLE IT UP b.g. 11 Buckskin (FR) - The Hofsa by Varano A H Mactaggart

1995 3(15),3(20),U(-),1(20),6(0),2(18),P(0),1(19)

50	4/2	Alnwick	(L)	CON 3m	9	G	*prog 6th, clse up til 12th, no prog 3 out*	5	14
610	23/3	Friars Haugh	(L)	CON 3m	11	G	*alwys twrds rr*	6	0
1251	27/4	Balcormo Ma'	(R)	OPE 3m	6	GS	*ld til 5th, disp frm 13th until outpcd frm 2 out*	2	16
1351	4/5	Mosshouses	(L)	CON 3m	11	GS	*ld to 3rd, lost plc & rdn 8th, btn 13th, p.u. 2 out*	P	0
1513	12/5	Hexham Poin'	(L)	CON 3m	6	HY	*ld/disp til apr 3 out, blnd badly nxt, rallied last, onepcd*	2	20

2 win last 13 starts; stays and needs mud; can win again when conditions suit. 18

BUCKLELONE b.m. 7 Buckley - Speakalone by Articulate Mrs J H Docker

1995 P(0)

241	25/2	Southwell P'	(L)	MDO 3m	15	HO	*sn rear, t.o. & p.u. 12th*	P	0
332	3/3	Market Rase'	(L)	MDO 3m	8	G	*rear & rmndrs 6th, no ch 13th, t.o.*	3	0
541	17/3	Southwell P'	(L)	MDO 3m	9	GS	*ld to 2 out, ev ch last, not qckn flat*	3	12
727	31/3	Garthorpe	(R)	MDO 3m	12	G	*in tch in rear to 11th, wll bhnd 13th, t.o. & p.u. 3 out*	P	0
898	6/4	Dingley	(R)	MDN 2m 5f	10	GS	*2nd frm 4th, chsd wnnr last m, no imp*	2	0
1104	14/4	Guilsborough	(L)	MDN 3m	18	G	*rear frm 7th, t.o. & p.u. 15th*	P	0

Only beaten 51/2 lengths at Southwell; disappointing otherwise and likely to prove frustrating. 12

BUCKLE UP (Irish) — I 245P

BUCKLEY'S COURT b.g. 7 Buckley - Wing On by Quayside R Weston

1995 **P(NH),P(NH)**

150	17/2	Erw Lon	(L)	MDN 3m	8	G	*cls up, went 2nd 14th, poor jmps nxt 2, onepcd*	3	0
551	17/3	Erw Lon	(L)	MDN 3m	8	GS	*sttld mid-div, prog 4 out, ld last, styd on well*	1	12
840	6/4	Maisemore P'	(L)	RES 3m	9	GF	*slw jmp 5th,prog to ld apr 2 out,slw jmp & hdd last,no ext*	3	17
1038	13/4	St Hilary	(R)	RES 3m	15	G	*rear, prog to 4th at 14th, wkng whn ran out 3 out*	r	-
1197	21/4	Lydstep	(L)	MEM 3m	3	S	*chsd wnr, cls enough 2 out, no dang aft*	2	10
1490	11/5	Erw Lon	(L)	RES 3m	6	F	*cls up 3rd, ev ch whn f 14th*	F	-

Won weak race; ran well next time but let down by jumping; L/H essential; weak Restricted possible. .. 16

BUCK RELATED (Irish) — I 275¹

BUCK RIVER (Irish) — I 161P, I 224², I 343³

BUCKSFERN b.g. 9 Buckskin (FR) - Deep Fern by Deep Run E E Williams

1995 **2(NH),5(NH),1(NH),3(NH),2(NH)**

18	14/1	Tweseldown	(R)	MXO 3m	6	GS	*3rd whn mstk & u.r. 4th*	U	-
160	17/2	Weston Park	(L)	OPE 3m	16	G	*chsd ldrs, outpcd 3 out, onepcd*	3	19
459	9/3	Eyton-On-Se'	(L)	OPE 3m	11	G	*prom, 2nd 13th, in tch & ev ch 3 out, no ex*	3	22
854	6/4	Sandon	(L)	OPE 3m	4	GF	*prom, lft 2nd 7th, cls up & ev ch 11th, not qckn frm 2 out*	2	21
1043	13/4	Bitterley	(L)	OPE 3m	9	G	*(fav) cls up til ld 12th, hrd prssd 2 out, drew clr last*	1	23
1333	1/5	Cheltenham	(L)	HC 3m 1f 110yds	13	G	*chsd ldr to 9th, prom till wknd apr 18th.*	6	13

Ex-useful Irish pointer; disappointing & won weak Open; should find another chance; G-F 22

BUCKS FLEA b.m. 7 Buckley - Flea Pit by Sir Lark Miss S Sadler

1995 3(10),4(12)

688	30/3	Chaddesley '	(L)	MDN 3m	17	G	*ld 2nd-11th, ev ch & rdn 3 out, onepcd*	3	12
1045	13/4	Bitterley	(L)	MDO 3m	16	G	*(fav) alwys prom, ev ch til no ext frm 2 out*	3	14

Lightly raced; beaten in fair races; onepaced; deserves a win and should do it in 97. 14

BUCKSHEE (Irish) — I 440, , I 497⁴, I 661P

BUCKS IMAGE (Irish) — I 469P, I 510F

BUCKSKIN CLOVER(IRE) b.g. 8 Buckskin (FR) - Dewy Clover by Green Shoon R J Rowsell

606	23/3	Howick	(L)	MDN 3m	13	S	*cls 5th whn f 8th*	F	-

Did not make halfway; may do better. 10

BUCKSKINS BABE (Irish) — I 478P

BUCKS REWARD (Irish) — I 7P, I 506⁴, I 564, , I 640B

BUCKSUM(IRE) b.m. 5 Buckskin (FR) - Cothill Lady (IRE) by Orchestra Mrs P Grainger

590	23/3	Wetherby Po'	(L)	MDO 3m	16	S	*mid-div, f 4th*	F	-
689	30/3	Chaddesley '	(L)	MDN 3m	15	G	*schoold in rear til p.u. 11th*	P	0
1041	13/4	Bitterley	(L)	MEM 3m	6	G	*jmpd novicey, cls 4th at 10th, wknd 12th, p.u. nxt*	P	0

Only learning and looks capable of better. 0

BUCKWHEAT LAD(IRE) br.g. 8 Over The River (FR) - Buckwheat Lass by Master Buck — P Cheesbrough

1995 **F(NH),6(NH),6(NH)**

53	4/2	Alnwick	(L)	MDO 3m	13	G	*wth ldr, ld 9-12th, no ext 3 out*	4	0
80	11/2	Wetherby Po'	(L)	MDO 3m	12	GS	*cls up, disp 3 out, ld last, drvn out*	1	15
302	2/3	Great Stain'	(L)	MEM 3m	7	GS	*(fav) handy, ld 12th-nxt, disp last, hdd nr fin, fin 2nd, disq*	2D	14
403	9/3	Dalston	(R)	RES 3m	11	G	*prom, trckd ldrs frm 12th, wnt 2nd at 17th, no ch wth wnr*	2	14
584	23/3	Wetherby Po'	(L)	RES 3m	13	S	*alwys mid-div, btn whn f 3 out*	F	-
758	31/3	Great Stain'	(L)	RES 3m	17	GS	*alwys rear, rdn 11th, onepcd frm 4 out*	8	0

Poor hurdler; found his niche in points; won stamina test; need same to score again. G-S. 15

BUCKWYN br.g. 7 Buckley - Bronwyn by Green Shoon — J Bowen

1995 P(0),P(0),P(0),6(0)

390	9/3	Llanfrynach	(R)	MDN 3m	13	GS	*n.j.w. in tch in rear to 10th, wknd & p.u. 12th*	P	0
882	6/4	Brampton Br'	(R)	RES 3m	14	GF	*alwys trailing, no ch frm 13th*	6	0

Well beaten when completing and shows no ability. 0

BUDGET ch.g. 8 Bustino - Australia Fair (AUS) by Without Fear (FR) — Ms Susan Croft

1995 P(0),3(0),F(-),P(0)

1243	27/4	Woodford	(L)	MEM 3m	6	G	*chsd ldr to 6th, soon wll bhnd, u.r. 8th*	U	-

Of no account 0

BUFFALO HOUSE (Irish) — I 87^{F}, I 161^{P}, I 381^{F}, I 527^{P}

BUILDER BOY ch.g. 6 Sunley Builds - Geordie Lass by Bleep-Bleep — Mrs C E Whiteway

463	9/3	Eyton-On-Se'	(L)	MDN 2 1/2m	14	G	*rr 5th, prog to chs ldrs 5 out, sn wknd, p.u. 2 out*	P	0
660	24/3	Eaton Hall	(R)	MDN 3m	7	S	*mid-div, prog to 3rd 13th, f nxt*	F	-
949	8/4	Eyton-On-Se'	(L)	MDN 3m	5	GF	*alwys in tch, ev ch whn f 5 out*	F	-
1484	11/5	Bredwardine	(R)	MDO 3m	17	G	*rear frm 11th, no ch 15th, t.o. & p.u. 2 out*	P	0

Some hope but jumping problems at present. 0

BULADANTE (Irish) — I 8^{4}, I 69^{P}, I 117^{P}, I 334^{6}, I 374^{2}

BULA VOGUE (Irish) — I 11^{2}, I 64, , I 144^{1}, I 242^{6}, I 276^{P}, I 333^{P}, I 376^{6}

BULLAFORD FAIR b.g. 8 Sergeant Drummer (USA) - Clifton Fair by Vimadee — Mrs B E Miller

1995 P(0),F(-),P(0),P(0)

188	24/2	Friars Haugh	(L)	RES 3m	12	S	*sn bhnd, p.u. 12th*	P	0
398	9/3	Dalston	(R)	MEM 3m	13	G	*u.r. 1st*	U	-
502	16/3	Lanark	(R)	MDO 3m	7	G	*in tch whn u.r. 9th*	U	-
755	31/3	Lockerbie	(R)	MDN 3m	17	G	*5th hlfwy, sn wknd, b.d. 2 out*	B	-
1088	14/4	Friars Haugh	(L)	MDO 3m	10	F	*2nd hlfwy, cls up til wknd 15th, p.u. apr last*	P	0

Yet to get round and unpromising. 0

BUMPTIOUS BOY b.g. 12 Neltino - Bellardita by Derring-Do — R F Hanks

686	30/3	Chaddesley '	(L)	OPE 3m	6	G	*cls up til outpcd apr 12th, p.u. 14th*	P	0
837	6/4	Maisemore P'	(L)	CON 3m	4	GF	*j.w. disp til lft in ld 4th, hdded 15th, outpcd appr 2 out*	2	16
1043	13/4	Bitterley	(L)	OPE 3m	9	G	*blnd badly & u.r. 1st*	U	-
1170	20/4	Chaddesley '	(L)	CON 3m	9	G	*chsd ldr 6-12th, wknd 14th, t.o. & p.u. 3 out*	P	0
1212	24/4	Andoversford	(R)	MEM 3m	5	G	*chsd wnr, chal 2 out, one pcd*	2	10
1507	12/5	Maisemore P'	(L)	CON 3m	10	F	*chsd ldrs, outpcd & lft 3rd aft 13th, mstk 3 out, t.o.*	3	0

Winning hurdler; novice ridden; placed in poor races and not threatening to win. 12

BUNCHOFFIVES ch.g. 5 Nearly A Hand - Confetti Copse by Town And Country — Mrs J Woodward

1044	13/4	Bitterley	(L)	MDO 3m	15	G	*hit marker & u.r. apr 5th*	U	-
1319	28/4	Bitterley	(L)	MDN 3m	13	G	*alwys prom, 2nd & ev ch whn b.d. 3 out*	B	-
1621	27/5	Chaddesley '	(L)	MDO 3m	17	GF	*(fav) trckd ldrs til p.u. aft 10th, lame*	P	0

Rather unfortunate and problems last start; go close if fit in 97. 14

BUNGY BOURKE b.g. 8 Precocious - Nebiha by Nebbiolo — W M Burnell

1995 **P(NH),19(NH)**

79	11/2	Wetherby Po'	(L)	MDO 3m	12	GS	*cls up, 2nd at 8th, f 10th*	F	-

N o form under rules; not seen after debut fall in 96. 0

BUNNY LIGHTENING (Irish) — I 204^{P}, I 252^{4}, I 290^{F}, I 370^{P}, I 474^{P}, I 540,

BUONARROTI b.g. 9 Ela-Mana-Mou - Amiel by Nonoalco (USA) — J R Vail

1995 P(0),4(11),2(19),2(19),2(19),**4(16)**

6	13/1	Larkhill	(R)	OPE 3m	18	GS	*prom, ld 6-9th, 3rd & outpcd frm 15th, fair effort*	3	24
99	14/2	Lingfield	(L)	HC 3m	9	HY	*held up, left in 2nd apr 10th till 14th, left in second again 3 out, no impn on wnr.*	2	25
255	28/2	Taunton	(R)	HC 4 1/4m 110yds	15	GS	*prom till lost position 12th, t.o. when p.u. before 21st.*	P	0

Winning hurdler 93; able but not 100% genuine; have a good chance in Confineds; stays. 22

BURKEAN MELODY (Irish) — **I** 116^{F}, **I** 136^{P}, **I** 186^{P}, **I** 276^{P}, **I** 357^{P}, **I** 547, , **I** 593^{F}, **I** 648^{F}

BURRELL WHARF (Irish) — **I** 299^{F}, **I** 318^{2}

BURREN VALLEY (Irish) — **I** 42^{P}

BURROMARINER b.g. 12 Julio Mariner - Ever Joyful by Aureole — Mrs A Blaker

249	25/2	Charing	(L)	XX	3m	11	GS	*alwys prom, mostly 3rd final cct, chal 2 out, kpt on*	2	17
453	9/3	Charing	(L)	XX	3m	4	G	*cls up, jmpd slwly 3 out, sn chal, ld apr last, drvn out*	1	15
571	17/3	Detling	(L)	CON	3m	13	GF	*(Jt fav) cls up, ld 3 out, drvn out*	1	19
775	31/3	Penshurst	(L)	CON	3m	8	GS	*(fav) cls up, prssd ldr 14th, ld apr 2 out, rddn out*	1	21
918	8/4	Aldington	(L)	CON	3m	4	F	*cls up, prog to ld 3 out, clr apr last, easily*	1	22
1372	4/5	Peper Harow	(L)	OPE	3m	6	F	*(fav) in tch, 4th whn reluctant & j.s. 14th, lsng tch whn ref nxt*	R	-
1444	6/5	Aldington	(L)	OPE	3m	6	HD	*(fav) trckd ldr, lft in ld 11th, made rest, pushd clr flat*	1	20

Missed 95; quirky but well handled; one lapse in 96; can win again; G/S-HD. 11 if staying sweet 21

BUSHMILLER (Irish) — **I** 57^{P}, **I** 78^{3}, **I** 138^{P}, **I** 516^{P}

BUSH TELEGRAPH (Irish) — **I** 68^{P}, **I** 71^{2}, **I** 155^{1}, **I** 220^{1}

BUSMAN(IRE) ch.g. 7 Be My Guest (USA) - Cistus by Sun Prince — Keith R Pearce

1995 6(0),1(15),3(17),1(19),U(-)

154	17/2	Erw Lon	(L)	LAD	3m	14	G	*chsd wnr 10th, wknd apr last*	3	20
364	5/3	Leicester	(R)	HC	2m 1f	12	GS	*chasing gp, prog 7th, chsd ldr 2 out, no impn run-in.*	2	21
546	17/3	Erw Lon	(L)	LAD	3m	10	GS	*twrds rear to 8th, prog frm 13th, ran on gamely*	3	20
769	31/3	Pantyderi	(R)	LAD	3m	6	G	*mid-div, mstk 10th, rallied frm 2 out, nrst fin*	2	22
979	8/4	Lydstep	(L)	LAD	3m	9	G	*wth ldrs, in ld last, easily*	1	24
1202	21/4	Lydstep	(L)	LAD	3m	4	S	*(fav) sttld bhnd ldr, ld 12th, unchal aft*	1	23
1338	3/5	Bangor	(L)	HC	3m 110yds	8	S	*pulld hrd, chsd ldrs, went 2nd 7th, led after 9th, ran on, pushed clr run-in.*	1	24

Improved; won 5 of last 11; staying better; should win more Ladies in 97, at least; Any, best G-S 24

BUSTEELE b.g. 12 Bustino - Narration (USA) by Sham (USA) — R Hardy

139	17/2	Larkhill	(R)	CON	3m	11	G	*alwys last & y.o., p.u. 13th*	P	0
468	10/3	Milborne St'	(L)	OPE	3m	5	G	*ld/disp to 14th, wknd nxt*	3	15
1309	28/4	Little Wind'	(R)	OPE	3m	8	G	*(bl) slight ld to 8th, grad wknd, rear & p.u. 14th*	P	0

Missed 95; not regain form; hard to find another win. 14

BUSTERS SISTER b.m. 8 Hasty Word - Spartan's Girl by Spartan General — G I Cooper

1995 2(12),1(17),P(0)

12	14/1	Cottenham	(R)	RES	3m	12	G	*(fav) prom, chsd ldr 8th, rdn & btn 3 out, styd on agn flat*	2	17
181	18/2	Horseheath	(R)	RES	3m	5	G	*(fav) made all, mstk 9th, clr whn mstks 3 out & nxt, comf*	1	17

Lightly raced; successful stable; won weak Restricted but can improve. G-S. 19

BUSY GOING NOWHERE 6

1007	9/4	Flagg Moor	(L)	MEM	3m	7	G		2	0

.. 0

BUTLER BRENNAN (Irish) — **I** 16^{R}, **I** 81^{P}, **I** 217^{3}

BUTLER JOHN(IRE) b.g. 7 The Parson - Corrielek by Menelek — Nick Viney

1995 **4(NH),4(NH),1(NH),F(NH),4(NH),2(NH)**

40	3/2	Wadebridge	(L)	LAD	3m	5	GF	*j.w., ld 2nd, clr 14th, pshd out flat*	1	24
67	10/2	Great Treth'	(R)	LAD	3m	11	S	*(Jt fav) ld 4th-14th, sn fdd, p.u. 2 out*	P	0
378	9/3	Barbury Cas'	(L)	LAD	3m	6	GS	*(fav) ld til blnd & u.r. 5th*	U	-
530	16/3	Cothelstone	(L)	OPE	3m	7	G	*hld up, prog to trk ldr 12th, rddn & btn appr 3 out*	2	22
654	23/3	Badbury Rin'	(L)	OPE	3m	5	G	*rr, prog 8th, no ch wth wnnr*	2	21
818	6/4	Charlton Ho'	(L)	LAD	3m	6	GF	*chsd ldr, chal 13th, alwys held frm 3 out*	2	21
1126	20/4	Stafford Cr'	(R)	LAD	3m	7	S	*made all, lft wll clr frm 3 out*	1	25

Winning hurdler; speedy & best in Ladies over eaßy 3m; good stable; can win again; G/F-S, G/F best ... 25

BUTLERS MATCH(IRE) ch.g. 6 Matching Pair - Millys Last by Cheval — Mrs Helen Mobley

1995 P(0)

439	9/3	Newton Brom'	(R)	MDN	3m	7	GS	*alwys prom, ld 12th-nxt, ld 14th-last, outpcd*	3	0
1103	14/4	Guilsborough	(L)	MDN	3m	15	G	*(Jt fav) mstk 3rd, chsd ldrs, wknd 15th, t.o. & p.u. last*	P	0

Last when completing; ran poorly after; still young and can do better in time. 12

BUT NOT QUITE(IRE) b.g. 8 Nearly A Nose (USA) - Rosa Perfecta — Derek J Harding-Jones

1995 3(11),2(13),7(0),2(12),3(15)

423	9/3	High Easter	(L)	MDN	3m	8	S	*(fav) keen hold, chsd ldrs, cls 3rd whn blnd & u.r. 10th*	U	-
495	16/3	Horseheath	(R)	MDO	3m	12	GF	*ld to 7th, wknd rpdly 10th, t.o. & p.u. 4 out*	P	0
1326	28/4	Fakenham P-'	(L)	MDO	3m	7	G	*hld up, mstk 5th, sn lost tch, p.u. apr 7th*	P	0

1403 6/5 Northaw (L) MDO 3m 8 F *keen hold, prom til wknd qkly 15th, bhnd & p.u. appr nxt* P 0

Fair form in 95; changed hands and gone to pieces; pulls and no stamina in 96; best avoided. 10

BUTT AND BEN b.g. 12 Crofter (USA) - Aileen's Belle by The Parson N F K Pearse
1995 8(0),P(0)
157 17/2 Erw Lon (L) CON 3m 15 G *alwys 3rd/4th, wknd 3 out* 5 10
544 17/3 Erw Lon (L) MEM 3m 5 GS *alwys 2nd/3rd, btn 2 out, lame* 3 0

1 win since 87; problems last start and no prospects now. 13

BUTTON YOUR LIP b.g. 14 Le Bavard (FR) - High Energy by Dalesa Mrs J Enderby
1995 6(0),U(-),6(0),6(10),4(0),4(11),2(12)
27 20/1 Barbury Cas' (L) LAD 3m 15 GS *chsd ldrs til f 10th* F -
126 17/2 Kingston Bl' (L) LAD 3m 11 GS *chsd ldrs, 4th & lost tch aft 13th, styd on well apr last* 3 16
782 31/3 Tweseldown (R) XX 3m 6 G *ld 3-9th, chsd ldr til not qckn 4 out, styd on wll flat* 1 13
888 6/4 Kimble (L) LAD 3m 4 GF *last frm 4th, t.o. 13th* 4 0
1015 13/4 Kingston Bl' (L) MEM 3m 9 G *chsd wnr 6-7th, lost plc 10th, effrt 14th, onepcd* 4 10
1562 19/5 Mollington (R) MEM 3m 6 GS *sn bhnd, t.o. 6th, p.u. 11th* P 0
1611 26/5 Tweseldown (R) XX 3m 9 G *chsd ldrs, disp 3rd whn u.r. 10th* U -

School master now; dead-heated in Tweseldown special; most unlikely to win again. 13

BUXOM ORLOV (Irish) — **I** 443^P, **I** 471^P
BUZZ ABOUT (Irish) — **I** 226^P, **I** 417^P, **I** 522^4, **I** 528^F
BUZZARDS GRANGE b.g. 8 Buzzards Bay - Tinbah by Rambah S N Burt
172 18/2 Market Rase' (L) RES 3m 9 GF *alwys last, jmpd slwly, t.o. & p.u. 12th* P 0
331 3/3 Market Rase' (L) MDO 3m 9 G *prom to 7th, wknd 10th, last & p.u. 12th* P 0

No signs of ability. 0

BY CRIKEY(IRE) b.g. 6 Treasure Hunter - Jamie's Lady by Ashmore (FR) A J Wight
115 17/2 Lanark (R) MDO 3m 8 GS *ref 2nd* R -

Not a good start. 0

BYE BYE BABY(FR) b.m. 8 Baby Turk - Bustelda (FR) by Busted J R Young
1995 1(11),2(16)
247 25/2 Charing (L) MEM 3m 7 GS *sn wll bhnd,ran on strngly frm 4 out,2nd apr last,no ch wnr* 2 14
775 31/3 Penshurst (L) CON 3m 8 GS *trckd ldrs til mstk 7th, no dang aft, ran on frm 3 out* 4 16

Lightly raced; Members winner 95; consistent and deserves another win. Members best hope. 16

BYLAND PRINCESS b.m. 13 Potent Councillor - Another Pin by Pinza Capt H M A Cummins
307 2/3 Great Stain' (L) MDO 3m 17 GS *1st ride, prom, wknd 15th, t.o. 2 out* 9 0
1134 20/4 Hornby Cast' (L) MEM 3m 6 G *wth ldrs whn u.r. 3rd* U -
1451 6/5 Witton Cast' (R) MDO 3m 12 G *midfld to rear, made slght late hdwy* 5 10

Beaten 14 lengths last start; but a Maiden win at 14 most unlikely. 0

BYRON CHOICE(IRE) ch.g. 6 Le Bavard (FR) - Miss Cynthia by Dawn Review E B Swaffield
470 10/3 Milborne St' (L) MDO 3m 18 G *sn rear, some prog whn u.r. 14th* U -

May have something to write home about in 97. 0

CABBERY ROSE (Irish) — **I** 177^1, **I** 257^3, **I** 362^B, **I** 406^1, **I** 414^1, **I** 490^1
CABRA BOY (Irish) — **I** 172^P, **I** 255^P, **I** 282^P
CADDY MAN (Irish) — **I** 334^U
CADER IDRIS b.g. 7 St Columbus - Llanon by Owen Dudley G J Tarry
1995 F(-),P(0),2(14),U(-),2(14),1(0)
665 24/3 Eaton Hall (R) RES 3m 14 S *ld to 2nd, chsng grp to 4 out, no ch whn p.u. nxt* P 0
1102 14/4 Guilsborough (L) RES 3m 15 G *mstks, ld til blnd 9th, lost tch whn blnd 15th, styd on 2out* 3 14
1145 20/4 Higham (L) RES 3m 12 F *prom in chsng grp to 11th, los ttch nxt, t.o. & p.u. 2 out* P 0
1380 5/5 Dingley (R) RES 3m 11 GF *ld to 2nd,prom,ev ch 15th,not qckn,styd on to chs wnr last* 2 19
1564 19/5 Mollington (R) XX 3m 14 GS *prom, ld 11-13th, ev ch apr 2 out, sn btn, fin tired* 2 16
1641 2/6 Dingley (R) RES 3m 13 GF *(fav) trckd ldrs, rdn & not qckn 15th, styd on, nvr nr* 3 16

Maiden winner 95; capable & beaten by good horses but hard ride & may struggle to find Restricted; gd 18

CADRILLON(FR) br.g. 6 Le Pontet (FR) - Jenvraie (FR) by Night And Day Chester Bosomworth
1995 **10(NH),7(NH),F(NH),4(NH),11(NH)**
176 18/2 Market Rase' (L) MDO 2m 5f 10 GF *mid-div, 3rd at 11th, mstk nxt, rdn & ch last, kpt on flat* 2 15
408 9/3 Charm Park (L) MEM 3m 7 G *(fav) in tch, ld frm 4 out, hld off chal run-in* 1 13
758 31/3 Great Stain' (L) RES 3m 17 GS *mid-div, fdd frm 5 out* 9 0
983 8/4 Charm Park (L) RES 3m 13 GF *in tch, 8th 9th, onepcd frm 4 out* 5 12
1090 14/4 Whitwell-On' (R) RES 3m 17 G *alwys rear, nvr dang, t.o.* 11 0
1447 6/5 Witton Cast' (R) RES 3m 11 G *alwys rear, p.u. 3 out* P 0

1466 11/5 Easingwold (L) CON 3m 10 G *rear, rdn 10th, nvr on terms, p.u. 2 out, saddle slppd* P 0

Poor novice hurdler; won weak race & outclassed after; Members best hope again. 14

CAERFFILI'S BAY b.m. 6 Bold Owl - Irish Holiday by Simbir Miss S Prangley
1995 P(0)

391 9/3 Llanfrynach (R) MDN 3m 11 GS *sn wll bhnd, t.o. 7th, last whn p.u. 12th* P 0
509 16/3 Magor (R) MDN 3m 9 GS *mid-div til lost tch hlfwy, p.u. 13th* P 0

No promise to date 0

CAHERGOWAN (Irish) — I 297^{F}, I 367^{4}, I 431^{1}
CAHERLAG (Irish) — I 651^{F}
CAHERMONE LADY (Irish) — I 55^{P}, I 76^{3}, I 211^{4}, I 277^{P}, I 356^{P}, I 503^{1}, I 648,
CAHILLS HILL (Irish) — I 21^{3}, I 179^{2}, I 261^{U}, I 305^{F}, I 404^{3}
CAILIN CHUINNE (Irish) — I 609^{1}
CAIRNCROSS (Irish) — I 300^{F}, I 361^{1}, I 482^{1}
CAIRNDHU MISTY ch.m. 9 Abednego - Ah Well by Silver Cloud Mrs R Gee

77 11/2 Wetherby Po' (L) RES 3m 18 GS *cls up, fdd 11th, p.u. 4 out* P 0
243 25/2 Southwell P' (L) RES 3m 11 HO *mid-div, prog 13th, ld 3 out-nxt, sn no ext* 3 13

Ran fair race in testing ground but season lasted 2 weeks; best watched 14

CAIRNEYMOUNT b.g. 10 Croghan Hill - Glentoran Valley by Little Buskins Robert Williams

149 17/2 Erw Lon (L) MDN 3m 10 G *rear whn f 4th* F -
509 16/3 Magor (R) MDN 3m 9 GS *5l 2nd whn ran out 4th* r -
771 31/3 Pantyderi (R) MDN 3m 14 G *alwys mid-div* 4 12
976 8/4 Lydstep (L) MDO 3m 12 G *wth ldrs, 3rd & btn last* 3 0
1040 13/4 St Hilary (R) MDN 3m 12 G *rear trio whn u.r. 5th* U -
1161 20/4 Llanwit Maj' (R) MDO 3m 15 GS *cls up, chsd ldr 15th, rdn apr 2 out, no ext* 2 11
1269 27/4 Pyle (R) MDO 3m 9 G *(fav) ld til ran out & u.r. 5th* r -
1391 6/5 Pantyderi (R) MDO 3m 13 GF *trckd ldrs til ld 15th, sn clr, comf* 1 16
1557 18/5 Bassaleg (R) RES 3m 14 F *ldng grp, ld 12th-2 out, rallied to ld last, drvn out* 1 19
1602 25/5 Bassaleg (R) CON 3m 8 GS *(fav) 2nd til ld 10th, clr 13th, easily* 1 18
1636 1/6 Bratton Down (L) OPE 4m 11 G *in tch til outpcd 20th, no dang aft* 4 17

Improved rapidly late season; won modest races; not disgraced last start; can win more. 18

CALICO DRUM (Irish) — I 271^{P}
CALL AVONDALE br.g. 8 Homeboy - Collectors Girl by Mr Bigmore Mrs W J Coombes

138 17/2 Ottery St M' (L) RES 3m 18 GS *alwys mid-div, outpcd frm 4 out* 6 10
821 6/4 Charlton Ho' (L) MDN 3m 10 GF *(7s-3s), alwys rear, t.o. whn p.u. bfr 12th* P 0

Ran well debut; gound possibly wrong next time; go close in 97. 14

CALL COUP(IRE) b.m. 6 Callernish - Coumenole by Beau Chapeau E H Crow

660 24/3 Eaton Hall (R) MDN 3m 7 S *lost tch 7th, ran on steadily frm 4 out, no dang* 3 0

Tailed off last; successful stable and should do better. 0

CALLED TO ACCOUNT b.m. 7 Cool Guy (USA) - True Grit by Klairon Mrs L Marshall
1995 **15(NH)**,**P(NH)**

46 4/2 Alnwick (L) MEM 3m 7 G *last whn u.r. 3rd* U -
89 11/2 Alnwick (L) MDO 3m 9 GS *mstk 2nd,schoold & bhnd,some prog 11th,sn lost tch,p.u. 13th* P 0
192 24/2 Friars Haugh (L) MDN 3m 12 S *nvr nr ldrs* 7 0
405 9/3 Dalston (R) MDO 2 1/2m 16 G *prom, chsd ldrs frm 15th, nt quckn frm 2 out* 3 0
488 16/3 Newcastle (L) HC 2 1/2m 9 GS *alwys bhnd, t.o. when p.u. before 12th.* P 0
613 23/3 Friars Haugh (L) MDN 3m 15 G *2nd hlfwy, ld brfly 15th, no ext frm nxt.* 4 11
916 8/4 Tranwell (L) MDO 2 1/2m 8 GF *(fav) alwys prom, ev ch 4 out, lft 4l 2nd 2 out, outpcd* 2 0

Gradual improvement; form weak and 3 miles too far at present. 12

CALLEROSE b.g. 9 Callernish - Tarqogan's Rose by Tarqogan R J Bevis

219 24/2 Newtown (L) RES 3m 17 GS *mid-div, effrt 11th, lost tch 13th, p.u. 3 out* P 0
749 31/3 Upper Sapey (R) MDO 3m 17 GS *u.r. 2nd* U -
1196 21/4 Sandon (L) MDN 3m 17 G *cls up, ld 5 out, sn clr, eased nr fin* 1 16
1338 3/5 Bangor (L) HC 3m 110yds 8 S *rear, hdwy to go prom 13th, challenging when not fluent 2 out, soon one pace.* 2 21

Ability under Rules; trotted up in Maiden & Restricted should be formality; worth another H/Chase try 20

CALL HER LIB (Irish) — I 459^{P}
CALL HOME(IRE) b.g. 8 Callernish - Easter Beauty by Raise You Ten Maurice E Pinto

580 20/3 Towcester (R) HC 2 3/4m 5 G *chsd ldr, ld 12th, joined 2 out, driven out run-in.* 1 30
808 6/4 Towcester (R) HC 3m 1f 4 F *(fav) blnd 2nd, ld 3rd, soon clr, hdd 3 out, soon outpcd.* 2 28

Decent under Rules & excellent start in H/Chases; can win more if fit 97; G-F 29

CALLIEALLA (Irish) — I 94^{P}, I 170, , I 287^{U}, I 537^{P}

CALLING WILD(IRE) b.g. 6 Callernish - Chestnut Vale by Pollerton — J A Keighley

1995 1(18)

29 20/1 Barbury Cas' (L) RES 3m 12 GS *(fav) mstks, hld up, effrt 15th, styd on, not rch ldrs* 3 18
269 2/3 Didmarton (L) RES 3m 12 G *(Jt fav) mstks,hld up,prog 11th,chal & outjmpd last,qcknd to ld flat* 1 21
1112 17/4 Hockworthy (L) PPO 3m 9 GS *mstks, hld up, chsd wnr aft 2 out, hrd rdn & ran on* 2 24
1244 27/4 Woodford (L) INT 3m 12 G *(fav) chsd ldr til lft in ld 14th,slght mstk 3out,clr nxt,pshd out* 1 24

Exciting youngster; mistakes but jumped much better at Woodford; win Opens 97. G-S. 25

CALL ME CONNIE (Irish) — I 20^{1}, I 44^{2}, I 246^{P}

CALL ME PARIS (Irish) — I 137^{P}, I 352^{6}, I 507^{P}, I 565^{4}, I 608, , I 645^{P}

CALL QUEEN (Irish) — I 225^{1}, I 383^{P}

CALLYS RUN (Irish) — I 132^{B}, I 165^{5}

CAMAN br.m. 9 Callernish - Chilly For June by Menelek — J A V Duell

1995 **P(NH),P(NH),P(NH)**

78 11/2 Wetherby Po' (L) OPE 3m 10 GS *cls up, 2nd at 5th, wknd, p.u. 13th* P 0
224 24/2 Duncombe Pa' (R) RES 3m 12 GS *sn wll bhnd, t.o. frm 7th* 6 0
302 2/3 Great Stain' (L) MEM 3m 7 GS *cls up to 12th, wknd aft, poor 5th 2 out, fin 5th, promoted* 4 0
411 9/3 Charm Park (L) RES 3m 20 G *rr early, p.u. 10th* P 0
585 23/3 Wetherby Po' (L) RES 3m 13 S *t.o. 6th, fin own time* 5 0
1092 14/4 Whitwell-On' (R) CON 3m 10 G *rear & dtchd 3rd, sn t.o., p.u. 2 out* P 0
1131 20/4 Hornby Cast' (L) RES 3m 17 G *prom early, lost plc hlfwy, t.o. 11th* 9 0
1281 27/4 Easingwold (L) CON 3m 15 G *rear, mid-div whn u.r. 9th* U -
1446 6/5 Witton Cast' (R) CON 3m 7 G *rear, t.o. 14th, came home own time* 5 0
1466 11/5 Easingwold (L) CON 3m 10 G *rear, dtchd 7th, t.o. 10th* 7 0
1571 19/5 Corbridge (R) RES 3m 13 G *alwys bhnd* 8 0

Poor novice hurdler/chaser; novice ridden; mega safe but woefully slow. 0

CAMDEN LAMP (Irish) — I 42^{P}, I 128^{P}, I 206^{6}, I 253^{4}, I 291^{P}

CAMLA LAD (Irish) — I 36^{F}

CAMOGUE BRIDGE (Irish) — I 73^{5}, I 138^{P}, I 199^{2}, I 248^{1}, I 371^{P}, I 441^{P}, I 544,

CAMOGUE-VALLEY(IRE) b or br.g. 7 Rising - Pandos Pet by Dusky Boy — Dudley C Moore

12 14/1 Cottenham (R) RES 3m 12 G *rear, pshd alng 8th, blnd nxt, t.o. & p.u. 13th* P 0
95 11/2 Ampton (R) RES 3m 11 GF *blnd 8th, rmndrs nxt, jnd ldrs 11th, wknd 13th, t.o.* 5 0

Won Irish Maiden 94; well beaten & finished early 96; unpromising. 0

CANADIAN BOY(IRE) b.g. 7 Commanche Run - Canadian Guest by Be My Guest (USA) — Mrs J Shirley

1995 P(0),2(11),9(0)

91 11/2 Ampton (R) MDO 3m 10 GF *alwys prom, ev ch 16th, wknd apr 2 out* 4 0
233 24/2 Heythrop (R) MDN 3m 14 GS *(Jt fav) cls up to hlfwy, fdd & p.u. 2 out* P 0
341 3/3 Heythrop (R) MDN 3m 13 G *prom, ld 9th, clr 3 out, hdd & no ext flat* 2 14
495 16/3 Horseheath (R) MDO 3m 12 GF *alwys prom, ld 9th, prssd 4 out, ran on well, fin tired* 1 14
1102 14/4 Guilsborough (L) RES 3m 15 G *chsd ldrs, rdn 9th, mstk 14th, wll btn 3 out* 5 0
1292 28/4 Barbury Cas' (L) RES 3m 11 F *made most to 6th, wth ldrs whn f 9th, dead* F -

Dead. 15

CANDLE GLOW ch.m. 8 Capitano - Fused Light by Fury Royal — Mrs P J Hutchinson

1995 1(14)

361 5/3 Leicester (R) HC 2 1/2m 110yds 15 GS *ld to 4th, weakening when blnd 9th, t.o. when p.u. 3 out.* P 0
484 15/3 Fakenham (L) HC 2m 5f 110yds 13 GF *chsd ldrs till wknd 11th.* 9 0
904 6/4 Dingley (R) RES 3m 20 GS *ld to 5 out, ran on onepce whn hdd* 3 16
1145 20/4 Higham (L) RES 3m 12 F *made all, sn wll clr, 25l up final cct, unchal* 1 24
1329 30/4 Huntingdon (R) HC 3m 14 GF *made all, soon well clr, rdn run-in, all out.* 1 22
1548 18/5 Southwell (L) HC 3m 110yds 11 GF *ld till apr 3rd, led 7th till approaching 10th, ran on from 2 out.* 4 16

Much improved; front runner; Restricted class H/chase win makes life tough now. 22

CANDY IS DANDY (Irish) — I 7^{P}

CANGORT KING (Irish) — I 201,

CAN I COME TOO (Irish) — I 492^{P}

CANISTER CASTLE b.g. 8 Gypsy Castle - Vultop by Vulgan Slave — Miss Z A Green

1995 **P(0),P(0)**

51 4/2 Alnwick (L) MDO 3m 17 G *tckd ldrs, clse up 13th, one pace frm 3 out* 4 13
88 11/2 Alnwick (L) MDO 3m 11 GS *prom, ld 9-11th, 2nd whn mstk 13th, wknd* 3 0

192	24/2	Friars Haugh	(L)	MDN	3m	12	S	*alwys handy, no imp frm 3 out*	3	11
321	2/3	Corbridge	(R)	MDN	3m	12	GS	*mstk 1st, rear til prog 15th, styd on und pres frm last*	2	12
789	1/4	Kelso	(L)	HC	3m 1f	11	GF	*blnd 2nd, chsd ldrs till lost tch quickly and p.u. before 7 out.*	P	0
1087	14/4	Friars Haugh	(L)	MDO	3m	9	F	*(fav) alwys handy, ld apr last, kpt on well*	1	15

Consistent in weak Maidens and deserved win; well short of Restricted class. 14

CANNY CHRONICLE b or br.g. 8 Daring March - Laisser Aller by Sagaro — Miss C E J Dawson

110	17/2	Lanark	(R)	CON	3m	10	GS	*alwys wll bhnd, p.u. 4 out*	P	0
371	8/3	Ayr	(L)	HC	2m 5f 110yds	8	GF	*ld, clr till hfwy, hdd after 14th, 2nd and weakening when f 4 out.*	F	-
498	16/3	Lanark	(R)	CON	3m	10	G	*cls 4th at 11th, wknd 4 out, p.u. 2 out*	P	0

Very useful novice hurdler in 92 but has shown nothing since 10

CANNY CURATE(IRE) b.g. 7 The Parson - Lisa Martin by Black Minstrel — C J B Barlow

407	9/3	Dalston	(R)	MDO	2 1/2m	13	G	*mid-div whn b.d. 8th*	B	-
661	24/3	Eaton Hall	(R)	MDN	3m	9	S	*mid-div, 4th & ev ch 3 out, onepcd*	4	0
1033	13/4	Alpraham	(R)	MDO	2 1/2m	15	GS	*mid-div frm 6th, onepcd aft*	5	0

Beaten 22 lengths minimum; can go closer in 97. 11

CANNY'S FORT ch.m. 7 Fort Nayef - Canny's Tudor by Tudor Cliff — P F Gibbon

764	31/3	Great Stain'	(L)	MDN	3m	16	GS	*chsd ldrs til wknd hlfwy, t.o. & p.u. 14th*	P	0
1095	14/4	Whitwell-On'	(R)	MDO	2 1/2m 88yds	14	G	*mid-div whn f 7th*	F	-
1137	20/4	Hornby Cast'	(L)	MDN	3m	13	G	*alwys wth ldrs, no prog frm 3 out, onepcd*	5	0
1452	6/5	Witton Cast'	(R)	MEM	3m	7	G	*pulld hrd, cls up whn f 10th*	F	-

Well beaten when completing; stamina looks a problem and well short of a win yet. 0

CAN SHE DO IT (Irish) — I 479P

CANTANGO(IRE) b.g. 6 Carlingford Castle - Judy Can Dance by Northern Guest (USA) — W J Turcan

62	10/2	Cottenham	(R)	MDO	3m	6	GS	*(fav) in tch, trckd ldr 10th-3 out, effrt apr last, no ext flat*	2	14
241	25/2	Southwell P'	(L)	MDO	3m	15	HO	*(fav) mid-div, effrt to 6th whn f 4 out*	F	-
542	17/3	Southwell P'	(L)	MDO	3m	15	GS	*(fav) hld up, nvr rchd ldrs*	3	0
900	6/4	Dingley	(R)	MDN	2m 5f	8	GS	*4th, lft 3rd 6 out, f nxt*	F	-

Good debut; seemed to lose confidence after; time on his side; novice-ridden & needs better handling 13

CANTANTIVY b.m. 11 Idiot's Delight - Ivy Hill by Cantab — T N Bailey

1995 P(0),P(0),U(-),4(0),4(13),P(0),2(16),3(15),5(17),3(19),P(0)

216	24/2	Newtown	(L)	LAD	3m	13	GS	*rear, mstk 8th, p.u. nxt*	P	0
603	23/3	Howick	(L)	LAD	3m	8	S	*chsd wnr to 12th, wknd & p.u. 3 out*	P	0
879	6/4	Brampton Br'	(R)	LAD	3m	9	GF	*mid-div, 21l 5th at 11th, wknd frm 14th, t.o.*	9	0
1415	6/5	Cursneh Hill	(L)	RES	3m	11	GF	*ld frm 2nd til hdd aft 15th, wknd frm nxt*	3	16
1508	12/5	Maisemore P'	(L)	LAD	3m	6	F	*2nd brfly 9th,poor 3rd frm 12th,styd on 3 out,lft in ld last*	1	15
1614	27/5	Hereford	(R)	HC	3m 1f 110yds	16	G	*handily pld, rdn 15th, outpcd 3 out.*	5	16
1635	1/6	Bratton Down	(L)	LAD	3m	13	G	*ld 6th til aft 3 out, wknd nxt, walked in*	11	0

Lucky ladies winner (runner up remounted); outclassed normally and need luck to win again.G-F. 15

CANTELIER (Irish) — I 500P

CANTORIAL ch.g. 15 Cantab - Signal Melody by Bleep-Bleep — Mrs A M G Church

1995 U(-),P(0)

249	25/2	Charing	(L)	XX	3m	11	GS	*rear til p.u. 11th*	P	0
270	2/3	Parham	(R)	MEM	3m	5	GF	*in tch, effrt 13th, ld brfly nxt, kpt on onepcd*	3	10

Winning chaser; not disgraced in Members but surely too old now. 0

CAPE COTTAGE ch.g. 12 Dubassoff (USA) - Cape Thriller by Thriller — D J Caro

1995 2(28),**2(27)**,3(26)

98	12/2	Hereford	(R)	HC	3m 1f 110yds	12	HY	*prom, weakening when left in 2nd pl and ref 2 out.*	R	-
256	29/2	Ludlow	(R)	HC	3m	14	G	*in tch 6th, styd on from 4 out, tk 2nd run-in, no ch with wnr.*	2	24
483	14/3	Cheltenham	(L)	HC	3 1/4m 110yds	17	G	*bhnd, hmpd 3rd, struggling from hfwy, well t.o. when p.u. between last 2.*	P	0

H/Chase winner 94; lightly raced; declined in 96 and need a return to points before winning again. 24

CAPE HENRY b.g. 9 Dubassoff (USA) - Cape Mandalin by Mandamus — T F Sage

1995 U(-)

139	17/2	Larkhill	(R)	CON	3m	11	G	*sttld rear, prog to ld 13th-15th, wknd nxt*	3	18

Ran a stormer on only start; only ever ran twice but a Maiden at his mercy if fit in 97. 17

CAPPAGH GLEN (Irish) — I 12[2]

CAPPAJUNE (Irish) — **I** 84^{4}, **I** 106^{2}, **I** 164^{1}, **I** 230^{1}, **I** 389^{1}

CAPPANAGRANE HILL (Irish) — **I** 579^{P}, **I** 605^{4}, **I** 636^{P}, **I** 647^{6}

CAPRICE DE COTTE(FR) ch.g. 6 Olmeto - Rafale de Cotte (FR) by Italic (FR) — Brian Coles

689 30/3 Chaddesley ' (L) MDN 3m 15 G *schoold rear, p.u. 11th* P 0
1170 20/4 Chaddesley ' (L) CON 3m 9 G *rear, short-lived effrt 8th, wknd 12th, p.u. nxt* P 0

Only learning so far. **0**

CAPSTOWN BAY b.g. 5 Capitano - Calfstown Maid by Master Buck — Mrs J Alford

131 17/2 Ottery St M' (L) MDN 3m 10 GS *rear, some prog 14th, lft bttr by dfctns, nvr nrr* 2 0
630 23/3 Kilworthy (L) MDN 3m 10 GS *(fav) 2s-1/1, lost plc 7th, prog to ld 14th, mstk 3 out, drvn out* 1 15

Landed a gamble; not seen again; looks capable of upgrading; stays; both runs easy surface. **17**

CAPTAIN BEAL ch.g. 10 Ginger Boy - Bealsmead by Rugantino — Mrs G Drury

1995 P(0),P(0),P(0),2(0)
576 17/3 Detling (L) MDN 3m 18 GF *prom, 3rd at 14th, wknd 3 out* 4 0
964 8/4 Heathfield (R) RES 3m 7 G *in tch to 10th, wll bhnd whn p.u. appr 14th* P 0

Lightly raced; subsequent winner behind when 4th but will need fortune to win. **10**

CAPTAIN DIMITRIS ch.g. 11 Dubassoff (USA) - Proud Gipsy by Sky Gipsy — Mrs N M Coombe

1995 R(-),8(0),6(0),3(0),P(0)
472 10/3 Milborne St' (L) INT 3m 8 G *sn rear, t.o. & p.u. 3 out* P 0
649 23/3 Cothelstone (L) LAD 3m 3 S *(Jt fav) chsd ldr, 5l bhnd 3 out, rdn, no impn from last* 2 11
728 31/3 Little Wind' (R) MEM 3m 7 GS *prom to 11th, sn outpcd, kpt on onepcd frm 3 out* 3 13
867 6/4 Larkhill (R) MXO 4m 6 F *sn rear, outpcd 10th, t.o. 13th* 4 0
1311 28/4 Little Wind' (R) INT 3m 6 G *last but in tch whn u.r. 4th* U -

Dual winner 92; outclassed in competitive races and unlikely to win again. **14**

CAPTAIN EQUATY ch.g. 13 Captain Drake - Equa by Cheval — Mrs B J Harkins

1156 20/4 Llanwit Maj' (R) MEM 3m 7 GS *ld to 11th, sn wknd, p.u. 14th* P 0
1557 18/5 Bassaleg (R) RES 3m 14 F *in tch whn b.d. 7th* B -
1601 25/5 Bassaleg (R) RES 3m 12 GS *mid-div, lost tch hlfwy, p.u. 10th* P 0

Beaten last 24 starts and looks past it now. **0**

CAPTAIN GUINNESS (Irish) — **I** 30^{P}, **I** 87^{P}, **I** 161^{U}, **I** 345^{3}, **I** 420^{2}, **I** 528^{B}

CAPTAIN JIM b.g. 13 Proverb - Brave Jennifer by Brave Invader (USA) — Miss Christine Adams

140 17/2 Larkhill (R) CON 3m 17 G *sn t.o., p.u. last* P 0

Won Intermediate 94; only 1 run since and looks finished now. **13**

CAPTAIN KELLY b.g. 18 Netherkelly - Popover by Dumbarnie — P M Webb

1150 20/4 Whittington (L) MEM 3m 6 G *2nd 4-8th, wknd qckly, wnt round in own time* 4 0

Returned for a jaunt round in his Members.ew owner & looks finished **0**

CAPTAIN SCURLOUGH (Irish) — **I** 345^{P}, **I** 381^{P}, **I** 618^{P}

CAPTAINS VIEW (Irish) — **I** 104^{P}, **I** 272^{3}, **I** 298^{3}, **I** 395^{1}, **I** 477^{6}, **I** 627^{3}

CAPTIVA BAY b.m. 7 Scorpio (FR) - Leading Line by Leading Man — Miss D Hockenhull

167 17/2 Weston Park (L) MDN 3m 10 G *f 1st* F -
288 2/3 Eaton Hall (R) MDO 3m 17 G *u.r. 5th* U -
569 17/3 Wolverhampt' (L) MDN 3m 11 GS *prom to 14th, wknd, btn 4th whn p.u. 3 out* P 0
663 24/3 Eaton Hall (R) LAD 3m 8 S *prom to 4 out, sn btn* 4 14
1029 13/4 Alpraham (R) MDO 3m 8 GS *chsd ldr til ld 13th, hdd apr last, no ext* 2 14

Steady improvement; winner behind on last start; should score in 97; stays. **13**

CAPTURE THE MAGIC(IRE) b.m. 6 Tanfirion - Petty Session by Blakeney — H Morris

352 3/3 Garnons (L) MDN 2 1/2m 9 GS *ref to race* 0 0
389 9/3 Llanfrynach (R) MDN 3m 11 GS *t.d.e. ld to 2nd, jnd ldr whn bmpd & f 6th* F -
696 30/3 Llanvapley (L) MDN 3m 13 GS *alwys rear, dist 5th whn p.u. flat* P 0
883 6/4 Brampton Br' (R) MDN 3m 13 GF *cls 4th at 13th, ld 16th, jmpd lft 2 out, rdn out flat* 1 15
1222 24/4 Brampton Br' (R) RES 3m 11 G *s.a., alwys rr, p.u. 14th* P 0

Beat six other finishers at Brampton Bryan; temperamental and needs more for Restricted. **14**

CAPULET b.g. 13 Henbit (USA) - Lady Juliet (USA) by Gallant Man — Miss L Jones

1205 21/4 Heathfield (R) MEM 3m 4 F *last & in tch, prog to ld 10-16th, 2nd aft, onepcd, lame* 2 0

Beaten in dire Members(7lbs o.w.); barely worth a rating. **10**

CARACOL b.g. 7 Ore - Fit For A King by Royalty — C G Bolton

1995 3(13),1(15)

41	3/2	Wadebridge	(L)	XX	3m	9	GF	*hld up, prog 11th, hmprd 15th, styd on agn flat*	3	15
219	24/2	Newtown	(L)	RES	3m	17	GS	*4s-9/4, alwys prom, ld apr 2 out, hdd & wknd apr last*	2	19
386	9/3	Llanfrynach	(R)	RES	3m	10	GS	*(fav) not fluent, ld, 1l up whn ran off course aft 11th*	r	-
549	17/3	Erw Lon	(L)	RES	3m	11	GS	*(fav) 2nd til ld 13th, sn in cmmnd*	1	17
1013	13/4	Ascot	(R)	HC	3m 110yds	11	GS	*hdwy 11th, wknd 3 out, t.o. when p.u. before last, taild off.*	P	0
1211	23/4	Chepstow	(L)	HC	3m	13	S	*mstk 2nd, hdwy 10th, wknd 13th, bhnd when p.u. before 4 out.*	P	0

Won 2 weak easily 95/96; outclassed in H/chases; young and capable of upgrading in 97. 19

CARBERY ARCTIC b.g. 11 Le Bavard (FR) - Arctic Straight by Straight Lad — John Eaton

1995 1(17),2(15),2(17),3(20)

687	30/3	Chaddesley '	(L)	CON	3m	10	G	*in tch, outpcd 13th, 5th 2 out, ran on well flat*	3	17
1046	13/4	Bitterley	(L)	LAD	3m	9	G	*(fav) prog 9th, trckd ldrs 12th, ev ch 14th, kpt on frm 3 out*	3	19
1244	27/4	Woodford	(L)	INT	3m	12	G	*prom in chsng grp, 4th & rddn 16th, onepcd*	3	18
1435	6/5	Ashorne	(R)	CON	3m	12	G	*mid-div,7th & out of tch 11th,ran on wll frm 14th,tk 2nd fin*	2	20
1478	11/5	Bredwardine	(R)	CON	3m	12	G	*w.w. prog 11th, chsd wnr 3 out, clsng flat*	2	23

Restricted winner 95; consistent; finishes well but normally to later; can win a weak Confined/Inter. ... 20

CARBERY BOY (Irish) — I 118[P], I 155[3], I 228[P], I 327[3], I 516[F], I 614[2], I 642[2]

CARBERY MINSTREL (Irish) — I 8[1], I 153[U], I 212[6], I 378[P], I 463[3]

CARDAN b.g. 10 Mandalus - Roamaway by Gala Performance (USA) — Mrs R Welch

1995 r(-),10(0),**4(0),4(12),P(0),P(0)**

132	17/2	Ottery St M'	(L)	MDN	3m	9	GS	*alwys prom, ld 7th-15th, lost tch 4 out, onepcd aft*	3	10
200	24/2	Lemalla	(R)	MDO	3m	12	HY	*ld 6th-9th, wknd, p.u. 3 out*	P	0
558	17/3	Ottery St M'	(L)	MDO	3m	9	G	*prom, 2nd whn u.r. 7th*	U	-
1014	13/4	Kingston Bl'	(L)	MEM	3m	4	G	*ld, blnd 9th, hdd nxt, ld 13th-nxt, wknd, virt p.u. flat*	4	0
1532	13/5	Towcester	(R)	HC	2m 110yds	16	GF	*nvr better than mid div.*	8	15
1638	1/6	Bratton Down	(L)	MDO	3m	13	G	*ld 6th, clr 15th, 6l up last, wknd & hdd nr fin*	2	15
1651	8/6	Umberleigh	(L)	MDO	3m	11	GF	*(fav) prom, ld 6th til ran out & u.r. 10th*	r	-

Basically a non-stayer; just caught at Bratton; frustrating & will prove hard to win with. 14

CARDINAL BIRD(USA) b.g. 9 Storm Bird (CAN) - Shawnee Creek (USA) by Mr Prospector (USA) — F R Bown

42	3/2	Wadebridge	(L)	CON	3m	8	GF	*rlct to race, t.o. whn tried to ref 5th, p.u. nxt*	P	0
134	17/2	Ottery St M'	(L)	CON	3m	12	GS	*alwys mid-div, nvr on terms*	5	0
196	24/2	Lemalla	(R)	CON	3m	14	HY	*(bl) t.o. 3rd, p.u. 13th*	P	0
560	17/3	Ottery St M'	(L)	CON	3m	7	G	*(bl) ref 1st*	R	-
623	23/3	Kilworthy	(L)	MEM	3m	4	GS	*(bl) 1st ride, s.s. last til ref 5th*	R	-
873	6/4	Higher Kilw'	(L)	CON	3m	4	GF	*(bl) prog to cls 3rd 9th, in tch til outpcd aft 14th*	3	16
1142	20/4	Flete Park	(R)	CON	3m	11	S	*prog 9th,rpd prog to ld aft 4 out,wknd & hdd apr 2 out,p.u.*	P	0
1275	27/4	Bratton Down	(L)	OPE	3m	8	GF	*(bl) bhnd, out of tch 13th, t.o. & p.u. last*	P	0
1427	6/5	High Bickin'	(R)	CON	3m	10	G	*(bl) t.o. whn ref 6th*	R	-
1636	1/6	Bratton Down	(L)	OPE	4m	11	G	*(bl) wll in tch til outpcd 20th, wknd 2 out, last whn p.u. flat*	P	0
1650	8/6	Umberleigh	(L)	CON	3m	7	GF	*(bl) reluc to race, ref 2nd*	R	-

Winning hurdler; does not enjoy pointing. 10

CARDINAL COURT(IRE) ch.g. 8 Cardinal Flower - Scarlet Wind by Whistling Wind — A G Bonas

77	11/2	Wetherby Po'	(L)	RES	3m	18	GS	*ran out 2nd*	r	-

Dead 12

CARDINAL RED b.g. 9 The Parson - Rose Ravine by Deep Run — J M Turner

1995 **8(NH),6(NH),8(NH),6(NH),4(NH),4(NH)**

31	20/1	Higham	(L)	CON	3m	9	GF	*prom, ld 5th-9th, rddn & no ex appr 2 out*	3	21
102	17/2	Marks Tey	(L)	CON	3m	17	G	*prom to 12th, grad wknd, p.u. 2 out*	P	0
418	9/3	High Easter	(L)	CON	3m	10	S	*keen hold,disp ld til 7th,chsd ldr til ld 2 out,clr last*	1	20
622	23/3	Higham	(L)	CON	3m	10	GF	*unruly start, mstks, rdn to ld 11th, hdd 15th, sn btn*	6	0
832	6/4	Marks Tey	(L)	LAD	3m	8	G	*prom/disp, wknd rpdly 15th, t.o. 17th*	4	16
1065	13/4	Horseheath	(R)	CON	3m	4	F	*keen hold,ld/disp to 12th,ev ch 3 out,3rd & btn whn u.r. nxt*	U	-
1324	28/4	Fakenham P-'	(L)	LAD	3m	6	G	*disp til lft in ld 11th-12th, rdn 3 out, ld last, all out*	1	21
1538	16/5	Folkestone	(R)	HC	3 1/4m	6	G	*ld into start, in tch, chsd ldr apr 2 out, rdn approaching last, led run-in, just held on.*	1	20

Quite able at best but inconsistent & hard ride; should win again but cannot be trusted; F-S 21

CARDINALS LADY (Irish) — I 176[B], I 259[P], I 301[F], I 315[F]

CARDSCHOOL b.m. 7 Senang Hati - Game Reserve by Doeskin — W E Smith

1995 **14(NH)**

640	23/3	Siddington	(L)	LAD	3m	9	S	*ld & hit 6th, blnd bdly 8th, pulld out nxt*	P	0
890	6/4	Kimble	(L)	MDN	3m	11	GF	*hld up, mstk 8th, rear 12th, wll bhnd whn p.u. 2 out*	P	0
1018	13/4	Kingston Bl'	(L)	LAD	3m	8	G	*alwys bhnd, t.o. last whn p.u. 11th*	P	0

Ex novice hurdler; no signs of hope in points yet. 0

CARHOO SURPRISE (Irish) — I 460[F]

CARIBO EXPRESS (Irish) — **I** 14^{P}, **I** 57^{4}, **I** 78^{F}, **I** 156^{U}, **I** 227^{P}, **I** 437^{P}

CARLINGFORD GALE (Irish) — **I** 76^{F}, **I** 119^{2}, **I** 380^{1}

CARLINGFORD LAD(IRE) b.g. 6 Carlingford Castle - Raby by Pongee — A J Brazier

1006 9/4 Upton-On-Se' (R) MDN 3m 11 F *sn wl bhnd, 10th whn r.o. & u.r. 4th* r -

Unpromising start. **0**

CARLING LASS (Irish) — **I** 44^{P}

CARLOWITZ(USA) b.g. 8 Danzig (USA) - Aunt Carol (USA) by Big Spruce (USA) — Mrs J Sidebottom
1995 **P(NH),0(NH)**

146 17/2 Erw Lon (L) MEM 3m 7 G *rear, prog to 3rd 10th, wknd, p.u. 15th* P 0
545 17/3 Erw Lon (L) CON 3m 10 GS *s.s. p.u. 3rd* P 0
547 17/3 Erw Lon (L) OPE 3m 10 GS *2nd outing, mstks, ld 10th, lkd wnr whn f 2 out* F -
766 31/3 Pantyderi (R) CON 3m 6 G *s.s. ref 2nd* R -
768 31/3 Pantyderi (R) OPE 3m 10 G *2nd outing, ld 13th-4 out, agn nxt, comf, lame* 1 19
1488 11/5 Erw Lon (L) OPE 3m 4 F *2nd/3rd thruout, 3rd whn ref last, (sore)* R -

Remarkable season; best runs on 2nd outing of day! temperamental & has problems now **15**

CARLSAN ch.g. 10 Carlingford Castle - Lovely Sanara by Proverb — Mrs A Price
1995 2(17),F(-),2(12),F(-)

386 9/3 Llanfrynach (R) RES 3m 10 GS *prom, chsd ldr 10th, lft clr nxt, hdd & no ext last* 2 14
880 6/4 Brampton Br' (R) XX 3m 8 GF *prom, ld 9th-15th, no ext whn hdd, kpt on onepcd* 2 18
1048 13/4 Bitterley (L) MDO 3m 12 G *alwys chsng ldrs, styd on to ld 2 out, rdn out flat* 1 15
1223 24/4 Brampton Br' (R) RES 3m 11 G *trckd ldrs, prog 14th, lft 2nd 16th, died aft race* 2 13

Dead. **16**

CARLY BRRIN br.g. 11 Carlin - Bios Brrin by Pitpan — J R Buckley

168 18/2 Market Rase' (L) MEM 3m 7 GF *mstks, made most to 15th, blnd nxt, sn rdn & btn* 2 15
326 3/3 Market Rase' (L) OPE 3m 14 G *ld 4th til apr 14th, rdn & onepcd frm nxt* 2 20
410 9/3 Charm Park (L) OPE 3m 17 G *cls up, 4th at 6th, rr whn p.u. 9th* P 0
632 23/3 Market Rase' (L) CON 3m 10 GF *ld, 12l clr 11th, ct 4 out, hdd flat, came again* 1 21
1024 13/4 Brocklesby ' (L) OPE 3m 6 GF *(fav) cont to 6 out, chsd wnnr nxt, 3l down whn f 3 out* F -
1330 30/4 Huntingdon (R) HC 2 1/2m 110yds 8 GF *disp ld to 4th, mstks 6th and 7th, rdn 10th, no ch when p.u. before last.* P 0
1462 10/5 Market Rasen (R) HC 2 3/4m 110yds 11 G *ld 2nd, hit 7th, hdd next, in tch till wknd apr 3 out.* 6 14

Won 3, placed 12, last 17 points; outclassed in H/chases; should find another race. **19**

CARLY CLEVER CLOGS(IRE) ch.m. 7 Carlingford Castle - Goccia D'Oro (ITY) by Bolkonski — Mrs P A Gaskin
1995 5(0),3(13),2(11),U(-)

175 18/2 Market Rase' (L) MDO 2m 5f 8 GF *pllng, hld up, squeezed thro' & ld apr last, drvn out* 1 14
329 3/3 Market Rase' (L) RES 3m 12 G *(Jt fav) w.w. prog & ev ch apr 14th, wknd nxt* 5 0
825 6/4 Stainton (R) RES 3m 7 GF *rear, prog 6th, ev ch 2 out, btn whn mstk last* 2 14
1131 20/4 Hornby Cast' (L) RES 3m 17 G *chsd ldrs, mstk 4th, outpcd 13th, kpt on frm 3 out* 4 14

Won short Maiden (well ridden); barely stays; may find weak Restricted on easy course.G-F. **16**

CARLY'S CASTLE b.m. 9 Carlingford Castle - Ann Advancer by Even Money — J T Jones
1995 3(19),3(20),**U(-)**,4(18),2(0),4(15),6(13),1(18),**7(14),6(0)**

162 17/2 Weston Park (L) OPE 3m 16 G *prom, outpcd by ldng pair frm 4 out* 3 18
255 28/2 Taunton (R) HC 4 1/4m 110yds 15 GS *chasing ldrs when f 6th, dead.* F -

Dead. **20**

CARN COUNT ch.g. 9 Carlingford Castle - Glencarrig Lady by Fortina — P Senter
1995 P(0),5(0),**F(-)**

1314 28/4 Bitterley (L) MEM 3m 13 G *rdn & no prog 11th, p.u. 13th* P 0

Maiden winner 93; hardly seen since and can only be watched now. **0**

CARNMORE HOUSE (Irish) — **I** 138^{P}, **I** 201^{P}, **I** 237^{P}, **I** 431^{P}, **I** 585^{P}

CAROLE'S DELIGHT b.m. 9 Idiot's Delight - Fishermans Lass by Articulate — C Holden
1995 2(20),2(20),2(20),P(0),1(19),1(21),2(17),3(13)

76 11/2 Wetherby Po' (L) LAD 3m 8 GS *mid-div, effrt 13th, onepcd aft* 5 14
227 24/2 Duncombe Pa' (R) LAD 3m 6 GS *ld to 10th, chsd wnr aft, rallied gamely flat* 2 18
412 9/3 Charm Park (L) LAD 3m 7 G *(fav) ld 13th, wknd, rnwd chal, disp last, drvn out* 1 20
514 16/3 Dalton Park (R) LAD 3m 8 G *ld til apr 15th, 4th & btn 3 out* 4 17
827 6/4 Stainton (R) LAD 3m 7 GF *(fav) trckd ldr, disp 2 out, ld last, ran on well* 1 20
1132 20/4 Hornby Cast' (L) LAD 3m 9 G *p.u. bef 1st, rider thought false start* P 0
1283 27/4 Easingwold (L) LAD 3m 10 G *sttld 3rd, ev ch frm 3 out, not qckn nxt* 3 20
1449 6/5 Witton Cast' (R) LAD 3m 10 G *hndy,disp 4th-5 out,rlld apr 2 out,no ext last,lost 2nd flat* 3 18

Consistent; 7 wins,13 places, last 25 starts; best on easy courses; can win again. Any. **20**

CAROL STYLE (Irish) — I 330^{P}

CAROUSEL CALYPSO ch.g. 10 Whistling Deer - Fairy Tree by Varano — A Saccomando

318	2/3	Corbridge	(R)	LAD	3m 5f	10	GS	*2nd early, lost plc, wll bhnd whn p.u. 2 out*	P	0
499	16/3	Lanark	(R)	LAD	3m	10	G	*2nd at 11th, lost tch 3 out, poor 4th whn p.u. last*	P	0
611	23/3	Friars Haugh	(L)	LAD	3m	10	G	*alwys rr.*	8	0
752	31/3	Lockerbie	(R)	LAD	3m	10	G	*cls 2nd whn u.r. 6th*	U	-

Last on only completion & looks to have no prospects now 0

CAROUSEL ROCKET ch.g. 13 Whistling Deer - Fairy Tree by Varano — A Saccomando

1995 **4(NH),5(NH),5(NH),2(NH),2(NH),5(NH),7(NH),2(NH),5(NH),P(NH)**

37	3/2	Wetherby	(L)	HC	3m 110yds	11	GS	*soon well bhnd, t.o..*	6	0
259	1/3	Kelso	(L)	HC	3m 1f	8	GS	*soon chasing ldrs, pushed along after 15th, kept on und pres from last.*	3	24
487	16/3	Newcastle	(L)	HC	3m	10	GS	*(Co fav) settld towards rear, rdn along from 10th, soon outpcd, no dngr after.*	4	14
1119	18/4	Ayr	(L)	HC	3m 3f 110yds	9	GS	*ld or disp ld till outpcd after 14th, rallied after 17th, kept on well und pres from 3 out.*	2	26
1337	1/5	Kelso	(L)	HC	3m 1f	9	S	*prom, rdn after 11th, soon lost pl, styd on from 2 out.*	3	24

Tough, staying chaser; mixed handicaps & H/Chases in 96; stays 4m; likes Carlisle; hard to win now ... 22

CARRAMORE HILL (Irish) — I 38^{P}, I 90^{P}, I 124^{P}, I 367^{P}, I 429^{2}, I 554^{4}

CARRAREA (Irish) — I 30^{P}, I 511^{P}, I 635^{P}

CARRICK LANES b.g. 9 Oats - Once Bitten by Brave Invader (USA) — David Brace

5	13/1	Larkhill	(R)	LAD	3m	10	GS	*mid-div, prog 11th, chsd wnr aft 3 out, outpcd apr last*	2	22
40	3/2	Wadebridge	(L)	LAD	3m	5	GF	*(fav) in tch, chsd wnr 11th, hld whn blndrd 2 out, kpt on*	2	22
384	9/3	Llanfrynach	(R)	OPE	3m	16	GS	*(fav) alwys prom, ld 15th, slw jmp last, drvn out flat*	1	22

Ex-Irish; decent performances & consistent; finished early; win Opens if fit 97; G/S-G/F 23

CARRICKMINES ch.g. 11 Deep Run - Gallant Breeze (USA) by Mongo — Lee Bowles

1995 **P(0),4(18)**,1(23),**2(26)**

183	19/2	Musselburgh	(R)	HC	3m	5	GF	*held up, rdn and hdwy before 14th, soon chasing wnr, ridden and no impn from 2 out.*	2	22
256	29/2	Ludlow	(R)	HC	3m	14	G	*prom, one pace from 15th.*	5	21
799	3/4	Ludlow	(R)	HC	3m	8	GF	*chsd ldrs, in tch when blnd 3 out, soon one pace.*	3	24

Fair H/Chaser at best but below form 96; finished early; points best chance at 12; R/H best; G-F 21

CARRIGANS LAD (Irish) — I 103^{3}, I 235^{P}, I 392^{U}, I 491^{P}, I 584^{4}, I 626^{2}

CARRIG CONN (Irish) — I 101^{5}, I 270^{1}, I 525^{P}

CARRIGEEN LAD b.g. 9 Mandalus - Monread by Le Tricolore — Mrs Julie Read

8	14/1	Cottenham	(R)	CON	3m	10	G	*trckd ldrs going wl,jnd ldr & hit 2 out,ld last,rdn out*	1	23
102	17/2	Marks Tey	(L)	CON	3m	17	G	*(Jt fav) w.w.11th & in tch hlfwy, outpcd 13th, no dang after*	4	18
367	6/3	Catterick	(L)	HC	3m 1f 110yds	12	G	*mid div, effort after 16th, styd on to go 2nd at last, no impn on wnr.*	2	23
581	21/3	Wincanton	(R)	HC	2m 5f	13	S	*chsd ldrs to 5 out, weakening when f 4 out.*	F	-
677	30/3	Cottenham	(R)	OPE	3m	11	GF	*mstk 9th, chsd ldr 14th-3 out, chal last, onepcd flat*	3	22
907	8/4	Fakenham	(L)	HC	3m 110yds	11	G	*(bl) prog to go 2nd twelfth, p.u. before 5 out, fin lame.*	P	0

Winning hurdler; fit early 96 ; seemed to train off later; can win again; easy track prefered. 20

CARRIGFERN (Irish) — I 239^{P}

CARRIGLAWN ch.g. 11 Buckskin (FR) - Sonlaru by Deep Run — Mrs Sheila Lousada

1995 P(0)

1222	24/4	Brampton Br'	(R)	RES	3m	11	G	*mid-div til wknd 13th, p.u. 16th*	P	0

Lightly raced; of no real account now. & no promise only point so far 0

CARRIGLEGAN GEM (Irish) — I 33^{P}, I 80^{P}, I 166^{P}

CARRIGMORE LADY (Irish) — I 385^{P}, I 479^{F}

CARROLLS ROCK (Irish) — I 6^{P}, I 34^{P}, I 126^{P}, I 212,

CARTON b.g. 9 Pollerton - Wild Deer by Royal Buck — Mrs A P Kelly

1995 **U(-)**

37	3/2	Wetherby	(L)	HC	3m 110yds	11	GS	*lost tch from hfwy, t.o. when p.u. before 12th.*	P	0
160	17/2	Weston Park	(L)	OPE	3m	16	G	*cls up, ld 12th-nxt, sn btn, p.u. 3 out*	P	0
293	2/3	Eaton Hall	(R)	INT	3m	11	G	*chsd ldrs to 6th, lost tch 14th, p.u. 2 out*	P	0

Ex-Irish; outclassed in 96 and has no real prospects. 0

CARUMU b.m. 7 Henricus (ATA) - Flame Song by True Song — Mrs S A Murch

1995 P(0),6(0)

284	2/3	Clyst St Ma'	(L)	MDN	3m	11	S	*mid-div til lost tch 14th, p.u. nxt*	P	0
447	9/3	Haldon	(R)	MDO	3m	13	S	*prog 6th, disp 8th-10th, wknd 13th, p.u. 3 out*	P	0
1432	6/5	High Bickin'	(R)	MDO	3m	9	G	*bhnd til p.u. apr 17th*	P	0
1554	18/5	Bratton Down	(L)	MDO	3m	16	F	*s.u. bnd apr 6th*	S	-
1593	25/5	Mounsey Hil'	(R)	MDO	3m	11	G	*mstk 1st, chsd ldrs to 10th, bhnd frm 13th, t.o.*	5	0
1637	1/6	Bratton Down	(L)	MDO	3m	11	G	*ld 2-6th, wknd 13th, t.o. 16th*	7	0
1652	8/6	Umberleigh	(L)	MDO	3m	10	GF	*prog 8th, ld 11th-13th, btn frm nxt*	3	0

Well-beaten when completing and looks a non-stayer. 10

CASCUM LAD (Irish) — I 318[P], I 450[P]
CASHEL MOSS (Irish) — I 118[P], I 154[P], I 197[P], I 268[P]
CASH FLOW (Irish) — I 440, , I 645[B]
CASH FOR BASH (Irish) — I 139[P], I 267[F], I 387[1]
CASS ch.g. 9 Stanford - Autumn Supreme by Supreme Sovereign — N P Williams

12	14/1	Cottenham	(R)	RES	3m	12	G	*alwys mid-div, nvr able to chal*	7	0
243	25/2	Southwell P'	(L)	RES	3m	11	HO	*mstk 6th, alwys bhnd, t.o. & p.u. 2 out*	P	0
396	9/3	Garthorpe	(R)	RES	3m	9	G	*mostly 4th, mstk 11th, in tch whn f 5 out*	F	-
635	23/3	Market Rase'	(L)	RES	3m	8	GF	*12s-6s, w.w. prog 6 out, ran on well to ld last*	1	12
899	6/4	Dingley	(R)	MEM	3m	4	GS	*cls up, chal 2 out, ran on onepce*	4	0

Won bad Maiden 94; missed 95; landed a touch in dire Restricted; Members only hope now. 13

CASTING TIME(NZ) br.g. 12 Drums Of Time (USA) - In Haste (NZ) by In The Purple (FR) — D H Barons
1995 **F(NH)**

64	10/2	Great Treth'	(R)	CON	3m	7	S	*(fav) prom til wknd 14th*	5	0
134	17/2	Ottery St M'	(L)	CON	3m	12	GS	*alwys mid-div, nvr on terms*	7	0

Season lasted a week & beat only one other finisher; prospects grim 0

CASTLE AVENUE (Irish) — I 275[P], I 332[5], I 458[P], I 565[1]
CASTLE BAILEY (Irish) — I 114[P]
CASTLEBAY LAD br.g. 13 Crozier - Carbery Star by Kelmal (FR) — Rob McGready
1995 P(0),7(0),1(23),1(25),r(-),P(0),**P(0)**

125	17/2	Kingston Bl'	(L)	OPE	3m	10	GS	*prom, chsd wnr 12-14th, wknd, poor 3rd whn ref last*	R	-
290	2/3	Eaton Hall	(R)	OPE	3m	6	G	*prom, ev ch 4 out, onepcd*	4	15
537	17/3	Southwell P'	(L)	OPE	3m	7	GS	*chsd ldrs, ev ch 4 out, not qckn*	2	22
1052	13/4	Penshurst	(L)	OPE	3m	7	G	*alwys prom, chsd wnr 11th, nvr on terms, 3rd & wknd 4 out*	3	15
1231	27/4	Weston Park	(L)	OPE	3m	6	G	*mstly 2nd/3rd, ev ch 3 out, not qckn*	3	14
1598	25/5	Garthorpe	(R)	OPE	3m	6	G	*cls up in 3rd to 11th, 4th & outpcd frm nxt*	4	14

Able but needs mud (not available 96); may stiill surprise when conditions suit. 18

CASTLECONNER (Irish) — I 231[2], I 300[3], I 478[2], I 559,
CASTLE CROSS ch.g. 9 Carlingford Castle - Siba Vione by Dusky Boy — K O'Meara

290	2/3	Eaton Hall	(R)	OPE	3m	6	G	*cls up to 12th, lost tch nxt, p.u. 3 out*	P	0
567	17/3	Wolverhampt'	(L)	MEM	3m	4	GS	*cls up in 3rd whn f 11th*	F	-
1009	9/4	Flagg Moor	(L)	CON	3m	7	G	*chsd ldr to 11th, t.o. frm 15th, p.u. 2 out*	P	0
1093	14/4	Whitwell-On'	(R)	MXO	4m	19	G	*alwys rear, blnd 15th, p.u. nxt*	P	0
1419	6/5	Eyton-On-Se'	(L)	OPE	3m	4	GF	*rr early, lost tch 8th, t.o. 13th*	4	0

Winning chaser; showed no aptitude for pointing. 10

CASTLEDELL (Irish) — I 171[B], I 285[1], I 360[4]
CASTLE GEM ch.m. 10 Kemal (FR) - Paddys Flyer by Paddy's Stream — S Clark
1995 P(0),P(0),4(17),2(18),2(12),**8(0)**,3(16),1(0),3(0)

49	4/2	Alnwick	(L)	OPE	3m	14	G	*chsd ldrs, outpcd 12th, kpt on agn frm 3 out*	5	18
118	17/2	Witton Cast'	(R)	INT	3m	9	S	*prom to 10th, wknd 12th, kpt on onepcd aft*	4	11

Won Restricted 95; finished early 96; could win modest Confined if fit 97.G/S-F. 19

CASTLE HERO (Irish) — I 272[F], I 481[U]
CASTLE JESTER gr.g. 11 Castle Keep - Peters Pleasure by Jimsun — Mrs C F Elliott
1995 U(-)

1288	28/4	Barbury Cas'	(L)	MEM	3m	5	F	*ld 6-10th, sn outpcd, t.o. whn ref 2 out*	R	-

Unlucky in Members 95; hardly runs now and most unlikely to win again. 0

CASTLE KATE (Irish) — I 348[P], I 385[3]
CASTLELACK (Irish) — I 10[F]
CASTLELAKE LADY (Irish) — I 427[F], I 469[3], I 499[6]
CASTLEMORE LEADER (Irish) — I 308[F], I 434[P], I 459[F], I 502[P], I 564[P]

CASTLEPOOK (Irish) — **I** 230^{F}, **I** 389^{2}, **I** 429^{F}, **I** 500^{6}, **I** 626^{U}

CASTLE ROYAL (Irish) — **I** 260^{P}, **I** 288^{1}, **I** 362^{F}, **I** 405^{4}, **I** 537^{4}, **I** 596^{1}

CASTLE SHELLEY (Irish) — **I** 70^{P}, **I** 118^{3}, **I** 244^{P}, **I** 311^{P}, **I** 374^{1}

CASTLE TIGER BAY (Irish) — **I** 187^{3}, **I** 293^{3}, **I** 366^{5}, **I** 552^{3}, **I** 630^{P}

CASTLE TYRANT b.m. 7 Idiot's Delight - Coolek by Menelek — S Clark

1995 3(10),2(14),2(14),U(-),3(10)

53	4/2	Alnwick	(L)	MDO	3m	13	G	*ld to 9th & frm 12th, clr 3 out, wknd & hd nr fin*	2	14
122	17/2	Witton Cast'	(R)	MDO	3m	8	S	*(fav) ld to 4th, cls 2nd aft, disp last, styd on best flat*	1	15
303	2/3	Great Stain'	(L)	CON	3m	11	GS	*ld til 16th, rallied apr last, styd on wll to ld flat*	1	20
409	9/3	Charm Park	(L)	CON	3m	11	G	*alwys prom, 4th 4 out, outpcd by ldr after*	4	17
588	23/3	Wetherby Po'	(L)	INT	3m	17	S	*made msot to 4 out, onepcd aft*	4	15
761	31/3	Great Stain'	(L)	INT	3m	7	GS	*disp to 4th, chsd wnr aft, ev ch 2 out, no ext last*	2	21
1092	14/4	Whitwell-On'	(R)	CON	3m	10	G	*disp to 5 out, rallied to ld 3 out, rdn & ran on well*	1	21
1337	1/5	Kelso	(L)	HC	3m 1f	9	S	*held up, joined ldrs 12th, wknd before 14th, lost tch and p.u. after 2 out.*	P	0

Improved & consistent; best at easy 3m; could reach Open standard in 97; G-S 22

CASTLE UNION (Irish) — **I** 269^{P}, **I** 395^{5}, **I** 429^{F}, **I** 557^{4}, **I** 581^{P}

CASTLE VENTRY (Irish) — **I** 311^{P}, **I** 377^{2}, **I** 567^{P}

CATBROOK CHANCE b.g. 9 Don Enrico (USA) - Red Pansy by Indian Ruler — A P Gent

1995 R(-),P(0),6(0),F(-),F(-),P(0)

349	3/3	Garnons	(L)	MEM	3m	4	GS	*cls up whn hit 12 & 13th, lost tch nxt, t.o. whn u.r. 2 out*	U	-
1272	27/4	Pyle	(R)	MDO	3m	9	G	*cls 4th at 10th, 1l 2nd whn ran out 14th*	R	-

Has ability but a poor jumper; stering problems also; may surprise one day. 10

CATCHAPENNY br.g. 11 True Song - Quickapenny by Espresso — W Tellwright

1995 **7(NH),2(NH),6(NH),2(NH),1(NH)**

94	11/2	Ampton	(R)	OPE	3m	8	GF	*(Jt fav) rear, in tch til outpcd 15th, no ch whn tried ref & u.r.17th*	U	-
290	2/3	Eaton Hall	(R)	OPE	3m	6	G	*(bl) wll in tch til outpcd 4 out, no ext nxt*	3	16
372	8/3	Market Rasen	(R)	HC	3m 1f	6	G	*(bl) chsd ldrs, blnd 10th, driven and outpcd 3 out, soon no dngr.*	3	20
854	6/4	Sandon	(L)	OPE	3m	4	GF	*sn outpcd, nvr dang*	3	10
1108	17/4	Cheltenham	(L)	HC	4m 1f	14	GS	*(bl) alwys prom, lost pl 4 out, styd on after 2 out.*	3	28

Winning chaser; thorough stayer; hard to win with; slog on long course best hope; blinkers. 20

CATCH ME KISS (Irish) — **I** 550,

CATCH THE CROSS gr.g. 10 Alias Smith (USA) - Juliette Mariner by Welsh Pageant — Reg Hand

1995 **5(NH),7(NH),P(NH),P(NH)**

294	2/3	Great Treth'	(R)	CON	3m	10	G	*(bl) made most aft 6th til wknd & hdd aft 2 out*	3	14
442	9/3	Haldon	(R)	CON	3m	6	S	*(bl) prom, cls 3rd hlfwy, wknd grad frm 3 out*	3	14
625	23/3	Kilworthy	(L)	CON	3m	11	GS	*ld to 8th, chsd wnr to 14th, fdd frm nxt*	7	12
715	30/3	Wadebridge	(L)	CON	3m	8	GF	*(bl) prog 11th,lft 2nd nxt,ld brfly aft 14th,hmpd bnd aft nxt,kpt*	2	16
1069	13/4	Lifton	(R)	CON	3m	9	S	*(bl) sn rear, poor 7th 14th, nvr nr to chal*	4	18
1138	20/4	Flete Park	(R)	MEM	3m	4	S	*(bl) trckd ldr 6th til ld 14th, clr 3 out, kpt on*	1	17
1361	4/5	Flete Park	(R)	CON	3m	9	G	*(bl) ld til 4th, ld 15th, disp & ev ch 2 out, wknd*	3	15
1525	12/5	Ottery St M'	(L)	CON	3m	9	GF	*(bl) rear, some late prog, nvr nr to chal*	5	14
1624	27/5	Lifton	(R)	LAD	3m	9	GS	*(bl) hld up, prog 14th, ev ch aft 3 out, not qckn und pres*	2	21
1635	1/6	Bratton Down	(L)	LAD	3m	13	G	*sn rdn & reluc, still in tch 15th, no ch aft nxt, walked in*	10	0
1648	8/6	Umberleigh	(L)	LAD	3m	11	GF	*(bl) wll bhnd, t.o. 11th, ran on frm 15th, tk 3rd 2 out*	3	20

Formerly good chaser; ungenuine now and unlikely to win a competitive race; blinkers; Any. 18

CATCH THE MOUSE (Irish) — **I** 383^{P}

CATHGAL b.g. 11 Crozier - Mawnie by Mon Capitaine — Richard Mathias

156	17/2	Erw Lon	(L)	RES	3m	13	G	*prom to hlfwy, wknd rpdly, p.u. 14th*	P	0
213	24/2	Newtown	(L)	MEM	3m	7	GS	*(bl) ld til hrd rdn & hdd 2 out, ev ch whn blnd last, not rcvr*	2	14
432	9/3	Upton-On-Se'	(R)	MDO	3m	17	GS	*alwys prom, lost tch & 4th 3 out, lft poor 3rd last*	3	0
482	13/3	Newton Abbot	(L)	HC	2m 5f 110yds	14	S	*ld to 3rd, wknd 10th, t.o..*	4	0
674	30/3	Hereford	(R)	HC	2m	8	S	*held up, hdwy 6th, ld next, mstk and hdd 2 out, kept on one pace.*	3	17
908	8/4	Hereford	(R)	HC	2m 3f	12	GF	*blnd and u.r. 3rd.*	U	-
1047	13/4	Bitterley	(L)	MDO	3m	13	G	*prog 9th, went 10l 2nd 14th, not get on terms wnr*	2	15
1161	20/4	Llanwit Maj'	(R)	MDO	3m	15	GS	*(fav) cls 4th whn hit by loose horse & u.r. 11th*	U	-
1319	28/4	Bitterley	(L)	MDN	3m	13	G	*w.w. prog 14th, lft in clr ld 3 out, hng lft flat*	1	15
1341	4/5	Warwick	(L)	HC	2 1/2m 110yds	12	GF	*started slowly, effort 8th, wknd 11th.*	6	16

Tricky ride and barely stays; placed in dire H/chase(2 miles); restricted looks tough at 12. 15

CAUNDLE STEPS b.g. 9 Impecunious - Caundle Break by Rugantino — P J Doggrell

1995 P(0),P(0),6(10),5(0),4(16),2(12)

656	23/3	Badbury Rin'	(L)	RES	3m	11	G	*front rank, ld 13th-16th, not qckn 2 out*	3	0
1313	28/4	Little Wind'	(R)	RES	3m	14	G	*mid-div, cls 6th at 13th, outpcd nxt, bhnd & p.u. last*	P	0

1345 4/5 Holnicote (L) RES 3m 11 GS *ld 14th-last, kpt on und pres* 2 18
1497 11/5 Holnicote (L) RES 3m 10 G *prom, cls 2nd 4 out til aft 2 out,wknng in 3rd whn f last* F -

Placed in weak Restricteds; likes Holnicote(now defunct); may have missed his chance; G-F. 16

CAUSEWAY CRUISER ch.g. 10 Crested Lark - Andromeda II by Romany Air J Tredwell

1995 **4(14)**,**P(0)**,5(15),3(20),2(20),2(23),**2(22)**,1(21)

170 18/2 Market Rase' (L) XX 3m 8 GF *hld up pling, hit 14th, 5th & rdn 3 out, kpt on* 4 19
230 24/2 Heythrop (R) MEM 3m 12 GS *hld up, chsd ldrs hlfwy, 2nd 12th, ld 16th, drew clr* 1 22
434 9/3 Newton Brom' (R) CON 3m 11 GS *hld up rear, prog 12th, ld 3 out, made rest, comf* 1 27
639 23/3 Siddington (L) OPE 3m 12 S *(fav) w.w. prog 10th, mod 3rd & rddn 3 out, ran on, nt rch wnnr* 2 22
1435 6/5 Ashorne (R) CON 3m 12 G *(fav) hld up, prog 5th, ld 10th, clr 13th, easily* 1 28
1565 19/5 Mollington (R) OPE 3m 8 GS *(fav) hld up, 5th whn mstk & u.r. 5th* U -
1630 31/5 Stratford (L) HC 3 1/2m 16 GF *started slowly, hdwy 6th, lost pl after 14th, taied off when p.u. before 17th.* P 0

Useful; settling better now and improved; could still win small H/chase;G/S-F. 26

CAUTEEN RIVER (Irish) — **I** 541[P]

CAUTIOUS REBEL ch.g. 9 Shy Groom (USA) - Riot Girl by Right Boy Mrs L Roberts

137 17/2 Ottery St M' (L) RES 3m 15 GS *mid-div, prog 12th, ld 14th, sn clr* 1 17
472 10/3 Milborne St' (L) INT 3m 8 G *in tch to 12th, outpcd nxt* 4 0
721 30/3 Wadebridge (L) INT 3m 3 GF *(fav) chsd wnr,not alwys fluent,ld brfly 12th,drvn & no imp,eased* 2 15
1079 13/4 Cothelstone (L) INT 3m 5 GF *(fav) well in rear, n.j.w. p.u. 2 out* P 0
1278 27/4 Bratton Down (L) INT 3m 12 GF *in tch, 5th at 12th, btn whn f 16th* F -
1632 1/6 Bratton Down (L) MEM 3m 3 G *(vis) made all, clr 12th, mstks 16th & nxt, unchal* 1 16

Won 2 weak races; disappointing in between; probably best fresh; more needed for Confined. 17

CAVISS b.m. 11 Corvaro (USA) - Ike's Mistress (USA) by Master Derby (USA) H Powell

214 24/2 Newtown (L) CON 3m 21 GS *alwys bhnd, t.o. last whn f 10th* F -
349 3/3 Garnons (L) MEM 3m 4 GS *ld to 10th, wknd, t.o. & u.r. 13th* U -

Of no account. 0

CAWKWELL DEAN b.g. 10 Boco (USA) - Cawkwell Duchess by Duc D'Orleans J N Hutchinson

1995 4(13),4(13),2(19),1(19),r(-),2(17)

124 17/2 Kingston Bl' (L) CON 3m 17 GS *prom in chsng grp, effrt 14th, chsd wnr 3 out, sn outpcd* 2 21
230 24/2 Heythrop (R) MEM 3m 12 GS *rear to hlfwy, styd on onepcd aft, tk 3rd flat* 3 14
538 17/3 Southwell P' (L) XX 3m 6 GS *chsd ldr to 13th, onepcd frm 4 out, lft poor 2nd 2 out* 2 10
683 30/3 Chaddesley ' (L) MEM 3m 17 G *chsd ldrs, ev ch & rdn 15th, lft 2nd last, onepcd* 2 20
1015 13/4 Kingston Bl' (L) MEM 3m 9 G *(fav) ld to 2nd & frm 4th, clr 15th, easily* 1 19
1176 21/4 Mollington (R) MEM 3m 6 F *prom til ran wd bnd apr 11th, sn wll bhnd, kpt on 2 out* 3 12
1438 6/5 Ashorne (R) XX 3m 14 G *ld to 2nd,mstk 4th,chsd wnr 12th,mstk nxt,kpt on onepcd flat* 3 19
1500 11/5 Kingston Bl' (L) CON 3m 7 G *(fav) made all, drew clr apr last, comf* 1 20

Won 6 placed 10 from last 19 starts; below Open class and needs careful placing now; F-S. 21

CAWKWELL WIN b.m. 5 Boco (USA) - Cawkwell Duchess by Duc D'Orleans Mrs Susan McDonald

904 6/4 Dingley (R) RES 3m 20 GS *t.o. last til p.u. 8th* P 0
1026 13/4 Brocklesby ' (L) MDN 3m 6 GF *n.j.w., t.o. 4th, f 6th* F -
1378 5/5 Dingley (R) MDO 2 1/2m 16 GF *alwys rear, 12th & no ch whn f 9th* F -

Needs to jump better before living up to her name. 0

CEBU GALE (Irish) — **I** 22[P]

CEDARBELLE (Irish) — **I** 129[4], **I** 159, , **I** 220[P], **I** 342[3], **I** 383[5], **I** 419[5], **I** 525[P]

CEDAR SQUARE(IRE) b.h. 5 Dancing Dissident (USA) - Freidnly Ann by Artaius (USA) A J Rhead

550 17/3 Erw Lon (L) MDN 3m 13 GS *mid-div, prog to hld ev ch 3 out, ran green* 3 0
772 31/3 Pantyderi (R) MDN 3m 8 G *made all, unchal* 1 16
974 8/4 Lydstep (L) MEM 3m 10 G *(fav) ld 4th, unchal frm 16th* 1 23
1199 21/4 Lydstep (L) OPE 3m 5 S *(fav) made all, unchal, imprssv* 1 25

Highly promising; cantered home in all victories; one to watch; G-S 26

CEFFYL GWYN gr.g. 9 Scallywag - Must Improve by Lucky Brief F H Williams

147 17/2 Erw Lon (L) MDN 3m 8 G *8s-3s, alwys last, u.r. 6th* U -

Only went a mile and gave his supporters no encouragement. 0

CEFN WOODSMAN b or br.g. 5 Tigerwood - Orange Pop by Gimlet D R Thomas

547 17/3 Erw Lon (L) OPE 3m 10 GS *alwys rear, p.u. 12th* P 0
770 31/3 Pantyderi (R) RES 3m 9 G *in rear whn p.u. 14th* P 0
1201 21/4 Lydstep (L) MDN 3m 9 S *nvr nrr than 7th, p.u. 12th* P 0
1272 27/4 Pyle (R) MDO 3m 9 G *cls up til outpcd frm 13th* 4 0
1390 6/5 Pantyderi (R) MDO 3m 15 GF *nvr nrr, nvr dang* 7 0

Well beaten when completing; only learning and can do better. 0

CELESTIAL STREAM ch.g. 9 Paddy's Stream - Starlight Beauty by Scallywag — L J Williams
1995 5(0)

849	6/4	Howick	(L) MDN	3m	14 GF	*made all, drew clr 13th, easily*	1	16
1160	20/4	Llanwit Maj'	(R) RES	3m	12 GS	*(fav) hngng on bnds, ld 6th-3 out, immed btn, p.u. last*	P	0

Lightly raced; hacked up in poor Maiden; excuses after; can upgrade; L/H essential. 17

CELIA'S PRIDE (Irish) — I 144U, I 152P, I 434P, I 507,

CELTIC ABBEY b.g. 8 Celtic Cone - Cagaleena by Cagirama — G J Powell
1995 **2(30),3(28),F(-),4(31),4(15),2(29)**

1478	11/5	Bredwardine	(R) CON	3m	12 G	*(fav) mid-div, prog to cls 2nd 10th, hmpd 12th, ld 3 out, kpt on*	1	24
1631	1/6	Stratford	(L) HC	3 1/2m	14 GF	*in tch, ld 17th to 3 out, ran on cl home.*	2	34

Late appearing; fine run at Stratford; win H/chases when avoiing top horses.G-F. 29

CELTICAIR (Irish) — I 481P

CELTIC BERRY gr.m. 7 Celtic Cone - Rockin Berry by Daybrook Lad — J T Jackson

353	3/3	Garnons	(L) MDN	2 1/2m	7 GS	*ld/disp til drew clr frm 3 out*	1	13
425	9/3	Upton-On-Se'	(R) MEM	3m	7 GS	*(fav) ld whn tried to ref & f 3rd*	F	-
882	6/4	Brampton Br'	(R) RES	3m	14 GF	*mid-div, effrt 14th, wknd 16th, p.u. nxt*	P	0
1481	11/5	Bredwardine	(R) RES	3m	14 G	*rear, mstk 5th, no ch 14th, t.o. & p.u. 2 out*	P	0

Easy winner; stamina problems now and Restricted needs much more. 15

CELTIC BIZARRE b.m. 8 Celtic Cone - Charity Bazzar by Native Bazaar — R R Smedley
1995 3(10),2(0),4(10),1(14)

156	17/2	Erw Lon	(L) RES	3m	13 G	*hld up, prog to 3rd 2 out, tk 2nd last, no ch wth wnr*	2	10
387	9/3	Llanfrynach	(R) RES	3m	11 GS	*chsd ldrs, not qckn apr 15th, onepcd aft*	4	11
548	17/3	Erw Lon	(L) RES	3m	8 GS	*alwys mid-div, onepcd*	3	12
765	31/3	Pantyderi	(R) MEM	3m	3 G	*(fav) ld 3rd, sn clr, unchal*	1	11
1160	20/4	Llanwit Maj'	(R) RES	3m	12 GS	*alwys rear, nvr trbld ldrs, p.u. 2 out*	P	0
1388	6/5	Pantyderi	(R) RES	3m	7 GF	*trckd ldr to hlfwy, wknd 11th, lame*	3	0

Won 2 weak races 95/96; struggling in better company; problems last start. 14

CELTIC BUCK (Irish) — I 468[1]

CELTIC CABER b.g. 10 Pragmatic - Cruises Royal by Pitpan — Miss T Habgood
1995 5(10)

1014	13/4	Kingston Bl'	(L) MEM	3m	4 G	*last til prog 14th, ld 2 out-last, not qckn*	2	10

2nd in Pegasus Members; say no more. 10

CELTIC DAUGHTER b.m. 7 Celtic Cone - Onaea by Prince de Galles — Mrs E A Webber
1995 **18(NH),2(NH),3(NH),5(NH)**

152	17/2	Erw Lon	(L) MDN	3m	11 G	*alwys cls up, disp 2nd frm 14th, alwys hld, fin 2nd, prmtd*	1	13
386	9/3	Llanfrynach	(R) RES	3m	10 GS	*mstks, outpcd in mid-div, ran on 14th, rdn to ld last,sn clr*	1	16
604	23/3	Howick	(L) INT	3m	7 S	*rear, prog to 3rd at 13th, tired & p.u. 3 out*	P	0
766	31/3	Pantyderi	(R) CON	3m	6 G	*ld 11th, hdd & onepcd last*	3	18
981	8/4	Lydstep	(L) INT	3m	5 G	*alwys 4th, tired whn lft 3rd last*	3	0
1211	23/4	Chepstow	(L) HC	3m	13 S	*t.o. from 7th, p.u. before 11th.*	P	0
1385	6/5	Pantyderi	(R) CON	3m	6 GF	*hld up, prog 12th, ld aft 15th, comf*	1	19
1614	27/5	Hereford	(R) HC	3m1f 110yds	16 G	*held up in rear when blnd and u.r. 5th.*	U	-

Placed under Rules; inconsistent & fair at best; should win Confined; blinkers worth a try; G/F-G/S 20

CELTIC DEMON ch.g. 8 Celtic Cone - Kelpie by Import — Mrs K A Blackman

478	10/3	Tweseldown	(R) RES	3m	9 G	*rear, prog & ch in 4th whn f 15th*	F	-

Won poor Maiden 94; only one run since; still young enough for weak Restricted if fit 97. 15

CELTIC FLAME ch.g. 15 Celtic Cone - Dandy's Last by Prefairy — Bryan Allen
1995 1(24),6(14),4(14),3(16),3D(16),2(20),2(20)

124	17/2	Kingston Bl'	(L) CON	3m	17 GS	*mid-div, lost tch aft 13th, t.o. & p.u. 2 out*	P	0
312	2/3	Ampton	(R) OPE	3m	6 G	*bhnd & pshd alng 8th, lst tch 10th, no ch 15th*	6	0
885	6/4	Kimble	(L) MEM	3m	5 GF	*1st ride, ld to 2 out, ld last, ran on well*	1	16
1186	21/4	Tweseldown	(R) LAD	3m	6 GF	*outpcd,styng on whn lft clr 2nd 3 out,btn whn u.r. last,lame*	U	-

Gallant veteran; novice ridden when winning; problems last start; could be the end now. 17

CELTIC GOBLIN b.m. 8 Swinging Rebel - Goblins Thimbles by Roi Soleil — M H Dare
1995 P(0),5(0)

135	17/2	Ottery St M'	(L) LAD	3m	11 GS	*mid-div whn blnd & u.r. 10th*	U	-
205	24/2	Castle Of C'	(R) MDO	3m	9 HY	*prom, ld 4-11th, wknd, t.o. & p.u. 4 out*	P	0

A little ability but rarely runs and not thretening to win. 10

CELTIC HAWK ch.g. 6 Celtic Cone - Khatti Hawk by Hittite Glory — A Chinery

1995 3(0),R(-),R(-),P(0),P(0),3(0),P(0),P(0)

835	6/4 Marks Tey	(L) MEM 3m	4 G	*rshd to ld 10th, hdd apr last, onepcd*	3	0
1063	13/4 Horseheath	(R) MDO 3m	5 F	*ld 1st, drpd rr 3rd, prog & ev ch 13th, 3rd & btn whn f 15th*	F	-
1149	20/4 Higham	(L) MDO 3m	10 F	*sn in tch, 4th & outpcd whn mstk 16th, kpt on*	3	0

Doing better now (could hardly do worse); novice ridden and need luck to win. 10

CELTIC KING ch.g. 12 Kingshaven - Celtic Siren by Welsh Pageant — John E Needham

1995 3(18)

72	11/2 Wetherby Po'	(L) CON 3m	18 GS	*alwys rear, p.u. 4 out*	P	0
303	2/3 Great Stain'	(L) CON 3m	11 GS	*mid-div, prog 11th, ev ch 2 out, onepcd apr last*	3	16
515	16/3 Dalton Park	(R) XX 3m	12 G	*mstk 7th, in tch, prog to ld 4 out, hdd last, kpt on*	2	18
725	31/3 Garthorpe	(R) OPE 3m	9 G	*trckd ldrs, prog 14th, ld last, rdn out flat*	1	22
1133	20/4 Hornby Cast'	(L) OPE 3m	14 G	*mstk 1st, mid-div, no prog frm 14th, sn wknd*	4	14
1457	8/5 Uttoxeter	(L) HC 3 1/4m	16 G	*in tch, bhnd when blnd 11th, t.o. when p.u. before 2 out.*	P	0
1594	25/5 Garthorpe	(R) MEM 3m	10 G	*3rd frm 10th, chsd wnr 3 out, no imp*	2	19

Safe & consistent but onepaced; did well in 96; may find Confined at 13; G/S-F 19

CELTIC KINSHIP (Irish) — I 112[P], I 166[3], I 346[4]

CELTIC LANE b.m. 9 Welsh Captain - Cottagers Lane by Farm Walk — W R Wilson

304	2/3 Great Stain'	(L) OPE 3m	10 GS	*mid-div, wknd 2 out, p.u. last*	P	0

Short Maiden winner 94; only one run since; stamina doubts; can only be watched now. 16

CELTIC PARK (Irish) — I 5[2], I 78[1]

CELTIC SPARK ch.g. 8 Celtic Cone - Kohinoor Diamond by Roman Warrior — M D Reed

1995 1(26),1(25),1(21),3(17),F(-),1(20),1(19),2(17),3(17)

104	17/2 Marks Tey	(L) OPE 3m	14 G	*made all, clr 16th, rddn aft 2 out, blnd last,styd on wll*	1	26
274	2/3 Parham	(R) OPE 3m	12 GF	*(fav) wll plcd, ld apr 3 out, styd on well*	1	26
595	23/3 Parham	(R) OPE 3m	12 GS	*(fav) mid-div,mstk 5th,nvr thrntd,some prog to 3rd 4 out,eased flt*	5	15
833	6/4 Marks Tey	(L) OPE 3m	4 G	*chsd ldr, clsd 16th, ran on to disp last, ld flat, lame,disq*	1D	22

Changed hands; useful; won 11 of last 18 (disqualified in one); goes well fresh; Good. 24

CELTIC SPORT br.g. 11 Celtic Cone - Bell-Amys by Blandford Lad — Mrs A C Martin

1995 2(16),1(24),1(23),1(23),4(21),U(-),1(23),4(17)

198	24/2 Lemalla	(R) OPE 3m	12 HY	*(bl) ld to 3 out, no ext aft*	3	24
296	2/3 Great Treth'	(R) OPE 3m	5 G	*(bl) made all, dictated pace, clr 3 out, styd on well*	1	24
529	16/3 Cothelstone	(L) LAD 3m	5 G	*(bl) trkd ldr, ld appr 4 out, drw clr appr last, styd on wll*	1	25

Decent staying pointer; won 8 of last 16; sure to win more; blinkers; G-Hy. 26

CELTIC TOKEN ch.g. 7 Celtic Cone - Ready Token (SWE) by Record Token — Mrs Kin Lundberg-Young

1995 **5(NH),6(NH),U(NH)**

145	17/2 Larkhill	(R) MDO 3m	13 G	*ld to 5th, sn wknd, p.u. 8th*	P	0
267	2/3 Didmarton	(L) MDN 3m	11 G	*ld til blnd & u.r. 4th*	U	-
471	10/3 Milborne St'	(L) MDO 3m	16 G	*ld to 4th, cls up whn u.r. 7th*	U	-
1060	13/4 Badbury Rin'	(L) MDO 3m	14 GF	*ld to 14th, wknd & onepcd aft*	7	0
1349	4/5 Holnicote	(L) MDO 3m	8 GS	*ld to 7th, ld 10th, made rest, ran on well*	1	16

Improved & easy winner of weak Maiden; novice-ridden; Restricted looks hard to find 15

CENTENARY STAR b.g. 11 Broadsword (USA) - Tina's Gold by Goldhill — G K Hullett

1995 3(0),5(0)

133	17/2 Ottery St M'	(L) OPE 3m	18 GS	*ld til 5 out, wknd nxt, p.u. 3 out*	P	0

Winning chaser; only 3 rhns 95/6; unlikely to win now. 14

CENTRAL LASS gr.m. 8 Glasgow Central - Fast Gold by Goldfella — K Bayliss

1006	9/4 Upton-On-Se'	(R) MDN 3m	11 F	*t.d.e., in tch to 11th, t.o. 14th, p.u. 3 out*	P	0
1618	27/5 Chaddesley '	(L) CON 3m	14 GF	*alwys last trio, t.o. & p.u. 11th*	P	0

No signs of ability yet. 0

CENTRE STAGE b.g. 10 Pas de Seul - All Beige by Ballyciptic — L J Bowman

1995 P(0)

274	2/3 Parham	(R) OPE 3m	12 GF	*last & nvr going wll, t.o. 7th, p.u. 12th*	P	0
480	11/3 Plumpton	(L) HC 3m 1f 110yds	6 GS	*blnd 2nd, alwys bhnd, t.o. from 11th.*	4	0
595	23/3 Parham	(R) OPE 3m	12 GS	*alwys rear, nvr going wll, p.u. 13th*	P	0
776	31/3 Penshurst	(L) OPE 3m	6 GS	*hndy, 2nd aft 3 out, chal last, ld cls home*	1	20
1052	13/4 Penshurst	(L) OPE 3m	7 G	*rear, prog 11th, 2nd 4 out, not pace to chal*	2	20

Won 4 points 94-96; likes Penshurst; best in mud; win again when conditions suit. 20

CERTAIN RHYTHM b.g. 13 Ascertain (USA) - Jungle Rhythm by Drumbeg — R G Watson

1995 3(15),P(0),P(0)

583 23/3 Wetherby Po' (L) MEM 3m 6 S *prom, wknd 12th, t.o. 14th, p.u. 3 out* P 0
984 8/4 Charm Park (L) MXO 3m 7 GF *mid-div, 4th 4 out, styd on onepcd* 4 17

Formerly useful; lightly raced now and unlikely to win again. 15

CHACER'S IMP b.g. 7 Noble Imp - Chacer by Quartette — Michael Farnan

1995 **P(NH),P(NH)**

241 25/2 Southwell P' (L) MDO 3m 15 HO *prom, ld 12th, jnd 4 out, hdd & no ext last 100 yrds* 2 13
361 5/3 Leicester (R) HC 2 1/2m 110yds 15 GS *prom till f 5th.* F -
727 31/3 Garthorpe (R) MDO 3m 12 G *jmpd lft, ld til hng lft & hdd 2 out, rdn & wknd last* 4 10
1103 14/4 Guilsborough (L) MDN 3m 15 G *(Jt fav) alwys prom, ld 3 out, clr nxt, hld on nr fin* 1 16
1456 8/5 Uttoxeter (L) HC 2m 5f 11 G *ld till after 8th, led 10th till after 12th, soon wknd, bhnd when p.u. before 3 out.* P 0

Won fair Maiden (good time); stays; L/H looks essential; should find a Restricted; G-S. 17

CHALVEY GROVE b.g. 8 New Member - My Molly by Averof — G Ivall

269 2/3 Didmarton (L) RES 3m 12 G *crawld 2nd, t.o. whn u.r. nxt* U -
522 16/3 Larkhill (R) MDO 3m 12 G *bhnd, prog 10th, 3rd 12th, wknd & p.u. nxt* P 0
997 8/4 Hackwood Pa' (L) MDO 3m 11 GF *rear til p.u. aft 9th* P 0

A glimmer of hope but much more needed. 0

CHALWOOD (Irish) — **I** 54^{2}, **I** 65^{3}, **I** 313^{1}

CHAMPAGNE RUN b.g. 11 Runnett - Tolaytala by Be My Guest (USA) — A G Sims

1995 **5(NH),5(NH),P(NH)**

141 17/2 Larkhill (R) MEM 3m 6 G *alwys bhnd, t.o. whn p.u. 4 out* P 0
381 9/3 Barbury Cas' (L) XX 3m 9 GS *sn bhnd, nvr a fctr, t.o.* 5 0
524 16/3 Larkhill (R) INT 3m 11 G *sn rear, t.o. & p.u. 14th* P 0
863 6/4 Larkhill (R) MEM 3m 4 F *cls up, lft ld 7th til hmp 11th, outpcd frm nxt & sn btn* 3 0
1167 20/4 Larkhill (R) MEM 3m 9 GF *jmp poorly in rear whn p.u. 4th* P 0
1393 6/5 Cotley Farm (L) XX 3m 10 GF *mid-div, lost tch 10th, t.o. & p.u. 3 out* P 0

Winning hurdler; last when completing and of no account now. 0

CHAMSY (Irish) — **I** 351^{P}

CHANAULEY (Irish) — **I** 259^{P}, **I** 319^{P}

CHANCY OATS ch.g. 8 Oats - Chancer's Last by Foggy Bell — Keith Lewis

1995 F(-)

552 17/3 Erw Lon (L) MDN 3m 10 GS *mid-div, prog whn blnd 4 out, not rcvr* 4 0
771 31/3 Pantyderi (R) MDN 3m 14 G *trckd ldrs, f 13th, dead* F -

Dead. 12

CHANDIGARH br.g. 8 High Top - Lady Zi by Manado — F R Bown

1995 **P(0)**,3(0),**U(-),U(-)**,r(-),3(12),4(11),**U(-)**,3(15),2(16)

64 10/2 Great Treth' (R) CON 3m 7 S *prom til lost tch 13th, p.u. 15th* P 0
133 17/2 Ottery St M' (L) OPE 3m 18 GS *sn rear, t.o. & p.u. 3 out* P 0
198 24/2 Lemalla (R) OPE 3m 12 HY *alwys bhnd, p.u. 2 out* P 0
625 23/3 Kilworthy (L) CON 3m 11 GS *alwys bhnd, t.o. 13th* 8 0
874 6/4 Higher Kilw' (L) OPE 3m 6 GF *last whn ran out 7th* r -
1069 13/4 Lifton (R) CON 3m 9 S *disp 6th til slght ld 14th, hdd & wknd 3 out* 6 16
1276 27/4 Bratton Down (L) LAD 3m 7 GF *in tch, 2nd frm 6th til wknd frm 3 out* 3 13
1454 7/5 Newton Abbot (L) HC 2m 5f 110yds 8 GS *in rear from 10th.* 5 12
1526 12/5 Ottery St M' (L) LAD 3m 5 GF *prom, disp 2nd mostly, ev ch til no ext aft 3 out* 3 20
1628 27/5 Lifton (R) MEM 3m 5 GS *(fav) f 4th,rmntd,2f bhnd,clsd,ld apr 2 out* 1 10
1635 1/6 Bratton Down (L) LAD 3m 13 G *prom, wll there 3 out, immed outpcd frm nxt* 4 16
1648 8/6 Umberleigh (L) LAD 3m 11 GF *s.s. ran in sntchs, in tch to 13th, sn wll bhnd* 6 13

Selling hurdle winner 94; won joke race after remounting; not 100% genuine and barely stays. 16

CHANGE THE PACE (Irish) — **I** 1^{P}, **I** 63^{6}, **I** 151^{2}, **I** 354^{4}, **I** 564^{5}, **I** 646^{3}

CHANNEL ISLAND b.m. 7 Cisto (FR) - Channel Ten by Babu — Mrs P M Williams

1270 27/4 Pyle (R) MDO 3m 9 G *trailing frm 4th,short-lived effrt apr 14th, t.o. & p.u.3out* P 0

Only learning on debut; may do better. 10

CHAPEL ISLAND b.g. 9 Glen Quaich - Cashelgarran by Never Say Die — E W & M Tuer

1995 P(0),5(0),1(16),3(10),F(-),S(-),F(-),**6(0)**

121 17/2 Witton Cast' (R) RES 3m 11 S *mid-div, effrt 2 out, no ext apr last* 4 15
411 9/3 Charm Park (L) RES 3m 20 G *bhnd early, 8th 11th, rn on lt, nvr nrr* 5 15
757 31/3 Great Stain' (L) MEM 3m 5 GS *sttld in tch,went 2nd 8th,ld 3 out,clr last,idld flat* 1 18
825 6/4 Stainton (R) RES 3m 7 GF *hld up, mstk 11th, prog 15th, ev ch 2 out, no ext* 3 14
1131 20/4 Hornby Cast' (L) RES 3m 17 G *mid-div, prog 12th, ev ch 4 out, kpt on frm 2 out* 2 18

1284 27/4 Easingwold (L) RES 3m 14 G *sttld mid-div, prog 10th, trckd ldrs 14th, onepcd frm 3 out* 4 15
1447 6/5 Witton Cast' (R) RES 3m 11 G *midfld, efft 3 out, no imp* 4 13
1466 11/5 Easingwold (L) CON 3m 10 G *mid-div, mstk 5th, prog 11th, ev ch 2 out, not qckn* 2 17
1586 25/5 Hexham (L) HC 2 1/2m 110yds 14 GF *settld with chasing gp, challenging for 2nd when not fluent 3 out, one pace after.* 3 12

Consistent but barely stays; weak Restricted on short track only possible; G/S-F. 17

CHAPERALL LADY br.m. 10 Mansingh (USA) - El Chaperall by Scottish Rifle — A R Campbell

109 17/2 Lanark (R) MEM 3m 5 GS *disp to 5th, t.o. 10th, p.u. 4 out* P 0

Of no account. 0

CHARACTERISTIC b.g. 8 Reformed Character - Far Coriander Vii — D H Godfrey
1995 P(0),1(17)

213 24/2 Newtown (L) MEM 3m 7 GS *(fav) chsd ldr frm 8th, ld 2 out, lft clr last, styd on* 1 15

Won modest Members; not seen after; capsble of upgrading if fit in 97; 18

CHARDEN b.g. 10 Touching Wood (USA) - Fighting Lady by Chebs Lad — Lt-Col R I Webb-Bowen
1995 1(21),5(23),**U(NH),1(28),4(22),5(0),3(19),5(26)**

1 13/1 Larkhill (R) XX 3m 7 GS *ld to 4th & agn nxt, sn wll clr, wknd & hdd 15th, fin tired* 4 14
185 23/2 Kempton (R) HC 3m 9 GS *blnd 4th, bhnd, hdwy into 5th when blunded and u.r. 14th.* U -
255 28/2 Taunton (R) HC 4 1/4m 110yds 15 GS *tk str hold, chsd ldrs 13th, ld after 19th, hdd 21st, styd on from 3 out but not pace to chal.* 4 20
1334 1/5 Cheltenham (L) HC 3 1/4m 110yds 3 G *steadied in 3rd, left 2nd 10th to 11th, blnd 15th and 19th, chsd wnr 2 out, driven and ran on well flat.* 2 23
1544 17/5 Stratford (L) HC 3m 10 GF *held up bhnd, blnd 13th, styd on well from 4 out, nvr nrr.* 5 19

Won H/chase 95; pulls; decent but hindered by poor rider; can win weak H/chase-Open; G/S-G/F. 23

CHARIOT DEL (Irish) — **I** 92^{P}, **I** 534^{1}, **I** 597^{F}

CHARLCOT STORM b.g. 5 Respect - Bantel Bouquet by Red Regent — R Walker

72 11/2 Wetherby Po' (L) CON 3m 18 GS *bhnd til p.u. 4th* P 0
223 24/2 Duncombe Pa' (R) CON 3m 16 GS *ran out 1st* r -
303 2/3 Great Stain' (L) CON 3m 11 GS *ref 1st* R -
584 23/3 Wetherby Po' (L) RES 3m 13 S *ref 1st* R -
758 31/3 Great Stain' (L) RES 3m 17 GS *(bl) ref 1st* R -
824 6/4 Stainton (R) CON 3m 11 GF *strng rmndrs to jmp 1st, ref nxt* R -

Horrible. 0

CHARLESFIELD (Irish) — **I** 102^{F}

CHARLES QUAKER ch.g. 6 Oats - Petite Mirage by Hittite Glory — F C Richens
1995 P(0),C(-),2(15),U(-)

151 17/2 Erw Lon (L) MDN 3m 8 G *(fav) rear, prog 3 out, 3rd nxt, wknd aft* 4 10
848 6/4 Howick (L) MDN 3m 14 GF *(fav) s.s. rear til steady prog 11th,3rd 3 out,styd on,nt rch wnr* 2 13
1511 12/5 Maisemore P' (L) MDO 3m 14 F *(fav) mid-div, prog to 4th at 11th til p.u. in tch at 15th, dsmntd* P 0

Unlucky 95; expensive to follow and problems last start; young enough to recoup losses if fit 97. 14

CHARLESTON LAD b.g. 11 Bali Dancer - Rodway Belle by Phebus — P A Bull
1995 U(-),P(0),P(0),F(-),P(0),**U(-)**

247 25/2 Charing (L) MEM 3m 7 GS *chsd ldrs, 3rd final cct, wll btn whn p.u. last* P 0
449 9/3 Charing (L) RES 3m 13 G *ld to 7th, agn 10-15th, 3rd & btn 2 out, tired, walked in* 6 0
679 30/3 Cottenham (R) RES 3m 15 GF *in tch, outpcd 16th, 4th & btn whn mstk 2 out, p.u. last* P 0
1371 4/5 Peper Harow (L) RES 3m 5 F *prom,ld 13th, hmpd 2 out, sn hdded, no ex* 2 13

Beaten in poor race; only form 95/96 and looks to have a problem. 13

CHARLIE ANDREWS ch.g. 6 Teofane - Royal Feature by King's Equity — R Andrews
1995 P(0)

107 17/2 Marks Tey (L) MDN 3m 15 G *mid div til f 11th* F -
424 9/3 High Easter (L) MDN 3m 10 S *prom, hit 11th, wknd appr 14th, t.o. & p.u. 16th* P 0
830 6/4 Marks Tey (L) MDN 3m 14 G *prom, cls up 4th at 12th, wknd nxt, rear 16th, p.u. 2 out* P 0

Still learning and may do better. 0

CHARLIE CHALK b.g. 9 Le Bavard (FR) - Blissful Hour by Hardicanute — Mrs R A Schofield
1995 4(0),P(0),3(17),2(18),1(17),1(17)

159 17/2 Weston Park (L) CON 3m 22 G *mid to rear, outpcd, p.u. 2 out* P 0
293 2/3 Eaton Hall (R) INT 3m 11 G *nvr bttr than mid-div, ran on onepcd* 7 0
735 31/3 Sudlow Farm (R) MEM 3m 7 G *not fluent, chsd ldr 6-12th, ev ch & blndrd 2 out, wknd* 3 11
1009 9/4 Flagg Moor (L) CON 3m 7 G *ld to 5th & 14th, jnd app 2 out, kpt on gmly flat* 1 19
1032 13/4 Alpraham (R) CON 3m 9 GS *alwys bhhd, t.o. 6th, p.u. 2 out* P 0
1369 4/5 Gisburn (R) CON 3m 10 G *lft 3l 2nd 15th, ev ch aft, no ext* 2 17

Won 5 points; moderate; stays and needs long course; makes mistakes; may win again; Any. 18

CHARLIE HAWES (Irish) — **I** 394^{U}, **I** 430^{U}, **I** 470^{4}, **I** 581^{4}, **I** 636^{U}, **I** 652^{4}

CHARLIE KELLY b.g. 7 Netherkelly - Changan by Touch Paper — T P Whales

1995 2(12),4(0)

13	14/1	Cottenham	(R) MDO 3m	10	G	*in tch, wnet 3rd 14th, chsd wnr 3 out-flat, fin 4th, disq*	4D	0
107	17/2	Marks Tey	(L) MDN 3m	15	G	*mid div, outpcd 14th, 3rd & no ch 17th, went 2nd last*	2	10

Safe and completed all starts; looks slow but can find a win; finished early 96. .... **13**

CHARLIE'S HIDEAWAY(IRE) ch.g. 7 Seclude (USA) - Lapeer by Young Emperor — D Branton

1995 **P(NH),P(NH)**

44	3/2	Wadebridge	(L) MDO 3m	9	GF	*prom, ld 8-10th, wknd rpdly, t.o. & p.u. 15th*	P	0
556	17/3	Ottery St M'	(L) MDO 3m	15	G	*rear whn u.r. 7th*	U	-
718	30/3	Wadebridge	(L) MDO 3m	11	GF	*sn rear, 6th at 16th, p.u. apr last, schooling*	P	0
1070	13/4	Lifton	(R) MDN 3m	9	S	*keen hold & ld to 12th,wknd qckly & mstk 13th,rear,p.u.15th*	P	0

Far too headstrong at present. **11**

CHARLOTTE'S OLIVER b.g. 11 Tumble Gold - Candy Belle by Candy Cane — Mrs C M A Dook

1995 P(0),4(0),7(0),5(0),2(0)

239	25/2	Southwell P'	(L) MDO 3m	9	HO	*cls up, ev ch 4 out, wknd apr nxt*	3	0
330	3/3	Market Rase'	(L) MDO 3m	7	G	*chsd ldrs til 5th & wkng 13th, t.o.*	5	0
636	23/3	Market Rase'	(L) MDN 3m	11	GF	*mostly 6th til f 12th (ditch)*	F	-
972	8/4	Thorpe Lodge	(L) MDO 3m	9	GF	*(bl) 3rd til 8th, fdd, t.o. 6 out, p.u. 2 out*	P	0

No rateable form and unimproved by blinkers. **0**

CHARLTON YEOMAN b.g. 11 Sheer Grit - Bell Walks Breeze by Flaming Breeze (CAN) — Mrs D Rowell

1995 **3(NH),6(NH)**

475	10/3	Tweseldown	(R) CON 3m	9	G	*pllng, prom to 9th, t.o. whn p.u. 3 out*	P	0
786	31/3	Tweseldown	(R) LAD 3m	8	G	*outpcd in rear, nvr able to chal*	4	10
962	8/4	Heathfield	(R) XX 3m	4	G	*chsd wnr 5th, 3l down 4 out, rdn & wknd 2 out*	2	14
1297	28/4	Bexhill	(R) LAD 3m	7	F	*wth ldr to 15th, steadily wknd 3 out*	5	0

Chase winner 93; does not stay 3m & a win at 12 in points highly unlikely **12**

CHARMERS WISH b.m. 12 Beau Charmeur (FR) - Velvet's Wish by Three Wishes — J R Thomas

1995 3(0),7(0),1(13)

198	24/2	Lemalla	(R) OPE 3m	12	HY	*alwys bhnd*	6	0
530	16/3	Cothelstone	(L) OPE 3m	7	G	*in tch, last & rddn 11th, t.o. & p.u. 2 out*	P	0
1343	4/5	Holnicote	(L) OPE 3m	6	GS	*nvr nrr*	3	12
1498	11/5	Holnicote	(L) OPE 3m	5	G	*hdwy to disp 9th, ld 12-15th, wknd qckly 2 out*	3	13
1550	18/5	Bratton Down	(L) CON 3m	8	F	*sn rear, hit 13th, bhnd whn p.u. apr nxt*	P	0
1632	1/6	Bratton Down	(L) MEM 3m	3	G	*chsd wnr to 4th & 14th-3 out, no imp*	3	0

Members winner 95; very moderate and easily beaten in competitive races. **12**

CHASE THE SUN (Irish) — **I** 217^{U}, **I** 255^{U}, **I** 287^{P}, **I** 361^{F}

CHASING CHARLIE ch.g. 6 Nearly A Hand - Bride by Remainder Man — Mrs S Hooper

806	4/4	Clyst St Ma'	(L) MDO 3m	7	GS	*tubed, chsd ldrs, prog 3 out, ld nxt, pshd clr*	1	15
1313	28/4	Little Wind'	(R) RES 3m	14	G	*handy, cls 6th at 9th, rdn & lost plc 13th, no ch 15th*	7	10

Beat 2 subsequent winners; tubed; breathing problems a worry; more needed for Restricted. **14**

CHAS RANDALL (Irish) — **I** 421^{F}, **I** 526^{P}, **I** 616^{P}

CHAT RUN (Irish) — **I** 409^{P}

CHATTERLEY b.g. 10 Oats - Non Such Valley by Colonist II — Mrs J Bloom

97	11/2	Ampton	(R) MEM 3m	2	GF	*(fav) ld til jnd 4th, ld agn 9th, lft solo nxt*	1	0
258	29/2	Nottingham	(L) HC 3m 110yds	10	G	*settld in tch, bustled along when pace qcknd final cct, no impn from 4 out.*	3	0

Dual winner 94; missed 95; problems mean he will not fulfill his potential; best watched now. **17**

CHE AMIGO (Irish) — **I** 256^{P}, **I** 318^{P}

CHECK ON TESSA b.m. 7 All Systems Go - Songful by Song — Miss Linda Wonnacott

1995 **11(NH)**

1530	12/5	Ottery St M'	(L) MDO 3m	8	GF	*s.s. schoold & well bhnd, blnd & u.r. 7th*	U	-
1628	27/5	Lifton	(R) MEM 3m	5	GS	*3rd whn blnd & u.r. 2nd*	U	-

No signs of ability. **0**

CHEEKY CHEVAL ch.g. 11 Cheval - Miss Charlottgoir by Charlottesvilles Flyer — Mrs D Buckett

1995 U(-),5(13),5(0),U(-),1(17),3(10)

140	17/2	Larkhill	(R) CON 3m	17	G	*prom early, wknd frm 13th, t.o.*	7	0
573	17/3	Detling	(L) OPE 4m	9	GF	*in tch til wknd 14th, wll bhnd whn p.u. 22nd*	P	0
998	8/4	Hackwood Pa'	(L) CON 3m	5	GF	*mstks, nvr a factor*	3	0
1246	27/4	Woodford	(L) OPE 3m	6	G	*prog 10th, lft 3rd 15th, rdn & btn 3 out, tk 2nd cls home*	2	14

1372 4/5 Peper Harow (L) OPE 3m 6 F *hld up, prog 12th, ev ch nxt, sn strugg, no ch frm 3 out* 3 11

1609 26/5 Tweseldown (R) MXO 3m 9 G *mstk 7th, in tch in rear til last frm 10th, bhnd & p.u.2 out* P 0

Won weak Open 95; well beaten when placed and need luck to win again. 13

CHEEKY FOX b.g. 10 King Of Spain - Diamond Talk by Counsel K O'Meara

1995 **8(NH),4(NH),P(NH)**

78 11/2 Wetherby Po' (L) OPE 3m 10 GS *mid-div, fdd, p.u. 11th* P 0

184 23/2 Haydock (L) HC 3m 9 GS *(bl) bhnd, tailing off when ref 9th.* R -

460 9/3 Eyton-On-Se' (L) LAD 3m 10 G *rr 6th, t.o. hlfwy, p.u. 13th* P 0

1032 13/4 Alpraham (R) CON 3m 9 GS *(bl) mid-div, 5th whn f 4th* F -

1193 21/4 Sandon (L) OPE 3m 8 G *(bl) alwys rear, losing tch whn p.u. 8th* P 0

No completions in 96 & no prospects now 0

CHEEKY POT b.g. 8 Petoski - Pato by High Top Mrs E I L Tate

1995 **3(NH),5(NH),2(NH),3(NH),8(NH),2(NH),8(NH),1(NH),7(NH),4(NH)**

759 31/3 Great Stain' (L) LAD 3m 10 GS *prom, 3rd hlfwy, kpt on onepcd frm 4 out* 4 18

827 6/4 Stainton (R) LAD 3m 7 GF *mid-div, prog 16th, onepcd frm 2 out* 3 17

1132 20/4 Hornby Cast' (L) LAD 3m 9 G *p.u. bef 1st, rider thought false start* P 0

1283 27/4 Easingwold (L) LAD 3m 10 G *rear, jmpd slwly 6th, wknd 10th, t.o. 13th* 6 12

1449 6/5 Witton Cast' (R) LAD 3m 10 G *outpcd in midfld, made slight late hdwy* 5 13

1469 11/5 Easingwold (L) LAD 3m 6 G *(bl) ld to 15th, ld nxt-apr last, switched rght flat, ld nr fin* 1 20

Winning hurdler 95; disappointing till blinkers re-applied; can win again with headgear; G-F 20

CHEERIO FIDEL VI (Irish) — **I** 178[P], **I** 215[P], **I** 286[5], **I** 401[2]

CHENE ROSE (Irish) — **I** 17[P], **I** 171[F], **I** 257[P], **I** 316[F], **I** 362[3], **I** 454[3], **I** 537[1]

CHERISHTHELADY (Irish) — **I** 464[P], **I** 510[P]

CHERI'S RIVAL (Irish) — **I** 97[P]

CHERRY ANNE ch.m. 12 Nearly A Hand - Cherry Fizz by Master Buck Mrs G Drury

781 31/3 Penshurst (L) MDN 3m 11 GS *alwys towrds rear, wll bhnd whn p.u. 13th* P 0

Lightly raced elderly maiden; will stay that way. 0

CHERRY CHAP b.g. 11 Kabour - Mild Wind by Porto Bello J M Bowles

1995 3(20),**P(0)**,2(19),**F(-)**,1(17),**5(18)**

620 23/3 Higham (L) LAD 3m 9 GF *sttld off pace, prog to 5th at 12th, ev ch 14th, no ext nxt* 5 12

678 30/3 Cottenham (R) LAD 3m 6 GF *hld up, lost tch 13th, went 3rd 15th, no imp aft* 3 18

1147 20/4 Higham (L) LAD 3m 9 F *mid-div, effrt 12th, chsd wnr 2 out, no imp flat* 2 22

1259 27/4 Cottenham (R) LAD 3m 5 F *(fav) chsd ldrs,prog to 2nd 13th,disp 15th til ld apr last,rdn out* 1 21

1546 18/5 Fakenham (L) HC 3m 110yds 13 G *mid div to 12th, p.u. in rear before last.* P 0

Won 2 weak races 95/96; tries hard but barely stays; may win again late season; G-F. 18

CHERRYFLAME (Irish) — **I** 99[P], **I** 180[6], **I** 216[F], **I** 259[P], **I** 319[P], **I** 535[P], **I** 601[P]

CHERRYGAYLE(IRE) b or br.m. 6 Strong Gale - Julia's Pauper by Pauper P Mercer

575 17/3 Detling (L) MDO 3m 10 GF *rear, poor 4th apr 3 out, styd on strngly to ld last* 1 10

Luckily beat a bunch of non-stayers; could be anything; more needed for Resricted. 13

CHERRY GLEN (Irish) — **I** 308[P], **I** 460[3], **I** 609[3], **I** 631[2]

CHERRY ISLAND(IRE) ch.g. 8 King Persian - Tamar Di Bulgaria (ITY) by Duke Of Marmalade (USA) Mrs Heather Gibbon

552 17/3 Erw Lon (L) MDN 3m 10 GS *(fav) alwys prom, ld 3 out, easily* 1 15

768 31/3 Pantyderi (R) OPE 3m 10 G *alwys prom, ev ch last, no ext flat* 3 16

980 8/4 Lydstep (L) RES 3m 11 G *(fav) prom, 2nd & onepcd frm last* 2 13

1197 21/4 Lydstep (L) MEM 3m 3 S *(fav) made all, easily* 1 18

1263 27/4 Pyle (R) CON 3m 9 G *(fav) cls up til ld 8th, kicked clr 14th, unchal* 1 22

Improved & good stable; beat modest rivals but should upgrade to Opens; G-S 22

CHERRY STREET b.m. 7 Cruise Missile - New Cherry by New Brig Mrs J E Purdie

1995 P(0)

3 13/1 Larkhill (R) MDO 3m 10 GS *n.j.w. chsd ldrs, 3rd whn f 11th* F -

281 2/3 Clyst St Ma' (L) RES 3m 11 S *ld to 7th, lost tch 14th, t.o. & p.u. 3 out* P 0

No real signs yet; may do better. 0

CHESHAM LORD (Irish) — **I** 102[3], **I** 162[P]

CHESTNUT SHOON (Irish) — **I** 641[U], **I** 647[P]

CHEVIN LAD (Irish) — **I** 612[6]

CHIASSO FORTE(ITY) b.g. 13 Furry Glen - Cassai (ITY) by Mduedo Mrs Pauline Adams

436 9/3 Newton Brom' (R) LAD 3m 10 GS *alwys prom, 2nd til outpcd frm 4 out, styd on* 5 15

723 31/3 Garthorpe (R) CON 3m 19 G *alwys rear, 11th hlfwy, nvr nrr* 7 0
1179 21/4 Mollington (R) LAD 3m 10 F *chsd ldrs, in tch to 11th, outpcd aft, no ch frm 13th* 5 13
1377 5/5 Dingley (R) CON 3m 12 GF *(bl) ld 3rd, sn clr, hdd 14th, grad fdd* 6 12
1520 12/5 Garthorpe (R) LAD 3m 8 GF *(bl) mid to rear, u.r. 6th* U -
1639 2/6 Dingley (R) MEM 3m 7 GF *(bl) ld 3rd, sn clr, mstks 4th & 12th, hdd 14th, one pace* 3 12

Winning chaser; safe but does not stay; win looks impossible at 14. .... **14**

CHIBOUGAMA(USA) br.g. 9 Alla Breva (USA) - Pie Chart (USA) by Nodouble (USA) R T Jones
1995 4(16),3(19),2(19),5(0),4(16),2(20),P(0)

6 13/1 Larkhill (R) OPE 3m 18 GS *alwys wll bhnd, t.o. frm 14th* 6 14
157 17/2 Erw Lon (L) CON 3m 15 G *8th at 9th, no prog aft* 9 0
505 16/3 Magor (R) PPO 3m 7 GS *cls up in 2nd frm 7-15th, 3rd & onepcd aft* 3 14
601 23/3 Howick (L) CON 3m 10 S *mid-div, ld 11th-14th & 3 out-nxt, onepcd aft* 2 16
671 28/3 Taunton (R) HC 3m 13 S *prom early, bhnd when mstks 7th and next, soon t.o..* 8 0
1043 13/4 Bitterley (L) OPE 3m 9 G *alwys last, not keen to jn ldrs, no ch 13th, late prog* 5 11
1111 17/4 Hockworthy (L) MXO 3m 13 GS *cls up, chsd ldr 10th, sn outpcd & no ch* 7 14
1158 20/4 Llanwit Maj' (R) OPE 4m 9 GS *in tch til outpcd 17th, no ch frm 20th* 6 13

Won 6 in 94; beaten last 16 and looks ungenuine; unlikely to consent to win again. **13**

CHICKCHARNIE ch.g. 6 Stanford - Lucky Angel by Lucky Wednesday Mrs D Cockburn

49 4/2 Alnwick (L) OPE 3m 14 G *t.o. last til f 5th* F -

An over ambitious start; not seen again. **0**

CHILDSWAY b.g. 8 Salmon Leap (USA) - Tharita by Thatch (USA) S J Robinson
1995 5(0),P(0),P(0),P(0),r(-)

4 13/1 Larkhill (R) MDO 3m 9 GS *pllng, ld til ran wd aft 12th, ld 14th-apr last, wknd* 2 12
253 25/2 Charing (L) MDO 3m 10 GS *plld into ld 3rd til u.r. 8th* U -
275 2/3 Parham (R) MDN 3m 15 GF *pllng,chsd ldr,ld 13th,mstk & hdd 3 out,wknd rpdly,p.u.last* P 0
997 8/4 Hackwood Pa' (L) MDO 3m 11 GF *held up, 2nd frm 11th, chal 2 out, wandered & no imp flat* 2 12
1164 20/4 Larkhill (R) MDN 3m 12 GF *tckd awy, prog 12th, ch 14th, wknd nxt* 4 10
1374 4/5 Peper Harow (L) MDO 3m 8 F *restrained in rr, prog to 2nd 3 out, ld nxt, drvn out flat* 1 12
1501 11/5 Kingston Bl' (L) RES 3m 10 G *hld up bhnd, prog 10th, rdn 12th, sn wknd, p.u. 15th* P 0
1607 26/5 Tweseldown (R) MEM 3m 3 G *(fav) hld up, ld 9th, qcknd 3 out, rdn out flat* 1 11

Hard puller; barely stays; amazingly won twice(well ridden); may find another local race. **15**

CHILIPOUR gr.g. 9 Nishapour (FR) - Con Carni by Blakeney Nick Viney
1995 1(23),1(22),1(24),1(24),1(25),1(25)

66 10/2 Great Treth' (R) OPE 3m 8 S *ld til last, no ext flat* 2 25
133 17/2 Ottery St M' (L) OPE 3m 18 GS *(fav) hld up, prog 15th, ld 3 out, qcknd clr last* 1 25
277 2/3 Clyst St Ma' (L) OPE 3m 4 S *(fav) hld up, blnd 14th, prog 17th, ld 3 out, sn clr, easily* 1 24
559 17/3 Ottery St M' (L) OPE 3m 7 G *(fav) w.w. prog 13th, ld 3 out, easily* 1 25
626 23/3 Kilworthy (L) OPE 3m 12 GS *(fav) w.w. trckd ldrs 12th, 4th & btn whn blnd 3 out, p.u. last* P 0
802 4/4 Clyst St Ma' (L) OPE 3m 2 GS *(fav) lft solo 2nd, jmpd slwly 3rd & 4th, grad warmed up* 1 0
1073 13/4 Lifton (R) OPE 3m 10 S *hld up in tch, hdwy 12th, ld 3 out, sn qcknd clr, imp* 1 27
1275 27/4 Bratton Down (L) OPE 3m 8 GF *(fav) hld up,2nd 12th,chal last,hld whn switchd flat,fin 2nd,prmtd* 1 25
1382 6/5 Exeter (R) HC 2m 7f 110yds 8 GF *(fav) alwys prom, ld 10th, ran on well.* 1 26
1541 16/5 Folkestone (R) HC 2m 5f 8 G *(fav) waited with, prog to chase ldr after 10th, mstk next, rdn to ld after 2 out, driven clr run-in.* 1 29
1613 27/5 Fontwell (R) HC 3 1/4m 110yds 12 G *(fav) in tch, chsd ldr 11th, ld 2 out, styd on well.* 1 30

Useful pointer/H/chaser; tough; best on easy courses; sure to win again; G/F-S. **30**

CHIP'N'RUN gr.g. 10 Cruise Missile - Fairytale-Ending by Sweet Story F D Cornes
1995 **P(0)**,2(21),r(-),P(0),2(21),2(20),**U(-),F(-)**

25 20/1 Barbury Cas' (L) OPE 3m 14 GS *prom to 10th, btn frm 12th, t.o. & p.u. 2 out* P 0
162 17/2 Weston Park (L) OPE 3m 16 G *chsd ldrs, ev ch 13th, sn wknd, p.u. 3 out* P 0
215 24/2 Newtown (L) OPE 3m 20 GS *prom til 4th & btn apr 14th, 5th whn p.u. 2 out* P 0
459 9/3 Eyton-On-Se' (L) OPE 3m 11 G *cls up, ld 13th, ran on und pres frm 4 out* 1 22
662 24/3 Eaton Hall (R) OPE 3m 10 S *prom, disp 2nd whn u.r. 5 out* U -
950 8/4 Eyton-On-Se' (L) OPE 3m 4 GF *(fav) ld to 6th, steadd, ld 4 out, ran on strgly* 1 24
1171 20/4 Chaddesley ' (L) OPE 3m 15 G *trckng ldrs whn u.r. 5th* U -
1220 24/4 Brampton Br' (R) OPE 3m 10 G *(fav) 3rd whn msd mrkr bef 8th, p.u.* P 0
1316 28/4 Bitterley (L) OPE 3m 5 G *trckd ldrs, went 4l 2nd 12th, chal last, drew clr flat* 1 24
1419 6/5 Eyton-On-Se' (L) OPE 3m 4 GF *made all sttng strng pace, ran on whn rnnr-up clsd 3 out* 1 23
1545 18/5 Bangor (L) HC 3m 110yds 8 G *in tch, ld briefly after 9th, wknd 14th, t.o. when p.u. before 2 out.* P 0

Won 3 in 94; revived in 96; Eyton specialist; can win Opens there at 11; G/F-S **23**

CHIP PAN b.g. 5 Pitpan - Harbour Girl by Quayside Sir John Barlow Bt

1033 13/4 Alpraham (R) MDO 2 1/2m 15 GS *nvr bynd mid-div, 6th whn p.u. last* P 0
1476 11/5 Aspatria (L) MDO 3m 16 GF *prom, mstk 8th, 5th & wknng 14th, p.u. 3 out* P 0

Only learning; promise on 2nd start; do much better in 97. .... **11**

CHISM(IRE) br.g. 5 Euphemism - Melody Gayle Vii by Damsire Unregistered — N R Freak

1511 12/5 Maisemore P' (L) MDO 3m 14 F *schoold & bhnd, some prog 8th, nvr rchd ldrs, p.u. 15th* P 0
1554 18/5 Bratton Down (L) MDO 3m 16 F *(Jt fav) handy,5th at 13th,lft 2nd 15th,ld aft last,ran on strngly* 1 16

Good stable & won fair race; should prosper - Restricted early 97 if acting on Soft, Firm so far 18

CHITA'S CONE gr.m. 9 Celtic Cone - Conchita II by Hardraw Scar — I M Ham

1995 5(17),2(22),2(18),1(20)

335 3/3 Heythrop (R) INT 3m 9 G *prom, trckd ldng pair 12th, btn 2 out, hit last, eased* 3 14
644 23/3 Cothelstone (L) MEM 3m 6 S *(fav) hndy, ld 6th, clr 12th, easily* 1 20
732 31/3 Little Wind' (R) INT 3m 6 GS *(fav) trckd ldr til ld brfly 14th,disp nxt til outpcd 3 out,eased* 3 15
989 8/4 Kingston St' (R) CON 3m 6 F *(fav) hld up in tch, 2nd at 10th, ld aft 14th, comf* 1 21

2 modest wins but beaten by good horses; c stays; can win more; G/F-Hy. 21

CHOCOLATE BUTTONS b.m. 7 Button Bright (USA) - Man Maid by Mandamus — J R Thomas

1995 P(0),2(10)

201 24/2 Lemalla (R) MDO 3m 13 HY *mid-div, s.u. bend apr 4th* S -
447 9/3 Haldon (R) MDO 3m 13 S *gd prog to 3rd at 13th, wknd 15th, p.u. 2 out* P 0
1115 17/4 Hockworthy (L) MDO 3m 10 GS *cls up, chsd ldr 15th, lft in ld 2 out, sn hdd & wknd* 2 12
1347 4/5 Holnicote (L) MDO 3m 16 GS *chsd ldrs til u.r. 10th* U
1592 25/5 Mounsey Hil' (R) MDO 3m 9 G *w.w. blnd 12th, 5th & in tch whn f 17th* F -
1638 1/6 Bratton Down (L) MDO 3m 13 G *(fav) 6s-2s, wll bhnd 7th,effrt 13th, nvr able to rch ldrs* 7 0

Placed in weak races; more needed to win. 12

CHOCTAW gr.g. 12 Great Nephew - Cheyenne by Sovereign Path — Mrs Anthea L Farrell

1995 **7(NH),7(NH),R(NH),9(NH),P(NH)**

305 2/3 Great Stain' (L) LAD 3m 11 GS *cls up, disp ld til outpcd 3 out, styd on onepcd* 4 16
1010 9/4 Flagg Moor (L) LAD 3m 6 G *j.w., made all, rdn 2 out, styd on strngly* 1 23
1516 12/5 Hexham Poin' (L) LAD 3m 2 HY *(fav) reluc to line up, disp til ld 13th, grad drew clr* 1 16

Winning chaser; thorough stayer; beat good horse at Flagg; quirky; win again in 97. 21

CHOICE COMPANY (Irish) — I 494P

CHORETINE LADY (Irish) — I 132P, I 223F, I 348F, I 385, , I 5225, I 616P

CHRISTIAN ch.g. 10 Baptism - Kalangali by Double-U-Jay — Miss E P Tomkinson

1995 P(0),F(-),4(13),1(13),5(0)

159 17/2 Weston Park (L) CON 3m 22 G *prom til outpcd 13th, sn btn* 9 0
457 9/3 Eyton-On-Se' (L) INT 3m 11 G *2nd to 8th, sn btn, p.u. 4 out* P 0

Won poor Confined 95; well beaten other starts; need luck to win again. 12

CHRISTIMATT (Irish) — I 260U, I 365P, I 4093, I 450P, I 495F, I 5993

CHRISTMAS BASH b.m. 13 Shaab - Christmas Fun by Tangle — G Chambers

1995 P(0),P(0),3(15),5(13),1(16),2(14)

1361 4/5 Flete Park (R) CON 3m 9 G *lft in ld 7th, hit 11th, hdd 15th, wknd rpdly 17th* 5 0
1526 12/5 Ottery St M' (L) LAD 3m 5 GF *in tch til outpcd 15th* 4 17
1624 27/5 Lifton (R) LAD 3m 9 GS *twrds rear, some prog 15th, not nr to chal* 5 15
1648 8/6 Umberleigh (L) LAD 3m 11 GF *rear til u.r. aft 4th* U

Won Restricted 95; stays; not threatening to win in better class. G-F. 13

CHRISTMAS HOLS b.g. 10 Young Generation - Foston Bridge by Relkino — Mrs V Greatrex

870 6/4 Higher Kilw' (L) MEM 3m 5 GF *ld/disp to 9th, 4th & rdn 15th, no ch aft* 4 0
1142 20/4 Flete Park (R) CON 3m 11 S *t.o. & p.u. 13th* P 0
1361 4/5 Flete Park (R) CON 3m 9 G *twrds rear, 6th at 14th, bhnd frm 15th, p.u. last* P 0
1525 12/5 Ottery St M' (L) CON 3m 9 GF *twrds rear frm hlfwy* 6 12

Unreliable;&of no real account now. 0

CHRISTY'S GIRL (Irish) — I 28U, I 163P

CHUCK (Irish) — I 528P, I 655F

CHUCKLEBERRY b.g. 7 Chukaroo - Pink Ebony by Indianira (USA) — Mrs D Ibbotson

1995 P(0),F(-),7(0)

409 9/3 Charm Park (L) CON 3m 11 G *prom early, wknd hlfwy, p.u. 3 out* P 0
762 31/3 Great Stain' (L) MDN 3m 11 GS *mid-div, mstk 6th, prom hlfwy, wknd 3 out, t.o. & p.u. last* P 0
1094 14/4 Whitwell-On' (R) MDO 2 1/2m 88yds 16 G *prom til onepcd frm 4 out* 5 0
1287 27/4 Easingwold (L) MEM 3m 5 G *prom til lost ground 10th, sn rdn & wknd, t.o.* 4 0
1470 11/5 Easingwold (L) MDO 3m 10 G *alwys prom, cls 3rd 14th, mstk nxt, ld 3 out-last, not qckn* 2 13

Gradually improved & ran best race last start; stamina still in doubt; may win late 97 13

CHUKAMILL b.g. 8 Chukaroo - Mill Straight by Straight Lad — Robin Mills

1995 P(0),3(10),P(0),2(0),2(12),P(0),F(-),5(0),**P(0)**

70 10/2 Great Treth' (R) MDO 3m 14 S *ld to 13th, sn btn* 3 0
131 17/2 Ottery St M' (L) MDN 3m 10 GS *alwys prom, lft in ld 3 out, easily* 1 16
199 24/2 Lemalla (R) RES 3m 17 HY *ld/disp to 9th, wknd rpdly, p.u. 2 out* P 0
445 9/3 Haldon (R) RES 3m 9 S *prom, disp 10-13th, sn outpcd, wll btn in 4th whn p.u. 2 out* P 0
482 13/3 Newton Abbot (L) HC 2m 5f 110yds 14 S *in tch to 6th, t.o. when p.u. before 4 out.* P 0
926 8/4 Bishopsleigh (R) RES 3m 9 G *ld 3rd & 8th til no ext 4 out* 3 14

Fortunate when winning & overall form modest; Restricted looks hard to find 14

CHUMMY'S LAST b.m. 6 Palm Track - Chumolaori by Indian Ruler — R Tate

77 11/2 Wetherby Po' (L) RES 3m 18 GS *rear early, t.o. & p.u. 7th* P 0
308 2/3 Great Stain' (L) MDO 3m 12 GS *rear whn bkd & u.r. 4th* U -
762 31/3 Great Stain' (L) MDN 3m 11 GS *rear, prog 12th, ev ch whn f 14th* F -
828 6/4 Stainton (R) MDO 3m 7 GF *rear, mstk 4th, ran wd & ran out bef nxt* r -
987 8/4 Charm Park (L) MDN 3m 13 GF *alwys wll in rear, outpcd, p.u. 14th* P 0
1137 20/4 Hornby Cast' (L) MDN 3m 13 G *in rear whn u.r. 3rd* U -
1285 27/4 Easingwold (L) MDO 3m 9 G *alwys rear, t.o. 8th, p.u. aft 10th* P 0
1451 6/5 Witton Cast' (R) MDO 3m 12 G *rear whn f 2nd* F -
1470 11/5 Easingwold (L) MDO 3m 10 G *rear,prog 5th,mstk 9th,outpcd 13th,kpt on wll 3 out,improve* 4 10

Beaten 15 lengths; getting round was a step in right direction; can do better. 12

CHURCHILL STAR ch.g. 8 Scorpio (FR) - Moya's Star by Top Star — G Moir

1995 4(18),P(0),5(0),3(12),P(0)

214 24/2 Newtown (L) CON 3m 21 GS *ld 2-4th, p.u. 10th, dead* P 0

Dead. 16

CHURCHTOWN CHANCE(IRE) b.m. 6 Fine Blade (USA) - Churchtown Breeze by Tarqogan — Miss Kim Tripp

138 17/2 Ottery St M' (L) RES 3m 18 GS *mid-div, wknd 14th, p.u. 3 out* P 0
268 2/3 Didmarton (L) MDN 3m 10 G *mstks, prom, blnd 9th, ev ch 14th, sn outpcd* 4 0
645 23/3 Cothelstone (L) MDO 3m 3 S *(fav) hrd hld, ld or disp till wnt clr appr last, easily* 1 12
822 6/4 Charlton Ho' (L) RES 3m 7 GF *held up, prog 13th, disp 3 out til hdd line* 2 18
1242 27/4 Woodford (L) RES 3m 18 G *chsd ldrs, 3rd hlfwy, ld 15-16th, grdly wknd* 5 15

Won feeble race but ran well after & Restricted looks very possible in 97; G/F-S 17

CIANICLO (Irish) — I 532^{P}

CIRVIN (Irish) — I 322^{P}, I 375^{P}

CISTOLENA ch.m. 10 Cisto (FR) - Keep Shining by Scintillant — P Barbrook

1995 P(0),3D(14),1(13),F(-)

695 30/3 Llanvapley (L) RES 3m 13 GS *rear, no ch whn p.u. 10th* P 0
844 6/4 Howick (L) RES 3m 10 GF *rear, some prog 12th, no ch 14th, p.u. nxt* P 0
1156 20/4 Llanwit Maj' (R) MEM 3m 7 GS *in tch, blndrd 10th, 4th & outpcd frm 16th* 4 0
1266 27/4 Pyle (R) RES 3m 10 G *cls up til lost plc & rdn 10th, t.o. 15th* 5 0
1557 18/5 Bassaleg (R) RES 3m 14 F *cls up til wkd 12th, t.o. & p.u. 15th* P 0

Won poor Maiden 95; tailed off when completing 96; unlikely to win again. 0

CITY BUZZ(IRE) br.g. 6 Phardante (FR) - Tourin Neofa by Teofane — Victor Ogden

1995 **5(NH),P(NH)**

74 11/2 Wetherby Po' (L) MDO 3m 11 GS *alwys prom, 2nd at 13th, f nxt* F -
117 17/2 Witton Cast' (R) MEM 3m 9 S *in tch to 12th, wknd nxt, poor 5th 2 out* 5 10
228 24/2 Duncombe Pa' (R) MDO 3m 9 GS *ld, drew clr 12th, lft 30l clr nxt, tired flat, all out* 1 12
411 9/3 Charm Park (L) RES 3m 20 G *b.d. 2nd* B -
983 8/4 Charm Park (L) RES 3m 13 GF *alwys rear, onepcd thruout* 9 0
1091 14/4 Whitwell-On' (R) XX 3m 6 G *disp ld til mstk 4th, lost plc 7th, wknd 10th, p.u. 4 out* P 0

Just lasted home in poor Maiden; much more needed for Restricted hopes 12

CITY ENTERTAINER br.g. 15 Tycoon II - Border Mouse by Border Chief — Keith Smith

1995 8(0),**P(0)**,P(0),**F(-)**,F(-)

157 17/2 Erw Lon (L) CON 3m 15 G *ld early, 3rd at 9th, lost plc aft* 10 0

Deserves retirement 0

CITY RHYTHM b.g. 6 Librate - Star City by Royal Boxer — C S Packer

1995 **P(NH)**

849 6/4 Howick (L) MDN 3m 14 GF *last to 7th, p.u. 10th* P 0
1039 13/4 St Hilary (R) MDN 3m 14 G *rear, fin own time* P 0
1248 27/4 Woodford (L) MDN 3m 15 G *ld til hdd & f 15th* F -
1416 6/5 Cursneh Hill (L) MDO 3m 9 GF *alwys rear, lost tch frm 11th, styd on frm 2 out* 5 0
1484 11/5 Bredwardine (R) MDO 3m 17 G *mid-div, lost plc 11th, wknd & p.u. 14th* P 0

Beaten 20l when completing & needs more stamina; may do better 10

CLAIRE ME (Irish) — I 257^{1}, I 315^{F}, I 452^{4}

CLANDON LAD b.g. 6 Impecunious - Madam's Choice by New Member — J G Crumpler

1995 1(16)

68	10/2 Great Treth'	(R)	RES	3m	14 S	*steady prog frm 14th, onepcd frm 2 out*	2	18
465	10/3 Milborne St'	(L)	RES	3m	11 G	*(fav) cls up whn u.r. 3rd*	U	-
656	23/3 Badbury Rin'	(L)	RES	3m	11 G	*(fav) settld mid-div, prog 15th, ev ch when f 2 out*	F	-
1114	17/4 Hockworthy	(L)	RES	3m	4 GS	*(fav) hld up, chsd wnr 12th, clse up 2 out, sn btn, eased*	2	15
1313	28/4 Little Wind'	(R)	RES	3m	14 G	*rear whn f 2nd*	F	-
1345	4/5 Holnicote	(L)	RES	3m	11 GS	*rear whn b.d. 6th*	B	-
1497	11/5 Holnicote	(L)	RES	3m	10 G	*(fav) prog 11th, cls 3rd & ev ch 4 out, wnt 2nd apr last, no ext*	2	18

Maiden winner only start 95; chapter of accidents 96 & disappointing; should win Restricted; G-S 17

CLANMANY (Irish) — I 22P, I 111P, I 180P, I 237P

CLARE LAD ch.g. 13 Garda's Revenge (USA) - Sea Dike by Dike (USA) — Dr M P Tate

1995 5(17),4(15),3(14),3(17),2(18),1(19),**4(11)**,1(18),2(15),4(0)

170	18/2 Market Rase'	(L)	XX	3m	8 GF	*ld 2nd-8th, last frm 11th, no ch 14th*	7	0
410	9/3 Charm Park	(L)	OPE	3m	17 G	*f 2nd*	F	-
894	6/4 Whittington	(L)	OPE	3m	5 F	*(3s-2s), alwys rear, t.o. 6th*	4	0
1093	14/4 Whitwell-On'	(R)	MXO	4m	19 G	*mid-div, wll bhnd frm 18th, t.o.*	7	0
1133	20/4 Hornby Cast'	(L)	OPE	3m	14 G	*twrds rear, mstk 4th, outpcd 7th, t.o. 3 out, u.r. last*	U	-
1304	28/4 Southwell P'	(L)	OPE	3m	5 GF	*(bl) chsg grp to 7th, sn t.o., fin own time, tk 4th on line*	4	0
1367	4/5 Gisburn	(R)	OPE	3m	4 G	*(vis) alwys rear, t.o. 14th*	4	0

Changed hands & schoolmaster in 96; showed minimum interest; unlikely to figure now win at 13 10

CLARE MAN(IRE) b.g. 8 Remainder Man - Bell Walks Rose by Decent Fellow — M P Wareing

99	14/2 Lingfield	(L)	HC	3m	9 HY	*chsd ldr till rider tk wrong course apr 10th, p.u..*	P	0
184	23/2 Haydock	(L)	HC	3m	9 GS	*(Jt fav) cl up, left in ld 5th, made rest, driven clr after last.*	1	26
483	14/3 Cheltenham	(L)	HC	3 1/4m 110yds	17 G	*cl up, ld 8th, jmpd right 10th, hdd 12th, driven along and mstk 3 out, fd from next.*	7	25
672	29/3 Aintree	(L)	HC	2 3/4m	26 G	*f 1st.*	F	-
1108	17/4 Cheltenham	(L)	HC	4m 1f	14 GS	*prom, weakening when mstks 21st and next, t.o. when p.u. before 2 out.*	P	0
1584	24/5 Towcester	(R)	HC	3m 1f	11 GS	*chsd ldr from 7th, went 2nd 6 out, ev ch 3 out, soon rdn and one pace.*	3	26

Winning H/Chaser 94; missed 95; mostly outclassed 96; professionally-trained but may need points ... 23

CLARKES CROSS (Irish) — I 27P, I 160P

CLARKES GORSE (Irish) — I 35P, I 62[2], I 114[1]

CLASHBRIDANE (Irish) — I 238[3], I 612P

CLASH OF THE GALES (Irish) — I 274P, I 322P

CLASSIC EDITION ch.m. 5 Type Edition - Cartress Blue Vii by Damsire Unregistered — R T Jones

1995 **13(NH)**

772	31/3 Pantyderi	(R)	MDN	3m	8 G	*twrds rear, ran green, p.u. 11th*	P	0
849	6/4 Howick	(L)	MDN	3m	14 GF	*rear, f 3rd*	F	-
1271	27/4 Pyle	(R)	MDO	3m	15 G	*w.w. prog to 5l 3rd 14th, no ext frm nxt*	3	0
1484	11/5 Bredwardine	(R)	MDO	3m	17 G	*rdn alng in rear 12th, lost tch 14th, p.u. 3 out*	P	0

Beaten long way only completion & no signs of stamina yet 0

CLASSIE CLAIRE (Irish) — I 210P

CLASSIS KING (Irish) — I 47P, I 79P, I 358[6], I 432[2], I 574P, I 594,

CLASS MEO ch.g. 11 Enryco Mieo - Carlton Bridge by Vivify — H Hill

972	8/4 Thorpe Lodge	(L)	MDO	3m	9 GF	*prog 11th, 2nd 6 out, ld 5 out-3 out, outpcd bef nxt*	2	12
1326	28/4 Fakenham P-'	(L)	MDO	3m	7 G	*ld 4th-13th, 4th & btn whn hmpd & u.r. 2 out*	U	-

Ex-eventer; not disgraced but very onepaced & unlikely to win 12

CLASTINIUM (Irish) — I 53P

CLATTER BROOK b.m. 7 Nearly A Hand - Court Bridge by Mandamus — D J Eckley

1116	17/4 Hockworthy	(L)	MDO	3m	9 GS	*trckd ldrs, cls 3rd whn f 13th, dead*	F	-

Dead 0

CLAUDIA ELECTRIC (Irish) — I 208[4], I 274[5], I 380[6]

CLAYWALLS b.g. 5 Meadowbrook - Lady Manello by Mandrake Major — Ian Hamilton

503	16/3 Lanark	(R)	MDO	3m	10 G	*alwys bhnd*	5	0
1135	20/4 Hornby Cast'	(L)	MDN	3m	10 G	*ld to 5th, prom, mstk 11th, no ext frm 3 out*	4	0

Beaten 30l minimum but should do better in time 10

CLEAN SWEEP br.g. 9 Deep Run - The Charwoman by Menelek — Miss Janet Menzies

1995 P(0),3(0),2(11),**U(-)**

454 9/3 Charing (L) MDN 3m 10 G *mid-div whn f 7th* F -
966 8/4 Heathfield (R) MDO 3m 7 G *chsd ldrs, rdn to chall 2 out, wknd appr last* 4 10
1300 28/4 Bexhill (R) MDO 3m 7 F *patiently rdn, prog to ld 14th, hrd prssd 3 out, hld on wll* 1 11

Deserved a win (poor race) but much more needed for Restricted chances 13

CLEAR CALL(FR) br.g. 11 Bikala - Catacomb (USA) by Halo (USA) J Vickers
1995 2(13),P(0),P(0),P(0)

1427 6/5 High Bickin' (R) CON 3m 10 G *towrds rear, bhnd whn p.u. apr 15th* P 0
1622 27/5 Lifton (R) CON 3m 14 GS *pllng, ld 1st, prom til lost plc 10th, bhnd & p.u. 2 out* P 0

6 runs in last 3 seasons & only one completion; looks finished now 0

CLEASBY HILL ch.g. 11 Avocat - Strandhill by Bargello Robert Ogden

303 2/3 Great Stain' (L) CON 3m 11 GS *mid-div whn u.r. 6th* U -
512 16/3 Dalton Park (R) CON 3m 10 G *prom til outpcd frm 14th, 6th 4 out, kpt on* 4 11
826 6/4 Stainton (R) OPE 3m 8 GF *nvr going wll, lost tch 8th, p.u. aft nxt* P 0
1281 27/4 Easingwold (L) CON 3m 15 G *prom, rdn 9th, sn lost plc, t.o. & p.u. 13th* P 0

Dual winner 92 but missed 95 & looks past it now 10

CLEDDAU KING b.g. 10 Push On - Karatina (FR) by Dilettante II James Buckle
1995 6(0),P(0),5(0),3(16),F(-),U(-),P(0),P(0),P(0),8(0),P(0)

621 23/3 Higham (L) INT 3m 12 GF *ld to 5th, lost tch 12th, sn t.o.* 4 0
1144 20/4 Higham (L) MEM 3m 4 F *ld to 8th, cls 2nd whn blnd & u.r. 12th* U -

Front-runner; never involved where it matters; Members only hope 10

CLERIC ON BROADWAY(IRE) b.m. 8 The Parson - L O Broadway by Crash Course R H Fox
1995 **9(NH),4(NH),U(NH),5(NH),3(NH)**

80 11/2 Wetherby Po' (L) MDO 3m 12 GS *cls up whn f 11th* F -
440 9/3 Newton Brom' (R) MDN 3m 10 GS *hld up rear, prog to cls 4th 3 out, not rch wnr* 2 0
723 31/3 Garthorpe (R) CON 3m 19 G *20s-8s, f 2nd* F -
1104 14/4 Guilsborough (L) MDN 3m 18 G *mstks, alwys bhnd, t.o. 11th, p.u. 3 out* P 0

Placed in novice hurdles 95; yet to learn to jump & barmy gamble; well beaten when 2nd 10

CLIFFORD (Irish) — I 299P, I 337P, I 365P

CLOBEEVER BOY b.g. 6 Shaab - Clover Bee Mrs J Spear

3 13/1 Larkhill (R) MDO 3m 10 GS *hld up bhnd, t.o. 13th, fin well, crashed thro rail aft fin* 4 13
1044 13/4 Bitterley (L) MDO 3m 15 G *chsg grp whn b.d. 4th* B -

Unfortunate start & should go close with better fortune in 97 13

CLOBRACKEN LAD ch.g. 8 Shaab - Clover Bee by The Bo'sun T J Swaffield
1995 P(0),4(14),2(15),P(0),1(17),P(0),2(15)

524 16/3 Larkhill (R) INT 3m 11 G *mid-div whn p.u. 8th* P 0
709 30/3 Barbury Cas' (L) OPE 3m 15 G *alwys mid-div, no ch frm 3 out* 5 17
1061 13/4 Badbury Rin' (L) INT 3m 3 GF *j.w. ld/disp til went clr 2 out, hld on und pres* 1 18
1335 1/5 Cheltenham (L) HC 2m 5f 10 G *mstk 5th, 4th and outpcd 12th, styd on from 3 out, went 2nd run-in, not trbl wnr.* 2 20
1533 14/5 Chepstow (L) HC 3m 6 F *in rear, hdwy 5 out, styd on to go 2nd apr last, kept on run-in.* 2 19
1614 27/5 Hereford (R) HC 3m 1f 110yds 16 G *(fav) n.j.w., in tch, reminders 10th, wknd 14th, t.o. when p.u. before 3 out.* P 0

Restricted winner 95; ran passably in H/Chases but moderate at best; often pulls-up; Confined 97 20

CLODAGH RIVER (Irish) — I 664, I 1952, I 3253

CLODIAGHRANGER (Irish) — I 466B, I 582F, I 607P

CLOGHEEN LASS (Irish) — I 120F, I 279F, I 3351

CLONAGEERA (Irish) — I 208F, I 2746, I 432P

CLONATTIN LADY(IRE) b.m. 7 Sandalay - Cold Arctic by Bargello Darren Page

61 10/2 Cottenham (R) MDO 3m 8 GS *raced wd, alwys bhnd, t.o. last whn p.u. 13th* P 0
182 18/2 Horseheath (R) MDO 3m 11 G *blnd 8th, in tch to 12th, t.o. 14th, p.u. 3 out* P 0
253 25/2 Charing (L) MDO 3m 10 GS *t.o. 7th* 4 0
575 17/3 Detling (L) MDO 3m 10 GF *sn wll in rear, t.o. 3 out* 4 0

Beaten miles & looks hopeless 0

CLONCANNON BELL (Irish) — I 2911, I 326F, I 4672, I 577U

CLON CAW (Irish) — I 3456, I 636P

CLONE(IRE) b.g. 8 Final Straw - Highland Girl (USA) by Sir Ivor Mrs J W Furness
1995 P(0),P(0),1(17),2(17)

47 4/2 Alnwick (L) XX 3m 14 G *prom til blndrd & u.r. 3rd* U -
121 17/2 Witton Cast' (R) RES 3m 11 S *rear, prog 10th, strng chal 2 out, onepcd apr last* 3 16
328 3/3 Market Rase' (L) RES 3m 9 G *prom, ld 13th, rdn 2 out, hdd last, kpt on* 2 19

726 31/3 Garthorpe (R) RES 3m 16 G *(fav) 4s-5/2,n.j.w. nvr gong well, effrt 11th, sn btn, no ch 15th* 11 0
983 8/4 Charm Park (L) RES 3m 13 GF *prom early, 2nd 11th, wknd, rear whn p.u. 2 out* P 0

Maiden winner 95; 2 fair shows 96 but ran badly last two (ground?); could find Restricted 97; G-S 16

CLONEA (Irish) — **I** 649P

CLONEE LANE (Irish) — **I** 31P, **I** 832, **I** 2254

CLONEENVERB (Irish) — **I** 615P, **I** 6602

CLONOGHILL(IRE) b.g. 7 Soughaan (USA) - Port-O-Call by Import G I Cooper

314 2/3 Ampton (R) MDO 3m 10 G *cls up, 4th & wkng whn u.r. 16th* U -
597 23/3 Parham (R) MDO 3m 9 GS *trckng ldrs whn u.r. 2nd* U -

No real signs yet but could improve 0

CLONROCHE GAZETTE ch.g. 16 Pauper - Clonrochess by London Gazette H W Wheeler

1995 4(0)

942 8/4 Andoversford (R) MEM 3m 8 GF *carried 14st, alwys wll bhnd, fin own time* 4 0

Superannuated now 0

CLONROCHE LUCKY(IRE) b.g. 6 Strong Statement (USA) - Clonroche Artic by Pauper Mrs C Handel

1995 P(0),P(0)

70 10/2 Great Treth' (R) MDO 3m 14 S *prom, ld 13th-15th, outpcd frm nxt* 2 11
207 24/2 Castle Of C' (R) MDO 3m 15 HY *(fav) handy, ev ch 2 out, no ext last* 2 13
534 16/3 Cothelstone (L) MDN 3m 10 G *(fav) in tch, jnd ldrs 12th, p.u. 14th, dsmntd* P 0

Good enough for a win but problems last start; should find a race if fit in 97 14

CLONROSH SLAVE (Irish) — **I** 29P, **I** 824, **I** 1041, **I** 158, , **I** 1983, **I** 2214

CLONTOURA(IRE) b.g. 8 Salluceva - Clara Novello by Maciver (USA) Mrs C A Coward

226 24/2 Duncombe Pa' (R) OPE 3m 10 GS *(Jt fav) in tch til blnd & u.r. 5th* U -
304 2/3 Great Stain' (L) OPE 3m 10 GS *alwys abt 3rd, styd on onepcd frm 2 out* 3 18
410 9/3 Charm Park (L) OPE 3m 17 G *mid-div to 14th, prog nxt, styd on 2 out, nvr nrr* 5 15
513 16/3 Dalton Park (R) OPE 3m 9 G *rear, nvr put in race, lft poor 4th 4 out, no ch* 4 12

Modest Irish points winner 95; struggling in England; finished early; Confined only possible; Good 18

CLOSE CONTROL(IRE) b.g. 8 Mummy's Treasure - Melika Iran by Fine Blade (USA) A Hollingsworth

430 9/3 Upton-On-Se' (R) MDO 3m 15 GS *mstks, rear whn p.u. 14th* P 0
688 30/3 Chaddesley ' (L) MDN 3m 17 G *alwys rear, last at 12th, p.u. 4 out* P 0
1047 13/4 Bitterley (L) MDO 3m 13 G *prom til wknd 13th, t.o. 3 out* 5 0
1319 28/4 Bitterley (L) MDN 3m 13 G *ld 12th, hdd aft 14th, 3rd whn b.d. 3 out, dead* B -

Dead. 14

CLOUD COVER gr.h. 8 Scallywag - Misty Sky by Hot Brandy C J B Barlow

1995 F(-),P(0)

79 11/2 Wetherby Po' (L) MDO 3m 12 GS *prom early, b.d. 10th* B -
217 24/2 Newtown (L) RES 3m 17 GS *rear, prog 9th, lost tch aft 13th, mstk 15th, p.u., dsmntd* P 0

No completions from 5 runs in 3 seasons & problems as well 0

CLOUD DANCING b.g. 8 Jupiter Island - Preobrajenska by Double Form John Connolly

1995 U(-),6(0),F(-),3(10)

288 2/3 Eaton Hall (R) MDO 3m 17 G *disp whn ran out aft 7th* r -
462 9/3 Eyton-On-Se' (L) RES 3m 12 G *trckd ldrs, ld brfly 4 out, ran on onepcd frm 2 out* 2 14
740 31/3 Sudlow Farm (R) MDN 3m 16 G *(fav) prog 9th, disp ld 3 out, lft clr nxt, wknd, hdd & f last* F -
1234 27/4 Weston Park (L) MDO 3m 13 G *mid-div, chsd ldr frm 5 out, ran on onepce* 2 13
1423 6/5 Eyton-On-Se' (L) MDO 3m 7 GF *(Jt fav) chsng grp, drvn to chal 3 out, not qckn* 2 0

Consistent but beaten in modest races & barely stays; may scrape a win eventually 13

CLOUGHAN BOY (Irish) — **I** 1034, **I** 162P, **I** 2302, **I** 299, , **I** 337U, **I** 4792, **I** 5521, **I** 6263, **I** 633P

CLOVER COIN ch.m. 9 St Columbus - Clover Doubloon by Tudor Treasure M E T Davies

1995 1(17),2(19),1(16)

273 2/3 Parham (R) LAD 3m 11 GF *alwys prom, chal 2 out, und pres & drft lft, just ld flat* 1 22
572 17/3 Detling (L) LAD 3m 10 GF *alwys prom, chsd wnr frm 15th, not pace to chal* 2 18
963 8/4 Heathfield (R) MXO 3m 7 G *trkd ldrs, 3rd & ev ch 16th, outpcd nxt, tk 2nd flat* 2 20

Lightly-raced; stays & consistent; placed last 17 starts; can win again; G/F-S 21

CLOVER NOOK (Irish) — **I** 244P, **I** 296P, **I** 358P

CLUB CARIBBEAN (Irish) — **I** 330,

CLYDE EMPEROR (Irish) — **I** 170P

C-MAC (Irish) — **I** 98P

COCH-BREAC (Irish) — I 457[P], I 610[P]

COACHROADSTARBOY b.g. 8 Vital Season - Millstar by Military — F G Gingell

1995 P(0)

471	10/3	Milborne St'	(L)	MDO 3m	16	G	*mid-div, hmpd 5th, chsd ldr 15th, no imp 2 out*	3	0
653	23/3	Badbury Rin'	(L)	MDO 3m	9	G	*ld 6th-9th and 12th to appr last, ran on run-in*	2	13
821	6/4	Charlton Ho'	(L)	MDN 3m	10	GF	*held up, prog 13th, efft 3 out, ld nxt, ran on wll*	1	18
1168	20/4	Larkhill	(R)	RES 3m	8	GF	*mid-div,chsd ldr 14th,hrd rdn to ld apr last,pshd out flat*	1	19
1553	18/5	Bratton Down	(L)	XX 3m	10	F	*(fav) prog 12th, 2nd frm 15th, cls up whn f 3 out, dead*	F	

Dead 18

COCK FINCH b.g. 7 Tout Ensemble - French Palace by Royal Palace — Miss Kim Tripp

208	24/2	Castle Of C'	(R)	LAD 3m	14	HY	*sn t.o., m bhnd whn p.u. 4 out*	P	0

Nothing to sing about yet 0

COCKPIT (Irish) — I 323[P]

COCKSTOWN LAD b.g. 10 Main Reef - Pasadena Girl by Busted — Mrs E R Featherstone

1995 5(0),F(-),4(12),1(0),1(13),2(18),4(17),1(20)

312	2/3	Ampton	(R)	OPE 3m	6	G	*blnd 2 nd, cls up til 3rd & outpcd appr 17th, no dang aft*	3	21
420	9/3	High Easter	(L)	OPE 3m	9	S	*disp til ld 4th-12th, blnd nxt, no ch frm 16th*	5	13
619	23/3	Higham	(L)	OPE 3m	10	GF	*rear of main grp, mstks 2nd & 8th, rdn 12th, styd on 3 out*	5	12
677	30/3	Cottenham	(R)	OPE 3m	11	GF	*in tch,prog 16th,ld 2 out-last,rallied flat,lkd to fin 2nd*	1	23
811	6/4	Charing	(L)	OPE 3m	9	F	*(fav) sn rear, hdwy 15th, 3rd 2 out, nvr nrr*	3	19
1146	20/4	Higham	(L)	OPE 3m	7	F	*outpcd, wll bhnd frm 4th, t.o. & u.r. 9th*	U	-
1565	19/5	Mollington	(R)	OPE 3m	8	GS	*n.j.w. last & t.o. til p.u. 12th*	P	0

Won 3 Opens 95; lucky only success 96; fast ground essential; moderate at best; deteriorating 16

CODDINGTON STAR ch.m. 6 Lighter - Emancipated by Mansingh (USA) — Miss H S Chapman

1995 P(0)

431	9/3	Upton-On-Se'	(R)	MDO 3m	17	GS	*10th hlfwy, styd on frm 15th, no dang*	7	0

Not disgraced but only two outings in two seasons to date 11

CODDINGTON VILLAGE b.g. 11 Bonnova - Hidden Melody by Melodic Air — A C McKay

1995 1(10),F(-),5(0),P(0)

659	24/3	Eaton Hall	(R)	MEM 3m	6	S	*cls up til lost tch 12th, sn btn, p.u. 14th*	P	0

Won poor Members 95 & well beaten since 0

CODGER b.g. 16 Kinglet - Oca by O'Grady — Miss J E Thame

1995 5(15),2(12),2(15),5(0),2(13)

126	17/2	Kingston Bl'	(L)	LAD 3m	11	GS	*mstk 6th, cls up to 9th, wll t.o. 13th*	6	0
234	24/2	Heythrop	(R)	LAD 3m	6	GS	*chsd ldr til ld 8th, jnd 3 out, hdd nxt, onepcd*	3	14
792	2/4	Heythrop	(R)	LAD 3 3/4m	7	F	*mid-div, no imp on ldrs 4 out, wknd 2 out*	5	0
1015	13/4	Kingston Bl'	(L)	MEM 3m	9	G	*cls up, chsd wnr 13th, no imp 15th, kpt on*	2	16
1179	21/4	Mollington	(R)	LAD 3m	10	F	*rear frm 5th, t.o. & p.u. 12th*	P	0

Gallant old stager; still runs well occasionally but will not win again 12

CODOLOGY (Irish) — I 19[P], I 107[P], I 164[P], I 631, , I 651[3]

COED CANLAS b.g. 7 Sizzling Melody - Hello Honey by Crepello — C Jenkins

1995 P(0),6(0),3(0),U(-)

202	24/2	Lemalla	(R)	MDO 3m	12	HY	*sn bhnd, p.u. aft 4th*	P	0
299	2/3	Great Treth'	(R)	MDO 3m	13	G	*bhnd til p.u. 16th*	P	0
629	23/3	Kilworthy	(L)	MDN 3m	11	GS	*in tch to 10th, t.o. frm 14th*	5	0
1118	17/4	Hockworthy	(L)	MDO 3m	14	GS	*mstk 2nd, alwys bhnd, mstk 11th, t.o. & p.u. nxt*	P	0

Ran one decent race in 95 but all other efforts poor 0

COGITATE ch.m. 7 Oats - Snow Time by Deep Run — J E Brockbank

194	24/2	Friars Haugh	(L)	MDN 3m	11	S	*sn t.o., p.u. 12th*	P	0
405	9/3	Dalston	(R)	MDO 2 1/2m	16	G	*prom early, lost plce frm 10th, t.o. & p.u. 13th*	P	0
756	31/3	Lockerbie	(R)	MDN 3m	14	G	*prom early, t.o. whn p.u. 11th*	P	0

Yet to go more than two miles; good stable & may improve 0

COLCOMBE CASTLE gr.g. 13 Persian Plan (AUS) - Vet's Bill by Hardraw Scar — B F W Rendell

1995 **P(0),R(-)**,P(0),3(0)

559	17/3	Ottery St M'	(L)	OPE 3m	7	G	*handy, ev ch 5 out, outpcd frm nxt*	3	20
709	30/3	Barbury Cas'	(L)	OPE 3m	15	G	*(bl) rear, nvr on terms frm 12th, outpcd*	6	15
1125	20/4	Stafford Cr'	(R)	OPE 3m	7	S	*rear til some late prog frm 3 out*	4	16

Remarkably revived 96; not threatening to win Opens but may find small opening at 14 16

COLIN'S HATCH (Irish) — I 18[3], I 100[5], I 168,

COLLARD TOR ch.g. 7 Smackover - Maksoufa by English Prince — Mrs M E Turner

1995 F(-),2(10),P(0)

629	23/3	Kilworthy	(L)	MDN	3m	11	GS	*in tch to 10th, sn wknd, p.u. 13th*	P	0
876	6/4	Higher Kilw'	(L)	MDN	3m	11	GF	*ld to 8th, lost plc rpdly 11th, t.o. & p.u. 3 out*	P	0

Only finished one of 10 races 94-6 & a breif season 96 0

COLLEGE LAND (Irish) — **I** 274^{1}

COLLIGAN RIVER (Irish) — **I** 10^{P}, **I** 67, , **I** 152^{2}, **I** 209^{2}, **I** 329^{P}, **I** 378^{2}, **I** 520^{F}, **I** 591^{P}

COLLON DIAMOND (Irish) — **I** 535^{1}

COLLON MISSION (Irish) — **I** 340^{U}, **I** 483^{P}, **I** 562^{4}, **I** 625^{P}

COLLOONEY SQUIRE (Irish) — **I** 337^{F}, **I** 395^{P}

COLMANS HATCH (Irish) — **I** 62^{F}

COLMANS HOPE (Irish) — **I** 9^{P}, **I** 52^{F}

COLNE VALLEY KID ch.g. 11 Homing - Pink Garter by Henry The Seventh — Mrs B D Welsh

776	31/3	Penshurst	(L)	OPE	3m	6	GS	*trckd ldrs, wknng whn p.u 13th*	P	0
920	8/4	Aldington	(L)	OPE	3m	6	F	*chsd ldr to 10th, wknd rpdly 15th, t.o. & p.u. 3 out*	P	0
1375	4/5	Peper Harow	(L)	CON	3m	9	F	*mid-div til lst pl appr 7th, t.o. whn p.u. 10th*	P	0

Of no account 0

COLONEL FAIRFAX gr.g. 8 Alias Smith (USA) - Mistress Meryll by Tower Walk — Mrs N R Matthews

1995 P(0),P(0),U(-),B(-),2(10),U(-),U(-),P(0),P(0)

643	23/3	Siddington	(L)	MDN	3m	16	S	*made most to 15th, wknd rpdly nxt*	5	0
791	2/4	Heythrop	(R)	MEM	3m	5	F	*hld up, nvr on terms, no dang*	3	0
947	8/4	Andoversford	(R)	MDN	3m	11	GF	*disp to 2nd, ld 4-6th, agn 8-13th, wknd, p.u. last*	P	0
1341	4/5	Warwick	(L)	HC	2 1/2m 110yds	12	GF	*mstk 1st, bhnd and hit 6th, t.o. when p.u. before 2 out.*	P	0
1434	6/5	Ashorne	(R)	MDO	3m	15	G	*hld up bhnd, prog frm 12th, ev ch 3 out, wknd rpdly nxt*	4	10
1569	19/5	Mollington	(R)	MDO	3m	10	GS	*20s-6s,prom,ld 9-13th,ld agn 2 out,clr last,all out flat*	1	14

Won at 20th attempt (7 mins race) after showing no stamina in previous 19! Restricted needs more 15

COLONEL FRAZER(IRE) b.g. 8 Buckskin (FR) - Tabitha Bay by Laurence O — Ray Perkins

1995 P(0),6(0),3(0),P(0)

504	16/3	Magor	(R)	MEM	3m	5	GS	*3rd til lost tch 12th, p.u. last*	P	0
605	23/3	Howick	(L)	MDN	3m	13	S	*rear, wknd 7th, p.u. 11th*	P	0
1040	13/4	St Hilary	(R)	MDN	3m	12	G	*prom in 3rd whn f 13th*	F	-
1162	20/4	Llanwit Maj'	(R)	MDO	3m	12	GS	*ld/disp to 5th, til ld 14-16th, kpt on und pres flat*	2	13
1272	27/4	Pyle	(R)	MDO	3m	9	G	*(fav) ld/disp til rdn clr frm 14th, kpt on und pres flat*	1	12
1557	18/5	Bassaleg	(R)	RES	3m	14	F	*ld to 4th, prom whn f nxt*	F	-
1601	25/5	Bassaleg	(R)	RES	3m	12	GS	*prom, 4th hlfwy, wknd, poor 5th whn p.u. last*	P	0

Looked hopeless but perked up mid-season; won dire Maiden & most unlikely to win Restricted 12

COLONEL JAMES br.g. 14 Captain James - Faraday Girl by Frigid Aire — R M Thorne

112	17/2	Lanark	(R)	LAD	3m	8	GS	*u.r. 5th*	U	-
499	16/3	Lanark	(R)	LAD	3m	10	G	*ld to 4th, wll bhnd whn p.u. 4 out*	P	0

Of no account 0

COLONEL KENSON ch.g. 10 Avocat - Bryophila (FR) by Breakspear II — Robert Barr

106	17/2	Marks Tey	(L)	RES	3m	12	G	*mid div, prog & ev ch 12th, wknd appr 17th*	4	0
419	9/3	High Easter	(L)	RES	3m	10	S	*disp ld to 4th, blnd 13th, sn stgglng, no ch frm 16th*	3	0
616	23/3	Higham	(L)	MEM	3m	3	GF	*ld & mstk 1st, mstk 5th, disp 9th til hdd last, ran on*	2	14
1329	30/4	Huntingdon	(R)	HC	3m	14	GF	*bhnd and rdn 10th, kept on from 2 out, n.d..*	5	0
1539	16/5	Folkestone	(R)	HC	3m 7f	9	G	*mstk 2nd, well bhnd 4th, t.o..*	7	0

Maiden winner 94; missed 95; just beaten in Members but outclassed apart; safe 13

COLONEL O'KELLY(NZ) br.g. 12 Kirrama (NZ) - Gold Coast (NZ) by Palm Beach — J L Dunlop

1995 1(16),3(16),1(17),1(21),1(21)

19	14/1	Tweseldown	(R)	CON	3m	9	GS	*rear, mstk 8th, lost tch 12th, ran on frm 2 out, nvr nrr*	3	18
271	2/3	Parham	(R)	CON	3m	15	GF	*prom til u.r. 14th*	U	-
592	23/3	Parham	(R)	MEM	3m	4	GS	*(fav) trckd ldrs, 2nd 9th, mstk 11th, chsng wnr whn u.r. 13th*	U	-
962	8/4	Heathfield	(R)	XX	3m	4	G	*trkd ldrs, 10l 3rd & outpcd 13th, no dang aft, kpt on flat*	3	14
1207	21/4	Heathfield	(R)	CON	3m	9	F	*in rear whn u.r. 6th*	U	-

Changed hands 96; proved handful for novice rider; no penalty 97 & may win Confined; G-Hy 15

COLONEL POPSKI ch.g. 14 Niniski (USA) - Miss Jessica by Milesian — J O Barr

1995 P(0),3(15),3(16)

305	2/3	Great Stain'	(L)	LAD	3m	11	GS	*alwys mid-div, nvr a fctr, p.u. last*	P	0
759	31/3	Great Stain'	(L)	LAD	3m	10	GS	*mid-div, went prom 6th, styd on frm 15th, disp 3 out,onepcd*	3	19
827	6/4	Stainton	(R)	LAD	3m	7	GF	*mid-div, gd prog to go prom 14th, wknd 3 out*	6	11

283 27/4 Easingwold (L) LAD 3m 10 G *mid-div, drppd rear 7th, t.o. 13th* 7 0
615 27/5 Wetherby (L) HC 2 1/2m 110yds 11 G *soon well bhnd, t.o. when p.u. before 4 out.* P 0

Ladies winner 94; well beaten in 96 & win at 15 looks impossible 12

COLONIAL KELLY ch.g. 8 Netherkelly - Nepal by Indian Ruler — Alan Cowing
1995 1(27),**2(28)**
179 18/2 Horseheath (R) OPE 3m 5 G *(fav) ld,blnd 9th,mstk & hdd nxt,ld agn 12th,ran on gamely flat* 1 30
260 1/3 Newbury (L) HC 3m 6 GS *(Jt fav) chsd ldr, hit 10th, ld 14th, hit 2 out, driven and kept on well.* 1 25
483 14/3 Cheltenham (L) HC 3 1/4m 110yds 17 G *hit 1st, cl up when f 3rd.* F -
670 28/3 Aintree (L) HC 3m 1f 9 G *cl up, mstk 4th, ld 11th, mistake and hdd next, kept on from 2 out.* 2 27
107 15/4 Southwell (L) HC 3m 110yds 10 G *(fav) made all, hit 4th, hrd pressed final 3, gamely.* 1 23

Top-class pointer & fair H/Chaser; should win more H/Chases; makes mistakes; G-S 29

COLONIAL KING b.g. 13 Dalsaan - Norfolk Bonnet by Morston (FR) — T Walker
365 4/5 Gisburn (R) MDO 3m 17 G *alwys rear, t.o. 10th* 7 0

.... 0

COLONIAN KING ch.g. 9 Scallywag - Colonian Queen by Colonist II — D Barnes
287 2/3 Eaton Hall (R) MDO 3m 11 G *s.s. last whn f 3rd* F -
589 23/3 Wetherby Po' (L) MDO 3m 16 S *f 1st* F -

Shows no ability 0

COLOURED THYME (Irish) — **I** 177^F, **I** 231^F, **I** 320^F, **I** 408^P, **I** 449^3

COLOURFUL BOY b.g. 7 Afzal - Jolly Girl by Jolly Me — H J Manners
1995 **9(NH),8(NH),9(NH),6(NH)**
713 30/3 Barbury Cas' (L) MDO 3m 10 G *alwys rear, t.o. 10th, p.u. 4 out* P 0
959 8/4 Lockinge (L) MDN 3m 6 GF *alwys rear, t.o. whn p.u. 5 out* P 0
217 24/4 Andoversford (R) MDO 3m 16 G *cl up to 4th, grad lost plc, mid-div & f 14th* F -
293 28/4 Barbury Cas' (L) MDO 3m 11 F *prom, mstk 9th, 2nd frm 11th, pshd into ld last, rdn out* 1 14
564 19/5 Mollington (R) XX 3m 14 GS *cls up til outpcd 14th, disp 3rd aft 3 out, onepcd* 4 11
612 26/5 Tweseldown (R) RES 3m 11 G *lost plc 8th, effrt 12th, ev ch 15th, grad wknd 3 out* 4 12

Just landed weak Maiden & struggled after; more needed for Restricted; does not impress in paddock 14

COLUMBIQUE ch.g. 13 Tobique - Lady Columbus by St Columbus — S D Moffett
1995 P(0),P(0),P(0),3(0)
209 24/2 Castle Of C' (R) OPE 3m 8 HY *ld to 5th, cls up aft, wknd & lost tch frm 14th* 4 0
647 23/3 Cothelstone (L) CON 3m 6 S *alwys rear* 3 0
125 20/4 Stafford Cr' (R) OPE 3m 7 S *ld to 4th, prom til mstk 11th, lost tch frm 4 out* 6 0
307 28/4 Little Wind' (R) MEM 3m 1 G *walked over* 1 0
397 6/5 Cotley Farm (L) CON 3m 4 GF *alwys last, no ch frm 13th* 4 0

Still safe but well past it now 0

COMEDIE FLEUR b.m. 8 Martinmas - Welsh Flower by Welsh Saint — Miss Caroline Nicholas
1995 1(16),1(16),P(0)
877 6/4 Brampton Br' (R) MEM 3m 1 GF *walked over* 1 0
881 6/4 Brampton Br' (R) CON 3m 9 GF *prog frm 14th, disp 3 out, wknd & p.u. last* P 0

Dual winner 95; season over in one day 96 & out of sorts; could revive; Any 17

COMERS GATE b.g. 11 Impecunious - Opt Out by Spartan General — R Fielder
1995 2(0)
252 25/2 Charing (L) INT 3m 7 GS *chsd wnr, wkng whn p.u. 11th* P 0
477 10/3 Tweseldown (R) MDO 3m 15 G *sn bhnd, t.o. & p.u. 4 out* P 0

No longer of any account 0

COMIC ACT (Irish) — **I** 312^P, **I** 358^5, **I** 515, , **I** 618^F, **I** 651,

COMING SOON (Irish) — **I** 550^4, **I** 604^F, **I** 651^5

COMMAND (Irish) — **I** 192^P

COMMANDER SWAINE ch.g. 10 Tepukei - Hannah Swaine Vii — R W Pitcher
096 14/4 Whitwell-On' (R) MEM 3m 9 G *chsd ldrs, wknd 8th, sn t.o.* 5 0

Rarely appears & shows nothing 0

COMMON COIN (Irish) — **I** 37^F, **I** 87^P, **I** 124^P, **I** 159^4

COMPUTER PICKINGS b.m. 9 Taufan (USA) - Ricciola (USA) by Stage Door Johnny — John E Wright
1995 **12(NH),13(NH),7(NH),7(NH)**

117 17/2 Witton Cast' (R) MEM 3m 9 S *rear of ldrs, smooth prog to 2nd 2 out, no ext apr last* 2 1
303 2/3 Great Stain' (L) CON 3m 11 GS *cls up, outpcd frm 2 out* 5 1
585 23/3 Wetherby Po' (L) RES 3m 13 S *alwys twrds rear, no ch whn p.u. 3 out* P
758 31/3 Great Stain' (L) RES 3m 17 GS *mid-div, went prom hlfwy, no prog aft, wknd 5 out, t.o.* 10
1452 6/5 Witton Cast' (R) MEM 3m 7 G *hndy, ld 4 out, lft wll clr 2 out, cruised home* 1 1

Irish Maiden winner 93; disappointing since; easy task when winning; not one to trust; Good 16

CONDONSTOWN (Irish) — I 390^{P}, I 469^{5}, I 501^{F}

CONFUSED EXPRESS bl.m. 14 Confused - Dawn Express by Pony Express — Mrs Janita Sco

64 10/2 Great Treth' (R) CON 3m 7 S *ld til u.r. 4th* U
196 24/2 Lemalla (R) CON 3m 14 HY *ld to 3rd, grad wknd, sn bhnd* 10

Very useful pointer at her best but sadly looks finished now 12

CONNAUGHT BOY (Irish) — I 109^{P}, I 236^{P}

CONNIE LEATHART b.m. 5 El Conquistador - Busy Quay by Quayside — D Sundi

115 17/2 Lanark (R) MDO 3m 8 GS *t.o. 4th, p.u. 10th* P

An uninspiring beginning 0

CONNOR THE SECOND b.g. 8 Pollerton - Pinkworthy Pond by Le Bavard (FR) — R H Blac

1995 **P(NH)**

116 17/2 Lanark (R) MDO 3m 10 GS *prom early, bhnd whn p.u. 11th* P
319 2/3 Corbridge (R) RES 3m 16 GS *bhnd whn p.u. 6th* P

Shows nothing to date 0

CONOR MAC (Irish) — I 52^{F}, I 114^{P}, I 352^{P}

CONORS BLUEBIRD (Irish) — I 457^{F}, I 502^{P}, I 645^{P}

CONSTANT AMUSEMENT b.m. 8 Funny Man - Common City by Comandeer — Mrs Karen Woodhea

1995 **4(NH)**

223 24/2 Duncombe Pa' (R) CON 3m 16 GS *jmpd slwly 1st, t.o. 5th, p.u. 12th* P
303 2/3 Great Stain' (L) CON 3m 11 GS *handy, wknd 12th, p.u. 3 out* P
488 16/3 Newcastle (L) HC 2 1/2m 9 GS *soon well bhnd, p.u. 7th.* P
1000 9/4 Wetherby (L) HC 3m 110yds 10 G *(bl) soon t.o., p.u. before 10th.* P

Showed nothing in 96 & her future already looks all behind her 0

CONSTANT SULA gr.m. 8 Sula Bula - Conchita II by Hardraw Scar — Derward Robert

1995 P(0)

520 16/3 Larkhill (R) MDO 3m 11 G *rear, prog 14th, ran on well frm 2 out, nrst fin* 3 1
733 31/3 Little Wind' (R) MDO 3m 13 GS *midfld til hdwy 15th, tk 3rd whn blndrd & u.r. 3 out* U
1047 13/4 Bitterley (L) MDO 3m 13 G *(fav) rear of mid-div, some prog 13th, styd on 3 out, nrst fin* 3 1
1248 27/4 Woodford (L) MDN 3m 15 G *(fav) chsd ldr til blnd 5th, rdn & strglng 13th, no ch & p.u. last* P

Well-bred; improved till disappointing favourite last start; should win in 97 15

CONSTRUCTION KING br.g. 10 Score Twenty Four (USA) - Teleprity by Welsh Pageant — Mrs J E Hawkin

1995 P(0),P(0),P(0),1(15),2(14),3(0),3(18),3(16)

157 17/2 Erw Lon (L) CON 3m 15 G *rear, some late prog, no dang* 7
255 28/2 Taunton (R) HC 4 1/4m 110yds 15 GS *soon well bhnd, t.o. when p.u. before 21st.* P
508 16/3 Magor (R) INT 3m 5 GS *(Jt fav) n.j.w. last & lost tch 10th, ran on own pace, no dang* 2
545 17/3 Erw Lon (L) CON 3m 10 GS *tongue-strap, 3rd/4th to 12th, no dang aft* 5 1
693 30/3 Llanvapley (L) LAD 3m 6 GS *rear, t.o. 13th, p.u. 3 out* P
845 6/4 Howick (L) CON 3m 12 GF *last pair, no ch whn p.u. 3 out* P
1413 6/5 Cursneh Hill (L) INT 3m 6 GF *drppd rear 6th, in tch til outpcd frm 13th* 4
1487 11/5 Erw Lon (L) CON 3m 4 F *trckd ldr til bad mstk 13th, renewd aft 2 out, not trbl wnr* 2 1
1558 18/5 Bassaleg (R) CON 3m 6 F *sn t.o. in 5th, nrly ref 8th, p.u. 15th* P
1648 8/6 Umberleigh (L) LAD 3m 11 GF *alwys wll bhnd, t.o. frm 13th* 9

Restricted winner 95; below par 96 & ran badly; best watched 10

CONTACT KELVIN br.g. 14 Workboy - Take My Hand by Precipice Wood — G Smit

1995 P(0),4(0),1(18),3(15),2(19),U(-)

9 14/1 Cottenham (R) OPE 3m 13 G *raced wd, lost tch 12th, p.u. 3 out* P
22 20/1 Barbury Cas' (L) XX 3m 19 GS *chsd ldrs til wknd 9th, p.u. 12th* P

Open winner 95; only lasted a week in 96 & probably finished now 0

CONTRADICT b.g. 6 Derring Rose - Contrary Lady by Conwyn — M H Westo

1423 6/5 Eyton-On-Se' (L) MDO 3m 7 GF *rr, t.o. 9th, btn over 1 fence* 4

Well-beaten & can only do better 0

CONVAMORE QUEEN (Irish) — I 7^{P}, I 144^{P}, I 522^{P}, I 550^{3}, I 575^{5}, I 654^{P}

CONVINCING ch.g. 12 Formidable (USA) - Star Of Bagdad (USA) by Bagdad — J Cornforth

1995 7(0),3(20),**U(-)**,2(17),**6(10)**,**P(0)**

72	11/2	Wetherby Po'	(L)	CON	3m	18	GS	*alwys prom, disp 6-8th, styd on onepcd frm 4 out*	5	15
326	3/3	Market Rase'	(L)	OPE	3m	14	G	*mid-div, mod 5th & rdn 13th, no prog, p.u. last*	P	0
410	9/3	Charm Park	(L)	OPE	3m	17	G	*ld to 4th, trckd ldr, disp 4 out to last, jst btn*	2	20
826	6/4	Stainton	(R)	OPE	3m	8	GF	*(vis) alwys prom, ev ch 4 out, wknd und pres 2 out*	4	13
1093	14/4	Whitwell-On'	(R)	MXO	4m	19	G	*(vis) alwys wll there, ev ch 4 out, wknd nxt*	4	12
1461	9/5	Sedgefield	(L)	HC	2m 5f	10	F	*(vis) ld to 3rd, led 9th till hdd 13th, gradually wknd.*	4	13

Unlucky 3rd start but most inconsistent & 1 win from last 37 races; unlikely to break the trend 17

COOKIE BOY b.g. 5 Ra Nova - Gypsy Heather by Bivouac — J S Delahooke

916	8/4	Tranwell	(L)	MDO	2 1/2m	8	GF	*alwys rear, remote 5th at 11th, t.o. & p.u. nxt*	P	0
1155	20/4	Whittington	(L)	MDN	3m	14	G	*4th whn f 4th*	F	-
1450	6/5	Witton Cast'	(R)	MDO	3m	14	G	*alwys rear, p.u. 12th*	P	0
1517	12/5	Hexham Poin'	(L)	MDN	3m	10	HY	*ld/disp to 10th, ev ch til wknd apr 3 out, p.u. 2 out*	P	0

Yet to complete the course but may do better in time 0

COOLADERRA LADY (Irish) — I 54[P], I 209[P], I 278[P], I 331[6], I 523[3]

COOLAFINKA (Irish) — I 130[2], I 158[3], I 342[2], I 383[2], I 422[2], I 525[2], I 619[1], I 633[1]

COOL AND EASY b.g. 10 King's Ride - Princess Grand by Kashiwa — H T Pelham

1995 **3(NH)**,**5(NH)**

99	14/2	Lingfield	(L)	HC	3m	9	HY	*in tch, wknd 7th, left mod 3rd 3 out.*	3	19
255	28/2	Taunton	(R)	HC	4 1/4m 110yds	15	GS	*chsd ldrs, ld 10th to after 19th, styd pressing lders till wknd 3 out, p.u. before last.*	P	0

Winning chaser; looks remarkably slow now & even points may tax him if fit in 97 17

COOL APOLLO(NZ) b.g. 9 Gay Apollo - Maple Leaf (NZ) by King's Troop — G W Plenderleith

1995 4(0),F(-),3(0),2(10),4(0),2(0),1(13),2(13)

36	20/1	Higham	(L)	RES	3m	12	GF	*wth ldr to 10th, wknd 12th*	7	0
106	17/2	Marks Tey	(L)	RES	3m	12	G	*alwys bhnd, nvr dang*	5	0
309	2/3	Ampton	(R)	MEM	3m	6	G	*ld 5th-8th, lft disp ld 13th til 16th, wknd next*	3	0
419	9/3	High Easter	(L)	RES	3m	10	S	*rr, lst tch 9th, p.u. 11th*	P	0
484	15/3	Fakenham	(L)	HC	2m 5f 110yds	13	GF	*nvr nrr.*	6	14
679	30/3	Cottenham	(R)	RES	3m	15	GF	*chsd ldrs til wknd frm 16th*	5	0
907	8/4	Fakenham	(L)	HC	3m 110yds	11	G	*bhnd from 11th, p.u. before 4 out.*	P	0
1145	20/4	Higham	(L)	RES	3m	12	F	*alwys rear of main grp, t.o. 16th*	6	0

Won poor Maiden 95; predictably struggling now; safe enough but forutne needed for another win 11

COOL BANDIT (Irish) — I 15[R], I 51[P]

COOLBAWN BRAMBLE (Irish) — I 7[P]

COOL CAILIN (Irish) — I 85[P]

COOL CHIC (Irish) — I 224[P]

COOL CORMACK (Irish) — I 612[P]

COOL DAWN(IRE) br.g. 8 Over The River (FR) - Aran Tour by Arapaho — The Hon Miss D Harding

1995 1(28),1(28),**2(23)**,1(31),**1(29)**,**U(-)**

185	23/2	Kempton	(R)	HC	3m	9	GS	*made all, hit 5 out, ran on strly from last.*	1	38
483	14/3	Cheltenham	(L)	HC	3 1/4m 110yds	17	G	*soon ld, hdd 8th, led again 12th, hded 3 out, outpcd 2 out, kept on from last.*	2	33

Top-class H/Chaser; also 3rd in Irish National; could win major prizes with right handling; G/S-F 38

COOL DELLA (Irish) — I 428[2], I 499[F], I 579[P], I 604[P]

COOLE ABBEY (Irish) — I 518[P]

COOLE CHERRY (Irish) — I 72[P], I 116[P], I 310[1]

COOLFLUGH HERO (Irish) — I 147[P], I 244[5], I 275[2], I 440[F], I 571[6]

COOL GINGER b.g. 10 Ginger Boy - Cool Straight by Straight Lad — C J R Sweeting

1995 P(0),P(0)

235	24/2	Heythrop	(R)	RES	3m	10	GS	*nvr a fctr, p.u. 12th*	P	0
676	30/3	Cottenham	(R)	INT	3m	13	GF	*prom til wknd frm 3 out*	5	13
868	6/4	Larkhill	(R)	RES	3m	4	F	*down early, outpcd 11th, btn frm 13th*	3	0
1260	27/4	Cottenham	(R)	RES	3m	3	F	*(fav) ld,wd bnd aft 3rd,hdd 4 out,ld agn 2 out,hdd flat,ld nr fn*	1	16
1609	26/5	Tweseldown	(R)	MXO	3m	9	G	*mstk 4th & last,effrt 12th,lost plc 15th,kpt on agn 2 out*	4	13

Maiden winner 94; chjanged hands 96; retains ability; should find Confined chance 97; G-F 17

COOLGREEN (Irish) — I 241[4], I 331[P], I 505[1]

COOLING CHIMES (Irish) — I 297[P], I 437, , I 567[1]

COOL IT (Irish) — **I** 82, , **I** 102^{U}, **I** 272^{P}, **I** 336^{2}, **I** 477^{4}

COOL IT A BIT b.g. 11 Mandalus - Burlington Miss by Burlington II — P A D Scouller

1995 2(0)

19 14/1 Tweseldown (R) CON 3m 9 GS *mstk 2nd, mid-div, lost tch 11th, wll bhnd whn p.u. last* P 0
124 17/2 Kingston Bl' (L) CON 3m 17 GS *mid-div, lost tch 13th, t.o. & p.u. 3 out* P 0
251 25/2 Charing (L) OPE 3m 10 GS *ld 9th, made rest, styd on well* 1 18
451 9/3 Charing (L) OPE 3m 11 G *mid-div whn b.d. 9th* B -
594 23/3 Parham (R) CON 3m 13 GS *nvr bttr than mid-div, losing tch whn p.u. 14th* P 0
996 8/4 Hackwood Pa' (L) MXO 3m 4 GF *ld to 14th, hrd rdn, outpcd* 3 14
1265 27/4 Pyle (R) OPE 3m 8 G *alwys rear, cls 7th at 6th, outpcd 8th, p.u. 13th* P 0

Popped up in bad Open at 25-1 & may be able to spring another surprise at 12 14

COOLMOREEN(IRE) ch.g. 8 Carlingford Castle - Sirrahdis by Bally Joy — Derek Baxter

1995 P(0),2(11),P(0),5(10),5(14),2(14),1(0)

642 23/3 Siddington (L) RES 3m 15 S *w.w. mstks 7th & 8th, lsing tch whn p.u. 13th* P 0
840 6/4 Maisemore P' (L) RES 3m 9 GF *hld up in rr, 7th & rddn 14th, no prog* 7 0
1242 27/4 Woodford (L) RES 3m 18 G *w.w, prog to 7th & in tch hlfwy, wknd 16th, p.u. 3 out* P 0
1415 6/5 Cursneh Hill (L) RES 3m 11 GF *midfld whn mstk 6th, lost tch frm 13th, p.u. nxt* P 0
1506 12/5 Maisemore P' (L) MEM 3m 5 F *pllng, trckd wnr til f 3rd* F -
1619 27/5 Chaddesley ' (L) OPE 3m 7 GF *alwys last, pair, blnd 9th, t.o. 12th* 4 12
1649 8/6 Umberleigh (L) RES 3m 14 GF *mid-div, hmpd 10th, no ch aft nxt, p.u. 2 out* P 0

Maiden winner 95; mistakes & showed little 96; best watched 11

COOL NATIVE (Irish) — **I** 347^{F}, **I** 386^{F}

COOL RASCAL gr.m. 10 Scallywag - Cool Gipsy by Romany Air — J Owen

1995 P(0),4(0),4(11),P(0),4(0)

266 2/3 Didmarton (L) LAD 3m 13 G *in tch in rear to 13th, wll bhnd whn p.u. 2 out* P 0
525 16/3 Larkhill (R) RES 3m 7 G *nvr trbld ldrs, t.o.* 3 0
788 31/3 Tweseldown (R) MDO 3m 8 G *mid-div, prog hlfwy, pshd alng 14th, ev ch last, onepcd* 2 14
1015 13/4 Kingston Bl' (L) MEM 3m 9 G *cls up, chsd wnr 7-13th, 3rd & outpcd 15th, no prog aft* 3 10
1183 21/4 Mollington (R) MDN 3m 10 F *trckd ldr, ld apr 13th-14th, onepcd frm 2 out* 2 13
1433 6/5 Ashorne (R) MDO 3m 16 G *in tch til outpcd 13th, ran on 15th, not rch ldrs, wknd flat* 4 0
1562 19/5 Mollington (R) MEM 3m 6 GS *4th til chsd ldng pair 11th, no imp, fin tired* 3 0

Placed 12 times 94/6 but does not really stay & will need fortune to win 12

COOLREE LORD (Irish) — **I** 16^{P}, **I** 36^{1}, **I** 276^{P}, **I** 371^{3}, **I** 463^{P}

COOL RELATION ch.g. 10 Brotherly (USA) - Celtic Ice by Celtic Cone — D J Caro

1995 **1(35),1(40),1(36),1(31)**

668 26/3 Sandown (R) HC 2 1/2m 110yds 8 GS *(fav) trckd ldrs, ld 8th, left clr 5 out, blnd 2 out, shaken up and ran on well from last.* 1 30

Top-class H/Chaser; late to appear 96; best under 3m; G/F-Hy, best Soft 35

COOLRENY(IRE) ch.g. 7 Bon Sang (FR) - Random Thatch by Random Shot — Mrs V Thompson

88 11/2 Alnwick (L) MDO 3m 11 GS *immed t.o. & schoold, f 2 out* F -
488 16/3 Newcastle (L) HC 2 1/2m 9 GS *nvr far away, hit 5th, ld 5 out, hit next, hdd after 2 out, five l 2nd when f last.* F 19
1456 8/5 Uttoxeter (L) HC 2m 5f 11 G *bhnd 4th, jmpd left 6th, p.u. before 12th.* P 0

Showed ability but calamitous & should stick to Maidens - good enough to win one 14

COOL ROCKET (Irish) — **I** 23^{3}, **I** 99^{F}, **I** 179^{3}

COOLSHAMROCK (Irish) — **I** 369^{P}, **I** 510^{1}

COOLSYTHE ch.m. 12 Avocat - Lindenise by London Gazette — C R Millington

241 25/2 Southwell P' (L) MDO 3m 15 HO *in tch til rdn & strggling 11th, t.o. & p.u. 4 out* P 0
904 6/4 Dingley (R) RES 3m 20 GS *alwys rear div, t.o. 8th, p.u. 6 out* P 0
1103 14/4 Guilsborough (L) MDN 3m 15 G *alwys bhnd, t.o. & p.u. 10th* P 0
1376 5/5 Dingley (R) MEM 3m 7 GF *ld to 2nd & 9-12th, 3rd & outpcd 2 out, onepcd* 4 10
1599 25/5 Garthorpe (R) MDO 3m 7 G *(bl) ld/disp to 11th, 4th & fdng whn f aft 4 out* F -
1639 2/6 Dingley (R) MEM 3m 7 GF *(bl) last til p.u. 6th, dsmntd* P 0

Aged maiden & sure to stay that way 0

COOLTEEN HERO (Irish) — **I** 4^{F}, **I** 56^{5}, **I** 236^{2}

COOLVAWN LADY(IRE) b.m. 7 Lancastrian - African Nelly by Pitpan — W R Halliday

1995 **P(NH),F(NH),P(NH),6(NH)**

242 25/2 Southwell P' (L) RES 3m 12 HO *trckd ldrs, mstk 10th, wknd frm 13th, t.o. & p.u. 3 out* P 0
393 9/3 Garthorpe (R) CON 3m 7 G *3rd frm 9th, 2nd 4 out, ev ch whn f 2 out* F 16
539 17/3 Southwell P' (L) RES 3m 11 GS *chsng grp, no ext whn wnr went clr* 2 10
904 6/4 Dingley (R) RES 3m 20 GS *alwys prom, 3rd frm 5th, 2nd 6 out, ld 4 out, ran on wll* 1 22
1100 14/4 Guilsborough (L) OPE 3m 9 G *ld 6-7th & frm 15th, jnd 2 out, ld last, hld on gamely* 1 23
1329 30/4 Huntingdon (R) HC 3m 14 GF *(fav) chsd ldr to 14th, wknd 16th, t.o..* 6 0
1379 5/5 Dingley (R) MXO 3m 7 GF *(fav) 5/4-4/6, ld 6th, just in ld whn f 14th* F -

519 12/5 Garthorpe (R) OPE 3m 7 GF *(fav) cls up, ld 7th & frm 10th, sn in cmnd, ran on* 1 23
598 25/5 Garthorpe (R) OPE 3m 6 G *2nd til ld 5th, hdd 3 out, outpcd frm nxt* 3 24
643 2/6 Dingley (R) OPE 3m 13 GF *lft 2nd app 9th, ld 13th, lft clr nxt, hdd aft 2 out, no ex* 2 26

Changed hands & much improved 96; best with forcing tactics; should win more Opens 97; G/S-G/F ... 24

COOL VIEW ch.m. 7 Kinglet - Cool Kit by Saucy Kit Mrs D Walton
1995 7(0)
89 11/2 Alnwick (L) MDO 3m 9 GS *trckd ldrs til f 5th* F -
323 2/3 Corbridge (R) MDN 3m 12 GS *cls 4th early,2nd frm 13th, und pres 2 out, ld last,hdd flat* 2 14
405 9/3 Dalston (R) MDO 2 1/2m 16 G *(fav) prom til outpcd frm 3 out* 4 0
614 23/3 Friars Haugh (L) MDN 3m 10 G *6th hlfwy, strgglng whn ref 13th* R -

Good enough for a win at best but struggling to stay & ominous signs last start 12

COOL WORK b.g. 8 Teamwork - Fabice by Vonice Christopher Cox
200 24/2 Lemalla (R) MDO 3m 12 HY *alwys prom, ld 9th-4 out, wknd, fin tired* 5 0
529 23/3 Kilworthy (L) MDN 3m 11 GS *sttld rear, prog 10th, sn outpcd, ran on 15th, no imp aft* 3 10

Not disgraced either start but more needed & time passing by 12

COOL YULE (Irish) — **I** 28², **I** 92ᵁ, **I** 234, , **I** 257ᴾ, **I** 452³

COOMBESBURY LANE b.m. 10 Torus - Nimble Rose by Furry Glen N F Williams
1995 P(0),1(19),P(0),3(0),3(15)
215 24/2 Newtown (L) OPE 3m 20 GS *prom, 4th whn f 13th* F -
744 31/3 Upper Sapey (R) OPE 3m 5 GS *mstk 12th, disp frm 15th, outpcd frm 3 out* 3 10
945 8/4 Andoversford (R) OPE 3m 3 GF *hld up rear, prog to ld 13th, qcknd clr frm 2 out* 1 17
1171 20/4 Chaddesley ' (L) OPE 3m 15 G *mid-div, lost tch frm 12th, p.u. 14th* P 0
1504 25/5 Bassaleg (R) OPE 3m 6 GS *cls up to 9th, wknd rpdly, almost ref & f nxt* F -
1643 2/6 Dingley (R) OPE 3m 13 GF *chsd ldr 4th til s.u. bnd app 9th* S -

Has ability but inconsistent; best R/H; won slowly-run race 96; struggle to win again 17

COOME HILL(IRE) b.g. 7 Riot Helmet - Ballybrack by Golden Love W W Dennis
1995 1(21),1(21),**1(23)**
370 7/3 Wincanton (R) HC 3m 1f 110yds 5 GF *alwys prom, ld 16th, clr 4 out, unchal.* 1 33
569 27/3 Chepstow (L) HC 3m 10 S *(fav) in tch till jmpd slowly and lost pl 11th, rallied to go 2nd 5 out, rdn and ran on run-in, just faild.* 2 35

Won 7 of 8 races & top-class H/Chaser now; stays & genuine; hard to beat 97; G/F-Hy 34

COOPER'S CLAN (Irish) — **I** 526ᴾ

COPPER AND CHROME(IRE) ch.m. 7 Sandalay - Dusky Jo by Dusky Boy J M Bowen
138 17/2 Ottery St M' (L) RES 3m 18 GS *alwys rear, t.o. & p.u. 3 out* P 0
199 24/2 Lemalla (R) RES 3m 17 HY *nvr a fctr, p.u. 8th* P 0
298 2/3 Great Treth' (R) RES 3m 13 G *raced wd, cls up, 5th aft 17th, kpt on* 3 15
562 17/3 Ottery St M' (L) XX 3m 12 G *cls up to 8th, wknd, t.o. & p.u. 4 out* P 0
720 30/3 Wadebridge (L) RES 3m 9 GF *sn rear, bhnd til p.u. 15th* P 0
871 6/4 Higher Kilw' (L) RES 3m 9 GF *tongue-strap, sn prom, ld 15th, jnd 3 out, hrd rdn, not qckn* 2 19

Improved last start when just beaten by subsequent H/Chase winner; should find Restricted 97 if fit ... 17

COPPER BANK b.g. 8 True Song - Copperclown by Spartan General Mrs H Hutsby
438 9/3 Newton Brom' (R) MDN 3m 10 GS *sn prom, going wll in 5th whn u.r. 15th* U -
641 23/3 Siddington (L) RES 3m 20 S *in tch,disp ld appr 15th,ld 3 out,clr nxt,rddn out,impress* 1 20
1098 14/4 Guilsborough (L) CON 3m 17 G *hld up, mstks 6th & nxt, bhnd frm 9th, t.o. & p.u. 13th* P 0

Lightly-raced; beat large field impressively; can progress if racing regularly 97; Soft 21

COPPER DIAL ch.g. 10 My Chopin - Copper Tinsell by Crooner G H D Hopes
503 16/3 Lanark (R) MDO 3m 10 G *sn bhnd, t.o. & p.u. 11th* P 0

No sign of talent 0

COPPER FRIEND (Irish) — **I** 284ᴾ, **I** 363⁵, **I** 412ᴾ, **I** 453ᴾ, **I** 491ᴾ

COPPER PAN ch.m. 9 True Song - Copperclown by Spartan General J Hutsby
1995 **P(NH),F(NH),P(NH),P(NH),P(NH)**
21 20/1 Barbury Cas' (L) MEM 3m 16 GS *prom, f 3rd* F -
129 17/2 Kingston Bl' (L) MDN 3m 15 GS *rear, lost tch whn u.r. 13th* U -
233 24/2 Heythrop (R) MDN 3m 14 GS *mid-div til prog 11th, 3rd & ev ch 15th, onepcd* 3 10
341 3/3 Heythrop (R) MDN 3m 13 G *prom til wknd 3 out* 4 0

Does not stay & will need great fortune to win 10

COPPER ROSE HILL b.m. 9 Cruise Missile - Lucibella by Comedy Star (USA) H M F McCall
1995 4(13),1(17),**7(0)**,2(19),3(17),1(19),U(-)
19 14/1 Tweseldown (R) CON 3m 9 GS *prog 6th, chsd ldr 12th, ld 3 out, clr nxt,hdd & no ext last* 2 21

Dual winner 95; ran well only start 96; finished 1st weekend; best watched start of 97 19

COPPER THISTLE(IRE) b.g. 8 Ovac (ITY) - Phantom Thistle by Deep Run — M G Sheppar

1995 2(20),1(24),1(24),1(25),1(0),1(26),**4(0)**

8	14/1	Cottenham	(R)	CON	3m	10	G	*(fav) in tch,ld apr 3 out,jnd & lft in ld 2 out, hdd & onepcd last*	2	2
90	11/2	Ampton	(R)	CON	3m	5	GF	*(fav) made all, drew clr 3 out, not extndd*	1	2
179	18/2	Horseheath	(R)	OPE	3m	5	G	*chsd wnr, disp 11th-nxt, 3l down 2 out, kpt on well aft*	2	2
312	2/3	Ampton	(R)	OPE	3m	6	G	*(fav) made all, drw clr appr 2 out,rddn & styd on wll appr last*	1	2
492	16/3	Horseheath	(R)	OPE	3m	3	GF	*(fav) j.w. made all at steady pace, qcknd clr last, easily*	1	2
1000	9/4	Wetherby	(L)	HC	3m 110yds	10	G	*(fav) ld 2nd till before 4 out, soon outpcd, fin tired.*	2	1
1180	21/4	Mollington	(R)	OPE	3m	5	F	*(fav) j.w. made all, wll clr 13th, easily*	1	2
1333	1/5	Cheltenham	(L)	HC	3m 1f 110yds	13	G	*ld, blnd 11th, hdd and blunded 15th, wknd quickly, t.o. and p.u. before 2 out.*	P	

Top-class pointer; front-runner; flopped in H/Chases; sure to win more points 97; F-S 28

COPPINGER'S CAVE b.g. 8 Kinglet - Versina by Leander — A W K Merria

34	20/1	Higham	(L)	MDN	3m	11	GF	*s.s. alwys bhnd, 5th & no ch whn p.u. 16th*	P
108	17/2	Marks Tey	(L)	MDN	3m	17	G	*in tch 11th, kpt on wll frm 3 out, nt rch ldrs*	3

Has ability but rarely seen; subsequent winners behind when 3rd & could win with regular racing 14

COPTIC DANCER b.m. 7 Sayf El Arab (USA) - Copt Hall Royale — J J Greenwoo

1102	14/4	Guilsborough	(L)	RES	3m	15	G	*alwys bhnd, t.o. & p.u. 13th*	P

No signs of ability only start 0

COQ AU VIN (Irish) — **I** 407P

COQ HARDI DANCER (Irish) — **I** 110P, **I** 172P, **I** 2551, **I** 287F, **I** 411F

COQUALLA (Irish) — **I** 480P

CORAL EDDY b.g. 9 Current Magic - Blue Coral by Long Till — D Mars

1995 4(0)

273	2/3	Parham	(R)	LAD	3m	11	GF	*twrds rear, 6th & no ch whn u.r. 13th*	U
455	9/3	Charing	(L)	MDN	3m	10	G	*nvr nr ldrs, 5th frm 15th*	5
576	17/3	Detling	(L)	MDN	3m	18	GF	*ld to 3rd, prom whn u.r. 6th*	U
676	30/3	Cottenham	(R)	INT	3m	13	GF	*alwys last pair, t.o. 9th*	8
1445	6/5	Aldington	(L)	MDO	3m	8	HD	*alwys towrds rear, in tch in 5th & btn whn u.r. 4 out*	U

Well beaten only two completions & has no winning prospects 0

CORBY KNOWE b.g. 10 Pragmatic - Easter Noddy by Sir Herbert — Dr L D Sincl

1995 **P(NH),P(NH),F(NH),11(NH)**

111	17/2	Lanark	(R)	RES	3m	6	GS	*wll bhnd whn u.r. 4th*	U
501	16/3	Lanark	(R)	RES	3m	12	G	*nvr dang, bhnd whn u.r. 3 out*	U
1249	27/4	Balcormo Ma'	(R)	RES	3m	10	GS	*bhnd by hlfwy, t.o.*	6
1353	4/5	Mosshouses	(L)	RES	3m	11	GS	*alwys last trio, no ch 11th, t.o. & p.u. 3 out*	P

Last & miles behind only completion - no chances 0

CORMEEN LORD(IRE) ch.g. 7 Mister Lord (USA) - Sand-Pit Cross by Pitpan — J C Sha

182	18/2	Horseheath	(R)	MDO	3m	11	G	*schoold in last, t.o. 14th, p.u. 2 out*	P
241	25/2	Southwell P'	(L)	MDO	3m	15	HO	*jmpd slwly, in tch, chsd 1st pair apr 3 out, no imp*	3
438	9/3	Newton Brom'	(R)	MDN	3m	10	GS	*hld up mid-div, prssd ldrs & mstk 14th, not rcvr*	4
899	6/4	Dingley	(R)	MEM	3m	4	GS	*(fav) cls up, hrd hld, chal 2 out, sn outpcd*	3
1103	14/4	Guilsborough	(L)	MDN	3m	15	G	*prom, chal & mstk 3 out, rallied aft nxt, just faild*	2
1381	5/5	Dingley	(R)	MDO	3m	16	GF	*(Jt fav) prom, 5th & wll outpcd 14th, kpt on 2 out, no dang*	5

Just touched off penultimate start; ran poorly after (fast ground); should win in 97; G-G/S 14

CORNAMONA b.m. 10 Head For Heights - Cliona (FR) by Ballymore — Miss Carol Richards

242	25/2	Southwell P'	(L)	RES	3m	12	HO	*ld to f 3rd*	F
329	3/3	Market Rase'	(L)	RES	3m	12	G	*set mad gallop, hdd & blnd 7th, sn wknd, p.u. 11th*	P
367	6/3	Catterick	(L)	HC	3m 1f 110yds	12	G	*keen, soon ld, blnd 5th, p.u. before 8th.*	P
542	17/3	Southwell P'	(L)	MDO	3m	15	GS	*mid-div, lost tch whn p.u. 3 out*	P

Dead 0

CORNISH COSSACK(NZ) br.g. 9 Wolverton - Cotton Bud (NZ) by Balkan Knight — J M B Pu

1995 2(20),1(21),1(22),F(-),2(0),**U(NH)**,**6(NH)**

384	9/3	Llanfrynach	(R)	OPE	3m	16	GS	*wll in tch til outpcd aft 15th, no ch aft*	8
547	17/3	Erw Lon	(L)	OPE	3m	10	GS	*chsd ldrs, lft 2nd 2 out, onepcd*	2
768	31/3	Pantyderi	(R)	OPE	3m	10	G	*alwys mid-div, no dang*	7
1037	13/4	St Hilary	(R)	OPE	3m	5	G	*alwys cls up, prog to disp 15th til wknd 3 out*	3
1265	27/4	Pyle	(R)	OPE	3m	8	G	*cls up til outpcd frm 13th, no ch frm 15th*	5
1488	11/5	Erw Lon	(L)	OPE	3m	4	F	*2nd/3rd thruout, nvr nrr to chal*	2

1604 25/5 Bassaleg (R) OPE 3m 6 GS *prom to 9th, lost plc, remote 4th 3 out* 3 0

Changed hands & declined alarmingly; busy career & best avoided now 12

CORNISH HARP br.g. 7 Prince Of Peace - Gold Harp by Tormento — M B Ogle

1361 4/5 Flete Park (R) CON 3m 9 G *went 3rd 9th, in tch til lost ground 15th, bhnd & p.u. last* P 0
1622 27/5 Lifton (R) CON 3m 14 GS *not fluent, t.o. & p.u. aft 11th* P 0

Late to appear & showed nothing 0

CORNISH WAYS b.g. 8 Foolish Ways - Decoyanne by Decoy Boy — R J S Linne

1995 P(0),**P(0)**,F(-)

720 30/3 Wadebridge (L) RES 3m 9 GF *sn rear, last frm 7th, t.o.* 4 0
937 8/4 Wadebridge (L) INT 3m 4 F *alwys trckng ldr, strng run to ld last stride* 1 13
1142 20/4 Flete Park (R) CON 3m 11 S *rear whn f 9th* F -
1625 27/5 Lifton (R) INT 3m 8 GS *t.o. & p.u. 13th, lame* P 0

Maiden winner 94; found a poor Intermediate; problems last start; best watched 13

CORN KINGDOM b.g. 10 Oats - Rosa Ruler by Gambling Debt — D W Clark

1995 4(14)

36 20/1 Higham (L) RES 3m 12 GF *in tch, rmndrs 11th, grad wknd frm 13th* 6 10
105 17/2 Marks Tey (L) RES 3m 11 G *(bl) cls up til f 14th* F -
419 9/3 High Easter (L) RES 3m 10 S *(bl) cls up til outpcd 13th, t.o.* 5 0
621 23/3 Higham (L) INT 3m 12 GF *alwys rear, mstk 4th, t.o. & p.u. 2 out* P 0
834 6/4 Marks Tey (L) RES 3m 11 G *(bl) ld til jnd aft 15th,hdd nxt,lft disp 2 out,hdd last,kpt on* 2 16

Maiden winner 94; acquiired blinkers in 96; L/H best; may find weak Restricted 15

CORPORAL CHARLIE b.g. 7 Sergeant Drummer (USA) - Palmid by Charlie's Pal — Mrs C Lawrence

1995 **P(NH)**

70 10/2 Great Treth' (R) MDO 3m 14 S *nvr on terms, p.u. bef 13th* P 0

Lightly raced & nothing yet 0

CORRIANNE ch.m. 9 Balidar - Serdarli by Miami Springs — Mrs P A Wallis

1995 F(-)

6 13/1 Larkhill (R) OPE 3m 18 GS *(vis) prom to 10th, t.o. whn p.u. 3 out* P 0
232 24/2 Heythrop (R) OPE 3m 10 GS *in tch, wknd hlfwy, t.o. & p.u. 12th* P 0
427 9/3 Upton-On-Se' (R) OPE 3m 6 GS *(vis) j.w. disp til onepcd frm 3 out* 3 15
687 30/3 Chaddesley ' (L) CON 3m 10 G *(vis) wth ldr 4th til lost plc 8th, last frm 10th, p.u. 3 out* P 0
880 6/4 Brampton Br' (R) XX 3m 8 GF *prom to 4th, grad lost tch frm 12th* 5 0
1437 6/5 Ashorne (R) MXO 3m 13 G *(vis) ld brfly 4th, wknd rpdly 8th, t.o. & p.u. 13th* P 0
1478 11/5 Bredwardine (R) CON 3m 12 G *(bl) ld 2nd-nxt, cls up til wknd 12th, p.u. 15th* P 0
1614 27/5 Hereford (R) HC 3m 1f 110yds 16 G *(vis) ld till after 7th, lost ground quickly, soon bhnd, t.o. when p.u. before 4 out.* P 0

Dual winner 94; only one good run since & looks safely ignored now 0

CORRIES HILL (Irish) — **I** 23^{P}, **I** 26^{F}, **I** 124^{P}, **I** 297^{P}, **I** 554^{P}

CORSAGE ch.g. 5 Good Times (ITY) - Carnation by Runnymede — P Stonehouse

704 30/3 Tranwell (L) MDO 3m 16 GS *mstk 6th, wll bhnd whn p.u. 3 out* P 0
910 8/4 Tranwell (L) MEM 3m 4 GF *3rd til chsd wnr 12th, no imp 4 out, wknd last* 3 0

Last when finishing & season lasted 9 days 0

CORVIEW(IRE) b.g. 5 Corvaro (USA) - Rich View by Candy Cane — P T Cartridge

1045 13/4 Bitterley (L) MDO 3m 16 G *cls up at 10th, ev ch whn blnd 13th, p.u. 15th* P 0

Showed enough on debut to suggest he should go close in 97 11

CORYMANDEL (Irish) — **I** 15^{2}

COSA NOSTRA b.g. 10 Furry Glen - The Very Thing — K Cousins

1995 P(0),P(0),1(0),P(0),P(0)

844 6/4 Howick (L) RES 3m 10 GF *prom to 8th, grad lost tch* 5 0
1034 13/4 St Hilary (R) MEM 3m 3 G *ld 6-12th, chsd wnr, alwys hld* 2 0
1266 27/4 Pyle (R) RES 3m 10 G *ld to 2nd, cls 2nd at 14th, wknd nxt, p.u. last* P 0

Failed in hat-trick bid for Members & outclassed outside that company now 10

COSHLA EXPRESSO (Irish) — **I** 23^{P}, **I** 40^{4}, **I** 69^{6}, **I** 206^{3}, **I** 237^{2}, **I** 446^{3}, **I** 511^{2}, **I** 579^{1}, **I** 626, , **I** 629^{P}

COSIE CARTEL (Irish) — **I** 83^{F}, **I** 308^{F}

COSSACK STRIKE(IRE) b.g. 8 Siberian Express (USA) - My Destiny (USA) by L'enjoleur (CAN) — S Currey

1995 P(0),U(-)

210 24/2 Castle Of C' (R) INT 3m 10 HY *rear til s.u. bend aft 13th* S -
388 9/3 Llanfrynach (R) RES 3m 20 GS *prom to 10th, mid-div by 13th, steadily wknd* 8 0
598 23/3 Howick (L) MEM 3m 6 S *cls 4th whn u.r. 9th* U -

694 30/3 Llanvapley (L) RES 3m 9 GS *lost tch 6th, p.u. 10th* P 0
844 6/4 Howick (L) RES 3m 10 GF *rear, 25l down 14th, ran on late* 4 0
1160 20/4 Llanwit Maj' (R) RES 3m 12 GS *s.s., last whn f 12th* F -

Members winner 93; shown nothing since 0

COSTERMONGER br.g. 7 Rymer - Pearly Miss by Space King A D W Griffith

166 17/2 Weston Park (L) MDN 3m 10 G *rear, prog frm 4 out, nrst fin* 3 10
286 2/3 Eaton Hall (R) MDO 3m 14 G *(fav) sttld mid-div, mstks, losing tch whn p.u. 11th* P 0
463 9/3 Eyton-On-Se' (L) MDN 2 1/2m 14 G *nvr btr thn mid-div, p.u. 3 out* P 0
1195 21/4 Sandon (L) XX 3m 9 G *mid to rear, p.u. 4 out* P 0
1234 27/4 Weston Park (L) MDO 3m 13 G *cls up, ld 10-12th, ev ch til wknd 3 out* 3 10
1365 4/5 Gisburn (R) MDO 3m 17 G *hrd rdn to jn ldr 15th, wknd & p.u. 2 out* P 0
1457 8/5 Uttoxeter (L) HC 3 1/4m 16 G *prom, blnd and lost pl 10th, wknd 14th, bhnd when p.u. before 16th.* P 0
1535 16/5 Aintree (L) HC 3m 1f 11 GF *(bl) trckd ldr, mstk 3rd, f next.* F -

Beaten 16l minimum when completing & short of stamina at present; much more needed for chances .. 10

CO-TACK ch.g. 11 Connaught - Dulcidene by Behistoun Mrs J L Livermore
1995 3(11),4(0),3(12)

691 30/3 Llanvapley (L) CON 3m 15 GS *rear, lost tch 8th, p.u. 10th* P 0
843 6/4 Howick (L) MEM 3m 7 GF *3rd/4th, rpd prog 15th, 2nd 2 out, alwys hld* 2 12

Members winner 94; ran well in same 96 but outclassed in better company 11

COT LANE ch.g. 11 Remainder Man - Smokey Princess by My Smokey J W Walmsley
1995 4D(21),**U(-),P(0),2(23),1(23),5(16)**

583 23/3 Wetherby Po' (L) MEM 3m 6 S *cls up, ld 13th, ran on well 2 out* 1 20
760 31/3 Great Stain' (L) OPE 3m 8 GS *(bl) nvr going wll, rear & rdn 11th, nvr dang* 6 0
1000 9/4 Wetherby (L) HC 3m 110yds 10 G *(bl) chsd ldrs till wknd after 11th.* 4 10
1093 14/4 Whitwell-On' (R) MXO 4m 19 G *(fav) (bl) prom,disp 7th-16th,ran on to ld 4 out,hdd last,rallied fin* 2 22
1573 19/5 Corbridge (R) OPE 3m 12 G *prom, disp 8th, styd prom til fdd 4 out* 7 12

H/Chase winner 95; stays well; becoming inconsistent; should win again on long course; F-S 20

COTTAGE LIGHT b.g. 8 Lighter - Flavias Cottage by Marcus Superbus Mrs S M Foale
1995 R(-),4(0),9(0)

132 17/2 Ottery St M' (L) MDN 3m 9 GS *(bl) cls up early, lost tch 12th, p.u. 4 out* P 0
557 17/3 Ottery St M' (L) MDN 3m 10 G *(bl) 2nd til lost plc 14th, ran on agn frm 3 out* 2 12
875 6/4 Higher Kilw' (L) MDN 3m 6 GF *(Jt fav) (bl) trckd ldr til aft 14th, sn wknd* 4 0
1362 4/5 Flete Park (R) MDO 3m 9 G *(bl) ld 6th til apr 3 out, onepcd* 3 10

Ran well 2nd start but proving frustrating & not progressed; always blinkered 12

COTTAGE RAIDER(IRE) b or br.g. 7 Roselier (FR) - Eleika by Camden Town Robert Vowles
1995 S(-),U(-),P(0),U(-),r(-),1(14),3(10)

600 23/3 Howick (L) RES 3m 14 S *ld til f 6th* F -
695 30/3 Llanvapley (L) RES 3m 13 GS *rear, prog to chal 14th, sn ld, wknd & jnd whn f 2 out* F -
1038 13/4 St Hilary (R) RES 3m 15 G *3rd til lft 2nd apr 12th, ld 15th, 3l up nxt, hdd & u.r.last* U 16
1160 20/4 Llanwit Maj' (R) RES 3m 12 GS *mid-div whn f 6th* F -
1266 27/4 Pyle (R) RES 3m 10 G *ld 3rd-3 out, rallied nxt, ld last, hdd flat* 2 17
1490 11/5 Erw Lon (L) RES 3m 6 F *ld to 12th, cont to chal til btn 2 out* 2 16

Only completed 4 of 13 starts 95/6; best runs at Pyle; could win Restricted if all went well; G-F 16

COTTON EYED JIMMY (Irish) — **I** 559[4]
COTTONEYEJOE (Irish) — **I** 21[U], **I** 38[P], **I** 367[F], **I** 511[P], **I** 557[F], **I** 581[1]
COULD BE A'NTIN (Irish) — **I** 70[P], **I** 143[P], **I** 550[P], **I** 608[6], **I** 651[6]
COUNT BALIOS(IRE) b.g. 7 Trojan Fen - Soyez Sage (FR) by Grundy M H Wood
1995 P(0),F(-),4(0),3(13)

145 17/2 Larkhill (R) MDO 3m 13 G *mid-div, 3rd at 12th, wknd & p.u. 3 out* P 0
267 2/3 Didmarton (L) MDN 3m 11 G *lft in ld 4th-8th, lft in ld 13th-15th, ld last, ran on* 1 16
641 23/3 Siddington (L) RES 3m 20 S *(Jt fav) jnd ldrs 11th, disp ld appr 15th, wknd qkly appr 3 out* 6 11

Fulfilled last year's prediction when winning; finished early; may upgrade if fit 97; Good 16

COUNTERBID gr.g. 9 Celio Rufo - Biddy The Crow by Bargello J M Turner
1995 1(21),2(22),2(19),2(20),2(20),**1(23)**

33 20/1 Higham (L) LAD 3m 9 GF *trkd ldrs, chall last, nt pace of wnnr flat* 2 22
103 17/2 Marks Tey (L) LAD 3m 7 G *(fav) trkd ldrs going wll, 2nd & rddn appr last, not qckn* 2 20
421 9/3 High Easter (L) LAD 3m 5 S *cls up, rddn 12th, lst tch appr 14th, p.u. last* P 0
620 23/3 Higham (L) LAD 3m 9 GF *(fav) (bl) ld at fast pace, hdd 3 out, wknd rpdly* 4 14
907 8/4 Fakenham (L) HC 3m 110yds 11 G *(bl) chsd ldr, ev ch 5 out, wknd from next.* 4 0
1330 30/4 Huntingdon (R) HC 2 1/2m 110yds 8 GF *(bl) trckd ldrs, disp ld 8th to 9th, 3rd and rdn 3 out, well btn next.* 4 17

1541 16/5 Folkestone (R) HC 2m 5f 8 G *(bl) chsd ldrs, went 2nd 9th to next, 3rd and outpcd from next.* 3 17

H/Chase winner 95; able but needs to have matters his own way; could win when fresh 97; G/S-F 21

COUNTESSA ch.m. 8 Royal Vulcan - Warwick Air by True Song — John Brown
1995 P(0),P(0),P(0),P(0)

314 2/3 Ampton (R) MDO 3m 10 G *prom to 5th, bhnd 9th, t.o. & p.u. 16th* P 0
618 23/3 Higham (L) MDO 3m 14 GF *in rear, mstk 1st, dtchd 4th, t.o. & p.u. 12th* P 0

8 starts - 8 pulled-ups 0

COUNTRY BLUE b.g. 5 Town And Country - Blue Breeze (USA) by Blue Times (USA) — J A Keighley

145 17/2 Larkhill (R) MDO 3m 13 G *(fav) sttld rear, rpd prog 12th, sn wknd, p.u. 15th* P 0
819 6/4 Charlton Ho' (L) MDN 3m 10 GF *held up, prog 12th, 3rd nxt, btn whn f last* F -

Top stable but no stamina yet 12

COUNTRY BREW ch.m. 8 Country Retreat - Totally Tiddly by French Vine — Major C Marriott
1995 P(0)

233 24/2 Heythrop (R) MDN 3m 14 GS *alwys bhnd, p.u. 12th* P 0
340 3/3 Heythrop (R) MDN 3m 12 G *trckd ldrs, blnd 13th, sn lost tch, p.u. last* P 0
797 2/4 Heythrop (R) MDN 3m 11 F *prom til outpcd aft 2 out* 4 10
946 8/4 Andoversford (R) RES 3m 10 GF *ld to 2nd, sn lost plc, rear hlfwy, p.u. last* P 0

Not disgraced only finish 96 but 6 runs in 3 seasons & no real stamina 10

COUNTRY CHALICE ch.g. 9 Moor House - Purple Chalice by Kadir Cup — Victor Ogden

121 17/2 Witton Cast' (R) RES 3m 11 S *2nd whn ran out 3rd* r -
223 24/2 Duncombe Pa' (R) CON 3m 16 GS *bhnd 5th, t.o. 8th* 8 0
416 9/3 Charm Park (L) MDO 3m 13 G *prom early, wkn 13th, outpcd frm 4 out* 7 0
588 23/3 Wetherby Po' (L) INT 3m 17 S *t.o. 10th, fin own time* 9 0
986 8/4 Charm Park (L) MDN 3m 10 GF *ld to 2nd agn 9th, lost saddle & u.r. apr 10th* U -

Beaten miles each completion & looks unpromising 0

COUNTRY FESTIVAL b.m. 10 Town And Country - Festive Season by Silly Season — Miss Janet Menzies
1995 10(0),B(-),1(15)

450 9/3 Charing (L) XX 3m 8 G *in tch,3rd whn blnd 11th,sn rdn,poor 4th whn p.u. last,lame* P 0

Won novice riders race 95; problems now & can only be watched 12

COUNTRY LIFE(USA) br.g. 10 Key To Content (USA) - Roseliere (FR) by Misti IV — G C Lloyd

263 2/3 Didmarton (L) INT 3m 18 G *t.o. frm 4th, p.u. 13th* P 0
380 9/3 Barbury Cas' (L) CON 3m 11 GS *t.o. 2nd, btn 2 fences* 5 0
606 23/3 Howick (L) MDN 3m 13 S *t.o. 8th, fin own time* 5 0
848 6/4 Howick (L) MDN 3m 14 GF *rear, fin own time, t.o.* 10 0
1243 27/4 Woodford (L) MEM 3m 6 G *chsd ldrs to 3rd, soon bhnd, t.o. 7th, fin lame, (disq)* 4D 0

Plods round for veteran rider & has no prospects 0

COUNTRY LOCH b.m. 7 Town And Country - Voolin by Jimmy Reppin — Mrs S Gill
1995 P(0),P(0),P(0)

1234 27/4 Weston Park (L) MDO 3m 13 G *mstks, mid to rear, t.o. whn p.u. 5 out* P 0

Still learning but no signs of ability yet 0

COUNTRY STYLE ch.m. 7 Town And Country - Win Green Hill by National Trust — N J Tory
1995 2(15),2(14),1(18)

139 17/2 Larkhill (R) CON 3m 11 G *ld to 5th, alwys prom, ran on frm 2 out* 2 21
467 10/3 Milborne St' (L) MEM 3m 8 G *(fav) handy, chsd ldr 12th, wknd 3 out* 4 11
1061 13/4 Badbury Rin' (L) INT 3m 3 GF *(fav) ld/disp til blnd 2 out, rdn aft last, alwys hld* 2 17
1313 28/4 Little Wind' (R) RES 3m 14 G *keen hold, ld 9-10th, lost plc 15th, ran on agn clsg stgs* 5 11

Maiden winner 95; not progressed 96; may perk up 97; should stick to Resttricteds; G/S-F 17

COUNTRY TARROGEN b.g. 7 Town And Country - Sweet Spice by Native Bazaar — Mrs M Cooper
1995 1(22),1(25),**1(27)**,**3(30)**,**1(27)**

184 23/2 Haydock (L) HC 3m 9 GS *(Jt fav) ld till blnd and u.r. 5th.* U -
483 14/3 Cheltenham (L) HC 3 1/4m 110yds 17 G *went handy 8th, mstk and driven along 14th, lost tch 6 out, t.o..* 11 0
119 18/4 Ayr (L) HC 3m 3f 110yds 9 GS *in tch, pushed along before 14th, outpcd after 16th, rallied after 4 out, wknd after next.* 5 19

Useful 95; stable out of form 96 & ran badly; hopefully will revive 97 - still young enough 26

COUNTRY VET b.m. 10 Town And Country - Ginnett by Owen Anthony — Miss Maud Ryder
1995 P(0),3(21),2(18),1(20),3(15),1(20),2(20)

252 25/2 Charing (L) INT 3m 7 GS *chsd wnr, niggld alng hlfwy, kpt on, nvr able to chal* 2 19
271 2/3 Parham (R) CON 3m 15 GF *prom,blnd & lost plc 4th, nvr going wll aft, bhnd & p.u.2out* P 0

450 9/3 Charing (L) XX 3m 8 G *chsd wnr frm 8th, outpcd frm 4 out* 2 18
594 23/3 Parham (R) CON 3m 13 GS *alwys twrds rear, lost tch 11th, p.u. last* P (

Dual winner 95; below best 96 & finished early; could win Confined but best watched; G-S 18

COUNTRYWIDE LAD ch.g. 7 Lancastrian - Minor Furlong by Native Bazaar Miss J Smit

1995 **9(NH)**

352 3/3 Garnons (L) MDN 2 1/2m 9 GS *ld 4th-7th, cls 3rd whn f 10th* F
748 31/3 Upper Sapey (R) MDO 3m 11 GS *prog 11th, 2nd at 15th, ev ch til outpcd 2 out* 3
1044 13/4 Bitterley (L) MDO 3m 15 G *t.o. in 3rd whn ref 15th* R
1417 6/5 Cursneh Hill (L) MDO 3m 14 GF *ld 7-14th, wknd frm nxt, p.u. last* P

Beaten 15l in poor Maiden only completion; doubtful stamina 10

COURIER'S WAY (Irish) — **I** 52^{F}, **I** 62^{P}, **I** 590^{1}

COUSIN AMOS b.g. 9 Obadiah - Double Surprise by Surprise Again L Bon

1995 P(0)

556 17/3 Ottery St M' (L) MDO 3m 15 G *ld to 3rd, cls up to 12th, wknd & p.u. 15th* P
1115 17/4 Hockworthy (L) MDO 3m 10 GS *chsd ldrs, 3rd at 11th, p.u. bef nxt* P
1432 6/5 High Bickin' (R) MDO 3m 9 G *n.j.w., bhnd til p.u. apr 17th* P

Yet to complete the course from 9 starts 94-6 0

COUTURE COLOR br.g. 13 Wolver Hollow - Home Sweet Home by Royal Palace S P D Tear

1995 F(-),F(-),P(0)

1150 20/4 Whittington (L) MEM 3m 6 G *cls 2nd whn u.r. 4th* U

No longer of any account 0

COUTURE QUALITY ro.g. 10 Absalom - Miss Couture by Tamerlane Mrs T W Bridge

1995 4(17),F(-),4(12),**4(0)**,U(-),**7(12)**,F(-),3(15),**3(16)**

10 14/1 Cottenham (R) INT 3m 10 G *ld to 7th, chsd ldrs til btn apr 3 out* 5
309 2/3 Ampton (R) MEM 3m 6 G *cls up, ld 11th, rddn clr 12th, blnd & u.r. nxt* U
361 5/3 Leicester (R) HC 2 1/2m 110yds 15 GS *(bl) chsd ldr, ld 5th, soon clr, hdd apr 3 out, btn and blnd 2 out.* 5 1
484 15/3 Fakenham (L) HC 2m 5f 110yds 13 GF *(bl) ld, hit 7th, hdd 12th, wknd 3 out.* 7 1
621 23/3 Higham (L) INT 3m 12 GF *(bl) chsd ldrs to 11th, wknd nxt, t.o. & p.u. last* P
906 8/4 Fakenham (L) HC 2m 5f 110yds 11 G *(bl) with ldrs, bad mstk 11th, t.o. when p.u. before next.* P
1068 13/4 Horseheath (R) INT 3m 7 F *blnd 4th, 5th & rdn 12th, no hdwy, wll btn whn u.r. 15th* U

Dual winner 94; likes Higham but lost last 17 starts & looks disinterested now 11

COUTURE TIGHTS b.g. 11 Mummy's Game - Miss Couture by Tamerlane M A Lloy

1995 1(23),1(23),2(22),1(23),2(21),**5(12)**,**F(-)**,1(16)

163 17/2 Weston Park (L) LAD 3m 10 G *mid-div, nvr dang* 6
460 9/3 Eyton-On-Se' (L) LAD 3m 10 G *hld up in rr, some late prog, no dang* 4 1
1420 6/5 Eyton-On-Se' (L) LAD 3m 3 GF *2nd 3-12th, clr 2nd 13th, chal whn lft in ld 4 out* 1 1
1480 11/5 Bredwardine (R) LAD 3m 12 G *chsd ldrs to 12th, went dist 3rd 2 out* 3 1
1619 27/5 Chaddesley ' (L) OPE 3m 7 GF *in tch, chsd wnr 10th, no imp frm 15th* 2 2

Solid pointer at best but interrupted season 96 & below best; goes well fresh; may revive 20

COWAGE BROOK b.g. 13 Paddy's Stream - Willie's Sister by Even Money D J La

1995 P(0),U(-),4(15),5(0),2(0),P(0)

36 20/1 Higham (L) RES 3m 12 GF *prom, chsd ldr 12-15th, wknd 2 out* 4 1
106 17/2 Marks Tey (L) RES 3m 12 G *in tch, 5th & rddn 11th, no ch whn ref 17th* R
620 23/3 Higham (L) LAD 3m 9 GF *lost tch ldrs 7th, t.o. 11th, p.u. 14th* P
679 30/3 Cottenham (R) RES 3m 15 GF *mid-div, b.d. 5th* B

Members winner 93; ran well 1st start 96 but non-stayer & another win hard to see 12

COZY COTTAGE (Irish) — **I** 289^{F}, **I** 325^{P}, **I** 444^{2}, **I** 510^{P}, **I** 545^{4}, **I** 625^{1}

CRABEG HAZEL (Irish) — **I** 151^{P}, **I** 252^{2}, **I** 369^{1}, **I** 544^{P}, **I** 623^{5}, **I** 629^{P}

CRACKER ALLEY (Irish) — **I** 222^{P}, **I** 343^{P}, **I** 421^{P}

CRAFTSMAN b.g. 10 Balinger - Crafty Look by Don't Look G W Pa

1995 1(20),1(23),2(11),1(24),2(16),F(-),B(-)

31 20/1 Higham (L) CON 3m 9 GF *cls up, ld 10th-11th & again 15th, clr nxt, ran on strngly* 1 2
93 11/2 Ampton (R) LAD 3m 7 GF *(fav) made all, hit 8th, drew clr 3 out, v easily* 1 2
832 6/4 Marks Tey (L) LAD 3m 8 G *ld 3rd, made most to 16th, wknd & no ext nxt* 3 2
1144 20/4 Higham (L) MEM 3m 4 F *(fav) not fluent, ld 8th, lft wll clr 12th, idld 2 out, pshd out* 1 1
1324 28/4 Fakenham P-' (L) LAD 3m 6 G *chsd ldrs, lft 2nd 11th, ld 13th, rdn 3 out, hdd last,onepcd* 2 2

Useful pointer at best; likes to dictate; best fresh & wins first time out; G-S 25

CRAGGAUNOWEN CHIEF(IRE) b.g. 8 Beau Charmeur (FR) - Deenside Vulgan by Aristocracy Mrs E A Taylo

967 8/4 Thorpe Lodge (L) MEM 3m 7 GF *prom, ld 9th-6 out, fdd, p.u. 3 out* P 0

Unpromising 0

CRAIG BURN b.m. 7 Arkan - Burning Mirage by Pamroy N M L Ewart

614 23/3 Friars Haugh (L) MDN 3m 10 G *u.r. 7th* U -
753 31/3 Lockerbie (R) OPE 3m 2 G *chsd wnnr til wknd rpdly frm 13th* 2 0
1085 14/4 Friars Haugh (L) OPE 3m 6 F *2nd til 9th, sn lost tch* 4 0
1355 4/5 Mosshouses (L) MDO 3m 10 GS *rear, lost tch 13th, sn no ch, kpt on frm 2 out* 6 0

Well beaten to date & only beaten one other finisher; may improve in 97 10

CRAIGELLE (Irish) — **I** 180[P], **I** 261[3], **I** 288[2], **I** 321[F], **I** 361[P], **I** 494[P]

CRANAGH MOSS(IRE) ch.g. 7 Le Moss - Cranagh Lady by Le Bavard (FR) Iwan Thomas

1995 U(-),4(0),U(-)

148 17/2 Erw Lon (L) MDN 3m 9 G *ld 6th, prssd 15th, rdn & ran on well* 1 14
770 31/3 Pantyderi (R) RES 3m 9 G *chsng grp, ev ch 3 out, onepcd aft* 3 15
980 8/4 Lydstep (L) RES 3m 11 G *mid-div, u.r. 10th* U -
1266 27/4 Pyle (R) RES 3m 10 G *cls up, 10l 5th at 14th, wknd frm 3 out* 4 0
1490 11/5 Erw Lon (L) RES 3m 6 F *nvr nrr to chal* 3 0

Fair performance when winning but not progressed; more needed for Restricted chances 13

CRAWN HAWK br.g. 11 Croghan Hill - Gin An Tonk by Osprey Hawk P C Shires

1995 4(0),P(0),1(14),4(11),**6(10)**,2(18),F(-),2(0),**3(NH),U(NH),2(NH)**

726 31/3 Garthorpe (R) RES 3m 16 G *prom til f 12th* F -
1101 14/4 Guilsborough (L) RES 3m 16 G *(fav) ld 5th, 2l up whn blnd & u.r. 13th* U -
1181 21/4 Mollington (R) RES 3m 10 F *ld to 3rd, prom til 3rd & outpcd 12th, kpt on onepcd 3 out* 4 15

Maiden winner 95; placed in novice chases summer 95; brief season; makes mistakes; best watched now 17

CRAZY DREAMS (Irish) — **I** 15[P], **I** 140[2], **I** 186[2], **I** 313[3]

CRAZY OTTO ch.g. 10 Nearly A Hand - Papa's Paradise by Florus Miss Louise Allan

1995 7(0),U(-),3(11),**7(0)**,4+(17),3(0),1(14)

33 20/1 Higham (L) LAD 3m 9 GF *in tch, ev ch appr 3 out, onpcd* 4 18
103 17/2 Marks Tey (L) LAD 3m 7 G *in tch, chsd ldr & ev ch 17th, onepcd 2 out* 3 18
347 3/3 Higham (L) LAD 3m 10 G *mid-div, wkng 11th, p.u. 13th* P 0
536 17/3 Southwell P' (L) LAD 3m 9 GS *mid to rear, alwys strgglng to keep in tch* 6 0

Ladies winner 95; ran well 1st two starts 96 but does not stay; fortunate to win again 14

CREDIT TRANSFER (Irish) — **I** 29[1]

CREDO IS KING (Irish) — **I** 22[2], **I** 87[3], **I** 108[1]

CREEVES NEPHEW b or br.g. 12 Trimmingham - Charlotts Fancy by Charlottesvilles Flyer Captain D R Parker

1995 F(-)

230 24/2 Heythrop (R) MEM 3m 12 GS *alwys well bhnd, t.o. & p.u. 12th* P 0
637 23/3 Siddington (L) MEM 3m 14 S *rr, sme prog 10th, nvr trbld ldrs* 8 0
1567 19/5 Mollington (R) INT 3m 12 GS *alwys bhnd, t.o. 10th, p.u. last* P 0

No longer of any account 0

CREIGHTON (Irish) — **I** 96[P], **I** 176[U]

CREME ZAHILLA b.m. 8 Afzal - Hill Straight by Graig Hill Master B R W Phillips

387 9/3 Llanfrynach (R) RES 3m 11 GS *schoold, last to 11th, t.o. 14th, p.u. 2 out* P 0
749 31/3 Upper Sapey (R) MDO 3m 17 GS *mstks, cls up til outpcd frm 3 out* 7 10
884 6/4 Brampton Br' (R) MDN 3m 12 GF *ld 9th til jnd apr 2 out, wknd last* 5 0

Improved each start & may go closer in 97 if showing more stamina 11

CRESTAFAIR ch.m. 8 Crested Lark - Karafair by Karabas J H Busby

1995 P(0),P(0),8(0),5(0)

233 24/2 Heythrop (R) MDN 3m 14 GS *alwys prom, disp frm hlfwy, ld 14th-16th, wknd* 4 0
438 9/3 Newton Brom' (R) MDN 3m 10 GS *chsd ldrs til f 9th* F -
959 8/4 Lockinge (L) MDN 3m 6 GF *(fav) held up, prog 9th, ld 11th-4 out, wknd qckly nxt, outpcd* 4 10
1103 14/4 Guilsborough (L) MDN 3m 15 G *rear, lost tch hlfwy, t.o. & p.u. 14th* P 0
1504 11/5 Kingston Bl' (L) MDO 3m 13 G *in tch, prog to ld 8th, clr 13th, wknd 2 out, hdd last,tired* 3 15
1621 27/5 Chaddesley ' (L) MDO 3m 17 GF *hld up, bhnd, blnd & u.r. 3rd* U -
1644 2/6 Dingley (R) MDO 3m 16 GF *hld up, prog 7th, ld 3 out, lkd wnr til wknd & hdd nr fin* 3 15

Improved; stamina gave out when twice looking likely to win; should find a race in 97 14

CRIMSON BOW b.m. 6 Balinger - Crimson Flag by Kinglet Mrs G C Owen

1045 13/4 Bitterley (L) MDO 3m 16 G *trckng ldrs whn u.r. 5th* U -
1155 20/4 Whittington (L) MDN 3m 14 G *bhnd, nvr dang, p.u. 12th* P 0

Not yet of any account 0

CRIMSON MARY ch.m. 10 Lucifer (USA) - Mary Ran Away by Great White Way (USA) — Sir Sanderson Temple

665	24/3	Eaton Hall	(R) RES	3m	14	S	*mid to rear, no ch frm hlfwy, p.u. 5 out*	P	0
751	31/3	Lockerbie	(R) CON	3m	12	G	*ran out 2nd*	r	-
891	6/4	Whittington	(L) MEM	3m	6	F	*3l 2nd whn u.r. 11th*	U	-
1014	13/4	Kingston Bl'	(L) MEM	3m	4	G	*pllng, mstks, in tch, pshd into ld last, styd on*	1	10
1152	20/4	Whittington	(L) CON	3m	9	G	*held up, 3rd 14th, ran on wll frm 2 out*	2	16
1369	4/5	Gisburn	(R) CON	3m	10	G	*cls up in 3rd whn f 15th*	F	-

Won a joke race but ran better next start; Restricted only possible 97; Good 14

CROCK D'OR b.g. 6 Heights Of Gold - Pegleg by New Member — H Macdonald

1995 **6(NH)**

653	23/3	Badbury Rin'	(L) MDO	3m	9	G	*prom, ld 10th, going well whn ran out 12th*	r	-
819	6/4	Charlton Ho'	(L) MDN	3m	10	GF	*(fav) held up, prog 10th, chsd wnnr vainly aft*	2	10

2nd in weak race but shows promise & should certainly go close if ready in 97 14

CROCKET LASS b.m. 13 Cagirama - Lady Crocket by Arrigle Valley — Miss Fiona M Hunter

316	2/3	Corbridge	(R) MEM	3m	10	GS	*bhnd frm 3rd, blnd & u.r. 8th*	U	-
511	16/3	Dalton Park	(R) MEM	3m	3	G	*pllng, ld 5-8th, last by 12th, sn t.o., lft poor 2nd 16th*	2	0
633	23/3	Market Rase'	(L) LAD	3m	10	GF	*rear, last & outpcd frm 7th*	8	0
1023	13/4	Brocklesby '	(L) LAD	3m	3	GF	*alwys last, t.o. frm 7th*	3	0
1132	20/4	Hornby Cast'	(L) LAD	3m	9	G	*p.u. bef 1st, restrted 10 fences bhnd wnr, compltd own time*	2	0
1366	4/5	Gisburn	(R) LAD	3m	12	G	*alwys rear, t.o. 10th*	8	0

Dual winner 92; missed 94/5; safe but no rateable form now 0

CROCKET PRINCE ch.g. 7 Mirror Boy - Lady Crocket by Arrigle Valley — A E Brown

1995 F(-),P(0)

1451	6/5	Witton Cast'	(R) MDO	3m	12	G	*rear whn p.u. 11th*	P	0

Shows no ability 0

CROFT COURT b.g. 5 Crofthall - Queen Of Dara by Dara Monarch — Barry J Cockerell

575	17/3	Detling	(L) MDO	3m	10	GF	*rear, t.o. 9th, p.u. 12th*	P	0
597	23/3	Parham	(R) MDO	3m	9	GS	*rear, 50l 6th at 12th,prog aft,3rd 4 out,styd on to ld last*	1	13
964	8/4	Heathfield	(R) RES	3m	7	G	*(fav) w.w. prog to 2nd 16th, 5l down 4 out,rdn & btn appr nxt*	2	14

Quite promising; won weak Maiden but ran well next time; Restricted on cards 97, at least 16

CROFT MILL b.g. 10 Furry Glen - Aplomb by Ballymore — T H J Bannister

1995 9(0),F(-),3(0)

326	3/3	Market Rase'	(L) OPE	3m	14	G	*n.j.w. sn wll bhnd, t.o. & p.u. 15th*	P	0
587	23/3	Wetherby Po'	(L) OPE	3m	15	S	*mstks, rear, t.o. & p.u. 11th*	P	0

Novice chase winner 93; gone to pieces now 0

CROKERS COTTAGE VI (Irish) — **I** 476[2]

CROMOGUE MINSTREL (Irish) — **I** 247[3]

CROMWELL POINT gr.h. 10 Another Realm - Miss Eliza by Mountain Call — P Sadler

1995 16(0),1+(19),3(16),4(10),2+(22),2(22),**13(NH),5(NH),P(NH),3(NH)**

56	10/2	Cottenham	(R) OPE	3m	12	GS	*(fav) n.j.w. ld to 2nd lft in ld 5th, hdd 7th, wknd 4 out*	7	0
367	6/3	Catterick	(L) HC	3m 1f 110yds	12	G	*bhnd, t.o. when p.u. before 3 out.*	P	0
410	9/3	Charm Park	(L) OPE	3m	17	G	*mid-div, 9th at 8th, styd on sm pc*	7	14
513	16/3	Dalton Park	(R) OPE	3m	9	G	*chsd ldrs, rdn frm 8th, no ch frm 14th, t.o.*	6	0
824	6/4	Stainton	(R) CON	3m	11	GF	*prom, pshd alng 9th, 2nd 16th, styd on onepcd*	2	19
1092	14/4	Whitwell-On'	(R) CON	3m	10	G	*mid-div, prog to jn ldrs 12th, onepcd frm 4 out*	3	18
1133	20/4	Hornby Cast'	(L) OPE	3m	14	G	*nvr bttr than mid-div, t.o. 3 out*	6	10
1457	8/5	Uttoxeter	(L) HC	3 1/4m	16	G	*alwys bhnd, t.o. when p.u. before 4 out.*	P	0
1548	18/5	Southwell	(L) HC	3m 110yds	11	GF	*slight mstks, kept on one pace from 3 out.*	5	14
1585	25/5	Cartmel	(L) HC	3 1/4m	14	GF	*soon well bhnd.*	6	0
1643	2/6	Dingley	(R) OPE	3m	13	GF	*rr & rdn 4th, 8th & no ch hlfwy, lft 3rd by dfctns*	3	15

Confined winner 95; disappointing since & beaten last 19 races; best avoided now 15

CROOKED STREAK bl.g. 11 Majestic Streak - Hartfell by Lord Nelson (FR) — John Shearer

109	17/2	Lanark	(R) MEM	3m	5	GS	*clr frm 6th, blnd 2 out, rider lost irons, r.o. last, rjnd*	2	12
188	24/2	Friars Haugh	(L) RES	3m	12	S	*bhnd whn p.u. 14th*	P	0

Lightly raced & lost golden opportunity 1st start 96 - novice ridden; unlikely to get another 0

CROSSOFSPANCILHILL ch.g. 10 Duky - Cappahard by Record Run — Mrs Jane Evans

668	26/3	Sandown	(R) HC	2 1/2m 110yds	8	GS	*keen hold, ld 4th to 7th, soon outpcd, t.o. when p.u. before 6 out.*	P	0
1213	24/4	Andoversford	(R) CON	3m	5	G	*ld to 3rd & 13-15th, rdn & wknd app 2 out*	3	10

1327 30/4 Huntingdon (R) HC 3m 6 GF *u.r. before start, prom, lost iron 2nd, weakening and blnd 13th, t.o..* 5 0
No stamina & totally outclassed in H/Chases 11

CROSSWELL STAR(IRE) ch.g. 5 Salluceva - Margaret Hulse by Arctic Chevalier — A J Sendell
711 30/3 Barbury Cas' (L) MDO 3m 8 G *n.j.w. rear til f 7th* F -
No star material yet 0

CROWNHILL CROSS ch.g. 5 Dutch Treat - Royal Cross by Royal Smoke — F R Bown
71 10/2 Great Treth' (R) MDO 3m 15 S *in rear whn p.u. aft 4th* P 0
A brief debut 0

CRUCIS(IRE) gr.g. 5 Kalaglow - Brave Advance (USA) by Bold Laddie (USA) — J W Haydon
301 2/3 Great Treth' (R) MDO 3m 13 G *blnd badly 7th, t.o. & p.u. 16th* P 0
1075 13/4 Lifton (R) RES 3m 12 S *not fluent early, prog to 6th 3 out, nrst at fin,shld imprv* 4 10
1279 27/4 Bratton Down (L) MDO 3m 14 GF *5s-5/2, plld hrd, cls up whn f 11th* F -
1396 6/5 Cotley Farm (L) MDO 3m 11 GF *mid-div, prog 10th, ev ch 3 out, btn 4th whn f last* F -
Previous owners shocked to find him running over jumps - has ability but not up to the rigours 12

CRUISE A HOOP b.g. 7 Cruise Missile - Hoopoe by Tower Walk — W M A Davies
1995 2(13),2(13),5(0),5(0)
218 24/2 Newtown (L) MDN 3m 14 GS *alwys rear, t.o. & p.u. 12th* P 0
431 9/3 Upton-On-Se' (R) MDO 3m 17 GS *effrt frm 13th, went 3rd 2 out, styd on onepcd* 3 12
748 31/3 Upper Sapey (R) MDO 3m 11 GS *(fav) 5th whn f 10th* F -
1044 13/4 Bitterley (L) MDO 3m 15 G *chsng grp whn f 4th* F -
1225 24/4 Brampton Br' (R) MDO 3m 18 G *trckd ldrs, eff 14th, ld nxt, wknd 2 out* 6 0
1417 6/5 Cursneh Hill (L) MDO 3m 14 GF *held up, prog 13th, ev ch 15th, wknd frm 2 out* 5 0
1483 11/5 Bredwardine (R) MDO 3m 15 G *prog 8th, ld frm 11th til jnd last, no ext flat* 2 14
1621 27/5 Chaddesley ' (L) MDO 3m 17 GF *hld up,gd prog frm 12th,clsng whn lft in ld 2 out,all out* 1 16
Modest; lucky winner of poor Maiden; barely stays & below Restricted standard 14

CRUISE ANN b.m. 7 Cruise Missile - Andantino by Another River — D R Bevan
1995 P(0),2(12)
221 24/2 Newtown (L) MDN 3m 12 GS *cls up to 8th, losing tch whn mstk 12th, p.u. 15th* P 0
390 9/3 Llanfrynach (R) MDN 3m 13 GS *chsd ldr to 15th, 3rd & wll btn aft* 3 0
696 30/3 Llanvapley (L) MDN 3m 13 GS *(Jt fav) 3rd at 11th, 5th 13th, wknd & p.u. 3 out* P 0
884 6/4 Brampton Br' (R) MDN 3m 12 GF *cls up at 8th, hit 13th, wknd 15th, p.u. 3 out* P 0
1410 6/5 Cursneh Hill (L) MEM 3m 4 GF *alwys last, t.o. frm 6th, btn 1 1/2 fences* 3 0
Placed 3 times 95/6 but well beaten each time & much more needed for a win 10

CRUISE FREE b.g. 7 Cruise Missile - Lyons Charity by Impecunious — P Dixon Smith
440 9/3 Newton Brom' (R) MDN 3m 10 GS *mid-div, nvr rchd ldrs* 5 0
617 23/3 Higham (L) MDO 3m 11 GF *mid-div, wknd 11th, lft poor 3rd last* 3 0
523 12/5 Garthorpe (R) MDO 3m 11 GF *rear, prog & cls up 4 out, not rch wnr* 3 10
644 2/6 Dingley (R) MDO 3m 16 GF *nvr gng well, alwys bhnd* 7 0
Safe but placed in modest Maidens & ran badly last start; may improve - needs to 12

CRUISING ON b.m. 9 Cruise Missile - Snipe Shooter by Le Coq D'Or — Mrs J E Goodall
1995 **P(0),P(0)**
394 9/3 Garthorpe (R) LAD 3m 6 G *ld frm 3rd til 3 out, chsd wnr gamely, no imp* 2 19
633 23/3 Market Rase' (L) LAD 3m 10 GF *(Jt fav) j.w. ld frm 3rd, ran on well last m, well rdn* 1 20
853 6/4 Sandon (L) LAD 3m 7 GF *j.w., made all, 8l clr 2 out, idld apr last, cght run in* 2 23
194 21/4 Sandon (L) LAD 3m 7 G *ld til hdd aft 2 out, ran on onepcd, no ext flat* 3 21
Much revived in 96 & ran well; front-runner; barely stays; win more Ladies if retaining form; G-F 22

CRUISIN ON CREDIT (Irish) — **I** 35[F], **I** 199[P], **I** 247[F], **I** 424[P]

CUCKOO PEN br.g. 11 Swing Easy (USA) - Peachy by Reliance II — Miss Janet Menzies
1995 P(0),P(0),4(0),8(0),3(11),**8(0)**
449 9/3 Charing (L) RES 3m 13 G *alwys rear, p.u. 13th* P 0
Maiden winner 93; showed little in 95 & finished early 96; prospects grim 0

CUCKROO (Irish) — **I** 528[F], **I** 618[P], **I** 634[P]

CUKEIRA ch.m. 7 Cruise Missile - Keira by Keren — R Paisley
1995 F(-),5(0),U(-)
51 4/2 Alnwick (L) MDO 3m 17 G *f 1st* F -
115 17/2 Lanark (R) MDO 3m 8 GS *(Jt fav) hld up, 4th at 10th, went 2nd 3 out, alwys hld* 2 11
321 2/3 Corbridge (R) MDN 3m 12 GS *cls up whn f 6th* F -
407 9/3 Dalston (R) MDO 2 1/2m 13 G *prom, wnt 2nd at 12th, tk ld 14th, ran on wl* 1 15
501 16/3 Lanark (R) RES 3m 12 G *alwys handy, prssd wnr frm 3 out, just hld* 2 16

1472 11/5 Aspatria (L) RES 3m 8 GF *(fav) prog 11th,5th & outpcd nxt,kpt on frm 2 out,fin 3rd plcd 2nd* 2 1

Improving; absent 8 weeks before final run; should find Restricted; G-S 17

CULLAUN (Irish) — I 645[2]

CUMBERLAND BLUES(IRE) b.g. 7 Lancastrian - Tengello by Bargello Mrs A Lockwoo

1995 3(14),1(12),U(-),P(0)

411 9/3 Charm Park (L) RES 3m 20 G *alwys prom, 2nd 13th, wknd rpdly, p.u. 4 out* P
584 23/3 Wetherby Po' (L) RES 3m 13 S *ld to 12th, in tch whn f 14th* F
825 6/4 Stainton (R) RES 3m 7 GF *ld, blnd 7th, hdd 2 out, wknd* 5
1132 20/4 Hornby Cast' (L) LAD 3m 9 G *whppd round start, ref to race* 0
1283 27/4 Easingwold (L) LAD 3m 10 G *rear, prog 5th, no hdwy 13th, wknd, t.o. & p.u. 2 out* P
1468 11/5 Easingwold (L) RES 3m 1 G *walked over* 1
1548 18/5 Southwell (L) HC 3m 110yds 11 GF *ld apr 3rd to 5th, led approaching 10th to 15th, wknd quickly 3 out, t.o..* 8
1586 25/5 Hexham (L) HC 2 1/2m 110yds 14 GF *chsd wnr most of way, not fluent 4 out and next, kept on, no impn.* 2 1

Maiden winner 95; disappointing 96 until last start & W/O makes future success hard to find 14

CUMBERLAND GAP b.g. 5 Broadsword (USA) - Pearl Bride by Spartan General George Tobi

779 31/3 Penshurst (L) RES 3m 13 GS *f 1st* F
1055 13/4 Penshurst (L) MDO 3m 11 G *schoold in rear til p.u. 12th* P
1504 11/5 Kingston Bl' (L) MDO 3m 13 G *s.s. schoold rear, blnd 7th, t.o. & p.u. aft 13th* P

Learning so far, but slowly 0

CUNNINGHAMS FORD(IRE) b.g. 8 Pollerton - Apicat by Buckskin (FR) Edward Harve

1995 **8(NH),4(NH),3(NH)**

177 18/2 Horseheath (R) CON 3m 8 G *prom, ld 11-12th & 15th-nxt, onepcd aft, lame* 3 2

Decent winning hurdler; good enough for Open points but problems on only start 22

CURRADUFF MOLL (Irish) — I 163[P], I 385[P], I 533[1]

CURRAGH RANGER (Irish) — I 266[P], I 299[6], I 481[P], I 559,

CURRAHEEN BRIDE (Irish) — I 7[P], I 50[P], I 354[2], I 504[1], I 613[P], I 659[P]

CURRASILLA (Irish) — I 271[F], I 391[P]

CURRENT ATTRACTION b.m. 10 Paddy's Stream - Chorabelle by Choral Society R H Fo

77 11/2 Wetherby Po' (L) RES 3m 18 GS *mid-div, onepcd, nvr nrr* 7
622 23/3 Higham (L) CON 3m 10 GF *chsd ldrs,prog to ld 9th,mstk nxt,hdd 11th,3rd whn f 3 out* F
897 6/4 Dingley (R) CON 3m 15 GS *cls up 5th/6th 2 m, wknd qckly 5 out* 9
1100 14/4 Guilsborough (L) OPE 3m 9 G *chsd ldrs, outpcd frm 15th, no imp on ldrs aft* 5
1256 27/4 Cottenham (R) MEM 3m 6 F *ld 2nd, hdd brfly 4th, hdd 10th, ld 4 out, rdn clr flat* 1

Missed 95; changed hands & found poor race; Members again best chance 97; Firm 15

CUSH MAID (Irish) — I 508[P], I 593[P], I 613[P]

CUSTARDORCREAM b.m. 9 Daring March - Bird's Custard by Birdbrook R F Walklir

1995 R(-)

576 17/3 Detling (L) MDN 3m 18 GF *prom to 11th, bhnd whn p.u. 17th* P

Shows some speed but has only run twice in two seasons 0

CUT A NICHE ch.g. 6 Callernish - Cut And Thrust by Pardal Miss Jennifer Pidgec

461 9/3 Eyton-On-Se' (L) RES 3m 15 G *mstks, lost tch frm 12th, p.u. 4 out* P
956 8/4 Lockinge (L) MDN 3m 7 GF *held up, 3rd 10th, chsd wnr frm 4 out, no imp frm 2 out* 2

Good stable & not disgraced 2nd start; should improve in 97 13

CUTSDEAN CROSS(IRE) br.g. 8 Roselier (FR) - Holy Cross by Arcticeelagh Mrs H Clark

1995 P(0),F(-),P(0),4(16),1(17),F(-)

269 2/3 Didmarton (L) RES 3m 12 G *trckd ldrs til lost tch frm 13th, t.o. & p.u. 2 out* P
428 9/3 Upton-On-Se' (R) RES 3m 17 GS *alwys prom, cls 2nd & ch 3 out, onepcd* 4
642 23/3 Siddington (L) RES 3m 15 S *cls up, outpcd appr 15th, 3rd & btn whn blnd 2 out* 3
1002 9/4 Upton-On-Se' (R) RES 3m 8 F *c.u., chsd wnr 12-13th, sn outpcd, kpt on mod 2nd last* 2
1178 21/4 Mollington (R) RES 3m 7 F *(Jt fav) made virt all, clr 13th, rdn apr last, all ot fin, lame* 1

Maiden winner 95; slow to find form 96; won weak Restricted & problems; best watched; G-F 17

CUTTER'S WHARF (Irish) — I 94[P], I 175[2]

CUT THE CORN ch.g. 8 Oats - Celtic Blade by Celtic Cone C J Benne

1995 P(0)

28 20/1 Barbury Cas' (L) RES 3m 14 GS *pllng, prom til f 8th* F
160 17/2 Weston Park (L) OPE 3m 16 G *chsng grp, outpcd frm 14th, p.u. 2 out* P
430 9/3 Upton-On-Se' (R) MDO 3m 15 GS *ld, lft clr 15th, hdd & unable qckn last* 2

Lightly raced but beat subsequent winner last start; could win over easy 3m if fit 97 14

CWM BYE ch.g. 5 Hubbly Bubbly (USA) - To Oneiro by Absalom — Ms B Brown

1995 **11(NH),16(NH),6(NH),11(NH),P(NH)**

1218	24/4	Brampton Br'	(R)	MEM	3m	4	G	*ld/disp til u.r. 6th*	U -
1485	11/5	Bredwardine	(R)	MDO	3m	15	G	*trckd ldrs frm 11th, ld 14th, rdn, hdd & no ext flat*	2 14

Poor novice hurdler but just caught in modest race last start & should go one better in 97 14

CYNICAL WIT (Irish) — **I** 270, , **I** 348^{F}, **I** 384^{P}, **I** 521^{P}, **I** 530^{P}

CZARYNE ch.m. 8 Czarist - Tyne Bridge by Red Bridge — Mrs J D Percy

1473	11/5	Aspatria	(L)	LAD	3m	7	GF	*chsd ldr 3rd til aft 11th, sn wknd*	5 0
1575	19/5	Corbridge	(R)	MDO	3m	10	G	*prom, cls 3rd at 12th, ld 14th-3 out, no ch wnr aft*	2 11

Missed 95 & started late 96; ran well in weak Maiden but more stamina needed for a win 11

CZERMNO br.g. 13 Strong Gale - Aquamanda by Bleep-Bleep — M A Lloyd

1995 **6(NH),5(NH),P(NH),4(NH)**

879	6/4	Brampton Br'	(R)	LAD	3m	9	GF	*ld to 9th, lost plc aft 16th, rallied frm 2 out*	2 20
1232	27/4	Weston Park	(L)	LAD	3m	6	G	*ld/disp to 11th, hdd 12th, ran on onepce*	2 16
1579	19/5	Wolverhampt'	(L)	LAD	3m	9	G	*ld to 14th, wknd frm 16th*	5 0

Ultra-safe & consistent but lost pace now & a win at 14 looks beyond him 15

DADDY WARBUCKS (Irish) — **I** 345^{5}, **I** 634^{3}, **I** 655^{4}

DAD'S PIPE b.g. 6 Nearly A Hand - Paddy's Pipe by Paddy's Stream — Terry Smith

1995 U(-),P(0)

275	2/3	Parham	(R)	MDN	3m	15	GF	*handy, cls 3rd 3 out, just outpcd aft, styd on*	3 13
473	10/3	Tweseldown	(R)	MEM	3m	5	G	*(fav) cls up, effrt 4 out, ld aft nxt, all out*	1 12
787	31/3	Tweseldown	(R)	RES	3m	9	G	*prom, mstly 2nd frm 12th, ev ch last, no ext flat*	2 15

Improved 96; form modest; young enough for more & weak area offers plenty of chances 15

DAFFYDOWN BREEZE VI (Irish) — **I** 125^{P}, **I** 430^{P}

DAISY LANE b.m. 7 Mart Lane - Alto Sax by Prince de Galles — Miss P Kerby

432	9/3	Upton-On-Se'	(R)	MDO	3m	17	GS	*f 3rd*	F -

A breif debut 0

DAISY POND(IRE) ch.m. 6 Long Pond - Cooladerry Lassy by Laurence O — W Murdoch

1995 **13(NH),15(NH),3(NH)**

1257	27/4	Cottenham	(R)	CON	3m	5	F	*rear,mstks 10 & 11th, lost tch 13th, crawld 2 out, ref last*	R -

An inauspicious pointing debut 0

DAISY'S PAL b.m. 5 Governor General - Pallomere by Blue Cashmere — A Bunn

220	24/2	Newtown	(L)	MDN	3m	12	GS	*in tch til eased & p.u. aft 11th*	P 0
430	9/3	Upton-On-Se'	(R)	MDO	3m	15	GS	*mid-div til wknd 12th, p.u. 14th*	P 0

Learning, to date 0

DALUSAWAY(IRE) b.m. 7 Mandalus - Head Away by Regular Guy — L Oakes

1995 4(0)

953	8/4	Eyton-On-Se'	(L)	MDO	2 1/2m	10	GF	*chsd ldrs, disp 3 out, hdd by wnr 2 out, onepcd*	3 0

Very lightly raced & needs improvement for winning chances in future 10

DAMERS TREASURE ch.g. 10 General Ironside - Dalmond by Diamonds Are Trump (USA) — O P J Meli

1995 P(0),3(15),1(17),2(15),**F(-)**,F(-)

726	31/3	Garthorpe	(R)	RES	3m	16	G	*prom to 6th,bhnd & rdn 10th,effrt to mid-div 13th,sn btn*	9 0
1001	9/4	Upton-On-Se'	(R)	MEM	3m	6	F	*chsd ldrs, rdn & lost tch frm 9th, mstk 12th, kpt on*	3 0
1173	20/4	Chaddesley '	(L)	RES	3m	18	G	*nvr bynd mid-div, 8th at 14th, kpt on frm 16th*	6 11
1464	11/5	Warwick	(L)	HC	3 1/4m	6	F	*ld till blnd and hdd 13th, wknd 5 out.*	3 10
1614	27/5	Hereford	(R)	HC	3m 1f 110yds	16	G	*held up, struggling 11th, t.o..*	7 0

Members winner 95; moderate at best & lacked enthusiasm 96; blinkers worth a try; G/F-S 15

DAMNIFICATION ch.g. 10 Sandalay - Damascus Sky by Skymaster — J W Hope

1995 **3(19)**,P(0)

789	1/4	Kelso	(L)	HC	3m 1f	11	GF	*in tch, left to chase lding pair after 8 out, kept on same pace from 3 out.*	3 15

Massive potential blighted by injury & time now slipping away - still showed plenty only start 96 22

DAMOLLY ROSE (Irish) — **I** 178^{F}, **I** 258^{P}, **I** 340^{F}, **I** 449^{U}, **I** 562^{P}

DANBURY LAD(IRE) b.g. 8 Bustinetto - Clyzari by Pinzari — Dr P P Brown

1995 4(14),P(0),1(16),2(18)

428	9/3	Upton-On-Se'	(R)	RES	3m	17	GS	*(fav) prog 14th, 5th & ch 2 out, unable to sustain effrt*	3	16
946	8/4	Andoversford	(R)	RES	3m	10	GF	*(fav) hld up rear,prog whn slw jmp 15th, disp 3 out,sn ld,pshd out*	1	21
1213	24/4	Andoversford	(R)	CON	3m	5	G	*(fav) trckd ldng pair 6th, ld 16th, drw clr 2 out, easily*	1	21
1413	6/5	Cursneh Hill	(L)	INT	3m	6	GF	*(fav) 3l 3rd 12th, prog to ld 3 out, clr last*	1	20
1620	27/5	Chaddesley '	(L)	XX	3m	8	GF	*(fav) not fluent, cls up, jnd wnr 3 out, outjmpd last, not qckn*	2	18

Won 4 of last 7 & continues to improve; sticks to easy courses; Ladies on cards 97; G/F-S 23

DANCING DESSIE (Irish) — **I** 2[P], **I** 53[4], **I** 73[P], **I** 114[F], **I** 142[P], **I** 375[2], **I** 502[4], **I** 541[P]

DANCING DORIS b.m. 12 Pony Express - Dance Partner by Manicou — John J Smith

1995 P(0),P(0),4(0),2(11),4(14),**P(0)**

140	17/2	Larkhill	(R)	CON	3m	17	G	*alwys bhnd ldng grp, p.u. 15th*	P	0
262	2/3	Didmarton	(L)	MEM	3m	11	G	*chsd ldrs, mstk 7th, lost tch 11th, 5th & no ch whn u.r.last*	U	-
604	23/3	Howick	(L)	INT	3m	7	S	*hld up, prog to 2nd at 9th, wknd frm 12th, lft 3rd 3 out*	3	0
866	6/4	Larkhill	(R)	INT	3m	4	F	*trckd wnnr, outpcd frm apr 13th, wnt 2nd nxt, no ch wth wnnr*	2	13

Dual winner 93; well below form since & beat only one other finisher 96; fortune needed to win again .. 13

DANCING LEGEND(IRE) b.g. 8 Lyphard's Special (USA) - Princess Nabila (USA) by King Pellinore (USA) — Mrs J Potts

1995 11(0),P(0),U(-),4(0),4(0)

187	24/2	Friars Haugh	(L)	CON	3m	12	S	*(bl) ld to 7th, sn wknd, p.u. 10th*	P	0
317	2/3	Corbridge	(R)	CON	3m	11	GS	*mid-div, clsd up hlfwy, chsng ldrs und pres whn f 2 out*	F	-
911	8/4	Tranwell	(L)	CON	3m	9	GF	*prom to hlfwy, not rch ldrs frm 14th*	5	0
1083	14/4	Friars Haugh	(L)	CON	3m	10	F	*alwys bhnd*	7	0
1351	4/5	Mosshouses	(L)	CON	3m	11	GS	*in tch to 12th, wknd rpdly, t.o. & p.u. 15th*	P	0
1513	12/5	Hexham Poin'	(L)	CON	3m	6	HY	*trckd ldrs til lost tch 14th, last & reluc 16th, p.u. 2 out*	P	0

Has his own ideas & one to avoid 0

DANCING SUPREME ch.g. 6 Nestor - Vulgan's Joy by Vulgan Slave — Mrs B Stokes

1995 **11(NH),10(NH)**

1241	27/4	Clifton On '	(L)	MDO	3m	8	GF	*prom, ld 10-12th, 7th & wkng whn f nxt*	F	-

Some speed but lightly raced & nothing concrete 0

DANE ROSE b.m. 10 Full Of Hope - Roella by Gold Rod — P J Sheppard

1995 P(0),P(0),U(-),1(15)

219	24/2	Newtown	(L)	RES	3m	17	GS	*prom to 6th, wknd rpdly, p.u. 12th*	P	0
382	9/3	Llanfrynach	(R)	MEM	3m	7	GS	*ld to 12th, outpcd 4 out, btn whn mstk 2 out*	4	0
882	6/4	Brampton Br'	(R)	RES	3m	14	GF	*prog frm 13th, rdn 16th, chal whn mstk last, no ext flat*	3	15
1223	24/4	Brampton Br'	(R)	RES	3m	11	G	*prog to 3rd at 14th, lft in ld nxt, clr last*	1	17
1478	11/5	Bredwardine	(R)	CON	3m	12	G	*hld up, prog 11th, no ext frm 15th*	4	15

Improved; won modest Restricted; likes Brampton Bryan; more needed for Confined but may have scope 17

DANGEROSA b.m. 7 Aragon - Faster Still by Giolla Mear — Mrs R J Burrow

1995 P(0),U(-),2(0),P(0),P(0),4(0),1(12),P(0)

59	10/2	Cottenham	(R)	RES	3m	9	GS	*prom til wknd sddnly & p.u. 13th*	P	0
965	8/4	Heathfield	(R)	INT	3m	6	G	*ld, hd prssd whn u.r. 14th*	U	-
1208	21/4	Heathfield	(R)	LAD	3m	6	F	*wll in tch, cls 3rd 4 out, rdn & wknd nxt*	5	0

Won bad Maiden 95 & predictably out of his depth in 96 10

DANNIGALE b.g. 10 Strong Gale - No Bella Lady by No Time — E Haddock

1995 **3(NH),7(NH)**

162	17/2	Weston Park	(L)	OPE	3m	16	G	*mid to rear, p.u. aft 12th*	P	0
662	24/3	Eaton Hall	(R)	OPE	3m	10	S	*nvr bynd mid-div, t.o. 12th, p.u. 4 out*	P	0
685	30/3	Chaddesley '	(L)	LAD	3m	9	G	*raced wd, prom til u.r. 9th*	U	-
855	6/4	Sandon	(L)	CON	3m	6	GF	*mid-div, disp 4th whn u.r. last*	U	-
1011	9/4	Flagg Moor	(L)	OPE	3m	4	G	*chsd ldr 3-5th, lost tch 11th, t.o. frm 14th*	3	0
1191	21/4	Sandon	(L)	MEM	3m	5	G	*ld 2-8th, chsd wnr, no imp*	2	0
1236	27/4	Clifton On '	(L)	CON	3m	8	GF	*ld/disp to 12th, 4th & outpcd nxt, no prog aft*	4	0
1333	1/5	Cheltenham	(L)	HC	3m 1f 110yds	13	G	*f 1st.*	F	-
1532	13/5	Towcester	(R)	HC	2m 110yds	16	GF	*soon t.o., p.u. before 2 out.*	P	0
1578	19/5	Wolverhampt'	(L)	OPE	3m	7	G	*chsd ldr 6th-8th, lost tch 14th, t.o. & p.u. 3 out*	P	0

Ex-Irish pointer; well beaten when completing; novice ridden; most unlikely to win 10

DANNYS GIRL (Irish) — **I** 42[P], **I** 85[P], **I** 163[P], **I** 233,

DANRIBO b.g. 13 Riboboy (USA) - Sheridans Daughter by Majority Blue — John Whyte

1995 5(0),P(0),**P(0)**,8(0),5(0),**P(NH)**,**6(NH)**

9	14/1	Cottenham	(R)	OPE	3m	13	G	*hmpd & u.r. 2nd*	U	-
32	20/1	Higham	(L)	OPE	3m	15	GF	*alwys bhnd t.o.*	5	0

96 11/2 Ampton (R) XX 3m 11 GF *prom, blnd 6th, bhnd frm 9th, p.u. 14th* P 0
258 29/2 Nottingham (L) HC 3m 110yds 10 G *well t.o. from 9th, cont 2 fences bhnd till p.u. before two out.* P 0
619 23/3 Higham (L) OPE 3m 10 GF *prom early, lost plc aft 4th, blnd 10th, t.o. & p.u. 3 out* P 0

No longer of any account 0

DANTE ALAINN (Irish) — I 615^{P}, I 655,
DANTE LAD (Irish) — I 8^{P}, I 71^{3}, I 167^{1}, I 212^{P}
DANTE'S PRIDE(IRE) ch.g. 7 Phardante (FR) - Una's Pride by Raise You Ten P J Millington

174 18/2 Market Rase' (L) MDO 2m 5f 7 GF *rear 8th, sn outpcd, p.u. 11th* P 0
333 3/3 Market Rase' (L) MDO 3m 11 G *hmpd 6th, 4th & rdn 11th, sn wknd, p.u. 15th* P 0
397 9/3 Garthorpe (R) MDN 3m 9 G *cls up til fdd 10th, bhnd whn p.u. 4 out* P 0
542 17/3 Southwell P' (L) MDO 3m 15 GS *schoold rear, p.u. 6 out* P 0
727 31/3 Garthorpe (R) MDO 3m 12 G *prom til wknd rpdly 12th, p.u. nxt* P 0
1103 14/4 Guilsborough (L) MDN 3m 15 G *chsd ldr to 6th, wknd rpdly 9th, t.o. & p.u. 13th* P 0
1381 5/5 Dingley (R) MDO 3m 16 GF *in tch to 11th, sn wknd, t.o.* 6 0

Barely stays two miles & looks hopeless - BUT sold to maestro Baimbridge & anything possible 13

DANTE'S REWARD (Irish) — I 57^{P}, I 78^{F}, I 188^{P}, I 312^{3}, I 462^{P}, I 543, , I 574^{3}
DANTE'S SKIP (Irish) — I 64, , I 119^{F}, I 149^{P}, I 308^{F}, I 353,
DANTE'S WHISTLE (Irish) — I 77^{P}, I 119^{F}
DAPHNI(FR) ch.g. 5 Bad Conduct (USA) - Ragniole (FR) by Mondain (FR) Mrs L M Boulter

14 14/1 Cottenham (R) MDO 3m 10 G *w.w. blnd 11th, b.d. nxt* B -
60 10/2 Cottenham (R) MDO 3m 7 GS *in tch to 11th, last & no ch whn f 14th* F -
1511 12/5 Maisemore P' (L) MDO 3m 14 F *alwys well in rear, t.o. & p.u. 15th* P 0
1638 1/6 Bratton Down (L) MDO 3m 13 G *rear & just in tch, 6th 3 out, gd prog nxt, drvn to ld nr fn* 1 15

33/1 when winning weak race; hard to assess but should improve - needs to for Restricteds 15

DARA KNIGHT (Irish) — I 305^{P}, I 404^{U}, I 455^{3}, I 488^{F}
DARA'S COURSE(IRE) b.m. 7 Crash Course - Sliabh Dara by Prince Hansel J T Jones
1995 **6(NH),7(NH),2(NH),3(NH),6(NH)**

1421 6/5 Eyton-On-Se' (L) RES 3m 11 GF *u.r. in rr 2nd, rmntd & cont 3 fncs bhnd, p.u. 5 out* P 0
1482 11/5 Bredwardine (R) RES 3m 13 G *alwys prom, rdn 14th, ld 3 out, drew wll clr* 1 19
1629 30/5 Uttoxeter (L) HC 2m 5f 13 GS *held up in tch, wknd apr 4 out.* 4 13

Ex-Irish; late to appear but bolted home 2nd start; Intermediate likely if same form 97 19

DARE SAY b.g. 13 Kris - Pampered Dancer by Pampered King Miss R Williams
1995 F(-),P(0),6(0)

154 17/2 Erw Lon (L) LAD 3m 14 G *alwys 4th/5th, wknd frm 13th* 6 0
385 9/3 Llanfrynach (R) LAD 3m 14 GS *prom, wkng whn mstk 3 out, sn btn* 6 12
603 23/3 Howick (L) LAD 3m 8 S *prom til 4th at 15th, wknd, lft poor 3rd 3 out* 3 12
769 31/3 Pantyderi (R) LAD 3m 6 G *u.r. 1st* U -
979 8/4 Lydstep (L) LAD 3m 9 G *prom, hrd rdn in 3rd aft last* 3 18

Winning chaser 94; ran better in 96 but unlikely to win now 14

DARING DAISY b.m. 8 Balinger - Avado by Cleon T B Brown

129 17/2 Kingston Bl' (L) MDN 3m 15 GS *alwys well in rear, lost tch whn p.u. 13th* P 0

Only four runs to date & no real signs of ability 0

DARINGLY b.h. 7 Daring March - Leylandia by Wolver Hollow Michael Appleby
1995 **P(NH),18(NH),7(NH),7(NH)**

6 13/1 Larkhill (R) OPE 3m 18 GS *mid-div, no ch frm 12th, t.o. & p.u. aft 3 out* P 0
124 17/2 Kingston Bl' (L) CON 3m 17 GS *1st ride, rear, gd prog 14th, ran on onepcd frm 2 out* 3 21
336 3/3 Heythrop (R) LAD 3m 5 G *hld up in tch, ld 14th, sn prssd, hdd last, not qckn* 2 18
523 16/3 Larkhill (R) MXO 3m 8 G *alwys cls up, ld aft 2 out, ran on well flat* 1 22
672 29/3 Aintree (L) HC 2 3/4m 26 G *held up, struggling 9th, well bhnd after.* 9 15
1013 13/4 Ascot (R) HC 3m 110yds 11 GS *mstk 3rd, bhnd from 11th, t.o. when p.u. before last.* P 0
1215 24/4 Andoversford (R) OPE 3m 5 G *chsd ldr to 8th, 3rd & rdn 16th, no prog, last whn ref last* R -
1502 11/5 Kingston Bl' (L) LAD 3m 7 G *ld 2-8th, outpcd frm 10th, t.o. 15th* 4 10

Winning hurdler; able but inconsistent; won chase in June 96 22

DARING TROUBLE b.m. 7 Tremblant - Daring Damsel by Daring March Mrs C Hicks
1995 **P(NH),P(NH),P(NH)**

787 31/3 Tweseldown (R) RES 3m 9 G *mid-div, prog 8th, wknd 12th, bhnd whn p.u. 3 out* P 0
947 8/4 Andoversford (R) MDN 3m 11 GF *rear, last at 13th, ran on, lft 3rd at last* 3 0
1217 24/4 Andoversford (R) MDO 3m 16 G *w.w., mid-div, prog to ch wnr 3 out-nxt, one pcd* 2 13
1501 11/5 Kingston Bl' (L) RES 3m 10 G *raced wd, cls up to 7th, bhnd frm 11th, t.o. & p.u. last* P 0
1610 26/5 Tweseldown (R) MDO 3m 5 G *hld up, in tch til last & n.j.w. frm 11th, t.o. & p.u.2 out* P 0

Placed in poor Maidens; stamina doubtful & more needed for a win 12

DARKBROOK b.g. 9 Green Shoon - Pitpan Lass by Pitpan — J P Bosley

1995 **9(NH)**

451	9/3	Charing	(L)	OPE	3m	11	G	*in tch, nggld alng 12th, wknd und pres 4 out*	7 0
595	23/3	Parham	(R)	OPE	3m	12	GS	*mstks, mid-div, rmndrs hlfwy, 7th & no ch whn f 12th*	F -
811	6/4	Charing	(L)	OPE	3m	9	F	*mid-div, strgglng 12th, rear whn p.u. 14th*	P 0

Chasing winner 94; last on only completion 96 & safely ignored now 0

DARK DAWN b.g. 12 Pollerton - Cacodor's Pet by Chinatown — Mrs J M Newitt

1995 **U(-),2(29),1(30),3(31),3(27)**

37	3/2	Wetherby	(L)	HC	3m 110yds	11	GS	*chsd ldrs till wknd before 4 out, losing tch when p.u. before 2 out.*	P 0
487	16/3	Newcastle	(L)	HC	3m	10	GS	*held up, hdwy hfwy, ld apr 3 out, soon clr, kept on.*	1 28
672	29/3	Aintree	(L)	HC	2 3/4m	26	G	*chsd ldrs till bumped and u.r. 5th.*	U -

Useful H/Chaser; best below 3m; could win again at 13; out of depth in handicaps; G/S-F 26

DARKER STILL (Irish) — I 305P

DARK FRIEND (Irish) — I 608P

DARK RECORD br.g. 13 Black Minstrel - Bonny Prepack by Gala Performance (USA) — Mrs C P Lees-Jones

1995 P(0),P(0),P(0)

159	17/2	Weston Park	(L)	CON	3m	22	G	*mid to hlfwy, sn btn, p.u. 4 out*	P 0

No longer of any account 0

DARK REFLECTION b.g. 10 Looking Glass - Ellers Gorse by Jock Scot — J D Curnow

562	17/3	Ottery St M'	(L)	XX	3m	12	G	*sn rear, t.o. & p.u. 13th*	P 0
714	30/3	Wadebridge	(L)	MEM	3m	3	GF	*(fav) made all, drew clr frm 14th, unchal*	1 12
937	8/4	Wadebridge	(L)	INT	3m	4	F	*(fav) ld 1st til cght cls home*	2 13

Standing dish in Members (won three times) and ran well last start; outclassed in fair company 15

DARK RHYTHAM br.g. 7 True Song - Crozanna by Crozier — G Coombe

1995 P(0)

727	31/3	Garthorpe	(R)	MDO	3m	12	G	*prom to 13th, sn lost plc, t.o. & p.u. 3 out*	P 0
901	6/4	Dingley	(R)	MDN	2m 5f	9	GS	*(fav) 6l 2nd whn f 4th*	F -
1104	14/4	Guilsborough	(L)	MDN	3m	18	G	*ld 3rd-12th, chsng aft, no imp frm 3 out*	3 10
1378	5/5	Dingley	(R)	MDO	2 1/2m	16	GF	*(fav) made all, 1l up & lkd wnr whn lft clr last*	1 15
1518	12/5	Garthorpe	(R)	MEM	3m	6	GF	*(Jt fav) made all, set str pace, ran on wll und pres 2 out*	1 15

Improving; front-runner; may need easy 3m; little more needed for Restricted success 17

DARK SIRONA b.m. 13 Pitskelly - Step You Gaily by King's Company — Miss Carolyn A B Allsopp

955	8/4	Lockinge	(L)	MEM	3m	5	GF	*prom early, lost tch frm 14th*	4 0
1246	27/4	Woodford	(L)	OPE	3m	6	G	*chsd ldr to 7th, wll bhnd frm 13th, t.o.*	4 0
1608	26/5	Tweseldown	(R)	CON	3m	6	G	*immed outpcd in 4th, t.o. 8th, lft dist 3rd 3 out*	3 0

Does not stay & is of no account 0

DARKTOWN STRUTTER ch.g. 10 Pas de Seul - Princess Henham by Record Token — R W Pincombe

1995 P(0),R(-),3(0),2(10),2(0),P(0)

138	17/2	Ottery St M'	(L)	RES	3m	18	GS	*cls up, f 7th*	F -
202	24/2	Lemalla	(R)	MDO	3m	12	HY	*ld to 3rd, sn wll bhnd, p.u. 10th*	P 0
446	9/3	Haldon	(R)	MDO	3m	13	S	*(bl) ld/disp to 12th,cls 2nd nxt,lkd btn til rallied to ld cls hm*	1 13
804	4/4	Clyst St Ma'	(L)	INT	3m	3	GS	*(bl) chsd wnr, outpcd 3 out*	2 12
926	8/4	Bishopsleigh	(R)	RES	3m	9	G	*(bl) midfld, bad mstk 12th, wknd rpdly, p.u. 17th whn wll bhnd*	P 0
1274	27/4	Bratton Down	(L)	MEM	3m	7	GF	*(bl) prom to 14th, wknd & outpcd frm nxt*	3 0
1587	25/5	Mounsey Hil'	(R)	MEM	3m	7	G	*(bl) ld to 7th, 4th & in tch whn p.u. 11th, dsmntd*	P 0

33-1 when winning at 25th attempt & that should be the limit of his success day - has enough choice! 12

DARSHABA (Irish) — I 285F, I 415P

DARTON RI b.g. 13 Abednego - Boogie Woogie by No Argument — Mrs S Maxse

1995 2(22)

19	14/1	Tweseldown	(R)	CON	3m	9	GS	*in tch,3rd & pshd alng 12th,chsd ldr 2 out,ld last,styd on*	1 21
140	17/2	Larkhill	(R)	CON	3m	17	G	*(fav) prom, ld 13th-2 out, not able to qckn*	2 19
475	10/3	Tweseldown	(R)	CON	3m	9	G	*(fav) disp til ld 3rd, made rest, mstk last, drvn out*	1 21
785	31/3	Tweseldown	(R)	OPE	3m	5	G	*(fav) trckd ldr, 2l 2nd whn u.r. 14th*	U -
1609	26/5	Tweseldown	(R)	MXO	3m	9	G	*bckwrd,chsd ldrs,outpcd 11th,kpt on to mod 3rd at last*	3 14

Tweseldown specialist & retains form well; could win there at 14; G/F-G/S 21

DASHBOARD LIGHT b.g. 6 Idiot's Delight - Good Lady by Deep Run — A D Cooke

1995 F(-),F(-)

13	14/1	Cottenham	(R)	MDO	3m	10	G	*hld up, jmpd big 1st, in tch, slght mstk 14th,p.u.nxt,imprve*	P 0

240 25/2 Southwell P' (L) MDO 3m 15 HO *trckd ldrs, prog 12th, chsd wnr & ev ch 3 out, no ext nxt* 2 14
541 17/3 Southwell P' (L) MDO 3m 9 GS *(fav) w.w. 3rd 4 out, disp 2 out, ld last, ran on well* 1 14
679 30/3 Cottenham (R) RES 3m 15 GF *blnd 1st, rear, prog 10th, chsd wnr 16th, no imp apr last* 3 17
1025 13/4 Brocklesby ' (L) XX 3m 9 GF *(fav) w.w, prog 8th, 2nd imprvng whn f 12th* F -
1380 5/5 Dingley (R) RES 3m 11 GF *j.w. in tch, chal 15th, wknd rpdly 2 out, p.u. last* P 0

Has ability but error-prone & stamina suspect; may find easy Restricted 97; G/S-G/F 16

DASHING BROOK b.g. 9 Over The River (FR) - Salty Sea by Sir Herbert Mrs Vanessa Ramm
1995 2(15),5(0)
22 20/1 Barbury Cas' (L) XX 3m 19 GS *ld til jnd & f 13th* F -

Won 2 Irish points 93; only 3 runs 94/6 & has that tell-tale look of the non-stayer 13

DAUPHIN BLEU(FR) b.g. 10 Direct Flight - Shabby (FR) by Carmarthan (FR) Miss Victoria Roberts
607 23/3 Howick (L) MDN 3m 12 S *ld & clr by 4th, drew wll away 10th, easily* 1 15
1113 17/4 Hockworthy (L) RES 3m 11 GS *made all, clr 12th, blndrd 2 out, impressive* 1 22
1316 28/4 Bitterley (L) OPE 3m 5 G *(fav) cls 2nd til ld 6th, 2-3l up aft til wknd apr last, hdd flat* 2 22
1508 12/5 Maisemore P' (L) LAD 3m 6 F *(fav) mstks,ld 3rd,sn clr,dist up whn f last,rmntd,just faild* 2 26

Much improved & goes real rattle now; likes to dominate; could be hard to beat in Ladies; S-F 24

DAVIDS PRIDE (Irish) — I 522^{P}, I 533^{P}, I 622^{P}, I 631^{P}
DAVIDS SISTER (Irish) — I 564^{P}, I 637^{6}, I 651^{F}
DAVIMPORT ch.g. 7 Import - Davett by Typhoon W Aitken
1995 7(0),P(0)
610 23/3 Friars Haugh (L) CON 3m 11 G *nvr dngrs, bhnd whn p.u. 4 out.* P 0
1087 14/4 Friars Haugh (L) MDO 3m 9 F *made most til 9th, sn wknd, t.o. & p.u. 4 out* P 0

No signs of ability yet 0

DAVY LAMP (Irish) — I 61^{3}, I 137^{1}
DAVY'S LAD b.g. 5 Respect - Colisfare by Coliseum Mrs E Borthwick
114 17/2 Lanark (R) MDO 3m 12 GS *in tch to 10th, bhnd whn p.u. 4 out* P 0
502 16/3 Lanark (R) MDO 3m 7 G *cls 2nd at 11th, wknd & p.u. apr nxt* P 0
614 23/3 Friars Haugh (L) MDN 3m 10 G *ld untl wknd quckly 4 out, p.u. aftr 2 out.* P 0

No stamina yet but time on his side & should do better 10

DAWN COYOTE(USA) ch.g. 13 Grey Dawn II - Beanery (USA) by Cavan William P Hay
113 17/2 Lanark (R) OPE 3m 6 GS *not fluent, t.o. 10th, p.u. 3 out* P 0
318 2/3 Corbridge (R) LAD 3m 5f 10 GS *(vis) prom early, lost plc & bhnd frm 14th* 8 0
610 23/3 Friars Haugh (L) CON 3m 11 G *6th hlfwy, sn lost tch, p.u. bfr last* 0 0
699 30/3 Tranwell (L) CON 3m 8 GS *(bl) not fluent, 4th at 12th, sn outpcd* 6 0
1351 4/5 Mosshouses (L) CON 3m 11 GS *(bl) in tch to 12th, sn outpcd, no imp frm 3 out* 6 0
1515 12/5 Hexham Poin' (L) OPE 3m 6 HY *(bl) in tch, rdn apr 3 out, 2nd whn blnd 3 out, wknd rpdly, p.u.* P 0
1573 19/5 Corbridge (R) OPE 3m 12 G *mid-div early, bhnd whn p.u. aft 10th* P 0

Beat two other finishers & is well past his sell-by date now 0

DAWN LAD (Irish) — I 13^{P}, I 69^{4}, I 185^{2}, I 245^{F}, I 377^{1}
DAYBROOK'S GIFT b.g. 13 Daybrook Lad - Current Gift by Current Coin Miss N K Allan
1995 P(0),U(-),2(18),F(-),1(20),F(-),1(23)
5 13/1 Larkhill (R) LAD 3m 10 GS *prom, mstk 6th, wknd rpdly 14th, t.o. & p.u. last* P 0
136 17/2 Ottery St M' (L) LAD 3m 9 GS *rear, prog 14th, styd on frm 4 out, nvr nrr* 2 19
208 24/2 Castle Of C' (R) LAD 3m 14 HY *alwys rear, nvr on terms* 9 0
469 10/3 Milborne St' (L) LAD 3m 8 G *bhnd, prog 14th, ld 2 out, sn clr* 1 21
655 23/3 Badbury Rin' (L) LAD 3m 8 G *rr untl ran on one pace from 16th* 4 16
863 6/4 Larkhill (R) MEM 3m 4 F *(fav) hld up, cls 2nd frm 12th, ld 3 out, rddn out flat, unimprssv* 1 16
1165 20/4 Larkhill (R) LAD 3m 7 GF *(fav) rear, prog, ld 10-12th, qcknd into clr ld frm 3 out* 1 21
1346 4/5 Holnicote (L) LAD 3m 5 GS *nvr trbld ldrs* 4 17
1552 18/5 Bratton Down (L) LAD 3m 7 F *went 3rd 10th, tk 2nd 3 out, no imp wnr* 2 20
1635 1/6 Bratton Down (L) LAD 3m 13 G *wll bhnd in last pair til ran on 14th, nvr on terms* 7 0

Capable in minor company & won 5 of last 13; can win easy Ladies at 14; G-F 20

DAY GIRL ch.m. 8 Extra - Day Bird by Court Feathers G F Beazley
883 6/4 Brampton Br' (R) MDN 3m 13 GF *trckng ldrs whn f 8th* F -
1224 24/4 Brampton Br' (R) MDO 3m 17 G *in tch in mid-div til wknd 14th, p.u. 3 out* P 0

No real signs yet 0

DAYTIME DANCER (Irish) — I 77^{3}, I 120^{F}, I 151^{P}, I 252^{F}, I 291^{P}, I 444^{P}
DEAL ME ONE ch.g. 7 Push On - Martian Wisdom by Aggressor R Jukes
146 17/2 Erw Lon (L) MEM 3m 7 G *cls 4th, prog to disp whn u.r. 6th* U -
217 24/2 Newtown (L) RES 3m 17 GS *mstk 3rd, alwys bhnd, t.o. & p.u. 14th* P 0
1601 25/5 Bassaleg (R) RES 3m 12 GS *cls up, gd 3rd at 9th, wknd rpdly & p.u. 11th* P 0

Maiden winner 94; missed 95; interrupted season 96 & no form; best watched 11

DEAR JEAN ch.m. 6 Exorbitant - High Jean by Arrigle Valley M E Sowersby
1995 P(0),P(0)

72 11/2 Wetherby Po' (L) CON 3m 18 GS *cls up, ld 9th-12th, fdd rpdly, p.u. 3 out* P 0
175 18/2 Market Rase' (L) MDO 2m 5f 8 GF *cls up, disp ld 3 out til apr last, no ext flat* 4 13
238 25/2 Southwell P' (L) MDO 3m 9 HO *hld up,mstk 8th,prog 11th,hmpd 13th,hrd rdn & ld last,allout* 1 15
411 9/3 Charm Park (L) RES 3m 20 G *alwys wl in rr, p.u. 4 out* P 0

Beat subsequent winner when scoring; finished early & more needed for Restricteds 15

DEARMISTERSHATTER (Irish) — **I** 81P, **I** 161³, **I** 267P, **I** 300⁴, **I** 390¹, **I** 482P, **I** 498F
DEBONAIR DUDE (Irish) — **I** 430¹, **I** 454²
DEBONAIR DUKE (Irish) — **I** 40F, **I** 109P
DECENT GOLD b or br.g. 13 Decent Fellow - Blaze Gold by Arizona Duke J W Stephenson
1995 B(-),2(19),2(16),6(0),8(0),2(0)

490 16/3 Horseheath (R) XX 3m 7 GF *mid-div, prog to 4th at 10th, lost tch ldrs 13th, t.o. 4 out* 4 0
725 31/3 Garthorpe (R) OPE 3m 9 G *nvr going wll, alwys last, t.o. & p.u. 9th* P 0
1098 14/4 Guilsborough (L) CON 3m 17 G *bhnd & sn drvn alng, t.o. 9th, nvr on terms* 8 0
1237 27/4 Clifton On ' (L) OPE 3m 5 GF *jmpd rght, ld 3-5th, last & outpcd 13th, no ch aft* 4 0
1521 12/5 Garthorpe (R) INT 3m 7 GF *mid to rear, no ext whn asked to qckn 4 out* 5 0
1595 25/5 Garthorpe (R) CON 3m 15 G *last til p.u. 11th* P 0
1639 2/6 Dingley (R) MEM 3m 7 GF *prog & cl up 13th, chsd wnr aft nxt, no imp, mstk last* 2 12

Declined in 96; lost last 16 starts & likely to extend sequence if appearing at 14 0

DECENT SCOTCH (Irish) — **I** 327P, **I** 516P, **I** 607U, **I** 636P
DECIDING DANCE (Irish) — **I** 149P, **I** 211⁵, **I** 308P, **I** 503³, **I** 572², **I** 610³
DECOR (Irish) — **I** 297¹
DEDAY gr.g. 9 Liberated - Pandoras Box Mrs H O Graham

47 4/2 Alnwick (L) XX 3m 14 G *ld 3rd-4th, wknd 7th, t.o. & p.u. 3 out* P 0
84 11/2 Alnwick (L) RES 3m 11 GS *alwys rear, wll bhnd hlfwy, t.o. & p.u. 13th* P 0
188 24/2 Friars Haugh (L) RES 3m 12 S *ld to 10th, grad wknd* 5 0
298 2/3 Great Treth' (R) RES 3m 13 G *ld 2nd til 9th, lost plc 11th, 8th whn f 17th* F -
486 16/3 Newcastle (L) HC 3m 9 GS *prom, ld 7th, blnd 12th, hdd after last, not qckn.* 2 21
789 1/4 Kelso (L) HC 3m 1f 11 GF *pressed ldr, blnd and u.r. 8 out.* U -
1000 9/4 Wetherby (L) HC 3m 110yds 10 G *disp ld when blnd 8th, weakening when blunded 10th, p.u. before next.* P 0
1249 27/4 Balcormo Ma' (R) RES 3m 10 GS *t.o. by 5th, p.u. aft 12th* P 0
1340 4/5 Hexham (L) HC 3m 1f 13 S *in tch when blnd and u.r. 8th.* U -
1515 12/5 Hexham Poin' (L) OPE 3m 6 HY *j.w. made all, drew clr apr 3 out, easily* 1 20
1573 19/5 Corbridge (R) OPE 3m 12 G *prom, made most frm 8th, jnd last, no ext und pres nr fin* 2 21

Missed 95; won poor Open; ran better last start; inconsistent; should win again; Any 20

DEE LIGHT ch.m. 7 Scorpio (FR) - Francis Lane by Broxted J M Tomlinson
1995 6(0),4(0),4(0)

288 2/3 Eaton Hall (R) MDO 3m 17 G *mid-div, prog 5 out, ev ch 3 out, no ext* 3 12

Completes but placed in poor Maiden 96 & disappeared; more needed for a win 12

DEEP IN GREEK b.g. 10 Deep Run - Dancing Doe by Royal Buck Bonsal/Kinsley (Usa)

378 9/3 Barbury Cas' (L) LAD 3m 6 GS *sn wll bhnd, t.o. frm 11th* 4 0
1547 18/5 Fakenham (L) HC 2m 5f 110yds 11 G *towards rear to hfwy, lost tch from 12th, t.o..* 5 0

Distant last both starts & has no prospects now 0

DEEP ISLE ch.g. 10 Deep Run - Baby Isle by Samantha Star B J Llewellyn
1995 **P(NH),F(NH),P(NH),13(NH)**

368 6/3 Lingfield (L) HC 3m 7 S *held up, lost tch after 10th, t.o. 5 out.* 5 0

The briefest of seasons & looks finished now 0

DEEP MOSS(IRE) b.g. 8 Le Moss - Why Ask by Deep Run J Pembroke
1995 2(0),3(0),3(0),2(12)

4 13/1 Larkhill (R) MDO 3m 9 GS *mid-div, outpcd 12th, plodded on* 4 0

Finished on oppening day; ungenuine & unlikely to win now 10

DEEP SALMON (Irish) — **I** 417P
DEEP SONG ch.g. 6 True Song - Rapagain by Deep Run P A Pritchard
1995 **16(NH),P(NH)**

1182 21/4 Mollington (R) MDN 3m 10 F *wll in rear, prog 12th, chsd wnr aft 3 out, wknd apr last* 4 0

No ability under Rules; well beaten in weak Maiden but gave some encouragement 11

DEEP WAVE (Irish) — **I** 39^{F}, **I** 121^{4}, **I** 156^{5}, **I** 206^{5}, **I** 334^{2}, **I** 368^{F}, **I** 474^{F}, **I** 543^{3}, **I** 574^{5}

DEERPARK KING (Irish) — **I** 86^{P}, **I** 446^{4}

DEEYEHFOLLYME (Irish) — **I** 423^{F}

DEFINITE MAYBE(IRE) b.g. 6 The Parson - Tumble Ria by Tumble Wind (USA) — B C Kilby

1995 **3(NH)**

144	17/2	Larkhill	(R)	MDO	3m	15	G	*(fav) rear, not fluent, t.o. & p.u. 12th*	P	0
268	2/3	Didmarton	(L)	MDN	3m	10	G	*(fav) s.s. prog 6th,prssd wnr 12th,ld apr last,sn hdd,ran on flat*	2	14
521	16/3	Larkhill	(R)	MDO	3m	6	G	*(fav) n.j.w. no ch whn lft in ld last, lucky*	1	14
822	6/4	Charlton Ho'	(L)	RES	3m	7	GF	*(bl) in tch, ev ch 3 out, outpcd aft, rlld aft last*	3	18
1113	17/4	Hockworthy	(L)	RES	3m	11	GS	*(bl) w.w., rmnds 4th, chsd wnr 13th, no imp 2 out, wknd, eased*	2	14
1395	6/5	Cotley Farm	(L)	RES	3m	8	GF	*alwys prom, ld 11th-2 out, outpcd aft*	3	20

Top stable & has ability but hard ride & disappointing; one to treat with caution start of 97; Good 18

DE GREY gr.g. 9 Grey Ghost - A Certain Lusty by Ascertain (USA) — Mrs H O Graham

1995 r(-),6(0),4(0)

1082	14/4	Friars Haugh	(L)	MEM	3m	3	F	*plld hrd, ld 8-10th, 3l 2nd whn f nxt*	F	-

Of no account 0

DEISE CRUSADER b.g. 9 Farhaan - Rugged Maid by Rugged Man — J P Henderson

1995 P(0),1(12),**8(0)**

316	2/3	Corbridge	(R)	MEM	3m	10	GS	*prom early, bhnd frm 6th, nvr dang aft*	6	0

Maiden winner 95; more needed for Restricteds & soon vanished in 96 12

DELGANY DEER (Irish) — **I** 130^{4}, **I** 220,

DELIGHTFILLY b.m. 5 Idiot's Delight - All Risks by Pitcairn — D T Goldsworthy

386	9/3	Llanfrynach	(R)	RES	3m	10	GS	*sn wll bhnd, t.o. & p.u. 9th*	P	0
600	23/3	Howick	(L)	RES	3m	14	S	*rear, p.u. 6th*	P	0

No sign of ability yet 0

DEMAMO(IRE) ch.g. 8 Denel (FR) - Ma Duchesse by Mon Capitaine — H Bricknell

1995 P(0),7(0),2(12),U(-),5(0)

221	24/2	Newtown	(L)	MDN	3m	12	GS	*chsd ldrs, outpcd whn lft poor 3rd 14th, no imp aft*	3	0
431	9/3	Upton-On-Se'	(R)	MDO	3m	17	GS	*6th at 12th, not pace to chal frm 4 out*	4	10
607	23/3	Howick	(L)	MDN	3m	12	S	*(fav) cls 2nd whn f 9th*	F	-
796	2/4	Heythrop	(R)	MDN	3m	11	F	*prom, ld 9th, clr last, all out nr fin*	1	15
1222	24/4	Brampton Br'	(R)	RES	3m	11	G	*cl up to 11th, lost tch frm 14th*	5	11
1582	19/5	Wolverhampt'	(L)	RES	3m	10	G	*12s-4s, whppd round & u.r. start*	U	-
1601	25/5	Bassaleg	(R)	RES	3m	12	GS	*rear, some prog to 5th apr 10th where p.u. rpdly*	P	0

Beat two subsequent winners when scoring; barely stays & problems last start; Restricted unlikely 14

DENBY HOUSE LAD(CAN) br.h. 9 Assert - Queens Club (USA) by Cyane (USA) — K J Shone

852	6/4	Sandon	(L)	MDN	3m	9	GF	*cls order 10th, tk ld 14th, ran on wll frm 3 out*	1	16

Won a weak race decisively & may have scope for Restricteds at 10 15

DENEL DE (Irish) — **I** 178^{P}, **I** 259^{P}, **I** 302^{U}, **I** 408^{F}, **I** 448^{P}, **I** 535^{F}, **I** 622^{P}

DENFIELD (Irish) — **I** 255^{P}, **I** 300^{1}, **I** 411^{P}

DENIM BLUE ch.g. 7 Mandrake Major - Delphinium by Tin King — Mrs L Walby

1995 P(0),U(-),2(11),F(-)

406	9/3	Dalston	(R)	MDO	2 1/2m	12	G	*(fav) mid-div,hdwy hlfwy,chal frm 2 out,hrd rdn run-in, jst faild*	2	14
502	16/3	Lanark	(R)	MDO	3m	7	G	*(fav) wnet 2nd 12th, clsd on wnr frm 3 out, not quite get up*	2	12
755	31/3	Lockerbie	(R)	MDN	3m	17	G	*(fav) alwys hndy, 4th hlfwy, ld 4 out, kpt on wll*	1	16
1447	6/5	Witton Cast'	(R)	RES	3m	11	G	*(fav) midfld, slght hdwy 3 out, no ext apr last*	3	14
1472	11/5	Aspatria	(L)	RES	3m	8	GF	*prog 8th, prssd ldr 12th, ld 2 out, clr whn blnd & u.r. last*	U	-

Improving; stays; unlucky last start & compensation should await early 97; G/F-G 18

DENNISTOWNTHRILLER (Irish) — **I** 17^{1}, **I** 54^{P}, **I** 129^{1}, **I** 221^{5}, **I** 349^{F}, **I** 382^{3}, **I** 529^{P}

DEPARTURE ch.m. 9 Gorytus (USA) - La Gravotte (FR) by Habitat — W H Whitley

1995 7(12)

133	17/2	Ottery St M'	(L)	OPE	3m	18	GS	*sn bhnd, t.o. & p.u. 14th*	P	0
198	24/2	Lemalla	(R)	OPE	3m	12	HY	*bhnd frm 6th, ran on agn frm 2 out*	5	14
279	2/3	Clyst St Ma'	(L)	LAD	3m	7	S	*alwys rear, no ch frm 13th*	4	15
554	17/3	Ottery St M'	(L)	MEM	3m	5	G	*ld 6-8th, ld agn 11th, clr aft 14th, comf*	1	15
717	30/3	Wadebridge	(L)	OPE	3m	3	GF	*j.w. made all, drew clr aft 15th, easily*	1	20
874	6/4	Higher Kilw'	(L)	OPE	3m	6	GF	*(fav) sn prom, disp 4-12th, wknd 15th, sn btn, eased*	3	13
1343	4/5	Holnicote	(L)	OPE	3m	6	GS	*mostly 3rd/4th, prog 15th, efft short-lived, sn fdd*	4	12
1525	12/5	Ottery St M'	(L)	CON	3m	9	GF	*handy, ld 16th, hdd aft 2 out, no ext*	2	18

1589	25/5 Mounsey Hil'	(R) OPE	3m	12	G	*f 3rd*	F	-

Has ability but inconsistent; likes to dictate; can win again in small field 97; Any 19

DEPLETE b.g. 13 Deep Run - Elite Lady by Prince Hansel — T W B Smalley

1995 F(-)

50	4/2 Alnwick	(L) CON	3m	9	G	*plld to ld 4th, hdd aft 12th, wknd, p.u. 2 out*	P	0
82	11/2 Alnwick	(L) MEM	3m	4	GS	*(fav) ld 2nd, drew clr frm 3 out, comf, cllpsd & died aft race*	1	16

Dead 16

DERALI (Irish) — I 197^{2}

DERBY O'GILL (Irish) — I 80^{5}, I 159^{P}

DEREENAVURRIG (Irish) — I 151^{P}, I 183^{P}

DERNAMAY (Irish) — I 169^{P}, I 215^{P}, I 258^{P}, I 281^{3}, I 320^{3}, I 364^{3}, I 397^{3}

DERRI BRIDE ch.m. 5 Vital Season - Summer Bride by Harvest Sun — Derward Roberts

144	17/2 Larkhill	(R) MDO	3m	15	G	*mid-div, u.r. 2nd*	U	-
522	16/3 Larkhill	(R) MDO	3m	12	G	*rear whn f 7th*	F	-

Could do better but needs to learn to jump first 0

DERRING ANN (Irish) — 883^{5}, 1161^{F}, 1416^{P}, 1485^{1}, 1601, , I 659^{4}

DERRING BUD br.g. 12 Derring Rose - Tarune by Tarqogan — Lady Susan Brooke

1995 **3(NH)**

216	24/2 Newtown	(L) LAD	3m	13	GS	*s.s. hld up wll bhnd, prog 13th, ran on 2 out, fin strngly*	3	17
356	3/3 Garnons	(L) LAD	3m	12	GS	*s.v.s. prog frm 13th, nrst fin*	3	18

Old character; ran badly under Rules after pointing; may consent in weak point at 13; Soft 18

DERRING FLOSS b.m. 6 Derring Rose - Win Green Hill by National Trust — Miss Jill Wormall

1995 P(0),6(0)

240	25/2 Southwell P'	(L) MDO	3m	15	HO	*5th whn f 7th*	F	-
332	3/3 Market Rase'	(L) MDO	3m	8	G	*rear, blnd & u.r. 5th*	U	-
518	16/3 Dalton Park	(R) MDO	3m	15	G	*wll in tch til wknd frm 16th, t.o.*	4	0
681	30/3 Cottenham	(R) MDO	3m	12	GF	*prom, ld 8-15th, 4th & wkng whn mstk 2 out*	5	0

Shows no stamina & beaten in modest races nowhere near a winning chance yet 10

DERRING KNIGHT b.g. 6 Derring Rose - Arctic Servant by Goldhill — N J Pomfret

1995 P(0),P(0),5(0),P(0),P(0),P(0)

14	14/1 Cottenham	(R) MDO	3m	10	G	*mid-div, lost tch 12th, lft 3rd 3 out, lft 2nd last*	2	0
60	10/2 Cottenham	(R) MDO	3m	7	GS	*ld to 12th, lft in ld apr 3 out, mstk 2 out, hdd & wknd*	3	10
182	18/2 Horseheath	(R) MDO	3m	11	G	*in tch, blnd 12th,ev ch whn mstk 3 out,wknd rpdly, p.u.last*	P	0
727	31/3 Garthorpe	(R) MDO	3m	12	G	*chsd ldrs, rdn 10th, sn lost tch, ref 14th*	R	-
1378	5/5 Dingley	(R) MDO	2 1/2m	16	GF	*(vis) last & t.o. 8th, p.u. 11th*	P	0
1568	19/5 Mollington	(R) MDO	3m	9	GS	*in tch til rdn & wknd 10th, ref nxt*	R	-

Ungenuine & throws in towel when pressure applied; safely ignored 0

DERRING RIVER (Irish) — I 470^{P}, I 531^{P}, I 607^{R}

DERRING RULER b.g. 6 Derring Rose - Born Bossy by Eborneezer — T N Bailey

1995 P(0),P(0),F(-),7(0)

218	24/2 Newtown	(L) MDN	3m	14	GS	*trckd ldrs, ev ch 14th, sn wknd, fin tired*	3	0
353	3/3 Garnons	(L) MDN	2 1/2m	7	GS	*chsd ldng pair frm 7th, no ch wth wnr, tk 2nd cls home*	2	0

Well beaten when placed & season lasted 8 days; stamina lacking but could improve 12

DERRING RUN b.m. 6 Derring Rose - Corbitt Coins by Deep Run — Mrs L Danton

1995 **U(-)**

579	20/3 Ludlow	(R) HC	2 1/2m	17	G	*started slowly, mstk and hmpd 1st, t.o. when p.u. before 10th.*	P	0

2 runs in 2 seasons & should try a Maiden for starters 0

DERRYGALLON FANCY (Irish) — I 379^{P}, I 457^{P}, I 572^{F}, I 650^{3}

DERRYGRA FOUNTAIN (Irish) — I 379^{P}, I 504, , I 569, , I 649^{P}

DERRY'S DIAMOND (Irish) — I 6^{P}, I 44^{P}

DERYN Y CWM(IRE) b.g. 6 Soughaan (USA) - Little Upstart by On Your Mark — T M Morris

358	3/3 Garnons	(L) RES	3m	18	GS	*bhnd frm 3rd, t.o. & p.u. 12th*	P	0
552	17/3 Erw Lon	(L) MDN	3m	10	GS	*alwys bhnd, t.o. & p.u. 11th*	P	0
771	31/3 Pantyderi	(R) MDN	3m	14	G	*mstks 2nd & 4th, p.u. aft 8th*	P	0
1269	27/4 Pyle	(R) MDO	3m	9	G	*last frm 6th, ran off course apr 9th, p.u. 11th*	P	0
1391	6/5 Pantyderi	(R) MDO	3m	13	GF	*b.d. 1st*	B	-

Looks hopeless 0

DESERT HERO br.g. 22 Menelek - Mrs Brady by Ossian II — Mrs P Grainger

176 18/2 Market Rase' (L) MDO 2m 5f 10 GF *w.w. 4th & rdn 11th, ev ch 3 out, onepcd* 4 12

.... **12**

DESERTMORE (Irish) — **I** 49F, **I** 78F, **I** 437¹, **I** 463¹

DESERT WALTZ(IRE) ch.h. 7 Gorytus (USA) - Desert Pet by Petingo — H B Geddes

1995 2(13),1(17),1(18),1(19),2(23)

1 13/1 Larkhill (R) XX 3m 7 GS *(fav) mstks 2nd & 3rd,chsd ldrs,disp 15th-2 out,rallied to ld fin* 1 24
141 17/2 Larkhill (R) MEM 3m 6 G *(fav) bhnd ldrs, smooth prog to ld 4 out, mstk last, ran on* 1 22
262 2/3 Didmarton (L) MEM 3m 11 G *(fav) w.w. mstk 10th, ld 12th, sn clr, slw last, pshd out* 1 23
524 16/3 Larkhill (R) INT 3m 11 G *mid-div, smooth prog to ld 14th, pshd clr apr last* 1 26
710 30/3 Barbury Cas' (L) CON 3m 6 G *(fav) hld up, prog 12th, chsd ldr aft, outpcd frm 2 out* 2 22
1247 27/4 Woodford (L) CON 3m 7 G *(fav) prog 8th, lft in ld 11-14th, chsd wnr, rdn 2 out, onepcd* 2 22
1526 12/5 Ottery St M' (L) LAD 3m 5 GF *(fav) hld up, prog & rdn 15th, cls 2nd & ev ch 2 out, no ext* 2 25
1588 25/5 Mounsey Hil' (R) LAD 3m 6 G *chsd wnr 7th, ld 13-16th,ld 3 out, hrd rdn flat, hdd post* 2 25
1635 1/6 Bratton Down (L) LAD 3m 13 G *w.w. rpd prog to ld aft 2 out, hdd & no ext flat* 2 25

Consistent; won hot Intermediate; beaten by good horses; onepaced; win Ladies in 97; G/S-F 26

DESMARFRAN (Irish) — **I** 89P, **I** 112⁴, **I** 167P

DES THE ARCHITECT (Irish) — **I** 117P, **I** 142P, **I** 185P, **I** 244⁴, **I** 437⁶

DETERMINED MAN (Irish) — **I** 52P, **I** 198P

DETERMINED OKIE (Irish) — **I** 59, , **I** 83⁶, **I** 198P, **I** 224³, **I** 347⁵, **I** 521²

DETINU ch.g. 5 Hasty Word - Knocksharry by Palm Track — M J Jackson

741 31/3 Upper Sapey (R) MEM 3m 4 GS *2nd whn f 2nd* F -
749 31/3 Upper Sapey (R) MDO 3m 17 GS *2nd outing, t.o. til p.u. 11th* P 0
1569 19/5 Mollington (R) MDO 3m 10 GS *ld to 9th, outpcd 13th, effrt agn 3 out, wknd nxt* 5 0

Well beaten last start but young enough to have hopes in 97 12

DEVILS ELBOW ch.g. 12 Remezzo - Spartan's Legacy by Spartan General — W J Donaldson

1247 27/4 Woodford (L) CON 3m 7 G *sn clr ld, 30l clr whn f 9th* F -
1507 12/5 Maisemore P' (L) CON 3m 10 F *sn clr, blnd 4th, hdd 12th, 3rd & wkng whn s.u. bnd aft 13th* S -

Winning hurdler; blazes off but no chance of staying there now 0

DEVIL'S STING(IRE) ch.g. 7 Henbit (USA) - Hells Mistress by Skymaster — R C Harper

1995 **P(NH),5(NH),3(NH)**

334 3/3 Heythrop (R) MEM 3m 6 G *chsd ldrs, 3rd & outpcd 12th, p.u. 2 out* P -
477 10/3 Tweseldown (R) MDO 3m 15 G *prom to 10th, wknd nxt, p.u. 2 out* P 0
797 2/4 Heythrop (R) MDN 3m 11 F *prom, ld 12-13th, outpcd frm 2 out* 5 10

Short of stamina at present but may do better in 97 10

DEVIOSITY(USA) b.g. 9 Spectacular Bid (USA) - Reinvestment (USA) by Key To The Mint (USA) — Merv Rowe

1995 **4(NH),P(NH),4(NH),5(NH),5(NH),11(NH),P(NH)**

278 2/3 Clyst St Ma' (L) CON 3m 9 S *bhnd, no ch frm 14th, outpcd* 5 0
531 16/3 Cothelstone (L) CON 3m 12 G *alwys rr div, 5th & no ch 15th* 4 11
801 4/4 Clyst St Ma' (L) CON 3m 2 GS *(bl) disp til slght ld aft 14th, pshd 3l clr apr 2 out* 1 17

Blinkered when winning match & unlikely to figure in competitive races 15

DEVONIA(NZ) ch.m. 11 Kutati (NZ) - Reese's Pride (NZ) by Trelay (NZ) — Mrs J M Bailey

1995 4(13),P(0),P(0),P(0)

815 6/4 Charlton Ho' (L) MEM 3m 8 GF *ld/disp to 12th, lost tch 4 out, p.u. apr last* P 0
1166 20/4 Larkhill (R) OPE 3m 6 GF *ldng grp throut til wknd frm 14th, t.o.* 3 11
1408 6/5 Hackwood Pa' (L) INT 3m 2 F *ld to 12th, cls up to 2 out, no ch wth wnr, eased flat* 2 0

Well beaten & flattered by placings; of no real account now 0

DEVONSHIRE LAD b.g. 5 Sergeant Drummer (USA) - Alice Rairthorn by Romany Air — Mrs D B Lunt

282 2/3 Clyst St Ma' (L) MDN 3m 8 S *cls up, ev ch 14th, wknd & f heavily 2 out* F -
719 30/3 Wadebridge (L) MDO 3m 7 GF *hld up rear, not fluent 12th, sn lost tch, p.u. 15th, school* P 0
1279 27/4 Bratton Down (L) MDO 3m 14 GF *prom, disp whn c.o. by loose horse 8th* C -
1348 4/5 Holnicote (L) MDO 3m 9 GS *nvr a fctr, p.u. 14th* P 0

Unfortunate to date but only schooling & should do better in time 10

DEWLINER gr.g. 11 Henbit (USA) - Farmers Daughter by Red Slipper — P Barbrook

1995 5(0),4(10),3(10),6(11),3(10),3(13)

385 9/3 Llanfrynach (R) LAD 3m 14 GS *t.o. 4th, 2 fences bhnd whn p.u. 11th* P 0
506 16/3 Magor (R) CON 3m 8 GS *last at hlfwy, t.o. & p.u. 2 out* P 0

Dual winner 92 but looks well past it now 0

DHARAMSHALA(IRE) b.g. 8 Torenaga - Ambitious Lady by Status Seeker — P D Jones

1995 2(12),**7(NH)**

44	3/2	Wadebridge	(L)	MDO	3m	9	GF	*trckd ldrs, rdn & outpcd aft 14th, no imp aft*	5	10
132	17/2	Ottery St M'	(L)	MDN	2	14				
1651	8/6	Umberleigh	(L)	MDO	3m	11	GF	*w.w. in tch, effrt to chs ldr aft 3 out, ld last, drvn out*	1	14

Does not look 100% genuine but improved & won modest Maiden; more needed for Restricted chances;F-GS 15

DIAMOND FLIER(IRE) b.g. 7 Kambalda - Cappagh Flier by Lock Diamond — Miss J Spear

1995 F(-),P(0),P(0),P(0),3(0)

941	8/4	Wadebridge	(L)	MDN	3m	5	F	*ld/disp to 12th, grdly fdd, p.u. 3 out*	P	0

Placed in 95 but brief appearance 96 bodes ill - young enough to revive yet 11

DIAMOND LIGHT ch.g. 9 Roman Warrior - Another Jo by Hotfoot — V R Bishop

1225	24/4	Brampton Br'	(R)	MDO	3m	18	G	*prom to 4th, cls up 9th, grad wknd frm 14th*	7	0
1477	11/5	Bredwardine	(R)	MEM	3m	3	G	*w.w. in 2nd, effrt to ld 15th, no ext frm nxt*	2	0

Late to appear; 2nd in feeble race but may have scope for better 12

DIAMOND VALLEY(IRE) b.g. 8 Bustinetto - Dalmond by Diamonds Are Trump (USA) — Robert Thame

1995 4(17)

235	24/2	Heythrop	(R)	RES	3m	10	GS	*rear, gd prog hlfwy, ld 2 out, hdd last, no ext flat*	2	17
428	9/3	Upton-On-Se'	(R)	RES	3m	17	GS	*smooth prog 14th, ev ch 2 out, outpcd by wnr*	2	18
593	23/3	Parham	(R)	RES	3m	11	GS	*(fav) ld to 2nd, mid-div aft, 7th whn u.r. 10th*	U	-

Maiden winner 94; ran really well 2nd start 96 but lightly raced now; good enough for Restricted win ... 19

DIANA MOSS(IRE) b.m. 7 Le Moss - El Diana by Tarboosh (USA) — J S Papworth

1995 P(0),P(0),r(-)

202	24/2	Lemalla	(R)	MDO	3m	12	HY	*ld 3rd-6th, wknd & p.u. 9th*	P	0
301	2/3	Great Treth'	(R)	MDO	3m	13	G	*prom whn hit 11th (broke fence), no ch 14th*	5	0
629	23/3	Kilworthy	(L)	MDN	3m	11	GS	*prom, chsd wnr 10-12th, wknd, poor 4th whn u.r. 3 out*	U	-
941	8/4	Wadebridge	(L)	MDN	3m	5	F	*ld/disp to 8th, drppd back, came agn run in*	2	12
1118	17/4	Hockworthy	(L)	MDO	3m	14	GS	*mid-div, 6th & btn at 11th, b.d. nxt*	B	-
1429	6/5	High Bickin'	(R)	MDO	3m	8	G	*hndy, qcknd to ld 16th, cght last*	2	15
1626	27/5	Lifton	(R)	MDO	3m	13	GS	*mid-div, 7th at 13th, went 3rd 3 out, lost 3rd cls home*	4	14
1637	1/6	Bratton Down	(L)	MDO	3m	11	G	*plng, prom, chsd ldr 15th, ld last, rdn clr*	1	14
1649	8/6	Umberleigh	(L)	RES	3m	14	GF	*w.w. prog 11th, chal & mstk 14th,chal 2 out,ld last,rdn out*	1	17

Much improved late season & did well; more needed when upgraded; makes mistakes; G-F 16

DIBLOOM b.g. 8 Nomination - Tosara by Main Reef — Mrs P J Lee

1995 **F(NH),5(NH),P(NH),4(NH),4(NH),7(NH),1(NH),7(NH),9(NH),8(NH)**

1111	17/4	Hockworthy	(L)	MXO	3m	13	GS	*in tch to 10th, lost pl, t.o. & p.u. 14th*	P	0
1204	21/4	Lydstep	(L)	CON	3m	3	S	*alwys rear, p.u. 12th*	P	0
1265	27/4	Pyle	(R)	OPE	3m	8	G	*cls up til lost plc 8th, wknd & p.u. 12th*	P	0

Winning hurdler; no sign of stamina in points & can only be watched 12

DICE OFF ch.m. 8 Dubassoff (USA) - Diceabed by Push On — H A Shone

1995 2(12),1(14),5(0),1(14),U(-)

163	17/2	Weston Park	(L)	LAD	3m	10	G	*mid to rear, lost tch frm 12th, p.u. 4 out*	P	0
735	31/3	Sudlow Farm	(R)	MEM	3m	7	G	*chsd ldr til ld 6th, hdd apr last, no ext*	2	16
1012	9/4	Flagg Moor	(L)	XX	3m	7	G	*chsd ldr 3rd, lft dsptng ld 13th, hrd rdn flat, ld cls home*	1	18
1195	21/4	Sandon	(L)	XX	3m	9	G	*ld to 4 out, no ch wth wnr frm nxt*	2	17
1545	18/5	Bangor	(L)	HC	3m 110yds	8	G	*alwys bhnd, blnd 12th, struggling when mstk next, no ch when f 3 out, dead.*	F	-

Dead 19

DICK'S CABIN (Irish) — **I** 99^{P}, **I** 180^{P}, **I** 260^{P}, **I** 305^{5}, **I** 360^{2}, **I** 404^{1}, **I** 537^{P}, **I** 596^{5}

DICKS DELIGHT(IRE) b.g. 8 Miner's Lamp - Fannie Farmer by Royal Avenue — M D P Butler

1995 F(-),5(0)

788	31/3	Tweseldown	(R)	MDO	3m	8	G	*ld to 11th, sn rdn, t.o. & p.u. last*	P	0
1404	6/5	Hackwood Pa'	(L)	MEM	3m	2	F	*u.r. paddock, plld hrd disp ld til f 10th*	F	-

No delight & none likely 0

DIFFICULT DECISION (Irish) — **I** 30^{5}, **I** 101^{2}, **I** 192^{2}, **I** 266^{2}

DIGACRE (Irish) — **I** 69, , **I** 124^{F}, **I** 167^{F}, **I** 250^{6}, **I** 289^{1}, **I** 441^{4}

DIGIN FOR GOLD (Irish) — **I** 110^{F}, **I** 267^{3}, **I** 478^{P}

DILKUSH b.g. 7 Dunbeath (USA) - Good Try by Good Bond — S C Wells

1995 3(0)

233	24/2	Heythrop	(R)	MDN	3m	14	GS	*nvr rchd ldrs, p.u. aft 11th*	P	0

Hardly ever runs & is of no real account 0

DILLY'S LAST br.m. 8 Saunter - Delilah Dell by The Dell — Mrs S Buckler

1995 P(0),4(0),1(13),F(-),3(0),7(0),6(10)

396	9/3	Garthorpe	(R)	RES	3m	9	G	*twrds rear whn u.r. 3rd (ditch)*	U	-
539	17/3	Southwell P'	(L)	RES	3m	11	GS	*mid-div, in tch to 12th, wknd rpdly, p.u. 6 out*	P	0
726	31/3	Garthorpe	(R)	RES	3m	16	G	*rear, prog to 7th hlfwy, rchd 4th 3 out, sn btn*	5	12
971	8/4	Thorpe Lodge	(L)	RES	3m	4	GF	*mostly last, cls up til outpcd 4 out, p.u. flat*	P	0

Maiden winner 95; does not stay & outclassed in 96; future prospects not bright 10

DI MODA ch.g. 9 Buzzards Bay - Diamond Talk by Counsel — Miss Sharon Firmin

1995 **4(NH),4(NH),3(NH),P(NH),7(NH)**

236	24/2	Heythrop	(R)	MDN	3m	13	GS	*cls 2nd to 7th, lost plc, 5th whn f 13th*	F	-
641	23/3	Siddington	(L)	RES	3m	20	S	*alwys wll bhnd, t.o. frm 10th*	12	0
1217	24/4	Andoversford	(R)	MDO	3m	16	G	*bhnd til kpt on frm 3 out, nvr dang*	5	0
1438	6/5	Ashorne	(R)	XX	3m	14	G	*alwys bhnd, t.o. 8th*	11	0

Placed novice chases 94/5; novice ridden & beat only two other finishers in points 0

DINAN (Irish) — I 289^{P}, I 366^{6}, I 464^{3}

DINKIES QUEST b.m. 8 Sergeant Drummer (USA) - Tinker's Quest by Romany Air — Mrs D J Cocks

1995 P(0),U(-)

1075	13/4	Lifton	(R)	RES	3m	12	S	*prom til lost plc hlfwy, rear whn f 16th*	F	-
1342	4/5	Holnicote	(L)	MEM	3m	7	GS	*alwys prom, unable to chal frm 3 out*	3	16
1527	12/5	Ottery St M'	(L)	RES	3m	8	GF	*cls 5th hlfwy, went 3rd 3 out, ran on to tk 2nd nr fin*	2	14
1625	27/5	Lifton	(R)	INT	3m	8	GS	*handy, cls 3rd 15th, effrt & cls 2nd 3 out, fdd, p.u. last*	P	0

Maiden winner 94; lightly raced; fair efforts 96; Restricted possible with blinkers 97 15

DIORRAING (Irish) — I 87^{P}, I 108^{3}, I 162^{1}, I 304^{2}, I 482^{P}, I 560^{1}, I 627^{1}

DIP THE LIGHTS b.m. 6 Lighter - Honey Dipper by Golden Dipper — J A T de Giles

1995 **6(NH),10(NH)**

233	24/2	Heythrop	(R)	MDN	3m	14	GS	*mid-div til f 4th*	F	-
267	2/3	Didmarton	(L)	MDN	3m	11	G	*jmpd all over the pl, sn wll bhnd, lft 3rd by dfctns*	3	0
479	10/3	Tweseldown	(R)	MDO	3m	10	G	*sn bhnd, lft remote 2nd 3 out, tired & lost plc flat*	3	0
643	23/3	Siddington	(L)	MDN	3m	16	S	*rear, rdn 7th, crashed thro' wing 9th*	r	-
796	2/4	Heythrop	(R)	MDN	3m	11	F	*chsd ldrs til grad wknd frm 15th*	5	0

Well beaten when finishing & jumps poorly; unlikely to win 0

DIRECT b.g. 13 The Parson - Let The Hare Sit by Politico (USA) — J A C Edwards

212	24/2	Castle Of C'	(R)	CON	3m	7	HY	*(fav) rear, went 3rd at 14th, no ch frm nxt*	3	10
368	6/3	Lingfield	(L)	HC	3m	7	S	*held up, mstk 11th, hdwy 4 out, ld apr last, driven out run-in.*	1	22
672	29/3	Aintree	(L)	HC	2 3/4m	26	G	*f 1st.*	F	-
1119	18/4	Ayr	(L)	HC	3m 3f 110yds	9	GS	*lost tch from 12th, t.o. when p.u. before 3 out.*	P	0

Winning chaser; made experience count in mud-bath at Lingfield; unlikely to win at 14 17

DIRECTLY b.g. 13 Bay Express - Veracious by Astec — J H Busby

1995 P(0)

245	25/2	Southwell P'	(L)	LAD	3m	8	HO	*mstk 2nd, mstk & u.r. nxt*	U	-
436	9/3	Newton Brom'	(R)	LAD	3m	10	GS	*wll bhnd til prog 9th, 3rd nxt & mstk, wknd 4 out*	6	0
903	6/4	Dingley	(R)	LAD	3m	7	GS	*(fav) jmp slwly in rear til ref 8th*	R	-
1100	14/4	Guilsborough	(L)	OPE	3m	9	G	*jmpd badly, t.o. & p.u. 7th*	P	0

No longer of any account 0

DIRRA MINSTREL (Irish) — I 439^{P}, I 572^{P}, I 602^{P}

DIRTY DANCER b.g. 7 Sizzling Melody - Stratch (FR) by Thatch (USA) — Miss J Smith

1995 **11(NH),5(NH),11(NH)**

207	24/2	Castle Of C'	(R)	MDO	3m	15	HY	*bhnd, t.o. & p.u. 12th*	P	0
865	6/4	Larkhill	(R)	CON	3m	3	F	*not fluent, trckd wnnr 2nd til outpcd frm 13th*	2	0

Ex-NH Flat; beaten distance when last of two to finish 0

DISCAIN BOY b.g. 16 Bargello - Another Romney by Malfaiteur — P Mercer

1995 P(0),P(0),2(0),**P(0)**

570	17/3	Detling	(L)	MEM	3m	6	GF	*chsd ldr til mstk 11th, outpcd 4 out, kpt on frm 2 out*	4	0
1441	6/5	Aldington	(L)	MEM	3m	4	HD	*ld hdd 11th, rddn & cls aft, chal 2 out, no ext last*	2	11

Too old now but plodded on gamely in both Members 0

DISCIPLINE b.m. 11 Roman Warrior - Steadily by Whitstead — Mrs K Lawther

1293	28/4	Barbury Cas'	(L)	MDO	3m	11	F	*chsd ldrs, 5th & in tch whn blnd & u.r. 9th*	U	-

Rarely appears & shows nothing 0

DISCO DAN br.g. 14 Torenaga - Corbally Hope by Milan — Miss Anne Barnett

1995 6(0),P(0)
1173 20/4 Chaddesley ' (L) RES 3m 18 G *s.s. rear til mod prog frm 14th* 7 0

Lightly raced & safely ignored **0**

DISNEYS HILL b.g. 9 Le Bavard (FR) - Keep The Day by Master Buck G J Smith
972 8/4 Thorpe Lodge (L) MDO 3m 9 GF *alwys last trio, t.o. last frm 6 out, p.u. 3 out* P 0

No sign of ability **0**

DISRESPECT b.m. 6 Respect - Miss Sunny by Sunyboy W G Macmillan
1995 P(0)
405 9/3 Dalston (R) MDO 2 1/2m 16 G *mid-div, hdwy frm 14th, nvr nrr, improve* 5 0
1254 27/4 Balcormo Ma' (R) MDO 3m 14 GS *bhnd whn p.u. aft 12th* P 0
1352 4/5 Mosshouses (L) LAD 3m 10 GS *u.r. 3rd* U -

Still learning & hopefully will do better **10**

DI STEFANO b.g. 8 Chief Singer - Doree Moisson (FR) by Connaught Mike Gifford
1995 1(21),1(22),4(13)
214 24/2 Newtown (L) CON 3m 21 GS *(fav) hld up, rpd prog aft 13th, ld 2 out, pshd clr last* 1 23
350 3/3 Garnons (L) CON 3m 11 GS *(fav) conf rdn, hld up til prog 9th, ld 3 out, drew clr last* 1 23
746 31/3 Upper Sapey (R) CON 3m 3 GS *(fav) smooth prog to disp 3 out, sn qcknd clr, easily* 1 25
944 8/4 Andoversford (R) LAD 3m 4 GF *(fav) hld up in tch,mstk 15 & 16th, ld aft 3 out, qcknd clr* 1 25
1214 24/4 Andoversford (R) LAD 3m 4 G *(fav) w.w., chsd ld 13th, ld 3 out, sn clr, easily* 1 26
1414 6/5 Cursneh Hill (L) LAD 3m 9 GF *(fav) held up, prog to ld aft 15th, lft clr last* 1 25
1566 19/5 Mollington (R) LAD 3m 7 GS *(fav) not fluent early, w.w., chsd ldr 13th,ld 15th,sn clr,easily* 1 27

Top-class Ladies horse; quickens; top stable; hard to beat in 97; G/S-G/F **29**

DIVALI (Irish) — **I** 37^{2}, **I** 54^{P}, **I** 202^{3}

DIVINE CHANCE(IRE) b.g. 8 The Parson - Random What by Random Shot J M Turner
1995 **14(NH),4(NH),F(NH),8(NH),13(NH),14(NH)**
177 18/2 Horseheath (R) CON 3m 8 G *ld til mstk 2nd, 5th & in tch whn u.r. 11th* U -
251 25/2 Charing (L) OPE 3m 10 GS *(fav) chsd wnr frm 12th, rdn to chal apr 2 out, wknd flat* 2 16
420 9/3 High Easter (L) OPE 3m 9 S *in tch, ld 13th to nxt, ev ch til wknd qkly 3 out* 6 11
906 8/4 Fakenham (L) HC 2m 5f 110yds 11 G *alwys bhnd, t.o..* 8 0

Does not stay & finished just as stable found its form **14**

DIVINE PROBLEM gr.g. 14 Roselier (FR) - Group Problem by Divine Gift A Coveney
1995 2(0),P(0)
1051 13/4 Penshurst (L) MEM 3m 5 G *t.o. 5th, fin own time* 4 0

Of no account **0**

DIVINE RAPTURE (Irish) — **I** 149^{P}, **I** 211^{F}

DIVINE SAINT (Irish) — **I** 27^{P}, **I** 90^{P}, **I** 167^{P}

DIVINE THYME (Irish) — **I** 164^{F}

DIXONS HOMEFINDER b.g. 12 Strong Gale - Julia Too by Golden Horus J L Barnett
1995 4(0),U(-),P(0)
428 9/3 Upton-On-Se' (R) RES 3m 17 GS *wll bhnd whn p.u. 15th* P 0
904 6/4 Dingley (R) RES 3m 20 GS *mid-div whn f 7th* F -
1436 6/5 Ashorne (R) MEM 3m 7 G *mstks, in tch, chsd wnr 13th, wll btn in 2nd whn f 15th* F -
1507 12/5 Maisemore P' (L) CON 3m 10 F *chsd ldr to 2nd,mstk 4th,strgglng frm 7th,t.o. 9th,p.u.3 out* P 0
1641 2/6 Dingley (R) RES 3m 13 GF *raced wd, in tch, outpcd 2 out, kpt on* 4 16

Maiden winner 94; ran two fair races but win at 13 beyond him **11**

DIXON VARNER (Irish) — **I** 4^{1}, **I** 37^{1}, **I** 67^{1}

DIZZY DEALER b.m. 9 Le Bavard (FR) - Dizzy Dot by Bargello Mrs R E Barr
1995 **6(NH),1(NH),11(NH)**
227 24/2 Duncombe Pa' (R) LAD 3m 6 GS *in tch, rdn 11th, blnd nxt, t.o. & p.u. 13th* P 0

Novice chase winner 95; will struggle to win in points now **10**

DOC-HALLIDAY (Irish) — **I** 409^{P}, **I** 630^{5}

DOCKMAID (Irish) — **I** 469^{F}, **I** 501^{P}, **I** 556^{R}, **I** 581^{P}

DOC LODGE b.m. 10 Doc Marten - Cooling by Tycoon II S Baker
100 16/2 Fakenham (L) HC 2m 5f 110yds 9 G *(bl) ld, hit 5th, hdd after 10th, soon wknd, p.u. before 3 out.* P 0
364 5/3 Leicester (R) HC 2m 1f 12 GS *(bl) alwys rear, t.o. when p.u. 4 out.* P 0
674 30/3 Hereford (R) HC 2m 8 S *(bl) started slowly, f 1st.* F -

1120 20/4 Bangor (L) HC 2 1/2m 110yds 13 S *(bl) prom till f 6th.* F -

Does not stay 3m & totally outclassed in H/Chases 0

DOC SPOT b.g. 6 Doc Marten - Detonate by Derring-Do S J Robinson
1995 F(-),B(-),2(10),3(13),P(0),P(0)

52 4/2 Alnwick (L) MDO 3m 11 G *prom, mstk 9th, blndrd 12th, not rcvr, p.u. nxt* P 0
308 2/3 Great Stain' (L) MDO 3m 12 GS *1st ride, mid-div, wknd 15th, t.o. 3 out* 5 0
407 9/3 Dalston (R) MDO 2 1/2m 13 G *bhnd 6th, mid-div whn f 8th* F -
704 30/3 Tranwell (L) MDO 3m 16 GS *disp 5th, styd prom til wknd 15th, p.u. 2 out* P 0
829 6/4 Stainton (R) MDO 3m 9 GF *mid-div, prog 7th, wknd 4 out* 3 0

Placed three times 95/6 but does not stay & a win looks impossible 10

DOCTER MAC br.m. 9 Strong Gale - Miss Lacemore by Red Alert Neil Allen
1995 **F(NH)**

426 9/3 Upton-On-Se' (R) CON 3m 16 GS *ld frm 10th til hdd & wknd 2 out* 2 16
687 30/3 Chaddesley ' (L) CON 3m 10 G *blnd 1st, ld nxt, clr 6th, hdd apr last, no ext flat* 2 20

Ex-Irish; ran well both times & Confined win over easy 3m likely if fit 97 19

DOCTOR DICK(IRE) b.g. 7 Orchestra - Miss Allright by Candy Cane B Kennedy
1995 U(-),1(11)

35 20/1 Higham (L) RES 3m 16 GF *cls up whn f 2nd* F -
59 10/2 Cottenham (R) RES 3m 9 GS *blnd & u.r. 2nd* U -
105 17/2 Marks Tey (L) RES 3m 11 G *alwys bhnd, 5th & no ch 16th, went poor 3rd last* 3 10
313 2/3 Ampton (R) RES 3m 9 G *pllng, ld 7th til appr 3 out, wknd appr 2 out* 4 11
419 9/3 High Easter (L) RES 3m 10 S *pllng, in tch til outpcd 13th, t.o. & p.u. 2 out* P 0

Maiden winner 95; mistakes, headstrong & outclassed in Restricteds 11

DODGY DEALER(IRE) ch.g. 6 Salluceva - Donna Chimene by Royal Gunner (USA) Gerard Nock
1995 **6(NH),P(NH)**

29 20/1 Barbury Cas' (L) RES 3m 12 GS *prom til wknd 3 out, not disgraced* 5 0
129 17/2 Kingston Bl' (L) MDN 3m 15 GS *(Jt fav) ld 3rd-14th, lft 2nd 3 out, wknd, fin tired* 3 0

Ran reasonably both times but insufficient stamina; finished early; best watched 13

DO DROP IN (Irish) — **I** 220[P], **I** 420[P]
DOHNEY BOY (Irish) — **I** 68[5], **I** 117[P], **I** 243[2], **I** 334[3]
DOLLYBAT b.m. 7 Battle Hymn - Come On Doll by True Song Mrs Carolyn Atyeo
1995 P(0)

278 2/3 Clyst St Ma' (L) CON 3m 9 S *alwys rear, t.o. & p.u. 15th* P 0
534 16/3 Cothelstone (L) MDN 3m 10 G *in tch to 12th, outpcd nxt, no dang aft* 6 0
819 6/4 Charlton Ho' (L) MDN 3m 10 GF *alwys midfld, nvr on terms wth ldrs* 4 0
1129 20/4 Stafford Cr' (R) MDO 3m 11 S *mid-div til 10th, wnt 3rd 3 out, not trbl 1st 2* 3 0
1347 4/5 Holnicote (L) MDO 3m 16 GS *prom early, fdng whn p.u. 3 out* P 0
1495 11/5 Holnicote (L) MDO 3m 11 G *rear til p.u. 15th* P 0
1554 18/5 Bratton Down (L) MDO 3m 16 F *made most til s.u. apr 15th* S -
1638 1/6 Bratton Down (L) MDO 3m 13 G *rear whn hmpd 8th, p.u. nxt, dsmntd* P 0

Well beaten when completing & problems last start to boot 10

DOLLY BLOOM b.m. 8 Crested Lark - Lucky Sandy by St Columbus G B Tarry

236 24/2 Heythrop (R) MDN 3m 13 GS *rear whn f 5th* F -
341 3/3 Heythrop (R) MDN 3m 13 G *mid-div, no ch 13th, p.u. 2 out* P 0
495 16/3 Horseheath (R) MDO 3m 12 GF *mstk 3rd, in tch to 10th, t.o. & p.u. 4 out* P 0
682 30/3 Cottenham (R) MDO 3m 9 GF *w.w.prog to ld aft 3 out,hmpd loose hrs apr last,rallied flt* 2 13
1381 5/5 Dingley (R) MDO 3m 16 GF *(Jt fav) prom,chsd wnr 10th,outpcd 15th,no imp,fin 4th,promoted* 3 11
1599 25/5 Garthorpe (R) MDO 3m 7 G *(fav) w.w. prog 8th, chsd wnr 5 out, blnd nxt, no ch aft* 2 10
1644 2/6 Dingley (R) MDO 3m 16 GF *(fav) lost pl 6th, prog 10th, chsd ldr 2 out, hrd rdn, not qckn* 2 15

Unlucky 4th start but looked less than genuine last start & may struggle to win 14

DOMINANT LADY (Irish) — **I** 120[3], **I** 165[2], **I** 225[P], **I** 515[1]
DONAL'S CHOICE (Irish) — **I** 30[4], **I** 109[2], **I** 191[P]
DONARD SON (Irish) — **I** 255[2]
DONICKMORE (Irish) — **I** 2[5], **I** 53, , **I** 61[2], **I** 114[F]
DONNA (Irish) — **I** 650[F]
DONS PRIDE (Irish) — **I** 207[F]
DON'TCALLMEGEORGE b.g. 5 Lighter - Pennulli by Sir Nulli H J Jarvis

1055 13/4 Penshurst (L) MDO 3m 11 G *schoold in rear, blnd 5th, some prog 10th, p.u. 12th* P 0

Can only do better 0

DONT TELL NELL (Irish) — I 609, , I 653^{P}

DONT WASTE IT (Irish) — I 44^{P}

DOONEAL HERO (Irish) — I 38^{3}, I 111^{3}, I 206^{P}, I 328^{P}

DOON RIVER (Irish) — I 514^{P}

DO POP IN (Irish) — I 636^{1}

DORGAN (Irish) — I 35^{P}, I 213^{U}, I 248^{F}

DORMSTON LAD b.g. 8 Pragmatic - March At Dawn by Nishapour (FR) Mrs B N Hicks

1995 P(0),5(0),4(0),P(0),P(0)

140	17/2	Larkhill	(R)	CON	3m	17	G	*alwys mid-div, wknd 12th, p.u. nxt*	P	0
272	2/3	Parham	(R)	RES	3m	13	GF	*prom til wknd 14th*	6	0
471	10/3	Milborne St'	(L)	MDO	3m	16	G	*alwys mid-div, no ch whn p.u. last*	P	0
651	23/3	Badbury Rin'	(L)	MEM	3m	4	G	*rr, bhnd 10th, ran on frm 15th, kpt on flat*	3	10
997	8/4	Hackwood Pa'	(L)	MDO	3m	11	GF	*ld to 5th, outpcd hlfwy, ran on last 2*	3	11
1164	20/4	Larkhill	(R)	MDN	3m	12	GF	*prom, ld 9-12th, wknd nxt, p.u. 3 out*	P	0

Placed in weak Hackwood Maiden & will need a desperate race to hold any chance 10

DORN RETREAT ch.g. 9 Country Retreat - March Maid by Marmaduke Mrs C M Righton

747	31/3	Upper Sapey	(R)	MDO	3m	11	GS	*25l last whn u.r. last*	U	-
947	8/4	Andoversford	(R)	MDN	3m	11	GF	*hld up,prog to 10l 2nd at 15th, wll btn 3rd whn u.r. last*	U	-

Yet to complete the course from 9 outings 93-6 0

DOUBLE OPPORTUNITY (Irish) — I 269^{P}, I 394^{P}, I 500^{P}

DOUBLE SILK b.g. 12 Dubassoff (USA) - Yellow Silk by Counsel R C Wilkins

1995 **1(40),1(43),3(27),5(24)**

98	12/2	Hereford	(R)	HC	3m 1f 110yds	12	HY	*(fav) ld after 2nd, left clr 2 out, unchal.*	1	33
261	2/3	Warwick	(L)	HC	3 1/4m	5	G	*(fav) ld to 2nd, chsd wnr after, chal from 16th, outpcd from 3 out, eased run-in, t.o..*	2	33
1332	1/5	Cheltenham	(L)	HC	3m 1f 110yds	11	G	*(fav) j.w, made all, drew clr from 3 out, easily.*	1	36

Still high-class H/Chaser; can win decent races if back in 97; G/F-S 36

DOUBLE THE STAKES(USA) b.g. 7 Raise A Man (USA) - Je'da Qua (USA) by Fleet Nasrullah Mrs J M Whitley

1995 **1(NH),3(NH),9(NH)**

134	17/2	Ottery St M'	(L)	CON	3m	12	GS	*alwys prom, ld 8-14th, wknd nxt*	4	0
196	24/2	Lemalla	(R)	CON	3m	14	HY	*t.d.e. rear til prog to chal 3 out, sn wknd, p.u. last*	P	0

Selling chase winner 95 (2m); finished early & unpromising pointer 12

DOUBLE-U-GEE(IRE) b.g. 6 Flash Of Steel - Blink by Dike (USA) F L Matthews

256	29/2	Ludlow	(R)	HC	3m	14	G	*n.j.w., t.o. 10th, p.u. after 12th.*	P	0
1336	1/5	Cheltenham	(L)	HC	2m 110yds	9	G	*well bhnd from 6th, t.o. and f 11th.*	F	-
1580	19/5	Wolverhampt'	(L)	MDO	3m	8	G	*jmpd bdly, sn wll bhnd, t.o. & p.u. aft 10th, dsmntd*	P	0

Silly campaign & a waste of time 0

DOUBTING DONNA gr.m. 10 Tom Noddy - Dewy's Quince by Quorum Mrs D Hughes

153	17/2	Erw Lon	(L)	OPE	3m	15	G	*alwys mid-div, no ch frm 14th*	7	0
351	3/3	Garnons	(L)	OPE	3m	14	GS	*prom til ld 14th-nxt, outpcd frm 3 out, lost 2nd flat*	3	18
384	9/3	Llanfrynach	(R)	OPE	3m	16	GS	*ld to 2nd, sn mid-div, wknd aft 14th*	10	0
768	31/3	Pantyderi	(R)	OPE	3m	10	G	*nvr nrr enough to chal*	6	11
846	6/4	Howick	(L)	OPE	3m	7	GF	*2nd to 10th, wknd rpdly, p.u. 14th*	P	0
1199	21/4	Lydstep	(L)	OPE	3m	5	S	*rear whn b.d. 12th*	B	-
1262	27/4	Pyle	(R)	MEM	3m	6	G	*8s-7/2, 10l 4th at 10th, rdn 14th, styd on to 2nd flat*	2	13
1386	6/5	Pantyderi	(R)	OPE	3m	5	GF	*ld 2nd til aft 15th, prssd wnr aft, no ext flat*	2	19

H/Chase winner 93; missed 95; inconsistent now; Confined just possible in 97; G/F-S 18

DOUCE ECLAIR b.m. 10 Warpath - Sweet Clare by Suki Desu J F Thompson

1995 F(-),4(0),2(10),2(0),P(0),P(0),1(15),4(16)

11	14/1	Cottenham	(R)	LAD	3m	7	G	*ld/disp in clr ld to 9th,ld 14-15th,3rd & btn 3 out,styd on*	2	16
47	4/2	Alnwick	(L)	XX	3m	14	G	*(fav) ld to 3rd, ld 9th till app 3 out, sn wknd*	4	11
536	17/3	Southwell P'	(L)	LAD	3m	9	GS	*mstks in rear, ran on onepcd frm 4 out, nrst fin*	3	13
586	23/3	Wetherby Po'	(L)	LAD	3m	8	S	*cls up til wknd 10th, no dang aft*	6	11
895	6/4	Whittington	(L)	RES	3m	5	F	*chsd ldrs, lost plc 14th, styd on wll frm 2 out*	3	10
1090	14/4	Whitwell-On'	(R)	RES	3m	17	G	*drppd out rear, imprvd 9th, no prog aft, wknd 14th*	8	0
1284	27/4	Easingwold	(L)	RES	3m	14	G	*ld to 4th, sn lost plc, t.o.*	8	0

Maiden winner 95; stable out of form 96; front-runner; may have Restricted chance on easy 3m 97; G-F 15

DOUJAS b.m. 6 Nearly A Hand - Doucement by Cheval Mrs B C Bloomfield

1995 **8(NH),10(NH)**

864	6/4	Larkhill	(R)	MDN 2 1/2m	9	F	*ld in, bhnd whn bldrd & u.r. 1st*	U	-
1291	28/4	Barbury Cas'	(L)	LAD 3m	5	F	*mstks, ld 2-12th, wknd 14th, t.o.*	3	10
1502	11/5	Kingston Bl'	(L)	LAD 3m	7	G	*prom til f 5th*	F	-

Needs to jump better, develop some stamina & stick to Maidens 0

DOVEDON PRINCESS gr.m. 9 Baron Blakeney - Grace Of Langley by Foggy Bell — D Stephens

1995 P(0),3(10),R(-)

201	24/2	Lemalla	(R)	MDO 3m	13	HY	*alwys rear, p.u. 2 out*	P	0
300	2/3	Great Treth'	(R)	MDO 3m	10	G	*in tch, went 3rd apr 2 out, not qckn*	3	13
447	9/3	Haldon	(R)	MDO 3m	13	S	*twrds rear, 10th hlfwy, p.u. 12th*	P	0
718	30/3	Wadebridge	(L)	MDO 3m	11	GF	*in tch,cls 4th hlfwy,mstk 14th,4th nxt til strng burst flat*	2	15
941	8/4	Wadebridge	(L)	MDN 3m	5	F	*(fav) ld/disp til ld 12th, made rest, ran on wll*	1	13
1139	20/4	Flete Park	(R)	RES 3m	14	S	*mid-div, 6th at 10th, bhnd whn p.u. 17th*	P	0
1358	4/5	Flete Park	(R)	RES 3m	8	G	*6th hlfwy, not pace to chal*	4	12
1428	6/5	High Bickin'	(R)	RES 3m	10	G	*prog & ev ch 15th, ran on onepce*	3	15
1528	12/5	Ottery St M'	(L)	RES 3m	10	GF	*bhnd frm 13th, t.o.*	7	0
1634	1/6	Bratton Down	(L)	INT 3m	15	G	*in tch to hlfwy, bhnd frm 12th, t.o.*	9	0
1649	8/6	Umberleigh	(L)	RES 3m	14	GF	*rear, mstk 7th, wll bhnd 12th, p.u. 14th*	P	0

Won slowly-run Maiden; likes Wadebridge but inconsistent & fortune needed for another win 12

DOVEHILL gr.g. 10 Pragmatic - Arconist by Welsh Pageant — D Rhys-Jones

1995 P(0),1(12),4(14),3(10),9(0),P(0)

247	25/2	Charing	(L)	MEM 3m	7	GS	*mstks, lost tch 15th, lft 3rd by dfctns*	3	0

Maiden winner 95; finished early 96 & best watched now 11

DOWHATYOUHAVETODO (Irish) — **I** 418^{F}, **I** 478^{3}, **I** 562^{F}, **I** 601,

DOWNHILL RACER b.m. 6 Grey Desire - Daring Delight by Daring March — Mrs J Barber

1995 3(0),P(0)

553	17/3	Erw Lon	(L)	MDN 3m	3	GS	*(fav) made all, unchal*	1	10
770	31/3	Pantyderi	(R)	RES 3m	9	G	*tried to ref 4th, u.r. 6th*	U	-
980	8/4	Lydstep	(L)	RES 3m	11	G	*f 6th*	F	-
1160	20/4	Llanwit Maj'	(R)	RES 3m	12	GS	*alwys rear, no ch 11th, p.u. 14th*	P	0
1267	27/4	Pyle	(R)	RES 3m	7	G	*prom in chsng grp til 9th, wknd 11th, p.u. 14th*	P	0
1490	11/5	Erw Lon	(L)	RES 3m	6	F	*in rear whn p.u. 11th*	P	0

Won joke race run at a crawl; downhill since; no future prospects 0

DOWN THE MINE b.g. 10 Le Moss - Zauditu by Menelek — R T Baimbridge

1995 1(22),1(22),1(23)

27	20/1	Barbury Cas'	(L)	LAD 3m	15	GS	*(fav) j.w. made all, ran on strngly apr last*	1	26
161	17/2	Weston Park	(L)	LAD 3m	11	G	*(fav) made all, ran on well whn prssd frm 4 out*	1	27
1003	9/4	Upton-On-Se'	(R)	LAD 3m	4	F	*(fav) ld, shkn up & hdd app last, eased whn btn*	2	22
1172	20/4	Chaddesley '	(L)	LAD 3m	3	G	*(fav) j.w. ld, 5l up aft 17th, jnd & no ext frm 2 out*	2	25

Lightly raced & very useful; top stable; jumps well; sure to win more; G-S, not Firm 27

DOWNTOWN br.g. 10 Good Thyne (USA) - Gentle Down (USA) by Naskra (USA) — R F Rimmer

293	2/3	Eaton Hall	(R)	INT 3m	11	G	*t.o. 8th, p.u. 14th*	P	0
458	9/3	Eyton-On-Se'	(L)	INT 3m	11	G	*ld/disp 5th, ld 6th-9th, 2nd & bd mstk 12th, p.u. 2 out*	P	0
735	31/3	Sudlow Farm	(R)	MEM 3m	7	G	*ld to 5th, grdly wknd, t.o. frm 13th*	5	0

Beaten miles only completion & no hopes now 0

DO YOU KNOW(IRE) b.m. 6 Creative Plan (USA) - Corrib Agreement by Lucifer (USA) — P J Millington

1995 P(0),P(0),U(-)

13	14/1	Cottenham	(R)	MDO 3m	10	G	*bhnd whn jmpd slwly 8th & 9th, p.u. nxt*	P	0

Yet to complete the course & finished 1st weekend 96 0

DRAGON'S BLOOD(USA) ch.g. 12 Nijinsky (CAN) - Rare Mint (USA) by Key To The Mint (USA) — N Lowe

1995 P(0),5(12)

427	9/3	Upton-On-Se'	(R)	OPE 3m	6	GS	*lost tch ldrs 12th, p.u. 14th*	P	0

Flat winner 87; rarely runs now & non-stayer 0

DRAGONS LADY b.m. 7 Dragon Palace (USA) - Lady Hamshire by Proverb — J S Warner

1995 **3(NH),8(NH),4(NH),3(NH),5(NH),5(NH)**

143	17/2	Larkhill	(R)	MDO 3m	14	G	*prom whn u.r. 4th*	U	-
221	24/2	Newtown	(L)	MDN 3m	12	GS	*ld to 10th, wknd 12th, t.o.*	4	0
796	2/4	Heythrop	(R)	MDN 3m	11	F	*ld to 9th, prom aft, ev ch 3 out, no ext frm nxt*	4	13
947	8/4	Andoversford	(R)	MDN 3m	11	GF	*(fav) hld up mid-div, prog 10th, ev ch 15th, outpcd*	2	11
1161	20/4	Llanwit Maj'	(R)	MDO 3m	15	GS	*cls up, ld 8th, 6l clr 2 out, hit last, pushd out, comf*	1	15

Gradually improving & beat subsequent winner when scoring; Restricted possible in 97; G/S-G/F 16

DRAKEWRATH(IRE) b.g. 6 Good Thyne (USA) - Velpol by Polyfoto R A Bartlett

115 17/2 Lanark (R) MDO 3m 8 GS *(Jt fav) in tch, 2nd frm 10th, ld apr 3 out, comf* 1 13
319 2/3 Corbridge (R) RES 3m 16 GS *(fav) mid-div whn f 14th* F -
501 16/3 Lanark (R) RES 3m 12 G *(fav) alwys handy, slght ld apr 3 out, hld on well* 1 17

Progressive youngster; won modest races; ran in jumping 96; should upgrade if pointing in 97 19

DRAWN'N'QUARTERED b.g. 9 Decent Fellow - Pencil Lady by Bargello Mrs E W Wilson
1995 3(16),8(0),P(0)

169 18/2 Market Rase' (L) CON 3m 15 GF *hld up, prog 3 out, chsd ldng pair apr last, onepcd flat* 3 20
327 3/3 Market Rase' (L) CON 3m 15 G *f 2nd* F -
632 23/3 Market Rase' (L) CON 3m 10 GF *(fav) s.s. 7th 6 out, ran on past btn horses* 4 15

Dual winner 94; disappointing since & frustrating now; may surprise; G-S 17

DREAM FLIGHT ch.m. 5 Nicholas Bill - Run'n Fly by Deep Run Mrs Lorraine Lomax

740 31/3 Sudlow Farm (R) MDN 3m 16 G *bhnd til p.u. 10th* P 0
1029 13/4 Alpraham (R) MDO 3m 8 GS *bhnd, prog 14th, 3rd 2 out, nrst fin* 3 13
1364 4/5 Gisburn (R) MDO 3m 11 G *(fav) 5/2-6/4, ld 7th, clr 3 out, ran on strngly* 1 16

Landed the gamble impressively; stays well; should progress; Restricted likely 97; Soft 18

DREAM GALE (Irish) — I 510B, I 5452, I 5754, I 6311, I 6486
DREAMING IDLE (Irish) — I 371P, I 485P, I 5551, I 5804
DREAM PACKET b.g. 6 Pablond - Glorious Jane by Hittite Glory A Howland Jackson
1995 F(-),U(-),1(13)

12 14/1 Cottenham (R) RES 3m 12 G *mid-div, in tch til outpcd apr 14th* 9 0
95 11/2 Ampton (R) RES 3m 11 GF *trckd ldrs going wll 9th, ld 3 out, clr nxt, imprssv* 1 20
310 2/3 Ampton (R) CON 3m 13 G *wth ldrs, ev ch 17th, no ex und press frm 3 out* 4 19
778 31/3 Penshurst (L) INT 3m 6 GS *(fav) hld up, imprvd to ld 12th, hdd brfly 3 out, drew clr last* 1 20
934 8/4 Marks Tey (L) CON 3m 6 G *(fav) hld up, prog 8th, mstks 12 & 13th, ld apr last, rdn out* 1 20

Improving & won 4 of last 6; stays; should upgrade to Opens in 97; G/F-G/S 22

DRESS HIRE (Irish) — I 4812, I 559F
DREWITTS DANCER b.g. 9 Balboa - Vermillon (FR) by Aureole Mrs A A Hawkins
1995 U(-),U(-),P(0),U(-),F(-),1(14),**2(16)**

592 23/3 Parham (R) MEM 3m 4 GS *pllng,cls up,ld aft 8th,lft dist clr 13th,hacked round* 1 13
1054 13/4 Penshurst (L) RES 3m 8 G *chsng grp,lft in ld 12th,clr 14th,wknd rpdly 3 out,hdd nxt* 4 0
1122 20/4 Stratford (L) HC 2m 5f 110yds 16 GF *nvr near to chal.* 7 13

Maiden winner 95; won joke race 96; does not stay but may find easy Restricted 97 14

DRIBS AND DRABS (Irish) — I 195P, I 224P, I 348P
DRIMEEN (Irish) — I 190P, I 346P, I 3874, I 5161, I 5935, I 629U
DRIMINAMORE (Irish) — I 79P, I 156P
DROMGURRIHY LAD (Irish) — I 6P, I 209P
DROMHANA (Irish) — I 252, I 1301, I 194P, I 2211, I 3441, I 4223
DROMINARGLE (Irish) — I 334P
DROMIN CHAT(IRE) b.g. 8 Miner's Lamp - Coolishall Again by Push On R J Rowsell

600 23/3 Howick (L) RES 3m 14 S *3rd to 6th, wknd & p.u. 12th* P 0
695 30/3 Llanvapley (L) RES 3m 13 GS *ld to 6th, wknd rpdly, p.u. 9th* P 0

No signs of stamina & season lasted a week 0

DROMIN LEADER b.g. 11 Crash Course - Astral Fairy by Prefairy J M Turner
1995 4(10),2(22),1(22),**3(19)**

347 3/3 Higham (L) LAD 3m 10 G *prom to 7th, lost plc & bhnd nxt, kpt on frm 2 out* 3 16
678 30/3 Cottenham (R) LAD 3m 6 GF *j.w. chsd ldr, ld 12th-3 out, ld agn brfly nxt, kpt on flat* 2 23
907 8/4 Fakenham (L) HC 3m 110yds 11 G *cl up when u.r. 10th.* U -
1147 20/4 Higham (L) LAD 3m 9 F *ld 3-4th & frm 10th, mstk 2 out, clr last, rdn out flat* 1 23
1546 18/5 Fakenham (L) HC 3m 110yds 13 G *lding gp, chsd ldr 13th to 3 out, outpcd from next.* 4 17

Fair Ladies horse at best; needs easy 3m; can win again in right conditions at 12; G-F 22

DROMIN PRIDE (Irish) — I 44P, I 72F, I 153P, I 246, , I 333P, I 441P, I 4733, I 5421, I 6051
DROMLAR (Irish) — I 5005, I 543P
DROMOD MAGIC (Irish) — I 9P, I 5653
DROMROE DANTE (Irish) — I 380F
DROMROE LADY (Irish) — I 309P

DROP THE ACT (Irish) — I 172^{2}, I 300^{F}, I 429^{3}, I 495^{1}, I 586^{1}

DROUM ROSS (Irish) — I 52^{3}, I 199^{P}

DRUID BLUE gr.g. 14 Padro - Beauty's Pal by Charlie's Pal — Miss E J Kessler

871	6/4	Higher Kilw'	(L)	RES	3m	9	GF	*slght ld to 12th, lost plc steadily, bhnd & p.u. 3 out*	P	0
1139	20/4	Flete Park	(R)	RES	3m	14	S	*mstk 2nd, nvr dang, bhnd whn p.u. 14th*	P	0

No longer of any account 0

DRUID'S BROOK b.g. 7 Meadowbrook - Struide by Guide — Mrs D B Johnstone

862	6/4	Alnwick	(L)	MDN	3m	8	GF	*w.w., hdwy 10th, ld 3 out, sn drew clr, imprv further*	1	16
1353	4/5	Mosshouses	(L)	RES	3m	11	GS	*(fav) hld up, prog 9th, ld 14th-nxt, ld apr 2 out, sn clr, imprssv*	1	21

Ideal start & shows right attributes; stays; should do well in 97 22

DRUID'S LODGE b.g. 9 Wolverlife - Taralote by Tarboosh (USA) — D J Lay

1995 F(-),3(10),F(-),3(16),2(16),3(15),3(10),2(17)

12	14/1	Cottenham	(R)	RES	3m	12	G	*rear div, kpt on frm 16th, nvr nrr*	5	15
96	11/2	Ampton	(R)	XX	3m	11	GF	*w.w. prog 8th, rdn to ld 17th, hrd rdn 2 out, hld on flat*	1	16
310	2/3	Ampton	(R)	CON	3m	13	G	*in tch, rddn 15th, blnd nxt, kpt on onpcd aft*	7	17
422	9/3	High Easter	(L)	INT	3m	3	S	*trkd ldrs, went 2nd 16th, rddn 2 out, sn btn*	2	15
676	30/3	Cottenham	(R)	INT	3m	13	GF	*mid-div, effrt 3 out, styd on well apr last, just hld*	2	20
831	6/4	Marks Tey	(L)	CON	3m	6	G	*hld up in tch, prog 15th, chal 2 out, ran on last, just hld*	2	20
1148	20/4	Higham	(L)	CON	3m	5	F	*mstks, in tch, 4th whn u.r. bnd apr 16th*	U	-
1323	28/4	Fakenham P-'	(L)	OPE	3m	8	G	*alwys abt same plc, onepcd und pres frm 3 out*	5	16

Improved 96; consistent but onepaced; 2 wins, 11 places last 23 starts; may find Confined; G/F-S 19

DRUMARD(IRE) b.g. 8 Fidel - Miss Maraise by Grange Melody — N Frankham

1995 1(17),**3(10)**,11(0)

98	12/2	Hereford	(R)	HC	3m 1f 110yds	12	HY	*ld till after 1st, remained prom till wknd 4 out, left poor 2nd 2 out.*	2	15
365	5/3	Leicester	(R)	HC	3m	10	GS	*waited with, in tch, outpcd 14th, btn and blnd 4 out, p.u. next.*	P	0

Restricted winner 95; short season 96 & outclassed; could win Confined if fit 97; G-Hy 18

DRUMBANES PET ch.g. 7 Tina's Pet - Confetti Copse by Town And Country — Mrs C Lawrence

1995 5(0),5(0),P(0)

446	9/3	Haldon	(R)	MDO	3m	13	S	*alwys in tch, ev ch til onepcd frm 3 out*	4	10
558	17/3	Ottery St M'	(L)	MDO	3m	9	G	*bhnd, plgd on frm 4 out, not trbl 1st pair*	3	0
733	31/3	Little Wind'	(R)	MDO	3m	13	GS	*hdwy frm rear aft 14th, tk 3rd aft 3 out, fin tired*	3	0

Safer now but beaten distance when 3rd & not enough stamina; luck needed for a win 11

DRUMCAIRN (Irish) — I 26^{6}, I 134^{1}, I 218^{U}, I 339^{1}

DRUMCEVA b or br.g. 10 Salluceva - Drumvision by Brave Invader (USA) — M S Wilesmith

1995 7(10),2(0),2(18),4(15),P(0),1(19)

24	20/1	Barbury Cas'	(L)	XX	3m	12	GS	*f 1st*	F	-
216	24/2	Newtown	(L)	LAD	3m	13	GS	*chsd ldrs, 6th & outpcd whn blnd & u.r. 12th*	U	-
351	3/3	Garnons	(L)	OPE	3m	14	GS	*ld 7th-12th, outpcd aft nxt*	6	0
744	31/3	Upper Sapey	(R)	OPE	3m	5	GS	*ran out & u.r. apr 2nd*	r	-
836	6/4	Maisemore P'	(L)	MEM	3m	7	GF	*mstk 2nd, trckd ldrs til ld 8th, 12l clr 13th, unchall*	1	20
1043	13/4	Bitterley	(L)	OPE	3m	9	G	*disp 9-10th, rdn & lost plc 13th, chal 3 out-nxt, blnd last*	2	18
1221	24/4	Brampton Br'	(R)	LAD	3m	6	G	*chsd ldr, hit 12th, 2l 2nd nxt, chal whn f 16th*	F	-

Cantered home in Members but makes mistakes & problems for novice rider; may win again; G-F 19

DRUMCOLLIHER ch.g. 9 Bustomi - Red House Lady by Manor Farm Boy — R L Black

1128	20/4	Stafford Cr'	(R)	RES	3m	17	S	*sn last, t.o. & p.u. 12th*	P	0
1424	6/5	High Bickin'	(R)	MEM	3m	4	G	*ld/disp til wknd 15th, sn btn*	3	0
1555	18/5	Bratton Down	(L)	MDO	3m	13	F	*mid-div whn u.r. 4th*	U	-
1593	25/5	Mounsey Hil'	(R)	MDO	3m	11	G	*disp to 8th, chsd ldr apr 2 out, kpt on flat*	2	14
1651	8/6	Umberleigh	(L)	MDO	3m	11	GF	*mstks, rear, gd prog 13th, rdn & outpcd 3 out, kpt on*	3	10

Ex-Irish; late start 96 but showed enough to suggest a win possible; Good 14

DRUMLINE CASTLE (Irish) — I 122^{F}, I 148^{P}, I 205^{2}, I 424^{P}

DRUMORGAN (Irish) — I 281^{S}

DRUMRIGA (Irish) — I 341^{P}

DRUMRIZA (Irish) — I 394^{F}

DRY HIGHLINE (Irish) — I 322^{2}

DRY HILL LAD b.g. 5 Cruise Missile - Arctic Lee by Arctic Judge — David Ibbotson

78	11/2	Wetherby Po'	(L)	OPE	3m	10	GS	*alwys rear, p.u. 4 out*	P	0
172	18/2	Market Rase'	(L)	RES	3m	9	GF	*chsd ldrs, rdn to chal 2 out, wknd rpdly apr last, fin tired*	2	12
635	23/3	Market Rase'	(L)	RES	3m	8	GF	*(Jt fav) overjmpd & f 1st*	F	-
727	31/3	Garthorpe	(R)	MDO	3m	12	G	*sttld last,prog frm 12th, ran on frm 2 out, nrst fin,improve*	3	11

Strange campaign & finished when looking imminent winner; good enough for Maiden if fit 97 15

DUAL OR BUST (Irish) — I 114^{P}, I 213^{2}

DUBALEA b.g. 13 Dubassoff (USA) - Thirkleby Kate Vii by Bivouac — P J Millington

395	9/3	Garthorpe	(R)	OPE	3m	7	G	*cls 2nd til mstk 10th, wknd rpdly, p.u. 6 out*	P	0
537	17/3	Southwell P'	(L)	OPE	3m	7	GS	*ld to 9th, wknd rpdly, p.u. 12th*	P	0
902	6/4	Dingley	(R)	OPE	3m	4	GS	*ld to 11th, wknd qckly, t.o. 5 out, fin 4th, promoted*	3	0
1024	13/4	Brocklesby '	(L)	OPE	3m	6	GF	*3rd to 8th, fdd, t.o. 5th 6 out, p.u. 4 out*	P	0
1192	21/4	Sandon	(L)	CON	3m	11	G	*cls 3rd at 7th, lost tch 12th, no ch aft*	5	0
1303	28/4	Southwell P'	(L)	CON	3m	7	GF	*mid-div, p.u. apr 12th, dead*	P	0

Dead 0

DUBATA b.g. 10 Dubassoff (USA) - Desiderata by Dairialatan — R Winslade

1995 1(14),7(12),5(15)

528	16/3	Cothelstone	(L)	MEM	3m	8	G	*w.w. prog 11th, 4th & blnd 14th, sn btn, p.u. 2 out*	P	0
990	8/4	Kingston St'	(R)	OPE	3m	6	F	*j.w. prog to cls 2nd 12th, ev ch til outpcd aft 15th*	2	20

Maiden winner 95; lightly raced; ran well last start; could win Restricted if fit 97 17

DUBIT b.g. 11 Dubassoff (USA) - Flippit by Dairialatan — R Winslade

1995 2(22),**U(-),3(27),2(23),2(24),1(30),1(31),3(29)**

260	1/3	Newbury	(L)	HC	3m	6	GS	*ld to 14th, rallied and kept on from 2 out.*	3	24
370	7/3	Wincanton	(R)	HC	3m 1f 110yds	5	GF	*ld to 14th, 3rd when p.u. before 17th.*	P	0
1584	24/5	Towcester	(R)	HC	3m 1f	11	GS	*held up, hdwy 12th, soon pushed along, styd on one pace but no ch after 4 out.*	4	21
1631	1/6	Stratford	(L)	HC	3 1/2m	14	GF	*(vis) chsd ldrs, wknd rpdly and p.u. before 4 out.*	P	0

Dual H/Chase winner 95; interrupted season 96 & looked in trouble last start; best watched; Firm 23

DUBLIN HILL (Irish) — I 8^{2}, I 56^{2}, I 71^{1}

DUCHESS OF PADUA (Irish) — I 24^{1}, I 44^{3}, I 82^{U}, I 141^{P}, I 202^{U}, I 246^{3}, I 295^{P}, I 468^{2}, I 512^{3}

DUCHESS OF TUBBER(IRE) b.m. 8 Buckskin (FR) - Unforgetabubble by Menelek — R J S Linne

1995 **6(NH),6(NH),3(NH),7(NH)**

67	10/2	Great Treth'	(R)	LAD	3m	11	S	*nvr a fctr, p.u. aft 14th*	P	0
197	24/2	Lemalla	(R)	LAD	3m	13	HY	*wll in rear till ran past tired horses*	4	14
716	30/3	Wadebridge	(L)	LAD	3m	6	GF	*prog 12th, cls 3rd 14th, ld 3 out, pshd out, ran on gamely*	1	20
940	8/4	Wadebridge	(L)	LAD	3m	4	F	*2nd best frm start, nvr engh to chal*	2	22
1382	6/5	Exeter	(R)	HC	2m 7f 110yds	8	GF	*joined wnr 10th, ev ch 4 out, one pace from next.*	3	22

Winning chaser; stays; won weak race but ran well last start & should win again; G-F 22

DUCKY POOL(IRE) b.g. 6 Cataldi - Good Court by Takawalk II — Capt T A Forster

1116	17/4	Hockworthy	(L)	MDO	3m	9	GS	*(fav) mstk 4th, trckd ldrds, cls 4th whn bdly hmprd 13th & p.u.*	P	0
1280	27/4	Bratton Down	(L)	MDO	3m	14	GF	*w.w. prog 14th, 3rd & chal whn u.r. flat, dead*	U	-

Dead 13

DUIRSE DAIRSE (Irish) — I 19^{F}, I 33^{F}, I 84, , I 423^{2}, I 531^{P}

DUKE OF HADES (Irish) — I 34^{F}

DUKE OF IMPNEY b.g. 9 Roscoe Blake - Top Secret by Manacle — Peter Saville

1995 B(-),P(0),U(-),3(0),F(-),6(0),U(-)

25	20/1	Barbury Cas'	(L)	OPE	3m	14	GS	*alwys bhnd, blnd 8th, t.o. & p.u. 14th*	P	0
159	17/2	Weston Park	(L)	CON	3m	22	G	*alwys mid-div, no dang*	8	0
459	9/3	Eyton-On-Se'	(L)	OPE	3m	11	G	*ld to 12th, grd wknd frm 4 out*	6	0
567	17/3	Wolverhampt'	(L)	MEM	3m	4	GS	*2nd frm 8-15th, wknd rpdly*	3	0
1028	13/4	Alpraham	(R)	MEM	3m	5	GS	*rider lost irons 1st, veered lft & ran out 2nd*	r	-
1154	20/4	Whittington	(L)	OPE	3m	7	G	*bhnd, 4th 3 out, styd on wll frm nxt*	3	15
1230	27/4	Weston Park	(L)	CON	3m	7	G	*rear early, cls order 13th, unable to qckn frm 3 out*	3	16
1422	6/5	Eyton-On-Se'	(L)	CON	3m	3	GF	*in tch, ld 5-6th, outpcd frm 13th, ran on frm 2 out*	3	0
1535	16/5	Aintree	(L)	HC	3m 1f	11	GF	*held up, hdwy into midfield when f 12th.*	F	-

Ran well late season but beaten in last 21 outings & likely to extend the sequence 14

DUKE'S CASTLE (Irish) — I 46^{2}

DUKES CASTLE (Irish) — I 2^{P}, I 74^{1}, I 313^{P}

DUKES SON ch.g. 9 The Parson - Dukes Darling by Duky — D P Smith

22	20/1	Barbury Cas'	(L)	XX	3m	19	GS	*rear, prog 13th, kpt on frm 2 out, nrst fin*	3	16
337	3/3	Heythrop	(R)	OPE	3m	10	G	*prom til lost plc 10th, wknd 14th, t.o. & p.u. last*	P	0
638	23/3	Siddington	(L)	CON	3m	16	S	*hld up, bhnd, ran on wll frm 15th, nvr nrr*	3	14

Novice-ridden; not disgraced twice but finished early; best watched 16

DUKES TOWN (Irish) — I 518^{P}

DUKY RIVER (Irish) — I 53^{F}, I 114^{P}

DULA MODEL b.m. 8 Latest Model - Mandula by Mandamus — J E Fear

1995 P(0),P(0),r(-),P(0)

280	2/3	Clyst St Ma'	(L)	RES 3m	11	S	*alwys mid-div, lost tch 13th, p.u. nxt*	P	0
470	10/3	Milborne St'	(L)	MDO 3m	18	G	*plld hrd, ld 4th til u.r. nxt*	U	-
1349	4/5	Holnicote	(L)	MDO 3m	8	GS	*ld 8-9th, sn fdd, p.u. 13th*	P	0
1396	6/5	Cotley Farm	(L)	MDO 3m	11	GF	*mid-div whn blndrd & u.r. aft 3rd*	U	-
1554	18/5	Bratton Down	(L)	MDO 3m	16	F	*rear whn mstk 7th, 10th hlfwy, bhnd whn u.r. last*	U	-
1592	25/5	Mounsey Hil'	(R)	MDO 3m	9	G	*hld up rear, ran off course apr 5th*	r	-
1637	1/6	Bratton Down	(L)	MDO 3m	11	G	*trckd ldrs til f 11th*	F	-

Yet to complete the course in 12 outings 94-6 0

DUMONT LADY (Irish) — I 66^{3}

DUNAMASE DANDY (Irish) — I 229^{P}, I 349^{1}

DUNBEACON (Irish) — I 154^{P}, I 416^{P}

DUN BELLE (Irish) — I 26^{P}, I 89^{1}, I 160^{1}

DUNBOY CASTLE(IRE) b.g. 8 Carlingford Castle - Many Miracles by Le Moss — Miss Gi Chown

310	2/3	Ampton	(R)	CON 3m	13	G	*ld 4th, made rest, blnd 17th, styd on strngly frm 2 out*	1	22
421	9/3	High Easter	(L)	LAD 3m	5	S	*(fav) cls up, pshd along & hit 15th, ev ch 2 out,hld whn u.r. last*	U	-
777	31/3	Penshurst	(L)	LAD 3m	7	GS	*trckd ldrs, 4th final ctt, ran on wll frm 3 out to ld flat*	1	23
1099	14/4	Guilsborough	(L)	LAD 3m	9	G	*(fav) trckd ldrs, ld 16th, clr 2 out, comf*	1	21
1324	28/4	Fakenham P-'	(L)	LAD 3m	6	G	*(fav) disp ld til blnd & u.r. 11th*	U	-
1401	6/5	Northaw	(L)	LAD 3m	4	F	*(fav) ld til u.r. 8th*	U	-

Winning Irish chaser; decent Ladies horse; unbeaten when completing; can win again; F-G/S 23

DUNCAHA HERO (Irish) — I 88^{3}, I 133^{2}, I 166^{P}, I 268^{P}, I 485,

DUNCAN b.g. 11 Cut Above - Tristan Du Cunha (USA) by Sir Ivor — C R Saunders

1995 **2(26),2(30),2(26),4(16),2(27),1(29)**

100	16/2	Fakenham	(L)	HC 2m 5f 110yds	9	G	*well pld, chsd wnr 12th, ran on one pace from 3 out.*	3	24

Fair H/Chaser; best under 3m; disappeared early 96 & may find a win at 12 hard to achieve; G-S 26

DUNCANS DREAM b.g. 11 Ayyabaan - Clifton Frolic by Ballynockan — Ms C Wilson

1995 U(-),P(0)

109	17/2	Lanark	(R)	MEM 3m	5	GS	*mod 2nd frm 9th, no imp whn lft clr last*	1	0
498	16/3	Lanark	(R)	CON 3m	10	G	*sn bhnd, some late prog, nvr dang*	5	0
754	31/3	Lockerbie	(R)	RES 3m	8	G	*sn strggLng in rear, p.u. 3 out*	P	0

Lucky in a joke race & of no account now 0

DUNDEE PRINCE(NZ) ch.g. 8 Defecting Dancer - Camelot Queen (NZ) by Danseur Etoile (FR) — Nicholas Alexander

49	4/2	Alnwick	(L)	OPE 3m	14	G	*s.v.s., prog frm hlfwy, disp 4th whn f 13th*	F	-
500	16/3	Lanark	(R)	OPE 3m	6	G	*reluc to race, abt 2 fences bhnd by 4th, p.u. 13th*	P	0
612	23/3	Friars Haugh	(L)	OPE 3m	8	G	*s.s. 8l bhnd ldr whn f 13th*	F	-
1085	14/4	Friars Haugh	(L)	OPE 3m	6	F	*reluc to race, ref 1st*	R	-

Able but horrible under Rules & repeated antics in points; not worth persevering with 0

DUNKEL (Irish) — I 40^{P}, I 88^{P}, I 124^{2}, I 155^{4}, I 296^{P}

DUNKITT LADY (Irish) — I 650^{P}

DUNLOUGHAN ch.g. 11 Torus - Polrevagh by Bargello — Peter H Neal

1995 P(13)

438	9/3	Newton Brom'	(R)	MDN 3m	10	GS	*mid-div, prog 13th, 2nd apr 2 out, styd on*	2	10
642	23/3	Siddington	(L)	RES 3m	15	S	*disp ld 3rd-6th, wknd 14th, p.u. 2 out*	P	0
890	6/4	Kimble	(L)	MDN 3m	11	GF	*mid-div, prog to ld 13-15th, wknd rpdly aft 3 out, p.u. last*	P	0

Very lightly raced & unlikely to achieve much at 12 10

DUNLUCE CASTLE (Irish) — I 175^{P}

DUNMOON LADY (Irish) — I 64^{P}, I 143^{P}, I 522, , I 575^{2}

DUNTIME br.g. 12 Reformed Character - Dunreekann by Fidalgo — Mrs S Gray

325	3/3	Market Rase'	(L)	LAD 3m	6	G	*jmpd rght, ld to 10th, prom til outpcd apr 14th*	4	16
633	23/3	Market Rase'	(L)	LAD 3m	10	GF	*(Jt fav) trckd ldrs, mstk 6 out, 3rd nxt, ran on onepcd*	3	17
1132	20/4	Hornby Cast'	(L)	LAD 3m	9	G	*p.u. bef 1st, rstrtd 10 fences bhnd wnr, p.u. agn 3rd*	P	0
1283	27/4	Easingwold	(L)	LAD 3m	10	G	*trckd ldr, disp 7th, ld nxt, qcknd 2 out, ran on strngly*	1	22
1449	6/5	Witton Cast'	(R)	LAD 3m	10	G	*(fav) ld til jmp rght 4th, wknd 5th, p.u. nxt (broke down)*	P	0

Missed 95; Fair Ladies horse at best but real problems last start & may be finished now 21

DUNTREE ch.g. 11 Day Is Done - Bay Tree (FR) by Relko — C J Macmillan

402	9/3	Dalston	(R)	XX	3m	13	G	*prom early, t.o. frm 11th, p.u. nxt*	P	0
500	16/3	Lanark	(R)	OPE	3m	6	G	*chsd wnr frm 12th, no real imp*	2	15
912	8/4	Tranwell	(L)	OPE	3m	8	GF	*mid-div whn f 3rd, dead*	F	-

Dead 15

DUPREY (Irish) — **I** 170^{3}, **I** 214^{1}, **I** 298^{B}, **I** 338^{2}

DUQUES b.m. 9 Duky - Golden Mela by Golden Love — I Sinton

1995 P(0),5(0),2(13),3(0),4(0)

264	2/3	Didmarton	(L)	INT	3m	12	G	*cls up til p.u. 9th*	P	0
477	10/3	Tweseldown	(R)	MDO	3m	15	G	*n.j.w. sn rear, t.o. 10th, p.u. 14th*	P	0
947	8/4	Andoversford	(R)	MDN	3m	11	GF	*in tch early, wknd, rear whn p.u. 15th*	P	0
1217	24/4	Andoversford	(R)	MDO	3m	16	G	*rr, prog & rmndrs 12th, no hdwy frm 15th*	7	0
1511	12/5	Maisemore P'	(L)	MDO	3m	14	F	*mstk 3rd, mid-div, prog 12th, 3rd 2 out,lft 2nd last, kpt on*	2	13

Some ability but non-stayer; only one flash of form 96; may strike lucky eventually 12

DURBO b.g. 12 Bustino - Durun by Run The Gantlet (USA) — Mrs E J Champion

1995 2(16),U(-),B(-)

250	25/2	Charing	(L)	LAD	3m	12	GS	*trckd ldrs, chal 2 out, ld last, rdn out*	1	19
421	9/3	High Easter	(L)	LAD	3m	5	S	*ld to 10th, disp ld 15th to 3 out, wknd*	3	14
572	17/3	Detling	(L)	LAD	3m	10	GF	*alwys prom, mstk 7th, 3rd 2 out, wknd last*	4	11
812	6/4	Charing	(L)	LAD	3m	6	F	*alwys prom, jmpd rght, effrt apr 4 out, 4th & btn 2 out*	3	18
1297	28/4	Bexhill	(R)	LAD	3m	7	F	*ld 4th, hdd 15th, chal 2 out, no ext flat*	3	15

Won 3 Ladies 94; always goes well fresh; 1st time out best chance of a win at 13; F-G/S 18

DURHAM HORNET ch.g. 9 Import - Salira by Double Jump — Mrs J Horner

1995 P(0),P(0),4(14),1(15),1(20),1(21)

306	2/3	Great Stain'	(L)	INT	3m	12	GS	*ld 1st til jnd 15th, disp aft til wknd apr last*	3	16
409	9/3	Charm Park	(L)	CON	3m	11	G	*ld to 11th, in tch 3rd 3 out, no extr nxt*	3	18
1000	9/4	Wetherby	(L)	HC	3m 110yds	10	G	*chsd ldrs early, wknd before 10th, t.o. when p.u. before 4 out.*	P	0
1092	14/4	Whitwell-On'	(R)	CON	3m	10	G	*disp to 5 out, wknd rpdly, t.o. & p.u. 2 out*	P	0
1132	20/4	Hornby Cast'	(L)	LAD	3m	9	G	*p.u. bef 1st, rider thought false start*	P	0
1283	27/4	Easingwold	(L)	LAD	3m	10	G	*chsd ldrs, mstk 2nd, outpcd 10th, sn no dang*	5	17
1449	6/5	Witton Cast'	(R)	LAD	3m	10	G	*outpcd in midfld, nvr a dang*	6	10

Won three in 95 but disappointing & struggled in 96; may find another Confined; G-F 18

DURZI b.g. 11 High Line - Sookera (USA) by Roberto (USA) — Mrs R E Walker

683	30/3	Chaddesley '	(L)	MEM	3m	17	G	*chsd ldrs to 7th, wknd 10th, p.u. 13th*	P	0
942	8/4	Andoversford	(R)	MEM	3m	8	GF	*chsd ldrs, cls 2nd at 16th, wknd rpdly, p.u. 2 out*	P	0
1318	28/4	Bitterley	(L)	XX	3m	8	G	*trckd ldrs, cls 2nd at 13th, ev ch nxt, wknd 15th*	4	10
1618	27/5	Chaddesley '	(L)	CON	3m	14	GF	*s.s. sn mid-div, wknd rpdly & p.u. 14th*	P	0

Lightly race dnow & does not stay 10

DUSKY DAY br.g. 10 Strong Gale - Arctic Rhapsody by Bargello — C J Hitchings

263	2/3	Didmarton	(L)	INT	3m	18	G	*wll in rear til prog frm 14th, nvr nrr, improve*	4	12
428	9/3	Upton-On-Se'	(R)	RES	3m	17	GS	*last hlfwy, steady run 14th, nvr nrr*	5	11
525	16/3	Larkhill	(R)	RES	3m	7	G	*ld/disp, slght ld whn lft clr last*	1	19
792	2/4	Heythrop	(R)	LAD	3 3/4m	7	F	*(fav) n.j.w. rear,prog to ld 15-17th,ran on agn flat,just faild*	3	17

Maiden winner 94; missed 95; improved but hated ground last start; can win again if fit 97; Good 20

DUSKY RUN (Irish) — **I** 105^{P}, **I** 163^{P}

DUSTY FURLONG b.g. 8 Button Bright (USA) - Poppy Furlong by Armagnac Monarch — Miss Katie Perry

1995 P(0),4(0),2(12),6(0)

446	9/3	Haldon	(R)	MDO	3m	13	S	*mid-div, 8th at 13th, bhnd aft*	6	0
807	4/4	Clyst St Ma'	(L)	MDO	3m	10	GS	*poor 5th at 14th, ran on clsng stgs, nrst fin*	2	10
928	8/4	Bishopsleigh	(R)	MDN	3m	9	G	*ld 1st-4th, stil frnt rank whn f 13th*	F	-
1070	13/4	Lifton	(R)	MDN	3m	9	S	*several postns, 5th 10th, wnt poor 4th 16th, no ch*	4	0

Placed in poor races & does not threaten to win 10

DUSTY MAID (Irish) — **I** 192^{F}, **I** 224^{4}, **I** 578^{4}

DUSTY'S DELIGHT (Irish) — **I** 76^{F}, **I** 119^{P}, **I** 210^{P}, **I** 239^{F}, **I** 290^{P}, **I** 324^{P}, **I** 503^{P}

DUSTYS TRAIL(IRE) b.g. 7 Seclude (USA) - Another Coup by Le Patron — G Morris

1995 P(0),P(0)

430	9/3	Upton-On-Se'	(R)	MDO	3m	15	GS	*conf rdn, just ld whn f 15th*	F	-
550	17/3	Erw Lon	(L)	MDN	3m	13	GS	*4th/5th, onepcd frm 3 out*	5	0
771	31/3	Pantyderi	(R)	MDN	3m	14	G	*(fav) mid-div, und pres 15th, hrd rdn to ld nr fin*	1	15
980	8/4	Lydstep	(L)	RES	3m	11	G	*alwys mid-div*	4	0
1388	6/5	Pantyderi	(R)	RES	3m	7	GF	*sttld cls up, rmndr aft 10th, prog to 2nd 13th, no ch wnr*	2	15
1490	11/5	Erw Lon	(L)	RES	3m	6	F	*(fav) ld frm 12th, drew clr frm 2 out*	1	20

1558	18/5 Bassaleg	(R) CON	3m	6	F	*rdn to prss wnr,ld 8-15th & 3 out til nrly ref last,not rcvr*	2	17

Much improved; needs plenty of driving & well-ridden; summer jumping 96; could win Confined; G-F ... 20

DUSTY TRACK (Irish) — I 31^{P}, I 81^{P}, I 131^{F}, I 161^{P}, I 223^{3}, I 343, , I 386^{5}, I 423^{4}

DYNAMITE DAN(IRE) b.g. 8 Ballinamona Boy - Aliceion by Tanfirion — B Kennedy

1995 F(-),P(0),P(0),1(16),1(18)

10	14/1 Cottenham	(R) INT	3m	10	G	*blnd & u.r. 1st*	U	-
101	17/2 Marks Tey	(L) MEM	3m	3	G	*made all, blnd & jnd brfly 17th, in cmmnd whn lft solo last*	1	18

Dual winner 95; changed hands; won weak race; finished early; can win again if fit 97; best easy 3m ... 19

DYSART O'DEA (Irish) — I 35^{F}, I 62^{4}, I 147^{4}, I 205^{1}

EADIE (Irish) — I 163^{F}, I 225^{P}

EAGLES WITCH (Irish) — I 144^{P}

EAGLE TRACE b.g. 13 Derring Rose - Vulvic by Vulgan — P L Southcombe

1995 U(-),P(0),3(0),4(0),**4(NH)**

136	17/2 Ottery St M'	(L) LAD	3m	9	GS	*alwys rear, last whn p.u. 12th*	P	0
210	24/2 Castle Of C'	(R) INT	3m	10	HY	*alwys rear, t.o. & p.u. last*	P	0
481	11/3 Taunton	(R) HC	3m	11	G	*alwys bhnd, t.o. from 9th.*	7	0

No longer of any account ... 0

EARL BOON gr.g. 8 Baron Blakeney - Miss Boon by Road House II — J A Keighley

1995 5(11),P(0),2(16),1(20),1(24),2(21)

7	13/1 Larkhill	(R) CON	3m	10	GS	*(fav) trckd ldrs, prog to disp 14th-2 out, no ch wth wnr aft*	2	22
139	17/2 Larkhill	(R) CON	3m	11	G	*(fav) w.w. ld 15th, sn clr, not extndd*	1	26
469	10/3 Milborne St'	(L) LAD	3m	8	G	*(fav) ld/disp to 12th, lost tch 4 out, b.b.v.*	5	12
817	6/4 Charlton Ho'	(L) OPE	3m	5	GF	*last thruout, lost tch 12th, p.u. apr 5 out*	P	0

Decent pointer; needs fast ground, problems last 2 starts; can win Opens if fit 97 ... 24

EARL GRAY gr.g. 9 Baron Blakeney - Conveyor Belle by Gunner B — J Dodsworth

1995 P(0),P(0),7(0),4(0),6(0),3(15),4(10),5(12)

72	11/2 Wetherby Po'	(L) CON	3m	18	GS	*alwys mid-div, nvr dang*	6	13
121	17/2 Witton Cast'	(R) RES	3m	11	S	*mid-div to 12th, rear aft*	8	0
222	24/2 Duncombe Pa'	(R) MEM	3m	6	GS	*(bl) w.w. jmpd lft 11th, sn strgglng, t.o.*	4	0
328	3/3 Market Rase'	(L) RES	3m	9	G	*(bl) disp 3rd, ld 7th, hdd 12th, wknd, no ch whn u.r. 3 out*	U	-
514	16/3 Dalton Park	(R) LAD	3m	8	G	*last whn mstk 9th, t.o. 12th, p.u. 2 out*	P	0
759	31/3 Great Stain'	(L) LAD	3m	10	GS	*(bl) rear, dtchd 9th, rdn 11th, t.o. & p.u. 14th*	P	0
827	6/4 Stainton	(R) LAD	3m	7	GF	*(bl) rear, mstk 8th, outpcd 10th, lost tch 14th, t.o.*	7	0
1090	14/4 Whitwell-On'	(R) RES	3m	17	G	*(bl) trckd ldrs, onepcd frm 13th*	6	0
1131	20/4 Hornby Cast'	(L) RES	3m	17	G	*chsd ldrs, lost plc 11th, t.o. 13th, p.u. 2 out*	P	0
1284	27/4 Easingwold	(L) RES	3m	14	G	*(bl) alwys bhnd, mod prog frm 4 out*	5	13
1447	6/5 Witton Cast'	(R) RES	3m	11	G	*(bl) alwys rear, t.o. 14th, p.u. last*	P	0
1466	11/5 Easingwold	(L) CON	3m	10	G	*(bl) keen hld, alwys mid-div, onepcd frm 4 out*	6	10

Members winner 94; lost last 24 races & looks disinterested now ... 0

EARL OF MIRTH (Irish) — I 14^{4}, I 311^{P}, I 445^{3}, I 462^{P}, I 564^{3}, I 594^{5}, I 637^{3}, I 655^{P}

EARLYDUE VI (Irish) — I 3^{1}, I 48^{2}, I 67^{3}, I 75^{1}

EARLY NEWS (Irish) — I 106^{F}, I 150^{P}, I 211^{2}, I 379^{F}

EARLY TO RISE b.g. 6 Don't Forget Me - Foreno by Formidable (USA) — W H Whitley

1995 **2(NH),5(NH),7(NH),8(NH),6(NH),6(NH),7(NH)**

42	3/2 Wadebridge	(L) CON	3m	8	GF	*tckd ldrs, eff & ev ch app 4 out, no ext*	3	17
130	17/2 Ottery St M'	(L) MEM	3m	6	GS	*prom, virt c.o. aft 7th, outpcd frm 4 out*	3	10
277	2/3 Clyst St Ma'	(L) OPE	3m	4	S	*ld to 3 out, outpcd aft*	2	17
482	13/3 Newton Abbot	(L) HC	2m 5f 110yds	14	S	*chsd ldrs till f 4 out.*	F	-

Ran passably but finished early & not threatening to win competitive races now ... 15

EARTHMOVER(IRE) ch.g. 5 Mister Lord (USA) - Clare's Crystal by Tekoah — R M Penny

69	10/2 Great Treth'	(R) MDO	3m	12	S	*mid-div, prog 14th, chal nxt, sn ld, readily*	1	14
466	10/3 Milborne St'	(L) RES	3m	13	G	*in tch, ld 9th, ran on well frm 3 out*	1	18
657	23/3 Badbury Rin'	(L) INT	3m	3	G	*(fav) ld/disp til 16th, not qckn whn hdd, kpt on*	2	16
1244	27/4 Woodford	(L) INT	3m	12	G	*held up, prog to chs wnr 16th, ev ch nxt, no ext*	2	22

Useful recruit, top stable; beaten by good horses; sure to progress; G-S ... 23

EASBY ROC(IRE) b.g. 8 Bulldozer - Lady Mell by Milan — Mrs C M A Dook

1995 P(0),P(0),1(16)

327	3/3 Market Rase'	(L) CON	3m	15	G	*alwys mid-div, no ch frm 14th, fin 4th, pld 3rd*	3	10

Lightly raced; well beaten only start 96; inconsistent & below Confined standard; Any ... 15

EASTERN EVENING gr.g. 11 Runnett - Sacola by Busted — Miss Sue Widdicombe

576 17/3 Detling (L) MDN 3m 18 GF *nvr bttr than mid-div, wll bhnd whn p.u. aft 4 out* P 0

Rarely runs & is of no account now 0

EASTERN FOX (Irish) — I 133[P], I 228[P], I 269[P], I 341[P], I 416[5], I 531[P], I 618[P]

EASTERN STATESMAN gr.g. 11 El-Birillo - Eastern Faith by Crown Again — Miss S L Bailey

1995 P(0),P(0)

539 17/3 Southwell P' (L) RES 3m 11 GS *mid-div, mostly 4th/5th, onepcd frm 12th* 5 0

Won poor Maiden 94; only 3 runs since; last in only start 96 & no real chances now 0

EASTER PRINCE ch.g. 6 Soldier Rose - Polka Dot by Flandre II — H V Jordan

1995 P(0)

947 8/4 Andoversford (R) MDN 3m 11 GF *alwys bhnd, p.u. 13th* P 0
1435 6/5 Ashorne (R) CON 3m 12 G *last whn mstk 7th, t.o. & p.u. 11th* P 0

Yet to complete & shows nothing 0

EASTLANDS HI-LIGHT ch.g. 7 Saxon Farm - Light O' Love by Lighter — J G Staveley

1995 P(0),R(-),3(0),5(0),2(14),2(13)

51 4/2 Alnwick (L) MDO 3m 17 G *ld 4-12th, ld 2 out, 1l up whn blndrd & u.r. last* U 16
114 17/2 Lanark (R) MDO 3m 12 GS *(fav) made most frm 9th, drew clr frm 3 out* 1 15
319 2/3 Corbridge (R) RES 3m 16 GS *mid-div, prog hlfwy, chsd ldrs 15th, onepcd* 4 13
404 9/3 Dalston (R) RES 3m 7 G *ld 2nd, dispute frm 4th & ev chnc last, outpcd nr fin* 3 15
608 23/3 Friars Haugh (L) RES 3m 13 G *4th hlfwy, wnt 2nd 2 out, no impr on wnnr* 2 16
858 6/4 Alnwick (L) RES 3m 7 GF *mid-div,prog to 3rd hlfwy, clsd appr last, just outpcd flat* 2 17
1086 14/4 Friars Haugh (L) RES 3m 7 F *(fav) alwys bhnd, plenty to do whn blnd 15th, no ch aft* 5 0
1353 4/5 Mosshouses (L) RES 3m 11 GS *chsd ldr 9th, ld 15th-apr 2 out, no ch wnr aft* 2 15
1585 25/5 Cartmel (L) HC 3 1/4m 14 GF *mstks, chsd ldrs, effort and blnd 13th and next, styd on flat, no ext near fin.* 2 18

Deserved win; genuine but onepaced; beaten by good horses in Restricted & should win one 97; G/S-F 18

EAST RIVER b.g. 12 Midland Gayle - French Note by Eton Rambler — Mrs Helen Mobley

1995 3(16),4(17),3(18),2(17),2(13),3(19)

1099 14/4 Guilsborough (L) LAD 3m 9 G *rear, pshd alng & prog 13th, chsd ldng pair 2 out, onepcd* 3 15

Ladies winner 94; barely stays & hard to win with; brief show 96 & win at 13 beyond him now 15

EASTSHAW b.g. 14 Crash Course - What A Duchess by Bargello — M P Wiggin

1995 **1(NH),4(NH),3(NH),5(NH)**

161 17/2 Weston Park (L) LAD 3m 11 G *alwys chsng wnr, ev ch 4 out, no ext frm 2 out* 2 24
216 24/2 Newtown (L) LAD 3m 13 GS *(fav) w.w. rmndrs 9th, chsd ldng pair 13th, no imp nxt, fin tired* 4 16

Winning chaser; ran well pointing debut but finished after disappointing 2nd effort; win at 15 tough 21

EASY CATCH (Irish) — I 110[F], I 327[2], I 446[1], I 514[1], I 586[F]

EASY LIFE(IRE) ch.g. 7 Boyne Valley - Manna Rose by Bonne Noel — Miss Jill Wormall

1995 U(-),2(14),F(-),1(12),6(0)

539 17/3 Southwell P' (L) RES 3m 11 GS *mid-div, late prog, nvr dang* 4 0
726 31/3 Garthorpe (R) RES 3m 16 G *handy to 12th, sn outpcd & btn* 8 0
1025 13/4 Brocklesby ' (L) XX 3m 9 GF *(bl) made most, ran on whn jnd 3 out, just outpcd flat* 3 15
1305 28/4 Southwell P' (L) LAD 3m 4 GF *(bl) 3rd & cls up, went 2nd 3 out, onepcd* 2 12

Maiden winner 95; acquired blinkers 96 & weak finisher; best watched; G/F-S 14

EASY OVER(USA) ch.g. 10 Transworld (USA) - Love Bunny (USA) by Exclusive Native (USA) — B Dowling

90 11/2 Ampton (R) CON 3m 5 GF *pllng, chsd wnr to 12th, outpcd 15th, no ch 3 out* 4 14
102 17/2 Marks Tey (L) CON 3m 17 G *ld to 5th, chsd ldr to 14th, grad wknd* 6 17
359 4/3 Doncaster (L) HC 2m 3f 110yds 10 G *chsd ldrs, mstk and lost pl quickly 7th, t.o. from hfwy.* 5 0
622 23/3 Higham (L) CON 3m 10 GF *alwys rear, blnd 8th, no ch wth ldrs 4 out* 4 11
906 8/4 Fakenham (L) HC 2m 5f 110yds 11 G *made most to 6th, blnd 8th, soon bhnd, t.o. when p.u. 12th.* P 0
1379 5/5 Dingley (R) MXO 3m 7 GF *ld 2-6th, mstk 12th, wknd, poor 4th whn hmpd apr 2 out* 5 0
1546 18/5 Fakenham (L) HC 3m 110yds 13 G *(bl) jmpd slowly in rear most of way, t.o. 14th.* 9 0

Missed 95; deteriorated & non-stayer; outclassed in competitive races & Members best hope 97 12

EATONS br.m. 5 Daring March - Party Game by Red Alert — P B Shaw

1995 **5(NH),P(NH)**

864 6/4 Larkhill (R) MDN 2 1/2m 9 F *pulld hrd, cls 2nd til wknd frm 5 out, u.r. 3 out* U -
1345 4/5 Holnicote (L) RES 3m 11 GS *plld hrd, rear whn p.u. 14th* P 0

Too headstrong at present 0

EAZY PEAZY(IRE) b.g. 8 Indian King (USA) - Dane Valley by Simbir — Brett Badham

540	17/3	Southwell P'	(L)	MDO	3m	9	GS	*chsng grp, ld 10-12th, onepcd whn hdd*	4	0
1104	14/4	Guilsborough	(L)	MDN	3m	18	G	*rear,prog & in tch 11th, 5th & btn 4 out, t.o. & p.u. 2 out*	P	0

Beaten miles on debut but shows a little ability; more stamina needed 10

EBBZEADO WILLFURR (Irish) — **I** 2^{4}, **I** 35^{3}, **I** 61^{U}, **I** 200^{1}

EBONY GALE br.g. 10 Strong Gale - Vanessa's Princess by Laurence O — Ken Liscombe

1995 **P(NH)**,**F(NH)**,**P(NH)**,**4(NH)**

159	17/2	Weston Park	(L)	CON	3m	22	G	*mid to rear, p.u. 3 out*	P	0
289	2/3	Eaton Hall	(R)	CON	3m	10	G	*mid-div, no ch wth 1st pair frm 5 out*	3	11
664	24/3	Eaton Hall	(R)	CON	3m	15	S	*mid to rear, no ch whn p.u. 4 out*	P	0
738	31/3	Sudlow Farm	(R)	LAD	3m	5	G	*chas ldrs, whn 2nd 13th, kpt on, not trbl wnnr*	2	15
1153	20/4	Whittington	(L)	LAD	3m	10	G	*alwys rear, wll btn 5th whn p.u. 2 out*	P	0
1230	27/4	Weston Park	(L)	CON	3m	7	G	*ld to 2nd, chsng grp to 12th, onepcd frm 5 out*	6	13
1369	4/5	Gisburn	(R)	CON	3m	10	G	*mid-div, 5th whn f 15th*	F	-

Winning chaser; inconsistent under Rules & shows little interest now 11

EBONY STAR br.g. 13 Irish Star - Rainy Season by Silly Season — P J Collicutt

1995 **5(20)**,**P(0)**,6(15),P(0),P(0),3(10),P(0),**P(0)**

908	8/4	Hereford	(R)	HC	2m 3f	12	GF	*p.u. before 1st.*	P	0

Appears to have retired himself now 0

ECOLOGIC (Irish) — **I** 187^{2}

EDDIE WALSHE b.g. 11 Smackover - Ashmore Lady by Ashmore (FR) — M J Footer

251	25/2	Charing	(L)	OPE	3m	10	GS	*ld to 9th, rear & btn whn p.u. 14th*	P	0
577	19/3	Fontwell	(R)	HC	2m 3f	5	GF	*pulld hrd, led apr 3rd, hdd 11th, f next.*	F	-
1052	13/4	Penshurst	(L)	OPE	3m	7	G	*ld to 11th, fdd, p.u. 13th*	P	0

Winning chaser; of no account now 0

EDERMINE SUNSET (Irish) — **I** 163^{P}, **I** 348^{F}

EDGED WEAPON(FR) ch.h. 11 Magesterial (USA) - Latin League by Sallust — Miss J C Aungiers

449	9/3	Charing	(L)	RES	3m	13	G	*prom to 5th, last by 7th, p.u. nxt*	P	0
1210	21/4	Heathfield	(R)	MDO	3m	13	F	*sn prom, wknd 8th, t.o. & p.u. 13th*	P	0
1442	6/5	Aldington	(L)	RES	3m	7	HD	*chsd ldr, 3rd whn u.r. 10th*	U	-

No cutting edge & of no account 0

EDINBURGH REEL ALE b.m. 5 Scottish Reel - Report 'em (USA) by Staff Writer (USA) — R T Dennis

229	24/2	Duncombe Pa'	(R)	MDO	3m	13	GS	*alwys rear, tk mod 3rd flat, ran on*	3	0
1365	4/5	Gisburn	(R)	MDO	3m	17	G	*bhnd, prog to 3l 3rd 16th, onepcd aft*	3	0

3 months between races; ran well enough each time but nmo subsequent winners behind; go closer 97 12

EDUCATE ME (Irish) — **I** 122^{P}, **I** 200^{6}, **I** 366^{3}, **I** 541^{6}, **I** 582^{6}

EIGHTY EIGHT b.g. 11 Doctor Wall - Pennulli by Sir Nulli — Mrs H B Dowson

1995 **P(NH)**,**9(NH)**,**11(NH)**,**5(NH)**,**6(NH)**,**4(NH)**,**4(NH)**,**3(NH)**

240	25/2	Southwell P'	(L)	MDO	3m	15	HO	*4th whn f 3rd*	F	-
340	3/3	Heythrop	(R)	MDN	3m	12	G	*prom, ld 11th-2 out, wknd last*	4	10
749	31/3	Upper Sapey	(R)	MDN	3m	17	GS	*alwys prom, disp 14th til outpcd flat*	2	15
1006	9/4	Upton-On-Se'	(R)	MDN	3m	11	F	*c.u., chsd ldr 10-14th, rdn & one pace frm 3 out*	3	13
1217	24/4	Andoversford	(R)	MDO	3m	16	G	*prom, lft in ld 14th, made rest, hrd prssd & lft clr last*	1	15
1522	12/5	Garthorpe	(R)	RES	3m	12	GF	*mid-div going wll whn u.r. 12th*	U	-
1548	18/5	Southwell	(L)	HC	3m 110yds	11	GF	*mid div, no ch from 4 out.*	6	14

Placed in chases; finally won Maiden (probably lucky); woefully onepaced; hard to win again 15

EILID ANOIR ch.g. 7 King Goldwyn - Hartfell by Lord Nelson (FR) — J Shearer

1995 P(0),P(0),2(0),4(0)

115	17/2	Lanark	(R)	MDO	3m	8	GS	*ld til apr 3 out, sn wknd*	3	0
193	24/2	Friars Haugh	(L)	MDN	3m	10	S	*ld til 3 out, wknd rpdly, p.u. nxt*	P	0
371	8/3	Ayr	(L)	HC	2m 5f 110yds	8	GF	*chsd ldr, ld after 14th, hdd after 2 out, soon wknd.*	3	12
488	16/3	Newcastle	(L)	HC	2 1/2m	9	GS	*disp ld to 8th, soon pushed along, struggling last 5.*	4	0
859	6/4	Alnwick	(L)	MDO	2 1/2m	5	GF	*disp ld til ld 4th, clr 8th, hdded & lft clr 2 out*	1	12

Lucky winner of short Maiden; does not stay 3m & Restricted prospects very slim 13

EL BAE b.g. 10 Lord Ha Ha - Shanaway by Moss Court — John Brown

1995 P(0)

31	20/1	Higham	(L)	CON	3m	9	GF	*nvr bttr than mid-div, t.o. & p.u. 2 out*	P	0
94	11/2	Ampton	(R)	OPE	3m	8	GF	*rear, lost tch 12th,, t.o. & p.u. last*	P	0
102	17/2	Marks Tey	(L)	CON	3m	17	G	*alwys rr div, nvr dang*	11	0

310	2/3	Ampton	(R) CON	3m	13	G	*w.w. prog 12th, chal 3 out, wknd appr last*	5	17
418	9/3	High Easter	(L) CON	3m	10	S	*w.w. blnd & lst pl 9th, lst tch 13th, p.u. 15th*	P	0
619	23/3	Higham	(L) OPE	3m	10	GF	*wth ldrs early, rmndrs 10th, grad lost tch 13th*	6	10
677	30/3	Cottenham	(R) OPE	3m	11	GF	*alwys last, t.o. & p.u. 10th*	P	0
1399	6/5	Northaw	(L) CON	3m	8	F	*w.w. in tch, outpcd 13th, no dang frm 15th*	6	0
1546	18/5	Fakenham	(L) HC	3m 110yds	13	G	*alwys rear gp, lost tch 12th.*	10	0
1595	25/5	Garthorpe	(R) CON	3m	15	G	*5th 1st m, fdd, bhnd whn p.u. 4 out*	P	0

Winning Irish hurdler; ran one good race but best avoided 10

ELDER PRINCE ch.g. 10 Final Straw - Particular Miss by Luthier — Brian Gee

1995 F(-),1(15),1(19),1(19)

170	18/2	Market Rase'	(L) XX	3m	8	GF	*(fav) pllng, trckd ldrs going wll, chal & ld last, comf*	1	22
326	3/3	Market Rase'	(L) OPE	3m	14	G	*(fav) alwys going well, prog 10th, ld apr 2 out, eased flat*	1	24
634	23/3	Market Rase'	(L) OPE	3m	6	GF	*(fav) w.w. cls up, chal 4 out, 2nd nxt, no ext frm 2 out*	3	17
1258	27/4	Cottenham	(R) OPE	3m	3	F	*(fav) ld 3-5th, ld 8th, qcknd 4 out, hdd & outpcd flat*	2	17
1546	18/5	Fakenham	(L) HC	3m 110yds	13	G	*chsd ldrs till blnd 9th, no impn after.*	5	14

Improved; won modest Open; struggles to stay in competitive races; should win again; likes M Rasen .. 23

ELECTRIC ARC(FR) b.g. 10 Electric - Ananiyya (FR) by Faristan — R W Green

1995 P(0),P(0),U(-),2(12),P(0)

194	24/2	Friars Haugh	(L) MDN	3m	11	S	*ld 5th, sn clr, unchal*	1	14
319	2/3	Corbridge	(R) RES	3m	16	GS	*ld 1st til f 14th*	F	

Romped home in fair Maiden; lightly raced & season lasted a week; can win Restricted if fit 97 16

ELECTRIC CAN (Irish) — I 239P, I 309P, I 351P, I 438P, I 504P

ELECTROFANE(IRE) b or br.g. 8 Teofane - Clanwilla by Pauper — Mrs R J Manning

1995 **16(NH),P(NH),P(NH),P(NH)**

206	24/2	Castle Of C'	(R) MDO	3m	10	HY	*prom to 3 out, wknd & p.u. last*	P	0
301	2/3	Great Treth'	(R) MDO	3m	13	G	*alwys prom, disp 14th-nxt, 3rd & onepcd 17th, lft 2nd 2 out*	2	11
533	16/3	Cothelstone	(L) MDN	3m	13	G	*prom to 10th, sn strugg, 3rd & no ch 4 out*	3	0

Placed Irish Maidens 94; disappointing sort & may struggle to win 11

ELECTROLYTE b.g. 6 Electric - This Sensation by Balidar — G Austin

1995 **11(NH),3(NH),11(NH),9(NH)**

23	20/1	Barbury Cas'	(L) XX	3m	11	GS	*mstk 7th, prom til wknd 10th, p.u. nxt*	P	0
153	17/2	Erw Lon	(L) OPE	3m	15	G	*u.r. 2nd*	U	-
215	24/2	Newtown	(L) OPE	3m	20	GS	*alwys rear, t.o. 13th, p.u. 2 out*	P	0
384	9/3	Llanfrynach	(R) OPE	3m	16	GS	*rear, lost tch 14th, mod late prog, nvr dang*	7	11
547	17/3	Erw Lon	(L) OPE	3m	10	GS	*u.r. 2nd*	U	-
768	31/3	Pantyderi	(R) OPE	3m	10	G	*alwys wll in rear*	9	0
978	8/4	Lydstep	(L) OPE	3m	6	G	*alwys mid-div, p.u. 3 out*	P	0
1199	21/4	Lydstep	(L) OPE	3m	5	S	*(bl) prog 12th, blnd 14th, fdd aft*	3	0
1529	12/5	Ottery St M'	(L) OPE	3m	7	GF	*(bl) ld til jmpd slwly 2nd, ran in sntchs, no ch frm 15th*	5	0
1636	1/6	Bratton Down	(L) OPE	4m	11	G	*(bl) prom, disp 15th-17th, cls up whn u.r. 19th*	U	-
1647	8/6	Umberleigh	(L) OPE	3m	7	GF	*(bl) jmpd slwly, rear frm 6th, last whn f 12th*	F	-

Well beaten when completing & no real prospects in even modest company 11

ELEGANT BERTIE ch.g. 7 Relkino - Arctic Elegance by Articulate — Lady Blyth

334	3/3	Heythrop	(R) MEM	3m	6	G	*n.j.w. blnd 9th & lost tch, t.o. & p.u. 13th*	P	0
842	6/4	Maisemore P'	(L) MDN	3m	17	GF	*mstks, mid-div, prog to 4th 15th, wknd nxt, 6th whn f last*	F	-
1621	27/5	Chaddesley '	(L) MDO	3m	17	GF	*rear, wll bhnd whn p.u. 10th*	P	0

Needs to learn to jump but not yet entirely without hope 0

ELEGANT FRIEND ch.g. 8 Music Boy - Cardinal Palace by Royal Palace — T R Darlington

1995 **2(NH),F(NH),5(NH),P(NH),7(NH),13(NH),5(NH)**

1120	20/4	Bangor	(L) HC	2 1/2m 110yds	13	S	*in tch, rdn and wknd before 9th, t.o. when mstk next, p.u. before 11th.*	P	0

Winning hurdler; outclassed in H/Chase on only appearance 0

ELEGANT GUEST ch.g. 13 Be My Guest (USA) - Countess Eileen by Sassafras (FR) — Miss J Tindale

1995 P(0),1(21)

410	9/3	Charm Park	(L) OPE	3m	17	G	*prom early, wknd 9th, p.u. 12th*	P	0
701	30/3	Tranwell	(L) OPE	3m	8	GS	*alwys rear, last at 9th, p.u. 13th*	P	0
1092	14/4	Whitwell-On'	(R) CON	3m	10	G	*trckd ldrs til lost plc 10th, wkng whn u.r. 13th*	U	-

Won 3 94/5; lightly raced; showed nothing in 96 & looks too old now 11

ELEGANT LORD (Irish) — I 18[1]

ELEGANT SUN ch.g. 14 Sunyboy - Arctic Elegance by Articulate — Mrs F Lockyer

1995 2(0),P(0),1(13),4(0)
651 23/3 Badbury Rin' (L) MEM 3m 4 G *prom early, wknd 10th, tk 2nd 15th, hld on* 2 10
1058 13/4 Badbury Rin' (L) LAD 3m 5 GF *alwys last, losing tch whn f 14th* F -

Won a match in 95; no hopes at 15 10

ELITE GOVERNOR(IRE) b.g. 7 Supreme Leader - Lishpower by Master Buck Paul Gardner
17 14/1 Tweseldown (R) MDN 3m 11 GS *(fav) ld 4th, made rest, mstks 3 out & last, drvn out flat* 1 18
68 10/2 Great Treth' (R) RES 3m 14 S *trckd ldrs, p.u. bef 4 out, bandages loose* P 0
361 5/3 Leicester (R) HC 2 1/2m 110yds 15 GS *(fav) chsd ldrs till u.r. 3rd.* U -
642 23/3 Siddington (L) RES 3m 15 S *(fav) prog to 2nd 11th, blnd badly 14th, nt rcvr, p.u nxt* P 0
1288 28/4 Barbury Cas' (L) MEM 3m 5 F *(fav) n.j.w. ld 4-6th & frm 10th, sn wll clr, blnd last* 1 12
1501 11/5 Kingston Bl' (L) RES 3m 10 G *(fav) made virt all, in cmmnd frm 2 out, easily* 1 20
1608 26/5 Tweseldown (R) CON 3m 6 G *(fav) mstks,jmpd lft,ld aft 10-13th,outpcd 3 out,btn whn blnd last* 2 18

Missed 94; improved; sketchy jumper; quite able & worth trying in Ladies 21

ELLE FLAVADOR b.m. 6 El Conquistador - Flavirostris by Grisaille Mrs A B Watts
283 2/3 Clyst St Ma' (L) MDN 3m 7 S *hld up in rear, t.o. & p.u. 14th, improve* P 0
819 6/4 Charlton Ho' (L) MDN 3m 10 GF *j.w., ld 4th, styd on wll frm 3 out, easily* 1 15
1345 4/5 Holnicote (L) RES 3m 11 GS *(fav) ld 7-14th, grad fdd* 3 12
1591 25/5 Mounsey Hil' (R) RES 3m 15 G *chsd ldrs,5th & wkng 16th,lft 3rd 2 out,fin 3rd,plcd 2nd* 2 10

Romped home in slow Maiden; well beaten after; should improve - needs to for Restricteds 15

ELLENMAE ROSE (Irish) — I 59[F]

ELLER'S REFLECTION b.m. 6 Looking Glass - Ellers Gorse by Jock Scot Ken Webb
740 31/3 Sudlow Farm (R) MDN 3m 16 G *schoold, rear of main grp til p.u. 12th* P 0
1033 13/4 Alpraham (R) MDO 2 1/2m 15 GS *rear, t.o. 7th, p.u. 10th* P 0

Only learning to date 0

ELLERTON HILL br.g. 13 Potent Councillor - Kenny by Royal Pennant T W Thompson
1995 **P(0)**,1(24),**2(24)**,**3(0)**,P(0)
120 17/2 Witton Cast' (R) OPE 3m 7 S *(Jt fav) j.w. made all, qcknd clr apr last, imprssv* 1 26
790 1/4 Kelso (L) HC 3m 1f 11 GF *ld till hdd and hit 2 out, wknd quickly before last.* 6 18
1133 20/4 Hornby Cast' (L) OPE 3m 14 G *alwys wth ldrs, ld 13th, hdd 4 out, ev ch whn f 2 out* F -
1448 6/5 Witton Cast' (R) OPE 3m 5 G *(fav) (4/6-6/4)cls 2nd,ld 14th-apr 4 out, outpcd by wnnr* 2 22

Formerly useful; front-runner; retains much of his ability & can win at 14; S-F 23

ELLERTON PARK b.g. 9 Politico (USA) - Sweet Clare by Suki Desu J F Thompson
411 9/3 Charm Park (L) RES 3m 20 G *ld to 2 out, hdd appr last, no ex flat* 4 17
539 17/3 Southwell P' (L) RES 3m 11 GS *(Jt fav) set str pace, hdd 13th, u.r. nxt* U -
983 8/4 Charm Park (L) RES 3m 13 GF *(bl) ld to 15th, disp nxt, hdd, no ext aft* 4 14
1447 6/5 Witton Cast' (R) RES 3m 11 G *(bl) pulld hrd,ld, 20l clr 7th, wknd 12th, rear whn p.u. 3 out* P 0

Missed 95; blazes the trail; runs well fresh & may surprise in modest Restricted early 97 16

ELLESMERE (Irish) — I 142[P], I 324[P], I 434[B], I 504[F], I 569[P], I 660[4]

ELLIES NELSON (Irish) — I 247[P], I 332[4], I 375[3], I 458[1]

ELLIES PRIDE (Irish) — I 95[5], I 214[3], I 301[F], I 319[P], I 448[4]

ELMORE ch.g. 9 Le Moss - Be Nice by Bowsprit Mrs R R Day
780 31/3 Penshurst (L) MDN 3m 12 GS *(fav) (5s-5/2),hndy, ld 4 out, rddn out whn chal last* 1 13
1206 21/4 Heathfield (R) RES 3m 8 F *(fav) mid-div, rmndrs 14th, btn 16th, p.u. nxt lame* P 0

Beat Hermes Harvest in novice chase two seasons ago & landed punt in weak Maiden; problems after 13

ELWILL GLORY (Irish) — I 5[4], I 47[1], I 72[6], I 116[4], I 212[4], I 333[5], I 463[P], I 576[1]

ELY ISLAND b.g. 9 Teofane - Court Fancy by Little Buskins J G Thatcher
1995 7(12),4(19)
656 23/3 Badbury Rin' (L) RES 3m 11 G *in rear untl rpd prog 14th, left 2nd 2 out, ran on well* 2 18

Irish Maiden winner 94; lightly raced but ran well only start 96 & can win Restricted if fit 97 18

EMBU-MERU b.g. 8 Scorpio (FR) - Rosie Tudor by Tudor Treasure R G Owen
1995 P(0),2(0)
462 9/3 Eyton-On-Se' (L) RES 3m 12 G *mstks, rr early, r.o. one pc frm 4 out* 7 0
659 24/3 Eaton Hall (R) MEM 3m 6 S *ld/disp to 12th, lost plc nxt, rallied 3 out, just faild* 2 13
740 31/3 Sudlow Farm (R) MDN 3m 16 G *mid-div, mod 6th 14th, styd on wll aft, ld flat* 1 14
1009 9/4 Flagg Moor (L) CON 3m 7 G *tbd, rear, 6th & pshd alng whn u.r. 12th* U -
1152 20/4 Whittington (L) CON 3m 9 G *rear, t.o. 6th, p.u. 8th* P 0

Stayed on dourly to win Maiden; outclassed after; tubed & Members best hope in 97 14

EMERALD GALE (Irish) — I 156[3], I 311[1]

EMERALD GEM b.g. 10 Henbit (USA) - Mary Arden by Mill Reef (USA) Mrs K J Buckley

426 9/3 Upton-On-Se' (R) CON 3m 16 GS *t.o. & p.u. 9th* P 0
880 6/4 Brampton Br' (R) XX 3m 8 GF *(bl) alwys rear, lost tch 14th, t.o.* 6 0
1159 20/4 Llanwit Maj' (R) LAD 3m 5 GS *(bl) s.s., sn wll bhnd, t.o.* 3 0
1264 27/4 Pyle (R) LAD 3m 10 G *(bl) rear 2nd, dist 9th whn u.r. flat apr 7th* U -
1507 12/5 Maisemore P' (L) CON 3m 10 F *(bl) chsd ldr 2-9th, outpcd frm 12th, t.o.* 5 0

Beaten miles when completing & has no prospects in points 0

EMERALD KNIGHT(IRE) ch.g. 6 Sandalay - Fort Etna by Be Friendly Peter Henley
1995 P(0),3(0),1(14)

465 10/3 Milborne St' (L) RES 3m 11 G *in tch, rdn 3 out, lft clr nxt, drvn out* 1 20
732 31/3 Little Wind' (R) INT 3m 6 GS *hld up in tch, wnt 2nd 3 out, no ext frm 2 out* 2 21

Maiden winner 95; beat dual H/Chase winner in Restricted; should reach Open class 97; good stable .. 24

EMERALD LAKE (Irish) — I 309^{P}, I 353^{P}

EMERALD QUEEN b.m. 7 Idiot's Delight - Corbitt Coins by Deep Run Miss B M Neal

324 3/3 Market Rase' (L) MEM 3m 4 G *set seady pace to 15th, no ext* 3 0
898 6/4 Dingley (R) MDN 2m 5f 10 GS *ld jmpng lft til ran out 4th* r -
1027 13/4 Brocklesby ' (L) MDN 3m 7 GF *nvr dang, 5th frm 8th, outpcd 3 out* 4 0

Well beaten in dire Maiden last start & prospects look remote 0

EMERALD STATEMENT (Irish) — I 56^{4}, I 117^{1}, I 333^{2}

EMILY'S NIECE b.m. 11 Balinger - Great Aunt Emily by Traditionalist (USA) T Woolridge

466 10/3 Milborne St' (L) RES 3m 13 G *alwys bhnd, t.o. 15th* 7 0
999 8/4 Hackwood Pa' (L) RES 3m 6 GF *ld 7th, hdd 9-16th, ld agn 2 out, ran on strgly* 1 16

Maiden winner 94; missed 95; game but weak Restricted win makes life hard in 97 if fit 16

EMMABELLA m. 10 A Hollingsworth
1995 4(0)

431 9/3 Upton-On-Se' (R) MDO 3m 17 GS *disp ld 12th til f 15th* F -

Hardly ever seen (7 runs in 5 seasons) & time slipping by now 11

EMMA CLEW(IRE) ch.m. 8 Remainder Man - Supple by Poynton E R Hughes

285 2/3 Eaton Hall (R) MEM 3m 5 G *prom, cls up & ev ch whn u.r. 13th* U -
564 17/3 Wolverhampt' (L) RES 3m 8 GS *s.s. ld 5th-13th, wknd, p.u. 3 out* P 0
1107 15/4 Southwell (L) HC 3m 110yds 10 G *bhnd when blnd and u.r. 11th.* U -
1192 21/4 Sandon (L) CON 3m 11 G *mid-div, u.r. 11th* U -

Irish Maiden winner 94; a disaster in England 0

EMPTY WAGON (Irish) — I 603^{F}

EMSEE-H b.g. 11 Paddy's Stream - Kincsem by Nelcius J M Turner
1995 P(0),2(22),3(10),2(20),**2(19)**,**5(12)**,**2(21)**

180 18/2 Horseheath (R) LAD 3m 3 G *ld 2nd-6th, wth wnr 10-14th, sn outpcd* 2 16
309 2/3 Ampton (R) MEM 3m 6 G *(fav) w.w. 4th & rddn appr 17th, no rspnse* 4 0
907 8/4 Fakenham (L) HC 3m 110yds 11 G *alwys bhnd, n.d..* 5 0
1148 20/4 Higham (L) CON 3m 5 F *wth ldr, ld 10th, qcknd clr aft 16th, rdn & hld on flat* 1 20
1539 16/5 Folkestone (R) HC 3m 7f 9 G *held up bhnd, n.d..* 6 0

Generally looks disinterested but broke losing sequence of 23 at Higham; best watched; G/S-G/F 16

EMU PARK gr.g. 8 Mansingh (USA) - Gun Tana (FR) by Tanerko J D Thompson
1995 U(-),P(0),F(-)

188 24/2 Friars Haugh (L) RES 3m 12 S *prom early, bhnd whn p.u. 14th* P 0
403 9/3 Dalston (R) RES 3m 11 G *disp 3rd, prom 8th-12th, lost plc & p.u. aft 3 out* P 0
611 23/3 Friars Haugh (L) LAD 3m 10 G *3rd hlfwy, sn wknd* 7 0
756 31/3 Lockerbie (R) MDN 3m 14 G *nvr dang, p.u. 3 out* P 0
1450 6/5 Witton Cast' (R) MDO 3m 14 G *alwys midfld, kpt on onepce* 4 0
1571 19/5 Corbridge (R) RES 3m 13 G *last early, prog 9th, gd hdwy 15th, rdn & ev ch 2 out,outpcd* 2 16
1585 25/5 Cartmel (L) HC 3 1/4m 14 GF *prom to 6th, soon lost pl and bhnd from 12th, t.o..* 8 0

Beat 8 others when 2nd & good enough for Maiden win on that form if it is not a flash in the pan 14

EMYVALE BOY (Irish) — I 155^{P}

ENCHANTED MAN b.g. 12 Enchantment - Queen's Treasure by Queen's Hussar Mrs J M Morris

384 9/3 Llanfrynach (R) OPE 3m 16 GS *prom til f 7th* F -
691 30/3 Llanvapley (L) CON 3m 15 GS *rear whn p.u. 9th* P 0
908 8/4 Hereford (R) HC 2m 3f 12 GF *prom, rdn 9th, styd on same pace from 4 out.* 3 12
1220 24/4 Brampton Br' (R) OPE 3m 10 G *25l 5th at 12th, rdn 14th, no ch whn p.u. 2 out* P 0
1509 12/5 Maisemore P' (L) OPE 3m 4 F *chsd ldr, ld aft 9th, clr 15th, wknd & hdd aft last* 2 16

Does not stay & too old now 12

ENDLESS GLEE b.g. 11 Gleason (USA) - Sleepytime Girl by Immortality — D P Smith

1995 4(0),5(0),5(10),U(-),6(0),4(12),U(-),4(10)

20	14/1	Tweseldown	(R)	RES	3m	9	GS	*chsd ldr til blnd & u.r. 10th*	U	-
231	24/2	Heythrop	(R)	XX	3m	10	GS	*in tch early, wkng whn p.u. 12th*	P	0
338	3/3	Heythrop	(R)	RES	3m	9	G	*mstk 4th, sn last & bhnd, t.o. & p.u. 12th*	P	0
641	23/3	Siddington	(L)	RES	3m	20	S	*mid div til rddn 10th, sn bhnd*	11	0
840	6/4	Maisemore P'	(L)	RES	3m	9	GF	*sn clr ld, 12l clr 14th, hdded appr 2 out, wknd rpdly*	5	12

Members winner 93; non-stayer; lost last 19 races & sure to extend the sequence 0

END OF THE RUN b.g. 5 Pragmatic - Its Now Up To You by Deep Run — E F Birchall

688	30/3	Chaddesley '	(L)	MDN	3m	17	G	*twrds rear, f 9th*	F	-

Not yet of any account 0

ENGAGING b.g. 9 Black Minstrel - Ko Mear by Giolla Mear — A Jackson

1995 P(0),4(10),**U(-)**

333	3/3	Market Rase'	(L)	MDO	3m	11	G	*ld, clr apr 14th, hdd apr last, no ext*	2	11
415	9/3	Charm Park	(L)	MDO	3m	13	G	*prom to hlfwy, wknd 12th, one pcd 4 out*	6	0
823	6/4	Stainton	(R)	MEM	3m	6	GF	*disp til wknd 5th, p.u. 7th*	P	0
1136	20/4	Hornby Cast'	(L)	MDN	3m	11	G	*ld to 5th, wth ldrs til not qckn frm 3 out*	3	13
1365	4/5	Gisburn	(R)	MDO	3m	17	G	*ld/disp to 12th, wknd rpdly, p.u. 15th*	P	0
1470	11/5	Easingwold	(L)	MDO	3m	10	G	*ld to 8th, fdd, t.o. & p.u. 3 out*	P	0

Ran passably twice in 96 but stamina problems; more needed for a win 11

ENSIGN EWART(IRE) ch.g. 5 Buckskin (FR) - Clonea Fog by Laurence O — Major M W Sample

82	11/2	Alnwick	(L)	MEM	3m	4	GS	*jmpd slwly early, alwys 3rd, lost tch 13th, t.o.*	3	0
319	2/3	Corbridge	(R)	RES	3m	16	GS	*alwys abt same plc*	5	10
705	30/3	Tranwell	(L)	MDO	3m	9	GS	*mid-div, prog 14th, disp nxt, ld 2 out, ran on well*	1	16
1249	27/4	Balcormo Ma'	(R)	RES	3m	10	GS	*(fav) 5th hlfwy, hdwy to ld aft 3 out, sn clr*	1	17

Promising, stays well & safe; should upgrade in 97; G/S, so far 20

EOSTRE b.g. 7 Saxon Farm - Herald The Dawn by Dubassoff (USA) — Mrs J M Lancaster

1995 4(0)

89	11/2	Alnwick	(L)	MDO	3m	9	GS	*(fav) hld up, prog to chs ldr 12th, wknd 3 out, lft 2nd nxt*	2	10
755	31/3	Lockerbie	(R)	MDN	3m	17	G	*midfld whn f 13th*	F	-
1254	27/4	Balcormo Ma'	(R)	MDO	3m	14	GS	*alwys hndy, 4th hlfwy, ld apr 2 out, no ext flat*	2	14
1355	4/5	Mosshouses	(L)	MDO	3m	10	GS	*(fav) trckd ldng pair, ld apr 2 out, rdn out flat*	1	14

Consistent but barely stays & finds little; more needed for Restricted win 97; G/S 15

EPILENY br.g. 12 Random Shot (USA) - Charming Hostess by Khalkis — N A Whittle

1247	27/4	Woodford	(L)	CON	3m	7	G	*lft in ld 9th til ran wd apr 11th, 3rd & outpcd frm 14th*	4	12
1584	24/5	Towcester	(R)	HC	3m 1f	11	GS	*blnd and u.r. 1st.*	U	-

Only 3 runs in last 3 seasons; ran passably at Woddford; unlikely to score again 13

EQUATIME b.m. 10 Turn Back The Time (USA) - Equa by Cheval — T K Williams

1995 P(0),6(0),F(-),P(0),P(0)

155	17/2	Erw Lon	(L)	RES	3m	9	G	*hld up, 5th at 10th, wknd rpdly, p.u. 13th*	P	0
387	9/3	Llanfrynach	(R)	RES	3m	11	GS	*ld to 10th, wknd rpdly, t.o. & p.u. 2 out*	P	0
549	17/3	Erw Lon	(L)	RES	3m	11	GS	*u.r. 1st*	U	-
604	23/3	Howick	(L)	INT	3m	7	S	*2nd early, wknd frm 6th, t.o. & p.u. 12th*	P	0
1160	20/4	Llanwit Maj'	(R)	RES	3m	12	GS	*chsd ldrs til wknd 15th, 4th whn f last, remntd*	4	0
1486	11/5	Erw Lon	(L)	MEM	3m	4	F	*ld to 13th, wknd*	3	0

Maiden winner 94; rarely completes now & tailed off when she does 0

EQUINOCTIAL b.g. 11 Skyliner - Night Rose by Sovereign Gleam — John Sisterson

83	11/2	Alnwick	(L)	CON	3m	10	GS	*trckd ldrs til mstk & u.r. 8th*	U	-
226	24/2	Duncombe Pa'	(R)	OPE	3m	10	GS	*ld to 5th, prom til wknd apr 4 out*	6	0
304	2/3	Great Stain'	(L)	OPE	3m	10	GS	*rear, chsd alng 11th, no imp, wknd 15th*	5	13
587	23/3	Wetherby Po'	(L)	OPE	3m	15	S	*handy til wknd 14th*	6	12
701	30/3	Tranwell	(L)	OPE	3m	8	GS	*prom,ld 4-9th,chsd ldr 15th,hrd rdn to ld apr last,drvn out*	1	18
912	8/4	Tranwell	(L)	OPE	3m	8	GF	*trckd ldr to 14th, going wll whn p.u. aft 3 out, dead*	P	0

Dead 18

ERA'S IMP ch.g. 7 Noble Imp - Goldys Era by Langton Gold Abbot — R E Baskerville

1995 P(0),2(17),3(17)

77	11/2	Wetherby Po'	(L)	RES	3m	18	GS	*cls up, u.r. 11th*	U	-
225	24/2	Duncombe Pa'	(R)	RES	3m	12	GS	*(fav) ld 4th, made rest, blnd 6th & 2 out, styd on strngly flat*	1	17
586	23/3	Wetherby Po'	(L)	LAD	3m	8	S	*prom whn p.u. 11th, dead*	P	0

Dead 19

ERINS BAR(IRE) b.g. 7 Erin's Hope - Vultellobar by Bargello — N Frankham

1995 2(13),P(0),3(0),1(14)

100	16/2	Fakenham	(L)	HC	2m 5f 110yds	9	G	*chsd ldr, mstk 8th, ld 10th till after 12th, soon wknd.*	6	11
484	15/3	Fakenham	(L)	HC	2m 5f 110yds	13	GF	*held up, imp 7th, cld on ldrs from 11th, ev ch 3 out, one pace apr last.*	3	21
670	28/3	Aintree	(L)	HC	3m 1f	9	G	*held up rear, mstk 5th, effort to chase ldrs hfwy, struggling when hit 5 out, t.o. when p.u. before 3 out.*	P	0

Maiden winner 95; ran well weak H/Chase but unlikely to win one; best below 3m; G/F-S 18

ERINSBOROUGH (Irish) — I 112^{P}, I 268^{R}

ERME ROSE(IRE) br.m. 7 Callernish - Rose Money by Roselier (FR) — Mrs B C Willcocks

1995 3(0),3(14)

145	17/2	Larkhill	(R)	MDO	3m	13	G	*alwys prom, chal 2 out, not qckn flat, improve*	2	17
299	2/3	Great Treth'	(R)	MDO	3m	13	G	*(fav) in tch, ld 15th, qcknd clr 2 out, comf*	1	18
627	23/3	Kilworthy	(L)	RES	3m	13	GS	*(fav) blnd 3rd & lost plc,prog und pres 13th,kpt on 3 out,nrst fin*	3	16
868	6/4	Larkhill	(R)	RES	3m	4	F	*(fav) hld up, stdy prog frm 11th, disp & blndrd last, no ext*	2	19
1114	17/4	Hockworthy	(L)	RES	3m	4	GS	*made all, rdn clr app last, ran on well*	1	18
1278	27/4	Bratton Down	(L)	INT	3m	12	GF	*ld/disp to 8th, cls up til not qckn frm last*	3	21

Steadily improving; consistent; makes mistakes; best when dictating; should upgrade; G/S-F 22

ERNIE FOX ch.g. 6 True Song - Castelira by Castle — Mrs B Hitchcock

1995 P(0),F(-)

34	20/1	Higham	(L)	MDN	3m	11	GF	*rr div, 5th & no ch whn ref & u.r. 13th*	R	-
108	17/2	Marks Tey	(L)	MDN	3m	17	G	*rr, in tch, wkng whn r.o. & u.r. 14th*	r	-
343	3/3	Higham	(L)	MDO	3m	11	G	*ld to 7th, ev ch whn ref 14th*	F	
423	9/3	High Easter	(L)	MDN	3m	8	S	*(bl) chsd ldrs,blnd 12th,ld 15th,j.s.3 out,hdded nxt,hld&ref last*	R	11
618	23/3	Higham	(L)	MDO	3m	14	GF	*rear of main grp whn ref 8th*	R	-
830	6/4	Marks Tey	(L)	MDN	3m	14	G	*mid-div til ref 5th*	R	-

Has ability but more than matched by temperament 10

ERRIGAL BAY (Irish) — I 99^{3}

ESCHEAT (Irish) — I 65, , I 116^{5}, I 141^{4}, I 160^{5}, I 198^{2}, I 263,

ESERIE DE CORES(USA) b.g. 6 Gold Crest (USA) - April Blues by Cure The Blues (USA) — F R Bown

1995 2(17),2(13),F(-),4(14)

69	10/2	Great Treth'	(R)	MDO	3m	12	S	*(fav) alwys prom, blnd 14th, p.u. nxt*	P	0
200	24/2	Lemalla	(R)	MDO	3m	12	HY	*prssd ldrs til blnd & u.r. 12th*	U	-
300	2/3	Great Treth'	(R)	MDO	3m	10	G	*hld up rear, 5th & clsng 3 out, not chal ldrs*	4	12
555	17/3	Ottery St M'	(L)	MDO	3m	15	G	*sn bhnd, t.o. 14th*	4	0

Placed 3 times 95 but declined 96; not 100% genuine; good enough for a win but best watched 11

ESKIMO STAR b.m. 6 Morgans Choice - Eskimo Slave by New Member — A J Cottle

1995 **12(NH),10(NH)**

1431	6/5	High Bickin'	(R)	MDO	3m	9	G	*rear whn blnd bdly & u.r. 8th*	U	-
1555	18/5	Bratton Down	(L)	MDO	3m	13	F	*crashed through wing 2nd*	r	-
1652	8/6	Umberleigh	(L)	MDO	3m	10	GF	*rear, lost tch whn p.u. 7th*	P	0

Ex-NH Flat; best left in the cold at present 0

ESPY b.g. 13 Pitpan - Minorette by Miralgo — C James

1995 **1(32),3(27),2(27),2(21),P(0),P(0)**

22	20/1	Barbury Cas'	(L)	XX	3m	19	GS	*(fav) (bl) prom,lft 2nd 13th,ev ch apr 2 out,rdn & not run on,f last*	F	22
127	17/2	Kingston Bl'	(L)	MEM	3m	6	GS	*(fav) w.w. chsd wnr 14th, no imp whn blnd 3 out, wknd*	3	12
994	8/4	Hackwood Pa'	(L)	MEM	3m	4	GF	*(fav) trckd ldr frm 6th, ld last, qcknd easily*	1	16
1510	12/5	Maisemore P'	(L)	XX	3m	8	F	*rear, rmndr 5th, rdn 10th, last & no ch whn p.u. aft 15th*	P	0
1611	26/5	Tweseldown	(R)	XX	3m	9	G	*prom, cls 2nd whn f 11th*	F	-

Former good chaser; declined considerably 96; best fresh; novice-ridden; best watched; Any 18

EUROMILL STAR ch.m. 6 White Mill — Mrs C Howells

1201	21/4	Lydstep	(L)	MDN	3m	9	S	*twrds rear whn f 6th*	F	-
1273	27/4	Pyle	(R)	MDO	3m	9	G	*mostly last, t.o. whn blnd 10th & p.u.*	P	0
1388	6/5	Pantyderi	(R)	RES	3m	7	GF	*s.s. t.o. whn ref 3rd*	R	-

No signs of hope 0

EVEN CALL (Irish) — I 227^{P}, I 523^{P}, I 594^{1}, I 613^{P}

EVENING EMPIRE (Irish) — I 528^{P}, I 607^{P}, I 635^{P}

EVENTSINTERNASHNAL ch.g. 7 Funny Man - Tamorina by Quayside — T C Court

1485	11/5	Bredwardine	(R)	MDO	3m	15	G	*ran out 1st*	r	-

Not the best of starts 0

INDEX TO POINT-TO-POINT RUNNERS 1996

EVERLAUGHING (Irish) — I 150P, I 277U, I 309P, I 459P, I 610P, I 650B

EVERSO IRISH b.g. 7 Hatim (USA) - Ever So by Mummy's Pet — F J Brennan

1995 1(11),P(0),**P(0),10(0),U(NH),5(NH),F(NH),4(NH),4(NH),7(NH)**

707	30/3	Barbury Cas'	(L)	RES	3m	18	G	*sn bhnd, t.o. & p.u. 4 out*	P	0
960	8/4	Lockinge	(L)	RES	3m	9	GF	*mid-div, prog 14th, ev ch 5 out til wknd apr 3 out, onepcd*	5	10
1292	28/4	Barbury Cas'	(L)	RES	3m	11	F	*mstks, bhnd, gd prog 13th, ev ch 15th, wknd apr last*	4	13
1547	18/5	Fakenham	(L)	HC	2m 5f 110yds	11	G	*towards rear and rdn 6th, nvr on terms after.*	4	14

Maiden winner 95 but not threatening since; sold June 96; best watched 13

EVER TRUE (Irish) — I 5073

EVIE'S PARTY (Irish) — I 75, I 49P, I 1283

EWHONOSEBEST ch.g. 9 Lir - Cornish Susie by Fair Season — B R J Young

1995 3(16),P(0),**P(0)**,4(0),4(0),P(0),1(15),2(16)

41	3/2	Wadebridge	(L)	XX	3m	9	GF	*10s-5s, wth wnr to 13th, outpcd 15th, kpt on*	4	14
199	24/2	Lemalla	(R)	RES	3m	17	HY	*sn bhnd, p.u. 12th*	P	0
625	23/3	Kilworthy	(L)	CON	3m	11	GS	*prom til outpcd 14th, ran on frm 2 out, fin well*	3	19

Maiden winner 95; ran well in good Confined but vanished after; Restricted certain if fit 97; G/S-F 19

EXCLUSIVE EDITION(IRE) ch.m. 6 Bob Back (USA) - Nielsine by Czaravich (USA) — Robert J Foster

1995 **P(NH),1(NH),8(NH),8(NH),3(NH)**

32	20/1	Higham	(L)	OPE	3m	15	GF	*prom, disp ld 4th-15th, sn wknd*	4	15
56	10/2	Cottenham	(R)	OPE	3m	12	GS	*mstks, hld up in tch, prog & in tch 3 out, not qckn, kpt on*	4	20
101	17/2	Marks Tey	(L)	MEM	3m	3	G	*(fav) pllng, alwys 2nd, rddn 2 out, hld whn f last*	2	16
420	9/3	High Easter	(L)	OPE	3m	9	S	*w.w. prog gng wll 12th, ev ch 3 out, wknd appr nxt*	3	19
619	23/3	Higham	(L)	OPE	3m	10	GF	*hld up rear,prog to cls on ldrs 11th,chal 3 out,onepcd flat*	2	17
935	8/4	Marks Tey	(L)	MEM	3m	3	G	*(fav) made all, clr 6th, jnd 10th, drew clr 16th, lft alone 3 out*	1	16
1146	20/4	Higham	(L)	OPE	3m	7	F	*hld up, no prog in 5th whn p.u. 13th*	P	0

Hurdles winner; tries hard but stamina problems blight hopes & won joke race; likely to struggle 17

EXCUSE ME (Irish) — I 451F

EXECUTIVE BILL (Irish) — I 107P, I 2324, I 298F, I 340U

EXECUTIVE CHIEF (Irish) — I 267F, I 3902, I 477,

EXECUTIVE CLASS (Irish) — I 62P, I 114P, I 148P, I 2482, I 2932, I 3662, I 4711

EXECUTIVE FOX (Irish) — I 2085

EXILE RUN(IRE) ch.g. 8 Deep Run - Castle Treasure by Perspex — Michael Davidson

1088	14/4	Friars Haugh	(L)	MDO	3m	10	F	*f 6th*	F	-
1253	27/4	Balcormo Ma'	(R)	MDO	3m	16	GS	*prom to hlfwy, sn wknd*	8	0
1356	4/5	Mosshouses	(L)	MDO	3m	12	GS	*mstk 6th, rear, wll bhnd 13th, p.u. 3 out*	P	0

Tailed off on only completion to date 0

EXPENSIVE PLEASURE (Irish) — I 427F

EXPRESSMENT br.g. 12 Battlement - Ruby Express by Pony Express — Miss A S Ross

1995 1(20),**3(23)**

134	17/2	Ottery St M'	(L)	CON	3m	12	GS	*alwys mid-div, nvr in tch, bttr for race*	6	0
195	24/2	Lemalla	(R)	INT	3m	7	HY	*chsd ldrs, lft 2nd 3 out, outpcd by wnr*	2	20
671	28/3	Taunton	(R)	HC	3m	13	S	*bhnd, mstk 13th, hdwy 15th, one pace 3 out.*	3	19
1110	17/4	Hockworthy	(L)	CON	3m	9	GS	*rr, eff to 5th hlfwy, sn lost tch, walked in*	5	12
1277	27/4	Bratton Down	(L)	CON	3m	15	GF	*in tch, chsd ldrs 4 out, not qckn frm last*	3	20
1344	4/5	Holnicote	(L)	CON	3m	4	GS	*trckd ldr, ld 8th, made rest, kpt on well*	1	18
1464	11/5	Warwick	(L)	HC	3 1/4m	6	F	*held up, hdwy when hit 14th, went 2nd 5 out, kept on one pace from 2 out.*	2	20
1614	27/5	Hereford	(R)	HC	3m 1f 110yds	16	G	*held up, hdwy 12th, went 2nd 4 out, ld after next, soon drew clr, easily.*	1	22

Tough & reliable; stays; modest H/Chase success poses problems for winning at 13; G-Hy 21

EXPRESS REALE b.g. 11 Al Sirat (USA) - Real Path Vii — Mrs F Marner

994	8/4	Hackwood Pa'	(L)	MEM	3m	4	GF	*cls up to 10th, wknd qckly, t.o.*	4	0

No prospects 0

EXTRASPECIAL BREW br.g. 9 Afzal - Totally Tiddly by French Vine — Mrs T Ritson

1995 P(0),P(0),3(12),P(0)

165	17/2	Weston Park	(L)	RES	3m	9	G	*chsd ldrs, fdd & p.u. 3 out*	P	0
739	31/3	Sudlow Farm	(R)	RES	3m	11	G	*rear & blndrd 8th, some late prog, nvr dang*	5	10
1030	13/4	Alpraham	(R)	RES	3m	10	GS	*chsd ldng pair, hmp & u.r. 5th*	U	-

Maiden winner 93; nothing special since & unlikely to win again 10

EXTRA STOUT (Irish) — I 3654

FAHA GIG (Irish) — I 48^{3}, I 67^{2}, I 115^{1}, I 140^{1}, I 152^{3}, I 184^{2}, I 278^{1}

FAHA MOSS (Irish) — I 187^{P}

FAHA POINT (Irish) — I 238^{F}

FAHOORA (Irish) — I 610^{P}, I 649^{P}

FAIR ALLY gr.g. 6 Scallywag - Fair Kitty by Saucy Kit — A Milner

1995 5(14),P(0)

176	18/2	Market Rase'	(L)	MDO	2m 5f	10	GF	*(fav) jmpd rght,pllng,ld 11th,wd & hdd aft 2 out,rallied flat*	3	15
240	25/2	Southwell P'	(L)	MDO	3m	15	HO	*hld up in poor last,gd prog frm 9th,ev ch 4 out,outpcd nxt*	3	10
413	9/3	Charm Park	(L)	MDO	3m	12	G	*(fav) jmpd rght,cls up,25l clr wth ldr 4 out,hit 2 out,no ch aft*	2	0
516	16/3	Dalton Park	(R)	MDO	3m	11	G	*(fav) hld up bhnd, prog 8th, ld 14th-2 out, hrd rdn & not qckn*	2	12
987	8/4	Charm Park	(L)	MDN	3m	13	GF	*mid-div, prog 12th, hit 14th & p.u.*	P	0
1286	27/4	Easingwold	(L)	MDO	3m	13	G	*(bl) nvr going wll, bhnd whn p.u. 12th*	P	0

Good enough to win but frustrating; blinkers no help; still young but best watched 97 13

FAIR AVOCA (Irish) — I 99^{F}, I 180^{P}, I 215^{P}, I 321^{P}, I 448^{P}

FAIR CROSSING ch.g. 10 Over The River (FR) - Golden Chestnut by Green Shoon — Michael Emmanuel

1995 **1(NH),2(NH),P(NH),8(NH)**

22	20/1	Barbury Cas'	(L)	XX	3m	19	GS	*chsd ldr,lft in ld 13th,in cmmnd whn lft clr last,ran on wll*	1	24

Winning hurdler; lightly raced; goes well fresh; decent win & could repeat if ready 97 23

FAIR GRAND b.g. 6 Primitive Rising (USA) - Grand Queen by Grand Conde (FR) — A G Knowles

1995 P(0),P(0),3(0),P(0),3(0)

53	4/2	Alnwick	(L)	MDO	3m	13	G	*n.j.w., rear, t.o. & p.u. 10th*	P	0
75	11/2	Wetherby Po'	(L)	MDO	3m	8	GS	*in tch to 10th, outpcd whn u.r. 13th*	U	-
123	17/2	Witton Cast'	(R)	MDO	3m	11	S	*rear whn p.u. 10th*	P	0
229	24/2	Duncombe Pa'	(R)	MDO	3m	13	GS	*chsd ldr to 4th, lost plc & rear 8th, p.u. 12th*	P	0

Placed in poor races 95; showed nothing 96 & looks a lost cause 0

FAIR ISLAND (Irish) — I 172^{4}

FAIR LARK b.g. 6 All Fair - Little Lark by Sir Lark — Miss K Stevens

1995 P(0),P(0)

928	8/4	Bishopsleigh	(R)	MDN	3m	9	G	*f 1st*	F	-
1117	17/4	Hockworthy	(L)	MDO	3m	8	GS	*out of tch in rr, 5th & rdn 10th, p.u. aft nxt*	P	0
1280	27/4	Bratton Down	(L)	MDO	3m	14	GF	*alwys mid-div, no ch whn p.u. last*	P	0
1347	4/5	Holnicote	(L)	MDO	3m	16	GS	*ld/disp 4th til wknd & u.r. 15th*	U	-

Yet to complete & unpromising 0

FAIR MANE (Irish) — I 608^{P}

FAIR REVIVAL (Irish) — I 355, , I 436^{4}, I 505^{5}, I 547^{4}, I 593^{4}, I 613^{P}, I 658^{P}

FAIR TREE (Irish) — I 455^{P}

FAIRY THORN (Irish) — I 291^{F}

FAITHFUL STAR b.g. 11 Tilden - Star Relation by Star Gazer — M C Pipe

1995 1(25),1(26),**P(0)**,1(27),1(0),1(26),**1(38),4(26)**

26	20/1	Barbury Cas'	(L)	OPE	3m	12	GS	*(fav) blnd 6th,effrt 10th,outpcd 12th,lft 3rd nxt,wknd 3 out,tired*	3	12
39	3/2	Wadebridge	(L)	OPE	3m	7	GF	*(fav) msk 5th, last whn u.r. 8th*	U	-
133	17/2	Ottery St M'	(L)	OPE	3m	18	GS	*hld up, prog 15th, went 3rd 2 out, no ext flat*	3	22
468	10/3	Milborne St'	(L)	OPE	3m	5	G	*(fav) hld up, prog 12th, ld 4 out, sn clr*	1	25
988	8/4	Kingston St'	(R)	MEM	3m	7	F	*(fav) hld up in tch, ld 12th, pshd clr 14th*	1	28
1110	17/4	Hockworthy	(L)	CON	3m	9	GS	*(fav) prog 5th, trckd ldr 10th, ld 15th, drvn out flat*	1	28
1276	27/4	Bratton Down	(L)	LAD	3m	7	GF	*(fav) mstks, ld 6th, sn clr, easily*	1	31
1346	4/5	Holnicote	(L)	LAD	3m	5	GS	*(fav) ld 14th, made rest, not extnd*	1	29
1552	18/5	Bratton Down	(L)	LAD	3m	7	F	*(fav) handy, mstk 4th, ld 14th, sn clr, unchal, eased flat*	1	30
1631	1/6	Stratford	(L)	HC	3 1/2m	14	GF	*prom, mstks 2nd and 9th, ld 12th to 17th, second when blnd and u.r. 4 out.*	U	-

Top pointer; won 15 of last 18; sulking early season; hard to beat again 97; G/S-F 33

FALAS LAD (Irish) — I 231, , I 256^{P}, I 492^{P}, I 583^{1}, I 596^{2}

FALCONBRIDGE BAY ch.g. 9 Buzzards Bay - Swaynes Princess by St Chad — S Williams

359	4/3	Doncaster	(L)	HC	2m 3f 110yds	10	G	*struggling to stay in tch hfwy, t.o. when p.u. before 6 out.*	P	0
579	20/3	Ludlow	(R)	HC	2 1/2m	17	G	*prom to 6th, t.o. from from 12th.*	6	0
1100	14/4	Guilsborough	(L)	OPE	3m	9	G	*mstk 1st, chsd ldrs, in tch whn blnd 15th, t.o. & p.u. 2 out*	P	0
1235	27/4	Clifton On '	(L)	MEM	3m	4	GF	*jmpd slwly 4th, jnd wnr 7th, hrd rdn & ev ch 2 out, sn btn*	2	12
1379	5/5	Dingley	(R)	MXO	3m	7	GF	*prom, chal & lft in ld 14th, hdd nxt, wknd 2 out, fin tired*	2	0
1519	12/5	Garthorpe	(R)	OPE	3m	7	GF	*rear, clsd on ldrs 11th, 4th & hld whn p.u. 2 out, lame*	P	0

Tries hard but does not stay 3m, problems last start & Members only hope if fit 97 13

FALSE ECONOMY ch.g. 11 Torus - Vulvic by Vulgan — Miss G Green

1995 4(14),R(-),1(16),B(-),P(0),4(10)

135 17/2 Ottery St M' (L) LAD 3m 11 GS *in tch, 3rd at 14th, outpcd frm 4 out, lft 3rd 2 out* 3 20
467 10/3 Milborne St' (L) MEM 3m 8 G *cls up whn u.r. 7th* U -
561 17/3 Ottery St M' (L) LAD 3m 12 G *in tch til lost plc 12th, ran on frm 4 out, went 3rd nxt* 3 16
655 23/3 Badbury Rin' (L) LAD 3m 8 G *prom early, wknd 10th, ran on frm 4 out* 3 19
991 8/4 Kingston St' (R) LAD 3m 8 F *twrds rear, 25l 6th at 10th, nvr dang* 5 14
124 20/4 Stafford Cr' (R) CON 3m 7 S *cls up til ld 9-10th, prom til wknd 4 out* 5 14
310 28/4 Little Wind' (R) LAD 3m 4 G *ld to 7th, chsd wnr, no imp* 2 18
393 6/5 Cotley Farm (L) XX 3m 10 GF *mid-div, 5th at 10th, lost tch 4 out, p.u. app last* P 0
552 18/5 Bratton Down (L) LAD 3m 7 F *made most til aft 5th, lost plc 10th, poor 4th frm nxt* 4 10
635 1/6 Bratton Down (L) LAD 3m 13 G *mid-div, lost tch 12th, kpt on onepcd frm 2 out, no dang* 6 11

Safe & solid but lost last 13 now & likely to extend the sequence at 12 16

FAMILIAR FRIEND gr.g. 10 John French - Bidula M H G Lang

1995 P(0),P(0),P(0),B(-),5(10),P(0),2(18),7(0),**5(10)**

12 14/1 Cottenham (R) RES 3m 12 G *(bl) rear, effrt & blnd 11th, no ch aft, p.u. apr 14th* P 0
58 10/2 Cottenham (R) RES 3m 7 GS *(bl) trckd ldrs, mstk 16th, ld 2 out, hdd & wknd last* 4 13
361 5/3 Leicester (R) HC 2 1/2m 110yds 15 GS *(bl) rear, prog 6th, blnd 10th, disp ld 3 out, wknd quickly.* 6 0
484 15/3 Fakenham (L) HC 2m 5f 110yds 13 GF *(bl) mid div, gd hdwy from 12th, wknd from 2 out.* 5 17
674 30/3 Hereford (R) HC 2m 8 S *(bl) held up, hdwy 4 out, ld 2 out, clr when hit last, rdn out.* 1 19
908 8/4 Hereford (R) HC 2m 3f 12 GF *(bl) held up, hdwy 6th, ld 4 out, rdn out.* 1 20
1227 26/4 Ludlow (R) HC 2 1/2m 16 G *(bl) held up, hdwy 10th, wknd apr last.* 4 16
1339 4/5 Hereford (R) HC 2m 3f 7 F *(bl) held up in tch, mstk 10th, ld after next, hdd apr 3 out, soon wknd.* 4 18

Well-placed to win 2 weak H/Chases; not stay 3m; suspect in a finish; hard to win again 19

FANCYTALKINTINKER(IRE) b.g. 6 Bold Owl - Our Ena by Tower Walk J N Dalton

1044 13/4 Bitterley (L) MDO 3m 15 G *alwys rear, in tch whn f 9th* F -
1225 24/4 Brampton Br' (R) MDO 3m 18 G *rr 9th, sm prog frm 14th, not rch ldrs, p.u. 3 out* P 0

Only learning & should do better 10

FARAS FLIGHT (Irish) — **I** 32^{P}, **I** 83^{P}, **I** 105^{F}

FAR EAST(NZ) gr.g. 7 Veloso (NZ) - East (USA) by Shecky Greene (USA) Mrs F Walwyn

1995 **3(NH),7(NH),5(NH),4(NH),9(NH),5(NH)**

132 17/2 Ottery St M' (L) MDN 3m 9 GS *rear early, prog 12th, 2nd at 16th, no ch wnr aft* 2 12
199 24/2 Lemalla (R) RES 3m 17 HY *mid-div, 5th & no ch whn p.u. last* P 0

Beaten by good prospect on debut but season lasted only a week; should win if fit 97 14

FARINGO b.g. 11 Rustingo - Royal Marie by Alba Rock Fred Farrow

1995 P(0),3(0),1(14),1(19),**1(23),7(0)**

100 16/2 Fakenham (L) HC 2m 5f 110yds 9 G *in tch till outpcd 10th, t.o. when p.u. before 12th.* P 0
345 3/3 Higham (L) OPE 3m 3 G *(fav) cls 2nd til ld 8-11th, ld agn 14th, pshd clr, ran on well* 1 17
372 8/3 Market Rasen (R) HC 3m 1f 6 G *in tch, reminders apr 12th, t.o. approaching 4 out.* 4 0
485 16/3 Hereford (R) HC 3m 1f 110yds 13 S *cl up when blnd and u.r. 1st.* U -
907 8/4 Fakenham (L) HC 3m 110yds 11 G *(Jt fav) chsd ldr, no ext after 4 out.* 2 12
1108 17/4 Cheltenham (L) HC 4m 1f 14 GS *alwys bhnd, t.o..* 10 0
1323 28/4 Fakenham P-' (L) OPE 3m 8 G *prom going wll, ld 15th, rdn apr last, styd on* 1 21

H/Chase winner 95; outclassed 96 but won only two contested points; could win another 97; G/F 20

FARLOUGH LADY (Irish) — **I** 99^{U}, **I** 258^{P}, **I** 415^{3}, **I** 448^{P}

FARMLEA DANCER (Irish) — **I** 93^{P}, **I** 174^{P}

FARM LODGE (Irish) — **I** 456^{P}, **I** 534^{P}

FARNEY GLEN (Irish) — **I** 18^{P}, **I** 82^{3}, **I** 94^{1}, **I** 129^{2}

FARRAN GARRETT (Irish) — **I** 64^{R}, **I** 149^{F}, **I** 210^{P}, **I** 309^{P}, **I** 351^{2}, **I** 522^{3}

FARRIERS FAVOURITE gr.m. 7 Alias Smith (USA) - Farm Consultation by Farm Walk J W Hope

1995 3(11),1(14),2(16),6(15)

47 4/2 Alnwick (L) XX 3m 14 G *hld up, prog 11th, disp app 3 out til lft clr last drvn out* 1 19
112 17/2 Lanark (R) LAD 3m 8 GS *(fav) 5th at 10th, some prog 4 out, no imp on wnr* 2 18
399 9/3 Dalston (R) CON 3m 9 G *hld up, imprv 10th, chsd wnr frm 3 out, ev ch 2 out,not qckn* 3 19

Maiden winner 95; handed Restricted 1st start 96; finds little; blinkers worth a try; finished early 19

FAR RUN b.g. 9 Farhaan - Ballynavin Run by Deep Run Paul C N Heywood

1995 **7(NH)**

44 3/2 Wadebridge (L) MDO 3m 9 GF *hld up, prog 10th, ld aft 14th-2 out, no ext* 2 16
131 17/2 Ottery St M' (L) MDN 3m 10 GS *(fav) cls up, slppd bnd 9th, rcvrd, slppd agn 16th, ev ch & f 3out* F -

300 2/3 Great Treth' (R) MDO 3m 10 G *(Jt fav) cls 2nd at 10th, wknd 12th, 8th whn p.u. 15th* P

Lightly raced; good enough for a win but unfortunate & finished early after poor run 14

FAR TOO LOUD b.g. 9 Taufan (USA) - Octet by Octavo (USA) G W Penfol
1995 **9(NH),6(NH),6(NH),5(NH),8(NH)**

66 10/2 Great Treth' (R) OPE 3m 8 S *nvr bttr than 4th/5th, no ch frm 3 out* 5 1
278 2/3 Clyst St Ma' (L) CON 3m 9 S *alwys mid-div, nvr any ch, outpcd* 4 1
559 17/3 Ottery St M' (L) OPE 3m 7 G *in tch, 5th hlfwy, outpcd frm 4 out* 5
626 23/3 Kilworthy (L) OPE 3m 12 GS *ref & u.r. 1st* R
731 31/3 Little Wind' (R) OPE 3m 5 GS *ref 3rd* R
927 8/4 Bishopsleigh (R) OPE 3m 7 G *ref 1st* R
1073 13/4 Lifton (R) OPE 3m 10 S *ref 1st* R

When he is good he is not very good & when he is bad he is horrid 0

FAR VIEW(IRE) ch.g. 7 Phardante (FR) - Whosview by Fine Blade (USA) H B Hodg
1995 F(-),2(14),1(15),2(15),3(16)

12 14/1 Cottenham (R) RES 3m 12 G *mstks, prog to 3rd 13th, btn apr 2 out, ran on agn flat* 4 1

Maiden winner 95; brief season 96 though ran well; best on easy 3m; Good 17

FAST FREEZE b.g. 10 Vision (USA) - Gohar (USA) by Barachois (CAN) Mrs J E Hawkin
1995 P(0),3(17),3(10),4(0),3(0),4(14),1(17),4(13),S(-),R(-)

154 17/2 Erw Lon (L) LAD 3m 14 G *rear, late prog, nrst fin* 4 1
266 2/3 Didmarton (L) LAD 3m 13 G *ld to last, ran on onepcd flat* 3 2
383 9/3 Llanfrynach (R) CON 3m 13 GS *ld til hdd, stumbld & u.r. 13th* U
546 17/3 Erw Lon (L) LAD 3m 10 GS *nvr clsr than mid-div* 5 1
769 31/3 Pantyderi (R) LAD 3m 6 G *nvr rchd ldrs* 4
1202 21/4 Lydstep (L) LAD 3m 4 S *prom, nvr able to chal wnr* 2 1

1 win from 22 starts 94-6 (lucky) & modest at best; disappointing after 2nd run 96; best watched 17

FAST RECOVERY b.g. 11 Cruise Missile - Poynton Kate by Gracious Melody Mrs E M Bousquet-Payn
1995 **U(NH),3(NH),3(NH)**

619 23/3 Higham (L) OPE 3m 10 GF *ld 3rd-4 out, wknd rpdly, cllpsd flat, dead* P

Dead 10

FAST STUDY b.g. 11 Crash Course - Mary May by Little Buskins Simon J Robinso
1995 **U(-)**,6(11),1(20),**8(0)**,1(15),4(14),1(18),3(0)

120 17/2 Witton Cast' (R) OPE 3m 7 S *cls up til outpcd 3 out, styd on onepcd aft* 3 1
401 9/3 Dalston (R) OPE 3m 6 G *mid-div early, last at 8th, cls 2nd frm 15th, outpcd* 2 1
701 30/3 Tranwell (L) OPE 3m 8 GS *(fav) prog to disp 10th, ld 14th til hdd apr last, no ext flat* 2 1
912 8/4 Tranwell (L) OPE 3m 8 GF *6th hlfwy, nvr on terms wth ldrs* 4 1
1133 20/4 Hornby Cast' (L) OPE 3m 14 G *mid-div, rdn 8th, lost tch 13th, blnd 2 out & p.u.* P
1515 12/5 Hexham Poin' (L) OPE 3m 6 HY *chsd wnr to 5th & frm 8th til blnd 11th, p.u. nxt* P
1573 19/5 Corbridge (R) OPE 3m 12 G *alwys mid-div* 5 1

Won 3 modest races 95; inconsistent & struggling now; need fortune to score again 15

FATHER DOWLING br.g. 9 Teofane - Stream Flyer by Paddy's Stream Mrs E A Haycoc
1995 **6(NH)**

481 11/3 Taunton (R) HC 3m 11 G *held up, hdwy 11th, wknd 15th.* 5 1
668 26/3 Sandown (R) HC 2 1/2m 110yds 8 GS *alwys bhnd, lost tch from 8th, t.o..* 4 1

Winning chaser; disappointing in H/Chases & ran better in handicaps after 17

FATHER FLATTERY ch.g. 9 Sousa - Love Girl by Irish Love Miss A V Hande
1995 P(0),3(10),5(11)

471 10/3 Milborne St' (L) MDO 3m 16 G *ld 5th til u.r. 15th* U
533 16/3 Cothelstone (L) MDN 3m 13 G *5/2-1/1,ld to 11th,lft in ld 15th til 3 out,lft in ld last* 1 1

Landed gamble but needed fortune to do so; finished lame & more needed for Restricted if fit 97 15

FATHER FORTUNE b.g. 8 The Parson - Irish Mint by Dusky Boy D Hia
1995 P(0),P(0)

337 3/3 Heythrop (R) OPE 3m 10 G *bolted bef start, last frm 6th, t.o. & p.u. 10th* P
812 6/4 Charing (L) LAD 3m 6 F *cls up, prssd wnr 13th til wknd 2 out, 3rd whn ran out last* r
1165 20/4 Larkhill (R) LAD 3m 7 GF *unruley lost 30l stt, prog & ld 13-14th, wknd nxt* 3 1
1328 30/4 Huntingdon (R) HC 3m 4 GF *ld till joined 13th, hdd 16th, rallied to ld run-in, drew clr.* 1 1

Hurdles winner 93; won poor H/Chase; hard ride & impossible to place in 97 17

FATHER LIAM b.g. 13 The Parson - Irish Master by Master Owen M G Appleyar
1995 P(0),2(18),3(0),2(0),P(0),2(14)

632 23/3 Market Rase' (L) CON 3m 10 GF *4th for 2m, cls enough whn ran out 5 out* r
1133 20/4 Hornby Cast' (L) OPE 3m 14 G *ld to 5th, rmnd prom til wknd 4 out* 5 1

1304 28/4 Southwell P' (L) OPE 3m 5 GF *lft 2nd at 3rd, clsd 13th, ld 5 out, ran on well* 1 20
1515 12/5 Hexham Poin' (L) OPE 3m 6 HY *(fav) chsd wnr 5-8th & 13-16th & apr 2 out, no imp* 2 0

Inconsistent but beat subsequent H/Chase winner at Southwell; may pop up at 14 17

FATHER MALONE(IRE) b.g. 7 Ovac (ITY) - Belle Fillette by Beau Chapeau D Luxton
132 17/2 Ottery St M' (L) MDN 3m 9 GS *mid-div til p.u. 11th, missed marker* P 0
284 2/3 Clyst St Ma' (L) MDN 3m 11 S *alwys mid-div, no ch whn p.u. 15th* P 0
534 16/3 Cothelstone (L) MDN 3m 10 G *prom, chsd ldr 9-12th, sn wknd, p.u. 14th* P 0

Shows a glimmer of hope but time already passing 0

FATHER PRESCOTT (Irish) — I 266[5]
FATHERS FOOTPRINTS b.g. 8 Roc Imp - Mayo Melody by Highland Melody Mrs J A Thomson
1995 **P(NH),P(NH),U(NH),P(NH)**
28 20/1 Barbury Cas' (L) RES 3m 14 GS *alwys rear, t.o. & p.u. 14th* P 0
204 24/2 Castle Of C' (R) MDO 3m 11 HY *rear til prog 14th, ev ch last, outpcd* 2 11
430 9/3 Upton-On-Se' (R) MDO 3m 15 GS *chsd ldrs til 13th, bhnd & p.u. 2 out* P 0
557 17/3 Ottery St M' (L) MDN 3m 10 G *mid-div, 4th at 14th, outpcd frm 4 out* 3 10
788 31/3 Tweseldown (R) MDO 3m 8 G *cls up, ld 11th, qcknd 13th, styd on well 2 out, pshd out* 1 15
1013 13/4 Ascot (R) HC 3m 110yds 11 GS *ld to 2nd, with ldrs 10th, wknd from 4 out, t.o..* 5 0
1335 1/5 Cheltenham (L) HC 2m 5f 10 G *raced wd, cl up to 4th, bhnd from 8th, t.o..* 8 0
1540 16/5 Folkestone (R) HC 2m 5f 10 G *chsd ldrs, ld apr 9th to 3 out, wknd approaching last.* 2 16
1641 2/6 Dingley (R) RES 3m 13 GF *ld to 5th, chsd ldr til mstk 11th, wknd, p.u. 2 out* P 0

Won weak Maiden; outclassed in H/Chases apart from Folkestone; stamina suspect; Restricted likely 97 18

FATHER'S GIFT b.m. 8 Lochnager - Pretty Lass by Workboy Mrs J Riby
333 3/3 Market Rase' (L) MDO 3m 11 G *bhnd, blnd 5th & 10th, p.u. 13th* P 0
517 16/3 Dalton Park (R) MDO 3m 10 G *prom to 6th, wknd rpdly, t.o. & p.u. aft 10th* P 0
589 23/3 Wetherby Po' (L) MDO 3m 16 S *mid-div to 10th, sn rear, p.u. 14th* P 0

No signs of ability or stamina 0

FAULTY RAP (Irish) — I 7[2], I 49[1], I 75[4], I 141[P], I 242[1], I 376[P]
FAVLIENT b.m. 6 Farajullah - Valiant Dancer by Northfields (USA) Miss C Sparkes
375 9/3 Barbury Cas' (L) MDN 3m 14 GS *alwys prom, ld 13-15th, f nxt* F -
711 30/3 Barbury Cas' (L) MDO 3m 8 G *ld to 4 out, outpcd frm nxt* 2 0
1217 24/4 Andoversford (R) MDO 3m 16 G *prom, mstks 3rd & 6th, lost pl 12th, b.d. 14th* B -

Beaten a distance when 2nd; should improve - needs to 11

FAVOURED VICTOR(USA) ch.g. 9 Diesis - Northern Walk (CAN) by Nijinsky (CAN) Mrs A E Lee
523 16/3 Larkhill (R) MXO 3m 8 G *plld hrd, prom, wknd 12th, p.u. nxt* P 0
1016 13/4 Kingston Bl' (L) CON 3m 6 G *pllng, mstks, bhnd frm 9th, sn t.o.* 4 0

No prospects now 0

FAY LIN (Irish) — I 175[3], I 254[U]
FAYS FOLLY (Irish) — I 101[3]
FEARLESS BERTIE b.g. 5 Fearless Action (USA) - Rambert by Mandamus Miss J Johnston
1501 11/5 Kingston Bl' (L) RES 3m 10 G *schoold in last pair, t.o. & p.u. 11th* P 0

Just an educational run so far 0

FEARLESS HUNTER (Irish) — I 21[P], I 111[P]
FEARSOME gr.g. 10 Formidable (USA) - Seriema by Petingo G W Penfold
1995 5(0),3(12),2(17),5(14),3(15),4(16),5(0),2(19),4(16)
66 10/2 Great Treth' (R) OPE 3m 8 S *alwys rear, no ch frm 3 out* 4 16
134 17/2 Ottery St M' (L) CON 3m 12 GS *alwys mid-div, prog 15th, no ext frm 3 out* 3 16
296 2/3 Great Treth' (R) OPE 3m 5 G *handy, 2nd at 14th, 3rd & onepcd frm 16th* 3 19
441 9/3 Haldon (R) MEM 3m 6 S *(Jt fav) hld up in tch, rmndrs aft 13th, lft 2nd 3 out, ld cls home* 1 14
927 8/4 Bishopsleigh (R) OPE 3m 7 G *raced at rear til cls order frm 13th, ld 3 out, easy* 1 20
1124 20/4 Stafford Cr' (R) CON 3m 7 S *(fav) bhnd, prog frm 3 out, nrst at fin* 3 18
1309 28/4 Little Wind' (R) OPE 3m 8 G *hld up, 4th & off pace 15th, styd on to 2nd 2 out, no ch wnr* 2 20
1427 6/5 High Bickin' (R) CON 3m 10 G *(fav) held up, prog 14th, 2nd 3 out, drvn to ld last 75 yards* 1 21
1525 12/5 Ottery St M' (L) CON 3m 9 GF *alwys prom, cls 3rd & ev ch 2 out, just outpcd* 3 19
1551 18/5 Bratton Down (L) OPE 3m 8 F *w.w. in tch, 3rd frm 16th, kpt on to tk 2nd cls home* 2 19
1636 1/6 Bratton Down (L) OPE 4m 11 G *cls up til outpcd 20th, sn rdn & no imp* 6 15

Most consistent & broke losing sequence of 21 at Haldon; always finishes & should find a race 97; any 20

FEILE NA HINSE b.g. 13 Cidrax (FR) - Hildamay by Cantab Or Sale Time Miss Anna Bucknall
1995 **U(NH),5(NH),2(NH)**
530 16/3 Cothelstone (L) OPE 3m 7 G *mstks, in tch to 12th, no ch whn p.u. & dism 4 out* P 0

Winning chaser but looks finished now 0

FELL MIST b.g. 13 Silly Prices - Minimist by Bilsborrow — Mrs W D Sykes

1995 3(19),2(20),2(22),4(20),4(18),3(20)

663	24/3	Eaton Hall	(R)	LAD	3m	8	S	*cls up, tried to chal last, alwys hld*	2	22
951	8/4	Eyton-On-Se'	(L)	LAD	3m	6	GF	*(fav) mstly 2nd to 12th, ld 13th-3 out, not qckn*	2	18
1221	24/4	Brampton Br'	(R)	LAD	3m	6	G	*(fav) made all, prsd whn lft wl clr 16th*	1	21
1457	8/5	Uttoxeter	(L)	HC	3 1/4m	16	G	*prom, wknd 14th, t.o. when p.u. before 4 out.*	P	0
1545	18/5	Bangor	(L)	HC	3m 110yds	8	G	*handily pld, rdn after 13th, fd.*	4	13
1585	25/5	Cartmel	(L)	HC	3 1/4m	14	GF	*not fluent, chsd ldrs till wknd 12th, t.o. when p.u. before 3 out.*	P	0

Still consistent & game in Ladies; no chance in H/Chases but could win point at 14; Any 19

FELLOW SIOUX ch.g. 9 Sunley Builds - Sue Lark by Sir Lark — T B Stevens

1995 P(0),P(0),3(14)

1278	27/4	Bratton Down	(L)	INT	3m	12	GF	*alwys mid-div, ev ch 4 out, outpcd frm nxt*	5	13
1342	4/5	Holnicote	(L)	MEM	3m	7	GS	*alwys going wll, trckd ldrs, ld 2 out, ran on well*	1	18
1497	11/5	Holnicote	(L)	RES	3m	10	G	*hdwy 9th, cls up til ld 3 out, ran on strgly*	1	19
1590	25/5	Mounsey Hil'	(R)	INT	3m	8	G	*(fav) hld up in tch til f 11th*	F	-
1634	1/6	Bratton Down	(L)	INT	3m	15	G	*mid-div,prog 11th,3rd 3 out,hung lft & wknd flat*	5	12

Back to form 96; won competitive Restricted; hangs & L/H essential; may win Confined; Good 19

FENNELLS BAY (Irish) — **I** 71^{P}, **I** 353^{P}, **I** 374^{P}, **I** 654^{P}

FENNORHILL b or br.g. 12 Al Sirat (USA) - Choralgina by Choral Society — R Ward-Dutton

1995 P(0),P(0),P(0),3(0),P(0),P(0),3(0),P(0),R(-)

462	9/3	Eyton-On-Se'	(L)	RES	3m	12	G	*ld to 3rd, cls up til outpcd 12th, p.u. 3 out*	P	0
684	30/3	Chaddesley '	(L)	RES	3m	14	G	*bhnd frm 4th, t.o. & p.u. 12th*	P	0
879	6/4	Brampton Br'	(R)	LAD	3m	9	GF	*rear frm 6th, t.o. 9th*	8	0
1173	20/4	Chaddesley '	(L)	RES	3m	18	G	*mid-div, lost tch 10th, p.u. 17th*	P	0

Maiden winner 92; no chance of another win now 0

FERGAL'S DELIGHT b.g. 13 Welsh Chanter - Telamonia by Ballymoss — Mrs Caroline Chadney

1995 P(0),4(11),6(0),P(0),**6(0)**,5(12)

362	5/3	Leicester	(R)	HC	2 1/2m 110yds	8	GS	*(bl) ld to 3rd, wknd 11th, t.o..*	5	0
426	9/3	Upton-On-Se'	(R)	CON	3m	16	GS	*ld to 10th, 2nd til wknd rpdly 3 out*	5	0
743	31/3	Upper Sapey	(R)	LAD	3m	7	GS	*(bl) clr ldr to 7th, 4th aft til wknd 14th*	6	0
1001	9/4	Upton-On-Se'	(R)	MEM	3m	6	F	*(bl) ld to 8th, chsd ldr to 14th, rlld to ld app 2 out, all out*	1	15
1316	28/4	Bitterley	(L)	OPE	3m	5	G	*(bl) set fast pace til hdd 6th, wknd frm 12th*	3	12
1411	6/5	Cursneh Hill	(L)	CON	3m	5	GF	*ld 1st & 6-9th, ld 13th til hdd & onepcd aft nxt*	3	11
1565	19/5	Mollington	(R)	OPE	3m	8	GS	*(bl) outpcd frm 5th, t.o. 7th*	4	0

Winning chaser; does not stay but carried home by rider in Members; only prospect again 97 13

FERNBOY (Irish) — **I** 500^{F}, **I** 551^{4}, **I** 615^{P}, **I** 642^{P}

FERNHILL (Irish) — **I** 43^{1}, **I** 65^{4}

FERNHILL HOUSE (Irish) — **I** 213^{P}, **I** 458^{P}

FERNHILL WAY (Irish) — **I** 321^{U}, **I** 365, , **I** 403, , **I** 455^{F}, **I** 539^{4}, **I** 596,

FERN LEADER(IRE) b.g. 6 Supreme Leader - Mossbrook by Le Moss — W R Ward

1995 P(0),F(-),4(0),5(0)

123	17/2	Witton Cast'	(R)	MDO	3m	11	S	*ld/disp til ld 12th, jnd 2 out, ran on well apr last*	1	13
306	2/3	Great Stain'	(L)	INT	3m	12	GS	*mid-div, prog 12th, cls 3rd 15th, disp nxt, ld last, ran on*	1	18
699	30/3	Tranwell	(L)	CON	3m	8	GS	*(fav) alwys prom, ld 10th, hrd rdn last, hld on flat*	1	22
1130	20/4	Hornby Cast'	(L)	CON	3m	13	G	*(fav) disp to 4th, prom, ev ch whn mstk 12th, onepcd frm 3 out*	4	13

Much improved & won well; below form last start but could reach Open standard 97; G/S-S 22

FESTIVAL LIGHT (Irish) — **I** 39^{P}, **I** 89^{P}, **I** 112^{P}, **I** 166^{4}, **I** 190^{P}, **I** 296^{3}, **I** 327^{P}, **I** 474^{3}

FETHARDONSEAFRIEND b.g. 9 Rymer - Shoa by Menelek — A W Wood

80	11/2	Wetherby Po'	(L)	MDO	3m	12	GS	*alwys wll in rear, p.u. 4 out*	P	0
307	2/3	Great Stain'	(L)	MDO	3m	17	GS	*mid-div, wknd 12th, t.o. 2 out*	11	0
1286	27/4	Easingwold	(L)	MDO	3m	13	G	*wth ldrs, steadily fdd frm 4 out*	5	0

Placed tiwce 94; missed 95 & unlikely to achieve anything now 0

FETHARD ORCHID (Irish) — **I** 392^{U}, **I** 441^{P}, **I** 467^{3}

FETTLE UP ch.g. 8 Lyphard's Special (USA) - Fire Risk by Thatch (USA) — Mrs D R Brotherton

1995 F(-),3(14),U(-),6(11),1(16),3(0),P(0),1(18),1(0)

325	3/3	Market Rase'	(L)	LAD	3m	6	G	*prog 12th, chsd ldr brfly apr 14th, onepcd aft*	3	16
514	16/3	Dalton Park	(R)	LAD	3m	8	G	*(bl) alwys prom, ld 3 out, just hdd whn f heavily nxt*	F	22
752	31/3	Lockerbie	(R)	LAD	3m	10	G	*(Jt fav) (bl) alwys hndy, 4th hlfwy, no ext frm 2 out*	3	17
913	8/4	Tranwell	(L)	LAD	3m	7	GF	*(fav) (bl) ld to 4th, ld nxt, jnd 13th, clr nxt, imprssv*	1	23

1462 10/5 Market Rasen (R) HC 2 3/4m 110yds 11 G *(bl) ld early, prom till wknd 4 out.* 5 15

Won 3 in 95; retained form; best on Firm with blinkers; should find another race 21

FIDDLERS BRAE b.g. 6 Baron Blakeney - Mildenstone by Milan — Miss D M M Calder

405 9/3 Dalston (R) MDO 2 1/2m 16 G *last at 4th, styd on frm 2 out* 7 0
1356 4/5 Mosshouses (L) MDO 3m 12 GS *cls up,2nd 14th,ld 3 out,going wll whn ran out nxt* r -

Took the soft option last start but sure to give veteran rider another winner if consenting in 97 15

FIDDLERS GLEN(IRE) b.g. 8 Fidel - Glenava by Avocat — Mrs L C Taylor

1013 13/4 Ascot (R) HC 3m 110yds 11 GS *blundred 6th, soon well bhnd, t.o. when p.u. before 15th.* P 0

Very lightly raced & looks unlikely to achieve anything now 0

FIDDLERS KNAP br.g. 6 Queen's Soldier (USA) - Sharp Reef by Milford — C P Hobbs

335 3/3 Heythrop (R) INT 3m 9 G *alwys last, t.o. & p.u. 14th* P 0
432 9/3 Upton-On-Se' (R) MDO 3m 17 GS *prom early, wkng whn f 14th* F -
797 2/4 Heythrop (R) MDN 3m 11 F *ld to 6th,lost plc & poor last 9th,rpd prog 2 out,just faild* 2 14
942 8/4 Andoversford (R) MEM 3m 8 GF *(fav) cls 2nd at 14th, wknd & p.u. last* P 0

Just failed in bad Maiden; no show after; novice-ridden; more needed to win 13

FIDDLER'S LANE b.g. 8 Mart Lane - Alto Sax by Prince de Galles — Miss P Kerby

1995 r(-),P(0),F(-)

1175 20/4 Chaddesley ' (L) MDN 3m 9 G *s.s. alwys last, lost tch & p.u. aft 16th* P 0
1225 24/4 Brampton Br' (R) MDO 3m 18 G *mid-div til prog 16th, strng run frm last to ld flat* 1 14

Beat 2 subsequent winners on 1st ever completion; hard to assess but should improve 15

FIDDLERS THREE ch.g. 13 Orchestra - Kirin by Tyrant (USA) — Ian Wynne

1995 4(22),2(22)

159 17/2 Weston Park (L) CON 3m 22 G *(bl) chsng grp, str chal 3 out, sn ld, ran on well* 1 24
662 24/3 Eaton Hall (R) OPE 3m 10 S *(bl) trckd ldrs, 2nd 7th til ld apr last, ran on well, comf* 1 27
1121 20/4 Bangor (L) HC 3m 110yds 8 S *(bl) held up in tch, lost pl 11th, no dngr after, t.o..* 6 13

Lightly raced now but still useful; won good races 96; blinkers essential; cna win at 14; G-S 24

FIDDLING THE FACTS (Irish) — **I** 417[1]

FIDOON (Irish) — **I** 99[P], **I** 179[P], **I** 261[4], **I** 288[4], **I** 320[5], **I** 415[2], **I** 448[P]

FIDSPRIT (Irish) — **I** 24[P], **I** 92[P], **I** 214[P], **I** 259[2], **I** 320[U], **I** 406[P], **I** 448[2], **I** 535[3], **I** 601[3]

FIELD OF DESTINY (Irish) — **I** 393[2], **I** 425[1], **I** 584[6], **I** 623[3]

FIERY SUN b.g. 11 Sexton Blake - Melanie Jane by Lord Gayle (USA) — Mrs R E Barr

1995 **4(NH),3(NH),7(NH),3(NH),3(NH),2(NH),4(NH),3(NH),4(NH),3(NH)**

760 31/3 Great Stain' (L) OPE 3m 8 GS *ld to 5 out, rallied to ld 2 out, sn clr* 1 22
826 6/4 Stainton (R) OPE 3m 8 GF *(fav) prom, went 2nd apr 14th, chal last, qcknd to ld flat* 1 20
1282 27/4 Easingwold (L) OPE 3m 8 G *(fav) ld to 10th, sn lost plc, onepcd frm 4 out* 4 15
1449 6/5 Witton Cast' (R) LAD 3m 10 G *outpcd in midfld, nvr a dang* 7 0

Start well but lost interest after; may revive early 97 but best watched for signs; G/F-G/S 20

FIFTH GENERATION (Irish) — **I** 40[F], **I** 137, , **I** 250[2], **I** 328, , **I** 511[3]

FIGHTING FOR GOOD(IRE) b.g. 6 Lancastrian - Breeze Dancer by Torus — C N Nimmo

1568 19/5 Mollington (R) MDO 3m 9 GS *trckd ldrs, pshd alng & wknd 10th, p.u. nxt* P 0

Stopped quickly on debut at halfway 0

FIGHTING MARINER b.g. 9 Julio Mariner - Dark Pearl by Harwell — Mrs J H Westrope

1995 P(0),P(0),1(19),4(12),3(15),2(20)

125 17/2 Kingston Bl' (L) OPE 3m 10 GS *in tch til pshd alng & wknd 10th, p.u. nxt* P 0

Surprise (25/1) winner 95 but disappeared quickly 96; front-runner; best watched 17

FILEO (Irish) — **I** 185[P], **I** 308[F], **I** 351[3], **I** 459[1], **I** 508[F]

FILL YOUR BOOTS (Irish) — **I** 22[P], **I** 90[P], **I** 98[F], **I** 219[P], **I** 261, , **I** 321[U], **I** 341[U], **I** 415[P], **I** 456[R]

FILTHY REESH b.g. 7 Reesh - Not Enough by Balinger — Robert Grove

1995 P(0),5(0)

3 13/1 Larkhill (R) MDO 3m 10 GS *prssd ldr til wknd 13th, p.u. 15th* P 0
144 17/2 Larkhill (R) MDO 3m 15 G *sttld bhnd ldrs, some prog 13th, wkng whn u.r. 3 out* U -

Shows some ability but more stamina needed 0

FINAL ABBY b.m. 8 Push On - Final Answer by Honour Bound — Mrs E A Thomas

1995 2(12),4(0),2(12)

432 9/3 Upton-On-Se' (R) MDO 3m 17 GS *(fav) conf rdn, ld 13th, mstks last 2, easily* 1 17
549 17/3 Erw Lon (L) RES 3m 11 GS *cls up til wknd 2 out* 3 0
1002 9/4 Upton-On-Se' (R) RES 3m 8 F *(fav) w.w., prog 9th, chsd wnr 14th, sn outpcd, mstk 2 out* 3 0

Beat large field & ran fair races after; should find Restricted if ready 97; G-S 17

FINAL CRUISE ch.m. 7 Cruise Missile - Final Answer by Honour Bound Mrs Elizabeth Thomas

1995 2(14),r(-),F(-),P(0)

147 17/2 Erw Lon (L) MDN 3m 8 G *(Jt fav) alwys prom, ld 13th-nxt, chal 2 out, outpcd* 2 14
367 6/3 Catterick (L) HC 3m 1f 110yds 12 G *in tch, slightly hmpd 15th, bhnd when f 2 out.* F -
772 31/3 Pantyderi (R) MDN 3m 8 G *(fav) prom whn u.r. 13th* U -
975 8/4 Lydstep (L) MDO 3m 9 G *3rd/4th, mstk 10th, ev ch 2 out, onepcd* 2 11
1201 21/4 Lydstep (L) MDN 3m 9 S *prom to 14th, fdd, p.u. 2 out* P 0

Runner-up 3 times from 9 starts 95-6 (only completions); becoming disappointing; may strike lucky 13

FINAL EXPRESS ch.m. 8 Pony Express - Sansem by New Member J A G Meaden

1995 **11(NH),6(NH),7(NH)**

470 10/3 Milborne St' (L) MDO 3m 18 G *handy, ev ch 3 out, not qckn frm nxt* 4 13
653 23/3 Badbury Rin' (L) MDO 3m 9 G *settld mid-div, left 2nd 12th, ld appr last, ran on.* 1 14
729 31/3 Little Wind' (R) RES 3m 12 GS *mid-div, 6th & pshd alng 12th, nvr dang* 6 14
1056 13/4 Badbury Rin' (L) RES 3m 10 GF *in tch to 13th, lost plc, renewed effrt 2 out, styd on* 2 18
1528 12/5 Ottery St M' (L) RES 3m 10 GF *alwys rear, t.o. & p.u. 4 out* P 0
1551 18/5 Bratton Down (L) OPE 3m 8 F *ld/disp to 6th, cls up til lost plc 14th, no ch frm 16th* 6 14
1611 26/5 Tweseldown (R) XX 3m 9 G *n.j.w. last pair til nrly u.r. 5th, p.u. nxt* P 0
1636 1/6 Bratton Down (L) OPE 4m 11 G *last & rdn 10th, ran on 20th, went 3rd 4 out, tk 2nd nr fin* 2 21

Has ability but novice-ridden to no good effect; easily good enough for Restricteds; stays; L/H; good ... 18

FINAL HOPE(IRE) ch.g. 8 Burslem - Mesnil Warren by Connaught R Tate

1995 4(10),1(20),4(15),U(-),4(13),**1(22)**,**1(25)**,**4(NH)**

76 11/2 Wetherby Po' (L) LAD 3m 8 GS *rear early, prog 11th, ld 14th-last, no ext flat* 3 20
117 17/2 Witton Cast' (R) MEM 3m 9 S *(fav) rear, prog 7th, 2nd at 9th, ld 12th, clr 2 out, kpt on well* 1 20
305 2/3 Great Stain' (L) LAD 3m 11 GS *(fav) hld up, prog 15th, disp 2 out, sn ld & clr, easily* 1 22
582 22/3 Kelso (L) HC 3 1/2m 8 G *held up in rear, steady hdwy 12th, trckd ldrs when f next.* F -
673 29/3 Sedgefield (L) HC 3m 3f 7 GF *(fav) settld in tch, chsd wnr 4 out, driven 2 out, no impn.* 2 19
1328 30/4 Huntingdon (R) HC 3m 4 GF *(fav) in tch, joined ldr 13th, ld 16th, pushed clr apr 2 out, rdn approaching last, hdd run-in, soon btn.* 2 17
1366 4/5 Gisburn (R) LAD 3m 12 G *bhnd, 3rd frm 2 out, nvr nrr* 3 19
1572 19/5 Corbridge (R) LAD 3m 8 G *disp 4th, prom til outpcd 14th, lft 2nd nxt, no ext apr last* 2 18

Won 2 H/Chases 95; consistent but disappointing 96 & below form last 5 races; Ladies in 97; Any 20

FINAL ISSUE (Irish) — **I** 235[6], **I** 338[5]

FINALLY FANTAZIA ch.m. 7 True Song - Catherine Bridge by Pitpan Miss K Holmes

1995 2(17),F(-),4(12)

266 2/3 Didmarton (L) LAD 3m 13 G *wll bhnd til prog frm 11th, kpt on, nvr dang* 5 10
436 9/3 Newton Brom' (R) LAD 3m 10 GS *hld up rear, some prog to 4th 3 out, fdd, walked in* 8 0

Placed twice in 95 but no stamina & hard to see a win in points 14

FINAL NOD b.g. 9 Tom Noddy - Gemmerly Jane by Bally Russe C T Pogson

173 18/2 Market Rase' (L) RES 3m 6 GF *w.w. in tch, outpcd apr 14th, wll btn nxt* 5 0
241 25/2 Southwell P' (L) MDO 3m 15 HO *prom, 3rd & ev ch 4 out, wknd apr nxt* 4 0
397 9/3 Garthorpe (R) MDN 3m 9 G *alwys rear hlf, outpcd 6 out, p.u. 3 out* P 0
636 23/3 Market Rase' (L) MDN 3m 11 GF *alwys prom, lft in ld 3 out, jnd last, just outpcd* 2 0
1026 13/4 Brocklesby ' (L) MDN 3m 6 GF *mid-div, prog 9th, chal ld & f 6 out, (dead)* F -

Dead 15

FINAL OPTION(IRE) b.g. 8 Quayside - Death Or Glory by Hasdrubal G A Fynn

1995 P(0),5(0),U(-),P(0)

17 14/1 Tweseldown (R) MDN 3m 11 GS *ld 3-4th, sn rear, t.o. 12th, p.u. 2 out, dsmntd* P 0
29 20/1 Barbury Cas' (L) RES 3m 12 GS *rear, lost tch 10th, t.o. whn blnd & u.r. 12th* U -
255 28/2 Taunton (R) HC 4 1/4m 110yds 15 GS *effort 13th, soon wknd, t.o. when p.u. before 21st.* P 0
391 9/3 Llanfrynach (R) MDN 3m 11 GS *bhnd til prog 7th,went poor 3rd 13th,no imp,.lft 2nd flat* 2 0
607 23/3 Howick (L) MDN 3m 12 S *cls 4th at 11th, wknd, fin own time* 4 0
695 30/3 Llanvapley (L) RES 3m 13 GS *alwys rear, fin own time* 4 0
848 6/4 Howick (L) MDN 3m 14 GF *ld chsng grp til wknd 10th, t.o. 13th* 9 0

Well beaten when finishing & nowhere near a win yet 0

FINAL ROSE b.m. 6 Derring Rose - Final Flirtation by Clear Run D H Llewellyn

1995 F(-)

548 17/3 Erw Lon (L) RES 3m 8 GS *mid-div, p.u. 10th* P 0

1200 21/4 Lydstep (L) MDN 3m 10 S *rear to 6th, prog 10th, nvr able to chal* 3 12

Beaten less than 3l when 3rd & should go close in 97 13

FINAL STATEMENT (Irish) — I 26, , I 88^{P}

FIND OUT MORE (Irish) — I 17^{3}, I 104^{3}, I 235^{F}, I 298^{2}, I 317^{2}, I 363^{1}, I 412^{3}, I 453^{2}, I 536^{P}

FINE AFFAIR (Irish) — I 212^{P}, I 276^{2}, I 357^{5}, I 576^{2}, I 613^{3}

FINE TIMING b.g. 9 Roscoe Blake - Off The Pill by Marshall Pil Miss D Hughes

1995 P(0),**F(-)**

485 16/3 Hereford (R) HC 3m 1f 110yds 13 S *chsd ldrs, wknd 11th, t.o. when p.u. before 15th.* P 0

1341 4/5 Warwick (L) HC 2 1/2m 110yds 12 GF *mid div, hdwy to chase ldrs 7th, wknd 12th, t.o. when p.u. before 2 out.* P 0

No prospects & a waste of time in H/Chases 0

FINGERHILL (Irish) — I 103^{P}, I 158^{6}, I 392, , I 561^{3}, I 584^{2}, I 626^{1}

FINNIGAN FREE ch.g. 6 Los Cerrillos (ARG) - Philly-Free by Avocat G E Rich

1995 **P(NH)**

137 17/2 Ottery St M' (L) RES 3m 15 GS *handy, ld 13th-nxt, wknd frm 4 out* 3 13

Ran well only start & Maiden most likely if able to run regularly 97 15

FINNOW THYNE (Irish) — I 4^{P}, I 39^{F}, I 79^{3}, I 146^{2}, I 306^{2}, I 334^{5}, I 457^{2}

FINNUALA SUPREME (Irish) — I 55^{5}, I 63^{F}, I 120^{S}, I 144^{P}, I 277^{1}

FINNURE (Irish) — I 518^{5}, I 571^{4}

FIREHALMS b.g. 9 Reesh - Halmsgiving by Free State A Beedles

1995 **P(0)**,2(18),2(17),**5(0)**,**P(0)**

159 17/2 Weston Park (L) CON 3m 22 G *prom in chsng grp, fdd, p.u. 2 out* P 0

457 9/3 Eyton-On-Se' (L) INT 3m 11 G *ld to 12th, wknd qkly, no ch whn p.u. 2 out* P 0

Looks finished now 0

FIRE OF TROY br.m. 8 Ilium - Rekindle by Relkino C Blank

718 30/3 Wadebridge (L) MDO 3m 11 GF *in tch to 8th, lost plc rpdly aft 11th, p.u. nxt* P 0

1143 20/4 Flete Park (R) MDN 3m 17 S *prog to 5th at 12th, 4th whn slw jmp 3 out, no ch nxt* 4 0

Last & well beaten when 4th, stamina doubtful & much more needed 0

FIREWATER STATION br.g. 13 Buckskin (FR) - Gamonda by Gala Performance (USA) Mrs D B A Silk

272 2/3 Parham (R) RES 3m 13 GF *alwys rear, p.u. 13th* P 0

574 17/3 Detling (L) RES 3m 14 GF *mid-div, some prog to 4th 3 out, no ch whn p.u. nxt* P 0

779 31/3 Penshurst (L) RES 3m 13 GS *prom to 11th, bhnd whn p.u. aft 13th* P 0

1051 13/4 Penshurst (L) MEM 3m 5 G *2nd at 7th, wth wnr 14th, wknd nxt, fin tired, walked in* 2 0

Missed 95 & looks well past it now 0

FIRST BASH (Irish) — I 156^{P}, I 236^{F}, I 634^{F}, I 651^{2}

FIRST COMMAND(NZ) b.g. 9 Captain Jason (NZ) - Lady Of The Dawn (NZ) by Princely Note R Newey

1995 **P(NH)**

358 3/3 Garnons (L) RES 3m 18 GS *in ldng grp, chal & ev ch 13th, wknd apr nxt* 5 0

749 31/3 Upper Sapey (R) MDO 3m 17 GS *prom til grad outpcd frm 15th* 8 0

1041 13/4 Bitterley (L) MEM 3m 6 G *disp 5th, chal 13-14th, wknd apr 3 out* 3 0

1319 28/4 Bitterley (L) MDN 3m 13 G *hld up, effrt & prog 14th, wknd frm 3 out* 3 10

1416 6/5 Cursneh Hill (L) MDO 3m 9 GF *(fav) chsd ldr, ld aft 2 out, pushd clr apr last* 1 15

Safe & found poor race over easy 3m; more stamina needed for Restricted chance 13

FIRST DESIGN b.g. 9 Rustingo - Designer by Celtic Cone P D Jones

1995 **3(NH)**,**P(NH)**,**2(NH)**

130 17/2 Ottery St M' (L) MEM 3m 6 GS *chsd wnr frm 8th, no imp frm 2 out* 2 12

297 2/3 Great Treth' (R) INT 3m 10 G *cls 4th whn f 9th* F -

Maiden winner 93; lightly raced now & may have problems after the fall 14

FIRST HARVEST b.g. 9 Oats - Celtic Blade by Celtic Cone C J Bennett

365 5/3 Leicester (R) HC 3m 10 GS *mstks, ld 5th, clr 9th, hdd apr 2 out, wknd.* 4 18

524 16/3 Larkhill (R) INT 3m 11 G *ld til 13th, wknd rpdly, onepcd* 6 0

878 6/4 Brampton Br' (R) OPE 3m 5 GF *ld 3rd, rmndrs 7th, 8l clr 13th, rdn & clr 3 out* 1 20

1228 27/4 Worcester (L) HC 2m 7f 17 G *left in ld 4th, hdd 10th, wknd four out.* 5 17

1479 11/5 Bredwardine (R) OPE 3m 8 G *(fav) ld frm 5th, rdn 15th, ran wd & hdd 2 out, wknd flat* 3 18

Missed 95; front-runner; likes Brampton Bryan; should find another Open; G/F-S 21

FISCAL POLICY b.g. 8 Politico (USA) - Moschata by Star Moss A R Trotter

88	11/2	Alnwick	(L)	MDO	3m	11	GS	*sn wll bhnd, t.o. 6th, p.u. last*	P	0
116	17/2	Lanark	(R)	MDO	3m	10	GS	*sn bhnd, rpd prog frm 14th, chal last, just hld*	2	15
186	24/2	Friars Haugh	(L)	MEM	3m	7	S	*made most frm 8th, jnd apr last, hdd cls home*	2	15
323	2/3	Corbridge	(R)	MDN	3m	12	GS	*(fav) mid-div 6th, prog 4 out, strng run to ld flat, ran on*	1	15
608	23/3	Friars Haugh	(L)	RES	3m	13	G	*(fav) alwys rr*	7	0
858	6/4	Alnwick	(L)	RES	3m	7	GF	*prom,ld 10th-12th,lkd btn 3 out, strng run flat, ld cls hme*	1	18
1252	27/4	Balcormo Ma'	(R)	INT	3m	5	GS	*ld til 6th, last & plenty to do 13th,styd on wll frm 4 out*	2	16
1351	4/5	Mosshouses	(L)	CON	3m	11	GS	*prog 9th, ld 13th-2 out, kpt on onepcd*	2	19
1448	6/5	Witton Cast'	(R)	OPE	3m	5	G	*rear by 5th, t.o. 14th, p.u. 3 out*	P	0

Missed 95; improved staedily 96; won weak races but Confined likely 97; stays; G-S 19

FISHERMAN'S QUAY ch.g. 12 Music Boy - Golconda by Matador — D J Fairbairn

1995 10(0),9(0),P(0),P(0)

1353	4/5	Mosshouses	(L)	RES	3m	11	GS	*in tch til 7th & outpcd hlfwy, no ch whn mstk 13th & p.u.*	P	0
1461	9/5	Sedgefield	(L)	HC	2m 5f	10	F	*ld 3rd till hdd 9th, chsd ldrs till gradually wknd from 3 out.*	5	12
1571	19/5	Corbridge	(R)	RES	3m	13	G	*prom early, mstk 11th, no dang aft*	10	0
1586	25/5	Hexham	(L)	HC	2 1/2m 110yds	14	GF	*driven along to go pace, t.o. when p.u. before 4 out.*	P	0

Maiden winner 92 but no prospects now 0

FISH QUAY ch.g. 13 Quayside - Winkle by Whistler — Mrs K M Lamb

1995 **P(NH),8(NH),7(NH),P(NH),10(NH),P(NH)**

48	4/2	Alnwick	(L)	LAD	3m	9	G	*last til eff app 3 out, kpt on, nvr able to chal*	4	17
85	11/2	Alnwick	(L)	LAD	3m	11	GS	*in tch,ld 10th,jmpd rght nxt,hdd 12th,disp 2nd 3 out,no ext*	4	18
183	19/2	Musselburgh	(R)	HC	3m	5	GF	*in tch, lost pl after 14th, kept on from 3 out.*	3	19
317	2/3	Corbridge	(R)	CON	3m	11	GS	*sn last, some prog 13th, nvr nrr*	6	12
402	9/3	Dalston	(R)	XX	3m	13	G	*bhnd tl hdwy 14th, styd on, nvr nrr*	4	16
487	16/3	Newcastle	(L)	HC	3m	10	GS	*bhnd, mstk 14th, soon struggling, t.o..*	5	10
673	29/3	Sedgefield	(L)	HC	3m 3f	7	GF	*alwys prom, left in ld 12th, hdd next, struggling 5 out, btn when ref last.*	R	-
861	6/4	Alnwick	(L)	CON	3m	7	GF	*alwys bhnd, nvr dang*	3	13
1226	25/4	Perth	(R)	HC	3m	7	S	*n.j.w., soon lost tch, t.o. when p.u. after 11th.*	P	0
1352	4/5	Mosshouses	(L)	LAD	3m	10	GS	*mstks, rear, lost tch 13th, effrt 3 out, sn wknd*	6	0
1546	18/5	Fakenham	(L)	HC	3m 110yds	13	G	*struggling in rear most of way, t.o. 13th.*	11	0

Last won in 94 & looks disinterested now; best avoided 11

FIVE CIRCLES (Irish) — I 39[1], I 425[P]

FIXED ASSETS (Irish) — I 242, , I 329[4]

FIXED LIABILITY ch.g. 9 Slippered - Adamstown Girl by Lucifer (USA) — T D B Underwood

574	17/3	Detling	(L)	RES	3m	14	GF	*badly hmpd 1st, rear aft, nvr able to get into race,p.u.12th*	P	0
593	23/3	Parham	(R)	RES	3m	11	GS	*handy, mstk 13th, prog to chs wnr 4 out, ev ch 2 out, wknd*	2	16
889	6/4	Kimble	(L)	RES	3m	7	GF	*chsd ldrs, mstk 14th, 3rd & btn frm 3 out*	3	12
1295	28/4	Bexhill	(R)	RES	3m	7	F	*(bl) 2nd whn u.r. 6th*	U	-
1371	4/5	Peper Harow	(L)	RES	3m	5	F	*(fav) (bl) mstks, chsd ldr 15th, chal on inner 2 out, ld last, rdn out*	1	14
1564	19/5	Mollington	(R)	XX	3m	14	GS	*(bl) in tch to 13th, 7th & no ch 3 out*	8	0

Irish Maiden winner 94; won bad Restricted; will struggle in better company; G/S-F 15

FLAHERTY'S BEST VI (Irish) — I 33[P], I 83[4], I 127[5]

FLAIRLINE BAY (Irish) — I 21[F], I 124[1], I 153[P], I 441[2], I 514[2]

FLAKED OATS b.g. 7 Oats - Polly Toodle by Kabale — E B Swaffield

1995 3(19),1(22),3(21),1(22)

5	13/1	Larkhill	(R)	LAD	3m	10	GS	*(fav) w.w. chsd ldr 9th, ld 3 out, qcknd apr last, imprssv*	1	28
135	17/2	Ottery St M'	(L)	LAD	3m	11	GS	*(fav) j.w. hld up, prog 7th, ld 4 out, 10l clr whn u.r. 2 out*	U	27
266	2/3	Didmarton	(L)	LAD	3m	13	G	*(fav) trckd ldrs, mstk 9th, chal 3 out, ld last, ran on well*	1	23
655	23/3	Badbury Rin'	(L)	LAD	3m	8	G	*(fav) bhnd, prog 13th, 2nd when mstk 3 out, no chnc wth wnnr*	2	23
1111	17/4	Hockworthy	(L)	MXO	3m	13	GS	*(fav) early rmndrs, rr, prog to ld aft 13th, clr last, rdn out*	1	26

Very useful pointer now; not the easiest of rides; quickens; worth trying in H/Chase; G/F-S 27

FLAME O'FRENSI b.m. 10 Tudor Flame - Regal Rage by Fury Royal — P J Clarke

1995 F(-),2(25),**4(14)**,6(10),3(21),1(23),1(22)

21	20/1	Barbury Cas'	(L)	MEM	3m	16	GS	*made all, rdn whn lft clr 2 out, fin tired*	1	26
135	17/2	Ottery St M'	(L)	LAD	3m	11	GS	*ld/disp to 4 out, wknd nxt, lft 2nd 2 out*	2	22
362	5/3	Leicester	(R)	HC	2 1/2m 110yds	8	GS	*(Jt fav) chsd ldr, ld 4th to 7th and 10th to 11th, led again 3 out, kept on gamely und pres.*	1	25
529	16/3	Cothelstone	(L)	LAD	3m	5	G	*(fav) ld til 15th, rlld & disp 3 out, wknd appr last*	2	23
708	30/3	Barbury Cas'	(L)	LAD	3m	10	G	*j.w. ld til hdd final 50 yrds*	2	24
925	8/4	Bishopsleigh	(R)	CON	3m	6	G	*(fav) ld 2nd, front rank til clr 11th, clvrly*	1	23
1110	17/4	Hockworthy	(L)	CON	3m	9	GS	*ld to 15th, 3rd & btn frm 2 out, wknd*	4	20
1331	1/5	Cheltenham	(L)	HC	2m 5f	9	G	*ld to 5th, chsd ldrs till wknd 11th, t.o..*	5	0
1526	12/5	Ottery St M'	(L)	LAD	3m	5	GF	*made all, j.w. ran on gamely*	1	26
1624	27/5	Lifton	(R)	LAD	3m	9	GS	*(fav) j.w. made all, ran on gamely*	1	23
1648	8/6	Umberleigh	(L)	LAD	3m	11	GF	*ld 2-4th, chal 13th til mstk nxt, wknd aft 3 out*	5	14

Useful, game & consistent; won 16 of 28 points 93-6 & 2 H/Chases; more in 97; vulnerable to top ones 25

FLASHING ROCK (Irish) — I 275P

FLASHLIGHT ch.g. 5 Lighter - Altun Ha by Morston (FR) — A G Bonas

764	31/3	Great Stain'	(L) MDN 3m	16 GS	*mid-div whn mstk 8th, sn lost tch, p.u. 14th*	P	0
1365	4/5	Gisburn	(R) MDO 3m	17 G	*cls up, mstks 6th & 8th, sn wknd, t.o. & u.r. 10th*	U	-

Needs to jump better & shows nothing yet 0

FLASHMANS MISTRESS b.m. 9 Stan Flashman - Blue Mist by New Member — Gerald Gwynne

1248	27/4	Woodford	(L) MDN 3m	15 G	*alwys rear, last hlfwy, p.u. 13th*	P	0
1506	12/5	Maisemore P'	(L) MEM 3m	5 F	*jmpd v slwly, t.o. 7th, fence bhnd 14th, fin fast*	3	0
1605	25/5	Bassaleg	(R) MDO 3m	8 GS	*33s-5s, cls up to 9th, lost tch nxt, p.u. 12th*	P	0

Shows no real ability & very optimistic punt last start 0

FLASH OF WHITE (Irish) — I 154P

FLASHY LEADER (Irish) — I 144F, I 5213

FLAXRIDGE b.g. 11 Amoristic (USA) - Pitpans Star by Pitpan — Miss E J Tamplin

1995 P(0),1(13),4(0),2(16),r(-),2(17)

24	20/1	Barbury Cas'	(L) XX 3m	12 GS	*rear whn u.r. 1st*	U	-
156	17/2	Erw Lon	(L) RES 3m	13 G	*prom, 2nd 10th, 15l down whn f 15th*	F	-
388	9/3	Llanfrynach	(R) RES 3m	20 GS	*mid-div, pshd alng & no prog 12th, nvr on terms*	6	0
695	30/3	Llanvapley	(L) RES 3m	13 GS	*ld 7-8th, cls 4th whn b.d. 13th*	B	-
1038	13/4	St Hilary	(R) RES 3m	15 G	*ld til s.u. flat apr 12th*	S	-
1223	24/4	Brampton Br'	(R) RES 3m	11 G	*prom, ld 6th til f 16th*	F	-
1481	11/5	Bredwardine	(R) RES 3m	14 G	*(fav) ld 1st, trckd ldr til mstk 13th, rallied 3 out, wknd flat*	9	0
1557	18/5	Bassaleg	(R) RES 3m	14 F	*prom, prssd ldr 10th-12th, sn wknd, p.u. 3 out*	P	0

Maiden winner 95; mostly novice-ridden & disappointing 96; some ability still but best watched; G-F ... 12

FLAXTON KING(IRE) ch.g. 5 Good Thyne (USA) - Velpol by Polyfoto — Mrs S E Hight

176	18/2	Market Rase'	(L) MDO 2m 5f	10 GF	*alwys rear, last whn p.u. 10th*	P	0
328	3/3	Market Rase'	(L) RES 3m	9 G	*mstks, prog to mod 3rd & blnd 14th, p.u. 3 out*	P	0
518	16/3	Dalton Park	(R) MDO 3m	15 G	*alwys wll bhnd, t.o. hlfwy, p.u. 3 out*	P	0
1027	13/4	Brocklesby '	(L) MDN 3m	7 GF	*cls up, 2nd 12th-4 out, wknd bfr nxt*	5	0
1285	27/4	Easingwold	(L) MDO 3m	9 G	*prom, chsd ldr 10th, losing tch whn f 14th*	F	-
1470	11/5	Easingwold	(L) MDO 3m	10 G	*mid-div, mstk 5th, clsd 7th, no prog aft, wknd 13th,p.u. nxt*	P	0

Last in bad Maiden & stamina the problem 0

FLEECED b.g. 6 Gambler's Cup (USA) - Shepherd Valley by Arrigle Valley — A D Crichton

1995 U(-),P(0)

589	23/3	Wetherby Po'	(L) MDO 3m	16 S	*prom, mstk 4th, wknd 10th, rear & p.u. 14th*	P	0
987	8/4	Charm Park	(L) MDN 3m	13 GF	*alwys mid-div, 5th 15th, no ext*	4	0
1095	14/4	Whitwell-On'	(R) MDO 2 1/2m 88yds	14 G	*mid-div til wknd 5 out*	7	0
1364	4/5	Gisburn	(R) MDO 3m	11 G	*alwys rear, t.o. 9th, p.u. 3 out*	P	0

Well beaten when completing & shorn of any ability yet 0

FLEMINGS FLEUR b.f. 7 Manor Farm Boy - Ashmo by Ashmore (FR) — Mrs C St V Fox

1995 P(0),P(0),U(-)

988	8/4	Kingston St'	(R) MEM 3m	7 F	*last whn u.r. 11th*	U	-
1118	17/4	Hockworthy	(L) MDO 3m	14 GS	*mid-div, 8th & btn 11th, hmprd & u.r. nxt*	U	-
1279	27/4	Bratton Down	(L) MDO 3m	14 GF	*prom whn u.r. 4th*	U	-
1348	4/5	Holnicote	(L) MDO 3m	9 GS	*bhnd til some prog 14th, went 3rd nxt, no imp aft*	3	0
1495	11/5	Holnicote	(L) MDO 3m	11 G	*(vis) towrds rear, hit 9th, no ch frm hlfwy*	6	0

Failed to finish first 6 races & beaten 35l when 3rd; much more needed for any hope 10

FLIGHT OF LOVE gr.m. 7 Cruise Missile - Jack's Love by Grey Love — James Buckle

1995 4(0),F(-),P(0),7(0)

618	23/3	Higham	(L) MDO 3m	14 GF	*plld to ld 2nd, p.u. aft 3rd*	P	0
622	23/3	Higham	(L) CON 3m	10 GF	*2nd outing, wth ldrs til wknd 8th, t.o. 11th, p.u. aft nxt*	P	0
1064	13/4	Horseheath	(R) MDO 3m	3 F	*made all, ran on wll flat*	1	10
1144	20/4	Higham	(L) MEM 3m	4 F	*1st ride, last, t.o. 10th, lft 2nd 12th, ran on frm 2 out*	2	13

Won one of season's worst Maidens; ran better next time; Restricted chances negligible 10

FLIGHTS LANE b.m. 6 Norwick (USA) - Farceuse by Comedy Star (USA) — B J Vernoum

1995 R(-),**14(NH)**

207	24/2	Castle Of C'	(R) MDO 3m	15 HY	*rear til p.u. 12th*	P	0
558	17/3	Ottery St M'	(L) MDO 3m	9 G	*bhnd, lost tch 12th, outpcd*	4	0

Only beat a rejoiner when 4th & looks unpromising 0

FLIMSY FLAME br.g. 7 Lighter - Flimsy Jacky by David Jack — M H Weston

214 24/2 Newtown (L) CON 3m 21 GS *prom, chsd ldr 6th-13th, wknd, p.u. 2 out* P 0
432 9/3 Upton-On-Se' (R) MDO 3m 17 GS *ld frm 11th til f 13th* F -

Has the speed; finished after fall but may go close if fit & stays in 97 12

FLINTERS b.g. 9 Deep Run - En Clair by Tarqogan — John Halewood

1995 **5(NH),4(NH),9(NH),P(NH),9(NH),12(NH),8(NH)**

164 17/2 Weston Park (L) RES 3m 11 G *mid to rear, losing tch whn u.r. 11th* U -
288 2/3 Eaton Hall (R) MDO 3m 17 G *(bl) chsng grp, prog to ld/disp 11-13th, not qckn frm nxt* 2 14
568 17/3 Wolverhampt' (L) MDN 3m 9 GS *(fav) ld to 3 out, mstk nxt, outpcd* 2 12
740 31/3 Sudlow Farm (R) MDN 3m 16 G *(bl) ld 3rd-12th, lft 8l 2nd 2 out, ld last, sn hdd* 2 14
1029 13/4 Alpraham (R) MDO 3m 8 GS *(fav) (bl) ld to 13th & apr last, rddn & held on wll* 1 15
1233 27/4 Weston Park (L) RES 3m 14 G *(bl) chsng grp, in tch whn p.u. qckly bfr 10th* P 0

Plodded home in 7 1/2mins Maiden & problems last start; more needed if fit 97; best in blinkers; soft .. 14

FLIP THE LID(IRE) b or br.m. 7 Orchestra - Punters Gold by Yankee Gold — Peter Sawney

121 17/2 Witton Cast' (R) RES 3m 11 S *mid-div, prog to disp 10th-2 out, rallied flat, just faild* 2 19
328 3/3 Market Rase' (L) RES 3m 9 G *(fav) in tch, rdn to chal 3 out, ld last, hld on well* 1 19
588 23/3 Wetherby Po' (L) INT 3m 17 S *cls up, outpcd 4 out, styd on onepcd frm nxt* 3 16
761 31/3 Great Stain' (L) INT 3m 7 GS *(fav) j.w. disp til ld 4th, qcknd clr apr last* 1 23
824 6/4 Stainton (R) CON 3m 11 GF *(fav) chsd ldrs, ld 8th, drew clr 3 out, comf* 1 22
1281 27/4 Easingwold (L) CON 3m 15 G *(fav) hld up, prog to chs ldrs 5th, ld 10th, jnd flat, ran on wll* 1 23

Irish Maiden winner 95; progressive & consistent; quickens; Opens in reach 97; G/F-S 24

FLO AGAIN (Irish) — **I** 41^{P}

FLODART (Irish) — **I** 288^{P}, **I** 321^{F}, **I** 365^{2}, **I** 403^{F}

FLO JO'S BOY (Irish) — **I** 234^{P}, **I** 313^{P}, **I** 629^{U}, **I** 659^{P}

FLOOD MARK ch.g. 12 High Line - Crystal Fountain by Great Nephew — R A Ford

1995 4(0),5(13),4(12),F(-)

1344 4/5 Holnicote (L) CON 3m 4 GS *chsd wnr 8th, no real imp* 2 15
1499 11/5 Holnicote (L) CON 3m 8 G *last, outpcd thruout, mstk 13th, p.u. nxt* P 0
1543 17/5 Newton Abbot (L) HC 3 1/4m 110yds 8 G *held up, lost tch apr 14th, t.o. when p.u. before 16th.* P 0

Last won 94; late start 96 & more wins beyond him now 13

FLOOD RELIEF (Irish) — **I** 40^{P}, **I** 57^{P}, **I** 121^{3}, **I** 368^{2}, **I** 430^{2}, **I** 540^{3}, **I** 607^{P}

FLORIDA LIGHT (Irish) — **I** 509^{U}

FLORIDA OR BUST (Irish) — **I** 97^{6}, **I** 173^{F}, **I** 260^{P}, **I** 300^{F}, **I** 365^{5}, **I** 409^{2}

FLORIDA PEARL (Irish) — **I** 208^{1}

FLORUCEVA (Irish) — **I** 178^{P}, **I** 258^{U}, **I** 286^{2}

FLOWER OF GRANGE (Irish) — **I** 101^{F}

FLOWERY FERN (Irish) — **I** 650^{F}

FLY FOR US b.m. 10 Cut Above - Flying Spice by Charlottown — C G Taylor

853 6/4 Sandon (L) LAD 3m 7 GF *w.w., cls order 14th, 2nd 2 out, no ext, will imprv* 3 22
1153 20/4 Whittington (L) LAD 3m 10 G *held up, ld 3 out til outpcd flat* 2 21
1366 4/5 Gisburn (R) LAD 3m 12 G *chal 14th, wknd rpdly nxt, btn 5th whn f last* F -

Ladies winner 94; missed 95; brief campaign 96; can win Ladies if fit 97 20

FLYING FELLOW (Irish) — **I** 190^{P}, **I** 293^{B}, **I** 386^{3}, **I** 465^{P}, **I** 497^{3}

FLYING LION b.g. 11 Flying Tyke - Comedy Spring by Comedy Star (USA) — John Mackley

1995 14(0),4(13),8(12),3(13),10(0),10(0),1(12)

302 2/3 Great Stain' (L) MEM 3m 7 GS *1st ride, cls up, ev ch 2 out, onepcd, fin 3rd, promoted* 2 12
758 31/3 Great Stain' (L) RES 3m 17 GS *alwys prom, prog to 2nd 4 out, onepcd frm nxt* 3 17
824 6/4 Stainton (R) CON 3m 11 GF *alwys prom, rdn 15th, styd on frm 2 out* 2 18
1130 20/4 Hornby Cast' (L) CON 3m 13 G *chsd ldrs til u.r. 11th* U -
1281 27/4 Easingwold (L) CON 3m 15 G *rear, pshd alng 7th, nvr on terms* 5 16
1447 6/5 Witton Cast' (R) RES 3m 11 G *midfld, prog 14th, 2l 2nd 3 out, ld nxt, ran on wll* 1 17
1573 19/5 Corbridge (R) OPE 3m 12 G *bhnd at 9th, some prog 14th, nvr nrr* 4 18

3 wins last 27 races (only 1 non-completion); easy 3m best; hard to find Confined win 18

FLYING MARIA br.m. 5 Neltino - Flying Mistress by Lear Jet — J S Papworth

629 23/3 Kilworthy (L) MDN 3m 11 GS *10s-3s, ran out 1st* r -
719 30/3 Wadebridge (L) MDO 3m 7 GF *not fluent, some prog aft 14th, no imp whn pckd 2 out* 4 0
1431 6/5 High Bickin' (R) MDO 3m 9 G *rear, hdwy 15th, ev ch 2 out, no ext apr last* 2 14

Not beaten far when placed in poor Maidens & should recoup debut losses in 96 15

FLYING PAN b.m. 7 Pitpan - Flying Flynn by Vaigly Great — P Needham

1995 P(0),P(0),P(0),2(0),2(11),U(-),F(-),4(0)

73	11/2 Wetherby Po'	(L) MDO 3m	15 GS *in tch, 5th at 10th, u.r. 12th*	U	-
229	24/2 Duncombe Pa'	(R) MDO 3m	13 GS *chsd ldrs til f 5th*	F	-
308	2/3 Great Stain'	(L) MDO 3m	12 GS *mid-div, prog 15th, ld nxt, 5l clr 4 out, wknd 2 out, onepcd*	3	11
488	16/3 Newcastle	(L) HC 2 1/2m	9 GS *settld in tch, challenging when u.r. 3 out.*	U	-
763	31/3 Great Stain'	(L) MDN 3m	11 GS *(fav) rear, prog hlfwy, ev ch whn f 14th*	F	-
828	6/4 Stainton	(R) MDO 3m	7 GF *chsd ldrs, ld 6 out, going wll whn p.u. 5 out, dead*	P	0

Dead 11

FLYING ROOFER b.m. 10 Jester - Forest Glen by Tarqogan — Mrs C Day

605	23/3 Howick	(L) MDN 3m	13 S *t.o. 8th, p.u. 11th*	P	0
997	8/4 Hackwood Pa'	(L) MDO 3m	11 GF *2nd whn mstk 10th, f nxt*	F	-

No signs yet 0

FLYING WILD b.g. 10 Another Hoarwithy - Valrina Miy by Carnival Boy — W J Bryan

1995 4(0),2(0),P(0)

1047	13/4 Bitterley	(L) MDO 3m	13 G *alwys rear, losing tch whn p.u. 11th*	P	0
1224	24/4 Brampton Br'	(R) MDO 3m	17 G *ld to 3rd, lost pl 8th, t.o. & p.u. 3 out*	P	0
1484	11/5 Bredwardine	(R) MDO 3m	17 G *chsng ldrs whn blnd & u.r. 6th*	U	-

Placed in poor races 95; showed nothing in 96 & prospects nil 0

FLYING ZIAD(CAN) ch.g. 13 Ziad (USA) - Flying Souvenir (USA) by Flying Relic — H J Manners

1995 **3(NH),3(NH),4(NH),P(NH),4(NH),4(NH),4(NH),3(NH),2(NH),8(NH),5(NH),8(NH),5(NH)**

265	2/3 Didmarton	(L) OPE 3m	6 G *in tch to 11th, sn bhnd, t.o. 14th*	5	10
639	23/3 Siddington	(L) OPE 3m	12 S *wll bhnd frm 9th*	7	0
943	8/4 Andoversford	(R) CON 3m	9 GF *chsd ldrs to hlfwy, wknd, last whn p.u. aft 12th*	P	0
1122	20/4 Stratford	(L) HC 2m 5f 110yds	16 GF *alwys in rear.*	9	0
1227	26/4 Ludlow	(R) HC 2 1/2m	16 G *bhnd 9th.*	10	0

Well beaten in points (does not stay) but placed in summer jumping after 0

FLYPIE b.g. 8 Current Magic - Southlandmargarete Vii — C Storey

1995 7(0),4(0),5(14),F(-),U(-),**P(0)**

190	24/2 Friars Haugh	(L) LAD 3m	7 S *alwys abt same plc, no ext frm 4 out*	4	10
488	16/3 Newcastle	(L) HC 2 1/2m	9 GS *soon well bhnd till styd on last 2, n.d..*	3	0
913	8/4 Tranwell	(L) LAD 3m	7 GF *nvr on terms, disp 5th hlfwy, no imp aft*	4	13
1084	14/4 Friars Haugh	(L) LAD 3m	8 F *ran out apr 6th*	r	-
1461	9/5 Sedgefield	(L) HC 2m 5f	10 F *in tch, 6th and no ch when blnd and u.r. 2 out.*	U	-
1572	19/5 Corbridge	(R) LAD 3m	10 G *trckd ldrs, disp brfly 9th, outpcd frm 13th*	4	11
1586	25/5 Hexham	(L) HC 2 1/2m 110yds	14 GF *with chasing gp, struggling to go pace hfwy, n.d..*	9	0

Unlucky in Maiden 95 but out of his depth 96 & does not stay; hard to see a win now 13

FLY THE WIND b.m. 11 Windjammer (USA) - Eagle's Quest by Legal Eagle — Mrs Pam Pengelly

1995 P(0),2(22),1(21),1(24)

528	16/3 Cothelstone	(L) MEM 3m	8 G *(fav) chsd ldrs, disp ld 12th til ld 15th, clr 3 out, easy*	1	23
924	8/4 Bishopsleigh	(R) LAD 3m	7 G *(fav) disp ld 1st-2nd, chsd nwr aft, nvr able to chal aft last*	2	24
1228	27/4 Worcester	(L) HC 2m 7f	17 G *with ldr, ld 12th to 4 out, hrd rdn and one pace from next.*	4	20
1635	1/6 Bratton Down	(L) LAD 3m	13 G *trckd ldrs, rdn 15th, cls up 3 out, immed outpcd aft nxt*	3	19

Useful pointer; best late season; won novice chase June 96 & worth trying in H/Chases 97; G-F 23

FOHERISH MIST (Irish) — **I** 63F, **I** 774, **I** 243F, **I** 280P, **I** 380P, **I** 475P

FOLK DANCE b.g. 14 Alias Smith (USA) - Enchanting Dancer (FR) by Nijinsky (CAN) — F R Jackson

1995 U(-),P(0),4(0),U(-),1(10),S(-),**6(0)**

274	2/3 Parham	(R) OPE 3m	12 GF *alwys bhnd, t.o. frm 12th*	5	0
451	9/3 Charing	(L) OPE 3m	11 G *handy, ld apr last, rdn out*	1	18
595	23/3 Parham	(R) OPE 3m	12 GS *in tch to 14th, bhnd whn p.u. 3 out*	P	0
1209	21/4 Heathfield	(R) OPE 3m	5 F *prom, outpcd & no dang frm 16th*	3	0
1333	1/5 Cheltenham	(L) HC 3m 1f 110yds	13 G *bhnd from 7th, t.o..*	7	0
1538	16/5 Folkestone	(R) HC 3 1/4m	6 G *(vis) prog and cl up 11th, wknd apr 13th, t.o. next.*	5	0

Won a joke race 95 but 25/1 winner of poor Open 96; novice ridden; usually outclassed 14

FOLLOW YOUR DREAM (Irish) — **I** 176⁵, **I** 285³

FOLLY ROAD (Irish) — **I** 218³, **I** 337², **I** 481¹

FOOLISH FANTASY b.g. 8 Idiot's Delight - In A Dream by Caruso — Jack Taylor

1995 P(0),F(-),P(0),P(0),P(0),1(13),7(0)

164 17/2 Weston Park (L) RES 3m 11 G *chsng grp, 4th at 15th, wknd rpdly, p.u. 2 out* P 0
243 25/2 Southwell P' (L) RES 3m 11 HO *in tch, rdn 13th, sn btn, t.o. 2 out* 7 0
564 17/3 Wolverhampt' (L) RES 3m 8 GS *alwys rear, nvr dang* 5 0
856 6/4 Sandon (L) RES 3m 9 GF *(bl) alwys rear, p.u. 2 out* P 0

Maiden winner 95 (blinkers); struggling & finished early 96 0

FOOLISH SOPRANO b or br.m. 10 Idiot's Delight - Indian Diva by Indian Ruler — Mrs G V Mackay

1995 F(-),3(11),2(13),2(15),**6(12)**

1105 14/4 Guilsborough (L) MDN 3m 12 G *w.w. prog to ld 15th, hdd & wknd 3 out* 3 0
1241 27/4 Clifton On ' (L) MDO 3m 8 GF *(fav) hld up last, prog 13th, 3rd 4 out, found nil frm 2 out* 3 11
1436 6/5 Ashorne (R) MEM 3m 7 G *ld 4-11th, wknd 13th, t.o. & p.u. last* P 0

Placed 3 times 95 but late to appear 96 & disappointing; can only be watched in 97 11

FOOLS COURAGE (Irish) — **I** 9ᴾ, **I** 60ᶠ, **I** 120ᴾ, **I** 210⁴

FOOLS WITH HORSES (Irish) — **I** 35ᴾ, **I** 53¹

FOOTSY MURRAY (Irish) — **I** 194ᴾ, **I** 267ᴾ, **I** 466ᴾ

FOR CATHAL (Irish) — **I** 53ᴾ, **I** 73¹

FOR CHRISTIE(IRE) ch.g. 7 Lancastrian - Lovenos by Golden Love — Miss A V Handel

1995 F(-),U(-)

1347 4/5 Holnicote (L) MDO 3m 16 GS *ld 14th, made rest, ran on wll whn chal* 1 16

Promising 94; only 3 runs since; won modest Maiden but can upgrade if running regularly 97; G/S 16

FORDSTOWN(IRE) ch.g. 7 Le Bavard (FR) - Gortroe Queen by Simbir — Jamie Alexander

1995 **9(NH),1(NH),P(NH),P(NH),P(NH),P(NH),3(NH)**

49 4/2 Alnwick (L) OPE 3m 14 G *alwys bhnd, t.o. hlfwy* 7 0
110 17/2 Lanark (R) CON 3m 10 GS *steady prog frm 10th, just ld whn lft clr 2 out* 1 21
187 24/2 Friars Haugh (L) CON 3m 12 S *mid-div, styd on frm 4 out, not rch wnr* 2 17
498 16/3 Lanark (R) CON 3m 10 G *ld to 5th, 20l 5th at 11th, styd on frm 4 out* 3 13
610 23/3 Friars Haugh (L) CON 3m 11 G *5th hlfwy, styd on frm 3 out, nrst fin.* 4 18
751 31/3 Lockerbie (R) CON 3m 12 G *ld 10th, made rest, 2l ld whn lft clr last* 1 23
1083 14/4 Friars Haugh (L) CON 3m 10 F *bhnd til some late prog, nvr dang* 4 16
1255 27/4 Balcormo Ma' (R) MEM 3m 2 GS *(fav) made all, unchal* 1 16

Ex-Irish; quite useful; novice ridden; burdened by penalties; try Opens 97; G-S 22

FOREIGN COVER (Irish) — **I** 220⁴

FOREST FOUNTAIN(IRE) b or br.g. 5 Royal Fountain - Forest Gale by Strong Gale — J D Callow

356 3/3 Garnons (L) LAD 3m 12 GS *chsd ldrs to 8th, wknd frm 10th, p.u. aft 13th* P 0
688 30/3 Chaddesley ' (L) MDN 3m 17 G *chsd ldrs going wll, prog to ld 2 out, sn clr, comf* 1 16
1173 20/4 Chaddesley ' (L) RES 3m 18 G *(fav) 2s-1/1, hld up, gd prog 15th, ld 2 out, sn clr* 1 19

Ex-Irish; useful recruit; hacked up in large fields (winners behind); could go far; Good, so far 22

FOREST MUSK (Irish) — **I** 49ᴾ, **I** 61ᴾ, **I** 122ᶠ, **I** 147³, **I** 244³, **I** 306³

FOREST POPPY b.m. 5 Derring Rose - Star Of Corrie by Ballynockan — J D Thomas

391 9/3 Llanfrynach (R) MDN 3m 11 GS *sn wll bhnd, t.o. 7th, last whn crawld 13th & u.r.* U -

An inauspicious debut but still has time on her side 0

FOREST RANGER b.g. 14 The Parson - Nora Grany by Menelek — Barrington M Robinson

1995 6(0),**P(0),P(0),5(11),P(0)**

153 17/2 Erw Lon (L) OPE 3m 15 G *m.n.s, p.u.* P 0

No longer of any account 0

FOREST ROSE b.m. 6 Derring Rose - Star Of Corrie by Ballynockan — J D Thomas

389 9/3 Llanfrynach (R) MDN 3m 11 GS *last whn ref & u.r. 1st* R -
747 31/3 Upper Sapey (R) MDO 3m 11 GS *t.o. whn p.u. 11th* P 0
1225 24/4 Brampton Br' (R) MDO 3m 18 G *t.o. frm 4th, ran out 6th* r -

Full sister to Forest Poppy (qv) & the pair not setting the scene alight yet 0

FOREST SUN ch.g. 11 Whistling Deer - Sun Spray by Nice Guy — J C Peate

1995 **P(NH)**

452 9/3 Charing (L) LAD 3m 8 G *(fav) handy, ld 9th-15th, agn 3 out, rdn & hdd flat* 2 18

596 23/3 Parham (R) LAD 3m 8 GS *prom, ld aft 4 out, clr 2 out, wknd aft, hdd flat* 2 17
777 31/3 Penshurst (L) LAD 3m 7 GS *hndy, ld apr 2 out, und press & hdd flat* 2 22

Former high-class hurdler; plagued by injury; could still win modest point at 12; G-S 19

FOREVER FREDDY b.g. 8 Lepanto (GER) - My Belleburd by Twilight Alley — A Witcomb

217 24/2 Newtown (L) RES 3m 17 GS *rear, lost tch 8th, t.o. & p.u. 12th* P 0
397 9/3 Garthorpe (R) MDN 3m 9 G *last & jmpd slwly til p.u. 12th* P 0
540 17/3 Southwell P' (L) MDO 3m 9 GS *prom, ld 8-9th, sn btn aft mstks 12 & 13th, p.u. 3 out* P 0
726 31/3 Garthorpe (R) RES 3m 16 G *wll bhnd, 11th hlfwy, styd on frm 15th, nrst fin* 4 14
904 6/4 Dingley (R) RES 3m 20 GS *mid-div, abt 7th whn u.r. 5 out* U -
1329 30/4 Huntingdon (R) HC 3m 14 GF *bhnd and rdn 11th, t.o. when p.u. before 14th.* P 0
1523 12/5 Garthorpe (R) MDO 3m 11 GF *cls up, 2nd at 12th, 3l 2nd & lkd hld whn f 2 out* F -
1599 25/5 Garthorpe (R) MDO 3m 7 G *cls up,ld 10th-6 out,3rd & outpcd 4 out, tired whn ref 3 out* R -
1644 2/6 Dingley (R) MDO 3m 16 GF *prom til rdn & reluc 9th, stpd aft nxt* P 0

Has some ability but increasingly mulish; can only be watched now 11

FOREVER GOLD (Irish) — I 104P, I 179S, I 413F

FOREVER IN DEBT b.m. 6 Pragmatic - Deep In Debt by Deep Run — E R Clough

1995 P(0),P(0),P(0)

150 17/2 Erw Lon (L) MDN 3m 8 G *5th whn ref 6th* R -
219 24/2 Newtown (L) RES 3m 17 GS *in tch to 8th, rdn & wknd 11th, t.o. & p.u. 15th* P 0
505 16/3 Magor (R) PPO 3m 7 GS *last pair whn p.u. 7th* P 0
551 17/3 Erw Lon (L) MDN 3m 8 GS *ran out 3rd* r -

Yet to complete & unpromising 0

FORGOODNESSJAKE VI (Irish) — I 252F, I 280P, I 370P, I 4445, I 471S, I 545F, I 581P

FOR JOSH (Irish) — I 403, I 691, I 184P

FORMAL b.g. 10 Cidrax (FR) - Late Challange by Tekoah — R A Owen

1995 P(0),8(0),P(0),3(16)

159 17/2 Weston Park (L) CON 3m 22 G *nvr bynd mid-div, no dang* 4 15
293 2/3 Eaton Hall (R) INT 3m 11 G *chsng grp, strgglng 4 out* 6 0

Ran well 1st start but finished early; does not stay & unlikely to win again 12

FOR MICHAEL b.g. 9 Orchestra - Pampered Sue by Pampered King — Mrs L A Syckelmoore

137 17/2 Ottery St M' (L) RES 3m 15 GS *mid-div, lost tch 12th, p.u. 14th* P 0

Maiden winner 94; only 1 run since & can only be watched if returning 97 11

FOROLD (Irish) — I 155P, I 250P, I 297F, I 327P, I 4702, I 500F

FORT ALICIA b.m. 9 Helluvafella - Fortalice by Saucy Kit — Mrs W H O Hutchison

756 31/3 Lockerbie (R) MDN 3m 14 G *3rd hlfwy, kpt on wll but no ch wth wnnr* 3 12

Late starter but fair debut; can go close in 97 if racing regularly 13

FORT DEELY (Irish) — I 1224, I 1471

FORT DIANA br.g. 10 Julio Mariner - Blue Delphinium by Quorum — J H Berwick

35 20/1 Higham (L) RES 3m 16 GF *blnd & u.r. 4th* U -
91 11/2 Ampton (R) MDO 3m 10 GF *n.j.w. ld to 3rd, grad lost plc, t.o. & p.u. 16th* P 0
178 18/2 Horseheath (R) INT 3m 11 G *bhnd, 10th whn f 9th* F -
253 25/2 Charing (L) MDO 3m 10 GS *in tch, 3rd frm 15th, btn 3 out* 3 0
275 2/3 Parham (R) MDN 3m 15 GF *nvr on terms, wll bhnd whn p.u. 4 out* P 0
576 17/3 Detling (L) MDN 3m 18 GF *alwys wll in rear, p.u. 14th* P 0
921 8/4 Aldington (L) MDO 3m 8 F *mstks, ld to 2nd, chsd ldr, ld 11th-aft 2 out, immed btn* 2 0
1300 28/4 Bexhill (R) MDO 3m 7 F *wth ldr whn f 4th* F -
1445 6/5 Aldington (L) MDO 3m 8 HD *alwys prom, prssd ldr 4 out, ld 2 out, drvn out flat* 1 12
1553 18/5 Bratton Down (L) XX 3m 10 F *in tch, cls 4th at 12th til f 15th* F -
1591 25/5 Mounsey Hil' (R) RES 3m 15 G *prog 6th, chsd ldrs 8-12th, bhnd whn p.u. 14th* P 0
1625 27/5 Lifton (R) INT 3m 8 GS *chsd ldr to 6th, grad wknd, rear & mstk 13th, p.u. nxt* P 0

Won a desperate contest; does not stay & will need great fortune to win again 10

FORTINAS FLYER b.m. 10 Helluvafella - Fortalice by Saucy Kit — Paul Reid

612 23/3 Friars Haugh (L) OPE 3m 8 G *(bl) 4th hlfwy, u.r. 11th* U -

Always lightly raced & signs not promising now 0

FORT ROUGE (Irish) — I 127P, I 309P, I 444P, I 545P

FORTYNINE PLUS (Irish) — I 108P, I 161P, I 2315, I 4205, I 4794

FORTYTIMES MORE ch.g. 10 True Song - Avado by Cleon — T B Brown

1995 P(0),2(10),U(-)

129 17/2 Kingston Bl' (L) MDN 3m 15 GS *alwys rear, t.o. 13th, p.u. 2 out* P 0
438 9/3 Newton Brom' (R) MDN 3m 10 GS *chsd ldr to 8th, fdd, rear 11th, p.u. 14th* P 0

2nd in 95 but light season 96 & showed nothing; unlikely to win at 11 10

FORTYTWO DEE(IRE) b.m. 6 Amazing Bust - Maggie's Way by Decent Fellow — B R Evans

1995 P(0)

175	18/2	Market Rase'	(L)	MDO 2m 5f	8 GF	*pling, prom to 11th, no dang aft*	6	0
330	3/3	Market Rase'	(L)	MDO 3m	7 G	*prog to 4th whn blnd 12th, outpcd nxt, lft 3rd 3 out*	3	0
425	9/3	Upton-On-Se'	(R)	MEM 3m	7 GS	*b.d. 3rd*	B	-
653	23/3	Badbury Rin'	(L)	MDO 3m	9 G	*ld to 5th, alwys prom untl one pace from 15th*	3	10

Beaten 13l last start & going the right way; more needed for a win in 97 13

FORT ZEDDAAN (Irish) — **I** 162^{F}, **I** 205^{3}, **I** 250^{F}

FORWARD ON (Irish) — **I** 526^{P}, **I** 616^{4}, **I** 630^{P}, **I** 644^{5}

FOSABUD b.g. 10 Dubassoff (USA) - Two Mm's by Manicou — G T Kittow

988	8/4	Kingston St'	(R)	MEM 3m	7 F	*twrds rear, last whn f 12th*	F	-
1118	17/4	Hockworthy	(L)	MDO 3m	14 GS	*alwys bhnd, t.o. & p.u. 12th*	P	0
1349	4/5	Holnicote	(L)	MDO 3m	8 GS	*in 5th & no ch whn ref last*	R	-
1527	12/5	Ottery St M'	(L)	RES 3m	8 GF	*twrds rear, bhnd frm 14th*	5	0

Missed 95 & no signs of any ability left in 96 0

FOSBURY b.g. 11 Kambalda - Joyful Luck by Master Buck — Mrs Susan Humphreys

1995 2+(22),**P(0)**,1(26),1(24),1(27),1(25),U(-),**P(0)**

27	20/1	Barbury Cas'	(L)	LAD 3m	15 GS	*mid-div & outpcd, styd on frm 14th, nrst fin*	4	17
142	17/2	Larkhill	(R)	MXO 3m	9 G	*alwys cls up, not pace of ldng pair to chal*	3	18
468	10/3	Milborne St'	(L)	OPE 3m	5 G	*hld up, ev ch 14th, not qckn frm 4 out*	4	0
1059	13/4	Badbury Rin'	(L)	OPE 3m	5 GF	*ld 3rd-3 out, rallied aft last, just faild*	2	25
1126	20/4	Stafford Cr'	(R)	LAD 3m	7 S	*held up, 3rd & in tch whn f 12th*	F	-
1333	1/5	Cheltenham	(L)	HC 3m 1f 110yds	13 G	*bhnd and hit 4th, t.o. 12th, ran on from 3 out, fin well.*	5	22
1496	11/5	Holnicote	(L)	LAD 3m	4 G	*(fav) hld up, prog 11th, ld 16th, comf*	1	24
1589	25/5	Mounsey Hil'	(R)	OPE 3m	12 G	*steady prog 7th, went 3rd 13th, chal last, sn ld, drew clr*	1	28
1636	1/6	Bratton Down	(L)	OPE 4m	11 G	*(fav) w.w. gd prog to ld 20th, clr 4 out, heavily eased flat*	1	29
1648	8/6	Umberleigh	(L)	LAD 3m	11 GF	*(fav) w.w. prog 6th, ld 11th, drew clr 3 out, easily*	1	30

Very useful pointer at best; problems early season; stays very well; could win H/Chase; G-F 29

FOUNTAIN HOUSE (Irish) — **I** 71^{F}, **I** 245^{P}, **I** 356^{P}, **I** 589^{3}, **I** 660^{3}

FOUNTAIN LADY (Irish) — **I** 434^{P}, **I** 503^{P}

FOUNTAIN MOSS (Irish) — **I** 457^{P}, **I** 637,

FOUNTAIN OF FIRE(IRE) b.m. 8 Lafontaine (USA) - Mil Pesetas by Hotfoot — R M Bluck

1995 **P(0)**,2(13),5(0),4(0)

341	3/3	Heythrop	(R)	MDN 3m	13 G	*(fav) 8s-5/2, mid-div, effrt & prog 13th, chsd ldrs 3 out, no imp*	3	10
430	9/3	Upton-On-Se'	(R)	MDO 3m	15 GS	*effrt to go 4th 3 out, no further prog, disq*	4D	0
796	2/4	Heythrop	(R)	MDN 3m	11 F	*(fav) cls up to 13th, wknd nxt, t.o. & p.u. 3 out*	P	0
1315	28/4	Bitterley	(L)	MDO 3m	10 G	*7th & just in tch 10th, kpt on frm 13th, no ch ldrs*	4	0
1433	6/5	Ashorne	(R)	MDO 3m	16 G	*cls up til outpcd 13th, styd on wll frm 2 out, tk 3rd nr fin*	3	0

Placed 10 times 94-6 but ungenuine & sure to furstrate in future; blinkers no help in 95 11

FOUNTAIN PAGE (Irish) — **I** 274^{3}, **I** 424^{2}

FOUNTAIN VIEW(IRE) b.f. 8 Royal Fountain - Madam's Well — Mrs Elizabeth Easton

1995 **9(NH)**

764	31/3	Great Stain'	(L)	MDN 3m	16 GS	*prom til fdd hlfwy, p.u. 3 out*	P	0

Lightly raced & showed nothing in 96 0

FOURACRE br.g. 12 Frigid Aire - Mezlam Queen by Terrific (NZ) — Mrs E Dodds

1995 F(-),F(-),P(0),8(0),5(0),1(15),1(15)

10	14/1	Cottenham	(R)	INT 3m	10 G	*in tch to 14th, p.u. & dsmntd last*	P	0

Dual winner 95 (modest races); problems & finished 1st weekend 96; hard to see a wwin at 13; Firm ... 12

FOUR FROM HOME (Irish) — **I** 330^{F}, **I** 438^{2}, **I** 612^{F}

FOUR HEARTS(IRE) br.g. 7 Mandalus - Daisy Owen by Master Owen — T D B Barlow

1995 **U(NH),8(NH),2(NH),2(NH)**

463	9/3	Eyton-On-Se'	(L)	MDN 2 1/2m	14 G	*(Jt fav) nvr shwd, p.u. 8th*	P	0
896	6/4	Whittington	(L)	MDO 3m	5 F	*2nd til ld apr 13th, kpt on wll whn chal flat*	1	15
1151	20/4	Whittington	(L)	INT 3m	12 G	*mid-div, fdd final ctt, p.u. 2 out*	P	0
1421	6/5	Eyton-On-Se'	(L)	RES 3m	11 GF	*chsng grp, 2nd frm 8th-3 out, not qckn nr fin*	3	16
1629	30/5	Uttoxeter	(L)	HC 2m 5f	13 GS	*(bl) ld after 1st till blnd and hdd 4th, wknd 9th, t.o. when p.u. before 11th.*	P	0

Placed in chases 95; just beaten 4th start & Restricted possible in 97; G-F 17

FOUR LEAF CLOVER ch.m. 9 Sunyboy - National Clover by National Trust D G L Llewellin
1995 P(0),4(0),5(0),3(11),2(13)

734 31/3 Little Wind' (R) MDO 3m 11 GS *prom,slght ld whn carrd wd by lose horse apr 2 out,not rcvr* 2 14
807 4/4 Clyst St Ma' (L) MDO 3m 10 GS *(fav) in tch, ld 12th, assured wnr whn f 2 out* F 15
1075 13/4 Lifton (R) RES 3m 12 S *disp 3rd-10th, outpcd 15th, disp 3rd whn u.r. last* U -
1308 28/4 Little Wind' (R) MDO 3m 6 G *prog 15th, 4th 3 out, styd on onepcd* 2 14
1432 6/5 High Bickin' (R) MDO 3m 9 G *(fav) in tch, wnt 2nd 16th, ld brfly run in, no ext cls home* 2 15
1554 18/5 Bratton Down (L) MDO 3m 16 F *(Jt fav) prom, ld brfly aft 13th, cls up whn c.o. 15th* C -
1638 1/6 Bratton Down (L) MDO 3m 13 G *trckd ldrs, not qckn frm 15th, btn 2 out* 4 11

Placed 8 times & unfortunate at least twice; no good luck charm but may get it right in 97 14

FOUR NORTH (Irish) — I 455P, I 492P

FOUR RIVERS b.g. 11 Relkino - Crystal Fountain by Great Nephew M W Redman
1995 P(0),1(10),1(16),**3(20)**

581 21/3 Wincanton (R) HC 2m 5f 13 S *chsd ldr, weakening when mstk 9th, p.u. before 5 out.* P 0
798 3/4 Ascot (R) HC 2m 3f 110yds 10 GF *alwys bhnd, t.o. when p.u. before 4 out.* P 0
1505 11/5 Kingston Bl' (L) MEM 3m 5 G *pllng, ld 6th til u.r. bend apr 9th* U -
1609 26/5 Tweseldown (R) MXO 3m 9 G *prom til outpcd 11th,chsd ldng pair 14th,no imp,wknd last* 5 13

Won 2 weak races 95; below form & outlcassed 96; win at 12 looks tough; Members best hope; G-F 14

FOUR STAR LINE ch.g. 11 Capricorn Line - Florida Girl by Owen Dudley Richard Hawker

140 17/2 Larkhill (R) CON 3m 17 G *alwys bhnd, p.u. 15th* P 0

Dead 0

FOUR ZEROS (Irish) — I 23P, I 88P, I 1024, I 1945, I 3413, I 3945, I 4775, I 563P

FOWLING PIECE ch.g. 11 Kinghaven - Bonny Hollow by Wolver Hollow Mrs J Horner
1995 P(0),P(0),F(-),9(0),1(0),3(0)

72 11/2 Wetherby Po' (L) CON 3m 18 GS *rear, nvr a fctr* 7 13
223 24/2 Duncombe Pa' (R) CON 3m 16 GS *prom to 9th, no ch whn u.r. 3 out* U -
303 2/3 Great Stain' (L) CON 3m 11 GS *disp til wknd 15th, styd on onepcd aft* 4 14
588 23/3 Wetherby Po' (L) INT 3m 17 S *rear by 10th, t.o. 12th, fin own time* 8 0
761 31/3 Great Stain' (L) INT 3m 7 GS *rear, outpcd 4th, bhnd 6th, t.o. & p.u. aft 11th* P 0
1091 14/4 Whitwell-On' (R) XX 3m 6 G *disp,ld 3rd at slw pace,qcknd clr 13th,hdd aft 14th,kpt on* 3 17
1130 20/4 Hornby Cast' (L) CON 3m 13 G *disp to 4th, jmpd slwly 8th, onepcd whn lft 2nd 3 out* 2 14
1281 27/4 Easingwold (L) CON 3m 15 G *prom, ld 3rd til disp 7th, grad fdd, wll btn whn f 2 out* F -
1369 4/5 Gisburn (R) CON 3m 10 G *bhnd, rear whn p.u. 15th* P 0
1446 6/5 Witton Cast' (R) CON 3m 7 G *cls up, wknd 3 out, kpt on onepce* 4 15
1466 11/5 Easingwold (L) CON 3m 10 G *chsd ldrs, lost plc 10th, kpt on onepcd 4 out* 5 14

Finished alone when winning 95; ran better 96 but most unlikely to score again in competitive races ... 13

FOX POINTER b.g. 11 Healaugh Fox - Miss Warwick by Stupendous Mrs L T J Evans
1995 2(20),P(0)

578 20/3 Ludlow (R) HC 3m 7 G *in rear when hmpd and u.r. bend after 11th.* U -
1227 26/4 Ludlow (R) HC 2 1/2m 16 G *bhnd, staying on when blnd and u.r. 4 out.* U -
1544 17/5 Stratford (L) HC 3m 10 GF *ld to last, soon wknd.* 4 24
1584 24/5 Towcester (R) HC 3m 1f 11 GS *ld 5th til hdd 2 out, rdn and styd on one pace between last two.* 2 27
1613 27/5 Fontwell (R) HC 3 1/4m 110yds 12 G *ld, hdd and jmpd right 2 out, rdn and kept on gamely.* 2 25

H/Chase winner 94; revived well late 96; front-runner; can win Opens if fit 97; G/S-F 24

FOXWOODS VALLEY (Irish) — I 187P, I 311P, I 358P, I 4623, I 5672, I 6143

FOXY BLUE b.g. 11 Fine Blue - Moxy Mrs M M Evans
1995 4(0),P(0),3(13),3(13),3(13),P(0)

462 9/3 Eyton-On-Se' (L) RES 3m 12 G *chsd ldrs, ld 4th-8th & agn 5 out-3 out, onepcd aft* 3 10
665 24/3 Eaton Hall (R) RES 3m 14 S *prom to hlfwy, sn btn, p.u. 4 out* P 0
739 31/3 Sudlow Farm (R) RES 3m 11 G *rear div, no ch 13th, u.r. 2 out* U -
952 8/4 Eyton-On-Se' (L) RES 3m 7 GF *ld to 5th, cls up til lost tch 13th, no ch whn p.u. 3 out* P 0
1151 20/4 Whittington (L) INT 3m 12 G *nvr bynd mid-div* 6 0
1233 27/4 Weston Park (L) RES 3m 14 G *ld/disp to 4th, mid-div to 12th, lost tch, p.u. bfr last* P 0
1421 6/5 Eyton-On-Se' (L) RES 3m 11 GF *ld 1st, ldng 4 thro'out, ev ch whn outpcd fr 3 out* 4 15
1582 19/5 Wolverhampt' (L) RES 3m 10 G *in tch, went 3rd 10th, rdn & wknd apr 14th, t.o. & p.u. 3out* P 0

Maiden winner 92; struggling since & much luck needed to find a Restricted 13

FOYLESIDE (Irish) — I 935, I 174P

FRAGMENT(IRE) b.g. 6 Glint Of Gold - Mouletta by Moulton Mrs V Simpson
1995 P(0),P(0),3(0)

103 17/2 Marks Tey (L) LAD 3m 7 G *rr, lst tch appr 11th, t.o. & p.u. 17th* P 0
344 3/3 Higham (L) MDO 3m 12 G *prom, mstk 4th, sn bhnd, p.u. 11th, stewards* P 0
417 9/3 High Easter (L) MEM 3m 4 S *(bl) disp til blnd bdly & u.r. 9th* U -

Placed in poor race 95 & showed nothing in 96 0

FRAGRANT FELLOW ch.g. 12 Hello Handsome - Fragrant Story by Sweet Story — Mrs Lorraine Lamb

1995 **P(0),U(-)**,5(0),3(13),5(0),5(0),P(0)

173 18/2 Market Rase' (L) RES 3m 6 GF *ld to 3rd, ld agn 14th, rdn apr 2 out, blnd last, hdd nr fin* 2 14

Unlucky only start 96 but vanished; hard to see a win at 13 14

FRAGRANT LORD b.g. 7 Germont - Tiger Feet by Pongee — Mrs V Jackson

1253 27/4 Balcormo Ma' (R) MDO 3m 16 GS *bhnd whn p.u. aft 12th* P 0

No show on debut 0

FRAMPTON HOUSE b.g. 14 Fine Blue - Frampton Close by Punchinello — A D Peachey

1995 P(0),**U(-)**,3(10),4(0),**9(0),5(0),7(0)**

215 24/2 Newtown (L) OPE 3m 20 GS *mid-div, rdn 11th, sn btn, t.o. & p.u. 2 out* P 0
426 9/3 Upton-On-Se' (R) CON 3m 16 GS *last frm hlfwy* 11 0
746 31/3 Upper Sapey (R) CON 3m 3 GS *ld 6-8th, outpcd frm 12th* 3 0
1383 6/5 Towcester (R) HC 2 3/4m 7 GF *mstk 8th, alwys bhnd, t.o. when p.u. before 4 out.* P 0

Of no account 0

FRANGAPINI (Irish) — I 9^{P}, I 43^{P}, I 253^{P}, I 291^{P}

FRANK RICH b.g. 9 King's Ride - Hill Invader by Brave Invader (USA) — D J Lay

1995 4(15),P(0),5(16),4+(17),6(0)

31 20/1 Higham (L) CON 3m 9 GF *prom, ld 12th-14th, sn wknd, p.u. 3 out* P 0
102 17/2 Marks Tey (L) CON 3m 17 G *in tch, rddn 11th, no ch whn u.r. 16th* U -
345 3/3 Higham (L) OPE 3m 3 G *alwys cls up, effrt 2 out, slw jmp last, sn btn* 2 14
418 9/3 High Easter (L) CON 3m 10 S *(bl) mid div, prog 10th, 3rd appr 2 out, wknd* 5 12

Hurdles winner 93; not 100% genuine & stamina doubtful; should try Members in 97 13

FRANK THE SWANK b.g. 5 Dunbeath (USA) - Dark Amber by Formidable (USA) — T C Gittins

167 17/2 Weston Park (L) MDN 3m 10 G *f 1st* F -
287 2/3 Eaton Hall (R) MDO 3m 11 G *mid to rear, nvr in race, p.u. 13th* P 0
463 9/3 Eyton-On-Se' (L) MDN 2 1/2m 14 G *prom early, fdd & sn btn 5 out, p.u. 3 out* P 0
884 6/4 Brampton Br' (R) MDN 3m 12 GF *ld to 8th, wknd frm 13th, p.u. 16th* P 0
1044 13/4 Bitterley (L) MDO 3m 15 G *ld 5-8th, wknd rpdly 10th, p.u. nxt* P 0
1225 24/4 Brampton Br' (R) MDO 3m 18 G *alwys mid-div, wknd 13th, p.u. 16th* P 0
1418 6/5 Eyton-On-Se' (L) MEM 3m 7 GF *rr early, 2nd 8th, ld 10-11th, wknd qckly* 5 0

No stamina & looks unpromising 0

FRAZER ISLAND (Irish) — I 198^{1}, I 235^{1}, I 310^{2}, I 329^{2}, I 426^{F}

FREDDIE FOX b.g. 10 Scallywag - Gouly Duff by Party Mink — Mrs A B Garton

1995 3(13),**2(19)**,2(19),1(19),**3(17),5(15),P(0)**

361 5/3 Leicester (R) HC 2 1/2m 110yds 15 GS *mid div, prog to dispute ld 3 out, wknd next, blnd last.* 3 15
735 31/3 Sudlow Farm (R) MEM 3m 7 G *(fav) in tch, gng wll, chsd ldr 13th, ld last, rddn clr* 1 18
1009 9/4 Flagg Moor (L) CON 3m 7 G *(fav) in tch, ld 11-13th, disp 2 out, unable to qckn und pres* 2 19
1456 8/5 Uttoxeter (L) HC 2m 5f 11 G *prog 9th, with ldr apr 4 out, ld last, driven out.* 1 20
1535 16/5 Aintree (L) HC 3m 1f 11 GF *held up, hmpd 4th, reminders 8th, pushed along and hdwy 11th, wknd 13th, t.o..* 5 0

Stays, onepaced but ultra-safe; won weak H/Chase & hard to place for a win in 97; G/F-S 19

FREDDY OWEN b.g. 10 Le Moss - Arctic Snow Cat by Raise You Ten — John R White

1995 **U(NH),2(NH),F(NH),P(NH)**

476 10/3 Tweseldown (R) OPE 3m 7 G *rear, jmpd lft 3rd, p.u. nxt, dsmntd* P 0

No longer of any account & problems 0

FRED SPLENDID b.g. 13 Piaffer (USA) - How Splendid by John Splendid — Ian Snowden

1995 **7(NH),3(NH),4(NH),P(NH)**

133 17/2 Ottery St M' (L) OPE 3m 18 GS *alwys mid-div, no ch whn p.u. 3 out* P 0
278 2/3 Clyst St Ma' (L) CON 3m 9 S *prom early, lost tch 12th, t.o. & p.u. 17th* P 0
559 17/3 Ottery St M' (L) OPE 3m 7 G *prom, disp 9-10th, wknd 13th, t.o. & p.u. 3 out* P 0
654 23/3 Badbury Rin' (L) OPE 3m 5 G *cl up untl wknd and t.o. frm 15th* 5 0
709 30/3 Barbury Cas' (L) OPE 3m 15 G *ld 4-6th, wknd nxt, t.o. 13th* 7 0
815 6/4 Charlton Ho' (L) MEM 3m 8 GF *hndy to 12th, lost tch frm 4 out* 5 0

Winning chaser but of no account now 0

FREE BEAR b.g. 13 Liberated - Buccoo Bear by Ragstone — Mrs Colin Chisholm

1995 P(0),5(0),3(0),3(0)

140 17/2 Larkhill (R) CON 3m 17 G *ld to 2nd, qckly wknd, t.o. 12th* 10 0
262 2/3 Didmarton (L) MEM 3m 11 G *alwys last pair, t.o. hlfwy* 7 0

848 6/4 Howick (L) MDN 3m 14 GF *alwys rear, some late prog* 6 0
1217 24/4 Andoversford (R) MDO 3m 16 G *rr div, prog 12th, blndrd & u.r. nxt* U

Placed in 95 but nothing in 96 & too old now 0

FREEMOUNT MINSTREL(IRE) ch.g. 8 Black Minstrel - List To Me by Pamroy J P Rawlins
1995 6(0),P(0),U(-),P(0)
471 10/3 Milborne St' (L) MDO 3m 16 G *alwys rear, no ch frm 14th* 8 0
652 23/3 Badbury Rin' (L) MDO 3m 13 G *mid-div untl wknd, t.o. 15th* 6 0

Tailed off when completing & appears to have no prospects 0

FREE TRANSFER(IRE) b.g. 7 Dara Monarch - Free Reserve (USA) by Tom Rolfe D J Fairbairn
699 30/3 Tranwell (L) CON 3m 8 GS *mid-div, prog 14th, chal 2 out, came again nr fin* 2 22
861 6/4 Alnwick (L) CON 3m 7 GF *(fav) w.w. prog to chs wnnr 16th, hd rddn & ev ch whn f last* U 21
1083 14/4 Friars Haugh (L) CON 3m 10 F *4th hlfwy, ld 4 out, clr 2 out* 1 21
1351 4/5 Mosshouses (L) CON 3m 11 GS *(fav) hld up, prog 9th, ev ch apr 2 out, wknd* 3 14
1542 16/5 Perth (R) HC 2 1/2m 110yds 8 F *prom, ld 8th to next, cl up and ev ch 3 out, not qckn run-in.* 2 23

Winning hurdler; able but needs easy 3m; not 100% genuine; good enough for Opens; G-F 24

FRENCH INVASION b.m. 7 Nader - Lyme Bay II by Incredule Mrs Marilyn Burrough
1494 11/5 Holnicote (L) MDO 3m 8 G *towrds rear, nvr dang, p.u. 15th* P 0
1626 27/5 Lifton (R) MDO 3m 13 GS *twrds rear whn blnd & u.r. 7th (ditch)* U -

No signs of ability 0

FRENCH LADY (Irish) — **I** 217[1], **I** 257[P], **I** 298[P], **I** 362[P]

FRENCHLANDS WAY ch.g. 12 Kinglet - Sylv by Calpurnius R E Young
1995 1(19),3(18),2(16)
494 16/3 Horseheath (R) RES 3m 10 GF *prom til f 4th* F -

Maiden winner 95; always lightly raced & vanished quickly 96; best watched if returning 15

FRENCH PLEASURE gr.m. 10 Dawn Johnny (USA) - Perfect Day by Roan Rocket A J Mason
264 2/3 Didmarton (L) INT 3m 12 G *cls up, ev ch frm 3 out, pshd into ld flat, comf* 1 17
380 9/3 Barbury Cas' (L) CON 3m 11 GS *(fav) prom, ch 14th, unable to qckn aft, onepcd* 3 10
794 2/4 Heythrop (R) CON 3m 6 F *not fluent, in tch, prog to chs wnr aft 3 out, no imp* 3 16

Has had a varied career; lightly raced now; could struggle to win Confined at 11; G-F 17

FRENCH STICK ch.g. 8 Sula Bula - French Highway by Duc D'Orleans Mrs J P Spencer
1995 4(10),1(14),F(-)
683 30/3 Chaddesley ' (L) MEM 3m 17 G *chsd ldr, blnd 3rd, wknd 7th, t.o. & p.u. 14th* P 0
1222 24/4 Brampton Br' (R) RES 3m 11 G *ld frm 5th til aft 16th, rlld frm 2 out* 2 17

Maiden winner 95; lightly raced; placed in weak Restricted; can win one if fit 97; G-F 17

FRERE HOGAN(FR) b.g. 14 Matahawk - Hantelle (FR) by Rose Laurel P A D Scouller
1995 P(0),6(0),2(15),P(0),P(0),4(12),1(16)
16 14/1 Tweseldown (R) MEM 3m 2 GS *made all, clr to 12th, kpt on gamely aft last* 1 16

Emerged to beat non-stayer in match & may well have gone out on a high note 14

FRESH ICE(IRE) ch.g. 6 Aristocracy - Quefort by Quayside G Vergette
15 14/1 Cottenham (R) MDN 3m 14 G *w.w. prog & ev ch 14th, btn & eased apr 3 out, p.u. nxt* P 0
60 10/2 Cottenham (R) MDO 3m 7 GS *prom, wth ldr whn f 11th* F -
182 18/2 Horseheath (R) MDO 3m 11 G *(fav) prom, ld 10th, blnd nxt, drvn & kpt on flat, jnd fin* 1 14
726 31/3 Garthorpe (R) RES 3m 16 G *prom, ld 11-15th, outpcd 3 out, kpt on flat* 2 17

Dead-heated in weak race but ran much better after; should win Restricted if fit 97; R/H so far 17

FRESH PRINCE b.g. 8 Balinger - Lasses Nightshade by Deadly Nightshade Mrs Vanessa Ramm
1995 1(15),P(0)
26 20/1 Barbury Cas' (L) OPE 3m 12 GS *ld, 3l up whn f 13th* F -
235 24/2 Heythrop (R) RES 3m 10 GS *(fav) ld to 2nd, cls up til ld 14th, hdd 2 out, wknd last* 5 0
599 23/3 Howick (L) RES 3m 7 S *(fav) ld to 4th, lost plc, lost tch 11th, p.u. 3 out* P 0
1038 13/4 St Hilary (R) RES 3m 15 G *clr 3rd whn p.u. 9th* P 0
1212 24/4 Andoversford (R) MEM 3m 5 G *(fav) made all at stdy pace, pshd clr app last, comf* 1 12
1439 6/5 Ashorne (R) RES 3m 11 G *made virt all, qcknd clr 12th, blnd 2 out, all out, well rdn* 1 19
1604 25/5 Bassaleg (R) OPE 3m 6 GS *ld to 9th, 2nd aft, grad wknd 13th, p.u. 2 out* P 0

Only completed 4 of 9 races (3 wins); breathing problems & unpredictable; should win again; Good 18

FRIARY LAD(IRE) ch.g. 7 Arapahos (FR) - Mylie's Response by Moyrath Response D Rogers
1995 4(13),P(0),3(16)
665 24/3 Eaton Hall (R) RES 3m 14 S *rear, some late prog, nrst fin* 4 0

952 8/4 Eyton-On-Se' (L) RES 3m 7 GF *held up, cls order 12th, hndy, ld 3 out, ran on strgly* 1 18
1219 24/4 Brampton Br' (R) CON 3m 9 G *w.w., prog 13th, nvr rch ldr, lft clr 2nd at last* 2 18

Irish Maiden winner 94; improved 96; ran well last start & Confined likely 97; lightly raced; Good 20

FRIC FACILE (Irish) — I 27F

FRIDAY THIRTEENTH (Irish) — I 17S, I 34P

FRIENDLY BID (Irish) — I 177F, I 233P, I 3012, I 427F, I 587P

FRIENDLY LADY b.m. 12 New Member - Friendly Glow by Pal O Mine J Grant Cann

1995 **4(NH),P(NH),P(NH),2(NH),9(NH)**

136 17/2 Ottery St M' (L) LAD 3m 9 GS *in tch til f 12th* F -
266 2/3 Didmarton (L) LAD 3m 13 G *hld up rear, t.o. 11th, ran on 3 out, nvr in race* 8 10
561 17/3 Ottery St M' (L) LAD 3m 12 G *alwys rear, nvr nrr* 6 11
655 23/3 Badbury Rin' (L) LAD 3m 8 G *nvr bttr than mid-div* 5 0
1110 17/4 Hockworthy (L) CON 3m 9 GS *sn mid-div, 4th & outpcd 12th, kpt on to mod 3rd post* 3 20
1277 27/4 Bratton Down (L) CON 3m 15 GF *prom, 4th at 12th, btn 4th whn u.r. last* U -
1342 4/5 Holnicote (L) MEM 3m 7 GS *(fav) ld/disp to 15th, ld 16th-2 out, ev ch til just outpcd nr fin* 2 18
1525 12/5 Ottery St M' (L) CON 3m 9 GF *in tch, cls 3rd 3 out, ld apr last, drew clr* 1 20

Formerly top-class; schoolmaster in 96 & partnership could win again at 13; G/F-S 19

FRIENDLY VIKING ch.g. 6 Viking (USA) - Ale Water by Be Friendly B R J Young

1995 6(0),P(0)

71 10/2 Great Treth' (R) MDO 3m 15 S *nvr bttr than mid-div, p.u. 13th* P 0
195 24/2 Lemalla (R) INT 3m 7 HY *mid-div whn ref 10th* R -
297 2/3 Great Treth' (R) INT 3m 10 G *bhnd frm 7th til f 11th* F -

No form & only one completion from 5 starts 95-6 0

FRIGHTENING CHILD (Irish) — I 47P, I 643, I 71P, I 354, , I 4593, I 5036

FROME BOY ch.g. 11 New Member - Groundsel by Reform Peter Johnson

1995 7(0),7(0),1(16)

826 6/4 Stainton (R) OPE 3m 8 GF *mid-div, mstk 2nd, p.u. nxt* P 0
1093 14/4 Whitwell-On' (R) MXO 4m 19 G *s.v.s. rear whn b.d. 6th* B -
1282 27/4 Easingwold (L) OPE 3m 8 G *n.j.w. sn dtchd, ran out & u.r. 10th* r -
1467 11/5 Easingwold (L) OPE 3m 6 G *prom to 7th, lost plc, wknd 10th, t.o. & f last* F -

Formerly useful; won weak race 95; lost interest now 0

FRONT COVER b.m. 6 Sunyboy - Roman Lilly by Romany Air Stewart Pike

1995 U(-),F(-),2(15)

2 13/1 Larkhill (R) MDO 3m 17 GS *prom whn u.r. 3rd* U -
447 9/3 Haldon (R) MDO 3m 13 S *(fav) hld up, prog 9th, 3rd & ev ch 15th, unable to chal aft* 3 15
652 23/3 Badbury Rin' (L) MDO 3m 13 G *(fav) mid-div, ld 4 out, going well whn f. next.* F -
1060 13/4 Badbury Rin' (L) MDO 3m 14 GF *(fav) hld up, prog 14th, ld 4 out, sn clr, easily* 1 16
1395 6/5 Cotley Farm (L) RES 3m 8 GF *(fav) w.w., prog frm 11th, ld app last, not qckn whn hdd* 2 20
1564 19/5 Mollington (R) XX 3m 14 GS *(fav) alwys prom, ld 13th, drew clr 2 out, ran on strngly* 1 20

Improving; good stable; bolted up last start & jumping improved; could prove useful; G/S-G/F 23

FRONTRUNNER ch.m. 8 Royal Match - Talarea by Takawalk II Ms Julia Louise Wyllie

1995 **7(NH),6(NH),4(NH),P(NH)**

1040 13/4 St Hilary (R) MDN 3m 12 G *cls up, 6th whn p.u. 9th* P 0
1201 21/4 Lydstep (L) MDN 3m 9 S *nvr nrr than 5th, p.u. 9th* P 0
1271 27/4 Pyle (R) MDO 3m 15 G *cls up to 7th, no ch 10th, p.u. 12th* P 0
1391 6/5 Pantyderi (R) MDO 3m 13 GF *u.r. 1st* U -
1486 11/5 Erw Lon (L) MEM 3m 4 F *in tch to 8th, fdd, fin t.o.* 4 0
1561 18/5 Bassaleg (R) MDO 3m 8 F *lost tch 7th, t.o. 10th, p.u. aft 3 out as rest fin* P 0

Not living up to her name; last & beaten miles on only completion 0

FROSTY MORN (Irish) — I 280P, I 379P

FROSTY RECEPTION ch.g. 11 What A Guest - Stormy Queen by Typhoon R J Baker

1588 25/5 Mounsey Hil' (R) LAD 3m 6 G *(bl) keen hold, in tch to 11th, t.o. frm 14th* 4 0
1635 1/6 Bratton Down (L) LAD 3m 13 G *not fluent, alwys rear, no ch frm 14th, t.o.* 12 0
1650 8/6 Umberleigh (L) CON 3m 7 GF *(bl) in tch, prog to chs ldr 15th, styd on to ld post* 1 18

Winning hurdler; novice ridden; shock winner (33/1); follow up looks tough; Firm 18

FROZEN MINSTREL b.g. 12 Black Minstrel - Arctic Sue by Arctic Slave R M Billing

1995 P(0),P(0),P(0)

203 24/2 Castle Of C' (R) MEM 3m 4 HY *sn t.o., btn 3 fences* 3 0

No longer of any account 0

FROZEN PIPE b.m. 8 Majestic Maharaj - Celtic Ice by Celtic Cone Alan P Brewer

1995 r(-),F(-),F(-),U(-)

357	3/3 Garnons	(L) RES 3m	14 GS	*trckd ldrs, effrt 13th, ev ch nxt, wknd apr last*	2	15
641	23/3 Siddington	(L) RES 3m	20 S	*w.w. mstks 3rd & 7th, prog 11th, 7th & in tch whn f 14th*	F	-
742	31/3 Upper Sapey	(R) RES 3m	9 GS	*effrt to disp 15th, qckned clr apr last*	1	17
1413	6/5 Cursneh Hill	(L) INT 3m	6 GF	*held up til prog 14th, slw jmp & no ch frm 2 out*	5	0
1478	11/5 Bredwardine	(R) CON 3m	12 G	*hld up rear, prog 13th, no ext frm 15th, p.u. last*	P	0

Maiden winner 93; won modest Restricted; poor jumper; more needed for Confined; G/S 16

FROZEN STIFF(IRE) ro.g. 8 Carlingford Castle - Run Wardasha by Run The Gantlet (USA) A J Brown

1995 F(-),R(-)

52	4/2 Alnwick	(L) MDO 3m	11 G	*trckd ldr, ld 9th, clr whn blndrd 2 out, ran on well*	1	15
84	11/2 Alnwick	(L) RES 3m	11 GS	*(fav) hld up,prog & mstk 9th,sn 2nd,rdn to ld 2 out,styd on well*	1	19

Vastly improved to complete early season double; vanished after; Confined likely if fit 97; G-S ... 20

FRUIDS PARK bl.m. 13 Royal Fountain - Cregg Park by Orchardist Jas D Wyllie

1995 6(0),4(0),U(-),5(0),4(0),8(0)

404	9/3 Dalston	(R) RES 3m	7 G	*4th at 6th, t.o. frm 11th*	5	0
608	23/3 Friars Haugh	(L) RES 3m	13 G	*bhnd 4th, u.r. 14th*	P	0
750	31/3 Lockerbie	(R) MEM 3m	2 G	*not alwys fluent, nvr lkd like wnng*	2	0
860	6/4 Alnwick	(L) MXO 4m 1f	7 GF	*bhnd 8th, blnd 14th, t.o. & p.u. 3 out*	P	0
1086	14/4 Friars Haugh	(L) RES 3m	7 F	*last hlfwy, t.o. whn p.u. 2 out*	P	0

Beaten in a match & of no account now 0

FRUIT TOWN (Irish) — **I** 69F, **I** 1254, **I** 2062, **I** 250P

FULL ALIRT ch.m. 8 Lir - Full Tan by Dairialatan B R J Young

1995 1(14),P(0),1(18),2(21),1(21),2(23)

42	3/2 Wadebridge	(L) CON 3m	8 GF	*(fav) u.r. 1st*	U	-
63	10/2 Great Treth'	(R) MEM 3m	6 S	*(fav) ld 4th,made rest, rdn out*	1	20
671	28/3 Taunton	(R) HC 3m	13 S	*trckd ldrs, ld 7th, mstks 9th and 14th, f next.*	F	-
1111	17/4 Hockworthy	(L) MXO 3m	13 GS	*w.w, prog 12th, outpcd 15th, kpt on one pace*	4	19

Won 3 in 95; quite useful & beaten in hot race last start; Confineds, at least, possible 97; G/F-Hy 23

FULL OF BOUNCE (Irish) — **I** 2P, **I** 36F, **I** 521, **I** 1162

FULL SCORE(IRE) b.g. 7 Orchestra - Country Character by Furry Glen Miss Anne Holloway

17	14/1 Tweseldown	(R) MDN 3m	11 GS	*ld to 3rd, chsd wnr & mstks 12,13 & nxt,drppd out & p.u.3out*	P	0

Disqualified when winning Irish Maiden 95; vanished after 1st weekend 96; best watched 11

FULL SONG b.m. 8 Idiot's Delight - Into Song by True Song G Coombe

1995 U(-),6(0),U(-),4(0),3(0),P(0)

726	31/3 Garthorpe	(R) RES 3m	16 G	*hld up last trio, nvr put in race*	10	0
967	8/4 Thorpe Lodge	(L) MEM 3m	7 GF	*nvr dang, last trio, prog 11th, 3rd & outpcd 4 out*	3	0
1103	14/4 Guilsborough	(L) MDN 3m	15 G	*hld up bhnd, steady prog frm 13th, kpt on to tk 3rd aft last*	3	10
1240	27/4 Clifton On '	(L) MDO 3m	10 GF	*alwys prom, ev ch 15th, wknd apr 3 out*	4	0
1381	5/5 Dingley	(R) MDO 3m	16 GF	*hld up,prog 11th,sn outpcd,kpt on frm 3 out,fin 3rd,disq*	0	0
1523	12/5 Garthorpe	(R) MDO 3m	11 GF	*chsd ldrs, alwys cls up, ev ch 4 out, not qckn*	2	12
1569	19/5 Mollington	(R) MDO 3m	10 GS	*(fav) 4s-9/4, w.w. rear, effrt whn outpcd 12th, no imp ldrs 3 out*	4	0
1644	2/6 Dingley	(R) MDO 3m	16 GF	*rr, mstk 5th, in tch whn hmprd 12th, sn btn, p.u. 2 out*	P	0

Stays better now but placed in modest races & not certain to find an opening in 97 13

FUMI D'ORO ch.m. 8 Lighter - Golden Murry by Murrayfield R E Evans

1995 **12(NH)**

771	31/3 Pantyderi	(R) MDN 3m	14 G	*nvr nr to chal, p.u. 15th*	P	0
976	8/4 Lydstep	(L) MDO 3m	12 G	*f 9th*	F	-
980	8/4 Lydstep	(L) RES 3m	11 G	*2nd outing, twrds rear, p.u. 13th*	P	0
1390	6/5 Pantyderi	(R) MDO 3m	15 GF	*rear, p.u. 8th*	P	0
1492	11/5 Erw Lon	(L) MDO 3m	10 F	*wth ldrs til 13th, fdd, p.u. 2 out*	P	0

Yet to complete & showed nothing in 96 0

FUNCHEN VIEW ch.g. 16 Mon Capitaine - Clontinty by Menelek Steven Astaire

1995 P(0),P(0),7(0),6(0),U(-),P(0),5(0),P(0),8(0),U(-),4(0)

1562	19/5 Mollington	(R) MEM 3m	6 GS	*1st ride, last, t.o. 6th, tk poor 4th apr 2 out*	4	0
1611	26/5 Tweseldown	(R) XX 3m	9 G	*last pair, t.o. 9th, retired*	4	0

Retired 0

FUNDY (Irish) — **I** 473, **I** 1182, **I** 1555, **I** 2431, **I** 3331, **I** 6472

FUNNY FARM ch.g. 6 Funny Man - Ba Ba Belle by Petit Instant Mrs Jane Walter

521	16/3 Larkhill	(R) MDO 3m	6 G	*schoold in rear, t.o. & p.u. 3 out*	P	0
1280	27/4 Bratton Down	(L) MDO 3m	14 GF	*16s-10s, plld hrd, ran wd bnd aft 2nd, ran out nxt*	r	-
1430	6/5 High Bickin'	(R) MDO 3m	8 G	*held up bhnd, late hdwy to take 2nd cls home*	2	13

Beaten a length in poor race; only learning & should win 97; problems L/H 14

FUNNY FEELINGS b.g. 6 Feelings (FR) - Miami Star by Miami Springs — Mrs A A Scott

194 24/2 Friars Haugh (L) MDN 3m 11 S *ld til 5th, grad lost tch frm 11th* 4 0
406 9/3 Dalston (R) MDO 2 1/2m 12 G *ld 3rd, und pres apr last, hld on gmly nr fin* 1 14
608 23/3 Friars Haugh (L) RES 3m 13 G *made most til f 7th* F -
1086 14/4 Friars Haugh (L) RES 3m 7 F *2nd mostly, ld brfly 2 out, sn hdd & outpcd* 2 15
1353 4/5 Mosshouses (L) RES 3m 11 GS *chsd ldr to 9th, grad outpcd frm 14th, no ch 2 out* 5 0
1472 11/5 Aspatria (L) RES 3m 8 GF *ld 9th, blndrd & hdd 2 out, btn whn lft clr last, disq* 1D 17
1572 19/5 Corbridge (R) LAD 3m 8 G *cls up 7th, disp 9th, 2nd nxt til blnd & u.r. 15th* U -

Fair start; makes mistakes & needs easy 3m; can win Restricted (again) 97; G-F 17

FUNNY HABITS (Irish) — **I** 76^P^, **I** 380^F^

FUNNY WORRY b.g. 7 Jester - Concern by Brigadier Gerard — Mrs M J Thorogood
1995 **8(NH)**
107 17/2 Marks Tey (L) MDN 3m 15 G *cls up til f 14th* F -
682 30/3 Cottenham (R) MDO 3m 9 GF *plld to ld 4th,sn clr,nrly u.r.10th,hdd 12th,wknd,p.u.16th* P 0

Some ability but needs to settle; may do better 97 0

FURIOUS AVENGER ch.g. 7 True Song - Furious Babs by Fury Royal — L R Gasson
1995 P(0),P(0)
797 2/4 Heythrop (R) MDN 3m 11 F *ld 6-12th, wknd 3 out* 7 0

Last in poor Maiden & much more needed 0

FURIOUS OATS(IRE) ch.m. 8 Oats - Fury Spirit by Fury Royal — J A C Sheppard
1995 P(0)
358 3/3 Garnons (L) RES 3m 18 GS *mid-div, just in tch whn f 12th* F -

No real signs of ability in annual outing 0

FURRY FOX(IRE) b.g. 8 Furry Glen - Pillow Chat by Le Bavard (FR) — E H Crow
1995 P(0),2(14),2(14),P(0),3(11),2(13),1(12)
564 17/3 Wolverhampt' (L) RES 3m 8 GS *chsd ldrs, ld 13th-15th, onepcd* 3 10
1102 14/4 Guilsborough (L) RES 3m 15 G *prom, ld 9-13th, ld agn aft 2 out, forged clr* 1 19
1230 27/4 Weston Park (L) CON 3m 7 G *(fav) ld/disp 3rd-3 out, qcknd 2 out, ran on wll* 1 19
1422 6/5 Eyton-On-Se' (L) CON 3m 3 GF *(fav) ld to 4th, cl up, ld 10th-5 out, not qckn frm 4 out* 2 11
1618 27/5 Chaddesley ' (L) CON 3m 14 GF *ld to 5th, chsd wnr aft, btn 15th, lost 2nd 2 out* 3 20

Improved; safe; won weak Confined & struggling in better races after; should find more chances; Any .. 20

FURRY KNOWE b.g. 11 Furry Glen - I Know by Crespino — David Pritchard
1995 **4(NH),4(NH),4(NH),P(NH),3(NH)**
226 24/2 Duncombe Pa' (R) OPE 3m 10 GS *in tch, pshd alng 10th, lft mod 4th 4 out, kpt on* 4 11
359 4/3 Doncaster (L) HC 2m 3f 110yds 10 G *in tch, mstk and reminders 5th, struggling from hfwy, t.o..* 4 0
513 16/3 Dalton Park (R) OPE 3m 9 G *pshd alng in tch, blnd 12th, sn bhnd & no ch* 5 12
587 23/3 Wetherby Po' (L) OPE 3m 15 S *prom to 10th, sn outpcd* 5 13
672 29/3 Aintree (L) HC 2 3/4m 26 G *hmpd and useated rider 1st.* U -
1133 20/4 Hornby Cast' (L) OPE 3m 14 G *alwys rear, bhnd whn u.r. 11th* U -
1584 24/5 Towcester (R) HC 3m 1f 11 GS *soon struggling in rear, t.o. after 9th, p.u. after 6 out.* P 0
1647 8/6 Umberleigh (L) OPE 3m 7 GF *prom, slw jmp 5th, nrly u.r. 10th, p.u. nxt, sddle slppd* P 0

Winning chaser; well beaten for new owner-rider & Members only hope 97 12

FURRY LOCH b.g. 10 Furry Glen - Loreto Lady by Brave Invader (USA) — Mrs R E Parker
1995 U(-),P(0),F(-),U(-),S(-),U(-),3(0)
533 16/3 Cothelstone (L) MDN 3m 13 G *f 1st* F -

Of no account 0

FURRY VENTURE b.m. 11 Furry Glen - Multeen by Deep Run — Miss D M M Calder
1995 P(0),2(14),12(0),P(0),4(0)
318 2/3 Corbridge (R) LAD 3m 5f 10 GS *last early, nvr rchd ldrs, blnd & u.r. 16th* U -
611 23/3 Friars Haugh (L) LAD 3m 10 G *sn bhnd, some late hdwy, nrst fin* 5 13
752 31/3 Lockerbie (R) LAD 3m 10 G *sn strgglng in rear, p.u. 3 out* P 0
913 8/4 Tranwell (L) LAD 3m 7 GF *outpcd, poor 6th at 13th, plodded on* 5 0
1084 14/4 Friars Haugh (L) LAD 3m 8 F *sn strgglng in rear, lft 3rd at last* 3 10

Won 3 in 94; struggling since & outclassed in Ladies; unlikely to win again 12

GABRIELLE'S BOY (Irish) — **I** 372^P^

GAELIC GLEN (Irish) — **I** 421^5^, **I** 500^P^, **I** 559^B^

GAELIC WARRIOR b.g. 9 Belfort (FR) - Practicality by Weavers' Hall — Mrs D Ibbotson
1995 1(20),**F(-)**,4(10),6(11),3(22),**3(18),6(14),P(0),P(0)**
587 23/3 Wetherby Po' (L) OPE 3m 15 S *mid-div, no ch whn p.u. 3 out* P 0
760 31/3 Great Stain' (L) OPE 3m 8 GS *prom, 2nd hlfwy, chal 5 out, ld 3 out-nxt, onepcd* 2 19

1093 14/4 Whitwell-On' (R) MXO 4m 19 G *rear, prog 9th, no hdwy aft, fdng whn u.r. 15th* U -
1287 27/4 Easingwold (L) MEM 3m 5 G *(fav) ld til jnd last, hdd & no ext nr fin* 2 15
1467 11/5 Easingwold (L) OPE 3m 6 G *chsd ldrs, mstk 5th, lft in ld apr 7th, hdd 15th, onepcd* 2 20
1615 27/5 Wetherby (L) HC 2 1/2m 110yds 11 G *cl up till wknd after 8th, poor 4th when f four out.* F -

Open winner 95; onepaced & lost last 14; likely to extend sequence; G-Hy 17

GALADINE gr.g. 14 Gaberdine - Spring Gala by Ancient Monro — Mrs E A Chapplehow

112 17/2 Lanark (R) LAD 3m 8 GS *blnd 6th, alwys wll bhnd aft* 5 0
398 9/3 Dalston (R) MEM 3m 13 G *2nd early, stdd, chsd ldrs frm hlfwy, one-pcd* 9 0
499 16/3 Lanark (R) LAD 3m 10 G *sn wll bhnd* 5 0

Winning chaser - looks finished now 0

GAL-A-DOR br.g. 9 Soldier Rose - Turleigh Cynara Vii — C D Bradley

1995 P(0),P(0)

160 17/2 Weston Park (L) OPE 3m 16 G *t.o. hlfwy, p.u. 14th* P 0
239 25/2 Southwell P' (L) MDO 3m 9 HO *prom til f 5th* F -
334 3/3 Heythrop (R) MEM 3m 6 G *prssd wnr, ev ch 2 out, wknd last* 2 0
432 9/3 Upton-On-Se' (R) MDO 3m 17 GS *ld brfly 7-8th, 2l 2nd at 15th, sn btn* 4 0
904 6/4 Dingley (R) RES 3m 20 GS *prom for 2 m, 2nd 5-11th, wknd qckly, p.u. 4 out* P 0
1433 6/5 Ashorne (R) MDO 3m 16 G *ld to 3rd & 6-8th, wknd 12th, t.o. & p.u. 15th* P 0

Last when completing & looks devoid of stamina 0

GALAROI(IRE) b.g. 7 Supreme Leader - Bank Rate by Deep Run — D C Robinson

454 9/3 Charing (L) MDN 3m 10 G *(fav) ld 10th, just hdd whn f 13th* F -
576 17/3 Detling (L) MDN 3m 18 GF *alwys prom, chsd ldr 14th, chal whn lft clr last* 1 14
810 6/4 Charing (L) RES 3m 6 F *disp 6th til ld 13th, hdd apr 3 out, rallied, no ext flat* 2 18
964 8/4 Heathfield (R) RES 3m 7 G *chsd ldr til 7th, made rest, drw clr appr 3 out, impress* 1 20
1207 21/4 Heathfield (R) CON 3m 9 F *(fav) disp 6-8th, ld nxt, made rest, pshd clr 2 out, blnd last* 1 20
1375 4/5 Peper Harow (L) CON 3m 9 F *(fav) 3/1-1/1,prom, ld 13th til appr last, no ex* 2 19

Placed Irish Maidens 95; progressive; veteran ridden; could reach Open class 97; G-F 20

GALATASORI JANE (Irish) — **I** 43^{P}, **I** 204^{2}, **I** 469^{2}, **I** 545^{1}

GALA VOTE (Irish) — **I** 42^{4}, **I** 127^{P}, **I** 232^{5}, **I** 427^{3}

GALAXY HIGH b.g. 9 Anita's Prince - Regal Charmer by Royal And Regal (USA) — Ronald Bracken

1995 **5(NH),8(NH)**

67 10/2 Great Treth' (R) LAD 3m 11 S *nvr on terms* 9 0
208 24/2 Castle Of C' (R) LAD 3m 14 HY *alwys mid-div, 4th at 14th, no ch frm nxt* 3 16
469 10/3 Milborne St' (L) LAD 3m 8 G *bhnd, late prog frm 4 out, not rch ldrs* 4 14
730 31/3 Little Wind' (R) LAD 3m 6 GS *(vis) rmmndrs aft 6th, in tch, 8l 3rd whn blndrd & u.r. 3 out* U -
1309 28/4 Little Wind' (R) OPE 3m 8 G *(bl) in tch til outpcd aft 13th, sn btn* 5 13
1394 6/5 Cotley Farm (L) MXO 3m 5 GF *alwys bhnd, no ch frm 14th* 3 10

Winning hurdler but not threatening to win a point 14

GALEBREAKER (Irish) — **I** 139^{2}, **I** 148^{5}, **I** 245^{4}, **I** 352^{2}, **I** 438^{1}, **I** 544^{4}

GALE GRIFFIN (Irish) — **I** 24^{P}, **I** 92^{3}, **I** 170^{2}, **I** 254^{3}, **I** 315^{1}, **I** 406^{2}, **I** 453^{3}

GALE TAN (Irish) — **I** 335^{P}, **I** 460^{P}

GALLANT DREAM (Irish) — **I** 510^{P}

GALLANT GALE (Irish) — **I** 185^{P}, **I** 614^{P}

GALLERY LADY(IRE) b.m. 8 Tender King - London Spin by Derring-Do — Miss J Howarth

924 8/4 Bishopsleigh (R) LAD 3m 7 G *towrds rear frm 1st, f 4th* F -
1117 17/4 Hockworthy (L) MDO 3m 8 GS *n.j.w., sn last, t.o. & blndrd 10th & 11th, p.u. nxt* P 0

Not likely to make the frame yet 0

GALLIC BELLE b.m. 10 Roman Warrior - Belle Lutine by Relkino — T J Sunderland

1995 P(0),P(0),1(16),1(16),P(0)

639 23/3 Siddington (L) OPE 3m 12 S *in tch til appr 10th, no dang aft* 6 13
944 8/4 Andoversford (R) LAD 3m 4 GF *chsd ldr to 8th, wknd 12th, last nxt, p.u. 2 out* P 0

Won 5 points 93-5; changed hands; outclassed in Opens; fortune to win again 12

GALLIC TWISTER (Irish) — **I** 387^{P}, **I** 416^{P}

GALLOPING GIGGS (Irish) — **I** 27^{P}, **I** 133^{P}, **I** 237^{U}, **I** 272^{F}, **I** 388^{P}

GALLOWAY RAIDER br.g. 12 Skyliner - Whispering Breeze by Caliban — Russell Page

1995 2(14),P(0),5(0),5(14),5(0),3(0),4(15),2(15),6(0),2(13)

310 2/3 Ampton (R) CON 3m 13 G *ld til f 3rd* F -

Dual winner 94 vanished after brief appearance 96 & can only be watched 11

GALZIG b.g. 8 Alzao (USA) - Idabella (FR) by Carwhite Mrs D E H Turne

10	14/1	Cottenham	(R)	INT	3m	10	G	*cls up, wkng whn blnd 15th, p.u. last*	P	
96	11/2	Ampton	(R)	XX	3m	11	GF	*prom,ld 10-11th,chsd ldr 3 out,kpt on wll und pres,jst faild*	2	16
244	25/2	Southwell P'	(L)	CON	3m	13	HO	*prom, mstk 11th, sn wknd, poor 5th 4 out, p.u. 3 out*	P	
327	3/3	Market Rase'	(L)	CON	3m	15	G	*chsd ldrs, 3rd & outpcd 14th, tk 2nd last, promoted*	1	17
484	15/3	Fakenham	(L)	HC	2m 5f 110yds	13	GF	*soon tracking ldrs, hit 3rd, rdn and no ext from 3 out.*	4	19

Won 2 Irish points 95; awarded only win 96; ran well weak H/Chase; may find samll chance 97; G-F 19

GAMAY b.g. 6 Rymer - Darling Rose by Darling Boy Mrs L M Boulte

1995 r(-),P(0),3(12),2(13)

375	9/3	Barbury Cas'	(L)	MDN	3m	14	GS	*mid-div whn u.r. 3rd*	U	
643	23/3	Siddington	(L)	MDN	3m	16	S	*w.w. prog 10th, cls 4th & running on whn blnd & u.r. 2 out*	U	
1115	17/4	Hockworthy	(L)	MDO	3m	10	GS	*hld up bhnd, prog 12th, lft 2nd 2 out, sn ld, drvn out*	1	1

Won 3 finisher Maiden (no winners behind); hard ride; L/H essential; needs more for Restricteds 15

GAMBLERS REFRAIN b.g. 11 Blue Refrain - Blue Fire Lady by Pitcairn R W Pincombe

1995 P(0),P(0),P(0),P(0),P(0)

718	30/3	Wadebridge	(L)	MDO	3m	11	GF	*rear & strgglng frm 7th, t.o. & p.u. 3 out*	P	
927	8/4	Bishopsleigh	(R)	OPE	3m	7	G	*ld 1st til hdd 11th, frnt rank whn u.r. 13th*	U	
1117	17/4	Hockworthy	(L)	MDO	3m	8	GS	*mstk 4th, ld to 13th, 3rd & wkng whn ref 15th*	R	
1432	6/5	High Bickin'	(R)	MDO	3m	9	G	*prom til lost plc & rmmndrs 11th, ref 13th*	R	
1495	11/5	Holnicote	(L)	MDO	3m	11	G	*in tch til wknd 12th, t.o.*	7	
1651	8/6	Umberleigh	(L)	MDO	3m	11	GF	*ld to 6th, lft in ld 10th, hdd & no ext last*	2	1

Shocked himself last start (only 2nd completion last 13 starts) & unlikely to repeat the trick 11

GAME FAIR b.g. 9 Lighter - Stagbury by National Trust Mrs D Burtor

1995 P(0),5(0),3(13),3(10),U(-),5(10)

377	9/3	Barbury Cas'	(L)	OPE	3m	5	GS	*prom early, sn wknd, p.u. 15th*	P	
519	16/3	Larkhill	(R)	CON	3m	5	G	*nvr trbld ldrs*	4	
707	30/3	Barbury Cas'	(L)	RES	3m	18	G	*alwys rear, t.o. & p.u. 4 out*	P	
863	6/4	Larkhill	(R)	MEM	3m	4	F	*ld til mstk 3rd, ld agn 9th til pckd 3 out, rlld flat*	2	1
1166	20/4	Larkhill	(R)	OPE	3m	6	GF	*prom til wknd qckly frm 13th, p.u. 3 out*	P	
1290	28/4	Barbury Cas'	(L)	OPE	3m	5	F	*alwys chsng wnr, outpcd 3 out, no imp aft*	2	1
1405	6/5	Hackwood Pa'	(L)	CON	3m	6	F	*alwys cls up, 3l 3rd 2 out, wknd*	3	1
1567	19/5	Mollington	(R)	INT	3m	12	GS	*ld to 2nd, rear whn mstk 5th, t.o. 11th, p.u. 2 out*	P	

Members winner 94; beaten all 14 starts 95-6; runs well occasionally but hard to win again; G-F 14

GAME SET ch.g. 10 Carlingford Castle - Star Set by Sunny Way Graham Treglow

1995 P(0),P(0),P(0),2(11),4(10)

426	9/3	Upton-On-Se'	(R)	CON	3m	16	GS	*prom til wknd aft hlfwy*	7	
745	31/3	Upper Sapey	(R)	INT	3m	6	GS	*alwys strgglng frm 10th*	4	
1213	24/4	Andoversford	(R)	CON	3m	5	G	*in tch, 4th & outpcd 6th, t.o. frm 13th*	4	
1328	30/4	Huntingdon	(R)	HC	3m	4	GF	*in tch till rdn and lost touch 14th, t.o..*	3	
1521	12/5	Garthorpe	(R)	INT	3m	7	GF	*chsng grp, 4th at 9th, lost tch apr 12th, onepcd*	6	

Dual winner 94; disappointing since; stamina doubtful & unlikely to win again 11

GAN AWRY b.m. 9 Kabour - Wedded Bliss by Relko A D Peachey

1995 P(0),6(0),1(0),3(14),F(-)

216	24/2	Newtown	(L)	LAD	3m	13	GS	*chsd ldrs til wknd 12th, p.u. nxt*	P	
1122	20/4	Stratford	(L)	HC	2m 5f 110yds	16	GF	*hdwy 5th, wknd 12th, bhnd when p.u. before 3 out.*	P	
1228	27/4	Worcester	(L)	HC	2m 7f	17	G	*mid div when f 8th.*	F	
1455	8/5	Uttoxeter	(L)	HC	2m 5f	9	G	*in tch, wknd 11th, t.o. when p.u. before 4 out.*	P	
1508	12/5	Maisemore P'	(L)	LAD	3m	6	F	*blnd 4th, last aft, t.o. & p.u. 13th*	P	

Walked over for Restricted 95; changed hands (again); totally outclassed 96 0

GARDA SPIRIT br.m. 10 Garda's Revenge (USA) - Next-Of-Kin by Great Nephew D L William

27	20/1	Barbury Cas'	(L)	LAD	3m	15	GS	*alwys t.o. last, p.u. 14th*	P	
266	2/3	Didmarton	(L)	LAD	3m	13	G	*mid-div til f 8th*	F	

Professionally trained but showed nothing in points 0

GARETHSON (Irish) — **I** 16[F], **I** 109[F], **I** 174[P], **I** 300[1], **I** 411[1]

GARRYLUCAS ch.g. 10 Bishop Of Orange - Susy Karne by Woodville II J D Loma

1995 1(20),R(-),P(0),4(12),P(0),P(0),3(22)

162	17/2	Weston Park	(L)	OPE	3m	16	G	*chsng grp, chsd wnr 13th, nvr able to chal*	2	2
215	24/2	Newtown	(L)	OPE	3m	20	GS	*prom, prog to ld 14th, clr 2 out, rdn out*	1	2
459	9/3	Eyton-On-Se'	(L)	OPE	3m	11	G	*(fav) chsng grp, ran on und pres frm 2 out, not rch wnr*	2	2
686	30/3	Chaddesley '	(L)	OPE	3m	6	G	*w.w. prog to ld 12th, hdd last, onepcd*	2	2

Revived by change of rider 96; ran sweetly & won good Open; win again if retaining enthusiasm 97; GS 24

GARRYNISK (Irish) — **I** 30^{1}

GARRYROSS (Irish) — **I** 356^{F}, **I** 374^{4}, **I** 517^{3}, **I** 608,

GARWELL (Irish) — **I** 391^{F}

GASMARK (Irish) — **I** 62^{P}, **I** 81^{U}, **I** 157^{3}, **I** 223^{U}, **I** 323^{3}, **I** 541^{3}, **I** 603^{2}, **I** 644^{3}

GATTEN'S BRAKE b or br.g. 8 Impecunious - Troijoy by Troilus — D W Parker

152 17/2 Erw Lon (L) MDN 3m 11 G *rear whn f 6th* F -
388 9/3 Llanfrynach (R) RES 3m 20 GS *wll in rear til p.u. 7th* P 0
544 17/3 Erw Lon (L) MEM 3m 5 GS *alwys rear, p.u. 15th* P 0
772 31/3 Pantyderi (R) MDN 3m 8 G *mid-div whn f 14th* F -

No sing of ability yet 0

GAWCOTT WOOD bl.m. 7 True Song - Dane Hole by Past Petition — Mrs E C Cockburn
1995 2(0),P(0)

4 13/1 Larkhill (R) MDO 3m 9 GS *hld up, prog to 3rd 14th, kpt on onepcd, hit last* 3 11
438 9/3 Newton Brom' (R) MDN 3m 10 GS *chsd ldr til ran wd apr 9th & ran out* r -
688 30/3 Chaddesley ' (L) MDN 3m 17 G *cls up, ld 12th-3 out, wknd* 4 12
890 6/4 Kimble (L) MDN 3m 11 GF *cls up, prog to ld 15th, clr last, ran on well* 1 15
1173 20/4 Chaddesley ' (L) RES 3m 18 G *prom, cls 3rd whn u.r. 6th* U -
1292 28/4 Barbury Cas' (L) RES 3m 11 F *mid-div, rdn & btn aft 11th, t.o. & p.u. 2 out* P 0
1620 27/5 Chaddesley ' (L) XX 3m 8 GF *mstk 4th, cls up, ld 12th til ran out & u.r. 14th* r -

Improved to win modest Maiden; disappointing after; may do better in 97 - needs to for Restricteds 16

GAWN INN (Irish) — **I** 22^{F}, **I** 93^{1}, **I** 170^{U}, **I** 257^{2}, **I** 316^{U}, **I** 411^{1}

GAY BOOTS b.m. 9 Doc Marten - Gay Desire by Dragonara Palace (USA) — P Quail

636 23/3 Market Rase' (L) MDN 3m 11 GF *t.o. in 8th at 6th, f 8th, rmntd* 4 0
1306 28/4 Southwell P' (L) MEM 3m 4 GF *ld to 6th, 3rd frm nxt, sn lost tch, t.o. & f 5 out* F -

Looks hopeless 0

GAY MUSE b.m. 7 Scorpio (FR) - La Tricoteuse by Le Tricolore — J G Charlton
1995 5(0),F(-)

71 10/2 Great Treth' (R) MDO 3m 15 S *alwys bhnd, p.u. 3 out* P 0

A hint of ability in 95 but vanished quickly in 96 0

GAY RUFFIAN b.g. 10 Welsh Term - Alcinea (FR) by Sweet Revenge — Mrs D J Dyson
1995 **13(NH),2(NH),8(NH),7(NH),4(NH),5(NH),P(NH)**

1042 13/4 Bitterley (L) CON 3m 9 G *cls up, chsd wnr 12th, no ext frm 15th* 2 17
1170 20/4 Chaddesley ' (L) CON 3m 9 G *(fav) mid-div, effrt 12th, 3l 3rd 14th, ev ch 16th, wknd nxt* 4 16
1463 10/5 Stratford (L) HC 3m 6 GF *lost tch 11th, t.o..* 6 0

Fair chaser under Rules but modest in points; win looks unlikely; novice ridden 15

GAYTON WILDS b.g. 7 Lightning Dealer - Seven Year Itch by Jimsun — Miss C Elderton

315 2/3 Ampton (R) MDO 3m 10 G *mstks,rmdrs 2nd,prom 7th ev ch til wknd 17th,3rd & p.u.last* P 0
542 17/3 Southwell P' (L) MDO 3m 15 GS *f 2nd* F -
618 23/3 Higham (L) MDO 3m 14 GF *(Jt fav) 5s-3s, mid-div whn f 2nd* F -
1522 12/5 Garthorpe (R) RES 3m 12 GF *s.s. ref 1st* R -

Promise on debut; fell to pieces after; best watched initially 97 10

GAY VIXEN VI ch.m. 11 Campaigner - Nregistered by Unregistered — Mrs Susan Corbett
1995 4(0),3(0),5(0),r(-),3(0),3(12),1(15),**F(-)**,F(-)

609 23/3 Friars Haugh (L) PPO 3m 7 G *3rd hlfwy, lost tch 15th, p.u. next.* P 0
702 30/3 Tranwell (L) XX 3m 3 GS *alwys last, outpcd frm 12th* 3 0
911 8/4 Tranwell (L) CON 3m 9 GF *ld/disp til wknd rpdly aft 2 out* 6 0
1353 4/5 Mosshouses (L) RES 3m 11 GS *made most to 14th, 3rd & outpcd nxt, fin tired* 3 11
1472 11/5 Aspatria (L) RES 3m 8 GF *ld to 4th, bhnd frm 12th, t.o.* 4 0
1586 25/5 Hexham (L) HC 2 1/2m 110yds 14 GF *well bhnd hfwy, t.o..* 10 0

Won poor Maiden 95; well beaten now upgraded & another win looks impossible 11

G DEREK br.g. 13 Derek H - Bonnie Lorraine by Sea Wolf — P M Halder
1995 5(0),1(13),r(-)

408 9/3 Charm Park (L) MEM 3m 7 G *md-div, lft 3rd 3 out, n.d.* 3 0
585 23/3 Wetherby Po' (L) RES 3m 13 S *t.o. 6th, p.u. 2 out* P 0
982 8/4 Charm Park (L) MEM 3m 3 GF *trckd to 12th, no ext aft, nvr nrr* 2 10
1093 14/4 Whitwell-On' (R) MXO 4m 19 G *rear & lost tch 12th, sn t.o., p.u. 2 out* P 0

Outclassed outside Members & finally defeated there as well (had completed nap-hand in 95) 10

GEATA BAWN (Irish) — **I** 14^{F}, **I** 47^{P}, **I** 190^{1}, **I** 313^{5}, **I** 326^{1}, **I** 426^{4}

GEE DOUBLE YOU ch.g. 10 Tap On Wood - Repicado Rose (USA) by Repicado (CHI) — J D Watkins

1995 P(0),P(0),5(0),1(14),5(0)

215	24/2	Newtown	(L)	OPE	3m	20	GS	*hld up wll bhnd, no prog 12th, t.o. & p.u. 3 out*	P	0
350	3/3	Garnons	(L)	CON	3m	11	GS	*ld/disp til ld 12th-nxt, sn outpcd*	6	0
506	16/3	Magor	(R)	CON	3m	8	GS	*rear, styd on frm 3 out, hrd rdn & nvr nrr*	4	0
598	23/3	Howick	(L)	MEM	3m	6	S	*(fav) cls 2nd, ld 10th, clr aft, easily*	1	14
845	6/4	Howick	(L)	CON	3m	12	GF	*12s-6s, rear, prog to ld 11th, chal frm 3 out, ran on well*	1	20
1211	23/4	Chepstow	(L)	HC	3m	13	S	*hdwy to ld 8th, hdd and wknd 9th, t.o. when p.u. after 13th.*	P	0
1246	27/4	Woodford	(L)	OPE	3m	6	G	*in tch, ld 9th, drew clr 2 out, comf*	1	21
1533	14/5	Chepstow	(L)	HC	3m	6	F	*prom, mstk 3rd, ld after 7th, mistakes 12th and 13th, blnd and u.r. 3 out.*	U	22

Members winner 95; improved 96; unlucky in weak H/Chase; best late season; should win again; G-F .. 20

GEE-GEE (Irish) — **I** 352[4], **I** 546[2]

GEMMA LAW b.m. 6 Germont - Lawsuitlaw by Cagirama — W Hodge

407	9/3	Dalston	(R)	MDO	2 1/2m	13	G	*nvr sn wth ch, p.u. 11th*	P	0
503	16/3	Lanark	(R)	MDO	3m	10	G	*sn bhnd, t.o. & p.u. 11th*	P	0
756	31/3	Lockerbie	(R)	MDN	3m	14	G	*sn bhnd, p.u. 3 out*	P	0

Yet to get competitive 0

GENERAL ARI (Irish) — **I** 122[P], **I** 472[3], **I** 541[5]

GENERAL BRANDY b.g. 10 Cruise Missile - Brandy's Honour by Hot Brandy — E Tuer

1995 **9(NH),U(NH),P(NH),2(NH)**

49	4/2	Alnwick	(L)	OPE	3m	14	G	*chsd ldrs, 3rd frm 10th-3 out, 5th & btn, f last*	F	-

Ran reasonably in decent Open but vanished after; best watched if returning 97 18

GENERAL DELIGHT gr.g. 9 General Ironside - Mistress Anna by Arapaho — Mrs A R Wood

1995 P(0),2(14),2(14),U(-)

316	2/3	Corbridge	(R)	MEM	3m	10	GS	*mid-div, prog 10th, 2nd 12th, ld nxt, lft clr 15th, styd on*	1	16
608	23/3	Friars Haugh	(L)	RES	3m	13	G	*nvr bttr thn mdfld*	6	0

Lightly raced; fortunate winner; outclassed in better company; more needed to win Restricted 14

GENERAL HIGHWAY b.g. 13 General Ironside - Highway Mistress by Royal Highway — C D Dawson

1995 **3(17)**,1(22),1(23),**4(10)**,B(-),1(23),**13(14)**,2(20),1(24),1(24)

394	9/3	Garthorpe	(R)	LAD	3m	6	G	*(fav) w.w. on outer, 2nd 6 out, chal 3 out, ld nxt, comf*	1	24
724	31/3	Garthorpe	(R)	LAD	3m	5	G	*ld to 3rd, trckd ldr aft, ld 2 out, rdn out nr fin*	1	25
1238	27/4	Clifton On '	(L)	LAD	3m	6	GF	*(fav) ld to 2nd, ld 14th, sn wll clr, hvly eased flat*	1	23
1520	12/5	Garthorpe	(R)	LAD	3m	8	GF	*(fav) ld to 4th, disp 2nl3rd til hit 15th, p.u. lame nxt*	P	0

Won 8 of 11 points 95-6 & useful; well-ridden; problem last start; win more if fit at 14; Any 23

GENERAL JACK b.g. 8 Liberated - Ganges Trial by Kadir Cup — Miss Nicola Dixon

1995 P(0),5(0)

192	24/2	Friars Haugh	(L)	MDN	3m	12	S	*prom early, lost tch frm hlfwy, p.u. 4 out*	P	0
321	2/3	Corbridge	(R)	MDN	3m	12	GS	*alwys mid-div, u.r. 15th*	U	-

Finished 2 out of 9 points & unpromising 0

GENERAL PICTON b.g. 10 Cut Above - Bodnant by Welsh Pageant — Mrs C S Knowles

1995 F(-),2(19),3(18),3(18)

180	18/2	Horseheath	(R)	LAD	3m	3	G	*restrained, t.o. 5th, u.r. 9th*	U	-
313	2/3	Ampton	(R)	RES	3m	9	G	*chsd ldr 7th, rddn to ld appr 3 out, hdd appr last, wknd*	3	14
419	9/3	High Easter	(L)	RES	3m	10	S	*(Jt fav) ld to 4th, rddn to ld 11th, hdded 13th,hrd rddn & wknd 2 out*	2	17
621	23/3	Higham	(L)	INT	3m	12	GF	*mid-div, prog to 2nd at 14th, chal 3 out, sn outpcd*	2	17
907	8/4	Fakenham	(L)	HC	3m 110yds	11	G	*chsd ldrs, ld 4 out, going well when f 2 out.*	F	22
1145	20/4	Higham	(L)	RES	3m	12	F	*chsg grp, pshd alng hlfwy, chsd wnr 12th, no imp*	2	16
1402	6/5	Northaw	(L)	RES	3m	5	F	*(fav) trkd ldrs,2nd & blnd 9th,ld 14th,rdn 2 out,forged clr flat*	1	16

Maiden winner 92; placed 9 times prior to weak Restricted win; ungenuine; able but hard to win more 18

GENERALS BOY b.g. 14 General Ironside - Even More by Even Money — P F Craggs

1995 2(20),1(27),1(24),1(27)

401	9/3	Dalston	(R)	OPE	3m	6	G	*(fav) hld up, trckng ldrs whn bdly hmprd & u.r. 11th*	U	-
612	23/3	Friars Haugh	(L)	OPE	3m	8	G	*(fav) ld 8th-15th, 3rd & wkng whn f 3 out, dead*	F	-

Dead 24

GENERATOR BOY b or br.g. 8 My Treasure Chest - Barley Fire by Prince Barle — T King

1995 P(0),P(0),P(0),1(0)

350	3/3	Garnons	(L)	CON	3m	11	GS	*mid-div til lost tch 11th, t.o. & p.u. 14th*	P	0
840	6/4	Maisemore P'	(L)	RES	3m	9	GF	*chsd ldrs, 5th whn f 11th*	F	-
1173	20/4	Chaddesley '	(L)	RES	3m	18	G	*7th at 9th, mstk nxt, lost tch 15th, p.u. 3 out*	P	0

Won a dire race in 95; changed hands & safely ignored now 0

GENEROUS SCOT b.g. 12 Rarity - Galloping Santa by Santa Claus — C D Humphrey
1995 U(-),U(-),3(11),2(14),2(14),1(16),U(-)

445	9/3 Haldon	(R) RES	3m	9	S	*keen hold,cls 5th hlfwy,cls 2nd 13th, wknd 15th,p.u. 2 out*	P	0

Maiden winner 95; barely stays & brief appearance 96; getting old to win again now 14

GENEVA STEELE (Irish) — I 195^{3}, I 232^{2}, I 475^{2}

GENIAL GENT (Irish) — I 97^{1}

GEN-TECH b.g. 9 Star Appeal - Targa (GER) by Stani — Dick Chapman

292	2/3 Eaton Hall	(R) RES	3m	15	G	*mid-div, outpcd frm hlfwy*	8	0
665	24/3 Eaton Hall	(R) RES	3m	14	S	*cls up, ld 5th, made rest, comf*	1	19
855	6/4 Sandon	(L) CON	3m	6	GF	*(Jt fav) chsd wnnr, ev ch til outpcd 5 out*	3	15
151	20/4 Whittington	(L) INT	3m	12	G	*alwys ldng grp & cls up, onepcd frm 3 out*	4	18
338	3/5 Bangor	(L) HC	3m 110yds	8	S	*alwys bhnd, struggling final cct.*	5	13
535	16/5 Aintree	(L) HC	3m 1f	11	GF	*midfield, lost pl 5th, struggling final cct.*	4	0
585	25/5 Cartmel	(L) HC	3 1/4m	14	GF	*blnd 7th, soon bhnd, t.o. hfwy.*	7	0

20/1 when bombing home at Eaton; safe but slow & stamina Confined looks best hope 97; Soft 17

GENTLE LEADER (Irish) — I 147^{P}, I 210^{3}, I 280^{P}, I 374^{3}

GENTLEMAN'S JIG(CAN) gr.g. 11 Jig Time (USA) - Sunny Season (USA) by Haveago (USA) — Mrs Jane Hadden-Wight
1995 3(16),4(15),3(15),1(13),3(16),3(14)

23	20/1 Barbury Cas'	(L) XX	3m	11	GS	*chsd ldrs, 3rd frm 14th, no imp frm 3 out*	3	15

Members winner 95; finished early 96; consistent; novice ridden; best watched at 12 14

GENTLE MOSSY (Irish) — I 222^{P}, I 343^{2}, I 518^{2}, I 630^{1}

GEO POTHEEN br.g. 12 Healaugh Fox - Sally Potheen by Aberdeen — T H Sheppard
1995 P(0),P(0),5(14),S(-),U(-),4(0),2(14)

154	17/2 Erw Lon	(L) LAD	3m	14	G	*rear & no ch frm hlfwy*	10	0
350	3/3 Garnons	(L) CON	3m	11	GS	*chsd ldrs, hit 7th & 15th, no ch frm 3 out, kpt on*	4	11
383	9/3 Llanfrynach	(R) CON	3m	13	GS	*rear, prog to mid-div hlfwy, outpcd 13th, no prog aft*	5	10
881	6/4 Brampton Br'	(R) CON	3m	9	GF	*mid-div, prog 16th, styd on to ld last, pshd out*	1	19
042	13/4 Bitterley	(L) CON	3m	9	G	*mid-div, prog 12th, chsd 2nd frm 3 out*	3	16
219	24/4 Brampton Br'	(R) CON	3m	9	G	*rpd prog to ch ldr 14th, disp btn 2nd whn f 3 out, dead*	F	-

Dead 17

GEORGE FINGLAS (Irish) — I 559^{5}, I 585^{4}, I 628^{F}

GEORGE THE GREEK(IRE) ch.g. 6 Erin's Hope - Tempo Rose by Crash Course — George Prodromou

97	11/2 Ampton	(R) MEM	3m	2	GF	*disp 5-8th, cls up whn stmbld & u.r. 10th*	U	-
182	18/2 Horseheath	(R) MDO	3m	11	G	*ld to 10th, blnd 12th, onepcd frm 15th*	3	0
495	16/3 Horseheath	(R) MDO	3m	12	GF	*prom, chal wnr 4 out, no ext frm 2 out*	2	12
681	30/3 Cottenham	(R) MDO	3m	12	GF	*trckd ldrs, chsd wnr 3 out, ev ch nxt, wknd apr last*	3	0
063	13/4 Horseheath	(R) MDO	3m	5	F	*(fav) cls up, ld 7th-14th, unable to qkn und press frm nxt*	2	13
325	28/4 Fakenham P-'	(L) MDO	3m	6	G	*(fav) prom, lft 2nd 5th, ld apr 4 out, lft wll clr 2 out*	1	12

Gained reward for consistent efforts in bad race; safe but needs to improve for Restricteds 14

GERAGH ROAD (Irish) — I 52^{P}, I 74^{P}, I 275^{P}, I 642^{P}

GERONE (Irish) — I 61^{1}

GERRY AND TOM (Irish) — I 56^{3}, I 78^{P}, I 113^{4}, I 312^{4}, I 356^{1}, I 519, , I 576^{3}

GERRY O'MALLEY (Irish) — I 500^{F}, I 634^{F}

GERRY'S DELIGHT (Irish) — I 20^{P}, I 84^{6}, I 233^{P}, I 301^{P}, I 449,

GERRY'S ROSE (Irish) — I 106^{F}, I 165^{P}, I 232^{P}

GETAWAY BLAKE b.g. 9 Baron Blakeney - Lady Hamshire by Proverb — Mrs C Mackness

24	20/1 Barbury Cas'	(L) XX	3m	12	GS	*chsd ldr, ld 14th, lft clr nxt, unchal*	1	25
230	24/2 Heythrop	(R) MEM	3m	12	GS	*(fav) mid-div to hlfwy, ev ch 13th, wkng 3rd whn f 16th*	F	-
355	3/3 Garnons	(L) INT	3m	10	GS	*ld/disp to 12th, 2l down last, rallied to ld nr fin*	1	21
709	30/3 Barbury Cas'	(L) OPE	3m	15	G	*sttld mid-div, prog 12th, ev ch 3 out, not qckn aft*	4	17
112	17/4 Hockworthy	(L) PPO	3m	9	GS	*ld to 3rd, outpcd 12th, ran on agn 14th, btn whn mstk 2 out*	5	17
216	24/4 Andoversford	(R) INT	3m	7	G	*disp to 3rd, 2nd 13th-3 out, rlld undr pres to ld flat*	1	19

Very lightly raced to 96; quite able but inconsistent; may be best fresh; Confined likely 97; G-S 21

GET CRACKING (Irish) — I 70^{P}, I 143^{1}, I 212^{P}, I 242^{P}

GET INTO IT (Irish) — I 345^{4}, I 416^{U}, I 470^{1}, I 555^{U}, I 617^{F}

GET REAL (Irish) — I 2^{1}

GET STEPPING ch.g. 10 Posse (USA) - Thanks Edith by Gratitude — W H Whitle

555 17/3 Ottery St M' (L) MDO 3m 15 G *cls up til blnd & u.r. 14th* U
876 6/4 Higher Kilw' (L) MDN 3m 11 GF *in tch, cls 3rd 13-15th, wknd nxt, t.o. & p.u. 2 out* P
1555 18/5 Bratton Down (L) MDO 3m 13 F *in tch, went 3rd 15th, 4th frm 3 out, tk 3rd cls home* 3 1

Missed 95; beaten 9l in bad Maiden & does not stay; win looks unlikely **12**

GHOFAR ch.g. 13 Nicholas Bill - Royale Final by Henry The Seventh — Lady Dunda

42 3/2 Wadebridge (L) CON 3m 8 GF *jmpd errctclly, bhnd frm 9th, kpt on frm 2 out* 5 1
63 10/2 Great Treth' (R) MEM 3m 6 S *twrds rear til prog 14th, kpt on onepcd* 3 1
196 24/2 Lemalla (R) CON 3m 14 HY *unruly start, nvr trbld ldrs* 7 1
873 6/4 Higher Kilw' (L) CON 3m 4 GF *lost tch frm 8th, t.o.* 4

Formerly very sueful chaser; enjoying his old age now **12**

GIGI BEACH(IRE) ch.g. 5 Roselier (FR) - Cranagh Lady by Le Bavard (FR) — Mrs Susan Humphrey

70 10/2 Great Treth' (R) MDO 3m 14 S *s.s. mstk 1st, bhnd whn u.r. 13th* U
470 10/3 Milborne St' (L) MDO 3m 18 G *bhnd, some late prog, nrst fin* 6 1
653 23/3 Badbury Rin' (L) MDO 3m 9 G *(fav) patiently rdn, nvr plcd to chall* 4
1129 20/4 Stafford Cr' (R) MDO 3m 11 S *(8s-3s),w.w.,prog 11th,2nd 14th,disp nxt til wnt clr aprlast* 1 1

Steady improvement & beat subsequent winner; should upgrade; top stable; G-S **18**

GILLIE'S FOUNTAIN b.g. 5 Baron Blakeney - Florella by Royal Fountain — J D Callov

357 3/3 Garnons (L) RES 3m 14 GS *in tch in rear til no prog frm 12th, kpt on steadily* 5
1484 11/5 Bredwardine (R) MDO 3m 17 G *(fav) w.w. 8th at 11th, chal 15th, disp nxt, wknd apr last* 4 1

Shows promise; 2 months between races & not disgraced in either; should go close 97 if staying **14**

GILLOWAY PRINCESS (Irish) — I 169^P, I 258^P, I 286^4, I 319^4, I 397^1, I 454^F, I 489^P

GILSON'S COVE b.g. 9 Netherkelly - Realm Wood by Precipice Wood — A Merriar

1995 5(10),P(0),2(19),5(15),P(0),1(16),P(0),5(0)

616 23/3 Higham (L) MEM 3m 3 GF *(fav) ld 3rd-10th, chal 3 out, ld last, ran on well* 1 1
832 6/4 Marks Tey (L) LAD 3m 8 G *mid-div, dist 5th at 11th, no ch aft, t.o.* 5
1208 21/4 Heathfield (R) LAD 3m 6 F *ld 6-9th,disp til ld 14th,blnd 16th & hdd,chal nxt,no ex las* 3 1
1259 27/4 Cottenham (R) LAD 3m 5 F *alwys prom, ld 4th, jnd 4 out, hdd apr last, wknd flat* 4
1520 12/5 Garthorpe (R) LAD 3m 8 GF *mid-div whn u.r. 6th* U

Ladies winner 95; struggling to add another now; barely stays; mistakes; Firm **15**

GINGE b.g. 7 Sulaafah (USA) - Bernigra Girl by Royal Match — Neil Alle

841 6/4 Maisemore P' (L) MDN 3m 9 GF *t.d.e. unruly start, ref to race* 0
1045 13/4 Bitterley (L) MDO 3m 16 G *ld 9th til jnd 15th, wknd & p.u. last* P
1224 24/4 Brampton Br' (R) MDO 3m 17 G *cls up frm 8th, chsd ldrs til wknd 2 out* 4 1
1433 6/5 Ashorne (R) MDO 3m 16 G *5s-7/2, unruly start, s.s. alwys bhnd, t.o. & p.u. 9th* P

Placed twice 94; missed 95 & changed hands; has ability but moody & best avoided **10**

GINGER PINK b.g. 10 Strong Gale - Zitas Toi by Chinatown — C Cottinghar

1995 1(0),6(0),2(14)

171 18/2 Market Rase' (L) RES 3m 5 GF *(bl) ld 2nd, jnd 4 out, hdd 2 out, btn apr last* 2 1
329 3/3 Market Rase' (L) RES 3m 12 G *(bl) rear, some prog 11th, nvr nr ldrs* 4
515 16/3 Dalton Park (R) XX 3m 12 G *ld 5th-12th, prom aft, 6th & btn whn u.r. 3 out* U
723 31/3 Garthorpe (R) CON 3m 19 G *ld 3-4th & 5-7th, 6th whn blnd 9th, sn strgglng* 10
1025 13/4 Brocklesby ' (L) XX 3m 9 GF *(bl) cls up 2nd-4 out,cls 4th nxt,ran on wll frm 2out,ld cls home* 1 1
1302 28/4 Southwell P' (L) INT 3m 10 GF *(bl) cls up, ld 9-12th, drppd away tamely nxt* 6

Improved to win poor Restricted; inconsistent & usually gives up; hard to win again; needs blinkers **14**

GINGER TRISTAN ch.g. 10 Ginger Boy - Also Kirsty by Twilight Alley — D C Robinsc

1995 **2(NH),4(NH),5(NH)**

247 25/2 Charing (L) MEM 3m 7 GS *(fav) ld to 4th, agn 10th, drew well clr aft 15th, easily* 1 2
451 9/3 Charing (L) OPE 3m 11 G *(fav) 2s-4/6, ld to 7th, agn 9th, hdd apr last, onepcd* 4
573 17/3 Detling (L) OPE 4m 9 GF *2nd til u.r. 10th* U
595 23/3 Parham (R) OPE 3m 12 GS *sn chsng ldng pair, nvr on terms, rdn out flat* 4
811 6/4 Charing (L) OPE 3m 9 F *alwys wth ldrs, prssd wnr 4 out-2 out, onepcd* 2 2
963 8/4 Heathfield (R) MXO 3m 7 G *ld til appr 4 out, sn outpcd, lst 2nd flat* 3 2
1209 21/4 Heathfield (R) OPE 3m 5 F *(fav) made virt all, chal 4 out, rdn clr nxt* 1
1296 28/4 Bexhill (R) OPE 3m 4 F *(fav) ld to apr 7th, agn aft 11th, made rest, drew clr 2 out* 1 2
1372 4/5 Peper Harow (L) OPE 3m 6 F *ld 8-12th, jmpd to ld nxt, made rest, clr 3 out, comf, lame* 1 2

Winning chaser; fair pointer; veteran ridden; jumps & stays; problem last start; can win again;G/S-F ... **22**

GIORGIONE (Irish) — I 180^P, I 287^P, I 321^P, I 403^2, I 599^1

GIPSULA ch.m. 8 Sula Bula - Proud Gipsy by Sky Gipsy — Granville Tayl

1995 B(-),5(0),P(0)

3 13/1 Larkhill (R) MDO 3m 10 GS *chsd ldrs, ld 13th-aft 2 out, onepcd* 3
70 10/2 Great Treth' (R) MDO 3m 14 S *mid-div whn f 11th* F

299 2/3 Great Treth' (R) MDO 3m 13 G *ld til 15th, ev ch til outpcd apr 2 out* 2 14
Ex-Barber horse; improved; beaten by fair prospect when 2nd & should win if fit 97 14

GIRLS IN BUSINESS b.m. 6 Sula Bula - Grade Well by Derring-Do Mrs V Barber
733 31/3 Little Wind' (R) MDO 3m 13 GS *bhnd & jmp nvcy til p.u. apr 16th, schoold* P 0
993 8/4 Kingston St' (R) MDO 3m 17 F *schoold round in mid-div, late prog, nrst fin, improve* 5 0
1396 6/5 Cotley Farm (L) MDO 3m 11 GF *mstk 1st, sn rr, t.o. whn p.u. 13th* P 0
Top stable; very green so far; should do better 12

GITCHE GUMME b.g. 15 Warpath - Enchanting by Behistoun Mrs T R Kinsey
1995 3(16),P(0),4(0)
735 31/3 Sudlow Farm (R) MEM 3m 7 G *rmndrs 4th, rddn & lost tch 7th, p.u. 13th* P 0
1032 13/4 Alpraham (R) CON 3m 9 GS *alwys rear, sn t.o., p.u. 7th* P 0
Too old now 0

GIVE ALL b.g. 10 Try My Best (USA) - Miss Spencer by Imperial Fling (USA) M Appleby
5 13/1 Larkhill (R) LAD 3m 10 GS *jmpd v slwly 1st, t.o. whn nrly ref 6th & p.u.* P 0
Lightly raced & looks hopeless 0

GIVE IT A BASH(IRE) b.m. 8 Gianchi - Marzia Fabbricotti by Ribero Miss S Wilson
1995 P(0),P(0),F(-),4(0),F(-),F(-)
92 11/2 Ampton (R) MDO 3m 7 GF *trckd ldrs going wl, disp 14th, ld 2 out, jmpd lft last,easy* 1 13
313 2/3 Ampton (R) RES 3m 9 G *pllng, in tch blnd 14th, rddn & wknd appr 3 out* 5 0
834 6/4 Marks Tey (L) RES 3m 11 G *mid-div, not pace to rch ldrs, styd on onepcd frm 3 out* 4 10
1145 20/4 Higham (L) RES 3m 12 F *20s-8s,chsng grp,strggling whn mstk 13th,wknd,p.u.2 out* P 0
Won poor Maiden; jumping better now but weak Restricted needed for another win 14

GIVE IT A LASH (Irish) — **I** 221P
GIVE IT A LAUGH (Irish) — **I** 343F
GIVE IT A WHIRL ch.g. 7 Revolutionary (USA) - No Love by Bustiki Ross Haddow
1995 **7(NH),P(NH),P(NH)**
239 25/2 Southwell P' (L) MDO 3m 9 HO *made most to 4 out, 2l 2nd whn lft in ld 2 out, ran on well* 1 13
635 23/3 Market Rase' (L) RES 3m 8 GF *(Jt fav) ld, 50l clr frm 6th, still wll clr whn f 12th (ditch)* F -
1025 13/4 Brocklesby ' (L) XX 3m 9 GF *cls up 3rd til u.r. 6th (ditch)* U -
1181 21/4 Mollington (R) RES 3m 10 F *cls up, trckd wnr 11th, blnd 14th, wknd 3 out, p.u. last* P 0
Front-runner & doubtful stamina; lucky when winning & same needed for Restricted 15

GIVEMEYOURHAND (Irish) — **I** 269[6], **I** 394[2], **I** 429[1]
GIVE US A LEAD (Irish) — **I** 173[2]
GIVOWER b.g. 8 Kinglet - River Valley by Apollonius A J Smith
1995 P(0),2(14),3(14)
403 9/3 Dalston (R) RES 3m 11 G *al mid-div* 6 0
754 31/3 Lockerbie (R) RES 3m 8 G *ld frm 9th til wknd 15th* 3 0
1471 11/5 Aspatria (L) MEM 3m 4 GF *(fav) ld aft 7th, hit 10th, hdd 11th, ld 14th, clr 16th, v easy* 1 12
Changed hands; interrupted season; won bad Members; go close in Restricted 97; G-F 14

GIVUS A HAND ch.g. 6 Nearly A Hand - Chanelle by The Parson Mrs J M Bailey
143 17/2 Larkhill (R) MDO 3m 14 G *sn rear, p.u. 6th* P 0
268 2/3 Didmarton (L) MDN 3m 10 G *mid-div, lost plc 7th, t.o. & p.u. 9th* P 0
1118 17/4 Hockworthy (L) MDO 3m 14 GS *mid-div, 7th & btn at 11th, b.d. nxt* B -
No real signs yet 0

GLAMDRING ch.m. 8 Broadsword (USA) - Fairies First by Nulli Secundus G Wellings
1995 F(-),U(-),F(-),F(-)
460 9/3 Eyton-On-Se' (L) LAD 3m 10 G *ld to 11th, wkng whn u.r. 4 out* U -
663 24/3 Eaton Hall (R) LAD 3m 8 S *ld to 9th, mstks aft, no ch whn f 3 out* F -
851 6/4 Sandon (L) MEM 3m 6 GF *cls up, ld 6th til u.r. 14th* U -
4 falls, 3 unseated riders - 7 outings 95-6 0

GLAMOROUS GUY ch.g. 9 Orchestra - Glamorous Night by Sir Herbert David M G Fitch-Peyton
465 10/3 Milborne St' (L) RES 3m 11 G *sn bhnd, t.o. 8th* 5 0
645 23/3 Cothelstone (L) MDO 3m 3 S *ld or disp til outpcd appr last* 2 0
993 8/4 Kingston St' (R) MDO 3m 17 F *sn rear, bhnd & alwys strgglng* 8 0
1113 17/4 Hockworthy (L) RES 3m 11 GS *rr frm 8th, t.o. & p.u. 13th* P 0
1393 6/5 Cotley Farm (L) XX 3m 10 GF *sn bhnd, t.o. 14th, p.u. 2 out* P 0
Beaten in 2 finisher Maiden & shows no real ability 0

GLEEMING LACE (Irish) — **I** 518P

GLENABOY (Irish) — I 74^{4}, I 113^{P}, I 356^{3}, I 466^{P}, I 502, , I 546^{1}

GLENARD(IRE) b.g. 7 Bulldozer - Tumble Heather by Tumble Wind (USA) R J Webb
269 2/3 Didmarton (L) RES 3m 12 G *b.d. 1st* B -
437 9/3 Newton Brom' (R) RES 3m 9 GS *alwys rear, t.o. & p.u. 2 out* P 0
642 23/3 Siddington (L) RES 3m 15 S *rr, prog & in tch 8th, outpcd 13th, no dang aft* 5 10
960 8/4 Lockinge (L) RES 3m 9 GF *ld/disp til wnt clr 3 out, styd on wll* 1 18
1176 21/4 Mollington (R) MEM 3m 6 F *(fav) ld 3rd, made most aft, jnd 12th-last, styd on well flat* 1 19
Irish Maiden winner 95; improving; stays; novice ridden; Confined likely 97; G-F 20

GLENAVEY b.g. 15 Cantab - Dancing Flame by Dead Ahead C J Hal
1995 F(-),1(12)
571 17/3 Detling (L) CON 3m 13 GF *alwys rear, t.o. 14th* 10
675 30/3 Cottenham (R) MEM 3m 6 GF *last pair, clsd 3 out, styd on well flat, nrst fin* 3 11
961 8/4 Heathfield (R) MEM 3m 5 G *last & detached, stdy prog 13th, wnt 2nd 2 out,ld flat* 1 13
1375 4/5 Peper Harow (L) CON 3m 9 F *bhnd 3rd, p.u. 5th* P
Schoolmaster now; won Members 95-6 & only chance of another win at 16 12

GLENBOWER QUEEN (Irish) — I 568^{U}, I 593, , I 641^{4}, I 658^{P}

GLENBRICKEN b.g. 10 Furry Glen - Kilbricken Money by Even Money H R Barke
1995 4(11),7(11),5(10),1(12),7(11),2(16)
224 24/2 Duncombe Pa' (R) RES 3m 12 GS *ld to 9th, grad wknd, 5th & no ch 13th* 5
411 9/3 Charm Park (L) RES 3m 20 G *mid-div, n.d., p.u. 4 out* P
758 31/3 Great Stain' (L) RES 3m 17 GS *mid-div, mstk 11th, outpcd frm 3 out* 6 12
905 8/4 Carlisle (R) HC 3 1/4m 5 F *alwys prom, chal twelfth and ev ch till rdn and one pace apr last.* 2 16
1134 20/4 Hornby Cast' (L) MEM 3m 6 G *w.w. prog 7th, ld nxt, kpt on strngly* 1 15
1457 8/5 Uttoxeter (L) HC 3 1/4m 16 G *bhnd 5th, t.o. when p.u. before 4 out.* P
1571 19/5 Corbridge (R) RES 3m 13 G *mid-div, prog 4 out, styd on apr last, no ext flat* 3 16
Modest & Members winner only in 95-6; placed in bad H/Chase; hat-trick best chance in 97 16

GLENBRIDE BOY (Irish) — I 110^{P}, I 162^{P}

GLENBRIN (Irish) — I 96^{F}, I 176^{P}, I 259^{P}, I 285^{F}, I 319^{3}, I 410^{F}, I 490^{3}

GLENBROWNE (Irish) — I 38^{P}, I 154^{P}

GLEN CHERRY b.g. 10 Furry Glen - Our Cherry by Tarqogan P A D Scoulle
1995 P(0),P(0),1(17),1(13)
127 17/2 Kingston Bl' (L) MEM 3m 6 GS *made all, clr aft 3 out, styd on well* 1 1
Winning chaser; found 3 modest races 95-6; finished early; may find another local win 17

GLENCOE BOY b.g. 13 Pry - Rainella by Bahrain P D Jones
1995 **3(NH)**,**4(NH)**,**6(NH)**
554 17/3 Ottery St M' (L) MEM 3m 5 G *1st ride, ld to 2nd, ld agn 4th, blnd & u.r. 5th* U
No longer of any account 0

GLENCOMMON ch.g. 15 Forties Field (FR) - Deep Pearl by Deep Run R W Pincomb
1274 27/4 Bratton Down (L) MEM 3m 7 GF *in tch to 11th, wknd & p.u. 14th* P
1587 25/5 Mounsey Hil' (R) MEM 3m 7 G *alwys bhnd, t.o. & p.u. 9th, dsmntd* P
Too old & problems last start 0

GLENDARRAGH (Irish) — I 299^{P}

GLEN DEAL (Irish) — I 319^{P}, I 401^{U}, I 535^{P}, I 601^{6}

GLENDINE (Irish) — I 23^{P}, I 86^{4}, I 125^{5}, I 157^{4}, I 190^{2}, I 236^{P}, I 554^{1}

GLEN EMPRESS (Irish) — I 330^{3}, I 434^{1}

GLENFONTAINE (Irish) — I 228^{5}, I 345^{F}, I 388^{3}, I 530^{2}, I 635^{P}

GLENFORM b.g. 9 Glenstal (USA) - In Form by Formidable (USA) A Col
1995 P(0),3(0)
296 2/3 Great Treth' (R) OPE 3m 5 G *in tch til wknd 14th* 4
626 23/3 Kilworthy (L) OPE 3m 12 GS *rear, poor 9th whn nrly u.r. 11th, t.o. aft, fin well* 5 1
1361 4/5 Flete Park (R) CON 3m 9 G *twrds rear, 7th at 14th, poor 5th 3 out, nvr nr* 4 1
1529 12/5 Ottery St M' (L) OPE 3m 7 GF *mid-div, 5th at 13th, nvr dang* 4 1
1589 25/5 Mounsey Hil' (R) OPE 3m 12 G *chsd ldrs, 4th & outpcd 11th, no ch frm 14th* 4 1
1622 27/5 Lifton (R) CON 3m 14 GS *(bl) ld 6th-8th & agn 13th-2 out, no ext apr last* 3 1
Safe but not 100% genuine; ran best in blinkers & could find weak Confined in them 97 16

GLENGARRA MAID (Irish) — I 113^{P}, I 144^{P}, I 207^{P}

GLENISLA ch.m. 8 Sunyboy - Sirenia by Biskrah Miss S M Morri
341 3/3 Heythrop (R) MDN 3m 13 G *t.o. last til p.u.9th* P
478 10/3 Tweseldown (R) RES 3m 9 G *slw jmp 1st, tried to ref & rdr lost irons 2nd, p.u.* P

719 30/3 Wadebridge (L) MDO 3m 7 GF *keen hold, cls 3rd 12th, mstk 14th, blnd 3 out, mstk last* 3 0

Improved but 3rd in poor Maiden & still makes mistakes; could go closer if jumping better 97 12

GLENMAVIS b.g. 9 King's Ride - Pink Quay by Quayside Mrs J Irish

27 20/1 Barbury Cas' (L) LAD 3m 15 GS *chsd ldrs to 9th, t.o. & p.u. 15th* P 0
350 3/3 Garnons (L) CON 3m 11 GS *ld/disp to 11th, wknd, t.o. & p.u. 2 out* P 0
048 13/4 Bitterley (L) MDO 3m 12 G *chsd ldrs, grad wknd 12th, p.u. last* P 0

Of no account 0

GLENMERE PRINCE b.g. 10 Prince Tenderfoot (USA) - Ashbourne Lass by Ashmore (FR) P J Ikin

568 19/5 Mollington (R) MDO 3m 9 GS *rear, lost tch 10th, t.o. & p.u. 13th* P 0
644 2/6 Dingley (R) MDO 3m 16 GF *pllng, hmprd 3rd, in tch, 7th whn f 13th* F -

Revived after long absence but showed no real signs 0

GLENMORE STAR (Irish) — I 90[P], I 198[F], I 349[4], I 522[6], I 530[5], I 621, , I 656[5]

GLEN OAK b.g. 11 Glenstal (USA) - Neeran by Wollow Paul Rackham

1995 2(23),2(23),3(19),2(20),5(22),4(22),4(15)

94 11/2 Ampton (R) OPE 3m 8 GF *alwys prom, drvn alng 15th, onepcd frm 3 out* 6 16
102 17/2 Marks Tey (L) CON 3m 17 G *mid div, 9th hlfwy, styd on wll frm 16th, nvr nrr* 3 19
420 9/3 High Easter (L) OPE 3m 9 S *in tch, rddn alng 11th, sn strgglng, no ch frm 15th* 7 0
490 16/3 Horseheath (R) XX 3m 7 GF *hld up, 6th & rdn aft 11th, prog 4 out, ev ch nxt, wknd 2out* 3 19
723 31/3 Garthorpe (R) CON 3m 19 G *rear, 9th hlfwy, styd on frm 15th, no dang, nrst fin* 4 11
100 14/4 Guilsborough (L) OPE 3m 9 G *mid-div, rdn 11th, outpcd 14th, kpt on* 4 18

Finished all races 95-6 but disappointing & no wins; very onepaced; hard to win again; G-S 16

GLEN OF BARGY (Irish) — I 521[P], I 528[5], I 636[F]

GLEN OG LANE (Irish) — I 382[4], I 422[S], I 620[2]

GLENPINE (Irish) — I 478[P], I 562[P]

GLENROE GAL (Irish) — I 385, , I 417[P], I 483[U], I 621[S], I 632[4]

GLENROWAN LAD b.g. 7 Netherkelly - Maid Of Honor II by Honour Bound R G Russell

28 20/1 Barbury Cas' (L) RES 3m 14 GS *cls up, effrt to chs wnr 2 out, styd on, no imp nr fin* 2 18
243 25/2 Southwell P' (L) RES 3m 11 HO *(Jt fav) trckd ldrs, chal 4 out, btn nxt, 4th whn f 2 out* F -
437 9/3 Newton Brom' (R) RES 3m 9 GS *hld up mid-div, cls up 4 out, styd on onepcd* 3 16
679 30/3 Cottenham (R) RES 3m 15 GF *(fav) hld up, in tch whn b.d. 5th* B -
904 6/4 Dingley (R) RES 3m 20 GS *(fav) abt 6th for 2 m, 4th 6 out, fdd, p.u. 2 out* P 0
181 21/4 Mollington (R) RES 3m 10 F *prom til p.u. aft 10th, lame* P 0

Maiden winner 94; missed 95; disappointing after 96 debut & more problems now; best watched 14

GLENSELIER (Irish) — I 8[P], I 47[P], I 71[6], I 154[5], I 188[4]

GLENSHANE LAD b.g. 10 Fidel - Molly Dancer by Choral Society Mrs R A Schofield

162 17/2 Weston Park (L) OPE 3m 16 G *prom to hlfwy, outpcd 13th, p.u. 3 out* P 0
215 24/2 Newtown (L) OPE 3m 20 GS *5th whn u.r. 8th* U -
662 24/3 Eaton Hall (R) OPE 3m 10 S *chsd ldrs to 8th, fdd, p.u. 5 out* P 0
950 8/4 Eyton-On-Se' (L) OPE 3m 4 GF *prom, ld 13th til apr 4 out, onepcd* 3 14
192 21/4 Sandon (L) CON 3m 11 G *ld 6-10th, wknd rpdly* 4 0
419 6/5 Eyton-On-Se' (L) OPE 3m 4 GF *cls up, 2nd to 13th, ran on one pce frm 5 out* 3 11

Chasing winner 93/4; looks disinterested now 0

GLEN TAYLOR 10 Mrs G A Spencer

1995 8(0),8(0),4(0),6(0),8(0),8(0),2(0)

239 25/2 Southwell P' (L) MDO 3m 9 HO *prom til wknd 12th, hmpd nxt, t.o.* 4 0
458 9/3 Eyton-On-Se' (L) INT 3m 11 G *t.o. frm hlfwy, jmpd rnd in own tm, btn 2 fncs* 6 0
566 17/3 Wolverhampt' (L) LAD 3m 5 GS *cls up 1st cct, wknd aft* 4 0
852 6/4 Sandon (L) MDN 3m 9 GF *ld to 2nd, in tch, ld 9-13th, onepce frm 4 out* 4 0
029 13/4 Alpraham (R) MDO 3m 8 GS *mid-div, 6th whn blndrd & u.r. 8th* U -
196 21/4 Sandon (L) MDN 3m 17 G *mid to rear & outpcd, no ch ldrs* 5 0
229 27/4 Weston Park (L) MEM 3m 2 G *made all, steadd pce, jmp rght, lft solo 3 out* 1 0
579 19/5 Wolverhampt' (L) LAD 3m 9 G *prom, losing plc whn mstk 9th, t.o. & p.u. 14th* P 0

Left solo when winning; safe but another miracle needed to win again 0

GLEN THYNE (Irish) — I 95[U], I 215[P], I 320[P]

GLENTORALDA (Irish) — I 311[P], I 420[P], I 500[P]

GLENVIEW ROSE (Irish) — I 42[1], I 54[P], I 141[P], I 376[F]

GLENVILLE BREEZE (Irish) — I 387[P], I 635[P], I 654[P]

GLIC GO LEOR (Irish) — I 644[P]

GLITTERBIRD br.m. 9 Glint Of Gold - Dovetail by Brigadier Gerard Mrs C J Chadney

173 20/4 Chaddesley ' (L) RES 3m 18 G *ld frm 3rd til hit 10th, ld 13th, hdd 2 out, rgnd 2nd flat* 2 17

1564 19/5 Mollington (R) XX 3m 14 GS *hld up, prog & cls up whn blnd 13th, sn wknd, p.u. 3 out* P

Maiden winner 94; missed 95; ran well both starts but needs to run regularly to win Restricted 16

GLITTER GIRL (Irish) — **I** 306^P

GLITZY LADY(IRE) b.m. 7 Strong Gale - Shady Lady by Proverb G Smit

10 14/1 Cottenham (R) INT 3m 10 G *7s-4s, w.w. in tch, prog to 3rd 2 out, nvr able to chal* 3 1
23 20/1 Barbury Cas' (L) XX 3m 11 GS *4s-3s, prom, ld 12th, clr aft 3 out, mstk nxt, ran on well* 1 2
169 18/2 Market Rase' (L) CON 3m 15 GF *wll bhnd, prog 11th, chal 3 out, kpt on* 2 2
244 25/2 Southwell P' (L) CON 3m 13 HO *mstks, chsd ldrs, 3rd at 12th, btn frm 14th, p.u. 3 out* P
515 16/3 Dalton Park (R) XX 3m 12 G *w.w. prog 12th, rdn 16th, ev ch 2 out, onepcd* 4 1
725 31/3 Garthorpe (R) OPE 3m 9 G *cls up, prssd ldr 13th til aft 3 out, onepcd* 4 1

Winning Irish pointer 94/5; won modest race; novice ridden; form tailed off; could win Confined 97 19

GLORIKI ch.m. 13 London Glory - Mykiki by Vicky Joe Mrs S C Willco

448 9/3 Haldon (R) MDO 3m 10 S *bhnd til p.u. apr 6th* P

An elderly maiden who did not last long 0

GLORIOUS GALE (Irish) — **I** 8^P, **I** 70^5, **I** 652^2

GLUAIS LINN (Irish) — **I** 55^P, **I** 63^P, **I** 210^P

GOBLINS LIGHT b.m. 9 Lighter - Liza Paul by Ron Miss Kim Trip

821 6/4 Charlton Ho' (L) MDN 3m 10 GF *ld til 8th, wknd 10th, p.u. apr 13th* P

Showed promise 94 but missed 95 & unable to fulfil it only start 96 11

GODOR SPIRIT ch.g. 6 Plenty Spirit - Godor Alice by Meldrum Mrs S M Grave

1995 **22(NH),15(NH)**

456 9/3 Eyton-On-Se' (L) MEM 3m 2 G *ld tl hdd 12th, lft solo 13th, f 14th* F
953 8/4 Eyton-On-Se' (L) MDO 2 1/2m 10 GF *mid-div, onepcd frm 3 out, nvr dang* 4
1423 6/5 Eyton-On-Se' (L) MDO 3m 7 GF *mid-div whn f 6th* F

Blew a gift on pointing debut; well beaten when completing & much more needed 0

GOLD CHOICE b.g. 11 Crooner - Coffee Bob by Espresso Victor Ogde

824 6/4 Stainton (R) CON 3m 11 GF *ld to 8th, fdng whn blnd 12th, p.u. 15th* P
1092 14/4 Whitwell-On' (R) CON 3m 10 G *prom til lost plc 7th, sn t.o., p.u. 4 out* P
1134 20/4 Hornby Cast' (L) MEM 3m 6 G *ld to 5th, sn lost plc, t.o.* 4
1363 4/5 Gisburn (R) MEM 3m 5 G *chsng ldr whn u.r. 13th* U

Well beaten on only completion 96 & has no winning prospects now 0

GOLD CODE b.m. 5 Gold Song - Dialling Code by Don't Look W Hodg

405 9/3 Dalston (R) MDO 2 1/2m 16 G *mid-div early, wl btn whn u.r. 13th* U

No real signs on debut 0

GOLD DIVER ch.g. 9 Main Reef - Ice Baby by Grundy Linden Roger

1995 P(0),F(-),8(0),P(0),3(12),1(16),1(17),1(18),**4(0)**

266 2/3 Didmarton (L) LAD 3m 13 G *prom to 10th, wknd rpdly aft nxt, t.o. 3 out* 9
545 17/3 Erw Lon (L) CON 3m 10 GS *ld to 13th, fdd, fin tired* 4 1
979 8/4 Lydstep (L) LAD 3m 9 G *mid-div, p.u. 14th* P
1157 20/4 Llanwit Maj' (R) CON 3m 11 GS *disp ld til ld 4-7th, wknd qckly & p.u. apr 11th* P
1387 6/5 Pantyderi (R) LAD 3m 6 GF *alwys prom, mstk 10th, ld 15th, comf* 1 1
1489 11/5 Erw Lon (L) LAD 3m 4 F *settld 2nd/3rd, outpcd aft 13th, no dang aft* 4 1

Won 3 in 95; no form 96 till won weak Ladies; best late season & R/H; should win again; G/F-F 17

GOLDEN ARCTIC b.g. 11 Golden Love - Arctic Jungle by Arctic Slave Robert Vowle

1157 20/4 Llanwit Maj' (R) CON 3m 11 GS *prom, lft in ld 14th, hdd & blndrd 2 out, wknd,bttr for race* 3 1
1263 27/4 Pyle (R) CON 3m 9 G *5l 3rd at 10th, not qckn 13th, wknd 15th, p.u. 2 out* 5

Ran well 1st start but 2nd came too quickly; very lightly raced now & struggle to win at 13 14

GOLDEN CLOGS b.g. 9 Lochnager - Dutch Girl by Workboy Mrs G Moor

327 3/3 Market Rase' (L) CON 3m 15 G *disp til p.u. aft 5th, dead* P

Dead 0

GOLDEN COMPANION b.g. 12 Torus - Carrigart by Bargello Mrs J Marle

1995 U(-),B(-),P(0),P(0),P(0),P(0)

231 24/2 Heythrop (R) XX 3m 10 GS *ld/disp to 9th, wknd rpdly, last at 11th & p.u.* P
684 30/3 Chaddesley ' (L) RES 3m 14 G *chsd ldrs til wknd 11th, bhnd whn p.u. 13th* P
946 8/4 Andoversford (R) RES 3m 10 GF *(bl) cls up, ld 10th, sn clr, wknd & hdd 14th, p.u. last* P
1292 28/4 Barbury Cas' (L) RES 3m 11 F *(bl) drppd last & lost tch 10th, t.o. & p.u. 14th* P
1564 19/5 Mollington (R) XX 3m 14 GS *(bl) ld to 11th, stppd bef nxt* P

No longer of any account **0**

GOLDEN CYGNETURE (Irish) — I 113P, I 521P

GOLDEN DROPS(NZ) b.g. 8 Dorchester (FR) - Super Maric (NZ) by Super Gray (USA) — Mrs D N Harris

201	24/2	Lemalla	(R)	MDO	3m	13	HY	*mid-div, prog to ld 3 out, ran on strngly*	1	15
298	2/3	Great Treth'	(R)	RES	3m	13	G	*handy, cls 4th at 15th, ev ch whn lft 2nd 2 out,no ext,imprv*	2	17

Won modest Maiden but ran better next time; finished early; should win Restricted if fit 97; G-Hy **17**

GOLDEN EYE(NZ) gr.g. 8 Kingsbridge (CAN) - Points II (AUS) by Crowned Prince (USA) — D H Barons

202	24/2	Lemalla	(R)	MDO	3m	12	HY	*prog to tck ldrs 4 out, onepcd frm nxt, improve*	3	12
446	9/3	Haldon	(R)	MDO	3m	13	S	*(fav) alwys wll plcd, effrt & 2nd aft 2 out, fdd flat*	3	12
1326	28/4	Fakenham P-'	(L)	MDO	3m	7	G	*(fav) chsd ldr 9th, ld 14th, in cmmnd whn lft solo 2 out*	1	14
1540	16/5	Folkestone	(R)	HC	2m 5f	10	G	*mstk 5th, bhnd from next, t.o. and p.u. before 3 out.*	P	0
1546	18/5	Fakenham	(L)	HC	3m 110yds	13	G	*rear till imp from 14th, nvr nrr.*	6	14

Changed hands mid-season; left solo in bad Maiden; not disgraced last start; sharp track best **15**

GOLDEN FARE ch.g. 11 Scallywag - Katie Fare by Ritudyr — W I Owens

385	9/3	Llanfrynach	(R)	LAD	3m	14	GS	*t.o. 4th, mls bhnd aft, p.u. last*	P	0
579	20/3	Ludlow	(R)	HC	2 1/2m	17	G	*mid div, lost tch hfwy, t.o. and p.u. before 2 out.*	P	0
879	6/4	Brampton Br'	(R)	LAD	3m	9	GF	*hld up, nvr rchd ldrs, no ch frm 16th*	6	0
1046	13/4	Bitterley	(L)	LAD	3m	9	G	*cls up til not qckn frm 13th, no ch frm 15th*	5	11
1221	24/4	Brampton Br'	(R)	LAD	3m	6	G	*(vis) cl up til outpcd 13th, lft 2nd, no ch frm 16th*	3	10
1314	28/4	Bitterley	(L)	MEM	3m	13	G	*(vis) cls 5th whn mstk 5th, in tch 11th, outpcd frm nxt*	6	0
1420	6/5	Eyton-On-Se'	(L)	LAD	3m	3	GF	*2nd 3-12th, lost tch 13th, lft 2nd 4 out*	2	11
1617	27/5	Chaddesley '	(L)	LAD	3m	8	GF	*mstk 3rd, t.o. 6th, p.u. 10th*	P	0

Beat 5 finishers in 5 completions & shows no stamina or fire any more **10**

GOLDEN FELLOW(IRE) ch.g. 8 Buckskin (FR) - Miss Argument by No Argument — Keith Coe

1995 2(15)

91	11/2	Ampton	(R)	MDO	3m	10	GF	*(fav) ld 4th, made rest, clr whn blnd bdly 2 out, rdn out flat*	1	15
348	3/3	Higham	(L)	RES	3m	12	G	*cls up in 3rd/4th til f 13th*	F	-

Very lightly raced; won weak Maiden; go close in weak Restricted if fit 97 .... **15**

GOLDEN FREEZE b.g. 14 Golden Love - Freezeaway by Vulgan — Mrs Amanda Bowlby

1995 1(27),7(0),**1(23),R(-),2(22),P(0)**

185	23/2	Kempton	(R)	HC	3m	9	GS	*alwys bhnd, lost tch from 13th, t.o..*	5	12
485	16/3	Hereford	(R)	HC	3m 1f 110yds	13	S	*chsd ldr from 5th to 4 out, soon wknd, t.o..*	4	10
671	28/3	Taunton	(R)	HC	3m	13	S	*prom, jmpd slowly 5th and 14th, chsd wnr from next, one pace.*	2	21
1215	24/4	Andoversford	(R)	OPE	3m	5	G	*jmpd slwly & drpd last 5th, rlctnt 12th, t.o. & ref 14th*	R	-

H/Chase winner 95; moody & unlikely to win at 15 .... **16**

GOLDEN HUNTRESS ch.m. 12 Golden Dipper - Medway Melody by Romany Air — Miss M Walter

1053	13/4	Penshurst	(L)	LAD	3m	5	G	*(bl) rear, lost tch 11th, p.u. 13th*	P	0
1297	28/4	Bexhill	(R)	LAD	3m	7	F	*(bl) blnd 1st, plld into ld 2nd, slppd & u.r. bnd aft 3rd*	U	-

Of no account **0**

GOLDEN MAC ch.g. 9 Court Macsherry - Prett Damsel by Prince Hansel — R L Fanshawe

1995 5(0),2(12),4(0),3(11),11(0)

1	13/1	Larkhill	(R)	XX	3m	7	GS	*alwys bhnd, t.o. 8th, p.u. last*	P	0
128	17/2	Kingston Bl'	(L)	RES	3m	14	GS	*alwys rear, lost tch 10th, t.o. 13th*	5	0
235	24/2	Heythrop	(R)	RES	3m	10	GS	*rear,poor 5th at 14th,styd on,still 5th last,ld 50 yrds out*	1	18
373	8/3	Sandown	(R)	HC	3m 110yds	4	G	*in 3rd pl msot of way, hit 12th, effort apr 3 out, soon oiutp aced.*	3	15
637	23/3	Siddington	(L)	MEM	3m	14	S	*(fav) mid div, 8th & rddn 13th, no dang aft*	6	10
793	2/4	Heythrop	(R)	OPE	4m	10	F	*mstk 9th, lost tch 14th, p.u. 17th*	P	0
1216	24/4	Andoversford	(R)	INT	3m	7	G	*disp til ld 4-7th, 4th & one pcd frm 3 out*	4	12

Safe enough but a plodder & won 7 1/2mins race; luck needed to find another chance **16**

GOLDEN MIST (Irish) — I 479P, I 562P

GOLDEN MOSS ch.g. 11 Le Moss - Call Bird by Le Johnstan — C Cottingham

1995 3(0),F(-),3(22),3(15),1(23),4(14)

169	18/2	Market Rase'	(L)	CON	3m	15	GF	*wth ldr to 4th, 6th whn f 8th*	F	-
634	23/3	Market Rase'	(L)	OPE	3m	6	GF	*ld to 5 out & frm 3 out, ran on gamely*	1	19
725	31/3	Garthorpe	(R)	OPE	3m	9	G	*mstk 3rd, prssd ldr, ld 11th, hdd last, unable qckn flat*	2	22
1024	13/4	Brocklesby '	(L)	OPE	3m	6	GF	*nvr dang, 25l 4th 4 out, ran on into rmte 2nd 2 out*	2	15
1462	10/5	Market Rasen	(R)	HC	2 3/4m 110yds	11	G	*in rear when f 4th.*	F	-
1595	25/5	Garthorpe	(R)	CON	3m	15	G	*ld to 9th, cls up til wknd rpdly frm 6 out*	7	0

Open winner 95; quite able but inconsistent; may win again at 12 19

GOLDEN NECTAR ch.g. 6 Relkino - Mizzie Lizzie by Netherkelly — J R Suthern

1995 **11(NH),15(NH),6(NH)**

841	6/4	Maisemore P'	(L)	MDN 3m	9	GF	*ld to 11th, wknd appr 13th, last frm 15th, p.u. appr last*	P	0
1319	28/4	Bitterley	(L)	MDN 3m	13	G	*prom to 10th, outpcd 12th, t.o. & p.u. 15th*	P	0
1378	5/5	Dingley	(R)	MDO 2 1/2m	16	GF	*ldng grp, 6th & still in tch whn f heavily 4 out*	F	-

No ability under Rules; gave a little hope but more stamina needed 0

GOLDEN PELE b.g. 15 Golden Love - Feale-Side Nook by Laurence O — Mrs B Ansell

1995 P(0),9(0),9(0),4(0)

248	25/2	Charing	(L)	RES 3m	12	GS	*alwys rear, t.o. & p.u. aft 14th*	P	0
449	9/3	Charing	(L)	RES 3m	13	G	*twrds rear whn f 2nd*	F	
574	17/3	Detling	(L)	RES 3m	14	GF	*mid-div early, wll whn p.u. 13th*	P	0
810	6/4	Charing	(L)	RES 3m	6	F	*in tch, und pres 13th, last nxt, wll bhnd whn p.u. aft 2 out*	P	0
1442	6/5	Aldington	(L)	RES 3m	7	HD	*alwys rear, wll bhnd whn p.u. bfr 15th*	P	0

No longer of any account 0

GOLDEN PERFORMANCE (Irish) — **I** 131^{P}, **I** 194^{P}

GOLDEN SAVANNAH b.g. 6 Presidium - Golden Pampas by Golden Fleece (USA) — A Reynard

1995 **6(NH),3(NH),10(NH),8(NH)**

170	18/2	Market Rase'	(L)	XX 3m	8	GF	*cls up, chsd ldr 7th, ld 9th-3 out, onepcd*	3	19
226	24/2	Duncombe Pa'	(R)	OPE 3m	10	GS	*prom to 8th, wknd nxt, p.u. 12th*	P	0
410	9/3	Charm Park	(L)	OPE 3m	17	G	*ld 5-14th, disp 4 out to last, drvn out flat*	1	20
515	16/3	Dalton Park	(R)	XX 3m	12	G	*(fav) ld to 5th & 12th-4 out, ev ch 2 out, onepcd*	3	17
984	8/4	Charm Park	(L)	MXO 3m	7	GF	*(fav) disp to 2 out, ld to last, hdd & just btn flat*	2	21
1281	27/4	Easingwold	(L)	CON 3m	15	G	*alwys prom, 2nd at 15th, no prog aft, onepcd*	3	20
1462	10/5	Market Rasen	(R)	HC 2 3/4m 110yds	11	G	*alwys prom, mstks, ld 8th, hdd soon after 4 out, no impn from next.*	2	21
1615	27/5	Wetherby	(L)	HC 2 1/2m 110yds	11	G	*chsd ldrs, mstk 7th, lost tch and p.u. before 9th.*	P	0

Winning hurdler; consistent in points; moderate form; could improve; worth another H/Chase try;G-G/F 21

GOLDEN SOUND b.g. 12 Goldhill - Regal Sound by Royal Palace — R Sparks

1995 7(0)

641	23/3	Siddington	(L)	RES 3m	20	S	*prom til wknd 11th, p.u. 14th*	P	0

Maiden winner 92; only 9 runs since & of no account now 0

GOLDEN START (Irish) — **I** 176^{2}, **I** 259^{P}, **I** 301^{F}, **I** 413^{5}, **I** 493^{2}, **I** 535^{2}, **I** 601^{2}

GOLDEN WALK (Irish) — **I** 108^{P}, **I** 161^{5}, **I** 266^{U}

GOLD LEADER (Irish) — **I** 19^{F}, **I** 177^{P}

GOLD PROFIT ch.m. 16 Rubor - Night Profit by Carnival Night — W G Young

109	17/2	Lanark	(R)	MEM 3m	5	GS	*(fav) f 2nd*	F	

An elderly maiden but started favourite! 0

GOLD TALISMAN b.m. 7 Scorpio (FR) - Jyponica by Wabash — P T Hollins

569	17/3	Wolverhampt'	(L)	MDN 3m	11	GS	*jmpd bdly in rear, p.u. 9th*	P	0
1029	13/4	Alpraham	(R)	MDO 3m	8	GS	*held up, 3rd 10th-3 out, wknd & p.u. nxt*	P	0
1365	4/5	Gisburn	(R)	MDO 3m	17	G	*alwys rear, p.u. 9th*	P	0

Showed a hint of ability at Alpraham & may do better 0

GOLD TIP ch.m. 10 Billion (USA) - Gamblers Ace — P Riddick

390	9/3	Llanfrynach	(R)	MDN 3m	13	GS	*last trio, t.o. 8th, p.u. 12th*	P	0
1040	13/4	St Hilary	(R)	MDN 3m	12	G	*2nd to 12th, wknd rpdly, p.u. 3 out*	P	0
1162	20/4	Llanwit Maj'	(R)	MDO 3m	12	GS	*wll bhnd, prog & in tch 11th, wknd 15th, p.u. 3 out*	P	0
1272	27/4	Pyle	(R)	MDO 3m	9	G	*mostly 3rd/4th, lft chsng wnr 14th, kpt on onepcd frm 3 out*	2	
1391	6/5	Pantyderi	(R)	MDO 3m	13	GF	*ld 7th-15th, wknd 2 out*	3	10
1484	11/5	Bredwardine	(R)	MDO 3m	17	G	*ld to 3rd, ev ch 15th, wknd & p.u. 2 out*	P	0
1561	18/5	Bassaleg	(R)	MDO 3m	8	F	*hld up, prog 5th, ld 7th-3 out, not run on und pres*	2	12
1606	25/5	Bassaleg	(R)	MDO 3m	7	GS	*ld til aft 9th, wknd rpdly, t.o. 3 out*	4	0
1651	8/6	Umberleigh	(L)	MDO 3m	11	GF	*in tch, cls enough 14th, wknd 3 out, p.u. flat, dsmntd*	P	0

Has some ability but also highly suspect & best avoided; form R/H only 11

GOLD TOP ch.m. 5 Precious Metal - Vilmax by Anax — G L Edwards

740	31/3	Sudlow Farm	(R)	MDN 3m	16	G	*schoold in last trio til p.u. 10th*	P	0
1008	9/4	Flagg Moor	(L)	MDO 2 1/2m	7	G	*in tch, 4th whn f 6th*	F	
1365	4/5	Gisburn	(R)	MDO 3m	17	G	*mstks, rear, u.r. 6th*	U	
1580	19/5	Wolverhampt'	(L)	MDO 3m	8	G	*n.j.w. t.o. & jmpd slwly 14th, p.u. nxt*	P	

Needs a major jumping overhaul 0

GOLDTOPPER ch.m. 9 Royal Vulcan - Cut And Thrust by Pardal — Mrs P Nichols
1995 7(0),2(12),1(16)

641	23/3	Siddington	(L)	RES	3m	20	S	*ld/disp to 6th, prom til grad wknd frm 14th*	10	0
889	6/4	Kimble	(L)	RES	3m	7	GF	*(fav) cls up, chsd wnr 10th, mstk 2 out, hrd rdn flat,just faild*	2	18
1181	21/4	Mollington	(R)	RES	3m	10	F	*outpcd,last & mstk 4th,wll bhnd 8th,ran on 15th,nvr nrr*	2	16

Maiden winner 95; stays, safe & slow; needs long trip; likes Kimble; may find Restricted; G-F 17

GOLDWREN (Irish) — I 84^{P}, I 178, , I 259^{3}, I 320^{1}, I 490^{P}, I 600^{2}

GOLESA b.g. 10 Goldhill - Bolesa — R C Turcan

1084	14/4	Friars Haugh	(L)	LAD	3m	8	F	*chsd wnr to 10th, sn wknd*	4	0
1250	27/4	Balcormo Ma'	(R)	LAD	3m	5	GS	*chsd wnr til wknd frm 11th, t.o. whn p.u. apr 3 out*	P	0
1473	11/5	Aspatria	(L)	LAD	3m	7	GF	*in tch til wknd 12th, t.o. & p.u. bfr 16th*	P	0

No longer of any account 0

GO MAGIC b.g. 7 Rustingo - Ruths Magic by Current Magic — Mrs E A Squirrell

314	2/3	Ampton	(R)	MDO	3m	10	G	*alwys bhnd, t.o. & p.u. 14th*	P	0
617	23/3	Higham	(L)	MDO	3m	11	GF	*mid-div, wknd 7th, bhnd & p.u. 10th*	P	0
929	8/4	Marks Tey	(L)	MDO	3m	5	G	*trckd ldrs, mstk 13th, ch whn mstk 4 out, wknd rpdly,p.u.nxt*	P	0

Nees more stamina but may do better 0

GO MEEKLY (Irish) — I 229^{4}

GO MILETRIAN b.g. 12 Sonnen Gold - Chestnut Hill by Sassafras (FR) — T H J Bannister
1995 **15(NH),P(NH)**

306	2/3	Great Stain'	(L)	INT	3m	12	GS	*cls up til wknd 10th, t.o. 3 out*	7	10
588	23/3	Wetherby Po'	(L)	INT	3m	17	S	*rear frm 10th, p.u. 14th*	P	0
892	6/4	Whittington	(L)	CON	3m	4	F	*held up, cls 2nd 3 out, outpcd aft*	2	12
1152	20/4	Whittington	(L)	CON	3m	9	G	*nvr bynd mid-div*	4	0

Restricted winner 94; only beat one horse in 96 & unlikely to win again 10

GONALSTON PERCY gr.g. 8 Dawn Johnny (USA) - Porto Louise by Porto Bello — F S Jackson
1995 U(-),P(0)

542	17/3	Southwell P'	(L)	MDO	3m	15	GS	*rear whn p.u. 13th*	P	0
968	8/4	Thorpe Lodge	(L)	CON	3m	5	GF	*alwys last, t.o. 9th, p.u. 4 out*	P	0

Yet to complete & unpromising 0

GOOD APPEAL ch.m. 11 Star Appeal - Good Larker by Some Hand — Roy Bolitho
1995 2(12),7(0),3(0),2(0)

131	17/2	Ottery St M'	(L)	MDN	3m	10	GS	*cls 4th whn f 12th*	F	-
282	2/3	Clyst St Ma'	(L)	MDN	3m	8	S	*handy, ld 12th-4 out, wknd frm nxt*	3	0
557	17/3	Ottery St M'	(L)	MDN	3m	10	G	*cls up to 13th, wknd, p.u. 3 out*	P	0
806	4/4	Clyst St Ma'	(L)	MDO	3m	7	GS	*handy, ld & hmpd apr 12th, ld agn aft 3 out-nxt, no ext*	2	12
431	6/5	High Bickin'	(R)	MDO	3m	9	G	*towrds rear, lost tch 15th, p.u. apr 17th*	P	0
530	12/5	Ottery St M'	(L)	MDO	3m	8	GF	*prom til ld 15th, lft clr last*	1	16
622	27/5	Lifton	(R)	CON	3m	14	GS	*prom, losing ground whn mstk 6th, p.u. nxt*	P	0

Modest & inconsistent; placed 5 times prior to win & Restricted at 12 looks tough; G/S-G/F 15

GOOD BOY CHARLIE ch.g. 5 Wonderful Surprise - Jenny's Joy by Le Bavard (FR) — N B Jones

201	21/4	Lydstep	(L)	MDN	3m	9	S	*alwys rear, p.u. 14th*	P	0
390	6/5	Pantyderi	(R)	MDO	3m	15	GF	*alwys bhnd, p.u. 3 out*	P	0
605	25/5	Bassaleg	(R)	MDO	3m	8	GS	*hld up,prog to chs wnr 10th,chal 2 out,lkd hld whn u.r. last*	U	-

Ran well in poor race last start; young & should go close in 97 with right progress 13

GOOD FOR BUSINESS b.g. 8 Sula Bula - Santan by Dairialatan — R G Williams
1995 2(21),1(20)

25	20/1	Barbury Cas'	(L)	OPE	3m	14	GS	*w.w. prog 10th, chsd wnr 15th, styd on strngly aft last*	2	29
65	10/2	Great Treth'	(R)	INT	3m	13	S	*(fav) mid-div, prog 7th, mstk nxt, no imp whn p.u. 2 out*	P	0
211	24/2	Castle Of C'	(R)	INT	3m	5	HY	*(fav) cls up, 2nd whn blnd & u.r. 13th*	U	-
472	10/3	Milborne St'	(L)	INT	3m	8	G	*(fav) hld up, prog 14th, went 2nd nxt, rdn & not qckn last*	2	20
816	6/4	Charlton Ho'	(L)	INT	3m	7	GF	*in tch to 15th, lost ch whn hit 2 out, onepcd aft*	3	20

Ran really well 96 debut but disappointing after; top stable & could revive but best watched; stays 21

GOOD HOLIDAYS b.m. 10 Good Times (ITY) - Mistress Bowen by Owen Anthony — Caleb Davies
1995 8(0),3(10),P(0),3(10)

6	13/1	Larkhill	(R)	OPE	3m	18	GS	*ld to 6th, wknd 8th, t.o. & p.u. 15th*	P	0
154	17/2	Erw Lon	(L)	LAD	3m	14	G	*alwys mid-div, no ch frm hlfwy*	7	0
385	9/3	Llanfrynach	(R)	LAD	3m	14	GS	*p.u. 3rd, tack problems*	P	0
546	17/3	Erw Lon	(L)	LAD	3m	10	GS	*prom til wknd 3 out*	7	15
204	21/4	Lydstep	(L)	CON	3m	3	S	*ld/disp til ld 2 out, blnd last, all out*	1	12
263	27/4	Pyle	(R)	CON	3m	9	G	*ld 5-7th, wth wnr til outpcd frm 14th*	2	11

Very little substantial form 95-6 & won slowly-run 2 finisher Confined; hard to find another 14

GOOD KING HENRY b.g. 10 St Columbus - Cooks' Knife by Perhapsburg — Miss S Garcia-Olmc
1995 P(0),U(-),2(10),1(16),**3(18)**,**P(0)**

554 17/3 Ottery St M' (L) MEM 3m 5 G *hld up, ld brfly 8-9th, lost tch frm 14th* 3
805 4/4 Clyst St Ma' (L) RES 3m 7 GS *nvr dang, poor 4th at 8th, t.o. & p.u. 13th* P
1139 20/4 Flete Park (R) RES 3m 14 S *cls up in 3rd to 14th, rdn & no ext frm 17th* 3 12
1275 27/4 Bratton Down (L) OPE 3m 8 GF *in tch to 12th, outpcd frm 14th, walked in* 4 12
1454 7/5 Newton Abbot (L) HC 2m 5f 110yds 8 GS *chsd ldrs, wknd 5 out.* 4 13
1543 17/5 Newton Abbot (L) HC 3 1/4m 110yds 8 G *alwys in tch, chal from 2 out, ev ch when not fluent last, ran on.* 2 20
1630 31/5 Stratford (L) HC 3 1/2m 16 GF *in tch to 16th, t.o. when p.u. before 2 out.* P

Maiden winner 95; modest form 96 but should have won poor H/Chase; may frustrate in Restricteds 97;G 17

GOOD LOOKING GUY ch.g. 7 Cruise Missile - Saxon Belle by Deep Run — Mrs Judy Youn
144 17/2 Larkhill (R) MDO 3m 15 G *alwys mid-div, nvr nr to chal* 6 1
236 24/2 Heythrop (R) MDN 3m 13 GS *rear to hlfwy, prog 12th, 3rd at 14th, styd on onepcd* 3 1
267 2/3 Didmarton (L) MDN 3m 11 G *u.r. 3rd* U
375 9/3 Barbury Cas' (L) MDN 3m 14 GS *alwys mid-div, onepcd frm 3 out* 3
641 23/3 Siddington (L) RES 3m 20 S *alwys mid div, kpt on frm 15th, nvr dang* 7 1
796 2/4 Heythrop (R) MDN 3m 11 F *ran in sntchs,outpcd frm 15th,mod 4th 2 out,fin strngly* 2 1
1164 20/4 Larkhill (R) MDN 3m 12 GF *(Jt fav) tckd awy, smooth prog to ld 3 out, ran on wll* 1 1
1464 11/5 Warwick (L) HC 3 1/4m 6 F *in tch till blnd badly and u.r. 12th.* U

Onepaced & stays & won weak Maiden; should be able to go close in Restricteds 97; G/S-F 17

GOOD OLD CHIPS b.g. 9 Oats - Etoile de Lune by Apollo Eight — John Whyt
1995 **8(NH)**

10 14/1 Cottenham (R) INT 3m 10 G *chsd ldrs to 4th, grad lost plc, last whn p.u. 11th* P
94 11/2 Ampton (R) OPE 3m 8 GF *wth wnr, ld brfly 14th, disp 3 out, unable qckn nxt* 2 2
178 18/2 Horseheath (R) INT 3m 11 G *ld 4-11th & 13-15th, wknd rpdly nxt* 4

Ran well 2nd start but tailed off last outing & disappeared; best watched 16

GOOD PROFIT ch.g. 7 Meadowbrook - Night Profit by Carnival Night — W G Youn
1995 **13(NH)**,**5(NH)**,**15(NH)**,**13(NH)**,**P(NH)**,**2(NH)**,**P(NH)**,**4(NH)**,**P(NH)**

193 24/2 Friars Haugh (L) MDN 3m 10 S *4th hlfwy, bhnd whn p.u. 4 out* P
371 8/3 Ayr (L) HC 2m 5f 110yds 8 GF *f 7th.* F
755 31/3 Lockerbie (R) MDN 3m 17 G *bhnd whn f 2 out* F
1087 14/4 Friars Haugh (L) MDO 3m 9 F *lost tch by 12th, p.u. 4 out* P
1253 27/4 Balcormo Ma' (R) MDO 3m 16 GS *nvr rch ldrs* 5
1356 4/5 Mosshouses (L) MDO 3m 12 GS *trckd ldrs, 5th & wll in tch whn u.r. 12th* U
1476 11/5 Aspatria (L) MDO 3m 16 GF *bhnd 11th, styd on frm 16th, wnt poor 3rd last, nvr dang* 3

Poor hurdler; well beaten & looks slow 0

GOODSHOT RICH b.g. 12 Roscoe Blake - Hunter's Treasure by Tudor Treasure — Mrs S Towle
1995 **P(NH)**,**2(NH)**

185 23/2 Kempton (R) HC 3m 9 GS *jmpd left, chsd ldrs to 12th, t.o. when p.u. before 3 out.* P
261 2/3 Warwick (L) HC 3 1/4m 5 G *(bl) held up, hdwy apr 4th, blnd 10th, soon wknd, t.o..* 3 1
368 6/3 Lingfield (L) HC 3m 7 S *(bl) chsd ldrs, ev ch 5 out, rdn and one pace after 2 out.* 3 1

Winning chaser; beaten in modest H/Chase last start & disappeared; prospects at 13 not good 15

GOOD TEAM b.g. 11 Furry Glen - Zohra by Proud Chieftain — D Crosslan
1995 P(0),4(15),**r(-)**,F(-),1(12),3(15),**P(0)**

9 14/1 Cottenham (R) OPE 3m 13 G *prom to 11th, losing tch whn u.r. 14th* U
512 16/3 Dalton Park (R) CON 3m 10 G *prom, ld 6th-9th, grad wknd frm 16th* 6
583 23/3 Wetherby Po' (L) MEM 3m 6 S *cls up, 2nd & ev ch 3 out, wknd nxt* 3 1
968 8/4 Thorpe Lodge (L) CON 3m 5 GF *mostly 3rd til effrt & ld 3 out, ran on well* 1 1
1281 27/4 Easingwold (L) CON 3m 15 G *rear, mstk 5th, wknd 11th, sn lost tch* 7 1
1467 11/5 Easingwold (L) OPE 3m 6 G *rear, dtchd 7th, nvr dang* 4 1

Members winner 95; won poor Confined & outclassed in competitive races; struggle to score again 14

GOODWILL HILL b.g. 8 State Diplomacy (USA) - Cessy by Burglar — Mrs S J Gosp
1995 P(0),P(0),P(0),7(0),7(0),P(0)

225 24/2 Duncombe Pa' (R) RES 3m 12 GS *in tch, blnd 10th, no ch frm 14th* 7
307 2/3 Great Stain' (L) MDO 3m 17 GS *cls up, outpcd 16th, onepcd frm 2 out* 6
416 9/3 Charm Park (L) MDO 3m 13 G *in tch, ld frm 3 out, hld off chal flat* 1
584 23/3 Wetherby Po' (L) RES 3m 13 S *mid-div, wknd 3 out, p.u. last* P
758 31/3 Great Stain' (L) RES 3m 17 GS *mid-div, outpcd frm 14th, t.o.* 12
983 8/4 Charm Park (L) RES 3m 13 GF *cls up, 5th 10th, no ext 4 out* 6
1368 4/5 Gisburn (R) RES 3m 9 G *alwys rear, nvr dang* 4

Won weak Maiden at 14th attempt; struggling in Restricteds after & unlikely to win one 13

GOOLDS GOLD ch.g. 10 Le Moss - Marie Goold by Arapaho — David Brace

1995 **5(16)**,**7(NH)**

153	17/2	Erw Lon	(L)	OPE	3m	15	G	*alwys prom, 3rd 14th, ran on 2 out, ld last*	1	25
483	14/3	Cheltenham	(L)	HC	3 1/4m 110yds	17	G	*held up, pushed along towards rear 6 out, nvr able to chal.*	6	27
546	17/3	Erw Lon	(L)	LAD	3m	10	GS	*(fav) 2nd/3rd til ld 2 out, unchal*	1	27
669	27/3	Chepstow	(L)	HC	3m	10	S	*prom till lost pl apr 8th, effort approaching 5 out, n.d..*	3	21
769	31/3	Pantyderi	(R)	LAD	3m	6	G	*(fav) ld chsng grp, ct ldr 4 out, sn clr, easily*	1	26
979	8/4	Lydstep	(L)	LAD	3m	9	G	*(fav) u.r. 2nd*	U	-
1036	13/4	St Hilary	(R)	LAD	3m	6	G	*(fav) cls 2nd til ld 11th, clr 14th, easily*	1	26
1211	23/4	Chepstow	(L)	HC	3m	13	S	*(fav) joined ldrs 6th, mstk and lost pl 12th, no ch after.*	4	18
1387	6/5	Pantyderi	(R)	LAD	3m	6	GF	*(fav) mid-div, s.u. flat aft 7th*	S	-

Ex-Irish; quite useful & won all completed points; win more 97; below form H/Chases; G-S 25

GOONGOR(IRE) ch.g. 7 Gorytus (USA) - Mettle (USA) by Pretendre — P Foran

75	11/2	Wetherby Po'	(L)	MDO	3m	8	GS	*ran out 1st*	r	-
117	17/2	Witton Cast'	(R)	MEM	3m	9	S	*rear whn b.d. 6th*	B	-
589	23/3	Wetherby Po'	(L)	MDO	3m	16	S	*cls up to 10th, rear whn p.u. 12th*	P	0
763	31/3	Great Stain'	(L)	MDN	3m	11	GS	*chsd ldrs, went 3rd hlfwy, no prog aft, wknd*	5	0
915	8/4	Tranwell	(L)	MDO	3m	7	GF	*lft clr 2nd at 4th, chsd wnr aft, no ch frm 15th, tired*	2	10

Beaten 12l when 2nd in bad Maiden; stamina doubtful & more needed to win 10

GORMLESS(IRE) b.g. 8 Torus - Fine Thing by Camden Town — Miss Jane Cooper

1995 P(0),1(14),1(15)

476	10/3	Tweseldown	(R)	OPE	3m	7	G	*handy, mstks frm 13th & wknd, p.u. 4 out*	P	0
816	6/4	Charlton Ho'	(L)	INT	3m	7	GF	*midfld, cls 3rd 12th, wknd frm 5 out*	5	13
1290	28/4	Barbury Cas'	(L)	OPE	3m	5	F	*n.j.w. in tch to 12th, bhnd frm 14th, t.o. & p.u. last*	P	0
1408	6/5	Hackwood Pa'	(L)	INT	3m	2	F	*(fav) 2nd to 12th, ld aft, 10l clr last, canter*	1	13

Dual winner 95; disappointing 96 & meaningless win; best watched; Firm 15

GOSPEL ROCK(NZ) br.g. 12 Church Parade - Leopard Rock (NZ) by Rocky Mountain (FR) — M A Humphreys

826	6/4	Stainton	(R)	OPE	3m	8	GF	*s.s. bhnd whn p.u. 3rd*	P	0
984	8/4	Charm Park	(L)	MXO	3m	7	GF	*disp 4th-2 out, hdd apr last, drvn out to line*	1	20
1133	20/4	Hornby Cast'	(L)	OPE	3m	14	G	*ld 5th, jnd 11th, hdd 13th, sn lost plc, t.o. & p.u. 2 out*	P	0
1446	6/5	Witton Cast'	(R)	CON	3m	7	G	*ld til ran wd apr 6th, cls up til wknd 13th, p.u. 3 out*	P	0

Chase winner 91-2; returned from long absence 96; 33/1 when winning; no other form; hard to win 97 15

GOTSOMEOFTHAT (Irish) — **I** 404^{P}, **I** 495^{P}

GO WEST b.g. 12 Akarad (FR) - Western Goddess by Red God — G C Fox

136	17/2	Ottery St M'	(L)	LAD	3m	9	GS	*(bl) n.j.w. alwys rear, no ch frm 12th*	6	0
279	2/3	Clyst St Ma'	(L)	LAD	3m	7	S	*(bl) alwys rear, t.o. & p.u. 2 out*	P	0
469	10/3	Milborne St'	(L)	LAD	3m	8	G	*(bl) sn rear, t.o. whn p.u. 15th*	P	0
730	31/3	Little Wind'	(R)	LAD	3m	6	GS	*just in tch til outpcd aft 14th, t.o. p.u. aft 3 out*	P	0
1078	13/4	Cothelstone	(L)	MXO	3m	6	GF	*rear, und pres whn p.u. aft 10th*	P	0

No longer of any account 0

GOZONE ro.h. 9 Carwhite - Perlesse by Bold Lad (USA) — S Turner

1995 P(0),2(19),**11(0)**,P(0),1(17)

214	24/2	Newtown	(L)	CON	3m	21	GS	*ld to 2nd, chsd ldrs aft, outpcd frm 13th*	8	0
1219	24/4	Brampton Br'	(R)	CON	3m	9	G	*rr frm 6th, lost tch 14th, p.u. aft nxt*	P	0

Members winner 95; changed hands & no form 96; best watched now 12

GRACEMARIE KATE (Irish) — **I** 65^{5}, **I** 72^{F}, **I** 141^{1}, **I** 246^{1}

GRAFY HILL (Irish) — **I** 267^{2}

GRAIGNAMANAGH (Irish) — **I** 351^{4}, **I** 616^{2}, **I** 645^{1}

GRAIGUESALLAGH (Irish) — **I** 109^{P}, **I** 158^{P}, **I** 266^{F}

GRAIN MERCHANT b.g. 10 Blakeney - Epilogue by Right Royal V — J W Walmsley

14	14/1	Cottenham	(R)	MDO	3m	10	G	*in tch, went 3rd 14th, lft 2nd 3 out, 4l down whn f last*	F	15
1286	27/4	Easingwold	(L)	MDO	3m	13	G	*(Jt fav) in tch, prog 4 out, ld 2 out, hrd prssd flat, hld on wll*	1	14
1597	25/5	Garthorpe	(R)	XX	3m	9	G	*alwys rear hlf, last & outpcd 6 out*	7	0

Lightly raced; won decent Maiden but ran badly next; may struggle to find Restricted at 11; Good 15

GRANBY GAP b.g. 9 Politico (USA) - Bravade by Blast — M G Chatterton

172	18/2	Market Rase'	(L)	RES	3m	9	GF	*w.w. prog & in tch 11th, mstk nxt, outpcd 14th*	5	11
328	3/3	Market Rase'	(L)	RES	3m	9	G	*disp to 2nd, grad lost plc, no ch apr 14th*	3	0

Maiden winner 94; missed 95; finished early 96 & best watched now 13

GRAND VALUE ch.g. 13 Kambalda - Candy Slam by Candy Cane — Mrs S J Coupe
1995 1(15),2(14),B(-),4(12),3(12),3(13),5(0),U(-)

245	25/2	Southwell P'	(L) LAD	3m	8 HO	*in tch to 9th, t.o. 12th*	4	0
336	3/3	Heythrop	(R) LAD	3m	5 G	*ld 5th-14th, outpcd 3 out*	3	0
474	10/3	Tweseldown	(R) LAD	3m	7 G	*outpcd, dtchd 4th whn u.r. 4th*	U	-
792	2/4	Heythrop	(R) LAD	3 3/4m	7 F	*3rd whn f 5th*	F	-

Won 1 of last 30 starts; looks past it now 10

GRANGE GRACIE b.m. 7 Oats - Song Of Grace by Articulate — L Turnbull
1995 3(0),P(0)

516	16/3	Dalton Park	(R) MDO	3m	11 G	*prom, lft in ld aft 10th, hdd 14th, sn wknd*	4	0
589	23/3	Wetherby Po'	(L) MDO	3m	16 S	*ld to 12th, cls up whn f 14th*	F	-
1094	14/4	Whitwell-On'	(R) MDO	2 1/2m 88yds	16 G	*mid-div whn u.r. 7th*	U	-
1135	20/4	Hornby Cast'	(L) MDN	3m	10 G	*mid-div, lost plc 9th, t.o. & p.u. 2 out*	P	0

Well beaten on only completion 96 & shows no ability 0

GRANGE MISSILE b.m. 8 Cruise Missile - Peticienne by Mummy's Pet — Ian Gilbert
1995 F(-),6(0),P(0)

904	6/4	Dingley	(R) RES	3m	20 GS	*alwys rear hlf, outpcd 6 out, p.u. 3 out*	P	0
1101	14/4	Guilsborough	(L) RES	3m	16 G	*rear, prog & in tch 14th, sn wknd, t.o.*	8	0

Last when completing 95-6 & no signs of real ability 0

GRANGE PRIZE ch.g. 10 Le Bavard (FR) - Queen's Prize by Random Shot — R Greenway
1995 3(0),4(0),F(-),3(0),2(15),5(0),3(10)

292	2/3	Eaton Hall	(R) RES	3m	15 G	*w.w. prog 5 out, styd on, nrst fin*	4	12

Maiden winner 94; struggling in Restricteds after; brief season 96; unlikely to win again 12

GRANNY BID (Irish) — **I** 43[5]

GRANNY'S BAY b.g. 13 Tycoon II - Lorien Wood by Precipice Wood — Mrs P C Stirling
1995 P(0),P(0),10(0),6(10),1(10),3(0)

112	17/2	Lanark	(R) LAD	3m	8 GS	*2nd til 7th, sn wknd, p.u. 13th*	P	0

No longer of any account 0

GRANNYS COTTAGE (Irish) — **I** 444[F], **I** 578[S], **I** 604[P], **I** 649[1]

GRANSTOWN LAKE (Irish) — **I** 292[1]

GRANTS CAROUSE (Irish) — **I** 34[P], **I** 72[P], **I** 441[3], **I** 544[3], **I** 605[3], **I** 659[6]

GRANVILLE GRILL b.g. 11 Furry Glen - Glamorous Night by Sir Herbert — E W Smith
1995 U(-),P(0),P(0),1(17),1(18),1(20),1(17),3(20)

262	2/3	Didmarton	(L) MEM	3m	11 G	*ld 3rd-12th, sn outpcd, rallied last, no ext flat*	2	21
638	23/3	Siddington	(L) CON	3m	16 S	*(fav) ld, clr 3rd, hdded 3 out, ld appr last, in comm whn lft clr*	1	22
795	2/4	Heythrop	(R) XX	3m	4 F	*(fav) jmpd lft, ld to 14th, btn frm 2 out*	2	21
943	8/4	Andoversford	(R) CON	3m	9 GF	*(fav) ld/disp to 12th, outpcd frm 3 out, lost 2nd flat*	3	17
1215	24/4	Andoversford	(R) OPE	3m	5 G	*made all, jmpd lft, styd on wl frm 2 out*	1	25
1437	6/5	Ashorne	(R) MXO	3m	13 G	*jmpd lft,ld apr 5th,narrow ld aft,pshd out flat*	1	24

Solid, consistent pointer; won 7 of last 11; front-runner; can win Opens at 12; G-F 24

GRANVILLE GUEST ch.g. 10 Deep Run - Miss Furlong by Fury Royal — Mrs Bridget Nicholls
1995 U(-)

7	13/1	Larkhill	(R) CON	3m	10 GS	*in tch, prog 13th, disp nxt til ld 2 out, sn clr, rdn out*	1	26
265	2/3	Didmarton	(L) OPE	3m	6 G	*prom, ld 8th, hrd rdn 2 out, hdd flat, ran on*	2	29
481	11/3	Taunton	(R) HC	3m	11 G	*(fav) in tch, ld 10th, hdd 4 out, wknd next.*	4	16

Chase winner 93; very useful performances 96 but disappointed in H/Chase; should win points 97; G-S 27

GRASSINGTON(IRE) gr.g. 7 Roselier (FR) - Private Affair by Julio Mariner — Scott Patrick Quirk
1995 **10(NH),7(NH),F(NH)**

60	10/2	Cottenham	(R) MDO	3m	7 GS	*1st ride,pllng,hld up last,kpt on to go 2nd flat,no ch wnr*	2	12
455	9/3	Charing	(L) MDN	3m	10 G	*(fav) s.s. t.o. 11th, ran on frm 4 out*	4	0
576	17/3	Detling	(L) MDN	3m	18 GF	*wll bhnd hlfwy, some late prog*	5	0
681	30/3	Cottenham	(R) MDO	3m	12 GF	*rear, mod 5th & no ch 3 out, kpt on, nrst fin*	4	0
966	8/4	Heathfield	(R) MDO	3m	7 G	*chsd ldrs, wnt 2nd 13th, ld last, hdd & no ex flat*	3	11
1210	21/4	Heathfield	(R) MDO	3m	13 F	*(fav) rear, steady prog 9th, 3rd 16th, ld 3 out, ran on wll last*	1	13

Safe, stays & modest; novice ridden; found poor Maiden & more needed for Restricteds 13

GRATUITY b.g. 11 Torus - Craeve by Crash Course — Robin Barwel

1109	17/4	Hockworthy	(L) MEM	3m	4 GS	*ld to 4th, wth wnr to 12th, btn 14th, lft 2nd 2 out*	2	10
1275	27/4	Bratton Down	(L) OPE	3m	8 GF	*handy to 13th, lost tch, p.u. 3 out, dsmntd*	P	0

Career has had many setbacks & this looks like curtains now 10

GRAY ROSETTE b.m. 7 Scallywag - Lady St Clair by Young Generation — Dr G M Thelwall Jones

1995 **P(NH),3(NH),P(NH)**

464	9/3	Eyton-On-Se'	(L)	MDN	2 1/2m	13	G	*mid-div,prog 4 out, styd on to disp & lft in ld flat,readily*	1	13
665	24/3	Eaton Hall	(R)	RES	3m	14	S	*mid-div to 10th, prog 12th, ev ch whn u.r. 2 out*	U	-
856	6/4	Sandon	(L)	RES	3m	9	GF	*rear early, prog 5 out to join chsng grp, ev ch last no ext*	2	16
1030	13/4	Alpraham	(R)	RES	3m	10	GS	*(fav) last to 11th, steadd prog to 4l 3rd 15th, lft 2nd last*	2	10
1458	8/5	Uttoxeter	(L)	HC	3 1/4m	8	G	*mstks, bhnd 8th, last when p.u. and dismntd before 13th.*	P	0
1535	16/5	Aintree	(L)	HC	3m 1f	11	GF	*soon bhnd, lost tch final cct, t.o. when p.u. before 3 out.*	P	0

Won modest race & struggling to stay; may go close in Restricted 97; G-S 16

GREATFULL FRED ch.g. 11 Reppin Castle - Kellet Lane by Sandford Lad — Howard J Pickersgill

1995 5(0),4(0),5(0)

986	8/4	Charm Park	(L)	MDN	3m	10	GF	*prom early, 2nd 7th, onepcd frm 13th*	5	0
1135	20/4	Hornby Cast'	(L)	MDN	3m	10	G	*plld hrd, prom, ld 4th til mstk & hdd 7th, ld 9-14th,onepcd*	2	0
1465	11/5	Easingwold	(L)	MEM	3m	4	G	*sttld 2nd, mstk 11th, outpcd nxt, lft 2nd 14th, sn wknd*	3	0

Well beaten when placed; safe but unlikely to win at 12 10

GREAT IMPOSTOR ch.g. 8 Vaigly Great - Lady Waverton by Huntercombe — Commander G Greaves

1995 P(0),P(0),4(0),P(0),1(15),3(11),**6(NH)**

41	3/2	Wadebridge	(L)	XX	3m	9	GF	*(bl) blndrd 2nd & 3rd, prom whn u.r. 5th*	U	-
138	17/2	Ottery St M'	(L)	RES	3m	18	GS	*alwys rear, t.o. & u.r. 14th*	U	-
281	2/3	Clyst St Ma'	(L)	RES	3m	11	S	*alwys mid-div, no ch frm 14th*	4	10
532	16/3	Cothelstone	(L)	RES	3m	12	G	*rr & hit 4th, t.o. frm 11th*	5	0
729	31/3	Little Wind'	(R)	RES	3m	12	GS	*(bl) mstk 4th, 8th 12th, nvr near*	7	0
992	8/4	Kingston St'	(R)	RES	3m	6	F	*nvr dang, hit 8th, tk 4th 3 out, nvr nr ldrs*	4	0
1113	17/4	Hockworthy	(L)	RES	3m	11	GS	*rr, t.o. 10th, kpt on late*	5	0
1312	28/4	Little Wind'	(R)	XX	3m	6	G	*nvr going wll, t.o. 12th*	5	0

Maiden winner 95; not 100% genuine & unlikely to win Restricted now 10

GREAT LEGEND ch.h. 10 Vaigly Great - Chinese Legend by Shantung — Phillip Taylor

334	3/3	Heythrop	(R)	MEM	3m	6	G	*last & sn bhnd, t.o. 9th, u.r. 14th*	U	-
897	6/4	Dingley	(R)	CON	3m	15	GS	*u.r. 1st*	U	-
904	6/4	Dingley	(R)	RES	3m	20	GS	*2nd outing, rear div whn f 7th (ditch)*	F	-
1105	14/4	Guilsborough	(L)	MDN	3m	12	G	*trckd ldrs, cls 5th whn u.r. 13th*	U	-
1240	27/4	Clifton On '	(L)	MDO	3m	10	GF	*12s-8s, made most to 12th, ev ch 15th, wknd, 6th whn f 2 out*	F	-

Novice ridden; poor jumper & non-stayer; unpromising 0

GREAT POKEY b or br.g. 11 Uncle Pokey - Mekhala by Menelek — Miss Nell Courtenay

1995 P(0),3(16),5(0),6(18),2(19),P(0),**3(14),F(-)**

67	10/2	Great Treth'	(R)	LAD	3m	11	S	*nvr bttr than mid-div, no ch frm 3 out*	5	19
135	17/2	Ottery St M'	(L)	LAD	3m	11	GS	*alwys mid-div, nvr on terms*	4	11
279	2/3	Clyst St Ma'	(L)	LAD	3m	7	S	*ld 5th-13th, hdd, easily hld frm 3 out*	2	17
561	17/3	Ottery St M'	(L)	LAD	3m	12	G	*made all, ran on well whn chal 3 out*	1	21
988	8/4	Kingston St'	(R)	MEM	3m	7	F	*ld to 12th, 6l 2nd 14-15th, fdd*	2	18
1346	4/5	Holnicote	(L)	LAD	3m	5	GS	*ld 8-14th, no imp wnr aft*	2	22
1532	13/5	Towcester	(R)	HC	2m 110yds	16	GF	*alwys prom, ld 3rd to 4th, led apr 2 out till final 100 yards.*	2	23

Consistent 96; novice ridden; needs to dominate; best easy 3m; may win again at 12; Any 21

GREAT PRECOCITY b.g. 9 Precocious - Rip Roaring by Royal And Regal (USA) — Richard Jones

1995 P(0),U(-),P(0),F(-),U(-)

44	3/2	Wadebridge	(L)	MDO	3m	9	GF	*mstk 2nd, alwyd bhnd, t.o. & p.u. 12th*	P	0
152	17/2	Erw Lon	(L)	MDN	3m	11	G	*mid-div, 4th at 14th, onepcd aft, fin 4th, plcd 3rd*	3	10
205	24/2	Castle Of C'	(R)	MDO	3m	9	HY	*rear til f 7th*	F	-
387	9/3	Llanfrynach	(R)	RES	3m	11	GS	*alwys rear, t.o. 14th, p.u. 3 out*	P	0
550	17/3	Erw Lon	(L)	MDN	3m	13	GS	*twrds rear, p.u. 11th*	P	0
848	6/4	Howick	(L)	MDN	3m	14	GF	*last pair, no ch frm 11th*	8	0
1040	13/4	St Hilary	(R)	MDN	3m	12	G	*rear, p.u. 9th*	P	0
1390	6/5	Pantyderi	(R)	MDO	3m	15	GF	*(vis) chsd ldrs to hlfwy, wknd frm 15th*	6	0

One passable run but nothing apart & unlikely to figure in 97 0

GREAT UNCLE b.g. 8 Uncle Pokey - Petrinella by Mummy's Pet — Miss E Oram

1995 4(13),P(0),P(0),1(14),3(13),4(13),1(14),**5(NH),4(NH),3(NH),2(NH)**

361	5/3	Leicester	(R)	HC	2 1/2m 110yds	15	GS	*soon well bhnd, t.o. from 7th.*	7	0
581	21/3	Wincanton	(R)	HC	2m 5f	13	S	*mstks 5th and 11th, t.o. when p.u. before 4 out.*	P	0
818	6/4	Charlton Ho'	(L)	LAD	3m	6	GF	*in tch til 9th, t.o. frm 13th*	3	10
1058	13/4	Badbury Rin'	(L)	LAD	3m	5	GF	*handy til lost tch 12th, onepcd frm 4 out*	3	11
1552	18/5	Bratton Down	(L)	LAD	3m	7	F	*sn twrds rear, bhnd frm 12th*	5	0

Dual winner 95 but totally out of his depth 96 & little hope of another success 14

GRECIAN LARK b.g. 8 Crested Lark - Grecian Lace by Spartan General — G B Tarry

1995 P(0),5(0),1(14),7(0)

339 3/3 Heythrop (R) RES 3m 10 G *rear,prog 14th,mod 3rd 3 out,styd on wll to ld last,rdn out* 1 17
667 24/3 Eaton Hall (R) INT 3m 11 S *hld up, prog 2 out, lvl last, sn ld, ran on well* 1 23
1019 13/4 Kingston Bl' (L) INT 3m 6 G *(fav) chsd ldrs, went 2nd 14th, ld 3 out, rdn out flat* 1 18
1458 8/5 Uttoxeter (L) HC 3 1/4m 8 G *(fav) cl up, ld 14th, drew clr apr 2 out, f last.* F 24

Maiden winner 95; much improved; stays well; unlucky last start; Confineds/Opens possible 97; G-S ... 23

GRECIANLID gr.g. 8 Lidhame - Grecian Charter by Runnymede L A E Hopkins
1995 P(0),1(12)

461 9/3 Eyton-On-Se' (L) RES 3m 15 G *chsd ldrs, ev ch 13th, lost tch frm 4 out, p.u. bfr last* P 0
665 24/3 Eaton Hall (R) RES 3m 14 S *t.o. & p.u. 11th* P 0
1030 13/4 Alpraham (R) RES 3m 10 GS *2nd 5th-2 out, onepcd & wll btn whn u.r. last* U -
1233 27/4 Weston Park (L) RES 3m 14 G *mid-div, nvr dang* 7 0
1368 4/5 Gisburn (R) RES 3m 9 G *alwys prom, lft 2nd 13th, wknd rpdly nxt* 5 0
1582 19/5 Wolverhampt' (L) RES 3m 10 G *chsd ldr 5th til apr 8th, lost tch apr 14th, t.o.* 5 0

Won a terrible race 95 & unsurprisingly floundering in Restricteds 10

GREEDY JOHNO (Irish) — **I** 30F, **I** 86P, **I** 131 4, **I** 161 2, **I** 228 2, **I** 381 3, **I** 421P, **I** 527 4, **I** 582 2, **I** 635 4

GREEK CHIME(IRE) gr.g. 7 Bellypha - Corinth Canal by Troy N A Smith

686 30/3 Chaddesley ' (L) OPE 3m 6 G *blnd 1st, jmpd dtckly in rear, t.o. & ref 13th* R -

Irish Flat winner 92; needs to learn to jump 0

GREENACRE GIRL b.m. 6 Lightning Dealer - Deep Love by Deep Run J R Kearsley

522 16/3 Larkhill (R) MDO 3m 12 G *bhnd & jmpd bdly, ref 3rd* R -

Not the best of starts 0

GREEN ARCHER b.g. 13 Hardgreen (USA) - Mittens by Run The Gantlet (USA) Mrs S D Walter
1995 2(23),2(24),**1(26)**,2(24),1(25),2(24)

436 9/3 Newton Brom' (R) LAD 3m 10 GS *(fav) alwys prom, chsd ldr frm 4th, ld 9th, clr 3 out, idld flat* 1 21
640 23/3 Siddington (L) LAD 3m 9 S *(fav) 4th & pshd alng 11th, ch appr 15th, no prog,wll btn & f last* F -
888 6/4 Kimble (L) LAD 3m 4 GF *trckd ldr, ld 13th-aft 3 out, outpcd frm nxt* 2 20
1179 21/4 Mollington (R) LAD 3m 10 F *prom, ld 4-6th, outpcd 11th, kpt on onepcd frm 3 out* 4 19
1459 8/5 Uttoxeter (L) HC 4 1/4m 8 G *rear, in tch till u.r. 13th.* U -
1566 19/5 Mollington (R) LAD 3m 7 GS *in tch til outpcd 12th, no ch nxt, kpt on slwly* 3 19

Useful in 95 but declined after debut 96; needs real stamina test & Soft ground; may revive early 97 ... 21

GREENFIELD GEORGE (Irish) — **I** 146 1

GREENFIELD LASS (Irish) — **I** 95 6, **I** 177P, **I** 259P

GREENFIELD LODGE (Irish) — **I** 531F

GREENFIELD TIGER (Irish) — **I** 17 4, **I** 25, , **I** 129F, **I** 136 3

GREEN HILL b.g. 11 Hillandale - Green Path by Hardraw Scar P C Pocock

199 24/2 Lemalla (R) RES 3m 17 HY *mid-div, styd on onepcd frm 2 out, nvr nrr* 4 14
280 2/3 Clyst St Ma' (L) RES 3m 11 S *hld up, prog 12th, ev ch 3 out, onepcd nxt* 2 18
528 16/3 Cothelstone (L) MEM 3m 8 G *w.w. prog to 2nd 15th, rddn appr 3 out, wknd* 4 11
627 23/3 Kilworthy (L) RES 3m 13 GS *in tch,prog 11th,ld 13th,sn clr,blnd & hdd 2 out,wknd* 4 13
871 6/4 Higher Kilw' (L) RES 3m 9 GF *hld up in tch, prog to disp 3 out, just ld last, drvn out* 1 19
1127 20/4 Stafford Cr' (R) INT 3m 4 S *w.w., prog 12th, ld 3 out, sn clr, easily* 1 20
1454 7/5 Newton Abbot (L) HC 2m 5f 110yds 8 GS *held up in rear, hdwy 8th, ld 6 out, shaken up apr last, ran on.* 1 22

Rarely seen till 96; most consistent; just stays 3m; H/Chase win makes future success hard; G-Hy 22

GREENHILL FLY AWAY b.g. 8 Cruise Missile - April Fortune by Maystreak Mrs S P Dench
1995 F(-),2(0),1(0),1(11)

449 9/3 Charing (L) RES 3m 13 G *prom, ld aft 7th til u.r. 10th* U -
571 17/3 Detling (L) CON 3m 13 GF *cls up whn u.r. 11th* U -
779 31/3 Penshurst (L) RES 3m 13 GS *rear, prog 11th, 3rd 3 out, wknd & p.u. last* P 0

Dual winner 95; lightly raced; showed nothing 96; best watched now; G-Hd 13

GREENHILL LADY b.m. 10 Mart Lane - Red Hill Lady by Hoarwithy K Jones
1995 P(0),F(-),U(-),P(0)

358 3/3 Garnons (L) RES 3m 18 GS *mid-div til prog twrds ldrs whn f 12th* F -
694 30/3 Llanvapley (L) RES 3m 9 GS *ld 6th til f 13th* F -
976 8/4 Lydstep (L) MDO 3m 12 G *mstk 3rd, alwys mid-div, unable to chal* 4 0
1162 20/4 Llanwit Maj' (R) MDO 3m 12 GS *hmp & f 2nd* F -
1270 27/4 Pyle (R) MDO 3m 9 G *cls up, ev ch whn u.r. 11th* U -
1417 6/5 Cursneh Hill (L) MDO 3m 14 GF *rear frm 4th, t.o. 13th, p.u. 15th* P 0
1485 11/5 Bredwardine (R) MDO 3m 15 G *mstk 7th, last frm nxt, t.o. & u.r. 14th* U -

Last on only completion from 11 starts 95-6 although showed a rare spark 2nd outing 0

GREENHILLS RUBY br.m. 5 Green Ruby (USA) - Tiki's Affair by Bustiki — Mrs G Lancina

239 25/2 Southwell P' (L) MDO 3m 9 HO *f 2nd* F -
430 9/3 Upton-On-Se' (R) MDO 3m 15 GS *losing tch whn p.u. 14th* P 0
1045 13/4 Bitterley (L) MDO 3m 16 G *prom to 10th, in tch til no ext frm 15th* 7 0

A hint of ability last start & may do better 10

GREENMOUNT LAD(IRE) ch.g. 8 Fidel - Deep Chariot by Deep Run — J Cornforth

1995 **3(NH),6(NH),5(NH),15(NH)**

223 24/2 Duncombe Pa' (R) CON 3m 16 GS *f 4th* F -
411 9/3 Charm Park (L) RES 3m 20 G *bhnd early, p.u. 8th* P 0
632 23/3 Market Rase' (L) CON 3m 10 GF *rear, prog 10th, 3rd 5 out, outpcd nxt* 3 16
1130 20/4 Hornby Cast' (L) CON 3m 13 G *rear, prog frm 3 out, kpt on well frm nxt* 3 14
1287 27/4 Easingwold (L) MEM 3m 5 G *prom, chsd ldr 10th, chal last, ran on gamely to ld nr fin* 1 15
1447 6/5 Witton Cast' (R) RES 3m 11 G *in tch in midfld whn bad mstk 7th, nvr a dang aft* 6 0
1571 19/5 Corbridge (R) RES 3m 13 G *mstk 9th, prog & prom 16th, onepcd frm nxt* 4 14

Irish Maiden winner 94; modest but tries; hard to win Restricted - Members best hope again 97; Good 16

GREEN'S GAME ch.g. 8 Vital Season - Iced Lolly by Master Stephen — M A Green

471 10/3 Milborne St' (L) MDO 3m 16 G *u.r. 2nd* U -
658 23/3 Badbury Rin' (L) MDO 3m 8 G *(fav) patiently rdn, 2nd at 11th, wknd, t.o. frm 15th* 5 0
1118 17/4 Hockworthy (L) MDO 3m 14 GS *prssd ldr to 11th, wknd, mstks 13th & nxt, p.u. 3 out* P 0

No signs of 2nd race support being justified 0

GREEN'S VAN GOYEN(IRE) b.g. 8 Lyphard's Special (USA) - Maiden Concert by Condorcet (FR) — Mrs D H McCarthy

1995 1(25),F(-),1(18),5(12),1(18),1(23)

9 14/1 Cottenham (R) OPE 3m 13 G *ld 1st, sn hdd, jnd ldr 9th, ld 12th-3 out, eased whn btn* 5 21
179 18/2 Horseheath (R) OPE 3m 5 G *trckd ldrs, ld 10th til jnd & f nxt* F -
920 8/4 Aldington (L) OPE 3m 6 F *ld to 15th,3rd & outpcd aft nxt,rallied to ld last,drvn out* 1 24
1327 30/4 Huntingdon (R) HC 3m 6 GF *ld to 15th, blnd and u.r. next.* U -

Useful pointer; won 5 of 9 95-6; front-runs & fights; win more 97; G-F 24

GREEN TIMES ch.g. 11 Green Shoon - Time And A Half by No Time — Major General C A Ramsay

1995 **3(16),1(23),7(NH),4(0),U(NH),4(14),9(NH),P(0)**

86 11/2 Alnwick (L) OPE 3m 8 GS *prom, mstk 12th, ev ch 14th, wknd rpdly, t.o.* 4 11
187 24/2 Friars Haugh (L) CON 3m 12 S *alwys handy, ld apr 2 out, just hdd whn lft clr last* 1 19
487 16/3 Newcastle (L) HC 3m 10 GS *alwys prom, ld briefly after 4 out, styd on one pace.* 3 22
790 1/4 Kelso (L) HC 3m 1f 11 GF *struggling to keep up after one cct, t.o..* 7 16
860 6/4 Alnwick (L) MXO 4m 1f 7 GF *chsd ldrs, ev ch 3 out, onepcd* 3 19
1121 20/4 Bangor (L) HC 3m 110yds 8 S *handily pld, not fluent 4 out, fd.* 4 22
1337 1/5 Kelso (L) HC 3m 1f 9 S *made most to 3 out, ev ch till wknd apr last.* 4 22
1615 27/5 Wetherby (L) HC 2 1/2m 110yds 11 G *soon well bhnd, t.o. when p.u. before 9th.* P 0

H/Chase winner 95; outclassed in same in 96 but could win another Confined at 12; G-S lower sights .. 20

GREENWINE(USA) br.h. 10 Green Dancer (USA) - Princesse Margo by Targowice (USA) — T Winzer

1995 4(18),2(19),2(16),2(19),3(11),1(16),**P(0)**

198 24/2 Lemalla (R) OPE 3m 12 HY *chsd ldrs til no ext frm 4 out* 4 21
481 11/3 Taunton (R) HC 3m 11 G *bhnd from 14th, t.o. when p.u. before 3 out.* P 0
716 30/3 Wadebridge (L) LAD 3m 6 GF *(Co fav) hld up rear, nvr dang, went 3rd 2 out, nrst fin* 3 18
924 8/4 Bishopsleigh (R) LAD 3m 7 G *mstk 9th, cls order frm 13th, no ext frm 3 out* 3 20
1141 20/4 Flete Park (R) LAD 3m 8 S *4th hlfwy, disp 2nd frm 15th, no ch wnr* 2 19
1426 6/5 High Bickin' (R) LAD 3m 3 G *(fav) cls up, ld 16th, clr 2 out, comf* 1 16
1588 25/5 Mounsey Hil' (R) LAD 3m 6 G *prog to jn ldrs 6th, 3rd & strggling 12th, t.o. 14th* 3 14

Safe but ungenuine & found 2 soft races 95-6; easily beaten in competitive events 17

GREET THE GREEK b.g. 7 Formidable (USA) - Yelney by Blakeney — Mrs G M Brooke

1995 **9(NH),16(NH)**

73 11/2 Wetherby Po' (L) MDO 3m 15 GS *cls up, disp 9th, ld nxt-4 out, sn no ext* 5 0
228 24/2 Duncombe Pa' (R) MDO 3m 9 GS *(fav) chsd ldr, outpcd 12th, 13l 3rd whn f nxt* F -
331 3/3 Market Rase' (L) MDO 3m 9 G *n.j.w. lost tch 13th, lft poor 3rd 3 out, kpt on* 3 0
589 23/3 Wetherby Po' (L) MDO 3m 16 S *alwys mid-div, nvr dang* 6 0
896 6/4 Whittington (L) MDO 3m 5 F *(4s-2s), ld to 12th, grdly wknd aft* 3 0

Beaten 19 lengths minimum when completing & more needed if losses are to be recouped 10

GREY GORDEN(IRE) gr.g. 8 Mister Lord (USA) - Grey Squirrell by Golden Gorden — R H W Major

1995 1(18),1(19),P(0)

293 2/3 Eaton Hall (R) INT 3m 11 G *rear, nrly t.o. til styd on frm 14th, nvr rchd ldrs* 5 12
736 31/3 Sudlow Farm (R) CON 3m 9 G *(fav) made virtly all, 4l clr 2 out, styd on und pres* 1 20
1032 13/4 Alpraham (R) CON 3m 9 GS *w.w., rddn 13th, ran on wll 4 out, ld bfr last* 1 23
1152 20/4 Whittington (L) CON 3m 9 G *(fav) f 1st* F -

1578 19/5 Wolverhampt' (L) OPE 3m 7 G *(fav) prog to chs ldr 9-10th, 4th & outpcd 14th, no dang aft* 3 15

Dual winner 95; still progressing; stays; should reach Open standard 97; G-Hy 22

GREY GUESTINO gr.g. 10 Ivotino (USA) - Wedding Guest by Sanbal Mrs A Delve

1995 2(13),1(15),2(14),P(0),4(10),7(0),8(0)

67 10/2 Great Treth' (R) LAD 3m 11 S *ld to 4th, grad wknd* 6 15
197 24/2 Lemalla (R) LAD 3m 13 HY *disp to 3rd, sn btn, p.u. 2 out* P 0
445 9/3 Haldon (R) RES 3m 9 S *ld to 8th, disp til lost plc 13th, bhnd & jmpd slw aft* 4 0
1072 13/4 Lifton (R) LAD 3m 7 S *prom, cls 3rd 10th, lost grnd stdly frm 3 out* 3 13
1141 20/4 Flete Park (R) LAD 3m 8 S *ld to 4th, chsd ldr til wknd 12th, bhnd & strgglng 16th* 5 0
1624 27/5 Lifton (R) LAD 3m 9 GS *chsd ldr til hlfwy, lost ground frm 15th* 6 14
1648 8/6 Umberleigh (L) LAD 3m 11 GF *mid-div, outpcd frm 7th, t.o. 13th* 7 0

1 win from 29 starts; barely stays & outclassed in Ladies 14

GREY HUSSAR(NZ) gr.g. 10 War Hawk - Poi (NZ) by Native Turn (USA) Mrs S Gray

1995 4(16),P(0),P(0),3(0),4(11)

326 3/3 Market Rase' (L) OPE 3m 14 G *nvr trbld ldrs, bhnd whn blnd 12th, p.u. nxt* P 0
410 9/3 Charm Park (L) OPE 3m 17 G *c.u. 4th-13th, no ext, one-pcd aftr* 8 13
511 16/3 Dalton Park (R) MEM 3m 3 G *(fav) not fluent or keen, in tch, rdn to ld & lft clr 16th, unchal* 1 10

Winning hurdler 93; most unimpressive in Members & best avoided in competitive events 12

GREY JERRY gr.g. 5 Kinglet - Orphan Grey by Crash Course Miss Jane Cooper

284 2/3 Clyst St Ma' (L) MDN 3m 11 S *alwys rear, t.o. & p.u. 15th* P 0
652 23/3 Badbury Rin' (L) MDO 3m 13 G *midfld until wknd 12th, p.u. 14th* P 0
1060 13/4 Badbury Rin' (L) MDO 3m 14 GF *alwys mid-div, t.o. & p.u. 15th* P 0

Only learning to date 0

GREY REALM ch.m. 8 Grey Desire - Miss Realm by Realm R E Barr

1995 F(-),2(12),1(13),3(18),2(12),P(0),3(17),**3(NH),8(NH)**

119 17/2 Witton Cast' (R) LAD 3m 4 S *disp to 8th, lft in ld 11th, 2l clr last, wknd & hdd flat* 2 18
305 2/3 Great Stain' (L) LAD 3m 11 GS *mid-div, prog 15th, styd on wll aft 2 out, nrst fin* 3 17
412 9/3 Charm Park (L) LAD 3m 7 G *u.r. 1st* U -
514 16/3 Dalton Park (R) LAD 3m 8 G *chsd ldrs, 5th & outpcd 4 out, hmpd 2 out, styd on* 3 20
759 31/3 Great Stain' (L) LAD 3m 10 GS *(fav) mid-div, rdn 8th, mstk 11th, mod prog frm 3 out, no dang* 5 15
827 6/4 Stainton (R) LAD 3m 7 GF *mid-div, mstk 7th, wknd apr 2 out* 5 15
1130 20/4 Hornby Cast' (L) CON 3m 13 G *mid-div, prog to ld 13th, lft clr 3 out, easily* 1 21
1446 6/5 Witton Cast' (R) CON 3m 7 G *prom, ld 6th til wknd 3 out, onepcd aft* 3 17

Members winner 95; improved 96; barely stays & easy 3m essential; could find another Ladies; Good .. 20

GREY ROCK (Irish) — **I** 319[P], **I** 365[P], **I** 415[P], **I** 456[2], **I** 492[P], **I** 535[P]

GREY SONATA gr.m. 9 Horage - The Grey (GER) by Pentathlon Miss Anna Bucknall

528 16/3 Cothelstone (L) MEM 3m 8 G *rr & hit 11th, rddn & lst tch 12th, p.u. appr 13th* P 0
709 30/3 Barbury Cas' (L) OPE 3m 15 G *alwys bhnd, t.o. & p.u. 2 out* P 0
990 8/4 Kingston St' (R) OPE 3m 6 F *(bl) in tch, cls 4th at 14th, wknd* 4 0
1080 13/4 Cothelstone (L) XX 3m 2 GF *wth wnr to 13th, sn no imp* 2 0
1331 1/5 Cheltenham (L) HC 2m 5f 9 G *(bl) mstk 5th, t.o. from 8th till u.r. 2 out.* U -
1498 11/5 Holnicote (L) OPE 3m 5 G *(bl) chsd ldr, not fluent, rddn & lost grnd 16th* 4 11
1633 1/6 Bratton Down (L) XX 3m 8 G *(bl) prom to 10th, rdn & strgglng 12th, p.u. 16th* P 0

Winning hurdler 92; does not stay & no prospects in points 10

GREY TUDOR gr.g. 9 Import - Grey Morley by Pongee Noel Warner

125 17/2 Kingston Bl' (L) OPE 3m 10 GS *s.s. pllng, in tch to 11th, t.o. 13th, p.u. 15th* P 0
214 24/2 Newtown (L) CON 3m 21 GS *last whn p.u. 6th* P 0
426 9/3 Upton-On-Se' (R) CON 3m 16 GS *mid-div, f 11th* F -
744 31/3 Upper Sapey (R) OPE 3m 5 GS *2nd/3rd til outpcd 11th, 50l 4th whn p.u. last* P 0
838 6/4 Maisemore P' (L) OPE 3m 4 GF *chsd ldrs, ev ch 12th, wkng & blnd nxt, t.o.* 4 10
1122 20/4 Stratford (L) HC 2m 5f 110yds 16 GF *mid div, hit 4th, gradually lost pl, bhnd when p.u. before 12th.* P 0
1236 27/4 Clifton On ' (L) CON 3m 8 GF *rdr lost irons 4th, bhnd frm 11th, 6th & t.o. whn u.r. 16th* U -

Flat winner; of no account in points 0

GREY WATCH gr.m. 6 Petong - Royal Custody by Reform Lady Susan Brooke

221 24/2 Newtown (L) MDN 3m 12 GS *rear, 8th whn mstk & u.r. 8th* U -
356 3/3 Garnons (L) LAD 3m 12 GS *15l 7th at 10th, wknd 12th, p.u. nxt* P 0
385 9/3 Llanfrynach (R) LAD 3m 14 GS *mid-div whn u.r. 2nd* U -
388 9/3 Llanfrynach (R) RES 3m 20 GS *2nd outing, alwys rear grp, t.o. & p.u. 2 out* P 0
693 30/3 Llanvapley (L) LAD 3m 6 GS *mostly 4th/5th, lost plc hlfwy, p.u. 3 out* P 0
879 6/4 Brampton Br' (R) LAD 3m 9 GF *rear til prog 14th, cls up 16th, no ext aft 3 out* 5 15
1221 24/4 Brampton Br' (R) LAD 3m 6 G *cl 4th whn hit 12th, wnt 2nd 3 out, no ch wth wnr* 2 15
1414 6/5 Cursneh Hill (L) LAD 3m 9 GF *cls up to 13th, wknd frm nxt, p.u. aft 15th* P 0

Ran well when 2nd in weak Ladies but no guarantee of Maiden success based on that 14

GREYWOOD (Irish) — I 14^{P}, I 86^{P}, I 296^{P}

GRIFFIN LARK b.m. 9 Crested Lark - Aimeeze by Huntercombe — Mrs K D Day

1995 P(0),P(0),P(0),F(-),B(-)

541	17/3	Southwell P'	(L)	MDO	3m	9	GS	*rear, mstks, prog frm 8th to trck ldrs, wknd & p.u. 3 out*	P	0
972	8/4	Thorpe Lodge	(L)	MDO	3m	9	GF	*alwys rear hlf, 5th & outpcd frm 6 out*	5	0

Of no account 0

GRIMLEY GALE(IRE) br.m. 7 Strong Gale - Zauditu by Menelek — R M Phillips

1995 1(17),3(16),F(-)

1380	5/5	Dingley	(R)	RES	3m	11	GF	*(fav) mstk 5th, trckd ldrs, ld aft 12th, drew clr apr last, comf*	1	23
1567	19/5	Mollington	(R)	INT	3m	12	GS	*mstk 3rd, in tch, chal & ev ch 15th, rdn & no ext aft 3 out*	3	19
1645	2/6	Dingley	(R)	INT	3m	5	GF	*(fav) prom, ld 9th til blnd 12th, ld 2 out, sn clr, comf*	1	19

Maiden winner 95; late start 96 & progressing; beaten in hot race; Confineds likely 97; G/S-F 22

GROMIT(NZ) gr.g. 8 Captain Jason (NZ) - Larksleve (NZ) by Grey Bird (NZ) — Miss Sarah Eaton

1995 U(-),P(0),8(0),U(-)

749	31/3	Upper Sapey	(R)	MDO	3m	17	GS	*w.w. strng run frm 3 out, disp last, ran on wll flat*	1	15
1216	24/4	Andoversford	(R)	INT	3m	7	G	*in tch, blndrd 12th, sn strglng, t.o. & p.u. app 2 out*	P	0
1415	6/5	Cursneh Hill	(L)	RES	3m	11	GF	*cls 4th 11th,wnt 2nd 2 out,lft in ld bfr last,drew clr flat*	1	19
1597	25/5	Garthorpe	(R)	XX	3m	9	G	*prog 11th, chsd ldr 4 out, ld aft 2 out, comf*	1	19

Much improved; needs strong handling; won fair race last start & Confineds likely 97; best easy 3m 20

GROVE VICTOR (Irish) — I 174^{6}, I 282^{P}, I 318^{4}, I 365^{3}, I 413^{3}, I 451^{3}, I 534^{P}, I 598^{3}

GT HAYES POMMARD b.g. 6 Trampler - Great Hayes Bene by Night Thought — D Howells

1995 P(0),U(-),P(0)

22	20/1	Barbury Cas'	(L)	XX	3m	19	GS	*t.o. til u.r. 5th*	U	-
128	17/2	Kingston Bl'	(L)	RES	3m	14	GS	*alwys bhnd, t.o. 11th, p.u. 15th*	P	0
376	9/3	Barbury Cas'	(L)	MEM	3m	4	GS	*2nd whn u.r. 5th*	U	-
713	30/3	Barbury Cas'	(L)	MDO	3m	10	G	*ld/disp to 12th, lost tch 3 out, tired whn f last*	F	-
956	8/4	Lockinge	(L)	MDN	3m	7	GF	*plld hrd, ld 4-14th, wknd & onepcd aft*	4	0
1248	27/4	Woodford	(L)	MDN	3m	15	G	*s.s., jmp bdly, fence bhnd whn p.u. aft 5th*	P	0

Last on only completion from 9 starts 95-6 0

GUARENA(USA) b.g. 11 Run The Gantlet (USA) - Trenton North (USA) by Herbager — M Lewis

1415	6/5	Cursneh Hill	(L)	RES	3m	11	GF	*alwys rear, short lived efft 9th, t.o. & p.u. aft 13th*	P	0
1620	27/5	Chaddesley '	(L)	XX	3m	8	GF	*n.j.w. rear, t.o. 13th, p.u. 3 out*	P	0

Missed 94/5 & of no account now 0

GUILD STREET b.m. 11 Hasty Word - Mickley Vulstar by Sea Moss — I D James

1995 P(0),4(13),**P(0)**

161	17/2	Weston Park	(L)	LAD	3m	11	G	*mid-div, no ch wth ldrs frm 11th, onepcd*	5	0
536	17/3	Southwell P'	(L)	LAD	3m	9	GS	*prom early, no ch frm 12th*	7	0
903	6/4	Dingley	(R)	LAD	3m	7	GS	*in tch 4th/5th til p.u. qckly 6 out*	P	0

Lightly raced in recent seasons & no sign of any ability left 0

GUIRNS SHOP (Irish) — I 37^{F}, I 124^{P}, I 167^{6}, I 206^{4}, I 250^{4}, I 296^{U}, I 470^{F}, I 513^{2}

GUITING GRAY gr.g. 9 Carlingford Castle - Very Pleased (USA) by Al Hattab (USA) — A M Mason

1995 U(-),2(0),1(14),2(17),1(16),**3(18)**

217	24/2	Newtown	(L)	RES	3m	17	GS	*(fav) trckd ldrs, ld 12th, drew clr 2 out, easily*	1	20
524	16/3	Larkhill	(R)	INT	3m	11	G	*(fav) prom, brfly ld 13th, unable to qckn frm 2 out*	4	18
794	2/4	Heythrop	(R)	CON	3m	6	F	*(fav) j.w. ld 10th, clr 2 out, v easy*	1	24
1216	24/4	Andoversford	(R)	INT	3m	7	G	*(fav) pllng, hit 7th, ld nxt, sn clr, wknd 2 out, hd flat*	2	19
1510	12/5	Maisemore P'	(L)	XX	3m	8	F	*(fav) made all, blnd 12th, wll clr nxt, mstk 14th, imprssv*	1	27

Much improved by Baimbridge; very useful now; swallowed tongue in defeats; Ladies likely 97; G/S-F .. 26

GUNNER BE A LADY ch.m. 6 Gunner B - Jeanne Du Barry by Dubassoff (USA) — Mrs C T Forber

953	8/4	Eyton-On-Se'	(L)	MDO	2 1/2m	10	GF	*rear, t.o. 8th, p.u. 3 out*	P	0
1094	14/4	Whitwell-On'	(R)	MDO	2 1/2m 88yds	16	G	*rear, t.o. & p.u. 4 out*	P	0
1196	21/4	Sandon	(L)	MDN	3m	17	G	*outpcd early, ran on frm 2 out, nrst fin*	3	0

Well beaten last start but distinct promise shown; should go much closer in 97 13

GUNNER BOON b.g. 6 Gunner B - Miss Boon — David Brace

4	13/1	Larkhill	(R)	MDO	3m	9	GS	*blnd 2nd, ran out nxt*	r	-
152	17/2	Erw Lon	(L)	MDN	3m	11	G	*2nd til lft in ld 13th, clr nxt, ran on, fin 1st, disq*	6D	14
552	17/3	Erw Lon	(L)	MDN	3m	10	GS	*ld to 3 out, onepcd*	2	12
771	31/3	Pantyderi	(R)	MDN	3m	14	G	*ld to 9th, agn 15th, jnd last, hrd rdn, just ct*	2	15
1039	13/4	St Hilary	(R)	MDN	3m	14	G	*(fav) cls 3rd, went 2nd at 8th, f nxt*	F	-

Desperately unlucky so far; sure to make amends early in 97 16

GUNNER STREAM ch.g. 12 Gunner B - Golfers Dream by Carnoustie — A G Sims

1995 P(0),9(0),F(-),U(-),**8(NH)**,F(-),**U(NH)**,4(11),4(0),**5(0)**,P(0)

139	17/2	Larkhill	(R)	CON	3m	11	G	*u.r. in mid-div 2nd*	U	-
1059	13/4	Badbury Rin'	(L)	OPE	3m	5	GF	*n.j.w. alwys rear, t.o. & p.u. 4 out*	P	0
1166	20/4	Larkhill	(R)	OPE	3m	6	GF	*sn wll bhnd, t.o. frm 12th, btn one fence*	4	0
1394	6/5	Cotley Farm	(L)	MXO	3m	5	GF	*alwys rr, no ch frm 11th*	4	0

No longer of any account 0

GUSHER ch.g. 7 Ore - Free Credit by Deep Run — T B Brown

340	3/3	Heythrop	(R)	MDN	3m	12	G	*mstks, in tch to 14th, 4th & btn nxt*	5	0

A little promise on debut & may do better in 97 10

GUS MCCRAE gr.g. 10 Parole - Golden Grove by Roan Rocket — Miss P Philipps

1995 2(12),1(13),4(13)

544	17/3	Erw Lon	(L)	MEM	3m	5	GS	*ld to 11th, wth wnr last, onepcd flat*	2	14
980	8/4	Lydstep	(L)	RES	3m	11	G	*disp, in ld apr last, easily*	1	17
1263	27/4	Pyle	(R)	CON	3m	9	G	*nvr rchd front rank, 10l 5th at 13th, no ch frm nxt*	4	0
1389	6/5	Pantyderi	(R)	INT	3m	5	GF	*alwys rear, onepcd, p.u. 11th*	P	0

Maiden winner 95; lightly raced; both wins at Lydstep; more needed for Confineds at 11; G-F 17

GYMCRAK DAWN b.g. 11 Rymer - Edwina's Dawn by Space King — A W Perkins

1995 P(0),2(14),P(0),2(16),P(0)

38	3/2	Wadebridge	(L)	MEM	3m	4	GF	*mstks, hld up, lost tch 11th, t.o. aft til fin fast*	4	0
198	24/2	Lemalla	(R)	OPE	3m	12	HY	*nvr seen wth a ch, p.u. 2 out*	P	0
294	2/3	Great Treth'	(R)	CON	3m	10	G	*alwys prom, disp 2 out-last, no ext*	2	16
560	17/3	Ottery St M'	(L)	CON	3m	7	G	*(bl) cls up, ld 8th-3 out, btn 2nd whn handed race nxt*	1	17
625	23/3	Kilworthy	(L)	CON	3m	11	GS	*(bl) trckd ldrs going wll, effrt 14th, sn outpcd, no imp aft*	6	14
938	8/4	Wadebridge	(L)	OPE	3m	3	F	*(fav) (bl) ld 8-11th, mstk 15th, no imp aft*	2	13
1069	13/4	Lifton	(R)	CON	3m	9	S	*(bl) plld hrd, 4th 13th, 5th & pshd alng 3 out, t.o., p.u. last*	P	0
1140	20/4	Flete Park	(R)	OPE	4m	6	S	*(bl) rear, losing tch whn p.u. 20th*	P	0
1427	6/5	High Bickin'	(R)	CON	3m	10	G	*towrds rear, bhnd whn p.u. apr 15th*	P	0
1529	12/5	Ottery St M'	(L)	OPE	3m	7	GF	*trckd ldr til ld 3 out, disp nxt, ev ch til no ext last*	2	18
1623	27/5	Lifton	(R)	OPE	3m	5	GS	*lost tch frm 14th, p.u. apr 2 out, lame*	P	0

Inconsistent; fortunate winner & finds little; problems last start & lucky to score again 16

GYPSEY ROYLE b.m. 6 Majestic Streak - Touch O' Rama by Cagirama — Mrs F Busby

755	31/3	Lockerbie	(R)	MDN	3m	17	G	*sn bhnd, p.u. 13th*	P	0

No signs yet 0

GYPSY GERRY (Irish) — **I** 131[P], **I** 161[F], **I** 228[3]

GYPSY KING(IRE) b.g. 8 Deep Run - Express Film by Ashmore (FR) — Mrs Nigel Wrighton

8	14/1	Cottenham	(R)	CON	3m	10	G	*in tch, 5th & rdn 16th, kpt on well apr last*	3	20
100	16/2	Fakenham	(L)	HC	2m 5f 110yds	9	G	*lding gp, mstk 3rd, rdn and not qckn from 2 out.*	2	26
360	4/3	Windsor	(R)	HC	3m	8	GS	*held up bhnd ldrs, rdn 4 out, soon btn.*	4	20

Ran well all starts but finished early; can win Confined if fit 97; G-S 21

GYPSY LUCK b.m. 7 Sula Bula - Pine Gypsy by Workboy — J Grant Cann

1995 P(0),1(14)

1428	6/5	High Bickin'	(R)	RES	3m	10	G	*prom til f 4th*	F	-
1528	12/5	Ottery St M'	(L)	RES	3m	10	GF	*mid-div, 5th at 13th, not able to chal*	5	11

Maiden winner 95; lightly raced & late to appear 96; could win Restricted if fit 97 15

GYPSY RACE(IRE) ch.m. 6 Good Thyne (USA) - Dambydale by Deep Run — M W Easterby

1995 **4(NH)**

229	24/2	Duncombe Pa'	(R)	MDO	3m	13	GS	*w.w. steady prog to 10l 2nd whn f 4 out*	F	-

4th in NH Flat 95; going well when departing only start 96 & win Maiden if fit 97 14

HACKETT'S FARM ch.g. 11 Deep Run - Anitacat by No Argument — Miss Barbara Wilce

1995 3(11),3(0),5(12),P(0),9(0),1(21)

96	11/2	Ampton	(R)	XX	3m	11	GF	*cls up, ld 7-9th & 13-16th, wknd apr 2 out*	4	14
161	17/2	Weston Park	(L)	LAD	3m	11	G	*f 4th*	F	-
264	2/3	Didmarton	(L)	INT	3m	12	G	*in tch, made most 11th-last,sn ld agn,hdd & no ext flat*	2	16
425	9/3	Upton-On-Se'	(R)	MEM	3m	7	GS	*smooth run to ld 14th, clr nxt, easily*	1	18
687	30/3	Chaddesley '	(L)	CON	3m	10	G	*ld 1st, sn hdd, outpcd 13th, kpt on agn frm 2 out*	5	17
1043	13/4	Bitterley	(L)	OPE	3m	9	G	*cls 5th at 11th, not qckn frm nxt, styd on into 4th at 15th*	4	13
1314	28/4	Bitterley	(L)	MEM	3m	13	G	*chsd ldrs, went 3rd 14th, no ch 1st pair, wknd flat*	5	14
1413	6/5	Cursneh Hill	(L)	INT	3m	6	GF	*made most til hdd & mstk 3 out, kpt on onepce*	2	18
1567	19/5	Mollington	(R)	INT	3m	12	GS	*chsd ldrs, 5th & outpcd 14th, no imp ldrs aft*	4	15
1620	27/5	Chaddesley '	(L)	XX	3m	8	GF	*ld 3-12th, lft in ld 14th, gd jmp last, drvn out*	1	19

Steady performer now; goes best for Julian Pritchard; should find another race; G/S-F 20

HAGLER br.g. 13 Silly Prices - Reigate Head by Timber King R D Griffiths

1995 3(12),P(0)

162	17/2	Weston Park	(L)	OPE	3m	16	G	*mid-div, nvr dang, p.u. 2 out*	P 0
214	24/2	Newtown	(L)	CON	3m	21	GS	*prom, chsd ldr 14th, ev ch 2 out, onepcd*	2 20
547	17/3	Erw Lon	(L)	OPE	3m	10	GS	*prom til lft in ld 2 out, unchal aft*	1 18
1041	13/4	Bitterley	(L)	MEM	3m	6	G	*hld up, p.u. 8th, lame*	P 0

Open winner 94; revived 96; won bad Open; problems last start & could be finished 17

HALENS MATCH (Irish) — I 92[P]

HALF A SOV b.g. 12 Kinglet - Hudsons Hill by Eborneezer Mrs Anne Butler

1995 1(11),F(-),P(0),1(0),P(0)

58	10/2	Cottenham	(R)	RES	3m	7	GS	*prom til wknd aft 3 out, p.u. last*	P 0
621	23/3	Higham	(L)	INT	3m	12	GF	*alwys bhnd, slight prog 15th, sn btn, p.u. last*	P 0
835	6/4	Marks Tey	(L)	MEM	3m	4	G	*(fav) trckd ldr, ld apr last, ran on flat, just hld on*	1 10
1322	28/4	Fakenham P-'	(L)	RES	3m	5	G	*chsd ldrs, 3rd & btn whn u.r. 3 out*	U -
1547	18/5	Fakenham	(L)	HC	2m 5f 110yds	11	G	*soon bhnd, lost tch from 4th, p.u. before 13th.*	P 0

Won 2 bad races 95-6 & no chance in competitive events 11

HALF BRANDY (Irish) — I 283[P]

HALF SCOTCH (Irish) — I 92[P], I 215[3], I 258[2], I 360[3], I 448[3], I 494[R], I 601[5]

HALHAM TARN(IRE) b.g. 6 Pennine Walk - Nouniya by Vayrann H J Manners

1995 **3(NH),4(NH),3(NH),7(NH),11(NH),5(NH),2(NH),3(NH),3(NH)**

232	24/2	Heythrop	(R)	OPE	3m	10	GS	*disp til hlfwy, wknd rpdly, p.u. 12th*	P 0
364	5/3	Leicester	(R)	HC	2m 1f	12	GS	*chsd clr ldr 2nd, ld apr 2 out, clear last, styd on well.*	1 26
958	8/4	Lockinge	(L)	MXO	3m	6	GF	*in tch til 13th, wknd nxt, t.o. & p.u. 5 out*	P 0
1336	1/5	Cheltenham	(L)	HC	2m 110yds	9	G	*chsd ldr 4th, ld 10th till 11th, rdn and blnd 2 out, fin tired.*	2 23

Winning hurdler; produced the Manners trick Leicester; non-stayer; few chances for another win; G-Hy 20

HALLO SENSATION ch.g. 9 Feelings (FR) - Artlight by Articulate Executors Of The Late Mrs J C Cookson

1995 F(-),4(13),2(19),8(0),**5(15),F(-)**,7(0),2(0)

50	4/2	Alnwick	(L)	CON	3m	9	G	*ld to 4th & aft 12th til 3 out, one pace*	3 17
85	11/2	Alnwick	(L)	LAD	3m	11	GS	*prom, 4th & outpcd 3 out, styd on strngly apr last, nrst fin*	2 20
190	24/2	Friars Haugh	(L)	LAD	3m	7	S	*(fav) hld up, some prog frm 4 out, nvr dang*	3 14

Dual winner 94; beaten last 12 & finished early 96; could win Confined 97; F-S 18

HALL'S MILL (Irish) — I 170[5], I 257[P], I 491[P]

HAMILTON LADY(IRE) b.m. 8 Zino - Villasanta by Corvaro (USA) Alex Fergusson

110	17/2	Lanark	(R)	CON	3m	10	GS	*prom early, losing tch whn p.u. 11th*	P 0
187	24/2	Friars Haugh	(L)	CON	3m	12	S	*mid-div whn u.r. 8th*	U -
497	16/3	Lanark	(R)	MEM	3m	2	G	*(fav) ld 10th, sn wll clr, fin alone*	1 10
751	31/3	Lockerbie	(R)	CON	3m	12	G	*3rd hlfwy, sn lost plc, p.u. 2 out*	P 0

Won a non-contest & showed nothing in proper races 0

HAMPER ch.g. 13 Final Straw - Great Care by Home Guard (USA) N J Hoare

1995 5(11),P(0),**4(0)**,1(0),1(18),**2(23)**,1(21)

257	29/2	Nottingham	(L)	HC	2 1/2m	11	G	*(bl) soon handily pld, joined ldrs final cct, ev ch till rdn and no ext from 2 out.*	4 20
577	19/3	Fontwell	(R)	HC	2m 3f	5	GF	*(fav) (bl) alwys in tch, challenging when hit 10th, ld next, left clr 12th, wknd run-in, fin tired.*	1 20
672	29/3	Aintree	(L)	HC	2 3/4m	26	G	*(bl) held up, struggling hfwy, nvr a factor.*	7 17
1309	28/4	Little Wind'	(R)	OPE	3m	8	G	*(bl) ld 10th til aft 14th, 3rd at 17th, fdd*	4 17
1339	4/5	Hereford	(R)	HC	2m 3f	7	F	*(bl) held up, bhnd from 10th.*	6 16
1623	27/5	Lifton	(R)	OPE	3m	5	GS	*(bl) cls up, ld 14th-3 out, sn outpcd*	3 20

Won 3 in 95; won weak H/Chase 96 & struggling under penalty; hard to find chances at 14; G-F 19

HAMSHIRE GALE (Irish) — I 640, , I 651[F]

HANDBALL (Irish) — I 182[P], I 226[F], I 291[2], I 469[1]

HANDSOME ANTHONY (Irish) — I 315[B]

HANDSOME GENT b.g. 7 Dunbeath (USA) - French Surprise by Hello Gorgeous (USA) John Threadgall

190	24/2	Friars Haugh	(L)	LAD	3m	7	S	*ld til 7th, wknd rpdly & p.u. 9th*	P 0
499	16/3	Lanark	(R)	LAD	3m	10	G	*sn bhnd, p.u. 4 out*	P 0

No signs yet 0

HANDSOME HARVEY b.g. 10 Push On - April Airs by Grey Mirage E L Harries

1995 1(21),1(21),1(20),1(23),1(23),1(22),1(23),1(25),1(25),1(0)

154	17/2	Erw Lon	(L)	LAD	3m	14	G	*(fav) ld 10th, made rest, clr last, easily*	1	26
385	9/3	Llanfrynach	(R)	LAD	3m	14	GS	*(fav) made all at fast pace, shkn up & ran on wll 2 out, clvrly*	1	26
603	23/3	Howick	(L)	LAD	3m	8	S	*(fav) made all, chal 2 out, qcknd away*	1	25
693	30/3	Llanvapley	(L)	LAD	3m	6	GS	*(fav) made all, qcknd flat*	1	23
1265	27/4	Pyle	(R)	OPE	3m	8	G	*(fav) ld frm 4th, prssd frm 14th, rdn & hld on flat*	1	23
1489	11/5	Erw Lon	(L)	LAD	3m	4	F	*(fav) svrl mstks, ld 7-13th, strgglng aft, eased flat*	2	18
1560	18/5	Bassaleg	(R)	OPE	3m	7	F	*(fav) ld 3rd, hrd prssd frm 15th, drvn & ran on well flat*	1	25
1630	31/5	Stratford	(L)	HC	3 1/2m	16	GF	*jmpd right, made all, mstk 2 out, styd on gamely run-in.*	1	26

Unbeaten in 10 points 95; not as invincible 96; well ridden for H/Chase win; more Ladies 97; S-F 27

HANDSOME MAID (Irish) — I 195[P], I 233[3], I 271[1]

HANDYFELLOW (Irish) — I 94[6]

HANDY SALLY (Irish) — I 164[P], I 233[P], I 469[4], I 499[3], I 579[4]

HANDY SPIDER ch.m. 8 Nearly A Hand - Lolly Spider by Rugantino — O Hemsley

728	31/3	Little Wind'	(R)	MEM	3m	7	GS	*rear, no ch whn blndrd 3 out, t.o. p.u. 2 out*	P	0
1060	13/4	Badbury Rin'	(L)	MDO	3m	14	GF	*alwys bhnd, nvr able to chal*	6	0
1128	20/4	Stafford Cr'	(R)	RES	3m	17	S	*u.r. 2nd*	U	-
1293	28/4	Barbury Cas'	(L)	MDO	3m	11	F	*cls up, f 2nd*	F	-

Only beat one other when finishing & not worth a rating yet 0

HANLEYS CALL (Irish) — I 97[P], I 173[P], I 287[P], I 321[P]

HANNIGAN'S BRIDGE (Irish) — I 2[P], I 9[S], I 61[F], I 213,

HANSOM MARSHAL br.g. 10 Daring March - Fille de Phaeton by Sun Prince — G D Mason

772	31/3	Pantyderi	(R)	MDN	3m	8	G	*prom til f 5th*	F	-
977	8/4	Lydstep	(L)	MDO	3m	8	G	*p.u. 8th*	P	0

Lightly raced & shows no ability 0

HANUKKAH b.m. 7 Oats - Badsworth Girl by Arch Sculptor — P Ansell

1995 P(0),P(0),P(0),F(-),P(0),4(0),F(-),4(0),0(0)

195	24/2	Lemalla	(R)	INT	3m	7	HY	*plld hrd, cls up whn u.r. 4th*	U	-
297	2/3	Great Treth'	(R)	INT	3m	10	G	*rear, p.u. 13th*	P	0
630	23/3	Kilworthy	(L)	MDN	3m	10	GS	*mid-div, outpcd aft 14th, no dang aft*	6	0
718	30/3	Wadebridge	(L)	MDO	3m	11	GF	*twrds rear, mstk 10th, poor 5th frm 14th*	5	0
1070	13/4	Lifton	(R)	MDN	3m	9	S	*chsd ldrs til wknd & onepcd frm 3 out*	3	10

Improved 96 but placed in poor Maiden; not threatening to win yet 12

HAPPY BREED b.g. 13 Bustino - Lucky Realm by Realm — Mrs A R Burt

1995 P(0)

169	18/2	Market Rase'	(L)	CON	3m	15	GF	*ld to 5th, disp to 8th, wknd 10th, p.u. 14th*	P	0
326	3/3	Market Rase'	(L)	OPE	3m	14	G	*prom til wknd 10th, t.o. & p.u. 2 out*	P	0
632	23/3	Market Rase'	(L)	CON	3m	10	GF	*cls up 2nd to 9th, 3rd & fdng whn f 12th (ditch)*	F	-

No longer of any account 0

HAPPY ENOUGH br.m. 9 Callernish - Tishoo by Frigid Aire — M Nelmes-Crocker

339	3/3	Heythrop	(R)	RES	3m	10	G	*in tch til lost plc & p.u. 12th*	P	0

Irish Maiden winner 95; vanished quickly 96; more evidence needed 11

HAPPY HANGOVER (Irish) — I 160[P], I 234, , I 477[3], I 558[2]

HAPPY HENRY(IRE) ch.g. 6 Arapahos (FR) - Pike Run by Deep Run — B Dennett

301	2/3	Great Treth'	(R)	MDO	3m	13	G	*(fav) no show, bhnd til p.u. 2 out*	P	0
864	6/4	Larkhill	(R)	MDN	2 1/2m	9	F	*plld, clsd up 5 out, narrow adv & gng wll whn f nxt*	F	-
1164	20/4	Larkhill	(R)	MDN	3m	12	GF	*(Jt fav) mid-div whn f 3rd*	F	-
1308	28/4	Little Wind'	(R)	MDO	3m	6	G	*rear, prog to 3rd aft 16th, ev ch nxt, 3rd & und pres,f 2out*	F	-
1554	18/5	Bratton Down	(L)	MDO	3m	16	F	*s.s. rear til gd prog 16th,3rd & ev ch whn blnd & u.r.2out*	U	-

Promising but very clumsy; pulls; should win if straightened out in 97 15

HAPPY HULA GIRL (Irish) — I 506[P], I 590[3], I 653[P]

HAPPY PADDY ch.g. 13 Paddy's Stream - Inch Tape by Prince Hansel — B R Summers

1995 P(0),**4(0)**

642	23/3	Siddington	(L)	RES	3m	15	S	*(bl) chsd ldrs to 10th, wkng & blnd 12th, p.u. nxt*	P	0
1002	9/4	Upton-On-Se'	(R)	RES	3m	8	F	*(bl) prog to ld 9-11th, sn btn, t.o. last 3 out*	4	0
1640	2/6	Dingley	(R)	RES	3m	9	GF	*rr, eff 11th, sn wknd, t.o. whn p.u. 3 out*	P	0

No longer of any account 0

HAPPY THOUGHT b.m. 9 Town And Country - Commander Alice by Spartan General — B Ayre

44	3/2	Wadebridge	(L)	MDO	3m	9	GF	*schoold rear, t.o. whn p.u. 2 out*	P	0

137 17/2 Ottery St M' (L) RES 3m 15 GS *rear whn u.r. 7th* U -
197 24/2 Lemalla (R) LAD 3m 13 HY *rear, rdn & no prog whn p.u. aft 12th* P 0
561 17/3 Ottery St M' (L) LAD 3m 12 G *mid-div whn u.r. 6th* U -
1072 13/4 Lifton (R) LAD 3m 7 S *wnt 4th 12th & just in tch, 5th whn blndrd & u.r. 13th* U -
1276 27/4 Bratton Down (L) LAD 3m 7 GF *ld/disp early, in tch aft, cls 4th whn u.r. 11th* U -
1530 12/5 Ottery St M' (L) MDO 3m 8 GF *in tch, 3rd & rdn 15th, wll btn whn lft 2nd last* 2 0
1587 25/5 Mounsey Hil' (R) MEM 3m 7 G *chsd ldr to 4th, 4th & rdn 13th, sn wknd, p.u. 16th* P 0
1652 8/6 Umberleigh (L) MDO 3m 10 GF *rear, lost tch whn p.u. 7th* P 0

Missed 95; beaten 25l when 2nd & shows no stamina 0

HAPPY VALLEY b.m. 8 Cruise Missile - Valley Mist by Perhapsburg — Captain M B Baker

294 2/3 Great Treth' (R) CON 3m 10 G *alwys bhnd* 6 0
556 17/3 Ottery St M' (L) MDO 3m 15 G *sn rear, t.o. frm 10th* 8 0
871 6/4 Higher Kilw' (L) RES 3m 9 GF *sn rear, nvr dang, t.o. & p.u. 3 out* P 0
1071 13/4 Lifton (R) MDN 3m 10 S *midfld, pckd bdly 16th, wnt poor 3rd apr 2 out* 3 10
1143 20/4 Flete Park (R) MDN 3m 17 S *in tch, 6th at 10th, prog to 2nd 3 out, ev ch nxt, no ext* 2 14

Gradually improved & 2nd in large but modest Maiden; novice ridden; may find a race; Soft 14

HARDEN GLEN b.g. 5 Respect - Polly Peril by Politico (USA) — R J Kyle

82 11/2 Alnwick (L) MEM 3m 4 GS *ld to 2nd, chsd wnr aft, ev ch apr 3 out, sn btn, fair debut* 2 10
321 2/3 Corbridge (R) MDN 3m 12 GS *rear early, styd on onepcd, nvr nr ldrs* 3 11
859 6/4 Alnwick (L) MDO 2 1/2m 5 GF *(fav) disp ld to 3rd, trkd ldr, ld & f 2 out* U -

Winner behind on debut & unlucky in poor Maiden; should win if fit in 97 14

HARDIHERO b.g. 10 Henbit (USA) - Hardirondo by Hardicanute — G F White

1995 2(19)

46 4/2 Alnwick (L) MEM 3m 7 G *(fav) trckd ldrs app 3 out, rdn & not qckn nxt* 2 17
402 9/3 Dalston (R) XX 3m 13 G *nvr btr thn mid-div* 6 0
609 23/3 Friars Haugh (L) PPO 3m 7 G *not fluent, nvr dngrs* 4 11

Winning hurdler 92; lightly raced now; good enough to win but finds little; 1st time out best hope 16

HARDTOBEGOOD (Irish) — I 384^{P}, I 418^{P}, I 532^{3}, I 621^{3}, I 631^{4}

HARDY BREEZE (Irish) — I 213^{3}, I 608^{F}, I 642^{B}, I 645^{F}

HARKEN PREMIER gr.g. 11 Hard Fought - Maraquiba (FR) by Kenmare (FR) — A Jeffries

1995 S(-),F(-),P(0)

601 23/3 Howick (L) CON 3m 10 S *t.o. 10th, p.u. nxt* P 0
845 6/4 Howick (L) CON 3m 12 GF *alwys rear, p.u. 13th* P 0
1157 20/4 Llanwit Maj' (R) CON 3m 11 GS *mid-div, prog to 3rd 10th, wknng whn f 14th* F -
1263 27/4 Pyle (R) CON 3m 9 G *cls up whn f 2nd* F -
1385 6/5 Pantyderi (R) CON 3m 6 GF *alwys rear, p.u. 11th* P 0
1556 18/5 Bassaleg (R) MEM 3m 6 F *jmpd slwly, t.o. whn nrly ref 8th, sntchd 4th on line* 4 0

Flat winner 89; no stamina for points 0

HARLEY ch.g. 16 Cranley - Harmony Rose by Drumbeg — Miss Judy Eaton

1152 20/4 Whittington (L) CON 3m 9 G *ld/disp to 6th,still cls up 11th,wknd, t.o. 14th,p.u. 3 out* P 0

Formerly decent but surely reached the end now 0

HARLIN LADY (Irish) — I 384^{P}, I 417^{P}, I 562^{P}

HARMONY'S CHOICE ch.g. 5 Morgans Choice - Beera Harmony by Shannon Boy — M E Hawkins

556 17/3 Ottery St M' (L) MDO 3m 15 G *mid-div til p.u. 12th* P 0
807 4/4 Clyst St Ma' (L) MDO 3m 10 GS *rear, prog 13th, ran on to 3rd whn f last* F -
1362 4/5 Flete Park (R) MDO 3m 9 G *in tch til lost ground frm 17th, tired whn mstk last* 5 0

Only beaten one other finisher so far but not without promise & should go closer in 97 13

HARMONY WALK(IRE) b.g. 8 Flair Path - Peaceful Girl by Keep The Peace — H Morton

1995 P(0),3(14),2(20),F(-),4(15),1(19),2(17)

244 25/2 Southwell P' (L) CON 3m 13 HO *chsng grp til wknd 11th, p.u. nxt* P 0
535 17/3 Southwell P' (L) CON 3m 10 GS *mid-div, prog 11th, outpcd frm 3 out* 4 0

Restricted winner 95; changed hands & brief 96 season of no form; can only be watched 11

HARPLEY gr.g. 9 Beldale Flutter (USA) - Jellygold by Jellaby — M A Lloyd

1995 **7(0),B(-)**

1221 24/4 Brampton Br' (R) LAD 3m 6 G *alws last, grad lost tch, t.o. whn p.u. aft 2 out* P 0
1366 4/5 Gisburn (R) LAD 3m 12 G *mstks, t.o. 9th* 7 0

Winning hurdler 92; beat only one other 95-6 & needs a drastic lowering of sights 10

HARPLEY DUAL(IRE) b.g. 8 Floriferous - Dual's Delight by Dual — R J Case

1995 F(-),1(14),P(0),P(0),U(-),P(0)

35 20/1 Higham (L) RES 3m 16 GF *bhnd frm 11th, t.o. & p.u. last* P 0

106 17/2 Marks Tey (L) RES 3m 12 G *in tch to 14th, 3rd & btn 16th, kpt on* 3 11
494 16/3 Horseheath (R) RES 3m 10 GF *hld up rear, ran on past btn horses frm 3 out, nvr nrr* 2 14
834 6/4 Marks Tey (L) RES 3m 11 G *rear, wll bhnd whn p.u. 18th* P 0
1320 28/4 Fakenham P-' (L) MEM 3m 3 G *(fav) made most til apr 2 out, rallied und pres to ld flat* 1 10

Maiden winner 95; won bad Members 96 & struggling in Restricteds; Members best hope again 97 13

HARRY FROM BARRY b.g. 8 Cree Song - Lyptosol Gold by Lepanto (GER) Gwyn R Davies
1995 **B(NH),5(NH)**
552 17/3 Erw Lon (L) MDN 3m 10 GS *prom til blnd 3 out, p.u. bef nxt* P 0
976 8/4 Lydstep (L) MDO 3m 12 G *mid-div, p.u. 2 out* P 0
1271 27/4 Pyle (R) MDO 3m 15 G *ld to 4th, cls up til chal 3 out, wknd frm nxt* 2 0
1390 6/5 Pantyderi (R) MDO 3m 15 GF *ld til f 4th* F -
1605 25/5 Bassaleg (R) MDO 3m 8 GS *4th til ld apr 10th, clr nxt, prssd 2 out, lft clr last* 1 13

Non-stayer but won bad Maiden; will struggle in Restricteds 12

HARRY-H b.g. 6 Les Morse Vii - Glasserton Girl by Ancient Monro H J Hopper
1995 P(0),3(0),P(0),P(0)
248 25/2 Charing (L) RES 3m 12 GS *alwys in rear* 7 0

Of no account 0

HARRY LAUDER(IRE) ch.g. 5 Noalto - Decent Debbie by Decent Fellow Christopher Sporborg
15 14/1 Cottenham (R) MDN 3m 14 G *alwys prom, 5th 2 out, kpt on, improve* 3 12
108 17/2 Marks Tey (L) MDN 3m 17 G *(fav) trkd ldrs, ld brfly 3 out, lft in ld last, hdd cls hme* 2 15

Quite promising; finished early but win awaits if ready in 97 15

HARRY'S SECRET (Irish) — **I** 23P, **I** 871, **I** 1303, **I** 304P
HARRY TARTAR b.g. 5 Cisto (FR) - Tartar Holly Vii by Damsire Unregistered J D Parker
643 23/3 Siddington (L) MDN 3m 16 S *rear & mstk 4th, bhnd whn p.u. 13th* P 0
1569 19/5 Mollington (R) MDO 3m 10 GS *rear, rdr lost irons 4th, p.u. nxt* P 0
1621 27/5 Chaddesley ' (L) MDO 3m 17 GF *last frm 3rd, lft 4th by dfctns* 4 0
1637 1/6 Bratton Down (L) MDO 3m 11 G *bhnd, last frm 10th, t.o. 15th* 6 0

Beaten miles when completing & much improvement needed 10

HARSH DECISION (Irish) — **I** 111P, **I** 228P
HARVEMAC (Irish) — **I** 26P, **I** 984, **I** 2194, **I** 272P, **I** 482P, **I** 5635, **I** 5995, **I** 628P
HARVEST DELIGHT (Irish) — **I** 50P, **I** 240P, **I** 354P, **I** 432P
HARVEST TIME (Irish) — **I** 587F, **I** 6252
HARVEY'S CREAM (Irish) — **I** 211P, **I** 280P, **I** 325P
HARWALL QUEEN b.m. 13 Tobique - Knights Queen by Arctic Chevalier E Tudor Harries
154 17/2 Erw Lon (L) LAD 3m 14 G *alwys last trio* 9 0
1263 27/4 Pyle (R) CON 3m 9 G *rear 5th, lost tch 11th, t.o. & p.u. 14th* P 0

No longer of any account 0

HASTY CRUISE b.g. 10 Cruise Missile - Hasena by Haven C Warde-Aldam
1995 5(10),P(0),U(-)
241 25/2 Southwell P' (L) MDO 3m 15 HO *prom til wknd 14th, t.o.* 5 0
1092 14/4 Whitwell-On' (R) CON 3m 10 G *rear & mstk 10th, mod prog 13th, sn wknd, t.o. & p.u. 2 out* P 0
1135 20/4 Hornby Cast' (L) MDN 3m 10 G *n.j.w. prom til wknd rpdly & p.u. 9th* P 0
1470 11/5 Easingwold (L) MDO 3m 10 G *prom whn s.u. flat apr 7th* S -

Looks devoid of stamina & finished only 2 of 7 outings 95-6 0

HATCHIT br.g. 7 Boyne - Minnie The Moocher by Prince Hansel Mrs Elaine Starr
922 8/4 Aldington (L) MEM 3m 4 F *1st ride, mod 3rd til ref & u.r. 6th* R -
1210 21/4 Heathfield (R) MDO 3m 13 F *last, lost tch 5th, jmpd slwly nxt, ref 7th* R -

Most unpromising 0

HA-TO-SIEE(IRE) b.g. 8 Burslem - Ingrid Volley (ITY) by Romolo Augusto (USA) Mrs Charlotte Cooke
1995 1(19),P(0),P(0),F(-)
36 20/1 Higham (L) RES 3m 12 GF *(fav) 5/2-1/1,ld,hit 4th,clr 12th,hdd 3 out,immed btn,p.u. nxt* P 0

Won Maiden debut 95; problems since & vanished early 96; can only be watched 12

HATTERILL RIDGE br.g. 6 Rustingo - Nun Owen by Owen Anthony A C James
690 30/3 Llanvapley (L) MEM 3m 4 GS *cls up in last til disp 3 out, ld nxt, clr last* 1 11
1038 13/4 St Hilary (R) RES 3m 15 G *alwys rear, p.u. 13th* P 0
1160 20/4 Llanwit Maj' (R) RES 3m 12 GS *wll bhnd, prog 8th, outpcd 12th, f 14th* F -
1267 27/4 Pyle (R) RES 3m 7 G *20l 6th at 10th, no prog nxt, t.o. & p.u. 14th* P 0
1482 11/5 Bredwardine (R) RES 3m 13 G *chsd ldrs til p.u. aft 8th* P 0

1582 19/5 Wolverhampt' (L) RES 3m 10 G *bhnd, prog to 5th & blnd 14th, wll btn nxt, t.o.* 4 0

Won poor Members; never in the hunt after; young but needs much more for Restricteds 10

HAVE A BRANDY (Irish) — **I** 158P, **I** 355[1]

HAVE A DROP (Irish) — **I** 8P, **I** 64[5], **I** 70[3], **I** 183P, **I** 374[6], **I** 459[4], **I** 569P, **I** 589[1], **I** 613P

HAVE ANOTHER (Irish) — **I** 14P, **I** 68P, **I** 124[4], **I** 328[3], **I** 446[6], **I** 500[3], **I** 530[3], **I** 607[3], **I** 655[2]

HAVEN ch.g. 6 North Street - Tandys Tonic by Full Of Beans B F W Rendell

1995 P(0),U(-)

1531 12/5 Ottery St M' (L) MDO 3m 9 GF *last whn ref 1st* R -

Yet to complete & all the wrong signs in 96 0

HAVEN LADY (Irish) — **I** 280P, **I** 353R

HAVEN LIGHT b.g. 9 Flower Robe - Points Review by Major Point Mrs J P Spencer

1995 3(15),2(17),P(0),1(19),3(15),5(14)

457 9/3 Eyton-On-Se' (L) INT 3m 11 G *chsd ldrs,prog 4 out,chal 3 out,ev ch nxt,btn whn u.r. last* U 19
741 31/3 Upper Sapey (R) MEM 3m 4 GS *(fav) made all, 10l clr hlfwy, unchal frm 15th* 1 16

Restricted winner 95; brief season 96; front runner & needs easy 3m; may find Confined if fit 97; Fm ... 19

HAVEN'T AN OCEAN (Irish) — **I** 192P, **I** 420[1]

HAWAIIAN GODDESS(USA) b.m. 9 Hawaii - Destiny's Reward (USA) by Executioner (USA) Mrs C W Pinney

1995 P(0),P(0),5(0),P(0)

536 17/3 Southwell P' (L) LAD 3m 9 GS *prom to 10th, wknd rpdly, t.o.* 8 0
631 23/3 Market Rase' (L) MEM 3m 3 GF *cls up on outer, effrt 2 out, ld last, ran on* 1 10
970 8/4 Thorpe Lodge (L) LAD 3m 6 GF *t.o. 4th, ran on past wkng rivals last m* 3 0
1305 28/4 Southwell P' (L) LAD 3m 4 GF *t.o. 4th* 3 0

Won a bad race & same again 97 offers only other chance 10

HAWAIIAN PRINCE b.g. 12 Hawaiian Return (USA) - Wrong Decision by No Argument Miss Tina Hammond

1995 P(0),**P(0)**

1516 12/5 Hexham Poin' (L) LAD 3m 2 HY *disp, blnd 7th, hit 12th, outpcd frm nxt* 2 0

Beaten a fence in a match & of no account 0

HAWAIIAN REEF b.g. 9 Henbit (USA) - Raffmarie by Raffingora M W Wells

236 24/2 Heythrop (R) MDN 3m 13 GS *in tch early, bhnd & p.u. 11th* P 0

Missed 94-5 & looks impossible to train 0

HAYDON HILL ch.m. 5 Hadeer - Coppice by Pardao Mrs E Kulbicki

1995 **5(NH),7(NH)**

268 2/3 Didmarton (L) MDN 3m 10 G *rear, prog & in tch 9th, outpcd 12th, poor 5th & p.u. 14th* P 0
850 6/4 Howick (L) MDN 3m 14 GF *mid-div,prog to 4th at 14th, ld nxt, mstk 3 out, ran on well* 1 15
1557 18/5 Bassaleg (R) RES 3m 14 F *hld up, prog 6th, cls up til wknd 12th, p.u. 15th* P 0
1601 25/5 Bassaleg (R) RES 3m 12 GS *ld 4th, 15l clr 10th, hdd 3 out, onepcd aft* 3 17

Fair start; won poor Maiden but ran well last start; young & Restricted likely in 97; G/S-G/F 17

HAYE BUSTER b.g. 11 Bustiki - Woodcote Lady by Bush Star M J Skuse

1995 P(0),6(0),B(-),4(0),8(0)

361 5/3 Leicester (R) HC 2 1/2m 110yds 15 GS *prom to 9th, rdn and wknd 11th, t.o. when p.u. last.* P 0
581 21/3 Wincanton (R) HC 2m 5f 13 S *t.o. when p.u. before 12th.* P 0
1169 20/4 Chaddesley ' (L) MEM 3m 9 G *cls up til wknd 14th, no ch nxt, t.o. & p.u. 17th* P 0
1227 26/4 Ludlow (R) HC 2 1/2m 16 G *(bl) bhnd hfwy.* 12 0

No longer of any account 0

HAYES CORNER (Irish) — **I** 491P, **I** 536P

HAZEL CREST b.g. 9 Hays - Singing Wren by Julio Mariner A Reynard

1995 P(0),4(0),C(-),**F(-)**

223 24/2 Duncombe Pa' (R) CON 3m 16 GS *cls up to 13th, no ch frm 3 out* 6 0
306 2/3 Great Stain' (L) INT 3m 12 GS *mid-div to 12th, rear whn p.u. 16th* P 0
985 8/4 Charm Park (L) INT 3m 9 GF *rear early, prog 10th, 3rd frm 13th, tk 2nd run in* 2 17
1287 27/4 Easingwold (L) MEM 3m 5 G *plld hrd, prom, cls 2nd whn u.r. 9th* U -
1461 9/5 Sedgefield (L) HC 2m 5f 10 F *held up, hdwy to track ldrs 8th, ld 13th, soon hdd, wknd before 2 out.* 3 14

Able but inconsistent & disappointing; unlikely to win now 14

HAZEL PARK b.f. 8 Broadsword (USA) - New Cherry by New Brig A J Morley

1995 P(0),P(0),U(-),7(11),P(0),8(0)

357 3/3 Garnons (L) RES 3m 14 GS *prom to 9th, wkng whn f 13th* F -

532 16/3 Cothelstone (L) RES 3m 12 G *rr div, lst tch 11th, t.o. & p.u. 15th* P 0
729 31/3 Little Wind' (R) RES 3m 12 GS *prom til lost plc 8th, bhnd whn hit 14th, fin tired* 8 0

Irish Maiden winner 94; has shown nothing in England 0

HAZEL RING (Irish) — I 32P, I 95P

HAZELS DREAM (Irish) — I 85P, I 132F, I 164P, I 195P, I 385⁵, I 621⁴, I 651¹

HAZY MIST (Irish) — I 292P

HAZY SUPREME (Irish) — I 2², I 9¹, I 65²

HEAD BOTTLE WASHER (Irish) — I 201⁶, I 250F, I 367P, I 543, , I 581,

HEALING THOUGHT (Irish) — I 660P

HEARNS HILL (Irish) — I 345¹, I 383⁴, I 482P, I 606¹

HEATHER BOY b.g. 7 Whistlefield - Calfstown Maid by Master Buck R G Westacott
1995 2(12),2(14),S(-)

2 13/1 Larkhill (R) MDO 3m 17 GS *prom to 10th, 8th & no ch 13th, wll bhnd whn p.u. 3 out* P 0
283 2/3 Clyst St Ma' (L) MDN 3m 7 S *(fav) ld 8th-3 out, onepcd frm nxt* 2 0
534 16/3 Cothelstone (L) MDN 3m 10 G *prom, ev ch 15th, wknd nxt* 3 13
712 30/3 Barbury Cas' (L) MDO 3m 10 G *cls 3rd whn f 2nd* F -
820 6/4 Charlton Ho' (L) MDN 3m 12 GF *ld 3rd-12th, rddn 4 out, onepcd aft* 5 0
1342 4/5 Holnicote (L) MEM 3m 7 GS *ld/disp to 15th, sn wknd* 4 16
1651 8/6 Umberleigh (L) MDO 3m 11 GF *prom, chsd ldr 11th til aft 3 out, wknd nxt, lame* 4 10

Placed 7 times from 13 starts; frustrating now & likely to remain so 13

HEATHERTON PARK b.m. 5 El Conquistador - Opt Out by Spartan General H Wellstead

653 23/3 Badbury Rin' (L) MDO 3m 9 G *jmpd poorly, crawld over 6th, u.r.* U -
820 6/4 Charlton Ho' (L) MDN 3m 12 GF *alwys rear, t.o. & p.u. 3 out* P 0
1118 17/4 Hockworthy (L) MDO 3m 14 GS *mstks,prog 9th,chsd wnr 14th,clsng whn ran out 2 out, rjnd* 3 14
1280 27/4 Bratton Down (L) MDO 3m 14 GF *(fav) w.w. prog 12th, ev ch 3 out, wknd nxt, btn 4th whn f last* F -

Headstrong & makes mistakes but shows ability & should win in 97 if settling better 15

HEATHER WOOD br.m. 6 Lighter - Irish Rose by Soldier Rose R Benbow
1995 U(-)

689 30/3 Chaddesley ' (L) MDN 3m 15 G *sn bhnd, t.o. 8th, p.u. 14th* P 0

Rarely seen & no signs of ability 0

HEATHFIELD(USA) b.g. 6 Procida (USA) - Mlle Judy (USA) by Silent Screen (USA) Miss J Galvin
1995 **4(NH),2(NH),5(NH)**

703 30/3 Tranwell (L) RES 3m 7 GS *s.s. last frm 9th, f 14th* F -

A brief appearance of no promise 0

HEAVENLY HOOFER b.g. 13 Dance In Time (CAN) - Heavenly Chord by Hittite Glory Miss E Johnston

400 9/3 Dalston (R) LAD 3m 10 G *2nd early, mstk 5th, lost pl, t.o. 10th, p.u. 3 out* P 0
893 6/4 Whittington (L) LAD 3m 4 F *chsd ldrs to 13th, wknd & t.o. nxt* 3 0

No longer of any account 0

HEDERA HELIX b or br.g. 12 Major Point - Salary by Faberge II Mrs K Sheilds
1995 U(-),P(0),1(10),F(-),U(-)

281 2/3 Clyst St Ma' (L) RES 3m 11 S *ld til f 2nd* F -
445 9/3 Haldon (R) RES 3m 9 S *mid-div, rmndrs 10th, mstk 12th, no ch nxt, p.u. 2 out* P 0
992 8/4 Kingston St' (R) RES 3m 6 F *some prog 12th, wkng whn hit 14th, t.o. & p.u. 2 out* P 0
1139 20/4 Flete Park (R) RES 3m 14 S *sn rear, wll bhnd til p.u. last* P 0
1493 11/5 Holnicote (L) MEM 3m 5 G *not fluent, ld 12th, slght ld til hdd & wknd qckly apr last* 3 0
1591 25/5 Mounsey Hil' (R) RES 3m 15 G *jmpd rght, alwys rear, t.o. & p.u. 15th* P 0

Won a desperate race in 95 & no chance of a repeat 0

HEDLEY MILL b.m. 8 Meadowbrook - Hope Of Oak by Leander J W Hope
1995 **6(NH),7(NH),4(NH)**

50 4/2 Alnwick (L) CON 3m 9 G *(fav) hld up, prog 12th, mstk nxt, ld 2 out, v easily* 1 23
113 17/2 Lanark (R) OPE 3m 6 GS *(fav) alwys handy, 2nd 4 out, ld apr 2 out, sn clr* 1 27
359 4/3 Doncaster (L) HC 2m 3f 110yds 10 G *waited with, imp to go handy before 4 out, effort next, 3rd and one pace when badly hmpd by faller and u.r. 2 out.* U 28
790 1/4 Kelso (L) HC 3m 1f 11 GF *(fav) patiently rdn, hdwy 5 out, ld briefly last, ridden and not qckn run-in, broke down.* 3 28

Chase winner; very useful pointer; quickens; best at easy 3m; real problem last start; G/S-G/F 28

HEHAS b.g. 6 True Song - Shewill by Evening Trial Mrs E C Cockburn

439 9/3 Newton Brom' (R) MDN 3m 7 GS *alwys rear, bhnd whn p.u. 16th* P 0
689 30/3 Chaddesley ' (L) MDN 3m 15 G *rear of main grp, prog to 5th 4 out, styd on, nvr nrr* 2 14
1104 14/4 Guilsborough (L) MDN 3m 18 G *(fav) alwys prom, ld apr 3 out, styd on well und pres* 1 15

1239 27/4 Clifton On ' (L) RES 3m 9 GF *w.w., going wll 12th, outpcd nxt, no imp on ldrs 4 out* 5 11
1436 6/5 Ashorne (R) MEM 3m 7 G *rear, t.o. & rdn 12th,ran on 15th,chsd wnr 2 out,nrst fin* 2 16

Improved to win modest race; below best after; should improve; stays; Restricted likely; Good 17

HE IS ch.g. 6 Gunner B - Barvadel by Le Bavard (FR) T Hamlin
1995 4(11)
207 24/2 Castle Of C' (R) MDO 3m 15 HY *rear, prog 12th, ev ch 2 out, no ext, promising* 3 12
555 17/3 Ottery St M' (L) MDO 3m 15 G *hld up,prog 14th,cls 3rd & blnd 3 out,hld whn lft in ld last* 1 15

Fortunate winner but improving each run & scope for more if ready 97; Restricted likely 16

HEKNOWYOU(IRE) b.g. 8 Remainder Man - Kilbride Lady VI Mrs Lynn Campion
1155 20/4 Whittington (L) MDN 3m 14 G *ld thruout, ran on whn chal 2 out* 1 14
1585 25/5 Cartmel (L) HC 3 1/4m 14 GF *ld to 2nd, cl up till blnd 4 out and next, weakening when f last.* F -

Impressed when winning but out of his depth other start; Restricted likely if ready 97; Good 17

HELLBRUNN ch.g. 10 Hotfoot - Midnight Music by Midsummer Night II N R J Bell
1995 U(-)
897 6/4 Dingley (R) CON 3m 15 GS *s.s., mid-div frm 11th, outpcd 6 out* 6 10
1376 5/5 Dingley (R) MEM 3m 7 GF *ld 2-5th, cls up til outpcd 3 out, kpt on agn apr last* 3 10

Very lightly raced & 3rd in terrible race - no prospects of a win 10

HELLCATMUDWRESTLER b.g. 15 Tumble Wind (USA) - Fairy Books by King's Leap Henry Bell
1995 4(12),P(0),**U(-)**,2(19),2(21),U(-),3(0),**10(0)**
827 6/4 Stainton (R) LAD 3m 7 GF *jmpd lft, ld til jnd 2 out, hdd last, kpt on well* 2 20
1132 20/4 Hornby Cast' (L) LAD 3m 9 G *raced solo for 10 fences, unchal* 1 0
1283 27/4 Easingwold (L) LAD 3m 10 G *ld til jnd 7th, disp 10th til wknd bef 2 out* 4 18
1449 6/5 Witton Cast' (R) LAD 3m 10 G *cls up, disp ld 4th til wknd 13th, rear whn p.u. 3 out* P 0
1465 11/5 Easingwold (L) MEM 3m 4 G *(fav) j.w. ld to 6th & frm 9th, lft clr 14th, unchal* 1 16

Game old stick who retired on the right note 19

HELUVA BATTLE b.g. 13 Battlement - Helset D H Llewellyn
1995 9(0),U(-),F(-),3(13),2(0)
157 17/2 Erw Lon (L) CON 3m 15 G *mid-div, 6th at 13th, onepcd aft* 6 0
547 17/3 Erw Lon (L) OPE 3m 10 GS *ld til u.r. 9th* U -
767 31/3 Pantyderi (R) INT 3m 7 G *ld 4-9th, outpcd aft 4 out* 5 0

Has not won for 7 years & sure to extend the sequence if running in 97 10

HELUVA SEASON b.m. 14 High Season - Helset Mrs Susan L Stratton
40 3/2 Wadebridge (L) LAD 3m 5 GF *ld to 2nd, p.u. aft 4th, lame* P 0

Of no account 0

HENBITS DREAM (Irish) — **I** 43[4], **I** 64[2], **I** 290[P]

HENCEYEM(IRE) ch.g. 8 Fine Blade (USA) - What Vision by Golden Vision David F Smith
79 11/2 Wetherby Po' (L) MDO 3m 12 GS *(fav) mid-div, 5th at 12th, fdd, p.u. 4 out* P 0
415 9/3 Charm Park (L) MDO 3m 13 G *mid-div, prog 11th, 4th 2 out, no extr* 4 0
757 31/3 Great Stain' (L) MEM 3m 5 GS *(fav) last & outpcd frm 8th, rdn hlfwy, sn t.o., p.u. 14th* P 0

Good stable but well beaten on only completion; expensive to follow; best watched 10

HENDORA(IRE) b.m. 5 Henbit (USA) - Araglin Dora by Green Shoon D L Claydon
830 6/4 Marks Tey (L) MDN 3m 14 G *in tch to 12th, wll in rear whn p.u. 16th* P 0
1063 13/4 Horseheath (R) MDO 3m 5 F *ld 2nd-nxt, prom til wknd 13th, p.u. nxt* P 0

No signs of any real ability yet 0

HENFIELD b.g. 12 Henbit (USA) - Dingle Bay by Petingo G G Tawell
1995 P(0),1(0),P(0),11(0),9(0),P(0)
433 9/3 Newton Brom' (R) MEM 3m 3 GS *ld/disp til mstk 11th, 12l 2nd nxt, lft clr 3 out* 1 0
1239 27/4 Clifton On ' (L) RES 3m 9 GF *mstks, raced wd, rear, outpcd 13th, kpt on* 6 0
1402 6/5 Northaw (L) RES 3m 5 F *alwys bhnd, mstk 7th, lst tch 14th, t.o.* 5 0
1501 11/5 Kingston Bl' (L) RES 3m 10 G *in tch til lost plc & mstk 6th, sn bhnd, t.o. & p.u. last* P 0

Bumbled home to complete Members double but of no account in proper races 10

HENLEYDOWN (Irish) — **I** 6[P]

HENNERWOOD OAK b.m. 6 Lighter - Welsh Log by King Log Cyril Thomas
1995 **4(NH),P(NH),F(NH),2(NH),F(NH),4(NH),U(NH),5(NH),U(NH),F(NH),4(NH),5(NH)**
213 24/2 Newtown (L) MEM 3m 7 GS *mstk 7th, prom til wknd 11th, sn t.o., p.u. 2 out* P 0
697 30/3 Llanvapley (L) MDN 3m 11 GS *ld & clr to 14th, wknd & hdd nxt, scrambld over last* 3 0
1044 13/4 Bitterley (L) MDO 3m 15 G *ld to 4th & frm 9th, jnd 13th, ev ch whn f 15th* F -
1315 28/4 Bitterley (L) MDO 3m 10 G *made all & sn clr, j.w. kpt on frm 3 out* 1 15

1411 6/5 Cursneh Hill (L) CON 3m 5 GF *ld 2nd-5th & 10-12th, wknd frm nxt, p.u. last* P 0
1481 11/5 Bredwardine (R) RES 3m 14 G *ld 2nd til hdd & wknd aft 15th* 5 12
1614 27/5 Hereford (R) HC 3m 1f 110yds 16 G *nvr far away, cl 3rd when blnd and u.r. 14th.* U -

Went clear to win modest Maiden but non-stayer & Restricted needs luck; hard career already; Good .. 15

HENRY DARLING b.g. 10 Tudorville - Custard by Darling Boy — Mrs B F Abraham

238 25/2 Southwell P' (L) MDO 3m 9 HO *ld, lft clr 13th, hmpd by loose horse & hdd last, no ext* 2 14
397 9/3 Garthorpe (R) MDN 3m 9 G *(fav) ld to 6 out, chsd ldr, in tch whn blnd 2 out, eased* 3 10
540 17/3 Southwell P' (L) MDO 3m 9 GS *(fav) hld up mid-div, smooth prog to ld 13th, ran on well 3 out* 1 15
723 31/3 Garthorpe (R) CON 3m 19 G *alwys rear, 10th hlfwy, no prog* 9 0
1518 12/5 Garthorpe (R) MEM 3m 6 GF *(Jt fav) chsd ldr, mostly 2nd, cls up but lkd hld whn f 2 out* F -

Missed 95; won modest Maiden; may have Restricted chances on right ground at 11; G/S-Hy 15

HENRYMYSON b.g. 8 Sunyboy - Toumanova by High Line — R Tate

371 8/3 Ayr (L) HC 2m 5f 110yds 8 GF *blnd and u.r. 3rd.* U -
488 16/3 Newcastle (L) HC 2 1/2m 9 GS *in tch, struggling before 6 out, soon btn.* 5 0

Very lightly raced & out of his depth in H/Chases 0

HENRY VAJRA b.g. 9 Henricus (ATA) - Vulganizer by Eborneezer — Mrs H M Bridges

1995 5(0),1(14),3(15),P(0),4(0),5(15)

65 10/2 Great Treth' (R) INT 3m 13 S *alwys bhnd, p.u. 2 out* P 0
140 17/2 Larkhill (R) CON 3m 17 G *prom, ld & tk cmmnd 2 out, ran on well* 1 21

Maiden winner 95; improved to win moderate Confined, then vanished; best watched early 97; G-S 19

HENSUE b.g. 7 Henricus (ATA) - Sue Ming Vii — Miss P J Boundy

1995 3(12),3(10),2(13),4(12),1(16),2(0)

138 17/2 Ottery St M' (L) RES 3m 18 GS *mid-div, no ch whn p.u. 3 out* P 0
280 2/3 Clyst St Ma' (L) RES 3m 11 S *(Co fav) rear, prog 12th, wknd 15th, t.o. & p.u. 3 out* P 0
650 23/3 Cothelstone (L) RES 3m 5 S *trckd ldr, ld aftr 3 out, rddn clr 2 out* 1 19
925 8/4 Bishopsleigh (R) CON 3m 6 G *wll bhnd til rppd hdwy 3 out, nvr nrr* 2 19
1080 13/4 Cothelstone (L) XX 3m 2 GF *(fav) made all, 4l clr 15th, easily* 1 16
1499 11/5 Holnicote (L) CON 3m 8 G *wnt 3rd 14th, rddn & disp 2nd apr 2 out, onepcd* 3 15
1553 18/5 Bratton Down (L) XX 3m 10 F *prog 7th, 4th at 16th, disp 2nd aft 3 out til wknd apr last* 3 15
1587 25/5 Mounsey Hil' (R) MEM 3m 7 G *(fav) cls up, blnd 3rd, disp 7th til blnd 16th, onepcd aft* 2 14

Maiden winner 95; genuine but onepaced; won weak races 96; should find another chance; F-S 18

HERB SUPERB (Irish) — **I** 300F, **I** 395P, **I** 481P

HERE COMES CHARTER b.g. 11 Le Moss - Windtown Fancy by Perspex — E Pennock

80 11/2 Wetherby Po' (L) MDO 3m 12 GS *ld to 5th, in tch to 4 out, outpcd* 5 0
224 24/2 Duncombe Pa' (R) RES 3m 12 GS *rear of main grp, steady prog to 3rd 15th, kpt on* 3 12
517 16/3 Dalton Park (R) MDO 3m 10 G *ld, qcknd 16th, hdd last, no ext flat* 2 13
764 31/3 Great Stain' (L) MDN 3m 16 GS *chsd ldng grp, rdn 13th, sn wknd, t.o.* 6 0
982 8/4 Charm Park (L) MEM 3m 3 GF *(fav) ld & made all, eased apr line* 1 13
1131 20/4 Hornby Cast' (L) RES 3m 17 G *keen hld, nvr bttr than mid-div, wknd 14th, t.o. & p.u. 3out* P 0

Disappointing under Rules; won poor Members; unlikely to win Restricted 13

HERE'S HUMPHREY b.g. 7 Le Moss - Bucketful by Brave Invader (USA) — J M Valdes-Scott

30 20/1 Higham (L) MEM 3m 4 GF *last whn ref & u.r. 2nd* R -
105 17/2 Marks Tey (L) RES 3m 11 G *ref 1st* R -
496 16/3 Horseheath (R) MDO 3m 10 GF *last whn ref 1st, cont, ref 2nd* R -

A complete waste of time, so far 0

HERE'S MARY b.m. 12 Amoristic (USA) - Pitpans Star by Pitpan — J F R Chapple

132 17/2 Ottery St M' (L) MDN 3m 9 GS *alwys bhnd, lost tch 10th* 4 0
282 2/3 Clyst St Ma' (L) MDN 3m 8 S *ld to 11th, in tch til wknd 13th, p.u. 3 out* P 0
558 17/3 Ottery St M' (L) MDO 3m 9 G *mid-div, out of tch 12th, t.o. & p.u. last* P 0
729 31/3 Little Wind' (R) RES 3m 12 GS *bhnd til p.u. apr 11th* P 0
1143 20/4 Flete Park (R) MDN 3m 17 S *6th at 12th, wknd 15th, t.o. & p.u. last* P 0
1277 27/4 Bratton Down (L) CON 3m 15 GF *cls up, 7th at 12th, outpcd 14th, t.o. & p.u. 3 out* P 0
1348 4/5 Holnicote (L) MDO 3m 9 GS *alwys well bhnd* 4 0
1530 12/5 Ottery St M' (L) MDO 3m 8 GF *mstk 6th, rear & rmndrs 11th, wll btn frm 15th* 3 0
1554 18/5 Bratton Down (L) MDO 3m 16 F *mid-div, 8th whn mstk 14th, no ch clsng stgs* 7 0

Well beaten when finishing & an old maid now 0

HERHORSE ch.m. 9 Royal Vulcan - Ditchling Beacon by High Line — Miss A Howard-Chappell

1995 R(-),P(0)

556 17/3 Ottery St M' (L) MDO 3m 15 G *handy to 13th, lost plc nxt, ran on agn frm 2 out* 4 11
876 6/4 Higher Kilw' (L) MDN 3m 11 GF *rear whn mstk 8th, p.u. nxt* P 0
1143 20/4 Flete Park (R) MDN 3m 17 S *prog to 6th at 14th,hit 17th,6l 2nd whn ran wd & p.u.2out* P 0

1362 4/5 Flete Park (R) MDO 3m 9 G *(bl) cls 4th at 10th, ran wd & plld herself up apr 11th* P 0

Some ability on only completion but a real madam & best avoided 0

HERIOT WATER(IRE) b.m. 7 Ovac (ITY) - Skillet by Fray Bentos Mrs C T Forber

286 2/3 Eaton Hall (R) MDO 3m 14 G *mid to rear, p.u. 11th* P 0
1033 13/4 Alpraham (R) MDO 2 1/2m 15 GS *last pair in rear, t.o. 4th, p.u. 8th* P 0
1196 21/4 Sandon (L) MDN 3m 17 G *p.u. aft 2nd* P 0

Slow & unpromising 0

HERMES HARVEST b.g. 8 Oats - Swift Messenger by Giolla Mear Miss B W Palmer

1995 **4(18),R(NH),F(-),2(29),1(30),2(31),1(29),1(32)**

362 5/3 Leicester (R) HC 2 1/2m 110yds 8 GS *(Jt fav) reminders 3rd, bhnd and pushed along 7th, blnd 11th, styd on from 3 out, not reach ldrs.* 3 21
483 14/3 Cheltenham (L) HC 3 1/4m 110yds 17 G *(vis) cl up when f 12th.* F -
808 6/4 Towcester (R) HC 3m 1f 4 F *alwys in tch, ld 3 out, pushed clr.* 1 33
1108 17/4 Cheltenham (L) HC 4m 1f 14 GS *not fluent, held up, hdwy 11th, mstk 4 out, ld apr 2 out, hdd before last, no ext.* 2 32
1584 24/5 Towcester (R) HC 3m 1f 11 GS *(fav) held up, hdwy 11th, pushed along after 5 out, ld 2 out, driven clr run-in.* 1 31
1631 1/6 Stratford (L) HC 3 1/2m 14 GF *(vis) held up bhnd ldrs, blnd 15th, rdn 17th, soon btn.* 4 25

Very useful H/Chaser; hard ride; best form late season; stays well; sure to win more; G/S-F 33

HEY CHIEF (Irish) — **I** 345P, **I** 421P, **I** 500F, **I** 557P

HEY HENRY b.g. 6 Hey Romeo - Whichford Lass by Indian Ruler Mrs N A Hedges

1995 P(0),P(0),4(0),5(0)

28 20/1 Barbury Cas' (L) RES 3m 14 GS *in tch, prog 11th, cls up 3 out, wknd* 4 10
129 17/2 Kingston Bl' (L) MDN 3m 15 GS *(Jt fav) rear, mstk 5th, lost tch 13th, t.o. & p.u. 2 out* P 0

Promise 95 & 1st start 96 but ran badly other outing & disappeared; best watched 11

HEYMOLL (Irish) — **I** 384U, **I** 464U

HICKELTON LAD ch.g. 12 Black Minstrel - Lupreno by Hugh Lupus Miss B W Palmer

1995 **P(NH)**

184 23/2 Haydock (L) HC 3m 9 GS *mstk 1st, in tch, wknd and p.u. before 15th.* P 0
374 9/3 Sandown (R) HC 2 1/2m 110yds 5 GS *chsd ldr, ld 7th till next, wknd apr 2 out.* 4 18
579 20/3 Ludlow (R) HC 2 1/2m 17 G *prom, mstk and lost pl 5 out, rallied 2 out, styd on to ld final 50 yards.* 1 20
908 8/4 Hereford (R) HC 2m 3f 12 GF *held up, hit 1st, mstks 3rd, f next.* F -

Moddest at best & fortunate when winning; best at 2 1/2m; prospects at 13 unappealing; Good 18

HIDDEN DOLLAR ch.g. 12 Buckskin (FR) - Famous Lady by Prefairy G Heal

1424 6/5 High Bickin' (R) MEM 3m 4 G *jmp wll, ld/disp til ld 14th, drew clr apr last* 1 13

Returned after 4 years absence to dot up in Members; same again 97?; G-S 15

HIDDEN PLAY (Irish) — **I** 177P

HIGH BURNSHOT br.g. 9 Cardinal Flower - Andonian by Road House II Mrs G M Gladders

1995 F(-),3(0),**6(NH)**

57 10/2 Cottenham (R) LAD 3m 9 GS *hmpd & u.r. 1st* U -
106 17/2 Marks Tey (L) RES 3m 12 G *pllng, ld, sn clr, blnd 10th, sn hdded & wknd, p.u. 12th* P 0
275 2/3 Parham (R) MDN 3m 15 GF *mid-div whn ran out 5th* r -
575 17/3 Detling (L) MDO 3m 10 GF *lft in ld 3rd, dist clr 10th, 20l up whn f 3 out* F -
921 8/4 Aldington (L) MDO 3m 8 F *(fav) plld to ld 2nd,stdd & hdd 11th,ld aft 2 out,sn clr,wll rdn* 1 15
1295 28/4 Bexhill (R) RES 3m 7 F *ld til f 2nd* F -
1442 6/5 Aldington (L) RES 3m 7 HD *pulld into ld 2nd, sn clr, stead & hdd 11th, ld & f 2 out* F 15
1540 16/5 Folkestone (R) HC 2m 5f 10 G *whipped round start, pulld hrd, led 3rd, mstk next, f 8th.* F -

Tearaway; brilliantly ridden to win bad Maiden; not for those of nervous disposition; G/F-Hd 13

HIGH CHARGES (Irish) — **I** 137P, **I** 213P

HIGH DEGREE b or br.g. 8 Superlative - St Colette by So Blessed Mrs Sarah Adams

1995 P(0),P(0),1(15),P(0),**7(0),11(0),P(0)**

41 3/2 Wadebridge (L) XX 3m 9 GF *prom to 11th, eff agn 15th, 3rd & btn whn blndrd last* 5 13
68 10/2 Great Treth' (R) RES 3m 14 S *nvr dang, p.u. aft 14th* P 0
197 24/2 Lemalla (R) LAD 3m 13 HY *nvr on terms, p.u. 2 out* P 0
716 30/3 Wadebridge (L) LAD 3m 6 GF *last but in tch whn u.r. 5th (ditch)* U -

Won short Maiden 95; does not stay 3m & hard to see another win 13

HIGHEST CALL (Irish) — **I** 5592

HIGHGATE MILD br.g. 11 Homeboy - Lady Jewel by Kibenka A R Hunt

1995 1(17),6(11)

248	25/2 Charing	(L) RES	3m	12 GS	*cls up, ld 15th, rdn 3 out, hld on gamely*	1	18
368	6/3 Lingfield	(L) HC	3m	7 S	*trckd ldrs, went 3rd after 6 out, wknd after 5 out, t.o..*	4	0
638	23/3 Siddington	(L) CON	3m	16 S	*chsd ldr, rddn to ld 3 out- nxt,2l dwn & hld whn f last,dead*	F	-

Dead **19**

HIGH HAM BLUES b.g. 14 White Prince (USA) - Gwentello by Cock Of The North — Mrs Christine Hardinge

1995 2(10),7(13)

215	24/2 Newtown	(L) OPE	3m	20 GS	*mid-div, no ch frm 13th, p.u. nxt*	P	0
349	3/3 Garnons	(L) MEM	3m	4 GS	*2nd til ld 11th, jnd 2 out, kpt on und pres whn hdd flat*	2	15

Rarely seen now; not disgraced in 2 finisher Members - only chance again at 15 .... **13**

HIGH HANDED(IRE) ch.g. 5 Roselier (FR) - Slaney Pride by Busted — T H Caldwell

1033	13/4 Alpraham	(R) MDO	2 1/2m	15 GS	*ld 6th til ran out thru wing 8th*	r	-
1196	21/4 Sandon	(L) MDN	3m	17 G	*mid-div, prog to 4th going wll whn ran out bnd apr 5 out*	R	-
1364	4/5 Gisburn	(R) MDO	3m	11 G	*rear whn hmpd & f 6th*	F	-

A little promise but plenty of steering problems so far **10**

HIGHLAND ARK (Irish) — **I** 31²

HIGHLAND BOUNTY b.g. 12 High Line - Segos by Runnymede — F R Jackson

249	25/2 Charing	(L) XX	3m	11 GS	*prom til jmpd slwly 10th, bhnd whn p.u. 14th*	P	0
271	2/3 Parham	(R) CON	3m	15 GF	*rear, some prog 8th, wknd 13th, bhnd whn p.u. 2 out*	P	0
450	9/3 Charing	(L) XX	3m	8 G	*f 5th in rear*	F	-
594	23/3 Parham	(R) CON	3m	13 GS	*alwys rear, rmndrs hlfwy, wll bhnd whn p.u. 13th*	P	0
963	8/4 Heathfield	(R) MXO	3m	7 G	*ld into start, in tch, blnd 13th, sn rdn & btn, p.u. 2 out*	P	0
1050	13/4 Penshurst	(L) CON	3m	8 G	*(vis) s.s. sn prom, 5th whn f 12th*	F	-
1444	6/5 Aldington	(L) OPE	3m	6 HD	*(bl) prom, rmmndrs 11th, feeling pce 3 out, wknd last*	4	15

Winning hurdler; ran reasonably last start but not threatening to win a point **12**

HIGHLAND BUCK (Irish) — **I** 112ᴾ, **I** 166ᴾ, **I** 179ᴾ, **I** 281ᶠ, **I** 321³, **I** 404ᵁ, **I** 451ᴾ, **I** 563ᴾ

HIGHLAND CALL (Irish) — **I** 354ᶠ, **I** 640,

HIGHLAND CHASE ch.g. 7 Kaytu - Thetford Chase by Relkino — M J Jackson

1995 P(0),**8(NH)**

842	6/4 Maisemore P'	(L) MDN	3m	17 GF	*chsd ldr 7th, lft in ld 11th-nxt, wknd 15th*	5	0
1234	27/4 Weston Park	(L) MDO	3m	13 G	*ld to 6th, lost tch 12th, fdd, p.u. 2 out*	P	0
1485	11/5 Bredwardine	(R) MDO	3m	15 G	*ld 1st, cls up til wknd 13th, p.u. 15th*	P	0

Beaten 25l when completing & needs more stamina **0**

HIGHLAND FRIEND ch.g. 8 Highlands - Friendly Wonder by Be Friendly — Henry Bell

1995 **6(NH),P(NH)**

308	2/3 Great Stain'	(L) MDO	3m	12 GS	*prom, outpcd 2 out, styd on onepcd aft*	4	11
589	23/3 Wetherby Po'	(L) MDO	3m	16 S	*(Jt fav) handy, ld 13th-4 out, styd on apr last, ld flat*	1	13
825	6/4 Stainton	(R) RES	3m	7 GF	*alwys abt same plc, not pace to chal*	4	12
1093	14/4 Whitwell-On'	(R) MXO	4m	19 G	*prom, disp 13th-16th, rallied to ld last, jnd fin,plcd 1st*	1	22
1340	4/5 Hexham	(L) HC	3m 1f	13 S	*in tch, effort before 3 out, soon btn.*	7	0
1573	19/5 Corbridge	(R) OPE	3m	12 G	*(bl) bhnd, prog 14th, styd on wll frm 2 out, not rch ldrs flat*	3	21
1630	31/5 Stratford	(L) HC	3 1/2m	16 GF	*(bl) in tch, mstk 15th, soon wknd, t.o. when p.u. before 3 out.*	P	0

Stays very well but very onepaced; ran well with blinkers; hard to place 96 - Open possible; G-S **20**

HIGHLAND LAIRD b.g. 12 Kampala - Bonny Hollow by Wolver Hollow — H Hill

1995 4(11),P(0),3(10),4(0),7(0),F(-),P(0),2(12),3(10)

54	10/2 Cottenham	(R) MEM	3m	3 GS	*ld to 5th, last & rdn 11th, sn lost tch*	2	0
96	11/2 Ampton	(R) XX	3m	11 GF	*in tch til outpcd 15th, no ch 17th*	5	0
310	2/3 Ampton	(R) CON	3m	13 G	*b.d. 3rd*	B	-
675	30/3 Cottenham	(R) MEM	3m	6 GF	*chsd wnr to til mstk 14th, went 2nd agn last, no ch*	2	11
970	8/4 Thorpe Lodge	(L) LAD	3m	6 GF	*4th, disp 3rd 11th-4 out, 4th agn & outpcd nxt*	4	0
1256	27/4 Cottenham	(R) MEM	3m	6 F	*alwys rear, mstks 2nd & 4th, strgglng 7th, t.o. 12th,f 4 out*	F	-

Very modest; usually goes well in Members (plenty of chances); not likely to win again now **11**

HIGHLAND MINSTREL b.f. 9 Black Minstrel - Quefort by Quayside — D J Miller

770	31/3 Pantyderi	(R) RES	3m	9 G	*nvr bttr than mid-div*	4	14
975	8/4 Lydstep	(L) MDO	3m	9 G	*(fav) prom to 10th, fdd, p.u. 2 out*	P	0
1200	21/4 Lydstep	(L) MDN	3m	10 S	*prom, ld 3 out, rdn out*	1	13
1266	27/4 Pyle	(R) RES	3m	10 G	*(fav) went 3l 3rd 13th, ld on inner 3 out, wknd aft nxt*	3	12

Won modest Maiden & may struggle to stay; well-ridden; Restricted may prove difficult; G-S **14**

HIGHLAND MISS gr.m. 6 Highlands - Umtali by Boreen (FR) — Mrs J Waggott

1285	27/4 Easingwold	(L) MDO	3m	9 G	*rear, t.o. 8th, p.u. aft 10th*	P	0
1450	6/5 Witton Cast'	(R) MDO	3m	14 G	*pulld hrd, cls up til wknd 10th, ran out nxt*	r	-

No encouragement & wrong signs 2nd start 0

HIGHLAND RALLY(USA) b.g. 9 Highland Blade (USA) - Fast Trek (FR) by Trepan (FR) — M W Ingle
1995 **6(NH),2(NH),6(NH)**

107 17/2 Marks Tey (L) MDN 3m 15 G *(fav) made all, drw wll clr frm 14th, drvn along frm 2 out* 1 18
489 16/3 Horseheath (R) MEM 3m 4 GF *(fav) rear, blnd & nrly u.r. 1st, mstk & u.r. 4th* U -

Placed in novice chases; romped home in good time; novice ridden other start; Restricted if fit 97 17

HIGHLAND RIVER b.m. 9 Salmon Leap (USA) - Sigtrudis by Sigebert — A Kane

755 31/3 Lockerbie (R) MDN 3m 17 G *nvr bttr then midfld* 5 0

Well beaten but conceivably could do better 10

HIGHLAND ROMANCE b.m. 7 Highlands - Lunar Romance by Julio Mariner — A M F Liegaux
1995 R(-),5(0),U(-)

576 17/3 Detling (L) MDN 3m 18 GF *rear til p.u. 15th* P 0

No signs of ability 0

HIGHLEEZE(IRE) ch.g. 6 Avocat - Cheramble by Wrekin Rambler — Mrs J Boucher
1995 2(13),1(16)

28 20/1 Barbury Cas' (L) RES 3m 14 GS *(fav) hld up, in tch in rear whn f 10th* F -
138 17/2 Ottery St M' (L) RES 3m 18 GS *(fav) mid-div, hmprd & u.r. 7th* U -
822 6/4 Charlton Ho' (L) RES 3m 7 GF *(Jt fav) mid-div,rmmndrs 7th,4th 12th,rddn nxt,f hvly 14th (dead)* F -

Dead 18

HIGH LUCY b.m. 8 Reformed Character - High Jean by Arrigle Valley — E F B Monck
1995 P(0)

21 20/1 Barbury Cas' (L) MEM 3m 16 GS *mstk 5th, alwys bhnd, t.o. & p.u. 13th* P 0

No sign of ability from 2 starts 95-6 0

HIGHLY DECORATED b.g. 11 Sharpo - New Ribbons by Ribero — Mrs C E Van Praagh
1995 **6(NH),4(NH),P(NH),3(NH)**

251 25/2 Charing (L) OPE 3m 10 GS *mid-div, chsd wnr frm 12th, fdd 3 out, p.u. nxt* P 0
451 9/3 Charing (L) OPE 3m 11 G *in tch til wknd 4 out, p.u. 2 out* P 0
963 8/4 Heathfield (R) MXO 3m 7 G *mstks, prom til lst pl & rmdrs 7th, bhnd frm 14th,p.u. 3 out* P 0
1209 21/4 Heathfield (R) OPE 3m 5 F *(bl) wth wnr to 10th, chal 16th, wknd apr 3 out* 2 13
1372 4/5 Peper Harow (L) OPE 3m 6 F *(bl) made most to 6th, lst pl & rmdrs 10th, no ch whn p.u. 15th* P 0

Chase winner 94; short on stamina; placed in slowly run race; no real prospects 13

HIGH MILL ch.g. 6 Primitive Rising (USA) - Cessy by Burglar — Mrs S J Gospel

518 16/3 Dalton Park (R) MDO 3m 15 G *t.o. last whn p.u. 4th* P 0
987 8/4 Charm Park (L) MDN 3m 13 GF *bhnd early, lost tch & p.u. 10th* P 0
1095 14/4 Whitwell-On' (R) MDO 2 1/2m 88yds 14 G *alwys rear, t.o. & p.u. 10th* P 0
1137 20/4 Hornby Cast' (L) MDN 3m 13 G *rear, prog 13th, ev ch nxt, sn wknd, p.u. 2 out* P 0

Showed a spark last outing but needs to do much more 0

HIGH PARK LADY (Irish) — **I** 77^{P}, **I** 142^{F}, **I** 279^{P}, **I** 434^{P}, **I** 610^{2}

HIGH REVS b.g. 12 Revlow - Pintary by Military — F S Harvey

1295 28/4 Bexhill (R) RES 3m 7 F *mstks, alwys rear, t.o. & p.u. aft 11th* P 0

Only 1 run since 94 & looks finished now 0

HIGH STAR (Irish) — **I** 179^{1}, **I** 287^{F}, **I** 316^{1}, **I** 405^{2}, **I** 452^{1}, **I** 491^{1}

HIGHWAY JIM b.g. 11 Dubassoff (USA) - Hilda's Way by Royal Highway — David Staddon
1995 P(0),4(11),1(14),P(0),6(0)

532 16/3 Cothelstone (L) RES 3m 12 G *prom,hit 13th, 4th & blnd bdly 15th, kpt on onpcd aft* 3 14
720 30/3 Wadebridge (L) RES 3m 9 GF *mid-div whn u.r. 6th* U -
992 8/4 Kingston St' (R) RES 3m 6 F *sn prom, 2nd mostly, ev ch til onepcd aft 3 out* 3 16
1077 13/4 Cothelstone (L) RES 3m 2 GF *(fav) made all, mstk 9th, 4l clr 12th, easily* 1 10
1141 20/4 Flete Park (R) LAD 3m 8 S *disp 2nd frm 15th, wkng in 4th whn blnd last* 4 14
1393 6/5 Cotley Farm (L) XX 3m 10 GF *alwys prom, 2nd at 10th, ev ch 3 out, outpcd aft* 3 17
1533 14/5 Chepstow (L) HC 3m 6 F *pulld hrd, prom when hit 9th, wknd next, blnd and u.r. 4 out.* U -

Schoolmaster now; won a match; safe but fortune needed to score again 14

HIGHWAY LAD b.g. 7 Nearly A Hand - Hilda's Way by Royal Highway — M White
1995 **12(NH),8(NH),13(NH)**

470 10/3 Milborne St' (L) MDO 3m 18 G *in tch, ev ch 15th, outpcd frm nxt* 5 12
993 8/4 Kingston St' (R) MDO 3m 17 F *mid-div, swrd & u.r. 7th* U -

No ability under Rules; subsequent winners behind when 5th & should go close if fit in 97 14

HIGHWAYS SISTER (Irish) — I 119⁴, I 150³, I 239⁴, I 335², I 459ᴾ, I 569³, I 640,

HI-JAMIE (Irish) — I 492ᴾ

HIL LADY b.m. 5 Arctic Lord - First Attempt by Proverb — A J Rhead

771	31/3 Pantyderi	(R) MDN 3m	14	G	*t.o. 7th, p.u. 9th*	P	0
976	8/4 Lydstep	(L) MDO 3m	12	G	*in rear, u.r. 12th*	U	-
1034	13/4 St Hilary	(R) MEM 3m	3	G	*cls 3rd to 9th, grad lost tch*	3	0

Tailed off last when completing & unpromising to date 0

HILL FORT(IRE) ch.g. 8 Carlingford Castle - Lismoyney Hill by Giolla Mear — David Pease

1995 P(0),3(14),U(-)

105	17/2 Marks Tey	(L) RES 3m	11 G	*(fav) mid div, rddn 13th, 4th & hd rddn 16th,no prog*	4	0
339	3/3 Heythrop	(R) RES 3m	10 G	*chsd ldrs, rdn 11th, outpcd frm 15th, no ch aft*	5	0
726	31/3 Garthorpe	(R) RES 3m	16 G	*bhnd, 12th & rdn hlfwy, kpt on frm 15th, no dang*	6	12
1101	14/4 Guilsborough	(L) RES 3m	16 G	*prom, lft in ld 13-15th & agn aft nxt-3 out,hrd rdn,onepcd*	3	16
1522	12/5 Garthorpe	(R) RES 3m	12 GF	*(fav) (bl) cls up, ld 8-12th, wknd rpdly, p.u. 3 out*	P	0

Maiden winner 94; disappointing since; blinkers & riding change no help; sold June 96; best watched .. 13

HILL ISLAND br.g. 9 Strong Gale - Affordalot by Fordham (USA) — Colin Gee

1995 F(-),2(19),2(17),2(19),5(11),1(0)

127	17/2 Kingston Bl'	(L) MEM 3m	6 GS	*5s-9/4, nvr going well, bhnd frm 5th, t.o. & p.u. 15th*	P	0
335	3/3 Heythrop	(R) INT 3m	9 G	*outpcd & alwys wll bhnd*	6	0
638	23/3 Siddington	(L) CON 3m	16 S	*in tch til u.r. 6th*	U	-
1098	14/4 Guilsborough	(L) CON 3m	17 G	*alwys prom, lft in ld 14th, hdd 4 out, drvn to ld flat*	1	23
1177	21/4 Mollington	(R) INT 3m	14 F	*(Jt fav) ld to 2nd, made most frm 5th, drew clr last, comf*	1	21
1563	19/5 Mollington	(R) CON 3m	8 GS	*(fav) ld 3rd til aft 3 out, rallied to ld last, all out*	1	23
1594	25/5 Garthorpe	(R) MEM 3m	10 G	*(fav) 2nd til ld 8th, drew away frm 2 out, comf*	1	22

Much improved 2nd half 96; won fair races; harder to place 97; could win Open if retains enthusiasm .. 24

HILL OF GRACE (Irish) — I 439ᴾ, I 457ᴾ

HILLVIEW LAD br.g. 10 Northern Tempest (USA) - Lady Grosvenor by Above Suspicion — Keith Thomas

1995 F(-),F(-)

77	11/2 Wetherby Po'	(L) RES 3m	18 GS	*alwys rear, p.u. 10th*	P	0
225	24/2 Duncombe Pa'	(R) RES 3m	12 GS	*prom to 10th, sn wknd, p.u. 13th*	P	0
461	9/3 Eyton-On-Se'	(L) RES 3m	15 G	*mid to rear, p.u. 5 out*	P	0
664	24/3 Eaton Hall	(R) CON 3m	15 S	*rear whn u.r. 7th*	U	-
891	6/4 Whittington	(L) MEM 3m	6 F	*ld til 6th, ran wd bnds, 2nd 13th, blndrd last*	2	0

Placed Irish Maidens 94; no form in England & Members only hope 97 10

HILLVIEW LIZZIE (Irish) — I 95ᴾ

HILLVIEW STAR(IRE) ch.m. 7 Lord Ha Ha - Wooden Minstrel by Black Minstrel — M F Harding

204	24/2 Castle Of C'	(R) MDO 3m	11 HY	*alwys rear, t.o. & p.u. 3 out*	P	0
352	3/3 Garnons	(L) MDN 2 1/2m	9 GS	*lost tch 7th, lft alone by many fallers*	1	0
805	4/4 Clyst St Ma'	(L) RES 3m	7 GS	*n.j.w. t.o. frm 9th*	4	0

LKeft solo in 9 runner Maiden; follow up looks highly unlikely 10

HILLVIEW SUSIE (Irish) — I 257ᴾ, I 319ᴾ, I 408ᶠ, I 490ᴾ

HILTON MILL (Irish) — I 17ᴾ, I 171ᴾ, I 315ᴮ

HILTONSTOWN LASS (Irish) — I 95¹, I 170ᴾ, I 218², I 287ᵁ, I 490²

HI MARBLE (Irish) — I 578ᶠ, I 604², I 632¹

HIT THE BID(IRE) b.g. 5 Buckskin (FR) - Dont Call Me Lady by Le Bavard (FR) — Peter Bonner

814	6/4 Charing	(L) MDO 2 1/2m	8 F	*rear, schoold, out of tch hlfwy, p.u. 4 out*	P	0
1261	27/4 Cottenham	(R) MDO 3m	10 F	*trckd ldrs, prog to 4th at 12th, mstk nxt,wknd, p.u. 4 out*	P	0

Good stable, schooling so far & should do better 10

HI-WAY'S GALE (Irish) — I 44⁴, I 127¹, I 246⁴, I 295, , I 371²

HIZAL b.g. 7 Afzal - Hi Darlin' by Prince de Galles — H J Manners

1995 P(0),U(-),3(11),2(10),F(-),1(13),**F(-),6(16),10(NH),P(NH),6(NH),U(NH),4(NH),2(NH),2(NH)**

377	9/3 Barbury Cas'	(L) OPE 3m	5 GS	*sn bhnd, nvr a fctr*	3	11
707	30/3 Barbury Cas'	(L) RES 3m	18 G	*mid-div, went 3rd 2 out, not trble 1st pair*	3	16
960	8/4 Lockinge	(L) RES 3m	9 GF	*(fav) rear early, prog 10th, outpcd frm 13th, p.u. 4 out*	P	0
1292	28/4 Barbury Cas'	(L) RES 3m	11 F	*wll in rear til gd prog 14th, styd on frm 2 out,tk 2nd fin*	2	16
1534	15/5 Hereford	(R) HC 3m 1f 110yds	4 F	*whipped round start, alwys well bhnd, t.o. when p.u. before 12th.*	P	0
1539	16/5 Folkestone	(R) HC 3m 7f	9 G	*in tch, 5th and rdn when blnd 16th, no ch after, p.u. before last.*	P	0

Maiden winner 95; ran well 4th start but inconsistent; no form in chases; likes Barbury; Firm 16

HOBNOBBER br.g. 9 True Song - Speakalone by Articulate J H Docker

327	3/3	Market Rase'	(L)	CON	3m	15	G	*ld to 10th, wknd apr 14th, p.u. last*	P	0
535	17/3	Southwell P'	(L)	CON	3m	10	GS	*(fav) alwys cls up, ld 11th til hdd nr fin*	2	17
683	30/3	Chaddesley '	(L)	MEM	3m	17	G	*(Jt fav) prog 11th, ld aft 2 out, in cmmnd whn ran out last*	r	22
1098	14/4	Guilsborough	(L)	CON	3m	17	G	*prog & prom 9th,chsd ldng pair 16th,styd on onepcd frm 3 out*	3	21
1456	8/5	Uttoxeter	(L)	HC	2m 5f	11	G	*(fav) cl up, ld apr 4 out, jmpd left next, blnd and hdd last, went left and no ext.*	2	19
1548	18/5	Southwell	(L)	HC	3m 110yds	11	GF	*hdwy 13th, slight ld last, hdd final 25 yards.*	2	19

Missed 95; should have won 4 races but hangs & ungenuine; L/H essential; try blinkers; one to oppose 20

HOD WOOD b.m. 5 Lighter - Pamaris by Pamroy A D Gale

44	3/2	Wadebridge	(L)	MDO	3m	9	GF	*last whn ran out 3rd, rjnd, p.u. aft 4th*	P	0
471	10/3	Milborne St'	(L)	MDO	3m	16	G	*sn rear, t.o. & p.u. 2 out*	P	0

Green, so far 0

HOGAN (Irish) — I 427^{U}, I 586^{P}, I 625^{P}

HOISTTHESTANDARD ch.m. 9 Stanford - Precious Mite by Tambourine II L Stephenson

1995 **12(0)**,P(0)

121	17/2	Witton Cast'	(R)	RES	3m	11	S	*alwys mid to rear, nvr a dang*	7	10
307	2/3	Great Stain'	(L)	MDO	3m	17	GS	*rear whn f 11th*	F	-
416	9/3	Charm Park	(L)	MDO	3m	13	G	*al prom, tk 2nd bfr last, styd on, jst btn*	2	13
762	31/3	Great Stain'	(L)	MDN	3m	11	GS	*(fav) mid-div, fdd hlfwy, t.o. & p.u. 11th*	P	0
1137	20/4	Hornby Cast'	(L)	MDN	3m	13	G	*disp to 14th, lost plc, onepcd aft*	4	0
1285	27/4	Easingwold	(L)	MDO	3m	9	G	*prom, jmpd slwly 3rd, lost plc 8th, blnd 13th, s.u. 2 out*	S	-
1451	6/5	Witton Cast'	(R)	MDO	3m	12	G	*(vis) ld 4-14th, grdly wknd aft*	6	0

Placed in 3 of 18 starts 93-6; beaten a length in bad Maiden; still unlikely to win 11

HOLDING THE ACES b.g. 6 Uncle Pokey - Carr-Daile by New Brig G Vergette

1995 **15(NH)**

35	20/1	Higham	(L)	RES	3m	16	GF	*mid-div whn hmpd 13th, nvr trbld ldrs, improve*	5	12
61	10/2	Cottenham	(R)	MDO	3m	8	GS	*(fav) mstks,poor 3rd frm 6th,lft in ld & blnd 15th,hdd & tired aft*	2	0
344	3/3	Higham	(L)	MDO	3m	12	G	*(fav) handy, ev ch in 4th whn f 13th*	F	-
681	30/3	Cottenham	(R)	MDO	3m	12	GF	*ld to 8th, cls 3rd whn f 12th*	F	-
1104	14/4	Guilsborough	(L)	MDN	3m	18	G	*bmpd & u.r. 1st*	U	-
1325	28/4	Fakenham P-'	(L)	MDO	3m	6	G	*ld, mstk 11th, hdd apr 4 out, blnd nxt,5l dwn whn u.r. 2 out*	U	-

Does not stay & jumping is calamitous; expensive to follow & best watched 11

HOLIDAY TIME (Irish) — I 12^{P}, I 335^{F}

HOLLAND HOUSE b.g. 10 Sunyboy - Norma Can by Normandy E Knight

1995 2(28),**U(-)**,2(28),**U(-)**,**2(32)**,**1(34)**

6	13/1	Larkhill	(R)	OPE	3m	18	GS	*trckd ldrs, blnd & u.r. 5th*	U	-
25	20/1	Barbury Cas'	(L)	OPE	3m	14	GS	*(Jt fav) mstk 3rd, rear, lost tch 12th, styd on frm 2 out, no dang*	4	24
99	14/2	Lingfield	(L)	HC	3m	9	HY	*(Jt fav) held up, hdwy after 6th, left in ld apr 10th, clr approaching 3 out, eased run-in.*	1	32
483	14/3	Cheltenham	(L)	HC	3 1/4m 110yds	17	G	*held up, pushed along from 6 out, styd on steadily from 3 out, nvr nrr.*	5	28
669	27/3	Chepstow	(L)	HC	3m	10	S	*held up, hdwy to go 2nd 7th, ld 13th, rdn run-in, just held on.*	1	35
1108	17/4	Cheltenham	(L)	HC	4m 1f	14	GS	*(fav) alwys prom, blnd 1st, ld after 3rd, mstk 12th, hdd 19th, challenging when hit 4 out, led apr last, ran on.*	1	35

High-class H/Chaser; stays extra-well; mistakes; won 4 of last 5; win more; G/F-Hylow best points 35

HOLLOW SUSPICION (Irish) — I 98^{5}, I 179^{P}, I 219^{P}, I 410^{1}

HOLLOW WOOD (Irish) — I 552^{2}

HOLLYBANK BUCK (Irish) — I 481^{3}

HOLLYBUCK (Irish) — I 32^{P}, I 163^{F}, I 196^{P}, I 385^{2}, I 621^{P}

HOLLY FARE b.g. 10 Holly Fern - Last Farewell by Palm Track D Bloomfield

1995 **P(0)**

63	10/2	Great Treth'	(R)	MEM	3m	6	S	*trckd ldrs til ref 7th*	R	-
68	10/2	Great Treth'	(R)	RES	3m	14	S	*2nd outing, bhnd whn p.u. aft 12th*	P	0
199	24/2	Lemalla	(R)	RES	3m	17	HY	*prom to 4th, sn bhnd, p.u. 2 out*	P	0
298	2/3	Great Treth'	(R)	RES	3m	13	G	*bhnd frm hlfwy*	6	0

Maiden winner 93; no form in 5 runs since; can only be watched 0

HOLLY LAKE (Irish) — I 42^{2}, I 85^{1}, I 159^{1}

HOLLY MOSS (Irish) — I 6^{P}, I 58^{3}, I 75^{3}, I 141^{P}, I 184^{P}, I 310^{4}, I 333^{4}

HOLMBY COPSE b.g. 6 Neltino - Truella by True Song C R Saunders

1378 5/5 Dingley (R) MDO 2 1/2m 16 GF *schoold,clsd hlfwy,prog to 3rd apr last,lost action & p.u.* P 0

Good stable & promise in weak Maiden; can do better if all's well 97 13

HOME TO TARA b.g. 12 Prince Tenderfoot (USA) - Gayshuka by Lord Gayle (USA) J Gallagher

641 23/3 Siddington (L) RES 3m 20 S *bhnd frm 11th, p.u appr 15th* P 0
748 31/3 Upper Sapey (R) MDO 3m 11 GS *4th at 14th, strng run frm 2 out, tk 2nd flat* 2 11
1102 14/4 Guilsborough (L) RES 3m 15 G *alwys rear, t.o. last 3 out, p.u. last* P 0

Placed AW Hurdle 89; 2nd in poor Maiden; unlikely to break duck at 13 10

HOMME D'AFFAIRE br.g. 13 Lord Gayle (USA) - French Cracker by Klairon N F Williams

1995 P(0),2(15),P(0),2(17)

214 24/2 Newtown (L) CON 3m 21 GS *prom, chsd ldr 13th-nxt, btn frm nxt* 5 13
350 3/3 Garnons (L) CON 3m 11 GS *trckd ldrs, effrt 14th, outpcd nxt, styd on frm last* 2 17
1314 28/4 Bitterley (L) MEM 3m 13 G *alwys mid-div, styd on onepcd frm 14th* 4 15
1411 6/5 Cursneh Hill (L) CON 3m 5 GF *w.w., efft 14th, chsd wnr frm nxt, alwys held* 2 17
1478 11/5 Bredwardine (R) CON 3m 12 G *mid-div whn u.r. flat bef 3rd* U -
1618 27/5 Chaddesley ' (L) CON 3m 14 GF *rear, effrt & prog 12th, no imp ldrs frm 15th* 4 17

Dual chasing winner 94; placed in 6 of 10 points 95-6 but will do well to win one at 14 15

HONEST EXPRESSION b.m. 6 Lochnager - Singing High by Julio Mariner M Lewis

1995 P(0),P(0),1(12)

224 24/2 Duncombe Pa' (R) RES 3m 12 GS *chsd ldrs til 4th & wkng 3 out* 4 0
306 2/3 Great Stain' (L) INT 3m 12 GS *mid-div, prog 10th, disp 15th, outpcd apr last* 2 17
411 9/3 Charm Park (L) RES 3m 20 G *cls up, 4th at 8th, no ext 14th, p.u. nxt* P 0
758 31/3 Great Stain' (L) RES 3m 17 GS *mid-div, prog to trck ldrs hlfwy, rdn 3 out, onepcd* 4 16
1090 14/4 Whitwell-On' (R) RES 3m 17 G *alwys prom, ld brfly 10th, onepcd frm 3 out* 3 14
1284 27/4 Easingwold (L) RES 3m 14 G *prom, ld 6th, jnd 3 out, hdd nxt, unable qckn* 2 17
1447 6/5 Witton Cast' (R) RES 3m 11 G *cls up, outpcd 14th, midfld whn p.u. 3 out, (lame)* P 0

Maiden winner 95; not disgraced in 96 but problems last start; should win Restricted if fit 97; Good 16

HOOFER SYD b.g. 8 Balinger - Sunny Cottage by Sunyboy Stuart Currie

1995 7(0),4(0),3(0),U(-),3(0)

79 11/2 Wetherby Po' (L) MDO 3m 12 GS *mid-div, 5th at 14th, nvr dang* 5 0

Placed in bad races 95; vanished early 96 & still well short of winning form yet 10

HOOK LINE'N'SINKER b.g. 10 Kabour - Valpolicella by Lorenzaccio Ian McLaughlin

1995 3(14),3(11),3(16),10(0)

579 20/3 Ludlow (R) HC 2 1/2m 17 G *mstk 3rd, alwys in rear, t.o. when p.u. before 2 out.* P 0
837 6/4 Maisemore P' (L) CON 3m 4 GF *cls up, 3rd & blnd 12th, outpcd appr 14th, no dang after* 3 15
1170 20/4 Chaddesley ' (L) CON 3m 9 G *trckd ldr til ld 5th, hdd & wknd 2 out* 3 17
1332 1/5 Cheltenham (L) HC 3m 1f 110yds 11 G *chsd ldrs, reminder 8th, blnd 9th, lost tch 11th, t.o. and p.u. before 3 out.* P 0
1507 12/5 Maisemore P' (L) CON 3m 10 F *w.w. prog to jn wnr 12-14th, rdn & no imp aft 3 out* 2 18
1618 27/5 Chaddesley ' (L) CON 3m 14 GF *rear, rdn 10th, no ch frm 14th* 5 0

Placed in 6 of 8 points 95-6 but not threatening to win; needs easy 3m & fortune to win again 16

HOOTENANY (Irish) — **I** 144P

HOPEFUL DEAL (Irish) — **I** 522P

HOPEFUL GAMBLE (Irish) — **I** 654,

HOPEFULL DRUMMER b or br.g. 7 Sergeant Drummer (USA) - Hopeful Leigh by Flandre II W Westacott

1995 4(10),1(15),1(15)

532 16/3 Cothelstone (L) RES 3m 12 G *hld up, prog 11th, in tch & gng wll whn f 14th* F -
1345 4/5 Holnicote (L) RES 3m 11 GS *ld to 7th, grad lost tch, p.u. 4 out* P 0

Dual winner 95 but problems 96; still young enough to revive & find Restricted; G-F 16

HOPEFULLY TRUE (Irish) — **I** 251F, **I** 372P, **I** 442², **I** 473², **I** 542³, **I** 580, , **I** 606, , **I** 611U

HOPE'S DELIGHT (Irish) — **I** 511P, **I** 588¹

HOPPERDANTE (Irish) — **I** 50P, **I** 63P, **I** 151³, **I** 239¹, **I** 376²

HORACE b.g. 11 True Song - Spartan Daisy by Spartan General Mrs A Vaughan-Jones

1995 P(0),3(11),P(0),5(13),2(20),4(16),2(16),1(16),**5(10)**,U(-)

10 14/1 Cottenham (R) INT 3m 10 G *prom, ld 8th, 6l clr whn f 3 out* F -

Members winner 95; disappeared after fall (would have won) 1st weekend 96 & can only be watched ... 17

HORCUM b or br.g. 11 Sweet Monday - Charlie's Sunshine by Jimsun Mrs Jayne Barton

341 3/3 Heythrop (R) MDN 3m 13 G *wll in tch til 4th & wkng whn f 3 out* F -
440 9/3 Newton Brom' (R) MDN 3m 10 GS *alwys cls up, 2nd 3 out, not qckn* 3 0
1020 13/4 Kingston Bl' (L) MDN 3m 10 G *hld up, prog 10th, chsd wnr 3 out, rdn & no imp aft nxt* 2 11
1183 21/4 Mollington (R) MDN 3m 10 F *in tch in rear, 7th & btn whn p.u. 15th* P 0

1434	6/5	Ashorne	(R)	MDO	3m	15	G	*in tch, clsd 13th, ld aft 2 out, styd on well*	1	16
1501	11/5	Kingston Bl'	(L)	RES	3m	10	G	*chsd ldrs, 4th & in tch 13th, same & btn nxt*	4	11

Did well for his age & deserved win; onepaced; placed, rather than win Restricted, 97; Good 15

HORGANS QUAY VI (Irish) — **I** 157^{P}, **I** 192^{P}, **I** 323^{P}

HORNBLOWER b.g. 9 Noalto - Hot Lips Moll by Firestreak — N J Barrowclough

1995 2(21),2(20),1(22)

163	17/2	Weston Park	(L)	LAD	3m	10	G	*ld to 3rd, in tch wth wnr 6th, onepcd aft*	2	21
291	2/3	Eaton Hall	(R)	LAD	3m	10	G	*ld to 2 out, rallied flat, just hld*	2	23
566	17/3	Wolverhampt'	(L)	LAD	3m	5	GS	*(fav) made all, alwys in cmmnd*	1	19
738	31/3	Sudlow Farm	(R)	LAD	3m	5	G	*(fav) made all, alwys in commd, pushd out flat*	1	22
1232	27/4	Weston Park	(L)	LAD	3m	6	G	*(fav) chsd ldrs, nvr gng wll, cls 3rd whn f 11th*	F	-

Decent Ladies horse; front-runs; best for Carrie Burgess; win more 97; G/S-G/F 23

HORN PLAYER(USA) ch.g. 9 The Minstrel (CAN) - Qualique (USA) by Hawaii — Stephen J Fletcher

1995 P(0),2(15),P(0),P(0),P(0)

98	12/2	Hereford	(R)	HC	3m 1f 110yds	12	HY	*alwys bhnd, t.o. when p.u. before 14th.*	P	0
155	17/2	Erw Lon	(L)	RES	3m	9	G	*prom, chsd wnr 9th-14th, wknd rpdly*	5	0
358	3/3	Garnons	(L)	RES	3m	18	GS	*(bl) chsd ldrs til not qckn aft 12th, no ch frm nxt*	6	0
388	9/3	Llanfrynach	(R)	RES	3m	20	GS	*(bl) mid-div, no ch frm 14th, t.o. & p.u. 2 out*	P	0
695	30/3	Llanvapley	(L)	RES	3m	13	GS	*cls up, 3rd & outpcd 15th, styd on*	2	16
882	6/4	Brampton Br'	(R)	RES	3m	14	GF	*ld to 4th, chsd ldrs, styd on frm 16th, ld flat*	1	16
1219	24/4	Brampton Br'	(R)	CON	3m	9	G	*chsd ldrs til lost pl 12th, no ch frm 15th, kpt on*	3	15
1413	6/5	Cursneh Hill	(L)	INT	3m	6	GF	*prom, ld brfly 8th, rddn & outpcd frm 15th*	3	14
1477	11/5	Bredwardine	(R)	MEM	3m	3	G	*(fav) ld to 14th, rdn & not qckn frm nxt*	3	0

Maiden winner 94; improved 2nd half 96; bare stayer; Confined chances not strong; G/F-S 15

HORTON COUNTRY br.m. 6 Town And Country - Horton Helen by Flatbush — R J Francome

375	9/3	Barbury Cas'	(L)	MDN	3m	14	GS	*schoold, p.u. 14th*	P	0
713	30/3	Barbury Cas'	(L)	MDO	3m	10	G	*mid-div, lost tch 12th, p.u. 4 out*	P	0
956	8/4	Lockinge	(L)	MDN	3m	7	GF	*alwys mid-div, wll bhnd frm 14th, not trbld 1st 2*	3	0
1409	6/5	Hackwood Pa'	(L)	MDO	3m	6	F	*last at 12th, p.u. 2 out*	P	0

Well beaten in bad race; may do better - needs to 0

HORWOOD GHOST gr.g. 12 — A W Congdon

1995 2(18),2(10),P(0),1(19),P(0),1(0)

1427	6/5	High Bickin'	(R)	CON	3m	10	G	*ld, wll clr til hdd & wknd 3 out, lost 3rd nr line*	5	17
1498	11/5	Holnicote	(L)	OPE	3m	5	G	*(fav) ld, hit 2nd, sn clr, slppd up bnd apr 7th*	S	-

Front-running non-stayer; season lasted 5 days 96; Members only real hope now; best L/H; G-F 15

HOSTETLER ch.g. 7 Fit To Fight (USA) - Diana's Bow by Great Nephew — Mrs Sally Norris

1995 **9(NH),10(NH),P(NH),11(NH)**

434	9/3	Newton Brom'	(R)	CON	3m	11	GS	*chsd ldrs to hlfwy, fdd, p.u. 2 out*	P	0
723	31/3	Garthorpe	(R)	CON	3m	19	G	*sn bhnd, 15th & t.o. hlfwy, p.u. 3 out*	P	0
1097	14/4	Guilsborough	(L)	MEM	3m	6	G	*bhnd frm 6th, t.o. 13th*	3	0
1236	27/4	Clifton On '	(L)	CON	3m	8	GF	*rear frm 5th, bhnd frm 12th, t.o.*	5	0
1377	5/5	Dingley	(R)	CON	3m	12	GF	*alwys last pair, t.o. frm 8th*	9	0
1643	2/6	Dingley	(R)	OPE	3m	13	GF	*t.o. 8th, last whn f 11th*	F	-

Winning Irish hurdler; no aptitude for pointing 0

HOT ADVICE(IRE) b.g. 7 Slip Anchor - La Grange by Habitat — Mrs Norma Barge

1995 P(0)

1008	9/4	Flagg Moor	(L)	MDO	2 1/2m	7	G	*w.w., prog 5th, chsd wnr 3 out, sn rdn & btn*	2	0

Beaten 30l only start 96; rarely seen & not worth a rating yet 0

HOTCHPOT (Irish) — **I** 75^{P}

HOT SCENT (Irish) — **I** 76^{F}, **I** 210^{2}, **I** 325^{P}

HOUSELOPE BECK ch.g. 6 Meadowbrook - Hallo Cheeky by Flatbush — F V White

1995 1(13),P(0)

84	11/2	Alnwick	(L)	RES	3m	11	GS	*mstk 4th,chsd ldrs,4th & outpcd 10th,no ch & p.u.15th,dsmntd*	P	0
319	2/3	Corbridge	(R)	RES	3m	16	GS	*mid-div, no ch whn p.u. 2 out*	P	0
403	9/3	Dalston	(R)	RES	3m	11	G	*4th frm 8th, outpcd frm 3 out*	4	0
700	30/3	Tranwell	(L)	LAD	3m	4	GS	*chsd wnr 3rd, outpcd whn f 15th*	F	-
913	8/4	Tranwell	(L)	LAD	3m	7	GF	*tongue-strap, 5l 4th hlfwy, 3rd frm 12th, outpcd 14th*	3	15
1250	27/4	Balcormo Ma'	(R)	LAD	3m	5	GS	*made all, drew clr 2 out*	1	17
1473	11/5	Aspatria	(L)	LAD	3m	7	GF	*chsd ldr apr 12th, rddn to chal apr last, unable to qckn*	2	20
1572	19/5	Corbridge	(R)	LAD	3m	8	G	*(fav) mid-div, prog to 3rd at 13th, cls up whn u.r. 15th*	U	-
1585	25/5	Cartmel	(L)	HC	3 1/4m	14	GF	*in tch, effort 12th, rdn and wknd 3 out.*	4	14

Improved in Ladies; modest form but could improve further; should win again; stays; S-G/F 19

HOWARYA HARRY (Irish) — I 37[4], I 251[3], I 378[F], I 442[3]

HOWARYASUN(IRE) b.g. 8 Derring Rose - Suny Salome by Sunyboy — M R Watkins

26 20/1 Barbury Cas' (L) OPE 3m 12 GS *in tch,lft 2nd 13th,lkd hld til styd on und pres to ld post* 1 21
98 12/2 Hereford (R) HC 3m 1f 110yds 12 HY *(vis) in tch, chsd wnr apr 9th, rdn when f 2 out.* F -
365 5/3 Leicester (R) HC 3m 10 GS *(fav) (vis) alwys going well, chsd ldr 9th, ld 2 out, clr and wandered last, rdn out.* 1 27
485 16/3 Hereford (R) HC 3m 1f 110yds 13 S *(fav) (vis) held up, hdwy 14th, ld last, ran on well.* 1 29
669 27/3 Chepstow (L) HC 3m 10 S *(vis) prom, jmpd badly right 13th, soon rcvred, rdn and wknd 4 out.* 4 18
1121 20/4 Bangor (L) HC 3m 110yds 8 S *(vis) held up, hdwy 11th, went 2nd 14th, outpcd by wnr from 3 out, lost second apr last.* 3 24
1341 4/5 Warwick (L) HC 2 1/2m 110yds 12 GF *(vis) alwys prom, mstk 4 out, ld run-in, styd on strly.* 1 28

Missed 95; very useful but hard ride; best R/H; should win more H/Chases 97; Any 28

HOWAYMAN b.g. 6 Faustus (USA) - Our Mable by Posse (USA) — Dennis Waggott
1995 3(0),1(17),1(16),P(0),1(17)

83 11/2 Alnwick (L) CON 3m 10 GS *(fav) trckd ldrs, ld apr 3 out, sn clr, rdn out flat* 1 19
317 2/3 Corbridge (R) CON 3m 11 GS *(fav) prom, disp 9th, ld 14th, clr 2 out, wkng nr fin* 1 19
612 23/3 Friars Haugh (L) OPE 3m 8 G *2nd hlfwy, ld 15th, pshd out flat* 1 0
1226 25/4 Perth (R) HC 3m 7 S *(fav) in tch, ev ch 15th, weakening when f 3 out.* F -

Capable & won 6 of last 7 points; yet to beat good horses; hard ride; should win more; G-S 23

HOWESSHECUTTING (Irish) — I 233[U], I 302[F], I 483[P]

HOW FRIENDLY ch.g. 6 Gabitat - Bucks Fizz Music by Be Friendly — R J Mansell
1995 P(0),3(12),4(0),1(14),3(0)

836 6/4 Maisemore P' (L) MEM 3m 7 GF *ld, blnd 4th, hdded appr 8th, cls up whn f 10th* F -
1415 6/5 Cursneh Hill (L) RES 3m 11 GF *(fav) ld 1st, alwys prom, not qckn frm 15th, styd on onepce* 2 17
1557 18/5 Bassaleg (R) RES 3m 14 F *prom, chsd ldr & blnd 8th, lost plc rpdly 12th, p.u. 14th* P 0
1603 25/5 Bassaleg (R) LAD 3m 4 GS *ld to 8th, 3rd frm 10th, no ch 3 out* 3 15
1649 8/6 Umberleigh (L) RES 3m 14 GF *hld up, outpcd & wll bhnd 12th, kpt on frm 2 out, nvr dang* 5 14

Maiden winner 95; late to appear 96 but showed fair form twice; could find Restricted 97; G/S-F 16

HOWLEY LAD b.g. 10 Coded Scrap - Rise by Fury Royal — T Jewitt
1995 P(0),P(0),r(-)

263 2/3 Didmarton (L) INT 3m 18 G *s.s. t.o. til u.r. 2nd* U -
428 9/3 Upton-On-Se' (R) RES 3m 17 GS *s.s. t.o. & p.u. 6th* P 0
707 30/3 Barbury Cas' (L) RES 3m 18 G *mid-div whn u.r. 2nd* U -
837 6/4 Maisemore P' (L) CON 3m 4 GF *hld up last, efft 13th, sn strugg, t.o. whn blnd last* 4 0

Of no account 0

HOWLIN' WOLF b.g. 9 Caribo - Lady Norefield by Milan — M Pennell
1995 P(0),3(0),5(10)

462 9/3 Eyton-On-Se' (L) RES 3m 12 G *prom, bd mstk 8th, u.r. 10th* U -
563 17/3 Wolverhampt' (L) XX 3m 4 GS *disp whn ref 4th* R -
664 24/3 Eaton Hall (R) CON 3m 15 S *mid-div, nvr rchd ldrs* 5 0
851 6/4 Sandon (L) MEM 3m 6 GF *(Jt fav) ld to 5th,trckd ldr lft in ld 14th,chal by wnr 3 out,outpcd* 2 0
1030 13/4 Alpraham (R) RES 3m 10 GS *cls up 13th, lost plc & wknd nxt, lft 3rd last* 3 0

Irish Maiden winner 92; beaten in bad Members & has no prospects now 0

HOWS YOUR LUCK (Irish) — I 93[U]

HUCKLEBERRY FRIEND ch.m. 8 Karlinsky (USA) - Katie Too by Amber Light — Mrs M G Howie
1995 P(0),P(0),U(-),3(0)

454 9/3 Charing (L) MDN 3m 10 G *lft in ld 8th, hdd 10th, strgglng aft, t.o. 4 out* 2 0
576 17/3 Detling (L) MDN 3m 18 GF *rear, p.u. 13th* P 0
779 31/3 Penshurst (L) RES 3m 13 GS *cls up, 3rd whn f 8th* F -
813 6/4 Charing (L) XX 3m 5 F *in tch to 3 out, wknd* 4 0

Well beaten when finishing & no prospects 0

HUGLI ch.g. 9 Relkino - Hors Serie (USA) by Vaguely Noble — G Hearse

602 23/3 Howick (L) OPE 3m 11 S *rear, prog to 3rd at 13th, chsd wnr 3 out, no imp* 2 18
978 8/4 Lydstep (L) OPE 3m 6 G *mid-div, p.u. 3 out* P 0
1559 18/5 Bassaleg (R) LAD 3m 4 F *in tch, ev ch 13th, outpcd by 1st pair frm 3 out* 3 14

Winning hurdler; lightly raced & disappointed last start; unlikely to win competitive point; G-F 16

HULLABALOO b.m. 7 Sula Bula - Newtonspirit by Salmonway Spirit — Miss Sophie Harrison

62 10/2 Cottenham (R) MDO 3m 6 GS *ld to 3 out, wknd apr last* 3 10
477 10/3 Tweseldown (R) MDO 3m 15 G *bhnd whn u.r. 9th* U -

Ran passably 1st start & may go closer if fit 97 12

HUM 'N' HAW (Irish) — **I** 466², **I** 644⁶

HUNGRY JACK b.g. 8 Germont - Kale Brig by New Brig — D G Atkinson

1995 3(0),3(0),6(0)

51	4/2 Alnwick	(L) MDO 3m	17	G	*alwys ldng grp, one pace app 3 out*	5	11
308	2/3 Great Stain'	(L) MDO 3m	12	GS	*(fav) mid-div, wkng whn blnd 14th, p.u. 3 out*	P	0
762	31/3 Great Stain'	(L) MDN 3m	11	GS	*prom, ld 3rd, disp 8th, ld agn 13th,hdd 15th,wknd,p.u. flat*	P	0
1136	20/4 Hornby Cast'	(L) MDN 3m	11	G	*hld up, prog 12th, ev ch whn blnd 2 out, not rcvr*	2	14
1286	27/4 Easingwold	(L) MDO 3m	13	G	*ld to 3rd, sn lost plc, outpcd 9th, kpt on frm 4 out*	4	10
1451	6/5 Witton Cast'	(R) MDO 3m	12	G	*ran in sntche,ld to 4th,rear by 11th,styd on 4 out,wknd last*	3	12
1470	11/5 Easingwold	(L) MDO 3m	10	G	*(fav) (bl) prom, ld 8th, disp 11th, hdd 3 out, ld last, ran on strngly*	1	15
1571	19/5 Corbridge	(R) RES 3m	13	G	*mstks, mid-div, wknd & p.u. 2 out*	P	0

Placed 8 times prior to blinkers working the oracle; need to work again for any Restricted hopes 14

HUNTERS CHORUS (Irish) — **I** 292ᶠ, **I** 323²

HUNTING COUNTRY b.h. 12 Wolver Hollow - Drag Line by Track Spare — Miss Tina Hammond

1995 **P(NH)**

1514	12/5 Hexham Poin'	(L) RES 3m	5 HY	*blnd 3rd, lost tch apr 9th, p.u. nxt*	P	0

No longer of any account 0

HUNTSBYDALE b.m. 8 Relkino - Bowery Babe by Tantivy — J R Knight

241	25/2 Southwell P'	(L) MDO 3m	15 HO	*hld up, prog to trck ldrs whn f 14th*	F	-
636	23/3 Market Rase'	(L) MDN 3m	11 GF	*cls up, ld 6 out, in cmmnd whn blnd & u.r. 3 out*	U	-

Missed 95; unfortunate 96 & should make amends if fit 97 14

HUNTSMAN'S LODGE (Irish) — **I** 231ᴾ

HURRICANE EDEN (Irish) — **I** 329⁶, **I** 468⁵, **I** 496ᶠ

HURRICANE GILBERT gr.g. 8 Neltino - Oakington by Henry The Seventh — Mrs A Villar

682	30/3 Cottenham	(R) MDO 3m	9 GF	*(fav) prom, 2nd whn blnd 3 out, lft in ld apr last, all out*	1	13
1101	14/4 Guilsborough	(L) RES 3m	16 G	*wll in tch, chsd ldrs 16th, ran on onepcd frm 2 out*	2	16
1145	20/4 Higham	(L) RES 3m	12 F	*(fav) chsd wnr 8-12th, no imp, onepcd frm 16th*	4	16
1322	28/4 Fakenham P-'	(L) RES 3m	5 G	*ld to 9th, rdn apr 15th, onepcd und pres*	2	17

Missed 95; fortunate to win & not 100% genuine; ran well in Restricteds but unlikely to win one 15

HURRICANE IRIS (Irish) — **I** 50ᵁ, **I** 70ᴾ, **I** 143ᴾ, **I** 149⁴, **I** 225⁵

HURRICANE LINDA b.m. 9 Strong Gale - El Reine by Bargello — Lady Hewitt

1995 1(19),3(19),P(0),1(19),2+(22)

1096	14/4 Whitwell-On'	(R) MEM 3m	9 G	*(Jt fav) hld up rear, f 2nd*	F	-
1130	20/4 Hornby Cast'	(L) CON 3m	13 G	*rear, prog hlfwy, 2nd & going wll whn f 3 out*	F	-

Improved & won 3 in 95; season lasted less than a week 96; should win if fit 97; stays; G/F-G/S 22

HURRICANE RYAN(IRE) b.g. 8 Lafontaine (USA) - Etesian by Tumble Wind (USA) — Mrs A J McMath

401	9/3 Dalston	(R) OPE 3m	6 G	*ld 4th til f 11th*	F	-

Rarely runs & can only be watched if back in 97 0

HURRICANE TOMMY ch.g. 9 Le Bavard (FR) - Graham Dieu by Three Dons — Mrs C Lawrence

1995 **P(NH),R(NH),P(NH),P(NH),5(NH),P(NH)**

444	9/3 Haldon	(R) OPE 3m	5 S	*sn prom, cls up til 12th, wknd nxt, p.u. 14th*	P	0
731	31/3 Little Wind'	(R) OPE 3m	5 GS	*in tch til outpcd aft 14th, bhnd whn ref 15th*	R	-

Winning chaser; looks of no account now 0

HUTCEL BELL b.m. 5 Belfort (FR) - Crammond Brig by New Brig — W H Jackson

1995 **15(NH),P(NH)**

307	2/3 Great Stain'	(L) MDO 3m	17 GS	*plld hrd, cls up til wknd 10th, t.o. 2 out*	10	0
408	9/3 Charm Park	(L) MEM 3m	7 G	*ld to 11th, hdd, fdng whn f 14th*	F	-
764	31/3 Great Stain'	(L) MDN 3m	16 GS	*last & sn t.o., p.u. 3 out*	P	0
1094	14/4 Whitwell-On'	(R) MDO 2 1/2m 88yds	16 G	*alwys twrds rear, bhnd frm 3 out*	6	0

Not disgraced last start but not enough stamina yet 0

HYDRO BROOK (Irish) — **I** 307ᴾ

HYDROPIC b.g. 9 Kabour - Hydrangea by Warpath — Mrs B E Miller

1995 1(18),2(18),12(0),3(11)

112	17/2 Lanark	(R) LAD 3m	8 GS	*chsd wnr frm 7th til wknd rpdly 4 out*	4	0
190	24/2 Friars Haugh	(L) LAD 3m	7 S	*ld 7th til wknd rpdly 15th*	6	0
498	16/3 Lanark	(R) CON 3m	10 G	*alwys wll bhnd*	7	0

751 31/3 Lockerbie (R) CON 3m 12 G *bhnd by 9th, t.o.* 6 0
1083 14/4 Friars Haugh (L) CON 3m 10 F *alwys bhnd* 8 0
1151 20/4 Whittington (L) INT 3m 12 G *chsd ldrs to 14th, wknd nxt* 5 10
1351 4/5 Mosshouses (L) CON 3m 11 GS *mstk 2nd, ld 5-9th, wknd 12th, sn bhnd* 7 0
1475 11/5 Aspatria (L) CON 3m 6 GF *chsd ldrs, mstk 11th, 4th whn blndrd 15th, no ch aft* 4 11

Won 1 of last 31 starts; barely stays & going downhill now 0

HYLUNA ch.m. 12 Hyrossi - Hello Luna by The Bo'sun T B Palmer

1206 21/4 Heathfield (R) RES 3m 8 F *t.o. whn p.u. aft 10th* P 0
1441 6/5 Aldington (L) MEM 3m 4 HD *alwys last, t.o. 8th* 4 0

Of no account 0

HYPERION SON gr.g. 9 Van Der Linden (FR) - Hyperion Palace by Dragonara Palace (USA) John Mackley

226 24/2 Duncombe Pa' (R) OPE 3m 10 GS *prom, ld 6th, lft clr 4 out, lkd wnr til tired & hdd flat* 3 14
304 2/3 Great Stain' (L) OPE 3m 10 GS *made most, 4l clr 4 out, 2l clr last, wknd flat, hdd cls hm* 2 20
488 16/3 Newcastle (L) HC 2 1/2m 9 GS *(fav) alwys well pld, chal 9th, mstk 11th, driven after 4 out, rallied to ld between last 2, left clr last.* 1 22
760 31/3 Great Stain' (L) OPE 3m 8 GS *(fav) chsd ldrs, 2nd 13th, disp 5 out, fdd 3 out, onepcd* 3 18
1093 14/4 Whitwell-On' (R) MXO 4m 19 G *wth ldrs, disp 7-13th, ld 16th-4 out, onepcd* 3 18
1282 27/4 Easingwold (L) OPE 3m 8 G *alwys chsng ldrs, pshd alng 15th, kpt on frm 2 out* 2 21

Winning Irish pointer; won weak H/Chase; best over easy 3m; hard to place now; G-G/S 21

IADES BOY(NZ) b.g. 5 Iades (FR) - Phero's Bay (NZ) by Brazen Boy (AUS) D H Barons

555 17/3 Ottery St M' (L) MDO 3m 15 G *mid-div, out of tch 14th, slght prog 4 out,nvr plcd to chal* 2 13

Encouraging debut but not seen after; sure to do better if racing regularly in 97 14

IAMA ZULU ch.g. 11 Son Of Shaka - Quick Sort by Henry The Seventh P Swaffield

7 13/1 Larkhill (R) CON 3m 10 GS *chsd ldr, lft in ld 10th, hdd 14th, 4th & btn whn f nxt* F -

Winning chaser; vanished after day 1; unlikely to stay 3m 17

IANOVITCH b.g. 8 Lightning Dealer - Misty Arch by Starch Reduced C Gillbard

201 24/2 Lemalla (R) MDO 3m 13 HY *u.r. 4th* U -
283 2/3 Clyst St Ma' (L) MDN 3m 7 S *(bl) sn 25l clr, wkng whn f heavily 8th* F -
556 17/3 Ottery St M' (L) MDO 3m 15 G *(bl) cls up to 13th, wknd, mid-div whn f 4 out* F -

Missed 95; useless 0

I BLAME THEPARENTS b.m. 9 Celtic Cone - Foxwell by Healaugh Fox P J Corbett

218 24/2 Newtown (L) MDN 3m 14 GS *in tch, ld 12-15th, ev ch 2 out, no ext apr last* 2 13
688 30/3 Chaddesley ' (L) MDN 3m 17 G *chsd ldrs, ev ch 12th, outpcd apr 15th* 5 0
1047 13/4 Bitterley (L) MDO 3m 13 G *trckd ldrs, prom 11th, chal whn f nxt* F -
1175 20/4 Chaddesley ' (L) MDN 3m 9 G *trckd dlrs, cls 2nd 14th, ld 16th, drew clr 2 out* 1 16
1482 11/5 Bredwardine (R) RES 3m 13 G *trckd ldrs, cls 4tha t 15th, kpt on onepcd frm 2 out* 4 13

Gradually improving; beat subsequent scorer when winning; should upgrade to Restricteds successfully 18

ICANTSAY (Irish) — **I** 187P, **I** 356P

I CANT WAIT (Irish) — **I** 131P, **I** 137P, **I** 193P, **I** 526P

ICECAPADE(BEL) b.g. 8 Moulouki - Furryrush by Furry Glen P Riddick
1995 2(11),P(0),3(0)

148 17/2 Erw Lon (L) MDN 3m 9 G *alwys rear, nvr dang* 6 0
391 9/3 Llanfrynach (R) MDN 3m 11 GS *ld to 2nd,chsd wnr,ev ch 14th,sn btn,tired 2nd whn p.u. flat* P 0
509 16/3 Magor (R) MDN 3m 9 GS *(fav) made all, wll clr frm 8th, easily* 1 10
695 30/3 Llanvapley (L) RES 3m 13 GS *ld 9-12th, grad lost tch* 3 0
844 6/4 Howick (L) RES 3m 10 GF *ld to 7th & frm 11th, disp 14th, went clr 3 out* 1 16
1157 20/4 Llanwit Maj' (R) CON 3m 11 GS *chsd ldrs, mstks 4th & 6th, lost plc 8th, bhnd & f 14th* F -
1263 27/4 Pyle (R) CON 3m 9 G *ld to 4th, lost plc 11th, t.o. & p.u. 14th* P 0
1558 18/5 Bassaleg (R) CON 3m 6 F *chsd ldng pair abt 15l down,unable to cls,wknd apr last* 3 0
1602 25/5 Bassaleg (R) CON 3m 8 GS *rear, steady prog to 4th at 10th, f nxt* F -

Tries but non-stayer & did well to find two races; hopes of Confined look slim; G/S 14

ICE HOUSE STREET(NZ) b.g. 8 Half Iced (USA) - Gai Pouliche (NZ) by Trictrac (FR) I A Balding

29 20/1 Barbury Cas' (L) RES 3m 12 GS *prom to 11th, wknd 13th, t.o. & p.u. 2 out* P 0
339 3/3 Heythrop (R) RES 3m 10 GS *cls up, chsd ldr 12th, ld aft 2 out, hdd & not qckn last* 2 16

Lightly raced & has ability; professionally-trained; finished early; could atone if fit 97 17

ICKY'S FIVE b.g. 12 Dawn Review - Reengaroga by Brave Invader (USA) Pat Callaghan
1995 P(0),3(0),5(11),U(-),2(0),8(0),U(-),1(18),6(12)

126 17/2 Kingston Bl' (L) LAD 3m 11 GS *alwys rear, last & wll t.o. 13th, p.u. 15th* P 0
336 3/3 Heythrop (R) LAD 3m 5 G *ld to 5th, strgglng frm 14th, t.o.* 4 0

436	9/3	Newton Brom'	(R)	LAD	3m	10	GS	*alwys twrds rear*	7	0
792	2/4	Heythrop	(R)	LAD	3 3/4m	7	F	*(bl) chsd ldrs to hlfwy, outpcd frm 15th, wknd 2 out*	4	10
995	8/4	Hackwood Pa'	(L)	XX	3m	8	GF	*mstk 2nd, alwys trlng*	4	0
1437	6/5	Ashorne	(R)	MXO	3m	13	G	*mid-div, prog to 5th at 11th, lost tch frm 13th*	8	0
1502	11/5	Kingston Bl'	(L)	LAD	3m	7	G	*(bl) chsd ldrs, lost tch frm 11th, t.o. 14th*	5	0
1566	19/5	Mollington	(R)	LAD	3m	7	GS	*(bl) prom to 12th, strggIng frm nxt*	4	15
1584	24/5	Towcester	(R)	HC	3m 1f	11	GS	*(bl) ld to 5th, wknd 9th, t.o. when p.u. before 12th.*	P	0
1642	2/6	Dingley	(R)	LAD	3m	6	GF	*chsd ldr to 4th, sn rr, wknd 3 out, t.o.*	5	10

Ladies winner 95 but declined 96; best late season; hard to win again; G/F-S 12

IDEAL b.g. 11 Salluceva - Hurry Miss by Royal Buck — Richard Mathias

1995 1(17),1(19),**F(-)**

674	30/3	Hereford	(R)	HC	2m	8	S	*ld, blnd and u.r. 2nd.*	U	-
745	31/3	Upper Sapey	(R)	INT	3m	6	GS	*ld, 20l clr hlfwy, still disp & ev ch til outpcd 2 out*	2	19
881	6/4	Brampton Br'	(R)	CON	3m	9	GF	*clr ldr til ct apr 16th, wknd rpdly nxt*	7	0
1158	20/4	Llanwit Maj'	(R)	OPE	4m	9	GS	*ld 2nd til blndrd 20th, sn hdd, rlld 3 out, onepcd*	3	18
1478	11/5	Bredwardine	(R)	CON	3m	12	G	*ld 4th-15th, wknd rpdly, p.u. nxt*	P	0

Dual winner 95; blazes the trail but disappointing 96; R/H essential; could win again; G-S 17

I DID IT MY WAY b.g. 11 The Parson - Entry Hill by Menelek — Mrs Jane Evans

1995 1(14),3(11),7(0),P(0)

242	25/2	Southwell P'	(L)	RES	3m	12	HO	*(bl) rdn & prog to jn ldrs 11th,4th & btn whn lft 3rd 3 out,kpton*	2	15
526	16/3	Larkhill	(R)	RES	3m	9	G	*(bl) alwys prom, onepcd frm 2 out, no ch whn ref last*	R	-

Maiden winner 95; best fresh & looks only chance in Restricted 97; 15

IDIOTIC br.g. 8 Idiot's Delight - Norma Can by Normandy — E Knight

1995 r(-),P(0),2(18)

1228	27/4	Worcester	(L)	HC	2m 7f	17	G	*hdwy 12th, blnd 2 out, ld apr last, driven out.*	1	26
1630	31/5	Stratford	(L)	HC	3 1/2m	16	GF	*mid div, smooth hdwy from 13th, tracking ldrs when b.d. 16th.*	B	-

Lightly raced; won modest H/Chase; going well other start; could win H/Chase debut 97; hard ride; Gd 27

IDIOT'S SURPRISE (Irish) — **I** 120^{P}, **I** 204^{F}, **I** 252^{3}, **I** 290^{2}, **I** 367^{2}

IF I FANCY b.m. 10 Davout - Sweet Chanteuse by Sweet Story — A Kane

1995 P(0),r(-),P(0),F(-)

399	9/3	Dalston	(R)	CON	3m	9	G	*bhnd frm 3rd, t.o. 11th, p.u. nxt*	P	0

Yet to complete the course from 6 starts 94-6 0

IF YOU SAY SO ch.g. 10 Say Primula - Vinovia by Ribston — I S G Lang

1995 **5(NH),7(NH)**

1111	17/4	Hockworthy	(L)	MXO	3m	13	GS	*sn last & nvr gng wl, t.o. & u.r. 7th*	U	-
1361	4/5	Flete Park	(R)	CON	3m	9	G	*plld hrd, ld apr 4th til ref & u.r. 7th (ditch)*	R	-
1553	18/5	Bratton Down	(L)	XX	3m	10	F	*rear til prog 11th, 2l 2nd whn f 15th*	F	-
1622	27/5	Lifton	(R)	CON	3m	14	GS	*hld up, prog to 4th at 13th, 3rd whn f 16th*	F	-

Holding chances when departing last two outings but can scarcely be recommended so far 14

I HAVEN'T A BUCK (Irish) — **I** 34^{2}, **I** 72^{4}, **I** 126^{1}, **I** 249^{U}

I HAVE YOU NOW (Irish) — **I** 38^{F}

I IS ch.g. 9 Pollerton - Gortroe Queen by Simbir — Mrs J Brook-Saunders

5	13/1	Larkhill	(R)	LAD	3m	10	GS	*chsd ldr 3-9th, wknd rpdly 12th, p.u. nxt*	P	0
26	20/1	Barbury Cas'	(L)	OPE	3m	12	GS	*bhnd frm 7th, t.o. & p.u. 12th*	P	0
207	24/2	Castle Of C'	(R)	MDO	3m	15	HY	*ld/disp to 10th, wknd & p.u. nxt*	P	0
364	5/3	Leicester	(R)	HC	2m 1f	12	GS	*prom in chasing gp till rdn and wknd apr 4 out, t.o..*	11	0
505	16/3	Magor	(R)	PPO	3m	7	GS	*ld to 7th, wkng whn f nxt*	F	-
1161	20/4	Llanwit Maj'	(R)	MDO	3m	15	GS	*prom to 11th, sn wknd, p.u. 3 out*	P	0
1273	27/4	Pyle	(R)	MDO	3m	9	G	*chsd ldrs, 10l 3rd whn f 13th, dead*	F	-

Dead 0

ILENGAR (Irish) — **I** 185^{3}, **I** 244^{1}, **I** 313^{P}, **I** 378^{P}

I LIKE THE DEAL b.m. 5 Lighter - Skidmore by Paddy's Stream — B Ayre

1278	27/4	Bratton Down	(L)	INT	3m	12	GF	*alwys rear, no ch whn p.u. 3 out*	P	0
1531	12/5	Ottery St M'	(L)	MDO	3m	9	GF	*bhnd til prog 14th, ran on to 3rd 2 out, promising*	3	10
1592	25/5	Mounsey Hil'	(R)	MDO	3m	9	G	*w.w. jmpd slwly 7th, rdn & btn 16th, p.u. 2 out*	P	0

Promise when 3rd; can be forgiven other outing; should go close in 97 14

I'LL SKIN THEM(IRE) br.m. 8 Buckskin (FR) - Stormy Wave by Gulf Pearl — M Lee

1995 P(0)

403	9/3	Dalston	(R)	RES	3m	11	G	*bhnd at 6th, nvr fctr*	P	0
756	31/3	Lockerbie	(R)	MDN	3m	14	G	*4th hlfwy, wnt 2nd 15th, no ext apr last*	4	11

Placed Irish Maidens 94; only 3 runs 95-6; beaten 12l when 4th & more needed 11

I'M A BUTE b.m. 6 Abutammam - Haselbech by Spartan General — T R R Fa

1995 F(-),P(0),P(0),7(0),3(0),P(0)

149 17/2 Erw Lon (L) MDN 3m 10 G *t.o. hlfwy, p.u. 15th* P

389 9/3 Llanfrynach (R) MDN 3m 11 GS *u.r. bef start,lft in ld 6-8th,ld 10-13th,wknd 3 out,tired* 5

606 23/3 Howick (L) MDN 3m 13 S *prom to 6th, wknd rpdly, p.u. 11th* P

848 6/4 Howick (L) MDN 3m 14 GF *alwys rear, p.u. 10th* P

1161 20/4 Llanwit Maj' (R) MDO 3m 15 GS *alwys rear, no ch whn f 14th* F

1271 27/4 Pyle (R) MDO 3m 15 G *mid-div, prog 8th, not qckn frm 13th, no ch frm 3 out* 4

1390 6/5 Pantyderi (R) MDO 3m 15 GF *ran out 7th* r

1492 11/5 Erw Lon (L) MDO 3m 10 F *nvr nrr to chal* 4

1561 18/5 Bassaleg (R) MDO 3m 8 F *prom, mstk & wknd 12th, sn t.o.* 4

Last & beaten miles when completing & no stamina at all 0

I'M A CHIPPY (Irish) — **I** 118[4], **I** 154[1], **I** 276[P]

IMAGE BOY(IRE) br.h. 8 Flash Of Steel - Gay Pariso by Sir Gaylord — Mrs R D Greenwoo

479 10/3 Tweseldown (R) MDO 3m 10 G *schoold rear, t.o. 4th, lft remote 4th 3 out, tk 2nd flat* 2

637 23/3 Siddington (L) MEM 3m 14 S *rr, lst tch 8th, t.o. & p.u. 13th* P

959 8/4 Lockinge (L) MDN 3m 6 GF *held up, prog 13th, disp 3 out til wknd apr last* 2 1

1187 21/4 Tweseldown (R) MDN 3m 11 GF *(fav) j.w. w.w. prog 8th, ld 14th, slw 2 out, pshd out* 1 1

Lightly raced; won poor Maiden; more needed for Restricteds but should find chances at Tweseldown 14

I'M-A-GYPSY b.g. 9 Balinger - Zingarella by Romany Air — Mrs B Whettam

1015 13/4 Kingston Bl' (L) MEM 3m 9 G *rear, mstk 11th, lost tch 13th, t.o. & f 2 out* F

Missed 95; does not stay & no prospects 0

I'M HAPPY NOW (Irish) — **I** 59[F], **I** 66[P], **I** 77[2], **I** 210[1]

IMIKE ch.g. 6 Gunner B - Joe's Fancy by Apollo Eight — N Poache

217 24/2 Newtown (L) RES 3m 17 GS *t.o. last til p.u. 8th* P

386 9/3 Llanfrynach (R) RES 3m 10 GS *in tch to 6th, t.o. 8th, p.u. 15th* P

Unpromising so far 0

I'MINONIT b.g. 6 Rolfe (USA) - Lorrensino by Laurence O — P S Macrae

521 16/3 Larkhill (R) MDO 3m 6 G *sttld wth chsng grp, bhnd whn f 4 out* F

734 31/3 Little Wind' (R) MDO 3m 11 GS *(fav) hdwy to 2nd 10th, ld apr 2 out, drvn out* 1 15

1242 27/4 Woodford (L) RES 3m 18 G *alwys rear, jmp lft 5th, no ch frm 11th, p.u. 3 out* P 0

Won slowly run Maiden (winner behind); no show in good Restricted but should do better in them 97 ... 16

I'M JOKING ch.g. 6 True Song - Sancal by Whistlefield — A R Trotter

1088 14/4 Friars Haugh (L) MDO 3m 10 F *nvr nr ldrs, p.u. 2 out* P 0

1254 27/4 Balcormo Ma' (R) MDO 3m 14 GS *prom to hlfwy, bhnd whn p.u. 2 out* P 0

No signs of ability yet 0

I'M NOT SHES GIRL (Irish) — **I** 84[P]

IM OK(IRE) br.m. 8 Creative Plan (USA) - How Are You by Brave Invander (USA) — Mrs Carol A Cowel

240 25/2 Southwell P' (L) MDO 3m 15 HO *started 5 fences bhnd, cont til p.u. 12th* P 0

333 3/3 Market Rase' (L) MDO 3m 11 G *chsd ldrs til wknd apr 14th, no ch whn u.r. 3 out* U -

367 6/3 Catterick (L) HC 3m 1f 110yds 12 G *well bhnd when mstk and u.r. 10th.* U -

541 17/3 Southwell P' (L) MDO 3m 9 GS *rear, prog 10th, ev ch 2 out, onepcd* 5 0

1010 9/4 Flagg Moor (L) LAD 3m 6 G *sn wl bhnd, p.u. 8th, stirrup broke* P 0

1090 14/4 Whitwell-On' (R) RES 3m 17 G *sttld mid-div, prog 8th, fdd frm 12th, sn wknd* 9 0

1286 27/4 Easingwold (L) MDO 3m 13 G *alwys rear, rdn 10th, sn t.o.* 7 0

1365 4/5 Gisburn (R) MDO 3m 17 G *ldng grp, rdn 3 out, fin tired* 6 0

1476 11/5 Aspatria (L) MDO 3m 16 GF *(bl) prom til b.d. 11th* B -

1629 30/5 Uttoxeter (L) HC 2m 5f 13 GS *(bl) bhnd till f 5th.* F -

Ran one fair race but devoid of stamina & no real prospects 0

IMPECCABLE BUCK (Irish) — **I** 559[1]

IMPLICITLY SUZIE b.m. 8 Wonderful Surprise - Swift Embrace by Enbrage — Mrs T Corrigan-Clark

1995 1(15),2(12),8(0),2(13)

77 11/2 Wetherby Po' (L) RES 3m 18 GS *mid-div, late prog, 5th 2 out, styd on well* 3 17

Maiden winner 95; fair run only start 96; likes Wetherby; stays well; could win Restricted if fit 97 16

INACTUALFACT (Irish) — **I** 236[P]

INCENSE DOLL (Irish) — **I** 178[F], **I** 285[P], **I** 364[F]

INCH CHAMPION (Irish) — **I** 565[F]

INCH CROSS (Irish) — **I** 466[F], **I** 497[P]

INCH EMPEROR (Irish) — I 51P, I 186P, I 241F

INCH EMPRESS(IRE) 7 — D J Miller

599 23/3 Howick (L) RES 3m 7 S *ld 4-10th, wknd rpdly, p.u. 3 out* P 0

Irish Maiden winner 94; unencouraging in 96 0

INCH FOUNTAIN(IRE) br.g. 5 Royal Fountain - The Priory by Oats — M J Parr

165 17/2 Weston Park (L) RES 3m 9 G *(fav) prom, prog to ld 3 out, comf* 1 18

Irish Maiden winner 95; ideal English debut; useful if returning 97; Good 20

INCH GALE br.m. 9 Strong Gale - Such Bliss by So Blessed — Mrs A T D Davies

1995 6(0),3(0),P(0),**7(0)**,3(10),**3(NH)**

348 3/3 Higham (L) RES 3m 12 G *t.o. frm 6th* 6 0
524 16/3 Larkhill (R) INT 3m 11 G *(bl) prom, 3rd at 6th, wknd 12th, t.o.* 7 0
679 30/3 Cottenham (R) RES 3m 15 GF *(bl) lft in ld 2nd, hdd 13th, sn wknd, poor 7th whn u.r. 2 out* U -
1380 5/5 Dingley (R) RES 3m 11 GF *(bl) wll in tch til wknd frm 14th* 8 0

Does not stay & well beaten all starts 94-6 0

INCH MAID b.m. 10 Le Moss - Annie Augusta by Master Owen — S A Brookshaw

1995 U(-)

663 24/3 Eaton Hall (R) LAD 3m 8 S *mid-div, cls up whn u.r. 6th* U -
855 6/4 Sandon (L) CON 3m 6 GF *mid-div,cls order 12th,up sides btwn last 2,outpcd cls home* 2 19
948 8/4 Eyton-On-Se' (L) MEM 3m 4 GF *made all to 2 out, ran on und pres frm last* 2 19
1194 21/4 Sandon (L) LAD 3m 7 G *steadied bhnd ldr, drvn to ld apr last, ran on well* 1 23
1232 27/4 Weston Park (L) LAD 3m 6 G *cls 3rd/4th til wnt on 12th, sn clr, easy* 1 23
1420 6/5 Eyton-On-Se' (L) LAD 3m 3 GF *(fav) ld stng stdy pce, qcknd frm 13th, chal whn ran out 4 out* r -
1545 18/5 Bangor (L) HC 3m 110yds 8 G *in tch, outpcd after 13th, hdwy after 3 out, left 2nd next, no impn on wnr.* 2 24
1617 27/5 Chaddesley ' (L) LAD 3m 8 GF *mstks,nrly u.r. 1st,pshd alng hlfwy,nvr able to chal,nvr nrr* 3 20

Useful but quirky & novice rider did well; can quicken & should win more 97; G-F 23

INCH VALLEY (Irish) — I 240F

IN DEMAND b.g. 5 Nomination - Romantic Saga by Prince Tenderfoot (USA) — A J Balmer

405 9/3 Dalston (R) MDO 2 1/2m 16 G *cls up frm 11th, lkd dang apr last, no ext nr fin* 2 13
613 23/3 Friars Haugh (L) MDN 3m 15 G *5th hlfwy, ld 4 out, sn clr, comf* 1 16
914 8/4 Tranwell (L) RES 3m 6 GF *(fav) hld up, prog 14th, disp nxt, qcknd to ld last, clvrly* 1 20
1252 27/4 Balcormo Ma' (R) INT 3m 5 GS *(fav) held up in tch til wknd qckly 4 out* 4 0

Promising; beat subsequent H/Chase winner 3rd start; ran badly on Soft; could reach Opens; G-F 21

INDIAN KNIGHT b.g. 11 Kinglet - Indian Whistle by Rugantino — C A Green

1995 2(23),2(23),U(-),**2(19)**,**P(0)**

523 16/3 Larkhill (R) MXO 3m 8 G *alwys prom, ld 13th til apr last, ran on, bttr for race* 2 18
709 30/3 Barbury Cas' (L) OPE 3m 15 G *hld up, prog 12th, ev ch 3 out, outpcd nxt* 3 18
865 6/4 Larkhill (R) CON 3m 3 F *(fav) narrow ld whn u.r. 2nd* U -
1290 28/4 Barbury Cas' (L) OPE 3m 5 F *mstks, cls up til not qckn 15th, no ch aft 3 out* 4 15
1453 7/5 Wincanton (R) HC 2m 5f 9 F *hdwy 10th, rdn 5 out, styd on one pace.* 4 20
1544 17/5 Stratford (L) HC 3m 10 GF *held up, mid div when blnd 4 out, wknd quickly.* 7 15

Last won in 93 & lost last 18 races; can run well but unlikely to break sequence at 12 16

INDIAN RABI gr.g. 6 Northern Game - Acoras Prediction by Scallywag — Mrs E M Roberts

1995 P(0)

626 23/3 Kilworthy (L) OPE 3m 12 GS *in tch, ran wd apr 7th, wkng whn mstk 12th,t.o. & p.u.15th* P 0
1430 6/5 High Bickin' (R) MDO 3m 8 G *(fav) in tch, outpcd 16th, lkd btn 2 out, lft in ld last* 1 14

Lucky winner of poor Maiden; young but lot more needed for Restricteds 13

INDIAN RIVER(IRE) b.g. 8 Indian King (USA) - Chaldea by Tamerlane — Robert Miller-Bakewell

1995 **P(NH)**,**P(NH)**

51 4/2 Alnwick (L) MDO 3m 17 G *7s-3s, ld to 4th, prom til wknd 13th, p.u. nxt* P 0
192 24/2 Friars Haugh (L) MDN 3m 12 S *in tch til grad wknd frm hlfwy* 6 0

An uninspired gamble 1st start; well beaten 2nd start & finished early 0

INDIE ROCK b.g. 6 Hadeer - Song Test (USA) by The Minstrel (CAN) — R Tate

1995 **5(NH)**,**F(NH)**,**8(NH)**,**2(NH)**,**2(NH)**,**4(NH)**,**1(NH)**,**2(NH)**,**6(NH)**,**3(NH)**,**3(NH)**

119 17/2 Witton Cast' (R) LAD 3m 4 S *hld up, smooth prog to ld 8th, going wll whn ran out 11th* r -
412 9/3 Charm Park (L) LAD 3m 7 G *rr early, prog 12th, ld 14th-2 out, hdd, no ext* 3 18
759 31/3 Great Stain' (L) LAD 3m 10 GS *hld up going wll,went 2nd 6th, qcknd to ld last, kpt on flat* 1 21
1132 20/4 Hornby Cast' (L) LAD 3m 9 G *(fav) p.u. bef 1st, rider thought false start* P 0
1283 27/4 Easingwold (L) LAD 3m 10 G *plld hrd in rear, prog 10th, going wll whn ran out 12th* r -
1449 6/5 Witton Cast' (R) LAD 3m 10 G *held up in rear, prog 8th, ld 5 out, 2l clr last, ran on wll* 1 20
1469 11/5 Easingwold (L) LAD 3m 6 G *(fav) prog 4th, ld 15th-nxt, ld apr last, hrd rdn & hdd cls hm* 2 20
1596 25/5 Garthorpe (R) LAD 3m 9 G *prog 7th, disp 10th-4 out, disp 3rd & ev ch whn f 2 out* F -

Useful but hard ride & barely stays; should win more Ladies on easy course 97; Good 22

INDIWAY ch.g. 8 Broadsword (USA) - Artalinda by Indiaro — Mrs S E Haydo

593 23/3 Parham (R) RES 3m 11 GS *alwys rear, p.u. 11th* P

1205 21/4 Heathfield (R) MEM 3m 4 F *in tch to 13th, bhnd whn blnd & u.r. 15th* U

No signs of ability 0

INGLEBROOK br.g. 5 Meadowbrook - Inglebrig by New Brig — D Williams

286 2/3 Eaton Hall (R) MDO 3m 14 G *mid-div, no ch whn p.u. 3 out* P

660 24/3 Eaton Hall (R) MDN 3m 7 S *ld to 6th, ld 11th, clr nxt, blnd & u.r. 13th* U

Going strongly when departing; every chance of recompense 97 14

INGLEBY FLYER b.m. 8 Valiyar - Fardella (ITY) by Molvedo — Mrs S Frank

1995 P(0),2(10),P(0),F(-)

80 11/2 Wetherby Po' (L) MDO 3m 12 GS *bhnd early, onepcd, p.u. 4 out* P

121 17/2 Witton Cast' (R) RES 3m 11 S *mid-div to 10th, rear aft, slght prog agn frm 2 out* 6 11

225 24/2 Duncombe Pa' (R) RES 3m 12 GS *in tch, chsd ldng pair 14th, blnd 3 out, fin tired* 3

415 9/3 Charm Park (L) MDO 3m 13 G *cls up, early, fdng whn b.d. 4 out* B

590 23/3 Wetherby Po' (L) MDO 3m 16 S *mid-div to 10th, t.o. whn f 12th* F

757 31/3 Great Stain' (L) MEM 3m 5 GS *chsd ldrs, wknd 14th, t.o.* 3

Well beaten when completing in 96 & not threatening to win; stamina suspect 11

INGLEBY LODGER ch.g. 7 Ardar - Orange Glint — Mrs S Frank

1995 U(-)

75 11/2 Wetherby Po' (L) MDO 3m 8 GS *alwys rear, p.u. 10th* P

123 17/2 Witton Cast' (R) MDO 3m 11 S *prom to 8th, wknd 10th, rear whn p.u. 13th* P

Lightly raced & shows nothing yet 0

INGLEBY WOT br.g. 8 Grey Ghost - Colishine by Coliseum — Mrs S Frank

411 9/3 Charm Park (L) RES 3m 20 G *cls up 7th, fdd, p.u. 10th* P

Missed 94/5 & scarcely seen 96; prospects grim 0

IN HAND ch.g. 16 Nearly A Hand - Miss India by Indian Ruler — Mrs J G Griffith

659 24/3 Eaton Hall (R) MEM 3m 6 S *alwys rear, t.o.* 4 0

No longer of any account 0

INHURST b.m. 7 Remezzo - Passionate by Dragonara Palace (USA) — D G Dixon

1995 6(0),6(0),P(0)

144 17/2 Larkhill (R) MDO 3m 15 G *mid-div whn f 6th* U -

No stamina in 95 & vanished quickly in 96 0

INK FLICKER(IRE) br.g. 6 Black Minstrel - Sand-Pit Cross by Pitpan — J M B Cookson

1351 4/5 Mosshouses (L) CON 3m 11 GS *alwys last, t.o. whn u.r. 10th* U -

1575 19/5 Corbridge (R) MDO 3m 10 G *ld 3rd-14th, f nxt* F -

Showed some speed at Corbridge & may improve at 7 10

INKY b or br.m. 7 Impecunious - Latanett by Dairialatan — M J Hart

1995 U(-),3(0),2(11),2(11),2(11)

1217 24/4 Andoversford (R) MDO 3m 16 G *in tch, prog to 5th 12th, ev ch til wknd app 2 out* 4 0

1621 27/5 Chaddesley ' (L) MDO 3m 17 GF *prom, ld apr 12th, 2l up whn f 2 out* F 16

Brief campaign 96; barely stays but unlucky last start; may win in 97; G-F 14

INNER SNU gr.m. 7 Vital Season - Grey Receipt by Rugantino — S L Mitchell

467 10/3 Milborne St' (L) MEM 3m 8 G *handy whn f 5th* F -

658 23/3 Badbury Rin' (L) MDO 3m 8 G *sn wll bhnd, ran through btn horses frm 4 out* 3 0

1129 20/4 Stafford Cr' (R) MDO 3m 11 S *rear til blndrd & u.r. 11th* U -

1308 28/4 Little Wind' (R) MDO 3m 6 G *rear, prog 14th, wknd frm 3 out* 4 0

1396 6/5 Cotley Farm (L) MDO 3m 11 GF *alwys mid-div, no ch whn p.u. app last* P 0

1554 18/5 Bratton Down (L) MDO 3m 16 F *hld up bhnd,prog to 5th 3 out,strng run to disp last,jst hld* 2 15

Missed 95; improved last start 96 & 2nd in fair race (winner behind); should win if maintaining 15

INNER TEMPLE b.g. 6 Shirley Heights - Round Tower by High Top — Capt T A Forster

1347 4/5 Holnicote (L) MDO 3m 16 GS *(fav) ld/disp til f 6th* P 0

1592 25/5 Mounsey Hil' (R) MDO 3m 9 G *(fav) u.r. 1st* U -

Placed NH Flat; jumping problems proving costly but should have chances with a clear round 12

INSPECTOR STALKER (Irish) — I 282P, I 365P, I 4882

NSTRUMENTAL (Irish) — I 83[F], I 107[1]

NSULATE ch.m. 6 Sula Bula - Penny Catcher by Barolo — Stephen March

108 17/2 Marks Tey (L) MDN 3m 17 G *f 2nd* F -

830 6/4 Marks Tey (L) MDN 3m 14 G *in rear whn blnd & u.r. 4th* U -

929 8/4 Marks Tey (L) MDO 3m 5 G *chsd ldrs, disp 7th, last by 9th, outpcd 15th,styd on 2 out* 2 10

Placed in a desperate contest run at a crawl; can do better 10

NTEGRITY BOY b.g. 9 Touching Wood (USA) - Powderhall by Murrayfield — Richard P Watts

1995 **2(NH),1(NH),4(NH),4(NH),5(NH)**

759 31/3 Great Stain' (L) LAD 3m 10 GS *sttld wth ldrs, disp 3 out, hdd last, rallied flat* 2 21

023 13/4 Brocklesby ' (L) LAD 3m 3 GF *(fav) dict pce, ran on wll whn chal 3 out, drew clr frm last* 1 19

283 27/4 Easingwold (L) LAD 3m 10 G *rear, prog 12th, ev ch 4 out, sn outpcd, ran on well flat* 2 21

Winning hurdler/chaser; useful in Ladies events; should win more 97; best L/H; G/F-G/S 22

NTERPRETATION(NZ) b.g. 10 Uncle Remus (NZ) - Misinterprate (NZ) by None Better — Nick Viney

1995 6(11)

379 9/3 Barbury Cas' (L) XX 3m 9 GS *rear, prog frm 14th, chal & ev ch whn f last* F -

708 30/3 Barbury Cas' (L) LAD 3m 10 G *in tch, 2nd frm 9th, strng chal apr last, ld nr fin* 1 25

110 17/4 Hockworthy (L) CON 3m 9 GS *prog 6th, chsd wnr 2 out, hrd rdn & ran on, just held* 2 28

276 27/4 Bratton Down (L) LAD 3m 7 GF *hld up, went 2nd 3 out, no further prog aft* 2 26

Brilliantly revived 96; twice beaten by Faithful Star; sure to win more 97; G/F-G/S 28

N THE BLOOD (Irish) — I 121[1], I 212[1]

N THE CHOIR b.m. 8 Chief Singer - In The Shade by Bustino — R J R Symonds

1995 **F(NH),10(NH),F(NH),P(NH)**

141 17/2 Larkhill (R) MEM 3m 6 G *alwys mid-div, nvr nrr* 4 10

Last & well beaten & prospects not good 10

N THE FUTURE (Irish) — I 19[P], I 105[P], I 364[4], I 408[2]

N THE NAVY b.g. 10 King's Ride - Fairy Run by Deep Run — M C Pipe

1995 **7+(NH),5(NH),U(NH),4(NH),P(NH)**

134 17/2 Ottery St M' (L) CON 3m 12 GS *n.j.w. mid-div, prog 14th, ld nxt, blnd last, hdd nr fin* 2 20

560 17/3 Ottery St M' (L) CON 3m 7 G *(fav) hld up, prog to ld 7-8th, ld 3 out, blnd bdly nxt,nt rcvr* 2 19

991 8/4 Kingston St' (R) LAD 3m 8 F *tongue-strap, ld 8-12th & 15th, 3l clr 3 out, hdd nxt,sn btn* 6 12

Right connections but problems clear; win weak race with no pressure if persevered with; G/S-F 19

N THE WATER ch.g. 9 Carlingford Castle - Cardamine by Indigenous — Mrs A Price

1995 **P(0)**,5(0),2(0)

879 6/4 Brampton Br' (R) LAD 3m 9 GF *alwys rear, t.o. 9th* 7 0

046 13/4 Bitterley (L) LAD 3m 9 G *prom til slppd bnd apr 8th, lost tch 13th, t.o. 15th* 6 0

218 24/4 Brampton Br' (R) MEM 3m 4 G *3l 3rd whn u.r. 6th* U -

318 28/4 Bitterley (L) XX 3m 8 G *blnd & u.r. 1st* U -

480 11/5 Bredwardine (R) LAD 3m 12 G *s.s. t.o. 2nd, p.u. aft 11th* P 0

Only once better than last & sure to reamin a maiden 0

NTO THE SWING (Irish) — I 268[1]

NTO THE TREES b.g. 12 Over The River (FR) - Diana's Flyer by Charlottesvilles Flyer — Michael D Abrahams

1995 P(0),3(12)

117 17/2 Witton Cast' (R) MEM 3m 9 S *mid-div whn f 6th* F -

326 3/3 Market Rase' (L) OPE 3m 14 G *nvr on terms, p.u. 13th* P 0

410 9/3 Charm Park (L) OPE 3m 17 G *alwys prom, 3rd at 13th, fdd rpdly* 11 11

No longer of any account 0

NTO THE WEB (Irish) — I 81[U], I 147[P], I 424[3], I 509[1]

NVINCIBLE LAD (Irish) — I 445[P]

NVITE D'HONNEUR(NZ) ch.g. 14 Guest Of Honour - Jillion's Joy (NZ) by Khan Sahib — M D M Evans

741 31/3 Upper Sapey (R) MEM 3m 4 GS *disp 2nd/3rd til outpcd frm 15th* 2 0

043 13/4 Bitterley (L) OPE 3m 9 G *6l 6th at 11th, lost tch nxt, t.o. & p.u. 15th* P 0

412 6/5 Cursneh Hill (L) OPE 3m 4 GF *remote 2nd til wknd frm 3 out* 4 0

577 19/5 Wolverhampt' (L) CON 3m 6 G *chsd ldrs 3-5th, lost tch 10th, t.o. & p.u. 3 out* P 0

618 27/5 Chaddesley ' (L) CON 3m 14 GF *alwys rear, wll bhnd whn p.u. 3 out* P 0

Winning hurdler; too old now 0

OLARA (Irish) — I 563[P]

ORWERTH b.g. 10 Rymer - Wicker Basket by Pamroy — Harry White

576 17/3 Detling (L) MDN 3m 18 GF *in tch til wknd 14th, wll bhnd whn p.u. 3 out* P 0

781 31/3 Penshurst (L) MDN 3m 11 GS *in tch, lft 2nd 14th, ld aft 3 out, kpt on* 1 12

1054 13/4 Penshurst (L) RES 3m 8 G *alwys rear, t.o. 7th, p.u. 12th* P
1294 28/4 Bexhill (R) MEM 3m 4 F *blnd 1st, 3rd & in tch frm 7th, btn whn r.o. 4 out, cont* 3
1442 6/5 Aldington (L) RES 3m 7 HD *alwys rear, t.o. 4 out* 3

Missed 95; won poor Maiden; unreliable & miracle needed for another win 10

IRENE'S CALL (Irish) — **I** 240^{F}, **I** 354^{1}, **I** 436^{1}

IRENES TREASURE (Irish) — **I** 22^{P}, **I** 87^{P}, **I** 97^{3}, **I** 172^{P}, **I** 219^{3}, **I** 300^{P}, **I** 450^{P}

IRIDOPHANES ch.g. 10 Import - Grouse by March Past Miss S P Knig
1995 **P(NH),P(NH)**

59 10/2 Cottenham (R) RES 3m 9 GS *prom til outpcd 14th, no ch 3 out, styd on agn flat* 3
238 25/2 Southwell P' (L) MDO 3m 9 HO *in tch to 10th, steadily wknd, t.o. 4 out* 4

Plods round safely but has no winning hopes now 10

IRISH COURT (Irish) — **I** 654^{P}

IRISH DISPLAY (Irish) — **I** 78^{P}, **I** 125^{P}, **I** 465^{U}, **I** 511^{P}

IRISH FROLIC (Irish) — **I** 439^{P}, **I** 638^{F}, **I** 653^{2}

IRISH GENIUS(IRE) ch.g. 7 Duky - Le-Mu-Co by Varano Rob Wood

61 10/2 Cottenham (R) MDO 3m 8 GS *alwys bhnd, t.o. & p.u. 14th* P
542 17/3 Southwell P' (L) MDO 3m 15 GS *mid to rear, p.u. 3 out* P
727 31/3 Garthorpe (R) MDO 3m 12 G *in tch til wknd rpdly 11th, p.u. 14th* P

No signs of ability 0

IRISH MARIE b.m. 7 Lighter - Irish Rose by Soldier Rose R Benbo
1995 P(0),**P(NH)**

353 3/3 Garnons (L) MDN 2 1/2m 7 GS *ld/disp til outpcd frm 3 out, wknd flat* 4

Last only start 96; much more needed 10

IRISH OATS (Irish) — **I** 409^{P}, **I** 451^{P}

IRISH PEACE (Irish) — **I** 344^{2}, **I** 620^{1}

IRISH PRIDE (Irish) — **I** 640^{P}

IRISH REEF (Irish) — **I** 16^{P}, **I** 31^{1}

IRISH SOCIETY (Irish) — **I** 39^{P}, **I** 57^{P}, **I** 117^{2}

IRISH STOUT (Irish) — **I** 16^{1}, **I** 92^{1}

IRISH THINKER b.g. 5 Derring Rose - Irish Holiday by Simbir W Tudo

696 30/3 Llanvapley (L) MDN 3m 13 GS *mid-div, losing tch whn p.u. 12th* P
975 8/4 Lydstep (L) MDO 3m 9 G *rear, u.r. 6th* U
1039 13/4 St Hilary (R) MDN 3m 14 G *mid-div, prog to 3rd whn u.r. 13th* U
1273 27/4 Pyle (R) MDO 3m 9 G *mstks, cls up, ev ch whn u.r. 12th* U

Shows some ability but partnership needs glue at present 11

IRON PRINCE gr.g. 10 General Ironside - Pry Princess by Pry D McCom

48 4/2 Alnwick (L) LAD 3m 9 G *clse up, eff & ev ch 13th, wknd nxt, fair effort* 7
116 17/2 Lanark (R) MDO 3m 10 GS *handy til wknd 4 out, p.u. 2 out* P

Ran passably at Alnwick but quickly disappeared & time passing now 0

IRREGULAR PLANTING (Irish) — **I** 36^{4}, **I** 110^{F}, **I** 630^{P}

ISABELLA MORN b.m. 6 War Hero - Dawn Cloud by Down Cloud B Hedge

1445 6/5 Aldington (L) MDO 3m 8 HD *wll detached whn ref 2nd* R

No the best of starts 0

ISE THE DRIVER (Irish) — **I** 642^{P}

ISLAND ECHO (Irish) — **I** 312^{P}, **I** 458^{P}, **I** 571^{3}

ISLAND HARRIET (Irish) — **I** 259^{U}, **I** 319^{R}, **I** 449^{P}, **I** 490^{P}

IS SHE QUICK ch.m. 6 Norwick (USA) - Get Involved by Shiny Tenth Mrs Anne Curti
1995 **7(NH)**

144 17/2 Larkhill (R) MDO 3m 15 G *prom, ld 8th-10th, wknd 4 out, onepcd* 5
375 9/3 Barbury Cas' (L) MDN 3m 14 GS *mid-div whn f 7th* F
711 30/3 Barbury Cas' (L) MDO 3m 8 G *in tch to 12th, outpcd aft* 3
1511 12/5 Maisemore P' (L) MDO 3m 14 F *10s-6s, alwys rear, no ch frm 14th, t.o. & p.u. last* P
1638 1/6 Bratton Down (L) MDO 3m 13 G *mid-div til f 8th* F

Beaten 14l on debut (subsequent winner behind); not progress but may have chances 97 11

ITA'S FELLOW(IRE) ch.g. 8 Decent Fellow - Castle Ita by Midland Gayle R Princ
1995 2(12),F(-),1(14)

461 9/3 Eyton-On-Se' (L) RES 3m 15 G *mid-div whn u.r. 7th* U -

564 17/3 Wolverhampt' (L) RES 3m 8 GS *hld up, ld 15th, ran on strngly frm 3 out* 1 17

1191 21/4 Sandon (L) MEM 3m 5 G *(fav) hld up, prog 8th, ld nxt, sn clr, easily* 1 17

Maiden winner 95; changed hands; won fair Restricted; looks sure to upgrade 96; G-G/S 20

IT'S A DEAL (Irish) — **I** 198^{4}, **I** 419^{4}, **I** 555^{2}

ITS A DODDLE ch.m. 6 Prince Of Peace - Bossy Cleo by Proud Challenge — Mrs J Marsh

1995 P(0),P(0),P(0),U(-)

301 2/3 Great Treth' (R) MDO 3m 13 G *nvr dang, t.o. & p.u. 13th* P 0

509 16/3 Magor (R) MDN 3m 9 GS *rear, poor 5th frm 11th, t.o. & p.u. last* P 0

696 30/3 Llanvapley (L) MDN 3m 13 GS *mid-div, no prog frm hlfwy, p.u. 15th* P 0

1156 20/4 Llanwit Maj' (R) MEM 3m 7 GS *chsd ldrs, strgglng & rmmdrs 9th, t.o. & f 14th* F -

Hopeless 0

IT'S A FIDDLE (Irish) — **I** 363^{P}, **I** 412^{4}, **I** 453^{P}

IT'S A GAMBLE (Irish) — **I** 311^{2}

ITSALLAMATTER(IRE) 8 — P Newth

1047 13/4 Bitterley (L) MDO 3m 13 G *rear frm 4th, lost tch & p.u. 10th* P 0

1244 27/4 Woodford (L) INT 3m 12 G *s.s., blnd 8th, 11th & no ch hlfwy, p.u. 14th* P 0

1506 12/5 Maisemore P' (L) MEM 3m 5 F *ld 5th-aft 9th, chsd wnr 14th, btn 3 out* 2 0

Promise in 94; missed 95; beaten 25l in bad race & no prospects now 0

ITS ALL OVER NOW b.g. 12 Martinmas - Devon Lark by Take A Reef — D J Renney

1995 **6(NH),15(NH),5(NH),11(NH)**

523 16/3 Larkhill (R) MXO 3m 8 G *alwys chsng ldrs, wknd 12th, t.o.* 7 0

1247 27/4 Woodford (L) CON 3m 7 G *mid-div, 4th & outpcd 14th, wnt mod 3rd cls home* 3 12

1507 12/5 Maisemore P' (L) CON 3m 10 F *chsd ldrs, outpcd aft 12th, no ch aft, t.o.* 4 0

Plodded round in 96 & could be aptly named now 11

ITSALLTHEONETODEV (Irish) — **I** 123^{1}, **I** 251^{1}

ITS A MUGS GAME b.m. 8 Petong - Naparima by Creetown — Miss S E Robinson

1995 4(0),5(0),5(0)

204 24/2 Castle Of C' (R) MDO 3m 11 HY *f 1st* F -

281 2/3 Clyst St Ma' (L) RES 3m 11 S *sn last, t.o. frm 12th* 6 0

Shows nothing & season lasted a week in 96 0

ITSCOUNTRYMAN b.g. 7 Itsu (USA) - Ambley Wood by Honour Bound — R G Westacott

1995 U(-),P(0),8(0),P(0)

69 10/2 Great Treth' (R) MDO 3m 12 S *ld to 7th, grad wknd, p.u. 3 out* P 0

713 30/3 Barbury Cas' (L) MDO 3m 10 G *alwys mid-div, no ch whn p.u. 4 out* P 0

1071 13/4 Lifton (R) MDN 3m 10 S *(fav) (7/2-2s),cls 3rd til outpcd 15th, sn btn & eased* 5 0

1280 27/4 Bratton Down (L) MDO 3m 14 GF *prom to 13th, wknd nxt, p.u. 15th, dsmntd* P 0

Well beaten when gambled on; problem last start & no real promise yet 10

ITSGONNASHINE ch.m. 7 Itsu (USA) - Shesheen by Lauso — John Jones

1995 P(0)

849 6/4 Howick (L) MDN 3m 14 GF *7th hlfwy, t.o. & p.u. last* P 0

No signs from 2 outings 95-6 0

ITS MURPHY MAN ch.g. 7 Itsu (USA) - Gaie Pretense (FR) by Pretendre — David J Murphy

1995 P(0),P(0)

175 18/2 Market Rase' (L) MDO 2m 5f 8 GF *prom, disp 9th til ld apr 11th, jnd 3 out, unable qckn flat* 3 14

712 30/3 Barbury Cas' (L) MDO 3m 10 G *alwys mid-div, no ch whn p.u. 13th* P 0

794 2/4 Heythrop (R) CON 3m 6 F *chsd ldrs til outpcd 14th, sn no ch* 4 10

1177 21/4 Mollington (R) INT 3m 14 F *prom, 3rd whn hit 13th, 4th & wkng whn p.u. nxt* P 0

Shows some promise but yet to prove he stays; may have chances in weak race 97 12

IT'SNOTSIMPLE (Irish) — **I** 285^{P}, **I** 400^{2}

IT'S SO SWEET br.m. 8 Sonnen Gold - Sweetheart by Reform — G W Jervis

1995 U(-),P(0),P(0)

607 23/3 Howick (L) MDN 3m 12 S *rear, p.u. 10th* P 0

1200 21/4 Lydstep (L) MDN 3m 10 S *9th whn u.r. 5th* U -

1270 27/4 Pyle (R) MDO 3m 9 G *chsd ldrs,chal 13th,ld apr 15th, sn jnd, no ext und pres* 2 10

1390 6/5 Pantyderi (R) MDO 3m 15 GF *nvr dang, bhnd whn p.u. aft 14th* P 0

Placed in bad Maiden on only completion from 7 starts 95-6; much more needed 10

ITSSTORMINGNORMA b.m. 6 Itsu (USA) - Norman Currency by Normandy — John Jones

1995 3(0)

205 24/2 Castle Of C' (R) MDO 3m 9 HY *sn rear, t.o. & p.u. 2 out* P
389 9/3 Llanfrynach (R) MDN 3m 11 GS *mstks, alwys prom, effrt 15th, sn wknd, fin tired* 3
848 6/4 Howick (L) MDN 3m 14 GF *ld to 9th, chsd nwr frm 13th, alwys hld* 4 1

Beat 6 other finishers last start & slowly improving; could go closer 97 11

ITS THE BIDDER(IRE) ch.g. 8 Bowling Pin - Liberties by Don S I Pittendrig
1995 **14(NH)**
86 11/2 Alnwick (L) OPE 3m 8 GS *wll bhnd frm 6th, t.o. & p.u. 10th* P
699 30/3 Tranwell (L) CON 3m 8 GS *(bl) bhnd 8th, prog to chs ldrs 14th, no ext frm 3 out* 5
912 8/4 Tranwell (L) OPE 3m 8 GF *handy 5th hlfwy, outpcd & wknd rpdly 14th, p.u. last* P

Well beaten on only completion & looks a forlorn hope now 0

ITTIHAAD gr.g. 13 Rusticaro (FR) - Perfect Bid (USA) by Baldric II T J Harri
1995 1(10),P(0)
153 17/2 Erw Lon (L) OPE 3m 15 G *alwys rear, t.o. & p.u. 15th* P
547 17/3 Erw Lon (L) OPE 3m 10 GS *(bl) nvr nrr than mid-div, u.r. 15th* U

No longer of any account 0

IVEAGH LAD br.g. 10 Irish Star - Lady McQuaid by Mick McQuaid Peter Sawne
1995 **P(0)**,5(17),5(13),**1(29)**
326 3/3 Market Rase' (L) OPE 3m 14 G *alwys prom, ev ch & rdn 3 out, unable qckn* 2 22

H/Chase winner 95; front-runs; vanished after debut 96; can win again if fit 97; G-F 23

IVEAGH LADY (Irish) — **I** 99^{P}, **I** 179^{P}, **I** 215^{4}, **I** 258^{4}, **I** 285^{4}, **I** 320^{4}, **I** 448^{U}

IVE CALLED TIME b.g. 8 Sergeant Drummer (USA) - Alice Rairthorn by Romany Air Mrs M de Burgh
1995 **2(NH)**
207 24/2 Castle Of C' (R) MDO 3m 15 HY *alwys mid-div, no ch whn p.u. last* P 0
447 9/3 Haldon (R) MDO 3m 13 S *prom, disp 13th-nxt, ld 3 out, jnd & blnd last, not rcvr* 2 15
646 23/3 Cothelstone (L) MDO 3m 5 S *(Jt fav) chsd ldrs, wnt 2nd 12th, styd on frm 3 out to ld cls home* 1 16
729 31/3 Little Wind' (R) RES 3m 12 GS *5th 12th, not rchd ldrs whn 3rd apr last* 3 19
1139 20/4 Flete Park (R) RES 3m 14 S *(fav) in tch, prog 14th, went 2nd 17th, strng run to ld 2 out,comf* 1 19
1311 28/4 Little Wind' (R) INT 3m 6 G *chsd wnr, mstk 13th, unable to get on terms* 2 16
1454 7/5 Newton Abbot (L) HC 2m 5f 110yds 8 GS *in tch early, wknd 9th, t.o. when p.u. before 2 out.* P 0
1590 25/5 Mounsey Hil' (R) INT 3m 8 G *w.w. prog 14th, ev ch 3 out, no ext apr last* 2 18
1634 1/6 Bratton Down (L) INT 3m 15 G *mid-div,prog frm 14th,went 2nd flat,no imp,fin 2nd,promoted* 1 19

Improved & consistent in points; stays; should find more chances in 97, Confineds; G-S 20

I'VE COPPED IT(IRE) br.g. 6 Corvaro (USA) - Diamond Glow Richard Mathias
1995 **5(NH)**,**7(NH)**,**6(NH)**,**6(NH)**,**7(NH)**
883 6/4 Brampton Br' (R) MDN 3m 13 GF *ld 9-12th, wknd frm 15th, p.u. flat* P 0

No sign of stamina 0

IVEGOTYOUNOW (Irish) — **I** 5^{P}, **I** 49^{P}, **I** 594^{6}

IVY BREEZE (Irish) — **I** 504^{4}, **I** 572^{1}

IVY GLEN (Irish) — **I** 41^{P}, **I** 128^{4}, **I** 203^{4}, **I** 233^{4}, **I** 431^{4}, **I** 585^{6}, **I** 632^{P}

JABBERWOCKY b.g. 7 Pablond - Annie Louise by Parthia R C Frankcom
139 17/2 Larkhill (R) CON 3m 11 G *alwys chsng ldrs, wknd & p.u. last* P 0
467 10/3 Milborne St' (L) MEM 3m 8 G *cls up, 3rd at 12th, outpcd frm 2 out* 3 14

Not disgraced 2nd start & may have prospects in 97 if fit 13

JACK DWYER br.g. 12 Mr Fordette - Daraheen Gate by Arcticeelagh D J Coates
1995 P(0),F(-),6(15),5(0),4(14),6(0),2(13),2(15),1(15),2(15)
118 17/2 Witton Cast' (R) INT 3m 9 S *disp to 12th, outpcd nxt, onepcd aft* 3 12
306 2/3 Great Stain' (L) INT 3m 12 GS *in tch til outpcd 3 out, styd on onepcd* 6 13
588 23/3 Wetherby Po' (L) INT 3m 17 S *handy wil wknd 4 out* 5 13
761 31/3 Great Stain' (L) INT 3m 7 GS *chsd ldrs til mstk 3 out, onepcd* 3 12
894 6/4 Whittington (L) OPE 3m 5 F *ld most, styd on wll whn chal 2 out* 1 18
1154 20/4 Whittington (L) OPE 3m 7 G *nvr dang, btn 5th whn blkd & u.r. apr 2 out* U -

Members winner 94-5; found poor Open 96 & Members best hope again at 13; S-F 15

JACKIE'S BOY (Irish) — **I** 407^{P}, **I** 450^{P}

JACK LITTLE b.g. 7 Miramar Reef - Responder by Vitiges (FR) M J Rozenbroek
416 9/3 Charm Park (L) MDO 3m 13 G *rr early, prog 10th, mstk 4 out, styd on 2 out* 4 0
590 23/3 Wetherby Po' (L) MDO 3m 16 S *mid-div whn f 12th* F -

Beaten 15l in poor race & much more needed to figure in 97 10

JACK'S CROFT b.g. 8 Damister (USA) - Smagiada by Young Generation R R Bainbridge

51	4/2	Alnwick	(L)	MDO	3m	17	G	*alwys bhnd, t.o. 9th, p.u. 11th*	P	0
89	11/2	Alnwick	(L)	MDO	3m	9	GS	*prom til outpcd aft 9th, lft poor 3rd 2 out*	3	0
116	17/2	Lanark	(R)	MDO	3m	10	GS	*sn wll bhnd, p.u. 4 out*	P	0
398	9/3	Dalston	(R)	MEM	3m	13	G	*cls up 7th, not go pc frm 12th*	8	0
756	31/3	Lockerbie	(R)	MDN	3m	14	G	*nvr dang, p.u. 3 out*	P	0
896	6/4	Whittington	(L)	MDO	3m	5	F	*alwys bhnd, nvr dang*	4	0
1155	20/4	Whittington	(L)	MDN	3m	14	G	*2nd whn f 4th*	F	-
1356	4/5	Mosshouses	(L)	MDO	3m	12	GS	*prom,lost plc 7th,ran on 3 out,lft disp nxt,hdd & no ext flt*	2	13
1476	11/5	Aspatria	(L)	MDO	3m	16	GF	*(bl) ld to 3rd, ld 12-15th, sn rddn, onepcd*	2	11
1574	19/5	Corbridge	(R)	MDO	3m	6	G	*(fav) made virt all, shakn up 2 out, hld on und pres flat*	1	14

Gradual improvement; won a poor race; lacks scope & much more needed for Restricteds 14

JACKSORBETTER (Irish) — **I** 108^{P}, **I** 173^{P}, **I** 231^{4}, **I** 409^{P}, **I** 415^{5}, **I** 552^{U}

JACK SUN br.g. 6 Sunyboy - Miss Craigie by New Brig — A J Morley

351	3/3	Garnons	(L)	OPE	3m	14	GS	*t.o. 3rd, m bhnd whn p.u. 15th*	P	0
638	23/3	Siddington	(L)	CON	3m	16	S	*nt fluent, rr, whn f 8th*	F	-

Well bred; shows nothing so far & needs to learn to jump 0

JACK'S WELL (Irish) — **I** 9^{P}, **I** 74^{P}, **I** 147^{P}, **I** 458^{F}, **I** 507^{4}, **I** 642^{P}

JACKY FLYNN (Irish) — **I** 244^{F}, **I** 311^{P}, **I** 352^{5}, **I** 438^{P}, **I** 458^{P}, **I** 565^{F}, **I** 571, , **I** 612^{1}

JACKY'S JAUNT b.m. 6 Sunley Builds - Just Jacky by David Jack — Mrs C E Whiteway

1995 F(-),F(-),U(-),U(-),F(-)

287	2/3	Eaton Hall	(R)	MDO	3m	11	G	*in tch, saddle slppd & p.u. 6th*	P	0
542	17/3	Southwell P'	(L)	MDO	3m	15	GS	*cls up, 2nd at 10th, sn btn, p.u. 13th*	P	0
953	8/4	Eyton-On-Se'	(L)	MDO	2 1/2m	10	GF	*ld til u.r. 4th*	U	-
1485	11/5	Bredwardine	(R)	MDO	3m	15	G	*in rear whn ref 8th*	R	-
1581	19/5	Wolverhampt'	(L)	MDO	3m	10	G	*mstks, in tch to 10th, t.o. & p.u. 14th*	P	0

No completions in 10 races 95-6 0

JADE SHOON b.g. 11 Green Shoon - Milparinka by King's Equity — J M B Cookson

1995 7(0),7(0),2(11),2(13),1(13),1(16)

610	23/3	Friars Haugh	(L)	CON	3m	11	G	*missed start, virt t.n.p., p.u. 8th*	P	0

Dual winner 95; all at sea 96 on only start; can only be watched; G-F 13

JADS LAD gr.g. 12 Warpath - Alexandra by Song — R D Pullar

1995 P(0),3(0),P(0),2(0),1(0),**P(0)**

84	11/2	Alnwick	(L)	RES	3m	11	GS	*mstk 1st, alwys bhnd, t.o. hlfwy*	7	0
111	17/2	Lanark	(R)	RES	3m	6	GS	*handy til lost tch 4 out*	4	0
501	16/3	Lanark	(R)	RES	3m	12	G	*sn bhnd, t.o.*	5	0
858	6/4	Alnwick	(L)	RES	3m	7	GF	*ld 3rd-5th, lst pl, mstk 14th, no dang aft*	6	0

Won bad Maiden 95; well beaten since upgrading 10

JAFFA MAN (Irish) — **I** 36^{F}, **I** 52^{F}

JAFFA'S BOY ch.g. 9 Broadsword (USA) - Lady Seville by Orange Bay — Dr Robert Sharpe

528	16/3	Cothelstone	(L)	MEM	3m	8	G	*chsd ldr to 11th, lst plc, 5th 4 out, styd on wll frm 3 out*	2	17
1076	13/4	Cothelstone	(L)	MEM	3m	2	GF	*(fav) ld 11th, wll clr 2 out, easily*	1	12

Placed in Members 95; ran blinder 1st run 96 & Restricted within scope if ambitiously campaigned 17

JAKES DILEMMA (Irish) — **I** 366^{P}

JAMARSAM(IRE) b.g. 8 The Parson - Park Blue by Levanter — Mrs J Waggott

1995 P(0),P(0),**F(-)**,**P(NH)**

53	4/2	Alnwick	(L)	MDO	3m	13	G	*mid-div, chsd ldrs 12th, sn btn, p.u. 3 out*	P	0
121	17/2	Witton Cast'	(R)	RES	3m	11	S	*prom til wknd 10th, rear whn p.u. 2 out*	P	0
224	24/2	Duncombe Pa'	(R)	RES	3m	12	GS	*f 2nd*	F	-
302	2/3	Great Stain'	(L)	MEM	3m	7	GS	*cls up, wknd 11th, styd on onepcd aft, fin 4th, promoted*	3	10
415	9/3	Charm Park	(L)	MDO	3m	13	G	*mid-div, wknd 10th, nvr fctr*	7	0
705	30/3	Tranwell	(L)	MDO	3m	9	GS	*ld 2-5th, prom til mstk 12th, no dang aft*	5	0
1286	27/4	Easingwold	(L)	MDO	3m	13	G	*mid-div, blnd 8th, sn t.o.*	8	0
1340	4/5	Hexham	(L)	HC	3m 1f	13	S	*(bl) mstks, soon well bhnd, t.o. when p.u. after 12th.*	P	0

Shows very little ability & looks destined to remain a maiden 10

JAMESWICK b.g. 6 Norwick (USA) - Auto Elegance by Brave Shot — R A Webb

1995 **1(NH)**,**7(NH)**,**5(NH)**,**F(NH)**,**4(NH)**,**7(NH)**

529	16/3	Cothelstone	(L)	LAD	3m	5	G	*chsd ldrs, lst tch 11th, 3rd & no ch whn ref & u.r. 3 out*	R	-
991	8/4	Kingston St'	(R)	LAD	3m	8	F	*prog 15th, cls 2nd & rdn nxt, 3rd 2 out, no ext und pres*	4	17
1496	11/5	Holnicote	(L)	LAD	3m	4	G	*hld up in tch, rddn & no response frm 17th*	3	16

NH Flat winner; ran well when completing but stamina suspect & may not be 100% genuine 15

JANEJOLAWRIECLAIRE ch.g. 6 Scorpio (FR) - Burton Princess by Prince Barle — Dave Dixon

653	23/3 Badbury Rin'	(L) MDO 3m	9 G	*alwys chsng ldng grp, t.o. from 13th, one pace*	5	0
1175	20/4 Chaddesley '	(L) MDN 3m	9 G	*cls last at 6th, losing tch whn f 8th*	F	-

Last & well beaten only completion & much more needed to figure 0

JANE'S FEELINGS b.g. 9 Feelings (FR) - Erroll's Elite by Saulingo — T L A Robson

52	4/2 Alnwick	(L) MDO 3m	11 G	*rear, lost tch 8th, t.o. & p.u. 13th*	P	0

Rarely runs & showed nothing in 96 0

JANICE PRICE (Irish) — **I** 77^P, **I** 120^P, **I** 210^F

JANICE PRIDE (Irish) — **I** 240^1

JANUARY DON (Irish) — 337^5, 744^2, 793^3, 943^2, 1158^P, 1332^P, 1412^3, 1506^1, 1560^3, **I** 648, , **I** 656^F

JASILU ch.m. 6 Faustus (USA) - Mosso by Ercolano (USA) — Mrs Susan E Mason

1995 P(0),2(0),P(0),P(0),3(0),2(13),1(14)

329	3/3 Market Rase'	(L) RES 3m	12 G	*(bl) w.w. steady prog to ld 2 out, rdn & hdd apr last, wknd*	3	14
515	16/3 Dalton Park	(R) XX 3m	12 G	*(bl) alwys prom, rdn & ev ch 2 out, wknd apr last*	5	15
585	23/3 Wetherby Po'	(L) RES 3m	13 S	*prom, ld 10th-aft 12th, lft in ld 4 out, hdd & no ext flat*	3	19
1000	9/4 Wetherby	(L) HC 3m 110yds	10 G	*(bl) mstks, in tch, hdwy hfwy, chsd clr ldrs from 11th, no impn.*	3	16
1096	14/4 Whitwell-On'	(R) MEM 3m	9 G	*(Jt fav) (bl) plldn hrd in rear, prog 10th, ev ch 2 out, kpt on flat*	2	17
1284	27/4 Easingwold	(L) RES 3m	14 G	*(bl) alwys prom, 2nd 4 out, chal nxt, ld 2 out, ran on wll flat*	1	19
1458	8/5 Uttoxeter	(L) HC 3 1/4m	8 G	*(bl) in tch, chsd ldr 16th, ev ch when blnd 3 out, held when left clr last.*	1	21
1548	18/5 Southwell	(L) HC 3m 110yds	11 GF	*(bl) rear till p.u. 4 out.*	P	0

Maiden winner 95; consistent but hard ride & finds little; lucky H/Chase win limits 97 options; G-S 20

JASPER JACK (Irish) — **I** 267^P

JAYANDOUBLEU(IRE) b.g. 7 Buckskin (FR) - Lucky House by Pollerton — W A Crozier

1995 F(-),10(0),3(14)

321	2/3 Corbridge	(R) MDN 3m	12 GS	*ld 1st, styd prom, disp til ld apr last, qcknd clr*	1	14
608	23/3 Friars Haugh	(L) RES 3m	13 G	*mid-div whn f 8th*	F	-

Lightly raced & confirmed promise when winning; disappeared after fall; could improve if fit 97 15

JAYBE'S FRIEND (Irish) — **I** 17^P, **I** 39^P, **I** 90^3, **I** 91^5, **I** 135^6, **I** 194^4, **I** 269^2, **I** 305^1

JAY CEEVEE b.g. 9 Cruise Missile - Till Brig by New Brig — Mrs Angela J Howie

1995 5(0),P(0),P(0)

862	6/4 Alnwick	(L) MDN 3m	8 GF	*mid-div 4th, grdly lost plc, bhnd & p.u. 2 out*	P	0

Has finished 2 of 5 starts & shows no ability 0

JAY EM ESS(NZ) b.g. 7 Blue Razor (USA) - Bonafide (FR) by Pharly (FR) — D H Barons

1995 **8(NH)**

69	10/2 Great Treth'	(R) MDO 3m	12 S	*u.r. 1st*	U	-
130	17/2 Ottery St M'	(L) MEM 3m	6 GS	*prom whn blnd & u.r. 6th*	U	-
195	24/2 Lemalla	(R) INT 3m	7 HY	*lft in ld 6th til u.r. 4 out*	U	-
299	2/3 Great Treth'	(R) MDO 3m	13 G	*hld up, gd prog to jnd ldrs 12th, wknd 15th, p.u. nxt*	P	0
557	17/3 Ottery St M'	(L) MDN 3m	10 G	*ld to 3 out, wknd nxt, fin tired*	4	10

Ran reasonably on only completion but finished early & best watched start of 97 12

J B LAD b.g. 10 Lighter - Cherry Fizz by Master Buck — Mrs M J Tuck

1995 6(0),1(15),**F(-)**,P(0),P(0),1(13),**2(18)**

142	17/2 Larkhill	(R) MXO 3m	9 G	*prom til wknd rpdly 11th, p.u. 4 out*	P	0

Won 2 modest races 95; vanished quickly 96; Members best hope if fit 97 13

J B SAUCY DORIS b.m. 10 Mljet - Saucy Lady by Saucy Kit — Mrs B Horan

287	2/3 Eaton Hall	(R) MDO 3m	11 G	*mid-div, no ch whn p.u. 4 out*	P	0
949	8/4 Eyton-On-Se'	(L) MDN 3m	5 GF	*wth ldrs to 10th, grdly wknd frm 3 out*	4	0

Has scant ability & revived to no effect in 96 0

JEEPERS (Irish) — **I** 36^3

JEFFERBY b.g. 9 Roscoe Blake - Darling Eve by Darling Boy — C T Pogson

1995 **6(NH)**,**8(NH)**,**5(NH)**,**6(NH)**,**1(NH)**,**5(NH)**

56	10/2 Cottenham	(R) OPE 3m	12 GS	*ld 2nd til ref 5th, cont t.o. til p.u. 13th*	P	0
120	17/2 Witton Cast'	(R) OPE 3m	7 S	*handy, 2nd 3 out, outpcd by wnr apr last*	2	19
304	2/3 Great Stain'	(L) OPE 3m	10 GS	*(fav) mid-div whn u.r. 6th, dead*	U	-

Dead 19

JELLARIDE (Irish) — **I** 521^P, **I** 528^F, **I** 587^6, **I** 622^P

JELLYBAND ro.g. 8 Baron Blakeney - General's Daughter by Spartan General — D Hiatt

1995 **P(NH)**

235	24/2	Heythrop	(R)	RES	3m	10	GS	*alwys bhnd, p.u. 12th*	P	0
269	2/3	Didmarton	(L)	RES	3m	12	G	*b.d. 1st*	B	-
684	30/3	Chaddesley '	(L)	RES	3m	14	G	*chsd ldr 5-9th, wkng whn blnd 11th, t.o. & p.u. 3 out*	P	0
792	2/4	Heythrop	(R)	LAD	3 3/4m	7	F	*alwys last pair, t.o. frm 15th*	6	0
1179	21/4	Mollington	(R)	LAD	3m	10	F	*mstk 5th, alwys wll bhnd, t.o. 10th*	7	0

Maiden winner 94; ex-Barber trained; novice ridden & showed nothing 96 10

JENSALEE (Irish) — **I** 16^{P}, **I** 43^{2}, **I** 85^{P}, **I** 203^{P}

JERRIGO b.g. 11 Reformed Character - High Jean by Arrigle Valley — S F Knowles

1995 7(0),4(14),1(14),2(14),5(11),2(13)

9	14/1	Cottenham	(R)	OPE	3m	13	G	*alwys rear, t.o. & p.u. 16th*	P	0
96	11/2	Ampton	(R)	XX	3m	11	GF	*ld to 2nd, bhnd 8th, mod 6th 17th, ran on strngly,just faild*	3	16
335	3/3	Heythrop	(R)	INT	3m	9	G	*chsd ldrs, 4th & outpcd 12th, wknd 3 out*	5	0
490	16/3	Horseheath	(R)	XX	3m	7	GF	*j.w. ld aft 1st, hdd aft 2 out, kpt on well*	2	20
897	6/4	Dingley	(R)	CON	3m	15	GS	*ld to 3rd, contd cls up, outpcd 4 out*	2	15
1097	14/4	Guilsborough	(L)	MEM	3m	6	G	*cls up til u.r. bnd apr 5th*	U	-

Steady but modest pointer; good ride for novice; likes Ampton; struggle to win again 16

JESTASTAR b.g. 5 Jester - Mickley Spacetrail by Space King — Mrs J Bush

375	9/3	Barbury Cas'	(L)	MDN	3m	14	GS	*rear whn u.r. 6th*	U	-
643	23/3	Siddington	(L)	MDN	3m	16	S	*schoold in rear, blnd 5th, p.u. 11th*	P	0

Schooling & showed nothing 0

JESTER JACK (Irish) — **I** 101^{B}, **I** 231^{P}

JEUNE GARCON(IRE) gr.g. 5 Roselier (FR) - Sailatel by Golden Love — M Hogg

1096	14/4	Whitwell-On'	(R)	MEM	3m	9	G	*mid-div, blnd 10th, p.u. nxt*	P	0
1301	28/4	Southwell P'	(L)	MDO	3m	10	GF	*hld up, prog 10th, chal 2 out, clr last, imprssv*	1	17

Bombed home in fair time; form yet to be substantiated but could prove useful 97 18

JIGG'S FORGE VI (Irish) — **I** 123^{P}, **I** 202^{R}, **I** 294^{P}, **I** 373^{4}

JIGTIME b.m. 7 Scottish Reel - Travel Again by Derrylin — J W Hughes

1995 5(0),1(15)

608	23/3	Friars Haugh	(L)	RES	3m	13	G	*disp ld frm 11th, ld 4 out, styd on wll*	1	18
1337	1/5	Kelso	(L)	HC	3m 1f	9	S	*mstk 1st, disp ld 4th till ld 3 out, hdd next, led last, styd on well.*	1	28

Massively promising; only raced 4 times but cantered home in H/Chase; sky the limit 97; G-S 30

JIM BOWIE b.g. 13 Yukon Eric (CAN) - Mingwyn Wood by Pirate King — Mrs Gail Davison

1995 6(0),2(16),U(-)

452	9/3	Charing	(L)	LAD	3m	8	G	*alwys prom, ld 3-5th, ev ch 4 out, wknd nxt*	5	15
572	17/3	Detling	(L)	LAD	3m	10	GF	*ld to 3rd, prom aft, outpcd 15th, styd on frm 2 out*	5	0

Winning hurdler; schoolmaster now; runs well without threatening to win. 14

JIM CROW b.g. 7 Bay Spirit - Sinsinawa VI by Menelek — J M Salter

1396	6/5	Cotley Farm	(L)	MDO	3m	11	GF	*mid-div, wknd 10th, t.o. whn p.u. 13th*	P	0
1593	25/5	Mounsey Hil'	(R)	MDO	3m	11	G	*in tch til bhnd & rdn 13th, t.o. & u.r. 2 out*	U	-

No signs yet; sopey and could improve. 0

JIMMY CONE ch.g. 13 Celtic Cone - True Member by New Member — Miss J Russell

1995 2(14),3(18),F(-),4(10),2(14),3(15)

140	17/2	Larkhill	(R)	CON	3m	17	G	*in rear whn u.r. 5th*	U	-
208	24/2	Castle Of C'	(R)	LAD	3m	14	HY	*rear whn f 13th*	F	-

Formerly decent; finished early 96 and looks past it now. 14

JIMMY MAC JIMMY b.g. 9 Carriage Way - Tuthill Bello by Porto Bello — D R Barnard

1995 P(0),P(0)

104	17/2	Marks Tey	(L)	OPE	3m	14	G	*bhnd 10th, t.o. & p.u. 13th*	P	0
312	2/3	Ampton	(R)	OPE	3m	6	G	*chsd ldr til 12th, 4th & rddn 15th, no ch frm nxt*	5	13
417	9/3	High Easter	(L)	MEM	3m	4	S	*disp ld til lft clr 9th, lft solo 12th*	1	0
491	16/3	Horseheath	(R)	CON	3m	5	GF	*j.w. made all, going wll 4 out, ran on strngly*	1	20
677	30/3	Cottenham	(R)	OPE	3m	11	GF	*mstk 7th, prom, mstk 14th, rdr lost irons & p.u. 3 out*	P	0
1067	13/4	Horseheath	(R)	OPE	3m	3	F	*ld /disp til ld 15th, hdd & wknd nxt*	3	16
1323	28/4	Fakenham P-'	(L)	OPE	3m	8	G	*chsd ldrs, went 2nd 15th, blnd 3 out, not qckn last*	2	19
1546	18/5	Fakenham	(L)	HC	3m 110yds	13	G	*chsd ldrs till wknd apr 14th, p.u. before 2 out.*	P	0

Revived in 96; won modest Confined; need luck to win Open; can find another win; any. 17

JIMMY O'GOBLIN ch.g. 9 Deep Run - Natural Shine by Indigenous — A J Cook

510	16/3	Magor	(R)	MDN	3m	9	GS	*(fav) prom, cls 3rd at 10th, outpcd 15th, improve*	3	0
606	23/3	Howick	(L)	MDN	3m	13	S	*just ld whn f 6th*	F	-
771	31/3	Pantyderi	(R)	MDN	3m	14	G	*ld 9-15th, fdd, p.u. 2 out*	P	0
1161	20/4	Llanwit Maj'	(R)	MDO	3m	15	GS	*ld to 7th, wth ldrs til wknd 16th*	5	0

Ex Irish N/H; beaten miles when completing and looks devoid of stamina. 11

JIMMY RIVER br.g. 13 Young Man (FR) - Mary Fox by Mummy's Pet — K Anderson

1995 P(0),2(26),3(22),1(25),1(24)

113	17/2	Lanark	(R)	OPE	3m	6	GS	*t.o. 10th, p.u. 3 out*	P	0
320	2/3	Corbridge	(R)	OPE	3m 5f	8	GS	*cls up early, nvr going wll, p.u. 11th*	P	0

Useful pointer; problems in 96; may revive but best watched initially in 97; any. 20

JIMMY THE FORGE (Irish) — I 343^{1}

JIMMY THE TAILOR (Irish) — I 311^{P}, I 375^{P}

JIMS CHOICE (Irish) — I 18^{P}, I 94^{5}, I 175^{1}, I 254^{1}, I 284^{1}, I 317^{3}, I 412^{2}, I 491^{2}, I 597^{1}

JIMSTRO b.g. 11 Jimsun - Bistro Blue by Blue Streak — K F Clutterbuck

1995 **8(NH)**

8	14/1	Cottenham	(R)	CON	3m	10	G	*cls up, disp 6-11th, blnd nxt, no ch whn f 2 out*	F	-
96	11/2	Ampton	(R)	XX	3m	11	GF	*disp til blnd 13th, losing tch whn blnd 15th, no ch aft*	6	0
177	18/2	Horseheath	(R)	CON	3m	8	G	*prom, rdn & strgglng 10th, sn lost tch, p.u. 2 out*	P	0
310	2/3	Ampton	(R)	CON	3m	13	G	*mid div, blnd 12th, lst tch 14th, t.o. whn s.u. appr 2 out*	S	-
1257	27/4	Cottenham	(R)	CON	3m	5	F	*alwys prom, disp to 8th & 9-12th, chal 3 out, blnd nxt,no ex*	3	12
1399	6/5	Northaw	(L)	CON	3m	8	F	*chsd ldr 4th-12th,3rd & rdn 3 out, strng run flat,ld cls hme*	1	17

Winning chaser; won weak Confined; goes best for T. Moore' hard to find another win; stays. 16

J J JIMMY b.g. 12 Lochnager - J J Caroline by Track Spare — A C Maylam

1995 **3(NH),6(NH),P(NH),6(NH)**

104	17/2	Marks Tey	(L)	OPE	3m	14	G	*pllng, wth ldr to 10th, wknd 12th, p.u. 17th*	P	0
668	26/3	Sandown	(R)	HC	2 1/2m 110yds	8	GS	*mstk 7th, soon bhnd, t.o. when mistake 9th, p.u. before 11th.*	P	0
922	8/4	Aldington	(L)	MEM	3m	4	F	*pllng, ld til p.u. aft 10th, lame*	P	0

Deteriorated rapidly & last start could spell the end 0

J J'S HOPE (Irish) — I 216^{P}, I 254^{P}, I 284^{P}, I 315^{B}, I 360^{5}, I 405^{P}, I 491^{P}

JOANNA MAY b.m. 5 Ardross - Ilton Moor by Bold Lad (IRE) — K Little

193	24/2	Friars Haugh	(L)	MDN	3m	10	S	*bhnd whn p.u. 10th*	P	0

Only learning on debut. 0

JOBINGO b or br.g. 8 Rustingo - Ruths Image by Grey Love — G M Price

1995 **F(NH),8(NH),6(NH)**

382	9/3	Llanfrynach	(R)	MEM	3m	7	GS	*hld up rear, lost tch & not pshd 12th, t.o. & p.u. 2 out*	P	0
849	6/4	Howick	(L)	MDN	3m	14	GF	*prom to 10th, grad lost tch*	6	0
1225	24/4	Brampton Br'	(R)	MDO	3m	18	G	*mid-div til prog frm 15th, fin wl frm 2 out*	5	10
1484	11/5	Bredwardine	(R)	MDO	3m	17	G	*6th & pshd alng 11th, no prog frm 14th*	5	0

No form under rules; only beaten 5 lengths at Brampton; needs a little more before winning. 12

JOBURN b.m. 13 Shua Jo - Glassburn by St Georg III — Mrs G V Mackay

1995 P(0),2(20),5(16),2(22)

232	24/2	Heythrop	(R)	OPE	3m	10	GS	*hld up mid-div,3rd 13th,ev ch nxt,wknd,poor 5th & p.u.last*	P	0
435	9/3	Newton Brom'	(R)	OPE	3m	7	GS	*sttld mid-div, 5th at 14th, prog 3 out, ld last, rdn clr*	1	21

Won 2 Opens 94; found another modest Open in 96; needs cut in ground; win at 14 looks tough. 22

JODESI (Irish) — I 121, , I 139^{1}

JOE PENNY gr.g. 7 Impecunious - Roberts Girl by Mount Hagen (FR) — Keith Kerley

1995 P(0),F(-)

468	10/3	Milborne St'	(L)	OPE	3m	5	G	*f 2nd*	F	-
733	31/3	Little Wind'	(R)	MDO	3m	13	GS	*6th 11th, wknd, t.o. p.u. apr 3 out*	P	0
993	8/4	Kingston St'	(R)	MDO	3m	17	F	*(vis) mid-div, 6th at 11th, nvr dang, p.u. 3 out*	P	0

Yet to complete; shows no ability. 0

JOE QUALITY b.g. 9 Smackover - Whangarei by Gold Rod — Miss Carron Nicol

106	17/2	Marks Tey	(L)	RES	3m	12	G	*alwys rr, t.o. & p.u. 17th*	P	0
254	25/2	Charing	(L)	MDO	3m	9	GS	*ld, hdd 8th, lft in ld 10th, jnd & f 14th*	F	-
477	10/3	Tweseldown	(R)	MDO	3m	15	G	*mid-div, jnd ldrs 12th, ev ch til onepcd frm 4 out*	4	0
575	17/3	Detling	(L)	MDO	3m	10	GF	*chsd clr ldr,clr of rest 4 out,lft in ld nxt,fdd & hdd nxt*	3	0
783	31/3	Tweseldown	(R)	MEM	3m	5	G	*w.w. prog to disp 12th,ld 3 out,rdn & hdd nxt,immed btn*	3	10
1055	13/4	Penshurst	(L)	MDO	3m	11	G	*ld til mstk 2nd, prom aft, ld 12th & 14th, 3rd nxt & btn*	3	0

1453 7/5 Wincanton (R) HC 2m 5f 9 F *t.o. when p.u. before 4 out.* P 0

Non stayer; handed race at Detling but stopped to nothing; very hard to find a win. 0

JOE'S BLACKJACK br.g. 8 Mansingh (USA) - Lyn Affair by Royal Palace — Mrs Eleanor Anderson

1995 6(0),8(0),1(12),P(0)

1452 6/5 Witton Cast' (R) MEM 3m 7 G *ld til wknd 4 out, lft 10l 2nd 2 out, kpt on onepce* 2 11

Won short Maiden (lucky) 95; does not stay and Restricted to hard; brief campaign in 96. 11

JOG-ALONG b.g. 7 Cool Guy (USA) - South Dakota by Patch — W McKeown

98 12/2 Hereford (R) HC 3m 1f 110yds 12 HY *ld after 1st till after next, chsd wnr till apr 9th, weakening when hit 10th, t.o. when p.u. before 14th.* P 0

Placed in H/chase 94; only one run since and can only be watched nowill young. 14

JOHN CORBET b.g. 13 Ascertain (USA) - Sweet Clare by Suki Desu — Tony Fawcett

1995 P(0),1(18),2(16),3(14),**4(18)**,5(12),2(15),**9(0)**

412 9/3 Charm Park (L) LAD 3m 7 G *alwys prom, disp last, styd on, jst btn* 2 19
759 31/3 Great Stain' (L) LAD 3m 10 GS *ld til hdd & wknd 3 out* 6 12
827 6/4 Stainton (R) LAD 3m 7 GF *prom til outpcd bef 2 out* 4 17
1449 6/5 Witton Cast' (R) LAD 3m 10 G *midfld, styd on wll apr 2 out, tk 2nd cls home* 2 18
1586 25/5 Hexham (L) HC 2 1/2m 110yds 14 GF *settld with chasing gp, kept on from 3 out, not pace to chal.* 5 11

Non-stayer; won 2 of last 25; tries hard but a win at 14 unlikely. 17

JOHNNY ROSE b.g. 12 Le Johnstan - The Rose Royale by Takawalk II — A Simpson

1995 4(13),U(-),3(13),2(17)

473 10/3 Tweseldown (R) MEM 3m 5 G *cls up til ld 12th, hdd aft 3 out, rallied last* 2 12
596 23/3 Parham (R) LAD 3m 8 GS *ld 6th til aft 4 out, kpt on same pace* 5 12
1373 4/5 Peper Harow (L) LAD 3m 3 F *ld, 12l clr 11th, hdded appr 3 out, rdn & btn apppr 2 out* 2 0

Placed in 7 of last 9 races ; barely stays and will need luck to win. 14

JOHNNY'S ECHO (Irish) — **I** 36^{P}, **I** 73^{U}, **I** 114^{P}, **I** 213^{P}

JOHNNY THE FOX (Irish) — **I** 10^{2}

JOHN O'DEE b.g. 13 Kambalda - Lady Parkhill by Even Money — Ian de Burgh Marsh

345 3/3 Higham (L) OPE 3m 3 G *ld to 8th, ld agn 12-14th, wknd 2 out* 3 12
668 26/3 Sandown (R) HC 2 1/2m 110yds 8 GS *ld till hdd 4th, bhnd from 6th, t.o. from 8th.* 5 0
1062 13/4 Horseheath (R) MEM 3m 3 F *ld til appr last, onepcd* 2 14
1538 16/5 Folkestone (R) HC 3 1/4m 6 G *chsd ldr 4th to 7th, soon bhnd, t.o. when u.r. 15th.* U -

Winning chaser; goes best fresh and needs easy course; unlikely to win again. 13

JOHN ROGER b.g. 10 Impecunious - Romany Serenade by Romany Air — H J Manners

1995 **4(NH),P(NH),P(NH),U(NH),3(NH),4(NH),3(NH),4(NH),3(NH),U(NH),7(NH)**

26 20/1 Barbury Cas' (L) OPE 3m 12 GS *f 2nd* F -
125 17/2 Kingston Bl' (L) OPE 3m 10 GS *alwys rear, mstk 11th, lost tch whn p.u. 13th* P 0
233 24/2 Heythrop (R) MDN 3m 14 GS *rear til prog to 4th at 14th, chal last, jnd ldr on line* 1 14

Disappointing till found his mark last start; more needed for Restricted; G/S 15

JOHN'S RIGHT (Irish) — **I** 2^{P}, **I** 46^{3}, **I** 71^{4}, **I** 148^{4}, **I** 213^{1}, **I** 378^{P}, **I** 519^{U}, **I** 549^{3}

JOINT ACCOUNT ch.g. 6 Sayyaf - Dancing Clara by Billion (USA) — Mrs F E Needham

1995 **11(NH),14(NH)**

332 3/3 Market Rase' (L) MDO 3m 8 G *mstks, sn t.o..p.u. 11th* P 0
414 9/3 Charm Park (L) MDO 3m 11 G *slw strt, prog, 6th at 10th, u.r. nxt* U -
987 8/4 Charm Park (L) MDN 3m 13 GF *f 1st* F -
1136 20/4 Hornby Cast' (L) MDN 3m 11 G *keen hold, mid-div whn u.r. 10th* U -
1450 6/5 Witton Cast' (R) MDO 3m 14 G *pulld hrd, cls up to 10th, wknd nxt, p.u. 12th* P 0
1465 11/5 Easingwold (L) MEM 3m 4 G *pllng,prom,ld 6th,wd & hdd 9th,blnd 11th,ev ch & f 14th* F -

No signs in bumpers; too headstrong at present; can do better. 12

JOKERS PATCH ch.g. 9 Hotfoot - Rhythmical by Swing Easy (USA) — Mrs D L Gillies

1995 **9(NH),P(NH),4(NH)**

197 24/2 Lemalla (R) LAD 3m 13 HY *alwys rear, p.u. 14th* P 0
295 2/3 Great Treth' (R) LAD 3m 6 G *in tch to 15th, sn wknd, walked in* 4 0
624 23/3 Kilworthy (L) LAD 3m 7 GS *mstk 9th, alwys last pair, t.o. 12th* 6 0
716 30/3 Wadebridge (L) LAD 3m 6 GF *in tch til lost plc steadily frm 13th, t.o. & p.u. 3 out* P 0
940 8/4 Wadebridge (L) LAD 3m 4 F *raced off the pce, til tk 3rd cls home* 3 0
1072 13/4 Lifton (R) LAD 3m 7 S *rear, wnt dist 4th 15th, hit last, virtly p.u. flat* 4 0
1276 27/4 Bratton Down (L) LAD 3m 7 GF *sn wll bhnd, t.o. 11th* 5 0
1624 27/5 Lifton (R) LAD 3m 9 GS *t.o. & p.u. 3 out* P 0

Schoolmaster & no stamina - just potters around the back 0

JOLI EXCITING b.m. 11 Tepukei - Merry Leap by Stephen George — Aj Carnegie

1995 P(0),6(11)

47	4/2	Alnwick	(L)	XX	3m	14 G	*mid-div, prog & in tch 12th, one pacd 3 out, lft 3rd last*	3	13
189	24/2	Friars Haugh	(L)	RES	3m	9 S	*hld up, kpt on frm 3 out, not rch ldrs*	4	13
608	23/3	Friars Haugh	(L)	RES	3m	13 G	*nvr bttr thn mdfld*	5	0
911	8/4	Tranwell	(L)	CON	3m	9 GF	*alwys rear, last at 9th, lost tch 12th*	8	0
1250	27/4	Balcormo Ma'	(R)	LAD	3m	5 GS	*not alwys fluent, chsd wnr frm 11th, no ext frm 2 out*	2	14
1352	4/5	Mosshouses	(L)	LAD	3m	10 GS	*jmpd slwly 6th, outpcd 13th, no prog frm 3 out*	5	10

Maiden winner 94; consistent, stays but moderate; Restricted at 12 looks hard. 13

JOLI HIGH NOTE b.m. 7 Senang Hati - Major Symphony by Trombone — Mrs C Barnett

993	8/4	Kingston St'	(R)	MDO	3m	17 F	*sn bhnd, t.o. til p.u. 15th*	P	0
1164	20/4	Larkhill	(R)	MDN	3m	12 GF	*rear whn u.r. 2nd*	U	-
1349	4/5	Holnicote	(L)	MDO	3m	8 GS	*wll bhnd, t.o. & p.u. 9th*	P	0
1555	18/5	Bratton Down	(L)	MDO	3m	13 F	*9th hlfwy, wll off pace til prog 2 out, fin wll*	2	12
1592	25/5	Mounsey Hil'	(R)	MDO	3m	9 G	*bhnd 8th, went poor 4th 3 out, nvr nrr*	3	10
1638	1/6	Bratton Down	(L)	MDO	3m	13 G	*hld up bhnd, rpd prog to jn ldrs 12th, wknd frm 15th*	8	0

Placed in weak Maidens; pulls and looks a hard ride tactically; more needed. 12

JOLLY BOAT br.g. 9 Lord Ha Ha - Mariner's Dash by Master Buck — Gareth Samuel

1995 2(20),1(18),U(-),1(17)

683	30/3	Chaddesley '	(L)	MEM	3m	17 G	*(Jt fav) chsd ldr 5th, ld 2 out, sn hdd, lft in ld last, drvn out*	1	21
1193	21/4	Sandon	(L)	OPE	3m	8 G	*(fav) w.w. ld 3 out, sn clr, comf*	1	22
1231	27/4	Weston Park	(L)	OPE	3m	6 G	*(fav) ld/disp to 4th,steadd,ld 10th,strng chal frm 3 out,ran onwll*	1	19
1419	6/5	Eyton-On-Se'	(L)	OPE	3m	4 GF	*(fav) 3rd in rr, clsr ordr 9th, 2nd 13th, chsd wnr, alwys hld*	2	17

Won 8 of last 14 races; consistent; stays well; sure to win more; best on G-Hy. 23

JOLLY FELLOW b.g. 12 Pimpernels Tune - Jolie Fille — J R Wiles

1995 P(0),P(0),P(0),P(0)

1281	27/4	Easingwold	(L)	CON	3m	15 G	*rear, sn bhnd, t.o.*	8	0
1447	6/5	Witton Cast'	(R)	RES	3m	11 G	*(bl) hndy, ld 14th-2 out, outpcd by wnnr*	2	16
1571	19/5	Corbridge	(R)	RES	3m	13 G	*(fav) (bl) hld up rear, prog 8th, nvr rchd ldrs*	6	12
1586	25/5	Hexham	(L)	HC	2 1/2m 110yds	14 GF	*(bl) waited with, steady hdwy when nearly u.r. 6 out, not rcvr, t.o..*	11	0
1641	2/6	Dingley	(R)	RES	3m	13 GF	*(bl) mid-div, prog to ch ldr 13th, not qckn 3 out,kpt on und pres*	2	17

Returned to form 96; placed 5 times 94-96 but last won in 87 and unlikely to change that; blinkers. 15

JOLLY FLIER br.g. 8 Prince Of Peace - Ceile by Galivanter — A L Hawkings

1995 P(0),2(12),4(0)

284	2/3	Clyst St Ma'	(L)	MDN	3m	11 S	*(fav) ld to 12th, prom aft, wknd 3 out*	3	0
534	16/3	Cothelstone	(L)	MDN	3m	10 G	*made most to 15th, rdn & wknd apr nxt*	5	0
807	4/4	Clyst St Ma'	(L)	MDO	3m	10 GS	*in tch, 3rd & rdn 14th, wknd, lft 3rd last*	3	0
990	8/4	Kingston St'	(R)	OPE	3m	6 F	*ld to 4th, wknd 8th, t.o. & p.u. 2 out*	P	0

Promise in 95; has not progressed; stamina looks the problem. 11

JOLLY GYPSY (Irish) — **I** 602P

JOLLY SENSIBLE gr.m. 7 Pragmatic - Jolly Regal by Jolly Good — W H Whitley

1995 r(-),P(0),P(0),3(10),P(0)

1347	4/5	Holnicote	(L)	MDO	3m	16 GS	*prom, 3rd & ev ch til outpcd frm 2 out*	4	12
1530	12/5	Ottery St M'	(L)	MDO	3m	8 GF	*(fav) not fluent, prog 6th, 3rd whn hit 12th, p.u. nxt*	P	0

Late to appear; placed in poor races; ran badly when favourite; more needed. 11

JOLLY SWAGMAN b.g. 5 Governor General - Armour Of Light by Hot Spark — B R Hughes

151	17/2	Erw Lon	(L)	MDN	3m	8 G	*t.o. 6th, p.u 12th*	P	0
552	17/3	Erw Lon	(L)	MDN	3m	10 GS	*nvr nr ldrs, p.u. 9th*	P	0
772	31/3	Pantyderi	(R)	MDN	3m	8 G	*in rear whn p.u. 9th*	P	0
976	8/4	Lydstep	(L)	MDO	3m	12 G	*nvr nrr than 4th, p.u. 14th*	P	0
1039	13/4	St Hilary	(R)	MDN	3m	14 G	*prom, 3rd whn f 11th*	F	-
1271	27/4	Pyle	(R)	MDO	3m	15 G	*prom, ev ch 13th, wknd nxt, p.u. 3 out*	P	0
1390	6/5	Pantyderi	(R)	MDO	3m	15 GF	*rear, prog 8th, ld 10-15th, fdd, fin tired*	4	10

Beaten 13 lengths in sub 6 minute Maiden; even that looked too far; young and may do better. 10

JOLLY TEAR (Irish) — **I** 642S

JONAH'S JEST(IRE) br.g. 7 Spin Of A Coin - Stormy Trip by Strong Gale — H R Barker

763	31/3	Great Stain'	(L)	MDN	3m	11 GS	*prom, mstk 11th, sn wknd, p.u. aft 14th*	P	0

No real signs on debut. 0

JORODEC (Irish) — **I** 245F, **I** 275F, **I** 3566

JOSALADY (Irish) — **I** 226F, **I** 3536, **I** 515U, **I** 531P, **I** 640S

JO-SU-KI b.g. 9 Strong Gale - Glenalass by Deep Diver — Peter Saville

564	17/3	Wolverhampt'	(L)	RES	3m	8	GS	*nvr bynd mid-div, p.u. 16th*	P	0
739	31/3	Sudlow Farm	(R)	RES	3m	11	G	*mid-div, outpcd 10th, no ch frm 13th*	6	0
1030	13/4	Alpraham	(R)	RES	3m	10	GS	*chas ldrs to 12th, wknd qckly, t.o. & p.u. 3 out*	P	0
1233	27/4	Weston Park	(L)	RES	3m	14	G	*prom, ldng grp thruout, not qckn frm 3 out*	4	0
1582	19/5	Wolverhampt'	(L)	RES	3m	10	G	*w.w. in tch, jnd ldrs 14th, ld apr last, drvn clr flat*	1	15
1614	27/5	Hereford	(R)	HC	3m 1f 110yds	16	G	*alwys bhnd, lost tch 14th, t.o. when p.u. before 3 out.*	P	0

Irish Maiden winner 95; won slowly run poor Restricted; stamina suspect; Confined looks very hard. ... 15

JOVEN TOP gr.g. 8 Mansingh (USA) - Jovenita by High Top — M H D Barlow

1995 F(-),P(0),6(0),**P(0)**,4(0)

959	8/4	Lockinge	(L)	MDN	3m	6	GF	*ld 4-10th, prom aft, disp 3 out til wknd apr last*	3	13

Hard puller and does not really stay; just beaten in poor race 96 need same to win. 12

JOYFUL HERO b.m. 6 War Hero - Joy Travel by Ete Indien (USA) — R Dench

35	20/1	Higham	(L)	RES	3m	16	GF	*sn bhnd, p.u. 9th*	P	0
254	25/2	Charing	(L)	MDO	3m	9	GS	*f 2nd*	F	-
921	8/4	Aldington	(L)	MDO	3m	8	F	*strtd 30l bhnd,schoold & t.o.,fin full of running,stewards*	4	0
1210	21/4	Heathfield	(R)	MDO	3m	13	F	*trckd ldrs, 3rd 13th, ld 16th, hdd nxt, wknd*	3	0
1445	6/5	Aldington	(L)	MDO	3m	8	HD	*(Jt fav) rr,jnd ldrs 10th,lft in ld 12th,hdd 2 out,rlld undpres,disq*	0	0

Placed in 3 dire contests (disqualified once); still young and can improve; needs to. 10

JOYFUL JOAN(IRE) b.m. 5 Viteric (FR) - Nana's Gift by Side Track — N W Padfield

681	30/3	Cottenham	(R)	MDO	3m	12	GF	*in tch in rear til f 9th*	F	-
1299	28/4	Bexhill	(R)	MDO	3m	7	F	*ld to 3rd, cls aft, 3rd frm 14th, wknd 4 out, p.u. 2 out*	P	0

Placed in Irish Maidens 95; no signs over here yet. 0

JOYNEY br.m. 9 Harlow (USA) - Whipper Snapper by Menelek — Miss Kathryn Guard

220	24/2	Newtown	(L)	MDN	3m	12	GS	*in tch til s.u. aft 8th*	S	-
357	3/3	Garnons	(L)	RES	3m	14	GS	*cls 2nd at 7th, wknd 12th, p.u. 3 out*	P	0
549	17/3	Erw Lon	(L)	RES	3m	11	GS	*twrds rear til p.u. 14th*	P	0
749	31/3	Upper Sapey	(R)	MDO	3m	17	GS	*prog frm 2 out, ev ch last, just outpcd flat*	3	14
1048	13/4	Bitterley	(L)	MDO	3m	12	G	*prog to lng grp 9th, ld 3 out, wknd frm nxt*	3	12
1315	28/4	Bitterley	(L)	MDO	3m	10	G	*(fav) hld up, last at 11th, prog 14th, 2nd 3 out, no ext last*	2	13
1417	6/5	Cursneh Hill	(L)	MDO	3m	14	GF	*(fav) cls up frm 11th, ev ch 15th, rddn & no ext frm nxt*	3	10

Good enough for a small win; stamina problems and short course looks essential. 14

JR-KAY(IRE) ch.g. 6 Tremblant - Promising Very Vii by Damsire Unregistered — N W A Bannister

758	31/3	Great Stain'	(L)	RES	3m	17	GS	*made all, drvn out flat*	1	19
1151	20/4	Whittington	(L)	INT	3m	12	G	*chsd ldr, lft in ld 14th, chal flat, just held on*	1	19
1369	4/5	Gisburn	(R)	CON	3m	10	G	*(fav) ld til f 15th whn going wll*	F	-
1585	25/5	Cartmel	(L)	HC	3 1/4m	14	GF	*(fav) trckd ldrs, hdwy to ld 4 out, driven out flat.*	1	19

Successful season but Restricted-standard H/Chase win means improvement needed for 97; G/S-G/F 21

JUDGEROGER b.g. 10 Decent Fellow - Carnation Cruise by Dual — Grant Lewis

146	17/2	Erw Lon	(L)	MEM	3m	7	G	*(fav) made all, 1l up 2 out, drew clr last*	1	17
384	9/3	Llanfrynach	(R)	OPE	3m	16	GS	*alwys prom, 3rd & rdn 15th, sn outpcd, no imp ldrs aft*	3	18

Won 5 in 94; missed 95; won weak Members; ran well after but obviously hard to train now; any. 20

JUDICIOUS CAPTAIN b.g. 9 New Member - Injudicious by Quorum — James R Adam

1995 **P(NH)**

49	4/2	Alnwick	(L)	OPE	3m	14	G	*mstk 4th, rear, lost tch 12th, t.o. & p.u. 3 out*	P	0
402	9/3	Dalston	(R)	XX	3m	13	G	*alwys abt sm plc*	8	0
612	23/3	Friars Haugh	(L)	OPE	3m	8	G	*3rd hlfwy, sn wknd.*	4	0
1354	4/5	Mosshouses	(L)	OPE	3m	4	GS	*66s-10s, mstks, ld 9-12th, ev ch 3 out, sn rdn & btn*	2	17

Disappointing till ran well last start & could have Confined chances in 97 18

JUDY LINE b.m. 7 Funny Man - Deirdre's Choice by Golden Love — K C Lewis

1995 6(0),3(13),3(12)

219	24/2	Newtown	(L)	RES	3m	17	GS	*last trio til prog 11th, poor 10th aft 13th, fin strngly*	4	10
358	3/3	Garnons	(L)	RES	3m	18	GS	*trckd ldrs, went cls 3rd 11th, lft 2nd 3 out, ld last,kpt on*	1	16
604	23/3	Howick	(L)	INT	3m	7	S	*rear, prog to 4th at 12th, styd on 3 out, nrst fin*	2	10
847	6/4	Howick	(L)	LAD	3m	9	GF	*1st ride, 15l 2nd whn u.r. 7th*	U	-
1244	27/4	Woodford	(L)	INT	3m	12	G	*prom in chsng grp til outpcd apr 16th*	5	13

Beat large field; well beaten in good races after; stays; should find another win. 18

JULY SCHOON (Irish) — **I** 333^{P}, **I** 436^{P}, **I** 519^{4}, **I** 549^{2}, **I** 611^{3}, **I** 639^{S}, **I** 648^{5}, **I** 656^{2}

JUMBEAU ch.g. 11 Beau Charmeur (FR) - My Hansel by Prince Hansel — Pell-Mell Partners

1995 **2(NH),10(NH),P(NH),B(NH),3(NH)**

672	29/3	Aintree	(L)	HC	2 3/4m	26	G	*held up, outpcd 9th, struggling when blnd 14th, t.o..*	10	14
1331	1/5	Cheltenham	(L)	HC	2m 5f	9	G	*waited with, prog 8th, outpcd 11th, no ch after.*	4	17
1544	17/5	Stratford	(L)	HC	3m	10	GF	*chsd ldr, rdn to ld last, soon hdd, not qckn.*	2	25
1615	27/5	Wetherby	(L)	HC	2 1/2m 110yds	11	G	*(fav) in tch till outpcd after 8th, no dngr after.*	4	18

Winning chaser; ran in good races & retains some ability; points best hope for 97 success; Good 23

JUNIOR MOSS (Irish) — **I** 297^{P}, **I** 388^{4}, **I** 416, , **I** 543^{5}, **I** 579^{3}

JUNIORS CHOICE br.g. 13 Bivouac - Lucky Number II by Lucky Sovereign — John Threadgall

1995 **5(0)**,6(0),U(-),3(13),5(0),1(12),P(0)

187	24/2	Friars Haugh	(L)	CON	3m	12	S	*wll bhnd p.u. 12th*	P	0
1350	4/5	Mosshouses	(L)	MEM	3m	2	GS	*(fav) sn wll clr, 15l up & wkng whn f 11th*	F	-

Won joke races 95/96; outclassed in proper races. 10

JUNIPER LODGE br.g. 8 Impecunious - Miss Ticklemouse by Rhodomantade — Mrs W Jarrett

1995 3(12),U(-)

204	24/2	Castle Of C'	(R)	MDO	3m	11	HY	*made most til 4 out, ev ch whn f nxt*	F	-
479	10/3	Tweseldown	(R)	MDO	3m	10	G	*6s-3s, disp to 6th, rdn & lkd hld whn f 3 out*	F	-
713	30/3	Barbury Cas'	(L)	MDO	3m	10	G	*ld/disp to 13th, outpcd frm 4 out*	3	0
1217	24/4	Andoversford	(R)	MDO	3m	16	G	*wth ldr, ld 12th, blndrd & hd 15th, not rcvr, kpt on 2 out*	3	10
1434	6/5	Ashorne	(R)	MDO	3m	15	G	*(fav) alwys prom, ld 11-12th, ev ch 14th, fdd frm 3 out*	3	12

Placed 4 times 95/96; stamina problems; may sneak a win one day. 13

JUPITER MOON b.g. 7 Jupiter Island - Troy Moon by Troy — Mrs I N McCallum

1995 **5(NH)**

212	24/2	Castle Of C'	(R)	CON	3m	7	HY	*cls up, ld 3rd til blnd & u.r. 13th*	U	-
262	2/3	Didmarton	(L)	MEM	3m	11	G	*wll in rear, no ch 11th, styd on aft, nrst fin*	5	0
785	31/3	Tweseldown	(R)	OPE	3m	5	G	*f 1st*	F	-
865	6/4	Larkhill	(R)	CON	3m	3	F	*not fluent & jmp lft, lft in ld 2nd, clr frm 5 out*	1	13
1167	20/4	Larkhill	(R)	MEM	3m	9	GF	*nvr bttr thn mid-div, not pce to chal*	4	14

Winning chaser 94; novice ridden in points; won non-contest; unlikely to win competitive races 14

JURANSTAN b.g. 11 Furry Glen - Atlantic Hope by Brave Invader (USA) — B W Holmes

231	24/2	Heythrop	(R)	XX	3m	10	GS	*nvr nr ldrs, mid-div whn blnd 10th, p.u. 15th*	P	0
338	3/3	Heythrop	(R)	RES	3m	9	G	*(bl) prom, mstk 10th, blnd 12th & wknd, ref 14th*	R	-
942	8/4	Andoversford	(R)	MEM	3m	8	GF	*chsd ldrs, ld bef 12th, almost ref nxt, 4th whn ref 14th*	R	-

Maiden winner 93; always ungenuine and looks gone now. 11

JUST A BREEZE (Irish) — **I** 6^{1}, **I** 44^{1}, **I** 140^{3}, **I** 198^{5}, **I** 295^{1}, **I** 442^{1}

JUST A MADAM(IRE) gr.m. 6 Roselier (FR) - La Bise by Callernish — M J Gingell

1995 U(-),7(0),4(12)

15	14/1	Cottenham	(R)	MDN	3m	14	G	*cls up, prog to ld 2 out, hdd apr last, no ext*	2	14
344	3/3	Higham	(L)	MDO	3m	12	G	*cls 2nd til ld 3rd-13th, prssd wnr aft, ran on, just faild*	2	13
522	16/3	Larkhill	(R)	MDO	3m	12	G	*ld to 2 out, ran on onepcd*	3	16
680	30/3	Cottenham	(R)	MDO	3m	11	GF	*made all, clr 13th, mstk last, unchal*	1	17
1380	5/5	Dingley	(R)	RES	3m	11	GF	*mstks, ld 2-3rd & 9-10th, btn frm 3 out*	5	10

Improved; easily won Maiden; novice ridden to no effect; also placed in NH Flat; potentially useful 17

JUST A PLAYBOY (Irish) — **I** 565^{P}

JUST AS HOPEFUL(NZ) b.g. 12 In The Purple (FR) - Bighearted (NZ) by Better Honey — I J Webber

1995 P(0),2(16),2(19),F(-),R(-),R(-)

1274	27/4	Bratton Down	(L)	MEM	3m	7	GF	*alwys last, t.o. whn ref 4th*	R	-

Able in 95 but 3 refusals on the trot now; best avoided. 0

JUST BALLYTOO b.g. 9 Fidel - Baringle by Bargello — P Scaramanga

1995 3(0),4(0),7(0),**8(0)**,3(10),P(0),r(-),U(-),4(12),2(10),2(0)

129	17/2	Kingston Bl'	(L)	MDN	3m	15	GS	*prom to 8th, sn outpcd, lft 4th 3 out, kpt on*	2	0
255	28/2	Taunton	(R)	HC	4 1/4m 110yds	15	GS	*wknd 13th, t.o. when p.u. before 21st.*	P	0
477	10/3	Tweseldown	(R)	MDO	3m	15	G	*disp to 5th, 2nd aft til outpcd 15th, styd on 2 out,not qckn*	2	13
637	23/3	Siddington	(L)	MEM	3m	14	S	*disp ld to 6th, prom til wknd appr 15th*	5	10
999	8/4	Hackwood Pa'	(L)	RES	3m	6	GF	*ld to 4th, 2nd to 8th, wknd, t.o.*	6	0

Slow; 4 2nds 95/96; easily beaten though and unlikely to win. 12

JUST BEN br.g. 8 Oats - Kayella by Fine Blade (USA) — Roger Persey

1995 P(0),7(0),3(15),2(12),1(16)

138	17/2	Ottery St M'	(L)	RES	3m	18	GS	*prom early, lost tch 4 out, p.u. 2 out*	P	0
280	2/3	Clyst St Ma'	(L)	RES	3m	11	S	*(Co fav) alwys prom, ld 14th, styd on well frm 3 out*	1	20

531 16/3 Cothelstone (L) CON 3m 12 G *bhnd frm 7th, t.o. & p.u. 15th* P 0
628 23/3 Kilworthy (L) INT 3m 7 GS *prom, mstk 8th, ld 11-12th, wknd rpdly apr 3 out* 4 13
1069 13/4 Lifton (R) CON 3m 9 S *hndy, outpcd 15th, wnt 3rd 3 out, ld last, pshd out* 1 20
1277 27/4 Bratton Down (L) CON 3m 15 GF *(fav) ld to 7th, cls up til wknd & outpcd frm 2 out* 5 15
1427 6/5 High Bickin' (R) CON 3m 10 G *chsd ldr, ld 3 out, cght in last 75 yards* 2 20
1625 27/5 Lifton (R) INT 3m 8 GS *(Jt fav) trckd ldr frm 8th, ld 4 out, styd on strngly und pres* 1 19

Improved; won 4 of last 9; inconsistent; best on sharp tracks; win more Confineds; S-G/F 21

JUST BERT(IRE) b.g. 6 Kambalda - Cappagh Flier by Lock Diamond Mrs J Alford

1995 F(-),1(16),U(-),2(16),1(18)

43 3/2 Wadebridge (L) INT 3m 5 GF *w.w., mstk 3rd, prog 11th, ld 14th, rdn out* 1 22
294 2/3 Great Treth' (R) CON 3m 10 G *(fav) w.w. prog 14th, cls 3rd whn u.r. 16th* U -
625 23/3 Kilworthy (L) CON 3m 11 GS *(fav) not fluent,lost plc 7th,prog to 2nd 14th,ev ch 2 out,nt qckn* 2 19
923 8/4 Bishopsleigh (R) MEM 3m 2 G *(fav) lft in ld 2nd,u.r. 9th, rider unable to remnt, injured* U -

Promising but won 3, failed to finish 4 of 9 starts 95/6; useful if mistakes ironed out; G-Hy 23

JUST CHARLIE b.g. 7 Bustino - Derring Miss by Derrylin Mrs Susan E Mason

1995 P(0),P(0),7(0),2(16),1(18),2(18),2(18)

223 24/2 Duncombe Pa' (R) CON 3m 16 GS *prog 9th, 6th & outpcd 3 out, styd on well aft* 3 19
409 9/3 Charm Park (L) CON 3m 11 G *alwys prom, ld frm 3 out, styd on wl* 1 23
588 23/3 Wetherby Po' (L) INT 3m 17 S *alwys mid-div, nvr a fctr* 6 11
985 8/4 Charm Park (L) INT 3m 9 GF *ld frm 7th, drew clr apr last, comf* 1 21
1092 14/4 Whitwell-On' (R) CON 3m 10 G *(fav) alwys prom, ld 5 out-3 out, no ext* 4 17
1281 27/4 Easingwold (L) CON 3m 15 G *ld to 3rd, prom, chsd wnr 3 out, chal flat, not qckn cls hm* 2 22

Solid, consistent and improved; best on easy course; can win again; G-F. 22

JUST DANNY ch.g. 6 Nijin (USA) - Del Mar by Orange Bay N K Thick

607 23/3 Howick (L) MDN 3m 12 S *rear, t.o. & p.u. 10th* P 0
842 6/4 Maisemore P' (L) MDN 3m 17 GF *alwys rr, last frm 9th til p.u. 13th* P 0
1174 20/4 Chaddesley ' (L) MDN 3m 10 G *(bl) alwys rear, in tch til not qckn 14th, no ch frm 17th* 4 0

Beaten over 30 lengths and much more needed. 10

JUST DONALD b.g. 9 Politico (USA) - Brox Treasure by Broxted M Garner

433 9/3 Newton Brom' (R) MEM 3m 3 GS *ld 1st-2nd, cls up til wknd 11th, lft 2nd 3 out* 2 0
494 16/3 Horseheath (R) RES 3m 10 GF *alwys mid-div, lost tch ldrs 12th, t.o. & p.u. 3 out* P 0
679 30/3 Cottenham (R) RES 3m 15 GF *chsd ldrs, mstk 13th, sn wknd, t.o.* 6 0
1345 4/5 Holnicote (L) RES 3m 11 GS *u.r. 2nd* U -
1395 6/5 Cotley Farm (L) RES 3m 8 GF *sn bhnd, t.o. frm 13th* 5 0
1497 11/5 Holnicote (L) RES 3m 10 G *keen hold, ld apr 8th til ran out 14th* r -
1625 27/5 Lifton (R) INT 3m 8 GS *5th at 15th, unable to chal, bhnd whn u.r. last* U -

Won weak Maiden 94; barely stays and no meaninful form in 96; need miracle to win again. 0

JUSTE JO b.m. 8 Joshua - Ribswood by Ribston C H Birch

1995 P(0)

164 17/2 Weston Park (L) RES 3m 11 G *bhnd & strggling, p.u. 11th* P 0
286 2/3 Eaton Hall (R) MDO 3m 14 G *u.r. 3rd* U -
458 9/3 Eyton-On-Se' (L) INT 3m 11 G *ld/disp to 5th, cls up whn u.r. 7th* U -
665 24/3 Eaton Hall (R) RES 3m 14 S *prom, ld 3rd-4th, fdd rpdly, p.u. 9th* P 0

Looks hopeless. 0

JUST EVE gr.m. 9 Alias Smith (USA) - Cupid's Delight by St Paddy The West Midland Racing Partnership

1416 6/5 Cursneh Hill (L) MDO 3m 9 GF *midfld, in tch til wknd 3 out, p.u. aft nxt* P 0
1644 2/6 Dingley (R) MDO 3m 16 GF *made most to 14th, wknd rpdly, well btn & p.u. last* P 0

Placed in poor novice hurdle 94; shows speed but not enough stamina so far. 10

JUST FOR A LARK ch.m. 6 Sunley Builds - Sue Lark by Sir Lark Ralph Morgans

1995 **P(NH)**,**P(NH)**,**P(NH)**

149 17/2 Erw Lon (L) MDN 3m 10 G *rear, lost tch frm 12th* 5 0

No form under rules; last on debut; not seen again. 0

JUSTFORGASTRIX(IRE) b.g. 8 Kemal (FR) - Up To Trix by Over The River (FR) Eddy Luke

516 16/3 Dalton Park (R) MDO 3m 11 G *hld up last, schoold & alwys t.o.* 6 0
591 23/3 Wetherby Po' (L) MDO 3m 14 S *alwys rear, p.u. 14th* P 0
764 31/3 Great Stain' (L) MDN 3m 16 GS *mid-div, wknd 14th, t.o. & p.u. 3 out* P 0
910 8/4 Tranwell (L) MEM 3m 4 GF *made all, j.w. 25l clr 14th, styd on strngly* 1 10
1130 20/4 Hornby Cast' (L) CON 3m 13 G *prom til steadily fdd frm 4 out* 5 10

Romped home in bad race; really up against it now; Members only hope again. 10

JUST HARVEY (Irish) — I 256P

JUST HORSEPLAY (Irish) — I 172F, I 255P, I 415U

JUST JACK br.g. 10 Ovac (ITY) - Precision Chopper by Menelek — P Jonason

1995 1(12),U(-),U(-),2(13),1(16),2(17),**1(19)**

8	14/1	Cottenham	(R)	CON	3m	10	G	*w.w. in tch, outpcd apr 14th, no dang aft*	7	0
100	16/2	Fakenham	(L)	HC	2m 5f 110yds	9	G	*held up in tch, effort 10th, outpcd from 12th.*	4	16
484	15/3	Fakenham	(L)	HC	2m 5f 110yds	13	GF	*u.r. 1st.*	U	-
906	8/4	Fakenham	(L)	HC	2m 5f 110yds	11	G	*n.d..*	5	14
1321	28/4	Fakenham P-'	(L)	CON	3m	5	G	*hld up going wll, 2nd whn blnd 13th & 15th, outpcd nxt*	2	18
1462	10/5	Market Rasen	(R)	HC	2 3/4m 110yds	11	G	*in tch to 10th, soon wknd, t.o. when p.u. before 3 out.*	P	0

Won weak H/chase 95; ran one passable race; hard to place now. needs to stick to Confineds; Good. .. 16

JUST JESSICA br.m. 7 State Diplomacy (USA) - Harpalyce by Don't Look — Lady Susan Watson

590	23/3	Wetherby Po'	(L)	MDO	3m	16	S	*f 2nd*	F	-
1095	14/4	Whitwell-On'	(R)	MDO	2 1/2m 88yds	14	G	*alwys rear, t.o. & p.u. 8th*	P	0
1137	20/4	Hornby Cast'	(L)	MDN	3m	13	G	*rear, not fluent, bhnd whn p.u. aft 5th*	P	0

No signs of ability. 0

JUST JOHNIE ch.g. 6 Meadowbrook - Just Diamonds by Laurence O — R G Watson

518	16/3	Dalton Park	(R)	MDO	3m	15	G	*schoold in last & t.o., poor 8th & running on whn p.u. 16th*	P	0
1095	14/4	Whitwell-On'	(R)	MDO	2 1/2m 88yds	14	G	*chsd ldrs til wknd 7th, t.o. & p.u. 3 out*	P	0

Only learning; successful stable and should do better. 11

JUST LIKE MADGE 6 — L R Gasson

904	6/4	Dingley	(R)	RES	3m	20	GS	*t.o. 19th frm 2nd, p.u. 8th*	P	0
1103	14/4	Guilsborough	(L)	MDN	3m	15	G	*(bl) t.d.e. alwys bhnd, t.o. & p.u. 13th*	P	0

Unpromising. 0

JUST MAISY b.m. 9 Broadsword (USA) - Quilpee Mai by Pee Mai — D L Claydon

1995 P(0),2(12),U(-),5(0)

343	3/3	Higham	(L)	MDO	3m	11	G	*handy in mid-div, chal 2 out, no ext cls home*	2	12
617	23/3	Higham	(L)	MDO	3m	11	GF	*sttld rear,prog 11th,styd on onepcd,u.r.4 out,saddle slppd*	U	-
1149	20/4	Higham	(L)	MDO	3m	10	F	*(fav) rear, outpcd 12th, styd on to chs wnr 3 out, no imp*	2	10
1326	28/4	Fakenham P-'	(L)	MDO	3m	7	G	*in tch, rdn 14th, 8l 3rd whn b.d. 2 out*	B	-
1403	6/5	Northaw	(L)	MDO	3m	8	F	*chsd ldr to 4th, in tch, ev ch 3 out, nt qkn flat*	2	12

Queen of the East Anglian maidens and happy to stay that way. 11

JUST MARMALADE ch.g. 7 Noalto - Kitty Come Home by Monsanto (FR) — J Tudor

1995 **4(NH),6(NH)**

147	17/2	Erw Lon	(L)	MDN	3m	8	G	*(Jt fav) cls up, rdn to ld 14th, jnd 2 out, ran on flat*	1	15
269	2/3	Didmarton	(L)	RES	3m	12	G	*trckd ldrs, 4th & outpcd whn mstk 15th, no dang aft*	4	16
387	9/3	Llanfrynach	(R)	RES	3m	11	GS	*(fav) trckd ldrs, mstk 11th, ld 13-15th, hrd rdn & no ext 2 out*	3	14
695	30/3	Llanvapley	(L)	RES	3m	13	GS	*(fav) hld up,prog 11th,ld & lft clr 14th,hdd 3 out,lft clr 2 out*	1	18
1198	21/4	Lydstep	(L)	INT	3m	5	S	*(fav) in tch, ev ch 5 out, onepcd frm 2 out*	3	15
1268	27/4	Pyle	(R)	INT	3m	8	G	*ld to 5th, chsd wnr, 4l down 14th, rdn & no ext frm nxt*	3	16
1385	6/5	Pantyderi	(R)	CON	3m	6	GF	*prom to hlfwy, rmndr 10th, mstk nxt, p.u. 12th*	P	0

Started well but not progressed; ran badly last start (G/F); may upgrade to Intermediates; G-S 17

JUST MASKARAIDER b.g. 11 Jester - Kalakan by Kalamoun — W M Aitchison

911	8/4	Tranwell	(L)	CON	3m	9	GF	*prom early, wknd into 7th hlfwy, lost tch 12th*	7	0
1513	12/5	Hexham Poin'	(L)	CON	3m	6	HY	*last frm 4th, t.o. & p.u. 6th*	P	0
1570	19/5	Corbridge	(R)	CON	3m	8	G	*alwys bhnd, styd on onepcd frm 2 out*	6	0

Restricted winner 94; missed 95; no form in 96 and best watched now. 0

JUST MY BILL ch.g. 10 Nicholas Bill - Misnomer by Milesian — Mrs K Heard

1995 U(-),2(15),U(-),2(16),5(0),1(16),5(15),5(0),4(17)

38	3/2	Wadebridge	(L)	MEM	3m	4	GF	*last til prog 6th, ld 9/11th, chsd wnr, no imp 2 out*	2	17
134	17/2	Ottery St M'	(L)	CON	3m	12	GS	*ref to race*	0	0
196	24/2	Lemalla	(R)	CON	3m	14	HY	*alwys prom, ld 3 out, hdd & outpcd nxt*	2	20
481	11/3	Taunton	(R)	HC	3m	11	G	*waited with, hdwy 6th, chsd wnr from 4 out, no impn from next.*	2	22
671	28/3	Taunton	(R)	HC	3m	13	S	*bhnd, hdwy 14th, wknd before 3 out.*	4	18

1 win last 19 starts; easily good enough for another win but quirky and frustrating; likes Lifton. 20

JUST MY HARRY (Irish) — **I** 557^F, **I** 603^5, **I** 630^F

JUST-N-JAMES (Irish) — **I** 56, , **I** 79^P, **I** 138^P, **I** 243^3, **I** 312^P, **I** 358^P

JUST PLACED (Irish) — **I** 42^P, **I** 128^P, **I** 150^4, **I** 290^5, **I** 325^P, **I** 475^P

JUST PRECIOUS b.m. 11 Ela-Mana-Mou - Border Squaw by Warpath — P Venner

347 3/3 Higham (L) LAD 3m 10 G *ld 3rd til hdd & wknd rpdly 3 out* 4 16
620 23/3 Higham (L) LAD 3m 9 GF *pllng, jnd ldrs 3rd, prom to 11th, wknd, p.u. 14th* P 0
1147 20/4 Higham (L) LAD 3m 9 F *u.r. 1st* U -

No stamina & no real prospects at 12 12

JUST ROSE ch.m. 12 Legal Eagle - Gambling Rose by Game Rights — B J Palfrey

1274 27/4 Bratton Down (L) MEM 3m 7 GF *in tch early, 6th at 12th, prog 14th, btn whn lft 2nd last* 2 0

Missed 95; of no real account. 0

JUST SILVER gr.g. 11 Persian Plan (AUS) - Vet's Bill by Hardraw Scar — B F W Rendell

1995 F(-),P(0),**P(0)**,**P(0)**,**P(0)**,P(0)

138 17/2 Ottery St M' (L) RES 3m 18 GS *alwys bhnd, t.o. & p.u. 15th* P 0
558 17/3 Ottery St M' (L) MDO 3m 9 G *(bl) ld til ran out 9th, rtrcd, cont t.o.* 5 0
711 30/3 Barbury Cas' (L) MDO 3m 8 G *(bl) cls up til blnd 10th, p.u. bef nxt* P 0
1128 20/4 Stafford Cr' (R) RES 3m 17 S *midfld til lost tch 10th, p.u. 12th* P 0
1528 12/5 Ottery St M' (L) RES 3m 10 GF *(bl) alwys prom, lft in ld 3 out, hdd last, collapsed & died aft* 3 16

Dead. 14

JUST SPELLBOUND (Irish) — **I** 173^{4}, **I** 256^{F}, **I** 409^{U}, **I** 410^{F}

JUST TAKETHE MICKY b.g. 6 Gay Meadow - Oujarater by Adropejo — Lady Susan Watson

413 9/3 Charm Park (L) MDO 3m 12 G *rr early, ht 1st, prog 9th, fdd 13th, p.u. 4 out* P 0
589 23/3 Wetherby Po' (L) MDO 3m 16 S *mid-div, btn whn mstk & u.r. 3 out* U -
1094 14/4 Whitwell-On' (R) MDO 2 1/2m 88yds 16 G *ld, mstk 4th, hdd nxt, sn lost plc, t.o. & p.u. 10th* P 0
1135 20/4 Hornby Cast' (L) MDN 3m 10 G *prom, ld 7th-9th, hld in 3rd whn f 3 out* F -

Some hope but needs to jump better. 0

JUST THE DUKE (Irish) — **I** 5^{P}, **I** 117^{P}, **I** 155^{P}

JUST US(IRE) b.g. 6 Muscatite - Bachelors Chant by Welsh Chanter — H E Peacock

15 14/1 Cottenham (R) MDN 3m 14 G *in tch to 12th, bhnd & p.u. 16th* P 0
91 11/2 Ampton (R) MDO 3m 10 GF *mstk 2nd, mid-div, lost tch 10th, p.u. 13th* P 0

Only learning; should do better. 0

JUVERNA RIVER (Irish) — **I** 351,

KAHLO b.m. 6 Jalmood (USA) - Five Farthings by Busted — Andrew Oliver

300 2/3 Great Treth' (R) MDO 3m 10 G *mid-div, 7th whn p.u. 16th* P 0
555 17/3 Ottery St M' (L) MDO 3m 15 G *(bl) ld 4th til blnd & u.r. 7th* U -
870 6/4 Higher Kilw' (L) MEM 3m 5 GF *16s-8s, rear, lost tch 13th* 5 0
1280 27/4 Bratton Down (L) MDO 3m 14 GF *alwys rear, no ch frm 4 out* 6 0

Last when completing and much more needed. 0

KAIM PARK b.g. 13 Ovac (ITY) - Liffey's Choice by Little Buskins — Mrs M D Reed

1995 5(12),P(0),4(14),2(15),5(0),3(14)

103 17/2 Marks Tey (L) LAD 3m 7 G *disp til ld 11th- 15th, rddn & outpcd nxt* 4 14
270 2/3 Parham (R) MEM 3m 5 GF *(Jt fav) ld to 3rd, in tch aft, 4th & no dang frm 15th* 4 0
573 17/3 Detling (L) OPE 4m 9 GF *rear, lost tch 10th, t.o. & p.u. 2 out* P 0
594 23/3 Parham (R) CON 3m 13 GS *rear, lost tch 12th, p.u. 2 out* P 0
832 6/4 Marks Tey (L) LAD 3m 8 G *twrds rear whn f 5th* F -
1207 21/4 Heathfield (R) CON 3m 9 F *sn rear, lost tch 14th* 7 0
1298 28/4 Bexhill (R) CON 3m 4 F *alwys 3rd, lost tch 12th* 3 0

Members winner 94; beaten last 19 including bad Members 96; hard to find another win. 11

KALA DAWN b.m. 9 Kala Shikari - Morning Heather by Langton Heath — Mrs B Everall

1057 13/4 Badbury Rin' (L) MEM 3m 4 GF *ld til hdd apr last, onepcd flat* 3 15
1348 4/5 Holnicote (L) MDO 3m 9 GS *2nd at 8th, chsd wnr at onepcd aft* 2 14
1638 1/6 Bratton Down (L) MDO 3m 13 G *mid-div, effrt to chs ldrs 14th, onepcd frm 2 out* 3 12
1651 8/6 Umberleigh (L) MDO 3m 11 GF *alwys in tch, not qckn frm 3 out* 5 0

Missed 95; improved; stamina doubts and win not easy to find; novice ridden. 12

KALAJO b.g. 6 Kala Shikari - Greenacres Joy by Tycoon II — M J McGovern

1995 P(0),P(0),P(0),P(0),2(13),1(12),2(10),4(10)

47 4/2 Alnwick (L) XX 3m 14 G *mid-div, prog 11th, disp app 3 out, just ld whn f last* F 19
189 24/2 Friars Haugh (L) RES 3m 9 S *2nd hlfwy, styd cls up til wknd 3 out* 5 10
319 2/3 Corbridge (R) RES 3m 16 GS *alwys mid-div* 7 0
608 23/3 Friars Haugh (L) RES 3m 13 G *5th hlfwy, styd on frm 3 out, nrst fin* 3 16
858 6/4 Alnwick (L) RES 3m 7 GF *(fav) disp ld 6-9th,ld 13th,clr 3 out, wknd rpdly last, hdded flat* 3 17
1082 14/4 Friars Haugh (L) MEM 3m 3 F *(fav) chal ldr frm 4 out, upsides last, ld flat* 1 15
1249 27/4 Balcormo Ma' (R) RES 3m 10 GS *bhnd whn p.u. bfr 12th* P 0

Unlucky 1st start; inconsistent; can win modest Restricted on best form; G-F. **15**

KALI SANA(IRE) b.g. 8 Fine Blade (USA) - Phayre Vulgan by Vulgan — M A Hill

1995 **9(NH),8(NH),P(NH),6(NH),P(NH),P(NH)**

173	18/2	Market Rase'	(L)	RES	3m	6	GF	*disp 4th til ld 7th, hit 9th, hdd 14th, wknd 3 out*	4	0
287	2/3	Eaton Hall	(R)	MDO	3m	11	G	*chsd ldrs to hlfwy, wknd, p.u. 4 out*	P	0
579	20/3	Ludlow	(R)	HC	2 1/2m	17	G	*blnd and u.r. 1st.*	U	-
683	30/3	Chaddesley '	(L)	MEM	3m	17	G	*chsd ldrs to 6th, sn wknd, t.o. & p.u. 12th*	P	0
799	3/4	Ludlow	(R)	HC	3m	8	GF	*(bl) bhnd, t.o. when p.u. before 9th.*	P	0

No stamina and prospects nil. **0**

KALOKAGATHOS b.g. 7 King Of Spain - Kip's Sister by Cawston's Clown — R H Pedrick

1995 **13(NH),7(NH),11(NH),P(NH),5(NH)**

131	17/2	Ottery St M'	(L)	MDN	3m	10	GS	*alwys mid-div, nvr on terms*	3	0
301	2/3	Great Treth'	(R)	MDO	3m	13	G	*handy, 4th at 16th, lft 3rd & hld whn hmpd 2 out*	3	0
557	17/3	Ottery St M'	(L)	MDN	3m	10	G	*alwys mid-div, t.o. & p.u. 2 out*	P	0
1139	20/4	Flete Park	(R)	RES	3m	14	S	*twrds rear, 8th hlfwy, bhnd whn p.u. 17th*	P	0

Not disgraced 2nd start but nothing after & unlikely to win in 97 .... **10**

KALOORE ch.g. 7 Ore - Cool Straight by Straight Lad — Mrs J Alford

1995 U(-),1(18),3(16),1(19),1(18),2(22)

65	10/2	Great Treth'	(R)	INT	3m	13	S	*mid-div til prog frm 13th, kpt on wll flat*	2	22
297	2/3	Great Treth'	(R)	INT	3m	10	G	*(fav) in tch, prog 14th, drvn to chal 2 out, ld last, sn clr*	1	25
628	23/3	Kilworthy	(L)	INT	3m	7	GS	*(fav) w.w. prog to ld 12th, clr 15th, shkn up flat, unchal*	1	23

Useful; still improving; win Opens and worth a try in novice H/chase 97ays; G-S. **25**

KAMADORA ch.g. 9 Kambalda - Icydora by Arctic Slave — Milson Robinson

1995 P(0),P(0),4(0),2(12),C(-),7(0),3(0),P(0)

79	11/2	Wetherby Po'	(L)	MDO	3m	12	GS	*cls up, ld 4 out, hld off chal flat*	1	14
172	18/2	Market Rase'	(L)	RES	3m	9	GF	*(fav) in tch, 3rd at 12th, rdn 4 out, btn nxt*	6	11
396	9/3	Garthorpe	(R)	RES	3m	9	G	*alwys rear hlf, outpcd in 6th whn f 5 out*	F	-
635	23/3	Market Rase'	(L)	RES	3m	8	GF	*prog 10th, 2nd 6 out, wknd nxt*	3	0
1090	14/4	Whitwell-On'	(R)	RES	3m	17	G	*mid-div, drppd rear 7th, rallied 11th, sn wknd, p.u. 3 out*	P	0
1303	28/4	Southwell P'	(L)	CON	3m	7	GF	*mid to rear, lost tch 8th, ran out 11th*	r	-

Won bad race (7 minutes plus); struggling after and Restricted looks too tough. **12**

KAMATRA EYRE (Irish) — **I** 504,

KAMBALDA RAMBLER b or br.g. 12 Kambalda - Stroan Lass by Brave Invader (USA) — H Morton

1995 **2(NH),4(NH),3(NH),5(NH),3(NH),5(NH),R(NH)**

57	10/2	Cottenham	(R)	LAD	3m	9	GS	*16s-7s, j.w. trckd ldr, ld 7th, wll clr frm 11th, unchal*	1	27
246	25/2	Southwell P'	(L)	OPE	3m	9	HO	*prom, ld 10th, blnd 13th, hdd & blnd nxt, p.u. 4 out*	P	0
362	5/3	Leicester	(R)	HC	2 1/2m 110yds	8	GS	*prom, chsd ldr 6th, disp ld 8th to next, ld 4 out till apr next, no ext.*	2	23
579	20/3	Ludlow	(R)	HC	2 1/2m	17	G	*mid div, hdwy 5 out, btn when left 4th last, kept on.*	3	21
672	29/3	Aintree	(L)	HC	2 3/4m	26	G	*alwys rear, t.o. hfwy, blnd and u.r. 13th (Valentine's)*	U	-
970	8/4	Thorpe Lodge	(L)	LAD	3m	6	GF	*(fav) disp til ld 4th, drew away 10th, v easily*	1	23

Winning chaser; needs easy 3 miles; good jumper; can win more Ladies. G/F-G/S. **22**

KAMEO STYLE b.g. 13 Kambalda - Smashing Style by Harwell — M A Lloyd

1995 **P(0),9(0),P(0)**,5(0),4(14),4(0),**9(17)**

161	17/2	Weston Park	(L)	LAD	3m	11	G	*f 1st*	F	-
426	9/3	Upton-On-Se'	(R)	CON	3m	16	GS	*disp 6th/7th til onepcd frm 14th*	8	0
738	31/3	Sudlow Farm	(R)	LAD	3m	5	G	*(bl) chsd 4-12th, sn outpcd*	3	0
880	6/4	Brampton Br'	(R)	XX	3m	8	GF	*rear & lost tch 11th, t.o. 16th, tk 4th on line*	4	10
1195	21/4	Sandon	(L)	XX	3m	9	G	*rear, styd on onepcd frm 3 out*	4	0
1318	28/4	Bitterley	(L)	XX	3m	8	G	*cls up til outpcd 12th, styng on in 3rd whn f 3 out*	F	-
1460	8/5	Uttoxeter	(L)	HC	2m 7f	5	G	*bhnd, lost tch 10th, tk poor 3rd run-in, t.o..*	3	10
1616	27/5	Chaddesley '	(L)	MEM	3m	1	GF	*walked over*	1	0

Winning hurdler; does not stay and not thretening to win. **13**

KAMTARA br.g. 10 Kambalda - Taralote by Tarboosh (USA) — Ken Edwards

1995 P(0),2(11),8(0),4(11),3(0),P(0)

264	2/3	Didmarton	(L)	INT	3m	12	G	*last pair, wll bhnd whn f 9th*	F	-
381	9/3	Barbury Cas'	(L)	XX	3m	9	GS	*sn t.o., f last*	F	-
525	16/3	Larkhill	(R)	RES	3m	7	G	*sn t.o., p.u. 15th*	P	0
960	8/4	Lockinge	(L)	RES	3m	9	GF	*sn bhnd, t.o. frm 12th, p.u. 4 out*	P	0
1242	27/4	Woodford	(L)	RES	3m	18	G	*chsd ldrs to 7th, soon lost plc, p.u. apr 11th*	P	0
1407	6/5	Hackwood Pa'	(L)	XX	3m	5	F	*last to hlfwy, prog 12th, sn outpcd*	3	0
1564	19/5	Mollington	(R)	XX	3m	14	GS	*n.j.w. wll bhnd frm 4th, t.o. aft, kpt on frm 3 out*	9	0
1612	26/5	Tweseldown	(R)	RES	3m	11	G	*mstks, wll bhnd, t.o. 11th, ran on 15th, nrst fin*	6	0

Ex Irish; changed hands; well beaten when completing and prospects bleak. **10**

KANANN (Irish) — I 320[P], I 364[P]

KANJO OLDA gr.m. 6 Scallywag - Devine Lady by The Parson — M A Lloyd

70	10/2	Great Treth'	(R)	MDO	3m	14	S	*bhnd whn p.u. 8th*	P	0
220	24/2	Newtown	(L)	MDN	3m	12	GS	*mstks, chsd ldrs, wknd 13th, poor 4th whn p.u. 2 out*	P	0

Only lasted a fortnight; some hope on 2nd start. **10**

KARAMAZOV br.g. 20 High Top - Over The Water II by Doutelle — Peter Finnegan

1621	27/5	Chaddesley '	(L)	MDO	3m	17	GF	*s.v.s. last til ran out 3rd*	r	-

Poor old thing **0**

KARENS LEADER (Irish) — I 284[P], I 449[P]

KARICLEIGH BOY ch.g. 8 Nearly A Hand - Duvessa by Glen Quaich — Philip Rogers

1995 **15(NH),P(NH),19(NH)**

195	24/2	Lemalla	(R)	INT	3m	7	HY	*chsd ldrs, ld 4 out, jnd & f nxt*	F	-
441	9/3	Haldon	(R)	MEM	3m	6	S	*(Jt fav) slght ld at slow pace til drew clr 14th, 20l clr whn f 3 out*	F	18
628	23/3	Kilworthy	(L)	INT	3m	7	GS	*hld up,hmpd 4th,prog 11th,chsd wnr aft 15th,no real imp*	2	19

Able but error prone; ran well last start & should win if fit 97; Soft **20**

KARLIMAY b.m. 6 Karlinsky (USA) - Mayspring by Silly Season — Mrs R Fell

1995 P(0),5(0),P(0)

69	10/2	Great Treth'	(R)	MDO	3m	12	S	*prom, losing tch whn p.u. 14th*	P	0
132	17/2	Ottery St M'	(L)	MDN	3m	9	GS	*alwys rear, t.o. whn f 3 out*	F	-
300	2/3	Great Treth'	(R)	MDO	3m	10	G	*prog 10th, ld 14th til wknd rpdly apr 2 out*	5	10
630	23/3	Kilworthy	(L)	MDN	3m	10	GS	*hld up wll bhnd,rpd prog 15th,clsd & blnd last,too mch to do*	3	11
875	6/4	Higher Kilw'	(L)	MDN	3m	6	GF	*(Jt fav) hld up in tch, qcknd to ld apr 2 out, comf*	1	15
1075	13/4	Lifton	(R)	RES	3m	12	S	*conf rddn, wnt 3rd 16th, qcknd to ld 2 out, sn clr comf*	1	17
1138	20/4	Flete Park	(R)	MEM	3m	4	S	*(fav) hld up rear, went 2nd 16th, effrt apr last, not qckn*	2	15
1361	4/5	Flete Park	(R)	CON	3m	9	G	*(fav) hld up, prog 3 out, short-lived effrt whn blnd last, sn btn*	2	17

Improving; stays but given lot to do in races; Confined likely 97; G-S **20**

KASPAIR ARROW (Irish) — I 93[P]

KATE GALE (Irish) — I 477[P], I 560[3]

KATES CASTLE b.m. 9 Carlingford Castle - Nadezda by Menelek — Ben Van Praagh

104	17/2	Marks Tey	(L)	OPE	3m	14	G	*rr, prog & in tch 12th, btn appr 15th, p.u. 3 out*	P	0
271	2/3	Parham	(R)	CON	3m	15	GF	*ld to 5th, cls up aft, prssd wnr 14th, wknd last*	4	17
594	23/3	Parham	(R)	CON	3m	13	GS	*ld, blnd 10th, hdd 12th, 3rd frm 14th, btn 3 out*	3	14
962	8/4	Heathfield	(R)	XX	3m	4	G	*(fav) made all, blnd 10th & 3 out, rdn & drw clr 2 out, comf*	1	19
1298	28/4	Bexhill	(R)	CON	3m	4	F	*(fav) ld til disp 13-16th, advtg 3 out, ran on well*	1	19
1375	4/5	Peper Harow	(L)	CON	3m	9	F	*(fav) ld to 10th, 4th whn p.u. qkly aft 12th*	P	0
1539	16/5	Folkestone	(R)	HC	3m 7f	9	G	*mid div, prog 13th, blnd 18th, ev ch 2 out, unable to qckn und pres.*	3	19

Irish points winner; easily won modest races; stays well; should find another opening; G/F-S. **19**

KATIE PARSON ch.m. 9 The Parson - Little Welly by Little Buskins — Mrs S E Vaughan

1995 P(0),P(0)

882	6/4	Brampton Br'	(R)	RES	3m	14	GF	*cls 2nd at 9th, ev ch 16th, wknd frm 3 out*	4	11

Only 4 runs 94-96; Restricted chance is passing her by. **13**

KATIES ARGUMENT br.m. 11 St Columbus - Royaldyne by No Argument — Mrs J Milburn

1995 B(-),8(0),15(0),P(0),P(0),P(0)

76	11/2	Wetherby Po'	(L)	LAD	3m	8	GS	*alwys rear, nvr dang*	4	15
222	24/2	Duncombe Pa'	(R)	MEM	3m	6	GS	*disp to 4th, sn lost plc, no ch 15th, ran on flat*	3	11
318	2/3	Corbridge	(R)	LAD	3m 5f	10	GS	*prom to 9th, lost plc 14th, nvr dang aft*	6	13
515	16/3	Dalton Park	(R)	XX	3m	12	G	*alwys rear, t.o. 16th, kpt on*	7	0
586	23/3	Wetherby Po'	(L)	LAD	3m	8	S	*handy, outpcd 3 out, styd on well, tk 2nd nr fin*	2	19
1093	14/4	Whitwell-On'	(R)	MXO	4m	19	G	*mid-div whn b.d. 6th*	B	-
1130	20/4	Hornby Cast'	(L)	CON	3m	13	G	*mid-div whn u.r. 4th*	U	-
1366	4/5	Gisburn	(R)	LAD	3m	12	G	*rear, t.o. 7th, p.u. 13th*	P	0

Lost last 14 starts; needs a real stamina test; getting old now. **15**

KATIES KISSES VI (Irish) — I 253[P], I 572[F]

KATY COUNTRY MOUSE b.m. 10 Push On - Princess Mouse by Royal Goblin — Alex Rhodes

1995 P(0),F(-),P(0),R(-),P(0)

146	17/2	Erw Lon	(L)	MEM	3m	7	G	*3rd early, grad lost plc, p.u. 13th*	P	0
772	31/3	Pantyderi	(R)	MDN	3m	8	G	*1st ride, trckd ldr to 8th, fdd rpdly, p.u. 11th*	P	0
975	8/4	Lydstep	(L)	MDO	3m	9	G	*mid-div, p.u. aft 6th, b.b.v.*	P	0
1200	21/4	Lydstep	(L)	MDN	3m	10	S	*prom to 11th, p.u. 14th*	P	0
1273	27/4	Pyle	(R)	MDO	3m	9	G	*ld to 7th,wknd 11th,p.u. aft nxt,cont, fin aft evone lft*	P	0
1492	11/5	Erw Lon	(L)	MDO	3m	10	F	*in tch to 9th, wknd & p.u. 11th*	P	0

Everyone had gone home when she finally completed (how unfair); hopeless. 0

KEELER RIDER(USA) b.g. 13 Cresta Rider (USA) - Keeler — Neil Allen

1435	6/5	Ashorne	(R) CON	3m	12 G	*mid-div, out of tch, effrt nxt, wknd 13th, p.u. 3 out*	P	0
1618	27/5	Chaddesley '	(L) CON	3m	14 GF	*w.w. prog going wll 12th, wknd rpdly 14th, p.u. 3 out*	P	0

Dual winner 93; only 3 runs since and too old now. 14

KEELSON (Irish) — **I** 192P, **I** 2231

KEEP FLOWING (Irish) — **I** 113P, **I** 465P

KEEPITSAFE (Irish) — **I** 131F, **I** 2311

KEEP ON DREAMING b.m. 6 Sunyboy - Nearly A Lady by Nearly A Hand — J J Barber

1995 2(0),F(-),P(0),1(14)

20	14/1	Tweseldown	(R) RES	3m	9 GS	*mstks, alwys rear, no ch whn f 3 out*	F	-

Won poor race 95; top stable; not seen after day one and plenty to prove yet. 13

KEEP ON TRYING b.m. 9 New Member - Flippit by Dairialatan — Miss S Pilkington

1995 **7(NH)**

239	25/2	Southwell P'	(L) MDO	3m	9 HO	*prom,disp 4 out,outpcd nxt,lft 2nd 2 out,btn whn blnd last*	2	10
640	23/3	Siddington	(L) LAD	3m	9 S	*w.w. lst tch & p.u. 10th*	P	0
787	31/3	Tweseldown	(R) RES	3m	9 G	*alwys prom, ld 11th, qcknd 13th, hdd apr last, no ext*	3	14
999	8/4	Hackwood Pa'	(L) RES	3m	6 GF	*alwys in rear, rddn hlfwy, t.o.*	5	0
1187	21/4	Tweseldown	(R) MDN	3m	11 GF	*rear, outpcd hlfwy, styd on well frm 3 out, nrst fin*	2	13
1288	28/4	Barbury Cas'	(L) MEM	3m	5 F	*hld up, went mod 2nd 12th, no imp on wnr*	2	0
1485	11/5	Bredwardine	(R) MDO	3m	15 G	*(fav) 2nd whn blnd 2nd, t.o. 4th, p.u. nxt*	P	0
1610	26/5	Tweseldown	(R) MDO	3m	5 G	*(fav) prom til f 10th*	F	-
1644	2/6	Dingley	(R) MDO	3m	16 GF	*chsd ldrs, eff 14th, unble to chal frm 2 out*	4	11

Placed in poor races; not progressing and disappointing now; may find win elusive. 12

KEEP STRONG (Irish) — **I** 308P, **I** 352,

KEEP THE CHANGE (Irish) — **I** 309P

KEEP THEM KEEN(IRE) ch.g. 8 Carlingford Castle - Some Gift by Avocat — K O'Meara

1995 P(0),3(10),F(-),R(-)

80	11/2	Wetherby Po'	(L) MDO	3m	12 GS	*rear, nvr dang, p.u. 4 out*	P	0

Placed in weak race 95; only completion and vanished early in 96. 10

KEERAGH (Irish) — **I** 348P

KEIROSE b.m. 6 Derring Rose - Keira by Keren — R Paisley

323	2/3	Corbridge	(R) MDN	3m	12 GS	*ref 1st*	R	-
859	6/4	Alnwick	(L) MDO	2 1/2m	5 GF	*sn bhnd, t.o. & p.u. 3 out*	P	0
1476	11/5	Aspatria	(L) MDO	3m	16 GF	*n.j.w., bhnd til p.u. bfr 10th*	P	0

Needs a jumping overhaul; may do better. 0

KELBURNE LAD(IRE) ch.g. 7 Cardinal Flower - Ross Lady by Master Buck — Mrs D B A Silk

1995 **F(NH),3(NH),2(NH),3(NH),12(NH),F(NH)**

344	3/3	Higham	(L) MDO	3m	12 G	*mid-div, prog to 3rd at 11th, not qckn 15th, mstk 3 out*	3	0
576	17/3	Detling	(L) MDN	3m	18 GF	*prom, ld 9th til f 13th*	F	-
597	23/3	Parham	(R) MDO	3m	9 GS	*chsd ldr, clsd in 3rd whn f 10th*	F	-
814	6/4	Charing	(L) MDO	2 1/2m	8 F	*alwys prom, ld apr 9th, blnd & hdd 2 out, rallied to ld flat*	1	12
1145	20/4	Higham	(L) RES	3m	12 F	*u.r. 1st*	U	-
1206	21/4	Heathfield	(R) RES	3m	8 F	*rear, prog 12th, 3rd frm 15th, rdn 4 out, kpt on*	3	14
1540	16/5	Folkestone	(R) HC	2m 5f	10 G	*held up, mstk 2nd, prog 7th, joined ldrs next, wknd 2 out.*	4	12

Disappointing novice chaser; poor jumper and does not stay; Restricted looks tough. 14

KELLYS DIAMOND ch.g. 7 Netherkelly - Just Diamonds by Laurence O — Mrs P A Russell

1995 3(11),F(-),F(-),1(15),2(18)

72	11/2	Wetherby Po'	(L) CON	3m	18 GS	*mid-div, prog 13th, 4th 4 out, no ext*	4	17
121	17/2	Witton Cast'	(R) RES	3m	11 S	*(fav) rear, prog 11th, disp ld 13th til ld apr last, wknd nr fin*	1	19
327	3/3	Market Rase'	(L) CON	3m	15 G	*prom 7th,disp 13th til outpcd nxt,wknd 3 out,fin 3rd,prmtd*	2	14
538	17/3	Southwell P'	(L) XX	3m	6 GS	*nvr bttr than mid-div, found little und pres*	3	0
1096	14/4	Whitwell-On'	(R) MEM	3m	9 G	*mid-div, prog 7th, chal 2 out, onepcd*	3	15

Consistent but stamina suspect and a weak finisher; more needed for Confined;G/F-G/S best. 17

KELLY'S EYE b.g. 10 Netherkelly - Quilpee Mai by Pee Mai — Mrs M Kimber

1995 R(-),U(-),4(10),5(0),2(20),4(0),4(15)

55	10/2	Cottenham	(R) CON	3m	2 GS	*(bl) mstk 9th,disp,ld & mstk 14th,clr 16th,tried ref 2 out,allout*	1	12
124	17/2	Kingston Bl'	(L) CON	3m	17 GS	*(bl) chsng grp, effrt apr 14th, sn wknd*	10	0
434	9/3	Newton Brom'	(R) CON	3m	11 GS	*(bl) alwys rear, last & lost tch whn crawld 13th & p.u.*	P	0
638	23/3	Siddington	(L) CON	3m	16 S	*(bl) chsd ldrs til appr 10th, no ch frm 14th*	7	10

897 6/4 Dingley (R) CON 3m 15 GS *(bl) prog 8th, 6th brfly 11th, sn fdd* 8 0
1016 13/4 Kingston Bl' (L) CON 3m 6 G *(bl) cls up,disp apr 14th,hrd rdn & hdd last,rallied to ld flat* 1 17
1236 27/4 Clifton On ' (L) CON 3m 8 GF *nvr going wll, alwys rear, poor 5th whn p.u. 2 out* P 0
1503 11/5 Kingston Bl' (L) OPE 3m 3 G *(bl) chsd wnr to 5th, rmndrs 11th, no ch frm 13th* 3 0

Hard ride and normally unwilling; blinkers essential; hard to find another win; G/F-S. G/F-S 15

KELLYS NAP ch.g. 7 Netherkelly - Nepal by Indian Ruler Major E W O'F Wilson
1995 F(-),P(0)
34 20/1 Higham (L) MDN 3m 11 GF *chsd ldr 11th, ld 16th,1l ld whn blnd & u.r. last, rmtd* 3 16

Only 6 runs 94-96; has the ability to win a Maiden but hardly ever runs. 14

KELLY'S ORIGINAL b.g. 8 Netherkelly - The Beginning by Goldhill Mrs W J Tolhurst
1995 U(-),2(11),3(12),1(13)
347 3/3 Higham (L) LAD 3m 10 G *trckd ldrs, prog 3 out, chal last, no ext flat* 2 18
421 9/3 High Easter (L) LAD 3m 5 S *in tch, blnd 9th, outpcd 15th, mstk 3 out, kpt on frm nxt* 2 15
620 23/3 Higham (L) LAD 3m 9 GF *mid-div, prog 12th, 3rd 15th, mstk 4 out, ran on to 2nd flat* 2 17
931 8/4 Marks Tey (L) RES 3m 8 G *(fav) mid-div, prog to 2nd 14th, ld 16th-apr 2 out, onepcd aft* 2 15
1145 20/4 Higham (L) RES 3m 12 F *alwys rear, last at 12th, p.u. nxt* P 0

Maiden winner 95; novice ridden; tries hard but very onepaced; need weak race to win again. 16

KELLYS PAL b.g. 13 Netherkelly - Paladore by St Paddy P J Millington
1995 3(13),3(13),P(0),3(15),**P(0),6(NH),3(NH)**
897 6/4 Dingley (R) CON 3m 15 GS *cls up til mstk 5th, no ch frm 10th* 10 0
1100 14/4 Guilsborough (L) OPE 3m 9 G *ld til hdd & blnd 6th, sn rdn, t.o. & p.u. 13th* P 0
1376 5/5 Dingley (R) MEM 3m 7 GF *cls up til blnd 11th, not rcvr, t.o. & p.u. 2 out* P 0
1400 6/5 Northaw (L) OPE 3m 6 F *(bl) wth ldr, ld 12th, sn hdd, wknd 14th, t.o.* 4 0
1519 12/5 Garthorpe (R) OPE 3m 7 GF *(bl) mid-div, f heavily 3rd* F -

Changed hands 95; looks finished now. 0

KELLY'S PERK (Irish) — **I** 267P

KELLY'S TWILIGHT b.m. 11 Netherkelly - Flirt by Twilight Alley Mrs A Holman
1995 P(0),P(0),P(0),P(0)
490 16/3 Horseheath (R) XX 3m 7 GF *ld & mstk 1st, prom til wknd rpdly 12th, t.o. & p.u. 3 out* P 0
679 30/3 Cottenham (R) RES 3m 15 GF *bhnd frm 7th, t.o. 10th, p.u. aft 12th* P 0
1068 13/4 Horseheath (R) INT 3m 7 F *prom, ld 6th-8th, wknd appr 14th, no ch whn j.s. last 2* 4 0
1145 20/4 Higham (L) RES 3m 12 F *chsng grp, wknd 12th, t.o.* 7 0
1320 28/4 Fakenham P-' (L) MEM 3m 3 G *chsd wnr, disp & blnd 13th, ld 2 out, hdd & no ext flat* 2 10

Just beaten in awful Members; rarely finishers and will need a miracle to win. 10

KENALAN LAD b.g. 6 Pitpan - Hollomoore by Moorestyle Mrs Sally Thornton
1995 2(11),F(-),P(0),P(0),P(0)
901 6/4 Dingley (R) MDN 2m 5f 9 GS *made all, clr ld, hmp by loose horses 10th, ran on wll* 1 14
1098 14/4 Guilsborough (L) CON 3m 17 G *14s-8s, lft in ld 1st, blnd & hdd 14th, not rcvr* 5 13

Won bad Maiden; ran much better after; can improve and must have chances in Restricted. G-S. 18

KENDOR PASS (Irish) — **I** 334P, **I** 437P, **I** 507P, **I** 5512, **I** 574P

KENELLEN (Irish) — **I** 93P, **I** 1744, **I** 282P, **I** 534P

KENILWORTH(IRE) b.g. 8 Kemal (FR) - Araglin Dora by Green Shoon Mrs D D Osborne
584 23/3 Wetherby Po' (L) RES 3m 13 S *mid-div, prog 11th, cls up til wknd 4 out* 6 14
1090 14/4 Whitwell-On' (R) RES 3m 17 G *alwys prom, ld 4 out, sn clr, styd on strngly* 1 18
1340 4/5 Hexham (L) HC 3m 1f 13 S *in tch, ld 12th, styd on strly apr last.* 1 25
1535 16/5 Aintree (L) HC 3m 1f 11 GF *(fav) midfield, cld 8th, ld 14th, f next.* F -
1630 31/5 Stratford (L) HC 3 1/2m 16 GF *held up in tch, effort 3 out, wknd quickly last.* 8 14

Ex-novice hurdler; improved & clear-cut H/Chase winner; problem last start; should win if fit 97;G-S ... 25

KENSTOWN(IRE) ch.g. 8 Le Bavard (FR) - Maureens Dote by David Jack P J King
1531 12/5 Ottery St M' (L) MDO 3m 9 GF *mid-div, 5th at 14th, prog aft 3 out, should improve* 4 0
1637 1/6 Bratton Down (L) MDO 3m 11 G *blnd 1st, rear aft, lost tch & p.u. 14th* P 0

Prmising debut; too many mistakes next time; can do beter. 12

KERRY GLEN (Irish) — **I** 1423

KERRY HILL ch.g. 10 Scallywag - Katie Fare by Ritudyr N F Williams
1995 **2(21),5(18),3(12),P(0),4(10)**,P(0)
217 24/2 Newtown (L) RES 3m 17 GS *alwys rear, lost tch 13th, t.o. & p.u. 2 out* P 0
425 9/3 Upton-On-Se' (R) MEM 3m 7 GS *disp 14th, chal agn 2 out, outpcd* 2 14
684 30/3 Chaddesley ' (L) RES 3m 14 G *tubed, chsd ldrs, wknd apr 15th* 6 11
1173 20/4 Chaddesley ' (L) RES 3m 18 G *rear of main grp, styd on frm 15th, not rch ldrs* 5 13
1223 24/4 Brampton Br' (R) RES 3m 11 G *outpcd frm 13th, t.o. & p.u. 16th* P 0
1481 11/5 Bredwardine (R) RES 3m 14 G *mid-div 8th, rdn 11th, no prog frm 13th, t.o. 2 out* 8 0

Ran well 1st 2 starts 95; downhill since; has problems and unlikely to win again. 10

KERRY MY HOME ch.g. 9 Le Moss - Sno-Sleigh by Bargello — M J Norman

108	17/2	Marks Tey	(L)	MDN	3m	17 G	*rr & rmdrs 9th, bhnd whn p.u. 13th*	P	0
314	2/3	Ampton	(R)	MDO	3m	10 G	*mstks,rmndrs 2nd, jnd ldrs 12th, ev ch til wknd appr 3 out*	3	0
439	9/3	Newton Brom'	(R)	MDN	3m	7 GS	*chsd ldrs, cls 2nd at 14th, lost plc, ran on agn 2 out*	2	12
681	30/3	Cottenham	(R)	MDO	3m	12 GF	*in tch, rmndr 11th, prog to ld 15th, rdn out frm last*	1	14
904	6/4	Dingley	(R)	RES	3m	20 GS	*abt 10th 1st m, p.u. 10th*	P	0
1101	14/4	Guilsborough	(L)	RES	3m	16 G	*trckd ldrs, effrt & 4th apr 3 out, wknd nxt*	7	0
1256	27/4	Cottenham	(R)	MEM	3m	6 F	*(fav) prom, mstk 1st, ld brfly 4th, ld 10th-4 out, no ext 2 out*	2	10
1522	12/5	Garthorpe	(R)	RES	3m	12 GF	*(bl) mid to rear, nrst fin, nvr dang*	4	0
1597	25/5	Garthorpe	(R)	XX	3m	9 G	*mostly 5th for 2m, ran on well frm 4 out, not rch wnr*	2	17

2 subsequent winners behind when winning; needs plenty of driving and more needed for Retricted. ... 16

KERRY ORCHID (Irish) — 483^{3}, 672^{2}, I 10^{1}, I 48^{1}, I 100^{3}, I 145^{1}

KERRY SOLDIER BLUE gr.g. 7 Fine Blue - Kerry Maid by Maestoso — Mrs Margaret Price

1417	6/5	Cursneh Hill	(L)	MDO	3m	14 GF	*midfld til prog 9th, wknd 14th, p.u. nxt*	P	0

Only learning and gave some hope on debut. 0

KERRY STORY (Irish) — I 589^{P}

KERSTIN'S CHOICE b.m. 5 Abutammam - Kick About by Rugantino — Mrs B W D Llewellyn

150	17/2	Erw Lon	(L)	MDN	3m	8 G	*t.o. whn p.u. 5th*	P	0
388	9/3	Llanfrynach	(R)	RES	3m	20 GS	*alwys wll bhnd, t.o. & p.u. 12th*	P	0
1197	21/4	Lydstep	(L)	MEM	3m	3 S	*alwys rear, do better*	3	0
1391	6/5	Pantyderi	(R)	MDO	3m	13 GF	*in rear whn p.u. 10th*	P	0

Tailed off last when completing; may do better. 0

KETTLES b.m. 9 Broadsword (USA) - Penny's Affair by Chingnu — Mrs M R Daniell

1995 4(0),P(0),1(13),P(0),2(12),9(0),4(12)

217	24/2	Newtown	(L)	RES	3m	17 GS	*chsd ldrs, 5th hlfwy, outpcd 14th, ran on agn 2 out*	3	15
428	9/3	Upton-On-Se'	(R)	RES	3m	17 GS	*disp ld 3 out, qcknd to ld apr last, ran on strngly*	1	19
793	2/4	Heythrop	(R)	OPE	4m	10 F	*mstks,rear,prog 10th,prssd ldrs 4 out,rdn to ld last 100yrds*	1	22
1171	20/4	Chaddesley '	(L)	OPE	3m	15 G	*(fav) alwys rear, last at 10th, ran on onepcd frm 15th*	7	18
1630	31/5	Stratford	(L)	HC	3 1/2m	16 GF	*towards rear, styd on 4 out, nvr able to chal.*	4	23

Much improved; suited by long trips; ran well in H/chase; modest Open win makes placing hard now. .. 21

KEY DOOR (Irish) — I 196^{P}, I 225^{P}, I 270^{2}, I 348^{P}, I 384^{4}, I 417^{2}

KEY OF THE NILE (Irish) — I 385^{P}

KHANDYS SLAVE(IRE) ch.m. 8 Le Johnstan - Snow Sweet by Arctic Slave — K M Stanworth

1995 P(0),P(0)

149	17/2	Erw Lon	(L)	MDN	3m	10 G	*rear, 7th at 11th, p.u. nxt*	P	0
605	23/3	Howick	(L)	MDN	3m	13 S	*cls up early, lost plc frm 13th, tk 4th last*	4	0
848	6/4	Howick	(L)	MDN	3m	14 GF	*chsd ldr to 9th, lost plc, rdn to 2nd agn 12th, wknd rpdly*	5	0
1161	20/4	Llanwit Maj'	(R)	MDO	3m	15 GS	*prom, hrd rdn 9th, wknd 12th, p.u. 3 out*	P	0

Well beaten when completing; unpromising. 0

KHATTAF b.g. 12 Kris - Hanna Alta (FR) by Busted — Mrs H C Johnson

1995 P(0),1(22),1(21),1(23),4(22)

136	17/2	Ottery St M'	(L)	LAD	3m	9 GS	*(fav) handy, prog 10th, ld 4 out, easily*	1	23
356	3/3	Garnons	(L)	LAD	3m	12 GS	*went 5th at 7th, chsd ldrs 12th, chal 3 out, hld frm nxt*	2	24
443	9/3	Haldon	(R)	LAD	3m	10 S	*(fav) patiently rdn, prog to 2nd 3 out, ld nxt, drew clr, easily*	1	24
624	23/3	Kilworthy	(L)	LAD	3m	7 GS	*race wd, j.w. prom, ld 15th, clr nxt, ran on well*	1	24
924	8/4	Bishopsleigh	(R)	LAD	3m	7 G	*ld/disp til clr ldr 3rd, nvr hdd, ran on strngly*	1	25
1072	13/4	Lifton	(R)	LAD	3m	7 S	*(fav) wnt 2nd 9th, efft to chal 2 out, not qckn clsng stgs*	2	21
1291	28/4	Barbury Cas'	(L)	LAD	3m	5 F	*(fav) trckd ldrs, ld 13th, comf*	1	22

Still very useful & maintains form really well; won 8 of last 11; win more at 13; S-F 25

KIAMA BAY (Irish) — I 7^{P}, I 49^{4}, I 83^{U}, I 132^{3}

KIDSTUFF (Irish) — I 583,

KILANNADRUM (Irish) — I 417^{6}, I 522^{1}

KILBALLY CASTLE (Irish) — I 325^{P}, I 367^{P}

KILBRICKEN MAID (Irish) — I 84^{1}, I 344^{4}

KILBURRY (Irish) — I 194^{3}

KILCANNON HOUSE (Irish) — I 116^{P}, I 212^{F}

KILCANNON SOPHIE (Irish) — I 649^{4}

KILCLARE KING (Irish) — I 337^{P}

KILCULLY CARRIG (Irish) — I 208^{F}, I 518^{P}, I 589^{2}

KILCULLY NIGHT (Irish) — I 8^{P}, I 64^{P}, I 71^{P}, I 143^{P}, I 183^{P}, I 309^{U}

KILCULLY-PRIDE (Irish) — I 6^{P}, I 15^{3}, I 54^{P}, I 333^{P}, I 519^{6}, I 593^{1}, I 639^{3}, I 648^{4}

KILCULLY TALBOT (Irish) — I 208^{F}, I 307^{P}

KILDOWNEY LADY (Irish) — I 316^{2}, I 406^{3}, I 454^{4}, I 600^{1}

KILGOBBIN (Irish) — I 582^{P}, I 603^{4}, I 636^{B}, I 644^{4}

KILLALIGAM KIM (Irish) — I 270^{P}

KILLALIGAN KIM (Irish) — I 299^{3}, I 385^{6}, I 418^{P}, I 587^{3}, I 631^{3}

KILLARNEY MAN br.g. 10 Pragmatic - Lilly Of Killarney by Sunny Way — Miss V H Smith

1995 P(0),2(11),2(10),2(11),1(12),**6(0)**

449	9/3	Charing	(L)	RES	3m	13	G	*rear, nvr going well, t.o. 15th*	7 0
574	17/3	Detling	(L)	RES	3m	14	GF	*rear, prog to 5th at 10th, rmndrs nxt, 7th & btn whn f 15th*	F -

Won bad Maiden 95; well below Restricted class and need fortune to win again. 11

KILLASHEELAN (Irish) — I 193^{1}

KILLATTY PLAYER (Irish) — I 182^{3}, I 279^{P}, I 335^{3}, I 459^{5}, I 503^{F}, I 569^{4}, I 640^{1}, I 646^{2}

KILLBALLY CASTLE (Irish) — I 127^{P}, I 183^{P}

KILLEEN COUNTESS (Irish) — I 41^{P}

KILLELAN LAD br.g. 14 Kambalda - Dusky Glory by Dusky Boy — Miss K Di Marte

529	16/3	Cothelstone	(L)	LAD	3m	5	G	*chsd ldrs, hit 5th, lst tch 11th, t.o.*	3 10
649	23/3	Cothelstone	(L)	LAD	3m	3	S	*(Jt fav) made all, clr 12th, ran on wll whn chall 2 out*	1 12

Lightly raced now; gave novice rider 1st win in bad race; need same to score at 15. 12

KILLERK LADY (Irish) — I 36^{P}, I 271^{2}, I 324^{1}, I 376^{5}, I 467^{P}

KILLESHANDRA LASS(IRE) b or br.m. 7 King's Ride - Barbara's Dream by Continuation — Mrs B Eggo

1995 1(15)

188	24/2	Friars Haugh	(L)	RES	3m	12	S	*alwys handy, chal whn lft clr 3 out, fin lame*	1 18

Undefeated in 2 starts; 3 winners behind in 96; problems now; can upgrade if fit in 97. 18

KILLOSKEHAN QUEEN (Irish) — I 44^{F}, I 123^{2}, I 197^{F}

KILLULA KING br.g. 9 Black Minstrel - Ski Cap by Beau Chapeau — Mrs M Armstrong

1995 8(0),**P(0)**,**7(0)**,3(14)

317	2/3	Corbridge	(R)	CON	3m	11	GS	*ld 1st til mstk 6th, prom whn blnd 3 out, sn btn*	8 0
474	11/5	Aspatria	(L)	OPE	3m	3	GF	*ld til aft 1st,ld 8-10th,wknd 12th,v tired & stppd bfr last*	P 0

Winning chaser(2 miles); does not stay and prospects virtually nil. 0

KILLY'S FILLY b.m. 6 Lochnager - May Kells by Artaius (USA) — N Cook

1995 **5(NH),4(NH),4(NH),3(NH),P(NH),4(NH),3(NH),5(NH),6(NH),8(NH)**

220	24/4	Brampton Br'	(R)	OPE	3m	10	G	*23l 4th at 12th, t.o. frm 14th, p.u. 16th*	P 0
246	27/4	Woodford	(L)	OPE	3m	6	G	*trckd ldrs, jnd ldr 11th til ran out & u.r. 15th*	r -
437	6/5	Ashorne	(R)	MXO	3m	13	G	*in tch in mid-div til fdd frm 14th*	7 0
565	19/5	Mollington	(R)	OPE	3m	8	GS	*chsd ldrs, outpcd 12th, lft disp dist 2nd 3 out, kpt on*	2 15
619	27/5	Chaddesley '	(L)	OPE	3m	7	GF	*last frm 6th, t.o. 12th*	5 12

Some ability but not a fluent jumper & out of her depth in Opens 15

KILMACREW (Irish) — I 23^{F}, I 27^{P}, I 179^{F}, I 261^{F}, I 288^{P}, I 402^{1}

KILMACTHOMAS ch.g. 10 Buckskin (FR) - Deep Vallie by Deep Run — Mrs M J Dusting

66	10/2	Great Treth'	(R)	OPE	3m	8	S	*twrds rear, p.u. 13th*	P 0

Won Restricted 94; only one run since; good enough for Confined if fit. goes well fresh. 22

KILMAINHWOOD (Irish) — I 20^{P}, I 176^{F}, I 258^{1}, I 406^{4}

KILMAKEE b.m. 10 Mandalus - Welsh Symphony by Welsh Saint — B R Evans

171	18/2	Market Rase'	(L)	RES	3m	5	GF	*ld 1st, sn hdd, disp 3rd whn f 13th*	F -
328	3/3	Market Rase'	(L)	RES	3m	9	G	*disp to 6th, wknd 11th, t.o. & p.u. 2 out*	P 0
426	9/3	Upton-On-Se'	(R)	CON	3m	16	GS	*lost tch ldrs hlfwy*	10 0
656	23/3	Badbury Rin'	(L)	RES	3m	11	G	*ld to 5th, prom untl wknd 11th, t.o.*	8 0
742	31/3	Upper Sapey	(R)	RES	3m	9	GS	*mostly 2nd, disp ld frm 16th til outpcd flat*	2 15
173	20/4	Chaddesley '	(L)	RES	3m	18	G	*chsd ldrs to 12th, wknd 15th, p.u. 3 out*	P 0
314	28/4	Bitterley	(L)	MEM	3m	13	G	*nvr rchd ldrs, in tch til wknd 11th, p.u. 3 out*	P 0
415	6/5	Cursneh Hill	(L)	RES	3m	11	GF	*last 12th, t.o. & p.u. 14th*	P 0

Won Irish Maiden 94; placed in 3 finisher race; no other form and win looks hard to find. 13

KILMINFOYLE b.g. 9 Furry Glen - Loreto Lady by Brave Invader (USA) — Mrs S H Shirley-Beavan

49	4/2	Alnwick	(L)	OPE	3m	14	G	*blndrd 5th, prom to 11th, t.o. & p.u. 3 out*	P 0
191	24/2	Friars Haugh	(L)	OPE	3m	5	S	*chsd wnr frm 4th, mstks 13th & nxt, no ext frm 2 out*	3 19

320 2/3 Corbridge (R) OPE 3m 5f 8 GS *mstk 3rd, prom, disp ld whn f 18th (4 out)* F
752 31/3 Lockerbie (R) LAD 3m 10 G *blndrd 2nd, 3rd hlfwy, jnd ldr 2 out, ld last stride* 1 2
1121 20/4 Bangor (L) HC 3m 110yds 8 S *in tch till no dngr from 12th.* 5 2

Scrambled home in modest race in only start in Ladies; may win similar 97; G-S 19

KILMINGTON(IRE) gr.g. 7 Roselier (FR) - Hope You're Lucky by Quayside H T Pelha
1995 **9(NH)**,**U(NH)**,**P(NH)**

652 23/3 Badbury Rin' (L) MDO 3m 13 G *ld 4th-9th & 14-15th, upsides whn f 3 out* F
1163 20/4 Larkhill (R) MEM 3m 3 GF *n.j.w. early, ev ch 14th, wknd qckly nxt* 2

Poor novice hurdler; has ability but needs to jump better. 13

KILPEACON LADY VI (Irish) — **I** 476^{4}

KILSHEELAN LAD ch.g. 13 Kambalda - Lady Ashton by Anthony K To
1995 3(11),4(0),U(-),3(0),U(-),P(0),3(0),R(-),2(0),**4(0)**

571 17/3 Detling (L) CON 3m 13 GF *alwys rear, t.o. 14th* 9
811 6/4 Charing (L) OPE 3m 9 F *t.o. hlfwy* 7

Open winner 94; changed hands & awful since. 0

KILTONGA b or br.g. 9 Indian King (USA) - Miss Teto by African Sky Miss Laura J Horse
1995 P(0),5(0),10(0),3(16),3(0),5(0)

443 9/3 Haldon (R) LAD 3m 10 S *tubed, sn bhnd, t.o. frm 10th* 6
708 30/3 Barbury Cas' (L) LAD 3m 10 G *sn rear, t.o. & p.u. 9th* P
818 6/4 Charlton Ho' (L) LAD 3m 6 GF *in tch til f 8th* F
1110 17/4 Hockworthy (L) CON 3m 9 GS *rr, lost tch & p.u. aft 11th* P

Of no account 11

KILTROSE LAD b.g. 7 Soldier Rose - Kiltish by Pamroy Mrs Elizabeth Gutteridg
1995 P(0),3(0),B(-),P(0)

665 24/3 Eaton Hall (R) RES 3m 14 S *f 1st* F
689 30/3 Chaddesley ' (L) MDN 3m 15 G *ld 2nd-nxt, blnd 10th, outpcd 14th, kpt on frm 2 out* 3
884 6/4 Brampton Br' (R) MDN 3m 12 GF *rdn to chs ldr 15th, kpt on onepcd* 2
1175 20/4 Chaddesley ' (L) MDN 3m 9 G *ld til ran wd bnd apr 13th,ld 15th-nxt,no ext frm 2 out* 2
1224 24/4 Brampton Br' (R) MDO 3m 17 G *(fav) ld 4-7th & frm 13th, kpt on und pres frm 3 out* 1
1481 11/5 Bredwardine (R) RES 3m 14 G *prom, went 2nd 13th, ld 15th, hdd & kpt on onepcd 2 out* 2

Improved; staying better now; chances in late season Restricted; G-G/F. 17

KIMBER SISSONS (Irish) — **I** 421^{U}, **I** 527^{F}, **I** 634^{P}, **I** 655^{P}

KIMBRY (Irish) — **I** 179^{P}, **I** 404^{P}, **I** 450^{4}, **I** 534^{P}

KINCARDINE BRIDGE(USA) b.g. 7 Tiffany Ice (USA) - Priestess (USA) by Time To Explode (USA) J Bradburr
1995 **F(NH)**

755 31/3 Lockerbie (R) MDN 3m 17 G *ld 7th til u.r. 14th* U
1088 14/4 Friars Haugh (L) MDO 3m 10 F *(fav) made virt all, drew wll clr frm 2 out* 1
1252 27/4 Balcormo Ma' (R) INT 3m 5 GS *cls up til wknd qckly apr 13th, p.u. bfr nxt* P
1472 11/5 Aspatria (L) RES 3m 8 GF *trckd ldrs, lost plc qckly 10th, t.o. & p.u. bfr 12th* P

Romped home in weak race; problems and stopped quickly after; young enough to revive; best watched. 15

KINCORA (Irish) — **I** 541^{P}, **I** 582^{P}, **I** 644,

KINDLY LADY b.m. 8 Kind Of Hush - Welcome Honey by Be Friendly David Fishe

876 6/4 Higher Kilw' (L) MDN 3m 11 GF *(fav) keen hold, conf rdn, prog 15th, disp 3 out, pshd clr flat* 1

Beat a poor lot but did it well & should find Restricted if ready in 97 17

KINESIOLOGY(IRE) b or br.g. 8 Boreen (FR) - Ardellis Lady by Pollerton A J Sende
1995 2(18)

1128 20/4 Stafford Cr' (R) RES 3m 17 S *ld til 10th & agn 12th til hdd cls home* 2 2

Irish Maiden winner 93; lightly raced; just beaten in hot race; win Restricted if fit in 97. 22

KINGDOM LAD b.g. 5 Sizzling Melody - Parson's Child (USA) by Arts And Letters (USA) D Luxto
1995 **8(NH)**

805 4/4 Clyst St Ma' (L) RES 3m 7 GS *rear, not fluent, p.u. 8th* P

Did not make halfway om debut; can do better. 0

KINGEOCHY (Irish) — **I** 349^{F}, **I** 416^{P}, **I** 618, **I** 635^{1}, **I** 658^{4}

KINGFISHER BAY b.g. 11 Try My Best (USA) - Damiya (FR) by Direct Flight D W Chilco
1995 P(0),5(0),P(0),1(14),7(0),**4(0)**

256 29/2 Ludlow (R) HC 3m 14 G *ld till apr 12th, soon wknd, t.o. when p.u. before 4 out.* P
384 9/3 Llanfrynach (R) OPE 3m 16 GS *ld/disp 2nd-15th, sn wknd* 9

602	23/3	Howick	(L)	OPE	3m	11	S	*cls up to 8th, wknd, p.u. 12th*	P	0
846	6/4	Howick	(L)	OPE	3m	7	GF	*mid-div, drvn to cls 4th at 11th, wknd & no ch 14th*	4	13
037	13/4	St Hilary	(R)	OPE	3m	5	G	*disp til p.u. 12th, lame*	P	0
159	20/4	Llanwit Maj'	(R)	LAD	3m	5	GS	*chsd ldng pair, lost tch 15th, lft poor 2nd 2 out*	2	0
331	1/5	Cheltenham	(L)	HC	2m 5f	9	G	*cl up to 3rd, well bhnd when blnd 10th, t.o..*	6	0
479	11/5	Bredwardine	(R)	OPE	3m	8	G	*prom, rdn 12th, wknd frm 14th*	6	0
544	17/5	Stratford	(L)	HC	3m	10	GF	*chsd ldrs, wknd quickly after 11th, soon t.o..*	9	0

Won awful Open 95; outclassed in 96 and need another miracle to win again. 10

KINGFISHER BLUES(IRE) ch.g. 8 Quayside - Night Spot by Midsummer Night II — Paul Morris

1995 F(-),P(0),F(-),R(-),**P(NH),8(NH)**

287	2/3	Eaton Hall	(R)	MDO	3m	11	G	*mid to rear, no ch whn p.u. 4 out*	P	0
740	31/3	Sudlow Farm	(R)	MDN	3m	16	G	*mstks, nvr bttr thn mid-div*	5	0
234	27/4	Weston Park	(L)	MDO	3m	13	G	*mid-div whn u.r. 4th*	U	-
484	11/5	Bredwardine	(R)	MDO	3m	17	G	*rear til effrt 12th, no prog frm 14th*	6	0

Finally getting round but barely worth a rating yet. 10

KINGFISHER LAD br.g. 10 River Poaching - Royal Spring by Crown Again — Miss Rosalind Booth

1995 P(0),P(0)

460	9/3	Eyton-On-Se'	(L)	LAD	3m	10	G	*prom, sn btn aftr 12th, p.u. 3 out*	P	0
852	6/4	Sandon	(L)	MDN	3m	9	GF	*prom, ld 3rd-8th, in tch to 4 out, outpcd*	3	0

Beaten 32 lengths when placed; much more needed. 0

KING FLY ch.g. 6 Saxon Farm - Deep Goddess by Deep Run — J A Wales

414	9/3	Charm Park	(L)	MDO	3m	11	G	*alwys wl in rr, p.u. 4 out*	P	0
704	30/3	Tranwell	(L)	MDO	3m	16	GS	*bhnd to hlfwy, gd prog 14th, kpt on, no ext apr last*	2	15
094	14/4	Whitwell-On'	(R)	MDO	2 1/2m 88yds	16	G	*prom, ld 5th, hdd nxt, prom aft, und pres & btn whn f 2 out*	F	-
365	4/5	Gisburn	(R)	MDO	3m	17	G	*cls up, ld 12th til hdd & outpcd flat*	2	14

Beaten 3 lengths maximum; improvement likely and should win in 97. 14

KING KEITH ch.g. 7 Sunley Builds - The Flying Cleo by Native Admiral (USA) — Mrs C E Whiteway

1995 7(0),F(-),P(0),U(-)

166	17/2	Weston Park	(L)	MDN	3m	10	G	*mid-div, prog 4 out, styd on, nrst fin*	2	12
288	2/3	Eaton Hall	(R)	MDO	3m	17	G	*nvr going wl, p.u. 5 out*	P	0
661	24/3	Eaton Hall	(R)	MDN	3m	9	S	*mid-div, prog to disp 8-10th, chal 2 out, not qckn*	2	13
740	31/3	Sudlow Farm	(R)	MDN	3m	16	G	*mstks, in tch, 4th & ch whn blndrd 14th, wknd*	4	0
364	4/5	Gisburn	(R)	MDO	3m	11	G	*alwys prom, 5th whn u.r. 14th*	U	-

Placed in weak races; mistakes and suspect in a finish; hard to find a win. 11

KINGOFNOBLES(IRE) ch.g. 7 King Persian - Eau D'Amour by Tall Noble (USA) — K B Rogers

1995 2(13),1(14)

128	17/2	Kingston Bl'	(L)	RES	3m	14	GS	*trckd ldrs, hit rail aft 8th, not rcvr, t.o. & p.u. 14th*	P	0
339	3/3	Heythrop	(R)	RES	3m	10	G	*ld to 9th & 11th til aft 2 out, btn whn mstk last*	3	12
641	23/3	Siddington	(L)	RES	3m	20	S	*(Jt fav) disp ld to 4th, rmdrs & lst pl appr 10th, no dang aft*	8	10
019	13/4	Kingston Bl'	(L)	INT	3m	6	G	*(bl) ld to 14th, 3rd & outpcd nxt, rallied 2 out, clsng flat*	2	16
329	30/4	Huntingdon	(R)	HC	3m	14	GF	*(bl) soon well bhnd, last and t.o. when p.u. before 9th.*	P	0
505	11/5	Kingston Bl'	(L)	MEM	3m	5	G	*(fav) ld to 6th,lft in ld apr 9th,wd & hdd apr 2 out,not qckn*	2	13
567	19/5	Mollington	(R)	INT	3m	12	GS	*(bl) ld 2nd-9th, rdn & not run on, t.o. & p.u. 13th*	P	0

Maiden winner 95; changed hands; disappointing and looks ungenuine; likely to prove frustrating. 14

KING OF SHADOWS b or br.g. 9 Connaught - Rhiannon by Welsh Pageant — Ceri James

459	9/3	Eyton-On-Se'	(L)	OPE	3m	11	G	*mid-div early, lst tch, p.u. bfr 13th*	P	0
579	20/3	Ludlow	(R)	HC	2 1/2m	17	G	*bhnd from hfwy, t.o. when p.u. before 2 out.*	P	0
120	20/4	Bangor	(L)	HC	2 1/2m 110yds	13	S	*bhnd, reminders after 6th, soon t.o., p.u. before 11th.*	P	0
227	26/4	Ludlow	(R)	HC	2 1/2m	16	G	*mid div, effort apr 6 out, not reach ldrs.*	5	16
455	8/5	Uttoxeter	(L)	HC	2m 5f	9	G	*ld till after 12th, led after 3 out, clr last, rdn out.*	1	21
532	13/5	Towcester	(R)	HC	2m 110yds	16	GF	*alwys prom, ev ch apr 2 out, ran on one pace.*	3	23

Winning hurdler; revived late season; won poor H/Chase; best under 3m; needs to dominate; moderate 21

KING OF THE CLOUDS b.g. 11 Sonnen Gold - Misfired by Blast — R N Devereux

1995 6(0),S(-),5(0),P(0),P(0)

339	3/3	Heythrop	(R)	RES	3m	10	G	*prom, ld 9-11th, wknd rpdly 13th*	6	0
603	23/3	Howick	(L)	LAD	3m	8	S	*mid-div, wknd & p.u. 3 out*	P	0
005	9/4	Upton-On-Se'	(R)	CON	3m	6	F	*prog frm rear 13th, chsd wnr 15th, btn whn mstk 2 out*	2	16
173	20/4	Chaddesley '	(L)	RES	3m	18	G	*ld chsng grp, clsd 16th, ev ch til no ext aft 3 out*	3	17
481	11/5	Bredwardine	(R)	RES	3m	14	G	*mid-div at 8th, lost tch aft 15th, p.u. last*	P	0
567	19/5	Mollington	(R)	INT	3m	12	GS	*pllng, hld up, gd prog 9th, wth ldrs whn u.r. 13th*	U	-
634	1/6	Bratton Down	(L)	INT	3m	15	G	*alwys rear, t.o. 11th, blnd 14th, p.u. nxt*	P	0

Inconsistent but ran 2 excellent races; last won in 92 and getting on now. 15

KINGOFTHESWINGERS br.g. 9 Swinging Rebel - Fair Sara by McIndoe M Gallemo

1012 9/4 Flagg Moor (L) XX 3m 7 G *hdstr, ld, hrd prsd whn f 13th* F
1196 21/4 Sandon (L) MDN 3m 17 G *chsng grp whn f 5th* F

Headstrong and clumsy; unpromising. 0

KINGQUILLO(IRE) b.g. 7 Henbit (USA) - Friendly Polly by Be Friendly Mrs B Sha
1995 **18(NH)**,**8(NH)**

287 2/3 Eaton Hall (R) MDO 3m 11 G *j.w. made all, ran on well frm 2 out* 1
1482 11/5 Bredwardine (R) RES 3m 13 G *2nd whn f 3rd* F

Ex Irish; fine start but absent for 2 months after; should upgrade if right in 97. 17

KINGS ALIBI (Irish) — **I** 270[P], **I** 290[P]

KING'S BANKER (Irish) — **I** 465[4], **I** 603[1]

KINGS CAVE (Irish) — **I** 13[U], **I** 31[3], **I** 80[1], **I** 198[P]

KINGS GUNNER ch.g. 9 Kings Lake (USA) - Resooka by Godswalk (USA) P D J Litsto

203 24/2 Castle Of C' (R) MEM 3m 4 HY *j.w. ld to last, tired & hdd* 2
469 10/3 Milborne St' (L) LAD 3m 8 G *handy, ld 13th-2 out, not qckn aft* 2
655 23/3 Badbury Rin' (L) LAD 3m 8 G *front rank untl wknd 15th, mstk 16th, t.o.* 6
1126 20/4 Stafford Cr' (R) LAD 3m 7 S *2nd early, lost tch 12th, t.o. frm 3 out* 4
1453 7/5 Wincanton (R) HC 2m 5f 9 F *well bhnd, some hdwy from 4 out.* 5

Missed 95; won i of last 15 (weak Ladies); may find similar; G-F. 15

KINGSLAND (Irish) — **I** 471[P]

KING'S MAVERICK(IRE) b.g. 8 King's Ride - Lawless Secret by Meadsville C J El
1995 P(0),2(0),1(0)

449 9/3 Charing (L) RES 3m 13 G *rear, dived thro 8th, f 10th* F
574 17/3 Detling (L) RES 3m 14 GF *rear, wll bhnd whn p.u. 17th* P
779 31/3 Penshurst (L) RES 3m 13 GS *rear, gd prog to 3rd 10th, ld 4-2 out, rddn & no ext* 2
1054 13/4 Penshurst (L) RES 3m 8 G *(fav) hld up, gd prog 4 out, ld apr 2 out, drew wll clr* 1

Won 2 bad races 95/96; hard ride and needs more for Confineds; G/S-F. 15

KINGS MISCHIEF(IRE) b.g. 8 King's Ride - Silent Collection by Monksfield R J Owe
1995 F(-),2(13),3(10),1(15)

77 11/2 Wetherby Po' (L) RES 3m 18 GS *rear, u.r. 11th* U
219 24/2 Newtown (L) RES 3m 17 GS *cls up, mstk 10th & rmndrs, wknd 13th, p.u. 15th* P
665 24/3 Eaton Hall (R) RES 3m 14 S *mid-div, prog last m, nvr dang* 3
1030 13/4 Alpraham (R) RES 3m 10 GS *mid-div, 8l 4th & styng on wll whn u.r. 3 out* U
1151 20/4 Whittington (L) INT 3m 12 G *(bl) alwys rear, nvr dang* 8

Struggling now upgraded; onepaced and only hope is weak Restricted in the mud. 14

KING SPRING br.g. 11 Royal Fountain - K-King by Fury Royal Mrs D B Johnston
1995 3(17),3(11),2(22),1(20),2(20)

500 16/3 Lanark (R) OPE 3m 6 G *(fav) alwys rear, lost tch by 4 out* 4

Won 6 of last 17 races; not seen after running poorly 96en looks hard to win now;F-S. 20

KINGS RANK br.g. 11 Tender King - Jhansi Ki Rani (USA) by Far North (CAN) M H Da
1995 P(0)

67 10/2 Great Treth' (R) LAD 3m 11 S *clsd up 13th, no ext frm nxt* 4
561 17/3 Ottery St M' (L) LAD 3m 12 G *mid-div whn slowed 7th, p.u. bef nxt* P
655 23/3 Badbury Rin' (L) LAD 3m 8 G *(bl) front rank, 2nd 10th, hmpd 12th, t.o.* 7
815 6/4 Charlton Ho' (L) MEM 3m 8 GF *alwys rear, t.o. 14th, p.u. & dismntd 4 out* P
1111 17/4 Hockworthy (L) MXO 3m 13 GS *(bl) prom, ld 9-12th, wknd rpdly, t.o. & ref 15th* R

Winning hurdler; beaten 71/2 lengths in good Ladies; lost interest after; best watched. 15

KINGS REWARD b.g. 10 King's Ride - Mancha Lady by Milan Mrs W S Coc
1995 2(17),8(0),4(15),4(10)

137 17/2 Ottery St M' (L) RES 3m 15 GS *in tch, ld 8-11th, outpcd by wnr 3 out* 2
199 24/2 Lemalla (R) RES 3m 17 HY *prom til wknd & p.u. 2 out* P

Members winner 94; stays but onepaced; Restricted hard to find; Soft. 16

KINGS ROMANCE b.m. 6 Rakaposhi King - Rymer's Fancy by Rymer J G Fry
1995 **P(NH)**,**R(NH)**

680 30/3 Cottenham (R) MDO 3m 11 GF *mid-div, wknd 8th, t.o. & p.u. 15th* P
1102 14/4 Guilsborough (L) RES 3m 15 G *drppd out aft 6th, t.o. 9th, p.u. 11th* P

Refused over hurdles and looks unpromising. 0

KINGS SUCCESS (Irish) — **I** 330, , **I** 502[1]

INGSTHORPE ch.g. 8 Brotherly (USA) - Miss Kewmill by Billion (USA) Mervyn Jones

2 13/1 Larkhill (R) MDO 3m 17 GS *in tch to 10th, 9th & wll bhnd whn p.u. 13th* P 0
31 9/3 Upton-On-Se' (R) MDO 3m 17 GS *8th 7 wll btn whn b.d. 3 out* B -
47 31/3 Upper Sapey (R) MDO 3m 11 GS *mid-div, effrt to go 3rd brfly 15th, sn no ext* 4 11
06 9/4 Upton-On-Se' (R) MDN 3m 11 F *c.u., trckd ldr 14th, ld aft 2 out, hrd rdn, hld on wl* 1 15
33 27/4 Weston Park (L) RES 3m 14 G *chsd ldrs, hndy whn f hvly 4th* F -
81 11/5 Bredwardine (R) RES 3m 14 G *mid-div & going wll 11th, effrt 13th, wknd 15th, p.u. 2 out* P 0
18 27/5 Chaddesley ' (L) CON 3m 14 GF *rear, mstk 12th, sn no ch, t.o.* 7 0

No ability under rules; beat 2 subsequent winners; needs easy 3 miles and life looks tough now. 14

INGS TOKEN b.g. 6 Rakaposhi King - Pro-Token by Proverb J B Walton

94 24/2 Friars Haugh (L) MDN 3m 11 S *sn t.o., p.u. 12th* P 0
06 9/3 Dalston (R) MDO 2 1/2m 12 G *bhnd early, sm hdwy 7th, nvr nrr* 5 0
05 30/3 Tranwell (L) MDO 3m 9 GS *(fav) prom, disp 12th, hrd rdn 3 out, hdd nxt, no ext apr last* 3 13
54 27/4 Balcormo Ma' (R) MDO 3m 14 GS *(fav) ld/disp frm 4th til wknd qckly 15th, p.u. 2 out* P 0
17 12/5 Hexham Poin' (L) MDN 3m 10 HY *wll bhnd, steady prog to 2nd 3 out, no ext frm nxt* 4 13
75 19/5 Corbridge (R) MDO 3m 10 G *(fav) mid-div, prog 9th, ld 3 out, comf, improve* 1 15

Steady improvement; won poor race and needs to improve; good stable. 15

ING'S TREASURE(USA) b.g. 7 King Of Clubs - Crown Treasure (USA) by Graustark I A Balding

1995 **3(NH)**

37 3/3 Heythrop (R) OPE 3m 10 G *tubed,w.w. prog 12th, jnd wnr 14th, ld going wll & u.r. last* U 23
81 21/3 Wincanton (R) HC 2m 5f 13 S *alwys prom, ev ch apr 3 out, not qckn.* 2 26
13 13/4 Ascot (R) HC 3m 110yds 11 GS *pushed along 9th, hdwy 14th, chsd ldrs 3 out, kept on from next but no ch with wnr.* 2 22
36 1/5 Cheltenham (L) HC 2m 110yds 9 G *prog 6th, cld up 10th, ld after 4 out, drew clr 2 out, blnd last, pushed out.* 1 30
62 10/5 Market Rasen (R) HC 2 3/4m 110yds 11 G *(fav) held up in rear, hmpd by faller 4th, steady hdwy from 9th, ld soon after four out, clr 2 out, comf.* 1 30
44 17/5 Stratford (L) HC 3m 10 GF *held up, hdwy 12th, went 3rd after 4 out, chal last, qcknd and soon ld, held on well.* 1 29

Winning hurdler; improved with tubing; useful H/Chaser now; quickens; win more 97; 2-3m; S-G/F 30

ING TORUS (Irish) — **I** 86^{3}, **I** 162^{3}, **I** 191^{1}, **I** 264^{3}
ING TYRANT (Irish) — **I** 190^{4}, **I** 377^{5}, **I** 470^{3}, **I** 500^{1}, **I** 613, , **I** 633^{P}
INKY LADY (Irish) — **I** 529^{F}, **I** 580^{2}, **I** 605^{2}

INLEA b.g. 6 Meadowbrook - Faskin by Fez Peter Diggle

1995 U(-),4(0),1(15)

84 11/2 Alnwick (L) RES 3m 11 GS *ld 4th-2 out, ran on onepcd aft* 2 17
11 17/2 Lanark (R) RES 3m 6 GS *(fav) cls up, chal 3 out, ld last, all out* 1 18

Progressive youngster; stays; finished early 96; can win Confined if fit in 97. 20

INLOGH GALE(IRE) b.g. 8 Strong Gale - Kinlogh Maid by Random Shot W J Evans

1995 **4(NH)**

49 17/2 Erw Lon (L) MDN 3m 10 G *(fav) ld, 5l clr 13th, wknd aft 2 out, hdd & no ext flat* 2 13
50 17/3 Erw Lon (L) MDN 3m 13 GS *disp 8th-4 out, fdd aft* 6 0
73 31/3 Pantyderi (R) MDN 3m 8 G *(fav) ld to 11th, onepcd frm 2 out* 3 11
75 8/4 Lydstep (L) MDO 3m 9 G *alwys mid-div, no dang* 4 0
36 13/4 St Hilary (R) LAD 3m 6 G *(bl) ld to 10th, hdd & wknd aft* 3 12

Moderate and disappointing under rules; same story in points; safe but win only possible. 12

INNAHALLA (Irish) — **I** 464^{6}, **I** 518^{U}
INROSS (Irish) — **I** 165^{4}, **I** 196^{P}, **I** 348^{P}, **I** 381^{5}, **I** 529^{P}
IPPINS (Irish) — **I** 73^{3}

IRBY'S CHARM ch.g. 7 Nearly A Hand - Vulgan's Flight by Vulgan Slave Bill Hall

73 31/3 Pantyderi (R) MDN 3m 8 G *alwys mid-div, ran green, improve* 4 10
77 8/4 Lydstep (L) MDO 3m 8 G *(Jt fav) alwys mid-div* 4 0
90 6/5 Pantyderi (R) MDO 3m 15 GF *3rd/4th til wknd 15th, p.u. last* P 0
92 11/5 Erw Lon (L) MDO 3m 10 F *alwys towrds rear, p.u. 2 out* P 0

Yet to beat another horse but looks capable of better. 10

IRCHWYN LAD b.g. 8 Kirchner - Gowyn by Goldhill Dr Bernard Lawley

56 31/3 Lockerbie (R) MDN 3m 14 G *jmp wll, made all, styd on wll* 1 15

Beat subsequent dual winner in 71/2 minutes plus race; surely able to progress. 16

ITES HARDWICKE b.g. 9 Sunyboy - Kitty Stobling by Goldhill S Lynch

1995 1(15),P(0),2(15),**U(-)**,U(-)

19 14/1 Tweseldown (R) CON 3m 9 GS *u.r. 1st* U -
22 20/1 Barbury Cas' (L) XX 3m 19 GS *rear til prog 10th, styd on frm 3 out, lft 2nd last* 2 19

124	17/2	Kingston Bl'	(L)	CON	3m	17	GS	*s.v.s. last til u.r. aft 4th*	U
234	24/2	Heythrop	(R)	LAD	3m	6	GS	*ld to 8th, chsd ldr, 3rd at 15th, chal last, got up nr fin*	1
369	7/3	Towcester	(R)	HC	3m 1f	6	G	*well bhnd from 12th, t.o..*	4
638	23/3	Siddington	(L)	CON	3m	16	S	*last whn u.r. 7th*	U
710	30/3	Barbury Cas'	(L)	CON	3m	6	G	*ld to 2nd, lost tch 12th, outpcd aft*	3

Changed hands; novice ridden; dead-heated in weak Ladies; stays; need same to win again;G-S. 17

KITZBERG (Irish) — I 96^{P}, I 169^{F}

KIWI EXILE(NZ) b.g. 7 Ivory Hunter (USA) - Kaymarg (NZ) by Attalas — N W Padfi

1995 P(0),P(0)

34	20/1	Higham	(L)	MDN	3m	11	GF	*bhnd, blnd 8th, p.u. nxt, dead*	P

Dead. 10

KIZZY ROSE (Irish) — I 44^{P}, I 202^{4}, I 295^{2}, I 372^{4}, I 473^{P}, I 512^{P}

KNIGHTS CREST (Irish) — I 131^{3}, I 327^{1}, I 425^{F}, I 482^{P}

KNIGHTS PLEASURE (Irish) — I 33^{P}, I 96, , I 178^{2}, I 259^{1}, I 298^{B}, I 338^{P}

KNIGHT'S SPUR(USA) b.g. 9 Diesis - Avoid (USA) by Buckpasser — Mrs Mary Henders

1995 4(14),4(23),2(22),3(19),5(18),5(0)

126	17/2	Kingston Bl'	(L)	LAD	3m	11	GS	*prom, ev ch apr 14th, 3rd & btn nxt, wknd*	4
436	9/3	Newton Brom'	(R)	LAD	3m	10	GS	*chsd ldrs, effrt apr last, ran on, just faild*	2
685	30/3	Chaddesley '	(L)	LAD	3m	9	G	*w.w. prog 11th, 4th & hit 3 out, lft 2nd last, no imp*	2
1227	26/4	Ludlow	(R)	HC	2 1/2m	16	G	*chsd ldrs, rdn 3 out, wknd next.*	6

Winning chaser; good enough for modest Ladies but frustrating; G/S-F. running 96 18

KNOCANS PRIDE (Irish) — I 98^{F}, I 340^{U}, I 403^{4}, I 448^{5}, I 534^{U}, I 601^{1}

KNOCK DERK (Irish) — I 252^{P}

KNOCK LEADER (Irish) — I 565^{2}, I 653^{3}

KNOCKNACARRA LAD (Irish) — I 3^{3}

KNOCK RANGER (Irish) — I 236^{P}, I 430^{F}

KNOCKTORAN LADY (Irish) — I 203^{P}, I 253^{F}, I 324^{F}, I 369^{4}, I 441^{1}, I 629^{P}

KNOCKUMSHIN ch.g. 13 Kambalda - Vina's Last by Royal Buck — Sidney J Sm

1995 **1(28),4(26),2(24),6(19),2(NH)**

256	29/2	Ludlow	(R)	HC	3m	14	G	*hdwy 12th, chsd ldrs 15th, wknd 4 out.*	7
799	3/4	Ludlow	(R)	HC	3m	8	GF	*held up, pushed along and outpcd apr 2 out.*	4
909	8/4	Towcester	(R)	HC	2 3/4m	6	F	*bhnd, mstk 10th, hdwy next, chsd wnr apr 2 out, no impn.*	2
1327	30/4	Huntingdon	(R)	HC	3m	6	GF	*in tch, left 3rd 16th, rdn and btn apr 2 out.*	3
1532	13/5	Towcester	(R)	HC	2m 110yds	16	GF	*hdwy apr 2 out, nvr on terms.*	6

Formerly good H/chaser; in decline now and a win at 14 looks tough; R/H only;G-F. 18

KNOWE HEAD b.g. 12 Beau Charmeur (FR) - Niagara Lass by Prince Hansel — J Hodgs

1995 1(22),1(23),1(23),**3(19),2(23)**

826	6/4	Stainton	(R)	OPE	3m	8	GF	*ld til last, onepcd*	3
1304	28/4	Southwell P'	(L)	OPE	3m	5	GF	*(fav) ld 4th, sn clr, breather 13th, ct 5 out, not qckn*	2
1448	6/5	Witton Cast'	(R)	OPE	3m	5	G	*ld til hdd 14th, wknd nxt, poor 3rd 3 out*	3
1467	11/5	Easingwold	(L)	OPE	3m	6	G	*j.w. ld til s.u. apr 7th*	S
1586	25/5	Hexham	(L)	HC	2 1/2m 110yds	14	GF	*(Jt fav) j.w, made all, clr thrght, unchal.*	1

Hacked up in poor H/chase; front runs; needs easy 3 miles; harder to place now.G-F. 21

KNOWING gr.m. 9 Lochnager - Caroline Lamb by Hotfoot — P G Watk

1995 P(0),**P(0)**

25	20/1	Barbury Cas'	(L)	OPE	3m	14	GS	*rear, lost tch & p.u. 11th*	P
155	17/2	Erw Lon	(L)	RES	3m	9	G	*ld to 8th, wknd rpdly, p.u. 13th*	P
219	24/2	Newtown	(L)	RES	3m	17	GS	*blnd 7th, alwys bhnd, p.u. 13th*	P
364	5/3	Leicester	(R)	HC	2m 1f	12	GS	*alwys rear, nvr on terms.*	7
908	8/4	Hereford	(R)	HC	2m 3f	12	GF	*held up, hdwy 7th, joined ldrs 10th, wknd 2 out.*	4
1336	1/5	Cheltenham	(L)	HC	2m 110yds	9	G	*mstk 1st, prog to 5th 10th, styd on one pace.*	4
1532	13/5	Towcester	(R)	HC	2m 110yds	16	GF	*soon well bhnd, t.o. when p.u. before 2 out.*	P

Short Maiden winner 94; does not stay 3 miles and outclassed in H/chase; win is very hard to find. 13

KNOW SOMETHING VI (Irish) — I 78^{F}, I 138^{F}, I 156^{4}, I 311^{3}, I 358^{P}, I 457^{1}

KOCHNIE (Irish) — I 119^{P}, I 149^{5}, I 204^{F}, I 289^{F}, I 369^{S}, I 443^{4}, I 581^{5}

KOLMAN-K (Irish) — I 373^{2}

KOMORI (Irish) — I 311^{P}, I 429^{F}, I 543^{P}

ORBELL(IRE) ch.m. 7 Roselier (FR) - Chipmunk by Apollo Eight — K J Mitchell

1995 F(-),1(18),1(21),F(-),1(19),1(19),1(21),1(23),U(-)

159	17/2	Weston Park	(L)	CON	3m	22	G	*(fav) ld to aft 3 out, sn btn whn hdd, bttr for race*	2	21
289	2/3	Eaton Hall	(R)	CON	3m	10	G	*(fav) n.j.w. mid-div,ld 8-11th,hit nxt 3,ld 2 out,jnd last,ran on*	1	23
664	24/3	Eaton Hall	(R)	CON	3m	15	S	*(fav) handy, ld 3 out, sn clr, hdd last, no ext*	2	24
687	30/3	Chaddesley '	(L)	CON	3m	10	G	*(fav) chsd ldr 8-14th, hrd rdn 3 out, ld last, gamely*	1	23
195	21/4	Sandon	(L)	XX	3m	9	G	*(fav) hld up, prog 11th, ld 3 out, sn clr, easily*	1	23
577	19/5	Wolverhampt'	(L)	CON	3m	6	G	*(fav) ld to 5th & 8-10th, ld apr 3 out, sn drew clr*	1	20

Won 10 points 95/96; tough & genuine; not always fluent; can win Opens; any.eting; win more; Any 23

UMADA b.g. 9 Vision (USA) - Fan The Flame by Grundy — Miss Lisa Llewellyn

1995 2(10),1(16),1(18),**4(16)**,**7(10)**

767	31/3	Pantyderi	(R)	INT	3m	7	G	*ld to 3rd, agn 9th-4 out, no ext aft*	3	16
981	8/4	Lydstep	(L)	INT	3m	5	G	*alwys disp, hrd rdn whn lft clr last*	1	18
157	20/4	Llanwit Maj'	(R)	CON	3m	11	GS	*(fav) disp ld to 3rd, ld 8th til f 14th*	F	-
414	6/5	Cursneh Hill	(L)	LAD	3m	9	GF	*ld til hdd aft 15th, btn frm 2 out, lft 2nd last*	2	20
489	11/5	Erw Lon	(L)	LAD	3m	4	F	*ld to 7th & agn 14th, no threat aft, easy*	1	21
559	18/5	Bassaleg	(R)	LAD	3m	4	F	*(fav) ld til nrly ref 8th,sn outpcd,ran on to jn wnr 15th,just hld*	2	20
635	1/6	Bratton Down	(L)	LAD	3m	13	G	*ran in sntchs, ld to 4th, in tch 15th, sn wknd, walked in*	9	0

Only horse to beat Handsome Harvey 95/96; needs easy 3 miles and likes to dictate; G-F. 19

USHDALAY(IRE) br.g. 7 Sandalay - Cushla by Zabeg — David Wales

1995 **P(NH)**,**4(NH)**,**2(NH)**

182	18/2	Horseheath	(R)	MDO	3m	11	G	*6s-7/2, trckd ldrs to 15th, no ch whn p.u. 2 out*	P	0

Poor placed form under Rules; well backed but showed little & disappeared 10

WALK ch.m. 6 K-Battery - Burri Walk by Tower Walk — Mrs M Armstrong

322	2/3	Corbridge	(R)	MDN	3m	10	GS	*sn bhnd, t.o. & p.u. 8th*	P	0
405	9/3	Dalston	(R)	MDO	2 1/2m	16	G	*al bhnd*	8	0
253	27/4	Balcormo Ma'	(R)	MDO	3m	16	GS	*ld til wknd frm 12th, p.u. 4 out*	P	0

Showed speed; needs more stamina before going close. 0

YLE LAMP (Irish) — I 533^{R}

YLNHILL (Irish) — I 169^{P}, I 219^{1}, I 281^{2}, I 315^{2}, I 405^{6}, I 537^{6}, I 597,

ABURNUM gr.g. 8 Glint Of Gold - Lorelene (FR) by Lorenzaccio — Robert Barr

1995 **7(NH)**

32	20/1	Higham	(L)	OPE	3m	15	GF	*rr whn hmpd bnd appr 4th, t.o. & p.u. 12th*	P	0
104	17/2	Marks Tey	(L)	OPE	3m	14	G	*mid div, prog & cls up 11th, wknd appr 16th, p.u. 3 out*	P	0
484	15/3	Fakenham	(L)	HC	2m 5f 110yds	13	GF	*in 7th pl to hfwy, bhnd when p.u. before 11th.*	P	0
619	23/3	Higham	(L)	OPE	3m	10	GF	*sttld mid-div, mstk 8th, prog to disp 4 out, ld 2 out,hld on*	1	18
833	6/4	Marks Tey	(L)	OPE	3m	4	G	*hld up in 4th, rdn & btn 17th, fin 4th, plcd 3rd*	3	15
228	27/4	Worcester	(L)	HC	2m 7f	17	G	*mstks, t.o. when p.u. before 4 out.*	P	0
400	6/5	Northaw	(L)	OPE	3m	6	F	*blnd & rmdr 1st,prom 5th,lst pl & rdn 11th,last & p.u. 13th*	P	0

Winning hurdler; quirky and not 100% genuine; needs easy track; may surprise again. 16

A CIENAGA (Irish) — I 37^{F}, I 140^{P}, I 202^{P}

ACKEN BEAU (Irish) — I 94^{2}, I 216^{1}, I 254^{2}, I 317^{1}, I 399^{1}, I 453^{1}

AD LANE b or br.g. 12 Proverb - Quarry Lane by Bargello — J Borradaile

169	18/2	Market Rase'	(L)	CON	3m	15	GF	*rear 10th, t.o. & p.u. 15th*	P	0
244	25/2	Southwell P'	(L)	CON	3m	13	HO	*lost tch 6th, t.o. aft*	4	0
392	9/3	Garthorpe	(R)	MEM	3m	6	G	*mostly 3rd, outpcd by 1st pair 4 out*	3	0
723	31/3	Garthorpe	(R)	CON	3m	19	G	*sn bhnd, 14th & wll bhnd hlfwy, t.o.*	12	0
098	14/4	Guilsborough	(L)	CON	3m	17	G	*alwys rear, t.o. 12th*	9	0

Moderate ex chaser; mega safe but too slow now. 0

ADY BARBAROSA(IRE) b.m. 6 Sylvan Barbarosa - The Blue Pound by Even Money — Mrs C J Black

1995 P(0),P(0)

954	8/4	Eyton-On-Se'	(L)	MDO	2 1/2m	6	GF	*prom to hlfwy, t.o. & no ch whn p.u. 3 out*	P	0
033	13/4	Alpraham	(R)	MDO	2 1/2m	15	GS	*prog 8th, wknd 11th, 7th whn p.u. last*	P	0
225	24/4	Brampton Br'	(R)	MDO	3m	18	G	*eff frm mid-div 9th, prom 12th, wknd 14th, p.u. 3 out*	P	0

Pulled up all 5 starts so far. 0

ADY BREMUR (Irish) — I 325^{P}, I 418^{P}, I 527^{P}

ADY BRIGIDA (Irish) — I 210^{P}

ADY CLARINA (Irish) — I 149^{3}, I 253^{F}, I 443^{5}, I 556^{F}, I 578^{2}, I 604^{1}, I 659^{1}

ADY ELISE (Irish) — I 20^{P}, I 60^{1}, I 116^{3}, I 220^{5}, I 333^{3}, I 419^{1}, I 525^{4}

ADY FOUNTAIN (Irish) — I 144^{P}, I 183^{U}, I 309^{P}, I 353, , I 432^{P}, I 550^{P}

LADY GOLDRUSH ch.m. 9 Remezzo - Jock's Darling by Jock Scot C Rus

875 6/4 Higher Kilw' (L) MDN 3m 6 GF *rear but in tch til blnd 11th, t.o. & p.u. 14th* P
1139 20/4 Flete Park (R) RES 3m 14 S *twrds rear whn blnd & u.r. 4th* U
1362 4/5 Flete Park (R) MDO 3m 9 G *alwys rear, no ch frm 15th, t.o. & p.u. last* P
1429 6/5 High Bickin' (R) MDO 3m 8 G *rear til p.u. apr 16th* P
1626 27/5 Lifton (R) MDO 3m 13 GS *not fluent, bhnd til p.u. 16th* P

No signs of ability. 0

LADY KAY-LEE b.m. 6 Cruise Missile - Arctic Lee C A Harne

1016 13/4 Kingston Bl' (L) CON 3m 6 G *s.s. prog & cls up 11th, wknd 13th, t.o. nxt, fin tired* 3

Beaten miles only start in points & unlikely to achieve anything 0

LADY LIR ch.m. 7 Lir - Kimberley Ann by St Columbus B R J Youn

1995 **9(NH)**,**P(NH)**

65 10/2 Great Treth' (R) INT 3m 13 S *ld to 2nd, disp to 8th, wknd, p.u. aft 12th* P
197 24/2 Lemalla (R) LAD 3m 13 HY *rear, t.o. 3 out* 6
562 17/3 Ottery St M' (L) XX 3m 12 G *alwys rear, t.o. 14th* 6
627 23/3 Kilworthy (L) RES 3m 13 GS *alwys rear, t.o. & p.u. 14th* P
1070 13/4 Lifton (R) MDN 3m 9 S *cls 2nd 6th til ld 12th, wll clr 3 out, unchal* 1 1

Won weak Maiden; 1st ever signs of ability; more needed for Restricted. 16

LADY LLANFAIR b.m. 10 Prince Tenderfoot (USA) - Picnic Time by Silly Season N G Anderso

1995 1(21),**P(0)**,2(17),**P(0)**,4(13),F(-),**P(0)**

39 3/2 Wadebridge (L) OPE 3m 7 GF *prom til lost pl 12th, outpcd 15th, fin well* 3 2
154 17/2 Erw Lon (L) LAD 3m 14 G *mid-div, no show frm hlfwy, p.u. 14th* P
385 9/3 Llanfrynach (R) LAD 3m 14 GS *alwys prom, outpcd aft 13th, effrt 2 out, kpt on* 4 1
603 23/3 Howick (L) LAD 3m 8 S *rear, gd prog 13th, 8l 3rd nxt, p.u. 3 out, lame* P

Formerly decent; ran well debut 95/96; problems last start; still win weak Ladies if fit in 97; F-S. 18

LADY MEDUSA(IRE) b or br.m. 5 Yashgan - Fine Artist by Fine Blade (USA) Lee Bowle

391 9/3 Llanfrynach (R) MDN 3m 11 GS *schoold in last pair, going easily whn p.u. aft 11th* P
697 30/3 Llanvapley (L) MDN 3m 11 GS *hld up, 4th at 14th, p.u. 3 out* P
1391 6/5 Pantyderi (R) MDO 3m 13 GF *ran out 3rd* r

Educational start; shrewd stable; should do better. 13

LADY OF MEANS (Irish) — I 8^U, I 63^P, I 70^4, I 119^P, I 279^3, I 433^P, I 608^U, I 655^6

LADY ORR(IRE) ch.m. 5 Ore - Better Again by Deep Run D W Evan

848 6/4 Howick (L) MDN 3m 14 GF *rear, no ch whn p.u. 14th* P

Only learning on debut. 0

LADY POKEY br.m. 6 Uncle Pokey - Lady Buttons by New Brig S Edward

288 2/3 Eaton Hall (R) MDO 3m 17 G *mid-div, wknd & p.u. 4 out* P
457 9/3 Eyton-On-Se' (L) INT 3m 11 G *cls up in 4th at 13th, wknd rpdly 4 out, p.u. 2 out* P

Shows speed but not enough stamina so far. 0

LADY ROMANCE(IRE) b.m. 8 Brewery Boy (AUS) - Romantic Rhapsody by Ovac (ITY) M G Jone

1995 F(-),P(0),U(-),F(-),P(0),3(10)

152 17/2 Erw Lon (L) MDN 3m 11 G *alwys prom, disp 2nd frm 14th, hld last, fin 3rd, plcd 2nd* 2 1
204 24/2 Castle Of C' (R) MDO 3m 11 HY *cls up to 12th, sn bhnd, styd on agn 3 out, no ext flat* 3 1
390 9/3 Llanfrynach (R) MDN 3m 13 GS *trckd ldrs, 4th & in tch whn f 12th* F
773 31/3 Pantyderi (R) MDN 3m 8 G *ld 12th, hdd flat, kpt on well* 2 1
842 6/4 Maisemore P' (L) MDN 3m 17 GF *ld bfly 1st, prom, 3rd & ev ch 2 out, wknd appr last* 3 1
1161 20/4 Llanwit Maj' (R) MDO 3m 15 GS *held up, some prog 9th, nvr rchd ldrs, p.u. 16th* P
1269 27/4 Pyle (R) MDO 3m 9 G *prog 10th, 3rd frm 13th, rdn & not rch ldrs frm 15th* 3 1

Placed 6 times from 13 starts; not progressing and looks one to oppose. 13

LADY ROSEBURY b.m. 6 Derring Rose - Foxbury by Healaugh Fox Mrs C W Middleto

218 24/2 Newtown (L) MDN 3m 14 GS *rear whn f 5th* F

Not a good start. 0

LADY SALLY (Irish) — I 33^P

LADY SANDALAY (Irish) — I 417^P, I 479^P, I 562^P, I 622^5, I 631^P

LADY STEEL (Irish) — I 113^5, I 207^6, I 379^1

LADY SYLVIE (Irish) — I 464^2, I 501^P, I 653^5

LADY WINDGATES (Irish) — I 417^P, I 533^P, I 622^P

LAERGY CRIPPERTY (Irish) — I 180^F, I 260^P, I 288^P, I 341^P

LAGANBRAE b.g. 10 White Christmas - Camus Abbey by Peacock (FR) Michael Ralph

511	16/3	Dalton Park	(R)	MEM	3m	3 G	*ld to 5th, ld 8th til hdd & u.r. 16th*	U	-
983	8/4	Charm Park	(L)	RES	3m	13 GF	*mid-div, fdd 11th, p.u. 13th*	P	0
1131	20/4	Hornby Cast'	(L)	RES	3m	17 G	*disp early, ld 3rd-8th, wknd 11th, t.o. & p.u. aft 13th*	P	0
1302	28/4	Southwell P'	(L)	INT	3m	10 GF	*(bl) chsd ldrs, going wll to 9th, wknd rpdly, p.u. 12th*	P	0

Ex-Irish; does not stay and has no prospects. 0

LAKEFIELD LEADER (Irish) — I 36^{2}, I 114^{3}, I 424^{1}

LAKELAND VENTURE ch.m. 6 Respect - Miss Lakeland by Pongee P E Clark

72	11/2	Wetherby Po'	(L)	CON	3m	18 GS	*rear whn ran out 6th*	r	-
242	25/2	Southwell P'	(L)	RES	3m	12 HO	*in tch til wknd 10th, t.o. & p.u. 12th*	P	0
413	9/3	Charm Park	(L)	MDO	3m	12 G	*mid-div, 4th at 11th, styd on one-pcd*	5	0
591	23/3	Wetherby Po'	(L)	MDO	3m	14 S	*(bl) cls up to 12th, wknd nxt, p.u. 4 out*	P	0

Lasdt and well beaten when completing; much more needed. 0

LAKE MAJESTIC (Irish) — I 176^{P}, I 215^{P}, I 258^{P}, I 319^{F}

LAKE MARINER b.m. 9 Julio Mariner - Lillytip by Tepukei Mrs Lyn Brafield

1995 P(0),U(-),U(-)

206	24/2	Castle Of C'	(R)	MDO	3m	10 HY	*mid-div to 12th, ev ch 3 out, no ext aft*	2	10
448	9/3	Haldon	(R)	MDO	3m	10 S	*handy, disp 11th, cls up going wll 13th, ld 15th, sn clr*	1	13
707	30/3	Barbury Cas'	(L)	RES	3m	18 G	*alwys mid-div, no ch whn p.u. 2 out*	P	0
989	8/4	Kingston St'	(R)	CON	3m	6 F	*handy til blnd 7th, bhnd frm 12th, p.u. 2 out*	P	0

Won poor Maiden (slow time); only completed 2 of 12 outings 94/96; needs to improve for Restricted. .. 14

LAKENHEATHER(NZ) b.g. 10 Lakenheath (USA) - Monanne by Pharamond Mrs Pat Mullen

1995 P(0),P(0),P(0),3(17),**6(0)**,U(-),4(0)

292	2/3	Eaton Hall	(R)	RES	3m	15 G	*mid-div whn u.r. 14th*	U	-
458	9/3	Eyton-On-Se'	(L)	INT	3m	11 G	*mid-div, clsr ordr to go 2nd at 12th, ran on one pce*	2	13
567	17/3	Wolverhampt'	(L)	MEM	3m	4 GS	*(fav) hld up, 2nd at 15th, ev ch til onepcd aft*	2	0
880	6/4	Brampton Br'	(R)	XX	3m	8 GF	*cls 2nd whn u.r. 6th*	U	-
1233	27/4	Weston Park	(L)	RES	3m	14 G	*mid-div, cls order 12th, ran on frm 3 out,lkd held bfr last*	1	13

Fortunate Restricted winner; barely stays and will struggle to win again. 15

LAKE TOUR (Irish) — I 63^{1}, I 116^{1}, I 141^{F}

LAKEVIEW LAD (Irish) — I 72^{P}, I 126^{P}, I 425^{2}

LA MAJA (Irish) — I 20^{F}, I 106^{3}, I 176^{1}, I 257^{P}, I 304^{F}, I 414^{2}

LA MEZERAY b.m. 8 Nishapour (FR) - La Pythie (FR) by Filiberto (USA) C C Morgan

1995 2(19),4(16),3(11),1(20),2(18),1(18),2(20),F(-),4+(19),3(0)

98	12/2	Hereford	(R)	HC	3m 1f 110yds	12 HY	*alwys bhnd, blnd and u.r. 7th.*	U	-
356	3/3	Garnons	(L)	LAD	3m	12 GS	*ld to 12th, not qckn frm nxt, wknd 2 out*	4	15
385	9/3	Llanfrynach	(R)	LAD	3m	14 GS	*alwys prom, chsd wnr 13th til apr last, onepcd*	3	21
506	16/3	Magor	(R)	CON	3m	8 GS	*(fav) hld up, prog to 2nd 14th, ld 2 out, easily*	1	20
603	23/3	Howick	(L)	LAD	3m	8 S	*mstk 8th, 2nd frm 13th, chal 2 out, alwys hld*	2	21
847	6/4	Howick	(L)	LAD	3m	9 GF	*(fav) handy,2nd 12th,ld nxt,clr 15th,blnd nxt,not run on,hdd last*	2	18
979	8/4	Lydstep	(L)	LAD	3m	9 G	*alwys twrds rear*	5	16
1414	6/5	Cursneh Hill	(L)	LAD	3m	9 GF	*chsd ldr, ev ch til outpcd frm 15th*	3	19
1489	11/5	Erw Lon	(L)	LAD	3m	4 F	*in rear til ran on 2 out, nvr able to chal*	3	16
1586	25/5	Hexham	(L)	HC	2 1/2m 110yds	14 GF	*settld bhnd, styd on from 3 out, nearest fin.*	4	12
1635	1/6	Bratton Down	(L)	LAD	3m	13 G	*alwys rear, 11th & rdn at 13th, no ch aft*	8	0

Won weak Confined; consistent but onepaced; hard to win with; mqay win again.; any. 19

LAMH EILE (Irish) — I 18^{P}

LA MON DERE (Irish) — I 122^{P}, I 147^{P}, I 205^{4}, I 440^{1}, I 568^{2}, I 658^{2}

LANCASTRIAN LASS (Irish) — I 127^{P}, I 239^{P}, I 291^{P}, I 324^{3}, I 380^{P}

LANCASTRIAN PRIDE (Irish) — I 109^{F}, I 161^{1}, I 234^{1}

LAND OF WONDER(USA) b.g. 9 Wind And Wuthering (USA) - Heat Haze (USA) by Jungle Savage (USA) N J Hughes

258	29/2	Nottingham	(L)	HC	3m 110yds	10 G	*soon well bhnd, relentless prog final cct, effort and blnd last, ran on to ld last stride.*	1	19
485	16/3	Hereford	(R)	HC	3m 1f 110yds	13 S	*bhnd, t.o. when p.u. before 6th.*	P	0

Lightly raced; just got up to land poor H/chase; stays; very hard to place now; G-S. 21

LANDSKER ALFRED ch.g. 10 Push On - April Fooldus by Haven Dr P P Brown

1995 P(0),P(0),P(0),P(0),2(10),P(0)

293	2/3	Eaton Hall	(R)	INT	3m	11 G	*(Jt fav) hld up, prog 13th, ld 5 out, ran on well 2 out*	1	19

667	24/3	Eaton Hall	(R)	INT	3m	11	S	*(fav) w.w. prog 7th, ld 3 out, clr nxt, hdd & onepcd flat*	2	23
837	6/4	Maisemore P'	(L)	CON	3m	4	GF	*(fav) disp ld til blnd 4th, ld 15th, drw clr appr 2 out, easy*	1	22
1243	27/4	Woodford	(L)	MEM	3m	6	G	*(fav) blndrd 3rd, chsd ldr 6th, ld apr 16th, clr 3 out, easy*	1	21
1507	12/5	Maisemore P'	(L)	CON	3m	10	F	*(fav) in tch, prog 9th, ld 12th, clr 3 out, comf*	1	22

Baimbridge magic works again; well placed; L/H looks essential; sure to win more; F-S. 22

LANEAST LORE b.g. 13 Shannon Boy - Laneast Lass by True Code — Mrs J Farrow

1995 7(0),7(0),P(0),P(0)

196	24/2	Lemalla	(R)	CON	3m	14	HY	*alwys bhnd, p.u. 13th*	P	0
294	2/3	Great Treth'	(R)	CON	3m	10	G	*bhnd frm hlfwy*	7	0
560	17/3	Ottery St M'	(L)	CON	3m	7	G	*ld to 7th, outpcd frm 13th*	4	0

of little account now. 0

LANEAST PRINCE ch.g. 12 Shannon Boy - Laneast Lass by True Code — Mrs J Farrow

199	24/2	Lemalla	(R)	RES	3m	17	HY	*sn wll bhnd, p.u. 12th*	P	0

Of no account 0

LANGRETTA (Irish) — **I** 380^{S}, **I** 504^{F}, **I** 609^{2}

LANGTON PARMILL b.g. 11 Pardigras - Millie Langton by Langton Heath — Miss J Hodgkinson

1995 P(0)

138	17/2	Ottery St M'	(L)	RES	3m	18	GS	*u.r. 2nd*	U	-
207	24/2	Castle Of C'	(R)	MDO	3m	15	HY	*mid-div, prog 14th, ev ch 3 out, outpcd aft*	4	12
282	2/3	Clyst St Ma'	(L)	MDN	3m	8	S	*6s-5/2, cls up til f 3rd*	F	-
556	17/3	Ottery St M'	(L)	MDO	3m	15	G	*alwys mid-div, outpcd frm 13th*	5	0
658	23/3	Badbury Rin'	(L)	MDO	3m	8	G	*ld to 5th, again from 4 out, pushed out flat*	1	12
728	31/3	Little Wind'	(R)	MEM	3m	7	GS	*mid-div, effт 3 out, no ch ldrs*	4	13
1056	13/4	Badbury Rin'	(L)	RES	3m	10	GF	*ld 3rd-7th, in tch aft, 4th whn b.d. 3 out*	B	-
1168	20/4	Larkhill	(R)	RES	3m	8	GF	*mid-div whn u.r. 11th*	U	-
1393	6/5	Cotley Farm	(L)	XX	3m	10	GF	*mid-div early, 3rd at 10th, 2nd 12th, ev ch & f last*	F	-

Won bad & slowly run Maiden; makes mistakes; Restricted at 12 looks to tough. 15

LANGUEDOC b.g. 9 Rousillon (USA) - Can Can Girl by Gay Fandango (USA) — Mrs J Smethurst

303	2/3	Great Stain'	(L)	CON	3m	11	GS	*alwys rear, p.u. 11th*	P	0
699	30/3	Tranwell	(L)	CON	3m	8	GS	*not fluent, ld 2nd til f 10th*	U	-

A brief season of no promise 0

LANTERN LOTTO (Irish) — **I** 12^{P}, **I** 43^{P}

LANTERN PIKE ch.g. 10 Full Of Hope - Tiddles Twopence by Royal Bay — A H L Michael

1995 6(10),6(12),1(14),**5(0)**,10(0)

105	17/2	Marks Tey	(L)	RES	3m	11	G	*ld 4th, 12l clr 15th, hdded last, onepcd*	2	16
348	3/3	Higham	(L)	RES	3m	12	G	*ld 3rd, made rest, ran on well last*	1	19
528	16/3	Cothelstone	(L)	MEM	3m	8	G	*ld to 14th, 3rd & blnd 3 out, no ex*	3	14
621	23/3	Higham	(L)	INT	3m	12	GF	*bhnd, prog to ld 4th, clr 9th, chal 3 out, sn qcknd away*	1	20
906	8/4	Fakenham	(L)	HC	2m 5f 110yds	11	G	*chsd ldrs, mstk 4th, ld after 9th, hdd before 3 out, no ext from next.*	2	21
1146	20/4	Higham	(L)	OPE	3m	7	F	*(Jt fav) ld 4th, made rest, drvn & hld on well flat*	1	24
1329	30/4	Huntingdon	(R)	HC	3m	14	GF	*outpcd in mid div, prog 11th, chsd wnr 15th to next, wknd 2 out.*	4	13

Benefited from move to weaker area; novice ridden; game; likes Higham; harder to place now; F-G/S. .. 22

LANTERN SPARK (Irish) — **I** 11^{3}, **I** 43^{P}, **I** 204^{4}, **I** 252^{F}, **I** 335^{P}, **I** 369^{P}, **I** 427^{P}, **I** 510^{2}, **I** 545^{3}

LANTINA (Irish) — **I** 107^{U}, **I** 165^{P}, **I** 193^{F}, **I** 347^{3}, **I** 385^{1}

LA PRINCESSE b.m. 9 Le Bavard (FR) - Morry's Lady by The Parson — M H B Portman

1995 2(17),3(14)

140	17/2	Larkhill	(R)	CON	3m	17	G	*prom, 3rd at 10th, wknd, p.u. 14th*	P	0

Hurdles winner 93; only 3 runs 95/96 and time passing her by. 17

LARA'S PRINCESS b.m. 7 Pragmatic - Shanlaragh by Gaberdine — R W Gardiner

1325	28/4	Fakenham P-'	(L)	MDO	3m	6	G	*jmpd lft & u.r. 1st*	U	-
1403	6/5	Northaw	(L)	MDO	3m	8	F	*prom, disp ld 10th, ld 13th, made rest,styd on wll frm 2 out*	1	12

Some promise in 94; missed 95; gamely won poor Maiden; can improve; needs to. 12

LA RIVIERA (Irish) — **I** 181^{P}

LARKIN GIRL ch.m. 6 Bootsman Bains (GER) - Meadowlark by Marmaduke — W M Aitchison

1512	12/5	Hexham Poin'	(L)	MEM	3m	6	HY	*jmpd badly rght, bhnd til u.r. 6th*	U	-

Looked clueless on debut. 0

LARKIN'S CROSS (Irish) — **I** 105^{P}, **I** 164^{P}

LARKY MCILROY b.m. 10 Rymer - Forest Row by Royal Highway — D Luxton

1995 U(-),P(0),3(11),1(15),P(0),**P(0)**,1(15),P(0)

278	2/3	Clyst St Ma'	(L)	CON	3m	9	S	*cls up, ld 13th-16th, outpcd frm 3 out*	2	18
531	16/3	Cothelstone	(L)	CON	3m	12	G	*mid div, prog to disp 2nd 10th, ev ch & rddn 4 out, no ex*	3	16
801	4/4	Clyst St Ma'	(L)	CON	3m	2	GS	*(fav) disp to 14th, ev ch til outpcd apr nxt, eased whn btn*	2	15
1109	17/4	Hockworthy	(L)	MEM	3m	4	GS	*ld 4th, made most aft, mstk 14th, lft wl clr 2 out*	1	17
1344	4/5	Holnicote	(L)	CON	3m	4	GS	*(fav) ld til u.r. 8th*	U	-
1499	11/5	Holnicote	(L)	CON	3m	8	G	*hndy, chsd wnnr und strng pres 3 out, no real imp*	2	18

More consistent in 96; only modest & onepaced; can win weak Confined; F-S. 17

LARQUILL b.m. 8 Crested Lark - Menquilla by Menelek — G T Ingleton

1995 U(-),F(-),4(0),P(0),P(0)

455	9/3	Charing	(L)	MDN	3m	10	G	*prom til wknd 14th*	6	0
572	17/3	Detling	(L)	LAD	3m	10	GF	*alwys rear, t.o. 10th*	7	0
919	8/4	Aldington	(L)	LAD	3m	4	F	*chsd ldr to 6th, last frm nxt, blnd 11th,t.o.14th,p.u. 2 out*	P	0

Tailed off when completing; no signs of ability. 0

LARRY'S PENNY (Irish) — I 225F

LARRY THE LAMB ch.g. 11 St Columbus - Florence Eliza by Floriana — Mrs F E Chown

1995 3(21),U(-),3(20),2(21),1(23),1(23),2(20),1(25),2(17),2(22),2(21)

311	2/3	Ampton	(R)	LAD	3m	4	G	*(fav) trkd ldrs, sltly outpcd appr 3 out, rlld & ch last, no ex*	2	21
493	16/3	Horseheath	(R)	LAD	3m	4	GF	*sttld in 2nd, hrd rdn to ld last, ld flat, lkd to hld on*	1	24
888	6/4	Kimble	(L)	LAD	3m	4	GF	*(fav) trckd ldrs, mstk 11th, ld aft 3 out, clr nxt, eased nr fin*	1	23
1179	21/4	Mollington	(R)	LAD	3m	10	F	*(fav) w.w. prog 11th, effrt 3 out, rdn to ld last, ran on strngly*	1	25
1502	11/5	Kingston Bl'	(L)	LAD	3m	7	G	*(fav) in tch, chsd wnr 11th, nvr able to chal*	2	23
1596	25/5	Garthorpe	(R)	LAD	3m	9	G	*(fav) prog 7th, 3rd frm 9th, rdn & disp 3rd whn f 2 out*	F	-
1642	2/6	Dingley	(R)	LAD	3m	6	GF	*(fav) w.w., in tch whn blndrd 14th, chsd wnr 2 out, not qckn last*	2	19

Useful but hard ride; stays and can quicken; sure to win more; G/F-S. 24

LARTINGTON LAD ch.g. 10 Dalsaan - Rarest Flower (USA) by Carlemont — Miss J Goodyear

1995 P(0),P(0),7(0),8(0)

79	11/2	Wetherby Po'	(L)	MDO	3m	12	GS	*wll in rear, t.o. 11th, some late prog*	4	0
118	17/2	Witton Cast'	(R)	INT	3m	9	S	*dwelt, t.o. 7th, fin own time*	6	0
225	24/2	Duncombe Pa'	(R)	RES	3m	12	GS	*alwys rear, t.o. frm 14th. walked in*	6	0

Well beaten when completing and barely worth a rating; finished early 96. 10

LATE CALL (Irish) — I 41²

LATE START ch.m. 9 Tudorville - Rosatpura by Mugatpura — P Andrews

59	10/2	Cottenham	(R)	RES	3m	9	GS	*last & n.j.w. t.o. & p.u. 11th*	P	0
181	18/2	Horseheath	(R)	RES	3m	5	G	*jmpd lft, sn wll bhnd, p.u. 8th*	P	0
238	25/2	Southwell P'	(L)	MDO	3m	9	HO	*prom whn mstk 6th, lost tch whn mstk 8th, t.o. & p.u. nxt*	P	0
1326	28/4	Fakenham P-'	(L)	MDO	3m	7	G	*blnd 3rd & 5th, last frm 10th, p.u. 13th*	P	0
1523	12/5	Garthorpe	(R)	MDO	3m	11	GF	*s.s. rear, t.o. & p.u. 14th*	P	0

Poor jumper; shows no ability. 0

LATHERON(IRE) b.g. 6 Reference Point - La Romance (USA) by Lyphard (USA) — Mrs A M Easterby

73	11/2	Wetherby Po'	(L)	MDO	3m	15	GS	*(fav) rear, prog 12th, disp last, styd on well flat*	1	15
224	24/2	Duncombe Pa'	(R)	RES	3m	12	GS	*(fav) mid-div whn blnd & u.r. 7th*	U	-
411	9/3	Charm Park	(L)	RES	3m	20	G	*cls up, 2nd at 14th, chsd wnr to post, jst btn*	2	22
585	23/3	Wetherby Po'	(L)	RES	3m	13	S	*(fav) rear, prog 10th, 4th 4 out, ran on on outer to ld flat*	1	20
1091	14/4	Whitwell-On'	(R)	XX	3m	6	G	*(fav) hld up rear, prog to trck ldrs 4 out, rdn 2 out, ld nr fin*	1	19
1282	27/4	Easingwold	(L)	OPE	3m	8	G	*(bl) sttld mid-div, prog 13th, lft 2nd 3 out, ev ch & wd nxt*	3	20
1446	6/5	Witton Cast'	(R)	CON	3m	7	G	*(fav) rear, prog 13th, hrd rdn nxt,hdwy 4 out,ld 2 out,ran on wll*	1	20

Useful recruit; good stable; stays; should progress further; G-S. 22

LATTIN GENERAL b.g. 14 General Ironside - Lattins Lady by Happy New Year — Mrs S M Shone

1995 P(0),U(-),P(0),P(0)

289	2/3	Eaton Hall	(R)	CON	3m	10	G	*1st ride, mid-div, outpcd hlfwy*	4	0
659	24/3	Eaton Hall	(R)	MEM	3m	6	S	*in tch whn u.r. 7th*	U	-
736	31/3	Sudlow Farm	(R)	CON	3m	9	G	*prom to 11th, 5th & no ch 3 out*	4	0
1009	9/4	Flagg Moor	(L)	CON	3m	7	G	*pllng, chsd ldr til ld 6-10th, wknd app 15th*	4	0

Non stayer and too old now. 0

LAUNCHSELECT b.g. 5 Alleging (USA) - Polished Queen by Kings Lake (USA) — M J Brown

75	11/2	Wetherby Po'	(L)	MDO	3m	8	GS	*in tch, 3rd at 14th, tk 2nd flat, outpcd by wnr*	2	13
229	24/2	Duncombe Pa'	(R)	MDO	3m	13	GS	*chsd ldrs, lft 3rd 4 out, chal last, sn ld, styd on strngly*	1	15
411	9/3	Charm Park	(L)	RES	3m	20	G	*(fav) alwys prom, ld last, drvn out, styd on wl*	1	22
588	23/3	Wetherby Po'	(L)	INT	3m	17	S	*(fav) prom, rdn whn mstk 13th, not rcvr, p.u. last*	P	0

Useful youngster; not seen after poor last run; one to watch if fit 97; stays; G-S. 22

LAUNDRYMAN b.g. 13 Celtic Cone - Lovely Laura by Lauso — A J Chamberlain

24 20/1 Barbury Cas' (L) XX 3m 12 GS *alwys bhnd, t.o. 9th* 4 0
Dead 0

LAURA'S BEAU (Irish) — I 18², I 29⁵, I 103¹, I 158⁵, I 265²

LAURA'S FLUTTER b.m. 7 Beldale Flutter (USA) - Sweetcal by Caliban Mrs Nerys Dutfield
1995 **P(NH),P(NH),P(NH),5(NH)**
471 10/3 Milborne St' (L) MDO 3m 16 G *mid-div, ev ch 15th, outpcd frm nxt* 4 0
beaten 34 lengths in good Maiden; not seen after; can go closer if fit in 97. 11

LAURA'S LEAP (Irish) — I 11ᴾ, I 55⁴, I 183¹

LAURAS TEEARA(IRE) b.m. 8 Torus - Dusky Glory by Dusky Boy Neil Bennett
323 2/3 Corbridge (R) MDN 3m 12 GS *ref 1st* R -
704 30/3 Tranwell (L) MDO 3m 16 GS *mid-div til mstk 7th, f 10th* F -
862 6/4 Alnwick (L) MDN 3m 8 GF *(bl) m.n.s., p.u. 13th* P 0
Unpromising. 0

LAURENS PRIDE (Irish) — I 556ᴾ

LAVALIGHT b.g. 9 Lighter - Laval by Cheval Mrs J Frankland
1995 **13(NH),6(NH),5(NH),7(NH)**
27 20/1 Barbury Cas' (L) LAD 3m 15 GS *chsd ldrs til wknd 12th, t.o. & p.u. 2 out* P 0
250 25/2 Charing (L) LAD 3m 12 GS *ld to 3rd & frm 8th til aft 3 out, fdd, fin tired* 5 13
577 19/3 Fontwell (R) HC 2m 3f 5 GF *pulld hrd, in rear, left poor 2nd 12th, wknd 2 out.* 3 12
1227 26/4 Ludlow (R) HC 2 1/2m 16 G *n.d..* 7 12
1454 7/5 Newton Abbot (L) HC 2m 5f 110yds 8 GS *ld to 5th, led apr 8th, hdd 6 out, wknd quickly, p.u. before last.* P 0
Does not stay 3m & outclassed in H/Chases; prospects grim 12

LAVINS THATCH b.m. 10 Buckskin (FR) - Siba Vione by Dusky Boy Mrs J V Kehoe
1995 F(-),3(10)
315 2/3 Ampton (R) MDO 3m 10 G *f 3rd* F -
496 16/3 Horseheath (R) MDO 3m 10 GF *prom, jnd ldrs 10th, und pres 13th, ev ch 3 out, sn btn* 2 12
1261 27/4 Cottenham (R) MDO 3m 10 F *alwys rear, blnd 4th, last nxt, rdn 10th, onepcd aft* 5 0
Lightly raced; beat subsequent winner when 2nd; stamina doubtful and more needed to win. 11

LAWD OF BLISLAND ch.g. 7 Celtic Cone - Foxwell by Healaugh Fox Paul C N Heywood
1995 4(0),F(-),P(0)
138 17/2 Ottery St M' (L) RES 3m 18 GS *alwys mid-div, onepcd frm 3 out* 5 14
555 17/3 Ottery St M' (L) MDO 3m 15 G *alwys mid-div, lost tch 14th, t.o. & p.u. 3 out* P 0
1070 13/4 Lifton (R) MDN 3m 9 S *hld up, hdwy 16th, wnt 2nd 3 out, no imp* 2 11
1431 6/5 High Bickin' (R) MDO 3m 9 G *hdwy 14th, ev ch til wknd 17th* 4 0
1627 27/5 Lifton (R) MDO 3m 9 GS *(fav) ld til 5th, cls up til wknd 12th, no ch aft* 3 0
Beaten 12 lengths minimum and needs more; can find a small race. 13

LAYEDBACK JACK ch.g. 9 True Song - Hayburnwyke by Pretty Form C D Dawson
1995 U(-),2(23),1(22)
168 18/2 Market Rase' (L) MEM 3m 7 GF *(fav) cls up, hit 6th, wth ldr 9th, ld 4 out, sn clr* 1 26
325 3/3 Market Rase' (L) LAD 3m 6 G *(fav) chsd ldrs, went 2nd 14th, ld 2 out, sn clr* 1 25
536 17/3 Southwell P' (L) LAD 3m 9 GS *(fav) w.w. 2nd at 9th, ld 5 out, 4l clr 2 out, hdd & no ext flat* 2 24
Won 10 of last 14 races; lightly raced 95/96; L/H best; sure to win again; G/F-S. 26

LAYITONTHELINE (Irish) — I 287¹

LAYSTON D'OR ch.g. 7 Le Coq D'Or - Water Crescent by No Mercy J W Russel
1995 F(-),r(-),U(-)
349 3/3 Garnons (L) MEM 3m 4 GS *(fav) 3rd til chsd ldr 13th, ld last, pshd out flat* 1 16
684 30/3 Chaddesley ' (L) RES 3m 14 G *mstks, hld up, prog 9th, 4th & ch whn blnd 2 out, no ext* 4 15
Beat a veteran in 2 finisher Members; ran passable after; not fluent and needs more. 17

LAYSTON PINZAL b.m. 5 Afzal - Clever Pin by Pinza J W Russel
354 3/3 Garnons (L) MDN 2 1/2m 13 GS *rear whn s.u. bend aft 3rd* S -
842 6/4 Maisemore P' (L) MDN 3m 17 GF *prog to 4th 12th,prssd wnnr frm 15th,unable to qkn frm 2 out* 2 14
Just beaten (poor horses behind); looks the part and should go one better in 97. 15

LAZY ACRES (Irish) — I 156ᴾ, I 244ᴾ, I 437ᴾ, I 567³, I 594², I 654ᴾ

LAZZARETTO b.g. 8 Ballacashtal (CAN) - Florence Mary by Mandamus Mrs J Brook-Saunders
17 14/1 Tweseldown (R) MDN 3m 11 GS *alwys bhnd, t.o. 11th, p.u. 2 out* P 0
28 20/1 Barbury Cas' (L) RES 3m 14 GS *last frm 4th, t.o. & p.u. 13th* P 0
506 16/3 Magor (R) CON 3m 8 GS *t.o. 3rd, p.u. 6th* P 0
607 23/3 Howick (L) MDN 3m 12 S *mid-div, t.o. & p.u. 14th* P 0

695 30/3 Llanvapley (L) RES 3m 13 GS *alwys last pair, p.u. 10th* P 0

Of no account. 0

.EADERS VIEW (Irish) — I 40P, I 124F, I 236P

.EADING GUEST b.g. 11 What A Guest - Light House by Primera — Peter S Lloyd

246 25/2 Southwell P' (L) OPE 3m 9 HO *4th whn f 5th* F -

016 13/4 Kingston Bl' (L) CON 3m 6 G *prom til wknd 11th, 5th & no ch whn f 13th* F -

No prospects now 0

.EADTHEBOYS (Irish) — I 457P

.EAMLARA ROSE (Irish) — I 59R

.EANNES MAN (Irish) — I 219U, I 305F, I 404F, I 4131, I 454F, I 5343, I 597P

.EAPING THREE (Irish) — I 308P, I 351U, I 460P, I 5075

.EARNED MASTER b.g. 6 Neltino - Learned Lady by Crozier — John Brown

1995 **4(NH)**

92 11/2 Ampton (R) MDO 3m 7 GF *(fav) hmpd & u.r. 2nd* U -

315 2/3 Ampton (R) MDO 3m 10 G *n.j.w. bhnd til p.u. 14th* P 0

Placed in N/H flat; jumped badly so far; can do better. 10

.EATANSCEIL (Irish) — I 224P

.EAVE IT BE (Irish) — I 171F, I 298B, I 4822, I 4893

.EDWYCHE GATE b.g. 9 Roscoe Blake - Ledwyche by Pamroy — L Evans

1995 4(0),U(-),1(16),F(-),1(19),P(0)

293 2/3 Eaton Hall (R) INT 3m 11 G *prog 11th, ev ch 3 out, ran on onepcd* 4 16

457 9/3 Eyton-On-Se' (L) INT 3m 11 G *alwys bhnd, nvr nrr* 4 0

041 13/4 Bitterley (L) MEM 3m 6 G *(bl) made virt all, drew clr frm 3 out* 1 18

314 28/4 Bitterley (L) MEM 3m 13 G *(bl) cls up, not fluent 1st cct, chsd wnr 12th, hld frm 15th* 2 18

457 8/5 Uttoxeter (L) HC 3 1/4m 16 G *(bl) chaed ldr 12th, ld 14th to 3 out, rallied und pres run-in.* 2 23

630 31/5 Stratford (L) HC 3 1/2m 16 GF *(bl) chsd ldrs, wknd 11th, taild of when p.u. before 17th.* P 0

Improved; quirky and poor jumper; likes Bitterley (trained next door); L/H and blinkers; win again. 22

.EEMOUNT LAD (Irish) — I 2P, I 46P

.EE VALLEY LADY (Irish) — I 60P, I 120P, I 444P

.EGAL AFFAIR b.m. 5 El Conquistador - Legal Aid by Legal Eagle — P R Hill

806 4/4 Clyst St Ma' (L) MDO 3m 7 GS *not fluent, bhnd til p.u. 13th, schoold* P 0

116 17/4 Hockworthy (L) MDO 3m 9 GS *rr, prog & cls up whn b.d. 13th* B -

280 27/4 Bratton Down (L) MDO 3m 14 GF *sn rear, t.o. & ref 14th* R -

Shows some ability; possibly not like ground last start. 12

.EGAL BEAGLE b.g. 9 Law Society (USA) - Calandra (USA) by Sir Ivor — N J Pewter

1995 U(-),P(0),P(0),3(0),P(0)

347 3/3 Higham (L) LAD 3m 10 G *f 2nd* F -

832 6/4 Marks Tey (L) LAD 3m 8 G *sn rear, t.o. last at 9th, p.u. 11th* P 0

934 8/4 Marks Tey (L) CON 3m 6 G *prom, ld 11th, p.u. 13th, dsmntd* P 0

Winning hurdler; of no account and problems last start. 0

.EGAL PICNIC gr.g. 13 Roselier (FR) - Margo's Pal — J T Jackson

1995 P(0),P(0),1(19),4(0),F(-),F(-),1(16),1(0),3(16),2(17),U(-),3(14)

429 9/3 Upton-On-Se' (R) LAD 3m 4 GS *20l 3rd 3 out, fin well, nrly snatched 2nd* 3 12

743 31/3 Upper Sapey (R) LAD 3m 7 GS *last at 14th, fin strngly frm 2 out* 5 14

879 6/4 Brampton Br' (R) LAD 3m 9 GF *alwys 3rd, 5l down 10th, kpt on onepcd frm 16th* 3 18

Won 3 weak Ladies 95 (P.Bowen trained); changed hands; outclassed in competitive races. 13 17

.EGAL VISION b.m. 7 Town And Country - Legal Aid by Legal Eagle — A Dixon

1995 P(0),P(0),5(0),P(0),9(0),4(0),3(13),5(0),**P(NH)**

207 24/2 Castle Of C' (R) MDO 3m 15 HY *(bl) rear til p.u. 14th* P 0

533 16/3 Cothelstone (L) MDN 3m 13 G *(vis) in tch til rddn & outpcd 13th, no ch 4 out* 4 0

060 13/4 Badbury Rin' (L) MDO 3m 14 GF *alwys mid-div, no ch frm 4 out* 4 0

187 21/4 Tweseldown (R) MDN 3m 11 GF *mid-div, prog 9th, hit 12th, sn pshd alng & btn* 4 10

494 11/5 Holnicote (L) MDO 3m 8 G *(fav) prom til rddn & wknd aft 16th, sn btn* 4 0

592 25/5 Mounsey Hil' (R) MDO 3m 9 G *(bl) in tch, cls 3rd 14th, sn rdn, btn 3 out* 4 0

Still a Maiden after 15 starts; ungenuine and will stay that way. 10

.EGAL WHISPER (Irish) — I 292P, I 366, , I 424F, I 466, , I 509, , I 541, , I 582,

.E GERARD ch.g. 11 Le Bavard (FR) - Pauline Blue by Majority Blue — Lee Bowles

1995 F(-),P(0),2(0),P(0),6(0),F(-),P(0)

149 17/2 Erw Lon (L) MDN 3m 10 G *rear, styd on to 3rd 2 out, no ch wth 1st 2* 3 1
255 28/2 Taunton (R) HC 4 1/4m 110yds 15 GS *chsd ldrs 11th, wknd 18th, t.o. when p.u. before 21st.* P
848 6/4 Howick (L) MDN 3m 14 GF *chsng grp, 30l bhnd hlfwy, styd on frm 14th* 3
1269 27/4 Pyle (R) MDO 3m 9 G *cls up, cls 4th & ev ch 14th, wknd frm nxt* 5
1484 11/5 Bredwardine (R) MDO 3m 17 G *(bl) nvr rchd ldrs, no ch frm 3 out* 7

An absolute rogue and one to steer clear of. 10

LEGITMAN (Irish) — I 34P

LE HACHETTE (Irish) — I 20²

LEIGH BOY(USA) b.g. 10 Bates Motel (USA) - Afasheen by Sheshoon Mrs S Warne
1995 3(17),1(21)

426 9/3 Upton-On-Se' (R) CON 3m 16 GS *(fav) (vis) effrt to 3rd 2 out, styd on well* 3
838 6/4 Maisemore P' (L) OPE 3m 4 GF *chsd ldr to 12th, & agn 15th, kpt on wll frm 2 out* 3 2
1171 20/4 Chaddesley ' (L) OPE 3m 15 G *mid-div, rdn 14th, 4th 3 out, unable to chal* 5 2

Lightly raced; consistent but barely stays; could win another Confined; G/F-G/S. 20

LE LOUBEC ch.m. 11 Le Moss - Last Round by Lucky Guy J A Bulloc
1995 4(0),R(-),F(-),7(0),2(13),3(13),3(0)

236 24/2 Heythrop (R) MDN 3m 13 GS *s.s. sn t.o., p.u. 9th* P
358 3/3 Garnons (L) RES 3m 18 GS *prom to 7th, outpcd, kpt on onepcd frm 13th* 4
749 31/3 Upper Sapey (R) MDO 3m 17 GS *rear whn p.u. 8th, dsmntd* P

Unlucky but a Maiden after 20 starts; stamina problems and may have missed her chance. 12

LEND US A BUCK b.m. 6 Buckley - Queen May by Rugantino Mrs Gillian Duffie
682 30/3 Cottenham (R) MDO 3m 9 GF *bhnd frm 6th, no ch whn hit 12th, p.u. nxt* P
901 6/4 Dingley (R) MDN 2m 5f 9 GS *3rd/4th to 6 out, fdd, p.u. 4 out* P
1149 20/4 Higham (L) MDO 3m 10 F *ld to 8th, prom aft, 3rd whn s.u. bnd apr 3 out* S

A hint of ability and young enough to improve. 11

LENNIE THE LION b.g. 5 Krisinsky (USA) - Leaning Tower by Menelek T R R Fa
390 9/3 Llanfrynach (R) MDN 3m 13 GS *green, last trio, t.o. 8th, p.u. 12th* P
605 23/3 Howick (L) MDN 3m 13 S *cls up whn f 6th* F
1039 13/4 St Hilary (R) MDN 3m 14 G *cls 2nd whn f 8th* F
1556 18/5 Bassaleg (R) MEM 3m 6 F *f 1st* F

Needs to learn to jump. 0

LEO THE LODGER b.g. 6 Scorpio (FR) - Adeney Lass by Space King Ms M Teagu
288 2/3 Eaton Hall (R) MDO 3m 17 G *mid to rear, no ch whn p.u. 4 out* P
461 9/3 Eyton-On-Se' (L) RES 3m 15 G *rr, n.d., p.u. 3 out* P

Only learning so far. 0

LE PICCOLAGE b.g. 12 The Parson - Daithis Coleen by Carnival Night P H Morr
1995 **P(NH)**,**P(NH)**,**3(NH)**

1193 21/4 Sandon (L) OPE 3m 8 G *rear, some late prog frm 5 out, onepcd* 3
1231 27/4 Weston Park (L) OPE 3m 6 G *rear early,prog 11th,cls up 13th,strng chal 3 out, fdd last* 2
1422 6/5 Eyton-On-Se' (L) CON 3m 3 GF *cl up, ld 7-9th, in tch, ld 4 out, sn clr, comf* 1 2
1545 18/5 Bangor (L) HC 3m 110yds 8 G *cl up, mstk 11th (water), weakening when mistake 4 out, soon bhnd.* 5
1578 19/5 Wolverhampt' (L) OPE 3m 7 G *w.w. effrt to 3rd 14th, btn nxt, t.o. & p.u. 2 out* P

Revived & brief purple patch 96; ran baldy last start & will do well to recover form at 13; Good 17

LEPTON(IRE) gr.g. 5 Duca Di Busted - Amelioras Gran by Northern Guest (USA) M W Eastert
1995 **3(NH)**,**7(NH)**

228 24/2 Duncombe Pa' (R) MDO 3m 9 GS *w.w. steady prog to 12l 2nd going wll whn f 4 out* F
333 3/3 Market Rase' (L) MDO 3m 11 G *(fav) conf rdn, steady prog to ld apr last, easily* 1

PLPlaced in a bumper; cruised home in poor race; not seen again; should upgrade; good stable. 16

LESLIESHILL (Irish) — I 261P, I 283⁴

LETHEM LAIRD b.g. 5 Germont - Lawsuitlaw by Cagirama Tim Bu
1476 11/5 Aspatria (L) MDO 3m 16 GF *alwys rear, t.o. & p.u. bfr 13th* P

No signs on debut; time on his side. 0

LET HER RUN WILD (Irish) — I 176F, I 258P, I 301F, I 320U, I 364U, I 587U

LETS GO POLLY b.m. 6 Pollerton - Letitica by Deep Run Mrs S M Fa
1995 P(0)

45 3/2 Wadebridge (L) MDO 3m 10 GF *prom till u.r. 10th* U
148 17/2 Erw Lon (L) MDN 3m 9 G *prom, blnd 12th, p.u. 14th* P

510 16/3 Magor (R) MDN 3m 9 GS *mid-div, poor 4th 2 out, fin own time* 5 0
697 30/3 Llanvapley (L) MDN 3m 11 GS *prom to 14th, wknd & p.u. nxt* P 0
850 6/4 Howick (L) MDN 3m 14 GF *prom to 12th, wknd rpdly, p.u. 14th* P 0
1039 13/4 St Hilary (R) MDN 3m 14 G *rear, went 5th at 14th, p.u. 2 out* P 0

Well beaten when completing; looks devoid of stamina. **0**

LETS TWIST AGAIN (Irish) — **I** 38[F], **I** 446[P], **I** 465[P], **I** 500[4], **I** 528[P], **I** 581[3], **I** 607[4], **I** 635[3], **I** 655[3]

LEVEL VIBES (Irish) — **I** 39[2], **I** 89[P], **I** 190[P], **I** 327[P]

LE VIENNA(IRE) b.g. 7 Le Bavard (FR) - Northern Push by Push On — N W Padfield

108 17/2 Marks Tey (L) MDN 3m 17 G *cls up, blnd 7th, wknd 13th, p.u. 3 out* P 0
314 2/3 Ampton (R) MDO 3m 10 G *mid div, hit 6th, lst tch 10th, p.u. 14th* P 0
597 23/3 Parham (R) MDO 3m 9 GS *rear, wll bhnd whn p.u. 9th* P 0
830 6/4 Marks Tey (L) MDN 3m 14 G *cls up, trckd ldrs, 3rd at 14th, wknd nxt, no ch 16th* 5 0
1055 13/4 Penshurst (L) MDO 3m 11 G *(Jt fav) handy, ev ch 4 out, wknd nxt, fin tired* 2 0
1300 28/4 Bexhill (R) MDO 3m 7 F *(fav) ld to 5th, agn 8-14th, rdn to chal 3 out, ran on gamely* 3 11
1398 6/5 Northaw (L) MEM 3m 4 F *(fav) n.j.w. rmdrs 2nd, chsd wnr 5th,ev ch & rdn 3 out, sn btn* 2 0

Ex Irish; only beaten 4 horses & form is very weak; blew a gift in his Members; more needed. **10**

LEWESDON HILL b.g. 9 Sonnen Gold - Lewesdon Lass by My Lord — T C Frost

1995 **3(NH),7(NH),6(NH),2(NH)**

66 10/2 Great Treth' (R) OPE 3m 8 S *alwys going wll, ld last, ran on well* 1 25
209 24/2 Castle Of C' (R) OPE 3m 8 HY *(fav) handy, prog 13th, disp whn blnd & u.r. 4 out* U -
265 2/3 Didmarton (L) OPE 3m 6 G *(fav) prom,wth ldr 11th til blnd 13th,rallied to ld aft last,ranon* 1 28
483 14/3 Cheltenham (L) HC 3 1/4m 110yds 17 G *blnd in rear 6th, struggling final cct, t.o..* 9 18
730 31/3 Little Wind' (R) LAD 3m 6 GS *(fav) hld up in tch, ld 14th, clr 3 out, eased run in* 1 25
991 8/4 Kingston St' (R) LAD 3m 8 F *(fav) not fluent,hld up,lot to do 15th,ran on wll 3 out,just got p* 1 20
1310 28/4 Little Wind' (R) LAD 3m 4 G *(fav) ld 7th, made rest, easily, collapsed & died aft race* 1 25

Dead. **26**

LEWESDON PRINCESS b.m. 8 Kinglet - Lewesdon Lass by My Lord — M P Haigh

1995 1(11),P(0),U(-),F(-),P(0)

20 14/1 Tweseldown (R) RES 3m 9 GS *last & losing tch whn blnd & u.r. 7th* U -
248 25/2 Charing (L) RES 3m 12 GS *in tch to 10th, bhnd whn p.u. 13th* P 0
449 9/3 Charing (L) RES 3m 13 G *rear, lost tch 10th, t.o. & p.u. 3 out* P 0
593 23/3 Parham (R) RES 3m 11 GS *alwys wll in rear, t.o. & p.u. 3 out* P 0
1054 13/4 Penshurst (L) RES 3m 8 G *ld 2-4th, styd in tch til wknd 12th, p.u. 3 out* P 0
1206 21/4 Heathfield (R) RES 3m 8 F *(bl) wth ldr to 14th, fdd & p.u. 4 out* P 0
1371 4/5 Peper Harow (L) RES 3m 5 F *(bl) ld,clr 3-7th,hdded appr 13th,wknd 3 out,wl btn & blnd last* 4 0
1612 26/5 Tweseldown (R) RES 3m 11 G *(bl) mid-div, jmpd slwly 8th, wknd 12th, t.o. & p.u. last* P 0

Won bad race 95; outclassed since and prospects are nil. **0**

LEYDEN LADY gr.m. 8 Baron Blakeney - Stormbound by Perspex — Miss J Fisher

1995 P(0),5(0),P(0),1(13)

498 16/3 Lanark (R) CON 3m 10 G *alwys wll bhnd, p.u. 2 out* P 0
608 23/3 Friars Haugh (L) RES 3m 13 G *not fluent, 3rd hlfway, sn wknd, p.u. 4 out* P 0
1350 4/5 Mosshouses (L) MEM 3m 2 GS *mstks, sn 30l bhnd, 15l down & clsng whn lft alone 11th* 1 0
1571 19/5 Corbridge (R) RES 3m 13 G *sn prom, disp 7th til outpcd 15th, p.u. nxt* P 0

Shock winner 95 (33/1); won joke race 96 and produced no other rateable form. **12**

LIBERTY JAMES ch.g. 9 Remezzo - Lady Cheval by Cheval — Mrs J Brooks

1995 **13(NH),7(NH),4(NH),P(NH),6(NH),U(NH),7(NH),2(NH),4(NH),3(NH),7(NH),10(NH)**

532 16/3 Cothelstone (L) RES 3m 12 G *dashed into ld 2nd, wll clr whn f 7th* F -
821 6/4 Charlton Ho' (L) MDN 3m 10 GF *prom, ld 9-13th, grdly wknd frm 4 out* 5 0
1347 4/5 Holnicote (L) MDO 3m 16 GS *rear til gd prog 14th, fin well, just hld* 2 16
1495 11/5 Holnicote (L) MDO 3m 11 G *(fav) hld up,hdwy 11th,trckd wnr & ev ch til not qckn clsng stgs* 2 15
1549 18/5 Bratton Down (L) MEM 3m 4 F *hld up, went 2nd 2 out, no imp flat* 2 12
1637 1/6 Bratton Down (L) MDO 3m 11 G *hld up bhnd,rpd prog to ld 14th,mstk nxt,hdd & wknd last* 3 10

Good enough for a win but hard ride & non-stayer; may continue to frustrate **14**

LIDDINGTON BELLE b.m. 7 Reesh - Stephouette by Stephen George — P Goldsworthy

1995 P(0),P(0),U(-),P(0),F(-)

21 20/1 Barbury Cas' (L) MEM 3m 16 GS *alwys bhnd, t.o. 7th, p.u. 9th* P 0
152 17/2 Erw Lon (L) MDN 3m 11 G *alwys rear, p.u. 11th* P 0
974 8/4 Lydstep (L) MEM 3m 10 G *1st ride, rear, p.u. 3 out* P 0
1200 21/4 Lydstep (L) MDN 3m 10 S *alwys rear, p.u. 10th* P 0

Of no account **0**

LIGHTEN THE LOAD b.g. 9 Lighter - Princess Charybdis by Ballymoss — J S Payne

1995 2(15),1(15),2(16),**5(0)**

6 13/1 Larkhill (R) OPE 3m 18 GS *well in rear whn f 11th* F -

26	20/1	Barbury Cas'	(L)	OPE	3m	12	GS	*mstk 3rd, rear, prog & cls up whn f 11th*	F	-
219	24/2	Newtown	(L)	RES	3m	17	GS	*rear, gd prog frm 12th, ld apr last, ran on well*	1	21
507	16/3	Magor	(R)	MXO	3m	5	GS	*2s-6/4, hld up, rpd prog 12th, 2nd til ld 2 out, sn clr*	1	21
669	27/3	Chepstow	(L)	HC	3m	10	S	*soon well bhnd, t.o. when p.u. before 2 out.*	P	0
838	6/4	Maisemore P'	(L)	OPE	3m	4	GF	*w.w. prog to 2nd 13th-nxt, sn rddn, rallied 2 out, ld flat*	1	23
1171	20/4	Chaddesley '	(L)	OPE	3m	15	G	*hld up til gd prog 15th, ev ch nxt, wknd 3 out*	6	19

Improved; Open wins make him hard to place now; worth another try in novice H/chase; G/F-G-S. 21

LIGHTOAK LAD (Irish) — **I** 52[B], **I** 293[F], **I** 323[5], **I** 366[P], **I** 440[6], **I** 458[4], **I** 507[6], **I** 612[P]

LIGHTS OUT g. 10 — Mrs D Pyper

1995 6(0),U(-)

56	10/2	Cottenham	(R)	OPE	3m	12	GS	*hld up in tch, outpcd aft 16th, not pshd, promising*	5	17
681	30/3	Cottenham	(R)	MDO	3m	12	GF	*(fav) mstk 3rd, rear, lost tch 14th, no dang aft*	6	0
1261	27/4	Cottenham	(R)	MDO	3m	10	F	*(fav) chsd ldr, mstk 11th, ld 15th-4 out, ld last, hdd nr fin*	2	13

Lightly raced; showed real promise 1st start; disappointing after (ground?); good enough to win. 14

LIGHT THE BAY ch.m. 6 Presidium - Light The Way by Nicholas Bill — E Wonnacott

1995 P(0),P(0),6(0),1(12),1(15)

297	2/3	Great Treth'	(R)	INT	3m	10	G	*7th hlfwy, bhnd whn p.u. 13th*	P	0
560	17/3	Ottery St M'	(L)	CON	3m	7	G	*handy, mstks, 3rd at 14th, nvr able to chal*	3	15
671	28/3	Taunton	(R)	HC	3m	13	S	*not fluent, held up, hdwy from 12th, wknd 15th, t.o. when p.u. before 2 out.*	P	0
870	6/4	Higher Kilw'	(L)	MEM	3m	5	GF	*(fav) hld up, ld 13th, ev ch whn blnd last, not rcvr*	2	13
1127	20/4	Stafford Cr'	(R)	INT	3m	4	S	*alwys 3rd/4th, nvr on terms wth ldrs*	3	0
1311	28/4	Little Wind'	(R)	INT	3m	6	G	*4th whn hit 13th, nvr dang*	5	0

Won Intermediate 95; struggling under the penalty and another win looks difficult. 15

LIGHT THE WICK b.g. 10 Furry Glen - Ollie's Pet by Tiepolo II — Mark Roche

1995 U(-),P(0),**P(NH)**,**8(NH)**,**F(-)**,11(0),U(-),4(0),4(0)

6	13/1	Larkhill	(R)	OPE	3m	18	GS	*alwys bhnd, t.o. & p.u. 13th*	P	0
154	17/2	Erw Lon	(L)	LAD	3m	14	G	*alwys last pair*	11	0
208	24/2	Castle Of C'	(R)	LAD	3m	14	HY	*sn t.o., wll bhnd whn p.u. 4 out*	P	0
362	5/3	Leicester	(R)	HC	2 1/2m 110yds	8	GS	*reminders 3rd, soon bhnd, blnd 5th, t.o. when p.u. 8th.*	P	0
507	16/3	Magor	(R)	MXO	3m	5	GS	*t.o. 6th, fin own time*	4	0
603	23/3	Howick	(L)	LAD	3m	8	S	*alwys rear, t.o. 9th, p.u. 11th*	P	0
693	30/3	Llanvapley	(L)	LAD	3m	6	GS	*alwys last, t.o. 12th, p.u. 15th*	P	0
845	6/4	Howick	(L)	CON	3m	12	GF	*cls 3rd whn u.r. 6th*	U	-
1035	13/4	St Hilary	(R)	CON	3m	10	G	*rear, t.o. & p.u. 14th*	P	0
1157	20/4	Llanwit Maj'	(R)	CON	3m	11	GS	*alwys rear, t.o. 12th, p.u. 3 out*	P	0
1263	27/4	Pyle	(R)	CON	3m	9	G	*cls up til outpcd 11th, t.o. & p.u. 15th*	P	0
1414	6/5	Cursneh Hill	(L)	LAD	3m	9	GF	*chsd ldrs, cls 5th 9th, outpcd frm 13th, t.o.*	5	0
1600	25/5	Bassaleg	(R)	MEM	3m	3	GS	*chsd wnr to 10th, lft 2nd nxt, btn 2 fences*	2	0

Utterly hopeless now. 0

LILLOOET (Irish) — **I** 258[P], **I** 320[2], **I** 408[F]

LILY THE LARK b.m. 8 Crested Lark - Florence Eliza by Floriana — Miss H M Irving

1995 2(10),4(10),P(0),S(-),1(0)

128	17/2	Kingston Bl'	(L)	RES	3m	14	GS	*mid-div, mstk 8th, 6th & out of tch whn f 13th*	F	-
338	3/3	Heythrop	(R)	RES	3m	9	G	*(Co fav) prom, prssd ldr 3 out, drvn to ld flat*	1	16
794	2/4	Heythrop	(R)	CON	3m	6	F	*w.w. strgglng whn mstk 14th, no dang aft*	5	10
1377	5/5	Dingley	(R)	CON	3m	12	GF	*mstks, cls up til hit 13th, strgglng 3 out, kpt on*	3	14
1567	19/5	Mollington	(R)	INT	3m	12	GS	*prom til 5th & outpcd 13th, no ch whn blnd 2 out*	5	12
1642	2/6	Dingley	(R)	LAD	3m	6	GF	*chsd ldr 10th, ld 15th, styd on well app last*	1	20

Small and suited by Ladies weight; game; beat Larry The Lamb; can improve; G-F. 20

LINANTIC b.g. 8 Full Of Hope - Contessa (HUN) by Peleid — John Rees

1995 P(0),P(0),3(0),3(12),P(0),1(19)

217	24/2	Newtown	(L)	RES	3m	17	GS	*made most to 12th, wth wnr 14th, sn wknd*	5	10
383	9/3	Llanfrynach	(R)	CON	3m	13	GS	*prom,3rd & outpcd 14th,no imp ldng pair 3 out,fin 3rd,prmtd*	2	15
600	23/3	Howick	(L)	RES	3m	14	S	*(fav) ld 6-11th, hdd & fdd, p.u. 3 out*	P	0
694	30/3	Llanvapley	(L)	RES	3m	9	GS	*1/1-5/2, ld to 5th, 2nd til p.u. aft 13th, lame*	P	0

Members winner 95; mainly disappointing; problems last start; may win again; best on Good. 17

LINDALIGHTER bl.m. 6 Lighter - Linda's Wish by Harvest Spirit — The Far Hill Partnership

1995 F(-),F(-),**5(NH)**,**9(NH)**

176	18/2	Market Rase'	(L)	MDO	2m 5f	10	GF	*chsd ldrs, 3rd whn f 9th*	F	-
354	3/3	Garnons	(L)	MDN	2 1/2m	13	GS	*ld 4th til f 10th*	F	-
1169	20/4	Chaddesley '	(L)	MEM	3m	9	G	*patiently rdn, prog frm 9th, ev ch 16th, no ext frm nxt*	5	13
1417	6/5	Cursneh Hill	(L)	MDO	3m	14	GF	*midfld whn mstk 8th, no prog frm 12th, p.u. 15th*	P	0
1629	30/5	Uttoxeter	(L)	HC	2m 5f	13	GS	*alwys bhnd, t.o. when p.u. before 9th.*	P	0

Ran passably on only completion in points; young but needs to find more stamina. 11

LINDA'S PARADISE (Irish) — **I** 247^{F}, **I** 293^{F}, **I** 323^{F}, **I** 472^{6}, **I** 540^{5}, **I** 630^{P}, **I** 645^{F}, **I** 661^{P}

LINDON RUN b.g. 7 Cruise Missile - Trial Run by Deep Run — T D Donaldson

1995 P(0)

87	11/2	Alnwick	(L)	MDO	3m	7	GS	*ld 2nd-5th, bhnd frm 7th, t.o. & p.u. 11th*	P	0
114	17/2	Lanark	(R)	MDO	3m	12	GS	*ld 4th til 9th, losing tch whn f 2 out*	F	-
323	2/3	Corbridge	(R)	MDN	3m	12	GS	*ld 2nd til 13th, lost plc, f 3 out*	F	-
407	9/3	Dalston	(R)	MDO	2 1/2m	13	G	*clse 2nd early, grad wknd, no ch frm 13th*	5	0
755	31/3	Lockerbie	(R)	MDN	3m	17	G	*ld til 7th, ld agn 14th-4 out, styd on wll*	2	15
916	8/4	Tranwell	(L)	MDO	2 1/2m	8	GF	*made all, j.w. qcknd clr last, styd on well*	1	14

Easily won short Maiden; stays 3 miles; should have chances in Restricted. 16

LINDSEY DOYLE ch.m. 10 Stanford - Sans Blague by Above Suspicion — R Burgess

292	2/3	Eaton Hall	(R)	RES	3m	15	G	*mid-div, prog frm 13th, not qckn aft*	6	0
666	24/3	Eaton Hall	(R)	RES	3m	13	S	*alwys rear, t.o.*	3	0
1010	9/4	Flagg Moor	(L)	LAD	3m	6	G	*alwys 3rd, outpcd 10th, p.u. 12th*	P	0

Won Maiden 93; missed 94/95; not show anything rateable in 96; can only be watched. 10

LINEBACKER b.g. 12 High Line - Gay Trinket by Grey Sovereign — Miss S Leach

1995 5(13),**U(-)**,**3(19)**,**1(22)**,**3(16)**

305	2/3	Great Stain'	(L)	LAD	3m	11	GS	*1st ride, prom to 10th, wknd aft, rear whn p.u. 16th*	P	0
514	16/3	Dalton Park	(R)	LAD	3m	8	G	*in tch to 10th, wll bhnd frm 13th*	5	10
586	23/3	Wetherby Po'	(L)	LAD	3m	8	S	*33s-20s, made most to 4 o ut, wknd nxt*	4	16
759	31/3	Great Stain'	(L)	LAD	3m	10	GS	*mid-div, drppd rear 9th, bhnd whn u.r. 14th*	U	-
1093	14/4	Whitwell-On'	(R)	MXO	4m	19	G	*trckd ldng grp til wknd 14th, f 4 out*	F	-
1366	4/5	Gisburn	(R)	LAD	3m	12	G	*bhnd whn u.r. 7th*	U	-
1469	11/5	Easingwold	(L)	LAD	3m	6	G	*mstk 4th, mid-div, blnd 13th, sn strgglng, t.o.*	3	10

Won weak H/chase 95; schoolmaster now; stays well but another win looks tough. 12

LINEKER (Irish) — **I** 101^{6}, **I** 145^{4}

LINGCOOL b.m. 6 Uncle Pokey - Cooling by Tycoon II — R Morley

1995 P(0)

74	11/2	Wetherby Po'	(L)	MDO	3m	11	GS	*bhnd early, nvr a fctr, p.u. 4 out*	P	0
176	18/2	Market Rase'	(L)	MDO	2m 5f	10	GF	*prog 8th, 5th whn hmpd & u.r. nxt*	U	-
408	9/3	Charm Park	(L)	MEM	3m	7	G	*prom, ld 12-15, in tch whn f 3 out*	F	-
517	16/3	Dalton Park	(R)	MDO	3m	10	G	*w.w. in tch, prog to 4th & in tch whn p.u. 15th*	P	0
589	23/3	Wetherby Po'	(L)	MDO	3m	16	S	*mid-div, prog 12th, lft 2nd 14th, ld last, hdd & no ext flat*	2	12
1094	14/4	Whitwell-On'	(R)	MDO	2 1/2m 88yds	16	G	*chsd ldrs, mod prog 4 out, sn wknd, p.u. last*	P	0
1135	20/4	Hornby Cast'	(L)	MDN	3m	10	G	*alwys rear, t.o. & p.u. 12th*	P	0
1451	6/5	Witton Cast'	(R)	MDO	3m	12	G	*alwys rear, p.u. 14th*	P	0

Beaten 3 lengths in stamina test; only completion; may surprise in similar. 12

LINGER BALINDA ch.m. 10 Balinger - Artalinda by Indiaro — Mrs S E Haydon

1995 B(-),5(0),2(0),F(-)

454	9/3	Charing	(L)	MDN	3m	10	G	*mid-div to 10th, sn strgglng, t.o. & p.u. 4 out*	P	0

Ungenuine & vanished quickly in 96; no prospects. 0

LINGERING HOPE (Irish) — **I** 98^{2}, **I** 219^{1}, **I** 298^{F}, **I** 315^{B}

LINK COPPER ch.g. 7 Whistlefield - Letitica by Deep Run — Mrs E J Taplin

1995 P(0)

532	16/3	Cothelstone	(L)	RES	3m	12	G	*lft in ld 7th, hdded appr 4 out, wknd nxt,3rd whn p.u. 2 out*	P	0
926	8/4	Bishopsleigh	(R)	RES	3m	9	G	*ld 2nd & 5th til hdd 7th, fronk rank, no ext aft last*	2	18
1113	17/4	Hockworthy	(L)	RES	3m	11	GS	*chsd ldrs to 8th, sn strgglng, t.o. & p.u. 14th*	P	0
1497	11/5	Holnicote	(L)	RES	3m	10	G	*ld/disp til f 8th (ditch)*	F	-
1550	18/5	Bratton Down	(L)	CON	3m	8	F	*went 3rd at 10th, lost ground 14th, bhnd & p.u. 3 out*	P	0
1591	25/5	Mounsey Hil'	(R)	RES	3m	15	G	*ld to 15th, sn wknd, p.u. apr 2 out*	P	0
1634	1/6	Bratton Down	(L)	INT	3m	15	G	*alwys prom,ld 15th-3 out,ev ch apr last,wknd,fin 4th,prmtd*	3	15
1649	8/6	Umberleigh	(L)	RES	3m	14	GF	*prom, ld 7th-apr 2 out, not qckn aft, styd on*	3	16

Maiden winner 94; inconsistent; could land small race but is a weak finisher; dislikes Firm. 15

LINKS WAY (Irish) — **I** 171^{4}

LINLAKE LIGHTNING b.m. 9 St Columbus - Bright Exploit by Exploitation — Miss H M Irving

1995 F(-),P(0),4(0),P(0),3(15),4(12),r(-),P(0)

494	16/3	Horseheath	(R)	RES	3m	10	GF	*alwys bhnd, lst tch 6th, t.o. & p.u. 10th*	P	0
904	6/4	Dingley	(R)	RES	3m	20	GS	*rear div, 12th 10th, ran on passed btn horses last m*	4	14
1102	14/4	Guilsborough	(L)	RES	3m	15	G	*mstks, wll bhnd hlfwy, t.o. 16th, styd on wll frm 3 out*	4	10
1439	6/5	Ashorne	(R)	RES	3m	11	G	*in tch til outpcd 12th, onepcd aft*	5	13
1564	19/5	Mollington	(R)	XX	3m	14	GS	*in tch in rear til rdn & wknd 10th, t.o. & p.u. 14th*	P	0
1641	2/6	Dingley	(R)	RES	3m	13	GF	*slw jmp 2nd & rdn, in tch to 11th, t.o. whn p.u. last*	P	0

Maiden winner 94; makes mistakes and has not progressed; not threatening to win Restricted. 12

LINRED b.g. 11 Politico (USA) - Denwick Bambi by Hamood — Mike Roberts

1995 2(21),**F(-)**

94	11/2	Ampton	(R)	OPE	3m	8	GF	*svrl pstns, ev ch 3 out, wknd nxt*	5	18
346	3/3	Higham	(L)	INT	3m	6	G	*(fav) ld to 12th, rmnd prom til no ext 16th*	3	19
476	10/3	Tweseldown	(R)	OPE	3m	7	G	*handy, blnd badly 10th, styng on whn lft 2nd apr last, no ch*	2	19

Won 4 points in 93; only 5 runs since; onepaced; may need to try Confined to win again; any. 21

LION OF VIENNA b.g. 9 Bulldozer - Lucky Favour by Ballyciptic — A Dawson

1995 **5(NH),14(NH),4(NH),P(NH),8(NH)**

50	4/2	Alnwick	(L)	CON	3m	9	G	*hld up, prog 12th, disp 2nd & gng wl, f nxt*	F	-
1570	19/5	Corbridge	(R)	CON	3m	8	G	*last at 4th, nvr seen wth ch*	7	0

Winning hurdler; interupted season but showed at Alnwick that a win is possible if fit in 97. 15

LIOS NA MAOL (Irish) — **I** 279^{F}, **I** 433^{P}

LIPSTICK LADY (Irish) — **I** 165^{P}, **I** 196^{P}, **I** 224^{F}, **I** 384^{P}

LISADANTE (Irish) — **I** 355^{F}, **I** 378^{5}, **I** 435^{3}, **I** 512^{2}, **I** 547^{2}, **I** 606^{3}

LISAHANE LAD b.g. 10 Daring March - Puff Pastry by Reform — T Powell

1995 P(0),P(0),6(0)

465	10/3	Milborne St'	(L)	RES	3m	11	G	*sn rear, t.o. & p.u. 4 out*	P	0
656	23/3	Badbury Rin'	(L)	RES	3m	11	G	*prom early, wknd frm 10th, t.o.*	7	0
728	31/3	Little Wind'	(R)	MEM	3m	7	GS	*lost tch frm 14th, t.o.*	6	0
822	6/4	Charlton Ho'	(L)	RES	3m	7	GF	*mid-div, no ch frm 13th, outpcd*	5	0
1128	20/4	Stafford Cr'	(R)	RES	3m	17	S	*alwys midfld, nvr any ch*	5	0

Maiden winner 94; only beat one horse in 96 and prospects bleak now. 0

LISAS DELIGHT (Irish) — **I** 546^{F}

LISBAND LADY(IRE) ch.m. 6 Orchestra - Lisaniskey Lady by Varano — J Townson

228	24/2	Duncombe Pa'	(R)	MDO	3m	9	GS	*rear, t.o. & hmpd 5th, p.u. 9th*	P	0
405	9/3	Dalston	(R)	MDO	2 1/2m	16	G	*blndrd & u.r. 3rd*	U	-

No signs yet. 0

LISHILLAUN (Irish) — **I** 41^{3}, **I** 128^{2}, **I** 150^{2}, **I** 335^{5}, **I** 369^{3}, **I** 443^{1}

LISKILNEWABBEY (Irish) — **I** 120^{F}, **I** 210^{P}, **I** 279^{P}

LISLARY LAD br.g. 16 Gala Performance (USA) - Lady Manta by Bargello — Lee Bowles

1995 F(-),**U(-)**,**5(0)**,1(18),2(21),5(18),3(19),**5(22)**,1(19),**2(18)**,2(22),5(0)

153	17/2	Erw Lon	(L)	OPE	3m	15	G	*mid-div no prog frm 3 out*	8	0
383	9/3	Llanfrynach	(R)	CON	3m	13	GS	*cls up,prog to ld & lft clr 13th,hld on wll apr last,disq*	1D	21
485	16/3	Hereford	(R)	HC	3m 1f 110yds	13	S	*midfield, mstk 5th, hit 9th, some hdwy 12th, wknd before 14th, t.o..*	6	0
692	30/3	Llanvapley	(L)	OPE	3m	6	GS	*rear, prog to ld 11th, 2l up last, hdd & no ext nr fin*	2	20
845	6/4	Howick	(L)	CON	3m	12	GF	*(fav) cls up, 3rd 4 out, chal nxt, outpcd*	3	17
1199	21/4	Lydstep	(L)	OPE	3m	5	S	*alwys 2nd/3rd, chsd wnr frm 15th, no imp*	2	18
1264	27/4	Pyle	(R)	LAD	3m	10	G	*15l 3rd at 10th,prog to ld 15th,hdd aft 2 out,fin 4th,prmtd*	3	16
1386	6/5	Pantyderi	(R)	OPE	3m	5	GF	*nvr bttr than 3rd, onepcd*	3	18
1479	11/5	Bredwardine	(R)	OPE	3m	8	G	*prog to trck ldr 11th, ld 2 out, pshd clr flat*	1	21
1560	18/5	Bassaleg	(R)	OPE	3m	7	F	*w.w. in tch, hmpd & u.r. apr 9th*	U	-
1613	27/5	Fontwell	(R)	HC	3 1/4m 110yds	12	G	*hdwy 13th, chsd lding pair 18th, wknd 3 out.*	4	14

Retains ability; consistent; win at 17 still possible; G/F-S. 19

LISLOONEY (Irish) — **I** 110^{F}

LISMOY (Irish) — **I** 106^{P}, **I** 271^{F}

LISNAGAR LADY (Irish) — **I** 128^{P}, **I** 309^{4}, **I** 380^{2}, **I** 522^{2}, **I** 575^{1}

LISNAGREE BOY (Irish) — **I** 111^{F}, **I** 167^{P}, **I** 237^{F}

LISNAVARAGH b.g. 10 Kemal (FR) - Weaver's Fool by Weaver's Hall — Vince Dolan

259	1/3	Kelso	(L)	HC	3m 1f	8	GS	*prom till wknd after 14th, t.o. when ref 2 out.*	R	-
367	6/3	Catterick	(L)	HC	3m 1f 110yds	12	G	*bhnd, hdwy into midfield hfwy, wknd after 16th.*	5	11

Ex-Irish; season lasted 5 days & most disappointing; can only be watched 13

LISSELAN LASS (Irish) — **I** 502^{F}, **I** 572^{3}, **I** 649^{P}

LISTRAKELT (Irish) — **I** 169^{P}, **I** 539^{P}, **I** 585^{P}

LITTLE BOPPER (Irish) — **I** 258^{P}

LITTLE BY LITTLE b.g. 6 Derring Rose - April Fortune by Maystreak — G L Edwards

1995 U(-),r(-),r(-),2(12),**5(NH)**,**7(NH)**

287	2/3	Eaton Hall	(R)	MDO	3m	11	G	*(fav) hld up, prog 12th, ev ch til wknd 4 out*	3	10

464 9/3 Eyton-On-Se' (L) MDN 2 1/2m 13 G *ldng grp whn r.o. 3rd* r -
661 24/3 Eaton Hall (R) MDN 3m 9 S *mstks, mid-div, some prog 14th, ran on onepcd* 3 11
953 8/4 Eyton-On-Se' (L) MDO 2 1/2m 10 GF *(fav) chsng grp, cls order 9th, chal & wnt clr 2 out, readly* 1 13
1222 24/4 Brampton Br' (R) RES 3m 11 G *chsd ldrs to 11th, wknd frm 13th, t.o.* 6 0
1421 6/5 Eyton-On-Se' (L) RES 3m 11 GF *chsd ldrs to 4 out, no ex frm 3 out* 6 0

Won short Maiden; stamina doubts and struggling now upgraded. much more needed. 14

LITTLE CELIA (Irish) — **I** 360[R], **I** 404[U], **I** 599[P]

LITTLE COOMBE b.m. 10 Lir - Clover Bee by The Bo'sun M Wilkins

1995 1(19),4(13),**U(-)**,5(13),5(14),1(18),4(0),1(18)

196 24/2 Lemalla (R) CON 3m 14 HY *nvr bttr than mid-div, lost tch 5 out* 11 0
561 17/3 Ottery St M' (L) LAD 3m 12 G *mid-div, outpcd frm 13th* 8 10
626 23/3 Kilworthy (L) OPE 3m 12 GS *alwys bhnd, t.o. 12th, p.u. last* P 0
870 6/4 Higher Kilw' (L) MEM 3m 5 GF *in tch, went 2nd 15th, chal 2 out, ld last, sn clr* 1 16
938 8/4 Wadebridge (L) OPE 3m 3 F *mstk 2nd, ld to 8th agn 11th, made rest, ran on wll* 1 17
1360 4/5 Flete Park (R) OPE 3m 5 G *in tch, 4th & tail swishing 12th, bhnd whn p.u. 17th* P 0

Won 2 modest races 96; won 10 of last 25 starts; best L/H; Open penalty makes things hard now. 18

LITTLEDALE(USA) b.h. 10 Lypheor - Smeralda by Grey Sovereign John McManus

1995 F(-),U(-),P(0),P(0),P(0),7(0),F(-),P(0)

541 17/3 Southwell P' (L) MDO 3m 9 GS *chsng grp, cls 2nd 10th, no ext frm 2 out* 4 10
973 8/4 Thorpe Lodge (L) MDO 3m 7 GF *mostly 3rd til ld 5 out, hdd 2 out, ran on und pres* 2 12
1301 28/4 Southwell P' (L) MDO 3m 10 GF *(Jt fav) chsng grp til wknd 6 out, poor 6th whn p.u. 2 out* P 0
1381 5/5 Dingley (R) MDO 3m 16 GF *prom to 12th, sn wknd, t.o. & p.u. last* P 0

Placed in poor race; stamina suspect and need fortune to win. 11

LITTLE DOE (Irish) — **I** 232[B], **I** 301[F], **I** 340[P], **I** 483[P]

LITTLE FLO b.m. 7 Rolfe (USA) - Maiden Venture by Eastern Venture Mrs G Rowan-Hamilton

1995 F(-),P(0),U(-),P(0),U(-)

114 17/2 Lanark (R) MDO 3m 12 GS *ld til 4th, losing tch whn f 2 out* F
704 30/3 Tranwell (L) MDO 3m 16 GS *nvr nr ldrs, wll bhnd whn p.u. 2 out* P 0
1089 14/4 Friars Haugh (L) MDN 3m 10 F *bhnd by hlfwy, p.u. 4 out* P 0

Yet to complete the course 0

LITTLE FREDDIE ch.g. 7 Roman Warrior - Dawns Ballad by Balidar J D Parker

1995 P(0)

30 20/1 Higham (L) MEM 3m 4 GF *ld/disp til blnd 11th, ev ch last, onepaced* 2 12
344 3/3 Higham (L) MDO 3m 12 G *sn bhnd, t.o. 11th, p.u. 14th* P 0
618 23/3 Higham (L) MDO 3m 14 GF *mid-div, lost tch 11th, slight prog 13th, sn btn, t.o.* 3 0
681 30/3 Cottenham (R) MDO 3m 12 GF *wth ldr to 14th, cls 5th whn f 3 out* F -
1149 20/4 Higham (L) MDO 3m 10 F *rear, lsot tch 12th, t.o. & p.u. 16th* P 0
1261 27/4 Cottenham (R) MDO 3m 10 F *mid-div, lost tch ldrs 12th, wknd rpdly nxt, fin tired* 6 0

Just beaten in slowly run Members; does not stay in proper races. 10

LITTLE GENERAL ch.g. 13 General Ironside - Coolentallagh by Perhapsburg Mrs D McCormack

1995 **3(NH),4(NH),3(NH),3(NH)**

487 16/3 Newcastle (L) HC 3m 10 GS *blnd 3rd, towards rear, imp after 8th, struggling after 6 out, p.u. 3 out.* P 0
1515 12/5 Hexham Poin' (L) OPE 3m 6 HY *33s-10s, in tch, 2nd apr 3 out, sn wknd, no ch & p.u. last* P 0

Wiinning chaser; looks past it now. 0

LITTLE GLEN b.g. 8 Germont - Glendyke by Elvis A B Crozier

1995 7(0),4(13),1(19),3(16),5(0),3(10),2(20),F(-)

187 24/2 Friars Haugh (L) CON 3m 12 S *alwys twrds rear* 5 0
317 2/3 Corbridge (R) CON 3m 11 GS *4th frm 6th, chsd ldrs 15th, styd on* 4 15
498 16/3 Lanark (R) CON 3m 10 G *ld 6th-9th, 3rd frm nxt, went 2nd 2 out, no ch wth wnr* 2 14
610 23/3 Friars Haugh (L) CON 3m 11 G *3rd hlfwy, styd on to take 2nd cl home* 2 16
751 31/3 Lockerbie (R) CON 3m 12 G *ld 5th til 8th, rmnd cls up, 2l 2nd whn u.r. last* U -
1340 4/5 Hexham (L) HC 3m 1f 13 S *losing tch when blnd badly 12th, well t.o..* 9 0
1475 11/5 Aspatria (L) CON 3m 6 GF *mstks, in tch, chal & ld apr last, mstk & hdd, not rcvrd* 2 19
1570 19/5 Corbridge (R) CON 3m 8 G *(Jt fav) mstks, prog 13th, went 3rd nxt, fdd 3 out* 4 14

Consistent Confined horse; able but let down by his jumping; deserves another win; G-F. 18

LITTLE HAWK 6 John Carr

916 8/4 Tranwell (L) MDO 2 1/2m 8 GF *nvr going wll, p.u. 7th* P 0
1253 27/4 Balcormo Ma' (R) MDO 3m 16 GS *bhnd by hlfwy, p.u. aft 12th* P 0
1355 4/5 Mosshouses (L) MDO 3m 10 GS *mstk 5th & last, t.o. & p.u. 13th* P 0

No signs of ability. 0

LITTLE ISLAND b.m. 10 Noble Imp - Island Serenade by Easter Island Richard Hardman

1995 3(15),2(16),**8(0)**,1(14),3(17)

266	2/3	Didmarton	(L)	LAD	3m	13	G	*mid-div, prog to jn ldrs 10th, 5th & outpcd 13th, no ch aft*	7 10
640	23/3	Siddington	(L)	LAD	3m	9	S	*prom, lft in ld 9th, hdded 3 out, no ex*	2 15
782	31/3	Tweseldown	(R)	XX	3m	6	G	*(fav) trckd ldrs,pshd alng hlfwy,bhnd whn mstk 13th,p.u.nxt,dsmntd*	P 0

Moderate but consistent; finds weak races; problems last start; may fined another win if fit. 16

LITTLE-K (Irish) — **I** 227³, **I** 346², **I** 528¹, **I** 617¹

LITTLE LEN (Irish) — **I** 346ᴾ, **I** 388, , **I** 618ᴾ

LITTLE MARTINA(IRE) b.m. 8 The Parson - Little Welly by Little Buskins — Christopher Newport

1995 1(17),1(19)

21	20/1	Barbury Cas'	(L)	MEM	3m	16	GS	*prom,chsd wnr 10-15th,3rd & btn whn hmpd & u.r. 2 out*	U -
271	2/3	Parham	(R)	CON	3m	15	GF	*alwys wth ldrs, jst ld 12th, rdn 2 out, hld on, all out*	1 21
595	23/3	Parham	(R)	OPE	3m	12	GS	*sn wth ldr, ld 11th, clr 4 out, unchal*	1 25
1013	13/4	Ascot	(R)	HC	3m 110yds	11	GS	*(fav) held up, steady hdwy 15th, ld after 3 out, soon clr.*	1 27
1338	3/5	Bangor	(L)	HC	3m 110yds	8	S	*(fav) handy, 2nd when blnd and u.r. 4 out.*	U -

Useful and still improving; stays well; can win another H/chase; G-S. 27

LITTLE MINUTE (Irish) — **I** 33³, **I** 84², **I** 348², **I** 417⁴

LITTLE NOD ch.g. 7 Domynsky - Vikris by Viking (USA) — D Rolfe

1995 P(0),F(-),F(-),5(14),4(18),3(0)

33	20/1	Higham	(L)	LAD	3m	9	GF	*in tch, ev ch appr 3 out, wknd 2 out*	5 16
250	25/2	Charing	(L)	LAD	3m	12	GS	*prom, 5th & ev ch whn u.r. 14th*	U -
347	3/3	Higham	(L)	LAD	3m	10	G	*t.o. 4th, p.u. 3 out*	P 0
571	17/3	Detling	(L)	CON	3m	13	GF	*alwys prom, ld 12th, hdd 3 out, 2nd & ev ch whn blnd last*	3 17
920	8/4	Aldington	(L)	OPE	3m	6	F	*cls up, wth ldr 15th-3 out, 2nd & btn whn blnd nxt, nt rcvr*	3 13
1330	30/4	Huntingdon	(R)	HC	2 1/2m 110yds	8	GF	*cl up to 4th, bhnd and blnd 8th, t.o. when p.u. before 12th.*	P 0
1444	6/5	Aldington	(L)	OPE	3m	6	HD	*mstks, alwys wll in tch, nvr dang, wknd 2 out*	5 14

Hurdles winner; tries hard but does not stay; deserves a win but not easy to find. 15

LITTLE NOTICE(IRE) g. 5 — Capt T A Forster

1045	13/4	Bitterley	(L)	MDO	3m	16	G	*trckd ldrs, effrt 15th, ld nxt, rallied to chal last,ld post*	1 15

Gamely beat a subsequent winner; can only improve and should upgrade. 16

LITTLE PETHERICK b.m. 6 Town And Country - Hasty Retreat by Country Retreat — R Parker

814	6/4	Charing	(L)	MDO	2 1/2m	8	F	*schoold in rear, out of tch hlfwy*	4 0
1210	21/4	Heathfield	(R)	MDO	3m	13	F	*schoold in rear, lost tch & p.u. 13th*	P 0
1370	4/5	Peper Harow	(L)	MEM	3m	3	F	*cls up, disp ld 10-12th, onepcd frm 15th*	3 0

Yet to beat another horse; may do better. 0

LITTLE SIMBA (Irish) — **I** 379ᴾ

LITTLE SQUAW ch.m. 5 Buckskin (FR) - Slaveside

1384	6/5	Pantyderi	(R)	MEM	3m	2	GF	*(fav) sttld cls up, hrd rdn to ld aft last, ran green*	1 0

Won an awful match; huge improvement needed. 0

LITTLE THYNE br.g. 11 Good Thyne (USA) - You Never Know by Brave Invader (USA) — Mrs T Pritchard

1995 6(0),5(0),9(0)

27	20/1	Barbury Cas'	(L)	LAD	3m	15	GS	*t.o. 6th, mstk 8th, p.u. 14th*	P 0
126	17/2	Kingston Bl'	(L)	LAD	3m	11	GS	*last & strggling 8th, t.o. & p.u. 12th*	P 0
208	24/2	Castle Of C'	(R)	LAD	3m	14	HY	*alwys rear, nvr on terms*	8 0
443	9/3	Haldon	(R)	LAD	3m	10	S	*mid-div, lost tch 13th, poor 5th frm 3 out*	5 10
640	23/3	Siddington	(L)	LAD	3m	9	S	*jmpd slwly, wll bhnd frm 13th, t.o.*	5 0
924	8/4	Bishopsleigh	(R)	LAD	3m	7	G	*alwys rear, jmp big, fin race own pce*	4 0
1245	27/4	Woodford	(L)	LAD	3m	6	G	*chsd ldr to 3rd, lost tch 7th, lost iron 12th, p.u. 15th*	P 0
1480	11/5	Bredwardine	(R)	LAD	3m	12	G	*rear frm 6th, lost tch & p.u. 12th*	P 0

Winning hurdler; of no accont now. 0

LITTLE WENLOCK b.g. 12 Tycoon II - Oujarater by Adropejo — Mrs D S C Gibson

1995 2(13)

319	2/3	Corbridge	(R)	RES	3m	16	GS	*bhnd, prog 10th, prom & ev ch 3 out, outpcd*	3 15
754	31/3	Lockerbie	(R)	RES	3m	8	G	*in tch whn u.r. 9th*	U -
914	8/4	Tranwell	(L)	RES	3m	6	GF	*cls up, smooth prog to ld 3 out, hdd & outpcd last*	2 18
1086	14/4	Friars Haugh	(L)	RES	3m	7	F	*patiently rdn, 4th hlfwy, ld apr last, comf*	1 17
1226	25/4	Perth	(R)	HC	3m	7	S	*well bhnd early, hdwy after 14th, challenging when bumped run-in, styd on strly.*	1 24
1461	9/5	Sedgefield	(L)	HC	2m 5f	10	F	*(fav) held up, tk clr order hfwy, ld last, rdn and styd on.*	1 21

1542 16/5 Perth (R) HC 2 1/2m 110yds 8 F *held up and bhnd, outpcd till hdwy after 4 out, kept on one pace.* 4 20
1586 25/5 Hexham (L) HC 2 1/2m 110yds 14 GF *(Jt fav) patiently rdn, steady hdwy to go 4th when f 6 out.* F -
1615 27/5 Wetherby (L) HC 2 1/2m 110yds 11 G *mstks, soon bhnd, t.o. when p.u. before last.* P 0

Vastly improved & fairy-tale season; problem last start & hard to place even if fit 97; F-S 20

LIVELY LIL(IRE) b.m. 6 Borovansky - Welsh Cuckoo by Roxy (FR) J Townson

589 23/3 Wetherby Po' (L) MDO 3m 16 S *t.o. 6th, p.u. 10th* P 0
740 31/3 Sudlow Farm (R) MDN 3m 16 G *ran out 5th* r -

No signs yet. 0

LIVE RUST(IRE) ch.g. 6 Air Display (USA) - Regretable by Hard Fought Gary Thomas

146 17/2 Erw Lon (L) MEM 3m 7 G *1st ride, 2nd til lost plc hlfwy, t.o. 14th* 4 0

Tailed off last and well short of standard yet. 0

LIVE WIRE(IRE) b.g. 5 Electric - Green Gale by Strong Gale C C Trietline

430 9/3 Upton-On-Se' (R) MDO 3m 15 GS *alwys last, p.u. 14th* P 0
748 31/3 Upper Sapey (R) MDO 3m 11 GS *ld frm 14th, drew clr frm 2 out* 1 15
1318 28/4 Bitterley (L) XX 3m 8 G *trckd ldrs, outpcd 12th, prog 15th, not rch 1st pair* 3 14

Won poor Maiden but ran better after; stays and has chances in weak Restricted. 16

LIVING ON THE EDGE(IRE) ch.g. 7 Callernish - Clashdermot Lady by Shackleton Mrs D Ibbotson

75 11/2 Wetherby Po' (L) MDO 3m 8 GS *prom, disp 12th-nxt, wknd, p.u. 4 out* P 0
228 24/2 Duncombe Pa' (R) MDO 3m 9 GS *w.w. lost tch 12th, lft 2nd nxt, ran on well flat* 3 11
416 9/3 Charm Park (L) MDO 3m 13 G *f 2nd* F -
764 31/3 Great Stain' (L) MDN 3m 16 GS *strng hld, hld up, ev ch whn blnd & u.r. 12th* U -
1095 14/4 Whitwell-On' (R) MDO 2 1/2m 88yds 14 G *rear, prog rpdly to ld 7th, sn drew wll clr, easily* 1 17
1284 27/4 Easingwold (L) RES 3m 14 G *(fav) hld up, gd prog 10th, poised to chal whn u.r. nxt* U -

Placed in novice hurdle; easily won short Maiden; pulls and easy 3 miles is essential. 17

LLES LE BUCFLOW ch.g. 8 Little Wolf - Elsell by Grey Mirage Jeffrey A Smith

1995 1(13),3(11)

882 6/4 Brampton Br' (R) RES 3m 14 GF *chsd ldrs, just in tch 12th, wknd 14th, p.u. 3 out* P 0
1223 24/4 Brampton Br' (R) RES 3m 11 G *chsd ldrs to 13th, wknd nxt, p.u. 16th* P 0
1415 6/5 Cursneh Hill (L) RES 3m 11 GF *rear whn mstk 5th, no ch frm 13th* 6 0

Won Maiden 95; gone the wrong way since and best watched. 0

LLOYDS LOSER ch.g. 8 Crested Lark - Ducal Gold by Solar Duke Viscount H N Gage

1995 P(0),P(0),F(-),P(0),P(0),P(0)

439 9/3 Newton Brom' (R) MDN 3m 7 GS *ld aft 1st til 13th, dropped out, p.u. aft 16th* P 0
496 16/3 Horseheath (R) MDO 3m 10 GF *sn ld, clr 6th, mstk & f 8th* F -
1020 13/4 Kingston Bl' (L) MDN 3m 10 G *made most to 7th, wknd rpdly 12th, t.o. & p.u. 14th* P 0
1183 21/4 Mollington (R) MDN 3m 10 F *14s-8s, ld to apr 13th, sn wknd, t.o. & p.u. 3 out* P 0
1434 6/5 Ashorne (R) MDO 3m 15 G *ld to 8th, wknd 12th, t.o. & p.u. 2 out* P 0
1610 26/5 Tweseldown (R) MDO 3m 5 G *hld up,chsd ldr 12th,ev ch & f 15th,even rmntd & fin* F -
1644 2/6 Dingley (R) MDO 3m 16 GF *prom, ld 14th-3 out, wknd nxt* 5 0

1 completion from 13 starts; short of stamina; may yet improve. 0

LOCAL MANOR ch.g. 9 Le Bavard (FR) - Blackrath Girl by Bargello J L Dunlop

1995 **6(NH),P(NH)**

17 14/1 Tweseldown (R) MDN 3m 11 GS *1st ride, prom til 5th & outpcd 15th, no prog aft* 4 10
275 2/3 Parham (R) MDN 3m 15 GF *(fav) 9/2-5/2, prog 8th, jnd ldrs 13th, ld aft 3 out, ran on well* 1 15
593 23/3 Parham (R) RES 3m 11 GS *sn prom, 3rd frm 3 out, not pace to chal* 3 14
964 8/4 Heathfield (R) RES 3m 7 G *prom til squeezed & r.o. 8th, cont, pld 3rd, disq* r -
1206 21/4 Heathfield (R) RES 3m 8 F *trckd ldrs, chsd ldr 16th, styd on to ld line* 1 15
1440 6/5 Aldington (L) INT 3m 5 HD *ld 3rd-11th, 3rd frm 12th, kpt on same pce 2 out* 3 13
1540 16/5 Folkestone (R) HC 2m 5f 10 G *started slowly, soon in tch, cl 5th when u.r. 11th.* U -

Ex novice chaser; novice ridden; consistent, stays but modest; weak Confined possible; Hd-G/S. 16

LOCAL RACE (Irish) — **I** 563ᴾ, **I** 628,

LOCATION b.g. 9 Blakeney - Green Teable (FR) by Green Dancer (USA) J Down

1995 10(0),P(0)

1431 6/5 High Bickin' (R) MDO 3m 9 G *prom til lost plc 14th, onepcd* 3 11

Lightly raced; 1st signs of ability; go close in weak Maiden if fit in 97. 13

LOCH BRAN LAD (Irish) — **I** 516, , **I** 527ᴾ, **I** 582ᴾ

LOCH GARANNE br.m. 8 Lochnager - Raperon by Rapid River P G Watkins

1995 **7(NH),10(NH),11(NH),12(NH),14(NH),5(NH),0(NH)**

21	20/1	Barbury Cas'	(L)	MEM	3m	16	GS	*reluc to race, t.o. til p.u. 4th*	P	0
157	17/2	Erw Lon	(L)	CON	3m	15	G	*ld 3rd-12th, wknd rpdly*	12	0
215	24/2	Newtown	(L)	OPE	3m	20	GS	*left, t.n.p.*	0	0
351	3/3	Garnons	(L)	OPE	3m	14	GS	*ref to race*	0	0
382	9/3	Llanfrynach	(R)	MEM	3m	7	GS	*reluc to race, sn in tch, cls up & going wll 14th, btn nxt*	5	0
547	17/3	Erw Lon	(L)	OPE	3m	10	GS	*ref to race*	0	0
602	23/3	Howick	(L)	OPE	3m	11	S	*ref to race*	0	0
1219	24/4	Brampton Br'	(R)	CON	3m	9	G	*ref to race (again), stewards*	0	0
1480	11/5	Bredwardine	(R)	LAD	3m	12	G	*trotted twards 1st & stppd*	R	

Comment unnecessary 0

LOCH GARMAN HOTEL (Irish) — **I** 18^{F}, **I** 29^{P}, **I** 82^{2}, **I** 158^{1}, **I** 221^{2}, **I** 382^{2}, **I** 422^{1}, **I** 561^{2}, **I** 633^{1}

LOCHINGALL br.g. 11 Mljet - Petite Doutelle by Percy Dear — Miss P Morris

1995 P(0),1(19)

160	17/2	Weston Park	(L)	OPE	3m	16	G	*10s-9/2, hld up in tch, gd prog to ld apr last, ran on wll*	1	23
351	3/3	Garnons	(L)	OPE	3m	14	GS	*trckd ldrs, chal 14th, ld 3 out, sn drew clr*	1	24
686	30/3	Chaddesley '	(L)	OPE	3m	6	G	*(fav) hld up, smooth prog to chal 2 out, ld last, ran on, clvrly*	1	26

Lightly raced; useful now; quickens; win more in 97; G-S. 25

LOCHINVAR LORD b.g. 9 Callernish - Side Wink by Quayside — D J Renney

1995 P(0),7(0),5(0),3(0),2(0)

341	3/3	Heythrop	(R)	MDN	3m	13	G	*(bl) prom to 7th, lost plc hlfwy, t.o. & p.u. 14th*	P	0
712	30/3	Barbury Cas'	(L)	MDO	3m	10	G	*(bl) ld to 5th, wknd, lost tch 12th, outpcd aft*	3	0
959	8/4	Lockinge	(L)	MDN	3m	6	GF	*(bl) ld to 3rd, outpcd 12th, prog frm 5 out, ld apr last, ran on*	1	13
1168	20/4	Larkhill	(R)	RES	3m	8	GF	*(bl) nvr bttr thn mid-div, t.o. frm 14th, onepcd*	3	0
1380	5/5	Dingley	(R)	RES	3m	11	GF	*(bl) rear, lost tch 10th, bhnd aft, kpt on apr last*	7	0

Novice ridden; won weak Maiden; safe but slow; Restricted hard to find. 14

LOCH IRISH(IRE) b.m. 7 Lancastrian - Pure Spec by Fine Blade (USA) — N W Padfield

92	11/2	Ampton	(R)	MDO	3m	7	GF	*f 2nd*	F	-
423	9/3	High Easter	(L)	MDN	3m	8	S	*n.j.w. blnd 2nd, bhnd sme prog whn hmpd 11th, p.u. nxt*	P	0
495	16/3	Horseheath	(R)	MDO	3m	12	GF	*alwys rear, effrt 14th, sn wknd, virt p.u. flat*	6	0
780	31/3	Penshurst	(L)	MDN	3m	12	GS	*mid-div, mstk 7th, prog to ld 10th-4 out, wknd*	3	10
929	8/4	Marks Tey	(L)	MDO	3m	5	G	*(fav) set steady pace, clr 15th, hdd apr last, no ext flat*	3	0

Irish Maiden winner (later disqualified); only beat one horse 96; stamina doubts; more needed. 10

LOCHNAVER b.m. 7 Lochnager - Annamanda by Tycoon II — T Long

284	2/3	Clyst St Ma'	(L)	MDN	3m	11	S	*mid-div, lost tch 10th, p.u. 12th*	P	0
528	16/3	Cothelstone	(L)	MEM	3m	8	G	*rr, in tch whn f 6th*	F	-
733	31/3	Little Wind'	(R)	MDO	3m	13	GS	*hdwy to 5th whn mstk 13th, p.u. nxt*	P	0
993	8/4	Kingston St'	(R)	MDO	3m	17	F	*some prog to 8th at 11th, nvr dang, btn 7th whn p.u. 2 out*	P	0
1349	4/5	Holnicote	(L)	MDO	3m	8	GS	*alwys abt same pl*	4	0

Last beaten 50 lengths when completing; huge improvement needed. 0

LOCH SALAND (Irish) — **I** 320^{U}

LOCKHILL(IRE) b.g. 8 Beldale Flutter (USA) - Sumintra by El Gallo — Russell G Abrey

344	3/3	Higham	(L)	MDO	3m	12	G	*sn bhnd, t.o. 15th*	4	0

Promise in 94; only managed 2 runs in 3 seasons; time passing him by. 12

LOCKLAN (Irish) — **I** 112^{P}, **I** 157^{2}, **I** 294^{P}, **I** 394^{1}

LOFTUS LAD (Irish) — **I** 3^{2}, **I** 65, , **I** 152^{4}, **I** 278^{4}, **I** 566^{2}, **I** 591^{1}, **I** 611^{2}, **I** 648^{2}

LOGICAL FUN b.g. 8 Nishapour (FR) - Thimblerigger by Sharpen Up — Mrs R Crank

664	24/3	Eaton Hall	(R)	CON	3m	15	S	*ld/disp to 14th, sn lost tch & btn, p.u. 3 out*	P	0
1193	21/4	Sandon	(L)	OPE	3m	8	G	*cls up, ld 11th-3 out, ran on onepcd, improve*	2	19
1579	19/5	Wolverhampt'	(L)	LAD	3m	9	G	*w.w. nvr nr ldrs, no dang frm 16th*	4	10

Winning hurdler; ran well at Sandon; may need strong handling; still young; Confined possible. 17

LOLLIA PAULINA (Irish) — **I** 32^{P}

LOMOND HILL (Irish) — **I** 502^{F}

LONELY CASTLE (Irish) — **I** 81^{P}, **I** 192^{F}, **I** 386^{2}

LONESOME STEP b.m. 9 Pas de Seul - Phalaborwa by Oats — A Gardner

1995 1(12),1(14),P(0),P(0)

263	2/3	Didmarton	(L)	INT	3m	18	G	*rear, t.o. 12th, p.u. 2 out*	P	0
383	9/3	Llanfrynach	(R)	CON	3m	13	GS	*mid-div, pshd algn 11th, sn wknd, t.o. 15th*	7	0
604	23/3	Howick	(L)	INT	3m	7	S	*cls up to hlfwy, wknd rpdly, p.u. 3 out*	P	0
843	6/4	Howick	(L)	MEM	3m	7	GF	*(fav) alwys 2nd/3rd, 2l down 2 out, wknd apr last, lame*	3	0

Won 2 poor races 95; problems last start; struggles in competitive races; Members best hope if fit. 13

LONESOME TRAVELLER(NZ) b.g. 7 Danzatore (CAN) - Honey Doll by Rheingold — Reg Hand
1995 2(13),2(12),1(15),F(-),2(16),3(16),2(18),**P(0)**

68 10/2 Great Treth' (R) RES 3m 14 S *ld to 3rd, drppd back, styd on agn frm 3 out* 4 13
199 24/2 Lemalla (R) RES 3m 17 HY *alwys cls up, chal 2 out, no ext* 2 19
298 2/3 Great Treth' (R) RES 3m 13 G *(Jt fav) ld 1st, ld agn 9-15th, sn outpcd* 5 11
627 23/3 Kilworthy (L) RES 3m 13 GS *mid-div, mstk 5th & rmndr, effrt 13th, nvr rchd ldrs* 5 11
805 4/4 Clyst St Ma' (L) RES 3m 7 GS *ld to 4th, sttld 3rd, prog 3 out, ld nxt, styd on* 1 17
1108 17/4 Cheltenham (L) HC 4m 1f 14 GS *alwys bhnd, mstk 14th, t.o..* 9 0
1278 27/4 Bratton Down (L) INT 3m 12 GF *ld/disp to 13th, outpcd frm 3 out* 4 19
1359 4/5 Flete Park (R) LAD 4m 5 G *chsd wnr, no imp, wknd & lost 2nd 4 out* 3 14
1625 27/5 Lifton (R) INT 3m 8 GS *ld til 4 out, onepcd clsng stgs* 3 15

Won modest Restricted; safe, stays and likes mud; needs to improve for Confineds& should do; G-Hy .. 20

LONG DRIVE (Irish) — I 139^{P}, I 148^{P}, I 247^{2}, I 332^{6}, I 472^{P}

LONGMORE (Irish) — I 257^{P}, I 493^{P}, I 538^{F}, I 598^{1}

LONGMORE BOY (Irish) — I 97^{5}, I 173^{3}, I 256^{3}, I 413^{4}, I 494^{2}

LOOKING b.g. 9 Kinglet - Chance A Look by Don't Look — P Caudwell
1995 4(10),P(0),3(10),S(-),8(0)

17 14/1 Tweseldown (R) MDN 3m 11 GS *rear, lost tch 11th, kpt on frm 15th, no dang* 5 0
129 17/2 Kingston Bl' (L) MDN 3m 15 GS *prog 12th,2nd 15th,lft in ld 3 out,wknd,nrly ref & hdd last* 3 0
432 9/3 Upton-On-Se' (R) MDO 3m 17 GS *mid-div whn f 9th* F -
526 16/3 Larkhill (R) RES 3m 9 G *prom, 2nd at 9th, sn wknd, p.u. 15th* P 0

Threw away golden chance 2nd start & will not find another 12

LOOKING AHEAD (Irish) — I 141^{P}, I 209^{6}, I 246^{5}, I 295^{4}, I 468^{3}, I 566^{3}, I 591^{3}, I 647^{3}

LOOSE WHEELS b.g. 10 Strong Gale - Kylogue Daisy by Little Buskins — Miss K Makinson
1995 8(0),5(15),2(16),3(10),U(-),7(15)

397 9/3 Garthorpe (R) MDN 3m 9 G *cls up 2nd/3rd til fdd frm 10th* 4 0
633 23/3 Market Rase' (L) LAD 3m 10 GF *nvr dang, 7th & outpcd frm 7th, ran on onepcd* 5 0
903 6/4 Dingley (R) LAD 3m 7 GS *(bl) made most, ran on gamely frm 2 out* 1 15
1099 14/4 Guilsborough (L) LAD 3m 9 G *(bl) mstks, mid-div, outpcd 14th, kpt on onepcd frm 3 out* 4 11
1377 5/5 Dingley (R) CON 3m 12 GF *(vis) ld to 3rd, prom aft til wknd 15th* 7 0
1520 12/5 Garthorpe (R) LAD 3m 8 GF *(vis) rear 5th, nvr nr to chal* 4 0
1642 2/6 Dingley (R) LAD 3m 6 GF *ld to 15th, outpcd aft 3 out* 3 14

Lost maiden tag in dire Ladies; novice ridden; safe; need same to score again. 15

LORD AMETHYST (Irish) — I 31^{P}, I 86^{P}, I 162^{P}, I 388^{5}, I 528^{4}

LORD BASIL (Irish) — I 283^{P}, I 361^{P}

LORD EGROSS (Irish) — I 502^{P}

LORD ELLERTON b.g. 8 Cree Song - Kenny by Royal Pennant — Mrs T H Regis
1995 2(11),1(13),3(17),2(15),P(0)

29 20/1 Barbury Cas' (L) RES 3m 12 GS *chsd wnr, rdn 2 out, ld last, sn hdd & no ext flat* 2 20

Vanished after good seasonal debut; stays; win Resticted if ready 97; G/F-G/S. 20

LORD HARRY (Irish) — I 208^{3}, I 307^{F}, I 548^{1}

LORDINTHESKY (Irish) — I 138^{P}, I 244^{P}, I 458^{3}, I 502^{5}, I 571^{1}

LORD JESTER b.g. 7 Jester - Morlolly by Morston (FR) — Mrs Judith Glass
1995 P(0),r(-),P(0),P(0),5(0),F(-),6(0)

123 17/2 Witton Cast' (R) MDO 3m 11 S *in tch to 8th, wknd 10th, t.o. 13th* 6 0
308 2/3 Great Stain' (L) MDO 3m 12 GS *rear, gd prog 11th, wknd rpdly 14th, p.u. 16th* P 0
406 9/3 Dalston (R) MDO 2 1/2m 12 G *sm hdwy frm rr at 12th, n.d.* 8 0
764 31/3 Great Stain' (L) MDN 3m 16 GS *tubed, rear, lost tch 5th, t.o. & p.u. 3 out* P 0

Yet to beat another horse; looks hopeless. 0

LORD KILTON ch.g. 8 Crested Lark - Kilton Jill by Adropejo — Mrs D Cowley
1995 U(-),2(12),6(0)

1241 27/4 Clifton On ' (L) MDO 3m 8 GF *ld/disp to 12th, 6th & wkng whn crashed thro wing 14th* r -
1504 11/5 Kingston Bl' (L) MDO 3m 13 G *(bl) cls up to 11th, wknd & p.u. 13th* P 0
1621 27/5 Chaddesley ' (L) MDO 3m 17 GF *(bl) prom, mstk 12th, sn btn, wll bhnd whn p.u. 3 out* P 0

2nd in bad race 95; does not stay and has no prospects. 0

LORD KNOX (Irish) — I 108, , I 161, , I 387^{6}, I 420^{4}, I 500^{P}, I 527^{P}

LORD LANDER gr.g. 5 Alfie Dickins - Ladylander by Smokey Rockett — M E Sowersby

758 31/3 Great Stain' (L) RES 3m 17 GS *rdn & lost tch 7th, p.u. aft 11th* P 0

Successful stable; only learning on debut. 0

LORD LOVING (Irish) — I 99^{1}, I 169^{5}, I 218^{P}, I 398^{2}, I 405^{P}

LORD MACDUFF b.g. 7 Dixi (BEL) - Splash by Bivouac — Mrs Lou McQueen

1995 P(0)

128	17/2	Kingston Bl'	(L)	RES	3m	14	GS	*last frm 6th, t.o. & p.u. 11th*	P	0
335	3/3	Heythrop	(R)	INT	3m	9	G	*in tch to 7th, sn wknd, p.u. 11th*	P	0

No sign of ability yet. 0

LORD O'THE RYE (Irish) — **I** 366^{F}

LORD PAT (Irish) — **I** 73, , **I** 352^{U}, **I** 440, , **I** 571, , **I** 637^{2}, **I** 645^{F}

LORD RATTLE(IRE) ch.g. 6 Orchestra - Mary Mary by Moulton — J M I Evetts

1995 P(0)

688	30/3	Chaddesley '	(L)	MDN	3m	17	G	*mid-div, 6th & outpcd apr 12th, no ch aft*	7	0
1175	20/4	Chaddesley '	(L)	MDN	3m	9	G	*cls 6th at 12th, ev ch 14th, wknd 17th, p.u. 2 out*	P	0
1434	6/5	Ashorne	(R)	MDO	3m	15	G	*alwys rear, bhnd frm 10th, t.o. & p.u. 13th*	P	0

Last when completing but shows some ability; can improve. 10

LORD RICHARD ch.g. 10 Lord Ha Ha - Orient Sun Rise by Menelek — A Howland Jackson

1995 P(0),P(0)

620	23/3	Higham	(L)	LAD	3m	9	GF	*alwys bhnd, t.o. 8th, p.u. 14th*	P	0
934	8/4	Marks Tey	(L)	CON	3m	6	G	*ld to 11th, prom to 16th, wknd rpdly aft*	4	0
1144	20/4	Higham	(L)	MEM	3m	4	F	*blnd & u.r. 2nd*	U	-
1399	6/5	Northaw	(L)	CON	3m	8	F	*ld 3rd til appr last, onepcd und press*	3	16
1547	18/5	Fakenham	(L)	HC	2m 5f 110yds	11	G	*pressed ldrs to 5th, lost pl 8th, f 10th.*	F	-

Restricted winner 93; only 7 runs since; placed in poor races; hard to find a win; G-F. 14

LORD SAMMY (Irish) — **I** 98^{P}, **I** 401^{3}, **I** 403^{P}, **I** 599^{P}

LORD VINCE (Irish) — **I** 328^{P}, **I** 642^{P}

LORENZA LAD ch.g. 10 Royal Boxer - Lady Lorenza by Lorenzaccio — N E J Cook

1995 P(0)

882	6/4	Brampton Br'	(R)	RES	3m	14	GF	*t.o. 4th, u.r. 10th*	U	-
1173	20/4	Chaddesley '	(L)	RES	3m	18	G	*blnd & u.r. 3rd*	U	-
1433	6/5	Ashorne	(R)	MDO	3m	16	G	*sn wll bhnd, t.o. & p.u. aft 12th*	P	0

Of no account 0

LOSLOMOS (Irish) — **I** 289^{P}, **I** 509^{3}

LOST FORTUNE ch.g. 13 Nearly A Hand - Opt Out by Spartan General — H W Wheeler

1995 1(24),1(24),1(24),3(19),1(22)

427	9/3	Upton-On-Se'	(R)	OPE	3m	6	GS	*(fav) 3rd at 14th, sustained run to ld apr last, ran on well*	1	22
744	31/3	Upper Sapey	(R)	OPE	3m	5	GS	*(fav) effrt to disp 3 out, sn clr, pshd out flat*	1	23

Useful pointer; won 13 of last 17; well placed; quickens; win more at 14; G-S. 25

LOSTYNDYKE (Irish) — **I** 201,

LOTHIAN MAGIC (Irish) — **I** 252^{P}

LOUGHBRICKLAND ch.g. 10 Le Bavard (FR) - Glenroid by Polaroid — Ian de Burgh Marsh

1995 4(16),8(0),**5(16)**,3(19),**7(0)**

8	14/1	Cottenham	(R)	CON	3m	10	G	*ld/disp til ld 12th, jnd 14th, grad wknd frm 3 out*	4	17
96	11/2	Ampton	(R)	XX	3m	11	GF	*(fav) chsd ldrs, strgglng 12th, no ch frm 15th, dsmntd aft fin*	7	0

Irish pointing winner; has ability but owner-ridden topoor effect; problems and finished early 96. 18

LOUGH CULLEN (Irish) — **I** 616^{P}

LOUGHDOO (Irish) — **I** 21^{P}, **I** 26^{4}, **I** 89^{3}, **I** 111^{4}, **I** 180^{3}, **I** 260^{1}, **I** 537, , **I** 597^{P}, **I** 629^{4}, **I** 648, , **I** 658^{3}

LOUGHLINS PRIDE (Irish) — **I** 83^{F}, **I** 142^{P}, **I** 290^{P}, **I** 379^{P}, **I** 499^{1}

LOUGHLINSTOWN BOY b.g. 11 Ela-Mana-Mou - Tante Yvonne by Crowned Prince (USA) — J A Riddell

1995 4(0),U(-),**6(10),2(28),4(14),5(13),2(25),2(25),1 1(0)**

46	4/2	Alnwick	(L)	MEM	3m	7	G	*ld to 7th, grad wknd frm 10th*	5	0
83	11/2	Alnwick	(L)	CON	3m	10	GS	*prom til grad wknd frm 13th*	6	0
259	1/3	Kelso	(L)	HC	3m 1f	8	GS	*soon lost tch, t.o. when p.u. before 13th.*	P	0
487	16/3	Newcastle	(L)	HC	3m	10	GS	*ld to 4th, prom, blnd 8th, struggling when p.u. before 13th.*	P	0
790	1/4	Kelso	(L)	HC	3m 1f	11	GF	*chsd ldrs till p.u. before 12th.*	P	0
857	6/4	Alnwick	(L)	MEM	3m	4	GF	*ld/disp til 15th, styd on, unchall*	1	20
1085	14/4	Friars Haugh	(L)	OPE	3m	6	F	*sn ld, drew wll clr frm 2 out*	1	21
1354	4/5	Mosshouses	(L)	OPE	3m	4	GS	*made most to 9th, 3rd & outpcd 15th, eased whn no ch 2 out*	3	13
1475	11/5	Aspatria	(L)	CON	3m	6	GF	*(fav) j.w., ld 6th til apr last, gd jmp to ld agn, ran on*	1	19
1570	19/5	Corbridge	(R)	CON	3m	8	G	*(Jt fav) made most, styd on wll flat*	1	19
1631	1/6	Stratford	(L)	HC	3 1/2m	14	GF	*mid div, lost pl 11th, no dngr after.*	7	20

Slow to reach peak; consistent when doing so; best with strong handling; win more; F-G/S. 20

LOUGH TULLY (Irish) — I 318^{1}

LOUIS DE PALMER (Irish) — I 131^{P}, I 162^{P}, I 197^{F}, I 346, , I 388, , I 421^{4}, I 527, , I 581^{2}

LOUIS FARRELL br.g. 11 Furry Glen - Brave Light by Brave Invader (USA) J G Narduzzo
1995 1(13),**3(13),P(0)**

156	17/2	Erw Lon	(L)	RES	3m	13	G	*alwys rear, p.u. 13th*	P	0
428	9/3	Upton-On-Se'	(R)	RES	3m	17	GS	*clr ldr frm 10th til wknd apr 2 out*	7	0
599	23/3	Howick	(L)	RES	3m	7	S	*mostly 3rd, cls 2nd 11th, wknd 14th, poor 3rd aft*	3	0
844	6/4	Howick	(L)	RES	3m	10	GF	*2nd til ld 8-10th, disp 14th, outpcd frm 3 out*	2	10
1038	13/4	St Hilary	(R)	RES	3m	15	G	*cls 2nd til lft clr apr 12th, hdd 15th, wknd*	4	0

Hard puller; does not really stay and struggling now upgraded; win at 12 unlikely. 14

LOUIS FOURTEEN (Irish) — I 109^{F}, I 516^{4}, I 582^{3}, I 607^{2}

LOUNGING gr.m. 7 Pragmatic - Deep Coach by Deep Run Miss V J Peet
1995 **10(NH)**

82	11/2	Alnwick	(L)	MEM	3m	4	GS	*last, effrt 12th, outpcd frm nxt, t.o.*	4	0
322	2/3	Corbridge	(R)	MDN	3m	10	GS	*prom, disp 8th, ev ch 2 out, outpcd apr last*	2	12
407	9/3	Dalston	(R)	MDO	2 1/2m	13	G	*t.o. 6th, sm hdwy 11th, nvr nr*	6	0
613	23/3	Friars Haugh	(L)	MDN	3m	15	G	*alwys same pl*	5	10

Placed in a poor race; safe but slow and more needed. 12

LOVABLE OUTLAW (Irish) — I 193^{P}, I 224^{P}, I 343, , I 421^{1}, I 498^{1}

LOVEABLE LADY (Irish) — I 533^{P}, I 622^{F}, I 631^{P}

LOVE ACTINIUM (Irish) — I 9^{P}, I 42^{F}, I 60^{U}, I 64^{6}, I 120^{P}, I 151^{P}, I 203^{U}, I 253^{2}, I 290^{1}

LOVELY CITIZEN (Irish) — I 10^{5}, I 58^{P}, I 123^{3}, I 140, , I 184^{P}, I 378^{P}

LOVELY CLONMOYLE(IRE) b.m. 8 Mister Lord (USA) - Arctic Jungle by Arctic Slave Mrs Beryl Lockey

934	8/4	Marks Tey	(L)	CON	3m	6	G	*(bl) wth ldrs til lost plc 6th, bhnd whn p.u. aft 11th*	P	0
1068	13/4	Horseheath	(R)	INT	3m	7	F	*rear, lst tch 12th, t.o. & p.u. 14th*	P	0
1321	28/4	Fakenham P-'	(L)	CON	3m	5	G	*chsd ldr to 3rd, last frm 11th, t.o.*	5	0
1594	25/5	Garthorpe	(R)	MEM	3m	10	G	*4th/5th for 2m, 6th & outpcd 5 out, p.u. 2 out*	P	0

Won 3 Irish points 93; shows no interest now and best avoided. 0

LOVE ON THE ROCKS b.m. 11 Martinmas - Love Is Blind (USA) by Hasty Road Mrs Vanessa Stratton
1995 P(0),7(0),5(0),U(-),4(0),5(12),5(0),4(10)

161	17/2	Weston Park	(L)	LAD	3m	11	G	*mid-div, fdd, p.u. 4 out*	P	0

Won poor Ladies 94; does not stay & most unlikely to win again. 0

LOYAL GAIT(NZ) ch.g. 8 Gaiter (NZ) - Lotsydamus (NZ) by Auk (USA) A M Darlington

1182	21/4	Mollington	(R)	MDN	3m	10	F	*tubed, ld 2nd, made rest, wll clr 3 out, unchal*	1	16
1464	11/5	Warwick	(L)	HC	3 1/4m	6	F	*(fav) trckd ldrs, f 9th.*	F	-

Ex novice hurdler; easy winner of poor Maiden; hard to assess; may find weak Restricted; Firm. 16

LOYAL NOTE ch.g. 8 Royal Vulcan - Maynote by Maystreak R Andrews
1995 1(21),2(21),1(25),1(22)

102	17/2	Marks Tey	(L)	CON	3m	17	G	*in tch, 8th hlfwy,5th & wll btn 16th*	7	14
480	11/3	Plumpton	(L)	HC	3m 1f 110yds	6	GS	*j.w, ld 2nd till 10th, led 14th, clr apr last.*	1	22
671	28/3	Taunton	(R)	HC	3m	13	S	*(fav) ld to 3rd, regained ld 5th, hdd 7th, wknd 13th.*	5	14
932	8/4	Marks Tey	(L)	OPE	3m	3	G	*(fav) ld, jnd 13th, f nxt*	F	-

Won poor H/chase; stays well; can win Opens no problem in 97; G-S. 25

LUCAS COURT b.g. 10 Henbit (USA) - Boudoir by Klairon Mrs M Rigg

1375	4/5	Peper Harow	(L)	CON	3m	9	F	*bhnd til p.u. aft 6th*	P	0
1503	11/5	Kingston Bl'	(L)	OPE	3m	3	G	*chsd wnr 5th, 4l down 15th, btn nxt*	2	10

Won 2 mile novice chase 91; beaten in poor 3 runner Open; makes no appeal as future winner. 10

LUCIANO THE YUPPI (Irish) — I 8^{P}, I 68^{P}, I 70^{P}, I 155^{P}, I 244^{P}, I 312^{P}, I 358^{P}, I 462^{P}, I 551^{5}, I 589^{4}, I 608, , I 647,

LUCK MONEY b.g. 10 Gleason (USA) - Candy Princess by Candy Cane Miss C Holliday

11	14/1	Cottenham	(R)	LAD	3m	7	G	*chsd clr ldrs, clsd 9th, 2nd apr 3 out, sn outpcd*	3	15
250	25/2	Charing	(L)	LAD	3m	12	GS	*handy, ld aft 3 out til last, not qckn*	2	18
452	9/3	Charing	(L)	LAD	3m	8	G	*mstk 2nd, chsd ldrs frm 12th, 3rd whn pckd 3 out, no ch aft*	4	15

Ladies winner 91; lightly raced and disappointing since; may find weak Ladies in 97. 17

LUCKY CALL(NZ) b.g. 5 Lucky Ring - Afrea (NZ) by Imposing (AUS) D H Barons

301	2/3	Great Treth'	(R)	MDO	3m	13	G	*bhnd til ran on steadily clsng stgs, do better*	4	0
556	17/3	Ottery St M'	(L)	MDO	3m	15	G	*cls up til f 10th*	F	-

1279	27/4	Bratton Down	(L)	MDO	3m	14	GF	*handy, 3rd at 12th, disp 3 out til hdd last 100 yrds*	2	13

Improving youngster; just collared last start; should soon be winning in 97. 15

LUCKY CHRISTOPHER b.g. 11 St Columbus - Lucky Story by Lucky Sovereign — G B Tarry

1995 2(17),3(19),1(19),1(22),1(22),1(24),1(25),1(25),2(21),1(0)

125	17/2	Kingston Bl'	(L)	OPE	3m	10	GS	*hld up,outpcd 13th,effrt nxt,not rch ldrs,3rd 2 out,p.u.last*	P	0
312	2/3	Ampton	(R)	OPE	3m	6	G	*in tch,rdn to chal 3 out,unable to qkn,hld whn slw jmp last*	2	25
369	7/3	Towcester	(R)	HC	3m 1f	6	G	*chsd wnr from 14th till wknd apr last.*	3	20
490	16/3	Horseheath	(R)	XX	3m	7	GF	*(fav) trckd ldrs, 2nd 4 out, chal nxt, ld aft 2 out, rdn out*	1	24
662	24/3	Eaton Hall	(R)	OPE	3m	10	S	*(fav) w.w. mid-div, clsd 13th, ran on und pres 4 out, tk 2nd flat*	2	20
1017	13/4	Kingston Bl'	(L)	OPE	3m	4	G	*(fav) cls up, chsd ldr 13th, chal 2 out, ld last, rdn out*	1	24
1237	27/4	Clifton On '	(L)	OPE	3m	5	GF	*(fav) mstk 1st, cls up, ld 12th, drvn clr 2 out, ran on well*	1	22
1457	8/5	Uttoxeter	(L)	HC	3 1/4m	16	G	*(fav) prom, blnd 16th, ld 3 out, clr last, eased cl home.*	1	25
1598	25/5	Garthorpe	(R)	OPE	3m	6	G	*(fav) w.w. 2nd 6 out, ld 3 out, drew away und pres apr last*	1	28
1643	2/6	Dingley	(R)	OPE	3m	13	GF	*(fav) w.w., prog 11th, left 2nd 14th, ld 2 out, sn clr, impressv*	1	30

Very useful; won 13 of last 18; consistent, stays and can quicken; sure to win more; G/F-S. 27

LUCKY CREST ch.m. 9 Crested Lark - Lucky Sandy by St Columbus — Mrs N A Hedges

440	9/3	Newton Brom'	(R)	MDN	3m	10	GS	*cls up, fdd & p.u. 14th*	P	0
1103	14/4	Guilsborough	(L)	MDN	3m	15	G	*blnd badly 6th, wll bhnd hlfwy, t.o. & p.u. 15th*	P	0
1293	28/4	Barbury Cas'	(L)	MDO	3m	11	F	*n.j.w. in tch to 9th, t.o. frm 11th*	4	0

Missed 95; jumps poorly and tailed off when completing. 10

LUCKY DOMINO b.g. 6 Primo Dominie - Ruff's Luck (USA) by Ruffinal (USA) — D J Clapham

1224	24/4	Brampton Br'	(R)	MDO	3m	17	G	*rr frm 6th, lost tch 13th, p.u. 3 out*	P	0

No signs on debut. 0

LUCKY HERO (Irish) — **I** 526^{2}

LUCKY HOPE (Irish) — **I** 30^{P}, **I** 56^{1}

LUCKY OLE SON b.g. 9 Old Lucky - Drake's Beauty by Captain Drake — David Brace

1995 3(0),P(0),**F(-)**,P(0),7(0),2(0),1(0),2(15),3(11)

43	3/2	Wadebridge	(L)	INT	3m	5	GF	*ld to 11th, outpcd, rlld 15th, ev ch last, kept on*	2	20
157	17/2	Erw Lon	(L)	CON	3m	15	G	*(fav) rear, prog frm 13th, fin well, nvr nrr*	4	13
385	9/3	Llanfrynach	(R)	LAD	3m	14	GS	*s.s. alwys t.o. & mls bhnd*	8	0
508	16/3	Magor	(R)	INT	3m	5	GS	*(Jt fav) cls 3rd til went 2nd 12th, ld 15th, qcknd away*	1	18
603	23/3	Howick	(L)	LAD	3m	8	S	*last, lft remote 4th by dfctns 3 out*	4	0
766	31/3	Pantyderi	(R)	CON	3m	6	G	*alwys prom, ran on frm last, just hld*	2	18
847	6/4	Howick	(L)	LAD	3m	9	GF	*hld up,prog to 3rd at 14th, 15l 2nd nxt, clsd to ld apr last*	1	19
1035	13/4	St Hilary	(R)	CON	3m	10	G	*hld up, prog to 5l 4th 3 out, ran on apr last, jnd ldr line*	1	18
1158	20/4	Llanwit Maj'	(R)	OPE	4m	9	GS	*(fav) held up bhnd, rdn & no resp 20th, t.o. & p.u. 2 out*	P	0
1202	21/4	Lydstep	(L)	LAD	3m	4	S	*nvr nrr than 4th*	4	0
1262	27/4	Pyle	(R)	MEM	3m	6	G	*ld to 5th, cls up til wknd 13th, t.o. & u.r. 2 out*	U	-
1385	6/5	Pantyderi	(R)	CON	3m	6	GF	*sttld 5th, prog 15th, hrd rdn 2 out, onepcd aft*	3	16
1487	11/5	Erw Lon	(L)	CON	3m	4	F	*nvr nrr then dist 3rd*	3	0
1558	18/5	Bassaleg	(R)	CON	3m	6	F	*sn t.o. in last, mstk 3rd, p.u. 15th*	P	0

Busy in 96; moody; goes best for Pip Jones; wins modest races; can win again; G/S-F. 16

LUCKY ROSS (Irish) — **I** 248^{3}, **I** 289^{P}

LUCKY THURSDAY b.g. 6 Sousa - Horwood Spirit by Sir Lark — A W Congdon

1279	27/4	Bratton Down	(L)	MDO	3m	14	GF	*rear, blnd & u.r. 2nd*	U	-
1430	6/5	High Bickin'	(R)	MDO	3m	8	G	*bhnd & jmp novcy til p.u. apr 15th*	P	0
1494	11/5	Holnicote	(L)	MDO	3m	8	G	*not fluent, hndy til outpcd 16th, no ch clsng stgs*	3	0
1646	8/6	Umberleigh	(L)	MEM	3m	4	GF	*(fav) ld 7-11th & frm 15th, clr 2 out, rdn out*	1	10

Won poor and slowly run Members; not fluent and much more needed for Restricted.G-F. 11

LUCKY TOWN (Irish) — **I** 323^{1}

LUDERMAIN ch.m. 11 Oats - Peacock Vain by Shiny Tenth — Mrs C Dix

1995 2(0)

390	9/3	Llanfrynach	(R)	MDN	3m	13	GS	*in tch to 10th, wknd, p.u. 13th*	P	0
607	23/3	Howick	(L)	MDN	3m	12	S	*mod 5th whn f 13th*	F	-

Lightly raced and looks past it now. 10

LUDOVICIANA b.m. 7 Oats - Crafty Look by Don't Look — G W Paul

1995 **6(NH),8(NH),P(NH)**

34	20/1	Higham	(L)	MDN	3m	11	GF	*set fast pace to 15th,lft in ld last, sn hdd,rlld gmly flat*	2	16

Ex novice hurdler; not seen after gutsy debut (beaten by good horse); sure to win if fit in 97. 16

LUKE'S THE BIZZ(IRE) br.g. 8 Ovac (ITY) - Precision Chopper by Menelek — E R Hughes

461	9/3	Eyton-On-Se'	(L)	RES	3m	15	G	*cls up, ld 7th-13th, sn btn, p.u. 2 out*	P	0

579 20/3 Ludlow (R) HC 2 1/2m 17 G *prom to 10th, bhnd when p.u. before 5 out.* P 0
1227 26/4 Ludlow (R) HC 2 1/2m 16 G *n.j.w., ld to 11th, wknd 5 out, bhnd when f 2 out, dead.* F -

Dead. 10

LUMBERJACK(USA) b.g. 12 Big Spruce (USA) - Snip by Shantung — Tony Hill
1995 **7(NH)**
257 29/2 Nottingham (L) HC 2 1/2m 11 G *(bl) settld in tch, effort after one cct, struggling before 6 out, no ch when blnd and u.r. 3 out.* U -
1120 20/4 Bangor (L) HC 2 1/2m 110yds 13 S *(bl) trckd ldrs, no ch with front 2 from 4 out.* 3 14

Formerly useful chaser; does not stay 3 miles and will not win H/chase. 18

LUNAR APPROACH (Irish) — **I** 63^{P}, **I** 240^{2}, **I** 354^{5}, **I** 521^{F}

LUNAR LUNACY(IRE) b.m. 8 Ahonoora - Flinging Star (USA) by Northern Fling (USA) — Harry Hobson
34 20/1 Higham (L) MDN 3m 11 GF *disp ld whn u.r. 3rd* U -

Not seen after debut; unpromising. 0

LURRIGA GLITTER (Irish) — **I** 473^{4}, **I** 542^{F}, **I** 606^{4}, **I** 648, , **I** 659^{2}

LUSMAGH RIVER (Irish) — **I** 85^{F}, **I** 120^{F}, **I** 149^{2}, **I** 211^{1}

LUTHIER GIRL (Irish) — **I** 223^{F}, **I** 385^{4}, **I** 521^{U}, **I** 532^{P}

LUVLY BUBBLY b.g. 8 Carlingford Castle - Mill Shine by Milan — Miss Carolyn Hall
754 31/3 Lockerbie (R) RES 3m 8 G *2nd whn f 3rd* F -
858 6/4 Alnwick (L) RES 3m 7 GF *not fluent, 4th hlfwy, wll bhnd whn p.u. 3 out* P -
1088 14/4 Friars Haugh (L) MDO 3m 10 F *5th hlfwy, styd on frm 4 out, no ch wth wnr* 2 10

Beaten 20l in poor Maiden; should go closer in 97 12

LYDEBROOK b.g. 7 Scallywag - Bahama by Bali Dancer — John R Wilson
463 9/3 Eyton-On-Se' (L) MDN 2 1/2m 14 G *chsng grp, ld 9th-3 out, 2l 2nd whn slppd & u.r. last* U -
1033 13/4 Alpraham (R) MDO 2 1/2m 15 GS *(fav) ld sn 10l clr, u.r. flat several strides aft 4th* U -
1196 21/4 Sandon (L) MDN 3m 17 G *(fav) ld til wknd & hdd 5 out, onepcd* 4 0

Missed 95; only beaten one other finisher so far & needs more stamina 10

LYFORD CAY(IRE) ch.g. 6 Waajib - Island Goddess by Godswalk (USA) — R Bewley
1995 P(0),6(13),2(18)
317 2/3 Corbridge (R) CON 3m 11 GS *mstks, last at 3rd, lost tch 8th, wll bhnd whn f 14th* F -

Flat winner 92; lightly raced now & not one to trust 13

LYNINGO ch.g. 9 Rustingo - Lyns Legend by Marengo — Mrs M J Ward
1995 P(0),P(0),2(0),5(0)
516 16/3 Dalton Park (R) MDO 3m 11 G *prom, 3rd whn f 9th* F -
757 31/3 Great Stain' (L) MEM 3m 5 GS *ld til 3 out, sn rdn, kpt on well cls home* 2 15
986 8/4 Charm Park (L) MDN 3m 10 GF *ld 3rd-8th, disp 12th-3 out, ld nxt, drew clr comf* 1 15
1284 27/4 Easingwold (L) RES 3m 14 G *mid-div, nvr a dang* 6 10
1447 6/5 Witton Cast' (R) RES 3m 11 G *cls up, outpcd 14th, made slght hdwy frm 2 out* 5 12
1571 19/5 Corbridge (R) RES 3m 13 G *alwys mid-div, nvr able to chal* 5 13

Improved 96; won poor Maiden; struggling in Restrictgeds but safe enough now & may strike lucky 15

LYNX MARINE (Irish) — **I** 283^{R}

MABOY LADY 9 — S W Reddaway
1995 **F(NH)**
197 24/2 Lemalla (R) LAD 3m 13 HY *ran wd aft 2nd, bhnd whn p.u. 4 out* P 0
1128 20/4 Stafford Cr' (R) RES 3m 17 S *rear whn f 4th* F -
1277 27/4 Bratton Down (L) CON 3m 15 GF *rear whn blnd & u.r. 5th* U -
1358 4/5 Flete Park (R) RES 3m 8 G *keen hld, ld early & agn brfly 10th, rear nxt, blnd last* 5 10
1622 27/5 Lifton (R) CON 3m 14 GS *11th hlfwy, nrst fin* 6 13

Irish Maiden winner; not disgraced last start but more needed for Restricted hopes 13

MACAABEE SPECIAL(IRE) ch.g. 8 Orchestra - Lady Machree by Octavo (USA) — Miss A Meakins
215 24/2 Newtown (L) OPE 3m 20 GS *t.o. & p.u. 7th* P 0
351 3/3 Garnons (L) OPE 3m 14 GS *t.o. 7th, p.u. 10th* P 0
386 9/3 Llanfrynach (R) RES 3m 10 GS *bhnd frm 5th, poor 6th whn f 10th* F -
510 16/3 Magor (R) MDN 3m 9 GS *mid-div, lost tch frm 15th* 6 0
975 8/4 Lydstep (L) MDO 3m 9 G *rear, p.u. 5th* P 0

Tailed off last on only completion 0

MACCARRONS RUN (Irish) — **I** 96^{3}, **I** 259^{4}

MAC-DUAGH (Irish) — **I** 327, , **I** 465^{P}, **I** 543^{2}, **I** 607^{F}, **I** 635^{2}

MACKABEE(IRE) b or br.g. 7 Supreme Leader - Donegal Queen by Quayside — P B Williams

1995 **P(NH),5(NH),13(NH)**

147	17/2	Erw Lon	(L)	MDN 3m	8	G	*t.o. 6th, fin own time*	4	0
382	9/3	Llanfrynach	(R)	MEM 3m	7	GS	*trckd ldrs, mstks 2nd & 15th, rdn to ld last, jnd fin*	1	15
548	17/3	Erw Lon	(L)	RES 3m	8	GS	*nvr nrr than mid-div, f 11th*	F	-
882	6/4	Brampton Br'	(R)	RES 3m	14	GF	*trckd ldrs, effrt 16th, lft in ld 3 out, jnd last, no ext*	2	16
1222	24/4	Brampton Br'	(R)	RES 3m	11	G	*prog frm rr 8th, ev ch 12th, not qckn frm 15th*	4	14
1482	11/5	Bredwardine	(R)	RES 3m	13	G	*mid-div whn s.u. bnd bef 6th*	S	-

Disappointing under Rules; did well to win Members but Restricted hopes not looking good; G/S 15

MACKEN MONEY (Irish) — **I** 456^{P}

MACKLETTE (Irish) — **I** 211^{P}, **I** 459^{P}, **I** 507^{2}

MACKS MOSS (Irish) — **I** 459^{B}

MAC'S BOY b.g. 7 Macmillion - Tender Manx by Owen Dudley — Julian P Allen

1995 **11(NH)**

2	13/1	Larkhill	(R)	MDO 3m	17	GS	*mid-div, 7th & lost tch 13th, running on whn p.u. 15th*	P	0
70	10/2	Great Treth'	(R)	MDO 3m	14	S	*(fav) 6s-6/4, mid-div, prog to ld 15th, drew clr aft*	1	15
219	24/2	Newtown	(L)	RES 3m	17	GS	*trckd ldrs going wll, lft in ld 12th, hdd & wknd apr 2 out*	3	17
388	9/3	Llanfrynach	(R)	RES 3m	20	GS	*(fav) w.w. out of tch, kpt on frm 14th, nvr any dang*	5	0
549	17/3	Erw Lon	(L)	RES 3m	11	GS	*mid-div, p.u. 14th*	P	0
1528	12/5	Ottery St M'	(L)	RES 3m	10	GF	*(fav) not alwys fluent, tried to make all, clr whn blnd & u.r.3out*	U	-
1629	30/5	Uttoxeter	(L)	HC 2m 5f	13	GS	*mid div when f 5th.*	F	-

Landed punt after gentle debut; unlucky penultimate start & should find Restricted; mistakes; G/F-S ... 18

MAC'S LEGEND (Irish) — **I** 332^{3}

MADAGANS GREY gr.g. 8 Carwhite - Cheri Berry by Air Trooper — Mrs Jane Kennedy

1995 P(0)

177	18/2	Horseheath	(R)	CON 3m	8	G	*rear, effrt to chs ldrs 13th, p.u. aft nxt, lame*	P	0

Flat winner; only two runs 95-6 & problems; can only be watched 0

MADAM ASIDE (Irish) — **I** 238^{P}

MADAME BECK b.m. 7 Meadowbrook - My Mimosa by Cagirama — R Michael Smith

114	17/2	Lanark	(R)	MDO 3m	12	GS	*cls up frm 11th, losing tch whn f 2 out*	F	-
503	16/3	Lanark	(R)	MDO 3m	10	G	*sn bhnd, p.u. 11th*	P	0
905	8/4	Carlisle	(R)	HC 3 1/4m	5	F	*held up in rear when f 6th, rmt and t.o. after.*	4	0
1253	27/4	Balcormo Ma'	(R)	MDO 3m	16	GS	*alwys hndy, ev ch til no ext frm 2 out*	4	13
1355	4/5	Mosshouses	(L)	MDO 3m	10	GS	*cls up, mstk 12th, chsd wnr 2 out, unable qckn last*	2	13
1476	11/5	Aspatria	(L)	MDO 3m	16	GF	*tubed, chsd ldrs til blnd & u.r. 7th*	U	-
1542	16/5	Perth	(R)	HC 2 1/2m 110yds	8	F	*tubed, not fluent, lost tch after 8th, last when blnd and u.r. 10th.*	U	-

Placed on long tracks but makes mistakes & a win still hard to find 14

MADE OF TALENT br.m. 7 Supreme Leader - Cedor's Daughter by Pallard Court — E H Crow

1995 P(13),1(15),P(0)

665	24/3	Eaton Hall	(R)	RES 3m	14	S	*(fav) w.w. in rear, prog to prss wnr 4 out, onepcd & hld last*	2	16
856	6/4	Sandon	(L)	RES 3m	9	GF	*(fav) ld to 2nd,restrain in rear 4th,rpd hdwy to cls whn f2 out*	F	-
1368	4/5	Gisburn	(R)	RES 3m	9	G	*bhnd, prog 14th, 3rd nxt, rdn & styd on onepcd*	2	16

Maiden winner 95; not progressed & disappointing; may need more enterprise; G/F-S 16

MADIYAN(USA) ch.g. 7 Sharastani (USA) - Meadow Glen Lady (USA) by Believe It (USA) — Peter Scott

1995 P(0),P(0)

706	30/3	Barbury Cas'	(L)	MEM 3m	7	G	*in tch to 14th, onepcd frm nxt*	3	12
960	8/4	Lockinge	(L)	RES 3m	9	GF	*hndy, 4th 10th, outpcd frm 4 out*	3	12
1139	20/4	Flete Park	(R)	RES 3m	14	S	*5th hlfwy, in tch to 14th, no ch clsng stgs*	4	12
1278	27/4	Bratton Down	(L)	INT 3m	12	GF	*rear, some prog 14th, outpcd frm 3 out*	6	12

Won poor Maiden 94; modest & outclassed in better company 12

MAESGWYN BACH b.m. 8 Leading Man - Fairlina by Quality Fair — Miss Jane Powis

1995 U(-)

287	2/3	Eaton Hall	(R)	MDO 3m	11	G	*prom to 13th, losing tch whn p.u. 3 out*	P	0
666	24/3	Eaton Hall	(R)	RES 3m	13	S	*mid to rear, no ch whn p.u. 5 out*	P	0
1225	24/4	Brampton Br'	(R)	MDO 3m	18	G	*nvr rch ldrs, lost tch 14th, p.u. 16th*	P	0

No signs of ability 0

MAES GWYN DREAMER b.g. 6 Dreams To Reality (USA) - Fairlina by Quality Fair — Ms M Teague

661	24/3	Eaton Hall	(R)	MDN 3m	9	S	*prom to 6th, wknd rpdly, p.u. 8th*	P	0
882	6/4	Brampton Br'	(R)	RES 3m	14	GF	*t.o. 3rd, p.u. 12th*	P	0
1224	24/4	Brampton Br'	(R)	MDO 3m	17	G	*prom, fair 6th whn f 14th*	F	-
1418	6/5	Eyton-On-Se'	(L)	MEM 3m	7	GF	*prom early, lost tch 6th, t.o. 5 out, p.u. 2 out*	P	0

A glimmer of hope 3rd start but stamina looks major problem 0

MAGGIES FELLOW(IRE) ch.g. 7 Decent Fellow - Gentle Maggie by Tarqogan — John Eaton

689 30/3 Chaddesley ' (L) MDN 3m 15 G *in tch, disp 12th, ld 3 out, clr nxt, rdn out* 1 16

Only 2 runs 94-6; beat subsequent winners when scoring; Restricted likely if fit 97 17

MAGICAL APPROACH (Irish) — I 516²

MAGICAL CRUISE b.m. 6 Cruise Missile - Magic Coin by Damsire Unregistered — Mrs R W Hall

267 2/3 Didmarton (L) MDN 3m 11 G *mstks, wll bhnd frm 6th, t.o. & p.u. 13th* P 0
520 16/3 Larkhill (R) MDO 3m 11 G *mid-div whn f 8th* F -

No signs of ability 0

MAGICAL MORRIS ch.g. 14 Balinger - River Spell by Spartan General — Mrs D M Grissell

1995 1(19),2(21),3(18),4(18),**4(18)**

250 25/2 Charing (L) LAD 3m 12 GS *wll in rear, steady prog frm 12th, styd on well frm 2 out* 4 17
452 9/3 Charing (L) LAD 3m 8 G *rear, prog final cct, 4th 3 out, kpt on* 3 17
777 31/3 Penshurst (L) LAD 3m 7 GS *alwys rear, styd on, nvr nrr* 4 17
1208 21/4 Heathfield (R) LAD 3m 6 F *alwys prom, 5th 4 out, chal 2 out, styd on wll to ld flat* 1 16
1373 4/5 Peper Harow (L) LAD 3m 3 F *(fav) chsd ldr, clsd appr 13th, ld appr 3 out, clr nxt, easy* 1 16
1443 6/5 Aldington (L) LAD 3m 4 HD *last & detached, ran on frm 12th, nvr dang, eased flat, lame* 3 10

Consistent but onepaced; novie ridden; found weak Ladies races; similar if fit at 15; F-Hy 16

MAGIC CALLER (Irish) — I 236ᴾ, I 635ᴾ, I 652ᴾ

MAGIC FOUNTAIN(IRE) b.m. 8 Royal Fountain - Magic Money by Even Money — Mrs Caroline Allen

1995 P(0)

107 17/2 Marks Tey (L) MDN 3m 15 G *alwys bhnd last whn p.u. 12th* P 0

No sign of ability 0

MAGIC RIPPLE b.m. 8 Current Magic - Splash by Bivouac — Mrs H Jones

767 31/3 Pantyderi (R) INT 3m 7 G *in rear, mstk 13th, p.u. nxt* P 0
974 8/4 Lydstep (L) MEM 3m 10 G *1st ride, mid-div, u.r. 4th* U -
1200 21/4 Lydstep (L) MDN 3m 10 S *nvr nrr than 8th, p.u. 14th* P 0

Looks unpromising 0

MAGIC SONG b.m. 8 Cree Song - Magic Chat by Le Bavard (FR) — R W Swiers

590 23/3 Wetherby Po' (L) MDO 3m 16 S *mid-div, ran out 9th* r -
763 31/3 Great Stain' (L) MDN 3m 11 GS *mid-div, mstk 4th, prom hlfwy, no prog aft, tk 3rd nr fin* 3 0
986 8/4 Charm Park (L) MDN 3m 10 GF *rear early, 7th 9th, p.u. 3 out* P 0

Well beaten when placed; much more needed 0

MAGNETIC IMAGE (Irish) — I 347ᴾ, I 385ᶠ

MAGNETIC REEL ch.g. 5 Scottish Reel - Miss Magnetism by Baptism — Mrs E A Webber

151 17/2 Erw Lon (L) MDN 3m 8 G *alwys chsng wnr, clsd 2 out, alwys hld* 2 14
1390 6/5 Pantyderi (R) MDO 3m 15 GF *(fav) ld/disp, hdd brfly aft 2 out, drvn out flat* 1 14
1557 18/5 Bassaleg (R) RES 3m 14 F *(fav) prom, ld 4th-12th, chsd wnr aft, rdn & btn 3 out* 3 10

Won modest race; well beaten after; good stable & may improve; may prefer easy 3m; G/F 15

MAGNOLIA MAN b.g. 10 Red Man - Roman Candy by Roman Candle — Mrs D B Lunt

1995 1(19),**2(21)**,**U(-)**,3(0),1(19),**5(0)**,1(20)

43 3/2 Wadebridge (L) INT 3m 5 GF *(fav) prom, clse 3rd whn slppd & f 14th* F -
134 17/2 Ottery St M' (L) CON 3m 12 GS *hld up, prog 13th, disp 4 out, ev ch last, just got up* 1 20
444 9/3 Haldon (R) OPE 3m 5 S *(fav) j.w. disp frm 11th, ld aft 13th, drew clr 3 out, imprssv* 1 23
717 30/3 Wadebridge (L) OPE 3m 3 GF *(fav) hld up in tch, effrt & hmpd 15th, unable qckn clsng stgs* 2 17
927 8/4 Bishopsleigh (R) OPE 3m 7 G *(fav) alwys frnt rank til clr 11th, no ext frm 3 out* 2 17
1109 17/4 Hockworthy (L) MEM 3m 4 GS *(fav) w.w., tckd wnr 12th, mstk 14th, ev ch whn f 2 out* F 16
1140 20/4 Flete Park (R) OPE 4m 6 S *hld up, prog to 3rd 3 out, ev ch til wknd nxt* 3 18
1425 6/5 High Bickin' (R) OPE 3m 4 G *held up, jmp lft, ev ch 14th, wknd, no ch whn lft 2nd last* 2 17
1529 12/5 Ottery St M' (L) OPE 3m 7 GF *alwys last & nvr going wll, p.u. 13th* P 0
1589 25/5 Mounsey Hil' (R) OPE 3m 12 G *mid-div, blnd 8th, no ch 13th, p.u. 17th* P 0

Consistent & tough; best early season & L/H; win Opens 97; dislikes Hockworthy; Soft 22

MAGNUM BULLUM (Irish) — I 347ᴾ, I 384¹

MAGNUS PYM b.g. 11 Al Nasr (FR) - Full Of Reason (USA) by Bold Reason (USA) — Tony Millard

1995 P(0),3(0),6(0),7(0),P(0)

356 3/3 Garnons (L) LAD 3m 12 GS *prom to 3rd, outpcd frm 6th, t.o. & p.u. aft 12th* P 0
383 9/3 Llanfrynach (R) CON 3m 13 GS *prom til lost plc & u.r. 7th* U -
843 6/4 Howick (L) MEM 3m 7 GF *alwys rear, no ch hlfwy, poor 5th whn p.u. flat* P 0
1035 13/4 St Hilary (R) CON 3m 10 G *(bl) ld 6th-12th, wknd rpdly, p.u. 14th* P 0

No longer of any account 0

MAGS SUPER TOI (Irish) — I 8[P], I 71[5], I 118[P], I 531[3], I 614[1], I 658[1]

MAHANA b.g. 12 Tepukei - Easby Saint by Saintly Song — D J Coates

72	11/2	Wetherby Po'	(L)	CON	3m	18	GS	*mid-div, prog 12th, tk 2nd 14th, chsd wnr*	2	20
304	2/3	Great Stain'	(L)	OPE	3m	10	GS	*rear, prog 15th, styd on wll 2 out, 2l 2nd last, ld cls hm*	1	20
410	9/3	Charm Park	(L)	OPE	3m	17	G	*mid-div, 3rd 4 out, styd on one-pcd*	4	16

Missed 95; did well to win at 12 but finished early & may struggle if back at 13; G/S-F 18

MAHANKHALI (Irish) — I 112[5], I 166[6], I 237[P], I 341[4], I 395[2], I 563[4], I 579[P]

MAHON RIVER (Irish) — I 66[2], I 91[4], I 135[P], I 187[P], I 327[4], I 523[6]

MAID O'TULLY (Irish) — I 95[F], I 258[P], I 535[U]

MAJESTIC RIDE b.g. 12 Palm Track - Lakeland Lady by Leander — Rob Woods

1995 P(0),3(0),2(13),1(13),P(0),**5(0)**,9(0),6(0),P(0)

59	10/2	Cottenham	(R)	RES	3m	9	GS	*withdrawn start - deemed to have come und orders*	0	0
1173	20/4	Chaddesley '	(L)	RES	3m	18	G	*rear frm 10th, t.o. & p.u. 16th*	P	0
1239	27/4	Clifton On '	(L)	RES	3m	9	GF	*mstk 6th,in tch,outpcd & mstk 14th,ran on 3 out,tk 2nd flat*	2	14
1380	5/5	Dingley	(R)	RES	3m	11	GF	*in tch, gd prog to chal wnr 2 out, wknd rpdly apr last*	6	10
1522	12/5	Garthorpe	(R)	RES	3m	12	GF	*w.w. rear, grad prog to 3rd 3 out, 20l 3rd whn lft clr last*	1	14
1595	25/5	Garthorpe	(R)	CON	3m	15	G	*alwys last trio, no ch frm 6 out*	9	0
1645	2/6	Dingley	(R)	INT	3m	5	GF	*pllng, in tch, outpcd 10th, stynd on 2 out, nrst fin*	3	15

Very lucky winner & does not stay; ran well last start but hard to win again; hard ride 15

MAJESTIC RING(CAN) b.g. 14 Majestic Prince - Savage Call (USA) by Jungle Savage (USA) — Miss A C Bowie

615	23/3	Friars Haugh	(L)	MEM	3m	9	G	*(fav) 2nd hlfwy, cl up untl wknd 4 out.*	3	0

No longer of any account 0

MAJESTIC SPIRIT gr.g. 10 Majestic Maharaj - Runquest by Runnymede — Alan Raymond

1995 P(0),1(14),2(15),U(-),P(0)

137	17/2	Ottery St M'	(L)	RES	3m	15	GS	*(fav) ld to 7th, wknd 14th, bhnd whn p.u. 2 out*	P	0
197	24/2	Lemalla	(R)	LAD	3m	13	HY	*alwys prom, unable to chal frm 2 out*	3	14
443	9/3	Haldon	(R)	LAD	3m	10	S	*ld/disp frm 7th til wknd aft 13th, p.u. 15th*	P	0
466	10/3	Milborne St'	(L)	RES	3m	13	G	*alwys mid-div, outpcd frm 4 out*	6	14
1072	13/4	Lifton	(R)	LAD	3m	7	S	*j.w., ld apr 9th, ran on strgly whn chal frm 2 out*	1	22
1126	20/4	Stafford Cr'	(R)	LAD	3m	7	S	*chsd ldr til lost tch 12th, lft 2nd 3 out*	2	18
1346	4/5	Holnicote	(L)	LAD	3m	5	GS	*ld to 8th, kpt on onepcd aft*	3	21

Beat Khattaf at Lifton; inconsistent & well beaten apart; needs easy course; may surprise again;G-Hy .. 20

MAJIC BELLE b.m. 8 Majestic Maharaj - Ankerdine Belle by Paddy Boy — D J B Denny

1995 5(0),F(-),4(12),U(-),r(-)

600	23/3	Howick	(L)	RES	3m	14	S	*prom to 6th, wknd grad, p.u. 15th*	P	0
1048	13/4	Bitterley	(L)	MDO	3m	12	G	*last at 10th, reluc aft nxt & p.u.*	P	0
1225	24/4	Brampton Br'	(R)	MDO	3m	18	G	*(bl) cls up 11th, chal 3 out, ld nxt, hd flat*	3	13
1434	6/5	Ashorne	(R)	MDO	3m	15	G	*(vis) prom, ld brfly 12th, sn wknd, t.o.*	5	0
1485	11/5	Bredwardine	(R)	MDO	3m	15	G	*(vis) cls up 9th, ev ch til wknd 14th, p.u. 2 out*	P	0

Ran well in blinkers but form very weak & still looks unlikely to win 11

MAJOR BERT(IRE) b.g. 8 Kemal (FR) - African Nelly by Pitpan — G M Spencer

1995 6(0),2(12),1(15),1(13)

358	3/3	Garnons	(L)	RES	3m	18	GS	*alwys mid-div, lost tch wth ldrs frm 12th*	3	0
690	30/3	Llanvapley	(L)	MEM	3m	4	GS	*(fav) alwys cls up, ld 11th, jnd 3 out, outpcd frm nxt*	2	0
1211	23/4	Chepstow	(L)	HC	3m	13	S	*mstk 11th, t.o. when p.u. before 4 out.*	P	0
1481	11/5	Bredwardine	(R)	RES	3m	14	G	*nvr rchd ldrs, in tch 11th, wknd 14th, p.u. 2 out*	P	0

Dual winner 95; not progress 96; beaten in bad Members; can only be watched now 11

MAJOR BILL (Irish) — I 113[F], I 139[P], I 612[P], I 645[P]

MAJOR INQUIRY(USA) b.g. 10 The Minstrel (CAN) - Hire A Brain (USA) by Seattle Slew (USA) — N J Pewter

1995 P(0),F(-),**P(0)**,P(0),5(12),R(-),2(14),5(0),**5(0)**,**9(0)**

102	17/2	Marks Tey	(L)	CON	3m	17	G	*rr, prog & in tch 13th,sn outpcd*	9	0
309	2/3	Ampton	(R)	MEM	3m	6	G	*w.w. lft 3rd 13th, chsd wnr appr last, kpt on wll*	2	13
418	9/3	High Easter	(L)	CON	3m	10	S	*in tch, pshd along 11th, no ch 14th*	7	0
622	23/3	Higham	(L)	CON	3m	10	GF	*alwys rear, wknd 11th, t.o. 13th*	5	0
831	6/4	Marks Tey	(L)	CON	3m	6	G	*last pair, t.o. 15th, p.u. last*	P	0
1323	28/4	Fakenham P-'	(L)	OPE	3m	8	G	*blnd 3rd, in tch, pshd alng 10th, last & no frm 14th*	7	0
1613	27/5	Fontwell	(R)	HC	3 1/4m 110yds	12	G	*bhnd from 12th, t.o. 16th, p.u. before 18th.*	P	0

No wins from 17 starts 95-6 & sure to extend the sequence 10

MAJOR MAN (Irish) — I 345[P], I 420[3], I 559[P], I 618[2], I 660[1]

MAJOR MATCH(NZ) b.g. 14 Frassino - Burks Rainbow (NZ) by Weyand (USA) — Mrs M Wiggin
1995 1(24),1(22),1(23),2(20),F(-),1(22),4(20)

163 17/2 Weston Park (L) LAD 3m 10 G *(fav) prom, ld 6th, sn clr, unchal* 1 24

Good Ladies horse; won 5 of last 8; best fresh; vanished quickly 96; win at 15 if fit; G/S-F 22

MAJOR NEAVE b.g. 9 Royal Vulcan - Park Springs by Brigadier Gerard — J D Jamieson

36 20/1 Higham (L) RES 3m 12 GF *w.w. prog 12th, went 3rd apr last, no ext flat* 3 15
105 17/2 Marks Tey (L) RES 3m 11 G *prog 12th, chall & rmdrs 3 out, ld last, rddn clr* 1 17
676 30/3 Cottenham (R) INT 3m 13 GF *mstks 3 & 5th,prog 11th,jnd wnr 3 out,ran wd aft nxt,p.u.* P 0
1329 30/4 Huntingdon (R) HC 3m 14 GF *mstks, nvr on terms, t.o. when p.u. before 2 out.* P 0

Missed 95; much improved 96; won fair Restricted; could win again if consenting; L/H best 18

MAJOR PERIL ch.g. 6 Politico (USA) - Priceless Peril by Silly Prices — Tim Butt
1995 P(0),P(0)

115 17/2 Lanark (R) MDO 3m 8 GS *f 3rd* F -

Yet to complete & the briefest of seasons in 96 0

MAJOR ROUGE ch.g. 14 Mandrake Major - Red Form by Reform — S A Pinder
1995 P(0),S(-),P(0),B(-),S(-)

72 11/2 Wetherby Po' (L) CON 3m 18 GS *cls up til p.u. 7th* P 0

No longer of any account 0

MAJOR SCANDAL (Irish) — I 365^{P}

MAJOR WAYNE br.h. 13 Pony Express - Damside by Shackleton — Mrs S L Dando

380 9/3 Barbury Cas' (L) CON 3m 11 GS *sn wll bhnd, p.u. 12th* P 0
638 23/3 Siddington (L) CON 3m 16 S *rr & blnd 7th, t.o. frm 12th* 8 0
957 8/4 Lockinge (L) CON 3m 5 GF *ld 2nd-3rd, agn 12th-2 out, outpcd aft* 2 14
1167 20/4 Larkhill (R) MEM 3m 9 GF *alwys bhnd ldng grp, t.o. frm 13th* 6 0
1247 27/4 Woodford (L) CON 3m 7 G *last frm 7th, t.o.* 5 0

Won 3 in 91; lightly raced since & needs a miracle to win now 10

MAKE A LINE (Irish) — I 54^{P}, I 126^{3}

MAKIN' DOO(IRE) ch.g. 6 Black Minstrel - Ariannrun by Deep Run — R G Makin

1095 14/4 Whitwell-On' (R) MDO 2 1/2m 88yds 14 G *rear, t.o. 8th, p.u. 10th* P 0
1155 20/4 Whittington (L) MDN 3m 14 G *mid-div, 3rd 3 out, fin wll* 3 0

Season lasted 6 days but some promise last start & should go closer in 97 11

MAKING TIME gr.m. 9 Furry Glen - Arctic Border by Arctic Slave — R Shepherd
1995 **4(NH),4(NH),P(NH),6(NH),2(NH)**

232 24/2 Heythrop (R) OPE 3m 10 GS *mid-div, no ch whn p.u. 13th* P 0
338 3/3 Heythrop (R) RES 3m 9 G *(Co fav) prom, ld 9th-13th, wknd aft nxt, lost 3rd flat* 4 0
707 30/3 Barbury Cas' (L) RES 3m 18 G *ld/disp to 12th, wknd nxt, t.o. & p.u. 2 out* P 0
889 6/4 Kimble (L) RES 3m 7 GF *made all, mstks 14th & 3 out, rdn & just hld on flat* 1 18
1177 21/4 Mollington (R) INT 3m 14 F *prom, wth wnr frm 5th, mstk 15th, ev ch 2 out, onepcd* 2 18
1329 30/4 Huntingdon (R) HC 3m 14 GF *outpcd in mid div, styd on from 16th, went 3rd last, nvr nrr.* 3 19
1458 8/5 Uttoxeter (L) HC 3 1/4m 8 G *chsd ldrs, rdn and outpcd 15th, 4th and no ch from four out, fin tired.* 5 0
1614 27/5 Hereford (R) HC 3m 1f 110yds 16 G *cl up, ld after 7th till 15th, wknd quickly next, bhnd when p.u. before 3 out.* P 0

A disappointment till Kimble win; barely stays; outclassed in H/Chases; may find Intermediate; Firm ... 18

MAK'S DREAM (Irish) — I 192^{P}, I 223^{P}, I 386^{1}, I 525^{P}

MALACHITE GREEN b.g. 6 Lochnager - Rhiannon by Welsh Pageant — B Kennedy
1995 **6(NH),U(NH),5(NH),5(NH),5(NH),1(NH),3(NH)**

418 9/3 High Easter (L) CON 3m 10 S *w.w. prog to ld 14th, sn clr, hdded & blnd 2 out, no ex* 2 17
934 8/4 Marks Tey (L) CON 3m 6 G *hld up, mstk 6th, prog 10th, disp 16th-2 out, slw jmp last* 2 18

Winning selling hurdler; ran well both points; may prefer easy 3m; could win Confined 18

MALAHIDE MICHAEL (Irish) — I 174^{P}

MALAKIE(IRE) b.g. 6 Mandalus - Sartfield Princess by Le Bavard (FR) — Chris Grant

52 4/2 Alnwick (L) MDO 3m 11 G *chsd ldrs, 6th & lsng tch whn blndrd & u.r. 12th* U -
308 2/3 Great Stain' (L) MDO 3m 12 GS *rear, slw jmp 4th, p.u. nxt* P 0
414 9/3 Charm Park (L) MDO 3m 11 G *in tch to 12th, wknd 4 out, cmpltd own tm* 5 0
705 30/3 Tranwell (L) MDO 3m 9 GS *cls up frm 5th, disp 12th til f 14th* F -
1095 14/4 Whitwell-On' (R) MDO 2 1/2m 88yds 14 G *nvr bttr than mid-div* 4 0
1365 4/5 Gisburn (R) MDO 3m 17 G *f 1st* F -

Well beaten when completing; looks capable of better - needs to 11

MALI (Irish) — I 545P

MALINGERER gr.m. 5 Petong - Crystal Gael by Sparkler — R Thomson

1995 **3(NH),4(NH),6(NH)**

575	17/3 Detling	(L) MDO 3m	10 GF	*pllng, ld til ran out 3rd*	r	-
1210	21/4 Heathfield	(R) MDO 3m	13 F	*rear, hmpd & f 2nd*	F	-
1299	28/4 Bexhill	(R) MDO 3m	7 F	*last, t.o. & p.u. 9th*	P	0

Ungenuine on the Flat; no prospects as a pointer 0

MAL'S CASTLE(IRE) ch.m. 7 Heraldiste (USA) - Listooder Girl by Wolverlife — S Clark

73	11/2 Wetherby Po'	(L) MDO 3m	15 GS	*bhnd, outpcd, p.u. 13th*	P	0
123	17/2 Witton Cast'	(R) MDO 3m	11 S	*rear whn f 9th*	F	-

Season lasted 6 days & no signs of ability 0

MALTBY BOY b.g. 13 Royal Palace - Assel Zawie by Sit In The Corner (USA) — Mrs A Hickman

273	2/3 Parham	(R) LAD 3m	11 GF	*lft in ld 4th, hdd 6th, wknd frm 12th, wll bhnd & p.u.3 out*	P	0
596	23/3 Parham	(R) LAD 3m	8 GS	*in tch to 13th, wll bhnd p.u. 2 out*	P	0

Won 16 of 20 points to 94; missed 95 & ready for retirement after 96 efforts 0

MALT MAN (Irish) — I 93P

MALVERN CANTINA b.g. 8 Royal Vulcan - My Martina by My Swallow — M J Hill

80	11/2 Wetherby Po'	(L) MDO 3m	12 GS	*prom, 4th at 8th, fdd, p.u. 10th*	P	0
117	17/2 Witton Cast'	(R) MEM 3m	9 S	*mid-div to 6th, rear whn p.u. 12th*	P	0
331	3/3 Market Rase'	(L) MDO 3m	9 G	*prom, jnd ldr 14th, f 3 out*	F	-
590	23/3 Wetherby Po'	(L) MDO 3m	16 S	*prom, disp 12th til f 4 out*	F	-
829	6/4 Stainton	(R) MDO 3m	9 GF	*(fav) hld up rear,prog 12th,lft in ld 4 out,jnd 2 out,rdn to ld fn*	1	14

Unlucky prior to winning poor Maiden; more needed for Restricteds; lightly raced 14

MALVERN LAD ch.g. 6 Lighter - Jack's Love by Grey Love — T F G Marks

898	6/4 Dingley	(R) MDN 2m 5f	10 GS	*nvr dang, mstly 6th frm 10th, outpcd whn u.r. 3 out*	U	-
1104	14/4 Guilsborough	(L) MDN 3m	18 G	*rear, prog & in tch 11th, 6th & btn 4 out, p.u. nxt*	P	0
1261	27/4 Cottenham	(R) MDO 3m	10 F	*mid-div, mstks 6 & 8th, bhnd whn p.u. 12th, dsmntd*	P	0

A glimmer of hope but problems last start 10

MAMMY'S CHOICE(IRE) br.m. 6 Mandalus - Liffey's Choice by Little Buskins — David Young

1995 **10(NH),4(NH),6(NH),12(NH)**

205	24/2 Castle Of C'	(R) MDO 3m	9 HY	*(fav) alwys prom, ld 12th, prssd 3 out, ran on well frm nxt*	1	14
465	10/3 Milborne St'	(L) RES 3m	11 G	*ld til blnd & u.r. 2 out*	U	-
1056	13/4 Badbury Rin'	(L) RES 3m	10 GF	*(Jt fav) ld to 3rd, prom, 3rd & ev ch whn f 3 out*	F	-

Won good Maiden in mud; possibly unlucky in hot race next; stays; Restricted no problem if jumping ... 19

MANAOLANA b.m. 8 Castle Keep - Ladysave by Stanford — Mrs Georgina Worsley

1995 P(0),F(-),P(0)

272	2/3 Parham	(R) RES 3m	13 GF	*pllng, prom to hlfwy, bhnd whn p.u. 14th*	P	0
449	9/3 Charing	(L) RES 3m	13 G	*rear, gd prog 12th, ld 15th, drvn clr, jnd last, wknd flat*	3	16
779	31/3 Penshurst	(L) RES 3m	13 GS	*in tch to 10th, p.u. 12th*	P	0
1295	28/4 Bexhill	(R) RES 3m	7 F	*lft 2nd 9th, pshd alng to sty wth wnr 14th, wknd 2 out*	2	12
1537	16/5 Folkestone	(R) HC 3 1/4m	8 GF	*mstks, ld to 1st, in tch till wknd 15th, no ch when ref 3 out.*	R	-

Maiden winner 93; returned to form 96; fair efforts but weak Restricted needed; Members best hope .. 14

MANDENKA br.g. 10 Mandalus - Kimin by Kibenka — G I Cooper

781	31/3 Penshurst	(L) MDN 3m	11 GS	*(fav) (6s-5/2),ld 6-12th, lft in ld 14th, hdd 3 out, fdd*	3	0
930	8/4 Marks Tey	(L) MDO 3m	6 G	*(Jt fav) wth ldrs, lft 2nd 13th, outpcd frm 16th*	3	0

Ex-Irish; lightly raced; placed in 2 poor races; much more needed 10

MANDINGO (Irish) — I 539F

MANDYS LAD ch.g. 7 Sula Bula - Sweet Mandy by Normandy — Tony Walpole

1995 **10(NH),12(NH),P(NH)**

218	24/2 Newtown	(L) MDN 3m	14 GS	*ld to 3rd & 8th til hdd & mstk 10th, wknd rpdly, p.u. 14th*	P	0
542	17/3 Southwell P'	(L) MDO 3m	15 GS	*prom, ld 7th, ran on well, easily*	1	15
684	30/3 Chaddesley '	(L) RES 3m	14 G	*ld, 5l clr whn f 12th*	F	-
1001	9/4 Upton-On-Se'	(R) MEM 3m	6 F	*(fav) jmpd lft, ld 8th til app 2 out, immed btn, virt p.u.*	5	0
1173	20/4 Chaddesley '	(L) RES 3m	18 G	*ld to 2nd & 11th-nxt, cls 2nd til wknd 17th, p.u. 3 out*	P	0

Disappointment under Rules; romped home when winning but looks suspect now; best watched 15

MANDYS SPECIAL ch.m. 10 Roman Warrior - Petite Mandy by Mandamus — R M Thorne

1995 P(0),F(-)

48	4/2	Alnwick	(L)	LAD	3m	9	G	*in tch, mstk 8th & 9th, wknd, p.u. 13th*	P	0
400	9/3	Dalston	(R)	LAD	3m	10	G	*ld 1st, prom tl mstk 4 out, nt rcvr, p.u. 16th*	P	0
501	16/3	Lanark	(R)	RES	3m	12	G	*prom early, losing tch whn f 11th*	F	-
700	30/3	Tranwell	(L)	LAD	3m	4	GS	*not fluent, t.o. frm 14th, lft poor 2nd nxt*	2	0
1471	11/5	Aspatria	(L)	MEM	3m	4	GF	*rcd wd,ld to 7th,ld 11th,sn hdd,wknd 16th,last whn u.r.2 out*	U	-

Maiden winner 93; novice ridden & well beaten only completion 96 0

MANHATTAN JEWEL (Irish) — **I** 302[U], **I** 406[F], **I** 448[1]

MANHATTAN PRINCE (Irish) — **I** 22[1], **I** 136[4], **I** 170[4], **I** 257[P], **I** 287[5], **I** 454[P], **I** 489[P], **I** 586[2]

MANLEY GIRL (Irish) — **I** 41[P], **I** 128[P], **I** 289[3], **I** 443[B], **I** 475[3], **I** 632[2]

MAN OF FASHION ch.g. 10 Free State - Miss Hartnell by Ballymoss — Mrs E Coombes

1995 P(0),0(0),U(-),9(0)

332	3/3	Market Rase'	(L)	MDO	3m	8	G	*t.d.e. ld to 7th, sn wknd, last whn blnd 12th, p.u. 14th*	P	0

Of no account & temperamental 0

MAN OF ICE ch.g. 10 Remainder Man - Coolek by Menelek — Mrs S Keating-Coyne

1995 r(-),P(0),F(-)

1293	28/4	Barbury Cas'	(L)	MDO	3m	11	F	*cls up to 9th, eased & p.u. nxt*	P	0
1504	11/5	Kingston Bl'	(L)	MDO	3m	13	G	*mstk 6th, bhnd frm 10th, t.o. & p.u. 13th*	P	0
1536	16/5	Folkestone	(R)	HC	2m 5f	9	GF	*cl up, jmpd left 6th, wknd 9th, bhnd when p.u. before 3 out.*	P	0
1652	8/6	Umberleigh	(L)	MDO	3m	10	GF	*ld to 11th & 13th til aft nxt, stppd bef 3 out, lame*	P	0

Has some ability but never completed & problem last start; unlikely to win 10

MAN OF IRON (Irish) — **I** 413[2], **I** 570[3]

MAN OF MOREEF b.g. 9 Miramar Reef - Coliemore by Coliseum — Mrs A R Wood

1995 **6(NH),8(NH),F(NH)**

323	2/3	Corbridge	(R)	MDN	3m	12	GS	*prom frm 6th, went 3rd at 8th, ld 10th til hdd & no ext last*	3	13

Ran well in average Maiden & could win at 10 if fit 14

MANOR COTTAGE(IRE) b or br.g. 7 Black Minstrel - Orient Sun Rise by Menelek — D A Howes

1995 P(0),U(-),2(0),2(0)

15	14/1	Cottenham	(R)	MDN	3m	14	G	*pllng, ld til f 11th*	F	-
34	20/1	Higham	(L)	MDN	3m	11	GF	*(fav) alwys chsing lding grp, 4th & no ch whn p.u. 3 out*	P	0

Placed in poor races 95; only lasted a week in 96; win unlikely 11

MANOR MIEO b.g. 10 Enryco Mieo - Manor Farm Girl by Autre Prince — George Prodromou

1995 1(23),1(23)

1321	28/4	Fakenham P-'	(L)	CON	3m	5	G	*(fav) made all, blnd 7th, drew clr 3 out, easily*	1	21
1547	18/5	Fakenham	(L)	HC	2m 5f 110yds	11	G	*j.w, ld 3rd, left well clr 2 out, unchal, tried to pull up after last.*	1	23

Useful; won 6 of 7 starts 94-6; needs easy track; jumps well; win Opens if fit 97; F-S 26

MANOR RANGER b.g. 10 Deep Run - Tanarpa by Dusky Boy — M C Wells

455	9/3	Charing	(L)	MDN	3m	10	G	*ref to race*	0	0
576	17/3	Detling	(L)	MDN	3m	18	GF	*ld 3rd-9th, lft in ld 13th, clr apr 3 out, prssd & u.r. last*	U	-
780	31/3	Penshurst	(L)	MDN	3m	12	GS	*u.r. 1st*	U	-
966	8/4	Heathfield	(R)	MDO	3m	7	G	*ld til appr last, rallied gamely flat*	2	12
1187	21/4	Tweseldown	(R)	MDN	3m	11	GF	*ld 1st, hdd & mstk 2nd, sn strggling, p.u. 9th*	P	0
1341	4/5	Warwick	(L)	HC	2 1/2m 110yds	12	GF	*alwys in rear, bhnd when mstk 4th, t.o. and p.u. before 12th.*	P	0

Front-runs, some ability but poor jumper; could win with stronger handling 11

MAN'S BEST FRIEND b.g. 9 Mandalus - Tara Weed by Tarqogan — Mrs M Dickinson

401	9/3	Dalston	(R)	OPE	3m	6	G	*jmpd wl, ld 1st, prom frm 4th, lft ld 11th, md rst, easily*	1	22
587	23/3	Wetherby Po'	(L)	OPE	3m	15	S	*(fav) cls up, disp 14th til ld last, hdd flat, rallied to ld fin*	1	23
1154	20/4	Whittington	(L)	OPE	3m	7	G	*(fav) cls 3rd 15th, outpcd by wnr aft*	2	16

Lightly raced but still able; won 5 of last 8; stays well; can win more in 97; Soft 25

MANSUN b or br.g. 9 Sunyboy - Emancipated by Mansingh (USA) — Miss J Simmons

160	17/2	Weston Park	(L)	OPE	3m	16	G	*mid-div, lost tch & p.u. 4 out*	P	0
432	9/3	Upton-On-Se'	(R)	MDO	3m	17	GS	*5th hlfwy, grad lost tch, p.u. 3 out*	P	0
606	23/3	Howick	(L)	MDN	3m	13	S	*f 2nd*	F	-
797	2/4	Heythrop	(R)	MDN	3m	11	F	*14s-8s, blnd 9th, cls up to 12th, t.o. whn blnd 3 out & p.u.*	P	0
1506	12/5	Maisemore P'	(L)	MEM	3m	5	F	*n.j.w. prssd wnr aft 9th til blnd 11th, wknd 15th, walked in*	4	0

No stamina & prospects bleak 0

MAN WITH A PLAN VI (Irish) — **I** 656[F]

MAPALAK ch.m. 6 Buckley - Sound Run by Deep Run — A Dawson

1995 P(0),P(0),U(-)

53	4/2	Alnwick	(L)	MDO	3m	13	G	*t.d.e., plld into ld & ran out 3rd*	r	-
88	11/2	Alnwick	(L)	MDO	3m	11	GS	*immed t.o., p.u. aft 10th*	P	0
194	24/2	Friars Haugh	(L)	MDN	3m	11	S	*15l 3rd whn f 11th*	F	-
405	9/3	Dalston	(R)	MDO	2 1/2m	16	G	*wl bhnd whn p.u. 10th*	P	0
614	23/3	Friars Haugh	(L)	MDN	3m	10	G	*5th hlfwy, hdwy 4 out, no ext apr last*	3	10
756	31/3	Lockerbie	(R)	MDN	3m	14	G	*(fav) last hlfwy, nvr got into contention*	6	0
1089	14/4	Friars Haugh	(L)	MDN	3m	10	F	*(fav) ld brfly 10th, losing plc whn f 12th*	F	-
1254	27/4	Balcormo Ma'	(R)	MDO	3m	14	GS	*f 5th*	F	-
1517	12/5	Hexham Poin'	(L)	MDN	3m	10	HY	*t.d.e. in tch, wknd apr 3 out, p.u. 2 out*	P	0
1574	19/5	Corbridge	(R)	MDO	3m	6	G	*prom, chsd wnr 12th, outpcd 16th, rallied apr last, ran on*	2	13

Finished 3 of 13 starts 95-6 & hard ride; silly favourite twice; may hit jackpot in 97 12

MARA ASKARI b.g. 8 Night Shift (USA) - Madam Cody by Hot Spark — Mrs E R Stevens

32	20/1	Higham	(L)	OPE	3m	15	GF	*(vis) prom to 6th, sn lst plc, p.u. aft 11th*	P	0
93	11/2	Ampton	(R)	LAD	3m	7	GF	*(vis) blnd & u.r. 2nd*	U	-
271	2/3	Parham	(R)	CON	3m	15	GF	*(vis) mid-div, rdn & wknd 12th, wll bhnd whn p.u. 4 out*	P	0

Winning hurdler; poor jumper & showed no enthusiasm for pointing 0

MARDON (Irish) — **I** 222^{3}, **I** 324^{2}, **I** 610^{4}

MARGARETS TOCRACY (Irish) — **I** 223^{P}

MARIANS OWN (Irish) — **I** 631^{P}, **I** 649^{P}

MARIES CALL (Irish) — **I** 101^{P}, **I** 587^{2}

MARILLO (Irish) — **I** 41^{1}

MARINERS MAID b.m. 9 Julio Mariner - Copamour by Bold As Brass — J Hart

788	31/3	Tweseldown	(R)	MDO	3m	8	G	*prom, rmndrs 2nd, 2nd & ev ch 3 out, wknd nxt*	4	0

Missed 94-5; well beaten but not disgraced; worth a pot in her Members if fit 97 10

MARINER'S WALK ch.g. 9 Julio Mariner - Nunswalk by The Parson — Mrs V Miles

1995 P(0),P(0),r(-),3(13),r(-),4+(0),P(0),3(12)

749	31/3	Upper Sapey	(R)	MDO	3m	17	GS	*disp to 8th, wknd & p.u. 14th*	P	0
1006	9/4	Upton-On-Se'	(R)	MDN	3m	11	F	*ld to 6th, wknd 13th, t.o. & p.u. 2 out*	P	0
1319	28/4	Bitterley	(L)	MDN	3m	13	G	*ld to 11th, chsd ldrs til outpcd frm 15th*	4	0
1483	11/5	Bredwardine	(R)	MDO	3m	15	G	*ld to 3rd, cls up til chal 3 out, rdn to ld flat*	1	15

Non-stayer & looked on the way out till beat large, weak field; much more needed for Restricteds 15

MARKET GOSSIP b.g. 6 Rolfe (USA) - Buckbe by Ragstone — R J Tory

1995 **P(NH),P(NH),14(NH)**

144	17/2	Larkhill	(R)	MDO	3m	15	G	*alwys prom, gd prog to ld last, ran on well*	1	16
466	10/3	Milborne St'	(L)	RES	3m	13	G	*(fav) ld to 8th, cls up aft, outpcd 15th*	3	16
1242	27/4	Woodford	(L)	RES	3m	18	G	*in tch, chsd ldr 10th, ld 16th, styd on strgly frm 2 out*	1	22

No ability under Rules but real prospect in points; won good Restricted; one to note; Good 23

MARKSWAY BOY ch.g. 8 Prince Of Peace - Moor Park Lass by Pony Express — Mark Westaway

1995 P(0)

197	24/2	Lemalla	(R)	LAD	3m	13	HY	*ld aft 4th, ran wd aft 6th, f nxt*	F	-

Unpromising 0

MARSHALSTONESWOOD b.g. 11 Gorytus (USA) - Secret Isle (USA) by Voluntario III — Miss A C Bowie

1995 8(0),P(0),1D(15),2(15),1(19),**F(-)**

85	11/2	Alnwick	(L)	LAD	3m	11	GS	*alwys prom, chsd wnr 15th, onepcd frm 2 out*	3	19
112	17/2	Lanark	(R)	LAD	3m	8	GS	*3rd at 10th, kpt on well, no ch wth wnr*	3	18
318	2/3	Corbridge	(R)	LAD	3m 5f	10	GS	*mid-div, prog 11th, prom frm 17th, no ext apr last*	3	18
611	23/3	Friars Haugh	(L)	LAD	3m	10	G	*(fav) mdfld, some hdwy frm 13th, 5l 4th whn u.r. 3 out*	9	0
752	31/3	Lockerbie	(R)	LAD	3m	10	G	*7th hlfwy, nvr rchd ldrs*	5	14
1084	14/4	Friars Haugh	(L)	LAD	3m	8	F	*chsd wnr frm 11th, outpcd frm 2 out*	2	16
1352	4/5	Mosshouses	(L)	LAD	3m	10	GS	*cls up, ld aft 12th, made rest, clr 2 out, idld flat*	1	17
1473	11/5	Aspatria	(L)	LAD	3m	7	GF	*in tch til p.u. & dismntd bfr 10th*	P	0

Consistent; no match for good horses; best late season; problem last start; may find another race 17

MARTHA'S BOY (Irish) — **I** 275^{5}, **I** 438^{P}

MARTIYA b.m. 8 Martinmas - Tia Song by Acrania — R Williams

1995 **U(-)**,U(-),P(0)

384	9/3	Llanfrynach	(R)	OPE	3m	16	GS	*alwys rear, t.o. & p.u. last*	P	0
504	16/3	Magor	(R)	MEM	3m	5	GS	*chsd wnr, rdn to chal 15th, wknd rpdly aft*	3	0

Beaten 40l on 1st completion - no chance of a win 0

MARY BOROUGH gr.m. 10 Baron Blakeney - Risello by Raise You Ten — Mrs Judy Young

140	17/2	Larkhill	(R)	CON	3m	17	G	*sn rear, t.o. 13th*	9	0
235	24/2	Heythrop	(R)	RES	3m	10	GS	*mid-div whn u.r. 3rd*	U	-
262	2/3	Didmarton	(L)	MEM	3m	11	G	*s.s. last pair & wll bhnd,mod prog but still t.o. whn f last*	F	-
707	30/3	Barbury Cas'	(L)	RES	3m	18	G	*alwys mid-div, t.o. & p.u. 3 out*	P	0
946	8/4	Andoversford	(R)	RES	3m	10	GF	*in tch early, rear by hlfwy*	6	0
1292	28/4	Barbury Cas'	(L)	RES	3m	11	F	*last whn u.r. 1st*	U	-

Maiden winner 94; missed 95; slow & nothing in 96; prospects bleak 0

MARY'S DELIGHT (Irish) — I 224^{P}, I 348^{4}, I 532^{6}

MARYS FRIEND (Irish) — I 550^{6}, I 608^{F}

MAST (Irish) — I 478^{P}, I 559^{P}, I 624^{1}

MASTER ART b.g. 6 Scorpio (FR) - The Huyton Girls by Master Sing — J R Vail

1995 3(13),P(0)

2	13/1	Larkhill	(R)	MDO	3m	17	GS	*mstks, alwys chsng ldrs, outpcd frm 12th, no dang aft*	4	0
144	17/2	Larkhill	(R)	MDO	3m	15	G	*alwys mid-div, wknd 3 out, p.u. last*	P	0
652	23/3	Badbury Rin'	(L)	MDO	3m	13	G	*ld to 3rd, prom whn f 14th.*	F	-

Promise in 95; jumped poorly & not progress 96; young enought to step up 97 13

MASTER BERTIE b.g. 9 New Member - Sprightly Miss by Master Spiritus — Dr R Jowett

1995 4(11),F(-),P(0),U(-),P(0)

526	16/3	Larkhill	(R)	RES	3m	9	G	*mid-div, mstk 8th, wknd & p.u. 13th*	P	0

Only 1 completion in 11 starts; vanished quickly 96 0

MASTER BUCKLEY b.g. 6 Buckley - Ivy Hill by Cantab — Mrs V M Robinson

1995 **14(NH)**

1554	18/5	Bratton Down	(L)	MDO	3m	16	F	*schoold in rear til p.u. 14th*	P	0
1593	25/5	Mounsey Hil'	(R)	MDO	3m	11	G	*in tch, 6th & outpcd 14th, p.u. 17th, improve*	P	0

Only learning but looks the part & should do better in time 12

MASTER CHUZZLEWIT (Irish) — I 343^{P}, I 420^{F}, I 526^{4}, I 636^{3}

MASTER CROZINA br.g. 8 Uncle Pokey - Miss Crozina by Crozier — J Cornforth

1995 2(10),U(-),2(10),2(0)

415	9/3	Charm Park	(L)	MDO	3m	13	G	*(fav) ld 5-12, hdd, f 4 out, lkd btn*	F	-
828	6/4	Stainton	(R)	MDO	3m	7	GF	*(fav) ld to 3rd,ld 7th,hdd 6 out,lft in ld nxt,styd on well*	1	14
1131	20/4	Hornby Cast'	(L)	RES	3m	17	G	*prom, ld 8th, jnd 15th, wknd rpdly*	5	14
1284	27/4	Easingwold	(L)	RES	3m	14	G	*prom, ld 4th-6th, mstk & wknd 15th, t.o. & p.u. last*	P	0
1462	10/5	Market Rasen	(R)	HC	2 3/4m 110yds	11	G	*chsd ldrs till wknd quickly apr 3 out, p.u. before last.*	P	0

Placed 5 times prior to winning weak Maiden; barely stays & not a patch on mum 14

MASTER DANCER b.g. 9 Mashhor Dancer (USA) - Silent Dancer by Quiet Fling (USA) — Mrs D J Dyson

1995 1(22),U(-)

687	30/3	Chaddesley '	(L)	CON	3m	10	G	*blnd & rmndrs 4th, lost tch 12th, p.u. 3 out*	P	0
1046	13/4	Bitterley	(L)	LAD	3m	9	G	*chsd ldrs til not qckn 13th, p.u. last*	P	0
1437	6/5	Ashorne	(R)	MXO	3m	13	G	*alwys rear, lost tch 9th, t.o. & p.u. 15th*	P	0
1618	27/5	Chaddesley '	(L)	CON	3m	14	GF	*chsd ldrs, 3rd & wkng 15th, no ch whn p.u. last, dsmntd*	P	0

Confined winner 95; looks to have lost interest now & problem last start 0

MASTER DONNINGTON br.g. 8 Julio Mariner - Lor Darnie by Dumbarnie — M S Wilesmith

1995 4(0),P(0),1(15),1(17)

214	24/2	Newtown	(L)	CON	3m	21	GS	*prom, ld 4-6th, outpcd aft 13th, no dang aft*	7	10
381	9/3	Barbury Cas'	(L)	XX	3m	9	GS	*prom, 3rd at 8th, sn wknd, t.o.*	4	0
683	30/3	Chaddesley '	(L)	MEM	3m	17	G	*hld up, 11th hlfwy, nvr on terms*	5	15
836	6/4	Maisemore P'	(L)	MEM	3m	7	GF	*cls up, chsd ldr 10th, nvr able to chall*	2	14

Dual winner 95; not disgraced 96 but finished as stable hit form; best watched 15

MASTER ENBORNE ch.g. 12 Celtic Cone - Booterstown by Master Owen — J Young

240	25/2	Southwell P'	(L)	MDO	3m	15	HO	*mid-div, in tch 11th, wkng whn f 13th*	F	-
542	17/3	Southwell P'	(L)	MDO	3m	15	GS	*mid-div, wll bhnd whn p.u. 3 out*	P	0
1027	13/4	Brocklesby '	(L)	MDN	3m	7	GF	*cls up, last pair whn f 7th*	F	-

An elderly maiden with no prospects 0

MASTER FRISK ch.g. 10 Broadsword (USA) - Jenny Frisk by Sunacelli — R Dalton

1136	20/4	Hornby Cast'	(L)	MDN	3m	11	G	*s.s. jmpd poorly, alwys t.o., p.u. 8th*	P	0

No hope 0

MASTER FRITH gr.g. 8 Dutch Treat - Dromeden Janice by Andrea Mantegna — Alan Ferguson

1995 P(0),P(0)

431	9/3	Upton-On-Se'	(R)	MDO	3m	17	GS	*t.o. & p.u. 14th*	P 0
883	6/4	Brampton Br'	(R)	MDN	3m	13	GF	*(bl) cls up 9th, prom whn ran out 12th*	r -
1047	13/4	Bitterley	(L)	MDO	3m	13	G	*(bl) cls up to 10th, outpcd 13th, p.u. 2 out*	P 0
1224	24/4	Brampton Br'	(R)	MDO	3m	17	G	*(bl) rr frm 6th, p.u. 9th*	P 0
1319	28/4	Bitterley	(L)	MDN	3m	13	G	*(bl) hit 3rd, last at 10th, t.o. & p.u. 13th*	P 0

No sign of ability & unimproved by blinkers 0

MASTER JAKE (Irish) — I 275^{P}, I 374^{5}, I 608^{5}, I 644^{P}

MASTER JULIAN (Irish) — I 442^{P}

MASTER KEMAL (Irish) — I 124^{3}, I 188^{2}, I 245^{1}, I 276^{3}, I 357^{2}, I 568^{1}

MASTER KIT(IRE) b.g. 7 Lancastrian - Katie Proverb by Proverb — J N R Billinge

188	24/2	Friars Haugh	(L)	RES	3m	12	S	*2nd whn u.r. 4th*	U -
319	2/3	Corbridge	(R)	RES	3m	16	GS	*alwys prom, cls 2nd 11th, ld 3 out, ran on well, improve*	1 20
498	16/3	Lanark	(R)	CON	3m	10	G	*(fav) alwys handy, ld 9th, drew clr frm 3 out*	1 21
751	31/3	Lockerbie	(R)	CON	3m	12	G	*(fav) ld 8th til 10th, cls 2nd whn s.u. apr 12th*	S -
860	6/4	Alnwick	(L)	MXO	4m 1f	7	GF	*(fav) w.w. prog to ld 10th-13th,ld agn 21st, clr whn f last*	F -
1251	27/4	Balcormo Ma'	(R)	OPE	3m	6	GS	*(fav) disp ld frm 6th til wnt clr frm 2 out*	1 24
1354	4/5	Mosshouses	(L)	OPE	3m	4	GS	*(fav) cls up, ld 14th, clr 2 out, easily*	1 25
1542	16/5	Perth	(R)	HC	2 1/2m 110yds	8	F	*trckd ldrs going well, ev ch 4 out, ld apr last, qcknd run-in, comf.*	1 28

Ex-Irish; unbeaten when completing; very useful; novice ridden; hard to beat 97; best R/H; G/S-F 29

MASTER KIWI(NZ) b.g. 9 Bagwis (AUS) - Veela (NZ) by Oakville — F G Hollis

6	13/1	Larkhill	(R)	OPE	3m	18	GS	*mid-div, wknd 10th, t.o. & p.u. 15th*	P 0
45	3/2	Wadebridge	(L)	MDO	3m	10	GF	*prssdl ld to 12th, 4th whn hit 15th, rlld flat*	4 13
202	24/2	Lemalla	(R)	MDO	3m	12	HY	*alwys prom, not pace to chal frm 3 out*	4 11
482	13/3	Newton Abbot	(L)	HC	2m 5f 110yds	14	S	*alwys bhnd, t.o. when p.u. before 4 out.*	P 0
928	8/4	Bishopsleigh	(R)	MDN	3m	9	G	*ld 4th, nvr hdd, won readly*	1 15
1358	4/5	Flete Park	(R)	RES	3m	8	G	*(fav) handy, raced keenly, ld aft 10th, ran on strngly*	1 19

Improving; stays well; should upgrade in 97 - Confined likely; Good 19

MASTER MARIO b.g. 8 Julio Mariner - Mrs Stephens by Master Stephen — Mrs M A T Potter

1995 9(0)

471	10/3	Milborne St'	(L)	MDO	3m	16	G	*(fav) mid-div, prog 12th, chsd wnr vainly frm 15th*	2 14
520	16/3	Larkhill	(R)	MDO	3m	11	G	*(fav) sttld mid-div, prog 13th, ld apr last, ran on well*	1 18
729	31/3	Little Wind'	(R)	RES	3m	12	GS	*hdwy to 3rd 12th, onepcd frm 3 out, blndrd last*	4 16
1168	20/4	Larkhill	(R)	RES	3m	8	GF	*frnt rank,lft in ld 14th,tired,hdd & wandered apr last*	2 18
1457	8/5	Uttoxeter	(L)	HC	3 1/4m	16	G	*mid div, rdn 15th, went poor 3rd 2 out, not trbl ldrs.*	3 18

Consistent; beaten by good horses; Restricted very likely 97; G/F-G/S 19

MASTER MISCHIEF br.g. 9 Zambrano - Merry Missus by Bargello — Mrs F T Walton

1995 1(12),3(12),1(17),**10(0)**,**P(0)**,**P(0)**

83	11/2	Alnwick	(L)	CON	3m	10	GS	*ran in snatches, in tch 15th, sn wknd*	7 0
317	2/3	Corbridge	(R)	CON	3m	11	GS	*mid-div early, prog 9th, cls up 15th, styd on onepcd*	2 18
699	30/3	Tranwell	(L)	CON	3m	8	GS	*mid-div, prog 9th, cls up 15th, rdn & wknd 2 out*	3 17
911	8/4	Tranwell	(L)	CON	3m	9	GF	*ran in sntchs, 10l 6th at 14th, prog 2 out, ran on wll flat*	2 19
1513	12/5	Hexham Poin'	(L)	CON	3m	6	HY	*nvr going wll, wll bhnd frm 7th, nvr dang*	4 13
1570	19/5	Corbridge	(R)	CON	3m	8	G	*mid-div, prog 3 out, gd hdwy apr last, not qckn flat*	2 17

Dual winner 95; not 100% genuine & hard ride; likely to frustrate in future; Good 16

MASTER PUG b.g. 5 Puget (USA) - Miss Curiso — Miss Jan Woolley

901	6/4	Dingley	(R)	MDN	2m 5f	9	GS	*(bl) alwys last pair, p.u. 9th*	P 0
1183	21/4	Mollington	(R)	MDN	3m	10	F	*last pair, in tch to 12th, no ch nxt, p.u. 3 out*	P 0

Blinkers on debut a worry & no signs of ability yet 0

MASTERS NEPHEW br.g. 7 Tout Ensemble - Pembridge by Master Sing — Richard Barber

1995 P(0),U(-)

206	24/2	Castle Of C'	(R)	MDO	3m	10	HY	*(fav) in tch, disp 11th-4 out, wknd nxt, p.u. last*	P 0
1347	4/5	Holnicote	(L)	MDO	3m	16	GS	*cls 3rd whn ran out 6th*	r -
1495	11/5	Holnicote	(L)	MDO	3m	11	G	*in tch, 3rd mstly, mstk 17th, onepcd frm 3 out*	4 0
1638	1/6	Bratton Down	(L)	MDO	3m	13	G	*pllng, chsd ldr 7th, no imp apr 2 out, wnd apr last*	6 0

Top stable but headstrong & no stamina; surprise if they persist in 97 10

MASTER SWILLBROOK b.g. 12 Kinglet - Pin Hole by Parthia — M H Wood

1995 **6(16)**,**P(0)**

264	2/3	Didmarton	(L)	INT	3m	12	G	*prom, ld 5th-11th, wknd 3 out*	5 0
524	16/3	Larkhill	(R)	INT	3m	11	G	*t.o. 6th*	8 0
637	23/3	Siddington	(L)	MEM	3m	14	S	*prom til appr 10th, no ch frm 14th*	7 10

995 8/4 Hackwood Pa' (L) XX 3m 8 GF *remote 4th aft 3 out, no imp* 3 0
1244 27/4 Woodford (L) INT 3m 12 G *blnd 1st, lost tch 11th, t.o. & p.u. 3 out* P 0

Schoolmaster now & safe at the job 10

MASTER TROOPER(IRE) b.g. 6 Mandalus - Sunrise Highway Vii by Damsire Unregistered J R Weston
432 9/3 Upton-On-Se' (R) MDO 3m 17 GS *mid-div whn mstk 9th, p.u. dead* P 0

Dead 0

MASTIFF LANE b or br.g. 10 Cisto (FR) - Latch Opener by Good Light W Probin
1995 R(-),4(11),1(14),P(0)
164 17/2 Weston Park (L) RES 3m 11 G *nvr bttr than mid-div, p.u. 12th* P 0
461 9/3 Eyton-On-Se' (L) RES 3m 15 G *cls up 13th, lsng tch wth 1st 4 whn f 4 out* F -
564 17/3 Wolverhampt' (L) RES 3m 8 GS *alwys rear, p.u. 3 out* P 0
856 6/4 Sandon (L) RES 3m 9 GF *chsd ldrs, ev ch to 2 out, wknd* 6 0
1195 21/4 Sandon (L) XX 3m 9 G *mid to rear, p.u. 3 out* P 0
1233 27/4 Weston Park (L) RES 3m 14 G *mid to rear* 8 0
1421 6/5 Eyton-On-Se' (L) RES 3m 11 GF *mid-to-rr, t.o. & trd whn u.r. last* U -
1582 19/5 Wolverhampt' (L) RES 3m 10 G *bhnd, lost tch 9th, t.o. & p.u. 12th* P 0

Surprise winner 95; unreliable & reverted to bad habits 96; will not win again 0

MATCHLESSLY b.g. 13 Royal Match - Mayfield Girl by Le Prince Mrs R E Walker
1995 3(12),F(-),P(0)
340 3/3 Heythrop (R) MDN 3m 12 G *ld to 6th & 10-11th, ev ch 2 out, wknd, walked in* 6 0
747 31/3 Upper Sapey (R) MDO 3m 11 GS *ld til wknd 9th* 5 0
947 8/4 Andoversford (R) MDN 3m 11 GF *cls up, ld 6th, sn hdd, grad wknd frm 11th* 5 0
1217 24/4 Andoversford (R) MDO 3m 16 G *rcd wd, prom to 13th, t.o. & p.u. last* P 0
1381 5/5 Dingley (R) MDO 3m 16 GF *chsd wnr to 10th, wknd frm 12th, t.o.* 7 0
1511 12/5 Maisemore P' (L) MDO 3m 14 F *chsd ldrs to 11th, sn strggling* 5 0
1621 27/5 Chaddesley ' (L) MDO 3m 17 GF *mid-div, outpcd frm 11th, kpt on frm 15th, nrst fin* 3 10

Maiden after 23 attempts; does not stay & no prospects of a win at 14 10

MATCHMAKER (Irish) — **I** 332P
MATCHMAKER SEAMUS (Irish) — **I** 113P
MATRACE ch.m. 11 Mummy's Game - Sospirae by Sandford Lad K Little
1473 11/5 Aspatria (L) LAD 3m 7 GF *ld to 15th, 3rd & wknng nxt, fin tired* 4 10

Lightly raced now & prospcts of following up 92 Maiden win nil 0

MATTELLA(IRE) b.m. 8 Mandalus - Marand by Prefairy Mrs A E Speke
755 31/3 Lockerbie (R) MDN 3m 17 G *nvr dang, p.u. 3 out* P 0

Rarely seen & shows nothing 0

MATT MOSS (Irish) — **I** 358F, **I** 564P
MAURADONNA (Irish) — **I** 835, **I** 1076, **I** 2525, **I** 290P
MAVERICK'S CREEK(NZ) ro.g. 10 Kutati (NZ) - Lady Nella (NZ) by Lord Kearsey D Stephens
719 30/3 Wadebridge (L) MDO 3m 7 GF *raced keenly, jmpd boldy, ld 2nd-apr 8th, p.u. 12th, dsmntd* P 0
1362 4/5 Flete Park (R) MDO 3m 9 G *ld to 6th, wll in tch til wknd 16th, t.o. & p.u. last* P 0
1651 8/6 Umberleigh (L) MDO 3m 11 GF *bhnd frm 6th, t.o. & p.u. 11th* P 0

Shows speed but no stamina so far 0

MAXXUM PLUS (Irish) — **I** 345, , **I** 3811, **I** 4671
MAYPOLE FOUNTAIN (Irish) — **I** 133, **I** 78P, **I** 1381
MAY RUN b.f. 10 Cruise Missile - Trial Run by Deep Run W R Middleton
1995 3(0),4(15),P(0)
400 9/3 Dalston (R) LAD 3m 10 G *bhnd hlfwy, improve 14th, nvr nrr* 4 13
698 30/3 Tranwell (L) MEM 3m 5 GS *(fav) trckd ldrs, prog 15th, ld 2 out, ran on strngly* 1 13
913 8/4 Tranwell (L) LAD 3m 7 GF *nvr going wll, last at 13th, p.u. nxt* P 0

Beat a 14yo in Members; lightly raced & no chance in Ladies 13

MAY RUNNER b.m. 6 Risk Me (FR) - Bit O' May by Mummy's Pet N Lowe
1995 U(-),P(0),R(-),P(0)
352 3/3 Garnons (L) MDN 2 1/2m 9 GS *12l 4th & wkng whn f 11th* F -

Yet to complete the course 0

MAYTOWN ch.g. 10 Town And Country - Mayotte by Little Buskins R Nolan
1995 U(-),4(0),U(-),P(0),4(0),2(0),**P(0)**,3(0)
389 9/3 Llanfrynach (R) MDN 3m 11 GS *not fluent, rear, lost tch 12th, t.o. & p.u. 2 out* P 0
843 6/4 Howick (L) MEM 3m 7 GF *(bl) 2nd til ld 13th, hdd 3 out, 3rd & hld whn u.r. last* U -

1272 27/4 Pyle (R) MDO 3m 9 G *(bl) last at 5th, t.o. 12th, styd on frm 14th* 3 0
1561 18/5 Bassaleg (R) MDO 3m 8 F *rear frm 6th, t.o. 10th, sntchd dist 3rd nr fin* 3 0
1606 25/5 Bassaleg (R) MDO 3m 7 GS *(vis) disp whn u.r. 4th* U -

Placed in bad races; novice ridden & miracle needed to win 0

MCCARTNEY b.g. 10 Tug Of War - Red Cross by Pitpan — Miss Sharon Goodhand
1995 1(13),4(14)

244 25/2 Southwell P' (L) CON 3m 13 HO *mstk 3rd, alwys rear, t.o. 11th, p.u. 15th* P 0
327 3/3 Market Rase' (L) CON 3m 15 G *alwys wll bhnd, t.o. whn blnd badly 14th, fin 6th* 5 0
512 16/3 Dalton Park (R) CON 3m 10 G *keen hold, ld to 6th, 9-14th & 4 out-apr 2 out, wknd* 5 10
634 23/3 Market Rase' (L) OPE 3m 6 GF *cls up, 2nd frm 11th, chal 4 out, f nxt* F -
1000 9/4 Wetherby (L) HC 3m 110yds 10 G *in tch till outpcd after 11th, t.o..* 6 0
1302 28/4 Southwell P' (L) INT 3m 10 GF *hld up, prog to 2nd 5 out, ran on, not rch wnr* 2 16
1462 10/5 Market Rasen (R) HC 2 3/4m 110yds 11 G *held up, hdwy 11th, went 3rd apr 3 out, one pace.* 3 20

Restricted winner 95; slow to reach form 96; ran well last 2; Confined chance if held up 96 18

MC CLATCHEY (Irish) — **I** 256[P], **I** 283[2], **I** 400[1], **I** 452[P], **I** 537[F]

MCFEPEND (Irish) — **I** 239[F], **I** 507[1], **I** 641[2], **I** 658[P]

MCMAHON'S RIVER ch.m. 9 Over The River (FR) - Kanndaya (FR) by Venture Vii — J V C Davenport
1995 1(15),2(18),1(21),P(0),P(0),2(18),2(19),**P(0)**

157 17/2 Erw Lon (L) CON 3m 15 G *last trio, p.u. 14th* P 0
365 5/3 Leicester (R) HC 3m 10 GS *disp ld till mstk 4th, weakening and blnd 12th, t.o. when p.u. 2 out.* P 0
382 9/3 Llanfrynach (R) MEM 3m 7 GS *(fav) in tch, chsd ldr 12th-2 out, hrd rdn & onepcd* 3 13
1035 13/4 St Hilary (R) CON 3m 10 G *prom, ld brfly 15th, ev ch 2 out, no ext* 3 16
1158 20/4 Llanwit Maj' (R) OPE 4m 9 GS *w.w., prog to jn ldr 22nd, rdn to ld apr last, held on wll* 1 19
1318 28/4 Bitterley (L) XX 3m 8 G *ld,jmpd rght 3 & 11th,mstk & hdd 14th,wknd,p.u. 3 out* P 0

Dual winner 95; below form 96; won poor stamina test; R/H essential; hard to place now; Soft 18

MCNAY b.g. 9 Montreal Boy - Zo-Zo by Hamood — Christopher Graham
1995 4(0)

46 4/2 Alnwick (L) MEM 3m 7 G *bhnd, prog & in tch 8th, no imp frm 12th* 4 0

Runs annually now & nowhere near winning chances 10

MEADOW COTTAGE ch.g. 10 Callernish - Miss Madam by Black Tarquin — N F Williams
1995 **6(NH),4(NH),2(NH),3(NH)**

688 30/3 Chaddesley ' (L) MDN 3m 17 G *f 1st* F -
842 6/4 Maisemore P' (L) MDN 3m 17 GF *w.w. prog to ld 14th, made rest, gd jmp last, hld on wll* 1 14
1482 11/5 Bredwardine (R) RES 3m 13 G *alwys prom, ev ch 15th, outpcd nxt, tk 2nd flat* 2 14
1601 25/5 Bassaleg (R) RES 3m 12 GS *(Jt fav) rear, steady prog 10th, 8l down 3 out, nrst fin* 2 18
1641 2/6 Dingley (R) RES 3m 13 GF *in tch in rr til s.u. bnd app 9th* S -

Placed in novice hurdles; fair 1st season; stays & onepaced; should find Restricted; G/F-G/S 17

MEADOW GRAY b.g. 8 Meadowbrook - Gray Loch by Lochnager — Mick Vernon

79 11/2 Wetherby Po' (L) MDO 3m 12 GS *ld to 14th, 3rd frm 2 out, no ext* 3 0
117 17/2 Witton Cast' (R) MEM 3m 9 S *cls up to 7th, wknd 12th, t.o. 2 out* 6 0
764 31/3 Great Stain' (L) MDN 3m 16 GS *ld to 7th, sn wknd, p.u. 3 out* P 0
829 6/4 Stainton (R) MDO 3m 9 GF *prom, went 2nd 8th, chal 2 out, ev ch flat, kpt on well* 2 14
1135 20/4 Hornby Cast' (L) MDN 3m 10 G *(fav) alwys handy, ev ch 4 out, onepcd* 3 0
1452 6/5 Witton Cast' (R) MEM 3m 7 G *(fav) cls up whn f 11th* F -

Touched off when 2nd; well beaten otherwise; no guarantee of a win yet 13

MEDIAS MAID b.m. 6 Mas Media - Silleys Maid by Continuation — R T Grant

558 17/3 Ottery St M' (L) MDO 3m 9 G *mid-div, out of tch whn f 13th* F -
928 8/4 Bishopsleigh (R) MDN 3m 9 G *towrds rear til hdwy 10th, lft 2nd 3 out, nvr trbld wnnr* 2 10
1118 17/4 Hockworthy (L) MDO 3m 14 GS *6th whn f 6th* F -
1279 27/4 Bratton Down (L) MDO 3m 14 GF *in tch, 5th at 12th, lost plc & wknd 4 out* 6 0
1348 4/5 Holnicote (L) MDO 3m 9 GS *mstks, 3rd at 8th, grad wknd, p.u. 3 out* P 0
1555 18/5 Bratton Down (L) MDO 3m 13 F *4th hlfwy,ld apr 14th til cls 3rd 2 out,ld flat,drvn out* 1 13

Won a poor Maiden (8 finishers but bad lot); could improve - needs to for Restricteds 15

MEDIATOR b.g. 7 Valiyar - Blushing Cousin by Great Nephew — Paul Clifton
1995 **11(NH),9(NH),1(NH),P(NH)**

78 11/2 Wetherby Po' (L) OPE 3m 10 GS *(Jt fav) rmndrs 2nd, cls up at 10th, fdd rpdly, p.u. nxt* P 0
169 18/2 Market Rase' (L) CON 3m 15 GF *rear, prog to 5th apr 14th, no prog frm 3 out* 5 15
327 3/3 Market Rase' (L) CON 3m 15 G *w.w. hit 4th, effrt 11th, no prog 13th, p.u. 4 out* P 0

Claiming hurdle winner; stamina doubtful & no appeal in points 13

MEDIEVAL QUEEN ch.m. 11 Jester - Cookstown Lady — Mrs J Mathias

1995 P(0),P(0),2(11),P(0),1(14)

546 17/3 Erw Lon (L) LAD 3m 10 GS *t.o. 4 out, rpd late prog, nrst fin* 6 16
768 31/3 Pantyderi (R) OPE 3m 10 G *ld to 13th, fdd* 4 15
974 8/4 Lydstep (L) MEM 3m 10 G *mid-div til prog 15th, ran on, unable to chal* 2 16
1204 21/4 Lydstep (L) CON 3m 3 S *(fav) ld/disp til blnd badly 3 out, mstk 2 out, rallied flat* 2 11

Dual winner 93; won 1 of 18 races since; fortune needed to win again 15

MEGANS MYSTERY(IRE) b.g. 6 Corvaro (USA) - Megans Choice by Furry Glen J S Haldane
1995 P(0)

192 24/2 Friars Haugh (L) MDN 3m 12 S *(fav) some prog 15th, mstk nxt, wll hld whn p.u. 2 out* P 0
407 9/3 Dalston (R) MDO 2 1/2m 13 G *(Jt fav) hdwy frm hlfwy, cls up 13th, no ext apr last* 3 11
614 23/3 Friars Haugh (L) MDN 3m 10 G *(fav) 7th hlfwy, hdwy to have ch 3 out, no ext frm 2 out* 4 0
1253 27/4 Balcormo Ma' (R) MDO 3m 16 GS *bhnd early, wnt hndy 4 out, wknd qckly frm nxt* 6 0

Ran best in short Maiden; struggles to stay 3m; needs to improve to win 11

MEGS LAW (Irish) — **I** 510B, **I** 545,

MEGS MOMENT (Irish) — **I** 483P, **I** 6253, **I** 631P

MELDANTE VI (Irish) — **I** 2P, **I** 46P, **I** 292U, **I** 3234, **I** 4402, **I** 4722, **I** 5414, **I** 6425

MELDAP (Irish) — **I** 12P, **I** 105F, **I** 163F, **I** 196P, **I** 348P, **I** 3845, **I** 6224

MELLING b.g. 5 Thowra (FR) - Miss Melmore by Nishapour (FR) Miss R Dobson
1995 **18(NH),19(NH)**

282 2/3 Clyst St Ma' (L) MDN 3m 8 S *cls up early, lost plc 12th, ran on 4 out, no ch wnr* 2 0
534 16/3 Cothelstone (L) MDN 3m 10 G *keen hold, disp to 4th, wknd 11th, t.o. & p.u. 2 out* P 0
712 30/3 Barbury Cas' (L) MDO 3m 10 G *handy, ld 6-8th, cls up whn f 10th* F -
820 6/4 Charlton Ho' (L) MDN 3m 12 GF *j.w., hndy, ev ch 14th-3 out, no ext frm nxt* 4D 14
1279 27/4 Bratton Down (L) MDO 3m 14 GF *prom whn c.o. by loose horse 5th* C -
1308 28/4 Little Wind' (R) MDO 3m 6 G *made most, hdd 3 out, no ext und pres* 3 13

No ability under Rules; steady improvement in points; should find a win at 6 15

MELODIC LADY (Irish) — **I** 178P, **I** 2155, **I** 259F, **I** 3024, **I** 403P

MELODY MINE br.m. 10 Torus - Sun Chimes by Roi Soleil R R Watson

534 16/3 Cothelstone (L) MDN 3m 10 G *rear, prog 10th, wkng whn blnd 13th, t.o. & p.u. 4 out* P 0
928 8/4 Bishopsleigh (R) MDN 3m 9 G *towrds rear early, p.u. aft 11th* P 0
1115 17/4 Hockworthy (L) MDO 3m 10 GS *lft in ld 6th, hdd 14th, btn whn lft 3rd 2 out* 3 0
1431 6/5 High Bickin' (R) MDO 3m 9 G *in tch til wknd 15th* 5 0
1555 18/5 Bratton Down (L) MDO 3m 13 F *prog 12th,disp 15th,jst ld nxt-2 out,cls 3rd,blnd & u.r.last* U -

Running well last start but only beat one other when completing; much more needed in average Maiden 12

MELSONBY br.g. 14 Politico (USA) - Melmin by Comandeer R Hankey

735 31/3 Sudlow Farm (R) MEM 3m 7 G *cls up, ev ch 15th, wknd 2 out* 4 10
1032 13/4 Alpraham (R) CON 3m 9 GS *rear, last & t.o. 6th, p.u. aft 11th* P 0
1192 21/4 Sandon (L) CON 3m 11 G *rear 7th, lost tch 10th, p.u. 13th* P 0

Consistent in 94; missed 95; not disgraced in Members but too old now 0

MEL'S ROSE ch.g. 11 Anfield - Ragtime Rose by Ragstone R H York
1995 U(-),U(-),P(0)

571 17/3 Detling (L) CON 3m 13 GF *nvr trbld ldrs* 8 0
775 31/3 Penshurst (L) CON 3m 8 GS *alwys rear, lost tch 14th* 5 0
1050 13/4 Penshurst (L) CON 3m 8 G *mid-div, nvr dang, wknd 3 out* 6 11

No longer of any account 0

MELTON PARK b.g. 12 Decent Fellow - Taggs Castle by Levmoss A J Papworth
1995 6(14),8(13),3(19),3(17),P(0),3(22),**P(0)**,2(19),1(17),4(14)

90 11/2 Ampton (R) CON 3m 5 GF *in tch, chsd wnr 16th, outpcd apr 3 out, lost 2nd last* 3 20
104 17/2 Marks Tey (L) OPE 3m 14 G *j.s. 1st, mid div, styd on frm 15th, nvr nrr, lkd to fin 3rd* 4 24
310 2/3 Ampton (R) CON 3m 13 G *nvr going, last & j.s. 5th, t.o. & p.u. 16th* P 0
420 9/3 High Easter (L) OPE 3m 9 S *(bl) nt alwys fluent,prom,chall 2 out,wnt lft flat, no ex cls hme* 2 22
491 16/3 Horseheath (R) CON 3m 5 GF *(fav) (bl) mid-div, last at 5th, mstks 8 & 9th, ev ch 4 out, onepcd* 3 17
932 8/4 Marks Tey (L) OPE 3m 3 G *(bl) trckd ldr, mstk 11th, disp 13th, lft clr nxt, fin alone* 1 20
1067 13/4 Horseheath (R) OPE 3m 3 F *(bl) last & pshd alng, clsd appr 15th, chsd wnr 2 out, kpt on* 2 23
1595 25/5 Garthorpe (R) CON 3m 15 G *(bl) alwys rear hlf, prog past btn horses last m* 6 10

Grand servant, now retired 18

MEMBERING ch.g. 8 New Member - Ringcreevy Lass by Push On Miss P Sutton
1995 4(0),P(0)

473 10/3 Tweseldown (R) MEM 3m 5 G *pllng, ld til apr 12th, wknd & btn 4 out* 3 0

Lightly raced; well bveaten in poor Members; may do better if racing regularly 10

MEMBERS CRUISE ch.g. 6 Cruise Missile - Members Joy by New Member — E W Smith

375	9/3	Barbury Cas'	(L)	MDN	3m	14	GS	*sn rear, f 9th*	F	-
1216	24/4	Andoversford	(R)	INT	3m	7	G	*rr, prog 8th, 4th whn f 15th*	F	-

Showed promise 2nd start; should go close when jumping better 12

MEMBERS RIGHTS ch.m. 11 New Member - Mistress Rights by Master Spiritus — M Keel

1995 U(-),U(-),P(0),F(-)

428	9/3	Upton-On-Se'	(R)	RES	3m	17	GS	*disp ld til wknd frm 8th*	8	0
1002	9/4	Upton-On-Se'	(R)	RES	3m	8	F	*ld 2nd-6th, wknd qckly 12th, p.u. nxt*	P	0
1169	20/4	Chaddesley '	(L)	MEM	3m	9	G	*ld to 10th, outpcd frm 16th, won race for 3rd*	3	14
1415	6/5	Cursneh Hill	(L)	RES	3m	11	GF	*cls up til outpcd frm 15th, no ch frm nxt*	4	0

Maiden winner 93; finished 5 of 16 races 93-6; ran better late 96 but unlikely to win again 11

MEMORY HARBOUR (Irish) — **I** 19[P], **I** 106[F], **I** 232[F]

MENATURE(IRE) ch.g. 7 Meneval (USA) - Speedy Venture by Bargello — J D V Seth-Smith

1995 **U(NH),4(NH),5(NH),P(NH)**

897	6/4	Dingley	(R)	CON	3m	15	GS	*mid-div to 8th, fdd, p.u. aft 4 out*	P	0
1102	14/4	Guilsborough	(L)	RES	3m	15	G	*rear hlfwy,lost tch 13th,kpt on,disp poor 4th whn blnd last*	8	0
1522	12/5	Garthorpe	(R)	RES	3m	12	GF	*prom, ld 14th, disp whn f nxt*	F	-
1564	19/5	Mollington	(R)	XX	3m	14	GS	*mid-div, outpcd frm 13th, kpt on onepcd frm 2 out*	6	0
1639	2/6	Dingley	(R)	MEM	3m	7	GF	*in tch, chsd ldr 10th, ld 14th, clr 2 out, unchal*	1	17

Irish Maiden winner 94; late appearing & won bad Members; summer jumping after; Restricted possible 15

MEND b.g. 10 Busted - Sound Type by Upper Case (USA) — Mrs Julie Read

1995 **P(0)**,1(14)

11	14/1	Cottenham	(R)	LAD	3m	7	G	*ref to race*	0	0
33	20/1	Higham	(L)	LAD	3m	9	GF	*hld up, in tch, ch 16th, btn appr 2 out*	6	14
93	11/2	Ampton	(R)	LAD	3m	7	GF	*trckd ldrs going wll, ev ch 17th, sn outpcd*	3	13
346	3/3	Higham	(L)	INT	3m	6	G	*cls up til wknd 15th, no ch nxt*	5	14
418	9/3	High Easter	(L)	CON	3m	10	S	*in tch til outpcd appr 14th, no dang aft*	6	0
619	23/3	Higham	(L)	OPE	3m	10	GF	*ld to 3rd, mstk & rdn 10th, btn aft 13th*	7	10

Restricted winner 95; well beaten in 96; Members looks only hope in 97 14

MENDIP MUSIC br.g. 12 Sousa - Track Music — Miss E Crawford

1995 8(0),2(19),R(-),2(14)

208	24/2	Castle Of C'	(R)	LAD	3m	14	HY	*1st ride, alwys mid-div, nvr on terms*	5	0
693	30/3	Llanvapley	(L)	LAD	3m	6	GS	*alwys 2nd, strng chal 15th, just hld*	2	22
847	6/4	Howick	(L)	LAD	3m	9	GF	*mid-div, hmpd & p.u. 9th, saddle slppd*	P	0
1036	13/4	St Hilary	(R)	LAD	3m	6	G	*mostly 5th, prog to 7l 4th whn u.r. 14th*	U	-
1264	27/4	Pyle	(R)	LAD	3m	10	G	*w.w. prog 13th, rdn to ld last, kpt on*	1	18
1414	6/5	Cursneh Hill	(L)	LAD	3m	9	GF	*chsd ldrs, styd on frm 15th, 2nd & lkd held whn u.r. last*	U	21
1559	18/5	Bassaleg	(R)	LAD	3m	4	F	*pllng, cls up, ld 8th, qcknd 11th, jnd 14th-last, ran on wll*	1	20
1603	25/5	Bassaleg	(R)	LAD	3m	4	GS	*(fav) cls up, ld apr 10th, made rest, alwys in cmmnd*	1	21

Changed hands & novice ridden 96; retains ability; stays well; can win again; G/S-F 20

MENDIP SON b.g. 6 Hallgate - Silver Surprise by Son Of Silver — Nick Shutts

1995 **2(NH),14(NH),2(NH)**

71	10/2	Great Treth'	(R)	MDO	3m	15	S	*(fav) chsng grp til mstk 10th, p.u. bef nxt*	P	0
590	23/3	Wetherby Po'	(L)	MDO	3m	16	S	*rear til p.u. 9th*	P	0
748	31/3	Upper Sapey	(R)	MDO	3m	11	GS	*(bl) clr ldr to 10th, wknd rpdly, last whn p.u. 15th*	P	0
1041	13/4	Bitterley	(L)	MEM	3m	6	G	*(bl) tk str hld, ran out 4th*	r	-

Placed in hurdles; a nightmare ride in points 0

MENEDREAM (Irish) — **I** 381[P], **I** 418[P], **I** 533[P]

MENEDUKE (Irish) — **I** 368[U], **I** 476[3], **I** 578[5]

MERCHANT MILE b.g. 9 Idiot's Delight - Mary Mile by Athenius — Mrs S E D Voller

376	9/3	Barbury Cas'	(L)	MEM	3m	4	GS	*ld til 7th, wknd rpdly 11th, p.u. nxt*	P	0

Of no account 0

MERINO WALTZ(USA) b.h. 10 Nijinsky (CAN) - Bethamane by Wajima (USA) — Lee Bowles

1995 3(18),2(16),**U(-)**,P(0),**3(23)**,**U(-)**

98	12/2	Hereford	(R)	HC	3m 1f 110yds	12	HY	*not fluent, alwys bhnd, t.o. when p.u. before 15th.*	P	0
384	9/3	Llanfrynach	(R)	OPE	3m	16	GS	*prom, cls up 15th, sn outpcd, kpt on apr last*	5	18
846	6/4	Howick	(L)	OPE	3m	7	GF	*hld up, prog to ld 12th, hdd 3 out, styd on, no ch wnr*	2	18
1385	6/5	Pantyderi	(R)	CON	3m	6	GF	*(fav) trckd ldrs to 13th, mstk nxt, wknd, tired*	4	0

Irish bumper winner 90; beaten all starts 95-6 & continues to frustrate; best watched 16

MERITMOORE b.g. 13 Moorestyle - More Treasure by Ballymore — K Tork

104 17/2 Marks Tey (L) OPE 3m 14 G *alwys bhnd, p.u. 13th* P 0
273 2/3 Parham (R) LAD 3m 11 GF *immed dtchd, t.o. hlfwy, p.u. 3 out* P 0
572 17/3 Detling (L) LAD 3m 10 GF *mid-div to hlfwy, wll bhnd 4 out* 8 0
1053 13/4 Penshurst (L) LAD 3m 5 G *jnd ldrs 10th, lost plc 13th, ran on strngly 2 out, ld last* 1 16

25/1 shock winner of soft race; hard to see another at 14 13

MERLINS GIRL ch.m. 10 Feelings (FR) - Raver — Mrs Helen Lynch
1995 1(14),2(0),7(0),6(0),U(-),7(0)
726 31/3 Garthorpe (R) RES 3m 16 G *f 1st* F -
904 6/4 Dingley (R) RES 3m 20 GS *rear div til floundd p.u. 8th* P 0
1025 13/4 Brocklesby ' (L) XX 3m 9 GF *last pair for 2 m,prog 4 out,slght ld 2 out,cght clse home* 2 16
1302 28/4 Southwell P' (L) INT 3m 10 GF *sn rear, t.o. & p.u. 5 out* P 0
1518 12/5 Garthorpe (R) MEM 3m 6 GF *chsd ldrs, alwys 2nd/3rd, lft 2nd 3 out, ran on* 2 13
1595 25/5 Garthorpe (R) CON 3m 15 G *abt 7th 1st m, fdd, bhnd whn p.u. 2 out* P 0

Maiden winner 95; placed in weak races 96; needs easy 3m; Restricted still unlikely 14

MERLYNS CHOICE b.g. 12 Ovac (ITY) - Liffey's Choice by Little Buskins — A Woodward
1995 U(-),P(0),5(0),5(14),2(14),5(0),4(11),2(13),9(0),3(0),3(10)
96 11/2 Ampton (R) XX 3m 11 GF *alwys wll bhnd, t.o. & p.u. 15th* P 0
244 25/2 Southwell P' (L) CON 3m 13 HO *sn t.o. in last, p.u. 4 out* P 0
395 9/3 Garthorpe (R) OPE 3m 7 G *alwys last pair, t.o. frm 10th* 5 0
537 17/3 Southwell P' (L) OPE 3m 7 GS *(bl) mid-div, lost tch, t.o.* 5 0
723 31/3 Garthorpe (R) CON 3m 19 G *s.s. alwys last grp, t.o. 7th* 11 0

No longer of any account 0

MERRY CASTLE (Irish) — **I** 150^{5}, **I** 240^{F}, **I** 609^{5}

MERRY JERRY b or br.g. 10 Montreal Boy - Very Merry by Lord Of Verona — Robert Neill
1995 6(0),1(15),F(-)
84 11/2 Alnwick (L) RES 3m 11 GS *rear, effrt 9th, outpcd nxt, sn wll bhnd* 6 0
186 24/2 Friars Haugh (L) MEM 3m 7 S *wll in tch til outpcd frm 2 out* 4 12
858 6/4 Alnwick (L) RES 3m 7 GF *(bl) bhnd 6th, pshd alng 9th, ran on frm 2 out, no dang* 4 0

Members winner 95; lightly raced; outclassed in Restricteds; Members only hope again 12

MERRY NUTKIN ch.g. 10 Jalmood (USA) - Merry Cindy by Sea Hawk II — Robert F S Newall
316 2/3 Corbridge (R) MEM 3m 10 GS *last til prog 5th, ld brfly nxt, btn 3rd whn u.r. last* U -

Formerly useful on Flat & hurdles but looks finished now 0

MERRY RIVER (Irish) — **I** 503^{2}, **I** 608^{3}

MERRY SCORPION ch.g. 7 Scorpio (FR) - Merry Jane by Rymer — T D Marlow
1995 **F(NH)**
164 17/2 Weston Park (L) RES 3m 11 G *chsd ldr to 11th, in tch in 3rd whn u.r. 5 out* U -
288 2/3 Eaton Hall (R) MDO 3m 17 G *ld, set str pace, carried by loose horses 10th* C -
464 9/3 Eyton-On-Se' (L) MDN 2 1/2m 13 G *mid-div, nvr rchd ldrs, lft 3rd aftr last* 3 11
659 24/3 Eaton Hall (R) MEM 3m 6 S *cls up, disp frm 11th, ld 13th, prssd last, ran on well* 1 13
1220 24/4 Brampton Br' (R) OPE 3m 10 G *wnt 2nd 10th, clsd on ldr til ld 16th, just hld on* 1 16

Improvingst prevailed both wins; poor Open win limits winning choices in 97; G-S 17

METAL MISS (Irish) — **I** 144^{P}, **I** 243^{P}, **I** 354^{P}, **I** 506^{U}

METROSTYLE gr.g. 13 Roselier (FR) - Changing Gears by Master Owen — C H Warner
157 17/2 Erw Lon (L) CON 3m 15 G *alwys prom, ld 12th, hdd & no ext flat* 2 17
263 2/3 Didmarton (L) INT 3m 18 G *mid-div, lost tch 12th, no ch aft, p.u. last* P 0
545 17/3 Erw Lon (L) CON 3m 10 GS *mid-div, prog frm 4 out, no ch wth wnr* 2 16
767 31/3 Pantyderi (R) INT 3m 7 G *alwys prom, chsd wnr 4 out, no imp* 2 18
978 8/4 Lydstep (L) OPE 3m 6 G *nvr nrr enough to chal* 3 14
1211 23/4 Chepstow (L) HC 3m 13 S *bhnd from 7th, t.o. when p.u. before 4 out.* P 0

Ex-Irish pointer; ran some solid races but will find it hard to win at 14 15

MIAMI BEAR b.g. 10 Miami Springs - Belinda Bear by Ragstone — Mrs L M Fahey
1995 **4(NH),3(NH),3(NH),5(NH),5(NH)**
222 24/2 Duncombe Pa' (R) MEM 3m 6 GS *ld/disp til ld 7th, made rest, clr & hit 3 out, comf* 1 17

Winning chaser; enjoyed drop in class; ran under Rules after win 19

MICHAEL UGENE (Irish) — **I** 199^{F}

MICHELLES CRYSTAL b.m. 5 Ovac (ITY) - Lochlairey by Lochnager — Paul Wise
1995 **19(NH)**
167 17/2 Weston Park (L) MDN 3m 10 G *mstks, t.o. 8th, p.u. 12th* P 0
464 9/3 Eyton-On-Se' (L) MDN 2 1/2m 13 G *nvr btr thn mid-div, btn 8th, p.u. 3 out* P 0

Only learning & shows nothing yet 0

MICHERADO(FR) ch.g. 6 Un Desperado (FR) - Quality Stripe (USA) by Lyphard (USA) — Stanley W Clarke

364	5/3	Leicester	(R)	HC	2m 1f	12	GS	*(fav) taken down early, ld, soon well clr, blnd 2nd, hdd apr 2 out, wknd.*	3	19
1336	1/5	Cheltenham	(L)	HC	2m 110yds	9	G	*taken steadily to start, ld 2nd, soon clr, hit 3rd, hdd 10th, wknd apr 3 out.*	5	14

Has two speeds - flat out & stop; won novice chase after H/Chases & future lies there 20

MICKEY'S DREAM (Irish) — I 52[2], I 74[P]

MICKLEY JUSTTHEONE b.m. 7 Rymer - Mickley Love Story by Eastern Lyric — Mrs G M Brookshaw

1995 P(0),F(-),F(-)

166	17/2	Weston Park	(L)	MDN	3m	10	G	*cls up, ld 5th-nxt, wknd rpdly, p.u. 13th*	P	0
463	9/3	Eyton-On-Se'	(L)	MDN	2 1/2m	14	G	*c.u. to hlfwy, fdd 5 out, p.u. 3 out*	P	0
660	24/3	Eaton Hall	(R)	MDN	3m	7	S	*chsng grp, in tch wth ldrs whn f heavily 10th*	F	-

Yet to complete & shows no abilty yet 0

MICKSDILEMMA b.g. 9 Mick The Lark (USA) - Lovely Sister by Menelek — Nick Shutts

286	2/3	Eaton Hall	(R)	MDO	3m	14	G	*mid-div, prog 4 out, fin well*	3	11
589	23/3	Wetherby Po'	(L)	MDO	3m	16	S	*mid-div, prog 12th, disp whn f 2 out*	F	-
896	6/4	Whittington	(L)	MDO	3m	5	F	*(fav) w.w., 2nd 14th, mstk last, drvn to chal flat, outpcd*	2	14
1048	13/4	Bitterley	(L)	MDO	3m	12	G	*cls 3rd at 8th, ev ch 15th, not qckn 3 out, tk 2nd flat*	2	13
1319	28/4	Bitterley	(L)	MDN	3m	13	G	*ld 1st, alwys prom, hit 14th, lft 2nd 3 out*	2	12
1484	11/5	Bredwardine	(R)	MDO	3m	17	G	*cls 3rd at 10th, ld 14th, jnd 3 out, rdn nxt, just hld on*	1	15

Consistent; onepaced; beat subsequent winner when scoring; summer jumping after; Restricted likely 16

MIDAS MAN ch.g. 5 Gold Claim - Golden Starfish by Porto Bello — Mrs K Russell

109	17/2	Lanark	(R)	MEM	3m	5	GS	*u.r. 1st*	U	-

Could not have done less 0

MIDGE b.m. 9 Reformed Character - Alpro by Count Albany — Mrs P P Wright

1995 F(-),U(-),8(11),3(13),S(-)

172	18/2	Market Rase'	(L)	RES	3m	9	GF	*w.w. prog & in tch 11th, wknd apr 14th, p.u. aft 2 out*	P	0
329	3/3	Market Rase'	(L)	RES	3m	12	G	*alwys bhnd, t.o. 11th, p.u. last*	P	0
411	9/3	Charm Park	(L)	RES	3m	20	G	*mid-div, nvr fctr, p.u. 3 out*	P	0
515	16/3	Dalton Park	(R)	XX	3m	12	G	*blnd 7th, alwys rear, t.o. & p.u. aft 3 out*	P	0
985	8/4	Charm Park	(L)	INT	3m	9	GF	*mid-div, prog hlfwy, nvr dang*	5	14
1025	13/4	Brocklesby '	(L)	XX	3m	9	GF	*cls up for 2 m,cont 3 out,on terms whn bldnrd & u.r.last*	U	15
1284	27/4	Easingwold	(L)	RES	3m	14	G	*alwys mid-div, rdn 10th, hmpd & c.o. 4 out*	C	-
1368	4/5	Gisburn	(R)	RES	3m	9	G	*6th whn f 8th*	F	-

1 win from 25 starts; mistakes & another success looks impossible 10

MIDI MINSTREL (Irish) — I 107[U], I 176[3], I 259[P], I 320[U], I 397[P], I 490[4], I 535[P]

MIDNIGHT RUNNER b.m. 6 Good Times (ITY) - Miss Jade by Hardgreen (USA) — A P Garland

1301	28/4	Southwell P'	(L)	MDO	3m	10	GF	*ref 1st*	R	-
1434	6/5	Ashorne	(R)	MDO	3m	15	G	*rear, 13th whn u.r. 8th*	U	-
1523	12/5	Garthorpe	(R)	MDO	3m	11	GF	*mid to rear, no ch whn p.u. 13th*	P	0

Gradually getting further but no sign of ability yet 0

MIDNIGHT SERVICE (Irish) — I 21[2], I 90[1], I 159[3], I 477[2]

MIDNIGHT SOCIETY (Irish) — I 149[P], I 203[5]

MIGHTY FALCON b.g. 11 Comedy Star (USA) - Lettuce by So Blessed — R J Tory

1995 **4(NH),5(NH),3(NH),7(NH),6(NH)**

467	10/3	Milborne St'	(L)	MEM	3m	8	G	*1st ride, chsd ldrs, 4th at 15th, styd on frm 2 out, nrst fn*	2	14
519	16/3	Larkhill	(R)	CON	3m	5	G	*alwys prom, rallied frm 2 out, no ext flat*	2	20
730	31/3	Little Wind'	(R)	LAD	3m	6	GS	*in tch til aft 14th, no ch clsng stgs*	4	12
1058	13/4	Badbury Rin'	(L)	LAD	3m	5	GF	*in tch to 4 out, 3rd & wkng whn mssd marker aft last, rtrcd*	4	0
1167	20/4	Larkhill	(R)	MEM	3m	9	GF	*frnt rank, ld 6-14th, ran on to chs wnr frm 2 out*	2	17

Good schoolmaster for rider & ran well; could go one better in Members 97; Good 17

MIGHTY HAGGIS b.g. 9 Glen Quaich - Willie Pat by Pitpan — Sir Sanderson Temple

1995 F(-),4(13),2(13),P(0)

292	2/3	Eaton Hall	(R)		3m	15	G	*mid to rear, sn btn, p.u. 3 out*	P	0

Irish Maiden winner 92; finished early 96 & unlikely to achieve anything now 10

MIGHTY TRUST (Irish) — I 68[3], I 117[4], I 157[1], I 220[6]

MIGHTY WIZARD br.g. 6 Doc Marten - Powder Horn by Scottish Rifle — J O Barr

764	31/3	Great Stain'	(L)	MDN	3m	16	GS	*mid-div, wknd 12th, p.u. 3 out*	P	0

No magic on debut 0

MIKE STAN (Irish) — I 247[1]

MILBIRD ch.g. 15 Milford - Gulf Bird by Gulf Pearl — W W Sim

1995 2(0)

1370	4/5	Peper Harow	(L)	MEM	3m	3 F	*tubed, cls up, ld 13th, clr 3 out, eased flat,*	1	12

Popped up to win Members at 15; probably ready for retirement now 11

MILE MILL (Irish) — I 110[P], I 193[3]

MILENKEH (Irish) — I 68[U], I 124[F], I 154[6], I 250[U], I 269[F], I 296[P]

MILES MORE FUN b.m. 7 Idiot's Delight - Mary Mile by Athenius — Mrs Sarah Adams

1995 1(0),P(0),4(10)

554	17/3	Ottery St M'	(L)	MEM	3m	5 G	*plld hrd, ld aft 2nd til p.u. aft nxt, stewards*	P	0
720	30/3	Wadebridge	(L)	RES	3m	9 GF	*2nd whn blnd & u.r. 5th (ditch)*	U	-
1647	8/6	Umberleigh	(L)	OPE	3m	7 GF	*hld up, prog 7th, cls 3rd whn hmpd & u.r. 3 out*	U	-

Walked over for Members 95; brief but unfortunate 96; short of Restricted standard 12

MILEY PIKE b.g. 9 Amboise - Cornetta by Cornuto — Mrs K Tutty

1995 **P(NH),4(NH),6(NH)**

77	11/2	Wetherby Po'	(L)	RES	3m	18 GS	*alwys prom, 3rd at 12th, rnwd chal 2 out, nvr nrr*	4	17
225	24/2	Duncombe Pa'	(R)	RES	3m	12 GS	*ld to 3rd, chsd wnr, rdn to chal last, no ext flat*	2	15
825	6/4	Stainton	(R)	RES	3m	7 GF	*chsd ldrs, grad wknd frm 6 out, t.o.*	6	0

Ex-novice chaser; lightly raced; needs stamina test; can win Restricted if fit 97; G-S 16

MILEY SWEENEY (Irish) — I 329[3], I 359[6], I 486[4], I 553[1]

MILFORD ROAD (Irish) — I 213[P], I 293[F], I 323[F], I 375[1]

MILITARY TWO STEP b.g. 14 Rarity - Jasusa by Cantab — M H D Barlow

1995 4(14),7(0),3(16),4(18),1(13)

126	17/2	Kingston Bl'	(L)	LAD	3m	11 GS	*ld/disp til lost plc 10th, no ch 13th, 6th whn p.u. 2 out*	P	0
436	9/3	Newton Brom'	(R)	LAD	3m	10 GS	*ld to 4th, chsd ldrs til lost plc 9th, styd on well frm 2out*	4	16
792	2/4	Heythrop	(R)	LAD	3 3/4m	7 F	*ld to 15th & frm 17th, 5l clr 2 out, hdd nr fin*	2	17
1015	13/4	Kingston Bl'	(L)	MEM	3m	9 G	*chsd ldrs, outpcd 14th, no prog aft*	7	10
1457	8/5	Uttoxeter	(L)	HC	3 1/4m	16 G	*rdn and lost pl after 12th, t.o. when p.u. before 4 out.*	P	0

Members winner 95; mostly outclassed now but just pipped in weak race at Heythrop 15

MILITATION (Irish) — I 137[P], I 162[P]

MILLAROO b.g. 7 Chukaroo - Mill Straight by Straight Lad — Robin Mills

1995 U(-),P(0),3(0)

68	10/2	Great Treth'	(R)	RES	3m	14 S	*ld to 3rd, sn bhnd, p.u. aft 12th*	P	0
134	17/2	Ottery St M'	(L)	CON	3m	12 GS	*sn bhnd, t.o. & p.u. 4 out*	P	0
448	9/3	Haldon	(R)	MDO	3m	10 S	*ld til apr 3rd, lost plc frm 7th, bhnd & p.u. 13th*	P	0
1115	17/4	Hockworthy	(L)	MDO	3m	10 GS	*in tch til wknd & p.u. 14th*	P	0
1143	20/4	Flete Park	(R)	MDN	3m	17 S	*alwys bhnd, t.o. & p.u. last*	P	0

Finished 1 of 8 races 95-6 & shows no ability 0

MILLBAY(IRE) br.g. 8 Pollerton - Night Course by Crash Course — Mrs C Bailey

177	18/2	Horseheath	(R)	CON	3m	8 G	*prom,ld 7th-11th,effrt & ev ch 3 out,mstk nxt,onepcd aft*	2	23
422	9/3	High Easter	(L)	INT	3m	3 S	*(fav) disp ld, hit 13th, ld nxt drw clr appr last, easy*	1	20
831	6/4	Marks Tey	(L)	CON	3m	6 G	*(fav) cls up, trckd ldr 16th, ld last, ran on, just hld on*	1	20

Won 5 in 94; missed 95; useful but below best last start; Opens if fit 97; G-S 25

MILLER KING (Irish) — I 111[6], I 167[1]

MILLERMAN (Irish) — I 407[P], I 492[P], I 583[F]

MILLFRONE (Irish) — I 86[1]

MILL KNOCK b.g. 14 Park Row - Barlocco Bay by Cantab — J D Thompson

1995 **6(0)**,2(0),**7(0)**,**P(0)**,F(-)

911	8/4	Tranwell	(L)	CON	3m	9 GF	*alwys rear, last whn mstk 12th, t.o.*	9	0
1512	12/5	Hexham Poin'	(L)	MEM	3m	6 HY	*(fav) trckd ldr 6th, ld apr 10th, grad drew clr, canter*	1	11
1576	19/5	Corbridge	(R)	MEM	3m	4 G	*blnd 1st, sn rcvrd, chsd wnr 9th, no ch*	2	14

Only effective in Members now & beat a bunch of hunters when winning 10

MILWAUKEE (Irish) — I 196[1]

MINEHILL (Irish) — I 4[P], I 13[4], I 69[3], I 154[2], I 187[1]

MINELLA LASS (Irish) — I 515[U]

MINELLA MIDGET (Irish) — I 79[P]

MINELLA MILLER (Irish) — I 57[3], I 78[P], I 328[2]

MINELLA STAR (Irish) — I 296[2], I 445[4]

MINERAL AL (Irish) — **I** 162[F], **I** 223[5]

MINERS FORTUNE(IRE) b.g. 8 Miner's Lamp - Banish Misfortune by Master Owen — J A C Edwards

691 30/3 Llanvapley (L) CON 3m 15 GS *prom, 2nd at 8th, ld 13th, made rest, hit 2 out, ran on flat* 1 22
1042 13/4 Bitterley (L) CON 3m 9 G *(fav) hit 4th, mid-div whn s.u. bend apr 8th* S -
1171 20/4 Chaddesley ' (L) OPE 3m 15 G *alwys cls up, ev ch 16th, 5th & btn 2 out, p.u. last* P 0

Irish Maiden winner 93; fastest time of day when winning; stays but lightly raced; should win again 21

MINERS MEDIC(IRE) b.g. 5 Miner's Lamp - Suny Furlong by Sunyboy — Dr D B A Silk

105 17/2 Marks Tey (L) RES 3m 11 G *rr, lsing tch whn p.u. appr 15th* P 0

No show on debut but may do better 0

MINERS REST b.m. 8 Sula Bula - Miners Lodge by Eborneezer — Mrs K J Gilmore

1995 P(0),3(0),4(0),P(0),3(0),8(0),4(10)

129 17/2 Kingston Bl' (L) MDN 3m 15 GS *cls up to 6th, t.o. 13th, no ch aft* 5 0
236 24/2 Heythrop (R) MDN 3m 13 GS *chsd ldrs to 11th, rear whn p.u. 2 out* P 0
640 23/3 Siddington (L) LAD 3m 9 S *rr, prog & in tch 13th, wknd appr 15th* 4 10
903 6/4 Dingley (R) LAD 3m 7 GS *cls up, 3rd 6 out, chsd wnnr 3 out, alwys held* 2 13
1018 13/4 Kingston Bl' (L) LAD 3m 8 G *bhnd frm 9th, t.o. & p.u. 3 out* P 0
1240 27/4 Clifton On ' (L) MDO 3m 10 GF *w.w. cls up 12th, ev ch 15th, outpcd frm 3 out* 3 10
1504 11/5 Kingston Bl' (L) MDO 3m 13 G *in tch to 12th, wll btn aft nxt, no real prog* 5 0

Placed 7 times 95-6 but does not stay & chances of a win still minimal 11

MINER'S SUNSET (Irish) — **I** 132[P]

MINERS VALLEY (Irish) — **I** 98[P], **I** 180[P], **I** 260[P]

MINE'S A GIN(IRE) gr.g. 5 Roselier (FR) - Cathedral Street by Boreen Beag — Mrs H C Johnson

711 30/3 Barbury Cas' (L) MDO 3m 8 G *schoold in rear til p.u. 12th* P 0
1075 13/4 Lifton (R) RES 3m 12 S *in tch til lost grnd stdly frm 12th,p.u. apr 2 out,schld,imp* P 0
1293 28/4 Barbury Cas' (L) MDO 3m 11 F *jmpd slwly, wll bhnd frm 8th, t.o. & p.u. 10th* P 0
1431 6/5 High Bickin' (R) MDO 3m 9 G *prom til lost plc 9th, bhnd frm 15th* 6 0
1627 27/5 Lifton (R) MDO 3m 9 GS *blnd 7th,prog to 2nd at 13th,lft in ld 3 out, pshd clr flat* 1 15

Slowly got to grips; beat subsequent winner when scoring; good stable & should improve 15

MINIBRIG b.m. 10 Le Coq D'Or - Millymeeta by New Brig — Mrs Jane Clark

1995 1(22),2(19)

400 9/3 Dalston (R) LAD 3m 10 G *bhnd 7th,hdwy 9th,clsd up app 2 out,strng brst flt,ld nr ln* 1 21
499 16/3 Lanark (R) LAD 3m 10 G *(fav) hld up, went 2nd brfly 4 out, no imp whn lft 2nd agn 2 out* 2 12
789 1/4 Kelso (L) HC 3m 1f 11 GF *settld with chasing gp, 5th and one pace when f 6 out.* F -
1250 27/4 Balcormo Ma' (R) LAD 3m 5 GS *(fav) bhnd, some hdwy frm 3 out, nvr nrr* 3 11
1352 4/5 Mosshouses (L) LAD 3m 10 GS *drppd last 6th, mstk 11th, ran on 15th, kpt on und pres flat* 3 15
1572 19/5 Corbridge (R) LAD 3m 8 G *mid-div, prog to chs ldrs hlfwy, nvr nrr* 3 13

Useful at best but best fresh & form trails off after; win Ladies debut 97; stays; Good 22

MINOR KEY (Irish) — **I** 250[3], **I** 296[1], **I** 425[U], **I** 544[5], **I** 629[1]

MINSTRALS BOYO ch.g. 9 Black Minstrel - Sweater Girl by Blue Cashmere — A Cole

299 2/3 Great Treth' (R) MDO 3m 13 G *prom, 4th whn f 14th* F -

Fair debut but not seen after 11

MINSTREL MADAME (Irish) — **I** 50[4], **I** 151[U], **I** 182[1]

MINSTREL PADDY b.g. 13 Black Minstrel - Lin-A-Dee by Linacre — W M Burnell

326 3/3 Market Rase' (L) OPE 3m 14 G *wll bhnd 10th, p.u. 2 out* P 0
410 9/3 Charm Park (L) OPE 3m 17 G *cls up early, wknd hlfwy, onepcd aft* 12 0
587 23/3 Wetherby Po' (L) OPE 3m 15 S *rear frm 10th, bhnd whn p.u. 14th* P 0
1092 14/4 Whitwell-On' (R) CON 3m 10 G *rear whn mstk 8th, wknd 13th, t.o. & p.u. 2 out* P 0
1282 27/4 Easingwold (L) OPE 3m 8 G *(vis) rear, mstk 5th, lost tch 7th, t.o. & p.u. 14th* P 0

Winning Irish chaser; returned from 3 year absence; of no account now 0

MINSTREL SAM (Irish) — **I** 276[P], **I** 333[P], **I** 461[P], **I** 505[4], **I** 591[4]

MINSTRELS JAZZ ch.m. 6 Black Minstrel - Tom's Lass by Proverb — Mrs G L Lee

1995 U(-),P(0)

745 31/3 Upper Sapey (R) INT 3m 6 GS *mid-div whn f 4th* F -
884 6/4 Brampton Br' (R) MDN 3m 12 GF *hit 6th, wknd 14th, p.u. 16th, lame* P 0

Yet to complete & problems to boot 0

MINSTRELS JOY(IRE) ch.g. 8 Black Minstrel - Enco's Lek by Menelek — M J Jerram

1995 P(0)

31 20/1 Higham (L) CON 3m 9 GF *ld to 4th, wknd appr 13th, t.o. & p.u. appr last, dead* P 0

Dead 0

MINSTREL'S NIGHT(IRE) b.g. 5 Black Minstrel - Enchanted Evening by Warpath — T P Whales

898 6/4 Dingley (R) MDN 2m 5f 10 GS *in tch last pair whn blkd by loose horse 7th* B -
1381 5/5 Dingley (R) MDO 3m 16 GF *in tch to 10th, t.o. & f 13th, dead* F -

Dead **0**

MINSTREL'S QUAY (Irish) — I 458, , I 516, , I 589[P], I 608, , I 645[3]

MIRACLE ME (Irish) — I 638[P], I 653[1]

MIRPUR b.g. 14 Leander - Malina by Astec — Miss Kim Smith

1995 U(-),3(0),7(10),2(18),1(0)

1316 28/4 Bitterley (L) OPE 3m 5 G *chsd ldrs til outpcd 12th, wknd & p.u. 15th* P 0
1437 6/5 Ashorne (R) MXO 3m 13 G *cls up to 10th, sn wknd, t.o. & p.u. 13th* P 0
1510 12/5 Maisemore P' (L) XX 3m 8 F *mstk 6th, t.o. last whn ref 9th* R -

Easily won poor Ladies 95; back to normal in 96 & looks finished now **0**

MIRROMARK (Irish) — I 446[P]

MIS-E-FISHANT b.m. 8 Sunyboy - Alpine Orchid by Mon Capitaine — H Turberfield

1995 U(-),2(0)

221 24/2 Newtown (L) MDN 3m 12 GS *mstk 5th, last whn p.u. 7th* P 0
432 9/3 Upton-On-Se' (R) MDO 3m 17 GS *last whn f 3 out* F -
689 30/3 Chaddesley ' (L) MDN 3m 15 G *prom to 10th, sn wknd, t.o.* 5 0
883 6/4 Brampton Br' (R) MDN 3m 13 GF *strtd fence bhnd, p.u. 5th* P 0
1048 13/4 Bitterley (L) MDO 3m 12 G *made most to 4th, wknd 11th, t.o. 15th* 5 0

In-e-fishant; unpromising **0**

MISGIVINGS (Irish) — I 7[1]

MISS ANNAGAUL (Irish) — I 101[U]

MISS BEAL b.m. 8 Full Of Hope - Bealsmead by Rugantino — Mrs G Drury

779 31/3 Penshurst (L) RES 3m 13 GS *b.d. 1st* B -
965 8/4 Heathfield (R) INT 3m 6 G *sn wll bhnd, blnd 5-6th, hmpd nxt, t.o. & p.u 9th* P 0
1055 13/4 Penshurst (L) MDO 3m 11 G *alwys rear, p.u. 12th* P 0

No signs of ability **0**

MISS BERTAINE (Irish) — I 433[P], I 504[5], I 575[U], I 640[B]

MISS CATHERINE (Irish) — I 592[2], I 640, , I 661[4]

MISS CLARE b.m. 8 Cruise Missile - Claredel by Saucy Kit — I D S Jones

391 9/3 Llanfrynach (R) MDN 3m 11 GS *nrly u.r. 6th, alwys bhnd, 7th & t.o. 11th, p.u. nxt* P 0
694 30/3 Llanvapley (L) RES 3m 9 GS *rear, blnd 7th, lost tch 11th, p.u. 3 out* P 0
1161 20/4 Llanwit Maj' (R) MDO 3m 15 GS *mstks, wll bhnd til f 14th* F -
1485 11/5 Bredwardine (R) MDO 3m 15 G *cls up 9th, lost tch ldrs 11th, t.o. & p.u. 2 out* P 0
1606 25/5 Bassaleg (R) MDO 3m 7 GS *hld up, lost plc 8th, drvn to cls 5th whn f 11th* F -

Jumps poorly & offers no encouragement yet **0**

MISS CONSTRUE b.m. 9 Rymer - Miss Behave by Don't Look — Mrs Kit Martin

36 20/1 Higham (L) RES 3m 12 GF *in tch, jnd ldr 16th, ld nxt, rdn out* 1 17
346 3/3 Higham (L) INT 3m 6 G *cls up on outer, prog 14th, styd on onepcd 2 out* 4 15
484 15/3 Fakenham (L) HC 2m 5f 110yds 13 GF *alwys towards rear, lost tch from 10th, mstk 2 out.* 10 0
934 8/4 Marks Tey (L) CON 3m 6 G *hld up,prog 6th,blnd 9th,4th & ev ch 15th,sn outpcd,virt p.u* 3 13

Missed 95; beat subsequent winners when scoring; likes Higham; may have Confined chance there 97; GF **17**

MISS CORINTHIAN br.m. 9 Cardinal Flower - Buck's Fairy by Master Buck — G M Flynn

1995 P(0),2(0),4(0)

264 2/3 Didmarton (L) INT 3m 12 G *u.r. 2nd* U -
379 9/3 Barbury Cas' (L) XX 3m 9 GS *sn rear, t.o. 11th, btn 2 fences* 5 0
598 23/3 Howick (L) MEM 3m 6 S *alwys 3rd/4th, onepcd frm hlfwy* 4 0
850 6/4 Howick (L) MDN 3m 14 GF *hld up, prog to 4th at 11th, 3rd 3 out, chal nxt, alwys hld* 2 12
1079 13/4 Cothelstone (L) INT 3m 5 GF *disp 2nd, effrt und pres 14th, no imp wnr* 2 13
1293 28/4 Barbury Cas' (L) MDO 3m 11 F *(fav) mstks, trckd ldrs, rdn to chal last, ev ch, just hld* 2 14
1511 12/5 Maisemore P' (L) MDO 3m 14 F *prom,mstk 12th,ld aft 15th,clr apr 2 out,hdd & ref last,lame* R 15

Improved 96 but hard ride & disaster struck when elusive win seemed likely **13**

MISS CRESTA b.m. 7 Master Willie - Sweet Snow (USA) by Lyphard (USA) — R Wale

1995 3(0),F(-),6(0),2(11)

340 3/3 Heythrop (R) MDN 3m 12 G *mstk 6th, trckd ldrs, prog to ld 2 out, hdd & wknd flat* 3 12
617 23/3 Higham (L) MDO 3m 11 GF *alwys prom, mstk 6th, ld nxt, clr 9th, lft clr 3 out* 1 15
1101 14/4 Guilsborough (L) RES 3m 16 G *mstk 3rd, rear, no imp on ldrs 16th, kpt on* 6 11
1239 27/4 Clifton On ' (L) RES 3m 9 GF *pllng, prom, wth wnr 4 out, wknd aft nxt* 4 12

1439 6/5 Ashorne (R) RES 3m 11 G *t.d.e. prom,mstk 11th,outpcd nxt,chsd wnr 15th-2 out, wknd* 6 1

Lucky winner of poor Maiden & stamina problems; consistent but Restricted looks unlikely 15

MISS CULLANE(IRE) b.m. 8 Duky - Cheeky Dame by Golden Love Robert Ne

1995 2(10)

51 4/2 Alnwick (L) MDO 3m 17 G *in tch to 9th, no ch 13th, virt p.u. flat* 8
116 17/2 Lanark (R) MDO 3m 10 GS *alwys handy, ld last, hld on well* 1 1
404 9/3 Dalston (R) RES 3m 7 G *f 3rd* F
501 16/3 Lanark (R) RES 3m 12 G *sn bhnd, p.u. 12th* P
703 30/3 Tranwell (L) RES 3m 7 GS *mid-div, rmndrs 9th, ran in sntchs, outpcd 3 out* 3 1
1353 4/5 Mosshouses (L) RES 3m 11 GS *sn last, t.o. 9th, p.u. 2 out* P

Won decent Maiden but moody & not progressed; best watched now 13

MISS DOTTY gr.m. 6 Baron Blakeney - Don't Ring Me by Exdirectory M C Pip

1995 P(0),P(0)

470 10/3 Milborne St' (L) MDO 3m 18 G *mid-div til p.u. 15th* P
1614 27/5 Hereford (R) HC 3m 1f 110yds 16 G *bhnd, struggling 11th, styd on from 3 out, nvr nrr.* 4 1

Showed nothing till last start in weak H/Chase; summer jumping after; Maiden chances if back 97 14

MISS ELIZABETH (Irish) — **I** 96^{1}, **I** 171^{1}, **I** 235^{P}, **I** 262^{1}, **I** 303^{3}, **I** 363^{2}

MISS ENRICO b.m. 10 Don Enrico (USA) - Mill Miss by Typhoon Miss E C A Nobl

1995 3(16),1(15),1(18),1(21),1(0),**1(24)**,**4(NH)**,**F(NH)**

1085 14/4 Friars Haugh (L) OPE 3m 6 F *(fav) 3rd frm 10th, nvr rchd chal pstn* 3 1
1354 4/5 Mosshouses (L) OPE 3m 4 GS *cls up, ld 12-14th, btn whn blnd 3 out, t.o. & u.r. last* U

Won 5 races 95 (including H/Chase); not recover form 96; best watched now; Firm 16

MISS EROS b.m. 11 Royal Fountain - Final Victory by Flatbush B Spek

1995 4(14),P(0)

47 4/2 Alnwick (L) XX 3m 14 G *rear, in tch 11th, eff 3 out, 4th whn hmprd & u.r. last* U
84 11/2 Alnwick (L) RES 3m 11 GS *rear, prog 8th, outpcd 10th, no imp aft, fin tired* 5

Maiden winner 93; lightly raced 95/6 & time running out for Restricted hopes 14

MISSFITZ (Irish) — **I** 509^{P}

MISSILE MAN b.g. 7 Cruise Missile - Into Song by True Song Tony Fawcet

1995 P(0),1(13),5(12),P(0),P(0)

77 11/2 Wetherby Po' (L) RES 3m 18 GS *in tch, 3rd at 13th, no ext 4 out* 8 15
411 9/3 Charm Park (L) RES 3m 20 G *rr early, prog 10th, 5th 4 out, tk 3rd run-in* 3 19
584 23/3 Wetherby Po' (L) RES 3m 13 S *cls up, outpcd4 out, styd on wll 2 out, no ext flat* 5 14
758 31/3 Great Stain' (L) RES 3m 17 GS *prom, mstk 6th, chsd ldr hlfwy, ev ch 3 out, onepcd* 5 14
983 8/4 Charm Park (L) RES 3m 13 GF *alwys prom, 6th 12th, 3rd 2 out, drvn out* 3 15

Finished alone when winning 95; onepaced; stays well; weak Restricted in testing conditions 97 17

MISSING LADY (Irish) — **I** 24^{3}, **I** 104^{4}, **I** 169^{2}, **I** 265^{3}, **I** 426^{5}, **I** 483^{5}, **I** 558^{1}, **I** 623^{2}, **I** 633^{P}

MISS ISLE ch.m. 10 Cruise Missile - Madge Spartan by Spartan General M F Clifford

1995 2(10),1(13),2(16),U(-)

599 23/3 Howick (L) RES 3m 7 S *cls 2nd til ld 11th, ran on well whn chal 3 out* 1 18
1177 21/4 Mollington (R) INT 3m 14 F *(Jt fav) in tch, outpcd 11th, styd on to 3rd 14th, no imp apr 2 out* 3 15
1436 6/5 Ashorne (R) MEM 3m 7 G *(fav) mstk 3rd & rmndr,prog to ld 11th,sn wll clr,wknd 2 out,unchl* 1 18

Improved further 96; needs easy 3m; tries hard but may have reached peak now; Confined possible;G-S 20

MISS JCB(IRE) b.f. 6 Bulldozer - Busted Angel A Oliver

1995 **15(NH)**

1417 6/5 Cursneh Hill (L) MDO 3m 14 GF *started 3 fences bhnd, p.u. aft 5th* P 0
1483 11/5 Bredwardine (R) MDO 3m 15 G *ref to race* 0 0
1580 19/5 Wolverhampt' (L) MDO 3m 8 G *lft in ld apr 8th,sn hdd,lft in ld 12th-nxt,btn & u.r. 16th* U -

Temperamental & best avoided 0

MISS JOSEPHINE (Irish) — **I** 277^{P}, **I** 353^{3}

MISSKEIRA ch.m. 8 Cruise Missile - Keira by Keren R Paisley

1995 P(0),2(10)

52 4/2 Alnwick (L) MDO 3m 11 G *tckd ldrs, eff 3 out, no imp wnr aft nxt* 2 12
862 6/4 Alnwick (L) MDN 3m 8 GF *(fav) cls up til p.u. 11th, dismntd* P 0

Lightly raced; possibly good enough to win but problems last start 13

MISS KENMAC br.m. 7 Southern Music - Burl's Sister by Burlington II S Clark

1995 r(-),5(0),3(0),4(0),2(12),P(0),P(0)

890 6/4 Kimble (L) MDN 3m 11 GF *ld 5-8th, outpcd apr 3 out, no dang aft* 4 0

1434 6/5 Ashorne (R) MDO 3m 15 G *in tch to 12th, lost plc whn p.u. 14th* P 0
1504 11/5 Kingston Bl' (L) MDO 3m 13 G *ld 5-8th, prom aft to 13th, sn lost tch & no dang* 4 10

Placed in poor Maidens 95-6 & short on stamina; unlikely to win 10

MISS LURGAN (Irish) — I 33^P, I 132^P, I 225^3, I 530^4, I 622^3, I 632^P

MISS LYNCH (Irish) — I 253^P, I 291^P

MISS MADGE b.m. 8 Cruise Missile - Madge Spartan by Spartan General — Mrs P A Wallis

1995 P(0),4(0),4(0),P(0)

688 30/3 Chaddesley ' (L) MDN 3m 17 G *s.v.s. jmpd badly, t.o. til p.u. 9th* P 0
747 31/3 Upper Sapey (R) MDO 3m 11 GS *t.o. whn ref 15th* R -

Well-beaten 95 & weekend of horror in 96 0

MISS METAL (Irish) — I 280^U, I 335, , I 354^P, I 460^P

MISS MILLBROOK b.m. 8 Meadowbrook - Broadwater by Cawston's Clown — D T Goldsworthy

1995 F(-),1(16),3(17),P(0),U(-)

21 20/1 Barbury Cas' (L) MEM 3m 16 GS *mid-div, 7th & lost tch 11th, p.u. 15th* P 0
157 17/2 Erw Lon (L) CON 3m 15 G *mid-div, rpd prog 3 out, styd on to ld flat* 1 18
215 24/2 Newtown (L) OPE 3m 20 GS *bhnd, prog to poor 5th aft 13th, kpt on, no dang* 3 15
604 23/3 Howick (L) INT 3m 7 S *6s-4s, cls up, went 2nd 10th, ld 14th, drew clr* 1 18
845 6/4 Howick (L) CON 3m 12 GF *3rd/4th, went 2nd 11th, chal 3 out, just hld frm nxt* 2 19
1211 23/4 Chepstow (L) HC 3m 13 S *ld 9th, ran on well.* 1 28
1332 1/5 Cheltenham (L) HC 3m 1f 110yds 11 G *chsd ldr 10th, mstks 12th and 14th, ev ch and hit 17th, btn 2nd when f last.* F 28

Much improved 96; change of rider helped; romped home Chepstow but hard to place 97; Soft essential 25

MISS MONTANA ch.m. 13 Spartan Jester - Lady Sue by Kadir Cup — W J G Hughes

1995 P(0)

545 17/3 Erw Lon (L) CON 3m 10 GS *twrds rear til p.u. 14th* P 0
767 31/3 Pantyderi (R) INT 3m 7 G *nvr trbld ldrs* 6 0
974 8/4 Lydstep (L) MEM 3m 10 G *chsd ldrs to 13th, fdd aft* 4 0
1198 21/4 Lydstep (L) INT 3m 5 S *alwys rear, p.u. 11th* P 0

Restricted winner 94 but looks past it now 0

MISS MONTGOMERY(IRE) b.m. 5 Montekin - Cherry Avenue by King's Ride — Mrs S M Farr

150 17/2 Erw Lon (L) MDN 3m 8 G *cls up whn f 8th* F -
391 9/3 Llanfrynach (R) MDN 3m 11 GS *chsd ldng pair to 13th, wll btn frm 15th* 4 0
607 23/3 Howick (L) MDN 3m 12 S *9th at 11th, ran on own pace, lft 3rd by dfctns* 3 0
847 6/4 Howick (L) LAD 3m 9 GF *rear, t.o. 12th* 4 0
1039 13/4 St Hilary (R) MDN 3m 14 G *mid-div, went 4th at 14th, wknd, lft poor 3rd 16th* 3 0
1162 20/4 Llanwit Maj' (R) MDO 3m 12 GS *w.w., prog 11th, cls 3rd whn f 3 out* F -
1391 6/5 Pantyderi (R) MDO 3m 13 GF *blnd 2nd, p.u. 8th* P 0
1492 11/5 Erw Lon (L) MDO 3m 10 F *settld mi-div to 8th, rpd prog frm 3 out, no dang to wnr* 2 10

Mostly well-beaten but may have won 6th start; improved stamina should see weak win in 97 13

MISS MOONY b.m. 12 Rapid Pass - First Express by Pony Express — I J Widdicombe

1995 8(0),4(10),5(13),7(0),4(0)

298 2/3 Great Treth' (R) RES 3m 13 G *bhnd til p.u. 17th* P 0
628 23/3 Kilworthy (L) INT 3m 7 GS *f 4th* F -
1361 4/5 Flete Park (R) CON 3m 9 G *alwys rear, last hlfwy, t.o. frm 3 out* 6 0
1553 18/5 Bratton Down (L) XX 3m 10 F *mid-div, rmndrs 12th, 6th at 14th, no dang* 5 0
1591 25/5 Mounsey Hil' (R) RES 3m 15 G *bhnd frm 6th, t.o. & p.u. 14th* P 0

Maiden winner 94; well-beaten since & win at 13 impossible 0

MISS NIVELS (Irish) — I 499^P

MISS PALEFACE (Irish) — I 507^F, I 531^1

MISS PENNAL b.m. 10 Oats - Zaratella by Le Levanstell — V Y Gethin

1995 8(0),1(13),F(-),4(0)

172 18/2 Market Rase' (L) RES 3m 9 GF *in tch, jnd ldr going wl 9th, ld 11th, hit 14th,clr apr last* 1 15
355 3/3 Garnons (L) INT 3m 10 GS *ld/disp, hit 4th, ld 15th, hdd nr fin* 2 20
745 31/3 Upper Sapey (R) INT 3m 6 GS *effrt to disp 15th, 2nd & ch whn f 2 out* F -
1005 9/4 Upton-On-Se' (R) CON 3m 6 F *(fav) tckd ldrs, not qckn 15th, no ch & p.u. last, lame* P 0

Maiden winner 95; much improved 96; ran well till disaster last race; win again if fit 97; Soft 19

MISS PERNICKITY b.m. 8 Balinger - Perplexity by Pony Express — Mrs K J Cumings

1995 P(0),3(11),P(0),2(11),3(0),2(10),5(0)

69 10/2 Great Treth' (R) MDO 3m 12 S *alwys bhnd, t.o.* 4 0
138 17/2 Ottery St M' (L) RES 3m 18 GS *alwys bhnd, t.o. frm 14th* 8 0
284 2/3 Clyst St Ma' (L) MDN 3m 11 S *handy, outpcd & no ch frm 14th* 4 0
556 17/3 Ottery St M' (L) MDO 3m 15 G *alwys mid-div, t.o. frm 15th* 7 0
928 8/4 Bishopsleigh (R) MDN 3m 9 G *alwys wll bhnd, t.o. frm 13th* 4 0

1118 17/4 Hockworthy (L) MDO 3m 14 GS *chsd ldrs, 4th & rdn 10th, sn wknd, lft dist 2nd 2 out* 2 0
1349 4/5 Holnicote (L) MDO 3m 8 GS *alwys prom, no ext frm 2 out* 3 0
1494 11/5 Holnicote (L) MDO 3m 8 G *prom til wknd 14th, no ch frm 16th* 5 0
1593 25/5 Mounsey Hil' (R) MDO 3m 11 G *disp to 4th, bhnd 12th, t.o. 3 out* 4 0
1652 8/6 Umberleigh (L) MDO 3m 10 GF *strgglng frm 8th, t.o. & p.u. 12th* P 0

Placed 15 times but getting worse & will not win 0

MISS PLAYTOI (Irish) — I 544P, I 6475, I 659P

MISS PRECOCIOUS b.m. 8 Precocious - Hissy Missy by Bold Lad (IRE) R C Harper
1995 P(0),P(0),U(-),F(-),U(-),2(12)
129 17/2 Kingston Bl' (L) MDN 3m 15 GS *rear, lost tch & mstk 11th, p.u. nxt* P 0
522 16/3 Larkhill (R) MDO 3m 12 G *nvr bttr than mid-div, p.u. 13th* P 0

2nd on only completion from 8 starts 95-6 but showed nothing 96 & can only be watched 10

MISS RICUS b.m. 5 Henricus (ATA) - Sue Ming Vii by Damsire Unregistered Miss P J Boundy
1081 13/4 Cothelstone (L) MDN 3m 4 GF *alwys rear, p.u. last* P 0
1347 4/5 Holnicote (L) MDO 3m 16 GS *prom early, sn bhnd, p.u. 2 out* P 0
1495 11/5 Holnicote (L) MDO 3m 11 G *midfld, ran on steadd clsng stgs, tk 3rd run in* 3 10
1592 25/5 Mounsey Hil' (R) MDO 3m 9 G *cls up, hit 8th, rdn 2 out, ld last, ran on well* 1 14

Steadily improved to win poor Maiden; should have scope for more progress - needs to for Restricteds 16

MISS SHAW b.m. 10 Cruise Missile - Fernshaw by Country Retreat Dr G M Thelwall Jones
1995 2(10),F(-),1(15),2(19),3(14),**3(17)**
165 17/2 Weston Park (L) RES 3m 9 G *ld/disp to 3 out, no ext aft* 2 15
292 2/3 Eaton Hall (R) RES 3m 15 G *ld to 4th, ld 12th-nxt, ev ch 4 out, outpcd aft* 3 15
666 24/3 Eaton Hall (R) RES 3m 13 S *prom, ld 8th til hdd apr last, onepcd* 2 10
952 8/4 Eyton-On-Se' (L) RES 3m 7 GF *chsd ldrs, ld 13th-4 out, ran on onepce* 3 11
1223 24/4 Brampton Br' (R) RES 3m 11 G *ld to 6th, chsd ldr, ev ch whn hmprd 16th, not rcvr* 3 12
1456 8/5 Uttoxeter (L) HC 2m 5f 11 G *in tch, strugling when f 12th.* F -
1582 19/5 Wolverhampt' (L) RES 3m 10 G *chsd ldr apr 8-13th, ld 3 out-apr last, wknd und pres* 3 12

Won 1, placed 10, last 13 starts; consistent but finds little; sure to frustrate in future 15

MISS SOLITAIRE ch.m. 8 St Columbus - Tlucky Diamond by Eborneezer Mrs M Goodwin
1995 P(0),1(14),6(0),F(-),P(0)
128 17/2 Kingston Bl' (L) RES 3m 14 GS *rear & pshd alng, t.o. 13th, p.u. 15th* P 0
242 25/2 Southwell P' (L) RES 3m 12 HO *f 1st* F -
313 2/3 Ampton (R) RES 3m 9 G *mstks, prog 12th, chsd wnr appr last, no impr flat* 2 15
494 16/3 Horseheath (R) RES 3m 10 GF *mid-div, prog 13th, lft remote 2nd 2 out, tired & dmtd flat* 3 11
1639 2/6 Dingley (R) MEM 3m 7 GF *(fav) not flnt, outpcd frm 6th, nvr nr ldrs* 4 11

Maiden winner 95; interrupted 96 & not improved; jumps sketchily; Restricted needs more 14

MISS THIMBLE (Irish) — I 503,

MISS THORNTON (Irish) — I 308P, I 353, , I 614P

MISS TOP (Irish) — I 1764, I 258P, I 3972, I 562F, I 5874

MISS TORNADO (Irish) — I 132P, I 197P, I 422P, I 5315, I 581P, I 6212, I 6613

MISS TROUT (Irish) — I 20P, I 33P, I 84P

MISTER BLACK (Irish) — I 922, I 1712, I 3981, I 489, , I 5363

MISTER CHIPPENDALE b.g. 9 Floriferous - Midi Skirt by Kabale Mrs D S R Watson
168 18/2 Market Rase' (L) MEM 3m 7 GF *chsd ldrs, 3rd & strgglng whn hit 12th, last whn p.u. 2 out* P 0
327 3/3 Market Rase' (L) CON 3m 15 G *nvr bttr than mid-div, no ch 13th, p.u. 2 out* P 0
543 17/3 Southwell P' (L) MEM 3m 2 GS *(fav) alternated ld til lft alone 13th* 1 12
1022 13/4 Brocklesby ' (L) CON 3m 6 GF *alwys abt 4th, cls up til outpcd 3 out* 4 10
1303 28/4 Southwell P' (L) CON 3m 7 GF *mid-div, going wll whn f 11th* F -

Dual winner 94; missed 95; showed little 96 & finished alone when winning; best watched; G/F-S 12

MISTER CHRISTIAN(NZ) b.g. 15 Captain Jason (NZ) - Grisette (NZ) by Arctic Explorer C James
1995 5(11),4(17),2(17),2(14)
19 14/1 Tweseldown (R) CON 3m 9 GS *(bl) chsd ldr to 12th, 4th & btn frm 14th* 4 12
127 17/2 Kingston Bl' (L) MEM 3m 6 GS *(bl) chsd wnr to 14th & agn apr 2 out, no imp* 2 14

Safe as houses but ungenuine & unlikley to win again 13

MISTER GEBO b.g. 11 Strong Gale - Miss Goldiane by Baragoi Mrs D J Dyson
1995 U(-),4(16),1(22),3(19),**F(-)**,3(20)
685 30/3 Chaddesley ' (L) LAD 3m 9 G *blnd 8th,ld/disp to 11th, ev ch 4 out, blnd 2 out, no ext* 3 18
1172 20/4 Chaddesley ' (L) LAD 3m 3 G *cls up til outpcd frm 6th* 3 0
1480 11/5 Bredwardine (R) LAD 3m 12 G *disp 5th, chsd ldr 11th, wknd frm 14th* 6 14
1617 27/5 Chaddesley ' (L) LAD 3m 8 GF *prom,not qckn 12th,lft 2nd 15th,ev ch last,no ext flat* 2 21

2 wins, 11 places, 94-6; able but needs things his own way; likes Chaddesley; F-S 19

MISTER GOODGUY(IRE) b.g. 7 Supreme Leader - Mislay by Henbit (USA) E H Crow
1995 P(0)

292	2/3	Eaton Hall	(R) RES	3m	15	G	*hld up, ld 5th-11th, wth ldrs whn f 5 out*	F	-
1421	6/5	Eyton-On-Se'	(L) RES	3m	11	GF	*(Jt fav) ld frm 2nd, set gd pce, clr whn mstk last, rcvrd wl*	1	17

Maiden winner 94; only 3 points since; modest win 96; should upgrade if fit 97 18

MISTER HORATIO b.g. 6 Derring Rose - Miss Horatio by Spartan General W D Lewis
1995 2(16),1(16),2(15)

156	17/2	Erw Lon	(L) RES	3m	13	G	*made all, wll clr 13th, easily*	1	20
263	2/3	Didmarton	(L) INT	3m	18	G	*(fav) made most, hrd prssd frm 2 out, kpt on, hdd nr fin*	2	22
545	17/3	Erw Lon	(L) CON	3m	10	GS	*(fav) sttld in 2nd, ld 13th, nvr trbld aft*	1	20
767	31/3	Pantyderi	(R) INT	3m	7	G	*(fav) alwys prom, ld 4 out, easily*	1	23
978	8/4	Lydstep	(L) OPE	3m	6	G	*(fav) alwys chsng wnr, nvr able to chal*	2	15
1335	1/5	Cheltenham	(L) HC	2m 5f	10	G	*blnd badly 3rd, bhnd and blunded 7th, n.d., t.o..*	6	0

Maiden winner 95; maintained progress; front-runner; novice ridden; should win Opens if fit 97; G-S ... 23

MISTER JAY DAY b.g. 6 Domitor (USA) - Habille by On Your Mark William John Day

148	17/2	Erw Lon	(L) MDN	3m	9	G	*cls up to 14th, wknd & p.u. 2 out*	P	0
390	9/3	Llanfrynach	(R) MDN	3m	13	GS	*prom, disp 2nd aft 14th, btn 3 out, eased & p.u. nxt*	P	0
696	30/3	Llanvapley	(L) MDN	3m	13	GS	*alwys cls up, 3rd 13th, chsd ldr 3 out, ev ch last, not qckn*	3	10
1162	20/4	Llanwit Maj'	(R) MDO	3m	12	GS	*(fav) trckd ldrs, 4th whn hmp 3 out, not rcvr, p.u. nxt*	P	0

Taken steadily but met trouble when the money went down; should atone in 97 with little improvement 14

MISTER MAIN MAN(IRE) ch.g. 8 Remainder Man - Mainstown Belle by Peacock (FR) Sir Chippendale Keswick

6	13/1	Larkhill	(R) OPE	3m	18	GS	*sn prom, chsd ldr brfly 13th, outpcd 15th, fair effort*	5	23
102	17/2	Marks Tey	(L) CON	3m	17	G	*(Jt fav) in tch, chsd ldr vainly frm 15th, no imp*	2	21
310	2/3	Ampton	(R) CON	3m	13	G	*(fav) cls up going wll,chsd ldr 14th,outpcd 3 out,ran on agn flat*	3	20

Top prospect 94 but broke down; ran well but not same sparkle 96; should win if fit 97; G-S 22

MISTER MCGASKILL ch.g. 7 Itsu (USA) - Deep Depression by Weathercock P L Thomas

151	17/2	Erw Lon	(L) MDN	3m	8	G	*mid-div, wknd 11th, p.u. 13th*	P	0
976	8/4	Lydstep	(L) MDO	3m	12	G	*mid-div, p.u. 2 out*	P	0
1161	20/4	Llanwit Maj'	(R) MDO	3m	15	GS	*in tch til 5th & outpcd 14th, t.o.*	6	0
1273	27/4	Pyle	(R) MDO	3m	9	G	*cls up til chal 14th, ld nxt, lft solo 3 out*	1	14

Steady improvement prior to solo in Maiden; needs to do more for Restricteds but should have scope .. 14

MISTER RAINMAN br.g. 7 Morston's Heir - Artwogan by Tarqogan G H Barber

101	17/2	Marks Tey	(L) MEM	3m	3	G	*hld up, in tch til f 14th*	F	-
343	3/3	Higham	(L) MDO	3m	11	G	*rear, mstks, p.u. 13th*	P	0
930	8/4	Marks Tey	(L) MDO	3m	6	G	*hld up,mstk 9th,prog 11th,ld 4 out-nxt,ev ch last, no ext*	2	12
1325	28/4	Fakenham P-'	(L) MDO	3m	6	G	*w.w. prog 10th, 5l 3rd whn f 4 out*	F	-

Beaten in bad race when 2nd; should improve, especially when jumping ironed out 11

MISTER ROSS (Irish) — **I** 28[F], **I** 162[2], **I** 345[P], **I** 582[1]

MISTER SALVO (Irish) — **I** 465[P], **I** 559[P]

MISTER SPECTATOR(IRE) br.g. 7 Mandalus - Focal Point by Hawaiian Sound (USA) P Hughes
1995 F(-)

61	10/2	Cottenham	(R) MDO	3m	8	GS	*ld, drew away 13th, fence up & f 15th*	F	-
454	9/3	Charing	(L) MDN	3m	10	G	*2nd, clr wth ldr whn ran out 8th*	r	-
597	23/3	Parham	(R) MDO	3m	9	GS	*(fav) ld, clr to 10th, just hdd whn f 14th*	F	-

More fun to watch than ride; has ability (would have won 1st start) but needs controlling 13

MISTER TINKER b.g. 6 Pollerton - Misty Lough by Deep Run Mrs A P Glassford

167	17/2	Weston Park	(L) MDN	3m	10	G	*t.o. 3rd, p.u. 10th*	P	0
286	2/3	Eaton Hall	(R) MDO	3m	14	G	*mid-div hlfwy, fdd, p.u. 4 out*	P	0
1028	13/4	Alpraham	(R) MEM	3m	5	GS	*alwys rear, t.o. 12th, crawld over nxt, cont & ref 2 out*	R	-
1233	27/4	Weston Park	(L) RES	3m	14	G	*mid-div, p.u. qckly & dismntd bfr 10th*	P	0

Unpromising & problems last start 0

MISTRESS ROSIE b.m. 9 Dubassoff (USA) - Somerford Glory by Hittite Glory Martin Hill
1995 **1(NH),3(NH),3(NH),2(NH),P(NH),6(NH),2(NH)**

1141	20/4	Flete Park	(R) LAD	3m	8	S	*prog to 3rd brfly 10th, wkng whn hit 13th, p.u. aft 3 out*	P	0
1426	6/5	High Bickin'	(R) LAD	3m	3	G	*raced outer, made most til hdd 16th, onepce*	2	11
1524	12/5	Ottery St M'	(L) MEM	3m	3	GF	*(fav) cls up, slght ld 14th, disp nxt til forged clr apr last*	1	10
1552	18/5	Bratton Down	(L) LAD	3m	7	F	*ld apr 6th til 14th, lost 2nd 3 out, grad fdd*	3	13

Hurdle winner 95; late to appear & disappointing; struggling in Ladies; Members best hope again 97 ... 16

MISTY(NZ) b.g. 9 Ivory Hunter (USA) - Our Loaming (NZ) by Sovereign Edition Mrs J E Milne

1995 P(0),R(-),**7(0)**,**P(0)**,**7(0)**,**3(0)**
207 24/2 Castle Of C' (R) MDO 3m 15 HY *cls up, ld 13th, styd on well frm 2 out* 1 14
361 5/3 Leicester (R) HC 2 1/2m 110yds 15 GS *bhnd, prog 11th, chsd ldrs and rdn 3 out, no further progress.* 4 15
526 16/3 Larkhill (R) RES 3m 9 G *sn t.o., nvr nrr* 5 0
707 30/3 Barbury Cas' (L) RES 3m 18 G *n.j.w. mid-div, cls 4th 4 out, wknd nxt* 4 14
1056 13/4 Badbury Rin' (L) RES 3m 10 GF *mid-div, prog 10th, prom to 4 out, wknd & blnd last* 4 0
1292 28/4 Barbury Cas' (L) RES 3m 11 F *ld to 2nd & 7-14th, slw jumps aft, virt p.u. flat* 5 0
1458 8/5 Uttoxeter (L) HC 3 1/4m 8 G *ld to 14th, rdn and wknd 16th, tk poor 2nd run-in.* 2 0
1614 27/5 Hereford (R) HC 3m 1f 110yds 16 G *prom till lost pl quickly before 7th, bhnd when p.u. before next.* P 0

Plodded home in mud; reluctant & hard ride; another win needs luck 14

MITCHELLS BEST br.g. 10 True Song - Emmalina by Doubtless II — A Hollingsworth
1995 4(12),4D(14),4(15),P(0),3(18),6(0),2(19)
234 24/2 Heythrop (R) LAD 3m 6 GS *mostly rear, went 4th at 15th, p.u. last* P 0
426 9/3 Upton-On-Se' (R) CON 3m 16 GS *effrt frm 10th, 4th 3 out, no ext* 4 11
687 30/3 Chaddesley ' (L) CON 3m 10 G *rear, prog 12th, chsd ldr & ev ch 15th, wknd 2 out* 4 17
943 8/4 Andoversford (R) CON 3m 9 GF *alwys in chsg grp, onepcd frm 3 out* 4 10
1042 13/4 Bitterley (L) CON 3m 9 G *cls up til outpcd frm 11th, styd on onepcd frm 3 out* 4 14
1169 20/4 Chaddesley ' (L) MEM 3m 9 G *cls up til lost plc 12th, styd on 16th, rdn to ld flat* 1 19
1435 6/5 Ashorne (R) CON 3m 12 G *prom, chsd wnr 11th, no imp 3 out, wknd flat, lost 2nd nr fn* 3 19
1478 11/5 Bredwardine (R) CON 3m 12 G *ld 1st, styd prom, rdn 12th, kpt on onepcd frm 15th* 3 19

Broke losing sequence of 19 when winning; consistent but Confineds difficult; Members again 97 18

MITE HAVE BEAN (Irish) — **I** 31[P], **I** 227[P], **I** 337[1]

M MACG (Irish) — **I** 268[F], **I** 394[U], **I** 563[2], **I** 579[2], **I** 634[1]

MODEL COUNTESS(IRE) b.m. 7 Niels - Gibson Girlee (USA) by Giboulee (CAN) — T Atkinson
1995 P(0),F(-),3(0)
820 6/4 Charlton Ho' (L) MDN 3m 12 GF *cls up til 7th, lost tch 9th, p.u. apr 12th* P 0
1187 21/4 Tweseldown (R) MDN 3m 11 GF *trckd ldrs, 3rd at 11th, wknd nxt, p.u. 15th* P 0
1348 4/5 Holnicote (L) MDO 3m 9 GS *bhnd whn u.r. 14th* U -

Placed in good Maiden 95; no other completions before or since & disappointing; best watched 12

MOGWAI(IRE) b.g. 7 Alzao (USA) - Maltese Pet by Dragonara Palace (USA) — H J Hopper
1995 **7(NH)**
249 25/2 Charing (L) XX 3m 11 GS *in tch til f 10th* F -
450 9/3 Charing (L) XX 3m 8 G *cls up, mstk 10th, wknd rpdly aft nxt, p.u. 14th, dsmntd* P 0

No stamina & a waste of time in points; problems last start 0

MOLL'S CHOICE (Irish) — **I** 33[P], **I** 81[2], **I** 165[1], **I** 241[3], **I** 313[4], **I** 383[P], **I** 519[5]

MONADANTE (Irish) — **I** 9[F], **I** 55[P], **I** 76[P], **I** 277[P], **I** 351, , **I** 438[3], **I** 502, , **I** 609[P]

MONAGURRA (Irish) — **I** 277[P], **I** 356[5]

MONA LITA (Irish) — **I** 204[P], **I** 232[P], **I** 291[P], **I** 427[P]

MONARROW(IRE) b.g. 8 Carlingford Castle - Christy's Arrow by Mon Capitaine — William Tellwright
1995 F(-),P(0),P(0),4(10),1(13)
292 2/3 Eaton Hall (R) RES 3m 15 G *chsd ldrs to 9th, wknd rpdly, p.u. 4 out* P 0
396 9/3 Garthorpe (R) RES 3m 9 G *mostly 3rd for 2m, chsd ldr 4 out, chal 2 out, outpcd flat* 2 14
722 31/3 Garthorpe (R) MEM 3m 4 G *(fav) ld arp 5th-9th, ld 12th, pshd out flat* 1 14
856 6/4 Sandon (L) RES 3m 9 GF *ld grp thruout, unable to qckn whn pce increased* 3 13

Members winner 95; stays but onepaced; completed double & same may offer best hope 97 14

MONAUGHTY MAN br.g. 10 Tower Walk - Springdamus by Mandamus — Mrs Karen Woodhead
1995 **5(13)**,**1(19)**,**2(24)**,**7(22)**,**5(0)**,**P(0)**
364 5/3 Leicester (R) HC 2m 1f 12 GS *alwys rear, some prog 4 out, nvr nrr.* 5 0

Won weak H/Chase 95; soon disappeared 96; best below 3m; best watched 16

MONDAY COUNTRY ch.g. 6 Sweet Monday - Penny's Affair by Chingnu — Mrs Joanna Daniell
1995 6(0),3(0)
28 20/1 Barbury Cas' (L) RES 3m 14 GS *in tch to 11th, last & no ch 15th, p.u. 2 out* P 0

Lightly raced & soon disappeared 96 0

MONDINO b or br.g. 11 Soudno - Ozy-Lass by Ozymandias — Mrs K Bamford
1995 5(0),5(0),U(-),5(0),6(14)
1511 12/5 Maisemore P' (L) MDO 3m 14 F *mstk 7th & rdr lost iron, rear til kpt on frm 14th, fin well* 3 10
1568 19/5 Mollington (R) MDO 3m 9 GS *n.j.w. rear 7th, rdn 10th, t.o. & p.u. 15th* P 0

Late to appear; 3rd in weak race; prospects of a win very slim; Firm 11

MONEYCARRAGH (Irish) — I 20^{P}, I 98^{F}, I 178^{P}, I 215^{F}, I 301^{F}

MONEYFROMAUSTRALIA (Irish) — I 290^{P}

MONEY LOW (Irish) — I 162^{P}, I 227^{4}, I 346^{3}, I 381^{2}, I 466^{1}, I 525^{P}

MONEY SAVED (Irish) — I 473^{P}

MONGIE (Irish) — I 98^{P}

MONKSFORT b.g. 10 Monksfield - Karamble by Karabas — Miss C Holliday

1995 **3(NH),2(NH)**

777	31/3	Penshurst	(L)	LAD	3m	7	GS	*ld, hdd aft 3 out, wknd & p.u. nxt*	P	0
1051	13/4	Penshurst	(L)	MEM	3m	5	G	*(fav) made all, blnd & nrly u.r. 1st, styd on, drew clr 3 out*	1	15
1566	19/5	Mollington	(R)	LAD	3m	7	GS	*ld to 12th, sn wknd, t.o. & p.u. last*	P	0
1609	26/5	Tweseldown	(R)	MXO	3m	9	G	*ju.w. made all, jmpd lft 11th, ran on gamely apr last*	1	24

Winning chaser; inconsistent; needs to dominate; not suited by Ladies; should win again; Good 20

MONKSLAND (Irish) — I 167^{F}

MONK'S MISTAKE ch.g. 14 Monksfield - Hardyglass Lass by Master Owen — K V Bonser

1995 4(15),5(0),5(0),F(-),r(-)

633	23/3	Market Rase'	(L)	LAD	3m	10	GF	*6th & in tch for 2m, fdd 6 out, p.u. 3 out*	P	0
970	8/4	Thorpe Lodge	(L)	LAD	3m	6	GF	*3rd to 11th, disp 3rd to 4 out, fdd, p.u. 2 out*	P	0
1377	5/5	Dingley	(R)	CON	3m	12	GF	*alwys last pair, t.o. frm 8th*	10	0
1518	12/5	Garthorpe	(R)	MEM	3m	6	GF	*rear frm 3rd, outpcd, nvr dang*	3	0

No longer of any account 0

MONKTON(IRE) ch.g. 8 The Parson - Poula Scawla by Pollerton — A J Scrimgeour

1995 F(-),1(15),3(17)

68	10/2	Great Treth'	(R)	RES	3m	14	S	*prom early, grad fdd, p.u. 5 out*	P	0
199	24/2	Lemalla	(R)	RES	3m	17	HY	*ld 9th-3 out, fdd aft*	3	18
298	2/3	Great Treth'	(R)	RES	3m	13	G	*hld up,prog to jn ldrs 12th,cls up whn lft in ld 2 out,hldon*	1	18
531	16/3	Cothelstone	(L)	CON	3m	12	G	*mid div whn blnd bdly 6th, nt rcvr, bhnd & p.u. 11th*	P	0
628	23/3	Kilworthy	(L)	INT	3m	7	GS	*(bl) ran in sntchs,mstk 4th,outpcd aft 14th,kpt on 2 out,no dang*	3	18
925	8/4	Bishopsleigh	(R)	CON	3m	6	G	*(bl) ld 1st, lsng grnd frm 7th, f 9th*	F	-
1277	27/4	Bratton Down	(L)	CON	3m	15	GF	*mid-div, p.u. 13th, dsmntd*	P	0

Maiden winner 95; fortunate winner 96; ran poorly after & wrong signs; best watched now 15

MONTEBA (Irish) — I 612^{5}

MONTEL EXPRESS (Irish) — I 386, , I 421^{P}, I 526^{3}, I 616^{1}

MONTIMEZZO b.g. 9 Remezzo - Jesstrapaul by Tycoon II — Mrs O Vaughan-Jones

13	14/1	Cottenham	(R)	MDO	3m	10	G	*ld/disp 5-9th, 4th & btn 2 out, tk 2nd flat, eased cls hm*	3	10
107	17/2	Marks Tey	(L)	MDN	3m	15	G	*trkd ldrs, going wll 10th, 2nd & outpcd 15th, lst 2nd flat*	4	0

Missed 95; placed 6 times now but finds little under pressure & frustrating 12

MONTOHOUSE (Irish) — I 120^{P}

MONTYKOSKY b.g. 9 Montekin - Reliable Rosie by Relko — A L Wallace

457	9/3	Eyton-On-Se'	(L)	INT	3m	11	G	*prom, ev ch 5 out, sn btn*	3	0
663	24/3	Eaton Hall	(R)	LAD	3m	8	S	*sn t.o., p.u. 11th*	P	0

Restricted winner 94; missed 95; showed nothing 96; best watched 12

MONYNUT ch.m. 7 Celtic Cone - Mount St Mary's by Lochnager — A J Wight

1995 **11(NH),6(NH)**

88	11/2	Alnwick	(L)	MDO	3m	11	GS	*cls up, 6th & in tch whn blnd 9th, wknd, p.u. 11th*	P	0
323	2/3	Corbridge	(R)	MDN	3m	12	GS	*last at 6th, p.u. 12th*	P	0
613	23/3	Friars Haugh	(L)	MDN	3m	15	G	*alwys mdfld.*	7	0
789	1/4	Kelso	(L)	HC	3m 1f	11	GF	*soon bhnd, p.u. before 7 out.*	P	0
1355	4/5	Mosshouses	(L)	MDO	3m	10	GS	*rear, lost tch 13th, p.u. 15th*	P	0

No sign of ability yet 0

MOONBAY LADY b.m. 6 State Diplomacy (USA) - Burntwood Lady by Royal Buck — Gary Andrew

1995 P(0),P(0),P(0),P(0),P(0)

200	24/2	Lemalla	(R)	MDO	3m	12	HY	*wll bhnd whn p.u. aft 12th*	P	0
301	2/3	Great Treth'	(R)	MDO	3m	13	G	*6th at 12th, p.u. 14th*	P	0
557	17/3	Ottery St M'	(L)	MDN	3m	10	G	*sn t.o., u.r. 14th*	U	-
937	8/4	Wadebridge	(L)	INT	3m	4	F	*bhnd, pshd alng frm 10th, grdly lost tch, btn 2 fences*	3	0
1074	13/4	Lifton	(R)	INT	3m	9	S	*bhnd whn p.u. apr 13th*	P	0
1432	6/5	High Bickin'	(R)	MDO	3m	9	G	*(bl) rear, blnd bdly 6th, strgglng til p.u. aft 13th*	P	0
1627	27/5	Lifton	(R)	MDO	3m	9	GS	*rear & rmndrs 12th, jmpd slwly nxt, p.u. 14th*	P	0

Hopeless 0

MOONCAPER (Irish) — I 37^{U}, I 58^{P}

MOONLIGHT CRUISE b.m. 8 Cruise Missile - Saucy Moon by Saucy Kit — W J G Hughes

1995 P(0),5(0),2(12),2(10)

152	17/2	Erw Lon	(L)	MDN	3m	11	G	*(fav) rear, some prog frm 13th, no ch 2 out, fin 5th, plcd 4th*	4	0
550	17/3	Erw Lon	(L)	MDN	3m	13	GS	*nvr dang, p.u. 11th*	P	0
772	31/3	Pantyderi	(R)	MDN	3m	8	G	*chsd ldrs, nvr thrtnd wnr*	2	10
977	8/4	Lydstep	(L)	MDO	3m	8	G	*(Jt fav) nvr nr enough to chal*	3	10
1201	21/4	Lydstep	(L)	MDN	3m	9	S	*sttld in 6th, prog frm 4 out, 3rd 2 out, tired*	3	13
1269	27/4	Pyle	(R)	MDO	3m	9	G	*ld 6-9th & 11-14th, rallied 3 out, ld last, ran on*	1	13

Placed 6 times prior to winning; game effort; needs to find more for Restricteds; G-S 14

MOONLIGHT SHIFT ch.g. 10 Night Shift (USA) - Rana by Welsh Pageant — C Lewis

1995 3(0)

695	30/3	Llanvapley	(L)	RES	3m	13	GS	*alwys rear, p.u. 3 out*	P	0
842	6/4	Maisemore P'	(L)	MDN	3m	17	GF	*ld 2nd,blnd 8th, clr whn p.u. & dism 11th*	P	0
1271	27/4	Pyle	(R)	MDO	3m	15	G	*prog to ld 11th, wknd & p.u. aft 13th*	P	0

Of no account 0

MOONVOOR (Irish) — **I** 517[4], **I** 644[2]

MOORECHURCH GLEN b.g. 10 Furry Glen - Sneem by Rum (USA) — H G Owen

1995 **F(NH),6(NH)**

946	8/4	Andoversford	(R)	RES	3m	10	GF	*plld hrd, ld aft 2nd, sn clr, hdd 10th, wknd, p.u. 13th*	P	0
1189	21/4	Tweseldown	(R)	RES	3m	10	GF	*ld in start, plld, ld 2nd, sn clr, tired & hdd aft 3 out*	3	0

Irish Maiden winner 93; placed in poor race; does not settle or stay 10

MOORES CROSS (Irish) — **I** 481[P], **I** 527[F]

MOORE VIEW b.m. 6 Germont - Slim View by Slim Jim — J J Dixon

1995 **10(NH),9(NH)**

613	23/3	Friars Haugh	(L)	MDN	3m	15	G	*t.o. hlfwy, p.u. 4 out*	P	0
896	6/4	Whittington	(L)	MDO	3m	5	F	*rear whn f 4th*	F	-

No form in NH Flat races or points yet 0

MOORLAND ABBOT b.g. 8 Lir - Moorland Heath Vii — Miss P D Mitchell

1995 4(11),4(13),2(13),F(-),7(0),P(0),3(13),U(-),4(0),2(14),F(-)

41	3/2	Wadebridge	(L)	XX	3m	9	GF	*in tchh to 13th, sn outpcd*	7	0
63	10/2	Great Treth'	(R)	MEM	3m	6	S	*bhnd til hmpd & u.r. 7th, rmntd, t.o. & p.u. 2 out*	P	0
196	24/2	Lemalla	(R)	CON	3m	14	HY	*prom early, grad wknd*	9	0
298	2/3	Great Treth'	(R)	RES	3m	13	G	*rear, 10th hlfwy, ran on steadily, nrst fin*	4	14
624	23/3	Kilworthy	(L)	LAD	3m	7	GS	*last to 10th, t.o. frm 12th, plodded on*	4	10
871	6/4	Higher Kilw'	(L)	RES	3m	9	GF	*6th hlfwy, nvr dang, nrst fin*	4	0
1075	13/4	Lifton	(R)	RES	3m	12	S	*mid-div thruout, not pce to chal*	5	0
1142	20/4	Flete Park	(R)	CON	3m	11	S	*sn rear, t.o. frm hlfwy, lft remote 3rd apr last*	3	0
1359	4/5	Flete Park	(R)	LAD	4m	5	G	*last & out of tch, sntchd remote 4th nr fin*	4	0
1622	27/5	Lifton	(R)	CON	3m	14	GS	*sn rear, bhnd til p.u. 2 out, lame*	P	0

Maiden winner 93; owner ridden to poor effect & beaten 25 times since 12

MOORLAND HIGHFLYER b or br.g. 5 Karlinsky (USA) - Moorland Heath Vii by Damsire Unregistered — Miss P D Mitchell

69	10/2	Great Treth'	(R)	MDO	3m	12	S	*prom, ld 14th-nxt, kpt on und pres*	3	11
202	24/2	Lemalla	(R)	MDO	3m	12	HY	*ld/disp 6th til 4 out, sn onepcd*	5	0
630	23/3	Kilworthy	(L)	MDN	3m	10	GS	*prssd ldr, lft in ld 12th, hdd 14th, ev ch 2 out, not qckn*	2	13
875	6/4	Higher Kilw'	(L)	MDN	3m	6	GF	*ld til hdd apr 2 out, kpt on onepcd*	2	13
1071	13/4	Lifton	(R)	MDN	3m	10	S	*prom, disp frm 12th, just ld cls home*	1	15
1139	20/4	Flete Park	(R)	RES	3m	14	S	*ld/disp to 17th, in tch til outpcd aft 3 out, ran on steadly*	2	15
1624	27/5	Lifton	(R)	LAD	3m	9	GS	*prom, 4th at 12th, in tch til onepcd frm 3 out*	4	17

Decent youngster; jumps & stays; owner ridden & deserves better handling - could prove useful 17

MOORSIDE LAD 10 — J E Stockton

1995 F(-),2(14),P(0),**P(0)**

231	24/2	Heythrop	(R)	XX	3m	10	GS	*ld/disp til ld 13th, jnd 15th, ld nxt, hdd 2 out, ran on*	2	12
665	24/3	Eaton Hall	(R)	RES	3m	14	S	*prom, chsd wnr 5-13th, grad fdd, p.u. 3 out*	P	0
739	31/3	Sudlow Farm	(R)	RES	3m	11	G	*(bl) mstks,chsd ldr to 7th, outpcd 12th, blndrd 2 out, p.u. last*	P	0
1030	13/4	Alpraham	(R)	RES	3m	10	GS	*(bl) ld to 2nd, still cls up whn f 5th*	F	-

Maiden winner 93; lightly raced since & not threatening to win Restricted now 12

MOPHEAD KELLY ch.g. 7 Netherkelly - Trois Filles by French Marny — N J Barrowclough

1995 P(0),4(10)

661	24/3	Eaton Hall	(R)	MDN	3m	9	S	*mid-div, blnd 11th & lost tch, p.u. 4 out*	P	0
1581	19/5	Wolverhampt'	(L)	MDO	3m	10	G	*chsd ldrs, mstk 5th, lost plc 9th, t.o. & p.u. 14th*	P	0
1621	27/5	Chaddesley '	(L)	MDO	3m	17	GF	*alwys prom, chsd ldr 11th-apr 3 out, lft 2nd nxt, no imp*	2	13

2nd in large but weak Maiden; may do better but more needed for win early 97 12

MORABITO (Irish) — I 389^{P}

MORAN BRIG ch.g. 6 Bustino - Aunt Judy by Great Nephew — K M H Podger

275	2/3	Parham	(R)	MDN	3m	15	GF	*wll in tch, wknd & p.u. 12th*	P	0
522	16/3	Larkhill	(R)	MDO	3m	12	G	*sn t.o., nvr nrr, p.u. 2 out*	P	0
997	8/4	Hackwood Pa'	(L)	MDO	3m	11	GF	*alwys rear, mstk 16th, nvr a factor*	6	0
1060	13/4	Badbury Rin'	(L)	MDO	3m	14	GF	*mid-div til u.r. 9th*	U	-
1189	21/4	Tweseldown	(R)	RES	3m	10	GF	*outpcd rear, nvr able to chal, some mod late prog*	4	0

Only beat one other finisher in 2 completions; needs more but local Maidens usually poor 10

MORCAT ch.m. 7 Morston (FR) - Ancat Girl by Politico (USA) — C I Ratcliffe

1995 **15(NH),5(NH)**

74	11/2	Wetherby Po'	(L)	MDO	3m	11	GS	*ld 8th-4 out, outpcd by wnr aft*	2	0
229	24/2	Duncombe Pa'	(R)	MDO	3m	13	GS	*pllng, jnd ldr 5th, wknd apr 10th, p.u. 12th*	P	0
416	9/3	Charm Park	(L)	MDO	3m	13	G	*cls up, 2nd at 14th, 3rd appr last, outpcd aftr*	3	10
986	8/4	Charm Park	(L)	MDN	3m	10	GF	*ld 10th-nxt, disp 12th-3 out, hdd, no ext*	2	11
1095	14/4	Whitwell-On'	(R)	MDO	2 1/2m 88yds	14	G	*alwys prom, remote 2nd 3 out, sn wknd*	6	0
1286	27/4	Easingwold	(L)	MDO	3m	13	G	*mstk 1st, prom, ld 8th til hdd 2 out, wknd rpdly*	6	0
1365	4/5	Gisburn	(R)	MDO	3m	17	G	*prog to 5th 3 out, lft 3rd last, no ext*	4	0

Safe but patently fails to stay; placed in 2m novice chase June & better off in them 12

MORCHARD MILLY br.m. 9 Remezzo - Border Gem by Border Chief — R T Grant

1995 P(0),2(11),P(0),4(0),2(14),3(10)

556	17/3	Ottery St M'	(L)	MDO	3m	15	G	*alwys rear, t.o. frm 13th*	6	0
1117	17/4	Hockworthy	(L)	MDO	3m	8	GS	*alwys prom, chsd wnr frm 13th, no imp app 2 out, wknd*	2	10
1274	27/4	Bratton Down	(L)	MEM	3m	7	GF	*handy, 3rd at 12th, 2nd 14th, ev ch whn blnd & u.r. last*	U	13
1347	4/5	Holnicote	(L)	MDO	3m	16	GS	*prom early, 2nd at 9th, grad lost tch*	5	11
1554	18/5	Bratton Down	(L)	MDO	3m	16	F	*cls 2nd mostly,lft in ld 15th,jnd aft 3 out,ev ch,wknd last*	3	13
1587	25/5	Mounsey Hil'	(R)	MEM	3m	7	G	*cls up, disp 7th, lft in ld 16th, clr 2 out, styd on*	1	16
1633	1/6	Bratton Down	(L)	XX	3m	8	G	*prom til rdn & outpcd 12th, ran on agn frm 16th, kpt on well*	3	19

Placed 12 times prior to win; ran well after; Restricted likely if maintaining trend 97 17

MORDELLA LASS (Irish) — I 105^{P}, I 164^{F}, I 230^{3}, I 302^{1}, I 389^{4}, I 414^{U}, I 558^{P}

MORDINGTON LASS b.m. 9 Torenaga - Mascarita by Final Problem — W A Crozier

755	31/3	Lockerbie	(R)	MDN	3m	17	G	*sn bhnd, p.u. 10th*	P	0
862	6/4	Alnwick	(L)	MDN	3m	8	GF	*t.o. 7th, p.u. apr 12th*	P	0
1512	12/5	Hexham Poin'	(L)	MEM	3m	6	HY	*last frm 3rd, t.o. frm 5th*	4	0

Of no account 0

MORE RAIN (Irish) — I 30^{P}, I 114^{5}, I 193^{2}, I 343^{4}, I 420^{F}, I 517^{2}, I 526^{P}

MORE THAN MOST (Irish) — I 92^{P}, I 257^{P}, I 362^{P}, I 454^{P}, I 489^{P}, I 537^{P}, I 596^{4}, I 658^{P}

MORGANS MAN b.g. 7 Morgans Choice - Mandover by Mandamus — Mrs Jane M Wickett

295	2/3	Great Treth'	(R)	LAD	3m	6	G	*n.j.w. bhnd til p.u. 13th*	P	0

A brief appearance of no promise 0

MORNAY DES GARNES (Irish) — I 101,, I 269^{3}

MORSTON AGAIN b.g. 7 Morston's Heir - Honourable Girl by Sunyboy — G H Barber

182	18/2	Horseheath	(R)	MDO	3m	11	G	*in tch til p.u. 11th, lame*	P	0

Barely made halfway & problems 0

MORSTONS EXPRESS b.g. 6 Morston's Heir - Saffron Lady by He Loves Me — G H Barber

932	8/4	Marks Tey	(L)	OPE	3m	3	G	*keen hold, alwys last, lft dist 2nd 14th, p.u. 2 out, lame*	P	0

Only learning & problems on debut 0

MO'S CHORISTER b.g. 10 Lir - Revelstoke by North Stoke — Mrs J Marsh

1995 9(0),3(10)

295	2/3	Great Treth'	(R)	LAD	3m	6	G	*ld/disp, hit 12th, 3rd & onepcd frm 14th*	3	13
506	16/3	Magor	(R)	CON	3m	8	GS	*chsng grp, 3rd 3 out, ran on to tk 2nd last*	2	15
691	30/3	Llanvapley	(L)	CON	3m	15	GS	*mid-div, wknd 12th, p.u. 15th*	P	0
845	6/4	Howick	(L)	CON	3m	12	GF	*ld to 10th, wknd aft, no ch frm 14th*	4	10

Dual winner 93; only 8 runs 94-6; placed in modest races; Confined unlikely; Any 14

MOSCOW MULE ch.g. 10 Nearly A Hand - Humbie's Pride by Guide — John A Dudgeon

1995 3(0),P(0),P(0)

116	17/2	Lanark	(R)	MDO	3m	10	GS	*in tch til wknd rpdly 3 out*	4	0
189	24/2	Friars Haugh	(L)	RES	3m	9	S	*bhnd whn p.u. 4 out*	P	0

Lightly raced now & well-beaten when completing 0

MOSES MAN (Irish) — I 493P, I 538P

MOSS CASTLE ch.g. 11 Le Moss - Distant Castle by Deep Run — G Jones

1995 1(24),1(24),1(21),1(24),2(16),1(24),1(22),2(22)

459	9/3	Eyton-On-Se'	(L)	OPE 3m	11 G	*hld up, clsr ordr 11th, in tch whn p.u. lame 13th*	P	0

Won 6 races 95 but disaster struck only run 96; can only be watched at 12; Any 19

MOSSIDE ch.g. 7 Le Moss - Eight Of Diamonds by Silent Spring — B W Gillbard

1995 **P(NH),P(NH)**

201	24/2	Lemalla	(R)	MDO 3m	13 HY	*mid-div til styd on onepcd clsng stgs*	3	13
446	9/3	Haldon	(R)	MDO 3m	13 S	*handy, ld 13th, pshd alng & lkd wnr 2 out, hdd cls hm*	2	13
718	30/3	Wadebridge	(L)	MDO 3m	11 GF	*handy,disp 8th-aft 14th,drvn to ld last 50 yrds,just hld on*	1	15
926	8/4	Bishopsleigh	(R)	RES 3m	9 G	*mid-div whn lsng grnd frm 16th, styd on onepcd*	4	11
1139	20/4	Flete Park	(R)	RES 3m	14 S	*cls 6th whn blnd & u.r. 9th*	U	-
1428	6/5	High Bickin'	(R)	RES 3m	10 G	*not fluent, rear 14th til p.u. apr 16th*	P	0
1649	8/6	Umberleigh	(L)	RES 3m	14 GF	*last & n.j.w. til p.u. 6th*	P	0

No form under Rules; won poor Maiden; looks suspect; struggling in Restricteds since 14

MOSSIMAN(IRE) b.g. 8 Le Moss - Suparoli by Super Sam — Mrs Cyril Alexander

1995 **P(NH),P(NH)**

1253	27/4	Balcormo Ma'	(R)	MDO 3m	16 GS	*not fluent, hndy til wknd qckly 4 out*	7	0

Well beaten only start in points & looks too slow even for pointing 0

MOSSLEN (Irish) — I 503,

MOSS'S BEAUTY (Irish) — I 308P, I 352F, I 503,

MOST RICH(IRE) b.g. 8 Dalsaan - Boule de Soie by The Parson — C E Sherry

220	24/2	Newtown	(L)	MDN 3m	12 GS	*jmpd rght, ld, clr frm 10th, wknd 2 out, hdd last*	2	10
542	17/3	Southwell P'	(L)	MDO 3m	15 GS	*prom, ld 4-6th, strgglng frm 12th, p.u. 3 out*	P	0
688	30/3	Chaddesley '	(L)	MDN 3m	17 G	*prom, 4th & rdn 4 out, kpt on, no ch wth wnr*	2	14
1048	13/4	Bitterley	(L)	MDO 3m	12 G	*(fav) prom til ld 12th, mstk 15th, hdd & wknd nxt*	4	0
1483	11/5	Bredwardine	(R)	MDO 3m	15 G	*cls up til wknd 14th, p.u. 3 out*	P	0

Shows some ability but not enough stamina & could frustrate in future 12

MOSTYN ch.g. 5 Astral Master - Temple Rock by Melody Rock — Mrs M E Weaver

143	17/2	Larkhill	(R)	MDO 3m	14 G	*sn t.o., nvr nrr*	4	0
385	9/3	Llanfrynach	(R)	LAD 3m	14 GS	*prssd wnr to 10th, wknd rpdly nxt, t.o.*	7	0
1117	17/4	Hockworthy	(L)	MDO 3m	8 GS	*mstks, prom, 4th & btn whn bkd 15th, cont'd*	3	0

Completes but tailed off & no stamina 10

MOTOR CLOAK b.g. 10 Motivate - Cavalry Cloak by Queen's Hussar — Mrs R J Burrow

1995 P(0),U(-),6(0),1(12),P(0)

33	20/1	Higham	(L)	LAD 3m	9 GF	*u.r. 1st*	U	-
57	10/2	Cottenham	(R)	LAD 3m	9 GS	*mstks, ld to 7th, chsd wnr aft, dist 2nd whn u.r. 2 out*	U	15
250	25/2	Charing	(L)	LAD 3m	12 GS	*sn rear, t.o. 14th, p.u. nxt*	P	0
272	2/3	Parham	(R)	RES 3m	13 GF	*alwys strgglng in rear, last whn blnd & u.r. 8th*	U	-
574	17/3	Detling	(L)	RES 3m	14 GF	*prom, 5th at 17th, kpt on*	3	11
779	31/3	Penshurst	(L)	RES 3m	13 GS	*alwys prom, 4th & mstk 3 out, no ch aft*	3	15
964	8/4	Heathfield	(R)	RES 3m	7 G	*w.w in tch, 4th & rdn appr 4 out, no prog*	4	13
1206	21/4	Heathfield	(R)	RES 3m	8 F	*ld, blnd 7th, rdn clr frm 16th, hdd line*	2	15
1329	30/4	Huntingdon	(R)	HC 3m	14 GF	*mstks, alwys well bhnd, t.o..*	8	0
1539	16/5	Folkestone	(R)	HC 3m 7f	9 G	*(bl) ld after 1st to 11th, blnd and u.r. 13th.*	U	-
1613	27/5	Fontwell	(R)	HC 3 1/4m 110yds	12 G	*(bl) mid div, wknd 15th, bhnd when p.u. after 17th.*	P	0

Maiden winer 95; very modest but nearly landed 8th start; novice ridden; struggle to win again 13

MOTOR TRADER b.g. 7 Pitpan - Altaghaderry Run by Deep Run — H C Pauling

268	2/3	Didmarton	(L)	MDN 3m	10 G	*alwys rear, t.o. & p.u. 12th*	P	0
638	23/3	Siddington	(L)	CON 3m	16 S	*mstk 5th, bhnd til p.u. 12th*	P	0

No real cause for optimism yet 0

MOUNTAICO b.g. 14 Paico - Mount Ranier by Danjoven — L J Bowman

596	23/3	Parham	(R)	LAD 3m	8 GS	*ld apr 3rd-6th, wknd 8th, rear & p.u. 11th*	P	0
961	8/4	Heathfield	(R)	MEM 3m	5 G	*(bl) lft in ld 11th, blnd 14th, sn hdd, rdn nxt,sn btn,p.u. 2 out*	P	0
1053	13/4	Penshurst	(L)	LAD 3m	5 G	*(bl) ran in sntchs, 2nd & btn 2 out*	3	10
1297	28/4	Bexhill	(R)	LAD 3m	7 F	*(bl) cls up, ld 15th, hrd prssd 3 out, hld on gamely flat*	1	16

Moody but gamely won modest Ladies; rarely runs now; win at 15 looks hard; G-F 14

MOUNTAIN FOX(IRE) b.g. 6 Riberetto - Ballyeel by Girandole — Mrs V Thompson

1337	1/5	Kelso	(L)	HC 3m 1f	9 S	*in tch when blundd and u.r. 9th.*	U	-
1455	8/5	Uttoxeter	(L)	HC 2m 5f	9 G	*chsd ldr 7th to 9th, wknd apr 12th.*	4	0

Tailed off both starts & sights need lowering considerably **0**

MOUNTAIN HALL (Irish) — I 312^{P}, I 358^{2}, I 462^{2}

MOUNTAIN-LINNET b.g. 9 Vital Season - Flavirostris by Grisaille — Major R P Thorman

1995 P(0),U(-),P(0)

555	17/3	Ottery St M'	(L)	MDO	3m	15	G	*mid-div, prog 13th, 4th whn f 15th*	F	-
733	31/3	Little Wind'	(R)	MDO	3m	13	GS	*not alwys fluent,gd hdwy to 3rd 15th,wknd 3 out,p.u. apr nxt*	P	0
821	6/4	Charlton Ho'	(L)	MDN	3m	10	GF	*in tch til 12th, outpcd frm 4 out*	4	0
1495	11/5	Holnicote	(L)	MDO	3m	11	G	*prom til mstk 12th, disp poor 3rd 4 out, fdd*	5	0
1593	25/5	Mounsey Hil'	(R)	MDO	3m	11	G	*(Jt fav) disp 5th til ld 8th, hdd 13th, 4th & btn 3 out*	3	11

Improved but beaten in weak race when favourite & still not enough stamina **12**

MOUNTAIN MASTER b.g. 10 Furry Glen - Leney Girl by Seminole II — Mrs Sue Rowe

1995 1(13),3(15),2(14),1(11)

137	17/2	Ottery St M'	(L)	RES	3m	15	GS	*prom early, lost tch 14th, no dang aft*	5	0
281	2/3	Clyst St Ma'	(L)	RES	3m	11	S	*(fav) 7/2-5/4, in tch, ld 8th-3 out, outpcd frm nxt*	2	16
482	13/3	Newton Abbot	(L)	HC	2m 5f 110yds	14	S	*bhnd till hdwy 6th, in tch when blnd and u.r. 10th.*	U	-
562	17/3	Ottery St M'	(L)	XX	3m	12	G	*mid-div, nvr on terms, p.u. 3 out*	P	0
720	30/3	Wadebridge	(L)	RES	3m	9	GF	*handy, chsd wnr 11th, outpcd 3 out, rallied flat, styd on*	2	19
805	4/4	Clyst St Ma'	(L)	RES	3m	7	GS	*(fav) disp 5th til ld 8th, hdd & blnd 11th, sn wknd & mstks*	3	11
1114	17/4	Hockworthy	(L)	RES	3m	4	GS	*chsd wnr to 12th, btn 15th, t.o. & u.r. last, rmntd*	3	0
1274	27/4	Bratton Down	(L)	MEM	3m	7	GF	*(fav) made all, lft clr last*	1	15
1528	12/5	Ottery St M'	(L)	RES	3m	10	GF	*in tch, 4th whn hit 16th, prog & ev ch 2 out, onepcd*	2	16

Dual winner 95; consistent but slow; Members double & best chance again 97; G/F-S **15**

MOUNTAINOUS VALLEY (Irish) — I 8^{F}, I 68^{6}, I 70^{U}, I 155^{P}, I 312^{P}, I 356^{2}, I 589^{F}, I 608^{1}, I 658^{P}

MOUNTAIN SLAVE b.m. 7 First Footman - Levotesse by Levmoss — Mrs June Howells

1271	27/4	Pyle	(R)	MDO	3m	15	G	*alwys rear, t.o. 4th, p.u. 7th*	P	0
1492	11/5	Erw Lon	(L)	MDO	3m	10	F	*in rear til 4th, imprvd 7-13th, wknd & p.u. 15th*	P	0

A glimmer last start & may do better **0**

MOUNT BUDA (Irish) — I 39^{P}, I 118^{1}

MOUNT DRUID (Irish) — I 250^{P}

MOUNT EATON FOX b or br.g. 13 Buckskin (FR) - Town Fox by Continuation — P J Cooper

490	16/3	Horseheath	(R)	XX	3m	7	GF	*alwys last, jmpd delib, lost tch 4th, t.o. & p.u. 10th*	P	0
675	30/3	Cottenham	(R)	MEM	3m	6	GF	*raced wd, 3rd til slw jmps 6 & 7th, p.u. nxt*	P	0
835	6/4	Marks Tey	(L)	MEM	3m	4	G	*ld, sn clr, wknd & hdd 10th, t.o. & p.u. nxt*	P	0
1258	27/4	Cottenham	(R)	OPE	3m	3	F	*ld to 2nd, lost tch 8th, t.o.*	3	0

No longer of any account **0**

MOUNT FABER b.g. 6 Headin' Up - Wise Lady by Law Of The Wise — R G Watson

1995 **13(NH)**

74	11/2	Wetherby Po'	(L)	MDO	3m	11	GS	*in tch, 3rd at 12th, fdd, p.u. 4 out*	P	0
174	18/2	Market Rase'	(L)	MDO	2m 5f	7	GF	*w.w. ev ch 11th, kpt on onepcd frm 2 out*	3	11
331	3/3	Market Rase'	(L)	MDO	3m	9	G	*hld up in tch, outpcd apr 14th, lft 2nd 3 out, fin tired*	2	11
1094	14/4	Whitwell-On'	(R)	MDO	2 1/2m 88yds	16	G	*prom, ld 10th, hdd 4 out, onepcd aft*	4	0
1136	20/4	Hornby Cast'	(L)	MDN	3m	11	G	*(bl) wth ldrs, ld 12th, qcknd 3 out, blnd nxt, styd on strngly*	1	16
1284	27/4	Easingwold	(L)	RES	3m	14	G	*(bl) alwys bhnd, blnd 5th, p.u. nxt*	P	0
1447	6/5	Witton Cast'	(R)	RES	3m	11	G	*(bl) hndy, wknd 14th, p.u. 3 out*	P	0

Blinkers worked when winning but not after; best watched now after last two starts **12**

MOUNT FALCON br.g. 14 Paico - Lady Mell by Milan — Miss Carolyn Morgan

1995 5(0),4(12),3(11),1(0),3(14),5(0),3(13),4(0),3(14),3(13),3(11)

154	17/2	Erw Lon	(L)	LAD	3m	14	G	*alwys rear*	8	0
356	3/3	Garnons	(L)	LAD	3m	12	GS	*cls up to 11th, wknd frm 13th*	6	0
546	17/3	Erw Lon	(L)	LAD	3m	10	GS	*nvr nr ldrs*	8	14
769	31/3	Pantyderi	(R)	LAD	3m	6	G	*in rear whn u.r. 13th*	U	-
979	8/4	Lydstep	(L)	LAD	3m	9	G	*alwys in rear*	6	0
1202	21/4	Lydstep	(L)	LAD	3m	4	S	*ld to 12th, onepcd aft*	3	10
1264	27/4	Pyle	(R)	LAD	3m	10	G	*s.v.s. fence bhnd frm 8th*	8	0
1387	6/5	Pantyderi	(R)	LAD	3m	6	GF	*alwys rear*	4	10
1603	25/5	Bassaleg	(R)	LAD	3m	4	GS	*s.s. cls 4th at 8th, grad lost tch*	4	0

Members winner 94/5; outclassed in Ladies & return to Members only hope in 97 .... **11**

MOUNTFOSSE gr.g. 8 Baron Blakeney - Spartella by Spartan General — J L Barnett

1995 P(0)

639	23/3	Siddington	(L)	OPE	3m	12	S	*j.s. 1st, sn wll bhnd, hit 5th, t.o. & p.u. 11th*	P	0
796	2/4	Heythrop	(R)	MDN	3m	11	F	*in tch to 12th, wll bhnd frm 3 out*	6	0

1020	13/4	Kingston Bl'	(L)	MDN	3m	10	G	*tubed, n.j.w. alwys bhnd, t.o. 13th, p.u. last*	P	0
1644	2/6	Dingley	(R)	MDO	3m	16	GF	*n.j.w., alwys wl bhnd, t.o. off*	8	0

Cannot jump & shows nothing 0

MOUNTHENRY LADY (Irish) — **I** 252^{P}, **I** 308^{P}

MOUNT NUGENT JACK (Irish) — **I** 80^{P}, **I** 157^{P}, **I** 193, , **I** 223^{4}, **I** 323^{P}, **I** 517^{P}

MOUNT PATRICK b.g. 12 Paddy's Stream - Hills Of Fashion by Tarqogan — C J Lawson

1995 5(10),4(17),6(11),3(0),4(0),P(0),2(13),4(0),U(-)

8	14/1	Cottenham	(R)	CON	3m	10	G	*alwys last, t.o. frm 6th*	8	0
36	20/1	Higham	(L)	RES	3m	12	GF	*sn t.o., p.u. 3 out*	P	0
95	11/2	Ampton	(R)	RES	3m	11	GF	*wll bhnd 4th, t.o. & p.u. 2 out*	P	0
102	17/2	Marks Tey	(L)	CON	3m	17	G	*prom to 12th, grad wknd*	10	0
420	9/3	High Easter	(L)	OPE	3m	9	S	*disp ld to 3rd, prom til wknd 13th, t.o. & p.u. 2 out*	P	0
622	23/3	Higham	(L)	CON	3m	10	GF	*mid-div whn mstk & u.r. 7th*	U	-
782	31/3	Tweseldown	(R)	XX	3m	6	G	*outpcd in rear, btn frm 4 out*	4	0
931	8/4	Marks Tey	(L)	RES	3m	8	G	*alwys prom, ld aft 4th-6th, ld 10th-16th, outpcd*	4	0
1148	20/4	Higham	(L)	CON	3m	5	F	*ld to 10th, last frm 15th, t.o.*	3	0
1398	6/5	Northaw	(L)	MEM	3m	4	F	*j.w. ld 3rd, made rest, clr 2 out, easy*	1	10

Broke losing sequence of 33 when winning; safe as houses but similar bad race needed to win again .. 11

MOUNTSHANNON b.g. 10 Pry - Tara Ogan by Tarqogan — Mrs T J Hill

1995 **4(NH),F(NH),7(NH),5(NH),2(NH),7(NH),6(NH)**

125	17/2	Kingston Bl'	(L)	OPE	3m	10	GS	*hld up, prog 10th, ev ch 14th, no imp wnr frm 3 out*	2	23
326	3/3	Market Rase'	(L)	OPE	3m	14	G	*prom, ld 14th-3 out, blnd nxt, no ext und pres*	4	22

Able but not genuine & finished early; 1st time out 97 best chance if fit; G-S 20

MOUNTVIEW SUE (Irish) — **I** 391^{4}

MOURNE MINER (Irish) — **I** 178^{F}, **I** 258^{P}

MOVING FORCE b.g. 9 Muscatite - Saint Simbir by Simbir — Mrs Louise Meyrick

1995 P(0),P(0),1(15),3(0),**F(-),5(0)**,3(13),**P(0)**

154	17/2	Erw Lon	(L)	LAD	3m	14	G	*prom, ld 5th-9th, wknd aft*	5	13
546	17/3	Erw Lon	(L)	LAD	3m	10	GS	*clr ldr to 3 out, tired 2nd whn u.r. last*	U	-
769	31/3	Pantyderi	(R)	LAD	3m	6	G	*clr ldr til 4 out, sn btn, kpt on frm 2 out*	3	22
979	8/4	Lydstep	(L)	LAD	3m	9	G	*made most til 4th & wkng at last*	4	18
1159	20/4	Llanwit Maj'	(R)	LAD	3m	5	GS	*(fav) disp ld to 3rd, ld 7th-3 out,3l down whn blndrd & u.r. 2 out*	U	-
1264	27/4	Pyle	(R)	LAD	3m	10	G	*ld 2-12th, ev ch 14th, outpcd frm nxt*	5	14
1385	6/5	Pantyderi	(R)	CON	3m	6	GF	*ld til aft 15th, breather, drvn & unable chal frm 2 out*	2	15
1488	11/5	Erw Lon	(L)	OPE	3m	4	F	*(fav) made all, clr 8th, unchal*	1	22
1617	27/5	Chaddesley '	(L)	LAD	3m	8	GF	*ld to 12th, cls 2nd whn hmpd & u.r. 14th*	U	-

Confined winner 95; does not stay but bombed home penultimate start; may find another chance 97; Fim 18

MOYA'S TIP TOP b.m. 10 Prince Titian - Moya's Star by Top Star — Kenneth R Owen

1995 P(0),P(0),P(0)

288	2/3	Eaton Hall	(R)	MDO	3m	17	G	*prom to 10th, grad lost tch, p.u. 5 out*	P	0
460	9/3	Eyton-On-Se'	(L)	LAD	3m	10	G	*nvr btr thn mid-div, sn btn, p.u. 4 out*	P	0
663	24/3	Eaton Hall	(R)	LAD	3m	8	S	*mid to rear, nvr bttr than 5th, p.u. 4 out*	P	0
853	6/4	Sandon	(L)	LAD	3m	7	GF	*msrly 2nd, in tch & ev ch whn u.r. 3 out*	U	-

Ran best last start but non-stayer or finisher & should concentrate on Maidens 12

MOYAVO LAD (Irish) — **I** 175^{F}, **I** 288^{P}, **I** 415^{P}, **I** 450^{5}, **I** 495^{P}

MOYAVO LADY (Irish) — **I** 171^{5}, **I** 284^{P}, **I** 316^{P}, **I** 406^{P}

MOYDANGANRYE (Irish) — **I** 270^{6}, **I** 336^{F}

MOYDRUM PRINCE ch.g. 10 Carlingford Castle - Chinese Queen by Tarim — A L Wallace

1995 P(0),P(0),P(0),4(0)

461	9/3	Eyton-On-Se'	(L)	RES	3m	15	G	*ld to 3rd, chsng grp tl wknd 4 out, p.u. 2 out*	P	0
666	24/3	Eaton Hall	(R)	RES	3m	13	S	*trckd ldrs to 6 out, wknd, p.u. 3 out*	P	0
1418	6/5	Eyton-On-Se'	(L)	MEM	3m	7	GF	*disp to 2nd, chsng grp to 4 out, wknd frm 3 out*	3	0
1620	27/5	Chaddesley '	(L)	XX	3m	8	GF	*ld to 3rd, cls up til wknd 14th*	5	0

Well beaten in 96 & is no little account now 0

MOYLENA (Irish) — **I** 92^{F}, **I** 168^{P}, **I** 273^{F}, **I** 314^{6}

MOYNALVY FUTURE VI (Irish) — **I** 558^{P}

MOYODE LADY (Irish) — **I** 428^{P}, **I** 545^{6}, **I** 632^{P}

MOZE TIDY b.g. 11 Rushmere - Church Belle by Spartan General — Denis Williams

1995 F(-),6(13),3(12),3(12),8(0),8(10)

39	3/2	Wadebridge	(L)	OPE	3m	7	GF	*cls up, eff aft 14th, sn outpcd*	5	16
130	17/2	Ottery St M'	(L)	MEM	3m	6	GS	*cls up, lft in ld aft 7th, made rest, comf*	1	17
554	17/3	Ottery St M'	(L)	MEM	3m	5	G	*(fav) in tch, chsd wnr 13th, outpcd 4 out, btn whn mstk last*	2	13
671	28/3	Taunton	(R)	HC	3m	13	S	*blnd 11th, nvr on terms.*	7	0

927	8/4	Bishopsleigh	(R)	OPE	3m	7	G	*mid-div til grdly wknd frm 16th*	3	12
1142	20/4	Flete Park	(R)	CON	3m	11	S	*in tch, ld 14th-nxt, sn wknd, poor 5th whn p.u. last*	P	0
1361	4/5	Flete Park	(R)	CON	3m	9	G	*hld up, steady prog to disp apr 2 out, ld last, pshd out*	1	19

Winning hurdler/chaser; revived 96; inconsistent; may find another chance at 12; Good 17

MR BARNEY (Irish) — **I** 373³, **I** 485ᵁ, **I** 595ᴾ

MR BEAK (Irish) — **I** 38ᴾ

MR BOBBIT(IRE) b.g. 6 Over The River (FR) - Orient Breeze by Deep Run — S J P Furniss

165	17/2	Weston Park	(L)	RES	3m	9	G	*cls up, losing tch whn f 12th*	F	-
288	2/3	Eaton Hall	(R)	MDO	3m	17	G	*prog frm mid-div to 2nd 13th, ld 5 out, ran on well 2 out*	1	16
564	17/3	Wolverhampt'	(L)	RES	3m	8	GS	*(fav) alwys prom, 2nd at 15th, ev ch 2 out, outpcd*	2	14
952	8/4	Eyton-On-Se'	(L)	RES	3m	7	GF	*(fav) ldng grp thruout, chsd wnr frm 3 out, outpcd*	2	16
1192	21/4	Sandon	(L)	CON	3m	11	G	*mid-div in tch, u.r. 13th*	U	-

Beat subsequent winner when scoring; ran well enough after & Restricted likely if fit 97; Good 17

MR BOOMALEEN (Irish) — **I** 114ᴾ, **I** 306⁶, **I** 332, , **I** 440ᴾ

MR BRANIGAN(IRE) b.g. 6 Cataldi - Silver Doll by Sovereign Gleam — G T H Bailey

1995 F(-),3(0),U(-)

238	25/2	Southwell P'	(L)	MDO	3m	9	HO	*prssd ldr, ev ch whn blnd & u.r. 13th*	U	-
439	9/3	Newton Brom'	(R)	MDN	3m	7	GS	*(fav) hld up rear,prog 14th,mod 4th 3 out,qcknd to ld last,sn clr*	1	14
726	31/3	Garthorpe	(R)	RES	3m	16	G	*w.w. prog 8th, ld 15th, qcknd clr apr last, imprssv*	1	24
1098	14/4	Guilsborough	(L)	CON	3m	17	G	*(fav) trckd ldrs,prog to ld 16th,1l up whn mstk last,sn hdd,ralld*	2	23

Improving; good stable; unlucky last start; should progress; Opens possible 97; G-G/S 24

MR BUSKER(IRE) b.g. 7 Orchestra - Kavali by Blakeney — C J B Barlow

1995 **4(NH),5(NH)**

75	11/2	Wetherby Po'	(L)	MDO	3m	8	GS	*(fav) prom, ld 14th, hdd & no ext last*	3	10
285	2/3	Eaton Hall	(R)	MEM	3m	5	G	*w.w. prog 4 out, chal whn u.r. 2 out, rmntd*	2	0
569	17/3	Wolverhampt'	(L)	MDN	3m	11	GS	*(fav) 3rd whn f 9th*	F	-
660	24/3	Eaton Hall	(R)	MDN	3m	7	S	*(fav) prom, blnd 5th, lft in ld 13th, prssd 2 out, ran on well*	1	15
1030	13/4	Alpraham	(R)	RES	3m	10	GS	*held up, impd & u.r. flat aft 5th*	U	-
1421	6/5	Eyton-On-Se'	(L)	RES	3m	11	GF	*cl up, dsp 5th, ev ch 4 out, not qckn*	5	14

Found a weak race when winning; may progress but more needed for Restricteds; G-S 15

MR CAMPUS (Irish) — **I** 200ᴾ, **I** 248ᴾ, **I** 440ᴾ

MR CHERRYPICKER(IRE) b.g. 6 Henbit (USA) - June Bug by Welsh Saint — D G Alers-Hankey

45	3/2	Wadebridge	(L)	MDO	3m	10	GF	*(fav) trckd ldrs gng wl, mstk 14th, sn wknd*	5	0
470	10/3	Milborne St'	(L)	MDO	3m	18	G	*alwys mid-div, outpcd frm 4 out, p.u. last*	P	0

Last & well beaten when completing; top stable; should do better 11

MR CONNIE VEE (Irish) — **I** 206ᴾ, **I** 250ᴾ, **I** 445ᴾ, **I** 652ᴾ

MR DENNEHY (Irish) — **I** 191ᴾ, **I** 228ᴾ, **I** 311⁴, **I** 430³, **I** 474ᶠ, **I** 530ᶠ

MR DICK gr.g. 6 Absalom - Red Spider by Red God — Mrs J Cooper

1995 **9(NH),P(NH)**

174	18/2	Market Rase'	(L)	MDO	2m 5f	7	GF	*prom, disp 6th-14th, rdn apr last, no ext*	2	12
307	2/3	Great Stain'	(L)	MDO	3m	17	GS	*(fav) rear of ldrs, prog 10th, 2nd 15th, onepcd frm 2 out*	4	12
413	9/3	Charm Park	(L)	MDO	3m	12	G	*prom, ld frm 13th, styd on wl, imprv*	1	16
588	23/3	Wetherby Po'	(L)	INT	3m	17	S	*mid-div whn f 4 out*	F	-
825	6/4	Stainton	(R)	RES	3m	7	GF	*(fav) prom & going wll, ld 2 out, sn qcknd clr*	1	18

Placed in novice hurdle; found his niche in points; improving; stays; should upgrade; Good 21

MR DIPLOMATIC b.g. 13 Cheval - Vulrain by Raincheck — J N Llewellen Palmer

1995 1(24),r(-),3(20)

487	16/3	Newcastle	(L)	HC	3m	10	GS	*(bl) cl up, ld 4th, stumbled and hdd after four out, p.u. next.*	P	0
582	22/3	Kelso	(L)	HC	3 1/2m	8	G	*(bl) rdn and hdd 16th, gradually wknd from 3 out.*	4	0
1226	25/4	Perth	(R)	HC	3m	7	S	*(bl) ld, mstk 10th, hdd next, soon wknd, t.o. when p.u. before 15th.*	P	0
1251	27/4	Balcormo Ma'	(R)	OPE	3m	6	GS	*ld/disp frm 5th til wknd frm 13th*	4	0

Looks finished now 0

MR DRAKE(IRE) b.g. 6 Salluceva - Salambos by Doon — M J Tuckey

641	23/3	Siddington	(L)	RES	3m	20	S	*schoold in rr til p.u. appr 15th*	P	0
890	6/4	Kimble	(L)	MDN	3m	11	GF	*ld to aft 3rd & 8th til mstk & hdd 13th, wknd 15th, p.u.2out*	P	0
1569	19/5	Mollington	(R)	MDO	3m	10	GS	*prom, ld 13th-2 out, wknd last*	3	12

Gradually improving & ran well enough in weak Maiden; should go close in 97 14

MR DUNCAN (Irish) — **I** 585ˢ, **I** 599ᴾ

M-REG b.g. 7 Politico (USA) - Heckley Surprise by Foggy Bell — Mrs C Egalton

1995 3(11),3(11),P(0),2(10),5(0),4(0)

558	17/3	Ottery St M'	(L)	MDO	3m	9	G	*handy, prog 13th, chal 4 out, disp nxt, qcknd clr flat*	1 15
926	8/4	Bishopsleigh	(R)	RES	3m	9	G	*(fav) alwys wll plcd, ld 3 out, won wll*	1 20
1590	25/5	Mounsey Hil'	(R)	INT	3m	8	G	*in tch, went 2nd 15th, ld 2 out, clr last, comf*	1 22
1634	1/6	Bratton Down	(L)	INT	3m	15	G	*(fav) in tch til p.u. 6th, saddle slpd*	P 0

Changed hands 96 & much improved; unextended when winning; sold Ascot June 96 21

MR ELK gr.g. 7 Bellypha - Shuteye by Shirley Heights — Peter Sawney

223	24/2	Duncombe Pa'	(R)	CON	3m	16	GS	*mid-div, lost tch 11th, t.o. & p.u. 14th*	P 0
411	9/3	Charm Park	(L)	RES	3m	20	G	*u.r. 2nd*	U
585	23/3	Wetherby Po'	(L)	RES	3m	13	S	*mid-div till f 14th*	F
1090	14/4	Whitwell-On'	(R)	RES	3m	17	G	*mid-div, blnd 10th, p.u. nxt*	P 0

Maiden winner 94; missed 95 & showed nothing in 96; best watched 10

MR FFITCH b.g. 10 Hays - Lady Topknot by High Top — M Howells

1995 P(0),P(0),U(-),P(0),2(0)

773	31/3	Pantyderi	(R)	MDN	3m	8	G	*trckd ldrs, wkng whn f 14th*	U
841	6/4	Maisemore P'	(L)	MDN	3m	9	GF	*rcd wd,chsd ldr 6th,disp ld bfly 12th,3rd & wkng appr 2 out*	3 0
1175	20/4	Chaddesley '	(L)	MDN	3m	9	G	*prom, chsd ldrs, 6l 3rd whn f 16th*	F
1390	6/5	Pantyderi	(R)	MDO	3m	15	GF	*prom til wknd frm 15th, kpt on apr last*	3 12

Gradually improving & beaten 6l last start; may win at 11 if finding a little more 12

MR FREEMAN (Irish) — I 200³, I 306,

MR GEE b.g. 11 Crooner - Miss Desla by Light Thrust — M W Conway

1995 **P(NH),7(NH),P(NH),4(NH),6(NH)**

856	6/4	Sandon	(L)	RES	3m	9	GF	*cls up,ld 2 out,hdd btwn last 2 fences,disp 3rd whn ro last*	r
1104	14/4	Guilsborough	(L)	MDN	3m	18	G	*prom, chsd wnr 3 out, chal frm nxt, not qckn apr last*	2 15
1240	27/4	Clifton On '	(L)	MDO	3m	10	GF	*(fav) cls up, chal 16th, not qckn nxt, styd on frm last to ld post*	1 15
1522	12/5	Garthorpe	(R)	RES	3m	12	GF	*ld/disp til ld 4th,hdd 7th, disp 3 out, going wll whn f last*	F 18
1597	25/5	Garthorpe	(R)	XX	3m	9	G	*cls up in 2nd/3rd to 9th, fdd, 8th & outpcd 6 out*	5 0
1641	2/6	Dingley	(R)	RES	3m	13	GF	*last whn jmpd slwly 2nd, mstk 8th, nvr on trms*	5 1

Fortunate to be given verdict when winning & not one to trust; likely to frustrate in Restricteds 15

MR GOLIGHTLY gr.g. 9 Lighter - Go Gently by New Member — Mrs B I Cobden

1995 **1(27),1(32),1(32)**

99	14/2	Lingfield	(L)	HC	3m	9	HY	*(Jt fav) ld till rider tk wrong course apr 10th, p.u..*	P
483	14/3	Cheltenham	(L)	HC	3 1/4m 110yds	17	G	*chsd ldrs, mstk 10th, 6th and driven along when u.r. 4 out.*	U
798	3/4	Ascot	(R)	HC	2m 3f 110yds	10	GF	*trckd ldrs, ld 8th, made rest, mstk last, styd on well.*	1 3
1122	20/4	Stratford	(L)	HC	2m 5f 110yds	16	GF	*alwys prom, ld 12th, hdd 3 out, mstk next, rallied to ld flat, styd on.*	1 3
1331	1/5	Cheltenham	(L)	HC	2m 5f	9	G	*(fav) prog to chase ldr 8th, mstk 11th, rdn apr last, drifted right run-in, just faild.*	2 3
1631	1/6	Stratford	(L)	HC	3 1/2m	14	GF	*chsd ldrs to 16th, soon wknd, t.o. when p.u. before 2 out.*	P

Very useful H/Chaser; won 5 of 6 completions 95/6; versatile; sure to win more; G/F-Hy 33

MR GOSSIP b.g. 14 Le Bavard (FR) - Regency View by Royal Highway — David Wale

1995 P(0),4(16),P(0),1(14),2(18),**4(19)**

93	11/2	Ampton	(R)	LAD	3m	7	GF	*jmpd slwly 3rd, prog to 3rd at 15th, outpcd 17th, 2nd last*	2 1
310	2/3	Ampton	(R)	CON	3m	13	G	*w.w. prog 7th, chsd wnr 2 out, kpt on onpcd*	2 2
491	16/3	Horseheath	(R)	CON	3m	5	GF	*w.w. rmndrs 5th, prog to jn ldrs 10th, ev ch 4 out, wknd*	5 1

Members winner 94/5; rarely consents to win & Members again best hope if back in 97 15

MR K'S WINTERBLUES (Irish) — I 63, , I 70ᴾ, I 149¹, I 376¹

MR LION ch.g. 14 Windjammer (USA) - Polly Darling by Darling Boy — G J Harri

1995 9(0),3(17),10(0),U(-)

66	10/2	Great Treth'	(R)	OPE	3m	8	S	*grad lost tch frm 10th, p.u. 2 out*	P
133	17/2	Ottery St M'	(L)	OPE	3m	18	GS	*rear whn blnd & u.r. 7th*	U
277	2/3	Clyst St Ma'	(L)	OPE	3m	4	S	*chsd ldr to 16th, wknd nxt, outpcd*	3 1
528	16/3	Cothelstone	(L)	MEM	3m	8	G	*rr & blnd 10th, no ch 14th, p.u. 2 out*	P
990	8/4	Kingston St'	(R)	OPE	3m	6	F	*prog to cls 2nd 9th, cls 3rd frm 13th, wknd steadily*	3 1

Still capable of occasional fair effort but too old now 12

MR LOVELY (Irish) — I 81⁴

MR MAD b.g. 8 Good Times (ITY) - Mistress Bowen by Owen Anthony — Gwynne Phillip

544	17/3	Erw Lon	(L)	MEM	3m	5	GS	*(fav) sttld rear, prog 11th, ld 13th, easily*	1 1
840	6/4	Maisemore P'	(L)	RES	3m	9	GF	*(fav) mstks,last trio frm 4th,rpd hdwy appr 2out,hit last,nvr nr*	2 1

Lightly raced; missed 95; unlucky last start; stays; should win Restricted 97; G/F-S 19

MR MATCHIT (Irish) — I 351ᶠ, I 548⁴

MR MAYFAIR b.g. 13 The Parson - Doe Royale by Royal Buck — R C Irving
1995 P(0),4(13),F(-),4(15),3(13),5(11),U(-),2(14)
381 9/3 Barbury Cas' (L) XX 3m 9 GS *nvr nr ldrs, t.o. & p.u. 12th* P 0
782 31/3 Tweseldown (R) XX 3m 6 G *sn rear, btn frm 4 out* 5 0
995 8/4 Hackwood Pa' (L) XX 3m 8 GF *alwys 1st trio, jnd ldr 14th, outpcd nxt, lft clr 2 out* 1 12
Broke a losing sequence of 18 when winning typical Hackwood race (lucky); similar miracle needed ... 12

MR MOSS TROOPER (Irish) — **I** 393^{P}, **I** 477^{P}, **I** 563^{F}, **I** 628^{3}

MR PADDY BELL b.g. 9 Paddy's Stream - My Bellebурd by Twilight Alley — Mrs Marian J Walters
1995 2(0),5(0),P(0)
23 20/1 Barbury Cas' (L) XX 3m 11 GS *blnd 6th & lost tch, t.o. & u.r. 11th* U -
218 24/2 Newtown (L) MDN 3m 14 GS *alwys bhnd, t.o. & p.u. 11th* P 0
688 30/3 Chaddesley ' (L) MDN 3m 17 G *mid-div, blnd 4th, strgglng whn u.r. 11th* U -
1006 9/4 Upton-On-Se' (R) MDN 3m 11 F *with ldr to 6th, wknd 11th, t.o. whn p.u. 14th* P 0
1174 20/4 Chaddesley ' (L) MDN 3m 10 G *(vis) chsd ldrs,cls 5th at 13th,rdn & ev ch 16th, wknd & p.u.3out* P 0
1433 6/5 Ashorne (R) MDO 3m 16 G *(vis) ld 5-6th, prom aft til wknd 13th, t.o.* 7 0
No stamina & no hopes; visor no help ... 0

MR PATRICK ch.g. 12 Import - Mrs Paddy by Acropolis — I McLaughlin
1995 5(0),2(0),1(14),2(13)
235 24/2 Heythrop (R) RES 3m 10 GS *(bl) ld 2nd-8th, wknd prdly, p.u. 11th* P 0
338 3/3 Heythrop (R) RES 3m 9 G *(Co fav) (bl) bhnd frm 9th, t.o. & p.u. 13th* P 0
1216 24/4 Andoversford (R) INT 3m 7 G *(bl) cl up, hit 3rd, lost pl 10th, last & p.u. 13th* P 0
Maiden winner 95; not genuine & disinterested 96; unlikely to achieve anything now ... 0

MR PEOPLES (Irish) — **I** 231^{P}, **I** 322^{P}

MR PIPEMAN (Irish) — **I** 6^{P}, **I** 58^{5}, **I** 140^{P}, **I** 241^{5}, **I** 331^{P}, **I** 435^{4}, **I** 547^{3}, **I** 593^{2}, **I** 613^{5}, **I** 646^{1}

MR RIGSBY(IRE) b.g. 8 Le Moss - Meadow Wings — Mrs Barbara Price
1995 P(0),9(0),4(14),1(19)
124 17/2 Kingston Bl' (L) CON 3m 17 GS *mid-div,rdn & prog 10th,ev ch apr 14th,wknd rpdly,p.u.2 out* P 0
434 9/3 Newton Brom' (R) CON 3m 11 GS *twrds rear til some prog frm 13th, nvr rchd ldrs* 6 0
724 31/3 Garthorpe (R) LAD 3m 5 G *f 2nd, dead* F -
Dead ... 19

MR ROBSTEE b.g. 5 Pragmatic - Miss Northwick by Remezzo — P H King
797 2/4 Heythrop (R) MDN 3m 11 F *ref 1st, cont, ref 2nd* R -
Scarcely the best of starts ... 0

MRS BEAN (Irish) — **I** 521^{P}, **I** 527^{P}

MRS BLOBBY(IRE) b.m. 6 Rontino - Allitess by Mugatpura — C N Nimmo
239 25/2 Southwell P' (L) MDO 3m 9 HO *(fav) hld up in tch, qcknd to ld 4 out, 2l up whn f 2 out* F 14
680 30/3 Cottenham (R) MDO 3m 11 GF *(fav) hld up bhnd, mstk 12th, no prog 14th, p.u. 3 out* P 0
1569 19/5 Mollington (R) MDO 3m 10 GS *cls up, mstk 7th, rdn & wknd 11th, p.u. 13th* P 0
Unlucky on debut in poor race but yet to repeat form; may do better but not one to back short odds 13

MRS CADOGAN gr.m. 11 Ring Bidder - Sandicroft by Colour Photo — Miss G Dewhurst
738 31/3 Sudlow Farm (R) LAD 3m 5 G *alwys last, losng tch & jmpd slwly 6th, p.u. nxt* P 0
1010 9/4 Flagg Moor (L) LAD 3m 6 G *chsd ldng trio, lost tch 10th, lft poor 3rd 12th* 3 0
Of no account ... 0

MRS GIGGS (Irish) — **I** 44^{P}, **I** 169^{3}, **I** 264^{4}

MR SHARP b.g. 7 Germont - Acton Littleeileen by Irish Edition — W Hodge
405 9/3 Dalston (R) MDO 2 1/2m 16 G *al in rr* 10 0
614 23/3 Friars Haugh (L) MDN 3m 10 G *alwys wll bhnd, t.o.* 5 0
755 31/3 Lockerbie (R) MDN 3m 17 G *alwys bhnd* 8 0
Gets round safely but only beaten one other finisher so far ... 0

MRS MAGINN (Irish) — **I** 325^{P}

MR SNAIL b.g. 8 Petorius - Spring Lane by Forlorn River — Stuart Currie
72 11/2 Wetherby Po' (L) CON 3m 18 GS *mid-div, rear whn u.r. 12th* U -
401 9/3 Dalston (R) OPE 3m 6 G *3rd frm 4th, wth ldrs whn u.r. 13th* U -
662 24/3 Eaton Hall (R) OPE 3m 10 S *mstks in rear, t.o. & p.u. 5 out* P 0
736 31/3 Sudlow Farm (R) CON 3m 9 G *prog & cls up 11th, outpcd 14th, 4th & wll btn whn u.r. last* U -
Flat winner 91; poor jumper with no prospects in points ... 0

MRS TWEED b.m. 10 Rusticaro (FR) - Bumpkin by Free State — W J Warner

333 3/3 Market Rase' (L) MDO 3m 11 G *8s-4s, cls up, ev ch apr 14th, wknd 3 out* 4 0

Placed in novice chase 94; well beaten & not seen again; good stable but barely worth a rating 10

MR SUNNYSIDE b.g. 10 Sunyboy - Firella by Firestreak S J Claisse
1995 **3(NH),P(NH),10(NH),4(NH),5(NH),4(NH),U(NH),5(NH)**

574 17/3 Detling (L) RES 3m 14 GF *wth ldrs whn f 1st* F -
787 31/3 Tweseldown (R) RES 3m 9 G *trckd ldrs, outpcd frm 12th, t.o. 2 out* 6 0
999 8/4 Hackwood Pa' (L) RES 3m 6 GF *last to hlfwy, ran on, no imp* 3 11
1189 21/4 Tweseldown (R) RES 3m 10 GF *w.w. prog to dist 2nd hlfwy, onepcd frm 14th* 5 0
1371 4/5 Peper Harow (L) RES 3m 5 F *chsd ldr 7-10th,strng chall whn bmpd & u.r. appr 2 out* U -
1612 26/5 Tweseldown (R) RES 3m 11 G *in tch to 13th, no ch whn blnd 16th, t.o. & p.u. 2 out* P 0

Maiden winner 92; poor form under Rules 94/5 & beaten in bad races 96; unlikely to win again 11

MRS WUMPKINS(IRE) b.m. 5 Phardante (FR) - Mr Jersey by Crash Course David Brace

45 3/2 Wadebridge (L) MDO 3m 10 GF *alwys rear, lost tch & p.u. 12th, dsmtd* P 0
149 17/2 Erw Lon (L) MDN 3m 10 G *hld up, 4th at 12th, 2nd 3 out, ran on to ld flat* 1 14
339 3/3 Heythrop (R) RES 3m 10 G *(Jt fav) w.w. mstk 6th, effrt 13th, btn whn blnd nxt & p.u.* P 0
549 17/3 Erw Lon (L) RES 3m 11 GS *in 3rd/4th til mstk 10th, p.u. nxt* P 0
844 6/4 Howick (L) RES 3m 10 GF *(fav) 5th hlfwy, no prog, p.u. 3 out* P 0
1038 13/4 St Hilary (R) RES 3m 15 G *rear, no prog whn p.u. 14th* P 0
1490 11/5 Erw Lon (L) RES 3m 6 F *prom to 9th, wknd, p.u. 13th* P 0
1557 18/5 Bassaleg (R) RES 3m 14 F *last whn u.r. 7th* U -

Won weak Maiden on only completion & struggled badly after; can only be watched 12

MR TITTLE TATTLE b.g. 10 Le Bavard (FR) - Mille Fleurs (USA) by Floribunda H A Shone
1995 1(23),1(19),3(16),3(18),**8(0)**

162 17/2 Weston Park (L) OPE 3m 16 G *(bl) ld to 5th, ld 8-11th, fdd rpdly 3 out, p.u. nxt* P 0
290 2/3 Eaton Hall (R) OPE 3m 6 G *ld to 12th, chal frm 4 out, ld last, hdd post* 2 23
565 17/3 Wolverhampt' (L) OPE 3m 6 GS *chsd ldrs, 7l 3rd at 14th, wknd aft* 3 12
737 31/3 Sudlow Farm (R) OPE 3m 4 G *(bl) ld to 7th & agn 11th, 2l ld 2 out, kpt on wll* 1 25
1154 20/4 Whittington (L) OPE 3m 7 G *(bl) ld thruout, wnt clr 15th, easily* 1 19
1367 4/5 Gisburn (R) OPE 3m 4 G *(bl) ld to 14th, sn btn* 2 19

Able but needs things his own way; front-runner; blinkers when winning; should win again; G-S 21

MR TOM TOM (Irish) — **I** 35^{P}, **I** 53^{2}, **I** 74^{2}, **I** 122^{2}, **I** 366^{4}, **I** 472^{4}

MR WEISER (Irish) — **I** 138^{P}, **I** 147^{P}

MR WENDYL b.g. 8 Celtic Cone - Run In Tune by Deep Run R M Emmanuel
1995 **5(NH),F(NH),P(NH),P(NH),4(NH)**

221 24/2 Newtown (L) MDN 3m 12 GS *mstk 2nd, prom til outpcd aft 13th, lft poor 2nd nxt, no imp* 2 10
479 10/3 Tweseldown (R) MDO 3m 10 G *cls up, ld 13th, 2l up whn u.r. 3 out* U -
680 30/3 Cottenham (R) MDO 3m 11 GF *prom, chsd wnr 10-16th, went 2nd agn last, no imp* 2 11
890 6/4 Kimble (L) MDN 3m 11 GF *(Jt fav) prom til lost plc 12th,8th at 14th,ran on & 3rd 2 out,no imp* 3 0
1241 27/4 Clifton On ' (L) MDO 3m 8 GF *prom, chsd wnr 13th, chal & lvl 2 out-last, not qckn flat* 2 14
1504 11/5 Kingston Bl' (L) MDO 3m 13 G *prom til ran out 4th* r -
1568 19/5 Mollington (R) MDO 3m 9 GS *(fav) prom, chsd wnr 14th, 2l down whn u.r. nxt* U -

Good enough for Maiden win but owner/ridden to poor effect & could continue to frustrate 14

MR WIDEAWAKE ch.g. 9 Royal Match - Dorriba by Ribero C J Wilton Jnr

70 10/2 Great Treth' (R) MDO 3m 14 S *chsd ldrs til lost ground & p.u. 13th* P 0
629 23/3 Kilworthy (L) MDN 3m 11 GS *ld to 3rd, chsd wnr frm 12th, rdn & btn 15th* 2 10
876 6/4 Higher Kilw' (L) MDN 3m 11 GF *in tch, prog 15th, ev ch til wknd 2 out* 3 13
1143 20/4 Flete Park (R) MDN 3m 17 S *(Co fav) mid-div, til p.u. aft 10th, lame* P 0

Missed 95; placed 4 times but not threatening a win & problmes last start 11

MSADI MHULU (Irish) — **I** 130^{P}, **I** 164^{P}, **I** 386^{P}

M T POCKETS (Irish) — **I** 101^{F}, **I** 160^{P}, **I** 268^{F}

MUCKLE JACK ch.g. 6 Nearly A Hand - Sparkling Tarqua by Never Die Dancing A P Gent

954 8/4 Eyton-On-Se' (L) MDO 2 1/2m 6 GF *rear early, prog 5 out, ran on, nrst fin* 4 0

Beaten over 30l on only start; should be capable of better if racing regularly 97 10

MUCK OR MONEY b.g. 12 Slim Jim - Karena III by Rubor Charles Yule

30 20/1 Higham (L) MEM 3m 4 GF *alwys 3rd, lst tch 12th, t.o. whn ref 3 out* R -

No longer of any account 0

MUDDLE HEAD(IRE) br.g. 7 Royal Fountain - Cairita by Pitcairn B Kennedy
1995 F(-),P(0),P(0),3(10),4(0)

14 14/1 Cottenham (R) MDO 3m 10 G *pllng, went prom 4th til f 12th* F -
61 10/2 Cottenham (R) MDO 3m 8 GS *wth ldr & clr of rest,blnd 11th, wknd rpdly & p.u. 14th* P 0
495 16/3 Horseheath (R) MDO 3m 12 GF *pllng, disp 6th, lost plc 10th, wknd 13th, p.u. 4 out* P 0

680	30/3	Cottenham	(R)	MDO	3m	11	GF	*(bl) plling, prom to 10th, sn wknd, t.o. & p.u. 15th*	P	0

Finished 2 of 9 races 95/6 & grinds himself to a halt after pulling; no chances 0

MULCAIRE BOY VI (Irish) — **I** 476^{P}

MULDERS FRIEND (Irish) — **I** 505^{3}

MULLABAWN (Irish) — **I** 418^{1}, **I** 529^{3}

MULLINELLO (Irish) — **I** 27^{P}, **I** 112^{P}

MULTI LINE ch.m. 6 High Line - Waterford Cream by Proverb — Mrs S Brazier

890	6/4	Kimble	(L)	MDN	3m	11	GF	*mid-div, prog 10th, outpcd apr 3 out, no dang aft*	5	0
1183	21/4	Mollington	(R)	MDN	3m	10	F	*trckd ldrs, chal 15th, ev ch 2 out, wknd apr last, tired*	3	11

Not disgraced on either start but well beaten so far; should go close in 97 14

MULTI PURPOSE ch.g. 9 Say Primula - Ribera by Ribston — Neil Bennett

763	31/3	Great Stain'	(L)	MDN	3m	11	GS	*ld to 8th, wknd rpdly 10th, p.u. 3 out*	P	0
910	8/4	Tranwell	(L)	MEM	3m	4	GF	*1st ride, alwys last, blnd & u.r. 7th*	U	-
1286	27/4	Easingwold	(L)	MDO	3m	13	G	*rear, rmndr 3rd, t.o. 6th, p.u. 11th*	P	0

Missed 95 & unpromising performances 96 0

MUMMY'S SONG b.g. 11 Mummy's Pet - Welsh Miniature by Owen Anthony — Miss S Prangley

153	17/2	Erw Lon	(L)	OPE	3m	15	G	*mid-div, 10l 5th at 13th, no ch aft*	5	11
351	3/3	Garnons	(L)	OPE	3m	14	GS	*10l 7th at 12th, lost tch frm 14th*	7	0
506	16/3	Magor	(R)	CON	3m	8	GS	*ld to 10th, wknd, t.o. & p.u. last*	P	0
602	23/3	Howick	(L)	OPE	3m	11	S	*ld to 7th, wknd rpdly, p.u. 13th*	P	0
768	31/3	Pantyderi	(R)	OPE	3m	10	G	*prom to 8th, fdd, p.u. 11th*	P	0
1532	13/5	Towcester	(R)	HC	2m 110yds	16	GF	*mid div when f 2 out.*	F	-
1619	27/5	Chaddesley '	(L)	OPE	3m	7	GF	*chsd wnr til p.u. 10th, lame*	P	0

No chance of staying & no prospects now 0

MUM'S THE WORD (Irish) — **I** 340^{F}, **I** 428^{P}

MURBERRY(IRE) b or br.m. 6 Strong Statement (USA) - Lady Tarsel by Tarqogan — M H D Barlow

272	2/3	Parham	(R)	RES	3m	13	GF	*5s-3s,handy,smooth prog to jn ldr 4 out,ld & clr 2 out*	1	20
594	23/3	Parham	(R)	CON	3m	13	GS	*(fav) cls up til mstk 11th, 4th frm 14th, no ch frm 3 out*	4	12
1050	13/4	Penshurst	(L)	CON	3m	8	G	*(fav) mid-div, clsd up 13th, wth ldr aft, ld 2 out-last,kpt on wll*	2	21

Ex-Irish; ran well twice; sold end of season; summer jumping 96; win more points; G-F 22

MURCHEEN DURKEN (Irish) — **I** 111^{5}, **I** 166^{2}, **I** 237^{1}, **I** 477^{P}

MURCOT MELODY ch.m. 7 Brotherly (USA) - Baynton Melody by Romany Air — Mrs Corp

1995 P(0),P(0),P(0)

354	3/3	Garnons	(L)	MDN	2 1/2m	13	GS	*nvr rchd ldrs, lost tch 9th, t.o. nxt*	6	0

Of no account 0

MURDER MOSS(IRE) ch.g. 6 Doulab (USA) - Northern Wind by Northfields (USA) — S Coltherd

88	11/2	Alnwick	(L)	MDO	3m	11	GS	*sn wll bhnd, t.o. 6th, p.u. 2 out*	P	0
193	24/2	Friars Haugh	(L)	MDN	3m	10	S	*sn bhnd, p.u. 10th*	P	0
406	9/3	Dalston	(R)	MDO	2 1/2m	12	G	*prom early, sn mid-div, n.d.*	7	0
756	31/3	Lockerbie	(R)	MDN	3m	14	G	*wnt 4th 4 out, kpt on wll, no imp on wnnr*	2	12
1254	27/4	Balcormo Ma'	(R)	MDO	3m	14	GS	*nvr dang, p.u. 3 out*	P	0
1353	4/5	Mosshouses	(L)	RES	3m	11	GS	*mstk 2nd, rear, 8th & lost tch hlfwy, t.o. & p.u. 2 out*	P	0
1517	12/5	Hexham Poin'	(L)	MDN	3m	10	HY	*in tch, ld 2 out, styd on*	1	15
1571	19/5	Corbridge	(R)	RES	3m	13	G	*mstk 3rd, prog hlfwy, ld aft 2 out, ran on wll, improve*	1	18

Much improved last two starts; stays; novice ridden; should progress to Confineds; G-Hy 18

MURPHYS LADY (Irish) — **I** 206^{1}, **I** 246^{2}, **I** 295^{P}

MUSBURY CASTLE br.m. 7 Henricus (ATA) - Belle Flare by Right Flare — Martin Rowswell

1995 U(-),U(-),P(0),R(-)

283	2/3	Clyst St Ma'	(L)	MDN	3m	7	S	*rear til p.u. 6th*	P	0
446	9/3	Haldon	(R)	MDO	3m	13	S	*bhnd til p.u. 10th*	P	0
719	30/3	Wadebridge	(L)	MDO	3m	7	GF	*mid-div, 5th & no ch 14th*	5	0
928	8/4	Bishopsleigh	(R)	MDN	3m	9	G	*mid-div whn f 9th*	F	-
1129	20/4	Stafford Cr'	(R)	MDO	3m	11	S	*sn rear, t.o. & p.u. 9th*	P	0
1429	6/5	High Bickin'	(R)	MDO	3m	8	G	*rear til p.u. apr 16th*	P	0
1494	11/5	Holnicote	(L)	MDO	3m	8	G	*wll in tch til lost plc 16th, mstk nxt, t.o.*	6	0

Of no account 0

MUSCOATES b.g. 5 Domynsky - Mescalin by Politico (USA) — W Brown

73	11/2	Wetherby Po'	(L)	MDO	3m	15	GS	*rear, p.u. 6th*	P	0
222	24/2	Duncombe Pa'	(R)	MEM	3m	6	GS	*last whn u.r. 5th*	U	-

307	2/3	Great Stain'	(L)	MDO 3m	17 GS	*jmpd stickily, t.o. 3rd, p.u. 6th*	P	0
414	9/3	Charm Park	(L)	MDO 3m	11 G	*2nd whn r.o. 5th*	r	-
590	23/3	Wetherby Po'	(L)	MDO 3m	16 S	*rear whn p.u. 12th*	P	0
987	8/4	Charm Park	(L)	MDN 3m	13 GF	*mid-div, 5th 13th, onepcd aft*	6	0
1285	27/4	Easingwold	(L)	MDO 3m	9 G	*rear, jmpd slwly 2nd, lost tch 5th, t.o. & p.u. 7th*	P	0

Last when completing & looks pretty hopeless 0

MUSICAL MAIL b.g. 9 Rymer - Blue Mail by Pony Express — J R Sutcliffe

1995 P(0),3(10),4(0)

128	17/2	Kingston Bl'	(L)	RES 3m	14 GS	*25s-8s, chsd ldrs, lost tch 11th, f 13th*	F	-
241	25/2	Southwell P'	(L)	MDO 3m	15 HO	*prom, wkng whn blnd & u.r. 14th*	U	-
357	3/3	Garnons	(L)	RES 3m	14 GS	*prom to 10th, lost tch 12th, p.u. 3 out*	P	0
1047	13/4	Bitterley	(L)	MDO 3m	13 G	*mid-div to 10th, wknd & p.u. aft 12th*	P	0
1196	21/4	Sandon	(L)	MDN 3m	17 G	*ldng trio clr of rest whn s.u. flat apr 13th*	S	-
1417	6/5	Cursneh Hill	(L)	MDO 3m	14 GF	*nvr rchd ldrs, styd on onepcd frm 14th*	4	10
1485	11/5	Bredwardine	(R)	MDO 3m	15 G	*cls up frm 8th, hmpd 13th, cls 2nd 3 out, kpt on onepcd nxt*	4	0

Placed 4 times 95-6 but does not stay & not threatening to win 10

MUSICAL PATCH (Irish) — **I** 176^{F}, **I** 258^{3}

MUSIC IN THE NIGHT ch.g. 8 True Song - Look Back by Country Retreat — Mrs Caroline Price

1995 P(0),F(-),3(11)

20	14/1	Tweseldown	(R)	RES 3m	9 GS	*ld, mstks 13 & 15th, hdd last, kpt on, no ch wth wnr*	2	18

Lightly raced; vanished after opening weekend; best watched early 97 17

MUSIC MINSTREL ch.g. 13 Orchestra - Victorian Era by High Hat — Mrs Yda Morgan

1995 P(0),P(0),3(0),F(-),F(-),R(-),P(0)

401	9/3	Dalston	(R)	OPE 3m	6 G	*(bl) last & undr pres 11th, t.o.*	3	0
701	30/3	Tranwell	(L)	OPE 3m	8 GS	*(bl) prom early, bhnd frm 11th*	5	0
861	6/4	Alnwick	(L)	CON 3m	7 GF	*(bl) mid-div, pshd alng 9th, t.o. 13th*	5	0
1083	14/4	Friars Haugh	(L)	CON 3m	10 F	*(bl) sn wll bhnd, t.o. whn u.r. last*	U	-

No longer of any account 0

MUSKERRY EXPRESS (Irish) — **I** 567^{4}, **I** 642^{P}

MUSKERRY MOYA(IRE) ch.m. 7 Rising - Muskerry Mary by Mon Capitaine — N W Rimington

1995 P(0),P(0),P(0),2(13),P(0)

2	13/1	Larkhill	(R)	MDO 3m	17 GS	*rear whn f 6th*	F	-
45	3/2	Wadebridge	(L)	MDO 3m	10 GF	*alwys rear, lost tch 11th, t.o. & p.u. 2 out*	P	0
145	17/2	Larkhill	(R)	MDO 3m	13 G	*rear whn u.r. 6th*	U	

Just beaten in weak race 95 but showed nothing in 96 & finished early 0

MUSKIN MORE (Irish) — **I** 131^{2}, **I** 192^{1}

MUST BE MURPHY(IRE) br.g. 5 Gallic Heir - Tricias Pet by Mandalus — Mrs J K Peutherer

220	24/2	Newtown	(L)	MDN 3m	12 GS	*t.o. in last pair til p.u. 11th*	P	0
747	31/3	Upper Sapey	(R)	MDO 3m	11 GS	*losing tch whn p.u. aft 11th*	P	0

No signs of ability but young enough to improve 0

MUTUAL AGREEMENT ch.m. 9 Quayside - Giolla's Bone by Pitpan — Edward Darke

1995 **P(NH),4(NH),2(NH)**

1143	20/4	Flete Park	(R)	MDN 3m	17 S	*(Co fav) hld up bhnd, mstk 5th, prog 3 out, strng run to ld last,comf*	1	15
1358	4/5	Flete Park	(R)	RES 3m	8 G	*w.w. prog 12th, ev ch til not qckn frm 2 out*	2	18
1528	12/5	Ottery St M'	(L)	RES 3m	10 GF	*rear frm hlfwy, blnd 14th, t.o.*	6	10

Placed in novice chases; good start; stays; ran badly on fast; should find Restricted; G-S 18

MYALUP (Irish) — **I** 15^{P}, **I** 67^{6}, **I** 115^{4}, **I** 209^{4}, **I** 355^{4}, **I** 435^{2}, **I** 468^{4}

MY BEST MAN br.g. 9 True Song - Eventime by Hot Brandy — Alan Hill

1995 P(0),4(17),F(-),4(12)

231	24/2	Heythrop	(R)	XX 3m	10 GS	*hld up, prog 13th, blnd nxt, chsd ldr 16th, ld nxt, ran on*	1	15
365	5/3	Leicester	(R)	HC 3m	10 GS	*mstks, bhnd and rdn along apr 9th, n.d..*	7	0
639	23/3	Siddington	(L)	OPE 3m	12 S	*jnd ldr 7th, kicked clr 11th, 15l ld 14th, blnd last, kpt on*	1	24
886	6/4	Kimble	(L)	CON 3m	5 GF	*(fav) chsd ldr,mstk 8th,rdn 14th,outpjmpd aft,ld last,all out*	1	19

Improved; makes mistakes & owes much to rider; harder to place now; cna win again; G-S 21

MY BOY BARNEY ro.g. 6 Baron Blakeney - Amy Gwen by Master Buck — Mrs A T Lodge

1995 **6(NH)**

29	20/1	Barbury Cas'	(L)	RES 3m	12 GS	*f 3rd*	F	
267	2/3	Didmarton	(L)	MDN 3m	11 G	*t.o. whn crawld 1st & 2nd, cont til p.u. last*	P	0
505	16/3	Magor	(R)	PPO 3m	7 GS	*hld up, prog to clr 2nd frm 15th, wknd flat*	2	16
643	23/3	Siddington	(L)	MDN 3m	16 S	*(fav) mid div, chall & rddn 3 out, lft in ld nxt, kpt on und press*	1	15

1038 13/4 St Hilary (R) RES 3m 15 G *rear, prog to cls 3rd 15th, ev ch whn ran out 3 out* r -
Dead 16

Y BOY BUSTER b.g. 7 Kind Of Hush - Happy Donna by Huntercombe — Miss L J Smale
718 30/3 Wadebridge (L) MDO 3m 11 GF *mstk 3rd, bolted clr aft nxt, u.r. 5th (ditch)* U -
1277 27/4 Bratton Down (L) CON 3m 15 GF *bhnd, t.o. 12th, outpcd* 6 0
1427 6/5 High Bickin' (R) CON 3m 10 G *rear whn f 7th* F -
1591 25/5 Mounsey Hil' (R) RES 3m 15 G *t.d.e. blnd 1st, alwys bhnd, t.o. & p.u. 14th* P 0
1638 1/6 Bratton Down (L) MDO 3m 13 G *last pair & wll bhnd, t.o. 14th, fin strngly* 5 0
1652 8/6 Umberleigh (L) MDO 3m 10 GF *t.d.e. prog 6th, ld & mstk 15th, clr 2 out, ran on well* 1 13
Hard puller; easy winner of bad race; can upgrade if going right way; G-F 15

MY GUITAR (Irish) — **I** 403[F], **I** 588[F], **I** 599[P]

MYHAMET b.g. 9 Gorytus (USA) - Honey Bridge by Crepello — Paul C N Heywood
1995 **7(NH),F(NH),4(NH),4(NH),6(NH),1D(NH)**
38 3/2 Wadebridge (L) MEM 3m 4 GF *(fav) ld to 9th & frm 11th, pshd out flt, comf* 1 20
134 17/2 Ottery St M' (L) CON 3m 12 GS *(fav) in tch, 3rd whn f 13th* F -
482 13/3 Newton Abbot (L) HC 2m 5f 110yds 14 S *alwys in tch, ld 6th out, hdd next, led and mstk 3 out, hrd rdn and hded last, no ext.* 2 24
671 28/3 Taunton (R) HC 3m 13 S *mid div, mstk 6th, effort 13th, wknd after next, t.o..* 10 0
1073 13/4 Lifton (R) OPE 3m 10 S *alwys prom, cls up & ev ch 3 out, outpcd clsng stgs* 4 22
Winning hurdler; fair start but lost way; goes well fresh & Confined early 97; G/F-S 22

MY HARVINSKI b.g. 6 Myjinski (USA) - Autumn Harvest by Martinmas — I R Jones
1995 B(-),2(12),F(-),2(11),1(15)
155 17/2 Erw Lon (L) RES 3m 9 G *rear, gd prog to 3rd at 11th, wknd & p.u. 13th* P 0
357 3/3 Garnons (L) RES 3m 14 GS *mstks, prom at 9th, not qckn frm 12th, p.u. 2 out* P 0
549 17/3 Erw Lon (L) RES 3m 11 GS *alwys rear, nvr dang* 5 0
770 31/3 Pantyderi (R) RES 3m 9 G *mstk 3rd, plodded round* 5 12
980 8/4 Lydstep (L) RES 3m 11 G *(bl) nvr nr to chal* 3 0
1156 20/4 Llanwit Maj' (R) MEM 3m 7 GS *(bl) mstks, prog to 3rd 11th, hrd rdn 3 out, no prog* 3 0
Game winner 95; lost interest 96 & beaten in poor races; placed hurdles after; best watched 11

MYITSU ch.g. 7 Itsu (USA) - Maella (FR) by Traffic — John Jones
1995 **20(NH)**
850 6/4 Howick (L) MDN 3m 14 GF *cls up whn f heavily 9th* F -
Not the best of starts 0

MY LAST BUCK(IRE) b.g. 8 Buckskin (FR) - Laiton Peni by Laurence O — Mrs H Clarke
264 2/3 Didmarton (L) INT 3m 12 G *last pair, wknd 11th, p.u. 13th* P 0
Of no account 0

MY LAST PENNY(IRE) ch.m. 8 Le Moss - Leah's Luck Penny by Deep Run — B M Gray
617 23/3 Higham (L) MDO 3m 11 GF *alwys rear, rdn aft 3rd, lost tch 7th, t.o. & p.u. 11th* P 0
Unpromising start 0

MYLIEGE b.g. 12 Lord Gayle (USA) - My Natalie by Rheingold — J Scott
1995 4(16),3+(15),**P(0)**,1(17),F(-),2(20),2(20),**3(19)**,1(23)
141 17/2 Larkhill (R) MEM 3m 6 G *ld to 6th, prom aft, onepcd frm 3 out* 2 20
255 28/2 Taunton (R) HC 4 1/4m 110yds 15 GS *pressed ldrs from 9th, ld 21st to 4 out, led again 3 out, ran on gamely.* 1 24
531 16/3 Cothelstone (L) CON 3m 12 G *(fav) hit 6th, prog 11th, ld 13th til appr 4 out, sn btn* 5 0
1309 28/4 Little Wind' (R) OPE 3m 8 G *in tch, cls 4th at 12th, 4l 2nd whn hit 3 out, sn outpcd* 3 18
1459 8/5 Uttoxeter (L) HC 4 1/4m 8 G *waited with in tch, mstk 10th, reminders 15th, lost touch 18th, t.o. and p.u. before 2 out.* P 0
1551 18/5 Bratton Down (L) OPE 3m 8 F *ld 6th, clr 16th, styd on wll whn chal flat* 1 22
1636 1/6 Bratton Down (L) OPE 4m 11 G *prom/disp,chsd wnr 20th,mstk nxt,sn outpcd,lost 2nd nr fin* 3 21
Thorough stayer; likes Bratton Down; H/Chase win makes life hard at 13; Any 20

MYLORDMAYOR ch.g. 9 Move Off - Sharenka by Sharpen Up — T G Price
1995 P(0),F(-)
389 9/3 Llanfrynach (R) MDN 3m 11 GS *1st ride, j.w. raced wd,prom 7th,ld 3 out,sn wll clr* 1 13
548 17/3 Erw Lon (L) RES 3m 8 GS *u.r. 3rd* U -
695 30/3 Llanvapley (L) RES 3m 13 GS *mid-div, prog to 2nd 11th, ld nxt til f 13th* F -
770 31/3 Pantyderi (R) RES 3m 9 G *twrds rear, p.u. aft 15th* P 0
980 8/4 Lydstep (L) RES 3m 11 G *mid-div, rear whn u.r. last* U -
1038 13/4 St Hilary (R) RES 3m 15 G *rear, t.o. whn f 14th* F -
Won bad Maiden; fell apart after; can only be watched 10

MY MEADOWSWEET ch.g. 6 Meadowbrook - My Mimosa by Cagirama — Roland W Telford

193 24/2 Friars Haugh (L) MDN 3m 10 S *poor 5th hlfwy, went cls 2nd 3 out, outpcd frm nxt* 2 1
613 23/3 Friars Haugh (L) MDN 3m 15 G *4th hlfwy, no ex. frm 15th* 6 0
862 6/4 Alnwick (L) MDN 3m 8 GF *mid-div early, prog 9th, outpcd frm 14th* 3 0

Last twice but not without some hope & ought to go closer in 96 12

MY MELLOW MAN ch.g. 13 Malicious - Mincy by No Mercy W G Gooder

1995 **3(16),U(-),U(-),6(11)**,2(18),2(20),1(22),2(16),**1(23)**

208 24/2 Castle Of C' (R) LAD 3m 14 HY *(bl) in tch, disp 4 out til ld 2 out, ran on* 1 22
360 4/3 Windsor (R) HC 3m 8 GS *(bl) blnd and u.r. 1st.* U
481 11/3 Taunton (R) HC 3m 11 G *(bl) jmpd left, held up, hdwy apr 5th, blnd badly next, outpcd 4 out, kept on again from 2 out.* 3 22
669 27/3 Chepstow (L) HC 3m 10 S *t.o. 7th, p.u. before 11th.* P 0
1059 13/4 Badbury Rin' (L) OPE 3m 5 GF *ld to 2nd, cls up to 12th, lost tch frm 4 out* 3 18
1111 17/4 Hockworthy (L) MXO 3m 13 GS *(bl) whpd rnd strt, in tch, hrd rdn to ld 12th, hdd & btn nxt* 5 18
1332 1/5 Cheltenham (L) HC 3m 1f 110yds 11 G *(bl) mid div, prog to 3rd 11th, soon lost tch, blnd 2 out, left third last.* 3 2
1496 11/5 Holnicote (L) LAD 3m 4 G *(bl) ld til 9th,in tch til rmdrs & no imp 16th,no ch clsng stgs* 4 14

Able but cantankerous; blinkers essential; needs to stick to points for a win at 14; G-Hy 19

MY NEW MERC (Irish) — **I** 204[P], **I** 253[5], **I** 291[P], **I** 443[6], **I** 510[P]

MY NOMINEE b.g. 8 Nomination - Salala by Connaught D E Nicholls

1995 **P(0)**,P(0),6(0),4(16),1(18),1(22),**1(29),1(30),2(26)**

160 17/2 Weston Park (L) OPE 3m 16 G *(fav) (bl) chsd ldrs, 2nd 13th, ld nxt, hdd 3 out, fdd, p.u. nxt* P
256 29/2 Ludlow (R) HC 3m 14 G *(bl) mstk 4th, hdwy 12th, mistake next, wknd.* 9
459 9/3 Eyton-On-Se' (L) OPE 3m 11 G *(bl) mid-div, clsr ordr 4 out, ev ch 3 out, nt qckn* 5 1
565 17/3 Wolverhampt' (L) OPE 3m 6 GS *(bl) ld 14th-3 out, no ext* 2 22
672 29/3 Aintree (L) HC 2 3/4m 26 G *(bl) chsd ldrs, 3rd when blnd 7th, losing pl when f 9th.* F
854 6/4 Sandon (L) OPE 3m 4 GF *(fav) (bl) ld/disp to 7th whn lft clr,hld off chal frm 6 out,ran on wll* 1 24
1011 9/4 Flagg Moor (L) OPE 3m 4 G *(bl) ld 6th, rdn 2 out, sn hdd, no ex* 2 24
1120 20/4 Bangor (L) HC 2 1/2m 110yds 13 S *(bl) prom, ld 8th, clr from 4 out till rdn 2 out, hdd last, rallied to regain ld flat, kept on.* 1 28
1331 1/5 Cheltenham (L) HC 2m 5f 9 G *(bl) chsd ldrs, ld 6th, made rest, hrd rdn run-in, just held on.* 1 3
1460 8/5 Uttoxeter (L) HC 2m 7f 5 G *(bl) chsd ldr,mstk 11th, ld 4 out, clr last, comf.* 1 3
1545 18/5 Bangor (L) HC 3m 110yds 8 G *(fav) (bl) ld, raced wd and hdd briefly after 9th, hded 4 out, soon und pres, btn apr 2 out.* 3 2
1615 27/5 Wetherby (L) HC 2 1/2m 110yds 11 G *(bl) ld after 1st till hdd after 9th, wknd from 4 out.* 3 2

Slow to find form 95-6 but purple patches late season; very able at best; L/H; win more H/Chases 97 ... 26

MYOWN TREASURE (Irish) — **I** 97[P], **I** 173[P], **I** 409[P]

MY PILOT b.g. 12 Al Sirat (USA) - Dandyville by Vulgan J Turnbu

1995 2(15),1(16),7(0),1(17),1(0)

157 17/2 Erw Lon (L) CON 3m 15 G *alwys rear* 11
355 3/3 Garnons (L) INT 3m 10 GS *chsd ldrs, cls 5th at 11th, ran on frm 3 out* 3 1

Completed Lydstep hat-trick 95; finished early 96; hard to win at 13; G/F-S 16

MY PRIDES WAY b.m. 7 Prince Of Peace - My Always by Kalimnos M G Gloy

1995 8(0)

200 24/2 Lemalla (R) MDO 3m 12 HY *rear, t.o. & f 3 out* F
301 2/3 Great Treth' (R) MDO 3m 13 G *mstk 5th, 6th hlfwy, nvr dang* 6
630 23/3 Kilworthy (L) MDN 3m 10 GS *alwys last pair, wkng whn f 11th* F

Last on both completions 95/6 0

MY SENOR b.g. 7 Jalmood (USA) - San Marguerite by Blakeney J N Dalto

1995 **6(NH),3(NH),3(NH),4(NH),2(NH),4(NH)**

459 9/3 Eyton-On-Se' (L) OPE 3m 11 G *mid-div, nvr trbld ldrs, p.u. 3 out* P

A brief appearance in points & most unlikely to stay 3m 0

MY SON JOHN ch.g. 13 Plenty Spirit - Lady Keeper by Worden II Miss Alexandra Whitfield Jone

1995 **F(-)**

158 17/2 Weston Park (L) MEM 3m 11 G *t.o. hlfwy, p.u. 12th* P
458 9/3 Eyton-On-Se' (L) INT 3m 11 G *mid-div, s-lvd effort to rch ldrs 13th, fdd, p.u. 2 out* P
568 17/3 Wolverhampt' (L) MDN 3m 9 GS *mid-div, 8l 3rd whn f 3 out* F
1048 13/4 Bitterley (L) MDO 3m 12 G *in tch in rear til wknd 11th, p.u. nxt* P

Of no account 0

MYSTERIOUS RUN(IRE) ch.g. 8 Deep Run - Misty Venture Mrs D C Samwort

171 18/2 Market Rase' (L) RES 3m 5 GF *cls up til blnd & u.r. 4th* U
392 9/3 Garthorpe (R) MEM 3m 6 G *alwys rear hlf, last & t.o. 12th, p.u. 4 out* P
542 17/3 Southwell P' (L) MDO 3m 15 GS *mid-div, nrst fin* 4
973 8/4 Thorpe Lodge (L) MDO 3m 7 GF *w.w. cls up, well-timed chal 3 out, ld nxt, ran on gamely* 1 1

1380 5/5 Dingley (R) RES 3m 11 GF *mstk 8th, sn lost tch, t.o. & p.u. 11th* P 0

Won poor Maiden & Restricted chances very slim 12

MYSTERY ARISTOCRAT (Irish) — I 79P, I 118P, I 156F

MYSTERY BELLE gr.m. 6 Baron Blakeney - Bredon Belle by Conwyn — Mrs S M Newell

1995 P(0),P(0)

388 9/3 Llanfrynach (R) RES 3m 20 GS *sn mid-div, lost tch 13th, no ch aft, t.o.* 9 0
1315 28/4 Bitterley (L) MDO 3m 10 G *prom in chsg grp, 20l 4th whn f 12th* F -
1483 11/5 Bredwardine (R) MDO 3m 15 G *ld 4th, prom til wknd 15th, p.u. 2 out* P 0

Shows some speed but tailed off on only completion from 5 starts 95/6 10

MYSTERY PAT (Irish) — I 501P, I 578R

MYSTERY PET (Irish) — I 479,

MYSTIC GALE(IRE) b.m. 8 Strong Gale - Tou Wan by Grand Roi — Mrs Lorna Bertram

1073 13/4 Lifton (R) OPE 3m 10 S *j.w., slght ld mstly, hdd aft 16th, kpt on wll* 3 23

Chase winner 94; ran really well in hot Open; wins certain if fit 97 25

MY SUNNY WAY (Irish) — I 355³, I 520², I 573²

MYTHICAL APPROACH (Irish) — I 117³, I 188¹

MY TRUE CLOWN ch.g. 10 True Song - Tudor Clown by Ritudyr — Mrs Peter Seels

1995 2(0),P(0),7(0),3(0),6(0),P(0),7(0)

81 11/2 Wetherby Po' (L) MEM 3m 4 GS *ld to 6th, agn 14th, disp 3 out, drew clr apr last* 1 0
584 23/3 Wetherby Po' (L) RES 3m 13 S *t.o. 3rd, p.u. 10th* P 0

Won joke Members run at a crawl; no chance in proper races 0

MYVERYGOODFRIEND b.g. 9 Swing Easy (USA) - Darymoss by Ballymoss — S Cobden

271 2/3 Parham (R) CON 3m 15 GF *mid-div, no dang frm 14th* 5 14
379 9/3 Barbury Cas' (L) XX 3m 9 GS *prom, wkng whn u.r. 3 out* U -
595 23/3 Parham (R) OPE 3m 12 GS *rear, sn strgglng to stay in tch, bhnd whn p.u. 12th* P 0

Fair start but soon in trouble & can only be watched 12

NADANNY(IRE) ch.g. 7 The Noble Player (USA) - Bradden by King Emperor (USA) — M E David

697 30/3 Llanvapley (L) MDN 3m 11 GS *last trio, t.o. & p.u. 10th* P 0

No show on only run 96 0

NAGLE RICE (Irish) — I 43P, I 279P, I 354F, I 380, , I 575⁶

NAIDA (Irish) — I 42P

NAMESTAKEN ch.g. 10 Sandalay - Darling's Double by Menelek — Mrs A M Berry

45 3/2 Wadebridge (L) MDO 3m 10 GF *prom til wknd 12th, t.o. & p.u. 15th* P 0
841 6/4 Maisemore P' (L) MDN 3m 9 GF *in tch, ld 12th-nxt, rddn & wknd appr 3 out* 4 0
1174 20/4 Chaddesley ' (L) MDN 3m 10 G *cls up, cls 2nd whn u.r. 13th* U -
1319 28/4 Bitterley (L) MDN 3m 13 G *prom, ev ch 14th, wknd bef nxt, t.o. & p.u. last* P 0
1417 6/5 Cursneh Hill (L) MDO 3m 14 GF *rear frm 9th, t.o. frm 13th, p.u. 15th* P 0

Ex-Irish; last when completing; looks sort of stamina 0

NA MOILLTEAR (Irish) — I 348⁵

NAMOILLTEAR (Irish) — I 224P

NAMOOS br.g. 15 Thatching - Little Firefly (USA) by Bold Ruler — Mrs D H McCarthy

1995 P(0),2(14),P(0),1(10)

104 17/2 Marks Tey (L) OPE 3m 14 G *w.w. prog 8th, outpcd 12th, p.u. 17th* P 0
271 2/3 Parham (R) CON 3m 15 GF *nvr nr ldrs, wll bhnd whn p.u. 2 out* P 0
476 10/3 Tweseldown (R) OPE 3m 7 G *hld up, rear whn p.u. aft 9th, rein broke* P 0
775 31/3 Penshurst (L) CON 3m 8 GS *alwys rear, in tch to 14th, p.u. 2 out* P 0

Formerly useful; looks ready for retirement now 0

NANCY HILL (Irish) — I 319P, I 408P, I 449P, I 492P

NANDA MOON b.g. 9 Henbit (USA) - Red Nanda by Status Seeker — N G Herrod

1995 **P(NH),P(NH),2(NH),P(NH),P(NH),P(NH)**

1309 28/4 Little Wind' (R) OPE 3m 8 G *prom, ld brfly 9th, sn pshd alng, lost tch 14th, p.u. nxt* P 0
1394 6/5 Cotley Farm (L) MXO 3m 5 GF *ld to 5th, prom to 11th, wknd & p.u. 14th* P 0

Placed in poor novice chase 95; season lasted 8 days & completely out of his depth 0

NANOOK b.g. 7 Ayyabaan - Sarah's Joy by Full Of Hope — S Gallagher

550 17/3 Erw Lon (L) MDN 3m 13 GS *f 2nd, dead* F -

Dead 0

NAN'S DREAM VI (Irish) — I 476[1]

NANS PET (Irish) — I 119[P], I 143[4], I 182[F], I 459[2], I 640[4]

NASH BRAKES b.g. 11 Torenaga - Mascarita by Final Problem — A W Forman

636	23/3 Market Rase'	(L) MDN 3m	11 GF	*t.o. 1st, p.u. 6 out*	P	0
1021	13/4 Brocklesby '	(L) MEM 3m	3 GF	*alwys last, t.o. frm 7th*	3	0

Of no account **0**

NASH NA HABHAINN (Irish) — I 348[P]

NATHAN BLAKE gr.g. 11 Sexton Blake - Nana by Forlorn River — Mrs M S Teversham

1995 **P(NH)**

7	13/1 Larkhill	(R) CON 3m	10 GS	*(bl) ld til blnd 3rd, blnd nxt, sn last, t.o. & p.u. 3 out*	P	0

Looks finished now **0**

NATIONAL CASE b.m. 7 Push On - Kitty Case by Saucy Kit — Nigel Lilley

1995 **10(NH)**

431	9/3 Upton-On-Se'	(R) MDO 3m	17 GS	*effrt frm 14th to disp 2 out, ld last, ran on well*	1	16

Beat 4 subsequent winners when scoring; not seen after but interesting prospect if fit 97 ...... **17**

NATIONAL CHOICE b.g. 10 National Trust - Wrong Choice by Royal Smoke — A D Wardall

1228	27/4 Worcester	(L) HC 2m 7f	17 G	*mstks, hdwy 6th, blnd and wknd 10th, t.o. when p.u. before 4 out.*	P	0

Very lightly raced; 3 runs 93-6; hard task 96 & could win point if fit 97; easy 3m **18**

NATIVE MISSILE b.m. 7 Cruise Missile - Native Star by Go Native — Mrs Colin Sinclair

1995 P(0)

353	3/3 Garnons	(L) MDN 2 1/2m	7 GS	*6l 4th at 5th, lost tch 9th, t.o. & p.u. last*	P	0
696	30/3 Llanvapley	(L) MDN 3m	13 GS	*2nd to 13th, wknd rpdly, p.u. 3 out*	P	0
1045	13/4 Bitterley	(L) MDO 3m	16 G	*cls 5th at 7th, ldng grp til not qckn 14th, kpt on*	5	0
1224	24/4 Brampton Br'	(R) MDO 3m	17 G	*prom to 6th, rdn 12th, no resp, p.u. 14th*	P	0

Beat 4 finishers when completing but barely worth a rating **10**

NATIVE SUCCESS (Irish) — I 42[F]

NATIVE VENTURE (Irish) — I 553[2], I 584[1]

NATTADON-HILL ch.m. 7 Queen's Soldier (USA) - La Chimie by Levanter — J B Shears

800	4/4 Clyst St Ma'	(L) MEM 3m	3 GS	*jmpd lft 1st, ref & u.r. 2nd*	R	-
1143	20/4 Flete Park	(R) MDN 3m	17 S	*f 1st*	F	-
1626	27/5 Lifton	(R) MDO 3m	13 GS	*last whn ref 2nd*	R	

Cleared 2 fences in 3 starts **0**

NATURAL LADY (Irish) — I 196[P], I 222[P], I 348[F], I 501[F]

NAUGHTY NELLIE b.m. 5 Neltino - Hayburnwyke by Pretty Form — C D Dawson

898	6/4 Dingley	(R) MDN 2m 5f	10 GS	*(Co fav) ld (safest plc) frm 4th, mstk 5 out, ran on wll*	1	13
1324	28/4 Fakenham P-'	(L) LAD 3m	6 G	*keen hold, disp to 8th, cls 3rd whn f nxt*	F	-
1640	2/6 Dingley	(R) RES 3m	9 GF	*pllng, mstks, lost pl rpdly 10th, last & p.u. 14th*	P	0

Easy winner of weak Maiden; headstrong & needs to settle for progress in 97; good stable **15**

NAWRIK(IRE) ch.g. 7 Orchestra - Rustic Rose by Rusticaro (FR) — Mrs J K Peutherer

1995 **F(NH),5(NH),1(NH),5(NH),10(NH),P(NH)**

215	24/2 Newtown	(L) OPE 3m	20 GS	*ptom to 12th, sn wknd, t.o. & p.u. 2 out*	P	0
351	3/3 Garnons	(L) OPE 3m	14 GS	*ld to 3rd, ev ch til not qckn 14th, kpt on onepcd 3 out*	4	18

Winning chaser; ran well Garnons; worth trying in Confineds if fit 97 ...... **17**

NEARCTIC BAY(USA) b.g. 10 Explodent (USA) - Golferette (USA) by Mr Randy — G B Barlow

1995 P(0),P(0),3(14),3(11)

159	17/2 Weston Park	(L) CON 3m	22 G	*mid to rear, no ch whn p.u. 14th*	P	0
735	31/3 Sudlow Farm	(R) MEM 3m	7 G	*tubed, sn wll bhnd, t.o. frm 5th*	6	0

Of no account **0**

NEARHAAN (Irish) — I 49[P], I 78[P], I 328[P], I 368[P], I 652[P], I 661[P]

NEARLY A BROOK b.m. 6 Nearly A Hand - Bybrook by Border Chief — Mrs S J Maltby

471	10/3 Milborne St'	(L) MDO 3m	16 G	*rear, prog 12th, outpcd frm 4 out, improve*	5	0
993	8/4 Kingston St'	(R) MDO 3m	17 F	*7th at 11th, prog to 15l 4th 4 out, kpt on to 3rd flat*	3	0

Beaten over 30l both starts; dam winning chaser & sure to go much closer 97 ...... **14**

NEARLY ALL RIGHT ch.g. 7 Nearly A Hand - Solhoon by Tycoon II — Miss A Rawle

1995 2(0),P(0),P(0),3(0),4(0),P(0)

533 16/3 Cothelstone (L) MDN 3m 13 G *f 2nd* F -

Changed hands 96 & the briefest of campaigns; no prospects **0**

NEARLY AMABOOBALEE ch.m. 7 Nearly A Hand - Martini Girl by Vilmoray Brian Moore

841 6/4 Maisemore P' (L) MDN 3m 9 GF *sn wll bhnd, t.o & p.u. appr 13th* P 0

.... **0**

NEARLY A MERMAID b.m. 7 Nearly A Hand - Mermaids Daughter by Crozier R E Nuttall

466 10/3 Milborne St' (L) RES 3m 13 G *prom til u.r. 7th* U -
1056 13/4 Badbury Rin' (L) RES 3m 10 GF *mid-div to 9th, lost tch 11th, t.o. & p.u. 4 out* P 0
1345 4/5 Holnicote (L) RES 3m 11 GS *rear til some prog 9-10th, ev ch 3 out, wknd clsng stgs* 4 11
1497 11/5 Holnicote (L) RES 3m 10 G *ld/disp to 7th, lost plc 15th, no ch frm 3 out* 4 10

Won a modest race (lucky) but should have plenty of improvement in her; Restricted more than possible **14**

NEARLY AT SEA ch.m. 7 Nearly A Hand - Culm Port by Port Corsair C J Down

1995 3(15)

1115 17/4 Hockworthy (L) MDO 3m 10 GS *(fav) prom, ld 14th, 1l up whn f 2 out* F -
1279 27/4 Bratton Down (L) MDO 3m 14 GF *(fav) w.w. 6th at 12th, prog 3 out, strng run to ld last 100 yrds* 1 14

Confimred 95 promise when winning; very lightly raced but should have Restricted chances in 97 ..... **16**

NEARLY FIVE TOO b.m. 9 Lepanto (GER) - Five To by Nearly A Hand Richard Hawker

711 30/3 Barbury Cas' (L) MDO 3m 8 G *f 2nd* F -
1060 13/4 Badbury Rin' (L) MDO 3m 14 GF *mid-div whn u.r. 5th* U -
1128 20/4 Stafford Cr' (R) RES 3m 17 S *sn bhnd, t.o. whn p.u. 12th* P 0
1248 27/4 Woodford (L) MDN 3m 15 G *blnd 4th, 12th & no ch hlfwy, f 14th* F -

No ability under Rules or in points & needs to jump better **0**

NEARLY SPLENDID br.g. 11 Nearly A Hand - Splentynna by John Splendid S R Stevens

6 13/1 Larkhill (R) OPE 3m 18 GS *mid-div, outpcd 13th, kpt on frm 3 out, bttr for race* 4 26
66 10/2 Great Treth' (R) OPE 3m 8 S *disp brfly 3rd, fdng whn blnd 11th, p.u. 13th* P 0
276 2/3 Clyst St Ma' (L) MEM 3m 4 S *(fav) made all, clr 15th, easily* 1 20
626 23/3 Kilworthy (L) OPE 3m 12 GS *prom, ld 11th, hrd rdn flat, hld on gamely nr fin* 1 28
1108 17/4 Cheltenham (L) HC 4m 1f 14 GS *alwys in tch, ld 19th, hdd after 3 out, mstk next, soon wknd.* 4 25
1275 27/4 Bratton Down (L) OPE 3m 8 GF *hld up, prog 13th, ev ch 4 out, not qckn frm 2 out* 3 21

Not as good as he was but still useful at best; stays well; can win Opens at 12; Any **25**

NEARLY THERE(IRE) ch.m. 6 Convinced - Owen's Shadow by Master Owen W Murdoch

632 23/3 Market Rase' (L) CON 3m 10 GF *t.o. last til p.u. 8th* P 0
1105 14/4 Guilsborough (L) MDN 3m 12 G *t.o. 9th, p.u. 11th* P 0

No signs of ability yet **0**

NECTAR BLOOM (Irish) — **I** 84P, **I** 132P

NEE-ARGEE ch.m. 11 Rymer - Royal Pam by Pamroy Miss Carole Baylis

1995 7(0),P(0),4(11)

676 30/3 Cottenham (R) INT 3m 13 GF *alwys last pair, t.o. 9th, p.u. 2 out* P 0
1027 13/4 Brocklesby ' (L) MDN 3m 7 GF *mstly 3rd, ran wll frm 3 out, chal last, ran on* 1 14
1376 5/5 Dingley (R) MEM 3m 7 GF *alwys bhnd, no ch whn nrly u.r. 3 out, walked in* 5 0

Won at 28th attempt; chances of another win nil **10**

NEED A LADDER b.g. 9 Highlands - Munster Glen by Furry Glen Mrs J Waggott

1995 U(-),6(0),3(10),F(-),F(-)

51 4/2 Alnwick (L) MDO 3m 17 G *mid-div, wknd 11th, bhnd & p.u. 13th* P 0
118 17/2 Witton Cast' (R) INT 3m 9 S *mid-div til wknd 8th, hrd rdn nxt, rear & p.u. 12th* P 0
416 9/3 Charm Park (L) MDO 3m 13 G *mid-div, one pcd, p.u. 4 out* P 0
915 8/4 Tranwell (L) MDO 3m 7 GF *(bl) mid-div, b.d. 4th* B -
1451 6/5 Witton Cast' (R) MDO 3m 12 G *(bl) jmpng errors, sn in rear, t.o. 13th, p.u. nxt* P 0

A parachute would be useful as well **0**

NEEDWOOD NEPTUNE b.g. 6 Rolfe (USA) - Needwood Nymph by Bold Owl P A Bennett

397 9/3 Garthorpe (R) MDN 3m 9 G *prog 10th, ld 4 out, clr whn blnd last, just ct* 2 15
727 31/3 Garthorpe (R) MDO 3m 12 G *(fav) w.w. in rear,prog 11th,ld 2 out,clr last,rdn & all out fin* 1 15
1239 27/4 Clifton On ' (L) RES 3m 9 GF *(fav) cls up, jnd wnr 14th, blnd 16th, hrd rdn & onepcd frm 2 out* 3 14

Quite promising but finds little in closing stages; should upgrade in 97 .... **17**

NEELISAGIN (Irish) — **I** 53P, **I** 1215, **I** 213P, **I** 472F, **I** 5094, **I** 557P

NEELY (Irish) — **I** 1805, **I** 288P, **I** 321U, **I** 403P, **I** 4502

NEIL'S WAY b.g. 8 Prince Of Peace - My Always by Kalimnos P D Rogers

1995 5(0),F(-),1(15),3(15),P(0)

199	24/2	Lemalla	(R)	RES	3m	17 HY	*mid-div til prog 4 out, sn wknd, p.u. 2 out*	P	0
445	9/3	Haldon	(R)	RES	3m	9 S	*prom, disp frm 8th til outpcd aft 13th, 2nd agn 3 out,no imp*	3	14
627	23/3	Kilworthy	(L)	RES	3m	13 GS	*trckd ldrs, mstk 11th, sn wknd, no ch whn p.u. 15th*	P	0
1138	20/4	Flete Park	(R)	MEM	3m	4 S	*6s-3s, 2l 2nd whn blnd & u.r. 6th*	U	-
1358	4/5	Flete Park	(R)	RES	3m	8 G	*prom, cls 2nd frm 12th, wknd 3 out, onepcd*	3	15

Maiden winner 95; struggled in Restricteds 96; may strike lucky 97; G-Hy 15

NELADAR b.m. 9 Ardar - Caravan Centre by Nelcius — T D Smith

1995 **P(NH)**

415	9/3	Charm Park	(L)	MDO	3m	13 G	*al prom, ld 13th to 2 out, disp last, jst btn*	2	15
517	16/3	Dalton Park	(R)	MDO	3m	10 G	*hld up, prog 9th, rdn & effrt 4 out, no imp frm 2 out*	4	12
823	6/4	Stainton	(R)	MEM	3m	6 GF	*(fav) alwys handy, prog 4 out, ev ch nxt, sn onepcd*	3	10
1135	20/4	Hornby Cast'	(L)	MDN	3m	10 G	*reluc to race,clsd 3rd,prog 11th,ld 14th,qcknd wll clr*	1	17

Disappointing till scooting home in weak race; could upgrade if in the mood; Good 16

NELLOES PET(IRE) b.m. 7 Bustinetto - Northern Gift by Northern Guest (USA) — A Grazebrook

1995 **10(NH),16(NH)**

1212	24/4	Andoversford	(R)	MEM	3m	5 G	*v rlctnt to race, ref 1st*	R	-

Could not have been less impressive 0

NELSON RIVER(USA) br.g. 11 Green Forest (USA) - Maple River (USA) by Clandestine — G Herrod

1995 U(-)

442	9/3	Haldon	(R)	CON	3m	6 S	*sn rear, bhnd frm 4th til p.u. 11th*	P	0
802	4/4	Clyst St Ma'	(L)	OPE	3m	2 GS	*tried to ref, blnd & u.r. 2nd*	U	-
989	8/4	Kingston St'	(R)	CON	3m	6 F	*5th & just in tch 9th, wknd, t.o. & p.u. 12th*	P	0

Flat winner 89; no aptitude for pointing 0

NENNI(FR) ch.g. 17 Urf (FR) - Carentonne (FR) by Dark Tiger — Mrs Phyl Robertson

1995 1(12)

891	6/4	Whittington	(L)	MEM	3m	6 F	*(fav) ld 11th, clr 13th, rasily*	1	14

Retired with all guns blazing after his 9th win at his home meeting 14

NESSELNITE br.m. 10 Nesselrode (USA) - Melinite by Milesian — M A Binnersley

637	23/3	Siddington	(L)	MEM	3m	14 S	*s.s. hit 1st, u.r. 3rd*	U	-
794	2/4	Heythrop	(R)	CON	3m	6 F	*s.s. t.o. last til mstk & u.r. 6th*	U	-
943	8/4	Andoversford	(R)	CON	3m	9 GF	*last whn u.r. 1st*	U	-
1213	24/4	Andoversford	(R)	CON	3m	5 G	*n.j.w., t.o. 6th til p.u. 11th*	P	0

A poor jumper of no account 0

NETHERBY CHEESE b.g. 9 Say Primula - Netherby Maid by Derek H — Mrs K Smith

778	31/3	Penshurst	(L)	INT	3m	6 GS	*immed detached, t.o. whn p.u. 10th*	P	0
921	8/4	Aldington	(L)	MDO	3m	8 F	*mod 4th til went 3rd frm 11th, kpt on, nvr rchd 1st pair*	3	0
1210	21/4	Heathfield	(R)	MDO	3m	13 F	*prom, ld brfly 9th, cls 5th at 16th, 3rd 2 out, wknd flat*	4	0
1300	28/4	Bexhill	(R)	MDO	3m	7 F	*ld 7th,ran wd & hdd bnd bef nxt,chal 3 out,not qckn flat*	2	11
1445	6/5	Aldington	(L)	MDO	3m	8 HD	*(Jt fav) cls up til ran wd bnd bfr 11th, 3rd aft, btn whn p.u.2 out*	P	0

Placed in poor Maidens; needs more stamina but could scrape a win at 10 11

NETHER GOBIONS br.g. 10 Netherkelly - Madame de Luce by Don't Look — P Clutterbuck

1995 3(15),F(-),1(20),2(19),1(21),F(-)

215	24/2	Newtown	(L)	OPE	3m	20 GS	*ld to 14th, wknd, fin tired*	5	11
355	3/3	Garnons	(L)	INT	3m	10 GS	*(fav) n.j.w. trckd ldrs, ev ch whn hit 3 out, p.u. nxt*	P	0
683	30/3	Chaddesley '	(L)	MEM	3m	17 G	*ld to 3 out, onepcd und pres aft*	3	20
943	8/4	Andoversford	(R)	CON	3m	9 GF	*ld/disp til ld aft 12th, made rest, drew clr frm 2 out*	1	23
1244	27/4	Woodford	(L)	INT	3m	12 G	*ld, blnd 8th, f 14th*	F	-
1412	6/5	Cursneh Hill	(L)	OPE	3m	4 GF	*(fav) made all, clr frm 6th, fence ahd frm 13th*	1	23
1619	27/5	Chaddesley '	(L)	OPE	3m	7 GF	*(fav) made all, clr 15th, blnd 3 out, unchal*	1	25

Fiar pointer; won 5 of last 11; top stable; front-runs; makes mistakes; sure to win again; G/F-S 23

NETHERTARA b.m. 9 Netherkelly - Asphaltara by Scallywag — Alan Cowing

1995 4(10),1(20),2(19),1(20),1(18),1(19),3(16)

10	14/1	Cottenham	(R)	INT	3m	10 G	*w.w. prog to 4th 3 out, lft 2nd nxt, kpt on und pres flat*	2	21
178	18/2	Horseheath	(R)	INT	3m	11 G	*4s-2s,mstks,prog 11th,disp & hit 2 out,lft clr last,rdn out*	1	24
450	9/3	Charing	(L)	XX	3m	8 G	*(fav) wll plcd, ld aft 8th, made rest, ran on strngly, clr 4 out*	1	22
594	23/3	Parham	(R)	CON	3m	13 GS	*mid-div, smooth prog to ld 12th, ran on strngly 3 out,sn clr*	1	24
963	8/4	Heathfield	(R)	MXO	3m	7 G	*(fav) prssd ldr til ld 4 out, qknd clr, impress*	1	26
1547	18/5	Fakenham	(L)	HC	2m 5f 110yds	11 G	*(fav) in tch till ran on to chase wnr 10th, cl 2nd when blnd and u.r. 2 out.*	U	23

Very useful now; stays & hard to beat points 97; should win H/Chase; G-S 27

NEVER BE GREAT b.g. 14 Merrymount - Contrivance by Vimy — Keith R Pearce
1995 F(-),2(16),F(-),U(-),4(0),1(15),5(0)

544	17/3	Erw Lon	(L)	MEM	3m	5	GS	*ld 11-13th, wkng whn u.r. 15th*	U	-
1036	13/4	St Hilary	(R)	LAD	3m	6	G	*cls up, 2nd frm 12th, wknd rpdly 16th, fin tired*	4	0
1159	20/4	Llanwit Maj'	(R)	LAD	3m	5	GS	*disp til ld 4-6th, ld aft 3 out, lft wll clr nxt*	1	19
1264	27/4	Pyle	(R)	LAD	3m	10	G	*cls 4th at 11th, ev ch til not qckn frm 2 out,fin 3rd,promtd*	2	16
1387	6/5	Pantyderi	(R)	LAD	3m	6	GF	*sttld off pace, prog frm 15th, hrd rdn 3 out, no ch wnr*	2	15
1543	17/5	Newton Abbot	(L)	HC	3 1/4m 110yds	8	G	*chsd wnr till wknd 15th, t.o..*	5	0
1603	25/5	Bassaleg	(R)	LAD	3m	4	GS	*cls up, 2nd frm 10th, clsd 3 out, alwys hld*	2	18

Modest Ladies pointer; easily beaten by good horses; tries & may find another chance at 15 15

NEVER HEARD (Irish) — **I** 53[3], **I** 61[P], **I** 114[4], **I** 146[4], **I** 213[4]

NEVER SO HIGH b.g. 9 Never So Bold - High Gait by High Top — Mrs G J Hamer

148	17/2	Erw Lon	(L)	MDN	3m	9	G	*ld to 5th, cls 2nd til 3 out, no ext apr last*	3	11
390	9/3	Llanfrynach	(R)	MDN	3m	13	GS	*rear main grp, lost tch 13th, t.o. & p.u. 3 out*	P	0
551	17/3	Erw Lon	(L)	MDN	3m	8	GS	*twrds rear, no ch 2 out, fin fast*	3	0

Missed 94/5; not beaten far when placed but finished early & more needed for a win 11

NEVER SO LOST ch.g. 6 Never So Bold - Lost In France by Northfields (USA) — P W Hiatt

340	3/3	Heythrop	(R)	MDN	3m	12	G	*in tch to hlfwy, p.u. 12th*	P	0
522	16/3	Larkhill	(R)	MDO	3m	12	G	*alwys mid-div, wknd 13th, p.u. 15th*	P	0
1105	14/4	Guilsborough	(L)	MDN	3m	12	G	*prom til wknd 13th, t.o.*	5	0
1378	5/5	Dingley	(R)	MDO	2 1/2m	16	GF	*wth ldrs, prog to chal 2 out, 1l down & lkd btn whn u.r.last*	U	-

1st form last start in poor Maiden; should improve in 97 & have winning chances if staying 3m 14

NEVILLE br.g. 10 Full Of Hope - Viduli by Firestreak — J F Heslop
1995 P(0),3(15)

319	2/3	Corbridge	(R)	RES	3m	16	GS	*nvr nr ldrs, no ch whn u.r. 2nd cct*	U	-
399	9/3	Dalston	(R)	CON	3m	9	G	*cls 2nd early, lst plc 11th, wl btn whn p.u. 2 out*	P	0
699	30/3	Tranwell	(L)	CON	3m	8	GS	*last early, prog hlfwy, cls up 4 out, wknd aft nxt*	4	12
911	8/4	Tranwell	(L)	CON	3m	9	GF	*alwys prom in chsng grp, 3rd frm 9-14th, no ext frm 2 out*	4	16

Maiden winner 94; lightly raced & disappointing since; hard to win again 13

NEWBRANO gr.m. 9 Zambrano - Fanny Adams by Sweet Ration — Ian Carmichael
1995 P(0),P(0),6(0),4(0),P(0)

698	30/3	Tranwell	(L)	MEM	3m	5	GS	*(bl) 4th at 10th, nvr nrr*	3	0
089	14/4	Friars Haugh	(L)	MDN	3m	10	F	*(bl) ld 14th til 4 out, no ext apr last*	3	12
254	27/4	Balcormo Ma'	(R)	MDO	3m	14	GS	*(bl) prom early, bhnd whn p.u. 4 out*	P	0

Ran better 2nd start but only 5 completions from 15 starts 94-6 & more needed for a win 11

NEW CRUISER b.m. 6 Cruise Missile - New Dawning by Deep Run — G L Edwards

740	31/3	Sudlow Farm	(R)	MDN	3m	16	G	*schoold, last trio, nvr dang*	6	0
033	13/4	Alpraham	(R)	MDO	2 1/2m	15	GS	*held up, stead prog 11th, rddn & no ext frm 3 out*	4	0

A steady introduction & should be ready to fire in 97 13

NEW DAY(IRE) b.m. 8 Bustinetto - Last Day by Night And Day — W J Turcan

178	18/2	Horseheath	(R)	INT	3m	11	G	*20s-10s, mstk 10th, prom to 12th, bhnd 14th, p.u. last*	P	0

Ex-Irish; a silly gamble & disappeared after 12

NEW LEGISLATION (Irish) — **I** 107[P], **I** 164[P], **I** 233[6], **I** 271[P], **I** 340[P], **I** 562[3], **I** 625[F]

NEW LINE GIRL (Irish) — **I** 238[1]

NEW MILL HOUSE ch.g. 13 Tobique - Ascess by Eastern Venture — Miss S E Cook
1995 **4(NH)**,**8(NH)**

261	2/3	Warwick	(L)	HC	3 1/4m	5	G	*soon well bhnd, t.o. when blnd and u.r. 3 out.*	U	-
671	28/3	Taunton	(R)	HC	3m	13	S	*bhnd from 13th, t.o. when p.u. before 3 out.*	P	0
808	6/4	Towcester	(R)	HC	3m 1f	4	F	*lost tch 9th, t.o. when hit 12th.*	3	12
108	17/4	Cheltenham	(L)	HC	4m 1f	14	GS	*t.o. 9th, p.u. before 19th.*	P	0

Winning chaser; outclassed in H/Chases & unlikely to do much at 14 0

NEW PROBLEM b.m. 9 New Member - Light Of Zion by Pieces Of Eight — R Michael Smith

193	24/2	Friars Haugh	(L)	MDN	3m	10	S	*10l 2nd whn s.u. aft 10th*	S	-
319	2/3	Corbridge	(R)	RES	3m	16	GS	*prom, cls up 15th, wknd & u.r. nxt*	U	-

Season lasted a week; showed speed but nothing concrete 0

NEWSKI EXPRESS bl.m. 11 Newski (USA) - Mint Express by Pony Express — John Lister
1995 3(12)

276	27/4	Bratton Down	(L)	LAD	3m	7	GF	*ld/disp til u.r. 5th*	U	-

1362 4/5 Flete Park (R) MDO 3m 9 G *(fav) w.w. in rear, prog 3 out, slght ld nxt, drew clr apr last* 1 15
1634 1/6 Bratton Down (L) INT 3m 15 G *well in rear,prog 11th,ran on 3 out,nvr nrr,fin 3rd,promoted* 2 17

Lightly raced; beat subsequent winner & ran well next time; could win Restricted in same form at 12 ... 17

NEWS REVIEW b.g. 13 Pony Express - Channel Ten by Babu Mrs S E Mathias
1995 2(18),4(0),1(20),4(12),2(18),P(0)
266 2/3 Didmarton (L) LAD 3m 13 G *in tch til outpcd 13th, kpt on onepcd frm 2 out* 4 12
546 17/3 Erw Lon (L) LAD 3m 10 GS *mid-div, prog frm 15th, no ch wth wnr* 2 21
979 8/4 Lydstep (L) LAD 3m 9 G *prom, 2nd at last, unable to chal* 2 18
1034 13/4 St Hilary (R) MEM 3m 3 G *(fav) ld to 5th & frm 13th, drew clr* 1 17
1264 27/4 Pyle (R) LAD 3m 10 G *ld 1st,rstrnd,prog to 3rd 14th,styd on apr last,fin 2nd,disq* 0 17
1480 11/5 Bredwardine (R) LAD 3m 12 G *cls up to 11th, outpcd frm 14th* 5 14

Ladies winner 95; schoolmaster & gradually deteriorating; Members best hope again 97 16

NEWSTARSKY b.g. 10 New Member - Star Beauty by Jock Scot R G Westacot
1995 4(0),P(0),**P(0)**
70 10/2 Great Treth' (R) MDO 3m 14 S *nvr a serious threat, p.u. aft 14th* P
137 17/2 Ottery St M' (L) RES 3m 15 GS *alwys rear, t.o. & p.u. 2 out* P
361 5/3 Leicester (R) HC 2 1/2m 110yds 15 GS *f 1st.* F

Placed 6 times 93-5 but showed nothing 96 & makes no appeal now 0

NEWTOWN RAMBLER (Irish) — **I** 86[P], **I** 227[P]
NEWTOWN ROAD (Irish) — **I** 421[F], **I** 478[P], **I** 559[P], **I** 624[F]
NEWTOWN ROSIE (Irish) — **I** 102[1], **I** 264[2], **I** 304[1]
NEW YEARS EVE b.g. 7 Ballacashtal (CAN) - Almadena by Dairialatan Miss V C Sturgi
28 20/1 Barbury Cas' (L) RES 3m 14 GS *mstk 7th, prom to 12th, wknd, p.u. 3 out* P
143 17/2 Larkhill (R) MDO 3m 14 G *mid-div whn f 5th* F
205 24/2 Castle Of C' (R) MDO 3m 9 HY *sn bhnd, t.o. & p.u. 2 out* P
268 2/3 Didmarton (L) MDN 3m 10 G *mid-div til f 8th* F
375 9/3 Barbury Cas' (L) MDN 3m 14 GS *nvr trbld ldrs, t.o. & p.u. 15th* P
1293 28/4 Barbury Cas' (L) MDO 3m 11 F *s.s. rear til hmpd & u.r. 2nd* U
1409 6/5 Hackwood Pa' (L) MDO 3m 6 F *hld up, wnt 2nd 12th, qknd clr 3 out, easy* 1 1

Won Hackwood special; form worthless & Restricted chances nil based on achievements so far 11

NEXT RIGHT (Irish) — **I** 75[P], **I** 140[F], **I** 436[P], **I** 505[6], **I** 566[U]
NGALA (Irish) — **I** 96[P], **I** 178[3], **I** 286[P], **I** 408[P], **I** 535[P], **I** 601[P]
NIAD b.g. 12 Lighter - Taxi Freight by Brave Invader (USA) Robert Johnso
1995 **P(NH)**,**4(NH)**,**P(NH)**
87 11/2 Alnwick (L) MDO 3m 7 GS *last & t.o. til p.u. 10th* P
316 2/3 Corbridge (R) MEM 3m 10 GS *alwys bhnd* 5
764 31/3 Great Stain' (L) MDN 3m 16 GS *alwys prom, ld 12th til hdd & wknd 2 out* 4 1
1106 15/4 Hexham (L) HC 3m 1f 9 GF *chasing ldrs when blnd 10th (water), soon lost tch, p.u. before 13th.* P
1450 6/5 Witton Cast' (R) MDO 3m 14 G *midfld, prog 4 out, gng wll whn bad mstk 2 out, not rcvrd* 3 1

Gradually found his feet but a win at 13 will need fortune 12

NIAL(IRE) b.g. 8 Niels - Cailin Deas Emma by Import Mrs B Hardin
288 2/3 Eaton Hall (R) MDO 3m 17 G *mid to rear, nvr dang, p.u. 4 out* P
563 17/3 Wolverhampt' (L) XX 3m 4 GS *disp to 13th, wknd* 2

Ex-Irish; last in a match & not worth a rating 0

NIBBLE b.g. 8 Nicholas Bill - Sigh by Highland Melody G I Coope
108 17/2 Marks Tey (L) MDN 3m 17 G *cls up,ld & blnd 2 out,blnd & hdd last,rallied to ld nr fin* 1 1
593 23/3 Parham (R) RES 3m 11 GS *cls up, jmpd slwly 14th whn 3rd, 4th & no dang frm 4 out* 4 1
931 8/4 Marks Tey (L) RES 3m 8 G *trckd ldrs, ld 6th-10th, rdn 15th, ld apr 2 out, blnd last* 1 1

Late starter; showed stamina when winning; mistakes; more needed for Confined; Good 19

NICENAMES (Irish) — **I** 306[P], **I** 324[P], **I** 457[P]
NICE TO NO ch.g. 8 Cisto (FR) - Noneed by Duneed G M Leeve
1112 17/4 Hockworthy (L) PPO 3m 9 GS *s.s., t.o. & jmpd bdly til p.u. 11th* P
1277 27/4 Bratton Down (L) CON 3m 15 GF *mid-div, lost tch 11th, t.o. & p.u. 14th* P
1493 11/5 Holnicote (L) MEM 3m 5 G *in tch, ev ch whn pckd 16th, wknd* 4
1554 18/5 Bratton Down (L) MDO 3m 16 F *sn rear, not alwys fluent, t.o. 13th* 5
1637 1/6 Bratton Down (L) MDO 3m 11 G *cls up, ld 10-14th, chsd ldrs til wknd 2 out* 5

Showed some improvement but well short of winning standard yet 10

NICK DUNDEE (Irish) — **I** 330, , **I** 518[1]

NICKNAVAR ch.g. 11 Raga Navarro (ITY) - Bay Girl by Persian Bold — Mrs P A Tetley

32 20/1 Higham (L) OPE 3m 15 GF *chsd ldrs, hit 8th, 4th & lsing grnd whn f 14th* F -

Very lightly raced last three seasons & looks finished now **0**

NICK THE BRIEF b.g. 14 Duky - Roman Twilight by Romulus — John R Upson

1995 **3(20)**,**3(17)**,2(17)

1435 6/5 Ashorne (R) CON 3m 12 G *1st ride, alwys bhnd, t.o. 13th* 6 0

Formerly top-class chaser; looks ready for retirement now **11**

NICOLINSKY b.m. 6 Krisinsky (USA) - Game Spinney by Precipice Wood — Mrs S J Biggin

1244 27/4 Woodford (L) INT 3m 12 G *alwys bhnd, last hlfwy, t.o. & p.u. 3 out* P 0
1511 12/5 Maisemore P' (L) MDO 3m 14 F *trckd ldrs til nrly ran off course & p.u. bef 6th* P 0

No signs of ability yet & wayward last run **0**

NIGHTS IMAGE(IRE) br.g. 6 Corvaro (USA) - Lysanders Lady by Saulingo — T H Caldwell

1995 **16(NH)**,**11(NH)**,**P(NH)**

286 2/3 Eaton Hall (R) MDO 3m 14 G *s.s. prog last m, nrst fin* 7 0
463 9/3 Eyton-On-Se' (L) MDN 2 1/2m 14 G *chsng grp, 10l 3rd whn u.r. 4 out* U -
660 24/3 Eaton Hall (R) MDN 3m 7 S *chsng grp, ld 7-10th, in tch aft, chal 2 out, onepcd* 2 12

No ability under Rules; only beaten one other finisher but improving & should go closer 97 .... **12**

NIGHT WIND b.g. 9 Strong Gale - Kylogue Lady by London Gazette — Mrs P Tollit

1995 **F(NH)**

1046 13/4 Bitterley (L) LAD 3m 9 G *ld to 11th, cls up, chal aft 2 out, not qckn flat* 2 20
1264 27/4 Pyle (R) LAD 3m 10 G *(fav) chsd ldr, ld 13th, hdd & wknd 3 out* 6 12
1579 19/5 Wolverhampt' (L) LAD 3m 9 G *chsd ldr to 5th, ld 15th-nxt, onepcd und pres 2 out* 2 18
1617 27/5 Chaddesley ' (L) LAD 3m 8 GF *cls up, lft 2nd 14th, ev ch whn f nxt* F -

Chase winner 94; ran fair races in points; needs easy 3m; may find modest race **18**

NINEFIVEO ch.m. 8 Kabour - Underbarrow Rose by Andrea Mantegna — Ms S J Wharton

416 9/3 Charm Park (L) MDO 3m 13 G *al wl bhnd, p.u. 11th* P 0
591 23/3 Wetherby Po' (L) MDO 3m 14 S *t.o. 7th, p.u. nxt* P 0
1026 13/4 Brocklesby ' (L) MDN 3m 6 GF *2nd to 8th, fdd, t.o. 10th, f 5 out (ditch)* F -

No signs of ability **0**

NINE OUT OF TEN (Irish) — **I** 290^{S}, **I** 335^{P}

NIORD b.g. 6 Nishapour (FR) - Pro Scania by Niniski (USA) — B Davies

1995 **8(NH)**,**4(NH)**,**3(NH)**,**8(NH)**,**B(NH)**,**5(NH)**,**5(NH)**,**3(NH)**,**9(NH)**,**2(NH)**,**10(NH)**

167 17/2 Weston Park (L) MDN 3m 10 G *trckd ldrs, 3rd at 11th, fdd rpdly, p.u. 4 out* P 0
463 9/3 Eyton-On-Se' (L) MDN 2 1/2m 14 G *ld to 8th, wknd quckly aftr 11th, p.u. 4 out* P 0
568 17/3 Wolverhampt' (L) MDN 3m 9 GS *s.s. bhnd whn f 8th* F -
1033 13/4 Alpraham (R) MDO 2 1/2m 15 GS *rear thruout, some late prog, nvr nrr* 6 0
1196 21/4 Sandon (L) MDN 3m 17 G *mid-div, btn whn f 5 out* F -
1423 6/5 Eyton-On-Se' (L) MDO 3m 7 GF *cl up, ev ch 4 out, ran on one pce, cght for 2nd flat* 3 0

Hard career already & beaten distance when 3rd - no stamina or prospects **0**

NISHKINA b.g. 8 Nishapour (FR) - Varishkina by Derring-Do — C J Cundall

1995 **P(0)**,2(19),B(-),7(15),2(17),P(0),6(12),1(17),2(18),U(-)

78 11/2 Wetherby Po' (L) OPE 3m 10 GS *cls up, 4th frm 4 out, onepcd aft* 4 13
226 24/2 Duncombe Pa' (R) OPE 3m 10 GS *prog to jn ldrs 10th, 2nd & ev ch whn f 4 out* F -
410 9/3 Charm Park (L) OPE 3m 17 G *rr early, prog 12th, n.d.* 6 15
512 16/3 Dalton Park (R) CON 3m 10 G *prom, ld 14th-4 out, ld agn apr 2 out, sn hdd & onepcd* 3 12
587 23/3 Wetherby Po' (L) OPE 3m 15 S *mid-div, blnd 12th, t.o. 3 out* 7 0
984 8/4 Charm Park (L) MXO 3m 7 GF *cls up, 3rd 2 out, no ext aft* 5 16

Confined winner 95; outclassed in 96; finds little under pressure; another win hard to find; Any **16**

NISHVAMITRA gr.g. 6 Nishapour (FR) - Red Nanda by Status Seeker — C D Dawson

1995 **4(NH)**,**1(NH)**,**3(NH)**,**4(NH)**,**2(NH)**,**3(NH)**,**9(NH)**

970 8/4 Thorpe Lodge (L) LAD 3m 6 GF *disp to 4th, chsd wnr, outpcd 10th, fair 1st effort* 2 0
1469 11/5 Easingwold (L) LAD 3m 6 G *handy, outpcd 14th, sn btn, t.o.* 4 0

NH Flat winner 95; good stable but outclassed in Ladies & hard to place at present; best watched **13**

NISSAN STAR (Irish) — **I** 238^{F}, **I** 307^{4}, **I** 433^{P}

NOBBUTJUST(IRE) ch.m. 6 Sandalay - Kam Hill by Kambalda — C H Birch

174 18/2 Market Rase' (L) MDO 2m 5f 7 GF *prom, 3rd & rdn 3 out, no ext* 4 10
463 9/3 Eyton-On-Se' (L) MDN 2 1/2m 14 G *rr, p.u. 3 out* P 0
1150 20/4 Whittington (L) MEM 3m 6 G *2nd 8th, mssd marker apr 14th, ld 3 out, held on wll,disq* 1D 10
1581 19/5 Wolverhampt' (L) MDO 3m 10 G *w.w. steady prog to 2nd 14th, ld 16th, clr 2 out, rdn out* 1 13

Won modest race to gain compensation; stays; should improve - needs to for Restricteds 15

NOBLE ANGEL(IRE) b.g. 8 Aristocracy - Be An Angel by Be Friendly — N J Barrowclough

565 17/3 Wolverhampt' (L) OPE 3m 6 GS *ld to 14th, wknd & p.u. 3 out, fair effort* P 0
666 24/3 Eaton Hall (R) RES 3m 13 S *ld/disp to 8th, hmpd by loose horse, p.u. 11th* P 0
674 30/3 Hereford (R) HC 2m 8 S *left in ld 2nd, mstk and hdd 5th, 4th when f 7th.* F -
1423 6/5 Eyton-On-Se' (L) MDO 3m 7 GF *ld to 6th whr sdle slpd, in tch, lkd hld whn u.r. 2 out* U -
1629 30/5 Uttoxeter (L) HC 2m 5f 13 GS *chsd ldrs, weakening when blnd 10th, t.o. when p.u. before 12th.* P 0

Ex-Irish; no luck so far; may go close in 97 if sticking to Maidens 14

NOBLE AUK(NZ) b.g. 8 Le Grand Seigneur (CAN) - Lady Auk (NZ) by Auk (USA) — D H Barons

447 9/3 Haldon (R) MDO 3m 13 S *mid-div, mstk 11th, 7th whn p.u. 14th* P 0

Just a glimmer of hope & time passing 0

NOBLE COMIC b.g. 5 Silly Prices - Barony by Ribston — R E Dimond

1995 **7(NH),P(NH)**

646 23/3 Cothelstone (L) MDO 3m 5 S *schoold in rr till p.u. 4 out* P 0
820 6/4 Charlton Ho' (L) MDN 3m 12 GF *in tch, 3rd 11th, ld 3 out til hdd aft nxt, not qckn aft* 3 14
1129 20/4 Stafford Cr' (R) MDO 3m 11 S *prom to 14th, lost tch nxt, p.u. apr 2 out* P 0

Beaten 10l in reasonable Maiden & sure to go closer 97; best run on G/F 14

NOBLE KNIGHT (Irish) — **I** 21[P], **I** 133[3], **I** 166[P], **I** 416[2], **I** 585[2], **I** 618[3], **I** 655[5]

NOBLE MELODY (Irish) — **I** 418[P], **I** 527[F]

NOBLE MINISTER gr.g. 9 Rusticaro (FR) - Nofert (USA) by Graustark — J H Forbes

1995 2(10),3(0)

203 24/2 Castle Of C' (R) MEM 3m 4 HY *cls up early, lost tch 11th, t.o. & p.u. 4 out* P 0
645 23/3 Cothelstone (L) MDO 3m 3 S *alwys 3rd, lst tch 14th, t.o. whn p.u. 2 out* P 0
1081 13/4 Cothelstone (L) MDN 3m 4 GF *disp, ld brfly 13th, hdd 2 out, no ext last* 2 0
1248 27/4 Woodford (L) MDN 3m 15 G *alwys rear, 11th hlfwy, t.o. & p.u. 3 out (lame)* P 0
1347 4/5 Holnicote (L) MDO 3m 16 GS *nvr on terms, p.u. 2 out* P 0
1510 12/5 Maisemore P' (L) XX 3m 8 F *in tch, 4th whn s.u. bend apr 7th* S -
1555 18/5 Bratton Down (L) MDO 3m 13 F *ld 9th til wd bnd apr 14th,ran on to ld 2 out,hdd & fdd flat* 4 0
1621 27/5 Chaddesley ' (L) MDO 3m 17 GF *prom til wknd 12th, wll btn whn p.u. 3 out* P 0
1638 1/6 Bratton Down (L) MDO 3m 13 G *ld 4-6th,mstk & wknd 12th,exhausted aft,f heavily 16th* F -

Placed in bad races; does not stay & given terrible ride last start 0

NOBLE NORMAN b.g. 5 Grey Desire - Pokey's Pet by Uncle Pokey — M S Vernon

1137 20/4 Hornby Cast' (L) MDN 3m 13 G *mid-div, drppd rear 7th, sn t.o.* 7 0

Last & beaten long way on debut 0

NOBLE PROTECTOR (Irish) — **I** 154[P]

NOBLE STREET (Irish) — **I** 266[6], **I** 479[P]

NOBODYS BOY (Irish) — **I** 386[P], **I** 420[P], **I** 616[P]

NOBODYWANTSME (Irish) — **I** 200[5], **I** 272[B], **I** 300[P]

NODDY'S STORY b.m. 9 Tom Noddy - Sharp Story by Sharpen Up — John Nicholls

1995 P(0),F(-),F(-)

294 2/3 Great Treth' (R) CON 3m 10 G *rear til p.u. apr 13th* P 0
560 17/3 Ottery St M' (L) CON 3m 7 G *cls up early, lost plc 7th, t.o. 10th* 5 0
625 23/3 Kilworthy (L) CON 3m 11 GS *alwys bhnd, t.o. 13th* 9 0
876 6/4 Higher Kilw' (L) MDN 3m 11 GF *ld 8th til aft 14th, lost plc 3 out* 4 10
1071 13/4 Lifton (R) MDN 3m 10 S *not fluent, 7th & outpcd 13th, t.o., p.u. aft 3 out* P 0

Beaten 15l when 4th - first concrete form; stick to Maidens & sound surface 97 - may have chances ... 11

NODFORMS DILEMMA(USA) ch.g. 13 State Dinner (USA) - Princess Jo Jo — S A Brookshaw

163 17/2 Weston Park (L) LAD 3m 10 G *hld up, late prog, fin well, nrst fin* 4 17
291 2/3 Eaton Hall (R) LAD 3m 10 G *w.w. prog frm 4 out, nrst fin* 3 18
460 9/3 Eyton-On-Se' (L) LAD 3m 10 G *chsng grp, outpcd frm hlfwy til ran on frm 3 out, nrst fin* 3 18
853 6/4 Sandon (L) LAD 3m 7 GF *chsng grp, not qckn whn pce increased 4 out* 4 18

Won 9 points 92-4; missed 95; looked after novice rider 96; hard to win at 14; G/F-S 16

NOISY WELCOME b.g. 10 The Parson - Lady Pitpan by Pitpan — M P Jones

1995 F(-),P(0),1(16),4(12),4(10)

153 17/2 Erw Lon (L) OPE 3m 15 G *rear, prog frm 3 out, nvr nrr* 6 0
214 24/2 Newtown (L) CON 3m 21 GS *f 2nd* F -
383 9/3 Llanfrynach (R) CON 3m 13 GS *wll bhnd frm 9th, t.o. 15th, mod late prog* 6 0
601 23/3 Howick (L) CON 3m 10 S *rear, lost irons 12th, fin well* 6 0
691 30/3 Llanvapley (L) CON 3m 15 GS *(bl) alwys last, fin own time* 5 0
981 8/4 Lydstep (L) INT 3m 5 G *alwys rear, f 13th* F -

Won weak Restricted 95; never involved in 96 & best watched now **10**

NO JOKER(IRE) b.g. 8 Jester - Canta Lair by The Parson — Brigadier R W S Hall

1995 P(0),4(13),2(20),**P(0)**,1(19),2+(19),2(0)

258	29/2	Nottingham	(L)	HC	3m 110yds	10	G	*blnd and u.r. 3rd.*	U	-
360	4/3	Windsor	(R)	HC	3m	8	GS	*soon ld, blnd 5th, hdd, mstk and rider lost irons 3 out, one pace.*	3	21
373	8/3	Sandown	(R)	HC	3m 110yds	4	G	*made most till hdd and mstk 15th, challenging wnr when f 18th.*	F	-
1227	26/4	Ludlow	(R)	HC	2 1/2m	16	G	*alwys bhnd, t.o. when blnd and u.r. 4 out.*	U	-
1453	7/5	Wincanton	(R)	HC	2m 5f	9	F	*with ldr, ld 11th to 12th, rdn 5 out, ev ch 3 out, hit 2 out, no impn.*	2	21
1547	18/5	Fakenham	(L)	HC	2m 5f 110yds	11	G	*ld to 3rd, with ldrs, hit 9th, blnd 11th, soon outpcd, left poor 2nd 2 out.*	2	20
1614	27/5	Hereford	(R)	HC	3m 1f 110yds	16	G	*bhnd, blnd 10th, hdwy 4 out, staying on in fourth when mstk and u.r. 2 out.*	U	-

Won 4 points 94/5; blunders round in H/Chases & novice rider no help; could win points 97; F-S **21**

NOLLAIG (Irish) — **I** 39^{P}, **I** 139^{P}, **I** 201^{F}, **I** 250^{P}

NOLUCKMATE (Irish) — **I** 365^{1}

NO MATTER (Irish) — **I** 603^{P}

NO MISTAKE VI (Irish) — **I** 23^{2}, **I** 27^{2}, **I** 88^{5}, **I** 112^{2}

NO MORE NICE GUY(IRE) b.g. 7 Remainder Man - Vaguely Decent by Decent Fellow — Reg Hand

1995 r(-),3(11),1(15),3(12),1(15),2(15),2(15)

138	17/2	Ottery St M'	(L)	RES	3m	18	GS	*rear, onepcd frm 13th*	7	0

Dual winner 95; disappeared early 96; stays; young enough top revive; Any, best Soft **15**

NO MORE THE FOOL ch.g. 10 Jester - Prima Bella by High Hat — Brian Brennan

1227	26/4	Ludlow	(R)	HC	2 1/2m	16	G	*mstk 3rd, alwys rear.*	11	0
1460	8/5	Uttoxeter	(L)	HC	2m 7f	5	G	*prog into 3rd 6th, lost tch apr 11th, t.o..*	4	0

No prospects in H/Chases or points now **0**

NONEOFYOURBUSINESS (Irish) — **I** 60^{P}, **I** 77^{P}, **I** 151^{P}, **I** 309^{U}, **I** 432^{P}, **I** 590^{2}, **I** 610^{P}, **I** 660^{P}

NO ONE KNOWS (Irish) — **I** 24^{2}, **I** 25^{3}, **I** 101^{1}, **I** 338^{P}, **I** 623^{4}

NO OTHER HILL (Irish) — **I** 390^{5}

NO PANIC b.g. 12 Pitpan - Scirea by Cantab — Mrs S Y Johnson

1995 6(0),P(0),4(15),U(-),5(12),**3(16)**,2(10)

157	17/2	Erw Lon	(L)	CON	3m	15	G	*mid-div, t.o. hlfwy, p.u. 3 out*	P	0
383	9/3	Llanfrynach	(R)	CON	3m	13	GS	*lft, t.o. & u.r. 1st*	U	-
545	17/3	Erw Lon	(L)	CON	3m	10	GS	*in rear, p.u. 13th*	P	0
1035	13/4	St Hilary	(R)	CON	3m	10	G	*alwys rear, p.u. 14th*	P	0

Changed hands 96 & can only be watched now **0**

NO PAROLE gr.g. 13 Parole - Princess Etoile by Le Levanstell — Mrs C E Van Praagh

1294	28/4	Bexhill	(R)	MEM	3m	4	F	*chsd ldr til f 5th*	F	-

Dual winner 93; only one run since & probably finished now **0**

NO PLANNING (Irish) — **I** 460^{B}, **I** 504^{F}, **I** 604^{P}, **I** 640, , **I** 651^{P}

NO PROBLEM (Irish) — **I** 275^{3}, **I** 438^{F}, **I** 565^{U}, **I** 571^{F}, **I** 603^{3}

NO QUITTING(IRE) b.g. 6 Sheer Grit - Curraheen Quiz by Quisling — M A Kemp

1995 R(-),P(0)

314	2/3	Ampton	(R)	MDO	3m	10	G	*ld to 2nd & agn 5th, made rest, drw clr appr 2 out, easy*	1	16
494	16/3	Horseheath	(R)	RES	3m	10	GF	*sn ld, 4l clr 4 out, in cmmnd whn f 2 out*	F	-

Potentially useful; won modest race; sure to upgrade; good stable; stays; Good **19**

NORDROSS b.m. 8 Ardross - Noreena by Nonoalco (USA) — M A Lloyd

1995 P(0),**P(0)**,P(0),R(-),P(0),**6(NH)**,**10(NH)**

688	30/3	Chaddesley '	(L)	MDN	3m	17	G	*mstks, bhnd 11th, t.o. & p.u. 3 out*	P	0
1196	21/4	Sandon	(L)	MDN	3m	17	G	*mid-div & out of tch, prog 3 out, ran on, nrst fin*	2	13
1483	11/5	Bredwardine	(R)	MDO	3m	15	G	*prog frm rear 6th, kpt on steadily frm 15th, nrst fin*	4	10

Improved & not disgraced last 2 starts; may go close on long track **13**

NO REPLY b.g. 10 Tumble Gold - Santa Luna by Saint Crespin — A Simpson

1995 3(0),P(0),7(0)

477	10/3	Tweseldown	(R)	MDO	3m	15	G	*disp to 5th, sn lost plc, p.u. 4 out*	P	0
597	23/3	Parham	(R)	MDO	3m	9	GS	*alwys rear & outpcd, dist 4th 4 out, plodded round*	4	0
788	31/3	Tweseldown	(R)	MDO	3m	8	G	*sn rear, t.o. 4 out*	5	0
997	8/4	Hackwood Pa'	(L)	MDO	3m	11	GF	*nvr bttr thn 4th, onepcd*	5	0

1187 21/4 Tweseldown (R) MDN 3m 11 GF *trckd ldrs, 4th & rdn 15th, sn btn* 3 10
1374 4/5 Peper Harow (L) MDO 3m 8 F *keen hold, chsd ldr 4-12th, rdn & wknd appr 2 out* 4 0
1567 19/5 Mollington (R) INT 3m 12 GS *prom to 8th, wknd, 7th & no ch whn blnd 12th, p.u. 3 out* P 0
1607 26/5 Tweseldown (R) MEM 3m 3 G *jmpd slwly, ld to 4th & 7-8th, outpcd frm 3 out* 3 0

Placed 10 times 94-6; beaten in poor events & win looks beyond him 0

NORMANS PROFIT ch.g. 6 Meadowbrook - Night Profit by Carnival Night W G Young
1995 **13(NH),13(NH),8(NH),6(NH),P(NH),8(NH),5(NH),P(NH)**

115 17/2 Lanark (R) MDO 3m 8 GS *2nd to 10th, sn wknd* 5 0
194 24/2 Friars Haugh (L) MDN 3m 11 S *sn t.o., p.u. 12th* P 0

No sign of ability under Rules or in points yet 0

NORMSKI b.g. 8 Petoski - Aiglon (HOL) by Shamaraan (FR) N F K Pearse

156 17/2 Erw Lon (L) RES 3m 13 G *alwys rear, p.u. 14th* P 0

Maiden winner 94; only one run since; best watched now 11

NORMUS (Irish) — **I** 108U, **I** 174, , **I** 267P, **I** 300U, **I** 430P, **I** 481P, **I** 559P
NORRISMOUNT (Irish) — **I** 103P, **I** 175P
NORTHERN BLUFF b.g. 6 Precocious - Mainmast by Bustino Mrs Heather Gibbon
1995 **15(NH),16(NH),11(NH)**

550 17/3 Erw Lon (L) MDN 3m 13 GS *mid-div, prog 3 out, nrst fin, improve* 2 12
771 31/3 Pantyderi (R) MDN 3m 14 G *twrds rear whn u.r. 5th* U -
1201 21/4 Lydstep (L) MDN 3m 9 S *(fav) ld/disp til ld 2 out, hrd rdn flat* 1 16
1388 6/5 Pantyderi (R) RES 3m 7 GF *(fav) made all, wll clr last, eased flat* 1 20
1487 11/5 Erw Lon (L) CON 3m 4 F *(fav) made all, in no dang frm 13th* 1 16
1558 18/5 Bassaleg (R) CON 3m 6 F *(fav) hanging lft,ld to 8th & 15-3 out,wd nxt,lft in ld last,kpton* 1 19
1629 30/5 Uttoxeter (L) HC 2m 5f 13 GS *ld till after 1st, left in ld 4th, made rest, just held on.* 1 25

Good stable & much improved; L/H best; harder to place in 97 but Opens within range; S-F 25

NORTHERN BRIDE ch.m. 8 Northern Game - Brampton Bride by Bribe Mrs J Wheatley

137 17/2 Ottery St M' (L) RES 3m 15 GS *rear whn p.u. 13th* P 0
200 24/2 Lemalla (R) MDO 3m 12 HY *cls up to hlfwy, wknd & p.u. 11th* P 0
447 9/3 Haldon (R) MDO 3m 13 S *rear & rmndrs 2nd, t.o. til p.u. 11th* P 0
1587 25/5 Mounsey Hil' (R) MEM 3m 7 G *alwys bhnd, t.o. & p.u. 13th* P 0

Of no account 0

NORTHERN GRANITE (Irish) — **I** 179P, **I** 395P, **I** 5882
NORTHERN KATIE (Irish) — **I** 150P, **I** 210P, **I** 309P, **I** 351, , **I** 3793, **I** 460P
NORTHERN OPTIMIST b.m. 8 Northern Tempest (USA) - On A Bit by Mummy's Pet Graham Hunt
1995 **2(NH),5(NH),2(NH),1(NH),4(NH),1(NH),U(NH),2(NH)**

482 13/3 Newton Abbot (L) HC 2m 5f 110yds 14 S *in tch till wknd 9th, p.u. before next.* P 0

Winning chaser; showed noting in H/Chase & reverted back to handicaps 17

NORTHERN REEF(FR) b.g. 5 Darshaan - North Cliff (FR) by Green Dancer (USA) Mrs P King

34 20/1 Higham (L) MDN 3m 11 GF *in tch til f 5th* 0 0
107 17/2 Marks Tey (L) MDN 3m 15 G *alwys rr div, p.u. 13th* P 0
343 3/3 Higham (L) MDO 3m 11 G *in rear til f 13th* F -

Let down by jumping but could do better when learning 0

NORTHERN SENSATION b.m. 7 Northern Game - Dark Sensation by Thriller J Down
1995 4(0),1(13),P(0),F(-)

532 16/3 Cothelstone (L) RES 3m 12 G *prom til p.u. qkly appr 13th* P 0
1075 13/4 Lifton (R) RES 3m 12 S *ld/disp frm 4th,ld apr 11th til hdd 3 out,btn whn blnd 2 out* 3 12
1428 6/5 High Bickin' (R) RES 3m 10 G *(fav) held up, 2nd & rddn 13th, sn wknd, p.u. apr 17th* P 0
1590 25/5 Mounsey Hil' (R) INT 3m 8 G *prom, mstk 14th, rdn nxt, btn 3 out, lft 3rd last* 3 10

Maiden winner 95; needs easy 3m; not threatening in Restricteds; should try Members; G-F 12

NORTH HOLLOW b.g. 11 Tyrnavos - Philigree by Moulton Andrew Kempster
1995 **12(NH),P(NH),P(NH)**

288 2/3 Eaton Hall (R) MDO 3m 17 G *prog last m, nrst fin* 5 0
740 31/3 Sudlow Farm (R) MDN 3m 16 G *(bl) alwys rear, last frm 11th, t.o. & p.u. last* P 0
1029 13/4 Alpraham (R) MDO 3m 8 GS *(bl) 4th whn u.r. 4th* U -

Of no account 0

NO SAY ch.g. 11 Parva Stella - Overproud by Flyover J S S Hollins

452 9/3 Charing (L) LAD 3m 8 G *ld 5th-9th, wth ldr whn p.u. qckly 11th* P 0

Only 2 starts 94-6; more problems now & could be finished 0

NOSSI BE b.g. 7 Just A Monarch - Beau Wonder by Veiled Wonder (USA) — Mrs T Arthur

No	Date	Course		Type	Dist	Ran	Going	Comment	Pl	Pts
956	8/4	Lockinge	(L)	MDN	3m	7	GF	*alwys last, schoold til p.u. 11th*	P	0
1164	20/4	Larkhill	(R)	MDN	3m	12	GF	*sn rear, nvr a factor, t.o.*	5	0
1504	11/5	Kingston Bl'	(L)	MDO	3m	13	G	*s.s. bhnd,prog 9th,poor 3rd aft 13th,styd on,tk 2nd nr fin*	2	15
1644	2/6	Dingley	(R)	MDO	3m	16	GF	*mid-div, prog 14th, 3rd at last, ran on well, ld nr fin*	1	15

Showed right attitude when winning; improving & stays; should have Restricted hopes 97 16

NO SUCH PARSON (Irish) — I 78[P]

NO SWAP (Irish) — I 127[P], I 291[3], I 428[1]

NO TAKERS b.m. 9 Carlingford Castle - La Perla by Majority Blue — Miss C A Blakeborough

No	Date	Course		Type	Dist	Ran	Going	Comment	Pl	Pts
80	11/2	Wetherby Po'	(L)	MDO	3m	12	GS	*ld 6th-13th, 4th 2 out, no ext*	4	10
330	3/3	Market Rase'	(L)	MDO	3m	7	G	*(fav) blnd 5th, ld/disp to 15th, 3rd & lkd btn whn f nxt*	F	-
415	9/3	Charm Park	(L)	MDO	3m	13	G	*bhnd early, errors, n.d., p.u. 4 out*	P	0
829	6/4	Stainton	(R)	MDO	3m	9	GF	*prom, ld aft 6th til u.r. 4 out*	U	-
1451	6/5	Witton Cast'	(R)	MDO	3m	12	G	*cls up in 2nd, disp ld 3 out, ld nxt, ran on wll*	1	15

Makes mistakes but well ridden by S Swiers to win modest race; more needed for Restricted chances 15

NOTANOTHERONE(IRE) b.g. 8 Mazaad - Maltese Pet by Dragonara Palace (USA) — R Light

1995 P(0),2(12),3(12),1(16),2(18),8(0),4(16)

No	Date	Course		Type	Dist	Ran	Going	Comment	Pl	Pts
156	17/2	Erw Lon	(L)	RES	3m	13	G	*mid-div, lost tch 12th*	5	0
235	24/2	Heythrop	(R)	RES	3m	10	GS	*wll bhnd, prog 11th, 3rd 2 out, slight ld last, outpcd flat*	4	13
361	5/3	Leicester	(R)	HC	2 1/2m 110yds	15	GS	*chsd ldr 7th, ev ch 4 out, wknd apr next, t.o. when p.u. last.*	P	0
581	21/3	Wincanton	(R)	HC	2m 5f	13	S	*t.o. when p.u. before 4 out.*	P	0
840	6/4	Maisemore P'	(L)	RES	3m	9	GF	*chsd ldr to 3 out, gd jmp to ld last, ran on wll*	1	19
1171	20/4	Chaddesley '	(L)	OPE	3m	15	G	*ld 1st, chsd ldrs aft, not qckn 14th, styd on frm 17th*	4	21

Maiden winner 95; ground against early 96; ran well last start; Confined, at least if fit 97; G-F 21

NOT A RAZU (Irish) — I 266[1]

NOTARY-NOWELL b.g. 10 Deep Run - Hamers Flame by Green Shoon — Mrs Richard Pilkington

1995 P(0),3(11),P(0),P(0),P(0),7(11),3(12),2(11),5(0),3(0),3(10),R(-)

No	Date	Course		Type	Dist	Ran	Going	Comment	Pl	Pts
93	11/2	Ampton	(R)	LAD	3m	7	GF	*chsd wnr to 11th, last frm 15th, p.u. 2 out*	P	0
311	2/3	Ampton	(R)	LAD	3m	4	G	*wth wnr til rddn & outpcd appr 3 out, kpt on onepcd aft*	3	18
491	16/3	Horseheath	(R)	CON	3m	5	GF	*alwys in tch, 2nd & ev ch 3 out, wknd nxt*	4	14
906	8/4	Fakenham	(L)	HC	2m 5f 110yds	11	G	*chsd ldrs to 11th, soon well bhnd.*	7	12
1257	27/4	Cottenham	(R)	CON	3m	5	F	*mid-div, prog to cls 3rd 13th, chal 3 out, ev ch last, hld*	2	14
1541	16/5	Folkestone	(R)	HC	2m 5f	8	G	*(bl) pressed ldr to 9th, 4th and well btn from 11th.*	4	0
1596	25/5	Garthorpe	(R)	LAD	3m	9	G	*(bl) 3rd to 9th, 5th & outpcd frm 11th, lft remote 3rd 2 out*	3	12

Mega-safe but beaten all 19 starts 95/6; ungenuine; changed hands before last two starts 12

NOT CONVINCED (Irish) — I 38[P]

NOT FOR PARROT (Irish) — I 571[U]

NOTHING TO FEAR b.g. 8 Day Is Done - Pembridge by Master Sing — Miss A S White

No	Date	Course		Type	Dist	Ran	Going	Comment	Pl	Pts
646	23/3	Cothelstone	(L)	MDO	3m	5	S	*last at 6th, styd on for 3rd from 2 out, not trble 1st 2.*	3	0
1081	13/4	Cothelstone	(L)	MDN	3m	4	GF	*disp til ld 2 out, hld on wll und pres*	1	10
1277	27/4	Bratton Down	(L)	CON	3m	15	GF	*handy, 5th at 12th, wknd whn crashd thro wing 4 out*	r	-
1493	11/5	Holnicote	(L)	MEM	3m	5	G	*(Jt fav) cls up, ev ch til outpcd 16th, ran on stdly, tk 2nd run in*	2	0
1636	1/6	Bratton Down	(L)	OPE	4m	11	G	*prom, disp 7th, f nxt*	F	-

Won desperate Maiden; struggling after & Restricted some way off yet 12

NOTHINGTOTELLME(IRE) gr.g. 5 Roselier (FR) - Tower Road by Polaroid — R A Bartlett

No	Date	Course		Type	Dist	Ran	Going	Comment	Pl	Pts
1253	27/4	Balcormo Ma'	(R)	MDO	3m	16	GS	*ev ch frm 4 out, no ext run in*	2	14
1517	12/5	Hexham Poin'	(L)	MDN	3m	10	HY	*(fav) trckd ldrs going wll, ld 3 out, rdn & hdd nxt, wknd*	3	13

Promising start; beat 7 horses when placed; should get off the mark early 97 15

NOTHING VENTURED 8 — Mrs Susie Farquhar

No	Date	Course		Type	Dist	Ran	Going	Comment	Pl	Pts
165	17/2	Weston Park	(L)	RES	3m	9	G	*mid-div, no ch whn p.u. 4 out*	P	0
464	9/3	Eyton-On-Se'	(L)	MDN	2 1/2m	13	G	*mid-div, sm prog frm 3 out, nrst fin*	4	0
747	31/3	Upper Sapey	(R)	MDO	3m	11	GS	*disp 3 out, cls 2nd til outpcd frm 2 out*	2	14
954	8/4	Eyton-On-Se'	(L)	MDO	2 1/2m	6	GF	*made virt all, ran on strgly frm 3 out, comf*	1	14
1418	6/5	Eyton-On-Se'	(L)	MEM	3m	7	GF	*hld up in 9th, ld 5 out, ran on strngly frm 3 out, easily*	1	16

Improved fast & wide margin winner; Restricted on the cards early 97; G/S-G/F 18

NOT MISTAKEN b.g. 7 Sulaafah (USA) - Before Long by Longleat (USA) — Mrs S A Turner

1995 P(0),P(0),3(0),U(-),2(13),1(0)

No	Date	Course		Type	Dist	Ran	Going	Comment	Pl	Pts
1313	28/4	Little Wind'	(R)	RES	3m	14	G	*hld up mid-div, prog 9th, ld 13th, ran on strngly whn prssd*	1	19
1510	12/5	Maisemore P'	(L)	XX	3m	8	F	*mstk 4th, 4th whn u.r. 8th*	U	-
1567	19/5	Mollington	(R)	INT	3m	12	GS	*prom, ld 9-14th, mstk 3 out, ld nxt, drvn clr*	1	24

1633	1/6	Bratton Down	(L)	XX	3m	8 G	*hld up, prog 9th, chsd wnr 14th, blnd nxt, no imp aft*	2	20
1648	8/6	Umberleigh	(L)	LAD	3m	11 GF	*ld to 2nd, mstks 10 & 12th, ev ch 15th, sn btn, fin tired*	2	23

Maiden winner 95; much improved; beaten by decent horses; can progress; F-G/S 24

NOT MY LINE(IRE) gr.g. 7 Entre Nous - Uno Navarro by Raga Navarro (ITY) — P Caudwell

1995 2(19)

7	13/1	Larkhill	(R)	CON	3m	10 GS	*ld 3rd til f 10th*	F	-

Irish Maiden winner 94; only two runs 95/6 & finished 1st day 96; best watched 15

NOT QUITE WHITE gr.g. 7 Absalom - Angelic Appeal by Star Appeal — Mrs D H McCarthy

1995 1(23)

258	29/2	Nottingham	(L)	HC	3m 110yds	10 G	*(fav) pricker off side, settld in tch, p.u. lame before 7th.*	P	0

Highly regarded but only 4 runs 94-6; more problems now 21

NOTTAREX b.g. 7 Right Regent - Baresca by Bargello — B J C Wright

1995 4(0),4(0),6(0),6(0)

557	17/3	Ottery St M'	(L)	MDN	3m	10 G	*mid-div whn u.r. 7th*	U	-
819	6/4	Charlton Ho'	(L)	MDN	3m	10 GF	*rear, no ch frm 12th, u.r. 14th*	U	-
1129	20/4	Stafford Cr'	(R)	MDO	3m	11 S	*alwys midfld, nvr on terms wth ldrs*	5	0
1493	11/5	Holnicote	(L)	MEM	3m	5 G	*ld til 12th, wknd, lost tch 14th*	5	0
1555	18/5	Bratton Down	(L)	MDO	3m	13 F	*alwys bhnd, u.r. last*	U	-
1637	1/6	Bratton Down	(L)	MDO	3m	11 G	*ld to 2nd & 6th-10th, 7th & btn whn u.r. 15th*	U	-
1651	8/6	Umberleigh	(L)	MDO	3m	11 GF	*alwys bhnd, t.o. & p.u. 13th*	P	0

Changed hands; novice ridden; does not stay & has no prospects 0

NOT THE NADGER b.g. 5 Aragon - Broken Accent by Busted — R T Dennis

413	9/3	Charm Park	(L)	MDO	3m	12 G	*bhnd early, 7th at 14th, no ext, p.u. 4 out*	P	0
590	23/3	Wetherby Po'	(L)	MDO	3m	16 S	*f 1st*	F	-
829	6/4	Stainton	(R)	MDO	3m	9 GF	*prom whn blnd 5th, outpcd 9th, t.o. & p.u. 14th*	P	0

Not yet of any account 0

NOT TO BE TRUSTED br.g. 6 Ra Nova — Mrs S Brazier

1020	13/4	Kingston Bl'	(L)	MDN	3m	10 G	*mstks 2nd & 3rd, f 5th*	F	-
1182	21/4	Mollington	(R)	MDN	3m	10 F	*in tch, 3rd & outpcd 14th, rdn & kpt on frm 3 out*	2	10
1403	6/5	Northaw	(L)	MDO	3m	8 F	*(fav) in tch, blnd 13-14th, 5th & strugg nxt, no dang aft*	5	0
1569	19/5	Mollington	(R)	MDO	3m	10 GS	*alwys prom,ev ch whn mstk 3 out,kpt on und pres,not rch wnr*	2	13

Placed in modest Maidens & should find an opportunity in 97; stays 15

NOVA NITA b.m. 6 Ra Nova - Jovenita by High Top — Robert Black

192	24/2	Friars Haugh	(L)	MDN	3m	12 S	*alwys handy, mstk 2 out, kpt on well to ld cls home*	1	13
754	31/3	Lockerbie	(R)	RES	3m	8 G	*(fav) chsd wnnr frm 16th, no imp frm 2 out*	2	16

Fair start; stays & should have Restricted chance if ready in 97 16

NOVA STAR gr.m. 5 Ra Nova - Tullymore Dew Vii by Damsire Unregistered — B P Sillis

930	8/4	Marks Tey	(L)	MDO	3m	6 G	*mid-div, mstk 1st, prog 11th, ld nxt, going wll whn u.r. nxt*	U	
1381	5/5	Dingley	(R)	MDO	3m	16 GF	*n.j.w. alwys rear, t.o. & p.u. 9th*	P	0

Promise on debut but felll apart other run; plenty to prove yet 10

NOWHISKI b.g. 8 Petoski - Be Faithful by Val de Loir — Tim Tarratt

394	9/3	Garthorpe	(R)	LAD	3m	6 G	*ld to 2nd, cls 2nd til wknd rpdly 12th, p.u. nxt*	P	0
536	17/3	Southwell P'	(L)	LAD	3m	9 GS	*ld to 5 out, wknd frm 3 out*	5	0
633	23/3	Market Rase'	(L)	LAD	3m	10 GF	*ld to 3rd, cls up til outpcd frm 10th*	4	0
906	8/4	Fakenham	(L)	HC	2m 5f 110yds	11 G	*u.r. 2nd.*	U	
1147	20/4	Higham	(L)	LAD	3m	9 F	*mstk 3rd, chsd ldrs til wknd 11th, p.u. 13th*	P	0
1305	28/4	Southwell P'	(L)	LAD	3m	4 GF	*made all, set strng pace, breather 5 out, ran on wll 3 out*	1	18
1520	12/5	Garthorpe	(R)	LAD	3m	8 GF	*cls 3rd to 12th, 2nd nxt, ld apr last, ran on well*	1	20
1596	25/5	Garthorpe	(R)	LAD	3m	9 G	*alwys ld/disp, qcknd gamely flat to ld cls home*	1	23

Found form with a vengeance late season; game; won modest races well; can win more 97; G-F 22

NUN ON THE RUN ch.m. 10 The Parson - Fortrition by David Jack — K Wellman-Smith

1995 **P(NH),U(NH),6(NH),P(NH),P(NH)**

91	11/2	Ampton	(R)	MDO	3m	10 GF	*mid-div, mod 6th & rdn 14th, no prog, p.u. 3 out*	P	

Placed in hurdle 95; disappointing & showed nothing in only point; shows temperament 0

NURNEY MINSTREL (Irish) — I 32^{2}, I 106^{F}, I 192^{P}

NURSERY STORY ch.g. 8 Ayyabaan - Sharp Story by Sharpen Up — A Aldridge

1995 **21(NH),6(NH)**

348 3/3 Higham (L) RES 3m 12 G *sn rear, bhnd whn p.u. 12th* P 0
618 23/3 Higham (L) MDO 3m 14 GF *alwys wll plcd, disp 7th til tired & f last* F 12
680 30/3 Cottenham (R) MDO 3m 11 GF *wth wrn to 8th, wknd 10th, t.o. & p.u. 16th* P 0
1149 20/4 Higham (L) MDO 3m 10 F *prom to 12th, wknd 15th, wll bhnd whn p.u. 2 out* P 0

Finished 1 of 9 points 93-6; capsized when holding best chance; makes little appeal 10

NUTCASE b.m. 7 Idiot's Delight - Real Beauty by Kinglet N Shutts

1995 F(-),3(11),2(13),4(0)

431 9/3 Upton-On-Se' (R) MDO 3m 17 GS *(fav) prog frm 12th, disp ld 2out-last, outpcd flat* 2 15
591 23/3 Wetherby Po' (L) MDO 3m 14 S *(fav) mid-div, prog 12th, ld 4 out, ran on well* 1 15
895 6/4 Whittington (L) RES 3m 5 F *(fav) held up,2nd 11th,ev ch whn chal 3 out,mstks last 3,eased flt* 2 10

Changed hands 96; improved; thorough stayer; Restricted possible; looked unhappy on Firm; G-S 16

NUTSIL b.m. 6 Dubassoff (USA) - Sunlit by Warpath O A Little

607 23/3 Howick (L) MDN 3m 12 S *rear, p.u. 9th* P 0
697 30/3 Llanvapley (L) MDN 3m 11 GS *last trio, t.o. & p.u. 10th* P 0
850 6/4 Howick (L) MDN 3m 14 GF *last pair, f 3rd* F -
1162 20/4 Llanwit Maj' (R) MDO 3m 12 GS *hmp & f 2nd (dead)* F -

Dead 0

NUTTY SOLERA (Irish) — **I** 139P, **I** 162P, **I** 2272, **I** 3461

OAKERS HILL b.h. 10 Majestic Maharaj - Just Jacky by David Jack J Todd

1995 P(0),2(13)

881 6/4 Brampton Br' (R) CON 3m 9 GF *last at 12th, t.o. 15th, p.u. 2 out* P 0
1268 27/4 Pyle (R) INT 3m 8 G *prom, cls 3rd whn hit 11th, wknd 13th, p.u. 15th* P 0
1478 11/5 Bredwardine (R) CON 3m 12 G *prom to 10th, wknd & p.u. 14th* P 0

Dual winner 94; nothing in 96; best watched now 10

OAKLANDS FRED b.g. 7 Palm Track - Redmarshall Folly by Carnival Dancer R G Russ

1995 U(-),P(0)

229 24/2 Duncombe Pa' (R) MDO 3m 13 GS *blnd 1st, alwys bhnd, t.o. 12th* 4 0
307 2/3 Great Stain' (L) MDO 3m 17 GS *alwys mid-div* 7 0
589 23/3 Wetherby Po' (L) MDO 3m 16 S *alwys mid-div, nvr dang* 5 0
1093 14/4 Whitwell-On' (R) MXO 4m 19 G *t.o. 7th, p.u. 17th* P 0
1364 4/5 Gisburn (R) MDO 3m 11 G *mid-div, blnd 11th, 3rd frm 13th-last, onepcd* 4 0

Safe but slow & never threatens to win 0

OAKLANDS WORD br.g. 7 Hasty Word - Salvo's Grace (FR) by Salvo F P Luff

1995 P(0),P(0),2(11)

150 17/2 Erw Lon (L) MDN 3m 8 G *alwys cls up, 2nd 2 out, chal last, outpcd flat* 2 14
263 2/3 Didmarton (L) INT 3m 18 G *chsng grp, prog 12th, chal apr last, ran on to ld nr fin* 1 22
581 21/3 Wincanton (R) HC 2m 5f 13 S *alwys prom, ld 4 out, ran on well.* 1 28
799 3/4 Ludlow (R) HC 3m 8 GF *in tch, ld 11th, drew clr between last 2, pushed out.* 1 28

Vastly improved; smart prospect now; won fair races; finished early; more H/Chases 97; G-S 29

OAKSEY b.g. 9 Buckskin (FR) - Sunny Sunset by Sunny Way D Crossland

587 23/3 Wetherby Po' (L) OPE 3m 15 S *rear frm 10th, bhnd whn p.u. 13th* P 0
1093 14/4 Whitwell-On' (R) MXO 4m 19 G *mid-div, prog 14th, ev ch whn f nxt* F -

H/Chase winner 94; missed 95; changed hands & brief season 96; best watched; G-S 18

OATS FOR NOTES b.m. 6 Oats - Run In Tune by Deep Run Mrs R F Knipe

1995 4(0)

354 3/3 Garnons (L) MDN 2 1/2m 13 GS *5s-3s, cls 5th & ev ch whn b.d. 10th* B -
749 31/3 Upper Sapey (R) MDO 3m 17 GS *(Jt fav) prog frm 15th, ev ch 2 out, wknd apr last* 4 13

Lightly raced & not disgraced last start; could go closer 97; NH Flat summer 96 13

OBERONS BUTTERFLY b.g. 9 Full Of Hope - Y I Oyston by Dublin Taxi Miss H Peck

1995 4(0),R(-)

252 25/2 Charing (L) INT 3m 7 GS *last & strgglng frm 7th, p.u. 10th* P 0
275 2/3 Parham (R) MDN 3m 15 GF *nvr nr ldrs, blnd 11th, p.u. nxt* P 0
575 17/3 Detling (L) MDO 3m 10 GF *in chsng grp, blnd 12th, wkng whn p.u. 4 out* P 0
781 31/3 Penshurst (L) MDN 3m 11 GS *alwys detached, t.o. whn p.u. aft 12th* P 0

Does not stay & no prospects 0

OBIE'S TRAIN ch.g. 10 Buckskin (FR) - Whisper Moon by Chinatown Mrs A E Lee

1995 3(11),P(0),P(0),4(0),5(12),5(0),3(11),3(16),4(12)

897 6/4 Dingley (R) CON 3m 15 GS *cls up, rnng wd, outpcd by 1st trio 3 out* 5 13

Placed 5 times in 95; does not threaten to win in points & brief season 96 13

OCEAN LAD b.g. 13 Windjammer (USA) - Elixir by Hard Tack Mrs C Bevar

266	2/3	Didmarton	(L)	LAD	3m	13	G	*u.r. 1st*	U	
638	23/3	Siddington	(L)	CON	3m	16	S	*mstk 2nd, bhnd til p.u. 12th*	P	
1005	9/4	Upton-On-Se'	(R)	CON	3m	6	F	*last pair, t.o. 13th, p.u. 15th*	P	
1214	24/4	Andoversford	(R)	LAD	3m	4	G	*chsd ldr to 6th, sn bhnd, t.o.*	4	
1414	6/5	Cursneh Hill	(L)	LAD	3m	9	GF	*t.o. frm 7th, f 10th*	F	

No longer of any account 0

OCEAN ROSE gr.m. 9 Baron Blakeney - Deep Ocean by Deep Run W M Burne

1995 P(0),3(13),1(14),2(14),2(10),5(16),**6(14)**,6(0)

77	11/2	Wetherby Po'	(L)	RES	3m	18	GS	*prom, ld 14th-3 out, outpcd aft*	6	1
173	18/2	Market Rase'	(L)	RES	3m	6	GF	*prom, jnd ldrs 14th, 2nd & hrd rdn 2 out, ld cls hm*	1	1
306	2/3	Great Stain'	(L)	INT	3m	12	GS	*mid-div, styd on well frm 2 out, onepcd last*	4	1
583	23/3	Wetherby Po'	(L)	MEM	3m	6	S	*(fav) prom, outpcd 14th, styd on onepcd aft*	2	1

Maiden winner 95; stays but very onepaced; 2 wins, 8 plces, last 17 starts; Members best hope in 97 .. 16

OCEAN SOVEREIGN b.g. 10 Smackover - Pacific Crown Vii Mrs Fiona Denni

1995 1(14),P(0)

243	25/2	Southwell P'	(L)	RES	3m	11	HO	*prom to 13th, sn outpcd & no dang*	6	
329	3/3	Market Rase'	(L)	RES	3m	12	G	*prom to 12th, t.o. & p.u. 2 out*	P	
726	31/3	Garthorpe	(R)	RES	3m	16	G	*alwys bhnd, t.o. & p.u. 15th*	P	
1306	28/4	Southwell P'	(L)	MEM	3m	4	GF	*3rd til prssd wnr 7th, duelld wth wnr, onepcd apr last*	2	1
1380	5/5	Dingley	(R)	RES	3m	11	GF	*ld 3-9th & 10th-aft 12th, wknd rpdly, walked in*	9	

Won weak Maiden 95; struggling since & unlikely to find Restricted chance 11

OCTOBER (Irish) — **I** 17^P, **I** 170,

ODDS ON (Irish) — **I** 293^P, **I** 440^4, **I** 472^P

ODYSSEUS b or br.g. 10 Deep Run - Russian Wings by Zabeg Miss E Inma

1995 P(0),3(11),2(13),5(0),3(10),P(0)

92	11/2	Ampton	(R)	MDO	3m	7	GF	*ld/disp to 13th, ev ch til onepcd apr 2 out*	2	1
392	9/3	Garthorpe	(R)	MEM	3m	6	G	*(fav) made all at steady pace, drew away 2 out, comf*	1	1
904	6/4	Dingley	(R)	RES	3m	20	GS	*cls up 1st m, sn fdd, p.u. 5 out*	P	
1181	21/4	Mollington	(R)	RES	3m	10	F	*rear, 8th & wll bhnd 8th, t.o. aft til p.u. last*	P	
1303	28/4	Southwell P'	(L)	CON	3m	7	GF	*disp whn u.r. 11th*	U	
1522	12/5	Garthorpe	(R)	RES	3m	12	GF	*ld/disp to 4th, cls up til outpcd 4 out, sn btn*	5	

Won bad Members & does not really stay; same race again only hope 97 11

OFFENSIVE WEAPON ch.g. 9 Homing - Chuchilla by Comedy Star (USA) Mrs J P Biss

1995 P(0),6(0),1(16)

263	2/3	Didmarton	(L)	INT	3m	18	G	*chsng grp, 3rd apr 12th, lost tch aft nxt*	5	

Maiden winner 95; well beaten in hot race; not seen after; Restricted chances if fit 97st watched 16

OFF THE BRU b.g. 11 General Ironside - Amelieranne by Daybrook Lad J G Bradburr

1995 **5(NH),U(NH),P(NH)**

37	3/2	Wetherby	(L)	HC	3m 110yds	11	GS	*(vis) chsd ldrs till wknd before 4 out, no ch when blnd 2 out, t.o..*	5	1
86	11/2	Alnwick	(L)	OPE	3m	8	GS	*prssd ldr, chal 2 out, ev ch aft last, not qckn*	3	2
113	17/2	Lanark	(R)	OPE	3m	6	GS	*2nd til ld 8th, hdd apr 2 out, sn outpcd*	2	2
259	1/3	Kelso	(L)	HC	3m 1f	8	GS	*j.w, made all, hrd pressed final 100 yards, held on well.*	1	2
672	29/3	Aintree	(L)	HC	2 3/4m	26	G	*hmpd 1st, rear when f 3rd (Chair).*	F	
790	1/4	Kelso	(L)	HC	3m 1f	11	GF	*pressed lea der, ld 2 out, hdd briefly last, rallied, hded and one pace run-in.*	2	2
1119	18/4	Ayr	(L)	HC	3m 3f 110yds	9	GS	*j.w, ld or disp ld till hdd 12th, remained cl up, weakening when hit 2 out.*	4	2

Winning chaser; maintained ability; onepaced; may need points to win at 12; G/F-G/S 23

OFF YOU SAIL (Irish) — **I** 324^P, **I** 499^P

O'FIAICH'S HOPE (Irish) — **I** 23^4, **I** 97^4, **I** 281^1, **I** 405^1

OFLAHERTY'S BABE(IRE) b.g. 7 Arapahos (FR) - Glittering Steel by Golden Love Derek J Harding-Jone

1995 P(0),P(0),6(0),F(-)

35	20/1	Higham	(L)	RES	3m	16	GF	*alwys prom, ev ch 16th, wknd 2 out*	4	

Irish Maiden winner 94; finished early 96; needs easy 3m; mistakes; good enough for Restricted 17

OH LORD(IRE) b.g. 7 Mister Lord (USA) - Arctic Survivor by Hard Run J A C Edwarc

29	20/1	Barbury Cas'	(L)	RES	3m	12	GS	*alwys bhnd, t.o. & p.u. 13th*	P	
207	24/2	Castle Of C'	(R)	MDO	3m	15	HY	*mid-div, ev ch 4 out, onepcd frm nxt*	5	

Beaten 14l when completing (last); professionally trained; should do better 11

OH SO WINDY b.m. 9 Oats - Tempest Girl by Caliban — Rupert Cottrell

No.	Date	Course		Race	Dist	Rnrs	Going	Comment	Pos	Rtg
897	6/4	Dingley	(R)	CON	3m	15	GS	*prog 8th, 4th 4 out, ran on, not rch 1st 2*	3	14
1105	14/4	Guilsborough	(L)	MDN	3m	12	G	*(fav) prom, ld 9-15th & frm 3 out, sn clr, unchal*	1	15
1236	27/4	Clifton On '	(L)	CON	3m	8	GF	*(fav) trckd ldrs, 2nd 13th, rdn to ld 2 out, clr last, all out*	1	20
1377	5/5	Dingley	(R)	CON	3m	12	GF	*(Co fav) mid-div, prog 9th, cls up 13th, rdn 15th, sn btn*	5	13

Poor under Rules; short but busy season in points; stays; beaten in good race last; should win again ... 19

OKDO (Irish) — **I** 153[1], **I** 263, , **I** 461[3], **I** 595[B], **I** 639[2]

OKEETEE b.g. 13 Raise You Ten - Peppardstown by Javelot — B T Crawford

1995 P(0),2(23),1(22),5(17),3(20),2(19)

No.	Date	Course		Race	Dist	Rnrs	Going	Comment	Pos	Rtg
326	3/3	Market Rase'	(L)	OPE	3m	14	G	*prom to 9th, sn wknd, p.u. 14th*	P	0
633	23/3	Market Rase'	(L)	LAD	3m	10	GF	*alwys prom, prssd wnr 5 out, outpcd bef last*	2	18
723	31/3	Garthorpe	(R)	CON	3m	19	G	*chsd ldrs, 7th hlfwy, prog 15th, 6th & btn whn nrly u.r.2out*	5	11
1099	14/4	Guilsborough	(L)	LAD	3m	9	G	*prom, ld 9-11th, outpcd 14th, rallied apr 3 out, onepcd nxt*	2	17
1238	27/4	Clifton On '	(L)	LAD	3m	6	GF	*chsd ldrs, 3rd & outpcd 13th, chsd wnr 2 out, no imp*	3	15
1519	12/5	Garthorpe	(R)	OPE	3m	7	GF	*ld to 6th, cls up, tk 2nd 10th, not qckn cls home*	2	18

Still tries hard but 1 win, 7 places in 95/6 & hard to find another chance at 14; G/F-S ... 17

OLD CAVALIER (Irish) — **I** 465[P], **I** 644[1]

OLD COMRADES ch.g. 9 Music Boy - Miss Candine by King Emperor (USA) — Ian Carmichael

No.	Date	Course		Race	Dist	Rnrs	Going	Comment	Pos	Rtg
317	2/3	Corbridge	(R)	CON	3m	11	GS	*bhnd frm 8th, p.u. 12th*	P	0
699	30/3	Tranwell	(L)	CON	3m	8	GS	*sn rear, t.o. & p.u. 14th*	P	0
1083	14/4	Friars Haugh	(L)	CON	3m	10	F	*bhnd whn u.r. 9th*	U	-

Flat winner; no prospects in points ... 0

OLD DUNDALK b.g. 12 Derrylin - Georgiana by Never Say Die — R Oliver Smith

1995 5(13),1(19),2(21),1(23),F(-),F(-)

No.	Date	Course		Race	Dist	Rnrs	Going	Comment	Pos	Rtg
90	11/2	Ampton	(R)	CON	3m	5	GF	*(bl) alwys last, lost tch 14th, no ch 3 out*	5	14
102	17/2	Marks Tey	(L)	CON	3m	17	G	*(bl) alwys rr, nvr dang*	12	0
309	2/3	Ampton	(R)	MEM	3m	6	G	*(bl) ld til jmpd slw 4th,lft disp 13th,ld 17th,sn clr,pshd out*	1	15
420	9/3	High Easter	(L)	OPE	3m	9	S	*(bl) rr, styd on wll frm 3 out, nvr nrr*	4	16
622	23/3	Higham	(L)	CON	3m	10	GF	*sttld rear of grp, prog 14th, chal 3 out, mstk last, no ext*	2	20

Moody & needs things his own way; 3 wins at Ampton; can win again 97; G-S ... 18

OLDE CRESCENT br.g. 10 Kambalda - Bush Mistress by Will Somers — T D B Underwood

No.	Date	Course		Race	Dist	Rnrs	Going	Comment	Pos	Rtg
16	14/1	Tweseldown	(R)	MEM	3m	2	GS	*(fav) pllng, hld up, clsd 12th, rdn & ev ch last, not qckn flat*	2	14
141	17/2	Larkhill	(R)	MEM	3m	6	G	*plld hrd, ld 7th til mstk & hdd 15th, wknd*	3	17
475	10/3	Tweseldown	(R)	CON	3m	9	G	*hld up rear, nvr in chal postn, p.u. 4 out*	P	0
594	23/3	Parham	(R)	CON	3m	13	GS	*rear whn u.r. 2nd*	U	-
784	31/3	Tweseldown	(R)	CON	3m	5	G	*hld up, prog 7th, 2nd 4 out, wknd 2 out, p.u. last*	P	0
998	8/4	Hackwood Pa'	(L)	CON	3m	5	GF	*rear early, ld 10th, strchd clr 12th, rddn out*	1	19
1190	21/4	Tweseldown	(R)	MEM	3m	3	GF	*(fav) plld hrd in 2nd, rdn to disp last, drvn out flat*	1	17
1375	4/5	Peper Harow	(L)	CON	3m	9	F	*hld up, efft 13th, 5th & btn whn p.u. aft 3 out*	P	0
1405	6/5	Hackwood Pa'	(L)	CON	3m	6	F	*reluctant, alwys bhnd, p.u before last*	P	0

Ex-Irish; inconsistent; won small races; struggles to stay; ominous last start; best watched; G-F ... 15

OLDHAM JOKER b.g. 8 Old Jocus - Miss Canada by Larkhill Lad — W R Britton

No.	Date	Course		Race	Dist	Rnrs	Going	Comment	Pos	Rtg
1074	13/4	Lifton	(R)	INT	3m	9	S	*bhnd, p.u. apr 13th*	P	0
1143	20/4	Flete Park	(R)	MDN	3m	17	S	*mstk 2nd, 12th hlfwy, mstks 15th & nxt, p.u. 17th*	P	0
1555	18/5	Bratton Down	(L)	MDO	3m	13	F	*nvr dang, t.o. & p.u. last*	P	0
1628	27/5	Lifton	(R)	MEM	3m	5	GS	*(bl) tubed, lost tch 10th, t.o. & p.u. 13th*	P	0

Of no account ... 0

OLD HARRY'S WIFE b.m. 6 Idiot's Delight - Blakesware Gift by Dominion — Mrs J E Purdie

No.	Date	Course		Race	Dist	Rnrs	Going	Comment	Pos	Rtg
820	6/4	Charlton Ho'	(L)	MDN	3m	12	GF	*midfld, 4th 11th, ev ch 14th, no ext frm 2 out, imprv*	4	0
1129	20/4	Stafford Cr'	(R)	MDO	3m	11	S	*2nd til 9th, lost tch & p.u. 13th*	P	0
1531	12/5	Ottery St M'	(L)	MDO	3m	9	GF	*(fav) mstks, 2nd whn blnd 15th, no ch frm nxt*	5	0

Promising debut; not yet progressed but should do better in 97 ... 12

OLD ROAD(USA) b.g. 10 Regal And Royal (USA) - Raise Me (USA) by Mr Prospector (USA) — Mrs Cherry McGready

1995 **3(NH),2(NH),P(NH),3(NH),4(NH),9(NH)**

No.	Date	Course		Race	Dist	Rnrs	Going	Comment	Pos	Rtg
25	20/1	Barbury Cas'	(L)	OPE	3m	14	GS	*ld 2-4th, wkng whn blnd 11th, p.u. 13th*	P	0
124	17/2	Kingston Bl'	(L)	CON	3m	17	GS	*(bl) ld 2nd-9th & 11-15th, wknd rpdly*	9	0
337	3/3	Heythrop	(R)	OPE	3m	10	G	*(bl) prom to 11th, t.o. 15th*	7	0
785	31/3	Tweseldown	(R)	OPE	3m	5	G	*(bl) trckd ldrs to 12th, outpcd 4 out, t.o. 2 out, lft 2nd last*	2	0
958	8/4	Lockinge	(L)	MXO	3m	6	GF	*(bl) ld til 9th, wknd & outpcd frm 12th*	5	0
1405	6/5	Hackwood Pa'	(L)	OPE	3m	6	F	*(bl) ld 1st, cls up to 2 out, wknd qkly*	5	10
1607	26/5	Tweseldown	(R)	MEM	3m	3	G	*hld up, ld 8-9th,not qckn 3 out, rdn & effrt apr last,kpt on*	2	10
1647	8/6	Umberleigh	(L)	OPE	3m	7	GF	*prom til mstk 13th, btn whn lft 2nd 3 out, no imp*	2	13

Winning chaser; does not stay & beat only 3 other finishers all season ... 0

OLDSON (Irish) — **I** 22^{P}, **I** 26^{3}, **I** 111^{P}, **I** 305^{F}, **I** 563^{3}, **I** 585^{1}

OLD SPORT b.g. 7 Myjinski (USA) - Eucryphia by Avgerinos — S H Gribble

247 25/2 Charing (L) MEM 3m 7 GS *ref 1st,clmbrd over 3rd try,f 2nd,rmntd & jmpd 3rd,p.u.* F -

Action-packed debut **0**

OLD STEINE b.g. 8 Elegant Air - Brightelmstone by Prince Regent (FR) — Carl Evans

1995 **P(0)**,4(0),3(0)

219 24/2 Newtown (L) RES 3m 17 GS *mstk 3rd, prom to 8th, t.o. 12th, p.u. 15th* P 0
360 4/3 Windsor (R) HC 3m 8 GS *held up, hdwy 9th, wknd next, t.o..* 6 0
485 16/3 Hereford (R) HC 3m 1f 110yds 13 S *bhnd, t.o. from 7th.* 7 0
605 23/3 Howick (L) MDN 3m 13 S *cls up, lost tch wth 1st 3 frm 12th, fin tired* 5 0
691 30/3 Llanvapley (L) CON 3m 15 GS *rear, went 6th at 13th, wknd rpdly, p.u. 3 out* P 0
850 6/4 Howick (L) MDN 3m 14 GF *chsd ldr to 13th, ld brfly til hdd & onepcd frm nxt* 3 0
1272 27/4 Pyle (R) MDO 3m 9 G *p.u. lame apr 4th* P 0

Does not threaten to win; no stamina & problems last start **0**

OLDTOWN GLEN (Irish) — **I** 283^{5}, **I** 365^{P}

OLD TRAFFORD (Irish) — **I** 306^{5}

OLIVE BASKET b.m. 5 Neltino - Casket by Pannier — Miss Jane Cooper

520 16/3 Larkhill (R) MDO 3m 11 G *dwelt & lost 30l start, p.u. 8th* P 0
653 23/3 Badbury Rin' (L) MDO 3m 9 G *mid-div til lost plc 11th, t.o. & f last* F -
819 6/4 Charlton Ho' (L) MDN 3m 10 GF *alwys midfld, outpcd frm 5 out* 5 0
1280 27/4 Bratton Down (L) MDO 3m 14 GF *j.w. alwys prom, 3rd at 12th, wknd frm 3 out, improve* 5 11
1552 18/5 Bratton Down (L) LAD 3m 7 F *blnd & u.r. 3rd* U -
1588 25/5 Mounsey Hil' (R) LAD 3m 6 G *ld to 6th, lost tch 11th, t.o. & p.u. 15th* P 0

Showed promise in weak race 4th start but no chance to capitalise yet; may do better **12**

OLIVE BRANCH br.m. 8 Le Moss - Olive Press by Ragapan — A H Mactaggart

1995 3(11),U(-)

53 4/2 Alnwick (L) MDO 3m 13 G *rear, lost tch 8th, ran on frm 3 out, nrst fin* 3 10
116 17/2 Lanark (R) MDO 3m 10 GS *(fav) alwys handy, ld 11th til last, no ext flat* 3 14
192 24/2 Friars Haugh (L) MDN 3m 12 S *alwys prom, no imp frm 3 out* 4 11

Well-bred but only 6 runs 94-6 & disappeared early 95/6; slow & disappointing **13**

OLIVER HIMSELF b.g. 5 Strong Gale - Sparticone by Celtic Cone — Mrs Judy Wilson

900 6/4 Dingley (R) MDN 2m 5f 8 GS *last jmpng slwly til p.u. 9th* P 0
1105 14/4 Guilsborough (L) MDN 3m 12 G *prom, ld 7-9th, mstk 11th, ev ch apr 3 out, wknd, improve* 4 0
1433 6/5 Ashorne (R) MDO 3m 16 G *(fav) w.w. rear, prog 11th, cls 3rd 15th, wknd nxt* 6 0
1644 2/6 Dingley (R) MDO 3m 16 GF *prom, ld gng well whn f 12th* F -

Good stable; going well last start & should win in 97 providing he gets the trip **14**

OLLARDALE(IRE) b.g. 8 Abednego - Kauai-Ka-Zum by Kauai King — Wilfred S Littleworth

1995 P(0),1(14),F(-),2(12),1(17)

217 24/2 Newtown (L) RES 3m 17 GS *in tch, prog 12th, chsd wnr 2 out, kpt on, no imp* 2 17
461 9/3 Eyton-On-Se' (L) RES 3m 15 G *(fav) chsng grp, ev ch 3 out, nt qckn clsng stgs* 3 14
684 30/3 Chaddesley ' (L) RES 3m 14 G *w.w. prog 11th, rdn apr 3 out, kpt on well flat* 3 17

Dual winner 95; consistent & ran well all starts 96; finished early; win Restricted if fit 97; G/F-S **18**

OLLAR LADY (Irish) — **I** 259^{P}, **I** 286^{6}, **I** 364^{P}

OLUMO (Irish) — **I** 172^{3}, **I** 282^{P}

OLYMPIC CLASS b.g. 6 Strong Gale - Olympic Course — Simon J Robinson

1995 **9(NH)**,**14(NH)**

87 11/2 Alnwick (L) MDO 3m 7 GS *cls up til wknd 11th, no ch whn f hvly 4 out* F -
307 2/3 Great Stain' (L) MDO 3m 17 GS *alwys mid-div* 8 0
406 9/3 Dalston (R) MDO 2 1/2m 12 G *hdwy 8th, ev ch frm 3 out, nt pc of frst 2* 3 13
1095 14/4 Whitwell-On' (R) MDO 2 1/2m 88yds 14 G *rear whn f 7th* F -
1452 6/5 Witton Cast' (R) MEM 3m 7 G *hndy, cls 2nd 4 out, 5l 2nd & held whn f nxt* F -
1575 19/5 Corbridge (R) MDO 3m 10 G *mid-div whn hmpd 15th, not rcvr* 5 0

2 subsequent winners behind when placed; jumping problems hampering progress; best watched **12**

O'MOSS (Irish) — **I** 97^{P}

ON ALERT(NZ) ch.g. 9 Double Trouble (NZ) - Stand By (NZ) by Oakville — V G Greenway

1995 P(0),1(14),1(18),**U(-)**

65 10/2 Great Treth' (R) INT 3m 13 S *nvr thrtnd ldrs, kpt on onepcd frm 3 out* 4 17
297 2/3 Great Treth' (R) INT 3m 10 G *trckd ldr til ld 16th, hdd & blnd badly last* 3 22
482 13/3 Newton Abbot (L) HC 2m 5f 110yds 14 S *in tch, ld 6th, hdd 8th, led 10th to next, led 5 out to 3 out, wknd apr next.* 3 16

671 28/3 Taunton (R) HC 3m 13 S *ld 3rd, jmpd slowly and hdd 5th, left in clr ld 15th, unchal.* 1 26

Dual winner 95; improved 96; modest H/Chase win makes harder to place 97 but should win again; Soft 25

ONCE IN A LIFETIME (Irish) — **I** 429F, **I** 636P

ONEEDIN GLORY (Irish) — **I** 538U, **I** 583,

ONE ELEVEN (Irish) — **I** 456F, **I** 493P, **I** 5834

ONE EYED GER VI (Irish) — **I** 251

ONE FOR NAVIGATION (Irish) — **I** 3071

ONE FOR THE CHIEF b.g. 8 Chief Singer - Action Belle by Auction Ring (USA) R M Whitaker

1995 **F(NH)**

77 11/2 Wetherby Po' (L) RES 3m 18 GS *alwys wll in rear, p.u. 4 out* P 0
292 2/3 Eaton Hall (R) RES 3m 15 G *mid to rear, nvr dang* 5 10
409 9/3 Charm Park (L) CON 3m 11 G *alwys mid-div, styd on sm pc* 6 16
583 23/3 Wetherby Po' (L) MEM 3m 6 S *rear whn ran out 8th* r -
1368 4/5 Gisburn (R) RES 3m 9 G *(vis) chsd ldrs, lft in ld 13th, clr 2 out* 1 18
1466 11/5 Easingwold (L) CON 3m 10 G *(vis) alwsy abt same plc, onepcd frm 4 out* 4 14

Dual winner 94; improved by visor when winning 96; little scope; Confined hard; Good 17

ONE FOR THE CROSS(IRE) ch.g. 8 The Parson - Dora-Elliven by Sweet Revenge L W Wickett

1995 6(0),4(0),3(0),2(10),3(0)

447 9/3 Haldon (R) MDO 3m 13 S *ld to 5th, prom whn mstk 10th, wknd 13th, p.u. 15th* P 0
926 8/4 Bishopsleigh (R) RES 3m 9 G *t.o. whn p.u. 5 out* P 0

Placed 5 times 94/5 but non-stayer & will be fortunate to find a win 11

ONEMAN'S CHOICE (Irish) — **I** 321P, **I** 3656, **I** 4023

ONEMOREANWEGO b.m. 8 Celtic Cone - Foxwell by Healaugh Fox P J Corbett

1314 28/4 Bitterley (L) MEM 3m 13 G *sttld mid-div, cls 8th at 10th, wknd 12th, p.u. 15th* P 0
1417 6/5 Cursneh Hill (L) MDO 3m 14 GF *cls 3rd 8th, prog to ld 15th, kpt on wll frm nxt* 1 16

Beat a soft lot but in fair time & should progress - Restricted likely in 97 18

ONE MORE RUN ch.g. 9 Deep Run - Mawbeg Holly by Golden Love Mrs C S Hall

1995 **3(NH),P(NH)**

677 30/3 Cottenham (R) OPE 3m 11 GF *ld to 2 out, wknd apr last* 5 16

Chase winner 94; always lightly raced; ran passably only start but unlikely to achieve much in 97 15

ONEOFOUROWN (Irish) — **I** 199P, **I** 375P, **I** 466U, **I** 5095, **I** 5402, **I** 6302

ONEOFTHECLAN (Irish) — **I** 163P, **I** 5273, **I** 632P

ONEOVERTHEIGHT br.g. 11 Sousa - Western Melody by West Partisan Miss K Cook

1995 5(12),2(17),**P(0)**,F(-),3(15),3(0),3(0),P(0),P(0)

42 3/2 Wadebridge (L) CON 3m 8 GF *ld 8-11th & 13th-aft nxt, kpt on frm 2 out* 2 17
134 17/2 Ottery St M' (L) CON 3m 12 GS *n.j.w. lost tch frm 14th* 8 0
199 24/2 Lemalla (R) RES 3m 17 HY *wll bhnd whn p.u. 12th* P 0
562 17/3 Ottery St M' (L) XX 3m 12 G *ld to 14th, no ext & onepcd frm 3 out* 5 10
720 30/3 Wadebridge (L) RES 3m 9 GF *prom til lost ground 12th, 5th & wkng 14th, p.u. nxt* P 0
805 4/4 Clyst St Ma' (L) RES 3m 7 GS *disp frm 5th, mstk 8th, ld 11th til hdd aft 2 out, no ext* 2 15
1069 13/4 Lifton (R) CON 3m 9 S *7th & just in tch 12th, bhnd frm 3 out* 7 0
1528 12/5 Ottery St M' (L) RES 3m 10 GF *mid-div, plenty to do 15th, styd on wll clsng stgs* 4 15
1591 25/5 Mounsey Hil' (R) RES 3m 15 G *prssd ldr,ld 15th-17th,sn wknd,lft poor 2nd 2 out,promoted* 1 11
1634 1/6 Bratton Down (L) INT 3m 15 G *bhnd, 12th whn p.u. 8th, dsmntd* P 0
1650 8/6 Umberleigh (L) CON 3m 7 GF *in tch, pshd alng 11th, ld 13th-15th, wknd nxt* 3 10

Maiden winner 94; broke losing sequence of 19 in highly fortunate way; hard to see another win 13

ON HIS OWN br.g. 13 Paico - Luvvy Duvvy by Levmoss P L Southcombe

1995 P(0),P(0),9(0)

135 17/2 Ottery St M' (L) LAD 3m 11 GS *rear til p.u. 3 out* P 0
208 24/2 Castle Of C' (R) LAD 3m 14 HY *alwys prom, disp 4 out-2 out, no ext aft* 2 20
443 9/3 Haldon (R) LAD 3m 10 S *in tch, went 2nd brfly at 15th, 4th & onepcd frm 3 out* 4 17
523 16/3 Larkhill (R) MXO 3m 8 G *ld to 13th, styd on frm 3 out* 3 17
728 31/3 Little Wind' (R) MEM 3m 7 GS *tried to make all, j.w., 5l clr 2 out, cght last, wknd rpdly* 2 16
991 8/4 Kingston St' (R) LAD 3m 8 F *hld up in tch, cls 5th at 15th, ld 2 out, ct nr post* 2 20
1126 20/4 Stafford Cr' (R) LAD 3m 7 S *sn rear, wll bhnd & no ch frm 4 out* 3 16
1310 28/4 Little Wind' (R) LAD 3m 4 G *3rd whn blnd 10th, 6l 3rd 3 out, fdd* 4 16
1394 6/5 Cotley Farm (L) MXO 3m 5 GF *j.r., ld 5th, clr 10th, easily* 1 21

Revived in 96; likes to dictate; easily beaten by decent horses; Ladies at 14 tough to find; best RH 17

ONLY ONE (Irish) — **I** 22U, **I** 87P, **I** 109P, **I** 2991

ONLY TIME (Irish) — **I** 42, **I** 701

ON THE BEER(IRE) b.g. 8 Kemal (FR) - Mad For Her Beer by Proverb H D Hill

1995 F(-),F(-),2(19),2(19),**2(19)**

35	20/1	Higham	(L)	RES	3m	16	GF	*(fav) prog to 4th at 11th, ev ch 3 out, rdn nxt, onepcd*	2	21
346	3/3	Higham	(L)	INT	3m	6	G	*cls up, ran on 3 ut, chal last, ld nr fin*	1	21
374	9/3	Sandown	(R)	HC	2 1/2m 110yds	5	GS	*cl up, ld 10th till next, one pace from 3 out.*	3	20
622	23/3	Higham	(L)	CON	3m	10	GF	*(fav) j.w. alwys prom, ld 15th, qcknd clr last, comf*	1	21
906	8/4	Fakenham	(L)	HC	2m 5f 110yds	11	G	*(fav) bhnd early, prog 5th, styd on one pace clsg stgs.*	4	19
1148	20/4	Higham	(L)	CON	3m	5	F	*(fav) trckd wnr 12th, outpcd 16th, ran on 2 out, not qckn flat*	2	18

Consistent & deserved wins; needs easy 3m; likes Higham; should win another Confined; G/F-S 21

ON THE BOOK ch.m. 7 Sunley Builds - Levanter Rose by Levanter — T G Price

553	17/3	Erw Lon	(L)	MDN	3m	3	GS	*2nd whn u.r. 14th*	U	-
771	31/3	Pantyderi	(R)	MDN	3m	14	G	*u.r. 3rd*	U	-
1039	13/4	St Hilary	(R)	MDN	3m	14	G	*alwys last pair, p.u. 15th*	P	0

Showed signs on debut but needs to jump better 0

ON THE OTHER HAND b.g. 13 Proverb - Saltee Star by Arapaho — Robert Ogden

1995 **5(26),1(29),10(0)**

183	19/2	Musselburgh	(R)	HC	3m	5	GF	*(fav) held up, steady hdwy to ld 14th, styd on well.*	1	24
373	8/3	Sandown	(R)	HC	3m 110yds	4	G	*(fav) held up in 4th, hit 12th, hdwy four out, str chal apr last, ran on, just faild.*	2	24
672	29/3	Aintree	(L)	HC	2 3/4m	26	G	*held up, losing tch when pkd 10th (Becher's), well bhnd after.*	12	0
1615	27/5	Wetherby	(L)	HC	2 1/2m 110yds	11	G	*(vis) soon well bhnd, p.u. before 7th.*	P	0

H/Chase winner 95; declined 96; won weak event; points only real option at 14; G/F-S 21

ON THE WAY HOME (Irish) — I 272[P], I 300[P], I 337[P]

ON YOUR WAY b.g. 14 Ragapan - Fourteen Carat by Sterling Bay (SWE) — A A Gilby

1995 P(0),7(0),P(0)

289	2/3	Eaton Hall	(R)	CON	3m	10	G	*mid to rear, no ch whn p.u. 5 out*	P	0
892	6/4	Whittington	(L)	CON	3m	4	F	*ld 8th to 3 out, wknd qckly*	3	0
1150	20/4	Whittington	(L)	MEM	3m	6	G	*rear, sn t.o., tk 4th aft 3 out*	3	0
1369	4/5	Gisburn	(R)	CON	3m	10	G	*mstks, rear 9th, t.o. nxt*	4	0

No longer of any account 0

OPEN AGENDA(IRE) b.g. 7 Ajdal (USA) - Metair by Laser Light — Miss D E Bastin

1995 P(0),P(0)

355	3/3	Garnons	(L)	INT	3m	10	GS	*prom whn f 8th*	F	-
807	4/4	Clyst St Ma'	(L)	MDO	3m	10	GS	*sn bhnd, t.o. & p.u. 10th*	P	0
908	8/4	Hereford	(R)	HC	2m 3f	12	GF	*ld to 6th, wknd 8th, t.o. when p.u. before 10th.*	P	0

Yet to complete & looks devoid of stamina 0

OPEN CHAMPION (Irish) — I 237[P], I 481[P]

OPENING QUOTE (Irish) — I 283[P], I 318[P], I 409[P], I 456[P]

OPUS WINWOOD(IRE) ch.g. 8 Orchestra - Atlantic Hope by Brave Invader (USA) — Bryan Allen

1995 P(0),P(0),P(0),2(0)

129	17/2	Kingston Bl'	(L)	MDN	3m	15	GS	*sn rear, wll bhnd 13th, no real prog aft, p.u. 2 out*	P	0
315	2/3	Ampton	(R)	MDO	3m	10	G	*in tch, j.s. 8th, ld 12th, clr frm 17th, easy*	1	13
494	16/3	Horseheath	(R)	RES	3m	10	GF	*cls up, 3rd whn f 11th*	F	-

Improved & romped home in weak event; finished early; Restricted will need more if fit 97 14

ORAFENO (Irish) — I 348[P], I 384[P], I 418[2], I 533[3]

ORAGAS b.g. 10 Sagaro - Maranatha by Le Prince — G J L Orchard

1995 7(0),P(0)

666	24/3	Eaton Hall	(R)	RES	3m	13	S	*chsng grp, 20l 3rd 5 out, ran on to ld apr last*	1	19
1041	13/4	Bitterley	(L)	MEM	3m	6	G	*(fav) w.w. cls 3rd at 10th, effrt 14th, not qckn nxt, btn 2 out*	2	12
1219	24/4	Brampton Br'	(R)	CON	3m	9	G	*mid-div, rdn 14th, kpt on, disp 2nd whn f last*	F	18
1411	6/5	Cursneh Hill	(L)	CON	3m	5	GF	*outpcd thruout, no ch frm 15th*	4	0
1604	25/5	Bassaleg	(R)	OPE	3m	6	GS	*cls up in 3rd/4th, chsd wnr 11th, styd on, no imp*	2	14
1645	2/6	Dingley	(R)	INT	3m	5	GF	*ld to 5th, rdn 10th, no ch whn nrly ref 2 out, t.o.*	5	0

Members winner 93; nothing after till 50/1 shock 1st time out; needs real slog to win again 16

ORANGE DREAM (Irish) — I 133[P]

ORA PRONOBIS b.g. 10 Kambalda - Let's Compromise — R Hancox

1174	20/4	Chaddesley '	(L)	MDN	3m	10	G	*went prom 6th, ev ch 17th, wknd 3 out*	3	11

Rarely seen; not disgraced only start 96 but time already passing him by 12

ORCHARD LADY ch.m. 6 Rich Charlie - Ballagarrow Girl by North Stoke — Laurie Snook

1995 **P(NH)**

204 24/2 Castle Of C' (R) MDO 3m 11 HY *in tch, 4th at 12th, wknd nxt, p.u. 3 out* P 0
470 10/3 Milborne St' (L) MDO 3m 18 G *rear whn u.r. 5th* U -
658 23/3 Badbury Rin' (L) MDO 3m 8 G *wth ldng grp until wknd whn u.r. 14th* U -
993 8/4 Kingston St' (R) MDO 3m 17 F *in tch, wll plcd til lost ground frm 15th* 9 0

Shows some speed but not enough stamina yet 0

ORCHESTRAL SUITE(IRE) br.g. 8 Orchestra - Sweetly Stung by Master Rocky G Pidgeon
1995 1(19),1(21),2(22)

457 9/3 Eyton-On-Se' (L) INT 3m 11 G *(fav) tkd ldrs gng esly,ld 13th,in cmd whn lft clr last* 1 21

Imposing sort but very lightly raced; 4 wins from 5 starts 93-6; win more if fit 97; G-S 23

ORCHESTRATED CHAOS(IRE) ch.m. 7 Orchestra - Quit The Hassle by Deep Run J H Mead

471 10/3 Milborne St' (L) MDO 3m 16 G *in tch to 14th, wknd nxt, outpcd aft* 7 0

No form under Rules 93/4; well beaten on pointing debut but not entirely without hope yet 10

ORDAIN (Irish) — **I** 112^{P}, **I** 169^{6}, **I** 288^{5}, **I** 321^{4}, **I** 413^{P}, **I** 450^{3}, **I** 599^{6}
ORE ENGINEERESS (Irish) — **I** 12^{1}, **I** 141^{P}, **I** 153^{P}, **I** 242^{4}, **I** 295^{5}, **I** 376^{P}
ORE GALORE (Irish) — **I** 143^{P}
ORELSE b.g. 8 Ore - Star Ruler by Indian Ruler Mrs D Barnett

440 9/3 Newton Brom' (R) MDN 3m 10 GS *m.n.s. rear whn ref 7th* R -

Lightly raced - missed 95 - & wrong signs on 96 run 0

ORIEL FLIGHT (Irish) — **I** 93^{P}
ORIENTAL BLAZE (Irish) — **I** 253^{3}, **I** 444^{4}
ORIENTAL PLUME br.g. 12 Nishapour (FR) - Yellow Plume by Home Guard (USA) J F Weldhen
1995 4(13)

64 10/2 Great Treth' (R) CON 3m 7 S *ld 6th-14th, prssd wnr til outpcd last* 2 19
197 24/2 Lemalla (R) LAD 3m 13 HY *alwys prom, ld 9th, made rest, kpt on well* 1 20
295 2/3 Great Treth' (R) LAD 3m 6 G *(fav) in tch, ld 14th, sn clr, easily* 1 22

Prolific winner to 93; well revived 96; stays; can win again if fit 97; G-Hy 22

ORIGAMI ch.g. 11 Horage - Demeter by Silly Season Alex Rhodes
1995 P(0),3(15),3(0),P(0)

146 17/2 Erw Lon (L) MEM 3m 7 G *rear, prog to chal 2 out, no ext aft* 2 13
547 17/3 Erw Lon (L) OPE 3m 10 GS *(bl) mid-div, rpd prog 4 out, fdd 2 out* 3 13
768 31/3 Pantyderi (R) OPE 3m 10 G *(bl) mid-div, prog to ld 4 out, hdd nxt, onepcd aft* 5 13
978 8/4 Lydstep (L) OPE 3m 6 G *(bl) mid-div, p.u. 3 out* P 0
1198 21/4 Lydstep (L) INT 3m 5 S *twrds rear,steady prog frm 12th,hrd rdn 2 out,ld flat,hld on* 1 18
1268 27/4 Pyle (R) INT 3m 8 G *drppd rear 5th, lost tch 13th, t.o. & p.u. 2 out* P 0
1389 6/5 Pantyderi (R) INT 3m 5 GF *rear, effrt 3 out, onepcd nxt, ref last, cont* 3 10

Won 2 of last 24 starts; inconsistent & needs everything to go right; may win again; Any 15

ORLAS FANCY (Irish) — **I** 33^{P}, **I** 85^{U}, **I** 105^{U}, **I** 164^{P}, **I** 195^{P}
ORMOND BEACH (Irish) — **I** 49^{P}, **I** 243^{P}
ORPHAN OLLY b.g. 6 Relkino - Austrian Maid by Faberge II R H York

254 25/2 Charing (L) MDO 3m 9 GS *alwys wll dtchd, jmpd bdly, strggld round* 3 0
479 10/3 Tweseldown (R) MDO 3m 10 G *rear, t.o. 13th, lft remote 3rd 3 out, disp 2nd whn f last* F -
780 31/3 Penshurst (L) MDN 3m 12 GS *prom til f 11th* F -
1164 20/4 Larkhill (R) MDN 3m 12 GF *sn in rear, t.o., p.u. 13th* P 0
1299 28/4 Bexhill (R) MDO 3m 7 F *strng hld, cls up til f 14th whn 3rd* F -
1409 6/5 Hackwood Pa' (L) MDO 3m 6 F *cls up til u.r 15th* U -

Beaten miles on only completion & cannot jump at present 0

ORTON ACTRESS b.m. 6 Scallywag - Fixby Story by Sweet Story R Harvey

1103 14/4 Guilsborough (L) MDN 3m 15 G *mstks, rear til prog & in tch 13th, wknd & p.u. 15th* P 0

A glimmer of hope on debut & should do better if appearing regularly in 97 10

ORTON HOUSE b.g. 9 Silly Prices - Who's Free by Sit In The Corner (USA) Mrs A P Kelly
1995 **7(NH)**

458 9/3 Eyton-On-Se' (L) INT 3m 11 G *alwys prom, ev ch 4 out, no ext frm 2 out* 3 10
485 16/3 Hereford (R) HC 3m 1f 110yds 13 S *jmpd slowly thrght, soon t.o., p.u. before 12th.* P 0
740 31/3 Sudlow Farm (R) MDN 3m 16 G *ld to 2nd, chsd ldr til ld 13th, jnd 3 out, f nxt* F -
1000 9/4 Wetherby (L) HC 3m 110yds 10 G *bhnd hfwy, t.o. when p.u. before 12th.* P 0
1195 21/4 Sandon (L) XX 3m 9 G *w.w. prog 4 out, outpcd frm nxt* 3 15

1234 27/4 Weston Park (L) MDO 3m 13 G *(fav) w.w., cls order 10th, ld 5 out, ran on strgly, comf* 1 15
1457 8/5 Uttoxeter (L) HC 3 1/4m 16 G *prom, ev ch 16th, soon rdn, wknd quickly after 4 out.* 6 0
1535 16/5 Aintree (L) HC 3m 1f 11 GF *trckd ldrs, wknd 12th, t.o. when blnd and u.r. 2 out.* U -

Peculiar campaign; no winners behind when scoring; outclassed in H/Chases & Restricted needs more 14

ORTY b.g. 11 Wolverlife - Diana's Choice by Tudor Music Miss J Short

432 9/3 Upton-On-Se' (R) MDO 3m 17 GS *disp 4th-5th, wknd 8th, p.u. 12th* P 0
1224 24/4 Brampton Br' (R) MDO 3m 17 G *ld 8-12th, wknd frm 15th, t.o. 3 out* 6 0
1416 6/5 Cursneh Hill (L) MDO 3m 9 GF *chsng ldrs whn slppd & f aft 3rd* F -

Lightly raced & of no real account 0

ORUJO(IRE) b.g. 8 Try My Best (USA) - Oyace (ITY) by Hogarth (ITY) Miss C Gordon

209 24/2 Castle Of C' (R) OPE 3m 8 HY *cls up, ld 14th-nxt, disp nxt, ev ch 2 out, wknd* 2 17
364 5/3 Leicester (R) HC 2m 1f 12 GS *chasing gp, rdn and blnd 4 out, n.d..* 9 0
523 16/3 Larkhill (R) MXO 3m 8 G *nvr bttr than mid-div* 6 10
1059 13/4 Badbury Rin' (L) OPE 3m 5 GF *handy to 15th, lost tch frm 4 out, onepcd* 4 10

Non-stayer & well beaten on all starts - hard to see a winning chance 13

OSCEOLA b.g. 10 Sunyboy - Chance A Look by Don't Look J Bryant

600 23/3 Howick (L) RES 3m 14 S *alwys prom, clr 2nd 12th, drvn to ld 3 out, hld on* 1 18
981 8/4 Lydstep (L) INT 3m 5 G *chsd ldng pair, lft 2nd & ev ch last, no ext flat* 2 17
1211 23/4 Chepstow (L) HC 3m 13 S *ld 4th to 8th, ev ch 13th, one pace from four out.* 3 19

Maiden winner 94; missed 95; ran well on return; Confined possible if fit 97; G-Hy 20

OSGATHORPE ch.g. 9 Dunbeath (USA) - Darlingka by Darling Boy R Tate
1995 P(0),U(-),F(-),1(20),**2(20),4(14),4(NH)**

170 18/2 Market Rase' (L) XX 3m 8 GF *chsd ldr 4th-6th, prom til wknd 14th, p.u. last* P 0
514 16/3 Dalton Park (R) LAD 3m 7 G *hld up, prog & wth ldrs whn f 13th* F -
984 8/4 Charm Park (L) MXO 3m 7 GF *rear early, prog 4 out, late chal, nvr nrr* 3 17
1023 13/4 Brocklesby ' (L) LAD 3m 3 GF *cls up, chal frm 3 out, outpcd flat* 2 17
1281 27/4 Easingwold (L) CON 3m 15 G *alwys rear, lost tch 11th, p.u. 14th* P 0
1462 10/5 Market Rasen (R) HC 2 3/4m 110yds 11 G *in tch, outpcd 4 out, wknd next.* 4 16

Ladies winner 95; below best 96; needs easy 3m; may win again; G-F 18

O SO BREEZY (Irish) — **I** 9^P, **I** 506^P

O'SULLIVAN'S CHOISE (Irish) — **I** 38^P, **I** 89, , **I** 125^F

OTTER MILL b.g. 8 Harvest Spirit - Jolly Music by Money Business O J Carter

1118 17/4 Hockworthy (L) MDO 3m 14 GS *cls up, ld 12th, 2l up whn lft wl clr 2 out* 1 15
1128 20/4 Stafford Cr' (R) RES 3m 17 S *in tch til 11th, btn whn blndrd & u.r. 14th* U -
1456 8/5 Uttoxeter (L) HC 2m 5f 11 G *prom, blnd 7th, lost pl 10th, rdn and rallied 12th, btn next.* 5 16
1527 12/5 Ottery St M' (L) RES 3m 8 GF *ld 1st & agn 9-16th, sn rdn & no ext* 3 14

Lightly raced; popped up 1st time out; ran passably after & may find Restricted 97 16

OUL LARRY ANDY (Irish) — **I** 87^4

OUNAVARRA CREEK (Irish) — **I** 104^5

OUR BLOSSOM (Irish) — **I** 113^1, **I** 209^P, **I** 276^P, **I** 357^4, **I** 508^P

OUR JACKIE b.g. 11 Pony Express - Corniche Rose by Punchinello T J Driscoll

133 17/2 Ottery St M' (L) OPE 3m 18 GS *bolted to start, in tch til wknd 14th, p.u. 4 out* P 0
263 2/3 Didmarton (L) INT 3m 18 G *f 1st* F -
472 10/3 Milborne St' (L) INT 3m 8 G *chsd wnr to 11th, lost tch 13th, p.u. 15th* P 0
531 16/3 Cothelstone (L) CON 3m 12 G *ld, sn clr, hdded & wknd qkly 13th, wll bhnd whn u.r. 15th* U -

Dual winner 91; hardly seen since & looks finished now 0

OUR OWN WAY (Irish) — **I** 351, , **I** 502^P

OUR SURVIVOR b.g. 12 Trimmingham - Lougharue by Deep Run Harry White

273 2/3 Parham (R) LAD 3m 11 GF *ld, mstk 2nd, c.o. by loose horse 4th* C -
452 9/3 Charing (L) LAD 3m 8 G *mid-div, prog to ld 15th-3 out, rallied & ld flat* 1 18
596 23/3 Parham (R) LAD 3m 8 GS *ld to 3rd, prom aft, outpcd 12th, 4th 2 out, styd on strngly* 3 17
812 6/4 Charing (L) LAD 3m 6 F *(fav) alwys rear, nvr going wll, wll bhnd whn p.u. 2 out* P 0
1297 28/4 Bexhill (R) LAD 3m 7 F *(fav) cls up, ev ch 3 out, mstk & btn nxt* 4 12
1613 27/5 Fontwell (R) HC 3 1/4m 110yds 12 G *bhnd, mstk 10th, t.o. when p.u. after 19th.* P 0

Chase winner 93; missing till 96; won modest Ladies; hard to score again at 13; Good 15

OUR TEDDIS b.g. 6 Henricus (ATA) - Ted's Choice by Royal Smoke E Sussex
1995 9(0),U(-),8(0)

137 17/2 Ottery St M' (L) RES 3m 15 GS *alwys bhnd, last whn f 3 out* F -

556	17/3	Ottery St M'	(L)	MDO	3m	15	G	*mid-div, prog 10th, 2nd at 13th, ld nxt-4 out, wknd*	3	11
629	23/3	Kilworthy	(L)	MDN	3m	11	GS	*(fav) ld 3rd, drew wll clr 15th, unchal, eased flat*	1	14
871	6/4	Higher Kilw'	(L)	RES	3m	9	GF	*(fav) mid-div, outpcd 12th, ran on steadily frm 3 out, sore*	3	14

Improved & easy winner of weak Maiden; ran well but problem after; should find Restricted if fit 97 15

OUT FOR FUN ch.g. 10 Relkino - Cherry Picking by Queen's Hussar — Miss G A March

99	14/2	Lingfield	(L)	HC	3m	9	HY	*in tch, chsd wnr from 14th, 2nd and held when f 3 out.*	F	-
485	16/3	Hereford	(R)	HC	3m 1f 110yds	13	S	*in tch, mstk 2nd, blnd 10th, soon lost pl, hdwy 12th, 3rd when f next (water).*	F	-

Impressive debut winner 94; missed 95; very able but unfortunate 96; win H/Chase if fit 97; G-S 28

OUT THE DOOR(IRE) br.g. 7 Lepanto (GER) - Pejays Princess by Pumps (USA) — M Mann

245	25/2	Southwell P'	(L)	LAD	3m	8	HO	*keen hld, hld up last, hmpd & u.r. 3rd*	U	-
325	3/3	Market Rase'	(L)	LAD	3m	6	G	*disp ld 4th til ld 11th, clr nxt, hdd & hit 2 out, no ext*	2	22
460	9/3	Eyton-On-Se'	(L)	LAD	3m	10	G	*hld up rr,prog frm 12th to ld 3 out,ran on wll frm nxt*	1	22
536	17/3	Southwell P'	(L)	LAD	3m	9	GS	*hld up, prog 8th, trckd ldr aft, qcknd to ld flat*	1	24
693	30/3	Llanvapley	(L)	LAD	3m	6	GS	*mostly 3rd, clsd 3 out, unable qckn frm nxt*	3	20
853	6/4	Sandon	(L)	LAD	3m	7	GF	*(fav) hld up in rear,cls order 10th,rlld apr last,ld flat,all out*	1	24
1194	21/4	Sandon	(L)	LAD	3m	7	G	*(fav) trckd ldr, ld aft 2 out, slw jmp last, hdd flat*	2	22
1317	28/4	Bitterley	(L)	LAD	3m	2	G	*(Jt fav) trckd ldr, pace qckng whn lft solo 13th*	1	18
1473	11/5	Aspatria	(L)	LAD	3m	7	GF	*(fav) conf rddn, ld 15th, shaken up apr last, rddn out flat*	1	22
1579	19/5	Wolverhampt'	(L)	LAD	3m	9	G	*(fav) hld up, smooth prog to ld 16th, rdn out flat, comf*	1	22

Successful season; tricky ride & well handled; all form L/H; should win more in 97; G/S-G/F 24

OVAC STAR ch.g. 10 Ovac (ITY) - Cora's Pryde by Pry — S M Shefras

1995 P(0),4(0),P(0),P(0),2(16),U(-),1(0),2(18),3(15)

676	30/3	Cottenham	(R)	INT	3m	13	GF	*chsd ldrs, effrt 13th, wknd 16th, no ch whn p.u. 2 out*	P	0
903	6/4	Dingley	(R)	LAD	3m	7	GS	*cls up 3rd/4th til outpcd 6 out*	5	0
1259	27/4	Cottenham	(R)	LAD	3m	5	F	*mid-div, prog 12th, outpcd 14th, styd on 2 out, tk 2nd flat*	2	19
1595	25/5	Garthorpe	(R)	CON	3m	15	G	*alwys rear hlf, outpcd 6 out, p.u. 3 out*	P	0

Can run well but needs easy 3m & Firm; R/H best; Members best hope if conditions right 97 15

OVER DECENT (Irish) — I 12^{F}, I 41^{P}, I 85^{P}, I 150^{F}

OVER IN MCGANNS (Irish) — I 125^{3}, I 156^{P}, I 367^{F}, I 554^{3}

OVERSTEP ch.g. 10 Over The River (FR) - Madam Exbury by Homeric — R Douglas

1995 P(0),3(13)

322	2/3	Corbridge	(R)	MDN	3m	10	GS	*alwys prom, ld 7th, ran on wll frm 3 out*	1	14
501	16/3	Lanark	(R)	RES	3m	12	G	*sn bhnd, p.u. 13th*	P	0

Lightly raced; won weak Maiden (slow time); finished early; more needs for Restricted hopes 14

OVER THE BARROW (Irish) — I 228^{P}, I 388^{F}, I 420^{6}, I 516^{P}, I 527^{6}

OVER THE CLOVER(IRE) ch.m. 6 Over The River (FR) - Clover Doubloon by Tudor Treasure — M E T Davies

1995 P(0)

455	9/3	Charing	(L)	MDN	3m	10	G	*twrds rear, lost ground 7th, t.o. & p.u. 10th*	P	0
576	17/3	Detling	(L)	MDN	3m	18	GF	*rear, p.u. 10th*	P	0
781	31/3	Penshurst	(L)	MDN	3m	11	GS	*(10s-9/2),prom,rddn final ctt,lft 3rd 14th,kpt on,2nd 2 out*	2	10
1055	13/4	Penshurst	(L)	MDO	3m	11	G	*(bl) alwys rear, p.u. 12th*	P	0

Beaten in bad race when punted; blinkers no help next time; well bred but may not recover the losses 10

OVER THE EDGE ch.g. 10 Over The River (FR) - Banish Misfortune by Master Owen — Christopher Sporborg

1995 1(24),P(0),**P(NH)**

1	13/1	Larkhill	(R)	XX	3m	7	GS	*ld 4-5th, chsd ldr, disp 15th til ld 2 out, hdd post*	2	24
94	11/2	Ampton	(R)	OPE	3m	8	GF	*(Jt fav) j.w. made virt all, shkn up & drew clr 2 out, comf*	1	23
373	8/3	Sandown	(R)	HC	3m 110yds	4	G	*pressed ldr, ld 15th, narrow ld when left clr 18th, driven and held on well run-in.*	1	23
672	29/3	Aintree	(L)	HC	2 3/4m	26	G	*jmpd slowly rear, struggling hfwy, t.o. 6 out.*	11	11
1067	13/4	Horseheath	(R)	OPE	3m	3	F	*(fav) ld/disp, hit 12th, ld 3 out, clr nxt rddn out*	1	24
1323	28/4	Fakenham P-'	(L)	OPE	3m	8	G	*(fav) ld to 4th, prom til 5th & rdn 13th, no dang aft*	6	13
1400	6/5	Northaw	(L)	OPE	3m	6	F	*ld to 11th, ld agn 14th, hld on gamely und press flat*	1	23
1539	16/5	Folkestone	(R)	HC	3m 7f	9	G	*ld till after 1st, chsd ldr, led 11th to 15th, led 2 out, rdn, styd on well.*	1	22

Much revived 96; showed ability & resolution; stays well; should win Opens, at least, 97; G-F 25

OVER THE LAKE(IRE) ch.m. 7 Over The River (FR) - Castle Lake by Orchardist — D W Ratcliff

1995 P(0),P(0),U(-),P(0)

1357	4/5	Flete Park	(R)	MEM	3m	3	G	*chsd wnr, lost tch 15th, onepcd*	2	0

Of no account 0

OVER THE MAINE (Irish) — I 17^{F}, I 92^{4}, I 171^{3}, I 218^{1}, I 412^{P}

OVER THE TAVERN (Irish) — I 348^{P}

OVER THE WALL (Irish) — **I** 19^{1}, **I** 82^{P}, **I** 141^{P}

OVER THE WAY (Irish) — **I** 173^{1}, **I** 284^{2}

OWD HENRY b.g. 13 Rymer - Jo-Marie by Master Buck — Mrs F Macfarlane

622	23/3	Higham	(L)	CON	3m	10	GF	*alwys prom, disp 4th, mstk & f 7th*	F	-
677	30/3	Cottenham	(R)	OPE	3m	11	GF	*prog & prom 10th, wknd 16th, no ch whn p.u. 2 out*	P	0
831	6/4	Marks Tey	(L)	CON	3m	6	G	*cls up, 2nd 12th, ld aft 15th-17th, btn 3rd whn f last*	F	-
1148	20/4	Higham	(L)	CON	3m	5	F	*trckd ldrs, 3rd & outpcd 16th, btn whn p.u. 2 out, lame*	P	0

Won 3 in 93; missed 95; needs Firm but problem on it last start & could be finished now 12

OWER FARM b.m. 7 Coronash - Royal Tudor by Tudor Treasure — Mrs J E Purdie

1995 F(-),P(0),P(0)

143	17/2	Larkhill	(R)	MDO	3m	14	G	*mid-div whn b.d. 5th*	B	-
206	24/2	Castle Of C'	(R)	MDO	3m	10	HY	*cls up, ld 4 out, ran on frm 2 out*	1	13
562	17/3	Ottery St M'	(L)	XX	3m	12	G	*cls 2nd til u.r. 10th*	U	-
656	23/3	Badbury Rin'	(L)	RES	3m	11	G	*sn in rr, t.o. 11th*	9	0
1128	20/4	Stafford Cr'	(R)	RES	3m	17	S	*prom early, lsng tch whn ref 13th*	R	-
1527	12/5	Ottery St M'	(L)	RES	3m	8	GF	*n.j.w. in tch til 14th, bhnd whn ref 16th*	R	-

Slogged home in 2 finisher race; fell to pieces after; can only be watched 10

OWNING (Irish) — **I** 5^{3}, **I** 57^{2}

OZIER HILL (Irish) — **I** 28^{1}

PABELO (Irish) — **I** 470^{U}, **I** 500^{2}

PABLOWMORE b.g. 6 Pablond - Carrowmore by Crozier — R W Green

114	17/2	Lanark	(R)	MDO	3m	12	GS	*wll bhnd 8th, gd prog 4 out, went 2nd flat*	2	11
407	9/3	Dalston	(R)	MDO	2 1/2m	13	G	*mid-div, gd hdwy 10th, lft 2nd at 14th, no ex appr last*	2	12
755	31/3	Lockerbie	(R)	MDN	3m	17	G	*towrds rear til hdwy frm 14th, no ext run in*	3	14

Knocking on the door & beaten less than 3l last start; should find an opening if ready in 97 14

PABREY gr.g. 10 Pablond - Grey Receipt by Rugantino — S L Mitchell

1995 2(16),1(15),5(0),3(17),1(16),1(0)

657	23/3	Badbury Rin'	(L)	INT	3m	3	G	*ld/disp untl 16th, wknd next, no ch with 1st 2*	3	14
816	6/4	Charlton Ho'	(L)	INT	3m	7	GF	*in tch to 12th, rddn nxt, outpcd frm 4 out*	7	0

Won 3 in 95; last in hot races 96; will struggle to win at 11; G/S-F 14

PACIFIC SOUND b.g. 13 Palm Track - Pacific Dream by Meldrum — Mrs C E Van Praagh

1995 **12(NH)**

450	9/3	Charing	(L)	XX	3m	8	G	*cls up, 3rd at 12th, wknd 15th, p.u. 2 out*	P	0
813	6/4	Charing	(L)	XX	3m	5	F	*ld to 2nd, disp 3-10th, 3rd frm 12th, rmndrs nxt,wknd 2 out*	3	0
1052	13/4	Penshurst	(L)	OPE	3m	7	G	*in tch to 13th, fdd*	4	0

Well beaten on both completions & no prospects now 0

PACO'S BOY b.g. 11 Good Thyne (USA) - Jeremique by Sunny Way — R H York

1995 P(0),P(0),1(11),1(16),1(16),4(16)

18	14/1	Tweseldown	(R)	MXO	3m	6	GS	*alwys last, t.o. 8th, btn 2f*	3	0
125	17/2	Kingston Bl'	(L)	OPE	3m	10	GS	*wth ldr to 5th, sn lost plc, t.o. 13th, btn a fence*	3	0
260	1/3	Newbury	(L)	HC	3m	6	GS	*hit 2nd, in tch, chasing ldrs 12th, mstk 13th and soon wknd, t.o..*	4	11
480	11/3	Plumpton	(L)	HC	3m 1f 110yds	6	GS	*hdwy 11th, ev ch after, one pace from 3 out.*	3	19
595	23/3	Parham	(R)	OPE	3m	12	GS	*in tch, nvr on terms, styd on well apr last*	3	18
798	3/4	Ascot	(R)	HC	2m 3f 110yds	10	GF	*bhnd, mstk 7th, cld 11th, soon lost tch, t.o..*	6	15
1108	17/4	Cheltenham	(L)	HC	4m 1f	14	GS	*well bhnd from 18th, t.o..*	6	10
1370	4/5	Peper Harow	(L)	MEM	3m	3	F	*(fav) made most to 13th, rdn appr 3 out, no resp*	2	10
1463	10/5	Stratford	(L)	HC	3m	6	GF	*(bl) in tch till wknd apr 5 out.*	5	11

Won 3 poor races 95; out of his depth 96 & no chance in H/Chases; little chance at 12; R/H 13

PACTOLUS(USA) b.g. 13 Lydian (FR) - Honey Sand (USA) by Windy Sands — Lease Terminated

481	11/3	Taunton	(R)	HC	3m	11	G	*blnd 3rd, alwys bhnd, t.o. when tried to refuse 5th, soon p.u..*	P	0
708	30/3	Barbury Cas'	(L)	LAD	3m	10	G	*bhnd, t.o. 11th, p.u. 3 out*	P	0
1078	13/4	Cothelstone	(L)	MXO	3m	6	GF	*tried to ref & u.r. 1st*	U	-
1111	17/4	Hockworthy	(L)	MXO	3m	13	GS	*reluct to race, bhnd & nrly ref 7th, t.o. & f 9th*	F	-

An old character who has reached the end of the road 0

PADDY HAYTON br.g. 15 St Paddy - Natenka by Native Prince — S J Leadbetter

86	11/2	Alnwick	(L)	OPE	3m	8	GS	*bhnd frm 6th, t.o. & p.u. 12th*	P	0
186	24/2	Friars Haugh	(L)	MEM	3m	7	S	*ld til 8th, grad lost tch*	6	0
317	2/3	Corbridge	(R)	CON	3m	11	GS	*alwys bhnd, schoolmaster*	7	0
498	16/3	Lanark	(R)	CON	3m	10	G	*alwys wll bhnd*	6	0
610	23/3	Friars Haugh	(L)	CON	3m	11	G	*sn bhnd.*	7	0

Good winner in his day but well past it now 0

PADDY IN PARIS ch.g. 13 Paddy's Stream - Wrekin Rose by Master Owen J L Needham
1995 **3(NH),1(NH),P(NH),P(NH),P(NH),P(NH)**

214 24/2 Newtown (L) CON 3m 21 GS *rear, lost tch & p.u. 13th* P 0
425 9/3 Upton-On-Se' (R) MEM 3m 7 GS *wth ldrs til wknd 15th* 3 0

Winning chaser 95 but brief season when schoolmaster in 96 0

PADRIGAL ch.m. 13 Paddy's Stream - Peaceful Madrigal by Blue Cliff J N Cheatle

395 9/3 Garthorpe (R) OPE 3m 7 G *mid-div, 4th & outpcd at 11th, ran on well last m* 2 13
725 31/3 Garthorpe (R) OPE 3m 9 G *ld to 5th, wknd rpdly 12th, t.o.* 8 0
1099 14/4 Guilsborough (L) LAD 3m 9 G *bhnd frm 8th, t.o. & p.u. 16th* P 0

H/Chase winner 93; missed 95; uninspired revival 0

PAID ELATION m. 11 Pia Fort - Dellation J H Wingfield Digby

482 13/3 Newton Abbot (L) HC 2m 5f 110yds 14 S *alwys bhnd, t.o. when p.u. before 10th.* P 0
733 31/3 Little Wind' (R) MDO 3m 13 GS *rear til p.u. apr 2 out* P 0
821 6/4 Charlton Ho' (L) MDN 3m 10 GF *cls up early, rear frm 9th, outpcd* 6 0
1164 20/4 Larkhill (R) MDN 3m 12 GF *prom, ld 7th til c.o. by loose horse 9th* C -
1453 7/5 Wincanton (R) HC 2m 5f 9 F *mstks, t.o. from 12th.* 7 0
1555 18/5 Bratton Down (L) MDO 3m 13 F *ld to 9th, lost ground steadily frm 14th, no ch* 8 0

Lightly raced until 96 & last on all 3 completions 0

PAKENHAM b.g. 10 Deep Run - Hazy Dawn by Official J G Nicholson
1995 P(0),1(12),1(19),1(21)

178 18/2 Horseheath (R) INT 3m 11 G *cls up,ld 11-13th & 15th, 1l up whn blnd & u.r. last* U 24
244 25/2 Southwell P' (L) CON 3m 13 HO *(fav) hld up,prog 8th,chsd wnr 4 out,kpt on,nvr able to chal* 2 23
393 9/3 Garthorpe (R) CON 3m 7 G *(fav) rear hlf whn s.u. apr 5th, dead* S -

Dead 24

PALACE KING(IRE) ch.g. 7 Great Eastern - Fancy Girl by Mon Capitaine Mrs P Strawbridge
1995 P(0),P(0),1(0)

280 2/3 Clyst St Ma' (L) RES 3m 11 S *sn bhnd, t.o. & p.u. 12th* P 0
445 9/3 Haldon (R) RES 3m 9 S *rear til p.u. 14th* P 0
656 23/3 Badbury Rin' (L) RES 3m 11 G *sn bhnd, t.o. 11th, p.u. 14th* P 0
992 8/4 Kingston St' (R) RES 3m 6 F *in tch til lost plc 15th, t.o.* 5 0
1114 17/4 Hockworthy (L) RES 3m 4 GS *mstks 4th & 6th, in tch to 10th, p.u. aft nxt* P 0
1392 6/5 Cotley Farm (L) MEM 3m 5 GF *chsd ldr, prog 10th, disp nxt til outpcd app last, rlld flat* 2 18
1497 11/5 Holnicote (L) RES 3m 10 G *just in tch 13th, outpcd frm 15th* 6 0
1634 1/6 Bratton Down (L) INT 3m 15 G *mstk 1st, prssd wnr til wknd & mstk 14th, no ch aft* 8 0

Fortunate Members winner 95; one good run 96 (same race) & again looks only hope 97 12

PALAMAN br.g. 9 Mandalus - Pallas Breeze by Shackleton C D Aikenhead
1995 P(0),4(0),3(0),4(0),1(11)

140 17/2 Larkhill (R) CON 3m 17 G *sn bhnd, p.u. 13th* P 0
272 2/3 Parham (R) RES 3m 13 GF *alwys rear* 5 0
478 10/3 Tweseldown (R) RES 3m 9 G *mostly 2nd to 12th, 4th & lkd btn whn u.r. 3 out* U -
593 23/3 Parham (R) RES 3m 11 GS *rear, mstk 3rd, lost tch whn p.u. aft 13th* P 0
1189 21/4 Tweseldown (R) RES 3m 10 GF *ld to 2nd, chsd ldr til mstk 12th, wknd rpdly, p.u. 2 out* P 0
1404 6/5 Hackwood Pa' (L) MEM 3m 2 F *(fav) disp ld til lft alone 10th* 1 0

Won 2 dire contests 95/6; does not stay & no chance in competitive races 10

PALLINGHAM STAR(IRE) b.g. 6 Le Bavard (FR) - Biddy Spatters by Raise You Ten Mrs Carrie Zetter-Wells
1995 P(0)

252 25/2 Charing (L) INT 3m 7 GS *out of tch hlfwy, 4th frm 14th, kpt on, tk 3rd apr last* 3 10
275 2/3 Parham (R) MDN 3m 15 GF *rear, steady prog fnl cct, 2nd aft 3 out, not pace to chal* 2 13
576 17/3 Detling (L) MDN 3m 18 GF *(fav) mid-div, nvr trbld ldrs, styd on* 3 0
597 23/3 Parham (R) MDO 3m 9 GS *2nd, clsd on clr ldr 9th, ld & lft clr 14th, hdd last,tired* 2 11
1228 27/4 Worcester (L) HC 2m 7f 17 G *alwys bhnd, t.o..* 10 0
1374 4/5 Peper Harow (L) MDO 3m 8 F *(fav) chsd ldrs, disp ld 13th, ld 15th-2 out, onepcd und press* 2 12
1540 16/5 Folkestone (R) HC 2m 5f 10 G *bhnd and rdn 8th, t.o. from 3 out.* 7 0
1610 26/5 Tweseldown (R) MDO 3m 5 G *ld to 3rd,rdn & outpcd 12th,ran on to ld & mstk last,drvnout* 1 11

Desperately onepaced; beat non-stayer in 2 finisher race & much more needed for another chance 12

PALMA D'OR (Irish) — I 23P

PALM READER b.g. 12 Palm Track - Carbia by Escart III Lord Mostyn

158 17/2 Weston Park (L) MEM 3m 11 G *chsng grp, no ext frm 3 out* 5 0
1577 19/5 Wolverhampt' (L) CON 3m 6 G *hld up, prog to mod 3rd 14th, no real hdwy nxt, tk 2nd last* 2 15

Ran passably after 3 month gap but no real prospects at 13 12

PALMROCK QUEEN (Irish) — **I** 233^{P}

PALMURA (Irish) — **I** 17^{P}, **I** 28^{4}, **I** 82^{P}, **I** 392^{1}, **I** 480^{P}, **I** 496^{6}, **I** 626^{4}

PAMELA'S LAD ch.g. 10 Dalsaan - La Margarite by Bonne Noel — M A Lloyd

1995 9(0),5(21),F(-),P(0),P(0),**2(14)**,**2(19)**,**5(NH)**

27	20/1	Barbury Cas'	(L)	LAD	3m	15	GS	*mstk 6th, rear, prog 10th, lft 2nd aft 2 out, onepcd*	3	19
160	17/2	Weston Park	(L)	OPE	3m	16	G	*mid-div, prog to chal 4 out, no ext frm nxt*	4	16
361	5/3	Leicester	(R)	HC	2 1/2m 110yds	15	GS	*held up, smooth prog to ld 3 out, rdn last, ct cl home.*	2	21
579	20/3	Ludlow	(R)	HC	2 1/2m	17	G	*held up, hdwy 10th, 3rd when f 4 out.*	F	-
878	6/4	Brampton Br'	(R)	OPE	3m	5	GF	*(fav) hld up, prog 14th, chsd wnr nxt, nvr on terms*	2	16
1456	8/5	Uttoxeter	(L)	HC	2m 5f	11	G	*bhnd, prog 9th, 3rd and rdn apr last, one pace.*	3	18
1620	27/5	Chaddesley '	(L)	XX	3m	8	GF	*w.w. prog 12th, jnd wnr 15th, not qckn 3 out*	3	16

Has ability but lost last 17; placed in 4 H/Chases 95/6 & sub 3m event offers best hope in 97 19

PAMPERED SOCIETY (Irish) — **I** 132^{F}, **I** 164^{P}

PANDANDY b.g. 5 Pitpan - Platinum Blond by Warpath — Mrs J Provan

1088	14/4	Friars Haugh	(L)	MDO	3m	10	F	*sn bhnd, p.u. aft 7th*	P	0
1254	27/4	Balcormo Ma'	(R)	MDO	3m	14	GS	*bhnd whn p.u. aft 12th*	P	0
1355	4/5	Mosshouses	(L)	MDO	3m	10	GS	*mstks 7 & 8th & lost tch, t.o. & p.u. aft 11th*	P	0

No signs of ability 0

PANDA NOVA (Irish) — **I** 260^{P}, **I** 318^{P}, **I** 407^{3}, **I** 451^{2}, **I** 493^{4}, **I** 538^{3}

PANDA SHANDY b.m. 8 Nearly A Hand - Panda Pops by Cornuto — Mrs R H Woodhouse

1995 F(-),1(17),1(19),F(-),1(20)

657	23/3	Badbury Rin'	(L)	INT	3m	3	G	*rstrnd in last, prog to ld 4 out, qckn clr*	1	21
793	2/4	Heythrop	(R)	OPE	4m	10	F	*(fav) hld up,prog to disp whn blnd 18th,nt rcvr,no ch whn p.u.flat*	P	0
1188	21/4	Tweseldown	(R)	OPE	3m	6	GF	*(fav) ld to 3rd & 13th-aft 2 out, all out to ld agn nr fin*	1	21

Won 3 in 95; remains promising; wrong choice of races 96; worth try in H/Chases; Good 24

PANTARA PRINCE(IRE) b.g. 7 Ovac (ITY) - Clara Girl by Fine Blade (USA) — David Carr

110	17/2	Lanark	(R)	CON	3m	10	GS	*alwys prom, no ext frm 3 out*	3	15
319	2/3	Corbridge	(R)	RES	3m	16	GS	*trckd ldrs, prog 15th, rdn 2 out, 2nd at last, no ext flat*	2	17

Irish Maiden winner 95; split H/Chase winners when 2nd & should win Restricted if fit 97; G/S 17

PANTO LADY br.m. 10 Lepanto (GER) - Dusky Damsel by Sahib — Mrs K M Lamb

1995 P(0),P(0),5(0),P(0),P(0),6(0),P(0),1(11),7(0),4(10),**8(NH)**,**4(NH)**,**5(NH)**,**5(NH)**,**5(NH)**,**5(NH)**

189	24/2	Friars Haugh	(L)	RES	3m	9	S	*sn bhnd, p.u. 4 out*	P	0
400	9/3	Dalston	(R)	LAD	3m	10	G	*last frm 2nd, blndrd & u.r. 15th*	U	-
486	16/3	Newcastle	(L)	HC	3m	9	GS	*held up in tch, hdwy 8th, struggling 13th, t.o..*	9	0
789	1/4	Kelso	(L)	HC	3m 1f	11	GF	*soon struggling, t.o..*	5	0
857	6/4	Alnwick	(L)	MEM	3m	4	GF	*soon last, t.o. whn p.u. 3 out*	P	0
1461	9/5	Sedgefield	(L)	HC	2m 5f	10	F	*bhnd from 10th, n.d..*	7	0

Won a poor Maiden in 95 & totally out of her depth in 96; no real prospects now 0

PAPER DAYS b.g. 6 Teenoso (USA) - April Days by Silly Season — Michael Kent

1995 1(20),2(18),2(20),P(0)

139	17/2	Larkhill	(R)	CON	3m	11	G	*mid-div, wknd frm 13th, p.u. last*	P	0
262	2/3	Didmarton	(L)	MEM	3m	11	G	*mstk 1st, trckd ldrs, effrt 13th, clsd apr last, onepcd flat*	3	20
377	9/3	Barbury Cas'	(L)	OPE	3m	5	GS	*j.w. alwys prssng wnr, no ext apr last*	2	23
1332	1/5	Cheltenham	(L)	HC	3m 1f 110yds	11	G	*bhnd and blnd 6th, nvr on terms after, t.o..*	4	10
1533	14/5	Chepstow	(L)	HC	3m	6	F	*trckd ldrs, disp ld apr 8th, lost pl 11th, rallied 3 out, kept on.*	3	18
1547	18/5	Fakenham	(L)	HC	2m 5f 110yds	11	G	*held up in mid div when blnd and u.r. 9th.*	U	-

Confined winner 95; quite able but lost last 9; below best H/Chases; likes Barbury; G/S-F 21

PAPER FAIR b.m. 11 Paper Cap - Trefair by Graig Hill Master — W C D James

690	30/3	Llanvapley	(L)	MEM	3m	4	GS	*ld to 11th, cls up til wknd rpdly 15th, p.u. nxt*	P	0
1038	13/4	St Hilary	(R)	RES	3m	15	G	*rear, no ch 15th, lft 3rd by dfctns*	3	0
1160	20/4	Llanwit Maj'	(R)	RES	3m	12	GS	*mid-div til outpcd 12th, t.o. & p.u. last*	P	0

Lightly raced & no form since Members win 92 0

PARADISE ROW(IRE) b.g. 6 Gunner B - Great Aunt Emily by Traditionalist (USA) — Mrs J A Youdan

1995 **6(NH)**,**9(NH)**,**5(NH)**,**2(NH)**,**3(NH)**

540	17/3	Southwell P'	(L)	MDO	3m	9	GS	*ld to 7th, in tch, 2nd 2 out, ran on onepcd*	2	13
727	31/3	Garthorpe	(R)	MDO	3m	12	G	*chsd ldr til apr 3 out, styd on to tk 2nd agn flat*	2	12
1027	13/4	Brocklesby '	(L)	MDN	3m	7	GF	*(fav) ld to 3 out, wknd whn hdd frm nxt*	3	11

Placed hurdles 95; ran well twice but beaten in very poor race after; may disappoint 14

PARAHANDY (Irish) — I 110[1], I 194[2], I 220[3], I 264[1]

PAR-BAR(IRE) gr.m. 8 The Parson - Baranee by My Swanee — Mrs Judy Wilson

1995 P(0),10(0),5(10),U(-),P(0)

24	20/1	Barbury Cas'	(L)	XX	3m	12	GS	*bhnd frm 8th, t.o. & p.u. 2 out*	P	0
95	11/2	Ampton	(R)	RES	3m	11	GF	*not fluent, last frm 6th, t.o. & p.u. 15th*	P	0

Good stable but shows no inclination & not worth persevering with 0

PARDITINO b.g. 8 Pardigras - Happy Tino by Rugantino — Mrs K R J Nicholas

1995 P(0),1(13),5(0),2(12),P(0)

28	20/1	Barbury Cas'	(L)	RES	3m	14	GS	*rear til u.r. 8th*	U	-
281	2/3	Clyst St Ma'	(L)	RES	3m	11	S	*unruly paddock, alwys mid-div, ran on frm 3 out, nrst fin*	3	12

Maiden winner 95; brief season 96 & signs not good; improvement needed for Restricteds; Soft 13

PARDON ME MUM ch.g. 11 The Parson - Please Mum by Kabale — Dr D B A Silk

1995 **6(NH)**,**6(NH)**

57	10/2	Cottenham	(R)	LAD	3m	9	GS	*(fav) (bl) hmpd & u.r. 1st*	U	-
347	3/3	Higham	(L)	LAD	3m	10	G	*ld to 2nd, trckd ldrs, chal 2 out, ld last, ran on well*	1	20
572	17/3	Detling	(L)	LAD	3m	10	GF	*(fav) hld up,smth prog to 2nd 13th,ld 15th,drew clr apr last,easy*	1	21
777	31/3	Penshurst	(L)	LAD	3m	7	GS	*(fav) sn cls up, chal 3 out, 3rd & btn nxt*	3	20
1147	20/4	Higham	(L)	LAD	3m	9	F	*(fav) w.w. prog to 3rd at 11th, mstk 15th, no prog frm nxt*	4	20

Chase winner 93; looked good when winning but failed to maintain; best easy 3m; win at 12; Good 20

PARISH RANGER (Irish) — I 9[U], I 52[P], I 73[6], I 207[1]

PARIS OF TROY b.h. 8 Trojan Fen - Little Loch Broom by Reform — H W Wheeler

429	9/3	Upton-On-Se'	(R)	LAD	3m	4	GS	*ld to 15th, 20l 2nd whn p.u. 2 out, sore*	P	0

Unbeaten in 3 hurdles autumn 92; unraced after till 96; problems again, unfortunately 15

PARKBHRIDE b.g. 10 Wolver Hollow - Gulistan by Sharpen Up — H J Jarvis

1995 6(0),5(0),1(0),2(18),2(18),2(16),2(17),2(19),7(12),3(0)

490	16/3	Horseheath	(R)	XX	3m	7	GF	*rear of main grp, mstk 9th, und pres whn f heavily 12th*	F	-
619	23/3	Higham	(L)	OPE	3m	10	GF	*mid-div,prog to 2nd 9th, und pres 12th, wknd 14th, p.u.2 out*	P	0
1209	21/4	Heathfield	(R)	OPE	3m	5	F	*wll in tch, blnd 9th, last & btn 13th, p.u. 4 out*	P	0
1296	28/4	Bexhill	(R)	OPE	3m	4	F	*trckd ldrs, 4th & btn 14th, p.u. 4 out*	P	0

Has travelled all over the place in his time but looks to have reached the end of his journey now 0

PARK DRIFT ch.g. 10 Say Primula - Kerera by Keren — G Thornton

1995 3(12),4(16),2(19),1(20),3(20),1(20),**3(18)**

170	18/2	Market Rase'	(L)	XX	3m	8	GF	*w.w. prog to 3rd going wl 10th,hit 12th,btn & eased apr last*	5	17
513	16/3	Dalton Park	(R)	OPE	3m	9	G	*w.w. went 3rd & outpcd 14th, ran on to chs wnr 2 out,no imp*	2	21
1024	13/4	Brocklesby '	(L)	OPE	3m	6	GF	*w.w., prog 6 out, ld nxt, ran on strgly last m*	1	25
1133	20/4	Hornby Cast'	(L)	OPE	3m	14	G	*prom, prog to jn ldr 11th, hdd 13th, onepcd frm 3 out*	3	22
1282	27/4	Easingwold	(L)	OPE	3m	8	G	*keen hold,alwys prom,ld 10th-12th,ld 14th,clr 2 out,easily*	1	23
1448	6/5	Witton Cast'	(R)	OPE	3m	5	G	*cls up in 3rd,outpcd 14th,styd on wll 3 out,ld nxt,ran on wl*	1	24
1467	11/5	Easingwold	(L)	OPE	3m	6	G	*(fav) prom, lft 2nd apr 7th, disp 14th, ld nxt, sn clr, eased flat*	1	24
1548	18/5	Southwell	(L)	HC	3m 110yds	11	GF	*(fav) nvr going well, alwys rear, p.u. 4 out.*	P	0

Useful; won 6 of last 12; easy 3m best; likes Easingwold; needs a run; no show H/Chases; G/S-F 23

PARK DUKE (Irish) — I 13[P], I 56[F], I 79[P], I 117[P], I 156[P], I 267[5], I 389[P], I 445[P], I 615[P]

PARKERS HILLS(IRE) b.g. 7 Mister Lord (USA) - Annies Pet by Normandy — Christopher Sporborg

1995 5(0),P(0),5(0),P(0)

12	14/1	Cottenham	(R)	RES	3m	12	G	*ld 1st, sn hdd, prom til no prog frm 15th*	6	10
106	17/2	Marks Tey	(L)	RES	3m	12	G	*rr div, last & rmdrs 11th, no resp, p.u. 17th*	P	0
313	2/3	Ampton	(R)	RES	3m	9	G	*1st ride, disp ld to 4th, grad lst pl, t.o. frm 16th*	6	0
494	16/3	Horseheath	(R)	RES	3m	10	GF	*prom, rdn 4 out, btn 2nd whn lft clr 2 out, all out*	1	17
831	6/4	Marks Tey	(L)	CON	3m	6	G	*ld to 15th, wknd steadily, bhnd 3 out*	4	16
1068	13/4	Horseheath	(R)	INT	3m	7	F	*prom, hit 6th, lst pl & bhnd 8th,rdn & no resp 12th,p.u 14th*	P	0
1399	6/5	Northaw	(L)	CON	3m	8	F	*ld to 2nd, lst pl appr 8th, t.o frm 15th*	7	0

Lucky winner; disappointing & looks disinterested; both wins Horeseheath; Confined unlikely 13

PARKINSON'S LAW b.g. 8 Idiot's Delight - Morgan's Money by David Jack — P R Whiston

1995 P(0),P(0)

569	17/3	Wolverhampt'	(L)	MDN	3m	11	GS	*alwys rear, p.u. 14th*	P	0
1227	26/4	Ludlow	(R)	HC	2 1/2m	16	G	*mid div, lost pl hfwy, t.o. when p.u. before 3 out.*	P	0

Yet to complete the course 0

PARK SERENADE (Irish) — I 572[P]

PARK SLAVE b.g. 14 Park Row - Cool Date by Arctic Slave — Mrs V S Jackson

698	30/3	Tranwell	(L)	MEM	3m	5	GS	*ld, jnd 15th, hdd & onpcd und pres 2 out*	2	0

Only seen in Members now & a win at 15 beyond him 11

PARKS PRIDE b.m. 5 Hubbly Bubbly (USA) - Valentine Song by Pas de Seul — R Evans

1995 **P(NH)**

147	17/2	Erw Lon	(L)	MDN	3m	8 G	*ld to 13th, wknd, f 15th*	F	-
550	17/3	Erw Lon	(L)	MDN	3m	13 GS	*alwys rear, p.u. 9th*	P	0
1045	13/4	Bitterley	(L)	MDO	3m	16 G	*nvr rchd ldrs, wknd frm 13th*	9	0
1200	21/4	Lydstep	(L)	MDN	3m	10 S	*5th whn f 10th*	F	-
1390	6/5	Pantyderi	(R)	MDO	3m	15 GF	*sttld rear,prog 9th,mstk nxt,ld aft 2 out,sn hdd & no ext*	2	13
1561	18/5	Bassaleg	(R)	MDO	3m	8 F	*not fluent, cls up, mstk 12th, 4th & btn whn f nxt*	F	-

Beat 5 others when 2nd but non-stayer so far; may improve & go close in 97 13

PARLEBIZ b.m. 7 Parliament - That's Show Biz by The Parson — A J Wight

1995 4(10),5(0),6(0),P(0)

89	11/2	Alnwick	(L)	MDO	3m	9 GS	*mstks, prom frm 5th, chsd ldr 3 out, ev ch whn lft clr nxt*	1	14
186	24/2	Friars Haugh	(L)	MEM	3m	7 S	*wll in tch til outpcd frm 2 out*	3	12
371	8/3	Ayr	(L)	HC	2m 5f 110yds	8 GF	*bhnd, lost tch after 12th, hdwy after 2 out, styd on well und pres to ld final 30 yards.*	1	15
582	22/3	Kelso	(L)	HC	3 1/2m	8 G	*held up, blnd 2nd, hit 7th, blunded 11th, hdwy 14th, rdn 3 out and one pace.*	3	10
790	1/4	Kelso	(L)	HC	3m 1f	11 GF	*settld off the pace, f 5th.*	F	-

Dead 16

PARLIAMENT HALL gr.g. 10 Piling (USA) - Miss Carribean by Sea Hawk II — S H Shirley-Beavan

1995 **6(NH),U(NH),4(NH),2(NH),F(NH),4(NH),4(NH)**

112	17/2	Lanark	(R)	LAD	3m	8 GS	*made all, drew wll clr apr last*	1	24
400	9/3	Dalston	(R)	LAD	3m	10 G	*(fav) prom, ld 3rd & 8th, md rst tl cght cls hm*	2	21
1120	20/4	Bangor	(L)	HC	2 1/2m 110yds	13 S	*ld, hdd 8th, blnd next, wknd quickly 10th, t.o. when p.u. before 4 out.*	P	0
1449	6/5	Witton Cast'	(R)	LAD	3m	10 G	*sn in rear, t.o. 7th, p.u. 10th*	P	0

Ex-useful winning chaser; started well but went badly amiss; unreliable; may revive early 97; G/S 21

PARMAN (Irish) — **I** 318[P], **I** 451[P]

PARSON FLYNN b.g. 9 Mandalus - Flynn's Field by The Parson — Mrs M J Trickey

1995 2(14),2(16),r(-),6(0)

71	10/2	Great Treth'	(R)	MDO	3m	15 S	*prog frm mid-div 13th, rdn nxt, no imp wnr*	2	14
201	24/2	Lemalla	(R)	MDO	3m	13 HY	*(fav) ld 9th til 3 out, no ext und pres*	2	15
447	9/3	Haldon	(R)	MDO	3m	13 S	*cls 5th hlfwy, just in tch whn slw jmp 14th, btn & p.u. 2out*	P	0
533	16/3	Cothelstone	(L)	MDN	3m	13 G	*prom, ld 12th til f nxt*	F	-
1431	6/5	High Bickin'	(R)	MDO	3m	9 G	*(fav) hdwy 12th, ld 15th, slight ld 2 out, drvn clr*	1	16

Placed 6 times prior to winning modest race; may do better but Restricted win odds against; G-Hy 16

PARSON RIVER (Irish) — **I** 60[2], **I** 64[P]

PARSON'S CORNER b.g. 9 The Parson - Arctic Rhapsody by Bargello — W D Oakes

600	23/3	Howick	(L)	RES	3m	14 S	*alwys rear, p.u. 3 out*	P	0
771	31/3	Pantyderi	(R)	MDN	3m	14 G	*alwys twrds rear*	5	0
976	8/4	Lydstep	(L)	MDO	3m	12 G	*ld til tired & in 2nd last, no ext*	2	0
1040	13/4	St Hilary	(R)	MDN	3m	12 G	*mid-div, cls 4th at 14th, no ext aft*	3	0

Beat subsequent winner when 2nd but well beaten all completions & stamina looks suspect 12

PARSONS FORT (Irish) — **I** 543[F], **I** 579[5]

PARSONS SON b.g. 11 The Parson - Ripperidge by Knotty Pine — Miss Kathryn Guard

1995 P(0),**7(15),U(-)**,3(20),**4(15),P(0)**

160	17/2	Weston Park	(L)	OPE	3m	16 G	*mid to rear, p.u. 14th*	P	0

Disappointing in 95 & breif season 96 could spell the end 11

PARSON'S WAY b.g. 9 The Parson - Daithis Coleen by Carnival Night — Paul C N Heywood

1995 **P(NH),P(NH),7(NH),5(NH),6(NH)**

626	23/3	Kilworthy	(L)	OPE	3m	12 GS	*rear, 8th & rdn aft 10th, sn t.o., rdn rght out*	6	0
1140	20/4	Flete Park	(R)	OPE	4m	6 S	*(bl) ld/disp til wknd 20th, bhnd whn p.u. last*	P	0
1425	6/5	High Bickin'	(R)	OPE	3m	4 G	*(bl) made all, ran on wll und pres whn chal*	1	20
1623	27/5	Lifton	(R)	OPE	3m	5 GS	*(bl) ld til 13th & agn 3 out, hrd rdn & ran on gamely nxt*	1	23

Chase winner 94; looks ungenuine but blinkers worked; well ridden; an enigma; may win again; G-S ... 21

PARTING HOUR b or br.g. 9 Top Ville - Cri de Coeur (USA) by Lyphard (USA) — R Adderson

1995 U(-),4(13)

433	9/3	Newton Brom'	(R)	MEM	3m	3 GS	*(fav) ld/disp til ld aft 12th, sn clr, 3l up whn u.r. 3 out*	U	-
492	16/3	Horseheath	(R)	OPE	3m	3 GF	*alwys last, lost tch 12th, t.o. 4 out*	3	0
743	31/3	Upper Sapey	(R)	LAD	3m	7 GS	*wkng in 5th whn u.r. 2 out*	U	-
886	6/4	Kimble	(L)	CON	3m	5 GF	*j.w. ld 2nd til mstk & hdd last, just hld nr fin*	2	18

Very lightly raced & put up best performance final start; Members 97 if keeping his feet 15

PARTYONJASON (Irish) — I 554^{P}, I 582^{4}, I 628^{P}, I 636^{P}

PASSER-BY (Irish) — I 496^{P}, I 580^{1}, I 657^{P}

PASSING FAIR b.m. 5 Pablond - Joyful's Girl by White Prince (USA) — Mrs C Wilson

470 10/3 Milborne St' (L) MDO 3m 18 G *mid-div, prog 12th, ld 4 out-2 out, outpcd aft* 3 14
820 6/4 Charlton Ho' (L) MDN 3m 12 GF *(Jt fav) held up in midfld, gng wll whn f 11th* F -
1396 6/5 Cotley Farm (L) MDO 3m 11 GF *(fav) hld up, prog to disp 10th, hdd 4 out, no ex aft* 2 12
1626 27/5 Lifton (R) MDO 3m 13 GS *(fav) handy, prog to 2nd 4 out, ev ch til rdn & no ext 2 out* 2 15

Fair form & may have been unlucky to date; should find a Maiden 97 if she has the desire 16

PASS THE BASKET (Irish) — I 11^{P}, I 47^{P}, I 128^{P}, I 354^{P}

PASTORAL PRIDE(USA) b.g. 12 Exceller (USA) - Pastoral Miss by Northfields (USA) — M R Scott

257 29/2 Nottingham (L) HC 2 1/2m 11 G *alwys handy, ld 3rd, clr hfwy, hdd 5 out, fd und pres last 2.* 5 17
579 20/3 Ludlow (R) HC 2 1/2m 17 G *(fav) ld, clr 4 out, f last.* F 22
1336 1/5 Cheltenham (L) HC 2m 110yds 9 G *(fav) raced wd, chsd ldrs, pkd 10th, ev ch 11th, wknd apr 2 out.* 3 21
1532 13/5 Towcester (R) HC 2m 110yds 16 GF *ld 2nd to 3rd, led 4 out till wknd apr 2 out.* 7 15

Nursed back to health & fell with race at mercy 2nd start; fragile & may have lost last chance now 19

PAT ALASKA b.g. 13 Ovac (ITY) - Indicate by Mustang — Miss C Wates

1995 1(12),U(-)

270 2/3 Parham (R) MEM 3m 5 GF *(Jt fav) ld 3rd, disp 9th-nxt, 2nd aft, chal & blnd 3 out, no ext nxt* 2 11
474 10/3 Tweseldown (R) LAD 3m 7 G *u.r. 1st* U -
594 23/3 Parham (R) CON 3m 13 GS *mid-div to hlfwy, wll bhnd whn p.u. 3 out* P 0
1539 16/5 Folkestone (R) HC 3m 7f 9 G *mid div, prog when mstk 15th, outpcd next, styd on from 2 out.* 4 16
1584 24/5 Towcester (R) HC 3m 1f 11 GS *bhnd, lost tch after 12th, t.o. when p.u. before 2 out.* P 0

Ran well at Folkestone but has only won in Members last 4 seasons & will struggle to do so again 97 ... 11

PAT BARRY (Irish) — I 324^{F}, I 501^{S}, I 533^{F}, I 578^{P}

PAT CULLEN b.g. 11 The Parson - Duhallow Hazel — D C White

1995 4(0),1(17),**7(0)**

691 30/3 Llanvapley (L) CON 3m 15 GS *3rd/4th til wknd frm 14th* 3 12
846 6/4 Howick (L) OPE 3m 7 GF *ld to 11th, grad wknd, 3rd frm 15th* 3 15
1211 23/4 Chepstow (L) HC 3m 13 S *prom till wknd 4 out.* 5 12

Confined winner 95; lightly raced; well beaten 96; likes Llanvapley & best chance there 97 16

PATEY COURT gr.m. 5 Grey Desire - Mrs Meyrick by Owen Dudley — D Gill

1995 **11(NH),9(NH)**

763 31/3 Great Stain' (L) MDN 3m 11 GS *mid-div, lost tch 10th, p.u. nxt* P 0
987 8/4 Charm Park (L) MDN 3m 13 GF *rear early, fdd & p.u. 10th* P 0
1285 27/4 Easingwold (L) MDO 3m 9 G *not fluent, rear, t.o. & p.u. aft 10th* P 0
1450 6/5 Witton Cast' (R) MDO 3m 14 G *alwys rear, p.u. 13th* P 0

Yet to show any ability 0

PATS CROSS (Irish) — I 111^{2}, I 180^{1}, I 257^{F}, I 304^{3}, I 405^{U}, I 537,

PAT THE HAT (Irish) — I 4^{P}, I 13^{P}, I 79^{P}, I 118^{P}, I 155^{P}, I 188^{P}, I 358^{F}, I 574^{2}, I 637^{1}

PATTY'S PRIDE (Irish) — I 197^{P}, I 346^{P}, I 447^{P}

PAULS POINT (Irish) — I 288, , I 321^{U}, I 455^{2}, I 495^{U}

PAUPER BOICE (Irish) — I 190^{F}, I 269^{4}, I 531^{P}, I 618^{1}

PAVI'S BROTHER ch.g. 8 Politico (USA) - May Moss by Sea Moss — C J R Sweeting

1995 2(16),1(14),r(-),**2(21),3(16)**

29 20/1 Barbury Cas' (L) RES 3m 12 GS *5s-7/2, trckd ldrs til wknd 13th, t.o. & p.u. 2 out* P 0
269 2/3 Didmarton (L) RES 3m 12 G *8s-5s, ld 3rd til ran off course apr 8th* r -
478 10/3 Tweseldown (R) RES 3m 9 G *(fav) trckd ldrs,blnd 8th,2nd 13th,ev ch til onepcd frm 3 out* 3 10
960 8/4 Lockinge (L) RES 3m 9 GF *sn bhnd, shrt livd efft 14th, outpcd frm 4 out* 6 0
1548 18/5 Southwell (L) HC 3m 110yds 11 GF *hdwy 6th, ld 15th to last, rallied to ld final 25 yards.* 1 19

Maiden winner 95; out of form in Restricteds but found H/Chase; struggle to win again; G-F 20

PAY-U-CASH b.g. 10 Winden - Abbots Delight by Welsh Abbot — W T D Perkins

1995 F(-),P(0),2(0),4(10),3(0),1(13),5(0),1(16)

133 17/2 Ottery St M' (L) OPE 3m 18 GS *prom to 13th, lost tch 4 out* 7 13

Won 2 in 95 but brief appearance 96 & prospects of another win now slight 13

PEACEFULL RIVER (Irish) — I 340^{P}

PEACHY GIRL (Irish) — **I** 572[P], **I** 604[5]

PEAJADE b.g. 12 Buckskin (FR) - Kaminaki by Deep Run — Mrs Janine Hall

1995 3(17),1(22),1(23),1(23),1(23),1(22),2(17),2(20)

245	25/2	Southwell P'	(L)	LAD	3m	8	HO	*(fav) ld to 3rd,wth ldr on innr aft, ld aft 4 out, jnd last,hld on*	1	21
363	5/3	Leicester	(R)	HC	3m	3	GS	*disp ld till ld 6th to 8th, outpcd apr 3 out, regained 2nd and blnd last, one pace.*	2	25
514	16/3	Dalton Park	(R)	LAD	3m	8	G	*(fav) prom, ld apr 15th, hdd 3 out, ld & lft clr 2 out, pshd out*	1	23
1010	9/4	Flagg Moor	(L)	LAD	3m	6	G	*(fav) not alwys fluent, chsd ldr, ev ch 15th, one pace frm 2 out*	2	22
1121	20/4	Bangor	(L)	HC	3m 110yds	8	S	*prom, lost pl 12th, soon und pres and outpcd, kept on to take 2nd apr last, no ch with wnr.*	2	24
1366	4/5	Gisburn	(R)	LAD	3m	12	G	*(fav) chsd ldrs, ld 14th, ran on well, eased flat*	1	24
1459	8/5	Uttoxeter	(L)	HC	4 1/4m	8	G	*with ldr, ld after 5th to 15th, led 20th, clr apr next, hdd 3 out, no ext.*	3	24

Useful Ladies horse; won 8 of last 11 points; thorough stayer; win more at 13; G-S, prefers Soft 23

PEANUTS PET b.g. 11 Tina's Pet - Sinzinbra by Royal Palace — J W Walmsley

1995 **4(NH),3(NH),13(NH)**

9	14/1	Cottenham	(R)	OPE	3m	13	G	*prom, disp ld 10-12th, ev ch til no ext apr last*	2	25
49	4/2	Alnwick	(L)	OPE	3m	14	G	*w.w., prog 11th, blndrd nxt, chsd wnr 2 out, no imp*	2	22
410	9/3	Charm Park	(L)	OPE	3m	17	G	*mid-div, nvr fctr*	10	12
587	23/3	Wetherby Po'	(L)	OPE	3m	15	S	*mid-div, prog 12th, disp 14th-last, ld flat, hdd nr fin*	2	23
1092	14/4	Whitwell-On'	(R)	CON	3m	10	G	*rear, prog 7th, effrt 4 out, rdn & styd on nxt*	2	20
1133	20/4	Hornby Cast'	(L)	OPE	3m	14	G	*alwys cls up, went 2nd apr 3 out, ld nxt, ran on strngly*	1	25
1598	25/5	Garthorpe	(R)	OPE	3m	6	G	*cls up, 3rd 12th-3 out, chsd wnr nxt, no imp*	2	25

Ex-useful hurdler; consistent & deserved win in decent race; should find another Open at 12; G-S 23

PEARL BRIDGE b.g. 8 Loch Pearl - Emralbridge by Precipice Wood — Mrs G D Moore

1995 F(-),C(-),P(0),F(-),5(0)

416	9/3	Charm Park	(L)	MDO	3m	13	G	*cls up, 4th at 8th, mid-div whn u.r. 12th*	U	-
515	16/3	Dalton Park	(R)	XX	3m	12	G	*rear, lost tch 15th, kpt on frm 3 out, nrst fin*	6	14
591	23/3	Wetherby Po'	(L)	MDO	3m	14	S	*mid-div, wkng whn ref 3 out*	R	-
986	8/4	Charm Park	(L)	MDN	3m	10	GF	*bhnd early, onepcd, nvr a factor, p.u. 4 out*	P	0

Ran one passable race but only 2 completions in 9 races 95/6 & winning prospects bleak 11

PEARL DANTE (Irish) — **I** 39[5], **I** 108[P], **I** 430[P], **I** 511[5], **I** 557[1]

PEARL OF ORIENT (Irish) — **I** 109[P], **I** 266[3], **I** 478[P], **I** 583[F]

PEAT POTHEEN b.g. 6 Derring Rose - Sally Potheen — P J Sheppard

2	13/1	Larkhill	(R)	MDO	3m	17	GS	*in tch whn blnd 6th, rear whn u.r. 9th*	U	-
149	17/2	Erw Lon	(L)	MDN	3m	10	G	*mid-div, prog to 2nd brfly 14th, mstk nxt & wknd*	4	0
1225	24/4	Brampton Br'	(R)	MDO	3m	18	G	*ld to 3rd, wth ldrs to 11th, wkng whn hit 14th, p.u. nxt*	P	0

Shows some speed but needs more stamina before any winning chance 10

PEAT STACK gr.g. 7 Petong - Delnadamph by Royal Palace — Joseph Brown

1995 **18(NH),P(NH),13(NH)**

87	11/2	Alnwick	(L)	MDO	3m	7	GS	*chsd ldrs, mstk 9th, wknd, t.o. & p.u. 3 out*	P	0
189	24/2	Friars Haugh	(L)	RES	3m	9	S	*made most til wknd rpdly 4 out*	7	0
405	9/3	Dalston	(R)	MDO	2 1/2m	16	G	*ld 2nd, mstks, prom tl wknd rpdly appr 13th, p.u. & dismnt*	P	0

No stamina & problems last start 0

PEBBLE ROCK b.g. 8 Uncle Pokey - Hejera by Cantab — E G Dilworth

1995 3(11),3D(0),2(13),3(0)

286	2/3	Eaton Hall	(R)	MDO	3m	14	G	*handy, ld 7th-2 out, ran on onepcd*	2	13

Placed all 5 starts 95/6 & beat subsequent winner 96; could win if fit 97 14

PEDLAR'S CROSS (Irish) — **I** 518[P], **I** 612[3]

PEELINICK b.g. 6 Meadowbrook - Jed Again by Cagirama — Mrs R L Elliot

1995 5(0)

194	24/2	Friars Haugh	(L)	MDN	3m	11	S	*(fav) mod 5th whn s.u. aft 13th*	S	-
322	2/3	Corbridge	(R)	MDN	3m	10	GS	*(fav) mstks, nvr going wll*	5	0

Showed a little promise only start 95 but nothing in brief 96 & expensive to follow 0

PEGGYS LEG (Irish) — **I** 30[P], **I** 81[P], **I** 211[P]

PEJAWI br.m. 9 Strong Gale - Beau St by Will Somers — Miss J Winch

1995 5(0),3(0),5(0),4(0)

40	3/2	Wadebridge	(L)	LAD	3m	5	GF	*chsd wnr 2nd-11th, outpcd 12th, kpt on*	4	18
273	2/3	Parham	(R)	LAD	3m	11	GF	*mid-div, prog to chs ldng trio 11th, 3rd & no ch, r.o. last*	r	-
708	30/3	Barbury Cas'	(L)	LAD	3m	10	G	*alwys rear, t.o. & p.u. last*	P	0
995	8/4	Hackwood Pa'	(L)	XX	3m	8	GF	*rear to hlfwy, mstk 15th, ran on*	2	10
1373	4/5	Peper Harow	(L)	LAD	3m	3	F	*blnd & u.r. 1st*	U	-

1407 6/5 Hackwood Pa' (L) XX 3m 5 F *ld to 2nd, cls up, ran on wll* 2 14
1564 19/5 Mollington (R) XX 3m 14 GS *rear, lost tch 12th, kpt on agn frm 14th, no dang* 7 0
1640 2/6 Dingley (R) RES 3m 9 GF *1st ride, rr, no ch whn mstk 14th, kpt on* 5 14

Irish Maiden winner 93; finished 9 of 12 races but no threat in England; Hackwood special best hope .. 13

PEJAYS DUCA (Irish) — **I** 193^{F}, **I** 222^{P}, **I** 322^{F}

PEN-ALISA b.m. 6 Al Amead - Cornish Mona Lisa P Mann

70 10/2 Great Treth' (R) MDO 3m 14 S *wll bhnd whn p.u. aft 7th* P 0
198 24/2 Lemalla (R) OPE 3m 12 HY *t.o. 2nd, p.u. 6th* P 0
294 2/3 Great Treth' (R) CON 3m 10 G *jmpd lft, ld til wd aft 6th, bhnd nxt, p.u. 13th* P 0
555 17/3 Ottery St M' (L) MDO 3m 15 G *mid-div til u.r. 7th* U -
714 30/3 Wadebridge (L) MEM 3m 3 GF *(bl) strgglng in 3rd & reluc thro'out* 3 0

Looks hopeless 0

PENDIL'S DELIGHT b.m. 7 Scorpio (FR) - Pendella by Pendragon Dave Dixon
1995 **0(NH),P(NH),3(NH),9(NH)**

552 17/3 Erw Lon (L) MDN 3m 10 GS *alwys prom, onepcd frm 3 out, improve* 3 12
975 8/4 Lydstep (L) MDO 3m 9 G *sttld mid-div, prog 8th, ld 2 out, easily* 1 14
1203 21/4 Lydstep (L) RES 3m 5 S *(fav) trckd ldr til ld 4 out, in cmmnd aft, unchal* 1 19
1389 6/5 Pantyderi (R) INT 3m 5 GF *(fav) prom, ld aft 15th, hrd rdn 2 out, all out* 1 20

Much improved in points; won modest races; Confined no problem 97 & could win Opens; G-S 21

PENDIL'S JOY b.g. 10 Roscoe Blake - Pendella by Pendragon C Carman

342 3/3 Higham (L) MEM 3m 4 G *(fav) ld 4th, made rest, ran on flat* 1 10
1322 28/4 Fakenham P-' (L) RES 3m 5 G *alwys last, lost tch 5th, t.o.* 4 0

Maiden winner 91; lightly raced & won joke contest 96 11

PENDIL'S PLEASURE b.m. 8 Scorpio (FR) - Pendle Princess by Broxted J R Heatley
1995 2(13),1(15),F(-)

106 17/2 Marks Tey (L) RES 3m 12 G *chsd ldrs, ld 11th clr & hit 2 out, sn rcvd, easy* 1 18

Maiden winner 95; very lightly raced; waltzed home only start 96; could upgrade if fit 97; G-S 19

PENDLE WITCH b.m. 8 Majestic Current (USA) - My Bridget Vii by Damsire Unregistered Miss Carol Richardson

539 17/3 Southwell P' (L) RES 3m 11 GS *lft a fence, t.o. til p.u. 8th* P 0
588 23/3 Wetherby Po' (L) INT 3m 17 S *mstks, t.o. 4th, p.u. 8th* P 0
763 31/3 Great Stain' (L) MDN 3m 11 GS *rear & mstk 5th, t.o. 9th, p.u. 14th* P 0
1090 14/4 Whitwell-On' (R) RES 3m 17 G *mid-div, mstk 3rd, drppd rear 6th, t.o. & p.u. 3 out* P 0
1155 20/4 Whittington (L) MDN 3m 14 G *alwys rear, t.o. 7th, p.u. last* P 0

Cannot jump & shows no aptitude 0

PENLET b.g. 8 Kinglet - Pensun by Jimsun R G Weaving
1995 1(14),4(0),1(16),5(15),3(15),1(18)

124 17/2 Kingston Bl' (L) CON 3m 17 GS *chsd ldrs, clsd 14th, ld nxt, clr 2 out, ran on well* 1 25
434 9/3 Newton Brom' (R) CON 3m 11 GS *(fav) hld up last, prog hlfwy, chsd ldrs 14th, ev ch 2 out, onepcd* 2 16
537 17/3 Southwell P' (L) OPE 3m 7 GS *(fav) hld up, prog to ld 5 out, sn wll clr, unchal* 1 23
686 30/3 Chaddesley ' (L) OPE 3m 6 G *chsd ldr, disp 8-11th, ev ch til onepcd frm 3 out* 3 21
1017 13/4 Kingston Bl' (L) OPE 3m 4 G *trckd ldr, ld 11th, 3l clr whn blnd 3 out, hdd last, onepcd* 2 23
1437 6/5 Ashorne (R) MXO 3m 13 G *(fav) rear, prog 10th, cls 3rd 15th, rdn to chal apr last, styd on* 2 22

Won 3 in 95; improved 96; consistent; won 5 of 12 95/6; win more Opens 97; stays; G/F-S 25

PENLLYNE'S PRIDE ch.g. 15 Tachypous - Fodens Eve by Dike (USA) J S Chilton
1995 F(-),P(0),P(0),P(0),10(0),P(0)

1194 21/4 Sandon (L) LAD 3m 7 G *cls up, p.u. qckly apr 6th* P 0
1219 24/4 Brampton Br' (R) CON 3m 9 G *ld 2nd-10th, wknd 12th, p.u. aft 15th* P 0
1232 27/4 Weston Park (L) LAD 3m 6 G *cls up, ld/disp til bad mstk & u.r. 12th* U -
1418 6/5 Eyton-On-Se' (L) MEM 3m 7 GF *prom, ld 3-7th, cl up & ev ch whn u.r. 12th* U -
1577 19/5 Wolverhampt' (L) CON 3m 6 G *race wd, ld 6-8th, & 10th-apr 3 out, sn btn* 3 14
1618 27/5 Chaddesley ' (L) CON 3m 14 GF *cls up whn u.r. 4th* U -
1643 2/6 Dingley (R) OPE 3m 13 GF *s.s., alwys bhnd, t.o. 9th* 6 0

Only finished 3 of 13 races 95/6 & much too old now 0

PENLY b.g. 6 Netherkelly - Pensun by Jimsun R G Weaving
1995 P(0)

61 10/2 Cottenham (R) MDO 3m 8 GS *out of tch, lft 2nd aft 15th, lft clr 2 out, all out* 1 10
437 9/3 Newton Brom' (R) RES 3m 9 GS *sn prom, ld aft 10th, jnd 12th, outpcd frm 2 out* 7 0
642 23/3 Siddington (L) RES 3m 15 S *chsd ldrs til appr 10th, sn wknd, p.u. 13th* P 0
1181 21/4 Mollington (R) RES 3m 10 F *alwys rear, no ch frm 10th, t.o. & p.u. 15th* P 0

Lucky winner of desperate Maiden & struggling after; half-brother to Penlet & could improve 11

PENNINE VIEW ch.g. 9 Slim Jim - Salvia by Salvo J J Dixon

1995 2(0),1(11),4(13),U(-),**13(0)**,3(13),3(0)

47	4/2	Alnwick	(L)	XX	3m	14	G	*ld 4-9th, grad wknd frm 13th*	7	0
188	24/2	Friars Haugh	(L)	RES	3m	12	S	*bhnd til styd on frm 4 out, nvr dang*	4	14
398	9/3	Dalston	(R)	MEM	3m	13	G	*(fav) alwys prom, ld 6th & agn 3 out, wnt clr 2 out, unchal*	1	15
501	16/3	Lanark	(R)	RES	3m	12	G	*clsd up 4 out, no real imp on ldng pair aft*	3	14
895	6/4	Whittington	(L)	RES	3m	5	F	*ld 4th, clr aft 3 out, easily*	1	17
1151	20/4	Whittington	(L)	INT	3m	12	G	*(fav) bhnd, prog 14th, 2nd aft 2 out, ran on strgly*	2	19
1585	25/5	Cartmel	(L)	HC	3 1/4m	14	GF	*blnd 1st, alwys bhnd, t.o. 5th, p.u. before 13th.*	P	0

Members winner 95; improved 96; stays & onepaced; could win Confined; Any 18

PENNY LARK b.g. 9 Mick The Lark (USA) - Paula's Pride by Even Money — A J Rhead

1995 P(0),2(11),2(12),1(14),7(0),P(0)

549	17/3	Erw Lon	(L)	RES	3m	11	GS	*ld to 13th, tired aft*	4	0
694	30/3	Llanvapley	(L)	RES	3m	9	GS	*4th at 7th, wknd rpdly & p.u. 11th*	P	0
1203	21/4	Lydstep	(L)	RES	3m	5	S	*rear, prog 3 out, hrd rdn last to tk 2nd flat*	2	15
1267	27/4	Pyle	(R)	RES	3m	7	G	*hld up, prog 9th, rdn & clsng frm 15th, hit last, wknd flat*	4	0

Maiden winner 95; novice ridden & well beaten 96; will struggle in Restricteds at 10; G-S 13

PENNYMAN(IRE) b.g. 6 Mandalus - Maggie's Penny by Woodville II — C Dawson

859	6/4	Alnwick	(L)	MDO	2 1/2m	5	GF	*nvr nr ldrs, p.u. 11th*	P	0

May do better with experience 0

PENNY'S PRINCE b.g. 6 White Prince (USA) - Windfall Penny by Blast — J Sprake

204	24/2	Castle Of C'	(R)	MDO	3m	11	HY	*f 1st*	F	
734	31/3	Little Wind'	(R)	MDO	3m	11	GS	*4th whn mstk 12th, hdwy 16th, not rch ldrs, do bttr*	4	10
1115	17/4	Hockworthy	(L)	MDO	3m	10	GS	*prom to u.r. 4th*	U	-
1280	27/4	Bratton Down	(L)	MDO	3m	14	GF	*w.w. prog 14th, chal aft last, ran on wll to ld flat*	1	16

Going right way & beat large but poor field last start; more needed for Restricteds; improve; G/S-GF ... 16

PENYLAN JACK (Irish) — **I** 321[P], **I** 415[P], **I** 455[P], **I** 599[P]

PEPPERBOX b.m. 8 King Of Spain - Bunduq by Scottish Rifle — Mrs C T Forber

1995 F(-),1(13),7(0),P(0),P(0),U(-),5(12),**U(-)**

291	2/3	Eaton Hall	(R)	LAD	3m	10	G	*u.r. 2nd*	U	-
461	9/3	Eyton-On-Se'	(L)	RES	3m	15	G	*alwys rear, p.u. 13th*	P	0
666	24/3	Eaton Hall	(R)	RES	3m	13	S	*mid to rear, nvr in race, p.u. 4 out*	P	0
952	8/4	Eyton-On-Se'	(L)	RES	3m	7	GF	*s.s., t.o., p.u. 13th*	P	0
1090	14/4	Whitwell-On'	(R)	RES	3m	17	G	*chsd ldrs til wknd 12th, t.o.*	12	0
1195	21/4	Sandon	(L)	XX	3m	9	G	*mid-div, u.r. 5th*	U	-
1421	6/5	Eyton-On-Se'	(L)	RES	3m	11	GF	*mid-to-rr, one pce, t.o.*	8	0

Won short Maiden 95; only finished 5 of 20 races & no form in 96 0

PEPPERMILL LANE ch.g. 8 True Song - Bow Lane by Idiot's Delight — W E Donohue

1995 4(0)

674	30/3	Hereford	(R)	HC	2m	8	S	*blnd 4th, alwys bhnd, t.o. from 7th, p.u. before last.*	P	0
1107	15/4	Southwell	(L)	HC	3m 110yds	10	G	*in tch, blnd 9th, soon struggling, t.o. when p.u. before 3 out.*	P	0
1248	27/4	Woodford	(L)	MDN	3m	15	G	*mid-div, 8th hlfwy, rdn & lost tch 13th, p.u. 2 out*	P	0

Only 5 runs in 4 seasons & silly campaign 96; should stick to Maidens 10

PEPTIC LADY(IRE) b.m. 6 Royal Fountain - In The Wood by Proverb — Dr D B A Silk

1995 **7(NH)**

106	17/2	Marks Tey	(L)	RES	3m	12	G	*alwys rr, t.o. & p.u. 17th*	P	0

Ex-Irish; brief appearance & showed nothing 0

PERCY HANNON (Irish) — **I** 13[P], **I** 57[F], **I** 188[P]

PERCY THROWER gr.g. 9 Oats - Arctic Advert by Birdbrook — The Double Octagon Partnership

257	29/2	Nottingham	(L)	HC	2 1/2m	11	G	*ld to 3rd, 2nd when jmpd right and u.r. 5th.*	U	-
372	8/3	Market Rasen	(R)	HC	3m 1f	6	G	*(fav) ld, mstk 5 out, hdd 3 out, rallied to ld next, pushed clr apr last.*	1	26
578	20/3	Ludlow	(R)	HC	3m	7	G	*chsd ldr, f bend after 11th.*	F	-
669	27/3	Chepstow	(L)	HC	3m	10	S	*ld 2nd, hit 7th, hdd 13th, wknd quickly, t.o. when p.u. before last.*	P	0
1122	20/4	Stratford	(L)	HC	2m 5f 110yds	16	GF	*prom, ld 5th to 9th, ev ch when blnd and u.r. 4 out.*	U	-
1382	6/5	Exeter	(R)	HC	2m 7f 110yds	8	GF	*f 3rd.*	F	-

Winning chaser; calamitous apart from win; won hurdles after & better off under Rules 25

PERFECT STRANGER b.g. 12 Wolver Hollow - Mrs Walmsley by Lorenzaccio — T A J McCoy

1995 P(0),2(22),P(0)

874	6/4	Higher Kilw'	(L)	OPE	3m	6	GF	*7s-3s, hld up in tch, outpcd aft 13th, no ch clsng stgs*	4	0

125	20/4	Stafford Cr'	(R)	OPE	3m	7	S	*held up, prog 12th, styd on frm 3 out, not trbld wnr*	2	20
589	25/5	Mounsey Hil'	(R)	OPE	3m	12	G	*alwys bhnd, t.o. frm 14th*	5	0
635	1/6	Bratton Down	(L)	LAD	3m	13	G	*ld 4-6th, prssd ldr, ld brfly apr 2 out, sn hdd & btn*	5	14

Runs well on occasions but not up to competitive races now; Members best hope at 13 16

ERISH THE THOUGHT b.g. 6 Remezzo - Pretty Fast by Firestreak — C M Oakes

1995 r(-),5(0),F(-)

28	20/1	Barbury Cas'	(L)	RES	3m	14	GS	*mstk 7th, rear whn hmpd & u.r. 10th*	U	

Of no account 0

ERKY LAD (Irish) — **I** 208^{2}, **I** 330^{6}

ERRYLINE b.m. 7 Capricorn Line - Perryville by New Brig — R Fellows

1995 P(0),3(0)

220	24/2	Newtown	(L)	MDN	3m	12	GS	*mstk 4th, prog frm rear 12th, lost tch & p.u. 15th*	P	0
354	3/3	Garnons	(L)	MDN	2 1/2m	13	GS	*w.w. prog 9th, chsd ldrs 3 out, rdn to ld cls home*	1	15
742	31/3	Upper Sapey	(R)	RES	3m	9	GS	*hld up, effrt frm 3 out, ev ch whn f last*	F	-
946	8/4	Andoversford	(R)	RES	3m	10	GF	*mid-div whn u.r. 5th*	U	-

Improved & won weak Maiden; only 7 races to date & may find Restricted if fit 97; G/S 16

ERRYMAN (Irish) — **I** 267^{F}, **I** 337^{P}, **I** 479^{3}, **I** 497^{1}

ERSEVERANCE b.g. 10 Pardigras - Perplexity by Pony Express — D H Bennett

1995 P(0),U(-),6(12),2(17)

262	2/3	Didmarton	(L)	MEM	3m	11	G	*prom til outpcd 12th, no ch frm 15th*	4	11
526	16/3	Larkhill	(R)	RES	3m	9	G	*j.w. ld to 3 out, onepcd aft*	3	12
684	30/3	Chaddesley '	(L)	RES	3m	14	G	*t.d.e. prom, lft 2nd 12th, ld 4 out, rdn 2 out, hld on flat*	1	17
112	17/4	Hockworthy	(L)	PPO	3m	9	GS	*in tch til outpcd 12th, no ch aft, t.o. & p.u. last*	P	0
244	27/4	Woodford	(L)	INT	3m	12	G	*tkn down early,8th hlfwy,lost tch 14th,styd on 3 out,nvrdang*	4	17

Maiden winner 94; held on well to win Restricted; tries but a win at 11 hard to find; Good 18

ERSIAN AMORE (Irish) — **I** 562^{2}, **I** 631^{P}

ERSIAN PACKER (Irish) — **I** 1^{F}, **I** 147^{P}, **I** 188^{P}, **I** 506^{3}, **I** 546^{4}, **I** 564^{6}, **I** 646^{P}, **I** 660^{P}

ETCHBURI ROAD(IRE) ch.g. 5 Remainder Man - Jasmine Melody by Jasmine Star — Nick Viney

555	17/3	Ottery St M'	(L)	MDO	3m	15	G	*hld up, prog 15th, chal 3 out, lft clr nxt, f last*	F	16

Top stable & most unlucky on debut; Maiden just the start in 97 - one to watch 18

ETE'S SAKE b.g. 11 Scorpio (FR) - Pete's Money (USA) by Caucasus (USA) — Mrs Michael Ennever

1995 3(16),1(15),1(20)

271	2/3	Parham	(R)	CON	3m	15	GF	*nvr trbld ldrs*	6	11
998	8/4	Hackwood Pa'	(L)	CON	3m	5	GF	*(fav) 2nd to 8th, outpcd, no imp*	2	13
185	21/4	Tweseldown	(R)	CON	3m	4	GF	*trckd ldrs, ld 10-14th, rdn 2 out, ld flat, all out*	1	20
405	6/5	Hackwood Pa'	(L)	CON	3m	6	F	*(fav) hld up, chall 2 out, ld last, ran on wll*	1	20

Dual winner 95; solid performer; won 4 of last 6; could find weak Open at 12; Firm 21

ETOSKI BAY b.g. 6 Petoski - Palace Tor by Dominion — Mrs F Kehoe

1995 **6(NH),9(NH)**

438	9/3	Newton Brom'	(R)	MDN	3m	10	GS	*last early, rpd prog to 3rd hlfwy, wknd & p.u. 13th*	P	0
495	16/3	Horseheath	(R)	MDO	3m	12	GF	*mid-div, prog to jn ldrs 5th, wknd 9th, t.o. & p.u. 3 out*	P	0
104	14/4	Guilsborough	(L)	MDN	3m	18	G	*trckd ldrs, cls 5th whn f 14th*	F	-

No sign of stamina yet 0

ETRIANA ch.m. 7 Petrizzo - Pete's Fancy by Chabrias (FR) — E Andrews

176	18/2	Market Rase'	(L)	MDO	2m 5f	10	GF	*1st ride, j.w. ld to 10th, ld on innr apr last, kpt on*	1	15
329	3/3	Market Rase'	(L)	RES	3m	12	G	*alwys prom, 4th & ev ch whn f 2 out*	F	-

Ex-Team chaser; game winner of modest Maiden; jumps well; finished early; chances if fit 97 15

ETT LAD b.g. 8 Remainder Man - Winter Lodge by Super Slip — J S Homewood

1995 U(-),2(10)

454	9/3	Charing	(L)	MDN	3m	10	G	*ld, ran wd bend bef 8th, styd wide & ran out 8th*	r	-
780	31/3	Penshurst	(L)	MDN	3m	12	GS	*plld to ld 2nd, sn clr, ran out bnd aft 7th, rddr baild out*	r	-

Promise in 95; went haywire 96; has ability but best watched at present 0

HANTOMS GIRL (Irish) — **I** 32^{P}, **I** 84^{P}, **I** 533^{2}, **I** 621^{P}

HANTOM SLIPPER gr.g. 6 Pragmatic - Tender Soul by Prince Tenderfoot (USA) — R H York

781	31/3	Penshurst	(L)	MDN	3m	11	GS	*prom til p.u. 8th*	P	0
814	6/4	Charing	(L)	MDO	2 1/2m	8	F	*alwys rear, lost tch 6th, p.u. aft 11th*	P	0
187	21/4	Tweseldown	(R)	MDN	3m	11	GF	*schoold rear, hng lft & ran out bnd aft 9th, u.r.*	r	-
300	28/4	Bexhill	(R)	MDO	3m	7	F	*(bl) cls up, mstk 6th, und pres & wkng 13th, p.u. 3 out*	P	0
374	4/5	Peper Harow	(L)	MDO	3m	8	F	*(bl) n.j.w. mid-div, lst tch appr 13th, p.u. 14th*	P	0

Unpromising **0**

PHARBROOK LAD (Irish) — **I** 174[F], **I** 217[2], **I** 282[P], **I** 407[P]

PHARDANTE'S WAY (Irish) — **I** 8[P], **I** 138[2]

PHAR DESERT (Irish) — **I** 332, , **I** 612[4], **I** 636[4]

PHARDING (Irish) — **I** 325[P], **I** 433[P]

PHARDITU (Irish) — **I** 12[3], **I** 55[1], **I** 72[P], **I** 141[3], **I** 184[P], **I** 242[P], **I** 278[3], **I** 376[4], **I** 520[1], **I** 657[P]

PHARLENG (Irish) — **I** 60[P], **I** 119[F], **I** 352[U]

PHARMACY PROPHET (Irish) — **I** 528[P], **I** 604[P], **I** 640,

PHARRAGO(IRE) ch.g. 7 Phardante (FR) - Garry Move On by Le Bavard (FR) — Mark Roch

1995 **16(NH),P(NH),14(NH)**

3	13/1	Larkhill	(R)	MDO	3m	10	GS	*rear, bhnd 10th, t.o. whn ran out 14th*	r
22	20/1	Barbury Cas'	(L)	XX	3m	19	GS	*alwys bhnd, t.o. 12th, p.u. last*	P
156	17/2	Erw Lon	(L)	RES	3m	13	G	*p.u. 2nd*	P
210	24/2	Castle Of C'	(R)	INT	3m	10	HY	*in rear til p.u. 12th*	P
361	5/3	Leicester	(R)	HC	2 1/2m 110yds	15	GS	*soon well bhnd, t.o. 5th.*	8
607	23/3	Howick	(L)	MDN	3m	12	S	*chsd wnr frm 9th, styd on, no imp*	2
697	30/3	Llanvapley	(L)	MDN	3m	11	GS	*mid-div whn u.r. 6th*	U
848	6/4	Howick	(L)	MDN	3m	14	GF	*alwys rear, no ch hlfwy, p.u. 3 out*	P
1039	13/4	St Hilary	(R)	MDN	3m	14	G	*rear, prog to 4th at 14th, 2nd 2 out, ld flat*	1 1
1268	27/4	Pyle	(R)	INT	3m	8	G	*rear frm 3rd, no ch frm 12th, t.o. & p.u. 3 out*	P
1415	6/5	Cursneh Hill	(L)	RES	3m	11	GF	*chsd ldrs, rddn & lost tch frm 14th, p.u. nxt*	P
1602	25/5	Bassaleg	(R)	CON	3m	8	GS	*mid-div, poor 3rd 3 out, lft dist 2nd nxt*	2

Stable star (!) but bad Maiden success offers only Members hopes in future **10**

PHAR TOO TOUCHY ch.m. 9 Mister Lord (USA) - Bridgitte Browne by Mon Fetiche — Miss R A Franci

1995 2(18),1(16),2(16),4(15),F(-),2(15)

23	20/1	Barbury Cas'	(L)	XX	3m	11	GS	*u.r. 1st*	U
41	3/2	Wadebridge	(L)	XX	3m	9	GF	*made virt all, jnd 3 out, ran on gmly flat*	1 1
65	10/2	Great Treth'	(R)	INT	3m	13	S	*ld 2nd, ld agn 8th, made rest, all out*	1 2
195	24/2	Lemalla	(R)	INT	3m	7	HY	*(fav) ld til carried wd aft 6th, ld agn 3 out, sn clr, easily*	1 2
279	2/3	Clyst St Ma'	(L)	LAD	3m	7	S	*(fav) prom, ld 14th, sn clr, easily*	1 2
381	9/3	Barbury Cas'	(L)	XX	3m	9	GS	*(fav) prom, lft in ld 13th, in cmmnd aft, easily*	1 2
624	23/3	Kilworthy	(L)	LAD	3m	7	GS	*(fav) ld to 4th & 9-11th,blnd nxt,rallied to chs wnr 3 out,no imp*	2 2
803	4/4	Clyst St Ma'	(L)	LAD	3m	4	GS	*(fav) hld up in tch, disp 9th til drew clr frm 12th, easily*	1 2
940	8/4	Wadebridge	(L)	LAD	3m	4	F	*(fav) made all, 10l clr 2nd, raced clr, ran on wll*	1 2
1141	20/4	Flete Park	(R)	LAD	3m	8	S	*(fav) ld 4th, sn clr, unchal*	1 2
1359	4/5	Flete Park	(R)	LAD	4m	5	G	*(fav) made all, wll clr final cct, unchal*	1 2
1549	18/5	Bratton Down	(L)	MEM	3m	4	F	*(fav) made all, clr 3 out, easily*	1 2

Maiden winner 95; changed hands; top-class now; stays well; novice ridden; win good races 97; Any ... **28**

PHARYNX b.g. 9 Pharly (FR) - Pamina by Brigadier Gerard — Mrs C Lawrence

65	10/2	Great Treth'	(R)	INT	3m	13	S	*nvr a fctr, p.u. 10th*	P
299	2/3	Great Treth'	(R)	MDO	3m	13	G	*6th hlfwy, no prog, p.u. 3 out*	P

Brief season & prospects already look poor **0**

PHELIOFF ch.g. 12 Dubassoff (USA) - Darymoss by Ballymoss — Miss Sarah A Dawso

1995 3(18),5(13),3(15),1(17),2(18)

234	24/2	Heythrop	(R)	LAD	3m	6	GS	*(fav) hld up, chsd ldrs 12th, ld 2 out, jnd nr fin*	1 1
474	10/3	Tweseldown	(R)	LAD	3m	7	G	*outpcd, t.o. 13th, nvr plcd to chal, stewards*	4
786	31/3	Tweseldown	(R)	LAD	3m	8	G	*chsd ldrs til pshd alng hlfwy, sn bhnd, t.o. 13th*	6
944	8/4	Andoversford	(R)	LAD	3m	4	GF	*made most to 13th, cls 2nd to 3 out, outpcd*	3 1
1186	21/4	Tweseldown	(R)	LAD	3m	6	GF	*disp 1st, chsd wnr til u.r. 7th*	U
1259	27/4	Cottenham	(R)	LAD	3m	5	F	*wth ldrs til wknd frm 15th, btn whn mstk nxt, t.o.*	5 1
1566	19/5	Mollington	(R)	LAD	3m	7	GS	*last frm 5th, t.o. & p.u. 11th*	P

Useful performer in his time but age caught up now; may have outside chance early 97 .... **14**

PHILELWYN(IRE) br.m. 5 Strong Gale - Miss Kamsy by Kambalda — P E Griffiths

689	30/3	Chaddesley '	(L)	MDN	3m	15	G	*in tch, blnd 9th & 10th, last frm nxt, p.u. 15th*	P
1044	13/4	Bitterley	(L)	MDO	3m	15	G	*in tch til eased 10th, p.u. aft nxt*	P

No real signs of ability yet **0**

PHILIPINTOWN 9 — A Hickmai

1995 3(10),8(0)

272	2/3	Parham	(R)	RES	3m	13	GF	*(vis) ld to 3rd, bhnd frm 7th, u.r. 12th*	U

Irish Maiden winner 93; very lightly raced since & not promising to win again **0**

PHILIPPASTONE ch.m. 5 Sousa - Stoneyard by The Parson — Miss L D Delve

1074 13/4 Lifton (R) INT 3m 9 S *s.s., sn t.o. & jmp slwly, fin in own time* 5 0
1626 27/5 Lifton (R) MDO 3m 13 GS *u.r. going to start, t.o. whn p.u. 7th* P 0
1652 8/6 Umberleigh (L) MDO 3m 10 GF *t.d.e. crawld fnces, 2l bhnd whn u.r. 10th* U -

Yet to learn to jump 0

PHIL'S DREAM b.g. 8 Scorpio (FR) - Wayward Pam by Pamroy Mrs Amanda Bowlby

17 14/1 Tweseldown (R) MDN 3m 11 GS *w.w. clsd 12th,went 3rd & outpcd 4 out,styd on,improve* 3 15
236 24/2 Heythrop (R) MDN 3m 13 GS *(fav) sn bhnd, prog to 3rd hlfwy, wknd 14th* 4 0
521 16/3 Larkhill (R) MDO 3m 6 G *prom, ld 13th, 8l clr but tiring whn f last, rmntd* 2 16
788 31/3 Tweseldown (R) MDO 3m 8 G *(fav) cls 4th whn u.r. 9th* U -
1107 15/4 Southwell (L) HC 3m 110yds 10 G *in tch, rdn along after 12th, outpcd last 4.* 5 16

Unlucky 3rd start & deserves a win; should come in 97 if all's well; easy 3m best 15

PHILS PRIDE b.g. 12 Sunotra - La Furze by Winden M Cubberley

6 13/1 Larkhill (R) OPE 3m 18 GS *nvr nr ldrs, t.o. & p.u. 15th* P 0
42 3/2 Wadebridge (L) CON 3m 8 GF *last whn u.r. 8th* U -
134 17/2 Ottery St M' (L) CON 3m 12 GS *prom, ld 2nd-7th, disp til blnd 13th, p.u. aft* P 0
278 2/3 Clyst St Ma' (L) CON 3m 9 S *ld 4th-15th, wknd & outpcd aft* 6 0
625 23/3 Kilworthy (L) CON 3m 11 GS *nrly u.r. 3rd & ran off course, p.u. nxt* P 0
923 8/4 Bishopsleigh (R) MEM 3m 2 G *ld 1st, ran out 2nd* r -
1069 13/4 Lifton (R) CON 3m 9 S *cls 6th whn mstk 13th,blndrd bdly nxt,last whn p.u. apr 15th* P 0

Novice ridden & doing his own thing now 0

PHOZA MOYA(IRE) b.g. 5 Lancastrian - Annes Grove by Raise You Ten J N Llewellen Palmer

322 2/3 Corbridge (R) MDN 3m 10 GS *last at 6th, t.o. & p.u.* P 0
407 9/3 Dalston (R) MDO 2 1/2m 13 GS *mid-div early, lost plc, bhnd whn ref 9th* R -
1253 27/4 Balcormo Ma' (R) MDO 3m 16 GS *bhnd whn p.u. aft 12th* P 0
1356 4/5 Mosshouses (L) MDO 3m 12 GS *alwys rear, no ch 14th, kpt on* 6 0

Last on only completion but may do better with experience 10

PHROSE b.g. 6 Pharly (FR) - Rose Chanelle by Welsh Pageant A W Pickering

1995 **1(NH),4(NH),10(NH),13(NH)**

327 3/3 Market Rase' (L) CON 3m 15 G *prom, hit 4th, wknd 8th, bhnd frm 11th, fin 5th, pld 4th* 4 0
535 17/3 Southwell P' (L) CON 3m 10 GS *chsd ldrs, no ext frm 3 out* 3 15

Hurdles winner 95; brief season 96; may do better without penalty in 97; Soft 16

PIBARA (Irish) — I 361P

PICK'N HILL(IRE) b.g. 8 Kind Of Hush - Shagra by Sallust A R Price

1995 P(0),1(15),4(0),7(10),4(12),4(13)

155 17/2 Erw Lon (L) RES 3m 9 G *mid-div, styd on frm hlfwy, nvr nrr* 4 0
269 2/3 Didmarton (L) RES 3m 12 G *ld to 2nd, lft in ld 8th, hdd 10th, wknd 14th, t.o.* 5 10
548 17/3 Erw Lon (L) RES 3m 8 GS *4th whn u.r. 11th* U -

Maiden winner 95; beaten in 7 races since & finished early 96; Restricted unlikely 12

PICTURE THIS b.g. 10 Tack On - Arctic Lass II by Straight Lad Mrs J Griffin

1995 3(0)

181 18/2 Horseheath (R) RES 3m 5 G *alwys 4th, lost tch 10th, p.u. aft 12th* P 0

2 runs in 2 seasons & no signs of any real ability 0

PIGEON ISLAND b.g. 14 General Ironside - Brown Cherry by Master Buck Miss Annabel Wilson

1995 1(0),P(0),3(14)

32 20/1 Higham (L) OPE 3m 15 GF *v.s.a. t.o. til p.u. 11th* P 0
56 10/2 Cottenham (R) OPE 3m 12 GS *33s-14s, ld 7-9th, wknd 13th, sn no ch* 8 0

Moody old chaser & silly gamble - looks finished now 0

PIGEONSTOWN (Irish) — I 431F, I 557P

PIKEMAN b.g. 14 Turnpike - Cavallina by Vulgan Bruce Knox

1995 R(-),r(-),P(0),R(-)

420 9/3 High Easter (L) OPE 3m 9 S *rr, last whn ref 13th* R -

No longer of any account 0

PIKE'S GLORY b.g. 12 Slippered - Croziers Glimmer B C Upchurch

1995 P(0),P(0),P(0),11(0),F(-),4(0)

1257 27/4 Cottenham (R) CON 3m 5 F *prom to 3rd, last by nxt, mstk 5th, sn lost tch, t.o.* 4 0
1400 6/5 Northaw (L) OPE 3m 6 F *last frm 3rd, t.o. whn p.u. 8th* P 0
1519 12/5 Garthorpe (R) OPE 3m 7 GF *(bl) rear to 5th, t.o. & p.u. 8th* P 0

No longer of any account 0

PILBARA (Irish) — I 110^P, I 174^3, I 413^P, I 539^1

PILLMERE LAD b.g. 6 Karlinsky (USA) - La Jolie Fille by Go Blue — Miss J Du Plessis

1995 F(-)

296	2/3	Great Treth'	(R)	OPE	3m	5	G	*last til p.u. 3 out*	P	0
447	9/3	Haldon	(R)	MDO	3m	13	S	*mid-div whn mstk 6th, sn rear, blnd 12th, p.u. nxt*	P	0

Yet to show any ability 0

PILLOW SPIN ch.g. 12 Deep Run - Miss Furlong by Fury Royal — Mrs P S S Hullett

1995 4(11),3(13)

68	10/2	Great Treth'	(R)	RES	3m	14	S	*u.r. 3rd*	U	-

Maiden winner 94; only 3 races 95/6 & looks finished now 10

PILS INVADER (Irish) — I 132^F, I 165^3, I 302^U, I 340^1

PINBER b.m. 8 New Member - Dicopin by Deauville II — G W Giddings

520	16/3	Larkhill	(R)	MDO	3m	11	G	*mid-div whn u.r. 1st*	U	-
712	30/3	Barbury Cas'	(L)	MDO	3m	10	G	*alwys mid-div, no ch whn p.u. 14th*	P	0
1060	13/4	Badbury Rin'	(L)	MDO	3m	14	GF	*mid-div, lost tch 10th, t.o. & p.u. 13th*	P	0
1163	20/4	Larkhill	(R)	MEM	3m	3	GF	*alwys chsng ldng 2, t.o. frm 13th*	3	0

Beaten miles in bad race & has no prospects 0

PINEHILL (Irish) — I 19^P, I 83^P, I 106^P

PINES EXPRESS(IRE) b.g. 6 Mister Lord (USA) - Autumn Spirit by Deep Run — Mrs Audrey Kley

1995 6(0),F(-),U(-),1(15)

298	2/3	Great Treth'	(R)	RES	3m	13	G	*(Jt fav) w.w. gd prog 14th, ld 17th, cls 2nd whn b.d. 2 out*	B	-
526	16/3	Larkhill	(R)	RES	3m	9	G	*(fav) alwys mid-div, wknd rpdly 13th, p.u. last*	P	0
656	23/3	Badbury Rin'	(L)	RES	3m	11	G	*ld 6th-12th, fdd next, one pace from 4 out*	6	0
868	6/4	Larkhill	(R)	RES	3m	4	F	*(bl) chsd wnnr til wknd frm 12th, sn bhnd, p.u. 4 out*	P	0
1189	21/4	Tweseldown	(R)	RES	3m	10	GF	*(fav) (bl) n.j.w. in mid-div, strgglng 10th, btn 5th whn p.u. 2 out*	P	0
1395	6/5	Cotley Farm	(L)	RES	3m	8	GF	*(bl) cl up to 10th, wknd nxt, p.u. 14th*	P	0

Maiden winner 95; fell to pieces 96 & blinkers no help; can only be watched now 11

PINE TIMBER b.g. 9 Winden - Pine Melody by Melodic Air — R E Barnett

849	6/4	Howick	(L)	MDN	3m	14	GF	*hld up, 6th at 13th, ran on, nrst fin*	2	10
1156	20/4	Llanwit Maj'	(R)	MEM	3m	7	GS	*(fav) held up, f 2nd*	F	-

Very lightly race - missed 95; beat future winners when 2nd; could win if fit 97 13

PINEWOOD LAD b.g. 9 Caribo - Rose Of The West by Royal Buck — Chris Grant

117	17/2	Witton Cast'	(R)	MEM	3m	9	S	*handy, ld 6th-11th, 2nd aft til outpcd 2 out*	4	15
305	2/3	Great Stain'	(L)	LAD	3m	11	GS	*j.w. cls up, ld 7th til jnd 2 out, outpcd by wnr apr last*	2	18
412	9/3	Charm Park	(L)	LAD	3m	7	G	*in tch 14th, wknd, effrt 2 out, nvr nrr*	4	17
487	16/3	Newcastle	(L)	HC	3m	10	GS	*in tch, lost pl 9th, soon struggling, t.o..*	7	0
824	6/4	Stainton	(R)	CON	3m	11	GF	*chsd ldrs, blnd 16th, no prog frm 4 out*	4	14
1281	27/4	Easingwold	(L)	CON	3m	15	G	*mid-div, lost plc 11th, nvr dang aft*	6	13
1594	25/5	Garthorpe	(R)	MEM	3m	10	G	*alwys last, t.o. 10th, p.u. 2 out*	P	0

Irish chase winner 94; ran well 2nd start but disappointing overall; best watched start of 96 15

PIN'S PRIDE b.g. 14 Hardboy - La Capitana by Mon Capitaine — Mrs E C Pinto

1995 U(-)

26	20/1	Barbury Cas'	(L)	OPE	3m	12	GS	*alwys last, t.o. & p.u. 13th*	P	0
270	2/3	Parham	(R)	MEM	3m	5	GF	*prom, disp 9th-nxt, made most aft, ran on well 2 out*	1	14
571	17/3	Detling	(L)	CON	3m	13	GF	*mid-div, prog 12th, 4th 3 out, onepcd*	5	16

Winning chaser; did well to pop up in Members & could repeat in 96 14

PINTAIL BAY b.g. 10 Buzzards Bay - Pin Hole by Parthia — J C Sweetland

1995 P(0),2(18)

1125	20/4	Stafford Cr'	(R)	OPE	3m	7	S	*(bl) in tch, 2nd 12th, wknd & no ch frm 2 out*	3	19
1397	6/5	Cotley Farm	(L)	CON	3m	4	GF	*hld up, ev ch 10th, outpcd frm 12th*	3	10
1498	11/5	Holnicote	(L)	OPE	3m	5	G	*(vis) w.w. in tch, hdwy to 2nd 2 out, ld aft last, pushd clr*	1	15

Placed 7 times from 10 starts 94-6 prior to winning bad Open (well-ridden); sure to frustrate 97 16

PIN UP BOY b.g. 7 Afzal - Clever Pin by Pinza — Mrs P Tollit

585	23/3	Wetherby Po'	(L)	RES	3m	13	S	*mid-div to 10th, rear whn p.u. 13th*	P	0
1030	13/4	Alpraham	(R)	RES	3m	10	GS	*ld 2nd, clr 3 out, styd on wll, impress*	1	18
1151	20/4	Whittington	(L)	INT	3m	12	G	*ld thruout, gng wll & 2l up whn f 14th*	F	-
1478	11/5	Bredwardine	(R)	CON	3m	12	G	*trckd ldrs, effrt apr 14th, no ext frm nxt, p.u. 2 out*	P	0

Maiden winner 94; missed 95; bombed home 2nd start & should upgrade 97; stays; G-S 20

PIPER O'DRUMMOND ch.g. 9 Ardross - Skelbrooke by Mummy's Pet — Mrs L Walby

316 2/3 Corbridge (R) MEM 3m 10 GS *(fav) alwys prom, ld 9th, going well whn f 15th* F -
498 16/3 Lanark (R) CON 3m 10 G *chsd wnr frm 9th, wknd 3 out* 4 11
1153 20/4 Whittington (L) LAD 3m 10 G *not alwys fluent, 3rd 11th, hrd rdn 2 out, ld flat* 1 22
1352 4/5 Mosshouses (L) LAD 3m 10 GS *(fav) prom, 2nd whn blnd 15th & lost plc, not qckn und pres,kpt on* 4 15

Winning chaser 93; able but unreliable & will disappoint more times than winning in 97; Good 19

PIPTONY b.g. 6 Rakaposhi King - Domtony by Martinmas R J Owen

166 17/2 Weston Park (L) MDN 3m 10 G *chsng grp, in tch 13th, wknd rpdly, p.u. 4 out* P 0
406 9/3 Dalston (R) MDO 2 1/2m 12 G *cls up frm 5th til f 10th* F -
1033 13/4 Alpraham (R) MDO 2 1/2m 15 GS *bhnd whn ref 8th* R -

No signs of ability or stamina 0

PITHY ch.g. 14 Orange Bay - Pranky by Bold Lad (IRE) Miss De La Pasture

216 24/2 Newtown (L) LAD 3m 13 GS *alwys wll bhnd, t.o. & p.u. 11th* P 0

No longer of any account 0

PITMAR (Irish) — **I** 20^{F}, **I** 85^{P}, **I** 107^{F}, **I** 270^{P}

PIXIE IN PURPLE(IRE) ch.g. 5 Executive Perk - Glint Of Baron by Glint Of Gold D Stephens

1430 6/5 High Bickin' (R) MDO 3m 8 G *rear til crashed thru wing 4th* r -
1554 18/5 Bratton Down (L) MDO 3m 16 F *alwys strgglng in rear* 8 0
1626 27/5 Lifton (R) MDO 3m 13 GS *ld 10th-nxt, agn 14th, mstk 16th, styd on well* 1 17

Amazing improvement to win fair race - no fluke - & could prove useful in 97 18

PLAIN SAILING(FR) b.g. 6 Slip Anchor - Lassalia by Sallust M J Sluggett

276 2/3 Clyst St Ma' (L) MEM 3m 4 S *chsd wnr to 15th, wknd nxt, t.o. 3 out* 3 0
872 6/4 Higher Kilw' (L) LAD 3m 3 GF *lost tch aft 5th, t.o. & p.u. 11th* P 0

Selling hurdle winner 94; finds pointing anything but plain sailing 0

PLAN-A(IRE) br.g. 6 Creative Plan (USA) - Faravaun Rose by Good Thyne (USA) R J Bullock

1995 P(0),1(13),P(0)

210 24/2 Castle Of C' (R) INT 3m 10 HY *in tch, wknd 13th, t.o. & p.u. last* P 0
298 2/3 Great Treth' (R) RES 3m 13 G *prom, ld 14th, ran wd apr 3 out, came agn, ld & f 2 out* F -
525 16/3 Larkhill (R) RES 3m 7 G *(fav) alwys wth wnr, upsides but tired whn f last* F 17
707 30/3 Barbury Cas' (L) RES 3m 18 G *w.w. prog 13th, ev ch 2 out, wknd, rallied wll flat* 2 19
1057 13/4 Badbury Rin' (L) MEM 3m 4 GF *(fav) n.j.w. last til 13th, prom nxt, rdn 3 out, chal flat, hld* 2 16
1313 28/4 Little Wind' (R) RES 3m 14 G *9th hlfwy, steady prog, cls 4th 15th, kpt on well* 3 13

Maiden winner 95; has ability but looks hard ride now; may find Restricted - don't bank on it 16

PLAS-HENDY ch.g. 10 Celtic Cone - Little Cindy II by Nine One J D Watkins

358 3/3 Garnons (L) RES 3m 18 GS *clsd on ldrs 7th, sn wknd, p.u. aft 12th* P 0
508 16/3 Magor (R) INT 3m 5 GS *2nd at 6th, lft in ld 9th, hdd 15th, wknd, p.u. last* P 0
599 23/3 Howick (L) RES 3m 7 S *alwys last, p.u. 13th* P 0
848 6/4 Howick (L) MDN 3m 14 GF *prom in ldng grp til wknd frm 14th* 7 0
1040 13/4 St Hilary (R) MDN 3m 12 G *cls 4th/5th till f 12th* F -

Well beaten on only completion & looks no-hoper 0

PLAT DU JOUR ch.m. 7 Starch Reduced - Secret Ingredient by Most Secret Mrs J Butt

1381 5/5 Dingley (R) MDO 3m 16 GF *mid-div til f 8th* F -
1434 6/5 Ashorne (R) MDO 3m 15 G *alwys bhnd, t.o. & p.u. 11th* P 0
1599 25/5 Garthorpe (R) MDO 3m 7 G *2nd/disp to 11th, outpcd nxt, completed own time* 3 0

Beaten miles when completing; no dish of the day yet 0

PLATEMAN ch.g. 9 True Song - Spartan Clover by Spartan General K Hutsby

689 30/3 Chaddesley ' (L) MDN 3m 15 G *u.r. 2nd* U -
1103 14/4 Guilsborough (L) MDN 3m 15 G *clr ldr til wknd & hdd 3 out, lame* 4 10
1438 6/5 Ashorne (R) XX 3m 14 G *ld 2-7th, chsd wnr, mstk 11th, wknd nxt, p.u. 15th* P 0
1568 19/5 Mollington (R) MDO 3m 9 GS *hld up, prog 8th, ld 14th, lft wll clr nxt, solo 3 out* 1 11
1640 2/6 Dingley (R) RES 3m 9 GF *hld up, prog 10th, 3rd whn mstk 15th, wknd, p.u. last* P 0

Very lightly raced to 96; solo round to win bad Maiden; stamina suspect; more needed for Restricteds 13

PLAX ch.g. 9 The Noble Player (USA) - Seapoint by Major Point Mrs M Baimbridge

263 2/3 Didmarton (L) INT 3m 18 G *mid-div, lost tch 13th, t.o.* 6 0
428 9/3 Upton-On-Se' (R) RES 3m 17 GS *u.r. apr 1st* U -
641 23/3 Siddington (L) RES 3m 20 S *ld 7th-13th, wknd appr 15th* 9 0
840 6/4 Maisemore P' (L) RES 3m 9 GF *jmpd slwly 4th, disp 2nd 8th-14th,kpt on onepcd frm 3 out* 4 13
1002 9/4 Upton-On-Se' (R) RES 3m 8 F *mstks, in tch, outpcd 13th, poor 4th whn p.u. last* P 0

Maiden winner 94; missed 95; mistakes in 96 & not threatening to win Restricted; G-S 14

PLAYBOY 9

1995 8(0)
1096 14/4 Whitwell-On' (R) MEM 3m 9 G *alwys wll in rear, u.r. 9th* U -
.. 0

PLAYFUL PRINCESS (Irish) — **I** 226P, **I** 347P

PLAYING THE FOOL b.m. 6 Idiot's Delight - Celtic Blade by Celtic Cone — C J Bennett
1995 P(0),P(0),2(12),F(-),P(0)
354 3/3 Garnons (L) MDN 2 1/2m 13 GS *went cls 3rd 8th, ld & blnd 3 out, sn hdd, p.u. last* P 0
953 8/4 Eyton-On-Se' (L) MDO 2 1/2m 10 GF *mid-div, lkd btn in 4th whn f 4 out* F -
1483 11/5 Bredwardine (R) MDO 3m 15 G *prom to 11th, wknd 13th, p.u. 15th* P 0
1581 19/5 Wolverhampt' (L) MDO 3m 10 G *chsd ldr 5th, ld 13th, clr nxt, hdd 16th, sn wknd, tired* 4 0
Placed in short Maiden 95; only finished 2 of 8 races 95/6 & even 2 1/2m looks beyond her 11

PLAYPEN b.g. 12 Sit In The Corner (USA) - Blue Nursery by Bluerullah — Miss S E Crook
1995 4(0),3(14),P(0),1(17),P(0)
295 2/3 Great Treth' (R) LAD 3m 6 G *1st ride, prom, 2nd whn mstk 14th, kpt on onepcd* 2 14
443 9/3 Haldon (R) LAD 3m 10 S *ld/disp to 15th, mstk nxt, 3rd & onepcd frm 2 out* 3 18
561 17/3 Ottery St M' (L) LAD 3m 12 G *handy, 2nd at 12th, wknd frm 4 out* 4 15
872 6/4 Higher Kilw' (L) LAD 3m 3 GF *disp til outpcd 15th, no ext* 2 16
1141 20/4 Flete Park (R) LAD 3m 8 S *mid-div, ran on steadily, tk remote 3rd apr last* 3 16
1359 4/5 Flete Park (R) LAD 4m 5 G *went 2nd apr 4 out, no ch wnr* 2 17
1496 11/5 Holnicote (L) LAD 3m 4 G *slght ld frm 9th til hdd aft 15th, blndrd 16th,kpt on onepce* 2 18
Ladies winner 95; schoolmaster 96 & ideal for job; could find weak opening at 13 16

PLAY POKER(IRE) ch.g. 8 Buckskin (FR) - Trulos by Three Dons — Mrs M J Dusting
1995 P(0),2(24)
298 2/3 Great Treth' (R) RES 3m 13 G *twrds rear whn f 4th* F -
466 10/3 Milborne St' (L) RES 3m 13 G *hld up, prog 12th, chal 2 out, alwys hld* 2 17
532 16/3 Cothelstone (L) RES 3m 12 G *(fav) keen hold, trkd ldrs, chall gng wll 2 out, sn rddn & fnd nil* 2 16
1591 25/5 Mounsey Hil' (R) RES 3m 15 G *w.w. prog to ld 17th,hdd aft 3 out,ev ch whn f nxt* F -
Maiden winner 94; quite able but irresolute & will need fortune for Restricted win; Good 17

PLAY RISKY(IRE) b.g. 7 Risk Me (FR) - Palucca (GER) by Orsini — P H Guard
1274 27/4 Bratton Down (L) MEM 3m 7 GF *rear, mstk 7th, wll bhnd 15th* 4 0
1495 11/5 Holnicote (L) MDO 3m 11 G *bhnd, blndrd bdly 16th, t.o.* 8 0
1627 27/5 Lifton (R) MDO 3m 9 GS *7th at 10th, rear whn u.r. 14th (ditch)* U -
1646 8/6 Umberleigh (L) MEM 3m 4 GF *prom, ld 11-14th, chsd wnr nxt, not qckn 2 out* 2 0
Lightly raced; late to appear 96 & last in desperate Members 0

PLEASING MELODY (Irish) — **I** 195, **I** 833, **I** 290P, **I** 325P, **I** 469P, **I** 5563, **I** 604,

PLENARY b.g. 13 Proverb - Sinarga by Even Money — D G Congdon
1995 U(-),P(0),C(-),6(0),4(0),P(0)
629 23/3 Kilworthy (L) MDN 3m 11 GS *alwys bhnd, t.o. 9th* 7 0
936 8/4 Wadebridge (L) MEM 3m 2 F *chsd wnnr frm start, no imp, wknd clsng stgs* 2 0
No longer of any account 0

PLOWSHARE TORTOISE b.g. 6 Buckley - Bally Small by Sunyboy — C E Ward
102 17/2 Marks Tey (L) CON 3m 17 G *schoold, last frm 11th, p. u. 3 out* P 0
Only learning; looks the part & may defy his name in time 0

PLUCKY PUNTER b.g. 8 Idiot's Delight - Birds Of A Feather by Warpath — Mrs Anne Henson
1995 **9(NH),P(NH),3(NH),2(NH)**
218 24/2 Newtown (L) MDN 3m 14 GS *ld 3-8th & 10-12th, wknd aft nxt, p.u. 15th* P 0
Placed in hurdles 95 but brief appearance 96 could spell problems; time passing 10

PLUMBRIDGE ch.g. 8 Oats - Hayley by Indian Ruler — D R Chamings
522 16/3 Larkhill (R) MDO 3m 12 G *prom, ev ch apr last, ran on well flat* 2 17
713 30/3 Barbury Cas' (L) MDO 3m 10 G *(fav) hld up, prog 11th, ld 14th, sn clr, easily* 1 17
Ex-Irish; waltzed home from modest field & Restricted certain if fit 97; Good 18

PLUNDERING STAR(IRE) b or br.g. 8 The Parson - Laud by Dual — D A Malam
1995 2(12),1(13),P(0)
217 24/2 Newtown (L) RES 3m 17 GS *prom to 7th, lost plc, prog 11th, no imp 15th, p.u. last* P 0
357 3/3 Garnons (L) RES 3m 14 GS *chsd ldrs, ld brfly 11th, not qckn frm nxt, kpt on onepcd* 3 12
Maiden winner 95; season lasted 8 days in 96; more needed for Restricted hopes 13

POACHER'S DELIGHT ch.g. 10 High Line - Moonlight Night (FR) by Levmoss — Mrs Lorna Bertram

1142 20/4 Flete Park (R) CON 3m 11 S *(fav) ld 3rd til 14th, wknd rpdly, p.u. 16th* P 0
1525 12/5 Ottery St M' (L) CON 3m 9 GF *(fav) 4s-2s, chsd ldr til ld 13th, blnd & lost plc 16th, f nxt* F -

Novice chase winner 93; unraced after; optimistic gambles after such an absence 11

POACHERS LAMP (Irish) — I 61U, I 74P, I 147P, I 275[4], I 352P, I 546[3], I 660P

PO CAP EEL b.m. 6 Uncle Pokey - Hejera by Cantab — Mrs T R Kinsey

1995 **P(NH)**

463 9/3 Eyton-On-Se' (L) MDN 2 1/2m 14 G *mid to rear, no dang, p.u. 3 out* P 0
660 24/3 Eaton Hall (R) MDN 3m 7 S *mid to rear, lost tch whn p.u. 3 out* P 0

Shows nothing, so far 0

POCKET PEST ch.m. 10 Balinger - Alpine Orchid by Mon Capitaine — Ms S West

1995 2(10)

842 6/4 Maisemore P' (L) MDN 3m 17 GF *rr, prog & in tch 8th, lst pl 10th, last frm 14th* 7 0
1165 20/4 Larkhill (R) LAD 3m 7 GF *mid-div whn u.r. 2nd* U -
1293 28/4 Barbury Cas' (L) MDO 3m 11 F *prom, disp 5th til ld 10th, mstk 3 out, hdd last, kpt on wll* 3 14
1511 12/5 Maisemore P' (L) MDO 3m 14 F *alwys 1st trio, chsd ldr 3 out, ld & lft clr last, rdn out* 1 15

Im,proved to win weak Maiden (probably lucky); more needed for Restricted chance at 11; Firm 14

POCKET WATCH b.g. 7 Good Times (ITY) - Votsala by Tap On Wood — I P Crane

900 6/4 Dingley (R) MDN 2m 5f 8 GS *2nd frm 1st til wknd 2 out* 3 0

Very lightly raced - missed 95 & no stamina only start 96 0

POKEY GRANGE b.g. 8 Uncle Pokey - Sudden Surrender by The Brianstan — S N Burt

1995 2(0),P(0),2(12),5(0),4(0),2(12),**5(0)**

168 18/2 Market Rase' (L) MEM 3m 7 GF *wth ldr to 6th, wknd apr 11th, t.o. 13th* 5 0
518 16/3 Dalton Park (R) MDO 3m 15 G *(fav) chsd ldr, ld 5 out til apr 2 out, onepcd* 2 11
1021 13/4 Brocklesby ' (L) MEM 3m 3 GF *(fav) made all, drew clr frm 8th* 1 10

Safe, slow & reliable; found one of season's worst contests; Restricted impossible; Any 12

POLAR ANA(IRE) b.m. 7 Pollerton - O Ana by Laurence O — Mrs P A McIntyre

1995 P(0),3(0),3(0)

254 25/2 Charing (L) MDO 3m 9 GS *f 2nd* F -
455 9/3 Charing (L) MDN 3m 10 G *s.s. t.o. 11th* 7 0
576 17/3 Detling (L) MDN 3m 18 GF *wll in rear, some prog in 10th whn u.r. 15th* U -
780 31/3 Penshurst (L) MDN 3m 12 GS *alwys wll in rear, p.u. 13th* P 0
809 6/4 Charing (L) MEM 3m 4 F *prom, ld 14th til hdd & outpcd apr 4 out* 3 10
1055 13/4 Penshurst (L) MDO 3m 11 G *alwys prom, qcknd to ld 4 out, sn clr, easily* 1 12
1297 28/4 Bexhill (R) LAD 3m 7 F *mstks in rear, clsd up 4 out, chal 2 out, ran on,jst faild* 2 16
1442 6/5 Aldington (L) RES 3m 7 HD *(fav) rear,hdwy to cls 3rd 15th,chal 2 out,level last,not qckn flt* 2 14

Improved after looking hopeless; touched off in poor Ladies & worth persevering in them; G-F 16

POLAR HAT ch.g. 8 Norwick (USA) - Sky Bonnet by Sky Gipsy — Miss J E Foster

1995 F(-),1(14),U(-),P(0),6(0),6(0)

84 11/2 Alnwick (L) RES 3m 11 GS *prom whn f 2nd* F -
224 24/2 Duncombe Pa' (R) RES 3m 12 GS *rear 8th, prog nxt, in tch whn f 13th* F -
515 16/3 Dalton Park (R) XX 3m 12 G *alwys rear, last & no ch 14th, t.o. & p.u. 2 out* P 0
584 23/3 Wetherby Po' (L) RES 3m 13 S *(bl) cls up til wknd 10th, rear whn p.u. 14th* P 0
758 31/3 Great Stain' (L) RES 3m 17 GS *mid-div, u.r. 15th* U -
983 8/4 Charm Park (L) RES 3m 13 GF *alwys rear, 11th 9th, nvr dang* 8 0
1363 4/5 Gisburn (R) MEM 3m 5 G *hld up, ld 14th, clr 2 out* 1 10
1571 19/5 Corbridge (R) RES 3m 13 G *not fluent, alwys bhnd, p.u. 2 out* P 0

Maiden winner 95; totally outclassed 96 till handed bad race on plate - only chance again 97 10

POLAR RIDGE (Irish) — I 222[4]

POLECROFT b.g. 13 Crofter (USA) - Grange Kova by Allangrange — E J Hance

885 6/4 Kimble (L) MEM 3m 5 GF *1st ride, chsd wnr to 12th, 4th & wkng whn u.r. nxt* U -
1505 11/5 Kingston Bl' (L) MEM 3m 5 G *alwys last, t.o. & u.r. 13th, rmntd, ref last, cont* 4 0
1608 26/5 Tweseldown (R) CON 3m 6 G *alwys last, t.o. 6th* 5 0

Winning hurdler; of no account now 0

POLISHED DIAMOND (Irish) — I 39P

POLISHING ch.g. 9 Touching Wood (USA) - Loveshine (USA) by Gallant Romeo (USA) — Mrs R E Barr

1995 **6(NH),P(NH)**

1093 14/4 Whitwell-On' (R) MXO 4m 19 G *ref 1st* R -

Not taken a shine to pointing 0

POLITICAL FIELD b.m. 6 Politico (USA) - Miss Broadfields by Bivouac — R G Watson

1995 F(-),P(0),P(0)

516 16/3 Dalton Park (R) MDO 3m 11 G *rear, effrt 15th, sn wknd, t.o.* 5 0
987 8/4 Charm Park (L) MDN 3m 13 GF *cls up early, 3rd 4 out, lft 2nd last, no ch wth wnnr* 2 11
1137 20/4 Hornby Cast' (L) MDN 3m 13 G *rear, prog 10th, rmndrs 12th, ran on to ld 3 out, kpt on* 1 15

Improving; just hung on to win & must have Restricted chances in 97; Good 16

POLITICAL ISSUE b.g. 12 Politico (USA) - Red Stockings by Red Pins T L A Robson
1995 2(16),**F(-)**,2(24),**U(-)**

49 4/2 Alnwick (L) OPE 3m 14 G *in tch, chsd wnr 11th, no imp aft 13th, one pace* 3 21
320 2/3 Corbridge (R) OPE 3m 5f 8 GS *(fav) disp 2nd til outpcd frm 15th, wknd & p.u. 3 out* P 0
582 22/3 Kelso (L) HC 3 1/2m 8 G *alwys prom, blnd 10th, effort and ld 3 out, soon rdn, hdd and no ext flat.* 2 19
1119 18/4 Ayr (L) HC 3m 3f 110yds 9 GS *lost tch and p.u. before 13th.* P 0

H/Chase winner 92; only 10 runs since; occasionally runs well but Confineds only hope 97; G-S 19

POLITICAL MAN b.g. 12 Mandalus - Worth A Vote by Vilmoray J E Holroyd
1995 P(0),4(0),7(0),2(16),1(11),P(0)

917 8/4 Aldington (L) RES 3m 4 F *ld 3-6th,chsd wnr 15th,no imp 2 out,p.u.last,dsmntd* P 0
1207 21/4 Heathfield (R) CON 3m 9 F *rear, in tch to 14th, p.u. 2 out* P 0
1441 6/5 Aldington (L) MEM 3m 4 HD *alwys 3rd,8l down 15th,clsd 3 out,ev ch nxt,no ext flat,lame* 3 11
1612 26/5 Tweseldown (R) RES 3m 11 G *ld to 3rd, sn lost plc, t.o. & p.u. 12th* P 0

Members winner 95; all sorts of problems 96 & could be finished now 10

POLITICAL SAM ch.g. 7 Politico (USA) - Samonia by Rolfe (USA) J W Barker
1995 4(0),P(0),P(0)

75 11/2 Wetherby Po' (L) MDO 3m 8 GS *cls up, ld 4 out, prssd 2 out, drew clr flat, comf* 1 16
306 2/3 Great Stain' (L) INT 3m 12 GS *alwys last, t.o. 11th, blnd & u.r. 15th* U -
585 23/3 Wetherby Po' (L) RES 3m 13 S *rear, prog 12th, 3rd 4 out, no imp til rallied wll flat* 2 19
1093 14/4 Whitwell-On' (R) MXO 4m 19 G *alwys bhnd, t.o. 17th* 6 0
1369 4/5 Gisburn (R) CON 3m 10 G *alwys bhnd, lft poor 3rd 15th* 3 0

Improved; twice ran well at Wetherby; badly placed after; Restricted early 97; stays; onepaced; Soft ... 17

POLITICAL SKIRMISH b.m. 7 Politico (USA) - Bridgits' Girl by New Brig Mrs C Park
1995 P(0),F(-),P(0)

307 2/3 Great Stain' (L) MDO 3m 17 GS *rear, effrt 10th, mid-div whn blnd & u.r. 12th* U -
406 9/3 Dalston (R) MDO 2 1/2m 12 G *cls 2nd at 3rd, mstk 7th, lost plc, t.o. & p.u. 2 out* P 0
916 8/4 Tranwell (L) MDO 2 1/2m 8 GF *u.r. 1st* U -

Yet to complete the course 0

POLITICAL STAR (Irish) — **I** 288^P, **I** 410^P, **I** 494^P

POLITICAL TROUT ch.m. 6 Politico (USA) - Elf Trout by Elf-Arrow R W Stephenson

1466 11/5 Easingwold (L) CON 3m 10 G *n.j.w. last & sn t.o., p.u. 13th* P 0

Fish out of water in points 0

POLITICIANS PRAYER b.m. 9 Politico (USA) - Mary McQuaker by Acer Mrs J A Charlton
1995 5(0),3(0),S(-)

171 18/2 Market Rase' (L) RES 3m 5 GF *w.w. hit 8th, ev ch 14th, sn rdn & btn* 3 0
225 24/2 Duncombe Pa' (R) RES 3m 12 GS *rear, brf effrt 10th, wkng whn blnd 14th, p.u. nxt* P 0
408 9/3 Charm Park (L) MEM 3m 7 G *cls up whn u.r. 7th* U -
518 16/3 Dalton Park (R) MDO 3m 15 G *hld up wll bhnd,prog hlfwy,cls up 5 out,outpcd aft 3 out* 3 10

Placed 3 times from 7 starts 95/6 but stamina lacking & finished early 12

POLITICO POT br.g. 9 Politico (USA) - Another Pin by Pinza Charlie Peckitt
1995 3(13),3(10),1(15),**U(-)**,12(0),3(19),U(-),**2(22)**

37 3/2 Wetherby (L) HC 3m 110yds 11 GS *bhnd from hfwy, lost tch and p.u. before 4 out.* P 0
78 11/2 Wetherby Po' (L) OPE 3m 10 GS *(Jt fav) ld to 3 out, disp last, drvn out to ld flat* 1 19
226 24/2 Duncombe Pa' (R) OPE 3m 10 GS *(Jt fav) prom to 5th,prog 12th,lft 2nd nxt,styd on to ld flat,all out* 1 18
367 6/3 Catterick (L) HC 3m 1f 110yds 12 G *in tch, hdwy after 12th, chsd ldrs from 16th, wknd after 2 out.* 4 18
587 23/3 Wetherby Po' (L) OPE 3m 15 S *cls up, ld 11-14th, outpcd nxt, onepcd* 4 15
673 29/3 Sedgefield (L) HC 3m 3f 7 GF *not fluent, bhnd, t.o. when p.u. before 3 out.* P 0
984 8/4 Charm Park (L) MXO 3m 7 GF *disp to 3rd, fdd, last frm 10th, p.u. 2 out* P 0

Maiden winner 95; found 2 poor Opens & struggling in better company; hard to win 97; G-S 18

POLLY PRINGLE ch.m. 11 Scallywag - Pollywella by Welham Mrs C E Goldsworthy
1995 P(0),P(0)

387 9/3 Llanfrynach (R) RES 3m 11 GS *rear, prog 10th, effrt to chs wnr 2 out, no imp, fair effrt* 2 16
600 23/3 Howick (L) RES 3m 14 S *mid-div, styd on to 4th at 15th, wknd aft* 5 13
694 30/3 Llanvapley (L) RES 3m 9 GS *(fav) 7/2-7/4, cls up 2nd at 11th, lft in ld 13th, sn clr, easily* 1 20
1037 13/4 St Hilary (R) OPE 3m 5 G *prom in 3rd, disp 15th, ld 3 out, wknd & hdd nxt* 2 19

1157 20/4 Llanwit Maj' (R) CON 3m 11 GS *in tch, lft 2nd 14th, rdn to ld 2 out, held on wll flat* 1 18
1268 27/4 Pyle (R) INT 3m 8 G *10l 6th at 10th, effrt 13th, rdn into 2nd last, no ch wnr* 2 19
1600 25/5 Bassaleg (R) MEM 3m 3 GS *(fav) ld, mstk 2nd, clr 10th, easily* 1 15

Maiden winner 93; vastly improved 96; consistent; just stays; can win Confined at 12; G-S 19

POLLY'S CORNER gr.m. 6 Pollerton - Uncornered (USA) by Silver Series (USA) D C Emmett
1995 P(0),P(0),P(0),0(0)
871 6/4 Higher Kilw' (L) RES 3m 9 GF *twrds rear, not fluent, t.o. & p.u. 3 out* P 0
1109 17/4 Hockworthy (L) MEM 3m 4 GS *in tch to 12th, btn 14th, lft 3rd 2 out* 3 0
1280 27/4 Bratton Down (L) MDO 3m 14 GF *mid-div, prog 14th, nrst fin, fin 4th, promoted* 3 12
1530 12/5 Ottery St M' (L) MDO 3m 8 GF *mid-div, 4th whn f 13th* F -

Ran her best race 3rd start but weak contest & more needed for a win; novice ridden 12

POLO PRINCE gr.13 Nishapour (FR) - Trepoless Mrs K Bamford
1995 P(0)
1102 14/4 Guilsborough (L) RES 3m 15 G *in tch to 8th, sn wknd, t.o. & p.u. 12th* P 0

No longer of any account 0

POLYNTH b.g. 7 Politico (USA) - Miss Trixie by Le Tricolore Mrs V Cunningham
1995 1(16),3(15),6(14)
77 11/2 Wetherby Po' (L) RES 3m 18 GS *ld 9th-13th, 2nd 2 out, hrd rdn, just btn* 2 18
224 24/2 Duncombe Pa' (R) RES 3m 12 GS *wth ldr, ld apr 10th, made rest, hit 3 out, styd on strngly* 1 18
409 9/3 Charm Park (L) CON 3m 11 G *mid-div, nvr dang, styd on one pc* 7 14
588 23/3 Wetherby Po' (L) INT 3m 17 S *alwys mid-div, no ch whn p.u. last* P 0
1091 14/4 Whitwell-On' (R) XX 3m 6 G *mid-div, prog 11th, chal 5 out, ld nxt, mstk last, hdd flat* 2 18
1130 20/4 Hornby Cast' (L) CON 3m 13 G *mid-div, wknd 14th, t.o. & p.u. 3 out* P 0

Maiden winner 95; stays & onepaced; disappointing after win; Confined likely early 97; Soft 20

PONTABULA b.g. 6 Sula Bula - Lady Penstone by Jimsun H J Manners
1995 **5(NH),P(NH)**
375 9/3 Barbury Cas' (L) MDN 3m 14 GS *sttld mid-div, prog & ev ch last, not qckn* 2 14
643 23/3 Siddington (L) MDN 3m 16 S *trkd ldrs, ev ch 3 out, lft 2nd nxt, no ex und press flat* 2 15
864 6/4 Larkhill (R) MDN 2 1/2m 9 F *(fav) trckd ldng pair, cls 2nd 10th, lft ld 4 out, pushd out* 1 15
1168 20/4 Larkhill (R) RES 3m 8 GF *alwys frnt rank, ld 13th, gng wll whn f nxt* F -
1292 28/4 Barbury Cas' (L) RES 3m 11 F *(fav) cls up,ld 14th,rdn & hdd aft 2 out,lft in ld last,all out* 1 17
1540 16/5 Folkestone (R) HC 2m 5f 10 G *(fav) chsd ldr apr 9th, ld 3 out, jmpd left next, clr last, driven out.* 1 19

Improved gradually; found weak H/Chase; life much harder in 97 & hard to place; G-F 19

PONT DE PAIX b.g. 10 Cheval - Mattie B by Sea Moss G Pidgeon
1995 F(-),1(24),**U(-)**,3(25),**3(18)**
26 20/1 Barbury Cas' (L) OPE 3m 12 GS *trckd ldrs til wknd 11th, t.o. & p.u. 13th* P 0
1215 24/4 Andoversford (R) OPE 3m 5 G *(fav) w.w., chsd ldr 9th, rdn 2 out, ev ch last, no ex* 2 24
1341 4/5 Warwick (L) HC 2 1/2m 110yds 12 GF *ld, hit 7th, hdd 5 out, wknd apr 2 out.* 5 17
1563 19/5 Mollington (R) CON 3m 8 GS *cls up til wknd 12th, poor 4th whn p.u. 3 out* P 0

Won 6 of 8 points prior to 96 but disappointing in new yard; may revive but best watched; G/S-F 18

POOR RECEPTION (Irish) — **I** 105^{F}, **I** 163^{1}, **I** 220^{P}

POPESWOOD b.g. 13 Nicholas Bill - Villarrica (FR) by Dan Cupid W G R Wightman
1995 8(0),1(17)
475 10/3 Tweseldown (R) CON 3m 9 G *mid-div, u.r. 2nd* U -
654 23/3 Badbury Rin' (L) OPE 3m 5 G *cl up untl outpcd from 13th* 3 0
709 30/3 Barbury Cas' (L) OPE 3m 15 G *mid-div, no ch frm 13th, t.o. & p.u. last* P 0
995 8/4 Hackwood Pa' (L) XX 3m 8 GF *in rear whn u.r. 7th* U -
1184 21/4 Tweseldown (R) MEM 3m 4 GF *disp til made most frm 6th, hdd & onepcd frm 14th* 2 10
1406 6/5 Hackwood Pa' (L) MXO 3m 5 F *alwys bhnd, p.u. 15th* P 0

Members winner 95; old now & another win unlikely 11

POPPY CLEO br.m. 8 Prince Of Peace - Bossy Cleo by Proud Challenge R K H May
806 4/4 Clyst St Ma' (L) MDO 3m 7 GS *bhnd & strgglng til p.u. 12th, schoold* P 0

No sign of ability 0

PORTAVOGIE b.g. 12 Kambalda - Mary's Honour by Honour Bound Mrs Jean Brown
1995 4(18),3(15),5(14),3(11),**6(0)**
1132 20/4 Hornby Cast' (L) LAD 3m 9 G *p.u. bef 1st, restrtd 11 fences bhnd wnr, cmpltd own time* 3 0

Chase winner 93; deteriorated 95 & not the ideal season 96 12

PORTAWAUD (Irish) — **I** 169^{F}

PORTKNOCKIE b.m. 8 Rymer - Vulpine Lady by Green Shoon David Pearson

1995 P(0),P(0),F(-),P(0),P(0)

1009 9/4 Flagg Moor (L) CON 3m 7 G *last frm 8th, t.o. & ref 13th* R -

Yet to complete the course 0

PORTMAN ROAD b.g. 7 Show-A-Leg - Ascen Mary by Ascendant — Miss S Wilson

424 9/3 High Easter (L) MDN 3m 10 S *prom 5th-7th, last & lsng tch whn f 10th* F -
830 6/4 Marks Tey (L) MDN 3m 14 G *plld into ld 3rd, jnd & blnd 11th, not rcvr, p.u. 13th* P 0

Shows speed but needs much more before scoring 10

POSY HILL(IRE) ch.m. 5 Strong Statement (USA) - Beggs Meadow by Quayside — M A Lloyd

22 20/1 Barbury Cas' (L) XX 3m 19 GS *t.o. in last trio til u.r. 10th* U -
740 31/3 Sudlow Farm (R) MDN 3m 16 G *mid-div, rddn 11th, no ch 13th, p.u. apr last* P 0
1368 4/5 Gisburn (R) RES 3m 9 G *8l 3rd at 10th, wknd 14th, p.u. 2 out* P 0
1484 11/5 Bredwardine (R) MDO 3m 17 G *mid-div til p.u. 9th, dsmntd* P 0

Interrupted season of no promise & problem last start 0

POTATO FOUNTAIN(IRE) b.m. 6 Royal Fountain - Ski Cap by Beau Chapeau — P J Millington
1995 R(-),P(0)

240 25/2 Southwell P' (L) MDO 3m 15 HO *rear, t.o. 8th, p.u. aft 11th* P 0
1174 20/4 Chaddesley ' (L) MDN 3m 10 G *(bl) prom whn u.r. 6th* U -
1376 5/5 Dingley (R) MEM 3m 7 GF *(bl) ld 5-9th & 12th-aft last, immed outpcd by wnr* 2 10

Easily beaten in bad race & shows little ability; blinkers poor sign & much more needed 11

POTENTIAL THREAT (Irish) — **I** 196^{P}
POTENTILLA(IRE) b.m. 5 Good Thyne (USA) - Mary Mary by Moulton — Jeremy Hancock

423 9/3 High Easter (L) MDN 3m 8 S *rr of mn grp, lst tch 12th, p.u. appr 14th* P 0
830 6/4 Marks Tey (L) MDN 3m 14 G *mid-div, prog to 3rd 12th, ev ch til wknd aft 2 out,promoted* 2 11

Ran reasonably in weak race & should have prospects at 6 13

POTIPHAR br.g. 10 Warpath - Zulaika Hopwood by Royalty — Mrs J M Worthington
1995 P(0),P(0)

1152 20/4 Whittington (L) CON 3m 9 G *bhnd, some prog 9th, fdd 14th, p.u. 3 out* P 0

Pulled up all 3 starts 95/6 & looks in trouble now 0

POULGILLIE (Irish) — **I** 161^{P}, **I** 265^{P}, **I** 387^{2}
PRAYON PARSON (Irish) — **I** 68^{4}, **I** 88^{4}, **I** 142^{2}, **I** 297^{F}, **I** 328^{F}, **I** 437^{4}, **I** 474^{1}, **I** 544^{2}
PRECIS b.m. 8 Pitpan - Ottery News by Pony Express — O J Carter

581 21/3 Wincanton (R) HC 2m 5f 13 S *t.o. when p.u. before 5 out.* P 0
1126 20/4 Stafford Cr' (R) LAD 3m 7 S *in tch til 10th, wknng whn f 14th* F -
1455 8/5 Uttoxeter (L) HC 2m 5f 9 G *waited with, prog 10th, blnd 12th, soon wknd, t.o. when p.u. 2 out.* P 0

Sights need drastic lowering 0

PRESELI VIEW b.m. 5 Still Time Left - Jacqueline by Harvest Sun — W D Lewis

151 17/2 Erw Lon (L) MDN 3m 8 G *alwys rear, no ch frm hlfwy* 6 0
551 17/3 Erw Lon (L) MDN 3m 8 GS *alwys in rear* 5 0
765 31/3 Pantyderi (R) MEM 3m 3 G *chsd wnr, ran green t.o.* 2 0
1390 6/5 Pantyderi (R) MDO 3m 15 GF *3rd/4th til wknd 15th* 5 0

Last in 1st 3 races & well beaten final start; at least completes & may do better 10

PRESENT TIMES b.g. 10 Sayf El Arab (USA) - Coins And Art (USA) by Mississipian (USA) — A J Taylor
1995 **11(NH)**

961 8/4 Heathfield (R) MEM 3m 5 G *ld 1st, sn hdd, chsd ldr, disp 14th-16th, wknd 4 out* 3 0

No longer of any account 0

PRESSURE GAME b.g. 13 Miami Springs - Cheena by Le Levanstell — Paul Maine
1995 **P(NH),4(NH),6(NH),4(NH),P(NH),5(NH),8(NH)**

1193 21/4 Sandon (L) OPE 3m 8 G *cls up to 8th, wknd rpdly, p.u. 10th* P 0

No longer of any account 0

PRESTIGIOUS MAN (Irish) — **I** 375^{5}
PRICELESS BUCK (Irish) — **I** 419^{2}, **I** 519^{2}
PRICELESS SAM b.m. 5 Silly Prices - Samonia by Rolfe (USA) — J W Barker
1995 **5(NH)**

73 11/2 Wetherby Po' (L) MDO 3m 15 GS *rear, late prog, nvr nrr* 4 0
307 2/3 Great Stain' (L) MDO 3m 17 GS *rear, prog 10th, gd hdwy 2 out, ev ch last, no ext flat* 2 14
764 31/3 Great Stain' (L) MDN 3m 16 GS *(fav) mid-div, prog hlfwy, 2nd 12th, ld aft 2 out, hdd flat,no ext* 2 14

1137 20/4 Hornby Cast' (L) MDN 3m 13 G *(fav) mid-div,prog to jn ldrs 11th,ld 15th,hdd & p.u. 3 out,dsmntd* P 0

2nd in big fields twice & must win in 97 if ready; G-S 15

PRICE WAR b.g. 7 Silly Prices - Verona Queen by Majestic Streak — J G Bell

1254 27/4 Balcormo Ma' (R) MDO 3m 14 GS *ld/disp frm 8th til no ext frm 2 out* 4 11

Only beaten about 11 lengths & should go much closer in 97 13

PRICKLY TROUT ch.m. 7 Politico (USA) - Elf Trout by Elf-Arrow — R W Stephenson

1995 U(-)

415 9/3 Charm Park (L) MDO 3m 13 G *alws wl bhnd, mstk 12th, p.u. 4 out* P 0

518 16/3 Dalton Park (R) MDO 3m 15 G *wll in tch to 4 out, 4th & no ch whn p.u. last* P 0

985 8/4 Charm Park (L) INT 3m 9 GF *mid-div, fdd 4 out, p.u. apr last* P 0

Well-bred but shows very little so far 0

PRIDES DELIGHT b.m. 6 Idiot's Delight - My Pride by Petit Instant — Les Bennett

446 9/3 Haldon (R) MDO 3m 13 S *prom, 3rd at 9th, sn wknd, mstk 11th, p.u. nxt* P 0

807 4/4 Clyst St Ma' (L) MDO 3m 10 GS *mid-div, 5th whn blnd & u.r. 13th* U -

1129 20/4 Stafford Cr' (R) MDO 3m 11 S *mid-div whn u.r. 11th* U -

Yet to complete the course 0

PRIDEWOOD TARGET ch.g. 8 Oats - Quick Reply by Tarqogan — Mrs B Morris

748 31/3 Upper Sapey (R) MDO 3m 11 GS *alwys last, mod prog frm hlfwy* 6 0

1225 24/4 Brampton Br' (R) MDO 3m 18 G *cls 3rd at 11th, ev ch 14th, wknd & p.u. 3 out* P 0

Not disgraced & may improve but time already passing by 10

PRIME COURSE(IRE) b.g. 7 Crash Course - Prime Mistress by Skymaster — E J Farrant

1995 **15(NH),10(NH),8(NH)**

35 20/1 Higham (L) RES 3m 16 GF *prom to 10th, wkng whn f 13th* F -

182 18/2 Horseheath (R) MDO 3m 11 G *cls up, prssd ldr 12th, styd on wll flat, got up fin* 1 14

1054 13/4 Penshurst (L) RES 3m 8 G *prom in chsng grp, 3rd frm 3 out, onepcd* 3 0

Forced dead-heat in weak Maiden; absent 8 weeks prior last start; could improve for Restricteds 15

PRIMITIVE PENNY ch.m. 5 Primitive Rising (USA) - Penny Pink by Spartan General — M J Brown

72 11/2 Wetherby Po' (L) CON 3m 18 GS *s.s. t.o. & p.u. 10th* P 0

225 24/2 Duncombe Pa' (R) RES 3m 12 GS *prom to 10th, 4th & outpcd 14th, kpt on, improve* 4 0

308 2/3 Great Stain' (L) MDO 3m 12 GS *mid-div,prog 10th,cruised to ld apr last,ran on well,imprssv* 1 15

515 16/3 Dalton Park (R) XX 3m 12 G *mstk & u.r. 2nd* U -

584 23/3 Wetherby Po' (L) RES 3m 13 S *alwys prom, onepcd frm 2 out* 3 17

Going right way & ran well enough last start for clear Restricted hopes in 97; G-S 18

PRIMITIVE STAR b.m. 5 Primitive Rising (USA) - Bill's Daughter by Nicholas Bill — J Cornforth

78 11/2 Wetherby Po' (L) OPE 3m 10 GS *rear, p.u. 13th* P 0

636 23/3 Market Rase' (L) MDN 3m 11 GF *rear, t.o. 10th, p.u. 12th* P 0

829 6/4 Stainton (R) MDO 3m 9 GF *mid-div, prog 9th, no hdwy aft, sn wknd* 5 0

Last on only completion & no real signs yet - could improve 0

PRINCE AMANDA ch.g. 10 Deep Run - Cool Amanda by Prince Hansel — G T Govier

1995 P(0),P(0),7(0),5(10),2(17),F(-),P(0)

822 6/4 Charlton Ho' (L) RES 3m 7 GF *rear, outpcd & no ch frm 14th* 4 10

1113 17/4 Hockworthy (L) RES 3m 11 GS *mstk 1st, last whn u.r. 2nd* U -

1551 18/5 Bratton Down (L) OPE 3m 8 F *wll in tch, 4th at 16th, fdd* 7 10

1591 25/5 Mounsey Hil' (R) RES 3m 15 G *in tch to 9th, bhnd & p.u. 14th* P 0

Maiden winner 94; beaten in 11 races since & showed little in 96; best watched at 11 12

PRINCE BUCK(IRE) b.g. 6 Buckskin (FR) - Rechime by Prince Regent (FR) — Mike Roberts

966 8/4 Heathfield (R) MDO 3m 7 G *(fav) blnd 1st, rr hit 7th, prog 12th, jnd ldrs & r.o. 16th* r -

1299 28/4 Bexhill (R) MDO 3m 7 F *(fav) trckd ldrs, 2nd frm 14th, ev ch 3 out, ran on same pace* 2 12

Last of two finishers but should do much better in 97 - win more than possible 13

PRINCE ITSU b.g. 8 Itsu (USA) - Beige Princess by French Beige — John Jones

1995 F(-),r(-)

206 24/2 Castle Of C' (R) MDO 3m 10 HY *bhnd, t.o. & p.u. 10th* P 0

Lightly raced & shows nothing 0

PRINCE METTERNICH ch.g. 15 Tall Noble (USA) - Coloressa by Le Tricolore — Miss C Arthers

1995 7(0),4(10),7(0)

22 20/1 Barbury Cas' (L) XX 3m 19 GS *in tch to 5th, sn strgglng, t.o.* 7 0

57 10/2 Cottenham (R) LAD 3m 9 GS *hmpd & u.r. 1st* U -

394 9/3 Garthorpe (R) LAD 3m 6 G *mid-div on innr til 4th & outpcd 6 out, lft remote 3rd 4 out* 3 0
1238 27/4 Clifton On ' (L) LAD 3m 6 GF *pllng,ld 2-10th,4th & outpcd 13th,kpt on 2 out,tk 2nd flat* 2 16
1596 25/5 Garthorpe (R) LAD 3m 9 G *t.o. frm 7th, f 10th* F -

Ran reasonably at Clifton but no winning hopes now 10

PRINCE NEPAL b.g. 12 Kinglet - Nepal by Indian Ruler — Terry Hopkins

1995 U(-),7(0),6(0),P(0),3(0),r(-)

208 24/2 Castle Of C' (R) LAD 3m 14 HY *rear til u.r. last* U -
385 9/3 Llanfrynach (R) LAD 3m 14 GS *alwys prom, onepcd frm 3 out, fair effrt* 5 18
507 16/3 Magor (R) MXO 3m 5 GS *ld to 12th, wknd rpdly, p.u. 2 out* P 0
601 23/3 Howick (L) CON 3m 10 S *cls up, ld 14th-nxt, wknd rpdly aft* 5 11
845 6/4 Howick (L) CON 3m 12 GF *rear til prog to 4th at 14th, wll btn whn p.u. 3 out* P 0
1078 13/4 Cothelstone (L) MXO 3m 6 GF *2nd early, 3rd at 15th, no ext und pres aft* 3 12
1243 27/4 Woodford (L) MEM 3m 6 G *chsd ldrs, 3rd & outpcd 15th, no ch whn blndrd last* 3 11
1343 4/5 Holnicote (L) OPE 3m 6 GS *mostly 2nd, effrt 3 out, kpt on onepcd* 2 16
1560 18/5 Bassaleg (R) OPE 3m 7 F *lost tch 8th, wll t.o. whn ref 15th* R -
1602 25/5 Bassaleg (R) CON 3m 8 GS *ld to 9th, 15l 2nd whn s.u. apr 3 out* S -

Slightly revived & ran odd fair race; no chance of a win at 13, though 12

PRINCE OF THYNE (Irish) — I 237^{5}, I 311^{P}, I 334, , I 431^{P}

PRINCE OWEN (Irish) — I 358^{P}, I 574^{P}

PRINCE RONAN(IRE) ch.g. 8 Carlingford Castle - Kalanshoe by Random Shot — J A C Ayton

272 2/3 Parham (R) RES 3m 13 GF *alwys mid-div, btn whn p.u. aft 14th* P 0
574 17/3 Detling (L) RES 3m 14 GF *b.d. 1st* B -
774 31/3 Penshurst (L) MEM 3m 3 GS *cls up, ld 12th, made rest, rddn out flat* 1 10
1054 13/4 Penshurst (L) RES 3m 8 G *ld to 2nd, prom in chsng grp aft, 4th 3 out, ran on onepcd* 2 0

Maiden winner 94; missed 95; won a ghastly Members & beaten a distance when 2nd 12

PRINCE ROSSINI(IRE) br.g. 8 Roselier (FR) - Auragne (FR) by Crowned Prince (USA) — R Thorburn

1995 P(0)

116 17/2 Lanark (R) MDO 3m 10 GS *sn bhnd, f 8th* F -
321 2/3 Corbridge (R) MDN 3m 12 GS *cls up early, lost plc 6th, t.o. frm 10th, f 14th* F -
403 9/3 Dalston (R) RES 3m 11 G *last at 6th, p.u. 11th* P 0
614 23/3 Friars Haugh (L) MDN 3m 10 G *alwys wll bhnd, t.o.* 6 0
756 31/3 Lockerbie (R) MDN 3m 14 G *alwys towrds rear* 8 0

Last on both completions & shows no ability 0

PRINCE RUA ch.g. 10 Wrens Hill - Oldtown Princess VI by Chou Chin Chou — C G Martin

1995 0(0),12(0),8(0),6(0),10(0),1(0),4(0)

272 2/3 Parham (R) RES 3m 13 GF *alwys wll in rear, p.u. 15th* P 0
574 17/3 Detling (L) RES 3m 14 GF *whppd round start, sn t.o., p.u. 10th* P 0
774 31/3 Penshurst (L) MEM 3m 3 GS *ld 6-9th, 3rd aft, ev ch 3 out, rddn & btn nxt* 3 0
917 8/4 Aldington (L) RES 3m 4 F *ld to 3rd & 6-13th, wth wnr whn u.r. 15th* U -
1206 21/4 Heathfield (R) RES 3m 8 F *prom to hlfwy, t.o. 4 out* 4 0

Won a dreadful Members 95 & shows no ability outside that class now 0

PRINCE SABI (Irish) — I 108^{6}

PRINCE'S COURT b.g. 13 Kinglet - Court Scene by Royal Levee (USA) — S Kimber

1995 7(0),4(11)

995 8/4 Hackwood Pa' (L) XX 3m 8 GF *rear early,cls up hlfwy,1l 3rd whn mstk leather brk u.r.16th* U -
1238 27/4 Clifton On ' (L) LAD 3m 6 GF *alwys bhnd, kpt on frm 2 out, nvr nrr* 5 12
1438 6/5 Ashorne (R) XX 3m 14 G *mid-div out of tch, 9th hlfwy, effrt 12th, nvr on terms* 7 11
1579 19/5 Wolverhampt' (L) LAD 3m 9 G *in tch, chsd ldr 10-15th, cls 3rd & btn whn u.r. 3 out* U -
1642 2/6 Dingley (R) LAD 3m 6 GF *in tch til slpd & u.r. bnd app 9th* U -

Winning hurdler; just going through the motions now 10

PRINCE'S GIFT b.g. 7 Scorpio (FR) - Burton Princess by Prince Barle — Dave Dixon

1995 U(-),1(14),7(11)

58 10/2 Cottenham (R) RES 3m 7 GS *(fav) blnd & u.r. 2nd* U -
231 24/2 Heythrop (R) XX 3m 10 GS *(fav) alwys rear, p.u. 6th* P 0
525 16/3 Larkhill (R) RES 3m 7 G *prom til wknd 12th, p.u. nxt* P 0
1173 20/4 Chaddesley ' (L) RES 3m 18 G *nvr bynd mid-div, no ch 15th, p.u. 3 out* P 0

Impressive Maiden winner 95; fell to pieces 96 & can only be watched 10

PRINCE SOLOMAN br.g. 10 Lir - Cornish Princess by True Code — W G Turner

444 9/3 Haldon (R) OPE 3m 5 S *disp,mstk 11th,3rd frm 13th,btn whn slw 2 out,hng lft flat* 3 0
625 23/3 Kilworthy (L) CON 3m 11 GS *wll in tch til outpcd 14th, styd on onepcd frm 3 out* 4 16
715 30/3 Wadebridge (L) CON 3m 8 GF *handy,lft in ld 12th,tried to p.u. aft 14th,ld nxt,all out* 1 17
1069 13/4 Lifton (R) CON 3m 9 S *cls 3rd mstly, mstk 3 out, ev ch 2 out, ran on onepce* 3 18
1142 20/4 Flete Park (R) CON 3m 11 S *handy,blnd 4th,drvn 13th,ld brfly 4 out,tired 4th & p.u.last* P 0

333 1/5 Cheltenham (L) HC 3m 1f 110yds 13 G *mstks, bhnd and rdn 7th, t.o. and p.u. before 12th.* P 0
529 12/5 Ottery St M' (L) OPE 3m 7 GF *3rd & rdn 15th, outpcd* 3 11
622 27/5 Lifton (R) CON 3m 14 GS *7th hlfwy, went 5th 3 out, not pace to chal ldrs* 4 16

Promising till missed 94/5; generally struggling 96 & hard to find another Confined; G-S 16

PRINCESS BREDA (Irish) — I 264P, I 383P, I 419³, I 496³, I 525⁵, I 617³

PRINCESS DIGA (Irish) — I 120F, I 150P, I 211B, I 279P, I 650U

PRINCESS GUILLAUME (Irish) — I 449P

PRINCESS HENRY (Irish) — I 204¹, I 249²

PRINCESS LENA (Irish) — I 6P, I 65, , I 72P

PRINCESS LETITIA br.m. 6 Kinglet - Lady Scamp by Scallywag J W Stephenson

797 2/4 Heythrop (R) MDN 3m 11 F *mstk 1st, t.o. whn ref 2nd* R -
1182 21/4 Mollington (R) MDN 3m 10 F *jmpd v slwly, t.o. til ref 5th* R -

Help 0

PRINCE THEO b.g. 9 Teofane - Clyda Princess by Pry Miss E F Goldsworthy

980 8/4 Lydstep (L) RES 3m 11 G *mid-div, p.u. 14th* P 0
1201 21/4 Lydstep (L) MDN 3m 9 S *prog 9th, mstk 14th, wknd, p.u. 3 out* P 0
1271 27/4 Pyle (R) MDO 3m 15 G *14s-8s, ld 5-10th, wknd aft 13th, no ch whn p.u. 2 out* P 0
1391 6/5 Pantyderi (R) MDO 3m 13 GF *c.o. 3rd* C -

Clearly though to have some ability but yet to show it 0

PRINCE TINO b.g. 8 Bustino - Northern Empress by Northfields (USA) N J Hughes

1995 **10(NH),2(NH),P(NH),6(NH),4(NH),5(NH)**

25 20/1 Barbury Cas' (L) OPE 3m 14 GS *prom to 9th, sn lost tch, t.o. & p.u. 2 out* P 0
209 24/2 Castle Of C' (R) OPE 3m 8 HY *rear til p.u. 13th* P 0

Looks a lost cause now - even at a youngish age 0

PRINCE ZEUS br.g. 17 Prince de Galles - Zeus Girl by Zeus Boy D G Knowles

1995 1(12),1(10),U(-)

922 8/4 Aldington (L) MEM 3m 4 F *(fav) chsd ldr til lft m clr aft 10th, lft alone nxt* 1 10
1208 21/4 Heathfield (R) LAD 3m 6 F *in tch, prog to ld 4 out, hrd prssd aft, hdd flat* 2 16
1541 16/5 Folkestone (R) HC 2m 5f 8 G *b.d. 3rd.* B -

Grand old servant; virtual solo in Members & could win again at 18; Firm 14

PRINCIPAL PEACE (Irish) — I 449P, I 492P

PRINCIPLE MUSIC(USA) ch.g. 8 Palace Music (USA) - Principle (USA) by Viceregal (CAN) N Shutts

1995 **4(NH),9(NH),9(NH),4(NH),6(NH)**

158 17/2 Weston Park (L) MEM 3m 11 G *(bl) mid-div, clsd up 12th, onepcd frm 2 out* 3 16

Irish hurdle winner 93; poor form latterly & disappeared early 96 14

PRI NEUKIN br.g. 9 Mufrij - Cessy by Burglar Mrs S J Gospel

223 24/2 Duncombe Pa' (R) CON 3m 16 GS *sn bhnd, t.o. 5th, p.u. 12th* P 0
762 31/3 Great Stain' (L) MDN 3m 11 GS *rear, prog und pres 11th, no frthr hdwy, wknd 14th, p.u.last* P 0
1365 4/5 Gisburn (R) MDO 3m 17 G *chsd ldrs to 12th, wknd & p.u. 3 out* P 0

No stamina & no promise 0

PRINTEMPS(USA) b.g. 9 Roberto (USA) - Golden Lamb (USA) by Graustark Ms K Rosser

264 2/3 Didmarton (L) INT 3m 12 G *in tch in rear, prog 15th, ev ch apr last, onepcd* 3 14
641 23/3 Siddington (L) RES 3m 20 S *mid div, stdy prog 14th, 3rd & hit 2 out, nt rch ldrs* 4 16

Ran more than adequately both starts in fair races & should certainly win in 97 if fit 16

PRINZAL b or br.g. 9 Afzal - Delvin Princess by Aglojo Mrs Pam Froud

906 8/4 Fakenham (L) HC 2m 5f 110yds 11 G *chsd ldrs, hdwy 4th, ld before 7th, hdd after 9th, mstk next, led again before 3 out, soon clr, impressive.* 1 30
1228 27/4 Worcester (L) HC 2m 7f 17 G *(fav) alwys prom, ld 10th to 12th, led 4 out, hit next 2, hdd apr last, not qckn.* 3 24

Missed 95; primed for spanking H/Chase win (well-backed) but below that after; best at 2 1/2m; Good 25

PRIOR CONVICTION(IRE) b.g. 7 Monksfield - Locked Up by Garda's Revenge (USA) Richard Johnson

1995 **8(NH)**

47 4/2 Alnwick (L) XX 3m 14 G *rear, prog 9th, chsd ldrs 3 out, lft 2nd last, no ext* 2 18
77 11/2 Wetherby Po' (L) RES 3m 18 GS *(fav) mid-div, prog 14th, ld 2 out, drvn out* 1 18
306 2/3 Great Stain' (L) INT 3m 12 GS *(fav) hld up, prog 10th, effrt 2 out, wknd apr last* 5 14
586 23/3 Wetherby Po' (L) LAD 3m 8 S *alwys mid-div, no dang* 5 14
1012 9/4 Flagg Moor (L) XX 3m 7 G *(fav) chsd ldr to 2nd, lost pl nxt, nvr gng wl aft, no ch 15th* 5 0

1134 20/4 Hornby Cast' (L) MEM 3m 6 G *prom,jmpd slwly 7th,lost tch 9th,t.o. & u.r.last,rmntd* 5

Maiden winner 94; started well 96 but fell apart after; may revive; could try blinkers; G-S 16

PRIORY STREET (Irish) — **I** 533^{F}

PRIVATE JET(IRE) b.g. 7 Dara Monarch - Torriglia (USA) by Nijinsky (CAN) P H Sanders

1995 P(0),P(0)

123 17/2 Witton Cast' (R) MDO 3m 11 S *prom to 10th, wknd nxt, kpt on in rear aft* 5
222 24/2 Duncombe Pa' (R) MEM 3m 6 GS *prom, hit 7th, chsd wnr 12th, btn 3 out, fin tired* 2 12
764 31/3 Great Stain' (L) MDN 3m 16 GS *prom, mstk 8th, chsd ldrs til wknd 4 out, t.o.* 5
1094 14/4 Whitwell-On' (R) MDO 2 1/2m 88yds 16 G *mid-div whn f 7th* F
1286 27/4 Easingwold (L) MDO 3m 13 G *handy, wth ldrs 4 out, not qckn 2 out, kpt on wll flat* 3 14
1461 9/5 Sedgefield (L) HC 2m 5f 10 F *nvr far away, ld before 3 out, mstk and hdd last, no ext.* 2 15
1548 18/5 Southwell (L) HC 3m 110yds 11 GF *held up, styd on from 4 out, nearest fin.* 3 16

Modest maiden but ran well in weak H/Chases; Maiden win certain if that can be relied upon 16

PRIVATE YASHKAN (Irish) — **I** 17^{2}, **I** 103^{2}, **I** 170^{1}, **I** 287^{4}, **I** 304^{F}

PRO BONO(IRE) ch.g. 6 Tale Quale - Quality Suite by Prince Hansel P C Caudwel

1995 **3(NH),7(NH),1(NH),11(NH),8(NH),4(NH),F(NH),3(NH),P(NH),2(NH),5(NH)**

6 13/1 Larkhill (R) OPE 3m 18 GS *prom to 10th, t.o. & p.u. 15th* P 0
257 29/2 Nottingham (L) HC 2 1/2m 11 G *soon handy, jmpd ahd 5 out, hrd pressed last 3, hdd and one pace run-in.* 2 23
484 15/3 Fakenham (L) HC 2m 5f 110yds 13 GF *chsd ldr, ld 12th, rdn and styd on well from last.* 1 22

Winning hurdler; found a weak H/Chase & disappeared; tough tasks in 97 if fit 21

PROCEEDWITHCAUTION (Irish) — **I** 219^{P}, **I** 288^{P}

PROFESSOR LONGHAIR br.g. 9 Strong Gale - Orient Conquest by Dual Huw Davies

1995 4(14),3(15),4(11),F(-),r(-),1(13),**5(17)**,**1(20)**

100 16/2 Fakenham (L) HC 2m 5f 110yds 9 G *mid div, hit 4th, bhnd from 6th.* 5 16
184 23/2 Haydock (L) HC 3m 9 GS *chsd wnr 5th to 15th, fd.* 3 16
672 29/3 Aintree (L) HC 2 3/4m 26 G *n.j.w., alwys rear, t.o. hfwy.* 13 0
1108 17/4 Cheltenham (L) HC 4m 1f 14 GS *alwys bhnd, t.o..* 7 10
1332 1/5 Cheltenham (L) HC 3m 1f 110yds 11 G *mid div, lost tch 11th, t.o. and p.u. before 18th.* P 0
1464 11/5 Warwick (L) HC 3 1/4m 6 F *trckd ldr, left in ld 13th, styd on from 2 out.* 1 21
1613 27/5 Fontwell (R) HC 3 1/4m 110yds 12 G *prom, outpcd 13th, no hdwy from 18th.* 5 15

H/Chase winner 95; found another weak contest 96; modest but stays; G-F; sold July 96 21

PROFILER(IRE) b.g. 5 Rontino - Ash Copse by Golden Love H L Thompson

414 9/3 Charm Park (L) MDO 3m 11 G *ld 4-5th, 2nd at 8th, wknd 14th, p.u. 4 out* P 0
518 16/3 Dalton Park (R) MDO 3m 15 G *alwys rear, t.o. 14th, p.u. 2 out* P 0

1st season lasted a week but just a faint hope on debut 0

PROFLIGATE ch.h. 11 Shack (USA) - Reshuffle by Sassafras (FR) R Dench

1995 P(0),P(0),2(17),2(15),3(16),1(16),**3(19)**

57 10/2 Cottenham (R) LAD 3m 9 GS *hld up, effrt hlfwy, no imp wnr, lft poor 2nd 2 out* 2 14
347 3/3 Higham (L) LAD 3m 10 G *mid-div, outpcd 11th, bhnd 15th* 6 10
452 9/3 Charing (L) LAD 3m 8 G *alwys rear, nvr thrtnd, 6th & wll btn whn p.u. last* P 0
809 6/4 Charing (L) MEM 3m 4 F *ld to 2nd, ld 11th-14th, agn apr 4 out-nxt, no ext 2 out* 2 12

Ladies winner 95; well beaten when 2nd & another win at 12 looks beyond him; Firm 12

PROLOGUE (Irish) — **I** 386^{P}

PROMETHEAN SINGER b.g. 10 Chief Singer - Patraana by Nishapour (FR) R Newey

1995 P(0),P(0),U(-),2(13)

218 24/2 Newtown (L) MDN 3m 14 GS *prom, ev ch 14th, sn wknd* 4 0
431 9/3 Upton-On-Se' (R) MDO 3m 17 GS *clr ldr to 10th, renewed effrt 3 out, wknd* 5 0

Promise last start 95; not disgraced 96 but a win at 11 looks hard to find 11

PROMITTO ch.m. 6 Roaring Riva - I Don't Mind by Swing Easy (USA) N Shutts

1995 **2(NH),2(NH),2(NH),2(NH)**

1044 13/4 Bitterley (L) MDO 3m 15 G *whppd round start, tk no part* 0 0
1315 28/4 Bitterley (L) MDO 3m 10 G *mid-div, 20l 5th at 12th, kpt on steadily frm 14th* 3 10
1485 11/5 Bredwardine (R) MDO 3m 15 G *trckd ldrs, effrt 13th, no prog & p.u. nxt* P 0

Has shown ability under Rules & in points but unreliable & may well continue to disappoint 12

PROM'S MOHOCK br.g. 7 Scallywag - Eastern Promise by Eastern Lyric Miss J H Wickens

1995 F(-),P(0),3(0)

14 6/4 Charing (L) MDO 2 1/2m 8 F *nvr fluent & jmpd rght, ld 4th-apr 9th, chal 3 out, wknd nxt* 3 10
55 13/4 Penshurst (L) MDO 3m 11 G *prom, jmpd rght, jmpd rght 6th & f* F -

Ran best race 1st start but season lasted a week; should at least try R/H course 10

ROPHET'S CHOICE gr.g. 10 Warpath - Queen's Melody by Highland Melody Mrs R A Alderton

79 11/2 Wetherby Po' (L) MDO 3m 12 GS *f 1st* F -
24 24/2 Duncombe Pa' (R) RES 3m 12 GS *s.s. t.o. til f 13th* F -
16 9/3 Charm Park (L) MDO 3m 13 G *al mid-div, 6th at 14th, nvr fctr* 5 0
17 16/3 Dalton Park (R) MDO 3m 10 G *mstk 2nd, in tch whn no room & ran out 4th* r -
86 8/4 Charm Park (L) MDN 3m 10 GF *in tch, 3rd 10th, fdd rpdly, p.u. 4 out* P 0
96 14/4 Whitwell-On' (R) MEM 3m 9 G *alwys prom, ev ch til fdd 3 out* 4 11
85 27/4 Easingwold (L) MDO 3m 9 G *alwys prom, steadily wknd frm 13th, lft remote 2nd 2 out* 2 0
70 11/5 Easingwold (L) MDO 3m 10 G *mstk 1st, alwys handy, disp 11th-3 out, onepcd* 3 13

Very lightly raced till 96; shows some ability but barely stays & win at 11 unlikely 11

ROPHETS THUMB (Irish) — **I** 1^{2}, **I** 49^{2}, **I** 69^{5}, **I** 117^{P}, **I** 243^{F}, **I** 311^{5}

ROPLUS ch.g. 14 Proverb - Castle Treasure by Perspex Mrs A E Lee

1995 5(12)

57 8/4 Lockinge (L) CON 3m 5 GF *ld to 2nd, prom til wknd & onepcd frm 5 out* 4 0

No longer of any account 0

ROSPECT STAR (Irish) — **I** 323^{P}, **I** 583^{2}

ROUD DRIFTER br.g. 9 Crash Course - Purlane (FR) by Kashmir II D R Thomas

1995 3(10),3(0),5(12),2(16),3(10),P(0),F(-),3(15),2(13),2(17),1(17)

57 17/2 Erw Lon (L) CON 3m 15 G *mid-div, prog to 2nd 2 out, onepcd* 3 15
55 3/3 Garnons (L) INT 3m 10 GS *alwys cls up, outpcd frm 3 out* 4 13
45 17/3 Erw Lon (L) CON 3m 10 GS *trckd ldrs, tiring whn p.u. aft 2 out, lame* P 0

Restricted winner 95; struggling in better class & problems last start 13

ROUD LADY (Irish) — **I** 181^{5}

ROUD PRINCESS (Irish) — **I** 106^{P}, **I** 164^{P}, **I** 196^{P}, **I** 271^{P}, **I** 481^{P}, **I** 604, , **I** 632^{3}, **I** 654^{P}

ROUD SLAVE b.m. 13 Crozier - Lady Actress by Arctic Slave J Colston

215 24/2 Newtown (L) OPE 3m 20 GS *1st ride, alwys rear, last whn u.r. 12th* U -
355 3/3 Garnons (L) INT 3m 10 GS *lost tch 5th, t.o. & p.u. 3 out* P 0

No longer of any account 0

ROUD SUN ch.g. 8 Sunyboy - Roman Lilly by Romany Air Stewart Pike

1995 2(27),**1(26),F(-),1(35),1(30),1(36)**

185 23/2 Kempton (R) HC 3m 9 GS *(fav) held up, hmpd and f 12th.* F -
483 14/3 Cheltenham (L) HC 3 1/4m 110yds 17 G *whipped round start, hmpd 3rd, n.j.w. after, blnd 9th and 13th, styd on from 2 out, n.d..* 4 30
798 3/4 Ascot (R) HC 2m 3f 110yds 10 GF *(fav) keen hold, held up, f 8th.* F -
544 17/5 Stratford (L) HC 3m 10 GF *(fav) held up, hdwy after 6 out, mstk 4 out, soon rdn, mistake 2 out, styd on well run-in.* 3 27
631 1/6 Stratford (L) HC 3 1/2m 14 GF *(fav) towards rear, hdwy 14th, ld 3 out, all out run-in, fin lame.* 1 38

Top H/Chaser; hard ride; stays well; quickens; probably miss 97; G/F-S 39

ROUD TOBY (Irish) — **I** 220^{F}, **I** 346^{5}, **I** 527^{1}

ROVENCE ch.g. 9 Rousillon (USA) - Premier Rose by Sharp Edge A J Thomas

1995 **5(NH),7(NH),12(NH),1(NH),7(NH)**

602 23/3 Howick (L) OPE 3m 11 S *alwys rear, some prog to 5th at 11th, wknd & p.u. 3 out* P 0
692 30/3 Llanvapley (L) OPE 3m 6 GS *(bl) 3rd/4th til clr 3rd frm 14th, 15l down whn u.r. nxt* U -

Hurdles winner 95; brief appearance in points & signs looks ominous 14

ROVEN SCHEDULE (Irish) — **I** 446^{P}

ROVERB PRINCE ch.g. 12 Proverb - Swallow Lass by Le Prince Mrs D C Samworth

1995 U(-),6(0),2(18),2(19),4(17)

325 3/3 Market Rase' (L) LAD 3m 6 G *chsd ldr to 3rd, last frm 7th, t.o.* 6 0
066 13/4 Horseheath (R) LAD 3m 2 F *(fav) ld, sn clr, hdd 15th, wknd appr nxt* 2 0
330 30/4 Huntingdon (R) HC 2 1/2m 110yds 8 GF *mstks, t.o. from 8th, p.u. before 12th.* P 0

Consistent but modest in 95 & deteriorated in 96; looks finished 0

UBLIC APPEAL b.g. 7 Law Society (USA) - Vacherin (USA) by Green Dancer (USA) T R Darlington

1995 R(-),R(-),**7(NH),9(NH),5(NH),5(NH),4(NH),P(NH),7(NH),P(NH)**

288 2/3 Eaton Hall (R) MDO 3m 17 G *alwys rear, p.u. 5 out* P 0

1234 27/4 Weston Park (L) MDO 3m 13 G *plld hrd, mid to rear, diff ride, p.u. 5 out* P

Refused twice in 95 & scarcely did better in 96 0

PULLTHEPLUG b.g. 5 Reesh - Stop Gap by Hasty Word Mrs J A Burt

882 6/4 Brampton Br' (R) RES 3m 14 GF *mid-div whn f 10th* F
1222 24/4 Brampton Br' (R) RES 3m 11 G *wth ldrs til wknd 12th, p.u. 15th* P
1314 28/4 Bitterley (L) MEM 3m 13 G *chsd ldrs, cls up whn f 12th* F

Going well last start & some clear rounds 97 should see him go close 12

PUNCHING GLORY b.g. 12 Idiot's Delight - Hitting Supreme by Supreme Sovereign Miss S E Brew

1995 P(0),5(16),3(16),3(17),2(19),4(0),**6(0)**

24 20/1 Barbury Cas' (L) XX 3m 12 GS *chsd ldrs, 3rd frm 11th, no ch wth 1st pair whn u.r. 14th* U
214 24/2 Newtown (L) CON 3m 21 GS *alwys rear, t.o. & p.u. 3 out* P
683 30/3 Chaddesley ' (L) MEM 3m 17 G *bhnd frm 7th, t.o. & p.u. last* P
836 6/4 Maisemore P' (L) MEM 3m 7 GF *cls up, 4th & outpcd 11th, no dang after, wnt 3rd appr last* 3
1314 28/4 Bitterley (L) MEM 3m 13 G *rear frm 6th, losing tch 11th, no ch nxt* 7
1507 12/5 Maisemore P' (L) CON 3m 10 F *bhnd whn nrly u.r. 3rd, t.o. 9th* 6
1611 26/5 Tweseldown (R) XX 3m 9 G *raced wd, chsd ldrs, 4th frm 12th, lft poor 3rd last* 3

Just a schoolmaster now & lost last 21 races 0

PUNTEILLE (Irish) — **I** 7F, **I** 12P

PUNTERS FORTUNE (Irish) — **I** 222P, **I** 343P, **I** 421³, **I** 526P

PURE MADNESS(USA) b.g. 6 Northern Prospect (USA) - Icy Oddsmaker (USA) by Icecapade (USA) M J Brow

1995 P(0),P(0),F(-),P(0),3(0),2(11),2(0)

74 11/2 Wetherby Po' (L) MDO 3m 11 GS *(bl) ld to 7th, wknd, p.u. 12th* P
122 17/2 Witton Cast' (R) MDO 3m 8 S *rear whn ref 6th* R
987 8/4 Charm Park (L) MDN 3m 13 GF *(bl) ld to 9th, hdd, cls up up to 4 out, outpcd aft* 3
1095 14/4 Whitwell-On' (R) MDO 2 1/2m 88yds 14 G *(bl) keen hold, chsd ldrs, outpcd 5 out, kpt on 2 out* 3
1137 20/4 Hornby Cast' (L) MDN 3m 13 G *keen hold, alwys prom, ev ch 3 out, onepcd* 3
1286 27/4 Easingwold (L) MDO 3m 13 G *mid-div, prog 10th, ev ch 2 out, drvn & kpt on wll flat* 2
1450 6/5 Witton Cast' (R) MDO 3m 14 G *midfld,prog 14th,2l 2nd 2 out,hrd rdn & rld flat,ld nr line* 1
1466 11/5 Easingwold (L) CON 3m 10 G *(Jt fav) hld up going wl,prog 8th,chal 2 out,rdn & qcknd clr apr last* 1
1585 25/5 Cartmel (L) HC 3 1/4m 14 GF *n.j.w., soon bhnd, t.o. when p.u. before last.* P

Looked ungenuine till vastly improved late season; 16 runs in 2 seasons but could upgrade; G-F 20

PURPLE MELODY(IRE) ch.g. 6 Orchestra - Violate by Continuation V Hughe

148 17/2 Erw Lon (L) MDN 3m 9 G *mid-div, prog to chal 15th, ev ch 2 out, styd on onepcd* 2
550 17/3 Erw Lon (L) MDN 3m 13 GS *(fav) mid-div, prog to ld 4 out, ran on gamely* 1

Won what turned out to be hottest Welsh Maiden of season & Restricted on the cards if fit 96; G-S 18

PUSH ALONG ch.g. 9 Push On - Pollywella by Welham G T Goldswort

1995 1(15),6(0),2(17),P(0),P(0)

156 17/2 Erw Lon (L) RES 3m 13 G *alwys 3rd/4th, wknd frm 14th* 4
219 24/2 Newtown (L) RES 3m 17 GS *prom, cls 4th at 14th, sn btn* 5
388 9/3 Llanfrynach (R) RES 3m 20 GS *prom, ld 13th, kicked clr nxt, in no dang frm 2 out, unchal* 1
601 23/3 Howick (L) CON 3m 10 S *(fav) hld up, went 3rd 3 out, not rch ldng pair* 3
691 30/3 Llanvapley (L) CON 3m 15 GS *cls up, 3rd at 13th, chsd wnr 15th, 5l dwn 3 out, just hld* 2
1035 13/4 St Hilary (R) CON 3m 10 G *(fav) ld til f 6th* F

Maiden winner 95; good Restricted win 96; likes Llanfrynach - win Confined there 97; Soft 20

PUSH GENTLY (Irish) — **I** 20P, **I** 84P, **I** 107², **I** 165P, **I** 195P, **I** 270⁴, **I** 381⁴

PUSHLYN b.m. 9 Push On - Shylyn by Hay Chas P Goldsworth

1995 U(-),P(0),F(-)

149 17/2 Erw Lon (L) MDN 3m 10 G *prom til wknd rpdly hlfwy, p.u. 14th* P
386 9/3 Llanfrynach (R) RES 3m 10 GS *bhnd frm 6th, t.o. & p.u. 10th* P

Yet to complete the course 0

PUTTINGONTHESTYLE ch.g. 9 Enchantment - Straightaway Style by Anax John Nichola

1995 P(0),P(0)

605 23/3 Howick (L) MDN 3m 13 S *mid-div, wknd 9th, p.u. 11th* P
850 6/4 Howick (L) MDN 3m 14 GF *t.o. 10th, p.u. 12th* P
1272 27/4 Pyle (R) MDO 3m 9 G *ld/disp til wknd aft 13th, dist 3rd whn ref 2 out* R
1492 11/5 Erw Lon (L) MDO 3m 10 F *ld/disp til ran out 13th* r
1556 18/5 Bassaleg (R) MEM 3m 6 F *16s-6s, chsd wnr, clsd 14th, lost 2nd nxt, wknd 3 out* 3

Ran his best ever race last start but still no conceivable chance of winning 0

PYRO PENNANT b.g. 11 Official - Courtney Pennant by Angus Mrs J Brook-Saunde

1995 **P(0)**,7(0),**U(-)**,2(12),5(0),2(0),U(-),P(0),P(0)

20 14/1 Tweseldown (R) RES 3m 9 GS *rear, last whn u.r. 10th* U -
27 20/1 Barbury Cas' (L) LAD 3m 15 GS *t.o. 5th, p.u. 10th* P 0
157 17/2 Erw Lon (L) CON 3m 15 G *alwys rear, no dang* 8 0
211 24/2 Castle Of C' (R) INT 3m 5 HY *sn wll bhnd, t.o. & p.u. 14th* P 0
509 16/3 Magor (R) MDN 3m 9 GS *prom early, wknd frm 11th* 4 0
606 23/3 Howick (L) MDN 3m 13 S *ld/disp to 11th, 2nd til wknd 13th, fin tired* 4 0
669 27/3 Chepstow (L) HC 3m 10 S *prom till blnd 7th, soon t.o., p.u. before 9th.* P 0
844 6/4 Howick (L) RES 3m 10 GF *alwys last pair, fin own time* 6 0
1040 13/4 St Hilary (R) MDN 3m 12 G *mid-div til wknd frm 13th* 4 0
1270 27/4 Pyle (R) MDO 3m 9 G *alwys prom, ev ch 14th, rdn & onepcd frm nxt* 4 0
1600 25/5 Bassaleg (R) MEM 3m 3 GS *3rd til dist 2nd frm 10th, u.r. nxt, rmntd* 3 0

Well beaten all 20 races 95/6 & a waste of time 0

QAJAR gr.g. 12 Nishapour (FR) - Gravina by Godswalk (USA) Lady Stucley
1995 4(11),6(0),7(0),2(11),P(0),2(13)
443 9/3 Haldon (R) LAD 3m 10 S *rear til p.u. 3 out* P 0

No longer of any account 0

QANNAAS br.g. 12 Kris - Red Berry by Great Nephew Mrs Ann Leat
1995 1(20),**1(23)**
474 10/3 Tweseldown (R) LAD 3m 7 G *(fav) (bl) made all, qcknd clr frm 2 out, easily* 1 22
786 31/3 Tweseldown (R) LAD 3m 8 G *(fav) (bl) cls up, lft in ld 10th, clr 12th, pshd out flat* 1 25
1186 21/4 Tweseldown (R) LAD 3m 6 GF *(fav) (bl) j.w. rdn to disp 1st, made rest, imprssv* 1 25
1330 30/4 Huntingdon (R) HC 2 1/2m 110yds 8 GF *(fav) (bl) made virtually all, rdn clr 2 out, easily.* 1 26

Able & won last 7 starts; needs to dominate; well-ridden; win more at 13; G-F 25

QUAKER PEP ch.g. 6 Scallywag - Jo Matanza by Adropejo T H Gibbon
1995 **P(NH),5(NH),18(NH)**
977 8/4 Lydstep (L) MDO 3m 8 G *twrds rear, p.u. 14th* P 0
1269 27/4 Pyle (R) MDO 3m 9 G *n.j.w. dtchd last til some prog 7th, no ch 10th, p.u. 2 out* P 0

Shows nothing yet 0

QUALIFIED ch.g. 13 Over The River (FR) - Arctic Lou by Arctic Slave Mrs Lucia Boscawen
1995 2(25),1(25),1(27),**7(0)**
18 14/1 Tweseldown (R) MXO 3m 6 GS *nvr going well, t.o. 10th, poor 4th whn ran out & u.r. 12th* r -
67 10/2 Great Treth' (R) LAD 3m 11 S *alwys cls up, kpt on onepcd frm 2 out, no imp wnr* 2 24

Very useful pointer at best; ran well 2nd start but will find it hard to revive at 14; G-Hy 22

QUALITAIR MEMORY(IRE) ch.g. 7 Don't Forget Me - Whist Awhile by Caerleon (USA) C Tizzard
1995 **11(NH),10(NH),3(NH),U(NH),6(NH),2(NH),15(NH),6(NH)**
7 13/1 Larkhill (R) CON 3m 10 GS *in tch whn mstk 6th, bhnd whn hmpd 10th, no ch aft* 5 0
133 17/2 Ottery St M' (L) OPE 3m 18 GS *mid-div, prog 12th, went 2nd 2 out, alwys hld* 2 22
278 2/3 Clyst St Ma' (L) CON 3m 9 S *(fav) hld up, prog 12th, ld 16th, ran on well frm 3 out* 1 20
531 16/3 Cothelstone (L) CON 3m 12 G *alwys prom, ld appr 3 out, clr nxt, easy* 1 21
731 31/3 Little Wind' (R) OPE 3m 5 GS *(Jt fav) cls up thruout, disp aft 14th til blndrd 3 out, not rcvr* 3 24
817 6/4 Charlton Ho' (L) OPE 3m 5 GF *chsd ldr, btn 3rd whn f 14th* F -
1125 20/4 Stafford Cr' (R) OPE 3m 7 S *prom, ld 5th til wnt clr 3 out, easily* 1 23
1343 4/5 Holnicote (L) OPE 3m 6 GS *(fav) made all, not extnd* 1 22

Hurdles winner 94; decent pointer now; well-ridden; consistent; win more 2nd class Opens; G-S 24

QUARTER MARKER(IRE) br.g. 8 Celio Rufo - Palatine Lady by Pauper K Tork
451 9/3 Charing (L) OPE 3m 11 G *rear, blnd 8th, p.u. nxt* P 0
595 23/3 Parham (R) OPE 3m 12 GS *prom, mstk 2nd, wknd rpdly 8th, bhnd whn p.u. 10th* P 0
778 31/3 Penshurst (L) INT 3m 6 GS *ld to 10th, bhnd whn p.u. aft 11th* P 0
965 8/4 Heathfield (R) INT 3m 6 G *hdstrng, chsd ldr 3rd til f 7th* F -
1052 13/4 Penshurst (L) OPE 3m 7 G *wll in tch to 11th, wknd aft, p.u. aft 13th* P 0
1209 21/4 Heathfield (R) OPE 3m 5 F *wll in tch, 4th whn f 14th* F -
1296 28/4 Bexhill (R) OPE 3m 4 F *trckd ldrs, rmndrs aft 4th, 3rd & ev ch whn u.r. 4 out* U -
1372 4/5 Peper Harow (L) OPE 3m 6 F *keen hold, hld up, lst tch appr 13th, p.u. 15th* P 0
1400 6/5 Northaw (L) OPE 3m 6 F *in tch, hit 9th, ld 13th, hdd & blnd nxt, sn wknd* 3 0
1541 16/5 Folkestone (R) HC 2m 5f 8 G *held up, rdn and lost tch apr 9th, t.o. when p.u. before 3 out.* P 0

Beaten a fence on only completion & no stamina for points 0

QUATTRO (Irish) — **I** 31[F], **I** 86[U], **I** 109[1], **I** 194[1], **I** 263[2]
QUAYFIELD (Irish) — **I** 170[6], **I** 254[U], **I** 287[3], **I** 401[1], **I** 485[4]
QUAY FLY (Irish) — **I** 92[P]
QUAYSIDE COTTAGE(IRE) b or br.g. 8 Quayside - Polly's Cottage by Pollerton B Marley
1995 P(0),F(-),P(0),r(-),4(15)
78 11/2 Wetherby Po' (L) OPE 3m 10 GS *alwys prom, 2nd at 13th, 3rd 4 out, onepcd* 3 15
118 17/2 Witton Cast' (R) INT 3m 9 S *rear early, prog 10th, ld 12th, ran on well* 1 18

303 2/3 Great Stain' (L) CON 3m 11 GS *(fav) hld up, prog 11th, ld 16th til jnd last, outpcd flat* 2 19
588 23/3 Wetherby Po' (L) INT 3m 17 S *hld up, prog 14th, ran on well 2 out, disp last, ld flat* 1 20
1106 15/4 Hexham (L) HC 3m 1f 9 GF *(fav) well bhnd early, steady hdwy after hfwy, ev ch 3 out, wknd after next and p.u. lame.* P 0

Much improved 96; stays well; unwise risk last start (ground); Opens if fit 97; Soft 22

QUEEN OF CLUBS (Irish) — **I** 71P, **I** 150P, **I** 210P
QUEEN OF EAGLES (Irish) — **I** 88P, **I** 143P
QUEEN OF THE GALES (Irish) — **I** 243P, **I** 351U
QUEEN OF THE SUIR (Irish) — **I** 42F, **I** 204U, **I** 253P, **I** 309³, **I** 427F

QUEEN'S CHAPLAIN b.g. 12 The Parson - Reginasway by Flair Path E F Astley-Arlington
1995 5(14),R(-)
93 11/2 Ampton (R) LAD 3m 7 GF *prom, chsd wnr 12-13th, rdn 15th, sn lost tch* 4 12
227 24/2 Duncombe Pa' (R) LAD 3m 6 GS *in tch to 12th, last & jmpd slwly 3 out & nxt* 4 0
536 17/3 Southwell P' (L) LAD 3m 9 GS *alwys rear, nvr going, p.u. 5 out* P 0
673 29/3 Sedgefield (L) HC 3m 3f 7 GF *hit 2nd, in tch, f heavily 12th.* F -
1121 20/4 Bangor (L) HC 3m 110yds 8 S *rear, jmpd slowly 3rd, rdn after next, ref 6th.* R

No longer of any account 0

QUEENS DAY b.m. 8 Balinger - Brave Remark by Brave Invader (USA) J Grant Cann
477 10/3 Tweseldown (R) MDO 3m 15 G *rear of ldng grp to hlfwy, p.u. 4 out* P 0

Rarely seen & shows nothing 0

QUEEN'S EQUA b or br.m. 6 Queen's Soldier (USA) - Equa by Cheval Mrs B J Harkins
388 9/3 Llanfrynach (R) RES 3m 20 GS *bhnd, blnd 6th, t.o. & p.u. 8th* P 0
696 30/3 Llanvapley (L) MDN 3m 13 GS *alwys rear, p.u. 11th* P 0
849 6/4 Howick (L) MDN 3m 14 GF *mid-div, f 4th* F -
1271 27/4 Pyle (R) MDO 3m 15 G *rear, losing tch 8th, t.o. 10th, p.u. 12th* P 0
1557 18/5 Bassaleg (R) RES 3m 14 F *alwys bhnd, t.o. & p.u. 12th* P 0
1605 25/5 Bassaleg (R) MDO 3m 8 GS *cls up til lost plc 8th, p.u. 13th* P 0

Shows no ability 0

QUEENS TOUR b.g. 11 Sweet Monday - On Tour by Queen's Hussar Mrs A P Kelly
159 17/2 Weston Park (L) CON 3m 22 G *prom early, fdd, p.u. 14th* P 0
291 2/3 Eaton Hall (R) LAD 3m 10 G *mid-div, lost tch 10th, p.u. 14th* P 0
908 8/4 Hereford (R) HC 2m 3f 12 GF *bhnd from 6th, t.o. when p.u. before 2 out.* P 0
1194 21/4 Sandon (L) LAD 3m 7 G *alwys rear, t.o. & p.u. 8th* P 0

No longer of any account 0

QUENBY GIRL(IRE) ch.m. 8 Remainder Man - Beyond The Rainbow by Royal Palace Miss E B Godfrey
57 10/2 Cottenham (R) LAD 3m 9 GS *chsd ldrs, lost tch 12th, nrly u.r. nxt, t.o.* 3 12
394 9/3 Garthorpe (R) LAD 3m 6 G *mostly 3rd/4th, 3rd & outpcd whn f 4 out* F -
566 17/3 Wolverhampt' (L) LAD 3m 5 GS *chsd wnr, ev ch 3 out, styd on onepcd* 2 15

Missed 95; ran well enough last start but outclassed; should try Maidens 13

QUENTIN DURWOOD gr.g. 10 Mr Fluorocarbon - Donallan by No Mercy Peter Bonner
56 10/2 Cottenham (R) OPE 3m 12 GS *hld up in tch, prog to ld 13th, hdd & no ext 2 out* 2 20
249 25/2 Charing (L) XX 3m 11 GS *(fav) hld up, jnd issue 4 out, rdn & btn in 4th nxt* 4 13
571 17/3 Detling (L) CON 3m 13 GF *rear til p.u. 10th, lame* P 0

Winning hurdler; non-stayer in points; disappointing & problems last start 16

QUERRIN LODGE b.g. 10 Furry Glen - Opel Kadett by Steel Heart P J Gratton
1995 P(0),P(0),2(16),1(16),4(11),2(18),2(0)
277 2/3 Clyst St Ma' (L) OPE 3m 4 S *sn bhnd, t.o. & p.u. 16th* P 0
444 9/3 Haldon (R) OPE 3m 5 S *alwys last, t.o. frm 7th til p.u. 3 out* P 0
804 4/4 Clyst St Ma' (L) INT 3m 3 GS *alwys last, strgglng final ctt* 3 10
925 8/4 Bishopsleigh (R) CON 3m 6 G *bhnd frm 10th, t.o. p.u. 3 out* P 0
1074 13/4 Lifton (R) INT 3m 9 S *disp 3rd 10th, poor 5th 13th, t.o., p.u. apr 2 out* P 0
1425 6/5 High Bickin' (R) OPE 3m 4 G *lost tch 14th, t.o.* 3 0
1625 27/5 Lifton (R) INT 3m 8 GS *4th at 10th, lost ground steadily frm 14th* 4 0

Restricted winner 95; reverted to type in 96; can only be watched now 10

QUICKLY (Irish) — **I** 286P

QUICK OPINION ch.g. 11 Deep Run - Kilbrack by Perspex J F Weldhen
200 24/2 Lemalla (R) MDO 3m 12 HY *ld to 6th, prom aft, no imp ldrs frm 4 out* 3 11
446 9/3 Haldon (R) MDO 3m 13 S *in tch, ev ch whn cls 3rd 3 out, sn wknd* 5 0
629 23/3 Kilworthy (L) MDN 3m 11 GS *c.o. by loose horse 2nd* C -
1071 13/4 Lifton (R) MDN 3m 10 S *cls 2nd 7th, disp frm 12th, hrd rddn, no ext cls home* 2 15

1432 6/5 High Bickin' (R) MDO 3m 9 G *ld to 4th, cls 3rd whn p.u. & dismntd apr 8th* P 0

Lightly raced & missed 95; just touched off at Lifton but have lost best chance of a win now 13

QUICK QUICK SLOE b.m. 7 Scallywag - Cherry Morello by Bargello Dr S G F Cave
1995 1(15)
684 30/3 Chaddesley ' (L) RES 3m 14 G *(fav) bmpd & u.r. 1st* U -
1075 13/4 Lifton (R) RES 3m 12 S *(fav) hld up,wnt 2nd 16th,ld nxt,lkd wnr til hdd & no ext 2 out* 2 15
1482 11/5 Bredwardine (R) RES 3m 13 G *(fav) s.s. u.r. 2nd* U -
1591 25/5 Mounsey Hil' (R) RES 3m 15 G *chsd ldr to 6th, lost plc nxt, bhnd & p.u. 2 out* P 0

Maiden winner only start 95; unfortunate season 96; may do better 97; G-S 17

QUICK RAPOR b.g. 11 Rapid Pass - Dark Sensation by Thriller D G Alers-Hankey
25 20/1 Barbury Cas' (L) OPE 3m 14 GS *ld 4th til hdd & mstk 15th, wknd rpdly, p.u. 2 out* P 0
257 29/2 Nottingham (L) HC 2 1/2m 11 G *bhnd and struggling to go pace after one cct, styd on from 3 out, nearest fin.* 3 20
672 29/3 Aintree (L) HC 2 3/4m 26 G *(bl) jmpd slowly rear, well bhnd when blnd 13th (Valentine's), t.o.* 14 0

Chase/points winner 94; missed 95; not disgraced 96 but on the slide; Confineds 97 best bet 19

QUIET ARROGANCE(USA) b.m. 10 Greek Sky (USA) - Figurative (USA) by Bolinas Boy D H Brown
1026 13/4 Brocklesby ' (L) MDN 3m 6 GF *ld to 12th, wknng whn broke leg bfr 4 out, (dead)* P 0

Dead 0

QUIET CONFIDENCE(IRE) b.m. 6 Pennine Walk - Northern Wisdom by Northfields (USA) Mrs Sally Mullins
1995 6(0),P(0),1(12)
136 17/2 Ottery St M' (L) LAD 3m 9 GS *ld to 4 out, onepcd frm nxt* 3 17
273 2/3 Parham (R) LAD 3m 11 GF *3rd whn u.r. 3rd* U -
527 16/3 Larkhill (R) MEM 3m 4 G *(fav) made all, 10l clr 14th, unchal* 1 15
868 6/4 Larkhill (R) RES 3m 4 F *j.w., made all, sn clr, slow 4 out, jnd last, ran on gamely* 1 19

Won poor Maiden 95; much improved last start 96; only won small races; could upgrade; G-F 19

QUIRINA MAJANO (Irish) — I 47[P], I 118[P], I 507[P]

QUITE A CHARACTER b.m. 8 Reformed Character - Tawny Eagle by The Tystan Mrs J Raw
1995 P(0),R(-)
80 11/2 Wetherby Po' (L) MDO 3m 12 GS *mid-div, fdd 12th, p.u. 4 out* P 0
308 2/3 Great Stain' (L) MDO 3m 12 GS *handy, ld 2 out til ran wd apr last, outpcd by wnr flat* 2 12
415 9/3 Charm Park (L) MDO 3m 13 G *in tch, mstks 8th & 11th, styd on same pace aft* 5 0
764 31/3 Great Stain' (L) MDN 3m 16 GS *prom, ld 7th-hlfwy, wknd rpdly, p.u. 3 out* P 0
1135 20/4 Hornby Cast' (L) MDN 3m 10 G *rear, mstk 3rd, sn strgglng, p.u. 2 out* P 0

Good enough for a win on her 2nd but no improvement; may do better 97 12

QUITE A MISS b.m. 6 True Song - Nitty's Girl by Spartan General C W Loggin
1641 2/6 Dingley (R) RES 3m 13 GF *jmpd badly, last frm 3rd, t.o. & p.u. 9th* P 0

An inauspicious debut 0

QUITE SO br.m. 12 Mansingh (USA) - Chiquitita by Reliance II F L Matthews
159 17/2 Weston Park (L) CON 3m 22 G *(bl) ref to start* 0 0
459 9/3 Eyton-On-Se' (L) OPE 3m 11 G *alwys bhnd, t.o. whn p.u. 12th* P 0
684 30/3 Chaddesley ' (L) RES 3m 14 G *s.v.s. t.o. til f 9th* F -

No longer of any account & unpleasant 0

QUIXALL CROSSETT b.g. 11 Beverley Boy - Grange Classic by Stype Grange Mrs Karen Woodhead
1995 **4(0),4(0),5(17),U(NH),P(NH),5(NH)**
37 3/2 Wetherby (L) HC 3m 110yds 11 GS *hmpd before 1st, lost tch from hfwy, t.o..* 7 0
226 24/2 Duncombe Pa' (R) OPE 3m 10 GS *prom, outpcd 12th, lft 3rd nxt, styd on und pres flat* 2 16
367 6/3 Catterick (L) HC 3m 1f 110yds 12 G *(bl) in tch till outpcd after 11th, bhnd after.* 6 11
486 16/3 Newcastle (L) HC 3m 9 GS *held up, hit 8th, rallied 11th, ev ch 3 out, one pace last.* 3 20
1340 4/5 Hexham (L) HC 3m 1f 13 S *bhnd most of way.* 6 10
1542 16/5 Perth (R) HC 2 1/2m 110yds 8 F *(bl) pressed ldrs, mstk 7th, wknd after 6 out, bhnd when p.u. before 3 out.* P 0

Has some ability but stupidly campaigned; would have fair shot if aimed at Maidens 14

RABBLE ROUSER b.g. 9 Politico (USA) - Penny Pink by Spartan General M J Brown
79 11/2 Wetherby Po' (L) MDO 3m 12 GS *alwys prom, 2nd 2 out, chsd wnr, alwys hld* 2 13
222 24/2 Duncombe Pa' (R) MEM 3m 6 GS *(fav) cls up, ev ch whn blnd 14th, not rcvr, no ch & u.r. 2 out* U -
516 16/3 Dalton Park (R) MDO 3m 11 G *n.j.w. mid-div & drvn alng, no ch whn ran out 3 out* r -
591 23/3 Wetherby Po' (L) MDO 3m 14 S *cls up, ld 11th-4 out, onepcd aft* 2 12
764 31/3 Great Stain' (L) MDN 3m 16 GS *chsd ldrs, prog 4 out, chal whn mstk last, sn ld, ran on wll* 1 16

1130	20/4	Hornby Cast'	(L)	CON	3m	13	G	*not fluent, alwys strgglng, t.o. & p.u. 3 out*	P	0

Missed 95; well ridden to beat large, weak field; much more needed for Restricted; jumps poorly 14

RACE AGAINST TIME b.m. 10 Latest Model - Gemini Miss by My Swanee — Mrs D D Scott

729	31/3	Little Wind'	(R)	RES	3m	12	GS	*sn bhnd, t.o. p.u. apr 11th*	P	0
1128	20/4	Stafford Cr'	(R)	RES	3m	17	S	*rear whn f 4th*	F	-
1652	8/6	Umberleigh	(L)	MDO	3m	10	GF	*in tch, prog 11th, rdn nxt, wknd 14th, f heavily 3 out*	F	-

Gave it a go last start but yet to show any tangible ability 0

RACHELS PLAN (Irish) — **I** 621[S]

RADIANT MONARCH b.g. 9 Kinglet - Sunyone by Sunyboy — S H Marriage

1995 P(0),P(0)

181	18/2	Horseheath	(R)	RES	3m	5	G	*cls up, chsd wnr 9th, mstk 12th, btn whn mstk 2 out, wknd*	3	10
494	16/3	Horseheath	(R)	RES	3m	10	GF	*alwys rear, prog 4 out, wknd rpdly nxt, t.o.*	4	0
679	30/3	Cottenham	(R)	RES	3m	15	GF	*in tch in rear, outpcd 15th, no imp on ldrs 3 out*	4	11
1260	27/4	Cottenham	(R)	RES	3m	3	F	*sttld rear,2nd at 9th,rdn 13th,outpcd frm 4 out*	3	0

Maiden winner 94; slight revival 96 but beaten 20l minimum & Restricted chances slim 12

RADICAL DUAL (Irish) — **I** 22[4], **I** 89[4]

RADICAL RIVER (Irish) — **I** 14[2], **I** 47[2], **I** 113[2], **I** 462[1]

RADICAL-TIMES (Irish) — **I** 243, , **I** 311[P], **I** 564[2], **I** 607[P], **I** 642[3]

RADICAL VIEWS b.g. 11 Radical - Regency View by Royal Highway — M A Walter

1995 P(0),**U(-)**,**8(17)**

364	5/3	Leicester	(R)	HC	2m 1f	12	GS	*chsd ldr to 2nd, prom in chasing gp till rdn 6th, no ch 4 out, t.o..*	8	0
435	9/3	Newton Brom'	(R)	OPE	3m	7	GS	*chsd ldrs til ld 14th, hdd 3 out, wknd*	5	10
885	6/4	Kimble	(L)	MEM	3m	5	GF	*hld up, chsd wnr aft 12th, ld 2 out-last, no ext*	2	15
1505	11/5	Kingston Bl'	(L)	MEM	3m	5	G	*w.w. trckd ldr 9th, ld on innr apr 2 out, sn clr*	1	16
1595	25/5	Garthorpe	(R)	CON	3m	15	G	*3rd 6 out, chsd wnr 4 out, ld brfly 2 out, no ext last*	2	18
1647	8/6	Umberleigh	(L)	OPE	3m	7	GF	*hld up, prog 13th, went 2nd & b.d.3 out*	B	-

Staged slight revival 96; needs gap between races; could win small race at 12; G/F-S 19

RADIO DAYS (Irish) — **I** 343[P]

RAGGED RIVER (Irish) — **I** 229[1], **I** 349[2]

RAGGETY MAN (Irish) — **I** 118[P], **I** 142[P], **I** 244[2], **I** 312[P], **I** 377[4], **I** 567[P]

RAGTIME b.g. 9 Pas de Seul - Boldella by Bold Lad (IRE) — A S Reid

143	17/2	Larkhill	(R)	MDO	3m	14	G	*mid-div whn f 2nd*	F	-

.. 0

RAGTIME BOY b.g. 8 Sunyboy - Ragtime Dance by Ragstone — Mrs Jo Clarke

1995 **3(NH)**,**9(NH)**,**P(NH)**,**4(NH)**,**2(NH)**,**3(NH)**,**2(NH)**,**2(NH)**

370	7/3	Wincanton	(R)	HC	3m 1f 110yds	5	GF	*held up, lost pl 13th, rallied 16th, f next.*	F	-
1277	27/4	Bratton Down	(L)	CON	3m	15	GF	*mid-div, prog 15th, 2nd apr last, no ch wth wnr*	2	20
1591	25/5	Mounsey Hil'	(R)	RES	3m	15	G	*(fav) chsd ldrs,ld apr 2 out,lft wll clr nxt,fin 1st, disq*	1D	20
1629	30/5	Uttoxeter	(L)	HC	2m 5f	13	GS	*held up, rdn along 11th, 5th and no ch when f 4 out.*	F	-

Has ability & very unlucky 3rd start; should gain compensation 97 if sensibly campaigned; Good 20

RAGTIME COWBOY JOE gr.g. 11 Alias Smith (USA) - Repel by Hardicanute — Miss R Knight

214	24/2	Newtown	(L)	CON	3m	21	GS	*hld up bhnd, nvr nr to chal*	9	0
426	9/3	Upton-On-Se'	(R)	CON	3m	16	GS	*alwys strgglng in rear*	9	0
638	23/3	Siddington	(L)	CON	3m	16	S	*mid div, rddn appr 10th, kpt on frm 14th, nvr trbld ldrs*	5	14
687	30/3	Chaddesley '	(L)	CON	3m	10	G	*cls up, rdn 10th, outpcd nxt, p.u. 14th*	P	0
1001	9/4	Upton-On-Se'	(R)	MEM	3m	6	F	*5th til p.u. 7th*	P	0
1437	6/5	Ashorne	(R)	MXO	3m	13	G	*last at 4th, alwys bhnd aft*	9	0

Schoolmaster & going through the motions now 0

RAGTIMER b.g. 6 Nearly A Hand - Ragtime Dance by Ragstone — W Bush

956	8/4	Lockinge	(L)	MDN	3m	7	GF	*cls up til 12th, wknd, t.o. & p.u. 5 out*	P	0
1248	27/4	Woodford	(L)	MDN	3m	15	G	*mid-div, mstk & rmmdr 9th, 6th whn hmp & u.r. 15th*	U	-

Young but yet to threaten; should do better 10

RAGTIME SOLO b.g. 12 Raga Navarro (ITY) - Solentown by Town Crier — Mrs Fiona Britten

1995 3(10),4(14),1(15),2(0)

133	17/2	Ottery St M'	(L)	OPE	3m	18	GS	*(bl) alwys mid-div, bhnd whn p.u. 3 out*	P	0
212	24/2	Castle Of C'	(R)	CON	3m	7	HY	*handy, lost tch 14th, t.o. & p.u. last*	P	0
561	17/3	Ottery St M'	(L)	LAD	3m	12	G	*(bl) prom early, lost tch 13th, bhnd whn p.u. 3 out*	P	0
991	8/4	Kingston St'	(R)	LAD	3m	8	F	*(bl) 7th at 10th, f 12th*	F	-

Won 2 of last 34 & showed nothing in 96; could be finished now 0

RAHEEN RIVER (Irish) — I 195P, I 3481

RAH WAN(USA) ch.g. 10 Riverman (USA) - Thorough by Thatch (USA) Mrs J Hadden-Wight

1995 **P(0)**

798 3/4 Ascot (R) HC 2m 3f 110yds 10 GF *held up, f 8th.* F -

1532 13/5 Towcester (R) HC 2m 110yds 16 GF *hdwy 6th, 7th when mstk and wknd 4 out, p.u. before 2 out.* P 0

1541 16/5 Folkestone (R) HC 2m 5f 8 G *started slowly, prog and in tch when f 8th.* F -

H/Chase winner 94 (2m); only 4 runs since & no completions; hard to place & best watched 14

RAIDO ch.g. 11 Black Minstrel - Fair Songstress by Compensation Miss Anne Barnett

683 30/3 Chaddesley ' (L) MEM 3m 17 G *blnd 1st, in tch, 6th & outpcd 12th, p.u. 3 out* P 0

1043 13/4 Bitterley (L) OPE 3m 9 G *ld 5-8th, 3l 2nd & ev ch 13th, onepcd frm 15th* 3 17

1316 28/4 Bitterley (L) OPE 3m 5 G *feeling pace frm 3rd, 10l 5th 11th, remote 4th 13th* 4 0

1480 11/5 Bredwardine (R) LAD 3m 12 G *ld to 3rd, cls up whn r.o. & u.r. 6th* r -

1579 19/5 Wolverhampt' (L) LAD 3m 9 G *chsd ldr 5-10th, wknd apr 14th, t.o. & p.u. 3 out* P 0

One fair performance in modest Open but most unlikely to win at 12 14

RAIKE IT IN b.m. 6 Silly Prices - Caravan Centre by Nelcius J Hugill

1995 U(-)

330 3/3 Market Rase' (L) MDO 3m 7 G *in tch, blnd 8th, 6th & outpcd 13th, p.u. nxt* P 0

704 30/3 Tranwell (L) MDO 3m 16 GS *mid-div whn mstk 13th, no dang aft* 4 12

823 6/4 Stainton (R) MEM 3m 6 GF *sttld rear, prog 4 out, ld nxt til hdd & hit last, not rcvr* 2 12

Gradually improving; more needed for Maiden win but should still have scope 13

RAINBOW FANTASIA(IRE) b.g. 7 Orchestra - Rovral Flo by Whistling Deer P J Millington

92 11/2 Ampton (R) MDO 3m 7 GF *n.j.w. wll bhnd frm 3rd, ref 7th* R -

239 25/2 Southwell P' (L) MDO 3m 9 HO *hld up in tch, 5th whn f 13th* F -

392 9/3 Garthorpe (R) MEM 3m 6 G *2nd frm 7th, chal 3 out, outpcd nxt* 2 10

540 17/3 Southwell P' (L) MDO 3m 9 GS *mid-div, lost tch aft 12th, p.u. 3 out* P 0

901 6/4 Dingley (R) MDN 2m 5f 9 GS *nvr dang, kpt gng whn rest stopped* 3 0

1008 9/4 Flagg Moor (L) MDO 2 1/2m 7 G *(fav) chsd ldr 7-11th, rdn app 3 out, 3rd & btn whn blndrd last* 4 0

1174 20/4 Chaddesley ' (L) MDN 3m 10 G *prom, ld 12th til hdd 17th, wknd frm nxt* 6 0

1378 5/5 Dingley (R) MDO 2 1/2m 16 GF *mid-div, 8th & btn whn nrly f 11th, no ch aft* 4 0

Beat 3 other finishers in 5 completions & a staggering favourite once 0

RAINBOW RIOT (Irish) — I 5982, I 630F

RAIN DOWN b or br.g. 9 Miner's Lamp - Queen McQuaid by Mick McQuaid Mrs Ian McKie

128 17/2 Kingston Bl' (L) RES 3m 14 GS *(fav) hld up bhnd, prog 10th, no imp 13th, 5th & btn whn p.u. 14th* P 0

1102 14/4 Guilsborough (L) RES 3m 15 G *prom, ld 13th til aft 2 out, no ch wth wnr aft* 2 16

Promising in 94; missed 95; ran well 2nd start but blighted by his fragility; G-S 18

RAIN MARK b.g. 15 Politico (USA) - Rightful Ruler by Sovereign Lord M G Chatterton

1995 5(14)

169 18/2 Market Rase' (L) CON 3m 15 GF *nvr bttr than mid-div* 9 0

326 3/3 Market Rase' (L) OPE 3m 14 G *nvr nr ldrs, 6th & no ch apr 14th, t.o.* 5 0

722 31/3 Garthorpe (R) MEM 3m 4 G *ld to apr 5th, ld 11th-12th, rdn & kpt on frm 2 out* 2 12

1022 13/4 Brocklesby ' (L) CON 3m 6 GF *ld for 2 m, ran on onepce, 3rd outpcd frm 3 out* 3 11

1377 5/5 Dingley (R) CON 3m 12 GF *prom til wknd 10th, poor 8th whn u.r. 15th* U -

Just makes up the numbers now 0

RAINPROOF (Irish) — I 475P

RAIN SPIRIT (Irish) — I 79P, I 13744, I 146F

RAINY MISS(IRE) b.m. 8 Cheval - Vulrain by Raincheck Neil Allen

1995 U(-),P(0),4(0),P(0),P(0),P(0),6(0),4(13),F(-)

21 20/1 Barbury Cas' (L) MEM 3m 16 GS *alwys rear, t.o. & p.u. 12th* P 0

Irish Maiden winner; not threatening to win in 95 & finished 2nd Saturday of 96 10

RAISE A DOLLAR br.m. 6 Primitive Rising (USA) - Gregory's Lady by Meldrum Mrs D W Hill

1995 **10(NH)**

123 17/2 Witton Cast' (R) MDO 3m 11 S *rear, smooth prog to trck ldrs 12th, ev ch 2 out, no ext aft* 2 10

Ran a decent race & disappeared; may do better if fit 97 13

RAISE A LOAN br.g. 6 Impecunious - Lizzie The Twig by Precipice Wood Mrs C Bailey

424 9/3 High Easter (L) MDN 3m 10 S *(fav) j.w. ld 7th, made rest drw clr appr last, v. easy* 1 15

834 6/4 Marks Tey (L) RES 3m 11 G *(fav) trckd ldr going wll, ld 16th, in cmmnd whn f 2 out* F -

1181 21/4 Mollington (R) RES 3m 10 F *(fav) ld 3rd, wll clr frm 15th, unchal* 1 19

Promising; speedy; won with minimum of fuss; should reach Opens in 97; F-S 22

RAISE AN ARGUMENT b.g. 17 No Argument - Ten Again by Raise You Ten Mrs J H Docker
1995 1(20),2(21),2(20),2(19),2(20),1(19),3(18),1(20),1(20)

246 25/2 Southwell P' (L) OPE 3m 9 HO *mid-div, lost tch 9th, t.o. 12th* 3 0
395 9/3 Garthorpe (R) OPE 3m 7 G *(fav) made all, drrew away frm 4 out, comf* 1 18
725 31/3 Garthorpe (R) OPE 3m 9 G *(fav) wth ldr, ld 5-11th, outpcd 15th, rallied 2 out, no ext last* 3 19
902 6/4 Dingley (R) OPE 3m 4 GS *(fav) 2nd til ld 12th, battld back whn hdd 2 out, remarkable* 1 20
1379 5/5 Dingley (R) MXO 3m 7 GF *trckd ldrs, chal 14th, ld nxt, clr 2 out, ran on strngly* 1 20
1519 12/5 Garthorpe (R) OPE 3m 7 GF *prom, ld 8-9th, n.j.w. frm hlfwy, onepcd frm 3 out* 3 15
1598 25/5 Garthorpe (R) OPE 3m 6 G *ld to 5th, 2nd til squeezed out apr 11th* r -

Most consistent veteran; unplaced twice in 25 starts 94-6; remarkable indeed; can win at 18; Any 19

RAKISH QUEEN b.m. 9 Joshua - Cognac Queen by Armagnac Monarch R W Phizacklea

1101 14/4 Guilsborough (L) RES 3m 16 G *6th whn u.r. 6th* U -
1181 21/4 Mollington (R) RES 3m 10 F *alwys rear, blnd 11th, p.u. 13th* P 0

Maiden winner 94; missed 95; showed nothing in 96 0

RALEAGH MUGGINS (Irish) — **I** 256U, **I** 2995, **I** 4072, **I** 4921, **I** 5966

RALLYE STRIPE gr.g. 12 Buckskin (FR) - Petit Bleu by Abernant Miss J F Holmes

240 25/2 Southwell P' (L) MDO 3m 15 HO *set mad gallop to 5th, wknd 9th, t.o. & p.u. 12th* P 0
333 3/3 Market Rase' (L) MDO 3m 11 G *chsd ldrs 7th-12th, grad wknd* 5 0
633 23/3 Market Rase' (L) LAD 3m 10 GF *nvr dang, last pair frm 6th, outpcd nxt* 6 0
726 31/3 Garthorpe (R) RES 3m 16 G *sn ld, hdd 11th, stppd to nil, p.u. 3 out* P 0
973 8/4 Thorpe Lodge (L) MDO 3m 7 GF *alwys prom, ld 6th-5 out, cls up whn f 2 out* F -
1301 28/4 Southwell P' (L) MDO 3m 10 GF *ld & f 1st* F -
1523 12/5 Garthorpe (R) MDO 3m 11 GF *s.s. prog & cls up 12th, sn btn, p.u. 4 out* P 0
1569 19/5 Mollington (R) MDO 3m 10 GS *s.s. last & wll bhnd, t.o. 11th* 6 0

Does not stay 0

RALLYING CRY(IRE) b.g. 8 Last Tycoon - Clarina by Klairon Mrs J Seymour
1995 **3(NH),7(NH),9(NH)**

501 16/3 Lanark (R) RES 3m 12 G *nvr dang, p.u. 2 out* P 0
789 1/4 Kelso (L) HC 3m 1f 11 GF *struggling to keep up after one cct, t.o..* 4 0
1087 14/4 Friars Haugh (L) MDO 3m 9 F *lost tch 12th, p.u. 4 out* P 0
1450 6/5 Witton Cast' (R) MDO 3m 14 G *midfld thruout, nvr a dang* 6 0

Disappointing & beaten long way on both completions 0

RAMBLING ECHO b.g. 15 Rymer - Tarquann by Elegant Stephen Miss C Greenwood
1995 P(0),8(0)

139 17/2 Larkhill (R) CON 3m 11 G *sn rear & jmpd slwly, p.u. 7th* P 0

Of no account 0

RAMBLING LORD(IRE) b.g. 8 Mister Lord (USA) - Vickies Gold by Golden Love J Betteridge
1995 **14(NH)**

244 25/2 Southwell P' (L) CON 3m 13 HO *rear, 12th whn u.r. 5th* U -
329 3/3 Market Rase' (L) RES 3m 12 G *in tch, jnd ldrs 4 out, ld apr last, styd on* 1 16
515 16/3 Dalton Park (R) XX 3m 12 G *in tch, 6th whn mstk 16th, ran on nxt, ld last, drvn out* 1 20

Ex-Irish; novice ridden to beat fair rivals; could win Opens if fit 97; Good 21

RAMLOSA(NZ) b.g. 12 Uncle Remus (NZ) - Sereniwai (NZ) by Golden Plume R Cope
1995 8(0),9(0),4(0),4(0),6(0),11(0),6(0)

124 17/2 Kingston Bl' (L) CON 3m 17 GS *1st ride, alwys bhnd, last frm 6th, t.o. 14th* 11 0
231 24/2 Heythrop (R) XX 3m 10 GS *in tch, chsd ldrs 12th, tk 3rd cls home* 3 12
478 10/3 Tweseldown (R) RES 3m 9 G *u.r. 3rd* U -
642 23/3 Siddington (L) RES 3m 15 S *wll bhnd frm 13th, t.o.* 6 0
885 6/4 Kimble (L) MEM 3m 5 GF *in tch in rear, 5th & btn whn u.r. 13th* U -
1019 13/4 Kingston Bl' (L) INT 3m 6 G *bhnd frm 6th, t.o. 13th, fin well* 4 0
1177 21/4 Mollington (R) INT 3m 14 F *(bl) alwys wll in rear, 10th hlfwy, t.o. & p.u. 2 out* P 0
1505 11/5 Kingston Bl' (L) MEM 3m 5 G *chsd ldrs, pshd alng 7th, outpcd 13th, onepcd aft* 3 0
1567 19/5 Mollington (R) INT 3m 12 GS *alwys bhnd, t.o. 11th, styd on* 6 0

Schoolmaster now & no longer of any account 0

RANDY ROSE (Irish) — **I** 196P, **I** 324F, **I** 3842

RAPID RASCAL b.h. 11 Rapid Pass - Sue Ming Vii Miss P J Boundy
1995 P(0),3(13),2(17),10(0),1(15),3(19),F(-),4(0)

135 17/2 Ottery St M' (L) LAD 3m 11 GS *prom early, lost tch 7th, t.o. 14th* 7 0
279 2/3 Clyst St Ma' (L) LAD 3m 7 S *prom to 14th, lost tch frm 3 out* 5 12
531 16/3 Cothelstone (L) CON 3m 12 G *chsd ldr 5th, disp bfly 6th, wknd 11th, u.r. 13th* U -

803 4/4 Clyst St Ma' (L) LAD 3m 4 GS *slght ld til aft 8th, disp 11th-nxt, sn wknd.* 4 0
991 8/4 Kingston St' (R) LAD 3m 8 F *ld to 7th, ld 12-15th, 5th 2 out, ran on agn cls home* 3 17
1078 13/4 Cothelstone (L) MXO 3m 6 GF *ld to 8th, b.d. bend aft 10th* B -
1264 27/4 Pyle (R) LAD 3m 10 G *8l 3rd at 6th, wknd 14th, no ch whn f 2 out* F -
1406 6/5 Hackwood Pa' (L) MXO 3m 5 F *2nd til wknd frm hlfwy* 4 12
1499 11/5 Holnicote (L) CON 3m 8 G *pullng & sn prom, ld brfly 9th, lost plc 15th* 5 14
1550 18/5 Bratton Down (L) CON 3m 8 F *ld to 3rd & frm 5th-14th, cls up til outpcd frm 3 out* 5 14
1611 26/5 Tweseldown (R) XX 3m 9 G *prom to 9th, sn outpcd, t.o. & p.u. 15th* P 0
1650 8/6 Umberleigh (L) CON 3m 7 GF *ld to 12th, wknd nxt* 4 0

Open winner 95; novice ridden 96; heavily campaigned & outclassed 96; unlikely to win again; Any 12

RAP UP FAST(USA) b.g. 7 Eskimo (USA) - Naomi's Flash (USA) by Ray Jeter (USA) R T Baimbridge

1995 4(0),6(0),5(0),P(0)

749 31/3 Upper Sapey (R) MDO 3m 17 GS *(Jt fav) ld/disp til wknd frm 2 out* 5 12
1319 28/4 Bitterley (L) MDN 3m 13 G *(fav) w.w. prog 13th, ld 15th, 2l up whn f nxt* F -
1637 1/6 Bratton Down (L) MDO 3m 11 G *(fav) w.w. mstk 9th,5th 3 out,prog nxt,in tch apr last,wknd flat* 4 10

Possibly unlucky 2nd start but non-stayer & even Baimbridge magic failed to work 13

RARE FIRE b.g. 12 Rarity - El Diana by Tarboosh (USA) Mrs R Davison

1995 **U(NH),15(NH),P(NH)**

305 2/3 Great Stain' (L) LAD 3m 11 GS *1st ride, t.o. 8th, p.u. 13th* P 0
499 16/3 Lanark (R) LAD 3m 10 G *sn well bhnd, p.u. 10th* P 0

No longer of any account 9

RARE FLUTTER b.m. 9 Sunyboy - Wings Ground by Murrayfield Richard Barber

1995 2(16),1(16),1(18)

379 9/3 Barbury Cas' (L) XX 3m 9 GS *(fav) sttld rear, limited prog 10th, wknd & p.u. 15th* P 0
732 31/3 Little Wind' (R) INT 3m 6 GS *towrds rear, lost tch aft 14th* 4 0
989 8/4 Kingston St' (R) CON 3m 6 F *went 2nd & mstk 9th, u.r. 10th* U -
1127 20/4 Stafford Cr' (R) INT 3m 4 S *ld til 10th, bndrd nxt, rmmdrs, t.o. & p.u. 4 out* P 0
1393 6/5 Cotley Farm (L) XX 3m 10 GF *rr early, prog 8th, ld nxt, ran on wl frm 2 out* 1 19
1550 18/5 Bratton Down (L) CON 3m 8 F *in tch, cls 5th at 16th, outpcd aft 3 out* 4 16
1590 25/5 Mounsey Hil' (R) INT 3m 8 G *cls up, rdn 15th, 3rd & btn whn u.r. last* U -

Dual winner 95; top stable but moderate at best; novice ridden; may find another chance 17

RARE GIFT(USA) ch.g. 5 Bounding Basque (USA) - Cherie's Hope (USA) by Flying Paster (USA) Raymond Tooth

1581 19/5 Wolverhampt' (L) MDO 3m 10 G *jmpd slwly 1st, sn wll bhnd, t.o. 5th* 5 0
1599 25/5 Garthorpe (R) MDO 3m 7 G *3rd 1st m, 5th whn f 9th* F -

Late to appear & showed nothing 0

RARE HOUSE (Irish) — I 16^{F}

RARE KNIGHT b.g. 8 Bohemond - Barera by Baragoi Mrs E A Vickers

1995 P(0)

434 9/3 Newton Brom' (R) CON 3m 11 GS *mid-div to hlfwy, wknd & wll bhnd whn p.u. 2 out* P 0
632 23/3 Market Rase' (L) CON 3m 10 GF *mid-div, 8th & outpcd 6 out* 5 0
897 6/4 Dingley (R) CON 3m 15 GS *(bl) last pair to 8th, stdy prog, nrst at fin* 4 13

Ran surprisingly well last start but more needed - should concentrate on Maidens 12

RARELY AT ODDS b.g. 12 Tyrnavos - Carol Service by Daring Display (USA) Major General C A Ramsay

1995 P(0),2(14),P(0),7(0),3(0),3(16),2(0),4(13),4(0)

85 11/2 Alnwick (L) LAD 3m 11 GS *mstks 3rd & 8th, rear, lost tch 10th, t.o.* 8 0
186 24/2 Friars Haugh (L) MEM 3m 7 S *nvr dang* 7 0
499 16/3 Lanark (R) LAD 3m 10 G *nvr a dang* 4 0
609 23/3 Friars Haugh (L) PPO 3m 7 G *2nd hlfwy, sn wknd* 5 0
860 6/4 Alnwick (L) MXO 4m 1f 7 GF *alwys abt same pl* 4 0
1250 27/4 Balcormo Ma' (R) LAD 3m 5 GS *alwys bhnd* 4 0
1352 4/5 Mosshouses (L) LAD 3m 10 GS *alwys rear, last by 13th, t.o.* 7 0
1570 19/5 Corbridge (R) CON 3m 8 G *cls up, disp 4th, sn lost plc, t.o. 16th* 8 0

Safe but no longer of any account 0

RARE SPREAD (Irish) — I 201^{F}, I 368^{1}, I 473^{1}

RASCAL STREET LAD (Irish) — I 7^{6}, I 11^{F}, I 50^{P}, I 144^{F}, I 182^{S}, I 239^{B}, I 309^{2}, I 353^{2}, I 433^{3}, I 503^{4}, I 575^{S}, I 615^{2}, I 640^{2}, I 654^{2}

RASHEE LADY (Irish) — I 261^{P}, I 286^{P}, I 364^{P}, I 495^{P}

RATH AN UISCE (Irish) — I 22^{P}, I 86^{P}, I 131^{1}

RATHCARRICK LASS (Irish) — I 19^{P}, I 105^{2}, I 232^{3}, I 391^{1}

RATHCORE LADY (Irish) — I 391^{P}, I 587^{5}, I 625^{P}

RATHFARDON (Irish) — I 220^{F}

RATHKERRY (Irish) — I 248^{F}

RATH MEAR (Irish) — **I** 288[P], **I** 320[P], **I** 494[P], **I** 599[4]

RATHMICHAEL b.g. 10 Petorius - Always Smiling by Prominer — P C N Heywood

1995 2(19),2(20),1(19),1(18),3(18),2(19),P(0)

63	10/2	Great Treth'	(R)	MEM	3m	6	S	*(bl) ld til apr 4th, in tch whn mstk 13th, sn btn*	4	0
721	30/3	Wadebridge	(L)	INT	3m	3	GF	*(bl) ld,sn drvn,hdd brfly 12th,6l clr 3 out,drvn out*	1	19
873	6/4	Higher Kilw'	(L)	CON	3m	4	GF	*(bl) ld, jmpd hstntly 5th & 12th (ditch), hdd apr 15th, no ext*	2	18
1427	6/5	High Bickin'	(R)	CON	3m	10	G	*(bl) prom in chsng grp til wknd 14th*	4	17

Dual winner 95; tough & consistent but no more than moderate; should win again; G-Hynow 19

RATHVENTURE (Irish) — **I** 235[P]

RATHWILADOON (Irish) — **I** 205[5]

RAT RACE (Irish) — **I** 31[P], **I** 87[P], **I** 110[2], **I** 162[4], **I** 201[F], **I** 267[1], **I** 336[1]

RAVENSDALE LAD ch.g. 8 Balinger - Minimint by Menelek — Miss S Hogbin

128	17/2	Kingston Bl'	(L)	RES	3m	14	GS	*ld aft 5th-13th, stdly wknd frm nxt*	4	10
432	9/3	Upton-On-Se'	(R)	MDO	3m	17	GS	*effrt from 15th, went 2nd 3 out, not trbl wnr*	2	14
712	30/3	Barbury Cas'	(L)	MDO	3m	10	G	*in tch, ld 8th, clr 4 out, easily*	1	14
999	8/4	Hackwood Pa'	(L)	RES	3m	6	GF	*(fav) ld 9-16th, outpcd*	2	14
1192	21/4	Sandon	(L)	CON	3m	11	G	*prom, 3rd at 11th, ld 14th, sn clr, hdd 3 out, onepcd*	2	18

Missed 95; wide-margin winner of Maiden; Restricted probable if all goes well 97; Good 18

RAVENS HASEY MOON gr.g. 11 Even Say - Benwell Girl by Random Shot — A Aldridge

1995 4(0),F(-)

33	20/1	Higham	(L)	LAD	3m	9	GF	*pllg, chsd ldr blnd 10th, wknd appr 12th, p.u. 3 out*	P	0
105	17/2	Marks Tey	(L)	RES	3m	11	G	*chsd ldrs til lst pl appr 11th, p.u. 12th*	P	0
419	9/3	High Easter	(L)	RES	3m	10	S	*ld 5th-6th, prom til 13th, 3rd & no ch appr 2 out*	4	0
676	30/3	Cottenham	(R)	INT	3m	13	GF	*wll in tch til wknd 3 out*	7	0
931	8/4	Marks Tey	(L)	RES	3m	8	G	*hld up rear, in tch whn p.u. qckly 11th*	P	0
1328	30/4	Huntingdon	(R)	HC	3m	4	GF	*chsd ldr to 10th, f 13th.*	F	-
1547	18/5	Fakenham	(L)	HC	2m 5f 110yds	11	G	*lding gp, rdn and wknd 8th, t.o. when p.u. before 13th.*	P	0

Showed no real form 96 & looks well past winning standard now 10

RAYMAN(IRE) ch.g. 8 Callernish - Clare's Hansel by Prince Hansel — Miss Julie Naylor

1995 **F(-),2(21),3(NH),3(NH)**

242	25/2	Southwell P'	(L)	RES	3m	12	HO	*mstks, trckd ldrs til wknd rpdly 12th, p.u. 14th*	P	0
525	16/3	Larkhill	(R)	RES	3m	7	G	*nvr able to rch ldrs, lft poor 2nd last*	2	0
707	30/3	Barbury Cas'	(L)	RES	3m	18	G	*prom to 4 out, wkng whn f nxt*	F	-
946	8/4	Andoversford	(R)	RES	3m	10	GF	*mostly mid-div, nvr nrr*	5	12
1341	4/5	Warwick	(L)	HC	2 1/2m 110yds	12	GF	*prom to 10th, gradually lost pl, kept on from 2 out.*	4	19
1547	18/5	Fakenham	(L)	HC	2m 5f 110yds	11	G	*mstk 1st, chsd ldrs till outpcd 12th, left poor 3rd 2 out.*	3	17
1614	27/5	Hereford	(R)	HC	3m 1f 110yds	16	G	*midfield, hdwy to chase ldrs 4 out, wknd 2 out.*	6	14

Changed hands 96; non-stayer & only slim prospects in sub 3m H/Chase 17

RBF ARIANNE b.m. 8 Cruise Missile - Boherash by Boreen (FR) — H M F McCall

1995 2(10)

17	14/1	Tweseldown	(R)	MDN	3m	11	GS	*8s-5s, hld up, lost tch 11th, nvr on terms aft*	7	0

A little ability but rarely seen now & finished 1st weekend in 96 10

READY STEADY ch.g. 14 Bivouac - Very Merry by Lord Of Verona — Lady Temple

1995 1(21),S(-),1(22),1(22),**3(16)**,3(19),2(19),F(-)

49	4/2	Alnwick	(L)	OPE	3m	14	G	*alwys outpcd in rear, nvr nr*	6	12
86	11/2	Alnwick	(L)	OPE	3m	8	GS	*prog to jn ldrs 7th, 5th & in tch whn f 12th*	F	-
113	17/2	Lanark	(R)	OPE	3m	6	GS	*bhnd frm 10th, nvr dang*	4	0
318	2/3	Corbridge	(R)	LAD	3m 5f	10	GS	*j.w. made all, wkng nr fin*	1	20
400	9/3	Dalston	(R)	LAD	3m	10	G	*w.w., hdwy 8th, wnd 2nd 13th, u.r. nxt*	U	-
499	16/3	Lanark	(R)	LAD	3m	10	G	*cls up til ld 7th, made rest, lft wll clr 2 out*	1	22
700	30/3	Tranwell	(L)	LAD	3m	4	GS	*(fav) ld 2nd, lft clr 15th, unchal*	1	21
860	6/4	Alnwick	(L)	MXO	4m 1f	7	GF	*w.w. prog to ld 14th, mstk & hdd nxt, no ex frm 2 out*	2	21
1153	20/4	Whittington	(L)	LAD	3m	10	G	*(Jt fav) 4th whn f 8th*	F	-

Won 3 in 95; maintains some ability; novice ridden early 96; can win at 15 with right handling; Any 21

REAL CLASS b.g. 13 Deep Run - Our Cherry by Tarqogan — J W Evans

1995 3(12),2(20),1(21),1(22),1(22),**P(0)**

158	17/2	Weston Park	(L)	MEM	3m	11	G	*(fav) cls up, chsd wnr frm 5 out, not qckn cls home*	2	18
402	9/3	Dalston	(R)	XX	3m	13	G	*(fav) j.w. alwys prom, ld 14th til hdd & no ext flat*	2	19
664	24/3	Eaton Hall	(R)	CON	3m	15	S	*mid to rear, onepcd, nvr dang*	6	0
1012	9/4	Flagg Moor	(L)	XX	3m	7	G	*in tch, prog 7th, lft dsptng ld 14th, no ex und pres flat*	2	17
1031	13/4	Alpraham	(R)	MXO	3m	5	GS	*alwys prom, ld 14th-2 out, outpcd aft*	2	19

1152 20/4 Whittington (L) CON 3m 9 G *prom, ld aft 3 out, eased flat* 1 18

Won 3 in 95; consistent, stays & onepaced; deserved win & may find another in 97; G-Hy 18

REAL GENT br.g. 6 Mandalus - Gentle Madam by Camden Town — Jonathan A Lee
1995 P(0),P(0)
158 17/2 Weston Park (L) MEM 3m 11 G *f 1st* F -

Yet to complete the course from 3 starts 95/6 0

REALLY AN ANGEL b.m. 9 Baron Blakeney - Busy Quay by Quayside — B Bevan
428 9/3 Upton-On-Se' (R) RES 3m 17 GS *t.o. whn p.u. 14th* P 0
840 6/4 Maisemore P' (L) RES 3m 9 GF *alwys rr, last & blnd 12th, t.o. & p.u. 3 out* P 0
1002 9/4 Upton-On-Se' (R) RES 3m 8 F *mstk 7th, last & stgng 9th, t.o. whn p.u. 11th* P 0
1173 20/4 Chaddesley ' (L) RES 3m 18 G *rear frm 10th, nvr nr ldrs* 9 0
1510 12/5 Maisemore P' (L) XX 3m 8 F *t.o. til u.r. 7th* U -
1618 27/5 Chaddesley ' (L) CON 3m 14 GF *alwys last, sn t.o.* 8 0

No longer of any account 0

REAL RASCAL (Irish) — **I** 240[P]
REAL TO REAL (Irish) — **I** 540[P]
REAPER b.g. 8 Lightning Dealer - Deep Love — G Vergette
36 20/1 Higham (L) RES 3m 12 GF *jmpd slwly 3rd, bhnd 8th, p.u. 12th* P 0

No sign of hope from only start in 96 0

REBEL TOM b.g. 6 Southern Music - Secret Rebel by Rebel Prince — C G Yule
1995 P(0),P(0),3(0),P(0),P(0)
91 11/2 Ampton (R) MDO 3m 10 GF *rear, steady prog 7th, went 2nd 2 out, not rch wnr* 2 14
107 17/2 Marks Tey (L) MDN 3m 15 G *mstks, prog 9th, poor 3rd whn f 16th* F -
314 2/3 Ampton (R) MDO 3m 10 G *(fav) ld 3-4th, disp ld 16th til rddn & btn appr 2 out* 2 10
680 30/3 Cottenham (R) MDO 3m 11 GF *rear, kpt on to poor 4th at 14th, nvr dang* 4 0

Slight improvement 96 & ran best 1st start; could go close in 97 but more needed to win 13

RECKLESS LORD(IRE) ch.g. 6 Mister Lord (USA) - Strelorus by Black Minstrel — E H Crow
1995 P(0),1(12)
666 24/3 Eaton Hall (R) RES 3m 13 S *ld to 4th, cls up whn u.r. 7th* U -
739 31/3 Sudlow Farm (R) RES 3m 11 G *(fav) lost 30l at start, prog to 5th 15th, no ext, p.u. apr last* P 0

Maiden winner 95; highly thought of by connections but 96 season lasted week; best watched 15

RECTORY BOY b.g. 13 Rustingo - Ron's Girl by Ron — B J Llewellyn
1995 **P(0),P(0),3(15),P(NH)**
216 24/2 Newtown (L) LAD 3m 13 GS *t.o. last, 3 fences bhnd whn u.r. last* U -
356 3/3 Garnons (L) LAD 3m 12 GS *in tch til wknd 8th, t.o. & p.u. 13th* P 0
383 9/3 Llanfrynach (R) CON 3m 13 GS *sn bhnd, t.o. & p.u. 10th* P 0
1122 20/4 Stratford (L) HC 2m 5f 110yds 16 GF *ld 2nd to 5th, gradually lost pl, t.o. when p.u. before 9th.* P 0
1336 1/5 Cheltenham (L) HC 2m 110yds 9 G *bhnd and blnd 5th, t.o. and p.u. before last.* P 0

No longer of any account 0

REDBEN ch.g. 11 Red Man - Bonham Hill by Armagnac Monarch — Mrs L J Gundry
685 30/3 Chaddesley ' (L) LAD 3m 9 G *s.s. alwys wll bhnd, t.o. frm 11th* 4 0

No longer of any account 0

RED BRONZE (Irish) — **I** 62[P], **I** 114[2], **I** 332[2]
RED CONKER (Irish) — **I** 559[B]
REDEDIVER b.g. 14 Tudor Diver - Redetwig by Carlton Grange — D Scott
1995 10(0)
610 23/3 Friars Haugh (L) CON 3m 11 G *(bl) t.o. hlfwy.* 8 0
860 6/4 Alnwick (L) MXO 4m 1f 7 GF *(bl) sn last, t.o. & p.u. appr 15th* P 0
1351 4/5 Mosshouses (L) CON 3m 11 GS *rear, wll bhnd frm 7th, t.o.* 8 0

No longer of any account 0

REDELVA b.m. 9 Fidel - Whisky Afric by African Sky — Mrs D Rowell
1995 F(-),3(14),P(0),2(0),1(10),P(0)
274 2/3 Parham (R) OPE 3m 12 GF *twrds rear, prog 14th, 4th frm 3 out, nvr dang* 4 18
782 31/3 Tweseldown (R) XX 3m 6 G *mstks, plld, ld to 3rd, outpcd frm 13th, styd on wll 2 out* 3 12
1053 13/4 Penshurst (L) LAD 3m 5 G *sn cls up, 2nd 4 out, wknd* 4 0
1207 21/4 Heathfield (R) CON 3m 9 F *alwys prom, 4th 4 out, styd on to tk 2nd flat* 2 17
1298 28/4 Bexhill (R) CON 3m 4 F *in tch to 11th, wll bhnd whn u.r. 15th* U -

1375 4/5 Peper Harow (L) CON 3m 9 F *chsd ldr, ld 11th til appr 13th, wknd 3 out* 4 10

Restricted winner 95; ran better in 96 but 1 win, 7 places 95/6 & ratio will continue 14

RED EXPRESS VI (Irish) — **I** 104^{2}, **I** 158, , **I** 235^{4}, **I** 303^{2}, **I** 338^{4}, **I** 426^{3}, **I** 447^{P}, **I** 561^{1}, **I** 643^{4}

RED FURLONG ch.g. 13 Cidrax (FR) - Nells Birthday by Royal Buck C P Hobbs

1995 P(0),P(0)

428 9/3 Upton-On-Se' (R) RES 3m 17 GS *wll bhnd whn p.u. 13th* P 0

Maiden winner 91; lightly raced since & of no account now 0

RED HOT BOOGIE(IRE) b.g. 7 Abednego - Boogie Woogie by No Argument Mrs J M Hollands

613 23/3 Friars Haugh (L) MDN 3m 15 G *prom til wknd frm hlfwy* 8 0
1088 14/4 Friars Haugh (L) MDO 3m 10 F *4th hlfwy, styd in tch til wknd 4 out, p.u. 2 out* P 0
1355 4/5 Mosshouses (L) MDO 3m 10 GS *made most to apr 2 out, wknd, crawld last, improve* 5 0

Not enough stamina yet but showed promise last start & should have chances in 97 13

RED HUGH (Irish) — **I** 628^{P}, **I** 655^{1}

RED MOLLIE (Irish) — **I** 26^{P}, **I** 271^{P}, **I** 483^{F}, **I** 600^{3}

REDORAN b.m. 5 Gildoran - Red Spirit by Starch Reduced G Gamage

152 17/2 Erw Lon (L) MDN 3m 11 G *alwys last, t.o. & p.u. 11th* P 0
549 17/3 Erw Lon (L) RES 3m 11 GS *mid-div, f 6th* F -
773 31/3 Pantyderi (R) MDN 3m 8 G *nvr nr ldrs, u.r. 13th* U -
1039 13/4 St Hilary (R) MDN 3m 14 G *alwys rear, p.u. 16th* P 0

Yet to complete the course 0

RED RORY b.g. 7 Idiot's Delight - Waterside by Shackleton Mrs D H McCarthy

1995 **12(NH),13(NH)**

60 10/2 Cottenham (R) MDO 3m 7 GS *mstk 4th,cls up,ld 12th,2l up whn hmpd & u.r. apr 3 out* U -
254 25/2 Charing (L) MDO 3m 9 GS *(fav) trckd ldrs, wth wnr on bridle frm 14th, rdn & found nil 2out* 2 0
617 23/3 Higham (L) MDO 3m 11 GF *(fav) pling in rear,last at 4th,prog 11th,rdn 13th,lft 2nd last* 2 10

Has ability but does not stay & finds little; good stable but may frustrate in 97 12

RED RUSSE b.g. 10 Sunyboy - Royal Russe by Bally Russe A K Leigh

1995 P(0)

1242 27/4 Woodford (L) RES 3m 18 G *p.u. 5th, (lame)* P 0

Maiden winner only start 94; problems since & can only be watched 10

RED SCOT b.g. 6 Scottish Reel - May Fox by Healaugh Fox Mrs M E Anderson

756 31/3 Lockerbie (R) MDN 3m 14 G *sn bhnd, p.u. 12th* P 0
1087 14/4 Friars Haugh (L) MDO 3m 9 F *cls up whn f 14th* F -
1476 11/5 Aspatria (L) MDO 3m 16 GF *prog 8th, wll in tch whn f 11th* F -
1574 19/5 Corbridge (R) MDO 3m 6 G *not fluent, alwys abt same plc* 4 0

Last when completing but not without hope if jumping better in 97 10

RED SHOON (Irish) — **I** 301^{F}, **I** 483^{P}, **I** 585^{5}, **I** 625^{6}

RED STAR QUEEN b.m. 6 State Diplomacy (USA) - Star's Silver Face by Smokey Rockett Geoff Stevenson

1995 U(-),U(-),4(0),P(0)

73 11/2 Wetherby Po' (L) MDO 3m 15 GS *alwys rear, p.u. 13th* P 0
307 2/3 Great Stain' (L) MDO 3m 17 GS *rear whn saddle slppd & u.r. flat apr 2nd* U -
413 9/3 Charm Park (L) MDO 3m 12 G *mid-div, 6th at 11th, outpcd aftr, p.u. 3 out* P 0
759 31/3 Great Stain' (L) LAD 3m 10 GS *keen hld, prom til wknd rpdly 9th, t.o. & p.u. 3 out* P 0
829 6/4 Stainton (R) MDO 3m 9 GF *plldn hrd, ld & ran wd apr 5th, blnd 7th, wknd, p.u. 15th* P 0

Only completed 1 of 9 starts 95/6 & no stamina 0

REDWOOD BOY ch.g. 6 Highlands - October Woods by Precipice Wood C B Taylor

763 31/3 Great Stain' (L) MDN 3m 11 GS *rear, wknd 6th, t.o. & p.u. 10th* P 0
1450 6/5 Witton Cast' (R) MDO 3m 14 G *jmpng errors, sn in rear, t.o. whn p.u. 10th* P 0

No sign that he can challenge yet 0

REED b.h. 11 Dara Monarch - Angelica (SWE) by Hornbeam Mrs J Provan

1995 **2(NH),U(NH),P(NH),8(NH)**

187 24/2 Friars Haugh (L) CON 3m 12 S *bhnd, kpt on frm 3 out, nvr dang* 3 11
402 9/3 Dalston (R) XX 3m 13 G *mid-div through't, n.d.* 5 13
610 23/3 Friars Haugh (L) CON 3m 11 G *2nd hlfwy, clse up untl wknd 2 out* 5 13
1083 14/4 Friars Haugh (L) CON 3m 10 F *nvr rchd ldrs* 6 0
1251 27/4 Balcormo Ma' (R) OPE 3m 6 GS *3rd hlfwy, sn lost tch* 5 0

Dual winner 93; safe in 96 but not threatenig to win again now 13

REEDFINCH b.g. 7 Rabdan - Tangara by Town Crier — Mrs P Robeson

61 10/2 Cottenham (R) MDO 3m 8 GS *out of tch,poor 4th 13th,lft in ld aft 15th,u.r 2 out,rmntd* 3 0
727 31/3 Garthorpe (R) MDO 3m 12 G *lost plc 7th, wll bhnd frm 13th, t.o. & p.u. 3 out* P 0

Unlucky in terrible race but showed nothing on other start **10**

REEF LARK b.g. 11 Mill Reef (USA) - Calandra (USA) by Sir Ivor — Mrs Jane Galpin
1995 **P(NH),P(NH)**

561 17/3 Ottery St M' (L) LAD 3m 12 G *alwys mid-div, nvr on terms* 5 12

Not disgraced only start but will find it hard to achieve much if fit at 12 .... **12**

REEFSIDE(IRE) ch.g. 7 Quayside - Brownstown Lady by Charlottesvilles Flyer — David Jones
1995 **F(NH),19(NH)**

74 11/2 Wetherby Po' (L) MDO 3m 11 GS *rear, prog 11th, lft dist 3rd at 14th, no ext* 3 0
229 24/2 Duncombe Pa' (R) MDO 3m 13 GS *s.v.s. rear whn b.d. 5th* B -

Dead **0**

REEL HIM IN (Irish) — **I** 167⁵, **I** 237ᴾ, **I** 268ᴾ

REEL RASCAL gr.m. 6 Scallywag - My Music by Sole Mio (USA) — Miss D B Stanhope
1995 P(0),F(-)

539 17/3 Southwell P' (L) RES 3m 11 GS *t.o. whn f 2nd* F -
636 23/3 Market Rase' (L) MDN 3m 11 GF *mid-div, prog 10th, 2nd 3 out, fdd frm nxt* 3 10
898 6/4 Dingley (R) MDN 2m 5f 10 GS *(Co fav) mid-div, 4th 5 out, lft 3rd 3 out, ran on onepce* 3 0
1103 14/4 Guilsborough (L) MDN 3m 15 G *s.s. mstks, alwys rear, t.o. & p.u. 15th* P 0

Only beat 1 other finisher in 2 completions & much more needed to win **10**

REEN-O-FOIL (Irish) — **I** 142ᴾ, **I** 185¹, **I** 461ᴾ

REFORMED QUEEN br.m. 12 Reformed Character - Pernod Queen by Green Whistle — Cooper Wilson

13 14/1 Cottenham (R) MDO 3m 10 G *bhnd til p.u. 11th* P 0

Of no account **0**

REGAL ABSENCE (Irish) — **I** 565ᶠ

REGAL BAY b.g. 6 Scorpio (FR) - Pendle Princess by Broxted — David Wales

108 17/2 Marks Tey (L) MDN 3m 17 G *blnd 1st, bhnd til p.u. 16th* P 0
424 9/3 High Easter (L) MDN 3m 10 S *w.w. in tch, outpcd appr 14th, no dang aft, kpt on* 3 0
727 31/3 Garthorpe (R) MDO 3m 12 G *sttld rear, prog to 5th aft 15th, kpt on onepcd, improve* 5 0

Learning to date & ran well enough last start to give hopes if fit in 97 .... **13**

REGAL SHADOW gr.g. 7 Scorpio (FR) - Pendle Princess by Broxted — David Wales

418 9/3 High Easter (L) CON 3m 10 S *rr, hit 10th, lst tch 13th, p.u. 16th* P 0
495 16/3 Horseheath (R) MDO 3m 12 GF *pllng, hld up, lost tch 10th, t.o. & p.u. 4 out* P 0

Rarely runs & shows nothing **0**

REGENT SON b.g. 10 Right Regent - Moorland Gal by Baragoi — Mrs M A Simpson
1995 R(-)

555 17/3 Ottery St M' (L) MDO 3m 15 G *sn rear, t.o. & p.u. 10th* P 0
1075 13/4 Lifton (R) RES 3m 12 S *towrds rear, bhnd 11th til p.u. aft 3 out* P 0
1143 20/4 Flete Park (R) MDN 3m 17 S *some prog to 7th at 12th, sn wknd, t.o. & p.u. last* P 0

Change of tack in 96 - usually refuses **0**

REGGIE b.g. 14 Impecunious - Vixens Surprise by Eastern Venture — R H Wilkinson
1995 F(-)

20 14/1 Tweseldown (R) RES 3m 9 GS *(vis) 3rd til lft 2nd 10th, 3rd agn frm 14th, dist bhnd & f last* F -
272 2/3 Parham (R) RES 3m 13 GF *(vis) alwys cls up, ld 3rd-4th, 3rd frm 3 out, onepcd* 3 15
774 31/3 Penshurst (L) MEM 3m 3 GS *(fav) (vis) ld to 6th, agn 9-12th, chal 4 out, no ext last* 2 0

Maiden winner 92; only 7 outings 94-6; Members only real hope at 15 .... **10**

REGULAR BEAT (Irish) — **I** 394ᵁ

REGULAR ROSE (Irish) — **I** 417ᴾ, **I** 622ᴾ

REHAB VENTURE ch.g. 12 Deep Run - Hansels Princess by Prince Hansel — Mrs Helen Lynch
1995 **P(0),P(0)**,3(14)

32 20/1 Higham (L) OPE 3m 15 GF *prom to 8th, sn bhnd p.u. appr 16th* P 0
169 18/2 Market Rase' (L) CON 3m 15 GF *chsd ldrs to 10th, sn wknd* 11 0
395 9/3 Garthorpe (R) OPE 3m 7 G *3rd frm 7th, 2nd frm 11th, outpcd 4 out* 3 11
725 31/3 Garthorpe (R) OPE 3m 9 G *in tch in mid-div to 13th, sn strggling, t.o.* 7 0
1333 1/5 Cheltenham (L) HC 3m 1f 110yds 13 G *mstk 1st, jmpd slowly 3rd, t.o. when p.u. before 12th.* P 0
1518 12/5 Garthorpe (R) MEM 3m 6 GF *wll in tch to 9th, wknd & p.u. 12th* P 0

Well beaten in 96 & no prospects now **0**

REHEY LADY (Irish) — **I** 417[5], **I** 499[P], **I** 556[1], **I** 577[1]

REIGN DANCE ch.g. 5 Kinglet - Gay Criselle by Decoy Boy — Mrs D H McCarthy

58 10/2 Cottenham (R) RES 3m 7 GS *schoold & t.o. til p.u. 12th* P 0
253 25/2 Charing (L) MDO 3m 10 GS *alwys rear, lost tch 10th, p.u. 14th* P 0
781 31/3 Penshurst (L) MDN 3m 11 GS *ld to 6th, wth ldr aft, ld agn 12th til p.u. 14th* P 0

Showed 1st signs of ability last start but may have a problem **10**

REINSKEA (Irish) — **I** 296[P], **I** 370[P], **I** 428[4], **I** 469[P], **I** 511[P]

REJECTS REPLY b.g. 6 Balliol - Fair Dino by Thatch (USA) — Alan Goodwin

167 17/2 Weston Park (L) MDN 3m 10 G *mid-div, btn whn lft poor 2nd 2 out* 2 0
464 9/3 Eyton-On-Se' (L) MDN 2 1/2m 13 G *md no shw, p.u. 4 out* P 0
1234 27/4 Weston Park (L) MDO 3m 13 G *held up mid-div, some late prog, ran on, nrst fin* 4 0

Well beaten on both completions but suggested better to come last start **11**

RELATIVELY HIGH b.m. 5 Persian Heights - Kissin' Cousin by Be Friendly — T G Price

1390 6/5 Pantyderi (R) MDO 3m 15 GF *alwys wll bhnd, t.o. & p.u. 3 out* P 0
1492 11/5 Erw Lon (L) MDO 3m 10 F *settld towrds rear, impvd frm 13th, mstk 3 out, no ch aft* 3 10
1606 25/5 Bassaleg (R) MDO 3m 7 GS *hld up, gd prog to 3rd at 10th, disp 3 out,no ext apr last* 2 12

Late to appear & steadily improved; ran well last start & should go closer 97 .... **14**

RELISHING b.m. 7 Relkino - Sizzle by High Line — W Shand Kydd

240 25/2 Southwell P' (L) MDO 3m 15 HO *(fav) trckd ldrs, prog to disp 4 out, btn apr nxt* 4 0
438 9/3 Newton Brom' (R) MDN 3m 10 GS *(fav) ld, 20l clr 5th, wknd & hdd 3 out, walked in* 5 0

Expensive to follow & does not stay, so far **10**

REMAINDER STAR (Irish) — **I** 16[F], **I** 81[1]

REMALONE ch.m. 7 Remezzo - Marilone by Maris Piper — Miss T A Aucott

1995 R(-),P(0),P(0)

540 17/3 Southwell P' (L) MDO 3m 9 GS *(bl) u.r. 1st* U -
688 30/3 Chaddesley ' (L) MDN 3m 17 G *(bl) t.o. 8th, last whn p.u. 11th* P 0
901 6/4 Dingley (R) MDN 2m 5f 9 GS *3rd til rddn & wknd 8th, t.o. 6 out* 4 0
1104 14/4 Guilsborough (L) MDN 3m 18 G *ld to 3rd, wknd 8th, t.o. whn blnd 10th, p.u. 12th* P 0
1240 27/4 Clifton On ' (L) MDO 3m 10 GF *alwys bhnd, t.o. last whn ran out apr 9th* r -
1378 5/5 Dingley (R) MDO 2 1/2m 16 GF *alwys bhnd, t.o. & p.u. 10th* P 0
1644 2/6 Dingley (R) MDO 3m 16 GF *s.s., alwys bhnd, t.o. whn p.u. 11th* P 0

A Waste of time **0**

REMEMBER MAC b.g. 8 My Dad Tom (USA) - Sur Les Roches by Sea Break — Mrs J Hayes

1995 3(0),R(-),5(0),2(11)

562 17/3 Ottery St M' (L) XX 3m 12 G *sn rear, t.o. & p.u. 11th* P 0
926 8/4 Bishopsleigh (R) RES 3m 9 G *(bl) bhnd frm 1st, p.u. 5th whn t.o.* P 0
1112 17/4 Hockworthy (L) PPO 3m 9 GS *(bl) mstk 1st, prom, rdn & wknd 10th, p.u. 12th* P 0
1277 27/4 Bratton Down (L) CON 3m 15 GF *mid-div, lost tch 9th, t.o. & p.u. 13th* P 0
1345 4/5 Holnicote (L) RES 3m 11 GS *nvr seen wth ch* 5 0
1549 18/5 Bratton Down (L) MEM 3m 4 F *(bl) chsd wnr, cls up til wknd aft 3 out* 3 10
1587 25/5 Mounsey Hil' (R) MEM 3m 7 G *(bl) in tch, went 3rd 10th, lost tch 15th, ref 2 out, cont* 3 0
1633 1/6 Bratton Down (L) XX 3m 8 G *(bl) cls up to 14th, sn wknd* 6 0
1649 8/6 Umberleigh (L) RES 3m 14 GF *(bl) chsd ldrs til outpcd 13th, wknd 3 out, p.u. last* P 0

Maiden winner 94; has shown no form 95/6 & has no further prospects **0**

REMEMBERTOM b.g. 9 New Member - Vespers II by The Monk — M J Parr

1995 2(16),P(0),3(15),F(-),5(14),4(0)

461 9/3 Eyton-On-Se' (L) RES 3m 15 G *hld up, ld 14th tl cght flat, fin lame* 2 16

Good enough to win Restricted but hard ride & problems 96; best watched **16**

REMILAN(IRE) b.g. 5 Remainder Man - Alice Milan by Milan — M G Sheppard

1063 13/4 Horseheath (R) MDO 3m 5 F *j.s. 1st & 3rd, in tch to 13th, lft poor 3rd 15th, t.o.* 3 0
1381 5/5 Dingley (R) MDO 3m 16 GF *alwys rear, t.o. last whn p.u. 10th* P 0

Shows nothing so far but should do better **0**

REMMY CRUZ (Irish) — **I** 312[P], **I** 332[P]

REMRAR (Irish) — **I** 88[1]

RENARD QUAY b or br.g. 13 Quayside - Donegal Lady by Indigenous — B Wilberforce

1995 2(17),4(0),1(19),2(19),**7(11)**

163 17/2 Weston Park (L) LAD 3m 10 G *chsd ldrs, no ext frm 4 out* 5 13
291 2/3 Eaton Hall (R) LAD 3m 10 G *mid-div, nrst fin* 5 13

663 24/3 Eaton Hall (R) LAD 3m 8 S *rear, out of tch wth ldrs, late prog, nrst fin* 3 15
1032 13/4 Alpraham (R) CON 3m 9 GS *nvr bynd mid-div* 3 12
1192 21/4 Sandon (L) CON 3m 11 G *outpcd, ran on frm 3 out, nrst fin* 3 11
1366 4/5 Gisburn (R) LAD 3m 12 G *alwys 4th/5th, nvr dang* 5 15

Declining veteran; consistent & safe but will struggle to find a race at 14 13

RENSHAW INGS ch.g. 7 Kirchner - Spot On Pink by Perhapsburg R Barrow

533 16/3 Cothelstone (L) MDN 3m 13 G *f 1st* F -
734 31/3 Little Wind' (R) MDO 3m 11 GS *3rd whn f 9th* F -
993 8/4 Kingston St' (R) MDO 3m 17 F *in tch, 5th at 11th, wknd nxt, rear & p.u. 15th* P 0

Not yet of any account 0

REPLY b.m. 9 Derrylin - Repoussee by Jimmy Reppin Mrs P Jones
1995 P(0),U(-),P(0),2(12)

264 2/3 Didmarton (L) INT 3m 12 G *in tch in rear, wknd 12th, p.u. 14th* P 0
387 9/3 Llanfrynach (R) RES 3m 11 GS *sn rear, last whn p.u. 7th* P 0

A little ability 94/5 but season lasted a week in 96 & looks to have problems now 0

REPTILE PRINCESS b.m. 10 Majestic Maharaj - Daring Liz by Dairialatan Miss Wizzy Hartnoll
1995 P(0),P(0),P(0),4(0),5(0)

131 17/2 Ottery St M' (L) MDN 3m 10 GS *alwys wll bhnd, t.o. 13th* 4 0
299 2/3 Great Treth' (R) MDO 3m 13 G *t.o. hlfwy* 5 0
470 10/3 Milborne St' (L) MDO 3m 18 G *sn bhnd, t.o. frm 14th* 9 0
629 23/3 Kilworthy (L) MDN 3m 11 GS *last whn jmpd slwly 3rd, sn t.o., nvr nrr* 4 0

Bumbles around miles behind with novice rider 0

RESKUE LINE ro.g. 6 Respect - Kiku by Faberge II Allan Shaw

403 9/3 Dalston (R) RES 3m 11 G *bhnd 11th, nvr sn wth ch* 8 0

Last of finish & of no account yet 0

RETAIL RUNNER b.g. 11 Trimmingham - Deep Rose by Deep Run Maurice E Pinto

125 17/2 Kingston Bl' (L) OPE 3m 10 GS *made most til mstk & u.r. 12th* U -
274 2/3 Parham (R) OPE 3m 12 GF *ld to 6th, agn 10th til aft 4 out,qcknd wth wnr, no ext last* 2 24
595 23/3 Parham (R) OPE 3m 12 GS *ld/disp to 11th, 2nd aft, outpcd 4 out, wknd last* 2 20
1052 13/4 Penshurst (L) OPE 3m 7 G *(fav) handy, ld frm 11th, made rest, clr 4 out, easily* 1 23
1541 16/5 Folkestone (R) HC 2m 5f 8 G *ld, went clr 11th, hdd after 2 out, no ext run-in.* 2 26

Winning chaser; quite useful pointer 96; best easy 3m; ran well H/Chase & could win one at 12; G/F-S 25

REVELS HILL(IRE) b.g. 6 Le Moss - Loverush by Golden Love N R Freak
1995 R(-),P(0)

143 17/2 Larkhill (R) MDO 3m 14 G *schoold in rear, t.o. whn f last* F -
470 10/3 Milborne St' (L) MDO 3m 18 G *alwys mid-div, no ch whn p.u. last* P 0
652 23/3 Badbury Rin' (L) MDO 3m 13 G *nvr trbld ldrs, wknd 11th, p.u. 14th* P 0

Still learning but yet to complete in 5 starts 95/6 0

REVILLER'S GLORY b.g. 12 Hittite Glory - Zulaika Hopwood by Royalty Miss Sara Jane Rodgers
1995 2(19),**U(-)**,P(0),**P(0)**

12 14/1 Cottenham (R) RES 3m 12 G *ld 2nd, went clr 13th, hdd 2 out, wknd rpdly* 8 0
47 4/2 Alnwick (L) XX 3m 14 G *rear, blndrd 8th, eff 12th, wknd, p.u. 3 out* P 0
243 25/2 Southwell P' (L) RES 3m 11 HO *made most to 3 out, sn outpcd* 4 10
371 8/3 Ayr (L) HC 2m 5f 110yds 8 GF *chsd ldrs, hdwy before 4 out, ld after 2 out, hdd final 30 yards, no ext.* 2 14
488 16/3 Newcastle (L) HC 2 1/2m 9 GS *disp ld, went on 8th, hdd 5 out, left remote 2nd last.* 2 10

Maiden winner 94; lost golden chance in season's worst H/Chase at Ayr & no prospects now 13

REXY BOY b.g. 9 Dunbeath (USA) - Coca by Levmoss P Swift
1995 **11(NH)**

327 3/3 Market Rase' (L) CON 3m 15 G *alwys chsng grp, no ch whn ran out 4 out* r -
632 23/3 Market Rase' (L) CON 3m 10 GF *mid-div, 6th whn b.d. 12th* B -
969 8/4 Thorpe Lodge (L) OPE 3m 4 GF *3rd til chsd wnr frm 12th, 5l down 6 out-last, outpcd flat* 2 15
1022 13/4 Brocklesby ' (L) CON 3m 6 GF *cls up, mstly 3rd til ld 5 out, hdd & no ext bfr 2 out* 2 14
1306 28/4 Southwell P' (L) MEM 3m 4 GF *(fav) 2nd til ld 7th, duelld frm 8th, ran on well* 1 12
1467 11/5 Easingwold (L) OPE 3m 6 G *pllng,rear,prog 8th,trckd 1st 2,outpcd 12th,blnd 15th,onepcd* 3 17

Winning hurdler; modest pointer; ran best last start & may have Confined chance at 10; G-F 16

RHETORIC HOUSE (Irish) — **I** 39P, **I** 121P, **I** 5401

RHINE RIVER(USA) br.g. 6 Riverman (USA) - Fruhlingstag (FR) by Orsini Brian Eardley
1995 U(-),3(0),7(0),1(11)

292 2/3 Eaton Hall (R) RES 3m 15 G *prom, outpcd hlfwy, p.u. 3 out* P 0
563 17/3 Wolverhampt' (L) XX 3m 4 GS *set slow pace til clr aft 13th, easily* 1 10

667 24/3 Eaton Hall (R) INT 3m 11 S *prom early, lost tch, p.u. 4 out* P 0
851 6/4 Sandon (L) MEM 3m 6 GF *(Jt fav) held up, cls order 11th, ld 3 out, ran on srgly apr last* 1 10
1192 21/4 Sandon (L) CON 3m 11 G *mid to rear, outpcd, p.u. 4 out* P 0

Maiden winner 95; changed hands 96; has won 3 desperate races & no show in proper contests 11

RHYME AND CHIME b.g. 5 Rymer - Belle Deirdrie by Mandamus Mrs R Kennen

876 6/4 Higher Kilw' (L) MDN 3m 11 GF *sn bhnd, t.o. & p.u. 11th* P 0
1071 13/4 Lifton (R) MDN 3m 10 S *blndrd & u.r. 3rd* U -
1430 6/5 High Bickin' (R) MDO 3m 8 G *rear whn hmpd by loose horse & rddr k/o on bnd* U -

No signs yet 0

RHYMING MOPPET b.m. 7 Rymer - Deep Moppet by Deep Run Exors Of The Late Capt W H Bulwer-Long
1995 P(0)

108 17/2 Marks Tey (L) MDN 3m 17 G *prog 10th, blnd 13th, 5th & ch whn blnd 17th, wlkd in* 7 0

2 runs in 2 seasons & regular racing has to be the first aim 0

RIBERETTO'S GIRL (Irish) — **I** 16^{F}, **I** 81^{5}, **I** 122^{P}, **I** 150^{F}, **I** 292^{4}, **I** 390^{6}, **I** 424^{5}, **I** 557^{5}, **I** 583^{3}

RICHARD HUNT b.g. 12 Celtic Cone - Member's Mistress by New Member Mrs P Rowe
1995 2(23),1(25),1(25),1(25),**F(-)**,1(26),1(25),1(23),**2(26)**

11 14/1 Cottenham (R) LAD 3m 7 G *(fav) chsd clr ldrs,clsd 9th,ld 15th,drew clr & blnd 2 out,easily* 1 26
33 20/1 Higham (L) LAD 3m 9 GF *(fav) alwys going wll, ld appr last, pushed out flat, clvrly* 1 24
180 18/2 Horseheath (R) LAD 3m 3 G *(fav) not fluent, ld to 2nd & frm 6th, clr 3 out, easily* 1 22
347 3/3 Higham (L) LAD 3m 10 G *(fav) hld up, u.r. 3rd* U -
369 7/3 Towcester (R) HC 3m 1f 6 G *mstk 1st, hdwy 12th, went poor 2nd apr last, ran on.* 2 23
493 16/3 Horseheath (R) LAD 3m 4 GF *(fav) ld at gd pace, hdd last, ran on well flat* 1 24
678 30/3 Cottenham (R) LAD 3m 6 GF *(fav) w.w. prog 11th,ld 3 out,outjmpd & hdd nxt,sn ld agn,rdn out* 1 25
832 6/4 Marks Tey (L) LAD 3m 8 G *(fav) hld up, chsd ldrs 11th, 2nd 15th, chal 2 out, no ext flat* 2 23

Very useful pointer; won 23 of last 31 ; should win more in 97; G/F-S 25

RICH ASSET(IRE) b.g. 6 Treasure Kay - Pride And Joy (FR) by Miami Springs I A Brown

414 9/3 Charm Park (L) MDO 3m 11 G *ld to 3rd, lst tch 12th p.u. 4 out* P 0
517 16/3 Dalton Park (R) MDO 3m 10 G *mstks, rear, 8th whn blnd & u.r. 7th* U -
763 31/3 Great Stain' (L) MDN 3m 11 GS *mid-div whn blnd 6th, sn prom, wknd frm 2 out* 4 0
987 8/4 Charm Park (L) MDN 3m 13 GF *(bl) alwys wll in rear, nvr dang, completed own time* 5 0
1094 14/4 Whitwell-On' (R) MDO 2 1/2m 88yds 16 G *mid-div, late prog frm 3 out, styd on to tk 2nd cls hm* 2 11
1451 6/5 Witton Cast' (R) MDO 3m 12 G *alwys abt same plc, styd on onepce* 4 11

A little ability but already looks a potential disappointment 12

RICKHAM BAY b.m. 12 Snow Warning - Grandanna by My Swanee G Burr

340 3/3 Heythrop (R) MDN 3m 12 G *t.o. til p.u. 4th* P 0
525 16/3 Larkhill (R) RES 3m 7 G *sn rear, f 10th* F -
796 2/4 Heythrop (R) MDN 3m 11 F *jmpd slwly, alwys last, t.o. 12th* 8 0

Of no account 0

RIDEMORE BALLADEER gr.g. 5 Malaspina - Balitree by Balidar D Barron

734 31/3 Little Wind' (R) MDO 3m 11 GS *hdwy frm rear 12th, 4th 3 out, bad mstk 2 out, should imprv* 3 11
820 6/4 Charlton Ho' (L) MDN 3m 12 GF *alwys prom, ld 13-15th, outpcd nxt, rlld apr last* 2 15
1308 28/4 Little Wind' (R) MDO 3m 6 G *(fav) hld up in tch, ld 3 out, ran on well* 1 15

Top stable & promising start; won modest race but should progress in 97; Good 18

RIDWAN b.g. 9 Rousillon (USA) - Ring Rose by Relko K V Bonser
1995 **12(NH)**,**P(NH)**

76 11/2 Wetherby Po' (L) LAD 3m 8 GS *cls up, 2nd at last, just hld flat* 2 21
245 25/2 Southwell P' (L) LAD 3m 8 HO *ld 3-6th, wth ldrs aft, chal frm 3 out, lvl last, just hld* 2 21
536 17/3 Southwell P' (L) LAD 3m 9 GS *mid-div, no ch wth 1st 2 from 3 out* 4 10
724 31/3 Garthorpe (R) LAD 3m 5 G *jmpd slwly, lost tch ldng pair 8th, t.o.* 3 12

Winning hurdler; stays all day & twice went close; may have chances early 97; Soft 21

RIGGLEDOWN REGENT b.g. 10 Right Regent - Blinding Light by Fury Royal R W Pincombe
1995 P(0)

1115 17/4 Hockworthy (L) MDO 3m 10 GS *jmpd bdly, ld til ran out 6th* r -
1652 8/6 Umberleigh (L) MDO 3m 10 GF *in tch to 11th, t.o. & p.u. 2 out* P 0

8 pulled-ups, 3 refusals, & a run-out, all starts 93-6 0

RIGHT POCKET (Irish) — **I** 324^{P}

RIGHT ROSY br.m. 7 Riberetto - Novelty Girl by Ben Novus Rhys Jenkins
1995 P(0),P(0)

220 24/2 Newtown (L) MDN 3m 12 GS *rear, poor last 14th, ran on aft, ld last, sn clr* 1 12

388 9/3 Llanfrynach (R) RES 3m 20 GS *mid-div, effrt 14th, styd on well frm 2 out, no ch wth wnr* 2 14
600 23/3 Howick (L) RES 3m 14 S *mid-div, mstk 9th, ran on 15th, 3l down 2 out, just hld* 3 18
1223 24/4 Brampton Br' (R) RES 3m 11 G *lost tch 12th, ran on strngly frm 3 out* 4 0
1242 27/4 Woodford (L) RES 3m 18 G *mstks, alwys rear div, 12th hlfwy, t.o. & p.u. 3 out* P 0

Improved; very onepaced & stays well; could win early season Restricted 97; Soft 18

RINGAHEEN (Irish) — I 222^{P}, I 343^{F}, I 386^{P}, I 465^{P}, I 526^{P}, I 616^{5}, I 630^{P}

RING BANK b.g. 5 Humdoleila - Butchers Barn by Space King — S Edwards
667 24/3 Eaton Hall (R) INT 3m 11 S *rear, p.u. 10th* P 0
736 31/3 Sudlow Farm (R) CON 3m 9 G *ref to race* R -
852 6/4 Sandon (L) MDN 3m 9 GF *chsng grp to 10th, lost tch wth ldrs 13th* 5 0
1008 9/4 Flagg Moor (L) MDO 2 1/2m 7 G *t.d.e., w.w., hmprd 6th, lost tch 8th, crwld 3 out & p.u.* P 0
1196 21/4 Sandon (L) MDN 3m 17 G *nvr bttr than mid-div, p.u. 3 out* P 0
1364 4/5 Gisburn (R) MDO 3m 11 G *rear whn hmpd & u.r. 6th* U -
1581 19/5 Wolverhampt' (L) MDO 3m 10 G *ld apr 5th-13th, 6th & wknd whn f nxt* F -

Unpleasant 0

RINGHILL BEAUTY (Irish) — I 631^{P}, I 650^{2}

RING MAM (Irish) — I 43^{3}, I 309^{P}, I 370^{2}, I 443^{F}, I 475^{P}, I 610^{P}

RINGMORE ch.g. 14 Porto Bello - Dirrie Star by Dunoon Star — Ms P Wilkin
226 24/2 Duncombe Pa' (R) OPE 3m 10 GS *in tch, wknd 11th, t.o. & p.u. 4 out* P 0
410 9/3 Charm Park (L) OPE 3m 17 G *in tch to 4 out, fdd rpdly, cmpltd own tm* 13 0
826 6/4 Stainton (R) OPE 3m 8 GF *twrds rear, dtchd by 11th, t.o. 4 out* 5 0

No longer of any account 0

RINKY DINKY DOO b.g. 10 Oats - County Clare by Vimadee — Miss Denise Foode
1995 P(0),P(0),U(-),1(13),4(0),3(11),F(-),2(15),**4(0)**
164 17/2 Weston Park (L) RES 3m 11 G *chsd ldrs, cls up 4 out, sn no ext* 4 0
292 2/3 Eaton Hall (R) RES 3m 15 G *prom, chsng grp til outpcd 5 out, sn btn, p.u. 2 out* P 0
366 6/3 Bangor (L) HC 3m 110yds 4 GS *slight ld to 9th, struggling to hold pl 4 out, t.o. next.* 3 0
564 17/3 Wolverhampt' (L) RES 3m 8 GS *ld to 5th, still cls up to 15th, no ext* 4 0
739 31/3 Sudlow Farm (R) RES 3m 11 G *mid-div, blndrd 5th, f 7th* F -
952 8/4 Eyton-On-Se' (L) RES 3m 7 GF *prom, disp 5th, ld 6-10th, wknd 2 out, p.u. last* P 0
1233 27/4 Weston Park (L) RES 3m 14 G *(bl) ld/disp to 4th, cls up 12th, outpcd* 6 0
1535 16/5 Aintree (L) HC 3m 1f 11 GF *(bl) ld till apr 8th, reminders 10th, mstk next, soon wknd, t.o. when mistake 13th, p.u. before next.* P 0

Maiden winner 95; outclassed & showed little 96; Good 10

RIO CISTO ch.m. 7 Cisto (FR) - Rio Princess by Prince Hansel — Mrs B J Harkins
386 9/3 Llanfrynach (R) RES 3m 10 GS *s.s. schoold & jmpd badly til p.u. 5th* P 0
510 16/3 Magor (R) MDN 3m 9 GS *t.o. whn p.u. 12th* P 0
605 23/3 Howick (L) MDN 3m 13 S *mid-div, dtchd at 10th, p.u. nxt* P 0

Learning - & not very quickly yet 0

RIO STAR (Irish) — I 8^{F}, I 50^{F}, I 71^{P}, I 144^{P}, I 183^{U}, I 240^{6}, I 353^{U}, I 433^{4}

RIOT LADY (Irish) — I 151^{P}, I 308^{2}, I 380^{3}, I 434^{3}, I 503^{F}

RIP THE CALICO(IRE) b.m. 8 Crash Course - Rocky's Dream by Aristocracy — Mrs Jo Duckett
1995 **U(NH),12(NH)**
234 24/2 Heythrop (R) LAD 3m 6 GS *mostly rear, some prog 11th, wknd frm 15th, p.u. nxt* P 0
266 2/3 Didmarton (L) LAD 3m 13 G *in tch, jnd ldrs 12th, wknd frm 15th* 6 10
708 30/3 Barbury Cas' (L) LAD 3m 10 G *sn bhnd, some prog frm 13th, not trbl 1st 3* 4 12
1018 13/4 Kingston Bl' (L) LAD 3m 8 G *in tch to 10th, 4th & btn 13th, t.o.* 5 0

Selling hurdles winner 94; outclassed & not stay in Ladies 12

RIP VAN WINKLE br.g. 9 Le Bavard (FR) - Flying Silver by Master Buck — Dr P P Brown
1995 2(17)
219 24/2 Newtown (L) RES 3m 17 GS *(fav) ld til f 12th* F -
292 2/3 Eaton Hall (R) RES 3m 15 G *(fav) w.w. smooth prog to ld 14th, sn clr, easily* 1 21
745 31/3 Upper Sapey (R) INT 3m 6 GS *(fav) hld up, smooth prog to disp 3 out, just ld whn lft clr nxt* 1 22
1247 27/4 Woodford (L) CON 3m 7 G *lft 2nd 11th, ld 15th, clr nxt, hung rght frm 3 out,kpt on* 1 24
1480 11/5 Bredwardine (R) LAD 3m 12 G *(fav) ld frm 4th, clr wth wnr 14th, hdd & no ext frm 2 out* 2 25
1588 25/5 Mounsey Hil' (R) LAD 3m 6 G *(fav) ld 6th-13th, ld 16th-nxt, rallied flat, ld post* 1 25

Able & top stable; well-placed & sure to win plenty more Ladies; G-S 26

RISE ABOVE IT(IRE) ch.g. 6 Aristocracy - Castle Tyne by Good Thyne (USA) — Mrs P M Jibson
1995 **7(NH),9(NH),5(NH)**
174 18/2 Market Rase' (L) MDO 2m 5f 7 GF *raced wd, plIng, ld 3rd, jnd 6th, blnd 11th, wknd,p.u.3out* P 0
542 17/3 Southwell P' (L) MDO 3m 15 GS *wth ldrs to 5th, cls up til fdd 4 out, p.u. 2 out* P 0
987 8/4 Charm Park (L) MDN 3m 13 GF *ld 11th-nxt, hdd, 2nd whn f last, lkd btn* F -

1095 14/4 Whitwell-On' (R) MDO 2 1/2m 88yds 14 G *(fav) ld til wd & hdd apr 7th,sn drppd bck,prog 5 out,2nd 2 out* 2 0
1301 28/4 Southwell P' (L) MDO 3m 10 GF *(Jt fav) cls up, ld/disp 5th til blnd 2 out, ran on und pres* 2 15

Some ability but hard ride & well beaten when 2nd; L/H looks essential; may frustrate 14

RISE IN POLITICS ch.m. 6 Politico (USA) - Rise by Fury Royal R G Brader

327 3/3 Market Rase' (L) CON 3m 15 G *alwys bhnd, t.o. 7th, p.u. 13th* P 0
413 9/3 Charm Park (L) MDO 3m 12 G *in tch to 10th, fdd rpdly 12th, p.u. 3 out* P 0

Season of no promise which lasted 6 days 0

RISEUPWILLIEREILLY ch.g. 10 Deep Run - Sinarga D F Bassett

1432 6/5 High Bickin' (R) MDO 3m 9 G *ld 4th til hdd brfly run in, rlld to ld cls home* 1 15

Poor under Rules; popped up to land weak Maiden on debut; hard to assess future prospects 15

RISING PADDY (Irish) — **I** 30^{P}, **I** 157^{5}, **I** 191^{U}, **I** 517^{F}, **I** 603^{P}

RISING SAP 6 Queen Elizabeth

883 6/4 Brampton Br' (R) MDN 3m 13 GF *rear til ran on frm 16th, fin well, not rch wnr* 2 13
1174 20/4 Chaddesley ' (L) MDN 3m 10 G *(fav) hld up, rpd prog 16th, chal & pckd 2 out, pshd into ld flat* 1 15

Won weak race but ideal start & should find Restricted, at least, in 97; Good 17

RISKY BID b.m. 6 Risk Me (FR) - Crammond Brig by New Brig J R Thomas

1995 **13(NH)**

533 16/3 Cothelstone (L) MDN 3m 13 G *rr, lst tch 11th, t.o. & p.u. 13th* P 0
1279 27/4 Bratton Down (L) MDO 3m 14 GF *mid-div, 4th at 12th, outpcd frm 3 out* 5 0
1349 4/5 Holnicote (L) MDO 3m 8 GS *mid-div, effrt 14th, kpt on onepcd frm nxt* 2 12
1593 25/5 Mounsey Hil' (R) MDO 3m 11 G *(Jt fav) bhnd, some prog 12th, nvr on terms, p.u. 16th* P 0

Well beaten in weak races & lots more needed to threaten in 97 10

RISKY DEE b.g. 7 Risk Me (FR) - Linn O' Dee by King Of Spain James Hepburn

1995 1(20),**2(24)**,**U(-)**,**2(18)**,**F(NH)**,**5(10)**,**9(NH)**,**4(NH)**

371 8/3 Ayr (L) HC 2m 5f 110yds 8 GF *(fav) blnd and u.r. 6th.* U -
673 29/3 Sedgefield (L) HC 3m 3f 7 GF *alwys handy, ld 5 out, pushed clr after next.* 1 21
1542 16/5 Perth (R) HC 2 1/2m 110yds 8 F *alwys chasing ldrs, hit 7th, ev ch when mstk 4 out, soon btn.* 5 15

Change of rider produced desired effect when winning; well beaten in handicaps after; hard to win 97 20

RISZARD (Irish) — **I** 184^{4}, **I** 310^{F}, **I** 355^{2}, **I** 461^{2}

RIVER BARGY (Irish) — **I** 228^{P}, **I** 517^{P}, **I** 527^{P}

RIVERDALE EXPRESS (Irish) — **I** 47, , **I** 125^{F}, **I** 154^{P}, **I** 306^{F}, **I** 567^{5}, **I** 614^{P}, **I** 637^{4}

RIVERDANCE ROSIE (Irish) — **I** 493^{F}, **I** 534^{F}

RIVER GALAXY ch.g. 13 Billion (USA) - River Severn by Henry The Seventh Mrs Ann Taylor

1995 6(0)

1003 9/4 Upton-On-Se' (R) LAD 3m 4 F *chsd ldr 6-14th, wknd rpdly, t.o.* 3 0
1238 27/4 Clifton On ' (L) LAD 3m 6 GF *prom, ld 10-14th, outpcd by wnr aft, wknd 2 out* 4 12
1439 6/5 Ashorne (R) RES 3m 11 G *rear of main grp, outpcd 12th, effrt 14th, sn no prog* 8 12
1508 12/5 Maisemore P' (L) LAD 3m 6 F *chsd ldr aft 9th,no imp, lft ev ch last, wknd, dead* 3 14

Dead 14

RIVER MAGNET (Irish) — **I** 171^{P}, **I** 262^{3}

RIVER MELODY ch.m. 9 Over The River (FR) - Deep Solare by Deep Run T W Moore

1995 1(24),2(24),4(21),2(22),1(22),3(23),1(21),2(20),1(20),**4(12)**

177 18/2 Horseheath (R) CON 3m 8 G *(fav) prom, ld 12th-15th & agn 3 out, ran on well flat* 1 27
677 30/3 Cottenham (R) OPE 3m 11 GF *(fav) w.w. prog 3 out,ld last,rdn & found lttl flat,lkd to fin 1st* 2 23
833 6/4 Marks Tey (L) OPE 3m 4 G *(fav) mostly 3rd, no ext frm 17th, btn 2 out, fin 3rd, plcd 2nd* 2 19
1065 13/4 Horseheath (R) CON 3m 4 F *(fav) alwys gng wll, ld 13th-15th, qknd to ld 2 out, pshd clr* 1 23
1258 27/4 Cottenham (R) OPE 3m 3 F *hld up, ld 5th-8th, chal last, bttr pace flat* 1 18
1400 6/5 Northaw (L) OPE 3m 6 F *(fav) trkd ldrs, chal 3 out, rdn nxt, unable to qkn flat* 2 21

Most consistent; 6 wins, 8 places, all points 95/6; goes well fresh; win more Opens 97; F-S 26

RIVER OF DREAMS (Irish) — **I** 234^{4}

RIVER RAMBLE b.m. 6 Rambling River - Oregano by Track Spare Mrs G Sunter

1995 **13(NH)**

229 24/2 Duncombe Pa' (R) MDO 3m 13 GS *mid-div whn f 5th* F -
414 9/3 Charm Park (L) MDO 3m 11 G *mid-div, lft 4th 4 out, nvr nrr* 4 0
590 23/3 Wetherby Po' (L) MDO 3m 16 S *alwys mid-div, no ch whn p.u. 4 out* P 0
762 31/3 Great Stain' (L) MDN 3m 11 GS *prom, mstk 11th, prog to ld 15th, hdd & no ext 2 out* 2 12

1094 14/4 Whitwell-On' (R) MDO 2 1/2m 88yds 16 G *alwys prom, no prog frm 3 out, onepcd* 3 11

Placed in modest races & shows enough to suggest a win possible in 97 14

RIVERRUNSTHROUGHIT (Irish) — I 222ᴾ, I 347ᴾ, I 417, , I 532ᴾ

RIVERSIDE LOVE ch.m. 7 Remezzo - River Valley by Apollonius C W Foulkes

1995 U(-),P(0),2(12),F(-)

241 25/2 Southwell P' (L) MDO 3m 15 HO *made most 3rd-12th, sn wknd, t.o. & p.u. 3 out* P 0
333 3/3 Market Rase' (L) MDO 3m 11 G *alwys mid-div, lost tch 12th, p.u. 14th* P 0

2nd in poor Maiden in 95 but showed nothing in brief season 96 10

RIVER SPIRIT(USA) ch.g. 11 Arts And Letters - Norma Teagarden by Jukebox G J Smith

1402 6/5 Northaw (L) RES 3m 5 F *ld to 5th, ld 10-11th,ev ch frm 3 out, no ex flat* 2 15

Maiden winner 94; missed 95; changed hands; ran well enough but Restricted hard to find at 12 14

RIVER STREAM b.m. 9 Paddy's Stream - River Belle by Divine Gift Mrs Sarah Faulks

1995 P(0),P(0),7(0),**7(0)**,P(0)

283 2/3 Clyst St Ma' (L) MDN 3m 7 S *in tch to 14th, wknd nxt, p.u. 2 out* P 0
533 16/3 Cothelstone (L) MDN 3m 13 G *alwys rr, t.o. & p.u. 13th* P 0
646 23/3 Cothelstone (L) MDO 3m 5 S *ld to 6th, in tch to 12th, wknd 3 out, fin tired* 4 0
993 8/4 Kingston St' (R) MDO 3m 17 F *mid-div, 8th at 15th, nvr dang* 7 0
1116 17/4 Hockworthy (L) MDO 3m 9 GS *pllng, cls up til rdn 10th, t.o. & p.u. last* P 0
1429 6/5 High Bickin' (R) MDO 3m 8 G *ld til blnd 5th, sn strllng, t.o. p.u. aft 13th* P 0

Tailed off when completing & of no account 0

RIVER TROUT ch.g. 15 Le Bavard (FR) - Lovely Ana by Tit For Tat II Mrs S J Coupe

1995 9(0),8(0),6(0),2(12),3(18)

566 17/3 Wolverhampt' (L) LAD 3m 5 GS *s.s. nvr in race* 3 0
685 30/3 Chaddesley ' (L) LAD 3m 9 G *ld 3-4th, sn wknd, t.o. frm 12th* 5 0
951 8/4 Eyton-On-Se' (L) LAD 3m 6 GF *prom to 8th, fdd 10th, no ch whn p.u. 3 out* P 0

No longer of any account 0

RIVER WATER (Irish) — I 3ᴾ, I 212ᴾ

R LAD b.g. 12 Rushmere - Brismaid by Flandre II Alan P Brewer

1995 5(11),U(-)

358 3/3 Garnons (L) RES 3m 18 GS *s.s. p.u. bef 3rd, lame* P 0
642 23/3 Siddington (L) RES 3m 15 S *prom til wknd appr 10th, bhnd & p.u 14th* P 0

An old maiden & sure to stay that way now 0

R N COMMANDER b.g. 10 Full Of Hope - Dectette by Quartette J R Cornwall

1995 6(13),P(0),4(12),**5(10)**,5(0),P(0),**P(0)**

258 29/2 Nottingham (L) HC 3m 110yds 10 G *alwys handy, ld 5th to 8th, chsd wnr after, 2nd and staying on when blnd and u.r. 4 out.* U -
372 8/3 Market Rasen (R) HC 3m 1f 6 G *trckd ldrs, jmpd slowly 7th, lost tch 13th, soon t.o..* 5 0
1000 9/4 Wetherby (L) HC 3m 110yds 10 G *ld to 2nd, bhnd hfwy.* 5 0
1107 15/4 Southwell (L) HC 3m 110yds 10 G *chsd ldrs, lost pl before 10th, soon struggling, p.u. before 13th.* P 0
1462 10/5 Market Rasen (R) HC 2 3/4m 110yds 11 G *(bl) slowly away, some hdwy 8th, bhnd when p.u. before 12th.* P 0
1522 12/5 Garthorpe (R) RES 3m 12 GF *mid-div, outpcd frm 13th, t.o. & p.u. 4 out* P 0
1595 25/5 Garthorpe (R) CON 3m 15 G *alwys abt 5th, outpcd by 1st pair frm 4 out* 5 13

Shock winner 94; totaly outclassed 96 & another win looks impossible 10

ROADRUNNER ch.g. 6 Sunley Builds - Derraleena by Derrylin W G R Wightman

145 17/2 Larkhill (R) MDO 3m 13 G *prom, losing tch whn ref 14th* R -

May do better 0

ROAMING SHADOW gr.g. 9 Rymer - Silver Shadow by Birdbrook J D Hankinson

1995 3(10),P(0),1(13),4(10),1(15),2(16),2(13),F(-)

25 20/1 Barbury Cas' (L) OPE 3m 14 GS *alwys bhnd, kpt on frm 15th, nrst fin* 6 15
140 17/2 Larkhill (R) CON 3m 17 G *sttld mid-div, ran on frm 3 out, nrst fin* 3 13
215 24/2 Newtown (L) OPE 3m 20 GS *rear, styd on frm 11th, no dang, nrst fin* 4 14
376 9/3 Barbury Cas' (L) MEM 3m 4 GS *(fav) ld 7th, pshd clr 3 out, ran on flat* 1 15
710 30/3 Barbury Cas' (L) CON 3m 6 G *alwys bhnd, t.o. & p.u. 4 out* P 0
866 6/4 Larkhill (R) INT 3m 4 F *trckd wnnr, rddn apr 13th, btn & wknd rpdly nxt, p.u. last* P 0
1216 24/4 Andoversford (R) INT 3m 7 G *w.w., prog 4th, 2nd app 2 out, one pcd* 3 17
1289 28/4 Barbury Cas' (L) CON 3m 8 F *last til 10th, outpcd 13th, 6th & btn whn u.r. 3 out* U -
1437 6/5 Ashorne (R) MXO 3m 13 G *last pair, wll bhnd 10th, kpt on frm 13th, nrst fin* 6 12
1564 19/5 Mollington (R) XX 3m 14 GS *hld up, prog 13th, nvr rchd ldrs, onepcd frm 3 out* 5 10

Dual winner 95; onepaced & modest but completed Members double & best chance again 97; G/S-G ... 15

ROARK'S CHUKKA 9 D P Smith

643 23/3 Siddington (L) MDN 3m 16 S *in tch til wknd rpdly 10th, p.u. nxt* P 0
797 2/4 Heythrop (R) MDN 3m 11 F *cls up, wknd whn mstk 11th, p.u. nxt* P 0
947 8/4 Andoversford (R) MDN 3m 11 GF *mid-div, btn whn p.u. 15th* P 0
1182 21/4 Mollington (R) MDN 3m 10 F *prom, mstk 13th, sn wknd, t.o. & p.u. 2 out* P 0
1434 6/5 Ashorne (R) MDO 3m 15 G *alwys rear, lost tch 11th, t.o. & p.u. 13th* P 0

No real signs of ability 0

ROBBIE'S BOY b.g. 9 Sunley Builds - Lucys Willing by Will Hays (USA) J L Brown
1995 1(14),2(0)

155 17/2 Erw Lon (L) RES 3m 9 G *rear til prog to 2nd at 15th, no ch wnr* 2 10
256 29/2 Ludlow (R) HC 3m 14 G *chsd ldrs to 14th.* 8 13
600 23/3 Howick (L) RES 3m 14 S *3rd/4th til ld 12th, hdd 3 out, ran on last, alwys hld* 2 18
770 31/3 Pantyderi (R) RES 3m 9 G *(fav) ld chsng grp, ld 2 out, easily* 1 18
1037 13/4 St Hilary (R) OPE 3m 5 G *(fav) last til prog 11th, ld/disp til f 16th* F -
1265 27/4 Pyle (R) OPE 3m 8 G *chsd ldrs til outpcd 14th* 4 13

Maiden winner 95; fair performances 96; should find Confined chances 97; G-S 19

ROBCOURT HILL br.g. 11 Callernish - Cooney Island by Distinctly (USA) H J Hopper

455 9/3 Charing (L) MDN 3m 10 G *chsd ldrs, disp 3rd & btn whn f 2 out* F -

Very lightly raced & little chance of breaking his duck at 12 0

ROBENKO(USA) b.g. 7 Roberto (USA) - Kendra Road (USA) by Kennedy Road (USA) Paul C N Heywood
1995 2(14),U(-),3(10),U(-)

201 24/2 Lemalla (R) MDO 3m 13 HY *prom til no ext frm 2 out* 4 10
556 17/3 Ottery St M' (L) MDO 3m 15 G *hld up,prog 10th, ld 13th-4 out, disp nxt, drew clr apr last* 1 15
720 30/3 Wadebridge (L) RES 3m 9 GF *(fav) rear, steady prog 11th, 3rd 13th, 5l 3rd whn f 15th* F -

Won decent Maiden & good enough for Restricteds but not trustworthy; finished early; G-Hy 16

ROBIN OF LOXLEY (Irish) — **I** 73P, **I** 213P, **I** 2756, **I** 3516, **I** 5026

ROBIN OF SHERWOOD ch.g. 14 Pollerton - Oriental Roo by Amazon Keith R Pearce
1995 **3(14)**

146 17/2 Erw Lon (L) MEM 3m 7 G *last til prog to 3rd 14th, ch 2 out, onepcd* 3 10
356 3/3 Garnons (L) LAD 3m 12 GS *rear frm 6th, t.o. 13th* 7 0

Lightly raced 95/6 & could be finished now 10

ROBOTIC (Irish) — **I** 300U, **I** 3953

ROBUSTI ch.g. 14 Bustino - Juliette Marny by Blakeney S Turner
1995 5(13),**R(-)**,2(21),1(20),**7(0)**,3(11)

22 20/1 Barbury Cas' (L) XX 3m 19 GS *alwys t.o.* 8 0
153 17/2 Erw Lon (L) OPE 3m 15 G *cls up, disp 8th-10th, outpcd frm 3 out* 4 15

Ladies winner 95; beaten in hot Open but winning chances at 15 slim; Soft 15

ROCHESTER gr.g. 10 Entre Nous - Satan's Daughter by Lucifer (USA) Robert & Elizabeth Hitchins

24 20/1 Barbury Cas' (L) XX 3m 12 GS *last whn u.r. 1st* U -
230 24/2 Heythrop (R) MEM 3m 12 GS *ld til 16th, grad wknd, lost 3rd flat* 4 13
362 5/3 Leicester (R) HC 2 1/2m 110yds 8 GS *held up, chasing ldrs when blnd and u.r. 7th.* U -
1544 17/5 Stratford (L) HC 3m 10 GF *chsd lding gp, wknd 13th, soon bhnd, t.o..* 8 0

Winning hurdler; lightly raced; disappointing in points; best watched 15

ROCK COTTAGE (Irish) — **I** 493P

ROCKET RADAR b.g. 5 Vouchsafe - Courtney Pennant by Angus Miss J Bunn

1006 9/4 Upton-On-Se' (R) MDN 3m 11 F *schoold & alws wl bhnd, nvr nrr* 6 0
1484 11/5 Bredwardine (R) MDO 3m 17 G *prom frm 6th, ev ch 15th, 2nd at last, no ext flat* 3 14

Beaten less than 4l in large field & should find certainly a chance in 97 16

ROCKVIEW SUPREME (Irish) — **I** 9F, **I** 593, **I** 77F, **I** 119P, **I** 203F, **I** 2404, **I** 3256, **I** 370S, **I** 443P

ROCKY ROSE b.m. 6 Nader - Hawthorn Summer by Comedy Star (USA) Mrs R Jowett

145 17/2 Larkhill (R) MDO 3m 13 G *rear whn u.r. 3rd* U -
1060 13/4 Badbury Rin' (L) MDO 3m 14 GF *last whn bkd 3rd* R -
1168 20/4 Larkhill (R) RES 3m 8 GF *prom early, wknd frm 7th, t.o. & p.u. 10th* P 0

Shows nothing yet 0

RODO (Irish) — **I** 440, , **I** 502,

ROGERSON ch.g. 8 Green-Fingered - Town Belle by Town Crier — S H Sweetland

1995 2(10)

284	2/3	Clyst St Ma'	(L)	MDN	3m	11	S	*mid-div, prog 12th, ev ch 15th, wknd 3 out, p.u. nxt*	P	0
558	17/3	Ottery St M'	(L)	MDO	3m	9	G	*bhnd & mstks, t.o. & p.u. 3 out*	P	0
1128	20/4	Stafford Cr'	(R)	RES	3m	17	S	*sn bhnd, t.o. & p.u. 11th*	P	0
1347	4/5	Holnicote	(L)	MDO	3m	16	GS	*2nd & ev ch whn u.r. 3 out*	U	-
1494	11/5	Holnicote	(L)	MDO	3m	8	G	*hld up, gd hdwy 15th, ld 2 out til last, no ext*	2	12

Improved late season; ran well enough when 2nd & may go one better in 97 14

ROLIER (Irish) — **I** 93[4], **I** 219[F], **I** 256[2], **I** 282[3], **I** 410[2]

ROLL-A-DANCE b.g. 7 Mashhor Dancer (USA) - Sandi's Gold by Godswalk (USA) — Peter Saville

1995 P(0),P(0),4(0),3(10),1(14)

29	20/1	Barbury Cas'	(L)	RES	3m	12	GS	*chsd ldrs to 8th, t.o. p.u. 12th*	P	0
165	17/2	Weston Park	(L)	RES	3m	9	G	*mid-div whn f 10th*	F	-
292	2/3	Eaton Hall	(R)	RES	3m	15	G	*mid-div, nvr dang, p.u. 3 out*	P	0
461	9/3	Eyton-On-Se'	(L)	RES	3m	15	G	*mid-div, sn btn, p.u. 4 out*	P	0
578	20/3	Ludlow	(R)	HC	3m	7	G	*started slowly, soon prom, rdn when blnd and u.r. 10th.*	U	-
739	31/3	Sudlow Farm	(R)	RES	3m	11	G	*alwys rear, lost tch 11th, p.u. last*	P	0

Maiden winner 95; showed nothing in 96; can only be watched 0

ROLLESTON BLADE ch.g. 9 Broadsword (USA) - Pearl Bride by Spartan General — H J Jarvis

1995 F(-),5(12),3(15)

348	3/3	Higham	(L)	RES	3m	12	G	*prom, hit 1st, f 2nd*	F	-
574	17/3	Detling	(L)	RES	3m	14	GF	*chsd wnr, 3rd & btn 3 out*	4	0
917	8/4	Aldington	(L)	RES	3m	4	F	*(fav) hld up, ld 13th, clr 2 out, pshd out flat*	1	16
1329	30/4	Huntingdon	(R)	HC	3m	14	GF	*mid div, blnd 5th and 12th, fifth when f next.*	F	-
1537	16/5	Folkestone	(R)	HC	3 1/4m	8	GF	*ld 1st till after 3rd, chsd ldr 10th to 12th and again 16th, led 2 out, hdd and one pace run-in.*	2	17

Maiden winner 94; won weak Restricted; best run in poor H/Chase; may find weak Confined; G-F 17

ROLLING BALL(FR) b.g. 13 Quart de Vin (FR) - Etoile Du Berger III by Farabi — Mrs H J Clarke

261	2/3	Warwick	(L)	HC	3 1/4m	5	G	*ld 2nd, made rest, drew clr from 3 out, v easily.*	1	44
672	29/3	Aintree	(L)	HC	2 3/4m	26	G	*(fav) raced freely, soon ld, clr when ran wd 12th (Canal Turn), hdd 4 out, rallied to ld last, edged right run-in, held on well.*	1	34
1460	8/5	Uttoxeter	(L)	HC	2m 7f	5	G	*(fav) ld to 4 out, switched right next, 2 l bhnd when blnd two out, no ch after.*	2	28
1631	1/6	Stratford	(L)	HC	3 1/2m	14	GF	*ld to 12th, wknd quickly 14th, t.o. when p.u. before 16th.*	P	0

Former top novice chaser; returned from wilderness with sensational run at Warwick; may revive 97 ... 34

ROLY PRIOR b.g. 7 Celtic Cone - Moonduster by Sparkler — Ian Hamilton

1995 **9(NH)**,**6(NH)**

51	4/2	Alnwick	(L)	MDO	3m	17	G	*in tch, lost pl 11th, prog 4 out, mstk nxt, fin well*	3	14
189	24/2	Friars Haugh	(L)	RES	3m	9	S	*4th hlfwy, went 2nd flat, not rch wnr*	2	15
321	2/3	Corbridge	(R)	MDN	3m	12	GS	*(fav) trckng ldrs whn f 7th*	F	-
407	9/3	Dalston	(R)	MDO	2 1/2m	13	G	*(Jt fav) alwys prom, with ldrs tl outpcd frm 14th*	4	0
613	23/3	Friars Haugh	(L)	MDN	3m	15	G	*(fav) mid-div, prog 4 out, went 2nd apr last, no imp on wnr*	2	15
704	30/3	Tranwell	(L)	MDO	3m	16	GS	*(fav) trckd ldrs, 2nd frm 13th, lft in ld 15th, ran on well*	1	16
1131	20/4	Hornby Cast'	(L)	RES	3m	17	G	*mostly mid-div, no prog frm 4 out*	6	13
1249	27/4	Balcormo Ma'	(R)	RES	3m	10	GS	*3rd hlfwy, lost tch by 3 out, p.u. bfr last*	P	0

Proved expensive till winning; disappointing after; may struggle to win Restricted; G-S 15

ROMAN GALE (Irish) — **I** 54[P]

ROMANO HATI b.m. 11 Senang Hati - Bella Romano by Roman Warrior — R G A Brown

204	24/2	Castle Of C'	(R)	MDO	3m	11	HY	*cls up early, sn lost tch, p.u. 11th*	P	0
358	3/3	Garnons	(L)	RES	3m	18	GS	*t.o. whn f 7th*	F	-
510	16/3	Magor	(R)	MDN	3m	9	GS	*t.o. whn p.u. 13th*	P	0
605	23/3	Howick	(L)	MDN	3m	13	S	*t.o. 5th, p.u. nxt*	P	0

Of no account 0

ROMANY ANNE b.m. 8 Button Bright (USA) - Romany Charm by Romany Air — L Bond

1995 P(0),P(0),2(0)

298	2/3	Great Treth'	(R)	RES	3m	13	G	*bhnd til p.u. 14th*	P	0
557	17/3	Ottery St M'	(L)	MDN	3m	10	G	*sn rear, t.o. & p.u. 11th*	P	0
629	23/3	Kilworthy	(L)	MDN	3m	11	GS	*chsd ldrs to 10th, sn wknd, t.o.*	6	0
875	6/4	Higher Kilw'	(L)	MDN	3m	6	GF	*cls 3rd mostly, 5l 3rd 3 out, no ext, blnd last*	3	11
1118	17/4	Hockworthy	(L)	MDO	3m	14	GS	*alwys rr, lft poor 5th 12th, stppd aft 3 out*	P	0
1424	6/5	High Bickin'	(R)	MEM	3m	4	G	*(fav) w.w. in tch, efft 3 out, not qckn*	2	10

Placed 3 times 95/6 but non-stayer & winning prospects very slim 10

ROMANY GOLD ch.m. 10 Pauper - Travellers Pride by Pry — Mrs J Tarran

221	24/2	Newtown	(L)	MDN	3m	12	GS	*(bl) mstk 6th, alwys rear, t.o. & p.u. 13th*	P	0

432 9/3 Upton-On-Se' (R) MDO 3m 17 GS *wll bhnd til p.u. 2 out* P 0

Missed 95 & could be finished now 0

ROMANY KING br.g. 12 Crash Course - Winsome Lady by Tarqogan Urs E Schwarzenbach
1995 **5(NH),3(NH),6(NH),5+(NH),4(NH)**

256 29/2 Ludlow (R) HC 3m 14 G *prom, lost pl 11th, kept on from 4 out.* 6 21
1226 25/4 Perth (R) HC 3m 7 S *trckd ldrs, ld 15th, clr 2 out, wknd, edged left und pres and hdd run-in, no ext.* 2 23
1382 6/5 Exeter (R) HC 2m 7f 110yds 8 GF *held up, steady hdwy 10th, ev ch 2 out, rdn and not qckn after last.* 2 25
1543 17/5 Newton Abbot (L) HC 3 1/4m 110yds 8 G *(fav) held up bhnd ldrs, rdn when mstk 3 out, soon btn.* 3 14

Decent chaser in his day but disappointing in H/Chases; declining; best watched; Good 20

ROMEO'S BROTHER (Irish) — I 458P, I 612P

RONEO(USA) ch.g. 8 Secretariat (USA) - Zaizafon (USA) by The Minstrel (CAN) R Parker

479 10/3 Tweseldown (R) MDO 3m 10 G *4th & pshd alng whn f 10th* F -

Not bred for it & unlikely to enjoy it 0

RONLEES b.g. 9 Rontino - Ballinlonig Lass by Diritto Mrs P H Parris
1995 4(0),F(-)

91 11/2 Ampton (R) MDO 3m 10 GF *jmpd bdly, t.o. whn ref & u.r. 11th* R -
417 9/3 High Easter (L) MEM 3m 4 S *(bl) alwys last, j.s. 1st & 6th, t.o. whn ref 10th* R -

Worthless 0

RONSON ROYALE ch.g. 9 Lighter - Mosquito River by River Beauty Miss S Springall

240 25/2 Southwell P' (L) MDO 3m 15 HO *hld up, plld to disp 6th-9th, sn wknd, t.o. & p.u. 3 out* P 0
681 30/3 Cottenham (R) MDO 3m 12 GF *mstk 4th, alwys rear, no ch 15th, t.o.* 7 0
1196 21/4 Sandon (L) MDN 3m 17 G *mid to rear, p.u. 5 out* P 0

Last on only completion 0

RONTOM (Irish) — I 98[1], I 216[3], I 262P, I 315[3]

ROOM TO MANOUVER(IRE) ch.g. 7 Le Bavard (FR) - She's A Model by Caribo R Lush

34 20/1 Higham (L) MDN 3m 11 GF *jmpd badly, sn t.o. p.u. 16th* P 0
62 10/2 Cottenham (R) MDO 3m 6 GS *in tch to 12th, no ch 15th, blnd 2 out* 4 0
108 17/2 Marks Tey (L) MDN 3m 17 G *in tch to 10th, t.o. whn p.u. appr last* P 0
424 9/3 High Easter (L) MDN 3m 10 S *prom til u.r. 3rd* U -
496 16/3 Horseheath (R) MDO 3m 10 GF *bhnd til ran on onepcd frm 2 out, nvr nrr* 4 0

Tailed off on both completions & unpromising 0

RORY'M(IRE) ch.g. 7 Remainder Man - First In by Over The River (FR) Mrs J Waring
1995 P(0),P(0)

2 13/1 Larkhill (R) MDO 3m 17 GS *rear whn f 2nd* F -
45 3/2 Wadebridge (L) MDO 3m 10 GF *jmpd bdly in last til p.u. 6th* P 0
150 17/2 Erw Lon (L) MDN 3m 8 G *rear, t.o. & p.u. 5th* P 0
1495 11/5 Holnicote (L) MDO 3m 11 G *sn bhnd, last whn ref 6th* R -

Yet to complete the course from 6 starts 95/6 0

ROSANDA b.m. 6 Derring Rose - Ananda by Majestic Maharaj J G Charlton

653 23/3 Badbury Rin' (L) MDO 3m 9 G *sn bhnd, nvr nvr, p.u. 10th* P 0
819 6/4 Charlton Ho' (L) MDN 3m 10 GF *u.r. 1st* U -
1060 13/4 Badbury Rin' (L) MDO 3m 14 GF *rear whn ref & u.r. 3rd* R -

Unpromising 0

ROSA'S REVENGE b or br.m. 8 Pony Express - Royal Brief by Eborneezer G W Johnson
1995 P(0),3(0),P(0),P(0),P(0)

71 10/2 Great Treth' (R) MDO 3m 15 S *prom early, losing tch whn p.u. aft 13th* P 0
202 24/2 Lemalla (R) MDO 3m 12 HY *prom til rdn 12th, no response* 6 0
300 2/3 Great Treth' (R) MDO 3m 10 G *(bl) made most til hdd 14th, renewed effrt 2 out,ld last,drvn out* 1 14
627 23/3 Kilworthy (L) RES 3m 13 GS *prom to 12th, sn lost plc, kpt on onepcd frm 2 out* 6 11

Improving; won modest Maiden; beaten in hot Restricted after & will find easier chances if fit 97 15

ROSCOE'S GEMMA b.m. 12 Roscoe Blake - Ash Copse by Golden Love N K Thick
1995 **P(NH),P(NH),9(NH)**

350 3/3 Garnons (L) CON 3m 11 GS *alwys rear, lost tch 8th, t.o. & p.u. 2 out* P 0
431 9/3 Upton-On-Se' (R) MDO 3m 17 GS *t.o. 1st cct, mod late prog* 6 0
606 23/3 Howick (L) MDN 3m 13 S *rear, prog steadily frm 13th, 3rd 3 out, tk 2nd flat* 2 12
836 6/4 Maisemore P' (L) MEM 3m 7 GF *prom to 3rd, sn bhnd, last frm 7th, no ch frm 12th* 5 0

Gave novice jockey good ride at Howick but no real chances at 13 10

ROSEBERRY STAR b.m. 8 Alfie Dickins - Sweet Roseberry by Derek H — P Cowey

1995 P(0),P(0),7(0),P(0),6(0)

225	24/2	Duncombe Pa'	(R)	RES	3m	12	GS	*in tch til f 6th*	F	-
332	3/3	Market Rase'	(L)	MDO	3m	8	G	*prog to 4th at 11th, sn outpcd, lft poor 2nd 3 out, tired*	2	0
516	16/3	Dalton Park	(R)	MDO	3m	11	G	*prom, disp 2nd 16th, wknd 3 out*	3	0
589	23/3	Wetherby Po'	(L)	MDO	3m	16	S	*hmpd 1st, alwys rear, t.o. 10th, p.u. 14th*	P	0
828	6/4	Stainton	(R)	MDO	3m	7	GF	*chsd ldrs, outpcd 10th, sn t.o.*	4	0
137	20/4	Hornby Cast'	(L)	MDN	3m	13	G	*mid-div, rmndrs 9th, sn wknd, t.o.*	6	0

Ran better in 96 but does not stay & well beaten each completion 10

ROSE KING b.g. 9 King's Ride - Choral Rose by Blue Refrain — Maurice E Pinto

920	8/4	Aldington	(L)	OPE	3m	6	F	*(fav) nt fluent early,prog 12th,ld 15th,hrd rdn & hdd last,nt qckn*	2	24
330	30/4	Huntingdon	(R)	HC	2 1/2m 110yds	8	GF	*waited with, mstks 8th and 9th, well btn 3 out, walked in.*	5	0

Winning chaser; disappointing both starts & may struggle to win; Confineds best hope 20

ROSEL WALK (Irish) — I 166^{1}

ROSELYNHILL (Irish) — I 178^{P}

ROSENTHAL b.m. 8 Green Ruby (USA) - Demetria (GER) by Basalt (GER) — M P Jones

218	24/2	Newtown	(L)	MDN	3m	14	GS	*mstks, alwys bhnd, t.o. 10th, p.u. 15th*	P	0
391	9/3	Llanfrynach	(R)	MDN	3m	11	GS	*chsd ldng quartet, no imp & no ch 14th, kpt on*	3	0
605	23/3	Howick	(L)	MDN	3m	13	S	*mid-div, prog to 3rd 12th, disp 14th-3 out, ld flat, all out*	1	12
222	24/4	Brampton Br'	(R)	RES	3m	11	G	*outpcd frm 10th, t.o. frm 14th*	7	0
266	27/4	Pyle	(R)	RES	3m	10	G	*rear frm 5th, t.o. & p.u. 9th*	P	0
482	11/5	Bredwardine	(R)	RES	3m	13	G	*rdn alng in rear 4th, t.o. & ref 6th*	R	-

Won bad Maiden & did nothing after; much more needed for Restricteds; Soft 12

ROSE OF STRADBALLY (Irish) — I 521^{P}

ROSES IN MAY b.m. 10 Mummy's Game - Ma Famille by Welsh Saint — R J S Linne

1995 P(0),1(11),3(10),P(0),5(0)

715	30/3	Wadebridge	(L)	CON	3m	8	GF	*mid-div, hmpd & lft 3rd 12th, sn rdn & wknd*	3	0
939	8/4	Wadebridge	(L)	RES	3m	2	F	*ld to 8th, mstk 9th, ld agn 15th, made rest, comf*	1	13
141	20/4	Flete Park	(R)	LAD	3m	8	S	*sn rear, t.o. & p.u. 12th*	P	0

Won bad Maiden 95; beat an unwilling rival in Restricted match & further chances unlikely 11

ROSE'S LADY DAY b.m. 5 Old Jocus - Rose's Final by Crawter — Mrs J Goudge

941	8/4	Wadebridge	(L)	MDN	3m	5	F	*bhnd whn u.r. 12th*	U	-
071	13/4	Lifton	(R)	MDN	3m	10	S	*imdly t.o., p.u. apr 13th*	P	0
429	6/5	High Bickin'	(R)	MDO	3m	8	G	*bhnd til p.u. apr 17th*	P	0
626	27/5	Lifton	(R)	MDO	3m	13	GS	*t.o. til p.u. 13th*	P	0

Consistent, at least 0

ROSE'S LUCK (Irish) — I 120^{P}, I 149^{P}, I 239, , I 460^{1}

ROSETOWN GIRL (Irish) — I 369^{P}, I 428^{F}, I 471^{2}, I 556^{P}

ROSEVALLEY (Irish) — I 87^{P}, I 201, , I 296^{4}, I 367^{3}

ROSEY ELLEN (Irish) — I 609^{P}, I 650^{1}

ROSIEPLANT b.m. 6 Queen's Soldier (USA) - Sweet Saskia by Spitsbergen — A Plant

976	8/4	Lydstep	(L)	MDO	3m	12	G	*twrds rear, p.u. 10th*	P	0
039	13/4	St Hilary	(R)	MDN	3m	14	G	*schoold, styd on late*	4	0
271	27/4	Pyle	(R)	MDO	3m	15	G	*alwys prom, ld 13th, rdn clr 3 out*	1	14

Benefited from education with wide-margin win; has every chance of improving for Restricteds 97 16

ROSIE'S PRIDE (Irish) — I 59^{1}, I 436^{2}, I 508^{3}, I 576^{P}

ROSKEEN BRIDGE (Irish) — I 139^{F}, I 199^{4}, I 375^{U}, I 457^{3}, I 502^{2}, I 571^{2}

ROSSI BEG (Irish) — I 661^{P}

ROSSI NOVAE (Irish) — I 10^{F}, I 67^{4}, I 115^{2}, I 158, , I 329, , I 496^{5}

ROSS QUAY (Irish) — I 79^{P}, I 118^{F}, I 139^{P}, I 517^{F}, I 551,

ROSS VENTURE b.g. 11 Monksfield - Fitz's Buck by Master Buck — Brian Brennan

160	17/2	Weston Park	(L)	OPE	3m	16	G	*ld to 11th, stppd qckly, p.u. nxt*	P	0
578	20/3	Ludlow	(R)	HC	3m	7	G	*ld, blnd 7th, hdd apr 4 out, no ch with wnr.*	2	20
031	13/4	Alpraham	(R)	MXO	3m	5	GS	*ld til hdd 14th, rddn & no ext frm 3 out*	3	11

Winning chaser; ran well at Ludlow but non-stayer & hard to see a win at 12 16

ROUGH AURA b.g. 6 Just A Monarch - Lucy Aura by Free State — C G Martin

1995 P(0),P(0),P(0)

450	9/3	Charing	(L)	XX	3m	8	G	*ld til blnd 7th, mstks & fdd aft, p.u. aft 12th*	P	0

No signs of ability & lightly raced 0

ROUGH ECHO b.g. 6 Rolfe (USA) - Gay Huntress by Hunter's Song — D P Constable

661 24/3 Eaton Hall (R) MDN 3m 9 S *mstks in rear, p.u. 8th, lame* P 0

Not the best of starts 0

ROUGH HOUSE b.g. 5 Homeboy - Course Weed by Crash Course — Robert Robinson

115 17/2 Lanark (R) MDO 3m 8 GS *nvr dang* 4 0
502 16/3 Lanark (R) MDO 3m 7 G *4th at 11th, nvr dang* 3 0
1356 4/5 Mosshouses (L) MDO 3m 12 GS *in tch til blnd 10th, sn bhnd, t.o. & p.u. 3 out* P 0

Tailed off both completions but should be able to do better in time 10

ROUGH LIGHT(IRE) b.g. 7 Supreme Leader - Liberty Calling by Caliban — Bruce Sarson

898 6/4 Dingley (R) MDN 2m 5f 10 GS *mid-div, chsd 1st pair 6 out, u.r. 3 out* U -

Not disgraced but nothing substantive yet 10

ROUGHSHOD (Irish) — I 518^{3}
ROUND POUND (Irish) — I 79^{P}, I 187^{P}, I 306^{P}, I 462^{F}
ROUND TOWER LADY (Irish) — I 60^{P}, I 66^{F}, I 77^{P}, I 119^{P}, I 211^{3}, I 434^{4}, I 521^{F}, I 550^{1}, I 593^{6}
ROVET (Irish) — I 237^{3}, I 429^{P}, I 559^{R}
ROVING REBEL b.g. 9 Prince Of Peace - Proven Gypsy by Ampney Prince — Mrs A P Wakeham
1995 P(0),U(-),3(11)

68 10/2 Great Treth' (R) RES 3m 14 S *nvr trbld ldrs, p.u. aft 14th* P 0
138 17/2 Ottery St M' (L) RES 3m 18 GS *mid-div, p.u. 12th* P 0

Maiden winner 94; season lasted a week in 96 & can only be watched now 0

ROVING REPORT gr.g. 9 Celio Rufo - Black Rapper by Le Tricolore — Mrs A Rucker
1995 S(-),3(20),2(21),1(19),2(22)

163 17/2 Weston Park (L) LAD 3m 10 G *chsd ldrs to 5 out, wknd & p.u. 3 out* P 0
266 2/3 Didmarton (L) LAD 3m 13 G *alwys prom, 3rd & not qckn whn mstk 3 out, ran on wll last* 2 21
378 9/3 Barbury Cas' (L) LAD 3m 6 GS *nvr able to chal wnr, onepcd* 2 14
743 31/3 Upper Sapey (R) LAD 3m 7 GS *3rd at 15th, effrt to disp nxt, ld 2 out, hdd & outpcd flat* 2 22
944 8/4 Andoversford (R) LAD 3m 4 GF *last early, 2nd at 9th, ld 14th til hdd 3 out, unable qckn* 2 20
1169 20/4 Chaddesley ' (L) MEM 3m 9 G *(fav) trckd ldrs, ld 16th, jnd & not qckn flat* 2 19
1411 6/5 Cursneh Hill (L) CON 3m 5 GF *(fav) 3rd til clsd up 11th, ld 15th, in commd frm 3 out* 1 19
1596 25/5 Garthorpe (R) LAD 3m 9 G *ref to race* 0 0
1618 27/5 Chaddesley ' (L) CON 3m 14 GF *in tch,mstk 6th,outpcd 13th,ran on to 2nd 2 out,no ch wnr* 2 21

Consistent; hard to win with now; 2 wins, 9 places, last 13 starts; should find another race; F-S 20

ROVING VAGABOND b.g. 12 Newski (USA) - Proven Gypsy by Ampney Prince — Mrs A P Wakeham
1995 5(0),P(0),1(12)

137 17/2 Ottery St M' (L) RES 3m 15 GS *alwys bhnd, t.o. & p.u. 2 out* P 0
298 2/3 Great Treth' (R) RES 3m 13 G *rear whn f 11th* F -
445 9/3 Haldon (R) RES 3m 9 S *rear & rmndr 10th, bhnd whn p.u. 14th* P 0
926 8/4 Bishopsleigh (R) RES 3m 9 G *lost grnd frm 5th, t.o. whn p.u. 4 out* P 0
1138 20/4 Flete Park (R) MEM 3m 4 S *ld til 14th, wll bhnd frm 17th* 3 0
1358 4/5 Flete Park (R) RES 3m 8 G *(bl) prom, 3rd at 12th, sn lost plc, last whn f 15th (ditch)* F -

Finished alone in slow Maiden in 95 & predictably outclassed since 0

ROWLANDSONS BRIDGE (Irish) — I 511^{P}
ROYAL ARCTIC (Irish) — I 342^{P}, I 420^{F}, I 528^{3}
ROYAL ARISTOCRAT (Irish) — I 258^{P}, I 286^{1}, I 315^{B}, I 362^{2}, I 414^{4}
ROYAL BARGE b.g. 6 Nearly A Hand - April Airs by Grey Mirage — E L Harries

977 8/4 Lydstep (L) MDO 3m 8 G *twrds rear, p.u. 14th* P 0
1162 20/4 Llanwit Maj' (R) MDO 3m 12 GS *t.d.e., mid-div whn ref 2nd* R -
1270 27/4 Pyle (R) MDO 3m 9 G *rear whn ran out & u.r. 3rd* r -

Good stable but unpromising so far 0

ROYAL BASIS (Irish) — I 31^{F}
ROYAL BAV(IRE) ch.g. 8 Le Bavard (FR) - Polly's Cacador by Royal Buck — A J Poulton

618 23/3 Higham (L) MDO 3m 14 GF *alwys bhnd, lost tch 5th, t.o. til p.u. 2 out* P 0
682 30/3 Cottenham (R) MDO 3m 9 GF *mid-div, last & outpcd 16th, kpt on* 3 0

Broke down only start 94; missed 95; 3rd in poor race - only form in 96 10

ROYAL BULA b.g. 8 Sula Bula - Clan Royal by Royal Smoke — G I Isaac
1995 P(0),F(-)

156	17/2	Erw Lon	(L)	RES	3m	13	G	*alwys last pair, p.u. 12th*	P	0
391	9/3	Llanfrynach	(R)	MDN	3m	11	GS	*jmpd badly, alwys rear, 6th & no ch 11th, p.u. 15th*	P	0
771	31/3	Pantyderi	(R)	MDN	3m	14	G	*rear whn p.u. 2 out*	P	0
341	6/4	Maisemore P'	(L)	MDN	3m	9	GF	*hld up, in tch,outpcd 14th, 3rd & wll btn whn u.r. 2 out*	U	-
162	20/4	Llanwit Maj'	(R)	MDO	3m	12	GS	*in tch, last & strggling 14th, lft poor 3rd 3 out*	3	0
271	27/4	Pyle	(R)	MDO	3m	15	G	*(fav) trckd ldrs, cls up 11th, p.u. nxt*	P	0

Last on only completion from 8 starts 95/6 & amazing favourite last start 0

OYAL CHAPEAU (Irish) — **I** 8^F, **I** 63^4

OYAL CREDIT ch.m. 6 Royal Vulcan - Free Credit by Deep Run — T B Brown

434	6/5	Ashorne	(R)	MDO	3m	15	G	*bhnd, prog to 7th & in tch 10th, lost tch 13th, p.u. 2 out*	P	0

Not totally disgraced on debut & may do better 10

OYAL ENTERTAINER ch.g. 8 Royal Blend - Feodora by Songedor — G L Edwards

1995 P(0),P(0),1(12),r(-)

462	9/3	Eyton-On-Se'	(L)	RES	3m	12	G	*prom, ld 9th-10th, lost plc nxt, no chnc frm 4 out*	6	0
566	24/3	Eaton Hall	(R)	RES	3m	13	S	*f 1st*	F	-

Won poor Maiden in 95 & showed little in brief 96 12

OYAL EXHIBITION ch.g. 12 Le Bavard (FR) - The Brown Link by Rugged Man — Mrs Jayne Barton

1995 P(0),P(0),P(0),3(0),4(0),2(12),4(0)

340	3/3	Heythrop	(R)	MDN	3m	12	G	*rear, rdn hlfwy, styd on frm 15th, ld flat, kpt on well*	1	13

Found a poor race to open his account & Restricted beyond him even if fit at 13 13

OYAL FIFE br.m. 10 Royal Fountain - Aunt Bertha by Blandford Lad — Mrs C G Braithwaite

112	17/2	Lanark	(R)	LAD	3m	8	GS	*4th at 10th, disp 2nd whn f 3 out*	F	-
501	16/3	Lanark	(R)	RES	3m	12	G	*sn bhnd, t.o.*	4	0
611	23/3	Friars Haugh	(L)	LAD	3m	10	G	*5th hlfwy, u.r. 11th.*	U	-
700	30/3	Tranwell	(L)	LAD	3m	4	GS	*ptchd & u.r. 1st*	U	-
089	14/4	Friars Haugh	(L)	MDN	3m	10	F	*patiently rdn, ld 4 out til hdd & no ext apr last*	2	13
254	27/4	Balcormo Ma'	(R)	MDO	3m	14	GS	*last early, steadd prog to ld last, drvn out*	1	15
353	4/5	Mosshouses	(L)	RES	3m	11	GS	*last trio, poor 9th hlfwy, prog to 6th at 14th, styd on*	4	11
571	19/5	Corbridge	(R)	RES	3m	13	G	*cls up at 11th, outpcd frm 14th*	7	10

Slogged to victory in 7 3/4mins Maiden; similar needed for Restricted hopes 97; Soft 15

OYAL FIREWORKS ch.g. 9 Royal Vulcan - Bengal Lady by Celtic Cone — Berkshire Commercial Components Ltd

263	2/3	Didmarton	(L)	INT	3m	18	G	*mid-div, wknd 13th, t.o. & p.u. last*	P	0
383	6/5	Towcester	(R)	HC	2 3/4m	7	GF	*blnd 6th, bhnd from 8th, t.o. when f 12th.*	F	-

Maiden winner 94; very lightly raced & showed nothing in 96 0

OYAL GLEASON b.g. 12 Gleason (USA) - Royal Treasure by Royal Buck — Mrs L P Vaughan

1995 U(-),1(12),**2(14)**,P(0)

364	5/3	Leicester	(R)	HC	2m 1f	12	GS	*prom in chasing gp till wknd 11th, t.o..*	10	0

Members winner 95; non-stayer & beaten miles only start 96 10

OYAL IRISH ch.g. 12 Le Bavard (FR) - Leuze by Vimy — Dr G Madan Mohan

1995 **3(NH),F(NH),P(NH),2(NH)**

258	29/2	Nottingham	(L)	HC	3m 110yds	10	G	*alwys handy, ld 8th, clr after next, rdn along from 4 out, ct last stride.*	2	19
480	11/3	Plumpton	(L)	HC	3m 1f 110yds	6	GS	*(fav) ld till 2nd, led 10th till 14th, ev ch 2 out, one pace.*	2	19
674	30/3	Hereford	(R)	HC	2m	8	S	*(fav) (bl) prom, ld 5th, hdd 7th, rdn after 4 out, chal 2 out, kept on one pace run-in.*	2	18
013	13/4	Ascot	(R)	HC	3m 110yds	11	GS	*(bl) in tch 10th, lost touch 15th, no ch when went badly left last, t.o..*	4	0
335	1/5	Cheltenham	(L)	HC	2m 5f	10	G	*(bl) bhnd and rdn along 5th, t.o. and p.u. before 3 out.*	P	0
457	8/5	Uttoxeter	(L)	HC	3 1/4m	16	G	*(bl) mid div, rdn 14th, some prog next, no hdwy 4 out.*	7	0

Placed under Rules; very slow & no trip; deteriorating; hard to see a win now 14

OYALIST(CAN) b.g. 10 Commemorate (USA) - Hangin Round (USA) by Stage Door Johnny — R J Kyle

83	11/2	Alnwick	(L)	CON	3m	10	GS	*mstk 2nd,trckd ldrs,cls up 15th,wknd nxt,fin tired*	5	0
191	24/2	Friars Haugh	(L)	OPE	3m	5	S	*chsd wnr to 4th & frm 2 out, no ch wth wnr*	2	18
399	9/3	Dalston	(R)	CON	3m	9	G	*2nd frm 4th, strng chal to jn wnr last, no ex flat*	2	19
609	23/3	Friars Haugh	(L)	PPO	3m	7	G	*2nd frm 11th, strng chal frm 2 out, no ext flat*	2	18
789	1/4	Kelso	(L)	HC	3m 1f	11	GF	*struggling to stay in tch after one cct, t.o. when ref last.*	R	-
905	8/4	Carlisle	(R)	HC	3 1/4m	5	F	*prom till lost pl quickly 6th, t.o. 10th, p.u. before 2 out.*	P	0
351	4/5	Mosshouses	(L)	CON	3m	11	GS	*in tch til 5th & outpcd aft 13th, kpt on und pres frm 3 out*	5	10
570	19/5	Corbridge	(R)	CON	3m	8	G	*alwys prom, cls 2nd at 13th, chsd wnr til wknd 2 out*	3	16

1586 25/5 Hexham (L) HC 2 1/2m 110yds 14 GF *settld bhnd, imp final cct, staying on fin.* 6

Missed 95; consistent but struggling to find another win; may find chance early 97; G/F-S 18

ROYAL JESTER b.g. 12 Royal Fountain - Tormina by Tormento — Mrs A D Wauchop

1995 **2(32)**,1(27),**8(0)**,**2(28)**,**2(28)**,**1(29)**

86 11/2 Alnwick (L) OPE 3m 8 GS *(fav) ld, rdn 3 out, slw nxt, styd on, hdd nr fin* 2
259 1/3 Kelso (L) HC 3m 1f 8 GS *(fav) chsd ldrs, kept on well from last, no ext und pres near fin.* 2
582 22/3 Kelso (L) HC 3 1/2m 8 G *(fav) trckd ldrs, hdwy 11th, ld 16th, blnd badly and hdd 3 out, rallied to chal last, led flat and ran on.* 1
790 1/4 Kelso (L) HC 3m 1f 11 GF *settld with chasing gp, imp before 5 out, outpcd after next, styd on strly to ld run-in.* 1
1119 18/4 Ayr (L) HC 3m 3f 110yds 9 GS *(fav) trckd ldrs, ld 12th, styd on well from 3 out.* 1
1337 1/5 Kelso (L) HC 3m 1f 9 S *(fav) cl up, disp ld from 12th, slight lead 2 out, hdd last, no ext.* 2

Useful H/Chaser; won 7 of last 13 (6 at Kelso); genuine; stays well; should win at 13; G/F-S 27

ROYAL LEADER (Irish) — **I** 541P

ROYAL MILE b.g. 11 Tyrnavos - Royal Rib by Sovereign Path — F S Jackso

967 8/4 Thorpe Lodge (L) MEM 3m 7 GF *4th til fdd 6th, t.o. 10th* 4
1304 28/4 Southwell P' (L) OPE 3m 5 GF *chsd ldr to 5 out, wknd rpdly* 5

Chase winner 91; very lightly raced since & last both starts 96 - no hope now 0

ROYAL OATS b.m. 11 Oats - Knights Queen by Arctic Chevalier — E Tudor Harrie

1995 P(0)

151 17/2 Erw Lon (L) MDN 3m 8 G *alwys 3rd/4th, styd on frm 13th, no ch 1st 2* 3
387 9/3 Llanfrynach (R) RES 3m 11 GS *prom, ld 10-13th, ld 15th, drvn & styd on wll frm 2 out* 1
766 31/3 Pantyderi (R) CON 3m 6 G *(fav) ld to 11th, fdd, no ext frm 15th* 4
974 8/4 Lydstep (L) MEM 3m 10 G *ld to 3rd, sn mid-div, no prog* 5
1198 21/4 Lydstep (L) INT 3m 5 S *ld to 6th, agn 11th til flat, just hld* 2
1268 27/4 Pyle (R) INT 3m 8 G *8l 4th at 8th, just outpcd frm 12th, no ch frm 14th* 4
1488 11/5 Erw Lon (L) OPE 3m 4 F *in rear whn p.u. 9th* P

Vastly improved 96; stays & could win stamina Confined at 12; Soft 17

ROYAL PITTANCE b.g. 7 Pitpan - Sheba Queen by Pongee — D R Gre

144 17/2 Larkhill (R) MDO 3m 15 G *sn t.o., p.u. 12th* P
275 2/3 Parham (R) MDN 3m 15 GF *rear, mstks, wll bhnd whn f 11th* F
520 16/3 Larkhill (R) MDO 3m 11 G *jmpd bdly, sn t.o., p.u. 9th* P

No sign of ability in running or jumping 0

ROYAL QUARRY b.g. 10 Royal Fountain - True Friend by Bilsborrow — A Edmund

396 9/3 Garthorpe (R) RES 3m 9 G *6th 1st m, fddd, t.o. 10th, p.u. 12th* P
973 8/4 Thorpe Lodge (L) MDO 3m 7 GF *6th & strgglng whn u.r. 11th* U
1149 20/4 Higham (L) MDO 3m 10 F *1st ride, alwys bhnd, t.o. 10th* 5
1261 27/4 Cottenham (R) MDO 3m 10 F *wth ldrs til outpcd frm 14th, wknd 4 out* 4
1403 6/5 Northaw (L) MDO 3m 8 F *in tch,lst pl 11th, prog to 2nd 15th, onepcd frm 2 out* 3

Not beaten far in poor race last start for novice rider but will find a win very difficult 11

ROYAL RECRUIT(IRE) b.g. 8 Prince Tenderfoot (USA) - Sandford Lass by Sandford Lad — I A Brow

80 11/2 Wetherby Po' (L) MDO 3m 12 GS *cls up, wknd 4th, p.u. 10th* P

Rarely runs & shows nothing 0

ROYAL ROAD (Irish) — **I** 387P, **I** 531P

ROYAL RUPERT ro.g. 9 Royal Match - Bidula by Manacle — R Chelt

1995 5(0),2(11),1(13),S(-),2(11)

20 14/1 Tweseldown (R) RES 3m 9 GS *rear, mstk 9th, effrt 14th, sn wknd* 4
248 25/2 Charing (L) RES 3m 12 GS *prom to 15th, fdd* 6
379 9/3 Barbury Cas' (L) XX 3m 9 GS *prom early, wknd & t.o. frm 14th* 4
656 23/3 Badbury Rin' (L) RES 3m 11 G *alwys prom, not qckn frm 4 out* 4
1056 13/4 Badbury Rin' (L) RES 3m 10 GF *in tch to 10th, outpcd frm 14th* 5

Won weak Maiden 95; safe but tailed off all starts 96 10

ROYAL STAR (Irish) — **I** 83F, **I** 1633, **I** 2703, **I** 3011, **I** 393, , **I** 4833, **I** 5614, **I** 6272

ROYAL STREAM br.g. 9 Royal Fountain - Struide by Guide — Mrs D B Johnstor

1995 1(20),1(24),2(20),F(-),**1(24)**

49 4/2 Alnwick (L) OPE 3m 14 G *(fav) j.w., made all, wl clr 3 out, eased flat* 1
191 24/2 Friars Haugh (L) OPE 3m 5 S *(fav) j.w. sn clr, unchal* 1
483 14/3 Cheltenham (L) HC 3 1/4m 110yds 17 G *midfield, hmpd 12th, bhnd when blnd 15th, p.u. before 3 out.* P

1119 18/4 Ayr (L) HC 3m 3f 110yds 9 GS *prom, disp ld 14th, rdn and wknd before 17th, lost tch and p.u. before 3 out.* P 0

Useful; goes well fresh; won 7 of last 10 points & sure to win more; H/Chases possible; G-S 28

ROYAL SURPRISE b.g. 9 Royal Fountain - Miss Craigie by New Brig J Walby

1995 5(0),P(0),5(0),2(10),2(0),1(15),5(0),4(0),4(11),U(-)

84 11/2 Alnwick (L) RES 3m 11 GS *prom til 3rd & strgglng 13th, sn lost plc, kpt on apr last* 4 0
188 24/2 Friars Haugh (L) RES 3m 12 S *bhnd til styd on frm 4 out, nvr dang* 3 15
319 2/3 Corbridge (R) RES 3m 16 GS *nvr nr ldrs* 6 0
611 23/3 Friars Haugh (L) LAD 3m 10 G *4th hlfwy, chal apr last, no ext flat* 2 15
703 30/3 Tranwell (L) RES 3m 7 GS *chsd wnr 4th, ev ch 3 out, wnd apr last* 2 15
914 8/4 Tranwell (L) RES 3m 6 GF *chsd ldr til ld 11th, hdd 4 out, sn btn* 3 15
1249 27/4 Balcormo Ma' (R) RES 3m 10 GS *rmmndrs aft 4th, 2nd hlfwy, ld 13th til outpcd aft 3 out* 2 14
1340 4/5 Hexham (L) HC 3m 1f 13 S *in tch, effort before 3 out, driven along between last 2, kept on, no impn on wnr.* 2 21
1514 12/5 Hexham Poin' (L) RES 3m 5 HY *(fav) disp aft 2nd, blnd nxt, blnd & u.r. 5th* U -

Maiden winner 95; onepaced, slow & struggling to find Restricted; lost last 13; Soft 16

ROYAL SURVIVOR ch.g. 9 Deep Run - Royal Escort by Royal Highway A Godrich

1995 F(-),F(-),P(0),S(-),F(-)

242 25/2 Southwell P' (L) RES 3m 12 HO *j.w. lft in ld 3rd, hdd 4 out, lft in ld nxt, ran on well* 1 19
535 17/3 Southwell P' (L) CON 3m 10 GS *wth ldr 2nd til f 6th* F -
676 30/3 Cottenham (R) INT 3m 13 GF *ld til mstk & hdd 7th, mstk 9th, sn lost plc, no dang aft* 6 13
1098 14/4 Guilsborough (L) CON 3m 17 G *ld, blnd & u.r. 1st* U -
1302 28/4 Southwell P' (L) INT 3m 10 GF *ld til f 8th, dead* F -

Dead 15

ROYAL SWINGER ch.m. 8 Royal Match - Easy Swinger by Swing Easy (USA) E Lord

206 24/2 Castle Of C' (R) MDO 3m 10 HY *alwys bhnd, no ch whn p.u. 4 out* P 0
263 2/3 Didmarton (L) INT 3m 18 G *chsng grp, lost tch 11th, 10th & no ch whn u.r. 13th* U -
606 23/3 Howick (L) MDN 3m 13 S *prom to hlfwy, wknd & p.u. 3 out* P 0
842 6/4 Maisemore P' (L) MDN 3m 17 GF *prom, blnd 11th, wknd appr 15th, no ch whn b.d. last* B -
1248 27/4 Woodford (L) MDN 3m 15 G *chsd ldr 6-10th, outpcd apr 16th, no dang aft* 4 10
1511 12/5 Maisemore P' (L) MDO 3m 14 F *alwys last trio, t.o. & p.u. 14th* P 0
1621 27/5 Chaddesley ' (L) MDO 3m 17 GF *in tch, prog 12th, 4th & btn whn p.u. 3 out, dsmntd* P 0

One fair run but not progressing & not threatening to win 10

ROYAL TURN b.g. 9 Turn Back The Time (USA) - Royal Blast by Royal Palm John Honeyball

1396 6/5 Cotley Farm (L) MDO 3m 11 GF *alwys rr, t.o. frm 14th, outpcd* 5 0
1527 12/5 Ottery St M' (L) RES 3m 8 GF *alwys last, t.o. hlfwy* 7 0
1554 18/5 Bratton Down (L) MDO 3m 16 F *mid-div,prog to 4th 3 out,kpt on onepcd* 4 12
1626 27/5 Lifton (R) MDO 3m 13 GS *prog 15th, styd on steadily clsng stgs, tk 3rd nr fin* 3 14

Late to appear; steadily improved & beat subsequent winner last start; could go close 97; G/S-F 14

ROYAL ZIERO (Irish) — **I** 34³, **I** 202¹, **I** 249¹, **I** 513¹

ROYELLA b.m. 12 Royal Fountain - Crella by Cagirama Mrs V Scott Watson

1995 1(19)

50 4/2 Alnwick (L) CON 3m 9 G *prom til lost pl 11th, ran on agn 2 out, fin well* 2 19

Very lightly raced now; goes well fresh & chances if fit 1st time out 97 19

ROYLE BURCHLIN b.g. 10 Roscoe Blake - Miss Evelin by Twilight Alley R A Royle

1995 P(0),P(0),P(0),2(17),2(17),P(0),P(0),**9(0)**

893 6/4 Whittington (L) LAD 3m 4 F *ld, mssd marker aft 13th, p.u. apr 3 out* P 0
1032 13/4 Alpraham (R) CON 3m 9 GS *chsd ldr to 4 out, wknd nxt, p.u. last* P 0
1153 20/4 Whittington (L) LAD 3m 10 G *2nd whn u.r. 2nd* U -
1233 27/4 Weston Park (L) RES 3m 14 G *chsng grp, outpcd frm 12th, styd on, nrst fin* 3 0
1582 19/5 Wolverhampt' (L) RES 3m 10 G *prom, went 2nd 14th, ld 16th-3 out, onepcd und pres* 2 13

Maiden winner 92; still runs the odd fair race but not threatening to win now 14

ROYLE SPEEDMASTER ch.g. 12 Green Shoon - Cahermone Ivy by Perspex Miss S J Cutcliffe

1995 P(0),7(10),P(0),10(0)

639 23/3 Siddington (L) OPE 3m 12 S *f 2nd* F -
709 30/3 Barbury Cas' (L) OPE 3m 15 G *hld up, prog 10th, ld 12th, ran on well frm 3 out* 1 22
958 8/4 Lockinge (L) MXO 3m 6 GF *in tch, wnt 2nd 3 out, alwys held frm 2 out* 2 23
1290 28/4 Barbury Cas' (L) OPE 3m 5 F *(fav) hld up, prog 10th, not qckn 15th, no ch whn mstk 2 out* 3 15
1551 18/5 Bratton Down (L) OPE 3m 8 F *prom, disp brfly 10th, lost plc 15th, onepcd* 4 19

Well-revived 96; won fair Open; lost form after; best watched at 13 18

RUBER b.g. 9 Mljet - Chip Of Gold by Goldhill R W Thomson

1995 P(0),1(19),r(-),**1(24),2(22),6(13),1(25),P(0)**

259 1/3 Kelso (L) HC 3m 1f 8 GS *(bl) mstk 7th, soon bhnd, lost tch 13th, t.o..* 4 12

486 16/3 Newcastle (L) HC 3m 9 GS *chsd ldrs, lost pl 10th, no dngr after.* 6 0
612 23/3 Friars Haugh (L) OPE 3m 8 G *ld til mstk & lost plc 6th, wnt 2nd 4 out, no ex apr last* 2 20
790 1/4 Kelso (L) HC 3m 1f 11 GF *soon struggling, t.o..* 8 0
1084 14/4 Friars Haugh (L) LAD 3m 8 F *(fav) c.o. apr 6th* C -
1337 1/5 Kelso (L) HC 3m 1f 9 S *mstks, alwys bhnd, t.o..* 5 0

Won 2 H/Chases 95 but struggling in better company 96; best watched 17

RUBIKA(FR) b.g. 13 Saumon (FR) - Eureka III (FR) by Vieux Chateau — Mrs Sarah Shoemark

22 20/1 Barbury Cas' (L) XX 3m 19 GS *unruly paddock, alwys wll bhnd, t.o.* 6 0
955 8/4 Lockinge (L) MEM 3m 5 GF *(Jt fav) ld/disp til apr last, not qckn aft* 2 10
1165 20/4 Larkhill (R) LAD 3m 7 GF *prom, mstk 6th, wknd frm 13th, p.u. 3 out* P 0
1289 28/4 Barbury Cas' (L) CON 3m 8 F *prom to 10th, bhnd frm 12th, no ch aft* 6 0

2nd in bad Members & of no account now 0

RUBY BELLE (Irish) — **I** 7^{3}, **I** 142^{1}, **I** 209^{3}, **I** 461^{1}
RUBY INVITE (Irish) — **I** 49^{P}, **I** 211^{F}
RUECASTLE b.g. 8 Politico (USA) - Topazolite by Hessonite — Miss Simone Park
1995 **P(NH),F(NH),5(NH)**

705 30/3 Tranwell (L) MDO 3m 9 GS *cls up, ld 8-12th, lost plc 14th, p.u. 2 out* P 0
915 8/4 Tranwell (L) MDO 3m 7 GF *made all, clr 9th, v easily* 1 15
1353 4/5 Mosshouses (L) RES 3m 11 GS *chsd ldrs, 6th & strgglng 12th, sn btn, p.u. 3 out* P 0
1571 19/5 Corbridge (R) RES 3m 13 G *ld/disp til mstk 3 out, not rcvr* 9 0

Bombed home in poor race; showed nothing after; may have Restricted chances on Firm in 97 15

RUFF ACCOUNT b.g. 9 Ruffo (USA) - Dutch Account Vii — R G Brader
1995 P(0),5(0),P(0),P(0)

763 31/3 Great Stain' (L) MDN 3m 11 GS *prom, ld 10th, sn wll clr, unchal* 1 16
1096 14/4 Whitwell-On' (R) MEM 3m 9 G *made all, styd on strngly frm 2 out, gamely* 1 17
1131 20/4 Hornby Cast' (L) RES 3m 17 G *mid-div, prog 11th, blnd 15th, no ext* 7 11
1368 4/5 Gisburn (R) RES 3m 9 G *cls up, 2l 2nd 14th-2 out, no ext aft* 3 15

Much improved 96; beat subsequent H/Chase winner in Members; Restricted likely early 97; G-G/S 17

RUFF SONG ch.g. 10 True Song - Fury Run by Deep Run — N Jelley

329 3/3 Market Rase' (L) RES 3m 12 G *chsd ldr 4th, ld 7th-3 out, rallied apr last, kpt on* 2 16
535 17/3 Southwell P' (L) CON 3m 10 GS *ld 7-10th, in tch 4 out, fdd, p.u. 2 out* P 0
636 23/3 Market Rase' (L) MDN 3m 11 GF *(fav) ld 2nd-6 out, ran on agn frm 4th 4 out, chal last, ran on* 1 15
1098 14/4 Guilsborough (L) CON 3m 17 G *lft 30l start, rcvrd to jnd rear of grp, 10th whn u.r. 10th* U -

Missed 95; improved & found weak Maiden; question mark over Restricted chances at 11; Good 15

RUFO'S COUP br.g. 9 Celio Rufo - Wadowice by Targowice (USA) — J S Swindells

159 17/2 Weston Park (L) CON 3m 22 G *mid to rear, nvr a fctr* 11 0

Last to finish & of no account 0

RUGANS HOPE b.g. 7 Full Of Hope - Ruganmoss by Rugantino — Mrs G Drury

814 6/4 Charing (L) MDO 2 1/2m 8 F *rear, out of tch whn p.u. 8th* P 0

Not much hope yet 0

RUNABOUT (Irish) — **I** 248^{F}, **I** 330^{2}, **I** 439^{2}, **I** 472^{1}
RUN FOR BROWNIE (Irish) — **I** 55^{3}, **I** 245^{F}, **I** 277^{P}
RUNNING FRAU ch.m. 9 Deep Run - Suzi Hegi by Mon Capitaine — T R M Oakey

951 8/4 Eyton-On-Se' (L) LAD 3m 6 GF *rear, t.o. 6th, cont in own time, p.u. bfr last* P 0
1170 20/4 Chaddesley ' (L) CON 3m 9 G *s.s. prog twrds ldrs whn u.r. 4th* U -
1245 27/4 Woodford (L) LAD 3m 6 G *alwys rear, last frm 9th, t.o.* 4 0
1478 11/5 Bredwardine (R) CON 3m 12 G *cls 10th at 9th, kpt on steadily frm 14th* 5 14
1618 27/5 Chaddesley ' (L) CON 3m 14 GF *alwys well in rear, nvr nrr* 6 0

Schoolmaster & not theeatening to win now 12

RUNNING ON THYNE (Irish) — **I** 602^{P}
RUN ROSE RUN (Irish) — **I** 1^{1}, **I** 51^{P}
RUNTARRA (Irish) — **I** 601^{P}
RUN TO AU BON(IRE) b.g. 6 Commanche Run - Donna Sabina by Nonoalco (USA) — Mrs D H McCarthy
1995 **7(NH),10(NH),9(NH)**

14 14/1 Cottenham (R) MDO 3m 10 G *hld up, some prog 10th, 6th & no ch whn p.u. 16th, dsmntd* P 0
182 18/2 Horseheath (R) MDO 3m 11 G *20s-5s, in tch to 13th, losing tch whn p.u. 15th* P 0
454 9/3 Charing (L) MDN 3m 10 G *rear, jmpd slwly 8th, 9th & 10th, p.u. aft* P 0
496 16/3 Horseheath (R) MDO 3m 10 GF *(bl) restrnd, prog 11th, sn bhnd, ran on well flat* 5 0
1051 13/4 Penshurst (L) MEM 3m 5 G *(bl) strgglng to stay in tch 7th, 3rd & wknd 13th* 3 0
1210 21/4 Heathfield (R) MDO 3m 13 F *(bl) made most to 16th,rdn to ld nxt,hdd & mstk 3 out,wknd* 2 0

1374 4/5 Peper Harow (L) MDO 3m 8 F *(bl) ld to 14th, 3rd & rdn appr 2 out, wknd appr last* 3 10

Does not stay & blinkers only marginal help; beaten in poor races & will struggle to win 10

RUN TO FORM br.g. 11 Deep Run - Let The Hare Sit by Politico (USA) M S Wilesmith

1995 4(13),4(20),3(16)

23 20/1 Barbury Cas' (L) XX 3m 11 GS *lft in ld 4th, hdd 12th, wknd nxt, t.o. & p.u. 2 out* P 0
126 17/2 Kingston Bl' (L) LAD 3m 11 GS *s.v.s. jmpd slwly, bhnd til prog aft 13th, no imp nxt, wknd* 5 0
356 3/3 Garnons (L) LAD 3m 12 GS *prom to 9th, outpcd frm 11th* 5 12
743 31/3 Upper Sapey (R) LAD 3m 7 GS *ld 8th, disp 3 out til mstk nxt, outpcd* 3 20
1046 13/4 Bitterley (L) LAD 3m 9 G *chsd ldr frm 7th, ld 12th, kpt on well frm 2 out* 1 21
1167 20/4 Larkhill (R) MEM 3m 9 GF *(fav) ld to 6th, styd frnt rank, ld agn 14th, ran on wll* 1 23

Well-revived 96 (stable in good form); stays; can win at 12 in same form; G/S-G 21

RUN WITH JOY(IRE) b.g. 5 Sharrood (USA) - Durun by Run The Gantlet (USA) Richard House

1995 **P(NH),P(NH),9(NH),5(NH),2(NH),7(NH),6(NH),12(NH)**

69 10/2 Great Treth' (R) MDO 3m 12 S *nvr dang, p.u. 14th* P 0
280 2/3 Clyst St Ma' (L) RES 3m 11 S *mid-div, lost tch 12th, t.o. & p.u. 14th* P 0
533 16/3 Cothelstone (L) MDN 3m 13 G *in tch til wknd 12th, t.o. & p.u. appr last* P 0

Placed under Rules but a disappointment in points so far 0

RURAL OUTFIT b.g. 9 Town And Country - Miss Moss Bros by Sparkler Mrs Susan Humphreys

67 10/2 Great Treth' (R) LAD 3m 11 S *(Jt fav) alwys prom, ld 14th, made rest, comf* 1 26

Top-class Ladies horse; missed 95 & disappeared after easy win only start 96; G-S 28

RURAL RUN (Irish) — I 196²

RUSHALONG ch.g. 6 Rousillon (USA) - Mousquetade by Moulton George Ball

1995 5(0),C(-),P(0),P(0)

45 3/2 Wadebridge (L) MDO 3m 10 GF *hld up rear, prog 11th, eff 3 out, ld flat, ran on well* 1 15
445 9/3 Haldon (R) RES 3m 9 S *(fav) hld up, prog 11th, disp nxt, ld 14th & sn clr, easily* 1 20
1074 13/4 Lifton (R) INT 3m 9 S *hld up, gd hdwy to 3rd 15th,ran on wll und pres clsng stgs* 2 19

Changed hands & brilliantly improved; ran really well last start & Intermediate likely in 97 21

RUSHHOME gr.m. 9 Rushmere - Doon Silver by Doon P R Rodford

1995 **13(NH),R(NH)**

533 16/3 Cothelstone (L) MDN 3m 13 G *prog 12th, ld 3 out til walked thro' last & hdded, fin tired* 2 13
821 6/4 Charlton Ho' (L) MDN 3m 10 GF *held up in tch, wknng whn p.u. & dismntd 4 out* P 0

Lightly raced; unlucky 96 debutbut may have a problem now 12

RUSHING BURN b.m. 10 Royal Fountain - Money Penny by Even Money F D A Snowden

1995 6(10),2(20),5(0),2(16),3(17),2(13)

85 11/2 Alnwick (L) LAD 3m 11 GS *alwys rear, t.o. & p.u. 15th* P 0
190 24/2 Friars Haugh (L) LAD 3m 7 S *alwys handy, ld 11th til 15th, ld agn 2 out, drew clr last* 1 17
412 9/3 Charm Park (L) LAD 3m 7 G *in tch 13th, fdd, styd on onepcd* 5 12
611 23/3 Friars Haugh (L) LAD 3m 10 G *hld up, hdwy to ld 3 out, styd on wll* 1 16

Broke her duck 96; all best runs at Friars Haugh & could win Ladies there 97; form modest; G-S 18

RUSHING WATERS (Irish) — I 21ᶠ, I 124ᴾ, I 201, I 431³, I 465³, I 511⁴

RUSNETTO (Irish) — I 14ᴾ, I 56ᴾ, I 266ᴾ, I 377³, I 615¹

RUSSELL ROVER b or br.g. 11 Strong Gale - Cacador's Magnet by Chinatown Mrs Janet Ostler

709 30/3 Barbury Cas' (L) OPE 3m 15 G *sn rear, t.o. & p.u. 11th* P 0
990 8/4 Kingston St' (R) OPE 3m 6 F *ld 4th, slght ld to 11th, sn wknd* 5 0
1111 17/4 Hockworthy (L) MXO 3m 13 GS *prom to 7th, t.o. & p.u. 11th* P 0
1343 4/5 Holnicote (L) OPE 3m 6 GS *cls up early, fdd frm 15th, sn bhnd* 6 0
1498 11/5 Holnicote (L) OPE 3m 5 G *lft in ld 7th,disp 9-11th,ld agn 15th til hdd & no ext flat* 2 14

Just beaten in weak race last start but no stamina or real hopes of a win 12

RUSSIAN VISION b.g. 7 Petoski - Visible Form by Formidable (USA) Mrs Alexander Scott

12 14/1 Cottenham (R) RES 3m 12 G *mid-div whn f 6th* F -
36 20/1 Higham (L) RES 3m 12 GF *n.j.w. rear, brief effrt 12th, sn btn, p.u. 16th* P 0
105 17/2 Marks Tey (L) RES 3m 11 G *ld to 3rd, hit 6th, wknd 15th, p.u. appr last* P 0
348 3/3 Higham (L) RES 3m 12 G *prom til b.d. 2nd* B -
419 9/3 High Easter (L) RES 3m 10 S *w.w. lst tch 13th, no ch 15th, p.u. 2 out* P 0
679 30/3 Cottenham (R) RES 3m 15 GF *(bl) wth ldr, blnd 10th, ld 13th, clr 2 out, pshd out* 1 20
1068 13/4 Horseheath (R) INT 3m 7 F *(bl) ld to 5th, & agn 9th, hdd last, no ex* 2 19
1521 12/5 Garthorpe (R) INT 3m 7 GF *(bl) mid-div, mstk 3rd, chal whn mstk 11th, sn btn, p.u. 3 out* P 0

Missed 95; blinkers did trick 96; fair form; mistakes; may upgrade 97; G-F 19

RUSSKI ro.g. 13 Rusticaro (FR) - Hill Moss by Priamos (GER) D V A Willis

1995 4(17),2(21)

685 30/3 Chaddesley ' (L) LAD 3m 9 G *chsd ldng pair 10th,rdn 3 out,rnunning on whn lft in ld last* 1 22
1317 28/4 Bitterley (L) LAD 3m 2 G *(Jt fav) ld by 2-3l, going wll whn f 13th* F -

Fragile veteran but retains ability; could still win if returning at 14; Good 23

RUSTIC BRIDGE b.g. 7 Celestial Storm (USA) - Travel Legend by Tap On Wood J Love

1995 **10(NH),14(NH),P(NH)**

406 9/3 Dalston (R) MDO 2 1/2m 12 G *cls up 9th, styd prom tl wknd frm 2 out, improve* 4 10
503 16/3 Lanark (R) MDO 3m 10 G *(fav) alwys handy, disp 4 out, outpcd frm nxt, blnd last* 3 0
755 31/3 Lockerbie (R) MDN 3m 17 G *bhnd early, 6th hlfwy, wknd 4 out* 7 0
1087 14/4 Friars Haugh (L) MDO 3m 9 F *ld frm 9th til hdd & no ext apr last* 2 14
1254 27/4 Balcormo Ma' (R) MDO 3m 14 GS *5th hlfwy, bhnd whn p.u. 2 out* P 0
1476 11/5 Aspatria (L) MDO 3m 16 GF *tubed, chsd ldr 6-12th, sn strgglng, t.o.* 5 0
1575 19/5 Corbridge (R) MDO 3m 10 G *cls up, rmndrs 11th, hmpd 14th, no dang aft* 4 0

Some ability but problems clear & tubing not appear to work 10

RUSTIC RAMBLE br.g. 10 Rusticaro (FR) - Swizzle Stick by Tumble Wind (USA) Peter Tipples

1995 P(0),1(14)

1294 28/4 Bexhill (R) MEM 3m 4 F *hld up, ld 15th, clr 2 out, easily* 1 14
1440 6/5 Aldington (L) INT 3m 5 HD *(fav) reluctant ldr crawl 1st,ld 11-15th,chal 3 out,ld nxt,all out* 1 15
1536 16/5 Folkestone (R) HC 2m 5f 9 GF *waited with, rdn and no response 9th, no ch when p.u. before 2 out.* P 0
1609 26/5 Tweseldown (R) MXO 3m 9 G *in tch in rear, mstk & lost plc 10th, wll btn & p.u. 2 out* P 0

Restricted winner 95; lightly raced; needs ground like concrete; could win Confined 17

RUSTY BRIDGE b.g. 9 Rustingo - Bridge Ash by Normandy I K Johnson

1995 5(15),**3(26),3(16),U(-),5(19),4(NH),3(20),3(23),1(23),1(23),8(10),5(NH),3(NH),5(NH),3(NH),5(NH),5(NH)**

98 12/2 Hereford (R) HC 3m 1f 110yds 12 HY *mstk 5th, nvr on terms, t.o..* 3 15
255 28/2 Taunton (R) HC 4 1/4m 110yds 15 GS *in tch when b.d. 6th.* B -
485 16/3 Hereford (R) HC 3m 1f 110yds 13 S *n.j.w., bhnd from 7th, soon pushed along, lost tch 11th, t.o..* 5 0
669 27/3 Chepstow (L) HC 3m 10 S *alwys bhnd, t.o..* 5 0
799 3/4 Ludlow (R) HC 3m 8 GF *ld 4th, blnd next, hdd 8th, one pace from 3 out.* 5 22
1332 1/5 Cheltenham (L) HC 3m 1f 110yds 11 G *soon driven along, chsd ldrs, lost tch 12th, left 2nd last.* 2 23
1459 8/5 Uttoxeter (L) HC 4 1/4m 8 G *ld till after 5th, soon rdn along, chsd ldr 11th to 14th, outpcd 20th, styd on from 2 out.* 2 26
1534 15/5 Hereford (R) HC 3m 1f 110yds 4 F *ld to 12th, outpcd 14th, styd on again from 3 out.* 3 23
1631 1/6 Stratford (L) HC 3 1/2m 14 GF *(bl) blnd 10th, alwys bhnd.* 8 11

Hard as nails but getting slower; needs driving from start; hard to win another H/Chase; G-F 20

RUSTY FELLOW b.g. 6 Rustingo - Sallisses by Pamroy R J Shail

1995 P(0),F(-),R(-)

220 24/2 Newtown (L) MDN 3m 12 GS *mstks, prog frm rear 12th, in tch whn blnd & u.r. nxt* U -
432 9/3 Upton-On-Se' (R) MDO 3m 17 GS *mstks, wll bhnd whn b.d. 14th* B -
749 31/3 Upper Sapey (R) MDO 3m 17 GS *ref 3rd* R -
842 6/4 Maisemore P' (L) MDN 3m 17 GF *jmpd slwly 1st, ref & u.r. 2nd* R -
1006 9/4 Upton-On-Se' (R) MDN 3m 11 F *immediately t.o. & crawld fences, btn 3 fences* 7 0
1175 20/4 Chaddesley ' (L) MDN 3m 9 G *prom,lost plc 5th,cls 2nd 10th,ld 13th,tried ref & u.r.nxt* U -
1248 27/4 Woodford (L) MDN 3m 15 G *held up,10th hlfwy,prog to 2nd 16th,clsng whn blnd & u.r.nxt* U -
1417 6/5 Cursneh Hill (L) MDO 3m 14 GF *rear whn mstk 9th, gd prog frm 14th, fin wll, not rch wnr* 2 13

Has ability & penny finally dropping; only goes for D Mansell; could win in 97 if in the mood 15

RUSTY LIGHT(IRE) b.g. 6 Rustingo - Light And Shade by High Line Miss S Garcia-Olmo

1995 P(0),P(0),P(0),P(0)

1143 20/4 Flete Park (R) MDN 3m 17 S *hmpd & u.r. 1st* U -
1362 4/5 Flete Park (R) MDO 3m 9 G *1st ride, mid-div, 6th at 16th, nvr dang* 4 0

Best ever effort last start (only completion) but long way short of winning chances yet 0

RUTH'S BOY(IRE) br.g. 7 Lord Ha Ha - Club Belle by Al Sirat (USA) Capt T A Forster

1995 **2(NH),4(NH)**

733 31/3 Little Wind' (R) MDO 3m 13 GS *2nd til ld 12th,slght ld last,not qckn run in,gd efft* 2 16
1118 17/4 Hockworthy (L) MDO 3m 14 GS *(fav) 4/7-4/9, cls up till f 4th* F -
1129 20/4 Stafford Cr' (R) MDO 3m 11 S *(fav) ld til 4 out, disp nxt, outpcd apr last* 2 13
1348 4/5 Holnicote (L) MDO 3m 9 GS *(fav) set gd pace, made all, clr 3 out, styd on well* 1 17
1591 25/5 Mounsey Hil' (R) RES 3m 15 G *w.w. in tch whn f 12th* F -
1649 8/6 Umberleigh (L) RES 3m 14 GF *(fav) ld 2nd-7th, ld agn apr 2 out-last where mstk, no ext* 2 17

Right connections but expensive to follow; should find Restricted but no world beater; G-S 18

RU VALENTINO ch.g. 12 Deep Run - Tape Mary by Even Money M A Lloyd

1995 6(10),P(0),4(13),2(16),3(17),**R(-),3(18)**,4(15),**P(NH)**

26 20/1 Barbury Cas' (L) OPE 3m 12 GS *in tch, 3rd whn lft in ld 13th, clr aft til wknd & hdd post* 2 21
159 17/2 Weston Park (L) CON 3m 22 G *chsd ldr to 3 out, not run on* 5 10
427 9/3 Upton-On-Se' (R) OPE 3m 6 GS *disp frm 11th, 5l clr 3 out, wknd nxt, hdd apr last* 2 20
686 30/3 Chaddesley ' (L) OPE 3m 6 G *prom, ev ch 12th, wknd 3 out* 4 20
950 8/4 Eyton-On-Se' (L) OPE 3m 4 GF *cls up,ld 7-12th,chsd wnr frm 4 out,ran on, cllpsd & died* 2 20

Dead **19**

RYDE AGAIN ch.g. 13 Celtic Cone - Rydewell by Blast — Miss J E Hayward

1995 **2(29),2(30),F(-),6(16)**,1(26)

26 20/1 Barbury Cas' (L) OPE 3m 12 GS *j.w. prom, trckd ldr 8th, going wll whn b.d. 13th* B -
246 25/2 Southwell P' (L) OPE 3m 9 HO *(fav) w.w. prog 9th, ld 14th, all out* 1 22
363 5/3 Leicester (R) HC 3m 3 GS *disp ld to 5th, ld 9th, made rest, clr 3 out, rdn and kept on apr last.* 1 28
668 26/3 Sandown (R) HC 2 1/2m 110yds 8 GS *nvr far away, trckd wnr from 8th, 2 l 2nd when f 5 out.* F -
1120 20/4 Bangor (L) HC 2 1/2m 110yds 13 S *(fav) in tch till b.d. 6th.* B -
1334 1/5 Cheltenham (L) HC 3 1/4m 110yds 3 G *ld till slpd on lndg 10th, with wnr and blnd 12th, rdn apr 19th, wknd 3 out, virtually p.u. run-in.* 3 0

Still quite able but won 1 of 8 H/Chases 95/6 & will need points at 14; R/H best; G-S **22**

RYDER CUP (Irish) — **I** 322[F], **I** 518[4], **I** 602[1]

RYDERS WELLS gr.g. 9 Warpath - The Lathkill by Clear River — E F Astley-Arlington

1995 5(10),6(0),U(-),**6(0)**,S(-),P(0),**7(0)**

36 20/1 Higham (L) RES 3m 12 GF *mid-div, chsd ldrs apr 3 out, not pace to chal* 5 14
58 10/2 Cottenham (R) RES 3m 7 GS *made most to 2 out, ev ch last, just hld nr fin* 2 16
173 18/2 Market Rase' (L) RES 3m 6 GF *(fav) in tch, blnd 5th & 10th, 4th & btn 15th* 3 12
679 30/3 Cottenham (R) RES 3m 15 GF *ld til blnd & u.r. 2nd* U -
971 8/4 Thorpe Lodge (L) RES 3m 4 GF *cls up, ld 4 out til blnd 2 out, not rcvr* 2 14
1107 15/4 Southwell (L) HC 3m 110yds 10 G *pressed wnr, ev ch from 3 out, one pace after last.* 2 22
1329 30/4 Huntingdon (R) HC 3m 14 GF *n.j.w., outpcd and rdn 6th, nvr on terms, t.o. when p.u. before last.* P 0
1464 11/5 Warwick (L) HC 3 1/4m 6 F *alwys bhnd, t.o. hfwy, p.u. before 4 out.* P 0

Maiden winner 93; improved 96; fantastic run at Southwell; unreliable; may win Restricted; G-F **17**

RYE HEAD b.g. 5 Primitive Rising (USA) - Cornetta by Cornuto — Bisgrove Partnership

1995 **P(NH)**

73 11/2 Wetherby Po' (L) MDO 3m 15 GS *alwys prom, 2nd at 12th, 3rd 2 out, styd on onepcd* 3 13
238 25/2 Southwell P' (L) MDO 3m 9 HO *(fav) blnd 4th, mstk nxt, blnd & u.r. 6th* U -
589 23/3 Wetherby Po' (L) MDO 3m 16 S *(Jt fav) mstks, mid-div, styd on well 3 out, nrst fin* 3 11
1094 14/4 Whitwell-On' (R) MDO 2 1/2m 88yds 16 G *prom, ld 7th-10th, ld agn 4 out, drew wll clr, easily* 1 17

Flew home in weak race last start; stays; makes mistakes; should find Restricted; G-S **17**

RYME AND RUN b.m. 10 Rymer - Altaghaderry Run by Deep Run — P Venner

1995 3(17),U(-),P(0),P(0),4(0)

832 6/4 Marks Tey (L) LAD 3m 8 G *rear, n.j.w. t.o. 12th, p.u. 17th* P 0

Maiden winner 94; looks virtually finished now **0**

RYMEROLE 6 — C D Dawson

900 6/4 Dingley (R) MDN 2m 5f 8 GS *(fav) mid-div, ran on frm 6 out, no threat to wnnr* 2 0

Well beaten in poor race; good stable & may improve **12**

RYMER'S EXPRESS ch.g. 6 Rymer - Toi Figures by Deep Run — R M Jones

1995 **P(NH)**

206 24/2 Castle Of C' (R) MDO 3m 10 HY *sn rear, t.o. & p.u. 13th* P 0
550 17/3 Erw Lon (L) MDN 3m 13 GS *alwys mid-div, p.u. 15th* P 0
773 31/3 Pantyderi (R) MDN 3m 8 G *trckd ldrs til ran out 6th* r -
850 6/4 Howick (L) MDN 3m 14 GF *alwys last trio, fin own time* 7 0
1159 20/4 Llanwit Maj' (R) LAD 3m 5 GS *mstks, alwys 4th, t.o. whn ref 12th* R -

Inspires little confidence **0**

RYMING CUPLET b.g. 11 Rymer - Leisure Bay by Jock Scot — Gerald Tanner

1995 1(25),2(23),1(21),2(24),**1(29)**

530 16/3 Cothelstone (L) OPE 3m 7 G *(fav) backward,prom,rmdr 8th,4th & strugg whn blnd 15th,no ch aft* 4 15
731 31/3 Little Wind' (R) OPE 3m 5 GS *disp ld til aft 14th, rddn apr 3 out, styd on clsng stgs* 2 27
1059 13/4 Badbury Rin' (L) OPE 3m 5 GF *(fav) in tch, ld 3 out, slw jmp last, rdn & just hld on* 1 25

1333 1/5 Cheltenham (L) HC 3m 1f 110yds 13 G *mid div, prog to chase ldr 16th, disp ld apr 2 out, hrd rdn run-in, ld cl home, all out.* 1 33
1631 1/6 Stratford (L) HC 3 1/2m 14 GF *alwys bhnd, t.o. when blnd 14th, p.u. before next.* P 0

Tough, very useful H/Chaser; below best in points; win more at 12 if ift; G/F-S 32

RYMIN THYNE ch.g. 7 Good Thyne (USA) - Mrs Popple by Deep Run J M Turner
1995 P(0),3(0),2(10)
1038 13/4 St Hilary (R) RES 3m 15 G *prom, grad lost tch, p.u. 14th* P 0

Placed twice in 95 but showed nothing in 96 10

RYTON GUARD br.g. 11 Strong Gale - Gardez Le Reste by Even Money G B Barlow
1995 P(0),1(15),1(23),2(22),**U(-),4(19)**
162 17/2 Weston Park (L) OPE 3m 16 G *alwys rear, p.u. 4 out* P 0
459 9/3 Eyton-On-Se' (L) OPE 3m 11 G *cls up til outpcd 13th, sn btn, p.u. 3 out* P 0
1231 27/4 Weston Park (L) OPE 3m 6 G *prom, ld 5-9th, onepcd frm 4 out* 5 11
1367 4/5 Gisburn (R) OPE 3m 4 G *alwys 3rd, 5l down 14th, onepcd aft* 3 15
1578 19/5 Wolverhampt' (L) OPE 3m 7 G *w.w. in tch to 13th, sn strggling, t.o. & p.u. 3 out* P 0

Won 2 points 95 but declined sharply 96; best watched at 12; G-F 13

SAAHI(USA) b.g. 7 Lyphard (USA) - Dumtadumtadum (USA) by Grey Dawn II Mrs Jan Wood
1995 **P(NH),7(NH)**
161 17/2 Weston Park (L) LAD 3m 11 G *prom, outpcd frm 11th* 6 0

Beaten miles on only start 0

SABRE KING ch.g. 8 Broadsword (USA) - King's Lavender by King's Troop J Tredwell
1995 P(0),P(0),P(0),2(12),F(-),U(-)
236 24/2 Heythrop (R) MDN 3m 13 GS *alwys prom, 6th hlfwy, jnd ldrs 11th, ld nxt-14th, rallied f* 2 12
440 9/3 Newton Brom' (R) MDN 3m 10 GS *(fav) (bl) alwys prom, ld 12th, clr 2 out, ran on well* 1 14
642 23/3 Siddington (L) RES 3m 15 S *disp ld 7th,ld 10th- 3 out, gd jmp to ld nxt,hld on und pres* 1 18
1098 14/4 Guilsborough (L) CON 3m 17 G *(bl) chsd ldrs, in tch 13th, btn whn p.u.15th* P 0

Jumping sorted out & vastly improved; Confined possible if fit 97; Soft 19

SACROSANCT b.g. 12 The Parson - Cahernane Girl by Bargello J S S Hollins
1995 U(-),U(-),4(14),6(12),3(13),U(-),2(0)
103 17/2 Marks Tey (L) LAD 3m 7 G *disp ld til 10th, sn strggling, p.u. & dismntd 17th* P 0

No longer of any account 0

SADDLE HER WELL (Irish) — **I** 357[P], **I** 436[P]
SAFETY FACTOR (Irish) — **I** 13[P], **I** 47[P], **I** 68[P], **I** 71[P], **I** 374[F], **I** 437[3], **I** 551[1], **I** 593[3], **I** 613[6], **I** 659[P]
SAFFRON FLAME(IRE) b.g. 6 Sandalay - Tip The Gold by Harwell M G Sheppard
1995 5(0)
15 14/1 Cottenham (R) MDN 3m 14 G *cls up to 9th, outpcd 13th, 6th whn blnd 2 out, improve* 6 0
60 10/2 Cottenham (R) MDO 3m 7 GS *w.w. mstk 14th, lft 2nd apr 3 out, ld aft 2 out, ran on well* 1 15
313 2/3 Ampton (R) RES 3m 9 G *(fav) w.w. jnd ldrs 13th, 3rd & hit 17th, ld appr last, rddn out* 1 17
676 30/3 Cottenham (R) INT 3m 13 GF *(Jt fav) hld up, prog 13th, outpcd 16th, ran on 2 out, fin well* 3 20
1068 13/4 Horseheath (R) INT 3m 7 F *(fav) w.w. prog to chal 3 out, ld last, rdn out* 1 20
1377 5/5 Dingley (R) CON 3m 12 GF *(Co fav) w.w. effrt 13th, nvr rchd ldrs, btn apr 2 out* 4 13

Progressive; stays & consistent; Confineds, at least, in 97; G/S-F 22

SAFFRON GALE(IRE) br.g. 7 Strong Gale - Kilbrogan by Menelek H B Hodge
437 9/3 Newton Brom' (R) RES 3m 9 GS *alwys in tch, ld apr 14th, disp aft til not qckn 2 out, wknd* 4 10
1101 14/4 Guilsborough (L) RES 3m 16 G *prom, ld 15th til p.u. aft nxt, broke down* P 0

Very lightly raced & missed 95; has ability but problems last start; best watched 17

SAFFRON GLORY ch.g. 7 Duky - Boreen's Glory by Boreen (FR) Mrs C J Bibbey
1995 P(0),4(0),U(-),P(0),1(13),3(17)
217 24/2 Newtown (L) RES 3m 17 GS *alwys prom, cls up 14th, no imp frm nxt* 4 12
462 9/3 Eyton-On-Se' (L) RES 3m 12 G *t.o. hlfwy, sm lt prog, nrst fin* 5 0
666 24/3 Eaton Hall (R) RES 3m 13 S *mid-div, 3rd at 10th, grad wknd, p.u. 4 out* P 0
882 6/4 Brampton Br' (R) RES 3m 14 GF *(bl) ld 5th, 6l up whn f 16th* F -
1233 27/4 Weston Park (L) RES 3m 14 G *(bl) chsd ldrs to 10th, in tch to 3 out, onepcd* 5 0

Maiden winner 95; unlucky 4th start but disappointing generally; best watched; G/F 15

SAFFRON MOSS ch.g. 6 Le Moss - Saffron's Daughter by Prince Hansel T R R Farr
1995 P(0),2(0),1(12),F(-),P(0)
41 3/2 Wadebridge (L) XX 3m 9 GF *lost tch & msk 7th, sn t.o., btn 3 f* 8 0
219 24/2 Newtown (L) RES 3m 17 GS *sn wll bhnd, t.o. & p.u. aft 13th* P 0
600 23/3 Howick (L) RES 3m 14 S *last at 2nd, fin own time* 6 0
770 31/3 Pantyderi (R) RES 3m 9 G *nvr nr to chal* 6 10

844 6/4 Howick (L) RES 3m 10 GF *disp 3rd whn f 5th* F -
1038 13/4 St Hilary (R) RES 3m 15 G *rear, p.u. 3 out* P 0
1203 21/4 Lydstep (L) RES 3m 5 S *alwys prom, tired & lost 2nd aft last* 3 14
1388 6/5 Pantyderi (R) RES 3m 7 GF *sttld 4th/5th, prog 8th, fdd 11th, onepcd* 4 0
1556 18/5 Bassaleg (R) MEM 3m 6 F *mod 3rd til clsd 14th,chsd wnr nxt,ev ch last,not qckn* 2 13

Maiden winner 95; not progressed & struggling 96; Members may be best hope 97 13

SAFFRON QUEEN ch.m. 5 Morston's Heir - Saffron Lady by He Loves Me G H Barber

935 8/4 Marks Tey (L) MEM 3m 3 G *mstks 1st & 2nd, lost tch 6th, t.o. & p.u. aft 10th* P 0
1261 27/4 Cottenham (R) MDO 3m 10 F *withdrawn und orders start* 0 0

Shows nothing yet 0

SAIGON LADY(IRE) b.m. 8 Scorpio (FR) - Fair Detail by Fine Blade (USA) J C Clark

503 16/3 Lanark (R) MDO 3m 10 G *cls up til outpcd frm 3 out* 3 0
614 23/3 Friars Haugh (L) MDN 3m 10 G *4th hlfwy, blnd 12th, p.u. nxt.* 0 0
756 31/3 Lockerbie (R) MDN 3m 14 G *not fluent, some hdwy hlfwy, bhnd whn p.u. 3 out* P 0
1089 14/4 Friars Haugh (L) MDN 3m 10 F *f 6th* F -

Beaten a long way when 3rd & no show after; may do better 10

SAILOR'S DELIGHT b.g. 12 Idiot's Delight - Sarasail by Hitting Away Alan Bosley
1995 1(18),2(17),**U(NH)**,**5(NH)**,**6(NH)**

791 2/4 Heythrop (R) MEM 3m 5 F *(fav) made all, hrd rdn flat, kpt on* 1 15
1017 13/4 Kingston Bl' (L) OPE 3m 4 G *jmpd rght, ld to 11th, last & outpcd 14th, nrly ref last* 3 13
1437 6/5 Ashorne (R) MXO 3m 13 G *mstks, prom to 12th, wknd & p.u. 15th* P 0

Members winner 95; repeated trick in weak race; outclassed other starts; hat-trick possible 97 15

SAINT BENE'T(IRE) b.g. 8 Glenstal (USA) - Basilea (FR) by Frere Basile (FR) George Prodromou
1995 4(10),**6(11)**,4(14),**2(19)**,**6(14)**,**7(16)**,**2(17)**,**8(NH)**,**P(NH)**,**6(NH)**,**U(NH)**

94 11/2 Ampton (R) OPE 3m 8 GF *hld up, prog 13th, chsd ldrs & ev ch 3 out, no prog nxt* 4 19
100 16/2 Fakenham (L) HC 2m 5f 110yds 9 G *bhnd from 6th.* 7 0
312 2/3 Ampton (R) OPE 3m 6 G *cls up, rmdrs 13th, no ch frm 16th* 4 19
492 16/3 Horseheath (R) OPE 3m 3 GF *alwys 2nd, jnd wnr 13th, ev ch 3 out, mstk nxt, btn last* 2 18
677 30/3 Cottenham (R) OPE 3m 11 GF *alwys prom, cls 5th 2 out, onepcd aft* 4 19
833 6/4 Marks Tey (L) OPE 3m 4 G *ld 2nd,sn clr,10l clr 17th,jnd last,hdd flat,fin 2nd,promotd* 1 22
1323 28/4 Fakenham P-' (L) OPE 3m 8 G *(bl) disp 5th-12th, 3rd & rdn 3 out, kpt on flat* 3 19
1457 8/5 Uttoxeter (L) HC 3 1/4m 16 G *(vis) ld to 14th, wknd.* 4 16
1546 18/5 Fakenham (L) HC 3m 110yds 13 G *(vis) well pld till lost position 8th, t.o. from 14th.* 8 10

Has ability but needed Stewards for only win from 16 starts 95/6; more placings likely in 97 18

SAINT JOSEPH ch.g. 6 Lir - Kimberley Ann by St Columbus B R J Young

69 10/2 Great Treth' (R) MDO 3m 12 S *twrds rear, p.u. 14th* P 0
299 2/3 Great Treth' (R) MDO 3m 13 G *cls 5th at 12th, p.u. 14th, quiet run* P 0
1116 17/4 Hockworthy (L) MDO 3m 9 GS *prom til f 4th* F -
1279 27/4 Bratton Down (L) MDO 3m 14 GF *mid-div, lost tch 14th, p.u. last* P 0
1593 25/5 Mounsey Hil' (R) MDO 3m 11 G *mid-div, 7th whn ran wd apr 15th, t.o. & p.u. 2 out* P 0
1627 27/5 Lifton (R) MDO 3m 9 GS *rear til p.u. aft 10th* P 0

Yet to complete the course 0

SAKIL(IRE) b.g. 8 Vision (USA) - Sciambola by Great Nephew Mrs P G Etheridge

251 25/2 Charing (L) OPE 3m 10 GS *rear, prog to trck ldrs 6th, p.u. 9th* P 0
451 9/3 Charing (L) OPE 3m 11 G *mid-div whn f 9th* F -
619 23/3 Higham (L) OPE 3m 10 GF *plIng, prog to mid-div 12th, ev ch 3 out, wknd rpdly* 4 15
1052 13/4 Penshurst (L) OPE 3m 7 G *rear, losing tch whn p.u. bef 12th* P 0
1146 20/4 Higham (L) OPE 3m 7 F *w.w. rdn 12th, no prog, p.u. 15th* P 0

4th in modest Open & does not stay - winning hopes slim 12

SALACHY RUN(IRE) b.g. 7 Fine Blade (USA) - Just Had It by No Argument Mrs J P Gordon
1995 5(0),C(-),**8(NH)**

13 14/1 Cottenham (R) MDO 3m 10 G *plIng, prom, ld 10-16th, p.u. rpdly apr nxt* P 0
61 10/2 Cottenham (R) MDO 3m 8 GS *alwys bhnd, t.o. & p.u. 14th* P 0
254 25/2 Charing (L) MDO 3m 9 GS *pshd alng 12th, just ld 14th, forged clr 2 out, all out* 1 10
449 9/3 Charing (L) RES 3m 13 G *alwys prom, 3rd at 15th, chal 2 out, ld flat, hdd on line* 2 17
574 17/3 Detling (L) RES 3m 14 GF *chsd wnr, outpcd in 2nd frm 3 out* 2 13
810 6/4 Charing (L) RES 3m 6 F *trckd ldrs, 3rd frm 14th, rddn 4 out, no imp, wknd 2 out* 3 15
1054 13/4 Penshurst (L) RES 3m 8 G *s.i.s. sn in tch, 3rd & rmndrs 13th, wknd nxt, p.u. aft 2out* P 0

Changed hands & improved 96; won bad Maiden; not disgraced after; may find Restricted; barely stays 15

SALARAN (Irish) — **I** 96P, **I** 285,

SALCOMBE HARBOUR(NZ) ch.g. 12 English Harbour - Faux Leigh (NZ) by Harleigh Mrs T Pritchard

1995 P(0),5(15),**F(-)**,**P(0)**,R(-)
6 13/1 Larkhill (R) OPE 3m 18 GS *jmpd badly, t.o. 7th, p.u. 2 out* P 0
No longer of any account 0

SALEMHADY (Irish) — I 27^{1}, I 102^{F}, I 160^{P}

SALE RING ch.g. 10 Ring Bidder - Elfen Queen by Crozier T R Darlington
1995 P(0)
285 2/3 Eaton Hall (R) MEM 3m 5 G *in tch to 8th, p.u. 11th* P 0
568 17/3 Wolverhampt' (L) MDN 3m 9 GS *2nd to 13th, wknd rpdly, p.u. 3 out* P 0
Rarely seen now & safely ignored 0

SALLY GEE (Irish) — I 95^{S}

SALLY SMITH b.m. 7 Alias Smith (USA) - Salira by Double Jump Miss M J Benson
1995 P(0),9(0)
316 2/3 Corbridge (R) MEM 3m 10 GS *bhnd til ran on frm 2 out, nvr nrr* 4 0
1517 12/5 Hexham Poin' (L) MDN 3m 10 HY *wll bhnd frm 6th, blnd 13th, t.o. & p.u. 2 out* P 0
1574 19/5 Corbridge (R) MDO 3m 6 G *f 2nd* F
Well beaten on 2 completions 95/6 & no real signs of ability 0

SALLY'S SONG ch.m. 5 True Song - Creetown Sally by Creetown R J Cherry
1182 21/4 Mollington (R) MDN 3m 10 F *slw jmp 5th, last frm 8th, t.o. & p.u. 11th* P 0
1433 6/5 Ashorne (R) MDO 3m 16 G *bhnd frm 6th, t.o. & p.u. 9th* P 0
Unpromising so far 0

SALLY WILLOWS (Irish) — I 33^{P}, I 106^{P}, I 302^{2}

SALMON MEAD(IRE) b.g. 7 Lancastrian - New Brook by Paddy's Stream Christopher Sporborg
1995 P(0),P(0),1(16),5(0),U(-),2(16)
36 20/1 Higham (L) RES 3m 12 GF *f 1st* F
54 10/2 Cottenham (R) MEM 3m 3 GS *(fav) jmpd lft, wth ldr, ld 5th-aft 12th, jnd ldr & lft clr 3 out* 1 14
95 11/2 Ampton (R) RES 3m 11 GF *prom, ld 8th-16th, wknd nxt, p.u. 2 out* P 0
348 3/3 Higham (L) RES 3m 12 G *mid-div, prog to 4th 14th, btn whn mstk 3 out* 4 0
621 23/3 Higham (L) INT 3m 12 GF *disp to 4th, und pres 10th, wknd 12th, t.o. & p.u. 2 out* P 0
834 6/4 Marks Tey (L) RES 3m 11 G *4th/5th,lost plc 10th,rear 14th,styd on onepcd frm 3 out* 3 14
1065 13/4 Horseheath (R) CON 3m 4 F *cls up, ld appr 3 out til 2 out, onepcd und press* 2 17
1145 20/4 Higham (L) RES 3m 12 F *bhnd til prog 5th,chsng grp aft,styd on onepcd frm 16th* 3 16
Has won 3 weak races 94-6; struggling to find Restricted - may strike lucky in weak one eventually 17

SALMON POUTCHER ch.m. 7 Brando - Heythrop Vii Mrs J L Phelps
638 23/3 Siddington (L) CON 3m 16 S *schoold, in tch til appr 10th, p.u. 15th* P 0
712 30/3 Barbury Cas' (L) MDO 3m 10 G *in tch to 11th, rdn nxt, outpcd & p.u. 14th* P 0
1248 27/4 Woodford (L) MDN 3m 15 G *in tch, 4th 13th, outpcd 15th, lft 2nd 3 out, kpt on* 2 13
Going the right way & may well go close in 97 14

SALMON RIVER(USA) b.g. 5 Northern Baby (CAN) - Dream Play (USA) by Blushing Groom (FR) Mrs Julie Read
1995 **11(NH)**,**6(NH)**,**5(NH)**
31 20/1 Higham (L) CON 3m 9 GF *bhnd, kpt on stdly from 16th, nvr nrr, improve* 4 14
177 18/2 Horseheath (R) CON 3m 8 G *ld 2nd-7th, outpcd 15th, wknd 2 out* 4 13
622 23/3 Higham (L) CON 3m 10 GF *alwys rear, nvr rchd ldrs, lft poor 3rd 3 out* 3 12
831 6/4 Marks Tey (L) CON 3m 6 G *cls up til 5th at 14th, rdn 16th, kpt on onepcd,lft 3rd last* 3 18
1321 28/4 Fakenham P-' (L) CON 3m 5 G *chsd ldr 4th-12th, 4th & outpcd 15th, onepcd und pres* 3 15
1399 6/5 Northaw (L) CON 3m 8 F *(fav) in tch,wnt 2nd 13th,ld appr last,nt qkn und pres,hdd cls hme* 2 17
1537 16/5 Folkestone (R) HC 3 1/4m 8 GF *held up, mstk 2nd, prog to chase ldr 13th, one pace next.* 3 13
Ungenuine & lost golden chance at Northaw; will continue to frustrate 15

SALMON SPRING ch.g. 9 Salmon Leap (USA) - Bal D'Oa (FR) by Noir Et Or S T Stokes
1995 P(0),4(0),F(-)
288 2/3 Eaton Hall (R) MDO 3m 17 G *chsng grp, ld/disp 11-13th, fdd* 4 0
590 23/3 Wetherby Po' (L) MDO 3m 16 S *alwys mid-div, no ch whn p.u. 4 out* P 0
1155 20/4 Whittington (L) MDN 3m 14 G *(bl) cls up 3rd to 15th, wknd aft* 5 0
1234 27/4 Weston Park (L) MDO 3m 13 G *mid-div, not qckn, nvr trbld ldrs* 5 0
1364 4/5 Gisburn (R) MDO 3m 11 G *(bl) ld to 6th, 2nd to 15th, wknd rpdly aft* 5 0
Beat 2 others in 4 completions & blinkers no help - not stay 0

SALVATION (Irish) — I 170^{P}, I 262^{P}, I 304^{P}, I 316^{P}, I 362^{P}

SAMBRIAN b.g. 11 The Brianstan - Stolen Halo by Manacle David Pritchard
1995 R(-),P(0),P(0),P(0),R(-),P(0),R(-),P(0),R(-),R(-),R(-)
1365 4/5 Gisburn (R) MDO 3m 17 G *(bl) rear, ref 1st (twice)* R
16 pulled-ups, 11 refusals, 6 unseats, 1 fall, 2 finishes 93-6 - hopefully seen the last of him 0

SAMMY SUNSHINE (Irish) — **I** 121^{6}, **I** 155^{6}, **I** 250^{F}, **I** 297^{3}, **I** 377^{6}, **I** 446^{P}

SAM QUALE (Irish) — **I** 247^{P}, **I** 292^{2}, **I** 439^{F}

SAMS HERITAGE b.g. 12 National Trust - Taberella by Aberdeen — C G Smedley

1995 **3(25),6(23)**

215	24/2	Newtown	(L)	OPE	3m	20	GS	*blnd 2nd, alwys bhnd, no prog 12th, p.u. 3 out*	P	0
578	20/3	Ludlow	(R)	HC	3m	7	G	*slowly into stride, hdwy 6th, left 3rd bend after 11th, wknd next.*	3	0
1004	9/4	Upton-On-Se'	(R)	OPE	3m	3	F	*chsd wnr 8th, jmpd lft nxt, not qckn 15th, wl btn 2 out*	2	13
1171	20/4	Chaddesley '	(L)	OPE	3m	15	G	*cls up til not qckn aft 14th, no ch frm 17th*	8	16

Useful at best but deteriorated rapidly 96; can only be watched if returning at 13 15

SAM SHORROCK b or br.g. 14 Vivadari - To Windward by Hard Tack — Mrs G Thorner

1995 **5(NH),6(NH),4(NH)**

786	31/3	Tweseldown	(R)	LAD	3m	8	G	*1st ride, sn rear, t.o. 11th*	5	0
957	8/4	Lockinge	(L)	CON	3m	5	GF	*last til prog 14th, ran on frm 4 out, nrst fin*	3	11
1018	13/4	Kingston Bl'	(L)	LAD	3m	8	G	*rear frm 9th, t.o. 5th at 13th, no prog*	4	11
1289	28/4	Barbury Cas'	(L)	CON	3m	8	F	*chsd ldrs, 4th & outpcd 14th, kpt on to tk 3rd last*	3	14
1435	6/5	Ashorne	(R)	CON	3m	12	G	*alwys wll in rear, t.o. 13th*	7	0

Winning chaser; good schoolmaster but too old to win now 12

SAM'S MAN (Irish) — **I** 21^{F}, **I** 30^{F}, **I** 86^{F}, **I** 108^{4}, **I** 174^{P}, **I** 299^{2}, **I** 337^{P}

SAM'S SUCCESSOR b.g. 5 Old Jocus - Melanie Lass Vii by Damsire Unregistered — Mrs J R Hellier

282	2/3	Clyst St Ma'	(L)	MDN	3m	8	S	*rear, lost tch 10th, t.o. & p.u. 12th*	P	0
448	9/3	Haldon	(R)	MDO	3m	10	S	*sn bhnd & jmpd lft, t.o. & p.u. 10th*	P	0
819	6/4	Charlton Ho'	(L)	MDN	3m	10	GF	*alwys rear, t.o. & p.u. 12th*	P	0
1115	17/4	Hockworthy	(L)	MDO	3m	10	GS	*jmpd slwly, t.o. last whn p.u. 7th*	P	0

Plenty of work needed here 0

SAMSWORD ch.g. 7 Broadsword (USA) - True Divine by True Song — Brian Gurney

1995 1(14),4(14),8(0)

59	10/2	Cottenham	(R)	RES	3m	9	GS	*(fav) mstks,prom,lost plc 12th,styd on 2 out,ld apr last,all out*	1	15

Maiden winner debut 95; won poor Restricted only start 96; may go well 97 debut if fit 15

SAMUEL PERRY b.g. 11 Cashwyn - Sam's Baby by Sammy Davis — Mrs C A Samwells

431	9/3	Upton-On-Se'	(R)	MDO	3m	17	GS	*mstks, mid-div, p.u. 14th*	P	0

Old & shows nothing 0

SAMUEL PLIMSOL b.g. 9 Balinger - Mandycap by Mandamus — M W Ginn

1995 P(0),6(0),3(0),0(0),2(0),5(0)

91	11/2	Ampton	(R)	MDO	3m	10	GF	*prom, chsd wnr 5th, ev ch 16th, wknd nxt*	5	0

Safe but poor & a brief campaign 96 0

SAMULE gr.g. 6 Another Realm - Dancing Kathleen by Green God — Mrs M Harding

1995 F(-),P(0)

144	17/2	Larkhill	(R)	MDO	3m	15	G	*prom, ld 11th til apr last, no ext flat*	3	14

Beat subsequent winners only start 96; only run 3 times & should win if ready 97 15

SANAMAR ch.g. 12 Hello Gorgeous (USA) - Miss Markey by Gay Fandango (USA) — Miss T A Aucott

1995 F(-),5(0),5(0),P(0)

1099	14/4	Guilsborough	(L)	LAD	3m	9	G	*rear frm 10th, last & wll btn whn f 3 out*	F	-
1236	27/4	Clifton On '	(L)	CON	3m	8	GF	*alwys rear, wll bhnd frm 12th, t.o.*	6	0
1377	5/5	Dingley	(R)	CON	3m	12	GF	*alwys rear grp, t.o. 12th, p.u. 2 out*	P	0
1520	12/5	Garthorpe	(R)	LAD	3m	8	GF	*alwys 4th & just in tch, lft 3rd 3 out*	3	0
1579	19/5	Wolverhampt'	(L)	LAD	3m	9	G	*prom to 4th, bhnd 7th, t.o. 15th*	6	0
1596	25/5	Garthorpe	(R)	LAD	3m	9	G	*alwys last pair, t.o. last frm 7th, p.u. 3 out*	P	0

Outclassed & no prospects at 13 0

SANCREED b.g. 11 Shaab - St Barbe by Galeopsis — Miss L Long

1995 6(0),3(0),5(10),2(18),P(0),2(12),5(0),3(13),8(0),3(13)

42	3/2	Wadebridge	(L)	CON	3m	8	GF	*clse up til outpcd 12th, kpt on frm 2 out*	4	15
64	10/2	Great Treth'	(R)	CON	3m	7	S	*mid-div, prog past btn horses frm 15th*	3	0
196	24/2	Lemalla	(R)	CON	3m	14	HY	*alwys abt same pl*	6	15
294	2/3	Great Treth'	(R)	CON	3m	10	G	*4th hlfwy, steadily wknd*	5	0
625	23/3	Kilworthy	(L)	CON	3m	11	GS	*prom til outpcd 13th, sn rear, styd on frm 3 out*	5	14
715	30/3	Wadebridge	(L)	CON	3m	8	GF	*raced wd, mid-div, virt c.o. apr 10th & p.u.*	P	0
1069	13/4	Lifton	(R)	CON	3m	9	S	*rear, ran on stdly 5th 16th, nrst at fin*	5	17
1359	4/5	Flete Park	(R)	LAD	4m	5	G	*3rd/4th & nvr in cont, lost 4th nr fin*	5	0

Members winner 94; beaten in last 21 races (8 places) & will struggle to win again 14

SANDBROOK b.g. 12 Golden Love - Spinnys Love by Saulingo — R W J Willcox

1995 P(0),F(-)

153	17/2 Erw Lon	(L) OPE 3m	15	G	*prom til wknd rpdly 13th, p.u. 3 out*	P	0
351	3/3 Garnons	(L) OPE 3m	14	GS	*lost tch 7th, t.o. & p.u. 14th*	P	0

Dual winner 94; brief seasons 95/6 & showed nothing 0

SAND DE VINCE (Irish) — **I** 174^{2}, **I** 255^{3}

SANDFAIR (Irish) — **I** 83^{1}, **I** 141^{P}, **I** 220, , **I** 342^{4}

SANDFORD ORCAS b.g. 10 Shrivenham - Miss Rosewyn by Wynkell — P G Bevins

1995 U(-),P(0),2(10),1(11),**3(13)**,1(0)

376	9/3 Barbury Cas'	(L) MEM 3m	4	GS	*sttld rear, prog to 2nd at 11th, hrd rdn flat, alwys hld*	2	14

Dual winner 95; brief 96 & Members looks only hope if fit 97; stays 14

SANDMOOR PRINCE b.g. 13 Grundy - Princesse Du Seine (FR) by Val de Loir — Mrs T Pritchard

1995 **9(NH),8(NH),3(NH)**

1166	20/4 Larkhill	(R) OPE 3m	6	GF	*1st ride, ld pllng hrd til 9th, wknd 12th, p.u. 3 out*	P	0

Usually races under Rules & too old now 0

SANDSTONE ARCH b.g. 13 Niels - War Rain by Bahrain — Brian Brennan

1995 P(0),4(0)

289	2/3 Eaton Hall	(R) CON 3m	10	G	*mid to rear, nvr dang, p.u. 4 out*	P	0
565	17/3 Wolverhampt'	(L) OPE 3m	6	GS	*alwys rear, p.u. 14th*	P	0
736	31/3 Sudlow Farm	(R) CON 3m	9	G	*rear, blndrd 9th & 10th, t.o. & p.u. 12th*	P	0

No longer of any account 0

SANDY BEAU ch.g. 10 Beau Charmeur (FR) - Straight Sprite by Three Wishes — Mrs Vanessa Ramm

232	24/2 Heythrop	(R) OPE 3m	10	GS	*disp to 5th, chsd wnr aft to 2 out, styd on onepcd*	3	15
351	3/3 Garnons	(L) OPE 3m	14	GS	*prom til lost plc apr 14th, styd on frm 3 out*	2	20
507	16/3 Magor	(R) MXO 3m	5	GS	*(fav) 2nd til ld 13th, hdd nxt, onepcd aft*	3	0
602	23/3 Howick	(L) OPE 3m	11	S	*ld 8-10th, chsd wnr, onepcd frm 15th*	3	17
1037	13/4 St Hilary	(R) OPE 3m	5	G	*ld to 12th, disp to 15th, 5l down 3 out, ran on to ld nxt*	1	22
1111	17/4 Hockworthy	(L) MXO 3m	13	GS	*ld to 9th, outpcd frm 12th, no dang aft*	6	14
1215	24/4 Andoversford	(R) OPE 3m	5	G	*in tch til 4th & outpcd 13th, kpt on frm 2 out*	3	22

Dual winner 94; missed 95; onepaced & usually outclassed; could win again; G-S 20

SANDY ETNA(IRE) gr.m. 7 Sandalay - Fort Etna by Be Friendly — M H Dare

1995 P(0)

658	23/3 Badbury Rin'	(L) MDO 3m	8	G	*prom untl 14th, wknd 15th, t.o. from 3 out*	4	0
820	6/4 Charlton Ho'	(L) MDN 3m	12	GF	*ld to 3rd, lost tch 11th, t.o. & p.u. 2 out*	P	0
1592	25/5 Mounsey Hil'	(R) MDO 3m	9	G	*ld to 6th, chsd ldr, ld agn apr 2 out, hdd last, no ext*	2	14

Just beaten in poor race last start & should have prospects if improving in 97 14

SANDY JAY (Irish) — **I** 622^{1}

SANDY KING(IRE) ch.g. 7 Sandalay - Comeallye by Kambalda — A J Baillie

1995 3(0)

166	17/2 Weston Park	(L) MDN 3m	10	G	*chsd ldrs, in tch whn f 7th*	F	-
286	2/3 Eaton Hall	(R) MDO 3m	14	G	*chsng grp, ev ch 4 out, not qckn nxt*	5	0

Lightly raced & finished early 96; much more needed for a win 10

SANDY PEARL (Irish) — **I** 32^{1}

SANDY PEARL TWO (Irish) — **I** 159^{5}, **I** 198^{P}, **I** 577^{U}, **I** 619^{3}, **I** 629^{P}

SANDYROCK (Irish) — **I** 68, , **I** 268^{P}, **I** 346^{P}

SANDY'S CHOICE (Irish) — **I** 187^{P}

SANDY VALLEY (Irish) — **I** 137^{P}, **I** 345^{P}, **I** 388^{6}, **I** 528^{P}

SAN REMO b.g. 9 Sexton Blake - Rockwood Lady by Aeolian — Mrs D C Samworth

1995 P(0),P(0),7(0),1(13),5(0),**3(11)**,**2(16)**

169	18/2 Market Rase'	(L) CON 3m	15	GF	*alwys mid-div, nvr dang*	10	0
258	29/2 Nottingham	(L) HC 3m 110yds	10	G	*ld to 5th, lost tch quickly final cct, t.o. when p.u. before 5 out.*	P	0
535	17/3 Southwell P'	(L) CON 3m	10	GS	*mid-div, fdd, no ch whn p.u. 3 out*	P	0
897	6/4 Dingley	(R) CON 3m	15	GS	*cls up 5-8th, fdd, bhnd whn f 3 out*	F	-
1177	21/4 Mollington	(R) INT 3m	14	F	*ldng grp til wknd aft 12th, no ch frm nxt*	7	0
1303	28/4 Southwell P'	(L) CON 3m	7	GF	*cls up, ld 4th, jnd & lft clr 11th, ran on gamely 3 out*	1	14

Restricted winner 95; found a bad Confined last start & will struggle to win another 14

SANTANO gr.g. 10 Monsanto (FR) - Stance by Habat — Miss S Wilson

102	17/2 Marks Tey	(L) CON 3m	17	G	*cls up til 7th, bhnd whn p.u. appr 11th*	P	0
620	23/3 Higham	(L) LAD 3m	9	GF	*prom, wknd rpdly 7th, t.o. & p.u. 11th*	P	0

No longer of any account **0**

SANTIETOWN ch.g. 14 Bonne Noel - Irish Ville by Meadsville — Mrs F E Harvey

1995 F(-),P(0),P(0),4(16),1(11)

178 18/2 Horseheath (R) INT 3m 11 G *blnd 2nd, alwys rear, t.o. & p.u. 14th* P 0

Looks finished now **0**

SAOL SONA (Irish) — **I** 139^{3}, **I** 207^{2}, **I** 462^{P}, **I** 574^{4}

SAPPHIRE 'N' SILVER (Irish) — **I** 19^{F}, **I** 107^{P}, **I** 177^{U}, **I** 215^{P}, **I** 259^{F}, **I** 302^{3}, **I** 364^{1}, **I** 454^{P}, **I** 619^{P}, **I** 629^{P}

SARADANTE (Irish) — **I** 13^{2}, **I** 79^{2}, **I** 138^{F}, **I** 306^{1}

SARAH DREAM(IRE) b or br.m. 7 Strong Gale - Pampered Run by Deep Run — E B Swaffield

207 24/2 Castle Of C' (R) MDO 3m 15 HY *rear, prog 7th, cls up 11th, wknd & p.u. 13th* P 0

Should do better if racing regularly in 97 .... **11**

SARAH'S CHERRIE (Irish) — **I** 177^{P}, **I** 259^{F}, **I** 410^{P}

SARAZAR(USA) ch.g. 7 Shahrastani (USA) - Sarshara by Habitat — N J Pewter

1995 **4(NH)**

311 2/3 Ampton (R) LAD 3m 4 G *alwys last, lst tch 16th, t.o.* 4 0
493 16/3 Horseheath (R) LAD 3m 4 GF *prom, 2nd at 8th, mstk 12th, lost tch 13th, u.r. 4 out* U -
678 30/3 Cottenham (R) LAD 3m 6 GF *wll in tch til outpcd 14th, sn no ch* 4 16
933 8/4 Marks Tey (L) LAD 3m 3 G *chsd wnr til last frm 14th, btn whn mstk 16th* 3 12
1147 20/4 Higham (L) LAD 3m 9 F *in tch to 8th, t.o. 11th, p.u. nxt* P 0
1324 28/4 Fakenham P-' (L) LAD 3m 6 G *sn bhnd, t.o. frm 5th* 3 11
1401 6/5 Northaw (L) LAD 3m 4 F *j.s. 3rd, lst tch appr 11th, t.o. frm 13th* 3 0

Another addition to a stable of duds **0**

SARCOID (Irish) — **I** 118^{P}, **I** 156^{2}

SARGEANTS CHOICE b.g. 7 Le Solaret (FR) - Rose Dante by Tiran (HUN) — John Sargeant

1995 B(-),F(-),5(0),5(0),P(0),F(-),P(0)

167 17/2 Weston Park (L) MDN 3m 10 G *cls up, 2nd at 8th, 3rd at 13th, tired & p.u. 3 out* P 0
241 25/2 Southwell P' (L) MDO 3m 15 HO *wth ldr 3rd-12th, sn wknd, t.o. 3 out* 6 0
464 9/3 Eyton-On-Se' (L) MDN 2 1/2m 13 G *chsng grp, 2nd & ev ch whn c.o. by lse hrse 9th* C -
568 17/3 Wolverhampt' (L) MDN 3m 9 GS *mid-div, 12l 4th whn hmpd & ran out 3 out* r -
1033 13/4 Alpraham (R) MDO 2 1/2m 15 GS *lft in ld 8th, hdd bfr 3 out, outpcd* 2 12
1196 21/4 Sandon (L) MDN 3m 17 G *disp 3rd & no ch 1st pair whn u.r. apr last, (tack broke)* U -
1523 12/5 Garthorpe (R) MDO 3m 11 GF *ld/disp til lft clr 11th, ran on well, drew clr apr 3 out* 1 15
1597 25/5 Garthorpe (R) XX 3m 9 G *cls up, 2nd frm 7th-5 out, went backwards nxt* 8 0

Finished 4 of 13 starts prior to winning weak race; much more needed for Restricteds; G-F **14**

SARONA SMITH ch.m. 9 Alias Smith (USA) - Sarona by Lord Of Verona — Mrs F T Walton

1995 5(0),2(0),4(13),6(0),**P(NH)**

319 2/3 Corbridge (R) RES 3m 16 GS *last at 5th, t.o. & p.u. 2 out* P 0
703 30/3 Tranwell (L) RES 3m 7 GS *prom til mstk 12th, no dang aft* 4 11
1106 15/4 Hexham (L) HC 3m 1f 9 GF *soon well bhnd, t.o. when p.u. before 12th.* P 0
1249 27/4 Balcormo Ma' (R) RES 3m 10 GS *bhnd by 6th, nvr dang* 5 0
1514 12/5 Hexham Poin' (R) RES 3m 5 HY *ld til aft 1st, disp 7-9th, mstk 16th, ev ch 3 out, onepcd* 2 11
1576 19/5 Corbridge (R) MEM 3m 4 G *outpcd frm 9th, t.o. 15th* 3 0

Maiden winner 94; usually completes but slow & struggled in 95/6 .... **10**

SARONICA-R 6 .... L J Remnant

849 6/4 Howick (L) MDN 3m 14 GF *u.r. 1st* U -

The briefest of seasons **0**

SARSHILL LAP (Irish) — **I** 131^{5}

SARVO(IRE) br.g. 8 Pollerton - Promising Very Vii — C Gibbon

591 23/3 Wetherby Po' (L) MDO 3m 14 S *ld 3rd, 20l clr whn f nxt, dead* F -

Dead **0**

SATALDO (Irish) — **I** 157^{P}, **I** 195^{F}, **I** 271^{P}, **I** 324^{F}, **I** 418^{F}, **I** 532^{2}

SATCO SUPREME (Irish) — **I** 366^{U}, **I** 424^{P}

SATCOTINO (Irish) — **I** 271^{F}, **I** 347^{2}

SATIN EMMA (Irish) — **I** 103^{5}, **I** 230^{4}, **I** 295^{P}, **I** 483^{P}, **I** 558, , **I** 623^{P}

SATIN TALKER (Irish) — **I** 20^{P}, **I** 319^{1}, **I** 414^{3}

SAUCY POLL (Irish) — **I** 21^{P}

SAUCY'S WOLF ch.g. 6 Little Wolf - Barton Sauce by Saucy Kit — Mrs J Brooks

1995 **18(NH),11(NH)**

65 10/2 Great Treth' (R) INT 3m 13 S *wll bhnd whn p.u. 13th* P 0
465 10/3 Milborne St' (L) RES 3m 11 G *mid-div til lost tch 13th, blnd 15th & p.u.* P 0
734 31/3 Little Wind' (R) MDO 3m 11 GS *hdwy to 3rd 15th, outpcd 17th, 6th whn f 2 out* F -
1280 27/4 Bratton Down (L) MDO 3m 14 GF *rear, no show, t.o. & p.u. 13th* P 0

Not totally disgraced 3rd start but more stamina needed in 97 10

SAUN(CZE) b.g. 10 Silver - Szunda (HUN) by Suc (FR) Miss C J Elliott

597 23/3 Parham (R) MDO 3m 9 GS *1st ride, alwys rear & outpcd, dist 2nd frm 14th, 3rd 3 out* 3 0
780 31/3 Penshurst (L) MDN 3m 12 GS *mid-div whn u.r. 4th* U -
966 8/4 Heathfield (R) MDO 3m 7 G *in tch, lft 4th 16th, chall appr last, ran on wll, ld flat* 1 12

Missed 95; found poor race to give rider 1st winner; Restricted hopes at 11 negligible 11

SAUSALITO BOY b.g. 8 Idiot's Delight - Brown Sauce by Saucy Kit Mrs S L Winwood

482 13/3 Newton Abbot (L) HC 2m 5f 110yds 14 S *mid div till wknd 6th, p.u. before 9th.* P 0
1121 20/4 Bangor (L) HC 3m 110yds 8 S *in tch early, bhnd from 10th, t.o. when p.u. before 13th.* P 0

Winning hurdler 3 years ago but showed nothing in 96 & can only be watched 0

SAXON FAIR ch.g. 7 Saxon Farm - Fair Kitty by Saucy Kit A Milner

1995 3(15),1(19),1(21),F(-),2(19),1(21)

326 3/3 Market Rase' (L) OPE 3m 14 G *rshd into ld til ran wd apr 4th, p.u. 5th, bridle broke* P 0
409 9/3 Charm Park (L) CON 3m 11 G *(fav) ld 12th to 4 out, ht nxt, hld by wnr* 2 21
985 8/4 Charm Park (L) INT 3m 9 GF *(fav) ld to 6th, in tch, 2nd 3 out, hit nxt, lost 2nd on flat* 3 16
1282 27/4 Easingwold (L) OPE 3m 8 G *keen hld,trckd ldrs,ld 12th-14th, ev ch whn p.u. 3 out,lame* P 0

Won 3 in 95 & useful; unlucky 96 & problems last start; Confineds, at least, if fit 97; Good 20

SAXON LASS b.m. 8 Martinmas - Khatti Hawk by Hittite Glory M N J Sparkes

1995 2(0),F(-),4(0),P(0),3(0)

236 24/2 Heythrop (R) MDN 3m 13 GS *ld to 10th, wknd rpdly, p.u. 16th* P 0
341 3/3 Heythrop (R) MDN 3m 13 G *prom, chsd ldr 9th til wknd 15th, p.u. 2 out* P 0
477 10/3 Tweseldown (R) MDO 3m 15 G *rear of ldng grp, in tch to 4 out, p.u. 2 out* P 0
637 23/3 Siddington (L) MEM 3m 14 S *jmpd lft, ld/disp thro'out, slt ld & blnd last, no ex flat* 2 15
947 8/4 Andoversford (R) MDN 3m 11 GF *ld to 3rd, steadied, ld 13th, drew clr* 1 15
1242 27/4 Woodford (L) RES 3m 18 G *alwys prom, wth wnr 2 out, no ext und pres last* 2 21

Much improved & stays better; ran outstandingly last start & Restricted certain on that form; Good 19

SAXON SMILE b.g. 8 Saxon Farm - Columboola by Rapid River R Lee

1995 4(0)

221 24/2 Newtown (L) MDN 3m 12 GS *f 1st* F -
350 3/3 Garnons (L) CON 3m 11 GS *rear frm 4th, p.u. 12th* P 0
747 31/3 Upper Sapey (R) MDO 3m 11 GS *bhnd whn u.r. 11th* U -
836 6/4 Maisemore P' (L) MEM 3m 7 GF *cls up,jmpd right 6th,lft 3rd 10th,sn strugg,no ch frm 14th* 4 0

Well beaten only completions 95-6 & no signs of ability yet 0

SAXON SWINGER b.g. 9 Saxon Farm - Done Over by Road House II G T Ingleton

1995 6(0),5(0),6(0),P(0)

452 9/3 Charing (L) LAD 3m 8 G *last frm 8th, t.o. 13th* 6 0
574 17/3 Detling (L) RES 3m 14 GF *2nd to 11th, fdd, t.o. 3 out* 5 0

Won short Maiden 94; tailed off when completing since 0

SAYBRIGHT ch.g. 13 Sayfar - Bright Exploit by Exploitation G B Tarry

1995 2(22),6(0)

124 17/2 Kingston Bl' (L) CON 3m 17 GS *ld to 2nd, prssd ldr, ld 9-11th, ev ch 15th, wknd, fin tired* 7 0
434 9/3 Newton Brom' (R) CON 3m 11 GS *chsd ldrs, ev ch 15th, lost plc, ran on agn 2 out* 3 13
638 23/3 Siddington (L) CON 3m 16 S *chsd lding pr to 12th, 4th & onepcd aft, lft 3rd last* 4 14
887 6/4 Kimble (L) OPE 3m 2 GF *not fluent, ld til mstk 1st, chal last, alwys hld flat* 2 18
1016 13/4 Kingston Bl' (L) CON 3m 6 G *(fav) ld to 2nd, disp apr 14th til ld last, hdd & no ext flat* 2 16
1563 19/5 Mollington (R) CON 3m 8 GS *prom, chsd wnr 14th, ld aft 3 out-last, kpt on flat* 2 22
1596 25/5 Garthorpe (R) LAD 3m 9 G *alwys 1st 4, chal 3 out, ld last, just outpcd flat* 2 23

Deteriorated 96 till perking up late season; Confined at Kingston Blount at 14 possible; Any 19

SAY CHARLIE b.g. 9 Say Primula - Ellaron by Abwah T P Tory

1995 2(10),P(0)

70 10/2 Great Treth' (R) MDO 3m 14 S *bhnd whn p.u. aft 14th* P 0
284 2/3 Clyst St Ma' (L) MDN 3m 11 S *prom, ld 12th-3 out, outpcd aft* 2 0
470 10/3 Milborne St' (L) MDO 3m 18 G *alwys mid-div, no ch whn f last* F -
652 23/3 Badbury Rin' (L) MDO 3m 13 G *bhnd, prog 13th, strngly rdn run-in, just faild* 2 14
821 6/4 Charlton Ho' (L) MDN 3m 10 GF *alwys rear, t.o. whn p.u. 4 out* P 0

Placed in 4 of 10 starts 94-6; good enough to win weak Maiden if fit 97 14

SAYIN NOWT b.m. 8 Nicholas Bill - Greyburn by Saintly Song — Dennis Waggott
1995 P(0),3(11),P(0),1(14)

404 9/3 Dalston (R) RES 3m 7 G *w.w. prog hlfwy,cls up 3 out,qcknd & ran on to ld nr fin* 1 17
610 23/3 Friars Haugh (L) CON 3m 11 G *(fav) 4th hlfwy, ld apr 2 out, sn clr, comf* 1 19

Maiden winner 95; improved in brief 96; could reach Opens if fit 97; G-S 21

SAY MILADY ch.m. 7 Say Primula - Milady Rose by Weensland — W E Philipson
1995 1(14)

703 30/3 Tranwell (L) RES 3m 7 GS *mid-div, prog 13th, wknd rpdly 3 out, p.u. nxt* P 0
914 8/4 Tranwell (L) RES 3m 6 GF *whppd round start, tk no part* 0 0
1086 14/4 Friars Haugh (L) RES 3m 7 F *cls 3rd whn p.u. aft 10th* P 0

Maiden winner only start 95; problems 96 & can only be watched 12

SAYMORE ch.g. 10 Seymour Hicks (FR) - Huahinee (FR) by Riverman (USA) — P H Morris

158 17/2 Weston Park (L) MEM 3m 11 G *hld up, nrst fin* 4 12
364 5/3 Leicester (R) HC 2m 1f 12 GS *prom in chasing gp, rdn and effort apr 3 out, btn 2 out.* 4 14
460 9/3 Eyton-On-Se' (L) LAD 3m 10 G *in tch, ld 12th-4 out, 3l 2nd whn f 3 out* F -

Winning hurdler 93; finished early 96 & unlikely to achieve much at 11 15

SAYYURE(USA) b.g. 10 Lydian (FR) - Periquito (USA) by Olden Times — A G Harris
1995 **2(NH),3(NH),9(NH),9(NH),3(NH),4(NH),4(NH)**

203 24/2 Castle Of C' (R) MEM 3m 4 HY *(fav) chsd ldr, rdn 4 out, blnd nxt, ld last, styd on* 1 20
648 23/3 Cothelstone (L) OPE 3m 1 S *walked over* 1 0
817 6/4 Charlton Ho' (L) OPE 3m 5 GF *chsd ldr, ld aft 3 out, clr nxt, rddn out* 1 25
1246 27/4 Woodford (L) OPE 3m 6 G *(fav) raced wd, prom, ev ch 3 out, sn btn, eased cls home* 3 14

Useful pointer in 96; owner/ridden 1st & last starts; can win Opens with right handling 97; Any 23

SCALLY BLUE gr.g. 5 Scallywag - Blue Gift by Hasty Word — G L Edwards

1033 13/4 Alpraham (R) MDO 2 1/2m 15 GS *cls up 4th whn hmp & u.r. 8th* U -
1423 6/5 Eyton-On-Se' (L) MDO 3m 7 GF *(Jt fav) hld up, tk clsr ordr 10th, 2nd 13th, rng on whn f 2 out* F -

Possibly unlucky 2nd start (weak race) & should go close in 97 14

SCALLY HICKS ch.m. 5 Seymour Hicks (FR) - Scally Jenks by Scallywag — T Walker

166 17/2 Weston Park (L) MDN 3m 10 G *f 1st* F -

The briefest of starts 0

SCALLY HILL gr.m. 5 Scallywag - Madge Hill by Spartan General — Mrs B Johnson

1482 11/5 Bredwardine (R) RES 3m 13 G *s.s. t.o. frm 5th, p.u. 10th* P 0
1580 19/5 Wolverhampt' (L) MDO 3m 8 G *blnd 1st, bhnd & pshd alng 7th, lft poor 2nd 16th* 2 0

Beaten two fences in one of season's worst Maidens - can only improve 0

SCALLYKENNING gr.g. 8 Scallywag - Delegation by Articulate — J F Weldhen
1995 r(-),P(0),R(-),P(0),P(0),P(0)

301 2/3 Great Treth' (R) MDO 3m 13 G *nvr dang, bhnd whn p.u. 15th* P 0
448 9/3 Haldon (R) MDO 3m 10 S *in tch, disp 3rd at 14th, wkng whn blnd nxt, mstk nxt & p.u.* P 0
718 30/3 Wadebridge (L) MDO 3m 11 GF *hld up in tch, prog aft 14th, ld 15th-aft last, wknd rpdly* 4 14
806 4/4 Clyst St Ma' (L) MDO 3m 7 GS *(Jt fav) prom, cls 3rd whn blnd & u.r. 11th* U -
1070 13/4 Lifton (R) MDN 3m 9 S *(Jt fav) in tch, 2nd & mstk 13th, blndrd 15th, btn 6th p.u. apr 3 out* P 0
1430 6/5 High Bickin' (R) MDO 3m 8 G *wnt 2nd 6th, ld 2 out, lkd wnnr whn ran out last* r 14
1554 18/5 Bratton Down (L) MDO 3m 16 F *mid-div, prog 15th, cls 3rd whn blnd & u.r. nxt (ditch)* U -
1626 27/5 Lifton (R) MDO 3m 13 GS *mid-div, 7th at 11th, nvr able to chal ldrs* 6 0
1637 1/6 Bratton Down (L) MDO 3m 11 G *alwys in tch, effrt & prog 2 out, ran on, no imp wnr flat* 2 12

Good enough to win but 3 completions from 15 starts 95/6 & threw away golden chance 6th start 13

SCALLY LASS gr.m. 7 Scallywag - Wexford Lass Vii by Damsire Unregistered — R F Rimmer

1155 20/4 Whittington (L) MDN 3m 14 G *alwys bhnd, p.u. 11th* P 0

Not yet of any account 0

SCALLY MUIRE ro.m. 12 Scallywag - Coroin Muire by Perspex — G L Edwards
1995 1(24),1(20),2(22),1(23),1(20),1(22),2(23),1(23),1(23)

160 17/2 Weston Park (L) OPE 3m 16 G *dwelt, steady prog frm rear to ld 3 out, wknd & hdd apr last* 2 20
290 2/3 Eaton Hall (R) OPE 3m 6 G *(fav) cls up, ld 12th, duelld wth 2dn frm 4 out, hdd last,ld line* 1 22
565 17/3 Wolverhampt' (L) OPE 3m 6 GS *(fav) hld up, drvn to ld 3 out, sn clr* 1 21
737 31/3 Sudlow Farm (R) OPE 3m 4 G *(fav) ld 8-10th, disp ld 14-15th, rddn & onepcd aft* 2 23
1011 9/4 Flagg Moor (L) OPE 3m 4 G *(fav) ld to 5th, chsd ldr, rdn to ld app last, drw clr flat* 1 27
1031 13/4 Alpraham (R) MXO 3m 5 GS *(fav) held up, prog to 2nd 3 out, ld aft nxt, styd on wll* 1 24
1367 4/5 Gisburn (R) OPE 3m 4 G *(fav) chsd ldrs til ld 15th, clr 2 out, easily* 1 24

1545	18/5	Bangor	(L)	HC	3m 110yds	8	G	*held up, hdwy apr 13th, ld 4 out, left clr 2 out, easily.*	1 28
1630	31/5	Stratford	(L)	HC	3 1/2m	16	GF	*(fav) chsd ldrs, lost pl after 10th, rallied 16th, one pace 2 out.*	3 23

Very useful pointer; won 13 of last 17; stays; lame last start & may not return; G/F-Hy 27

SCALLY'S DAUGHTER gr.m. 12 Scallywag - Cedor's Daughter by Pallard Court — Mrs J Thomas

1995 1(25),1(25),1(24),1(26),1(21)

21	20/1	Barbury Cas'	(L)	MEM	3m	16	GS	*(fav) mstks,prog & prom 10th,outpcd 15th,lft 2nd 2 out,styd on wl*	2 24
153	17/2	Erw Lon	(L)	OPE	3m	15	G	*ld to 8th, cls up aft, blnd 15th, no ext*	3 16
662	24/3	Eaton Hall	(R)	OPE	3m	10	S	*ld til apr last, fdd flat*	3 20
838	6/4	Maisemore P'	(L)	OPE	3m	4	GF	*(fav) ld,jmpd rght 6th,qcknd 8l clr 15th,jmpd slwly last,hdd flat*	2 22

Unbeaten in 5 in 95 but deteriorated 96; may revive but best watched if returning 20

SCAMPTON b.g. 11 Cisto (FR) - Blue Relish by Saucy Kit — David Wharfedale

79	11/2	Wetherby Po'	(L)	MDO	3m	12	GS	*bhnd early, t.o. 11th, p.u. nxt*	P 0
224	24/2	Duncombe Pa'	(R)	RES	3m	12	GS	*in tch, rdn 10th, t.o. & p.u. 15th*	P 0
1093	14/4	Whitwell-On'	(R)	MXO	4m	19	G	*(bl) ld til f 6th*	F -

Lightly raced & shows nothing 0

SCARLET BERRY br.m. 8 Zambrano - Scarlet Letch by New Brig — Mrs C A Dance

1995 **5(NH),8(NH),9(NH)**

2	13/1	Larkhill	(R)	MDO	3m	17	GS	*rear, effrt 11th, nvr nr ldrs*	6 0
218	24/2	Newtown	(L)	MDN	3m	14	GS	*hld up, prog 10th, ld 15th, clr last, styd on well*	1 15
357	3/3	Garnons	(L)	RES	3m	14	GS	*ld aft 12th-nxt, ev ch til not qckn apr 3 out*	4 10
599	23/3	Howick	(L)	RES	3m	7	S	*hld up, prog frm 12th, 2l down 3 out, alwys hld*	2 16
946	8/4	Andoversford	(R)	RES	3m	10	GF	*alwys prom, not qckn frm 2 out*	4 15

Solid debut season; not disgraced in Restricted & could find one early 97; stays; G/S-S 18

SCARLET RISING b.m. 6 Primitive Rising (USA) - Royal Scarlet by Royal Fountain — A J Wight

53	4/2	Alnwick	(L)	MDO	3m	13	G	*rear, wl bhnd hlfwy, t.o. & p.u. 11th*	P 0
89	11/2	Alnwick	(L)	MDO	3m	9	GS	*mid-div, lost tch whn blnd 10th, p.u. nxt*	P 0

A brief season of no promise 0

SCARLET RIVER (Irish) — I 50^{P}, I 119^{3}, I 183^{2}, I 253^{1}, I 376^{P}, I 463^{P}, I 508^{1}

SCARNING GIZMO br.m. 11 Mandrake Major - Sew And Sew by Hard Tack — T F Greengrow

809	6/4	Charing	(L)	MEM	3m	4	F	*ld 2nd, clr 8th til u.r. 11th*	U -
966	8/4	Heathfield	(R)	MDO	3m	7	G	*t.d.e. alwys rr, lst tch 11th, t.o. frm 14th*	5 0
1210	21/4	Heathfield	(R)	MDO	3m	13	F	*alwys rear, lost tch 13th*	6 0
1300	28/4	Bexhill	(R)	MDO	3m	7	F	*rear & in tch til wknd 2 out*	4 0
1445	6/5	Aldington	(L)	MDO	3m	8	HD	*mid-div, imprvd to 2nd 13th, wknd 15th, fin 3rd prom 2nd*	2 11

Completions mean little & no hope of a win at 12 0

SCARRA DARRAGH (Irish) — I 120^{P}, I 143^{P}, I 203, , I 239^{F}, I 280^{P}, I 354^{P}, I 444^{6}, I 460^{P}, I 504, , I 550^{2}, I 604^{4}, I 640^{F}, I 661^{P}

SCAR STATEMENT (Irish) — I 133^{P}, I 167^{4}, I 228^{4}, I 416^{6}, I 531^{2}

SCARTEEN LOWER (Irish) — I 6^{P}, I 51^{F}, I 72, , I 153^{2}, I 212^{5}, I 242^{2}, I 313^{2}, I 331^{4}, I 508^{2}

SCARTH NICK br.g. 8 Ardar - French Look by Don't Look — Henry Bell

307	2/3	Great Stain'	(L)	MDO	3m	17	GS	*mid-div to 10th, rear whn p.u. 16th*	P 0
517	16/3	Dalton Park	(R)	MDO	3m	10	G	*pllng, cls up til wknd frm 16th*	5 0
829	6/4	Stainton	(R)	MDO	3m	9	GF	*alwys rear, t.o. & p.u. 2 out*	P 0

Shows little stamina & last when completing 0

SCARVEY BRIDGE (Irish) — I 390^{4}, I 497^{P}

SCHWEPPES TONIC (Irish) — I 18^{P}, I 94^{P}, I 216^{4}, I 298^{F}, I 317^{4}, I 399^{2}, I 453^{P}, I 536^{4}

SCORPIO SAM b.g. 11 Scorpio (FR) - Copocabana by Petingo — Major S D Oliver

1995 F(-)

65	10/2	Great Treth'	(R)	INT	3m	13	S	*nvr nr ldrs, p.u. aft 13th*	P 0
128	17/2	Kingston Bl'	(L)	RES	3m	14	GS	*alwys rear, t.o. hlfwy*	6 0

Maiden winner 93; lightly raced since & could be finished now 0

SCORPOTINA b.m. 7 Scorpio (FR) - Ablula by Abwah — Mrs T R Kinsey

1995 F(-),4(0)

953	8/4	Eyton-On-Se'	(L)	MDO	2 1/2m	10	GF	*ld 4th-4 out, ran on clsng stgs*	2 12

Ran reasonably but only 3 starts 95/6 & yet to prove she stays 3m 12

SCOTCHIE(IRE) ch.g. 6 Sandalay - Happy Hereford by Bonne Noel — Miss N C Hogg

122	17/2	Witton Cast'	(R)	MDO	3m	8	S	*mid-div, prog 14th, ld 2 out, jnd last, outpcd flat*	2 14

Just beaten by decent horse only start 96 & would surely win if fit 97 15

SCOTCH II(FR) ch.g. 12 Kaolin de Lyre (FR) - Alikame (FR) by Alize (FR) K O'Meara

162 17/2 Weston Park (L) OPE 3m 16 G *mid-div, t.o. & p.u. aft 12th* P 0

No longer of any account 0

SCOTCH LAW br.g. 8 Little Wolf - Scotch Dawn by Jock Scot B J Champion

1995 P(0),P(0)

596 23/3 Parham (R) LAD 3m 8 GS *pllng, prom to 10th, rear & strgglng 12th, u.r. 14th* U -
777 31/3 Penshurst (L) LAD 3m 7 GS *5th whn f 7th* F -

No completions & of no account 0

SCOTTISH DREAM ch.g. 18 Palm Track - Captain Frances by Captain's Gig (USA) A L Shaw

1220 24/4 Brampton Br' (R) OPE 3m 10 G *rr frm 4th, t.o. 6th, p.u. 8th* P 0

Returned to do his customary half lap of honour 0

SCOTTISH GOLD b.g. 12 Sonnen Gold - Calaburn by Caliban J M Craig

1995 **7(NH)**

110 17/2 Lanark (R) CON 3m 10 GS *alwys rear, t.o.* 7 0
320 2/3 Corbridge (R) OPE 3m 5f 8 GS *cls up early, mstks 4th & 7th, u.r. 16th* U -
751 31/3 Lockerbie (R) CON 3m 12 G *alwys wll bhnd* 5 0

Beaten miles both completions & of no account now 0

SCOTTISHHIGHLANDER b.g. 6 Broadsword (USA) - Athenmore Lass by Athenien II Michael H Ings

1995 P(0),P(0)

354 3/3 Garnons (L) MDN 2 1/2m 13 GS *cls 6th at 5th, lost tch frm 9th, p.u. 2 out* P 0
390 9/3 Llanfrynach (R) MDN 3m 13 GS *last trio, t.o. 8th, p.u. 12th* P 0
697 30/3 Llanvapley (L) MDN 3m 11 GS *2nd at 9th, wknd, 5th whn u.r. 13th* U -
1006 9/4 Upton-On-Se' (R) MDN 3m 11 F *rear, outpcd 12th, prog to 4th at 14th, not rch ldrs* 4 0

1st signs of ability last start & may do better if fit 97 11

SCOTTISH LAIRD b.g. 9 Callernish - Serene River by Over The River (FR) Mrs A B Garton

1995 P(0),5(0),3(0),3(12)

80 11/2 Wetherby Po' (L) MDO 3m 12 GS *(fav) prom, ld 14th-nxt, disp 3 out, hit last, just btn* 2 15
288 2/3 Eaton Hall (R) MDO 3m 17 G *(fav) hld up rear, nvr going wll, no ch whn p.u. 2 out* P 0

Placed 3 times 95/6 & good enough to win but problem last start; stays 14

SCOTTISH SOCKS (Irish) — **I** 252^P, **I** 353^F, **I** 379^P, **I** 444^P

SCOTTS CROSS (Irish) — **I** 319^P, **I** 409^P, **I** 448^P, **I** 494^P

SCOUT br.g. 7 Hunter's Delight - Master Suite by Master Owen A S Templeton

1995 P(0),P(0),P(0),2(10),P(0),B(-)

107 17/2 Marks Tey (L) MDN 3m 15 G *chsd ldrs til wknd 11th, t.o. & p.u. 16th* P 0
830 6/4 Marks Tey (L) MDN 3m 14 G *mid-div,prog to ld 14th,disp 15th,no ext last,fin 2nd,disq* 2D 12
1149 20/4 Higham (L) MDO 3m 10 F *mid-div, prog to prss wnr 13-16th, wknd nxt* 4 0
1403 6/5 Northaw (L) MDO 3m 8 F *ld to 12th, wknd appr 2 out* 4 0

Ran best ever race when disqualified but does not stay & great fortune needed to win 10

SCRATCH PLAYER(NZ) b.g. 9 Cocky Golfer (USA) - Nipaway (NZ) by Mellay Dave Dixon

1995 **P(NH),F(NH),5(NH),U(NH)**

17 14/1 Tweseldown (R) MDN 3m 11 GS *mstk 2nd, in tch to 10th, sn outpcd, no dang frm 12th* 6 0

Not totally disgraced but finished 1st weekend of season 10

SCRIVEN BOY b.g. 9 Lafontaine (USA) - Miss Bula by Master Buck Exors Of The Late Mrs J M Howell

1995 2(14),1(14),1(19)

160 17/2 Weston Park (L) OPE 3m 16 G *mid-div, nvr dang, p.u. 14th* P 0
293 2/3 Eaton Hall (R) INT 3m 11 G *prom, ld 10th til u.r. 14th* U -
457 9/3 Eyton-On-Se' (L) INT 3m 11 G *hld up mid-div, ran on one pc frm 4 out, lft poor 2nd last* 2 12
881 6/4 Brampton Br' (R) CON 3m 9 GF *prog to 3rd at 13th, chal 3 out, ld nxt, hdd & not qckn last* 2 18
948 8/4 Eyton-On-Se' (L) MEM 3m 4 GF *w.w. in tch, ev ch whn f 12th* F -

Dual winner 95; probably unlucky 96 but not improved; may find Confined if fit 97; G/S-G/F 18

SEABRIGHT SAGA b.g. 6 Ra Nova - Seabright Smile by Pitpan Dr L G Parry

324 3/3 Market Rase' (L) MEM 3m 4 G *pllng, in tch, reluc & lost plc aft 13th, p.u. nxt* P 0

Unpromising 0

SEACHEST ch.m. 7 Stanford - Seajan by Mandamus D G Stephens

1995 F(-),3(11),P(0)

145	17/2	Larkhill	(R)	MDO	3m	13	G	*chsd ldrs, wknd 12th, p.u. 16th*	P	0
300	2/3	Great Treth'	(R)	MDO	3m	10	G	*s.s. rear til p.u. 2 out*	P	0
993	8/4	Kingston St'	(R)	MDO	3m	17	F	*ld to 7th, handy til outpcd aft 15th, ran on agn 2 out*	2	14
1217	24/4	Andoversford	(R)	MDO	3m	16	G	*made most to 12th, grad lost pl, t.o. & p.u. 2 out*	P	0

Ran well 3rd start; should have chances in 97; needs Firm 14

SEA CLIPPER(IRE) ch.g. 7 Tale Quale - Daithis Coleen by Carnival Night — Miss E Powell

724	31/3	Garthorpe	(R)	LAD	3m	5	G	*s.s. alwys last, t.o. 11th, p.u. 3 out*	P	0
903	6/4	Dingley	(R)	LAD	3m	7	GS	*last pair frm 5th, no ch frm 6 out*	4	0
1104	14/4	Guilsborough	(L)	MDN	3m	18	G	*alwys well in rear, t.o. whn mstk 11th*	7	0

Beat only one other & just bumbling around so far 0

SEAHAWK RETRIEVER ch.g. 7 Treasure Hunter - Sister Claire by Quayside — H B Geddes

1995 **8(NH)**,**14(NH)**

267	2/3	Didmarton	(L)	MDN	3m	11	G	*prom,ld 8th til blnd 13th,ld 15th,hdd & lkd btn whn u.r.last*	U	15
375	9/3	Barbury Cas'	(L)	MDN	3m	14	GS	*(fav) sttld rear, smooth prog whn f 12th*	F	-
993	8/4	Kingston St'	(R)	MDO	3m	17	F	*(fav) alwys prom, cls 3rd 13th, ld 16th, sn clr, comf*	1	17
1395	6/5	Cotley Farm	(L)	RES	3m	8	GF	*hld up, prog frm 10th, ev ch 3 out, wknd nxt & p.u.*	P	0
1527	12/5	Ottery St M'	(L)	RES	3m	8	GF	*(fav) prom, went 2nd 15th, ld nxt, drew clr 2 out, easily*	1	20
1634	1/6	Bratton Down	(L)	INT	3m	15	G	*pllng, prog 8th,trckd ldrs til lost plc & 6th whn u.r. 15th*	U	-

Top stable & has ability but hard ride & makes mistakes; should upgrade but hardly bomb-proof; G-F ... 20

SEAN O'COININ (Irish) — **I** 615[P], **I** 642[P]

SEAN'S QUARTER (Irish) — **I** 222[1]

SEA OVAC (Irish) — **I** 99[F]

SEARCY b.g. 8 Good Times (ITY) - Fee by Mandamus — K Haynes

1995 2(20),1(20),1(21),**5(24)**,**6(0)**,2(21),2(22)

67	10/2	Great Treth'	(R)	LAD	3m	11	S	*chsd wnr 14th til last, wknd und pres*	3	22
197	24/2	Lemalla	(R)	LAD	3m	13	HY	*(fav) mid-div, prog to chal 3 out whn ran out*	r	-
365	5/3	Leicester	(R)	HC	3m	10	GS	*in tch till reminders and lost pl apr 9th, rdn and btn approaching 4 out.*	5	10
579	20/3	Ludlow	(R)	HC	2 1/2m	17	G	*prom, rdn 5 out, gradually wknd.*	5	13
1078	13/4	Cothelstone	(L)	MXO	3m	6	GF	*4th til prog 15th, ld last, rdn out*	1	20
1589	25/5	Mounsey Hil'	(R)	OPE	3m	12	G	*mstk 2nd, mid-div, rdn 9th, no ch 14th, p.u. last*	P	0

Fair at best (won 2 in 95) but below form 96; no real form in H/Chases; should win again; F-S 21

SEA SEARCH ch.g. 9 Deep Run - Gift Seeker by Status Seeker — C R Johnson

1995 U(-),3(0),2(0)

147	17/2	Erw Lon	(L)	MDN	3m	8	G	*mid-div, wknd 10th, p.u. 13th*	P	0
355	3/3	Garnons	(L)	INT	3m	10	GS	*cls up til blnd 12th, wknd nxt, p.u. 2 out*	P	0
550	17/3	Erw Lon	(L)	MDN	3m	13	GS	*chsd ldrs, prog 3 out, onepcd*	4	0
975	8/4	Lydstep	(L)	MDO	3m	9	G	*nvr nrr enough to chal*	5	0
1040	13/4	St Hilary	(R)	MDN	3m	12	G	*hld up, went 3rd at 13th, ran on to chal 2 out, just hld*	2	15
1200	21/4	Lydstep	(L)	MDN	3m	10	S	*mid-div whn f 6th*	F	-
1270	27/4	Pyle	(R)	MDO	3m	9	G	*(fav) trckd ldrs going wll, ld 3 out, sn in cmmnd*	1	13
1339	4/5	Hereford	(R)	HC	2m 3f	7	F	*held up, gd hdwy 8th, mstk next, rdn apr 3 out, wknd before next.*	3	18
1486	11/5	Erw Lon	(L)	MEM	3m	4	F	*prom, ld 14th-aft last, rallied und pres*	2	16
1557	18/5	Bassaleg	(R)	RES	3m	14	F	*cls up, prog 14th, sn chsd wnr, ld 2 out-last, not qckn*	2	18
1614	27/5	Hereford	(R)	HC	3m 1f 110yds	16	G	*held up, hdwy 5th, ld 15th till after 3 out, rdn when blnd next, one pace.*	3	18
1630	31/5	Stratford	(L)	HC	3 1/2m	16	GF	*nvr near to chal.*	7	20

Improved late 96; won weak Maiden but ran well after; not 100% reliable; summer jumping 96; G-F 17

SEA TARTH gr.m. 5 Nicholas Bill - Seajan by Mandamus — F P Luff

1271	27/4	Pyle	(R)	MDO	3m	15	G	*rear 6th, f 11th*	F	-
1391	6/5	Pantyderi	(R)	MDO	3m	13	GF	*alwys rear, ref 14th*	R	-
1557	18/5	Bassaleg	(R)	RES	3m	14	F	*in tch whn u.r. 7th*	U	-
1601	25/5	Bassaleg	(R)	RES	3m	12	GS	*mid-div, no ch whn u.r. 11th*	U	-

Unpleasant to date 0

SEATON MILL b.g. 8 Scorpio (FR) - Maygo — N P Morgan

1104	14/4	Guilsborough	(L)	MDN	3m	18	G	*mid-div, f 5th*	F	-
1240	27/4	Clifton On '	(L)	MDO	3m	10	GF	*pllng, prom, mstk 7th, mid-div whn u.r. bnd apr 9th*	U	-
1381	5/5	Dingley	(R)	MDO	3m	16	GF	*mid-div til f 6th*	F	-

Needs to learn to jump first 0

SEATTLE FOUNTAIN (Irish) — **I** 543,

SEATYRN (Irish) — **I** 253[P]

SEAVIEW STAR (Irish) — **I** 226[P], **I** 418[P], **I** 530[P]

SECOND TIME ROUND bl.g. 13 Genuine - Brinny River — Captain D R Parker

1995 5(0),2(10),2(11),P(0),4(0)
810 6/4 Charing (L) RES 3m 6 F *in tch, no dang final cct* 4 10
1189 21/4 Tweseldown (R) RES 3m 10 GF *outpcd rear, p.u. 10th* P 0
1371 4/5 Peper Harow (L) RES 3m 5 F *bhnd, lst tch appr 13th, styd on frm 3 out, nvr dang* 3 0
1501 11/5 Kingston Bl' (L) RES 3m 10 G *mstks, bhnd, t.o. & p.u. 9th* P 0
1649 8/6 Umberleigh (L) RES 3m 14 GF *alwys bhnd, t.o. & p.u. 2 out* P 0

Maiden winner 94; beaten in bad races 95/6 & no prospects now 0

SECRET MUSIC b.g. 5 Southern Music - Secret Rebel by Rebel Prince J D Parker
830 6/4 Marks Tey (L) MDN 3m 14 G *rear, f 5th* F -
1325 28/4 Fakenham P-' (L) MDO 3m 6 G *in tch, last & outpcd 12th, lft poor 2nd 2 out* 2 0
1620 27/5 Chaddesley ' (L) XX 3m 8 GF *mstk 8th, in tch to 11th, t.o. & p.u. 3 out* P 0

Distant last in poor race when 2nd & no real signs yet 0

SECRET PRINCE (Irish) — I 173[F], I 256[F], I 299[4], I 407[P], I 538[2], I 598[4]
SECRET SCEPTRE ch.g. 9 Kambalda - Secret Suspicion by Above Suspicion R A Bartlett
790 1/4 Kelso (L) HC 3m 1f 11 GF *driven along and outpcd after one cct, t.o. when p.u. before 2 out.* P 0
1083 14/4 Friars Haugh (L) CON 3m 10 F *3rd hlfwy, went 2nd 4 out, outpcd frm 3 out* 2 16
1226 25/4 Perth (R) HC 3m 7 S *prom, driven along after 13th, lost tch from 3 out, jmpd badly left and blnd next.* 4 10
1474 11/5 Aspatria (L) OPE 3m 3 GF *(fav) w.w., ld 10th, clr 12th, canter* 1 16
1573 19/5 Corbridge (R) OPE 3m 12 G *prom to 7th, disp 11th, outpcd frm 15th* 6 14

Ex-Irish staying hurdler; found terrible race & disappointing in better company; G-F 17

SECRET SIPHONER ch.g. 7 Flying Tyke - Sunshine State by Roi Soleil Miss L J Smale
1075 13/4 Lifton (R) RES 3m 12 S *sn towrds rear, bhnd, blndrd bdly 14th, p.u. apr nxt* P 0
1280 27/4 Bratton Down (L) MDO 3m 14 GF *sn rear, t.o. & p.u. 11th* P 0
1646 8/6 Umberleigh (L) MEM 3m 4 GF *in tch, mstk 9th, ev ch 13th, wknd & p.u. 15th, dsmntd* P 0

Shown nothing yet & unlikely to do so 0

SECRET SUMMIT(USA) b.g. 10 Diamond Shoal - Ygraine by Blakeney Mrs Vivien Hart
1995 **7(NH),5(NH),5(NH),2(NH),4(NH),P(NH),6(NH),4(NH)**
22 20/1 Barbury Cas' (L) XX 3m 19 GS *bhnd til some prog 13th, nvr on terms, t.o. & p.u. 2 out* P 0
161 17/2 Weston Park (L) LAD 3m 11 G *mid to rear, nvr rchd ldrs* 7 0

Winning chaser 94; brief season 96 & finished very early; best watched 0

SECRET TRUTH ch.m. 7 Nestor - Another Nitty by Country Retreat Andrew J Martin
233 24/2 Heythrop (R) MDN 3m 14 GS *mostly mid-div til wknd & p.u. 12th* P 0
1315 28/4 Bitterley (L) MDO 3m 10 G *plld hrd, 2nd at 4th, saddle slppd & p.u. nxt* P 0
1523 12/5 Garthorpe (R) MDO 3m 11 GF *ld/disp at gd pace til u.r. 11th (ditch)* U -
1568 19/5 Mollington (R) MDO 3m 9 GS *ld 3-5th, wknd 8th, t.o. last whn p.u. 11th* P 0

No stamina yet 0

SEEANDBESEEN (Irish) — I 10[P], I 58[P], I 65[P]
SEE JUST THERE (Irish) — I 79[P], I 117[P], I 156[1], I 212[3]
SEEMINGLY SO (Irish) — I 133[1], I 234, , I 560[5]
SEE THE LORD(IRE) ch.g. 6 Mister Lord (USA) - Segiolla by Giolla Mear A E Jones
900 6/4 Dingley (R) MDN 2m 5f 8 GS *6th til f 9th* F -
1097 14/4 Guilsborough (L) MEM 3m 6 G *chsd wnr to 9th, wkng whn mstk 11th, p.u. nxt* P 0
1381 5/5 Dingley (R) MDO 3m 16 GF *in tch til blnd 11th, not rcvr, p.u. nxt* P 0

Mistakes & no stamina so far 0

SEE YOU THERE ch.g. 14 Prominer - Mariner's Leap by King's Leap Mrs Peter Corbett
1995 2(15),P(0),2(13),2(12),1(14)
380 9/3 Barbury Cas' (L) CON 3m 11 GS *mid-div til wknd rpdly 14th, p.u. 2 out* P 0
706 30/3 Barbury Cas' (L) MEM 3m 7 G *cls up to 10th, lost tch & outpcd frm 13th* 4 0
998 8/4 Hackwood Pa' (L) CON 3m 5 GF *drppd away 4th, rddn 6th, cont slwly & rmtly* 4 0
1406 6/5 Hackwood Pa' (L) MXO 3m 5 F *mostly 2nd/3rd, ld bfly 13th, fdd 2 out* 3 14

Members winner 95; tries hard still but too old for anotehr win 10

SELKOLINE (Irish) — I 104[P], I 158[P], I 197[U], I 221[6], I 520[5]
SELL AND REGRET (Irish) — I 370[P]
SELM MARY (Irish) — I 7[P], I 127[2], I 203[2], I 252[1], I 295[P], I 441[P], I 514[3]
SENEGALAIS(FR) b.g. 12 Quart de Vin (FR) - Divonne (FR) by Vieux Chateau M S Venner
1995 5(10),4(12),4(13),4(16),3(11),2(13)
64 10/2 Great Treth' (R) CON 3m 7 S *ld 4th-nxt, wknd 9th, fin tired* 4 0
196 24/2 Lemalla (R) CON 3m 14 HY *mid-div, prog frm 14th, kpt on onepcd* 3 19

442 9/3 Haldon (R) CON 3m 6 S *went 4th at 13th, prog frm off pace to take 2nd flat, ran on* 2 17
560 17/3 Ottery St M' (L) CON 3m 7 G *2nd til f 6th* F -
800 4/4 Clyst St Ma' (L) MEM 3m 3 GS *(fav) ld at v slow pace, f heavily 15th (ditch)* F -
1073 13/4 Lifton (R) OPE 3m 10 S *towrds rear, 6th frm hlfwy, not able to chal* 6 15
1142 20/4 Flete Park (R) CON 3m 11 S *handy, cls 5th frm hlfwy, 2nd aft 3 out, ld nxt, sn clr* 1 21

Placed 8 times 95/6 prior to storming home last start; may consent in 97 - don't rely on it; Soft 17

SENORA D'OR br.m. 6 Le Coq D'Or - Eustacia Vye by Viking Chief Mrs Ann Rutherford

613 23/3 Friars Haugh (L) MDN 3m 15 G *3rd hlfwy, sn wknd, p.u. 4 out* P 0
755 31/3 Lockerbie (R) MDN 3m 17 G *sn bhnd, p.u. 3 out* P 0
1089 14/4 Friars Haugh (L) MDN 3m 10 F *alwys handy, kpt on wll frm 2 out to ld apr last* 1 14
1353 4/5 Mosshouses (L) RES 3m 11 GS *wth ldrs til wknd 14th, t.o.* 6 0
1472 11/5 Aspatria (L) RES 3m 8 GF *ld 4-9th,prom,wknd apr 3 out,lft 2nd last,fin 2nd plcd 1st* 1 14

Modest but improved on faster ground; lucky last win makes life hard in 97; Firm 15

SENOR TOMAS b.g. 13 Sparkler - Pearlemor by Gulf Pearl B J Trickey

1344 4/5 Holnicote (L) CON 3m 4 GS *chsd 1st pair, wknd frm 3 out* 3 0

Flat winner back in the mists of time; rarely seen now 0

SENTIMENTALITY(IRE) b.g. 8 Reasonable (FR) - Good Reliance by Good Bond Ms A J White

637 23/3 Siddington (L) MEM 3m 14 S *sn bhnd, t.o. frm 12th* 10 0

Of no account 0

SEPTEMBER STEPHEN (Irish) — **I** 40^F^, **I** 289^P^, **I** 367^F^, **I** 430^5^, **I** 474, , **I** 557^P^

SERENADE STAR (Irish) — **I** 122^3^, **I** 148^6^, **I** 440^P^

SERGEANT PEPPER ch.g. 6 Mandrake Major - Party Cloak by New Member Mrs D N B Pearson

413 9/3 Charm Park (L) MDO 3m 12 G *mid-div early, tk 3rd rn-in, nvr nrr* 3 0
591 23/3 Wetherby Po' (L) MDO 3m 14 S *mstks, mid-div, wknd 10th, p.u. 14th* P 0
1285 27/4 Easingwold (L) MDO 3m 9 G *(fav) mid-div,mstk 12th,went poor 2nd 4 out, btn whn lft clr 2 out* 1 11

Fortunate when winning but should have scope - needs to for Restricted chances; Good 14

SERGENT KAY b.g. 6 K-Battery - Kindly Night by Midsummer Night II Mrs C A Coward

1995 P(0),6(0)

74 11/2 Wetherby Po' (L) MDO 3m 11 GS *mid-div, fdd, f 12th* F -
122 17/2 Witton Cast' (R) MDO 3m 8 S *rear of ldrs, outpcd aft 3 out* 4 0
228 24/2 Duncombe Pa' (R) MDO 3m 9 GS *pllng, mid-div whn f 5th* F -
307 2/3 Great Stain' (L) MDO 3m 17 GS *mid-div, prog 15th, smooth run to ld apr last, styd on well* 1 15
411 9/3 Charm Park (L) RES 3m 20 G *mid-div, prog 12th, 3rd 4 out, u.r. nxt* U -
758 31/3 Great Stain' (L) RES 3m 17 GS *mstk 1st, mid-div, rdn 15th, sn no ext* 7 10
1287 27/4 Easingwold (L) MEM 3m 5 G *last & outpcd 7th, hmpd & lost ground 9th, sn t.o.* 3 0

Won competitive race but yet to progress; Restricted should be possible but best watched; G/S 15

SERIOUS NOTE (Irish) — **I** 171^6^, **I** 339^U^, **I** 414^P^, **I** 537^3^

SERIOUS TIME ch.h. 8 Good Times (ITY) - Milva by Jellaby P C Browne

1995 P(0),1(0)

133 17/2 Ottery St M' (L) OPE 3m 18 GS *rear whn f 6th* F -
198 24/2 Lemalla (R) OPE 3m 12 HY *bhnd whn p.u. aft 11th* P 0

Won a bad Members 95 & season lasted a week in 96 0

SETERALITE b.m. 9 Lighter - Arctic Servant by Goldhill M L Dale

1995 4(15),2(12),3(0)

188 24/2 Friars Haugh (L) RES 3m 12 S *nvr dang, p.u. 15th* P 0

Maiden winner 93; disappointing since & brief appearance 96 10

SET FOR FREE (Irish) — **I** 545^P^, **I** 575^U^

SEVEN CRUISE ch.g. 7 Cruise Missile - Seven Ways by Seven Bells C Biddle

1995 F(-),P(0),U(-),F(-),2(0),P(0)

883 6/4 Brampton Br' (R) MDN 3m 13 GF *prom til wknd 13th, p.u. 16th* P 0
1045 13/4 Bitterley (L) MDO 3m 16 G *outpcd & lost tch 11th, t.o. & p.u. 3 out* P 0
1218 24/4 Brampton Br' (R) MEM 3m 4 G *lft 2nd at 6th, chal 9th til lost irons 11th, p.u. nxt, cont* 2 0
1483 11/5 Bredwardine (R) MDO 3m 15 G *lost tch 8th, t.o. & p.u. 15th* P 0
1580 19/5 Wolverhampt' (L) MDO 3m 8 G *mid-div, disp poor 3rd 14th, exhausted frm 3 out, walked in* 4 0

Finished 3 of 11 starts in 95/6 & has no ability 0

SEVENS OUT ch.g. 14 Touch Paper - Rosie Probert by Captain's Gig (USA) Gerard Nock

1995 2(21),2(21),3(22),1(21),1(22),4(18),1(22),4(14)

22 20/1 Barbury Cas' (L) XX 3m 19 GS *prom til lost plc 5th,sn bhnd,kpt on frm 14th,no dang* 5 17
639 23/3 Siddington (L) OPE 3m 12 S *rr div, 8th & rddn appr 10th, kpt on frm 15th, nvr dang* 5 18

793 2/4 Heythrop (R) OPE 4m 10 F *prom,ld/disp 12-16th,ev ch whn blnd 2 out,not rcvr* 5 16
1098 14/4 Guilsborough (L) CON 3m 17 G *novie rdn, alwys wll bhnd, t.o. 9th, nvr nrr* 7 0
1318 28/4 Bitterley (L) XX 3m 8 G *alwys prom, chal 14th, chsd wnr, rallied apr last* 2 20
1438 6/5 Ashorne (R) XX 3m 14 G *prom, ld 7th, clr wth chsr 13th, rdn & all out flat,wll rdn* 1 21

Solid & ultra-safe; popped up last start & could win at 15 in modest company; Any 19

SEVENTH LOCK b.g. 10 Oats - Barge Mistress by Bargello — K L Dare

1995 4(10),P(0),U(-),6(0)

279 2/3 Clyst St Ma' (L) LAD 3m 7 S *rear, 4th at 11th, no ch frm 3 out, outpcd* 3 16
441 9/3 Haldon (R) MEM 3m 6 S *handy,2nd 13th,lft in ld 3 out,lkd wnr til hng lft flat,hdd* 2 13
716 30/3 Wadebridge (L) LAD 3m 6 GF *(Co fav) ld 5th til hdd 3 out, rnwd effrt cls home* 2 18
1124 20/4 Stafford Cr' (R) CON 3m 7 S *sn bhnd, out of tch 12th, mod late prog* 4 15

Consistent but struggles to stay & threw away race in Members; hard to win in 97; F-S 15

SEVENTH SYMPHONY (Irish) — I 2721

SEVERN INVADER b.g. 11 Al Sirat (USA) - Wunder Madchen by Brave Invader (USA) — Captain Miles Gosling

1995 2(20),1(21),**2(22)**

124 17/2 Kingston Bl' (L) CON 3m 17 GS *mid-div, lost tch wth ldrs 14th, kpt on frm 2 out* 5 16
1179 21/4 Mollington (R) LAD 3m 10 F *prom, ld & qcknd aft 10th, hdd 3 out, styd on onepcd* 3 22
1438 6/5 Ashorne (R) XX 3m 14 G *(fav) chsng grp,5th hlfwy,poor 5th 3 out,ran on strngly,just faild* 3 19
1502 11/5 Kingston Bl' (L) LAD 3m 7 G *ld to 2nd, lost plc 5th, 3rd frm 13th, kpt on* 3 22
1562 19/5 Mollington (R) MEM 3m 6 GS *(fav) cls up, jnd ldr 13th, ld 3 out, clr nxt, comf* 1 21
1608 26/5 Tweseldown (R) CON 3m 6 G *mstk 2nd,chsd ldr to 3rd,effrt & ld 13th,clr 3 out,ran on wl* 1 22

Useful pointer; consistent; stays; win more Confineds 97; G/S-F, best Firm 22

SEXTON GLEAM (Irish) — I 103^{P}, I 159^{P}, I 389^{P}

SEYMORE MONEY b.g. 7 Seymour Hicks (FR) - Morgan's Money by David Jack — E H Crow

1995 F(-),P(0),r(-),P(0)

464 9/3 Eyton-On-Se' (L) MDN 2 1/2m 13 G *ld 4th, jnd 2 out, hdd & p.u. flat, dead* P 0

Dead 12

SEYMOUR FIDDLES b.m. 5 King's Holt - Kidcello by Bybicello — J P Seymour

615 23/3 Friars Haugh (L) MEM 3m 9 G *4th hlfwy, went 2nd 13th, wknd quckly 4 out.* 4 0
1089 14/4 Friars Haugh (L) MDN 3m 10 F *in tch whn u.r. 12th* U -

Distant 4th in silly race & no concrete signs yet 0

SEYMOUR LAD (Irish) — I 169^{P}

SEZU (Irish) — I 7^{4}, I 50^{2}, I 144^{P}, I 309^{5}, I 353^{U}, I 504^{6}, I 550^{5}

SGEIR BANTIGHEARNA br.m. 9 Rough Lad - Oiseval by National Trust — Mrs H M Bridges

71 10/2 Great Treth' (R) MDO 3m 15 S *wll bhnd, p.u. 3 out* P 0
207 24/2 Castle Of C' (R) MDO 3m 15 HY *rear til p.u. 13th* P 0
658 23/3 Badbury Rin' (L) MDO 3m 8 G *ld 6th until 3 out, not able to qckn wth wnnr* 2 10

2nd in poor race & finished early; more needed for winning chances 11

SGT CHILDCRAFT b.g. 6 Sergeant Drummer (USA) - Palmid by Charlie's Pal — R T J Sexon

1995 **17(NH)**,**P(NH)**,7**(NH)**

928 8/4 Bishopsleigh (R) MDN 3m 9 G *towrds rear, some prog frm 12th, nvr nrr* 3 0

Beaten miles when 3rd & no real encouragement yet 0

SHAAB TURBO b.g. 10 Shaab - Argosa by No Argument — D Heath

15 14/1 Cottenham (R) MDN 3m 14 G *(fav) prom, chsd ldr 4th, lft in ld 11th, hdd apr 2 out, wknd* 4 12
108 17/2 Marks Tey (L) MDN 3m 17 G *pllng, jnd ldrs 10th,ld 16th til appr 3 out,sn wkd,p.u. last* P 0
344 3/3 Higham (L) MDO 3m 12 G *ld to 3rd,cls 2nd aft til ld agn 13th,made rest,just hld on* 1 13

Barely stays but beat subsequent winner; finished early; Restricted chance if fit 97; Good 14

SHADOWGRAFF b.m. 6 Scorpio (FR) - Panatate by Panco — A Hollingsworth

352 3/3 Garnons (L) MDN 2 1/2m 9 GS *6l 3rd at 11th, lft 2l 2nd 3 out, ld & f nxt* F -
689 30/3 Chaddesley ' (L) MDN 3m 15 G *(fav) mid-div til f 5th* F -
749 31/3 Upper Sapey (R) MDO 3m 17 GS *4th at hlfwy, still 4th til wknd 2 out* 6 11
947 8/4 Andoversford (R) MDN 3m 11 GF *sn rear, ran on thro' btn horses* 4 0

Not beaten far when 6th but more needed for chances in 97; should improve 11

SHADOW WALKER b.g. 12 Bigivor - Panatate by Panco — A Hollingsworth

1995 2(18),2(20),3(10),3(16),5(17),P(0),3(21),1(23),**P(0)**

232 24/2 Heythrop (R) OPE 3m 10 GS *alwys wll bhnd, t.o. & p.u. 13th* P 0
265 2/3 Didmarton (L) OPE 3m 6 G *ld to 8th, outpcd aft 11th, sn no ch* 3 18
427 9/3 Upton-On-Se' (R) OPE 3m 6 GS *disp to 8th, onepcd aft* 4 0
683 30/3 Chaddesley ' (L) MEM 3m 17 G *mid-div, 10th & pshd alng hlfwy, nvr trbld ldrs* 4 15

945 8/4 Andoversford (R) OPE 3m 3 GF *hld up bhnd ldrs, ran on frm 2 uot, unable to chal* 3 14
1046 13/4 Bitterley (L) LAD 3m 9 G *cls up til outpcd frm 12th, lost tch & p.u. 15th* P 0
1171 20/4 Chaddesley ' (L) OPE 3m 15 G *nvr rchd ldrs, bhnd frm 13th* 9 0
1437 6/5 Ashorne (R) MXO 3m 13 G *rear til prog 11th, 5th & in tch 15th, chal apr last, wknd* 5 19
1479 11/5 Bredwardine (R) OPE 3m 8 G *cls up til not qckn frm 14th* 5 12

Has ability still but 1 win from 18 starts 95/6 & deteriorated 96; struggle to win again 17

SHADY PRINCE (Irish) — **I** 71P, **I** 139P, **I** 311P

SHAKE FIVE(IRE) br.g. 5 Tremblant - Five Swallows by Crash Course Mrs C H Sporborg

34 20/1 Higham (L) MDN 3m 11 GF *chsd lding pr 12th, qknd to chall last, sn ld, clvrly* 1 17
348 3/3 Higham (L) RES 3m 12 G *(fav) sweating, rear, nvr going wll, nvr dang* 5 0
679 30/3 Cottenham (R) RES 3m 15 GF *w.w. prog to 3rd 16th, mstk 2 out, styd on to 2nd flat* 2 18
1062 13/4 Horseheath (R) MEM 3m 3 F *(fav) chsd ldr, qknd to ld last, rdn out* 1 16

Quite promising; looks awkward ride but should find Restricted 97; stays; Firm 19

SHAKER MAKER ch.g. 8 Noalto - Something To Hide by Double-U-Jay J C Collett

1995 P(0)

426 9/3 Upton-On-Se' (R) CON 3m 16 GS *chsng ldrs whn b.d. 7th* B -
683 30/3 Chaddesley ' (L) MEM 3m 17 G *alwys bhnd, t.o. & p.u. 13th* P 0
1048 13/4 Bitterley (L) MDO 3m 12 G *mid-div, outpcd apr 13th, p.u. 15th* P 0
1217 24/4 Andoversford (R) MDO 3m 16 G *(fav) w.w., prog to 3rd 12th, wknd app 3 out, p.u. last* P 0

Never completes & amazing favourite last start 0

SHAKEY THYNE(IRE) ch.m. 6 Good Thyne (USA) - Captain's Flat by Mon Capitaine Miss Carol Richardson

238 25/2 Southwell P' (L) MDO 3m 9 HO *s.s. t.o. til p.u. aft 11th* P 0
331 3/3 Market Rase' (L) MDO 3m 9 G *bhnd frm 8th, p.u. 14th* P 0
540 17/3 Southwell P' (L) MDO 3m 9 GS *mid-div, prog frm 4 out, nrst fin* 3 0
1008 9/4 Flagg Moor (L) MDO 2 1/2m 7 G *chsd ldr to 6th, outpcd app 8th, no ch 11th, tk 3rd on post* 3 0

Well beaten in both completions & much more needed for any chances in 97 10

SHALCHLO BOY gr.g. 12 Rusticaro (FR) - Mala Mala by Crepello Miss Linda Wonnacott

1995 **U(NH),6(NH),4(NH),3(NH),2(NH),9(NH),5(NH)**

874 6/4 Higher Kilw' (L) OPE 3m 6 GF *lost ground frm 10th, t.o. 13th* 5 0
1073 13/4 Lifton (R) OPE 3m 10 S *rear, jmp slwly 13th, hit 14th, p.u. apr nxt* P 0
1142 20/4 Flete Park (R) CON 3m 11 S *bhnd & strgglng frm 10th, t.o.* 4 0
1525 12/5 Ottery St M' (L) CON 3m 9 GF *ld til hdd & wknd rpdly 12th, t.o. 16th* 7 0
1624 27/5 Lifton (R) LAD 3m 9 GS *twrds rear whn u.r. 4th* U -

Winning chaser; looks finished now; Firm 0

SHAMROCK LUBE (Irish) — **I** 335P

SHAMROCK STAR ch.g. 10 Horage - Alfarouse by Home Guard (USA) A C Ayres

1995 P(0),4(14),6(0),5(0),U(-)

919 8/4 Aldington (L) LAD 3m 4 F *cls up to 13th, t.o. 16th* 3 0
1186 21/4 Tweseldown (R) LAD 3m 6 GF *immed outpcd, t.o.8th, lft v remote 3rd last* 3 0

Won 3 poor contests in 94 & predictably struggling since 0

SHAMRON (Irish) — **I** 12P, **I** 66B, **I** 120P

SHANAGORE WARRIOR (Irish) — **I** 181³, **I** 502³

SHANBALLYMORE(IRE) b.g. 7 Teofane - Greenhall Madam by Lucifer (USA) Mrs W J N Tilley

1995 2(10),P(0),2(0)

464 9/3 Eyton-On-Se' (L) MDN 2 1/2m 13 G *mid-div,ran on frm 5 out, disp 2 out, not qckn, lft 2nd flat* 2 12
659 24/3 Eaton Hall (R) MEM 3m 6 S *(fav) chsd ldrs, ev ch 2 out, not qckn* 3 11
856 6/4 Sandon (L) RES 3m 9 GF *mid-div in tch, no ext frm 2 out* 4 12
1033 13/4 Alpraham (R) MDO 2 1/2m 15 GS *alwys prom, ld apr 3 out, drew clr aft nxt* 1 15
1228 27/4 Worcester (L) HC 2m 7f 17 G *alwys bhnd.* 7 0
1341 4/5 Warwick (L) HC 2 1/2m 110yds 12 GF *prom to 10th, soon wknd.* 7 0

Improved to win short Maiden; no chance in H/Chases - Restricted needs more in 97; G/S 14

SHANECRACKEN (Irish) — **I** 405⁵, **I** 489¹

SHANNON KING(IRE) ch.g. 8 Boyne Valley - Miss Royal by King's Company Mrs C A Dance

388 9/3 Llanfrynach (R) RES 3m 20 GS *prom, rdn & wknd 10th, p.u. 12th* P 0
742 31/3 Upper Sapey (R) RES 3m 9 GS *clr ldr til wknd 14th, p.u. 2 out* P 0
1223 24/4 Brampton Br' (R) RES 3m 11 G *chsd ldrs rdn 14th, hmprds 16th, t.o. 2 out* 5 0

Maiden winner 94; missed 95 & not able to recover form for new connections; best watched 11

SHANNON RUGBY CLUB (Irish) — **I** 50F, **I** 142P

SHARED FORTUNE(IRE) b or br.g. 8 Strong Gale - Reaper's Run by Deep Run R Gould

1995 P(0),P(0),4(0),U(-),3(0),3(12)

253	25/2	Charing	(L)	MDO	3m	10	GS	*(fav) ld to 3rd, prom aft, wkng in 4th whn p.u. 4 out*	P	0
470	10/3	Milborne St'	(L)	MDO	3m	18	G	*cls up early, lost tch 14th, t.o. & p.u. last*	P	0
1187	21/4	Tweseldown	(R)	MDN	3m	11	GF	*ld 2nd til f 8th*	F	-
1374	4/5	Peper Harow	(L)	MDO	3m	8	F	*f 1st*	F	-
1608	26/5	Tweseldown	(R)	CON	3m	6	G	*st fast pace til hdd aft 10th,3rd frm 13th,btn whn f 3out*	F	-
1638	1/6	Bratton Down	(L)	MDO	3m	13	G	*ld to 4th, wknd 13th, t.o. & p.u. 2 out*	P	0

Placed in 95 but no completions 96 & likely to remain a maiden 0

SHAREEF STAR b.g. 8 Shareef Dancer (USA) - Ultra Vires by High Line — Paul Wise

1995 **U(-),F(-),P(0)**

256	29/2	Ludlow	(R)	HC	3m	14	G	*t.o. 6th, p.u. before 15th.*	P	0
369	7/3	Towcester	(R)	HC	3m 1f	6	G	*(vis) started slowly, t.o. till f 2 out.*	F	-
664	24/3	Eaton Hall	(R)	CON	3m	15	S	*mid to rear, no ch whn p.u. 5 out*	P	0
1120	20/4	Bangor	(L)	HC	2 1/2m 110yds	13	S	*bhnd, f 8th (water).*	F	-
1233	27/4	Weston Park	(L)	RES	3m	14	G	*s.s., alwys rear, grdly lost tch, btn 1 fence*	9	0
1544	17/5	Stratford	(L)	HC	3m	10	GF	*alwys last, t.o. after 5th.*	10	0
1578	19/5	Wolverhampt'	(L)	OPE	3m	7	G	*(vis) s.s. sn prom, rmndrs 7th, bhnd 11th, t.o. & p.u. 2 out*	P	0

Selling hurdle winner 92; waste of time in H/Chases 0

SHAREZA RIVER (Irish) — **I** 38^{2}, **I** 121^{2}, **I** 155^{P}, **I** 445^{1}, **I** 544^{F}

SHARIMAGE (Irish) — **I** 173^{S}, **I** 260^{2}, **I** 299^{F}, **I** 493^{1}, **I** 617^{4}

SHARING THOUGHTS b.m. 11 Tickled Pink - Fantasy Royale by Breeders Dream — R H P Williams

1995 7(0),U(-),P(0)

1262	27/4	Pyle	(R)	MEM	3m	6	G	*ld 6-12th, p.u. lame aft nxt*	P	0

Dual winner 92; shows nothing now 0

SHARINSKI ch.g. 9 Niniski (USA) - Upanishad by Amber Rama (USA) — Mrs Jo Yeomans

1995 3(18),1(18),2(20),1(20),2(18),1(22),**P(0)**

351	3/3	Garnons	(L)	OPE	3m	14	GS	*trckd ldrs, effrt to 3l 4th at 14th, no ext nxt*	5	15
1004	9/4	Upton-On-Se'	(R)	OPE	3m	3	F	*(fav) ld 3rd, mstks 11-12th, clr aft 15th, easily*	1	21
1171	20/4	Chaddesley '	(L)	OPE	3m	15	G	*trckd ldrs, prog to ld 17th, styd on wll frm nxt*	1	25
1509	12/5	Maisemore P'	(L)	OPE	3m	4	F	*(fav) cls up, wth ldr 11-13th, wknd frm nxt, t.o. & p.u. last*	P	0

Won 3 in 95; maintained progress; won competitive Open; ground against last; Opens in 97; G-S 24

SHAROUJACK (Irish) — **I** 143^{2}, **I** 183^{4}, **I** 207^{4}, **I** 309^{1}, **I** 331^{5}, **I** 463^{2}, **I** 519^{3}, **I** 568^{3}, **I** 641^{3}, **I** 647^{1}

SHARPE EXIT b.g. 7 Say Primula - Kerera by Keren — Ms J Sharpe

321	2/3	Corbridge	(R)	MDN	3m	12	GS	*mstk 2nd, t.o. & p.u. 11th*	P	0
704	30/3	Tranwell	(L)	MDO	3m	16	GS	*t.o. & p.u. 14th*	P	0
916	8/4	Tranwell	(L)	MDO	2 1/2m	8	GF	*alwys strgglng, lost tch 10th, f nxt*	F	-
1575	19/5	Corbridge	(R)	MDO	3m	10	G	*last at 4th, t.o. & p.u. 9th*	P	0

Shows nothing 0

SHARP OPINION b.g. 13 Le Bavard (FR) - Arctic Tack by Arctic Slave — Mrs L Walby

1995 4(14),1(19),**4(19)**,1(22)

50	4/2	Alnwick	(L)	CON	3m	9	G	*in tch to 7th, t.o. & p.u. 11th*	P	0
110	17/2	Lanark	(R)	CON	3m	10	GS	*(Jt fav) early rmndrs, cls up, no imp on wnr frm 2 out*	2	19
399	9/3	Dalston	(R)	CON	3m	9	G	*prom early, lost plc hlfwy, ran on agn 3 out, no dang*	4	10
751	31/3	Lockerbie	(R)	CON	3m	12	G	*nvr nr ldrs*	4	10
1251	27/4	Balcormo Ma'	(R)	OPE	3m	6	GS	*sn last, lost tch by 12th, p.u. apr 3 out*	P	0
1513	12/5	Hexham Poin'	(L)	CON	3m	6	HY	*trckd ldrs going wll, 3rd & outpcd 3 out, no ch frm nxt*	3	13

Solid Confined horse up to 95 but deteriorating now & will do well to revive at 14; G-Hy 13

SHARPRIDGE ch.g. 12 Nearly A Hand - Maria's Piece by Rose Knight — M B Mawhinney

1995 2(12),2(13),1(14),3(15),1(17),2(16),**5(0)**,**7(NH)**

223	24/2	Duncombe Pa'	(R)	CON	3m	16	GS	*ld to 11th, 5th & wkng 14th, no ch aft*	5	12
761	31/3	Great Stain'	(L)	INT	3m	7	GS	*alwys rear, t.o. & p.u. 8th*	P	0
985	8/4	Charm Park	(L)	INT	3m	9	GF	*rear early, outpcd frm 11th, p.u. nxt*	P	0
1130	20/4	Hornby Cast'	(L)	CON	3m	13	G	*prom, ld 4th-11th, wknd rpdly, t.o. & u.r. 3 out*	U	-
1281	27/4	Easingwold	(L)	CON	3m	15	G	*nvr bttr than mid-div, wknd 10th, t.o. & p.u. 15th*	P	0
1448	6/5	Witton Cast'	(R)	OPE	3m	5	G	*rear by 5th, t.o. 14th, p.u. nxt*	P	0
1465	11/5	Easingwold	(L)	MEM	3m	4	G	*nvr going wl,jmpd slwly 3rd,sn t.o.,lft 3rd 14th,tk 2nd 2out*	2	0
1595	25/5	Garthorpe	(R)	CON	3m	15	G	*cls up in 3rd til chsd ldr 12th, wknd nxt, f 4 out*	F	-
1645	2/6	Dingley	(R)	INT	3m	5	GF	*alwys rr, lost tch 12th, t.o., sntchd 4th nr fin*	4	0

Dual winner 95 when improved; gone to pieces now & no further winning hopes 0

SHARP TACTICS gr.g. 6 Broadsword (USA) - Speckle by King Sitric — Mrs Jill McVay

92	11/2	Ampton	(R)	MDO	3m	7	GF	*jmpd lft, ld/disp, mstks 12th & 15th, wknd 2 out*	3	10
830	6/4	Marks Tey	(L)	MDN	3m	14	G	*pllng, cls up til lost plc 10th, rear whn p.u. 13th*	P	0

Last in weak Maiden when 3rd & much more needed in 97 .... **10**

SHARP TO OBLIGE ch.g. 9 Dublin Taxi - Please Oblige by Le Levanstell — Miss S J Rodgers

14	14/1	Cottenham	(R)	MDO	3m	10	G	*(fav) ld 5th, blnd 9th, hdd apr 3 out where f*	F	-
52	4/2	Alnwick	(L)	MDO	3m	11	G	*(fav) hld up wll bhnd, prog 10th, not rch ldrs, wknd 2 out*	5	0
240	25/2	Southwell P'	(L)	MDO	3m	15	HO	*hld up, prog & in tch 11th, 5th & btn 4 out, p.u. nxt*	P	0
1026	13/4	Brocklesby '	(L)	MDN	3m	6	GF	*w.w., rpd prog 6 out, 2nd 5 out, ld 3 out, sn clr*	1	15
1284	27/4	Easingwold	(L)	RES	3m	14	G	*alwys rear, wll bhnd whn p.u. 14th*	P	0
1522	12/5	Garthorpe	(R)	RES	3m	12	GF	*chsd ldrs, prog 3 out, upsides whn f last*	F	18
1597	25/5	Garthorpe	(R)	XX	3m	9	G	*(fav) rpd prog 9th, disp 10-11th, 3rd 6 out, outpcd 4 out*	4	10

Non-stayer; found dire race; unlucky 6th start but likely to frustrate in future; G/F **16**

SHARROW BAY(NZ) ch.g. 9 Sovereign Parade (NZ) - Minella (NZ) by Causeur — D H Barons

1995 **P(NH)**

70	10/2	Great Treth'	(R)	MDO	3m	14	S	*nvr bttr than mid-div, p.u. aft 14th*	P	0
200	24/2	Lemalla	(R)	MDO	3m	12	HY	*nvr bttr than 4th, no dang frm 3 out*	4	0
448	9/3	Haldon	(R)	MDO	3m	10	S	*(fav) prom til lost plc 6th, bhnd whn p.u. 10th, dsmntd*	P	0
1143	20/4	Flete Park	(R)	MDN	3m	17	S	*went 3rd 10th, ld 15th, clr 3 out, hdd & wknd apr last*	3	12

Ground to a halt last start (large but weak field); may find race over easy 3m; Soft **13**

SHARSMAN(IRE) b.g. 6 Callernish - Another Dutchess by Master Buck — E H Crow

1995 S(-),P(0)

463	9/3	Eyton-On-Se'	(L)	MDN	2 1/2m	14	G	*w.w., rng on 3rd bt lkd hld whn f 3 out*	F	-
1581	19/5	Wolverhampt'	(L)	MDO	3m	10	G	*mid-div, prog 13th, prssd wnr 16th, rdn & hit nxt, no ext*	2	10

Good stable but lightly raced & more needed for a win in 97 .... **13**

SHAWN CUDDY ch.g. 5 Hubbly Bubbly (USA) - Quick Kick by Saritamer (USA) — R T Jones

1995 **9(NH)**

390	9/3	Llanfrynach	(R)	MDN	3m	13	GS	*w.w. in tch,hmpd 12th,prog 14th,ld 2 out,rdn & all out flat*	1	14
1482	11/5	Bredwardine	(R)	RES	3m	13	G	*rdn 11th, lost tch frm 15th, p.u. 2 out*	P	0

Poor under Rules; found weak Maiden; absent 2 months after & more needed for Restricted hopes **14**

SHAWS CROSS (Irish) — **I** 465^{2}, **I** 526^{1}

SHAYNA MAIDEL ch.m. 7 Scottish Reel - Revisit by Busted — N Shutts

569	17/3	Wolverhampt'	(L)	MDN	3m	11	GS	*prog to 5l 2nd at 15th, wknd rpdly, p.u. 2 out*	P	0
954	8/4	Eyton-On-Se'	(L)	MDO	2 1/2m	6	GF	*cls up to 9th, sn wknd & t.o., p.u. 3 out*	P	0

No stamina yet **0**

SHEER HOPE ro.g. 8 Hope Anchor - Sheer Romance by Precipice Wood — D Hays

1995 P(0)

34	20/1	Higham	(L)	MDN	3m	11	GF	*(bl) chsd ldr to 10th, sn wknd, p.u. 12th*	P	0
343	3/3	Higham	(L)	MDO	3m	11	G	*(bl) in rear, jnd main grp 11-13th, wknd 4 out*	5	0

Last in bad race on only completion & signs not good **0**

SHEER INDULGENCE (Irish) — **I** 180^{4}, **I** 219^{U}, **I** 288^{3}, **I** 402, , **I** 539^{3}

SHEER JEST b.g. 11 Mummy's Game - Tabasheer (USA) by Indian Chief II — Mrs Judy Wilson

1995 **5(27),1(32),2(27),1(32),2(NH),F(-)**

9	14/1	Cottenham	(R)	OPE	3m	13	G	*(fav) w.w. smooth prog to 2nd 13th, ld apr 2 out, clr last, easily*	1	32
100	16/2	Fakenham	(L)	HC	2m 5f 110yds	9	G	*(fav) held up, hdwy 10th, ld after 12th, clr last.*	1	36
359	4/3	Doncaster	(L)	HC	2m 3f 110yds	10	G	*(fav) patiently rdn, smooth hdwy on bit 4 out, nosing ahd when f 2 out.*	F	35
1122	20/4	Stratford	(L)	HC	2m 5f 110yds	16	GF	*(fav) held up, hdwy 9th, ld 3 out, hdd and no ext flat.*	2	32
1333	1/5	Cheltenham	(L)	HC	3m 1f 110yds	13	G	*(fav) held up, steady prog to 4th 13th, joined ldrs 3 out, hrd rdn run-in, wknd cl home.*	2	33
1546	18/5	Fakenham	(L)	HC	3m 110yds	13	G	*(fav) held up rear, prog 12th, ld 3 out, driven and held on cl home.*	1	30
1631	1/6	Stratford	(L)	HC	3 1/2m	14	GF	*held up, hdwy 12th, rdn apr 2 out, kept on same pace.*	3	33

Very good H/Chaser still; won 4 of last 12 H/Chases; finds little in finish now; win again at 12;G-F **34**

SHEER MISCHIEF (Irish) — **I** 332^{F}, **I** 458^{P}, **I** 608^{2}

SHEER MYSTERY (Irish) — **I** 112^{3}, **I** 167^{P}

SHEER POWER(IRE) b.g. 7 Exhibitioner - Quality Blake by Blakeney — Mrs J L Games

1995 P(0),3(0)

548	17/3	Erw Lon	(L)	RES	3m	8	GS	*p.u. 5th*	P	0
697	30/3	Llanvapley	(L)	MDN	3m	11	GS	*4th at 7th, wkng whn p.u. 14th*	P	0
842	6/4	Maisemore P'	(L)	MDN	3m	17	GF	*rr of mn grp, 10th & outpcd 12th, no ch aft*	6	0

1162 20/4 Llanwit Maj' (R) MDO 3m 12 GS *disp ld til ld 6-13th, wknd 15th, p.u. 2 out* P 0

Beat only one other when finishing & shows no stamina 0

SHE GOES ch.m. 9 Royal Boxer - Village Beauty by Gregalach's Nephew William John Day
1995 P(0),3(10),3(10),4(10)
848 6/4 Howick (L) MDN 3m 14 GF *rear, clsd frm 14th, 15l down 3 out, p.u. nxt* P 0

Weak form in 95 & looks to have a problem now 10

SHELLEY'S DREAM b.m. 6 Impecunious - Badinage by Brigadier Gerard D J Dando
375 9/3 Barbury Cas' (L) MDN 3m 14 GS *rear whn f 1st* F -

Could not have done less 0

SHELLEY STREET b.m. 7 Sula Bula - Kerry Street by Dairialatan R H York
253 25/2 Charing (L) MDO 3m 10 GS *sn cls up, lft in clr ld 8th, still in ld whn p.u. 12th* P 0
477 10/3 Tweseldown (R) MDO 3m 15 G *schoold in rear, t.o. 11th, p.u. 4 out* P 0

Strange start but can only do better 10

SHELTER b.g. 9 Teenoso (USA) - Safe House by Lyphard (USA) Major R G Wilson
1995 P(0),2(10),3(10),**P(0)**,3(10)
681 30/3 Cottenham (R) MDO 3m 12 GF *blnd 1st, last pair til hmpd & u.r. 9th* U -
834 6/4 Marks Tey (L) RES 3m 11 G *blnd 3rd & p.u.* P 0
1149 20/4 Higham (L) MDO 3m 10 F *alwys rear, bhnd frm 12th, t.o. & p.u. 3 out* P 0
1261 27/4 Cottenham (R) MDO 3m 10 F *ld at gd pace to 15th, ld 4 out-last, no ext flat* 3 12

Ran best ever race last start; does not stay; may hit lucky late 97; Firm 11

SHEPPIE'S REALITY b.g. 6 Dreams To Reality (USA) - Manshecango by Saucy Kit Mrs Jane Smith
1995 **13(NH),19(NH),9(NH)**
738 31/3 Sudlow Farm (R) LAD 3m 5 G *chsd ldr to 3rd, blndrd nxt, bhnd frm 7th, p.u. 12th* P 0
853 6/4 Sandon (L) LAD 3m 7 GF *sn t.o., no ch whn p.u. 12th* P 0
1196 21/4 Sandon (L) MDN 3m 17 G *rear frm 3rd, t.o. & p.u. 13th* P 0
1234 27/4 Weston Park (L) MDO 3m 13 G *alwys rear, t.o. frm 8th* 6 0

Beaten miles when last in a poor race - no encouragement yet 0

SHERBROOKS b.g. 10 Millfontaine - Candolcis by Candy Cane M Hoskins
1995 1(12),5(0),P(0),2(14),6(0),3(14)
41 3/2 Wadebridge (L) XX 3m 9 GF *in tch to 13th, rdn & outpcd aft nxt* 6 13
68 10/2 Great Treth' (R) RES 3m 14 S *nvr seen wth ch, p.u. 14th* P 0
281 2/3 Clyst St Ma' (L) RES 3m 11 S *alwys mid-div, nvr on terms* 5 0
532 16/3 Cothelstone (L) RES 3m 12 G *in tch, blnd 10th, rddn & onpcd frm 14th* 4 14
1061 13/4 Badbury Rin' (L) INT 3m 3 GF *alwys 3rd, wll bhnd frm 15th* 3 0
1312 28/4 Little Wind' (R) XX 3m 6 G *rear, prog 16th, cls 3rd & ev ch 3 out, no ext* 3 16
1497 11/5 Holnicote (L) RES 3m 10 G *midfld, no ch & jmp lft clsng stgs* 5 0

Maiden winner 95; beaten in 12 races since (placed in 5) & will struggle to find Restricted; G-S 13

SHESHIA (Irish) — I 43[P], I 369[5]

SHE WONT STOP (Irish) — I 12[P], I 253[P], I 291[P], I 379[4], I 528[P], I 578[3], I 604[P]

SHILDON(IRE) b.g. 8 Ovac (ITY) - Hal's Pauper by Official Cooper Wilson
1995 P(0),F(-),P(0),P(0)
416 9/3 Charm Park (L) MDO 3m 13 G *ld 3rd-3 out, hdd, fdd rpdly aftr* 6 0
518 16/3 Dalton Park (R) MDO 3m 15 G *ld to 15th, 4th & in tch whn blnd & u.r. nxt* U -
585 23/3 Wetherby Po' (L) RES 3m 13 S *ld til nrly c.o. 10th, wknd nxt, p.u. 14th* P 0
986 8/4 Charm Park (L) MDN 3m 10 GF *cls up, 3rd 13th, 4th frm 4 out, nvr nrr* 4 0
1286 27/4 Easingwold (L) MDO 3m 13 G *mid-div, u.r. 2nd* U -
1462 10/5 Market Rasen (R) HC 2 3/4m 110yds 11 G *ld apr 1st, hit and hdd next, rdn approaching 9th, soon wknd, t.o. when p.u. after 12th.* P 0

Completed only 2 of 10 races 95/6 & beat 2 other finishers; much more needed 10

SHILGROVE PLACE ch.g. 14 Le Bavard (FR) - Petmon by Eudaemon Col S R Allen
1995 3(11),F(-),4(23),2(22),2(19),P(0),P(0),2(17)
1 13/1 Larkhill (R) XX 3m 7 GS *reluc to race, t.o. whn f 1st* F -

Disappeared 1st fence of season & looks finished now 0

SHILLELAGH OAK (Irish) — I 31[P], I 109[P], I 227[P], I 266[P], I 388[2], I 528[2]

SHILLELEGH OAK (Irish) — I 481[4]

SHIMANO (Irish) — I 27[P], I 89[5], I 133[4], I 228[P], I 345[2], I 416[4], I 500[F], I 618[P]

SHIMNA RIVER (Irish) — I 174[U], I 407[P], I 450[P], I 493[P], I 598[F]

SHIMSHEK(USA) b.g. 12 Gold Stage (USA) - Marie de Retz by Reliance II Mrs P King

9 14/1 Cottenham (R) OPE 3m 13 G *knckd over 2nd* F -
104 17/2 Marks Tey (L) OPE 3m 14 G *prom to 11th, bhnd & p.u. appr 15th, lame* P 0

Broke down in 94 & suffered again in 96 - looks finished now 0

SHINE A LIGHT ch.g. 6 K-Battery - Lady Jay by Double Jump — Neil Bennett

1136 20/4 Hornby Cast' (L) MDN 3m 11 G *prom til lost plc 9th, t.o. & p.u. 12th* P 0
1356 4/5 Mosshouses (L) MDO 3m 12 GS *mstk 8th, rear, no ch 14th, styd on frm 2 out* 4 0

Well beaten in weak race but should do better with experience 10

SHINING GEM b.m. 10 Sunyboy - Tourmalina by Ragstone — Ms Sally Page-Ratcliff

1187 21/4 Tweseldown (R) MDN 3m 11 GF *prom, hit 2nd, wknd 9th, f heavily 12th, winded* F -
1504 11/5 Kingston Bl' (L) MDO 3m 13 G *sn last, t.o. & p.u. 10th* P 0

Rarely runs & does not finish 0

SHINING MINSTREL (Irish) — I 13P

SHIPMATE ch.g. 14 Be Friendly - Maytide by Vimadee — R S Hunnisett

1995 P(0),5(0),1(12),9(0),4(12),7(0),7(0)

179 18/2 Horseheath (R) OPE 3m 5 G *t.o. 7th, btn over 2 fences* 3 0
392 9/3 Garthorpe (R) MEM 3m 6 G *last pair frm 7th, t.o. 12th* 4 0
538 17/3 Southwell P' (L) XX 3m 6 GS *rear, prog to 4th & in tch 12th, sn wknd, t.o. & p.u. 3 out* P 0
793 2/4 Heythrop (R) OPE 4m 10 F *lost tch 10th, t.o. 14th* 6 0
1022 13/4 Brocklesby ' (L) CON 3m 6 GF *alwys rear, last whn hit 8th & t.o.* 5 0
1179 21/4 Mollington (R) LAD 3m 10 F *1st ride, prom to 3rd, rear whn u.r. 8th* U -
1379 5/5 Dingley (R) MXO 3m 7 GF *last pair, t.o. 12th, styd on apr last* 4 0
1520 12/5 Garthorpe (R) LAD 3m 8 GF *t.o. 12th, ran on own pace* 5 0

No longer of any account 0

SHIP THE BUILDER ch.g. 7 Politico (USA) - Early Run by Deep Run — T R Calam

1995 **10(NH),18(NH)**

229 24/2 Duncombe Pa' (R) MDO 3m 13 GS *f 4th* F -
1095 14/4 Whitwell-On' (R) MDO 2 1/2m 88yds 14 G *rear, gd prog to chs ldrs 10th, no imp aft* 5 0
1286 27/4 Easingwold (L) MDO 3m 13 G *(Jt fav) mid-div, mstk 5th, s.u. apr 9th* S -
1451 6/5 Witton Cast' (R) MDO 3m 12 G *rear, prog 8th, cls up 4 out, 2nd aft 2 out, outpcd by wnnr* 2 13

Beat subsequent winner when 2nd & should certainly go close in 97 14

SHIRDANTE (Irish) — I 63F

SHIREOAK'S FLYER ch.g. 8 Hell's Gate - Velocidad by Balidar — D J W Edmunds

1995 U(-),F(-)

636 23/3 Market Rase' (L) MDN 3m 11 GF *broke leather 1st, p.u. 4th* P 0
726 31/3 Garthorpe (R) RES 3m 16 G *s.s. last til u.r. 3rd* U -

Yet to complete the course & managed 5 fences in 96 0

SHOCKING SCOUSE (Irish) — I 571P

SHOON WIND b.g. 13 Green Shoon - Gone by Whistling Wind — J N Dalton

1995 3(14)

159 17/2 Weston Park (L) CON 3m 22 G *hld up in tch, ran on clsng stgs, nrst fin* 3 16
289 2/3 Eaton Hall (R) CON 3m 10 G *prog 6th, ld 12th-2 out, ev ch last, no ext nr line* 2 22
664 24/3 Eaton Hall (R) CON 3m 15 S *mid-div, styd on frm 3 out, no ch 1st pair* 3 14
880 6/4 Brampton Br' (R) XX 3m 8 GF *(fav) mid-div, prog 9th, trckd ldr 12th, ld 3 out, easily* 1 23
1042 13/4 Bitterley (L) CON 3m 9 G *cls 2nd til ld 8th, gd jmp & drew clr frm 15th* 1 23
1171 20/4 Chaddesley ' (L) OPE 3m 15 G *ld 2nd, cls 2nd til ld 14th, hdd & no ext 17th, kpt on* 2 24
1219 24/4 Brampton Br' (R) CON 3m 9 G *(fav) ld 1st & frm 11th, drw clr aft nxt, unchal* 1 22
1618 27/5 Chaddesley ' (L) CON 3m 14 GF *(fav) chsd ldr til ld 5th, clr 15th, unchal* 1 25
1643 2/6 Dingley (R) OPE 3m 13 GF *fast away, ld to 13th, with ldr whn f nxt* F -

Winning chaser; revived well 96; solid form; can win more at 14; G-F 23

SHORE LANE ch.g. 7 Mirror Boy - Derry Island by Varano — G C Musgrave

1995 P(0),U(-)

328 3/3 Market Rase' (L) RES 3m 9 G *lost tch 13th, t.o. & p.u. last* P 0
411 9/3 Charm Park (L) RES 3m 20 G *in tch to hlfwy, wknd 13th, p.u. 4 out* P 0
1094 14/4 Whitwell-On' (R) MDO 2 1/2m 88yds 16 G *mid-div, prog 7th, ev ch 5 out, wknd nxt, p.u. last* P 0
1470 11/5 Easingwold (L) MDO 3m 10 G *bhnd frm 8th, strgglng 14th, t.o.* 5 0

Last on only completion from 6 starts 95/6 0

SHORTCASTLE ch.g. 10 Lucifer (USA) - Skivvy by Nice Guy — T J Sunderland

1995 P(0),13(0),U(-)

230 24/2 Heythrop (R) MEM 3m 12 GS *cls up to hlfwy, wknd, t.o. & p.u. last* P 0
337 3/3 Heythrop (R) OPE 3m 10 G *cls up to 12th, sn outpcd, wll btn whn slw jmp 2 out* 6 0

537 17/3 Southwell P' (L) OPE 3m 7 GS *chsng grp, nvr dang* 4 0
709 30/3 Barbury Cas' (L) OPE 3m 15 G *cls up to 9th, lost tch 11th, t.o. & u.r. 13th* U -
1015 13/4 Kingston Bl' (L) MEM 3m 9 G *cls up, rider lost irons svrl fences, outpcd 14th, no ch aft* 6 10
1180 21/4 Mollington (R) OPE 3m 5 F *s.s. last til p.u. aft 8th* P 0
1438 6/5 Ashorne (R) XX 3m 14 G *alwys bhnd, t.o. 7th, ref 13th, lame* R -

Novice ridden & no form 0

SHORT CIRCUIT (Irish) — **I** 148[2], **I** 243[P], **I** 438[4]
SHORT OF A BUCK (Irish) — **I** 85[F], **I** 165[P], **I** 232[F], **I** 417[F], **I** 581[6]
SHORT SHOT b.g. 10 Young Generation - Blessed Damsel by So Blessed Mrs C Howell

263 2/3 Didmarton (L) INT 3m 18 G *s.v.s. t.o. til p.u. 13th* P 0
549 17/3 Erw Lon (L) RES 3m 11 GS *ref to race* 0 0
844 6/4 Howick (L) RES 3m 10 GF *ref 1st* R -

Unfortunately revived in 96 - hopefully seen the last of him 0

SHOTIVOR b.g. 10 Official - Penny's Daughter by Angus M A Humphreys

72 11/2 Wetherby Po' (L) CON 3m 18 GS *alwys rear, p.u. 3 out* P 0

Maiden winner 94; missed 95 & soon vanished 96 0

SHOULDOFDONE gr.g. 7 Alias Smith (USA) - Snare by Poaching Miss H Vickers
1995 **P(NH)**

245 25/2 Southwell P' (L) LAD 3m 8 HO *raced wd, made most frm 6th til aft 4 out, sn wknd* 3 11

Ran well in decent race but vanished after 15

SHOW THE LIGHT (Irish) — **I** 526[F]
SHOW YOUR HAND (Irish) — **I** 393[1], **I** 498[2], **I** 525[P], **I** 560[4]
SHRULE HILL (Irish) — **I** 228[P], **I** 269[5], **I** 403[1]
SHUIL DAINGEAN (Irish) — **I** 22[3], **I** 172[1], **I** 287[2]
SHUIL MOR (Irish) — **I** 173[P], **I** 282[P]
SHUILNAMON (Irish) — **I** 353,
SHUIL POIPIN(IRE) b or br.m. 7 Buckskin (FR) - Shuil Comeragh by Laurence O Wickfield Farm Partnership

1212 24/4 Andoversford (R) MEM 3m 5 G *last & jmpd slwly 2nd & 3rd, blndrd 4th, ref & u.r. 5th* R -

Disaster in only point but ran much better under Rules after 14

SHUIL'S STAR(IRE) b.g. 5 Henbit (USA) - Shuil Run by Deep Run Bob Mason

553 17/3 Erw Lon (L) MDN 3m 3 GS *rear, nvr thrtnd wnr, ran on frm last* 2 0
773 31/3 Pantyderi (R) MDN 3m 8 G *s.s. rear, prog 4 out, hrd rdn to ld flat* 1 13
1038 13/4 St Hilary (R) RES 3m 15 G *(fav) rear, gd prog 14th, disp 2 out, ld last & lft clr* 1 18

Promising; Restricted win in fair time; slightly suspect but should progress; Good 20

SIAMSA BRAE (Irish) — **I** 89[P], **I** 269[P], **I** 305[4], **I** 388[P]
SIDCUP HILL (Irish) — **I** 66[1], **I** 72[3], **I** 141[2]
SIDE BRACE(NZ) gr.g. 12 Mayo Mellay (NZ) - Grey Mist (NZ) by Karayar J S Swindells

76 11/2 Wetherby Po' (L) LAD 3m 8 GS *alwys wll in rear, p.u. 4 out* P 0
291 2/3 Eaton Hall (R) LAD 3m 10 G *mid-div, prog 6th, onepcd frm 4 out* 4 15
486 16/3 Newcastle (L) HC 3m 9 GS *in tch, lost pl before 9th, rallied 11th, struggling last 3.* 4 13
736 31/3 Sudlow Farm (R) CON 3m 9 G *chsd wnnr to 12th & agn 2 out, onepcd und pres* 2 18
1028 13/4 Alpraham (R) MEM 3m 5 GS *chsd ldrs, not alwys fluent, ev ch frm 3 out, just btn* 2 16
1457 8/5 Uttoxeter (L) HC 3 1/4m 16 G *mstk 3rd, in tch till outpcd 15th.* 5 12

Missed 95; placed in 13 of last 17 points & ungenuine 14

SIDELINER ch.g. 8 Green Shoon - Emmalina by Doubtless II A Hollingsworth
1995 3(10),3(10),1(15),P(0)

231 24/2 Heythrop (R) XX 3m 10 GS *rear, prog to 3rd at 12th, grad wknd* 5 0
428 9/3 Upton-On-Se' (R) RES 3m 17 GS *svrl pstns 1st cct, 4th at 15th, onepcd* 6 0
684 30/3 Chaddesley ' (L) RES 3m 14 G *mid-div, pshd alng 11th, 5th & ch 3 out, onepcd* 5 15
946 8/4 Andoversford (R) RES 3m 10 GF *alwys prom, ld 14th til jnd 3 out, sn hdd, onepcd* 3 15
1173 20/4 Chaddesley ' (L) RES 3m 18 G *mid-div, 25l 6th aft 14th, wknd frm 3 out* 8 0
1481 11/5 Bredwardine (R) RES 3m 14 G *cls up til not qckn frm 14th* 4 12

Maiden winner 95; safe but non-stayer & Restricted looking most unlikely 13

SIDE STEPPER (Irish) — **I** 222[P], **I** 343[F], **I** 420[P]
SIDEWAYS SALLY (Irish) — **I** 19[F], **I** 96[P], **I** 177[4], **I** 214[2], **I** 285[2], **I** 408[1], **I** 490[5]
SIGN PERFORMER ch.g. 9 Longleat (USA) - Grandgirl by Mansingh (USA) Miss Charlotte Wolstenholme
1995 **8(NH),7(NH)**

15	14/1	Cottenham	(R)	MDN 3m	14	G	*bhnd frm 10th, p.u. 16th*	P 0
419	9/3	High Easter	(L)	RES 3m	10	S	*lst pl qkly aft 5th, p.u. nxt*	P 0
930	8/4	Marks Tey	(L)	MDO 3m	6	G	*alwys bhnd, lost tch 12th, t.o. 16th*	4 0
1261	27/4	Cottenham	(R)	MDO 3m	10	F	*mid-div whn u.r. 1st*	U -

Tailed off last in poor race on only completion 0

SILENT POND (Irish) — I 275P, I 440, , I 541P, I 571P, I 6454

SILENT SNEEZE (Irish) — I 83, I 503, I 632, I 1191, I 2091, I 242, , I 3312

SILKEN ASH (Irish) — I 494F, I 539P

SILK OATS ch.m. 6 Oats - Celtic Silk by Celtic Cone — M S Wilesmith

842	6/4	Maisemore P'	(L)	MDN 3m	17	GF	*sttld rr, blnd 4th, lst tch 9th, bhnd & p.u. appr 13th*	P 0
1315	28/4	Bitterley	(L)	MDO 3m	10	G	*chsd clr ldr, effrt 12th, 15l down 14th, wknd nxt*	5 0

Last when completing but not disgraced & should improve 11

SILKS DOMINO ch.g. 11 Dominion - Bourgeonette by Mummy's Pet — W G Good

1995 6(0)

383	9/3	Llanfrynach	(R)	CON 3m	13	GS	*mstks, rear, lost tch 13th, sn t.o.*	8 0
506	16/3	Magor	(R)	CON 3m	8	GS	*cls up in 2nd/3rd to 13th, wknd rpdly, p.u. last*	P 0
691	30/3	Llanvapley	(L)	CON 3m	15	GS	*5th/6th to hlfwy, lost plc & p.u. 15th*	P 0
845	6/4	Howick	(L)	CON 3m	12	GF	*(bl) alwys rear, t.o. hlfwy, p.u. 3 out*	P 0
1157	20/4	Llanwit Maj'	(R)	CON 3m	11	GS	*rear til blndrd & u.r. 11th*	U -

Placed in Confined 94 but looks finished now 0

SILLY SOVEREIGN b.m. 9 Just A Monarch - Minalto by Thriller — Mrs Angus Campbell

1995 P(0),3(0),P(0),r(-)

572	17/3	Detling	(L)	LAD 3m	10	GF	*rear, t.o. & p.u. 12th*	P 0
780	31/3	Penshurst	(L)	MDN 3m	12	GS	*(bl) ld to 2nd, styd in tch, wknng in 6th whn p.u. 13th*	P 0
921	8/4	Aldington	(L)	MDO 3m	8	F	*raced in 5th/6th wth stablemate, t.o. 10th, p.u. 15th*	P 0

No signs of any ability 0

SILVER BLEND (Irish) — I 36P, I 52P, I 438P

SILVER BOW (Irish) — I 74P

SILVER BUCKLE (Irish) — I 143, I 265, I 1111, I 160P, I 2292, I 349P

SILVER CONCORD gr.g. 8 Absalom - Boarding House by Shack (USA) — Mrs D E Cheshire

221	24/2	Newtown	(L)	MDN 3m	12	GS	*10s-4s, hld up, prog aft 12th, sn lost tch, p.u. 2 out*	P 0
479	10/3	Tweseldown	(R)	MDO 3m	10	G	*dist 5th hlfwy, prog 11th, lft clr 3 out, fin tired*	1 10
787	31/3	Tweseldown	(R)	RES 3m	9	G	*8s-4s,w.w. prog 12th,styd on wll to ld apr last,all out*	1 16
1188	21/4	Tweseldown	(R)	OPE 3m	6	GF	*cls up frm 12th, rdn 4 out, ld aft 2 out, hdd nr fin*	2 19

Missed 95; improved & enterprising campaign; could find Tweseldown Open in 97; G-F 19

SILVER FIG ch.m. 9 True Song - Spartan Clown by Spartan General — J Mahon

1995 2(16),B(-),6(0),P(0)

688	30/3	Chaddesley '	(L)	MDN 3m	17	G	*(fav) mounted on course, w.w. mid-div, lsot tch 11th, p.u. 13th*	P 0
1047	13/4	Bitterley	(L)	MDO 3m	13	G	*ld 3rd, lft clr 12th, kpt on frm 2 out*	1 16
1222	24/4	Brampton Br'	(R)	RES 3m	11	G	*2nd/3rd til chsd ldr 3 out, no ex nxt, lost 2nd flat*	3 17
1439	6/5	Ashorne	(R)	RES 3m	11	G	*t.d.e. prom til lost plc & outpcd 12th,ran on 2 out,nrst fin*	2 18

Has ability but hard ride; good enough for Restricteds but may struggle to win one; G-S 17

SILVER HOLLOW gr.g. 11 True Song - Wilspoon Hollow by Wolver Hollow — Mrs P M Pile

1995 P(0),U(-),P(0)

642	23/3	Siddington	(L)	RES 3m	15	S	*tubed, wll bhnd frm 5th, t.o. whn ref 10th*	R -

Dead 0

SILVER SHILLING gr.g. 9 Sonnen Gold - Continental Divide by Sharp Edge — Mrs D Cockburn

1995 **4(NH),8(NH),P(NH)**

51	4/2	Alnwick	(L)	MDO 3m	17	G	*alwys bhnd, t.o. & p.u. 3 out*	P 0

Brief appearance & time passing 0

SILVER SIROCCO (Irish) — I 4641

SILVER STEP gr.g. 10 Step Together (USA) - Rainsky by Bahrain — Mrs D Thomas

1995 **U(-)**,P(0),P(0)

1038	13/4	St Hilary	(R)	RES 3m	15	G	*alwys rear, p.u. 3 out*	P 0
1203	21/4	Lydstep	(L)	RES 3m	5	S	*rear, p.u. 4th*	P 0
1266	27/4	Pyle	(R)	RES 3m	10	G	*chsd ldr to 8th, wknd 12th, p.u. 14th*	P 0

Irish Maiden winner; no completions from 6 starts 95/6 0

SIMPLY A STAR(IRE) ch.g. 6 Simply Great (FR) - Burren Star by Hardgreen (USA) — M W Easterby

72	11/2	Wetherby Po'	(L)	CON	3m	18	GS	*bhnd early, prog 14th, 3rd 4 out, chal whn u.r. 2 out*	U	-
169	18/2	Market Rase'	(L)	CON	3m	15	GF	*(fav) w.w. prog 10th, hit 12th, 3rd & rdn apr 2 out, no ext*	4	17
223	24/2	Duncombe Pa'	(R)	CON	3m	16	GS	*(fav) w.w. prog 9th, chal apr last, drew clr und pres flat*	1	21
410	9/3	Charm Park	(L)	OPE	3m	17	G	*(fav) rr early, prog 12th, 20l 3rd 2 out, too much to do*	3	19

Right connections & quite able; finished early but should wina gain if fit 97; G-S 21

SIMPLY JOYFUL b.m. 9 Idiot's Delight - Royal Pam by Pamroy — Mrs G Greenwood

1995 4(0),P(0)

200	24/2	Lemalla	(R)	MDO	3m	12	HY	*chsd ldrs, 2nd frm 4 out, no ch wth wnr*	2	12
471	10/3	Milborne St'	(L)	MDO	3m	16	G	*mid-div, lost tch 15th, onepcd aft*	6	0
658	23/3	Badbury Rin'	(L)	MDO	3m	8	G	*whipped round and u.r. start*	U	-
1140	20/4	Flete Park	(R)	OPE	4m	6	S	*cls 3rd til lost plc 14th, bhnd whn p.u. 4 out*	P	0
1396	6/5	Cotley Farm	(L)	MDO	3m	11	GF	*alwys mid-div, 3rd 4 out, not trble 1st 2*	3	0

Placed 5 times 94-6 but well beaten each time & improvement needed for any chance 11

SIMPLY PERFECT b.g. 10 Wassl - Haneena by Habitat — J S Swindells

1995 P(0),R(-),3(16),U(-),1(21),**U(-),2(23)**

184	23/2	Haydock	(L)	HC	3m	9	GS	*in tch, chsd wnr from 15th, ev ch 2 out, no ext.*	2	22
460	9/3	Eyton-On-Se'	(L)	LAD	3m	10	G	*(fav) mid-div, 3rd at 12th, lft 2nd 3 out,ran on onepcd clsng stgs*	2	21
487	16/3	Newcastle	(L)	HC	3m	10	GS	*(Co fav) settld in tch, chsd ldrs 7th, outpcd final 3.*	6	0
893	6/4	Whittington	(L)	LAD	3m	4	F	*(fav) lft 1l 2nd 3 out, rddn & no ext*	2	18
1120	20/4	Bangor	(L)	HC	2 1/2m 110yds	13	S	*bhnd, mstk 4th, t.o. 7th, kept on steadily from four out, n.d..*	4	12
1330	30/4	Huntingdon	(R)	HC	2 1/2m 110yds	8	GF	*prog 9th, blnd next, rdn apr 2 out, went 2nd run-in, not trbl wnr.*	2	20
1463	10/5	Stratford	(L)	HC	3m	6	GF	*cld 12th, rdn 4 out, one pace.*	3	17
1615	27/5	Wetherby	(L)	HC	2 1/2m 110yds	11	G	*in tch, went 2nd between last 2, no ch with wnr.*	2	20

Ladies winner 95; retains ability but very hard to win with now; H/Chase places likely 97; G/F-S 20

SIMPLY STANLEY b.g. 9 Ovac (ITY) - C Jay's Lady by Red Alert — B Henton

1995 P(0),U(-),r(-),5(0)

541	17/3	Southwell P'	(L)	MDO	3m	9	GS	*prom, chsng grp to 3 out, btn whn p.u. last*	P	0

Has a hint of ability but soon disappeared in 96 0

SINBERTO b.m. 9 - Silberto — M A Connolly

1101	14/4	Guilsborough	(L)	RES	3m	16	G	*ld to 5th, prom til wknd rpdly & p.u. 13th*	P	0
1242	27/4	Woodford	(L)	RES	3m	18	G	*ld to 14th, wknd rpdly & p.u. nxt*	P	0

Maiden winner 93; absent since & looks to have met more problems now 12

SINEAD'S JOY (Irish) — **I** 223^{P}, **I** 347^{P}

SINERGIA (Irish) — **I** 21^{P}, **I** 109^{P}, **I** 169, , **I** 283^{3}, **I** 395^{P}, **I** 413^{P}, **I** 554^{2}, **I** 585, , **I** 599^{P}

SINGH SONG b.m. 6 True Song - Regal Ranee by Indian Ruler — Richard Chandler

1105	14/4	Guilsborough	(L)	MDN	3m	12	G	*rear, effrt 9th, rdn 12th, sn wknd & p.u. nxt*	P	0

No real promise but cleverly named 0

SINGING CLOWN ch.m. 11 True Song - Copperclown by Spartan General — R Jeffrey

1995 P(0),P(0),P(0),4+(0),5(0)

129	17/2	Kingston Bl'	(L)	MDN	3m	15	GS	*mid-div,outpcd 13th,styd on und pres 2 out,lft in ld last*	1	12
437	9/3	Newton Brom'	(R)	RES	3m	9	GS	*chsd ldr til ld/disp 9th-2 out, styd on onepcd*	2	16
641	23/3	Siddington	(L)	RES	3m	20	S	*chsd ldrs, strugg 13th, no ch whn p.u. 2 out*	P	0
1101	14/4	Guilsborough	(L)	RES	3m	16	G	*mstk 3rd, alwys bhnd, t.o. & p.u. 13th*	P	0
1176	21/4	Mollington	(R)	MEM	3m	6	F	*1st ride, t.o. 4th, nrly ref 7th & p.u.*	P	0

Handed a bad race on a plate; ran well next time but unlikely to figure in 97 12

SINGING SEAL ch.g. 15 Privy Seal - Blue Song by Majority Blue — H Wilson

1995 P(0),P(0)

394	9/3	Garthorpe	(R)	LAD	3m	6	G	*last frm 7th, t.o. 9th*	4	0
722	31/3	Garthorpe	(R)	MEM	3m	4	G	*prom, ld 9-11th, 3rd & btn whn u.r. 14th*	U	-
970	8/4	Thorpe Lodge	(L)	LAD	3m	6	GF	*nvr dang, t.o. 10th, p.u. flat*	P	0

No longer of any account 0

SIOUX PERFICK b.m. 7 Blakeney - Siouxsie by Warpath — P Downes

1995 4(11),P(0)

748	31/3	Upper Sapey	(R)	MDO	3m	11	GS	*rmndrs 2nd, t.o. whn p.u. 16th*	P	0
884	6/4	Brampton Br'	(R)	MDN	3m	12	GF	*prom at 8th, in tch til wknd aft 16th, p.u. last*	P	0
1224	24/4	Brampton Br'	(R)	MDO	3m	17	G	*rr frm 6th, lost tch & p.u. 12th*	P	0

Ran reasonably on debut in 95 but disappointing since with no completions 0

SIR-EILE (Irish) — **I** 184^{3}, **I** 378^{4}, **I** 505^{S}, **I** 573^{1}, **I** 611^{F}, **I** 648^{F}

SIR FREDERICK (Irish) — I 56^{P}, I 79^{4}, I 188^{P}

SIR GALEFORCE(IRE) br.g. 6 Mister Lord (USA) - Forest Gale by Strong Gale — E H Crow

569	17/3	Wolverhampt'	(L)	MDN	3m	11	GS	*ld 9th, clr 3 out, styd on well*	1	13
684	30/3	Chaddesley '	(L)	RES	3m	14	G	*plld hrd, chsd ldr 4th til u.r. 6th*	U	-
1223	24/4	Brampton Br'	(R)	RES	3m	11	G	*(fav) rr til prog 14th, not rch ldrs, p.u. 3 out*	P	0

Won a bad race & not progressed; may do better with forcing tactics; improvement needed 14

SIR GALLOP (Irish) — I 288^{P}, I 341^{U}, I 402^{4}, I 403^{P}, I 495^{P}, I 561^{U}, I 588, , I 599^{P}

SIR GEORGE CHUFFY(IRE) b.g. 8 Welsh Term - Grand Legacy by Relko — T D B Barlow

1995 3(10),1(14),F(-)

1028	13/4	Alpraham	(R)	MEM	3m	5	GS	*ld most to 10th, qckly p.u. apr nxt*	P	0

Maiden winner 95; ungenuine & soon disappeared 96 11

SIR HARRY RINUS ch.g. 10 Golden Love - Teresa Jane by My Swanee — Mrs Andrea Fisher

398	9/3	Dalston	(R)	MEM	3m	13	G	*cls up frm 8th, styd prom, chsd ldr frm 3 out, styd on sm pc*	2	10
755	31/3	Lockerbie	(R)	MDN	3m	17	G	*alwys hndy, 3rd hlfwy, wknd 3 out*	4	0

Not disgraced but beaten long way last start & hard to win at 11 10

SIRISAT ch.g. 12 Cisto (FR) - Gay Ruin by Master Spiritus — Miss T O Blazey

1995 1(22),2(21),1(21),**F(-)**

139	17/2	Larkhill	(R)	CON	3m	11	G	*prom, ld 5th-7th, wknd frm 15th, onepcd*	5	18
262	2/3	Didmarton	(L)	MEM	3m	11	G	*trckd ldrs, outpcd whn blnd 12th, wknd*	6	0
792	2/4	Heythrop	(R)	LAD	3 3/4m	7	F	*prssd ldr to 13th, 3rd aft til ran on last, ld nr fin*	1	17
958	8/4	Lockinge	(L)	MXO	3m	6	GF	*mstly 4th, nvr on terms wth 1st 2*	3	14
1165	20/4	Larkhill	(R)	LAD	3m	7	GF	*ld til 10th, styd prom, ev ch 3 out, not qckn*	2	19
1291	28/4	Barbury Cas'	(L)	LAD	3m	5	F	*prog & cls up 11th, ld 12th-nxt, chsd wnr, no imp 2 out*	2	19
1394	6/5	Cotley Farm	(L)	MXO	3m	5	GF	*(fav) w.w., 4th at 10th, 2nd 12th, outpcd frm 3 out*	2	15

Changed hands; novice ridden 96; won weak race; hard to find another at 13; Any 15

SIR LARRY (Irish) — I 162^{F}, I 223^{P}, I 267^{4}

SIR NODDY ch.g. 13 Tom Noddy - Pinzarose by Pinzan — G W Briscoe

485	16/3	Hereford	(R)	HC	3m 1f 110yds	13	S	*ld, clr to 11th, clear again 14th, joined 3 out, hdd last, soon btn.*	3	21
672	29/3	Aintree	(L)	HC	2 3/4m	26	G	*pressed ldr, ld 4 out to last, kept on well till no ext cl home.*	3	30
1032	13/4	Alpraham	(R)	CON	3m	9	GS	*(fav) ld til hdd apr last, no ext*	2	22

Dead 29

SIRRAH ARIS (Irish) — I 74^{F}, I 114^{P}, I 148^{P}, I 351^{1}, I 505^{U}, I 547^{1}, I 611^{4}

SIR WAGER b.g. 15 Immortal Knight - Fine Flutter by Flush Royal — Mrs B Ansell

1995 P(0),6(0),3(0),7(0),3(0),6(0),4(0)

249	25/2	Charing	(L)	XX	3m	11	GS	*(bl) t.o. 6th, p.u. 8th*	P	0
453	9/3	Charing	(L)	XX	3m	4	G	*(bl) ld to 4th, lost tch 7th, wll bhnd whn p.u. aft 11th*	P	0
813	6/4	Charing	(L)	XX	3m	5	F	*(bl) sn last, jmpd slwly & nvr going, p.u. aft 6th*	P	0

Deserves retirement 0

SISTER EMU b.m. 9 Buckskin (FR) - Hill Master by Master Owen — M D Gichero

1995 P(0)

243	25/2	Southwell P'	(L)	RES	3m	11	HO	*lost plc 4th,prog frm rear 4 out,ld 2 out,sn clr, drvn out*	1	19
563	17/3	Wolverhampt'	(L)	XX	3m	4	GS	*(fav) rear, mstk & u.r. 2nd*	U	-
1009	9/4	Flagg Moor	(L)	CON	3m	7	G	*prog 10th, ev ch 15th, wknd qckly app 2 out*	3	13
1302	28/4	Southwell P'	(L)	INT	3m	10	GF	*(Jt fav) hld up, hrd rdn 6 out, no imp*	5	0

Disappointing till ploughed through mud 1st start; nothing since & best watched start of 97; Soft 14

SISTER LARK ch.m. 7 True Song - Seeker's Sister by Ashmore (FR) — N B Jones

1995 F(-)

4	13/1	Larkhill	(R)	MDO	3m	9	GS	*ld til aft 1st, t.o. last 7th, plodded on*	5	0
44	3/2	Wadebridge	(L)	MDO	3m	9	GF	*ld to 3rd, mid-div & rdn 12th, sn outpcd, fin well*	4	10
152	17/2	Erw Lon	(L)	MDN	3m	11	G	*ld, 5l clr 9th, p.u. qckly 13th*	P	0
207	24/2	Castle Of C'	(R)	MDO	3m	15	HY	*alwys mid-div, t.o. & p.u. 14th*	P	0
390	9/3	Llanfrynach	(R)	MDN	3m	13	GS	*(bl) clr ldr til hdd 2 out, rallied & ev ch last, just hld*	2	14
551	17/3	Erw Lon	(L)	MDN	3m	8	GS	*(fav) ld to 4 out, wknd*	4	0
696	30/3	Llanvapley	(L)	MDN	3m	13	GS	*(Jt fav) (vis) alwys prom, 2nd 13th-3 out, ev ch last, wknd, tired*	4	0
849	6/4	Howick	(L)	MDN	3m	14	GF	*3rd/4th til chsd wnr 15th, no imp, lost 2nd flat*	3	10
1039	13/4	St Hilary	(R)	MDN	3m	14	G	*ld, clr 14th, tired 3 out, ct flat*	2	12
1335	1/5	Cheltenham	(L)	HC	2m 5f	10	G	*chsd ldrs 7th, rdn and lost pl 8th, blnd 11th, t.o..*	7	0
1492	11/5	Erw Lon	(L)	MDO	3m	10	F	*(fav) ld/disp til ld 14th, easily*	1	13
1602	25/5	Bassaleg	(R)	CON	3m	8	GS	*prom to 5th, wknd 9th, p.u. nxt*	P	0

Non-stayer but eventually found her chance; Restricted looks almost impossible 13

SISTERLY b.m. 10 Brotherly (USA) - Wee Jennie by Vimadee — Peter Nash
1995 P(0),4(14),3(15)

21 20/1 Barbury Cas' (L) MEM 3m 16 GS *blnd 8th,prssd wnr to 10th,wknd 14th,lft 3rd 2 out,f last* F -
170 18/2 Market Rase' (L) XX 3m 8 GF *ld 1st, sn hdd, prom, ld 2 out, hdd & onepcd last* 2 20
214 24/2 Newtown (L) CON 3m 21 GS *ld 6th, clr 13th, hdd & wknd 2 out* 3 19
426 9/3 Upton-On-Se' (R) CON 3m 16 GS *effrt frm 11th, disp 2 out, sn ld & clr* 1 19

Dual winner 94; consistent but needs easy 3m; finished early; can win Confined if fit 97; G/S-F 20

SISTER SEAT b.m. 10 Cisto (FR) - Quay Seat by Quayside — T R Darlington

569 17/3 Wolverhampt' (L) MDN 3m 11 GS *mid-div, no ch whn p.u. 14th* P 0
852 6/4 Sandon (L) MDN 3m 9 GF *chsdng grp to hlf way, fdd qckly, wll btn* 6 0

Beaten miles when completing 0

SISTER SEVEN (Irish) — I 222^{P}, I 347^{1}, I 406^{5}

SIT TIGHT b.g. 7 Buckley - Chaise Longue by Full Of Hope — Miss S Pilkington
1995 F(-),5(0),4(0),2(0)

2 13/1 Larkhill (R) MDO 3m 17 GS *chsd ldrs, outpcd frm 12th, no dang aft* 5 0
143 17/2 Larkhill (R) MDO 3m 14 G *alwys prom, ran on wll frm last, tk 2nd nr fin* 2 14
268 2/3 Didmarton (L) MDN 3m 10 G *prom til blnd & u.r. 6th* U -
643 23/3 Siddington (L) MDN 3m 16 S *disp whn blnd 11th, ld 3 out, blnd & u.r. nxt* U -
997 8/4 Hackwood Pa' (L) MDO 3m 11 GF *(fav) nvr in contention, p.u. aft 13th* P 0
1242 27/4 Woodford (L) RES 3m 18 G *chsd ldrs, 4th hlfwy, wknd apr 3 out, 6th whn p.u. 2 out* P 0
1381 5/5 Dingley (R) MDO 3m 16 GF *in tch, went 3rd & outpcd 14th, kpt on to chs wnr apr last* 2 11

Placed 4 times 95/6 but not threatening & more needed for a win 13

SIX OF SPADES (Irish) — I 127^{P}, I 203^{1}

SIXTH IN LINE(IRE) ch.g. 8 Deep Run - Yellow Lotus by Majority Blue — R G Chapman
1995 F(-),P(0),P(0),P(0),F(-)

71 10/2 Great Treth' (R) MDO 3m 15 S *bhnd frm 4th, p.u. 7th* P 0
201 24/2 Lemalla (R) MDO 3m 13 HY *prom early, losing tch whn p.u. aft 11th* P 0
299 2/3 Great Treth' (R) MDO 3m 13 G *twrds rear til p.u. 16th* P 0
630 23/3 Kilworthy (L) MDN 3m 10 GS *prom, mstk 8th, 3rd & outpcd 15th, no imp ldrs aft* 4 0
1071 13/4 Lifton (R) MDN 3m 10 S *mid-div, 4th & no ch frm 3 out, walked in* 4 0
1430 6/5 High Bickin' (R) MDO 3m 8 G *ld/disp, lft in ld whn blnd badly last, not rcvrd* 4 13
1554 18/5 Bratton Down (L) MDO 3m 16 F *mid-div, 7th & wd bnd aft 13th, no dang clsg stgs* 6 0
1627 27/5 Lifton (R) MDO 3m 9 GS *sn prom, slght ld 12th til f 3 out* F -

Finished only 4 of 13 starts 95/6 & threw away chance 6th outing; improving & may strike lucky 97 13

SIXTY-ONE (Irish) — I 85^{P}, I 195^{P}, I 226^{P}

SKERRY MEADOW b.g. 12 Anfield - Mi Tia by Great Nephew — O J Carter
1995 P(0),**2(NH),P(0),2(NH),P(0),P(0),3(0)**

669 27/3 Chepstow (L) HC 3m 10 S *ld to 2nd, bhnd from 6th, t.o. when p.u. before 12th.* P 0
924 8/4 Bishopsleigh (R) LAD 3m 7 G *in front rank chal whn u.r. 14th* U -
1123 20/4 Stafford Cr' (R) MEM 3m 3 S *disp to 4th, cls up til lost tch 4 out* 3 0
1382 6/5 Exeter (R) HC 2m 7f 110yds 8 GF *alwys well bhnd.* 5 15
1459 8/5 Uttoxeter (L) HC 4 1/4m 8 G *in tch, mstk 9th, lost touch 18th, t.o. and p.u. before 4 out.* P 0

Formerly useful but struggling 95/6 & no real hopes now 12

SKIN GRAFT (Irish) — I 302^{B}, I 336^{3}, I 391^{5}, I 449^{P}, I 558^{5}, I 625^{5}

SKINNHILL b.g. 12 Final Straw - Twenty Two (FR) by Busted — Mrs T Binnington
1995 5(0),5(10),**3(12),P(0)**,3(14),2(15),2(14),5(10),2(15),2(14),2(15)

7 13/1 Larkhill (R) CON 3m 10 GS *(bl) mstk 6th, prom to 14th, wknd rpdly* 7 0
140 17/2 Larkhill (R) CON 3m 17 G *(bl) bhnd til prog 4 out, nrst fin* 4 11
271 2/3 Parham (R) CON 3m 15 GF *(bl) nvr bttr than mid-div, wknd 4 out* 7 11
475 10/3 Tweseldown (R) CON 3m 9 G *(bl) 2nd til mstk 10th, wknd rpdly, ran on agn cls home* 5 15
784 31/3 Tweseldown (R) CON 3m 5 G *(bl) chsd wnr to 11th, sn wknd, lft 3rd apr last* 3 15
995 8/4 Hackwood Pa' (L) XX 3m 8 GF *(fav) ld frm 7th,ran in sntchs,qcknd up 15th,3l clr whn u.r.2 out* U 15
1184 21/4 Tweseldown (R) MEM 3m 4 GF *(fav) (bl) ran in sntchs, disp til rdn 6th, ld 14th, pshd out* 1 16
1289 28/4 Barbury Cas' (L) CON 3m 8 F *(bl) ld, rdn 11th, hdd 14th, prssd wnr aft, alwys hld* 2 19
1375 4/5 Peper Harow (L) CON 3m 9 F *(bl) prom to 8th, last & pshd alng 11th, styd on frm 3 out, n.d.* 3 16
1405 6/5 Hackwood Pa' (L) CON 3m 6 F *(bl) reluctant, hd rdn thro'out, nvr dang* 4 13

Placed 9 times 95/6 but shocked himself when winning; reverted to type after; novice ridden; G-F 15

SKI NUT b.g. 9 Sharpo - Saint Cynthia by Welsh Saint — K D Wright
1995 P(0),8(0),7(0),P(0),4(16),U(-),r(-),2(18),5(10)

5 13/1 Larkhill (R) LAD 3m 10 GS *mid-div, lost tch 12th, poor 6th whn u.r. 3 out* U -
27 20/1 Barbury Cas' (L) LAD 3m 15 GS *wll bhnd frm 8th, t.o. & p.u. 2 out* P 0
216 24/2 Newtown (L) LAD 3m 13 GS *rear, lost tch 10th, no prog 14th, p.u. 2 out* P 0
474 10/3 Tweseldown (R) LAD 3m 7 G *chsd wnr, clr 2nd frm 13th, ch whn blnd 3 out* 2 18
561 17/3 Ottery St M' (L) LAD 3m 12 G *alwys last, t.o. 13th* 7 10

867 6/4 Larkhill (R) MXO 4m 6 F *ld til jnd 5th, hdd 13th, rddn 5 out, no ext, sn btn* 3 0
1186 21/4 Tweseldown (R) LAD 3m 6 GF *immed outpcd, t.o. 8th, lft remote 2nd last* 2 11

Tries but will need very weak race to win; novice ridden; beaten all 16 starts 95/6 14

SKIP'N'TIME b.g. 6 Idiot's Delight - Skipton Bridge by Harwell M S Rose
1995 2(0),2(15)

145 17/2 Larkhill (R) MDO 3m 13 G *ld 6th, hrd rdn apr last, styd on well* 1 18
269 2/3 Didmarton (L) RES 3m 12 G *(Jt fav) trckd ldrs, ld 15th, jnd & bttr jmp last, hdd & outpcd flat* 2 20
1168 20/4 Larkhill (R) RES 3m 8 GF *(fav) ld & gng wll til lost action & p.u. lame aft 12th* P 0

Very promising till problems last start; could go far if fit again 97; Good 21

SKIPPING CHICK (Irish) — **I** 71P, **I** 149P, **I** 507F, **I** 5695, **I** 6094, **I** 650F

SKIPPING GALE b.g. 11 Strong Gale - Skiporetta by Even Money G W Barker
1995 P(0)

304 2/3 Great Stain' (L) OPE 3m 10 GS *cls up to 5th, lost tch 10th, p.u. 15th* P 0
587 23/3 Wetherby Po' (L) OPE 3m 15 S *ld to 10th, wknd 12th, p.u. 14th* P 0
760 31/3 Great Stain' (L) OPE 3m 8 GS *blnd 1st, chsd ldrs til rdn & fdd frm 13th* 5 11
826 6/4 Stainton (R) OPE 3m 8 GF *alwys prom, mstk 13th, kpt on well frm 2 out* 2 19
1134 20/4 Hornby Cast' (L) MEM 3m 6 G *(fav) rear, prog 8th, hit nxt, 2nd 15th, no hdwy aft, onepcd* 3 13
1466 11/5 Easingwold (L) CON 3m 10 G *disp til hdd & onepcd 2 out* 3 15

Revived 96; just beaten 4th start but will find it hard to win again 15

SKIP TRACER b.g. 8 Balliol - Song To Singo by Master Sing Mrs J M Whitley

202 24/2 Lemalla (R) MDO 3m 12 HY *not alwys fluent, p.u. aft 9th* P 0
447 9/3 Haldon (R) MDO 3m 13 S *prog to 3rd whn crashed thro wing 7th* r -

Finished 2 of 14 races 93-6 & showed nothing in 96 0

SKULLDUGERY (Irish) — **I** 385, **I** 124F, **I** 1552

SKY MISSILE b.m. 7 Cruise Missile - Over Dinsdale by Rubor Gavin Douglas

192 24/2 Friars Haugh (L) MDN 3m 12 S *nvr nr ldrs* 5 0
406 9/3 Dalston (R) MDO 2 1/2m 12 G *bhnd, hdwy frm 12th, sm pc frm 13th* 6 0
613 23/3 Friars Haugh (L) MDN 3m 15 G *nvr dang* 9 0

Safe at least but yet to get competitive in any sense 0

SKY RUNNER ch.g. 5 Scallywag - Space Drama by Space King R G E Owen

1033 13/4 Alpraham (R) MDO 2 1/2m 15 GS *last pair in rear, t.o. 4th, p.u. 8th* P 0
1319 28/4 Bitterley (L) MDN 3m 13 G *mid-div, in tch 11th, lost tch 13th, t.o. & p.u. 3 out* P 0
1621 27/5 Chaddesley ' (L) MDO 3m 17 GF *bolted bef start, alwys rear, t.o. & p.u. 11th* P 0

No signs of promise yet 0

SKYVAL ch.m. 6 Domynsky - Derry Island by Varano T Peace
1995 **10(NH),P(NH)**

73 11/2 Wetherby Po' (L) MDO 3m 15 GS *mid-div, 3rd at 13th, onepcd aft* 6 0
176 18/2 Market Rase' (L) MDO 2m 5f 10 GF *prog 9th, 4th & ch whn blnd 3 out, wknd* 5 0
330 3/3 Market Rase' (L) MDO 3m 7 G *chsd ldrs, hit 10th, chal 3 out, ld apr last, rdn clr* 1 13
1025 13/4 Brocklesby ' (L) XX 3m 9 GF *t.o. last frm 7th, p.u. 11th* P 0

Found a bad race when winning & looks to have met a problem after; best watched 12

SKY VENTURE ch.g. 12 Paddy's Stream - Mijette by Pauper Barry Briggs
1995 1(20),2(19),5(12),4(13),3(15),1(14),2(19),1(15)

250 25/2 Charing (L) LAD 3m 12 GS *wll in rear, gd prog 12th, 4th 4 out, kpt on* 3 18
474 10/3 Tweseldown (R) LAD 3m 7 G *outpcd in rear, rdn frm hlfwy, t.o. 13th* 5 0
573 17/3 Detling (L) OPE 4m 9 GF *alwys prom, rdn to ld apr 2 out, hdd last, rallied & ld fin* 1 21
811 6/4 Charing (L) OPE 3m 9 F *alwys mid-div, 8l 3rd 4 out, onepcd* 4 15
1208 21/4 Heathfield (R) LAD 3m 6 F *(fav) rear, clsd up 10th, 2nd 14th-4 out, onepcd* 4 13
1372 4/5 Peper Harow (L) OPE 3m 6 F *prom, ld bfly appr 13th, outpcd nxt, kpt on und press 2 out* 2 17

Won 3 in 95; consistent & Solid & deserved win; struggle to find another at 13; G-F 16

SLADE VALLEY LADY (Irish) — **I** 195F, **I** 232B

SLANEY BEEF (Irish) — **I** 525P, **I** 606P, **I** 647U

SLANEY FOOD (Irish) — **I** 158P, **I** 2213, **I** 3443, **I** 3821, **I** 4121, **I** 5291

SLANEY GODDESS (Irish) — **I** 261

SLANEY GOODNESS (Irish) — **I** 3571, **I** 4261, **I** 5534, **I** 620S, **I** 6483, **I** 657P

SLANEY STANDARD (Irish) — **I** 184, **I** 292

SLANEY SUPREME (Irish) — **I** 658P

SLANEY WIND (Irish) — **I** 17P, **I** 802, **I** 1602, **I** 2202, **I** 342S, **I** 3831, **I** 4231, **I** 584S, **I** 620F, **I** 6563

SLAVICA (Irish) — **I** 2331, **I** 294F, **I** 3763

SLEEPY ROCK (Irish) — I 212^{2}, I 378^{3}, I 508^{P}

SLEETMORE GALE (Irish) — I 354^{3}, I 427^{1}

SLEMISH MIST (Irish) — I 33^{1}, I 102^{P}, I 264^{P}, I 483^{2}

SLIEVE NA BAR(IRE) ch.g. 7 Jamesmead - Ah Well by Silver Cloud — C Dawson

302 2/3 Great Stain' (L) MEM 3m 7 GS *rear, effrt 11th, no imp, poor 6th 2 out, fin 6th, promoted* 5 0
405 9/3 Dalston (R) MDO 2 1/2m 16 G *nvr sn wth chnc* 6 0
704 30/3 Tranwell (L) MDO 3m 16 GS *prom, ld 4th til jnd & f 10th* F -
916 8/4 Tranwell (L) MDO 2 1/2m 8 GF *alwys prom, trckd wnr til wknd und pres 3 out, f nxt,dead* F -

Dead 0

SLIEVENAMON MIST ch.g. 10 Thatching - La Generale by Brigadier Gerard — Nick Viney

1995 4(21),4(12),1(19)

5 13/1 Larkhill (R) LAD 3m 10 GS *chsd ldrs til wknd rpdly 11th, t.o. & p.u. 13th* P 0
1277 27/4 Bratton Down (L) CON 3m 15 GF *hld up, prog 10th, 2nd 12th, disp 15th til clr 2 out, easily* 1 24
1615 27/5 Wetherby (L) HC 2 1/2m 110yds 11 G *ld till after 1st, chsd ldrs, led after 9th, drew well clr from 4 out.* 1 33

Lightly raced but very useful; romped home in H/Chase; can win another; best under 3m; Good 29

SLIGHT PANIC b.m. 8 Lighter - Midnight Panic by Panco — M B Bent

1995 F(-),P(0),1(11),9(0)

742 31/3 Upper Sapey (R) RES 3m 9 GS *6th whn f 10th* F -
1178 21/4 Mollington (R) RES 3m 7 F *hld up, prog to 3rd at 11th, no imp 1st pair frm 3 out* 3 12
1481 11/5 Bredwardine (R) RES 3m 14 G *cls 5th at 7th, chsd ldrs til not qckn frm 13th* 6 10

Maiden winner 95; does not really stay & will struggle to win again 12

SLIM KING b.g. 8 Slim Jim - Bromley Rose by Rubor — Mrs S E Woodward

757 31/3 Great Stain' (L) MEM 3m 5 GS *prom, jmpd rght 4th, mstk 11th, wknd nxt, t.o. & p.u. 2 out* P 0
829 6/4 Stainton (R) MDO 3m 9 GF *alwys rear, jmpd lft 3rd, wll bhnd frm 5 out* 4 0

Well beaten in poor race & well below a rating yet 0

SLIP ALONG SALLY (Irish) — I 196^{P}, I 515^{2}, I 530^{P}, I 604^{U}

SLOOTHAK b.g. 9 Pollerton - Patrician Maid by Milan — A J Wight

1995 5(12)

111 17/2 Lanark (R) RES 3m 6 GS *ld til wknd rpdly apr 3 out* 3 10

Irish Maiden winner 93; only 5 runs 94-6 & looks to have problems now 13

SLOWLY BUT SURELY (Irish) — I 309^{P}, I 380,

SLUMBER HILL (Irish) — I 185^{P}, I 332,

SMART PAL b.g. 11 Balinger - Smart Bird by Stephen George — Bruce Knox

346 3/3 Higham (L) INT 3m 6 G *handy to 11th, wknd 14th, t.o. 16th, p.u. 2 out* P 0
1521 12/5 Garthorpe (R) INT 3m 7 GF *mid to rear, nvr on terms wth ldrs, not qckn* 4 11
1595 25/5 Garthorpe (R) CON 3m 15 G *2nd til ld 10th-6 out, 3rd & outpcd 3 out* 4 13

Dual winner 94; missed 95; changed hands; interrupted season 96; best watched now 13

SMART RHYTHM ch.m. 8 True Song - Clear Thinking by Articulate — R H Woodward

1995 4(10),2(11),2(0)

397 9/3 Garthorpe (R) MDN 3m 9 G *alwys prom, ld 5 out-nxt, hld til rvl blnd last, ld nr fin* 1 15
904 6/4 Dingley (R) RES 3m 20 GS *last trio frm 5th, t.o. 8th, p.u. 12th* P 0
1101 14/4 Guilsborough (L) RES 3m 16 G *in tch to 13th, t.o. & p.u. 3 out* P 0
1235 27/4 Clifton On ' (L) MEM 3m 4 GF *cls up to 8th, last & no ch frm 12th* 4 0

Deserved her win (fortunate) but out of her depth since & Restricted win looks beyond her 11

SMART SONG b.g. 5 True Song - New World by St Columbus — Mrs S Cartridge

688 30/3 Chaddesley ' (L) MDN 3m 17 G *mstk 3rd, in tch to 11th, p.u. apr 4 out* P 0
1433 6/5 Ashorne (R) MDO 3m 16 G *schoold, lost tch 13th, no ch whn hit 2 out & p.u.* P 0

Not competitive yet but should do better in 97 0

SMART TEACHER(USA) b or br.h. 6 Smarten (USA) - Finality (USA) by In Reality — Mrs N R Matthews

1995 **5(NH),5(NH),P(NH)**

943 8/4 Andoversford (R) CON 3m 9 GF *chsd ldrs til aft 12th, wknd & p.u. 14th* P 0

Unencouraging on only display in points 0

SMART WORK ch.m. 8 Giacometti - Highwood Princess by Crooner — M C Wells

248 25/2 Charing (L) RES 3m 12 GS *wll bhnd, steady prog frm 15th, 5th & no ch whn f last* F -
573 17/3 Detling (L) OPE 4m 9 GF *t.o. 8th, p.u. 21st* P 0

Won a dreadful Maiden in 93; missed 94/5 & not well campaigned 96 0

SMILING MINSTREL (Irish) — I 61^P^

SMOOTH ESCORT b.g. 12 Beau Charmeur (FR) - Wishing Trout by Three Wishes — Mrs Ann Lea

1995 6(0),1(20),**2(20)**,7(0),2(12),**3(20)**,**9(0)**

140	17/2	Larkhill	(R)	CON	3m	17	G	*made most to 7th, wknd frm 13th, t.o.*	6	0
475	10/3	Tweseldown	(R)	CON	3m	9	G	*hld up,prog 10th,rdn 3 out,styd on onepcd frm nxt*	3	19
867	6/4	Larkhill	(R)	MXO	4m	6	F	*cls up, lost plc & rddn frm 11th, t.o. 17th, p.u. 3 out*	P	0
1185	21/4	Tweseldown	(R)	CON	3m	4	GF	*(bl) made most to 7th, sn lost tch whn hdd, t.o. 15th*	3	0
1407	6/5	Hackwood Pa'	(L)	XX	3m	5	F	*rdn along, cls up to 11th, fdd*	4	0

Retired **16**

SMOULDER(USA) b.g. 8 Glow (USA) - Whitethroat by Artaius (USA) — R J Rowsell

601	23/3	Howick	(L)	CON	3m	10	S	*mid-div, lost plc 10th, p.u. 12th*	P	0
846	6/4	Howick	(L)	OPE	3m	7	GF	*10s-4s, alwys last, lost tch 9th, p.u. 14th*	P	0

An uninspired gamble & unlikely to burst into flames **12**

SNAPPER b.g. 5 Gunner B - Fortalice by Saucy Kit — R H Black

705	30/3	Tranwell	(L)	MDO	3m	9	GS	*mstk 4th, trckd ldrs frm 13th, ev ch 2 out, not pace of wnr*	2	14
1253	27/4	Balcormo Ma'	(R)	MDO	3m	16	GS	*(fav) ld aft 12th, made rest, held on wll*	1	15

Did nothing wrong & landed 7 3/4mins Maiden; should be fishing for Restriced in 97; G/S **16**

SNIPE LODGE (Irish) — I 41^P^, I 127^F^, I 143^P^, I 203^3^, I 370^P^

SNIPPETOFF b.g. 8 Dubassoff (USA) - Snippet by Ragstone — Mrs P Lucy

849	6/4	Howick	(L)	MDN	3m	14	GF	*2nd/3rd to 13th, drppd out rpdly*	7	0
1161	20/4	Llanwit Maj'	(R)	MDO	3m	15	GS	*bhnd, steady prog to 4th 14th, no prog frm 3 out*	3	0
1248	27/4	Woodford	(L)	MDN	3m	15	G	*rear div, some prog whn f 8th*	F	-

Not disgraced but more needed & vanished after the fall **10**

SNOWFIRE CHAP ch.g. 13 Salluceva - Fainne Nua by Paddy's Birthday — T D B Underwood

1995 3(17),U(-),4(20),2(20),4(17)

142	17/2	Larkhill	(R)	MXO	3m	9	G	*alwys bhnd, t.o. & p.u. 14th*	P	0
271	2/3	Parham	(R)	CON	3m	15	GF	*(bl) prog to trck ldrs hlfwy, fdd 14th*	8	11
451	9/3	Charing	(L)	OPE	3m	11	G	*(bl) cls up, chal 2 out, lvl last, no ext flat*	2	15
795	2/4	Heythrop	(R)	XX	3m	4	F	*(bl) cls up to 12th, btn whn blnd nxt, kpt on*	3	15
996	8/4	Hackwood Pa'	(L)	MXO	3m	4	GF	*(bl) sweating,3rd til cls up 2 out, hrd rdn, ld last, ran on wll*	1	17

Changed hands 96; deteriorating but found weak opening; unlikely to win again; G-F **15**

SNUGGLE ch.m. 9 Music Boy - Sinzinbra by Royal Palace — Mrs J S Wootton

1073	13/4	Lifton	(R)	OPE	3m	10	S	*ref 1st*	R	-
1139	20/4	Flete Park	(R)	RES	3m	14	S	*ref 1st, cont, t.o. & ref 2nd*	R	-
1358	4/5	Flete Park	(R)	RES	3m	8	G	*ref 1st (twice), cont, ref 2nd, cont, t.o. & p.u. 11th*	P	0
1528	12/5	Ottery St M'	(L)	RES	3m	10	GF	*bhnd til p.u. apr 12th, dead*	P	0

Dead **0**

SNUGGLEDOWN (Irish) — I 104^P^, I 140^U^, I 152^P^

SOCIAL CLIMBER b or br.g. 12 Crash Course - What A Duchess by Bargello — Mrs M Kimber

1995 **4(NH)**,**2(NH)**,**3(NH)**,**2(NH)**

257	29/2	Nottingham	(L)	HC	2 1/2m	11	G	*chsd ldrs for over a cct, struggling before 6 out, t.o..*	7	0
668	26/3	Sandown	(R)	HC	2 1/2m 110yds	8	GS	*cl up, ld briefly 7th, outpcd 9th, t.o..*	3	13
798	3/4	Ascot	(R)	HC	2m 3f 110yds	10	GF	*keen hold early, trckd ldr to 7th, cl up till rdn and wknd apr 3 out.*	5	15
1122	20/4	Stratford	(L)	HC	2m 5f 110yds	16	GF	*prom to 8th, bhnd when p.u. before 12th.*	P	0
1435	6/5	Ashorne	(R)	CON	3m	12	G	*prom, ld 6-10th, wknd 13th, wll bhnd whn p.u. last*	P	0
1532	13/5	Towcester	(R)	HC	2m 110yds	16	GF	*alwys prom, rdn 3 out, one pace from 2 out.*	4	20

Non-stayer & outlcassed in H/Chases; ran passably but no real chances at 13 .... **15**

SOCIAL VISION(IRE) b.g. 6 Parliament - Elegant Miss by Prince Tenderfoot (USA) — R Fellows

1995 P(0)

430	9/3	Upton-On-Se'	(R)	MDO	3m	15	GS	*mid-div to 11th, wknd, p.u. 3 out*	P	0

2 runs in 2 seasons & nothing yet **0**

SO EASY ro.m. 6 Cavalier Servente - Casual Kate by Don Enrico (USA) — Mrs E Weaver

213	24/2	Newtown	(L)	MEM	3m	7	GS	*sn wll bhnd, t.o. & p.u. 7th*	P	0
354	3/3	Garnons	(L)	MDN	2 1/2m	13	GS	*rear frm 6th, p.u. aft 9th*	P	0
749	31/3	Upper Sapey	(R)	MDO	3m	17	GS	*prom to hlfwy, wknd, p.u. 14th*	P	0
1044	13/4	Bitterley	(L)	MDO	3m	15	G	*nvr nr ldrs, eased & p.u. 10th*	P	0

Schooling & yet to show any ability **0**

SOHAIL(USA) ch.g. 13 Topsider (USA) - Your Nuts (USA) by Creme Dela Creme — Mrs Carrie Janaway
1995 **1(NH),2(NH),2(NH),5(NH),P(NH),5(NH)**

136	17/2	Ottery St M'	(L)	LAD	3m	9	GS	*w.w. prog 14th, onepcd frm 4 out*	4	15
381	9/3	Barbury Cas'	(L)	XX	3m	9	GS	*sttld mid-div, prog 4 out, unable to chal*	2	15
708	30/3	Barbury Cas'	(L)	LAD	3m	10	G	*in tch, effrt 13th, ev ch 3 out, onepcd aft*	3	21
958	8/4	Lockinge	(L)	MXO	3m	6	GF	*sn bhnd, nvr on terms to chal*	4	13
1165	20/4	Larkhill	(R)	LAD	3m	7	GF	*prom thruout til ran on onepce frm 4 out*	4	15
1407	6/5	Hackwood Pa'	(L)	XX	3m	5	F	*(fav) lft in ld 7th, made rest, all out*	1	18
1589	25/5	Mounsey Hil'	(R)	OPE	3m	12	G	*wll bhnd 12th, t.o. & p.u. 14th*	P	0

Winning hurdler/chaser; old character & handed poor race on plate; same needed at 14 15

SOLAR CASTLE (Irish) — **I** 12^{P}, **I** 42^{3}, **I** 64, , **I** 143^{P}, **I** 183^{3}, **I** 306^{4}, **I** 379^{2}, **I** 433^{2}, **I** 504^{3}, **I** 569^{2}, **I** 615^{3}, **I** 640^{6}

SOLAR ROCKET b.m. 9 St Columbus - Solar Fox by Solar Duke — Miss F M Tarry
1995 1(18),1(22)

640	23/3	Siddington	(L)	LAD	3m	9	S	*pllng, cls up, ev ch 3 out, onepcd*	3	14

Won both starts 95; brief appearance 96; can win if fit 97; G/F-S 21

SOLARS SISTER b.m. 8 High Season - Seeker's Sister by Ashmore (FR) — Colin Pritchard

1269	27/4	Pyle	(R)	MDO	3m	9	G	*rear 7th, no ch 11th, t.o. & p.u. 13th*	P	0
1391	6/5	Pantyderi	(R)	MDO	3m	13	GF	*u.r. 1st*	U	-

Of no account 0

SOLDIERS DUTY(USA) b.g. 12 Golden Act (USA) - Fuzier (USA) by Crozier (USA) — David A Smith
1995 P(0),5(0),U(-),4(13)

163	17/2	Weston Park	(L)	LAD	3m	10	G	*mid-div, styd on frm 4 out, nrst fin*	3	18
687	30/3	Chaddesley '	(L)	CON	3m	10	G	*w.w. prog & in tch 10th, wknd 13th, p.u. 2 out*	P	0
879	6/4	Brampton Br'	(R)	LAD	3m	9	GF	*4th/5th til effrt & ch apr 16th, no prog frm 3 out*	4	15
1230	27/4	Weston Park	(L)	CON	3m	7	G	*held up, 3rd 10th, mstk 13th, not qckn frm 3 out*	5	15
1480	11/5	Bredwardine	(R)	LAD	3m	12	G	*chsd ldrs til outpcd frm 13th, styd on frm 3 out*	4	14

Won 3 in 93; missed 94 & struggling since; lost speed & very hard to win at 13 15

SOLITARY REAPER b.g. 11 Valiyar - Fardella (ITY) by Molvedo — R King

237	25/2	Southwell P'	(L)	MEM	3m	4	HO	*3rd til went 2nd apr 3 out, not qckn flat, fin 2nd, promoted*	1	0
327	3/3	Market Rase'	(L)	CON	3m	15	G	*alwys rear, p.u. 14th*	P	0
535	17/3	Southwell P'	(L)	CON	3m	10	GS	*(bl) in tch whn u.r. 6th*	U	-
969	8/4	Thorpe Lodge	(L)	OPE	3m	4	GF	*(bl) chsd wnr to 12th, outpcd 4 out, mstk 2 out, lost 2nd nr fin*	4	0
1303	28/4	Southwell P'	(L)	CON	3m	7	GF	*(bl) prom, chsg grp, not qckn frm 4 out*	3	0

Won a joke race & outicassed in other company; Members only chance at 12 10

SOLITARY SPIRIT (Irish) — **I** 134^{U}, **I** 268^{P}, **I** 305^{6}, **I** 416,

SOLO MINSTREL (Irish) — **I** 291^{P}, **I** 356^{P}, **I** 652^{P}

SOLVANG (Irish) — **I** 571^{U}, **I** 612,

SOLWAYSANDS b.g. 6 Germont - Castle Point by Majestic Streak — K Little
1995 P(0),U(-),8(0),P(0),4(0)

114	17/2	Lanark	(R)	MDO	3m	12	GS	*alwys handy, ld brfly 11th, outpcd frm 3 out*	3	10
323	2/3	Corbridge	(R)	MDN	3m	12	GS	*mstks, last frm 7th, bhnd aft*	5	0
503	16/3	Lanark	(R)	MDO	3m	10	G	*alwys handy, disp 4 out, drew clr apr nxt*	1	14
750	31/3	Lockerbie	(R)	MEM	3m	2	G	*(fav) abt 4l clr thruout, eased cls home*	1	12
1249	27/4	Balcormo Ma'	(R)	RES	3m	10	GS	*4th hlfwy, sn lost tch, p.u. 4 out*	P	0

Improved & wide margin winner of poor race; more needed for Restricteds - could improve further 15

SOME DAY (Irish) — **I** 150^{P}

SOME FLASH b.g. 9 Quayside - Sirrahdis by Bally Joy — S J Robinson
1995 P(0),U(-),5(16),9(0),F(-),P(0)

118	17/2	Witton Cast'	(R)	INT	3m	9	S	*prom, cls up whn f 12th*	F	-
306	2/3	Great Stain'	(L)	INT	3m	12	GS	*alwys rear, p.u. 16th*	P	0
760	31/3	Great Stain'	(L)	OPE	3m	8	GS	*alwys mid-div, onepcd frm 3 out*	4	14
824	6/4	Stainton	(R)	CON	3m	11	GF	*twrds rear, rdn 6th, u.r. nxt*	U	-
1091	14/4	Whitwell-On'	(R)	XX	3m	6	G	*trckd ldrs, disp 9th, mstk nxt, sn fdd, t.o. & p.u. last*	P	0
1130	20/4	Hornby Cast'	(L)	CON	3m	13	G	*handy, ld brfly 11th, wknd frm 4 out, t.o. & p.u. last*	P	0
1461	9/5	Sedgefield	(L)	HC	2m 5f	10	F	*mstks, in tch, blnd 5th, hdwy to join ldrs hfwy, hit 11th, soon wknd.*	8	0
1586	25/5	Hexham	(L)	HC	2 1/2m 110yds	14	GF	*alwys well bhnd, t.o. when pulld before 6 out.*	P	0

Silly campaign & of no account now 0

SOME MAN (Irish) — **I** 110^{P}, **I** 456^{F}

SOME OBLIGATION b.g. 11 Gleason (USA) - Happy Lass by Tarqogan — D E Wilson

1995 **3(22),6(11),7(0)**

362 5/3 Leicester (R) HC 2 1/2m 110yds 8 GS *in tch, blnd 4th, 3rd and btn four out, t.o. when p.u. last.* P 0
374 9/3 Sandown (R) HC 2 1/2m 110yds 5 GS *ld, mstk 3rd, hdd 7th, led 8th till 10th, weakening when mistake 13th, p.u. before 3 out.* P 0
579 20/3 Ludlow (R) HC 2 1/2m 17 G *(bl) mid div when blnd and u.r. 5th.* U -
1330 30/4 Huntingdon (R) HC 2 1/2m 110yds 8 GF *(bl) prom, disp ld 5th to 9th and 11th to 3 out, wknd next.* 3 19

Change of rider & brief revival last start but shadow of former self now 16

SOMERBY b.g. 9 Tudorville - Nautique by Windjammer (USA) C G Sanderson

1995 1(15),3(12),F(-),1(15),2(0)

168 18/2 Market Rase' (L) MEM 3m 7 GF *in tch, outpcd 10th, t.o. 13th* 4 0

Dual winner 95; no show only start 96 & best watched now 13

SOMETHING SHEER (Irish) — **I** 11[F], **I** 127[F], **I** 151[1], **I** 246[P]

SOME TOURIST (Irish) — **I** 116[P], **I** 313[P], **I** 357[3], **I** 435[P], **I** 547[6], **I** 657[P]

SOME-TOY ch.g. 10 Arkan - Cedar Of Galaxy by Bauble John Squire

135 17/2 Ottery St M' (L) LAD 3m 11 GS *hld up, prog 13th, 2nd & hld whn lft clr 2 out* 1 23
624 23/3 Kilworthy (L) LAD 3m 7 GS *prom, ld 11-15th, 3rd & wkng whn blnd 2 out* 3 17
872 6/4 Higher Kilw' (L) LAD 3m 3 GF *(fav) j.w. disp til drew clr aft 15th, canter* 1 25
1013 13/4 Ascot (R) HC 3m 110yds 11 GS *chsd ldrs 7th, still with lders when mstk and u.r. 4 out.* U -
1111 17/4 Hockworthy (L) MXO 3m 13 GS *mstks, w.w., prog 13th, 3rd & in tch whn blndrd 2 out, no ex* 3 20
1335 1/5 Cheltenham (L) HC 2m 5f 10 G *(fav) mid div, prog to dispute ld 14th, ld apr 2 out, clr last, rdn out.* 1 25

Missed 95; useful & deserved modest H/Chase win; can win points in 97; mistakes; G/F-S 25

SONNY'S SONG b.g. 10 True Song - Zaratune by Badedas Alan Clarke

1995 **P(NH),P(NH),P(NH)**

341 3/3 Heythrop (R) MDN 3m 13 G *nvr dang, t.o. & p.u. 14th* P 0
431 9/3 Upton-On-Se' (R) MDO 3m 17 GS *disp 3rd til wknd frm 9th* 8 0
688 30/3 Chaddesley ' (L) MDN 3m 17 G *alwys rear, some late prog, nvr dang* 6 0
1319 28/4 Bitterley (L) MDN 3m 13 G *cls up to 8th, lost tch ldrs 14th* 5 0
1434 6/5 Ashorne (R) MDO 3m 15 G *alwys bhnd, t.o. 14th* 6 0
1485 11/5 Bredwardine (R) MDO 3m 15 G *prog to ld 7th, hdd 14th, wknd & p.u. 3 out* P 0
1621 27/5 Chaddesley ' (L) MDO 3m 17 GF *(bl) mid-div, in tch til wknd 14th, wll bhnd & p.u. 2 out* P 0

Beat only 3 others in 4 completions & blinkers no help 0

SONNY SULLIVAN (Irish) — **I** 445[P]

SONOFAGIPSY b.g. 12 Sunyboy - Zingarella by Romany Air Mrs B Whettam

1995 **3(23),2(25),3(26),16(0),4(18),1(26),3(26)**

185 23/2 Kempton (R) HC 3m 9 GS *trckd ldrs till wknd apr 13th, t.o..* 3 24
370 7/3 Wincanton (R) HC 3m 1f 110yds 5 GF *prom, rdn 13th, lost pl 16th, went remote 2nd 2 out.* 2 21
672 29/3 Aintree (L) HC 2 3/4m 26 G *chsd ldrs, outpcd hfwy, driven along from 5 out, no impn 3 out.* 6 21
1327 30/4 Huntingdon (R) HC 3m 6 GF *chsd ldr, driven to ld 15th, hdd apr 2 out, kept on und pres run-in.* 2 23
1382 6/5 Exeter (R) HC 2m 7f 110yds 8 GF *ld to 10th, wknd apr 4 out.* 4 19
1539 16/5 Folkestone (R) HC 3m 7f 9 G *(fav) prom, blnd 10th, 4th and rdn when mstk 16th, btn 3 out.* 5 12

H/Chase winner 95; outclassed early 95 & reluctant after; win at 13 beyond him; Firm 19

SON OF ANUN ch.g. 7 Norwick (USA) - Sister Rosarii (USA) by Properantes (USA) Richard Hawker

1995 **9(NH),5(NH)**

205 24/2 Castle Of C' (R) MDO 3m 9 HY *handy to 8th, lost tch & p.u. 13th* P 0
267 2/3 Didmarton (L) MDN 3m 11 G *chsd ldrs til wknd 10th, wll bhnd whn u.r. 13th* U -
643 23/3 Siddington (L) MDN 3m 16 S *blnd 2nd, t.o. & p.u. 14th* P 0
956 8/4 Lockinge (L) MDN 3m 7 GF *n.j.w., hndy til lost tch 14th, t.o. & p.u. 3 out* P 0
1242 27/4 Woodford (L) RES 3m 18 G *nvr trbld ldrs, 10th hlfwy, t.o. & p.u. 16th* P 0

Yet to complete the course in points & does not jump well 0

SON OF ISHKA b.g. 8 Humdoleila - Ishka by Tribal Chief L A E Hopkins

1995 P(0)

568 17/3 Wolverhampt' (L) MDN 3m 9 GS *cls up in 3rd whn u.r. 8th* U -
740 31/3 Sudlow Farm (R) MDN 3m 16 G *cls up, wknd 7th, t.o. 13th* 7 0
852 6/4 Sandon (L) MDN 3m 9 GF *chsd ldrs to 11th, wknng & btn whn u.r. 14th* U -
1029 13/4 Alpraham (R) MDO 3m 8 GS *chsd ldrs to 9th, wknd nxt, t.o. 11th, p.u. 13th* P 0
1234 27/4 Weston Park (L) MDO 3m 13 G *ld 7-9th, cls up, ld 13th, wknd 4 out, p.u. 2 out* P 0

Last on only completion from 9 starts 94-6 0

SOONER STILL b.g. 12 Tachypous - Sooner Or Later by Sheshoon R F Rimmer

1995 **P(NH),P(NH),3(NH)**

161 17/2 Weston Park (L) LAD 3m 11 G *(bl) cls up til outpcd 4 out, onepcd aft* 3 13
291 2/3 Eaton Hall (R) LAD 3m 10 G *(bl) wll in tch til f 14th* F -
460 9/3 Eyton-On-Se' (L) LAD 3m 10 G *(bl) cls up to 8th, outpcd frm 4 out* 5 10
1153 20/4 Whittington (L) LAD 3m 10 G *(bl) ld 12th-3 out, outpcd aft* 3 11
1232 27/4 Weston Park (L) LAD 3m 6 G *(bl) held up, prog 2nd 13th, no ext frm 4 out* 3 14
1366 4/5 Gisburn (R) LAD 3m 12 G *(bl) made most to 14th, onepcd aft* 4 17

Winning chaser; scholmaster now & unlikely to win 14

SORRY SARAH (Irish) — **I** 134P

SOULDAN(IRE) b.g. 8 Trimmingham - Safe Return by Canisbay Mrs C Rimmer
1995 P(0),P(0),U(-),P(0),7(0),1(10)

248 25/2 Charing (L) RES 3m 12 GS *ld til jmpd rght 15th, grad wknd, 6th whn f last* F
478 10/3 Tweseldown (R) RES 3m 9 G *prom early, in pack whn p.u. aft 11th* P 0

Won dreadful Maiden 95 & struggled in brief campaign 96 0

SOUND GOLLY ch.g. 14 Fair Turn - Rock's Rose by Little Buskins J R Pike
1995 P(0),3(16),5(11)

214 24/2 Newtown (L) CON 3m 21 GS *wll bhnd til ran on frm 15th, nrst fin* 4 14
880 6/4 Brampton Br' (R) XX 3m 8 GF *ld to 8th, lost plc 13th, styd on frm 3 out* 3 17
1158 20/4 Llanwit Maj' (R) OPE 4m 9 GS *disp 2nd til chsd ldr 11th, ld 21st-2 out, just onepcd* 2 19

Safe & sprightly veteran; could still win Members at 15; G/F-G/S 15

SOUND PROFIT ch.m. 8 Scallywag - Night Profit by Carnival Night W G Young
1995 **12(NH),5(NH),P(NH)**

371 8/3 Ayr (L) HC 2m 5f 110yds 8 GF *mstks, lost tch from 11th, t.o..* 4 0

Of no account - tailed off in worst hunter chase of season 0

SOUNDSGOODTOME (Irish) — **I** 482P

SOUND STATEMENT(IRE) ch.g. 7 Strong Statement (USA) - Coolishall Again by Push On Maurice E Pinto
1995 3(11),2(0),1(14),B(-)

28 20/1 Barbury Cas' (L) RES 3m 14 GS *ld to 14th, lft in ld nxt, hdd aft 3 out, fdd* 3 13
128 17/2 Kingston Bl' (L) RES 3m 14 GS *prom,lft in ld 5th,sn hdd,chsd wnr 14th,styd on onepcd 2 out* 2 16
574 17/3 Detling (L) RES 3m 14 GF *(fav) made all, clr 13th, unchal* 1 18
918 8/4 Aldington (L) CON 3m 4 F *(fav) jmpd rght, ld to 12th, wth wnr 3 out, btn whn mstk nxt* 2 18

Maiden winner 95; changed hands; front-runner; barely stays; can win Confined if fit 97; G/F-G/S 19

SOUTH EAST SUN (Irish) — **I** 23P, **I** 389P, **I** 482P, **I** 563¹

SOUTHERLY BUSTER b.g. 13 Strong Gale - Southern Slave by Arctic Slave Mrs S C White
1995 P(0),1(17),4(14),1(13),2(0),6(14)

209 24/2 Castle Of C' (R) OPE 3m 8 HY *sn rear, t.o. whn blnd & u.r. 2 out* U -

Dual winner 95; brief appearance in 96 & hard to revive at 14 14

SOUTHERLY GALE b.g. 9 Strong Gale - Chestnut Belle by Even Money 405200 Racing
1995 **2(NH),P(NH),F(NH),P(NH)**

555 17/3 Ottery St M' (L) MDO 3m 15 G *(fav) handy, ld 10th to 3 out, disp whn hit marker & u.r apr nxt* U 16
1335 1/5 Cheltenham (L) HC 2m 5f 10 G *held up rear, prog 8th, wknd 13th, t.o..* 5 10
1454 7/5 Newton Abbot (L) HC 2m 5f 110yds 8 GS *nvr far away, went 2nd 4 out, rdn and no impn from 2 out.* 2 21
1543 17/5 Newton Abbot (L) HC 3 1/4m 110yds 8 G *made all, not fluent 3 out, all out.* 1 19
1630 31/5 Stratford (L) HC 3 1/2m 16 GF *held up in tch, rdn 17th, one pace after next.* 6 23

Able but ungenuine; won weak H/Chase to break duck; won chase in summer jumping & better off there 22

SOUTHERN FLIGHT b.g. 7 Southern Music - Fly Blackie by Dear Gazelle Mrs K J Cumings
1995 F(-),1(15),P(0),P(0)

29 20/1 Barbury Cas' (L) RES 3m 12 GS *rear,prog 11th,chsd ldrs 14th,fair 5th but btn whn u.r. last* U 17
199 24/2 Lemalla (R) RES 3m 17 HY *alwys prom, ld 3 out, styd on well* 1 20
442 9/3 Haldon (R) CON 3m 6 S *(fav) alwys wll plcd, ld 16th, drew clr nxt, comf, eased* 1 20

Maiden winner 95; much improved; stays & fair form; should upgrade if fit 97; S-Hy 22

SOUTHERN MINSTREL ch.g. 13 Black Minstrel - Jadida (FR) by Yelapa (FR) N Chamberlain

37 3/2 Wetherby (L) HC 3m 110yds 11 GS *in tch, effort after 12th, ev ch 4 out, soon wknd.* 4 24
76 11/2 Wetherby Po' (L) LAD 3m 8 GS *(fav) cls up, 3rd 4 out, drvn to ld flat, styd on well* 1 22
257 29/2 Nottingham (L) HC 2 1/2m 11 G *patiently rdn, steady hdwy from 5 out, drew level last, soon ld, styd on strly to go clr run-in.* 1 26
672 29/3 Aintree (L) HC 2 3/4m 26 G *hmpd 1st, alwys well bhnd, t.o. hfwy.* 8 16

1119 18/4 Ayr (L) HC 3m 3f 110yds 9 GS *held up, tk clr order hfwy, outpcd before 17th, styd on from 3 out.* 3 23
1226 25/4 Perth (R) HC 3m 7 S *trckd ldrs, mstk and ld 11th (water), hdd 15th, kept on same pace.* 3 22
1532 13/5 Towcester (R) HC 2m 110yds 16 GF *prom early, not trbl ldrs from 6th.* 9 15
1615 27/5 Wetherby (L) HC 2 1/2m 110yds 11 G *soon well bhnd, t.o..* 5 0

Winning chaser; ultra-safe & retains some ability; best L/H under 3m; may score again; G-S 23

SOUTH STACK b.g. 10 Daring March - Lady Henham by Breakspear II — T Laxton
1995 P(0),P(0),3(0)
402 9/3 Dalston (R) XX 3m 13 G *sn bhnd, mstk 13th, p.u. nxt* P 0
1152 20/4 Whittington (L) CON 3m 9 G *6l 4th 14th, wknd nxt, wll btn 4th whn p.u. & dismntd flat* P 0
1363 4/5 Gisburn (R) MEM 3m 5 G *chsd ldrs, cls up to 15th, onepcd aft* 2 0
1515 12/5 Hexham Poin' (L) OPE 3m 6 HY *bhnd,rdn 14th,no prog,p.u. 2 out, cont, blnd last, walked in* 3 0

Poor under Rules & in points as well - placings worthless 0

SOVEREIGNS MATCH b.g. 8 Royal Match - Sovereign's Folly by Sovereign Bill — J McKinnon
1995 P(0),P(0),3(10),2(13),P(0)
89 11/2 Alnwick (L) MDO 3m 9 GS *ld, prssd whn p.u. 2 out, dsmntd* P 0

Ran well only start 96 but obvious problem - best watched if returning 13

SOVEREIGN SPRAY(IRE) b.g. 6 Celio Rufo - Countess Spray by Even Say — S P Tindall
1995 **10(NH),4(NH)**
254 25/2 Charing (L) MDO 3m 9 GS *alwys rear, losing tch whn p.u. 14th* P 0
454 9/3 Charing (L) MDN 3m 10 G *rear, clsd up 10th, ld 13th, prssd whn lft clr 3 out* 1 12
810 6/4 Charing (L) RES 3m 6 F *(fav) wll plcd, ld apr 3 out, rdn out whn chal last* 1 19

Poor under Rules; improved & won average Restricted; should upgrade if fit 97; G-F 18

SPACE CAMP ch.g. 7 Kalaglow - Base Camp by Derring-Do — Richard House
1995 1(19)
27 20/1 Barbury Cas' (L) LAD 3m 15 GS *w.w. prog to chs wnr 10-13th, wknd 3 out, fin tired* 6 0
65 10/2 Great Treth' (R) INT 3m 13 S *nvr nr to chal, p.u. bef 2 out* P 0

Promising when winning only start 95 but problems 96; can only be watched when returning; G/S-G/F 17

SPACE CAPPA br.g. 8 Capitano - Space Speaker by Space King — D G Stephens
1995 P(0),1(15),3(17),2(16)
210 24/2 Castle Of C' (R) INT 3m 10 HY *made most, ran on well frm 2 out* 1 20
481 11/3 Taunton (R) HC 3m 11 G *prom, ld 4th to 10th, regained ld four out, in command when mstk 2 out, readily.* 1 24
670 28/3 Aintree (L) HC 3m 1f 9 G *soon ld, hdd 6th, dropped rear apr 9th, bhnd when blnd and u.r. 5 out.* U -

Maiden winner 95; improved; found modest H/Chase; more needed in better company 97; finished early 23

SPACE FAIR b.g. 13 Space King - Katie Fare by Ritudyr — Mrs R Fifield
359 4/3 Doncaster (L) HC 2m 3f 110yds 10 G *trckd ldr, feeling pace and rdn after 4 out, left 2nd 2 out, kept on one pace.* 2 24
1122 20/4 Stratford (L) HC 2m 5f 110yds 16 GF *chsd ldrs, ld 9th to 12th, wknd apr 2 out, dead.* 3 26

Dead 26

SPACE LAB b.g. 11 Tanfirion - Marzooga by Bold Lad (IRE) — Mrs C F M Fitchett
863 6/4 Larkhill (R) MEM 3m 4 F *ld 3rd til blndrd & u.r. 7th* U -
1167 20/4 Larkhill (R) MEM 3m 9 GF *sn in rear, t.o. frm 13th* 7 0

Tailed off last on only completion 0

SPACE MAN ch.g. 13 True Song - Perfect Day by Roan Rocket — Miss Scarlett J Crew
1995 4(16),3(13),3(18),2(17)
232 24/2 Heythrop (R) OPE 3m 10 GS *in tch, went 4th at 14th, chsd wnr 2 out, nvr nrr* 2 19
475 10/3 Tweseldown (R) CON 3m 9 G *mid-div, prog 14th, styd on frm 2 out, nrst fin* 2 19
637 23/3 Siddington (L) MEM 3m 14 S *in tch, chall & rddn 3 out, not much room flat,onepcd* 3 14
1108 17/4 Cheltenham (L) HC 4m 1f 14 GS *bhnd when mstk 8th, t.o..* 8 0
1438 6/5 Ashorne (R) XX 3m 14 G *mstk 4th, chsg grp out of tch, poor 4th 3 out, wknd* 6 11
1560 18/5 Bassaleg (R) OPE 3m 7 F *ld to 3rd, prssd wnr aft, ev ch 2 out, not qckn apr last* 2 23

Placed in 8 of 9 points 95/6; onepaced but ran really well last start; still struggle to win again 18

SPACE MARINER b.g. 9 Julio Mariner - Spaced Out by Space King — T N Bailey
1995 P(0),6(0),3(0),6(0),1(17),**7(0)**,**P(0)**,7(0)
213 24/2 Newtown (L) MEM 3m 7 GS *sn bhnd, t.o. frm 5th* 4 0

255	28/2	Taunton	(R)	HC	4 1/4m 110yds	15 GS	*bhnd from 15th, t.o. when p.u. before 3 out.*	P	0
601	23/3	Howick	(L)	CON	3m	10 S	*t.o. 6th, fin own time*	7	0
881	6/4	Brampton Br'	(R)	CON	3m	9 GF	*35l 3rd at 12th, kpt on onepcd frm 16th*	5	12
042	13/4	Bitterley	(L)	CON	3m	9 G	*tubed, prom to 4th, lost tch aft 12th, t.o. 14th*	7	0
412	6/5	Cursneh Hill	(L)	OPE	3m	4 GF	*alwys 3rd, chal for 2nd frm 15th, styd on*	2	12
507	12/5	Maisemore P'	(L)	CON	3m	10 F	*bhnd frm 5th, t.o. 9th*	7	0
636	1/6	Bratton Down	(L)	OPE	4m	11 G	*rear & rdn 12th, wknd rpdly 19th, t.o. & p.u. 21st*	P	0

No longer of any account 0

SPACE MOLLY b.m. 7 Capitano - Space Speaker by Space King — T Frost

1995 U(-)

236	24/2	Heythrop	(R)	MDN	3m	13 GS	*rear whn f 5th*	F	-
182	21/4	Mollington	(R)	MDN	3m	10 F	*rear, pshd alng 10th, sn btn, t.o. & p.u. 13th*	P	0
241	27/4	Clifton On '	(L)	MDO	3m	8 GF	*last frm 11th, t.o. & p.u. 16th*	P	0
434	6/5	Ashorne	(R)	MDO	3m	15 G	*mid-div, 10th whn u.r. 7th*	U	-
504	11/5	Kingston Bl'	(L)	MDO	3m	13 G	*made most to 5th, wknd 11th, t.o. 13th, p.u. 15th*	P	0
569	19/5	Mollington	(R)	MDO	3m	10 GS	*prom til rdn & wknd 10th, t.o. & p.u. 13th*	P	0

Yet to complete the course in points & no stamina 0

SPACIAL(USA) b.g. 12 Star Appeal - Abeer (USA) by Dewan (USA) — Richard J Hill

1995 4(11),5(15),3(0),1(20)

5	13/1	Larkhill	(R)	LAD	3m	10 GS	*ld to 3 out, sn btn*	3	20
378	9/3	Barbury Cas'	(L)	LAD	3m	6 GS	*lft in ld 5th, sn wll clr, unchal, canter*	1	24
655	23/3	Badbury Rin'	(L)	LAD	3m	8 G	*made all, jmpd well, ran on flat*	1	25
1058	13/4	Badbury Rin'	(L)	LAD	3m	5 GF	*(fav) made all, mstk last, unchal*	1	26

Revived strongly 96; best making all in small races on easy 3m; can win at 13; G-F 24

SPALEASE br.m. 6 Strong Gale - Batease by Quiet Fling (USA) — Mrs Judy Wilson

1995 2(0)

174	18/2	Market Rase'	(L)	MDO	2m 5f	7 GF	*(fav) not alwys fluent, prog to ld 12th, hit 2 out, clr last, comf*	1	15
437	9/3	Newton Brom'	(R)	RES	3m	9 GS	*hld up rear, prog to chal 4 out, btn whn blnd 2 out*	6	0

Confirmed promise when winning; disappointed next start; good stable & may improve 16

SPANISH ARCH(IRE) ch.g. 7 Ovac (ITY) - Castile's Rose by Ballyciptic — C R Millington

1995 **7(NH),12(NH),9(NH)**

176	18/2	Market Rase'	(L)	MDO	2m 5f	10 GF	*plling, mstks, prom to 9th, t.o. & p.u. 12th*	P	0

Looks of no account 0

SPANISH CASTLE (Irish) — **I** 213P, **I** 6421

SPANISH FLY(IRE) b.m. 7 Spanish Place (USA) - Quality Suite by Prince Hansel — C H A Denny

584	23/3	Wetherby Po'	(L)	RES	3m	13 S	*mid-div, f 6th*	F	-

Promise 94; missed 95 & a breif return 0

SPANISH MONEY gr.g. 9 Scallywag - Morgan's Money by David Jack — Russel H Lee

1995 P(0),1(10)

1340	4/5	Hexham	(L)	HC	3m 1f	13 S	*ld till hdd 9th, soon wknd, t.o. when p.u. before 14th.*	P	0

Won dire Maiden 95 & late appearance 96 showed nothing 0

SPANISH PAL (Irish) — **I** 6344

SPANISH ROUGE ch.g. 12 - Sparwood by Spartan General — A R Ford

1995 4(0),3(12)

213	24/2	Newtown	(L)	MEM	3m	7 GS	*mstks 3rd & 10th, in tch to 12th, sn t.o., btn 2 fences*	3	0
350	3/3	Garnons	(L)	CON	3m	11 GS	*trckd ldng pair to 11th, wknd 13th, t.o. & p.u. 2 out*	P	0
600	23/3	Howick	(L)	RES	3m	14 S	*4th/5th to 12th, wknd, fin own time*	7	0
1415	6/5	Cursneh Hill	(L)	RES	3m	11 GF	*prom, ld 3 out, lkd wnnr whn reins broke & ran out bfr last*	r	-

Maiden winner 93; placed 5 times 94-6 but struggles to stay & lost golden chance last start 13

SPANISH WHISPER b.g. 9 Aragon - Whisper Gently by Pitskelly — M Lane

1995 **6(NH),8(NH),7(NH),8(NH)**

535	17/3	Southwell P'	(L)	CON	3m	10 GS	*rear, mid-div by 12th, nvr rchd ldrs*	5	0
678	30/3	Cottenham	(R)	LAD	3m	6 GF	*chsd ldrs, lost plc whn pckd 10th, bhnd frm 13th*	6	0
897	6/4	Dingley	(R)	CON	3m	15 GS	*prom to 3rd, sn wknd, last trio frm 10th*	11	0
1377	5/5	Dingley	(R)	CON	3m	12 GF	*alwys rear, t.o. 13th*	8	0
1594	25/5	Garthorpe	(R)	MEM	3m	10 G	*alwys last trio, 7th & outpcd 6 out*	5	0
1639	2/6	Dingley	(R)	MEM	3m	7 GF	*alwys rr, t.o. 12th*	6	0

Last on 5 of the 6 starts - of no account now 0

SPAR COPSE ch.g. 13 Pablond - Ringarose by Rose Knight — P E Froud

1995 5(0),4(0),2(13),4(0),5(10),2(14),3(0)

815	6/4	Charlton Ho'	(L)	MEM	3m	8	GF	*sn rear, t.o. whn p.u. 12th*	P 0
1060	13/4	Badbury Rin'	(L)	MDO	3m	14	GF	*cls up, 3rd at 10th, wknd & outpcd frm 4 out*	5 0
1164	20/4	Larkhill	(R)	MDN	3m	12	GF	*ld to 6th & 13-15th, not able to qckn wth wnr*	2 12
1540	16/5	Folkestone	(R)	HC	2m 5f	10	G	*chsd ldrs, rdn 11th, hdwy 3 out, ev ch next, soon wknd.*	3 13
1610	26/5	Tweseldown	(R)	MDO	3m	5	G	*ld 3rd, lft clr 15th, tired 2 out, hdd last no ext*	2 10
1652	8/6	Umberleigh	(L)	MDO	3m	10	GF	*(fav) prom, disp 14th, chsd wnr aft, no imp 2 out, tired*	2 10

Tries really hard but does not stay & placed 8 times 95/6; great fortune needed at 14 12

SPARKLING CLOWN ch.m. 7 True Song - Copperclown by Spartan General — H Hutsby

1104	14/4	Guilsborough	(L)	MDN	3m	18	G	*mid-div, jmpd slwly 5th, in tch to 14th, no dang aft,improve*	6 0

Not disgraced & may sparkle if racing regularly in 97 11

SPARKY JOE (Irish) — I 1P

SPARKY'S DECISION(IRE) b.g. 5 Electric - Rainy Planet by Jupiter Pluvius — G E Dods

53	4/2	Alnwick	(L)	MDO	3m	13	G	*(Jt fav) hld up, prog 8th, ev ch aft 13th, wknd rpdly*	6 0

Suffering with rest of stable in 96 & should do better in time 12

SPARNOVA ch.m. 6 Ra Nova - Spartaca by Spartan General — V T Bradshaw

1995 P(0),F(-),5(0),9(0)

440	9/3	Newton Brom'	(R)	MDN	3m	10	GS	*mostly mid-div, wkng whn p.u. 3 out*	P 0
797	2/4	Heythrop	(R)	MDN	3m	11	F	*cls up, chsd ldr 2 out, chal last, ld nr fin*	1 14
1181	21/4	Mollington	(R)	RES	3m	10	F	*mid-div, 4th & wll outpcd 13th, ran on 3 out, nrst fin*	3 16
1402	6/5	Northaw	(L)	RES	3m	5	F	*in tch,lst pl appr 8th,pshd alng 10th,n.d. aft,wnt 3rd 3 out*	3 10
1501	11/5	Kingston Bl'	(L)	RES	3m	10	G	*mstk 3rd,in tch,effrt 11th,ch whn mstk 15th,wknd aft 2 out*	3 15

Improved & found poor race; slow but safe & may find Restricted in 97; Firm 16

SPARTAN ERIC b.g. 9 Oats - Miss Spartan by Spartan General — Mrs P Morris

884	6/4	Brampton Br'	(R)	MDN	3m	12	GF	*hld up, nvr rchd ldrs, p.u. 3 out*	P 0

Should be capable of better but time already passing him by 0

SPARTAN JULIET b.m. 8 Julio Mariner - Miss Spartan by Spartan General — H S Fletcher

1995 6(14),5(0),4(13),6(0)

225	24/2	Duncombe Pa'	(R)	RES	3m	12	GS	*in rear 9th, some late prog, nvr dang*	5 0
305	2/3	Great Stain'	(L)	LAD	3m	11	GS	*alwys rear, t.o. 7th, p.u. 13th*	P 0
411	9/3	Charm Park	(L)	RES	3m	20	G	*alwys wl in rr, t.o. & p.u. 10th*	P 0
825	6/4	Stainton	(R)	RES	3m	7	GF	*prom, pshd alng 6th, fdd 10th, t.o. 4 out*	7 0
1131	20/4	Hornby Cast'	(L)	RES	3m	17	G	*mid-div, prog 14th, styd on wll frm 3 out*	3 15
1284	27/4	Easingwold	(L)	RES	3m	14	G	*alwys prom, ev ch 3 out, styd on wll flat*	2 17

Maiden winner 94; finished 8 of 10 races 95/6 but gets going too late; may strike lucky; Good 15

SPARTAN PETE ch.g. 8 Peter Wrekin - Spartan Madam by Spartan General — Mrs J A Burton

159	17/2	Weston Park	(L)	CON	3m	22	G	*mid to rear, no ch whn p.u. 14th*	P 0
461	9/3	Eyton-On-Se'	(L)	RES	3m	15	G	*mid to rear, p.u. 4 out*	P 0
1219	24/4	Brampton Br'	(R)	CON	3m	9	G	*cl up til outpcd 14th, kpt on one pace frm nxt*	4 14

Placed 94; missed 95; not disgraced when 4th & drop to Maidens could see success in 97 if fit 14

SPARTAN'S CONQUEST b.g. 6 Baron Blakeney - Spartella — G I Cooper

15	14/1	Cottenham	(R)	MDN	3m	14	G	*n.j.w. sn bhnd, p.u. apr 13th*	P 0
105	17/2	Marks Tey	(L)	RES	3m	11	G	*schoold in rr til p.u. 15th*	P 0
618	23/3	Higham	(L)	MDO	3m	14	GF	*alwys bhnd, lost tch 4th, t.o. & p.u. 12th*	P 0
830	6/4	Marks Tey	(L)	MDN	3m	14	G	*prom, ld 11th-13th, disp 15th til forged clr flat*	1 13

Benefited from his education when winning weak race; should improve; Restricted possible; Good 15

SPARTANS DINA b.m. 5 Newski (USA) - Spartan Mariner by Spartan General — P D Rogers

70	10/2	Great Treth'	(R)	MDO	3m	14	S	*f 4th*	F -
131	17/2	Ottery St M'	(L)	MDN	3m	10	GS	*n.j.w. mid-div whn c.o. 10th*	C -
200	24/2	Lemalla	(R)	MDO	3m	12	HY	*strgglng frm 9th, p.u. 11th*	P 0
1070	13/4	Lifton	(R)	MDO	3m	9	S	*hd strng,restrained in rear,last 12th,bhnd whn f hvly16th*	F -
1143	20/4	Flete Park	(R)	MDN	3m	17	S	*plld hrd, ld 2-7th & 12-15th, wknd rpdly, p.u. 16th*	P 0
1530	12/5	Ottery St M'	(L)	MDO	3m	8	GF	*plld hrd, ld & sn clr, hdd 15th, sn wknd*	4 0

Problems obvious & tailed off last on only completion 0

SPARTAN'S SAINT b.g. 11 St Columbus - Spartan Lace by Spartan General — G B Tarry

1995 P(0),P(0)

642	23/3	Siddington	(L)	RES	3m	15	S	*n.j.w. bhnd frm 6th, p.u.10th*	P 0
1178	21/4	Mollington	(R)	RES	3m	7	F	*in tch, rdn 11th, sn wll bhnd, mod prog agn 2 out*	4 11
1522	12/5	Garthorpe	(R)	RES	3m	12	GF	*mid-div, running on onepcd & no ch whn lft 2nd last*	2 11

Maiden winner 93; only 7 runs since & not threatening to follow-up 12

SPEAKERS CORNER ch.g. 13 Politico (USA) - Gusty Lucy by White Speck M E Sowersby
1995 **2(23)**,4(17),1(22),2(24),1(23),**4(22)**
120 17/2 Witton Cast' (R) OPE 3m 7 S *cls up til outpcd 13th, onepcd aft* 4 14
304 2/3 Great Stain' (L) OPE 3m 10 GS *cls up til outpcd 3 out, styd on onepcd* 4 15
Formerly very useful; finished early in 96 & will struggle to win another; stays; G-F 18

SPECIAL COMPANY (Irish) — I 443^{P}, I 569^{1}, I 641^{1}
SPECIFIC IMPULSE b.h. 9 Star Appeal - Lead Me On by King's Troop C C B Mathew
1995 **P(NH)**
233 24/2 Heythrop (R) MDN 3m 14 GS *chsd ldr, cls up til wknd & p.u. 3 out* P 0
430 9/3 Upton-On-Se' (R) MDO 3m 15 GS *wll btn 6th whn virt p.u. flat* 7 0
796 2/4 Heythrop (R) MDN 3m 11 F *mstk 1st, prom, prssd wnr 14th, rdn & no ext apr last* 3 14
Lightly raced; best ever run in weak race last start but disappeared 13

SPECKLED GLEN (Irish) — I 30^{2}, I 87^{2}, I 162^{P}
SPECTRE BROWN (Irish) — I 137^{P}, I 174^{P}, I 300^{U}, I 337^{4}, I 394^{3}, I 495^{P}, I 559^{P}
SPECULATION ch.g. 14 New Member - Stockley Crystal by Dairialatan M J Gingell
1995 **4(NH),P(NH),2(NH),F(NH),3(NH),6(NH)**
11 14/1 Cottenham (R) LAD 3m 7 G *disp til wknd 13th, no ch whn f 16th, dead* F -
Dead 11

SPEECH ch.g. 13 Salluceva - Malone by Politico (USA) D J Fairbairn
1995 P(0),4(10),7(0),P(0),4(0)
183 19/2 Musselburgh (R) HC 3m 5 GF *ld 3rd, hit 9th, mstk and hdd 14th, lost tch from 2 out, t.o..* 4 0
701 30/3 Tranwell (L) OPE 3m 8 GS *mstks 6th, ld 2nd-10th, disp til wknd 14th, p.u. 2 out* P 0
085 14/4 Friars Haugh (L) OPE 3m 6 F *wll bhnd by 11th* 5 0
No longer of any account 0

SPEEDY DAN (Irish) — I 445^{P}, I 557^{F}, I 636^{P}, I 651^{4}
SPEEDY SIOUX ch.m. 7 Mandrake Major - Sioux Be It by Warpath M A Lloyd
1995 **8(NH),9(NH),11(NH),10(NH),10(NH)**
220 24/4 Brampton Br' (R) OPE 3m 10 G *alws rr, ref 4th* R -
Only 7 but future all behind her 0

SPERRIN VIEW ch.m. 10 Fidel - Baroness Vimy by Barrons Court Mrs Helen Mobley
1995 r(-),P(0),1(14),8(0),4(10),1(16),2(17)
126 17/2 Kingston Bl' (L) LAD 3m 11 GS *trckd ldrs, prog 10th, mstk 14th, ld on innr 2 out, drvn out* 1 21
336 3/3 Heythrop (R) LAD 3m 5 G *(fav) w.w. in tch, jnd ldr 3 out, ld last, rdn out* 1 20
640 23/3 Siddington (L) LAD 3m 9 S *trkd ldrs going wll 11th, ld 3 out, sn clr, easy* 1 22
018 13/4 Kingston Bl' (L) LAD 3m 8 G *w.w. chsd wnr 13th, qcknd to ld last, hdd post* 2 26
214 24/4 Andoversford (R) LAD 3m 4 G *ld, jmpd lft 7th, hd 3 out, sn rdn & btn* 2 22
502 11/5 Kingston Bl' (L) LAD 3m 7 G *prom, ld 8th, clr 14th, ran on well, comf* 1 26
566 19/5 Mollington (R) LAD 3m 7 GS *w.w. rdn & qcknd to ld 12th, hdd 15th, wknd apr 2 out* 2 19
Much improved; very useful Ladies horse; beaten by top horses; well ridden; win more at 11; G-S 26

SPIKEIE ROSE b.m. 6 Derring Rose - Ms Largesse by Goldhill P Morgan
1995 P(0),P(0)
148 17/2 Erw Lon (L) MDN 3m 9 G *alwys rear, t.o. & p.u. 3 out* P 0
696 30/3 Llanvapley (L) MDN 3m 13 GS *ld, 3l clr 2 out, wknd last, hdd flat* 2 13
039 13/4 St Hilary (R) MDN 3m 14 G *4th/5th, badly hmpd 9th, some prog 13th, p.u. 15th* P 0
273 27/4 Pyle (R) MDO 3m 9 G *(fav) mid-div,lft dist 3rd whn ref 13th,cont,fin aft evone left* R -
Only finished 1 of 6 races but ran well enough to suggest a win possible in 97 13

SPINANS HILL (Irish) — I 198^{P}, I 272^{P}, I 387,
SPINNING MELODY (Irish) — I 42^{P}
SPIRE HILL (Irish) — I 236^{1}, I 454^{1}, I 491^{3}
SPIRITED HOLME(FR) b.g. 11 Gay Mecene (USA) - Lyphard's Holme (USA) Miss Emma Masterson
153 17/2 Erw Lon (L) OPE 3m 15 G *alwys rear, p.u. 13th* P 0
No longer of any account 0

SPIRIT OF A KING (Irish) — I 62^{P}
SPIRIT OF SUCCESS b.g. 6 Rakaposhi King - Sweet Linda by Saucy Kit Paul Gardner
293 28/4 Barbury Cas' (L) MDO 3m 11 F *jmpd badly, t.o. til p.u. 6th* P 0
An inauspicious debut 0

SPITFIRE JUBILEE b.g. 10 Chief Singer - Altana by Grundy Mrs Z S Cla
1995 1(16),**8(0)**,**1(23)**,**4(17)**

651 23/3 Badbury Rin' (L) MEM 3m 4 G *(fav) made all, clr 15th, unchall, canter* 1 2
817 6/4 Charlton Ho' (L) OPE 3m 5 GF *in tch to 12th, outpcd frm 14th* 3
1166 20/4 Larkhill (R) OPE 3m 6 GF *front rank, ld 10th til no match for wnr whn chal last* 2 2
1406 6/5 Hackwood Pa' (L) MXO 3m 5 F *(fav) made most, j.w. qknd 4l clr aft 3 out, jnd last, ran on wll* 1 2
1647 8/6 Umberleigh (L) OPE 3m 7 GF *(fav) mstk 8th,prom to 10th,renewd effrt whn lft clr 3 out,unchal* 1

Speedy; best front-running in small fields; barely stays; should win again; G-F 22

SPLIT SECOND b.g. 7 Damister (USA) - Moment In Time by Without Fear (FR) Mrs P J Will
1995 1(16),1(20)

839 6/4 Maisemore P' (L) LAD 3m 2 GF *(fav) blnd 1st & 11th, disp til ld 15th, clr 2 out, easy* 1 2
1245 27/4 Woodford (L) LAD 3m 6 G *(fav) trckd ldrs, lft 2nd 9th, ld 3 out, easy* 1 2
1635 1/6 Bratton Down (L) LAD 3m 13 G *(fav) w.w. gd prog to ld 2 out, sn hdd, ld flat, ran on well* 1 2

Unbeaten in 5 starts 95/6 & showed class last start; hard to beat 97; top stable; Good 27

SPLIT THE WIND br.m. 10 Strong Gale - Dane-Jor's by Take A Reef Gareth W Evar

239 25/2 Southwell P' (L) MDO 3m 9 HO *alwys last, t.o. & p.u. 9th* P
540 17/3 Southwell P' (L) MDO 3m 9 GS *schoold rear, p.u. 9th* P
636 23/3 Market Rase' (L) MDN 3m 11 GF *t.o. in 9th at 6th, hmpd & u.r. 8th* U

Only learning but an elderly pupil 0

SPORTING LARK b.m. 9 Crested Lark - Florence Eliza by Floriana G B Tarr

1102 14/4 Guilsborough (L) RES 3m 15 G *alwys bhnd, t.o. & p.u. 14th* P
1239 27/4 Clifton On ' (L) RES 3m 9 GF *prom to 8th, sn rear, wll bhnd whn p.u. 15th* P
1439 6/5 Ashorne (R) RES 3m 11 G *in tch, outpcd 12th, wknd 14th, t.o. & p.u. 2 out* P
1501 11/5 Kingston Bl' (L) RES 3m 10 G *prom, chsd wnr 10th, 3l down last, no imp* 2 1
1612 26/5 Tweseldown (R) RES 3m 11 G *chsd ldrs, lft 2nd & hmpd 16th, outjmpd 2 out, btn aft* 2 1
1640 2/6 Dingley (R) RES 3m 9 GF *prom, chsd wnr 13th, chal 2 out, not qckn app last* 2 1

Maiden winner 94; missed 95; improved late 96; finished 5 of 18 races & Restricted hard to find; Gd ... 17

SPORTING VISION (Irish) — **I** 108^P, **I** 161^F, **I** 231^3, **I** 299^P, **I** 337^P

SPRING BAVARD ch.m. 9 Le Bavard (FR) - Welsh Cuckoo by Roxy (FR) K Jone

382 9/3 Llanfrynach (R) MEM 3m 7 GS *prom, ld 12th, rdn & hdd last, rallied, lkd to d/h* 2 1
882 6/4 Brampton Br' (R) RES 3m 14 GF *(fav) prog to chs ldr 15th, lft in ld nxt, 3l up whn f 3 out* F
1222 24/4 Brampton Br' (R) RES 3m 11 G *(fav) ld 2nd-4th, 4l 3rd 15th, rdn to ld 3 out, kpt on wl* 1

Maiden winner 94; missed 95; deserved success & could upgrade in 97; G-F 20

SPRING BEAU (Irish) — **I** 102^F, **I** 192^3

SPRINGCOMBE ch.m. 8 Vital Season - Triscombe Stone by Pharaoh Hophra Mrs E Eame
1995 3(0),P(0),2(11),6(0)

201 24/2 Lemalla (R) MDO 3m 13 HY *rear, no ch whn p.u. aft 11th* P
299 2/3 Great Treth' (R) MDO 3m 13 G *alwys rear* 4
532 16/3 Cothelstone (L) RES 3m 12 G *bhnd 8th, t.o. & p.u. last* P
627 23/3 Kilworthy (L) RES 3m 13 GS *alwys bhnd, t.o. & p.u. 15th* P
807 4/4 Clyst St Ma' (L) MDO 3m 10 GS *bhnd frm 8th, t.o.* 4
993 8/4 Kingston St' (R) MDO 3m 17 F *sn rear, t.o. frm hlfwy* 10
1079 13/4 Cothelstone (L) INT 3m 5 GF *rear, no ch whn p.u. 2 out* P
1392 6/5 Cotley Farm (L) MEM 3m 5 GF *prom early, 4th frm 5th, clsng whn blndrd & u.r. 13th* U
1494 11/5 Holnicote (L) MDO 3m 8 G *made most til hdd aft 2 out, rlld to ld agn last, ran on* 1 1
1591 25/5 Mounsey Hil' (R) RES 3m 15 G *wll bhnd frm 6th, t.o. & p.u. 14th* P
1636 1/6 Bratton Down (L) OPE 4m 11 G *blnd & u.r. 1st* U
1649 8/6 Umberleigh (L) RES 3m 14 GF *rear & pshd along, wll bhnd 12th, styd on wll apr 2 out* 4 1

Novice ridden to score on 15th attempt (poor race); Restricted needs stronger handling 14

SPRINGFARM RATH (Irish) — **I** 172^P, **I** 282^P, **I** 413^6, **I** 493^3

SPRINGFIELD LAD ch.g. 10 Golden Love - Barnaderg Lass by Bargello Miss L Robbin
1995 P(0),P(0),1(17),P(0)

942 8/4 Andoversford (R) MEM 3m 8 GF *carried 14st, wll bhnd to 13th, prog aft, nrst fin* 2 1
1170 20/4 Chaddesley ' (L) CON 3m 9 G *prog 10th, chsd ldr 12th, ld 2 out, drew clr last* 1 2
1332 1/5 Cheltenham (L) HC 3m 1f 110yds 11 G *veered right at start, jmpd badly right, t.o. from 3rd, p.u. before 2 out.* P
1507 12/5 Maisemore P' (L) CON 3m 10 F *alwys last & bhnd, t.o. 8th* 8
1620 27/5 Chaddesley ' (L) XX 3m 8 GF *trckd ldrs til easily outpcd frm 13th* 4 1

Restricted winner 95; good performance when winning but fell apart after; best watched 16

SPRINGFIELD PET b.m. 7 Oedipus Complex - Scarlet Coon by Tycoon II Mrs C W Pinne
1995 F(-),3(0),P(0),4(10),U(-)

541 17/3 Southwell P' (L) MDO 3m 9 GS *mid-div, fdng whn p.u. 3 out* P

631	23/3	Market Rase'	(L)	MEM	3m	3	GF	*cls up, outpcd 2 out*	3	0

Of no account - last in bad race 0

SPRINGFORD (Irish) — I 181[6]

SPRING FUN b.g. 13 Over The River (FR) - Russian Fun by Zabeg — David Young

265	2/3	Didmarton	(L)	OPE	3m	6	G	*cls up to 11th, sn btn, t.o. 3 out*	4	13
480	11/3	Plumpton	(L)	HC	3m 1f 110yds	6	GS	*prom till 9th, t.o. from 14th, p.u. before last.*	P	0
654	23/3	Badbury Rin'	(L)	OPE	3m	5	G	*prom till wknd 14th, one pace final m*	4	0
1057	13/4	Badbury Rin'	(L)	MEM	3m	4	GF	*j.w. chsd ldr, ld apr last, ran on well*	1	16
1167	20/4	Larkhill	(R)	MEM	3m	9	GF	*prom thruout, ch 4 out, no able to qckn*	3	15
1393	6/5	Cotley Farm	(L)	XX	3m	10	GF	*in tch, 4th at 9th, ev ch 4 out, one pace aft*	2	17
1543	17/5	Newton Abbot	(L)	HC	3 1/4m 110yds	8	G	*in tch till wknd apr 16th, t.o..*	4	0

H/Chase winner 94; missed 95; novice ridden to land bad Members & struggles in decent company now 15

SPRINGLARK(IRE) b.m. 5 Lafontaine (USA) - Yellow Canary by Miner's Lamp — Mrs Luisa Wrighton

13	14/1	Cottenham	(R)	MDO	3m	10	G	*rear & blnd 9th, t.o. & p.u. 13th*	P	0
107	17/2	Marks Tey	(L)	MDN	3m	15	G	*alwys bhnd, nvr nr ldrs*	3	0
424	9/3	High Easter	(L)	MDN	3m	10	S	*prom, chsd ldr 14th, ev ch whn u.r. 3 out*	U	-
680	30/3	Cottenham	(R)	MDO	3m	11	GF	*mid-div, mstk 11th, prog 14th, chsd wnr 16th-last, no imp*	3	10
933	8/4	Marks Tey	(L)	LAD	3m	3	G	*s.i.s. prog to cls 2nd 14th, outpcd 16th, styd on*	2	14

Shows a little but flattered by 2nd in Ladies & more needed for a win 12

SPRING SABRE ch.g. 6 Broadsword (USA) - Karafair by Karabas — J H Busby

439	9/3	Newton Brom'	(R)	MDN	3m	7	GS	*jmpd slwly 1st & 2nd, bhnd whn p.u. 2 out*	P	0
712	30/3	Barbury Cas'	(L)	MDO	3m	10	G	*33s-14s, rear, prog 10th, 3rd nxt, wkng whn ran out 4 out*	r	-
1104	14/4	Guilsborough	(L)	MDN	3m	18	G	*mstks, hld up, some prog 11th, nvr rchd ldrs*	5	0
1183	21/4	Mollington	(R)	MDN	3m	10	F	*jmpd sketchily, last pair in tch til ran out 9th*	r	-
1433	6/5	Ashorne	(R)	MDO	3m	16	G	*(bl) chsd ldrs til ran out bnd apr 11th*	r	-

Cannot jump & wayward 0

SPRING TOUR (Irish) — I 478[P]

SPRINGVILLA(IRE) b.g. 8 Invited (USA) - Rooske Loraine by Vulgan — C A Green

1995 F(-),F(-),U(-)

1060	13/4	Badbury Rin'	(L)	MDO	3m	14	GF	*hld up, prog 14th, 4th & ev ch whn f 3 out*	F	-

Placed in Irish Maiden 94; easily good enough to win but 1 finish from 8 starts 94-6 14

SPRITLY LADY (Irish) — I 132[B], I 222[P], I 348[3], I 381[P], I 532[4], I 622[2], I 649[5]

SPRUCEFIELD ch.g. 13 Pamroy - Vacuna by Bargello — M H D Barlow

1995 **P(0)**,7(0),7(0),3(18),1(19)

24	20/1	Barbury Cas'	(L)	XX	3m	12	GS	*sn wll bhnd, t.o. & p.u. 9th*	P	0
124	17/2	Kingston Bl'	(L)	CON	3m	17	GS	*chsd ldrs, effrt apr 14th, wknd nxt*	8	0
434	9/3	Newton Brom'	(R)	CON	3m	11	GS	*alwys prom, wknd frm 3 out*	5	0
886	6/4	Kimble	(L)	CON	3m	5	GF	*ld to 2nd, strgglng frm 5th, t.o. 12th*	4	0
1177	21/4	Mollington	(R)	INT	3m	14	F	*mid-div, 6th & effrt hlfwy, no prog frm 13th*	5	10
1438	6/5	Ashorne	(R)	XX	3m	14	G	*chsng grp,went mod 3rd 13th,ran on strngly 2 out,jst faild*	2	19

Intermediate winner 95; only form last start in 96; may have chances late season 97; G/F-S 16

SPURIOUS b.g. 10 The Parson - Lady Of Desmond by Polly's Jet — Mrs A P Kelly

1995 **F(NH),U(NH),3(NH),F(NH),8(NH),7(NH)**

165	17/2	Weston Park	(L)	RES	3m	9	G	*mid-div, prog 13th, 3rd & in tch whn f 3 out*	F	-
292	2/3	Eaton Hall	(R)	RES	3m	15	G	*mid-div, prog 13th, 3rd 4 out, fdd nxt*	7	0
366	6/3	Bangor	(L)	HC	3m 110yds	4	GS	*disp ld, ld 9th, joined and hit 2 out, soon hdd, mstk last, one pace.*	2	18
1193	21/4	Sandon	(L)	OPE	3m	8	G	*ld to 10th, not qckn frm 5 out*	4	13
1233	27/4	Weston Park	(L)	RES	3m	14	G	*disp frm 8th,lft ld 4 out,clr whn carred wd by loose horse*	2	16
1338	3/5	Bangor	(L)	HC	3m 110yds	8	S	*keen hold, mstk 2nd, in tch, effort 13th, btn 3 out.*	3	14
1456	8/5	Uttoxeter	(L)	HC	2m 5f	11	G	*cl up, ld apr 9th to next, wknd quickly 12th, bhnd when p.u. before 4 out.*	P	0

2nd in bad H/Chase; unlucky 5th start & should stick to Restricteds - could win 15

SPY DESSA br.g. 8 Uncle Pokey - Jeanne Du Barry by Dubassoff (USA) — Mrs Pamela Cann

1995 P(0)

448	9/3	Haldon	(R)	MDO	3m	10	S	*j.w. ld 3rd, disp 10-14th, wknd nxt, tired nr fin*	3	0
733	31/3	Little Wind'	(R)	MDO	3m	13	GS	*prom til outpcd 15th, v tired clsng stgs*	4	0
988	8/4	Kingston St'	(R)	MEM	3m	7	F	*keen hld, prog to cls 2nd 6th til u.r. 9th*	U	-
1128	20/4	Stafford Cr'	(R)	RES	3m	17	S	*midfld, wnt 4th 12th, nvr nrr*	4	0
1347	4/5	Holnicote	(L)	MDO	3m	16	GS	*cls up, disp 4-6th, chsd ldrs aft til fdd 14th, p.u. aft nxt*	P	0

Tailed off when completing & no stamina **0**

SQUEEZE PLAY b.g. 11 Gleason (USA) - Cherry Leaf by Vulgan — Mrs D M Grissell

217	24/2 Newtown	(L) RES	3m	17 GS	*alwys well bhnd, t.o. & p.u. 11th*	P	0
387	9/3 Llanfrynach	(R) RES	3m	11 GS	*(bl) prom til rdn & wknd 13th, t.o. & p.u. 2 out*	P	0
840	6/4 Maisemore P'	(L) RES	3m	9 GF	*(bl) alwys mid-div, nvr trbld ldrs*	6	0

Had ability but all gone now **0**

SQUIRRELLSDAUGHTER gr.m. 9 Black Minstrel - Grey Squirell by Golden Gorden — J W Beddoes
1995 U(-),1(15),1(18),1(21),1(21),3(17),2(21),U(-),1(23)

258	29/2 Nottingham	(L) HC	3m 110yds	10 G	*settld to track ldrs, blnd and u.r. 7th.*	U	-
366	6/3 Bangor	(L) HC	3m 110yds	4 GS	*(fav) patiently rdn, hdwy going well when hit 6 out, ld between last 2, readily.*	1	20
670	28/3 Aintree	(L) HC	3m 1f	9 G	*jmpd poorly, alwys rear, well bhnd from 4 out, t.o. when p.u. after 2 out.*	P	0
908	8/4 Hereford	(R) HC	2m 3f	12 GF	*(fav) held up, hdwy 6th, chsd ldr and mstk 9th, ev ch from 3 out, kept on run-in.*	2	19
1120	20/4 Bangor	(L) HC	2 1/2m 110yds	13 S	*rear, mstk 1st, hdwy to track ldrs 7th, outpcd from 4 out, fourth and btn when f heavily 2 out.*	F	-

Won 5 points in 95; found bad H/Chase; struggled apart & too many mistakes; return to points 97 ...... **20**

STAB IN THE DARK b.g. 8 Broadsword (USA) - Lucy Parker by Milan — J N Cheatle
1995 P(0),U(-)

1104	14/4 Guilsborough	(L) MDN	3m	18 G	*prom, ld 12th-3 out, wknd, fin tired*	4	0

Well-beaten in 2 completions from 6 starts 94-6 but best effort yet only start 96 .... **10**

STAFFY'S BOY (Irish) — **I** 110[F], **I** 174[1], **I** 257[4], **I** 489[2]

STAG FIGHT b.g. 6 Primitive Rising (USA) - Gamewood by Ascertain (USA) — Mrs P A Russell
1995 F(-),P(0),1(15)

77	11/2 Wetherby Po'	(L) RES	3m	18 GS	*cls up, 3rd 2 out, no ext aft*	5	16
118	17/2 Witton Cast'	(R) INT	3m	9 S	*(fav) rear, prog to 3rd at 12th, chsd wnr nxt, no imp aft*	2	17
224	24/2 Duncombe Pa'	(R) RES	3m	12 GS	*chsd wnr 12th, rdn to chal 2 out, unable qckn flat*	2	17
539	17/3 Southwell P'	(L) RES	3m	11 GS	*(Jt fav) prom, unable to qckn 14th, onepcd*	3	0
584	23/3 Wetherby Po'	(L) RES	3m	13 S	*(fav) 2nd til ld 12th, styd on well frm 2 out*	1	19
1091	14/4 Whitwell-On'	(R) XX	3m	6 G	*sttld mid-div, ev ch 5 out, onepcd nxt*	4	13
1369	4/5 Gisburn	(R) CON	3m	10 G	*4l 5th whn f 14th*	F	-

Maiden winner 95; onepaced & thorough stayer; should find stamina Confined; G-S **20**

STAG HUNT (Irish) — **I** 98[3], **I** 179[4], **I** 219[5], **I** 260[3], **I** 305[F], **I** 361[4], **I** 402[6], **I** 488[3], **I** 599[P]

STAGS ROCK (Irish) — **I** 332, , **I** 507[F]

ST AIDAN (Irish) — **I** 125[P], **I** 206[U], **I** 236[P], **I** 430[4]

STAINLESS STEEL ch.g. 9 Crawter - Culmleigh Princess by Solar Duke — S H Sweetland
1995 P(0),1(11)

276	2/3 Clyst St Ma'	(L) MEM	3m	4 S	*last til prog 15th, went 2nd nxt, no ch wth wnr*	2	10
926	8/4 Bishopsleigh	(R) RES	3m	9 G	*wll bhnd frm 10th, p.u. 4 out*	P	0
1123	20/4 Stafford Cr'	(R) MEM	3m	3 S	*disp to 4th, chsd ldr aft, no imp frm 3 out*	2	16

Members winner 95 & only effective in that company **12**

STALBRIDGE BILL b.g. 6 El Conquistador - Abridged by Nearly A Hand — Mrs J Frankland

375	9/3 Barbury Cas'	(L) MDN	3m	14 GS	*alwys prom, ld 4 out, pshd out flat*	1	16
707	30/3 Barbury Cas'	(L) RES	3m	18 G	*bhnd, some prog frm 12th, sn outpcd*	6	10

Beat subsequent winners on debut; disappointing other start but time to make amends **16**

STALBRIDGE GOLD ch.m. 7 Vital Season - Abridged by Nearly A Hand — C J Barnes
1995 2(15),P(0),**10(NH)**,**8(NH)**

17	14/1 Tweseldown	(R) MDN	3m	11 GS	*prom, 3rd & outpcd 15th, wknd, hit 2 out & p.u.*	P	0
45	3/2 Wadebridge	(L) MDO	3m	10 GF	*tckd ldrs, ld 15th, clr 3 out, wknd & hdd flat*	2	14
283	2/3 Clyst St Ma'	(L) MDN	3m	7 S	*cls up, ld 3 out, styd on well, easily*	1	14
562	17/3 Ottery St M'	(L) XX	3m	12 G	*in tch to 13th, wknd & p.u. 4 out*	P	0
1056	13/4 Badbury Rin'	(L) RES	3m	10 GF	*cls up to 7th, p.u. 9th, tack broke*	P	0
1497	11/5 Holnicote	(L) RES	3m	10 G	*wll in tch 14th, wknd 18th, lft 3rd last*	3	13

Easily won small race but struggling to follow up; onepaced; may go close on Soft in 97 .... **15**

STALBRIDGE RETURN b.m. 8 New Member - Abridged by Nearly A Hand — Mrs Marilyn Burrough

1395	6/5 Cotley Farm	(L) RES	3m	8 GF	*sn rr, t.o. whn p.u. 8th*	P	0
1495	11/5 Holnicote	(L) MDO	3m	11 G	*bhnd til p.u. 11th*	P	0

Of no account **0**

ST AMOUR b.g. 5 Broadsword (USA) - Mini Gazette by London Gazette — Mrs L M Boulter

62 10/2 Cottenham (R) MDO 3m 6 GS *blnd & u.r. 2nd* U -

A brief start 0

STAND ALONE (Irish) — **I** 543[4]

STANESHIEL b.g. 10 Royal Fountain - Mildenstone by Milan — Miss D M M Calder

186 24/2 Friars Haugh (L) MEM 3m 7 S *ld brfly 14th, styd in tch til outpcd frm 2 out* 5 11
321 2/3 Corbridge (R) MDN 3m 12 GS *mid-div, prog 10th, not rch ldrs* 4 10
614 23/3 Friars Haugh (L) MDN 3m 10 G *3rd hlfwy, ld 4 out, styd on wll* 1 13
754 31/3 Lockerbie (R) RES 3m 8 G *cls up whn p.u. lame aft 10th* P 0

Placed in 94; missed 95; won weak Maiden but problems after; more needed 13

STANFORD BOY b.g. 11 Stanford - Gothic Lady by Godswalk (USA) — D J & C B Clapham

350 3/3 Garnons (L) CON 3m 11 GS *hld up til effrt to ld 14th, jnd 3 out, wknd frm nxt* 5 0
523 16/3 Larkhill (R) MXO 3m 8 G *bhnd til ran on frm 4 out, nrst fin* 4 15
836 6/4 Maisemore P' (L) MEM 3m 7 GF *(fav) w.w. prog 9th, b.d. nxt* B -
1046 13/4 Bitterley (L) LAD 3m 9 G *hld up, prog 9th, effrt 12th, onepcd frm 15th* 4 16
1170 20/4 Chaddesley ' (L) CON 3m 9 G *prog 10th,hit 13th & lost plc,styd on 3 out,rdn to 2nd flat* 2 18
1332 1/5 Cheltenham (L) HC 3m 1f 110yds 11 G *bhnd, rdn and lost tch apr 12th, t.o.* 5 0

Dual winner 94; missed 95; retains ability but struggling to win again; Members best chance at 12 16

STANLEY STEAMER (Irish) — **I** 21[1]

STANWICK BELFRY ch.m. 8 Crested Lark - Rustic Princess by Devon Prince — T F G Marks

1995 P(0),6(0),P(0)

343 3/3 Higham (L) MDO 3m 11 G *rear, sn t.o., p.u. 3 out* P 0
496 16/3 Horseheath (R) MDO 3m 10 GF *hld up rear, nvr on trms, t.o. 10th* 6 0

Beaten miles on only completion 96 & not improving so far 0

STANWICK FARLAP ch.m. 10 St Columbus - Stanwick Twister by Netherkelly — T F G Marks

1995 F(-),2(18),3(14),2(19),2(16),3(16),7(0)

178 18/2 Horseheath (R) INT 3m 11 G *prom til wknd 15th, bhnd whn p.u. last* P 0
310 2/3 Ampton (R) CON 3m 13 G *prom, disp ld 9th-11th, ev ch til wknd 3 out* 8 17
436 9/3 Newton Brom' (R) LAD 3m 10 GS *wll bhnd til prog 14th, gd run frm 2 out, styd on* 3 17
723 31/3 Garthorpe (R) CON 3m 19 G *in tch, clsd frm 11th, chsd ldr aft 15th, ld last, rdn out* 1 18
1068 13/4 Horseheath (R) INT 3m 7 F *chsd ldr 10th-15th, rdn & onepcd frm 3 out* 3 15
1257 27/4 Cottenham (R) CON 3m 5 F *(fav) alwys prom, ld aft 12th, prssd 3 out, rdn out flat, comf* 1 15
1521 12/5 Garthorpe (R) INT 3m 7 GF *(fav) cls up, ld 4th til ct last, ran on onepcd* 2 16
1594 25/5 Garthorpe (R) MEM 3m 10 G *prog 6th, 2nd 10th-4 out, 3rd aft, just hld for 2nd* 3 18
1645 2/6 Dingley (R) INT 3m 5 GF *ld 5-9th, lft in ld 12th-2 out, kpt on one pace* 2 16

Onepaced & consistent; 2 wins, 10 places, 16 starts 95/6; ratio likely to continue; S-F 18

STANWICK FORT b.m. 7 Belfort (FR) - Allez Stanwick by Goldhill — J L Gledson

1995 P(0),P(0),F(-),2(0),r(-),3(0),U(-),F(-),**P(NH)**

407 9/3 Dalston (R) MDO 2 1/2m 13 G *f 3rd* F -

Showed a little ability 95 but blink & you missed him in 96 0

STANWICK LASS ch.m. 11 Netherkelly - Rustic Princess by Devon Prince — T F G Marks

1995 F(-),R(-)

344 3/3 Higham (L) MDO 3m 12 G *sn bhnd, t.o. & p.u. 11th* P 0
675 30/3 Cottenham (R) MEM 3m 6 GF *in tch, chsd wnr 14th-last, kpt on onepcd* 4 10
972 8/4 Thorpe Lodge (L) MDO 3m 9 GF *(fav) alwys rear hlf, outpcd in 6th 6 out, p.u. 3 out* P 0
1064 13/4 Horseheath (R) MDO 3m 3 F *(fav) alwys 2nd, ev ch 2 out, rdn & nt qkn flat* 2 0
1256 27/4 Cottenham (R) MEM 3m 6 F *hld up rear, mstk 10th, lost tch nxt, sn t.o.* 5 0
1403 6/5 Northaw (L) MDO 3m 8 F *(bl) rr, in tch til f 8th* F -
1523 12/5 Garthorpe (R) MDO 3m 11 GF *(fav) (bl) prom, 4th at 8th, 3rd frm 10th til wknd 4 out* 5 0

Basically useless yet favourite three times - bookmakers should send her some mints 0

STAR ACTOR b.g. 10 Pollerton - Play The Part by Deep Run — Miss S Cockburn

1995 P(0),P(0),3(15),1(20),3(18),**P(0)**

335 3/3 Heythrop (R) INT 3m 9 G *set fast pace til hdd 11th, wknd nxt, p.u. 14th* P 0
508 16/3 Magor (R) INT 3m 5 GS *cls up in 5l 2nd whn p.u. 11th, lame* P 0

Intermediate winner 95; changed hands 96; problems now 0

STAREMBER LAD b.h. 12 New Member - Star Beauty by Jock Scot — Miss J M Cumings

1995 1(19),**P(0)**,6(0),1(19),**5(0)**

27 20/1 Barbury Cas' (L) LAD 3m 15 GS *in tch, chsd wnr 13th, 2nd & hld whn p.u. aft 2 out, dead* P 0

Dead 23

STARLIGHT FOUNTAIN (Irish) — I 202P

STARLING LAKE (Irish) — I 105P

STARLIN SAM b.g. 7 Alias Smith (USA) - Czarosa by Czarist — John Sisterson

53	4/2 Alnwick	(L) MDO 3m	13 G	*alwys bhnd, t.o. & p.u. 13th*	P	0
323	2/3 Corbridge	(R) MDN 3m	12 GS	*prom early, jmpd lft thro'out, p.u. 12th*	P	0
705	30/3 Tranwell	(L) MDO 3m	9 GS	*mstks, last frm 3rd, nvr dang*	7	0
916	8/4 Tranwell	(L) MDO 2 1/2m	8 GF	*mid-div, handy 4th at 6th, wknd 11th, lost tch nxt*	3	0

Last on both completions & shows nothing **0**

STAR OF STEANE b.m. 7 Crested Lark - Lady Carinya by Heswall Honey — Sir Michael Connell

21	20/1 Barbury Cas'	(L) MEM 3m	16 GS	*lost tch whn f 7th*	F	-
233	24/2 Heythrop	(R) MDN 3m	14 GS	*alwys rear, p.u. 12th*	P	0

Unpromising **0**

STATELY LOVER b.g. 13 Free State - Maid In Love by Sky Gipsy — Mrs Jean R Bishop

961	8/4 Heathfield	(R) MEM 3m	5 G	*(fav) lft 2nd 11th,ld 4 out,8l clr nxt, rdn 2 out, wknd & hdd flat*	2	12

Returned from long absence but denied on possibly last chance **11**

STATION MAN (Irish) — I 269P, I 482P

STATOIL (Irish) — I 240, , I 306P, I 354P

STAY IN TOUCH (Irish) — I 5F, I 14[1], I 54[1]

STAYS FRESH b.g. 6 Gambler's Cup (USA) - Cassandra Moor Vii by Damsire Unregistered — D Westwood

516	16/3 Dalton Park	(R) MDO 3m	11 G	*rear, effrt aft 14th, sn wknd, p.u. 16th*	P	0
591	23/3 Wetherby Po'	(L) MDO 3m	14 S	*rear whn blnd & u.r. 10th*	U	-
1094	14/4 Whitwell-On'	(R) MDO 2 1/2m 88yds	16 G	*twrds rear, nvr a threat*	7	0
1301	28/4 Southwell P'	(L) MDO 3m	10 GF	*prom early, mid-div hlfwy, onepcd*	5	10
1450	6/5 Witton Cast'	(R) MDO 3m	14 G	*rear, gd hdwy 12th, cls 2nd 14th til wknd 3 out*	5	0
1575	19/5 Corbridge	(R) MDO 3m	10 G	*mid-div, prog hlfwy, chsd ldrs 14th, nvr dang*	3	0

Well beaten when 3rd & more stamina needed for a winning chance **10**

STEADY AWAY(IRE) b.g. 7 Salluceva - Sprightly's Last by Random Shot — Mrs J D Bulman

1995 5(0),F(-),F(-),3(12),2(14),**P(0)**

51	4/2 Alnwick	(L) MDO 3m	17 G	*rear, kpt on frm 3 out, nvr dang*	6	0
88	11/2 Alnwick	(L) MDO 3m	11 GS	*prom, ld 11th-nxt, rallied 3 out, ld last, styd on well*	1	16
189	24/2 Friars Haugh	(L) RES 3m	9 S	*alwys twrds rear*	6	0
398	9/3 Dalston	(R) MEM 3m	13 G	*prom whn mstk 7th, rmndrs 9th, nvr sn wth chnc*	6	0
754	31/3 Lockerbie	(R) RES 3m	8 G	*(bl) ld til ran out 9th*	r	-
895	6/4 Whittington	(L) RES 3m	5 F	*(bl) chsd ldrs to 11th, wknd & p.u. apr 14th*	P	0
1151	20/4 Whittington	(L) INT 3m	12 G	*(bl) nvr bynd mid-div*	7	0

Confirmed promise in modest race but fell apart & signs ominous now **11**

STEADY JOHNNY (Irish) — I 260P, I 288P, I 321[1], I 362P, I 489[4]

STEAMBURD b.m. 6 Dowsing (USA) - No Control by Bustino — M Hamilton

1995 r(-)

448	9/3 Haldon	(R) MDO 3m	10 S	*strng hld, prom, 3rd hlfwy, 4th & wkng 14th, p.u. 3 out*	P	0
630	23/3 Kilworthy	(L) MDN 3m	10 GS	*ld, narrow ld whn u.r. 12th*	U	-
1116	17/4 Hockworthy	(L) MDO 3m	9 GS	*ld to 11th, chsd wnr to 3 out, 3rd & btn aft*	3	0
1280	27/4 Bratton Down	(L) MDO 3m	14 GF	*ld/disp to 13th, chsd ldr aft, onepcd 2 out, fin 3rd, prmtd*	2	13

Gradually improving but not enough stamina & needs stronger handling; may go close 97 .... **13**

STEDE QUARTER b.g. 9 Cruise Missile - Dragon Lass by Cheval — Mrs S Dench

1995 5(12),5(0),2(15),1(17),2(16),1(17),**4D(18)**

32	20/1 Higham	(L) OPE 3m	15 GF	*chsd ldrs to 11th, wkng whn u.r. 13th*	U	-
56	10/2 Cottenham	(R) OPE 3m	12 GS	*prom, ld 9th-13th, cls 3rd 3 out, no imp wnr nxt*	3	20
249	25/2 Charing	(L) XX 3m	11 GS	*ld 6th-4 out, chal & ld 2 out, kpt on well*	1	18
453	9/3 Charing	(L) XX 3m	4 G	*(fav) ld 4th, blnd 11th & 15th, hdd apr last, no ext*	2	14
573	17/3 Detling	(L) OPE 4m	9 GF	*alwys prom, 4th whn jmpd slwly 4 out, no ch aft*	4	0
775	31/3 Penshurst	(L) CON 3m	8 GS	*in tch, hdwy 12th, cls up in 3rd whn f nxt*	F	-
813	6/4 Charing	(L) XX 3m	5 F	*(fav) clsd up 12th, disp 14-15th, 2nd aft, chal 2 out, ld last*	1	17
920	8/4 Aldington	(L) OPE 3m	6 F	*sttld last, lost tch 14th, t.o. & p.u. aft 16th*	P	0
1207	21/4 Heathfield	(R) CON 3m	9 F	*in tch, 6th & no ch 4 out, kpt on frm 2 out*	4	14
1440	6/5 Aldington	(L) INT 3m	5 HD	*cls up, ld 15th-2 out, kpt on gamely*	2	15
1537	16/5 Folkestone	(R) HC 3 1/4m	8 GF	*ld after 5th to 2 out, rallied gamely to ld run-in.*	1	18
1630	31/5 Stratford	(L) HC 3 1/2m	16 GF	*nvr on terms, t.o. when p.u. before 17th.*	P	0

Modest, stays & tough; H/Chase win spells problems for 97 chances; G/S-F **19**

STEEL BEE b.m. 7 Bee Alive (USA) - Steel Haven by Haven — Mrs M R Sullivan

1995 U(-),r(-),r(-),P(0)

147 17/2 Erw Lon (L) MDN 3m 8 G *rear, lost tch 10th, p.u. 13th* P 0
Yet to complete the course 0

STEEL DANCE b.g. 8 Mashhor Dancer (USA) - Damaska (USA) by Damascus (USA) Mrs D Burton
1995 P(0),2(10),F(-),3(11),1(14)
524 16/3 Larkhill (R) INT 3m 11 G *prom to 10th, t.o. whn u.r. 14th* U -
709 30/3 Barbury Cas' (L) OPE 3m 15 G *alwys mid-div, nvr on terms, t.o. & p.u. 2 out* P 0
Won a bad Maiden in 95 & brief 96 season showed nothing 0

STEELE JUSTICE ch.g. 12 Avocat - Strandhill by Bargello W Manners
1995 **5(10)**,3(19),3(18),5(13),2(17)
48 4/2 Alnwick (L) LAD 3m 9 G *tckd ldrs, eff 3 out, ev ch last, not qckn nr fin* 2 20
85 11/2 Alnwick (L) LAD 3m 11 GS *(fav) prom, ld 14th, clr 3 out, all out aft last* 1 21
318 2/3 Corbridge (R) LAD 3m 5f 10 GS *(fav) alwys abt same plc, nvr nrr* 5 15
Formerly useful; staged revival 96 but finished early; could win at 13 if fit 19

STEEL FAUCON(IRE) ch.g. 7 Nepotism - Le Agio by Le Bavard (FR) F D Cornes
1995 R(-),P(0),F(-)
219 24/2 Newtown (L) RES 3m 17 GS *f 1st, dead* F -
Dead 0

STEEL GUEST(IRE) b.g. 8 Flash Of Steel - Guess Who by Be My Guest (USA) A J Hogarth
1995 1(16),1(19),2(18)
1151 20/4 Whittington (L) INT 3m 12 G *mid-div, wknd 7th, rear & t.o. whn p.u. 11th* P 0
Won twice in 95 & promising; changed hands & can only be watched now 12

STEEL ICE ch.g. 8 Broadsword (USA) - Iced Tea by Pappatea Mrs A J McVay
1995 P(0)
107 17/2 Marks Tey (L) MDN 3m 15 G *chsd ldrs to 10th, wknd 12th, t.o. & p.u. 3 out* P 0
Rarely runs & shows nothing now 0

STEEL PLATE gr.g. 9 Pragmatic - Mid-Way Model by Royal Highway A W Froggatt
457 9/3 Eyton-On-Se' (L) INT 3m 11 G *mid to rear, no ch whn p.u. 4 out* P 0
Of no account 0

STEEL STREET(IRE) b.g. 6 The Parson - Lady Siobhan by Laurence O E J Parrott
145 17/2 Larkhill (R) MDO 3m 13 G *alwys rear, nvr nrr* 5 0
Last in a good Maiden & may do better if running regularly 10

STEEL VALLEY(IRE) ch.m. 8 Orchestra - Caddy Girl by Avocat T White
1995 **8(NH),F(NH)**
509 16/3 Magor (R) MDN 3m 9 GS *dist 2nd frm 9th, mstks 15th & nxt, lost 2nd 2 out* 3 0
607 23/3 Howick (L) MDN 3m 12 S *alwys 3rd/4th, wknd frm 13th, clr 3rd whn f 3 out* F -
850 6/4 Howick (L) MDN 3m 14 GF *rear, p.u. 6th* P 0
1156 20/4 Llanwit Maj' (R) MEM 3m 7 GS *w.w., prog to jn wnr 16th-nxt, sn outpcd* 2 10
1273 27/4 Pyle (R) MDO 3m 9 G *last at 5th, t.o. nxt, p.u. 11th* P 0
1561 18/5 Bassaleg (R) MDO 3m 8 F *mstks 3 & 4th,prog 11th, 3rd & ev ch whn s.u. apr 2 out* S -
1605 25/5 Bassaleg (R) MDO 3m 8 GS *(fav) 4/5-7/4, rear, prog to 3rd 10th, lost plc 12th,ran on late* 3 12
A little ability but not enough stamina & placed in poor races 11

ST ENTON b.g. 11 Record Token - Nuse Avella by Jimsun R Green
1995 P(0),P(0),P(0)
240 25/2 Southwell P' (L) MDO 3m 15 HO *alwys bhnd, t.o. 8th, p.u. aft 11th* P 0
333 3/3 Market Rase' (L) MDO 3m 11 G *alwys rear, t.o. 13th, jmpd slwly last* 6 0
518 16/3 Dalton Park (R) MDO 3m 15 G *6th whn blnd & u.r. 7th* U -
1021 13/4 Brocklesby ' (L) MEM 3m 3 GF *alwys 2nd, outpcd frm 8th* 2 0
Beaten a fence when 2nd & no hope of a win 0

STEP-ASIDE ch.g. 8 Miramar Reef - Purple Pride by Derek H Miss J F Holmes
635 23/3 Market Rase' (L) RES 3m 8 GF *alwys last pair, outpcd 11th, p.u. 4 out* P 0
Of no account 0

STEPASIDEBOY b.g. 6 Idiot's Delight - Waterside by Shackleton E H Crow
1995 r(-)
167 17/2 Weston Park (L) MDN 3m 10 G *5th whn ran out 4th* r -
568 17/3 Wolverhampt' (L) MDN 3m 9 GS *hld up, ld 3 out, styd on well* 1 15
1481 11/5 Bredwardine (R) RES 3m 14 G *s.s. clsd by 11th, strng run to ld 2 out, kpt on well* 1 19

Awkward ride but potentially useful; good performance last start; should upgrade; G-G/S 20

STEPHENS PET ch.g. 13 Piaffer (USA) - Mrs Stephens by Master Stephen — Dr P P Brown

1995 3(20),1(28),1(24),1(25),U(-)

291	2/3	Eaton Hall	(R)	LAD	3m	10	G	*(fav) hld up, prog 12th, ld 2 out, ran on well flat, just hld on*	1	23
429	9/3	Upton-On-Se'	(R)	LAD	3m	4	GS	*(fav) 2nd til qcknd to ld 15th, sn clr, easily*	1	24
663	24/3	Eaton Hall	(R)	LAD	3m	8	S	*(fav) hld up in tch, prog to ld 10th, comf*	1	24
743	31/3	Upper Sapey	(R)	LAD	3m	7	GS	*(fav) mstks, prog to disp 3 out-nxt, rnwd effrt to ld last, sn clr*	1	23

Ultra-consistent; won 19 of 24 from 91-6; well placed; can win more at 14; G-Hy 25

STEPHLEYS GIRL br.m. 9 New Member - Latanett by Dairialatan — D Gibbs

1995 4(12)

773	31/3	Pantyderi	(R)	MDN	3m	8	G	*mid-div, p.u. 11th, lame*	P	0

Fair run in 95 but obvious problems now - best watched if running 97 10

STEPPY BOY (Irish) — I 386F, I 517F

STERLING BUCK(USA) b.g. 9 Buckfinder (USA) - Aged (USA) by Olden Times — D J Clapham

1995 **9(NH),6(NH),P(NH),5(NH),P(NH),4(NH)**

841	6/4	Maisemore P'	(L)	MDN	3m	9	GF	*sttld, in tch, prog to chs wnnr 2 out, hit last, nt qkn flat*	2	14
1175	20/4	Chaddesley '	(L)	MDN	3m	9	G	*(fav) w.w. gd prog frm rear 16th, no ext frm 3 out*	4	10
1484	11/5	Bredwardine	(R)	MDO	3m	17	G	*prom til not qckn frm 15th, styd on 2 out, clsng flat*	2	15
1561	18/5	Bassaleg	(R)	MDO	3m	8	F	*(fav) ld to 7th, trckd ldr aft, ld 3 out, clr last, easily*	1	16
1601	25/5	Bassaleg	(R)	RES	3m	12	GS	*(Jt fav) ld to 4th, 2nd til prog to ld 3 out, ran on*	1	20

Not 100% genuine but found right chances late season; should win Confined 97; G/S-F 19

STEVIE BE (Irish) — I 37P

ST GREGORY b.g. 8 Ardross - Crymlyn by Welsh Pageant — A Howland Jackson

1995 4(14),U(-),P(0),1(22),4(14),P(0),**2(20)**

8	14/1	Cottenham	(R)	CON	3m	10	G	*w.w. in tch, no prog frm 16th, fin with no irons*	6	14
90	11/2	Ampton	(R)	CON	3m	5	GF	*mstk 2nd,rdn & chsd wnr 13th-15th,outpcd 3 out,2nd agn last*	2	20
102	17/2	Marks Tey	(L)	CON	3m	17	G	*mid div, 10th & rddn hlfwy, 4th & no ch 16th*	5	17
311	2/3	Ampton	(R)	LAD	3m	4	G	*(bl) mstks, made virt all, rddn & qknd clr appr 3 out, drvn out*	1	22
421	9/3	High Easter	(L)	LAD	3m	5	S	*(bl) rr,hit 2nd & 8th, pshd up to ld 11th,made rest,styd on wll*	1	20
493	16/3	Horseheath	(R)	LAD	3m	4	GF	*s.v.s mstks 1st & 2nd, nvr on terms, wknd 12th,lft 3rd 4 out*	3	14
832	6/4	Marks Tey	(L)	LAD	3m	8	G	*(bl) ld to 3rd, prog agn 13th, ld aft 15th, ran on whn chal flat*	1	24
933	8/4	Marks Tey	(L)	LAD	3m	3	G	*(fav) (bl) made all, drew clr 4 out, unchal*	1	20
1146	20/4	Higham	(L)	OPE	3m	7	F	*(Jt fav) (bl) chsd ldng pair,mstk 14th,chal 2 out,ran on flat,just hld*	2	24
1324	28/4	Fakenham P-'	(L)	LAD	3m	6	G	*(bl) 5th whn blnd & u.r. 7th*	U	-
1401	6/5	Northaw	(L)	LAD	3m	4	F	*(bl) chsd ldr 4th,lft disp 8th,ld 12th-15th,sn ld agn & drw clr*	1	20

Tough, stays & hard ride; blinkers worked; well-ridden; best L/H; should win again; Any, best Soft 23

ST HELENS BOY b.g. 14 Abwah - Cullen by Quorum — J Tudor

1995 P(0)

153	17/2	Erw Lon	(L)	OPE	3m	15	G	*last trio, no prog, p.u. 14th*	P	0
384	9/3	Llanfrynach	(R)	OPE	3m	16	GS	*lft, sn rcvrd, cls up til aft 14th, sn btn*	6	13
506	16/3	Magor	(R)	CON	3m	8	GS	*2nd til ld 10th, 5l clr 15th, hdd & onepcd 2 out*	3	10
878	6/4	Brampton Br'	(R)	OPE	3m	5	GF	*ld to 2nd, chsd wnr til slw jmp 15th, no ch aft*	4	11
1158	20/4	Llanwit Maj'	(R)	OPE	4m	9	GS	*in tch, 3rd & rdn 3 out, no hdwy aft*	4	15

Showed just a hint of his old ability but Members offers only hope if back at 15 13

STILL HOPEFUL b.m. 7 Broadsword (USA) - Still Marching by Riboboy (USA) — Mrs E W Rees

62	10/2	Cottenham	(R)	MDO	3m	6	GS	*chsd ldr to 10th, last whn f 13th*	F	-
175	18/2	Market Rase'	(L)	MDO	2m 5f	8	GF	*ld til jnd 9th, wknd apr 2 out*	5	0
237	25/2	Southwell P'	(L)	MEM	3m	4	HO	*last, t.o. 4 out, tk poor 3rd nr fin, promoted*	2	0
540	17/3	Southwell P'	(L)	MDO	3m	9	GS	*alwys rear, p.u. 4 out*	P	0
898	6/4	Dingley	(R)	MDN	2m 5f	10	GS	*imprvng 3rd whn u.r. 5th (ditch)*	U	-

No cause to be hopeful here 0

STILL IN BUSINESS b.g. 8 Don Enrico (USA) - Mill Miss by Typhoon — R G Williams

1995 1(22),1(22),1(23),**1(25)**

142	17/2	Larkhill	(R)	MXO	3m	9	G	*ld 3rd til 4 out, chal agn last, ran on well*	2	30
260	1/3	Newbury	(L)	HC	3m	6	GS	*(Jt fav) hit 1st, hdwy 5th, hit 10th, chal 14th, blnd 4 out, rallied from 2 out, rdn and not qckn run-in.*	2	25
370	7/3	Wincanton	(R)	HC	3m 1f 110yds	5	GF	*(fav) held up, mstk 2nd, hdwy 13th, ld next to 16th, wknd 4 out.*	3	19
581	21/3	Wincanton	(R)	HC	2m 5f	13	S	*(fav) hdwy 10th, wknd apr 3 out.*	5	15
990	8/4	Kingston St'	(R)	OPE	3m	6	F	*(fav) prom til ld 11th, drew clr 3 out, comf*	1	26
1125	20/4	Stafford Cr'	(R)	OPE	3m	7	S	*(fav) hndy whn f 2nd*	F	-
1309	28/4	Little Wind'	(R)	OPE	3m	8	G	*(fav) j.w. hld up, cls 3rd 14th, ld nxt, drew clr aft 3 out,easily*	1	25
1453	7/5	Wincanton	(R)	HC	2m 5f	9	F	*(fav) hdwy 6th, hrd rdn 12th, one pace from 3 out.*	3	21
1550	18/5	Bratton Down	(L)	CON	3m	8	F	*(fav) hld up, prog 14th, ld 3 out, ran on well whn chal flat*	1	24

1633 1/6 Bratton Down (L) XX 3m 8 G *(fav) j.w. ld 8th, clr 16th, eased flat* 1 28

Very useful pointer (won 7 of 9) but disappointing in H/Chases 96; should win more Opens; F-G/S 28

STILLMORE BUSINESS ch.g. 5 Don Enrico (USA) - Mill Miss by Typhoon R G Williams

520 16/3 Larkhill (R) MDO 3m 11 G *sn wll bhnd, jmpd slwly, p.u. 6th* P 0
555 17/3 Ottery St M' (L) MDO 3m 15 G *rear whn u.r. 4th* U -
734 31/3 Little Wind' (R) MDO 3m 11 GS *slght mstk 7th, towrds rear whn badly hmpd & u.r. 9th* U -
820 6/4 Charlton Ho' (L) MDN 3m 12 GF *n.j.w., alwys rear, t.o. whn p.u. 4 out* P 0
1347 4/5 Holnicote (L) MDO 3m 16 GS *mid-div, prog 3 out, no ext frm nxt* 3 15

1st form last start; should improve & every chance of a win early 97 15

STILL OPTIMISTIC (Irish) — **I** 84^{5}, **I** 165^{6}

STILLORGAN PARK (Irish) — **I** 131^{P}, **I** 161, , **I** 228^{F}, **I** 388^{1}, **I** 577^{2}

STILLTODO gr.m. 9 Grey Ghost - River Sirene by Another River W R Wilson
1995 6(11),P(0),1(13),**P(0)**

77 11/2 Wetherby Po' (L) RES 3m 18 GS *bhnd early, p.u. 4 out* P 0
242 25/2 Southwell P' (L) RES 3m 12 HO *prom til outpcd 4 out, no ch aft nxt* 4 0
702 30/3 Tranwell (L) XX 3m 3 GS *(fav) disp til ld 13th, hrd rdn last, jnd fin* 1 13
1106 15/4 Hexham (L) HC 3m 1f 9 GF *chsd ldrs, ld after 16th, just ahd when tk wrong course between last 2.* r -
1340 4/5 Hexham (L) HC 3m 1f 13 S *cl up, ld 9th, hdd 12th, chsd wnr after till wknd apr last.* 4 19
1535 16/5 Aintree (L) HC 3m 1f 11 GF *prom, ld apr 8th to 10th, hit next, struggling to go pace 15th.* 3 10
1585 25/5 Cartmel (L) HC 3 1/4m 14 GF *prom, effort 4 out, rdn flat and ev ch till no ext near fin.* 3 18

Maiden winner 95; dead-heated in poor race 96; ran well H/Chases but lucky to win one; easy 3m best 18

STIRRUP CUP b.g. 12 Majestic Maharaj - Gold Gift by Gold Rod C Goulding
1995 **3(NH),P(NH),3(NH)**

527 16/3 Larkhill (R) MEM 3m 4 G *alwys chsng wnr, unable qckn 3 out* 2 11
776 31/3 Penshurst (L) OPE 3m 6 GS *in tch in rear, nvr dang, mstk 2 out, kpt on* 4 15

Winning chaser; well past it now & even Members may be beyond him at 13 12

ST JULIEN(IRE) b.g. 6 Le Bavard (FR) - Johns County by Crash Course Mrs L M Boulter

28 20/1 Barbury Cas' (L) RES 3m 14 GS *in tch in rear to 11th, nrly u.r. 13th, p.u. nxt* P 0
637 23/3 Siddington (L) MEM 3m 14 S *prog 10th, chsd ldrs & ch appr 15th, wknd qkly 3 out* 9 0
1129 20/4 Stafford Cr' (R) MDO 3m 11 S *in tch, prog 11th, ev ch 14th, wknd frm 3 out* 4 0
1396 6/5 Cotley Farm (L) MDO 3m 11 GF *alwys mid-div, no ch frm 4 out, onepcd* 4 0

Safe enough but not enough stamina yet - could improve 12

ST LAYCAR b.g. 11 St Columbus - Lady Carinya by Heswall Honey D R Greig
1995 3(18),**3(12)**,1(23),3(20),**3(16)**,U(-),3(20),**2(23)**,**2(19)**

39 3/2 Wadebridge (L) OPE 3m 7 GF *hld up, ev ch aft 14th, sn not qckn* 6 15

Useful up to 95 but disappeared early 96 & can only be watched if returning 16

ST MARTIN b.g. 8 Martinmas - Cedar Shade by Connaught D E Fletcher

340 3/3 Heythrop (R) MDN 3m 12 G *blnd & lost plc 4th, rear & mstk 9th, p.u. 12th* P 0

Not bred to stay & showed nothing 0

ST MORWENNA b.m. 10 St Columbus - Crozanna by Crozier Mrs J M Whitley
1995 P(0),4(0),F(-),F(-),3(10),P(0)

941 8/4 Wadebridge (L) MDN 3m 5 F *pssd ldr 12th-last, no ext run in* 3 11
1349 4/5 Holnicote (L) MDO 3m 8 GS *(fav) nvr going wll, bhnd til p.u. 14th* P 0
1524 12/5 Ottery St M' (L) MEM 3m 3 GF *plld hrd,made most to 14th, disp & ev ch til no ext apr last* 2 0
1593 25/5 Mounsey Hil' (R) MDO 3m 11 G *in tch, prog to 3rd at 16th, wll btn 3 out, p.u. nxt* P 0
1651 8/6 Umberleigh (L) MDO 3m 11 GF *prom til wnd frm 14th, stppd aft 2 out* P 0

Non-stayer & has finished 6 of 19 races; luck needed to win 11

STOKE HAND b.g. 12 Some Hand - Stoke-Andre by Flandre II W C Bunt
1995 3(18),1(16),2(17),2(19),1(18),1(20),P(0)

39 3/2 Wadebridge (L) OPE 3m 7 GF *trckd ldr, ld 8th, rdn last, hdd & no ext flat* 2 22
133 17/2 Ottery St M' (L) OPE 3m 18 GS *cls up to 12th, lost tch 15th, p.u. 3 out* P 0

Won 3 in 95 but problems last start then & finished early 96; best watched at 13; F-S 17

STONE BROOM b.m. 10 Full Of Hope - Westamist by Malacate (USA) C T Pogson
1995 P(0),P(0),5(0),4(0)

973 8/4 Thorpe Lodge (L) MDO 3m 7 GF *rear hlf, prog to disp 9-13th, 5th & outpcd 6 out* 4 0

Promise in 93; not progressed & tailed off only start in 96 0

STONEWALL CURTIN (Irish) — **I** 268^{2}, **I** 462^{F}

STONEYACRE (Irish) — I 394P

STORM ALIVE(IRE) b.g. 5 Electric - Gaileen by Boreen (FR) T P Whales

901	6/4	Dingley	(R)	MDN	2m 5f	9	GS	*last jmpng slwly til p.u. 9th*	P	0
1181	21/4	Mollington	(R)	RES	3m	10	F	*alwys last, t.o. & p.u. 11th*	P	0

Shows nothing yet **0**

STORMHEAD ch.g. 8 Move Off - Young Lamb by Sea Hawk II Miss E Stubbs

1153	20/4	Whittington	(L)	LAD	3m	10	G	*2nd whn u.r. 1st*	U	-

Quite useful winning hurdler in 94; could not have done less in 96 .... **0**

STORMHILL PILGRIM b.g. 7 Politico (USA) - In A Dream by Caruso Mike Roberts

1995 P(0),2(12),1(13)

35	20/1	Higham	(L)	RES	3m	16	GF	*ld 3rd, clr 8th, ran on strngly whn chal 2 out*	1	22
1013	13/4	Ascot	(R)	HC	3m 110yds	11	GS	*prom till ld and u.r. 5th.*	U	-
1338	3/5	Bangor	(L)	HC	3m 110yds	8	S	*alwys rear, struggling 10th, t.o. when p.u. before 4 out.*	P	0

Good start to season but badly campaigned after; back to points & could progress 97; G-S **21**

STORMHILL RECRUIT b.g. 6 Welsh Captain - Miss Oxstall's by The Brianstan Mrs A Price

1995 P(0),5(0)

426	9/3	Upton-On-Se'	(R)	CON	3m	16	GS	*mid-div whn f 7th*	F	-
602	23/3	Howick	(L)	OPE	3m	11	S	*cls up whn u.r. 6th*	U	-
748	31/3	Upper Sapey	(R)	MDO	3m	11	GS	*chsd ldrs, nvr on terms, nrst fin*	5	0
884	6/4	Brampton Br'	(R)	MDN	3m	12	GF	*wth ldrs, ev ch til wknd aft 2 out*	3	10

Slowly getting closer & may be ready to strike if staying the trip in 97 .... **13**

STORMYFAIRWEATHER (Irish) — I 439³

STORMY FASHION b.g. 9 Strong Gale - Belle Chanel by Moyrath Jet R A Read

1995 **F(NH),P(NH)**

207	24/2	Castle Of C'	(R)	MDO	3m	15	HY	*rear til p.u. 13th*	P	0
471	10/3	Milborne St'	(L)	MDO	3m	16	G	*rear whn u.r. 8th*	U	-
652	23/3	Badbury Rin'	(L)	MDO	3m	13	G	*sn wll bhnd, t.o. whn p.u. 12th*	P	0
1494	11/5	Holnicote	(L)	MDO	3m	8	G	*tubed, hld up rear, mkng gd hdwy 4th whn f 3 out*	F	-
1543	17/5	Newton Abbot	(L)	HC	3 1/4m 110yds	8	G	*alwys bhnd, t.o. when p.u. after 6th.*	P	0

Possibly unlucky 4th start but yet to complete & remains suspect **10**

STORMY SUNSET br.m. 9 Strong Gale - Last Sunset by Deep Run Mrs Jill Dennis

1995 **R(NH)**

69	10/2	Great Treth'	(R)	MDO	3m	12	S	*1st ride, ld 7th til jnd & u.r. 14th*	U	-
132	17/2	Ottery St M'	(L)	MDN	3m	9	GS	*(fav) j.w. alwys prom, ld 4 out, sn clr, imprssv*	1	18
482	13/3	Newton Abbot	(L)	HC	2m 5f 110yds	14	S	*ld 3rd to 6th, led 8th to 10th, weakening when blnd and u.r. 3 out.*	U	-
625	23/3	Kilworthy	(L)	CON	3m	11	GS	*prom, ld 8th, made rest, clr last, drvn out flat*	1	20
1073	13/4	Lifton	(R)	OPE	3m	10	S	*(Jt fav) hld up in tch, gd hdwy to disp 16-17th, sn outpcd*	5	20
1335	1/5	Cheltenham	(L)	HC	2m 5f	10	G	*ld 2nd to 10th, led 14th till apr 2 out, wknd.*	3	17
1454	7/5	Newton Abbot	(L)	HC	2m 5f 110yds	8	GS	*(fav) trckd ldr, ld 5th, hdd apr 8th, f next*	F	-

Much improved; dodgy in H/Chases but progressive in points; could win Open; easy 3m best; Soft **23**

STORMY WITNESS(IRE) br.m. 8 Strong Gale - Revenue Reserve by Proverb D J Miller

150	17/2	Erw Lon	(L)	MDN	3m	8	G	*(fav) ld 2nd, made rrest, drvn clr flat*	1	15
388	9/3	Llanfrynach	(R)	RES	3m	20	GS	*in tch, chsd wnr 14th, 4l down 3 out, sn btn*	3	11
548	17/3	Erw Lon	(L)	RES	3m	8	GS	*chsd wnr, chal 13th, sn outpcd*	2	13
1458	8/5	Uttoxeter	(L)	HC	3 1/4m	8	G	*trckd ldrs, ev ch 4 out, soon rdn and btn, left remote 2nd at last, fin tired.*	3	0

Good stable & fair start; struggles to stay but should land Restricted on easy course; G-S **17**

STRADBALLY JANE (Irish) — I 270⁵, I 380⁵, I 521P, I 578¹

STRAIGHT BAT b.g. 13 Dragonara Palace (USA) - Camdamus by Mandamus Miss S Sadler

1995 4(12),P(0),1(17),6(0),3(13),6(0),7(10)

942	8/4	Andoversford	(R)	MEM	3m	8	GF	*carried 14st, ld to aft 8th, lost plc, ran on agn 16th*	3	0
1214	24/4	Andoversford	(R)	LAD	3m	4	G	*hld up, prog to ch ldr 8-12th, outpcd nxt, t.o.*	3	0
1435	6/5	Ashorne	(R)	CON	3m	12	G	*ld 2-6th, wknd rpdly 8th, t.o. & p.u. 13th*	P	0

No longer of any account **0**

STRAIGHT BRANDY b.g. 13 Sit In The Corner (USA) - Fair Spirit by Spiritus R J Metherell

1995 S(-)

628 23/3 Kilworthy (L) INT 3m 7 GS *wth ldr to 8th, wknd rpdly 11th, p.u. nxt* P 0
1646 8/6 Umberleigh (L) MEM 3m 4 GF *ld to 7th, ld 14th-15th, wknd nxt, p.u. last, dsmntd* P 0

No longer of any account **0**

STRATHBOGIE MIST(IRE) br.g. 8 Seclude (USA) - Devon Lark by Take A Reef — Colin Way

664 24/3 Eaton Hall (R) CON 3m 15 S *rear, p.u. 6th* P 0
736 31/3 Sudlow Farm (R) CON 3m 9 G *s.s, bhnd til p.u. 4th* P 0
894 6/4 Whittington (L) OPE 3m 5 F *2nd to 3 out, wknd rpdly, p.u. last* P 0
1150 20/4 Whittington (L) MEM 3m 6 G *(fav) w.w., cls 2nd & ev ch 3 out, no ext* 1 10

Handed bad race by Stewards & no other prospects **11**

STRATTON PARK (Irish) — I 66P, I 118P, I 139P

STRAY HARMONY ch.m. 6 Noalto - Kitty Come Home by Monsanto (FR) — Mrs S Connell

1995 **13(NH),9(NH)**

268 2/3 Didmarton (L) MDN 3m 10 G *prom, ev ch 14th, outpcd by 1st pair frm 3 out* 3 10

Not disgraced but not seen after - may go closer if fit in 97 .... **13**

STRIDE TO GLORY(IRE) b.g. 5 Superpower - Damira (FR) by Pharly (FR) — M J Brown

73 11/2 Wetherby Po' (L) MDO 3m 15 GS *rear, mstk 6th, outpcd, p.u. 4 out* P 0
123 17/2 Witton Cast' (R) MDO 3m 11 S *mid-div, prog 12th, styd on strngly apr last, improve* 3 0
414 9/3 Charm Park (L) MDO 3m 11 G *(fav) mid-div, 3rd frm 14th-last, styd on wl to line* 1 14
585 23/3 Wetherby Po' (L) RES 3m 13 S *mid-div whn blnd & u.r. 4th* U -
983 8/4 Charm Park (L) RES 3m 13 GF *(Jt fav) alwys wll in rear, nvr a factor* 10 0
1131 20/4 Hornby Cast' (L) RES 3m 17 G *twrds rear, mstk 5th, t.o. 5 out* 8 0

Competent start but ran badly after win; could perk up again 97 - time on his side; Good **15**

STRIKING CHIMES b.g. 9 Ahonoora - Arctic Chimes by Arctic Slave — Mrs L Burke

358 3/3 Garnons (L) RES 3m 18 GS *rear frm 4th, t.o. & p.u. 10th* P 0
795 2/4 Heythrop (R) XX 3m 4 F *t.o. 3rd, 2 fences bhnd whn p.u. 3 out* P 0

Of no account **0**

ST ROBERT b.g. 9 Taufan (USA) - Sainthill by St Alphage — D A Cundle

275 2/3 Parham (R) MDN 3m 15 GF *ld 1st, clr hlfwy, hdd 13th, wknd rpdly, p.u. aft nxt* P 0
455 9/3 Charing (L) MDN 3m 10 G *made all, drew clr 3 out* 1 13
779 31/3 Penshurst (L) RES 3m 13 GS *ld to 14th, fdd, tired & walked in* 5 0
964 8/4 Heathfield (R) RES 3m 7 G *ld til jmpd lft & hdd 6th, in tch til wknd appr 4 out* 5 0

Beat bad lot when winning & does not stay - restraining tactics may be worth a try **11**

STROLL HOME (Irish) — I 14F, I 575, I 78P, I 1133, I 1383, I 188F, I 3581, I 4674, I 5491, I 5661, I 5912, I 6333, I 6573

STRONG ACCOUNT(IRE) ch.g. 7 Strong Statement (USA) - Clare's Hansel by Prince Hansel — Andrew Mobley

1995 **7(NH)**

1105 14/4 Guilsborough (L) MDN 3m 12 G *prom whn u.r. 2nd* U -
1241 27/4 Clifton On ' (L) MDO 3m 8 GF *pllng, prom/disp to 10th, wknd 15th, t.o. & p.u. 2 out* P 0
1433 6/5 Ashorne (R) MDO 3m 16 G *mid-div, 10th whn u.r. 7th* U -

Shows no aptitude **0**

STRONG BEAU br.g. 11 Strong Gale - Red Pine by Khalkis — Mrs G Maxwell-Jones

1995 **6(NH),6(NH),5(NH),8(NH),P(NH)**

337 3/3 Heythrop (R) OPE 3m 10 G *prom til outpcd aft 12th, no imp ldrs aft* 4 11
475 10/3 Tweseldown (R) CON 3m 9 G *trckd ldrs, 3rd & rmndrs 13th, ch 3 out, sn wknd* 4 15
639 23/3 Siddington (L) OPE 3m 12 S *in tch, rmdrs 9th, chsd ldr appr 15th,styd on, nt rch wnnr* 3 20
793 2/4 Heythrop (R) OPE 4m 10 F *prom, ld 16th, hrd prssd frm 3 out, hdd last 100 yrds* 2 21
1180 21/4 Mollington (R) OPE 3m 5 F *cls up, outpcd 13th, mstk 15th, kpt on to mod 2nd flat* 2 19
1333 1/5 Cheltenham (L) HC 3m 1f 110yds 13 G *chsd ldrs, rdn 11th, soon lost tch, t.o. and p.u. before last.* P 0
1500 11/5 Kingston Bl' (L) CON 3m 7 G *chsd ldng pair, pshd alng hlfwy, chal 14th, 3rd & btn 2 out* 3 17

Winning chaser; onepaced & struggling to find a race in points; may win at 12; Any **20**

STRONG BREEZE b.g. 12 Strong Gale - Salty Breeze by Pitpan — I J Pocock

1995 2(14),U(-),5(0)

68 10/2 Great Treth' (R) RES 3m 14 S *alwys prom, unable to chal frm 2 out* 3 16
211 24/2 Castle Of C' (R) INT 3m 5 HY *in tch, outpcd frm 4 out* 3 10
280 2/3 Clyst St Ma' (L) RES 3m 11 S *(Co fav) ld/disp to 13th, chsd wnr frm nxt, ev ch 3 out, outpcd aft* 3 17
627 23/3 Kilworthy (L) RES 3m 13 GS *ld to 13th, outpcd frm nxt, sn no ch* 7 0
992 8/4 Kingston St' (R) RES 3m 6 F *j.w. made all, ran on gamely frm 2 out* 1 18
1124 20/4 Stafford Cr' (R) CON 3m 7 S *ld til 8th agn 11th-3 out, hdd, rlld to ld 2 out, rdn out* 1 20
1393 6/5 Cotley Farm (L) XX 3m 10 GF *(fav) ld til blndrd 9th, rdr lost irns, p.u. bef nxt* P 0
1499 11/5 Holnicote (L) CON 3m 8 G *(Jt fav) ld til 7th, mstk 8th, lost plc, no ch frm hlfwy* 4 14

Maiden winner 94; improved at 12; gamely won twice; hard to win again at 13; Any **18**

STRONG CHAIRMAN(IRE) br.g. 5 Strong Gale - The Furnituremaker by Mandalus — J A Keighley

522	16/3	Larkhill	(R)	MDO	3m	12	G	*w.w. prog 14th, cruising & lvl whn f last*	F	17
820	6/4	Charlton Ho'	(L)	MDN	3m	12	GF	*(Jt fav) held up, prog 12th, wnt 3rd 3 out, ld aft 2 out, ran on wll*	1	18
1242	27/4	Woodford	(L)	RES	3m	18	G	*(fav) held up, prog to 3rd 16th, not qckn nxt, kpt on flat*	3	21

Good start; top stable & should certainly improve; Restricted 1st step in 97 22

STRONG CHANCE b.g. 10 Strong Gale - Jabula by Sheshoon — W R Page

704	30/3	Tranwell	(L)	MDO	3m	16	GS	*nvr rchd ldrs, bhnd frm 10th, p.u. 3 out*	P	0
1253	27/4	Balcormo Ma'	(R)	MDO	3m	16	GS	*p.u. aft 4th, (broke leg)*	P	0

Dead 12

STRONG GOLD b.g. 13 Strong Gale - Miss Goldiane by Baragoi — Peter Bonner

1995 1(26),2(26),1(26),**5(14)**,1(25)

32	20/1	Higham	(L)	OPE	3m	15	GF	*(fav) (bl) ld/disp,rddn 12th,hd rdn to ld 3 out to flat,rlld to ld post*	1	25
274	2/3	Parham	(R)	OPE	3m	12	GF	*(bl) cls up, ld 6th-10th, outpcd in 3rd frm 3 out*	3	19
573	17/3	Detling	(L)	OPE	4m	9	GF	*(fav) (bl) ld to 3 out, rallied apr last, lame*	3	22
776	31/3	Penshurst	(L)	OPE	3m	6	GS	*(fav) (bl) ld, prssd frm 10th, styd on, hdd line*	2	21
811	6/4	Charing	(L)	OPE	3m	9	F	*(bl) sn prom, ld 9th, disp 13-15th, made rest, ran on wll 2 out*	1	23
1333	1/5	Cheltenham	(L)	HC	3m 1f 110yds	13	G	*(bl) cl up, reminders 11th, well bhnd from 14th, t.o. when p.u. before 18th.*	P	0
1538	16/5	Folkestone	(R)	HC	3 1/4m	6	G	*(fav) (bl) ld 2nd, rdn and hdd run-in, rallied cl home, just failed.*	2	22

Won 3 in 95; hard ride; best fresh; needs to dominate; could win if returning at 14; F-S 23

STRONG PERFORMANCE (Irish) — I 27^{3}, I 82^{P}, I 298^{P}, I 361^{P}

STRONG SECRET b.g. 9 Strong Gale - Shuil Na Greine by Deep Run — Peter Lewis

695	30/3	Llanvapley	(L)	RES	3m	13	GS	*alwys rear, p.u. 11th*	P	0
1077	13/4	Cothelstone	(L)	RES	3m	2	GF	*chsd wnr, 4l down 12th, mstk 15th, no ext 2 out*	2	0
1173	20/4	Chaddesley '	(L)	RES	3m	18	G	*mid-div, fair 8th at 9th, outpcd 14th, p.u. 3 out*	P	0

Beaten in a match & shows no form 0

STRONG STERN (Irish) — I 252^{F}, I 308^{P}, I 369^{F}, I 443^{2}

STRONG STUFF (Irish) — I 78^{P}, I 446^{5}, I 574^{1}, I 613^{2}

STRONG SUSPICION b.g. 12 Strong Gale - Shady Doorknocker by Mon Capitaine — T Grimley

1995 P(0),**F(-)**

452	9/3	Charing	(L)	LAD	3m	8	G	*ld to 3rd, cls up aft, wknd & p.u. 14th*	P	0
783	31/3	Tweseldown	(R)	MEM	3m	5	G	*made most til p.u. aft 9th, dsmntd*	P	0
812	6/4	Charing	(L)	LAD	3m	6	F	*alwys rear, blnd 4th, last & no ch whn u.r. 4 out*	U	-
1147	20/4	Higham	(L)	LAD	3m	9	F	*ran wd bnd apr 4th, strgglng aft, t.o.*	5	0

Does not stay & of no account now 0

STRONG TARQUIN(IRE) br.g. 6 Strong Gale - Trumpster by Tarqogan — Paul K Barber

1995 **10(NH)**

3	13/1	Larkhill	(R)	MDO	3m	10	GS	*(fav) hld up, rpd prog to 2nd 13th, ld aft 2 out, qcknd flat*	1	18
68	10/2	Great Treth'	(R)	RES	3m	14	S	*(fav) mid-div til prog 5 out, ld 3 out, ran on well*	1	19
264	2/3	Didmarton	(L)	INT	3m	12	G	*(fav) trckd ldrs, cls 3rd whn f 9th*	F	-
519	16/3	Larkhill	(R)	CON	3m	5	G	*(fav) restrnd, mstk 8th, prog to ld 13th, pshd out flat*	1	23
815	6/4	Charlton Ho'	(L)	MEM	3m	8	GF	*(fav) held up,mstk 11th & rmmndrs,prog nxt,3rd & outpcd frm 3 out*	3	13
1245	27/4	Woodford	(L)	LAD	3m	6	G	*chsd ldr 4th, disp 2nd whn f 9th*	F	-

Looks the part, top stable but yet to beat significant rivals; should find more chances 97; G-S 22

STRONG TRACE(IRE) b.g. 7 Strong Gale - Royal Inheritance by Will Somers — David Ian Tuckley

1995 **P(0)**,1(10),P(0)

172	18/2	Market Rase'	(L)	RES	3m	9	GF	*t.d.e. ld/disp to 8th, rmndrs apr 14th, sn wknd, p.u. nxt*	P	0

Won a short Maiden in 95; brief show 96 could spell problems 10

STRONG VIEWS b.g. 9 Remainder Man - Gokatiego by Huntercombe — E Haddock

1995 **4(NH)**

325	3/3	Market Rase'	(L)	LAD	3m	6	G	*chsd ldrs 6th-10th, wknd apr 14th*	5	10
566	17/3	Wolverhampt'	(L)	LAD	3m	5	GS	*alwys rear, wknd rpdly 15th, p.u. 3 out*	P	0

Winning chaser 93; looks a lost cause now 11

STRONG VISION (Irish) — I 35^{2}, I 148^{1}, I 313^{P}, I 441^{F}, I 544^{1}

STRONTINO b.g. 11 Rontino - Fair Pirouette by Fair Turn — C Jarvis

309	2/3	Ampton	(R)	MEM	3m	6	G	*cls up til 8th, last whn f 12th, dead*	F	-

Dead 11

STRUGGLES GLORY (Irish) — I 458^{2}, I 516^{3}

STUARTS POINT (Irish) — I 50F

SUBA LIN b.m. 7 Sula Bula - Tula Lin by Tula Rocket — Mrs Carolyn Atyeo

1995 P(0),P(0),R(-)

284	2/3 Clyst St Ma'	(L) MDN 3m	11	S	*sn rear, t.o. & p.u. 14th*	P	0
556	17/3 Ottery St M'	(L) MDO 3m	15	G	*alwys rear, t.o. & p.u. 13th*	P	0
820	6/4 Charlton Ho'	(L) MDN 3m	12	GF	*rear til blndrd & u.r. 7th*	U	-
1634	1/6 Bratton Down	(L) INT 3m	15	G	*9/4-33s (!), s.s. alwys last, t.o. & p.u. 11th*	P	0

Yet to complete the course 0

SUBSONIC(IRE) b.g. 8 Be My Guest (USA) - Broken Wide by Busted — Tim Tarratt

1995 **14(NH)**

535	17/3 Southwell P'	(L) CON 3m	10	GS	*sn t.o., poor 6th whn p.u. last*	P	0
897	6/4 Dingley	(R) CON 3m	15	GS	*cls up, chsd wnnr 6 out, wknd 2 out*	7	0

Well beaten when completing & prospects not good 12

SUDANOR(IRE) b.g. 7 Khartoum (USA) - Alencon by Northfields (USA) — Miss Jane Fellows

1995 U(-),1(15),3(17)

428	9/3 Upton-On-Se'	(R) RES 3m	17	GS	*ld/disp til wknd frm 13th, p.u. 3 out*	P	0
1002	9/4 Upton-On-Se'	(R) RES 3m	8	F	*ld to 2nd, agn 6-9th & frm 11th, drw wl clr 3 out, esd flat*	1	21

Maiden winner 95; bombed home 2nd start 96; easy 3m best; can upgrade if fit 97; G/F-S 21

SUE'S QUEST b.m. 6 El Conquistador - Parisian Piaffer by Piaffer (USA) — Mrs S E Wall

206	24/2 Castle Of C'	(R) MDO 3m	10	HY	*sn t.o., last whn p.u. 4 out*	P	0
465	10/3 Milborne St'	(L) RES 3m	11	G	*rear, wll bhnd 12th, kpt on same pace*	4	0
819	6/4 Charlton Ho'	(L) MDN 3m	10	GF	*rear til 10th, prog 12th, nvr on terms wth 1st 2*	3	0

Not disgraced but well beaten & more needed to go close 11

SUE WOOD BAY (Irish) — I 101P

SUGI g. 7 Oats - Ledee — A D W Griffith

217	24/2 Newtown	(L) RES 3m	17	GS	*f 5th*	F	-
463	9/3 Eyton-On-Se'	(L) MDN 2 1/2m	14	G	*f 1st*	F	-
569	17/3 Wolverhampt'	(L) MDN 3m	11	GS	*n.j.w. bhnd whn ran out 10th*	r	-
1364	4/5 Gisburn	(R) MDO 3m	11	G	*bhnd, late prog to 3rd apr last, nvr nrr*	3	10

Did better last start in weak race & more needed to win in 97 10

SUIL EILE ch.g. 9 Balboa - Divided Loyalties by Ballydar — Mrs A Connal

1995 P(0),F(-),P(0)

472	10/3 Milborne St'	(L) INT 3m	8	G	*mid-div til p.u. 9th, lame*	P	0

No prospects 0

SUIR SIDE (Irish) — I 6071

SUITE COTTAGE LADY (Irish) — I 119P, I 143P, I 335P, I 434P

SULA PRIDE b.g. 8 Sula Bula - My Pride by Petit Instant — J W Kwiatkowski

707	30/3 Barbury Cas'	(L) RES 3m	18	G	*sn rear, t.o. 5th, p.u. 3 out*	P	0
815	6/4 Charlton Ho'	(L) MEM 3m	8	GF	*midfld, styd on onepce frm 3 out*	4	13
1167	20/4 Larkhill	(R) MEM 3m	9	GF	*mid-div whn mstk & u.r. 5th*	U	-

Maiden winner only start 94; missed 95 & showed nothing in 96 10

SULASON b.g. 6 Sulaafah (USA) - Perrimay by Levanter — R N Miller

1995 P(0)

143	17/2 Larkhill	(R) MDO 3m	14	G	*prom til wknd frm 13th, p.u. 3 out*	P	0
520	16/3 Larkhill	(R) MDO 3m	11	G	*prom til wknd rpdly frm 14th, p.u. 2 out*	P	0
658	23/3 Badbury Rin'	(L) MDO 3m	8	G	*hmpd start, rpd prog whn f. 5th*	F	-
864	6/4 Larkhill	(R) MDN 2 1/2m	9	F	*w.w., clsd up 5 out, 2nd & ch whn hit 2 out, not rcvr*	3	11

First form when 3rd but finished last & looks non-stayer; improvement required 11

SULLIVANS CHOICE b.g. 10 The Parson - Rosamer by Vulgan's Air — A H Bulled

1995 3(18),P(0),2(14),2(17),6(0)

729	31/3 Little Wind'	(R) RES 3m	12	GS	*prom til rddn aft 12th, blndrd 13th, p.u. & destroyed*	P	0

Dead 17

SULTAN OF SWING (Irish) — I 39[4], I 90P, I 125F, I 289[2]

SUMAKANO (Irish) — I 380[4], I 564[1], I 606[5]

SUMMER DALLIANCE b.g. 6 Silver Season - Sandycroft by Sandford Lad — A Robson

1995 **P(NH)**

53	4/2 Alnwick	(L) MDO 3m	13	G	*prom to 6th, sn wknd, t.o. & p.u. 13th*	P	0

114 17/2 Lanark (R) MDO 3m 12 GS *nvr dang, p.u. 2 out* P 0

Showed nothing & finished early 0

SUMMERHILL EXPRESS (Irish) — **I** 141P, **I** 242³, **I** 295P, **I** 331³

SUNCZECH (Irish) — **I** 84³, **I** 163², **I** 291P, **I** 369², **I** 499⁴

SUNDAY PUNCH b.g. 10 The Parson - Darkina by Tarqogan Mrs C E Van Praagh

1995 U(-),P(0),r(-),2(15)

274 2/3 Parham (R) OPE 3m 12 GF *prom to 7th, bhnd whn p.u. 3 out* P 0
595 23/3 Parham (R) OPE 3m 12 GS *ref to race* 0 0
811 6/4 Charing (L) OPE 3m 9 F *ld to 9th, disp 13-15th, wknd & p.u. 4 out* P 0

Winning hurdler 92; front-runs; does not stay & showed nothing in 96 10

SUNLEY LINE ch.g. 9 Sunley Builds - Linescar by Hardraw Scar Mrs Angus Campbell

1995 P(0),P(0),P(0),P(0)

781 31/3 Penshurst (L) MDN 3m 11 GS *(bl) sn rear, p.u. 12th* P 0
921 8/4 Aldington (L) MDO 3m 8 F *(bl) raced in 5th/6th wth stablemate, t.o. 10th, p.u. 15th* P 0
1300 28/4 Bexhill (R) MDO 3m 7 F *(bl) prom, ld brfly 5-6th, steadily wknd, bhnd whn p.u. aft 11th* P 0

Yet to complete from 10 starts 94-6 0

SUNLEY STREET b.m. 8 Sunley Builds - Kerry Street by Dairialatan C R West

1995 P(0),2(0),F(-)

786 31/3 Tweseldown (R) LAD 3m 8 G *(vis) hld up rear, prog 7th, not qckn 12th, styd on frm last,no ch* 2 20
1058 13/4 Badbury Rin' (L) LAD 3m 5 GF *(bl) chsd wnr, blnd 15th, styd on onepcd frm 2 out* 2 22

Won 3 in 94; ran 2 fair races 96 (beaten by good horses) but lightly raced now 20

SUNNIE CRUISE ch.m. 8 Cruise Missile - Unmentionable by Vulgan Peter N Warcup

1995 P(0),F(-),3(0),6(0)

47 4/2 Alnwick (L) XX 3m 14 G *hld up last pair, nvr nr, imprv* 5 11
84 11/2 Alnwick (L) RES 3m 11 GS *hld up, prog to trck ldng pair 14th, btn nxt, wknd 2 out* 3 0
318 2/3 Corbridge (R) LAD 3m 5f 10 GS *cls 3rd frm 4th, styd prom, onepcd frm 3 out* 4 17
608 23/3 Friars Haugh (L) RES 3m 13 G *alwys rr* 8 0
752 31/3 Lockerbie (R) LAD 3m 10 G *8th hlfwy, nvr a dang* 7 0

Safe & has completed last 7 starts but should stick to Maidens; stamina? 12

SUNNYFIELD BOY b.g. 13 Sunyboy - Cherry Sauce by Saucy Kit R W Phizacklea

332 3/3 Market Rase' (L) MDO 3m 8 G *cls up, 3rd & wkng whn blnd & u.r. 14th* U -

Rarely seen & an elderly maiden 0

SUN OF CHANCE b.g. 12 Sunyboy - Chance A Look by Don't Look Miss M Ree

1995 3(13),2(15),1(18),F(-),5(13),2(17)

384 9/3 Llanfrynach (R) OPE 3m 16 GS *ld/disp 2nd-14th, sn outpcd, ran on agn flat, lkd 3rd* 4 18
601 23/3 Howick (L) CON 3m 10 S *mstk 4th, prom aft, rdn to 2nd 3 out, ld nxt, sn clr* 1 19
1386 6/5 Pantyderi (R) OPE 3m 5 GF *strng hld, trckd ldrs, mstk 10th, wknd aft, p.u. 12th* P 0
1619 27/5 Chaddesley ' (L) OPE 3m 7 GF *chsd ldrs til wknd 9th, t.o. & p.u. 13th* P 0

Restricted winner 95; did well to win Confined; ground against after; could win at 13; G-S 18

SUNSET REINS FREE b.g. 11 Red Sunset - Free Rein by Sagaro S G Payne

751 31/3 Lockerbie (R) CON 3m 12 G *u.r. 3rd* U -
1475 11/5 Aspatria (L) CON 3m 6 GF *mstk 3rd, prog to 2nd 12th, wknd qckly 14th, p.u. nxt* P 0

Looks of no account now 0

SUNSET RUN b.g. 10 Deep Run - Sunset Queen by Arctic Slave Miss Catherine Tuke

1995 2(10),2(14),4(0),U(-),1(12),3(0),r(-),**5(0)**

12 14/1 Cottenham (R) RES 3m 12 G *rear, prog 15th, went 2nd apr last, nvr nrr* 3 17
54 10/2 Cottenham (R) MEM 3m 3 GS *pllng, hld up, ld aft 12th, jnd & ran out 3 out, lame* r -

Poor Maiden winner 95; problem 96 & Restricted likely to be beyond him if fit 97; Any 14

SUN SETTING ch.g. 5 Sunyboy - Nosey's Daughter by Song C J R Sweeting

1485 11/5 Bredwardine (R) MDO 3m 15 G *l.w. rear whn f 3rd* F -

Decent stable & should do better 0

SUNSHINE MANOR ch.g. 12 Le Soleil - Manor Lady by Eastern Venture G B Tarry

1995 1(18),1(20),1(21),1(21),3(15)

639 23/3 Siddington (L) OPE 3m 12 S *ld to 3rd,2nd whn hit 10 & 12th,wknd 14th,5th whn p.u.2 out* P 0
1146 20/4 Higham (L) OPE 3m 7 F *ld to 4th, prssd wnr to 2 out, rdn & onepcd* 3 21
1437 6/5 Ashorne (R) MXO 3m 13 G *pllng,ld to 4th,mstk 8th,chal & mstk 3 out,ev ch last,no ext* 3 21
1565 19/5 Mollington (R) OPE 3m 8 GS *ld, clr 11th, 15l up & in cmmnd whn f 15th* F -
1609 26/5 Tweseldown (R) MXO 3m 9 G *(fav) prom, prssd wnr 10th, outjmpd aft, no ext apr last* 2 21

Won 4 in 95; struggling in Opens; can revert to Confineds with no penalty in 97 & win at 13; Good 21

SUNWIND b.g. 10 Windjammer (USA) - Mrewa by Runnymede — David Heath

1995 U(-),1(14),S(-)

720	30/3 Wadebridge	(L) RES 3m	9 GF	*in tch, cls 4th hlfwy, wknd, lft poor 3rd at 15th*	3	10
1428	6/5 High Bickin'	(R) RES 3m	10 G	*alwys mid-div, no ch frm 16th*	5	14
1527	12/5 Ottery St M'	(L) RES 3m	8 GF	*plld hrd, ld 2nd til mstk 9th, lost ground frm 15th*	4	12
1622	27/5 Lifton	(R) CON 3m	14 GS	*alwys rear grp*	7	0
1649	8/6 Umberleigh	(L) RES 3m	14 GF	*s.s. rear til b.d. 10th*	B	

Maiden winner 95; struggling in Restricteds & will need luck to win one 13

SUNY BERTIE b.g. 8 Sunyboy - St Lucian Breeze by Vivify — R Pollard

680	30/3 Cottenham	(R) MDO 3m	11 GF	*mid-div, ran wd aft 12th & lost tch, t.o. & p.u. 15th*	P	0

Unpromising 0

SUNY MILL b.g. 8 Sunyboy - Zaratella by Le Levanstell — Mrs J M Owen

642	23/3 Siddington	(L) RES 3m	15 S	*nt fluent, rr til p.u. 14th*	P	0

Not yet of any account 0

SUP A WHISKEY (Irish) — **I** 195U, **I** 6046, **I** 631P, **I** 650F

SUPER DEALER (Irish) — **I** 1811

SUPERFORCE b.g. 9 Superlative - Loup de Mer by Wolver Hollow — A B Coogan

108	17/2 Marks Tey	(L) MDN 3m	17 G	*t.o. whn p.u. 7th*	P	0
314	2/3 Ampton	(R) MDO 3m	10 G	*disp ld 8th, blnd 10th, wknd qkly 13th, p.u. 16th*	P	0
424	9/3 High Easter	(L) MDN 3m	10 S	*rr, blnd 9th, outpcd & blnd 14th, 4th & no ch whn p.u. last*	P	0
495	16/3 Horseheath	(R) MDO 3m	12 GF	*prom early, lost tch 11th, bhnd whn mstk & u.r. 13th*	U	-
929	8/4 Marks Tey	(L) MDO 3m	5 G	*rear whn slw jmp & nrly ref 1st, ref 2nd*	R	-

Cannot jump & yet to complete 0

SUPER FRED (Irish) — **I** 70P, **I** 114P, **I** 275P, **I** 352P

SUPER SECRETARY (Irish) — **I** 625F, **I** 632P

SUPERSONIA (Irish) — **I** 633, **I** 151P, **I** 2073, **I** 2802, **I** 3531, **I** 5253, **I** 6131

SUPREMCAN (Irish) — **I** 5P

SUPREME ARCTIC (Irish) — **I** 111, **I** 116P, **I** 141P, **I** 186P, **I** 463P

SUPREME ATHLETE (Irish) — **I** 3275, **I** 4624

SUPREME CAUTION (Irish) — **I** 569P, **I** 651P

SUPREME DEALER ch.g. 11 The Parson - Vul's Money by Even Money — L J Bowman

1995 3(10),P(0),2(16),2(19),U(-),**5(12)**

271	2/3 Parham	(R) CON 3m	15 GF	*ld 5th-12th, fdd, wll bhnd whn p.u. 2 out*	P	0

Dual winner 93; brief appearance 96 could spell problems 13

SUPREME DREAM(IRE) b.m. 7 Supreme Leader - Rock Solid by Hardboy — Mrs Pauline Adams

1995 6(0),6(0),3(12),U(-),4(10),U(-)

440	9/3 Newton Brom'	(R) MDN 3m	10 GS	*ld to 12th, lost plc, 5th 2 out, fin fast*	4	0
727	31/3 Garthorpe	(R) MDO 3m	12 G	*chsd ldrs til u.r. aft 8th*	U	-
1097	14/4 Guilsborough	(L) MEM 3m	6 G	*hld up,mod 3rd 12th,chsd wnr 2 out,clsng fast whn u.r. last*	U	18
1183	21/4 Mollington	(R) MDN 3m	10 F	*(fav) prom to 9th, lost plc, wll bhnd 3 out, fin fast*	5	10
1241	27/4 Clifton On '	(L) MDO 3m	8 GF	*cls up, ld 13th, jnd 2 out-last, found ext flat*	1	15
1380	5/5 Dingley	(R) RES 3m	11 GF	*chsd ldrs, mstk 12th, strgglng 3 out, styd on apr last*	3	16
1597	25/5 Garthorpe	(R) XX 3m	9 G	*alwys rear hlf, 7th whn f 5 out*	F	-
1641	2/6 Dingley	(R) RES 3m	13 GF	*prom to 14th, 7th & btn whn f 2 out*	F	-

Deserved win in modest race; unseated/fallen 6 of last 11 & Restricted unlikely 15

SUPREME FLYER (Irish) — **I** 384, **I** 78P, **I** 2505

SUPREME FRIEND (Irish) — **I** 530P, **I** 6216

SUPREME HOOKER (Irish) — **I** 56P, **I** 66P, **I** 117P

SUPREME ODDS (Irish) — **I** 47P, **I** 702, **I** 144P, **I** 640F, **I** 654P

SUPREME WARRIOR b.g. 10 Simply Great (FR) - Sindo by Derring-Do — Miss L Blackford

534	16/3 Cothelstone	(L) MDN 3m	10 G	*w.w. in tch, ch 15th, onepcd frm nxt*	4	10

Has some ability but missed 95 & time passing rapidly 11

SUPREMO (Irish) — **I** 6521

SURE PRIDE(USA) b.g. 8 Bates Motel (USA) - Coquelicot (CAN) by L'enjoleur (CAN) — A G Russell

1995 **4(NH),P(NH),2(NH),P(NH)**

594	23/3	Parham	(R)	CON	3m	13	GS	*mid-div, 5th & wkng 14th, wll bhnd whn p.u. 3 out*	P 0
963	8/4	Heathfield	(R)	MXO	3m	7	G	*hld up, effort to 4th 14th, wknd appr 4 out*	4 0
1228	27/4	Worcester	(L)	HC	2m 7f	17	G	*mid div when blnd and u.r. 10th.*	U -
1546	18/5	Fakenham	(L)	HC	3m 110yds	13	G	*trckd lding gp to 12th, lost tch from 14th.*	7 11
1613	27/5	Fontwell	(R)	HC	3 1/4m 110yds	12	G	*mid div, mstk 2nd, wknd 13th, bhnd when p.u. before 18th.*	P 0

Disappointing in points & a waste of time in H/Chases 10

SURRENDELL b.g. 7 Oats - Senlac by Paveh Star — R Hawker

1995 **P(NH),P(NH)**

352	3/3	Garnons	(L)	MDN	2 1/2m	9	GS	*ld to 3rd & frm 8th, 8l up whn f 3 out, dead*	F -

Dead 13

SUSIES MELODY(IRE) ch.g. 5 Carlingford Castle - Stardust Melody by Pas de Seul — C A Fuller

353	3/3	Garnons	(L)	MDN	2 1/2m	7	GS	*taken steadily in rear, prog 9th, nrst fin*	3 0
884	6/4	Brampton Br'	(R)	MDN	3m	12	GF	*trckd ldrs, went 2nd apr 3 out, wknd nxt*	4 0

Shows enough to suggest he should go much closer in 97 if staying 13

SUSTAINING b.g. 7 Oats - Chancebeg by Random Shot — Mrs J K Marriage

108	17/2	Marks Tey	(L)	MDN	3m	17	G	*mstks, made most 14th, sn wknd, t.o. whn p.u. 3 out*	P 0
423	9/3	High Easter	(L)	MDN	3m	8	S	*chsng grp, lst tch 12th, p.u. appr 14th*	P 0
617	23/3	Higham	(L)	MDO	3m	11	GF	*in rear whn mstk 2nd, prog 6th, ch 11th, wknd nxt, p.u. 3out*	P 0

No stamina yet 0

SUTTON LASS ch.m. 13 Politico (USA) - Selborne Lass by Deep Run — H C Harper

126	17/2	Kingston Bl'	(L)	LAD	3m	11	GS	*in tch to 10th, t.o. 13th, p.u. aft 15th*	P 0
999	8/4	Hackwood Pa'	(L)	RES	3m	6	GF	*ld early, 3rd hlfwy, wknd*	4 0
1238	27/4	Clifton On '	(L)	LAD	3m	6	GF	*rear, mstk 12th & sn strgglng, t.o.*	6 0
1501	11/5	Kingston Bl'	(L)	RES	3m	10	G	*chsd wnr to 10th, sn wknd & bhnd*	5 0
1612	26/5	Tweseldown	(R)	RES	3m	11	G	*chsd ldrs, mstk 11th, outpcd frm 13th, wknd 3 out*	5 0
1649	8/6	Umberleigh	(L)	RES	3m	14	GF	*ld to 2nd, prom to 10th, sn lost tch*	6 0

No longer of any account 0

SUTTON LIGHTER b.g. 6 Lighter - Happy Returns by Saucy Kit — E Turner

689	30/3	Chaddesley '	(L)	MDN	3m	15	G	*plld hrd, chsd ldr to 3rd, wknd 6th, t.o. & p.u. 12th*	P 0
1045	13/4	Bitterley	(L)	MDO	3m	16	G	*cls up til wknd 12th, t.o. & p.u. 3 out*	P 0
1319	28/4	Bitterley	(L)	MDN	3m	13	G	*jmpd novicey in rear, lost tch 10th, p.u. aft nxt*	P 0
1484	11/5	Bredwardine	(R)	MDO	3m	17	G	*alwys rear, t.o. 8th, p.u. 10th*	P 0

No signs of ability or stamina yet 0

SWAHILI RUN ch.g. 8 Ayyabaan - Nicolene by Nice Music — S Gallagher

1995 **P(NH),P(NH)**

384	9/3	Llanfrynach	(R)	OPE	3m	16	GS	*alwys last pair, t.o. whn blnd 14th, p.u. 2 out*	P 0
1220	24/4	Brampton Br'	(R)	OPE	3m	10	G	*ld, msd mrkr app 8th, hd 16th, fin 3rd, disq*	0 0
1479	11/5	Bredwardine	(R)	OPE	3m	8	G	*ld to 5th, ran out & u.r. nxt*	r -

Beaten a distance when 3rd & looks to have no prospects in points 10

SWANING AROUND (Irish) — **I** 261P, **I** 415F

SWANSEA GOLD(IRE) ch.m. 5 Torus - Show M How by Ashmore (FR) — Mrs H E North

534	16/3	Cothelstone	(L)	MDN	3m	10	G	*cls up, disp 5th-10th, ld 3 out, clr last, just hld on*	1 15

Ideal start but no winners emerged yet & form weak; time on her side 16

SWANS WISH (Irish) — **I** 721, **I** 1521

SWAPING LUCK (Irish) — **I** 195P, **I** 2261

SWEATSHIRT ch.g. 11 Leander - Roman Lilly by Romany Air — Stewart Pike

1995 **P(0),3(19),3(20),2(18),P(0)**

6	13/1	Larkhill	(R)	OPE	3m	18	GS	*w.w. effrt 13th, 6th & btn whn blnd & u.r. 15th*	U -
133	17/2	Ottery St M'	(L)	OPE	3m	18	GS	*hld up, prog 14th, ev ch 3 out, no ext aft*	5 19
255	28/2	Taunton	(R)	HC	4 1/4m 110yds	15	GS	*steady hdwy from 17th, chsd wnr from 3 out, edged left and no ext run-in.*	2 22
671	28/3	Taunton	(R)	HC	3m	13	S	*bhnd, gd hdwy 11th, blnd next, wknd 15th.*	6 0

H/Chase winner 93; no wins since & does not stay despite 3rd run; struggle to find a race at 12; G-S ... 18

SWEENEY LEE (Irish) — **I** 474P, **I** 540P, **I** 5825

SWEEPIN BENDS (Irish) — **I** 347P, **I** 385F, **I** 5014, **I** 533P

SWEET BLUE b.m. 6 Triple Sweet (USA) - Blue Sunday by Fine Blue — Miss R Cowen

696	30/3	Llanvapley	(L)	MDN	3m	13	GS	*rear, wkng whn ref 12th*	R -

1162 20/4 Llanwit Maj' (R) MDO 3m 12 GS *hmp & ref 2nd* R -
1271 27/4 Pyle (R) MDO 3m 15 G *prom, cls up whn f 11th* F -
1483 11/5 Bredwardine (R) MDO 3m 15 G *rear frm 4th, lost tch 14th, t.o. & p.u. last* P 0

An unpromising 1st season **0**

SWEET CASTLEHYDE (Irish) — I 63^{5}, I 76^{4}, I 142^{P}, I 290^{3}, I 325^{2}

SWEET JESTERDAY br.m. 6 Sweet Monday - Jestelle by Majestic Maharaj D J B Denny

953 8/4 Eyton-On-Se' (L) MDO 2 1/2m 10 GF *rear to 7th, t.o. & p.u. 10th* P 0
1224 24/4 Brampton Br' (R) MDO 3m 17 G *rr frm 6th, lost tch 13th, p.u. nxt* P 0
1417 6/5 Cursneh Hill (L) MDO 3m 14 GF *cls 4th 8th, in tch whn p.u. aft 12th* P 0
1581 19/5 Wolverhampt' (L) MDO 3m 10 G *sn bhnd, jmpd slwly 9th, t.o. whn blnd & u.r. 11th* U -

No signs of ability yet **0**

SWEET JOANNA b.m. 9 Escapism (USA) - Alto Sax by Prince de Galles Miss P Kerby
1995 P(0),6(0),U(-),P(0)

747 31/3 Upper Sapey (R) MDO 3m 11 GS *prom to hlfwy, wknd, p.u. 12th* P 0
884 6/4 Brampton Br' (R) MDN 3m 12 GF *alwys prom, kpt on to ld 2 out, drew clr flat* 1 13

Had shown nothing prior to winning weak Maiden last start; much more needed for Restricteds **13**

SWEET KILDARE ch.m. 9 Parole - Lady Royal by Sharpen Up V J Thomas
1995 P(0)

848 6/4 Howick (L) MDN 3m 14 GF *trckd ldrs, ld 13th, clr nxt, unchal* 1 16
1160 20/4 Llanwit Maj' (R) RES 3m 12 GS *chsd ldrs, prog to ld apr 2 out, sn clr, rddn out* 1 17
1389 6/5 Pantyderi (R) INT 3m 5 GF *strng hld, chsd ldr 9th, chsd wnr 3 out, kpt on flat* 2 19
1556 18/5 Bassaleg (R) MEM 3m 6 F *(fav) made all, clr 3-14th, kpt on whn prssd apr last* 1 14

Much improved 96; beaten by fair prospect when 2nd; should win Confined at 10; G/S-G/F **20**

SWEETLY SENSITIVE (Irish) — I 530^{P}, I 579^{P}

SWEET MERENDA (Irish) — I 9^{F}, I 50^{P}, I 64^{1}, I 116^{P}, I 212^{P}, I 461^{P}, I 520^{3}

SWEETMOUNT LAD (Irish) — I 31^{F}, I 193^{F}, I 224, , I 343^{6}, I 421^{F}, I 497^{2}, I 630^{4}

SWEET PETEL b.m. 9 Cardinal Flower - Findabair by Sunny Way Mrs Hilary Bubb

163 17/2 Weston Park (L) LAD 3m 10 G *mid-div, nvr nr ldrs, p.u. 4 out* P 0
213 24/2 Newtown (L) MEM 3m 7 GS *chsd ldr til blnd 8th & rider lost irons, p.u. nxt* P 0
358 3/3 Garnons (L) RES 3m 18 GS *chsd ldrs til no prog frm 12th, p.u. 2 out* P 0
432 9/3 Upton-On-Se' (R) MDO 3m 17 GS *ld brfly 3rd, rear hlfwy, p.u. 15th* P 0
748 31/3 Upper Sapey (R) MDO 3m 11 GS *effrt to ld brfly 13th, wkng in 5th whn f 2 out* F -
1048 13/4 Bitterley (L) MDO 3m 12 G *s.s. prog to disp whn u.r. 7th* U -
1225 24/4 Brampton Br' (R) MDO 3m 18 G *ld 4th, 4l up 9th, jnd app 15th, wknd & p.u. 3 out* P 0
1416 6/5 Cursneh Hill (L) MDO 3m 9 GF *ld frm 3rd, hit 10th, hdd & wknd aft 2 out* 2 13
1484 11/5 Bredwardine (R) MDO 3m 17 G *ld 3rd-13th, wknd & p.u. nxt* P 0

2nd in poor Maiden - only completion & only run on fast ground; does not stay **10**

SWEET ROSE br.m. 8 Tudor Rhythm - Lund Head Lady by Gracious Melody A Jackson
1995 P(0),3(0),U(-),4+(0),4(0)

79 11/2 Wetherby Po' (L) MDO 3m 12 GS *alwys rear, t.o. 11th, p.u. 4 out* P 0
121 17/2 Witton Cast' (R) RES 3m 11 S *mid-div to 11th, rear whn mstk & u.r. nxt* U -
225 24/2 Duncombe Pa' (R) RES 3m 12 GS *rear but in tch whn u.r. 5th* U -
305 2/3 Great Stain' (L) LAD 3m 11 GS *slw jmp 1st, t.o. 8th, p.u. 12th* P 0
518 16/3 Dalton Park (R) MDO 3m 15 G *alwys rear, t.o. 14th, p.u. 2 out* P 0
762 31/3 Great Stain' (L) MDN 3m 11 GS *alwys chsng ldrs, onepcd frm 3 out* 4 0
823 6/4 Stainton (R) MEM 3m 6 GF *disp til ld 5th, hdd 14th, lost plc & wknd 3 out* 4 0
1135 20/4 Hornby Cast' (L) MDN 3m 10 G *alwys rear, lost tch 9th, t.o.* 5 0
1286 27/4 Easingwold (L) MDO 3m 13 G *prom, ld 3rd- 8th, wknd 11th, t.o. & u.r. 2 out* U -
1450 6/5 Witton Cast' (R) MDO 3m 14 G *alwys rear, t.o. 4 out* 8 0
1469 11/5 Easingwold (L) LAD 3m 6 G *mstks, alwys bhnd, t.o. & p.u. 10th* P 0

Last on every completion in 96 & devoid of ability **0**

SWEET SERGEANT b.g. 8 Sergeant Drummer (USA) - Dolly Mixture by Sweet Ration Mrs S H Shirley-Beavan
1995 P(0)

192 24/2 Friars Haugh (L) MDN 3m 12 S *sn wll bhnd, p.u. 4 out* P 0
322 2/3 Corbridge (R) MDN 3m 10 GS *ld 1st, styd prom til wknd 14th* 7 0
613 23/3 Friars Haugh (L) MDN 3m 15 G *sn bhnd, p.u. 4 out* P 0
756 31/3 Lockerbie (R) MDN 3m 14 G *2nd hlfwy, rmnd cls up til no ext frm 3 out* 5 0
1082 14/4 Friars Haugh (L) MEM 3m 3 F *made most til jnd last, outpcd flat* 2 13
1356 4/5 Mosshouses (L) MDO 3m 12 GS *ld to 12th, wknd 3 out* 5 0

Stamina suspect & last of 2 finishers when 2nd - unlikely to win **10**

SWEET WYN ch.m. 9 Sweet Monday - Wyn-Bank by Green God B Heywood

415 9/3 Charm Park (L) MDO 3m 13 G *alws wl in rr, p.u. 11th* P 0
517 16/3 Dalton Park (R) MDO 3m 10 G *bhnd, t.o. 8th, p.u. 11th, dsmntd* P 0

636 23/3 Market Rase' (L) MDN 3m 11 GF *prom til wknd 10th, t.o. 6 out, p.u. nxt* P 0

Of no account 0

SWIFT MONDAY b.g. 6 Sweet Monday - Casha by Castlenik A J Chambers

352 3/3 Garnons (L) MDN 2 1/2m 9 GS *(fav) chsd ldr 11th,lft in ld nxt,hdd & lft clr 2 out,f last* F -
842 6/4 Maisemore P' (L) MDN 3m 17 GF *(fav) w.w. prog 11th, cls 6th whn f 14th* F -

Clearly has some ability but needs to finish first - best watched till he does 12

SWIFT REWARD b.m. 7 Kinglet - Swift Wood by Precipice Wood David Wales
1995 P(0),P(0),P(0),4(0),3(11),1(14)
35 20/1 Higham (L) RES 3m 16 GF *bhnd frm 10th, p.u. last* P 0

Maiden winner 95; swiftly disappeared 96; best watched 13

SWING FREE b.h. 14 Swing Easy (USA) - Failing Light by Ballymoss Mrs J Young
1995 U(-)
381 9/3 Barbury Cas' (L) XX 3m 9 GS *mstk 2nd, sn rear, t.o. & p.u. last* P 0
706 30/3 Barbury Cas' (L) MEM 3m 7 G *mid-div til blnd & u.r. 13th* U -
1185 21/4 Tweseldown (R) CON 3m 4 GF *s.s. sn rdn, alwys rear, t.o.14th* 4 0

No longer of any account 0

SWINGING SONG b.g. 9 True Song - Grissy by Grisaille Mrs F E Gilman
1995 **8(NH)**
33 20/1 Higham (L) LAD 3m 9 GF *pllg,jmpd rt, made most to 13th, sn wknd, p.u. 3 out* P 0
57 10/2 Cottenham (R) LAD 3m 9 GS *pllng, prom to 8th, strgglng 10th, t.o. & p.u. 3 out* P 0
618 23/3 Higham (L) MDO 3m 14 GF *alwys prom, lost plc 11th, styd on frm 3 out, lft 2nd last* 2 0
973 8/4 Thorpe Lodge (L) MDO 3m 7 GF *(fav) ld to 6th, cls up til outpcd by 1st pair frm 3 out* 3 0
1149 20/4 Higham (L) MDO 3m 10 F *rdn into fences,prom,ld 8th,made most aft,clr 3 out,rdn out* 1 15

Very modest & well ridden to win poor Maiden; Restricted looks beyond him 14

SWING TO THE LEFT(IRE) gr.m. 6 Corvaro (USA) - Ballinoe Lass by Captain James J Pryce
71 10/2 Great Treth' (R) MDO 3m 15 S *ld 3rd-4th, cls up til wknd 14th, p.u. 3 out* P 0
202 24/2 Lemalla (R) MDO 3m 12 HY *alwys handy, ld 2 out, rdn out* 1 14
562 17/3 Ottery St M' (L) XX 3m 12 G *mid-div, prog 11th, 3rd nxt, lost plc nxt, ran on agn 3 out* 3 13
1113 17/4 Hockworthy (L) RES 3m 11 GS *prom, chsd wnr 11-13th, 3rd & btn frm nxt* 3 11

Satisfactory start; not disgraced after win & Restricted possible in 97; G-Hy 16

SWISS COMFORT(IRE) b.m. 5 Henbit (USA) - Malozza Brig by New Brig Mrs Karen Woodhead
1995 **P(NH)**
828 6/4 Stainton (R) MDO 3m 7 GF *n.j.w. alwys bhnd, t.o. 13th, ref & u.r. nxt* R -

Not the best of starts 0

SWISS THYNE (Irish) — **I** 291P

SWORD-ASH ch.g. 14 Le Bavard (FR) - Roman Vulgan by Vulgan Robert J Williams
1995 r(-),P(0)
98 12/2 Hereford (R) HC 3m 1f 110yds 12 HY *alwys bhnd, t.o. when p.u. before 4 out.* P 0
383 9/3 Llanfrynach (R) CON 3m 13 GS *in tch til p.u. aft 4th* P 0

No longer of any account 0

SWORDELLA b.m. 8 Broadsword (USA) - Picotee by Pieces Of Eight Andrew J Martin
1995 F(-),1(18),1(19)
476 10/3 Tweseldown (R) OPE 3m 7 G *(fav) ld,blnd 12th,tired frm 4 out,hdd 2 out,p.u. aft,dsmntd* P 0

Dual winner 95; problem 96 & best watched start of 97; L/H; G/F-S 18

SYBILLABEE br.m. 8 Sula Bula - Upham Jubilee by Murrayfield R A Horne
1995 2(16),P(0)
248 25/2 Charing (L) RES 3m 12 GS *alwys prom, 3rd & blnd 4 out, no ch aft* 4 10
713 30/3 Barbury Cas' (L) MDO 3m 10 G *in tch, ev ch 13th, wknd whn f 2 out* F -
1060 13/4 Badbury Rin' (L) MDO 3m 14 GF *prom, ld 15th-4 out, outpcd frm 2 out* 3 10
1217 24/4 Andoversford (R) MDO 3m 16 G *hld up, prog 14th, 2nd 2 out, chal & lkd wnr whn f last* F 15
1504 11/5 Kingston Bl' (L) MDO 3m 13 G *(fav) rcd wd,cls up,rdn to chs ldr 13th,kpt on to ld last,all out* 1 16

Finally confirmed promise; should improve but would benefit from stronger handling 16

SYD GREEN(IRE) b.g. 8 Green Shoon - Gone by Whistling Wind P M Hodges
1995 F(-),1(19)
246 25/2 Southwell P' (L) OPE 3m 9 HO *pllng, prom to 9th, wknd & p.u. aft 11th* P 0
1024 13/4 Brocklesby ' (L) OPE 3m 6 GF *cont to 6 out, wknd qckly nxt, rmte 3rd whn u.r. last* U -
1302 28/4 Southwell P' (L) INT 3m 10 GF *(Jt fav) mid-div, prog 11th, ld 13th, sn in cmmnd, ran on well* 1 18

1535 16/5 Aintree (L) HC 3m 1f 11 GF *keen hold, midfield, hdwy 7th, ld 10th, mstk and hdd 14th, left in ld next, soon clr, easily.* 1 24
1630 31/5 Stratford (L) HC 3 1/2m 16 GF *alwys handy, effort 3 out, unable to qckn from last.* 2 25

Restricted winner 95; improved 96 & ran really well last start; may struggle early 97; G-F 23

SYDNEY BOON ch.g. 5 Newski (USA) - Bassinet by Sagaro — Mrs M E Doidge

1139 20/4 Flete Park (R) RES 3m 14 S *in tch til mstk 11th, eased & p.u. 13th, quiet run* P 0
1357 4/5 Flete Park (R) MEM 3m 3 G *(fav) made all at slow pace, forged clr 15th, easily* 1 0
1525 12/5 Ottery St M' (L) CON 3m 9 GF *in tch, mstk 12th, lost plc, t.o. & p.u. 2 out* P 0

Set up for dreadful race; should improve but more needed for Restricteds 13

SYLVAN SIROCCO b.g. 9 Known Fact (USA) - Juddmonte by Habitat — A G L Taylor

263 2/3 Didmarton (L) INT 3m 18 G *prssd ldr to 11th, wknd 14th, 5th & no ch whn u.r. last* U -
641 23/3 Siddington (L) RES 3m 20 S *mid div, in tch, kpt on onepcd frm 15th* 5 12
1122 20/4 Stratford (L) HC 2m 5f 110yds 16 GF *alwys bhnd.* 10 0
1332 1/5 Cheltenham (L) HC 3m 1f 110yds 11 G *bhnd and rdn 10th, t.o. and p.u. before 12th.* P 0

Beat 7 others when 5th & should try Maidens - would have a squeak 12

SYLVAN TEMPEST b or br.g. 10 Strong Gale - Hedwige by African Sky — N P Morgan

1995 3(0),4(0),3(0),U(-)

55 10/2 Cottenham (R) CON 3m 2 GS *(fav) jmpd slwly 4th, disp to 14th, btn 16th, slw 2 out, lame* 2 0

Flat winner; beaten by unwilling rival in match only start 96 & problems 13

SYNDERBOROUGH LAD ch.g. 10 Rymer - Roman Lilly by Romany Air — Stewart Pike

1995 **U(-),5(NH),4(17),1(27),1(NH),4(27),4(NH)**

257 29/2 Nottingham (L) HC 2 1/2m 11 G *(fav) held up in rear when f 1st.* F -
672 29/3 Aintree (L) HC 2 3/4m 26 G *patiently rdn, imp hfwy, hdwy to chal 2 out, ridden and one pace run-in.* 4 28
1331 1/5 Cheltenham (L) HC 2m 5f 9 G *soon pushed along, prog 10th, lost tch 14th, went poor 3rd apr last.* 3 21

Dead 29

SYRUS P TURNTABLE b.g. 10 King Of Spain - Lizabeth Chudleigh by Imperial Fling (USA) — Miss P Fitton

1995 P(0),6(0),P(0),1D(15),3(10),4(12),5(0)

78 11/2 Wetherby Po' (L) OPE 3m 10 GS *mid-div, prog 4 out, ld 2 out, disp last, just btn* 2 18
120 17/2 Witton Cast' (R) OPE 3m 7 S *rear, styd on well frm 2 out, nvr dang* 5 13
184 23/2 Haydock (L) HC 3m 9 GS *bhnd most of way, blnd 13th.* 5 11

Ran above himself when 2nd but finished early & unlikely to achieve much at 11 15

TACK ROOM LADY (Irish) — **I** 77[1], **I** 241[2], **I** 310[5], **I** 376[P]

TACKY LADY (Irish) — **I** 11[P]

TACMAHACK (Irish) — **I** 444[P]

TACOMENT b.m. 11 Battlement - Tacova by Avocat — Mrs H Hornby

446 9/3 Haldon (R) MDO 3m 13 S *rear & rmndrs 11th, t.o. & p.u. 2 out* P 0
718 30/3 Wadebridge (L) MDO 3m 11 GF *ld 2nd-4th, disp 7-8th, 5tha t 11th, wknd, p.u. 3 out* P 0
1075 13/4 Lifton (R) RES 3m 12 S *wll plc til lost grng 13th, mstk 14th, p.u. bfr nxt* P 0
1143 20/4 Flete Park (R) MDN 3m 17 S *rear, some prog to 7th at 14th, not rch ldrs, p.u. last* P 0
1524 12/5 Ottery St M' (L) MEM 3m 3 GF *keen hld, prom til outpcd 15th, bhnd whn blnd 2 out* 3 0

Last on only completion 96 & no stamina 0

TACOVA'S GIFT (Irish) — **I** 495[P]

TAKE ISSUE b.g. 11 Absalom - Abstract by French Beige — Jamie Poulton

1995 P(0),3(0),1(17),**P(0)**,6(0)

250 25/2 Charing (L) LAD 3m 12 GS *ld 3rd-8th, 2nd & wkng whn f 10th* F -

Confined winner 95 but soon disappeared 96 & best watched if returning 15

TAKE IT AWAY (Irish) — **I** 207[P], **I** 567[P]

TAKEITHANDY (Irish) — **I** 99[2], **I** 180[2], **I** 261[2], **I** 341[2], **I** 361[2], **I** 450[1]

TAKE THE PLEDGE (Irish) — **I** 250[F]

TAKE THE TOWN b.g. 11 Pollerton - Rose Of Spring by Golden Vision — Mrs O Hubbard

1995 P(0),3(14),U(-)

251 25/2 Charing (L) OPE 3m 10 GS *in tch, pshd alng 12th, btn 15th, p.u. last* P 0
274 2/3 Parham (R) OPE 3m 12 GF *6th whn f 6th* F -
451 9/3 Charing (L) OPE 3m 11 G *wth ldr, ld 8-9th, 4th aft, drvn to 2nd 4 out, sn btn* 6 0
776 31/3 Penshurst (L) OPE 3m 6 GS *2nd, prssd ldr frm 10th til rddn & wknd apr 2 out* 5 15
1050 13/4 Penshurst (L) CON 3m 8 G *ld, just hdd whn u.r. 12th* U -

Winning Irish chaser; well-beaten in points 10

TALBOT'S HOLLOW (Irish) — **I** 226², **I** 384ᴾ, **I** 417ᴾ, **I** 527⁵, **I** 621ᴾ, **I** 632⁵
TALBOY MAYE (Irish) — **I** 108ᴾ
TALK OF EXCITEMENT (Irish) — **I** 22ᴾ
TALK SENCE(IRE) ch.g. 8 Le Bavard (FR) - Jukella by Jukebox — P J King
1995 P(0),P(0),P(0),P(0)

95 11/2 Ampton (R) RES 3m 11 GF *(bl) alwys wll bhnd, nvr nrr* 4 0
177 18/2 Horseheath (R) CON 3m 8 G *(bl) alwys last, rdn 9th, sn t.o.* 5 0
313 2/3 Ampton (R) RES 3m 9 G *(bl) alwys bhnd, j.s. 10th, t.o. & p.u. appr 3 out* P 0
1527 12/5 Ottery St M' (L) RES 3m 8 GF *alwys rear* 6 0
1553 18/5 Bratton Down (L) XX 3m 10 F *sn rear, t.o. frm 10th* 6 0
1634 1/6 Bratton Down (L) INT 3m 15 G *alwys rear, t.o. & p.u. 2 out* P 0

Irish Maiden winner 94; changed hands mid season; never better than tailed off in England. 0

TALK TO YOU LATER (Irish) — **I** 158⁴, **I** 235³, **I** 298¹
TALL FELLOW(IRE) b.g. 6 Torus - Peaceful Girl by Keep The Peace — S B Clark
1995 **20(NH),P(NH),8(NH),5(NH),P(NH),P(NH)**

47 4/2 Alnwick (L) XX 3m 14 G *pllng, wth ld 4th-nxt, wknd rpdly, p.u. 10th* P 0

Ex novice hurdler; too keen and not seen after debut; unpromising. 0

TAMAIMO(IRE) b.g. 5 Electric - Tino's Love by Rugantino — Mrs Susan Humphreys

652 23/3 Badbury Rin' (L) MDO 3m 13 G *settld and schooled in rear, p.u. 12th* P 0
819 6/4 Charlton Ho' (L) MDN 3m 10 GF *alwys rear, p.u. & dismntd 14th* P 0

Top stable and only learning so far. 0

TAMAR LASS b.m. 11 Shaab - La Jolie Fille by Go Blue — David G Du Plessis
1995 **7(0),4(NH),6(NH)**

197 24/2 Lemalla (R) LAD 3m 13 HY *disp to 3rd & frm 6th-9th, chal 3 out, no ext apr last* 2 19
443 9/3 Haldon (R) LAD 3m 10 S *in tch, cls 4th at 13th, wknd rpdly & p.u. nxt, dead* P 0

Dead. 19

TAMBORITO(IRE) b.g. 7 Thatching - Vera Musica (USA) by Stop The Music (USA) — Mrs M Rigg

780 31/3 Penshurst (L) MDN 3m 12 GS *alwys rear, wll bhnd whn p.u. 13th* P 0
966 8/4 Heathfield (R) MDO 3m 7 G *pllng, disp ld 7-11th, wknd 13th, slpd & u.r. appr 16th* U -
1299 28/4 Bexhill (R) MDO 3m 7 F *ld aft 3rd-7th, wknd rpdly 12th, t.o. & p.u. 14th* P 0

Looks a non-stayer; unpromising. 0

TAMER'S RUN (Irish) — **I** 101ᴮ, **I** 268³, **I** 484ᶠ
TAMMY MY GIRL ch.m. 13 Timolin (FR) - Teasemenot by Doubtless II — Mrs P N Crookenden
1995 2(22),**U(-)**,3(11),5(11),B(-),3(10),4(0)

303 2/3 Great Stain' (L) CON 3m 11 GS *1st ride, handy to 11th, outpcd nxt, styd on onepcd* 6 12
587 23/3 Wetherby Po' (L) OPE 3m 15 S *alwys rear, t.o. 3 out* 8 0
760 31/3 Great Stain' (L) OPE 3m 8 GS *mid-div, u.r. 7th* U -
824 6/4 Stainton (R) CON 3m 11 GF *mid-div, rdn 6th, u.r. nxt* U -
1093 14/4 Whitwell-On' (R) MXO 4m 19 G *mid-div whn b.d. 6th* B -
1133 20/4 Hornby Cast' (L) OPE 3m 14 G *rear & pshd alng 2nd, sn strgglng, t.o.* 7 10
1366 4/5 Gisburn (R) LAD 3m 12 G *mid-div, nvr trbld ldrs* 6 11

Novice ridden mostly in 96; lost last 23 races and unlikely to win again. 11

TAMMY'S FRIEND b.g. 9 Deep Run - Cinderwood by Laurence O — John Ferguson
1995 **2(NH),P(NH),P(NH),3(NH),2(NH)**

9 14/1 Cottenham (R) OPE 3m 13 G *(bl) ld 2nd til jnd & hit 9th, outpcd 16th, styd on agn flat* 4 22

Winning chaserod enough to win pointsnished quickly; likes to dictate; blinkers. 20

TANGLE BARON gr.g. 8 Baron Blakeney - Spartangle by Spartan General — P J Clarke
1995 5(0),3(18),1(20),2(17),1(22),3(19)

25 20/1 Barbury Cas' (L) OPE 3m 14 GS *w.w. prog 10th, chsd ldrs aft, 3rd 3 out, wknd nxt* 5 20
65 10/2 Great Treth' (R) INT 3m 13 S *mid-div, no imp whn p.u. aft 13th* P 0
365 5/3 Leicester (R) HC 3m 10 GS *held up, prog 12th, chsd ldr and rdn 2 out, btn last.* 3 22
530 16/3 Cothelstone (L) OPE 3m 7 G *chsd ldr 5th-11th, 3rd & outpcd 15th, no dang aft* 3 14
816 6/4 Charlton Ho' (L) INT 3m 7 GF *chsd ldrs, lost tch 13th, outpcd frm nxt* 4 17
1453 7/5 Wincanton (R) HC 2m 5f 9 F *alwys bhnd, t.o..* 6 0
1499 11/5 Holnicote (L) CON 3m 8 G *ld 13th,drvn clr 2 out,clr whn trd to stop & hit rlls 50yout* 1 20
1550 18/5 Bratton Down (L) CON 3m 8 F *hld up, went 2nd 2 out, chal und pres last, no ext flat* 2 22
1634 1/6 Bratton Down (L) INT 3m 15 G *made most to 15th,ld agn 3 out,rdn clr aft last,fin 1st,disq* 1D 23
1650 8/6 Umberleigh (L) CON 3m 7 GF *(fav) prom, ld 12th, 3l clr & rdn 2 out, hdd post* 2 18

Fair pointer; best late season; likes fast ground; safe but needs more for Opens. 22

TANGLE KELLY b.g. 7 Netherkelly - Spartangle by Spartan General — Michael Lanz

1995 P(0),P(0),P(0),P(0)

627	23/3	Kilworthy	(L)	RES	3m	13	GS	*w.w. in rear til lost tch 12th, t.o. & p.u. 15th*	P	0
928	8/4	Bishopsleigh	(R)	MDN	3m	9	G	*(fav) mntng chal & hrd rddn whn f 3 out*	F	-
1279	27/4	Bratton Down	(L)	MDO	3m	14	GF	*ld/disp til hdd & outpcd aft last*	3	12
1429	6/5	High Bickin'	(R)	MDO	3m	8	G	*(Jt fav) j.w. cls up, outpcd 16th, styd on to ld last*	1	15
1591	25/5	Mounsey Hil'	(R)	RES	3m	15	G	*chsd ldrs to 14th, btn whn blnd bdly 17th, p.u. aft*	P	0
1632	1/6	Bratton Down	(L)	MEM	3m	3	G	*(fav) chsd wnr 4th til rdn & slwd 14th,2nd agn 3 out,no ch*	2	0
1649	8/6	Umberleigh	(L)	RES	3m	14	GF	*prom, disp brfly 8th, wknd 12th, t.o. & p.u. last*	P	0

Beat subsequent dual winner; disappointing after; mistakes; needs more for Restricted. 13

TANGLEWOOD BOY b.g. 5 Nomination - Eaves by Thatching — S Aspinall

62	10/2	Cottenham	(R)	MDO	3m	6	GS	*hld up,prog 12th,mstk 15th,qcknd to ld 3 out,drvn out flat*	1	14
428	9/3	Upton-On-Se'	(R)	RES	3m	17	GS	*losing tch whn p.u. 14th*	P	0

Won modest race (no winners behind) in good time; very young and looks the part; should upgrade. 16

TANGO TOM ch.g. 11 New Member - Dance Partner by Manicou — John J Smith

1995 P(0),3(17),2(16)

232	24/2	Heythrop	(R)	OPE	3m	10	GS	*wll bhnd to hlfwy, steady prog 11th, ran past btn hrss*	4	13
601	23/3	Howick	(L)	CON	3m	10	S	*rear of ldng grp, f 7th*	F	-
710	30/3	Barbury Cas'	(L)	CON	3m	6	G	*cls up to 12th, lost tch 4 out, p.u. last*	P	0
1079	13/4	Cothelstone	(L)	INT	3m	5	GF	*4th til 2nd frm 8th, rdn 12th, no ext*	3	10
1289	28/4	Barbury Cas'	(L)	CON	3m	8	F	*mstk 7th, chsd ldrs, rdn frm 11th, no prog frm 3 out*	5	12

Dual winner 93; only beat 2 horses in 96 and not threatening to win now. 14

TANNER b.g. 6 Impecunious - Tantaliser II by Tenterhooks — Mrs S E Vaughan

221	24/2	Newtown	(L)	MDN	3m	12	GS	*trckd ldrs going wll, mstk 11th, lost tch 13th, p.u. nxt*	P	0
463	9/3	Eyton-On-Se'	(L)	MDN	2 1/2m	14	G	*t.o. hlfwy, schooling, btn fnce*	2	0
1045	13/4	Bitterley	(L)	MDO	3m	16	G	*ld 5-8th, lost plc 13th, p.u. 3 out*	P	0
1218	24/4	Brampton Br'	(R)	MEM	3m	4	G	*(fav) chal 5th, lft in ld 6th, lft virt solo 12th*	1	10
1582	19/5	Wolverhampt'	(L)	RES	3m	10	G	*in tch, mstk 9th, sn wknd, t.o. & p.u. 11th*	P	0

Won joke Members; still has a lot to learn and really up against now. 11

TANNOCK BROOK b.g. 8 Meadowbrook - Miss Sunny by Sunyboy — W G Macmillan

1995 P(0),1(16),4(12)

400	9/3	Dalston	(R)	LAD	3m	10	G	*bhnd 8th, t.o. 9th, p.u. 3 out*	P	0
499	16/3	Lanark	(R)	LAD	3m	10	G	*3rd at 11th, chsd wnr frm 3 out, 4l down whn u.r. 2 out*	U	19
752	31/3	Lockerbie	(R)	LAD	3m	10	G	*5th hlfwy, lost tch by 13th, p.u. 3 out*	P	0

Lightly racediden winner 95; ran well 2nd start and would go very close in Resricted. 16

TAPALONG ch.m. 11 True Song - Spartan Clown by Spartan General — H Hutsby

1995 P(0),P(0),1(12),2(15),6(0)

21	20/1	Barbury Cas'	(L)	MEM	3m	16	GS	*mid-div, 8th & lost tch 11th, p.u. 14th*	P	0
124	17/2	Kingston Bl'	(L)	CON	3m	17	GS	*alwys bhnd, t.o. & p.u. 3 out*	P	0
338	3/3	Heythrop	(R)	RES	3m	9	G	*bhnd 9th, sn t.o., styd on to poor 3rd flat*	3	0
1101	14/4	Guilsborough	(L)	RES	3m	16	G	*bhnd, prog 12th, chsd ldrs 16th, kpt on, lame*	5	13

Won poor Maiden (33/1) 95; struggling now upgraded and unlikely to win at 12oblems now. 15

TAP DANCING ch.g. 10 Sallust - Amorak by Wolver Hollow — Neil Allen

1995 P(0),6(10),6(14),4(16),1(19),**3(21)**,3(19),2(0),**5(NH)**

1005	9/4	Upton-On-Se'	(R)	CON	3m	6	F	*tckd ldrs, mstk 10th, not qckn 12th, p.u. qckly 14th*	P	0
1171	20/4	Chaddesley '	(L)	OPE	3m	15	G	*s.s. prom at 8th, wknd 12th, p.u. 14th*	P	0
1314	28/4	Bitterley	(L)	MEM	3m	13	G	*rdn & prog 10th, lost tch 1st pair frm 13th, tk 3rd flat*	3	15
1457	8/5	Uttoxeter	(L)	HC	3 1/4m	16	G	*mstk 8th, prog and in tch 12th, soon rdn and btn, t.o. when p.u. before 16th.*	P	0

Confined winner 95; mostly outclassed in 96; stays; needs to stick to Confineds to win again.G-F. 16

TAPPIETOURIE ch.m. 7 Crofthall - Sharenka by Sharpen Up — Miss H G Dudgeon

1995 **11(NH)**

85	11/2	Alnwick	(L)	LAD	3m	11	GS	*last pair & t.o. til p.u. 12th*	P	0
111	17/2	Lanark	(R)	RES	3m	6	GS	*lost tch by 11th, p.u. 4 out*	P	0

Only learning and out of her depth so far. 0

TARA BOY b.g. 11 Rusticaro (FR) - Flosshilde by Rheingold — Mrs R Cambray

1995 3(16),U(-),P(0)

162	17/2	Weston Park	(L)	OPE	3m	16	G	*chsd ldrs, outpcd frm 3 out*	5	12
232	24/2	Heythrop	(R)	OPE	3m	10	GS	*chsd ldrs to hlfwy, 5th & wll btn whn f last*	F	-
459	9/3	Eyton-On-Se'	(L)	OPE	3m	11	G	*prom, 5th 4 out, styd on frm 2 out, nvr nrr*	4	18
662	24/3	Eaton Hall	(R)	OPE	3m	10	S	*mid-div in tch, not qckn frm 3 out, sn btn*	4	15
881	6/4	Brampton Br'	(R)	CON	3m	9	GF	*last frm 4th, fin well frm 3 out*	6	12
1043	13/4	Bitterley	(L)	OPE	3m	9	G	*(bl) ld to 4th, v slw jmp nxt, cls 4th at 11th, wknd 13th*	6	0

1193 21/4 Sandon (L) OPE 3m 8 G *(bl) rear of chsng grp, v onepcd frm 5 out* 5 0
1231 27/4 Weston Park (L) OPE 3m 6 G *(bl) chsng grp, outpcd frm 13th, nvr dang* 4 14
1418 6/5 Eyton-On-Se' (L) MEM 3m 7 GF *(bl) hld up in rr, 2nd 9th, ran on one pace* 2 0

Confined winner 94; lost his last 13 starts and likely to extend the sequence. 14

TARA LODGE (Irish) — **I** 44P

TARA RIVER (Irish) — **I** 26P, **I** 88P, **I** 129³, **I** 198P, **I** 347⁶, **I** 384, , **I** 423P, **I** 531P

TARGET TIME b.m. 6 Faustus (USA) - Alicia Markova by Habat B Neaves

250 25/2 Charing (L) LAD 3m 12 GS *mid-div, f 2nd* F -
454 9/3 Charing (L) MDN 3m 10 G *mstk 2nd, twrds rear whn p.u. 10th* P 0
575 17/3 Detling (L) MDO 3m 10 GF *t.o. 9th, jmpd slwly & u.r. 13th* U -
781 31/3 Penshurst (L) MDN 3m 11 GS *(bl) cls up til f 9th* F -
814 6/4 Charing (L) MDO 2 1/2m 8 F *(bl) prom, 4th & btn whn f 2 out* F -
1445 6/5 Aldington (L) MDO 3m 8 HD *(bl) cls up, ran wd bnd bfr 2nd, ld 6th til f 12th* F -

Shows speed but needs to learn to jump; unpromising. 0

TARRS BRIDGE (Irish) — **I** 352¹

TARRTINGO b.m. 6 Rustingo - Tarrcity Jane by Stetchworth Lad Mrs H A Miles

509 16/3 Magor (R) MDN 3m 9 GS *rear, losing tch whn p.u. 12th* P 0
771 31/3 Pantyderi (R) MDN 3m 14 G *in rear whn p.u. 13th* P 0

No signs yet. 0

TARRY AWHILE ch.g. 10 Crested Lark - Lucky Sandy by St Columbus Sir Michael Connell

1995 P(0),r(-),2(16),2(18),5(11)

338 3/3 Heythrop (R) RES 3m 9 G *(Co fav) ld to 9th, ld 13th til hdd & f nxt* F -
437 9/3 Newton Brom' (R) RES 3m 9 GS *alwys prom, ev ch 16th, wknd, walked in* 5 0
641 23/3 Siddington (L) RES 3m 20 S *chsd ldrs, 3rd & rddn 3 out, kpt on onepcd* 2 18
1101 14/4 Guilsborough (L) RES 3m 16 G *mstks, bhnd & pshd alng hlfwy, styd on frm 3 out, nrst fin* 4 14
1176 21/4 Mollington (R) MEM 3m 6 F *cls up, wth wnr 12th til wknd aft last* 2 17
1329 30/4 Huntingdon (R) HC 3m 14 GF *prom in chasing gp, went 2nd 3 out, rdn apr last, kept on.* 2 20
1455 8/5 Uttoxeter (L) HC 2m 5f 9 G *in tch, rdn 11th, 4th and outpcd apr four out, no dngr after.* 3 12
1595 25/5 Garthorpe (R) CON 3m 15 G *alwys mid-div, outpcd frm 6 out* 8 0
1640 2/6 Dingley (R) RES 3m 9 GF *prom, chsd wnr 9-13th, styd on undr pres frm 2 out* 3 18

Maiden winner 93; beaten 19 times since; desperately onepaced and win hard to find; stays;F-S. 17

TARRY NO MORE b.m. 7 Crested Lark - Lucky Sandy by St Columbus Sir Michael Connell

680 30/3 Cottenham (R) MDO 3m 11 GF *mstk 5th, trckd ldrs, blnd 13th, sn btn, p.u. 15th* P 0
1103 14/4 Guilsborough (L) MDN 3m 15 G *chsd ldrs, mstk 7th, wknd & p.u. 16th* P 0
1378 5/5 Dingley (R) MDO 2 1/2m 16 GF *chsd ldrs, in tch whn p.u. 10th* P 0

Only learning so far; good stable and should do better in time. 10

TARTAN GLORY b.m. 6 Roman Glory - Spartan Flame by Owen Anthony R R Ledger

780 31/3 Penshurst (L) MDN 3m 12 GS *prog frm rear 9th, 4th 12th, wknng & jmp slwly 14th & p.u.* P 0
1210 21/4 Heathfield (R) MDO 3m 13 F *rear, n.j.w. p.u. aft 9th* P 0

Too many mistakes at present; could do better. 0

TARTAN TORNADO b.g. 10 Strong Gale - Frankford Run by Deep Run W J Laws

1995 P(0),4(11),4(0),**1(21)**,1(22),**7(0)**

86 11/2 Alnwick (L) OPE 3m 8 GS *reluc to race, t.o. til p.u. 10th* P 0
191 24/2 Friars Haugh (L) OPE 3m 5 S *wll bhnd til kpt on frm 3 out* 4 18
320 2/3 Corbridge (R) OPE 3m 5f 8 GS *mid-div, lft 2nd at 18th, onepcd* 2 12
486 16/3 Newcastle (L) HC 3m 9 GS *not fluent in rear, nvr on terms.* 8 0
701 30/3 Tranwell (L) OPE 3m 8 GS *wll bhnd, prog 13th, outpcd frm nxt, ran on agn 2 out,no ext* 4 15
912 8/4 Tranwell (L) OPE 3m 8 GF *rear, prog to 4th hlfwy, styd on wll 4 out, not trbl ldrs* 3 18
1085 14/4 Friars Haugh (L) OPE 3m 6 F *chsd wnr frm 9th, outpcd frm 2 out* 2 13
1573 19/5 Corbridge (R) OPE 3m 12 G *wll bhnd 9th, t.o. & p.u. 12th* P 0
1586 25/5 Hexham (L) HC 2 1/2m 110yds 14 GF *chsd along to go pace, nvr reach challenging position.* 8 0

H/chase win in 95 causing problems now; ned very weak Open before winning again. 14

TA SE AG TEACHT (Irish) — **I** 25⁶

TASMANITE br.g. 7 Lighter - Minirocket by Space King Miss S Garratt

32 20/1 Higham (L) OPE 3m 15 GF *bhnd til p.u. 11th* P 0
106 17/2 Marks Tey (L) RES 3m 12 G *rr whn p.u. 5th* P 0
496 16/3 Horseheath (R) MDO 3m 10 GF *alwys rear, blnd & nrly u.r. 9th, t.o. 3 out, p.u. nxt* P 0
922 8/4 Aldington (L) MEM 3m 4 F *alwys last, t.o. 6th, 2 fences bhnd whn p.u. 11th* P 0
1299 28/4 Bexhill (R) MDO 3m 7 F *wll plcd, cls 4th whn f 14th* F -

1st signs on last start but still well short of winning. 0

TASMIN TYRANT(NZ) b.g. 7 Church Parade - Lovela (NZ) by Rapier II — Mrs C Egalton

71	10/2	Great Treth'	(R)	MDO	3m	15	S	*alwys prom, ld 3 out, drvn clr*	1	16
199	24/2	Lemalla	(R)	RES	3m	17	HY	*(fav) nvr going wll, strggling whn p.u. 2 out*	P	0
627	23/3	Kilworthy	(L)	RES	3m	13	GS	*alwys prom, chal whn lft in ld 2 out, styd on well, rdn out*	1	20
1074	13/4	Lifton	(R)	INT	3m	9	S	*(fav) j.w., 2nd til ld aft 14th, drew clr 3 out, easily*	1	21
1123	20/4	Stafford Cr'	(R)	MEM	3m	3	S	*(fav) ld 5th, wnt clr 3 out, easily*	1	22
1278	27/4	Bratton Down	(L)	INT	3m	12	GF	*(fav) prom, disp 9th til ld 14th, styd on wll frm 3 out*	1	24
1589	25/5	Mounsey Hil'	(R)	OPE	3m	12	G	*chsd ldr, ld 17th til aft last, wknd*	3	23

Missed 95; improving; ran blinder last start; exciting prospect; worth a try in H/chase 97; G/F-S. 25

TASSAGH BOY (Irish) — I 237^{4}, I 281^{4}, I 495^{P}

TASSE DU THE (Irish) — I 29^{P}, I 82^{P}, I 135^{3}, I 168^{2}, I 265^{1}, I 350^{2}, I 484^{P}

TASTE OF FREEDOM (Irish) — I 166^{P}, I 269^{P}, I 395^{6}, I 563^{P}, I 628^{P}

TATTLEJACK(IRE) ch.g. 8 Le Bavard (FR) - Bonne Fille by Bonne Noel — J M I Evetts

1995 4(11),2(19),1(20),**2(13)**,3(17),3(16),2(17)

23	20/1	Barbury Cas'	(L)	XX	3m	11	GS	*(fav) prom,blnd 10th,wth wnr 12-14th,wknd 2 out,nrly ref last*	5	0
98	12/2	Hereford	(R)	HC	3m 1f 110yds	12	HY	*f 5th.*	F	-
263	2/3	Didmarton	(L)	INT	3m	18	G	*mstk 2nd, chsd ldrs, wknd 13th, t.o.*	7	0
638	23/3	Siddington	(L)	CON	3m	16	S	*(vis) chsd lding pr & rddn 13th, kpt on frm 2 out, lft 2nd last*	2	16
1019	13/4	Kingston Bl'	(L)	INT	3m	6	G	*(vis) prssd ldr 6th, ld 14th-3 out, wknd apr last*	3	12
1244	27/4	Woodford	(L)	INT	3m	12	G	*chsd ldrs, 4th & blndrd 13th, sn rddn, outpcd apr 16th*	6	0
1435	6/5	Ashorne	(R)	CON	3m	12	G	*chsd ldrs, outpcd frm 12th, no ch nxt*	5	11

Restricted winner 95; disappointing since; stays; needs soft and Confined still possible. 15

TAU ch.g. 11 Kambalda - Mystry Tour by Master Buck — Miss Felicity McLachlan

1995 3(0),4(0),1(12),P(0),U(-),**P(0)**

272	2/3	Parham	(R)	RES	3m	13	GF	*alwys rear, wll bhnd whn p.u. 3 out*	P	0
593	23/3	Parham	(R)	RES	3m	11	GS	*prom til wknd 13th, wll bhnd whn p.u. 2 out*	P	0
779	31/3	Penshurst	(L)	RES	3m	13	GS	*in tch in mid-div, kpt on same pce*	4	12
964	8/4	Heathfield	(R)	RES	3m	7	G	*in tch, blnd 14th, rdn & onepcd frm 16th*	3	14
1442	6/5	Aldington	(L)	RES	3m	7	HD	*(12s-5s),hndy,ld 11th,hdd whn lft in ld 2 out,drvn out flat*	1	15
1537	16/5	Folkestone	(R)	HC	3 1/4m	8	GF	*in tch till pushed along and outpcd 16th.*	4	0

Moderate pointer; fortunate to collect weak Restricted; onepaced and follow up looks tough. 15

TAURA'S RASCAL b.g. 7 Scallywag - Centaura by Centaurus — P A Jones

1995 F(-),2(12)

463	9/3	Eyton-On-Se'	(L)	MDN	2 1/2m	14	G	*(Jt fav) w.w. in tch, tk ld 3 out, ran on well*	1	15

Won by a fence (2 finishers); hard to assess but should upgrade if staying. 15

TAURIAN PRINCESS b.m. 7 Electric - Facetious by Malicious — G D Hanmer

1995 P(0)

1194	21/4	Sandon	(L)	LAD	3m	7	G	*mid-div, 5th & in tch 4 out, wknd rpdly, p.u. nxt*	P	0
1579	19/5	Wolverhampt'	(L)	LAD	3m	9	G	*in tch, pckd 12th, ev ch 16th, lft 3rd nxt, onepcd*	3	16

Hurdles winner 92; lightly raced; ran well last start; worth a try in her Members. 16

TAVERN TALE (Irish) — I 47^{P}, I 312^{P}, I 334^{4}, I 445^{2}, I 517^{1}

TAYLORS TWIST (Irish) — I 43^{P}, I 204^{F}, I 232^{P}, I 428^{U}, I 475^{6}, I 578^{F}, I 625^{P}

TEA BOX (Irish) — I 466^{3}

TEACAKE b.g. 12 Deep Run - Another Adventure by Dual — J G Nicholson

1995 P(0),2(0),2(11),3(13),P(0)

246	25/2	Southwell P'	(L)	OPE	3m	9	HO	*last & bhnd frm 6th, p.u. 9th*	P	0
392	9/3	Garthorpe	(R)	MEM	3m	6	G	*(bl) 2nd til p.u. aft 5th, b.b.v.*	P	0
899	6/4	Dingley	(R)	MEM	3m	4	GS	*(bl) reluctant ldr slow pce, ran on gamely frm 2 out*	1	0
1098	14/4	Guilsborough	(L)	CON	3m	17	G	*(bl) alwys wll bhnd, t.o. 10th, p.u. 3 out*	P	0

Won a bad race run at a crawl (8 mins plus); has problems and meed same to win again. 12

TEA CEE KAY ch.g. 6 True Song - Fort Ditton by The Ditton — C O King

1995 P(0),3(0),2(13)

2	13/1	Larkhill	(R)	MDO	3m	17	GS	*ld 5th-3 out, no ext aft*	3	15
29	20/1	Barbury Cas'	(L)	RES	3m	12	GS	*hld up, prog frm 12th, styd on frm 3 out, nrst fin*	4	18
144	17/2	Larkhill	(R)	MDO	3m	15	G	*sttld bhnd, some prog 14th, sn onepcd*	4	14
267	2/3	Didmarton	(L)	MDN	3m	11	G	*(fav) mstks, chsd ldrs, clsd frm 3 uot, ev ch last, not qckn*	2	15
788	31/3	Tweseldown	(R)	MDO	3m	8	G	*trckd ldrs, not qckn & rdn 13th, styd on onepcd frm 2 out*	3	12
956	8/4	Lockinge	(L)	MDN	3m	7	GF	*(fav) ld til 3rd, cls up til ld 13th, ran on wll, easily*	1	15
1228	27/4	Worcester	(L)	HC	2m 7f	17	G	*hdwy 10th, wknd 14th.*	6	12
1383	6/5	Towcester	(R)	HC	2 3/4m	7	GF	*in tch, mstk 5th, jmpd slowly and lost pl 10th, no dngr after.*	3	16

Placed 7 times prior to winning & disappointing overall; no chance in H/Chases - stick to Restricted ... 17

TEAL BRIDGE (Irish) — I 18^{P}, I 29^{3}, I 82^{1}, I 94^{3}, I 168^{3}, I 303^{1}, I 350^{1}, I 480^{2}, I 595^{3}, I 643^{2}

TEAMTALK (Irish) — I 50^{P}, I 113^{P}, I 279^{F}

TEAPLANTER b.g. 13 National Trust - Miss India by Indian Ruler — R G Russel

1995 **1(34),2(31),U(-)**

25	20/1	Barbury Cas'	(L)	OPE	3m	14	GS	*(Jt fav) ld to 2nd, ld agn 15th, clr aft nxt, all out flat*	1 31
37	3/2	Wetherby	(L)	HC	3m 110yds	11	GS	*prom, ld 4 out, styd on well.*	1 34
185	23/2	Kempton	(R)	HC	3m	9	GS	*chsd wnr from 6th, hrd rdn apr 3 out, ev ch next, no ext approaching last.*	2 34
369	7/3	Towcester	(R)	HC	3m 1f	6	G	*(fav) ld 5th, clr 13th, easily.*	1 35
580	20/3	Towcester	(R)	HC	2 3/4m	5	G	*(fav) ld, mstk 11th, hdd next, str chal from 2 out, no ext run-in.*	2 32
909	8/4	Towcester	(R)	HC	2 3/4m	6	F	*(fav) ld to 7th, led apr 9th, mstk 12th, clr approaching 3 out, unchal.*	1 34
1121	20/4	Bangor	(L)	HC	3m 110yds	8	S	*(fav) made all, clr from 3 out, easily.*	1 34
1459	8/5	Uttoxeter	(L)	HC	4 1/4m	8	G	*(fav) chsd ldr 7th to 11th and 14th till ld 16th, hdd 20th, wknd apr next.*	4 20

Useful H/chaser; found 41/4 miles too far; win more at 14; won on firm but G-S best. 32

TEARAWAY KING (Irish) — I 4^{3}, I 40^{2}, I 78^{F}, I 125^{2}, I 250^{1}, I 294^{1}

TEARAWAY SARAH (Irish) — I 163^{P}, I 195^{4}, I 270^{P}

TEARFULL (Irish) — I 615^{P}, I 640^{5}, I 652^{5}

TEATIME GIRL br.m. 9 Royal Fountain - Pee Wee by Indian Ruler — W G Forster

399	9/3	Dalston	(R)	CON	3m	9	G	*u.r. 4th*	U -
698	30/3	Tranwell	(L)	MEM	3m	5	GS	*prom, disp 15th, cls up 2 out, btn whn f last*	F -
915	8/4	Tranwell	(L)	MDO	3m	7	GF	*alwys last, nvr going wll, t.o. & p.u. aft 9th*	P 0

Missed 94/95; ran passably in Members but not worth a rating yet. 0

TED'S KNIGHT(IRE) ch.g. 5 Mister Lord (USA) - Annie Panny by Take A Reef — Dave Dixon

521	16/3	Larkhill	(R)	MDO	3m	6	G	*sn t.o., f 11th*	F -
997	8/4	Hackwood Pa'	(L)	MDO	3m	11	GF	*mstk 1st, rear whn mstk & p.u. aft 8th*	P 0
1174	20/4	Chaddesley '	(L)	MDN	3m	10	G	*mid-div til prog 15th, ld 3 out, hdd & outpcd flat*	2 14
1536	16/5	Folkestone	(R)	HC	2m 5f	9	GF	*in tch to 8th, bhnd when p.u. before 13th, saddle slpd.*	P 0
1629	30/5	Uttoxeter	(L)	HC	2m 5f	13	GS	*alwys bhnd, t.o. when p.u. before 12th.*	P 0

placed in slowly run race; too ambitious after; every chance of Maiden success in 97. 15

TEEGA SUKU ch.g. 9 Sula Bula - Tizziwizzy Vii — C Wilson

217	24/2	Newtown	(L)	RES	3m	17	GS	*nvr nr ldrs, t.o. & p.u. 15th*	P 0
262	2/3	Didmarton	(L)	MEM	3m	11	G	*alwys wll bhnd, t.o. 12th*	8 0

No signs of ability. 0

TEELINE TERRAPIN (Irish) — I 614^{P}

TEETON MILL b.g. 7 Neltino - Celtic Well by Celtic Cone — C R Saunders

1995 U(-),F(-),1(17)

242	25/2	Southwell P'	(L)	RES	3m	12	HO	*(fav) trckd ldrs, ld 4 out, clr whn f nxt*	F 21
437	9/3	Newton Brom'	(R)	RES	3m	9	GS	*(fav) hld up mid-div, prog 14th, ld 2 out, qcknd clr*	1 20

Potentially useful; finished early 96; good stable and sure to upgrade if fit in 97; stays. 22

TEETON NISHABALL gr.m. 6 Nishapour (FR) - Charlton Athletic by Bustino — Mrs Joan Tice

438	9/3	Newton Brom'	(R)	MDN	3m	10	GS	*hld up, prog to 3rd at 11th, ld 3 out, drew clr*	1 15
1097	14/4	Guilsborough	(L)	MEM	3m	6	G	*(fav) prssd wnr 9th,ld 13th til mstk 15th,btn 3 out,lft 2nd last*	2 10

Romped home in modest race; well beaten after; young enough to regain the plot. 17

TEETON THOMAS b.g. 7 Sunley Builds - Royal Darwin by Royal Palm — Mrs Joan Tice

1995 **9(NH)**

182	18/2	Horseheath	(R)	MDO	3m	11	G	*jmpd badly, in tch to 13th, kpt on*	4 0

Very lightly raced; shows some hope and surely capable of better. 11

TEKLA(FR) b.g. 11 Toujours Pret (USA) - Hekla Des Sacart (FR) by Laniste — E H Lodge

1995 **4(NH),P(NH),F(NH),P(NH)**

26	20/1	Barbury Cas'	(L)	OPE	3m	12	GS	*33s-14s, cls up, 4th whn f 8th*	F -
139	17/2	Larkhill	(R)	CON	3m	11	G	*prom, ld 8th-12th, sn wknd, onepcd*	4 17
379	9/3	Barbury Cas'	(L)	XX	3m	9	GS	*made most to 11th, wknd nxt, t.o.*	3 0
505	16/3	Magor	(R)	PPO	3m	7	GS	*rear, blnd 12th, lost tch aft*	4 0
637	23/3	Siddington	(L)	MEM	3m	14	S	*ld/disp thro'out,rddn 2 out, lft in ld last, kpt on flat*	1 15
908	8/4	Hereford	(R)	HC	2m 3f	12	GF	*mid div, hit 5th, outpcd from 4 out.*	5 0
1108	17/4	Cheltenham	(L)	HC	4m 1f	14	GS	*prom, mstk 10th, wknd when mistake 17th, blnd 20th, p.u. before 22nd.*	P 0
1228	27/4	Worcester	(L)	HC	2m 7f	17	G	*prom to 9th.*	8 0

382 6/5 Exeter (R) HC 2m 7f 110yds 8 GF *with ldr till wknd 9th, t.o. when p.u. before 5 out.* P 0

Winning hurdler; needs easy 3 miles; won competitive race; outclassed after; hard to win again. 16

TEL D'OR b.g. 11 Le Coq D'Or - Tel Brig by New Brig P J Millington

35 20/1 Higham (L) RES 3m 16 GF *bhnd frm 11th, t.o. & p.u. last* P 0
95 11/2 Ampton (R) RES 3m 11 GF *disp to 7th, wknd 11th, p.u. 15th* P 0
242 25/2 Southwell P' (L) RES 3m 12 HO *bhnd frm 6th, t.o. & p.u. aft 11th* P 0
396 9/3 Garthorpe (R) RES 3m 9 G *alwys last, blnd 6th, t.o. 8th, p.u. 11th* P 0
195 21/4 Sandon (L) XX 3m 9 G *rear, t.o. 12th, p.u. 3 out* P 0
239 27/4 Clifton On ' (L) RES 3m 9 GF *mstk 4th, alwys rear, t.o. 14th* 7 0
518 12/5 Garthorpe (R) MEM 3m 6 GF *(bl) rear, t.o. 9th, p.u. 13th* P 0

Ex Irish pointer; last won in 92; looks well past it now. 0

TELEPHONE b.g. 7 Sonnen Gold - Bellekino by Relkino R J Hamer

148 17/2 Erw Lon (L) MDN 3m 9 G *(fav) 4s-6/4, rear, some late prog 3 out, nvr nrr* 5 0
386 9/3 Llanfrynach (R) RES 3m 10 GS *chsd ldrs,lft 2nd 11th,no imp,btn 3rd whn eased & p.u. 2 out* P 0
552 17/3 Erw Lon (L) MDN 3m 10 GS *nvr bynd mid-div, p.u. 15th* P 0
696 30/3 Llanvapley (L) MDN 3m 13 GS *hld up, mod 6th at 15th, prog nxt, qcknd to ld flat* 1 14
980 8/4 Lydstep (L) RES 3m 11 G *trckd ldrs, btn whn p.u. last* P 0
267 27/4 Pyle (R) RES 3m 7 G *(fav) w.w. effrt & prog 13th, rdn & kpt on onepcd frm 15th* 3 15

Ex novice hurdler; won slowly run race; inconsistent; just beaten in weak Restricted; can win one. 16

TELL YOU WHAT ch.g. 11 Crested Lark - Andromeda II by Romany Air R Freeman

1995 8(11),3(0),2(14),3(19)

230 24/2 Heythrop (R) MEM 3m 12 GS *cls up to hlfwy, bhnd whn p.u. 14th* P 0
943 8/4 Andoversford (R) CON 3m 9 GF *in tch til wknd frm 13th, t.o. 2 out* 5 0
180 21/4 Mollington (R) OPE 3m 5 F *chsd wnr to 12th, last & btn frm nxt* 4 14
236 27/4 Clifton On ' (L) CON 3m 8 GF *ld/disp to 12th, 3rd & outpcd frm nxt, kpt on* 3 14
436 6/5 Ashorne (R) MEM 3m 7 G *prom, outpcd 12th, lft 2nd 15th, no imp, fin tired* 3 13
500 11/5 Kingston Bl' (L) CON 3m 7 G *prssd wnr to 13th, chal agn 3 out, no ext apr last* 2 17
563 19/5 Mollington (R) CON 3m 8 GS *prom to 12th, sn strgglng, t.o.* 4 0

Hurdle winner 92; safe but beaten all 15 points; need luck to win. 16

TEMPERED POINT(USA) br.g. 10 Temperence Hill (USA) - Parissaul by Saulingo Mrs R Smith

1995 P(0),P(0),P(0),P(0),U(-),2(0),4(0),3(0)

542 17/3 Southwell P' (L) MDO 3m 15 GS *cls up, unable to cls on wnr frm 4 out* 2 0
972 8/4 Thorpe Lodge (L) MDO 3m 9 GF *cls up, 3rd 6 out, chal 3 out, ld nxt, ran on* 1 14
302 28/4 Southwell P' (L) INT 3m 10 GF *alwys 1st 3, outpcd frm 4 out* 3 14
522 12/5 Garthorpe (R) RES 3m 12 GF *chsd ldrs, ev ch til wknd 4 out, lft 3rd last, not qckn* 3 10
597 25/5 Garthorpe (R) XX 3m 9 G *ld to 9th, fdd, 6th & outpcd 4 out* 6 0
640 2/6 Dingley (R) RES 3m 9 GF *prom gng wl, not qckn 15th, no imp 2 out* 4 16

Improved; won bad Maiden; ran passably after but a weak finisher and another win looks hard; G-F. 14

TEMPEST MEAD(IRE) br.g. 7 Strong Gale - Honeytoi by Carlburg A G Fear

470 10/3 Milborne St' (L) MDO 3m 18 G *mid-div, no ch whn f 4 out* F -

Only learning; may do better. 0

TEMPLE KNIGHT b.g. 7 Never So Bold - Nelly Do Da by Derring-Do Miss E J Budden

469 10/3 Milborne St' (L) LAD 3m 8 G *mid-div, lost tch 12th, t.o. & p.u. 14th, lame* P 0
818 6/4 Charlton Ho' (L) LAD 3m 6 GF *in tch til 10th, t.o. & p.u. lame 3 out* P 0

Two disasters in 96 & can only be watched 0

TEMPORALE (Irish) — I 18P, I 235⁵, I 284³, I 392², I 412⁶, I 553³, I 584⁵, I 597P

TEMPORARY ch.g. 11 Croghan Hill - Pejays Princess by Pumps (USA) Philip Rogers

1995 P(0),2(13),2(15),2(15),5(10)

555 17/3 Ottery St M' (L) MDO 3m 15 G *prom, ld 6-10th, cls up to 4 out, outpcd aft* 3 10
718 30/3 Wadebridge (L) MDO 3m 11 GF *(fav) lft in ld 5th,ld/disp to aft 14th,styd on onepcd aft* 3 15
143 20/4 Flete Park (R) MDN 3m 17 S *(Co fav) handy,cls 3rd frm 13th, wknd aft 3 out, btn 5th whn p.u.last* P 0

Very frustrating; beaten favourite 4 times; weak finisher and win looks to have passed him by. 14

TEN BOB DOWN (Irish) — I 148P

TENDERMAN(IRE) b.g. 5 Tender King - Mayrhofen by Don J M Turner

834 6/4 Marks Tey (L) RES 3m 11 G *prom, wknd aft 14th, rear whn p.u. 2 out* P 0
145 20/4 Higham (L) RES 3m 12 F *rear of chsng grp, lost tch 12th, t.o. & p.u. 16th* P 0
260 27/4 Cottenham (R) RES 3m 3 F *chsd ldr to 9th,ld 15th,hdd 2 out,ld flat,hdd cls hm* 2 16

Battled away in virtual match last start & may be able to go one better in 97 15

TENELLA'S LAST ch.m. 8 Broadsword (USA) - Tenella by Wrekin Rambler Mrs M G Richardson

1995 3(0),P(0),1(13),U(-),U(-),**4(12)**

219	24/2	Newtown	(L)	RES	3m	17	GS	*mid-div, lost tch 13th, no ch aft*	7
338	3/3	Heythrop	(R)	RES	3m	9	G	*cls up, ld 14th til hdd & no ext flat*	2 1
889	6/4	Kimble	(L)	RES	3m	7	GF	*cls up to 12th, 4th & btn frm 16th*	4

Won 1 (poor Maiden) of 14 starts; ran well at Heythrop but very onepaced and win not easy to find. 15

TENELORD ch.g. 9 True Song - Tenella by Wrekin Rambler C R Saunder

1995 3(15),F(-),U(-),P(0)

22	20/1	Barbury Cas'	(L)	XX	3m	19	GS	*hld up,prog to chs ldng trio 12th,no imp frm nxt*	4 1
106	17/2	Marks Tey	(L)	RES	3m	12	G	*(fav) in tch, 4th & blnd 12th, wknd appr 16th, p.u. & dism 17th*	P
243	25/2	Southwell P'	(L)	RES	3m	11	HO	*prom to 12th, rnwd effrt 4 out, kpt on onepcd frm 2 out*	2 1
396	9/3	Garthorpe	(R)	RES	3m	9	G	*(fav) 2nd to 5 out, renewed chal 2 out, best spd flat, wll rdn*	1 1
723	31/3	Garthorpe	(R)	CON	3m	19	G	*ld 4-5th, chsd ldr 13th-aft 15th, not qckn 3 out, styd on*	3 1
1097	14/4	Guilsborough	(L)	MEM	3m	6	G	*mstk 7th,ld to 13th & frm 15th,clr 3 out,rdn & lft clr last*	1 1
1594	25/5	Garthorpe	(R)	MEM	3m	10	G	*cls up 1st m, wknd 7th, 7th at 10th, p.u. 12th*	P

Maiden winner 93; needs easy 3 miles; well ridden and placed; can win again. 18

TENNESSEE CRUISER b.g. 8 Cruise Missile - Tennessee II by Kribi A V Watkin

1995 P(0),r(-)

218	24/2	Newtown	(L)	MDN	3m	14	GS	*last & t.o. til p.u. 3 out*	P
690	30/3	Llanvapley	(L)	MEM	3m	4	GS	*cls up, wknd 10th, t.o. 13th, p.u. 3 out*	P
849	6/4	Howick	(L)	MDN	3m	14	GF	*t.o. whn ref 12th*	R
1483	11/5	Bredwardine	(R)	MDO	3m	15	G	*in tch til outpcd frm 12th, t.o. & p.u. 2 out*	P
1606	25/5	Bassaleg	(R)	MDO	3m	7	GS	*rear, lost tch 7th, poor 4th 3 out, tk 3rd flat*	3

Well beaten on 1st ever completion; huge improvement needed. 0

TEN OF SPADES b.g. 16 Raise You Ten - Hansel Money by Prince Hansel Mrs S A Sanson

9	14/1	Cottenham	(R)	OPE	3m	13	G	*chsd ldrs, wknd 16th, p.u. last*	P
249	25/2	Charing	(L)	XX	3m	11	GS	*ld to 6th, wth ldr til wknd 15th, bhnd whn u.r. 2 out*	U
570	17/3	Detling	(L)	MEM	3m	6	GF	*ld, prssd whn u.r. 3 out*	U
775	31/3	Penshurst	(L)	CON	3m	8	GS	*ld to apr 2 out, no ext flat*	2 1

Former very useful chaser; retains some ability; novice ridden after debut; Members possible at 17. ... 17

TEN PAST TEN (Irish) — **I** 531⁴, **I** 621⁵

TENPENCE PRINCESS (Irish) — **I** 37ᴾ, **I** 443ᴾ

TERALISA (Irish) — **I** 20ᶠ, **I** 32ᴾ, **I** 95⁴, **I** 215ᴾ, **I** 270,

TERRACOTTA WARRIOR ch.h. 10 Roman Warrior - Derek's Folly by Derek H John Sisterso

1995 P(0),4(0)

52	4/2	Alnwick	(L)	MDO	3m	11	G	*f 2nd*	F
89	11/2	Alnwick	(L)	MDO	3m	9	GS	*alwys last, t.o. hlfwy*	4
320	2/3	Corbridge	(R)	OPE	3m 5f	8	GS	*sn last, t.o.& u.r. 12th*	U
910	8/4	Tranwell	(L)	MEM	3m	4	GF	*(fav) chsd wnr, wknd to 3rd at 12th, tk remote 2nd last*	2
1136	20/4	Hornby Cast'	(L)	MDN	3m	11	G	*wth ldrs, outpcd 13th, sn t.o.*	6
1253	27/4	Balcormo Ma'	(R)	MDO	3m	16	GS	*prom early, lost tch frm hlfwy*	9
1517	12/5	Hexham Poin'	(L)	MDN	3m	10	HY	*in tch, lost plc & rdn 13th, rallied & ev ch 3 out, onepcd*	2 1

Only beaten 1 horse prior to last race; winner behind but makes little appeal as a future winner. 10

TERRANO STAR (Irish) — **I** 9², **I** 53, , **I** 147⁵, **I** 245ᴾ, **I** 432¹, **I** 646,

TEX MEX(IRE) b.g. 8 Deep Run - Polar Bee by Gunner B Mrs S Maxs

1995 1(16),P(0),3(15),P(0)

29	20/1	Barbury Cas'	(L)	RES	3m	12	GS	*ld, clr to 13th, rdn & hdd last, sn ld agn, ran on gamely*	1 2
252	25/2	Charing	(L)	INT	3m	7	GS	*made all, clr frm 4th, mstk 4 out, nvr chal*	1 2
784	31/3	Tweseldown	(R)	CON	3m	5	G	*(fav) made all, clr 4 out, eased flat, cllpsd & died*	1 2

Dead. 23

THADY'S REMEDY (Irish) — **I** 291ᴾ, **I** 324⁴

THAMESDOWN TOOTSIE b.m. 11 Comedy Star (USA) - Lizzie Lightfoot by Hotfoot Miss V S Lyo

1995 1(24),1(26),1(27),1(24),1(21)

27	20/1	Barbury Cas'	(L)	LAD	3m	15	GS	*prom til outpcd frm 13th, sn no ch*	5
126	17/2	Kingston Bl'	(L)	LAD	3m	11	GS	*(fav) raced wd,ld/disp til ld 10th,hdd 2 out,rallied flat,hld off*	2 2
216	24/2	Newtown	(L)	LAD	3m	13	GS	*ld, clr 12th, hdd 2 out, not qckn apr last*	2 2

Uesful Ladies horse; finished early 96; best on S-Hyice ridden; win again when conditions suit. 24

THANK THE LORD b.g. 5 Arctic Lord - Anitacat by No Argument Mrs J Lee

684	30/3	Chaddesley '	(L)	RES	3m	14	G	*schoold, bhnd, some prog whn f 12th*	F

Showed a little on debut; should do better. 0

THANK YOU (Irish) — **I** 164ᴾ, **I** 469ᴾ, **I** 532ᴾ, **I** 604ᵁ, **I** 631ᴾ

THARIF b.g. 8 Green Desert (USA) - Mrs Bacon by Balliol N J Pewter
1995 F(-),P(0),P(0),P(0),P(0),P(0),P(0),U(-),P(0)

344	3/3 Higham	(L) MDO 3m	12	G	*cls up til u.r. 6th*	U	-
423	9/3 High Easter	(L) MDN 3m	8	S	*clr wth ldr to 9th, wknd appr 14th, t.o. 3 out*	2	0
617	23/3 Higham	(L) MDO 3m	11	GF	*rear, prog 3 out, 2nd & btn whn ran out last*	r	11
682	30/3 Cottenham	(R) MDO 3m	9	GF	*ld to 4th, ld 12th, sn clr, wknd & hdd aft 3 out*	4	0
931	8/4 Marks Tey	(L) RES 3m	8	G	*alwys rear, mstk & rdn 10th, t.o. whn u.r. 12th*	U	-
1326	28/4 Fakenham P-'	(L) MDO 3m	7	G	*chsd ldrs to 7th, no ch 13th, p.u. 15th*	P	0

Last when completing; does not stay and needs a miracle to win. 0

THATS DIFFERENT gr.g. 7 My Rough Diamond - Easy Swinger by Swing Easy (USA) Miss A Cavanagh

842	6/4 Maisemore P'	(L) MDN 3m	17	GF	*jmpd badly, t.o. 3rd til ref 7th*	R	-

Awful on his debut. 0

THATS MY LUCK (Irish) — **I** 172^P, **I** 255^4
THATS MY WIFE (Irish) — **I** 532^P
THE AIRY MAN (Irish) — **I** 457^P
THEAIRYMAN (Irish) — **I** 118^P, **I** 146^P, **I** 507^B, **I** 564,
THE ALAMO (Irish) — **I** 36^P

THE APPRENTICE ch.g. 10 Torus - Bog View by African Sky Robert Williams
1995 **P(NH)**

151	17/2 Erw Lon	(L) MDN 3m	8	G	*made all, 20l clr 5th, 5l up 2 out, styd on*	1	15
388	9/3 Llanfrynach	(R) RES 3m	20	GS	*ld to 13th, sn wknd, p.u. 3 out*	P	0
770	31/3 Pantyderi	(R) RES 3m	9	G	*dist ldr til hdd 2 out, kpt on*	2	16
980	8/4 Lydstep	(L) RES 3m	11	G	*disp to 14th, p.u. 16th*	P	0
1267	27/4 Pyle	(R) RES 3m	7	G	*made all, clr 5th, tired apr last, hld on well*	1	16
1389	6/5 Pantyderi	(R) INT 3m	5	GF	*ld til aft 15th, wknd rpdly, p.u. 3 out*	P	0

Did well to win 2 but basically non-stayer; needs to get clear; weak Confined possible; Good 16

THE ARTFUL RASCAL b.g. 12 Scallywag - Quick Exit by David Jack M A Kemp
1995 5(19)

102	17/2 Marks Tey	(L) CON 3m	17	G	*prom, ld 6th 10l clr 15th, unchall*	1	26

Decent but hardly ever runs; stays well; can win again if fit in 97; likes Marks Tey; G-S. 25

THEATRE SISTER (Irish) — **I** 578^P, **I** 610^F, **I** 632^P

THE BARREN ARCTIC br.g. 10 Baron Blakeney - Arctic Granada by Arctic Slave David A Smith
1995 P(0),U(-),1(15),P(0)

165	17/2 Weston Park	(L) RES 3m	9	G	*rear, mstks, ran on frm 4 out, nrst fin*	3	12
292	2/3 Eaton Hall	(R) RES 3m	15	G	*hld up rear, prog 4 out, ran in 2 out, fin well*	2	15
685	30/3 Chaddesley '	(L) LAD 3m	9	G	*prom, cls 4th whn ran out 11th*	r	
951	8/4 Eyton-On-Se'	(L) LAD 3m	6	GF	*mid-div to 10th,smth prog to disp ld 3 out,clr 2 out,ran on*	1	20
1232	27/4 Weston Park	(L) LAD 3m	6	G	*w.w.,rear hlfwy,bad mstk 13th,onepcd,4th last,p.u.runin lame*	P	0

Maiden winner 95; improved & did well to win modest Ladies; problem last start; Firm 18

THE BATCHLOR b.g. 13 Sparkler - Proxy by Quorum J M B Pugh

153	17/2 Erw Lon	(L) OPE 3m	15	G	*rear, t.o. & p.u. 15th*	P	0
351	3/3 Garnons	(L) OPE 3m	14	GS	*f 1st*	F	-
545	17/3 Erw Lon	(L) CON 3m	10	GS	*nvr bttr than mid-div*	6	0
602	23/3 Howick	(L) OPE 3m	11	S	*mid-div, t.o. & p.u. 3 out*	P	0
845	6/4 Howick	(L) CON 3m	12	GF	*last pair, f 4th*	F	-
1035	13/4 St Hilary	(R) CON 3m	10	G	*rear, 20l 5th at 14th, p.u. 2 out*	P	0
1157	20/4 Llanwit Maj'	(R) CON 3m	11	GS	*prog 9th, lft 3rd 14th, wknd 3 out*	4	0
1263	27/4 Pyle	(R) CON 3m	9	G	*rear, cls 7th at 7th, went remote 3rd 14th, styd on*	3	0

Missed 95; won 1 of last 28 races; does not stay and win at 14 looks impossible. 10

THE BIG WHEEL ch.g. 13 Wolverlife - Rosie O'Grady by Barrons Court Milson Robinson
1995 P(0),3(0)

324	3/3 Market Rase'	(L) MEM 3m	4	G	*trckd ldr, ld 3 out, tried to ref & hdd nxt, onepcd*	2	0
513	16/3 Dalton Park	(R) OPE 3m	9	G	*ld to 2nd, chsd ldrs, 4th & btn whn f 4 out*	F	-
723	31/3 Garthorpe	(R) CON 3m	19	G	*mid-div, 8th hlfwy, prog to 4th aft 15th, btn 3 out*	6	0
968	8/4 Thorpe Lodge	(L) CON 3m	5	GF	*prog 7th, 2nd at 9th, ld 4 out, onepcd frm nxt*	3	11

Very moderate; ungenuine and need luck to win again. 12

THE BIRDIE SONG b.m. 6 Little Wolf - Katebird by Birdbrook Mrs G M Summers

1523	12/5 Garthorpe	(R) MDO 3m	11	GF	*mid to rear, no prog whn f 11th*	F	-

No signs yet. 0

THE BIRD O'DONNELL b.g. 10 Monksfield - Sheila's Flame Lady Sarah Barry

66	10/2	Great Treth'	(R)	OPE	3m	8	S	*chsd ldr til onepcd frm 3 out*	3 22
209	24/2	Castle Of C'	(R)	OPE	3m	8	HY	*hld up, prog 13th, disp 4 out til ld 2 out, sn clr*	1 26
483	14/3	Cheltenham	(L)	HC	3 1/4m 110yds	17	G	*mid div when hit 5th, hdwy to chase ldrs from 10th, disp 3rd when mstk 3 out, wknd apr next.*	8 24
672	29/3	Aintree	(L)	HC	2 3/4m	26	G	*held up, pushed along and outpcd hfwy, some hdwy apr 2 out, n.d..*	5 26

Useful ex Irish pointer; outclassed in top races; can win H/chase; well suited by S-Hy. 28

THE BLACK BISHOP(IRE) b.g. 8 The Parson - Darkina by Tarqogan — Martin F Edgar

1995 **8(NH),5(NH),P(NH)**

189	24/2	Friars Haugh	(L)	RES	3m	9	S	*5th hlfwy, ld 4 out, styd on well*	1 17
402	9/3	Dalston	(R)	XX	3m	13	G	*mid-div early, imprv 11th, chsd ldrs frm 3 out, one pace*	3 16

Won Irish Maiden 94; won fair race; stays; finished early; needs more for Confined; Soft. 18

THE BLEARY FLYER (Irish) — I 479^P, I 492^P

THE BLIND JUDGE b.g. 7 Baron Blakeney - Fernessa by Roman Warrior — Miss Scarlett J Crew

1995 P(0),P(0),B(-),P(0)

144	17/2	Larkhill	(R)	MDO	3m	15	G	*rear whn u.r. 1st*	U -
268	2/3	Didmarton	(L)	MDN	3m	10	G	*ld to 4th, wkng whn mstk 9th, t.o.*	5 0
643	23/3	Siddington	(L)	MDN	3m	16	S	*mid-div til f 6th*	F -
947	8/4	Andoversford	(R)	MDN	3m	11	GF	*alwys last, t.o. & p.u. 15th*	P 0

Looks hopeless. 0

THEBLONDEBARRISTER (Irish) — I 106^P, I 165^P, I 660^P

THE BOLD ABBOT b.g. 6 Derring Rose - Canford Abbas by Hasty Word — P J Millington

1995 **P(NH),12(NH)**

331	3/3	Market Rase'	(L)	MDO	3m	9	G	*lost tch 12th, p.u. 15th*	P 0
397	9/3	Garthorpe	(R)	MDN	3m	9	G	*cls up, disp 10th-6 out, wknd rpdly nxt*	5 0
541	17/3	Southwell P'	(L)	MDO	3m	9	GS	*prom, chal & ev ch whn f last*	F -
898	6/4	Dingley	(R)	MDN	2m 5f	10	GS	*(Co fav) in tch last pair whn blkd loose horse 7th*	B -
1026	13/4	Brocklesby '	(L)	MDN	3m	6	GF	*(fav) cls up, ld 5 out, hdd bfr 3 out, ran on onepce*	2 12
1217	24/4	Andoversford	(R)	MDO	3m	16	G	*in tch, chsd ldr 15-16th, wknd nxt*	6 0
1301	28/4	Southwell P'	(L)	MDO	3m	10	GF	*chsd ldrs, ev ch 3 out, not qckn*	4 11
1381	5/5	Dingley	(R)	MDO	3m	16	GF	*alwys rear, t.o. 14th*	8 0

Flattered by his placings; only beaten 2 other horses; well short of a win yet. 10

THE BREASER FAWL (Irish) — I 40^P, I 125, , I 294^P, I 371^P

THE BUACHAILL(IRE) ch.g. 7 Le Bavard (FR) - Many Views by Bargello — Mrs Alix Stevenson

1995 **4(NH)**

87	11/2	Alnwick	(L)	MDO	3m	7	GS	*(fav) hld up, trckd ldr 11th, ld apr 3 out, blnd nxt, easily*	1 14
189	24/2	Friars Haugh	(L)	RES	3m	9	S	*(fav) not fluent, 3rd hlfwy, no ext apr last*	3 15
1249	27/4	Balcormo Ma'	(R)	RES	3m	10	GS	*ld til 13th, grdly wknd*	4 10

Ex-Irish; easily won poor Maiden but not progressed; interrupted season; may do better in 97 15

THE BUCK PONY (Irish) — I 270^P, I 322^P, I 418^P, I 464^5

THE BUTLER ch.g. 10 Roman Warrior - Just Nicola by Eborneezer — Miss A L Barnett

1995 4(0),7(0),1(12),5(0),P(0),4(15),4(11),7(0)

281	2/3	Clyst St Ma'	(L)	RES	3m	11	S	*sn rear, no ch whn p.u. 12th*	P 0
715	30/3	Wadebridge	(L)	CON	3m	8	GF	*ld til f heavily 12th (ditch)*	F -
1075	13/4	Lifton	(R)	RES	3m	12	S	*ld til 3rd, 2nd 11-14th, sn wknd*	6 0
1128	20/4	Stafford Cr'	(R)	RES	3m	17	S	*midfld til lost tch 10th, p.u. 12th*	P 0

Maiden winner 95; does not stay and Restricted looks too tough. 12

THE CAFFLER (Irish) — I 227^P, I 312^1, I 357^P

THE CAMAIR FLYER(IRE) b.g. 6 Wylfa - Merrybash by Pinzari — Colin W German

704	30/3	Tranwell	(L)	MDO	3m	16	GS	*ld 2-4th, disp nxt, ld 11th til f 15th*	F -
915	8/4	Tranwell	(L)	MDO	3m	7	GF	*chsd ldr, disp 2nd whn f 4th*	F -
1517	12/5	Hexham Poin'	(L)	MDN	3m	10	HY	*disp ld til ld 11th, hdd 3 out, 5th & wll btn whn f nxt*	F -

Has ability but keeps crash landing; chances if learning in 97. 12

THE CASS MAN (Irish) — I 470^P

THE CHAP br.g. 13 Tanfirion - Bay Tree (FR) by Relko — Paul L Gill

1995 6(0),5(0),4(16),2(16),4(13),5(16)

329	3/3	Market Rase'	(L)	RES	3m	12	G	*alwys rear, no ch frm 12th*	7 0
411	9/3	Charm Park	(L)	RES	3m	20	G	*prom early, outpcd 11th, p.u. 3 out*	P 0
585	23/3	Wetherby Po'	(L)	RES	3m	13	S	*alwys mid-div, no ch whn p.u. last*	P 0
1093	14/4	Whitwell-On'	(R)	MXO	4m	19	G	*alwys trckng ldrs, lost plc frm 19th*	5 11
1131	20/4	Hornby Cast'	(L)	RES	3m	17	G	*alwys rear, t.o. & p.u. 2 out*	P 0
1368	4/5	Gisburn	(R)	RES	3m	9	G	*bhnd, t.o. 10th, p.u. 2 out*	P 0

Maiden winner 93; safe but lost last 15 and declined in 96; looks past it now. 11

THE CITY MINSTREL br.g. 11 Black Minstrel - Miss Diga by Tarqogan P Cave
1995 P(0),P(0),P(0),2(10),9(0),2(0)
1046 13/4 Bitterley (L) LAD 3m 9 G *cls up til lost plc 9th, wknd 13th, p.u. last* P 0
1291 28/4 Barbury Cas' (L) LAD 3m 5 F *cls up to 11th, sn wll bhnd, t.o. & p.u. last, lame* R -

Last won in 92; problems last start and prospects bleak now. 0

THE CLIENT (Irish) — I 283^{F}, I 492^{P}
THE CONAWAREY (Irish) — I 172^{F}, I 402^{5}
THE CONVINCER (Irish) — I 97^{P}, I 256^{1}, I 316^{F}, I 411^{4}, I 454^{P}, I 537^{2}
THE COPPER KEY b.g. 11 Park Row - Menhaden by Menelek Mrs S M Trump
1995 P(0),4(16),5(11),P(0),P(0)
137 17/2 Ottery St M' (L) RES 3m 15 GS *alwys rear, nvr on terms* 6 0
276 2/3 Clyst St Ma' (L) MEM 3m 4 S *2nd whn blnd & u.r. 3rd* U -
280 2/3 Clyst St Ma' (L) RES 3m 11 S *2nd outing, mid-div, lost tch 14th, t.o. nxt* 4 0
441 9/3 Haldon (R) MEM 3m 6 S *cls up,trckd ldr 6-13th,cls 3rd frm 3 out,blnd last,nt rcvr* 3 10
805 4/4 Clyst St Ma' (L) RES 3m 7 GS *mstk 1st, rear til p.u. aft 6th* P 0
1113 17/4 Hockworthy (L) RES 3m 11 GS *chsd ldrs, 4th & outpcd frm 13th, no prog aft* 4 0
1313 28/4 Little Wind' (R) RES 3m 14 G *ld 1st, styd prom til lost plc 12th, bhnd frm 15th* 10 0
1428 6/5 High Bickin' (R) RES 3m 10 G *ld til hdd aft 2 out, drvn to ld agn last 50 yards* 1 18
1622 27/5 Lifton (R) CON 3m 14 GS *6th at 13th, went 3rd 3 out, effrt und pres nxt, just faild* 2 19
1634 1/6 Bratton Down (L) INT 3m 15 G *n.j.w. mid-div, lost tch frm 14th* 7 0

Won weak Restricted; stays but inconsistent; good enough for modest Confined if in the mood; G-S. ... 17

THE COUNTRY TRADER br.g. 10 Furry Glen - Lady Girand by Raise You Ten P J Hobbs
1995 **1(NH),1(NH),2(NH),4(NH)**
672 29/3 Aintree (L) HC 2 3/4m 26 G *(bl) f 1st.* F -

Winning chaser autumn 95 but can only be watched after the briefest of attempt sin H/Chases 20

THE CRIOSRA (Irish) — I 51^{3}, I 72, , I 186^{4}, I 436^{3}
THE DANCE (Irish) — I 166^{F}, I 272^{P}
THE DANCING PARSON b.m. 9 The Parson - Quayville by Quayside T B Brown
1995 7(14)
725 31/3 Garthorpe (R) OPE 3m 9 G *bhnd, lost tch hlfwy, ran on 14th, 5th 3 out, no more prog* 5 16
1098 14/4 Guilsborough (L) CON 3m 17 G *mstks, prom to 12th, sn strggLng, kpt on agn frm 2 out* 4 14
1438 6/5 Ashorne (R) XX 3m 14 G *chsd ldrs, clsd 10th, wknd 13th, t.o.* 8 0

Won 3 Irish points 93; lightly raced; beaten 15 lengths minimum and not threatening to win. 13

THE DARK WATCH br.g. 13 Our Mirage - Dusky Shue by Dusky Boy E A Thomas
691 30/3 Llanvapley (L) CON 3m 15 GS *last pair, t.o. & p.u. 15th* P 0
1042 13/4 Bitterley (L) CON 3m 9 G *trckd ldrs, 8l 3rd 13th, outpcd frm nxt* 5 11
1170 20/4 Chaddesley ' (L) CON 3m 9 G *chsd ldrs, 5th & in tch 13th, outpcd nxt, p.u. 3 out* P 0

Maiden winner 89; of little account now. 11

THE DEANE DELEGATE (Irish) — I 429^{5}
THE DEFENDER (Irish) — I 88^{P}, I 111^{P}, I 206^{P}, I 368^{3}, I 431^{2}, I 511^{1}
THE DIFFERENCE b.g. 9 Cruise Missile - Brandy's Honour by Hot Brandy M G Chatterton
1995 3(10),7(12),3(14),3(12),2(15),1(17),4(13)
244 25/2 Southwell P' (L) CON 3m 13 HO *alwys rear, t.o. 11th, styd on aft, poor 5th whn p.u. 3 out* P 0
393 9/3 Garthorpe (R) CON 3m 7 G *5th & outpcd frm 7th, 4th & running on whn f 2 out* F -
535 17/3 Southwell P' (L) CON 3m 10 GS *hld up mid-div, clsd 5 out, ran on frm 2 out, ld nr fin* 1 17
723 31/3 Garthorpe (R) CON 3m 19 G *alwys rear, 12th & wll bhnd hlfwy, nvr dang* 8 0
1093 14/4 Whitwell-On' (R) MXO 4m 19 G *chsd ldrs til b.d. 6th* B -
1302 28/4 Southwell P' (L) INT 3m 10 GF *hld up rear, prog to ldrs whn u.r. 12th* U -
1521 12/5 Garthorpe (R) INT 3m 7 GF *ld to 2nd, hld up, prog 3 out, disp nxt, ld last, ran on wll* 1 17

Won 2 modest races; stays; penalties make life hard in 97; G/S-F. 18

THE DOORMAKER ch.g. 14 Balinger - Romany Queen by Romany Air B J Trickey
1995 3(0),P(0),3(13),1(18)
442 9/3 Haldon (R) CON 3m 6 S *in tch, blnd 3rd, lost ground frm 11th, wll bhnd clsng stgs* 5 0
1342 4/5 Holnicote (L) MEM 3m 7 GS *ld to 3rd, grad lost tch* 5 11
1589 25/5 Mounsey Hil' (R) OPE 3m 12 G *alwys rear, t.o. & p.u. 15th* P 0

Schoolmaster now; well beaten in 96 and most unlikely to win again. 15

THE EARLY BIRD b.m. 5 Bold Owl - Monsoon by Royal Palace Mrs V Nyberg
755 31/3 Lockerbie (R) MDN 3m 17 G *sn bhnd, p.u. 13th* P 0
1089 14/4 Friars Haugh (L) MDN 3m 10 F *nvr dang, t.o. & p.u. 2 out* P 0

1476 11/5 Aspatria (L) MDO 3m 16 GF *mstks, alwys last, t.o. & p.u. bfr 12th* P 0

No signs of catching the worm yet. 0

THE FINANCIER (Irish) — I 341^{U}, I 395^{P}, I 477^{P}, I 494^{1}

THEFIRSTONE (Irish) — I 543^{1}, I 606, , I 659^{3}

THE FOOLISH ONE b.m. 9 Idiot's Delight - The Ceiriog by Deep Diver R Alner

1995 4(0),1(15),2(16)

1557 18/5 Bassaleg (R) RES 3m 14 F *prom til wknd frm 3 out* 4 0

1601 25/5 Bassaleg (R) RES 3m 12 GS *mid-div, lost tch 9th, p.u. last* P 0

1641 2/6 Dingley (R) RES 3m 13 GF *ld 5th, clr 13th, hdd 2 out, wknd rpdly* 6 0

Won weak Maiden 95; late to appear and showed nothing in 96; Restricted looks hard; G-F. 13

THE FORTIES ch.g. 11 Bybicello - Fanny Adams by Sweet Ration N C Earnshaw

1995 **P(NH)**

56 10/2 Cottenham (R) OPE 3m 12 GS *alwys last, t.o. 12th* 9 0

274 2/3 Parham (R) OPE 3m 12 GF *alwys rear, t.o. 7th* 6 0

571 17/3 Detling (L) CON 3m 13 GF *alwys rear, t.o. 14th* 11 0

962 8/4 Heathfield (R) XX 3m 4 G *tubed, chsd wnr to 4th, lst tch 12th, t.o. frm 14th* 4 0

Winning staying chaser; novice ridden and of no account now. 0

THE FRAIRY SISTER (Irish) — I 19^{P}, I 83^{P}, I 164^{2}, I 481^{P}

THE FUN OF IT ch.g. 11 Ballymore - Aughalion by Pals Passage A Hazell

1995 P(0),3(0),4(10),2(0),4(0),3(0)

357 3/3 Garnons (L) RES 3m 14 GS *nvr rchd ldrs, no ch 13th, p.u. 2 out* P 0

390 9/3 Llanfrynach (R) MDN 3m 13 GS *ref 1st* R -

510 16/3 Magor (R) MDN 3m 9 GS *hld up, gd prog 13th, disp 15th, ld 2 out, ran on* 1 11

1266 27/4 Pyle (R) RES 3m 10 G *rear frm 4th, in tch 10th, wknd & p.u. 13th* P 0

Won a dire race (slow time); follow up looks impossible. 10

THE FUZZ BUZZ WUZZ (Irish) — I 292^{P}

THE GAFFER (Irish) — I 185^{4}, I 245^{3}, I 551^{3}, I 594^{3}, I 655^{P}

THE GENERAL'S DRUM b.g. 9 Sergeant Drummer (USA) - Scottswood by Spartan General Mrs R Fell

1995 P(0),1(16),1(19),2(20),1(21),4(17),1(19),2(22)

64 10/2 Great Treth' (R) CON 3m 7 S *bhnd, godd prog to ld 14th, made rest, readily* 1 21

196 24/2 Lemalla (R) CON 3m 14 HY *(fav) alwys going wll, ld 2 out, styd on well* 1 22

296 2/3 Great Treth' (R) OPE 3m 5 G *(fav) hld up, chsd wnr 16th, not qckn clsng stgs* 2 21

482 13/3 Newton Abbot (L) HC 2m 5f 110yds 14 S *held up in rear, steady hdwy from 10th, ld last, rdn out.* 1 26

626 23/3 Kilworthy (L) OPE 3m 12 GS *wll in rear to gd prog to chs wnr 15th,chal flat,just hld* 2 28

873 6/4 Higher Kilw' (L) CON 3m 4 GF *(fav) in tch, ld apr 15th, sn clr, comf* 1 24

1073 13/4 Lifton (R) OPE 3m 10 S *(Jt fav) in tch, ld brfly aft 16th, outpcd nxt, styd on clsng stgs* 2 25

1140 20/4 Flete Park (R) OPE 4m 6 S *(fav) hld up, prog 14th, trckd ldr 4 out til ld apr last, easily* 1 28

1360 4/5 Flete Park (R) OPE 3m 5 G *(fav) ld/disp til ld 15th, ran on gamely whn chal 2 out* 1 24

1551 18/5 Bratton Down (L) OPE 3m 8 F *(fav) in tch, went 2nd 15th, ev ch und pres apr last, not qckn* 3 20

1623 27/5 Lifton (R) OPE 3m 5 GS *(fav) in tch, prog to 2nd & rdn aft 3 out, ev ch til not qckn nxt* 2 22

1630 31/5 Stratford (L) HC 3 1/2m 16 GF *nvr near to chal.* 5 23

Tough & very useful stayer; consistent; win more Opens & H/Chases 97; given lot to do in races; G-Hy .. 29

THE GINGER TOM ch.g. 11 Record Run - Proviso by Golden Vision N W A Bannister

1995 1(0)

895 6/4 Whittington (L) RES 3m 5 F *in tch to 13th, wknd qckly aft* 4 0

1090 14/4 Whitwell-On' (R) RES 3m 17 G *f 1st* F -

Won joke match in 95; willnot win again. 0

THE GOLLY OLLYBIRD ch.g. 7 Ballacashtal (CAN) - Persian Air by Persian Bold J C Swinburn

123 17/2 Witton Cast' (R) MDO 3m 11 S *jmpd slwly 1st, last whn p.u. aft 11th* P 0

704 30/3 Tranwell (L) MDO 3m 16 GS *last frm 3rd, t.o. til p.u. aft 13th* P 0

No signs of ability. 0

THEGOOSE b.g. 11 Windjammer (USA) - Space Dancer by Roan Rocket A Palmer

1995 P(0),F(-),2(11),4(15),1(16)

466 10/3 Milborne St' (L) RES 3m 13 G *alwys mid-div, late prog frm 3 out, nvr nrr* 4 15

656 23/3 Badbury Rin' (L) RES 3m 11 G *tucked away, prog to ld 4 out, left clr 2 out, ran on* 1 19

816 6/4 Charlton Ho' (L) INT 3m 7 GF *held up, prog 12th, ev ch 3 out, onepcd aft* 2 22

1278 27/4 Bratton Down (L) INT 3m 12 GF *w.w. prog 4 out, ev ch 2 out, ran on wll frm last* 2 22

1392 6/5 Cotley Farm (L) MEM 3m 5 GF *(fav) j.w., hld up, disp 3 out, ld app last, rdn out* 1 19

Improved; lightly raced; consistent; placed in hot races; can win Confined; G-F. 22

THE GREEN FOOL ch.g. 9 Southern Music - Random Thatch by Random Shot Mrs V Thompson

1995 **5(NH),3(NH),6(NH)**

790 1/4 Kelso (L) HC 3m 1f 11 GF *chsd ldrs, effort hfwy, struggling when pace qcknd 5 out, no impn after.* 5 19

Modest under Rules & ran poorly in only attempt at H/Chases 14

THE GREY BOREEN gr.g. 11 Boreen (FR) - Grey Daisy by Bruni — Mrs Ann Nott

102 17/2 Marks Tey (L) CON 3m 17 G *cls up to 9th, bhnd whn p.u. 2 out* P 0
310 2/3 Ampton (R) CON 3m 13 G *hmpd & u.r. 3rd* U -
422 9/3 High Easter (L) INT 3m 3 S *disp ld to 13th, last frm 16th, t.o.* 3 0

Last when completing; need luck to win again. 12

THE HAPPY CLIENT (Irish) — **I** 518^{U}, **I** 565^{P}, **I** 653^{P}

THE HEALY b.m. 9 Blushing Scribe (USA) - Smitten by Run The Gantlet (USA) — Mrs M Sircus

1995 7(0),P(0),3(16),4(12),2(14),4(12),2(16)

46 4/2 Alnwick (L) MEM 3m 7 G *chsd ldr, ld 7th-nxt, outpcd 3 out, ran on nxt* 3 15
83 11/2 Alnwick (L) CON 3m 10 GS *ld to 14th, sn outpcd, kpt on frm 2 out* 4 14
318 2/3 Corbridge (R) LAD 3m 5f 10 GS *nvr a fctr* 7 0
609 23/3 Friars Haugh (L) PPO 3m 7 G *10l 4th whn u.r. 4 out.* U -
752 31/3 Lockerbie (R) LAD 3m 10 G *ld frm 10th, jnd 2 out, hdd last stride* 2 20
857 6/4 Alnwick (L) MEM 3m 4 GF *(Jt fav) chsd ldr, disp ld 10th-14th, no ex frm 3 out* 2 16
1084 14/4 Friars Haugh (L) LAD 3m 8 F *made all, drew clr frm 2 out* 1 19

Fulfilled last years prediction; safe & stays; may find another opening; best on Firm. 19

THE HOLLOW(IRE) b.m. 6 Phardante (FR) - Fairy Hollow by Furry Glen — C E Sherry

221 24/2 Newtown (L) MDN 3m 12 GS *prom, ld 10-12th, 2l bhnd wnr whn f 14th* F -
288 2/3 Eaton Hall (R) MDO 3m 17 G *rear, prog to 4th at 12th, fdd, p.u. 3 out* P 0

Shows some promise; can do better. 0

THE HOLY GOLFER br.g. 9 Avocat - Taitu by Menelek — C Smyth

1995 P(0),P(0),3(0),1(10),3(12),3(0),U(-)

142 17/2 Larkhill (R) MXO 3m 9 G *sn rear, p.u. 5th* P 0
265 2/3 Didmarton (L) OPE 3m 6 G *n.j.w. alwys last, t.o. 5th* 6 0
380 9/3 Barbury Cas' (L) CON 3m 11 GS *prom til wknd frm 13th, onepcd* 4 0
638 23/3 Siddington (L) CON 3m 16 S *nvr bttr than mid div, nvr dang* 6 11
955 8/4 Lockinge (L) MEM 3m 5 GF *in tch, efft 3 out, ld apr last, ran on* 1 11
1289 28/4 Barbury Cas' (L) CON 3m 8 F *in tch in rear, blnd 10th, last & no ch frm 12th* 7 0
1500 11/5 Kingston Bl' (L) CON 3m 7 G *last & well bhnd, t.o. 14th, fin strngly* 5 10
1563 19/5 Mollington (R) CON 3m 8 GS *sn last & wll bhnd, prog 10th, no imp aft, t.o. & p.u. 3 out* P 0
1611 26/5 Tweseldown (R) XX 3m 9 G *rear & in tch,prog to 3rd 12th,ld apr last where blnd,rdnout* 1 17

Found 3 weak races 95/96; barely stays and well beaten in competitive races;G-F. 15

THE HON COMPANY b.g. 10 Silly Prices - Derigold by Hunter's Song — Mrs R E Walker

1995 P(0)

339 3/3 Heythrop (R) RES 3m 10 G *prom, mstk 9th, wkng whn mstk 13th, p.u. nxt* P 0
742 31/3 Upper Sapey (R) RES 3m 9 GS *strgglng frm 13th, last whn p.u. 2 out* P 0

Maiden winner 94; lightly raced & shown nothing since; can only be watched now. 0

THE HUMBLE TILLER b.g. 13 Rarity - Bardicate by Bargello — Miss L Knights

1995 **3(NH),4(NH),6(NH),7(NH)**

467 10/3 Milborne St' (L) MEM 3m 8 G *1st ride, 33s-11s, made all, clr 12th, ran on well 4 out* 1 19
730 31/3 Little Wind' (R) LAD 3m 6 GS *ld til hdd 14th, kpt on wll, not qckn clsng stgs* 2 19
991 8/4 Kingston St' (R) LAD 3m 8 F *last & strgglng, nvr put into race, p.u. 12th* P 0
1312 28/4 Little Wind' (R) XX 3m 6 G *(fav) blnd 6th, prog 12th, ld apr 15th, mstk 2 out, kpt on* 1 18
1393 6/5 Cotley Farm (L) XX 3m 10 GF *rr, no ch 10th, btn 5th whn u.r. 2 out* U -

Revived for novice rider; stays well; moody but could find another small win; G-S. 16

THE ILLIAD (Irish) — **I** 392^{P}, **I** 480^{1}, **I** 496^{2}, **I** 561^{5}

THE JOGGER b.g. 11 Deep Run - Pollychant by Politico (USA) — Mrs P Tizzard

1995 2(20),**5(0)**,2(12)

24 20/1 Barbury Cas' (L) XX 3m 12 GS *chsd ldrs, 4th & no prog 13th, lft 3rd nxt, no imp ldrs* 3 12
138 17/2 Ottery St M' (L) RES 3m 18 GS *chsd ldr, ev ch 2 out, onepcd aft* 3 17
211 24/2 Castle Of C' (R) INT 3m 5 HY *handy, prog 12th, ld 14th til disp nxt, wknd 2 out* 2 17
465 10/3 Milborne St' (L) RES 3m 11 G *cls up, 3rd at 12th, ran on well frm 2 out, just hld* 2 20
532 16/3 Cothelstone (L) RES 3m 12 G *lft 2nd 7th, ld 4 out, kpt on und press frm 2 out* 1 18
815 6/4 Charlton Ho' (L) MEM 3m 8 GF *in tch, ld 12th, sn clr, easily* 1 22
1127 20/4 Stafford Cr' (R) INT 3m 4 S *(fav) hndy, ld 11th-3 out, onepcd whn hdd* 2 12
1453 7/5 Wincanton (R) HC 2m 5f 9 F *j.w, alwys prom, ld 12th, ran on well.* 1 23
1533 14/5 Chepstow (L) HC 3m 6 F *(fav) trckd ldr, rdn and held when left clr 3 out, ridden when mstk last, all out.* 1 20

Changed hands & much improved; consistent in 96; hard to place now; stays; any. 23

THE KIMBLER ch.g. 8 Lir - Kimberley Ann by St Columbus — B R J Young

1995 2(18)

68	10/2	Great Treth'	(R)	RES	3m	14	S	*nvr bttr than mid-div, p.u. 14th*	P	0
196	24/2	Lemalla	(R)	CON	3m	14	HY	*mid-div til some late prog, no dang, bttr for race*	5	17
294	2/3	Great Treth'	(R)	CON	3m	10	G	*hld up, prog 16th, styd on wll to ld last*	1	17
1074	13/4	Lifton	(R)	INT	3m	9	S	*in tch til lost plc 11th, 6th whn p.u. apr 13th*	P	0
1276	27/4	Bratton Down	(L)	LAD	3m	7	GF	*sn bhnd, t.o. 12th*	4	0
1588	25/5	Mounsey Hil'	(R)	LAD	3m	6	G	*jmpd lft, bhnd frm 7th, t.o. & p.u. 14th*	P	0
1622	27/5	Lifton	(R)	CON	3m	14	GS	*mid-div, 8th at 12th, rear whn p.u. 2 out*	P	0

Maiden winner 94; won fair Confined but fell apart after; stays; may revive but best watched.G-S. 16

THE LAGER LOUT b.g. 12 Rolfe (USA) - Fleora by Fleece — Nigel Benstead

247	25/2	Charing	(L)	MEM	3m	7	GS	*ld 4th-10th, chsd wnr aft, 3rd & wll btn whn ran out last*	r	-
1444	6/5	Aldington	(L)	OPE	3m	6	HD	*pulld into ld aft 1st til p.u. qckly apr 11th, dismntd*	P	0

Missed 94/95; more problems now and looks finished. 13

THE LAST JOSHUA b.g. 7 Joshua - Maidensgrove by Canadel II — E Haddock

166	17/2	Weston Park	(L)	MDN	3m	10	G	*hld up, prog 12th, unable to chal frm 4 out*	4	0
242	25/2	Southwell P'	(L)	RES	3m	12	HO	*rear, lost tch 8th, t.o. & p.u. 13th*	P	0
330	3/3	Market Rase'	(L)	MDO	3m	7	G	*sn wll bhnd, some late prog*	4	0
458	9/3	Eyton-On-Se'	(L)	INT	3m	11	G	*alwys rear, passed btn horses from 3 out*	5	0
569	17/3	Wolverhampt'	(L)	MDN	3m	11	GS	*prog to 2nd 4 out, styd on onepcd*	2	11
683	30/3	Chaddesley '	(L)	MEM	3m	17	G	*alwys wll bhnd, t.o. frm 4th*	6	0
1010	9/4	Flagg Moor	(L)	LAD	3m	6	G	*sn wl bhnd, t.o. frm 7th*	4	0
1196	21/4	Sandon	(L)	MDN	3m	17	G	*mid to rear, p.u. 4 out*	P	0
1580	19/5	Wolverhampt'	(L)	MDO	3m	8	G	*(fav) mid-div, lft 2nd 12th, ld apr 14th, drew wll clr nxt*	1	10

Novice ridden; safe but slow; won awful Maiden & much more needed to follow up. 12

THE LAST MISTRESS b.m. 9 Mandalus - Slinky Persin by Jupiter Pluvius — A J Cook

1995 3(10),**2(14)**,**3(0)**

384	9/3	Llanfrynach	(R)	OPE	3m	16	GS	*alwys last pair, t.o. 14th, p.u. 2 out*	P	0
1157	20/4	Llanwit Maj'	(R)	CON	3m	11	GS	*rear div til p.u. apr 12th*	P	0
1198	21/4	Lydstep	(L)	INT	3m	5	S	*ld 6th-11th, fdd, p.u. 2 out*	P	0
1268	27/4	Pyle	(R)	INT	3m	8	G	*rmndrs 10th, lost tch 12th, styd on und pres 3 out*	5	0

Dual winner 94; disappointing and last on only completion since; could still revive on Firm. but lat 12

THE LAST ONE (Irish) — **I** 506^{P}

THE LAZY CAT (Irish) — **I** 324^{P}, **I** 428^{U}

THE MAGIC SLABBER (Irish) — **I** 2^{F}, **I** 53^{P}, **I** 148^{3}, **I** 311^{P}, **I** 375^{4}

THE MAJOR GENERAL b.g. 9 Pollerton - Cornamucla by Lucky Guy — Robert Ogden

1995 **3(19)**,**3(23)**,**F(-)**,**2(21)**

184	23/2	Haydock	(L)	HC	3m	9	GS	*in tch, effort after 15th, no hdwy.*	4	12
374	9/3	Sandown	(R)	HC	2 1/2m 110yds	5	GS	*(fav) hdwy 9th, ld 11th, mstk next, clr 2 out, rdn out.*	1	22
1000	9/4	Wetherby	(L)	HC	3m 110yds	10	G	*held up, hdwy to track ldrs hfwy, ld before 4 out, soon clr.*	1	28

Lightly raced & improved further 96; scooted home last start & can more H/Chases if fit 97; G-S 27

THE MAN FROM CLARE(IRE) b.g. 8 Roselier (FR) - Restless Saint by Saint Denys — Mrs R C Matheson

341	3/3	Heythrop	(R)	MDN	3m	13	G	*ld to 9th, wkng whn blnd 12th, p.u. 14th*	P	0
479	10/3	Tweseldown	(R)	MDO	3m	10	G	*bhnd, some mod late prog whn f 3 out*	F	-
797	2/4	Heythrop	(R)	MDN	3m	11	F	*hld up, nvr plcd to chal*	6	0
1020	13/4	Kingston Bl'	(L)	MDN	3m	10	G	*prom, ld/disp 7th til ld 14th, clr 2 out, styd on*	1	14

Improving; won poor 3 finisher Maiden; should improve further; needs to. 14

THE MILL HEIGHT(IRE) ch.g. 6 Callernish - Cherry Gamble by Meadsville — Mrs J Mathias

147	17/2	Erw Lon	(L)	MDN	3m	8	G	*alwys cls up, ev ch 3 out, wknd nxt, improve*	3	11
551	17/3	Erw Lon	(L)	MDN	3m	8	GS	*2nd til ld 13th, hdd apr last, onepcd*	2	10
976	8/4	Lydstep	(L)	MDO	3m	12	G	*(fav) alwys ldng grp, in ld last, easily*	1	14

Gradually improved; clear cut winner & should upgrade; L/H only so far. 16

THE MINER'S FATE (Irish) — **I** 54^{3}

THE MINERS FATE (Irish) — **I** 65^{6}, **I** 115^{3}, **I** 140^{4}, **I** 184^{P}

THE MOSSES br.g. 11 Kinglet - Yutoi Lady by Arctic Slave — C J Sample

1995 **19(NH)**,**5(NH)**,**5(NH)**

317	2/3	Corbridge	(R)	CON	3m	11	GS	*hld up, prog 12th, outpcd frm 14th*	5	14
701	30/3	Tranwell	(L)	OPE	3m	8	GS	*prog 12th, cls up 3 out, ev ch last, no ext flat*	3	15
911	8/4	Tranwell	(L)	CON	3m	9	GF	*mid-div, prog to handy 3rd 2 out, styd on, not rch ldrs*	3	17

1120	20/4	Bangor	(L)	HC	2 1/2m 110yds	13	S	*rear, pushed along and t.o. from 7th, fin lame.*	6	0

Won 2 chases 91; beaten 8 lengths maximum in points; problems last start; stays but win not easy. 15

THE PARISH PUMP (Irish) — **I** 136^{2}, **I** 329^{1}

THE PEDLAR ch.m. 8 Riberetto - Scally Jenks by Scallywag — D Hurst

1995 P(0),6(16),6(11),6(13)

281	2/3	Clyst St Ma'	(L)	RES	3m	11	S	*handy, 3rd at 8th, ld 3 out, styd on well*	1	19
531	16/3	Cothelstone	(L)	CON	3m	12	G	*w.w.prog & in tch 13th,rddn 4 out, wnt 2nd flat,nt trbl wnr*	2	17
647	23/3	Cothelstone	(L)	CON	3m	6	S	*hld up, prog 12th, ld 15th, ran on wll whn chllg*	1	18
804	4/4	Clyst St Ma'	(L)	INT	3m	3	GS	*(fav) made all, mstk 6th, drew wll clr aft 3 out, easily*	1	20
1112	17/4	Hockworthy	(L)	PPO	3m	9	GS	*ld 3rd-6th & 9-15th, chsd wnr til wknd aft 2 out*	4	19
1228	27/4	Worcester	(L)	HC	2m 7f	17	G	*gd hdwy 4 out, mstk 2 out, ran on, not reach wnr.*	2	24
1589	25/5	Mounsey Hil'	(R)	OPE	3m	12	G	*chsd ldrs to 7th, lost plc 10th, p.u. 15th*	P	0
1633	1/6	Bratton Down	(L)	XX	3m	8	G	*w.w. last at 12th, effrt 15th, no imp frm 3 out*	4	15

Much improved; won modest races; consistent in 96 and win another Confined; L/H; G-S. 20

THE PODGER (Irish) — **I** 381^{P}, **I** 420^{P}, **I** 526^{P}, **I** 616^{3}, **I** 644^{P}

THE POINT IS ch.g. 9 Major Point - Babble by Forlorn River — P S Hewitt

1995 3(17),P(0)

244	25/2	Southwell P'	(L)	CON	3m	13	HO	*mstks, made all, sn clr, styd on well frm 3 out*	1	24
435	9/3	Newton Brom'	(R)	OPE	3m	7	GS	*(fav) ld to 14th, cls 2nd & going wll whn u.r. nxt*	U	-
538	17/3	Southwell P'	(L)	XX	3m	6	GS	*ld, clr & lkd wnr whn u.r. 2 out*	U	22
677	30/3	Cottenham	(R)	OPE	3m	11	GF	*f 1st*	F	-
969	8/4	Thorpe Lodge	(L)	OPE	3m	4	GF	*(fav) made all, waited in front, clvrly*	1	23

Revived in 96; won 4 of last 9 94/96; front runs; mistakes; win more in 97; G/F-S. 22

THE PORTSOY LOON b.g. 9 Miami Springs - Glittering Gem by Silly Season — Lease Terminated

1995 **P(NH),12(NH),4(NH),P(NH)**

32	20/1	Higham	(L)	OPE	3m	15	GF	*prom, 3rd at 12th, jnd ldr 16th- nxt,ld flat til hdd post*	2	25
104	17/2	Marks Tey	(L)	OPE	3m	14	G	*w.w. prog 10th, chsd ldr 16th, onepcd und press frm 2 out*	3	24
271	2/3	Parham	(R)	CON	3m	15	GF	*(fav) twrds rear, clsd up aft hlfwy, 3rd 14th, und pres & btn 2out*	3	19
594	23/3	Parham	(R)	CON	3m	13	GS	*alwys prom, chsd wnr 4 out, outpcd 2 out*	2	17
918	8/4	Aldington	(L)	CON	3m	4	F	*cls up in last, effrt apr 3 out, found nil*	4	13
1294	28/4	Bexhill	(R)	MEM	3m	4	F	*(fav) ld to 15th, rdn & chsd wnr aft, wknd 2 out*	2	0
1613	27/5	Fontwell	(R)	HC	3 1/4m 110yds	12	G	*(bl) bhnd, hdwy 10th, wknd 17th, t.o. when p.u. before 2 out.*	P	0

Novice chase winner; good start but gradually got worse; finds nothing under pressure; best avoided .. 15

THE PRIOR b.g. 10 Monksfield - Merry Rambler by Wrekin Rambler — P J Rowe

1995 U(-),F(-),4(0)

15	14/1	Cottenham	(R)	MDN	3m	14	G	*rear, prog to mid-div whn blnd & u.r. 14th*	U	-
31	20/1	Higham	(L)	CON	3m	9	GF	*alwys bhnd, t.o. & p.u. appr 16th*	P	0
107	17/2	Marks Tey	(L)	MDN	3m	15	G	*wl bhnd frm 6th, t.o. & p.u. 3 out*	P	0
315	2/3	Ampton	(R)	MDO	3m	10	G	*disp ld 5th-7th, chsd wnr aft, btn appr 3 out*	2	0

Novice ridden; beaten 25 lengths when 2nd; poor Maiden still a possibility. 11

THE PULPIT (Irish) — **I** 64^{4}, **I** 143^{3}, **I** 182^{4}, **I** 279^{1}, **I** 436^{P}

THE PUNTERS PAL (Irish) — **I** 22^{P}, **I** 88^{2}, **I** 236^{P}

THE RASKINS b.m. 9 Salluceva - Nymble Ann by Capistrano — J S R Nicholl

1995 P(0),F(-),U(-),P(0),R(-),2(0),F(-)

323	2/3	Corbridge	(R)	MDN	3m	12	GS	*alwys bhnd*	6	0
404	9/3	Dalston	(R)	RES	3m	7	G	*3rd at 4th, bd mstk 14th, p.u. nxt*	P	0
704	30/3	Tranwell	(L)	MDO	3m	16	GS	*prom, 4th at 13th, outpcd frm nxt*	5	0
915	8/4	Tranwell	(L)	MDO	3m	7	GF	*mid-div whn b.d. 4th*	B	-
1136	20/4	Hornby Cast'	(L)	MDN	3m	11	G	*mid-div whn u.r. 10th*	U	-
1476	11/5	Aspatria	(L)	MDO	3m	16	GF	*bhnd frm 6th, t.o. frm 13th*	7	0
1574	19/5	Corbridge	(R)	MDO	3m	6	G	*not fluent, lost plc 12th, f nxt*	F	-

Has not beaten another horse 95/96; prospects nil. 0

THE REAL UNYOKE b or br.g. 11 Callernish - Tudor Dancer by Balidar — Guy Luck

1995 **3(20),6(0)**

185	23/2	Kempton	(R)	HC	3m	9	GS	*held up in tch, chsd lding pair from 13th, outpcd from 5 out, t.o..*	4	15

Winning Irish chaser; lightly raced & flying to high; novice ridden; could win points. 23

THE RED DEVIL (Irish) — **I** 36^{P}, **I** 61^{F}, **I** 122^{1}, **I** 153^{P}, **I** 326^{2}, **I** 372^{2}, **I** 555^{4}

THEREWEGO(IRE) br.g. 8 Mandalus - Knockscovane by Carlburg — T D B Underwood

1995 **F(NH)**

210	24/2	Castle Of C'	(R)	INT	3m	10	HY	*mid-div, lost tch 14th, t.o. & p.u. 2 out*	P	0
571	17/3	Detling	(L)	CON	3m	13	GF	*(bl) rear, mstk 16th, prog 4 out, 3rd 2 out, wknd & eased*	7	0

Won 2 Irish points 94; eye catching 2nd run; vanished after; shrewd stable should find a win in 97. 16

THEREYOUGO b.g. 5 Touch Of Grey - Young Lady by Young Generation Mrs P King

108 17/2 Marks Tey (L) MDN 3m 17 G *alwys rr, last whn p.u. 15th* P

315 2/3 Ampton (R) MDO 3m 10 G *alws bhnd, p.u. appr 3 out* P

No signs yet; may do better. 0

THE RIGHT GUY ch.g. 11 Regular Guy - Vulgan's Law by Vulgan Keith Thomas

1995 P(0)

78 11/2 Wetherby Po' (L) OPE 3m 10 GS *rear, t.o. 7th, p.u. 11th* P

226 24/2 Duncombe Pa' (R) OPE 3m 10 GS *alwys rear, no ch frm 12th* 5

457 9/3 Eyton-On-Se' (L) INT 3m 11 G *rr 5th, t.o. 12th, p.u. 5 out* P

667 24/3 Eaton Hall (R) INT 3m 11 S *sn bhnd, t.o.* 5

891 6/4 Whittington (L) MEM 3m 6 F *alwys rear, sn t.o., crawld over 14th, immed p.u.* P

Intermediate winner 94 (lucky); shown nothing since; can only be watched. 0

THE RIGHT KIND br.g. 9 Kind Of Hush - Malmaison by Royal Palace M J Jerram

1995 F(-),3(16),1(18),1(18),1(17)

10 14/1 Cottenham (R) INT 3m 10 G *bhnd, prog & in tch 9th, lost tch 13th, ran on well frm 2out* 4 1

178 18/2 Horseheath (R) INT 3m 11 G *wth ldrs,lost plc 11th,rallied 3 out,lft 2nd last, styd on* 2 2

Improved but finished early; stays; can win Confined/Intermediate if fit in 97; G-S. 22

THE ROAD TO MOSCOW (Irish) — **I** 138^{P}, **I** 222^{F}, **I** 343^{5}, **I** 616^{B}, **I** 636^{2}, **I** 661^{1}

THE RUM MARINER (Irish) — 214^{P}, 383^{1}, 667^{P}, 881^{3}, 1005^{1}, 1171^{P}, 1314^{1}, 1510^{2}, 1578^{2}, **I** 657^{4}

THE SHADE MATCHER br.g. 10 Black Minstrel - Dursey Sound by Royal Highway Mrs Alix Stevenson

110 17/2 Lanark (R) CON 3m 10 GS *mid-div, clsd up 4 out, no ext frm nxt* 4 1

402 9/3 Dalston (R) XX 3m 13 G *ld 1st, prom frm 8th,strng chal appr last,ran on to ld flat* 1 2

751 31/3 Lockerbie (R) CON 3m 12 G *ld til 5th, lost plc, styd on agn frm 4 out, no imp* 2 1

Fair performances in 96 but nothing out of the ordinary & modest Confined only possible 97; Good 19

THE SNUFFMAN (Irish) — **I** 245^{P}, **I** 458^{P}

THE STAG (Irish) — **I** 213^{F}

THE TARTAN SPARTAN ch.g. 12 McIndoe - Themopolli by Spartan General Mrs Delyth Batchelor

1995 **5(NH),5(NH),P(NH),5(NH),P(NH)**

142 17/2 Larkhill (R) MXO 3m 9 G *prom early, wknd frm 13th, onepcd* 4 1

337 3/3 Heythrop (R) OPE 3m 10 G *in tch, prog 11th, ld 14th, hdd & lft clr last* 1 2

793 2/4 Heythrop (R) OPE 4m 10 F *trckd ldrs,rdn & lost tch aft 17th,t.o. & p.u. 2 out, dsmntd* P

Winning chaser; won good Open (lucky); problems after; stays well but a win at 13 not easy. 20

THE TERRITORIAN (Irish) — **I** 166^{5}

THE THIN FELLOW (Irish) — **I** 323^{P}, **I** 366^{P}, **I** 466^{P}, **I** 541^{P}

THETHREETOMS (Irish) — **I** 102^{P}

THE TONDY(IRE) gr.g. 8 Godswalk (USA) - Miss Kirby by Town Crier Charles Booth

240 25/2 Southwell P' (L) MDO 3m 15 HO *hld up bhnd, prog & in tch 11th, eased & p.u. 14th* P

1027 13/4 Brocklesby ' (L) MDN 3m 7 GF *w.w., prog 4 out, chal nxt, ld aft 2 out, just outpcd flat* 2 1

Beaten by an aged maiden; needs more before winning. 13

THE TOOR TRAIL (Irish) — **I** 102^{P}, **I** 161^{4}, **I** 267^{P}

THE UGLY DUCKLING br.g. 6 Lir - Dule Darkie by Bay Spirit D W Heard

131 17/2 Ottery St M' (L) MDN 3m 10 GS *in tch whn ran out & u.r. 10th* r

280 2/3 Clyst St Ma' (L) RES 3m 11 S *rear, t.o. & p.u. 14th* P

448 9/3 Haldon (R) MDO 3m 10 S *wll in tch, disp 10-11th, cls 3rd 14th, 2nd 2 out, no ch wnr* 2

623 23/3 Kilworthy (L) MEM 3m 4 GS *raced 3rd, losing tch whn blnd 12th, p.u. aft nxt* P

876 6/4 Higher Kilw' (L) MDN 3m 11 GF *prom, no prog frm 15th, 6th whn blnd & u.r. 2 out* U

1117 17/4 Hockworthy (L) MDO 3m 8 GS *chsd ldn quartet, wknd 9th, p.u. 11th* P

1429 6/5 High Bickin' (R) MDO 3m 8 G *made most frm 5th, not alwys fluent, hdd 16th, sn wknd* 3

1626 27/5 Lifton (R) MDO 3m 13 GS *mid-div, rdn 13th, no prog* 5

Has only beaten 3 horses and beaten 20 lengths minimum; stamina suspect & much more needed. 10

THE VENDOR (Irish) — **I** 19^{2}, **I** 107^{4}, **I** 177^{2}, **I** 340^{F}, **I** 562^{1}

THE VICARETTE (Irish) — **I** 44^{P}, **I** 58^{4}, **I** 75^{5}, **I** 184^{P}, **I** 295^{3}

THE VILLAGE WAY (Irish) — **I** 332,

THE WAY NORTH b.g. 7 Northern Game - Good Way by Good Apple Mrs A C Wakeham

1451 6/5 Witton Cast' (R) MDO 3m 12 G *midfld whn ran out 3rd* r

1476 11/5 Aspatria (L) MDO 3m 16 GF *tubed, prog 11th, cls 3rd 15th, wknd nxt, fin tired* 4

Ran passsably last start; has problems and still got plenty to find. **10**

THE WEE FELLOW (Irish) — I 80³, I 101⁴

THE WILD WAVE (Irish) — I 149ᴾ, I 240ᴾ, I 352ᴾ, I 460ᴾ, I 506ᴾ, I 632ᴾ, I 649ᴾ, I 660ᴾ

THE WOODEN HUT ch.g. 13 Windjammer (USA) - Bunduq by Scottish Rifle — Ms B Brown

1995 9(0),P(0),U(-),4(0),6(0)

384	9/3	Llanfrynach	(R)	OPE	3m	16 GS	*chsd ldrs to 14th, wknd nxt*	11	0
692	30/3	Llanvapley	(L)	OPE	3m	6 GS	*ld 3-9th, wknd rpdly, t.o. 13th, ref last*	R	-
878	6/4	Brampton Br'	(R)	OPE	3m	5 GF	*6l 3rd at 12th, cls enough 15th, wknd apr nxt*	5	0

Of no account **10**

THEY ALL FORGOT ME b.g. 9 Tender King - African Doll by African Sky — Mrs D J Dyson

216	24/2	Newtown	(L)	LAD	3m	13 GS	*alwys rear, t.o. & p.u. 13th*	P	0
429	9/3	Upton-On-Se'	(R)	LAD	3m	4 GS	*cls 3rd til wknd 13th, eased flat, almost lost 2nd*	2	12
743	31/3	Upper Sapey	(R)	LAD	3m	7 GS	*cls up in 4th til outpcd frm 15th*	4	16
839	6/4	Maisemore P'	(L)	LAD	3m	2 GF	*disp ld til hit 14th, 4l down whn jmpd slwly 2 out,no ch aft*	2	12
1194	21/4	Sandon	(L)	LAD	3m	7 G	*chsng grp til outpcd 4 out*	4	15
1642	2/6	Dingley	(R)	LAD	3m	6 GF	*chsd ldr 4-10th, outpcd frm 3 out*	4	14

Winning chaser; safe but easily beaten by good horses; barely stays & will struggle to find a win. **16**

THE YELLOW BOG (Irish) — I 441¹, I 513ᴾ, I 580³

THE YOKEL b.g. 10 Hays - Some Dame by Will Somers — T A Peake

164	17/2	Weston Park	(L)	RES	3m	11 G	*chsng grp to hlfwy, lost tch frm 3 out*	5	0
286	2/3	Eaton Hall	(R)	MDO	3m	14 G	*(bl) ld to 6th, in tch whn f 13th*	F	-
569	17/3	Wolverhampt'	(L)	MDN	3m	11 GS	*ld to 9th, wknd rpdly, p.u. 16th*	P	0
666	24/3	Eaton Hall	(R)	RES	3m	13 S	*cls up, 2nd at 12th, btn whn blnd 2 out, p.u. last*	P	0
852	6/4	Sandon	(L)	MDN	3m	9 GF	*(fav) held up,smth prog frm 12th to be up sides 3 out,no ext 2 out*	2	12
949	8/4	Eyton-On-Se'	(L)	MDN	3m	5 GF	*made all til bad mstk 3 out, hdd 2 out, onepcd*	2	14
1191	21/4	Sandon	(L)	MEM	3m	5 G	*ld & u.r. 1st*	U	-
1455	8/5	Uttoxeter	(L)	HC	2m 5f	9 G	*chsd ldr to 2nd and from 9th to 12th, rdn apr next, one pace 2 out.*	2	18
1586	25/5	Hexham	(L)	HC	2 1/2m 110yds	14 GF	*chsd lding pair 1st cct, rdn along before 3 out, one pace.*	7	0

Good enough for a win & ran well in poor H/Chase but finds little & may continue to frustrate at 11 ..... **14**

THIEF'S ROAD b.g. 9 Royal Fountain - Mildenstone by Milan — Miss D M M Calder

1995 P(0)

194	24/2	Friars Haugh	(L)	MDN	3m	11 S	*bhnd early, went 2nd 11th, nvr nr wnr*	2	0
1355	4/5	Mosshouses	(L)	MDO	3m	10 GS	*wth ldr til mstk 3 out, wknd aft nxt*	4	0

Placed 4 times 94/96; lightly raced and time passing him by. **11**

THIEVING SANDS (Irish) — I 347ᴮ, I 385ᴾ

THINKABOUTTHAT (Irish) — I 237ᴾ, I 470⁵

THINK IT OUT ch.m. 5 Master Willie - Fresh Thoughts by Young Generation — Miss D Banwell

733	31/3	Little Wind'	(R)	MDO	3m	13 GS	*rear whn f hvly 12th*	F	-

Unfortunate end to her debut. **0**

THINK PINK gr.g. 9 Import - Spot On Pink by Perhapsburg — Mrs M R Beaumont

763	31/3	Great Stain'	(L)	MDN	3m	11 GS	*mid-div, prog 6th, ld 8th-10th, wknd 2 out*	2	0
1155	20/4	Whittington	(L)	MDN	3m	14 G	*4th/5th frm 11th, nvr nrr*	4	0

Poor novice hurdler; well beaten when placed and well short of a win yet. **10**

THINK TWICE b.g. 6 Pollerton - Hammerhill by Grisaille — Mrs J P Spencer

748	31/3	Upper Sapey	(R)	MDO	3m	11 GS	*effrt frm hlfwy to 3rd at 15th, wknd apr last*	4	0
1045	13/4	Bitterley	(L)	MDO	3m	16 G	*chsd ldrs, ev ch 13th, wknd frm 15th*	8	0
1483	11/5	Bredwardine	(R)	MDO	3m	15 G	*trckd ldrs, cls up til wknd rdply 14th, p.u. nxt*	P	0

Beaten 16 lengths on debut; needs more stamina before going closer. **11**

THIRD TIME(IRE) b.m. 6 Royal Fountain - Zipkin by Sir Herbert — Miss J Green

1995 5(0)

74	11/2	Wetherby Po'	(L)	MDO	3m	11 GS	*mid-div, prog 12th, ld 3 out, drew clr, comf*	1	13

Won stamina test (slow time); not seen again but needs to improve for Restricteds. **15**

THIRTYSOMETHING (Irish) — I 35ᴾ, I 61ᴾ, I 73ᴾ

THIS I'LL DO US(IRE) ch.g. 8 Boyne Valley - Sweater Girl by Blue Cashmere — A J Morley

641	23/3	Siddington	(L)	RES	3m	20 S	*bhnd, ran on wll frm 15th, nvr pld to chall, improve*	3	17
1101	14/4	Guilsborough	(L)	RES	3m	16 G	*mid-div, 7th & in tch whn blnd & u.r. 14th*	U	-
1242	27/4	Woodford	(L)	RES	3m	18 G	*alwys rear, 13th hlfwy, nvr trbld ldrs*	6	11

Irish Maiden winner 93ssed 94/95; yet to get seriously involved but good enough for a small win. 16

THISTLE MONARCH b.g. 11 Rontino - Lavender Blue by Silly Season — S B Clark
1995 **6(NH),P(NH)**

48	4/2	Alnwick	(L)	LAD	3m	9	G	*sttld rear, prog 8th, ld 2 out, slow last, drvn out*	1	21
72	11/2	Wetherby Po'	(L)	CON	3m	18	GS	*(fav) cls up, ld 14th, hld off chal, styd on well*	1	24
119	17/2	Witton Cast'	(R)	LAD	3m	4	S	*(fav) mstk 1st, cls 4th at 7th, lft 2nd 11th, rallied to ld flat*	1	19
514	16/3	Dalton Park	(R)	LAD	3m	8	G	*rear, prog 11th, 3rd 4 out, hmpd & lft 2nd 2 out,unable chal*	2	22
1366	4/5	Gisburn	(R)	LAD	3m	12	G	*nvr bynd mid-div, t.o. 13th, p.u. nxt*	P	0

Winning hurdler; good start in points but not fluent jumper; last effort after break worrying; stays 21

THORN COTTAGE (Irish) — **I** 112^{F}, **I** 455^{P}

THORNHILL b.m. 6 Pollerton - Crowebrass by Crowned Prince (USA) — F L Matthews

184	23/2	Haydock	(L)	HC	3m	9	GS	*slowly into stride, soon in tch, tracking ldrs when blnd and u.r. 4th.*	U	-
674	30/3	Hereford	(R)	HC	2m	8	S	*bhnd when blnd 1st, f 3rd.*	F	-
799	3/4	Ludlow	(R)	HC	3m	8	GF	*ld after 2nd to 4th, midfield when f 7th.*	F	-
1225	24/4	Brampton Br'	(R)	MDO	3m	18	G	*(bl) last frm 9th, lost tch 14th, f nxt*	F	-

A confidence shattering start. 0

THORN HILL VALLEY (Irish) — **I** 551^{F}

THORNY BRIDGE (Irish) — **I** 204^{3}

THOUGHT READER (Irish) — **I** 101^{F}, **I** 161^{P}, **I** 266^{P}, **I** 387^{5}

THREE AND A HALF b.g. 7 Nearly A Hand - Miss Comedy by Comedy Star (USA) — J Scott
1995 5(0),4(0)

145	17/2	Larkhill	(R)	MDO	3m	13	G	*nvr bttr than mid-div*	4	10
1280	27/4	Bratton Down	(L)	MDO	3m	14	GF	*handy, 2nd at 12th, ld 14th til hdd cls hm, fin 2nd, disq*	0	16
1342	4/5	Holnicote	(L)	MEM	3m	7	GS	*alwys bhnd*	6	0
1637	1/6	Bratton Down	(L)	MDO	3m	11	G	*n.j.w. mid-div, lost tch 13th, t.o. 16th*	8	0

Interrupted season; beaten 1/2 length 2nd start (disqualified); disappointing after; best run on G/F 13

THREE HEADS (Irish) — **I** 390^{P}

THREE POTATO FOUR b.g. 9 Pablond - Capelena by Mon Fetiche — Sir John Barlow
1995 2(16),2(18),1(17),1(19),**3(18)**

293	2/3	Eaton Hall	(R)	INT	3m	11	G	*(Jt fav) w.w. jnd chsng grp 13th, 2nd 2 out, no imp wnr*	2	18
588	23/3	Wetherby Po'	(L)	INT	3m	17	S	*rear, gd prog 14th, ld 3 out, hdd & no ext flat*	2	19

Beaten by good horses 95/96; onepaced; needs long course; deserves another win; best Soft. 22

THREE TOWN ROCK (Irish) — **I** 360^{U}, **I** 415^{P}, **I** 494^{3}

THUNDER ROAD (Irish) — **I** 2^{3}, **I** 35^{F}, **I** 62^{3}, **I** 200^{2}, **I** 440^{5}, **I** 509^{2}

THURLES PICKPOCKET(IRE) b.g. 5 Hollow Hand - Sugar Lady by Dalsaan — G I Cooper

830	6/4	Marks Tey	(L)	MDN	3m	14	G	*rear, t.o. 4th, schoold til p.u. 16th*	P	0

Successful stable; only learning on debut and should do better. 0

THYNE PLEASE (Irish) — **I** 41^{P}, **I** 132^{5}, **I** 143^{P}

THYNE VALLEY (Irish) — **I** 364^{P}

TICKET TO THE MOON b.m. 6 Pollerton - Spring Rocket by Harwell — Mrs Janita Scott
1995 3(0),1(15),3(13)

199	24/2	Lemalla	(R)	RES	3m	17	HY	*mid-div, prog to chal 3 out, sn wknd, p.u. last*	P	0
562	17/3	Ottery St M'	(L)	XX	3m	12	G	*hld up, prog 12th, ld 4 out, ran on well*	1	17
1074	13/4	Lifton	(R)	INT	3m	9	S	*hld up, hdwy to cls 2nd 14th, ev ch til rddn & outpcd 3 out*	3	18

Improving; ran well last start & should progress further; stays; G-S. 19

TICKLEBAY b.m. 5 Rolfe (USA) - Profusion Of Pink by Tickled Pink — Keith Coe

314	2/3	Ampton	(R)	MDO	3m	10	G	*alwys bhnd,t.o. & p.u. 15th*	P	0

No encouragement on debut. 0

TIDY VILLAGE (Irish) — **I** 328^{P}, **I** 368^{P}, **I** 557^{3}

TIERFERGUS (Irish) — **I** 176^{P}

TIGER ch.g. 6 Primitive Rising (USA) - Forrester's Fling by Derwent — Philip Newton

175	18/2	Market Rase'	(L)	MDO	2m 5f	8	GF	*prog to 6th & in tch 11th, wknd 3 out*	7	0
440	9/3	Newton Brom'	(R)	MDN	3m	10	GS	*sn prom, cls up whn blnd 15th, fdd, p.u. nxt*	P	0
1104	14/4	Guilsborough	(L)	MDN	3m	18	G	*prom to 11th, wknd rpdly, t.o. & p.u. 3 out*	P	0
1378	5/5	Dingley	(R)	MDO	2 1/2m	16	GF	*prom, chsd wnr 6th-4 out, 4th & btn aft nxt, lft 2nd last*	2	10

Good stable; safe but stamina looks the problem; may do better. 11

TIGER DOLLY (Irish) — I 42^{P}, I 105^{4}, I 191^{F}

TIGERITSI ch.m. 6 Royal Vulcan - Maynote by Maystreak — N F Williams

354	3/3	Garnons	(L)	MDN	2 1/2m	13	GS	*mid-div whn mstk 8th, lost tch nxt, t.o.*	5	0
1044	13/4	Bitterley	(L)	MDO	3m	15	G	*mid-div, remote 4th whn p.u. 15th, cont, f 2 out*	F	-
1416	6/5	Cursneh Hill	(L)	MDO	3m	9	GF	*pllng, held up, efft & clsng 14th, no ext frm 3 out*	4	10

Beaten 13 lengths last start (weak race); stamina doubtful but young & can do better. 11

TIGER LORD bl.g. 5 Tigerwood - Roushane by Rustingo — William John Day

389	9/3	Llanfrynach	(R)	MDN	3m	11	GS	*mstks 1st & 2nd, in tch to 14th, t.o. & p.u. last*	P	0
607	23/3	Howick	(L)	MDN	3m	12	S	*t.o. hlfwy, p.u. 15th*	P	0
1039	13/4	St Hilary	(R)	MDN	3m	14	G	*prom to 12th, wknd & p.u. 3 out*	P	0
1483	11/5	Bredwardine	(R)	MDO	3m	15	G	*mstk 5th, rdn frm 7th, lost tch & p.u. 12th*	P	0

No signs of ability 0

TIGER PAWS(IRE) b.m. 6 Carlingford Castle - Miss Tarbow by Tarqogan — Mrs M Hope

1995 U(-)

14	14/1	Cottenham	(R)	MDO	3m	10	G	*cls up, f 7th*	F	-

Showed some promise in 95 but yet to complete & vanished after day 2 in 96. 12

TILLY LAMP (Irish) — I 397^{F}, I 495^{P}, I 587^{P}

TIMBER'S BOY b.g. 11 Nemorino (USA) - Ludorum's Praise by Song Of Praise — B G Clark

1995 P(0),2(14),2(13),R(-),1(17),2(17),1(18),1(20)

10	14/1	Cottenham	(R)	INT	3m	10	G	*(fav) w.w. prog & cls up 11th, lft in ld 3 out, kpt on*	1	22
31	20/1	Higham	(L)	CON	3m	9	GF	*(fav) w.w. stdy prog 9th, hit 10th, chsd ldr 2 out, no ext last*	2	23
178	18/2	Horseheath	(R)	INT	3m	11	G	*(fav) w.w. prog 12th, rdn & outpcd 3 out, styd on apr last*	3	20
346	3/3	Higham	(L)	INT	3m	6	G	*trckd ldrs, ld 12th, prssd last, hrd rdn, hdd nr fin*	2	22
621	23/3	Higham	(L)	INT	3m	12	GF	*(fav) hld up rear, blnd 5th, prog to 4th at 15th, no ext 2 out*	3	15
676	30/3	Cottenham	(R)	INT	3m	13	GF	*(Jt fav) hld up rear, outpcd 14th, ran on 3 out, too mch to do*	4	19
907	8/4	Fakenham	(L)	HC	3m 110yds	11	G	*bhnd early, gd hdwy after 9th, chsd ldr from 15th, left well clr 2 out, unchal.*	1	23
1107	15/4	Southwell	(L)	HC	3m 110yds	10	G	*held up, rdn and outpcd final cct, nvr able to chal.*	6	16
1383	6/5	Towcester	(R)	HC	2 3/4m	7	GF	*alwys bhnd, t.o..*	5	0

Fit early & consistent till last 2 runs; poor H/chase win (lucky) makes life harder now;G-F. 19

TIMBER TOPPER ch.g. 6 Crowning Honors (CAN) - Clairwood by Final Straw — P Wilkin

73	11/2	Wetherby Po'	(L)	MDO	3m	15	GS	*lost tch early, rear whn p.u. 4 out*	P	0
223	24/2	Duncombe Pa'	(R)	CON	3m	16	GS	*hmpd & u.r. 4th*	U	-
308	2/3	Great Stain'	(L)	MDO	3m	12	GS	*alwys rear, t.o. 15th*	7	0
591	23/3	Wetherby Po'	(L)	MDO	3m	14	S	*rear, p.u. 3rd, saddle slppd*	P	0

Last & beaten 40 lengths plus when completing; much more needed. 0

TIM BOBBIN b.h. 14 Swing Easy (USA) - Rosalia by Tower Walk — J G Scott

615	23/3	Friars Haugh	(L)	MEM	3m	9	G	*3rd hlfwy, wknd frm 11th.*	6	0

Of no account. 0

TIMEFORGOING (Irish) — I 81^{3}, I 106^{P}, I 163^{4}, I 418^{5}

TIME FOR OATS ch.g. 6 Oats - Scrambird by Dubassoff (USA) — Richard Barber

558	17/3	Ottery St M'	(L)	MDO	3m	9	G	*(fav) cls up, ld 10th-4out, disp til wknd apr last*	2	13

Top stablr; beaten by good horse in fast time; not seen again but sure to win if fit in 97. 15

TIMELESS RIVER (Irish) — I 17^{P}, I 28^{5}, I 103, , I 395^{4}

TIMELLS BROOK gr.g. 8 Balinger - Cherry Meringue by Birdbrook — Mrs G A Robarts

1995 **P(NH),R(NH),F(NH),P(NH),P(NH)**

734	31/3	Little Wind'	(R)	MDO	3m	11	GS	*prom, mstk 8th, lost plc 11th, p.u. aft 13th*	P	0
1115	17/4	Hockworthy	(L)	MDO	3m	10	GS	*prom to 8th, wknd, bhnd whn p.u. 12th*	P	0

Bad novice hurdler/chaser; no better in points. 0

TIME MODULE b.g. 12 Latest Model - Gemini Miss by My Swanee — Mrs D D Scott

1995 P(0),5(11),4(0),**P(0)**

466	10/3	Milborne St'	(L)	RES	3m	13	G	*n.j.w. lost tch 12th, t.o. & p.u. 14th*	P	0
652	23/3	Badbury Rin'	(L)	MDO	3m	13	G	*mid-div, wknd frm 14th, one pace aftr*	4	0
707	30/3	Barbury Cas'	(L)	RES	3m	18	G	*rear whn u.r. 7th*	U	-
1056	13/4	Badbury Rin'	(L)	RES	3m	10	GF	*n.j.w. alwys bhnd, t.o. 12th, p.u. 3 out*	P	0

Of no account 0

TIMES ARE CHANGING b.m. 9 Cruise Missile - Sparella by Spartan General — M J Footer

1995 P(0)
275 2/3 Parham (R) MDN 3m 15 GF *in tch til mstk 7th, wll bhnd whn p.u. 12th* P 0
574 17/3 Detling (L) RES 3m 14 GF *t.o. 6th, f 2 out* F -
781 31/3 Penshurst (L) MDN 3m 11 GS *in tch, hmpd 9th, rddn & wknd 12th, p.u. 14th* P 0

Of no account 0

TIME STAR(NZ) br.g. 12 Drums Of Time (USA) - Crescent Star (NZ) by Persian Garden — Mrs O Hubbard

247 25/2 Charing (L) MEM 3m 7 GS *in tch to 13th, wll bhnd whn p.u. aft 15th* P 0
275 2/3 Parham (R) MDN 3m 15 GF *ld & u.r. 1st* U -
455 9/3 Charing (L) MDN 3m 10 G *chsd wnr, nvr fluent, lost plc 15th, kpt on, tk 2nd 2 out* 2 0
597 23/3 Parham (R) MDO 3m 9 GS *alwys strgglng, wll bhnd whn p.u. 14th* P 0
1055 13/4 Penshurst (L) MDO 3m 11 G *ld 2nd, hdd 12th, hmpd aft nxt, wll bhnd whn p.u. 2 out* P 0
1210 21/4 Heathfield (R) MDO 3m 13 F *cls up, 4th at 16th, steadily wknd* 5 0

Does not stay; flattered by his placing & will not win at 13. 0

TIME TO SMILE (Irish) — **I** 196^{3}, **I** 271^{4}

TIMMY TUFF (Irish) — **I** 138^{P}, **I** 275^{P}, **I** 351^{5}, **I** 506^{5}

TIMS KICK(IRE) b.m. 5 Borovoe - La Paure by Pauper — Mrs L Richardson

152 17/2 Erw Lon (L) MDN 3m 11 G *alwys last pair, p.u. 15th* P 0
510 16/3 Magor (R) MDN 3m 9 GS *ld to 13th, wknd rpdly, p.u. 2 out* P 0
1162 20/4 Llanwit Maj' (R) MDO 3m 12 GS *chsd ldrs, ld 3 out, blndrd nxt & last, drvn out* 1 14
1388 6/5 Pantyderi (R) RES 3m 7 GF *mid-div, no ch whn p.u. 2 out* P 0

Beat subsequent winner but race poor and time slow; needs major improvement now. 13

TINAMONA (Irish) — **I** 162^{P}, **I** 197^{P}, **I** 328^{P}, **I** 500^{P}

TINA ORE (Irish) — **I** 113^{P}, **I** 151^{P}, **I** 207^{F}, **I** 354^{P}

TINAS LAD b.g. 13 Jellaby - Arbatina by Sallust — Salvo Giannini

1386 6/5 Pantyderi (R) OPE 3m 5 GF *trckd ldrs, mstk 12th, wknd, p.u. nxt, dead* P 0

Dead. 0

TINA'S MISSILE b.g. 9 Cruise Missile - Tina's Gold by Goldhill — M M Allen

1995 **U(NH),13(NH)**
165 17/2 Weston Park (L) RES 3m 9 G *ld/disp to 9th, sn btn, p.u. 4 out* P 0
332 3/3 Market Rase' (L) MDO 3m 8 G *chsd ldr, ld 8th, jnd & lft clr 3 out* 1 13
501 16/3 Lanark (R) RES 3m 12 G *disp til ld 11th, hdd aft 4 out, btn 4th whn f 2 out* F -
856 6/4 Sandon (L) RES 3m 9 GF *ld 3rd to 2 out, outpcd* 5 10

Won weak racein slow time (lucky); struggling now & follow most unlikely. 12

TINERANA BOY (Irish) — **I** 124^{F}, **I** 154^{4}, **I** 201^{1}, **I** 371^{1}

TINKER'S HILL br.g. 5 Dowsing (USA) - Open Country by Town And Country — David Ibbotson

75 11/2 Wetherby Po' (L) MDO 3m 8 GS *ld to 11th, disp to 13th, fdd rpdly, p.u. 4 out* P 0

Rran passably on debut; needs to find more stamina. 0

TINNECARRIG HILL (Irish) — **I** 347^{P}, **I** 385^{P}

TINOTOPS br.g. 6 Neltino - Topte by Copte (FR) — R H H Targett

1995 P(0),3(0),1(12),6(0)
28 20/1 Barbury Cas' (L) RES 3m 14 GS *chsd ldr, ld 14th, jnd & f nxt* F -
138 17/2 Ottery St M' (L) RES 3m 18 GS *mid-div, prog 12th, ev ch 3 out, wknd nxt* 4 16
357 3/3 Garnons (L) RES 3m 14 GS *(fav) cls 5th at 9th, ld 13th, drew clr frm 2 out* 1 18
524 16/3 Larkhill (R) INT 3m 11 G *rear til sustained prog frm 14th, fin well* 2 22
795 2/4 Heythrop (R) XX 3m 4 F *trckd ldr, ld 14th, clr 3 out, drvn out frm last* 1 25
1112 17/4 Hockworthy (L) PPO 3m 9 GS *(fav) cls up, ld 15th, clr last, drvn out* 1 25

Changed hands 96 & much improved; tough & useful now; sure to win more 97; G/S-F 26

TINSTREAMER JOHNNY b.g. 5 Teamwork - Little Stella by I'm Alright Jack — S P Long

202 24/2 Lemalla (R) MDO 3m 12 HY *bhnd frm 3rd, t.o. & p.u. 9th* P 0
300 2/3 Great Treth' (R) MDO 3m 10 G *lost plc rpdly aft 5th, last whn p.u. 9th* P 0
630 23/3 Kilworthy (L) MDN 3m 10 GS *mid-div, wknd 9th, last whn f 11th* F -
718 30/3 Wadebridge (L) MDO 3m 11 GF *twrds rear whn u.r. 4th* U -
1070 13/4 Lifton (R) MDN 3m 9 S *towrds rear, bad mstk 9th, bhnd, p.u. apr 13th* P 0
1279 27/4 Bratton Down (L) MDO 3m 14 GF *rear, no ch whn p.u. 4 out, dsmntd* P 0

Not a good start & problems last start. 0

TINSUN b.g. 5 Neltino - Pensun by Jimsun — R G Weaving

890 6/4 Kimble (L) MDN 3m 11 GF *hld up last trio, prog & in tch 15th, btn 3 out, improve* 6 0

Last beaten 32 lengths in poor race on debut; successful stable and should go closr in 97. 12

T'INT(IRE) b.m. 8 Camden Town - Rue Del Peru by Linacre — S Burley

1995 5(0),F(-),1(15),5(0),4(12),P(0),4(0)

No.	Date	Course		Type	Dist	Rnrs	Going	Comment	Pos	Rtg
584	23/3	Wetherby Po'	(L)	RES	3m	13	S	*mid-div, kpt on onepcd frm 2 out, nvr nrr*	4	17
971	8/4	Thorpe Lodge	(L)	RES	3m	4	GF	*mostly 3rd, chsd ldr & cls up 3 out, just outpcd frm nxt*	3	13

Won Maiden in mud 95; slow but weak Restricted in similar not impossible. 15

TIPP DOWN ch.g. 13 Crash Course - Caramore Lady by Deep Run — Mrs A E Astall

1995 U(-),P(0),6(0),2(0),4(0)

No.	Date	Course		Type	Dist	Rnrs	Going	Comment	Pos	Rtg
162	17/2	Weston Park	(L)	OPE	3m	16	G	*chsng grp, in tch to 13th, wknd rpdly, p.u. 3 out*	P	0
289	2/3	Eaton Hall	(R)	CON	3m	10	G	*ld to 7th, grad wknd, p.u. 4 out*	P	0
565	17/3	Wolverhampt'.	(L)	OPE	3m	6	GS	*alwys rear, no dang*	4	0
1007	9/4	Flagg Moor	(L)	MEM	3m	7	G		U	-
1227	26/4	Ludlow	(R)	HC	2 1/2m	16	G	*bhnd hfwy.*	9	0
1455	8/5	Uttoxeter	(L)	HC	2m 5f	9	G	*chsd ldr 3rd till u.r. 6th.*	U	-

Of no account 0

TIPPERARYENTEPRISE (Irish) — I 144^{P}, I 280^{P}, I 353^{P}

TIPPING TIM b.g. 11 King's Ride - Jeanarie by Reformed Character — Mrs J Mould

1995 **15(NH),5(NH)**

No.	Date	Course		Type	Dist	Rnrs	Going	Comment	Pos	Rtg
37	3/2	Wetherby	(L)	HC	3m 110yds	11	GS	*(fav) ld till hdd 4 out, no ext.*	3	25
99	14/2	Lingfield	(L)	HC	3m	9	HY	*held up, hdwy 7th, left in 4th apr 10th, wknd quickly four out.*	5	12
359	4/3	Doncaster	(L)	HC	2m 3f 110yds	10	G	*made most, hdd briefly when left with advantage again 2 out, styd on well.*	1	25
798	3/4	Ascot	(R)	HC	2m 3f 110yds	10	GF	*ld to 8th, rallied 10th, wknd next, t.o..*	7	10

Former very useful chaser; very much on the slide & fortunate when winning; best under 3m; Good 20

TIP THE SKIP (Irish) — I 23^{U}, I 89^{P}

TITCHWELL MILLY b.m. 7 Baron Blakeney - Zaratella by Le Levanstell — J Owen

No.	Date	Course		Type	Dist	Rnrs	Going	Comment	Pos	Rtg
263	2/3	Didmarton	(L)	INT	3m	18	G	*s.v.s. t.o. til p.u. 13th*	P	0
520	16/3	Larkhill	(R)	MDO	3m	11	G	*mid-div whn u.r. 6th*	U	-
787	31/3	Tweseldown	(R)	RES	3m	9	G	*rear, gd prog 3 out, 3rd & ev ch whn no room & u.r. last*	U	-
1164	20/4	Larkhill	(R)	MDN	3m	12	GF	*mid-div, prog 13th, onepce frm 3 out*	3	10
1439	6/5	Ashorne	(R)	RES	3m	11	G	*in tch, outpcd 12th, wknd & p.u. 14th*	P	0

2 subsequent winners behind when placed (beaten 18 lengths); sure to go closer in 97. 13

T J GOODTYME (Irish) — I 518^{F}, I 612^{2}

TOASTER CRUMPET b.g. 7 Seymour Hicks (FR) - Lady Letitia by Le Bavard (FR) — Miss P Robson

1995 4(0),1(14),P(0)

No.	Date	Course		Type	Dist	Rnrs	Going	Comment	Pos	Rtg
47	4/2	Alnwick	(L)	XX	3m	14	G	*mid-div, prog to trck ldr 12th, wknd 3 out*	6	0
111	17/2	Lanark	(R)	RES	3m	6	GS	*alwys handy, ld apr 3 out, hdd last, no ext flat*	2	17
403	9/3	Dalston	(R)	RES	3m	11	G	*(fav) mid-div early, impr 12th, onepcd frm 14th*	5	0
754	31/3	Lockerbie	(R)	RES	3m	8	G	*alwys hndy, ld 15th, styd on strngly*	1	18
1151	20/4	Whittington	(L)	INT	3m	12	G	*held up, hdwy 13th, lft 2nd nxt, ev ch frm 3 out, no ext*	3	18
1252	27/4	Balcormo Ma'	(R)	INT	3m	5	GS	*ld 6th til outpcd frm 3 out*	3	16
1475	11/5	Aspatria	(L)	CON	3m	6	GF	*ld 4-6th, chsd ldr 15-16th, wknd nxt*	3	14

Onepaced stayer; both wins at Lockerbie; safe now; can win Confined on long track; G-G/S. 18

TOBAR BHRIDE (Irish) — I 232^{F}, I 272^{P}

TOBARELLA (Irish) — I 6^{P}, I 378^{P}

TOBERMORE (Irish) — I 97^{2}, I 413^{F}

TOBIN BRONZE b.g. 9 Sexton Blake - Pampered Julie by Le Bavard (FR) — I Bray

1995 3(16),1(22)

No.	Date	Course		Type	Dist	Rnrs	Going	Comment	Pos	Rtg
120	17/2	Witton Cast'	(R)	OPE	3m	7	S	*(Jt fav) mid-div, wknd 13th, p.u. 2 out*	P	0
410	9/3	Charm Park	(L)	OPE	3m	17	G	*alwys wl in rr, p.u. 14th*	P	0
512	16/3	Dalton Park	(R)	CON	3m	10	G	*(fav) hld up rear, prog frm 14th, chal last, pshd out to ld flat*	1	18
587	23/3	Wetherby Po'	(L)	OPE	3m	15	S	*hld up, prog 14th, styd on well 3 out, no ext apr last*	3	20

Lightly raced; won 4 of last 11; stays; can still win modest Open. G-S. 20

TOBY'S FRIEND (Irish) — I 234^{3}, I 295^{6}, I 498^{4}, I 544, , I 577^{F}, I 606^{2}, I 629^{3}

TODCRAG b.g. 7 Feelings (FR) - Redetwig by Carlton Grange — Mrs D Scott

1995 5(0),2(0),2(10)

No.	Date	Course		Type	Dist	Rnrs	Going	Comment	Pos	Rtg
193	24/2	Friars Haugh	(L)	MDN	3m	10	S	*(fav) 3rd hlfwy, ld 3 out, drew clr apr last*	1	15
404	9/3	Dalston	(R)	RES	3m	7	G	*(fav) ld 4th, nt fuent, disp aft, ran on frm last, jst outpcd*	2	16
703	30/3	Tranwell	(L)	RES	3m	7	GS	*(fav) not alwys fluent, ld 2nd, made rest, comf*	1	19
911	8/4	Tranwell	(L)	CON	3m	9	GF	*trckd ldr til ld/disp 9th-2 out, just ld last, found ext*	1	20
1351	4/5	Mosshouses	(L)	CON	3m	11	GS	*mstk 2nd, alwys going wll, ld 2 out, sn clr, comf*	1	23
1513	12/5	Hexham Poin'	(L)	CON	3m	6	HY	*(fav) ld/disp til ld 3 out, clr whn jmpd rght last 2, rdn & ran on*	1	23

1576 19/5 Corbridge (R) MEM 3m 4 G *(fav) made all, clr 6th, eased flat* 1 22

Much improved; yet to meet decent horses; stays & quickens; one to watch; G/F-Hy. 23

TODDLIN HAME br.g. 14 Bronze Hill - Pandorana by Pandofell W Hodge
1995 P(0),P(0),5(0),F(-),P(0)

110 17/2 Lanark (R) CON 3m 10 GS *ld to 12th, sn wknd* 6 0
187 24/2 Friars Haugh (L) CON 3m 12 S *prom til hlfwy* 6 0
259 1/3 Kelso (L) HC 3m 1f 8 GS *chsd ldrs, outpcd 12th, well bhnd when blnd and u.r. 16th.* U -
500 16/3 Lanark (R) OPE 3m 6 G *2nd at 11th, wknd frm 13th* 5 0
582 22/3 Kelso (L) HC 3 1/2m 8 G *u.r. 2nd.* U -

Dead 0

TODDS HALL(IRE) gr.g. 8 Orchestra - Golden Robe by Yankee Gold Andrew Munro
1995 **5(NH)**

379 9/3 Barbury Cas' (L) XX 3m 9 GS *sn wll bhnd, btn 2 fences* 6 0
706 30/3 Barbury Cas' (L) MEM 3m 7 G *sn bhnd, t.o. 10th* 6 0
995 8/4 Hackwood Pa' (L) XX 3m 8 GF *ld to 6th, wknd qckly 9th, ref 12th* R -

Awarded Irish Maiden 95; most unpromising in England. 0

TOD LAW b.m. 8 Le Moss - Owenburn by Menelek J P Elliot
1995 3(11),5(11),2(15),3(0),1(14),4(15),3(18)

50 4/2 Alnwick (L) CON 3m 9 G *in tch, mstk 9th, ld 3 out-nxt, no ext* 4 16
187 24/2 Friars Haugh (L) CON 3m 12 S *nvr dang, p.u. 4 out* P 0

Restricted winner 95; finished early 96; ran well 1st start but Confined looks tough; Firm best. 17

TOKANDA ch.g. 12 Record Token - Andalucia by Rheingold Mrs C M Lucas

334 3/3 Heythrop (R) MEM 3m 6 G *chsd ldrs til wknd 12th, t.o. & p.u. 2 out* P 0
435 9/3 Newton Brom' (R) OPE 3m 7 GS *chsd ldrs to 8th, fdd, t.o. 13th, p.u. 3 out* P 0

Flat winner; unwilling & of no account now. 0

TOLMIN ch.g. 8 Topsider (USA) - Ivor's Honey by Sir Ivor P G Forster
1995 **P(NH),P(NH)**

705 30/3 Tranwell (L) MDO 3m 9 GS *sn mid-div, wll bhnd frm 13th* 6 0
1088 14/4 Friars Haugh (L) MDO 3m 10 F *6th hlfwy, nvr rchd ldrs* 4 0
1461 9/5 Sedgefield (L) HC 2m 5f 10 F *soon well bhnd.* 9 0
1514 12/5 Hexham Poin' (L) RES 3m 5 HY *jmpd slwly 1st, disp 11th-3 out, onepcd und pres aft* 3 10
1574 19/5 Corbridge (R) MDO 3m 6 G *trckd ldrs,rmndrs 9th,prog 14th,ev ch 2 out,styd on und pres* 3 13

Safe & placed in modest company; good enough for a small win; onepaced. 13

TOMALLEY b.g. 12 Reformed Character - High Jean by Arrigle Valley Steven Astaire
1995 P(0),P(0),U(-),5(10),4(12),P(0),6(0),P(0),4(0),**P(NH)**

19 14/1 Tweseldown (R) CON 3m 9 GS *(bl) 1st ride, alwys last pair, t.o. whn f 11th* F -

Won 3 in 94; changed hands after; of no account now. 0

TOMASINS CHOICE (Irish) — **I** 61P, **I** 734

TOM BOY br.g. 6 Sunyboy - Orphan Grey by Crash Course Miss Jane Cooper
1995 P(0),P(0),P(0)

137 17/2 Ottery St M' (L) RES 3m 15 GS *alwys mid-div, nvr nrr* 4 11
282 2/3 Clyst St Ma' (L) MDN 3m 8 S *(fav) 3rd whn ran out 3rd* r -
477 10/3 Tweseldown (R) MDO 3m 15 G *trckd ldrs, ev ch 14th, lost plc frm nxt, p.u. 2 out* P 0

Beaten 15 lengths in Restricted; not progress after but young and can make amends. 13

TOMCAPPAGH(IRE) br.g. 5 Riberetto - Shuil Suas by Menelek Miss S French

1378 5/5 Dingley (R) MDO 2 1/2m 16 GF *schoold in last trio, t.o. & p.u. 4 out* P 0

Learning on debut; may do better. 0

TOM DEELY (Irish) — **I** 121U, **I** 293F, **I** 332U, **I** 366P, **I** 440P, **I** 472P, **I** 5096, **I** 5404

TOMEKO (Irish) — **I** 4163, **I** 5301

TOM FURZE b.g. 9 Sula Bula - Bittleys Wood by Straight Lad R A Horne
1995 1(13),2(12),3(0)

1453 7/5 Wincanton (R) HC 2m 5f 9 F *ld to 11th, blnd and wknd 12th, t.o. when p.u. before 3 out.* P 0
1536 16/5 Folkestone (R) HC 2m 5f 9 GF *ld to 10th, mstk next, led last, driven clr.* 1 20

Lightly raced; barely stays; weak H/chase (2m 5f) means placing very hard now; G/F-F. 20

TOM LOG ch.g. 9 Politico (USA) - Shepherd Valley by Arrigle Valley Mrs C M Wardroper
1995 2(14),1(16),U(-),3(18),1(17),8(0),**5(16)**

49 4/2 Alnwick (L) OPE 3m 14 G *blndrd 9th, chsd wnr til blndrd 11th, one pace frm 13th* 4 20

72 11/2 Wetherby Po' (L) CON 3m 18 GS *ld to 5th, disp 6-8th, in tch to 4 out, outpcd aft* 3 18
223 24/2 Duncombe Pa' (R) CON 3m 16 GS *chsd ldrs, hit 9th, ld 15th, hdd und pres flat, wknd nr fin* 2 19
588 23/3 Wetherby Po' (L) INT 3m 17 S *alwys mid-div, nvr dang* 7 0
985 8/4 Charm Park (L) INT 3m 9 GF *rear early, outpcd 13th, nvr a factor* 6 0

2 wins 6 placings last 18 starts; onepaced & needs stamina test; good enough for Confined; G-Hy. 19

TOMMY O'DWYER(IRE) b.g. 7 Black Minstrel - Collective by Pragmatic A K Pritchard
1995 U(-),5(0)
129 17/2 Kingston Bl' (L) MDN 3m 15 GS *raced wd, mid-div till f 5th* F -
236 24/2 Heythrop (R) MDN 3m 13 GS *hld up rear, prog to 3rd at 12th, ld 14th, made rest,rdn out* 1 13
494 16/3 Horseheath (R) RES 3m 10 GF *(fav) sttld rear,prog to trck ldrs 12th,blnd 4 out,wknd,p.u.2 out* P 0
1564 19/5 Mollington (R) XX 3m 14 GS *hld up, prog 11th, cls up nxt, sn wknd, t.o. & p.u. 2 out* P 0
1597 25/5 Garthorpe (R) XX 3m 9 G *cls up, ld 12th, 10l clr 3 out, wknd rpdly & hdd nxt* 3 15

Beat 2 subsequent winners in stamina test; stopped quickly after; problems? best watched. 16

TOMMY SPRINGER b.g. 8 Zambrano - Carlton Jubilee by Derek H Mrs O Hubbard
780 31/3 Penshurst (L) MDN 3m 12 GS *mid-div, jnd ldrs 8th, wknd 3 out* 4 0
1051 13/4 Penshurst (L) MEM 3m 5 G *chsd ldr to 7th, steadily wknd, bhnd & p.u. 12th* P 0

Beaten 30 lengths on debut; more needed. 0

TOMMY TUFF (Irish) — **I** 565^{F}
TOMORROW'S TIMES b.g. 6 Neltino - Song Of Glory by True Song Miss F Robinson
618 23/3 Higham (L) MDO 3m 14 GF *hld up, prog to 3rd at 10th, chal 4 out til lft clr last* 1 13
1102 14/4 Guilsborough (L) RES 3m 15 G *trckd ldrs going wll, mstks 13 & 15th, btn frm nxt* 6 0

Good stable; won poor race; costly blunders after; can upgrade when gaining experience. 16

TOMPET b.g. 10 Le Bavard (FR) - Swanny Jane by Bargello Sir Michael Connell
1995 P(0),3(13),6(0),U(-),2(20),1(25),3(17),**4(13)**,**3(15)**,5(16)
435 9/3 Newton Brom' (R) OPE 3m 7 GS *nvr rchd ldrs, styd on onepcd* 4 12
677 30/3 Cottenham (R) OPE 3m 11 GF *prom to 11th, wknd frm 4 out* 6 10
1014 13/4 Kingston Bl' (L) MEM 3m 4 G *(fav) chsd ldr, ld 10-13th & 14th-2 out, not qckn* 3 0
1438 6/5 Ashorne (R) XX 3m 14 G *2nd meeting (!),rear of chsng grp,no ch frm 15th,kpt on* 5 14
1407 6/5 Hackwood Pa' (L) XX 3m 5 F *ld 3rd til r.o. 7th* r -
1563 19/5 Mollington (R) CON 3m 8 GS *prom, chsd wnr 11-14th, outpcd 3 out, styd on* 3 18
1643 2/6 Dingley (R) OPE 3m 13 GF *chsd ldrs, rdn hlfwy, poor 3rd whn s.u. bnd app 2 out* S -

Winning chaser; changed hands & novice ridden 96ody and unlikely to comsent to win again.G-F. 16

TOM'S APACHE br.g. 7 Sula Bula - Tom's Nap Hand by Some Hand O J Carter
1592 25/5 Mounsey Hil' (R) MDO 3m 9 G *jmpd lft, ld 6th, clr 10th, hdd aft 3 out, wknd, p.u. last* P 0

Placed on flat 92; hardly seen since but has ability and can win a race if fit in 97. 12

TOMS CHOICE(IRE) gr.g. 7 Mandalus - Prior Engagement by Push On M F Harding
1995 U(-),4(11)
143 17/2 Larkhill (R) MDO 3m 14 G *alwys prom, ch 3 out, unable to qckn, lost 2nd nr fin* 3 14
354 3/3 Garnons (L) MDN 2 1/2m 13 GS *(fav) ld to 3rd, jmpd to ld 3 out, hdd flat* 2 15

Lightly raced; placed on last 3 starts; stamina suspect but capable of a win. 15

TOM'S GEMINI STAR ch.g. 8 Celtic Cone - Je Dit by I Say O J Carter
1593 25/5 Mounsey Hil' (R) MDO 3m 11 G *w.w. prog to 5th at 14th, btn 16th, p.u. 2 out* P 0

No form in bumpers 92; showed promise on 1st run since; could win a race; summer jumping now. 0

TOM SMITH b.g. 6 Shrivenham - Troopial by King's Troop Arthur E Smith
1003 9/4 Upton-On-Se' (R) LAD 3m 4 F *j.s., t.o. 6th, 2 fences bhnd whn p.u. 2 out* P 0
1164 20/4 Larkhill (R) MDN 3m 12 GF *prom early, wknd frm 8th, t.o., p.u. 13th* P 0

No stamina or ability shown yet. 0

TOM SNOUT(IRE) b.g. 8 Kambalda - Nesford by Walshford J M Kinnear
1995 **6(NH)**,**3(NH)**,**7(NH)**,**F(NH)**,**3(NH)**,**1(NH)**
279 2/3 Clyst St Ma' (L) LAD 3m 7 S *disp til blnd & u.r. 8th* U -
561 17/3 Ottery St M' (L) LAD 3m 12 G *hld up, went 3rd 11th, chal 3 out, no ext und pres aft* 2 19
818 6/4 Charlton Ho' (L) LAD 3m 6 GF *(Jt fav) made all, ran on wll frm 4 out* 1 24
1186 21/4 Tweseldown (R) LAD 3m 6 GF *n.j.w. chsd wnr, blnd 6th, btn & wknd whn ref & u.r. 3 out* R -

Winning hurdler; fair form in points & could be useful but jumping problems & last start alarming 22

TOM'S TUNE (Irish) — **I** 366^{P}, **I** 541^{P}, **I** 582^{U}, **I** 636^{P}
TOM THE BOY VI (Irish) — **I** 49^{3}, **I** 243^{P}, **I** 311^{P}, **I** 432^{3}, **I** 574^{U}, **I** 642^{P}, **I** 661^{P}
TOM THE SAINT (Irish) — **I** 122^{F}, **I** 147,
TOM THE TANK b.g. 6 Skyliner - Mistral Magic by Crofter (USA) D Gill

1995 F(-),3(0),5(0),3(0),3(0)

413	9/3	Charm Park	(L)	MDO 3m	12 G	*prom 12th, lost tch 14th, no extr aftr*	4	0
518	16/3	Dalton Park	(R)	MDO 3m	15 G	*in tch, 3rd frm 10th til effrt to ld apr 2 out, lft clr,comf*	1	15
758	31/3	Great Stain'	(L)	RES 3m	17 GS	*chsd ldrs, ev ch 3 out, went 2nd nxt, styd on well flat*	2	19
983	8/4	Charm Park	(L)	RES 3m	13 GF	*(Jt fav) cls up, disp 4 out, ld nxt, drew clr, comf*	1	19
1281	27/4	Easingwold	(L)	CON 3m	15 G	*sn rear, mstk 11th, wll bhnd whn p.u. 14th*	P	0
1446	6/5	Witton Cast'	(R)	CON 3m	7 G	*prom, ld 3-2 out, no ext whn hdd*	2	18

Improving; safe & 2nd to good horse; still young & can progress further; G/S-G/F. 20

TOM TUCKER b.g. 16 Tack On - Festive Girl by Festino — S H Gribble

1995 P(0),13(0),P(0),6(0),P(0),4(0),2(0)

251	25/2	Charing	(L)	OPE 3m	10 GS	*rear, t.o. & p.u. 14th*	P	0

Safe but woefully slow; of little account. 0

TONI'S TIP (Irish) — I 330[1]

TONMARIE CHANCE (Irish) — I 307[P], I 322[P], I 548[3], I 602[3]

TOOTING TIMES ch.g. 10 Leading Man - Saucy by Saucy Kit — R Dalton

1995 U(-),F(-),2(15)

983	8/4	Charm Park	(L)	RES 3m	13 GF	*towrds rear, lost tch, p.u. 12th*	P	0

Lightly raced; Members winner 94; brief campaign 96 and can only be watched now. 12

TOP OF THE RANGE(IRE) ch.g. 6 Quayside - Dersina by Deep Run — P C Cornwell

423	9/3	High Easter	(L)	MDN 3m	8 S	*chsng grp,prog 9th,hit16th,ld 2 out,in comm whn lft clr last*	1	13
834	6/4	Marks Tey	(L)	RES 3m	11 G	*alwys rear, nvr going wll, p.u. 17th*	P	0
1145	20/4	Higham	(L)	RES 3m	12 F	*prom in chsng grp, onepcd frm 16th*	5	16

Placed 6 times in Irish Maidens; won poor 2 finisher race; struggling now upgraded. 15

TOPPING-THE-BILL b.g. 11 Nicholas Bill - Top-N-Tale by Sweet Story — Mrs Emma Coveney

1995 U(-),2(19),1(18),1(19),1(20)

103	17/2	Marks Tey	(L)	LAD 3m	7 G	*alwys going wll, ld 16th, qknd appr last, comf*	1	21
273	2/3	Parham	(R)	LAD 3m	11 GF	*(fav) alwys prom, ld 14th, rdn 2 out, hdd flat*	2	22
596	23/3	Parham	(R)	LAD 3m	8 GS	*(fav) rear, jnd ldrs 9th, mstks aft, chsd ldr 4 out, btn 2 out*	4	14
919	8/4	Aldington	(L)	LAD 3m	4 F	*(fav) steadied start,prog to jn ldr 11th,mstk 14th,ld last,pshdout*	1	18
1443	6/5	Aldington	(L)	LAD 3m	4 HD	*(fav) chsd wnnr frm 5th, chal 2 out, kpt on onepce*	2	19

Won 7 of last 13 starts; consistent, stays & can win more; any. 19

TOP THE BID b.g. 9 Auction Ring (USA) - Funicular by Arctic Slave — J Griffin

1995 U(-),P(0)

160	17/2	Weston Park	(L)	OPE 3m	16 G	*rear, t.o. & p.u. 13th*	P	0
542	17/3	Southwell P'	(L)	MDO 3m	15 GS	*chsng grp to hlfwy, fdd, p.u. 3 out*	P	0
972	8/4	Thorpe Lodge	(L)	MDO 3m	9 GF	*rear hlf, ran on onepcd into 4th, no ch wth 1st 3 5 out*	4	0
1240	27/4	Clifton On '	(L)	MDO 3m	10 GF	*prom, ld 12th til mstk 14th, wknd apr 3 out*	5	0

Well beaten in bad race at Thorpe; not thretening to win yet. 10

TOP TOR b.m. 6 — R H P Williams

1161	20/4	Llanwit Maj'	(R)	MDO 3m	15 GS	*bhnd & hit 5th, t.o. 12th, p.u. 2 out*	P	0
1269	27/4	Pyle	(R)	MDO 3m	9 G	*prom, ld 10th, agn 15th, jnd 2 out, hdd & no ext last*	2	12

Beaten 2 lengths (poor horses behind); surely can improve and should win in 97. 13

TOP TRUMP b.m. 5 Neltino - Rolling Dice by Balinger — Mrs L Redman

1020	13/4	Kingston Bl'	(L)	MDN 3m	10 G	*cls up, mstk 10th & pshd alng, wknd & t.o. 14th, p.u. nxt*	P	0

Only learning and should do better. 10

TOR (Irish) — I 79[P], I 117[P], I 156[P], I 528[F], I 574[P]

TORALI(IRE) ch.g. 8 Torus - Ali-Boo by Laurence O — Colin Gee

13	14/1	Cottenham	(R)	MDO 3m	10 G	*sn well bhnd, t.o. & f 9th*	F	-

Placed twice in 94; only 1 run since & can only be watched now. 13

TORDUFF EXPRESS (Irish) — I 386[P], I 420[P]

TORENAGA HILL (Irish) — I 303[P], I 389[5], I 483[P], I 555[5]

TORLOC (Irish) — I 614[P], I 637,

TORSONS COMET(IRE) ch.g. 8 Torus - Miss Fidget by Autre Prince — Mrs S Watts

2	13/1	Larkhill	(R)	MDO 3m	17 GS	*alwys bhnd, t.o. last whn p.u. 13th*	P	0

Jumped poorly on debut; vanished after. 0

TORTULA ch.m. 7 Good Times (ITY) - Bristle-Moss by Brigadier Gerard N S Bostock

590 23/3 Wetherby Po' (L) MDO 3m 16 S *ld to 11th, wknd, p.u. 4 out* P 0
1008 9/4 Flagg Moor (L) MDO 2 1/2m 7 G *made all, blndrd 10th, drew clr app 2 out, easily* 1 14

No form in bumpers; wide margin winner of poor race; can improve; needs to; front runs. 14

TORUS SPA (Irish) — I 191U, I 2222

TOSS UP (Irish) — I 3053

TOTALLY OPTIMISTIC b.g. 6 True Song - Wildly Optimistic by Hard Fact R C Hayward

641 23/3 Siddington (L) RES 3m 20 S *bhnd whn blnd 8th, p.u. appr 10th* P 0
796 2/4 Heythrop (R) MDN 3m 11 F *mstks, in tch to hlfwy, t.o. whn blnd 13th, p.u. 15th* P 0
1433 6/5 Ashorne (R) MDO 3m 16 G *prom to 14th, wll btn frm nxt* 5 0

Beaten 30 lengths plus when completing; needs more but time on his side. 0

TOT OF RUM ch.m. 6 Little Wolf - Decorum by Quorum Mrs C M Rogers

883 6/4 Brampton Br' (R) MDN 3m 13 GF *rear, still in tch 11th, wknd 13th, p.u. 15th* P 0

An educational debut. 0

TOUCHER(IRE) ch.g. 8 Fidel - Lealies Pride by Knotty Pine David Morris

1995 P(0),U(-),P(0),3(0),4(0)

150 17/2 Erw Lon (L) MDN 3m 8 G *ld 1st, disp whn u.r. 4th* U -
387 9/3 Llanfrynach (R) RES 3m 11 GS *in tch to 7th, last at 11th, t.o. & p.u. 15th* P 0
552 17/3 Erw Lon (L) MDN 3m 10 GS *mid-div, wknd & p.u. 14th* P 0
694 30/3 Llanvapley (L) RES 3m 9 GS *mid-div, 5th at 11th, wknd aft, p.u. 3 out* P 0
1161 20/4 Llanwit Maj' (R) MDO 3m 15 GS *in tch til u.r. 6th* U -
1270 27/4 Pyle (R) MDO 3m 9 G *cls up til lft in ld 10th, hdd apr 15th, rdn & wknd* 3 0
1483 11/5 Bredwardine (R) MDO 3m 15 G *nvr rchd ldrs, wknd 10th, p.u. 12th* P 0
1605 25/5 Bassaleg (R) MDO 3m 8 GS *alwys rear, fin own time* 4 0

Has only beaten one horse in 95/96; need a miracle to win. 0

TOUCH 'N' PASS ch.g. 8 Dominion - Hanglands by Bustino David Vaughan-Morgan

385 9/3 Llanfrynach (R) LAD 3m 14 GS *rear whn u.r. 2nd* U -
507 16/3 Magor (R) MXO 3m 5 GS *rear, hrd rdn & prog to ld 15th, hdd 2 out, fin tired* 2 12
766 31/3 Pantyderi (R) CON 3m 6 G *alwys in rear* 5 14
978 8/4 Lydstep (L) OPE 3m 6 G *made all, easily* 1 23
1211 23/4 Chepstow (L) HC 3m 13 S *prom till wknd 8th, t.o. when p.u. before 14th.* P 0
1265 27/4 Pyle (R) OPE 3m 8 G *trckd ldrs, chal und pres 14th, disp 2 out, just hld* 2 23
1386 6/5 Pantyderi (R) OPE 3m 5 GF *(fav) sttld rear, prog 10th, ld aft 15th, ran om gamely flat* 1 20
1560 18/5 Bassaleg (R) OPE 3m 7 F *chsd ldrs, prog & cls 3rd whn blnd & u.r. 12th* U -
1604 25/5 Bassaleg (R) OPE 3m 6 GS *(fav) hld up, prog to ld 10th, qcknd away nxt, easily* 1 21
1633 1/6 Bratton Down (L) XX 3m 8 G *ld to 2nd, f nxt* F -

Tough & battles hard but has problems with fences; should win more 2nd class Opens 97; G/S-G/F 21

TOUCH OF WIND b.m. 5 Whistlefield - Cosmic by Foggy Bell S J Rawlins

471 10/3 Milborne St' (L) MDO 3m 16 G *mid-div, losing tch whn f 13th* F -
807 4/4 Clyst St Ma' (L) MDO 3m 10 GS *sight ld til f 10th* F -
1129 20/4 Stafford Cr' (R) MDO 3m 11 S *sn rear, t.o. & p.u. 7th* P 0
1348 4/5 Holnicote (L) MDO 3m 9 GS *p.u. 2nd* P 0

No real signs yet. 0

TOUCH OF WINTER b or br.g. 10 Strong Gale - Ballyhoura Lady by Green Shoon M W Kwiatkowski

1995 **2(NH),6(NH),F(NH),F(NH)**

523 16/3 Larkhill (R) MXO 3m 8 G *(fav) alwys bhnd, nvr trbld ldng grp* 5 16
706 30/3 Barbury Cas' (L) MEM 3m 7 G *(fav) n.j.w. hld up, prog 10th, ld 3 out, sn clr, easily* 1 20
996 8/4 Hackwood Pa' (L) MXO 3m 4 GF *(fav) alwys trlld, wknd qckly 3 out* 4 12
1290 28/4 Barbury Cas' (L) OPE 3m 5 F *made all, kicked clr 3 out, rdn out, unchal* 1 20
1406 6/5 Hackwood Pa' (L) MXO 3m 5 F *hld up, 20l off pace aft 12th, prog 2 out, chall last, no ex* 2 22
1584 24/5 Towcester (R) HC 3m 1f 11 GS *u.r. after 3rd.* U -
1643 2/6 Dingley (R) OPE 3m 13 GF *mid-div, mstk 5th, 6th & btn hlfwy, wlkd in* 7 0

Quite useful at best but inconsistent & jumped indifferently in points; should win again; G-F 21

TOUGH MINDED ch.g. 7 Starch Reduced - Oujarater by Adropejo Mrs P King

1995 2(17)

35 20/1 Higham (L) RES 3m 16 GF *mid-div, poor 4th at 16th, rpd prog to chal 2 out, no ext* 3 20
95 11/2 Ampton (R) RES 3m 11 GF *(fav) mid-div, jnd ldrs 13th, ev ch & rdn 3 out, btn nxt, lame* 2 14

Maiden winner 94; only 3 runs since; needs easy 3 miles; can win Restricted if fit in 97. 19

TOURIG DANTE (Irish) — I 11P, I 55P, I 1202, I 150P, I 277P, I 3564, I 4342, I 569P

TOUSHTARI(USA) b.g. 10 Youth (USA) - Taduska (FR) by Daring Display (USA) L J Bowman

274 2/3 Parham (R) OPE 3m 12 GF *prom to 12th, 6th & wkng whn f 15th* F -

571 17/3 Detling (L) CON 3m 13 GF *prom til wknd 4 out* 6 1

Flat winner; only 5 runs 94/96; not threatening to win now. 0

TOYTOWN KING (Irish) — **I** 462P, **I** 507F, **I** 567P, **I** 608[4], **I** 642[4], **I** 652[3]

TRACK ANGEL ch.m. 13 Ardoon - Angels Hair by Le Haar P V Mendoz

708 30/3 Barbury Cas' (L) LAD 3m 10 G *cls up to 8th, wknd nxt, t.o. & p.u. 11th, lame* P

No longer of any account 0

TRACKMAN (Irish) — **I** 90P, **I** 167P, **I** 237P, **I** 297[2], **I** 429[4], **I** 579F, **I** 607[5]

TRACTORIAS(IRE) br.g. 8 Aristocracy - My Serena Mrs A Conna

281 2/3 Clyst St Ma' (L) RES 3m 11 S *sn rear, t.o. & p.u. 16th* P
997 8/4 Hackwood Pa' (L) MDO 3m 11 GF *alwys in 1st 4, onepcd* 4 1
1409 6/5 Hackwood Pa' (L) MDO 3m 6 F *ld 11th, hdd 3 out, ran on onepcd* 3

Ex Irish; beaten 9 lengths maximum but form is very weak & win still looks tough. 10

TRADERS CHOICE b.g. 11 Salluceva - Maeve's Choice by Double-U-Jay C R Millingto
1995 P(0),2(19),**6(0)**

393 9/3 Garthorpe (R) CON 3m 7 G *(vis) cls up 3rd til wknd 9th, last & outpcd frm 12th* 3
677 30/3 Cottenham (R) OPE 3m 11 GF *in tch to 14th, sn wknd, t.o. & p.u. 2 out* P

Lightly raced now; tailed off in 96 and best watched. 14

TRAKSWAYBOY (Irish) — **I** 642P, **I** 655P

TRANQUIL LORD(IRE) b.g. 7 Le Moss - Sedate by Green Shoon D P Smith

233 24/2 Heythrop (R) MDN 3m 14 GS *cls up, disp 5th, in tch whn u.r. 10th* U
340 3/3 Heythrop (R) MDN 3m 12 G *(fav) in tch,lost plc 10th,ran on 3 out,mstk last,ev ch flat,no ex* 2 1
643 23/3 Siddington (L) MDN 3m 16 S *prom, blnd 6th, wknd 13th, lft poor 3rd 2 out* 3 1
791 2/4 Heythrop (R) MEM 3m 5 F *trckd wnr, 4l down last, ran on flat, too much to do* 2 1
1020 13/4 Kingston Bl' (L) MDN 3m 10 G *(fav) w.w. prog to jn ldrs 11th til u.r. 13th* U
1183 21/4 Mollington (R) MDN 3m 10 F *prom, ld 14th, drew clr apr last, ran on well* 1 1

Ex Irish; novice ridden; steady improvement; weak Restricted possible; any. 17

TRANSPLANT BLUE b.g. 13 Buckskin (FR) - Slave Light by Arctic Slave S J Goodings
1995 4(0),U(-),1(11),P(0),2(10)

339 3/3 Heythrop (R) RES 3m 10 G *alwys last, t.o. 13th* 7
478 10/3 Tweseldown (R) RES 3m 9 G *trckd ldrs, prog 3 out, ld apr last, rdn out* 1 1
783 31/3 Tweseldown (R) MEM 3m 5 G *hld up, went 2nd & ev ch aft 2 out, no ext flat* 2 1
957 8/4 Lockinge (L) CON 3m 5 GF *(fav) prom, ld 4-11th, cls up til ld 2 out, ran on wll* 1 1
1188 21/4 Tweseldown (R) OPE 3m 6 GF *rear, outpcd 12th, styd on onepcd frm 3 out* 3 1
1537 16/5 Folkestone (R) HC 3 1/4m 8 GF *(fav) ld after 3rd till after 5th, lost pl quickly 12th, p.u. before next, broke blood vessel.* P (

Won 3 modest races 95/96; tries hard & could find another local race at 14; Firm. 14

TRASNA NA CUNGAIM (Irish) — **I** 347P

TRAVARIANS GOLD (Irish) — **I** 321P, **I** 456F, **I** 494P

TRAVISTOWN b.g. 14 Grange Melody - Ednamore by Vulgan P Richards
1995 P(0),P(0),3(0),P(0)

154 17/2 Erw Lon (L) LAD 3m 14 G *alwys rear, p.u. 14th* P (
356 3/3 Garnons (L) LAD 3m 12 GS *rear & lost tch frm 4th, t.o. & p.u. aft 6th* P (
847 6/4 Howick (L) LAD 3m 9 GF *alwys rear, t.o. 12th* 5 (
1414 6/5 Cursneh Hill (L) LAD 3m 9 GF *t.o. frm 7th, p.u. 13th* P (
1559 18/5 Bassaleg (R) LAD 3m 4 F *last frm 4th, t.o. 12th* 4 (

Won 3 in 92; not won since & looks past it now. 0

TREASSOWE OATS br.g. 8 Oats - Pic-A-Path by Warpath C P F Lawrey

201 24/2 Lemalla (R) MDO 3m 13 HY *nvr nrr* 5 (
299 2/3 Great Treth' (R) MDO 3m 13 G *8th hlfwy, went 3rd 16th, kpt on* 3 12

Beaten 16 lengths (winners behind) when placed; not seen again but can go closer if fit in 97. 14

TREASURESOX (Irish) — **I** 161[6]

TREATY BRIDGE ch.g. 9 Over The River (FR) - Diplomat's Tam by Tamariscifolia J A C Edwards
1995 6(10)

162 17/2 Weston Park (L) OPE 3m 16 G *prom, ld 6-7th, in tch to 5 out, fdd, p.u. 2 out* P (
351 3/3 Garnons (L) OPE 3m 14 GS *mid-div whn u.r. 9th* U

Winning chaser; shows nothing now. 15

TREBONKERS b.g. 12 Treboro (USA) - Sally Conkers by Roi Lear (FR) J C Swinburn

49 4/2 Alnwick (L) OPE 3m 14 G *alwys wl bhnd, t.o. & p.u. 3 out* P (

83 11/2 Alnwick (L) CON 3m 10 GS *alwys last, t.o. & p.u. 2 out* P 0
191 24/2 Friars Haugh (L) OPE 3m 5 S *alwys bhnd* 5 0
402 9/3 Dalston (R) XX 3m 13 G *c.u. 6th, sn lst plc, t.o. frm 12th* 9 0

No longer of any account 0

TRECOMETTI b.m. 8 Giacometti - Balitree by Balidar — J A T de Giles

477 10/3 Tweseldown (R) MDO 3m 15 G *ld, clr hlfwy, hdd 4 out, wknd rpdly* 5 0

Showed plenty of speed but no stamina on debut. 0

TREENS FOLLY (Irish) — **I** 158F, **I** 429P, **I** 482P, **I** 563P, **I** 5883, **I** 6285

TRELEVEN b.m. 11 Town And Country - Balitree by Balidar — Miss V Nicholls

1995 2(13),F(-),2(19)

67 10/2 Great Treth' (R) LAD 3m 11 S *alwys bhnd* 7 0
136 17/2 Ottery St M' (L) LAD 3m 9 GS *prom early, lost tch frm 13th* 5 11
295 2/3 Great Treth' (R) LAD 3m 6 G *sn rear, t.o. frm hlfwy* 5 0
624 23/3 Kilworthy (L) LAD 3m 7 GS *ld 4-9th, 4th & btn frm 11th til p.u. last, dsmntd* P 0

Maiden winner 93; lost his last 18 races & problems last start; prospects very slim. 14

TREMBLES CHOICE (Irish) — **I** 32P, **I** 107F, **I** 196P, **I** 2715, **I** 3254, **I** 522P

TREMBLE VALLEY (Irish) — **I** 418P, **I** 5321

TREMBLING LADY (Irish) — **I** 128F, **I** 2335

TREMBLING ROSE (Irish) — **I** 33P, **I** 163P, **I** 340U

TREMOLLINA (Irish) — **I** 301F, **I** 340P, **I** 478F

TRESILLIAN BAY b.g. 11 Torus - Ivory Silk by Shantung — M Barthorpe

1995 P(0),3(11),3(10),1(15),2(14)

169 18/2 Market Rase' (L) CON 3m 15 GF *(bl) ld brfly 3rd, prom to 10th, t.o. & p.u. 2 out* P 0
328 3/3 Market Rase' (L) RES 3m 9 G *(vis) in tch til 3rd & outpcd apr 14th, no ch aft* 3 0
484 15/3 Fakenham (L) HC 2m 5f 110yds 13 GF *well pld till hit 3 out, soon btn.* 8 0
631 23/3 Market Rase' (L) MEM 3m 3 GF *(fav) (vis) tried to make all, hdd apr last, no ext* 2 0

Won poor Maiden 95; beaten in bad Members & looked reluctant in 96; Members looks only hope now. 12

TREVELLA b.m. 8 Celtic Cone - Bell-Amys by Blandford Lad — O J Stephens

1995 P(0),P(0),**P(NH)**

204 24/2 Castle Of C' (R) MDO 3m 11 HY *mid-div to 14th, wknd nxt, p.u. 3 out* P 0
843 6/4 Howick (L) MEM 3m 7 GF *mstks 2nd & 11th, alwys rear, btn frm 13th* 4 0
1040 13/4 St Hilary (R) MDN 3m 12 G *rear whn f 13th* F -
1391 6/5 Pantyderi (R) MDO 3m 13 GF *(bl) nvr nrr than 4th, strgglng frm 14th* 4 0

Only managed to beat 1 horse so far and not worth a rating.No signs of ability 0

TREYFORD ch.g. 16 Deep Run - Bunkilla by Arctic Slave — M P Wareing

1995 3(11),5(12),P(0),P(0)

909 8/4 Towcester (R) HC 2 3/4m 6 F *prom, wknd apr 3 out.* 3 19
1169 20/4 Chaddesley ' (L) MEM 3m 9 G *alwys last, t.o. 8th, completed own time* 6 0

Formerly decent pointer but looks ready for retirement now. 0

TRIBUTE TO DAD b.g. 9 Aragon - Bourienne by Bolkonski — Miss P Fitton

1995 8(0),4(13),F(-)

80 11/2 Wetherby Po' (L) MDO 3m 12 GS *mid-div, prog 12th, went 3rd 2 out, nvr nrr* 3 13

Only 6 runs in 3 seasons; good enough for weak Maiden but time passing him by. 13

TRICKY DEX(USA) ch.g. 9 Bar Dexter (USA) - Faire Trixie (USA) by Hold Your Tricks (USA) — D Gibbs

1995 1(18)

767 31/3 Pantyderi (R) INT 3m 7 G *nvr bttr than mid-div* 4 15
1035 13/4 St Hilary (R) CON 3m 10 G *prom til ld 12th, hdd 15th, cls enough 3 out, not run on* 4 15
1262 27/4 Pyle (R) MEM 3m 6 G *(fav) w.w. prog 11th, ld 13th, hit 2 out, clr last* 1 17
1491 11/5 Erw Lon (L) XX 3m 2 F *ld 11th til aft 13th, p.u. lame* P 0

Probably reached his peak now; barely stays; problems last start; win Confined if fit in 97; any. 17

TRICYCLIC (Irish) — **I** 22F, **I** 111P

TRICYCLING(IRE) b.g. 8 Flash Of Steel - Stradavari by Stradavinsky — J Doyle

1995 **P(NH)**

591 23/3 Wetherby Po' (L) MDO 3m 14 S *alwys rear, p.u. 14th* P 0

No signs on only start. 0

TRIFAST LAD ch.g. 11 Scallywag - Cilla by Highland Melody — Mike Roberts

1995 2(24)

709 30/3 Barbury Cas' (L) OPE 3m 15 G *(fav) 7/2-6/4, in tch, chsd wnr 13th, chal 2 out, alwys hld aft* 2 19
1100 14/4 Guilsborough (L) OPE 3m 9 G *prom, ld 7-15th, jnd wnr 2 out, kpt on flat, just hld* 2 22

Very lightly raced; onepaced but still good enough for modest Open/Confined in 97; Good. 22

TRIMAGE(IRE) b.g. 8 Trimmingham - Lisfuncheon Adage by Proverb T R Newton
1995 **4(NH),P(NH)**

181 18/2 Horseheath (R) RES 3m 5 G *chsd wnr to 9th, lost tch 14th, styd on to go 2nd agn flat* 2 11
313 2/3 Ampton (R) RES 3m 9 G *disp til ld 4th to 6th, wknd 14th, blnd & u.r. 16th* U -

Irish Maiden winner 93; placed novice chases; novice ridden; capable of a small win. 14

TRIMBUSH ch.g. 11 Flatbush - Miss Flymo by Guide K J Sims

380 9/3 Barbury Cas' (L) CON 3m 11 GS *sn rear, p.u. 12th* P 0
527 16/3 Larkhill (R) MEM 3m 4 G *sn wll bhnd, t.o.* 3 0
821 6/4 Charlton Ho' (L) MDN 3m 10 GF *mid-div thruout, nvr on terms wth ldrs* 3 0

Missed 95; safe but beaten 30 lengths minimum and a win at 12 looks tough. 11

TRIMFOLD (Irish) — **I 174^{5}, I 219^{P}**

TRIMMER LADY (Irish) — **I 33^{P}, I 85^{P}, I 143^{P}, I 225^{6}, I 308^{P}, I 354^{P}, I 522^{P}**

TRIMMER PRINCESS (Irish) — **I 25^{5}, I 80^{6}, I 141^{P}, I 212, , I 276^{P}, I 423^{3}**

TRIMMER WONDER (Irish) — **I 3^{P}, I 24^{4}, I 58^{2}, I 158, , I 242^{5}, I 278^{2}, I 355^{6}, I 422^{4}, I 529^{2}, I 619^{2}**

TRINA'S COTTAGE (Irish) — **I 27^{P}**

TRIPLE BUSH (Irish) — **I 321^{2}, I 404^{F}, I 539^{2}**

TRIPLE VALUE b.m. 9 Royal Fountain - Super Valu by Golden Love Miss L E Foxton
1995 4(10)

307 2/3 Great Stain' (L) MDO 3m 17 GS *prom, ev ch 2 out, no ext apr last, improve* 5 11
416 9/3 Charm Park (L) MDO 3m 13 G *alwys rr, n.d., p.u. 3 out* P 0
590 23/3 Wetherby Po' (L) MDO 3m 16 S *mid-div, prog to 3rd 14th, lft poor 2nd nxt, no ch wnr* 2 0
1365 4/5 Gisburn (R) MDO 3m 17 G *alwys bhnd, p.u. 2 out* P 0

Has ability; beat 7 others on completions; needs a little more before winning. 12

TRIP YOUR TRIGGER(IRE) ch.g. 5 Kamehameha (USA) - Half Smashed by Belfalas Chris Grant

51 4/2 Alnwick (L) MDO 3m 17 G *schoold rear, lost tch hlfwy, nvr nr* 7 0
302 2/3 Great Stain' (L) MEM 3m 7 GS *j.w. mid-div, prog to ld 13th, jnd last, forged clr nr fin* 1 13

Scrambled home in bad race; very young but needs huge improvement now. 14

TRISTIORUM ch.g. 9 Crofthall - Annie-Jo by Malicious Mrs Jayne Spawton
1995 4+(0)

331 3/3 Market Rase' (L) MDO 3m 9 G *ld to 10th, wknd apr 14th, p.u. 2 out* P 0

Lightly raced; shows little now and prospects slim. 10

TROLLY gr.g. 5 Joli Wasfi (USA) - True Princess by Eastwood Prince D J Norman

871 6/4 Higher Kilw' (L) RES 3m 9 GF *bhnd til p.u. apr 15th, schoold* P 0
1279 27/4 Bratton Down (L) MDO 3m 14 GF *mid-div, lost tch 13th, t.o. & p.u. 3 out* P 0
1530 12/5 Ottery St M' (L) MDO 3m 8 GF *rear,hit 11th,bhnd 15th,ran on to 2nd 2 out,2l 2nd f last* F 15

1st signs on last start (weak race); normal improvement should give him every chance of a win in 97. .. 13

TROPICAL GABRIEL(IRE) ch.c. 8 Invited (USA) - Shimering Star by Mon Capitaine Ken Liscombe
1995 5(0),P(0),U(-),5(0),4(15),6(0),**P(0)**,5(0)

164 17/2 Weston Park (L) RES 3m 11 G *mid-div, some late prog, nvr nrr* 3 0

Irish point winner 94; well beaten in England & very brief campaign in 96. 0

TROY BOY b or br.g. 6 Wassl - Petrol by Troy A P Gent
1995 **10(NH)**

214 24/2 Newtown (L) CON 3m 21 GS *wll bhnd, brf effrt 13th, no dang* 11 0
384 9/3 Llanfrynach (R) OPE 3m 16 GS *hld up, alwys rear, lost tch 15th, p.u. 2 out* P 0
601 23/3 Howick (L) CON 3m 10 S *4th frm 11th, styd on onepcd aft* 4 12

A short season & showed little; stamina the problem; unlikely to win points 14

TRUE FAIR b.g. 13 Balinger - Aberfair by Honour Bound G F White
1995 4(0),2(15),1(16),1(16),3(0),1(0),**7(0),2(NH)**

187 24/2 Friars Haugh (L) CON 3m 12 S *5th hlfwy, nvr nr ldrs* 4 0
610 23/3 Friars Haugh (L) CON 3m 11 G *ld til apr 2 out, no ext apr last* 3 17
857 6/4 Alnwick (L) MEM 3m 4 GF *(Jt fav) alwys 3rd,mstk 13th, onepcd & no dang aft* 3 14
912 8/4 Tranwell (L) OPE 3m 8 GF *ld, outpcd & wknd into 3rd 3 out, lft 2nd apr nxt* 2 18
1083 14/4 Friars Haugh (L) CON 3m 10 F *2nd mostly til 10th, grad wknd* 5 0

Won 3 modest races 95; struggling under penalties in 96; needs Firm; win at 14 looks tough. 17

TRUE FORTUNE b.g. 6 True Song - Cost A Fortune by Silver Cloud D J Miller
1995 F(-),2(13),P(0)
4 13/1 Larkhill (R) MDO 3m 9 GS *(fav) in tch, blnd 6th, prog & ld 13-14th, ld apr last, styd on* 1 14
Beat 2 subsequent winners on day one; not seen after; good stable & can upgrade if fit in 97. 15

TRUE FRED ch.g. 7 True Song - Silver Spartan by Spartan General Mrs A Price
884 6/4 Brampton Br' (R) MDN 3m 12 GF *rear frm 5th, lost tch 15th, p.u. 3 out* P 0
1044 13/4 Bitterley (L) MDO 3m 15 G *dist 4th whn u.r. 12th* U -
1224 24/4 Brampton Br' (R) MDO 3m 17 G *wth ldrs, 5th whn p.u. lame app 14th* P 0
Missed 95; yet to show anything & problems last start. 0

TRUELY ROYAL b.g. 12 Royal Fountain - True Friend by Bilsborrow Peter Stevens
1995 **4(NH),7(NH),4(NH),6(NH),6(NH),5(NH),P(NH),2(NH),7(NH),4(NH),6(NH),3(NH),3(NH),4(NH)**
885 6/4 Kimble (L) MEM 3m 5 GF *w.w. chsd ldng pair 13th, onepcd frm 3 out* 3 12
1188 21/4 Tweseldown (R) OPE 3m 6 GF *hit 3rd & rmndrs, pshd alng hlfwy, outpcd 12th, sn bhnd* 6 0
1399 6/5 Northaw (L) CON 3m 8 F *nt fluent early, prog to 6th 12th, no imp on ldrs frm 15th* 5 10
Winning chaser; safe but very onepaced; ran passably on debut but win at 14 not easy to find. 14

TRUE MEASURE b.m. 9 Kala Shikari - Fair Measure by Quorum J C Window
348 3/3 Higham (L) RES 3m 12 G *pckd & u.r. 2nd* U -
1206 21/4 Heathfield (R) RES 3m 8 F *sn rear, wll bhnd whn p.u. 16th* P 0
1537 16/5 Folkestone (R) HC 3 1/4m 8 GF *in tch, last and struggling when f 13th.* F -
Maiden winner 93; missed 94/95; unfortunate season and most unlikely to win now. 0

TRUE SPARKLE ch.m. 7 True Song - Spartan Clown by Spartan General H Hutsby
340 3/3 Heythrop (R) MDN 3m 12 G *s.s. sn trckd ldrs, wknd 12th, p.u. 14th* P 0
Only 2 runs in 3 seasons; do better when appearing regularly. 0

TRUE STEEL b.g. 10 Deep Run - Aran Tour by Arapaho Jon Trice-Rolph
1 13/1 Larkhill (R) XX 3m 7 GS *hld up, lost tch 13th, bhnd whn p.u. 3 out* P 0
230 24/2 Heythrop (R) MEM 3m 12 GS *hld up, prog frm 11th, styd on frm 3 out, went 2nd nxt* 2 18
374 9/3 Sandown (R) HC 2 1/2m 110yds 5 GS *lost pl 8th, shaken up 14th, styd on well apr last.* 2 21
Won 3 in 94; missed 95; ungenuine & tricky ride; good enogh for Confined; G-S.Quite able but tricky ... 21

TRULY OPTIMISTIC b.m. 7 True Song - Wildly Optimistic by Hard Fact Mrs R C Hayward
1995 P(0)
1020 13/4 Kingston Bl' (L) MDN 3m 10 G *prom to 6th, last 9th, t.o. & p.u. 12th* P 0
1434 6/5 Ashorne (R) MDO 3m 15 G *chsd ldr, ld 8-11th, wknd rpdly, t.o. & p.u. 13th* P 0
1504 11/5 Kingston Bl' (L) MDO 3m 13 G *20s-7s, chsng grp, rdn & lost tch 11th, no ch whn f 13th* F -
Yet to complete; her name accurately sums up the last start plunge. 0

TRUMPET HILL b.g. 7 Feelings (FR) - Faughill by Bronze Hill H M Barnfather
322 2/3 Corbridge (R) MDN 3m 10 GS *cls up frm 10th, chsd ldrs 3 out, no ext nxt* 4 0
398 9/3 Dalston (R) MEM 3m 13 G *alwys hndy, cls up 7th, ld 11th-16th, no ex frm 2 out* 3 0
613 23/3 Friars Haugh (L) MDN 3m 15 G *alwys bhnd.* 10 0
1254 27/4 Balcormo Ma' (R) MDO 3m 14 GS *ld til 4th, grdly lost tch* 5 0
Gets round safely; beaten 13 lengths minimum & needs more before winning. 0

TRUST MERCI ch.m. 8 Julio Mariner - Trust Ann by Capistrano John Jones
1995 3(10),2(0),P(0)
151 17/2 Erw Lon (L) MDN 3m 8 G *prom early, lost plc frm 12th* 5 0
Lightly raced; well beaten when completing; finished early and win looks unlikely. 11

TRUST THE GYPSY br.g. 14 National Trust - Zingarella by Romany Air Mrs B Whettam
1995 **2(18),4(21),2(26),5(0),F(-),2(22),5(NH),6(NH),4(NH),3(NH),3(NH),4(NH)**
364 5/3 Leicester (R) HC 2m 1f 12 GS *rear and pushed along 5th, n.d..* 6 0
798 3/4 Ascot (R) HC 2m 3f 110yds 10 GF *trckd ldrs till wknd after 10th, soon driven along, styd on one pace.* 4 19
1336 1/5 Cheltenham (L) HC 2m 110yds 9 G *blnd 1st, alwys bhnd, t.o. from 8th.* 6 0
1538 16/5 Folkestone (R) HC 3 1/4m 6 G *ld to 2nd, chsd ldr 7th to 13th and from 15th till after 3 out, no ext next.* 3 18
1613 27/5 Fontwell (R) HC 3 1/4m 110yds 12 G *prom till wknd 18th, t.o. when virtually p.u. run-in.* 7 0
H/Chase winner 94; grand servant but age caught up with him; win at 15 unlikely;G-F. 18

TRUSTY FRIEND b.g. 14 True Song - Princess Camilla by Prince Barle James Oldring
1995 2(19),P(0),5(12)

169 18/2 Market Rase' (L) CON 3m 15 GF *alwys mid-div, nvr dang* 7 13
395 9/3 Garthorpe (R) OPE 3m 7 G *last trio frm 3rd, 5th & t.o. 10th* 4 0
725 31/3 Garthorpe (R) OPE 3m 9 G *in tch in rear, nrly u.r. 7th, outpcd 14th, onepcd aft* 6 14
1011 9/4 Flagg Moor (L) OPE 3m 4 G *in tch, 3rd & outpcd 12th, btn whn swrvd & u.r. aft 15th* U -
1235 27/4 Clifton On ' (L) MEM 3m 4 GF *ld to 2nd, 3rd & outpcd 12th, no ch whn nrly ref 15th* 3 0
1379 5/5 Dingley (R) MXO 3m 7 GF *last pair, t.o. 12th, styd on apr last* 3 0
1598 25/5 Garthorpe (R) OPE 3m 6 G *alwys last, t.o. frm 5th* 5 14
1643 2/6 Dingley (R) OPE 3m 13 GF *alwys bhnd, t.o. 7th* 5 0

Winning chaser; novice ridden; safe but declined now and another win looks impossible. 11

TRUTH TO TELL (Irish) — **I** 494[P]

TRYDAN ch.g. 8 Push On - Island Joy by Easter Island Malcolm W Davies
1995 P(0),P(0),P(0),P(0),4(0)

504 16/3 Magor (R) MEM 3m 5 GS *cls 4th whn ran out 4th* r -
605 23/3 Howick (L) MDN 3m 13 S *u.r. 2nd* U -
850 6/4 Howick (L) MDN 3m 14 GF *t.o. 8th, p.u. 10th* P 0

Completed 2 of 19 races (last both times); no prospects. 0

TRY GOD (Irish) — **I** 184[1], **I** 241[1], **I** 310[3], **I** 435[5]

TRY IT ALONE b.g. 14 Harvest Sun - Philemore by Philemon M Biddick
1995 3(10),5(10),F(-),1(18),**4(12)**,1(20),4(0)

874 6/4 Higher Kilw' (L) OPE 3m 6 GF *hld up in tch, prog 14th, went 2nd nxt, ld 2 out, drew clr* 1 25
1228 27/4 Worcester (L) HC 2m 7f 17 G *hdwy 10th, rdn and wknd 12th.* 9 0
1425 6/5 High Bickin' (R) OPE 3m 4 G *(fav) trckd ldr,3rd 14th,2nd apr 3 out,chal und pres whn f last* F -
1624 27/5 Lifton (R) LAD 3m 9 GS *prog to 2nd 12th, chsd wnr til wknd 16th, onepcd aft* 3 18
1648 8/6 Umberleigh (L) LAD 3m 11 GF *lost plc 5th, nvr on trms aft, 4th & no ch 13th, no prog* 4 18

Found 3 weak Opens 95/96; gallant old stager & could still win at 15; any. 18

TRYUMPHANT LAD gr.g. 12 Roselier (FR) - Blackbog Lass by Le Tricolore M J Deasley
1995 3(19),3(16),3(14),7(0),F(-),**6(12)**

99 14/2 Lingfield (L) HC 3m 9 HY *nvr on terms.* 4 10
249 25/2 Charing (L) XX 3m 11 GS *wll in tch to 15th, no dang aft* 5 13
573 17/3 Detling (L) OPE 4m 9 GF *f 4th* F -

Lost last 20 races; reluctent now and will extend the sequence. 12

TSAGAIRT PAROISTE b.g. 13 Captain James - Tanzanite by Mongo A J Paterson

23 20/1 Barbury Cas' (L) XX 3m 11 GS *u.r. 2nd* U -
426 9/3 Upton-On-Se' (R) CON 3m 16 GS *t.o. whn blnd 9th, p.u. 10th* P 0

Formerly good pointer; of no account now. 0

TUDOR HENRY b.g. 11 Tudor Rhythm - Grebe by Hot Brandy J W Mitchell
1995 P(0),3(0)

5 13/1 Larkhill (R) LAD 3m 10 GS *mstk 6th, in tch to 12th, wll bhnd whn p.u. 15th* P 0
474 10/3 Tweseldown (R) LAD 3m 7 G *chsd wnr to 13th, mstk 15th, sn btn* 3 15
786 31/3 Tweseldown (R) LAD 3m 8 G *cls up, chsd wnr 10th, outpcd 12th, no ext 2 out* 3 18
1018 13/4 Kingston Bl' (L) LAD 3m 8 G *ld to 11th, 3rd frm 13th, kpt on onepcd* 3 19
1245 27/4 Woodford (L) LAD 3m 6 G *ld to 16th, onepcd aft* 2 18
1508 12/5 Maisemore P' (L) LAD 3m 6 F *ld to 3rd, mstk nxt, wknd 9th, sn t.o.* 4 0

Revived in 96; tries hard but easily beaten by good horses; worth a try in Members. 16

TUDOR LORD br.g. 10 Tudor Rhythm - Lady Buttons by New Brig Mrs Jill Jones
1995 P(0),2(10),P(0),6(0)

308 2/3 Great Stain' (L) MDO 3m 12 GS *plld hrd, ld 4th til wknd 14th, rear whn p.u. 3 out* P 0
516 16/3 Dalton Park (R) MDO 3m 11 G *plld hrd, sn ld, p.u. aft 10th, lame* P 0

Showed a little in 95; problems now and prospects slim. 0

TUDOR OAKS b.m. 9 Ayyabaan - Sarah's Joy by Full Of Hope S Gallagher
1995 P(0),U(-),U(-),P(0),r(-),8(0),F(-),1(0),F(-)

357 3/3 Garnons (L) RES 3m 14 GS *prom to 8th, wknd 11th, t.o. 3 out* 7 0
388 9/3 Llanfrynach (R) RES 3m 20 GS *nvr bynd mid-div, no ch 14th, p.u. 2 out* P 0
600 23/3 Howick (L) RES 3m 14 S *alwys rear, p.u. 14th* P 0
843 6/4 Howick (L) MEM 3m 7 GF *rear, prog 10th, 2nd 15th, ld nxt, drvn out* 1 13
1160 20/4 Llanwit Maj' (R) RES 3m 12 GS *alwys rear, lost tch 12th, no ch frm 16th* 3 0
1267 27/4 Pyle (R) RES 3m 7 G *12l 3rd at 8th, outpcd frm 12th, no ch 14th* 5 0
1557 18/5 Bassaleg (R) RES 3m 14 F *mstk 3rd, sn wll in rear, t.o. 10th* 5 0

Won 2 dire races 95/96; only beat a remounter otherwise; both wins G/F-F. 11

TUFFNUT GEORGE ch.g. 9 True Song - Arenig by New Member P T Cartridge
1995 U(-),6(0),1(17),2(19),1(17),**U(-),2(18)**

24 20/1 Barbury Cas' (L) XX 3m 12 GS *(fav) clr ldr til hdd 14th, blnd nxt, no ch wth wnr aft* 2 16

65 10/2 Great Treth' (R) INT 3m 13 S *mostly abt 5th-6th, wknd 13th, p.u. 16th* P 0
579 20/3 Ludlow (R) HC 2 1/2m 17 G *held up, hdwy 5 out, left in ld flat, hdd final 50 yards.* 2 20
879 6/4 Brampton Br' (R) LAD 3m 9 GF *(fav) chsd ldr til ld 9th, 4l up 13th, styd on strngly 3 out* 1 23
1227 26/4 Ludlow (R) HC 2 1/2m 16 G *prom, driven along apr 2 out, styd on same pace.* 3 20
1339 4/5 Hereford (R) HC 2m 3f 7 F *alwys prom, ld 7th till after 11th, regained ld apr 3 out, mstk next, hdd last, rallied to lead again cl home.* 1 23

Consistent & maintained improvement; best under 3m; can win again; summer jumping 96 (won chase) 23

TUFTER'S GARTH b or br.g. 11 Maculata - Magic Minstrel by Pitpan Mrs M Rigg
1995 1(10),U(-),**F(-)**

593 23/3 Parham (R) RES 3m 11 GS *plld into ld 2nd,prssd frm 8th,hdd 14th,wll bhnd & p.u.2 out* P 0
961 8/4 Heathfield (R) MEM 3m 5 G *ld 2nd til u.r. 11th* U -
1205 21/4 Heathfield (R) MEM 3m 4 F *(fav) ld/disp to 6th, ld 9-10th, agn 16th, kpt on wll 2 out* 1 0
1295 28/4 Bexhill (R) RES 3m 7 F *lost tch 4th, fin own time* 3 0

Won 2 desperate races 95/96; jumps poorly & need same to win again. 11

TULLAGHFIN (Irish) — **I** 445^{P}, **I** 474^{2}, **I** 543,
TULLBEG BLOOM (Irish) — **I** 32^{F}, **I** 85^{3}, **I** 105^{F}
TULLEBARD BEETMAN (Irish) — **I** 87^{F}
TULLIBARDS AGAIN (Irish) — **I** 384^{6}, **I** 522, , **I** 532^{5}
TULLIBARDS RAINBOW (Irish) — **I** 30^{F}, **I** 62^{P}, **I** 81^{P}
TULLYKYNE BELLS gr.g. 7 Le Solaret (FR) - Cowbells by Mountain Call M A Kerley
1995 **P(NH),7(NH),8(NH)**

207 24/2 Castle Of C' (R) MDO 3m 15 HY *in tch to 7th, ld 11th-nxt, wknd, t.o. & p.u. 15th* P 0
471 10/3 Milborne St' (L) MDO 3m 16 G *rear whn u.r. 5th* U -
652 23/3 Badbury Rin' (L) MDO 3m 13 G *frnt rnk untl lost plc 13th, lost plc from 3 out* 3 0
864 6/4 Larkhill (R) MDN 2 1/2m 9 F *made most to 4 out, onepcd whn hdd, no ch with wnnr* 2 12
1409 6/5 Hackwood Pa' (L) MDO 3m 6 F *(fav) ld to 10th, outpcd aft* 4 0

3 placings but form is weak & last in bad race last start & not threatening to win yet. 11

TUL NA GCARN (Irish) — **I** 104^{P}, **I** 158^{P}, **I** 194^{P}, **I** 229^{3}, **I** 349^{3}
TUMBLE TIME b.g. 12 Tumble Wind (USA) - Odette Odile by Home Guard (USA) Captain Miles Gosling

264 2/3 Didmarton (L) INT 3m 12 G *made most to 5th, wth ldrs aft, ld last, sn hdd & no ext* 4 14
436 9/3 Newton Brom' (R) LAD 3m 10 GS *alwys wll bhnd* 9 0
1177 21/4 Mollington (R) INT 3m 14 F *wll bhnd, ran past btn horses to 6th 3 out, no dang* 6 0
1500 11/5 Kingston Bl' (L) CON 3m 7 G *chsd ldng trio, easily outpcd frm 13th, no ch aft* 4 11
1567 19/5 Mollington (R) INT 3m 12 GS *alwys last pair, t.o. 11th, poor 6th whn f last* F -

Missed 94/5 & returned with modest performances; unlikely to achieve anything at 13 12

TUMBRIL ch.g. 11 Legal Tender - Cartwheel by Escart III Major R P G Dill
1995 4(22),3(21),U(-)

230 24/2 Heythrop (R) MEM 3m 12 GS *mostly mid-div til prog hlfwy, wkng whn p.u. 13th* P 0
639 23/3 Siddington (L) OPE 3m 12 S *ld 4th, blnd 6th, hdded 10th, wknd 13th, p.u. appr 3 out* P 0
1098 14/4 Guilsborough (L) CON 3m 17 G *mid-div, ran wd bnd apr 9th, p.u. & dsmntd* P 0

Lightly raced; more problems last start and looks finished now. 13

TU PIECE b.g. 7 Kaytu - Bikini Top by Formidable (USA) P H Howse
1995 P(0),R(-)

637 23/3 Siddington (L) MEM 3m 14 S *j.s. 1st, in tch to 13th, p.u. appr 15th* P 0
842 6/4 Maisemore P' (L) MDN 3m 17 GF *in tch,outpcd 14th, ran on agn frm 2 out, fin wll.* 4 0

Beaten 19 lengths (poor horses behind); gradually learning & should go closer in 97. 12

TURBULENT GALE(IRE) br.g. 7 Strong Gale - Turbo Run E E Williams

20 14/1 Tweseldown (R) RES 3m 9 GS *(fav) nrly u.r. 1st,mstks,chsd ldng trio,outpcd frm 12th,t.o.* 3 0
158 17/2 Weston Park (L) MEM 3m 11 G *6s-3s, ld/disp, clr 3 out, ran on well* 1 18
1368 4/5 Gisburn (R) RES 3m 9 G *(fav) ld 4th, going wll whn c.o. by loose horse apr 13th* C -

Irish Maiden winner; scooted home 2nd start & unlucky after break; should find Restricted 97; Good ... 19

TURKISH ISLAND b.m. 9 Kemal (FR) - Island More by Mugatpura Mrs D Cowley

1104 14/4 Guilsborough (L) MDN 3m 18 G *alwys wll bhnd, t.o. & p.u. 14th* P 0
1182 21/4 Mollington (R) MDN 3m 10 F *prssd wnr 4th til mstk 7th, wknd 11th, t.o.* 5 0
1433 6/5 Ashorne (R) MDO 3m 16 G *alwys rear, lost tch & p.u. 9th* P 0
1504 11/5 Kingston Bl' (L) MDO 3m 13 G *sn mid-div, 9th whn u.r. 9th* U -
1621 27/5 Chaddesley ' (L) MDO 3m 17 GF *alwys wll in rear, t.o. & p.u. 12th* P 0

Of no account 0

TUROS (Irish) — **I** 267^{F}
TUSCANIA ch.m. 6 Faustus (USA) - The Shrew by Relko Mrs P Grainger

1995 **6(NH)**
354 3/3 Garnons (L) MDN 2 1/2m 13 GS *cls 4th at 7th, ev ch 10th, wkng whn u.r. 3 out* U -
977 8/4 Lydstep (L) MDO 3m 8 G *ld til hdd aft last, just hld* 2 13

Beaten a head in weak race; surely can improve & find similar in 97. 13

TWEED VALLEY b.g. 10 Le Coq D'Or - Tillside by Lucky Brief Mrs Susan Crawford
1995 5(14)
328 3/3 Market Rase' (L) RES 3m 9 G *rear & hit 8th, t.o. & p.u. 13th* P 0
539 17/3 Southwell P' (L) RES 3m 11 GS *(bl) mid-div, prog 12th, 4th & btn whn p.u. 3 out* P 0
967 8/4 Thorpe Lodge (L) MEM 3m 7 GF *(bl) prog 9th, 3rd nxt, 2nd 5 out, chal innr & ld 2 out, ran on* 1 12
1439 6/5 Ashorne (R) RES 3m 11 G *(bl) in tch, outpcd 12th, effrt to 4th 3 out, kpt on* 4 16

Maiden winner 93; won poor Members; ran passably after but Restricted still looks tough; blinkers. 13

TWELTH MAN b.g. 9 Remainder Man - Merry Cherry by Deep Run W G Dutton
159 17/2 Weston Park (L) CON 3m 22 G *chsd ldrs, fdd & p.u. 14th* P 0
666 24/3 Eaton Hall (R) RES 3m 13 S *alwys rear, p.u. 5 out* P 0

Maiden winner 94; lightly raced & shown nothing under rules or in points since; best watched. 0

TWENTYFIVEQUID (Irish) — **I** 16P, **I** 932, **I** 4922, **I** 5381

TWICE KNIGHTLY b.g. 5 Double Bed (FR) - Charter Belle by Runnymede W H Whitley
559 17/3 Ottery St M' (L) OPE 3m 7 G *last til some prog frm 4 out, btn whn f 2 out* F -

Poor on the Flat & no encouragement from pointing debut 0

TWILIGHT TOM ro.g. 7 Pragmatic - Starlight Beauty by Scallywag L J Williams
267 2/3 Didmarton (L) MDN 3m 11 G *rear til b.d. 4th* B -
598 23/3 Howick (L) MEM 3m 6 S *hld up, ran on onepcd frm 14th, tk 2nd 3 out* 2 0
697 30/3 Llanvapley (L) MDN 3m 11 GS *2nd/3rd til disp 15th, ld 2 out, ran on well* 1 15

Steady improvement; won 3 finisher race; can improve and every chance of upgrading. 15

TWO GUN TEX b.g. 6 Bairn (USA) - Relkisha by Relkino Martin F Edgar
47 4/2 Alnwick (L) XX 3m 14 G *t.o. in last pair til p.u. 8th* P -
193 24/2 Friars Haugh (L) MDN 3m 10 S *sn bhnd, p.u. 10th* P 0
502 16/3 Lanark (R) MDO 3m 7 G *in tch whn u.r. 6th* U -
615 23/3 Friars Haugh (L) MEM 3m 9 G *wll bhnd by 7th,* 8 0

Firing blanks at present; unpromising. 0

TWO JOHN'S(IRE) b or br.g. 7 King's Ride - No Honey by Dual Paul K Barber
2 13/1 Larkhill (R) MDO 3m 17 GS *(fav) pllng, mskts, ld 3-5th, disp whn ran out & u.r. 12th* r -
143 17/2 Larkhill (R) MDO 3m 14 G *(fav) j.w. made all, not extndd* 1 20

Ex novice hurdler; lightly raced; headstrong but obviously talented; sure to progress if fit in 97. 21

TYDELMORE b.g. 12 Tycoon II - Delcombe by Cracksman (NZ) R Loughlin
1995 3(0),F(-)
22 20/1 Barbury Cas' (L) XX 3m 19 GS *mstk 5th, alwys bhnd, t.o. & p.u. 12th* P 0
160 17/2 Weston Park (L) OPE 3m 16 G *chsd ldrs to 9th, fdd, p.u. 12th* P 0

Showed nothing in 96 & getting old now. 10

TYNDRUM GOLD br.g. 6 Sonnen Gold - Firwood by Touching Wood (USA) John L Holdroyd
1995 **17(NH),P(NH)**
74 11/2 Wetherby Po' (L) MDO 3m 11 GS *alwys rear, nvr dang, p.u. 14th* P 0
241 25/2 Southwell P' (L) MDO 3m 15 HO *n.j.w. alwys bhnd, t.o. & p.u. 3 out* P 0
518 16/3 Dalton Park (R) MDO 3m 15 G *mid-div to 8th, sn wll bhnd, t.o. & p.u. 3 out* P 0
589 23/3 Wetherby Po' (L) MDO 3m 16 S *rear, prog 14th, styd on frm 3 out, nvr nrr* 4 0
987 8/4 Charm Park (L) MDN 3m 13 GF *alwys wll in rear, nvr a factor, p.u. 3 out* P 0
1364 4/5 Gisburn (R) MDO 3m 11 G *ldng grp, 4th whn p.u. 13th* P 0

Beaten 20 lengths when completing; looks slow and more needed. 10

TYPOGRAPHER(IRE) b.g. 5 Never So Bold - Elabella by Ela-Mana-Mou D F Gillard
924 8/4 Bishopsleigh (R) LAD 3m 7 G *u.r. 1st* U -

A short season. 0

TYRELLA CLEAR VIEW (Irish) — **I** 96F, **I** 2144, **I** 261P, **I** 397B, **I** 4494, **I** 601P

TYTHERINGTON b or br.g. 12 New Member - Vespers II by The Monk G F Hammond
1995 2(16),2(19),**2(20)**
579 20/3 Ludlow (R) HC 2 1/2m 17 G *ref to race.* F -
793 2/4 Heythrop (R) OPE 4m 10 F *ld to 12th, prom til wknd 17th, t.o. & p.u. 2 out* P 0
1005 9/4 Upton-On-Se' (R) CON 3m 6 F *ld to 2nd, rdn 11th, 4th & outpcd 15th, no dang aft* 3 0

1169	20/4	Chaddesley '	(L)	MEM	3m	9	G	*disp frm 10th til ld 12th, hdd 16th, onepcd frm nxt*	4	14
1510	12/5	Maisemore P'	(L)	XX	3m	8	F	*chsd ldng pair 3rd, no ch aft 13th, plggd on*	3	14

Lost his last 9 starts & declined in 96; hard to find a win at 13; G-F. 15

UCKERBY LAD b.g. 5 Tobin Lad (USA) - Chomolonga by High Top — Roger Ford

1995 **6(NH)**

1071	13/4	Lifton	(R)	MDN	3m	10	S	*plling & ld 3rd-6th,jmp slwly 7th,bhnd frm 8th til p.u. 11th*	P	0

Tailed of in hurdle; ran too freely on point debut; unpromising. 0

UFANO(FR) b.g. 10 Toujours Pret (USA) - Osca (FR) by Taj Dewan — C C Bennett

1995 P(0),10(0),4(0),3(10),3(10),5(0),U(-),1(0),9(0)

25	20/1	Barbury Cas'	(L)	OPE	3m	14	GS	*mid-div, prog 11th, wknd 14th, no ch whn u.r. 3 out*	U	-
274	2/3	Parham	(R)	OPE	3m	12	GF	*lost tch 8th, t.o. & p.u. 3 out*	P	0
994	8/4	Hackwood Pa'	(L)	MEM	3m	4	GF	*ld to last, outpcd*	2	11

Won joke Open 95; no form in proper races & need another miracle to win again. 12

ULLSWATER b.g. 10 Waffl - Dignified Air (FR) by Wolver Hollow — Philip D Brougham

360	4/3	Windsor	(R)	HC	3m	8	GS	*chsd ldrs 2nd to 5th, wknd 9th, t.o..*	7	0
480	11/3	Plumpton	(L)	HC	3m 1f 110yds	6	GS	*prom till wknd 9th, t.o. from 13th.*	5	0
672	29/3	Aintree	(L)	HC	2 3/4m	26	G	*jmpd slowly, alwys well bhnd, t.o. hfwy.*	15	0
1382	6/5	Exeter	(R)	HC	2m 7f 110yds	8	GF	*t.o. from 6th, blnd 9th, p.u. before next.*	P	0

Winning chaser; outclassed in H/chases; needs to concentrate on points; will struggle to win one. 0

ULTRASON IV(FR) b.g. 10 Quart de Vin (FR) - Jivati (FR) by Laniste — David A Smith

1995 2(15),4(11),3(14)

159	17/2	Weston Park	(L)	CON	3m	22	G	*prom early, lost tch, not qckn frm 4 out*	6	0
458	9/3	Eyton-On-Se'	(L)	INT	3m	11	G	*chsd ldrs, ld 10th-4 out, 1l down whn lft in ld 2 out*	1	16
683	30/3	Chaddesley '	(L)	MEM	3m	17	G	*chsd ldrs to 11th, sn wknd, p.u. 3 out*	P	0
1012	9/4	Flagg Moor	(L)	XX	3m	7	G	*mid-div til u.r. 6th*	U	-

Dual winner 94; won weak Intermediate; stays but confined looks tough; G-S. 16

UNCLE ART (Irish) — I 109^{P}, I 173^{P}, I 283^{1}, I 411^{5}, I 537^{5}, I 586^{3}

UNCLE BRUCE b.g. 6 Sula Bula - Saxon Belle by Deep Run — Mrs Judy Young

1995 **21(NH),13(NH),6(NH),P(NH)**

711	30/3	Barbury Cas'	(L)	MDO	3m	8	G	*f 1st*	F	-
864	6/4	Larkhill	(R)	MDN	2 1/2m	9	F	*trckd ldrs til wknd frm 9th, t.o. whn ref 4 out*	R	-

Season lasted a week & unpromising 0

UNIQUE NEW YORK b.g. 13 Balinger - Credo's Daughter by Credo — Miss S L Offord

1995 1(0),2(0),**4(0)**

135	17/2	Ottery St M'	(L)	LAD	3m	11	GS	*(bl) alwys bhnd, t.o. 14th*	6	0
208	24/2	Castle Of C'	(R)	LAD	3m	14	HY	*disp to 5th, cls up to 12th, outpcd frm nxt*	7	0
378	9/3	Barbury Cas'	(L)	LAD	3m	6	GS	*sn rear, t.o. 11th*	3	10
730	31/3	Little Wind'	(R)	LAD	3m	6	GS	*(vis) prom til lost plc stdly frm 15th*	3	13
803	4/4	Clyst St Ma'	(L)	LAD	3m	4	GS	*(bl) prom, hit 8th, disp 11th-nxt, sn outpcd*	2	15
1165	20/4	Larkhill	(R)	LAD	3m	7	GF	*(vis) alwys ldng grp, prom whn ran out 12th*	r	-
1312	28/4	Little Wind'	(R)	XX	3m	6	G	*(bl) prom, ld brfly 14th, chsd wnr, ev ch 2 out, onepcd*	2	17

Winning chaser; novice ridden; safe but barely stays & Ladies at 14 most unlikely. 15

UNIQUE TRIBUTE b.g. 7 Celestial Storm (USA) - Fearless Felon (USA) by Bailjumper (USA) — Miss L Hollis

1995 2(17),2(18),3(12),3(15)

419	9/3	High Easter	(L)	RES	3m	10	S	*(Jt fav) prom, ld 14th, drw clr appr 2 out, styd on*	1	20

Won 2 placed 6 from 9 starts; stays well & best in Soft; can win Confined.G-S. 19

UNITYFARM OLTOWNER b.g. 12 Le Johnstan - Ribble Reed by Bullrush — Miss T McCurrich

67	10/2	Great Treth'	(R)	LAD	3m	11	S	*alwys bhnd, fin own time*	8	0
197	24/2	Lemalla	(R)	LAD	3m	13	HY	*nvr a fctr*	5	10
443	9/3	Haldon	(R)	LAD	3m	10	S	*5th hlfwy, lost ground frm 11th, t.o.*	7	0
647	23/3	Cothelstone	(L)	CON	3m	6	S	*clse up tll blun 7th, t.o. 13th, walked in*	5	0
988	8/4	Kingston St'	(R)	MEM	3m	7	F	*in tch to 11th, 20l 4th at 13th, t.o. & p.u. aft 15th*	P	0

Novice ridden; safe but too slow now. 11

UNLUCKY FOR SOME(IRE) b.g. 7 Dromod Hill - Red Gimmy Vii — Jeremy Mason

1995 **P(NH),5(NH)**

95	11/2	Ampton	(R)	RES	3m	11	GF	*ld/disp to 7th, prom, rdn to ld 17th-nxt, sn wknd*	3	12
231	24/2	Heythrop	(R)	XX	3m	10	GS	*alwys cls up, jnd ldr 12th, sn wknd, fdd flat*	4	11
621	23/3	Higham	(L)	INT	3m	12	GF	*alwys prom, cls up whn f 10th*	F	-
904	6/4	Dingley	(R)	RES	3m	20	GS	*nvr dang, remote 7th 2 out, p.u. last*	P	0

1239 27/4 Clifton On ' (L) RES 3m 9 GF *ld to 8th, prom til lost tch 15th, wll bhnd whn p.u. last* P

Maiden winner 95; ran passably 1st 2 starts but more needed; still young & could improve. 14

UNSCRUPULOUS GENT ch.g. 14 Over The River (FR) - Even Lass by Even Money Mrs E Huttinger
1995 2(10)
706 30/3 Barbury Cas' (L) MEM 3m 7 G *ld to 9th, grad wknd frm nxt, t.o. 3 out* 5
1288 28/4 Barbury Cas' (L) MEM 3m 5 F *carried 14st, ld to 4th, wll bhnd frm 9th, t.o.* 3
1502 11/5 Kingston Bl' (L) LAD 3m 7 G *sn wll bhnd, t.o. 5th, p.u. 15th* P
1608 26/5 Tweseldown (R) CON 3m 6 G *immed outpcd in 5th, t.o. frm 8th* 4

No longer of any account 0

UP AND COMING b.g. 13 Avocat - Cummin Hill by Wrekin Rambler Miss M C Bentham
1995 **14(NH)**
710 30/3 Barbury Cas' (L) CON 3m 6 G *j.w. ld 6th, went clr frm 2 out* 1 24
1018 13/4 Kingston Bl' (L) LAD 3m 8 G *prom, j.w. til blnd 10th, not rcvr, t.o. & p.u. 15th* P
1289 28/4 Barbury Cas' (L) CON 3m 8 F *(fav) cls up, ld 14th, alwys in cmmnd aft, clvrly* 1 21

Winning chaser; revived after long absence; 2 good performances & can win at 14 if fit; Good 21

UP AND OVER (Irish) — **I** 213^{P}, **I** 375^{P}
UP AND UNDER (Irish) — **I** 23^{F}, **I** 88^{F}
UP FOR RANSOME (Irish) — **I** 202^{2}, **I** 294^{2}, **I** 372^{1}, **I** 426^{2}, **I** 542^{P}
UPHAM CLOSE ch.m. 10 Oats - Real View by Royal Highway Reg Hand
1995 **3(22),4(22)**,5(21),2(19),3(12),1(20)
5 13/1 Larkhill (R) LAD 3m 10 GS *last pair, lost tch 7th, nvr nr ldrs aft* 4 12
Won 4 in 93; lost last 11; finished early 96; stays well; could still win if fit in 97. F-S. 20

UP IN THE AIR (Irish) — **I** 197^{P}
UPSHEPOPS (Irish) — **I** 265^{P}, **I** 294^{P}, **I** 441^{5}, **I** 468^{F}, **I** 656^{P}
UP THE BANNER VI (Irish) — **I** 292^{P}, **I** 373^{1}
UP THE ROCK (Irish) — **I** 227^{P}, **I** 266^{P}
UPTON GALE(IRE) br.g. 6 Strong Gale - Newtown Colleen by Golden Love W W Dennis
1995 **F(NH)**
71 10/2 Great Treth' (R) MDO 3m 15 S *disp to 3rd, grad wknd, p.u. 3 out* P

Only learning on debut; looks capable of better. 0

UPTON ORBIT b.g. 7 Riberetto - Well Starched by Starch Reduced J C Collett
1995 R(-),3(10),P(0),4(12)
2 13/1 Larkhill (R) MDO 3m 17 GS *mid-div, prog to 3rd 13th, chsd wnr apr last, ran on* 2 18
60 10/2 Cottenham (R) MDO 3m 7 GS *(fav) ld & f 1st* F
145 17/2 Larkhill (R) MDO 3m 13 G *prom, ev ch 2 out, ran on onepcd* 3 12
286 2/3 Eaton Hall (R) MDO 3m 14 G *mid-div, prog 12th, strng run to ld 2 out, ran on well* 1 15
684 30/3 Chaddesley ' (L) RES 3m 14 G *chsd ldr 11th, lft in ld nxt, hdd 4 out, kpt on wll flat* 2 17
1102 14/4 Guilsborough (L) RES 3m 15 G *(fav) mid-div, out of tch & rdn hlfwy, nvr rchd ldrs* 7

Improved; won slow race; inconsistent & showed no interest last start; could prove frustating. 17

UPTON STEAMER (Irish) — **I** 137^{P}, **I** 213^{F}
UP TRUMPS (Irish) — **I** 576^{P}, **I** 657^{P}
UPWELL b.g. 12 Tanfirion - Debnic by Counsel Robert Johnson
1995 **14(NH),4(NH),6(NH),2(NH),5(NH),4(NH),3(NH),2(NH),2(NH),3(NH),5(NH),6(NH)**
85 11/2 Alnwick (L) LAD 3m 11 GS *last pair & alwys t.o.* 9
316 2/3 Corbridge (R) MEM 3m 10 GS *alwys prom, lft 2nd 15th, styd on, not pace to chal* 2 11
759 31/3 Great Stain' (L) LAD 3m 10 GS *prom til fdd 4 out* 7

Maintained the modest level of performance that has characterised his career 11

VAGABOND COLLONGES (Irish) — **I** 557^{2}
VAIGLY GREY gr.m. 8 Zambrano - Dunlean by Leander J A Featherstone
1995 P(0),P(0),1(16),P(0)
411 9/3 Charm Park (L) RES 3m 20 G *alwys rr, sme pace thro'out, p.u. 4 out* P

Only 1 completion 94/96 (33/1 Maiden win); vanished quickly in 96; can only be watched. 14

VAIN PRINCESS (Irish) — **I** 370^{1}, **I** 512^{1}, **I** 542^{2}
VALASSY b.g. 13 Northern Value (USA) - Plum Sassy by Prince Tenderfoot (USA) Miss C A Blakeborough
1995 P(0),P(0),6(0),2(14),3(14),2(0),3(0)
72 11/2 Wetherby Po' (L) CON 3m 18 GS *(vis) alwys rear, f 12th* F

Last won in 91; ungenuine and past it now. 13

VALATCH ch.g. 8 Valiyar - Love Match (USA) by Affiliate (USA) — J H Henderson

1995 P(0),4(0)

723	31/3	Garthorpe	(R)	CON 3m	19	G	*blnd 3rd, sn wll bhnd, t.o. last whn p.u. 9th*	P	0
969	8/4	Thorpe Lodge	(L)	OPE 3m	4	GF	*last, t.o. 12th, stole 3rd on line*	3	0
1256	27/4	Cottenham	(R)	MEM 3m	6	F	*ld to 2nd, chsd ldng pair 8th, outpcd 4 out*	3	0
1399	6/5	Northaw	(L)	CON 3m	8	F	*chsd ldrs, 4th & outpcd 13th, kpt on onepcd frm 3 out*	4	12

Well beaten when placed in weak races & not threatening to win. **10**

VALE OF YORK gr.g. 8 Kabour - Amber Vale by Warpath — S B Clark

1995 **P(NH)**

409	9/3	Charm Park	(L)	CON 3m	11	G	*ht 3rd, cls up 4th-8th, fdd 12th, p.u. 4 out*	P	0
762	31/3	Great Stain'	(L)	MDN 3m	11	GS	*chsd ldr, disp 8th, hdd 13th, wknd rpdly, p.u. 3 out*	P	0
828	6/4	Stainton	(R)	MDO 3m	7	GF	*prom, ld 3rd-7th, onepcd frm 4 out*	2	11
1136	20/4	Hornby Cast'	(L)	MDN 3m	11	G	*chsd ldrs, ld 5th, hdd 12th, outpcd frm 2 out*	4	10

Placed in 2 weak Maidens; stamina doubtful and more needed to win. **10**

VALIANT FRIEND b.g. 9 Hell's Gate - Fleur-De-Chriose by Dragonara Palace (USA) — Mrs M E Barton

1995 F(-),7(0),3(10),5(0),3(0),5(0),6(0),2(13),P(0),5(0)

155	17/2	Erw Lon	(L)	RES 3m	9	G	*hld up, prog frm 3 out, nrst fin*	3	0
388	9/3	Llanfrynach	(R)	RES 3m	20	GS	*alwys bhnd, t.o. & p.u. 14th*	P	0

Finished alone in Members 94; beaten 15 times since and follow up unlikely now. **10**

VALIANT VICAR b.g. 9 Belfort (FR) - Shagra by Sallust — David Ford

227	24/2	Duncombe Pa'	(R)	LAD 3m	6	GS	*prom 6th-9th, last whn u.r. 12th*	U	-
412	9/3	Charm Park	(L)	LAD 3m	7	G	*alwys rr, last whn u.r. 9th*	U	-
512	16/3	Dalton Park	(R)	CON 3m	10	G	*alwys rear, nrly u.r. 14th, t.o. & p.u. last*	P	0
824	6/4	Stainton	(R)	CON 3m	11	GF	*last & lost tch 9th, blnd 13th, t.o. & p.u. 4 out*	P	0
1281	27/4	Easingwold	(L)	CON 3m	15	G	*sn rear, rdn 11th, lost tch, t.o. & p.u. 14th*	P	0

Flat winner 90; no prospects in points. **0**

VALIBUS(FR) b.g. 11 Labus (FR) - Valgrinette (FR) by Valdingran (FR) — P A D Scouller

1995 P(0),P(0),P(0),1(16),r(-),R(-)

1016	13/4	Kingston Bl'	(L)	CON 3m	6	G	*n.j.w. made most 2nd-apr 14th,wknd rpdly,poor 3rd & p.u.3out*	P	0
1298	28/4	Bexhill	(R)	CON 3m	4	F	*cls 2nd, disp 13-16th, 2nd aft, wknd 2 out*	2	10
1375	4/5	Peper Harow	(L)	CON 3m	9	F	*prog 9th, chsd ldr 13th, ld appr last, std on strngly*	1	20
1503	11/5	Kingston Bl'	(L)	OPE 3m	3	G	*(fav) made all, drew wll clr 2 out, ran on strngly*	1	15

Won 3 of 4 completions; best late season; can win again if right in 97; G-F. **18**

VALLEY ERNE (Irish) — I 9[P], I 46[1]

VALTORUS(IRE) b.g. 7 Torus - Barberstown's Last by Le Bavard (FR) — W J Turcan

1995 4(11),1(14),P(0),4(11),1(17),4(0)

393	9/3	Garthorpe	(R)	CON 3m	7	G	*ld frm 6th, lft clr 2 out*	1	19
723	31/3	Garthorpe	(R)	CON 3m	19	G	*(fav) wth ldrs til mstk 11th, sn drppd out, t.o. & p.u. 3 out*	P	0

Found 3 modest races 95/96; main rivals departed when winning Confined; well below Open class. **18**

VASILIKI (Irish) — I 208[P], I 330[P]

VATACAN BANK b.g. 11 The Parson - Little Credit by Little Buskins — C S Packer

1995 P(0),P(0),3(0),P(0),3(17),U(-)

355	3/3	Garnons	(L)	INT 3m	10	GS	*alwys rear, t.o. & p.u. 3 out*	P	0
691	30/3	Llanvapley	(L)	CON 3m	15	GS	*rear, no ch frm 10th, p.u. 15th*	P	0
845	6/4	Howick	(L)	CON 3m	12	GF	*alwys rear, fin own time*	5	0
1035	13/4	St Hilary	(R)	CON 3m	10	G	*alwys rear, t.o. 13th*	5	0
1245	27/4	Woodford	(L)	LAD 3m	6	G	*alwys rear, wnt poor 3rd 13th, nvr dang*	3	10
1414	6/5	Cursneh Hill	(L)	LAD 3m	9	GF	*rear frm 6th, lost tch 11th, styd on frm 14th*	4	0
1480	11/5	Bredwardine	(R)	LAD 3m	12	G	*rear frm 4th, rmndrs nxt, lost tch 7th, t.o. & u.r. 15th*	U	-

Safe but outclassed in Ladies/Confineds; no real prospects now. **10**

VELKA b or br.m. 7 Uncle Pokey - Miss Prague by Mon Capitaine — R V Mair

1995 **6(NH),7(NH),8(NH),3(NH),F(NH)**

575	17/3	Detling	(L)	MDO 3m	10	GF	*chsng grp,dist 3rd 4 out,lft 2nd nxt,ld 2 out,sn hdd & outpcd*	2	0
814	6/4	Charing	(L)	MDO 2 1/2m	8	F	*(fav) ld to 4th, cls aft, chal 3 out, ld nxt, hdd flat*	2	12
1299	28/4	Bexhill	(R)	MDO 3m	7	F	*rear, prog to ld apr 8th, clr 4 out, kpt on well*	1	13
1540	16/5	Folkestone	(R)	HC 2m 5f	10	G	*chsd ldr 3rd, left in ld 8th, soon hdd, no hdwy from 3 out.*	5	0

Placed in novice chase; consistent; won 2 finisher race and needs to improve for Restricteds. **14**

VENERDI SANTO (Irish) — I 266[4], I 395[F]

VENETIAN STAR (Irish) — I 90[P], I 166[F]

VENN BOY ch.g. 7 White Prince (USA) - Ace Chance by Blandford Lad — L G Tizzard

284	2/3	Clyst St Ma'	(L)	MDN 3m	11	S	*w.w. prog 10th, in tch 14th, ld 3 out, sn clr, improve*	1	16

562 17/3 Ottery St M' (L) XX 3m 12 G *(fav) 3s-1/1, not fluent, prog 12th, ld 5 out-nxt, outpcd aft* 4 12
650 23/3 Cothelstone (L) RES 3m 5 S *4s-2s, mostly 3rd, blnd 5 out, t.o. whn p.u. 2 out* P 0
1313 28/4 Little Wind' (R) RES 3m 14 G *in tch, cls 7th at 11th, lost plc aft 14th, bhnd & p.u. last* P 0

Hacked up in good time (poor race); disappointing after; young enough to revive; Soft. 16

VENTURE ON (Irish) — **I** 194^{P}, **I** 268^{P}, **I** 346^{P}

VERNOMETUM br.g. 10 Rapid River - Silver Thread by Sayfar J R Cornwall

14 14/1 Cottenham (R) MDO 3m 10 G *ld to 4th, cls up, ran wd apr 10th, wknd 13th, p.u. 3 out* P 0
172 18/2 Market Rase' (L) RES 3m 9 GF *raced wd, ld/disp to 15th, grad wknd* 4 12
241 25/2 Southwell P' (L) MDO 3m 15 HO *ld to 3rd, mid-div whn f 5th* F -

Placed in 94; missed 95; headstrong; novice ridden; more needed for small win. 10

VERY CAVALIER b.g. 5 Cavalier Servente - Wildly Optimistic by Hard Fact Mrs R C Hayward

943 8/4 Andoversford (R) CON 3m 9 GF *last whn f 4th* F -

Unpromising 0

VERY DARING b.g. 6 Derring Rose - La Verite by Vitiges (FR) Miss Rosalind Booth

1995 F(-),F(-),P(0),5(0),P(0),7(0),5(0),3(0),5(0),P(0)

1456 8/5 Uttoxeter (L) HC 2m 5f 11 G *alwys bhnd, t.o. when p.u. before 4 out.* P 0

Late start & hopelessly out of his depth; yet to show any rateable form. 0

VERY EVIDENT (Irish) — **I** 3^{4}, **I** 10^{3}, **I** 48^{P}

VERY TENSE (Irish) — **I** 19^{P}

VIA DEL QUATRO (Irish) — **I** 464^{4}, **I** 548^{2}, **I** 602^{2}, **I** 649^{3}

VIASCORIT ch.g. 14 Aristocracy - Mesena by Pals Passage Miss S French

230 24/2 Heythrop (R) MEM 3m 12 GS *chsd ldrs, wknd aft 7th, bhnd whn p.u. 10th* P 0
1246 27/4 Woodford (L) OPE 3m 6 G *keen hold, ld to 8th, sn bhnd, last & p.u. 13th* P 0
1509 12/5 Maisemore P' (L) OPE 3m 4 F *ld to aft 9th, last frm 12th, t.o. & p.u. 15th* P 0

Winning Irish chaser; well past it now. 0

VICE CAPTAIN (Irish) — **I** 323^{P}

VICTIM OF SLANDER (Irish) — **I** 11^{P}, **I** 42^{P}, **I** 119^{P}, **I** 203^{U}, **I** 239^{6}, **I** 335^{6}, **I** 370^{3}

VIENNA WOODS b.g. 9 Elegant Air - Grace Note by Parthia Miss F K Mudd

1995 **6(NH),F(NH)**

118 17/2 Witton Cast' (R) INT 3m 9 S *rear, prog 10th, 7th & in tch whn b.d. 12th* B -
245 25/2 Southwell P' (L) LAD 3m 8 HO *s.s. trckd ldrs 7th, 8l 4th whn mstk & u.r. 12th* U -
305 2/3 Great Stain' (L) LAD 3m 11 GS *rear whn u.r. 14th* U -
408 9/3 Charm Park (L) MEM 3m 7 G *cls up, lft 2nd 4 out, chsd wnr, jst btn* 2 13
588 23/3 Wetherby Po' (L) INT 3m 17 S *mid-div, blnd 12th, p.u. nxt* P 0
1283 27/4 Easingwold (L) LAD 3m 10 G *sn rear, mstk 5th, wll bhnd whn u.r. 13th* U -
1469 11/5 Easingwold (L) LAD 3m 6 G *prog 7th, fdd 11th, mstk nxt, strgglng whn f 14th* F -

Could not handle the fences & only form in modest Members; unlikely to win 12

VIEW POINT(IRE) br.g. 6 Point North - Dangan View by Bargello Peter Smith

343 3/3 Higham (L) MDO 3m 11 G *t.o. 4th, p.u. 15th* P 0
618 23/3 Higham (L) MDO 3m 14 GF *rear whn u.r. 2nd* U -
675 30/3 Cottenham (R) MEM 3m 6 GF *jmpd slwly, last pair, nrly u.r. 13th, effrt 3 out,wknd nxt* 5 0
898 6/4 Dingley (R) MDN 2m 5f 10 GS *3rd frm 7th, wknd 6 out, b.d. 3 out* B -
1378 5/5 Dingley (R) MDO 2 1/2m 16 GF *in tch, chsd wnr 4 out-aft nxt, wknd, lft 3rd last* 3 10

Only beaten 1 other horse so far; stamina's the problem. 11

VILLANELLA b.m. 6 Seymour Hicks (FR) - Timeless Flight by Prince Hansel Mrs M R Ridley

114 17/2 Lanark (R) MDO 3m 12 GS *in tch til wknd rpdly 4 out* 4 0

Well beaten but a reasonable debut; can do better. 10

VINTAGE LAD b.g. 13 Crash Course - Phaestus Sister by Seminole II A Chinery

418 9/3 High Easter (L) CON 3m 10 S *disp ld to 7th, wknd 11th, mstk 14th, t.o. & p.u. 15th* P 0

Winning hurdler; of no account now. 0

VIRGINIA'S BAY b.g. 10 Uncle Pokey - Carnation by Runnymede D Griffiths

1995 **P(0)**,5(0),7(0),U(-),P(0),C(-),U(-),**P(0)**

142 17/2 Larkhill (R) MXO 3m 9 G *chsd ldrs, wknd 12th, p.u. 14th* P 0
692 30/3 Llanvapley (L) OPE 3m 6 GS *alwys rear, lost tch 10th, p.u. 15th* P 0
1479 11/5 Bredwardine (R) OPE 3m 8 G *chsd ldrs 4th-8th, wknd 10th, p.u. 12th* P 0

No longer of any account 0

VISCOUNT THURLS (Irish) — **I** 23^{1}

VITAL APPROACH (Irish) — I 353F, I 4375, I 5042, I 569U, I 6403, I 6543

VITAL LEGACY b.g. 7 Vital Season - Unto Rose by Cornuto — J Bugg
1995 P(0),U(-),P(0)
254 25/2 Charing (L) MDO 3m 9 GS *f 2nd* F -
470 10/3 Milborne St' (L) MDO 3m 18 G *alwys mid-div, no ch frm 2 out* 7 11
652 23/3 Badbury Rin' (L) MDO 3m 13 G *alwys prom, left in ld 3 out, held on flat* 1 14
816 6/4 Charlton Ho' (L) INT 3m 7 GF *alwys rear, lost tch frm 14th* 6 12
1057 13/4 Badbury Rin' (L) MEM 3m 4 GF *3rd til 13th, lost tch nxt, ref 15th* R -
Fortunately beat 6 others; shown little else & suspect; follow up looks hard. 14

VITAL SHOT b.m. 7 Vital Season - Skilla by Mexico III — M C Hillier
1995 P(0),P(0),P(0)
234 24/2 Heythrop (R) LAD 3m 6 GS *mostly rear, nvr rchd ldrs* 4 0
430 9/3 Upton-On-Se' (R) MDO 3m 15 GS *alwys ldng grp, no ext frm 3 out* 5 0
713 30/3 Barbury Cas' (L) MDO 3m 10 G *alwys rear, t.o. & p.u. 4 out* P 0
997 8/4 Hackwood Pa' (L) MDO 3m 11 GF *ld frm 6th, jnd 2 out, held on, all out* 1 13
1189 21/4 Tweseldown (R) RES 3m 10 GF *4s-5/2, twrds rear whn p.u. aft 4th* P 0
Beat a subsequent winner but form is weak; problems last start; more needed for weak Restricted. 14

VITAL SONG 10 — M H Dare
1995 4(0),4(10),1(16),8(0)
65 10/2 Great Treth' (R) INT 3m 13 S *ld/disp 2nd-8th, no ext frm 3 out* 3 17
297 2/3 Great Treth' (R) INT 3m 10 G *ld to 16th, 3rd frm 3 out, styd on gamely flat* 2 23
472 10/3 Milborne St' (L) INT 3m 8 G *made all, ran on well frm 2 out* 1 22
654 23/3 Badbury Rin' (L) OPE 3m 5 G *(fav) made all, clr frm 14th, not extnd, easily* 1 24
817 6/4 Charlton Ho' (L) OPE 3m 5 GF *(fav) ld til aft 3 out, rlld apr last, not qckn aft* 2 24
1275 27/4 Bratton Down (L) OPE 3m 8 GF *ld til apr last,hdd,rallied & ran on wll,fin 1st,disq* 2 26
1589 25/5 Mounsey Hil' (R) OPE 3m 12 G *(fav) ld til hdd & pckd 17th, styd on onepcd frm 2 out* 2 24
Improved & now useful; front runs, game & stays; worth a try in H/chase; G/S-F. 25

VITAL WITNESS(CAN) b.g. 9 Val de L'orne (FR) - Friendly Witness (USA) by Northern Dancer — M C Ashton
1995 **10(NH),P(NH)**
435 9/3 Newton Brom' (R) OPE 3m 7 GS *cls 2nd til lost plc 14th,ran on 3 out,fin well* 3 18
Lightly raced; ran well only start (novice ridden) but promptly disappeared; best watched 17

VITAL WONDER ch.g. 8 Vital Season - Honey Wonder by Winden — J Parfitt
1995 **P(NH)**
1224 24/4 Brampton Br' (R) MDO 3m 17 G *jmpd nvcy in rr, nvr rch ldrs, p.u. 13th* P 0
1484 11/5 Bredwardine (R) MDO 3m 17 G *s.s. mstk & u.r. 3rd* U -
No signs yet. 0

VIVIENNES JOY (Irish) — I 5753

VOLCANIC DANCER(USA) b.g. 10 Northern Baby (CAN) - Salva (USA) by Secretariat (USA) — Mrs J Ashmole
880 6/4 Brampton Br' (R) XX 3m 8 GF *strtd 3 fences bhnd, p.u. 13th* P 0
1043 13/4 Bitterley (L) OPE 3m 9 G *(bl) started 3 fences bhnd (again), p.u. 2nd* P 0
1265 27/4 Pyle (R) OPE 3m 8 G *wppd round & u.r. start, rmntd, p.u. 13th* P 0
Winning hurdler; beyond recall now. 0

VOLDI (Irish) — I 18P, I 1754, I 2352, I 3034, I 338F, I 3633

VULCAN STAR ch.g. 10 Royal Vulcan - Star Shell by Queen's Hussar — G Morson
580 20/3 Towcester (R) HC 2 3/4m 5 G *soon t.o..* 3 12
1107 15/4 Southwell (L) HC 3m 110yds 10 G *in rear when blnd and u.r. 2nd.* U -
1228 27/4 Worcester (L) HC 2m 7f 17 G *t.o. when p.u. before 4 out.* P 0
Promise 92/4 but missed 95 & comeback singularly unsuccessful 11

VULGAN PRINCE b.g. 8 Scorpio (FR) - Burton Princess by Prince Barle — D R Greig
1995 3(11)
3 13/1 Larkhill (R) MDO 3m 10 GS *hld up, mstk 12th, prog to 3rd 14th, chal last,brshd aside* 2 14
477 10/3 Tweseldown (R) MDO 3m 15 G *(fav) bhnd, mstk 14th, styd on frm 4 out, nrst fin* 3 10
522 16/3 Larkhill (R) MDO 3m 12 G *prom, mstk 8th, unable qckn frm 3 out* 4 15
712 30/3 Barbury Cas' (L) MDO 3m 10 G *(fav) handy, chsd wnr 11th, outpcd frm 4 out* 2 0
994 8/4 Hackwood Pa' (L) MEM 3m 4 GF *in rear, jmp rght, rddn 12th, fdd* 3 0
1374 4/5 Peper Harow (L) MDO 3m 8 F *in tch til u.r. 6th* U -
Changed handsadually getting worse; may atone with stronger handling. 12

VULTORO b.g. 13 Torus - Vulace by Vulgan — T D B Underwood
1995 1(11),P(0),P(0),P(0),5(12),3(0),P(0),1(17),1(18),1(15),1(17),P(0)
251 25/2 Charing (L) OPE 3m 10 GS *s.s. alwys t.o., p.u. 2 out* P 0

476 10/3 Tweseldown (R) OPE 3m 7 G *2nd to 9th, grad wknd, t.o. 2 out* 3 10
595 23/3 Parham (R) OPE 3m 12 GS *alwys rear & strgglng to stay in tch, p.u. 13th* P 0
785 31/3 Tweseldown (R) OPE 3m 5 G *cls up, ld 6th, clr 4 out, 15l clr whn blnd & u.r. last* U 18
1188 21/4 Tweseldown (R) OPE 3m 6 GF *plld, ld 3rd, jmpd lft frm 10th, hdd 13th, wknd frm 4 out* 4 13
1296 28/4 Bexhill (R) OPE 3m 4 F *restrnd, ld apr 7th-aft 11th, wknd 2 out, fin 2nd, disq* 2D 17

Only effective in weak races (won 4 in 95); unlucky in same 96 & can win again; G-Hy. 17

WAIPIRO ch.g. 6 Doulab (USA) - Kundrie (GER) by Luciano Mrs C A Furse
1995 **16(NH),13(NH)**

4 13/1 Larkhill (R) MDO 3m 9 GS *last whn f 6th* F -
69 10/2 Great Treth' (R) MDO 3m 12 S *alwys cls up, ev ch 2 out, no ext, promising* 2 12
200 24/2 Lemalla (R) MDO 3m 12 HY *(fav) alwys going wll, ld 4 out, in cmmnd aft, easily* 1 15
466 10/3 Milborne St' (L) RES 3m 13 G *mid-div til blnd & u.r. 7th* U -
627 23/3 Kilworthy (L) RES 3m 13 GS *nvr nrr ldrs, lost tch 12th, p.u. 15th* P 0
707 30/3 Barbury Cas' (L) RES 3m 18 G *rear, outpcd frm 10th, t.o. & p.u. 3 out* P 0

Slogged home in mud; no form after & mud looks essential; win Restricted when conditions right. 15

WALKERS POINT b.g. 10 Le Moss - Saltee Star by Arapaho T D H Hughes
1995 0D(20),1(21),1(20),1(19),3(17),2(17)

42 3/2 Wadebridge (L) CON 3m 8 GF *ld to 8th, 11-13th & aft nxt, rdn clr 3 out, styd on* 1 20
196 24/2 Lemalla (R) CON 3m 14 HY *ld/disp frm 4th til hdd 3 out, onepcd aft* 4 19
623 23/3 Kilworthy (L) MEM 3m 4 GS *(fav) made all, slw jmps 3 & 11th (ditch), shkn up & drw clr 2 out* 1 16
715 30/3 Wadebridge (L) CON 3m 8 GF *(fav) prom, cls 2nd whn f 10th* F -
1069 13/4 Lifton (R) CON 3m 9 S *(fav) prom, disp 6-14th, slght ld und pres 2 out,hdd & no ext last* 2 18
1142 20/4 Flete Park (R) CON 3m 11 S *in tch, cls 3rd 14th, wknd grad frm 3 out* 2 14
1622 27/5 Lifton (R) CON 3m 14 GS *(fav) in tch, 4th 3 out, chal und pres & just ld last, drvn out* 1 20

Game & stays & likes to dictate; won 6 of last 12 but hard ride now; should win again; Good/Hy 20

WALKONTHEMOON ch.m. 7 Coquelin (USA) - Lunar Eclipse by Hot Spark M F Loggin

709 30/3 Barbury Cas' (L) OPE 3m 15 G *sn rear, t.o. & p.u. 11th* P 0
886 6/4 Kimble (L) CON 3m 5 GF *alwys last, t.o. 12th* 5 0
1500 11/5 Kingston Bl' (L) CON 3m 7 G *chsg grp, rdn 10th, no ch aft 13th* 6 0

.. 0

WALL GAME(USA) ch.g. 11 Quiet Fling (USA) - Eton Song (USA) by Etonian J S Delahooke
1995 4(17),2(17),4(14),1+(17),3(13)

85 11/2 Alnwick (L) LAD 3m 11 GS *mstk 8th, prom til wknd rpdly aft 3 out* 6 10
117 17/2 Witton Cast' (R) MEM 3m 9 S *ld to 6th, outpcd 8th, 4th 2 out, styd on apr last, 3rd flat* 3 16
227 24/2 Duncombe Pa' (R) LAD 3m 6 GS *in tch, 3rd & rdn 3 out, kpt on flat* 3 17
586 23/3 Wetherby Po' (L) LAD 3m 8 S *alwys rear, t.o. & p.u. 10th* P 0
824 6/4 Stainton (R) CON 3m 11 GF *(bl) mid-div, rdn 9th, sn strgglng, t.o. & p.u. last* P 0
1452 6/5 Witton Cast' (R) MEM 3m 7 G *cls up, wknd 4 out, rear whn ran out 2 out* r -

Formerly very useful; schoolmaster now & declined greatly; another win looks hard now. 15

WALLY'S GIRL b.m. 7 Nestor - Vallee Des Roses by Dubassoff (USA) D B Curran

1470 11/5 Easingwold (L) MDO 3m 10 G *dtchd 8th, t.o. & p.u. 14th* P 0

No signs of ability in 4 outings in 3 seasons. 0

WALLY WREKIN ch.g. 13 Peter Wrekin - Winning Venture by Eastern Venture Mrs C R Dutton
1995 3(13),**4(0)**,3(14),2(17),3(14),B(-),1(18),**P(0)**

285 2/3 Eaton Hall (R) MEM 3m 5 G *ld til u.r. 4th* U -
500 16/3 Lanark (R) OPE 3m 6 G *(bl) made all, kpt on wll* 1 17
894 6/4 Whittington (L) OPE 3m 5 F *(fav) (bl) held up, n.j.w., ev ch whn chal 2 out to last, no ext* 2 17
1031 13/4 Alpraham (R) MXO 3m 5 GS *(bl) in tch to 12th, t.o. nxt* 4 0

Formerly decent; found weak Opens 95/96; stays well but win at 14 may beyond him; not firm. 16

WALSHESTOWN (Irish) — **I** 103^{P}
WANCLASSTRAIN (Irish) — **I** 172^{P}, **I** 321^{P}, **I** 415^{P}, **I** 456^{P}, **I** 539^{P}
WANDERING CHOICE (Irish) — **I** 418^{P}, **I** 556^{P}
WANG HOW b.g. 8 Nishapour (FR) - Killifreth by Jimmy Reppin A J Barnett
1995 P(0),2(0)

194 24/2 Friars Haugh (L) MDN 3m 11 S *6th hlfwy, no imp on ldrs* 3 0
399 9/3 Dalston (R) CON 3m 9 G *cls 3rd at 4th, prom tl outpcd frm 15th* 5 0
503 16/3 Lanark (R) MDO 3m 10 G *mid-div whn u..r 9th* U -

Beaten a long way when completing; barely worth a rating. 10

WAR BARON ch.g. 7 Baron Blakeney - Red Lady by Warpath Mrs C E G Bonner

732 31/3 Little Wind' (R) INT 3m 6 GS *bhnd til p.u. apr 10th* P 0

1081	13/4	Cothelstone	(L)	MDN	3m	4	GF	*(fav) rear, mstk 15th, no ch whn p.u. last*	P	0

No signs of ability; even when favourite for dreadful race on last start. 0

WAR HEAD b.g. 13 Warpath - Foil by Bleep-Bleep — T Collins

409	9/3	Charm Park	(L)	CON	3m	11	G	*mid-div early, fdd, p.u. 11th*	P	0
512	16/3	Dalton Park	(R)	CON	3m	10	G	*rear frm 7th, t.o. & p.u. 13th*	P	0
588	23/3	Wetherby Po'	(L)	INT	3m	17	S	*rear by 10th, t.o. & p.u. 13th*	P	0

No missile now 0

WARKEY LADY (Irish) — I 132[P], I 225[2], I 417[3]

WARKSWOODMAN gr.g. 8 Zambrano - Amberama by Sweet Ration — Mrs Helen Dickson

321	2/3	Corbridge	(R)	MDN	3m	12	GS	*ld 4th, disp & ev ch til wknd 2 out*	5	0
704	30/3	Tranwell	(L)	MDO	3m	16	GS	*bhnd, prog 10th, styd on frm 3 out, not rch ldrs*	3	13
1087	14/4	Friars Haugh	(L)	MDO	3m	9	F	*3rd hlfwy, outpcd 3 out, styd on agn apr last*	3	14

Gets round safely but only better than last once; reliability may see him home one day. 13

WARLOCKFOE (Irish) — I 64[P], I 77[P], I 119[P], I 151[P]

WARM RELATION(IRE) b.g. 5 Nepotism - Summerello by Bargello — C C Trietline

431	9/3	Upton-On-Se'	(R)	MDO	3m	17	GS	*n.j.w. rear & p.u. 13th*	P	0
542	17/3	Southwell P'	(L)	MDO	3m	15	GS	*ld to 3rd, in tch to 13th, p.u. 4 out*	P	0
900	6/4	Dingley	(R)	MDN	2m 5f	8	GS	*3rd frm 1st, wknd qckly 10th, p.u. nxt*	P	0
1416	6/5	Cursneh Hill	(L)	MDO	3m	9	GF	*chsd ldrs, ev ch til not qckn frm 14th, kpt on*	3	10

Beaten 13 lengths when completing; young & needs to improve to win. 10

WARNER FORPLEASURE b.g. 10 Lighter - Gay Park by Pardigras — G W Briscoe

579	20/3	Ludlow	(R)	HC	2 1/2m	17	G	*(bl) prom to hfwy, soon bhnd, p.u. before 5 out.*	P	0
737	31/3	Sudlow Farm	(R)	OPE	3m	4	G	*(bl) chsd ldr to 7th & 11-12th, sn lost tch, p.u. 3 out*	P	0
908	8/4	Hereford	(R)	HC	2m 3f	12	GF	*(bl) prom, ld 6th, rdn and hdd 4 out, soon wknd.*	6	0
1221	24/4	Brampton Br'	(R)	LAD	3m	6	G	*(bl) cl up til wknd 13th, p.u. 15th*	P	0
1336	1/5	Cheltenham	(L)	HC	2m 110yds	9	G	*(bl) ld 1st, chsd ldr to 3rd, well bhnd 8th, t.o. and p.u. before 3 out.*	P	0
1338	3/5	Bangor	(L)	HC	3m 110yds	8	S	*(bl) ld, reminders after 3rd, clr to 8th, hdd after next, wknd quickly 12th, t.o. when mstk next, p.u. before 3 out.*	P	0
1455	8/5	Uttoxeter	(L)	HC	2m 5f	9	G	*in tch, rdn 9th, wknd apr 12th, t.o. when p.u. before 4 out.*	P	0

Selling hurdle winner 93; no prospects now. 0

WARNER FOR SPORT b.g. 7 Mandalus - Joy Travel by Ete Indien (USA) — R O Bishop

1995 **U(NH),14(NH)**

1149	20/4	Higham	(L)	MDO	3m	10	F	*bhnd frm 8th, t.o. & p.u. 11th*	P	0
1445	6/5	Aldington	(L)	MDO	3m	8	HD	*ld to 6th, last final cct, t.o. 4 out, u.r. last*	U	-

No signs of ability. 0

WARNING CALL (Irish) — I 13[P], I 57[1], I 72[5], I 186[3], I 276[1]

WARREN BOY b.g. 6 Hotfoot - Artaius Rose (FR) by Artaius (USA) — F J Ayres

1995 4(0),6(0),U(-)

391	9/3	Llanfrynach	(R)	MDN	3m	11	GS	*(fav) mstks, ld aft 1st, drew clr frm 15th, promising*	1	16
548	17/3	Erw Lon	(L)	RES	3m	8	GS	*(fav) made all, easily*	1	19
691	30/3	Llanvapley	(L)	CON	3m	15	GS	*(fav) ld to 13th, chsd wnr til wknd rpdly 15th, p.u. nxt*	P	0
1491	11/5	Erw Lon	(L)	XX	3m	2	F	*(fav) ld to 10th & agn aft 13th whn lft alone*	1	16

Progressive front runner; wide margin wins in modest races; looks sure to upgrade; S-F. 20

WARRENSTOWN LASS (Irish) — I 20[F]

WARRIOR BARD(IRE) ch.g. 6 Black Minstrel - Enco's War by Tug Of War — Mrs M A Puddick

1995 **P(NH),P(NH),P(NH)**

128	17/2	Kingston Bl'	(L)	RES	3m	14	GS	*hld up, prog 10th, ld 13th, clr 15th, styd on well*	1	19

Showed little under Rules but won well on pointing debut; vanished after & best watched 97 18

WASHAKIE gr.g. 11 Warpath - Super Satin by Lord Of Verona — Mrs F T Walton

1995 1(16),P(0),7(0),P(0)

46	4/2	Alnwick	(L)	MEM	3m	7	G	*trckd ldrs, ld 8th, rdn 2 out, hld on gmly*	1	21
86	11/2	Alnwick	(L)	OPE	3m	8	GS	*cls up,outpcd whn blnd 15th,rallied strngly 2 out,ld nr fin*	1	25
487	16/3	Newcastle	(L)	HC	3m	10	GS	*(Co fav) held up, gd hdwy 8th, outpcd after 3 out, hung left, styd on well from last.*	2	24
790	1/4	Kelso	(L)	HC	3m 1f	11	GF	*in tch one cct, soon outpcd and driven along, kept on from 3 out, no impn.*	4	19
912	8/4	Tranwell	(L)	OPE	3m	8	GF	*(fav) chsd ldng pair, cls up 4 out, ld & mstk nxt, clr 2 out*	1	22
1337	1/5	Kelso	(L)	HC	3m 1f	9	S	*mstks, in tch when blnd 13th, soon wknd, t.o..*	6	0
1573	19/5	Corbridge	(R)	OPE	3m	12	G	*(fav) mid-div, prog 4 out, disp last, drvn to ld nr fin gamely*	1	22

H/Chase winner 93; revived & decent now; goes well fresh & likes Alnwick; win more; G/F-G/S. 23

WASSL'S NANNY(IRE) b.m. 7 Wassl - Granny's Bank by Music Boy — Miss C Woodmass
1995 **8(NH),7(NH)**

53	4/2 Alnwick	(L) MDO 3m	13 G	*mid-div, 6th whn u.r. 11th*	U	-
123	17/2 Witton Cast'	(R) MDO 3m	11 S	*rear whn mstk & u.r. 9th*	U	-
322	2/3 Corbridge	(R) MDN 3m	10 GS	*cls 4th frm 8th, prom, strng chal 2 out, wknd last*	3	11
705	30/3 Tranwell	(L) MDO 3m	9 GS	*bhnd, prog 14th, disp nxt til bmpd 3 out, not rcvr*	4	11
915	8/4 Tranwell	(L) MDO 3m	7 GF	*(fav) nvr on terms wth ldrs, 20l 3rd hlfwy, und pres 5 out, no imp*	3	0

Poor novice hurdler; beaten 7 lengths minimum; poor run last start(ground); may find a small win. 11

WATCHIT LAD b.g. 6 El-Birillo - Watch Lady by Home Guard (USA) — Mrs A Price

256	29/2 Ludlow	(R) HC 3m	14 G	*t.o. 10th, no ch when f last.*	F	-
366	6/3 Bangor	(L) HC 3m 110yds	4 GS	*in tch, disp 3rd and staying on when f 7 out.*	F	-
799	3/4 Ludlow	(R) HC 3m	8 GF	*bhnd when blnd and u.r. 6th.*	U	-
1045	13/4 Bitterley	(L) MDO 3m	16 G	*alwys rear, late prog frm 15th*	6	0
1225	24/4 Brampton Br'	(R) MDO 3m	18 G	*rr & mstk 8th, mod prog 13th, no ch whn f 16th*	F	-

A glimmer of hope in Maidens but too clumsy so far. 10

WATERCOURSE (Irish) — **I** 496^{4}

WATER FONT (Irish) — **I** 274^{F}, **I** 307^{2}

WATERHAY b.g. 13 Callernish - Crookhaven by Arctic Slave — Mrs S Bailey
1995 5(14),6(0),U(-),r(-),7(0),5(10),3(0),1(15),P(0),4(11),5(11),5(0)

235	24/2 Heythrop	(R) RES 3m	10 GS	*prom til lost plc hlfwy, bhnd whn p.u. 14th*	P	0
338	3/3 Heythrop	(R) RES 3m	9 G	*wll bhnd 9th, sn t.o.*	5	0
437	9/3 Newton Brom'	(R) RES 3m	9 GS	*ld to 9th, 3rd hlfwy, btn whn f 15th*	F	-
1438	6/5 Ashorne	(R) XX 3m	14 G	*alwys bhnd, t.o. 7th*	9	0
1564	19/5 Mollington	(R) XX 3m	14 GS	*cls up to 12th, t.o. 3 out*	10	0
1595	25/5 Garthorpe	(R) CON 3m	15 G	*abt 6th 1st m, fdd 7th, mstk 12th, p.u. nxt*	P	0
1640	2/6 Dingley	(R) RES 3m	9 GF	*rr til u.r. 7th*	U	-

Won poor Maiden 95; follow up chances are virtually nil. 0

WATERLOO PRINCESS (Irish) — **I** 182^{P}

WATT A BUZZ (Irish) — **I** 41^{P}, **I** 59^{R}

WATTASUPRISEFORUS ch.g. 6 Wonderful Surprise - Miss Anax by Anax — Mrs J Neath

353	3/3 Garnons	(L) MDN 2 1/2m	7 GS	*alwys rear, lost tch 9th, p.u. 3 out*	P	0

No signs on debut. 0

WAY OF LIFE(FR) ch.g. 11 No Lute (FR) - My Beloved (FR) by Margouillat (FR) — John Ferguson
1995 2(14),1(14),3(16),5(12),3(16),**6(13)**,3(16),1(20),**5(0)**,**U(-)**

31	20/1 Higham	(L) CON 3m	9 GF	*nvr put in race, sme prog 13th, no dang*	5	10
104	17/2 Marks Tey	(L) OPE 3m	14 G	*chsd ldrs til blnd & u.r. 13th*	U	-
418	9/3 High Easter	(L) CON 3m	10 S	*prom, ld 8th-13th, grad wknd frm 16th*	4	13
489	16/3 Horseheath	(R) MEM 3m	4 GF	*sttld bhnd ldr, ld 7th-10th, ld 4 out, blnd 2 out, all out*	1	15
907	8/4 Fakenham	(L) HC 3m 110yds	11 G	*soon bhnd, mstk 13th, t.o. when p.u. before 2 out.*	P	0

Declined in 96n bad 2 finisher Members; barely stays & Members best hope again.Good. 16

WAYS AND MEANS b.m. 9 Oedipus Complex - Snow Mountain by Mountain Call — Mrs S Mollett
1995 F(-),1(18),1(17)

168	18/2 Market Rase'	(L) MEM 3m	7 GF	*trckd ldrs 7th, 4th & outpcd 11th, no ch aft*	3	14
324	3/3 Market Rase'	(L) MEM 3m	4 G	*(fav) trckd ldrs, hit 14th, ld 2 out, clr last, easily*	1	15
513	16/3 Dalton Park	(R) OPE 3m	9 G	*made most frm 3-15th, outpcd by wnr 4 out, kpt on*	3	20
632	23/3 Market Rase'	(L) CON 3m	10 GF	*alwys prom, 2nd frm 11th, chal 4 out, ld flat, just outpcd*	2	21
1022	13/4 Brocklesby '	(L) CON 3m	6 GF	*(fav) w.w., last pair for 2 m, prog 4 out, ld 2 out, comf*	1	20

Improved; well placed; consistent & can win more Confineds;4 wins at Market Rasen.G-G/F. 21

WAYSIDE BOY b.g. 11 Deep Run - Ciotog by Varano — D J Caro
1995 1(20),4(17),P(0)

260	1/3 Newbury	(L) HC 3m	6 GS	*hit 4th, t.o. 8th, p.u. after 13th.*	P	0
637	23/3 Siddington	(L) MEM 3m	14 S	*trkd ldrs, 4th & rddn 3 out, onepcd*	4	13

Restricted winner 95; has problems; ran passably in Members but win not easy now.G/S-S. 15

WAYSIDE SPIN (Irish) — **I** 173^{P}, **I** 283^{S}, **I** 409^{1}, **I** 537^{P}

WAYWARD EDWARD ch.g. 10 Takachiho - Portate by Articulate — J Turnbull
1995 **P(NH),7(NH),P(NH),U(NH),5(NH),5(NH),5(NH),5(NH),3(NH)**

1201	21/4 Lydstep	(L) MDN 3m	9 S	*ld/disp to 2 out, rallied flat, just hld*	2	15
1390	6/5 Pantyderi	(R) MDO 3m	15 GF	*alwys mid-div, p.u. 14th*	P	0

Poor & disappointing novice hurdler/chaser; 2nd to good horse; could win if he wanted to. 14

WAYWARD KING (Irish) — I 274², I 330⁴

WAYWARD SAILOR ch.g. 10 Julio Mariner - Tempest Girl by Caliban — Miss C Spearing

128	17/2	Kingston Bl'	(L)	RES	3m	14 GS	*sn prom, 4th & outpcd aft 13th, kpt on*	3	13
358	3/3	Garnons	(L)	RES	3m	18 GS	*ld 7th til jnd 13th, lft in ld nxt, hdd 2 out, kpt on well*	2	16
904	6/4	Dingley	(R)	RES	3m	20 GS	*(bl) prom bhnd ldrs, 5th 6 out, ran on, not rch wnnr*	2	19
1001	9/4	Upton-On-Se'	(R)	MEM	3m	6 F	*(bl) not fluent, chsd ld 14th, slpd app 3 out, ev ch, not qckn*	2	14
1178	21/4	Mollington	(R)	RES	3m	7 F	*(Jt fav) (bl) cls up, prssd wnr 9-11th, slw jmps aft & not qckn*	2	16
1439	6/5	Ashorne	(R)	RES	3m	11 G	*(bl) mstks, prom to 7th, outpcd 12th, no prog aft*	7	12
1641	2/6	Dingley	(R)	RES	3m	13 GF	*(bl) rr, mstk 8th, blndrd 11th, p.u. nxt*	P	0

Maiden winner 93; placed under rules since; ungenuine and unlikely to consent to win again. 14

WEAK MOMENT (Irish) — I 137³, I 188³, I 312², I 437²

WEDDICAR LADY b.m. 10 Strong Gale - Tip Your Toes by Prince Tenderfoot (USA) — Mrs M Armstrong

1995 **F(-)**,P(0),5(11),3(0),**12(0)**,P(0),U(-),4(0),**4(15)**

52	4/2	Alnwick	(L)	MDO	3m	11 G	*made most til 9th, prom aft, one pace 3 out*	3	10
183	19/2	Musselburgh	(R)	HC	3m	5 GF	*ld to 3rd, dropped rear after 10th, gradually lost tch, t.o..*	5	0
316	2/3	Corbridge	(R)	MEM	3m	10 GS	*disp 3rd, prom whn mstk 11th, styd on frm 2 out*	3	10
403	9/3	Dalston	(R)	RES	3m	11 G	*prom at 6th, nt go pc frm 14th*	7	0
789	1/4	Kelso	(L)	HC	3m 1f	11 GF	*settld with chasing gp, blnd and u.r. 11th.*	U	-
862	6/4	Alnwick	(L)	MDN	3m	8 GF	*prom, ld 7-15th, no ext*	2	10
1461	9/5	Sedgefield	(L)	HC	2m 5f	10 F	*soon bhnd, reminders after 7th, some late hdwy, n.d..*	6	10
1575	19/5	Corbridge	(R)	MDO	3m	10 G	*prom til rdn & wknd 10th, bhnd whn p.u. 2 out*	P	0

A maiden after 25 attempts; moody & need luck to win now. 11

WEEJUMPAWUD b.m. 6 Jumbo Hirt (USA) - Weewumpawud by King Log — Aj Carnegie

51	4/2	Alnwick	(L)	MDO	3m	17 G	*tckd ldrs, ld 12th-2 out, lft in ld last, all out*	1	15
188	24/2	Friars Haugh	(L)	RES	3m	12 S	*(fav) 2nd whn mstk 14th, lost plc & p.u. aft nxt*	P	0
1472	11/5	Aspatria	(L)	RES	3m	8 GF	*pullng, mstks, prom to 11th, t.o. whn p.u. 2 out*	P	0

Half-sister to Wudimp; won decent race in good time; struggling after but can improve. 13

WEJEM (Irish) — I 191², I 269¹

WELCOME CALL (Irish) — I 38¹, I 65¹

WELLANE BOY (Irish) — I 5¹, I 51¹

WELL ARMED (Irish) — I 224¹, I 278ᴾ

WELL DOCTOR (Irish) — I 293ᴾ

WELLINGTON BAY b.g. 10 Tachypous - Julie Emma by Farm Walk — L R Vine

1995 3(16),P(0)

250	25/2	Charing	(L)	LAD	3m	12 GS	*prom to 15th, wkng whn p.u. 4 out*	P	0
271	2/3	Parham	(R)	CON	3m	15 GF	*alwys rear, wll bhnd whn p.u. 2 out*	P	0
572	17/3	Detling	(L)	LAD	3m	10 GF	*rear, prog 10th, 5th & no ch whn u.r. 3 out*	U	-
596	23/3	Parham	(R)	LAD	3m	8 GS	*rear,out of tch 13th,rdn & styd on 4 out,2nd 2 out, ld flat*	1	17
919	8/4	Aldington	(L)	LAD	3m	4 F	*ld, jnd 12th, outjmpd wnr aft, hdd last, ran on und pres*	2	17

Won 4 in 94; revived in late season; consistent when right; may win again;G/S-F. 18

WELL RECOVERED (Irish) — I 89, , I 98ᴾ, I 268ᴾ, I 298ᴾ, I 628⁴, I 634ᴾ

WELL TIMED ch.g. 6 Relkino - Cherry Meringue by Birdbrook — Mrs G A Robarts

1995 **P(NH)**

132	17/2	Ottery St M'	(L)	MDN	3m	9 GS	*sn rear, t.o. & p.u. 3 out*	P	0
447	9/3	Haldon	(R)	MDO	3m	13 S	*ld/disp frm 5th, hdd 3 out, renewed effrt last, sn clr*	1	16
627	23/3	Kilworthy	(L)	RES	3m	13 GS	*mstk 3rd,cls up,outpcd 15th,styd on to chs wnr last,ran on*	2	18
1113	17/4	Hockworthy	(L)	RES	3m	11 GS	*(fav) rr, rdn 10th, 7th whn blndrd 11th, no ch & p.u. 14th*	P	0
1454	7/5	Newton Abbot	(L)	HC	2m 5f 110yds	8 GS	*held up in rear, hdwy when mstk 5 out, no impn from 3 out.*	3	19

Progressive & 2nd in hot Restricted but ran badly next time; easily good enough to win agian 97ft 19

WELSH CLOVER b.m. 8 Cruise Missile - National Clover by National Trust — Michael H Ings

1995 P(0),2(0),1(14),3(0),U(-),P(0)

217	24/2	Newtown	(L)	RES	3m	17 GS	*chsd ldrs, lost tch aft 13th, p.u. 15th*	P	0
357	3/3	Garnons	(L)	RES	3m	14 GS	*made most to 12th, outpcd frm nxt, tired whn ref 2 out*	R	-
387	9/3	Llanfrynach	(R)	RES	3m	11 GS	*cls up to 11th, sn wknd, t.o. & p.u. 2 out*	P	0
599	23/3	Howick	(L)	RES	3m	7 S	*mid-div, wknd hlfwy, p.u. 14th*	P	0
952	8/4	Eyton-On-Se'	(L)	RES	3m	7 GF	*cls up,disp 10th,ld 11-12th,wknd qckly frm 4 out,p.u. last*	P	0
1223	24/4	Brampton Br'	(R)	RES	3m	11 G	*prom to 12th, wknd nxt, p.u. 16th*	P	0
1314	28/4	Bitterley	(L)	MEM	3m	13 G	*mid-div, cls 5th at 10th, rdn 12th, wknd & p.u. 15th*	P	0
1410	6/5	Cursneh Hill	(L)	MEM	3m	4 GF	*chsd ldr, hit 4th & 11th, wknd 15th, lft 2nd last*	2	0
1601	25/5	Bassaleg	(R)	RES	3m	12 GS	*3rd at 7th, wknd rpdly, p.u. 10th*	P	0

Won poor Maiden 95; does not stay & awful in 96; can only be watched. 10

WELSH LANE (Irish) — I 603,

WELSH LEGION b.g. 11 Welsh Saint - Beau Jo by Joshua — G W Lewis

1995 **2(17)**,**8(0)**,1(22),**3(18)**,**4(0)**,**1(23)**,**P(0)**

25	20/1	Barbury Cas'	(L)	OPE	3m	14 GS	*hld up, prog frm 12th, disp 2nd aft 3 out, wknd last*	3	26
98	12/2	Hereford	(R)	HC	3m 1f 110yds	12 HY	*held up, hdwy 10th, wknd 15th, t.o. when p.u. before 3 out.*	P	0
256	29/2	Ludlow	(R)	HC	3m	14 G	*well bhnd 10th, some prog 13th, f next.*	F	-
602	23/3	Howick	(L)	OPE	3m	11 S	*(fav) hld up, prog to ld 11th, made rest, alwys in cmmnd*	1	23
846	6/4	Howick	(L)	OPE	3m	7 GF	*(fav) hld up, steady prog to 2nd 15th, ld nxt, easily*	1	24
1211	23/4	Chepstow	(L)	HC	3m	13 S	*ld to 4th, mstk and lost pl 11th, hdwy to chase wnr 14th, wknd 3 out.*	2	22
1333	1/5	Cheltenham	(L)	HC	3m 1f 110yds	13 G	*mid div, prog 12th, 4th and rdn apr 3 out, no progress.*	4	23
1534	15/5	Hereford	(R)	HC	3m 1f 110yds	4 F	*alwys prom, ld 12th, rdn out.*	1	27
1631	1/6	Stratford	(L)	HC	3 1/2m	14 GF	*not fluent, mid div when blnd 7th, bhnd when mstk 13th.*	6	21

Decent performer; won 3 of 4 points 95/6; fair H/Chaser but hard to place; should win more; G-F 27

WELSH LIGHTNING b or br.g. 8 Lighter - Welsh Log by King Log — B W Leighton

1995 P(0)

749	31/3	Upper Sapey	(R)	MDO	3m	17 GS	*disp to 11th, wknd rpdly frm 15th*	9	0
1047	13/4	Bitterley	(L)	MDO	3m	13 G	*in tch til no prog 11th, no ch 14th, p.u. 3 out*	P	0

Does not stay & of no account. 0

WELSHMANS CANYON(IRE) b.g. 6 Anita's Prince - Malibu Lady by Ragapan — Dr D B A Silk

275	2/3	Parham	(R)	MDN	3m	15 GF	*rear, losing tch whn p.u. 9th*	P	0
575	17/3	Detling	(L)	MDO	3m	10 GF	*bhnd whn f 13th*	F	-
781	31/3	Penshurst	(L)	MDN	3m	11 GS	*mstks in rear, wll bhnd whn p.u. 13th*	P	0
1210	21/4	Heathfield	(R)	MDO	3m	13 F	*in tch, blnd 10th, wll bhnd whn p.u. 14th*	P	0

Yet to show anything; successful stable and could do better. 0

WELSHMAN'S CREEK ch.g. 10 Orchestra - Malibu Lady by Ragapan — Dr D B A Silk

1995 P(0),2(15)

56	10/2	Cottenham	(R)	OPE	3m	12 GS	*sttld mid-div, effrt & in tch 15th, wknd nxt*	6	12

Dual winner 94; only 3 runs since; stamina doubtful; blinkers; best watched if returning; G-S. 17

WELSHMAN'S GULLY ch.g. 12 Jasmine Star - Malibu Lady by Ragapan — Dr D B A Silk

1995 P(0),**U(-)**,**3(23)**,**3(20)**

577	19/3	Fontwell	(R)	HC	2m 3f	5 GF	*alwys bhnd, t.o. when p.u. after 4 out.*	P	0
775	31/3	Penshurst	(L)	CON	3m	8 GS	*trckd ldrs, wknd 14th, bhnd whn p.u. aft 3 out*	P	0
918	8/4	Aldington	(L)	CON	3m	4 F	*prssd ldr, ld 12th til hdd & wknd 3 out*	3	14
1146	20/4	Higham	(L)	OPE	3m	7 F	*rear, lost tch 13th, wll bhnd whn p.u. 16th*	P	0

Formerly decent; declining now & another win looks unlikely. 14

WELSH ROYAL(IRE) b.g. 5 Welsh Term - Royal Miami — John L Lewis

1995 **16(NH)**,**10(NH)**

156	17/2	Erw Lon	(L)	RES	3m	13 G	*schoold rear, f 14th*	F	-

Ex Irish; learning on debut; not seen again. 0

WELSH SINGER ch.g. 10 Celtic Cone - Madam Butterfly by Deep Run — K B Rogers

1995 6(0),2(23),1(23),2(23),2(24),F(-)

32	20/1	Higham	(L)	OPE	3m	15 GF	*hit 2nd, alwys wll bhnd, kpt on from 16th, nvr nrr*	3	18
124	17/2	Kingston Bl'	(L)	CON	3m	17 GS	*mstks, hld up bhnd, gd prog 14th, onepcd & no imp frm nxt*	4	19
337	3/3	Heythrop	(R)	OPE	3m	10 G	*not fluent, hld up bhnd, prog 14th, lft 2nd last, no ch wnr*	2	18
435	9/3	Newton Brom'	(R)	OPE	3m	7 GS	*last til apr hlfwy,prog & cls 3rd 15th,ld aft 3 out,hdd last*	2	18
887	6/4	Kimble	(L)	OPE	3m	2 GF	*(fav) ld aft 1st, made rest, rdn out flat*	1	19
1180	21/4	Mollington	(R)	OPE	3m	5 F	*hld up,chsd wnr 12th,sn outpcd,mstk 3 out,wknd badly flat*	3	17

Quite decent but barely stays & tricky ride; should find another opening; G/F-G/S. 21

WELSH SITARA (Irish) — I 169F, I 364F, I 448F

WENDY JANE b.m. 11 Relkino - Syltung by Shantung — Mrs R Turnwell

1995 P(0),P(0),P(0),3(0),4(11),7(0),F(-)

273	2/3	Parham	(R)	LAD	3m	11 GF	*1st ride, rear, poor 5th frm 14th, lft 4th last*	4	11
572	17/3	Detling	(L)	LAD	3m	10 GF	*ld 3rd, jmpd rght, hdd 15th, fdd*	6	0
678	30/3	Cottenham	(R)	LAD	3m	6 GF	*jmpd rght, clr ldr til aft 12th, sn lost plc & btn*	5	12

Maiden winner 93; schoolmistress now; safe but not threatening to win. 0

WERGILD ch.g. 7 Ore - Zenaida by Lear Jet — Mrs J A C Lundgren

477	10/3	Tweseldown	(R)	MDO	3m	15 G	*u.r. 1st*	U	-
576	17/3	Detling	(L)	MDN	3m	18 GF	*rear, p.u. 9th*	P	0
592	23/3	Parham	(R)	MEM	3m	4 GS	*immed dtchd, t.o. whn ref 4th*	R	-

Has jumped dreadfully so far; dam won points. 0

WESTSHAUN b.m. 6 Shaunicken - Wessex Flyer by Pony Express — A G Sims

1995 U(-),F(-),P(0),U(-),**12(NH)**

144	17/2	Larkhill	(R)	MDO 3m	15	G	*in rear whn b.d. 6th*	B	-
375	9/3	Barbury Cas'	(L)	MDN 3m	14	GS	*sn well bhnd, f 8th*	F	-
519	16/3	Larkhill	(R)	CON 3m	5	G	*ld til wknd rpdly aft 12th, p.u. nxt*	P	0
864	6/4	Larkhill	(R)	MDN 2 1/2m	9	F	*alwys towrds rear, t.o. 9th, p.u. nxt*	P	0

Yet to complete the course and looks hopeless. 0

WESTCOTE LAD b.g. 7 Adonijah - Lady Lynx (USA) by Stop The Music (USA) — David A Smith

1995 F(-),2(13)

167	17/2	Weston Park	(L)	MDN 3m	10	G	*(fav) prom, prog to ld 4 out, lft clr nxt, easily*	1	15
462	9/3	Eyton-On-Se'	(L)	RES 3m	12	G	*(fav) w.w., clsr ordr 5 out, ld 3 out, ran out wll aft*	1	16
1418	6/5	Eyton-On-Se'	(L)	MEM 3m	7	GF	*(fav) ld to 2nd, cl up, ld 8-9th, trckd ldr, u.r. 12th, rmntd*	4	0

Impressively won modest races; can improve; needs to for Confineds; may prove useful in time. 19

WESTCOUNTRY LAD b.g. 6 General Surprise - Charmezzo by Remezzo — Mrs P Bond

1424	6/5	High Bickin'	(R)	MEM 3m	4	G	*lost tch aft 11th, t.o. p.u. aft 13th*	P	0

Showed nothing on debut. 0

WESTERN FORT (Irish) — I 4^{U}, I 31^{P}, I 511^{P}, I 543^{6}, I 574^{P}, I 634^{P}

WESTERN HARMONY ch.g. 8 Extra - Harmonica by St Paddy — R T Baimbridge

1995 P(0),P(0),U(-),P(0),P(0),3(0),P(0),P(0)

747	31/3	Upper Sapey	(R)	MDO 3m	11	GS	*disp frm 12th, qcknd clr apr last*	1	15

Awful until Baimbridge magic worked again; probably win again; needs easy 3 miles. 16

WESTERN PEARL(IRE) gr.g. 8 Sarab - Legs And Things by Three Legs — Mrs P J Price

1995 2(0),7(0),5(0),U(-)

220	24/2	Newtown	(L)	MDN 3m	12	GS	*(Jt fav) mstks, chsd ldng pair, wknd & p.u. 13th*	P	0

Showed a little ability in 95; brief 96 & not progress; could win if fit in 97. 12

WEST LYN (Irish) — I 69^{2}, I 125^{1}, I 153^{3}, I 186^{1}, I 241^{F}

WESTON GALE ch.m. 7 Tremblant - Trust Ann by Capistrano — N R J Bell

1178	21/4	Mollington	(R)	RES 3m	7	F	*alwys last, t.o. 8th, p.u. 11th*	P	0

2 runs in 3 seasons; shows nothing. 0

WESTON MOON(IRE) b.m. 7 Le Moss - Lady Bluebird by Arapaho — N R J Bell

900	6/4	Dingley	(R)	MDN 2m 5f	8	GS	*made all, 20l clr 6 out, unchal*	1	13

3 runs in 3 seasons; won bad race; very easily; hard to assess; needs to iprove for follow up. 15

WEST QUAY b.g. 10 Dubassoff (USA) - Elysium Dream Vii — C T Moate

530	16/3	Cothelstone	(L)	OPE 3m	7	G	*made all, in comm 3 out, eased flat, impress*	1	24
799	3/4	Ludlow	(R)	HC 3m	8	GF	*(fav) ld till after 2nd, blnd next, led 8th till mstk and hdd 11th, only horse to jump 15th, blunded 2 out, no ext.*	2	24
1333	1/5	Cheltenham	(L)	HC 3m 1f 110yds	13	G	*prog to 2nd 10th, ld 15th, hit 4 out, joined and hit next, btn apr last, eased run-in.*	3	23
1630	31/5	Stratford	(L)	HC 3 1/2m	16	GF	*prom till f 16th.*	F	-

Missed 95; improved & useful now; mistakes in H/chases; can win a modest one; G/F-S. 29

WESTWITHTHENIGHT (Irish) — I 17^{P}

WESTWOOD MARCH b.g. 8 Nestor - Ratley Lodge by Daring March — P R M Philips

683	30/3	Chaddesley '	(L)	MEM 3m	17	G	*rear, p.u. 9th*	P	0
884	6/4	Brampton Br'	(R)	MDN 3m	12	GF	*in tch to 12th, wknd 14th, p.u. 3 out*	P	0

Only learning; looks capable of better. 0

WE WILL SEE (Irish) — I 336^{U}, I 558^{U}, I 625^{4}

WEWILLSEE (Irish) — I 233^{U}, I 272^{P}, I 632^{6}

WHAT ABOUT THAT(IRE) ch.g. 8 Sandalay - Knockarone Star by Paddy's Stream — Miss Samantha Stuart-Hunt

1995 4(0),5(11),1(16),1(19),4(17)

125	17/2	Kingston Bl'	(L)	OPE 3m	10	GS	*(bl) prom til wknd 13th, t.o. & p.u. 15th*	P	0
262	2/3	Didmarton	(L)	MEM 3m	11	G	*(bl) ld to 3rd, chsd ldr to 11th, 4th & hld whn u.r. 3 out*	U	-
638	23/3	Siddington	(L)	CON 3m	16	S	*mid div, rddn 10th, no ch whn blnd & u.r. 14th*	U	-
1019	13/4	Kingston Bl'	(L)	INT 3m	6	G	*(bl) mstks, chsd ldrs, rdn 9th, 4th & btn whn p.u. 12th, dsmntd*	P	0

DUALwinner 95; struggling now upgraded; problems last start; weak Confined possible if fit in 97. 15

WHAT A CHOICE (Irish) — **I** 19^{4}

WHATAFELLOW(IRE) ch.g. 6 Arapahos (FR) - Dara's March by March Parade — Gareth Samuel

164	17/2	Weston Park	(L)	RES	3m	11	G	*(fav) hld up, rpd prog to ld aft 3 out, sn clr*	1	18
458	9/3	Eyton-On-Se'	(L)	INT	3m	11	G	*(fav) w.w., 3rd 13th, tk ld 3 out, 2l clr gng wl, u.r. 2 out*	U	19
667	24/3	Eaton Hall	(R)	INT	3m	11	S	*hld up rear, ran on frm 3 out, outpcd by ldng pair*	3	19
948	8/4	Eyton-On-Se'	(L)	MEM	3m	4	GF	*(fav) cls up, gng easily, ld 2 out, ran on wll frm last*	1	20
1192	21/4	Sandon	(L)	CON	3m	11	G	*(fav) hld up rear, smooth prog 11th, ld 3 out, ran on well*	1	20
1594	25/5	Garthorpe	(R)	MEM	3m	10	G	*w.w. 15l 5th 6 out, ran on 3 out, not rch 1st trio*	4	16

Ex-Irish; useful prospect; cna quicken but given lot to do; should reach Opens in 97; G-S 22

WHAT A GIG br.g. 13 Pardigras - Fizgig by Don't Look — Hugh Ellison

1995 1(20),2(20)

33	20/1	Higham	(L)	LAD	3m	9	GF	*prom, ld 14th til appr last, onepcd*	3	19
250	25/2	Charing	(L)	LAD	3m	12	GS	*(fav) mid-div, prog to cls 2nd 4 out, wknd nxt, p.u. 2 out*	P	0
572	17/3	Detling	(L)	LAD	3m	10	GF	*rear, prog 14th, 3rd 4 out, wknd nxt*	3	13
620	23/3	Higham	(L)	LAD	3m	9	GF	*hld up bhnd, gd prog to 3rd 12th, ev ch 3 out, no ext*	3	16
812	6/4	Charing	(L)	LAD	3m	6	F	*rear, clsd 13th, outpcd 15th, rdn & ran on 4 out,tk 2nd last*	2	21
1147	20/4	Higham	(L)	LAD	3m	9	F	*hld up, prog 5th, 6th whn s.u. bnd apr 9th*	S	-

Won weak Ladies 95; barely stays & L/H essential; declined in 96 & win at 14 looks hard. 17

WHAT A HAND ch.g. 8 Nearly A Hand - Kiki Star by Some Hand — Mrs L J Roberts

1995 1(28),**U(-)**,**1(30)**

6	13/1	Larkhill	(R)	OPE	3m	18	GS	*(fav) hld up,rpd prog 12th,2nd 14th,ld 3 out,slw last,ran on well*	1	31
142	17/2	Larkhill	(R)	MXO	3m	9	G	*(fav) tckd away, prog to ld 15th, ran on well frm last*	1	32
360	4/3	Windsor	(R)	HC	3m	8	GS	*(fav) patiently rdn, hdwy 12th, ld 2 out, ran on well.*	1	29
483	14/3	Cheltenham	(L)	HC	3 1/4m 110yds	17	G	*f 1st.*	F	-
1631	1/6	Stratford	(L)	HC	3 1/2m	14	GF	*alwys bhnd, t.o. when p.u. before 16th.*	P	0

Very useful; ground wrong last start; could still reach the top; quirky but quickens;G-S. 36

WHAT A MISS ch.m. 9 Move Off - Vinovia by Ribston — A Jackson

1995 3(0),4(0),P(0),1(11),6(0),1(17),**8(0)**

306	2/3	Great Stain'	(L)	INT	3m	12	GS	*cls up til wknd 10th, rear whn p.u. 14th*	P	0
409	9/3	Charm Park	(L)	CON	3m	11	G	*alwys wl in rr, p.u. 4 out*	P	0
761	31/3	Great Stain'	(L)	INT	3m	7	GS	*rear & lost tch 6th, p.u. aft 11th*	P	0
985	8/4	Charm Park	(L)	INT	3m	9	GF	*rear early, onepcd frm 12th, p.u. 3 out*	P	0
1130	20/4	Hornby Cast'	(L)	CON	3m	13	G	*mid-div, wknd frm 13th, t.o. & p.u. last*	P	0

Won 2 poor races 95; awful in 96 & best watched now. 12

WHATASHOT ch.g. 6 Gunner B - Lady Letitia by Le Bavard (FR) — Mrs R Aston

406	9/3	Dalston	(R)	MDO	2 1/2m	12	G	*rlctnt to line up, al bhnd, p.u. last*	P	0

No signs on debut. 0

WHAT A TO DO b.g. 12 Le Bavard (FR) - Alfie's Wish by Three Wishes — C J R Sweeting

1995 3(16),3(13),3(13),U(-),**2(19)**,4(14)

475	10/3	Tweseldown	(R)	CON	3m	9	G	*mid-div, prog to 3rd hlfwy, sn wknd, bhnd whn u.r. 3 out*	U	-
639	23/3	Siddington	(L)	OPE	3m	12	S	*p.u appr 3rd*	P	0
867	6/4	Larkhill	(R)	MXO	4m	6	F	*prom, disp 5-12th & 5 out til wnt on apr 2 out, cosily*	1	19
1435	6/5	Ashorne	(R)	CON	3m	12	G	*ld to 2nd, prom aft til 3rd & outpcd 13th, no dang aft*	4	17
1463	10/5	Stratford	(L)	HC	3m	6	GF	*ld to 3rd, led 6th, ran on well.*	1	23

Enjoyed best season; given intelligent ride to win H/Chase; hard to place at 13 now; G/F-S 19

WHAT CHANCE(IRE) ch.m. 8 Buckskin (FR) - Grainne Geal by General Ironside — Mrs Helen Mobley

1995 5(0),8(0),4(15)

341	3/3	Heythrop	(R)	MDN	3m	13	G	*alwys in tch, chsd ldr 3 out, mstk last, rdn to ld flat*	1	15
642	23/3	Siddington	(L)	RES	3m	15	S	*w.w. hit 8th, prog nxt, ld 3 out, outjmpd & hdded nxt,no ex*	2	18
1179	21/4	Mollington	(R)	LAD	3m	10	F	*w.w. going wll,trckd ldr 11th,ld 3 out,hdd & mstk last,eased*	2	23

Improved; lightly raced; Restricted no problem in 97 & can win Ladies; F-S. 23

WHATFORSURPRISE (Irish) — **I** 110^{P}

WHAT IS THE PLAN (Irish) — **I** 117^{5}, **I** 206^{P}, **I** 634^{2}, **I** 654^{1}

WHATOUPA ch.g. 9 All Systems Go - Fearless Lass by Import — Mrs J Collinson

1995 P(0),P(0)

323	2/3	Corbridge	(R)	MDN	3m	12	GS	*prom whn f 4th*	F	-
1131	20/4	Hornby Cast'	(L)	RES	3m	17	G	*last frm 3rd, sn trailing, t.o. 10th, p.u. aft 13th*	P	0

Yet to complete & looks hopeless. 0

WHATS ANOTHER ch.m. 9 Lord Ha Ha - Purranna by Mugatpura — D L Claydon

1995 **11(NH)**,**9(NH)**

105	17/2	Marks Tey	(L)	RES	3m	11	G	*chsd ldrs, wkng whn u.r. 15th*	U	-
313	2/3	Ampton	(R)	RES	3m	9	G	*chsd ldrs to 15th, wknd appr 3 out, p.u. last*	P	0
621	23/3	Higham	(L)	INT	3m	12	GF	*mid-div, rdn to cls 11th, wknd 14th, t.o. & p.u. 2 out*	P	0
931	8/4	Marks Tey	(L)	RES	3m	8	G	*s.v.s. t.o. 3rd, p.u. 12th*	P	0
1321	28/4	Fakenham P-'	(L)	CON	3m	5	G	*in tch, blnd 4th, 3rd & outpcd 15th, no dang aft*	4	13
1401	6/5	Northaw	(L)	LAD	3m	4	F	*lft disp ld 8th, blnd nxt,hdd 12th,ld bfly 15th,sn outpcd*	2	13

Irish Maiden winner 94; ran passably twice but not threatening to win. 10

WHATS MONEY gr.m. 5 Scallywag - What A Coup by Malicious — E H Crow

1234	27/4	Weston Park	(L)	MDO	3m	13	G	*mid to rear, lost cth, p.u. 4 out*	P	0

Successful stable; only learning on debut. 0

WHATS THE CRACK b.g. 13 The Parson - Mighty Crack by Deep Run — N Rossiter

1995 **4(14)**,**3(22)**,**6(0)**,**P(NH)**

626	23/3	Kilworthy	(L)	OPE	3m	12	GS	*(bl) rel to race, t.o. whn ref 1st*	R	-
715	30/3	Wadebridge	(L)	CON	3m	8	GF	*lost tch aft 7th, t.o. whn hmpd 10 & 12th*	4	0
1073	13/4	Lifton	(R)	OPE	3m	10	S	*ref to race*	R	-
1275	27/4	Bratton Down	(L)	OPE	3m	8	GF	*prom early, lost plc 9th, t.o. 13th*	6	0
1360	4/5	Flete Park	(R)	OPE	3m	5	G	*(bl) lost tch & reluc 11th, t.o.*	4	0

Former useful chaser; changed hands & most reluctant now. 0

WHATS YOUR GAME b.g. 13 Kambalda - Sugar Shaker by Quisling — J S Papworth

1995 P(0),P(0),3(12)

625	23/3	Kilworthy	(L)	CON	3m	11	GS	*(bl) rear, wknd rpdly 11th, t.o. & p.u. 14th*	P	0
715	30/3	Wadebridge	(L)	CON	3m	8	GF	*(bl) in tch til p.u. 10th, lame*	P	0

Ladies winner 94; lightly raced & more problems now; looks finished. 12

WHAT THING (Irish) — **I** 75^{P}, **I** 115^{P}, **I** 152^{P}, **I** 184^{P}, **I** 295, , **I** 331^{1}, **I** 378^{1}, **I** 447^{2}, **I** 487^{3}, **I** 523^{1}, **I** 595^{U}, **I** 643^{1}, **I** 656^{1}

WHATWILLBEWILLBE(IRE) b or br.g. 7 Long Pond - Cheap Fuel by Bluerullah — P S Burke

240	25/2	Southwell P'	(L)	MDO	3m	15	HO	*trckd ldrs, ld 13th, drew clr 2 out, ran on well*	1	17
666	24/3	Eaton Hall	(R)	RES	3m	13	S	*(fav) hld up in tch, going easily in 3rd whn f 13th*	F	-

Easily beat subsequent winner; unfortunate next time; looks sure to atone; stays; Soft. 18

WHERE'S NOEL (Irish) — **I** 61^{P}, **I** 114^{P}, **I** 200^{4}, **I** 247^{F}

WHINSTONE MILL b.g. 8 Pablond - Carrowmore by Crozier — Mrs Sally Thornton

1995 3(10),P(0),**5(10)**,P(0),**7(NH)**

242	25/2	Southwell P'	(L)	RES	3m	12	HO	*trckd ldrs 6th, 3rd whn blnd 12th, rdn & onepcd frm 4 out*	3	11
365	5/3	Leicester	(R)	HC	3m	10	GS	*in tch to 12th, well bhnd when p.u. 2 out.*	P	0
539	17/3	Southwell P'	(L)	RES	3m	11	GS	*cls up to 12th, sn btn, p.u. 3 out*	P	0
904	6/4	Dingley	(R)	RES	3m	20	GS	*prom bhnd ldrs, 3rd 6-3 out, fdd*	5	0
1102	14/4	Guilsborough	(L)	RES	3m	15	G	*wth ldrs til reluc frm 15th, t.o. & p.u. 2 out*	P	0
1239	27/4	Clifton On '	(L)	RES	3m	9	GF	*prom, ld/disp frm 8th, drvn clr 2 out, hng left flat*	1	17
1377	5/5	Dingley	(R)	CON	3m	12	GF	*mid-div,prog 10th,chsd wnr 3 out,ch whn slw jmp last,onepcd*	2	20
1535	16/5	Aintree	(L)	HC	3m 1f	11	GF	*rear, mstk 7th, hdwy 12th, und pres and chasing ldrs 4 out, went 2nd 2 out, no impn on wnr.*	2	17
1595	25/5	Garthorpe	(R)	CON	3m	15	G	*(fav) 3rd frm 11th, ld 6 out, ran on gamely whn hdd 2 out,ld last*	1	20
1643	2/6	Dingley	(R)	OPE	3m	13	GF	*7th & pshd alng hlfwy, nvr a dang, t.o.*	4	12

Revived late season; hard ride & well ridden; win another Confined if in the mood. G/F-G/S. 20

WHISPERS HILL ch.m. 5 Kind Of Hush - Snarry Hill by Vitiges (FR) — Roy Robinson

73	11/2	Wetherby Po'	(L)	MDO	3m	15	GS	*f 4th*	F	-
308	2/3	Great Stain'	(L)	MDO	3m	12	GS	*alwys rear, t.o. 15th*	6	0
414	9/3	Charm Park	(L)	MDO	3m	11	G	*cls up, 4th at 14th, ht wing 3 out*	F	-
762	31/3	Great Stain'	(L)	MDN	3m	11	GS	*mid-div, prog to chs ldrs hlfwy, ld 2 out, sn clr, easily*	1	15

Stady progress; won weak race; needs more but surely can improve further. 15

WHISTLING EDDY ch.g. 12 Whistling Deer - Silver Tongue by Salvo — S H Marriage

1995 P(0),6(0),3(0),U(-),4(0),4(0)

11	14/1	Cottenham	(R)	LAD	3m	7	G	*bhnd & pshd alng 5th, t.o. & p.u. 13th*	P	0
103	17/2	Marks Tey	(L)	LAD	3m	7	G	*prom, disp ld 9th til appr 11th, wknd 16th*	5	0

Restricted winner 93; novice ridden & of no real account now. 0

WHITEBARN CAILIN (Irish) — **I** 239^{5}

WHITEBARN GRIT (Irish) — **I** 5^{P}, **I** 55^{2}, **I** 108^{2}, **I** 201^{2}, **I** 227^{1}

WHITESTOWN BOY (Irish) — **I** 224^{P}, **I** 343^{P}, **I** 582^{U}, **I** 616^{P}, **I** 644^{P}

WHITE WYANDOTTE (Irish) — **I** 352^{P}, **I** 459^{F}

WHOD OF THOUGHT IT(IRE) b.g. 5 Cataldi - Granalice by Giolla Mear — P R Chamings

520 16/3 Larkhill (R) MDO 3m 11 G *nvr bttr than mid-div, no ch whn p.u. 14th* P 0
997 8/4 Hackwood Pa' (L) MDO 3m 11 GF *mstly rear, 10l 4th hlfwy, wknd qckly 16th, p.u.* P 0

No signs of stamina or ability yet. 0

WHO IS ED (Irish) — **I** 415[1]

WHOLESTONE(IRE) b.g. 8 Cataldi - Fiery Rose by Boreen (FR) D R Greig

17 14/1 Tweseldown (R) MDN 3m 11 GS *alwys prom, chsd wnr 13th, rdn apr last, onepcd flat* 2 17
44 3/2 Wadebridge (L) MDO 3m 9 GF *(fav) ld 3rd-8th & 10th-aft 14th, ld 2 out, rdn out* 1 17
272 2/3 Parham (R) RES 3m 13 GF *ld 4th-14th, styd cls up til wknd 2 out* 4 12
787 31/3 Tweseldown (R) RES 3m 9 G *(fav) n.j.w. blnd 3rd, wknd 12th, blnd 4 out & p.u.* P 0

Dead 14

WHO'S IN CHARGE b.g. 12 Proverb - I'm Grannie by Perspex Mrs M Armstrong

49 4/2 Alnwick (L) OPE 3m 14 G *rear, t.o. & p.u. aft 8th* P 0
1475 11/5 Aspatria (L) CON 3m 6 GF *ld to 4th, bhnd & reluctant frm 7th, t.o. & p.u. bfr 12th* P 0

No longer of any account 0

WHO'S NEXT b.g. 8 Oats - Kaotesse by Djakao (FR) Harry Hobson

1995 4(0),6(13),3(17),3(18),**1(22)**

8 14/1 Cottenham (R) CON 3m 10 G *(bl) in tch, prog to disp 14th, blnd 16th, rdn & btn nxt* 5 17

Won weak H/chase 95; gone novice chasing after Cottenham; win Confined if returning; blinkers. 21

WHOSTHAT b.g. 10 Politico (USA) - Muffler by Haris II D A Lamb

259 1/3 Kelso (L) HC 3m 1f 8 GS *bhnd when blnd and u.r. 9th.* U -
673 29/3 Sedgefield (L) HC 3m 3f 7 GF *jmpd right, ld and soon clr, mstk 3rd, blnd and u.r. 12th.* U -
905 8/4 Carlisle (R) HC 3 1/4m 5 F *ld till hdd twelfth, soon wknd.* 3 0

No longer of any account 0

WHO'S YOUR MAN (Irish) — **I** 21[P], **I** 86[5], **I** 346[6], **I** 387[U], **I** 421[2], **I** 527[2]

WHY EVER NOT br.g. 12 Nickel King - Black Patches by Klondyke Bill R E Baskerville

1995 P(0),P(0),**S(-)**,1(14)

889 6/4 Kimble (L) RES 3m 7 GF *chsd wnr 4-10th, 3rd whn blnd 15th, not rcvr, p.u. nxt* P 0

Won bad Maiden 95; does not stay; brief campaign 96 & follow up looks impossible. 13

WHY NOT FLOPSY b.m. 11 Quayside - Realinda by Realm A Charles-Jones

1995 4(0),P(0),9(0),6(0),4(14),5(0),7(10),3(0)

1102 14/4 Guilsborough (L) RES 3m 15 G *alwys wll bhnd, t.o. hlfwy, no real prog* 9 0

Dead 13

WICKED THOUGHTS b.g. 6 Domitor (USA) - Marigold by High Perch M J Coates

1995 P(0)

144 17/2 Larkhill (R) MDO 3m 15 G *tckd away, rpd prog 3 out, ev ch last, not qckn* 2 15
479 10/3 Tweseldown (R) MDO 3m 10 G *(fav) disp til ld 6th, hdd 13th, btn 4th whn f 4 out, winded* F -

Beaten by good horse (winners behind); ran poorly after; can win but looks a tricky ride. 14

WIDOW TWANKY (Irish) — **I** 347[P]

WIGTOWN BAY br.g. 13 Young Nelson - Bonnie Bladnoch by Lord Of Verona Mrs P C Stirling

611 23/3 Friars Haugh (L) LAD 3m 10 G *2nd frm 4th, remained clse up untl wknd 4 out* 6 0
702 30/3 Tranwell (L) XX 3m 3 GS *disp to 13th, chal und pres last, jnd ldr fin* 1 13
1084 14/4 Friars Haugh (L) LAD 3m 8 F *nvr dang, poor 3rd whn f last* F -
1352 4/5 Mosshouses (L) LAD 3m 10 GS *trckd ldrs, mstk 10th, chsd wnr 3 out, not qckn nxt, kpt on* 2 16
1573 19/5 Corbridge (R) OPE 3m 12 G *alwys mid-div, no ch & p.u. 4 out* P 0

Dead-heated in poor race & too old for competitive races now 15

WILD EXPRESSION ch.g. 6 Then Again - Pleasure Island by Dalsaan T Pickering

1137 20/4 Hornby Cast' (L) MDN 3m 13 G *mid-div, wknd 13th, t.o. & p.u. 15th* P 0

No signs on debut. 0

WILD FORTUNE b.g. 14 Free Boy - Hopeful Fortune by Autre Prince P Baring

955 8/4 Lockinge (L) MEM 3m 5 GF *(Jt fav) cls up, efft 4 out, ev ch nxt, wknd aft* 3 0
1177 21/4 Mollington (R) INT 3m 14 F *ld 2-5th, wkng whn mstk 11th, t.o.* 10 0
1500 11/5 Kingston Bl' (L) CON 3m 7 G *sn pshd alng, chsg grp to 12th, t.o. 14th* 7 0
1563 19/5 Mollington (R) CON 3m 8 GS *ld to 3rd, wknd 7th, t.o. & p.u. 13th* P 0

Winning pointer; novice ridden & looks well past it now. 0

WILD ILLUSION ch.g. 12 True Song - Fused Light by Fury Royal G Pidgeon

1995 1(30),**2(27)**,**2(32)**,**1(30)**,**2(NH)**,**1(32)**,**1(31)**,**2(23)**

18 14/1 Tweseldown (R) MXO 3m 6 GS *(fav) ld til hit 2nd, chsd wnr 11th, 2l down 3 out, rdn & btn nxt* 2 22
125 17/2 Kingston Bl' (L) OPE 3m 10 GS *(fav) j.w. trckd ldrs, lft in ld 12th, clr 2 out, easily* 1 28
256 29/2 Ludlow (R) HC 3m 14 G *(fav) prom, hit 9th, ld before 12th, hit 14th, drew clr from 4 out.* 1 30
363 5/3 Leicester (R) HC 3m 3 GS *(fav) hit 1st, trckd ldrs, went 2nd 4 out, rdn and btn apr 2 out.* 3 20
578 20/3 Ludlow (R) HC 3m 7 G *(fav) alwys prom, left 2nd bend after 11th, ld apr 4 out, soon clr.* 1 28
327 30/4 Huntingdon (R) HC 3m 6 GF *(fav) trckd ldrs, left 2nd 16th, ld apr 2 out, pushed out.* 1 28
534 15/5 Hereford (R) HC 3m 1f 110yds 4 F *(fav) alwys prom, rdn apr 4 out, styd on run-in.* 2 25

Very useful & consistent H/Chaser; below best 96 but still hard to beat; can win more at 13; G-F;R/H ... 30

VILD MOON b.m. 13 Belfalas - Keyed Up by Delirium A G Tutton

179 21/4 Mollington (R) LAD 3m 10 F *alwys bhnd, t.o. 10th* 8 0
291 28/4 Barbury Cas' (L) LAD 3m 5 F *ld to 2nd, last frm 8th, sn t.o.* 0 0
438 6/5 Ashorne (R) XX 3m 14 G *alwys bhnd, t.o. 7th* 10 0

Dual winner 90; disappointing since & too old now. 0

VILDNITE b.g. 12 Whealden - Melinite by Milesian Miss L Robbins
1995 3(16),1(17),**8(0)**,**3(11)**,8(0)

683 30/3 Chaddesley ' (L) MEM 3m 17 G *mid-div, no ch whn blnd 12th, p.u. 14th* P 0
942 8/4 Andoversford (R) MEM 3m 8 GF *alwys in tch, ld 13th, made rest, styd on* 1 14
413 6/5 Cursneh Hill (L) INT 3m 6 GF *cls up, ld 6th, wknd frm 14th, t.o. 3 out* 6 0

Won 2 of last 26 93/96; beat 3 heavyweights in Members; need same to score again. 13

VILLBROOK (Irish) — I 148^{P}, I 248^{F}, I 292^{3}, I 472^{F}

VILL DE-BROOKE b.g. 9 Broadsword (USA) - Julie de Fortisson by Entanglement D Nichols
1995 1(16),P(0)

030 13/4 Alpraham (R) RES 3m 10 GS *rear, p.u. bfr 5th, broke pelvis (dead)* P 0

Dead. 15

VILLIE BE BRAVE (Irish) — I 172^{P}, I 401^{4}

VILLIE MCGARR(USA) ch.g. 11 Master Willie - Pay T V (USA) by T V Commercial (USA) Mrs D Thomas
1995 **4(NH)**,**4(NH)**,**R(NH)**

215 24/2 Newtown (L) OPE 3m 20 GS *s.s. wll bhnd, some prog 13th, no ch whn p.u. 2 out* P 0
384 9/3 Llanfrynach (R) OPE 3m 16 GS *hld up rear,gd prog 14th,chsd wnr nxt,unable to qckn last* 2 21
768 31/3 Pantyderi (R) OPE 3m 10 G *(fav) s.s. ld brfly 11th, hrd rdn 2 out, no ext* 2 17

Old character; returned to points with good displays (well ridden) but finds little & hard to win 97 19

VILL I OR WONT I (Irish) — I 460^{P}, I 569^{P}, I 572^{F}

VILLOW BELLE(IRE) b.m. 8 Bustinetto - Light Belle by Light Brigade Mrs C Day
1995 P(0),U(-),2(0),R(-),4(0),U(-),F(-),P(0)

155 17/2 Erw Lon (L) RES 3m 9 G *alwys last, p.u. 12th* P 0
358 3/3 Garnons (L) RES 3m 18 GS *ld to 6th, sn wknd, p.u. aft 12th* P 0
509 16/3 Magor (R) MDN 3m 9 GS *rear, steady prog to 3rd at 11th, tk 2nd 2 out, no dang* 2 0
606 23/3 Howick (L) MDN 3m 13 S *alwys rear, p.u. 3 out* P 0
850 6/4 Howick (L) MDN 3m 14 GF *mid-div, prog to 5l down 14th, no imp aft* 4 0

Placed in 4 awful races; no other completions2& barely worth a rating so far. 10

VILLOWMERE (Irish) — I 169^{P}, I 258^{U}, I 285^{P}

VILLOWS ENGAGEMENT ch.m. 7 High Season - Willows Account by Stetchworth Lad D G Brace
1995 U(-),P(0),5(0),U(-)

550 17/3 Erw Lon (L) MDN 3m 13 GS *nvr dang, p.u. 14th* P 0
273 27/4 Pyle (R) MDO 3m 9 G *ld 8-14th, 2l down & lkd hld whn f 3 out* F -

Showed some signs in bad race on last start; much more needed; successful stable. 0

VILLOWS WONDERMAN b.g. 6 Balinger - Loch Rose by Tula Rocket D G Brace
1995 U(-),P(0)

509 16/3 Magor (R) MDN 3m 9 GS *alwys last, t.o. & p.u. 6th* P 0
976 8/4 Lydstep (L) MDO 3m 12 G *f 3rd* F -
270 27/4 Pyle (R) MDO 3m 9 G *last frm 5th, ran out wing nxt* r -

Successful stable but dreadful so far. 0

VILLSAN ch.g. 6 Nearly A Hand - Sanber by New Member R Winslade

554 18/5 Bratton Down (L) MDO 3m 16 F *s.s. gd prog 9th, cls 4th at 11th, fdd & p.u. aft 13th* P 0

A reasonable debut & can do better. 10

VILL TRAVEL (Irish) — I 89^{2}, I 167^{3}, I 227^{P}, I 387^{3}, I 416^{1}, I 617^{2}

VILLY WAFFLES(IRE) ch.g. 8 Orchestra - Gayles Approach by Strong Gale David Carr

1995 P(0),4(0),2(0),4(0)

88	11/2 Alnwick	(L) MDO 3m	11 GS	*ld to 7th, prom til wknd 4 out, t.o.*	4
116	17/2 Lanark	(R) MDO 3m	10 GS	*prom early, bhnd whn p.u. 12th*	P
862	6/4 Alnwick	(L) MDN 3m	8 GF	*chsd ldr, blndrd 8th-nxt, sn wknd, t.o. & p.u. 3 out*	P
1512	12/5 Hexham Poin'	(L) MEM 3m	6 HY	*last whn blnd & u.r. 3rd*	U
1575	19/5 Corbridge	(R) MDO 3m	10 G	*3rd at 6th, cls up whn f 15th*	F

Slow & well short of a win yet. 0

WILLY WEE (Irish) — I 409F

WINDGATES ZONE (Irish) — I 134P, I 340P

WINDMILL STAR (Irish) — I 106P, I 176P, I 455P

WINDOVER LODGE ch.g. 9 Don - Arabian Squaw Mrs S A Scra

23	20/1 Barbury Cas'	(L) XX 3m	11 GS	*ld til ran out & u.r. 4th*	r
140	17/2 Larkhill	(R) CON 3m	17 G	*prom, ld 7th-12th, wknd nxt, t.o.*	8
478	10/3 Tweseldown	(R) RES 3m	9 G	*j.w. ld, rdn 2 out, hdd apr last, no ext*	2
786	31/3 Tweseldown	(R) LAD 3m	8 G	*ld, dstrctd by loose horse & ran out 10th*	r

Irish Maiden winner 94; headstrong & needs strong handling; stamina doubts; need a poor race to win 13

WINDWHISTLE JOKER b.g. 6 Sharp Deal - Maius Dancer by Full Of Beans Mrs H J Church

1345	4/5 Holnicote	(L) RES 3m	11 GS	*rear whn f 6th*	F

Only went a mile on debut. 0

WINDY BEE (Irish) — I 191P

WINDY WAYS br.g. 11 Strong Gale - Woodville Grove by Harwell N J Henderso

1995 **2(NH),P(NH)**

808	6/4 Towcester	(R) HC 3m 1f	4 F	*ld to 3rd, styd chasing ldr till p.u. before 14th, lame.*	P

Dead 23

WINGED WHISPER(USA) ch.g. 7 Air Forbes Won (USA) - Soft Reply (USA) by Personality (USA) P R We

436	9/3 Newton Brom'	(R) LAD 3m	10 GS	*bolted bef start, rear til plld to ld 4th-9th,wknd,p.u. 14th*	P
633	23/3 Market Rase'	(L) LAD 3m	10 GF	*s.s. alwys last trio, outpcd frm 10th*	7
903	6/4 Dingley	(R) LAD 3m	7 GS	*alwys prom, cont 7-11th, 3rd reluctant 3 out*	3
1099	14/4 Guilsborough	(L) LAD 3m	9 G	*prom to 15th, sn wknd*	6

Flat winner; placed in poor Ladies; reluctant & unlikely to win; novice ridden. 10

WINKELWEG (Irish) — I 626F

WINNING SALLY (Irish) — I 483P

WINSOME BLENDS (Irish) — I 319P

WINTER BREEZE (Irish) — I 40P, I 125P, I 154P, I 206F, I 368[4], I 471[4], I 511P, I 579S

WINTER GEM b.m. 7 Hasty Word - Masami by King Log A Wrig

352	3/3 Garnons	(L) MDN 2 1/2m	9 GS	*cls up whn f 2nd*	F
953	8/4 Eyton-On-Se'	(L) MDO 2 1/2m	10 GF	*in tch whn f 6th*	F

Not a good start. 0

WINTERS COTTAGE(IRE) ch.g. 8 Sandalay - Hilltown Yvonne by Avocat M A Lloy

1995 **4(NH),P(NH),2(NH),5(NH),P(NH)**

158	17/2 Weston Park	(L) MEM 3m	11 G	*ld/disp to 10th, wknd, p.u. 3 out*	P
238	25/2 Southwell P'	(L) MDO 3m	9 HO	*trckd ldrs til wknd 11th, poor 3rd whn p.u. 4 out*	P
431	9/3 Upton-On-Se'	(R) MDO 3m	17 GS	*12th hlfwy, mod late prog, nrst fin*	9
949	8/4 Eyton-On-Se'	(L) MDN 3m	5 GF	*held up, cls order 10th, ld 2 out, ran on*	1
1173	20/4 Chaddesley '	(L) RES 3m	18 G	*prom in chsng grp, prog frm 15th, ev ch 3 out, wknd nxt*	4
1421	6/5 Eyton-On-Se'	(L) RES 3m	11 GF	*(Jt fav) hld up mid-div, prog 5 out, strng chal 2 out, ran on*	2

Placed novice hurdle; won weak race; ran better after; can follow up; needs easy 3 miles. 18

WINTER'S LANE ch.g. 12 Leander - Roman Lilly by Romany Air Stewart Pik

6	13/1 Larkhill	(R) OPE 3m	18 GS	*mid-div, prog 12th, chsd ldrs 14th, wknd nxt, p.u. last*	P
135	17/2 Ottery St M'	(L) LAD 3m	11 GS	*alwys mid-div, nvr on terms*	5
481	11/3 Taunton	(R) HC 3m	11 G	*held up in tch, wknd from 15th.*	6
655	23/3 Badbury Rin'	(L) LAD 3m	8 G	*prom and 2nd whn u.r. 6th,*	U
1124	20/4 Stafford Cr'	(R) CON 3m	7 S	*hndy, 2nd 12th, ld 3 out til wknd qckly frm 2 out*	6
1343	4/5 Holnicote	(L) OPE 3m	6 GS	*s.s. nvr a serious threat*	5
1525	12/5 Ottery St M'	(L) CON 3m	9 GF	*hld up, some prog to 4th 3 out, nvr dang*	4
1624	27/5 Lifton	(R) LAD 3m	9 GS	*rear, no ch whn blnd & u.r. last*	U
1647	8/6 Umberleigh	(L) OPE 3m	7 GF	*made most, 2l up whn f 3 out*	F

Formerly decent; declined now & hard to find another win. 17

WINTERS MELODY b.m. 6 Southern Music - Wintersgame by Game Warden E Pennoc

74	11/2	Wetherby Po'	(L)	MDO 3m	11 GS	*f whn hit wing 4th*	F	-
229	24/2	Duncombe Pa'	(R)	MDO 3m	13 GS	*jmpd lft, chsd ldng trio 5th, wd apr 9th, t.o. & p.u. 12th*	P	0
413	9/3	Charm Park	(L)	MDO 3m	12 G	*ld 6th-13th, hdd, u.r. 15th*	U	-
518	16/3	Dalton Park	(R)	MDO 3m	15 G	*plld hrd, mid-div til ran out 8th*	r	-

Shows speed but steering & breaks faulty at present. 0

WINTRY DAWN (Irish) — **I** 327[6], **I** 367[1]

WINTRY WILLOW (Irish) — **I** 147[6], **I** 424[4]

WIRED FOR SOUND b.g. 6 Sharpo - Swift Return by Double Form — Mrs Hazel Richardson

375	9/3	Barbury Cas'	(L)	MDN 3m	14 GS	*ld to 13th, wknd rpdly, p.u. 4 out*	P	0
643	23/3	Siddington	(L)	MDN 3m	16 S	*chsd ldr 6th, wkng whn blnd 12th, p.u. 14th*	P	0
864	6/4	Larkhill	(R)	MDN 2 1/2m	9 F	*alwys rear, no ch frm 10th, u.r. 4 out*	U	-
1164	20/4	Larkhill	(R)	MDN 3m	12 GF	*mid-div til wknd frm 12th, t.o. frm 14th*	6	0
1248	27/4	Woodford	(L)	MDN 3m	15 G	*blnd 3rd, bhnd, 9th hlfwy, kpt on frm 3 out, nvr nrr*	3	11

1st signs when beaten 16 lengths on last start; stamina doubts & more needed. 10

WIRE LASS b.m. 12 New Brig - Anotherwire by Cagirama — Mrs M Armstrong

1995 P(0),**11(0)**,**U(-)**,1(13),U(-),**P(0)**

914	8/4	Tranwell	(L)	RES 3m	6 GF	*ld/disp 4-10th, wknd 12th, p.u. 2 out*	P	0
1106	15/4	Hexham	(L)	HC 3m 1f	9 GF	*ld to 3rd, cl up, led 16th, soon hdd, wknd between last 2.*	3	12
1249	27/4	Balcormo Ma'	(R)	RES 3m	10 GS	*6th hlfwy, tk 3rd cls home, nvr dang*	3	10
1340	4/5	Hexham	(L)	HC 3m 1f	13 S	*in tch when blnd and u.r. 8th.*	U	-
1514	12/5	Hexham Poin'	(L)	RES 3m	5 HY	*10s-5s, ld/disp til ld 3 out, jmpd lft last, rdn out*	1	12
1570	19/5	Corbridge	(R)	CON 3m	8 G	*alwys mid-div, no dang*	5	11
1585	25/5	Cartmel	(L)	HC 3 1/4m	14 GF	*f 2nd.*	F	-

Won 2 bad races from 29 starts; well below Confined class; hard to find another race; mistakes. 14

WISHING VELVET (Irish) — **I** 132[2]

WISHING WILLIAM (Irish) — **I** 274[4]

WISTINO b.g. 11 Neltino - Pensive Princess by Kinglet — A W K Merriam

35	20/1	Higham	(L)	RES 3m	16 GF	*prom to 11th, grad lost plc frm nxt*	6	11
348	3/3	Higham	(L)	RES 3m	12 G	*alwys prom, onepcd apr last*	3	16
484	15/3	Fakenham	(L)	HC 2m 5f 110yds	13 GF	*chsd ldrs till blnd and u.r. 4th.*	U	-
620	23/3	Higham	(L)	LAD 3m	9 GF	*alwys prom, clr 2nd at 14th, ld 3 out, clr last, easily*	1	21
907	8/4	Fakenham	(L)	HC 3m 110yds	11 G	*(Jt fav) ld 3rd, bad mstk when hdd 4 out, no ext.*	3	0
1147	20/4	Higham	(L)	LAD 3m	9 F	*ld to 3rd & 4-10th, chsd wnr to 2 out, onepcd, lame*	3	20

Missed 95; ran consistently & won weak Ladies; likes Higham but more problems last start. 20

WITCH DOCTOR b or br.g. 8 Senang Hati - Cognac Queen by Armagnac Monarch — R W Phizacklea

1995 P(0),P(0),P(0),P(0)

1105	14/4	Guilsborough	(L)	MDN 3m	12 G	*made most to 7th, wknd rpdly, t.o. & p.u. 12th*	P	0
1183	21/4	Mollington	(R)	MDN 3m	10 F	*mstk 3rd, in tch til wknd 9th, last whn p.u. 11th*	P	0
1301	28/4	Southwell P'	(L)	MDO 3m	10 GF	*(vis) mid to rear, t.o. & p.u. 13th*	P	0
1580	19/5	Wolverhampt'	(L)	MDO 3m	8 G	*chsd ldrs to 9th, t.o. frm 14th*	3	0
1644	2/6	Dingley	(R)	MDO 3m	16 GF	*prom, ld & f 3rd*	F	-

Besten miles in dire Maiden; no prospects. 0

WITCHES PROMISE b.m. 6 Cruise Missile - Gregani by The Brianstan — Mrs K Lawther

1020	13/4	Kingston Bl'	(L)	MDN 3m	10 G	*prom, disp 10th-14th, lost 2nd 3 out, wknd, walked in*	3	0

Last & beaten a distance on debut; surely can do better. 12

WITCHIEWAH (Irish) — **I** 8[P], **I** 138[F], **I** 148[P], **I** 213[P]

WITH CREDIT (Irish) — **I** 305[F]

WITNESS OF TRUTH b.m. 6 Alias Smith (USA) - True Grit by Klairon — Mrs S Taylor

1995 **20(NH)**,**11(NH)**

193	24/2	Friars Haugh	(L)	MDN 3m	10 S	*sn bhnd, p.u. 10th*	P	0
322	2/3	Corbridge	(R)	MDN 3m	10 GS	*trckng ldrs whn f 4th*	F	-

No signs of ability now. 0

WOLFIE SMITH b.g. 6 Little Wolf - Gillie's Daughter by Hardiran — Mrs Jim Houldey

143	17/2	Larkhill	(R)	MDO 3m	14 G	*rear whn p.u. 4th*	P	0
354	3/3	Garnons	(L)	MDN 2 1/2m	13 GS	*alwys prom, ev ch 3 out, kpt on frm nxt*	3	14
606	23/3	Howick	(L)	MDN 3m	13 S	*(fav) ld/disp to 11th, wknd grad, p.u. 3 out*	P	0
1045	13/4	Bitterley	(L)	MDO 3m	16 G	*ld 2-4th, cls up to 14th, kpt on onepcd frm 3 out*	4	10

Beat 7 other horses in his placings; needs more to win though. 12

WOLF'S DEN ch.g. 7 Fools Holme (USA) - Tralee Falcon by Falcon — Mrs V Jackson

1995 6(0)
88 11/2 Alnwick (L) MDO 3m 11 GS *prom, ld 7-9th, wknd 11th, p.u. 2 out* P (
192 24/2 Friars Haugh (L) MDN 3m 12 S *ld til hdd nr fin* 2 13
407 9/3 Dalston (R) MDO 2 1/2m 13 G *ld 1st, rdn & disp 3 out, still there when f 2 out* F

Lightly raced; short headed in 7 minute plus race; fair chance of going one better; stays. 14

WOLF WINTER ch.g. 11 Wolverlife - Windara by Double-U-Jay Victor Dartnal
1995 **2(NH),1(NH),1(NH),3(NH)**
6 13/1 Larkhill (R) OPE 3m 18 GS *jmpd lft, prom, ld 9th-3 out, ev ch aft last, ran on onepcd* 2 29
39 3/2 Wadebridge (L) OPE 3m 7 GF *ld to 8th, chsd ldr, hrd rdn last, ran on to ld flat* 1 24
153 17/2 Erw Lon (L) OPE 3m 15 G *(fav) prom, ld 10th, hdd last, kpt on* 2 26
198 24/2 Lemalla (R) OPE 3m 12 HY *(fav) alwys prom, chal 3 out, ev ch nxt, no ext flat* 2 25
377 9/3 Barbury Cas' (L) OPE 3m 5 GS *(fav) made all, alwys in command, easily* 1 27
958 8/4 Lockinge (L) MXO 3m 6 GF *(fav) cls up, ld 10th, mstks 3 & 2 out, kpt on whn chal* 1 25

Winning chaser; very useful pointer; best L/H on galloping courses; should win more; G-Hy 28

WOLVERBANK (Irish) — **I** 95[3]
WOLVERCASTLE b.m. 8 Wolver Heights - Red Jenny by Red God Ian Wormald
409 9/3 Charm Park (L) CON 3m 11 G *rr early, tk 5th 3 out, nvr fctr* 5 16
590 23/3 Wetherby Po' (L) MDO 3m 16 S *mid-div, prog 11th, disp nxt, lft dist clr 4 out, easily* 1 14
1090 14/4 Whitwell-On' (R) RES 3m 17 G *(fav) mid-div, prog 13th, chal 4 out, sn onepcd, 2nd & btn, f last* F
1131 20/4 Hornby Cast' (L) RES 3m 17 G *mid-div whn u.r. 2nd* U
1284 27/4 Easingwold (L) RES 3m 14 G *prom, rdn 4 out, sn wknd* 7 0

Missed 95; romped home in 3 finisher stamina test; poor runs on easy tracks; more needed; Soft. 15

WOLVER'S PET(IRE) ch.g. 8 Tina's Pet - Wolviston by Wolverlife R W J Willcox
1995 P(0),4(12),2(14),4(14),2(13)
156 17/2 Erw Lon (L) RES 3m 13 G *twrds rear, prog hlfwy, 6th at 15th, fin well* 3 10
358 3/3 Garnons (L) RES 3m 18 GS *(fav) trckg ldrs whn f 2nd* F
388 9/3 Llanfrynach (R) RES 3m 20 GS *rear whn p.u. aft 4th* P 0

Maiden winner 93; lightly raced & below form in 96; Restricted still possible if fit in 97.G/F-S. 14

WONDER DAWN (Irish) — **I** 16[P]
WOODBINESANDROSES (Irish) — **I** 223[P], **I** 501[P]
WOODHAVEN LAD (Irish) — **I** 269[P], **I** 336[P], **I** 477[P], **I** 563[F], **I** 628[P]
WOODHAY HILL br.g. 11 Oats - Firs Park by Crozier J D V Seth-Smith
1995 **F(NH),P(NH),P(NH)**
25 20/1 Barbury Cas' (L) OPE 3m 14 GS *trckd ldrs, pshd alng 11th, wknd frm 13th* 7 14
178 18/2 Horseheath (R) INT 3m 11 G *prom til outpcd frm 15th, wll btn whn u.r. 2 out* U
365 5/3 Leicester (R) HC 3m 10 GS *bhnd 10th, styd on well from 4 out, nvr nrr.* 2 23

Ran well at Leicester but has never fulfilled promise in points or under Rules; best watched 97 19

WOODLAND CUTTING gr.g. 8 Pragmatic - Woodland Furbelow by Fury Royal Mrs P Glenn
2 13/1 Larkhill (R) MDO 3m 17 GS *alwys rear, t.o. & p.u. 13th* P 0
341 3/3 Heythrop (R) MDN 3m 13 G *in tch to hlfwy, no ch aft 13th, t.o. & p.u. 2 out* P 0
713 30/3 Barbury Cas' (L) MDO 3m 10 G *handy, 3rd at 11th, ev ch 4 out, no ext frm 2 out* 2 13

Gradual progress; beaten 8 lengths in 3 finisher race; improvement kikely & can go close in 97. 14

WOODLANDS GENHIRE ch.g. 11 Celtic Cone - Spartella by Spartan General Woodlands (Worcestershire) Ltd
1995 **5(NH),8(NH),4(NH),2(NH),8(NH),8(NH)**
909 8/4 Towcester (R) HC 2 3/4m 6 F *(vis) held up in tch, ld 7th, hdd apr 9th, wknd 11th.* 5 15
1108 17/4 Cheltenham (L) HC 4m 1f 14 GS *(vis) mid div when mstks 11th and 13th, bhnd final cct, t.o..* 5 14
1327 30/4 Huntingdon (R) HC 3m 6 GF *(vis) in tch, pushed along 5th, lost touch 14th, t.o..* 4 10
1539 16/5 Folkestone (R) HC 3m 7f 9 G *(vis) prom, chsd ldr 13th, ld after 15th to 2 out, one pace und pres.* 2 19

Slow plodder; nearly caused surprise in modest H/Chase last start - outclassed apart 18

WOODLIGHT DAWN ch.m. 7 St Columbus - Woodlight Fantasy by Happy Match W G Bevan
1384 6/5 Pantyderi (R) MEM 3m 2 GF *mstks, ld til aft last, no ext* 2 0
1492 11/5 Erw Lon (L) MDO 3m 10 F *alwys towrds rear, p.u. 11th* P 0

Beaten in a match run at a crawl; huge improvement needed. 0

WOOD LOUSE (Irish) — **I** 94[P]
WOODMANTON ch.m. 8 Brotherly (USA) - Vido by Vimadee Mark Hall
21 20/1 Barbury Cas' (L) MEM 3m 16 GS *alwys bhnd, t.o. & p.u. 15th* P 0
218 24/2 Newtown (L) MDN 3m 14 GS *in tch to 10th, wknd & p.u. 13th* P 0
841 6/4 Maisemore P' (L) MDN 3m 9 GF *prom til r.o. 5th* r
1048 13/4 Bitterley (L) MDO 3m 12 G *ld 4th til hdd & f 12th* F -

Shows speed but yet to complete; may do better. **10**

WOODROW CALL b.g. 10 Bishop Of Orange - Courtmac Fleur by Ragapan B Kennedy
1995 P(0),P(0),P(0),5(0)

35	20/1 Higham	(L) RES 3m	16 GF	*bhnd frm 12th, t.o.*	8	0
348	3/3 Higham	(L) RES 3m	12 G	*sn rear, t.o. 12th, p.u. 15th*	P	0
679	30/3 Cottenham	(R) RES 3m	15 GF	*in tch whn b.d. 5th*	B	-
935	8/4 Marks Tey	(L) MEM 3m	3 G	*alwys 2nd, rdn to disp brfly 10th, wknd 16th, p.u. 3 out*	P	0

Won weak Maiden & placed 6 times in 94; shown nothing since & looks troubled. **0**

WOODSIDE LADY(IRE) b.m. 8 Erin's Hope - Rose Almond by Stanford Denis Barry

3	13/1 Larkhill	(R) MDO 3m	10 GS	*ld to 13th, wknd rpdly & p.u. 15th*	P	0
205	24/2 Castle Of C'	(R) MDO 3m	9 HY	*nvr on terms, t.o. 13th, p.u. last*	P	0
652	23/3 Badbury Rin'	(L) MDO 3m	13 G	*alwys prom, ld 10th-14th, wknd next, t.o.*	5	0

Tailed off when completing & well short of stamina so far. **10**

WOODVILLE PRINCESS (Irish) — **I** 356, , **I** 459P

WOODWAY ch.g. 15 Tap On Wood - Clarina by Klairon Mrs C Bevan

266	2/3 Didmarton	(L) LAD 3m	13 G	*sn last, t.o. whn u.r. 11th*	U	-
640	23/3 Siddington	(L) LAD 3m	9 S	*ld 2nd til 5th, last frm 10th, t.o.*	6	0
1004	9/4 Upton-On-Se'	(R) OPE 3m	3 F	*ld to 3rd, last frm 8th, t.o. 11th, dsmntd aft fin*	3	0

Of no account **0**

WOODY DARE b.g. 6 Phardante (FR) - Woodland Pit by Pitpan P Needham

228	24/2 Duncombe Pa'	(R) MDO 3m	9 GS	*prom 8th til wknd apr 10th, p.u. nxt*	P	0
307	2/3 Great Stain'	(L) MDO 3m	17 GS	*mid-div, prog 11th, ld 15th til wknd apr last, onepcd flat*	3	14

beaten under 3 lengths (8 others behind); looks nailed on for a win in 97. .... **14**

WOODZEE b.g. 7 Durandal - Jeanne D'Accord by John de Coombe W J Bryan
1995 P(0)

883	6/4 Brampton Br'	(R) MDN 3m	13 GF	*cls up, ev ch 16th, wknd frm 2 out*	6	0
1272	27/4 Pyle	(R) MDO 3m	9 G	*trckd ldrs til p.u. lame aft 6th*	P	0

Showed some hope on 1st completion from 7 starts; problems next time & more needed. **12**

WOOLAW LASS(USA) b.m. 8 Full Extent (USA) - Current River (USA) by Little Current (USA) Mrs M E Anderson

52	4/2 Alnwick	(L) MDO 3m	11 G	*prom, ld brfly 5th, wkng whn mst 9th, p.u. 3 out*	P	0
89	11/2 Alnwick	(L) MDO 3m	9 GS	*prom til f 6th*	F	-
194	24/2 Friars Haugh	(L) MDN 3m	11 S	*bhnd whn p.u. 7th*	P	0
321	2/3 Corbridge	(R) MDN 3m	12 GS	*mid-div whn f 14th*	F	-
613	23/3 Friars Haugh	(L) MDN 3m	15 G	*bhnd whn p.u. 4th*	P	0

Of no account **0**

WOOLOOMOOLOO (Irish) — **I** 366[1]

WOOLSTONWOOD b.m. 7 Scallywag - Golden Valley by Hotfoot J E Bownes
1995 P(0),F(-),P(0),P(0)

158	17/2 Weston Park	(L) MEM 3m	11 G	*mid-div, some late prog, nvr dang*	6	0
502	16/3 Lanark	(R) MDO 3m	7 G	*lost tch by 12th, p.u. 2 out*	P	0
1008	9/4 Flagg Moor	(L) MDO 2 1/2m	7 G	*t.d.e., jmpd bdly, sn wl bhnd, t.o. & p.u. 10th*	P	0

Last on 1st completion; unpromising. **0**

WOOLY TOWN b.m. 9 Town And Country - Something Slinky by Chingnu W Williams

847	6/4 Howick	(L) LAD 3m	9 GF	*alwys last pair, t.o. & p.u. 15th*	P	0
1271	27/4 Pyle	(R) MDO 3m	15 G	*alwys rear, t.o. 10th, p.u. nxt*	P	0

Of no account **0**

WORKINGFORPEANUTS(IRE) ch.m. 6 Entitled - Tracy's Sundown by Red Sunset Mrs D A Smith
1995 3(20),1(19),U(-),F(-),1(18),4(17),3(16),2(21)

27	20/1 Barbury Cas'	(L) LAD 3m	15 GS	*hld up bhnd, gd prog frm 12th, chsd wnr last, no imp flat*	2	23
76	11/2 Wetherby Po'	(L) LAD 3m	8 GS	*in tch, ld 11th-13th, 2nd whn u.r. 3 out*	U	-
154	17/2 Erw Lon	(L) LAD 3m	14 G	*hld up, steady prog frm 10th, 2nd 2 out, no ch wnr*	2	22
385	9/3 Llanfrynach	(R) LAD 3m	14 GS	*sttld in tch,effrt 3 out,chsd wnr apr last,fin wll,alwys hld*	2	24
586	23/3 Wetherby Po'	(L) LAD 3m	8 S	*(fav) mid-div, gd prog to ld last, ran on well*	1	22
1003	9/4 Upton-On-Se'	(R) LAD 3m	4 F	*tckd ldr to 6th & frm 14th, ld app last, qckn clr flat*	1	24

Useful Ladies pointer now; beaten by good horses in 96; sure to win more if fit 97; G/F-S **25**

WORKING MAN(IRE) ch.g. 5 Duky - Candolcis by Candy Cane M W Hoskins

283	2/3 Clyst St Ma'	(L) MDN 3m	7 S	*hld up, prog 14th, ev ch 3 out, outpcd aft*	3	0
533	16/3 Cothelstone	(L) MDN 3m	13 G	*b.d. 2nd*	B	-

733	31/3 Little Wind'	(R) MDO 3m	13 GS	*not fluent, rear til p.u. apr 10th*	P	0
807	4/4 Clyst St Ma'	(L) MDO 3m	10 GS	*not fluent, alwys rear*	5	0

Beaten 25 lengths minimum & yet to beat another horse. can do better. 10

WORLESTON FARRIER b.g. 8 Looking Glass - Madame Serenity by What A Man — Mrs A J Flanders

1995 P(0),P(0),5(0),3(10),P(0),P(0)

164	17/2 Weston Park	(L) RES 3m	11 G	*ld to aft 3 out, sn outpcd by wnr*	2	0
293	2/3 Eaton Hall	(R) INT 3m	11 G	*ld to 9th, cls up & ev ch, no ext last*	3	17
667	24/3 Eaton Hall	(R) INT 3m	11 S	*ld to 3 out, outpcd aft*	4	10
739	31/3 Sudlow Farm	(R) RES 3m	11 G	*ld to 8th, chsd ldr, ld apr last, sn clr, rddn out*	1	18
855	6/4 Sandon	(L) CON 3m	6 GF	*(Jt fav) j.w., made all, conf rddn*	1	20

Improved; runs tubed; front runs, stays & should find another small Confined; G/F-S. 20

WORTHY MEMORIES b.m. 7 Don't Forget Me - Intrinsic by Troy — Mrs E M Bousquet-Payne

344	3/3 Higham	(L) MDO 3m	12 G	*handy, cls up 7th, p.u. nxt, saddle slppd*	P	0
423	9/3 High Easter	(L) MDN 3m	8 S	*made most til blnd 14th,wknd 3 out,3rd & no ch whn p.u. last*	P	0
618	23/3 Higham	(L) MDO 3m	14 GF	*ld 4th, still prom but und pres whn mstk & u.r. 13th*	U	-

Shows speed but no stamina so far. 11

WORTHY SPARK b.g. 11 Lighter - Sardan by Lauso — A J Balmer

1995 1(21),2(17),F(-)

187	24/2 Friars Haugh	(L) CON 3m	12 S	*ld 7th til apr 2 out, just ld agn whn f last*	F	19
399	9/3 Dalston	(R) CON 3m	9 G	*(fav) ld 2nd, clr at 8th tl jnd at last, qcknd away on flat*	1	22
609	23/3 Friars Haugh	(L) PPO 3m	7 G	*(fav) made all, blnd 13th, hrd prssd apr last, styd on gamely*	1	19
789	1/4 Kelso	(L) HC 3m 1f	11 GF	*(fav) j.w, ld to 6 out, led 3 out, hdd run-in, no ext.*	2	20
1083	14/4 Friars Haugh	(L) CON 3m	10 F	*(fav) ld til hdd & wknd 4 out*	3	16

Had a good season; front runs & needs easy 3 miles; goes well fresh; can win again; G/F-S. 20

WOT PET b.g. 13 Crozier - Annies Pet by Normandy — C G Taylor

1995 P(0),P(0),U(-),6(0),3(0),2(17),r(-),5(0)

289	2/3 Eaton Hall	(R) CON 3m	10 G	*chsd ldrs to 6th, outpcd frm 12th, p.u. 4 out*	P	0
664	24/3 Eaton Hall	(R) CON 3m	15 S	*mid-div whn u.r. 9th*	U	-
736	31/3 Sudlow Farm	(R) CON 3m	9 G	*sn wll bhnd, t.o. frm 6th*	5	0
855	6/4 Sandon	(L) CON 3m	6 GF	*sn rear, jmp round in own time, btn 2 fences*	5	0

Maiden winner 94; novice ridden & of no account now. 0

WREKIN HILL b.g. 14 Duky - Cummin Hill by Wrekin Rambler — Mrs J V Wilkinson

1995 3(10),4(14),1(12),2(18),2(16),S(-),**4(14),8(0),P(NH)**

273	2/3 Parham	(R) LAD 3m	11 GF	*alwys well in rear, t.o. final cct*	5	0
469	10/3 Milborne St'	(L) LAD 3m	8 G	*chsd ldrs, no ch & outpcd frm 3 out*	3	19
783	31/3 Tweseldown	(R) MEM 3m	5 G	*(fav) w.w. prog to ld 10th, jnd 12th, hdd 3out, ld nxt, pshd out*	1	14
867	6/4 Larkhill	(R) MXO 4m	6 F	*(fav) hndy,ld 13th,jnd 5 out,blndrd nxt,hd 2 out,ev ch last outpcd*	2	17
1190	21/4 Tweseldown	(R) MEM 3m	3 GF	*hld up in 3rd, blnd & u.r. 3rd, rmntd, ref 4th*	R	-
1310	28/4 Little Wind'	(R) LAD 3m	4 G	*rear, prog 15th, tk 3rd clsng stgs*	3	17
1463	10/5 Stratford	(L) HC 3m	6 GF	*in tch to 10th, soon bhnd.*	4	15
1613	27/5 Fontwell	(R) HC 3 1/4m 110yds	12 G	*well bhnd till hdwy 13th, chsd ldrs 18th, one pace from next.*	3	15

Grand old stager; won Members 94/96; stays well; every chance of Members again. 13

WRENBURY FARMER ch.g. 6 Say Primula - Willow Path by Farm Walk — K O'Meara

1044	13/4 Bitterley	(L) MDO 3m	15 G	*nvr going pace, t.o. & ref 4th*	R	-
1224	24/4 Brampton Br'	(R) MDO 3m	17 G	*v slw jmp 5th, t.o. frm 8th*	5	0
1378	5/5 Dingley	(R) MDO 2 1/2m	16 GF	*rear, prog & in tch hlfwy, sn btn, t.o. & p.u. last*	P	0

Yet to show anything. 0

WRITER'S QUAY ch.g. 13 Quayside - Chapter Four by Shuffleton — John Jones

1995 2(14),**2(22)**

1211	23/4 Chepstow	(L) HC 3m	13 S	*hdwy 9th, ev ch 13th, wknd next, p.u. before 4 out.*	P	0

Members winner 94; late start & vanished after in 96; can only be watched now. 16

WRITE THE MUSIC b.g. 15 Riboboy (USA) - Zither by Vienna — Miss E M Davison

1995 4(0),U(-),7(13),S(-),2(18),P(0),1(16),P(0),4(0)

632	23/3 Market Rase'	(L) CON 3m	10 GF	*(bl) rider hit by clod in eye & p.u. 4th*	P	0
634	23/3 Market Rase'	(L) OPE 3m	6 GF	*(bl) 2nd outing, rear in tch, 4th 2 out, ran on well, just hld*	2	18
723	31/3 Garthorpe	(R) CON 3m	19 G	*(bl) alwys bhnd, t.o. 7th, last whn u.r. 15th*	U	-
902	6/4 Dingley	(R) OPE 3m	4 GS	*(bl) cls up,jmp rght,3rd 6 out,lost wght clth 2 out,fin fast,disq*	3D	18
1237	27/4 Clifton On '	(L) OPE 3m	5 GF	*(bl) sn pshd alng, in tch, chsd 1st pair 4 out, sn outpcd*	3	11
1376	5/5 Dingley	(R) MEM 3m	7 GF	*(fav) (bl) in tch, mstk 3 out, sn trckd ldr, ld aft last, sn clr,easily*	1	13

Retains some ability; moody but fulfilled last years prediction in Members; same possible at 17. 17

WUDIMP b.g. 7 Import - Weewumpawud by King Log — C Storey

1995 1(16),1(19),1(21),**2(22)**,1(20)

37	3/2 Wetherby	(L) HC	3m 110yds	11 GS	*nvr far away, chsd wnr from 4 out, kept on, no impn.*	2	30
367	6/3 Catterick	(L) HC	3m 1f 110yds	12 G	*(fav) nvr far away, ld 16th, clr after 3 out, eased run-in.*	1	28
486	16/3 Newcastle	(L) HC	3m	9 GS	*(fav) held up in rear, blnd 12th, hdwy after 4 out, chal last, soon ld, kept on well.*	1	25
670	28/3 Aintree	(L) HC	3m 1f	9 G	*(fav) midfield, ld 12th, mstk next, driven clr apr last, kept on well und pres.*	1	29
1542	16/5 Perth	(R) HC	2 1/2m 110yds	8 F	*(fav) held up, hit 9th, driven along after 6 out, no impn apr 2 out.*	6	15
1630	31/5 Stratford	(L) HC	3 1/2m	16 GF	*mid div when blnd 15th, soon wknd, t.o. when p.u. before 2 out.*	P	0

Useful novice H/Chaser & won valuable prize Aintree; ran badly after break; should win more 97; G/S-F 29

WUNDERBAR b.g. 9 Strong Gale - Wunder Madchen by Brave Invader (USA) N J Pomfret
1995 P(0)

9	14/1 Cottenham	(R) OPE 3m	13 G	*b.d. 2nd*	B	-
26	20/1 Barbury Cas'	(L) OPE 3m	12 GS	*prom to 8th, wknd rpdly & p.u. 10th*	P	0

Of no account 0

WYLFA BOY (Irish) — **I** 125⁶, **I** 201, , **I** 250ᴾ

WYN WAN SOON (Irish) — **I** 81ᴾ, **I** 131, , **I** 139ᴾ, **I** 193ᵁ, **I** 223², **I** 386,

YABBADABBADOO b.g. 10 Royal Fountain - Annie Buskins by Little Buskins Mrs L Bedford

340	3/3 Heythrop	(R) MDN 3m	12 G	*prom, ld 6-10th, wknd aft nxt, p.u. 13th*	P	0
495	16/3 Horseheath	(R) MDO 3m	12 GF	*hld up bhnd, rmndrs 10th, t.o. frm 12th*	4	0
890	6/4 Kimble	(L) MDN 3m	11 GF	*rear, gd prog 14th, chsd wnr 3 out, btn whn mstk last*	2	11
1182	21/4 Mollington	(R) MDN 3m	10 F	*(fav) w.w. prog to jn wnr 14th, btn aft nxt, p.u. 2 out, lame*	P	0

Missed 94/95; placed in weak races; more problems now & win may have passed him by. 13

YAHOO b.g. 15 Trombone - Coolroe Aga by Laurence O Steven Astaire
1995 P(0),2(20),3(15),5(10),3(20),2(13),4(10),6(0),3(0),4(0)

19	14/1 Tweseldown	(R) CON 3m	9 GS	*raced wd, hit 2nd, wll bhnd hlfwy, plodded on*	5	12
377	9/3 Barbury Cas'	(L) OPE 3m	5 GS	*sn rear, t.o. frm 11th*	4	0
782	31/3 Tweseldown	(R) XX 3m	6 G	*16s-12s,cls up,ld 9th,qcknd clr 4 out,idld flat,jnd fin*	1	13
1015	13/4 Kingston Bl'	(L) MEM 3m	9 G	*last, prog hlfwy, outpcd 14th, no prog aft*	5	10
1190	21/4 Tweseldown	(R) MEM 3m	3 GF	*j.w. ld, jnd last, no ext flat, dead*	2	16

A great old campaigner who went out in the best possible manner 14

YANKIE LORD (Irish) — **I** 407ᴾ, **I** 493ᴾ

YARRON KING b.g. 10 Push On - Baming by Barbin Miss R Y Hamer
1995 **U(-)**

432	9/3 Upton-On-Se'	(R) MDO 3m	17 GS	*disp 3rd-9th, wknd & p.u. 3 out*	P	0
605	23/3 Howick	(L) MDN 3m	13 S	*(fav) (bl) ld to 13th, disp to 15th, wknd, fin v tired*	3	0
850	6/4 Howick	(L) MDN 3m	14 GF	*(fav) (bl) ld to 13th, wknd rpdly*	5	0

Placed 65 times 94/96; ungenuine, does not stay & will not win. 10

YASGOURRA (Irish) — **I** 203ᴾ, **I** 253ᶠ, **I** 290⁴, **I** 370⁴, **I** 471³, **I** 510⁴, **I** 631ᴾ

YASHGANS VISION (Irish) — **I** 324ᴾ, **I** 418⁴, **I** 521ᴾ

YENOORA(IRE) b.g. 7 Ahonoora - Beijing (USA) by Northjet Mrs Sue Bell
1995 **P(NH)**

83	11/2 Alnwick	(L) CON 3m	10 GS	*prom til p.u. 7th, dsmntd*	P	0
612	23/3 Friars Haugh	(L) OPE 3m	8 G	*sn bhnd, t.o. whn p.u. 11th*	P	0
701	30/3 Tranwell	(L) OPE 3m	8 GS	*prom to 8th, bhnd whn f 10th*	F	-
861	6/4 Alnwick	(L) CON 3m	7 GF	*ld 1st-2nd, lsng pl whn u.r. 10th*	U	-
1133	20/4 Hornby Cast'	(L) OPE 3m	14 G	*rear, sn strggling, t.o. & p.u. aft 12th*	P	0
1474	11/5 Aspatria	(L) OPE 3m	3 GF	*(bl) pulld hrd, ld aft 1st-8th, sn t.o., p.u. bfr 16th*	P	0
1573	19/5 Corbridge	(R) OPE 3m	12 G	*bhnd whn f 3rd*	F	-

A disaster in points & no prospects 0

YEOMAN CRICKETER ch.g. 11 Buckskin (FR) - Kates Princess by Pitpan M E Kirkham

1001	9/4 Upton-On-Se'	(R) MEM 3m	6 F	*last, t.o. frm 8th, fin well*	4	0

Only 2 runs in last 3 seasons & will not be winning again now. 12

YEOMAN FARMER br.g. 12 Trombone - Ballykeel Owen by Master Owen Miss P Wood
1995 P(0),1(17),3(14),1(0),6(12),2(16)

32	20/1 Higham	(L) OPE 3m	15 GF	*in tch to 11th, p.u. 13th*	P	0
251	25/2 Charing	(L) OPE 3m	10 GS	*wll in rear early, steady prog 13th, 4th & ev ch 4 out, wknd*	3	12
451	9/3 Charing	(L) OPE 3m	11 G	*w.w. dtchd 12th,rpd prog 4 out,wth wnr whn blnd last,nt rcvr*	3	16
776	31/3 Penshurst	(L) OPE 3m	6 GS	*in tch in rear, drvn up to 3rd 2 out, no ext flat*	3	18

811 6/4 Charing (L) OPE 3m 9 F *alwys rear, mstk 12th, nvr thrtnd* 6 14
1050 13/4 Penshurst (L) CON 3m 8 G *in tch, 4th & btn 4 out* 5 14
1444 6/5 Aldington (L) OPE 3m 6 HD *sttld off pce, efft 15th, 3rd aft 2 out, not pce to chal* 3 16

Consistent but moderate; needs a run to get fit; onepaced & win not easy to find now. 15

YET TO DANCE b.m. 6 Mashhor Dancer (USA) - Fayette by Dom Racine (FR) Michael Kent

206 24/2 Castle Of C' (R) MDO 3m 10 HY *ld to 9th, wknd & p.u. 13th* P 0
521 16/3 Larkhill (R) MDO 3m 6 G *ld, 20l clr 12th, p.u. nxt, lame* P 0

Shows plenty of speed; problems last start. 13

YORNOANGEL b.g. 7 Lochnager - Angel Dust by Pitskelly W Brown

1995 U(-),F(-),P(0)

122 17/2 Witton Cast' (R) MDO 3m 8 S *cls up, ld 4th, clr 6th-13th, wknd & hdd 3 out, onepcd aft* 3 11
415 9/3 Charm Park (L) MDO 3m 13 G *cls up, 2nd 3 out, r.o. nxt* r -
764 31/3 Great Stain' (L) MDN 3m 16 GS *rear, prog frm 7th, ev ch aft 2 out, not qckn* 3 13
986 8/4 Charm Park (L) MDN 3m 10 GF *(fav) mid-div, prog 9th, 3rd frm 3 out, outpcd aft* 3 10

Improved; beaten 11 lengths maximum in weak races; stamina doubtfulA& needs a little more to win. .. 13

YOUBETYA (Irish) — I 473^{5}, I 555^{3}

YOUBETYA(IRE) b.m. 5 Welsh Term - On The Bluff by Proverb Lady Sarah Barry

21 20/1 Barbury Cas' (L) MEM 3m 16 GS *mstk 5th, rear whn f 8th* F -
68 10/2 Great Treth' (R) RES 3m 14 S *nvr a fctr, p.u. aft 14th* P 0

Ex-Irish; top stable; should be up to winning but a brief season & nothing in 96 15

YOUCAT (Irish) — I 268^{4}, I 334^{1}, I 519^{1}

YOU KNOW BEST (Irish) — I 2^{P}, I 35^{1}, I 72^{2}, I 234^{2}

YOU NAME IT (Irish) — I 178^{1}, I 281^{F}

YOUNGANDFAIR (Irish) — I 392^{U}, I 561,

YOUNG BEBE (Irish) — I 302^{P}, I 340, , I 391^{P}, I 415^{4}, I 455^{F}

YOUNG BRAVE b.g. 10 Warpath - Mekhala by Menelek David Young

1995 3(19),1(23),1(21),**2(27),1(31),2(31),4(29)**

731 31/3 Little Wind' (R) OPE 3m 5 GS *(Jt fav) j.w., disp ld thruout til qcknd clr 2 out, imp* 1 29
1166 20/4 Larkhill (R) OPE 3m 6 GF *(fav) tckd awy in rear, prog frm 13th, ld apr last, easily* 1 28
1334 1/5 Cheltenham (L) HC 3 1/4m 110yds 3 G *(fav) with ldr, blnd 5th, left in ld 10th, clr 3 out, idld run-in, driven out.* 1 24
1459 8/5 Uttoxeter (L) HC 4 1/4m 8 G *held up, prog into 3rd 18th, ld 3 out, clr when mstk next, hit last, comf.* 1 30

Useful pointer/H/chaser; stays well; 4 miles ideal; needs more for top races; win more; G/S-F. 30

YOUNG CAL (Irish) — I 358^{P}

YOUNG ENTRY (Irish) — I 94^{P}, I 168^{P}, I 363^{4}, I 412^{5}, I 536^{1}, I 570^{1}, I 643,

YOUNG GUN b.g. 9 Le Moss - Bavardmore by Le Bavard (FR) J A Wales

1995 F(-),P(0),6(0),4(0),3(0)

95 11/2 Ampton (R) RES 3m 11 GF *mid-div, outpcd 12th, p.u. 3 out* P 0

Maiden winner 93; only 6 runs since; finished early 96 & can only be watched now. 10

YOUNG MOSS b.g. 10 Le Moss - Young Ash Linn by Deep Run S G Jones

1995 U(-),4(0),4(10),1(13),5(10)

77 11/2 Wetherby Po' (L) RES 3m 18 GS *alwys rear, nvr a fctr, p.u. 4 out* P 0
121 17/2 Witton Cast' (R) RES 3m 11 S *ld/disp to 10th, wknd nxt, kpt on in mid-div aft* 5 13
329 3/3 Market Rase' (L) RES 3m 12 G *alwys rear, nvr nr ldrs, some late prog* 6 0
585 23/3 Wetherby Po' (L) RES 3m 13 S *alwys mid-div, kpt on onepcd frm 3 out, no dang* 4 11

Won weak Maiden 95; stays but struggling now upgraded & follow up looks too tough. 15

YOUNG MRS KELLY (Irish) — I 126^{2}

YOUNG PARSON b.g. 10 The Parson - Dadooronron by Deep Run T D Marlow

1995 **11(NH),P(NH),U(NH),5(NH)**

882 6/4 Brampton Br' (R) RES 3m 14 GF *just in tch 12th, no ch frm 15th* 5 0

Placed in novice chase; well beaten on only start; more needed. 10

YOUNG TIGER ch.g. 6 Dubassoff (USA) - Lady Brooklyn by Streak E J Legg

1995 P(0),P(0),U(-)

734 31/3 Little Wind' (R) MDO 3m 11 GS *mstk 1st, ld & jmp slwly 3rd, 6th whn ref 6th* R -
993 8/4 Kingston St' (R) MDO 3m 17 F *prom, jmpd lft 4th, 3rd whn f 7th* F -
1531 12/5 Ottery St M' (L) MDO 3m 9 GF *6th hlfwy, wkng whn mstk 14th, wll btn 4 out* 8 0

Yet to complete & unpromising. 0

YOUR OPINION gr.g. 10 Cut Above - Dance Mistress by Javelot — C James

1995 U(-),U(-),6(12),4(15),2(15),5(11),5(0)

24	20/1	Barbury Cas'	(L)	XX	3m	12 GS	*mstks, blnd 4th & lost plc, t.o. & p.u. 15th*	P	0

Irish Maiden winner 90; non stayer & finished early in 96; need a poor race for a win. 14

YQUEM(IRE) ch.g. 6 Henbit (USA) - Silent Run by Deep Run — Mrs L M Boulter

1995 2(0)

1117	17/4	Hockworthy	(L)	MDO	3m	8 GS	*(fav) tckd ldrs, ld 13th, clr app 2 out, easily*	1	16
1313	28/4	Little Wind'	(R)	RES	3m	14 G	*(fav) hld up rear, prog to 5th at 14th, went 2nd 16th, not qckn*	2	17

Confirmed promise & ran well in decent Restricted after; only raced 3 times & sure to win if fit 97 19

YUKON GALE(IRE) br.g. 8 Strong Gale - Lou by Arctic Chevalier — J Aled Griffiths

1233	27/4	Weston Park	(L)	RES	3m	14 G	*(fav) cls up, ld/disp 5th, clr 12th, gng wll f 4 out*	F	17
1582	19/5	Wolverhampt'	(L)	RES	3m	10 G	*(fav) ld, slppd lndg 12th, hdd 16th, 4th & btn, p.u. nxt*	P	0

Irish Maiden winner 95; unlucky 1st start but stopped quickly next time; problems? best watched. 17

ZALLOT br.g. 9 Gleaming Wave - Zara by Sooner Peace — Miss M R Palmer

1995 P(0),5(0),P(0),2(0)

253	25/2	Charing	(L)	MDO	3m	10 GS	*prom to 8th, bhnd whn p.u. 12th*	P	0
275	2/3	Parham	(R)	MDN	3m	15 GF	*alwys well in rear, lost tch 13th*	4	0
576	17/3	Detling	(L)	MDN	3m	18 GF	*mid-div to 10th, bhnd whn p.u. 14th*	P	0

Of no account 0

ZAMANAYN(IRE) gr.g. 8 Mouktar - Zariya (USA) by Blushing Groom (FR) — Miss Carolyn Morgan

765	31/3	Pantyderi	(R)	MEM	3m	3 G	*bolted into ld, f 2nd*	F	-

Not a good start. 0

ZAM BEE br.g. 10 Zambrano - Brown Bee III by Marcus Superbus — Mrs A Bell

169	18/2	Market Rase'	(L)	CON	3m	15 GF	*j.w. jnd ldr 10th, ld 15th, bttr jmps last 2, hld on*	1	21
327	3/3	Market Rase'	(L)	CON	3m	15 G	*(fav) j.w. disp 4th, ld 11th, drew clr frm 14th, fin 1st, disq*	0D	22
513	16/3	Dalton Park	(R)	OPE	3m	9 G	*(fav) prssd ldr frm 3rd til ld 15th, clr 3 out, easily*	1	25
724	31/3	Garthorpe	(R)	LAD	3m	5 G	*(fav) s.s. rcvrd to ld 3rd, hdd 2 out, mstk last, rallied flat*	2	24
1133	20/4	Hornby Cast'	(L)	OPE	3m	14 G	*(fav) alwys handy, prog to ld 4 out, hdd & onepcd 2 out*	2	24
1463	10/5	Stratford	(L)	HC	3m	6 GF	*(fav) ld 3rd to 6th, chsd wnr after, hmpd apr 5 out, no impn.*	2	21
1546	18/5	Fakenham	(L)	HC	3m 110yds	13 G	*ld till hdd 3 out, rallied last, just failed.*	2	26
1631	1/6	Stratford	(L)	HC	3 1/2m	14 GF	*prom till wknd 10th.*	5	23

Winning chaser; novice ridden; jumps, stays but onepaced; could win weak H/chase; G-F. 26

ZANY GIRL b.m. 9 Idiot's Delight - Noble Leaf by Sahib — P Ansell

1995 P(0),P(0),P(0),P(0),P(0),P(0)

71	10/2	Great Treth'	(R)	MDO	3m	15 S	*(bl) nvr a fctr, p.u. 13th*	P	0
201	24/2	Lemalla	(R)	MDO	3m	13 HY	*(bl) alwys bhnd, p.u. aft 13th*	P	0
300	2/3	Great Treth'	(R)	MDO	3m	10 G	*(bl) mid-div, 6th whn mstk 14th, p.u. 16th*	P	0
557	17/3	Ottery St M'	(L)	MDN	3m	10 G	*(bl) alwys rear, no ch frm 15th*	5	0
714	30/3	Wadebridge	(L)	MEM	3m	3 GF	*(bl) chsd wnr, lkd reluc, some prog 13th, sn rdn & wknd*	2	0
1071	13/4	Lifton	(R)	MDN	3m	10 S	*(bl) n.j.w., lost tch 15th, reluctant & jmp slwly clsng stgs*	6	0
1362	4/5	Flete Park	(R)	MDO	3m	9 G	*twrds rear, 6th at 14th, bhnd frm 17th*	6	0

At least she's getting round now but ungenuine & need a miracle to win. 10

ZAP(IRE) b.m. 8 Pitskelly - Cookstown Lady by Linacre — Mrs Fiona Herbert

617	23/3	Higham	(L)	MDO	3m	11 GF	*prom, wknd rpdly 7th, t.o. & u.r. 10th*	U	-
682	30/3	Cottenham	(R)	MDO	3m	9 GF	*mid-div, blnd 13th, not rcvr, p.u. nxt*	P	0
931	8/4	Marks Tey	(L)	RES	3m	8 G	*slw jmp 1st, alwys rear, lost tch 10th, p.u. 13th*	P	0

No signs of ability yet. 0

ZENISKA(USA) b.g. 8 Cozzene (USA) - Istiska (FR) by Irish River (FR) — Mrs P King

1995 P(0),P(0),4(10),3(12),**P(0)**,6(0),5(0)

12	14/1	Cottenham	(R)	RES	3m	12 G	*chsd ldrs, went 2nd 3 out, ld nxt, clr & blnd last, rdn out*	1	19
178	18/2	Horseheath	(R)	INT	3m	11 G	*in tch to 7th, last by 9th, t.o. & p.u. 2 out*	P	0
395	9/3	Garthorpe	(R)	OPE	3m	7 G	*alwys last pair, t.o. last frm 7th, p.u. 4 out*	P	0
621	23/3	Higham	(L)	INT	3m	12 GF	*alwys rear, lost tch 8th, t.o. & p.u. last*	P	0

Changed hands after winning; does not stay & most unlikely to win again. 11

ZIEG (Irish) — **I** 288[6], **I** 321[P], **I** 404[2], **I** 495[3]

ZILFI(USA) b.g. 6 Lyphard (USA) - Over Your Shoulder (USA) by Graustark — Mrs L Worley

777	31/3	Penshurst	(L)	LAD	3m	7 GS	*prom early, wll bhnd whn p.u. 11th*	P	0
963	8/4	Heathfield	(R)	MXO	3m	7 G	*s.s. sn rcvd, lst tch 10th, t.o. & p.u. 4 out*	P	0
1208	21/4	Heathfield	(R)	LAD	3m	6 F	*ld to 6th & agn 9th, disp 10-13th, cls up whn ran out nxt*	r	-

1297	28/4 Bexhill	(R) LAD 3m	7 F	*ld to 2nd, cls up whn ran out bnd apr 4th*	r	-

Flat winner; shows speed (not unexpected) but wayward & unlikely to stay or win. 0

ZIN ZAN(IRE) br.g. 8 Strong Gale - Meanwood by Tap On Wood — M B Mawhinney

1995 P(0),r(-)

591	23/3 Wetherby Po'	(L) MDO 3m	14 S	*plld hrd, ld to 3rd, lft in ld nxt, wknd 10th, p.u. 14th*	P	0
762	31/3 Great Stain'	(L) MDN 3m	11 GS	*rear, prog 12th, styd on frm 3 out*	3	11
1137	20/4 Hornby Cast'	(L) MDN 3m	13 G	*disp mostly, ev ch flat, kpt on well*	2	15
1450	6/5 Witton Cast'	(R) MDO 3m	14 G	*(fav) made most, 2l clr 2 out, ran on flat, just hdd nr line*	2	15

Improved; beaten less than a length last 2 starts; front runs; novice ridden; should win. 15

ZOFLO b.m. 8 Zambrano - Aunt Bertha by Blandford Lad — Mrs F J Drysdale

1995 P(0),P(0),P(0),P(0),R(-),P(0)

503	16/3 Lanark	(R) MDO 3m	10 G	*ld til 4 out, wknd rpdly, t.o. & p.u. aft last*	P	0
756	31/3 Lockerbie	(R) MDN 3m	14 G	*5th hlfwy, no ext frm 4 out*	7	0
913	8/4 Tranwell	(L) LAD 3m	7 GF	*chsd ldng pair to hlfwy, wknd 13th, p.u. 3 out*	P	0
1089	14/4 Friars Haugh	(L) MDN 3m	10 F	*made most frm 3rd til 14th, no ext frm 3 out*	4	0
1253	27/4 Balcormo Ma'	(R) MDO 3m	16 GS	*prom to hlfwy, bhnd whn p.u. 4 out*	P	0

Completed 3 of 14 races; only beat one other horse in 96; much more needed. 10

ZORRO'S MARK b.g. 9 My Rough Diamond - Hawksbill by Tomahawk IV — Mrs J E Purdie

7	13/1 Larkhill	(R) CON 3m	10 GS	*in tch, effrt 12th, lost tch wth ldrs 14th, no dang aft*	6	0
210	24/2 Castle Of C'	(R) INT 3m	10 HY	*cls up to 14th, no ext aft*	4	12
467	10/3 Milborne St'	(L) MEM 3m	8 G	*p.u. before 3rd, lame*	P	0

Dual winner 93; missed 95; not recapture form & more problems now; can only be watched. 14

STATISTICAL LEADERS 1996

LEADING HUNTER CHASE WINNERS

Teaplanter	4
Royal Jester	3
King's Treasure (USA)	3
Wild Illusion	3
Wudimp	3
My Nominee	3
Howaryasun (IRE)	3
Holland House	3
Chilipour	3
Sheer Jest	2
Hermes Harvest	2
Colonial Kelly	2
Mr Golightly	2
Double Silk	2
Rolling Ball (FR)	2
Oaklands Word	2
Familiar Friend	2
The Major General	2
Young Brave	2
Little Wenlock	2
Beau Dandy	2
The Jogger	2
Over The Edge	2

LEADING HUNTER CHASE RIDERS

R White	7
C Storey	6
B Pollock	5
J Culloty	4
D S Jones	4
J Jukes	4
M Rimell	4
C Vigors	4
A Balding	3
A Griffith	3
N Harris	3
R Hicks	3
Capt A Ogden	3
Miss L Blackford	2
M Bradburne	2
A Charles-Jones	2
R Ford	2
P Hacking	2
A Hill	2
Mrs V Jackson	2
L Lay	2
T Marks	2
M Miller	2
A Phillips	2
Mrs J Reed	2
S Sporborg	2
R Sweeting	2
S Swiers	2
J Tizzard	2
R Treloggen	2

P-T-P LEADING GENTLEMEN RIDERS

J Jukes	34
A Crow	27
A Parker	22
P Hacking	20
T Mitchell	19
S Swiers	16
L Jefford	14
N Harris	13
J Tudor	13
A Dalton	12
R Sweeting	12
N Wilson	11
D S Jones	11
T Greed	11
G Hanmer	10
A Farrant	10
Julian Pritchard	10
S Sporborg	10
A Hill	10
R Ford	10
T Scott	10
M Miller	10
N Bloom	10

P-T-P LEADING LADY RIDERS

Miss A Dare	31
Miss P Curling	23
Miss P Jones	20
Miss J Cumings	19
Miss S Vickery	15
Miss G Chown	10
Miss R Francis	10
Miss S Baxter	8
Miss L Blackford	7
Miss L Hollis	7
Miss L Rowe	7
Miss P Robson	6
Mrs M Hand	6
Miss E James	6
Mrs J Dawson	6
Mrs F Needham	6
Miss C Spearing	6
Miss S Young	6
Miss C Holliday	6
Mrs K Sunderland	5
Miss A Goschen	5
Miss M Hill	5

LEADING P-T-P HORSES

Phar Too Touchy	10
Di Stefano	7
Out The Door (IRE)	6
Chilipour	6
Handsome Harvey	6
Todcrag	6
Faithful Star	6
Bankhead (IRE)	6
The General's Drum	5
St Gregory	5
Khattaf	5
Scally Muire	5
Lucky Christopher	5
Richard Hunt	5
African Bride (IRE)	5
Burromariner	5
Tasmin Tyrant (NZ)	5
Lewesdon Hill	5
Desert Waltz (IRE)	4
Sperrin View	4
Flame O'Frensi	4
Shoon Wind	4
Copper Thistle (IRE)	4
Korbell (IRE)	4
Flip The Lid (IRE)	4

Qualitair Memory (IRE)	4
Ginger Tristan	4
Latheron (IRE)	4
Park Drift	4
Fosbury	4
Nethertara	4
Landsker Alfred	4
Northern Bluff	4
Rip Van Winkle	4
Still In Business	4
Loughlinstown Boy	4
Stephens Pet	4
Goolds Gold	4
Master Kit (IRE)	4
Chip 'N' run	4
Washakie	4
Hill Island	4

LEADING P-T-P AND HUNTER CHASE SIRES

Strong Gale (IRE)	33
True Song	29
Celtic Cone	28
Deep Run	24
Le Bavard (FR)	24
The Parson	24
Le Moss (IRE)	23
Carlingford Castle (IRE)	21
Oats (IRE)	21
Cruise Missile	20
Mister Lord (USA)	20
Buckskin (FR)	18
Over The River (FR)	17
Roselier (FR)	17
Scallywag	17
Lancastrian (IRE)	16
Netherkelly (IRE)	16
Baron Blakeney	15
Kambalda	15
Nearly A Hand	15
Push On	15
Politico (USA)	14
Idiot's Delight	13
Julio Mariner	13
Nishapour (FR)	13
Royal Fountain	13
Supreme Leader	13
Balinger	12
Lighter	12
St. Columbus	12

AMATEUR RIDERS

The table below gives the weights of amateur riders, their number of winners of Hunter chases and Point-to-Points.
The criterion for inclusion is at least one winner in a Hunter chase or Point-to-Point.
All riders with weights had licences to ride under Rules.

	Weight	Hunter Chases	P-t-P
Mrs P Adams		0	1
D Alers-Hankey	10 12	0	3
J Alexander	12 0	0	3
Miss N Allan		0	3
Miss L Allan	9 4	0	1
S Andrews	11 7	1	4
E Andrewes	11 7	0	3
E Andrews		0	1
M Appleyard	10 7	0	1
Miss A Armitage	8 4	0	1
R Armson	10 7	0	1
M Armytage	10 4	1	0
S Astaire	11 7	0	1
P Atkinson	10 7	0	6
R Atkinson		0	2
P Atkins	11 7	0	1
Auvray		0	1
Miss K Baily		0	1
G Baines	9 7	0	1
Baker	9 7	0	1
A Balding	11 0	3	0
Mrs R Baldwin		1	0
N Bannister	11 7	1	2
G Barfoot-Saunt	10 7	0	3
R Barker	12 0	0	1
D Barlow	11 5	1	5
C Barlow	11 3	0	4
Barlow		0	3
Barnes		0	1
R Barrett	9 10	0	2
Barry	10 0	0	1
Miss B Barton		0	1
Miss S Baskerville		0	1
Miss S Baxter		0	8
Miss S Beddoes	9 7	1	0
Beadles		0	3
Mrs C Behrens	12 0	0	1
Bell	11 2	0	3
C Bennett	12 0	0	2
Miss M Bentham		0	2
Betteridge		0	2
R Bevis	10 0	0	5
Billinge	11 9	1	4
Miss L Blackford	10 9	2	7
Blackwell	10 2	0	5
Mrs A Blaker		0	1
Miss T Blazey		0	1
N Bloom	11 0	0	10
E Bolger		1	0
C Bonner	9 9	1	0
S Bowden		0	1
Miss A Bowie	9 7	0	2
M Bradburne	10 7	2	3
C Brader		0	1
N Bradley	9 7	0	1
S Brisby	10 10	1	1
Miss H Brookshaw		0	2
Miss S Brotherton	9 7	0	3
H Brown		0	1
Mrs M Bryan		0	2
W Bryan		0	4
J Buckle		0	1
T Bulgin	11 0	0	2
P Bull	10 7	0	6
Miss C Burgess	9 0	0	4
W Burnell	9 7	0	3
M Burrows	9 10	0	1
R Burton	9 12	0	3
Miss A Bush		0	1
Miss D Calder		0	1
C Carman		0	1
A Case		0	1
C Casey	12 0	0	1
Miss T Cave	9 7	0	1
A Charles-Jones	10 0	2	7
S Charlton		0	2
M Chatterton		0	2
Miss G Chown	9 5	0	10
Miss R Clark	9 7	0	3
D Coates		0	3
Miss S Cobden	9 7	0	1
A Coe	10 7	1	7
R Cole		0	1
E Collins	11 7	0	1
Miss M Coombe	9 7	0	1
G Cooper		0	3
Miss P Cooper	9 6	0	1
Miss A Corbett		0	1
J Cornes	11 0	0	4
P Cornforth	11 3	0	2
Miss N Courtenay	9 10	0	1
Mrs E Coveney	9 2	0	4

	Weight	*Hunter Chases*	*P-t-P*
S Cowell	10 10	0	7
T Cox		0	2
P Craggs	10 7	0	8
G Crank	11 7	0	2
Miss E Crawford		0	3
J Creighton	10 5	0	8
F Crew	11 7	0	1
D Crossland	10 4	0	1
A Crow	10 11	1	27
J Culloty	9 7	4	0
Miss J Cumings	9 7	1	19
Miss P Curling	10 10	0	23
D Curnow		0	1
D Curren		0	1
A Dalton	11 2	0	12
Miss A Dare	10 0	0	31
R Darke	10 7	0	2
Mrs J Dawson	9 7	0	6
Miss S Dawson		0	1
Miss A Deniel	9 0	0	1
Daniel Dennis	11 0	0	2
David Dennis	9 7	0	2
T Dennis	10 10	1	0
J Deutsch		0	3
Miss K Di Marte	9 7	0	1
P Diggle		0	2
B Dixon	10 7	0	1
J Docker	9 12	0	5
P Doorhof		0	1
I Dowrick	10 9	0	7
Miss S Duckett	9 7	0	2
Miss H Dudgeon	10 0	0	1
D Duggan		0	1
H Dunlop	11 0	0	2
Miss S Eames		0	1
D Easterby		0	2
Miss J Eastwood	9 0	0	2
R Edwards	10 7	0	8
Miss C Elliot		0	1
Maj O Ellwood	10 0	0	2
M Emmanuel		0	1
Mrs J Enderby		0	1
D Esden		0	2
J Evans		0	1
J Ewart		0	1
Capt R Fanshawe	12 0	0	1
A Farrant	11 0	1	10
Mrs A Farrell	8 7	0	2
D Featherstone	11 0	0	1
M Felton	11 0	0	6
J Ferguson	11 5	0	1
Miss H Fines		0	1
M Fitzgerald	10 0	0	3
R Ford	11 0	2	10
Miss S Forster	10 0	1	4
Miss J Foster		0	1
Miss R Francis		0	10
Miss S French	10 0	0	1
M Frith	9 10	0	3
S Garrott		0	1
T Garton	11 5	1	0
P Gee	10 0	0	3
Mrs L Gibbon		0	2
C Gibbon		0	1
K Giles		0	1
R Gill	11 9	1	1
Miss K Gilman		0	1
N Gittins		0	1
Miss S Gladders	9 7	0	1
S Goodings	10 0	0	2
M Gorman	11 2	0	4
Miss A Goschen	10 8	0	5
Miss H Gosling		0	2
Sgt W Goudie		0	1
Mrs S Grant	10 9	0	2
Miss J Grant		0	2
Miss T Gray		0	2
T Greed	10 10	0	11
R Green	10 0	0	1
K Green	10 0	0	3
A Greig	11 7	0	1
A Gribbin	10 0	0	1
A Griffith	10 5	3	2
S Griffiths		0	1
Miss C Grissell		0	3
Miss E Guest		0	1
Miss P Gundry		0	4
P Hacking	11 9	2	20
E Haddock	12 0	0	1
M Haigh	9 7	1	1
R Hale	10 2	0	3
C Hall		0	1
I Hambly		0	1
P Hamer	10 7	0	5
M Hammond	11 7	0	2
Miss L Hampshire		0	1
Mrs M Hand	10 5	0	6
J Hankinson		0	4
P Hanly	10 4	0	1
G Hanmer	11 0	0	10
P Harding-Jones	10 10	0	2
Miss D Harding	9 2	1	0
Mrs K Hargreave		0	2
N Harris	10 0	3	13
A Harris		0	1
M Harris	10 10	0	3
A Harvey	11 0	0	2
Miss F Hatfield		0	1
Mrs J Hawkins	10 7	0	1
C Heard	10 0	0	2
K Heard	11 7	1	7
P Henley	9 9	0	7
M Hewitt		0	2
K Hibbert		0	1
P Hickman	11 7	1	1
Mrs S Hickman	10 0	0	1

AMATEUR RIDERS 1996

	Weight	Hunter Chases	P-t-P
R Hicks	11 7	3	1
L Hicks	10 10	0	1
Miss S Higgins	8 12	1	0
Miss M Hill		0	5
A Hill	11 11	2	10
T Hills	11 4	1	6
B Hodkin		0	2
A Holdsworth	9 0	0	2
Miss C Holliday		0	6
Miss L Hollis	10 7	1	7
K Hollowell	10 2	0	1
J Holt		0	1
G Hopper	9 12	0	2
M Hoskins		0	1
P Howse	11 3	0	1
V Hughes		0	4
P Hutchinson	11 5	1	0
F Hutsby	9 10	0	2
Miss H Irving		0	4
R Irving		0	1
F Jackson	12 0	0	1
M Jackson	10 0	0	7
S Jackson	9 7	0	1
Miss S Jackson	10 0	0	2
T Jackson		0	1
Mrs V Jackson	10 0	2	2
E James	10 0	0	2
A James		0	1
Miss E James	9 7	0	6
L Jefford	9 12	0	14
N Jelley		0	1
P Jenkins		0	1
R Jenkins		0	1
D Jones	9 0	0	1
D S Jones	10 10	4	11
Miss E Jones	8 12	0	2
M Jones		0	1
M P Jones	11 7	0	3
Miss P Jones	9 0	0	20
R Jones		0	1
T Jones	11 7	0	8
J Jukes	10 0	4	34
J P Keen		0	8
N Kent	10 4	0	2
N King	10 10	0	2
P King	11 7	0	2
Miss S Kirkpatrick		0	1
Miss L Knights		0	2
T Lacey	11 7	0	6
Miss D Laidlaw	10 4	0	1
Miss A Lamb		0	1
T Lane	9 12	0	4
C Lawson		0	1
R Lawther	10 10	0	4
L Lay	11 0	2	6
Mrs N Ledger	9 7	0	1
G Lewis		0	3
M Lewis	10 8	0	4

	Weight	Hunter Chases	P-t-P
K Little		0	1
S Lloyd	11 7	0	2
I Lowe		0	1
Miss M Maher		0	1
Miss K Makinson		0	1
S March		0	2
Mrs P Marjoribanks		0	1
T Marks	11 5	2	7
T Marlow		0	1
A Martin	10 7	0	3
C Mason		0	1
Miss J Mathias		0	1
G Matthews		0	3
J Maxse	9 12	0	6
T McCarthy	10 0	0	4
Miss C Mee		0	1
Miss C Metcalfe	9 7	1	2
A Michael	9 8	0	3
M Miller	11 7	2	10
C Millington		0	1
R Mills	10 11	0	1
A Milner	11 0	0	1
Miss D Mitchell		0	1
N Mitchell	11 0	1	7
T Mitchell	11 12	1	19
D Moffett		0	1
T Moore	10 10	0	5
R Morgan	11 0	0	2
S Morris		0	8
T Morrison	10 0	0	4
G Morrison		0	1
S Mulcaire	10 0	0	1
C Mulhall	10 4	1	6
R Mumford	11 0	0	1
M Munrowd	10 7	0	1
Mrs F Needham	9 7	0	6
K Needham	11 7	0	1
R Neill		0	1
Miss S Nichol	9 7	0	1
H Nicholson		0	1
R Nuttall	10 5	1	6
B O'Doherty		0	1
P O'Keeffe	10 3	0	1
A Ogden	10 7	3	1
Miss D Olding	10 0	0	1
R Owen		0	1
R Page		0	1
A Parker	10 0	0	22
Capt D Parker	10 10	0	1
D Parravani	10 5	0	1
Miss L Parrott	9 4	0	1
Miss H Pavey	10 7	0	2
R Payne	10 12	0	1
Miss L Pearce		0	3
Miss M Peck		0	1
G Penfold	11 7	1	6
A Pennock		0	1
A Phillips	10 2	2	7

AMATEUR RIDERS 1996

	Weight	Hunter Chases	P-t-P
Miss H Phizacklea	10 9	0	1
A Pickering		0	1
P Picton-Warlow		0	1
D Pipe	11 7	0	3
Miss A Plunkett	9 7	0	3
Mrs R Pocock		0	2
B Pollock	10 4	5	5
Miss L Pope	9 2	0	1
B Potts		1	3
J Van Praagh		0	2
A Price	11 0	0	5
A W Price		0	1
J Price		0	2
Miss J Priest	8 10	0	2
S Prior	10 0	1	1
John Pritchard	11 7	0	5
Julian Pritchard	10 12	0	10
Dr P Pritchard	9 11	0	2
S Quirk		0	1
W Ramsay	11 7	1	3
A Rebori	11 0	0	2
Mrs J Reed	10 9	2	0
J Rees	9 10	0	1
D Renney		0	1
C Richards	11 0	0	3
M Rimell	10 0	4	0
W Ritson	10 7	0	2
S Roberts		0	1
Miss V Roberts		0	1
D Robinson	12 3	0	7
Capt S Robinson	11 0	0	3
S J Robinson		0	1
Miss P Robson	9 0	0	6
A Robson	10 10	1	1
Miss S Rodman		0	1
Miss L Rowe	10 0	0	7
H Rowsell		0	1
Mrs A Rucker		0	1
M Ruddy		0	2
Miss S Sadler		0	1
Miss S Samworth	8 9	0	2
A Sansome	10 7	1	6
Miss C Savell	10 4	0	2
Mrs F Scales		0	1
P Scholfield		0	5
J Scott		0	1
T Scott	11 2	0	10
P Scouller		0	5
J Seth-Smith		0	1
P Shaw		0	3
Mrs N Sheppard		0	2
R Shiels	11 5	0	6
S Shinton	10 10	0	3
Miss B Sillars		0	2
S Slade	11 5	0	1
T Smalley		0	1
D Smith		0	1
G Smith	12 0	0	1

	Weight	Hunter Chases	P-t-P
M Smith	10 7	0	1
R Smith	11 4	0	2
T Smith	10 7	0	1
C Smyth		0	2
Miss N Snowden		0	2
Miss W Southcombe	8 0	0	2
M Sowersby	11 7	0	5
Miss C Spearing	9 7	0	6
S Sporborg	11 0	2	10
L Squire	10 0	0	1
Miss D Stafford		0	2
D Stephens (Devon)		0	3
D Stephens (Wales)		0	1
Miss V Stephens	9 7	1	1
T Stephenson		0	9
Miss N Stirling		0	1
C Stockton	11 7	0	3
C Storey	10 0	6	4
Mrs K Sunderland	8 7	0	5
R Sweeting	11 0	2	12
S Swiers	10 5	2	16
Miss A Sykes	9 5	0	1
P Taiano	10 10	0	7
Miss E Tamplin		0	1
Miss C Tarratt	7 7	0	3
G Tarry	10 10	1	6
R Tate		0	4
W Tellwright	11 7	0	2
Miss C Thomas	9 0	0	2
V Thomas		0	1
J Thompson		0	1
R Thornton	9 0	0	8
J Tilley		0	1
J Tizzard	10 0	2	8
Miss E Tomlinson	9 7	0	1
Miss C Townsley	9 0	1	0
R Treloggen	10 10	2	9
J Trice-Rolph	11 10	0	3
H Trotter		0	1
J Tudor	11 10	0	13
G Tuer		0	1
B Tulloch	11 7	0	3
J Turcan		0	1
M Turner		0	1
W G Turner		0	1
A Tutton		0	1
N Tutty	10 10	0	7
T Underwood		0	5
M Venner		0	1
Miss S Vickery	9 7	0	15
C Vigors	10 2	4	5
C Wadland	11 2	0	2
R Wakeham	10 7	0	1
R Wakley	9 10	0	4
W Wales	11 0	0	2
E Walker	11 0	0	1
Miss E Walker	11 3	0	1
R Walker		0	1

	Weight	Hunter Chases	P-t-P
S Walker	9 7	1	8
Mrs M Wall		0	1
Miss S Wallin	9 7	0	1
R Walmsley	11 0	0	3
J Walton	11 10	0	7
C Ward	10 7	0	3
C Ward Thomas	10 5	1	4
Mrs L Ward	9 4	0	2
A Warr	11 0	0	2
C Way		0	1
T Weale		0	1
A Welsh	10 7	0	8
Maj G Wheeler	10 10	0	3
H Wheeler		0	6
S Whitaker	11 7	0	2
R White	10 7	7	8
I Widdicombe	11 7	0	2
A Wight		0	1

	Weight	Hunter Chases	P-t-P
Miss E Wilesmith		0	2
M Wilesmith		0	3
Mrs J Wilkinson	8 7	0	1
E Williams	10 7	1	5
P Williams		0	6
Mrs J Williamson	9 5	0	1
N Wilson	10 2	1	11
C Wilson	10 12	0	3
Miss C Wilson		0	1
A Wintle	10 7	0	5
D Wood	11 7	0	1
T Woolridge		0	1
Miss J Wormall	9 0	0	3
M Worthington	10 10	0	1
I Wynne	10 5	0	2
Miss S Young	10 7	0	6
J Young		0	4
Miss Y Young		0	1

LEADING POINT-TO-POINT RIDERS OF THE POST-WAR YEARS

	Wins
Turner, David	343
Llewellyn, John	270
Cunard, Sir Guy	268
Dare, Miss Alison	231
Felton, Mike	225
Ryall, Frank	218
Cann, Grant	217
Alner, Robert	211
Curling, Miss Polly	179
Miller, Richard	178
Scholfield, Philip	178
Daniell, John	175
Sheppard, Mrs. Josie (fly. Bothway née Turner)	173
Tollit, Mrs. Pat	171
Hacking, Robert (W.R.)	170
Sharp, John	164
Greenall, Peter	160
Tarry, James	157
Treloggen, Ron	151
Brookshaw, Steven	148
Bloom, Michael	145
Horton, Mrs. Sue (née Aston)	145
Rooney, Tim	144
Hill, Bertie (A.E.)	136
Guilding, Roger	135
Tatlow, David	133
Jones, Tim	130
Andrews, Simon	129
Hamer, Paul	128
Pidgeon, Miss Jenny	126
Crow, Alastair	124
Farthing, Justin	124
Williams, Michael (Wales)	124
Hacking, Paul	120
French, Mrs. Sheilagh	119
Bloom, Nigel	118
Dawson, Mrs. Jill	116
Down, Chris	116
Bryan, John	115
Jones, Bill	113
Craggs, Peter	112
McKie, Ian	112
Greenway, Robin	111
Wales, David	110
Wilkin, Tommy	109
Gibbon, Mrs. Lucy	107
Newton, Joey	107
Spencer, Col. C. R.	107
Scouller, Philip	105
Hand, Mrs Mandy (née Turner)	104
Williams, Michael (Devon)	103
Cooper, George	101

	Wins
Macmillan, Charlie	101
Pritchard, Julian	101
Edwards, Ron (R.J.)	100
Woolley, Bob	99
Barber, Mick (G.M.)	97
Crank, Simon	97
Davies, Bob	97
Tate, Robin	97
Jeanes, Stuart (T.S.)	95
Tutty, Nigel	95
Jones, Miss Pip	92
Gibson, David	91
Mathias, Fred	91
Moore, Tim	91
Anderson, Kevin	90
Bush, Nicky	90
Holland-Martin, Tim	89
Stephens, David	87
Chugg, Robert	84
Hill, Alan	85
Wheeler, Harry	85
Elliott, Harry (W.H.)	82
Shepherd, Richard	82
Fisher, Miss Pip	82
Ulyet, Alistair	82
Jukes, Jamie	81
Dickinson, A	80+
Blackford, Miss Linda	80
Charlton, Alistair	80
Chown, Mrs. "Fizz" (D.)	80
Duggan, Damien	80
Sowersby, Michael	80
Dufosee, John	79
Hickman, John	79
Arthers, Malcolm	78
Berry, Andrew	78
Bloomfield, R.A.	78
Cowell, Henry	77
Trice-Rolph, Jon	77
Frost, Jimmy	76
Docker, John	75
Bryan, Willie	74
Cowell, Bob	74
Crouch, Mrs. Mary	74
Kinsella, David	74
McCarthy, Tim	74
Philby, Tommy	74
Turner, George	74
Mathias, Philip	72
Morgan, Miss Shan	72
Warren, Bruce	71
Foulkes, Billy (C.W.)	70
Rowe, Hunter	70

WINNERS OF MAJOR POINT-TO-POINT RACES

Four-Mile Men's Open for Lord Ashton of Hyde's Cup at the Heythrop

	Owner	*Horse*	*Rider*
1953	L. A. Coville	Dark Stranger	I. Kerwood
1954	S. C. Turner	Nylon	G. Morgan
1955	H. Phillips	Chandie IV	J. Jackson
1956	H. M. Ballard	Cash Account	W. Foulkes
1957	S. L. Maundrell	Star Bar	Owner
1958	S. L. Maundrell	Kolpham	P. Dibble
1959	R. J. Horton	Andy Pandy	D. Horton
1960	R. I. Johnson	Mascot III	R. Woolley
1961	Major H. P. Rushton	Holystone Oak	A. Biddlecombe
1962	W. H. Firkins	Everything's Rosy	D. Tatlow
1963	C. D. Collins	Wild Legend	Owner
1964	W. J. A. Shepherd	Straight Lady	R. J. Shepherd
1965	Mrs J. Brutton	Snowdra Queen	H. Oliver
1966	Miss V. Diment	Bob Sawyer	G. Dartnall
1967	J. Jordan	Barley Bree	D. Tatlow
1968	Major P. Ormrod	Winter Willow	D. W. Williams-Wynn
1969	Miss L. Jones	Bartlemy Boy	J. Daniell
1970	Mrs. J. Brutton	Lord Fortune	G. Hyatt
1971	J. S. Townsend	Creme Brule	R. Knipe
1972	M. H. Ings	Dunsbrook Lass	Owner
1973	Major M. R. Dangerfield	All A Myth	R. N. Miller
1974	A. E. Cowan	False Note	Owner
1975	(Div. 1) J. W. Brown	Take Cover	Owner
	(Div. 2) M. R. Churches	Rich Rose	R. N. Miller
1976	Mrs. J. Brutton	Lord Fortune	D. Edmunds
1977	Mrs. J. Brutton	Lord Fortune	D. Edmunds
1978	Mrs. P. Morris	Sparkford	J. Bryan
1979	E. J. Bufton	Headmaster	A. James
1980	H. Wellon	Spartan Scot	T. Houlbrooke
1981	J. B. Sumner	Nostradamus	I. McKie
1982	H. Wellon	Spartan Scot	T. Houlbrooke
1983	J. B. Sumner	Nostradamus	I. McKie
1984	Mrs. E. Dowling	Lay-The-Trump	B. Dowling
1985	J. B. Sumner	Nostradamus	I. McKie
1986	A. Perry and J. Deutsch	Paddy's Peril	J. Deutsch
1987	P. Hemelek and P. Barnes	Political Whip	D. Naylor-Leyland
1988	A. Perry and J. Deutsch	Paddy's Peril	J. Deutsch
1989	C. Main	Lolly's Patch	Owner
1990	J. Cullen	Polar Glen	M. Felton
1991	J Deutsch	Dromin Joker	J Deutsch
1992	Mrs. M.E. Terry	Speedy Boy	T. McCarthy
1993	Mrs. P. White	Uncle Raggy	R. Lawther
1994	E. Knight	Holland House	C. Vigors
1995	G. Nock	Sevens Out	E. James
1996	Mrs. J. Daniell	Kettles	A. Phillips

From 1953 to 1982 the race was run at Fox Farm, Stow-on-the-Wold, and since then it has been run at Heythrop just outside Chipping Norton. For the last ten years it has been sponsored by *The Sporting Life*.

WINNERS OF MAJOR POINT-TO-POINT RACES

The Lady Dudley Cup (Men's Open) at the Worcestershire (First competed for in 1897)

	Owner	*Horse*	*Rider*
1946	E. Holland-Martin	Hefty	T. Holland-Martin
1947	A. W. Garfield	Arod	Dr. D. J. K. McCarthy
1948	P. Kerby	Vinty	P. J. Kerby
1949	G. Hutsby	Sir Isumbras	Owner
1950	P. T. Cartridge	Maybe II	Owner
1951	A. H. Thomlinson	Paul Pry	W. A. Stephenson
1952	G. R. Maundrell	Right Again	D. Maundrell
1953	(Div. 1) G. R. Maundrell	Cottage Lace	D. Maundrell
	(Div. 2) H. Sumner	Flint Jack	J. Fowler
1954	(Div. 1) C. S. Ireland	Blenalad	C. Harty
	(Div. 2) H. Sumner	Flint Jack	J. Fowler
1955	(Div. 1) H. M. Ballard	Cash Account	M. Tate
	(Div. 2) C. Nixon	Creeola II	C. Harty
1956	(Div. 1) H. M. Ballard	Cash Account	W. Foulkes
	(Div. 2) G. A. Miles	Galloping Gold	C. Nesfield
1957	(Div. 1) H. M. Ballard	Cash Account	W. H. Wynn
	(Div. 2) J. R. Hindley	Prospero	P. Brookshaw
1958	(Div. 1) C. Davies	Master Copper	Owner
	(Div. 2) J. R. French	Domabelle	Owner
	(Div. 3) T. D. Rootes	Some Baby	M. J. Thorne
1959	(Div. 1) G. C. Llewellin	Clover Bud	D. Llewellin
	(Div. 2) Miss L. Jones	Flippant Lad	J. Daniell
1960	(Div. 1) K. Small	Precious Gem	G. Small
	(Div. 2) Miss L. Jones	Culleenpark	J. Daniell
1961	(Div. 1) Miss L. Jones	Corn Star	J. Daniell
1962	(Div. 1) T. D. Holland-Martin	Midnight Coup	Owner
	(Div. 2) Major J. L. Davenport	Pomme De Guerre	P. Davenport
1963	(Div. 1) R. P. Cooper	Foroughona	Owner
	(Div. 2) W. Shand Kydd	No Reward	Owner
1964	W. J. A. Shepherd	Straight Lady	R. Willis
1965	Mrs. J. Brutton	Snowdra Queen	H. Oliver
1966	T. G. Cambridge	Handsel	Owner
1967	Mrs. D. L. Freer	Tailorman	P. Hobbs
1968	G. A. C. Cure	Bright Willow	R. Chugg
1969	Abandoned. Course waterlogged		
1970	Mrs. E. C. Gaze	Frozen Dawn	H. Oliver
1971	D. T. Surnam	Real Rascal	G. Hyatt
1972	G. A. C. Cure	Mighty Red	J. Chugg
1973	G. A. C. Cure	Mighty Red	R. Woolley
1974	P. A. Rackham	Lake District	M. Bloom
1975	P. T. Brookshaw	Mickley Seabright	P. Brookshaw, Jnr.
1976	Mrs. P. Morris	Jim Lad	J. R. Bryan
1977	R. Wynn	Little Fleur	J. R. Bryan
1978	Miss J. Hey	Sporting Luck	T. Smith
1979	Mrs. P. Morris	Sparkford	J. R. Bryan
1980	W. R. J. Everall	Major Star	S. Brookshaw
1981	W. Price	Petite Mandy	N. Oliver
1982	D. L. Reed	Norman Case	P. Mathias
1983	Mrs. P. M. Jones	Clear Pride	D. Trow
1984	M. F. Howard	Darlingate	T. Jackson
1985	R. A. Phillips	Ridgeman	I. K. Johnson
1986	P. Greenall	Highland Blaze	Owner
1987	J. Harris, B. Leighton, K. Brooke, E. Rees and S. Merrick	Pride Of Tullow	T. Bowen
1988	J. Palmer	North Key	A. Ulyet
1989	P. Deal	Border Sun	S. Sweeting
1990	Mrs. S. A. Potter	Turn Mill	M. Hammond

	Owner	*Horse*	*Rider*
991	P R Haley	The Red One	S Swiers
992	R. J. Mansell	Brunico	R. Treloggen
993	T. W. Raymond	Brunico	R. Treloggen
994	R. Jones	Yahoo	M. Rimell
995	P. Barber	Bond Jnr	T. Mitchell
996	Mrs. J. Yeomans	Sharinski	M. Jackson

rom 1946 to 1950, the race was run over a 3-mile course at Chaddesley Corbett, in 1951 and 1952 ver a 3½-mile course at Upton-on-Severn, from 1953 to 1968 over a 3¼-mile course at Upton-on-evern, in 1970 over a 3-mile 500 yds. course at Chaddesley Corbett, from 1971 to 1973 over a 3-mile 00 yds. course at Chaddesley Corbett, and from 1974 onwards over a 3-mile 520 yds. course at Chaddesley Corbett. For the last ten years it has been sponsored by *The Sporting Life*.

The Lord Grimthorpe Gold Cup (Men's Open) at the Middleton

	Owner	*Horse*	*Rider*
946	H. W. Metcalfe	San Michele	G. B. Metcalfe
947	H. W. Metcalfe	San Michele	C. Metcalfe
948	Mrs. H. M. Gilpin	Rolling River	Capt. C. MacAndrew
949	(Div. 1) C. Chapman	Finolly	Major G. Cunard
	(Div. 2) A. Simpson	The Joker VII	W. R. Simpson
950	W. A. Stephenson	General Ripple	Owner
951	A. H. Thomlinson	Paul Pry	W. A. Stephenson
952	G. F. Fawcett	Trusty	H. Elliott
953	Miss V. Porter-Hargreaves	Turkish Prince	A. Dickinson
954	Mrs. J. Makin	Kitty Brook	C. Smith
955	W. A. Stephenson	Mr. Gay	Owner
956	S. Webster	More Honour	Owner
957	H. M. Ballard	Cash Account	W. Wynn
958	R. W. Ratcliffe	Brown Sugar	P. Fox
959	S. Webster	More Honour	Owner
960	J. H. Thompson	Gay William	M. Thompson
961	J. Peckitt	Glann	T. Wilkin
962	R. Heaton	Brass Tacks	P. Brookshaw
963	F. T. Gibbon	Harrow Hall	R. Moody
964	Major G. Cunard	Ferncliffe	Owner
965	R. A. H. Perkins	Faruno	Owner
966	Mrs. R. G. Hutchison-Bradburne	Banjoe	J. Hutchinson-Bradburne
967	Major G. Cunard	Puddle Jumper	Owner
968	Mrs. A. E. Dickinson	Shandover	M. Dickinson
969	C. B. Harper	My Night	J. Leadbetter
970	D. E. Wilson	Young Highlander	D. Gibson
971	Capt. R. M. Micklethwait	Kangaroo Jim	A. Berry
972	J. W. Walton	Old Man Trouble	Owner
973	F. D. Nicholson	Moyleen	A. Nicholson
974	P. A. Rackham	Watch Night	M. Bloom
975	Mrs. J. Gilmour	Falling Leaves	J. Gilmour
976	L. H. Barker	Villa Court	L. Barker
977	J. B. Walker	Escamist	J. Barton
978	J. Scott-Aiton	Sea Petrel	I. Scott-Aiton
979	T. M. Wilson	Rakamar	T. Smith
980	A. W. Johnson	Scalby Cresta	G. Halder
981	J. A. Cooper	Mountain Lad	J. Peckitt
982	J. M. Evetts	Border Mark	Owner
983	A. Sanderson	Lady Buttons	N. Tutty
984	Race abandoned. Too firm ground		
985	J. D. Jemmeson	Salkeld	D. Kinsella

WINNERS OF MAJOR POINT-TO-POINT RACES

	Owner	Horse	Rider
1986	Mrs. M. F. Strawson	Freddie Teal	P. Strawson
1987	Race abandoned. Waterlogging		
1988	Mrs. S. Frank	Ingleby Star	N. Tutty
1989	T. P. Bell	Old Nick	S. Whitaker
1990	R. G. Watson	Certain Rhythm	M. Sowersby
1991	Meeting abandoned.		
1992	B. Heywood	Ocean Day	Mrs. A. Farrell
1993	B. Heywood	Ocean Day	H. Brown
1994	Mrs. D. R. Brotherton	Across The Lake	Miss S. Brotherton
1995	P. Sawney	Duright	N. Tutty
1996	H. Bell	Highland Friend	P. Atkinson

In 1952 the distance of this race was extended from 3½ miles to 4 miles; and in 1954, when it becam known as the point-to-point Grand National, to 4½ miles. In 1982 the distance was reduced to 4½ miles, in 1986 to 4 miles 1 furlong, and in 1989 to 3 miles 1 furlong. In 1990 the race was run over miles 50 yards. In 1992 the race reverted to 4 miles and became a mixed open. The venue is Whitwell on-the-Hill, mid-way between Malton and York.

The Sporting Life Classics Cup

	Owner	Horse	Points
1995	Grahame Barrett	Final Pride	84
1996	Mrs. J. Yeomans	Sharinski	70

LEADING HORSE AWARDS

	Owner	*Horse*	*Number of races won*

Grand Marnier Trophy

1970	A. Gordon-Watson	Barty	10
1971	C. Hancock	Golden Batman	8
1972	Mrs. H. P. Rushton	Pensham	11
1973	J. M. Turner	Master Vesuvius	11
1974	J. M. Turner	Boy Bumble	12
1975	J. M. Turner	Even Harmony	11
1976	J. M. Turner	Hardcastle	9
1977	J. M. Turner	Hardcastle	11
1978	R. Wynn	Little Fleur	12
1979	P. Tylor	Hargan	10
1980	T. Hunnable	Florida King	8
1981	J. Sumner	Nostradamus	9
1982	R. Bulgin	Mac Kelly	8
1983	Mrs. B. Perry	Seine Bay	8
1984	D. Llewellin	National Clover	9
1985	Mrs. C. Foote-Forster	Brigadier Mouse	9
1986	C. Dawson, M.F.H.	Sweet Diana	9
1987	Mrs. C. Nicholas	Mantinolas	8
1988	T. F. G. Marks	Stanwick Lad	10
1989	J. F. Weldhen	For A Lark	10

The Daily Telegraph Trophy

1990	W. J. Evans	Timber Tool	11
1991	Mrs L Wadham	Fort Hall	10
1992	R. J. Mansell	Brunico	12
1993	A. J. Papworth	Melton Park	12

Grand Marnier Trophy

1994	A. J. Papworth	Melton Park	7
1995	E. Harries	Handsome Harvey	10
1996	Miss R. A. Francis	Phar Too Touchy	10

(Cont. p. 748)

NATIONAL WINNERS 1996

Land Rover	G. Tanner	Ryming Cuplet
Vauxhall Monterey	Mrs. S. Mason	Jasilu

PPORA AWARDS 1996

Horse and Hound/PPORA Young Horse Award		
	M. Mann	Out The Door
PPORA Mares	Miss R. A. Francis	Phar Too Touchy
Leading Novice Riders	Joe Tizzard and Stuart Morris	

DAILY TELEGRAPH CUP: LEADING GENTLEMAN POINT-TO-POINT RIDER
Winners and Runners-up

	Wins
67	
avid Tatlow	24
oger Guilding	19
68	
avid Tatlow	18
avid Gibson	14
69	
ichael Bloom	19
ll Shand Kydd	18
70	
avid Turner	19
rant Cann	16
71	
ob Davies	29
ike Villiers	18
72	
ichard Miller	21
ohn Docker	14
David Turner	14
73	
ichard Miller	23
avid Turner	20
74	
avid Turner	26
ichard Miller	14
75	
avid Turner	24
Grant Cann	14
Robin Greenway	14
76	
avid Turner	22
hn Bryan	16
77	
avid Turner	29
hn Bryan	26
78	
hn Bryan	32
avid Turner	19

	Wins
1979	
David Turner	17
John Bryan	15
1980	
Ian McKie (tie)	20
David Turner (tie)	20
1981	
Ian McKie	18
Peter Greenall (tie)	16
Tim Rooney (tie)	16
1982	
Peter Greenall	24
Jimmy Frost	18
1983	
John Llewellyn	19
Peter Greenall	17
1984	
David Turner	20
Peter Greenall	19
1985	
Peter Greenall	23
David Turner	15
1986	
Peter Greenall	28
Mike Felton	24
1987	
Mike Felton	26
Philip Scholfield	18
1988	
Philip Scholfield	37
Mike Felton	28
1989	
Mike Felton	26
John Llewellyn	18
1990	
Mike Felton	27
Philip Scholfield	20
1991	
Justin Farthing	26
Philip Scholfield	23

	Wins
1992	
Robert Alner	31
Julian Pritchard	19
1993	
Alastair Crow	22
{Nigel Bloom	20
{Julian Pritchard	20
1994	
Nigel Bloom	22
Damien Duggan	21

	Wi
1995	
Alastair Crow	3
Jimmy Tarry	2
1996	
Jamie Jukes	3
Alastair Crow	2

THE SPORTING LIFE CUP: LEADING LADY POINT-TO-POINT RIDER
Winners and Runners-up

	Wins
1967	
Mrs Pat Hinch	11
{Mrs Pat Tollit	10
{Mrs Avril Williams	10
1968	
Miss Sue Aston	15
{Miss Rosemary Cadell	8
{Miss Josie Turner	8
1969	
Miss Josie Turner	14
Miss Sue Aston	13
1970	
Miss Sue Aston	14
{Mrs Pat Tollit	9
{Miss Anne Greenwood	9
1971	
Miss Sue Aston	14
Mrs Pat Tollit	11
1972	
{**Miss Sue Aston**	15
{**Mrs Pat Tollit**	15
1973	
Mrs Mabel Forrest	17
Mrs Josie Bothway (née Turner)	12
1974	
Mrs Josie Bothway	20
Miss Diana Bishop	16
1975	
Mrs Josie Bothway	17
{Mrs Mary Crouch	9
{Mrs Anne Sturdy	9
1976	
Mrs Josie Bothway	17
Mrs Mary Crouch	15
1977	
Mrs Josie Sheppard (fly. Bothway)	17
Mrs Mary Crouch	14
1978	
Mrs Rosemary White	11
Miss Amanda Jemmeson	9
1979	
Miss Pip Fisher	10
{Miss Katie Halswell	9
{Mrs Josie Sheppard	9
1980	
Miss Lucy King (now Mrs David Gibbon)	14
Miss Pip Fisher	11
1981	
Miss Lucy King	14
Miss Jenny Pidgeon	10
1982	
Miss Jenny Pidgeon	18
Mrs Jenny Hembrow	15
1983	
Miss Jenny Pidgeon	18
{Mrs Lucy Gibbon (née King)	8
{Miss Mandy Lingard	8
1984	
{**Miss Jenny Pidgeon**	13
{**Miss Mandy Lingard**	13
1985	
Miss Jenny Pidgeon	18
{Miss Lucy Crow	13
{Miss Alison Dare	13
1986	
Miss Alison Dare	17
Miss Amanda Harwood	14
1987	
Miss Alison Dare	17
{Miss Jenny Pidgeon	10
{Mrs Lucy Gibbon	10
1988	
Mrs Jenny Litston	16
Miss Amanda Harwood	15
1989	
Miss Lucy Crow	15
Miss Mandy Turner	14
1990	
Miss Alison Dare	20
{Miss Polly Curling	14
{Mrs Jill Dawson	14

	Wins
1991	
Miss Alison Dare	26
Mrs P Nash	22
1992	
Miss Alison Dare	21
Miss Linda Blackford	16
1993	
Miss Polly Curling	25
Miss Mandy Turner	20
1994	
Miss Polly Curling	35
Miss Alison Dare	17
1995	
Miss Polly Curling	40
{Miss Shirley Vickery	10
{Miss Pip Jones	10
1996	
Miss Alison Dare	31
Miss Polly Curling	23

POINT-TO-POINT COURSES

ALDINGTON Kent
6m SE of Ashford, S of A20
L/H; 19J; 7m 05s.
Undulating, galloping, test of stamina.
Good viewing.

ALNWICK Northumberland
3m E of Alnwick, near B1399
L/H; 18J; 6m 35s.
Slightly undulating, galloping.
Excellent viewing.

ALPRAHAM Cheshire
3m SE of Tarporley, off A51
R/H; 18J; 7m 20s.
Mostly flat, suits stayers.
Reasonable viewing.

AMPTON Suffolk
4m N of Bury St Edmunds, near A134
R/H; 20J; 6m 55s.
Undulating, sharp but suits stayers.
Poor viewing.

ANDOVERSFORD Glos.
6m SE of Cheltenham, signposted from A40
R/H; 19J; 6m 30s.
Undulating, uphill finish.
Reasonable viewing.

ASHORNE Warwicks
4m S of Warwick, off A41
R/H; 18J; 6m 20s.
Slightly undulating, uphill finish.
Very good viewing.

ASPATRIA Cumbria
2m NE of town, on A596, Carlisle to Maryport Road
L/H; 18J 6m 20s.
Undulating, galloping.
Good viewing.

BADBURY RINGS Dorset
5m SE of Blandford, Adj B3082
L/H; 19J; 6m 30s.
Undulating, rectangular.
Good viewing

BALCORMO MAINS Fife
3m NE of Leven, off A915
R/H; 18J; 7m 00s.
Gently undulating, galloping, suits stayers.
Good viewing.

BARBURY CASTLE Wilts
4m S of Swindon, Near Wroughton
L/H; 18J; 6m 25s.
Galloping.
Excellent viewing.

BASSALEG Gwent
2m NW Junction 28 M4, near A468.
R/H; 18J; 6m 45s.
Undulating, galloping.
Excellent viewing.

BEXHILL E Sussex
½m N of town, off A269
R/H; 19J; 7m 00s.
Undulating, stamina test, uphill finish.
Very good viewing.

BISHOPSLEIGH Devon
9m NE of Crediton, E of A377
R/H; 19J; 6m 25s.
Undulating, not as testing as previously.
Course Revised: Viewing improved

BITTERLEY Shropshire
4m NE of Ludlow, N of A4117
L/H; 18J; 6m 30s.
Almost flat, sharp, slight uphill finish.
Good viewing.

BRAMPTON BRYAN Hereford & Worcs.
10m W of Ludlow, near A4113
R/H; 18J; 6m 25s.
Flat, galloping.
Fair viewing.

BRATTON DOWN Devon
10m N of South Molton, Adj B3226
L/H; 18J; 6m 15s.
Undulating, long uphill finish.
Mostly good viewing.

BREDWARDINE Hereford & Worcs.
7m E of Hay-on-Wye, E of B4352
R/H; 18J; 6m 45s.
Flat, galloping.
Good viewing.

BROCKLESBY PARK Lincs.
10m W of Grimsby, Adj B1210.
L/H; 18J; 6m 25s.
Flat, slight uphill finish.
Good viewing.

CASTLE OF COMFORT Somerset
Off B3134, between Priddy & East Harptree
R/H; 18J; 6m 35s.
Undulating, sharp.
Good viewing.

CHADDESLEY CORBETT Hereford & Worcs.
6m W of Bromsgrove, Adj A448.
L/H; 18J; 6m 15s; 20J, 6m 40s.
Gently undulating, galloping.
Very good viewing.

CHARING Kent
6m NW of Ashford, Adj A20.
L/H; 19J; 6m 35s.
Undulating, suits stayers.
Good viewing.

CHARLTON HORETHORNE Somerset
Off B3145, 6m SW of Wincanton.
L/H; 18J; 6m 20s.
Slightly undulating.
Good viewing.

CHARM PARK Yorkshire
At Wykeham, Adj A170, 5m SW of Scarborough.
L/H; 19J; 6m 40s.
Flat, galloping.
Very good viewing.

CLIFTON-ON-DUNSMORE Warwicks
3m NW of Junc 18 of M1; Adj A5.
L/H; 19J; 6m 10s.
Slightly undulating, galloping, old Rugby racecourse.
Very good viewing.

CLYST ST MARY Devon
5m E of Exeter, Nr A3052
L/H; 22J; 7m 00s.
Mostly flat, sharp.
Very good viewing.

CORBRIDGE Northumberland
3m N of Town, near A68.
R/H; 18J; 6m 25s; (3m 5f, 22J, 8m 00s).
Undulating, galloping, uphill finish.
Good viewing.

COTHELSTONE Somerset
3m N of Taunton.
L/H; 18J; 6m 30s.
Undulating.
Good viewing.

COTLEY FARM Somerset
2m S of Chard, 1½m off A30
L/H; 18J; 6m 45s.
Undulating, galloping, suits stayers.
Very good viewing.

COTTENHAM Cambs.
5m N of Cambridge, E of B1049.
R/H; 19J; 6m 10s.
Flat, galloping.
Very good viewing (including grandstand).

CURSNEH HILL Hereford & Worcs.
1m W of Leominster, off A44.
L/H; 18J; 6m 15s.
Very sharp, undulating.
Good viewing.

DALSTON Cumbria
5m S of Carlisle, Adj B5299.
R/H; 18J; 6m 40s.
Flat, galloping.
Good viewing.

DALTON PARK Yorkshire
5m NW of Beverley, W of B1248.
R/H; 19J; 7m 05s.
Almost flat, stamina test.
Fairly good viewing.

DETLING Kent
3m NE of Maidstone, N of A249
L/H; 18J; 6m 30s; (4m, 24J, 8m 45s).
Almost flat, galloping, slight uphill finish.
Good viewing.

DIDMARTON Glos.
6m SW of Tetbury, Adj A433
L/H; 18J; 6m 15s.
Undulating, downhill finish.
Very good viewing.

DINGLEY Northants.
2m E of Market Harborough, Adj A427.
R/H; 18J; 6m 35s.
Almost flat, sharp bend before last.
Excellent viewing.

DUNCOMBE PARK Yorkshire
1m SW of Helmsley, W of A170.
R/H; 18J; 6m 15s.
Undulating, long uphill finish.
Good viewing.

EASINGWOLD Yorkshire
13m NW of York, off A419.
L/H; 18J; 6m 00s.
Almost flat, sharp, suits non-stayers.
Fair viewing.

EATON HALL Cheshire
4m S of Chester, off A483.
R/H; 18J; 6m 45s.
Flat, galloping, stamina needed.
Reasonable viewing.

ERW LON Dyfed
10m N of Carmarthen, near B4459.
L/H; 18J; 6m 25s.
Flat, galloping.
Poor viewing.

EYTON-ON-SEVERN Shropshire
6m SE of Shrewsbury, near B4380.
L/H; 18J; 6m 25s.
Big, flat, galloping.
Very good viewing.

FAKENHAM Norfolk
2n SW of town.
L/H; 18J; 6m 15s.
Undulating, sharp, inside/outside NH course.
Excellent viewing.

FLAGG MOOR Derbyshire
6m SE of Buxton, E of A515.
L/H; 20J; 7m 40s.
Undulating, very testing, uphill finish.
Good viewing.

FLETE PARK Devon
2m N of Modbury, N of A379.
R/H; 19J; 6m 55s.
Undulating, stayers' course.
Reasonable viewing.

FRIARS HAUGH Borders
1m W of Kelso, off A699.
L/H; 19J; 6m 50s.
Flat, one sharp rise/fall, galloping, finish up centre shute.
Good viewing.

GARNONS Hereford & Worcs.
7m W of Hereford, N of A438.
L/H; 18J; 6m 40s.
Undulating, sharp.
Good viewing.

GARTHORPE Leics.
5m E of Melton Mowbray, Adj B676.
R/H; 18J; 6m 30s.
Undulating, last 3f flat.
Very good viewing.

GISBURN Lancs.
1m SW of town, off A59.
R/H; 18J; 7m 15s.
Sharp undulating, suits stayers.
Poor viewing.

GREAT STAINTON, Co. Durham
5m SW of Sedgefield, Handy A1(M)
R/H; 18J; 6m 10s.
Galloping
Good viewing.

GREAT TRETHEW Cornwall
3m SE of Liskeard.
R/H; 22J; 6m 30s.
Very undulating, quite testing, uphill finish.
Good viewing.

GUILSBOROUGH Northants.
10m N of Northampton, Adj A50.
L/H; 19J; 6m 30s.
Flat, sharp bends.
Fair viewing.

HACKWOOD PARK Hampshire
2m SE of Basingstoke; E of A339.
L/H; 18J; 6m 25s.
Flat, sharp.
Unsatisfactory viewing.

HALDON Devon
6m SW of Exeter, Adj A38.
R/H; 18J; 6m 30s.
Undulating, inside NH course.
Very good viewing from grandstand.
Course reported closed.

HEATHFIELD Sussex
1m E of town, Adj A265.
R/H; 20J; 7m 10s.
Undulating, twisty, suits stayers.
Very good viewing.

HEXHAM Northumberland
Inside NH course.
L/H; 18J; 7m 20s.
Undulating, stayers course.
Very good viewing.

HEYTHROP Oxfordshire
2m E of Chipping Norton, off A34.
R/H; 20J; 7m 00s. (4m, 25J, 8m 20s).
Slightly undulating; long course but suits front-runners.
Good viewing.

HIGH BICKINGTON Devon
9m S of Barnstaple, off B3217.
R/H; 18J; 6m 35s.
Sharp, twisty.
Good viewing.

HIGHAM Essex
7m NE of Colchester, W of A12.
L/H; 19J; 6m 15s.
Flat, galloping, suits front-runners.
Fair viewing.

HIGH EASTER Essex
Off A1060, between Bishops Stortford & Chelmsford
L/H; 18J; 6m 20s.
Undulating, galloping, suits non-stayers.
Good viewing.

HIGHER KILWORTHY Devon
2m NE of Tavistock, N of A286.
L/H; 18J; 6m 35s.
Undulating, uphill finish.
Very good viewing.

HOCKWORTHY Devon
6m W of Wellington, between M5 & A361.
L/H; 18J; 6m 35s.
Undulating, uphill finish.
Good viewing.

HOLNICOTE Somerset
Adj. A39, 3m W of Minehead
L/H; 20J; 6m 30s.
Flat, sharp. Poor viewing.
Course reported closed.

HORNBY CASTLE Yorkshire
3m S of Catterick, W of A1.
L/H; 18J; 6m 40s.
Slightly undulating, suits stayers.
Unsatisfactory viewing.

HORSEHEATH Cambs.
3m E of Linton, Adj. A604.
R/H; 18J; 6m 30s.
Undulating, galloping, suits stayers.
Quite good viewing.

HOWICK Gwent
2m W of Chepstow, near B4235.
L/H; 18J; 6m 45s.
Undulating, sharp bends.
Good viewing, but not of finish.

KILWORTHY Devon
2m NE of Tavistock, N of A386.
L/H; 18J; 6m 40s.
Undulating, galloping, suits stayers.
Good viewing.

KIMBLE Bucks.
4m S of Aylesbury, near B4009.
L/H; 19J; 6m 35s.
Almost flat, galloping.
Reasonable viewing.

KINGSTON BLOUNT Oxfordshire
4m NE of Watlington; off B4009.
L/H; 18J; 6m 20s.
Undulating, steep rise/fall far end.
Good viewing.

KINGSTON ST MARY Somerset
3m N of Taunton, E of A358.
R/H; 18J; 6m 30s.
Undulating, twisting.
Reasonable viewing.

LANARK Strathclyde
1m E of town off A73 (old Lanark racecourse).
R/H; 18J; 6m 45s.
Galloping, suits stayers.
Good viewing.

LARKHILL Wiltshire
3m NW of Amesbury, W of A345.
R/H; 18J; 6m 10s.
Undulating, galloping, suits non-stayer.
Good but distant viewing.

LEMALLA Cornwall
6m SW of Launceston, S of A30.
R/H; 20J; 7m 00s.
Sharp, undulating.
Poor viewing.

LIFTON Devon
3m N of Launceston, 2m off A30
R/H; 19J; 6m 30s.
Undulating, sharp.
Very good viewing.

LITTLE WINDSOR Dorset
4m S of Crewkerne, 2m W of A3066.
R/H; 19J; 6m 45s.
Undulating, galloping, uphill finish.
Good viewing.

LLANFRYNACH Powys
3m SE of Brecon, off B4558.
R/H; 18J; 6m 40s.
Flat, twisty.
Reasonable viewing.

LLANTWIT MAJOR S. Glamorgan
1½m NW of town, off B4265.
R/H; 19J; 6m 15s (4m, 25J, 8m 10s).
Flat, sharp.
Reasonable viewing.

LLANVAPLEY Gwent
4m E of Abergavenny, off B4223.
L/H; 18J; 6m 25s.
Flat, twisty.
Excellent viewing.

LOCKERBIE Dumfries & Galloway
2m SW of town, S of A709.
R/H; 19J; 7m 30s.
Flat, sharp, long trip.
Good viewing.

LOCKINGE Oxfordshire
2m S of Wantage, Adj B4494.
L/H; 19J; 6m 25s.
Undulating, galloping, very short run-in.
Excellent viewing.

LYDSTEP Dyfed
3m SW of Tenby, off A4139.
L/H; 19J; 6m 35s.
Gently undulating, sharp.
Excellent viewing.

MAGOR Gwent
Adjacent Junction 23, M4.
R/H; 18J; 6m 00s.
Very undulating, sharp.
Poor viewing.

MAISEMORE PARK Glos.
2m NW of Gloucester, Adj A417.
L/H; 18J; 6m 45s.
Flat, fairly sharp.
Very good viewing.

MARKET RASEN Lincs
Inside N.H. Course
L/H; 18J; 6m 35s.
Sharp, undulating.
Excellent viewing.

MARKS TEY Essex
5m W of Colchester, Adj A12.
L/H; 19J; 6m 40s (3¼m, 20J, 7m 00s).
Galloping, uphill finish, suits stayers.
Good viewing.

MILBORNE ST ANDREW Dorset
4m E of Puddletown, S of A354
L/H; 19J; 6m 30s.
Galloping, fairly flat.
Fair viewing.

MOLLINGTON Oxfordshire
5m N of Banbury, Adj A423.
R/H; 18J; 6m 30s.
Undulating, galloping, uphill finish.
Excellent viewing.

MOSSHOUSES Borders
4m N of Melrose, W of A68.
L/H; 18J; 6m 50s.
Undulating, galloping, suits stayers.
Very good viewing.

MOUNSEY HILL GATE Somerset
4m N of Dulverton, Adj B3223.
R/H; 20J; 6m 33s.
Flat, sharp.
Very poor viewing.

NEWTON BROMSWOLD Northants.
3m SE of Rushden, E of A6.
R/H; 19J; 6m 50s.
Slightly undulating, galloping, suits stayers.
Good viewing.

NEWTOWN Hereford & Worcs.
7m NE of Hereford, Adj A417/A4103.
L/H; 18J; 6m 30s.
Undulating, suits stayers.
Good viewing.

NORTHAW Herts.
2m NE of Potters Bar, Adj B156.
L/H; 18J; 6m 25s.
Slightly undulating, suits stayers.
Course changed in 1994, viewing much improved.

OTTERY ST. MARY Devon
1m SW of town, off B3174.
L/H; 19J; 6m 25s.
Flat, sharp.
Excellent viewing.

PANTYDERI Dyfed
7m NE of Newcastle Enlyn, Adj B4332.
R/H; 18J; 6m 40s.
Mostly flat.
Good viewing.

PARHAM Sussex
3m SE of Pulbrough, Adj A283.
R/H; 18J; 6m 35s.
Flat, galloping.
Good viewing.

PENSHURST Kent
4m SW of Tonbridge, W of B2188.
L/H; 18J; 6m 45s.
Undulating, uphill finish.
Unsatisfactory viewing.

PEPER HAROW Surrey
2m W of Godalming, W of A3.
L/H; 18J; 6m 50s.
Flat, very sharp, finish up centre chute.
Very poor viewing.

PYLE W Glamorgan
At Margam Park, off M40, junction 38.
R/H; 18J; 6m 10s.
Undulating, sharp.
Good viewing.

SANDON Staffs.
4m SE of Stone, off A51.
L/H; 19J; 6m 50s.
Slightly undulating.
Excellent viewing.

SIDDINGTON Glos.
2m S of Cirencester, W of A419.
L/H; 18J; 6m 20s.
Flat, galloping.
Good viewing, but not of finish.

SOUTHWELL Notts.
1m SW of town.
L/H; 18J; 6m 30s.
Flat, sharp, inside of NH Course.
Excellent viewing.

STAFFORD CROSS Devon
3m W of Seaton, Adj A3052.
R/H; 18J; 6m 10s.
Flat, sharp, easy 3m.
Unsatisfactory viewing.

STAINTON Cleveland
1m S of Middlesbrough, off A19.
R/H; 18J; 6m 30s.
Sharp.
Fair viewing.

ST HILARY S Glamorgan
2m E of Cowbridge, S of A48.
R/H; 19J; 6m 20s.
Flat, sharp.
Good viewing.

SUDLOW FARM Cheshire
1m W of Knutsford, junction 19, M6.
R/H; 18J; 6m 50s.
Sharp, uphill finish, suits stayers.
Good viewing.

TALYBONT-ON-USK Powys
6m SE of Brecon, off B4558.
R/H; 18J; 6m 20s.
Undulating, galloping.
Good viewing.

THORPE LODGE Notts.
3m SW of Newark, S of A46.
L/H; 18J; 6m 40s.
Flat, fair.
Excellent viewing.

TRANWELL Northumberland
3m SW of Morpeth, S of B6524.
L/H; 18J; 6m 20s.
Flat, uphill finish in shute.
Reasonable viewing.

TWESELDOWN Hampshire
3m W of Aldershot, W of A325.
R/H; 19J; 6m 20s.
Undulating, triangular.
Excellent view of finish, but not much else.

UMBERLEIGH Devon
5m SE of Barnstaple, Adj A377.
L/H; 18J; 6m 25s.
Sharp, up & down side of hill.
Reasonable viewing, but mobility essential.

UPPER SAPEY Hereford & Worcs.
6m N of Bromyard, Adj B4203.
R/H; 18J; 6m 05s.
Very undulating.
Reasonable viewing.

UPTON-ON-SEVERN Hereford & Worcs.
5m N of Tewkesbury, W of A38.
R/H; 18J; 6m 35s.
Flat, galloping, suits stayers.
Excellent viewing.

WADEBRIDGE Cornwall
1m W of town, Adj A39 (Royal Showground).
L/H; 21J; 6m 30s.
Slightly undulating, twisty.
Reasonable viewing.

WESTON PARK Shropshire
6m E of Telford, S of A5.
L/H; 20J; 6m 35s.
Flat, sharp.
Reasonable viewing.

WETHERBY Yorkshire
8m SE of Harrogate, Adj A1.
L/H; 18J; 7m 00s.
Flat, suits stayers, inside NH course.
Excellent from grandstand.

WHITTINGTON Lancashire
2m S of Kirkby Lonsdale, off B6254.
L/H; 18J; 7m 10s.
Flat, galloping, stamina test.
Excellent viewing.

WHITWELL-ON-THE-HILL Yorkshire
6m SW of Malton, Adj A64.
R/H; 18J; 6m 45s.
Mainly flat, galloping, suits stayers.
Excellent viewing.

WITTON CASTLE Durham
3m W of Bishop Auckland, E of A68.
R/H; 21J; 6m 30s.
Flat, galloping.
Excellent viewing.

WOLVERHAMPTON Staffs.
Inside A/W Course.
L/H; 18J; 6m 40s.
Flat, sharp.
Excellent viewing.

WOODFORD Glos.
15m NE of Bristol, Adj A38.
L/H; 19J; 6m 25s.
Flat, galloping.
Fair viewing.

POINT-TO-POINT SECRETARIES' ASSOCIATION

CHAIRMAN: Major M. MacEwan, Urless Farm, Corscombe, Dorchester, Dorset. Tel. (01935) 891327
VICE CHAIRMAN: Andrew Merriam, Oaklawn House, Eye, Suffolk. IP23 7NN. Tel. (01379) 870362
ADMINISTRATOR/SECRETARY: The Jockey Club, 42 Portman Square, London. W1H 0EN. Tel. 0171 486 4921

AREA REPRESENTATIVES & ADDRESSES FOR AREA SCHEDULES

Each Schedule lists name, address and telephone number of each Point-to-Point Secretary in its Area, and gives full details of every meeting and race planned for 1997 in that Area. They may be obtained by sending a SAE (at least 7 × 5 ins) to the following or, where shown otherwise[★], to the address indicated.

DEVON & CORNWALL: P. Wakeham Esq, Torne House, Rattery, South Brent, Devon. ★Schedule: M. E. Hawkins Esq, Hunters Lodge, Newton St Cyres, Exeter, Devon. EX5 5BS. Tel. (01392) 851275.

EAST ANGLIA: Mrs. P. Rowe, Curles Manor, Clavering, Saffron Walden, Essex. CB11 4PW. Tel. (01799) 550283.

MIDLANDS (Lincolnshire, Northants & Notts): Mrs. E. Gilman, Coppice Farmhouse, Church Lane, Glaston, Oakham, Rutland. LE15 9BN. Tel. (01572) 823476.

NORTHERN (Northumberland, Scotland): C. J. Sample, ARICS, Estate Office, Bothal Castle, Morpeth, Northumberland. Tel. (01670) 513128. ★Schedule: A. J. Hogarth Esq, Mosshouses, Galashields, Selkirkshire. TD1 2PG. Tel. (01896) 860242.

NORTH WEST (Shropshire, Cheshire): J. R. Wilson Esq. Huntington House, Little Wenlock, Telford, Salop. TF6 5BW. Tel. (01952) 502354.

SANDHURST (Surrey, Hampshire & Isle of Wight): P. A. D. Scouller Esq, Bottom House, Bix, Henley-on-Thames, Oxon. RG9 6DF. Tel. (0118) 9874311. ★Schedule: Mrs. H. Murray, Kingston House, Kingston Blount, Oxon. OX9 4SH. Tel. (01844) 351216.

SOUTH EAST (Kent, Sussex & Surrey): J. C. S. Hickman Esq, Romney House, Ashford Market, Elwick Road, Ashford, Kent. TN23 1PG. Tel. (01233) 622222 (office); (01233) 720397 (home). ★Schedule: Mrs. Nicky Featherstone, 28 Exeter Close, Tonbridge, Kent. TN10 4NT. Tel. (01732) 353518.

SOUTH MIDLANDS (Warwickshire, Oxon, Berks, Bucks): Col. A. Clerke Brown, OBE, Kingston Grove, Kingston Blount, Oxon. OX9 4SQ. Tel. (01844) 351356. ★Schedule: Mrs. H. Murray (as Sandhurst).

SOUTH & WEST WALES: I. Prichard Esq. Karlyn, St Hilary, Cowbridge, S. Glamorgan. Tel. (01446) 772335 (home) (01446) 774603 (office).

TAUNTON (Somerset, Dorset, Wilts): Major M. MacEwan, Urless Farm, Corscombe, Dorchester, Dorset. Tel. (01935) 891327. ★Schedule: F. G. Mathews Esq, Peak Ashes, Penselwood, Wincanton, Somerset. BA9 8LY. Tel. (01747) 840412.

WELSH BORDER COUNTIES: F. J. A. Morgan Esq, 38 South Street, Leominster, Herefordshire. Tel. (01568) 611166. ★Schedule: J. R. Pike Esq, The Priory, Kilpeck, Hereford. HR2 9DN. Tel. (01981) 570366.

WEST MIDLANDS (Gloucestershire, Worcestershire & Warwickshire): Mrs. K. Smith-Maxwell, Phepson Manor, Himbleton, nr. Droitwich, Worcs. WR9 7JE. Tel. (01905) 391206.

WEST WALES: Mrs C. Higgon, Newton Hall, Crundale, Haverfordwest, Dyfed. SA62 4EB. Tel. (01437) 731239. ★Schedule: I. Prichard (as South & West Wales).

YORKSHIRE: Mrs. C. M. Wardroper, High Osgoodby Grange, Thirsk, N. Yorks. YO7 2AW. Tel. (01845) 597226.

If any changes are made for 1997 after the publication of this annual, those listed above will pass on correspondence to any successor.

THE POINT-TO-POINT OWNERS' & RIDERS' ASSOCIATION

CHAIRMAN: M. J. R. Bannister, MFH, Coniston Hall, Coniston Cold, Skipton, N. Yorkshire. (Tel: Skipton [01756] 749551 Home; Skipton [01756] 748136 Office).

PRESIDENT and CHAIRMAN OF POINT-TO-POINT COMMITTEE: J. Mahon Esq, Bishopton Hill House, Bishopton, Stratford-on-Avon, Warwicks. (Tel: Stratford-on-Avon [01789] 299029).

SECRETARY: Mrs Jeanette Dawson, Horton Court, Westbere Lane, Westbere, Canterbury, Kent. CT2 0HG. (Tel/Fax: [01227] 713080).

AREA REPRESENTATIVES

DEVON & CORNWALL: K. Cumings Esq, Eastwood, Bishops Nympton, South Molton, N. Devon. EX36 4PB. (Tel: [01769] 550528 Home; [01823] 432356 Office).

EAST ANGLIA: M. Bloom Esq, Kimberley Home Farm, Wymondham, Norfolk. NR18 0RW. (Tel: Wymondham [01953] 603137).

MIDLANDS: J. H. Docker Esq, Rookery Farm, Northbrook Road, Coundon, nr. Coventry, Warwicks. CV6 2AJ. (Tel: [01203] 332036).

NORTHERN: R. F. Minto Esq, Gilson, Spylaw Park, Kelso, Borders. TD5 8DS (Tel: [01573] 223162).

NORTH WEST: T. P. Brookshaw Esq, Mickley House Farm, Habberley, Pontesbury, Shrewsbury. SY5 0SQ. (Tel: [01743] 790083).

SANDHURST: C. Coyne Esq, Court Hill, Letcombe Regis, Wantage, Oxon. OX12 9JL. (Tel: Wantage [01235] 762399).

SOUTH EAST: W. A. Alcock Esq, The Willows, Brook, Ashford, Kent. TN25 5PD. (Tel: Wye [01233] 812613 Home; Wye [01233] 812761 Office).

SOUTH MIDLANDS: N. Price Esq, Manor Farmhouse, Maidford, nr. Towcester. NN12 8HB. (Tel: [01327] 860297).

SOUTH WALES: Mrs J. Tamplin, Cefn Llwyd Farm, Abertridwr, Caerphilly, Mid Glamorgan. (Tel: Caerphilly [01222] 830278).

TAUNTON: J. J. Barber Esq, Peckmore Farm, Henley, Crewkerne, Somerset. TA18 8PQ. (Tel: [01460] 74943) *and* L. Vickery Esq, Knowle End, South Barrow, Yeovil, Somerset. BA22 7LN. (Tel: [01963] 440043).

WELSH BORDERS: G. Snell Esq, Lower Lulham, Madley, Hereford. HR2 9JJ. (Tel: Golden Valley [01981] 251301 Home; Golden Valley [01981] 250253 Office).

WEST MIDLANDS: W. Bush Esq, Old Manor House, West Littleton, Chippenham, Wilts. SN14 8JE. (Tel: Bath [01225] 891683).

WEST WALES: Mrs C. Higgon, Newton Hall, Crundale, Haverfordwest, Dyfed. SA62 4EB. (Tel: Clarbeston [01437] 731239).

YORKSHIRE: M. J. R. Bannister, MFH, Coniston Hall, Coniston Cold, Skipton, N. Yorkshire. (Tel: Skipton [01756] 749551 Home; Skipton [01756] 748136 Office).

NORTHERN JOCKEYS REPRESENTATIVE: S. Whitaker Esq, Hellwood Farm, Hellwood Lane, Scarcroft, Leeds. LS14 3BP. (Tel: Leeds [0113] 2892265).

SOUTHERN JOCKEYS REPRESENTATIVE: J. G. Cann Esq, Newland, Cullompton, Devon. EX15 1QQ. (Tel: Cullompton [01884] 32284).

The Point-to-Point Owners' & Riders' Association are dedicated to the advancement and promotion of point-to-pointing. Annual Subscription £10.00. Life Membership £100. For further information contact the secretary (above).

NOTES

NOTES

NOTES

NOTES

NOTES

NOTES

NOTES

NOTES

NOTES

NOTES

NOTES

NOTES

NOTES

NOTES

NOTES

NOTES

NOTES

NOTES

NOTES

NOTES

NOTES

NOTES

NOTES

NOTES

NOTES

NOTES

NOTES

NOTES

NOTES